W9-BRR-221

Masterpieces of World Literature

Masterpieces
of
World Literature

Edited by
Frank N. Magill

Harper Collins *Publishers*

MASTERPIECES OF WORLD LITERATURE. Copyright © 1989 by Frank N. Magill. All rights reserved. Printed in the United States of America. No part of this book may be used or reproduced in any manner whatsoever without written permission except in the case of brief quotations embodied in critical articles and reviews. For information address HarperCollins Publishers, 10 East 53rd Street, New York, NY 10022.

FIRST EDITION

Library of Congress Cataloging-in-Publication Data

Masterpieces of world literature / edited by Frank N. Magill, editor.
    p.   cm.
  Includes indexes.
  ISBN 0-06-270050-2
    1. Literature—Stories, plots, etc. 2. Literature—History and criticism. I. Magill, Frank Northen, 1907–
PN44.M3448   1989
809—dc20   89-45052

96 97 RRD 10 9 8

Preface

Masterpieces of World Literature revives a publishing tradition. Following the publication of *Masterplots* in 1949 by Salem Press, Harper & Row released a trade reference edition titled *Masterpieces of World Literature*. The success of this publication led to three additional series and other related reference works which found their way into homes nationwide. Now, forty years later, a new generation of Americans, many of whom grew up with the original summaries and essays, will take the opportunity to have just such a reference in their home libraries for their own use and as an enhancement to their children's education.

The current *Masterpieces* presents standard essays on 270 classic works of world literature, arranged alphabetically by their best known English titles. Designed primarily for reference, the format is stylized and standardized to afford maximum information in the quickest time. For the 204 works which tell a story—novels, stories, plays, epic poems—the plot-summary format is employed. Each plot digest is preceded by carefully checked reference data that furnish at a glance the type of work, author, type of plot, time of plot, locale, and first publication date. Next, a brief summary of the narrative appears, which can be used either separately or in conjunction with the fuller treatment that follows. The first major section of each essay introduces to the reader the story's principal characters. In addition to a brief description of each character and his or her relationship to the other characters, a phonetic guide to the pronunciation of difficult names is presented. The text itself is divided into two sections. "The Story," a well-rounded synopsis of approximately 1,000 words, orients the new reader to the novel, story, play, or poem, and refreshes the memory of the reader who is reviewing a book read long ago. Immediately following the plot summary, the "Critical Evaluation" discusses, in some 1,000 words, the major critical and analytical approaches to the work, setting the course for formal or informal study.

The remaining 66 works, those that do not tell a story but impart important thoughts in prose or verse, are presented in the essay-review format. Following the ready-reference data (type of work, author, and publication date), a 2,000-word essay identifies the primary ideas and integrates them with a discussion of the literary merits of the work in a clear, expository style, making accessible to readers many of the ideas that form the foundation of Western thought.

Each of the 270 essays in this edition has been written to assure currency of the ideas presented, requiring an enormous amount of assistance from a carefully selected staff that included scores of English faculty members from universities and colleges throughout the United States. All of these contributors deserve recognition; in particular, we would like to acknowledge: Patrick Adcock, Raymond M. Archer, Stanley Archer, Jean Ashton, Bryan Aubrey, Melissa E. Barth, Wm. S. Brockington, Jr., Rebecca R. Butler, Joan E. Carr, John J. Conlon, Robert P. Ellis, David Marc Fisher, Dana Gerhardt, Daniel Guillory, Terry Heller, Richard Kelly, Eugene S. Larson, Leon Lewis, Robert A. Morace, Robert H. O'Connor, Robert M. Otten, William Pemberton, Betty Richardson, Joseph Rosenblum, Murray Sachs, Marjorie Smelstor, Gilbert G. Smith, James T. Sullivan, Roy Arthur Swanson, Eileen Tess Tyler, and Michael Witkoski.

The volume concludes with two indexes to aid the user in locating all works by author (author index) or title, including alternate titles (title index).

Some readers will find in the pages of *Masterpieces* a pleasant renewal of an old acquaintance, a chance meeting with an almost forgotten literary friend. Others may wish to pursue further an interest encountered here for the first time. The first instance would please me, but the second would please me even more.

FRANK N. MAGILL

ACKNOWLEDGEMENTS

The following plot summaries are used by permission of the publishers and copyright holders.

Absalom, Absalom! by William Faulkner (Random House, Inc., and William Faulkner, 1936).

The Ambassadors by Henry James (Harper & Brothers, 1902, 1903; Henry James, executor, 1930).

As I Lay Dying by William Faulkner (Random House, Inc., and William Faulkner, 1930).

Babbitt by Sinclair Lewis (Harcourt, Brace & Co., Inc., 1922).

Billy Budd, Foretopman by Herman Melville (Liveright Publishing Corp., 1928).

Buddenbrooks by Thomas Mann (Alfred A. Knopf, Inc., 1924).

Death in Venice by Thomas Mann (Alfred A. Knopf, Inc., 1930, 1931, 1934, 1935, 1936).

Dracula by Bram Stoker (Doubleday & Co., Inc., and Bram Stoker, 1897; Florence A. L. Bram Stoker, 1924).

East of Eden by John Steinbeck (The Viking Press, Inc., and John Steinbeck, 1952).

A Fable by William Faulkner (Random House, Inc. and William Faulkner, 1950, 1954).

A Farewell to Arms by Ernest Hemingway (Charles Scribner's Sons and Ernest Hemingway, 1929).

For Whom the Bell Tolls by Ernest Hemingway (Charles Scribner's Sons and Ernest Hemingway, 1940).

The Golden Bowl by Henry James (Charles Scribner's Sons, 1904; Henry James, executor, 1932).

The Good Earth by Pearl S. Buck (The John Day Co., Inc., and Pearl S. Buck, 1931).

The Grapes of Wrath by John Steinbeck (The Viking Press, Inc., and John Steinbeck, 1939).

The Great Gatsby by F. Scott Fitzgerald (Charles Scribner's Sons, 1925).

Hunger by Knut Hamsun (Alfred A. Knopf, Inc., 1920, 1948).

Jude the Obscure by Thomas Hardy (Harper & Brothers, 1895; Thomas Hardy, 1923).

Kim by Rudyard Kipling (Doubleday & Co., Inc., and Rudyard Kipling, 1900, 1901; Rudyard Kipling, 1927).

The Magic Mountain by Thomas Mann (Alfred A. Knopf, Inc., and Thomas Mann, 1927).

Main Street by Sinclair Lewis (Harcourt, Brace & Co., Inc., 1920; Sinclair Lewis, 1948).

Mrs. Dalloway by Virginia Woolf (Harcourt, Brace & Co., Inc., 1925).

Mourning Becomes Electra by Eugene O'Neill (Random House, Inc., and Horace Liveright, Inc., 1931).

My Ántonia by Willa Cather (Houghton Mifflin Co. and Willa S. Cather, 1918; Willa S. Cather, 1946).

Nostromo by Joseph Conrad (Harper & Brothers, 1904; Mrs. Jessie Conrad, 1931).

The Old Man and the Sea by Ernest Hemingway (Charles Scribner's Sons and Ernest Hemingway, 1952).

The Old Wives' Tale by Arnold Bennett (Doubleday & Co., Inc., 1911; Marie Margaret Bennett, 1938).

A Passage to India by E. M. Forster (Harcourt, Brace & Co., Inc., 1924).

The Plague by Albert Camus (Alfred A. Knopf, Inc., 1948).

A Portrait of the Artist as a Young Man by James Joyce (The Viking Press, Inc. and B. W. Huebsch, 1916; Nora Joyce, 1944).

The Red Badge of Courage by Stephen Crane (D. Appleton & Co., 1895; William H. Crane, 1923).

Remembrance of Things Past by Marcel Proust (Random House, Inc., and Thomas Seltzer, 1924, 1925; Random House, Inc., 1927, 1929, 1930, 1932; The Modern Library, Inc., 1934).

Sons and Lovers by D. H. Lawrence (The Viking Press, Inc., and Mitchell Kennerley, 1913).

The Sound and the Fury by William Faulkner (Random House, Inc., and William Faulkner, 1929).

To the Lighthouse by Virginia Woolf (Harcourt, Brace & Co., Inc., 1927).

The Trial by Franz Kafka (Alfred A. Knopf, Inc., 1937).

The Turn of the Screw by Henry James (The Macmillian Co., 1898; Henry James, executor, 1926).

Ulysses by James Joyce (Random House, Inc., and Nora Joseph Joyce, 1914, 1918, 1942, 1946).

Waiting for Godot by Samuel Beckett (Grove Press, Inc., 1954).

The Waves by Virginia Woolf (Harcourt, Brace & Co., Inc., 1933).

Key to Pronunciation

â	pare, stair	o͝o	book, push
ă	man, rang	o͞o	moor, move
ā	ale, fate	ou	loud, round
ä	calm, father	p	put, stop
b	bed, rub	r	red, try
ch	chin, reach	s	see, pass
d	day, bad	t	to, bit
ĕ	ten, ebb	th	thin, path
ē	equal, meat	t͟h	then, mother
ė	fern, bird	ŭ	up, dove
f	fill, off	ū	use, cube
g	go, rug	û	surge, burn
h	hot, hear	v	vast, above
ĭ	if, hit	w	will, away
ī	ice, right	y	yet, yam
j	joy, hedge	z	zest, amaze
k	keep, take	zh	azure, seizure
l	let, ball	ə	is a vowel occuring in an
l	man, him		unaccented syllable, as
n	now, ton	a	*in* above
ng	ring, English	e	*in* chapel
ŏ	lot, box	i	*in* veracity
ō	old, over	o	*in* connect
ô	order, shorn	u	*in* crocus
oi	boy, oil		

Foreign Sounds

à	pronounced as in the French *ami*
ll	usually pronounced like *y* in *yes* in Spanish America; in Spain like the *ll* in *million*
ṅ	a nasal *n* pronounced as in the French *bon*
ñ	pronounced like the *ny* in *canyon*
œ	pronounced as in the French *feu* or the German *böse*
r͞r	pronounced as in the Spanish *barranco*
ü	pronounced as in the French *du* or the German *grün*

CONTENTS

CONTENTS

CONTENTS

CONTENTS

Masterpieces of World Literature

ABSALOM, ABSALOM!

Type of work: Novel
Author: William Faulkner (1897–1962)
Type of plot: Psychological realism
Time of plot: Nineteenth century
Locale: Mississippi
First published: 1936

Instead of his usual sustained interior monologue technique, Faulkner here uses the device of three narrators, each of whom relates the family saga of Thomas Sutpen from his or her unique point of view. This device imparts to Absalom, Absalom!, *which is a metaphor for the rich and chaotic Southern experience, a complexity, a depth of psychological insight, and an emotional intensity which might have been lost in a narrative of more traditional format.*

Principal Characters

Thomas Sutpen, the owner of Sutpen's Hundred in Yoknapatawpha County, Mississippi. Born of a poor white family in the mountains of Western Virginia, he grows up to become an ambitious man of implacable will. After his arrival in Mississippi he thinks he can win his neighbors' respect by building a huge mansion and marrying the daughter of a respectable merchant. When he is not driving his wild African slaves and a kidnapped French architect to finish construction of his magnificent house, he seeks relaxation by fighting his most powerful slaves. Wishing to found a family dynasty, he wants, more than anything else, to have a male heir. When one son is killed and the other disappears, Sutpen, now aging, fathers a child by Milly, the granddaughter of Wash Jones, one of his tenants. After learning that the child is a girl, he rejects and insults Milly. Because of his callous rejection old Wash Jones kills him.

Ellen Coldfield, the wife chosen by Thomas Sutpen because he believes she is "adjunctive" to his design of founding a plantation family. A meek, helpless woman, she is completely dominated by her husband.

Henry Sutpen, the son born to Thomas and Ellen Sutpen. Unlike his sister Judith, he faints when he sees his father fighting with slaves. At first, not knowing that Charles Bon is also Sutpen's son, impressionable Henry idolizes and imitates that suave young man. Later he learns Bon's true identity and kills him, after their return from the Civil War, to keep Judith from marrying her half brother, who is part black.

Charles Bon, Thomas Sutpen's unacknowledged son by his earlier marriage in Haiti. A polished man of the world, he forms a close friendship with the more provincial Henry, whom he meets at college, and he becomes engaged to Judith Sutpen. When the two return from the Civil War, Bon's charming manner does not prevent his being killed by Henry, who has learned that his friend and sister's suitor is part black.

Judith Sutpen, Thomas Sutpen's daughter. After Charles Bon has been killed and Henry flees, she vows never to marry. She dies of smallpox contracted while nursing Charles Bon's black wife.

Goodhue Coldfield, a middle-class storekeeper in the town of Jefferson, the father of Ellen and Rosa Coldfield. When the Civil War begins, he locks himself in his attic and disdainfully refuses to have any part in the conflict. Fed by Rosa, who sends him food that he pulls up in a basket, he dies alone in the attic.

Wash Jones, a squatter on Thomas Sutpen's land and, after the Civil War, his drinking companion. While his employer is away during the Civil War, Wash looks after the plantation. Ignorant, unwashed, but more vigorous than others of his type, he serves Sutpen well until the latter rejects Milly and her child by declaring that if she were a mare with a foal he could give her a stall in his stable. Picking up a scythe, a symbol of time and change, Wash beheads Sutpen.

Rosa Coldfield, Goodhue Coldfield's younger daughter. She is an old woman when she tells Quentin Compson that Sutpen, whom she calls a ruthless demon, brought terror and tragedy to all who had dealings with him. A strait-laced person, she recalls the abrupt, insulting fashion in which Sutpen had proposed to her in the hope that she would be able to bear him a son after his wife's death. Never married, she is obsessed by memories of her brother-in-law.

Clytemnestra Sutpen, called **Clytie,** the daughter of Thomas Sutpen's former slave, who hides Henry Sutpen in the mansion when he returns, old and sick, years after the murder he committed. Fearing that he will be arrested, she sets fire to the house and burns herself and Henry in the conflagration which destroys that dilapidated monument to Thomas Sutpen's pride and folly.

Milly Jones, the granddaughter of Wash Jones. She and her child are killed by Wash after Sutpen's murder.

Charles Etienne de Saint Velery Bon, the son of Charles Bon and his octoroon mistress. He dies of smallpox at Sutpen's Hundred.

Jim Bond (Bon), the half-witted son of Charles Etienne de Saint Velery Bon and a full-blooded black woman. He is the only survivor of Sutpen's family.

Quentin Compson, the anguished son of a decaying Southern family. Moody and morose, he tells the story of the Sutpens to his uncomprehending roommate at Harvard. Driven by personal guilt, he is later to commit

suicide. Before leaving for Harvard he learns about Thomas Sutpen from Rosa Coldfield.

Shrevlin McCannon, called **Shreve,** a Canadian student at Harvard and Quentin Compson's roommate. With great curiosity but without much understanding, he listens to Quentin's strange tale of Southern passions and tragedy leading to decay and ruin.

The Story

In the summer of 1909, when Quentin Compson was preparing to go to Harvard, old Rosa Coldfield insisted upon telling him the whole infamous story of Thomas Sutpen, whom she called a demon. According to Miss Rosa, he had brought terror and tragedy to all who had dealings with him.

In 1833, Thomas Sutpen had come to Jefferson, Mississippi, with a fine horse and two pistols and no known past. He had lived mysteriously for a while among people at the hotel, and after a short time, he had disappeared from the area. He had purchased one hundred square miles of uncleared land from the Chickasaws and had had it recorded at the land office.

When he returned with a wagon load of wild-looking blacks, a French architect, and a few tools and wagons, he was as uncommunicative as ever. At once, he set about clearing land and building a mansion. For two years he labored, and during all that time he rarely saw or visited his acquaintances in Jefferson. People wondered about the source of his money. Some claimed that he had stolen it somewhere in his mysterious comings and goings. Then, for three years, his house remained unfinished, without windowpanes or furnishings, while Thomas Sutpen busied himself with his crops. Occasionally he invited Jefferson men to his plantation to hunt, entertaining them with liquor, cards, and savage combats between his giant slaves—combats in which he himself sometimes joined for the sport.

At last, he disappeared once more, and when he returned, he had furniture and furnishings elaborate and fine enough to make his great house a splendid showplace. Because of his mysterious actions, sentiment in the village turned against him. This hostility, however, subsided somewhat when Sutpen married Ellen Coldfield, daughter of the highly respected Goodhue Coldfield.

Miss Rosa and Quentin's father shared some of Sutpen's revelations. Because Quentin was away in college, many of the things he knew about Sutpen's Hundred had come to him in letters from home. Other details he had learned during talks with his father. He learned of Ellen Sutpen's life as mistress of the strange mansion in the wilderness. He learned how she discovered her husband fighting savagely with one of his slaves. Young Henry Sutpen fainted, but Judith, the daughter, watched from

the haymow with interest and delight. Ellen thereafter refused to reveal her true feelings and ignored the village gossip about Sutpen's Hundred.

The children grew up. Young Henry, so unlike his father, attended the university at Oxford, Mississippi, and there he met Charles Bon, a rich planter's grandson. Unknown to Henry, Charles was his half brother, Sutpen's son by his first marriage. Unknown to all of Jefferson, Sutpen had gotten his money as the dowry of his earlier marriage to Charles Bon's West Indian mother, a wife he discarded when he learned she was part black.

Charles Bon became engaged to Judith Sutpen. The engagement was suddenly broken off for a probation period of four years. In the meantime, the Civil War began. Charles and Henry served together. Thomas Sutpen became a colonel.

Goodhue Coldfield took a disdainful stand against the war. He barricaded himself in his attic and his daughter, Rosa, was forced to put his food in a basket let down by a long rope. His store was looted by Confederate soldiers. One night, alone in his attic, he died.

Judith, in the meantime, had waited patiently for her lover. She carried his letter, written at the end of the four-year period, to Quentin's grandmother. Sometime later on Wash Jones, a tenant on the Sutpen plantation, came to Miss Rosa's door with the crude announcement that Charles Bon was dead, killed at the gate of the plantation by his half brother and former friend. Henry fled. Judith buried her lover in the Sutpen family plot on the plantation. Rosa, whose mother had died when she was born, went to Sutpen's Hundred to live with her niece. Ellen was already dead. It was Rosa's conviction that she could help Judith.

Colonel Thomas Sutpen returned. His slaves had been taken away, and he was burdened with new taxes on his overrun land and ruined buildings. He planned to marry Rosa Coldfield, more than ever desiring an heir now that Judith had vowed spinsterhood and Henry had become a fugitive. His son, Charles Bon, whom he might, in desperation, have permitted to marry his daughter, was dead.

Rosa, insulted when she understood the true nature of his proposal, returned to her father's ruined house in the village. She was to spend the rest of her miserable life pondering the fearful intensity of Thomas Sutpen, whose nature, in her outraged belief, seemed to partake of the devil himself.

Quentin, during his last vacation, had learned more of the Sutpen tragedy. He now revealed much of the story to Shreve McCannon, his roommate, who listened with all of a Northerner's misunderstanding and indifference.

Quentin and his father had visited the Sutpen graveyard, where they saw a little path and a hole leading into Ellen Sutpen's grave. Generations of opossums lived there. Over her tomb and that of her husband stood a marble monument from Italy. Sutpen himself had died in 1869. In 1867, he had taken young Milly Jones, Wash Jones's granddaughter. After she bore a child, a girl, Wash Jones had killed Thomas Sutpen.

Judith and Charles Bon's son, his child by an octoroon woman who had brought her child to Sutpen's Hundred when he was eleven years old, died in 1884 of smallpox. Before he died, the boy had married a black woman, and they had had an idiot son, James Bond. Rosa Coldfield had placed headstones on their graves, and on Judith's gravestone she had caused to be inscribed a fearful message.

In the summer of 1910, Rosa Coldfield confided to Quentin that she felt there was still someone living at Sutpen's Hundred. Together the two had gone out there at night and had discovered Clytie, the aged daughter of Thomas Sutpen and a slave. More important, they discovered Henry Sutpen himself hiding in the ruined old house. He had returned, he told them, four years before; he had come back to die. The idiot, James Bond, watched Rosa and Quentin as they departed. Rosa returned to her home, and Quentin went back to college.

Quentin's father wrote to tell him the tragic ending of the Sutpen story. Months later, Rosa sent an ambulance out to the ruined plantation house, for she had finally determined to bring her nephew, Henry, into the village to live with her so that he could get decent care. Clytie, seeing the ambulance, was afraid that Henry was to be arrested for the murder of Charles Bon many years before. In desperation she set fire to the old house, burning herself and Henry Sutpen to death. Only the idiot, James Bond, the last surviving descendant of Thomas Sutpen, escaped. No one knew where he went, for he was never seen again. Miss Rosa took to her bed and died soon afterward, in the winter of 1910.

Quentin told the story to his roommate because it seemed to him, somehow, to be the story of the whole South, a tale of deep passions, tragedy, ruin, and decay.

Critical Evaluation

Absalom, Absalom! is the most involved of William Faulkner's works, for the narrative is revealed by recollections years after the events described have taken place. Experience is related at its fullest expression; its initial import is recollected, and its significance years thereafter is faithfully recorded. The conventional method of storytelling has been discarded. Through his special method, Faulkner is able to re-create human action and human emotion in its own setting. Sensory impressions gained at the moment, family traditions as powerful stimuli, the tragic impulses—these focus truly in the reader's mind so that a tremendous picture of the nineteenth century South, vivid down to the most minute detail, grows slowly in the reader's imagination.

This novel is Faulkner's most comprehensive attempt to come to terms with the full implications of the Southern experience. The structure of the novel, itself an attempt by its various narrators to make some sense of the seemingly chaotic experience, is indicative of the multifaceted complexity of that experience, and the various narrators' relationship to the material suggests the difficulty that making order of the past entails. Each narrator has, to begin with, only part of the total picture—and some parts of that hearsay or conjecture—at his disposal, and each of their responses is conditioned by their individual experiences and backgrounds. Thus, Miss Rosa's idea of Sutpen depends equally upon her Calvinist background and her failure to guess why Henry Sutpen killed Charles Bon.

Quentin's father responds with an ironic detachment, conditioned by his insistence upon viewing the fall of the South as the result of the workings of an inevitable Fate, as in Greek drama. Like Quentin and Shreve, the reader must attempt to coordinate these partial views of the Sutpen history into a meaningful whole—with the added irony that he must also deal with Quentin's romanticism. In effect, the reader becomes yet another investigator, but one whose concern is with the entire scope of the novel rather than only with the Sutpen family.

At the very heart of the novel is Thomas Sutpen and his grand design, and the reader's comprehension of the meaning of the work depends upon the discovery of the implications of this design. Unlike the chaos of history the narrators perceive, Sutpen's design would, by its very nature, reduce human history and experience to a mechanical and passionless process which he could control. The irony of Sutpen's failure lies in the fact that he could not achieve the design precisely because he was unable to exclude such human elements as Charles Bon's need for his father's love and recognition. Faulkner, however, gains more than this irony from his metaphor of design. In effect, Sutpen's design is based upon a formula of the antebellum South which reduces it to essentials. It encompasses the plantation, the slaves, the wife and family—all the external trappings of the plantation aristocracy Sutpen, as a small boy from the mountains, saw in his first encounter with this foreign world. Sutpen, who never really becomes one of the aristocracy his world tries to mirror, manages, by excluding the human element from his design, to reflect only what is worst in the South. Southern society is starkly revealed to have at its heart the simple fact of possession: of the land, of the slaves, and, in Sutpen's case, even of wife and children. Thus, Faulkner demonstrates here, as he does in his great story "The Bear," that the urge to possess is the fundamental evil from which other evils spring. Sutpen, trying to insulate himself from the pain of rejection that he encountered as a child, is driven almost mad by the need to possess the semblance of the world that denies his humanity, but in his obsession, he loses that humanity.

Once the idea of the design and the principle of possession in *Absalom, Absalom!* is established, Sutpen's treatment both of Charles Bon and Bon's mother is more easily understood. In Sutpen's distorted mind, that which is possessed can also be thrown away if it does not fit the design. Like certain other Faulkner characters—Benjy of *The Sound and the Fury* being the best example—Sutpen is obsessed with the need to establish a perfect order in the world into which he will fit. His first vision of tidewater Virginia, after leaving the timeless anarchy of the mountains, was the sight of perfectly ordered and neatly divided plantations, and, like a chick imprinted by its first contact, Sutpen spends his life trying to create a world that imitates that order and a dynasty that will keep his spirit alive to preserve it. His rejection of Bon is essentially emotionless, mechanical, and even without rancor because Bon's black blood simply excludes him from the design. Similarly, the proposal that Rosa have his child to prove herself worthy of marriage, and the

rejection of Milly when she bears a female child are also responses dictated by the design. Thus, Sutpen, and all whose lives touch his, ultimately become victims of the mad design he has created. Sutpen, however, is not its final victim: the curse of the design lives on into the present in Jim Bond, the last of Sutpen's bloodline.

Sutpen's rejection of Charles Bon and the consequences of that rejection are at the thematic center of *Absalom, Absalom!* In the fact that Charles is rejected for the taint of black blood, Faulkner very clearly points to the particularly Southern implication of his story. Bon must be seen, on one level, to represent the human element within Southern society that cannot be assimilated and will not be ignored. Faulkner implies that the system, which denies the rights and needs of some of its children, dehumanizes all it touches—master and victim alike. In asserting himself to demand the only recognition he can gain from his father—and that only at second hand through Henry—Charles Bon makes of himself an innocent sacrifice to the sin upon which the South was founded. His death also dramatizes the biblical admonition so relevant to *Absalom, Absalom!*: A house divided against itself cannot stand.

Sutpen's history is a metaphor of the South, and his rise and fall is Southern history written in one man's experience. The Sutpens, however, are not the only victims in the novel: The narrators too are victims and survivors of the Southern experience, and each of them seeks in Sutpen's history some clue to the meaning of his or her own relationship to the fall of the South. Their narratives seek to discover the designs which will impose some order on the chaos of the past.

THE ADVENTURES OF HUCKLEBERRY FINN

Type of work: Novel
Author: Mark Twain (Samuel L. Clemens, 1835–1910)
Type of plot: Humorous satire
Time of plot: Nineteenth century
Locale: Along the Mississippi River
First published: 1884

The title character of this famous novel tells his own story in a straightforward narrative laced with shrewd, sharp comments on human nature. The boy's adventures along the Mississippi form the framework of a series of moral lessons, revelations of a corrupt society, and contrasts of innocence and hypocrisy.

Principal Characters

Huckleberry Finn, a small-town boy living along the banks of the Mississippi in the 1800s before the American Civil War. Perhaps the best-known youthful character in world fiction, Huck has become the prototype of the boy who lives a life that all boys would like to live; he also helped to shape such diverse characters as Hemingway's Nick Adams and Salinger's Holden Caulfield. His adventurous voyage with the black slave Jim, when they drift down the Mississippi on a raft, is the trip every boy dreams of making, on his own, living by his adaptable wits and his unerring ingenuity. When he contrasts himself with his flamboyant and wildly imaginative friend, Tom Sawyer, Huck feels somewhat inadequate, but deep inside he has a triumphant reliance on the power of common sense. Thus the world of Huck's reality—his capture by and escape from old drunken Pap; the macabre pageant of his townsfolk searching the Mississippi for his supposedly drowned body; his encounters with the King and the Duke, two preposterous swindlers; his stay among the feuding Grangerfords and Shepherdsons; and his defense of the pure, benighted Wilks sisters—is proved to be far more imaginative than Tom Sawyer's imagination. Yet Huck is not some irresponsible wanderer through adolescence. He has a conscience. He knows it is wrong to be harboring a runaway slave, but his friendship with Jim makes him defy the law. His appreciation of the ridiculous allows him to go along with the lies and swindles of the King and the Duke until they seem ready to bring real harm to the Wilks sisters, and he himself will fib and steal to get food and comfort; but his code of boyhood rebels at oppression, injustice, hypocrisy. Mark Twain has created in Huckleberry Finn a magnificent American example of the romanticism that rolled like a great wave across the Atlantic in the nineteenth century.

Jim, the black slave of Miss Watson. Believing that he is about to be sold down the river for eight hundred dollars, he runs away and hides on Jackson's Island, where Huck also takes refuge after faking his own murder in order to escape from Pap. Jim has all the charm and the many inconsistencies of the Southern black. Ignorant, superstitious, gullible, Jim is nevertheless, in Huck's words, "most always right; he had an uncommon level head, for a nigger." He will laugh at everything comical, but he suffers poignantly when he thinks of the family he has left in bondage. He protects Huck physically and emotionally, feeling that the boy is the one white person he can trust, never suspecting that Huck is struggling with his conscience about whether to turn Jim in. When the two companions encounter the King and the Duke, Jim is completely taken in by their fakery, though at one point he asks, "Don't it 'sprise you, de way dem kings carries on, Huck?" Typically, Jim is subservient to and patient with the white man. Even when Tom Sawyer arrives at the Phelpses, where Jim has been caught and held, the slave goes through Tom's complicated and romantic ritual of escape with grumbling good nature. Jim is a sensitive, sincere man who seems to play his half-comic, half-tragic role in life because he is supposed to play it that way.

Tom Sawyer, Huck's friend, who can, with a lively imagination stimulated by excessive reading, turn a raid by his gang on a Sunday-School picnic into the highway robbery of "a whole parcel of Spanish merchants and rich A-rabs . . . with two hundred elephants, and six hundred camels, and over a thousand 'sumter' mules, all loaded down with di'monds. . . ." He is a foil to the practicality of Huck; he is the universal boy-leader in any small town who can sway his gang or his pal into any act of fancy, despite all grumbling and disbelief. His ritual for the rescue of the captured Jim (who he knows has already been set free by Miss Watson's last will) is a masterful selection of details from all the romantic rescues of fact and fiction.

Pap, Huck's father and the town drunkard. When he learns that Huck has been awarded in trust a share of the money derived from the box of gold found in the robber's cave, he shows up one night at Huck's room at the Widow Douglas'. He takes the pledge and stays in the Widow's spare room. Finding that Huck's share of the money is legally beyond his reach, he breaks the pledge and creates such havoc in the room that "they had to take soundings before they could navigate it." Pap kidnaps his son, keeping him prisoner in an old cabin. He then proceeds to go on a classic drunk, followed by a monumental case of delirium tremens. Snakes in abundance crawl all over him and one bites his cheek, though Huck, of course, can see nothing. The boy finally makes his escape from Pap by killing a pig and leaving bloody evidence of a most convincing murder. Jim discovers Pap's dead body in a flooded boat on the Mississippi.

The King and **The Duke,** two rapscallions and confidence men with whom Huck and Jim join up on their trip down the Mississippi. Their so-called play, "The Royal Nonesuch," finally leads to their just desserts: tarring, feathering, riding out of town on a rail.

The Widow Douglas and **Miss Watson,** unsuccessful reformers of Huck after he comes into his fortune.

Aunt Polly, Tom Sawyer's relative who at the end of the story sets straight the by-now complicated identities of Huck and Tom.

The Grangerfords and **The Shepherdsons,** two feuding families. Huck spends some time with the Grangerfords, who renew the feud when a Grangerford daughter elopes with a young Shepherdson.

Mr. and **Mrs. Phelps,** at whose farm the captured Jim is confined until Tom arrives to effect his "rescue."

Mary Jane, Susan, and **Joanna Wilks,** three sisters whom the King and the Duke set out to bilk; Huck thwarts the connivers.

Judge Thatcher, the "law" who protects Huck's interests.

The Story

Tom Sawyer and Huckleberry Finn had found a box of gold in a robber's cave. After Judge Thatcher had taken the money and invested it for the boys, each had a huge allowance of a dollar a day. The Widow Douglas and her sister, Miss Watson, had taken Huck home with them to try to reform him. At first, Huck could not stand living in a tidy house where smoking and swearing were forbidden. Worse, he had to go to school and learn how to read. He did, however, manage to drag himself to school almost every day, except for the times when he sneaked off for a smoke in the woods or to go fishing in the Mississippi.

Life was beginning to become bearable to him when one day he noticed some tracks in the snow. Examining them closely, he realized that they belonged to the worthless father whom Huck had not seen for more than a year. Knowing that his father would be back hunting him when the old man learned about the six thousand dollars, Huck rushed over to Judge Thatcher and persuaded the judge to take the fortune for himself. The judge was puzzled, but he signed some papers, and Huck was satisfied that he no longer had any money for his father to take from him.

Huck's father finally showed up one night in Huck's room at Widow Douglas' home. Complaining that he had been cheated out of his money, the old drunkard took Huck away with him to a cabin in the woods, where he kept the boy a prisoner, beating him periodically and half starving him. Before long, Huck began to wonder why he had ever liked living with the Widow. With his father, he could smoke and swear all he wanted, and his life would have been pleasant if it had not been for the beatings. One night, Huck sneaked away, leaving a bloody trail from a pig he had killed in the woods. Huck wanted everyone to believe he was dead. He climbed into a boat and went to Jackson's Island to hide until all the excitement had blown over.

After three days of freedom, Huck wandered to another part of the island, and there he discovered Jim, Miss Watson's black slave. Jim told Huck that he had run off because he had overheard Miss Watson planning to sell him down south for eight hundred dollars. Huck swore he would not report Jim. The two stayed on the island many days, Jim giving Huck an education in primitive superstition. One night, Huck rowed back to the mainland. Disguised as a girl, he called on a house near the shore. There he learned that his father had disappeared shortly after the townspeople had decided that Huck had been murdered. Since Jim's disappearance had occurred just after Huck's alleged death, there was now a three-hundred-dollar reward posted for Jim's capture, as most people believed that Jim had killed Huck.

Fearing that Jackson's Island would be searched, Huck hurried back to Jim, and the two headed down the Mississippi. They planned to leave the raft at Cairo and then go on a steamboat up the Ohio into free territory. Jim told Huck that he would work hard in the North and then buy his wife and children from their masters in the South. Helping a runaway slave bothered Huck's conscience, but he reasoned that it would bother him more if he betrayed such a good friend as Jim. One night, as they were drifting down the river on their raft, a large boat loomed before them, and Huck and Jim, knowing that the raft would be smashed under the hull of the ship, jumped into the water. Huck swam safely to shore, but Jim disappeared.

Huck found a home with a friendly family named Grangerford. The Grangerfords were feuding with the Shepherdsons, another family living nearby. The Grangerfords left Huck mostly to himself and gave him a young slave to wait on him. One day, the slave asked him to come to the woods to see some snakes. Following the boy, Huck came across Jim, who had been hiding in the woods waiting for an opportunity to send for Huck. Jim had repaired the broken raft. That night, one of the Grangerford daughters eloped with a young Shepherdson, and the feud broke out once more. Huck and Jim ran away during the shooting and set off down the river.

Shortly afterward, Jim and Huck met two men who pretended they were royalty and made all sorts of nonsensical demands on Huck and Jim. Huck was not taken in, but he reasoned that it would do no harm to humor the two men to prevent quarreling. The Duke and the King were clever schemers. In one of the small river towns, they staged a fake show which lasted long enough to net them a few hundred dollars. Then they ran off before the angered townspeople could catch them.

The Duke and the King overheard some people talking about the death of Peter Wilks, who had left considerable property and some cash to his three daughters. Wilks's two brothers, whom no one in the town had ever seen, were living in England. The King and the Duke went to the three daughters, Mary Jane, Susan, and Joanna, and presented themselves as the two uncles. They took a few thousand dollars of the inheritance and then put up the property for auction and sold the slaves. This high-handed deed caused great grief to the girls, and Huck could not bear to see them so unhappy. He decided to expose the two frauds, but he wanted to ensure Jim's safety first. Jim had been hiding in the woods waiting for his companions to return to him. Employing a series of lies, subterfuges, and maneuverings that were worthy of his ingenious mind, Huck exposed the Duke and King. Huck fled back to Jim, and the two escaped on their raft. Just as Jim and Huck thought they were on their way and well rid of their former companions, the Duke and King came rowing down the river toward them.

The whole party set out again with their royal plots to hoodwink the public. In one town where they landed, Jim was captured, and Huck learned that the Duke had turned him in for the reward. Huck had quite a tussle with his conscience. He knew that he ought to help return a slave to the rightful owner, but, on the other hand, he thought of all the fine times he and Jim had had together

and how loyal a friend Jim had been. Finally, Huck decided that he would help Jim to escape.

Learning that Mr. Phelps was holding Jim, he headed for the Phelps farm. There, Mrs. Phelps ran up and hugged him, mistaking him for the nephew whom she had been expecting to come for a visit. Huck wondered how he could keep Mrs. Phelps from learning that he was not her nephew. Then to his relief, he learned they had mistaken him for Tom Sawyer. Huck rather liked being Tom for a while, and he was able to tell the Phelps all about Tom's Aunt Polly and Sid, Tom's half brother, and Mary, Tom's cousin. Huck was feeling proud of himself for keeping up the deception. When Tom Sawyer really did arrive, he told his aunt that he was Sid.

At the first opportunity, Huck told Tom about Jim's capture. To his surprise, Tom offered to help him set Jim free. Huck could not believe that Tom would be a slave stealer, but he kept his feelings to himself. Huck had intended merely to wait until there was a dark night and then break the padlock on the door of the shack where Jim was kept; but Tom said the rescue had to be done according to the books, and he laid out a most complicated plan with all kinds of storybook ramifications. It took fully three weeks of plotting, stealing, and deceit to let Jim out of the shack. Then the scheme failed. A chase began after Jim escaped, and Tom was shot in the leg. After Jim had been recaptured, Tom was brought back to Aunt Sally's house to recover from his wound. Then Tom revealed the fact that Miss Watson had died, giving Jim his freedom in her will. Huck was greatly relieved to learn that Tom was not really a slave stealer after all.

To complicate matters still more, Tom's Aunt Polly arrived. She quickly set straight the identities of the two boys. Jim was given his freedom, and Tom gave him forty dollars. Tom told Huck that his money was still safely in the hands of Judge Thatcher, but Huck moaned that his father would likely be back to claim it again. Then Jim told Huck that his father was dead; Jim had seen him lying in an abandoned boat along the river.

Huck was ready to start out again because Aunt Sally said she thought she might adopt him and try to civilize him. Huck thought that he could not go through such a trial again after he had once tried to be civilized under the care of Widow Douglas.

Critical Evaluation

Little could Mark Twain have visualized in 1876 when he began a sequel to capitalize on the success of *The Adventures of Tom Sawyer* that *The Adventures of Huckleberry Finn* would evolve into his masterpiece and one of the most significant works in the development of the American novel. With an unerring instinct for American regional dialects, Twain elected to tell the story in Huck's own words. The skill with which Twain elevated the dialect of an illiterate village boy to the highest levels of

poetry established the spoken American idiom as a literary language and earned for Twain his reputation—proclaimed by Ernest Hemingway, William Faulkner, and others—as the father of the modern American novel. Twain also maintained an almost perfect fidelity to Huck's point of view in order to dramatize the conflict between Huck's own innate innocence and natural goodness and the dictates of a corrupt society.

As Huck's own story, the novel centers around several

major themes, including death and rebirth, freedom and bondage, the search for a father, the individual versus society, and the all-pervasive theme of brotherhood. Huck's character reflects a point in Mark Twain's development when he still believed man to be innately good but saw social forces as corrupting influences which replaced, with the dictates of a socially determined "conscience," man's intuitive sense of right and wrong. This theme is explicitly dramatized through Huck's conflict with his conscience over whether or not to turn Jim in as a runaway slave. Huck, on the one hand, accepts without question what he has been taught by church and society about slavery. In his own mind, as surely as in that of his Southern contemporaries, aiding an escaped slave was clearly wrong both legally and morally. Thus, Huck's battle with his conscience is a real trauma for him, and his decision to "go to Hell" rather than give Jim up is made with a certainty that such a fate awaits him for breaking one of society's laws. It is ironic that Huck's "sin" against the social establishment affirms the best that is possible to the individual.

Among the many forms of bondage that permeate the novel, ranging from the Widow's attempt to "civilize" Huck to the code of "honor," which causes Sherburn to murder Boggs and the law of the vendetta which absolutely governs the lives of the Grangerfords and Shepherdsons, slavery provides Twain his greatest metaphor for both bondage and institutionalized injustice and inhumanity. Written well after the termination of the Civil War, *The Adventures of Huckleberry Finn* is not an antislavery novel in the limited sense that *Uncle Tom's Cabin* is. Rather than simply attacking an institution already legally dead, Twain uses the idea of slavery as a metaphor for all social bondage and injustice. Thus, Jim's search for freedom, like Huck's own need to escape both the Widow and Pap Finn, is as much a metaphorical search for an ideal state of freedom as mere flight from slavery into free-state sanctuary. Thus, it is largely irrelevant that Twain has Huck and Jim running deeper into the South rather than north toward free soil. Freedom exists neither in the North nor the South but in the ideal and idyllic world of the raft and river.

The special world of raft and river is at the very heart of the novel. In contrast to the restrictive and oppressive social world of the shore, the raft is a veritable Eden where the evils of civilization are escaped. It is here that Jim and Huck can allow their natural bond of love to develop without regard for the question of race. It is here on the raft that Jim can become a surrogate father to Huck, and Huck can develop the depth of feeling for Jim which eventually leads to his decision to "go to Hell." But, while the developing relationship between Huck and Jim determines the basic shape of the novel, the river works in other structural ways as well. The picaresque form of the novel and its structural rhythm are based upon a series of episodes on shore, after each of which Huck and Jim return to the peaceful sanctuary of the raft. It is on shore that Huck encounters the worst excesses of which "the damned human race" is capable, but with each return to the raft comes a renewal of spiritual hope and idealism.

The two major thrusts of Twain's attack on the "civilized" world in *The Adventures of Huckleberry Finn* are against institutionalized religion and the romanticism which he believed characterized the South. The former is easily illustrated by the irony of the Widow's attempt to teach Huck religious principles while she persists in holding slaves. As with her snuff taking—which was all right because she did it herself—there seems to be no relationship between a fundamental sense of humanity and justice and her religion. Huck's practical morality makes him more "Christian" than the Widow, though he takes no interest in her lifeless principles. Southern romanticism, which Twain blamed for the fall of the South, is particularly allegorized by the sinking of the Walter Scott, but it is also inherent in such episodes as the feud where Twain shows the real horror of the sort of vendetta traditionally glamorized by romantic authors. In both cases, Twain is attacking the mindless acceptance of values which he believed kept the South in its dark ages.

Many critics have argued that the ending hopelessly flaws *The Adventures of Huckleberry Finn* by reducing its final quarter to literary burlesque. Others have argued that the ending is in perfect accord with Twain's themes. Nevertheless all agree that, flawed or not, the substance of Twain's masterpiece transcends the limits of literary formalism to explore those eternal verities upon which great literature rests. Through the adventures of an escaped slave and a runaway boy, both representatives of the ignorant and lowly of the earth, Twain affirms that true humanity is of men rather than institutions and that everyone can be aristocrats in the kingdom of the heart.

THE ADVENTURES OF TOM SAWYER

Type of work: Novel
Author: Mark Twain (Samuel L. Clemens, 1835–1910)
Type of plot: Adventure romance
Time of plot: Nineteenth century
Locale: St. Petersburg on the Mississippi River
First published: 1876

More than a book for boys, The Adventures of Tom Sawyer, *with its rich native humor and shrewd observations of human character, is an idyll of American village life, of that quieter age that had already vanished when Mark Twain re-created St. Petersburg from memories of his own boyhood.*

Principal Characters

Tom Sawyer, the mischievous ringleader of countless boyish adventures, who almost drives his long-suffering aunt to distraction with his pranks. If not fighting with other village urchins, the indolent boy plans numerous romantic and impractical escapades, many of which cost him hours of conscience-stricken torment. If he is not planning misdemeanors on the high seas, he is looking for buried treasure. Although unthinking, he is not really a bad boy; he is capable of generosity; occasionally, he surprises even himself with magnanimous acts.

Aunt Polly, Tom's warm, tender-hearted aunt. Sometimes this simple scripture-quoting old soul does not understand her mischievous charge. Even though she uses Tom's brother Sid as an example of a model youth, her frequent admonitions, emphasized by repeated thumps on the head with a thimble, fail to have a lasting effect on Tom. Believing herself endowed with subtle guile, she often tries to trap the boy into admitting his pranks. Rarely, however, is she successful. Tom usually manages to outwit her if Sid does not call her attention to certain inexactnesses in Tom's excuses.

Huckleberry Finn, one of Tom's best friends and a social pariah to the village mothers, but not to their sons. In the self-sufficient outcast the boys see everything they want to be. They long for his freedom to do as he pleases. Sometimes, to their regret, the other boys try to emulate their individualistic hero. Carefully, they mark the way he smokes strong tobacco in smelly old pipes and sleeps on empty hogsheads. Although he is not accepted by the mothers, Huck, even if he is vulgar, is a decent, honest lad. Happy only when he can sleep and eat where he pleases, Huck feels uncomfortable when the Widow Douglas takes him into her home.

Becky Thatcher, Tom's sweetheart. With her blue eyes, golden hair, and winsome smile, she captures his rather fickle heart at their first meeting. A little coquette, she, like Tom, alternately suffers from and enjoys their innocent love. Tom proves his generosity and love for her when he admits to the schoolteacher a crime he did not commit, thus astounding the rest of the class by his incredible folly.

Injun Joe, a half-breed. A murderous, sinister figure who lurks mysteriously in the background, the savagely vindictive killer stabs young Dr. Robinson and is subsequently exposed by Tom. In a cave Injun Joe, who had leaped from the court room window during Muff Potter's trial, almost has his revenge against the boy. Finally he pays for his many crimes when he is trapped in the cave and dies of starvation.

Muff Potter, a local ne'er-do-well and, along with Pap Finn, the town drunk. After helping Injun Joe and Dr. Robinson rob a grave, Muff Potter is accused of killing the doctor and almost pays with his worthless life. Had Tom not belatedly intervened, he would have been hanged and Injun Joe would have gone free. When the boys see a stray dog howling at the newly released Potter, asleep in a drunken stupor, they know that he is still doomed.

Sid, Tom's half brother and one of the model boys in the community. A quiet, rather calculating child, he exposes Tom's tricks whenever possible. However, when Tom is presumed drowned, Sid manages a few snuffles. To Tom, Sid's behavior is reprehensible; he keeps clean, goes to school regularly, and behaves well in church.

Mary, Tom's cousin. She is a sweet, lovable girl who often irritates him by insisting that he wash and dress carefully for church.

Judge Thatcher, Becky's pompous but kind-hearted father and the local celebrity.

Joe Harper, who runs away with Tom and Huck to Jackson's Island. Pretending to be pirates, they remain there for several days while the townspeople search for their bodies.

The Story

Tom Sawyer lived securely with the knowledge that his Aunt Polly loved him dearly. When she scolded him or whipped him, he knew that inside her breast lurked a hidden remorse. Often he deserved punishment he received, but there were times when he was the victim of his tale-bearing half brother, Sid. Tom's cousin, Mary, was kinder to him. Her worst duty toward him was to see to it that he washed and put on clean clothes, so that he would look respectable when Aunt Polly took Tom, Sid, and Mary to church on Sunday.

A new family had moved into the neighborhood. Investigating, Tom saw a pretty, blue-eyed girl with lacy pantalets. She was Becky Thatcher. Instantly the fervent love he had felt for Amy Lawrence fled from his faithless bosom to be replaced by devotion to the new girl he had just beheld.

Becky was in school the next day, sitting on the girls' side of the room with an empty seat beside her. Tom had come late to school that morning. When the schoolmaster asked Tom why he had been late, that empty seat beside Becky Thatcher caught Tom's eye. Recklessly he confessed he had stopped to talk with Huckleberry Finn, son of the town drunk. Huck wore castoff clothing, never attended school, smoked and fished as often as he pleased, and slept wherever he could. For associating with Huckleberry Finn, Tom was whipped by the schoolmaster and ordered to sit on the girls' side of the room. Amid the snickers of the entire class, he took the empty seat next to Becky Thatcher.

Tom first attracted Becky's attention by a series of drawings on his slate. At length, he wrote the words, "I love you," and Becky blushed. Tom urged her to meet him after school. Sitting with her on a fence, he explained to her the possibilities of an engagement between them. Innocently, she accepted his proposal, which Tom insisted must be sealed by a kiss. In coy resistance, she allowed Tom a brief chase before she yielded to his embrace. Tom's happiness was unbounded. When he mentioned his previous tie with Amy Lawrence, however, the brief romance ended. Becky left her affianced with a haughty shrug of her pretty shoulders.

That night, Tom heard Huck's whistle below his bedroom window. Sneaking out, Tom joined his friend, and the two went off to the cemetery, Huck dragging a dead cat behind him. They were about to try a new method for curing warts. The gloomy atmosphere of the burial ground filled the boys with apprehension, and their fears increased still more when they spied three figures stealing into the graveyard. They were Injun Joe, Muff Potter, and Doctor Robinson. Evidently they had come to rob a grave. When the two robbers had exhumed the body, they began to quarrel with the doctor about money, and in the quarrel, Potter was knocked out. Then Injun Joe took Potter's knife and killed the doctor. When Potter recovered from his blow, he thought he had killed Robinson, and Injun Joe allowed the poor old man to believe himself guilty.

Terrified, Tom and Huck slipped away from the scene they had just witnessed, afraid that if Injun Joe discovered them he would kill them too.

Tom brooded on what he and Huck had seen. Convinced that he was ill, Aunt Polly dosed him with Pain Killer and kept him in bed, but he did not seem to recover. Becky Thatcher had not come to school since she had broken Tom's heart. Rumor around town said that she was also ill. Coupled with this sad news was the fear of Injun Joe. When Becky finally returned to school, she cut Tom coldly. Feeling that there was nothing else for him to do, he decided to run away. He met Joe Harper and Huck Finn. Together they went to Jackson's Island and pretended to be pirates.

For a few days they stayed happily on the island and learned from Huck how to smoke and swear. One day they heard a boat on the river, firing a cannon over the water. Then the boys realized that the townspeople were searching for their bodies. This discovery put a new aspect on their adventure; the people at home thought they were dead. Gleeful, Tom could not resist the temptation to see how Aunt Polly had reacted to his death. He slipped back to the mainland one night and into his aunt's house, where Mrs. Harper and Aunt Polly were mourning the deaths of their mischievous but good-hearted children. When Tom returned to the island, he found Joe and Huck tired of their game and ready to go home. Tom revealed to them an attractive plan which they immediately decided to carry out.

With a heavy gloom overhanging the town, funeral services were held for the deceased Thomas Sawyer, Joseph Harper, and Huckleberry Finn. The minister pronounced a lengthy eulogy about the respective good characters of the unfortunate boys. When the funeral procession was about to start, Tom, Joe, and Huck marched down the aisle of the church into the arms of the startled mourners.

For a while, Tom was the hero of all the boys in the town. They whispered about him and eyed him with awe in the schoolyard. Becky, however, ignored him until the day she accidentally tore the schoolmaster's book. When the irate teacher demanded to know who had torn his book, Tom confessed. Becky's gratitude and forgiveness were his reward.

After Muff Potter had been put in jail for the murder of the doctor in the graveyard, Tom and Huck had sworn to each other they would never utter a word about what they had seen. Afraid Injun Joe would murder them for revenge, they furtively sneaked behind the prison and brought Muff food and other cheer; but Tom could not let an innocent man be condemned. At the trial, he appeared to tell what he had seen on the night of the murder. While

Tom spoke, Injun Joe, a witness at the trial, sprang through the window of the courtroom and escaped. For days Tom worried, convinced that Injun Joe would come back to murder him. As time went by and nothing happened, he gradually lost his fears. With Becky looking upon him as a hero, his world was filled with sunshine.

Huck and Tom decided to hunt for pirates' treasures. One night, ransacking an old abandoned house, they watched, unseen, while Injun Joe and a companion unearthed a chest of money buried under the floorboards of the house. The two frightened boys fled before they were discovered. The next day, they began a steady watch for Injun Joe and his accomplice, for Tom and Huck were bent on finding the lost treasure.

When Judge Thatcher gave a picnic for all the young people in town, Becky and Tom were supposed to spend the night with Mrs. Harper. One of the biggest excitements of the merrymaking came when the children went into a cave in the riverbank. The next day, Mrs. Thatcher and Aunt Polly learned that Tom and Becky were miss-

ing, for Mrs. Harper said they had not come to spend the night with her. Then everyone remembered that Tom and Becky had not been seen since the picnickers had left the cave. Meanwhile the two, having lost their bearings, were wandering in the cavern. To add to Tom's terror, he discovered that Injun Joe was also in the cave. Miraculously, after spending five days in the dismal cave, Tom found an exit that was five miles from the place where they had entered. Again he was a hero.

Injun Joe starved to death in the cave. After searchers had located his body, Tom and Huck went back into the cavern to look for the chest which they believed Injun Joe had hidden there. They found it and the twelve thousand dollars it contained.

Adopted shortly afterward by the Widow Douglas, Huck planned to retire with an income of a dollar a day for the rest of his life. He never would have stayed with the Widow or consented to learn her prim, tidy ways if Tom had not promised that he would form a pirates' gang and make Huck one of the bold buccaneers.

Critical Evaluation

Beginning his writing career as a frontier humorist and ending it as a bitter satirist, Mark Twain drew from his circus of experiences, as a child in a small Missouri town (who had little formal schooling), as a printer's apprentice, a journalist, a roving correspondent, a world traveler, silver prospector, Mississippi steamboat pilot, and lecturer. He was influenced, in turn, by Artemus Ward, Bret Harte, Augustus Baldwin Longstreet, and G. W. Harris. Beginning with the publication of his first short story, "The Celebrated Jumping Frog of Calaveras County," in 1865, and proceeding through his best novels—*Innocents Abroad* (1869); *Roughing It* (1872); *The Gilded Age* (1873), brilliant in concept but a failure in design and execution; *The Adventures of Tom Sawyer* (1876); *Life on the Mississippi* (1883); *The Adventures of Huckleberry Finn* (1885); *A Connecticut Yankee in King Arthur's Court* (1889); and *The American Claimant* (1892)—Twain developed a characteristic style which, though uneven in its productions, made him the most important and most representative nineteenth century American writer. His service as delightful entertainment to generations of American youngsters is equaled only by his influence on such twentieth century admirers as Gertrude Stein, William Faulkner, and Ernest Hemingway.

Twain's generally careful and conscientious style was both a development of the southwestern humor tradition of Longstreet and Harris and a departure from the conventions of nineteenth century literary gentility. It is characterized by the adroit use of exaggeration, stalwart irreverence, deadpan seriousness, droll cynicism, and pungent commentary on the human situation. All of this is masked in an uncomplicated, straightforward narrative

distinguished for its wholehearted introduction of the colloquial and vernacular into American fiction that was to have a profound impact on the development of American writing and also shape the world's view of America. Twain, according to Frank Baldanza, had a talent for "paring away the inessential and presenting the bare core of experience with devastating authenticity." The combination of childish rascality and innocence in his earlier writing gave way, in his later and posthumous works, to an ever darkening vision of man that left Twain bitter and disillusioned. This darker vision is hardly present in the three Tom Sawyer books (1876, 1894, 1896) and in his masterpiece, *The Adventures of Huckleberry Finn*.

Twain's lifelong fascination with boyhood play led to the creation of *The Adventures of Tom Sawyer*, a book of nostalgic recollections of his own lost youth that has been dismissed too lightly by some sober-sided academics as "amusing but thin stuff" and taken too analytically and seriously by others who seek in it the complexities—of carefully controlled viewpoint, multiple irony, and social social satire—found in *The Adventures of Huckleberry Finn*, begun in the year *The Adventures of Tom Sawyer* was published. Beyond noting that *The Adventures of Tom Sawyer* is a delicate balance of the romantic with the realistic, of humor and pathos, of innocence and evil, one must admit that the book defies analysis. In fact, Twain's opening statement in *The Adventures of Huckleberry Finn* is, ironically, more applicable to *The Adventures of Tom Sawyer*: "Persons attempting to find a motive in this narrative will be prosecuted; persons attempting to find a moral in it will be banished; persons attempting to find a plot in it will be shot." *The Adventures of Tom*

Sawyer is purely, simply, and happily "the history of a boy," or as Twain also called it, "simply a hymn, put into prose form to give it a worldly air." It should be read first and last for pleasure, first by children, then by adults.

For *The Adventures of Tom Sawyer* is also, as even Twain admitted, a book for those who have long since passed from boyhood: "It is *not* a boy's book at all. It will be read only by adults. It is written only for adults." Kenneth S. Lynn explicates the author's preface when he says that *The Adventures of Tom Sawyer* "confirms the profoundest wishes of the heart"; as does Christopher Morley, who calls the book "a panorama of happy memory" and who made a special visit to Hannibal because he wanted to see the town and house where Tom lived. During that visit, Morley and friends actually whitewashed Aunt Polly's fence. Certainly there can be no greater testimony to the effectiveness of a literary work than its readers' desire to reenact the exploits of its hero.

Tom is the archetypal all-American boy, defining in himself the very concept of American boyhood, as he passes with equal seriousness from one obsession to another: whistling, glory, spying, sympathy, flirtation, exploration, piracy, shame, fear—always displaying to the utmost the child's ability to concentrate his entire energies on one thing at a time (as when he puts the treasure hunt out of his mind in favor of Becky's picnic). Tom is contrasted to both Sid, the sanctimonious "good boy" informant who loses the reader's sympathies as immediately as Tom gains them, and to Huck. As opposed to Huck's self-reliant, unschooled, parentless existence, his love of profanity, his passive preference for being a follower, his abhorrence of civilization, Tom is shrewd in the ways of civilization, adventurous and a leader. He comes from the respectable world of Aunt Polly, with a literary mind, with a conscious romantic desire for experience and for the hero's part, an insatiable egotism which assists him in his ingenious schematizations of life to achieve his heroic aspirations—and a general love of fame, money, attention, and "glory." The relationship between the two boys may be compared to that between the romantic Don Quixote and the realist Sancho Panza. It was Twain's genius to understand that the games Quixote played out of "madness" were, in fact, those played by children with deadly seriousness. Lionel Trilling summarizes Twain's achievement in this book when he says that *The Adventures of Tom Sawyer* has the truth of honesty—what it says about things and feelings is never false and always both adequate and beautiful."

AENEID

Type of work: Poem
Author: Vergil (70–19 B.C.)
Type of plot: Heroic epic
Time of plot: The period immediately following the Trojan War
Locale: The Mediterranean region
First transcribed: Augustan manuscript

Written at the emperor's request as an endorsement of the newly established principate, this epic Latin poem celebrates the glory and heroism of the Roman race. In twelve books it traces the legendary founding of Rome, from the time of the Trojan War down to the establishment of the reign of Augustus Caesar.

Principal Characters

Aeneas (ē·nē′əs), the legendary progenitor of the Roman rulers whose son Ascanius, in fulfillment of a prophecy, founded Alba Longa and whose later descendants, Romulus and Remus, founded Rome. The son of Venus and Anchises, king of Dardanus, Aeneas is somewhat more diffident than the warrior heroes of other ancient epics, and he displays the Latin virtues of moderation and filial devotion. Only occasionally does he indulge in righteous indignation. Twice during the siege of Troy he is saved from death by the intervention of his divine mother. After the fall of the city he flees, carrying his aged father on his shoulders and leading his son Ascanius by the hand. In the confusion his devoted wife Creusa is lost. Aeneas searches for her in vain until her shade appears to tell him that he will find his destiny in a distant land. After long wandering, Aeneas and his small band of followers arrive in Italy. There he engages in warfare with the people of Latium and Rutuli. Eventually a truce is arranged and he marries Lavinia, the daughter of King Latinus. In her honor he founds the city of Lavinium.

Anchises (ăn·kī′sēz), king of Dardanus, King Priam's ally in the Trojan War, and the father of Aeneas. A man of great wisdom, he guides his son through many dangers during the wanderings of Aeneas and his followers from Troy to Sicily, where Anchises dies. From the underworld he foretells the greatness of Rome and commands Aeneas to end his travels at the place where he will eat his tables. Though he appears only as a shade within the poem, the old man figures as a sage patriarch in the recital of earlier events.

Ascanius (ăs·kā′nĭ·əs), sometimes called **Iulus,** the son of Aeneas. He fulfills Anchises' prophecy of the place to settle when he declares, while the Trojans are eating food heaped on large pieces of bread, that they are eating their tables. He takes part in one battle, in which he acquits himself with bravery befitting the future founder of a city and a kingdom.

Creusa (krē·ōō′sə), the wife of Aeneas. After she became separated from her husband and son during the flight from Troy, Aeneas searched for her despairingly until her shade appeared to tell him that she was lost to Troy forever and that in Italy an empire awaited him.

Dido (dī′dō), the queen of Carthage, whose love for Aeneas causes her death. When Jupiter sends Mercury, the messenger of the gods, to remind Aeneas of his mission, the hero prepares to continue his wanderings, in spite of the vows he has sworn and Dido's pathetic pleas that he remain with her. On the pretext of burning the love tokens he gave her, Dido prepares a funeral pyre and, lamenting her betrayal, kills herself after the departure of Aeneas and his band. Considered one of the most wronged women in all literature, Dido has beauty, charm, and character, though the latter she sacrifices to the whims of Venus.

Anna (ăn′ə), Queen Dido's sister and confidante.

Latinus (lətī′nəs), king of Latium. Because the oracles have foretold that a stranger will appear, marry his daughter, and rule his kingdom, Latinus befriends Aeneas and promises him the hand of Lavinia, the royal princess, in marriage. The prophecy is not immediately fulfilled, however, for Juno, the enemy of Aeneas, sends the Fury Alecto to turn Amata, the wife of Latinus, against Aeneas. Amata finds a confederate in Turnus, the leader of the Rutulians, her choice as a husband for Lavinia. Bewildered and grieved by this dissension, Latinus goes into retirement and Turnus takes command of the Latiums and Rutulians in the war with the Trojans and their allies.

Lavinia (lə·vĭ′nĭ·ə), the beautiful young daughter of King Latinus and his wife Amata. Loved by Turnus but betrothed to Aeneas, she becomes the prize for which the leaders contend in a bloody tribal war. She becomes the bride of Aeneas after the hero has killed Turnus in single combat and peace has been restored.

Turnus (tûr′nəs), the leader of the Rutulians and the enemy of Aeneas. A giant of a man, the favorite of Queen Amata for the hand of Lavinia, Turnus is a braggart warrior who makes good his boasts. Aided by Juno, he is almost successful in defeating the Trojan warriors led by Aeneas. When Turnus is decoyed away from the battle, Aeneas pursues and kills him. After the death of Turnus, according to the decision of the gods, Aeneas and his followers abandon Trojan ways and accept the customs of Latium.

Amata (ə·mä′tə), the wife of Latinus. Goaded by the Fury Alecto, she is moved to hate Aeneas and to plot against him.

Camilla (kə·mĭ′lə), a warrior maiden of the Rutulians brought up in the worship of Diana. She dies in battle, her exposed breast pierced by a Trojan spear, and her death incites Turnus to frenzied rage and even greater efforts against the warriors of Aeneas.

Aruns (ă′rəns), the slayer of Camilla.

Opis (ō′pĭs), the nymph charged by Diana to look over Camilla and protect her. Opis kills Aruns to avenge the death of the warrior maiden.

Evander (ə·văn′dĕr), the leader of an Arcadian colony and the ruler of the city of Pallanteum, built on the site of later Rome. In a dream, Tiber, the stream-god, directs Aeneas to seek the help of Evander in the coming battle with the Latium and Rutulian forces under Turnus. The Arcadian leader welcomes Aeneas to his city and sends a band of warriors, under the leadership of his son Pallas, to aid the Trojans.

Pallas (păl′əs), the son of Evander. During a hard-fought battle, Pallas, while trying to rally his followers, meets Turnus in single combat and is killed by the Rutulian. His death causes great grief among the Trojans, and Evander is heartbroken. In the conflict between Aeneas and Turnus, Aeneas is about to spare his enemy's life when he sees that Turnus is wearing a gold-studded sword belt stripped from the body of Pallas. Proclaiming that

Pallas really strikes the blow, Aeneas drives his sword through Turnus and kills the Rutulian leader.

Euryalus (ū·ri′ə·ləs) and **Nisus** (nī′səs), valiant young Trojan warriors. During the absence of Aeneas, who has gone to Pallanteum to ask Evander for aid, the two leave the beleaguered Trojan camp and steal into the tents of the besieging enemy. There they kill a number of the Latin soldiers and collect trophies of their exploits before they are surrounded and killed. The followers of Turnus parade the heads of the dead heroes before the Trojan camp.

Anius (ă′nĭ·əs), king of Ortygia, where Aeneas and his followers sail after the ghost of Polydorus has warned them not to settle in Thrace. At Ortygia the priest of Apollo prophesies that the descendants of Aeneas will rule over a world empire if the wanderers will return to the ancient motherland of Troy. Anchises mistakenly declares that the Trojans had come from Crete.

Celaeno (sə·lē′nō), Queen of the Harpies. When the Trojans land in the Strophades, they unknowingly offend her and she threatens them with famine.

Acestes (ə·sĕs′tēz), the son of a Trojan maiden and a river-god. He rules over that part of Sicily where Aeneas and his followers go ashore to hold funeral games in observance of Anchises' death. Aeneas awards Acestes first prize in the archery contest because he is "the favorite of the gods."

Nautes (nô′tēz), the wisest of the Trojan band. He advises Aeneas to leave the aged and infirm behind with Acestes when the Trojans continue their wanderings.

Palinurus (pă·lĭ·nōō′rəs), the helmsman drowned shortly after the Trojans sail away from the kingdom of Acestes. Venus has offered his life as a sacrifice if Neptune will grant safe convoy to her son and his followers.

The Story

Aeneas, driven by a storm to the shores of Libya, was welcomed gladly by the people of Carthage. Because Carthage was the favorite city of Juno, divine enemy of Aeneas, Venus had Cupid take the form of Ascanius, son of Aeneas, so that the young god of love might warm the heart of proud Dido and Aeneas would come to no harm in her land. At the close of a welcoming feast Aeneas was prevailed upon to recount his adventures.

He described the fall of his native Troy at the hands of the Greeks after a ten-year siege, telling how the armed Greeks had entered the city in the belly of a great wooden horse and how the Trojans had fled from their burning city, among them Aeneas with his father Anchises and young Ascanius. Not long afterward, Anchises had advised setting sail for distant lands. Blown by varying winds, the Trojans had at length reached Buthrotum, where had been foretold a long and arduous journey before Aeneas would reach Italy. Having set sail once more, they had

reached Sicily. There Anchises, who had been his son's sage counselor, had died and had been buried. Forced to leave Sicily, Aeneas had been blown by stormy winds to the coast of Libya. Here he ended his tale, and Dido, influenced by Cupid disguised as Ascanius, felt pity and admiration for the Trojan hero.

The next day Dido continued her entertainment for Aeneas. During a royal hunt a great storm drove Dido and Aeneas to the same cave for refuge. There they succumbed to the passion of love. Aeneas spent the winter in Carthage and enjoyed the devotion of the queen. But in the spring he felt the need to continue his destined course. When he set sail, the sorrowing Dido killed herself. The light of her funeral pyre was seen far out at sea.

Again on the shores of Sicily, Aeneas bade his men refresh themselves with food, drink, and games. First of all there was a boat race in which Cloanthus was the victor. The second event was a foot race, won by Euryalus. Entellus engaged Dares in a boxing match, which Aeneas stopped before the obviously superior Entellus achieved a knockout. The final contest was with bow and arrow. Eurytion and Acestes made spectacular showings and to each was awarded a handsome prize. Following the contests, Ascanius and the other young boys rode out to engage in war games. Meanwhile, the women were grieving the lost guidance of Anchises, and at the instigation of Juno set fire to the ships. Aeneas, sustained by the gods, bade his people repair the damage. Once more the Trojans set sail.

Finally, they reached the shores of Italy, at Cumae, famous for its sibyl. The Sibyl granted Aeneas the privilege of visiting his father in the underworld. After due sacrifice, the two of them began their descent into Hades. At length they reached the river Styx and persuaded the boatman Charon to row them across. Aeneas saw the spirits of many people he had known in life, including the ill-fated Dido. Then they came to the beginning of a forked road. One path led to the regions of the damned; the other led to the land of the blessed. Following this latter road, they came at last to Anchises, who showed Aeneas in marvelous fashion all the future history of Rome, and commanded him to found his kingdom at the place where he would eat his tables. On his return to the upper regions Aeneas revisited his men and proceeded to his own abode.

Again the Trojans set sail up the coast of Italy, to the ancient state of Latium, ruled over by Latinus. On the shore they prepared a meal, laying bread under their meat. As they were eating, Ascanius jokingly observed that in eating their bread they were eating their tables. This remark told Aeneas that here was the place Anchises had foretold. Next day the Trojans came to the city of King Latinus on the Tiber. Latinus had been warned by an oracle not to give his daughter Lavinia in marriage to any native man, but to wait for an alien, who would come to establish a great people. He welcomed Aeneas as that man of destiny.

A Latin hero, Turnus, became jealous of the favor Latinus showed Aeneas, and stirred up revolt among the people. Juno, hating Aeneas, aided Turnus. One day Ascanius killed a stag, not knowing that it was the tame favorite of a native family. There grew from the incident such a feud that Latinus shut himself up in his house and ceased to control his subjects. Meanwhile Aeneas made preparations for battle with the Latins under Turnus.

In a dream he was advised to seek the help of Evander, whose kingdom on the Seven Hills would become the site of mighty Rome. Evander agreed to join forces with Aeneas against the armies of Turnus and to enlist troops from nearby territories as well. Now Venus presented Aeneas with a fabulous shield made by Vulcan, for she feared for the safety of her son.

When Turnus learned that Aeneas was with Evander, he and his troops besieged the Trojan camp. One night Nisus and Euryalus, two Trojan youths, entered the camp of the sleeping Latins and slaughtered a great many of them before they were discovered and put to death. The enraged Latins advanced on the Trojans with fire and sword and forced them into open battle. When the Trojans seemed about to beat back their attackers, Turnus entered the fray and put them to flight. But the thought of Aeneas inspired the Trojans to such bravery that they drove Turnus into the river.

Aeneas, warned in a dream of this battle, returned and landed with his allies on the shore near the battlefield, where he encountered Turnus and his armies. Evander's troops were being routed when Pallas, Evander's beloved son, began to urge them on and himself rushed into the fight, killing many of the enemy before he was slain in combat with Turnus. Aeneas sought to take the life of Turnus, who escaped through the intervention of Juno.

Aeneas decreed that the body of Pallas should be sent back to his father with appropriate pomp during a twelve-day truce. The gods had watched the conflict from afar; now Juno relented at Jupiter's command, but insisted that the Trojans must take the Latin speech and garb before their city could rule the world.

Turnus led his band of followers against Aeneas in spite of a treaty made by Latinus. An arrow from an unknown source wounded Aeneas, but his wound was miraculously healed. The Trojan hero reentered the battle, was again wounded, but was able to engage Turnus in personal combat and strike him down. Aeneas killed his enemy in the name of Pallas and sacrificed his body to the shade of his dead ally. No longer opposed by Turnus, Aeneas was now free to marry Lavinia and establish his long-promised new nation. This was Rome, the mistress of the ancient world.

Critical Evaluation

Publius Vergilius Maro, better known as Vergil, was the greatest poet Rome produced. His finest work, the *Aeneid*, became the national epic and, when Rome collapsed, it survived to become the most influential book Rome contributed to Western culture. Dante drew direct inspiration from book 6 for *The Divine Comedy*, allowing the spirit of Vergil to guide him through the Inferno and up the heights of Purgatory. The work has been the cornerstone of liberal education from the Christian Middle Ages to the late nineteenth century. Even today it is still studied in universities and read for pleasure by a literate public.

Vergil himself was a modest, retiring man who preferred the seclusion of his country estate to life in the bustling metropolis of Rome. However, he was much liked and esteemed by important people, including the poet Horace and the Emperor Augustus. He won the patronage of the great, secured the wealth and leisure necessary to write, composed three supreme poems— the *Georgics*, the *Eclogues*, and the *Aeneid*—and died revered and honored. In his lifetime he saw the closing years of the Civil War that destroyed the Roman Republic, and the establishment of the Roman Empire under Augustus. To celebrate the *Pax Romana* and the leadership of Augustus, Vergil wrote the *Aeneid*, his patriotic epic dealing with the mythical Roman past.

According to legend, the Trojan hero Aeneas came to Italy after escaping the fall of Troy and became the ancestor of the Romans through his descendant, Romulus. Vergil took this material and, borrowing his structure from Homer, fashioned an epic of it. The first part of the poem, dealing with Aeneas' wanderings, resembles the *Odyssey* in form and content; while the second half, which treats Aeneas' war in Latium and its surroundings, imitates in some ways the *Iliad*. Certain poetic devices, such as the repeated epithet, are taken from Homer, as well as the way the gods interfere on behalf of their favorites. And yet the *Aeneid* is wholly original in concept, possessing a unity of its own.

The originality lies in its presentation of Aeneas, a hero who struggles and fights, not for booty, personal fame, or any existing country, but for a civilization that will exist in the distant future, that of Rome and Augustus. Time and again he sacrifices his personal comforts, leaving home after home because of the prodding of his inner sense of destiny. He knows that he is to be the founder of a new nation, but the details are revealed to him only gradually in the course of his journeying. Chronologically, the pattern is one of revelation and sacrifice, and each new revelation about his destiny imposes a greater burden of responsibility on him. The final revelation—when Aeneas descends with the Sibyl into the Cavern of Death and is shown the coming glory of Rome by his father, Anchises—prepares him spiritually and physically for the greatest fight of his life. And, finally, he is something greater than a man. In fulfilling his grand Fate he becomes a monument, an unstoppable force, an instrument of the gods, like the Roman Empire itself as Vergil visualized it.

When the poem opens and Aeneas and his men are shipwrecked at Carthage, the hero already knows two things: that he has an important mission to accomplish and that his future home lies on the western coast of Italy. This knowledge ensures, on his part, a limited commitment to Dido, whereas she falls completely in love with him, giving herself freely even though it ruins her as a woman and a queen when Aeneas is ordered by Jupiter

to sail on to Italy. In the coldness of his parting the founder of Rome draws upon himself all the wrath of Dido, the founder of Carthage, which points forward to the Punic Wars between those cities.

However, Aeneas is not hardhearted. He feels pity for those who are trying to prevent him from accomplishing his aim—Dido, Lausus the son of Mezentius, and even Turnus. The entire epic is weighted with the sadness of mortality. Aeneas' sense of destiny gives him courage, fortitude, patience, determination, and strength; yet it also makes him humorless, overbearing, and relentless. Still, without that inner conviction in the future destiny of his line and of his fellow Trojans, he would be nothing. Pity is the most that a person who knows he is doing right can feel for those who oppose him. Aeneas has a noble character, though somewhat inhuman, and he seems to embody the best traits of the Roman people.

The crux of the *Aeneid* comes, as Dante rightly perceived, in book 6, where Aeneas enters the realm of Death to gain enlightenment about his future. From the fall of Troy, where the ghost of Hector warns Aeneas, to this point, the dead are associated with revelation. And here Aeneas must purify himself ritually, enter the Cavern of Death, brave all the terrors of Hell, meet dead comrades, and finally, with a rite, enter the realms of the Blest to learn the truth about himself and his fate. Like Dante's Hell, Vergil's has various places assigned for various acts, sins, and crimes, but punishment there purges the soul to prepare it for the Elysium Fields, from which it may reincarnate.

In this section, Vergil delineates his view of the meaning of life and death. There is a Great Soul that gave birth to all living spirits, which incarnated themselves in flesh as assorted creatures, including man. The desires of these spirits hindered them from living up to their true purpose in bodily form, so that they must be cleansed after death, only to take on flesh again until they learn their rightful end and achieve it. Thus, death purifies and life tests one on the long road to perfection. This outlook—a mixture of Pythagorean reincarnation, Stoic pantheism, and Platonic mysticism—gives credence to everything Anchises shows Aeneas about his illustrious descendants and the rising power of Rome. Aeneas sees the souls of the future waiting their turn and he knows how much responsibility he really bears. Anchises' judgment of Aeneas is a fitting comment on Rome itself:

> "But yours, my Roman, is the gift of government,
> That is your bent—to impose upon the nations
> The code of peace; to be clement to conquered,
> But utterly to crush the intransigent!"

In those lines Vergil summed up the particular genius of Rome, together with its greatness and its terrors.

THE AGE OF REASON

Type of work: Theological study
Author: Thomas Paine (1737–1809)
First published: Part I, 1794; Part II, 1796

Thomas Paine earned lasting fame as one of history's most powerful and persuasive writers. Born in England as the son of an artisan, largely self-educated, he wrote robust, plain, emotionally intense English that crystallized thought and galvanized into action the common people of America, Great Britain, and France. Paine, a young English immigrant sponsored by Benjamin Franklin, became beloved in his adopted country after he wrote *Common Sense* (1776), an impelling force in persuading Americans to break their remaining ties with England. His *Crisis* papers, written during the American Revolution, buoyed American spirits, and his *The Rights of Man* (1791–1792), pleading for natural rights and republican principles, won for him admirers throughout the Western world.

Paine placed before the common people the Enlightenment ideas of intellectual circles. He possessed an uncanny ability to translate the abstractions of the well-educated elite into living ideas that moved the masses. He believed that just as Sir Isaac Newton revealed the natural laws governing the universe, he and others could use reason to uncover the natural rights of individuals, republican principles in politics, or the laws of the marketplace.

While millions of people responded positively to Paine's early writings calling for independence and individual liberty, *The Age of Reason* made him a hated and reviled figure. The once-beloved advocate of humane and gentle treatment of all God's creatures was now presented as a drunkard and moral degenerate—a "filthy little atheist," in the words of Theodore Roosevelt, almost a century after Paine's death.

Although thousands of ministers denounced Paine as an atheist, he clearly stated on the first page of *The Age of Reason* that "I believe in one God, and no more; and I hope for happiness beyond this life." He described his moral principles, those taught by many religious figures: "I believe in the equality of man; and I believe that religious duties consist in doing justice, loving mercy, and endeavoring to make our fellow-creatures happy."

Paine wrote *The Age of Reason* in 1793 in Paris during the French Revolution, which he had promoted and defended. Deeply troubled by the cruel excesses of a minority of revolutionaries, expecting arrest any day, he had seen reason overthrown and monarchy replaced with new despots. Similarly, in religion he saw the spread of atheism as a by-product of attacks on the established church. *The Age of Reason* was a blow against institutionalized religion on the one hand and an antidote to what Paine regarded as the poison of atheism on the other. As his fellow revolutionaries executed the French king and abolished the established church, Paine cautioned them not to dethrone reason, "lest in the general wreck of superstition, of false systems of government and false theology, we lose sight of morality, of humanity and of the theology that is true."

Paine outraged many former admirers not because he rejected God, which he did not do, but because he attacked the Christian church: "I do not believe in the creed professed . . . by any church that I know of. My own mind is my own church." Anticipating Karl Marx, Paine wrote: "All national institutions of churches . . . appear to me no other than human inventions, set up to terrify and enslave mankind, and monopolize power and profit." Government officials propped up the church for the benefit of greedy priests, and in return the church lent legitimacy to government, Paine said. He understood the danger of excess as the church-state edifice toppled, but he believed that reason would free humanity from the despotism of the clerics and protect it from the abyss of amoral anarchism.

Before Paine could present a theology appropriate to an age of reason, he had to strip away the false doctrine of Christianity. All existing religions claimed to be based on revelations from gods, but Paine argued that revelations could only occur between God and those to whom he directly revealed himself. After that, revelations, in the unlikely event that they had occurred, became mere hearsay and had been distorted to protect the position of the clerics.

The Bible was composed of hearsay, not revelation, Paine argued; using what would later be called biblical criticism, he found that many of the Old Testament stories were mere reworkings of ancient pagan tales. God's victory over Satan and the latter's confinement in the pit of fire reminded him of the tale of Jupiter's defeating a giant and confining him under Mount Etna, where he still belches fire. Christian mythologists did not settle the Satan problem so easily, Paine asserted:

> . . . they could not do without him; and after being at the trouble of making him, they bribed him to stay. They promised him ALL the Jews, ALL the Turks by anticipation, nine-tenths of the world beside, and Mahomet into the bargain.

Christian mythologists deified Satan, Paine charged, even

forcing God to capitulate to him by surrendering His Son on the cross.

The Old Testament degraded God by having Him order His people to engage in treachery, murder, and genocide, Paine wrote. It was full of confused chronology and fragments of non-Jewish writing. The books ascribed to Moses, Joshua, Samuel, and others could not have been written by them. That which was not absurd was an obscene history of wickedness. The Book of Job was interesting but was not Hebrew in origin; some of the Psalms properly exalted God but were not superior to other such writings before or since; the bits of wisdom in the Proverbs were not any wiser than those of Ben Franklin.

Paine then turned to the New Testament. It was not as full of brutality and blood as the Old Testament, but it was even more absurd, he believed. The Gospels of Matthew, Mark, Luke, and John were not revelations but anecdotal hearsay written by unknown figures long after the events they described. The biblical story of Jesus, a modest and humane man whose message was distorted by church mythologists, was an absurdity. The story of his birth was an obscene tale of the violation of a virgin by a ghost. Jesus' death, God dying on a cross, was even more ridiculous: "His historians, having brought him into the world in a supernatural manner, were obliged to take him out again in the same manner, or the first part of the story must have fallen to the ground."

Jesus was a good man, a reformer and revolutionist, who was killed because he posed a threat to greedy priests and power-hungry Romans. Subsequently, the church built myths about him to support and justify a priestly religion of pomp and revenue. It created a false concept of redemption to obscure the fact that all humans at all times occupy the same relation to God, needing no mediation by churches or ministers. The doctrine of redemption served the clerics by turning humans into outcasts living in a dunghill and needing the church to regain the kingdom. The Bible, books of hearsay written centuries after the events they described, was shaped to fit the needs of the church. Church leaders settled by majority vote what would make up the Bible. If the vote had been different, Paine said, then Christian belief would be different.

Reason taught a very clear lesson to Paine. All human languages were ambiguous, easily miscopied, or even forged. The word of God would never have been revealed in a human language, a changeable and varying vehicle. The word of God would be revealed in a way that could never be changed or distorted or misunderstood, and it would be revealed to all people in every generation.

"The Word of God IS THE CREATION WE BEHOLD and it is in *this word*, which no human invention can counterfeit or alter, that God speaketh universally to man." In God's creation of the earth and all the universe, we see His wisdom, power, munificence, and mercy, Paine said. The absurdities and creations of the Bible paled beside the workings of the universe in which God placed

humanity. The Bible was so inferior to the glory and power of God revealed in His creation that the church had to suppress philosophy and science that would reveal the true theology revealed in the creation. Christianity so offended reason that in order to survive the church had to suppress freedom of thought.

There was a religious creed suitable for an age of reason, Paine believed, the deistic creed of Ben Franklin and Thomas Jefferson, as well as Voltaire and other European Enlightenment leaders. Paine made his deistic beliefs clear:

> The only idea man can affix to the name of God is that of a *first cause*, the cause of all things. And incomprehensible and difficult as it is for a man to conceive what a first cause is, he arrives at the belief of it from the tenfold greater difficulty of disbelieving it.

People did not need the church and ministers to have access to the mind of God: "It is only by the exercise of reason that man can discover God." The Bible served only to diminish God and to make Him appear cruel and angry.

So Paine ended the first part of *The Age of Reason*. He did not have the leisure to worry about its reception. Maximilien Robespierre and his radical comrades imprisoned Paine and kept him locked up through most of 1794. They probably did not intend to execute him but wanted to keep his pen from being turned against their excesses. He nearly died of illness before James Monroe helped free him. As Paine recovered, he read attacks on the first part of *The Age of Reason*. He had not had access to a Bible in anticlerical France when he wrote the first part. Now he had a Bible at hand and, he wrote, found that it was worse than he remembered.

Paine did not develop new themes in part 2 of *The Age of Reason* but provided more details of biblical criticism to support his argument that Moses, Joshua, Samuel, and others could not have written the books ascribed to them, thus removing any authority that they had as revelation. Paine again hammered at the theme that the Bible reduced God and His holy disciples to barbaric evildoers. Only the Book of Job could be read without indignation and disgust, he said. The New Testament began with the debauchery of Mary and ended with the absurdity of men placing God on a cross. The heart of the New Testament was the often-conflicting Gospels of Matthew, Mark, Luke, and John, each of whom seemed to have known a different Jesus.

Paine reiterated his central message. God's glory and benevolence were not found in the Bible or in churches or in ministers' sermons. Humans did not need mediating institutions to reach God. All people could find God's revelation by looking at his creation, using reason.

Although *The Age of Reason* was a book of profound morality and ethics and a paean to the glories of God, it gained for Paine undying hatred throughout the Christian world. His message was derived from the thought of Isaac Newton and René Descartes. He did not add anything to the deistic thought of Voltaire, Franklin, and Jefferson. Paine's unforgivable sin was to take deistic theology out of the gentlefolk's drawing rooms and to place it in the plain language of the people. His book horrified many of the common people by its seeming blasphemy and frightened the elite by its threat of freeing the masses from religious control. *The Age of Reason* came at the close of the Enlightenment, as reason was being dethroned. A century would pass before Paine's message of political, religious, and economic freedom could again be clearly heard.

THE ALCHEMIST

Type of work: Drama
Author: Ben Jonson (1573?-1637)
Type of plot: Comedy of manners
Time of plot: Early seventeenth century
Locale: London
First presented: 1610

A masterpiece of plot construction, The Alchemist *marked the peak of Jonson's career. A delightful, entertaining satire on human greed, this play is free of the sermonizing that characterizes the dramatist's other work.*

Principal Characters

Subtle, the Alchemist, a moldy, disreputable cheat. Joining forces with Jeremy Butler and Dol Common, he uses his fund of scientific and pseudo-scientific jargon to fleece the gullible. He promises large returns from transmutation of metals, astrological prophecies, physical nostrums, or whatever seems most likely to entrap his victims. When the master of the house returns, he is forced to take flight without his gains.

Face (Jeremy Butler), Subtle's contact man, who furnishes his master's house as the Alchemist's headquarters. He is a resourceful, quick-witted improviser. Disguised as a rough, blunt captain, he entices victims to the house. When his master, Lovewit, returns home unexpectedly, he arranges a marriage between Lovewit and the Widow Pliant, thereby escaping punishment.

Dol Common, the third of the tricksters, common mistress of the other two. Her dominant personality keeps her quarrelsome cohorts in line. She can act various roles, such as an exotic lady or the Queen of the Fairies to carry out Subtle's various schemes. Along with Subtle she is forced to flee with the jeers of Face following her.

Sir Epicure Mammon, a fantastic voluptuary. He is a veritable fountain of lust and imagined luxury, and he seeks the philosopher's stone to help him to unbounded self-indulgence. When his investment is wiped out by the explosion of the Alchemist's furnace, planned and well-timed by Subtle, Sir Epicure confesses that he has been justly punished for his voluptuous mind.

Abel Drugger, a small-time tobacconist ambitious for commercial success. Engaged to the Widow Pliant, he brings her and her brother Kastril to the Alchemist. He is tricked out of not only his money but the widow.

Kastril, the angry boy, brother of the Widow Pliant. He has come up to London to learn to smoke and quarrel. Face uses him to get rid of the skeptic, Surly. He is much taken with old Lovewit, who quarrels well, and consents to his sister's marriage with him.

Pertinax Surly, a sour skeptic who prides himself on being too astute to be tricked. First coming to the Alchemist's as a friend of Sir Epicure, he returns disguised as a Spanish don, planning to save the Widow Pliant from Subtle and Face and to marry her. He is driven away by Kastril and loses the widow to Lovewit.

Tribulation Wholesome, an oily Puritan hypocrite from Amsterdam. Himself quite willing to compromise his conscience for profit, he has difficulty restraining his uncompromising companion, Deacon Ananias.

Ananias, a deacon, a hot-tempered zealot who considers even the word Christmas a Papist abomination. Quarrelsome at first, he finally agrees that counterfeiting is lawful if it is for the benefit of the faithful. Along with Tribulation he is driven away by Lovewit.

Dame Pliant, an easy-going, attractive young widow, affianced to Drugger, but perfectly willing to accept another husband. Subtle and Face both hope to marry her, but the latter decides that it is safer to hand her over to Lovewit, his master.

Lovewit, the master of the house who has left London because of the plague. His absence sets up the plot; his return resolves it. He drives away Subtle, Dol, and their victims, but forgives Jeremy Butler (Face) when he arranges a marriage between his master and the rich young widow, Dame Pliant.

The Story

Master Lovewit having left the city because of plague, his butler, Jeremy, known as Face to his friends of the underworld, invited Subtle, a swindler posing as an alchemist, and Dol Common, a prostitute, to join him in using the house as a base of operations for their rascally activities. Matters fared well for the three until a dispute arose between Face and Subtle over authority. Dol, seeing their money-making projects doomed if this strife continued, rebuked the two men and cajoled them back to their senses.

No sooner had Face and Subtle become reconciled than Dapper, a gullible lawyer's clerk given to gambling, called, by previous arrangement with Face, to learn from the eminent astrologer, Doctor Subtle, how to win at all games of chance. Dapper, in the hands of the two merciless rascals, was relieved of all his ready cash, in return for which Subtle predicted that Dapper would have good luck at the gaming tables. In order to gull Dapper further, Subtle told him to return later to confer with the Queen of Fairy, a mysterious benefactress who could promote Dapper's worldly success.

Abel Drugger, an ambitious young druggist who had been led on by Face, was the next victim to enter the house. To his delight, he learned from Subtle, who spoke in incomprehensible pharmaceutical and astrological jargon, that he would have a rich future.

Next arrived Sir Epicure Mammon, a greedy and lecherous knight, with his friend Pertinax Surly, a man versed in the ways of London confidence men. Having been promised the philosopher's stone by Subtle, Mammon had wild visions of transforming all of his possessions into gold and silver, but he was completely taken in by the duplicities of Subtle and Face. Subtle further aroused Mammon's greed by describing at length, in the pseudo-scientific gibberish of the alchemist-confidence man, the processes which led to his approximate achievement of the mythical philosopher's stone. Surly, quick to see what was afoot, scoffed at Subtle and at the folly of Mammon.

During the interview Mammon caught sight of Dol, who appeared inadvertently, and was fascinated. Thinking quickly, Face told Mammon that Dol was an aristocratic lady who, being mad, was under the care of Doctor Subtle but who in her moments of sanity was most affable. Before he left the house Mammon promised to send to the unprincipled Subtle certain of his household objects of base metal for the purpose of having them transmuted into gold.

The parade of victims continued. Elder Ananias of the Amsterdam community of extreme Protestants came to negotiate for his group with Subtle for the philosopher's stone. Subtle, with Face as his assistant, repeated his extravagant jargon to the impressionable Ananias, who, in his greed, declared that the brethren were impatient with the slowness of the experiment. Subtle, feigning professional indignation, frightened Ananias with a threat to put out forever his alchemist's fire.

Drugger reappeared to be duped further. Subtle and Face were delighted when he told them that a wealthy young widow had taken lodgings near his and that her brother, just come into an inheritance, had journeyed to London to learn how to quarrel in rakish fashion. The two knaves plotted eagerly to get brother and sister into their clutches.

Ananias returned with his pastor, Tribulation Whole-some. Both Puritans managed to wink at moral considerations as Subtle glowingly described the near completion of the philosopher's stone. Prepared to go to any ends to procure the stone, Ananias and Tribulation contracted to purchase Mammon's household articles, which, Subtle explained, he needed for the experiment; the proceeds of the sale would go toward the care of orphans for whom Subtle said he was responsible.

Subtle and Face also plotted to sell these same household articles to the young widow, who, having just moved to London, was probably in need of such items. In the meantime Face met in the streets a Spanish Don—Surly in clever disguise—who expressed a desire to confer with Subtle on matters of business and health.

Dapper returned to meet the Queen of Fairy. At the same time Drugger brought to the house Master Kastril, the angry young man who would learn to quarrel. Kastril was completely taken in. Subtle, promising to make him a perfect London gallant, arranged to have him instructed by Face, who posed as a city captain. Kastril was so pleased with his new acquaintances that he sent Drugger to bring his sister to the house.

Kastril having departed, Dol, Subtle, and Face relieved Dapper of all of his money in a ridiculous ritual in which Dapper was to see and talk to the Queen of Fairy. During the shameless proceedings Mammon knocked. Dapper, who had been blindfolded, was gagged and hastily put into a water closet at the rear of the house. Mammon entered and began to woo Dol, whom he believed to be a distracted aristocratic lady. Face and Subtle, in order to have the front part of the house clear for further swindles, shunted the amorous pair to another part of the house.

Young Kastril returned with his widowed sister, Dame Pliant; both were deeply impressed by Subtle's manner and by his rhetoric. When the Spanish Don arrived, Subtle escorted Kastril and Dame Pliant to inspect his laboratory. By that time both Subtle and Face were determined to wed Dame Pliant.

Face introduced the Spaniard to Dame Pliant, who, in spite of her objections to Spaniards in general, consented to walk in the garden with the Don.

Meanwhile, in another part of the house, Dol assumed madness. Subtle, discovering the distraught Mammon with her, declared that Mammon's moral laxity would surely delay completion of the philosopher's stone. Following a loud explosion, Face reported that the laboratory was a shambles. Mammon despondently left the house, and Subtle simulated a fainting spell.

In the garden Surly revealed his true identity to Dame Pliant and warned the young widow against the swindlers. When, as Surly, he confronted the two rogues, Face, in desperation, told Kastril that Surly was an impostor who was trying to steal Dame Pliant away. Drugger entered and, being Face's creature, insisted that he knew Surly to be a scoundrel. Then Ananias came to the house and all but wrecked Subtle's plot by talking indiscreetly of making counterfeit money. Unable to cope with the wily rascals, Surly departed, followed by Kastril.

Glad to be rid of his callers, Subtle placed Dame Pliant in Dol's care. But they were once more thrown into confusion when Lovewit, owner of the house, made an untimely appearance. Face, quickly reverting to his normal role of Jeremy, the butler, went to the door in an attempt to detain his master long enough to permit Subtle and Dol to escape.

Although warned by his butler that the house was infested, Lovewit suspected that something was amiss when Mammon and Surly returned to expose Subtle and Face. Kastril, Ananias, and Tribulation confirmed their account. Dapper, having managed to get rid of his gag, cried out inside the house. Deciding that honesty was the

only policy, Face confessed everything to his master and promised to provide him with a wealthy young widow as his wife, if Lovewit would have mercy on his servant.

In the house, meanwhile, Subtle concluded the gulling of Dapper and sent the young clerk on his way, filled with the belief that he would win at all games of chance. Subtle and Dol then tried to abscond with the threesome's loot, but Face, back in Lovewit's good graces, thwarted them in their attempt. They were forced to escape empty-handed by the back gate.

Lovewit won the hand of Dame Pliant and in his good humor forgave his crafty butler. When those who had been swindled demanded retribution, they were finally convinced that they had been mulcted as a result of their own selfishness and greed.

Critical Evaluation

For anyone interested in learning how to take in the gullible, Ben Jonson's *The Alchemist* is a fundamental text. "Cony-catching" was a popular practice in Elizabethan England, and Jonson, an intimate of London's jails, taverns, theaters, and places of even less repute, here reveals the technique on several of the most amusing and lucrative ploys. And his protagonist, it should be noted, gets off scot-free.

The complex and incongruous tone of life in London in the Elizabethan Age helped account for the widespread faith in astrology and alchemy and helped make them leading gimmicks. Commerce thrived, but people were not far from believing in the dragons slain by King Arthur's knights. Many believed also that the dawning age of science would discover a "Philosopher's Stone" which would transmute dross into gold. Jonson's London, the London of *The Alchemist*, was growing and glittering and slightly hysterical, and cozening was easy, widespread, and immensely successful.

The critical response to the play has been intriguing. Coleridge, presumably impressed by the play's adherence to the classical unities, praised it as having one of the most perfect plots in literature. Several modern commentators have contended that while *The Alchemist* does cleave to the classical ideals, it is not a proper comedy, it has no plot at all, and it consists merely of a series of linked incidents. Romantic and Victorian critics particularly, enchanted by Jonson's contemporary and diametric opposite, William Shakespeare, were put off by Jonson's classical forms, his satiric manner, and his coarseness. They also disliked his unemotional tone, controlled plots, and intellectual detachment. While *The Alchemist* lacks none of these features, they do not necessarily render it deficient.

The classical ideals are so well met in *The Alchemist* that the play is in its own way a small masterpiece. Jonson

observes unity of time in that the dramatic situation is enacted in the same amount of time that it would take in real life. Unity of place is maintained in that the scene, Lovewit's house in the Friars, is specific and limited. The discrete beginning, middle, and conclusion of the play provide for unity of action. The characters are types who behave consistently, doing nothing unexpected, and thus the ideal of decorum, the paramount classical precept, is met; Jonson's prostitute is bawdy, his churchmen sanctimonious.

Faithfulness to classical concepts, however, is not the only virtue of *The Alchemist*. A talented actor as well as a writer of poetry, masques, criticism, and tragic and comic plays, Jonson was a masterful manipulator of theatrical effects. The opening argument of *The Alchemist,* presented in antic verse, catapults the play headlong into a rollicking, boisterous, bawdy life of its own. The simple yet ingenious plot provides for the multiplicity of incident dear to the Renaissance heart; costume, disguise, and transmutation of identity are similarly exploited.

The internal development is more complex than some critics suggest. The characters are introduced in approximate order of both their social status and rapacity. As these advance, so does the degree of cozening inflicted by Face and Subtle, and this progression reinforces the cohesiveness of the play. Although the fates of the characters are not contingent, since all are frauds or dupes, they interact in complex and amusing ways. These interactions, which become so dense that eventually Face and Subtle have their victims cozening each other, engender organic unity and dramatic tension simultaneously. As the play advances, the number of characters on stage increases, the pace quickens, and the scenes grow shorter. The climax is predictable but impressive, the denouement tidy, and the entire proceeding animated by a genuine and hearty spirit.

Despite its qualifications as a well-wrought, clever, and entertaining play in the classical mode, *The Alchemist* owes much of its literary interest and charm to Jonson's rhetorical flourishes. The underworld slang and alchemical jargon used by the protagonists lend color and authenticity. Double entendres and simultaneous dialogue (which originated with Jonson) add to the effect. But most impressive, perhaps, is the way Subtle and Face use a debased eloquence in perpetrating their frauds. One of Subtle's elegant, highly rhetorical, pseudo-rational arguments, for example, seems unequivocally to establish the propensity of all metals to turn into gold. Surly's calm and earnest reasoning with Dame Pliant, on the other hand, seems but a pale counterfeit of Subtle's spirited equivocation.

The Alchemist dramatizes what might happen when moral order is suspended by plague in London. Lovewit, representing responsible society, jettisons civic responsibility and flees the city, leaving behind only knaves and fools. Although the reader is reminded early that order will eventually be restored, society in the hands of the unscrupulous degenerates into chaos. The servant supplants the master, science is overthrown by alchemy, reason is toppled by rhetoric, nature's secrets are transcended, and the moral order is subverted as churchmen become swindlers.

Jonson's vehicle, satire, was quite popular in Elizabethan England, and in *The Alchemist* its effect is intensified by the plague in the background. Jonson intended to be instructive, even if it meant instructing by ridicule. And the classicist in him wanted to restore to England some of the glory of Augustan Rome. To this end Jonson adopted Cicero's famous definition of tragedy: "a copy of life, a mirror of custom, a representation of truth." Accordingly, he anchors his play in contemporary London and reflects the speech, behavior, and attitudes of its citizens. The Renaissance saw a shift in emphasis from the world of the Church to the world of experience, but while Jonson set an extremely worldly stage, his morality was severe and almost medieval. His moral values, clear from the first scene on, are constantly reiterated as *The Alchemist* indicts vain and wishful thinking and directs the mind to the contemplation of virtue. It is a sign of Ben Jonson's genius that he does so both unequivocally and entertainingly.

ALICE'S ADVENTURES IN WONDERLAND

Type of work: Imaginative tale
Author: Lewis Carroll (Charles Lutwidge Dodgson, 1832–1898)
Type of plot: Fantasy
Time of plot: Victorian England
Locale: The dream world of an imaginative child
First published: 1865

Carroll's classic fantasy can be read on many levels and appreciated by diverse audiences: it is at once a biting social and political satire sufficiently complex to satisfy the most sophisticated adult, and a delightfully whimsical fairy tale to capture the fancy of the imaginative child.

Principal Characters

Alice, a curious, imaginative strong-willed, and honest young English girl. She falls asleep by the side of a stream in a meadow and dreams that she follows a White Rabbit down his hole. She has many adventures in a Wonderland peopled by all kinds of strange characters and animals.

The White Rabbit, anxious, aristocratic, dandified. Alice follows him down his hole, which leads to an enchanted house and garden. The White Rabbit is a Prime Minister of sorts in this Wonderland, for he has close contact with the royalty there and carries out their orders, although he does not institute policy.

The Queen of Hearts, the ill-tempered Queen of Wonderland. She constantly demands that everyone who crosses her to be beheaded. Fond of croquet, she orders Alice to take part in a game in which flamingos are used for mallets and hedgehogs for balls. She issues an order for Alice's execution at the end of the book, but this order is never carried out because Alice accuses the Queen and all her company of being only a pack of cards, an assertion that turns out to be true.

The King of Hearts, a timid, kindly man. Although he is completely under his wife's power because of her temper, he manages to pardon all her victims surreptitiously.

The Duchess, another member of royalty in Wonderland, a platitude-quoting, moralizing, ugly old woman who lives in a chaotic house. Deathly afraid of the Queen, she is ordered to be beheaded, but the sentence is never carried out.

The Cook, the Duchess' servant. She flavors everything with pepper, insults her mistress, and throws cooking pans at her.

The Cheshire Cat, the Duchess' grinning cat. Continually vanishing and reappearing, he is a great conversationalist, and he tells Alice much of the gossip in Wonderland.

The Duchess' Baby, a strange, howling, little infant. The baby turns into a pig when the Duchess entrusts it to Alice's care.

The Knave of Hearts, a timid, poetry-writing fellow accused of stealing some tarts that the Queen has made.

The March Hare, the rude host of a mad tea party to which Alice invites herself and then wishes that she had not.

The Mad Hatter, a riddle-making, blunt, outspoken guest at the tea party. He is a good friend of the March Hare, and at the party the two try to prove to Alice that she is stupid.

The Dormouse, another guest at the tea party. He is a sleepy creature, aroused long enough to recite for Alice and then pushed headfirst into the teapot.

The Gryphon, a mythical creature, half bird, half animal, who escorts Alice to the home of the Mock Turtle so that she may hear the recital of the Turtle's life story.

The Mock Turtle, an ever-sobbing animal. He recites his life's story to Alice and everyone else within earshot.

The Caterpillar, a hookah-smoking insect who perches on the top of a magic mushroom. Officious and easily offended, he tests Alice's intelligence with a series of ridiculous riddles.

Bill, The Lizard, an unfortunate fellow picked by the other animals to go down the chimney of the White Rabbit's house and try to force out Alice, who has assumed gigantic proportions after drinking a magic potion she found on the table.

The Mouse, who greets Alice in the pool of tears which she had made by crying while she was of gigantic size. Now of minute proportions, she is almost overwhelmed by the Mouse, a creature easily offended.

The Lorry, The Duck, The Dodo, The Eaglet, The Crab, and **The Baby Crab,** all creatures whom Alice meets in the pool of her tears and who swim around with her.

Father William and **His Son,** characters in a poem that Alice recites. The old man, a former athlete, can still balance an eel on his nose, much to the amazement of his curious and impertinent son. The poem is a parody of Robert Southey's "The Old Man's Comforts."

The Pigeon, a bird Alice meets after she has made

herself tall by eating part of the Caterpillar's mushroom.

The Fish Footman, the bearer of a note from the Queen inviting the Duchess to play croquet.

The Frog Footman, the impolite servant of the Duchess; his wig becomes entangled with that of the Fish Footman when the two bow in greeting each other.

The Puppy, a playful animal Alice meets while she is in her small state.

The Flamingo, the bird Alice uses for a croquet mallet in the game with the Queen.

The Hedgehog, the animal that acts as the ball in the croquet game.

Five, Two, and **Seven,** three quarrelsome gardeners of the Queen. When Alice meets them, they are painting red all the white roses in the garden to obliterate the mistake someone had made in ordering white ones.

Elsie, Lacie, and **Tillie,** three sisters in the Dormouse's story. They live at the bottom of a well and exist solely on treacle.

Dinah, Alice's pet cat in real life.

Alice's Sister, the wise older sister who is charmed by Alice's tales of her adventures in Wonderland.

The Story

Alice was quietly reading over her sister's shoulder when she saw a White Rabbit dash across the lawn and disappear into its hole. She jumped up to rush after him and found herself falling down the rabbit hole. At the bottom, she saw the White Rabbit hurrying along a corridor ahead of her and murmuring that he would be late. He disappeared around a corner, leaving Alice standing in front of several locked doors.

On a glass table, she found a tiny golden key that unlocked a little door hidden behind a curtain. The door opened upon a lovely miniature garden, but she could not get through the doorway because it was too small. She sadly replaced the key on the table. A little bottle mysteriously appeared. Alice drank the contents and immediately began to grow smaller, so much so that she could no longer reach the key on the table. Next, she ate a piece of cake she found nearby, and soon she began to grow to such enormous size that she could only squint through the door. In despair, she began to weep tears as big as raindrops. As she sat crying, the White Rabbit appeared, bewailing the fact that the Duchess would be angry if he kept her waiting.

The White Rabbit dropped his fan and gloves. Alice picked them up, and as she did so, she began to grow smaller. Again she rushed to the garden door, but she found it shut and the golden key once more on the table out of reach.

Then she fell into a pond of her own tears. Splashing along, she encountered a mouse who had stumbled into the pool. Alice tactlessly began a conversation about her cat Dinah, and the mouse became speechless with terror. Soon the pool of tears was filled with living creatures—birds and animals of all kinds. An old Dodo suggested that they run a Caucus Race to get dry. Having asked what a Caucus Race was, Alice was told that the best way to explain it was to do it, whereupon the animals ran themselves quite breathless and finally became dry.

Afterward, the mouse told a "Tail" to match its own appendage. Alice was asked to tell something, but the only thing she could think of was her cat Dinah. Fright-ened, the other creatures went away, and Alice was left alone.

The White Rabbit appeared once more, this time hunting for his gloves and fan. Catching sight of Alice, he sent her to his home to get him a fresh pair of gloves and another fan. In the Rabbit's house, she found the fan and gloves and also took a drink from a bottle. Instantly, she grew to be a giant size and was forced to put her leg up the chimney and her elbow out of the window in order to keep from being squeezed to death.

She managed to eat a little cake and shrink herself again. As soon as she was small enough to get through the door, she ran into a nearby wood where she found a caterpillar sitting on a mushroom. The caterpillar was very rude to Alice, and he scornfully asked her to prove her worth by reciting "You Are Old, Father William." Alice did so, but the words sounded very strange. Disgusted, he left her after giving her some valuable information about increasing or decreasing her size. She broke off pieces of the mushroom and found to her delight that by eating from the piece in her left hand she could become taller, and from the piece in her right hand, smaller.

She came to a little house among the trees. There a footman, who looked very much like a fish, presented to another footman, who closely resembled a frog, an invitation for the Duchess to play croquet with the Queen. The two amphibians bowed to each other with great formality, tangling their wigs together. Alice opened the door and found herself in the chaotic house of the Duchess. The cook was stirring a large pot of soup and pouring plenty of pepper into the mixture. Everyone was sneezing except the cook and a Cheshire cat, which sat on the hearth grinning. The Duchess herself held a sneezing, squalling baby and sang a blaring lullaby to it. Alice, in sympathy with the poor child, picked it up and carried it out into the fresh air, whereupon the baby turned slowly into a pig, squirmed out of her arms, and waddled into the forest.

Standing in bewilderment, Alice saw the grinning Cheshire cat sitting in a tree. He was able to appear and disappear at will, and after exercising his talents, he advised Alice to go to a tea party given by the Mad Hatter. The cat vanished, all but the grin. Finally, that, too, disappeared, and Alice left for the party.

There, Alice found she had to deal with the strangest people she had ever seen—a March Hare, a Mad Hatter, and a sleepy Dormouse. All were too lazy to set the table properly; dirty dishes were everywhere. The Dormouse fell asleep in its teacup; the Mad Hatter told Alice her hair needed cutting; the March Hare offered her wine and then told her there was none. They asked her foolish riddles that had no answers. Then, worse, they ignored her completely and carried on a ridiculous conversation among themselves. She escaped after the Dormouse fell asleep in the middle of a story he was telling.

Next, she found herself in a garden of talking flowers. Just as the conversation was beginning, some gardeners appeared with paintbrushes and began to splash red paint on a rosebush. Alice learned that the Queen had ordered a red bush to be placed in that spot, and the gardeners had made a mistake and planted a white one. Now they were busily and fearfully trying to cover their error before the Queen arrived. The poor gardeners, however, were not swift enough. The Queen caught them in the act, and the wretched gardeners were led off to be decapitated. Alice saved them by shoving them down into a large flowerpot, out of sight of the dreadful Queen.

A croquet game began. The mallets were live flamingos, and the balls were hedgehogs which thought nothing of uncurling themselves and running rapidly over the field. The Duchess cornered Alice and led her away to the seaside to introduce her to the Mock Turtle and the Gryphon.

While engaged in a Lobster Quadrille, they heard the news of a trial. A thief had stolen some tarts. Rushing to the courtroom where a trial by jury was already in session, Alice was called upon to act as a witness before the King and Queen of Hearts, but the excited child upset the jury box and spilled out all of its occupants. After replacing all the animals in the box, Alice said she knew nothing of the matter. Her speech infuriated the Queen, who ordered that Alice's head be cut off. The whole court rushed at her, and Alice defiantly called them nothing but a pack of cards. She awoke from her dream as her sister brushed away some dead leaves blowing over her face.

Critical Evaluation

One summer afternoon in 1862, the Reverend Charles Lutwidge Dodgson, an Oxford friend, and three little girls set out on a boat trip. Somewhere along the way, *Alice's Adventures in Wonderland* was born. Although it was not the first story that Dodgson had told the girls, children of Henry George Liddell, dean of Christ Church, Oxford, it was one that immediately captured Alice Liddell, the prototype for the fictional seven-year-old heroine. Her later requests for Dodgson to "write it down" were to turn him into one of the world's favorite authors, with his work translated into many languages and part of the heritage of most literate people.

Dodgson, who transposed his first two names into the pen name Lewis Carroll, was on the surface a shy but seemingly conventional Oxford mathematician. Today, however, his outwardly harmless affinity for little girls is viewed as the sign of a serious neurosis, an inability to grow up, which also revealed itself in his writings. Alice was only one of many young girls who would provide Carroll with the only love—innocent and sexless as it seemed—to which he could respond. As she matured, each child was replaced in Carroll's affections by another young lady who shared the secret world of childhood in which he spent much of his adult life.

Expressing itself in many ways, this attraction to fantasy gave rise to Carroll's love of whimsical letters, gadgets, theatricals, toys, and, of course, to the Alice stories. First prepared in a handwritten manuscript book for Alice Liddell (then called *Alice's Adventures Under Ground*), the book was published in its present form in 1865 and was almost immediately popular. Adding to its originality were the famous illustrations by Sir John Tenniel, who did not use the real Alice for his model. (She, unlike the pictured child, had short dark hair and bangs.)

Followed in 1871 by the even more brilliant sequel, *Through the Looking-Glass and What Alice Found There*, the book has always been enjoyed on several levels. Initially, it is a very special children's story, but it is also a book teeming with fascination for certain specialists—mathematicians, linguists, logicians, Freudians, and even those who envision the book as an example of a drug trip. Yet, perhaps its philosophical suggestions give the work most of its never-ending appeal for adults.

If readers examine the book as children's literature, readers see that it offered its young audience a charming new outlook, dispensing with the moralistic viewpoint then prevalent in almost all tales for youngsters. Alice is neither continuously nice nor thoroughly naughty, for she is simply a curious child whose queries lead her into strange situations, and in the end, she is neither punished nor rewarded. A moral, proposing that she do this or that, is absent. Departing even further from the saccharine stories praising standard virtues, Carroll pokes fun at many of the ideas with which Alice, a well-bred English child, has been imbued. The Mock Turtle, for example, chides the sacred subject of learning by terming the branches of arithmetic Ambition, Distraction, Uglification, and Derision. Children who read the book are permitted to see adults quite unlike the perfect beings usually portrayed. It is the story's adults rather than Alice who are rude, demanding, and ridiculous.

As a work for the specialist, *Alice's Adventures in Wonderland* touches on many puzzles more thoroughly presented in *Through the Looking-Glass and What Alice Found There*. Its playfulness with language, for example, involves puns, parodies, and clever phrasing, but it does not deal as fully with the basic nature of language as does its sequel. Even in *Alice's Adventures in Wonderland*, however, Carroll's casual amusement with words often has deeper meaning. When he parodies the well-known poems and songs of his day, he is again questioning their supercilious platitudes. When he makes a pun (the Gryphon tells the reader that boots and shoes under the sea are "done" with whiting rather than blacking and are, of course, made of soles and eels), Carroll is asserting the total logic of illogic. When he designs a Cheshire cat, he is taking a common but unclear phrase of his time ("Grin like a Cheshire cat" referred either to inn signs in the county of Cheshire depicting a grinning lion or to Cheshire cheeses modeled in the shape of a smiling cat) and turning it into a concrete reality. Logicians also find a multitude of tidbits. The Cheshire cat "proves" it is not mad by adopting the premise that if a dog is not mad, anyone who reacts in ways opposite to a dog must be. The March Hare offers a nice exercise in logic and language with his discussion of taking "more" versus taking "less" and his challenge as to whether "I mean what I say" is the same as "I say what I mean."

For Freudians, the book is also a mass of complicated mysteries. Freudians see significance in most of the characters and incidents, but the fall down the rabbit hole, the changes in size, the great interest in eating and drink-ing, the obnoxious mature females, and Alice's continual anxiety are some of the most revealing topics, all of them suggesting Carroll's neuroses about women and sex.

The larger philosophical questions raised by Alice center on the order of life as readers know it. Set in the context of the dream vision, a journey different from a conscious quest, the book asks whether there is indeed any pattern or meaning to life. Alice is the curious innocent who compares so favorably with the jaded and even wicked grown-ups. Always sensible and open to experience, she would seem the ideal messenger to bring readers a true concept, yet her adventures hint that all readers may know is the ridiculousness of logic and what readers imagine to be reality and the logic of nonsense. Readers see that Wonderland is no more incomprehensible than Victorian England, that the Mad Duchess lives next door, that as the Cheshire cat says, "We're all mad here."

Alice brings to Wonderland a strong belief in order and certain concepts, and she must continually refuse to accept the chaos that she finds there. When Wonderland turns her views askew, she can withstand the strain for only so long. Then she must rebel. The trial, which is the last refuge of justice in man's world, is the key factor in Alice's rejection of Wonderland, for it is a trial of Wonderland itself, with many of the earlier encountered creatures reassembled to assert forcefully, once more, that expectations and rules are meaningless. Like the child of the world that she is, Alice (and Carroll) must deny the truth that there is no truth. She must shout "Nonsense" to it all. As one critic has pointed out, she rejects "mad sanity in favor of the sane madness of the ordinary existence." Facing the same confusion and frightened by what it hints, the reader also rebels, laughing and turning to more serious considerations.

ALL'S WELL THAT ENDS WELL

Type of work: Drama
Author: William Shakespeare (1564–1616)
Type of plot: Romantic comedy
Time of plot: Sixteenth century
Locale: France and Italy
First presented: c. 1602

Uneven in tone, All's Well That Ends Well *ranges from scenes of farce to moments of serious insight. Helena's character, of rather dubious virtue in terms of her tactics with Bertram, sheds interesting ambiguity on the play's general theme of the blindness of prejudice and unreason.*

Principal Characters

Helena (hĕl′ə·nə), the orphaned daughter of Gerard de Narbon, a distinguished physician, and the ward of the Countess of Rousillon. She at first regards her love for Bertram, the countess' son, as hopeless; then, with the independence characteristic of the heroines of Shakespeare's comedies, she resolves to try to win him with her father's one legacy to her, a cure for the ailing king's mysterious malady. Her charm and sincerity win the love and admiration of all who see her except Bertram himself. Hurt but undaunted by his flight from her on their wedding day, she mourns chiefly that she has sent him into danger in the Florentine war and deprived his mother of his presence. She leaves the countess without farewell, hoping at least to free her husband to return to his home if she is not successful in fulfilling his seemingly impossible conditions for a reconciliation. She contrives through an ingenious trick, substituting herself for the Florentine girl he is trying to seduce, to obtain his ring and conceive his child. Thus she wins for herself a loving and repentant husband.

Bertram (bĕr′trəm), **Count Rousillon** (rōō·sĭl′yən, rōō·sē·yōn′), a rather arrogant, self-satisfied, impulsive young man. Proud of his noble blood, he feels degraded by the king's command that he marry Helena, and after the ceremony he flees with his dissolute companion, Parolles, to the army of the Duke of Florence to escape such ignominy. He wins fame as a soldier, but he fares less well in his personal relationships. First, Parolles' essential cowardice and disloyalty are exposed by his fellow soldiers to the young count who had trusted him. Then his attempt to seduce Diana brings about the very end he is trying to escape, union with his own wife. His antagonism for Helena melts when he hears reports of her death and recognizes the depth of the love he has lost, and he is willingly reconciled to her when she is restored to him.

The Countess of Rousillon, Bertram's mother, a wise and gracious woman who is devoted to both Bertram and Helena and welcomes the idea of their marriage. Her son's calloused rejection of his virtuous wife appalls her, and she grieves deeply for his folly, in spite of her protest to Helena that she looks upon her as her only remaining child. After Helena's reported death and Bertram's return, she begs the king to forgive her son's youthful rebelliousness.

Parolles (pā·rōl′ĕs), Bertram's follower and fellow soldier, who has no illusions about his own character: "Simply the thing I am shall make me live . . . every braggart shall be found an ass." His romantic illusions are nonexistent; he encourages Bertram to be off to the wars with him, and he aids and abets the attempted seduction of Diana. The quality of his loyalty to his patron becomes all too obvious in the hilarious drum scene, when he, blindfolded, insults and offers to betray all his countrymen to free himself from the enemies into whose hands he thinks he has fallen.

The King of France, a kindly old man who has almost resigned himself to the fact that his illness is incurable when Helena comes to court with her father's prescription, which heals him. He believes her the equal of any man in the kingdom and readily agrees to reward her service to him by letting her choose her husband from among the noblemen of the kingdom. Only the pleas of Lafeu and the countess and Bertram's late recognition of Helena's virtues prevent him from punishing the young man severely for his rebellious flight.

Lafeu (lä′fü′), an old lord, counselor to the king and the countess' friend. He is as much captivated by Helena's grace as his king is, but he blames Parolles chiefly for Bertram's ungentle desertion of his wife. Out of friendship for the countess, he arranges a marriage between Bertram and his own daughter in an attempt to assuage the king's anger against the count.

Lavache (lä·väsh′), the countess' servant, a witty clown who is expert in the nonsensical trains of logic spun by characters such as Touchstone and Feste.

Diana Capilet (dī·ăn′ə kăp′ĭ·lĕt), the attractive, virtuous daughter of a Florentine widow. She willingly agrees to help Helena win Bertram when she hears her story, and she wins a rich husband for herself as a reward from the king for her honesty.

A Widow, Diana's mother, who is concerned about the honor of her daughter and her house.

The Story

Bertram, the Count of Rousillon, had been called to the court to serve the king of France, who was ill of a disease that all the royal physicians had failed to cure. The only doctor in the entire country who might have cured the king was now dead. On his deathbed he had bequeathed to his daughter Helena his books and papers describing cures for all common and rare diseases, among them the one suffered by the king.

Helena was now the ward of the Countess of Rousillon, who thought of her as a daughter. Helena loved young Count Bertram and wanted him for a husband, not a brother. Bertram considered Helena only slightly above a servant, however, and would not consider her for a wife. Through her knowledge of the king's illness, Helena at last hit upon a plot to gain the spoiled young man for her mate, in such fashion as to leave him no choice in the decision. She journeyed to the court and, offering her life as forfeit if she failed, gained the king's consent to try her father's cure on him. If she won, the young lord of her choice was to be given to her in marriage.

Her sincerity won the king's confidence. She cured him by means of her father's prescription and as her boon asked for Bertram for her husband. That young man protested to the king, but the ruler kept his promise, not only because he had given his word but also because Helena had won him over completely.

The king ordered the marriage to be performed at once, yet Bertram, although bowing to the king's will, would not have Helena for a wife in any but a legal way. Pleading the excuse of urgent business elsewhere, he deserted her after the ceremony and sent messages to her and to his mother saying he would never belong to a wife forced upon him. He told Helena that she would not really be his wife until she wore on her finger a ring he now wore on his and carried in her body a child that was his; and these two things would never come to pass, for he would never see Helena again. He was encouraged in his hatred for Helena by his follower, Parolles, a scoundrel and a coward who would as soon betray one person as another. Helena had reproached him for his vulgar ways, and he wanted vengeance on her.

Helena returned to the Countess of Rousillon, as Bertram had commanded. The countess heard of her son's actions with horror, and when she read the letter he had written her, restating his hatred for Helena, she disowned her son, for she loved Helena as her own child. When Helena learned that Bertram had said he would never

Violenta (vē·ō·l'ĕn'tà) and **Mariana** (mä·rē·ä'nà), the widow's honest neighbors.

The Duke of Florence, the general whose army Bertram joins.

Rinaldo (rĭ·näl'dō), the countess' steward, who first tells her of Helena's love for Bertram.

return to France until he no longer had a wife there, she sadly decided to leave the home of her benefactress. Loving Bertram, she vowed that she would not keep him from his home.

Disguising herself as a religious pilgrim, Helena followed Bertram to Italy, where he had gone to fight for the Duke of Florence. While lodging with a widow and her daughter, a beautiful young girl named Diana, Helena learned that Bertram had seduced a number of young Florentine girls. Lately he had turned his attention to Diana, but she, a pure and virtuous girl, would not accept his attentions. Then Helena told the widow and Diana that she was Bertram's wife, and by bribery and a show of friendliness she persuaded them to join her in a plot against Bertram. Diana listened again to his vows of love for her and agreed to let him come to her rooms, provided he first gave her a ring from his finger to prove the constancy of his love. Bertram, overcome with passion, gave her the ring, and that night, as he kept the appointment in her room, the girl he thought Diana slipped a ring on his finger as they lay in bed together.

News came to the countess in France and to Bertram in Italy that Helena had died of grief and love for Bertram. Bertram returned to France to face his mother's and the king's displeasure, but first he discovered that Parolles was the knave everyone else knew him to be. When Bertram held him up to public ridicule, Parolles vowed he would be revenged on his former benefactor.

When the king visited the Countess of Rousillon, she begged him to restore her son to favor. Bertram protested that he really loved Helena, though he had not recognized that love until after he had lost her forever through death. His humility so pleased the king that his confession of love, coupled with his exploits in the Italian wars, won him a royal pardon for his offense against his wife. Then the king, about to betroth him to another wife, the lovely and wealthy daughter of a favorite lord, noticed the ring Bertram was wearing. It was the ring given to him the night he went to Diana's rooms; the king in turn recognized it as a jewel he had given to Helena. Bertram tried to pretend that it had been thrown to him in Florence by a high-born lady who loved him. He said that he had told the lady he was not free to wed, but that she had refused to take back her gift.

At that moment Diana appeared as a petitioner to the king and demanded that Bertram fulfill his pledge to recognize her as his wife. When Bertram tried to pretend that she was no more than a prostitute he had visited, she produced the ring he had given her. That ring convinced everyone present, especially his mother, that Diana was really Bertram's wife. Parolles added to the evidence against Bertram by testifying that he had heard his former master promise to marry the girl. Bertram persisted in his denials. Diana then asked for the ring she had given to him, the ring which the king thought to be Helena's. The king asked Diana where she had gotten the ring. When she refused to tell on penalty of her life, he ordered her taken to prison. Diana then declared that she would

sent for her bail. Her bail was Helena, now carrying Bertram's child within her, for it was she, of course, who had received him in Diana's rooms that fateful night. To her Diana gave the ring. The two requirements for his real wife being now fulfilled, Bertram promised to love Helena as a true and faithful husband. Diana received from the king a promise to give her any young man of her choice for her husband, with the king to provide the dowry. Thus the bitter events of the past made sweeter the happiness of all.

Critical Evaluation

All's Well That Ends Well belongs to the set of "problem plays" of Shakespeare—those works which approach traditional dramatic themes in an unconventional fashion, or which combine the outward forms of comedy with an inner sense of unease and disquiet. Undoubtedly the most famous and successful of these troubling comedies is *Measure for Measure*, and it is worth noting that it and *All's Well That Ends Well* were almost certainly written about the same time. This was also the period of Shakespeare's great tragedies, such as *Hamlet*, *Othello*, and *King Lear*. *All's Well That Ends Well* stands as the weakest work of the period; it is a masterpiece, but a flawed one.

Two major reasons contribute to the relative thinness of the play: Its characters are sketchily drawn and, with the exception of Helena, do not fully engage the audience's sympathies; the plot, taken from ancient folktales by way of Boccaccio, retains many of its magical aspects—such as Helena's miraculous cure of the king—yet these elements do not fit well with the spare, unromantic style of the play.

The language of *All's Well That Ends Well* is suited to the intelligent, skeptical view of this period of Shakespeare's art, but it is not lively enough for a true comedy, or elaborate enough for a fantasy based on folklore. There are moments of ribald interchange, including the one at the beginning of the play between Parolles and Helena, and there are the finely elegiac lines of the ill French king, when he speaks of old men "whose judgments are mere fathers of their garments." These and numerous other remarkable passages reveal that any fault lies not in Shakespeare's linguistic resources but in the link between language and the characters and actions of the play.

The prime weakness of the plot must consist in its brevity, a normal feature of folktales but one which makes it difficult to sustain action throughout a five-act play. Shakespeare's mastery of invention, so amply demonstrated in other works, seems to have been held in check here, perhaps deliberately so, according to many critics. While it is possible to speculate on his motives for restraining his plot, one should note that a conscious limitation of invention is typical of the problem plays.

The basic situation of the plot is familiar to any reader of folktales: A woman is set what seems to be an impossible task, which, if she completes it, will win her a desired reward. In *All's Well That Ends Well*, the reward for Helena will be Bertram as her true husband; to win him she must wear a ring from his finger and bear his child. Bertram attempts to forestall these actions by deserting Helena in France while he travels to Italy with his bombastic companion, Parolles. Such a task as Helena is given makes sense in a folktale, but in a full-length play it must be made believable through the nature of the characters.

Helena, a strong, capable, and lively young woman, is one of Shakespeare's most engaging heroines. Yet she has one inexplicable trait—perhaps even a flaw—in that she desires Bertram for her husband. Bertram, a self-centered, snobbish young nobleman, enters the play with no apparent qualities to recommend him to a generous woman such as Helena. Perhaps she sees in him some nature that is capable of being renewed; this is suggested during the play's Italian episodes, in which Bertram seems to redeem himself through personal valor in battle, and in which his conscience is stirred by a justly reproachful letter from his mother. Yet it is also in Italy that Bertram barters away his precious ring for a moment of lewd pleasure; back in France, he will promptly and ineptly lie about the exchange. This moral seesawing raises questions about Bertram's basic character. Still, without the love of Helena for Bertram, there would be no play, and as Helena remarks, "All's well that ends well yet/ Though time seem so adverse and means unfit." Perhaps here we should understand "time" as being the events of the play and Bertram as the "means unfit."

The other particularly notable character in the play is Parolles, a braggart soldier whose valor is all in the sound of his voice, and who carries into battle, tellingly enough, not a musket but a drum. Once again, there is the inevitable tendency to contrast characters, but between Sir John Falstaff and the rogue of this play there is no contest. Parolles is neither witty nor humorous in Falstaff's sense, although he is gifted with great verbal ingenuity, especially of the coarse and mocking sort—*parolles* means "words"—but his language repels rather than attracts the audience or reader.

Yet, in the end, Parolles speaks the lines that sum up the central mystery of *All's Well That Ends Well*, and of all the problem plays, when he defines his character and fate: "Simply the thing I am shall make me live." The supposedly simple thing that Shakespeare hints at throughout the play is the one point that he never fully reveals.

THE AMBASSADORS

Type of work: Novel
Author: Henry James (1843–1916)
Type of plot: Psychological realism
Time of plot: About 1900
Locale: Paris, France
First published: 1903

The Ambassadors marks a turning point in James's attitude toward his American characters. This novel contains none of the embarrassment found in many of the earlier works, which portray the author's fellow Americans as slightly barbaric in their inability to appreciate the fineness and subtlety of European culture.

Principal Characters

Lambert Strether, the chief ambassador of Mrs. Newsome, his betrothed, sent to summon her son Chad back from Paris to the family business in Wollett, Massachusetts. A fifty-five-year-old editor of a review, Lambert Strether has all the tact and diplomacy necessary to accomplish his task, but his sensitivity will not allow him either to complete it or to take advantage of Chad's situation to gain his own ends. He sees Chad as immeasurably better off in Paris, himself as somehow changed and strengthened by his sojourn abroad, though he will not allow himself to stay in Europe after having failed his benefactress. His heady experiences renew his earlier impressions, and he forms friendships, visits cathedrals, and lives easily for the first time since his wife died while bearing their son, also dead. His delicacy—in approaching young Newsome and his mistress, Mme. de Vionnet; in handling Chadwick's sister, brother-in-law, and childhood sweetheart, and in breaking off from Maria Gostrey, who loves him—is the more remarkable when one considers that his own hopes of a rich marriage and great influence have been shattered by his actions.

Chadwick Newsome, called **Chad,** the handsome, twenty-eight-year-old successor to a family business on the one hand and the heir to a modest income from another source. Candid and open-hearted, the graying young man has been so improved by his years in Europe, largely under the tutelage of Mme. de Vionnet, that no thought of his return can really be harbored by anyone who has seen him. Although he himself is willing to return for a visit and to consider taking over the advertising and sales promotion of the business he is well equipped to run, his proposed marriage to Mamie Pocock is unthinkable. His greatest triumph comes as the result of his mannerly presentation of his sister's group of ambassadors to his Parisian friends, while his saddest duty is to allow his good friend Lambert Strether to return to face the consequences of a diplomatic failure.

Maria Gostrey, a self-styled introducer and tour director and a chance acquaintance of Lambert Strether. A

sensitive, genial, and understanding woman, she proves to be the agent through whom the ambassador discovers the irony of Chad Newsome's situation. Her generosity and devotion to her new friend first touch him and then move him deeply when he sees her loyalty and love unencumbered by desire for personal gain.

Mme. Marie de Vionnet (mä·rē′ də vē·ôn·nä′), the beautiful Comtesse whose religion and social position will not allow her to divorce an unloved and faithless husband. Gravely lovely and charming, she has educated young Chad Newsome in the social graces and has won his heart and soul. Called a virtuous connection by intimate friends, the arrangement seems shabby to Mr. Waymarsh and Mrs. Pocock, typically closed-minded Americans. Through the efforts of good friends, especially those of Lambert Strether, Mme. de Vionnet is allowed to retain her younger lover in spite of the fact that they have no future beyond their immediate happiness. Her daughter, who was believed by some to be in love with Chad Newsome, settles on a marriage more reasonable and agreeable to all.

John Little Bilham, called **Little Bilham,** an American expatriate artist and Chad Newsome's close friend. A perceptive, bright young man, Little Bilham becomes the confidant of the ambassadors and, along with a friend, Miss Barrace, their interpreters of social and artistic life in Paris.

Miss Barrace, a shrewd, witty, understanding woman living in Paris. She asks Lambert Strether not to force the issue of Chad Newsome's return home.

Mr. Waymarsh, an American lawyer residing in England, Lambert Strether's friend. He accompanies Strether to Paris and directly involves himself in Chad Newsome's affairs when he writes a letter informing Mrs. Newsome that her ambassador is not fulfilling his mission.

Sarah Newsome Pocock, Chad Newsome's older sister. She, her husband, and her sister-in-law are also dispatched as Mrs. Newsome's ambassadors to make certain that Chad returns to America. She and Mr. Waymarsh join forces to separate Chad and Mme. de Vionnet.

James Pocock, Sarah's husband, who during Chad Newsome's absence is in control of the Newsome mills. He enjoys his trip to Paris, sympathizes with Chad, and becomes Lambert Strether's tacit ally.

Mamie Pocock, James Pocock's younger sister, the girl Mrs. Newsome has selected as a suitable wife for her son. Although she accompanies her brother and his wife on their mission to persuade Chad Newsome to return, she loses her personal interest in the young man after meeting John Little Bilham. Little Bilham's announced

intention of marrying Mamie helps Chad solve his own problems of loyalty and love in his affair with Mme. de Vionnet.

Jeanne de Vionnet, Mme. de Vionnet's daughter. For a time society assumed that Chad Newsome might be in love with the daughter. Jeanne becomes engaged to M. de Montbron.

M. Gloriani, a sculptor, Mme. de Vionnet's friend, famous in the artistic and fashionable circles of Parisian society.

Mme. Gloriani, his loving wife.

The Story

Lambert Strether was engaged to marry Mrs. Newsome, a widow. Mrs. Newsome had a son, Chadwick, whom she wanted to return home from Paris and take over the family business in Woollett, Massachusetts. She was especially concerned for his future after she had heard that he was seriously involved with a Frenchwoman. In her anxiety, she asked Strether to go to Paris and persuade her son to return to the respectable life she had planned for him.

Strether did not look forward to his task, for Chadwick had ignored all of his mother's written requests to return home. Strether also did not know what hold Chadwick's mistress might have over him or what sort of woman she might be. He strongly suspected that she was a young girl of unsavory reputation. Strether realized, however, that his hopes of marrying Mrs. Newsome depended upon his success in bringing Chad back to America, where his mother could see him married to Mamie Pocock.

Leaving his ship at Liverpool, Strether journeyed across England to London. On the way he met Miss Gostrey, a young woman who was acquainted with some of Strether's American friends, and she promised to aid Strether in getting acquainted with Europe before he left for home again. Strether met another old friend, Mr. Waymarsh, an American lawyer living in England, whom he asked to go with him to Paris.

A few days after arriving in Paris, Strether went to Chad's house. The young man was not in Paris, and he had temporarily given the house over to a friend, Mr. Bilham. Through Bilham, Strether got in touch with Chad at Cannes. Strether was surprised to learn of his whereabouts, for he knew that Chad would not have dared to take an ordinary mistress to such a fashionable resort.

About a week later, Strether, Miss Gostrey, and Waymarsh went to the theater. Between the acts of the play, the door of their box was opened and Chad entered. He was much changed from the adolescent college boy Strether remembered. He was slightly gray, although only twenty-eight years old.

Both Strether and Chad Newsome were pleased to see each other. Over coffee after the theater, the older man

told Chad why he had come to Europe. Chad answered that all he asked was an opportunity to be convinced that he should return.

A few days later, Chad took Strether and his friends to a tea where they met Mme. and Mlle. de Vionnet. The former, who had married a French count, turned out to be an old school friend of Miss Gostrey. Strether was at a loss to understand whether Chad was in love with the comtesse or with her daughter Jeanne. Since the older woman was only a few years the senior of the young man and as beautiful as her daughter, either was possibly the object of his affections.

As the days slipped by, it became apparent to Strether that he himself wanted to stay in Paris. The French city and its life were much calmer and more beautiful than the provincial existence he had known in Woollett, and he began to understand why Chad was unwilling to go back to his mother and the Newsome mills.

Strether learned that Chad was in love with Mme. de Vionnet, rather than with her daughter. The comtesse had been separated from her husband for many years, but their position and religion made divorce impossible. Strether, who was often in the company of the Frenchwoman, soon fell under her charm. Miss Gostrey, who had known Mme. de Vionnet for many years, had only praise for her and questioned Strether as to the advisability of removing Chad from the woman's continued influence.

One morning Chad announced to Strether that he was ready to return immediately to America. The young man was puzzled when Strether replied that he was not sure it was wise for either of them to return and that it would be wiser for them both to reconsider whether they would not be better off in Paris than in New England.

When Mrs. Newsome, back in America, received word of that decision on the part of her ambassador, she immediately sent the Pococks, her daughter and son-in-law, to Paris along with Mamie Pocock, the girl she hoped her son would marry. They were to bring back both Strether and her son.

Mrs. Newsome's daughter and her relatives did not

come to Paris with an obvious ill will. Their attitude seemed to be that Chad and Strether had somehow drifted astray, and it was their duty to set them right. At least that was the attitude of Mrs. Pocock. Her husband, however, was not at all interested in having Chad return, for in the young man's absence, Mr. Pocock controlled the Newsome mills. Mr. Pocock further saw that his visit was probably the last opportunity he would have for a spirited time in the European city, and so he was quite willing to spend his holiday going to theaters and cafés. His younger sister, Mamie, seemed to take little interest in the recall of her supposed fiancé, for she had become interested in Chad's friend, Mr. Bilham.

The more Strether saw of Mme. de Vionnet after the arrival of the Pococks, the more he was convinced that she was both noble and sincere in her attempts to make friends with her lover's family. Mrs. Pocock found it difficult to reconcile Mme. de Vionnet's aristocratic background with the fact that she was Chad's mistress.

After several weeks of hints and genteel pleading, the Pococks and Mamie went to Switzerland, leaving Chad to make a decision whether to return to America. As for Mr. Strether, Mrs. Newsome had advised that he be left alone to make his own decision, for the widow wanted to avoid the appearance of having lost her dignity or her sense of propriety.

While the Pococks were gone, Strether and Chad discussed the course they should follow. Chad was uncertain of his attitude toward Mamie Pocock. Strether assured him that the girl was already happy with her new love, Mr. Bilham, who had told Strether that he intended to marry the American girl. His advice, contrary to what he had thought when he had sailed from America, was that Chadwick Newsome should remain in France with the comtesse, despite the fact that the young man could not marry her and would, by remaining in Europe, lose the opportunity to make himself an extremely rich man. Chad decided to take his older friend's counsel.

Waymarsh, who had promised his help in persuading Chad to return to America, was outraged at Strether's changed attitude. Miss Gostrey, however, remained loyal, for she had fallen deeply in love with Strether during their time together in Paris. Strether, however, realizing her feelings, told her that he had to go back to America alone. His object in Europe had been to return Chad Newsome to his mother. Because he had failed in that mission and would never marry Mrs. Newsome, he could not justify to himself marrying another woman whom he had met on a journey financed by the woman he had at one time intended to marry. Only Mme. de Vionnet, he felt, could truly appreciate the irony of his position.

Critical Evaluation

In Henry James's *The Ambassadors*, plot is minimal; the story line consists simply in Mrs. Newsome sending Lambert Strether to Europe to bring home her son, Chad. The important action is psychological rather than physical; the crucial activities are thought and conversation. The pace of the novel is slow. Events unfold as they do in life: in their own good time.

Because of these qualities, James's work demands certain responses from the reader. He must not expect boisterous action, shocking or violent occurrences, sensational coincidences, quickly mounting suspense, or breathtaking climaxes; these devices have no place in a Henry James novel. Rather, the reader must bring to the work a sensitivity to problems of conscience, an appreciation of the meaning beneath manners, and an awareness of the intricacies of human relationships. Finally, and of the utmost importance, the reader must be patient; the power of a novel like *The Ambassadors* is only revealed quietly and without haste. This is why, perhaps more than any other modern author, James requires rereading—not merely because of the complexity of his style, but because the richly layered texture of his prose contains a multiplicity of meanings, a wealth of subtle shadings.

In *The Ambassadors,* which James considered his masterpiece, this subtlety and complexity is partially the result of his perfection of the technique for handling point of view. Departing from traditional eighteenth and nineteenth century use of the omniscient narrator, James experimented extensively with the limited point of view, exploring the device to discover what advantages it might have over the older method. He found that what was lost in panoramic scope and comprehensiveness, the limited viewpoint more than compensated for in focus, concentration, and intensity. It was a technique perfectly suited to an author whose primary concern was with presenting the thoughts, emotions, and motivations of an intelligent character, with understanding the psychological makeup of a sensitive mind and charting its growth.

The sensitive and intelligent character through whose mind all events in the novel are filtered is Lambert Strether. The reader sees and hears only what Strether sees and hears; all experiences, perceptions, and judgments are his. Strictly adhered to, this device proved too restrictive for James's purpose; therefore, he utilized other characters—called confidants—who enabled him to expand the scope of his narrative without sacrificing advantages inherent in the limited point of view. The basic function of these "listening characters" is to expand and enrich Strether's experience. Miss Gostrey, Little Bilham, Waymarsh, and Miss Barrace—all share with him attitudes and insights arising from their widely diverse backgrounds; they provide him with a wider range of knowledge than he could ever gain from firsthand experience. Maria Gostrey, Strether's primary confidante, illustrates the fact that James's listening characters are deep and memorable personalities in their own right. Miss Gostrey not only listens to Strether, but she also becomes an important figure in the plot, and as she gradually falls in love with Strether, she engages the reader's sympathy as well.

Lambert Strether interacts with and learns from the environment of Paris as well as from the people he meets there; thus, the setting is far more than a mere backdrop against which events in the plot occur. To understand the significance of Paris as the setting, the reader must appreciate the meaning that the author, throughout his fiction, attached to certain places. James was fascinated by what he saw as the underlying differences in the cultures of America and Europe and, in particular, in the opposing values of a booming American factory town such as Woollett and an ancient European capital such as Paris. In these two places, very different qualities are held in esteem. In Woollett, Mrs. Newsome admires practicality, individuality, and enterprise, while in Paris, her son appreciates good food and expensive wine, conversation with a close circle of friends, and leisure time quietly spent. Woollett pursues commercialism, higher social status, and rigid moral codes with untiring vigor; Paris values the beauty of nature, the pleasure of companionship, and an appreciation of the arts with studied simplicity. Thus, the implications of a native of Woollett, such as Lambert Strether, going to Paris at the end of his life are manifold; and it is through his journey that the theme of the novel is played out.

The theme consists of a question of conscience: Should Strether, in his capacity as Mrs. Newsome's ambassador, be faithful to his mission of bringing Chad home, once he no longer believes in that mission? That he ceases to believe is the result of his conversion during his stay in Paris. He is exposed to a side of life that he had not known previously; furthermore, he finds it to be good. As a man of noble nature and sensitive conscience, he cannot ignore or deny, as Sarah Newsome later does, that life in Paris has vastly improved Chad. Ultimately, therefore, he must oppose rather than promote the young man's return. The honesty of this action not only destroys his chance for financial security in marriage to Chad's mother but also prevents him from returning the love of Maria Gostrey. Although Strether's discovery of a different set of values comes too late in life for his own benefit, he at least can save Chad. The lesson he learns is the one he passionately seeks to impart to Little Bilham: "Live all you can; it's a mistake not to. It doesn't so much matter what you do in particular, so long as you have your life. . . . Don't, at any rate, miss things out of stupidity. . . . Live!"

If, in reading *The Ambassadors*, the reader's expectations are for keenness of observation, insight into motivations, comprehension of mental processes, and powerful characterizations, he will not be disappointed. If Henry James demands the effort, concentration, and commitment of his reader, he also—with his depth and breadth of vision and the sheer beauty of his craftsmanship—repays him a hundredfold.

ANDERSEN'S FAIRY TALES

Type of work: Fairy tales
Author: Hans Christian Andersen (1805–1875)
Type of plots: Folk tradition
Time of plots: Indeterminate
Locale: Denmark
First published: At intervals, 1835–1872

The Stories

The fairy tales written by Hans Christian Andersen include several which have become known and loved the world over, such as "The Red Shoes." The heroine of this story is Karen, who was such a poor little girl that she had to go barefoot in winter. An old mother shoemaker felt sorry for her and made Karen a clumsy pair of shoes out of pieces of red felt. When Karen's mother died, the girl had to wear the red shoes to the funeral. An old lady, seeing Karen walking forlornly behind her mother's coffin, pitied her and took the child home. The old lady thought that the red shoes were ugly, and she burned them.

One day, Karen saw the queen and the little princess. The princess was dressed all in white, with beautiful red morocco shoes.

When the time came for Karen's confirmation, she needed new shoes. The old lady, almost blind, did not know that the shoes Karen picked out were red ones just like those the princess had worn. During the confirmation, Karen could think of nothing but her red shoes.

The next Sunday, as Karen went to her first communion, she met an old soldier with a crutch. After admiring the red shoes, he struck them on the soles and told them to stick fast when Karen danced. During the service, she could think only of her shoes. After church, she started to dance. The footman had to pick her up and take off her shoes before the old lady could take her home.

At a ball in town, Karen could not stop dancing. She danced out through the fields and up to the church. There, an angel with a broad sword stopped her and told her she would dance until she became a skeleton, a warning to all other vain children.

She danced day and night until she came to the executioner's house. There she tapped on the window and begged him to come out and cut off her feet. When he chopped off her feet, they and the little red shoes danced off into the forest. The executioner made Karen wooden feet and crutches and taught her a psalm, and the parson gave her a home.

Karen thought she had suffered enough to go to church, but each time she tried she saw the red shoes dancing ahead of her and was afraid. One Sunday, she stayed at home. As she heard the organ music, she read her prayer book humbly and begged help from God. Then she saw the angel again, not with a sword but with a green branch covered with roses. As the angel moved the branch, Karen felt that she was being carried off to the church. There she was so thankful that her heart broke, and her soul flew up to heaven.

"The Ugly Duckling," another favorite Andersen tale, opens with a mother duck sitting on a clutch of eggs. When the largest egg did not crack with the rest, an old matriarchal duck warned the fowl that she should let that egg alone; it would probably turn out to be a turkey. The egg, however, finally cracked, and out of it came the biggest, ugliest duckling ever seen in the barnyard. The other ducklings pecked it and chased it and made it so unhappy that it felt comfortable only when it was paddling in the pond. The mother duck was proud only of the very fine paddling the ugly duckling did.

The scorn heaped on his head was so bitter that the duckling ran away from home. He spent a miserable winter in the marsh. When spring came, he saw some beautiful white swans settle down on the water. He moved out to admire them as they came toward him with ruffled feathers. He bent down to await their attack, but as he looked in the water he saw that he was no longer a gray ugly duckling but another graceful swan. He was so glad then that he never thought to be proud but smiled when he heard some children say that he was the handsomest swan they had ever seen.

"The Snow Queen" tells of a very wicked hobgoblin who invented a mirror that reflected everything good as trivial and everything bad as monstrous; a good thought became a grin in the mirror. His cohorts carried it all over the earth and finally up to heaven to test the angels. There, many good thoughts made the mirror grin so much that it fell out of their hands and splintered as it hit the earth.

Each tiny piece could cause the same distortions. One of the shards pierced Kay through the heart, and a tiny grain lodged in his eye. Kay had been a happy little boy before that. He had played with Gerda in their rooms high above the street, and they both had admired some rosebushes their parents had planted in boxes spanning the space between their houses. With the glass in his eye and heart, however, Kay saw nothing beautiful, and nothing pleased him.

One night, he went sledding in the town square. When a lady all in white drove by, he thought that she was so beautiful that he hitched his sled behind her sleigh as she drove slowly around the square. Suddenly, her horses galloped out of the town. The lady looked back at Kay and smiled each time he tried to loosen his sled. Then she stopped the sleigh and told Kay to get in with her. There she wrapped him in her fur coat. She was the Snow Queen. He was nearly frozen, but he did not feel cold after she kissed him, nor did he remember Gerda.

Gerda did not forget Kay; at last, she ran away from home to look for him. She went to the garden of a woman learned in magic and asked all the flowers if they had seen Kay, but the flowers knew only their own stories. She met a crow who led her to the prince and princess, but they had not heard of Kay. They gave her boots and a muff and a golden coach to ride in when they sent her on the way. Robbers stopped the golden coach. At the insistence of a little robber girl, Gerda was left alive, a prisoner in the robbers' house. Some wood pigeons in the loft told Gerda that Kay had gone with the Snow Queen to Lapland. Since the reindeer tethered inside the house knew the way to Lapland, the robber girl unloosed him to take Gerda on her way.

The Lapp and the Finn women gave Gerda directions to the Snow Queen's palace and told her that it was only through the goodness of her heart that Kay could be released. When Gerda found Kay, she wept so hard that she melted the piece of mirror out of his heart. Then he wept the splinter from his eye and realized what a vast and empty place he had been in. With thankfulness in her heart, Gerda led Kay out of the snow palace and home.

Less known, perhaps, is Andersen's story called "The Shepherdess and the Sweep." In the middle of the door of an old wooden parlor cupboard was carved a ridiculous little man with goat's legs, horns on his head, and a beard. The children called him Major-general-field-sergeant-commander-Billy-goat's-legs. He always looked at the china figure of a shepherdess. Finally, he asked the china figure of a Chinaman, who claimed to be her grandfather, if he could marry the shepherdess. The Chinaman, who could nod his head when he chose, nodded his consent.

The shepherdess had been engaged to the china figure of a chimneysweep. She begged him to take her away. That night, he used his ladder to help her get off the table. The Chinaman saw them leave and started after them.

Through the stove and up the chimney went the shepherdess and the chimneysweep. When she saw how big the world was, the shepherdess began to cry, and the chimneysweep had to take her back to the parlor. There they saw the Chinaman broken on the floor. The shepherdess was distressed, but the chimneysweep said the Chinaman could be mended and riveted.

Although the family had the Chinaman riveted so that he was whole again, he could no longer nod his head. When the Major-general-field-sergeant-commander-Billy-goat's-legs asked again for the shepherdess, the Chinaman could not nod, and so the shepherdess and the chimneysweep stayed together and loved each other until they were broken to pieces.

According to "The Emperor's New Clothes," once there was a foolish emperor who loved clothes so well that he spent all the kingdom's money to buy new ones. Two swindlers, who knew the Emperor's weakness, came to town with big looms. They told the people that they wove the most beautiful cloth in the world but that it had a magical property: If someone unworthy of his post looked at it, the cloth became invisible.

The Emperor gave them much gold and thread to make him a new outfit. The swindlers set up their looms and worked far into the night. Becoming curious about the materials, the Emperor sent his most trusted minister to see them. When the minister looked at the looms, he saw nothing; but, thinking of the magical property of the cloth, he decided that he was unworthy of his post. He said nothing to the swindlers and reported to the Emperor, praising the colors and pattern of the cloth as the swindlers had described it.

Others, looking at the looms, saw nothing and said nothing. Even the Emperor saw nothing when the material was finished and then was made into clothes, but he also kept silent. He wore his new clothes in a fine procession. All the people called out that his new clothes were beautiful—all the people except one little boy, who said that the Emperor did not have on any clothes at all.

Then there was a buzzing along the line of march. Soon everyone was saying that the Emperor wore no clothes. The Emperor, realizing the truth, held himself stiffer than ever until the procession ended.

"The Steadfast Tin Soldier" provides an image of love and constancy. A little boy had a set of twenty-five tin soldiers made out of the same tin spoon. Since there was not quite enough tin, one soldier had only one leg, but he stood as solidly as those with two legs. The one-legged soldier stood on a table and looked longingly at a paper castle, at the door of which stood a paper dancer who wore a gauze dress. A ribbon over her shoulder was held in position by a spangle as big as her face.

One morning, the little boy put the one-legged soldier on a windowsill. When the window opened, the soldier fell three stories to the ground. There he stuck, head down between two stones, until some boys found him. They made a paper boat for the soldier and sailed it down the gutter. After a time, the boat entered a sewer. Beginning to get limp, it settled deeper into the water. Just as the soldier thought he would fall into the water, a fish swallowed him.

When the fish was opened, the soldier found himself in the same house out of which he had fallen. Soon he was back on his table looking at the dancer. For no reason, the boy threw him into a roaring fire. Suddenly, a draft in the room whisked the dancer off the table and straight to the soldier in the fire. When the fire burned down, the soldier had melted to a small tin heart. All that was left of the dancer was her spangle, burned black.

Another popular Andersen tale is titled "The Tinder Box." A soldier was walking along the highroad one day when a witch stopped him and told him that he could have a lot of money if he would climb down a hollow tree and bring her up a tinder box. Thinking that was an easy way to get money, he tied a rope around his waist and the witch helped him to climb down inside the tree.

He took along the witch's apron, for on it he had to place the dogs that guarded the chests of money. The first dog, with eyes as big as saucers, guarded a chest full of coppers. The soldier placed the dog on the apron, filled his pockets with coppers, and walked on. The next dog, with eyes as big as millstones, guarded silver. The soldier placed the dog on the apron, emptied his pockets of coppers, and filled them with silver. The third dog had eyes as big as the Round Tower. He guarded gold. Placing the dog on the apron, he emptied his pockets of silver and filled them, his knapsack, his cap, and his boots with gold. Then he called to the witch to pull him up.

When she refused to tell him why she wanted the tinder box, he cut off her head and started for town. There he lived in splendor and gave alms to the poor, for he was goodhearted. He heard of a beautiful princess who was kept locked up because of a prophecy that she would marry a common soldier. Idly he thought of ways to see her.

When his money ran out and he had no candle, he remembered that there was a piece of candle in the tinder box. As he struck the box to light the candle, the door flew open and the dog with eyes like saucers burst in, asking what the soldier wanted. When he asked for money, the dog brought it back immediately. Then he found that he could call the second dog by striking the box twice, and the third dog by striking it three times. When he asked the dogs to bring the princess, she was brought to his room.

The king and queen had him thrown into prison when they caught him. There he was helpless until a little boy to whom he called brought the tinder box to him. When the soldier was about to be hanged, he asked permission to smoke a last pipe. Then he pulled out his tinder box and hit once, twice, three times. All three dogs came to rout the king's men and free the soldier. The people were so impressed that they made the soldier king and the princess his queen.

Critical Evaluation

Hans Christian Andersen's fairy tales are popular among both children and adults. The tales' power has its source in Andersen's use of the form to illumine the psychic wounds and scars of childhood that no adult ever forgets and to uphold the value of childhood purity against adult materialism. Andersen's stories are not self-consciously literary, nor are they usually set in the historical past. Instead, they are, with few exceptions, simple incidents with roots in events of his own life. As he develops them, they come to speak of the innocence of childhood, the falsity of adult rationality and materialism, the heartbreak of the sometimes futile search for unconditional love, and, above all, the need to transcend hardship— or to attempt to transcend it. When Andersen, still in his early teens, left his home for Copenhagen, he told his worried mother, "First one has to endure terrible adversity, then one becomes famous." The tales speak of the terror and adversity, if not always of the fame.

"The Red Shoes" has its source in new boots that Andersen himself wore for confirmation. In consternation and delight, he noticed that the squeaky boots distracted the congregation, and he, like Karen, could not concentrate despite the solemnity of the occasion. Karen, too, is ambitious, but the voices of law and church stifle and even cripple her, as they attempted to cripple Ander-

sen. Karen finds peace in heaven, where, says the story's ending, no one will be concerned about her red shoes— or a child's harmless vanity; Andersen found escape from pettiness and provincialism by fleeing Denmark into a wider world.

"The Ugly Duckling" is clearly autobiographical. The swan in the duck's nest is no more unlikely than was the future writer in the Odense nest of poverty, illiteracy, illegitimacy, and insanity from which he arose. The mother duck, like the author's own mother, makes a kindly but misguided effort to force him to conform; the hardships after leaving the nest are those that Andersen himself experienced as he created his career. Just as in Andersen's own life, the other swans caress the ugly duckling and welcome him as one of their own only after his hardships are over and his success is assured.

In "The Snow Queen," the queen is identified with the death, which came to take away Andersen's father when the child was eleven. As the tale progresses, however, the Snow Queen also becomes identified with adult reason and intellect, with the mathematics and geography that were imposed upon Andersen by a sadistic, and hated, schoolmaster who attempted to kill the boy's poetic gifts. Opposed to this sterility is emotion, embodied in Gerda, with her love and her tears, and the outlaw robbers and old crones, who advise her and the various flowers and beasts who see her on her way. When Gerda finds Kay, he is seated, quiet as death, in the Snow Queen's icy world, vainly trying to spell "eternity" with pieces of her frozen mirror. Gerda's tears free the boy. They return to springtime and to a world of steeples and church bells, as Grandmother reads, "Except ye become as little children, ye shall not enter the Kingdom of Heaven."

In "The Shepherdess and the Sweep," conflict also exists between the coldness and materialism of adulthood and the purity of innocence. The young porcelain lovers are thwarted by the worldly old Chinaman, who assumes authority he does not possess (the adult world is often arbitrary) and forbids the marriage between shepherdess and sweep. The girl is unwilling to risk the open, insecure world up beyond the chimney, just as the women Andersen adored would not risk marriage with the rootless and insecure artist. If in life unconditional love is rarely realized, the ending of a story can be happier. The authority of the old Chinaman is first broken and then rendered impotent, and the lovers are united.

The futility of adult wisdom likewise underlies "The Emperor's New Clothes." There, adults combine to reinforce the foolishness and vanity of the Emperor. Only the child in the crowd has the ability to see truth and the courage to express it. It is not stretching interpretation to see the Emperor's supposedly beautiful clothing as the equivalent of what Andersen perceived as second-rate art, which dominated the world into which he painfully tried to break. This art, perhaps also created by frauds, is that cultivated by fads, cliques, coteries, and place-seekers, while Andersen's own pure voice went unnoticed.

In "The Steadfast Tin Soldier," the topic turns back to the search, this time futile, for love. The tin soldier is another cripple, much as Andersen had been crippled by ungainly appearance and early adversity. The soldier, like his creator, is unwavering despite unspeakable hardships. He is rescued, but, unlike the successful Andersen, he is cast aside; the family prefers toys that are new and shiny to those that have been tested by life. The soldier is thrown into the fire, but chance, or God, ensures that there, finally, he is united with the paper doll he loves. The overcoming of hardship must in some way be rewarded, if only at the moment of extinction.

"The Tinder Box," too, deals with adversity, but its hero is spoiled in the process of overcoming it, much as Andersen, in his autobiographical writings, sometimes recorded his fear that he, also, would take his success too seriously. This story's hero forgets gratitude and kills the crone who helped him; he wastes the wealth he has gained and loses the friends who surrounded him when he was rich. Nonetheless, he can call upon the magic of the tinder box—the magic of art itself—to save him from his own folly. Ultimately, it saves him from death and wins him the hand of a princess.

ANNA KARENINA

Type of work: Novel
Author: Leo Tolstoy
Type of plot: Social criticism
Time of plot: Nineteenth century
Locale: Russia
First published: 1875–1877 (English translation, 1886)

The first of the dual plots in this novel relates the tragic story of Anna Karenina, who falls in love with a handsome young officer; eventually despairing of his love, she commits suicide by throwing herself under a train. The second plot, which centers on the happy marriage of Konstantine Levin and his young wife Kitty, is Tolstoy's vehicle for dramatizing a search for the meaning of life and a philosophy and manner of living similar to his own.

Principal Characters

Anna Karenina (än·nə′ kä·rĕ′nĭ·nə, Karenin's beautiful, wayward wife. After meeting the handsome officer Count Vronsky, she falls completely in love with him, even though she realizes what the consequences of this act of infidelity may be. In spite of her love for her child, she cannot give up Vronsky. Estranged from her husband, this unhappy woman, once so generous and respected, has an illegitimate child, runs off with Vronsky, and finally, when his love seems to wane, commits suicide by throwing herself in front of an approaching railway engine.

Count Alexey Kirilich Vronsky (ä·lĕk·sā′ kĭ·rĭ′lĭch vrŏn′skĭy), a wealthy army officer, who eagerly returns Anna Karenina's love. He is not a bad man; in fact, he is thoughtful and generous in many ways, as he proved when he gave part of his inheritance to his brother. Yet he thinks nothing of taking Anna away from her husband. Actually, such behavior is part of his code, which includes patronizing his inferiors. After Anna's death, he gloomily seeks death for himself.

Alexei Karenin (ä·lĕk·sā′ kä·rĕ′nĭn), a public official and a cold-blooded, ambitious man, whose main desire is to rise in government service. Seemingly incapable of jealousy or love (except self-love), he allows Anna to see Vronsky away from home. He is afraid only that his reputation will be blemished by his wife's infidelity. In spite of his cold temperament, he is a good official, who knows how to cut red tape and bureaucratic inefficiency.

Sergey Alexeyich Karenin (sĕr·gā′ ä·lĕksā′ĭch kä·rĕ′nĭn), called **Serezha** (sĕrĕ′zhə), Anna Karenina's bewildered young son. Recognizing the schism between his father and mother, he is often distraught by what he senses but does not understand.

Konstantine Levin (kôn·stän·tĭn′ lē′vĭn), a prosperous landowner. A fine, decent man, he intensely dislikes all forms of chicanery and hypocrisy. With his generous spirit and democratic outlook, he wants to help his peasants by giving them larger profits from their work on his estate. In return, he believes they will work harder for him. Forgetting his pride, he finally marries Kitty Shtcherbatskaya, and together they work hard to make his agricultural theories succeed.

Prince Stepan Oblonsky (stĕ·pän′ ôblŏn′skĭy), a high government official and Anna's brother. With his strong, well-fed body, he is the very picture of robust energy. A kind, often guilt-ridden man, he has a bachelor's temperament, and he finds it practically impossible to be true to his unattractive, jealous wife. After each affair, he strongly feels his guilt and tries to make amends, only to be smitten by the next pretty face he sees. He is so cheerful and happy that people like to be around him.

Princess Darya Oblonskaya (dä′ryə ŏblŏn′skə·yə), called **Dolly,** Oblonsky's long-suffering and unattractive wife. Faced with her husband's infidelity, she finds solace in her six children. Although she often threatens to leave him, she never does, and she becomes partly reconciled to his philandering.

Princess Catharine Shtcherbatskaya (schĕr·bät′skə·yə), called **Kitty,** Dolly's younger sister, who cannot choose between sober, generous Konstantine Levin and the more dashing Count Vronsky. When she learns that Vronsky obviously is not interested in marriage, she knows she has made an error in refusing Levin's proposal. After a short period of despondency, she, naturally buoyant and happy, realizes that the future is not completely gloomy, and she marries Levin.

Prince Alexander Shtcherbatsky (ä·lĕksän′dĕr shchĕr·bät′skĭy), a bluff, hardy man, the father of Kitty and Dolly. He likes Levin as Kitty's suitor because he is often suspicious of Vronsky's intentions toward his daughter. His cheerfulness lifts the spirits of his associates.

Princess Shtcherbatskaya (shchĕr·bät′skə·yə), Dolly and Kitty's ambitious mother. At first, she hopes Kitty will marry handsome Count Vronsky. Later, she is willing to accept Levin as Kitty's husband.

Nicholas Levin (nĭ·kô·lĭ′ lē′vĭn), Konstantine's brother.

A rather pitiful figure, he is aware of his approaching death from tuberculosis. Dreading his fate, he is a somber man, subject to violent rages and childish behavior.

Sergius Ivanich Koznyshev (sẻr′jĭ·ŭs ĭ·vän′ĭch kŏz′nĭy·shĕf), Konstantine Levin's half brother, a noted novelist and philosopher, whose favorite pastime is debating the issues of the day. Although he has many convincing arguments, it is doubtful that he understands the peasants as much as his more inarticulate brother.

Countess Vronskaya (vrōn′skə·yə), Count Vronsky's mother. An emaciated old woman, she tries to keep her favorite son under close watch. Failing in this effort, she withholds his allowance.

Marya Nikolavna (mä′ryə nĭ·kō′ləv·nə), called **Masha** (mä′shə), Nicholas Levin's mistress. She looks after the sick man as she would a child, even though he does not seem to appreciate her attempts to help them.

Tanya Oblonskaya (tän′yə ôb·lōn′skə·yə), Prince Oblonsky's daughter.

Grisha (grĭ′shə), Oblonsky's son.

Princess Elizabeth Fёdorovna Tvershaya (fyō′ dərəv·nə tvĕr·shä′yə), called **Betsy,** who acts as a go-between for Vronsky and Anna. Like many women in her social set, Betsy has a lover.

Agatha Mikhaylovna (mĭ·hī′lə·vnə), Levin's trusted housekeeper and confidante.

Princess Myagkaya (myäg·kä′yə), who likes to gossip and has a sharp, vituperative tongue.

Lieutenant Petritsky (pĕt·rĭt′skĭy), Count Vronsky's friend, a hard-drinking gambler. His commanding officer often threatens to expel him from the regiment.

Prince Yashvin (yä′shvĭn), Vronsky's friend. Like Petritsky, he is a hard drinker and an inveterate gambler.

Kuzma (kōōz·mä′), Levin's manservant.

Mikhail (mĭ·hä·ĭl′) and **Piotr** (pyō′tr), Vronsky's servants.

Piotr Ivanovich (pyō′tr ĭ·vä′nə·vĭch), a professor.

Petrov (pĕt·rôf′), an invalid artist dying of tuberculosis. He is infatuated with Kitty.

Anna Pavlovna (än′nə päv′ləv·nə), Petrov's jealous wife.

Sappho Stolz, a full-blown actress.

Lisa Merkalova (lĭ′sə mĕr·kä′lə·və), Betsy Tvershaya's friend. A beautiful, charming girl, she always has a number of ardent admirers following her.

Nicholas Ivanich Sviyazhsky (nĭ·kô·lĭ′ ĭ·vä′nĭch svĭ·yä′zh·skĭy), a wealthy landowner and a marshal of the nobility.

Mlle Varenka (vä·rĕn′kə), Kitty's friend. She is wholesome and pure, and her greatest pleasure is caring for the sick.

Mme Stahl, Mlle Varenka's malingering foster mother. According to one person, she never gets up because she has short legs and a bad figure.

Annushka (än·nūsh′kə), Anna Karenina's maid.

The Story

Anna Karenina, the sister of Stepan Oblonsky, came to Moscow in an attempt to patch up a quarrel between her brother and his wife, Dolly. There she met the handsome young Count Vronsky, who was rumored to be in love with Dolly's younger sister, Kitty.

Konstantine Levin, of an old Muscovite family, was also in love with Kitty, and his visit to Moscow coincided with Anna's. Kitty refused Levin, but to her chagrin she received no proposal from the count. Indeed, Vronsky had no intention of proposing to Kitty. His heart went out to Anna the first time he laid eyes on her, and when Anna returned to her home in St. Petersburg, he followed her.

Soon they began to be seen together at soirees and at the theater, apparently unaware of gossip which circulated about them. Karenin, Anna's husband, became concerned. A coldly ambitious and dispassionate man, he felt that his social position was at stake. One night, he discussed these rumors with Anna and pointed out the danger of her flirtation, as he called it. He forbade her to entertain Vronsky at home and cautioned her to be more careful. He was not jealous of his wife, only worried over the social consequences of her behavior. He reminded her of her duty to her young son, Serezha.

Anna said she would obey her husband, and there the matter rested.

Anna, however, was unable to conceal her true feelings when Vronsky was injured in a racetrack accident. Karenin upbraided her for her indiscreet behavior in public. He considered a duel, separation, and divorce but rejected all these courses. When he finally decided to keep Anna under his roof, he reflected that he was acting in accordance with the laws of religion. Anna continued to meet Vronsky in secret.

Levin had returned to his country estate after Kitty had refused him, and he busied himself there with problems of agriculture and peasant labor. One day, he went into the fields and worked with a scythe along with the serfs. He felt that he was beginning to understand the primitive philosophy of their lives. He planned new developments, among them a cooperative enterprise system. When he heard that Kitty was not married after all and that she had been ill but was soon returning to Moscow, he resolved to seek her hand once more. Secretly, he knew that she loved him. His pride, as well as hers, had kept them apart. Accordingly, Levin made the journey to Moscow with new hope that soon Kitty would be his wife.

Against her husband's orders, Anna Karenina sent for

Vronsky and told him that she was pregnant. Aware of his responsibilities to Anna, he begged her to petition Karenin for a divorce so that she would be free to marry him. Karenin informed her coldly that he would consider the child his and accept it so that the world should never know his wife's disgrace, but he refused to think of going through shameful divorce proceedings. Karenin reduced Anna to submission by warning her that he would take Serezha away if she persisted in making a fool of herself.

The strained family relationship continued unbroken. One night, Karenin had planned to go out, and Anna persuaded Vronsky to come to the house. As he was leaving, Karenin met Vronsky on the front steps. Enraged, Karenin told Anna that he had decided to get a divorce and that he would keep Serezha in his custody. Divorce proceedings, however, were so intricate, the scandal so great, the whole aspect of the step so disgusting to Karenin that he could not bring himself to go through the process. As Anna's confinement drew near, he was still undecided. After winning an important political seat, he became even more unwilling to risk his public reputation.

At the birth of her child, Anna became deathly ill. Overcome with guilt, Vronsky attempted suicide but failed. Karenin was reduced to a state of such confusion that he determined to grant his wife any request, since he thought she was on her deathbed. The sight of Vronsky seemed to be the only thing that restored her. After many months of illness, she went with her lover and baby daughter to Italy where they lived under strained circumstances. Meanwhile, Levin proposed once more to Kitty; after a flurry of preparations, they were married.

Anna Karenina and Vronsky returned to Russia and went to live on his estate. It was now impossible for Anna to return home. Although Karenin had not undertaken divorce proceedings, he considered himself separated from Anna and was everywhere thought to be a man of fine loyalty and unswerving honor, unjustly imposed upon by an unfaithful wife. Sometimes Anna stole into town to see Serezha, but her fear of being discovered there by her husband cut these visits short. After each visit, she returned bitter and sad. She became more and more demanding toward Vronsky, with the result that he spent less time with her. She took only slight interest in her child. Before long, she convinced herself that Vronsky was in love with another woman. One day, she could not stay alone in the house. She found herself at the railway station, and she bought a ticket. As she stood on the platform, gazing at the tracks below, the thunder of an approaching train roared in her ears. Suddenly, she remembered a man run over in the Moscow railroad station on the day she and Vronsky met. Carefully measuring the distance, she threw herself in front of the approaching train.

After her death, Vronsky joined the army. He had changed from a handsome, cheerful man to one who welcomed death; his only reason for living had been Anna.

For Levin and Kitty, life became an increasing round of daily work and everyday routine, which they shared with each other. At last, Levin knew the responsibility of wealth imposed upon him in his dealings with the peasants. Kitty shared with him this responsibility. Although there were many questions he could never answer satisfactorily for himself, he was nevertheless aware of the satisfying beauty of life—its toil, leisure, pain, and happiness.

Critical Evaluation

Leo Tolstoy spent almost six years composing *Anna Karenina*, from first draft (1873) through serial publication (1875–1877) to publication in one volume (1878). He constantly refined the structure, style, and content until he took unabashed "pride in the architectonics." The novel is perfectly symmetrical in balancing pairs of relationships, places, and events. The style is carefully crafted to suit the character and the event: famous scenes such as Levin's reaping of the harvest and Anna's suicide possess distinctive rhythm, syntax, and imagery. The novel tackles subjects that concerned its contemporary audience: the morality of divorce, the problem of managing land with freed serfs, and the wisdom of a recently declared war against Bulgaria.

The opening sentence of *Anna Karenina* simply, starkly announces the theme and predicts the symmetrical structure: "All happy families resemble one another, but each unhappy family is unhappy in its own way." Whether a family is happy or not depends upon the husband and wife, man and woman who are its nucleus. The happy family is that formed by the marriage of Konstantine Levin and Kitty Shtcherbatskaya. The unhappy family is composed of Anna Karenina and Alexei Karenin.

The happy family of Kitty and Levin does not happen spontaneously or easily. Kitty, her heart set on the charming Count Vronsky, refuses Levin's first proposal. When Vronsky finds another love, Levin makes a second, hesitant proposal. Kitty's acceptance is tentative because what she feels for Levin is more affection than passion. To ease his conscience of past sins, Levin shows Kitty his youthful diaries; their secrets are bitter to her but not barriers to their union. Their wedding day is joyous as is establishing their household on the estate that Levin manages. Inevitably, the honeymoon ends. Together, Levin and Kitty must care for his dying brother Nicholas and then open their house to her sister Dolly, who is estranged from her philandering husband. Now the established married couple, they play matchmaker for friends and relations. With Kitty in confinement with their first child, the lonely Levin wrestles with the questions of life's meaning and his own mortality. Then the birth of his son reminds him that he has the power to invest life with goodness and meaning. Kitty and Levin are thus a happy couple not because their life together is without sorrow but because they sacrifice for each other, pardon each other, and desire each other's happiness.

The family of the Karenins was possibly once happy. Anna and Karenin are among the elite of St. Petersburg society; they possess status, wealth, security, and reputation. Anna's first meeting with Vronsky is accidental; though the young count is handsome and her husband cold, she is not looking for a distracting passion. Yet he pursues Anna over her protestations, and eventually she returns his love. Their affair soon comes to Karenin's attention, but he only cautions her to conceal her actions. Even if the inward happiness of their relationship is destroyed, Karenin would be content with the outward appearance of happiness. Since passion is stronger than prudence, Anna and Vronsky continue to meet until the inevitable happens: She becomes pregnant. Karenin threatens a divorce but is afraid of public scandal. Anna almost dies giving birth to the child, and Vronsky attempts suicide. To convalesce, the lovers travel to Italy and live together—in open defiance of convention—when they return to Russia. As her world narrows, Anna grows jealous and suspicious. Thinking Vronsky has fallen in love with another woman, Anna commits suicide. Vronsky volunteers for the Bulgarian war, determined to die in battle. Their story is the classic tale of fatal attraction. For love—or perhaps for ego—Anna and Vronsky sacrifice family, reputation, health, and ultimately, life.

Tolstoy's contrast between these stories is neither a simple nor a simplistic one. Levin and Kitty are not unvaryingly good or is their marriage without its problems. Conversely, Anna and Vronsky are adulterers who possess intelligence, passion, and commitment; their relationship offers moments of peace and insight. Most surprisingly, the central contrast is neither between Levin and Vronsky or Karenin, nor between Anna and Kitty. The novel offers portraits of adulterers who are not punished and portraits of faithful husbands who are ignoble. Both marriages are, in fact, atypical of aristocratic society. Only by resisting the temptation to present Sunday-schoolish opposition between moral respectability and self-destructive sinfulness was Tolstoy able to invest *Anna Karenina* with a transcendent quality approaching wisdom.

What gives the novel its unusual power is the crucial juxtaposition of Levin to Anna. The dramatic similarity between Anna and Levin is that both are tempted to kill themselves. Both reach a moment in which they despair that life has no meaning. Anna succumbs but Levin does not. Neither can claim credit for their fate. At the last second, Anna attempts to stop herself from pitching beneath the wheels, but something forces her forward. Levin carries about the rope or gun that could end his life, but something prevents him. That something comes from the character's relationship to society and to nature.

Anna is a creature of St. Petersburg society, and Levin is a creature of Moscow society. They stand, however, in different relationship to their societies. To Anna, status is everything: her conversation, her dress, her thinking— all of her activities—have the sole purpose of distinguishing her from the other important women of St. Petersburg. To Levin, status is nothing: he cares little for the round of glittering parties and current fashions. He accepts society's characterization of him as a sweet but odd man.

Anna is a creature of the city. She lives in the artificial environments of the parlor, boudoir, and ballroom. She lives by the calendar of public events, and mixes only with those of her own social class. Levin, on the other hand, is a creature of the country. He lives in the natural environments of field and forest. He lives by the calendar of the seasons: sowing, hunting, and harvesting in turn. He works beside the laborers who tend his estate, sharing their physical exertions and pleasures.

Finally, Anna is a woman. Her intelligence and her will have two avenues of expression in St. Petersburg society. She may have status as a wife, binding her husband by giving him children and managing his house, or she may have reputation as a mistress, captivating her lover by passion and sensuousness. When she stops being a wife and no longer charms a paramour, she has no power or position left in society. As a man, Levin is more fortunate. He has a wider scope for exercising his intelligence and will. He can abjure political or military responsibility and content himself with managing his estate. He can live without a wife; he can postpone having a family and still have purpose and identity in life.

Tolstoy clearly respects both of his protagonists. His identity with Levin is easy to understand. The self-reflective nobleman has much in common with the author: His marriage is a portrait of Tolstoy's own marriage, with Sonya Bers; his fear of death is Tolstoy's own *memento mori*. Tolstoy's respect for Anna is more complex. He originally conceived her as a portrait of sexual corruption: She would be an object lesson about the wages of infidelity (a topic much on Tolstoy's mind). Then he came to conceive her as a character deserving sympathy, a pathetic figure rather than a monster. Actually, he presents her as a tragic figure. Like Oedipus or Antigone, she is trapped by fate. Unable to undo the effects of society and nature, she asserts herself by controlling the one thing she has power over, her life. Like Levin, she proves that she is ultimately free to invest her life with meaning.

ANTIGONE

Type of work: Drama
Author: Sophocles (495?–406 B.C.)
Type of plot: Classical tragedy
Time of plot: Remote antiquity
Locale: The city of Thebes
First presented: 441 B.C.

This play was so successful with its original Athenian audience that they rewarded the playwright with a generalship in the war against Samos. The tragedy in the play arises from the age-old conflict between individual moral responsibility (the necessity of proper burial) and the demands of the state (the obedience owed to Creon as the legitimate ruler).

Principal Characters

Antigone (ăn·tĭg′ə·nē), the daughter of Oedipus, sister of Eteocles, defender of Thebes, and Polynices, an exile from the city and one of its attackers. After Eteocles and Polynices have killed each other in battle, Creon, Antigone's uncle and now king of Thebes, decrees that Eteocles' body shall be buried with honors befitting a national hero but that Polynices' body shall be left unburied, a prey to scavengers. Divine law, Greek custom, and simple humanity demand, however, that Antigone see her brother buried; she must choose, therefore, between obedience to the temporal rule of Creon and the duty she owes to a brother she had loved. Although she knows that her fate will be death, she chooses to bury the body of her brother. She is undoubtedly strong-willed and defiant; having been apprehended by the guards posted to prevent the burial, she replies to Creon's wrathful accusations of treason with an equal ferocity. Yet she emerges as immensely heroic, for she alone seems clearly to understand that the king's law is inferior to divine law and that if sacrifice is required to follow the right, such sacrifice must be made. She is always aware of the glory of her deed and dies for love in the largest sense of the word, but her concurrent awareness of her youth and her loss of earthly love humanizes her and makes her a profoundly tragic figure.

Creon (krē′ŏn), king of Thebes. Although he gives lip service to the necessity for order and for obedience to the law, he is a tyrant who has identified the welfare of the state with his own self-interest and self-will. He commits hubris through his violent misuse of his temporal power; he too has a duty to bury the dead, and his unjust condemnation of Antigone to death is murder of a near relative, although he changes her sentence from stoning to burial alive in order to avoid the formal pollution which would accompany such a deed. He has a regard for the external forms of religion but no understanding of its essential meaning. When Tiresias brings the gods' curse on his actions, he relents, but too late to save Antigone or his son.

Haemon (hē′mŏn), Creon's son, engaged to wed Antigone. He attempts to placate his father. Failing, he declares his fidelity to Antigone. When Creon comes to release Antigone from the cave in which she has been entombed, he finds that she has hanged herself and that Haemon is embracing her suspended body. Haemon attempts to kill his father, then falls on his own sword.

Ismene (ĭs·mē′nē), Antigone's sister, as gentle and timid as Antigone is high-minded and strong. She pleads a woman's weakness when Antigone asks her to help with Polynices' burial, yet her love for her sister makes her willing to share the blame when Antigone is accused.

Eurydice (ū·rĭd′ĭ·sē), Creon's wife. She kills herself when she is informed of Haemon's death.

Tiresias (tī·rē′sĭ·əs), a prophet who brings to Creon a warning and a curse that cause him belatedly to revoke his decision to execute Antigone. He is the human in closest affinity with the divine; his intercession is therefore equivalent to divine sanction for Antigone's deeds.

The Story

Polynices and Eteocles, sons of the cursed family of King Oedipus, led two armies against each other before the gates of Thebes, and both brothers were killed in single combat with each other. Creon, their uncle, and now the tyrant ruler of the city, ordered that Eteocles be given full funeral rites, but that Polynices, who had attacked the city, be left unburied and unmourned. Anyone who broke this decree would be punished with death.

Antigone and Ismene, the sisters of Polynices and Eteocles, discussed this order, and with grief for the unburied brother tearing at her heart, Antigone asked Ismene to aid her in giving him burial. When Ismene refused to help in so dangerous a task, Antigone went defiantly to bury Polynices.

Shortly afterward, Creon learned from a sentry that the body had been buried. Angrily he ordered the sentry to find the perpetrator of the deed. The sentry returned to the grave and uncovered the body. During a dust storm Antigone came to look at the grave and, finding it open, filled the air with lamentation. Her cries attracted the attention of the guard, who captured her and took her to Creon.

Questioned by Creon, she said that to bury a man was to obey the laws of the gods, even if it were against the laws of a man. Her reply angered Creon. Antigone must die. Ismene tried to soften Creon's heart toward her sister by reminding him that Antigone was engaged to his son, Haemon. But Creon remained firm.

Haemon incurred his father's anger by arguments that Creon should soften his cruel decree because of popular sympathy for Antigone. Creon said that he cared nothing for the ideas of the town, and Haemon called his answer foolish. As a punishment, Creon ordered that Antigone be killed before Haemon's eyes. Haemon fled with threats of revenge. Creon ordered that Antigone be walled up in a cave outside Thebes and left there to die for her crime against his law.

When Antigone was led out of the city, the people of Thebes followed her, lamenting her fate. She was thrust into the cave while Polynices' body lay unburied outside the walls. The prophet Tiresias warned Creon that the gods had not been pleased with his action, and that the body should be buried. He foretold that before long Haemon would die if his father did not bury Polynices and rescue Antigone from the cave.

Creon, realizing that Tiresias' prophesies had never proved false, hurried to avert the fate the prophet had foretold. Quickly Creon ordered a tomb prepared for Polynices, and he set off to release Antigone. But the will of the gods could not be changed so easily. When he reached the cave, he heard his son's voice within, crying out in grief. Creon entered and saw that Antigone had hanged herself with a rope made from her own dress. Haemon, sword in hand, rushed at his father as if to attack him. He then fell on his sword and killed himself in sorrow over Antigone's death. The news of these events quickly traveled back to the city, and Creon's wife, hearing of so many misfortunes, died by her own hand.

On returning to Thebes with the body of his son, Creon learned of his wife's death. Seeing that his life could no longer have meaning, he had himself led out of the city into exile. He was, himself, the final victim of his harsh tyranny.

Critical Evaluation

Antigone is one of the finest, most moving tragedies ever written. It was very successful when it was first produced in 441 B.C., and tradition says that Sophocles was made an Athenian general in the war against Samos because of it. Modern audiences, too, find this play meaningful, particularly in the conflict between individual conscience and the state policy. The fundamental issue of the play, however, goes deeper than that conflict. It probes the nature of suffering, and finds in it a universal condition, one that exists at the very heart of the human experience.

Sophocles did not share Aeschylus' view that man learns by pain, or the Christian idea that we are purified by agony. Both opinions are ultimately optimistic because they are based on hope in some future vindication of our misery. In contrast, Sophocles faced the problem of pain without hope, as an essential fact of life that no one could escape. With this outlook he was keenly attuned to both the sadness and the tragedy inherent in living.

Ironically, Sophocles himself enjoyed the most fortunate life possible to a Greek. He was crowned with honors from early manhood on to the age of ninety, when he died. He was a skilled athlete, he achieved public position. Most important, he had an extremely creative and successful dramatic career, writing more than one hundred and twenty plays, ninety-six of which were awarded first place in the Athenian drama competitions. He was the foremost tragedian in an age of magnificent literary, artistic, and political genius—Periclean Athens. Moreover, he won a lasting reputation as one of the supreme playwrights of all time. *Antigone*, written when Sophocles was in his fifties, affords a penetrating look at his dramatic prowess.

The meaning of this play is to be found in the antithesis between Antigone and her uncle Creon. The issue of burying Polynices depends on a grasp of Greek ideas about death. An unburied body meant a soul condemned to torment. It was the profound obligation of the family, therefore, to see that a body was properly inhumed. This was more than a matter of family loyalty, it was an act of piety demanded by the gods. Antigone undertakes that obligation even though it means treason to the State, the rejection of her only sister Ismene, the renunciation of her fiancé, and her own death. She is absolutely uncompromising about it, knowing all the consequences beforehand. As it turns out, she is justified, but we do not know this until Tiresias appears and then it is too late to matter, for she has hanged herself.

Creon also has a valid stand. The traitor Polynices should be punished in death. A conscientious ruler, he is concerned about loyalty to the state. But in his position as king he confuses his own will with the good of Thebes.

In pursuing his edict, which says that anyone who buries Polynices will be put to death, he changes from a good king into a tyrant. His vanity is involved: he will not be put in the wrong by a young woman or his son in front of the chorus of Theban elders. His flaw lies in his stubborn, self-righteous inflexibility when the tide of evidence turns against him. He angrily maintains his stand in the face of Antigone's martyrdom, his son's pleading, the sympathy of the townspeople with Antigone, and Tiresias' warnings. He only relents because of the fear he feels after Tiresias has prophesied doom for his family and for the city. But, again, his penitence comes too late to save himself.

It is wrong, however, to see Antigone as a perfect heroine or Creon as a willing malefactor. The same passion that goes into Antigone's heroic treason in burying her brother makes her unjustly cruel to her gentle sister Ismene; and she has no thought whatever for Haemon, her fiancé. She is right, but she is also unbearably self-righteous. The only time we feel sympathy for her is when she laments that she will never have a husband or a child, but she made that choice freely and passionately. As far as character goes, there is no difference whatever between Antigone's self-righteousness and Creon's. Both are hard and unyielding.

The difference between the two lies in the principle by which they live. Antigone chooses to serve the gods, or divine law, while Creon makes the state his top priority. Both serve their principle with all the force of their being. But because Creon has chosen the lesser law, and because the state as he conceives it is indistinguishable from his own ego, he must bow in the end to the gods, and they crush him. Ironically, he faces the same suffering he meted out to Antigone. Just as he deprived her of the chance to have a husband and child, so he is bereft of his wife and son.

Creon's fate is sad because he blundered into it unwittingly, through stubbornly upholding a limited idea. The man lacked wisdom. Yet Antigone's death is tragic because she voluntarily accepted it as the consequence of her heroism. For all her hardness, there is something truly grand and edifying in her fate. When suffering is a part of every man's condition, there is a vast difference in how one takes it. A man can fumble into it through ignorance and flaws of character, as Creon does, which makes him merely pathetic. This is the normal human lot. Or a person can freely choose suffering with open eyes by taking on a divine obligation in spite of all obstacles. This way is intense and tragic, but in the end it is the only path that can enlarge our humanity. The greatness of *Antigone* lies in the clarity, the poignance, and the integrity with which Sophocles presented these two possibilities.

ANTONY AND CLEOPATRA

Type of work: Drama
Author: William Shakespeare (1564–1616)
Type of plot: Romantic tragedy
Time of plot: About 30 B.C.
Locale: Egypt and various parts of the Roman Empire
First presented: 1606–1607

Antony and Cleopatra *is the tragedy of a man destined to rule the world who instead brings himself to ruin through capitulation to desires of the flesh; deserted by friends and subjects, he is forced to seek the escape of ignoble suicide. Shakespeare's source for the play was Sir Thomas North's translation of Plutarch's* Lives. *It is interesting to note that for many years Dryden's version of the story,* All for Love, *was the more frequently performed of the two plays.*

Principal Characters

Mark Antony (märk ăn′tə·nē), also **Marcus Antonius,** the majestic ruin of a great general and political leader, a Triumvir of Rome. Enthralled by Cleopatra, he sometimes seems about to desert her for her real and dangerous rival: Rome. He marries Caesar's sister Octavia for political reasons, but returns to Cleopatra. His greatness is shown as much by his effect on others as by his own actions. His cynical, realistic follower Enobarbus is deeply moved by him; his soldier's adore him even in defeat; his armor-bearer remains with him to the death; even his enemy Octavius Caesar praises him in life and is shocked into heightened eulogy when he hears of his death. Antony is capable of jealous fury and reckless indiscretion; but he bears the aura of greatness. He dies by his own hand after hearing the false report of Cleopatra's death, but lives long enough to see her once more and bid her farewell.

Cleopatra (klē·ō·pā′trə), queen of Egypt. Considered by many critics Shakespeare's greatest feminine creation, she has the complexity and inconsistency of real life. Like Antony, she is displayed much through the eyes of others. Even the hard-bitten realist Enobarbus is moved to lavish poetic splendor by her charm and beauty. Only Octavius Caesar, of all those who come in contact with her, is impervious to her charms, but the nobility of her death moves even him. She is mercurial and self-centered, and there is some ambiguity in her love of Antony. It is difficult to be certain that her tragic death would have taken place had cold Octavius Caesar been susceptible to her fascination. She is most queenly in her death, which she chooses to bring about in "the high Roman fashion," calling the dead Antony "husband" just before she applies the asp to her bosom.

Octavius Caesar (äk·′ tā·vē·əs ′sē·zər), Triumvir of Rome, Antony's great rival. His youthfulness is set off against Antony's age; his coldness against Antony's passion; his prudence against Antony's recklessness. The result, from a dramatic point of view, is heavily in Antony's favor. Caesar's affection for his sister Octavia is almost the only warm note in his character; but his comments on the deaths of Antony and Cleopatra show unexpected generosity and magnanimity.

Domitius Enobarbus (dō·mĭsh′yŭs ē·nōbär′bŭs), Antony's friend and follower. Of the family of Shakespeare's loyal Horatio and Kent, he is a strong individual within the type. Though given to the disillusioned cynicism of the veteran soldier, he has a splendid poetic vein which is stimulated by Cleopatra. He knows his master well and leaves him only when Antony seems to have left himself. Miserable as a deserter, Enobarbus is moved so deeply by Antony's generosity that he dies of grief. He serves as a keen, critical chorus for about three-fourths of the play.

Marcus Aemilius Lepidus (mĭ′kŭs ēmĭl′ĭ·dŭs), the third Triumvir, a "poor third," as Enobarbus calls him. He tries to bring together Antony and Octavius and to quell the thunderstorms which their rivalry frequently engenders. He is the butt of some teasing by Antony when they are both drinking heavily on Pompey's galley. After the defeat of Pompey, Octavius Caesar destroys Lepidus, leaving himself and Antony to fight for control of the world.

Sextus Pompeius (Pompey) (sĕks′tŭs pŏm·pē′yŭs; ′päm·pē), the son of Pompey the Great. Ambitious and power-hungry, he has a vein of chivalric honor which prevents his consenting to the murder of his guests, the Triumvirs, aboard his galley. He makes a peace with the Triumvirs, largely because of Antony, but is later attacked and defeated by Caesar and loses not only his power but his life as well.

Octavia (äk·′tā·vēə), sister of Octavius Caesar. A virtuous widow, fond of her brother and strangely fond of Antony after their marriage, she serves as a foil to Cleopatra. She is not necessarily as dull as Cleopatra thinks her. There is pathos in her situation, but she lacks tragic stature.

Charmian, a pert, charming girl attending Cleopatra. Gay, witty, and risqué, she maintains a tragic dignity during the death of her queen. She tends Cleopatra's body, closes the eyes, delivers a touching eulogy, and then joins her mistress in death.

Iras, another of Cleopatra's charming attendants. Much like Charmian, but not quite so fully drawn, she dies just before Cleopatra.

Mardian, a eunuch, servant of Cleopatra. He bears the false message of Cleopatra's death to Antony, which leads Antony to kill himself.

Alexas, an attendant to Cleopatra. He jests wittily with Charmian, Iras, and the Soothsayer. Deserting Cleopatra and joining Caesar, he is hanged by Caesar's orders.

A Soothsayer. He serves two functions: one to make satirical prophecies to Charmian and Iras, which turn out to be literally true; the other to warn Antony against remaining near Caesar, whose fortune will always predominate. The second helps Antony to make firm his decision to leave Octavia and return to Egypt.

Seleucus (sĕ·lōō′kŭs), Cleopatra's treasurer. He betrays to Caesar the information that Cleopatra is holding back the greater part of her treasure. She indulges in a public temper tantrum when he discloses this; but since the information apparently lulls Caesar into thinking that the queen is not planning suicide, perhaps Seleucus is really aiding, not betraying, her.

A Clown, who brings a basket of figs to the captured queen. In the basket are concealed the poisonous asps. The clown's language is a mixture of simpleminded philosophy and mistaken meanings. The juxtaposition of his unconscious humor and Cleopatra's tragic death is reminiscent of the scene between Hamlet and the gravedigger.

Ventidius (vĕn·tĭd′ĭ·ŭs), one of Antony's able subordinates. A practical soldier, he realizes that it is best to be reasonably effective, but not spectacular enough to arouse the envy of his superiors; therefore, he does not push his victory to the extreme.

Eros (ē′rŏs), Antony's loyal bodyguard and armor bearer. He remains with his leader to final defeat. Rather than carry out Antony's command to deliver him a death stroke, he kills himself.

Scarus (skä′rŭs, skā′rŭs), one of Antony's tough veterans. Fighting heroically against Caesar's forces in spite of severe wounds, he rouses Antony's admiration. In partial payment, Antony requests the queen to offer him her hand to kiss.

Canidius (că·nĭd′ĭ·ŭs), Antony's lieutenant general. When Antony refuses his advice and indiscreetly chooses to fight Caesar's forces on sea rather than on land, and consequently meets defeat, Canidius deserts to Caesar.

Dercetas (der′cĕ·tə s), a loyal follower of Antony. He takes the sword stained with Antony's blood to Caesar, announces his leader's death, and offers either to serve Caesar or die.

Demetrius (də·mē′trĭ·ŭs) and **Philo** (fī′lō), followers of Antony. They open the play with comments on Antony's "dotage" on the Queen of Egypt.

Euphronius (ū·frō′nĭ·ŭs), Antony's old schoolmaster. He is Antony's emissary to Caesar asking for generous terms of surrender. Caesar refuses his requests.

Silius (sĭl′yŭs), an officer in Ventidius' army.

Menas (mē′năs), a pirate in the service of Pompey. He remains sober at the drinking bout on board Pompey's galley and offers Pompey the world. He intends to cut the cable of the galley and then cut the throats of the Triumvirs and their followers. Angered at Pompey's rejection of his proposal, he joins Enobarbus in drunken revelry and withdraws his support from Pompey.

Menecrates (mĕn·ĕk′rə·tēz) and **Varrius** (vä′rĭ·ŭs), followers of Pompey.

Maecenas (mē·sē′nəs), Caesar's friend and follower. He supports Agrippa and Lepidus in arranging the alliance between Caesar and Antony.

Agrippa (ə·grĭp′ə), Caesar's follower. He is responsible for the proposal that Antony and Octavia be married to cement the alliance. His curiosity about Cleopatra leads to Enobarbus' magnificent description of her on her royal barge.

Dolabella (dŏl·ə·bĕl′ə), one of Caesar's emissaries to Cleopatra. Enchanted by her, he reveals Caesar's plan to display her in a Roman triumph. This information strengthens her resolution to take her own life.

Proculeius (prō·kū·lē′ŭs), the only one of Caesar's followers whom Antony advises Cleopatra to trust. She wisely withholds the trust, for Proculeius is sent by Caesar to lull her into a false sense of security.

Thyreus (thī′rē·ŭs), an emissary of Caesar. Antony catches him kissing Cleopatra's hand and has him whipped and sent back to Caesar with insulting messages.

Gallus (găl′ŭs), another of Caesar's followers. He captures Cleopatra and her maids in the monument and leaves them guarded.

Taurus (tô′rŭs), Caesar's lieutenant general.

The Story

After the murder of Julius Caesar, the Roman Empire was ruled by three men, the noble triumvirs, Mark Antony, Lepidus, and Octavius, Caesar's nephew. Antony, having been given the Eastern sphere to rule, had gone to Alexandria and there he had seen and fallen passionately in love with Cleopatra, queen of Egypt. She was the flower of the Nile, but a wanton who had been the mistress of Julius Caesar and of many others. Antony was so filled with lust for her that he ignored his own counsel and the warnings of his friends, and as long as possible he ignored also a request from Octavius Caesar that he return to Rome. Sextus Pompeius, son of Pompey the Great, and a powerful leader, was gathering troops to seize Rome from the rule of the triumvirs, and Octavius Caesar wished to confer with the other two, Antony and Lepidus. At last the danger of a victory by Sextus Pompeius, coupled with the news that his wife Fulvia was dead, forced Antony to leave Egypt and Cleopatra and journey to Rome.

Pompeius was confident of victory so long as Antony stayed in Egypt, for Antony was a better general than either Lepidus or Octavius. When Pompeius heard that Antony was headed toward Rome, his hope was that Octavius and Antony would not mend their quarrels but would continue to fight each other as they had in the past. Lepidus did not matter; he sided with neither of the other two, and cared little for conquest and glory. Pompeius faced disappointment however, for Antony and Octavius mended their quarrels in the face of common danger. To seal their renewed friendship, Antony married Octavia, the sister of Octavius; through her, each general would be bound to the other. Thus it seemed that Pompeius' scheme to separate Antony and Octavius would fail. His last hope was that Antony's lust would send him back to Cleopatra; then he and Octavius would battle each other and Pompeius would conquer Rome. To stall for time, he sealed a treaty with the triumvirs. Antony, with his wife, went to Athens on business for the Empire. There word reached him that Lepidus and Octavius had waged war in spite of the treaty they had signed, and Pompeius had been killed. Octavius' next move was to seize Lepidus on the pretext that he had aided Pompeius. Now the Roman world had but two rulers, Octavius and Antony.

But Antony could not resist the lure of Cleopatra. Sending Octavia, his wife, home from Athens, he hurried back to Egypt. His return ended all pretense of friendship between him and Octavius. Each man prepared for battle, the winner to be the sole ruler of the world. Cleopatra joined her forces with those of Antony. At first Antony was supreme on the land, but Octavius ruled the sea and lured Antony to fight him there. Antony's friends and captains, particularly loyal Enobarbus, begged him not to risk his forces on the sea, but Antony, confident of victory, prepared to match his ships with those of Octavius at Actium. But in the decisive hour of the great sea fight Cleopatra ordered her fleet to leave the battle, and sail for home. Antony, leaving the battle and his honor and his glory, followed her. Because he had set the example for desertion, many of his men left his forces and joined the standard of Octavius.

Antony was sunk in gloom at the folly of his own actions, but his lust had made him drunk with desire, and everything, even honor, must bow to Cleopatra. She protested that she did not know that Antony would follow her when she sailed away. Antony had reason enough to know she lied, but he still wanted the fickle wanton at any cost.

Octavius sent word to Cleopatra that she might have all her wishes granted if she would surrender Antony to Octavius. Knowing that Octavius was likely to be the victor in the struggle, she sent him a message of loyalty and of admiration for his greatness. Although Antony had seen her receive the addresses of Octavius' messenger, and even though he ranted and stormed at her for her faithlessness, she was easily able to dispel his fears and jealousy and make him hers again. After a failure to sue for peace, Antony decided to march again against his enemy. At this decision even the faithful Enobarbus left him and went over to Octavius, for he thought Antony had lost his reason as well as his honor. But Enobarbus too was an honorable man who shortly afterward died of shame for deserting his general.

On the day of the battle, victory was in sight for Antony, in spite of overwhelming odds. But once more the flight of the Egyptian fleet betrayed him. His defeat left Octavius master of the world. Antony was like a madman, seeking nothing but revenge on treacherous Cleopatra. When the queen heard of his rage, she had word sent to him that she was dead, killed by her own hand out of love for him. Convinced once more that Cleopatra had been true to him, Antony called on Eros, his one remaining follower, to kill him so that he could join Cleopatra in death. But faithful Eros killed himself rather than stab his beloved general. Determined to die, Antony fell on his own sword. Even that desperate act was without dignity or honor, for he did not die immediately and he could find no one who loved him enough to end his pain and misery. While he lay there, a messenger brought word that Cleopatra still lived. He ordered his servants to carry him to her. There he died in her arms, each proclaiming eternal love for the other.

When Octavius Caesar heard the news of Antony's death, he grieved. Although he had fought and conquered Antony, he lamented the sorry fate of a great man turned weakling, ruined by his own lust. He sent a messenger to assure Cleopatra that she would be treated royally, that she should be ruler of her own fate. But the queen learned, as Antony had warned her, that Octavius would take her to Rome to march behind him in his triumphant procession, where she, a queen and mistress to two former rulers of the world, would be pinched and spat upon by rabble and slaves. To cheat him of his triumph, she put on her crown and all her royal garb, placed a poisonous asp on her breast, and lay down to die. Charmian and Iras, her loyal attendants, died the same death. Octavius Caesar, entering her chamber, saw her dead, but as beautiful and desirable as in life. There was only one thing he could do for his one-time friend and the dead queen: He ordered their burial in a common grave, so they were together in death as they had wished to be in life.

Critical Evaluation

In *Antony and Cleopatra* Shakespeare is not bound by the Aristotelian unities. He moves swiftly across the whole of the civilized world with a panorama of scenes and characters; he creates a majestic expanse suitable to the broad significance of the tragedy. The play, Shakespeare's longest, is broken up into small units which intensify the impression of rapid movement. Written immediately after the four great tragedies—*Julius Caesar*, *Hamlet*, *King Lear*, and *Macbeth*—it rivals them in tragic effect even though it has no plot which Aristotle would recognize. The story is taken from North's translation of Plutarch, but is refashioned into a complex rendering of a corruption which enobles as it destroys. It may lack the poignantly representative character of the great tragedies, but it extends its significance by taking the whole world for its canvas.

As a standard tragic figure, Antony leaves much to be desired. His actions are little more than a series of vacillations between commitment to a set of responsibilities, which are his by virtue of his person and his office, and submission to the overpowering passion which repeatedly draws him back to the fatal influence of Cleopatra. His nobility is of an odd sort. He commands respect and admiration as one of the two great rulers of the world, but we merely are told of his greatness; we do not see it represented in his actions. Antony travels, but he does not really do anything until his suicide—and he does not even do that very efficiently. His nobility, attested by his past deeds and his association with the glories of Rome, is a quality of which we are frequently reminded, but it is not something earned within the play.

Antony has another impediment to tragic stature: He is somewhat too intelligent and aware of what he is doing. Although it is true that he behaves irresponsibly, the fact remains, as Mark Van Doren has noted, that he lives "in the full light of accepted illusion." There is no duping of the hero: Cleopatra is not Antony's Iago. Nor is there any self-deception; Antony does not cheer himself up by pretending that their love is anything more than it is.

Nevertheless, their love is sufficiently great to endow Antony with whatever nobility he salvages in the play. It is not simply that he is a hero brought to disgrace by lust, although that much is true. Viewed from another angle, he is a hero set free from the limits of heroism by a love which frees him from a commitment to honor for a commitment to life. Of course, his liberation is also his humiliation and destruction because he is a Roman hero of great power and historical significance. Both noble and depraved, both consequential and trivial, Antony finds new greatness in the intense passion which simultaneously lays him low.

Cleopatra is an equally complex character, but her complexity is less the result of paradox than of infinite variation. Throughout the first four acts she lies, poses, cajoles, and entices, ringing manifold changes on her powers to attract. Yet she is not a coarse temptress, not a personification of evil loosed upon a helpless victim. As her behavior in the last act reminds us, she is also an empress, whose dignity should be recalled throughout her machinations. For Cleopatra too is swept along by overwhelming passion. She is not only a proud queen and conniving seducer, but a sincere and passionate lover. Despite her tarnished past, her plottings in *Antony and Cleopatra* are given the dignity of underlying love. Like Antony, she is not the sort of character who challenges the universe and transcends personal destruction. Rather, her dignity lies somewhere beyond, or outside, traditional heroism.

The complexity of Cleopatra is most apparent in the motivation for her suicide. Certainly one motive is the desire to avoid the humiliation of being led in a triumph through Rome by the victorious Octavius Caesar. But if that were all, then she would be nothing more than an egoistic conniver. However, she is also motivated by her sincere unwillingness to survive Antony. The two motives become intertwined, since the humiliation of slavery would also extend to Antony and taint his reputation. This mixture of motives is a model of the way in which the two lovers are simultaneously the undoing and the salvation of each other. Their mutual destruction springs from the same love that provides them with their antiheroic greatness. Love is lower than honor in the Roman world, but it can generate an intensity which makes heroism irrelevant. Antony is too intelligent, Cleopatra is too witty, and their love is too intricate for ordinary tragedy.

The structure of the plot also departs from the tragic norm. There is almost none of the complication and unraveling which we expect in tragedy. Rather, the action moves in fits and starts through the forty-two scenes of the play. These brief segments appear to be a series of unequal waves, sweeping over the characters and finally carrying them to destruction. The plethora of scenes and the rapid shifting of locations create a jerky dramatic movement. Although the action of the play must extend over a long period of time, the quick succession of scenes suggests an unsteady hurtling toward a conclusion.

The helter-skelter quality is reinforced by the language of the play. Few speeches are long, and there are many abrupt exchanges; there are also many quick, wide-ranging allusions. Finally, in his versification, Shakespeare uses feminine endings which metrically recreate the nervous vitality of the action. Thus, plot and language spread the drama over the whole world and hasten its conclusion in order to maximize the tensions of a "world well lost" for love.

THE ARABIAN NIGHTS' ENTERTAINMENTS

Type of work: Tales
Author: Unknown
Type of plots: Adventure romances
Time of plots: The legendary past
Locale: India, China, Persia, and Arabia
First transcribed: Fifteenth century

This group of tales, more properly called The Thousand and One Nights, *was passed down by word of mouth in many lands throughout the East and was eventually formalized and standardized by bazaar storytellers. Most scholars believe that the collection took its present form in Cairo in the fifteenth century; it was introduced to the West in Antoine Gallad's 1704 translation published in Paris. The stories often have striking parallels to Biblical tales and incidents from the* Iliad *and the* Odyssey.

Principal Characters

Shahriar, emperor of Persia and India. Convinced of the unfaithfulness of all women, he vows to marry a new woman every day and have her executed the next morning.

Scheherazade, his wise and beautiful bride. On the night of their wedding, she begins to tell him a tale which so fascinates him that he stays her execution for a day so that he can learn the end of the story. The stories are continued for a thousand and one nights. Then, convinced of her worthiness, he bids her live and makes her his consort. The following are characters in some of her stories:

The King of the Black Isles. He nearly kills the lover of his unfaithful queen, who gets revenge by turning her husband's lower half into marble and changing his town and all its people into a lake of fish. A neighboring sultan kills the lover and deceives the queen into undoing all her enchantments; then she too is killed.

Sindbad the Sailor, who, in the course of his voyages, visits an island that is really the back of a sea monster, a valley of diamonds, an island inhabited by cannibal dwarfs and black one-eyed giants, and an underground river.

The Caliph Harun-al-Rashid of Baghdad, Sindbad's ruler.

Houssain, Ali, and **Ahmed,** sons of the Sultan of India. They compete for the hand of their father's ward; after an archery contest Ali is proclaimed the winner, though Ahmed's arrow has gone so far that no one can find it.

Periebanou, a fairy living in a mountain, at whose door Ahmed finds his arrow. He marries her and with her help performs unreasonable tasks for his father, who has been persuaded by courtiers to be suspicious of his son, now secretive about his life and apparently rich and powerful. The sultan is killed by Periebanou's annoyed brother, and Ahmed succeeds him as sultan.

Princess Nouronnihar, the ward of the sultan. She is sought in marriage by the brothers. Ali wins her.

Ali Baba, a Persian woodcutter who happens upon a thieves' cave filled with riches.

Cassim, his greedy brother, who forgets the password, "Open Sesame," and so cannot get out of the cave. The thieves kill him.

Morgiana, Ali Baba's beautiful slave. She discovers that the thieves are hiding in oil jars brought by their disguised captain to Ali Baba's house. Morgiana kills the robbers, is rewarded with her freedom, and becomes Ali Baba's son's wife.

Aladdin, a young vagabond in China who gets possession of a magic lamp, and through the power of its genie, gains incredible wealth and wins the sultan's daughter as his wife.

The Stories

Convinced by the treachery of his brother's wife and his own that all women were unfaithful, Shahrir, Emperor of Persia and India, vowed that he would marry a new wife every day and have her executed the next day. Only Scheherazade, wise as well as beautiful, had the courage to try to save the young women of Persia. On the night of her marriage to Shahriar, she began to tell him a tale which fascinated him so much that he stayed her death for one more night so that he could learn the end of the story. Scheherazade told him stories for one thousand and one nights. At that time, convinced of her worthiness and goodness, he bade her live and made her his consort.

One tale Scheherazade told was "The History of the

Fisherman and the Genie": A poor Mussulman fisherman drew from the sea in his nets a strange box with a seal on top. When he pried off the top, a huge genie appeared and threatened him with death, offering the poor man no more than his choice in the manner of his death. The fisherman begged for his life because he had done the genie a favor by releasing him, but the genie declared that he had vowed death to the man who opened the box. Finally, the fisherman exclaimed that he could not believe anything as huge and terrible as the genie could ever have been in a space so small. Dissolving into a cloud of smoke, the genie shrank until he could slip back into the box, whereupon the fisherman clamped on the lid. Throwing the box back into the sea, he warned all other fishermen to beware if it should ever fall into their nets.

Another story was "The History of the Young King of the Black Isles": A fisherman caught four beautiful fish, one white, one red, one blue, and one yellow. They were so choice that he took them to the sultan's palace. While the fish were being cooked, a beautiful girl suddenly appeared and talked to the fish, after which they were too charred to take to the sultan. When the same thing happened two days in a row, the sultan was called. After asking where the fish came from, he decided to visit the lake. Nearby, he found a beautiful, apparently deserted palace. As he walked through the beautiful halls, he found one in which a king was sitting on a throne. The king apologized for not rising, explaining that his lower half was marble.

He was the King of the Black Isles. When he had learned that his queen was unfaithful to him, he had nearly killed her blackamoor lover. In revenge, the queen had cast a spell over her husband, making him half marble. She whipped him daily and then had him dressed in coarse goat's hair over which his royal robes were placed. In the meantime, while she had kept her lover barely alive, she had changed her husband's town and all its inhabitants into the lake full of fish.

The king told the sultan where the queen's lover was kept. There the sultan went, killed the lover, and put himself in the blackamoor's place. The queen, overjoyed to hear speaking the one she had kept from the edge of death so long, hastened to do all the voice commanded. She restored the king to his human form and the lake to its previous state as a populous town. The four colors of fish indicated the four different religions of the inhabitants.

When the queen returned to the sultan, whom she mistook for her lover, he killed her for her treachery. Thereafter, he took home with him the King of the Black Isles and rewarded the fisherman who had led him to the magic lake.

Shahriar was vastly entertained by "The History of Sindbad the Sailor": A poor porter in Baghdad, resting before the house of Sindbad, bewailed the fact that his lot was harder than that of Sindbad. Sindbad overheard him and invited the porter to dine with him. During the meal, he told of the hardships he had suffered in order to make his fortune.

On his first voyage to India by way of the Persian Gulf, Sindbad's ship was becalmed near a small green island. The sailors climbed upon the island, only to find that it was really a sea monster which heaved itself up and swam away. Sindbad was the only man who did not get back to the ship. After days of clinging to a piece of driftwood, he landed on an island where some men were gathered. They led him to a maharajah who treated Sindbad graciously. When he had been there some time, his own ship came into port, and he claimed his bales of goods, to the astonishment of the captain, who thought he had seen Sindbad killed at sea. Then Sindbad sailed home in the ship in which he had set out.

The porter was so impressed with the first tale that he came again to hear a second. On his second voyage, Sindbad was left asleep on an island where the sailors had rested. There he found a huge roc's egg. He waited, knowing that the parent bird would return to the nest at dusk. When it came, he used his turban to tie himself to the bird's leg. In the morning, the bird flew to a place surrounded by mountains. There Sindbad freed himself when the bird descended to pick up a serpent. The place seemed deserted, except for large serpents. Diamonds of great size were scattered throughout the valley.

Sindbad remembered that merchants were said to throw joints of meat into the diamond valley, from which big eagles carried the joints to their nests close to shore. At the nests, the merchants frightened away the birds and recovered diamonds which had stuck to the meat. Sindbad collected some large diamonds. With his turban, he fastened a piece of meat to his back and lay down. An eagle picked him up and carried him to its nest. When he was dropped into a nest, the merchant who claimed the nest was indignant and accused Sindbad of stealing his property. Sindbad offered him some choice diamonds. In return, the merchant was glad to take the adventurer back to civilization.

On his third voyage, Sindbad was wrecked on an island inhabited by cannibal dwarfs and huge black creatures with only one eye in the middle of their foreheads. Sindbad and his friends blinded one black giant, but two others helped the blind one to chase the sailors. By the time the giants and a large serpent had overtaken them, only Sindbad was lucky enough to escape.

On his fourth voyage, Sindbad sailed from a port in Persia. He and his friends were shipwrecked on an island inhabited by black cannibals who fattened the sailors before killing them. Sindbad refused the food, grew too thin to interest the black men, and finally found his way to the shore. There he met white men who took him to their kingdom. To please the king, Sindbad made a fine saddle. In appreciation, the king married Sindbad to a beautiful girl. In that country, a man or woman was buried alive if the spouse died. When Sindbad's wife died, he was put in a tomb with a small amount of bread and water. As he ate the last of his food, he heard an animal snuffling, then running away. Following the sound, he found himself on the shore and hailed a ship which carried him home.

On his fifth voyage, Sindbad used his own ship. After his sailors had broken open a roc's egg, the parent rocs hurled tremendous stones on the ship and broke it to pieces. Sindbad came under the power of the Old Man of the Sea and escaped only after making the old man so intoxicated that he loosed his death grip on Sindbad. Again, Sindbad found a ship to take him home, and he did much profitable trading on the way.

On the sixth voyage, all of his companions succumbed on a beautiful but lifeless coast. Expecting to die, Sindbad built a raft which he put in an underground river to drift where it would. When he reached the kingdom of Serendib, he had to be revived. He found the country exceedingly rich and the people kind. When he asked to be allowed to go home, the king sent him there with rich presents for Sindbad's ruler, the Caliph Harun-al-Rashid of Baghdad.

Sindbad made his seventh and final voyage to take gifts from the caliph to the King of Serendib. He carried them safely, but his return trip was delayed when corsairs seized his ship and sold the sailors into slavery. Sindbad was sold to an ivory merchant and was ordered to shoot an elephant a day. Annoyed at Sindbad's persistence, an elephant picked him up and took him to an elephant burial ground, to which Sindbad and his owner returned many times to gather ivory. As a reward, the merchant sent Sindbad home with rich goods.

Another diverting tale was "The History of Prince Ahmed": Houssain, Ali, and Ahmed, sons of the Sultan of India, were all in love with the Princess Nouronnihar, their father's ward. To determine who should be the bridegroom, the sultan sent them out to find the most extraordinary things they could. Whoever brought back the rarest object would win the hand of the princess.

Houssain found a magic carpet which would transport him wherever he wished. Ali found an ivory tube containing a glass which would show any object he wished to see. Ahmed found an artificial apple, the odor of which would cure any illness.

The three princes met before they journeyed home. As they displayed their gifts, Houssain, looking through the tube, saw the princess apparently at the point of death. They all jumped on his magic carpet and were whisked to her bedroom, where Ahmed used his magic apple to revive her. The sultan could not determine which article was the most unusual, for all had been of use to effect the princess' recovery. He suggested an archery contest. Prince Ali shot farther than Houssain, but Ahmed's arrow could not be found. The sultan decided in favor of Ali. Houssain retired to become a dervish. Instead of attending the wedding, Ahmed went in search of his arrow,

which he found at the foot of a mountain, much farther away than he could have shot. Looking around, he found a door into the mountain. When he passed through the door, he found a fairy called Periebanou, who pleased him so much that he married her.

When Ahmed went to visit his father, he refused to discuss where or how he lived, but he appeared to be so rich that the courtiers grew jealous and persuaded the sultan that it was dangerous to have his son so powerful a neighbor. The sultan asked Ahmed to perform unreasonable tasks, made possible only by Periebanou's help; but while fulfilling one request her brother became so annoyed with the sultan that he killed him. Ahmed became sultan and afterward dealt kindly with his brothers.

Scheherazade also pleased her lord with "The History of Ali Baba and the Forty Thieves": Ali Baba was a Persian woodcutter. One day, to hide from a band of strange horsemen, he climbed a tree under which they halted. When the leader cried, "Open, Sesame!" to a rock nearby, a door opened through which the men carried their heavy packs. After the men left, Ali Baba used the secret word to investigate the cave. He found such riches there that the gold he took could never be missed.

He and his wife were content with that amount, but his brother Cassim, to whom he had told his story, was greedy for more wealth. Without telling Ali Baba, Cassim went to the cave. He was so excited by the gold that he forgot the password and could not get out. The robbers found and murdered him.

The robbers tried to find Ali Baba in order to kill him and so keep the secret of their hoard. The leader brought his men, hidden in oil jars, to Ali Baba's house, but a beautiful slave, Morgiana, went in search of oil, discovered the ruse, and killed the bandits. Again the captain, disguised as a merchant, entered the house, but Morgiana saw through his disguise and killed him.

To reward Morgiana, Ali Baba not only made her a free woman but also gave her to his son in marriage. Ali Baba was then the only one who knew the secret of the cave. He used the hidden wealth in moderation and passed the secret on to his posterity.

No less pleasing was "The History of Aladdin, or the Wonderful Lamp": Aladdin was a youthful vagabond who lived in China. An African magician, sensing that Aladdin would suit his plans, and pretending to be the boy's rich uncle, took him to a secret place to get a magic lamp. Passing through halls stored with treasures, Aladdin filled his gown with so many things that he could not give the magician the lamp at the moment he wanted it, and the magician sealed him up in the earth. By chance, Aladdin rubbed a ring which the magician had given him. A genie appeared and escorted him home.

When Aladdin showed his mother the lamp, she tried to clean it to sell. As she rubbed, another genie appeared from whom Aladdin asked food. The food appeared on silver trays that Aladdin sold one by one to a Jewish chapman. When an honest jeweler stopped Aladdin one day and asked to buy the silver, Aladdin began to realize the great riches he had at his fingertips, enough to win him the sultan's daughter as his wife.

Because the grand vizier wanted his own son to marry the princess, he suggested many outrageous demands which the sultan made upon Aladdin before he could be considered a suitor. The genies produced slaves, costumes, jewelry, gold, and chargers in such profusion that the sultan gladly accepted Aladdin's suit. Overnight, Aladdin had the genie build a magnificent palace next to the sultan's.

Life went smoothly until the African magician, while Aladdin was away, persuaded the princess to trade the old lamp for a new one. Then the magician transported the great palace to Africa. When Aladdin came home, the sultan threatened him with arrest but allowed him forty days in which to find the palace with the princess therein. Rubbing his ring by chance and summoning its genie, Aladdin asked to be carried wherever his palace was. The princess was overjoyed to see him. After he had killed the magician by a ruse, he ordered the genie of the lamp to transport the palace back to China. There, after disposing of the magician's brother who had followed them, Aladdin and the princess lived happily ever after.

Critical Evaluation

The Arabian Nights' Entertainments is the title usually used in English to designate a group of tales more properly called *The Thousand and One Nights*. These stories, adapted and formalized by bazaar storytellers, had their origins in many lands throughout the East and were handed down by word of mouth for hundreds of years. Some present interesting parallels. In the story of "The Three Sisters," a baby is put in a basket to float down a river, a circumstance reminiscent of the biblical account of Moses in the bulrushes. In Sindbad's various journeys by sea, there are similarities to the wanderings of Ulysses as related by Homer, in one instance a close parallel to the Cyclops story. Some of the characters have been drawn from history; but whether the source is folklore, religious tradition, or history, the tales have a timeless quality appealing, from legendary times to the present, to authors of every sort. Most scholars believe that the collection took its present form in Cairo in the fifteenth century; it was introduced to the Western world in a translation by Antoine Galland, published in Paris in 1704. Traditionally, there were a thousand and one stories told by Scheherazade to her emperor-husband, but in extant manuscripts the tales are not always the same. Practically all modern editions contain only a small portion of the complete collection. Those most frequently reprinted have become minor classics of the world's literature.

The older title of the work refers to the implied dramatic situation in which Scheherazade tells a story (or part of one) to Shahriar every night for the famous number of nights in order to forestall her death on the following morning. The tales are embedded in a frame-story, in the tradition of Boccaccio's *Decameron* and Chaucer's *Canterbury Tales*. Like the *Canterbury Tales*, the *Arabian Nights* includes some tales which are enriched by the situation of their framework.

If readers keep in mind Shahriar's repeated vow to kill his wife in the morning, there is much more of a point to one of Scheherazade's first tales to her new husband and king. "The History of the Fisherman and the Genie" involves another powerful character, the genie, who has similarly vowed to kill. In both cases, the vow would involve the killing of one who has performed an act of charity or of love toward the avowed killer: in the fisherman's case, freeing the genie, and in Scheherazade's case, marrying the king. When the fisherman chastises the rebottled genie, predicting Allah's certain vengeance upon him for killing, the humble man is in fact a mask through which Scheherazade is speaking to Shahriar.

In "The History of the Young King of the Black Isles," other details of the framework are alluded to. It will be remembered that Shahriar's reason for his vow is rooted in his painful experience with his unfaithful wife, whom he discovered to be engaged in adultery with a black slave. The fact that his brother's case paralleled his would indicate that the societies in which this book took form were preoccupied with a sense of inadequacy when placed in sexual competition with blacks.

The racial, psychosexual problem amounts to the thematic focus of the story. The Young King has likewise discovered his wife's infidelity and is greatly disturbed at her fiercely expressed preference for her black lover. Throughout the story, black and white are pointedly juxtaposed. The king is described as extremely pale with only the smallest touch of black, a mole. His palace is black, perhaps an omen of his catastrophe. On the first two occasions of the spoiled fish (they are blackened), a fair lady comes out of the wall to upset the pan; on the third occasion, it is a black giant who performs the same act. The Young King's being turned to stone below the waist is part of the allegory signifying his impotence upon having his male ego destroyed by his wife's preference for the slave. The sympathy and vengeance provided by the sultan are obviously designed to further soothe Shahriar.

With "The History of Sindbad the Sailor," a smaller frame-story within the larger, readers come to the end of selections which contain pointed allusions to Shahriar's life and problems. All that can be said of the remaining selections' relationship to the framework is that they contain within their allegorical forms a wisdom about the ways of the world, which at one and the same time accords with Scheherazade's great learning and would no doubt impress Shahriar so much as to purge him of his unfortunate vision of all women as faithless and blind in their lust.

Sindbad, a wealthy man, tells his seven tales to a poor porter of the same name. The purpose of telling the tales is to justify the wealth of the rich Sindbad to the envious poor Sindbad. In each story, the wealth is justified by a different example of perils endured by the storyteller. Each of the seven stories follows a narrative pattern in which Sindbad, first, sets out to sea to make money; second, loses everything in a catastrophe; third, undergoes a frightening experience (usually underground); fourth, escapes by means of his wits; and, finally, escapes with far greater riches than would ever have been possible by ordinary trading. The most frightening part of each episode is invariably a close brush with death for Sindbad and is recognizably a descent into the mythic world of the dead. Sindbad returns from each descent with treasures commensurate with the risks he had taken.

In "The History of Prince Ahmed," the reader meets with the now-familiar motif of trials undergone to win the hand of a princess. In this case, however, there are two princesses, one mortal and one fairy. Ahmed and his brothers vie for the mortal princess, unaware of the fairy princess' love for Ahmed and of her having planned every detail of their adventures. The allegory involves Ahmed's being led unwittingly (and unwillingly) past the mortal princess and inexorably to the fairy princess (who is more beautiful and wise in the extreme). The story points to the superiority of spiritual riches over material wealth. The sultan is depicted as foolish (and so deserving of his ultimate overthrow) when he ignores the superiority of Ahmed's magic apple, when he disqualifies Ahmed's archery for his arrow's being unrecoverable by ordinary

mortal means, and when he demands material wealth of Ahmed.

"The History of Ali Baba and the Forty Thieves" depicts Ali Baba as a man who prospers through his lack of greed. He is contrasted with his brother Cassim in this; Cassim apparently married for money, while Ali Baba married a poor woman and was a woodcutter. When Ali Baba learns the magic formula for opening the door to wealth, he takes only as much as would not be missed. Cassim's greed, by contrast, causes him to become so excited by the wealth that he forgets the magic word and is killed. It is significant that Cassim, when he is trapped in the cave, has the entire treasure and, having it, has death along with it. When the threat of death for Ali Baba is resolved with the death of the thieves, the hero draws so temperately upon his secret cache that it supports his family for many generations. (The fact that Ali Baba's life and fortunes are preserved by a clever woman, Morgiana, would not be lost on Shahriar.)

This story is another example of riches obtained by a successful descent into the underworld, as is the next, "The History of Aladdin: Or, The Wonderful Lamp." Aladdin is another naif, not suspecting the great material value of the gold and silver trays, considering the food they had carried to be of the utmost importance. This sort of naïveté is the stuff of which wisdom is made, making him truly worthy of the Sultan's daughter and of the powerful lamp.

It is helpful in understanding and enjoying *The Arabian Nights' Entertainments* to keep in mind the parallel symbolism of wealth, power, and beautiful women: all are symbolic of spiritual fulfillment. The omnipresence of the three in this book is one clear indication of the work's purpose: to teach a moral lesson as well as to entertain. It is a storehouse of wisdom couched in the terms all cultures know best, the terms of sight, smell, and touch, and of the delightful forms those sensations take in the imagination.

AREOPAGITICA

Type of work: Philosophic address
Author: John Milton (1608–1674)
First published: 1644

Milton's impassioned argument for unlicensed printing, the *Areopagitica*, appeared in November, 1644, during a stormy period in English history. Parliament had rebelled against the authoritarian rule of King Charles I two years earlier, and its supporters, Puritans for the most part, were beginning to demonstrate their military superiority in periodic battles against the Royalist forces. Since Parliament had abolished the venerable Court of the Star Chamber, which previously had exercised control over the press, Milton for a time took advantage of the new freedom to publish a series of pamphlets against the episcopal form of church government inherited from Roman Catholicism. When Parliament convoked the Westminster Assembly of churchmen in 1643 to advise the lawmakers on religious reform, however, this freedom proved to be short-lived, for the Assembly soon recommended, and Parliament passed, a new licensing order which differed from the earlier one chiefly in that the responsibility passed from the bishops to a twenty-man Committee of Examinations.

In defiance of the order, Milton issued four pamphlets between 1643 and 1645 defending divorce, a subject in which he had a strong personal interest, as his own marriage to Mary Powell had turned out very unhappily. In the midst of this concern, Milton turned his attention to the issue of censorship; he addressed the *Aeropagitica*, itself another unlicensed pamphlet, to Parliament.

Milton's title derives ultimately from the Areopagus, a hill in Athens which served as a governmental meeting place from early in the city's history. Thus the name had been extended to the Athenian council, which exercised both civil and religious authority. Milton may well have intended to acknowledge similar jurisdiction by Parliament, for nowhere in the *Areopagitica* does he argue for the separation of church and state; as a matter of fact, he needed the support of those who opposed such separation. In addition, one of the political arguments of Socrates in the fourth century B.C. was called *Areopagiticus*; Milton's work was similar insofar as it was shaped like an oration but not actually delivered as a speech. Christian humanists of the English Renaissance regarded the oration as a species of poetry calculated to stir an audience and move it to the practice of virtue, as Sir Philip Sidney's *Apology for Poetry* (c. 1580), also a classical oration in form, illustrates. Finally, Milton probably also had in mind Saint Paul, who addressed the Areopagus as a gathering of religious men who nonetheless required further enlightenment (Acts 17:22-31). Milton alludes to

Saint Paul a number of times in the *Areopagitica*.

A thorough classical scholar, Milton knew intimately the techniques of the great orators of the ancient world and skillfully adapted them to the pamphlet form. The *Areopagitica* is much more than an oration, however; it is also a bold appeal by a patriotic Englishman who is eager that his nation increase its stature by granting intellectual liberty to its writers. As in the case of the divorce pamphlets, his motives were hardly disinterested. Nevertheless, he crafted the *Areopagitica* as a general defense of freedom of the press that could not be interpreted as mere special pleading, for its argument transcends his own difficulties with censors and the problems of intellectuals disenchanted with what, in the 1640s, looked like dangerous backsliding into the tyranny of the past. Milton deploys his immense learning, remarkable verbal facility, and diplomatic skill in composing a work designed to force the Lords and Commons to see the issue in the context of Parliament's—and England's—continuing struggle for liberty from oppression.

To gain the goodwill of the lawmakers, Milton applauds their concern about the press, "for Books are not absolutely dead things, but doe contain a potencie of life in them to be as active as that soule was whose progeny they are." For this reason, prior censorship is a terrible and destructive act: "Who kills a Man kills a reasonable creature, Gods Image; but hee who destroyes a good Booke, kills reason it selfe, kills the Image of God, as it were in the eye." Throughout the arguments that follow, he balances his sense of injustice already done against expressions of confidence that Parliament consists of rational men who will act to redress it.

His first argument consists of a survey of the history of licensing, which he judges the inevitable handmaiden of tyranny in the ancient world and particularly in the Roman Catholic church. He singles out the activities of the Inquisition and those of the sixteenth century Council of Trent, in its attempt to counter the effects of the Protestant Reformation by establishing an index of forbidden books and an elaborate system of imprimaturs (the term means "it may be printed") by ecclesiastical authorities. Milton acknowledges this argument as his weakest one by placing it first; still, it was bound to carry emotional weight in a society that had been cultivating fear of Rome for more than a century.

Conceding that a thing may possibly be good in itself despite its association with oppressive regimes of the sort Parliament has repudiated, Milton next argues the necessity of access to all manner of ideas, including bad ones. Even good books can be misused, and bad ones "to a discreet and judicious Reader serve in many respects to discover, to confute, to forewarn, and to illustrate." Throughout his essay, it should be noted, Milton has this "discreet and judicious Reader" in mind, for he is defending the rights of earnest seekers after truth, not recommending erroneous and dangerous books to the multitude. His essay *Of Education*, written in the same year, addresses the educational needs of "our choicest and hopefullest wits." In Milton's eyes, virtue worthy of the name is possible only to such a seeker, for it cannot thrive, cannot even exist, except by confronting the evil that lurks in the library:

> As therefore the state of man now is; what wisdom can there be to choose, what continence to forbeare without the knowledge of evill? He that can apprehend and consider vice with all her baits and seeming pleasures, and yet abstain, and yet distinguish, and yet prefer that which is truly better, he is the true warfaring Christian. I cannot praise a fugitive and cloister'd vertue, unexercis'd & unbreath'd, that never sallies out and sees her adversary, but slinks out of the race, where that immortall garland is to be run for, not without dust and heat. Assuredly we bring not innocence into the world, we bring impurity much rather: that which purifies us is triall, and triall is by what is contrary.

The printed text of this famous passage refers to "wayfaring" rather than "warfaring" Christians, but textual scholars have pointed out that Milton's *r*'s can easily be confused with his *y*'s, and "warfaring" accords with the militant context and with Milton's attitude toward Christianity generally.

A key qualifying clause is the first one in the passage: "as therefore the state of man now is." Book 9 of *Paradise Lost* (1667, 1674) attributes a similar argument to Satan as part of Eve's temptation, but such reasoning applies only in a fallen world. Such pursuits as Milton has Satan recommend in the later work here "are not temptations, nor vanities; but usefull drugs and materialls wherewith to temper and compose effect and strong med'cins, which mans life cannot want" (that is, cannot be without). In the latter-day warfare against Satan, Christians must turn his own duplicitous arguments against him, for in the world as it is, good and evil are always intermingled, and only moral choices can disentangle them. Virtue consists precisely in making such choices. To prevent man from choosing is to deny the possibility of virtue. Only by familiarity with evil can a person reject it in favor of the good.

Milton goes on to praise Sir Guyon, the hero of book 2 of a classic by another Christian humanist, Edmund Spenser. In *The Faerie Queene* (1590, 1596), Spenser "brings him in with his palmer through the cave of Mammon, and the bowr of earthly blisse that he might see and know, and yet abstain." It is significant that Milton has cited a character devoted to a "classical" virtue, temperance, governed by reason, as are justice and continence, which he also emphasizes in this part of his argument. God commands these virtues but "gives us minds that can wander beyond all limit and satiety." In *Paradise Lost* Milton would stress the temptation of pride in such minds, but here he presents warfaring Christians as people who exercise humanistic virtues and thus attain worthiness in the sight of God. This emphasis clearly diverges from the Calvinism in which Milton was reared and to which he still professes allegiance at the time of the writing of the *Areopagitica*.

Milton's third major argument concerns the futility of censorship. Books are, after all, only one way in which malign influences are propagated. Plato was more consistent in his *Republic* than is Parliament in its licensing order, for he regulated all manner of education and recreation to forestall the evil influences that reside in music, dance, conversation, and many other activities when left unscrutinized. Plato, however, was describing an ideal and not a real commonwealth. No discipline imposed from without can prevent real people from finding opportunities to indulge their moral weaknesses, and the effort will only remove the means by which the self-disciplined can test and develop their virtue. Furthermore, Milton adds, even the backlog of previously published books to be examined and judged imposes a Herculean burden on the censors. Could a committee of examiners wise enough and industrious enough be found, and if so, how could they be prevailed upon to spend all their working hours in such a negative occupation as reading suspect books in search of error? Thus Milton demonstrates the impossibility of controlling the circulation of evil and also the foolishness of a law that expects to dam the flow of opinion in this way.

Finally, Milton argues that licensing is the enemy of truth. Though absolute and knowable, men do not possess it in its fullness.

> Truth indeed came once into the world with her divine Master, and was a perfect shape most glorious to look on: but when he ascended, and his Apostles after him were laid asleep, then strait arose a wicked race of deceivers, who . . . took the virgin Truth, hewd her lovely form into a thousand peeces, and scatter'd them to the four winds. From that time ever since, the sad friends of Truth, such as durst appear, . . . went up and down gathering up limb by limb still as they could find them. We have not yet found them all, Lords and Commons, nor ever shall doe, till her Masters second comming.

Until such time as truth reappears in its wholeness, there remains a long task of recovery which licensing can only impede. Although Milton thinks of the available truth as largely the possession of Protestant Christendom, the capacities that can reassemble more pieces are diffused widely and require maximum encouragement. In contending that scholars will not suffer the funneling of their efforts through a censor, Milton is affirming what the situation was already demonstrating, as he and other writers disdained to recognize the authority of a committee which, he implies, inevitably must consist of their intellectual inferiors. To think that a mature, reflecting Christian could not without danger to his faith contemplate such books as came along was a patent insult. Having repudiated Roman Catholic authority in one century and the severities of the English episcopacy in the next, reformers would inevitably oppose a relapse into yet another form of passive obedience. For Milton, viewing the ongoing political and religious struggle, the Reformation was incomplete; in many respects it had scarcely begun in England. The head of the church was still nominally, if not effectively, Charles I, a monarch already repudiated and destined for execution, although it is unlikely that rational men in 1644 could have anticipated the reality of 1649.

After presenting his arguments, Milton envisions the fully reformed nation:

Methinks I see in my mind a noble and puissant Nation rousing herself like a strong man after sleep, and shaking her invincible locks: Methinks I see her as an Eagle muing her mighty youth, and kindling her undazl'd eyes at the full midday beam; purging and unscaling her long abused sight at the fountain it self of heav'nly radiance.

Milton uses all the weapons of his rhetorical arsenal to convince Parliament that its part in this consummation of a greater England is the promotion of intellectual freedom: "Give me the liberty to know, to utter, and to argue freely according to conscience, above all liberties." Milton would not, however, extend such liberty to all. He explicitly denies the free press to Roman Catholics; in his mind they would employ this freedom to destroy that of others. Only truth-seekers qualified, and Milton could define this concept only by this arbitrary exclusion.

At the end of his essay, Milton puts to Parliament a practical question which can be appreciated even better centuries later: "What Magistrate may not be mis-inform'd, and much the sooner, if liberty of Printing be reduc't into the power of a few[?]" He calls on the Lords and Commons to demonstrate their own capacity for virtue, "to redresse wilingly and speedily what hath bin err'd—that is to revoke the order which created the licensing committee.

Although Parliament did not rescind the licensing order for another half century, the *Areopagitica* endures as the first great defense of freedom of the press in English. John Locke's *Letters on Toleration* (1689–1692) and John Stuart Mill's *On Liberty* (1859) notably extended and enlarged the scope of Milton's argument, but from a literary standpoint the *Areopagitica* remains the greatest work of its kind.

ARS POETICA

Type of work: Poem
Author: Horace (Quintus Horatius Flaccus, 65–8 B.C.)
First published: *Epistula ad Pisones*, after 23 B.C.

The *Ars poetica*, the longest poem written by the Roman lyric poet Quintus Horatius Flaccus, is one of the foremost documents on ancient literary criticism in the Western world. Although this 476-line poem has profoundly influenced literature (especially drama) throughout the centuries, it has also sparked substantial controversy. Scholars have debated its title, its date of composition, and the identity of the Pisones, to whom the poem is addressed. Whether Horace originally titled his work *Epistula ad Pisones de arte poetica* (letter to the Pisones about the art of poetry) or simply *Epistula ad Pisones* (letter to the Pisones), the title had been abbreviated to *Ars poetica* by the first century A.D., as the Roman rhetorician and critic Marcus Fabius Quintilianus attests. No evidence exists within the poem or in other works that would allow its composition to be assigned to a specific year. While a few scholars have argued for a date early in Horace's poetic career, most critics believe that he probably wrote the poem sometime after the publication of his first three books of odes in 23 B.C. The identities of Piso and his two sons have also come into question. Pomponius Porphyrion, an early third century scholar who wrote a commentary on Horace, identifies the men as Lucius Calpurnius Piso and his two sons, but their dates do not coincide with the poem's internal evidence. Later commentators have suggested Gnaeus Calpurnius Piso and his sons, but their identities are subject to question as well. Although the ancient manuscripts display the *Ars poetica* by itself, its longer title and casual tone argue for its inclusion in book 2 of Horace's *Epistles*, where editors have long placed it.

Scholars also argue over more substantial matters, including the poem's exact purpose, its structure, and the question of its value as literary criticism. While the main theme of the *Ars poetica* is agreed to be poetry, scholars view its points of emphasis differently. Some contend that its treatment of poetry is opposed to works on rhetoric. Others state that Horace is presenting his ideas on what he considers great poetry and which of that great poetry is supreme. To others, the poem deals foremost with the unique difficulties of being a good poet.

Horace's desultory style of address makes it difficult to see any coherent organization in the poem. Although some critics have denied any deliberate arrangement, most scholars argue for either a bipartite or tripartite structure. One authority has suggested that, depending on the focus of study, the structure in the *Ars poetica* will appear different. The critical triad of *poema* (the technique of writing verse), *poesis* (the subject matter as organized in long poems), and *poeta* (the skill, training, and talent of the poet) reveals a division into three parts. A second, more balanced tripartite arrangement derives from the single unit of style and content, followed by the major Greek and Roman dramatic genres, and finally poetic theory. A case may also be made for a bipartite division, as the poem is first concerned with poetry as a technical craft, then with general poetic theory. Still other constructions are evident, and Horace may have intended the poem to be understood on different levels.

In his intent to write a poem rather than a textbook, Horace develops a seeming incoherence to his narrative. Gradual transitions, recurring themes, and a well-concealed philosophical framework all contribute to the poetry. Each section is connected to the preceding by a passage that can belong to either; in this way the end of one passage and the beginning of another are camouflaged. Character, propriety, training, and unity are the most outstanding among a larger number of recurring topics, crossing divisional barriers throughout and helping to maintain the poem's claim to literature. The philosophical structure surfaces in very few places.

In the first forty-one lines of the *Ars poetica*, Horace introduces his discussion of poetry by showing how laughable and repulsive are badly made works of art or poetry. The poem's first major axiom preaches simplicity in and unity to one's creation: "Finally, let it be whatever you wish, as long as it is simple and unified." The poet must choose a topic that is equal to his abilities, and if "the subject is capably chosen, then style and arrangement will never desert him" (lines 40–41). In this way Horace introduces the major components of subject matter (*res*), style (*facundia*), and arrangement (*ordo*). Since Horace has previously demanded unity in composition, these three elements come to support each other in Horace's own work to produce that unity.

In reverse order and increasing depth, Horace discusses subject, style, and structure. He briefly describes arrangement as occurring when the poet says what needs to be said at the time and puts off or omits other topics as the occasion demands (lines 43–44).

The next seventy-four lines focus on style. The poet must use words sparingly, but unusual circumstances make the creation of new words acceptable. Such words carry more conviction if they are formed from Greek. Meter, the second aspect of style, should remain in its appropriate genre. Comedy and tragedy exemplify the complete inability of one meter to substitute for another. Finally, the expression of various emotions in the proper phrasing is necessary to elicit the desired response from the audience. Language must fit not only the emotional circumstances, but also the character's age, sex, social class, and nationality.

So far, Horace's discussion has been of technical skill. He has avoided the prosaic role of a writer of textbooks by referring to historical figures, nature vignettes, and literary genres—especially comedy and tragedy—which will be quite familiar to his audience.

The next 176 lines (slightly more than one-third of the *Ars poetica*) explore a poem's subject matter. The abrupt change of topic appears at line 119, where Horace enjoins the poet either to keep to traditional stories or, if he must create a story, to invent something that is consistent within its own fictional realm. Familiar literary characters, such as Achilles and Medea, illustrate these principles since their characters must reflect the legends about them. While a writer should keep to familiar stories, such as those found in Homer, one must not simply imitate them; one should rework them to make them one's own. Nor must a story begin at an inappropriate place, but the poet must ensure that beginning, middle, and end are compatible. Next, the poet should create characters in their proper age and station of life. A substantial passage depicting the four ages of man (boy, youth, adult, old man) identifies the characteristics befitting each.

An even longer sequence of verses follows in which the qualities necessary to support a play's content are set forth. Actions must be proper to the stage and not offend the audience. The production of the play, its division into five acts, the use of only three speaking characters, the chorus' active participation in the plot, all further support the content. The satyr play must also be appropriately written and produced in order to fit at the end of a tragic performance. Meter likewise plays an important role. The section ends with a comparison of Greek and Roman drama.

Again, Horace avoids the tone of a textbook in his list of literary precepts. He interweaves elements of history and legend, repeats his maxim of writing about familiar themes, and again uses the Greeks as the standard of excellence. The theme of propriety (*decorum*) reappears and allows Horace to criticize or moralize about past events and playwrights.

The final 182 lines of the *Ars poetica* focus upon the function (*munus*) and obligations (*officium*) of the poet. In typical fashion, an eleven-line passage on insane poets, beginning at line 295, serves to conclude the previous section and to usher in Horace's last major theme. In the next two lines poetic function and obligation expand to include the origin of the poet's resources, his nourishment and shaping, the qualities befitting him, and the direction in which his virtues and faults will lead him. Next, wisdom appears a the primary fountainhead of good

writing. Acquired knowledge of human nature is as important to a poet as acquired knowledge of business is to an ordinary citizen. Another major axiom states that a poet must instruct as well as entertain in pleasing and suitable words if he is to appeal to the greatest number of people. Brevity and close adherence to truth aid poetic instruction. The perfection of the poet's skill is arrived at through revision of his verses, but he must avoid the advice of friends and instead seek impartial criticism even in the smallest details. Another maxim surfaces at lines 408 through 411: Talent (*natura*) and training (*ars*) must strike a balance in a writer. The poem concludes with a description of the mad poet whom all should avoid.

In this final third of the *Ars poetica*, Horace has maintained his penchant for familiar themes to illustrate literary points and to unite the section with the previous ones. He reiterates in slightly altered form his belief that words will follow logically from a chosen subject. He again portrays Greeks as models of genius. Mediocrity in everyday activities—book production, music, painting, law, parties, sports—serves to illustrate the necessity for perfection in the poet. Legend and history, from Orpheus to Homer, afford further examples of ancient perfection, and the story of Empedocles' suicide corroborates Horace's argument that the mad poet should be avoided.

Although authorities disagree about the locations of divisions in the early part of the *Ars poetica*, all concur that the final one takes place at line 295. The uncertainty regarding thematic division may derive in part from Horace's adaptation of Aristotelian and Alexandrian philosophical literary doctrine.

From the time of Aristotle, the fourth century Greek philosopher, certain literary principles had predominated in the field of literary criticism. The *Ars poetica* echoes many of those tenets. The importance of unity, the balance between a poet's talent and training, and pleasure and instruction as the aim of poetry are themes present in both authors. Horace follows Aristotle in discussion of subject, style, and arrangement and in focusing on tragedy and epic as the two preeminent literary genres. Like Aristotle, Horace believes in the superiority of tragedy. Horace's arrangement of topics and his emphasis on poetry differ so markedly from Aristotle's *Rhetoric* and *Poetics*, however, that scholars have supposed an intermediate source between the two. Porphyrion, in another statement on the *Ars poetica*, says that Horace brought together the most outstanding literary precepts of Neoptolemus of Parium, a third century B.C. Hellenistic writer. Thus, later critics have supposed that Horace borrowed Aristotelian rhetorical principles from the writings of Neoptolemus, following more closely the thematic structure and poetic emphasis of the Alexandrian than the rhetorical outlook of the Greek philosopher.

The impact of the *Ars poetica* on European literature since the fourteenth century has been substantial. From the time of the Italian Renaissance, literary authorities accepted the poem as a manual of classical standards in the fine arts and relied upon it as well as Aristotle's works for their discourses on literary criticism. In the seventeenth and eighteenth centuries, the *Ars poetica* was a major contributor to the development of the neoclassical movement. Authors of that time tended to ignore the poem's apparent inconsistencies, instead focusing on the precepts and advice it gives.

Since that time, scholars have valued the poem primarily for what it tells them of the history of literary criticism in classical times. From the maxims, rules, and conclusions of the *Ars poetica* critics have been able to understand more clearly the evolution from ancient to modern literary criticism.

AS I LAY DYING

Type of work: Novel
Author: William Faulkner (1897–1962)
Type of plot: Psychological realism
Time of plot: Early twentieth century
Locale: Mississippi
First published: 1930

Centering around the effect of Addie Bundren's death and burial on members of her family, this novel has a powerful unity not always found in Faulkner's longer works. Although his method of shifting between the multiple points of view of the different family members binds Faulkner's characters into a homogeneous unit through their common suffering, individual personalities with their special emotions and abnormalities nevertheless emerge.

Principal Characters

Anse Bundren, an ignorant poor white. When Addie, his wife, dies, he is determined to take her body to Jefferson, as he had promised, even though the town is forty miles away. In a rickety old wagon he and his sons must get across a flooding river which has destroyed most of the nearby bridges. Ostensibly, the shiftless and unlucky man is burying Addie there because of the promise. After a long trip with her unembalmed corpse, now dead more than a week, he arrives in Jefferson, pursued by a flock of buzzards which, like a grim chorus, hang apparently motionless against a sultry Mississippi sky. On reaching Jefferson, his family learns Anse's true reason for the trip: a set of false teeth and the "duck-shaped woman" whom he marries, to the surprise of his children.

Addie Bundren, Anse's overworked wife. Though dying, she wants to see her coffin finished. Anse does not know it, but she has always thought him to be only a man of words; and words, she thinks, are useless. Feeling isolated from him and her children, she has always tried to break through the wall of isolation surrounding her, but despairing, she never finds any meaning in her grinding existence. To her, sexual relationship means only violation, whereas, to Anse, it means love. Before her death she knows her father's words to be true: "The reason for living was to get ready to stay dead a long time."

Darl Bundren, Addie's strange son, thought by his family to be feebleminded. Unlike the others, he seems to have the gift of second sight. Knowing the true reasons why Anse and the others are going to Jefferson, he tries to burn the barn housing his mother's body. For this act of attempted purification, his family declares him insane, and he is taken to the asylum at Jackson.

Jewel Bundren, Preacher Whitfield's illegitimate son. A violent young man, he loves only his horse, which cost him many long hours of labor at night. Although devoted to the animal, he allows Anse to trade it to Snopes for a badly needed team of mules. Like the rest of the Bundrens, he tenaciously hauls his mother on the long eventful trip, all the while cursing and raging at his brothers. When Darl tries to burn the corpse, it is Jewel who manages to save her body for burial.

Cash Bundren, Anse's son, a carpenter. While his mother is dying, he busily saws and hammers away at her coffin, just outside her window. Carefully beveling the wood (he hates shoddy work) and showing his mother each board before nailing it in place, he finishes the job shortly after Addie's death. At the flooded river he desperately tries to save his treasured tools when the wagon overturns. His leg broken on the trip, he stoically endures the pain, even after his father uses cement to plaster the swollen and infected leg.

Vardaman Bundren, Anse's son. Constantly, he repeats to himself, "My mother is a fish."

Dewey Dell Bundren, Anse's daughter. A girl of seventeen, she has a reason for going to Jefferson. She is pregnant and wants to buy drugs which she hopes will cause a miscarriage.

Dr. Peabody, a fat, seventy-year-old country doctor. During his long practice he has ministered to many poor-white families like the Bundrens. When his unpaid bills reach fifty thousand dollars, he intends to retire.

Vernon Tull, Anse's helpful neighbor. He does what he can to help Bundren on his ghoulish journey.

Cora Tull, Vernon's fundamentalist wife. Constantly praying and singing hymns, she tries to make Addie repent.

Preacher Whitfield, Addie's former lover, the father of Jewel. Hearing of her sickness, this wordy man goes to confess his sin to Anse. On the way he decides that his fight against the elements, as he crosses the flooding river, helps to expiate his sins. After she dies, he does not feel that a public confession is necessary.

Lafe, a field hand, the father of Dewey Dell's unborn child.

Mr. Gillespie, in whose barn Addie's coffin lies when Darl attempts to burn it.

The Story

Addie Bundren was dying. She lay propped up in a bed in the Bundren farmhouse, looking out the window at her son Cash as he built the coffin in which she was to be buried. Obsessed with perfection in carpentry, Cash held up each board for her approval before he nailed it in place. Dewey Dell, Addie's daughter, stood beside the bed, fanning her mother as she lay there in the summer heat. In another room, Anse Bundren, Addie's husband, and two sons, Darl and Jewel, discussed the possibility of the boys making a trip with a wagonload of lumber to earn three dollars for the family. Because Addie's wish was that she be buried in Jefferson, the town where her relatives lay, Anse was afraid the boys might not get back in time to carry her body to the Jefferson graveyard. He finally approved the trip, and Jewel and Darl set out.

Addie died while the two brothers were gone and before Cash could finish the coffin. When it was obvious that she was dying, Dr. Peabody was summoned, but he came too late to help the sick woman. While Dr. Peabody was at the house, Vardaman, the youngest boy, arrived home with a fish he had caught in the river; his mother's death somehow became entangled in his mind with the death of the fish, and because Dr. Peabody was there when she died, Vardaman thought the doctor had killed her.

Meanwhile, a great rainstorm came up. Jewel and Darl, with their load of lumber, were delayed on the road by a broken wagon wheel. Cash kept working through the rain, trying to finish the coffin. At last it was complete, and Addie was placed in it, but the crazed Vardaman, who once had almost smothered in his crib, tried to let his mother out by boring holes through the top of the coffin.

After Jewel and Darl finally got back with the wagon, neighbors gathered at the Bundren house for the funeral service, which was conducted by Whitfield, the minister. Whitfield had once been a lover of Addie's after her marriage, and Jewel, the son whom she seemed to favor, had been fathered by the minister.

Following the service, Anse, his family, and the dead Addie started for Jefferson, normally one hard day's ride away. The rainstorm, however, had so swollen the river that the bridge had been broken and could not be crossed by wagon. After trying another bridge, which had also been washed out, they drove back to an old ford near the first bridge. Three of the family—Anse, Dewey Dell, and Vardaman, with the assistance of Vernon Tull, a neighboring farmer—got across the river on the ruins of the bridge. Then Darl and Cash attempted to drive the wagon across at the obliterated ford, with Jewel leading the way on his spotted horse. This horse was Jewel's one great possession; he had earned the money to purchase it by working all day at the Bundren farm and then by working all night clearing ground for a neighbor. When

the wagon was nearly across, a big log floating downstream upset the wagon. As a result, Cash broke his leg and nearly died; the mules were drowned; the coffin fell out, but was dragged to the bank by Jewel; and Cash's carpenter's tools were scattered in the water and had to be recovered one by one.

Anse refused the loan of anyone's mules, insisting that he must own the team that carried Addie to the grave. He went off to bargain for mules and made a trade in which he offered, without Jewel's consent, to give the spotted horse as part payment. When Jewel found out what his father had done, he rode off, apparently abandoning the group. Later it turned out that he had put the spotted horse in the barn of Snopes, who was dickering with Anse. Thus, they got their new mules, and the trip continued.

By the time they arrived in Mottson, a town on the way to Jefferson, Addie had been dead so long that buzzards followed the wagon. In Mottson, they stopped to buy cement to strengthen Cash's broken leg. The police and citizens, whose noses were offended, insisted that the wagon move on, but they would not budge until they bought the cement and treated the leg. While they were in the town, Dewey Dell left the wagon, went to a drugstore, and tried to buy medicine that would abort the illegitimate child she carried, for she had become pregnant by a man named Lafe, with whom she had worked on the farm. The druggist refused to sell her the medicine.

Addie Bundren had been dead nine days and was still not buried. The family spent the last night before their arrival in Jefferson at the house of Mr. Gillespie, who allowed them to put the odorous coffin in his barn. During the night, Darl, whom the neighbors had always thought to be the least sane of the Bundrens, set fire to the barn. Jewel rescued the coffin by carrying it out on his back. Anse later turned Darl over to the authorities at Jefferson; they sent him to the asylum in Jackson.

Lacking a spade and shovel to dig Addie's grave, Anse stopped at a house in Jefferson and borrowed these tools. The burial finally took place. Afterward, Dewey Dell again tried to buy medicine at a drugstore. One of the clerks pretended to be a doctor, gave her some innocuous fluid, and told her to come back that night for further treatment. The further treatment took the form of a seduction in the basement of the drugstore.

Cash's broken leg, encased in cement, had by now become so infected that Anse took him to Dr. Peabody, who said Cash might not walk for a year. Before starting on the trip home, Anse bought himself a set of false teeth that he had long needed. He then returned the borrowed tools. When he got back to the wagon, he had acquired not only the new teeth but also a new Mrs. Bundren, the woman who lent him the tools.

Critical Evaluation

Considered by many contemporary critics the greatest American fiction writer, William Faulkner was awarded the Nobel Prize in Literature for 1949, after a prolific career that included nineteen novels and two volumes of poetry. Although his formal education was limited, Faulkner read prodigiously in the Greek and Roman classics, the Bible, Shakespeare, the English Romantics, Conrad, Joyce, and Eliot. After relatively undistinguished early attempts in poetry and prose, Faulkner was advised by Sherwood Anderson to concentrate on his "own postage stamp of native soil." This led to the saga of Yoknapatawpha County, a partly true regional history (based on Oxford, Mississippi) merging imperceptibly into a coherent myth, introduced in *Sartoris* (1929) and continued in *The Sound and the Fury* (1929) and *As I Lay Dying* (1930).

In the Yoknapatawpha novels, Faulkner placed himself in the forefront of the avant-garde with his intricate plot organization, his bold experiments in the dislocation of narrative time, and his use of the stream-of-consciousness technique. His stylistic view of time was affected by his sense that past events continue into the present. As he once said, "There is no such thing as *was*; if *was* existed, there would be no grief or sorrow." These stylistic characteristics were undergirded by the development of a complex social structure that enabled Faulkner to explore the inherited guilt of the Southern past, the incapacity of the white aristocracy to cope with modern life, the relations between classes, and the relations between the races.

Starkly realistic, poignantly symbolic, grotesquely comic, and immensely complicated as an experiment in point of view, *As I Lay Dying* ranks with Faulkner's greatest novels: *The Sound and the Fury*, *Sanctuary* (1931), *Light in August* (1932), and *Absalom, Absalom!* (1936). The relative simplicity of its style, characterized by staccatolike sentences and repetitive dialogue, enhances the tragicomic effect. At the same time, the prosaic quality of the narrative often renders into poetry—as when Dewey Dell becomes the symbol of heedless motherhood by wiping everything on her dress, when Darl sees stars first in the bucket and then in his dipper, when Jewel's horse appears "enclosed by a glittering maze of hooves as by an illusion of wings," when the buzzards accompanying Addie's coffin are juxtaposed suddenly with the sparks that make the stars flow backward for Vardaman, or when Darl, in his visionary fashion, speculates: "It is as though the space between us were time: an irrevocable quality. It is as though time, no longer running straight before us in a diminishing line, now runs parallel between us like a looping string, the distance between the doubling accretion of the thread and not the interval between."

The novel's theme, in the very widest terms, is man's absurdly comic distinction between being and not-being.

Peabody describes death as "merely a function of the mind—and that of the ones who suffer the bereavement." The theme is stated most clearly in the single chapter narrated from Addie's viewpoint: "I could just remember how my father used to say that the reason for living was to get ready to stay dead a long time." Addie has long since considered Anse dead, because she realizes that he, like most humans, cannot distinguish between the "thin line" of words that float upward into nothingness and the terrible reality of "doing [that] goes along the earth, clinging to it." Her attitude is expressed tersely and succinctly when she comments, after allusively revealing her affair with Whitfield: "Then I found that I had Jewel. When I waked to remember to discover it, he was two months gone."

Nineteen of the fifty-nine chapters are narrated from Darl's viewpoint, making him the primary persona of the novel. His references to his family's conglomerate madness sets the tone: "In sunset we fall into furious attitudes, dead gestures of dolls." The novel proceeds in a jerky, doll-like movement, as the narration passes through the viewpoints of fifteen different characters, not without occasional retrogression and hiatus. Although Darl might be called the primary narrator, whose voice is most representative of the author's own, he is not the only interesting one. Vardaman, with ten chapters, displays a mentality reminiscent of Benjie's in *The Sound and the Fury*, showing readers the crazy events connected with the burial through the eyes of a confused and simple-minded child. The third chapter from his viewpoint consists of a single sentence: "My mother is a fish." Only three chapters present Anse's viewpoint, but that is enough to show that he is a bizarre combination of his sons' characteristics: Darl's imagination, Vardaman's insanity, Cash's stubborn practicality, and Dewey Dell's earthiness (which also sets her in contrast with the bitterness of Addie's outlook toward sex and motherhood).

As he does in *The Sound and the Fury*, with Jason's chapter, Faulkner achieves his greatest artistic success with the least intrinsically interesting character, Cash. The first chapter (of five) from Cash's viewpoint is an artistic *coup*. Until this point, readers have heard, through many different viewpoints, the steady buzzing of Cash's saw preparing his mother's coffin—a sound that provides the thread of continuity through the first half of the novel. Even through the rain and through the night, Cash will not cease his labor: "Yet the motion of the saw has not faltered, as though it and the arm functioned in a tranquil conviction that rain was an illusion of the mind." Finally, his own voice is heard in chapter 18: "I made it on the bevel." After this statement, Cash proceeds to explain what he means as Faulkner presents the carpenter's methodological mind in a straightforward list: "1. There is more surface for the nails to grip," ending with, "13. It makes a neater job." Cash's second chapter is a nine-line warning to his impatient father and brothers that the coffin "wasn't on a balance" in the wagon. When the tragedy in the river results from their ignoring his warning, Faulkner presents Cash's third chapter in three lines, beginning with, "It wasn't on a balance," and not even mentioning the fact that Cash's leg has been broken. Cash's single-minded craftsmanship and superhuman patience become a reflection of the author's own technique. The final chapter is Cash's.

AS YOU LIKE IT

Type of work: Drama
Author: William Shakespeare (1564–1616)
Type of plot: Pastoral romance
Time of plot: The Middle Ages
Locale: The Forest of Arden in medieval France
First presented: c. 1590-1600

A pastoral romantic comedy set in the Middle Ages, As You Like It *takes its plot from Thomas Lodge's popular romance,* Rosalyde *(1590). Involving the eventual union of four very different pairs of lovers who represent the diverse faces of love, the story is marked by its mood of kindliness, fellowship, and good humor.*

Principal Characters

Rosalind (rŏz′ə·lĭnd)—disguised as **Ganymede** (găn′ə·mēd) in the forest scenes—the daughter of the banished Duke Senior. A witty, self-possessed young woman, she accepts whatever fortune brings, be it love or exile, with gaiety and good sense. She is amused by the ironic situations arising from her disguise as a youth, and she wryly recognizes the humorous aspects of her growing love for Orlando, whose passion she pretends to be curing. Her central place in the lives of her companions is epitomized in the final scene where she sorts out the tangled skeins of romance and, with Orlando, joins three other couples before Hymen, the god of marriage.

Orlando (ôr·lăn′dō), youngest son of Sir Rowland de Boys, the late ally of Rosalind's father. Although his elder brother mistreats him and neglects his education, he reveals his gentle birth in his manner and appearance. His love for Rosalind provokes extravagantly romantic gestures, but the deeper feeling of which he is capable is evident in his concern for his faithful old servant Adam, as well as in his fidelity to his sweetheart.

Celia (sē′lĭ·ə), Rosalind's gentle cousin, who refuses to let her depart alone for the Forest of Arden. She, too, is gay and witty, ready to exchange quips with Touchstone and tease Rosalind about her love for Orlando. When she meets Orlando's brother Oliver, however, she succumbs to Cupid even more rapidly than did her cousin.

Touchstone, Duke Frederick's clever fool, who accompanies his master's daughter Celia and Rosalind into the Forest of Arden, much to the amusement of Jaques and to the consternation of the old shepherd Corin, who finds himself damned for never having been at court, according to Touchstone's logic. The fool, more than any of the other characters, remains at heart a courtier, even in Arcadia, but he returns from the forest with a country wench as his bride.

Jaques (jā′kwēz), a hanger-on of Duke Senior's court in Arden, a professional man of melancholy who philosophizes on the "seven ages of man." He is fascinated by the presence in the forest of a "motley fool," and he delights in Touchstone's explanations of court formalities. He remains in the forest when his lord recovers his dukedom, and he goes off to observe and comment on the unexpected conversion of Duke Frederick.

Oliver (ŏl′ĭ·vər), Orlando's greedy, tyrannical brother, who tries to deprive him of both wealth and life. Sent by Duke Frederick to find his brother or forfeit all his lands, he is rescued by Orlando from a lioness. This kindness from his mistreated brother gives him new humanity, and he becomes a worthy husband for Celia.

Duke Frederick, Celia's strong, self-centered father, the usurper. Fearing her popularity with the people, he arbitrarily sends Rosalind away to her exiled father. Later, equally unreasonably, he banishes Orlando for being the son of an old enemy and then sets Oliver wandering in search of the brother he despises. He is reported at the end of the play to have retired from the world with an old hermit.

Duke Senior, Rosalind's genial father, banished by his brother Duke Frederick, who holds court under the greenwood trees, drawing amusement from hunting, singing, and listening to Jaques' melancholy philosophy in the golden world of Arden.

Silvius (sĭl′vĭ·ŭs), a lovesick young shepherd. He asks "Ganymede" to help him win his scornful sweetheart Phebe.

Phebe (fē′bē), a disdainful shepherdess. Rebuked by "Ganymede" for her cruelty to Silvius, she promptly becomes enamored of the youth. She promises, however, to wed Silvius if she is refused Ganymede, and, of course, she does so once Rosalind reveals her identity.

Audrey (ô′drĭ), Touchstone's homely, stupid, good-hearted country wench.

William, Audrey's equally simple-minded rustic suitor.

Corin (kŏr′ĭn), a wide, well-meaning old shepherd. He gives good counsel to William and expresses the virtues of the simple life in his cross-purposes discussion of court and country with Touchstone.

Adam, a faithful old servant of Orlando's family. He accompanies his young master into the forest.

Jaques (jā′kwēz, jăk), the brother of Orlando and Oliver. He brings the news of Duke Frederick's retirement to the forest.

Sir Oliver Martext, a "hedge-priest" hired by Touchstone to marry him to Audrey in somewhat dubious rites.

Le Beau (lə bō), Duke Frederick's pompous attendant.

Charles, a champion wrestler challenged and defeated by Orlando.

Amiens (ā′mĭ·ĕnz), one of Duke Senior's lords.

Dennis, Oliver's servant.

Hymen (hī′mən), the god of marriage.

The Story

A long time ago the elder and lawful ruler of a French province had been deposed by his younger brother, Frederick. The old duke, driven from his dominions, fled with several faithful followers to the Forest of Arden. There he lived a happy life, free from the cares of the court and able to devote himself at last to learning the lessons nature had to teach. His daughter Rosalind, however, remained at court as a companion to her cousin Celia, the usurping Duke Frederick's daughter. The two girls were inseparable, and nothing her father said or did could make Celia part from her dearest friend.

One day Duke Frederick commanded the two girls to attend a wrestling match between the duke's champion, Charles, and a young man named Orlando, the special object of Duke Frederick's hatred. Orlando was the son of Sir Rowland de Boys, who in his lifetime had been one of the banished duke's most loyal supporters. When Sir Rowland died, he had charged his oldest son, Oliver, with the task of looking after his younger brother's education, but Oliver had neglected his father's charge. The moment Rosalind laid eyes on Orlando she fell in love with him, and he with her. She tried to dissuade him from an unequal contest with a champion so much more powerful than he, but the more she pleaded the more determined Orlando was to distinguish himself in his lady's eyes. In the end he completely conquered his antagonist, and was rewarded for his prowess by a chain from Rosalind's own neck.

When Duke Frederick discovered his niece's interest in Sir Rowland's son, he banished Rosalind immediately from the court. His daughter Celia announced her intention of following her cousin. As a consequence, Rosalind disguised herself as a boy and set out for the Forest of Arden, and Celia and the faithful Touchstone (the false duke's jester) went with her. In the meantime, Orlando also found it necessary to flee because of his brother's harsh treatment. He was accompanied by his faithful servant, Adam, an old man who willingly turned over his life savings of five hundred crowns for the privilege of following his young master.

Orlando and Adam also set out for the Forest of Arden, but before they had traveled very far they were both weary and hungry. While Adam rested in the shade of some trees, Orlando wandered into that part of the forest where the old duke was, and came upon the outlaws at their meal. Desperate from hunger, Orlando rushed upon the duke with a drawn sword and demanded food. The duke immediately offered to share the hospitality of his table, and Orlando blushed with shame over his rude manner. Moreover, he would not touch a mouthful until Adam had been fed. When the old duke found that Orlando was the son of his friend, Sir Rowland de Boys, he took Orlando and Adam under his protection and made them members of his band of foresters.

In the meantime, Rosalind and Celia also arrived in the Forest of Arden, where they bought a flock of sheep and proceeded to live the life of shepherds. Rosalind passed as Ganymede, Celia, as a sister, Aliena. In this adventure they encountered some real Arcadians—Silvius, a shepherd, and Phebe, a dainty shepherdess with whom Silvius was in love. But the moment Phebe laid eyes on the disguised Rosalind she fell in love with the supposed young shepherd and would have nothing further to do with Silvius. As Ganymede, Rosalind also met Orlando in the forest and twitted him on his practice of writing verses in praise of Rosalind and hanging them on the trees. Touchstone displayed, in the forest, the same willfulness and whimsicality he showed at court, even to his love Audrey, a country wench whose sole appeal was her unloveliness.

One morning, as Orlando was on his way to visit Ganymede, he saw a man lying asleep under an oak tree. A snake was coiled about the sleeper's neck, and a hungry lioness crouched nearby ready to spring. He recognized the man as his own brother, Oliver, and for a moment Orlando was tempted to leave him to his fate. But he drew his sword and killed the snake and the lioness. In the encounter he himself was wounded by the lioness. Because Orlando had saved his life, Oliver was duly repentant, and the two brothers were joyfully reunited.

His wound having bled profusely, Orlando was too weak to visit Ganymede, and he sent Oliver instead with a bloody handkerchief as proof of his wounded condition. When Ganymede saw the handkerchief, the supposed shepherd promptly fainted. The disguised Celia was so impressed by Oliver's concern for his brother that she fell in love with him, and they made plans to be married on the following day. Orlando was so overwhelmed by this news that he was a little envious. But when Ganymede came to call upon Orlando, the young shepherd promised to produce the lady Rosalind the next day. Meanwhile Phebe came to renew her ardent declaration of love for Ganymede, who promised on the morrow to unravel the love tangle of everyone.

In the meantime, Duke Frederick, enraged at the flight of his daughter, Celia, had set out at the head of an expedition to capture his elder brother and put him and all his followers to death. But on the outskirts of the Forest of Arden he met an old hermit who turned Frederick's head from his evil design. On the day following, as Ganymede had promised, with the banished duke and

his followers as guests, Rosalind appeared as herself and explained how she and Celia had posed as the shepherd Ganymede and his sister Aliena. Four marriages took place with great rejoicing that day—Orlando to Rosalind, Oliver to Celia, Silvius to Phebe, and Touchstone to Audrey. Moreover, Frederick was so completely converted by the hermit that he resolved to take religious orders, and he straightway dispatched a messenger to the Forest of Arden to restore his brother's lands and those of all his followers.

Critical Evaluation

As You Like It is a splendid comedy on love and alternate life-styles that more than fulfills the promise of its title. Its characters are, for the most part, wonderfully enamored of love, one another, and themselves. The play has a feeling of freshness and vitality, and although adapted from an older story full of artifice, suggests a world of spontaneity and life.

To understand *As You Like It*, one must understand the conventions it uses. *As You Like It* is often called a pastoral comedy because it engages the conventions of pastoral literature. Pastoral literature, beginning in the third century B.C. and popular in the late sixteenth century, enabled poets, novelists, and dramatists to contrast the everyday world's fears, anxieties, disloyalties, uncertainties, and tensions with the imagined, mythical world of a previous age when peace, longevity, contentment, and fulfillment reigned in men's lives. Each age develops its own manner of describing lost happiness, far removed from the normal toil of human existence. The pastoral was the dominant such vision in the late sixteenth century.

In the pastoral, the mythic, lost, "golden" world is set in a simple, rural environment, which then becomes the image of all things desirable to honest men. *As You Like It* is typical of this convention and it contains two contrasting worlds: the world of the court and the rural world—in this case the Forest of Arden. The court is inhabited by corrupt men; namely, Duke Frederick and Oliver. It is not significant that the gentle Duke, Orlando, Rosalind, and Celia once resided there. Rather, as the play develops, the court is the natural home of the wicked and ambitious. Yet, we do not witness the degeneration of Duke Frederick and Oliver; they are naturally wicked, and the court is their proper milieu.

The elder Duke, Orlando, Rosalind, and Celia, on the other hand, are naturally good, and the forest is their natural milieu. If the court represents elaborate artifice, ambition, avarice, cruelty, and deception, the forest represents openness, tolerance, simplicity, and freedom. In the pastoral, one does not find immensely complex characters such as Hamlet, who like most humans has both good and bad characteristics; instead, good and bad traits

are apportioned to separate characters. This allocation imposes a necessary artifice upon the play, which colors all actions, from falling in love to hating or helping a brother. In a play such as *As You Like It*, one does not expect naturalistic behavior. On the other hand, by using the conventions and artifice adroitly, Shakespeare achieved a remarkable exploration of love and its attendant values.

In the opening scene, Orlando, who has been denied an education and kept like an animal by his brother, is seen to be naturally good and decent. Talking to his brother Oliver, Orlando says, "You have train'd me like a peasant, obscuring and hiding from me all gentleman-like qualities. The spirit of my father grows strong in me, and I will no longer endure it: therefore allow me such exercises as may become a gentleman . . ." (I.i.71–76). Oliver, on the other hand, is just as naturally wicked as Orlando is decent. He says, "for my soul—yet I know not why—hates nothing more than he" (I.i.171–172). Logic has no necessary place in this world. Love, however, does.

Love is a natural part of the pastoral world. Practically at first glance, Rosalind and Orlando are in love. Shakespeare's magic in *As You Like It* is to take the contrived love that is the expected part of the pastoral convention, and make of it a deeply felt experience that the audience can understand and to which it can react. Shakespeare manages this not only through the extraordinary beauty of his language but also through the structure of his play.

As You Like It is full of parallel actions. Orlando and Rosalind meet and immediately fall in love. Silvius and Phebe are in love. Touchstone meets Audrey in the forest, and they fall in love. At the end of the play Celia meets the reformed Oliver, and they fall in love just as quickly as Rosalind and Orlando had at the beginning of the play. The love match at the play's end nicely sets off the love match at the beginning.

Each love pairing serves a particular purpose. The focus of the play is primarily upon the Rosalind-Orlando match. Rosalind is the more interesting of the pair, for while she recognizes the silliness of the lover's ardor, she is as much victim as those she scorns. In Act IV, while in boy's disguise, she pretends to Orlando that his Rosalind will not have him. He says, "Then . . . I die" (IV.i.93). Her response pokes fun at the expiring love: "No, faith, die by attorney. The poor world is almost six thousand years old, and in all this time there was not any man died in his own person, *videlicet,* in a love-cause. . . . Men have died from time to time and worms have eaten them, but not for love" (IV.i.93–108). She can toy with Orlando in her disguise as Ganymede, yet she is completely dominated by her love passion. Strong passion is a part of the love experience, but Rosalind's and Orlando's passion is highly refined; the passion others know is more earthly.

Touchstone, in his quest for Audrey, exemplifies this side of love. He at first wants to marry her out of church so when he tires of her, he can claim their marriage was invalid. The kind of love he represents is physical passion. The Phebe-Silvius pairing shows yet another face of love. Silvius exemplifies the typical pastoral lover, hopelessly in love with a fickle mistress. He sighs on his pillow and breaks off from company, forlornly calling out his mistress' name. Touchstone's and Silvius' brands of love are extreme versions of qualities in Rosalind's love. In the comedies Shakespeare often used this device of apportioning diverse characteristics to multiple characters rather than building one complete character. Without Touchstone, love in the play may be too sentimental to take seriously. Without Silvius, it may be too crude. With both, love as exemplified by Rosalind and Orlando becomes a precious balance of substance and nonsense, spirituality and silliness.

Curious things happen in *As You Like It*. Good men leave the honorable forest to return to the wicked court. Wicked men who enter the forest are instantly converted in their ways. At the end of the play Oliver, who came to the Forest of Arden to hunt down his brother Orlando, gives his estate to Orlando and marries Celia, vowing to remain in the forest and live and die a shepherd. Duke Frederick also came to the Forest of Arden in order to kill his brother. Meeting "an old religious man" in the forest, Duke Frederick "was converted/ Both from his enterprise and from the world." He too gives up his estate, and his crown, to his brother. The forest, the pastoral world, has the power to convert.

Why, then, do the elder Duke, Orlando, and Rosalind elect to return to the court, home of wickedness? They do so because in the end *As You Like It* is not a fairy tale, but an expression of humanly felt experiences. The forest ultimately is to be used as a cleansing and regenerative experience, a place to which one may retire in order to renew simplicity, honesty, and virtue. It is not, however, to be a permanent retreat. Good men stained by labor and trouble in their everyday world in the end must still participate in that world. They can retreat to the pastoral world in order to renew and reinvigorate themselves, but finally they must return, refreshed and fortified, to the community of men, to take on the responsibilities all must face.

THE AUTOBIOGRAPHY OF BENJAMIN FRANKLIN

Type of work: Autobiography
Author: Benjamin Franklin (1706–1790)
Time: 1706–1757
Locale: Boston, London, Philadelphia
First published: 1791; first printed in Paris, as *Mémoires*

Principal Personages

Benjamin Franklin
Josiah Franklin, his father
James Franklin, his brother and first employer
Sir William Keith, Governor of Pennsylvania
Mr. Denham, a merchant
Mr. Meredith, Franklin's partner in the print shop
Alexander Hamilton
Governor Morris

Addressing himself to his "Dear Son," Benjamin Franklin first began in Twyford, England, at the age of sixty-five, to set down reminiscences of his early days. For years he had been collecting data about his ancestors, who had lived in Ecton, Northamptonshire, as far back as 1555, the oldest date of the town records; and he thought that his son William Franklin (1731–1813) would someday be interested in the "circumstances" of his father's life, just as Franklin had delighted in anecdotes relating to his family.

The work was composed in installments. The first section, dealing with Franklin's first twenty-four years, was the product of a week of leisure in England in 1771. Then, because of his political activities abroad and at home, he had no further opportunity to continue his task until the urgings of friends persuaded him to resume his writing in 1783. The final section was probably written between November, 1789, and April, 1790. Titled *Mémoires,* it was first printed in France in 1791. No complete text appeared until 1868.

In spite of the lengthy period of composition, only Franklin's life before July, 1757, is covered, with a few comments on his activities in the following year. But the failure to complete the *Autobiography* beyond his fifty-first year does not mean that Franklin failed to write of his activities over the next thirty years. Some of his most important diplomatic missions are reported in individual compositions, such as the sample he showed to Jefferson of the "history of my life" that he said he was preparing. They cover "Negotiations in London for Effecting a Reconciliation between Great Britain and the American Colonies" and the "Journal of the Negotiations for Peace with Great Britain from March 21st to July 1st, 1782."

In addition, this indefatigable letter writer filled his correspondence (in many ways the most interesting part of his writing) with details and sketches. By combining the correspondence chronologically, a biographer can obtain Franklin's personal reactions to practically everything that happened to him. These letters show Franklin as the first real American who stood apart from European influences.

The Franklin family, whose ancestors had lived in the Northamptonshire village of Ecton from the time they assumed a surname originally signifying a middle-class landowner, was transplanted to Boston about 1682, when Benjamin's father Josiah brought his wife and several children to Massachusetts. After his wife's death, the older Franklin remarried. Benjamin, born of the second marriage, was the youngest son of seventeen children.

Fond of study and quickly learning to read, Benjamin was destined for the ministry until his father, a tallow-candler and soap-boiler by trade, began calculating the cost of education and the pitiable salary received by most ministers. So the boy was taken out of school to learn a trade. After a brief period as his father's assistant he was, at the age of twelve, apprenticed to his half brother James, a printer. In his brother's shop he saw his first writing in print, topical ballads written to be sold in the streets.

He continued to read: *The Pilgrim's Progress*, Plutarch's *Parallel Lives*, essays by Defoe, Burton, and Mather. A volume of the *Spectator*, acquired by chance, revealed to him the importance of style and, like Robert Louis Stevenson at a later date, he taught himself by rewriting and comparing sentences. From this printshop came the fifth—Franklin's mistakenly says the second—newspaper in America, the *New England Courant*, to which Franklin became an anonymous contributor.

Fights with his brother eventually sent the seventeen-year-old apprentice to Philadelphia looking for employment. His arrival early in the morning, with three-penny-worth of rolls in his mouth and under his arms as he walked up Market Street past the home of Miss Read, whom he was to marry later, was Philadelphia's first sight of one of its most distinguished citizens.

Neither Bradford nor Keimer, the only printers in Philadelphia, was very advanced. After the boy found a place in Keimer's shop, his wide reading and his ability to talk and to listen brought him many friends. Finally Governor Keith offered to send him to England to buy type and equipment for a shop of his own. Arriving in London, he learned that Keith, whose credit was not good, had provided nothing but promises. To support himself, Franklin found work in a printing house. After eighteen months he was happy to accept the offer of a merchant who wanted him to take back to America a consignment of merchandise. Back in Philadelphia, he worked for a time in Keimer's shop; then, finding a partner in Hugh Meredith, he and the Welsh Pennsylvanian set up their own establishment. They prospered and in 1729 Franklin became the sole proprietor, having bought out Meredith, whose drinking habits were distasteful to the temperate, frugal Franklin. He branched out as a stationer. In 1730 he founded the *Pennsylvania Gazette* and also married Miss Read. At this point the first section of the *Autobiography* ends.

In 1784, in Passy, France, Franklin again began to write his story, this time addressed more generally to the reading public than to his son. With friends interested in scientific and intellectual matters he had in 1743 founded a junto for their mutual exchange of ideas and intellectual improvement; this was later to become the American Philosophical Society. The members sponsored a library for the use of the public.

Now that he had educated himself, Franklin sought moral perfection. He set down twelve virtues, then added a thirteenth, Pride, at the suggestion of critical friends. But he had reason to be proud. He had learned to speak fluent French, Spanish, and Italian. His civic spirit, born when he was appointed postmaster of Philadelphia, induced him to reorganize the fire department, start a movement to pave and light the streets, and to establish an academy which later became the University of Pennsylvania. The death of a son from smallpox caused him to argue for inoculation against the disease. He invented an improved form of heating stove and offered it free for general use, only to learn that he had brought wealth to one stove manufacturer. Meanwhile, beginning in 1732, he published *Poor Richard's Almanack*, the usual collection of agricultural and astronomical data to which he added a compendium of practical wisdom and moral maxims. This venture also brought him wealth and enabled him to retire from active business in 1748.

His thoughts about defense caused him to campaign for the establishment of a militia, but this man who so candidly confessed his "errata," or mistakes, was too well acquainted with himself to accept appointment as their colonel. Civic improvements, when initiated by others, needed his approval before his fellow citizens would adopt them. Yale and Harvard awarded honorary degrees to this self-taught scholar, and he was elected to membership in cultural and scientific societies at home and abroad.

Braddock sought Franklin's advice in campaigning against the Indians, only to disregard it with disastrous results. After selling out his shop to his foreman, he occupied his time with philosophical concerns and scientific experiments, particularly those relating to electricity. His theories, when ignored or contradicted abroad, led to his experiments with lightning in 1752.

Having represented Pennsylvania at the Albany Congress in 1754, he was chosen to represent it in protests to the English crown. His arrival in England, July 27, 1757, is the last date in his story of himself.

THE AUTOBIOGRAPHY OF WILLIAM BUTLER YEATS

Type of work: Memoirs and journals
Author: William Butler Yeats (1865–1939)
First published: *Reveries over Childhood and Youth*, 1915; *Four Years*, 1921; *The Trembling of the Veil*, 1922; *Autobiographies*, 1926; *Estrangement*, 1926; *Reflections from a Diary Kept in 1909*, 1926; *The Death of Synge and Other Passages from an Old Diary*, 1928; *Dramatis Personae*, 1936

Yeats's *Autobiography* is important for several reasons, not the least of which is that it serves as an illuminating background to the greatest body of twentieth century poetry in English, *The Collected Poems of W. B. Yeats*. Yeats's poetry is about people: imaginary people (Michael Robartes, Crazy Jane), people of Irish legend (Cuchulain, Fergus), people of Irish history (Parnell, Robert Emmet), people to whom Yeats was related (the Middletons, the Pollexfens), people Yeats knew (Maud Gonne, Lady Gregory). All these, and many more, are celebrated in his poems. The main figure in the poems is, of course, "I, the poet William Yeats."

The poems themselves are not important as autobiography, for the people in them exist in art, not in life. There is a "Yeats country" just as there is a "Faulkner country," but whereas Faulkner changed the names (Oxford, Mississippi becoming "Jefferson"), Yeats did not. In the "Yeats country" Michael Robartes is as real as Maud Gonne; Cuchulain is as alive as Lady Gregory. Yet we are always aware that many of Yeats's people are taken from real life, and in the *Autobiography* we are afforded an extraordinary view into that life. We read about the places Yeats made famous: Sligo, Coole, Ballylee. We meet the Yeats family and Irish peasants, poets of the 1890s, patriots and revolutionaries, spiritualists, and Swedish royalty. We are presented with the real-life equivalent of the "Yeats country" of the *Collected Poems*, and we see it through the eyes and through the memory of the poet himself.

The first section of the *Autobiography*, "Reveries over Childhood and Youth," begins with Yeats's earliest memories and concludes with the publication of his first book of poems, *The Wanderings of Oisin and Other Poems* (1889). The chief locales are Sligo, London, and Dublin.

As a very young child Yeats stood in awe of his sea-captain grandfather, William Pollexfen, but it was his father, John Butler Yeats, whose influence was dominant throughout his childhood and adolescence. The elder Yeats, a none-too-successful painter and an opinionated skeptic, influenced his son in several ways. He fostered his interest in literature by reading to him from the works of James Fenimore Cooper, Walter Scott, Chaucer, Shelley, Thoreau, and many other writers, and in the theater by taking him to see Henry Irving in *Hamlet*. Until he was nearly twenty Yeats seems to have shared most of his father's opinions (and they were generally outspoken ones)

about art, education, and politics. It was only after he had begun to study psychical research and mystical philosophy that he finally was able to break away from his father's influence. But in some respects his father's influence was never broken; John Butler Yeats's hatred for abstractions, for example, was one opinion his son held to all his life, and it greatly influenced the younger Yeats's attitudes toward politics, art, and life itself. Moreover, Yeats was always conscious of being an artist's son and aware, therefore, that he must follow a career that would embrace the whole of life rather than provide a means to becoming well off and living pleasantly. The work that Yeats considered as embracing life was, of course, his poetry.

In this section we read of many things: Yeats's early interest in natural science (which he later grew to hate); his lack of scholarship and his resultant lack of anything like a systematic formal education; the influence on him of the Fenian leader, John O'Leary; and his continuing interest in legends of the Irish heroes, in stories of ghosts and omens, and in peasant tales of all kinds. It was only natural that Yeats was later to collect these stories (as in *The Celtic Twilight*, 1893), for he was never to forget his mother and a fisherman's wife telling each other stories such as Homer himself might have told.

This section of the *Autobiography* is a portrait of the artist as a young man. At first Yeats merely played the roles of sage, magician, poet. Sometimes he was Hamlet, or Byron's Manfred, or Shelley's Alastor; at other times he was Byron himself. Then he began to write poems in admiring imitation of Shelley and Spenser. All of his early work was derivative; it was not until years afterward that he began, deliberately, to reshape his style by discarding traditional metaphors, employing looser rhythms, communicating emotion that he described as "cold." But for now there was nothing "cold" about his emotion. Very much under the influence of his father's belief that only passionate poetry is important, he filled his early lyrics with imagery and color, a heritage from the Romantic poets.

The longest section of the *Autobiography*, "The Trembling of the Veil," deals with the period between 1887 and the turn of the century. On the one hand this section is a record of his friendships during these years. Nearly all of the famous literary figures of the 1890s are here: W. E. Henley, Oscar Wilde, William Morris, Lionel

Johnson, Ernest Dowson, George Bernard Shaw, George Russell ("A. E."), John Synge, Arthur Symons, Aubrey Beardsley, Max Beerbohm, William Sharp ("Fiona Mcleod"), Paul Verlaine—Yeats knew them all. On the other hand the section is a record of the coming to maturity of Yeats's own work and its chief importance is perhaps that it gives us insights into the development of his theories of poetry.

He did not forsake his interest in emotion, but he began to write poems combining personal feeling with larger patterns of myth and symbol. His interest in myth and symbol, an understanding of which is essential to an understanding of his mature poetry, led him into a series of esoteric studies. He was associated with the Theosophist, Madame Blavatsky; he experimented with the evocative power of symbols under the direction of Macgregor Mathers and later in conjunction with his uncle, George Pollexfen. He eventually realized that he had found only a variety of images. He had been searching for a tradition—for the centrality of a tradition—but he had hit upon its opposite: fragmentation.

Yeats envied Dante for having had a unified culture out of which to write. "Unity of Culture," a unity stemming from a universally accepted mythology, is precisely what, in Yeats's view, the modern world lacks. Symbolism he saw as the language of mythology. For years Yeats was occupied with the attempt to regain, in Ireland, that "Unity of Culture" which would make the language of symbolism intelligible. He hoped to find his mythology in peasant legendry. He hoped to encourage a national literature, one above politics and all temporal disputes, which would draw upon such a mythology. Finally he came to realize that his dream of a modern nation returned to Unity of Culture, was false. When this dream failed, he inevitably turned inward. Lacking a traditional mythology, he created one of his own, compounded from a complex variety of sources. He adopted myths and symbols from Christianity, from paganism, from the Orient, from Theosophy, and from Irish folklore.

In the third section of the *Autobiography*, "Dramatis Personae, 1896–1902," the main "Personae" are Edward Martyn, Arthur Symons, George Moore, and, above all, Lady Gregory. This section recounts the struggles of a small group of people to found in Ireland a native and national theater. But most of all it serves as Yeats's graceful and grateful tribute to Lady Gregory, his patron, collaborator, and friend. She encouraged him in his work and lent him money. Of even greater influence in the development of his art, as Yeats recalled years later, were the times he stayed at Coole, Lady Gregory's home, where Yeats spent the summers of twenty years. Among the trees and by the lake at Coole, Yeats was to do much of his greatest work, and the place itself, which he said he knew better than any spot on earth, became, like the people he knew, a familiar and important part of the world of his *Collected Poems*.

The *Autobiography* is far from being a complete account of Yeats's life. The first three sections cover the years 1865 to 1902, but Yeats was to live until 1939, and to do nearly all of his important work during the remaining years. Of the last three sections of the book, two ("Estrangement" and "The Death of Synge") are but fragmentary extracts from a diary Yeats kept in 1909. "Estrangement" is a collection of scattered and, at times, half-formed ideas about art, and is not, in the true sense of the word, autobiography. "The Death of Synge" is also largely a series of reveries about art; those reveries, in particular, which were induced by his friend's death. The final section of the book, "The Bounty of Sweden" (written in 1925), is a relaxed account of his trip to Stockholm in 1923 to receive the Nobel Prize.

BABBITT

Type of work: Novel
Author: Sinclair Lewis (1885–1951)
Type of plot: Social satire
Time of plot: 1920s
Locale: Zenith, a fictional midwestern town
First published: 1922

Babbitt is a pungent satire about a man who typifies complacent mediocrity. Middle-class businessman George F. Babbitt revels in his popularity, his automobile, and his ability to make money. He drinks bootleg whiskey, bullies his wife, and ogles his manicurist. Because he is firmly grounded in realism, Babbitt is one of American fiction's most memorable characters; his very name has entered the language as a synonym for the widespread phenomenon he represents.

Principal Characters

George F. Babbitt, a satirically portrayed prosperous real-estate dealer in Zenith, a typical American city. He is the standardized product of modern American civilization, a member of the Boosters' Club, hypnotized by all the slogans of success, enthralled by material possessions, envious of those who have more, patronizing toward those who have less, yet dimly aware that his life is unsatisfactory. His high moment comes when, after delivering a speech at a real-estate convention, he is asked to take part in a political campaign against Seneca Doane, a liberal lawyer who is running for mayor. As a result of his campaign efforts, Babbitt is elected vice-president of the Boosters. His self-satisfaction is shattered when his one real friend, Paul Riesling, shoots his nagging wife and is sent to prison. For the first time Babbitt begins to doubt the values of American middle-class life. He has a love affair with a client, Mrs. Judique, and becomes involved with her somewhat bohemian friends; he publicly questions some of the tenets of Boosterism; he refuses to join the Good Citizens' League. But the pressure of public opinion becomes too much for him; when his wife is taken ill, his brief revolt collapses, and he returns to the standardized world of the Boosters' Club.

Myra Babbitt, his colorless wife, whom he married because he could not bear to hurt her feelings. She lives only for him and the children.

Verona Babbitt, their dumpy daughter. Just out of college, she is a timid intellectual whose mild unconventionality angers her father. He is relieved when she marries Kenneth Escott.

Theodore (Ted) Babbitt, their son. A typical product of the American school system, he hates study and the thought of college. He elopes with Eunice Littlefield, thus winning his father's secret admiration, for he has at least dared to do what he wanted.

Paul Riesling, Babbitt's most intimate friend since college days. With the soul of a musician, he has been trapped into a lifetime of manufacturing tar-roofing and is burdened with a shrewish wife. Goaded to desperation, he shoots her and, though she lives, is sent to prison.

Zilla Riesling, Paul's nagging wife. With a vicious disposition that is made worse by having too much time on her hands, she finally drives Paul to the point of shooting her.

Mrs. Daniel (Tanis) Judique, a widow with whom Babbitt has a brief affair as a part of his revolt against conventionality.

Seneca Doane, a liberal lawyer, the anathema of all the solid businessmen of Zenith.

William Washington Eathorne, a rich conservative banker. He represents the real power behind the scene in Zenith.

Charles and **Lucille McKelvey,** wealthy members of Zenith's smart set. The Babbitts are hopeful of being accepted socially by the McKelveys but do not succeed.

Ed and **Mrs. Overbrook,** a down-at-heels couple. They are hopeful of being accepted socially by the Babbitts but do not succeed.

The Reverend Dr. John Jennison Drew, the efficient, high-powered pastor of Babbitt's church.

Vergil Gunch, a successful coal dealer. He is prominent in all the civic organizations to which Babbitt belongs.

T. Cholmondeley (Chum) Frink, a member of Babbitt's social group. He is a popular poet whose work is syndicated throughout the country.

Howard Littlefield, Babbitt's next-door neighbor. An economist for the Zenith Street Traction Company, he can prove to everyone's satisfaction that Zenith is the best of all possible worlds.

Eunice Littlefield, his flapper daughter. She elopes with Ted Babbitt to the public surprise and indignation of both families but to Babbitt's secret delight.

Kenneth Escott, a newspaper reporter. After a tepid courtship, he finally marries Verona Babbitt.

The Story

George F. Babbitt was proud of his house in Floral Heights, one of the most respectable residential districts in Zenith. Its architecture was standardized; its interior decorations were standardized; its atmosphere was standardized. Therein lay its appeal for Babbitt.

He bustled about in a tile and chromium bathroom during his morning ritual of getting ready for another day. When he went down to breakfast, he was as grumpy as usual. It was expected of him. He read the dull real-estate page of the newspaper to his patient wife, Myra. Then he commented on the weather, grumbled at his son and daughter, gulped his breakfast, and started for his office.

Babbitt was a real-estate broker who knew how to handle business with zip and zowie. Having closed a deal whereby he forced a poor businessman to buy a piece of property at twice its value, he pocketed part of the money and paid the rest to the man who had suggested the enterprise. Proud of his acumen, he picked up the telephone and called his best friend, Paul Riesling, to ask him to lunch.

Paul Riesling should have been a violinist, but he had gone into the tar-roofing business in order to support his shrewish wife, Zilla. Lately, she had made it her practice to infuriate doormen, theater ushers, or taxicab drivers, and then ask Paul to come to her rescue and fight them like a man. Cringing with embarrassment, Paul would pretend he had not noticed the incident. Later, at home, Zilla would accuse him of being a coward and a weakling.

So sad did Paul's affairs seem to Babbitt that he suggested a vacation to Maine together—away from their wives. Paul was skeptical, but with magnificent assurance, Babbitt promised to arrange the trip. Paul was humbly grateful.

Back in his office, Babbitt refused a raise for one of his employees. When he got home, he and his wife decided to give a dinner party, with the arrangements taken from the contents of a woman's magazine, and everything edible disguised to look like something else.

The party was a great success. Babbitt's friends were exactly like Babbitt. They all became drunk on prohibition gin, were disappointed when the cocktails ran out, stuffed themselves with food, and went home to nurse headaches.

Sometime later, Babbitt and Myra paid a call on the Rieslings. Zilla, trying to enlist their sympathy, berated her husband until he was goaded to fury. Babbitt finally told Zilla that she was a nagging, jealous, sour, and unwholesome wife, and he demanded that she allow Paul to go with him to Maine. Weeping in self-pity, Zilla consented. Myra sat calmly during the scene, but later she criticized Babbitt for bullying Paul's wife. Babbitt told her sharply to mind her own business.

On the train, Babbitt and Paul met numerous businessmen who loudly agreed with one another that what this country needed was a sound business administration. They deplored the price of motor cars, textiles, wheat, and oil; they swore that they had not an ounce of race prejudice; they blamed communism and socialism for labor unions that got out of hand. Paul soon tired of the discussion and went to bed. Babbitt stayed up late, smoking countless cigars and telling countless stories.

Maine had a soothing effect upon Babbitt. He and Paul fished and hiked in the quiet of the north woods, and Babbitt began to realize that his life in Zenith was not all it should be. He promised himself a new outlook on life, a more simple, less hurried way of living.

Back in Zenith, Babbitt was asked to make a speech at a convention of real-estate men, which was to be held in Monarch, a nearby city. He wrote a speech contending that real-estate men should be considered professionals and called realtors. At the meeting, he declaimed loudly that real estate was a great profession, that Zenith was God's own country—the best little spot on earth—and to prove his statements, he quoted countless statistics on waterways, textile production, and lumber manufacture. The speech was such a success that Babbitt instantly won recognition as an orator.

Babbitt was made a precinct leader in the coming election. His duty was to speak to small labor groups about the inadvisability of voting for Seneca Doane, a liberal, in favor of a man named Prout, a solid businessman who represented the conservative element. Babbitt's speeches helped to defeat Doane. He was very proud of himself for having Vision and Ideals.

On a business trip to Chicago, Babbitt spied Paul Riesling sitting at dinner with a middle-aged and pretty woman. Later, in his hotel room, Babbitt indignantly demanded an explanation for Paul's lack of morality. Paul told Babbitt that he could no longer stand living with Zilla. Babbitt, feeling sorry for his friend, swore that he would keep Paul's secret from Zilla. Privately, Babbitt envied Paul's independence.

Babbitt was made vice-president of the Booster's Club. He was so proud of himself that he bragged loudly when his wife called him at the office. It was a long time before he understood what she was trying to tell him; Paul had shot his wife.

Babbitt's world collapsed about him. Though Zilla was still alive, Paul was in prison. Babbitt began to question his ideas about the power of the dollar. Paul was perhaps the only person Babbitt had ever loved. Myra had long since become a habit, and the children were too full of new ideas to be close to their father. Babbitt felt suddenly alone. He began to criticize the minister's sermons. He no longer visited the Athletic Club and rarely ate lunch with any of his business acquaintances.

One day, the pretty widow Mrs. Judique came to his

office and asked him to find her a flat. Babbitt joined her circle of Bohemian friends. He drank more than he had ever drunk in his life. He spent money wildly. Two of the most powerful men in town requested that he join the Good Citizen's League—or else. Babbitt refused to be bullied. For the first time in his life, he was a human being. He actually made friends with his archenemy, Seneca Doane, and discovered that he liked his liberal ideas. He praised Doane publicly. Babbitt's new outlook on life appealed to his children, who at once began to respect him as they never had before. Babbitt, however, became unpopular among his business-boosting friends. When he again refused to join the Good Citizen's League,

he was snubbed in the streets. Gradually, Babbitt found that he had no real resources within himself. He was miserable.

When Myra became ill, Babbitt suddenly realized that he loved his colorless wife. He broke with Mrs. Judique and joined the Good Citizen's League. By the time Myra was well again, there was no more active leader in the town of Zenith than George F. Babbitt. Once more he announced his distrust of Seneca Doane. He became the best Booster the club ever had. His last gesture of revolt was private approval of his son's elopement. Outwardly he conformed.

Critical Evaluation

Zenith, "the Zip City—Zeal, Zest, and Zowie," is Sinclair Lewis' satirical composite picture of the typical progressive American "business city" of the 1920s, and middle-aged, middle-class midwesterner George F. Babbitt is its average prosperous citizen. Everything about Zenith is modern. A few old buildings, ramshackle witnesses of the city's nineteenth century origins, are embarrassing, discordant notes amid the harmony of newness produced by shining skyscrapers, factories, and railroads. One by one, the old buildings are surrounded and bulldozed. The thrust of all energies in the city is toward growth: One of Zenith's most booming businesses is real estate; one of its favorite occupations is the religious tallying and charting of population increase.

As Lewis presents his characters, however, the reader discovers that the prosperity and growth of Zenith has been inversely proportional to the intellectual bankruptcy and spiritual stagnation of its inhabitants. Because they subscribe to the values of Zenith's culture, which are all based on the "Dollar Ethic," Lewis' characters think in terms of production and consumption, judge people on the grounds of their purchasing power, and seek happiness in the earning and spending of money. This creed of prosperity permeates every aspect of society. It is evident not only in political and economic beliefs (discussion between Babbitt and his friends about government affairs is limited to the monotonous refrain, "What this country needs is a good, sound business administration") but in moral and religious attitudes as well. Thus, Dr. Drew attracts followers to his "Salvation and Five Percent" church with a combined cross-and-dollar-sign approach. Even more sinister is the facility with which the upright Babbitt carries through crooked deals in his real estate business. In one maneuver, he plots with a speculator to force a struggling grocer to buy the store building (which he has been renting for years) at a scalper's price. The money ethic is so elemental to Babbitt's conscience that he honestly feels nothing but delight and pride when the deal is completed; his only regret is that

the speculator carries off nine thousand dollars while Babbitt receives a mere four hundred and fifty dollar commission. At the same time, Babbitt—with no inkling of his hypocrisy—discourses on his virtue to his friend Paul Riesling, touting his own integrity while denigrating the morality of his competitors.

The value placed on money also determines Zenith's aesthetic standards. There is no frivolity about the city's architecture; the most important structures are the strictly functional business buildings. Other structures, such as the Athletic Club—where the businessmen go to "relax" and discuss weighty matters of finance—are gaudy, unabashed copies of past styles; the Club's motley conglomeration includes everything from Roman to Gothic to Chinese. The culmination of literary talent in Zenith is the work of Chum Frink, whose daily newspaper lyrics are indistinguishable from his Zeeco car ads. He comes to Babbitt's dinner party fresh from having written a lyric in praise of drinking water instead of poison booze; with bootleg cocktail in hand, he identifies the American genius as the fellow who can run a successful business or the man who writes the Prince Albert Tobacco ads.

Most important, the prosperity ethic is at the heart of social norms in Zenith; it is the basis upon which each citizen judges his individual worth. Lewis' novel includes caricatures of men in every major field of endeavor: Howard Littlefield is the scholar; T. Cholmondeley Frink, the poet; Mike Monday, the popular preacher; Jake Offut, the politician; Vergil Gunch, the industrialist. Yet despite their various professions, these men are identical in their values; they are united in their complacent pride at their own success and in their scorn for those who have not "made it." A man is measured by his income and his possessions. Thus, Babbitt's car is far more than his means of transportation, and his acquisition of gimmicks like the nickel-plated cigar cutter more than mere whim; both car and cigar cutter are affirmations of competence and virility. But the more Babbitt and his peers strive to distinguish themselves through ownership, the more alike they seem. Thus, the men of Zenith, since they are saturated day after day with the demands of the business life and its values, are even more alike than the women, who are not as immersed in the "rat race" as their husbands.

Mercilessly revealing and minutely detailed as its portrait of Zenith is, however, *Babbitt* would not be the excellent novel it is if Lewis had stopped at that. In addition to being an exposé of shallowness, the novel is the chronicle of one man's feeble and half-conscious attempt to break out of a meaningless and sterile existence. In the first half of the book, George Babbitt is the Zenithite par excellence; but in the realtor's sporadic bursts of discontent, Lewis plants seeds of the rebellion to come. Babbitt's complacency is occasionally punctured by disturbing questions: Might his wife be right that he bullied Zilla only to strut and show off his strength and virtue? Are his friends really interesting people? Does he really love his wife and enjoy his career? These nagging questions and the pressures in his life finally build sufficient tension to push Babbitt to the unprecedented step of taking a week's vacation in Maine without his wife and children. The trip relieves his tension and dissolves the questions, and he returns to another year in Zenith with renewed vigor and enthusiasm for Boosters, baseball, dinner parties, and real estate.

It takes the personal tragedy of his friend Paul Riesling to really shock Babbitt out of this routine way of life; Paul's shooting of his wife and consequent imprisonment, which occur approximately midway in the novel, shake Babbitt to his foundations. The Babbitt of the first half of the story is a parody; the Babbitt of the second half, a weak and struggling human being. After Paul goes to prison, Babbitt seems to throw off his previous life-style: he drinks, smokes, and curses; he frequents wild parties, befriends the city's bohemian set, adopts radical opinions, and has a love affair. All these things are part of his rebellion against stifling circumstances and his attempt to escape into individuality. The attempt fails because he lacks the inner strength to be independent, and his revolt is ultimately little more than a teapot tempest. Whether preaching the philosophy of the Elks or rebelliously praising the radical politics of Seneca Doane, whether giving a dinner party with his wife or sneaking out to see Mrs. Judique, Babbitt never truly acts on his own.

Thus, by the end of the novel, Babbitt has returned to the fold, joining the Good Citizen's League and redoubling his zeal in behalf of Zenith Booster activities. But even though Babbitt lacks the strength to break out of his mold, Lewis does not imply that he is unchanged by his experience. On the contrary, Babbitt rediscovers his love for his wife and learns something about himself. By the close of the novel he has grown in awareness, even if he has proven himself incapable of essentially changing his life. If he has lost his own individuality, he is still able to hope for better things for his son, Ted, of whose elopement he secretly approves.

THE BACCHAE

Type of work: Drama
Author: Euripides (480–406 B.C.)
Type of plot: Classical tragedy
Time of plot: Remote antiquity
Locale: Thebes, in Boeotia
First presented: c. 405 B.C.

This complex and disturbing drama has been the subject of interpretations so diverse as to be sometimes diametrically opposed. It has been treated, for example, on the one hand as a condemnation of religious excess, and on the other as the playwright's late acceptance of the Dionysian rites.

Principal Characters

Dionysus (dī′ə·nī′sûs), also called **Bromius, Evius,** and **Bacchus.** He is a god of the general fertility of nature and especially of wine. He has been traveling through the world spreading his teachings but has met with opposition at Thebes, where he appears disguised as his own prophet to take measures on the human level to overcome his opponents. He has driven his mother's sisters (he was the son of Semele by Zeus) to frenzy because they refused to recognize him as a god, and they now revel as thyrsus-bearing Bacchantes with the other women of Thebes on the slopes of Mount Citaeron. Chief of the god's enemy was young King Pentheus, who refuses to recognize Dionysus as a god. Appearing at first as the friend of mortals, he is joyful and willing to reason with the young king, even when Pentheus imprisons him in the royal stables. He frees himself and makes one last attempt to convince Pentheus that he must acknowledge Dionysus' divinity and power. Only when Pentheus determines to drive the Bacchantes from the hills by force does Dionysus reveal the opposite aspect of his character. Becoming cruel, ruthless, and cunning, he establishes control over the mind of Pentheus and leads him, disguised as a woman, through the streets of Thebes to Cithaeron, where he is torn apart by the maddened women of his own city, led by Pentheus' mother, Agave. At the end of the play, after Agave has returned and has realized what she has done, Dionysus appears to pass the sentence of exile on the family of Pentheus. The most terrible aspect of his character emerges as he extends Pentheus' fate to include the suffering of the old and the innocent.

Pentheus (pĕn′thūs), the young, still beardless king of Thebes. He is a puritan with something in his own mind which prevents his seeing any but the extreme aspects, the supposed sexual excesses, of the worship of Dionysus. His opposition of the god is adamant; he imprisons some of the women who follow Dionysus and even the disguised Dionysus himself. When the imprisoned women are miraculously released he remains angry and scornful. After he determines to move with armed force against the Bacchantes, Dionysus exerts control over him and the young king appears beastly drunk, losing all self-control and self-respect. Disguised as a woman, he is led off by Dionysus to spy, as he thinks, on the Bacchantes. The maddened women fall on him and tear him to pieces.

Agave (ə·gā′vē), the mother of Pentheus. In a frenzy she leads the Bacchantes as they tear her son limb from limb under the delusion that he is a lion. Still under her delusion, she first appears carrying her son's mangled head affixed to her thyrsus like a trophy. She praises the gods for guiding her in the deed, inquires after her father, Cadmus, and calls out to Pentheus to come and receive the trophy she has brought. When Cadmus slowly and painfully brings her back to sanity, dazed and perplexed, she realizes what she has done. She is condemned to exile by Dionysus.

Cadmus (kăd′mŭs), the father of Agave. He first appears on his way to worship Dionysus, whom he has conventionally accepted as a god for the good of the family, since Dionysus is reputed to be the cousin of Pentheus. He urges his grandson to do the same but is refuted. He next appears, after gathering the mangled remains of his grandson from the slopes of Cithaeron, to bring Agave back to sanity. He is condemned to exile by Dionysus, even though he protests that such action is too severe.

Tiresias (tī·rē′sĭ·əs), the blind prophet of Thebes. He appears with Cadmus as they prepare to worship Dionysus. He has cleverly accepted Dionysus while retaining his old beliefs. He is proud of his good sense; he has not reasoned dangerously. He urges Pentheus to do the same.

Ino (ī′nō) and **Autonoë** (ô·tōn′ō·ĭ), Agave's sisters who help her tear apart Pentheus' body.

Chorus of Asian Bacchae, followers of Dionysus. Their odes in praise of Dionysus present a picture of Dionysus worship in its purer form and contrast with Pentheus' warped ideas.

The Story

Visited by Zeus, Semele, daughter of Cadmus, the king of Thebes, conceived a child. While she was still carrying her unborn child, she prayed to see Zeus in all his regal splendor. Zeus accordingly appeared to her in the form of a bolt of lightning; Semele was killed instantly. Zeus took the prematurely born child he had fathered and placed him within himself.

In its proper time the child was born again and was named Dionysus. When he grew up and became the god of revelry and wine, men established a cult for his worship. The cult of Dionysus spread throughout western Asia, but it had not yet gained a real foothold in Europe. Dionysus, the god-man whom his devotees associated with the vine and with the ecstasies derived from the juice of the grape, decided that Thebes, home of his ancestors, would be the logical place for the beginning of his cult in the West. At first Theban resistance to Dionysiac behavior balked his efforts, and many Thebans refused to believe that he was a son of Zeus. Pentheus, grandson of Cadmus and cousin of Dionysus, ruled as king of Thebes. Dreading the disorders and madness induced by the new cult, he stubbornly opposed its mysteries, which hinged largely upon orgiastic and frenzied Nature-rites.

A group of Eastern women, devotees of Dionysus, called upon the Theban women to join them in the worship of their beloved god. During the ceremonies blind Tiresias, an ancient Theban prophet, summoned old Cadmus, now withdrawn from public life, to the worship of Dionysus. Performing the frenzied rites, the two old men miraculously regained youthful vigor.

Pentheus, enraged because some of his people had turned to the new religion, imprisoned all women who were caught carrying any of the Bacchic symbols: wine, an ivy crown, or a staff. He rebuked his aged grandfather and accused Tiresias of responsibility for the spread of the cult in Thebes. Tiresias championed Dionysus, declaring that wine provided men with a temporary release from the harshness and miseries of life. The Theban maidens, he said, were exalted and purified by the Bacchic ecstasies. Old Cadmus seconded the words of Tiresias and offered to place an ivy wreath on Pentheus' brow. Pentheus brushed it aside and ordered some of his soldiers to destroy Tiresias' house; others he directed to seize a mysterious stranger, a priest of Dionysus, who had a remarkable influence over Theban women.

When the stranger, Dionysus in disguise, was brought before the king, all the Theban women who had been jailed suddenly and mysteriously found themselves free in a forest where they were engaged in worship of Dionysus. Meanwhile, in the city, Pentheus asked the prisoner his name and his country. Dionysus answered that he was from Lydia, in Asia Minor, and that he and his followers had received their religion from Dionysus. He refused,

however, to tell his name. When Pentheus asked to know more about the strange religion, Dionysus said that this knowledge was reserved for the virtuous only. Pentheus impatiently ordered a soldier to cut off Dionysus' curls, which the prisoner had said were dedicated to his god. Then Pentheus seized Dionysus' staff and ordered him to be imprisoned. Dionysus, calm in spite of these humiliations, expressed confidence in his own welfare and pity at the blindness of Pentheus. Before the guards took Dionysus to be imprisoned in the royal stables, he predicted catastrophe for Pentheus. The king, unmindful of this prophecy, directed that the female followers of Dionysus be put to practical womanly labors.

From his place of imprisonment Dionysus called out encouragement to his devotees. Then he invoked an earthquake which shook the foundations of Pentheus' fortress. Flames danced on Semele's tomb. Dionysus appeared, mysteriously freed from his prison, and rebuked his followers for any doubts and fears they had expressed. He had cast a spell on Pentheus, who in his mad frenzy mistook a bull for Dionysus and chained the animal in its stall while the man-god looked on. Another earth tremor tumbled the royal fortress in ruins.

Pentheus, enraged at seeing Dionysus free, ordered his guards to shut the gates of the city. At the same time a messenger reported that many Theban women, among them Agave, mother of Pentheus, were on nearby Mount Cithaeron observing Dionysiac rites that were partly a dignified and beautiful Nature-worship, partly the cruel slaughter of cattle. A battle had taken place between the women and Boeotian peasants, but the frenzied women, although victorious over the peasants, did not harm them. Pentheus ordered the immediate suppression of the cult. Dionysus offered to lead the women back to the city, but he declared that if he did so the women would only grow more devoted to the man-god.

When Pentheus imperiously demanded that his orders be obeyed, Dionysus cast over him a spell which made the king express a desire to see the women at their worship. In a trance, he resisted only feebly when Dionysus dressed him in woman's clothes in order that he might not be detected by the women, who were jealous of the secrecy of their cult. Pentheus, in fact, was almost overcome by Dionysus' charms as the god led him to Mount Cithaeron.

On the mountain Pentheus complained that he could not see the rites because of the thick pine forest. Dionysus immediately bent a large pine tree to the ground, set Pentheus in its topmost branches, and gently let the tree return to its upright position. At that moment the man-god disappeared, but his voice boomed out to his ecstatic devotees that a great enemy of the cult was hidden in the tall tree. The women, wild with fury, felled the tree, Pentheus with it. Agave, in a Dionysiac frenzy, stood over her son. He frantically threw off his feminine dress and pleaded with her to recognize him, but in her Bacchic trance she imagined him to be a lion. With prodigious strength she tore off his left arm at the shoulder. Her sisters, Ino and Autonoë, joined her and together the three women broke Pentheus' body to pieces. Agave placed his severed head on her wand and called upon the revelers to behold the desert-whelped lion's head that she had taken.

Cadmus and his attendants carried the maimed body of his grandson back to the city. When Agave displayed her bloody trophy, the old man could only feel the deepest pity for his daughter in her blind excess. When Agave

awoke from her trance and recognized the head of her beloved son on her wand, she was bewildered and grief-stricken. Cadmus, mourning the violence that had occurred, urged all men to comply with the wishes of the Olympian deities.

Dionysus returned in his divine form and prophesied that Cadmus and his wife, Harmonia, transformed into dragons, would overcome many Grecian lands before they died. He showed no sympathy for Agave, who cried out that she had been guilty of sinning against him. He doomed her and her sisters to wander without respite until death overtook them.

Critical Evaluation

The Bacchae, written in Macedonia after the author's voluntary exile from Athens and produced posthumously, is one of Euripides' most poetically beautiful as well as thematically difficult dramas. The play abounds in passages of nature description unsurpassed in any of the playwright's other works; the lyrics of the chorus in praise of Dionysus and his gifts of wine and sensuality are particularly exquisite. The vivid landscapes and hymns to bacchanalian pleasure in the first part of the play are so intriguing, in fact, that Pentheus seems a combined brute and prude for opposing the spread of the Dionysian cult in Thebes. In the second half of the play, Euripides' descriptive talent turns to a different purpose with equal effectiveness, as he presents the grisly scene of Pentheus' slaughter by the revelers, terrifying in their mindless, maddened frenzy.

The fact that *The Bacchae* has been alternately interpreted as Euripides' approval of the Dionysian nature-worship cult and as his condemnation of religious excess, attests to the play's thematic complexity. Critics of the first persuasion can cite several undeniable facts as evidence. Perhaps the first thing one notices upon beginning the play is that the Chorus, which traditionally functions as the upholder of moral values and mouthpiece of social standards, in *The Bacchae* aligns itself with Dionysus and fully supports his attempt to introduce his cult into Thebes. Also a follower of the god-man is Tiresias, the familiar blind prophet of Greek tragedy, who vehemently exhorts Pentheus to accept the new cult and accompany him—along with Pentheus' grandfather, Cadmus—to the worship rites. But perhaps the strongest evidence that can be used to support this interpretation is that the doom foretold by the Chorus for Pentheus, if he persists in opposing what they view as the unquestionable right of

the gods to demand worship, comes true; the king of Thebes is killed by his own mother in a most savage and gruesome manner. And yet critics who feel that the play is Euripides' condemnation of excessive emotionalism and religious fanaticism can turn this same event of Pentheus' cruel death around: Is the author not portraying the king as a victim of an unnecessary, unreasoning frenzy? This reading can also be supported by pointing out that Pentheus is not an evil character by any means, but a king who has a duty to protect his city from disruptive social influences. Furthermore, this second interpretation would explain Agave's sentence of lifelong exile at the close of the play.

In view of Euripides' rational and humanistic stance throughout all his dramas, however, it would seem most likely that each interpretation contains some amount of truth, but that both are greatly oversimplified. It is true, for example, that Pentheus is not an evil king, but on the other hand he is unwise in his rejection of advice from his elders, his total reliance on his own reason. His insistence that the cult be destroyed is a denial of one powerful aspect of man's nature; Dionysus represents a force—man's animal nature which must be reckoned with. It is also true that Agave is banished, but she is banished, one must not forget, by Dionysus himself, against whom she has sinned; and her sin certainly is not in worshiping him, but in perverting her worship by carrying it to such excessive lengths that she kills her own son. Thus it would seem that in *The Bacchae*, as elsewhere, Euripides is arguing for moderation in all things. Pure reason which denies the animal element in man leads to destruction just as surely as pure sensuality unleashed without reasonable control.

BARCHESTER TOWERS

Type of work: Novel
Author: Anthony Trollope (1815–1882)
Type of plot: Social satire
Time of plot: Mid-nineteenth century
Locale: "Barchester," an English cathedral town
First published: 1857

This sequel to The Warden *is probably the best known of the novels in the Barsetshire series. Barchester Towers is a story of clerical intrigue centering on the power struggle between an obnoxious and imperious bishop's wife and her scheming, sneaking chaplain. Trollope's fine irony of tone, and his delightful characterizations create a light and purely entertaining novel unburdened by social comment or philosophical questioning.*

Principal Characters

Eleanor Bold, younger daughter of the Reverend Septimius Harding, the "Warden," and wealthy widow of John Bold. She lives with her baby son and her sister-in-law, Mary Bold. Much of the novel revolves around Eleanor's choice of one of her three suitors: Mr. Slope, Bertie Stanhope, and Mr. Arabin. Throughout a large portion of the novel, most of her ecclesiastical friends and relatives assume that she will choose Mr. Slope.

Dr. Proudie, the clergyman who becomes Bishop of Barchester after the death of Archdeacon Grantly's father. Dr. Proudie is a vain but weak man, dominated by his wife and by Mr. Slope. Although all Barchester expects him to offer the wardenship of Hiram's Hospital to Mr. Harding, Dr. Proudie allows Mr. Slope's chicanery to gain the appointment for Mr. Quiverful.

Mrs. Proudie, the aggressive and domineering wife of the Bishop of Barchester. She attempts to control Barchester by championing evangelical and Low Church causes, awarding church patronage, and manipulating people through the offices of Mr. Slope. She antagonizes the established ecclesiastical society in Barchester.

The Reverend Obadiah Slope, the Bishop's chaplain. An evangelical clergyman, Mr. Slope antagonizes most of the chapter with his initial fiery sermon at Barchester Cathedral. He first acts as Mrs. Proudie's agent, but, after he supports the claims of Mr. Harding in an attempt to gain favor with Eleanor Bold, Mrs. Proudie scorns him. Unable to win favor or Eleanor or the post of Dean of Barchester, he returns to London.

The Reverend Theophilus Grantly, the Archdeacon of Barchester and rector of Plumstead Episcopi. He strongly supports the claims of Harding, his father-in-law, to be reinstated as warden of Hiram's Hospital. When the nearby living of St. Ewold's becomes vacant, he goes to Oxford to obtain the post for the Reverend Francis Arabin. He also fears that his sister-in-law, Eleanor Bold, will marry the Low Churchman, Slope.

Susan Grantly, wife of Archdeacon Grantly and the elder daughter of Mr. Harding. She generally follows her husband, but attempts to mitigate his anger at her sister.

The Rev. Septimus Harding, former Warden of Hiram's Hospital. He desires his former charge but is denied it through the machinations of Mr. Slope and Mrs. Proudie, who make his appointment conditional on his assuming extra duties and administering evangelical Sunday Schools. Later he is offered the Deanship of Barchester Cathedral, but he refuses the post because of his advanced age.

The Reverend Francis Arabin, a scholarly High Church clergyman from Oxford who is brought into the living at St. Ewold's to strengthen forces against Bishop Proudie and Mr. Slope. He eventually becomes Dean of Barchester and marries Eleanor Bold.

Dr. Vesey Stanhope, holder of several livings in the Barchester area who has spent the preceding twelve years in Italy. He is summoned to Barchester by Dr. Proudie, through Slope, but has little interest in the political or ecclesiastical affairs of Barchester.

Mrs. Stanhope, his wife, interested chiefly in dress.

Charlotte Stanhope, the oldest daughter of the Stanhopes, who manages the house and the rest of the family with efficiency and intelligence. She, a friend of Eleanor Bold, urges her brother to propose to Eleanor.

La Signora Madeline Vesey Neroni, née **Stanhope,** the great beauty of the Stanhope family who has been crippled in a short, disastrous marriage to a brutal Italian. Although confined to her sofa, she attracts men easily. One of her victims is Mr. Slope, whose hypocrisy she exposes, but she is sufficiently generous to encourage Eleanor to marry Mr. Arabin.

Ethelbert Stanhope (Bertie), the amiable son of the Stanhopes, who has dabbled in law, art, and numerous religions. His family wishes to settle him with Eleanor and her money, but Bertie's proposal fails and he is sent back to Carrara by his father.

Mr. Quiverful, the genial clergyman and father who

is persuaded to accept the preferment at Hiram's Hospital in addition to his living at Puddingdale.

Mrs. Letty Quiverful, his wife and the mother of fourteen children, who begs Mrs. Proudie to bestow the preferment at Hiram's Hospital on her husband.

Miss Thorne of Ullathorne, the member of an old family at St. Ewold's who gives a large party at which both Mr. Slope and Bertie Stanhope propose to Eleanor. Miss Thorne, however, favors Arabin and invites both Arabin and Eleanor to stay until the engagement is settled.

Wilfred Thorne, Esq., of Ullathorne, the younger brother of Miss Thorne, a bachelor, and an authority on tradition and genealogy.

Dr. Gwynne, Master of Lazarus College, Oxford, the man instrumental in securing the Deanship for Mr. Arabin.

Olivia Proudie, the daughter of the Proudies, briefly thought to be engaged to Mr. Slope.

Mary Bold, the sister-in-law and confidante of Eleanor Bold.

Johnny Bold, the infant son of Eleanor and the late John Bold.

Griselda Grantly, the pretty daughter of Archdeacon Grantly.

Dr. Trefoil, Dean of Barchester Cathedral, who dies of apoplexy.

The Bishop of Barchester, the father of Archdeacon Grantly. He dies at the very beginning of the novel.

Dr. Omicron Pi, a famous doctor from London.

The Story

After the death of Bishop Grantly of Barchester, there was much conjecture as to his successor. Bishop Grantly's son, the Archdeacon, was ambitious for the position, but his hopes were deflated when Dr. Proudie was appointed to the diocese. Bishop Proudie's wife was of Low Church propensities. She was also a woman of extremely aggressive nature, who kept the bishop's chaplain, Obadiah Slope, in constant row.

On the first Sunday of the new bishop's regime, Mr. Slope was the preacher in the cathedral. His sermon was concerned with the importance of simplicity in the church service and the consequent omission of chanting, intoning, and formal ritual. The cathedral chapter was aghast. For generations, the services in the cathedral had been chanted; the chapter could see no reason for discontinuing the practice. In counsel, it was decreed that Mr. Slope never be permitted to preach from the cathedral pulpit again.

The Reverend Septimus Harding, who had resigned because of conscientious scruples from his position as warden of Hiram's Hospital, now had several reasons to believe that he would be returned to his post, although at a smaller salary than that he had drawn before. Mr. Harding, however, was perturbed when Mr. Slope, actually Mrs. Proudie's mouthpiece, told him that he would be expected to conduct several services a week and also manage some Sunday schools in connection with the asylum. Such duties would make arduous a preferment heretofore very pleasant and leisurely.

Another change of policy was effected in the diocese when the bishop announced, through Mr. Slope, that absentee clergymen should return and help in the administration of the diocese. For years, Dr. Vesey Stanhope had left his duties to his curates while he remained in Italy. Now he was forced to return, bringing with him an ailing wife and three grown children, spinster Charlotte, exotic Signora Madeline Vesey Stanhope Neroni, and ne'er-do-well Ethelbert. Signora Neroni, separated from her husband, was an invalid who passed her days lying on a couch. Bertie had studied art and had been at varying times a Christian, a Muslim, and a Jew. He had amassed some sizable debts.

The Proudies held a reception in the bishop's palace soon after their arrival. Signora Neroni, carried in with great ceremony, captured the group's attention. She had a fascinating way with men and succeeded in almost devastating Mr. Slope. Mrs. Proudie disapproved and did her best to keep Mr. Slope and others away from the invalid.

When the living of St. Ewold's became vacant, Dr. Grantly made a trip to Oxford and saw to it that the Reverend Francis Arabin, a High Churchman, received the appointment. With Mrs. Proudie and Mr. Slope advocating Low Church practices, it was necessary to build up the strength of the High Church forces. Mr. Arabin was a bachelor about forty years old. The question arose as to what he would do with the parsonage at St. Ewold's.

Mr. Harding's widowed daughter, Mrs. Eleanor Bold, had a good income and was the mother of a baby boy. Mr. Slope had his eye on her and attempted to interest Mrs. Bold in the work of the Sunday schools. At the same time, he asked Mr. Quiverful of Puddingdale to take over the duties of the hospital. Mr. Quiverful's fourteen children were reasons enough for his being grateful for the opportunity. Mrs. Bold, however, learned how her father felt about the extra duties imposed upon him, and she grew cold toward Mr. Slope. In the end, Mr. Harding decided that he simply could not undertake the new duties at his age, so Mr. Quiverful, a Low Churchman, was granted the preferment, much to Mrs. Proudie's satisfaction.

Mr. Slope was not the only man interested in Mrs. Bold. The Stanhope sisters, realizing that Bertie could never make a living for himself, decided that he should ask Mrs. Bold to be his wife.

Meanwhile, Mr. Slope was losing favor with Mrs.

Proudie. She was repulsed that he would throw himself at the feet of Signora Neroni, and his interest in Mr. Harding's daughter, who refused to comply with her wishes, was disgraceful.

The Thornes of Ullathorne were an old and affluent family. One day, they gave a great party. Mrs. Bold, driving to Ullathorne with the Stanhopes, found herself in the same carriage with Mr. Slope, whom by this time she greatly disliked. Later that day, as she was walking with Mr. Slope, he suddenly put his arm around her and declared his love. She rushed away and told Charlotte Stanhope, who suggested that Bertie should speak to Mr. Slope about his irregularity; but the occasion for this discussion never arose. Bertie himself told Mrs. Bold that his sister Charlotte had urged him to marry Mrs. Bold for her money. Naturally insulted, Mrs. Bold was angered at the entire Stanhope family. That evening, when Dr. Stanhope learned what had happened, he insisted that Bertie go away and earn his own living or starve. Bertie left several days later.

The Dean of Barchester was beyond recovery after a stroke of apoplexy. It was understood that Dr. Grantly would not accept the deanship. Mr. Slope wanted the position, but Mrs. Proudie would not consider him as a candidate. When the dean died, speculation ran high.

Mr. Slope felt encouraged by the newspapers, which said that younger men should be admitted to places of influence in the church.

After Bertie had gone, Signora Neroni wrote a note asking Mrs. Bold to come to see her. When Mrs. Bold entered the Stanhope drawing room, Signora Neroni told her that she should marry Mr. Arabin. With calculating generosity, she had decided that he would make a good husband for Mrs. Bold.

Meanwhile, Mr. Slope had been sent off to another diocese, for Mrs. Proudie could no longer bear having him in Barchester. Mr. Arabin, through Oxford influences, was appointed to the deanship—a victory for the High Churchmen. With Mr. Slope gone, the Stanhopes felt safe in returning to Italy.

Miss Thorne asked Mrs. Bold to spend some time at Ullathorne. She also contrived to have Mr. Arabin there. It was inevitable that Mr. Arabin should ask Mrs. Bold to be his wife. Dr. Grantly was satisfied. He had threatened to forbid the hospitality of Plumstead Episcopi to Mrs. Bold if she had become the wife of a Low Churchman. In fact, Dr. Grantly was moved to such generosity that he furnished the deanery and gave wonderful gifts to the entire family, including a cello to his father-in-law, Mr. Harding.

Critical Evaluation

As a young man, Anthony Trollope, son of a ne'er-do-well barrister of good family, seemed destined to further the decline of the family. An undistinguished student in two distinguished public schools, he had no hopes for university or career. His mother persuaded a family friend to find work for him in the London Post Office where his performance as a clerk was to be rated as "worthless." Indeed, the burdens of the family fell upon his indefatigable mother, who had converted a family business failure in Cincinnati, Ohio, into a literary career with her satiric study *Domestic Manners of Americans* (1832). Like his mother, the son found his way after a change of scenery. When the Post Office sent him to the south of Ireland to assist in a postal survey, his career in the postal service began to advance, he married happily, and he began to write.

Success as a novelist came when the Post Office sent Trollope to survey southwest England. A midsummer visit to the beautiful cathedral town of Salisbury produced the idea for *The Warden* (1855) and, more important, furnished the outlines for a fictional county, Barsetshire, which is as impressive as Hardy's Wessex or Faulkner's Yoknapatawpha. When he returned in *Barchester Towers* to the milieu of *The Warden*, which had been a modest success, he achieved resounding acclaim. Later he was to write four more novels in the series known as the Barsetshire Novels. This series is set in the chiefly agricultural county of that name, with its seat of Bar-

chester, a quiet town in the west of England noted for its beautiful cathedral and fine monuments but hardly for its commercial prosperity. Thus at middle age began the career of one of the most prolific of the Victorians and, until his last years, one of the most popular.

In his day, Trollope was admired as a realist. He was delighted with Hawthorne's appraisal that his novels were "just as real as if some giant had hewn a great lump out of the earth and put it under a glass case, with all its inhabitants going about their daily business, and not suspecting that they were being made a show of." Today, Trollope's novels are generally viewed as comic works. Instead of merely being people going about their daily affairs, Trollope's characters are in the grip of a firmly controlled irony.

The irony that Trollope perceives in the affairs of the men of Barchester arises from discrepancies between the ideals they uphold and the means by which they uphold their ideals. A layman with no special knowledge of the Church of England, Trollope vividly depicts the internecine war that breaks out between the party of the new Bishop of Barchester and that of the former bishop's son, Archdeacon Grantly. Both parties intend to preserve the integrity of the church. However, the church is vested in buildings, furnishings, livings; and these clergymen fight for power over the appurtenances, the worldly forms of the spiritual church.

Barchester Towers consists of a number of subplots,

all of which are related to the ecclesiastical power struggle. Since buildings, furnishings, and livings are occupied by human beings, the clerics who guard the Church must also dispose of the lives of men. The subplots involve characters who become mere objects in a dispute over power—for example, Mr. Harding and the Quiverfuls in the competition for wardenship of Hiram's Hospital or Eleanor Bold in the rivalry of two clergymen for her hand in marriage. Episodes not directly related to the ecclesiastical battles serve to underscore them—as in the parallel between the rivalry of Mrs. Lookaloft and Mrs. Greenacre and the absurd ploys of the higher orders that abound in the novel.

The main conflicts of the novel are those that engage the high and the mighty of Barchester. The strength of Trollope's satire lies in his refusal to oversimplify the motives of these worldlings of the church or to deny them sincerity in their defense of the church. Even as Slope genuinely believes Grantly and his type to be the enemies of religion, so also does the Archdeacon honestly believe that Slope is the kind who could well ruin the Church of England.

One of Trollope's devices for deflating these militant clerics is to treat their wars in the mock heroic vein. After the first meeting between the Archdeacon and the Proudies, the author declares, "And now, had I the pen of a mighty poet, would I sing in epic verse the noble wrath of the Archdeacon." In time, Mrs. Proudie is ironically compared to Juno, Medea, even Achilles, while the archdeacon's extravagance in celebrating Eleanor Bold's marriage to his champion, Arabin, is suggestive of the glorious warrior returning from the fields with his spoils.

Marital glory is satirized by a recurrent analogy with games, underscoring the truth that Barchester's leadership is really concerned with social rather than spiritual or moral issues. Slope's major defeats arise from his indecorous behavior with Madeline Neroni, who is alert to every possible move. Worse, he underestimates his other opponent, Mrs. Proudie, and at the end, he discovers that "Mrs. Proudie had checkmated him."

Human strife is incongruous with the idealized setting of peaceful Barchester, its venerable church and its rural villages round about, all endowed with a loveliness suggestive of the age-old pastoral tradition. The cathedral itself seems to judge the folly of its worldly champions. As the battles commerce, Archdeacon Grantly looks up to the cathedral towers as if evoking a blessing for his efforts. However genial the comedy played out beneath the Barchester towers, the outcome is not without serious significance; for the ultimate result is the further separation of man from his ideals. In the end, the bishop's wife finds that her "sphere is more extended, more noble, and more suited to her ambition than that of a cathedral city," while the bishop himself "had learnt that his proper sphere of action lay in close contiguity with Mrs. Proudie's wardrobe." As Mr. Slope makes his ignominious final departure from the city, "he gave no longing lingering look after the cathedral towers." As for the Archdeacon, it is sufficient for him to "walk down the High Street of Barchester without feeling that those who see him are comparing his claims with those of Mr. Slope."

Despite the futility of its human strivings, *Barchester Towers* is a cheerful novel, not merely because the satire provokes laughter, but also because occasionally, briefly, the real and the ideal meet. Mr. Harding, for example, is too peaceable, too naïve, too reticent to be effective in the world. Nonetheless, when prompted by his dedication to simple justice, Mr. Harding personally introduces Mr. Quiverful to his former charges at Hiram Hospital. This act, representing the union of his profession and practice, creates a consequence greater than the act would suggest, for it causes the Barchester world to treat Mr. Quiverful with more respect as he assumes his duties.

Quite appropriately, then, Trollope brings the novel to its close with pastoral serenity by offering a word of Mr. Harding, who functions not as a hero and not as a perfect divine but as a good, humble man without guile.

BENITO CERENO

Type of work: Novella
Author: Herman Melville (1819–1891)
Type of plot: Adventure romance
Time of plot: 1799
Locale: The harbor of St. Maria, off the coast of Chile, and Lima, Peru
First published: 1856

Superficially, this is a story of slavery and mutiny on the high seas, but beneath the adventure-charged plot lies Melville's examination of that subject which so fascinated him: the confrontation of extreme forces of good and evil in the universe. The irony of the tale is that goodhearted, naïve Delano is only victorious in rescuing the victimized Benito because he is too innocent to comprehend the horror and depravity into which he wanders.

Principal Characters

Amasa Delano (ä·mä′sä dĕl′ə·nō), an American sea captain. Off the coast of Chile he sees a ship in distress and sets out with food and water for her company. He finds a Spanish merchantman carrying slaves. Ship and crew are in deplorable condition, and their captain suffers from what appear to be severe mental disorders. A series of strange and sinister events lead Captain Delano to the knowledge that the Spanish captain is a prisoner of the slaves. He is able to rescue the captive and take him ashore.

Don Benito Cereno (dōn bā·nē′tō thärā′nō), the captain of a Spanish slave ship. His human cargo mutinies and makes him a prisoner, and he is forced to witness horrible atrocities on and murders of the Spanish crew. After his rescue by Captain Delano, he gives testimony concerning the mutiny and dies broken in mind and spirit.

Babo (bä′bō), a mutinous slave. He poses as the devoted servant of Captain Cereno and attempts to deceive Captain Delano concerning his master's true condition. Failing in this attempt, he is captured and hanged on Captain Cereno's testimony.

Don Alexandro Aranda (dōn ä·lä·ksän′drō ä·rän′dä), owner of the cargo of the Spanish slave ship. He is murdered and mutilated by the mutinous slaves.

Raneds (rä′nādz), the slave ship's mate, murdered by the mutinous slaves.

The Story

Captain Amasa Delano was commander of an American sealer called *Bachelor's Delight*, which was anchored in the harbor of St. Maria, on an island off the coast of southern Chile. While there, he saw a ship apparently in distress, and thinking it carried a party of monks, he sent out in a whaleboat to board the vessel and supply it with food and water. When he came aboard, he found that the ship, the *San Dominick*, was a Spanish merchant ship carrying slaves. The crew was parched and moaning; the ship itself was filthy; the sails were rotten. Most deplorable of all, the captain, the young Don Benito Cereno, seemed barely able to stand or to talk coherently. Aloof and indifferent, the Captain seemed ill both physically (he coughed constantly) and mentally. The Captain was attended by Babo, his devoted slave.

Delano sent the whaleboat back to his ship to get additional water, food, and extra sails for the *San Dominick*, while he remained aboard the desolate ship. He tried to talk to Cereno, but the Captain's fainting fits kept interrupting the conversation. The Spaniard seemed reserved and sour, in spite of Delano's attempts to assure the man

that he was now out of danger. Delano finally assumed that Cereno was suffering from a severe mental disorder. The Captain did, with great difficulty and after frequent private talks with Babo, manage to explain that the *San Dominick* had been at sea for 190 days. They had, Cereno explained, started out as a well-manned and smart vessel sailing from Buenos Aires to Lima but had encountered several gales around Cape Horn, lost many officers and men, and then had run into dreadful calms and the ravages of plagues and scurvy. Most of the Spanish officers and all the passengers, including the slave owner, Don Alexandro Aranda, had died of fever. Delano, who knew that the weather in recent months had not been as extreme as Cereno described it, simply concluded that the Spanish officers had been incompetent and had not taken the proper precautions against disease. Cereno continually repeated that only the devotion of his slave, Babo, had kept him alive.

Numerous other circumstances on the *San Dominick* began to make the innocent Delano more suspicious. Although everything was in disorder and Cereno was obviously ill, he was dressed perfectly in a clean uniform. Six black men were sitting in the rigging holding hatchets, although Cereno said they were only cleaning them. Two were beating up a Spanish boy, but Cereno explained that this deed was simply a form of sport. The slaves were not in chains; Cereno claimed they were so docile that they did not require chains. This notion pleased the humane Delano, although it also surprised him.

Every two hours, as they awaited the expected wind and the arrival of Delano's whaleboat, a large black in chains was brought before Cereno, who would ask him if he, the Captain, could be forgiven. The man would answer, "No," and be led away. At one point, Delano began to fear that Cereno and Babo were plotting against him, for they moved away from him and whispered together. Cereno then asked Delano about his ship, requesting the number of men and the strength of arms aboard the *Bachelor's Delight*. Delano thought they might be pirates.

Nevertheless, Delano joined Cereno and Babo in Cereno's cabin for dinner. Throughout the meal, Delano alternately gained and lost confidence in Cereno's story. He tried, while discussing a means of getting Cereno new sails, to get Babo to leave the room, but the man and master were apparently inseparable. After dinner Babo, while shaving his master, cut his cheek slightly despite the warning that had been given. Babo left the room for a second and returned with his own cheek cut in a curious imitation of his master's. Delano thought this episode curious and sinister, but he finally decided that the man was so devoted to Cereno that he had punished himself for inadvertently cutting his master.

At last, Delano's whaleboat returned with more supplies. Delano, about to leave the *San Dominick*, promised to return with new sails the next day. When he invited Cereno to his own boat, he was surprised at the Captain's curt refusal and his failure to escort the visitor to the rail. Delano was offended at the Spaniard's apparent lack of gratitude. As the whaleboat was about to leave, Cereno appeared suddenly at the rail. He expressed his gratitude profusely and then, hastily, jumped into the whaleboat. At first Delano thought that Cereno was about to kill him; then he saw Babo at the rail brandishing a knife. In a flash, he realized that Babo and the other slaves had been holding Cereno a captive. Delano took Cereno back to the *Bachelor's Delight*. Later they pursued the fleeing slaves. The slaves, having no guns, were easily captured by the American ship and brought back to shore.

Cereno later explained that the slaves, having mutinied shortly after the ship set out, had committed horrible atrocities and killed most of the Spaniards. They had murdered the mate, Raneds, for a trifling offense and had committed atrocities on the dead body of Don Alexandro Aranda, whose skeleton they placed on the masthead.

On his arrival in Lima, Don Benito Cereno submitted a long testimony, recounting all the cruelties the slaves had committed. Babo was tried and hanged. Cereno felt enormously grateful to Delano, recalling the strange innocence that had somehow kept the slaves from harming him, when they had the chance, aboard the *San Dominick*.

Don Benito Cereno planned to enter a monastery; however, broken in body and spirit, he died three months after he completed his testimony.

Critical Evaluation

Originally serialized in *Putnam's Monthly* in 1855, *Benito Cereno* first appeared, slightly revised, in book form as the first story in Herman Melville's *Piazza Tales* in 1856. It was not reprinted until 1924, when interest was being revived in Melville's writings. Since then it has often been praised as not only one of Melville's best fictional works but also one of the finest short novels in American literature. In 1964, Robert Lowell adapted *Benito Cereno* into verse-drama as the third act of his play *The Old Glory*.

Benito Cereno is Melville's version of a true story he had read in Amasa Delano's *Narrative of Voyages and Travels in the Northern and Southern Hemispheres* (1817). Melville freely adapted Delano's account to his own fictional purposes. The court depositions, which make up a considerable part of the latter half of *Benito Cereno*, have been shown to be close to those in Delano's account, though Melville omitted some of the court material. In contrast, the creation of atmosphere, the building of suspense, the development of the three main characters—

Delano, Cereno, and Babo—and the extended use of symbolism are among Melville's chief contributions to the original story. Also, the thematically important conversation between Delano and Cereno at the end of *Benito Cereno* was added by Melville.

The remarkable third paragraph of *Benito Cereno* illustrates Melville's careful combining of atmospheric detail, color symbolism, and both dramatic and thematic foreshadowing.

> The morning was one peculiar to that coast. Everything was mute and calm; everything grey. The sea, though undulated into long roods of swells, seemed fixed, and was sleeked at the surface like waved lead that has cooled and set in the smelter's mould. The sky seemed a grey surtout. Flights of troubled grey vapours among which they were mixed, skimmed low and fitfully over the waters, as swallows over meadows before storms. Shadows present, foreshadowing deeper shadows to come.

The description, with its repeated use of *grey* and

seemed, is important in setting the scene for a story the action of which will be, as seen through Delano's eyes, ambiguous and deceptive until the light of truth suddenly blazes upon the American captain's mind. Until that time, he will be seeing both action and character through a mist. The *grey* is symbolically significant also because Delano's clouded vision will cause him to misjudge both the whites and blacks aboard the *San Dominick*. In the light of the final revelations of the story, the *grey* has a moral symbolism too, perhaps for Melville and surely for the modern reader, since Cereno and Delano are not morally pure white or good, nor is Babo all black or bad. The Spaniard is a slaver and the American appears to condone the trade though he is not a part of it; the slave is certainly justified in seeking an escape from captivity for himself and his fellow blacks, though one cannot justify some of the atrocities consciously committed by Babo and his followers. The closing sentence of this mist-shrouded paragraph—"Shadows present, foreshadowing deeper shadows to come"—not only looks forward to the mystery that so long remains veiled but also anticipates the final words of the two captains, words that partly suggest the great difference in their characters. Delano says, "You are saved: what has cast such a shadow upon you?" Cereno replies, "The negro."

In reading *Benito Cereno*, one is caught up in the same mystery that Captain Delano cannot penetrate, and one longs for a final release of the suspense, a solution to the strange puzzle. Melville's hold upon the reader until the flash of illumination in the climax is maintained by his use of Delano's consciousness as the lens through which scene, character, and action are viewed. The revelation is so long delayed because of Delano's being the kind of man he is: "a person of a singularly undistrustful good nature, not liable, except on extraordinary and repeated incentives, and hardly then, to indulge in personal alarms, any way involving the imputation of malign evil in man." His heart is benevolent, but his mind is slow to perceive through the dragging hours from his boarding the *San Dominick* until he is finally shocked into recognition of the truth when Babo prepares to stab Don Benito with the dagger he had concealed in his hair. At one moment Delano is repelled by Don Benito's manner and suspicious of his intentions; at the next he is inclined to acquit Cereno of seeming rudeness because of his frail health and condemn himself for his suspicions with the excuse that "the poor invalid scarcely knew what he was about."

Just as Melville may have intended to portray Delano as representing a type of American—good-hearted, friendly, and helpful but rather slow-witted and naïve— so he may have delineated Don Benito as emblematic of eighteenth century Spanish aristocracy—proud, enfeebled, and, finally, troubled in conscience over such moral crimes as slave trading. To Delano, he first appears as "a gentlemanly, reserved-looking, and rather young man . . . dressed with singular richness, but bearing plain traces of recent sleepless cares and disquietudes." Later, Don Benito's manner "conveyed a sort of sour and gloomy disdain [which] the American in charity ascribed to the harassing effects of sickness." Further observation leads Delano to conclude that Don Benito's "singular alternations of courtesy and ill-breeding" are the result of either "innocent lunacy, or wicked imposture." He is finally undeceived and apologizes for having suspected villainy in Don Benito toward the end of the danger-filled encounter with the slaves. Delano is lighthearted and eager to dismiss the affair when the danger is over and his suspicions have been erased. Don Benito's mind, however, is of a different cast. He broods on the results in human experience of the confusing of appearance and reality: "You were with me all day," he says to Delano, "stood with me, sat with me, looked at me, ate with me, drank with me, and yet, your last act was to clutch for a monster, not only an innocent man, but the most pitiable of all men. To such degree may malign machinations and deceptions impose. So far may ever the best man err, in judging the conduct of one with the recesses of whose condition he is not acquainted."

The horrors resulting from the slave mutiny and the tensions and terror that follow Delano's kind offer to aid a ship in apparent distress, leave an already ill man a dejected and broken one. The shadow of "the negro" has been cast forever upon him. He retires to the monastery on the symbolically named Mount Agonia and, three months later, is released from his sufferings.

Babo, the third major character in *Benito Cereno*, is unforgettable, one of the first important black characters in American fiction (Mrs. Stowe's Uncle Tom had preceded him by only four years). He is one of the most striking of the "masked" characters who appear in Melville's work from beginning to end, hiding their true selves behind the semblance they present to the world. Captain Delano is completely deceived in his first sight of Babo with Don Benito: "By his side stood a black of small stature, in whose rude face, as occasionally, like a shepherd's dog, he mutely turned it up into the Spaniard's, sorrow and affection were equally blended." His attentiveness makes him seem "less a servant than a devoted companion" to Don Benito. Though he speaks little, his few brief speeches suggest the intelligence that enables him to lead the revolt on the *San Dominick*. He is capable of irony, as is clear when Benito explains that it is to Babo he owes his preservation and that Babo pacified "his more ignorant brethren, when at intervals tempted to murmurings." "Ah, master," he sighs, ". . . what Babo has done was but duty." The remark is as masked as Babo's bowed face, and the American is so completely taken in that, "As master and man stood before him, the black upholding the white, Captain Delano could not but bethink him of the beauty of that relationship which could present such a spectacle of fidelity on the one hand and confidence on the other."

With its many ironies—an aristocratic Spanish slaver captured by his slaves, a murderous black posing as a faithful servant, a naïve American protected from violent death through his own innocence and uncovering villainy by accident—*Benito Cereno* may be read as a magnificently contrived parable of limited, rational, well-ordered man struggling against evil in the social and natural universe and achieving at least a partial victory.

BEOWULF

Type of work: Poem
Author: Unknown
Type of plot: Heroic epic
Time of plot: c. Sixth century
Locale: Denmark, southern Sweden (land of the Geats)
First transcribed: c. 1000

In 3,200 lines of alliterative verse, this Anglo-Saxon epic is a pagan story overlaid with a veneer of Christian theology. Its content originated in a fusion of Norse legend and Danish historical events, which were passed on by oral tradition. When Danish invaders carried the tale to England, it gradually absorbed Christian influences, and was finally transcribed in Old English by a single, unknown poet.

Principal Characters

Beowulf (bā·ə·wōōlf), the nephew and thane of King Hygelac of the Geats. A warrior who proves his superhuman strength and endurance in his struggle with the monster Grendel, he exemplifies the ideal lord and vassal, rewarding his own men generously and accomplishing glorious deeds to honor his king, while he fulfills all the forms of courtesy at Hrothgar's court.

Hrothgar (hrōth′gär), the aging lord of the Danes, a good and generous ruler deeply distressed by Grendel's ravaging visits to Heorot, his great hall. He adopts his savior, Beowulf, as his son and parts with him tearfully in a moving scene, for he knows that he will not see the young warrior again.

Wealhtheow (wē′äl·thä·ō), his queen, a gracious, dignified hostess to the visiting Geats. She, too, grows fond of Beowulf and commends the welfare of her young sons into his hands.

Unferth (ōōn′fârth), Hrothgar's adviser, typical of the wicked counselors of folklore. Jealous of Beowulf and heated with wine, he taunts the Geat with his failure to defeat Breca in a youthful swimming match. He is won over by Beowulf's victory against Grendel and lends the hero his sword, Hrunting, for the undersea battle against Grendel's mother.

Grendel (grĕn′dəl), one of the monstrous descendants of Cain, condemned to wander alone in the wastelands of the world. Given pain by the light and merriment in Hrothgar's hall, he visits it and regularly carries off warriors to devour until he is mortally maimed in a struggle with Beowulf.

Grendel's Dam, another monster. She invades Heorot to avenge her dead son, and is herself killed by Beowulf after a long and difficult combat in her underwater cave.

Hygelac (hē′gə·läk), Beowulf's lord, the wise ruler of the Geats. He is killed while leading a raid in the Rhineland.

Hygd (hĭjd), his young, accomplished, intelligent queen. She offers the throne of her young son to Beowulf after Hygelac's death.

Hrothmund (hrōth′mōōnd) and **Hrethric** (hrāth′rēk), the sons of Hrothgar and Wealhtheow.

Hrothulf (hrōth′ōōlf), Hrothgar's nephew and ward. Although Wealhtheow professes trust in his care of her children, there are hints of his subsequent treachery to them.

Freawaru (frā′ä·wä·rōō), Hrothgar's daughter, about to be betrothed to Ingeld of the Heathobards as a political pawn. Beowulf prophesies that only unhappiness will arise from this alliance.

Wiglaf (wēg′läf), the last of Beowulf's kinsmen and his heir. He alone helps the old hero in his last fight against a ravaging dragon, and he later berates his companions for their cowardice.

Heardred (hĕ′ärd·rād), Hygelac's son, who succeeds his father as king of the Geats. Beowulf serves as his regent until the boy reaches maturity and replaces him after Heardred is killed in battle with the Swedes.

Ongentheow (ôn′yən·thē·ō), the Swedish King, slain by the Geats at the battle of Ravenswood.

Onela (ôn′ĕ·lə), **Ohthere** (ōht′ĕr·ə), **Eanmund** (ā′än·mōōnd), and **Eadgils** (ā′äd·gĭls), members of the Swedish royal family.

Wulfgar (woolf′gär), Hrothgar's messenger, famous for wisdom and courtesy.

Hrethel (hrāth′əl), Hygelac's father, who trained his grandson Beowulf.

Haethcynn (hăth′kĭn) and **Herebeald** (hĕr′ə·bā·äld), his sons, who brought tragedy to their father by Herebeald's accidental killing of Haethcynn.

Eofor (ā′ə·fôr), a warrior of the Geats, the slayer of Ongentheow.

Aeschere (ĕsh′hĕr·ə), Hrothgar's thane, a victim of Grendel and his mother.

Scyld (shēld) and **Beowulf** (bā′·ə·wōōlf), legendary Danish kings.

Breca (brĕk′ə) a prince of the Brondings, Beowulf's companion in a swimming marathon.

Daeghraefn (dāy′rāf·ən), a Frankish warrior whom

Beowulf crushes in his powerful grip.

Finn (fĭn), the Frisian ruler in a minstrel's legend.

Hildeburh (hĭl′də·bōōr), his Queen.

Sigemund (sĭg′ə·mōōnd) and **Fitela** (fĭt′ə·lə), the legendary Volsungs, uncle and nephew, whose valor is compared to Beowulf's.

Heremod (hĕr′ə·mōd), the minstrel's example of an evil, oppressive ruler.

Offa (ôf′fə), king of the Angles, another figure from an illustrative legend.

The Story

Once long ago in Hrothgar's kingdom a monster named Grendel roamed the countryside at night. Rising from his marshy home, Grendel would stalk to the hall of the king, where he would seize fifteen of Hrothgar's sleeping warriors and devour them. Departing, he would gather fifteen more into his huge arms and carry them back to his watery lair. For twelve years this slaughter continued.

Word of the terror spread. In the land of the Geats, ruled over by Hygelac, lived Beowulf, a man of great strength and bravery. When he heard the tale of Hrothgar's distress, he set sail for Denmark to rid the land of its fear. With a company of fourteen men he came ashore and asked a coast watcher to lead him to Hrothgar's high hall. There he was feasted in great honor while the mead cup went around. Unferth reminded Beowulf of a swimming contest which Beowulf was said to have lost. Beowulf said only that he had more strength and that he had also slaughtered many deadly monsters in the sea. At the close of the feast Hrothgar and his warriors went to their rest, leaving Beowulf and his band in the hall. Then came the awful Grendel and seized one of the sleeping warriors. But he was fated to kill no more that night, for Beowulf without shield or spear seized the dread monster and wrenched off his mighty right arm. Thus maimed, Grendel fled back to his marshland home. His bloody arm was hung in Hrothgar's hall.

The next night Grendel's mother came to avenge her son. Bursting into the great hall, she seized one of the warriors, Aeschere, Hrothgar's chief counselor, and fled with him into the night. She took with her also the prized arm of Grendel. Beowulf was asleep in a house removed from the hall, and not until morning did he learn of the monster's visit. Then, with Hrothgar leading the way, a mournful procession approached the dire marsh. At its edge they sighted the head of the ill-fated Aeschere and saw the stain of blood on the water. Beowulf prepared for descent to the home of the foe. Unferth offered Beowulf the finest sword in the kingdom, and thus forfeited his own chance of brave deeds.

As Beowulf sank beneath the waters of the marsh, he was beset on every hand by prodigious monsters. After a long swim he came to the lair of Grendel's mother.

Failing to wound her with Unferth's sword, he seized the monster by the shoulder and threw her to the ground. During a grim hand-to-hand battle, in which Beowulf was being worsted, he sighted a famous old sword of the giants, which he seized and thrust at Grendel's mother, who fell in helpless death throes. Then Beowulf turned and saw Grendel himself lying weak and maimed on the floor of the lair. Quickly he swung the sword and severed Grendel's head from his body. As he began to swim back up to the surface of the marsh, the sword with which he had killed his enemies melted until only the head and hilt were left. On his return, the Danes rejoiced and fêted him with another high feast. He presented the sword hilt to Hrothgar and returned Unferth's sword without telling that it had failed him.

The time came for Beowulf's return to his homeland. He left Denmark in great glory and sailed toward the land of the Geats. Once more at the court of his lord Hygelac, he was held in high esteem and was rewarded with riches and position. After many years Beowulf himself became king among the Geats. One of the Geats by accident discovered an ancient hoard, and, while its guardian dragon slept, carried away a golden goblet which he presented to Beowulf. The discovery of the loss caused the dragon to rise in fury and to devastate the land. Old man that he was, Beowulf was determined to rid his kingdom of the dragon's scourge. Daring the flames of the dragon's nostrils, he smote his foe with his sword, but without effect. Once more Beowulf was forced to rely on the grip of his mighty hands. Of his warriors only Wiglaf stood by his king; the others fled. The dragon rushed at Beowulf and sank its teeth deeply into his neck. But Wiglaf smote the dragon with his sword, and Beowulf with his war-knife gave the dragon its death blow.

Weak from loss of blood, the old hero was dying. His last act was to give Wiglaf a king's collar of gold. The other warriors now came out of hiding and burned with pagan rites the body of their dead king. From the dragon's lair they took the treasure hoard and buried it in the great mound they built over Beowulf's ashes. Then with due ceremony they mourned the passing of the great and dauntless Beowulf.

Critical Evaluation

Beowulf is the earliest extant heroic poem in any modern European language. The poem has come down to us in a single manuscript, which was damaged and almost destroyed in the 1731 fire in the Cotton Library. Although the manuscript dates from the tenth century, the poem was probably composed in the eighth century and deals with sixth century events, before the migration of the Germanic tribes to Britain.

The poem was composed and performed orally. Old English bards, or *scops*, most likely began by piecing together traditional short songs; they then gradually added to that base until the poem grew to its present size. The verse form is the standard Old English isochronic: each line contains four stresses; there is a strong caesura in the middle of the lines, and the resultant half lines are bound together by alliteration. Although little Old English poetry survives, *Beowulf*'s polished verse and reflective, allusive development suggest that it is part of a rich poetic tradition.

Besides having unusual literary merit, *Beowulf* also provides information about and insight into the social, political, and ethical systems of Anglo-Saxon culture. There is a strong emphasis on courage in battle, fidelity to one's word, and loyalty to kinsmen. This is a violent but highly principled society in which struggle is everywhere and honor is everything. The hero, bound by family ties, by his own word, and by a strict code of revenge, is surrounded by his *comitatus*, his band of devoted comrades in arms. Christianity enters into the poem—and into the society—but it is an Old Testament variety, stressing justice rather than love. There is controversy about whether the Christian elements are intrinsic or are interpolations by a tenth century monastic scribe. In any case, the Christianity of *Beowulf* does not much resemble that of the High Middle Ages or of the modern world. Frequently the poem seems a meditation on the traditional pagan value system from the moral point of view of the new, incompletely assimilated Christianity.

Despite the fact that the heroic poem centers on valorous exploits, *Beowulf* contains curiously little action. The plot is embedded in a mass of other materials which some critics have seen as irrelevant or peripheral. However, the poem is basically reflective and ruminative and the digressive materials provide the context in which the action of the poem is to be seen and interpreted. Consequently, *Beowulf* contains historical information, ceremonial descriptions, lengthy genealogies, elaborate speeches, and interspersed heroic songs which reveal much about the world in which Beowulf acts. For example, it is important that the action is entwined in a historical sequence of events, because complex loyalties and responsibilities are thereby implied: Beowulf helps Hrothgar because of the past links between their families and much later, when Beowulf succumbs to the dragon, it is clear that the future of his whole people is in jeopardy. In addition, the songs of the *scop* at Hrothgar's court indicate the value of poetry as a means of recording the past and honoring the brave. In like manner, the genealogies dignify characters by uniting them with revered ancestors, and the ceremonies underscore the importance of present deeds and past worth. Through these apparently extrinsic materials, the poet builds a continuity between past and present and extends the significance of his poem and characters to the whole of society.

In this context Beowulf meets a series of challenges embodied in the poem's three monsters. That Beowulf battles imposing monsters rather than human adversaries suggests that his actions bear larger meanings. The hero arrives at the court of Hrothgar at the height of his youthful abilities. Not a neophyte, he has already fought bravely and demonstrated his preternatural power and charisma. He has no doubts or hesitancies as he prepares to fight. Grendel, a descendant of the line of Cain, is hateful to God, a lonely and vicious outcast, who hates light and joy and exacts bloody vengeance on man. All the more terrifying because of his vague but imposing physique, Grendel is a representative of the physical evil which was so present in the lives and imaginations of the Anglo-Saxons, as witnessed in poems such as *The Wanderer* and *The Seafarer*. Beowulf confronts that physical evil and, bolstered by lineage and loyalty, routs the inimical force with which all men must contend.

However, Grendel, mortally wounded, escapes to his undersea lair, a submerged area devoid of light and appropriate to his joyless evil. Beowulf must, as a result, trace evil to its source if he is to be truly victorious. He ultimately returns with Grendel's head as a sign of victory, but to do that he must descend to the depths and exterminate the source of evil figured in Grendel's mother. This battle is more difficult and ominous: Beowulf doubts his capacities and his men almost give up on him. Naturally this battle is more arduous, because he is facing the intellectual or moral evil which is at the root of the physical evil that threatens human life and joy. The poem is not a moral allegory in which Beowulf roots evil out of the world, but an exemplum of how each man must face adversity.

One greater challenge remains for Beowulf, and it is significant that it is separated, by space and years, from these youthful encounters. As a young warrior, Beowulf faced evil in vigorous foreign exploits; as an old king in his own country, he faces the dragon, the ultimate test of his courage. The dragon is at once less horrible (he is not human) and more fearsome. Beowulf, as the representative of his society, must enter the battle in which he knows he will die. The nonhuman dragon is a figure of the metaphysical evil which is woven into the fabric of the universe. Physical and moral evil can be challenged and overcome, but the ultimate evil (perhaps, at its extremity, age and death) cannot be avoided. Beowulf slays his antagonist and transcends his own death. By dying as he lived, he is a model for triumph in the last struggle every man must face.

BEYOND GOOD AND EVIL

Type of work: Philosophical treatise
Author: Friedrich Wilhelm Nietzsche (1844–1900)
First published: 1886

In *Thus Spake Zarathustra* (1883–1884) Friedrich Nietzsche proclaimed in parable and pseudo-prophetical cries the philosophy of the Superman, the being who would transcend man in his will to power, going beyond conventional morality and making his own law. *Beyond Good and Evil* carries forward, in a somewhat more temperate style, the same basic ideas, but with particular attention to values and morality. The central thesis of the book is that the proud, creative individual goes beyond good and evil in action, thought, and creation.

Ordinary men are fearful, obedient, and slavelike. The true aristocrat of the spirit, the noble man, is neither slave nor citizen; he is the lawmaker, the one who determines by his acts and decisions what is right or wrong, good or bad. He is what the novelist Dostoevski in *Crime and Punishment* calls the "extraordinary" man.

To sharpen his image of the noble man Nietzsche describes two primary types of morality: master-morality and slave-morality. Moral values are determined either by the rulers or the ruled. The rulers naturally regard the terms "good" and "bad" as synonymous with "noble" and "despicable." They apply moral values to men, venerating the aristocrat; but those who are ruled, the subservient class, apply moral values primarily to acts, grounding the value of an act in its utility, its service to them. For the noble man pride and strength are virtues; for the "slaves" patience, self-sacrifice, meekness, and humility are virtues. The aristocrat scorns utility, cowardice, self-abasement, and the telling of lies; as a member of the ruling class he must seek the opposite moral qualities. According to Nietzsche:

> The noble type of man regards *himself* as a determiner of values; he does not require to be approved of; he passes the judgment: "What is injurious to me is injurious in itself"; he knows that it is he himself only who confers honour on things; he is a *creator of values*. He honours whatever he recognizes in himself: such morality is self-glorification.

Those who are ruled, the slaves, construct a morality which will make their suffering bearable. They are pessimistic in their morality and come to regard the "good" in man as the "safe" man, one who is "good-natured, easily deceived, perhaps a little stupid, *un bonhomme*."

Nietzsche concludes that in slave-morality "language shows a tendency to approximate the significations of the words 'good' and 'stupid.' " Perhaps because Nietzsche regarded love considered "*as a passion*" as of noble origin, he maintained in the chapter titled "Apophthegms and Interludes" that "What is done out of love always takes place beyond good and evil."

A proper interpretation of Nietzsche's work is possible only if one remembers that Nietzsche is not talking about actual political rulers and the ruled, although even in this particular case something of his general thesis applies. He is speaking instead of those who have the power and will to be a law to themselves, to pass their own moral judgments according to their inclinations, and of those who do not: the former are the masters, the latter, the slaves. A revealing statement of the philosophical perspective from which this view becomes possible is the apophthegm, "There is no such thing as moral phenomena, but only a moral interpretation of phenomena."

Nietzsche must be given credit for having anticipated to a considerable extent many of the prevailing tendencies in twentieth century philosophy. He is sophisticated about language: He understands the persuasive function of philosophy, and he is unrelenting in his naturalistic and relativistic interpretation of man's values and moralities. If he errs at all in his philosophic objectivity, it is in endorsing the way of power as if, in some absolute sense, that is *the* way, the only right way. This flaw in Nietzsche's disdain of dogmatism, this capitulation to dogmatism in his own case, is one cause of the ironic character of his book.

Another weakness in the author which makes something of a mockery out of his veneration of the Superman is his fear of failure and rejection. The fear is so strong that it comes to the surface of certain passages despite what must have been the author's desire to keep it hidden. Certainly he would not have appreciated the irony of having others discover that he himself is the slave he so much despises! For example, in the last few pages of the book Nietzsche writes that "Every deep thinker is more afraid of being understood than of being misunderstood." A little later, in describing the philosopher, he writes: "A philosopher: alas, a being who often runs away from himself, is often afraid of himself." He ends the book with a passage which begins, "Alas! what are you, after all, my written and painted thoughts!" and ends, "but nobody will divine . . . how ye looked in your morning, you sudden sparks and marvels of my solitude, you, my old, beloved—*evil* thoughts!" Although in context such passages seem to be part of Nietzsche's pose of superiority, out of context they take on another, revealing meaning.

Nietzsche begins his book with a chapter on the "Prejudices of Philosophers." He claims that philosophers pretend to doubt everything, but in the exposition of their views they reveal the prejudices they mean to communicate. Philosophers of the past have tried to derive human values from some outside source; the result has been that what they reveal is nothing more than their own dogmatic "frog perspective." Nietzsche, on the other hand, prides himself on being one of the "new" philosophers, one who suggests that the traditional values may be intimately related to their evil opposites.

Nietzsche argues that false opinions are often better than true ones, that the only test of an opinion is not whether it is true or false but whether it is "life-furthering, life-preserving, species-preserving, perhaps species-rearing." This is the point at which his own dogmatism shows itself: in making "species-rearing" the criterion of a worthy idea he shows his own prejudice in favor of the man of power. He is unabashed in his preference and argues that the recognition of the value of untruth impugns the traditional ideas of value and places his philosophy beyond good and evil. Nietzsche, declaring himself one who wishes to bring about a transvaluation of all values, argues that there is no more effective way than to begin by supposing that conventional morality is a sign of slavery and weakness. The free man, the man strong enough to be independent, sees through the pretenses of philosophers and moralists; he laughs, and creates a new world.

According to Nietzsche himself, there is danger in his philosophy. In fact, he takes pride in that danger. He identifies himself with the "philosophers of the dangerous 'Perhaps'"—that is, with philosophers who insist that "perhaps" everyone else is mistaken. He offers certain "tests" that one can use to determine whether he is ready for independence and command, and he says that one should not avoid these tests, "although they constitute perhaps the most dangerous game one can play." He chooses a dangerous name for the new philosophers: "tempters."

Speaking for the "philosophers of the future," the "opposite ones," Nietzsche writes: "we believe that severity, violence, slavery, danger in the street and in the heart, secrecy, stoicism, tempter's art and deviltry of every kind, that everything wicked, terrible, tyrannical, predatory, and serpentine in man, serves as well for the elevation of the human species as its opposite."

Considered coolly, what is this danger and deviltry of which Nietzsche is so fond? It is nothing more than the possibility of new lines of development for the human spirit. The danger and the deviltry are such only in relation to the rule-bound spirits of conventional men. Nietzsche is philosopher enough to know that the human being is too complex an organism ever to have been confined or exhausted by ways of life already tried and endorsed. He calls attention to the value of revolt by playing the devil or tempter. The "most dangerous game," or the "big hunt," is man's free search for new ways of being insofar as he has the power. The hunting domain is extensive; it is the entire range of man's experiences, both actual and possible. And there is no need or use in taking "hundreds of hunting assistants," Nietzsche tells us, for each man must search alone; each man must do everything himself in order to learn anything.

Nietzsche's objection to Christianity is that it has been a major force in limiting man by imposing on him a static morality. Since Nietzsche thinks of man's most important creative function as the creation of a new self, since he would urge each man, as artist, to use himself as material and fashion a new man, even a superman, he rejects as life-defeating any force that works against such a creative function. He argues that men with neither the strength nor the intelligence to recognize the differences among men, to distinguish the nobles from the slaves, have fashioned Christianity, with the result that man has become nothing more than "a gregarious animal, something obliging, sickly, mediocre."

Whether one agrees with Nietzsche in his estimate of Christianity and philosophy, no one can justifiably deny his claim that to look beyond good and evil, to throw over conventional modes of thought, is to provide oneself with a challenging, even a liberating, experience. The old "tempter" tempts us into a critical consideration of our values, and that is all to the good.

BILLY BUDD, FORETOPMAN

Type of work: Novel
Author: Herman Melville (1819–1891)
Type of plot: Symbolic tragedy
Time of plot: 1797
Locale: Aboard a British man-of-war
First published: 1924

In this last of Melville's works, published posthumously, the author dramatized the clash between natural goodness and innocence as personified by Billy Budd, and unprovoked evil as embodied in Claggart. Captain Vere, as his name suggests, is the upholder of truth and right in the story. When Billy inadvertently kills his antagonizer in a fight, Vere is caught between his love for Billy and his duty to uphold the law and maintain order; he opts for justice over mercy, and decides that he must hang the boy.

Principal Characters

Billy Budd, a youthful member of the crew of the merchantman *Rights-of-Man,* who is impressed into service aboard H.M.S. *Indomitable* during the last decade of the eighteenth century. Billy is twenty-one, "welkin-eyed," and possessed of great masculine beauty; he has no idea who his father and mother were, having been left a foundling in a basket on the doorstep of a "good man" in Bristol, England. Billy was a cheerful, stabilizing influence on the rough crew of the merchantman; when he is taken aboard the *Indomitable,* he is popular with all the officers and crew except John Claggart, the master-at-arms, who is envious of Billy's almost perfect physique and personality. Claggart falsely accuses Billy of fomenting a mutiny aboard the ship. When he repeats the charges in the Captain's quarters while Billy is present, the young man (who stutters under stress and sometimes suffers a total speech block) can say nothing in his own defense and hits Claggart on the forehead with his fist. Claggart falls and dies. In the subsequent trial at which the Captain is the sole witness, there can be no leniency because of the recent Great Mutiny in the fleet. Billy is sentenced to hang. At the execution his last words are, "God bless Captain Vere!" Honest, refreshing, ingenuous, uncomplaining—these adjectives may be applied to Billy Budd, who represents an innocent youth trapped by the brutality of fleet regulations or, perhaps, who represents truth and beauty trapped by the wickedness of the world.

Captain the Honourable Edward Fairfax Vere, of the *Indomitable.* He is known in the fleet as "Starry" Vere to distinguish him from a kinsman and officer of like rank in the navy. The nickname is a misnomer, however, for Captain Vere, a bachelor of about forty, is a quiet, brooding intellectual who reads a great deal. He is also a fine commander, but he lacks the flamboyance of the more famous Nelson. He suffers greatly at having to testify before the three-man court against Billy Budd, whom he recognizes as an efficient, attractive, impulsive seaman. He, too, seems trapped by regulations (tightened during the Great Mutiny) which state that striking an officer is a capital offense. When Claggart comes to Captain Vere with his foggy, unsubstantiated charges that Billy is mutinous, the Captain summons Billy to his quarters only to prove that Claggart is a false witness.

John Claggart, the master-at-arms of the ship. Since guns have replaced the many small arms used in naval fighting, his duties are mainly to oversee the crew and its work. When Claggart observes Billy Budd, he quickly becomes envious of the personal beauty of the young man. In this respect he is like Iago in "Othello"; Iago hates Cassio partly because he is an open, honest, handsome man. So with the Claggart-Budd relationship. The only basis for the charges Claggart makes against Billy is that an afterguardsman, a troublemaker, tries to be friendly and confidential with the foretopman. Because he joined the navy for no apparent reason and because he never makes any reference to his previous life ashore, Claggart is a man of mystery about whom many rumors are circulated on the ship.

The Dansker, an old veteran who serves as mainmastman in his watch. He likes Billy from the start and is the one who nicknames him "Baby." When Billy comes to him for counsel and to ask why his petty mistakes are getting him into trouble, the Dansker astutely remarks that "Jimmy Legs" (meaning the master-at-arms) is down on him.

The Afterguardsman, a troublemaking sailor. He approaches Billy and tries to tempt him to join an incipient mutiny. Billy angrily rebuffs him but does not report the incident to any officer.

Lieutenant Ratcliffe, the officer who goes aboard the *Rights-of-Man* and selects Billy to be impressed into his majesty's service.

The Story

In 1797, the British merchant ship *Rights-of-Man*, named after the famous reply of Thomas Paine to Edmund Burke's criticism of the French Revolution, was close to home after a long voyage. As it neared England, the merchant vessel was stopped by a man-of-war, H.M.S. *Indomitable*, and an officer from the warship went aboard the *Rights-of-Man* to impress sailors for military service. This practice was necessary at the time to provide men to work the large number of ships that Britain had at sea for protection against the French.

The captain of the *Rights-of-Man* was relieved to have only one sailor taken from his ship, but he was unhappy because the man was his best sailor, Billy Budd. Billy was what his captain called a peacemaker; because of his strength and good looks, he was a natural leader among the other sailors, and he used his influence to keep them contented and hard at work. Billy Budd seemed utterly without guile, a man who tried to promote the welfare of the merchant ship because he liked peace and was willing to work hard to please his superiors. When informed that he was not to return to England but was to head for duty with the fleet in the Mediterranean Sea, he did not appear disturbed; he liked the sea, and he had no family ties. He was an orphan who had been left as a tiny baby in a basket on the doorstep of a family in Bristol.

As the boat from the warship took him away from the merchant ship, Billy called farewell to the *Rights-of-Man* by name, a deed that greatly embarrassed the naval officer who had impressed him. The remark was unwittingly satirical of the treatment to which Billy was being subjected by the navy.

Once aboard the *Indomitable*, Billy quickly made himself at home with the ship and the men with whom he served in the foretop. Because of his good personality and his willingness to work, he soon made a place for himself with his messmates and also won the regard of the officers under whom he served.

At first, the master-at-arms, a petty officer named Claggart, seemed particularly friendly to Billy, a fortunate circumstance, Billy thought, for the master-at-arms was the equivalent of the chief of police aboard the warship. The young sailor was rather surprised, therefore, when he received reprimands for slight breaches of conduct which were normally overlooked. The reprimands came from the ship's corporals who were Claggart's underlings. Since the reprimands indicated that something was wrong, Billy grew perturbed; he had a deadly fear of being the recipient of a flogging in public. He thought he could never stand such treatment.

Anxious to discover what was wrong, Billy consulted an old sailor, who told him that Claggart was filled with animosity for the young man. The reason for the animosity was not known, and because the old man could give him no reason, Billy refused to believe that the master-at-arms was his enemy. Claggart had taken a deep dislike to Billy Budd on sight, however, and for no reason except a personal antipathy that the young man's appearance had generated. Sly as he was, Claggart kept, or tried to keep, his feelings to himself. He operated through underlings against Billy.

Not long after he had been warned by the old sailor, Billy spilled a bowl of soup in the path of Claggart as he was inspecting the mess. Even then, Claggart smiled and pretended to treat the incident as a joke, for Billy had done the deed accidentally. A few nights later, however, someone awakened Billy and told him to go to a secluded spot in the ship. Billy went and met a sailor who tried to tempt him into joining a mutiny. The incident bothered Billy, who could not understand why anyone had approached him as a possible conspirator. Such activity was not a part of his personality, and he was disgusted to find it in other men.

A few days later, the master-at-arms approached the captain of the ship and reported that he and his men had discovered that a mutiny was being fomented by Billy Budd. Captain Vere, a very fair officer, reminded Claggart of the seriousness of the charge and warned the master-at-arms that bearing false witness in such a case called for the death penalty. Because Claggart persisted in his accusations, Captain Vere ended the interview on deck, a place he thought too public, and ordered the master-at-arms and Billy Budd to his cabin. There Captain Vere commanded Claggart to repeat his accusations. When he did, Billy became emotionally so upset that he was tongue-tied. In utter frustration at being unable to reply to the infamous charges, Billy hit the master-at-arms. The petty officer was killed when he fell heavily to the floor.

Captain Vere was filled with consternation, for he, like everyone except the master-at-arms, liked Billy Budd. After the surgeon had pronounced the petty officer dead, the captain immediately convened a court-martial to try Billy for assaulting and murdering a superior officer. Because England was at war, and because two mutinies had already occurred in the British navy that year, action had to be taken immediately. The captain could not afford to overlook the offense.

The court-martial, acting under regulations, found Billy Budd guilty and sentenced him to be hanged from a yardarm the following morning. Even under the circumstances of Claggart's death, there was no alternative. The only person who could have testified that the charge of mutiny was false was the man who had been killed.

All the ship's company were dismayed when informed of the sentence. But Billy bore no animosity for the captain or for the officers who had sentenced him to die. When he was placed beneath the yardarm the following morning, he called out a blessing on Captain Vere, who, he realized, had no other choice in the matter but to hang him. It was quite strange, too, that Billy Budd's calm seemed even to control his corpse. Unlike most hanged men, he never twitched when hauled aloft by the neck. The surgeon's mate, when queried by his messmates, had no answer for this unique behavior.

Some months later, Captain Vere was wounded in action. In the last hours before his death, he was heard to murmur Billy Budd's name over and over again. Nor did the common sailors forget the hanged man. For many years, the yardarm from which he had been hanged was kept track of by sailors, who regarded it almost as reverently as Christians might revere the cross.

Critical Evaluation

According to Harrison Hayford and Merton M. Sealts, the editors of *Billy Budd, Sailor*, Herman Melville began the novel in 1886, developed and revised it through several stages, and then left it unpublished when he died in 1891. The Hayford-Sealts text, published in 1962, differs considerably from earlier ones published in 1924 and 1948. Among the noteworthy differences is the change of name for the ship on which the action occurs, from *Indomitable* to *Bellipotent*. The symbolism of the latter name relates it to the emphasis that Melville places in the novel on war, man's involvement in it, and the effects of war on the individual.

That Melville did not wish his readers to mistake the nature or the general intent of his novel is clear in his early warning that Billy "is not presented as a conventional hero" and "that the story in which he is the main figure is no romance." The story itself is extremely simple. A young sailor on a British merchant ship is impressed for service on a British warship. He offers no resistance but accepts his new assignment with good will and attempts to be an ideal sailor. The ship's master-at-arms takes an immediate and unwarranted dislike to the sailor, plots to cause him trouble, and then accuses him to the captain of having plotted mutiny. The captain summons the sailor, asks him to defend himself, and sees him strike and accidentally kill his accuser. The captain imprisons him, convenes a court-martial, condemns him to death, and has him hanged. This plot is the vehicle for Melville's extended use of moral symbolism throughout the novel.

Billy Budd, Claggart, and Captain Vere are all clearly symbolic characters, and Melville brings out the symbolism through information supplied about their backgrounds, language used to describe them, and authorial comment of moral, theological, and philosophical import.

Melville employs a double symbolism for Billy: He is both a Christ-figure and a representation of innocent or Adamic man. Before Billy is removed from the merchant ship, the Captain explains to the lieutenant from the warship that Billy has been most useful in quieting the "rat-pit of quarrels" that formerly infested his forecastle. "Not that he preached to them or said or did anything in particular; but a virtue went out of him, sugaring the sour ones." The captain's words echo Luke 6:19: "And the whole multitude sought to touch him: for there went virtue out of him, and healed them all." When the lieutenant

is adamant about Billy's impressment, the captain's last words to him are: "You are going to take away my peace-maker." Again, there is no mistaking the reference to the Prince of Peace. In describing Billy as he appears to the men and officers on the warship, Melville mentions "something in the mobile expression, and every chance attitude and movement, something suggestive of a mother eminently favored by Love and the Graces." An officer asks, "Who was your father?" and Billy answers, "God knows, sir." Though Billy explains that he was told he was a foundling, the hint has already been given of a divine paternity. Melville drops the Christ symbolism of Billy until the confrontation with Claggart when Billy, unable to reply to Captain Vere's request that he defend himself, shows in his face "an expression which was as a crucifixion to behold." At the hanging, Billy's last words are, "God bless Captain Vere!" and the reader recalls Christ's words on the Cross, "Father, forgive them; for they know not what they do." The symbolism continues with the hanging itself. Captain Vere gives a silent signal and "At the same moment it chanced that the vapory fleece hanging low in the East was shot through with a soft glory as of the fleece of the Lamb of God seen in mystical vision, and simultaneously therewith, watched by the wedged mass of upturned faces, Billy ascended; and, ascending, took the full rose of the dawn." In the final chapter, Melville adds that

> The spar from which the foretopman was suspended was
> for some few years kept trace of by the bluejackets. . . .
> To them a chip from it was as a piece of the Cross. . . .
> They recalled a fresh young image of the Handsome Sailor,
> that face never deformed by a sneer or subtler vile freak
> of the heart within. This impression of him was doubtless
> deepened by the fact that he was gone, and in a measure
> mysteriously gone.

Even in the verses which close the novel, with Billy's words, "They'll give me a nibble—bit o' biscuit ere I go./ Sure a messmate will reach me the last parting cup," one cannot miss the Last Supper reference.

Yet, though Billy is Christlike, he belongs to the race of man, and Melville repeatedly employs him as an archetype. His complete innocence is first suggested in Melville's comment that "Billy in many respects was little more than a sort of upright barbarian, much such perhaps as Adam presumably might have been ere the urbane Serpent wriggled himself into his company." Later, Captain Vere thinks of the handsome sailor as one "who in the nude might have posed for a statue of young Adam before the Fall." But innocence will not protect Billy. As Adam's human imperfection led to his fall, so an imperfection in Billy leads to his destruction. In times of stress, Billy stutters or is even speechless and, says Melville, "In this particular Billy was a striking instance that the arch interferer, the envious marplot of Eden, still has more or less to do with every human consignment to this planet of Earth."

The innocence that is his "blinder" causes Billy (or "Baby," as he is called) to fail to see and be on guard against the evil in Claggart, and his "vocal defect" deprives him of speech when he faces his false accuser. He strikes out as instinctively as a cornered animal, and his enemy dies. Billy did not intend to commit murder but, as Captain Vere tells his officers, "The prisoner's deed—with that alone we have to do." Billy does not live in an animal's instinctive world of nature. His life is bound by social law and particularly by naval law in a time of war. As Captain Vere explains, innocent Billy will be acquitted by God at "the last Assizes," but "We proceed under the law of the Mutiny Act." That act demands death for Billy's deed, and he dies in order that discipline may be maintained in the great navy which must protect Britain against her enemies.

As Billy symbolizes innocent man, Claggart represents the spirit of evil, the foe of innocence. There is a mystery in Claggart's enmity toward harmless Billy. For, says Melville, "what can more partake of the mysterious than an antipathy spontaneous and profound such as is evoked in certain exceptional mortals by the mere aspect of some other mortal, however harmless he may be, if not called forth by this very harmlessness itself?" Claggart's evil nature was not acquired, "not engendered by vicious training or corrupting books or licentious living, but born with him and innate." He can recognize the good but is "powerless to be it." His energies are self-destructive; his nature is doomed to "act out to the end the part allotted to it." Although he destroys an innocent man, he must himself be destroyed as well.

As Billy at one extreme is Christlike and childishly innocent and Claggart at the other is Satanic, Captain Vere represents the kind of officer needed to preserve such an institution as the navy he serves. He is a man of balance, "mindful of the welfare of his men, but never tolerating an infraction of discipline; thoroughly versed in the science of his profession, and intrepid to the verge of temerity, though never injudiciously so." His reading tastes incline toward "books treating of actual men and events . . . history, biography, and unconventional writers like Montaigne, who, free from cant and convention, honestly and in the spirit of common sense philosophize upon realities." More intellectual than his fellow officers, he seems somewhat "pedantic" to them, and Melville hints that, in reporting Vere's long speech to his junior officers of the drumhead court, he has simplified the phrasing of the argument. Yet elsewhere Captain Vere's speech is simple, brief, and direct.

Although Captain Vere is a thoughtful, reserved man, he is not without feeling. Quickly recognizing Billy's inability to speak when he has been ordered to defend himself, he soothingly says, "There is no hurry, my boy. Take your time, take your time." He is even capable of momentary vehemence as when he surprises the surgeon with the outburst, "Struck dead by an angel of God! Yet the angel must hang!"But he quickly regains control. Melville does not report what Captain Vere says to Billy when he informs him privately of the death sentence, though he suggests that Vere may have shown compassion by catching Billy "to his heart, even as Abraham may have caught young Isaac on the brink of resolutely offering him up." Vere is seemingly overcome after Billy's last words, "God bless Captain Vere!" and the echo from the crew, since "either through stoic self-control or a sort of momentary paralysis induced by emotional shock," he stands "rigidly erect as a musket." The final view of a man whose heart balanced his mind is given in the report of Captain Vere's dying words, "Billy Budd, Billy Budd," spoken not in "the accents of remorse." Though capable of fatherly feeling toward an unfortunate young man, he had caused to be carried out a sentence he believed was needed if the strength of order was to be maintained in the turmoil of war.

Although *Billy Budd* has occasionally been read as a veiled attack on the unjust treatment of a hapless man by an impersonal, authoritarian state, a close reading of the novel makes it seem more likely that Melville's intent was to show, especially through Captain Vere, that the protection of a state during a time of war must inevitably involve on occasion the sacrifice of an individual. Melville does include scattered satiric comments on the imperfections of both men and organizations, but his overwhelmingly favorable portrait of Captain Vere as a high-principled and dedicated representative of the state leaves the reader with the final impression that Melville had at last become sadly resigned to the fact that imperfect man living in an imperfect world has no guarantee against suffering an unjust fate. That Billy uncomplainingly accepts his end, even asking God's blessing upon the man who is sending him to death, suggests that Melville too had become reconciled to the eternal coexistence of good and evil in the world.

BIOGRAPHIA LITERARIA

Type of work: Intellectual autobiography
Author: Samuel Taylor Coleridge (1772–1834)
First published: 1817

Samuel Taylor Coleridge's *Biographia Literaria* begins as an account of the major influences on the development of his philosophy and his literary technique, but the total effect of the work is considerably less coherent than this plan would indicate. As he progressed the author apparently altered his purpose, and he discussed at considerable length intellectual problems of special interest to him and gave some of his standards of literary criticism with comments on specific works. In his opening paragraph he speaks of his work as "miscellaneous reflections"; the description seems appropriate.

The loose, rambling structure of the *Biographia Literaria* accords well with the picture of Coleridge that has been handed down, that of a man of great intellectual and poetic gifts who lacked the self-discipline to produce the works of which he seemed capable. Charles Lamb and William Hazlitt both characterized him as an indefatigable and fascinating talker, full of ideas, and this trait, too, plays its part in the creation of the *Biographia Literaria*, which is, in essence, a long conversation, ranging widely over the worlds of poetry, drama, philosophy, and psychology. The lack of a tight organizational plan in no way prevents the book from being both readable and profound in its content; Coleridge's comments on the nature of the poetic imagination have never been surpassed, and his criticism of Wordsworth's work is still perhaps the most balanced and judicious assessment available, a model for all scholars who seek to form general views on the basis of close examination of individual texts.

In the opening chapter Coleridge pays tribute to his most influential teacher, the Reverend James Bowyer of Christ's Hospital, who insisted that his students learn to think logically and use language precisely, in poetry as well as in prose. Coleridge also discusses the poetry he preferred in the years when his literary tastes were being formed; he turned toward the "pre-romantic" lyrics of minor writers rather than to the terse, epigrammatic intellectual poems of the best known eighteenth century literary men, most notably Alexander Pope and his followers. At an early stage he developed sound critical principles, looking for works that gained in power through rereading and for words that seemed to express ideas better than any phrases substituted for them could, and he quickly learned to distinguish between the virtues of works of original ideas and the faults of those that made their effect through novel phraseology. He confesses, however, that his critical judgment was better than his creative talent: his own early poems, though he thought highly of them when he wrote them, left much to be desired.

The harshness of critics in his time is a recurrent theme throughout Coleridge's autobiography, and in his second chapter he ponders on the tendency of the public to side with them rather than with the poets, who are considered to be strange, irritable, even mad. Yet the greatest writers, Chaucer, Shakespeare, Spenser, and Milton, seem to him unusually well balanced, and he suggests that the popular heresy results from the frustrations of the second-rate writer who pursues fame without real talent. These general comments are closely linked to Coleridge's sense of injustice at the vituperative attacks on him that issued regularly from the pages of the popular reviews, partly as a result of his association with Wordsworth and Robert Southey. The three poets were accused of trying to revolutionize, to vulgarize, poetry; they were avowedly interested in freeing poetry from the limitations of the eighteenth century poetic tradition. Coleridge denies that they deserved the abuses hurled at them.

After making some comments on the works of Wordsworth and Southey, Coleridge turns to a number of philosophical problems that fascinated him, questions of perception, sensation, and the human thought processes. It is this section of his work that provides the greatest difficulty for the uninitiated reader, for he assumes considerable familiarity with the works of German philosophers and English psychologists and mystics. He surveys the theories of Thomas Hobbes, David Hartley, Aristotle, Descartes, and others as they relate to problems of perception and of the development of thought through the association of ideas, and he assesses the influence of Immanuel Kant on his own philosophy.

Coleridge digresses from the complex history of his intellectual growth to describe his first literary venture into the commercial side of his world, his publication of a periodical called *The Watchman*. His attempts to secure subscriptions were ludicrous, and his project met with the failure that his friends had predicted; one of them had to pay his printer to keep him out of debtor's prison.

One of the most important periods in Coleridge's life was his 1798 trip to Germany, where he widened his knowledge of the literature and philosophy of that country. He returned to England to take a position with a newspaper, writing on literature and politics; he attacked Napoleon so vociferously that the French general actually sent out an order for his arrest while he was living in Italy as a correspondent for his paper. Coleridge evidently enjoyed his journalistic work, and he advises all would-be literary men to find some regular occupation rather than to devote all their time to writing.

Returning to his philosophical discussion, Coleridge lists several of his major premises about truth and knowledge. He is particularly concerned with distinguishing between the essence of the subject—the perceiver—and of the object—that which is perceived. Related to this distinction is the nature of the imagination, which Coleridge divides into two parts. The primary imagination is that power in man which perceives and recognizes objects; the secondary imagination acts on these initial perceptions to produce new thoughts: "It dissolves, diffuses, dissipates, in order to re-create."

Coleridge next turns to a presentation of his literary standards, referring especially to the *Lyrical Ballads*, the volume containing much of Wordsworth's poetry and some of his own. He tries to define poetry, pointing out that it has as its "immediate object pleasure, not truth," and that it delights by the effect of the whole, as well as of individual parts. In one of the most famous passages in the book he discusses the function of the poet who, by the power of his imagination, must bring unity out of diversity, reconciling "sameness, with differences; of the general, with the concrete; the idea, with the image; the individual, with the representative; the sense of novelty and freshness, with old and familiar objects; a more than usual state of emotion, with more than usual order; judgment ever awake and steady self-possession, with enthusiasm and feeling profound or vehement."

Coleridge applies these general tenets to specific works, analyzing Shakespeare's early poems, *The Rape of Lucrece* and *Venus and Adonis* to determine what in them reveals genius and what is the result of the poet's immaturity. He praises particularly Shakespeare's musical language and his distance from his subject matter, saying, with reference to the latter point, that the average youthful writer is likely to concentrate on his own sensations and experiences. Shakespeare's greatness seems to him to lie, too, in the vividness of his imagery and in his "depth, and energy of thought."

While he was closely associated with Wordsworth in the creation of the *Lyrical Ballads*, Coleridge does not hesitate to indicate the points at which he differed from his colleague. He takes issue most strongly with Wordsworth's assertion that the speech of low and rustic life is the natural language of emotion and therefore best for poetry. Coleridge stresses rather the choice of a diction as universal as possible, not associated with class or region,

and he says that it is this kind of language that Wordsworth has, in fact, used in almost all of his work. He feels that in the preface to the *Lyrical Ballads* Wordsworth was, to a certain extent, exaggerating in order to make clear advantages of natural, clear language over the empty poetic diction of the typical poetry of the time.

Coleridge's comments on Wordsworth lead him to an extended attack on the practices of the critical reviews, whose commentary on his friend's works seems to him both biased and absurd. He ridicules the tendency of anonymous reviewers to offer criticism without giving examples to support their assertions; they hardly seem to have read the works they lampoon. So as to counteract their ill-tempered, inconsistent judgments he sets down his own views on Wordsworth's most serious flaws and his outstanding talents. He criticizes his "inconstancy of the style," a tendency to shift from a lofty level to a commonplace one; his occasionally excessive attention to factual details of landscape or biography; his poor handling of dialogue in some poems; his "occasional prolixity, repetition, and an eddying instead of progression of thought" in a few passages; and, finally, his use of "thoughts and images too great for the subject."

With these defects in mind Coleridge commends Wordsworth's work for the purity and appropriateness of its language, the freshness of the thoughts, the "sinewy strength and originality of single lines and paragraphs," the accuracy of the descriptions of nature, the pathos and human sympathy, and the imaginative power of the poet.

The major portion of the *Biographia Literaria* ends with a final assessment of Wordsworth's work. However, Coleridge added, in order to give the reader a picture of his early maturity, a group of letters written to friends while he was traveling in Germany, containing amusing accounts of his shipboard companions, his meeting with the famous poet Klopstock, and some of his literary opinions. To show how little his critical standards had changed, he also included a long and devastating critique of a contemporary melodrama, *Bertram, or the Castle of St. Aldobrand*, an essay published just before the *Biographia Literaria*.

Coleridge's concluding chapter, as rambling in subject matter as the rest of the book, treats briefly the harsh critical reaction to his poem, *Christabel*, then turns to his affirmation of his Christian faith and his reasons for holding it. He makes no attempt to summarize his volume, which has presented a remarkably full portrait of his wide-ranging, questioning mind.

THE BIRDS

Type of work: Drama
Author: Aristophanes (c. 448–385 B.C.)
Type of plot: Social satire
Time of plot: Second Peloponnesian War
Locale: Athens and Nephelo-Coccygia, the city of the birds
First presented: 414 B.C.

On a political level, this comedy ridicules the disastrous Greek expedition to Sicily in 413 B.C. More generally, The Birds *is a rollicking commentary on man's eternal dissatisfaction with his lot; his habit of ignoring the divinities which shape his ends; his crowded, evil-breeding cities; and his tendency to disturb the equilibrium of the universe, Pisthetærus, with his irresistible rhetoric, surely is a forebear of the men who sell salvation or the world's goods with equal glibness and ease.*

Principal Characters

Pisthetærus (pĭs'thĕ·tī'rəs), an old man of Athens who has left his native city in disapproval because of the corruption, especially the litigiousness, of his countrymen. High-spirited, comically fantastic, and sometimes even vulgar, he nevertheless has an underlying vein of hardheaded good sense which makes him despise hypocrites and frauds. His oratorical skill convinces the birds that they are the superiors of the gods, and he proposes the creation of Nephelo-Coccygia (nĕ'fə·lō·kō·sĭ'jĭ·ə), or "Cloudcuckooland," the strategic location of which will give the birds power over both gods and men. For his pains he is awarded wings and a position of respect in the land of the birds. He adopts a very casual attitude toward the gods who come to negotiate a peace, and through shrewd dealing wins not only the scepter of Zeus for the birds but the hand of Basileia (bă·sĭlē'yə), or "Sovereignty," and celestial bounty for himself.

Euelpides (ū·ĕl'pĭ·dēz), another old Athenian, Pisthetærus' companion and foil. Not as sharply individualized, he is, like Pisthetærus, disgusted with Athenian life and ready to cooperate in his friend's schemes. He too has a broadly comic wit and a keen eye for a pretty courtesan.

Epops (ĕ'pŏps), the hoopoe. Now King of the Birds, he was once Tereus, a king of Thrace and the son of Ares, who, after his marriage to Procne, violated her sister Philomela and cut out her tongue so that she could not tell of the deed. All three were transformed by the gods: Tereus became a hoopoe (in the version of the myth followed by Aristophanes), Procne a nightingale, and Philomela a swallow. Epops is reunited with Procne in the land of the birds, where he has special status because he has human as well as bird knowledge. He is delighted with Pisthetærus' suggestion regarding the foundation of Nephelo-Coccygia.

Trochilus (trō'kĭ·ləs), the wren, a servant to Epops.

Phoenicopterus (fē'nĭ·kŏp'te·rəs), the flamingo, who attends the council of birds which votes to establish Nephelo-Coccygia.

A Priest. After the establishment of Nephelo-Coccygia he sacrifices to all the bird gods and goddesses.

A Poet, who addresses some rather bad verses to the new city.

A Prophet, Meton (mē'tŏn), a geometrician and astronomer, **An Inspector of Tributary Towns,** and **A Dealer in Decrees,** who also arrive for the inaugural ceremonies but are driven away by Pisthetærus, who knows them for frauds.

Iris (ī'rĭs), the messenger of Zeus who wanders into Nephelo-Coccygia on her way to command mankind to offer sacrifices to the gods. She is denied passage and treated impolitely because she has failed to get a safe conduct from the birds. She carries the news to Olympus that communication between gods and men has been cut off.

A Parricide, Cinesias (sĭ·nē'sĭ·əs), a dithyrambic poet, and **An Informer,** who come to Nephelo-Coccygia seeking wings to aid them in attaining their various objectives. The first is sent to Thrace to fight; the second and third are beaten.

Prometheus (prō·mē'thĭ·əs), the Titan, who tells Pisthetærus that the gods are ready to come to terms with the birds for the smoke of sacrifices has been cut off and the Olympians are starving.

Poseidon (pō·sī'dən), the god of the sea, **Heracles** (hĕ'rə·klēz), the demi-god, and **Triballus** (trĭ·bă'ləs), a barbarian god, who negotiate a truce with the birds by bargaining away the power of Zeus to Pisthetærus.

The Story

Euelpides and Pisthetærus, two disgruntled citizens, wanted to escape from the pettiness of life in Athens. They bought a jay and a crow, which Philocrates, the birdseller, told them could guide them to Epops—a bird not born of birds; from Epops they hoped to learn of a land where they could live a peaceful life.

The jay and the crow guided the pair into the mountains and led them to a shelter hidden among the rocks. They knocked and shouted for admittance. When Trochilus, Epops' servant, came to the door, Euelpides and Pisthetærus were prostrated with fear; they insisted that they were birds, not men, a species the birds intensely disliked. Epops, a hoopoe with a triple crest, emerged from the shelter to inform the Athenians that he had once been a man named Tereus, whom the gods had transformed into a hoopoe. At that particular time, however, Epops did not present a very colorful aspect, since he was molting.

When the Athenians revealed the purpose of their visit, Epops suggested that they move on to the Red Sea, but they said they were not interested in living in a seaport. Epops suggested several other places, but on one ground or another the pair objected to all suggestions which Epops had to offer. The truth was that they wanted to stay among the birds and establish a city. Interested in this novel idea, Epops summoned the birds that they too might hear of the plan.

The birds swarmed to the shelter from all directions until every species of Old World birds was represented at the gathering. The leader of the birds, fearful of all men, was dismayed when he learned that Epops had talked with Euelpides and Pisthetærus, and he incited all the birds to attack and to tear the Athenians to pieces. To defend themselves, Euelpides and Pisthetærus took up stewpots and other kitchen utensils. But Epops rebuked the birds for their precipitous behavior. Finally, heeding this suggestion that perhaps they could profit from the plan of the two men, they settled down to listen. Epops assured the birds that Euelpides and Pisthetærus had only the most honorable of intentions.

Pisthetærus told the birds that they were older than man. In fact, the feathered tribes had once been sovereign over all creation, and even within the memory of man birds were known to have been supreme over the human race. For that reason, he continued, men used birds as symbols of power and authority. For example, the eagle was the symbol of Zeus, the owl Athena's symbol, and the hawk, Apollo's.

Seeing that the birds were vitally interested in his words, Pisthetærus propounded his plan: The birds were to build a wall around their realm, the air, so that communication between the gods and men would be cut off. Both gods and men would then have to recognize the supremacy of the birds. If men proved recalcitrant, the sparrows would devour their grain and crows would peck out the eyes of their livestock. If men acceded, the birds would control insect plagues and would help men to store up earthly treasures.

The birds were delighted with his plan. Epops ushered the Athenians into his shelter, where the pair momentarily forgot their project when they saw Epops' wife, Procne, who had an uncanny resemblance to a desirable young maiden. Meanwhile the leader of the birds spoke of man's great debt to the birds. Urging mankind to look upon the birds as the true gods, he invited all men to join the birds and acquire wings.

Pisthetærus, winged like a bird, organized the building of the wall and arranged all negotiations with gods and men. As he prepared to make propitiatory offerings to the new gods, he was beset by opportunists who had heard of the great project. An indigent poetaster offered to glorify the project in verse. A charlatan offered worthless prophecies. But when Meton, a surveyor, offered to divide the realm of the air into the principal parts of a typical Greek city, Pisthetærus thrashed him. An inspector and a dealer in decrees importuned him and were likewise thrashed and dismissed. Annoyed by these money-seeking hangers-on, Pisthetærus retreated into Epops' shelter to sacrifice a goat. The leader of the birds again sang the praises of his kind and told how the birds were indispensable to the welfare of mankind.

The sacrifice was completed, and shortly thereafter the wall was finished, all the birds, using their various specialized organs, having cooperated in the construction. Then a messenger reported that a winged goddess, sent by Zeus, had got through to the bird kingdom in spite of the wall. Pisthetærus issued a call to arms—the birds would war with the gods. When Iris, the goddess of the rainbow, made her appearance, Pisthetærus was enraged at the ineffectualness of his wall. Oblivious of the importance assumed by the birds under Pisthetærus' influence, Iris declared that she was on her way to men to ask them to make a great sacrifice to the Olympian gods. When Pisthetærus inferred that the birds were now the only gods, Iris pitied him for his presumption and warned him not to arouse the ire of the Olympians.

A messenger who had been sent as an emissary from the birds to men returned and presented Pisthetærus with a gift, a golden chaplet. Men, it seemed, were delighted with the idea of the bird city; thousands were eager to come there to take wings and to live a life of ease. Pleased and flattered, the birds welcomed the men as they arrived.

First came a man with thoughts of parricide, who felt that he would at last be free to murder his father. Pisthetærus pointed out to the would-be parricide that the young bird might peck at his father, but that later it was his duty to administer to his father. He gave the youth wings and sent him off as a bird-soldier in order to make good use of his inclinations. Next a poet arrived and asked for wings so that he might gather inspiration for his verse from the upper air. Pisthetærus gave him wings and directed him to organize a chorus of birds. An informer arrived and asked for wings the better to practice his vicious profession; Pisthetærus whipped him and in despair removed the baskets of wings which had been placed at the gate.

Prometheus, the friend of mankind, made his appearance. Although he still feared the wrath of Zeus, he raised his mask and reported to Pisthetærus, who recognized him, that men no longer worshipped Zeus since the bird city, Nephelo-Coccygia, had been founded. He added that Zeus, deeply concerned, was sending a peace mission to the city and was even prepared to offer to Pisthetærus one of his maidservants, Basileia, for his wife. Prometheus then sneaked away to return to the abode of the gods.

Poseidon, Heracles, and Triballus, the barbarian god, came upon Pisthetærus as he was cooking a meal. Pisthetærus, visibly impressed by their presence, greeted them nonchalantly. They promised him plenty of warm weather and sufficient rain if he would drop his project.

Their argument might have been more effective had they not been so noticeably hungry. Pisthetærus declared that he would invite them to dinner if they promised to bring the scepter of Zeus to the birds. Heracles, almost famished, promised, but Poseidon was angered by Pisthetærus' audacity. Pisthetærus argued that it was to the advantage of the gods that the birds be supreme on earth since the birds, who were below the clouds, could keep an eye on mankind, while the gods, who were above the clouds, could not. The birds could, in fact, mete out to men the justice of the gods. The envoys agreed to this argument, but they balked when Pisthetærus insisted also upon having Basileia as his wife.

After a heated discussion Pisthetærus convinced Heracles, a natural son of Zeus, that he would receive nothing on the death of Zeus, and that Poseidon, as brother of Zeus, would get Heracles' share of Zeus's property. Heracles and Triballus prevailed over Poseidon in the hot dispute that followed and Basileia was conceded after much argument. The envoys then sat down to dinner. Pisthetærus, having received the scepter of Zeus, became not only the king of the birds but also the supreme deity.

Critical Evaluation

First shown at the City Dionysia festival in 414 B.C., *The Birds* is commonly regarded today as Aristophanes' finest work, although it only won second prize at the festival. Richly imaginative, full of scintillating wit and lovely lyrical songs, *The Birds* is unquestionably a comic masterpiece. In fact, it is unique in that it takes a fantastic and amusing idea and quite literally soars off into infinity with it. The entire play is a sustained and wonderful joke that carries one rollicking into heaven. And if that heaven is completely unconventional, what else could one expect from a genius such as Aristophanes?

Some critics have felt that this play satirizes the airy hopes of conquest that gripped Athens while the comedy was being written. In 415 B.C. a huge military expedition had sailed to subdue Sicily and establish an empire in the west. Two years later the expedition proved a fiasco, but in the meantime Athens was rife with grand rumors and expectations. *The Birds* does present a grand, crazy scheme of bringing both men and gods to heel, and it seems to convey some of the ebullience of the time. It uses fantasy as a means of delivering several well-aimed kicks at contemporary figures, at Athens, and at men and gods in general. A modern reader or audience can appreciate this comedy simply for its escapism and its beautiful lyrics, with no knowledge of its topical allusions. The important facts are contained within the play itself.

Here Aristophanes adapts an idea that appears in *The Clouds*, where Socrates explores the starry heavens in a basket, and makes it the basis of this comedy. Debt-

ridden, plagued by lawsuits in Athens, and seeking a restful retirement community, the hero, Pisthetærus, has a brainstorm. Why not found a kingdom in the sky with the help of the birds? By organizing the birds effectively he could subdue the gods through starving them, since the birds could intercept the sacred offerings. And he could bring men to their knees by using the birds to control harvests and livestock. Elderly, quick-witted, confident, Pisthetærus is likable as well, a kind of super-salesman. He convinces the birds and, by this through-the-looking-glass logic, he gains absolute mastery of the cosmos, winning a goddess for a bride in addition.

Yet his true glory rests in the kingdom to which he gives birth—Nephelo-Coccygia, or Cloudcuckooland. It is the equivalent of the Big Rock Candy Mountain, a place where all one's dreams come true. This Utopia is in harmony with nature, as represented by the birds, but it attracts idlers, parasites, nuisances. Bad poets, a false prophet, a father-beater, a magistrate, a process-server, an informer, a surveyor, a sycophant—all flock to Cloud-cuckooland, which gives Pisthetærus the chance to reform them or repel them. Pisthetærus' own companion, Euelpides, leaves of his own accord, sick of being ordered around. Even the gods are not really welcome. Thus the hero exercises his power mainly to exclude undesirables. When he finishes, his only comrades are the birds.

This rejection of human pests allows Aristophanes' satirical gift free play. These parasites are the usual types that the dramatist lampooned. Aristophanes seems to say that without these types a community could be a paradise. But he goes further than this. The birds, and particularly the chorus, sing some very beautiful songs that astonish one with their lyrical virtuosity. These songs are vastly superior to anything the poets in the play invent. Again, almost all of the birds have beautiful plumage, but the humans by contrast are shabbily dressed. And whereas the birds are friendly once Pisthetærus wins them over, the men are typically rapacious or looking for a hand-out. In short, the birds are altogether more desirable as companions than men. Even the gods come off poorly by comparison. They are merely immortal versions of the human species, full of greed and anxious to take advantage of their position.

The Birds is not completely misanthropic, for it pays ample tribute to man's eternal desire to achieve birdlike freedom and beauty, and to soar through the skies unimpeded by reality. It suggests that a man can best gain a Utopia by his own wits, and in friendly communion with nature. Pisthetærus founds his fabulous empire in a realm of sheer imagination, where any man can erect castles in the air, fashioned of daydreams and free of life's demands. This is the place where a person can find peace with friends of his own choosing, the kingdom where he can win out over the gods and his human foes alike. Imagination is the single area where a man can enthrone himself as ruler of the universe. And in a sense, *The Birds* is a dramatic hymn to the power of fantasy. All the shackles of reality and of human limitation are in abeyance, while the play sails straight up into the wild blue yonder. It is escapist, but a daring, witty, songful, exhilarating kind of escape.

THE BROTHERS KARAMAZOV

Type of work: Novel
Author: Fyodor Mikhailovich Dostoevski (1821–1881)
Type of plot: Impressionistic realism
Locale: Russia
First published: *Bratya Karamazovy*, 1879–1880 (English translation, 1912)

The anguish caused by man's dual nature reverberates throughout this powerful novel, which tells the story of the effects of greed, passion, and depravity on a father and his sons. Considered to be the author's best work, The Brothers Karamazov *is filled with brilliant characterizations which in turn are underpinned by the ethical and psychological probings for which Dostoevski is famous.*

Principal Characters

Fyodor Pavlovich Karamazov (fyō'dər päv'lô·vĭch kä·rä·mä'zəf), a crude buffoon of a father, the extremist, sensual, materialistic progenitor of a line of doomed sons. As an aging libertine, he is brought into competition with his sons over a woman, money, and status, and also by a sheer determination to live and control his destiny without interference. His manners are as threatening as his brooding appearance, and his debauchery is extreme, unabated even in his dwindling years. He is crafty, greedy, close-fisted, exhibiting a low cunning which speaks of a special kind of intelligence. His pose is artful; his lust for life and his voluptuousness are phenomenal. Obscene as he is, a malignant joker of low order, he has about him an air of magnificence gone to seed in an aging domestic tyrant.

Dmitri (dmĭ'trĭy), often called **Mitya,** his oldest son, who most resembles his father and most despises him for the wrong done the dead mother and himself. Morbidly fearful of his heredity, Dmitri reviles his father not so much for what he has done—cheated his son of both birthright and lover—as for what he is, a cruel, crafty despoiler of all that is decent. Like his father, he is muscular though slender; he is sallow, with large dark eyes. He is a kind of scapegoat, the one on whom the curse of sensuousness falls most heavily, given as he is to strong feelings and actions. He has a brooding Russian personality, an excitability, a violent nature capable of deep emotions and lasting love and antagonisms, though he has also simplicity, natural goodness, an open heart, directness, and awareness.

Ivan (ĭ·vän'), his half brother, an intellectual, poet, and atheist, given to visions and flights of fancy, secretiveness, and remote aloofness. Five years younger than Dmitri, he seems older, more mature, better poised. He has a subtle mind, both skeptical and idealistic, mercurial and unrealistic. Although none of the boys, having been cared for by relatives, is close to their tempestuous father, Ivan is the least known to Fyodor Karamazov and the one he most fears for qualities so remote from his own.

Though he wills his father's death, he is greatly shocked at the deed and his part in it, and he suffers a guilt complex so great that it unhinges his dualistic mind. He serves as the author's mouthpiece in the long Grand Inquisitor scene and the account of his private devil. Ivan is loved distantly and respected by his brothers for his lucidity and clairvoyance. He inherits the lust, the extremism, the egocentricity of his father, but in a refined, inward way.

Alyosha (ä·lyō'shə), or **Alexey** (ä·lĕk·sā'), Ivan's brother and Dmitri's half brother, the spiritual son who is the peacemaker, the sympathizer, the trusted and beloved brother if not son. Nineteen, healthy, bright, personable, good-looking, Alyosha, out of goodness and love, forms a bond with his unregenerate father and his distrustful brothers. His devotion to the good Father Zossima, his acceptance of his own worldliness at war with his spirituality, and his sheer love of life make him an attractive character, a natural, human person among grotesques.

Grushenka (grōō'shĕn·kə), beloved by father and son, an intemperate temptress, an earthy type who realizes more than she can communicate. She appears a hussy with all the tricks of her kind, but she is also devoted, loyal in her own way, and loving. Primitive, independent, free of the petty vindictiveness that plagues her lovers, Grushenka enlivens the story with a wholesome, womanly, even motherly quality.

Katerina Ivanovna (kä·tĕr·ĭn'ə ĭ·vä'nôv·nə), beloved by Ivan but engaged to Dmitri, an aristocrat and compulsive lover of great force of character. Willing to beg for love, to buy her beloved, she also has a fierce pride that flames up in revenge. Though she is attractive in a more austere way than Grushenka's, they share many eternally feminine traits.

Smerdyakov (smĕr·dyä'kəf), a half-witted servant, perhaps a natural son of Karamazov, and his murderer. He is scornful and sadistic. As the murderer who cannot live with his guilt, he is seen as more sinned against than sinning, the victim more than the antagonist. He hates his master and Dmitri, but he is curiously drawn to Ivan and in reality dies for him. Smerdyakov hangs himself.

Father Zossima (zō′sĕ·mə), a devout religious ascetic, Alyosha's teacher in the monastery to which the boy retires for a time. Aware of the sensual nature of the Karamazovs, the old priest advises the boy to go back to the world. Because of his holy example, his followers expect a miracle to occur when Father Zossima dies. Instead, his body decomposes rapidly, a circumstance viewed by other monks as proof that the aged man's teachings have been false.

Marfa (mär′fə), a servant in the Karamazov household and Smerdyakov's foster mother.

Grigory (grĭ·gô′rē), Marfa's husband.

Lizaveta (lyē·zä·vĕ′tə), the half-witted girl who died giving birth to Smerdyakov. Many people in the village believe that Fyodor Karamazov is the father of her child.

The Story

In the middle of the nineteenth century in Skotoprigonyevski, a town in the Russian provinces, Fyodor Karamazov fathered three sons: the eldest, Dmitri, by his first wife, and the other two, Ivan and Alexey, by his second. Fyodor, a good businessman but a scoundrel by nature, abandoned the children after their mothers died. A family servant, Grigory, saw that they were placed in the care of relatives.

Dmitri grew up believing that he would receive a legacy from his mother's estate. He served in the army, where he developed wild ways. Becoming a wastrel, he went to his father and asked for the money he believed to be due him. Ivan, morose but not timid, went from a *gymnasium* to a college in Moscow. Poverty forced him to teach and to contribute articles to periodicals, and he achieved modest fame when he published an article on the position of the ecclesiastical courts. Alexey, or Alyosha, a boy of a dreamy, retiring nature, entered a local monastery, where he became the pupil of a famous Orthodox church elder, Zossima. When Alyosha asked his father's permission to become a monk, Fyodor, to whom nothing was sacred, scoffed but gave his sanction.

When the brothers had all reached manhood, their paths converged in the town of their birth. Dmitri returned to collect his legacy. Ivan, a professed atheist, returned home for financial reasons.

At a meeting of the father and sons at the monastery, Fyodor shamed his sons by behaving like a fool in the presence of the revered Zossima. Dmitri, who arrived late, was accused by Fyodor of wanting the legacy money in order to entertain a local adventuress to whom he himself was attracted. Dmitri, who was betrothed at this time to Katerina, a colonel's daughter whom he had rescued from shame, raged at his father, saying that the old man was a great sinner and had no room to talk. Zossima fell down before Dmitri, tapping his head on the floor, and his fall was believed to be a portent of an evil that would befall the oldest son. Realizing that the Karamazovs were sensualists, Zossima advised Alyosha to leave the monastery and go into the world at Zossima's death. There was further dissension among the Karamazovs because of Ivan's love for Katerina, the betrothed of Dmitri.

Marfa, the wife of Grigory, Fyodor's faithful servant, had given birth to a deformed child. The night that Marfa's deformed baby died, Lizaveta, an idiot girl of the town, also died after giving birth to a son. The child, later to be called Smerdyakov, was taken in by Grigory and Marfa and was accepted as a servant in the household of Fyodor, whom everyone in the district believed the child's true father.

Dmitri confessed his wild ways to Alyosha. He opened his heart to his brother and told how he had spent three thousand rubles of Katerina's money in an orgy with Grushenka, a local woman of questionable character, with whom he had fallen passionately in love. Desperate for the money to repay Katerina, Dmitri asked Alyosha to secure it for him from Fyodor.

Alyosha found Fyodor and Ivan at the table, attended by the servant Smerdyakov, who was an epileptic. Entering suddenly in search of Grushenka, Dmitri attacked his father. Alyosha went to Katerina's house, where he found Katerina trying to bribe Grushenka into abandoning her interest in Dmitri. Grushenka, however, could not be compromised. Upon his return to the monastery, Alyosha found Zossima dying. He returned to Fyodor, to discover that his father had become afraid of both Dmitri and Ivan. Ivan wanted Dmitri to marry Grushenka so that he himself could marry Katerina. Fyodor wanted to marry Grushenka. The father refused to give Alyosha any money for Dmitri.

Spurned by Dmitri, Katerina dedicated her life to watching over him, although she felt a true love for Ivan. Ivan, seeing that Katerina was pledged to torture herself for life, nobly approved of her decision.

Later, in an inn, Ivan disclosed to Alyosha that he believed in God but that he could not accept God's world. The young men discussed the dual nature of man. Ivan disclosed that he hated Smerdyakov, who was caught between the wild passions of Dmitri and Fyodor and who, out of fear, worked for the interests of each against the other.

The dying Zossima revived long enough to converse once more with his devoted disciples. When he died, a miracle was expected. In the place of a miracle, however, his body decomposed rapidly, delighting certain of the monks, who were anxious that the institution of elders in the Orthodox church be discredited. They argued that the decomposition of his body proved that his teachings had been false.

In his disappointment at the turn of events at the monastery, Alyosha was persuaded to visit Grushenka, who wished to seduce him. He found Grushenka prepared to escape the madness of the Karamazovs by running off with a former lover. The saintly Alyosha saw good in Grushenka; she, for her part, found him an understanding soul.

Dmitri, eager to pay his debt to Katerina, made various fruitless attempts to borrow the money. Mad with jealousy when he learned that Grushenka was not at her home, he went to Fyodor's house to see whether she were there. He found no Grushenka, but he seriously injured old Grigory with a pestle with which he had intended to kill his father. Discovering that Grushenka had fled to another man, he armed himself and went in pursuit. He found Grushenka with two Poles in an inn at another village. The young woman welcomed Dmitri and professed undying love for him alone. During the lovers' subsequent drunken orgy, the police appeared and charged Dmitri with the murder of his father, who had been found robbed and dead in his house. Blood on Dmitri's clothing, his possession of a large sum of money, and passionate statements he had made against Fyodor were all evidence against him. Dmitri repeatedly protested his innocence, claiming that the money he had spent on his latest orgy was half of Katerina's rubles. He had saved the money to insure his future in the event that Grushenka accepted him, but the testimony of witnesses made his case seem hopeless. He was taken into custody and placed in the town jail to await trial.

Grushenka fell sick after the arrest of Dmitri, and she and Dmitri were plagued with jealousy of each other. As the result of a strange dream, Dmitri began to look upon himself as an innocent man destined to suffer for the crimes of humanity. Ivan and Katerina, in the meantime, worked on a scheme whereby Dmitri might escape to America.

Before the trial, Ivan interviewed Smerdyakov three times. The servant had once told Ivan that he was able to feign an epileptic fit; such a fit had been Smerdyakov's alibi during the search for the murderer of Fyodor. The third interview ended when Smerdyakov confessed to the murder, insisting, however, that he had been the instrument of Ivan, who by certain words and actions had led the servant to believe that the death of Fyodor would be a blessing for everyone in his household. Smerdyakov, depending on a guilt complex in the soul of Ivan, had murdered his master at a time when all the evidence would point directly to Dmitri. He had believed that Ivan would protect him and provide him with a comfortable living. At the end of the third interview, he gave the stolen money to Ivan, who returned to his rooms and fell ill with fever and delirium, during which he was haunted by a realistic specter of the devil that resided in his soul. That same night, Smerdyakov hanged himself.

The Karamazov case had attracted widespread attention throughout Russia, and many notables attended the trial. Prosecution built up what seemed to be a strong case against Dmitri, but the defense, a city lawyer, refuted the evidence piece by piece. Doctors declared Dmitri to be abnormal; in the end, however, they could not agree. Katerina had her woman's revenge by revealing to the court a letter Dmitri had written to her, in which he declared his intention of killing his father to get the money he owed her. Ivan, still in a fever, testified that Smerdyakov had confessed to the murder. Ivan gave the money to the court, but he negated his testimony when he lost control of himself and told the court of the visits of his private devil.

Despite the defense counsel's eloquent plea on Dmitri's behalf, the jury returned a verdict of guilty amid a tremendous hubbub in the courtroom.

Katerina was haunted by guilt because she had revealed Dmitri's letter; furthermore, she felt that she was responsible for the jealousy of the two brothers. She left Ivan's bedside and went to the hospital, where Dmitri, also ill of a fever, had been taken. Alyosha and Grushenka were present at their interview, when Katerina begged Dmitri for his forgiveness.

Later, Alyosha left Dmitri in the care of Grushenka and went to the funeral of a schoolboy friend. Filled with pity and compassion for the sorrow of death and the misery of life, Alyosha gently admonished the mourners, most of them schoolmates of the dead boy, to live for goodness and to love the world of man. He himself was preparing to go with Dmitri to Siberia, for he was ready to sacrifice his own life for innocence and truth.

Critical Evaluation

Fyodor Dostoevski published *The Brothers Karamazov* a year before he died. Almost a thousand pages long, the book was intended as the first volume in a fictional trilogy on the topics of religious faith, the nature of evil, and the existence of God. Like his contemporary Leo Tolstoy, Dostoevski believed that Russia had a divine mission: to bring to the world a renewed and invigorated Christianity. Both writers believed that the technological wonders of nineteenth century society had been accompanied by spiritual ills. Rationalism, socialism, nihilism, and other modern "isms" had alienated humanity from its spiritual dimension. To enable Russia to lead in the spiritual regeneration of Europe, Dostoevski took on the task of plumbing the depths of the Russian soul and revealing its powers as well as limitations. Once probed, ravaged, and cleansed, the nation's soul would be ready for its holy mission. Though Dostoevski did not live to complete the project, his ambitious plan and sense of high purpose make *The Brothers Karamazov* an extraordinary novel. Plotted as a sensational, intriguing detective story about the search for Fyodor Karamazov's murderer, it is also a profound inquiry into the great questions of psychology, philosophy, and theology.

Like good detective fiction, *The Brothers Karamazov* gradually—almost teasingly—reveals the circumstances of the crime. It follows the processes of a police investigation and criminal trial. Readers eavesdrop on the interrogations of suspects and listen as prosecutors and defense attorneys present their cases. Readers observe how individual delusions, peculiar motives, and accidental evidence all contribute to Dmitri's conviction—a verdict that is factually wrong. To neither the novelist nor the characters who know the truth is this misleading verdict a miscarriage of justice. For Dostoevski, the investigation into Fyodor's murder points to larger problems than the reliability of the criminal justice system: The Karamazov case bares the great difficulty that human reason has in determining truth. The cause of reason's limitation is the very nature of human beings.

The Karamazov family is Dostoevski's composite portrait of human nature. The name derives from the Russian word for dirt or earth; clearly, Fyodor represents humanity in its simple, physical state. He pursues money to ensure his security, and he pursues women and drink to ensure his pleasure. He watches out only for himself; he abandons his sons and does not—indeed cannot—participate civilly in society. Fyodor is the physical impulse to survive and pursue pleasure.

Fyodor's radically different sons represent the other aspects of human nature. Dmitri embodies the emotions: He knows the ecstasy of joy, the passions of lust and anger, and the misery of guilt. Ivan personifies the intellect, the rational ability to dissect and analyze the motives and ideals of human conduct. Alyosha incarnates spirituality, which strives to get beyond the self to touch divinity. Smerdyakov, who is probably Fyodor's bastard son, is closest to the father; he is the flesh which is weak, craven, unreliable, and ultimately rebellious. Though Smerdyakov actually kills Fyodor, all the brothers are implicated: Dmitri is legally guilty, and Ivan and Alyosha are morally guilty. In murder as in any other human action, the whole person participates.

Though this schema for the human soul seems Dostoevski's conclusion, it is actually only the springboard for the investigation of flesh, emotion, intellect, and spirit. Dostoevski's insight is that none of these dimensions of human nature is static. Traditional moral psychology, on the other hand, interpreted these dimensions as having a consistent value: The yearning spirit always strives to point the shortsighted emotions toward eternal goals; the prudent intellect prods the imprudent flesh to put off gratification. These constant parts of the self constantly war against each other. Dostoevski sees, however, that the battle is also joined *within* each dimension. All of Fyodor's sons experience inner as well as outer conflict. Through these internal struggles, Dostoevski explores issues of good, evil, morality, and faith.

Dmitri is a study in the puzzles of behavior and motivation. He is impulsively good and impulsively wicked. He is at times brave and generous, yet at other moments he is unable to control passion or anger. He is at a loss to explain his behavior. He hurts Katerina, whom he loves, and sinks to the sinfulness of his father, whom he hates. Is he a creature of heredity or a creature of environment? Is his inability to control his actions by his will a sign of moral corruption or of moral freedom?

Ivan is a study in the dilemmas of logic. The questions that torment him are more abstract but equally intense. His internal intellectual debate drives him one time into delirium, another time into literary creation. Is Christianity or socialism salvation for humanity? Is the church fated to outlive and replace the state, or will the state make the church redundant and obsolete? If there is no God, is everything and anything lawful? Unable to resolve such questions, the intellect alternates endlessly between confidence and doubt.

Alyosha is a study in the foundations of faith. The issues that perplex him are religious and transcendent. How is one to be saved, by the Christlike sacrifice of self for others in an admittedly corrupt world or by observation of the church's rules and doctrines away from the world? How does God manifest Himself to the world? Why does He seem to ignore the innocent suffering of children in war or natural disaster while concentrating on showy but ineffectual tricks like preserving a holy man's corpse? Dmitri, Ivan, and Alyosha show that in all aspects of human life, duality rather than unity is the reality.

Dostoevski's character and thematic complexities strain the limits of traditional narrative methods and force the novelist into a multilayered structure of storytelling. In some of the novel, the narrator is an eyewitness chronicler, an inhabitant of Skotoprigonyevski who knows the Karamazovs personally and witnesses the events of the investigation. This chronicler reports the outward appearance of things. At other times the storyteller is an omniscient narrator who enters the minds and hearts of lesser characters or focuses on the actions of various major characters, in turn, for extended stretches. Yet even the omniscient narrator cannot fully explore the recesses of Ivan, Dmitri, and Alyosha. Readers gain access there only through Dmitri's confession, Ivan's "Legend of the Grand Inquisitor," and Alyosha's transcription of Father Zossima's autobiography. If one judge's verdict cannot explain the full facts of Fyodor's murder, one narrator cannot describe the full truth of humanity's nature.

Dostoevski remains widely read. His approaches to

issues of behavior, ethics, and belief have attracted psychologists, philosophers, and theologians as well as literary critics. Ironically, *The Brothers Karamazov* was intended to pose questions that subsequent volumes would answer. Instead, it left questions that a century of investigation and inquiry has not yet resolved.

BUDDENBROOKS

Type of work: Novel
Author: Thomas Mann (1875–1955)
Type of plot: Social chronicle
Time of plot: Nineteenth century
Locale: Germany
First published: *Buddenbrooks: Verfall einer Familie*, 1901 (English translation, 1924)

An exposé of decadence in a materialistic society, this chronicle of a nineteenth century German industrial family follows its members from their peak of wealth and power into gradual decay and eventual ruin. Originally an exemplary family imbued with honesty, loyalty, and strong traditions, they succumb slowly but surely to decadence. Mann sees in a frail Hanno, the last of the Buddenbrook line, the culmination of a symbolic clash between the antithetical forces of art and life.

Principal Characters

Johann Buddenbrook (yō′hän bōō′děnbrōk), the stout, rosy-faced, benevolent-looking patriarch of the Buddenbrook family. He is the wealthy, successful senior partner of a grain-trading firm inherited from his father.

Johann (yō′hän) **Buddenbrook, Jr. (Jean, The Consul),** his serious-looking, aquiline-nosed, blond-bearded first son by his second wife. Jean combines the sentimentalist and the businessman. He rejoices over a happy family gathering, worries about the alienation of his half brother, Gotthold, from the family, and then advises coolly that Gotthold's request for money be denied because of likely future results to both family and firm. Jean's pietism seems foreign to the other Buddenbrooks, whose religion is superficial and confined to conventional sentiments proper to people of their class.

Antonie (än′tō·nē), **(Tony) Buddenbrook,** later **Frau Grünlich** and **Frau Permaneder,** Jean's oldest child. She has ash-blonde hair, gray-blue eyes, and finely shaped but stumpy hands. Impetuous in youth, she becomes conventional in maturity, but to her brother Tom she always remains a child in her reactions to the incidents in her life. She easily adapts herself to any situation; she is not humiliated by the dissolution of her marriage to Grünlich and is proud of the fact that she becomes a person of importance in the family. She adapts as readily to the breaking up of her marriage to Permaneder. As she develops a closer intimacy with her father following her first divorce, she recognizes and establishes closer ties with Tom after the death of their father. She sees the two of them as true Buddenbrooks, for their brother Christian does not really seem one of the family and young Clara remains an unimportant sister. The retention of dignity for both herself and the family becomes almost a religion with Tony.

Tom Buddenbrook, Jean's older son (modeled upon Thomas Mann's father). A quick-witted, intelligent, even-tempered boy, he becomes a strong, sturdy youth resembling his grandfather Johann. As he matures, he develops a stocky, broad-shouldered figure and a military air. His excessive clothes consciousness seems out of character for a Buddenbrook. An earnest, responsible businessman, he is proud of his burgher ancestry, and he contrasts his own desire to preserve the family name with the lack of imagination and idealism shown by Gotthold, his half brother. He is increasingly disgusted with Christian's business irresponsibility and his reputation as a strange kind of clown. He cannot forgive Christian's joking in public that all businessmen are swindlers. In his prime Tom is more aggressive than the earlier Buddenbrooks, but occasionally a little less scrupulous. His participation in public affairs and his interest in culture set him somewhat apart from his ancestors and his business associates. Early in his forties, he becomes increasingly aware that he has grown prematurely old, and he thinks more and more of death. At forty-eight he feels that death is stalking him. He dies not many months later following a fall in a snowy street after the partial extraction of a rotted tooth.

Christian (krĭs′tē·än) **Buddenbrook,** Jean's younger son. A born mimic, he is a moody, whimsical, sometimes extravagantly silly boy. As a youth he first betrays his weakness for pretty women and his deep interest in the theater. During an eight-year absence from home, principally in South America, he becomes lean and pallid, his large humped nose more prominent, his neck thinner, his hair sparse. Through association with Englishmen abroad he himself has grown to look like an Englishman. His self-absorption and his lack of dignity in his social manners disturb Tom Buddenbrook's sense of propriety. Christian becomes more and more a neurotic and a hypochondriac as he ages. After Tom's death Christian marries his mistress, who not long afterward has to put him in a mental institution. Like Tom's son Hanno, he symbolizes the decay of the Buddenbrook family.

Frau Consul Elizabeth Kröger (frou kŏn·sōōl′ ä·lē′sä·băt kroe′gėr) **Buddenbrook,** the wife of Jean Buddenbrook. A woman of the world and a lover of life, she becomes well known in her later years for her piety and her numerous charities. After a long life with her family, she dies of pneumonia.

Clara (clä′rä) **Buddenbrook,** the fourth and youngest child of Jean and Elizabeth. Hawk-nosed, dark-haired, and firm-mouthed, she is at times haughty. She marries Pastor Tiburtius, a minister from Riga, and dies childless a few years later.

Gotthold (gŏt′hôld) **Buddenbrook,** the elder Johann's unambitious son by his first wife. Having angered his father by a disapproved marriage and by becoming a shopkeeper, he is thereafter shunned by the family. He resents the favored treatment accorded his half brother Jean. After his father's death Gotthold retires and lives on the income from his inheritance and the sale of his shop. He dies at sixty of a heart attack.

Gerda Arnoldsen (gär′dä är′nŏld·sĕn) **Buddenbrook,** an aristocratic Dutch heiress who attends school with Tony. Her immense dowry later influences Tom's decision to marry her, though he declares to his mother at the time that he loves Gerda. The marriage is a happy one, but Gerda (perhaps modeled in part on Thomas Mann's mother), with her high degree of refinement, her detached nature, and her intense interest in music, remains somewhat a stranger among the Buddenbrooks.

Little Johann, or **Hanno** (hän′nō), **Buddenbrook,** the pathetic, sickly son of Tom and Gerda. He shares his mother's love of music and she thinks him a precocious genius. He dies in his teens of typhoid fever. Like his Uncle Christian, Hanno symbolizes the decadence of the family, and with his death the family itself comes to an end, for no male is left to carry on the Buddenbrook name.

Bendix Grünlich (bĕn′dĭks grün′lĭsh), Tony's first husband, a well-do-do Hamburg merchant and a pink-faced, blue-eyed, golden-whiskered, obsequious flatterer

and rascal. His bogus charm takes in Jean, who urges Tony to marry him despite her disgust for him. When his impending bankruptcy later leads him to seek money from Jean, Buddenbrook angrily discovers that Grünlich, even before marrying Tony, had unscrupulously capitalized on his supposed connection with the family. A divorce follows shortly after Tony's return to her parents' home with her daughter.

Morten Schartzkopf (mōr′tĕn schärts′kŏpf), a charming, serious-minded, liberal-thinking but naïve medical student whose brief romance with Tony is broken up when Grünlich reports to Morten's father a prior claim on Tony.

Alois Permaneder (ä′lō·ēs pėr′mä·nädėr), Tony's second husband, a bullet-headed, walrus-like, fat-cheeked, man of forty, a Munich brewer. Vulgar in speech and desirous of an easy life, he gets no sympathy from Tony regarding his decision to retire from the brewing business to live on his income from rents and investments. After Tony finds him one night drunkenly forcing his attentions on Babette, the cook, she leaves him. When she seeks a divorce, he willingly agrees to it and returns her dowry because he has no need of it.

Erica Grünlich (â′rĭ·kä grün′lĭsh), the daughter of Tony and her first husband. Tall, fresh-colored, pretty, healthy, and strong, she is occasionally inclined to melancholy moods. Her marriage, after the birth of a daughter, ends in disaster.

Hugo Weinschenk (hōō′gō wĭn′shănk), Erica's husband, a crude, pompous, self-made man, the middle-aged Silesian director of a fire insurance company. Convicted of unscrupulous business practices, he goes to prison. Upon his release and after a brief visit with the Buddenbrooks, he disappears.

Friederick Wilhelm Marcus (frē′dė·rĭk wĭl′hėlm mär′kŏs), Jean's confidential clerk. After Jean's death he becomes a junior partner in the Buddenbrook firm. His conservatism counteracts Tom's occasional tendency to overstretch himself.

The Story

In the year 1875, the Buddenbrook family was at its peak. Johann had maintained intact the business and wealth he had inherited from his father, and the Buddenbrook name was held in high esteem. Johann's oldest son, Jean, inherited the business when old Johann died. Antonie, Jean's first child, was born in the family home on Mengstrasse. Tony was an aristocrat by nature and temperament. The next child was Tom, followed by Christian, who seemed peculiar in his manners from birth. Tom displayed an early interest in the Buddenbrook business, but Christian seemed indifferent to all family responsibilities.

Tony grew into a beautiful woman. One day Herr Grünlich came to call on the family. Because of his obvious

interest in Tony, Jean investigated Grünlich's financial status. The headstrong girl, however, despised Grünlich and his obsequious manner. Having gone to the seashore to avoid meeting Grünlich when he called again, she fell in love with a young medical student named Morten Schartzkopf. Learning of Tony's interest in the student, Jean and Frau Buddenbrook hurried their daughter home, and Tony was too much bred with a sense of her family duties to ignore their arguments in favor of Grünlich when he asked for her hand. Her wedding date set, Grünlich received a promise of a dowry of eighty thousand marks.

Grünlich, after taking his twenty-year-old bride to the country, would not allow her to call on any of her city friends. Although she complained in her letters to her parents, Tony resigned herself to obeying her husband's wishes.

Tom held an important position in the business which was still amassing money for the Buddenbrooks. Christian's early distaste for business and his ill health had given him the privilege of going to South America.

When Grünlich found his establishment floundering, his creditors urged him to send to his father-in-law for help. Jean Buddenbrook learned then of Grünlich's motive in marrying Tony; the Buddenbrook reputation had placed Grünlich's already failing credit upon a sounder basis. Actually, Grünlich was a poor man who was depending upon Jean's concern for Tony to keep his son-in-law from financial failure. Tony herself assured her father that she hated Grünlich but that she did not wish to endure the hardships that bankruptcy would entail.

Jean brought Tony and his granddaughter, Erica Grünlich, back to the Buddenbrook home. The divorce, based on Grünlich's fraudulent handling of Tony's dowry, was easily arranged.

Jean Buddenbrook loved his family dearly and firmly believed in the greatness of the Buddenbrook heritage. Tony was once again happy in her father's home, although she bore her sorrows like a cross for everyone to notice and revere. Tom had grown quite close to his sister, who took pride in his development and in the progress of the Buddenbrook firm.

Christian, having failed in his enterprises in South America, had returned home. His father gave him a job and an office which Christian hated and avoided. His manners were still peculiar and his health poor. Serious Tom handled the business as well as Jean, and he remained fixed in his attachment to family customs. When Jean died and left the business to Tom, Tony felt that the family had lost its strongest tie. Tom, too, was greatly affected by his father's death, but the responsibility of his financial burdens immediately became of foremost importance.

Because Christian could not adjust himself to Buddenbrook interests, the ever-patient Tom sent him to Munich for his health. Reports from Munich that he was seen often in the company of a notoriously loose actress distressed his family. Then Tom made a satisfactory marriage with the daughter of a wealthy businessman. Gerda, whose dowry added to the Buddenbrook fortune, was an attractive woman who loved music. Parties were once more held at the Buddenbrook mansion on Mengstrasse.

Tony returned from a trip with hopes that a man whom she had met while traveling would come to call. Soon, Herr Permaneder did call. He was a successful beer merchant in Munich. Tom and Frau Buddenbrook thought that Permaneder, in spite of his crude manners and strange dialect, would make a satisfactory husband for Tony. Fortified with her second, smaller dowry, Tony went to Munich as Frau Permaneder. She sent Erica off to boarding school.

Once again Tony wrote passionate appeals to her family complaining of her married life. Finally she came home, weeping because Permaneder had betrayed her by making love to a servant. Tom protested against a second divorce, but Tony insisted. Prevailing upon Tom to write to Permaneder, Tony was surprised to learn that her husband would not fight the proceedings, that he felt the marriage had been a mistake, and that he would return Tony's dowry which he did not need.

Tom and Gerda had produced a son to carry on the family name. Little Johann, or Hanno, as he was called, inherited his mother's love for music, but he was pale and sickly from birth. Tom tried to instill in his son a love for the family business, but Hanno was too shy to respond to his father.

The death of Frau Buddenbrook brought Christian, Tony, and Tom together to haggle over the inheritance. Christian demanded his money, but Tom, as administrator, refused. Infuriated, Christian quarreled bitterly with Tom, all the pent-up feeling of the past years giving vent to a torrent of abuse against the cold, mercenary actions of Tom Buddenbrook.

Tom was not mercenary. He worked hard and faithfully, but despite his efforts the business had declined much in the past few years because of economic changes. In poor health, he felt that sickly Christian would outlive him.

Although Tony found a fine husband for her daughter, even the marriage of Erica and Herr Weinschenk was destined to end in disaster. Herr Weinschenk was caught indulging in some foul business practices and went to jail for three years. Accustomed to public scandal, Tony bore that new hardship with forbearance. Erica also adopted her mother's attitude.

Suddenly, Tom died. He had fallen in the snow, to be brought to his bed and die, a few hours later, babbling incoherently. His loss was greater to Tony than to any of the others. Christian, arriving from Munich for the funeral, had grown too concerned over his own suffering to show grief over the death of his brother. Gerda felt her own sorrow deeply, for her marriage with Tom had been a true love match.

After the will had been read, Christian returned to Munich to marry the mistress whom Tom's control had prevented him from marrying. Soon afterward, Christian's wife wrote to Tony that his illness had poisoned his mind. She had placed Christian in an institution.

Life at the Buddenbrook home continued. Little Hanno, growing up in a household of women, never gained much strength. Thin and sickly at fifteen years old, he died during a typhoid epidemic.

So passed the last of the Buddenbrooks. From the days of the first Johann, whose elegance and power had produced a fine business and a healthy, vigorous lineage, to the last pitiably small generation which died with Hanno, the Buddenbrooks had decayed into nothing.

Critical Evaluation

Buddenbrooks was Thomas Mann's first novel, and it was a great success. It is still one of his most popular works and has enjoyed international fame. Though not as complex or problematic as his later novels, it develops most of the major themes that came to occupy him throughout his career. The work had originally been planned as a novella about the boy Hanno Buddenbrook, but in assembling the material, Mann found himself compelled to trace the story back four generations. Thus, the novel became a family chronicle with a broad social milieu, a type of novel rare in German literature, which has tended to concentrate on the *Bildüngsroman*, or novel of development, a form that traces the growth of a single character. *Buddenbrooks* further departs from the tradition in that it reverses the emphasis on growth and development to concentrate on decay and decadence. In this, it represents a typical aspect of Mann's work, the fascination with the conflict between the life force and the death wish, especially as it appears in the artist type. Mann's artist figures are the product of robust bourgeois stock, families whose drive for work and achievement has led to prosperity and comfort. As the family, however, attains greater refinement and sensitivity, the life force slackens. At this stage, the artist figure appears, estranged from the bourgeois world and its values and curiously drawn toward disease and death. It is no accident that several of Mann's works take place in sanatoriums, or that typhus, syphilis, and tuberculosis figure prominently in his work.

The importance of this theme is perhaps best explained by the fact that it is essentially autobiographical, and *Buddenbrooks* is the most thoroughly autobiographical of Mann's novels. Every character in it can be traced to an actual prototype; the people of Lübeck were quite shocked when the novel appeared and protested what amounted to an invasion of privacy. The streets and houses, the seashore and the countryside were all identifiable as actual places, and the Buddenbrooks are, in fact, the Mann family. Yet Mann is obviously not Hanno, although parallels may be drawn—Thomas Mann was an artist, working in words rather than in music, and he rejected his family, a middle-class career, and the expectations of his community. He had left Lübeck for Italy, where, in fact, he began to write the Buddenbrooks chronicle. Thus, the stuff of the novel was intensely personal to him. Despite the autobiographical aspect, Mann has carefully structured the work so that the process of family decay proceeds in a clear and almost inevitable movement, by stages through the four generations, gathering momentum and expressing itself simultaneously in the business fortunes, physical characteristics, mannerisms, and psychological makeup of the four eldest sons, Johann, Jean, Thomas, and Hanno.

At each stage there is both a descent and an ascent.

Vitality and physical vigor decline and the business skill likewise is lost, as is evidenced by the steadily declining capital. This external decline, however, reflected even in such details as increasing susceptibility to tooth decay, is counterbalanced by an increase in sensitivity, an inclination toward art and metaphysics, and an increasingly active interior life. Johann may indeed play the flute—a necessary social grace for the eighteenth century gentleman—but he is not given to introspection. He lives to a ripe old age, and although he is an honest man, he has no scruples about the propriety of business and profit, and he has a sure sense of investment. His son Jean is far more concerned with moral principles, and business is no longer for him a natural drive but a responsibility. His health is diminished, and his life shorter, but his capacity for artistic enjoyment and religious emotion is greater. A tension between inner and outer begins to manifest itself, which becomes evident in Thomas. In him, refinement becomes elegance, and an inclination for the exotic manifests itself in his choice of a wife. Yet the strain of preserving his exterior form—a new house, high social position, and the fortunes of the business—show in his weakened physical constitution and in his attraction, late in his short life, to the philosophy of Schopenhauer, in which he sees the possibility of the dissolution of his embattled individuality into an eternal impersonal spiritual existence. Hanno, the last of the Buddenbrooks, dies while he is still a youth, his life filled with pain but rich in its inner creativity, expressed in his Wagnerian flights of musical composition. For Mann, Wagner was always linked with decadence and the death wish.

Many of the elements of this sequence recur in Mann's other works, especially his early works; the family is instantly recognizable. It is also clear that Mann is absorbed by the psychological development of his figures. The novel dwells more and more intensely on the inner states of the later characters. Hanno, the starting point of Mann's conception, retains a disproportionately large share of the novel's pages and remains one of Mann's most engaging and memorable creations. Yet it is also clear that Mann, for all of his understanding and sympathy toward the artistically inclined temperaments of the declining Buddenbrook family, drew a clear line between that sympathy and his own allegiance. Not only does he dwell on the increasingly difficult lives and demeaning deaths of the later characters—the eloquent and self-possessed Thomas collapsing and dying in a pool of filth on the street, Hanno's dying suddenly of typhus—but, in the case of Hanno, he also unequivocally attributes the death to a failure of the will to live. In one of the most remarkable chapters of the book, the narrator, who has generally retained his objectivity in chronicling the fortunes of the family, describes the course of a typical case of typhus, raising it to a mythical encounter between life and death:

At the crisis, the victim may either exert his will to live, and return, or proceed onward on the path to self-dissolution in death. Hanno, whose music has expressed this longing for release from the demands of life to which he is not equal, takes the latter course and dies. Here, any similarity between Mann and his characters ends. Although Mann as an artist felt himself estranged from the social world of the bourgeoisie, for him, unlike Hanno, art became the means by which he could retain his focus on life. *Buddenbrooks* may describe a family's loss of the will to live, but in so doing, it affirms the writer's most profound love of life.

CANDIDE

Type of work: Novel
Author: Voltaire (François-Marie Arouet de Voltaire, 1694–1778)
Type of plot: Social satire
Time of plot: Eighteenth century
Locale: Europe and South America
First published: *Candide: Ou, L'Optimisme*, 1759 (English translation, 1759)

This most popular of Voltaire's works is a masterful satire on the follies and vices of men, particularly of the belief embodied by Pangloss that "All is for the best in this best of all possible worlds." The author, through the outrageous misadventures of his hero, disproves this theory utterly, taking to task all of man's most prized institutions: science, philosophy, religion, government, and romance.

Principal Characters

Candide (kän·dēd′), a gentle, honest, and pleasant young man, reputed to be the illegitimate son of the sister of Baron Thunder-ten-tronckh and a decent man she was too proud to accept as a husband. Expelled from the Baron's castle after exploring the mysteries and pleasures of love with Cunegonde, the Baron's daughter, Candide travels all over the world. A dutiful young man who has been taught that this is the best of all possible worlds, Candide searches the globe for proof, meeting old friends and acquaintances in unexpected places and unusual circumstances. During his travels he has many misadventures and endures many hardships and pains. Impressed into the Bulgarian army, he discovers the horrors of war. He lives through the Lisbon Earthquake and is ordered flogged by officers of the Inquisition. He finds and loses his sweetheart Cunegonde. He discovers wealth and loses it. He kills men when he does not mean to do so. All of these experiences slowly convince Candide that this is really not the best of all possible worlds. After years of wandering he retires to a little farm where he lives with a small group of friends and his wife, Cunegonde, now old and far from pretty.

Cunegonde (kü·nä·gōńd′), the beautiful daughter of the Baron Thunder-ten-tronckh. With Candide she explores love, only to have her young lover dismissed violently from the castle. After his dismissal she endures much pain and many adventures. She is captured by the Bulgarians, raped, and wounded. She makes her way to Portugal, where she becomes the mistress of two men, a Jew and an officer of the Inquisition. She is reunited with Candide, only to be separated from him by another series of unhappy adventures. At last she and Candide are reunited. Married, they settle down on a small farm. By that time his ardor for her has been cooled by the adventures she has undergone and the effect they have had upon her. She becomes adept as a pastry cook, happy in that humble occupation.

Pangloss (pän·glôs′), Candide's tutor, a professor of metaphysico-theologo-cosmolonigology—in other words, abstract nonsense. Despite the terrible adventures that befall Candide and Pangloss' other friends, he is unwilling to forego theorizing or to admit that this is not the best of all possible worlds. He settles down with Candide on the latter's farm after undergoing many misadventures, including being hanged unsuccessfully by the Inquisition.

Baron Thunder-Ten-Tronckh (tün·dârtĕn·trŏńk′), Cunegonde's brother, who inherits his father's title. He is a proud young man, even in adversity and poverty, and he refuses again and again to give his consent to a marriage between his sister and Candide. Tired at last of the Baron's refusals, uttered with no regard for what Candide has endured on behalf of Cunegonde or the girl's changed condition, Candide causes the proud Baron to be shipped as a galley slave.

Jacques (zhäk′), a kindly Anabaptist who befriends Candide in Holland and travels with him to Portugal, only to be drowned at the time of the Lisbon Earthquake.

Martin (màr·tăn), a friend Candide meets in Surinam. Martin, accused by the church of being a Socinian heretic, admits to Candide that he is a Manichee, though none are supposed to be left in the world. Martin travels with Candide on the latter portion of Candide's wanderings and settles down with Candide on the young man's little farm.

Paquette (pà·kĕt′), a maid to the Baroness Thunder-ten-tronckh. Loved by Pangloss, she gives him venereal disease. After many misadventures of her own she turns up again in Candide's life and becomes a member of the little colony on his farm, where she earns her living by doing embroidery.

Friar Giroflée (jē·rô·flā′), a discontented friar who falls in love with Paquette during her travels and leaves his order for her sake. Befriended by Candide, he joins the colony on Candide's farm and turns carpenter.

The Old Woman, Cunegonde's servant. She relates

that she was once a beautiful princess, the daughter of the Princess Palestrina and a fictional pope, Urban X. The splendid life she expects is lost when she is captured by Moroccan pirates and condemned to a hard life as a slave. She clings to Cunegonde and Candide and settles with them on Candide's farm.

Cacambo (ká·käm′bō), Candide's servant. Separated from Candide in South America, he turns up later in

Venice as a slave belonging to the deposed Sultan Achmet III. Through Cacambo's intercession Candide and his party are allowed to visit Turkey.

A Contented Old Man, who has learned that hard work and minding one's own business are the best means to happiness. He avoids boredom, vice, and need by working a twenty-acre farm. Following his advice, Candide settles with his friends on a farm of his own.

The Story

Candide was born in Westphalia, the illegitimate son of Baron Thunder-ten-tronckh's sister. Dr. Pangloss, his tutor and a devout follower of Liebnitz, taught him metaphysico-theologo-cosmolonigology and assured his pupil that this is the best of all possible worlds. Cunegonde, the daughter of the baron, kissed Candide one day behind a screen. Candide was expelled from the noble baron's household.

Impressed into the army of the king of Bulgaria, Candide deserted during a battle between the King of Bulgaria and the king of Abares. Later, he was befriended by James the Anabaptist. He also met his old friend, Dr. Pangloss, now a beggar. James, Pangloss, and Candide started for Lisbon. Their ship was wrecked in a storm off the coast of Portugal. James was drowned, but Candide and Pangloss swam to shore just as an earthquake shook the city. The rulers of Lisbon, both secular and religious, decided to punish those people whose wickedness had brought about the earthquake, and Candide and Pangloss were among the accused. Pangloss was hanged, Candide thoroughly whipped.

While he was smarting from his wounds, an old woman accosted Candide and told him to have courage and to follow her. She led him to a house where he was fed and clothed. Then Cunegonde appeared. Candide was amazed because Pangloss had told him that Cunegonde was dead. Cunegonde related the story of her life from the time that she last saw Candide to their happy meeting. She was being kept by a Jew and an Inquisitor, but she held both men at a distance. Candide killed the Jew and the Inquisitor when they came to see her.

With the old woman, Cunegonde and Candide fled to Cadiz, where they were robbed. In despair, they sailed for Paraguay, where Candide hoped to enlist in the Spanish army which was fighting the rebellious Jesuits. During the voyage, the old woman told her story. They learned that she was the daughter of Pope Urban X and the princess of Palestrina.

The governor of Buenos Aires developed a great affection for Cunegonde, and through his scheming Candide was accused of having committed robbery while still in Spain. Candide fled with his servant, Cacambo; Cunegonde and the old woman remained behind. When Candide decided to fight for the Jesuits, he learned that the

commandant was in reality Cunegonde's brother. The brother, however, would not hear of his sister's marriage to Candide. They quarreled, and Candide, fearing that he had killed the brother, took to the road with Cacambo once more. Shortly afterward, they were captured by the Oreillons, a tribe of savage Indians, but when Cacambo proved they were not Jesuits, the two were allowed to go free. They traveled on to Eldorado. There life was simple and perfect, but Candide was not happy because he missed Cunegonde.

At last he decided to take some of the useless jeweled pebbles and golden mud of Eldorado and return to Buenos Aires to search for Cunegonde. He and Cacambo started out with a hundred sheep laden with riches, but they lost all but two sheep and the wealth these animals carried.

Candide approached a Dutch merchant and tried to arrange passage to Buenos Aires. The merchant sailed away with Candide's money and treasures, leaving Candide behind. Cacambo then went to Buenos Aires to find Cunegonde and take her to Venice to meet Candide. After many adventures, including a sea fight and the miraculous recovery of one of his lost sheep from a sinking ship, Candide arrived at Bordeaux. His intention was to go to Venice by way of Paris. Police arrested him in Paris, however, and Candide was forced to buy his freedom with diamonds. Later, he sailed on a Dutch ship to Portsmouth, England, where he witnessed the execution of an English admiral. From Portsmouth he went to Venice. There he found no Cacambo and no Cunegonde. He did, however, meet Paquette, Cunegonde's waiting maid. Shortly afterward, Candide encountered Cacambo, who was now a slave and who informed him that Cunegonde was in Constantinople. In the Venetian galley which carried them to Constantinople, Candide found Pangloss and Cunegonde's brother among the galley slaves. Pangloss related that he had miraculously escaped from his hanging in Lisbon because the bungling hangman had not been able to tie a proper knot. Cunegonde's brother told how he survived the wound which Candide had thought fatal. Candide bought both men from the Venetians and gave them their freedom.

When the group arrived at Constantinople, Candide bought the old woman and Cunegonde from their masters and also purchased a little farm to which they all retired. There each had his own particular work to do. Candide

decided that the best thing in the world was to cultivate one's garden.

Critical Evaluation

Candide, Voltaire's tour de force, goes beyond most other famous satires. Like Alexander Pope's *Rape of the Lock* (1714), it attacks the pretentiousness of the upper classes; like George Orwell's *Animal Farm* (1945), it undercuts political systems; like Jonathan Swift's ambitious *Gulliver's Travels* (1726), it sheds sharp light on man's grossness, his cupidity, and his stupidity, as well as on his crude and frequently cruel institutions. It goes beyond man and his society, however, to examine the entire world in which man finds himself. Its thesis is contrived in explicit response to Leibnitzian optimism that this is "the best of all possible worlds."

The problem of the existence of evil in the world has bothered man ever since he dared speculate about the nature of things. It is treated in the literature of the West at least as early as the book of Genesis, which attributes evil to man's disobedient nature. St. Augustine and, later, John Milton enlarged on this theory, claiming that God limited his own interference in the world when he created man "sufficient to stand though free to fall." The Book of Job in the Bible centers more specifically on the problem of suffering. Its answer is essentially no answer except for God's overwhelming (some have said obscene) demonstration of power, which humbles Job into acceptance. A third century Persian philosopher, Mani, devised the theory that earth is a field of dispute between two nearly matched powers—one of light, one of darkness—with man caught in the middle.

Most later explanations appear to be variations on these three. The seventeenth century Frenchman Blaise Pascal believed, like the author of Job, that man's vision cannot perceive the justice of God's overall plan. Gottfried Wilhelm von Leibnitz developed this explanation further. In his *Théodicée*, published in 1710, he described a harmonious universe in which all events are linked into a chain of cause and effect, and in which apparent evil is compensated by some greater good which may not be evident in the short run to the limited human mind. The English poet Alexander Pope expressed similar views in rhymed couplets:

> All Nature is but art, unknown to thee;
> All chance, direction, which thou canst not see;
> All discord, harmony not understood;
> All partial evil, universal good:
> And, in spite of pride, in erring reason's spite,
> One truth is clear: Whatever IS, IS RIGHT.

In his early life, Voltaire had been generally optimis-

tic. Beginning in 1752, however, his writings evidence growing pessimism. On November 1, 1755, an earthquake in Lisbon, Portugal, killed thirty to forty thousand people. This catastrophe provided Voltaire with a perfect springboard for his skepticism about the basic goodness of this world. "If Pope had been at Lisbon," he wrote, "would he have dared to say *All is well*?" His fellow Frenchman Jean Jacques Rousseau responded that man, not God, is to blame for evil, including earthquakes: that man brings misfortune upon himself by congregating in cities instead of living naturally in the country.

Voltaire continued the debate by composing *Candide*. He created a young, impressionable protagonist and set him upon an incredible series of adventures, many of which are drawn from real life, for example, the Lisbon earthquake and subsequent auto-da-fé; the political chaos of Morocco; and the execution of an admiral (Voltaire had tried to intercede in just such a situation). Like such other wandering heroes as Gulliver and Huckleberry Finn, Candide is naïve. For a time, like a schoolboy, he reacts to such events as torture, war, and catastrophe by recalling the favorite principles of his tutor, Pangloss: "Every effect has a cause," and "All is for the best in this best of all possible worlds." As horror piles on horror, however, his doubts increase. Pangloss reappears periodically to soothe his pupil with the most illogical logic imaginable, but hard experience takes its toll.

Candide's visit to Eldorado, the famed lost city of the New World, is a high-water mark. Here all is placid and serene. People live in absolute harmony. Suffering and poverty are unknown. There is no greed; the natives smile at Candide's interest in the gold and jewels which lie on the ground as "clay and pebbles." Eldorado is Utopia— as J. G. Weightman has put it, "a sunny interlude between two series of disasters to show us how happy and pious we might have been had God not given us our ungovernable natures and put us into a world containing inexplicable evil." In his desire to regain his lost love, Cunegonde, Candide leaves Eldorado; but having seen a truly harmonious world, he can no longer accept cruelty, catastrophe, and suffering as necessary ingredients for a universal good.

In the final chapter, Candide and his little band— including his former tutor, Pangloss; his more recent friend, the pessimistic Martin; and Cunegonde, now grown old and ugly—settle on a small farm "till the company should meet with a more favorable destiny." There they become almost as distressed by boredom as they previously were by disaster. Two neighbors, however, bring enlightenment to them. A dervish, questioned about the existence of evil, responds, "What signifies it whether there be evil or good? When his highness sends a ship to Egypt does he trouble his head whether the rats in the vessel are at their ease or not?" This echo of a metaphor Voltaire had contrived as early as 1736 briefly asserts the notion that the world may in the view of the "divine architect" be excellent indeed—but it is not designed for man, the "mouse" in the hold, any more than noses were designed for spectacles.

The second neighbor, a contented old farmer, advises Candide's group of the worthwhileness of labor, which "keeps off from us three great evils—idleness, vice, and want." For once, those philosophical opposites, Pangloss and Martin, agree; the little community settles down to work in earnest, each member doing his part with a good will and deriving satisfaction therefrom.

Candide, then, while an attack on philosophical optimism, is not a pessimistic work: Its ending, with the hero remarking that "we must cultivate our garden," reminds the reader of the words of another realistic, but hopeful, man, Anton Chekhov, who was to observe more than a century later, "If everyone in the world did all he was capable of on his own plot of land, what a beautiful world it would be!"

THE CANTERBURY TALES

Type of work: Poetry
Author: Geoffrey Chaucer (1340?–1400)
Types of plots: Chivalric romance, folktale, and saint's legend
Times of plots: Remote antiquity to fourteenth century
Locale: England
First transcribed: 1380–1390

In this great Middle English classic, Chaucer uses an imaginative frame-story format to present twenty-four tales: A group of pilgrims meet at a tavern on their way to the shrine of Becket at Canterbury and agree to pass the long hours of their journey in a storytelling contest to be judged by the innkeeper. The stories range from bawdy burlesques to tales of chivalry, from local folk legends to sermons. Chaucer's genius is such that the tales reveal the personalities of their tellers; in addition, the pilgrims grow as distinct personalities as they converse and argue between stories.

Principal Characters

The Knight, a courtly medieval fighting man who has served king and religion all over the known world. Modest in dress and speech, though the highest in rank of the pilgrims to Canterbury, he rides with only his son and a yeoman in attendance. He tells a metrical romance, the first of the stories in the series related by the various pilgrims. His is a tale of courtly love, the story of the love two young Theban noblemen, Palamon and Arcite, have for Emily, beautiful sister-in-law of Duke Theseus of Athens. The young men compete in a tourney for the girl's hand; Arcite wins but is killed in an accident, so that Palamon eventually has his love rewarded.

The Squire, the Knight's son. A young man of twenty, he has fought in several battles. Like his father, he is full of knightly courtesy, but he also enjoys a good time. He tells a story of adventure and enchantment in a distant land. The story he leaves unfinished tells of three gifts sent to Canacee, daughter of King Cambuscan. Each of the gifts has magical powers: a ring that enables the bearer to talk to birds, a brass horse that will take its rider anywhere, and a mirror that shows the truth and the future. The ring enables Canacee to learn the story of a lovelorn hawk, deserted by her mate.

The Yeoman, the Knight's attendant, a forester who takes excellent care of his gear. He wears a St. Christopher medal on his breast. Chaucer assigned no story to his telling.

The Prioress (Madame Eglentyn), who travels with another nun and three priests as her attendants to the shrine of St. Thomas à Becket at Canterbury. A woman of conscience and sympathy, she wears a curious brooch upon which appears the ambiguous statement, in Latin, "Love conquers all." Her story is that of a little schoolboy murdered for his religion by Jews. The child's death is discovered by a miracle of Our Lady. Like most of the stories told in the collection of tales, this one fits the personality of its narrator.

The Second Nun, who accompanies the Prioress. She also tells a Christian legend of the martyrdom of St. Cecilia, a story typical of medieval hagiography.

The Nun's Priest, whose name is **John.** He tells the beast epic relating the adventures of the cock Chanticleer and the fox. It is a didactic yet humorous story suitable for the Prioress' father confessor.

The Monk, a fat hedonist who prefers to be out of his cloister. No lover of books and learning, he prefers to hunt and eat. He defines tragedy as being the story of a man fallen from high degree and then offers many examples, including anecdotes of Lucifer, Adam, Samson, Hercules, Balthasar, Ugolino of Pisa, Julius Caesar, and Croesus. His lugubrious recital is interrupted by the Knight.

The Friar, named **Huberd.** He is a merry chap who knows barmaids better than the sick. Having the reputation of being the best beggar in his house, he appears to be a venal, worldly man. His story is a fabliau telling about a summoner who loses his soul to the devil; the story arouses the discomfiture of the Summoner in the group of pilgrims.

The Merchant, a tight-lipped man of business. Unhappily married, he tells a story of the evils of marriage between old men and young women. A variation of an old *märchen*, it relates how a super-annuated husband named January is deceived by his young and hearty spouse named May.

The Clerk of Oxford, a serious young scholar who heeds philosophy and prefers books to worldly pleasures. His tale is an answer to the Wife of Bath's idea that in marriage the woman ought to have dominion. The Clerk's tale is of an infinitely patient wife named Griselda, who endures all manner of ill-treatment from her husband.

The Sergeant of Law, a busy man who seems busier than he really is. He makes a great show of his learning, citing cases all the way back to William the Conqueror.

The Franklin, a rich landlord who loves to eat and keeps a ready table of dainties. In his time he has been sheriff of his county. His story is an old Breton lay, a tale of chivalry and the supernatural. He apologizes for his story and its telling, saying he is an uneducated man.

The Haberdasher, The Carpenter, The Weaver, The Dyer, and **The Tapestry Maker,** all members of a guild, each one rich and wise enough to be an alderman. None has been assigned a tale by Chaucer.

The Cook, named **Roger,** hired by the master workmen to serve them during their journey. He is a rollicking fellow. Pleased by the bawdy tales of the Miller and the Reeve, he insists upon telling a bawdy story of his own, one left unfinished by Chaucer.

The Shipman, captain of the *Maudelayne,* of Dartmouth. He is a good skipper and a smuggler. Like others of the company, he tells a fabliau, a bawdy tale. He relates the misadventures of a merchant of St. Denis, in Belgium, who is cheated of his wife's favors and his money by a sly monk named John.

The Doctor of Physick, a materialistic man greatly interested in money. He knows all the great medical authorities, as well as his astrology, though he seldom reads the Bible. His story, which he attributes to Livy, is the old tale of Appius and Virginia.

The Wife of Bath, named **Alice,** a clothmaker and five times a widow. Apparently wealthy from her marriages, she has traveled a great deal, including three trips to Jerusalem. She is well-versed in marriage and lovemaking. Her theory is that the woman must dominate in marriage, and to make her point tells a tale of an ugly lady who, when her husband is obedient, becomes fair.

The Parson, a poor but loyal churchman who teaches his parishioners by his good example. Refusing to tell an idle tale to his fellow pilgrims, he tells what he terms a merry tale about the Seven Deadly Sins.

The Plowman, an honest man, the Parson's brother. He tells no tale.

The Miller, a jolly, drunken reveler who leads the company, playing on his bagpipes. He tells a bawdy story about a carpenter named John who is cuckolded by his young wife, Alison, and her witty lover, Nicholas.

The Reeve, a slender, choleric man named **Oswald.** Having been a carpenter, he is incensed by Miller's tale. In retribution he tells a story about a miller cuckolded by two lusty students, who sleep with the miller's wife and daughter.

The Manciple, an uneducated man who is shrewd enough to steal a great deal from the learned lawyers who hire him to look after their establishments. He relates the old folktale of the tattling bird.

The Summoner, a lecherous, drunken fellow who loves food and strong drink. Angered by the Friar's tale about a summoner, he tells a tale about a friar who becomes the butt of coarse humor.

The Pardoner, a womanish man with long, blond hair. He tells a tale of three young men who seek death and find it. His story is actually a sermon on the evils of the unnatural love of money. He follows up the sermon with an attempt to sell phony relics to his fellow pilgrims.

Harry Bailey, the host at the Tabard Inn in Southwark. He organizes the storytelling among the pilgrims, with the winner to have a meal at his fellows' cost upon the company's return. He is a natural leader, as his words and actions show.

Geoffrey Chaucer, the author, who put himself into his poem as a retiring, mild-mannered person. He tries to recite the "Rime of Sir Thopas," a dreary tale which is interrupted as dull, whereupon he tells the story of Melibee and Dame Prudence.

The Canon, a traveler who joins the pilgrims briefly on the road to Canterbury. He leaves when it is hinted that he is a cheating alchemist.

The Canon's Yeoman, who remains with the pilgrim company and tells an anecdote about an alchemist, a canon like his master, who swindles a priest.

The Stories

Although a number of the individual tales of Geoffrey Chaucer's masterpiece, *The Canterbury Tales*, are themselves brilliant feats, the work as a whole—though an unfinished whole—is unique. No earlier collection of narratives is framed so imaginatively. The General Prologue gathers together thirty characters, most of whom are not mere storytellers but well-articulated personalities of various occupations and social levels. They meet at the Tabard, a real inn in Southwark, across the Thames River from London, for a purpose familiar to fourteenth century English folk: a pilgrimage to Canterbury Cathedral, where St. Thomas à Becket was murdered in 1170.

Chaucer devotes the bulk of the General Prologue to describing the pilgrims. He deftly sketches the Knight, who loves chivalry and has fought in many lands for his faith; his son, the Squire, blessed with blond curls and musical talent; the Prioress, who eats perhaps too heartily but nevertheless very daintily; the Monk, who escapes his monastery as often as possible to hunt; the begging Friar, lisper of easy penances to widows who open their pocketbooks wide; the Clerk of Oxford, a sober student of Aristotle; the Miller, a brawny chap with a wart on the end of his nose—and even Chaucer the pilgrim, a shy and rotund little man.

Harry Bailly, the proprietor of the Tabard, offers to accompany them and enliven their journey, which will take two days each way, by hosting a storytelling contest. As they ride along, each pilgrim will tell two tales outbound and two more on the return journey, at the end of which Harry will reward the teller of the tales he judges most instructive and entertaining with a free meal (the cost of which devolves upon the other pilgrims). The competition is never completed. In fact, Chaucer did not succeed in bringing his pilgrims into Canterbury, but he left two dozen richly diverse tales embedded in a context of lively interplay among the pilgrims.

The gentlemanly Knight appropriately begins the storytelling with a long, stately romance about two Theban knights, Palamon and Arcite, who, as prisoners of war in Athens, spot through a window of their cell Emily, the sister-in-law of their captor, Duke Theseus, and immediately fall in love with her. Later Arcite is released and Palamon escapes, and the two friends battle over the beautiful Emily. Theseus, coming upon this unseemly struggle, arranges a proper tournament for the purpose of determining her husband. Arcite wins but is mortally injured. On his deathbed he commends his friend to Emily, and Theseus confers her upon Palamon.

The Miller follows with a tale as earthy as the Knight's is elevated. Nicholas, an Oxford student boarding with a carpenter named John, lusts for Alison, the latter's young wife. He convinces his landlord that a great flood is imminent but assures him that they can escape if John will make three tubs, one for each of them, and hang them from the eaves of the house in readiness. When John falls asleep in his tub, Nicholas and Alison climb down from theirs and make love in John's bed. Toward morning, another admirer, Absalom, a dandified parish clerk, comes to the bedroom window and begs a kiss. Alison gleefully presents her posterior over the windowsill. When Absalom discovers which end of Alison he has kissed, he vows revenge. Returning from a blacksmith's forge with a hot coulter, he asks for another kiss. This time Nicholas decides to repeat the ruse. Absalom applies the smoking implement, the stricken Nicholas shouts "Water!" and John awakens. When he cuts loose his tub and crashes to the ground, the confusion brings out the neighbors in the gathering dawn, who laugh at the disorder, particularly at John's "madness."

This fabliau, as such a tale is called, brings the Knight's theme of contending lovers down to earth, with gross motives, language, and behavior replacing the courtly conduct of the previous tale. It also generates wrath in the Reeve, a carpenter by profession, who sees himself in the gulled husband. He thereupon tells a similar tale whose victim is naturally a miller. Thus, Chaucer sets in motion an intricate work in which tales can reflect their tellers, tellers often interact, and themes sometimes intersect.

The Wife of Bath introduces another theme. She is perhaps Chaucer's most complex creation: a virago who has outlived five husbands and is seeking a sixth, a champion of oppressed womanhood, an outrageous misinterpreter of the Bible, an experienced traveler, a skilled

clothmaker, a sinner who has nevertheless enjoyed her life and would not have had it otherwise. She tells an old fairy tale beautifully adapted to her purpose, the promotion of woman's sovereignty. An Arthurian knight has dishonored his calling by raping a woman. The queen prevails upon King Arthur to suspend the death penalty he has imposed if the knight can, in a year and a day, discover "what women most desire." Near the end of a fruitless quest, the knight meets an ugly old woman who reveals the secret extracting a promise that he will do the first thing she asks of him. The hag trails the knight to court and, upon his disclosure that women desire most sovereignty over their men, requests that he marry her. The appalled knight objects to her age, ugliness, poverty, and low social standing; she responds with a lecture on gentilesse, comprising the qualities of a true gentleman. He must fulfill his promise, but the hag unexpectedly gives him a choice: He can have her ugly and loyal, or beautiful and perhaps unfaithful. The knight avoids the dilemma by turning the choice over to her. By accepting her "governance," he is rewarded beyond his hopes, for she is transformed into a beautiful woman who will always be true to him.

This tale provokes several more on the sovereignty theme. In the Clerk's tale of patient Griselda, a marquis named Walter marries a peasant's daughter and soon begins to subject her to humiliations. He sends away their daughter because his lowborn wife is not a suitable mother. Later he removes their son also and eventually sends Griselda back to her father's house in rags. At length he announces that he is remarrying and orders Griselda back to his palace to minister to the young bride-to-be. Patient and diplomatic as ever, Griselda nevertheless counsels Walter not to subject his second wife to the same indignities, for she has been reared gently and could not endure adversity. At this point Walter confesses that the "bride" is in fact their own daughter. He has been testing Griselda's obedience, and since she has passed all the tests, the family is now reunited in happiness and prosperity.

The Merchant, a newlywed already regretting his own marriage, tells a cynical tale of a possessive old husband who, in the midst of guarding his young wife from temptation, is struck blind. In their secluded garden, she plays him false in his presence. When his sight is suddenly restored, she is still able to convince him of her fidelity against the evidence of his senses. The story ends with the befuddled old man doting on her.

After such extremities of marital disorder, the Franklin's story of Arveragus and Dorigen achieves a moral equilibrium. Dorigen rashly promises herself to a lover in order to promote her beloved husband's safety. When she confesses to Arveragus, he advises his distraught wife to be true to her word and reward her lover. The lover, Aurelius, in turn acknowledges Arveragus's magnanimity by releasing Dorigen from her promise. Finally, Aurelius is forgiven a huge debt he has incurred in his efforts to gain her love. Gentilesse, not sovereignty, turns out to be the last word in the marriage debate.

Several other tales, less obviously connected, are classics. The rapacious Pardoner's is an exemplum, a tale designed to illustrate the theme of a sermon. His unvarying theme—that avarice is the root of all evil (and, incidentally, an obstacle to his success as a con man)—he exemplifies by his tale of three carousers who seek to kill the "false traitor Death," the destroyer of many of their friends. A strange old man points the way to Death's abode; they follow it and find a pile of gold. Their original quest now forgotten, two of the revelers send the third for food and drink to celebrate their find. When he returns, they slay him to increase their share, then consume the poison he has brought back for them. Thus all three find Death.

The Nun's Priest contributes a rollicking beast fable about Chanticleer the proud rooster, who almost loses his life to a sly fox but outwits the beast in the climactic moments of a helter-skelter barnyard chase. The pilgrim Chaucer attempts a chivalric romance in clanging short lines, but his listeners disgustedly cut short his uproarious tale of Sir Thopas and force him to substitute a prose narrative. The Parson, similarly unable to manage the rhymed couplets and other verse forms which Chaucer the author was pioneering, tells the only other prose tale, actually a treatise on the Seven Deadly Sins.

At the end of the Parson's Tale, Chaucer purports to revoke all his writings of "worldly vanities" in a pious retraction that has produced much controversy. It stands as Chaucer's alternative to the fulfillment of an original plan which he recognized, late in his life, as beyond his capacity to complete. Neither the scribes who copied *The Canterbury Tales* nor its modern editors, however, have withdrawn from circulation even Chaucer's most "worldly" poems but have consigned to posterity in its fullness the work to which John Dryden later referred as "God's plenty."

Critical Evaluation

Geoffrey Chaucer, the first great poet in English literature, left behind him a work of perennial attraction and enjoyment. Not only was *The Canterbury Tales* popular from the time of its composition; it has been read ever since, edited, reprinted endlessly, taught in schools, adapted in part for the stage, and used for political parody.

Why should a work written in Middle English six centuries ago have such a hold upon subsequent generations? What does its author contribute in his collection of stories that appeals so to all classes of individuals down the years? Why is *The Canterbury Tales* considered one of the outstanding works of English literature? Answers to these questions are not difficult when one reads the tales either in their original language or in modern translation. Immediately one finds an author who had a tremendous feeling for life, understood human motivation, and could tell a story with great gusto.

The collection of pilgrims making their way to the shrine of Canterbury is a fair cross section of people from various walks of life and professions. Chaucer draws them with detailed individual characteristics but still with universal qualities that allow them to come alive in any generation. Moreover, he has taken consummate care to match these stories to their tellers.

No one, for example, can forget the brief portrait in the Prologue of the Wife of Bath, a florid woman, gaudy and bold in appearance. She is a lower-middle-class weaver from beside the town of Bath and has had five husbands; Chaucer slyly adds, "not to speak of other company in her youth." Yet the story she tells is an Arthurian romance stressing the virtues of courtesy and gentilesse. It has been termed a wish-fulfillment tale in which the ugly old woman wins sovereignty over her unwilling youthful husband and then turns young and beautiful. Careful study of this tale with the Wife's Prologue portrait, her conversation with other pilgrims, and her lusty confessional prologue reveals another side of this apparently crude and brash woman. She is more complex than one at first realizes, but Chaucer handles this point subtly without stating the fact.

Another pilgrim who fascinates readers is the Pardoner, a thorough charlatan, admittedly evil, who brags of his scandalous treatment of those he should serve. It is again important that Chaucer never says the Pardoner is a rogue; as with all the characters, he is allowed to reveal his character through quarrels with other pilgrims or by the type of story he relates.

The purposeful ambiguity in the portrait of the Nun, who concentrates on social concerns—feeding delicate morsels to her pet dogs and watching her table manners—instead of showing more Christian traits, makes a comment, though again indirect. Her tale reveals little human sympathy but is a typical miracle story she might have learned by rote.

Throughout *The Canterbury Tales*, Chaucer, who places himself along with other pilgrims as a naïve, unobservant traveling companion, uses this persona to effect satire and irony in the portraits. Seldom is the work didactic; Chaucer does not condemn clerics, tradespeople, or any other group. Instead, he allows them to reveal their own faults or makes clever asides to the reader to suggest a viewpoint. We see the pilgrims as they are with all their virtues and vices, and we can readily identify with their humanness.

Another reason for this great work's popularity lies in the variety of tales. Chaucer handles with equal facility different genres of medieval literature, from the courtly romance told by the Knight down to the bawdy tales of the Miller and Reeve. In the collection of twenty-four stories, there is something for everyone. If the reader does not care for one, Chaucer advises, "turn over the leaf and choose another tale." If anyone is offended by a tale of lechery, he can select a saint's legend or something in between.

Chaucer also handles with dexterity different levels of language: courtly speech, bawdy expressions, elegant prayers—language of the church, street and tavern. He can employ a clipped reporting style and turn out a parody of the excesses in metrical romance. He has at his command a whole bag of rhetorical tricks.

Critics and readers have attempted over the centuries to find an encompassing theme in *The Canterbury Tales*. Is the work a mere collection of unrelated stories or do they in one way or another deal with a single topic such as love (human or divine), or the question of who should have the upper hand in marriage? Attempts at making the tales conform to a single theme have mainly been unsuccessful; one can always find certain tales which do not fit the chosen category. It seems more likely that the Canterbury collection represents a panorama of representative humanity—a *comédie humaine*, not only of the fourteenth century but of all ages.

One other reason for the lasting quality of this first great work in English literature is that, like Shakespeare's drama, it opens innumerable possibilities to the reader. It poses questions about human motivation and aspirations. It probes into established attitudes, questions existing institutions. *The Canterbury Tales* reveals the tensions of Chaucer's time, the alternatives for man in a changing world, where many long-cherished customs and opinions were disintegrating.

Chaucer's pilgrims with their tales reveal the hopes and uncertainties of life, the heights to which man can climb as well as the depths to which he can descend. Perhaps all these qualities make *The Canterbury Tales* timeless.

CANTOS

Type of work: Poetry
Author: Ezra Pound (1885–1972)
First published: *Canto I*, 1925; *Canto CXX*, 1969

The common conceptions of Ezra Pound's *Cantos*, that they are obscure exhibits in the museum of Pound's prodigious memory rife with references to archaic cultures and unfamiliar languages, or that they are fatally infected with the pox of Pound's Fascist politics, are not entirely without truth but are also oversimplifications which distort the much greater truth that the *Cantos* contain some of the finest poetry and most fascinating and influential literary experiments of the twentieth century. Just as Walt Whitman's *Leaves of Grass* (1855) is a kind of epic of nineteenth century American life and a demonstration of the origins of poetry in American English, the *Cantos* are an epic of modernist thought in American life in the twentieth century and a measure of the growth of American poetic form to the middle of the century.

Building on Whitman's realization that an epic conception of a legendary hero was no longer viable, and acting in accordance with the Romantic emphasis on the creating artist as a cultural exemplar and heroic focus of a song of himself, Pound envisioned a work that would record the collision of an evolving poetic sensibility with the crucial historical events of his time. He believed that his essentially self-directed education was sufficient preparation for the project, and he believed as an article of faith that his mental energies were of significant proportions equal to the implicit demand that the mind of an epic poem is a concentration of the voices of history. Both "detesting" and admiring Whitman, he wanted to reach beyond the autobiographical vortex of Whitman's poem so that the convergence of scholarship, cultural theory, and poetic imagery in his own consciousness would range beyond an examination of the self not only to record history and its consequences but also to shape it. As a result, the *Cantos* have an open-ended aspect; Pound, unlike Dante, one of his most important precursors, had no specific charts for the unknown country he was entering.

Yet, even without a definite map in mind, Pound had extensive experience in a variety of poetic forms by the time he started, and he was convinced that structure was possible through, as Hugh Kenner explains, "the electrification of mute experiential filings into a manifestation of form." In addition to what Pound called "a coherent splendor" reachable through a poetic process that stressed the juxtaposition of related images, Pound was intensely aware of the work of painters, composers, and sculptors in Europe whose techniques led him to develop a method akin to what filmmaker Sergie Eisenstein called "ideological montage," in which diverse materials and languages are arranged so as to coalesce into new pat-

terns of meaning. The organizing principle behind Pound's data-collages derived from what Kenneth Rexroth describes as a "radical dissociation and recombination of elements," and while the connections between the various elements sometimes depended on a logic of association inherent in Pound's mind and not clear to anyone outside, from the perspective of an entire sequence of cantos, unifying patterns are clearly discernible. Another method of structural arrangement involves the use of voice—a prophetic voice that is primarily visionary in form and a pedagogic voice that is essentially summary in substance. Among the various insertions of speeches by historical figures, Pound also employs a kind of maverick Yankee dialect to contrast with the staggering erudition of the epic, and in moments of special feeling, what Kenner calls "lyric passages of intoxicated vision." The use of these different voices controls the tone of the poem and permits Pound to modulate mood and develop dramatic tension, another means of establishing structure within an essentially elastic frame.

The first announcement of Pound's intention to begin the *Cantos* came in 1915, when he wrote in a letter, "I am also at work on a cryselephantine poem of immeasurable length which will occupy me for the next four decades." Drafts of the three cantos were published in *Poetry* magazine in 1917, and much of what originally appeared in Canto III was revised into the opening lines of Canto I in the early 1920's. The poem begins with a descent into an *under* or *inner* world patterned after book 11 of Homer's *Odyssey*; the beginning of a mental voyage back into myth to recapitulate literary and cultural sources, which also moves inward toward the center of the poet's subconscious mind, the source of his image-making power. The poet's journey is intersected *in medias res*, specifically in the continuation of a sentence with no preliminary part ("And then went down to the ship . . ."), suggesting a mid-life launching. Canto II introduces key figures in Pound's cultural pantheon (Dionysus), crucial techniques (his use of the ideogramatic method for fashioning images), and special texts (Ovid's *Metamorphoses*). Canto III deals with the flow of history and visionary moments in time, anticipating other important moments in later cantos, while Canto IV extends this idea by examining the ruins of ancient cities with archaeological insight. Cantos V and VI consider the intersection of sexual power and political action, an important psychological theme, in Renaissance Europe and ancient Greece, while Canto VII establishes an autobiographical connection to the historical material by shifting the focus to the London that Pound and T. S. Eliot knew during the years of World War I. The first six cantos are primarily designed to establish a context and generate an energy field—to place the poet's consciousness into a realm in which an epic assessment of an epoch might become possible.

Pound published Cantos VIII to XI in Eliot's *The Criterion* in 1923 under the title "Maletesta Cantos" after Sigismundo Maletesta, a Renaissance artist and economic planner whose aesthetic integrity and political principles Pound saw as a model for an exceptional man living amid mundane times and hostile forces. Pound's admiration for Maletesta foreshadows his almost blind obeisance before other men of power and will, but in the poem, his questionable judgment was often balanced by an instinctive interest in figures who provided correction and balance. In Canto XIII, Pound introduced Confucius (Kung-fu-tsu) as another model of reason, insight, and refinement. This canto is one of Pound's clearest, an inventive translation of the Chinese classic *The Great Digest,* in which a just society is carefully and soberly described in stately cadences:

> If a man have not order within him
> He cannot spread order about him
> And if a man have not order within him
> His family will not act with due order;
>   And if a prince have not order within him
> He cannot put order in his dominions.

As the canto concludes, Kung warns, "Without character you will be unable to play on that instrument" (in other words, the poet will not be able to write), and he shows some of the consequences of a world in which character is notably absent among social leaders by describing a version of hell which he told his friend Wyndham Lewis was "a portrait of contemporary London." The urban landscape is full of people who represent the worst of the modern world—their names included in Pound's original manuscript but inked out to avoid libel suits—exploiters, speculators, and avaricious financiers who have produced an economic inferno that Albert Gelpi calls "a fetid, cloacal nightmare of oozing mud, pus, and excrement." These demons are the first in a long list of "obstructors of distribution" or "liars and loan lice" who have perverted Western economic systems so that commerce was not an extension of a natural process. They are, instead, the promoters of *usura*, Pound's root cause for economic malfunction, and are depicted in a nightmare region, since for Pound usury is "the power of hell." Cantos XV and XVI further illustrate this growing obsession, while Cantos XIII and XVII, which bracket the hellish modern world, offer alternatives. Canto XVII is an elevated vision of Venice, a city presented in positive images of light, air, water, and clean crafted stone, where a dream of utopia enters history, actualized by Venetian

artisans who temporarily overcame the usurers who tried to exploit their work. That canto concludes, however, with another return to the course of a history in which usurious oppressors ruin the efforts of craftsmen.

The poem continues with a rough alternation of groups of cantos documenting the effects of usury and groups illustrating heroic resistance to it. Throughout the 1930's, Pound, acting in what he considered to be the spirit of Confucius, celebrated early American politicians (Thomas Jefferson and John Adams in Cantos XXXI and XXXII) who governed with wisdom and direction or those (John Quincy Adams in Canto XXXIV, Andrew Jackson and Martin Van Buren in Canto XXVII) who acted with practical sense, and he described responsible monetary institutions which made credit available to all citizens (the Monte dei Paschi bank in Siena in Cantos XLIII and XLIV). Paralleling his accounts of heroic action by virtuous men, Pound celebrated the powers of light, which he often used as a symbol for the powers of love, in lyric paeans (almost prayers) to Aphrodite or Artemis, and investigated what he believed were both the destructive and the restorative powers of the feminine in passages concentrating on Odysseus and Circe. In one of the most famous sections of the poem, Canto XLV, he delivers a kind of sermon against usury, a rhetorical statement of what Gelpi calls "sustained outrage that usury has corrupted both economic and natural process, both Confucian order and Dionysian creativity." The field of the poem narrows here, as it did in the Kung canto, as it will in future cantos which concentrate energy into very specific concerns. With mounting intensity, Pound chants in bardic indignation:

> with usura the line grows thick
> with usura is no clear demarcation
> and no man can find site for his dwelling.
> Stone cutter is kept from his stone
> weaver is kept from his loom
> WITH USURA

It is CONTRA NATURAM, a plague against the natural order, Pound proclaims. This canto is followed by further examinations of the psychic voyage of Odysseus, as the archetypal explorer seeks knowledge that will permit self-expression through his encounters with Circe (sexual passion) and Tiresias (reflective wisdom). Odysseus continues to be a symbolic figure for Pound, his adventures a reflection of Pound's personal struggles with the artistic, intellectual, and social circumstances of his life.

The first fifty-two cantos move toward a kind of reconciliation, a state of calmness (or still point) in which the processes of the natural world provide the poet with images of visual beauty and psychological truth to be used against destructive external events and disruptive inner forces. In his own life, however, the fracture between the situation of the poem and Pound's personal turmoil as World War II approached prevented him from moving beyond a momentary serenity toward the projected Paradiso that would balance his Inferno. *The Fifth Decad of Cantos* (1937) was followed by three years of almost frantic poetic and political activity as Pound tried to influence the direction of American involvement in the flux of history by arranging an audience with Franklin Roosevelt so that he could explain to the president how to handle events in Europe. In 1940, Pound published *Cantos LII–LXXI*, ten cantos on Chinese history and ten on John Adams. Drawing on Joseph de Mailla's *Histoire Générale de la Chine* (1777–1785), Pound tried to explain how throughout Chinese history, whenever Confucian order controlled government, the state prospered. When Pound's enemies (militants, merchants, financiers) opposed order, "decadence supervened." In roughly parallel fashion, Pound yoked John Adams to Kung, Adams who left a "line of descendants who have steadily and without break felt their responsibility" and instituted Confucian principles in the American republic. The relatively undistinguished quality of the writing detracted from Pound's attempts to make Adams a pivotal figure in the middle of the entire sequence. The Kung and Adams cantos, though, while not covering new ground, are a kind of attempt to establish a strong historical foundation for the projected paradisiacal conclusion.

By 1940, Pound believed that the poem was essentially complete, lacking only a section that dealt with his spiritual beliefs. At the same time, he had doubts about the unity of his vision, writing, "As to the *form* of *The Cantos*: All I can say or pray is: *wait* till it's there." Yet his determination to convince Americans not to support capitalist corrupters against Benito Mussolini's new economic order turned, as Gelpi observes, "the prophet into a crank, if not a dupe, if not a crackpot." Pound spent the World War II years in Rapallo, making broadcasts on Rome radio which were considered treasonous by American authorities, and at the conclusion of the war he was incarcerated in a detention camp in Pisa for six months. A psychiatric evaluation in Washington determined that he was not sane enough to stand trial for his actions, and he was placed in St. Elizabeths Hospital for the next thirteen years. During the first three years of his confinement, he wrote *The Pisan Cantos* (1948), in which he stepped out from behind the various literary and historical masks through which he spoke to become the undisguised protagonist of his epic.

The *Cantos* had been derailed by the war. Aside from two unpublished cantos, LXXII and LXXIII, which he wrote in Italy, Pound's literary productivity was subordinated almost entirely to political invective from 1940 to 1945, a period in his life that could accurately be designated by his later term for the entire poem, "a botch." In St. Elizabeths, however, chastened by his treatment and forced to consider the dominant role of his ego in his life, he began to rebuild both his mind and his poetic

vision. In his first descriptions of his life in prison, he identified with slaves and criminals, an unprecedented act of humility and compassion. He confronted the need to recognize, admit, and confess his failures and misperceptions, most prominent among which was his inability to offer love unselfishly, and recognized vanity as a cause for his blindness—an especially adept formulation, considering his previous equation of love with light. As the sequence concluded with Canto LXXXI, in one of his finest passages, Pound offered the wisdom he had drawn from his experiences in a hell he deserved:

> What thou lovest well remains,
> $\qquad\qquad\qquad$ the rest is dross
> What thou lov'st well shall not be reft from thee
> What thou lov'st well is thy true heritage
> . . . .
> $\qquad$ Pull down thy vanity, I say pull down.
> Learn of the green world what can be thy place
> In scaled invention or true artistry,
> Pull down thy vanity,

In accordance with one of his earliest and firmest precepts, the operation of the poet's mind over the material of his life lifts him "out of hell, the pit/ out of dust and glare evil" in the direction of paradise, the early goal of the entire poem.

The next two segments of the *Cantos* were written while Pound was still in prison, and *Section: Rock-Drill* (1955) and *Thrones* (1959) recall his early attempts to outline an ideal society. "I've got to drill it into their beans," Pound wrote to his publisher James Laughlin, and in an unusually explicit explanation of his plans for *Thrones* (Cantos XCVI–CIX), he said, "The thrones in *The Cantos* are an attempt to move out from egoism and to establish some definition of an order possible or at any rate conceivable on earth." Ironically, these two books did not reach out very far, but represented Pound's enclosure within the proscribed bounds of his mind and vast educational experience. The pattern of arcane references and inward-directed linkages tended to seal the material away from easy external scrutiny. Pound may have realized that, and that realization, combined with the other frustrations of his life, may have led to a radically different style in the last cantos, which he called *Drafts and Fragments* and which he did not present for publication until 1969, several years after their completion.

Pound had returned to Europe after his release from confinement, but he found a very different land from the one he left. "The shock of no longer feeling oneself in the center of something is probably a part of it," he remarked. Combined with his awareness of how conventional critics had misunderstood and dismissed his work and the encroachments of old age, Pound offered the last cantos as hesitant and tentative gestures. "I cannot make it cohere," he lamented in Canto CXVI, and in the 1960's he settled into almost complete (but attentive) silence. Throughout the final, fragmentary poems, a feeling of placidity, of the calm vision of the ancient seer, balances the moods of discouragement. The questions he asks in Canto CXVI—"I have brought the great ball of crystal;/ who can lift it?/ Can you enter the great acorn of light?"— are answered by implication when Pound asserts, "it coheres all right/ even if my notes do not cohere." In other words, even if the poem did not fulfill the epic aim of explaining order on earth, the effort itself leads to a vision of beauty in poetic light. Moments of lyric radiance ("the great acorn of light") exhibit cohering propensity, just as there is a version of unity in "the replacement of para-

phraseable plot by rhythmic recurrence," as Kenner comments. The final canto, the shortest of the entire poem, is like a summary prayer of farewell and forgiveness:

> I have tried to write Paradise
> Do not move
>   Let the wind speak
>   that is paradise.
> Let the Gods forgive what I
>   have made
> Let those I love try to forgive
>   what I have made.

THE CAPTAIN'S DAUGHTER

Type of work: Novel
Author: Alexander Pushkin (1799–1837)
Type of plot: Historical romance
Time of plot: About 1774
Locale: Russia
First published: *Kapitanskaya dochka*, 1836 (English translation, 1878)

One of the first pure examples of Russian realism, The Captain's Daughter *is an exciting and concisely told narrative with a gallery of characters ranging from simple Maria to the cruel rebel Pougatcheff. The novel was written as the result of Pushkin's appointment to the office of crown historian, which gave him access to state archives and the private papers of Empress Catherine II.*

Principal Characters

Piotr Andreitch Grineff (pyō′tr än·drĕ′ĭch grĭ·nĕf′), a young officer in a Russian regiment. A kindly and generous young man who falls in love with the commandant's daughter, he goes to great lengths to protect her from harm and fights a duel when a fellow officer criticizes a love poem he has written for her. At first his parents do not approve of the girl, but they later give their consent to the marriage.

Maria Ivanovna (mä′ryə ĭ·vä′nəv·nə), the captain's daughter, a lovely girl very much in love with Piotr. When he sends her to his parents for her protection, she so impresses them that they change their minds about not allowing their son to marry her. She saves her lover from exile in Siberia by appealing to the empress.

Alexey Ivanitch Shvabrin (ä·lĕk·sä′ ĭ·vän′ĭch shvä′brĭn), an officer in the same regiment with Piotr. A suitor rejected by Maria, he is jealous of her love for Piotr. When the rebel Pougatcheff takes the Bailogorsk fortress, Shvabrin deserts to the rebel side. He does everything in his power to separate Maria and Piotr. He accuses Piotr of being a spy for the rebels and is responsible for his rival's sentence of exile.

Emelyan Pougatcheff (ĕ·mĕ·lyän′ pōōgä′chəf), a Cossack rebel leader who claims to be the dead Emperor Peter III. He is cruel and ruthless, but after the capture of the Bailogorsk fortress he spares Piotr's life and sends him away under safe conduct because the young officer had sometime before given the rebel, disguised as a traveler, a sheepskin coat to protect him during a snowstorm.

Savelitch (sä·vĕ′lĭch), Piotr's old servant, whose intervention saves his master from several predicaments. He is faithful, loyal, and shrewd.

Vassilissa Egorovna (vä·sĭ′lĭ·sə ĕ·gō′rəv·nə), the captain's wife, a very capable woman who runs her household and her husband's regiment with great efficiency. When she protests against her husband's murder by the Cossack rebels, she is killed.

Captain Ivan Mironoff, the commanding officer at the Bailogorsk fortress and Piotr's superior. Captured when Cossacks under Emelyan Pougatcheff seize the fortress, he and his aides are hanged by order of the rebel chief.

Captain Zourin, who rescues Piotr, his family, and Maria from death at the hands of the renegade Shvabrin.

The Story

Although Peter Andreitch Grineff was registered as a sergeant in the Semenovsky regiment when he was very young, he was given leave to stay at home until he had completed his studies. When he was nearly seventeen years old, his father decided that the time had arrived to begin his military career. With his parents' blessing, Peter set out for distant Orenburg, in the company of his faithful servant, Savelitch.

The trip was not without incident. One night, the travelers put up at Simbirsk. There, while his man went to see about some purchases, Peter was lured into playing billiards with a fellow soldier, Zourin, and quickly lost one hundred rubles. Toward evening of the following day, the young man and Savelitch found themselves on the snowy plain with a storm approaching. As darkness fell, the snow grew thicker, until finally the horses could not find their way and the driver confessed that he was lost. They were rescued by another traveler, a man with such sensitive nostrils that he was able to scent smoke from a village some distance away and to lead them to it. The three men and their guide spent the night in the village. The next morning, Peter presented his sheepskin jacket to his poorly dressed rescuer. Savelitch warned Peter that the coat would probably be pawned for a drink.

Late that day, the young man reached Orenburg and presented himself to the general in command. It was decided that he should join the Bailogorsk fortress garrison under Captain Mironoff, for his superior felt that the dull life at Orenburg might lead the young man into a career of dissipation.

The Bailogorsk fortress, on the edge of the Kirghis steppes, was nothing more than a village surrounded by a log fence. Its real commandant was not Captain Mironoff but his lady, Vassilissa Egorovna, a lively, strict woman who saw to the discipline of her husband's underlings as well as the running of her own household.

Peter quickly made friends with a fellow officer, Shvabrin, who had been exiled to the steppes for fighting a duel. He spent much time with his captain's family and grew deeply attached to the couple and to their daughter, Maria Ivanovna. After he had received his commission, he found military discipline so relaxed that he was able to indulge his literary tastes.

The quiet routine of Peter's life was interrupted by an unexpected quarrel with Shvabrin. One day, he showed his friend a love poem he had written to Maria. Shvabrin criticized the work severely and went on to make derogatory remarks about Maria until they quarreled and Peter found himself challenged to a duel for having called the man a liar.

The next morning, the two soldiers met in a field to fight but they were stopped by some of the garrison, for Vassilissa Egorovna had learned of the duel. Peter and his enemy, although apparently reconciled, intended to carry out their plan at the earliest opportunity. Discussing the quarrel with Maria, Peter learned that Shvabrin's actions could be explained by the fact that he was her rejected suitor.

Assuring themselves that they were not watched, Shvabrin and Peter fought their duel the following day. Wounded in the breast, Peter lay unconscious for five days after the fight. When he began to recover, he asked Maria to marry him. Shvabrin had been jailed. Then Peter's father wrote that he disapproved of a match with Captain Mironoff's daughter and that he intended to have his son transferred from the fortress so that he might forget his foolish ideas. As Savelitch denied having written a letter home, Peter could only conclude that Shvabrin had been the informer.

Life would have become unbearable for the young man after his father's letter arrived if the unexpected had not happened. One evening, Captain Mironoff informed his officers that the Yaikian Cossacks, led by Emelyan Pougatcheff, who claimed to be the dead Emperor Peter III, had risen and were sacking fortresses and committing outrages everywhere. The captain ordered his men to keep on the alert and to ready the cannon.

The news of Pougatcheff's uprising quickly spread through the garrison. Many of the Cossacks of the town sided with the rebel, so that Captain Mironoff did not know whom he could trust or who might betray him. It was not long before the captain received a manifesto from the leader of the Cossacks ordering him to surrender.

It was decided that Maria should be sent back to Orenburg, but the attack came early the next morning before she could leave. Captain Mironoff and his officers made a valiant effort to defend the town; but with the aid of Cossack traitors inside the walls, Pougatcheff was soon master of the fortress.

Captain Mironoff and his aides were hanged. Shvabrin deserted to the rebels. Peter, at the intercession of old Savelitch, was spared by Pougatcheff. The townspeople and the garrison soldiers had no scruples about pledging allegiance to the rebel leader. Vassilissa Egorovna was slain when she cried out against her husband's murderer.

When Pougatcheff and his followers rode off to inspect the fortress, Peter began his search for Maria. To his great relief, he found that she had been hidden by the wife of the village priest and that Shvabrin, who knew her whereabouts, had not revealed her identity. He learned from Savelitch that the servant had recognized Pougatcheff as the man to whom he had given his hareskin coat months before. Later, the rebel leader sent for Peter and acknowledged his identity.

The rebel tried to persuade Peter to join the Cossacks but respected his wish to rejoin his own forces at Orenburg. The next day, Peter and his servant were given safe conduct, and Pougatcheff gave Peter a horse and a sheepskin coat for the journey.

Several days later the Cossacks attacked Orenburg. During a sally against them, Peter received a disturbing message from one of the Bailogorsk Cossacks; Shvabrin was forcing Maria to marry him. Peter went at once to the general and tried to persuade him to raise the siege and go to the rescue of the village. When the general refused, Peter and Savelitch started out once more for the Bailogorsk fortress. Intercepted and taken before Pougatcheff, Peter persuaded the rebel to give Maria safe conduct to Orenburg.

On the way, they met a detachment of soldiers led by Captain Zourin, who persuaded Peter to send Maria, under Savelitch's protection, to his family, while he himself remained with the troops in Orenburg.

The siege of Orenburg was finally lifted, and the army began its task of tracking down rebel units. Some months later, Peter found himself near his own village and set off alone to visit his parents' estate. Reaching his home, he found the serfs in rebellion and his family and Maria captives. That day, Shvabrin swooped down upon them with his troops. He was about to have them all hanged, except Maria, when they were rescued by Zourin's men. The renegade was shot during the encounter and taken prisoner.

Peter's parents had changed their attitude toward the captain's daughter, and Peter was able to rejoin Captain Zourin with the expectation that he and Maria would be wed in a month. Then an order came for his arrest. He was accused of having been in the pay of Pougatcheff, of spying for the rebel, and of having taken presents from him. The author of the accusations was the captive, Shvabrin. Though Peter could easily have cleared himself by summoning Maria as a witness, he decided not to drag her into the matter. He was sentenced to spend the rest of his life in exile in Siberia.

Maria, however, was not one to let matters stand at that. Leaving Peter's parents, she traveled to St. Petersburg and went to Tsarskoe Selo, where the court was located. Walking in the garden there one day, she met a woman who declared that she went to court on occasion and would be pleased to present her petition to the empress. Maria was summoned to the royal presence the same day and discovered that it was the empress herself to whom she had spoken. Peter received his pardon and soon afterward married the captain's daughter.

Critical Evaluation

The longest of Alexander Pushkin's completed prose tales, *The Captain's Daughter* was based on true events which Pushkin wrote as history in his *Istoria Pugachev* (1834; *The History of the Pugachev Rebellion*). The astonishing quality about *The Captain's Daughter* is the style. Although written in 1836, and the first modern Russian novel, it possesses a brisk, lean style more suggestive of twentieth century fiction than that of the early nineteenth century. Pushkin wastes no words, yet his scenes are vivid, his characters fully fleshed and remarkably alive, and his tale recounted in a suspenseful and moving manner. The first-person narration is realistic and adds to the verisimilitude of the story. The naïve, romantic illusions of the young protagonist are described by the narrator in a thoroughly disarming and often humorous manner. The entire story is seen through Peter's eyes, allowing the reader to share his enthusiasms, his impetuousness, and his fears, as well as his youthful ardor and romantic spirit. A sense of the vitality of youth pervades the book.

The accounts of action, such as the duel or the siege of the Bailogorsk fortress, are vivid and well paced. Throughout the novel, Pushkin writes with extraordinary ease and vitality, bringing to life in a few strokes situations and characters. A sly humor is an integral part of the narrative. When the hero notes that his French tutor was sent from Moscow with the yearly supply of wine and olive oil, readers know precisely where that unlucky tutor fits into the household. Many of the characters possess a humorous side to their nature. The ill-fated, henpecked captain and his talkative but kindly tyrant of a wife are both portrayed with a light touch. Old Savelitch, Peter's servant, is the truest comic figure in the novel; devoted to his young master, as to Peter's father before, the old man would willingly sacrifice his life for Peter, but he never hesitates to talk back to Peter or even to the rebel Cossack leader if he feels that he is in the right. Even Pougatcheff, self-styled pretender to the throne, is presented with a great deal of humor; in a sense, he is the only character in the book who does not take himself completely seriously, and this, at least in part, is the result of an ironic realization of the precariousness of his existence.

Many scenes in the novel possess a double-edged humor, from the absurd, aborted, and then finished duel between Peter and Shvabrin to the moment, in the midst of horror, when old Savelitch dares to present an itemized list of destroyed and stolen goods to the man who holds all of their lives in his hands. The deaths of the captain and his wife are handled with a certain grotesque humor. As in Shakespeare's tragedies, this humor serves to heighten the horror of certain dramatic scenes, such as the fall of the fortress and the butchering of the innocent at the hands of the rebels. Despite the terrible events portrayed in the novel, the book is not grim. It is a romantic tale of action and romance, and the ending is appropriately happy. Even the conclusion, with its scenes of mistaken identity, possesses a charming humor.

At the same time, the realism of the portrayals of the duplicity of human nature, the traitorous villainy of Shvabrin, the cowardice of the garrison when they all throw down their arms in the face of the enemy, and the pettiness of many of the minor characters is shocking. The brilliant construction of the novel, the alternating light and dark scenes, sweeps the reader along, never letting him be quite sure of where he is. Pushkin seems to delight in catching the reader off guard, of making him laugh and then gasp with horror and then hurling a piece of slapstick at him before he has recovered from the shock. The scene of the captain's fat wife being dragged naked from her house to the gallows, screaming and shouting abuse at the Cossacks, is both funny and horrible. Shvabrin, completely despicable, is shown to be absurd as he struts and postures during his brief glory, and then, even more so, when he falls. Pushkin is extremely deft at showing both sides of human beings, the noble and the phony, the absurd and the courageous, the hateful and the loving.

The Russian land is an important part of this novel. The vast spaces almost become another character, as the hero flies across them in sleds and carriages or on horseback. Pushkin carefully builds a sense of intense patriotic fervor throughout the narrative, culminating in the scenes with the empress. The empress is seen as the Mother figure of all Russia, wise and warm, quick to understand and forgive and to come to the aid of her "children."

Frequently, in the course of the book, words and phrases refer to the Russian people as one large family; underlings call their masters and mistresses "Father" and "Mother," and the land is referred to as the Great Mother of them all. The empress and the land are inseparable. In the light of this powerful sentiment, the daring of Pougatcheff to attempt to usurp the throne becomes all the more shocking, as Pushkin intended, because to attack the throne is to attack all of Russia and to undermine the structure of the entire country.

The Captain's Daughter exerted a tremendous influence on Russian fiction; it showed novelists the possibilities of Russian themes and Russian settings, and, above all, it illustrated the narrative capabilities of the Russian language. Never before had Russian prose been used in fiction in such a lean, vigorous, and completely unpretentious manner. The perfection of the book was awesome but also inspiring to the writers who followed Pushkin. It can be said that the great period of Russian fiction begins with *The Captain's Daughter*. (The other great formative influence on Russian fiction, Nikolai Gogol's *Dead Souls*, did not appear until 1842.) The great tragedy for Russian literature and the world is that the year after writing this novel, Pushkin was killed at the age of thirty-seven in a duel.

THE CASTLE

Type of work: Novel
Author: Franz Kafka (1883–1924)
Type of plot: Philosophical and religious allegory
Time of plot: Anytime
Locale: Indefinite
First published: *Das Schloss,* 1926 (English translation, 1930)

In this unfinished novel, sometimes referred to as a modern Pilgrim's Progress, *K. seeks the grace of God to fulfill his life but finds his path beset with all the confusion of the modern world. His straightforward attack on the obstacles surrounding the castle and his unrelenting singleness of purpose are finally rewarded, but only at the moment of his death.*

Principal Characters

K., a young man seeking entrance to the castle. He is both puzzled and irritated by his inability to get to the castle where he had thought himself needed as a land surveyor. He never reaches the castle. Kafka intended, in a chapter planned but never written, to relate that K. was to be given permission to live and work in the village though not to enter the castle itself. K.'s efforts to reach the castle resemble Christian's struggle in *The Pilgrim's Progress* to reach the celestial city. Christian succeeded but K. did not.

Frieda, a fair-haired, sad-eyed, hollow-cheeked young barmaid; Klamm's mistress. She becomes K.'s fiancée and stays with him at the Bridge Inn and later at the schoolhouse. Jealous of his apparent interest in Olga and Amalia, she rejects K. for Jeremiah.

Barnabas, a white-clad young messenger who brings K. a letter from Klamm and introduces him to Barnabas' family. He is a servant at the castle.

Olga, his yellow-haired sister, a strapping girl with a hard-looking face. She shows kindness to K. and tells him much about the organization of the castle and about the village people.

Amalia, another sister who closely resembles both Olga and Barnabas.

Arthur, K.'s assistant, a slim, brown-skinned, jolly young man with a little pointed black beard, He and Jeremiah keep an almost constant watch on K.

Jeremiah, another assistant who looks so like Arthur that K., who says they are as alike as two snakes, calls him Arthur also.

Klamm, a chief at the castle who is often seen at the Herrenhof. He is plump, ponderous, and flabby-cheeked, and wears a pointed black mustache and a pince-nez.

Schwarzer, a young man who telephones the castle to check on K. He is in love with Gisa.

The Superintendent, a kindly, stout, clean-shaven man suffering from gout. He tries to explain to K. the intricacies of the management of the castle.

Gardana, the landlady at the Bridge Inn. She was once, briefly, Klamm's mistress.

Momus, the village secretary, a deputy of Klamm.

Gisa, the lady schoolteacher.

Sortini, a great official at the castle who once wrote an obscene letter to Amalia.

The Story

It was late in the evening when K. arrived in the town which lay before the castle of Count West-west. After his long walk through deep snow, K. wanted to do nothing so much as go to sleep. He went to an inn and fell asleep by the fire, only to be awakened by a man wanting to see his permit to stay in the town. K. explained that he had just arrived and that he had come at the count's request to be the new land surveyor. A telephone call to the castle established the fact that a land surveyor was expected. K. was allowed to rest in peace.

The next morning, although his assistant had not yet arrived, K. decided to go to the castle to report for duty. He set off through the snowy streets toward the castle, which as he walked seemed farther and farther away. After a while he became tired, and he stopped in a house for refreshment and directions. As he left the house, he saw two men coming from the castle. He tried to speak to them, but they refused to stop. As evening came on, K. got a ride back to the inn in a sledge.

At the inn, he met the two men he had seen coming from the castle. They introduced themselves as Arthur and Jeremiah and said that they were his old assistants. They were not, but K. accepted them, because he knew that they had come from the castle and therefore must have been sent to help him. Because the two men so greatly resembled each other, he could not tell the two men apart and therefore called them both Arthur. He ordered them to have a sledge to take him to the castle in the morning. When they refused, K. telephoned the castle. A voice told him that he could never come to the castle. Shortly afterward, a messenger named Barnabas arrived with a letter from Klamm, a chief at the castle. K. was ordered to report to the superintendent of the town.

K. arranged for a room in the inn. He asked Barnabas to let him go for a walk with him. Barnabas, a kind young man, agreed. He took K. to his home to meet his two sisters, Olga and Amalia, and his sickly old mother and father. K., however, was ill at ease; it was Barnabas, not he, who had come home. When Olga left to get some beer from a nearby inn, K. went with her. At the inn it was made clear that he would be welcome only in the bar. The other rooms were reserved for the gentlemen from the castle.

In the bar, K. quickly made friends with the barmaid, Frieda, who seemed to wish to save him from Olga and her family. She hid K. underneath the counter. K. did not understand what was happening. He learned that Frieda had been Klamm's mistress.

Frieda was determined to stay with K. from then on, if K. were willing. K. thought he might as well marry her. Determined to get through to the castle, he thought his chances would improve if he married a girl who had been a chief's mistress. Arthur and Jeremiah came into the room and watched them. K. sent the men away. Frieda decided to go to the inn where K. was staying.

K. went to call on the village superintendent, whom he found sick in bed with gout. K. learned from him that a land surveyor had been needed several years before but that nobody knew why K. had now come to fill the unnecessary post. When K. showed him Klamm's letter, the superintendent said that it was of no importance. The superintendent convinced him that his arrival in the town was a result of confusion. K. decided to remain and find work so that he could become an accepted citizen of the town.

By the time K. returned to the inn, Frieda had made his room comfortable. The schoolmaster came to offer K. the job of janitor at the school. At Frieda's insistence, K. accepted. That night K., Frieda, and the two assistants went to the school to live. The next morning, the assistants tricked K. into so many arguments with the teachers that K. dismissed both of them. After he had done his day's work, he slipped away from Frieda and went to Barnabas' house to see if he had received a message from the castle.

Barnabas was not at home. Olga explained that her family was an outcast group because of Amalia's refusal to become the mistress of one of the gentlemen of the castle. He had written her a very crude and obscene letter, which Amalia destroyed. Afterward the whole town had turned against them. K. was so interested in this story that he did not realize how late he had stayed. When he finally got ready to go, he saw that Jeremiah was outside spying on him.

K. slipped out the back way but came back down the street and asked Jeremiah why he was there. The man sullenly answered that Frieda had sent him. She had gone back to her old job at the tavern and never wanted to see K. again. Barnabas came up with the news that one of the most important men from the castle was waiting at the tavern to see K.

At the tavern, he learned that the gentleman had gone to sleep. As he stood in the hall, he saw Frieda going down another corridor. He ran after her to explain why he had stayed away so long with Olga, and he asked her to come back to him. Just as she seemed to relent, Jeremiah came from one of the rooms and persuaded Frieda to go with him. Frieda left K. forever.

At this point, the novel in its published form ends, and for the rest of the story we have only the few statements made by Kafka to his friends in conversation. K. was to continue his fight to live and work in the town and eventually to reach the castle. On his deathbed, he was to receive a call from the castle, a message granting him the right to live in the town in peace.

Critical Evaluation

The reader's efforts to approach Kakfa's last, longest, and most enigmatic novel prove no more successful than those of its elliptically named hero, K., to reach the castle for which it is named. Critics have read *The Castle* as religious allegory, as existential novel, as modernist text, as autobiography. The novel's dreamlike setting—out of time and space, distant yet disconcertingly close at hand (with telephones and electric lights)—invites this multiplicity of interpretive approaches on the part of both readers and characters. Against the village's blank snowscape, K. and the villagers seize and elaborate upon the few facts available to them, adding their own interpretive explanations in such a way as to make all efforts to distinguish fact from fiction problematic. Similar to the midrash practiced by Hebrew scholars who flesh out gaps in the biblical narrative with commentary that then becomes part of the narrative, Kafka's technique transforms the novel into less a network of meanings than a field of interpretive possibilities, in which it becomes as impossible as it is necessary to determine where the phenomenological castle "itself" leaves off and where the characters' conceptions and commentaries about it begin.

The novel poses a large number of unresolvable anti-nomies–castle and village, of course, as well as the village and the vague world from which K. comes, God and man, spirit and flesh, ideal and real, male and female, father and son, authority and freedom, order and accident—and as such poses for the reader the question of precisely where to place interpretive stress in so decentered a work and so decentered a world. Desperate for meaning, characters and readers alike grasp at whatever is at hand, giving it a meaning it may or may not have and turning it into the Ptolemaic center around which all else must, at least momentarily, revolve. This narrative relativism manifests itself in the way in which everything in the novel, even the simplest description, includes its opposite or at least the possibility of its opposite. Everything is qualified so that even the omnipotent castle itself may be nothing more than "a manner of speaking." Reaching into every corner of *The Castle,* the irony turns on itself—at least potentially—causing the reader to feel about the novel the way one character, Olga, feels about her sister, Amalia. "It's not easy to follow her, for often one can't tell whether she's speaking ironically or in earnest. Mostly she's in earnest but sounds ironical."

Given such a world, K.'s confusion is understandable, yet he too is ambiguously presented. He is the existential outsider, precursor of Roquentin in Jean-Paul Sartre's *Nausea* (1938) and Meursault in Albert Camus' *The Stranger* (1942), but he is also the comic schlemiel of Jewish fiction, who speaks with great authority despite his ignorance and who often ends his speeches by running away from his audience. Even his status as existential outsider proves double; he is ignorant of what the villagers know, yet privileged in that he is not blinded by the habits and myths by which they live.

K. questions and asserts, doubts and demands. Meanwhile, the castle remains remote and impregnable—the fit symbol of all that lies mysteriously beyond the merely human. Because it has no single, definable meaning—in fact, it may have no meaning at all—the castle can mean everything. It can be both peace and pandemonium, origin and projection, refuge and refusal; it is imperfect, even incompetent, in the workings of its functionaries, yet ultimately perfect and omnipotent in "itself." It is the perfect object of desire—the source, or home, where all is explained, decided, final—but its perfection depends upon its being forever unattainable. Thus, the castle represents not only the fulfillment K. desires but its opposite as well: the frustration of a perfect futility, fueled by K.'s discontent over the bleakness of the world in which he lives (a bleakness perceived against the contrasting background of the idealized castle). The circularity of K.'s quest becomes even more apparent when one considers that K. not only regards the castle as the source of his own identity; he also demands that the castle tell him that he is the land surveyor that he says he is.

He demands that it validate his existence and validate, too, the identity for which he prefers not to have to take responsibility.

If the castle did not exist it would have to be invented, which is to say imagined, projected, hypothesized. Life without hope of its existence and its power to validate is unimaginable for the villagers and, to a slightly lesser extent, for K. as well. They must believe in its existence in order to believe in their own. Further, they must believe in its arbitrary system of rewards and punishments in order not to have to confront their own insignificance—indeed, their invisibility—and, most disconcerting, their freedom. It is precisely this meaningless freedom—the very center of Sartre's later existentialism—which they reject in order to have their existences certified for them. They long to be named, even as wrongdoer, rather than see themselves as they are, or at least as they may be: unnecessary, even superfluous. Dismayingly, this feeling and this fear cause the characters to enact among themselves the system of inequality which they experience in all their dealings with the castle: exerting arbitrary power over an inferior other, whose worth and sometimes even whose existence they simply deny.

What is terrifying and yet so comical about K. and the others is precisely their capacity for hope, coupled with their inability to act in any way other than absurdly. The apparent baselessness of their hope is, however, the very basis of their faith and, of course, of their absurdity. The castle toward which, as well as against which, K. struggles may be a spiritual fact or a psychological delusion. Both possibilities exist; neither can be eliminated or denied, and it is from this intolerable coexistence that the novel derives much of its power to unsettle. "For the extremely ridiculous and the extremely serious are not far removed from each other." In the ending Kafka projected for this unfinished, perhaps unfinishable novel, K., worn down by the struggle and now on his deathbed, learns that although he has no right to stay in the village, the castle will now permit him to remain. Thus does Kafka's labyrinthine novel come full circle, leaving K. where he began: without any rights, without any hope of appeal, without either an identity (other than that of stranger) or a name (other than his lone initial), and still at the mercy of the whimsical (or, alternately, benevolent) castle. K. remains what he has been: inexplicably and existentially just there, perplexed yet persistent, paradoxically so. "What could have enticed me to this desolate country except the wish to stay here?" His wish granted, K. is now free to die, but whether he will die deluded or redeemed (his persistence rewarded), it is impossible to say. This much, however, is clear: In the world according to Kafka, belief has grown increasingly suspect, the prospect of life without faith terrifyingly bleak, and the individual absurdly, tragicomically free.

THE CID

Type of work: Drama
Author: Pierre Corneille (1606–1684)
Type of plot: Romantic tragedy
Time of plot: Eleventh century
Locale: Seville
First presented: 1636

Generally ranked as the best of Corneille's works, this tragedy is considered by many scholars to be the beginning of modern French drama. The playwright reputedly used as his source Guillén de Castro y Bellvis' treatment of the Cid legends, which form the basis of Spain's great medieval epic poem.

Principal Characters

Don Rodrigue (rô·drēg'), the Cid, son of aged Don Diègue. As his father's champion, he kills Don Gomès, mightiest swordsman of Castile. It appears he may eventually marry Chimène.

Don Diègue (dyĕg'), once Spain's greatest warrior.

Chimène (shē·mĕn'), the daughter of the slain Don Gomès, who demands Rodrigue's death in punishment. Later, when he determines to let Sanche kill him, she begs Rodrigue to defend himself.

Don Gomès (gô·mĕs'), the father of Chimène, who quarrels with Diègue over tutoring the king's son and is slain by Rodrigue.

Don Fernand (fĕr·nän'), king of Castile, who names Rodrigue "The Cid" (Lord) after his victory over the Moors in Seville.

Don Sanche (sänsh), a suitor of Chimène who challenges Rodrigue to avenge Gomès' death. The Cid magnanimously spares his life.

Doña Urraque (ü·räk'), the daughter of Fernand, who loves Rodrigue but yields to Chimène's prior claims.

The Story

Because she was the princess royal, the Infanta felt she could not openly love Rodrigue, a nobleman of lower rank. She encouraged, therefore, the growing attachment between Chimène and Rodrigue. Chimène asked her father, Don Gomès, to choose for his son-in-law either Rodrigue or Sanche. She awaited the choice anxiously; her father was on his way to court, and she would soon hear his decision. Don Gomès chose Rodrigue without hesitation, chiefly because of the fame of Don Diègue, Rodrigue's father.

A complication soon arose at court. The king had chosen Don Diègue as preceptor for his son, the heir apparent. Don Gomès felt that the choice was unjust. Don Diègue had been the greatest warrior in Castile, but he was now old. Don Gomès considered himself the doughtiest knight in the kingdom. In a bitter quarrel Don Gomès unjustly accused Don Diègue of gaining the king's favor through flattery and deceit. He felt the prince needed a preceptor who would be a living example, not a teacher who would dwell in the past. In the quarrel, Don Gomès slapped his older rival. Don Diègue, too feeble to draw his sword against Don Gomès, upbraided himself bitterly for having to accept the insult. His only recourse was to call on his young son to uphold the family honor.

Torn between love and duty, Rodrigue challenged Don Gomès to a duel. After some hesitation because of Rodrigue's youth and unproved valor, Don Gomès accepted the challenge of his daughter's suitor. To the surprise of the court, Rodrigue, the untried novice, killed the mightiest man in Castile, piercing with his sword the man whom he respected as his future father-in-law.

Chimène now felt herself in a desperate plight because her love for Rodrigue was mixed with hatred for the murderer of her father. She finally decided to avenge her father by seeking justice from the king. Since she had the right to petition the king, Don Fernand was forced to hear her pleas. In the scene at court, Don Diègue made a strong counter-plea for his son, reminding the king that Rodrigue had done only what honor forced him to do—uphold the family name.

The king was saved from the vexing decision when fierce Moors assaulted the walls of Seville. Chimène awaited the outcome of the battle with mixed emotions. The army of Castile returned in triumph, bringing as captives two Moorish kings. And the man who had inspired and led the Castilians by his audacity was Rodrigue. The grateful king gave the hero a new title, The Cid, a Moorish name meaning "lord." The Infanta was wretched. Although her high position would not allow her to love Rodrigue, she could love The Cid, a high noble and the hero of Castile. She showed her nobility by yielding to Chimène's prior right.

Chimène was still bound to seek redress. The king resolved to test her true feelings. When she entered the throne room, he told her gravely that Rodrigue had died from battle wounds. Chimène fainted. The king advised her to follow the promptings of her heart and cease her quest for vengeance.

Still holding duty above love, however, Chimène insisted on her feudal right of a champion. Sanche, hoping to win the favor of Chimène, offered to meet Rodrigue in mortal combat and avenge the death of Don Gomès. Chimène accepted him as her champion. The king decreed that Chimène must marry the victor.

In private, Rodrigue came to Chimène. Indignant at first, Chimène soon softened when she learned that Rodrigue had resolved to let himself be killed because

she wished it. Again wavering between love and duty, Chimène begged him to defend himself as best he could.

Sanche went bravely to meet Rodrigue who easily disarmed his opponent and showed his magnanimity by refusing to kill Chimène's champion. He sent his sword to Chimène in token of defeat. As soon as Chimène saw her champion approach with Rodrigue's sword in his hand, she immediately thought that Rodrigue was dead. She ran in haste to the king and begged him to change his edict because she could not bear to wed the slayer of her lover. When the king told her the truth, that Rodrigue had won, Don Diègue praised her for at last avowing openly her love. Still Chimène hesitated to take Rodrigue as her husband. The king understood her plight. He ordered The Cid to lead an expedition against the Moors. He knew that time would heal the breach between the lovers. The king was wise.

Critical Evaluation

The neoclassical tragedies of seventeenth century France are especially in need of introductions for a modern audience; Corneille's *The Cid* only a little less than most. The Renaissance had seen, among other things, an intensification of interest in the individual and in the self. This focusing of interest (amounting almost to a vision of the nature of man) was in conflict with the medieval view which perceived of man more as a race than as an individual. The individual was perceived, to be sure, but perceived as something like a component of society, reproducing it and assuring its integrity by maintaining binding interrelationships with other individual members of society both alive and dead. In Corneille's time, the more romantic tenets of the Renaissance had been displaced by the neoclassical adoption of the life of reason and order within a cohesive community; and with this life there came, understandably, a high regard for honor.

The twentieth century does not easily understand the classical and neoclassical concern for "honor" because our age is essentially a romantic one; our concerns are primarily for the immediate future and the physically alive, concerns of the individual. Romantic love, concerning itself as it does with physically alive individuals and their immediate futures, is of extreme importance to us. But honor is based not upon immediacy or subjectivity but upon loyalty to others (particularly those to whom one is related by blood ties, marriage, or a shared set of cultural assumptions) and concern for the opinions of others. It is not merely a matter of respectfully but radically differing with one's fellows on moral questions; one's fellows are a part of oneself; to differ radically with them is to be schizophrenic. The task then, in living a life of honor, is to live it so that others approve. For if others do not approve, no man (or woman) in such an age can approve of himself.

This is the situation of *The Cid*. The Infanta's dilemma is the keynote of the play; she must choose between her romantic love for Rodrigue (to whom she is impelled by her feelings as an individual) and her honor (as demanded by her ties to her father and her attendant position in society). Love urges that she make herself available for marriage to him, but honor insists that she not marry beneath her station. She chooses honor almost instinctively, even going so far as to take direct action to decrease her own romantic love; she brings Rodrigue and Chimène together so as to make him completely unavailable to herself as a lover. In act 5 she almost succumbs to love, thinking Rodrigue's newly won glories and title bring him nearly to her social station, but her lady in waiting (acting as her visible conscience on the stage) dissuades her. She goes on to aid in the final reconciliation of the principal pair.

Rodrigue and Chimène each must make the same choice, though their positions differ from the Infanta's in that theirs are seemingly impossible. While the Infanta's problem admits of the simplest (though not the easiest) of solutions, that of not declaring her love, Rodrigue cannot expect a loving response from the daughter of the man he has killed, and Chimène cannot give such a response. Both are acting in a typically honorable fashion, maintaining their fathers' reputations and foregoing their personal desires. To do less would be to make themselves less than human. Honor threatens the love affair of Chimène and Rodrigue, while love threatens the honor of the Infanta.

It will seem to some readers that love wins out in the end over honor, the honorable scruples of the principal pair having been overcome by reason and circumstances. But in fact love and honor are synthesized, neither force canceling out the other. The Infanta's moral position, being above reproach, is perfect for her role as a proponent of marriage for the pair. Had she surrendered to her own emotion, she could not have been nearly so effective a spokesperson on the part of love for others. Add to this Elvira's chiding and, indeed, the king himself in the role of matchmaker, and it will be seen that Corneille is at some pains to overcome excessive preoccupation with honor, but only in such a way as to leave real honor intact and alive.

Until we reach the denouement—Chimène's admission of her love—the heroine sees herself primarily as the daughter of Don Gomès; her admission of her feelings to the king and the resolution of the play are made possible by her being persuaded to see herself primarily as a member of the Castilian community. As a result of this shift in her perception of her role, she no longer sees Rodrigue as enemy and begins to see the Moors in that capacity. As principal bulwark against the common enemy, Rodrigue both lays the groundwork for this change in Chimène and is in a unique position to enjoy the benefits of it. Thus, while upholding the concept of honor in a humanly achievable form, the play uses a typically romantic process as the underpinnings of its plot: thesis and antithesis (honor and love) are synthesized.

Critics have seen in this play certain basic similarities to Shakespeare's *Romeo and Juliet*, foremost among which is the feud between the lovers' families. But a more essential similarity lies in the use of death by both dramatists as a threat to young love. Both Romeo and Rodrigue think of death (for themselves) as a solution to their problems, and both offer the solution with such alacrity as to give rise to speculations of a death wish on both their parts. Such speculations, however, have the distinct disadvantage of focusing our attention entirely upon the character, causing us to ignore the play's overall design.

Death is not initially the preoccupation of either hero. Both want simply to marry the ladies they love. Death presents itself to them as a solution only when this desire becomes both undeniable and impossible to satisfy. This renders life impossible, and when life begins to seem impossible the natural impulse is to consign it to a state of nonexistence (the natural state for any impossibility). Death is the inevitable threat. But death becomes truly inevitable only when the character is convinced that his life is indeed impossible, that there is no way out. Romeo is convinced of this on two occasions; Rodrigue repeatedly offers himself to Chimène for execution, believing there is no other solution.

Death, then, is not intrinsic to Rodrigue's character; it is a force from without, threatening the healthy love relationship with the ferocity of a tangible monster. There is a level at which most love comedies are fertility rites, celebrating and promoting the optimism and fecundity of a society. In such comedies the lovers' eventual wedding (or promise of one) affirms this social optimism. But when optimism and fertility are seriously threatened by death, as they are in this play, we revise our classification of the play and call it a "tragicomedy." The play ends happily with the promise of a marriage, the protagonists having avoided death's many invasions into their happiness. But death's attempts were persistent, and were overcome by the slimmest of margins.

The Cid is Corneille's first major play and is today often considered his finest. His plays are often compared with those of his younger contemporary, Racine. Both authors adhered strictly to the neoclassical unities (action, time, and place), though Racine evidently worked more comfortably within those restrictions; Corneille reminds us throughout *The Cid* that the action occurs within one day, but the day is an unnaturally full one.

COLLECTED POEMS, 1934–1952

Type of work: Poetry
Author: Dylan Thomas (1914–1953)
First published: 1952

When Dylan Thomas died at the age of thirty-nine he was, for a poet in the twentieth century, extraordinarily popular. His poetry had been read and admired for years; a paean of praise greeted his collected works, and still more appreciation was accorded him after his death. However, many reputable critics, fellow poets, and general readers have disliked, derided, and dismissed his work on the grounds that it is merely sibylline raving. These contradictory reactions are explained by the fact that Thomas was primarily a violently emotional poet. The strength of his feelings thus either forcibly attracts or repels his readers.

The poems make an emotional impact, on first reading, that subsequent analyses will not displace. With the exception of Ezra Pound, Thomas is probably the most obscure of the prominent poets of this century. Whether he is a major or a minor poet will be established only by the evaluation of critics in the future, as no contemporary can have the necessary perspective to place a poet accurately in such a hierarchy.

A poet who is both very obscure and very popular is an anomaly. Thomas is not in this position by virtue of belonging to a particular school of verse, nor by writing in a recognized poetic convention. Nor is he socially or politically committed. His poetry is an affirmation of life: "These poems are written for the love of man and in praise of God, and I'd be a damn' fool if they weren't." The truth of this assertion in the introductory note to his volume of collected verse is shown in every successful poem that he wrote. His early poetry is egocentric; he was writing of his own private feelings in these poems of birth, death, and sex, and the glory he found in these themes was entirely personal. His later poems show a far wider human interest and an increasing concern for mankind.

Throughout his work a unity of vision is apparent. He sees death in birth and resurrection in death. He is aware of the hate in all love and of the power of love to transcend suffering. He comprehends the simultaneous glory and corruption in life, and the fact that all forms of life are interdependent and inseparable. "I see the boys of summer" is a dialogue between the young poet who sees the destruction of the future in the present, and the adolescent boys living their first passionate and confusing loves. The successive images of light and dark, heat and cold, throughout the poem emphasize this contrast. The poem is filled with pleasure and pain conjoined, and with gain and loss. The polarity of these emotions is explicitly stated in the final, joyful image:

> O see the poles are kissing as they cross.

"If I were tickled by the rub of love" is a difficult poem, to be understood by remembering the comprehensiveness of Thomas' idea of life. In the context of the poem, "tickled" appears to mean completely involved with, or wholly absorbed by, but the term necessarily retains the connotations of amusement and enjoyment. "Rub," as well as having sensual implications, also means doubt, difficulty, or strain. The poet says that if he were "tickled by the rub of love," he would not fear the fall from Eden or the flood; if he were "tickled" by the birth of a child, he would not fear death or war. Desire is spoken of as devilish and is provoked by

> . . . the drug that's smoking in a girl
> And curling round the bud that forks her eye.

This harsh image is followed by a statement of the poet's consciousness that he carries his own old age and death already within him.

> An old man's shank one-marrowed with my bone,
> And all the herrings smelling in the sea,
> I sit and watch the worm beneath my nail
> Wearing the quick away.

The feeling of fear is strong, and neither love, sex, beauty, nor birth is the "rub"; the solution is in wholeness or unity:

> I would be tickled by the love that is:
> Man be my metaphor.

Thomas' poetical development is unusual in that the thought in his later poems is usually not at all obscure. These poems are also less clotted with material; there are fewer esoteric symbols; ideas are developed at greater length, and tension is relaxed. The close attention to rhythm and structure persists, and the evocative power of his language is enhanced. Thomas' genius lay in the brilliant and highly personal use of the words with which his penetrating perception is communicated. The ambiguity of his language parallels the reciprocal nature of his images. He delights in punning and the various meanings of a word or image will often reverberate throughout an entire stanza.

"Poem on his birthday" is a good example of Thomas' method. The last poems are often, as this one is, set in the Welsh countryside. The heron is always in his poems a religious or priestly symbol. In the first stanza "herons spire and spear"; in the third, "herons walk in their shroud," and in the ninth he writes of the "druid herons' vows" and of his "tumbledown tongue"—this last a beautifully fused image of the action of the tongue of a pealing bell and the impetuous voice of the poet. In the tenth stanza he speaks of the "nimbus bell" which is a magical goal. By this use of compound images Thomas explores and thoroughly penetrates his subject. All aspects of the experience are involved, and pain, happiness, grief, and joy are equally present in this expression of unified sensibility.

This inclusive view of the universe is sometimes incoherent in his early poems, sometimes illuminating. One of the finest of his early poems is titled "The force that through the green fuse drives the flower." The symbolism here is not obscure and the emotions are controlled by the form of the poem. The third line of each of the four five-line stanzas has only three or four words and is the main clause of the three-line sentence in which the theme of each stanza is stated. The last two lines of each stanza begin with the words "And I am dumb. . . ." After the dramatic first two lines the short solemn third lines ready the reader for the equally forceful antithesis. The poem ends with a rhyming couplet:

> And I am dumb to tell the lover's tomb,
> How at my sheet goes the same crooked
>   worm.

The theme of the poem is that the forces of nature are the same as those that drive man and that these forces both create and destroy. The careful structure of this poem is typical of Thomas' craftsmanship. He has been called undisciplined. He is not, but his unfettered imagination can confuse his meaning and his symbolism remains, in spite of painstaking analysis, almost inexplicable.

The sonnet sequence, "Altarwise by owl-light," is Thomas' most difficult poetry. The sonnets contain lines and passages of great beauty, and the overall movement, from horror and suffering toward the idea of the redemption of man by the Resurrection of Christ after the Crucifixion, is clear. But the sequence as a whole remains too compressed and fragmentary to be successful. Thomas has failed mainly to communicate the bases of the intense suffering and hope that he so obviously felt.

In "After the funeral," an elegy for a cousin, Ann Jones, Thomas expresses both his own grief and the character of the dead woman. It is, as the poet points out, written with a magniloquence that exceeds the subject's,

> Though this for her is a monstrous image blindly
> Magnified out of praise. . . .

This manner contrasts so sharply with the humble and suffering woman that the poignancy of the portrait is increased. His grief

> Shakes a desolate boy who slit his throat
> In the dark of the coffin and sheds dry leaves.

The clear-sighted description of the woman after the expression of such grief is very moving:

> I know her scrubbed and sour humble hands
> Lie with religion in their cramp, her thread-bare
> Whisper in a damp word, her wits drilled hollow,
> Her fist of a face died clenched on a round pain.

The sonnet sequence and the elegy give some indication of Thomas' later themes, where religious faith and a concern for mankind are evident.

During the second world war Thomas spent several years in London, where he was deeply moved by German air raids on the city. This reaction is very clear in his fourth volume, *Deaths and Entrances*. The well-known "A refusal to Mourn the Death, by Fire, of a Child in London" is both an affirmation of Christian faith and an expression of cold fury at such a death. The poet feels that the event was too great for grief and that no elegy should be written for the child until the end of the world. Writing of grief at the time would be as if to murder her again:

> I shall not murder
> The mankind of her going with a grave truth.

The child is representative of all mankind and of all London's dead, a view which gives her a certain greatness:

> Deep with the first dead lies London's daughter.

The last line of the poem is ambivalent; it communicates both the irrevocability, finality, and cruelty of death and the Christian belief of the deathlessness of the soul:

> After the first death there is no other.

After the war Thomas was concerned with recapturing in his poetry the world of his childhood. The rhythm of these poems is more relaxed and flowing than that of his early work, and the landscapes are glowing and full of color and wonder. These lyrics are poems in praise of the created world. Thomas' skill with words and rhythm evokes the whole Welsh countryside, and his unique imaginative vision makes the places his own. He has here communicated his great reverence and love of life. The unified vision of life remains, and Thomas is still aware of the presence of death in life, although this is no longer a cause of anguish as it was in the early poems.

In "Fern Hill," Thomas describes his youth on a farm.

He has re-created youthful feeling that the whole world was his; there is an atmosphere of timelessness, a lulling of the consciousness of time's destruction, which the poet in recapturing his youthful feeling has conveyed without negating his manhood's knowledge.

Dylan Thomas was a highly emotional poet whose lyrics express a unified vision of life. His poetry contains many of the aspects of birth and death, fear, grief, joy, and beauty. From the violent, anguished poems of his youth, his power over his "craft or sullen art" increased until he was able to channel his special mode of feeling in ways which enabled him to speak for all men:

> And you shall wake, from country sleep, this
>   dawn and each first dawn,
> Your faith as deathless as the outcry of the
>   ruled sun.

THE COMEDY OF ERRORS

Type of work: Drama
Author: William Shakespeare (1564–1616)
Type of plot: Comedy
Time of plot: First century B.C.
Locale: Ancient Greece
First presented: c. 1592

The Comedy of Errors is a farce-comedy bordering at times on slapstick. The basic plot, inherently confusing, involves two sets of twins and a family, separated for years, which is reunited at last in court. For his sources in this play, Shakespeare used The Twin Menaechmi *of the Roman playwright Plautus, and perhaps Plautus'* Amphitryon *as well.*

Principal Characters

Antipholus of Syracuse (ăn·tĭf'ō·lŭs of sĭr'ə·kūs), the son of Aegeon and Aemilia. Separated from his twin brother in his childhood, he meets him again under the most baffling circumstances. Shortly after he and his servant, Dromio of Syracuse, land in Ephesus, the whole series of comic errors begins. Antipholus meets his servant's lost twin brother, who is also bewildered by the ensuing conversation. Thinking this Dromio to be his own servant, Antipholus belabors the mystified man about his pate with great vigor. Finally, at the end, the puzzle is solved when he recognizes that he has found his identical twin.

Antipholus of Ephesus (ĕf'ĕ·sŭs), the identical twin brother of Antipholus of Syracuse. Equally bewildered by his mishaps, he is disgruntled when his wife locks him out of his house; she is blissfully unaware of the truth—that the man in her house is not her husband. In addition, a purse of money is received by the wrong man. Never having seen his own father, or at least not aware of the relationship, he is even more amazed when the old man calls him son. By this time the entire town believes him to be mad, and he, like his twin, is beginning to think that he is bewitched. It is with great relief that he finally learns the true situation and is reunited with his family.

Dromio of Syracuse (drō'mĭ·ō), the twin brother to Dromio of Ephesus and attendant to Antipholus of Syracuse. He is as much bewildered as his master, who, in the mix-up, beats both Dromios. To add to his misery, a serving wench takes him for *her* Dromio and makes unwanted advances. Much to his chagrin, she is "no longer from head to foot than from hip to hip. She is spherical, like a globe. . . ."

Dromio of Ephesus. When the two Antipholi were separated during a shipwreck, he, too, was separated from his identical twin. As is his brother, he is often drubbed by his master. In this case, if his master does not pummel him, his mistress will perform the same office. During all this time he is involved in many cases of mistaken identity. Sent for a piece of rope, he is amazed when his supposed master knows nothing of the transaction.

Aegeon (ē·jē'ŏn), a merchant of Syracuse. Many years before, he had lost his beloved wife and one son. Since then, his other son has left home to find his twin brother. Now Aegeon is searching for all his family. Landing in Ephesus, he finds that merchants from Syracuse are not allowed there on penalty of death or payment of a large ransom; the duke gives the old man a one-day reprieve. He finds his sons just in time, the ransom is paid, and the family is reunited.

Adriana (ā·drĭ·ānə), the wife of Antipholus of Ephesus. When her husband denies his relationship to her, she (unaware that he is the wrong man) thinks he is insane. Already suspicious of her husband because of supposed infidelities, she suspects him even more.

Aemilia (ē·mĭl'ĭ·ə), the wife of Aegeon, and abbess at Ephesus. In the recognition scene she finds her husband, who has been separated from her for many years.

Solinus (sō·lī'nŭs), duke of Ephesus.

Luciana (lōō·shē·ä'nə), Adriana's sister, wooed by Antipholus of Syracuse.

Angelo (ăn'jĕ·lō), a goldsmith.

Pinch, a schoolmaster, "a hungry lean-fac'd villain, a mere anatomy."

The Story

Aegeon, a merchant of Syracuse recently arrived in Ephesus, was to be put to death because he could not raise a thousand marks for payment of his fine. The law of the time was that a native of either land must not journey to the other on penalty of his life or the ransom of a thousand marks. When Solinus, duke of Ephesus, heard Aegeon's story, however, he gave the merchant one more day to try to raise the money.

It was a sad and strange tale Aegeon told. He had, many years ago, journeyed to Epidamnum. Shortly after his wife joined him there she was delivered of identical twins. Strangely enough, at the same time and in the same house, another woman also bore twin boys, both identical. The second wife and her husband were so poor that they could not care for their children, and so they gave them to Aegeon and his wife Aemilia, to be attendants to their two sons. On their way home to Syracuse, the six were shipwrecked. Aemilia and the two with her were rescued by one ship, Aegeon and the other two by a different ship. Aegeon did not see his wife and the two children in her company again. When he reached eighteen years of age, Antipholus, the son reared by his father, grew anxious to find his brother, and he and his attendant set out to find their missing twins. Now they too were lost to Aegeon, and he had come to Syracuse to seek them.

Unknown to Aegeon, his son and his attendant had just arrived in Ephesus. Antipholus and Dromio, his attendant, met first a merchant of the city, who warned them to say that they came from somewhere other than Syracuse, lest they suffer the penalty already meted out to Aegeon. Antipholus, having sent Dromio to find lodging for them, was utterly bewildered when the servant returned and said that Antipholus' wife waited dinner for him. What had happened was that the Dromio who came now to Antipholus was Dromio of Ephesus, servant and attendant to Antipholus of Ephesus. Antipholus of Syracuse had given his Dromio money to pay for lodging, and when he heard a tale of a wife about whom he knew nothing he thought his servant was trying to trick him. He asked the servant to return his money, but Dromio of Ephesus had been given no money and professed no knowledge of the sum. He was beaten soundly for dishonesty. Antipholus of Syracuse later heard that his money had been delivered to the inn; he could not understand his servant's joke.

A short time later, the wife and sister-in-law of Antipholus of Ephesus met Antipholus of Syracuse and, after berating him for refusing to come home to dinner, accused him of unfaithfulness with another woman. Not understanding a thing of which Adriana spoke, Antipholus of Syracuse went to her home to dinner, Dromio being assigned by her to guard the gate and allow no one to enter. Thus it was that Antipholus of Ephesus arrived at his home with his Dromio and was refused admittance. So incensed was he that he left his house and went to an inn. There he dined with a courtesan and gave her gifts intended for his wife.

In the meantime Antipholus of Syracuse, even though almost believing that he must be the husband of Adriana, fell in love with her sister Luciana. When he told her of his love, she called him an unfaithful husband and begged him to remain true to his wife. Dromio of Syracuse was pursued by a kitchen maid whom he abhorred; the poor girl mistook him for Dromio of Ephesus, who loved her.

Even the townspeople and merchants were bewildered. A goldsmith delivered to Antipholus of Syracuse a chain meant for Antipholus of Ephesus and then tried to collect from the latter, who in turn stated that he had received no chain and accused the merchant of trying to rob him.

Antipholus and Dromio of Syracuse decided to get out of the seemingly mad town as soon as possible, and the servant was sent to book passage on the first ship leaving the city. Dromio of Syracuse brought back the news of the sailing, however, to Antipholus of Ephesus, who by that time had been arrested for refusing to pay the merchant for the chain he had not received. Antipholus of Ephesus, believing the servant to be his own, sent Dromio of Syracuse to his house to get money for his bail. Before that Dromio returned with the money, Dromio of Ephesus came to Antipholus of Ephesus, naturally without the desired money. Meanwhile, Dromio of Syracuse took the money to Antipholus of Syracuse, who had not sent for money and could not understand what his servant was talking about. To make matters worse, the courtesan with whom Antipholus of Ephesus had dined had given him a ring. Now she approached the other Antipholus and demanded the ring. Knowing nothing about the ring, he angrily dismissed the wench, who decided to go to his house and tell his wife of his betrayal.

On his way to jail for the debt he did not owe, Antipholus of Ephesus met his wife. Wild with rage, he accused her of locking him out of his own house and of refusing him his own money for bail. She was so frightened that she asked the police first to make sure that he was securely bound and then to imprison him in their home so that she could care for him.

At the same time, Antipholus and Dromio of Syracuse were making their way toward the ship that would carry them away from this mad city. Antipholus was wearing the gold chain. The merchant, meeting them, demanded that Antipholus be arrested. To escape, Antipholus of Syracuse and his Dromio fled into an abbey. To the same abbey came Aegeon, the duke, and the executioners, for Aegeon had not raised the money for his ransom. Adriana and Luciana also appeared, demanding the release to them of Adriana's husband and his servant. Adriana, seeing the two men take refuge in the convent, thought they were Antipholus and Dromio of Ephesus. At that instant a servant ran in to tell Adriana that her husband and Dromio had escaped from the house and were even now on the way to the abbey. Adriana did not believe the servant, for she herself had seen her husband and Dromio enter the abbey. Then Antipholus and Dromio of Ephesus appeared before the abbey. Aegeon thought he recognized the son and servant he had been seeking, but they denied any knowledge of him. The confusion grew worse until the abbess brought from the convent Antipholus and

Dromio of Syracuse, who instantly recognized Aegeon. Then all the mysteries were solved. Adriana was reunited with her husband, Antipholus of Ephesus, and his Dromio had the kitchen maid once more. Antipholus of Syracuse was free to make love to Luciana. His Dromio was merely

freed. Still more surprising, the abbess turned out to be Aegeon's wife, the mother of the Antipholi. So the happy family was together again. Lastly, Antipholus of Ephesus paid his father's ransom and brought to an end all the errors of that unhappy day.

Critical Evaluation

The Comedy of Errors is not a subtle play. Although it is well constructed and highly amusing, it never really rises above the level of farce, largely because its characters remain the stock figures of traditional low comedy and exhibit none of the individual touches and personalities of Shakespeare's later characters. The humor of the play is broad, both in action and in language. These facts have caused many to see *The Comedy of Errors* as Shakespeare's first comedy, a work of genius perhaps, but of apprentice genius. To support this conjecture it should be noted that this is his shortest play in number of lines, and one of only two comedies without songs; the other is *All's Well That Ends Well*, another play which does not quite fit into the traditional framework.

The plot of *The Comedy of Errors* was taken from the Latin New Comedy farce by Plautus, *The Twin Menaechimi*, which follows the misadventures of identical twins separated at birth. In Shakespeare's comedy, these are the two brothers who share the name Antipholus. Shakespeare also borrowed from another of Plautus' plays, *Amphitryon*, for a second set of separated twins, the Dromio brothers, servants to the Antipholi. This doubling of twins and the confusions which result constitute almost the sole comic resources of the play.

In adapting the Plautine comedy, Shakespeare made a number of telling changes. He greatly softened the coarse, satirical approach of the ancient Roman farce, placing less emphasis on sexual gibes and more on witty wordplay. He was also more sympathetic and original with his characters; even as broadly drawn as Shakespeare's figures are in this work, they have much more life and appeal than the characters of Plautus. The two Antipholi are certainly not well-rounded persons, but they can be distinguished from one another: The brother from Syracuse is the more thoughtful of the two, while his Ephesian brother is a hardheaded businessman. Another change: Plautus had the twins' father die of grief over their loss, while Shakespeare keeps Aegeon and his wife alive so the family can be reunited at play's end. In these and numerous other touches, Shakespeare made the rough texture of his source more appealing and accessible.

Still, the play is a comedy of events rather than characters, and the humor springs from situations which are often bizarre or outrageous. *The Comedy of Errors* is heavily dependent upon two staples of much Elizabethan comedy, and indeed all broad comedy: wordplay and physical cruelty. The cruelty is humorous precisely because the characters are not individuals but only clowns, and

the numerous beatings administered to the bewildered Dromios are laughable since no real pain is inflicted. The verbal repartee, based on quibbles, puns, and feigned mistakings, is a central technique in Shakespeare, and in this play appears in its obvious forms; the lengthy exchange between Antipholus of Syracuse and his Dromio in act 2, scene 2 is typical. While these exchanges are amusing, they lack the linguistic energy and sustained intelligence of Shakespeare's later plays.

The genius of *The Comedy of Errors* is not, then, in its characters or language but rather in the deftness of its plot and the fast-paced perfection of its action. In addition to the basic situation of the play, Shakespeare brought from Plautus many of the conventions of this particular type of comedy; chief among these was that no character move beyond his or her role. On the most obvious level, this means that until the very end of the play, the characters never learn what the audience knows from the start; if they possessed such knowledge, there could be no misunderstandings and therefore no play. On a deeper level, adherence to this convention means that no character can assume a dominant role, either by having a superior knowledge of events (as Prospero does in *The Tempest*) or by possessing a more generous character (as Rosalind does in *As You Like It*). Since precisely such a situation is brilliantly created and then masterfully exploited in Shakespeare's later comedies, its omission in *The Comedy of Errors* is especially striking.

There can be no doubt, however, that this play is Shakespeare's. Its first performance, at the Gray's Inn Christmas Revels on December 28, 1594, is well documented; the play was also published in the Folio of 1623, so the text is considered to be as good as any we have for Shakespeare. Furthermore, this play introduces a theme which was to occupy Shakespeare throughout his dramatic career: a shipwreck which separates families or lovers, who must then pass through trials before a final reunion. From *The Comedy of Errors* to *The Tempest*, this shipwreck motif exerted a powerful, mysterious hold over Shakespeare's imagination.

In a sense, it is unfair to compare this early work with the masterpieces of Shakespeare's later career. *The Comedy of Errors* has many virtues, and its defects are perceived largely in retrospect. Further, even if we acknowledge that Shakespeare was working within a limited compass and at the start of his career, it must be admitted that *The Comedy of Errors* is filled with touches of genius and moments of greatness that are uniquely his.

CONFESSIONS

Type of work: Spiritual autobiography
Author: Saint Augustine (Aurelius Augustinus, 354–430)
Time: 354–399
Locale: Tagaste, Carthage, Rome, Milan
First transcribed: 397–401

"My *Confessions*, in thirteen books," wrote Saint Augustine, looking back from the age of sixty-three at his various writings, "praise the righteous and good God as they speak either of my evil or good, and they are meant to excite men's minds and affections toward him. . . . The first through the tenth books were written about myself, the other three about the Holy Scripture."

In the year before his death, writing to Darius, he declared: "Take the books of my *Confessions* and use them as a good man should. Here see me as I am and do not praise me for more than I am."

Many critics regard the *Confessions* as the first true autobiography in the modern sense of the word. Others, like Marcus Aurelius, had set down meditations, but this was more. Others had written accounts of their lives, but again Saint Augustine did not follow their model. His method went beyond a mere narrative of dates and events. He devoted more attention to his youthful thief of pears than to his seemingly more important actions because this incident, with its echoes of Adam and Eve in the Garden of Eden, revealed his bondage to Original Sin. Other episodes are selected because of their revelation of the grace and provision of God. As he wrote: "I pass over many things, hastening on to those which more strongly compel me to confess to thee." In fact, his life story might be looked on as a parallel to the parable of the Prodigal Son, with his heart "restless till it finds its rest in God"; and he brings his account to an end, after his struggles to free himself from pride and sensuality, with his return to his home at Tagaste. Half his life still lay ahead of him.

Although his friends, his teachers, and his mother appear in the *Confessions*, they lack any physical details by which one may visualize them. Two lines cover the death of his father. Neither name nor description is given to his mistress and the mother of his child, nor of the friend whose death drove him from his native city. Detail was of less importance to Saint Augustine than theological meditation and interpretation.

Taking his text from the psalmist who would "confess my transgressions unto the Lord," this work is one long prayer beginning, "Great art thou, O Lord, and greatly to be praised," and ending with the hope that "thus shall thy door be opened."

From the very first, the consolation of God's mercy sustained Saint Augustine. His memories of infancy made him wonder what preceded that period, as later he theorized about what had been before the creation. His pictures of himself crying and flinging his arms about because he could not make his wants known were symbols to him of the Christian life, even as the acquisition of facts about this early period from his mother impressed on him the need for help from others to gain self-knowledge.

Though his mother, Monica, was a devout Christian and her son had been brought up in that faith, young Aurelius Augustinus was more interested in Aeneas than in God. Once, at the point of death from a stomach ailment, he begged to be baptized, but his mother refused to have him frightened into becoming a Christian. So he went on, reading Latin and disliking Greek, and taking special delight in the theater. A frank but modest description of his many abilities—a gift from his God to one not yet dedicated to God—ends the first book of this revealing work.

Book 2 concentrates on the sixteenth year of lazy, lustful, and mischievous Aurelius. He and his companions robbed a pear tree, not because they wanted the fruit, since they threw it to the swine, but because it was forbidden. His confession that he loved doing wrong made him ponder his reasons for wandering from the path of good and becoming a "wasteland."

When he traveled to Carthage to study, at the age of nineteen, his chief delights were his mistress and the theater. In the course of his prescribed studies he read an essay by Cicero, *Hortensius*, now lost, urging the study of philosophy. Remembering his mother's hopes that he would become a Christian, he tried to read the Scriptures; but he found them inferior in style to Cicero. However he did become involved with a pseudo-Christian sect, founded by the Persian religious teacher Mani (c. 216–277), because he approved of their logical approach to the problems of evil and good, represented by the dualistic concept of the universe. During the nine years that he was a Manichaean, his mother, encouraged by a dream that he would eventually see his error, kept loyally by him.

Back in Tagaste, he wrote plays, taught rhetoric, and lived with a mistress. He had no patience with a bishop, sent by his mother, to instruct him in Christianity. He was equally scornful of a magician who offered to cast spells to ensure his success in a drama competition. He thought he was sufficient to himself, and by his own efforts he won a rhetoric contest.

His temporary interest in astrology ended when he was unable to prove that successful divinations were more than chance. The death of a dear friend, who during his last illness became a Christian and denounced the life Aurelius was leading, so profoundly affected him that he returned to Carthage. There, still following Manichaean beliefs, he wrote several essays, now lost. He was soon to be disillusioned. Faustus, reputed the most learned of Manichaean bishops, came to Carthage, and Aurelius Augustinus went to him to clear his religious doubts. But he found Faustus more eloquent than logical. Hoping to improve himself, this teacher of rhetoric then went to Rome, where students were reported to be less rowdy than those in his classes in Carthage. In Rome, malaria, the teaching of the skeptics who upset his confidence in the certainty of knowledge, and above all, the lack of classroom discipline induced him to accept the invitation of officials to go to Milan and resume his teaching career in that city.

In Milan he enjoyed the companionship of two friends from Tagaste, Alypius and Nebridius. His mother, coming to live with him, persuaded Bishop Ambrose to try to convert her son. About the same time efforts to get him married and to regularize his life caused a break with his mistress, who on her departure left him with his young son Adeodatus.

The group around the young rhetorician often discussed philosophy, and in Neoplatonism he found an answer to his greatest perplexity: If there is a God, what is the nature of His material existence? Now he was ready to study Christianity, especially the writings of Saint Paul. In book 7, which describes this period of his life, appears one of Saint Augustine's two ecstatic visions, a momentary glimpse of the One.

Book 8 recounts his conversion. Anxious to imitate those who had gained what he himself sought, he listened to an account of the conversion of the orator Marius Victorinus. While returning home, still upset and uncertain, he heard a child chanting: "Pick it up and read it." Taking these words as God's command, he opened the Bible at random and found himself reading Romans 8, 13: "Put on the Lord Jesus Christ." Convinced, he called Alypius, and they found Monica and reported to her their newly acquired convictions.

Giving up his teaching, Saint Augustine prepared for baptism, along with his friend and Adeodatus. He was baptized by Bishop Ambrose during Easter Week, A.D. 387. Then the party set out to return to Tagaste. During their journey, and following another moment of Christian ecstasy, Monica died at Ostia on the Tiber. Her son's *Confessions* contains touching chapters of affection and admiration for her; sure of his faith at the time of her death, however, he fell into no period of abject mourning such as that which had followed the death of his friend at an earlier time.

With book 10, Saint Augustine turned from episodes of his life to self-analysis, detailing the three steps of the soul's approach to God, passing from an appreciation of the beauties of the outside world to an introspective study of itself, and ending with an inexplicable anticipation of the blessedness of the knowledge of God, the "truth-given Joy," that crowns the soul's pilgrimage.

Book 11 represents one of Saint Augustine's great contributions to Christian thought, the analysis of time. Pondering the mysteries of creation in an "eternal world," he saw it not as measured by "the motion of sun, moon, and stars," but as determined by the soul, the past being its remembrance; the present, its attention; and the future, its anticipation. He wrote: "The past increases by the diminution of the future, until by the consumption of all the future, all is past."

The last two books present speculation on the methods of creation and on the truth of the Scriptures, with most of the chapters devoted to interpretation of the opening verses of Genesis. The Old Testament account is open to many interpretations, and the final book of the *Confessions* deals with both the material and allegorical possibilities of the story of the Creation. At the end, Saint Augustine acknowledges the "goodness" of creation, and meditates on verses describing the rest on the Seventh Day. He begs that God will bestow the rest and blessedness of that Sabbath in the life eternal that is to come.

The *Confessions*, a work filled with the spirit of a sincere, devout faith, lays the groundwork for Saint Augustine's more formal treatises, *On the Trinity* and *The City of God*.

CONFESSIONS

Type of work: Autobiography
Author: Jean Jacques Rousseau (1712–1778)
Time: 1712–1765
Locale: Switzerland, France, England
First published: 1784

Rousseau's *Confessions*, one of the most widely read autobiographies in world literature, is the result of the writer's self-avowed determination to speak fully and honestly of his own life. As a remembrance of things past, it is more revealing through its signs of passion and prejudice than through its recording of the facts of his experience; it must be checked against other, more objective, reports. Whatever its bias, however, the *Confessions* reflects Rousseau as he was at the time of its writing. With its emphasis on self-realization and its rejection of conventional society in favor of nature and natural man, Rousseau's *Confessions* became one of the seminal works of the Romantic movement in France.

To some extent Rousseau undoubtedly succeeded in his effort to write an autobiography of such character that he could present himself before "the sovereign Judge with this book in my hand, and loudly proclaim, Thus have I acted; these were my thoughts; such was I. With equal freedom and veracity have I related what was laudable or wicked, I have concealed no crimes, added no virtues." Only a person attempting to tell all would have revealed so frankly the sensual satisfaction he received from the spankings administered by Mlle. Lambercier, the sister of the pastor at Bossey, who was his tutor. Only a writer finding satisfaction either in truth or self-abasement would have gone on to tell that his passion for being overpowered by women continued throughout his adult life: "To fall at the feet of an imperious mistress, obey an imperious mistress, obey her mandates, or implore pardon, were for me the most exquisite enjoyments; and the more my blood was inflamed by the efforts of a lively imagination, the more I acquired the appearance of a whining lover." Having made this confession, Rousseau probably found it easier to tell of his extended affair with Madame de Warens at Annecy and of his experiences with his mistress and common-law wife, Thérèse Levasseur.

Rousseau records that he was born at Geneva in 1712, the son of Isaac Rousseau, a watchmaker, and Suzanne Bernard. His mother died at his birth, "the first of my misfortunes." According to the son's account of his father's grief, Isaac Rousseau had mixed feelings toward his son, seeing in him an image of Suzanne and, at the same time, the cause of her death. Rousseau writes, "Nor did he ever embrace me, but his sighs, the convulsive pressure of his arms, witnessed that a bitter regret mingled itself with his caresses. . . . When he said to me, 'Jean Jacques, let us talk of your mother,' my usual reply was, 'Yes, father, but then you know we shall cry,' and immediately the tears started from his eyes."

Rousseau describes his first experiences with reading. He turns to the romances that his mother had loved, and he and his father sometimes spent the entire night reading aloud alternately. His response to these books was almost entirely emotional, but he finally discovered other books in his grandfather's library, works which demanded something from the intellect: Plutarch, Ovid, Molière, and others.

He describes with great affection how his Aunt Suzanne, his father's sister, moved him with her singing; and he attributes his interest in music to her influence.

After his stay at Bossey with Pastor Lambercier, Rousseau was apprenticed to an engraver, Abel Ducommun, in the hope that he would succeed better in the engraver's workshop than he had with City Registrar Masseron, who had fired him after a brief trial. Ducommun is described as "a young man of a very violent and boorish character," who was something of a tyrant, punishing Rousseau if he failed to return to the city before the gates were closed. Rousseau was by this time, according to his account, a liar and a petty thief.

Returning from a Sunday walk with some companions, Rousseau found the city gates closing an hour before time. He ran to reach the bridge, but he was too late. Reluctant to be punished by the engraver, he suddenly decided to give up his apprenticeship.

Having left Geneva, Rousseau wandered aimlessly in the environs of the city, finally arriving at Confignon. There he was welcomed by the village curate, M. de Pontverre, who gave him a good meal and sent him on to Madame Louise de Warens at Annecy. Rousseau expected to find "a devout, forbidding old woman"; instead, he discovered "a face beaming with charms, fine blue eyes full of sweetness, a complexion whose whiteness dazzled the sight, the form of an enchanting neck." He was sixteen, she was twenty-eight. She became something of a mother to him (he called her "Maman") and something of a goddess, but within five years he was her lover, at her instigation. Her motive was to protect him and to initiate him into the mysteries of love. She explained what she intended and gave him eight days to think it over; her proposal was intellectually cool and morally motivated. Since Rousseau had long imagined the delights of making love to her, he spent the eight days enjoying thoughts more lively than ever; but when he finally found himself in her arms, he was miserable: "Was I happy? No: I felt I know not what invincible sadness which empoisoned my happiness: it seemed that I had committed an incest, and two or three times, pressing her eagerly in my arms, I deluged her bosom with my tears."

Madame de Warens was at the same time involved with Claude Anet, a young peasant with a knowledge of herbs who had become one of her domestics. Before becoming intimate with Rousseau she had confessed to him that Anet was her lover, having been upset by Anet's attempt to poison himself after a quarrel with her. Despite her generosity to the two young men, she was no wanton; her behavior was more a sign of friendship than of passion, and she was busy being an intelligent and gracious woman of the world.

Through her efforts Rousseau had secured a position registering land for the king in the office at Chambéry. His interest in music, however, led him to give more and more time to arranging concerts and giving music lessons; he gave up his job in the survey office.

This was the turning point of his life, the decision which threw him into the society of his times and made possible his growing familiarity with the world of music and letters. His friendship with Madame de Warens continued, but the alliance was no longer of an intimate sort, for he had been supplanted by Winzenreid de Courtilles during their stay at Les Charmettes. Winzenreid came on the scene after the first idyllic summer, a period in his life which Rousseau describes as "the short happiness of my life." He tells of rising with the sun, walking through the woods, over the hills, and along the valley; his delight in nature is evident, and his theories concerning natural man become comprehensible. On his arrival Winzenreid took over physical chores and was forever walking about with a hatchet or a pickax; for all practical purposes Rousseau's close relationship with Madame de Warens was finished, even if a kind of filial affection on his part survived. He describes other adventures in love, although some of them gave him extreme pleasure, he never found another "Maman."

Rousseau, having invented a new musical notation, went to Paris hoping to convince others of its value. The system was dismissed as unoriginal and too difficult, but Rousseau had by that time been introduced to Parisian society and was known as a young philosopher as well as a writer of poetry and operas. He received an appointment as secretary to the French ambassador at Venice,

but he and M. de Montaigu irritated each other and he left his post about a year later.

Returning to Paris, Rousseau became involved with the illustrious circle containing the encyclopedist Diderot, Friedrich Melchior Grimm, and Mme. Louise d'Épinay. He later became involved in a bitter quarrel with all three, stemming from a remark in Diderot's *Le Fils naturel*, but he was reconciled with Diderot and continued the novel he was writing at the time, *La Nouvelle Héloïse*. His account of the quarrel together with the letters that marked its progress is one of the liveliest parts of the *Confessions*.

As important an event as any in Rousseau's life was his meeting with Thérèse Levasseur, a needlewoman between twenty-two and twenty-three years of age, with a "lively yet charming look." Rousseau reports that "At first, amusement was my only object," but in making love to her he found that he was happy and that she was a suitable successor to "Maman." Despite the difficulties put in his way by her mother, and despite the fact that his attempts to improve her mind were useless, he was satisfied with her as his companion. She bore him five children, all of whom were sent to the foundling hospital, against Thérèse's will and to Rousseau's subsequent regret.

Rousseau describes the moment on the road to Vincennes when the question proposed by the Academy of Dijon—"Has the progress of sciences and arts contributed to corrupt or purify morals?"—so struck him that he "seemed to behold another world." The discourse that resulted from his inspired moment won him the prize and brought him fame. However, it may be that here, as elsewhere in the *Confessions*, the actual circumstances have been considerably altered in the act of recollection.

The *Confessions* carries the account of Rousseau's life to the point when, having been asked to leave Bern by the ecclesiastical authorities as a result of the uproar over *Emile*, he set off for England, where David Hume had offered him asylum.

Rousseau's *Confessions* offers a personal account of the experiences of a great writer. Here the events which history notes are mentioned—his literary triumphs, his early conversion, his reconversion, his romance with Madame d'Houdetot, his quarrels with Voltaire, Diderot, and churchmen, his musical successes—but they are all transformed by the passionate perspective from which Rousseau, writing years after most of the events he describes, imagines his own past. The result is that the *Confessions* leaves the reader with the intimate knowledge of a human being, full of faults and passions, but driven by ambition and ability to a significant position in the history of literature.

THE COUNT OF MONTE-CRISTO

Type of work: Novel
Author: Alexandre Dumas, *père* (1802–1870)
Type of plot: Historical romance
Time of plot: Nineteenth century
Locale: France
First published: *Le Comte de Monte-Cristo*, 1844–1845 (English translation, 1846)

The Count of Monte-Cristo tells the story of a young man on the threshold of a bright career and a happy marriage who is imprisoned in a dungeon for years on a false political charge. When he escapes and finds a treasure which makes him wealthy, he sets upon an implacable course of revenge against his old enemies. If the characterizations are sometimes set in conventional molds, the story is unforgettable for its suspenseful plot and the intriguing figure of the Count.

Principal Characters

Edmond Dantès (ĕd·môn' dän·tĕs'), a young man unjustly imprisoned in the grim Château D'If. He escapes fourteen years later, after he has learned where a vast fortune is amassed. He secures the fortune and assumes the title of Count of Monte-Cristo. He then sets about avenging himself on those who were instrumental in having him imprisoned.

M. Morrel (mə·syoe' mô·rĕl'), a merchant and shipowner, the friend of young Dantès and the benefactor of Edmond's father. He is later saved by Monte-Cristo from bankruptcy and suicide.

M. Danglars (mə·syoe' dän·glàr'), an employee of M. Morrel. He helps to betray Edmond Dantès to the authorities because of professional jealousy. He later amasses a fortune which Monte-Cristo causes him to lose. He is further punished by being allowed to starve almost to death as he had allowed Edmond's father to starve.

Mercédès (mĕr·sä·dĕz'), the betrothed of young Edmond Dantès. Believing him to be dead, she marries his rival, Fernand Mondego. In the end she leaves her husband's house, gives his fortune to charity, and lives on the dowry Edmond had saved for her in his youth.

Louis Dantès (lwē' dän·tĕs'), Edmond's father. He dies of starvation after his son is imprisoned.

Gaspard Caderousse (gàs·pàr' ka·dərōōs'), a tailor, innkeeper, and thief. One of Edmond's betrayers, he is killed while robbing Monte-Cristo's house.

Fernand Mondego, Count de Morcerf (fĕr·nän' môn·də·gō', kônt' də môr·sĕr'), a fisherman in love with Mercédès. He mails the letter which betrays Edmond to the authorities. He later marries Mercédès, becomes a soldier and a count. Monte-Cristo later brings about the revelation that Fernand got his fortune by selling out the Pasha of Janina to the enemy. His wife and son leave him and he commits suicide.

The Marquis and Marchioness de Saint-Méran (də sän'mä·rän'), the father and mother of M. Villefort's first wife, poisoned by his second wife.

Renée (rə·nä'), the daughter of the Marquis and Marchioness de Saint-Méran. She married Villefort.

M. Villefort (mə·syoe' vēl·fôr'), a deputy prosecutor, later attorney general, and a royalist. He causes Edmond to be imprisoned because he fears involvement in a Napoleonic plot. Monte-Cristo later discovers an attempted infanticide on the part of Villefort and causes this secret to be revealed publicly at a trial Villefort is conducting. After this public denunciation and the discovery that his second wife has poisoned several members of his household, then her son and herself, Villefort goes mad.

The Abbé Faria (à·bā' fà'ryà, Edmond's fellow prisoner, who dies of a stroke after educating Edmond and revealing to him the whereabouts of the vast lost fortune of the extinct family of Spada in the caverns of the isle of Monte-Cristo.

Emmanuel Herbaut (ā·mà·nü·ĕl'·ĕr·bō'), a clerk in Morrel's business establishment. He marries Julie Morrel.

Julie Morrel (zhü·lē' mô·rĕl'), the daughter of the merchant Morrel. She finds the purse in which Monte-Cristo had put money to repay the loan that Morrel had given his father, old Dantès, and thus saves her own father from bankruptcy. She later marries Emmanuel Herbaut.

Maximilian Morrel (màk·sē·mēl·yän' mô·rĕl'), the son of the merchant, a soldier and a loyal friend of Monte-Cristo. He marries Valentine de Villefort.

Viscount Albert de Morcerf (àl·bĕr' də môr·sĕr'), the son of Fernand and Mercédès. He leaves his disgraced father's house, gives his fortune to charity, and seeks his own fortune as a soldier.

Baron Franz d'Épinay (fräns dä·pē·nä'), the friend of Albert, about to be betrothed to Valentine de Villefort when the betrothal is called off after Franz discovers that her grandfather had killed his father.

Luigi Vampa (lwē'jē vàm'pà), a Roman bandit and

friend of Monte-Cristo. He kidnaps Albert but frees him at Monte-Cristo's order. Later he also kidnaps Danglars, robs, and almost starves him.

Peppino (pā·pē′nō), also known as **Rocca Priori** (rō′kà prē·ō·rē′), one of Vampa's band. Monte-Cristo saves him from being beheaded.

Countess Guiccioli (gwēt′chō·lē), the friend of Franz and Albert in Rome and later in Paris.

Giovanni Bertuccio (jō·vän′nē bĕr·tōōt′chyō), the steward of Monte-Cristo, who reveals to his master Villefort's attempted infanticide. Unknown to Villefort, he saves the child's life.

Lucien Debray (lü·syăn′ də·brē′), a friend of Albert, secretary to the Internal Department, and the lover of Mme. Danglars.

M. Beauchamp (mə·syoe′ bō·shän′), Albert's friend, a newspaper editor.

Count Château-Renaud (shà·tō′ rə·nō′), another of Albert's friends.

Eugénie Danglars (oe·zhā·nē′ dän·glàr′), the daughter of Danglars, about to be betrothed, first to Albert, then to Andrea Cavalcanti. She later runs away with her governess to go on the stage.

Assunta (à·sün′tà), Bertuccio's sister-in-law. She claims Villefort's child from the foundling home where Bertuccio had placed it.

Benedetto (bā·nā·dā′tō), also **Andrea Cavalcanti** (än·drā·à′ kà·väl·kän′tē), the illegitimate son of Villefort and Mme. Danglars. He does not know who his parents are, and they believe him to be dead. He is a forger, a thief escaped from the galleys, and the murderer of Caderousse. He discovers that Villefort is his father and reveals this fact at the trial. It is implied that the court will find "extenuating circumstances" in his new trial.

Haidée (ĕ·dā′), the daughter of Ali Tebelen, Pasha of Janina and Basiliki, captured and sold as a slave by Fer-

nand Mondego after he betrays her father. She is bought by Monte-Cristo, and they fall in love with each other.

Baptistin (bà·tēs·tăn′), the servant of Monte-Cristo.

Hermine Danglars (ĕr·mēn′ dän·glàr′), Danglars' wife and the mother of Benedetto and Eugénie.

Héloïse de Villefort (ā·lô·ēz′ də vēl·fôr′), the second wife of Villefort. She poisons the Saint-Mérans and tries to poison Noirtier and Valentine so that her son may inherit their vast wealth. Her guilt discovered, she kills her son and herself.

Edouard de Villefort (ā·dwàr′ də vēl·fôr′), the spoiled, irresponsible son of Héloïse and Villefort. He is killed by his mother.

Valentine de Villefort (và·län·tēn′ də vēl·fôr′), the daughter of Villefort and Renée Saint-Méran Villefort. She is poisoned by the second Mme. Villefort but is saved by Noirtier and Monte-Cristo after being given a sleeping potion that makes her appear dead. After her rescue she marries Maximilian Morrel.

Noirtier de Villefort (nwàr·tyā′ də vēl·fôr′), the father of Villefort and a fiery Jacobin of the French Revolution. Completely paralyzed by a stroke, he communicates with his eyes.

The Marquis Bartolomeo Cavalcanti (bàr·tō·lō·mā·ō′ kà·väl·kän′tē), the name assumed by a man pretending to be Andrea Cavalcanti's father.

Barrois (bà·rwà′), a faithful servant of old Noirtier, poisoned by drinking some lemonade intended for Noirtier.

Ali Tebelen (à·lē täb·lăn′), the father of Haidée, betrayed by Fernand.

Louise d'Armilly (lwēz′ dàr·mē·yē′), the governess to Eugénie Danglars. Together they run away in hopes they can go on the stage as singers.

Lord Wilmore and **Abbé Busoni** (à·bā′ bü·zō′·nē), aliases used by the Count of Monte-Cristo.

The Story

When Edmond Dantès sailed into Marseilles harbor that day in 1815, he was surrounded by enemies. His shipmate, Danglars, coveted his appointment as captain of the *Pharaon*. Ferdinand Mondego wished to wed Mercédès, who was betrothed to Edmond.

Danglars and Ferdinand wrote a note accusing Edmond of carrying a letter from Elba to the Bonapartist committee in Paris. Caderousse, a neighbor, learned of the plot but kept silent. On his wedding day, Edmond was arrested and taken before a deputy named Villefort, a political turncoat, who, to protect himself, had Edmond secretly imprisoned in the dungeons of the Château D'If. There Dantès' incarceration was secured by the plotting of his enemies outside the prison, notably Villefort, who wished to cover up his own father's connections with the Bonapartists.

Napoleon came from Elba, but Edmond lay forgotten in his cell. The cannonading at Waterloo died away. Years passed. Then one night Edmond heard the sound of digging from an adjoining cell. For days later, a section of the flooring fell in, and Edmond saw an old man in the narrow tunnel below. He was the Abbé Faria, whose attempt to dig his way to freedom had led him only to Edmond's cell. Thereafter the two met daily, and the old man taught Edmond history, mathematics, and languages. In Edmond's fourteenth year of imprisonment, Faria, mortally ill, told Edmond where to find a tremendous fortune should he escape after the old man's death. When death did come, the abbé's body was placed in a sack. Edmond conceived the idea of changing places with the dead man, whom he dragged through the tunnel into his own bed. Jailers threw the sack into the sea.

Edmond ripped the cloth and swam through the darkness to an islet in the bay.

At daybreak he was picked up by a gang of smugglers with whom he worked until a stroke of luck brought him to the island of Monte-Cristo, where Faria's fortune awaited him. He landed on the island with the crew of the ship. Feigning injury in a fall, he persuaded the crew to leave him behind until they could return for him. Thus, he was able to explore the island and to find his treasure hidden in an underground cavern. He returned to the mainland and sold some small jewels to provide himself with money enough to carry out his plans to bring his treasure from Monte-Cristo. There he learned that his father had died and Mercédès, despairing of Edmond's return, had married Ferdinand.

Disguised as an abbé, he visited M. Caderousse to seek information of those who had caused his imprisonment. M. Villefort had gained fortune and station in life. Danglars was a rich banker. Ferdinand had won wealth and a title in the Greek war. For this information, Edmond gave Caderousse a diamond worth fifty thousand francs.

He also learned that his old shipping master, M. Morrel, was on the verge of bankruptcy. In gratitude, because Morrel had given the older Dantès money to keep him from starvation, Edmond saved Morrel's shipping business.

Edmond took the name of his treasure island. As the Count of Monte-Cristo, he dazzled all Paris with his fabulous wealth and his social graces. He and his mysterious protégée, a beautiful girl named Haidée whom he had bought during his travels in Greece, became the talk of the boulevards.

Meanwhile he was slowly plotting the ruin of the four men who had caused him to be sent to the Château D'If. Caderousse was the first to be destroyed. Monte-Cristo had awakened his greed with the gift of a diamond. Later, urged by his wife, Caderousse had committed robbery and murder. Now, released from prison, he attempted to rob Monte-Cristo but was mortally wounded by an escaping accomplice. As the man lay dying, Monte-Cristo revealed his true name—Edmond Dantès.

In Paris, Monte-Cristo had succeeded in ingratiating himself with the banker, Danglars, and was secretly ruin-ing him. Ferdinand was the next victim on his list. Ferdinand had gained his wealth by betraying Pasha Ali in the Greek revolution of 1823. Monte-Cristo persuaded Danglars to send to Greece for confirmation of Ferdinand's operations there. Ferdinand was exposed, and Haidée, daughter of the Pasha Ali, appeared to confront him with the story of her father's betrayal. Albert, the son of Mercédès and Ferdinand, challenged Monte-Cristo to a duel to avenge his father's disgrace. Monte-Cristo intended to make his revenge complete by killing the young man, but Mercédès came to him and begged for her son's life. Aware of Monte-Cristo's true identity, she interceded with her son as well. At the scene of the duel, the young man publicly declared his father's ruin had been justified. Mother and son left Paris. Ferdinand shot himself.

Monte-Cristo had also become intimate with Madame Villefort and encouraged her desire to possess the wealth of her stepdaughter, Valentine, whom Maximilian Morrel, son of the shipping master, loved. The count had slyly directed Madame Villefort in the use of poisons, and the depraved woman murdered three people. When Valentine herself succumbed to poison, Maximilian went to Monte-Cristo for help. Upon learning that his friend Maximilian loved Valentine, Monte-Cristo vowed to save the young girl. Valentine, however, had apparently died. Nevertheless, Monte-Cristo promised future happiness to Maximilian.

Meanwhile Danglars' daughter, Eugénie, ran off to seek her fortune independently, and Danglars found himself bankrupt. He deserted his wife and fled the country. When Villefort discovered his wife's treachery and crimes, he confronted her with a threat of exposure. She then poisoned herself and her son Edward, for whose sake she had poisoned the others. Monte-Cristo revealed his true name to Villefort, who subsequently went mad.

Monte-Cristo, however, had not deceived Maximilian. He had rescued Valentine while she lay in a drugged coma in the tomb. Now he reunited the two lovers on his island of Monte-Cristo. They were given the count's wealth, and Monte-Cristo sailed away with Haidée, never to be seen again.

Critical Evaluation

The Count of Monte-Cristo, Alexandre Dumas' best-known novel after *The Three Musketeers* (1844), is, as improbable as it might seem, based on a true story. Dumas, who has become almost legendary for his prolific literary output of nearly three hundred volumes, maintained a corps of collaborators who were engaged in searching through earlier writers of memoirs for suitably exciting plots. Through this process, a volume entitled *Mèmoires tirès des archives de la Police de Paris* by Jacques Peuchet, the Keeper of the Archives at the Prefecture of Police, came to Dumas' attention.

In Peuchet's memoirs, which contained a treasure of potential plots for novels, was a record of a case of wrongful imprisonment and vengeance which strongly appealed to the French author. In 1807, there had been living in Paris a young shoemaker, François Picaud, who was engaged to marry Marguerite Vigoroux, a beautiful orphan with a fortune of one hundred thousand gold francs. Four of Picaud's friends, jealous of his good fortune, accused him of being an English agent. Picaud was spirited away in the night by the police, who at the time were worried about certain insurrectionary movements. The unfortunate man's parents and his betrothed made inquiries, but failed to obtain any satisfaction and resigned themselves to the inevitable. In 1814, with the fall of the Empire, Picaud was released from the castle of Fenestrelle where he had all that time been imprisoned. While in captivity, he had, with great devotion, looked after an Italian prelate who had been imprisoned on a political charge and had not long to live. The dying man bequeathed to Picaud a treasure hidden in Milan. After his release, the shoemaker recovered the treasure and returned under an assumed name to the district in which he had been living. Making inquiries, he soon discovered the plot against him by his jealous friends and spent ten years of his life engaged in an elaborate plot against the perpetrators of his suffering that resulted in the eventual destruction of his former friends.

Dumas delighted in the idea of creating a character possessed of a fabulous fortune and of making that character an avenger in some great cause. This impulse was natural, for Dumas, despite his exuberant exterior, harbored within himself many grievances against society at large, and individual enemies in particular. His father had been persecuted; he himself was harassed by creditors and slandered. He shared with other major writers, who had been unjustly treated, that longing for vengeance which has engendered so many masterpieces. The experiences of Picaud gave him the story for which he had been longing. Normal imagination, however, was not responsible for the stroke of genius that produced the name "Count of Monte-Cristo," which has come to be so romantically imbedded in the memories of countless readers. The mysterious creative forces which cause the birth of great works had been enriched one day when Dumas had gone boating among the islands which lie about Elba and his guide pointed out a beautiful island named Monte-Cristo.

The Count of Monte-Cristo had a greater success than any book which Dumas published prior to *The Three Musketeers*. Like most of Dumas' major novels, it was first serialized in the daily newspaper. In this way, he kept his public excited from one day to the next by means of romantic love affairs, intrigues, imprisonments, hairbreadth escapes, and innumerable duels. Dumas had great gifts of narrative and dialogue and a creative imagination but only a limited critical sense and an even smaller concern for historical accuracy. He did have a knack for seizing situations and characters that would render a satisfactory historical atmosphere. He wrote with a sincere gusto that action and love were the two essential things in life and thus in fiction. His writing was never complicated by analysis or psychological insights, and his best works, such as *The Count of Monte-Cristo* and *The Three Musketeers*, can be read with effortless enjoyment.

Critics point to the excessive melodrama of Dumas' work and his lack of psychological perception and careless style. The characters are one-dimensional, stranded in the conventional molds the author has set for them. There is no change, no sudden insight, and no growth in the players upon Dumas' stage. Despite many defects, however, this novel remains a great work in literature, for it is a breathtaking experience, a dramatic tale filled with mystery and intrigue. For thousands of years, the unhappy human race has found release in cathartic tales such as this one. The most popular characters have been the magician and the dispenser of justice. The injured and weak live with the hope, which no ill-success can weaken, of witnessing the coming of the hero who will redress all wrongs, cast down the wicked, and at long last give the good man his desserts.

At the time Dumas was writing, the magician had been confused with the rich man, with great vaults filled with jewels, whose wealth permits him to indulge his every whim and to use his treasure to provide justice for the innocent man and to punish the guilty. Dumas dreamed of becoming just such a distributor of earthly happiness, and *The Count of Monte-Cristo* gave him the framework for which he was looking: The hero is an implacable avenger who obtains his justice and disappears. *The Count of Monte-Cristo*, then, finds its audience among people of all ages and of all times who like a romantic adventure tale with a larger-than-life hero.

CRIME AND PUNISHMENT

Type of work: Novel
Author: Fyodor Mikhailovich Dostoevski (1821–1881)
Type of plot: Psychological realism
Time of plot: Mid-nineteenth century
Locale: Russia
First published: *Prestupleniye i nakazaniye*, 1866 (English translation, 1886)

Crime and Punishment *is a powerful story of sin, suffering, and redemption; Dostoevski's theme is that man inevitably pays for his crimes against his fellows by suffering, and by that suffering he may ultimately be purified. The character of Raskolnikov is a tremendous study of a sensitive intellectual driven by poverty to believe that he is exempt from moral law.*

Principal Characters

Rodion Romanovitch Raskolnikov (rôdĭ·ōn rô·mä′nə·vĭch räs·kōl′y·nĭ·kəf), called **Rodya,** a psychologically complex young law student who murders not for wealth but as an experiment, to see if he is one of those who can circumvent society's restrictions. Impoverished and weakened by illness and hunger, he decides to rid society of a worthless person in order to preserve his genius for posterity, to relieve his devoted mother and sister from compromising themselves, and to prove that he is above conscience. He kills Alonya Ivanovna, a miserly old crone, and her sister. Later, in his loss of illusions, of peace of mind, and of the wealth he sought, he learns through suffering. Important changes result from acceptance of his inward punishment. His humanitarian instincts are brought out; his deep love of family and friends is revealed, and his belief that life must be lived is renewed. The study of his psychoses from the time he conceives his mad theory to his attempt at expiation in Siberia is a masterfully drawn portrait of a tormented mind and shattered body. The study is one of contrasts, of good and evil, within all mankind.

Pulcheria Alexandrovna (pōōly·chě′rĭ·yə ä·lěk·sän′drəv·nə), his long-suffering mother whose faith in her son sustains her but whose mind gives way under the strain of his deed and guilt. A handsome, middle-aged woman of distinction, a widow who has supported her family and urged her son to make his way in life, Pulcheria is a study of motherhood thwarted, a woman tortured by her inability to fathom her favorite's depravity.

Avdotya Romanovna (äv·dōt′yə rô·mä′nəv·nə), called **Dounia** (dōō′nyə), her daughter and the younger sister who has aided in her mother's effort to make something of the brother through working and skimping. A mirror of her mother's fortitude and faith, Dounia is the beautiful, impoverished, clear-sighted savior of her family. In spite of attempted seductions, the devoted sister continues her efforts to sustain her beloved brother in his reversals and suffering.

Dmitri Prokofitch Razumihin (dmĭ′trĭ prô·kō′fĭch rä·zōō′mĭ·hĭn), Raskolnikov's devoted friend. Enamored of Dounia, he is the savior of the family honor. Like Dounia, he has all the normal responses of a generous nature and works unceasingly to discover and repair the tragic situation of his friend. Affianced to the beautiful Dounia, he founds a publishing company to aid the hapless girl, mother, and brother. He is one of the few characters with a sense of humor; his good deeds lighten a psychologically gloomy and depth-insighted plot.

Piotr Petrovitch Luzhin (pyō′tr pět·rō′vĭch lyōōz′hĭn), a minor government official betrothed to Dounia, a man filled with a sense of his own importance. Raskolnikov objects to his suit. Dounia herself loses interest in him after she meets Razumihin, whom she later marries.

Sofya Semyonovna Marmeladov (sō′fyə sě·myō′nəv·nə mär·mě′lä·dəf), called **Sonia,** the daughter of a drunken clerk and stepdaughter of the high-strung Katerina Ivanovna. It is her father who brings the luckless prostitute to Rodya's attention and whose funeral the unstable student finances. From gratitude the benevolent though soiled child of the streets comforts the murderer and supports him in his transgressions so that he finally will confess. Forced to support her father, her stepmother, and their three children, she remains unsullied and her spirit transcends these morbid conditions. With great depth of character and faith, Sonia follows the criminal to Siberia, where she inspires the entire prison colony with her devotion and goodness.

Marmeladov (mär·mě′lä·dəf), Sonia's father, an impoverished ex-clerk and drunkard. He is killed when struck by a carriage. Raskolnikov, who witnesses the accident, gives Marmeladov's wife some money to help pay for his friend's funeral expenses.

Katerina Ivanovna (kä·těr·ĭn′ə ĭ·vä′nôv·nə), Marmeladov's wife, slowly dying of tuberculosis. She collapses in the street and dies a short time later.

Arkady Ivanovitch Svidrigaïlov (är·kä′dĭy ĭ·vä′nə·

vĭch svĭ·drĭg′ĭ·ləf), the sensualist in whose house Dounia had been a governess. He is both the would-be seducer and savior of Dounia, and through her of Sonia's orphaned half sisters and brother, when he gives her money as atonement for his conduct. A complicated character, sometimes considered, with Raskolnikov, one of the alter egos of the writer, he is obsessed by guilt and driven by libido.

Porfiry Petrovitch (pôr·fĭ′rĭy pĕt·ro·vĭch), a brilliant detective more interested in the rehabilitation than the prosecution of the murderer. Somewhat disturbed and neurotic himself, Porfiry seconds Sonia's influence and causes Raskolnikov to confess his crime and thus begin his redemption.

Alonya Ivanovna (ä·lyō′nyə ĭ·vä′nôv·nə), a miserly old pawnbroker and usurer, murdered by Raskolnikov.

Lizaveta Ivanovna (lyē·zä·vĕ′tə ĭ·vä′nôv·nə), a seller of old clothes and Alonya Ivanovna's sister, also killed by Raskolnikov.

The Story

Rodion Raskolnikov, an impoverished student in St. Petersburg, dreamed of committing the perfect crime. He murdered an old widowed pawnbroker and her stepsister with an ax and stole some jewelry from their flat.

Back in his room, Raskolnikov received a summons from the police. Weak from hunger and illness, he prepared to make a full confession. The police, however, had called merely to ask him to pay a debt his landlady had reported to them. When he discovered what they wanted, he collapsed from relief. Upon being revived, he was questioned; his answers provoked suspicion.

Raskolnikov hid the jewelry under a rock in a courtyard. He returned to his room, where he remained for four days in a high fever. When he recovered, he learned that the authorities had visited him while he was delirious and that he had said things during his fever which tended to cast further suspicion on him.

Luzhin, betrothed to Raskolnikov's sister Dounia, came to St. Petersburg from the provinces to prepare for the wedding. Raskolnikov resented Luzhin because he knew his sister was marrying to provide money for her destitute brother. Luzhin visited the convalescent and left in a rage when the young man made no attempt to hide his dislike for him.

A sudden calm came upon the young murderer; he went out and read the accounts of the murders in the papers. While he was reading, a detective joined him. The student, in a high pitch of excitement caused by his crime and by his sickness, talked too much, revealing to the detective that he might well be the murderer. No evidence, however, could be found that would throw direct suspicion on him.

Later, witnessing a suicide attempt in the slums of St. Petersburg, Raskolnikov decided to turn himself over to the police; but he was deterred when his friend, a former clerk named Marmeladov, was struck by a carriage and killed. Raskolnikov gave the widow a small amount of money he had received from his mother. Later, he attended a party given by some of his friends and discovered that they, too, suspected him of complicity in the murder of the two women.

Back in his room, Raskolnikov found his mother and his sister, who were awaiting his return. Unnerved at their appearance and not wanting them to be near him, he placed them in the care of his friend, Razumihin, who, upon meeting Dounia, was immediately attracted to her.

In an interview with Porfiry, the chief of the murder investigation, Raskolnikov was mentally tortured by questions and ironic statements until he was ready to believe that he had been all but apprehended for the double crime. Partly in his own defense, he expounded his theory that any means justified the ends of a man of genius and that sometimes he believed himself a man of genius.

Raskolnikov proved to his mother and Dounia that Luzhin was a pompous fool, and the angry suitor was dismissed. Razumihin had by that time replaced Luzhin in the girl's affections.

Meanwhile Svidrigailov, who had caused Dounia great suffering while she had been employed as his governess, arrived in St. Petersburg. His wife had died, and he had followed Dounia, as he explained, to atone for his sins against her by settling upon her a large amount of money.

Razumihin received money from a rich uncle and went into the publishing business with Dounia. They asked Raskolnikov to join them in the venture, but the student, whose mind and heart were full of turmoil, declined; he said good-bye to his friend and to his mother and sister and asked them not to try to see him again.

He went to Sonia, the prostitute daughter of the dead Marmeladov. They read Sonia's Bible together. Raskolnikov was deeply impressed by the wretched girl's faith. He felt a great sympathy for Sonia and promised to tell her who had committed the murders of the old pawnbroker and stepsister. Svidrigailov, who rented the room next to Sonia's, overheard the conversation; he anticipated Raskolnikov's disclosure with interest.

Tortured in his own mind, Raskolnikov went to the police station, where Porfiry played another game of cat-and-mouse with him. His conscience and his imagined insecurity had resulted in immense suffering and torment of mind for Raskolnikov.

At a banquet given by Marmeladov's widow for the friends of her late husband, Luzhin accused Sonia of stealing money from his room. He had observed Raskolnikov's interest in Sonia, and he wished to hurt the student for having spoken against him to Dounia. The girl was saved by the report of a neighbor who had seen Luzhin slipping money into Sonia's pocket. Later, in Sonia's room, Raskolnikov confessed his crime and admitted that in killing the two women he had actually destroyed himself.

Svidrigailov had overheard the confession and disclosed his knowledge to Raskolnikov. Believing that Porfiry suspected him of the murder and realizing that Svidrigailov knew the truth, Raskolnikov found life unbearable. Then Porfiry told Raskolnikov outright that he was the murderer, at the same time promising Raskolnikov that a plea of temporary insanity would be placed in his behalf and his sentence would be mitigated if he confessed. Raskolnikov delayed his confession.

Svidrigailov had informed Dounia of the truth concerning her brother, and he now offered to save the student if Dounia would consent to be his wife. He made this offer to her in his room, which he had locked after tricking her into the meeting. He released her when she attempted unsuccessfully to shoot him with a pistol she had brought with her. Convinced at last that Dounia intended to reject him, Svidrigailov gave her a large sum of money and ended his life with a pistol.

Raskolnikov, after being reassured by his mother and his sister of their love for him, and by Sonia of her undying devotion, turned himself over to the police. He was tried and sentenced to serve eight years in Siberia. Dounia and Razumihin, now successful publishers, were married. Sonia followed Raskolnikov to Siberia, where she stayed in a village near the prison camp. In her goodness to Raskolnikov and to the other prisoners, she came to be known as Little Mother Sonia. With her help, Raskolnikov began his regeneration.

Critical Evaluation

Crime and Punishment was Fyodor Mikhailovich Dostoevski's first popularly successful novel after his nine-year imprisonment and exile for alleged political crimes (the charges were of doubtful validity) against the czar. After his release from penal servitude, Dostoevski published novels, short stories, novellas, and journalistic pieces, but none of these brought him the critical and popular acclaim which in 1866 greeted *Crime and Punishment*—possibly his most popular novel. This book is no simple precursor of the detective novel, no simplistic mystery story to challenge the minds of Russian counterparts to Sherlock Holmes's fans. It is a complex story of a man's turbulent inner life and his relationship to others and to society at large. The book must be considered within the matrix of Dostoevski's convictions at the time he wrote the novel, because Dostoevski's experience with czarist power made a lasting impression on his thinking. Indeed, Dostoevski himself made such an evaluation possible by keeping detailed notebooks on the development of his novels and on his problems with fleshing out plots and characters.

Chastened by his imprisonment and exile, Dostoevski shifted his position from the youthful liberalism (certainly not radicalism), which seemed to have precipitated his incarceration, to a mature conservatism which embraced many, perhaps most, of the traditional views of his time. Thus, Dostoevski came to believe that legal punishment was not a deterrent to crime because he was convinced that criminals demanded to be punished; that is, they had a spiritual need to be punished. Today, that compulsion might be called masochistic; but Dostoevski, in his time, related the tendency to mystical concepts of the Eastern Orthodox church, an establishment institution. With a skeptical hostility toward Western religion and culture, born of several years of living abroad, Dostoevski became convinced that the Western soul was bankrupt and that salvation—one of his major preoccupations—was possible only under the influence of the church and an ineffable love for Mother Russia, a devotion to homeland, to the native soil, which would brook neither logic nor common sense: a dedication beyond reason or analysis. Thus, expiation for sins was attained through atonement, a rite of purification.

The required expiation, however, is complicated in *Crime and Punishment* by the split personality—a typically Dostoevskian ploy—of the protagonist. The schizophrenia of Raskolnikov is best illustrated by his ambivalent motives for murdering the pawnbroker. At first, Raskolnikov views his heinous crime as an altruistic act which puts the pawnbroker and her sister out of their misery while providing him the necessary financial support to further his education and mitigate his family's poverty, thus relieving unbearable pressures on him. He does intend to atone for his misdeed by subsequently living an upright life dedicated to humanitarian enterprises. Raskolnikov, however, shortly becomes convinced of his own superiority. Indeed, he divides the human race into "losers" and "winners": the former, meek and submissive; the latter, Nietzschean supermen who can violate any law or principle to attain their legitimately innovative and presumably beneficial ends. Raskolnikov allies himself with the "superman" faction. He intends to prove his superiority by committing murder and justifying it on the basis of his own superiority. This psychological configuration is common enough, but, unlike most paranoid schizophrenics, Raskolnikov carries his design through—a signal tribute to the depth of his convictions.

The results are predictably confusing. The reader is as puzzled about Raskolnikov's motives as he is. Is it justifiable to commit an atrocity in the name of improvement of the human condition? This essential question remains unanswered in *Crime and Punishment*; Raskolnikov, egocentrically impelled by pride, cannot decide whether or not he is superior, one of those supermen entitled to violate any law or any principle to serve the cause of ultimate justice, however justice might be construed. In his notebooks, Dostoevski implied that he, too, was ambivalent about Raskolnikov's motives. Yet he added that he was not a psychologist but a novelist who plumbed the depths of men's souls; in other words, he had a religious not a secular orientation. He was thus more concerned with consequences than with causality. This carefully planned novel therefore expands upon a philosophical problem embodied in the protagonist.

The philosophical problem in *Crime and Punishment* constitutes the central theme of the novel: the lesson Raskolnikov has to learn, the precept he has to master in order to redeem himself. The protagonist finally has to concede that free will is limited. He has to admit that he cannot control and direct his life solely with his reason and intellect, as he tried to do, for such a plan leads only to emptiness and to sinful intellectual pride. The glorification of abstract reason precludes the happiness of a fully lived life; happiness must be earned, and it can be earned only through suffering—another typically Dostoevskian mystical concept. The climactic moment in the novel, therefore, comes when Raskolnikov confesses his guilt at the police station, for Raskolnikov's confession is tantamount to a request for punishment for the crime and acceptance of his need to suffer.

The epilogue—summarizing the fates of other characters; Raskolnikov's trial, his sentencing, and his prison term; and Sonia's devotion to Raskolnikov during his imprisonment—confirms the novel's central theme. Artistically, however, the epilogue is somewhat less than satisfactory or satisfying. First, Dostoevski's notes indicate that he had considered and rejected an alternate ending in which Raskolnikov committed suicide. Such a conclusion would have been logical in an existential sense, and it would have been psychologically sound. The very logicality of Raskolnikov's suicide, however, would have suggested a triumph of reason over the soul. That idea was not consonant with Dostoevski's convictions; thus, he dropped the plan. Second, the ending which Dostoevski finally wrote in the epilogue implies that the meek and submissive side of Raskolnikov's personality emerged completely victorious over the superman. Such an ending contradicts Raskolnikov's persistent duality throughout the novel. Raskolnikov's dramatic conversion thus strains credulity, for it seems too pat a resolution of the plot. For the sophisticated reader, however, it does not greatly detract from the powerful psychological impact of the novel proper or diminish the quality of a genuinely serious attempt to confront simultaneously a crucial social problem and a deeply profound individual, human one.

CRITIQUE OF PURE REASON

Type of work: Philosophical treatise
Author: Immanuel Kant (1724–1804)
First published: 1781

Kant's *Critique of Pure Reason* is a masterpiece in metaphysics designed to answer the question, "How are synthetic *a priori* judgments possible?" Since a synthetic judgment is one whose predicate is not contained in the subject, and an *a priori* judgment is one whose truth can be known independently of experience, Kant's question meant, in effect, "How can there be statements such that the idea of the subject does not involve the idea of the predicate and which, nevertheless, *must* be true and can be known to be true without recourse to experience?"

To make the question clearer, Kant offered examples of *analytic* and *synthetic* judgments. The statement that "All bodies are extended" is offered as an analytic judgment, since it would be impossible to think of a body—that is, of a physical object—that was not spread out in space; and the statement "All bodies are heavy" is offered as a synthetic judgment, since Kant believed that it is possible to conceive of something as a body without supposing that it has weight.

Perhaps even clearer examples are possible. The judgment that "All red apples are apples" is surely analytic, since it would be impossible to conceive of something as being red and as being an apple without supposing it to be an apple; the predicate is, in this sense, included in the subject. But the judgment "All apples are red" is surely synthetic, since it is possible to think of something as being an apple without supposing it to be red; in fact, some apples are green. Synthetic judgments can be false, but analytic judgments are never false.

A priori knowledge is knowledge "absolutely independent of all experience," and *a posteriori* knowledge is empirical knowledge, that is, knowledge possible only through experience. We can know *a priori* that all red apples are apples (and that they are red), but to know that a particular apple has a worm in it is something that must be known *a posteriori*.

The question of how synthetic *a priori* judgments are possible is, then, a question concerning judgments that must be true—since they are *a priori* and can be known to be true without reference to experience—even though, as synthetic, their predicates are not conceived in thinking of their subjects.

As an example of a synthetic *a priori* judgment Kant offers, "Everything which happens has its cause." He argues that he can think of something as happening without considering whether it has a cause; the judgment is, therefore, not analytic. Yet he supposes that it is necessarily the case that everything that happens has a cause, even though his experience is not sufficient to support his claim. The judgment must be *a priori*. How are such synthetic *a priori* judgments possible?

One difficulty arises at this point. Critics of Kant have argued that Kant's examples are not satisfactory. The judgment that everything that happens has a cause is regarded as being either an analytic, not synthetic, *a priori* judgment (every event being a cause relative to an immediately subsequent event, and an effect relative to an immediately precedent event), or as being a synthetic *a posteriori*, not *a priori*, judgment (leaving open the possibility that some events may be uncaused). A great many critics have maintained that Kant's examples are bound to be unsatisfactory for the obvious reason that no synthetic *a priori* judgments are possible. (The argument is that unless the predicate is involved in the subject, the truth of the judgment is a matter of fact, to be determined only by reference to experience.)

Kant's answer to the problem concerning the possibility of synthetic *a priori* judgments was that pure reason—that is, the faculty of arriving at *a priori* knowledge—is possible because the human way of knowing determines, to a considerable extent, the character of what is known. Whenever human beings perceive physical objects, they perceive them in time and space; time and space are what Kant calls "modes of intuition," that is, ways of apprehending the objects of sensation. Since human beings must perceive objects in time and space, the judgment that an object is in time must be *a priori* but, provided the element of time is no part of the conception of the object, the judgment is also synthetic. It is somewhat as if we were considering a world in which all human beings are compelled to wear green glasses. The judgment that everything seen is somewhat green would be *a priori* (since nothing could be seen except by means of the green glasses), but it would also be synthetic (since being green is no part of the conception of object).

In Kant's terminology, a *transcendental* philosophy is one concerned not so much with objects as with the mode of *a priori* knowledge, and a critique of pure reason is the science of the sources and limits of that which contains the principles by which we know *a priori*. Space and time are the forms of pure intuition, that is, modes of sensing objects. The science of all principles of *a priori* sensibility, that is, of those principles that make *a priori* intuitions (sensations) possible, Kant calls the *transcendental aesthetic*.

But human beings do more than merely sense or perceive objects; they also think about them. The study of how *a priori* concepts, as distinguished from intuitions, are possible is called *transcendental logic*. Transcendental logic is divided into *transcendental analytic*, dealing with the principles of the understanding without which no object can be thought, and *transcendental dialectic*, showing the error of applying the principles of pure thought to objects considered in themselves.

Using Aristotle's term, Kant calls the pure concepts of the understanding *categories*. The categories are of *quantity* (unity, plurality, totality), of *quality* (reality, negation, limitation), of *relation* (substance and accident, cause and effect, reciprocity between agent and patient), and of *modality* (possibility-impossibility, existence-nonexistence, necessity-contingency). According to Kant, everything which is thought is considered according to these categories. It is not a truth about things in themselves that they are one or many, positive or negative, but that all things fall into these categories because the understanding is so constituted that it can think in no other way.

Kant maintained that there are three subjective sources of the knowledge of objects: sense, imagination, and apperception. By its categories the mind imposes a unity on the manifold of intuition. What would be a mere sequence of appearances, were the mind not involved, makes sense as the appearance of objects.

The principles of pure understanding fall into four classes: axioms of intuition, anticipations of perception, analogies of experience, and postulates of empirical thought in general.

The principle of the axioms of intuition is that "All intuitions are extensive magnitudes," proved by reference to the claim that all intuitions are conditioned by the spatial and temporal mode of intuition.

The principle by which all perception is anticipated is that "the real that is an object of sensation has intensive magnitude, that is, a degree." It would not be possible for an object to influence the senses to *no* degree; hence various objects have different degrees of influence on the senses.

The principle of the analogies of experience is that "Experience is possible only through the representation of a necessary connection of perceptions." Our experience would be meaningless to us were it not ordered by the supposition that perceptions are of causally related substances which are mutually interacting.

Kant's postulates of empirical thought in general relate the *possibility* of things to their satisfying the formal conditions of intuition and of concepts, the *actuality* of things to their satisfying the material conditions of sensation, and the *necessity* of things to their being determined "in accordance with universal conditions of experience" in their connection with the actual.

A distinction which is central in Kant's philosophy is the distinction between the *phenomenal* and the *noumenal*. The phenomenal world is the world of appearances, the manifold of sensation as formed spatially and temporally and understood by use of the categories. The noumenal world is the world beyond appearance, the unknown and unknowable, the world of "things-in-themselves."

In the attempt to unify experience, the reason constructs certain ideas—of a soul, of the world, of God. But these ideas are transcendental in that they are illegitimately derived from a consideration of the conditions of reason, and to rely on them leads to difficulties which Kant's transcendental dialectic was designed to expose. The "Paralogisms of Pure Reason" are fallacious syllogisms for which the reason has transcendental grounds; that is, the reason makes sense out of its operations by supposing what, on logical grounds, cannot be admitted. The "Antinomies of Pure Reason" are pairs of contradictory propositions, all capable of proof provided the arguments involve illegitimate applications of the forms and concepts of experience to matters beyond experience.

Kant concludes the *Critique of Pure Reason* with the suggestion that the ideas of God, freedom, and immortality arise in the attempt to make moral obligation intelligible. This point was developed at greater length in his *Metaphysics of Morals* (1785) and his *Critique of Practical Reason* (1788).

CYRANO DE BERGERAC

Type of work: Drama
Author: Edmond Rostand (1868–1918)
Type of plot: Tragicomedy
Locale: France
First presented: 1897

In this play, based upon the life of seventeenth century French author and playwright Cyrano de Bergerac, a freethinker and soldier famed for his skill in duels as well as for his inordinately long nose, Rostand develops a character symbolizing magnanimity, unselfishness, and beauty of the soul in a seemingly bellicose and physically ugly individual. Rostand's tragicomedy ranks among the most popular plays of the modern French theater.

Principal Characters

Cyrano de Bergerac (sē·rȧ·nô′ dǝ bĕr·zhǝ·rȧk′), a historical poet-playwright-soldier who, as a contemporary of the three famous musketeers, creates an image of romance considerably heightened by his lines in the play. Although the possessor of an enormous nose, which its owner declared was a symbol of generosity and independence, Cyrano has a romantic heart and a gifted tongue as well as a spirit of fierce independence. He chooses as his symbol a white plume of unsullied integrity, never lowered for expediency's sake. While appearing boastful in the braggart warrior tradition, he is actually shy and diffident, especially when confronting beauty in any form. As the accomplice in a love plot, he never speaks for himself until wounded mortally. His name stands not only for an ugly handicap for which compensation must be made but also for all that is good, true, loyal, and fine in human nature. Such integrity is in the great tradition of Don Quixote, whom Cyrano admires because tilting at the windmills of pomposity and philistinism, while it may throw the challenger down, more often elevates.

Christian de Neuvillette (krēs·t'yän′ dǝ nœ·vē·yĕt′), Cyrano's protégé in love, who never learns the language of sentiment. Often mistaken for a silent lover, the young soldier has greater depths of feeling and finer sensibilities than he can express. He is undoubtedly handsome and generous, but his valor in battle is offset by this morbid shyness in love, and while he acts the dupe of his mentor, he resents very much his own inadequacies. He dies bravely, knowing that another man has won his wife but realizing also that he will not be betrayed by his beloved friend and poet.

Roxane (rôk·sȧn′), or **Madeleine Robin,** who as "précieuse" seems the prototype of thoughtless love, but who as suffering widow becomes the ideal of womanhood. Bright and beautiful, gay and youthful, Roxane is the symbol of beauty that all men desire. She insists that the amenities and conventions of love come before the character of the lover, only to learn that there is no substitute for sincerity of feeling and expression. She is also a romantic and somewhat silly heroine who becomes wise and thoughtful only after revelation.

Ragueneau (rȧ·gǝ·nō′), a pastry cook-poet who, as a bard of the oven, befriends the hero and holds a salon for destitute artists. While obviously the Silenus of the plot, this tippling pretender suffers the scorn of his wife and the appetite of his poets. He is loyal to an ideal and constant in his loyalties.

Le Bret (lǝ brā′), the friend and counselor of Cyrano and the author's commentator, who interprets the brave soldier's heart. Steadfast in his regard for the hero, Le Bret is the only one permitted to speak directly to him of his inconsistencies. He proves loyal and devoted always.

Montfleury (mōń·flœ·rē′), a famous actor whom Cyrano will not permit to play because of Montfleury's lack of refinement and sensitivity to language. As the pompous idol of his day, the actor represents popular tastes, a symbol of decadence that Cyrano cannot tolerate.

The Comte de Guiche (kōńt′ dǝ gēsh′), who woos Roxane without success and who has his revenge when he sends Christian, her husband, into battle and to his death. Though a representative of civil and military power, he displays some redeeming features even while he plays the villain of the play. He is a step above the fops and dandies, and he admires the bravery of Cyrano against the odds of life.

The Story

In the theater hall of the Hôtel de Burgundy, a young soldier named Christian de Neuvillette anxiously waited for the beautiful Roxane to appear in her box. Christian had fallen passionately in love with this girl whom he had never met. While he was waiting for her arrival, Christian became increasingly upset because he feared that he would never be able to summon sufficient courage to address her, for he believed she was as brilliant and as graceful as he was doltish and clumsy.

Also in the audience, waiting for the curtain to go up, was one Ragueneau, a romantic tavern keeper and tosspot poet, whose friends praised his verses to his face, while behind his back they helped themselves to the pastries that he made. Ragueneau inquired of another poet concerning the whereabouts of Cyrano de Bergerac. The actor Montfleury, Cyrano's enemy and one of Roxane's suitors, was to star in the play, and Cyrano had threatened him with bodily injury if he appeared for the performance. Cyrano, however, had not yet arrived.

At last Roxane appeared. The play began, and Montfleury came out on the stage to recite his lines. Suddenly, a powerful voice ordered him to leave the stage. After the voice came the man, Cyrano de Bergerac, one of the best swordsmen in France. The performance was halted abruptly.

Another of Roxane's suitors tried to provoke a fight with Cyrano by ridiculing his uncommonly big nose. Cyrano, sensitive about his disfiguring nose, became the insulter instead of the insulted. Words led to a duel. To show his contempt for his adversary, Cyrano composed a poem while he was sparring with his opponent, and when he had finished the last word of the last line, Cyrano staggered his man. Le Bret, Cyrano's close friend, cautioned the gallant swordsman against making too many enemies by his insults.

Cyrano confessed that he was exceptionally moody lately because he was in love with his lovely cousin Roxane, despite the fact that he could never hope to win her because of his ugliness. While Le Bret tried to give Cyrano confidence in himself, Roxane's chaperone appeared to give Cyrano a note from his cousin, who wanted to see him. Cyrano was overcome with joy.

The place selected for the meeting between Cyrano and Roxane was Ragueneau's tavern. Cyrano arrived early, and while he waited for his beautiful cousin, he composed a love letter, which he left unsigned because he intended to deliver it in person. When Roxane appeared, she confessed to Cyrano that she was in love. Cyrano thought for a moment that she was in love with him. He soon realized, however, that the lucky fellow was not he but Christian. Roxane asked Cyrano to take the young soldier under his wing, to protect him in battle. Cyrano sadly consented to do her bidding.

Later, when Christian dared jest with Cyrano concerning the latter's nose, Cyrano restrained himself for Roxane's sake. When he learned that Cyrano was Roxane's cousin, Christian confessed his love for Roxane and begged Cyrano's help in winning her. Christian was a warrior, not a lover; he needed Cyrano's ability to compose pretty speeches and to write tender, graceful messages. Although his heart was broken, Cyrano gave the young man the letter he had written in Ragueneau's tavern.

Cyrano visited Roxane to inquire about her love affair with Christian. Roxane, who had recently received a letter from Christian, was delighted by his wit. Cyrano did not tell her that he was the writer of the letter.

Shortly thereafter, Christian told Cyrano that he now wanted to speak for himself in his wooing of Roxane. Christian did try to speak for himself under Roxane's balcony one evening, but he became so tongue-tied that he had to ask the aid of Cyrano, who was lurking in the shadows. Cyrano, hidden, told Christian what to say, and Roxane was so delighted by these dictated protestations that she bestowed a kiss on Christian.

A friar appeared with a letter from the Comte de Guiche, commander of Cyrano's regiment, to Roxane. The comte wrote that he was coming to see her that night, even though by so doing he was deserting his post. Roxane deliberately misread the letter, which, she said, ordered the friar to marry her to Christian. Roxane asked Cyrano to delay de Guiche until after the ceremony, a request which he effectively carried out by making the comte think that he was mad. After learning that Roxane and Christian were already married, the duped de Guiche ordered Christian to report immediately to his regiment.

In a battle which followed, Cyrano and the other cadets were engaged against the Spanish. During the conflict, Cyrano risked his life to send letters to Roxane through the enemy's lines, and she never suspected that the author of these messages was not Christian. Later, Roxane joined her husband and confessed to him that his masterful letters had brought her to his side.

Realizing that Roxane was actually in love with the nobility and tenderness of Cyrano's letters, Christian begged Cyrano to tell Roxane the truth. Christian was killed in battle shortly afterward, however, and Cyrano swore never to reveal his friend's secret. Rallying the cadets, Cyrano charged bravely into the fight, and under his leadership the Spanish were defeated.

Fifteen years passed. Roxane, grieving for Christian, had retired to a convent. Each week, Cyrano visited her, but one day he came late. When he arrived, he concealed under his hat a mortal wound which one of his enemies had inflicted by dropping an object from a building onto his head. While talking about her dead husband, Roxane recited to Cyrano Christian's last letter, which she kept next to her heart. With Roxane's permission, Cyrano read the letter, which he himself had written, even though it had grown so dark that neither he nor Roxane could see the words.

Suddenly, Roxane realized that Cyrano knew the contents of the letter by heart and that he, not Christian, must have written it. With this realization came her conviction that for fifteen years she had unknowingly loved the soul of Cyrano. Roxane confessed her love for Cyrano, who died knowing that at last Roxane was aware of his love and that she returned it.

Critical Evaluation

Since the enthusiastic reception of its debut in Paris in 1897, Edmund Rostand's glittering historical drama *Cyrano de Bergerac* has taken its place in the world's theatrical repertoire as the most popular and most frequently performed verse play of modern times. Though serious students of drama have often been harshly critical of its facile sentimentality and bombastic diction, *Cyrano de Bergerac* continued to be a consistent source of enchantment and delight for a broadly diversified international public.

The sources of its original success in late nineteenth century Paris are readily understandable. At a time when the French theater was dominated by slice-of-life drama of the starkest naturalism, Rostand's attempt to revive the glories of Romantic drama in the grand manner of Victor Hugo, not seen in Paris for more than half a century, struck a sympathetic chord among a public nostalgic for heroes to admire. Moreover, a resurgent French nationalism created a receptive audience for a play that richly evoked the Paris of Louis XIII and idealized a relatively obscure seventeenth century French poet who was a patriot as well as an artist and whose language and imagination were elegantly original. It was true that Rostand took gross liberties with historical fact in his play, but the public took no notice of that, being more intent on the sheer pleasure of hearing brilliant wordplay and the unabashed expression of noble sentiments and patriotic spirit. *Cyrano de Bergerac* was thus exceptionally fortunate in its timing, for the French public had by 1897 been inundated with the dark solemnities of contemporary social issues and was thirsting for escape into the emotions and values of France's glorious past.

For subsequent generations, however, both in France and abroad, the particular appeal of Rostand's play seems rather to have been its witty verbal virtuosity, its bittersweet theme of unrequited love silently and nobly borne, and, above all, its compelling central character, Cyrano, who strikes audiences as a wonderfully volatile compound of public panache and private pain. Cyrano is on stage almost all of the time, has the best of all the dialogue, and dominates and controls the action throughout. His is a rich and varied role, much coveted by actors, but his commanding presence in the play has the dramaturgical consequence of rendering all the other characters dull and uninteresting by comparison. Indeed, Rostand's creative energy and inventiveness seem so heavily invested in the character of Cyrano that critics have long complained of the artificiality and flatness of his writing for the other characters, including the two key supporting figures: Cyrano's secret love, his cousin Roxane, who comes off as frivolous and empty-headed, and Roxane's successful suitor, Christian, who seems a handsome but tongue-tied dolt. The unfortunate effect, for viewer and reader alike, is that the scintillating Cyrano seems at all times to be surrounded by a cast of pasteboard figures.

It must nevertheless be emphasized that Rostand's writing for the part of Cyrano is sufficiently dazzling and inspired to rivet the audience's attention at all times and to carry the entire play alone. From the time he steps on stage, early in act 1 (which takes place in a theater), to interrupt the play that is about to be performed that day, Cyrano projects a masterful presence by both his words and his bearing. He orders the actor Montfleury, whom he has forbidden to perform for three weeks, to leave the stage, faces the angered crowd thus deprived of its entertainment, then ingratiates the crowd with a grand gesture: He throws down a purse containing all his money for that month, so the spectators might be refunded the price of admission. Thus, in a matter of moments, Cyrano impresses on the audience that he is the kind of person who takes charge of events, wherever he happens to be. There follows, still in act 1, the justly celebrated scene in which Cyrano displays his mastery of both word and sword—to a young man who makes an insulting reference to the size of his nose, Cyrano replies first with a brilliantly comic speech showing how a person of talent might have insulted his nose with imagination and wit, then announces, and proceeds to carry out, his intention to fight a duel with his insulter, while improvising a ballade, and to deliver the *coup de grâce* to his victim at the end of the last line of the ballade. It would be difficult to imagine a more spectacular introduction for a play's central figure. After such a first act, the audience can have eyes and ears only for Cyrano and will be eager to see what unpredictable gestures he will engage in next.

In the second act, the bold and daring public Cyrano reveals his private side: the worshipful but timid lover, lacking the courage to approach his beautiful cousin Roxane for fear that, with his monstrous nose, he is too ugly to be accepted as a suitor. For the rest of the play, the public and the private Cyrano function at ironic cross-purposes with each other, as Cyrano secretly provides the words of courtship his fellow soldier Christian needs to woo Roxane; keeps their enemy, the Comte de Guiche, at bay while Roxane and Christian get married; writes impassioned love letters to Roxane for Christian while their regiment does battle with the Spaniards; and finally, after Christian is killed in the battle, devotes himself loyally, for fifteen years, to making weekly visits to Roxane to comfort her in her widowhood, without ever hinting at the role he has played as Christian's "voice" and as silent admirer. Only by accident, during Cyrano's last dying visit to Roxane, does she discover the truth about the secret role he has played in her life.

The wit and brio of the public Cyrano are what create the most delightfully memorable scenes in the play, and those scenes are undoubtedly the basis for Rostand's decision to designate his play a "heroic comedy." Yet the poignancy of Cyrano's private suffering is never for a moment absent from the consciousness of the spectator or reader. Even the celebrated "nose speech" of act 1, so inventively comic, leaves the bitter aftertaste of ashes with Cyrano's audience, unable to miss the note of wounded pride in his cleverly impoverished self-mockery. Indeed, as Cyrano himself acknowledges in the play's closing scene, his whole life has been marked by apparently triumphant scenes of bravado and defiance, all of which only concealed the unfulfilled dreams and repeated failures which constituted the truth of his existence. Even his death is pitifully unheroic, the blow that kills him

being delivered, not in battle, but from behind with a block of wood. "I have missed everything,/ Even my death," he admits in his dying moments. Cyrano's painful awareness of his life as a failure has increasingly caught the attention of critics and has led to a revised estimate of the play as less a comedy than a deeply felt tragedy— the tragedy of unfulfilled greatness. Reinforcing that new interpretation has been the critical perception that all of Rostand's plays share that same poignant theme of the unfulfilled life and, indeed, that Rostand was consciously reproducing in his plays his own haunted vision of his career as an artist.

DAPHNIS AND CHLOË

Type of work: Tale
Author: Attributed to Longus (third century)
Type of plot: Pastoral romance
Time of plot: Indefinite
Locale: Island of Lesbos
First transcribed: Third century manuscript

A Greek pastoral poem generally ascribed to the third, fourth, or fifth century A.D. sophist Longus, Daphnis and Chloë *is a product of decadent Greek literature and one of the most popular of the early predecessors of the modern novel. As such it is highly romantic in both characterization and incident, alive with extravagant improbabilities, and laced with humor. The story centers on the innocent though passionate love of two children of nature, unspoiled by contact with city manners, amid idyllic scenes of natural beauty.*

Principal Characters

Daphnis (dăf'nĭs), found as a baby by Lamo and reared by him. Though he loves Chloë, Daphnis is unable to ask for her in marriage until he finds a purse of silver. He is discovered to be Philopoemen, lost son of Dionysophanes.

Chloë (klō'ē), found as an infant girl by Dryas in the Cave of the Nymphs, on Lesbos. She is discovered to be Agéle, the daughter of Megacles.

Lamo (lă'mō), a goatherd of Lesbos and the foster father of Daphnis.

Myrtale (mĭr'tə·lē'), his wife, who hides the purple cloak and ivory dagger found with Daphnis.

Dryas (drī'əs), a shepherd and the foster father of Chloë.

Nape (nă'pē), his wife, who brings up Chloë.

Dorco (dôr'kō), a fisherman who wants to marry Chloë

and tries to kidnap her. He later saves Daphnis after he has been captured by pirates.

Lampis (lăm'pĭs), another suitor of Chloë, who steals her.

Gnatho (nă'thō), Astylus' parasite, who rescues Chloë.

The Methymneans (mə·thĭm'nĭ·əns), who carry off Chloë but, frightened by Pan, return her.

Lycaenium (lī·sē'nĭ·əm), who teaches love to Daphnis.

Megacles (mĕ'gək·lēz), of Mitylene, the father of Chloë.

Dionysophanes (dī'ō·nĭ·sŏ'fə·nēz), owner of Lamo and the father of Daphnis.

Astylus (ăs·tīləs), the son of Dionysophanes and the young master of Lamo.

Eudromus (ū·drō'məs), Astylus' page.

The Story

On the Greek island of Lesbos, a goatherd named Lamo one day found a richly dressed infant boy being suckled by one of his goats. Lamo and his wife, Myrtale, hid the purple cloak and ivory dagger the boy had worn and pretended he was their own son. They named him Daphnis. Two years later, a shepherd named Dryas discovered an infant girl being nursed by one of his sheep in a cave of the Nymphs. This child also was richly dressed. Dryas and his wife Nape kept the girl as their own, giving her the name Chloë.

When the two children were fifteen and thirteen years old respectively, they were given flocks to tend. Daphnis and Chloë played happily together, amusing themselves in many ways. One day, while chasing a goat, Daphnis fell into a wolf pit, from which he was rescued unharmed by Chloë and a herdsman she had summoned to help her. Daphnis began to experience delightful but disturbing

feelings about Chloë. Dorco, a herdsman, asked permission to marry Chloë but was refused by Dryas. Disguising himself in a wolf skin, Dorco shortly afterward attempted to seize Chloë. Attacked by the flock dogs, he was rescued by Daphnis and Chloë, who innocently thought he had merely been playing a prank. Love, little understood by either, grew between Daphnis and Chloë.

In the autumn some Tyrian pirates wounded Dorco, stole some of his oxen and cows, and took Daphnis away with them. Chloë, who heard Daphnis calling to her from the pirate ship, ran to aid the mortally wounded Dorco. Dorco gave her his herdsman's pipe, telling her to blow upon it. When she blew, the cattle jumped into the sea and overturned the ship. The pirates drowned, but Daphnis, grasping the horns of two swimming cows, came safely to shore.

After the celebration of the autumn vintage, Daphnis

and Chloë returned to their flocks. They attempted in their innocence to practice the art of love, but they were not successful. Some young men of Methymne came to the fields of Mitylene to hunt. When a withe used as a cable to hold their small ship was gnawed in two by a goat, the Methymneans blamed Daphnis and set upon him. In a trial over the affair, Daphnis was judged innocent. The angry Methymneans later carried away Chloë. The god Pan warned the Methymnean captain in a dream that he should bring back Chloë, and she was returned. Daphnis and Chloë joyfully celebrated holidays in honor of Pan.

The two lovers were sad at being parted by winter weather, which kept the flocks in their folds. In the spring the lovers happily drove their flocks again to the fields. When a woman named Lycaenium became enamored of the boy, Daphnis finally learned how to ease the pains he had felt for Chloë; but Lycaenium warned him that Chloë would be hurt the first time she experienced the ecstasy of love. Fearing that he might harm his sweetheart, the tender Daphnis would not deflower Chloë. Meanwhile many suitors, Lampis among them, asked for the hand of Chloë, and Dryas almost consented. Daphnis brooded about his inability to compete successfully with the suitors because of his poverty. With the aid of the Nymphs, he then found a purse of silver, which he gave Dryas in order to become contracted to Chloë. In return,

Dryas asked Lamo to consent to the marriage of his son, but Lamo answered that first he must consult his master, Dionysophanes.

Lamo, Daphnis, and Chloë prepared to entertain Dionysophanes; but Lampis ravaged the garden they had prepared because he had been denied Chloë's hand. Fearing the wrath of his master, Lamo lamented his ill fortune. Eudromus, a page, helped to explain the trouble to Lamo's young master Astylus, who promised to intercede with his father and blame the wanton destruction on some horses in the neighborhood. Astylus' parasite, Gnatho, fell in love with Daphnis but was repulsed. Finally, the depraved Gnatho received Astylus' permission to take Daphnis with him to the city. Just in time, Lamo revealed the story of the finding of Daphnis, who was discovered to be Dionysophanes' son. Meanwhile, Lampis stole Chloë, who was later rescued by Gnatho. After Dryas told how Chloë had been found as a child, it was learned that she was the daughter of Megacles of Mitylene. Thus the supposed son and daughter of Lamo and Dryas were revealed as the children of wealthy parents who were happy to consent to their marriage. The wedding was celebrated amid the rural scenes dear to both bride and groom. Daphnis became Philopoemen, and Chloë was named Agéle. On her wedding night, Chloë at last learned from Daphnis how the delights of love might be obtained.

Critical Evaluation

The romance is the least "classical" of ancient literary genres. The name itself derives many centuries later, since the ancients apparently did not know what to call this prose that was not history, this adventure that was not epic, this love story that was neither tragedy nor comedy, this pastoral that was not bound by the verse forms of Theocritus and Vergil. Romance finds its origins perhaps in late Hellenistic times, having developed from erotic and exotic approaches to literature in Euripides, Menander, and Apollonius Rhodius, but it did not reach full bloom until the age of the Second Sophistic in the second century A.D., when rhetoricians encouraged their students to create improbable human situations rife with problems on which they might conduct debate.

Daphnis and Chloë is such an improbable theme, but the resolution of its incredible complications amid such faraway non-Roman places casts a unique charm deepened by the idealized devotion of the young lovers. The story provides an escape to a primeval state for a reader jaded by the violence and sophistication of the Roman Empire. Daphnis and Chloë personify innocent, ignorant love. They are taught by hard experience and the cruel selfishness of the real, urbane world, but they manage to survive and return to their idyllic, simple remove.

An intelligible structure is canonical in classical com-

position, and appropriately this work is divided into four "books" which define movements from spring to autumn, to winter and a second spring and summer, and finally to a second autumn. The blooming love of Daphnis and Chloë must be tested by the seasons, both of nature and of human life, before the matured lovers can reap the harvest. Longus uses the imagery of Philetas' and Lamon's gardens to convey the natural morality of the children's love, shaped and cultivated by experience, So, too, he entrusts them to the care of Pan and Dionysus, gods of natural sexuality, and to Eros, god of irresistible love. This is further enforced by the motif of milk and wine, symbolizing innocence and passion.

Longus' *Daphnis and Chloë* is an interesting example of an unusual genre, Greek romance. This is an identifiable, if evolving, genre that manifests certain structural elements. First of all, it is a prose narrative, and the subject is fictional rather than mythical; the pair of lovers fall into love at first sight, but their union is frustrated by internal and external obstacles; the gods are the agency of the final union of the lovers and the subsequent happy ending. *Daphnis and Chloë* contains all these elements, although some, such as the obstacles to the lovers' union and the intervention of the gods, are given more prominence. It is also a work that stresses parallels in its structure. From the mysterious birth of the heroes in nature to the recognition of their beauty to the threats to each to the final recognition of their true nature, one element is being set against another. This parallel structure is mirrored by the style, with its long strings of clauses and comparisons and juxtapositions.

The plot structure is clearly connected to Greek romance, but the world in which the book exists is a pastoral one and uses many of the elements from that literary tradition, especially those from the Greek poet who invented the pastoral, Theocritus. Daphnis and Chloë are both born in a rural setting; their lives are sustained by the care and nurturing of a goat and a sheep. Both of the main characters work, but their work, tending their flocks, seems less important than their piping and singing and their worship of the nature gods that surround them. Furthermore, nature is beneficent; the animals respond to the piping of their masters, and descriptions of flowers and gardens abound. It is important that Daphnis and Chloë return to the pastoral world after their true social position is recognized; they may be too noble for their foster parents, but they are not and cannot be too noble for the benign world of nature the pastoral portrays.

Another important element of the pastoral in *Daphnis and Chloë* is the seasons. They are rendered in great detail, and they mirror the waxing and waning of the love between Daphnis and Chloë. Winter obstructs their love, while spring is the time when Daphnis begins to perceive the possibilities of erotic love. Summer is a time when the new knowledge must be controlled; their anticipated union takes place in autumn, amid harvest festivals and the appearance of their lord. The natural rhythms mirror the development and attitude of the main characters.

The parents of Daphnis and Chloë and their neighbors are firmly located in the bucolic—or more realistic—aspects of the pastoral. Their work, rather than their singing or feelings, is stressed, and their origin is clearly human and simple, not noble. They worry about crops, survival, and the proper mates for their children. They do not have leisure for or interest in the worship of nature, although some minor characters, such as Philetas, who has seen and worships the god Eros, are taken directly from earlier pastorals.

Daphnis and Chloë are innocent, and that innocence is preserved in the pastoral world they inhabit. They often see each other in metaphors of nature, especially of flowers. Their world is full of natural beauty and wonder, especially the Cave of the Nymphs, which they visit, decorate, and use as a shrine. Also prominent is the time spent with the pipe; the tradition of the singing shepherd is taken directly from Theocritus and Vergil. There is a singing contest between Daphnis and Dorco, and Daphnis teaches Chloë how to play the pipe, as he later teaches her how to love. Their innocence extends to their sexuality; they do not know the ways of love, and when the first knowledge of this world comes to Daphnis and then Chloë it is disturbing and confusing.

The contrast between the world outside and the pastoral one within is very strong throughout Daphnis and Chloë. Pirates and raiders invade the green world and attempt to carry off first Daphnis and then Chloë. The suitors for the hand of Chloë are also seen as impeding the natural union of the lovers. They have wealth and property to offer—elements that have no place in the pastoral world. A prime example of the way such characters soil the pastoral world is the court parasite Gnathon, who has a homosexual longing for Daphnis and plots to take him to the city and away from Chloë.

The presence of the gods is a very important element of *Daphnis and Chloë*. They can be found in the Cave of the Nymphs and in Pan, who is worshipped by the people, especially the parents of Daphnis and Chloë. Pan also rescues Chloë at the urging of the Nymphs when she is taken as a slave. The god Dionysus is also an important figure in the book, since he is worshipped as the bringer of fertility to the land. The final recognition by a lord called Dionysophanes of the noble origins of Daphnis and Chloë is only a final manifestation of the gods' presence.

The most important theme in the book is love. Love moves from the brother-sister affection of the pair through early stirrings of affection and admiration to an erotic union; that union is natural and predestined, but it must be developed and tested. Eros, a god who is described as older than time, has, in fact, planned their union and guides and protects them from the assaults of others and their own premature sexual feelings. The act of love is described by Lycaenion as "bloody" and frightful to Chloë, and Daphnis' delicacy in resisting the urge to see sexuality as a merely natural element is crucial to his development. Their union can come only when they are recognized for what they truly are: nobles.

Daphnis and Chloë is a hybrid work; it is part Greek romance, part pastoral, and even part New Comedy. It blends these various genres to produce a work that portrays the movement from innocence to experience; this movement is seen as a natural and gratifying process rather than a threatening one. The tale also elevates and redeems nature. Its rural world is enhanced by the presence of characters from another realm who find a home there. It gives us a vision of a desirable world of nature, fertility, and nobility to which we can aspire if never reach.

DAVID COPPERFIELD

Type of work: Novel
Author: Charles Dickens (1812–1870)
Type of plot: Sentimental romance
Time of plot: Early nineteenth century
Locale: England
First published: 1849–1850

One of the best-loved novels in the English language, David Copperfield *is a devastating exposé of the treatment of children in the nineteenth century. Admittedly autobiographical, it is a work of art which can be read and reread, chiefly for its gallery of immortalized characters. Though the novel has flaws, it enjoys a kind of freshness and spontaneity stemming from the first-person recounting of events and the sympathetic treatment of characters.*

Principal Characters

David Copperfield, the orphaned hero-narrator whose story of his early years and growing maturity comprises one of the best-known works of fiction in the English language. A posthumous child, extremely sensitive in retrospect, he first experiences cruelty and tyranny when his young widowed mother marries stern Mr. Murdstone, and he quickly forms emotional alliances with the underprivileged and the victimized. His loyalties are sometimes misplaced, as in the case of Steerforth, his school friend who seduces Little Em'ly, but his heart remains sound and generous toward even the erring. As he passes from childhood to disillusioned adolescence, his perceptions increase, though he often misses the truth because he misreads the evidence before him. His trust is all the more remarkable when one considers the recurrence of error which leads him from false friends to false love and on to near catastrophe. Finally, unlike his creator, David finds balance and completion in his literary career, his abiding friendships, and his happy second marriage.

Clara Copperfield, David's childlike but understanding and beautiful mother, destined to an early death because of her inability to cope with life. Strong in her own attachments, she attributes to everyone motives as good and generous as her own. Misled into a second marriage to an unloving husband, she is torn between son and husband and dies soon after giving birth to another child. Mother and child are buried in the same coffin.

Edward Murdstone, Clara Copperfield's second husband and David's irascible stepfather, who cruelly mistreats the sensitive young boy. Self-seeking to an extreme degree, Murdstone has become a synonym for the mean and low, the calculating and untrustworthy. His cruelty is touched with sadism, and his egoism borders on the messianic.

Jane Murdstone, Edward Murdstone's sister. Like her brother, she is harsh and unbending. Her severe nature is symbolized by the somber colors and metallic beards she wears. Her suspicious mind is shown by her belief that the maids have a man hidden somewhere in the house.

Clara Peggotty, Mrs. Copperfield's devoted servant and David's nurse and friend. Cheerful and plump, she always seems about to burst out of her clothing, and when she moves buttons pop and fly in all directions. Discharged after the death of her mistress, she marries Barkis, a carrier.

Daniel Peggotty, Clara Peggotty's brother, a Yarmouth fisherman whose home is a boat beached on the sands. A generous, kind-hearted man, he has made himself the protector of a niece and a nephew, Little Em'ly and Ham, and of Mrs. Gummidge, the forlorn widow of his former partner. His charity consists of thoughtful devotion as much as material support.

Ham Peggotty, Daniel Peggotty's stalwart nephew. He grows up to fall in love with his cousin, Little Em'ly, but on the eve of their wedding she elopes with James Steerforth, her seducer. Some years later, during a great storm, Ham is drowned while trying to rescue Steerforth from a ship in distress off Yarmouth beach.

Little Em'ly, Daniel Peggotty's niece and adopted daughter, a girl of great beauty and charm and David's first love. Though engaged to marry her cousin Ham, she runs away with James Steerforth. After he discards her, Daniel Peggotty saves her from a life of further shame, and she and her uncle join a party emigrating to Australia.

Barkis, the carrier between Blunderstone and Yarmouth. A bashful suitor, he woos Peggotty by having David tell her that "Barkis is willin'!" This tag line, frequently repeated, reveals the carter's good and simple nature.

Mrs. Gummidge, the widow of Daniel Peggotty's fishing partner. After he takes her into his home she spends most of her time by the fire, meanwhile complaining sadly that she is a "lone, lorn creetur."

Miss Betsey Trotwood, David Copperfield's great-aunt, eccentric, sharp-spoken, but essentially kindhearted. Present on the night of David's birth, she has already made up her mind as to his sex and his name, her own. When she learns that the child is a boy, she leaves the house in great indignation. Eventually she becomes the benefactress of destitute and desolate David, educates him, and lives to see him happily married to Agnes Wickfield and established in his literary career.

Richard Babley, called **Mr. Dick,** a mildly mad and seemingly irresponsible man befriended by Miss Trotwood. He has great difficulty in keeping the subject of King Charles the First out of his conversation and the memorial he is writing. Miss Trotwood, who refuses to admit that he is mad, always defers to him as a shrewd judge of character and situation.

Dora Spenlow, the ornamental but helpless "child-wife" whom David loves protectively, marries, and loses when she dies young. Her helplessness in dealing with the ordinary situations of life is both amusing and touching.

Agnes Wickfield, the daughter of Miss Trotwood's solicitor and David's staunch friend for many years. Though David at first admires the father, his admiration is soon transferred to the sensible, generous daughter. She nurses Dora Copperfield at the time of her fatal illness, and Dora on her deathbed advises David to marry Agnes. The delicacy with which Agnes contains her love for many years makes her an appealing figure. Eventually she and David are married, to Miss Trotwood's great delight.

Uriah Heep, the hypocritical villain who, beginning as a clerk in Mr. Wickfield's law office, worms his way into the confidence of his employer, becomes a partner in the firm, ruins Mr. Wickfield, and embezzles Miss Trotwood's fortune. His insistence that he is a very humble person provides the clue to his sly, conniving nature. His villainy is finally uncovered by Wilkins Micawber, whom he has used as a pawn, and he is forced to make restitution. After Mr. Wickfield and Miss Trotwood refuse to charge him with fraud, he continues his sharp practices in another section of the country until he is arrested for forgery and imprisoned.

Wilkins Micawber, an impecunious man who is "always waiting for something to turn up" while spending himself into debtors' prison, writing grandiloquent letters, indulging in flowery rhetoric, and eking out a shabbily genteel existence on the brink of disaster. David Copperfield lodges with the Micawbers for a time in London, and to him Mr. Micawber confides the sum of his worldly philosophy: "Annual income twenty pounds; annual expenditure nineteen, nineteen, six—result happiness. Annual income twenty pounds; annual expenditure twenty pounds nought six—result misery." He tries a variety of occupations in the course of the novel and is for a time employed by Uriah Heep, whose villainy he contemptuously unmasks. Miss Trotwood aids him and his family to immigrate to Australia, where he becomes a magistrate. A figure of improvidence, alternating between high spirits and low, well-meaning but without understanding of the ways of the world, Mr. Micawber is one of Dickens' great comic creations.

Mrs. Emma Micawber, a woman of genteel birth (as she frequently insists) and as mercurial in temperament as her husband. She is capable of fainting over the prospect of financial ruin at three o'clock and of eating with relish breaded lamb chops and drinking ale, bought with money from two pawned teaspoons, at four. Loyal in nature, she says in every crisis that she will never desert Mr. Micawber.

Master Wilkins and **Miss Emma,** the Micawber children.

James Steerforth, David Copperfield's fellow student at Salem House. The handsome, spoiled son of a wealthy widow, he hides his true nature behind pleasing manners and a seemingly engaging disposition. Introduced by David into the Peggotty household at Yarmouth, he succeeds in seducing Little Em'ly and persuading her to elope with him on the eve of her marriage to Ham. Later he tires of her and plans to marry her off to Littimer, the servant who aids him in his amorous conquests. He is drowned when his ship breaks up during a storm off Yarmouth.

Mrs. Steerforth, James Steerforth's mother, a proud, austere woman, at first devoted to her handsome, wayward son but eventually estranged from him.

Rosa Dartle, Mrs. Steerforth's companion. Older than Steerforth but deeply in love with him, she endures humiliation and many indignities because of her unreasoning passion. Her lip is scarred, the result of a wound suffered when Steerforth, in a childish fit of anger, threw a hammer at her.

Littimer, Steerforth's valet, a complete scoundrel. Tired of Little Em'ly, Steerforth plans to marry her to his servant, but the girl runs away in order to escape this degradation.

Miss Mowcher, a pursy dwarf. A hairdresser, she makes herself "useful" to a number of people in a variety of ways. Steerforth avails himself of her services.

Markham and **Grainger,** Steerforth's lively, amusing friends.

Francis Spenlow, a partner in the London firm of Spenlow and Jorkins, proctors, in which David Copperfield becomes an articled clerk. During a visit at the Spenlow country place David meets Dora, Mr. Spenlow's lovely but childlike daughter and falls in love with her, but her father opposes David's suit after Miss Trotwood loses her fortune. Mr. Spenlow dies suddenly after a fall from his carriage and Dora is taken in charge by two maiden aunts. Following the discovery that Mr. Spenlow's business affairs were in great confusion and that he died almost penniless, David marries Dora.

Miss Clarissa and **Miss Lavina Spenlow,** Mr. Spenlow's sisters, who take Dora into their home after her father's death.

Mr. Jorkins, Mr. Spenlow's business partner.

Mary Anne Paragon, a servant to David and Dora during their brief married life.

Mr. Tiffey, an elderly, withered-looking clerk employed by Spenlow and Jorkins.

Mr. Wickfield, a solicitor of Canterbury and Miss Trotwood's man of business, brought to ruin by Uriah Heep's scheming and adroit mismanagement of the firm's accounts. He is saved from disaster when Wilkins Micawber exposes Heep's machinations. Mr. Wickfield is a weak, foolish, but high-principled man victimized by a scoundrel who exploits his weaknesses.

Mr. Creakle, the master of Salem House, the wretched school to which Mr. Murdstone sends David Copperfield. Lacking in scholarly qualities, he prides himself on his strict discipline. Years later he becomes interested in a model prison where Uriah Heep and Littimer are among the inmates.

Mrs. Creakle, his wife, the victim of her husband's tyranny.

Miss Creakle, their daughter, reported to be in love with Steerforth.

Charles Mell, a junior master at Salem House, discharged when Mr. Creakle learns that the teacher's mother lives in an almshouse. Immigrating to Australia, he eventually becomes the head of the Colonial Salem-House Grammar School.

Mr. Sharp, the senior master at Salem House.

George Demple, one of David Copperfield's schoolmates at Salem House.

Thomas Traddles, another student at Salem House. As an unhappy schoolboy he consoles himself by drawing skeletons. He studies law, marries the daughter of a clergyman, and eventually becomes a judge. He, with David Copperfield, acts for Miss Trotwood after Uriah Heep's villainy has been revealed.

Miss Sophy Crewler, the fourth daughter of a clergyman's family, a pleasant, cheerful girl who marries Thomas Traddles. Her husband always refers to her as "the dearest girl in the world."

The Reverend Horace Crewler, a poor clergyman and the father of a large family of daughters.

Mrs. Crewler, his wife, a chronic invalid whose condition mends or grows worse according to the pleasing or displeasing circumstances of her life.

Caroline, Sarah, Louisa, Lucy, and **Margaret,** the other Crewler daughters. They and their husbands form part of the family circle surrounding happy, generous Traddles.

Dr. Strong, the master of the school at Canterbury where Miss Trotwood sends her great-nephew to be educated. After Miss Trotwood loses her money, Dr. Strong hires David to help in compiling a classical dictionary.

Mrs. Strong, a woman much younger than her husband.

Mrs. Markleham, the mother of Mrs. Strong. The boys at the Canterbury school call her the "Old Soldier."

Mr. Quinion, the manager of the warehouse of Murdstone and Grinby, where David Copperfield is sent to do menial work after his mother's death. Miserable in these surroundings, David finally resolves to run away and look for his only relative, Miss Betsey Trotwood, in Dover.

Tipp, a workman in the Murdstone and Grinby warehouse.

Mealy Potatoes and **Mick Walker,** two rough slum boys who work with David at the warehouse of Murdstone and Grinby.

Miss Larkins, a dark-eyed, statuesque beauty with whom David Copperfield falls in love when he is seventeen. She disappoints him by marrying Mr. Chestle, a grower of hops.

Miss Shepherd, a student at Miss Nettingall's Establishment for Young Ladies and another of David Copperfield's youthful loves.

Mrs. Crupp, David Copperfield's landlady while he is an articled clerk in the firm of Spenlow and Jorkins. She suffers from "the spazzums" and takes quantities of peppermint for this strange disorder.

Martha Endell, the unfortunate young woman who helps to restore Little Em'ly to her uncle.

Janet, Miss Betsey Trotwood's servant.

Jack Maldon, Mrs. Strong's cousin, a libertine for whom her kindhearted husband finds employment.

The Story

David Copperfield was born at Blunderstone, in Suffolk, six months after his father's death. Miss Betsey Trotwood, an eccentric grandaunt, was present on the night of his birth, but she left the house abruptly and indignantly when she learned that the child was a boy who could never bear her name. David spent his early years with his pretty young mother, Clara Copperfield, and a devoted servant named Peggotty. Peggotty was plain and plump; when she bustled about the house, her buttons popped off her dress.

The youthful widow was soon courted by Mr. Murdstone, who proved to be stingy and cruel after marriage.

When his mother married a second time, David was packed off with Peggotty to visit her relatives at Yarmouth. There her brother had converted an old boat into a seaside cottage, where he lived with his niece, Little Em'ly, and his sturdy young nephew, Ham. Little Em'ly and Ham were David's first real playmates, and his visit to Yarmouth remained a happy memory of his lonely and unhappy childhood. After Miss Jane Murdstone arrived to take charge of her brother's household, David and his mother were never to feel free again from the dark atmosphere of suspicion and gloom the Murdstones brought with them.

One day in a fit of childish terror, David bit his stepfather on the hand. He was immediately sent off to Salem House, a wretched school near London. There his life was more miserable than ever under a brutal headmaster named Creakle; but in spite of the harsh system of the school and the bullyings of Mr. Creakle, his life was endurable because of his friendship with two boys whom he was to meet again under much different circumstances in later life—lovable Tommy Traddles and handsome, lordly James Steerforth.

His school days ended suddenly with the death of his mother and her infant child. When he returned home, he discovered that Mr. Murdstone had dismissed Peggotty. Barkis, the stage driver, whose courtship had been meager but earnest, had taken Peggotty away to become Mrs. Barkis, and David was left friendless in the home of his cruel stepfather.

David was put to work in an export warehouse in which Murdstone had an interest. As a ten-year-old worker in the dilapidated establishment of the wine merchants Murdstone and Grinby, David was overworked and half-starved. He loathed his job and associates such as young Mick Walker and Mealy Potatoes. The youngster, however, met still another person with whom he was to associate in later life: Wilkins Micawber, a pompous ne'er-do-well in whose house David lodged. The impecunious Mr. Micawber found himself in debtor's prison shortly afterward. On his release, he decided to move with his brood in Plymouth. Having lost these good friends, David decided to run away from the environment he detested.

When David decided to leave Murdstone and Grinby, he knew he could not return to his stepfather. The only other relative he could think of was his father's aunt, Miss Betsey Trotwood, who had flounced indignantly out of the house on the night of David's birth. Hopefully, he set out for Dover where Miss Betsey lived, but not before he had been robbed of all his possessions. Consequently, he arrived at Miss Betsey's home physically and mentally wretched.

At first, David's reception was not cordial. Miss Betsey had never forgotten the injustice done her when David was born a boy instead of a girl; however, upon the advice of Mr. Dick, a feebleminded distant kinsman who was staying with her, she decided to take David in, at least until he had been washed thoroughly. While she was deliberating further about what to do with her bedraggled nephew, she wrote to Mr. Murdstone, who came with his sister to Dover to claim his stepson. Miss Betsey decided she disliked both Murdstones intensely. Mr. Dick solved her problem by suggesting that she keep David.

Much to David's joy and satisfaction, Miss Betsey planned to let the boy continue his education and almost immediately sent him to a school in Canterbury, run by a Mr. Strong, a headmaster quite different from Mr. Creakle. During his stay at school, David lodged with Miss Betsey's lawyer, Mr. Wickfield. David became very fond of Agnes, Wickfield's daughter. At Wickfield's he also met Uriah Heep, Mr. Wickfield's cringing clerk, whose hypocritical humility and clammy handclasp filled David with disgust.

David finished school when he was seventeen years old. Miss Betsey suggested that he travel for a time before deciding on a profession. On his way to visit his old nurse Peggotty, David met James Steerforth and went home with his former schoolmate. There he met Steerforth's mother and Rosa Dartle, a girl passionately in love with Steerforth. Years before, the quick-tempered Steerforth had struck Rosa, who carried a scar as a reminder of Steerforth's brutality.

After a brief visit, David persuaded Steerforth to go with him to see Peggotty and her family. At Yarmouth, Steerforth met Little Em'ly. In spite of the fact that she was engaged to Ham, she and Steerforth were immediately attracted to each other.

At length, David told his grandaunt that he wished to study law. Accordingly, he was articled to the law firm of Spenlow and Jorkins. At this time, David saw Agnes Wickfield, who told him she feared Steerforth and asked David to stay away from him. Agnes also expressed a fear of Uriah Heep, who was on the point of entering into partnership with her senile father. Shortly after these revelations by Agnes, David encountered Uriah himself, who confessed that he wanted to marry Agnes. David was properly disgusted.

On a visit to the Spenlow home, David met and instantly fell in love with Dora Spenlow, his employer's pretty but childish daughter. Soon they became secretly engaged. Before this happy event, however, David heard some startling news—Steerforth had run away with Little Em'ly.

This elopement was not the only blow to David's happiness. Shortly after his engagement to Dora, David learned from his grandaunt that she had lost all her money, and Agnes informed him that Uriah Heep had become Mr. Wickfield's partner. David tried unsuccessfully to be released from his contract with Spenlow and Jorkins. Determined to show his grandaunt he could repay her, even in a small way, for her past sacrifices, he took a part-time job as secretary to Mr. Strong, his former headmaster.

The job with Mr. Strong, however, paid very little; therefore, David undertook to study for a position as a reporter of parliamentary debates. Even poor, simple Mr. Dick came to Miss Betsey's rescue, for Traddles, now a lawyer, gave him a job as a clerk.

The sudden death of Mr. Spenlow dissolved the partnership of Spenlow and Jorkins, and David learned to his dismay that his former employer had died almost penniless. With much study on his part, David became a reporter. At the age of twenty-one, he married Dora, who, however, never seemed capable of growing up. During these events, David had kept in touch with Mr. Micawber, now Uriah Heep's confidential secretary.

Though something had finally turned up for Mr. Micawber, his relations with David and even with his own family were mysteriously strange, as though he were hiding something.

David soon learned the nature of the trouble; Mr. Micawber's conscience got the better of him. At a meeting arranged by him at Mr. Wickfield's, he revealed in Uriah's presence and to an assembled company including Agnes, Miss Betsey, David, and Traddles, the criminal perfidy of Uriah Heep, who for years had robbed and cheated Mr. Wickfield. Miss Betsey discovered that Uriah was also responsible for her own financial losses. With the exposure of the villainous Uriah, partial restitution for her and for Mr. Wickfield was not long in coming.

Mr. Micawber's conscience was cleared by his exposure of Uriah Heep's villainy, and he proposed to take his family to Australia. There, he was sure something would again turn up. Mr. Peggotty and Little Em'ly also went to Australia; Little Em'ly had turned to her uncle in sorrow and shame after Steerforth had deserted her. David watched as their ship put out to sea. It seemed to him that the sunset was a bright promise for them as they sailed away to a new life in the new land. The darkness fell about him as he watched.

The great cloud now in David's life was his wife's delicate health. Day after day she failed, and in spite of his tenderest care, he was forced to see her grow more feeble and wan. Agnes Wickfield, like the true friend she had always been, was with him on the night of Dora's death. As in his earlier troubles, he turned to Agnes in the days that followed and found comfort in her sympathy and understanding.

Upon her advice, he decided to go abroad for a while. First, however, he went to Yarmouth to put a last letter from Little Em'ly into Ham's hands. There he witnessed the final act of her betrayal. During a storm, the heavy seas battered a ship in distress off the coast. Ham went to his death in a stouthearted attempt to rescue a survivor clinging to a broken mast. The bodies washed ashore by the rolling waves were those of loyal Ham and the false Steerforth.

David lived in Europe for three years. On his return, he discovered again his need for Agnes Wickfield's quiet friendship. One day, Miss Betsey Trotwood slyly suggested that Agnes might soon be married. Heavy in heart, David went off to offer her his good wishes. When she burst into tears, he realized that what he had hoped was true—her heart was already his. To the great delight of matchmaking Miss Betsey, Agnes and David were married, and David settled down to begin his career as a successful novelist.

Critical Evaluation

"But, like many fond parents, I have in my heart of hearts a favorite child. And his name is David Copperfield."

This is Charles Dickens' final, affectionate judgment of the work that stands exactly in the middle of his novelistic career, with seven novels before and seven after (excluding the unfinished *The Mystery of Edwin Drood*). When he began the novel, he was in his mid-thirties, secure in continuing success that had begun with *Sketches by Boz* (1836) and *Pickwick Papers* (1836–1837). It was a good time to take stock of his life and to make use of the autobiographical manuscript he had put by earlier; nor did he try to conceal the personal element from his public, which eagerly awaited each of the nineteen numbers of *David Copperfield*. The novel was issued serially from May, 1849, through November, 1850. Charles Dickens, writer, is readily identified with David Copperfield, writer, viewing his life through the "long Copperfieldian perspective," as Dickens called it.

Although much in the life of the first-person narrator corresponds to Dickens' own life, details are significantly altered. Unlike David, Dickens was not a genteel orphan but the eldest son of living and improvident parents; his own father served as the model for Micawber. Dickens' childhood stint in a shoeblacking factory seems to have been somewhat shorter than David's drudgery in the warehouse of the wine distributors Murdstone and Grinby, but the shame and suffering were identical. Young Dickens failed in his romance with a pretty young girl, but the author Dickens permits David to win his Dora. Dickens, however, inflicts upon Dora as Mrs. Copperfield the faults of his own Kate, who, unlike Dora, lived on as his wife until their separation in 1858.

However fascinating the autobiographical details, *David Copperfield* stands primarily on its merits as a novel endowed with the bustling life of Dickens' earlier works but controlled by his maturing sense of design. The novel in its entirety answers affirmatively the question posed by David himself in the opening sentence: "Whether I shall turn out to be the hero of my own life."

In addition to the compelling characterization of the protagonist, the novel abounds with memorable portrayals. The square face and black beard of Mr. Murdstone, always viewed in conjunction with that "metallic lady," Miss Murdstone, evoke the horror of dehumanized humanity. Uriah Heep's writhing body, clammy skin, and peculiarly lidless eyes suggest a subhuman form that is more terrifying than the revolting nature of his "umbleness." Above all the figures that crowd the lonely world of the orphan rises the bald head of Wilkins Micawber, flourishing the English language and his quizzing glass with equal impressiveness, confidently prepared in case some opportunity turns up.

David Copperfield, nevertheless, is very definitely the hero of his own story. This is a novel of initiation, organized around the two major cycles of the hero's development—first in childhood, then in early manhood. He makes his own choices, but each important stage of his moral progress is marked by the intervention of Aunt Betsey Trotwood.

Initially, David is weak simply because he is a child, the hapless victim of adult exploitation; but he is also heir to the moral weakness of his childish mother and his dead father, who was an inept, impractical man. Portentously, David's birth is the occasion of a conflict between his mother's Copperfieldian softness and Aunt Betsey's firmness, displayed in her rigidity of figure and countenance.

From a state of childish freedom, David falls into the Murdstone world. The clanking chains of Miss Murdstone's steel purse symbolize the metaphorical prison that replaces his innocently happy home. Indeed, for David, the world becomes a prison. After his five days of solitary confinement at Blunderstone, he enters the jail-like Salem House School. After his mother's death, he is placed in the grim warehouse, apparently for life; nor is his involvement with the Micawbers any real escape, for he is burdened with their problems and retains his place in the family even after their incarceration in the King's Bench Prison.

Although David repudiates the tyrannical firmness of which he is a victim, he does not actively rebel except for the one occasion when he bites Mr. Murdstone. Instead, like his mother, he indulges his weakness; he submits, fearfully to the Murdstones and Creakle, worshipfully to the arrogant Steerforth. In addition, he escapes into the illusory freedom of fantasy—through books and stories and through the lives of others, which he invests with an enchantment that conceals from him whatever is potentially tragic or sordid.

David's pliant nature, nevertheless, shares something of the resolute spirit of Aunt Betsey, despite her disappearance on the night of his birth. Looking back upon his wretched boyhood, David recalls that he kept his own counsel and did his work. From having suffered in secret, he moves to the decision to escape by his own act. The heroic flight is rewarded when Aunt Betsey relents and takes him in. Appropriately, she trusses up the small boy in adult clothes and announces her own goal of making him a "fine fellow, with a will of your own," with a "strength of character that is not to be influenced, except on good reason, by anybody, or by anything." The first cycle of testing is complete.

The conventionally happy years in Dover and Canterbury mark an interlude before the second major cycle of the novel, which commences with David's reentry into the world as a young man. Significantly, he at first resumes the docile patterns of childhood. Reunited with Steerforth, he once again takes pride in his friend's overbearing attitude. He allows himself to be bullied by various inferiors. He evades the obligation to choose his own career by entering into a profession that affects him like an opiate. In Dora's childlike charms, he recaptures the girlish image of his mother. At this point, however, the firm Aunt Betsey, having cut short his childhood trials, deliberately sets into motion his adult testing with her apparent bankruptcy.

In response to his new challenges, David is forced back upon his childhood resources. At first, he unconsciously imitates Murdstone in trying to mold Dora; but he again rejects tyranny, choosing instead resignation, understanding that she can be no more than his "child-wife." He responds with full sympathy to the tragedy of Little Em'ly's affair with Steerforth, but he is finally disenchanted with the splendid willfulness that had captivated his boyish heart. Most important, he recovers the saving virtue of his childhood, his ability to suffer in secrecy, to keep his own counsel, and to do his work. As his trials pile up—poverty, overwork, disappointment in marriage, his wife's death, and the tribulations of the friends to whom his tender heart is wholly committed—he conquers his own undisciplined heart.

The mature man who emerges from his trials profits from his experiences and heritage. His capacity for secret suffering is, for him as for Aunt Betsey, a source of strength; but his, unlike hers, is joined to the tenderheartedness inherited from his parents. Her distrust of mankind has made her an eccentric. His trusting disposition, though rendering him vulnerable, binds him to humanity.

While Aunt Betsey sets a goal of maturity before David, Agnes Wickfield is the symbol of the hard-won self-discipline which he finally achieves. She is from the beginning his "better angel." Like him, she is tenderhearted and compliant; yet, though a passive character, she is not submissive, and she is always in control of herself in even the most difficult human relationships. Moreover, her firmness of character is never distorted by fundamental distrust of mankind; thus hers is the only influence that David should accept, "on good reason," in his pursuit of the moral goal that Aunt Betsey sets before him.

By the time David has recognized his love for Agnes, he has also attained a strength of character like hers. The appropriate conclusion to his quest for maturity is his union with Agnes—who is from the beginning a model of the self-disciplined person in whom gentleness and strength are perfectly balanced. Furthermore, the home he builds with her is the proper journey's end for the orphaned child who has grasped at many versions of father, mother, family, and home: "Long miles of road then opened out before my mind, and toiling on, I saw a ragged way-worn boy forsaken and neglected, who should come to call even the heart now beating against him, his own." He has outgrown the child-mother, the

child-wife, the childhood idols, even the childhood terrors, and he is a mature man ready to accept love "founded
on a rock."

In the context of a successful completed quest, the
novel ends with a glimpse of the complete man, who
writes far into the night to erase the shadows of his past
but whose control of the realities is sufficient in the presence of the woman who is always, symbolically, "near
me, pointing upward!"

DEAD SOULS

Type of work: Novel
Author: Nikolai Gogol (1809–1852)
Type of plot: Social satire
Time of plot: Early nineteenth century
Locale: Russia
First published: *Myortvye dushi*, part 1, 1842; part 2, 1855 (English translation, 1887)

Dead Souls is unanimously considered one of the greatest novels in the Russian language for its characterizations, satiric humor, and style. The plot is not complex—a scheme to buy, from landlords, serfs who have died since the last census, in order to perpetrate the hero's own real estate deal in eastern Russia. The length of the novel is accounted for by numerous digressions adding up to a rich picture of provincial Russia. Whether Gogol's fiction is reality or fantasy, a topic much debated, he uses characterization, extravagant imagery, and hyperbolic language to color intensely his work.

Principal Characters

Pavel Ivanovich Chichikov (pävěl ĭ·vä′nə·vĭch chĕt′chĕ·kəf), an adventurer of early nineteenth century Russia. He buys "dead souls," that is, the names of serfs who have died since the last census but who still continue to cost their owners taxes until they can be written off in the next census. Using their names, he plans to get from his uncle's estate the money refused him in the old man's will, by mortgaging his own "estate," with its dead souls, to the Trustee Committee. To find dead souls, he rides from village to village visiting landowners and exerting his charm to obtain the names of dead serfs. The villagers begin to talk, however, and, not able to guess what he is up to, accuse him of all sorts of crimes. He has an encounter with the law and is arrested. He is finally aided by an unscrupulous lawyer who brings to light all the local scandals, so that the villagers are glad to get Chichikov out of town.

Selifan (sĕ′lĭ·vən), Pavel's coachman, through whose mistake about roads he visits Madame Korobochka. They are put onto the right road by her twelve-year-old maid, Pelageya.

Nastasya Petrovna Korobochka (nästä′syə pĕt·rov′nə kô·rō·bach′kə), an overnight hostess who sells Chichikov eighteen of her dead souls for fifteen rubles each.

Petrushka (pĕt·rōōsh′kə), Chichikov's valet, who shares his adventures.

Nozdryov (nōz′dryəf), a gambler and liar who meets Chichikov at an inn and finally denounces him to the police as a spy and forger. He himself is arrested for assaulting a friend, Maximov.

Manilov (mä·nĭ·lōf′), a genial landowner who offers hospitality to Chichikov and gives him his first dead souls.

Themistoclus (tĕ·mĭs′tə·kləs), one of Manilov's two children.

Mikhail Semyonovich Sobakevich (mĭhä·ĭl′ sĕ·myō′nə·vĭch sô·bä′kĕ·vĭch), a landowner who at first demands a hundred rubles apiece for his dead souls but finally settles for two and a half.

Plyushkin (plūsh′kĭn), a miser who haggles fiercely over 120 dead souls and 78 fugitives. He finally gives Chichikov a letter to the town president.

Ivan Grigoryevich (ĭ·vän′ grĭ·gō′ryěvĭch), the town president, who transfers Chichikov's purchased dead souls to the adventurer's imaginary estate in the Kherson province and makes the transactions legal.

Ivan Antonovich (ĭ·vän′ än·tō′nə·vĭch), a minor clerk who must be bribed to record the purchases.

The Governor, who entertains at a big ball.

The Governor's Daughter, with whom Chichikov is supposed to be eloping. His coach had previously collided with hers.

Captain Kopeikin (kô·pā′kĭn), a legendary soldier of the War of 1812, turned bandit. Some think he has returned disguised as Chichikov.

Andrey Ivanovich Tentetnikov (ändrā′ĭ·vä′nə·vĭch tyĕn·tyĕt′nĭ·kəf), a thirty-three-year-old bachelor who plays host to the adventurer. Chichikov aids him in his suit for a neighbor's daughter.

General Betrishchev (bĕt·rĭsh′chĕf), a neighbor of Tentetnikov, who gives the young landowner his daughter in marriage and sells more dead souls to Chichikov.

Ulinka (ōō·lĭn′kə), the general's daughter, in love with Tentetnikov.

Vishnepokromov (vĭsh·nyĕ·pōk′rə·məf), who tries to prevent Ulinka's engagement.

Petukh (pyĕ′tūk), a generous glutton who entertains Chichikov.

Platonov (plä′tə·nəf), a young friend who accompanies Chichikov on his travels and introduces him to his sister and his brother-in-law.

Kostanjoglo (kô·stän·zhō′glə), a prosperous landowner and the brother-in-law of Platonov. He lends Chichikov ten thousand rubles to buy an estate.

Khlobuyev (hlô·bōō′yĕf), a spendthrift whose land Chichikov wants to buy. By forging a will Chichikov tries to help him claim an inheritance from a rich aunt, but he forgets to cancel in it all earlier documents.

Alexey Ivanovich Lenitsyn (ä·lĕk·sā′ ĭ·vä′nə·vĭch lĕ·nĭ′tsōōn), a public official who discovers two wills of the old woman, one contradicting the other. He has Chi-

chikov jailed on a charge of forgery.

Ivan Andreyevich (ĭ·vän′ än·drā′yĕ·vĭch), the postmaster of N——.

Samosvistov (sä·mōs′vĭs·təf), who offers to get Chichikov out of jail for thirty thousand rubles.

Murazov (mōō·rä·zōf′), the shrewd, unscrupulous lawyer who gets Chichikov freed by raking up scandals against all those who have accused his client.

The Story

Pavel Ivanovich Chichikov had arrived in the town accompanied by his coachman, Selifan, and his valet, Petrushka. He had been entertained gloriously and had met many interesting people, who insisted on his visiting them in their own homes. Nothing could have suited Chichikov better. After several days of celebration in the town, he took his coachman and began a round of visits to the various estates in the surrounding country.

His first host was Manilov, a genial man who wined and dined him in a manner fit for a prince. When the time was ripe, Chichikov began to question his host about his estate. To his satisfaction, he learned that many of Manilov's souls, as the serfs were called, had died since the last census and that Manilov was still paying taxes on them and would continue to do so until the next census. Chichikov offered to buy these dead souls from Manilov and so relieve him of his extra tax burden. The contract was signed, and Chichikov set out for the next estate.

Selifan got lost and in the middle of the night drew up to a house which belonged to Madame Korobochka, from whom Chichikov also bought dead souls. When he left his hostess, he found his way to an inn in the neighborhood. There he met Nozdryov, a notorious gambler and liar. Nozdryov had recently lost a great deal of money at gambling, and Chichikov thought he would be a likely seller of dead souls. When he broached the subject, Nozdryov asked him the reason for his interest in dead souls. For every reason Chichikov gave, Nozdryov called him a liar. Then Nozdryov wanted to play at cards for the souls, but Chichikov refused. They were arguing when a police captain came in and arrested Nozdryov for assault on a man while drunk. Chichikov thought himself well rid of the annoying Nozdryov.

His next host was Sobakevich, who at first demanded the unreasonable sum of one hundred rubles for each name of a dead soul. Chichikov finally persuaded him to accept two and a half rubles apiece, a higher price than he had planned to pay.

Plyushkin, with whom he negotiated next, was a miser. From him Chichikov bought 120 dead souls and 78 fugitives after considerable haggling. Plyushkin gave him a letter to Ivan Grigoryevich, the town president.

Back in town, Chichikov persuaded the town president

to make his recent purchases legal. Since the law required that souls when purchased be transferred to another estate, Chichikov told the officials that he had land in the Kherson province. He had no trouble in making himself sound plausible. Some bribes to minor officials helped.

Chichikov proved to be such a delightful guest that the people of the town insisted that he stay on and on. He was the center of attraction at many social functions, including a ball at which he was especially interested in the governor's daughter. Soon, however, rumors spread that Chichikov was using the dead souls as a screen, that he was really planning to elope with the governor's daughter. The men, in consultation at the police master's house, speculated variously. Some said he was a forger; others thought he might be an officer in the governor-general's office; one man put forth the fantastic suggestion that he was really the legendary Captain Kopeikin in disguise. They questioned Nozdryov, who had been the first to report the story of the purchase of dead souls. At their interrogation, Nozdryov confirmed their opinions that Chichikov was a spy and a forger who was trying to elope with the governor's daughter.

The truth of the matter was that Chichikov had begun his career as a humble clerk. His father had died leaving no legacy for his son, who worked in various capacities, passing from customs officer to smuggler to pauper to legal agent. When he learned that the Trustee Committee would mortgage souls, he hit upon the scheme of acquiring funds by mortgaging dead souls that were still on the census lists. It was this purpose which had sent him on his current tour.

While the townsfolk debated his identity, Chichikov, having caught a cold, was confined to his bed. When at last he had recovered sufficiently to go out, he found himself no longer welcome at the houses of his former friends. He was, in fact, turned away by servants at the door. Chichikov realized that it would be best for him to leave town.

According to extant fragments, unpublished by Gogol, that have been assembled as part 2 of *Dead Souls*, Chichikov turned up next on the estate of Andrey Ivanovich Tentetnikov, a thirty-three-year-old bachelor who had retired from public life to vegetate in the country. Learning that Tentetnikov was in love with the daughter of his neighbor, General Betrishchev, Chichikov went to see the general and won his consent to Tentetnikov's suit. He brought the conversation around to a point where he could offer to buy dead souls from the general. He gave as his reason the story that his old uncle would not leave him an estate unless he himself already owned some property. The scheme so delighted the general that he gladly made the transaction.

Chichikov's next stop was with Petukh, a generous glutton whose table Chichikov enjoyed. There he met a young man named Platonov, whom Chichikov persuaded to travel with him and see Russia. The two stopped to see Platonov's sister and brother-in-law, Kostanjoglo, a prosperous landholder. Chichikov so impressed his host that Kostanjoglo agreed to lend him ten thousand rubles to buy the estate of a neighboring spendthrift named Khlobuyev. Khlobuyev said he had a rich old aunt who would give great gifts to churches and monasteries but would not help her destitute relatives. Chichikov proceeded to the town where the old woman resided and forged a will to his own advantage, but he forgot to insert a clause canceling all previous wills. On her death, he went to interview His Excellency Alexey Ivanovich Lenitsyn, who told him that two wills had been discovered, each contradicting the other. Chichikov was accused of forging the second will and was thrown into prison. In the interpretation of this mix-up, Chichikov learned a valuable lesson in deception from the crafty lawyer he consulted. The lawyer managed to confuse the affair with every public and private scandal in the province, so that the officials were soon willing to drop the whole matter if Chichikov would leave town immediately. The ruined adventurer was only too glad to comply.

Critical Evaluation

When part 1 of *Dead Souls*, Nikolai Gogol's most ambitious work, was first published in 1842, its author had already written such distinctive miniatures as "Diary of a Madman," "The Nose," and "The Overcoat," as well as his play *The Inspector General*. According to legend, the great poet Aleksandr Pushkin supplied Gogol with the book's premise, urging his younger compatriot to create an epic that would ensure him the same place in literature that *Don Quixote* had secured for Cervantes. In contrast with the Spanish author, who had completed the second part of his masterpiece a decade after the first was published, Gogol never finished the second and third portions, which he dreamed would somehow encompass all of Russia. Thus, despite the survival of fragments tracing Chichikov's adventures after escaping the town of N——, the masterpiece that is *Dead Souls* represents only the first part of an unfinished epic. The author's tortured attempts to complete it, culminating with his death by fasting in 1852, brought Gogol and *Dead Souls* added notoriety.

Critics are quick to point out that, since contemporary landowners commonly bartered their living serfs, Chichikov's paper trade in "dead souls" (the Russian word for "soul" also carried the meaning of "serf") is more of an ingenious literary device than an unforgivable crime. Pushkin's plot line, focusing on a smooth-talking stranger who tries to take advantage of a provincial town's inhabitants, afforded Gogol an opportunity to invent an unforgettable gallery of grotesques stepped in *poshlust* (utter banality and worthlessness of character). The deadbeats, ignoramuses, brutes, liars, and misers populating the vicinity of N—— embody various manifestations of this characteristic so well that some of their names have been incorporated into the Russian language. Gogol's depictions of these landowners suggest richly colored literary portraits in their skillful employment of dialogue and revealing details. In contrast, his portrayals of lesser figures, such as the town's bureaucrats (described as anonymous laboring jackets) and the gossips of the ninth chapter (coyly introduced as "a lady agreeable in all respects" and "a lady who was simply agreeable"), invite comparisons to clever caricatures.

In his extended essay *Nikolai Gogal*, Vladimir Nabokov voices a particular predilection for the many characters and situations created by Gogol via similes. Rather than briefly alighting on such descriptive conceits, Gogol expands upon them, punctuating his narrative, for example, with sketches of a man polishing his boots deep into the night and a police sentry who, awakened by the noisy arrival of Korobochka's carriage at the other end of town, crushes an insect on his thumbnail before falling asleep again.

The most audacious of Gogol's digressions is the interpolated tale of Captain Kopeikin, which the author thought so essential that he repeatedly implored his censors to have mercy on it. The story is introduced when the town postmaster, believing Chichikov to be Kopeikin, relates the double-amputee outlaw's exploits, only to be informed at the end of the tale that, since Chichikov is in full possession of all of his limbs, the two could not possibly be the same individual. In a letter to the censor Alexander Nikitenko, Gogol wrote that this tale was "essential not for the connection of events, but in order to distract the reader for a moment, to replace one impression with another," showing that the artist was conscious of the effect his digressions would have on his audience. Other notable excursions are those relating to the narrator's feelings about his book and his readers, as well as meditations on travel and the Russian state. Most famous of these is the concluding passage that follows Chichikov as he flees N——.

Alternately a spellbinding raconteur, a pedant, and an

apologist, Gogol assumed an elaborate succession of narrative voices to carry his story forward. Apparent to readers of the original Russian is the facility with which he employed his homeland's still nascent literary language. The work's lush lyrical passages are virtually unprecedented in Russian prose, and names such as Nozdryov (nostril), Sobakevich (dog), Korobochka (little box), and Manilov (combining "mannerism," "mistiness," and "dreamy attraction") are fully exploited for their comedic and symbolic potential.

After the publication of *Dead Souls*, Gogol struggled with chronic illness, insecurity, and, many believe, incipient insanity. Troubled by the possibility that his story might be considered too frivolous, the moralistic Gogol had established his tripartite plan (echoing the structure of Dante's *The Divine Comedy*) with the hope that it would imbue his epic with a moral context and thereby confirm the first book's "absolute usefulness and necessity." Yet he was never satisfied with his work on the second and third parts. Seeking to cure his physical, spiritual, and creative woes, he traveled compulsively throughout Europe, burning his work on the second part in 1845 before publishing *Selected Passages from Correspondence with Friends* in 1847. The abrasive harangues of this edition earned Gogol widespread criticism, most notably in a letter by the literary critic and journalist Vissarion Belinsky. When Fyodor Dostoevski was arrested in 1849, he was accused of having read this banned document.

Returning to Russia after a pilgrimage to Palestine in 1848, Gogol continued his struggles with *Dead Souls* until February 11, 1852. Told by the fanatical Father Matthew Konstantinovsky that his life's work had been mired in sin, the repentant and frustrated Gogol again incinerated his manuscript and then took to bed, refusing food. Suffering the agonies of contemporary medical practices as well as his own profound hunger, he died soon thereafter, on the morning of March 4.

DEATH COMES FOR THE ARCHBISHOP

Type of work: Novel
Author: Willa Cather (1873–1947)
Type of plot: Historical chronicle
Time of plot: Last half of the nineteenth century
Locale: New Mexico and Arizona
First published: 1927

Based on the lives of two eminent nineteenth century French clerics, this novel tells of the missionary efforts of the French bishop, Jean Latour, and his vicar, Father Joseph Vaillant, to establish a diocese in the territory of New Mexico. Besides a skillful reconstruction of these dedicated lives, the novel also provides a vivid picture of a particular region and culture. Tales and legends from Spanish colonial history and from the primitive tribal traditions of the Hopi and Navajo enter the chronicle at many points, creating an effect of density and variety.

Principal Characters

Father Jean Marie Latour, a devout French priest consecrated Vicar Apostolic of New Mexico and Bishop of Agathonica in Partibus in 1850. With Father Vaillant, his friend and fellow seminarian, he journeys from his old parish on the shores of Lake Ontario to Santa Fé, seat of the new diocese in territory recently acquired from Mexico. In those troubled times he finds many of the old missions in ruins or abandoned, the Mexican clergy lax and unlearned, the sacraments corrupted by native superstitions. The travels of these two dedicated missionary priests over a desert region of sand, arroyos, towering mesas, and bleak red hills, the accounts of the labors they perform and the hardships they endure to establish the order and authority of the church in a wild land, make up the story of this beautifully told chronicle. Father Latour is an aristocrat by nature and tradition. Intellectual, fastidious, reserved, he finds the loneliness of his mission redeemed by the cheerfulness and simple-hearted warmth of his old friend and by the simple piety he often encounters among the humblest of his people; from them, as in the case of old Sada, he learns lessons of humility and grace. For years he dreams of building a cathedral in Santa Fé, and in time his ambition is realized. By then he is an archbishop and an old man. In the end he decides not to return to his native Auvergne, the wet, green country of his youth that he had often remembered with yearning during his years in the hot desert country. He retires to a small farm outside Santa Fé, and when he dies his body rests in state before the altar in the cathedral he had built. Father Latour's story is based on the life of a historical figure, Jean Baptiste Lamy, the first archbishop of Santa Fé.

Father Joseph Vaillant, Father Latour's friend and vicar. The son of hardy peasant stock, he is tireless in his missionary labors. If Father Latour is an intellectual aristocrat, Father Vaillant is his opposite, the hearty man of feeling, able to mix with all kinds of people and to move them as much by his good humor and physical vitality as by his eloquence. Doctrine, he holds, is good enough in its place, but he prefers to put his trust in miracles and the working of faith. When the gold rush begins in Colorado, he is sent to Camp Denver to work among the miners. There he continues his missionary labors, traveling from camp to camp in a covered carriage that is both his sleeping quarters and an improvised chapel. Borrowing and begging wherever he can, he builds for the church and for the future. When he dies, the first Bishop of Denver, there is not a building in the city large enough to hold the thousands who come to his funeral. Like Father Latour, Father Vaillant is modeled after a real person, Father Joseph P. Machebeuf.

Padre Antonio José Martinez, the vigorous but arrogant priest at Taos credited with having instigated the revolt of the Taos Indians. A man of violence and sensual passions, he has lived like a dictator too long to accept the authority of Father Latour with meekness or reason. When Father Latour visits him in Taos, he challenges his Bishop on the subject of celibacy. After the Bishop announces his intention to reform lax practices throughout his diocese, Padre Martinez tells him blandly that he will found his own church if interfered with. As good as his promise, he and Padre Lucero defy Father Latour and Rome and try to establish a schism called the Old Holy Catholic Church of Mexico. Until his death a short time later Padre Martinez carries on his personal and ecclesiastical feud with Father Taladrid, appointed by Father Latour to succeed the old tyrant of Taos.

Padre Marino Lucero, the priest of Arroyo Hondo, who joins Padre Martinez in defying Father Latour's authority. Padre Lucero is said to have a fortune hidden away. After he repents of his heresy and dies reconciled to Rome, buckskin bags containing gold and silver coins valued at almost twenty thousand dollars are found buried under the floor of his house.

Padre Gallegos, the genial, worldly priest at Albuquerque, a lover of whiskey, fandangos, and poker. Although Father Latour likes him as a man, he finds him scandalous and impossible as a priest. As soon as possible he suspends Padre Gallegos and puts Father Vaillant in charge of the Albuquerque parish.

Manuel Lujon, a wealthy Mexican. During a visit at his ranch Father Vaillant sees and admires a matched pair of white mules, Contento and Angelica. The priest praises the animals so highly that Lujon, a generous, pious man, decides to give him one of them. But Father Vaillant refuses to accept the gift, saying that it would not be fitting for him to ride on a fine white mule while his Bishop rides a common hack. Resigned, Lujon sends the second mule to Father Latour.

Buck Scales, a gaunt, surly American at whose house Father Latour and his vicar stop on one of their missionary journeys. Warned away by the gestures of his frightened wife, they continue on to the next town. The woman follows them to tell that in the past six years her husband has murdered four travelers as well as the three children she has borne. Scales is arrested and hanged.

Magdalena, the Mexican wife of Buck Scales, a devout woman who reveals her husband's crimes. After her husband's hanging, she lives for a time in the home of Kit Carson. Later Father Latour makes her the housekeeper in the establishment of the Sisters of Loretto in Santa Fé. She attends the old archbishop in his last days.

Kit Carson, the American trapper and scout. He and Father Latour become friends when they meet after the arrest of Buck Scales.

Jacinto, an intelligent young Indian from the Pecos pueblo, often employed as Father Latour's guide on the priest's missionary journeys. On one of these trips the travelers are overtaken by a sudden snowstorm. Jacinto leads Father Latour into a cave which has obviously been used for ceremonial purposes. Before he builds a fire Jacinto walls up an opening in the cave. Waking later in the night, Father Latour sees his guide standing guard over the sealed opening. He realizes that he has been close to some secret ceremonial mystery of the Pecos, possibly connected with snake worship, but he respects Jacinto's confidence and never mentions the matter.

Don Antonio Olivares, a wealthy rancher who has promised to make a large contribution to Father Latour's cathedral fund. He dies suddenly before he can make good his promise, leaving his estate to his wife and daughter for life, after which his property is to go to the church. Two of his brothers contest the will.

Doña Isabella Olivares, the American wife of Father Latour's friend and benefactor. After her husband's death, two of his brothers contest the will on the grounds that Doña Isabella is not old enough to have a daughter of the age of Señorita Inez and that the girl is the child of one of Don Antonio's indiscreet youthful romances, adopted by Doña Isabella for the purpose of defrauding the brothers. Father Vaillant convinces the vain woman that it is her duty to tell the truth about her age in order for her and her daughter to win the case. Much against her will Doña Isabella confesses in court that she is fifty-three years old and not forty-two, as she has claimed. Later she tells Father Vaillant and Father Latour that she will never forgive them for having made her tell a lie about a matter as serious as a woman's age.

Señorita Inez, the daughter of Doña Isabella and Don Antonio Olivares. Her age and her mother's are questioned when the Olivares brothers try to break Don Antonio's will.

Boyd O'Reilly, a young American lawyer, the manager of Don Antonio Olivares' affairs.

Sada, the wretched slave of a Protestant American family. One December night she escapes from the stable where she sleeps and takes refuge in the church. Father Latour finds her there, hears her confession, blesses her, and gives her a holy relic and his own warm cloak.

Eusabio, a man of influence among the Navajos. Though he is younger than Father Latour, the priest respects him greatly for his intelligence and sense of honor. Father Latour grieves when the Navajos are forced to leave their country and rejoices that he has been able to live long enough to see them restored to their lands. When the old Archbishop dies, Eusabio carries word of his death to the Indians.

Bernard Ducrot, the young priest who looks after Father Latour in his last years. He becomes like a son to the gentle old man.

Padre Jesus de Baca, the white-haired, almost blind priest at Isleta. An old man of great innocence and piety, he lives surrounded by his tame parrots.

Trinidad Lucero, a slovenly young monk in training for the priesthood whom Father Latour meets in the house of Padre Martinez. He passes as Padre Lucero's nephew, but some say he is the son of Padre Martinez. When Padre Martinez and Padre Lucero proclaim their schism, Trinidad acts as a curate for both.

Padre Taladrid, the young Spanish priest whom Father Latour appoints to succeed Padre Martinez at Taos.

The Story

In 1851 Father Jean Marie Latour reached Santa Fé, where he was to become Vicar Apostolic of New Mexico. His journey from the shores of Lake Ontario had been long and arduous. He had lost his belongings in a shipwreck at Galveston and had suffered painful injury in a wagon accident at San Antonio.

Upon Father Latour's arrival, in company with his good friend, Father Joseph Vaillant, the Mexican priests refused to recognize his authority. He had no choice but to ride three thousand miles into Mexico to secure the necessary papers from the Bishop of Durango.

On the road he lost his way in an arid landscape of red hills and gaunt junipers. His thirst created vertigo, and he could blot out his agony only by repeating the cry of the Saviour on the Cross. As he was about to give up all hope, he saw a tree growing in the shape of a cross. A short time later he arrived in the Mexican settlement called *Aqua Secreta*, or Hidden Water. Stopping at the home of Benito, Bishop Latour first performed the marriage ceremonies and then baptized all the children.

At Durango he received the necessary documents and started the long trip back to Santa Fé. Meanwhile Father Vaillant had won over the inhabitants from enmity to amity and had set up the Episcopal residence in an old adobe house. On the first morning after his return to Santa Fé, the bishop heard the unexpected sound of a bell ringing the Angelus. Father Vaillant told him that he had found the bell, bearing the date 1356, in the basement of old San Miguel Church.

On a missionary journey to Albuquerque in March, Father Vaillant acquired as a gift a handsome cream-colored mule and another just like it for his bishop. These mules, Contento and Angelica, served the men in good stead for many years.

On another such trip the two priests were riding together on their mules. Caught in a sleet storm, they stopped at the rude shack of an American, Buck Scales. His Mexican wife warned the travelers by gestures that their lives were in danger, and they rode on to Mora without spending the night. The next morning the Mexican woman appeared in town. She told them that her husband had already murdered and robbed four travelers, and that he had killed her three babies. The result was that Scales was brought to justice, and his wife, Magdalena, was sent to the home of Kit Carson, the famous frontier scout. From that time on Kit Carson was a valuable friend of the bishop and his vicar. Magdalena later became the housekeeper and manager for the kitchens of the Sisters of Loretto.

During his first year at Santa Fé, the bishop was called to a meeting of the Plenary Council at Baltimore. On the return journey he brought back with him five nuns sent to establish the school of Our Lady of Light. Next, Bishop Latour, attended by the Indian Jacinto as his guide, spent some time visiting his own vicariate. Padre Gallegos, whom he visited at Albuquerque, acted more like a professional gambler than a priest, but because he was very popular with the natives Bishop Latour did not remove him at that time. At last he arrived at his destination, the top of the mesa at Acoma, the end of his long journey. On that trip he heard the legend of Fray Baltazar, killed during an uprising of the Acoma Indians.

A month after the bishop's visit, Latour suspended Padre Gallegos and put Father Vaillant in charge of the parish at Albuquerque. On a trip to the Pecos Mountains the vicar fell ill with an attack of the black measles. The bishop, hearing of his illness, set out to nurse his friend. Jacinto again served as guide on the cold, snowy trip. When Bishop Latour reached his friend's bedside, he found that Kit Carson had arrived before him. As soon as the sick man could sit in the saddle, Carson and the bishop took him back to Santa Fé.

Bishop Latour decided to investigate the parish of Taos, where the powerful old priest, Antonio José Martinez, was the ruler of both spiritual and temporal matters. The following year the bishop was called to Rome. When he returned, he brought with him four young priests from the Seminary of Montferrand and a Spanish priest to replace Padre Martinez at Taos.

Bishop Latour had one great ambition; he wanted to build a cathedral in Santa Fé. In that project he was assisted by the rich Mexican *rancheros*, but to the greatest extent by his good friend, Don Antonio Olivares. When Don Antonio died, his will stated that his estate was left to his wife and daughter during their lives, and after their decease to the church. Don Antonio's brothers contested the will on the grounds that the daughter, Señorita Inez, was too old to be Doña Isabella's daughter, and the bishop and his vicar had to persuade the vain, coquettish widow to swear to her true age of fifty-three, rather than the forty-two years she claimed. Thus the money was saved for Don Antonio's family and, eventually, the church.

Father Vaillant was sent to Tucson, but after several years Bishop Latour decided to recall him to Santa Fé. When he arrived, the bishop showed him the stone for building the cathedral. About that time Bishop Latour received a letter from the Bishop of Leavenworth. Because of the discovery of gold near Pike's Peak, he asked to have a priest sent there from Father Latour's diocese. Father Vaillant was the obvious choice.

Father Vaillant spent the rest of his life doing good works in Colorado, though he did return to Santa Fé with the Papal Emissary when Bishop Latour was made an archbishop. Father Vaillant became the first Bishop of Colorado. He died there after years of service, and Archbishop Latour attended his impressive funeral services.

After the death of his friend, Father Latour retired to a modest country estate near Santa Fé. He had dreamed during all his missionary years of the time when he could retire to his fertile green Auvergne in France, but in the end he decided that he could not leave the land of his labors. Memories of the journeys he and Father Vaillant had made over thousands of miles of desert country became the meaning of his later years. Bernard Ducrot, a young seminarian from France, became like a son to him.

When Father Latour knew that his time had come to die, he asked to be taken into town to spend his last days near the cathedral. On the last day of his life the church was filled with people who came to pray for him, as word that he was dying spread through the town. He died in the still twilight, and the cathedral bell, tolling in the early darkness, carried to the waiting countryside the news that at last death had come for Father Latour.

Critical Evaluation

When writing of her great predecessor and teacher, Sarah Orne Jewett, Willa Cather expressed her own belief that the quality that gives a work of literature greatness is the "voice" of the author, the sincere, unadorned, and unique vision of a writer coming to grips with his material. If any one characteristic can be said to dominate the writings of Willa Cather, it is a true and moving sincerity. She never tried to twist her subject matter to suit a preconceived purpose, and she resisted the temptation to dress up her homely material. She gave herself absolutely to her chosen material, and the result was a series of books both truthful and rich with intimations of the destiny of the American continent. By digging into the roots of her material, she found the greater meanings and expressed them with a deceptive simplicity. Her vision and craftsmanship were seldom more successfully joined than in *Death Comes for the Archbishop*. So completely did Willa Cather merge her "voice" with her material, that some critics have felt that the book is almost too polished, without the sense of struggle necessary in a truly great novel. But this, in fact, indicates the magnitude of the author's achievement and the brilliance of her technical skill. *Death Comes for the Archbishop* resonates with the unspoken beliefs of the author and the resolved conflicts that went into its construction. On the surface, it is cleanly wrought and simple, but it is a more complicated and profound book than it appears at first reading. Cather learned well from Jewett the secret of unadorned art, of craftsmanship that disarms by its very simplicity, but which is based in a highly sophisticated intelligence.

It is true that this novel is an epic and a regional history, but, much more than either, it is a tale of personal isolation, of one man's life reduced to the painful weariness of his own sensitivities. Father Latour is a hero in the most profound sense of the word, at times almost a romantic hero, with his virtues of courage and determination, but he is also a very modern protagonist, with his doubts and inner conflicts and his philosophical nature. His personality is held up in startling contrast to that of his friend and vicar, Father Vaillant, a more simple, although no less admirable, individual. Cather's austere style perfectly captures the scholarly and urbane religious devotion that compose Father Latour's character. Always in this book, the reader is aware of a sense of the dignity of human life. Cather was not afraid to draw a good man, a man who could stand above others because of his deeds and because of his innate quality. The novel must stand or fall on this character, and it stands superbly.

Although this book is based on a true sequence of events, it is not a novel of plot. It is a chronicle and a character study, and, perhaps more specifically, an interplay of environment and character. Throughout the book, the reader is aware of the reaction of men to the land, and of one man to the land he has chosen. Subtly and deeply, the author suggests that the soul of man is profoundly altered by the soul of the land, and Cather never doubts for a moment that the land does possess a soul or that this soul can transform a human being in complex and important ways. Willa Cather was fascinated by the way the rough landscape of the Southwest, when reduced to its essences, seemed to take human beings and reduce them to their essences. She abandoned traditional realism in this book, turning toward the directness of symbolism. With stark pictures and vivid styles, she created an imaginary world rooted in realism, but transcending realism. The rigid economy with which the book is written forces it to stand with a unique power in the reader's mind long after his reading. And the personality of Bishop Latour stands as the greatest symbol, like a wind-swept crag or precipice in the vast New Mexico landscape, suggesting the nobility of the human spirit, despite the inner conflicts against which it must struggle.

The descriptions of place set the emotional tone of the novel. The quality of life is intimately related to the landscape, and the accounts of the journeys and the efforts to survive despite the unfriendliness of the barren land, all help to create an odd warmth and passion in the narrative. The personalities of Bishop Latour and Father Vaillant establish a definite emotional relationship with the country, and if the other characters in the book are less vividly realized as individuals, perhaps it is because they do not seem to have this relationship with the land. Some of them have become part of the land, worn down by the elements like the rocks and riverbeds, and others have no relationship to it at all; but none of them is involved in the intense love-hate relationship with the land with which the two main characters struggle for so many years.

Although the chronology of the book encompasses many years, the novel is essentially static, a series of rich images and thoughtful moments highlighted and captured as by a camera. This quality of the narrative is not a fault; it is a fact of Cather's style. The frozen moments of contemplation, the glimpses into Father Latour's inner world and spiritual loneliness, are the moments that give the book its greatness. Despite the presence of Kit Carson, the novel is not an adventure story any more than it is merely the account of a pair of churchmen attempting to establish their faith in a difficult new terrain. The cathedral becomes the most important symbol in the final part of the book, representing the earthly successes of a man dedicated to nonworldly ambitions. This conflict between the earthly and the spiritual is at the heart of Bishop Latour's personality and at the heart of the book. But the reader understands, at the end, when the bell tolls for Father Latour, that the temptations were never very deep and that the good man's victory was greater than he ever knew. The author does not spell out her meaning, but the emotional impact of her narrative brings it home to the reader.

DEATH IN VENICE

Type of work: Novella
Author: Thomas Mann (1875–1955)
Type of plot: Symbolic realism
Time of plot: Early twentieth century
Locale: Italy
First published: *Der Tod in Venedig*, 1912 (English translation, 1925)

This novella of great psychological intensity and tragic power is permeated by the rich and varied symbolism of Mann's many conflicting themes—being and death, youth and age, sickness and health, beauty and decay, love and suffering, art and life, the German North and the Mediterranean South. The story of a middle-aged artist whose character deteriorates because of his hopeless passion for a young Polish boy, and whose death is the final irony of his emotional upheaval, Death in Venice *examines understandingly and critically the solitary position of the artist in modern society and uses the infatuation with the boy to dramatize symbolically the narcissism which can be one of the fatal qualities of art.*

Principal Characters

Gustave von Aschenbach (gōō′stäf fŏn ä′shĕn·bäch′), a middle-aged German writer. Small, dark, his bushy gray hair (thinning on top) is brushed back on his overlarge head. His mouth is large, his cheeks lean and furrowed, and his prominent chin slightly cleft. He wears rimless gold glasses on his thick, aristocratically hooked nose, and his eyes are weary and sunken. A widower, he has one child, a married daughter. Precocious, Aschenbach early longed for fame, which he has achieved through several works acclaimed by the general public and the critics as well. He is not a born artist but has made himself one through rigorous discipline and unwavering dedication. A solitary man, he has only a superficial, limited knowledge of the real world. In cultivating his intellect he has denied his feelings. His passion for Tadzio is symbolic of his narcissism, which first degrades and then destroys him. Aschenbach is a symbol of the artist in modern society.

Tadzio (täd′tsĭ·ō), a Polish boy of fourteen who possesses a perfect Greek classic beauty of face and form. To Aschenbach his beautiful head seems that of Eros and the boy himself the essence of beauty. When Aschenbach almost touches Tadzio and then draws back in panic, the action symbolizes the artist's fear of giving way to an emotion. Sometimes the artist sees in Tadzio the youth

Hyacinth, who died the victim of the rivalry of two gods. When after many days Tadzio finally smiles at Aschenbach, the smile is that of Narcissus looking in the pool, and the artist whispers his love. Tadzio's is the last face the artist sees before he dies.

A Stranger. Thin, beardless, snub-nosed, red-haired, freckled, and exotic-looking, he seems to Aschenbach to be bold, domineering, even ruthless.

Another Stranger, an old man masquerading as a youth on an old, dingy Italian ship. He is flashily dressed, his face and eyes are wrinkled, his cheeks rouged, his brown hair and yellow teeth false, and his turned-up mustaches and imperial are dyed. He becomes disgustingly drunk before the ship reaches Venice. When Aschenbach's desperate passion for Tadzio consumes him he, like the painted stranger, tries foolishly to hide his age.

A Strolling Player, a pale, thin-faced, snub-nosed, red-haired man of slight build whose singing is entertaining but obscene and who carries with him an odor of carbolic acid.

A Gondolier. Undersized, brutish-looking, an expert boatman, he is gruff and rude, and he disappears before Aschenbach returns with change to pay him. The gondolier represents Charon, and the artist's ride in the gondola portends his death in Venice.

The Story

Gustave von Aschenbach was a distinguished German writer whose work had brought him world fame and a patent of nobility from a grateful government. His career had been honorable and dignified. A man of ambitious nature, unmarried, he had lived a life of personal discipline and dedication to his art, and in his portrayal of heroes who combined the forcefulness of a Frederick the

Great with the selfless striving of a Saint Sebastian he believed that he had spoken for his race as well as for the deathless spirit of man. At the same time, his devotion to the ideals of duty and achievement had brought him close to physical collapse.

One day, after a morning spent at his desk, he left his house in Munich and went for a walk. His stroll took him as far as a cemetery on the outskirts of the city. While he waited for a streetcar to carry him back to town, he suddenly became aware of a man who stood watching him from the doorway of the mortuary chapel. The stranger, who had a rucksack on his back and walking staff in his hand, was evidently a traveler. Although no word passed between the watcher and the watched, Aschenbach felt a sudden desire to take a trip, to leave the cold, wet German spring for the warmer climate of the Mediterranean lands. His impulse was strengthened by a problem of technique which he had been unable to solve in his writing. At last, reluctantly, he decided to take a holiday and leave his work for a time in order to find relaxation for mind and body in Italy.

He went first to an island resort in the Adriatic, but before long, he became bored with his surroundings and booked passage for Venice. On the ship, he encountered a party of lively young clerks from Pola. With them was an old man whose dyed hair and rouged cheeks made him a ridiculous but sinister caricature of youth. In his disgust, Aschenbach failed to notice that the raddled old man bore a vague resemblance to the traveler he had seen at the cemetery in Munich.

Aschenbach's destination was Lido. At the dock in Venice, he transferred to a gondola which took him by the water route to his Lido hotel. The gondolier spoke and acted so strangely that Aschenbach became disturbed, and because of his agitation he never noticed that the man looked something like the drunk old scarecrow on the ship and the silent stranger at the cemetery. After taking his passenger to the landing stage, the gondolier, without waiting for his money, hastily rowed away. Other boatmen suggested that he might have been afraid of the law because he had no license.

Aschenbach stayed at the Hotel des Bains. That night, shortly before dinner, his attention was drawn to a Polish family—a beautiful mother, three daughters, and a handsome boy of about fourteen. Aschenbach was unaccountably attracted to the youngster, so much so that he continued to watch the family throughout his meal. The next morning, he saw the boy playing with some companions on the beach. His name, as Aschenbach learned while watching their games, was Tadzio.

Disturbed by the appeal the boy had for him, the writer announced his intention of returning home. On his arrival at the railroad station in Venice, however, he discovered that his trunks had been misdirected to Como. Since there was nothing for him to do but to wait for his missing luggage to turn up, he went back to the hotel. Although he despised himself for his vacillation, he realized that his true desire was to be near Tadzio. For Aschenbach there began a period of happiness and anguish, happiness in watching the boy, anguish in that they must remain strangers. One day he almost summoned up enough courage to speak to the youngster. A moment later, he became panic stricken for fear that Tadzio might be alarmed by the older man's interest. The time Aschenbach had set for his holiday passed, but the writer had almost forgotten his home and his work. One evening, Tadzio smiled at him as they passed each other. Aschenbach trembled with pleasure.

Guests began to leave the hotel; there were rumors that a plague had broken out in nearby cities. While loitering one day on the piazza, Aschenbach detected the sweetish odor of disinfectant in the air, for the authorities were beginning to take precautions against an outbreak of the plague in Venice. Aschenbach stubbornly decided to stay on despite the dangers of infection.

A band of entertainers came to the hotel to serenade the guests. In the troupe was an impudent, disreputable-looking street singer whose antics and ballads were insulting and obscene. As he passed among the guests to collect money for the performance, Aschenbach detected on his clothing the almost overpowering smell of disinfectant, an odor suggesting the sweetly corruptive taints of lust and death. The ribald comedian also had a strange similarity to the gondolier, the rouged old rake, and the silent traveler whose disturbing presence had given Aschenbach the idea for his holiday. Aschenbach was torn between fear and desire. The next day, he went to a tourist agency where a young clerk told him that people were dying of the plague in Venice. Even that confirmation of his fears failed to speed Aschenbach's departure from the city. That night, he dreamed that in a fetid jungle, surrounded by naked orgiasts, he was taking part in horrible, Priapean rites.

By that time his deterioration was almost complete. At last he allowed a barber to dye his hair and tint his cheeks, but he still refused to see the likeness between himself and the raddled old fop whose appearance had disgusted him on shipboard. His behavior became more reckless. One afternoon, he followed the Polish family into Venice and trailed them through the city streets. Hungry and thirsty after his exercise, he bought some overripe strawberries at an open stall and ate them. The odor of disinfectant was strong on the sultry breeze.

Several days later, Aschenbach went down to the beach where Tadzio was playing with three or four other boys. They began to fight, and one of the boys threw Tadzio to the ground and pressed his face into the sand. As Aschenbach was about to interfere, the other boy released his victim. Humiliated and hurt, Tadzio walked down to the water. He stood facing seaward for a time, as remote and isolated as a young Saint Sebastian, and then he turned and looked with a somber, secret gaze at Aschenbach, who was watching from his beach chair. To the writer it seemed as though the boy were summoning him. He started to rise but became so giddy that he fell back into his chair. Attendants carried him to his room. That night the world learned that the great Gustave von Aschenbach had died suddenly of the plague in Venice.

Critical Evaluation

Thomas Mann is ranked with James Joyce and Marcel Proust as one of the greatest writers of the early twentieth century. Mann was born into a wealthy German family. He was awarded the Nobel Prize in Literature in 1919. In 1933, he left Germany because of his opposition to Hitler and the Nazi party. He later came to the United States, where he taught and lectured. A scholar as well as an artist, Mann shows in his works the influence of such diverse thinkers as Friedrich Nietzsche, Arthur Schopenhauer, Richard Wagner, and Sigmund Freud. The problem of the artist's role in a decadent, industrialized society is a recurring theme in many of his works, such as *Buddenbrooks* (1901), *Tonio Kröger* (1903), *Death in Venice* (1912), and *The Magic Mountain* (1924).

Death in Venice, Mann's best-known novella, is a complex, beautifully wrought tale dealing with the eternal conflict of the forces of death and decay with man's attempts to achieve permanence through art. Mann portrays the final triumph of death and decay, but not before the hero, Aschenbach, has experienced an escape into the eternal beauty created by the imagination of the artist. The escape of the famous writer, Aschenbach, is accomplished, however, not by his own writings, but by the art of his creator, Thomas Mann. Form and order do finally impose themselves on the chaos of his life; corruption and death are transformed into the purity of artistic beauty. To accomplish this, Mann utilizes an elaborate technical skill in structure, characterization, and symbolism which establishes him among the great writers of Western literature.

The characterization of Aschenbach, the literary hero of his age, is subtle and complex. Author of prose epics, philosophical novels, novels of moral resolution, and aesthetics, Aschenbach has created the hero for his generation. He is aware that his success and talent rely on a basis of physical stamina as well as moral and mental discipline; his key word is *durchhalten* (endure). His work is a product of strain, endurance, intellectual tenacity, and spasms of will. He recognizes, however, that his writing has been to some degree a "pursuit of fame" at the expense of turning his back on a full search for truth. As the novella opens, Aschenbach, exhausted, finding no more joy in his craft, and aware of approaching old age and death, is faced with the fear of not having time to finish all the works he desired to write. Restlessly walking amid the beauty of the English Garden of Munich, Aschenbach is inspired to leave his relatively rootless life on a pilgrimage for artistic renewal in Venice, the perfect symbol of man's art imposed on nature's chaos. This journey motif begins with his glimpse of a stranger, a foreigner with a skull-like face and a certain animal ruthlessness, in a cemetery.

Arriving at the port of Venice, he discovers he is being taken out to sea, rather than into the city, by his gondolier, a figure whose physical description ominously echoes that of the stranger of the cemetery. The gondola itself is specifically compared to a black coffin. The trip, then, becomes the archetypal journey of life to death and of man into the depths of himself. Aschenbach discovers Venice, the symbol of perfect art in his memory, to be dirty, infected, corrupt, permeated by the odor of the human disease and pollution spread in the natural swamp on which the artifice is built. Aschenbach's own transformation to a "foreigner," one who belongs in Venice, is accomplished at an increasingly mad tempo after the moment when, turning his back on the possibility of escaping from Venice by train, he collapses at a fountain in the heart of the city. His death becomes almost self-willed; he dies not because of the plague, not because of his love of Tadzio, but because of his will to live and to create atrophy.

The exterior events of the story, which are minimal, can be properly explained only in terms of the inner conflict of the artist. To produce art, Aschenbach believes he must practice absolute self-denial, affirming the dignity and moral capacity of man in the face of a world of self-indulgence that leads to personal abasement. Yet the artist is also a man and, as such, has drives connecting him to the chaos of the formless elements of nature. This inner conflict is objectified in the boy Tadzio, who embodies all that Aschenbach has rejected in fifty long years of dedication to Apollonian art. As his desire for Tadzio becomes obsessive, disintegration sets in and death becomes irrevocable. Subconsciously, Aschenbach is choosing to pursue the sensual, Dionysian side of himself that he has always denied.

Mann uses dream visions to underline and clarify the subconscious conflicts of Aschenbach. Aschenbach's first hallucination of the crouching beast in the jungle is evoked by the glimpse of the stranger at the Byzantine chapel in Munich. This vision literally foreshadows the trip to Venice and metaphorically foreshadows the inner journey where Aschenbach discovers the jungle and beast within himself. The second vision on the beach in Venice, cast in the form of a Platonic dialogue, explores the interrelatedness of art, love, and beauty with the bestial in man. In a third major dream, Aschenbach is initiated into the worship of the Dionysian rite and finally glimpses "the stranger god" of sensual experience, of formless, chaotic joy, and excesses of emotion. The most striking vision occurs at the end of the novella, when Aschenbach, viewing the amoral beauty of perfection of form in Tadzio silhouetted against the amoral, formless beauty of the sea, accepts the promise inherent in the sea's chaos as the equivalent of the beauty produced by order and moral discipline. The reader assumes the vision to be objective reality until he is brought sharply and suddenly into the present reality of Aschenbach's dead body. Ernest Hemingway used this same technique later in his own novella-length study of death and art "The Snows of Kilimanjaro."

Mann's use of natural, geographical symbols also underlines the central conflicts of the novella. Aschenbach identifies the discipline of his art with Munich, a city of northern Europe, and with the snowy mountains. These places are associated with health, energy, reason, will, and Apollonian creative power. Against them, Mann juxtaposes the tropical marshes, the jungle animal and plant life, the Indian plague, the sun and the sea, which are associated with Dionysian excesses of emotion and ecstasy in art. The beast, the jungle, the plague, the chaos lie within the nature of man and art just as clearly as do the mountain, self-denial, will, and reason, qualities which enable man to construct artifice upon the chaos of nature. Great art, Nietzsche says in *The Birth of Tragedy*, is a product of the fusion rather than the separation of the calm, ordered, contemplative spirit of Apollo and the savage, sensual ecstasy of Dionysius. This is what both Aschenbach and the reader discover in Mann's great work *Death in Venice*.

THE DECAMERON

Type of work: Tales
Author: Giovanni Boccaccio (1313–1375)
Types of plots: Romantic tragedy, farce, and folk tradition
Times of plots: Greco-Roman times and the Middle Ages
Locale: Italy
First transcribed: c. 1348–1353

This collection of tales is set in 1348, the year of the Black Death. Seven ladies and three gentlemen meet in a Florentine church and decide to escape from the city and spend time in the hills of Fiesole; there they pass the time telling stories for ten days. Bocaccio broke free of past tradition and created a literature about ordinary people, and his novellas range from anecdotes and fabliaux to folk and fairy tales of ancient lineage. All are told with a wit carrying them above the range of the licentious, a term sometimes used unjustly about the tales. Their use and adaptations in literature, plays, operas, and paintings attest to their popularity throughout the ages.

The Story

A terrible plague was ravaging Florence, Italy. To flee from it, a group of seven young women and three young men, who had met by chance in a church, decided to go to a villa out of town. There they set up a working arrangement whereby each would be king or queen for a day. During the ten days they stayed in the country, each told a story following certain stipulations laid down by the daily ruler. The stories range from romance to farce, from comedy to tragedy.

Pampinea, for example, told a tale of three young men. When Messer Tedaldo died, he left all of his goods and chattels to his three sons. With no thought for the future, they lived so extravagantly that they soon had little left. The oldest son suggested that they sell what they could, leave Florence, and go to London, where they were unknown.

In London they lent money at a high rate of interest, and in a few years, they had a small fortune. Then they returned to Florence. There they married and began to live extravagantly again, while depending on the monies still coming to them from England.

A nephew named Alessandro took care of their business in England. At that time, there were such differences between the king and a son that Alessandro's business was ruined. He stayed in England, however, in hopes that peace would come and his business would recover. Finally he returned to Italy with a group of monks who were taking their young abbot to the pope to get a dispensation for him and a confirmation of the youthful cleric's election.

On the way, Alessandro discovered that the abbot was a girl, and he married her in the sight of God. In Rome, the girl had an audience with the pope. Her father, the king of England, wished the pope's blessing on her marriage to the old king of Scotland, but she asked the pope's blessing on her marriage to Alessandro instead.

After the wedding, Alessandro and his bride went to Florence, where she paid his uncles' debts. Two knights preceded the couple to England and urged the king to forgive his daughter. After the king had knighted Alessandro, the new knight reconciled the king and his rebellious son.

One of Fiammetta's stories had to do with Tancred, prince of Salerno, who loved his daughter Ghismonda so much that when she was widowed soon after her marriage he did not think to provide her with a second husband, and she was too modest to ask him to do so. Being a lively girl, however, she decided to have as her lover the most valiant man in her father's court. His name was Guiscardo. His only fault was that he was of humble birth.

Ghismonda noticed that Guiscardo returned her interest, and they met secretly in a cave, one entrance to which was through a door in the young widow's bedroom. Soon she was taking her lover into her bedroom, where they enjoyed each other frequently.

Tancred was in the habit of visiting his daughter's room at odd times. One day, when he went to visit, she was not there. He sat down to wait in a place where he was by accident hidden by the bed curtains from his daughter and her lover, who soon came in to use the bed.

Tancred remained hidden, but that night he had Guiscardo arrested. When he berated his daughter for picking so humble a lover, she defied him for letting so brave a man remain poor in his court. She begged nothing from Tancred except that he kill her and her lover with the same stroke.

The prince did not believe Ghismonda would be as resolute as she sounded. When her lover was killed, Tancred had his heart cut from his body and sent to her in a golden cup. Ghismonda thanked her father for his noble gift. After repeatedly kissing the heart, she poured poison in the cup and drank it. Then she lay down upon her bed with Guiscardo's heart upon her own. Tancred's own heart was touched when he saw her cold in death, and he obeyed her last request that she and Guiscardo be buried together.

Another of the storytellers was Filomena. Her heroine, Isabetta, lived in Messina with her three merchant brothers and a young man named Lorenzo, who attended to their business affairs. Isabetta and Lorenzo fell in love. One night, as she went to Lorenzo's room, her oldest brother saw her. He said nothing until the next morning, when the three brothers conferred to see how they could settle the matter so that no shame should fall upon them or upon Isabetta. Not long afterward, the three brothers set out with Lorenzo, claiming that they were going partway with him on a journey. Secretly, however, they killed and buried the young man.

After their return home, the brothers answered none of Isabetta's questions about Lorenzo. She wept and refused to be consoled in her grief. One night Lorenzo came to her in a dream and told her what had happened and where he was buried. Without telling her brothers, she went to the spot indicated in her dream and found her lover's body there. She cut off his head and wrapped it in a cloth to take home. She buried the head in a large flowerpot and planted basil over it. The basil flourished, watered by her tears.

She wept so much over the plant that her brothers took away the pot of basil and hid it. Because she asked about it often, the brothers grew curious. At last they investigated and found Lorenzo's head. Abashed, they left the city. Isabetta died of a broken heart.

Pamfilo wove a tale of Cimone, who became civilized through love. Galeso was the tallest and handsomest of Aristippo's children, but he was so stupid that the people of Cyprus called him Cimone, which means Brute. Cimone's stupidity embarrassed his father until the old man set the boy to the country to live. There Cimone was contented until one day he came upon a sleeping girl, Efigenia, whose beauty completely changed him.

He told his father that he intended to live in town. The news worried his father for a while, but Cimone bought fine clothes and associated only with worthy young men. In four years he was the most accomplished and virtuous young man on the island.

Although he knew she was promised to Pasimunda of Rhodes, Cimone asked Efigenia's father for her hand in marriage. He was refused. When Pasimunda sent for his bride, Cimone and his friends pursued the ship and took Efigenia off the vessel, after which they let the ship's crew go free to return to Rhodes. In the night, a storm arose and blew Cimone's ship to the very harbor in Rhodes where Efigenia was supposed to go. Cimone and his men were arrested.

Pasimunda had a brother who had been promised a wife, but this girl was loved by Lisimaco, a youth of Rhodes, as Efigenia was loved by Cimone. The brothers planned a double wedding.

Lisimaco made plans with Cimone. At the double wedding feast, Lisimaco and Cimone with many of their friends snatched the brides away from their prospective husbands. The young men carried their loved ones to Crete, where they lived happily in exile for a time until their fathers interceded for them. Then Cimone took Efigenia home to Cyprus, and Lisimaco took his wife back to Rhodes.

A story by Fiammetta concerned Federigo degli Alberighi, who was famed in Florence for his courtesy and his prowess in arms. He fell in love with Monna Giovanna, a woman who cared nothing for him, though he spent his fortune trying to please her. Finally he was so poor that he went to the country to live on his farm. There he entertained himself only by flying his falcon, which was considered the best in the world.

Monna's husband died, leaving her to enjoy his vast estates with one young son. The son struck up an acquaintance with Federigo and particularly admired the falcon. When the boy became sick, he thought he might get well if he could own Federigo's bird.

Monna, as a last resort, swallowed her pride and called upon Federigo. She told him she would stay for supper, but Federigo, desperately poor as he was, had nothing to serve his love except the falcon, which he promptly killed and roasted for her.

After the meal, with many apologies, Monna told her host that her son, thinking he would get well if he had the falcon, desired Federigo's bird. Federigo wept to think that Monna had asked for the one thing he could not give her.

The boy died soon after, and Monna was bereft. When her brothers urged her to remarry, she finally agreed to do so, but she would marry no one but the generous Federigo, who had killed his pet falcon to do her honor. So Federigo married into great riches.

Filostrato entertained his companions by telling them of Peronella, a Neapolitan wool comber married to a poor bricklayer. Together they made enough to live comfortably. Peronella had a lover named Strignario, who came to the house each day after the husband went to work.

One day, when the husband returned unexpectedly, Peronella hid Strignario in a butt. Her husband had brought home a man to buy the butt for five florins. Thinking quickly, Peronella told her husband that she already had a buyer who had offered seven florins for the butt and that he was at that moment inside the butt inspecting it.

Strignario came out, complaining that the butt was dirty. The husband offered to clean it. While the husband was inside scraping, Strignario cuckolded him again, paid for the butt, and went away.

According to another of Filostrato's tales, there was

once in Cathay a very rich and generous old man named Nathan. He had a splendid palace and many servants, and he entertained lavishly anyone who came his way.

In a country nearby lived Mitridanes, who was not nearly so old as Nathan but just as rich. Since he was jealous of Nathan's fame, he built a palace and entertained handsomely everyone who visited. One day a woman came thirteen times asking alms. Furious when Mitridanes called her to task, she told him that she had once asked alms of Nathan forty-two times in one day without reproof. Mitridanes decided that he would have to kill Nathan before his own fame could grow.

Riding near Nathan's palace, Mitridanes discovered Nathan walking alone. When he asked to be directed secretly to Nathan's palace, Nathan cheerfully took him there and established him in a fine apartment. Still not realizing Nathan's identify, Mitridanes revealed his plan to kill his rival. Nathan arranged matters so that Mitridanes came upon him alone in the woods.

Mitridanes, curious to see Nathan, caught hold of him before piercing him with a sword. When he discovered that Nathan was the old man who had first directed him to the palace, made him comfortable, and then arranged the meeting in the woods, Mitridanes realized that he could never match Nathan's generosity, and he was greatly ashamed.

Nathan offered to go to Mitridanes' home and become known as Mitridanes, while Mitridanes would remain to be known as Nathan. By that time, however, Mitridanes thought his own actions would tarnish Nathan's fame, and he went home humbled.

A tale of the Middle East was told by Pamfilo, who explained that in the time of Emperor Frederick the First, all Christendom united in a crusade for the recovery of the Holy Land. To see how the Christians were preparing themselves and to learn to protect himself against them, Saladin, the sultan of Babylon, took two of his best knights and made a tour through Italy to Paris. The travelers were disguised as merchants.

Outside the little town of Pavia, they came upon Messer Torello, who was on his way to his country estate. When they asked him how far they were from Pavia, he told them quickly that the town was too far to be reached that night and sent his servants with them to an inn. Messer Torello sensed that the three men were foreign gentlemen and wanted to honor them; he had the servants take them by a roundabout way to his own estate. Meanwhile he rode directly home. The travelers were surprised when they saw him in his own place, but, realizing that he meant only to honor them, they graciously consented to spend the night.

The next day, Messer Torello sent word to his wife in town to prepare a banquet. The preparations were made, and both Torellos honored the merchants that day. Before they left, the wife gave them handsome suits of clothes like those her husband wore.

When Messer Torello became one of the crusaders, he asked his wife to wait a year and a month before remarrying if she heard nothing from him. She gave him a ring with which to remember her. Soon afterward, a great plague broke out among the Christians at Acre and killed many men. Most of the survivors were imprisoned by the sultan. Messer Torello was taken to Alexandria, where he trained hawks for Saladin and was called Saladin's Christian. Neither man recognized the other for a long time, until at last Saladin recognized a facial gesture in Torello and made himself known as one of the traveling merchants. Torello was freed and lived happily as Saladin's guest. He expected daily to hear from his wife, to whom he had sent word of his adventures. His messenger had been shipwrecked, however, and the day approached when his wife would be free to remarry.

At last Torello told Saladin of the arrangement he and his wife had made. The sultan took pity on him and had Torello put to sleep on a couch heaped with jewels and gold. Then the couch, whisked off to Italy by magic, was set down in the church of which his uncle was abbot. Torello and the abbot went to the marriage feast prepared for Torello's wife and her new husband. No one recognized Torello because of his strange beard and oriental clothing until he displayed the ring his wife had given him. Then with great rejoicing they were reunited, a reward for their early generosity.

Dioneo embarked upon a tale of the patience of Griselda. Gualtieri, eldest son of the marquess of Saluzzo, was a bachelor whose subjects begged him to marry. Though he was not anxious to take a wife, he decided to wed poor Griselda, who lived in a nearby hamlet. When he went with his friends to bring Griselda home, he asked her if she would always be obedient and try to please him and never be angry. Upon her word that she would do so, Gualtieri had her stripped of her poor gown and dressed in finery becoming her new station.

With her new clothes, Griselda changed so much in appearance that she seemed to be a true noblewoman, and Gualtieri's subjects were pleased. She bore him a daughter and a son, both of whom Gualtieri took from her. In order to test her devotion, he pretended to have the children put to death, but Griselda sent them off cheerfully since that was her husband's wish.

When their daughter was in her early teens, Gualtieri sent Griselda home, clad only in a shift, after telling her that he intended to take a new wife. His subjects were sad, but Griselda remained composed. A short time later he called Griselda back to his house and ordered her to prepare it for his wedding, saying that no one else knew so well how to arrange it. In her ragged dress, she prepared everything for the wedding feast. Welcoming the guests, she was particularly thoughtful of the new bride.

By that time Gualtieri thought he had tested Griselda in every possible way. He introduced the supposed bride as her daughter and the little boy who had accompanied the girl as her son. Then he had Griselda dressed in her best clothes, and everyone rejoiced.

Critical Evaluation

Giovanni Boccaccio, Dante, and Petrarch were the leading lights in a century that is considered the beginning of the Italian Renaissance. Dante died while Boccaccio was a child, but Petrarch was Boccaccio's friend during his middle and later life. Dante's work was essentially of the spirit; Petrarch's was that of the literary man; Boccaccio's broke free of all tradition and created a living literature about ordinary people. *The Decameron* is his most famous work. Since its composition, readers and critics have made much of *The Decameron*'s hundred entertaining and worldly tales, comic and tragic, bawdy and courteous, satiric and serious. Unfortunately, much early criticism was moralistic, and Boccaccio was faulted for devoting his mature artistic skill to a collection of "immoral" stories. *The Decameron* has fared better in the latter half of the twentieth century, with more solid critical inquiries into the work's literary significance and style. Boccaccio's collection has been considered representative of the Middle Ages; it has also been viewed as a product of the Renaissance. The work is both. *The Decameron* not only encompasses literary legacies of the medieval world but also goes far beyond Boccaccio's own time, transcending in tone and style artistic works of previous as well as later periods.

The structure with its frame characters has many analogs in medieval literature; the frame story (a group of tales within an enclosing narrative) was a device known previously, in the Orient, as well as in the West. Two twelfth century examples are the collections *The Seven Sages of Rome* and the *Disciplina clericalis*. The material for many of Boccaccio's stories was gleaned from Indian, Arabic, Byzantine, French, Hebrew, and Spanish tales.

Although *The Decameron* is not escapist literature, the idea and nature of the framework have much in common with medieval romance. There is the idealistic, pastoral quality of withdrawal into the "pleasant place" or garden, away from the ugly, harsh reality of the surrounding world. The ten young people who leave Florence—a dying, corrupt city which Boccaccio describes plainly in all of its horrors—find only momentary respite from the charnel house of reality; but their existence for ten days is that of the enchanted medieval dreamworld: a paradise of flowers, ever-flowing fountains, shade trees, soft breezes, where all luxuries of food and drink abound. Furthermore, virtue reigns along with medieval gentilesse in its finest sense. There is no cynicism or lust in the various garden settings, where the pastimes are strolling, weaving garlands, or playing chess. Even Dioneo, who tells the most salacious stories, is as chaste in his conduct as Pampinea, Filomena, Filostrato, and the others. One critic

has even seen in these frame characters a progression of virtues, their stories groups of exempla praising such qualities as wisdom, prudence, or generosity.

Against this refined and idealized medieval framework are the stories themselves, the majority marked by intense realism in a world where dreams and enchanted gardens have little place. The locale of each novella is usually that of actual geography; the Italian cities of Pisa, Siena, and especially Florence figure largely as settings. The entire Mediterranean is represented with its islands of Sicily, Corfu, Rhodes, Cyprus, and Ischia. France, England, and Spain also serve as backgrounds. In one Oriental story, the Seventh Tale on the Second Day, beautiful Altiel, the Sultan of Babylon's daughter, after being kidnapped, travels in the spaces of four years over most of the Mediterranean, the islands, Greece, Turkey, and Alexandria. Boccaccio is also concerned with restricted spatial reality, and he sketches in close detail internal settings of abbeys, bedrooms, churches, marketplaces, castles, and inns. Different social classes are shown with their own language and clothing. Ciappelletto, living in profanation of the world; Rinaldo, abandoned in nakedness and cold by his fellowmen; Peronella, the deceitful Neapolitan wool comber cuckolding her husband; the whole convent of nuns eagerly lying with the youth Masetto—these characters Boccaccio describes in believable human conflicts.

Although he draws upon the entire arsenal of medieval rhetoric, the author of these one hundred novellas goes beyond figures of speech and linguistic tools in his modern paradoxical style and cynical tone. Although his satire often bites deep, his comic mood generally embraces evil and holiness alike with sympathy and tolerance. His treatment of theme, situation, and character is never didactic. Like Chaucer, he is indulgent, exposing moral and social corruption but leaving guilty characters to condemn themselves.

A novella like the comic tale of Chichibio, told on the Sixth Day, is pure farce, moving rapidly by question and answer, playfully rollicking to a surprise ending brought about by this impulsive, foolish cook. The story of Rossiglione and Guardastagno, Ninth Tale of the Fourth Day, has a tragic plot, but the narrators draw no moral in either case. The interaction of character, scene, and plot brings into relief forces that motivate the world of humanity and allow the reader to judge if he must. Again and again, characters in the tales are relieved from moral responsibility by the control of Fortune.

Throughout *The Decameron*, Boccaccio concerns himself primarily with presenting a very human world

With such tales the ten young people made their retreat in the country pass quickly and happily.

as he observed and understood it. In this presentation, there is no pedantry or reticence; he paints men and women in all of their rascality, faithlessness, nobility, and suffering, changing his Italian prose to suit the exigency of purpose, whether that results in a serious or comic, refined or coarse, descriptive or analytical style. Boccaccio has command of many styles; in fact, his "Commedia Umana" comprehends most, and its author changes easily from one to another.

It is true that in utilizing fables and anecdotes from many medieval sources, in employing figurative and rhythmic devices from books on medieval rhetoric, in structuring his framework according to the chivalric world of valor and courtesy, his work is a product of the Middle Ages. In its frank, open-minded treatment of flesh as flesh, its use of paradox, cynicism, and realistic handling of character, however, *The Decameron* transcends the medieval period and, going beyond the Renaissance, takes its place as universal art.

DEMOCRACY IN AMERICA

Type of work: Essays in political science
Author: Alexis de Tocqueville (1805–1859)
First published: Volume I, 1835; Volume II, 1840

Alexis de Tocqueville lived in a time of enormous political change, when every conceivable variety of political theory flourished. He was born shortly after the French Revolution had turned itself into the Empire, and in his lifetime occurred those further changes which transformed France, at least nominally, into a Republic. His object in writing *Democracy in America* was twofold: to write about the new nation that he so much admired and to establish a new way of examining ideas of politics. Instead of proceeding from ideas of right and responsibility, Tocqueville preferred to begin by analyzing social institutions as they functioned in reality. Instead of working, as Rousseau had worked, from an arbitrary picture of the beginnings of humanity in a "natural" condition, Tocqueville preferred to work from what was statistically observable. Thus, *Democracy in America* begins with a picture of the geography of the new continent, its weather, its indigenous tribes, its economy, and its natural resources. In this respect *Democracy in America* is the forerunner of the scientific spirit in the investigation of social structures.

Much of *Democracy in America* is concerned with institutions, and the first of these described by its author is that of the partition of property. He points out that it is customary in the nations of Europe to divide property by the laws of primogeniture. The result is that property remains fixed in extent and in possession; the family, no matter how changed in each generation, is linked to the wealth and political power of landed property. The family represents the estate, the estate the family, and naturally a strong inequality is carried from one generation to another. The foundations of American culture are to be found, Tocqueville points out, in the equal partition of land and fortune. Land is continually broken up into parcels, sold, developed, and transformed. The accompanying wealth and power is much more fluid than in societies in which descent really dominates fortune. The subsidiary effect of equal partition is the access of careers to men who might in another system be blocked from advancement.

Tocqueville was fascinated by the practice of equality, a phenomenon rarely encountered in France during his lifetime. His next series of chapters concerns political equality; he is one of the first great commentators on the democracy of the township and corporation in early nineteenth century America. He emphasizes that it is fundamental to understand the nature of the township, particularly in its New England tradition. The key to the nature of the American nation, he finds, is the wide and responsible nature of freedom at the level of municipal government. This gives the citizen direct voice in his government and trains him for the representative democracy of the Federal government. Tocqueville points out that under this form of government, power is actually concentrated in the hands of the voter; the legislative and executive branches have no power of their own, but merely represent those who appoint them. To us this fact is commonplace, but it was a new idea for the citizens of Europe.

Although much of this work is in praise of American democracy, Tocqueville makes some important qualifications. His first principle is that abuse in government occurs when one special interest is served to the exclusion of all others. This kind of abuse, he remarks, formerly occurred when the upper classes imposed their will on the lower, when the military, or feudal, or financial, or even religious values operate to the exclusion of all others. His great reservation concerning democracy is that in this form of government a kind of tyranny is also possible, that of the majority. He states that it is conceivable that the free institutions of America may be destroyed by forcing all minorities to give up their freedoms for what is supposedly the good of the majority. In that case, he concludes, democracy will give way first to despotism and then to anarchy. Above all things Tocqueville is taken with equality, and that principle, regardless of the greatest good for the greatest number, is what animates his opinion.

Democracy in America is of course principally about its great subject, but there are in it many reminders of a larger view that its author has. One constant theme of the book is that the Old World must learn from the New; in fact, the book functions not so much as an independent study of a unique phenomenon as a study of comparative political science.

Tocqueville suggests that democratic institutions need to be introduced in France; there will be independence for none, he adds, unless, as in the American republic, independence is granted for all. With uncommon clarity he predicts the totalitarian potentialities of the twentieth century, where unlimited power restricts itself not to a class, but first to a party, and then to a single man. The famous ending of the first volume carries this insight to a more elaborate and specific culmination. There are two nations, Tocqueville says, which will probably dominate the next century, the United States and Russia. One, he says, is driven by the desire for power and war, the other by the desire to increase domestic prosperity. He predicts that there will be no peace until the aggressiveness of Russia is checked by the peacefulness of the United States; in his own words, he looks to a future in which the principle of "servitude" will encounter that of "freedom."

The second volume of *Democracy in America* was published after a lapse of five years. The first volume had established its author as one of the best political thinkers in Europe. It won for him not only the esteem of the best minds of the Continent but financial and even political rewards, so that from the time of its publication Tocqueville was to take an active part as a member of the French government. The second volume is concerned not with the basic economic and social characteristics of America, but with subsidiary questions about the nature of American culture. He asks, for example, how Americans cultivate the arts and whether or not eloquence is to be encountered in the rhetoric of Congress. He covers the progress of science as well as that of poetry, the position of religious minorities, even the meaning of public monuments in a democracy. His general conclusion concerning the arts in America is that they do not flourish as they do in other political climates, for the arts require an atmosphere of privilege and an amount of money that a tax-conscious public is quite unlikely to spend. The useful, he says, is much preferred in a democracy to the beautiful. The artist becomes an artisan and, the author remarks with some delicacy, he tends to produce "imperfect commodities" rather than lasting works of art.

Nevertheless, Tocqueville suggests that a lowering of some standards is amply compensated by a heightening of others. Particularly in the matter of foreign policy does he admire the republican sense as well as form of government. Toward the end of *Democracy in America* he spends much thought on the inclinations toward war and peace of different forms of government. The democratic form, he judges, is predisposed to peace because of various influences: the rapid growth of personal wealth; the stake in property; the less material but equally important "gentleness of heart" which allows the citizens of a democracy a more humane view of life. Yet, when the democratic government is involved in war, the same application of ambition and energy that is so marked in commercial life results often in military success as well. Tocqueville's last thoughts about the democracy and its army deal with the danger to any society from its own standing army, and he covers substantially the same ground on this matter as do the authors of the *Federalist* papers.

Democracy in America ends with the restatement that despotism may be encountered even in republics. While democracies can, the author admits, on occasion be violent and unjust, he believes these occasions are exceptional. They will be more and more frequent, however, in the proportion that equality is allowed to lapse. Among the last of Tocqueville's animated descriptions is that of the "flock of timid and industrious animals" who have given up their individuality to a strong central government. He urges a balance between central and decentralized power, the constant consciousness of equality for all members of the polity.

THE DIALOGUES OF PLATO

Type of work: Philosophical dialogues
Author: Plato (427–347 B.C.)
Time: About 400 B.C.
Locale: Greece, principally Athens
First transcribed: c. 387–347 B.C.

Principal Personages

Socrates, the Athenian philosopher
Gorgias, a Sophist
Protagoras, a Sophist
Crito, Socrates' contemporary, an aged friend
Phaedrus, a defender of rhetoric
Aristophanes, a poet and playwright
Theaetetus, hero of the battle of Corinth
Parmenides, the philosopher from Elea
Philebus, a hedonist
Timaeus, a philosopher and statesman
Plato, Socrates' pupil

The Platonic *Dialogues* rank with the extant works of Aristotle as the most important collection of philosophical works so far produced in the Western world. Although Plato's influence is partly due to the fact that his works have survived, unlike many writings of earlier Greek philosophers, and also to the fact that at various times in the history of the Christian church his ideas have been utilized in one form or another in the process of constructing a Christian theology, the principal cause of his past and present effect on human thought is the quality of his work.

The distinctive character of Platonic thought finds adequate expression in the dialogue form. Although Plato, like all philosophers, had his favored perspectives from which he interpreted and, consequently, saw the world, he realized better than most philosophers that philosophy is more an activity of the mind than the product of an investigation. This is not to say that philosophy does not, in some legitimate sense, illuminate the world; it means that in the process of making sense out of experience the philosopher is restless: no one way of clarifying an idea or a view is entirely satisfactory, and there is always much to be said for some alternative mode of explanation. When distinctive Platonic conceptions finally become clear, they do so against a background of penetrating discussion by means of which alternative ideas are explored for their own values and made to complement the conception which Plato finally endorses. As an instrument for presenting the critical point counterpoint of ideas, the dialogue is ideal; and as a character in control of the general course and quality of the discussion, Socrates is unsurpassed.

Socrates was Plato's teacher, and it was probably out of respect for Socrates the man and philosopher that Plato first considered using him as the central disputant in his dialogues. Reflection must have enforced his decision, for Socrates was important more for his method than for his fixed ideas, more for his value as a philosophical irritant than as a source of enduring wisdom. The Socratic method is often described as a question-answer method designed to bring out the contradictions and omissions in the philosophical views of others; but it is better understood as a clever technique for so playing upon the ambiguities of claims as to lead others into changing their use of terms and, hence, into *apparent* inconsistency.

The question concerning the extent to which Plato uses the dialogues to record the ideas of Socrates and the extent to which he uses Socrates as a proponent of his own ideas will probably never be conclusively answered. The question is, of course, historical; philosophically speaking, it makes no difference whose ideas find their way into the dialogues. A fairly safe assumption is that Socrates emphasized the importance of philosophical problems of value, knowledge, and philosophy itself. He probably did argue that it is important to know oneself, that the admission of one's own ignorance is a kind of wisdom possessed by few men, and that virtue is knowledge.

Certainly Socrates must have had a devotion to his calling as philosopher and critic. No man who regarded philosophy as a game would have remained in Athens to face the charge that by philosophy he had corrupted the youth of Athens, nor would he have refused a chance to escape after having been condemned to death. The courage and integrity of Socrates are recorded with poignant power in the *Apology*, the dialogue in which Socrates defends himself and philosophy against the charges brought against him; the *Crito*, in which Socrates refuses to escape from prison; and the *Phaedo*, in which Socrates discusses the immortality of the soul before he drinks the hemlock poison and dies.

Of the ideas presented in the dialogues, perhaps none is more important than Plato's theory of Ideas or Forms. This idea is most clearly expressed in the *Republic*, in which the problem of discovering the nature of justice in man is resolved by considering the nature of justice in the state. Plato distinguished between particular things, the objects we experience in our daily living, and the characters that things have, or could have. Goodness, truth, beauty, and other universal characters—properties that can affect a number of individual objects—are eternal, changeless, beautiful, and the source of all knowledge. Although some critics have claimed that Plato was speaking metaphorically when he talked, through Socrates, about the reality of the Forms, speaking as if they enjoyed a separate existence, the dialogues leave the impression that Plato considered the Forms (Ideas) to be actually existing, in some sense peculiar to themselves, as universals or prototypes which things may or may not exemplify.

If one reviews, however inadequately, the range of questions and tentative answers to be found in the dialogues, a bare inkling of Plato's power as a philosopher is then realized. But the dialogues must be read before the depth of Plato's speculative mind and the skill of his dialectic can be appreciated. Furthermore, only a reading of the dialogues can convey Plato's charm, wit, and range of sympathy. Whether the final result may be in good part attributed to Socrates as Plato's inspiring teacher is not important. Socrates as the subject and Plato as the writer (and philosopher—in all probability more creative than Socrates) combine to leave us with an unforgettable image of the Hellenistic mind.

Although many of the dialogues concern themselves with more than one question, and although definitive answers are infrequent so that discussions centering about a certain subject may crop up in a number of different dialogues, it may be helpful to indicate the central problems and conclusions of the dialogues:

Charmides centers on the question, "What is temperance?" After criticizing a number of answers, and without finally answering the question, Socrates emphasizes the point that temperance involves knowledge. *Lysis* and *Laches* consider, respectively, the questions, "What is friendship?" and "What is courage?" The former discussion points out the difficulty of the question and of resolving conflicts of values: the latter distinguishes courage from a mere facing of danger and makes the point that courage, as one of the virtues, is a kind of

knowledge involving willingness to act for the good. The *Ion* exhibits Socratic irony at work on a rhapsodist who is proud of his skill in the recitation of poetry. Socrates argues that poetry is the result of inspiration, a kind of divine madness. In the *Protagoras* Socrates identifies virtue and knowledge, insisting that no one chooses evil except through ignorance. One of a number of attacks on the sophistical art of fighting with words is contained in the *Euthydemus*.

In the *Meno* the philosopher Socrates and his companions wonder whether virtue can be taught. The doctrine that ideas are implanted in the soul before birth is demonstrated by leading a slave boy into making the correct answers to some problems in geometry. At first it seems that since virtue is a good and goodness is knowledge, virtue can be taught. But since there are no teachers of virtue, it cannot be taught; and, in any case, since virtue involves right opinion, it is not teachable.

"What is piety?" is the question of the *Euthyphro*. Euthyphro's idea that piety is whatever is pleasing to the gods is shown to be inadequate.

The *Apology* is the most effective portrait of Socrates in a practical situation. No moment in his life had graver consequences than the trial resulting from the charge that he had corrupted the youth of Athens by his teachings, yet Socrates continued to be himself, to argue dialectically, and to reaffirm his love of wisdom and virtue. He pictured himself as a gadfly, stinging the Athenians out of their intellectual arrogance. He argued that he would not corrupt anyone voluntarily, for to corrupt those about him would be to create evil that might harm him.

Socrates is shown as a respecter of the law in the *Crito*; he refuses to escape after having been pronounced guilty. In the *Phaedo* he argues that the philosopher seeks death because his whole aim in life is to separate the soul from the body. He argues for the immortality of the soul by saying that opposites are generated from opposites; therefore, life is generated from death. Also, the soul is by its very nature the principle of life; hence, it cannot itself die.

The dialogue *Greater Hippias* does not settle the question, "What is beauty?" but it does show, as Socrates points out, that "All that is beautiful is difficult."

The subject of love is considered from various philosophic perspectives in the *Symposium*, culminating in the conception of the highest love as the love of the good, the beautiful, and the true.

Gorgias begins with a discussion of the art of rhetoric, and proceeds to the development of the familiar Socratic ideas that it is better to suffer evil than to do it, and it is better to be punished for evil-doing than to escape punishment.

The *Parmenides* is a fascinating technical argument concerning various logical puzzles about the one and the many. It contains some criticism of Plato's theory of Ideas. Plato's increasing interest in problems of philosophic method is shown by the *Cratylus*, which contains a discussion of language beginning with the question whether there are true and false names. Socrates is not dogmatic about the implications of using names, but he does insist that any theory of language allow men to continue to speak of their knowledge of realities.

The *Phaedrus* is another discourse on love. It contains the famous myth of the soul conceived as a charioteer and winged steeds. In the *Theaetetus* Socrates examines the proposal by Theaetetus that knowledge is sense perception. He rejects this idea as well as the notion that knowledge is true opinion.

The *Sophist* is a careful study of sophistical method with emphasis on the problem of Being and Not-being. In the *Statesman* Plato continues the study of the state he initiated in the *Republic*, introducing the idea—later stressed by Aristotle—that virtue is a mean.

Socrates argues in the *Philebus* that neither pleasure nor wisdom is in itself the highest good, since pleasure that is not known is worthless and wisdom that is not pleasant is not worth having; only a combination is wholly satisfactory.

A rare excursion into physics and a philosophical consideration of the nature of the universe are found in the *Timaeus*. Here Plato writes of God, creation, the elements, the soul, gravitation, and many other matters.

The *Critias*, an unfinished dialogue, presents the story of an ancient and mythical war between Athens and Atlantis; and with the *Laws*, the longest of the dialogues, Plato ranges over most of the areas touched on in his other dialogues, but with an added religious content: Soul is the source of life, motion, and moral action; and there is an evil soul in the universe with which God must deal.

THE DIVINE COMEDY

Type of work: Poem
Author: Dante Alighieri (1265–1321)
Type of plot: Christian allegory
Time of plot: The Friday before Easter, 1300
Locale: Hell, Purgatory, Paradise
First transcribed: c. 1320

Dante's greatest work, an epic poem in one hundred cantos, is divided equally after an introductory canto into sections, each thirty-three cantos in length, which see Dante and a guide respectively through Hell, Purgatory, and Paradise. The cosmology, angelology, and theology of the poem are based on St. Thomas Aquinas. Dante's literal journey is also an allegory of the progress of the human soul toward God and the progress of political and social mankind toward peace on earth. Characterization is drawn from ancient Roman history and from Dante's contemporary Italy, making the work a realistic picture and an intensely involved analysis of human affairs and life, even though in structure it appears to be a description of the beyond. It is, in essence, a compassionate, oral evaluation of human nature and a mystic vision of the Absolute toward which mankind strives, and it endures more through the universality of the drama and the lyric quality of the poetry than through specific doctrinal content.

Principal Characters

Dante (dän′tā), the exile Florentine poet, who is halted in his path of error through the grace of the Virgin, St. Lucy, and Beatrice, and is redeemed by his journey through Hell, Purgatory, and Paradise. He learns to submerge his instinctive pity for some sinners in his recognition of the justice of God, and he frees himself of the faults of wrath and misdirected love by participating in the penance for these sins in Purgatory. He is then ready to grow in understanding and love as he moves with Beatrice nearer and nearer the presence of God.

Beatrice (bĕ′ə·trē′chā), his beloved, who is transformed into an angel, one of Mary's handmaids. Through her intercession, her compassion, and her teaching, Dante's passion is transmuted into divine love, which brings him to a state of indescribable blessedness.

Virgil, Dante's master, the great Roman poet who guides him through Hell and Purgatory. The most favored of the noble pagans who dwells in Limbo without hope of heavenly bliss, he represents the highest achievements of human reason and classical learning.

St. Lucy, Dante's patron saint. She sends him aid and conveys him through a part of Purgatory.

Charon, traditionally the ferryman of damned souls.

Minos, the monstrous judge who dooms sinners to their allotted torments.

Paolo and **Francesca,** devoted lovers, murdered by Paolo's brother, who was Francesca's husband. Together even in hell, they arouse Dante's pity by their tale of growing affection.

Ciacco, a Florentine damned for gluttony, who prophesies the civil disputes which engulfed his native city after his death.

Plutus, the bloated, clucking creature who guards the entrance of the fourth circle of Hell.

Phlegyas, the boatman of the wrathful.

Filippo Argenti, another Florentine noble, damned to welter in mud for his uncontrollable temper.

Megaera, Alecto, and **Tisiphone,** the Furies, tower warders of the City of Dis.

Farinata Degli Uberti, leader of the Ghibelline party of Florence, condemned to rest in an indestructible sepulcher for his heresy. He remains concerned primarily for the fate of his city.

Cavalcante, a Guelph leader, the father of Dante's friend Guido. He rises from his tomb to ask about his son.

Nessus, Chiron, and **Pholus,** the courteous archer centaurs who guard the river of boiling blood which holds the violent against men.

Piero Delle Vigne, the loyal adviser to the Emperor Frederick, imprisoned, with others who committed suicide, in a thornbush.

Capaneus, a proud, blasphemous tyrant, one of the Seven against Thebes.

Brunetto Latini, Dante's old teacher, whom the poet treats with great respect; he laments the sin of sodomy which placed him deep in Hell.

Guido Guerra, Tegghiaio Aldobrandi, Jacopo Rusticucci, and **Guglielmo Borsiere,** Florentine citizens who gave in to unnatural lust.

Geryon, a beast with human face and scorpion's tail, symbolic of fraud.

Venedico Caccianemico, a Bolognese panderer.

Jason, a classical hero, damned as a seducer.

Alessio Interminei, a flatterer.

Nicholas III, one of the popes, damned to burn in a rocky cave for using the resources of the Church for worldly advancement.

Amphiaraus, Tiresias, Aruns, Manto, Eurypylus, Michael Scot, and **Guido Bonatti,** astrologers and diviners whose grotesquely twisted shapes reflect their distortion of divine counsel.

Malacoda, chief of the devils who torments corrupt political officials.

Ciampolo, one of his charges, who converses with Dante and Virgil while he plans to outwit the devils.

Catalano and **Loderingo,** jovial Bolognese friars, who wear the gilded leaden mantles decreed eternally for hypocrites.

Caiphas, the high priest who had Christ condemned. He lies naked in the path of the heavily laden hypocrites.

Vanni Fucci, a bestial, wrathful thief, the damned spirit most arrogant against God.

Agnello, Francisco, Cianfa, Buoso, and **Puccio,** malicious thieves and oppressors, who are metamorphosed from men to serpents, then from serpents to men, before the eyes of the poet.

Ulysses and **Diomed,** Greek heroes transformed into tongues of flame as types of the evil counselor. Ulysses retains the splendid passion for knowledge which led him beyond the limits set for men.

Guido de Montefeltro, another of the evil counselors, who became involved in the fraud and sacrilege of Pope Boniface.

Mahomet, Piero da Medicina, and **Bertran de Born,** sowers of schism and discord, whose bodies are cleft and mutilated.

Capocchio and **Griffolino,** alchemists afflicted with leprosy.

Gianni Schicchi and **Myrrha,** sinners who disguised themselves because of lust and greed, fittingly transformed into swine.

Master Adam, a counterfeiter.

Sinon and **Potiphar's Wife,** damned for malicious lying and treachery.

Nimrod, Antaeus, and **Briareus,** giants who rebelled against God.

Camincion de' Pazzi, Count Ugolino, Fra Alberigo, Judas Iscariot, Brutus, and **Cassius,** traitors to family, country, and their masters. They dwell forever in ice, hard and cold as their own hearts.

Cato, the aged Roman sage who was, for the Middle Ages, a symbol of pagan virtue. He meets Dante and Virgil at the base of Mount Purgatory and sends them on their way upward.

Casella, a Florentine composer who charms his hearers with a song as they enter Purgatory.

Manfred, a Ghibelline leader, **Belacqua, La Pia, Cassero,** and **Buonconte da Montefeltro,** souls who must wait many years at the foot of Mount Purgatory

because they delayed their repentance until the time of their death.

Sordello, the Mantuan poet, who reverently greets Virgil and accompanies him and his companion for part of their journey.

Nino Visconti and **Conrad Malaspina,** men too preoccupied with their political life to repent early.

Omberto Aldobrandesco, Oderisi, and **Provenzan Salvani,** sinners who walk twisted and bent over in penance for their pride in ancestry, artistry, and power.

Sapia, one of the envious, a woman who rejoiced at the defeat of her townspeople.

Guido del Duca, another doing penance for envy. He laments the dissensions which tear apart the Italian states.

Marco Lombardo, Dante's companion through the smoky way trodden by the wrathful.

Pope Adrian, one of those being purged of avarice.

Hugh Capet, the founder of the French ruling dynasty, which he castigates for its crimes and brutality. He atones for his own ambition and greed.

Statius, the author of the "Thebaid." One of Virgil's disciples, he has just completed his penance for prodigality. He tells Dante and Virgil of the liberation of the truly repentant soul.

Forese Donati, Dante's friend, and **Bonagiunta,** Florentines guilty of gluttony.

Guido Guinicelli and **Arnaut,** love poets who submit to the flames which purify them of lust.

Matilda, a heavenly lady who meets Dante in the earthly paradise at the top of Mount Purgatory and takes him to Beatrice.

Piccarda, a Florentine nun, a fragile, almost transparent spirit who dwells in the moon's sphere, the outermost circle of heaven, since her faith wavered, making her incapable of receiving greater bliss than this.

Justinian, the great Roman Emperor and law-giver, one of the champions of the Christian faith.

Charles Martel, the heir to Charles II, King of Naples, whose early death precipitated strife and injustice.

Cunizza, Sordello's mistress, the sister of an Italian tyrant.

Falco, a troubadour who was, after his conversion, made a bishop.

Rahab, the harlot who aided Joshua to enter Jerusalem, another of the many whose human passions were transformed into love of God.

Thomas Aquinas, the Scholastic philosopher. He tells Dante of St. Francis when he comes to the sphere of the sun, the home of those who have reached heaven through their knowledge of God.

St. Bonaventura, his companion, who praises St. Dominic.

Cacciaguida, Dante's great-great-grandfather, placed in the sphere of Mars as a warrior for the Church.

Peter Damian, a hermit, an inhabitant of the sphere of Saturn, the place allotted to spirits blessed for their temperance and contemplative life.

St. Peter, St. James, and **St. John,** representatives, for Dante, of the virtues of Faith, Hope, and Love. The three great disciples examine the poet to assure his understanding of these three qualities.

Adam, the prototype of fallen man, who is, through Christ, given the greatest redemption; he is the companion of the three apostles and sits enthroned at the left hand of the Virgin.

St. Bernard, Dante's guide during the last stage of his journey, when he comes before the throne of the Queen of Heaven.

The Story

Dante found himself lost in a dark and frightening wood, and as he was trying to regain his path, he came to a mountain which he decided to climb in order to get his bearings. Strange beasts blocked his way, however, and he was forced back to the plain. As he was bemoaning his fate, the poet Virgil approached Dante and offered to conduct him through Hell, Purgatory, and blissful Paradise.

When they arrived at the gates of Hell, Virgil explained that here were confined those who had lived their lives without regard for good or evil. At the River Acheron, where they found Charon, the ferryman, Dante was seized with terror and fell into a trance. Aroused by a loud clap of thunder, he followed his guide through Limbo, the first circle of Hell. The spirits confined there, he learned, were those who, although they had lived a virtuous life, had not been baptized.

At the entrance to the second circle of Hell, Dante met Minos, the Infernal Judge, who warned him to take heed how he entered the lower regions. Dante was overcome by pity as he witnessed the terrible punishment which the spirits were undergoing. They had been guilty of carnal sin, and for punishment they were whirled around without cessation in the air. The third circle housed those who had been guilty of the sin of gluttony. They were forced to lie deep in the mud, under a constant fall of snow and hail and stagnant water. Above them stood Cerberus, a cruel monster, barking at the helpless creatures and tearing at their flesh. In the next circle, Dante witnesses the punishment of the prodigal and the avaricious, and realized the vanity of fortune.

He and Virgil continued on their journey until they reached the Stygian Lake, in which the wrathful and gloomy were suffering. At Virgil's signal, a ferryman transported them across the lake to the city of Dis. They were denied admittance, however, and the gates were closed against them by the fallen angels who guard the city. Dante and Virgil gained admittance into the city only after an angel had interceded for them. There Dante discovered that tombs burning with a blistering heat housed the souls of heretics. Dante spoke to two of these tormented spirits and learned that all the souls in Hell, who knew nothing of the present, can remember the past, and dimly foresee the future.

The entrance to the seventh circle was guarded by the Minotaur, and only after Virgil had pacified him could the two travelers pass down the steep crags to the base of the mountain. There they discerned a river of blood in which those who had committed violence in their lifetimes were confined. On the other side of the river they learned that those who had committed suicide were doomed to inhabit the trunks of trees. Beyond the river they came to a desert in which were confined those who had sinned against God, or Art, or Nature. A stream flowed near the desert and the two poets followed it until the water plunged into an abyss. In order that they might descend to the eighth circle, Virgil summoned Geryon, a frightful monster, who conducted them below. There they saw the tortured souls of seducers, flatters, diviners, and barterers. Continuing along their way, they witnessed the punishment accorded hypocrites and robbers. In the ninth gulf were confined scandalmongers and spreaders of false doctrine. Among the writhing figures they saw Mahomet. Still farther along, the two discovered the horrible disease-ridden bodies of forgers, counterfeiters, alchemists, and all those who deceived under false pretenses.

They were summoned to the next circle by the soul of a trumpet. In it were confined all traitors. A ring of giants surrounded the circle, one of whom lifted both Dante and Virgil and deposited them in the bottom of the circle. There Dante conversed with many of the spirits and learned the nature of their particular crimes.

After this visit to the lowest depths of Hell, Dante and Virgil emerged from the foul air to the pure atmosphere which surrounded the island of Purgatory. In a little while, they saw a boat conducted by an angel, in which were souls being brought to Purgatory. Dante recognized a friend among them. The two poets reached the foot of a mountain, where passing spirits showed them the easiest path to climb its slope. On their way up the path they encountered many spirits who explained that they were kept in Ante-Purgatory because they had delayed their repentance too long. They pleaded with Dante to ask their families to pray for their souls when he once again returned to earth. Soon Dante and Virgil came to the gate of Purgatory, which was guarded by an angel. The two poets ascended a winding path and saw men, bent under the weight of heavy stones, who were expiating the sin of pride. They examined the heavily carved cornices, which they passed, and found them covered with inscriptions urging humility and righteousness. At the second cornice were the souls of those who had been guilty of envy.

They wore sackcloth and their eyelids were sewed with iron thread. Around them were the voices of angels singing of great examples of humility and the futility of envy. An angel invited the poets to visit the third cornice, where those who had been guilty of anger underwent repentance. Dante was astonished at the examples of patience which he witnessed there. At the fourth cornice he witnessed the purging of the sin of indifference or gloominess. He discussed with Virgil the nature of love. The Latin poet stated that there were two kinds of love, natural love, which was always right, and love of the soul, which might be misdirected. At the fifth cornice, avarice was purged. On their way to the next cornice, the two were overtaken by Statius, whose spirit had been cleansed and who was on his way to Paradise. He accompanied them to the next place of purging, where the sin of gluttony was repented, while voices sang of the glory of temperance. The last cornice was the place for purging by fire of the sin of incontinence. Here the sinners were heard to recite innumerable examples of praiseworthy chastity.

An angel now directed the two poets and Statius to a path which would lead them to Paradise. Virgil told Dante that he might wander through Paradise at his will until he found his love, Beatrice. As he was strolling through a forest, Dante came to a stream; on the other bank stood a beautiful woman. She explained to him that the stream was called Lethe and helped him to cross it. Then Beatrice descended from heaven and reproached him for his unfaithfulness to her during her life, but the virgins in the heavenly fields interceded with her on his behalf. Convinced of his sincere repentance and remorse, she agreed to accompany him through the heavens.

On the moon Dante found those who had made vows of chastity and determined to follow the religious life, but who were forced to break their vows. Beatrice led him to the planet Mercury, the second heaven, and from there to Venus, the third heaven, where Dante conversed with many spirits and learned of their virtues. On the sun, the fourth heaven, they were surrounded by a group of spirits, among them Thomas Aquinas. He named each of the spirits in turn and discussed their individual virtues. A second circle of blessed spirits surrounded the first, and Dante learned from each how he had achieved blessedness.

Then Beatrice and Dante came to Mars, the fifth heaven, where he saw the cherished souls of those who had been martyred. Dante recognized many renowned warriors and crusaders among them.

On Jupiter, the sixth heaven, Dante saw the souls of those who had administered justice faithfully in the world. The seventh heaven was on Saturn, where Dante found the souls of those who had spent their lives in meditation and religious retirement. From there Beatrice and her lover passed to the eighth heaven, the region of the fixed stars. Dante looked back over all the distance which extended between the earth and this apex of Paradise and was dazzled and awed by what he saw. As they stood there, they saw the triumphal hosts approaching, with Christ leading, followed by Mary.

Dante was questioned by the saints. Saint Peter examined his opinions concerning faith; Saint James, concerning hope, and Saint John, concerning charity. Adam then approached and told the poet of the first man's creation, of his life in Paradise, and of his fall and what had caused it. Saint Peter bitterly lamented the avarice which his apostolic successors displayed, and all the sainted host agreed with him.

Beatrice then conducted Dante to the ninth heaven, where he was permitted to view the divine essence and to listen to the chorus of angels. She then led him to the Empyrean, from the heights of which, and with the aid of her vision, he was able to witness the triumphs of the angels and of the souls of the blessed. So dazzled and overcome was he by this vision that it was some time before he realized Beatrice had left him. At his side stood an old man whom he recognized as Saint Bernard, who told him Beatrice had returned to her throne. He then told Dante that if he wished to discover still more of the heavenly vision, he must join with him in a prayer to Mary. Dante received the grace to contemplate the glory of God, and to glimpse, for a moment, the greatest of mysteries, the Trinity and man's union with the divine.

Critical Evaluation

Dante was born into an aristocratic Florentine family. Unusually well educated even for his time and place, he was knowledgeable in science and philosophy and was an active man of letters as well as an artist. He lived in politically tumultuous times and was active in politics and government. All of his knowledge, his experience, and his skill were brought to bear in his writings. During an absence from Florence in 1302, he was sentenced to exile for opposing the government then in power; he was never allowed to return to his beloved Florence. In exile, Dante wrote *The Divine Comedy*. He died in Ravenna.

This masterpiece was written in Italian, but Dante also wrote in Latin, the language of scholarship at that time. His Latin treatise *De Vulgari Eloquentia* (On the Vulgar Tongue)—a compelling defense of the use of the written vernacular, instead of Latin—argued in conventional Latin the superiority of unconventional written Italian as a medium of expression. His other major Latin treatise was *De Monarchia* (About Monarchy), a political essay. He also used Latin for some very important letters and for a few poems. But Dante's choice was his native Italian. His earliest major work—*La Vita Nuova* (The New Life), a mystical-spiritual autobiography, combining prose and poetry—was written in Italian. So, too, was *Il Convivio* (The Banquet), a scholarly and philosophical treatise. And he wrote a number of lyric poems in Italian as well. Standing above all as a tribute to the eloquence of written Italian is *The Divine Comedy*.

La Commedia—as it was first titled; *Divina* was added later—is an incredibly complex work. It is divided into three sections, or canticles, the *Inferno* (Hell), the *Purgatorio* (Purgatory), and the *Paradiso* (Heaven). The entire work is composed of 100 cantos, apportioned into segments of 34 (*Inferno*), 33 (*Purgatorio*), and 33 (*Paradiso*). The rhyme scheme is called *terza rima*—aba bab cbc dcd—an interlocking pattern which produces a very closely knit poem. This structure is neither arbitrary nor a mere intellectual exercise.

Number symbolism plays an important part in *The Divine Comedy*. As an essentially Christian poem, it relies heavily on mystical associations with numbers. Inasmuch as the poem deals with Christian religious concepts, it is not difficult to discern the relationship between one poem in three canticles and one God in Three Persons. So, too, terza rima becomes significant. But then more complex intricacies come into play. The unity or oneness of God is diffused on a metric basis: one is divided into one hundred cantos, for example. And two becomes the duality of nature: corporeal and spiritual, active and contemplative, Church and State, Old Testament and New, and so on. Three signifies Father, Son, Holy Ghost; Power, Wisdom, Love; Faith, Hope, Charity; and other combinations. Four—as in seasons, elements, humors, directions, cardinal virtues—combines with three to make a mystical seven: days of creation, days of the week (length of Dante's journey), seven virtues and seven vices (reflected in the seven levels of Purgatory), planets, and many more. Moreover, multiples of three—three times three equals nine—create further permutations: choirs of angels, circles of Hell, and the like. And adding the mystical unity of one to the product nine makes ten, the metric permutation of one discussed above.

These complex relationships of number symbolism were deliberately contrived by Dante and other medieval writers. Dante himself explained, in *Il Convivio*, his view of the four levels of interpretation of a literary work and by doing so legitimized such explanations of number symbolism. He proposed that a text be read literally, allegorically, morally, and anagogically. The literal reading attended to the story itself. The allegorical reading

uncovered hidden meanings in the story. The moral reading related to matters of human behavior. And the anagogical reading, accessible to only the most sophisticated, pertained to the absolute and universal truths contained in a work. Hence, *The Divine Comedy* can be appreciated on each of these four levels of interpretation.

As a literal story, it has the fascination of autobiographical elements as well as the features of high adventure. The protagonist Dante, led by Vergil, undertakes a journey to learn about himself, the world, and the relations between the two. In the course of his journey, he explores other worlds in order to place his own world in proper perspective. As his journey progresses, he learns.

As an allegorical story, *The Divine Comedy* traces the enlightenment of Dante's soul. It also delineates social, political, cultural, and scientific parables. By integrating all of these aspects into an intricately interwoven pattern, the poem becomes an allegory for the real and spiritual world order.

As a moral story, the work has perhaps its greatest impact as a cautionary tale to warn the reader about the consequences of various categories of behavior. In the process, it helps the reader to understand sin (Hell), penance (Purgatory), and salvation (Heaven). Thus, *The Divine Comedy* becomes a vehicle for teaching moral behavior.

As an anagogical story, the poem offers a mystical vision of God's grand design for the entire universe. The complex interdependency of all things—including the web of interrelationships stemming from number symbolism—is, in this view, all part of the Divine Plan, which humankind can grasp only partially and dimly. For God remains ineffable to the finite capacities of human beings, and His will can never be fully apprehended by humans, whose vision has been impaired by sin. The anagogical aspects of *The Divine Comedy* are therefore aids for the most spiritually enlightened to approach Eternal Truth.

To be sure, no brief explanation can do justice to the majesty of this monumental achievement in the history of Western poetry. The very encyclopedic nature of its scope makes *The Divine Comedy* a key to the study of medieval civilization. As such, it cannot be easily or properly fragmented into neat categories for discussion, and the reader must advance on tiptoe, as it were. Background in history and theology are strongly recommended. But, above all, the reader must recognize that no sweeping generalization will adequately account for the complexity of ideas or the intricacy of structure in *The Divine Comedy*.

DOCTOR FAUSTUS

Type of work: Drama
Author: Christopher Marlowe (1564–1593)
Type of plot: Romantic tragedy
Time of plot: Sixteenth century
Locale: Germany
First presented: c. 1588

This drama should be regarded as only the skeletal structure of the original play written by Marlowe, since the surviving manuscripts are so interspersed with comic scenes and lines revised at the whim of actors that one must sort and sift to discover Marlowe's original poetry. In addition to the adulterated poetry, there is the problem of altered symbolisms and reinterpreted characterizations; in places, Mephistophilis falls into a caricature, while the exploits of Faustus are frequently rendered as pure low comedy. Where the hand of Marlowe is discernible, however, the play enjoys considerable artistry, although it is never comparable in depth or scope to the treatment of the same theme in Goethe's Faust.

Principal Characters

Faustus (fous′tŭs, fôs′tŭs), a learned scholar and theologian. Ambitious for boundless knowledge, he abandons the accepted professions for black magic and sells his soul for knowledge and power. Though haunted by remorse, he is unrepentant. After he gains power, his character deteriorates, and he adds cruelty to cowardice in asking tortures for an old man who tries to save his soul. He shows a final flash of nobility in sending his friends away before the expected arrival of the devils, and he delivers a poignant soliloquy while awaiting his death and damnation.

Mephistophilis (mĕf′ĭ·stof′ĭ·lĭs), a tormented devil aware of the horror of being an outcast from the sight of God. He speaks frankly to Faustus before the signing of the bond; after that, he is not concerned with fair play, being sometimes tricky, sometimes savage. At the expired time, he carries Faustus off to hell.

Lucifer (lū′sĭ·fər), the commander of the fallen spirits. Eager for human souls to join him in misery, he puts forth great efforts to keep Faustus from escaping by repentance.

Belzebub (bĕl′zē·bŭb), the third evil spirit.

An Old Man, a godly elder concerned with saving Faustus' soul. Rejected by Faustus and made the physical prey of devils, he escapes them and rises to God by means of his great faith.

Alexander the Great, Alexander's Paramour, and **Helen of Troy,** spirits raised by Mephistophilis and Faustus. The beauty of Helen, "the face that launched a thousand ships," further entangles Faustus in evil and confirms his damnation.

Valdes (väl′dās) and **Cornelius,** learned magicians to whom Faustus turns for counsel when he decides to engage in black magic.

Wagner (väg′nər), the comical and impudent servant of Faustus. He follows his master in conjuring and furnishes a ridiculous contrast to the tragic Faustus.

Three Scholars, friends of Faustus for whom he produces the apparition of Helen and to whom he makes his confession just before his death.

The Pope, a victim of Faustus' playful trickery.

The Cardinal of Lorrain, an attendant to the pope.

Charles V, emperor of Germany. Faustus and Mephistophilis entertain him with magical tricks.

A Knight, a scornful skeptic whom Faustus abuses and infuriates by making stag horns grow on his head. He is restored to his normal state at the request of the emperor.

The Duke of Vanholt and **The Duchess of Vanholt,** patrons of Faustus whom he gratefully entertains.

The Good Angel and **the Evil Angel,** who contend for Faustus' soul, each urging him to choose his way of life.

Robin, an ostler, and **Ralph,** a serving man, comical characters who find Faustus' books and raise Mephistophilis, to their great terror.

A Vintner, the victim of Robin's and Ralph's pranks.

A Horse Courser, a trader deceived and abused by Faustus.

A Clown, the gullible victim of Wagner's conjuring.

Baliol (bā′lĭ·ŏl) and **Belcher,** evil spirits raised by Wagner to terrify the clown.

Pride, Covetousness, Wrath, Envy, Gluttony, Sloth, and **Lechery,** the Seven Deadly Sins, who appear in a pageant for Faustus.

The Chorus, which serves as prologue, commentator, and epilogue to the play.

The Story

Faustus had been born of base stock in Rhodes, Germany. In his maturity, while living with some relatives in Wittenberg, he studied theology and was called a doctor. However, Faustus was so swollen with conceit that, Daedalus-like, he strove too far, became glutted with learning, conspired with the Devil, and finally fell, accursed.

At the outset of his downward path, Doctor Faustus found himself a complete master of the fields of knowledge which men at that time studied. As a medical doctor he had already achieved huge success and great renown. After good health was obtained for men, however, no challenge remained in medicine except the quest for immortality. Law, Faustus concluded, was nothing but an elaborate moneymaking scheme. Only divinity remained, but theology led to a blind alley. Since the reward of sin was death and since no man could say he was without sin, then all men must sin and consequently die.

Necromancy greatly attracted Faustus. Universal power would be within his reach, the whole world at his command, and emperors at his feet, were he to become a magician. Summoning his servant Wagner, Faustus ordered him to summon Valdes and Cornelius, who could teach him their arts.

The Good Angel and the Evil Angel each tried to persuade Faustus, but Faustus was in no mood to listen to the Good Angel. He exulted over the prospect of his forthcoming adventures. He would get gold from India, pearls from the oceans, tasty delicacies from faraway places; he would read strange philosophies, cull from foreign kings their secrets, control Germany with his power, reform the public schools, and perform many other fabulous deeds. Eager to acquire knowledge of the black arts, he went away to study with Valdes and Cornelius.

Before long, the scholars of Wittenberg began to notice the doctor's prolonged absence. Learning from Wagner of his master's unhallowed pursuits, the scholars lamented the fate of the famous doctor.

Faustus' first act of magic was to summon Mephistophilis. At the sight of the ugly devil, he ordered Mephistophilis to assume the shape of a Franciscan friar. The docile obedience of Mephistophilis elated the magician, but Mephistophilis explained that magic had limits in the Devil's kingdom. Mephistophilis claimed that he had not actually appeared at Faustus' behest but had come, as he would have to any other person, because Faustus had cursed Christ and abjured the Scriptures. Whenever a man is on the verge of being doomed, a devil will appear.

Interested in the nature of Lucifer, Faustus questioned Mephistophilis about his master, the fallen angel, and about hell, Lucifer's domain. Mephistophilis was wary. He claimed that the fallen spirits, having been deprived of the glories of heaven, found the whole world hell. Mephistophilis urged Faustus to give up his scheme, but Faustus scorned the warning, saying that he would surrender his soul to Lucifer if the fallen angel would give to Faustus twenty-four years of voluptuous ease, with Mephistophilis to attend him.

While Faustus indulged in a mental argument concerning the relative merits of God and the Devil, the Good Angel and the Evil Angel, symbolic of his inner conflict, appeared once again, each attempting to persuade him. The result was that Faustus was more determined than ever to continue his course.

Mephistophilis returned to assure Faustus that Lucifer was agreeable to the bargain, which must be sealed in Faustus' blood. When Faustus tried to write, however, his blood congealed, and Mephistophilis had to warm the liquid with fire. The words "Fly, man" appeared in Latin on Faustus' arm. When Faustus questioned Mephistophilis about the nature of hell, the devil claimed that hell had no limits for the damned. Intoxicated by his new estate, Faustus disclaimed any belief in an afterlife. Thus he assured himself that his contract with Lucifer would never be fulfilled, in spite of the devil's warning that he, Mephistophilis, was living proof of hell's existence.

Faustus, eager to consume the fruits of the Devil's offering, demanded books that would contain varied information about the Devil's regime. When the Good Angel and the Evil Angel came to him again, he realized that he was beyond repentance. Again the opposing angels insinuated themselves into his mind, until he called on Christ to save him. As he spoke, wrathful Lucifer descended upon his prospective victim to admonish him never to call to God. As an appeasing gesture, Lucifer conjured up a vision of the Seven Deadly Sins.

Faustus traveled extensively throughout the world, and Wagner marveled at his master's rapid progress. In Rome, at the palace of the pope, Faustus, made invisible by his magic arts, astounded the pope by snatching things from the holy man's hands. Like a gleeful child, Faustus asked Mephistophilis to create more mischief. When Faustus returned home, the scholars questioned him eagerly about many things unknown to them. As his fame spread, the emperor invited him to the palace and asked him to conjure up the spirit of Alexander the Great. Because a doubtful knight scoffed at such a preposterous idea, Faustus, after fulfilling the emperor's request, spitefully placed horns on the head of the skeptical nobleman.

Foreseeing that his time of merriment was drawing to a close, Faustus returned to Wittenberg. Wagner sensed that his master was about to die when Faustus gave his faithful servant all his worldly goods.

As death drew near, Faustus spoke with his conscience, which assuming the form of an old man, begged him to repent before he died. When Faustus declared that he would repent, Mephistophilis cautioned him not to offend Lucifer. Faustus asked Mephistophilis to bring him Helen of Troy as a lover to amuse him during the final days of his life.

In his declining hours, Faustus conversed with schol-ars who had loved him, and the fallen theologian revealed to them his bargain with Lucifer. Alone, he uttered a final despairing plea that he be saved from impending misery, but in the end he was borne off by a company of devils.

Critical Evaluation

Although *Doctor Faustus* is a play of undoubted genius and one of the most powerful productions of the English Renaissance, there are four factors which must be considered in assessing its fundamental nature and in fully appreciating a work which is part burlesque, part moral and theological tragedy.

The first and most obvious point to consider is the corrupt nature of the text, which exists in two separate versions, the first printed in 1604 and the second, longer version in 1616. Modern scholars generally agree that neither version is satisfactory and that both are filled with interpolations and insertions by lesser talents which mar Marlowe's work. Even a beginning student will have little difficulty in separating the profound strains of Marlowe's lines from the inferior additions.

Yet this same student—and more experienced scholars—will not find in Marlowe's "mighty line" the same ease and naturalness discovered in Shakespeare's plays. This is the second factor that must be considered: that of style. Marlowe is generally regarded as the playwright who transformed English theatrical language from its crude and obvious pitch into the first semblance of Elizabethan blank verse. Indeed, many have considered that his greatest accomplishment comes not in *Doctor Faustus* or any single drama but in his overall achievement of providing the vehicle for an entire generation of dramatists, of whom Shakespeare was certainly the greatest. While it may be true that Marlowe provided the essential bridge to the medium of fully developed blank verse, it cannot be denied that his style remains stiff and formal, with a conscious air that can achieve lovely effects but which sometimes borders on the pompous. Still, in *Doctor Faustus* Marlowe's language is capable of great beauty and emotion, as when the doomed Faustus cries in vain for salvation: "See, see where Christ's blood streams in the firmament!-One drop would save my soul, half a drop." At his best, Marlowe is a master of blank verse at its highest pitch.

A third concern is the transitional nature of Marlowe's plays. *Doctor Faustus* stands poised between older, medieval traditions and the newer forms and concepts of the Renaissance. Both in style and in content, the play remains part of both worlds, and this division is seen most clearly in the two main characters, Faustus and Mephistophilis.

On one side, Faustus is a prototypical Renaissance man, desiring ultimate knowledge and infinite power, ready to assert, and if possible embody, the new and heady doctrine that "man is the measure of all things" and that there are no innate limits to human accomplishment. Such a view certainly followed the temper of the time, in which leaders consciously saw themselves as rediscovering and renewing all aspects of human life, including many areas long banned by religion. From another angle, however, Faustus remains firmly entrenched in medieval thought, since he feels responsible to follow not his own individual desires but the dictates of society, law, and religion. The tension between these two aspects of his personality, and his failure to resolve them, is a major source of the tragedy which overwhelms him.

Mephistophilis, like Faustus, is a divided character; he retains aspects of the old-fashioned devil while partaking of the new. Setting aside the ridiculous and clowning scenes which are clearly interpolations, the play gives a powerful and subtle view of Mephistophilis and the nature of evil. In his more traditional guise, Mephistophilis tempts Faustus with wiles and lures pitched to the traditional weaknesses of mortals: pride, envy, lust, and the whole panoply of the Seven Deadly Sins. At the same time, he is strictly limited by divine restrictions—for example, Mephistophilis cannot give Faustus a wife, for marriage is a sacrament and thus beyond the reach of the damned. In this respect, Mephistophilis is very much within the traditional doctrines of the Church. At times, however, he becomes more modern, almost existential, in his views. Whereas earlier writers such as Dante envisioned hell as a literal place, Marlowe concentrates upon the lack of love and absence of God; thus, Mephistophilis can stand in Faustus' study and state: "Why this is hell, nor am I out of it." Such a conjunction of old and new perspectives causes the play to resonate with real, if sometimes puzzling, power.

In many ways, *Doctor Faustus* represents the peak of Marlowe's dramatic achievements; many regard it as his best play. Yet—and here is the final problem for the modern reader—it is impossible to determine exactly what is Marlowe's best work, or what can be accurately said about a dramatic career that lasted only six years and produced but seven plays. Such a brief span makes it difficult to gauge the development of Marlowe's artistry or even evaluate his central concerns and techniques. There is a quantum leap in ability and expression from Marlowe's first major play, *Tamburlaine the Great* in 1587, to *Doctor Faustus*, written the following year. Tamburlaine's language is full of bombast and fustian;

Faustus, while still stiff and formal in many lines, displays much greater power and assurance. The major characters of *Doctor Faustus* achieve more individuality and become more immediately real in their presence. It was only in *Edward II* (written around 1591) that Marlowe again attained such dramatic heights. Had Marlowe not been killed in 1593, at the age of twenty-nine, where might his art have gone? It is impossible to tell, and the reader can only echo the epilogue of *Doctor Faustus*: "Cut is the branch that might have grown full straight,/ And burned is Apollo's laurel bough."

A DOLL'S HOUSE

Type of work: Drama
Author: Henrik Ibsen (1828–1906)
Type of plot: Social criticism
Time of plot: Nineteenth century
Locale: Norway
First presented: 1879

Nora Helmer, the central character of this play, realizing that after eight years of marriage her husband has never viewed her as anything more than a sheltered, petted doll, leaves him in order to learn to become a person in her own right. One of Ibsen's best-known and most popular works, A Doll's House *has become a classic expression of the theme of women's rights.*

Principal Characters

Nora, the "doll-wife" of Torvald Helmer. Seeking to charm her husband always, Nora is his "singing lark," his pretty "little squirrel," his "little spendthrift." She seems to be a spendthrift because secretly she is paying off a debt which she incurred to finance a year in Italy for the sake of Torvald's health. To get the money, she had forged her dying father's name to a bond at the bank. Now Krogstad, a bookkeeper at the bank where Torvald has recently been appointed manager, aware that the bond was signed after Nora's father's death, is putting pressure on Nora to persuade Torvald to promote him. Frightened, Nora agrees to help him. When her friend Christine Linde, a widow and formerly Krogstad's sweetheart, also asks for help, Nora easily persuades Torvald to give Christine an appointment at the bank. The position, unfortunately, is Krogstad's. Torvald, finding Krogstad's presumption unbearable, plans to discharge him. While Christine helps Nora prepare a costume for a fancy dress ball in which she will dance the tarantella, Krogstad writes a letter, following his dismissal, telling Torvald of Nora's forgery. Nora desperately keeps Torvald from the mailbox until after the dance. She decides to kill herself so that all will know that she alone is guilty and not Torvald. After the dance Torvald reads the letter and tells Nora in anger that she is a criminal and can no longer be his wife, although she may continue to live in his house to keep up appearances. When Krogstad, softened by Christine's promise to marry him and care for his motherless children, returns the bond, Torvald destroys it and is willing to take back his little singing bird. Nora, realizing the shallow basis of his love for her as a "doll-wife," leaves Torvald to find her own personality away from him. She leaves him with the faint hope that their marriage might be resumed if it could be a "real wedlock."

Torvald Helmer, the newly promoted manager of a bank. Concerned with business, he is unaware that his wife Nora, whom he regards as a plaything, is capable of making serious decisions. When he discovers her forgery, he is horrified and convinced that he will be blamed as the instigator, and he plans to try to appease Krogstad in order to forestall his own disgrace. As soon as the bond is returned, Torvald becomes himself again, wants his pet reinstated, and is eager to forget the whole affair. He is baffled when Nora says that she no longer loves him and is leaving him. At the end, he has a sudden hope that what Nora has called "the most wonderful thing of all" might really happen, the "real wedlock" which she wanted. But Nora has gone.

Nils Krogstad, a bookkeeper at the bank, dissatisfied with his appointment and with life in general. At first Krogstad appears as a sinister blackmailer threatening Nora with disaster if she does not help him gain a promotion at the bank. Later, when he finds the love of Christine Linde, whose loss had embittered him in the first place, he becomes a changed man and returns the bond.

Christine Linde, a widow and Nora's old schoolfriend. When Mrs. Linde first appears, she is quite worn and desperate for work. She had married for money which she needed to support her mother and two young brothers. Now husband and mother are dead and the brothers grown. In the end, when she and Krogstad have decided to marry, she is happy because she will have someone to care for. She decided that Nora cannot continue to deceive Torvald and that Krogstad should not retrieve his letter. presumably Krogstad will retain his position at the bank.

Doctor Rank, a family friend, in love with Nora. Suffering bodily for his father's sins, Dr. Rank is marked by death. Nora starts to ask Dr. Rank to help her pay off the debt, but after he reveals his love for her, she will not ask this favor of him. He tells Nora that he is soon to die and that when death has begun, he will send her his card with a black cross on it. The card appears in the mailbox with Krogstad's letter. Dr. Rank serves no purpose in the play except to show Nora's fidelity to Torvald when she refuses Rank's offer of help after she knows that he loves her.

The Story

On the day before Christmas, Nora Helmer was busying herself with last minute shopping, for this was the first Christmas since her marriage that she had not had to economize. Her husband, Torvald, had just been made manager of a bank and after the New Year their money troubles would be over. She bought a tree and plenty of toys for the children, and she even indulged herself in some macaroons, her favorite confection, but of which Torvald did not entirely approve. He loved his wife dearly, but he regarded her very much as her own father had seen her, as an amusing doll—a plaything.

It was true that she did behave like a child sometimes in her relations with her husband. She pouted, wheedled, and chattered because Torvald expected these things; he would not have loved his doll-wife without them. Actually, Nora was not a doll but a woman with a woman's loves, hopes, and fears. This was shown seven years before, just after her first child was born, when Torvald had been ill, and the doctor said that unless he went abroad immediately he would die. Nora was desperate. She could not seek Torvald's advice because she knew he would rather die than borrow money. She could not go to her father, for he himself was a dying man. She did the only thing possible under the circumstances. She borrowed the requisite two hundred and fifty pounds from Krogstad, a moneylender, forging her father's name to the note, so that Torvald could have his holiday in Italy.

Krogstad was exacting, and she had to think up ways and means to meet the regular payments. When Torvald gave her money for new dresses and such things, she never spent more than half of it, and she found other ways to earn money. One winter she did copying, but she kept this work a secret from Torvald, for he believed that the money for their trip had come from her father.

Then Krogstad, who was in the employ of the bank of which Torvald was now manager, determined to use Torvald to advance his own fortunes. But Torvald hated Krogstad, and was just as determined to be rid of him. The opportunity came when Christine Linde, Nora's old school friend, applied to Torvald for a position in the bank. Torvald resolved to dismiss Krogstad and hire Mrs. Linde in his place.

When Krogstad discovered that he was to be fired, he called on Nora and informed her that if he were dismissed he would ruin her and her husband. He reminded her that the note supposedly signed by her father was dated three days after his death. Frightened at the turn matters had taken, Nora pleaded unsuccessfully with Torvald to reinstate Krogstad in the bank. Krogstad, receiving from Torvald an official notice of his dismissal, wrote in return

a letter in which he revealed the full details of the forgery. He dropped the letter in the mailbox outside the Helmer home.

Torvald was in a holiday mood. The following evening they were to attend a fancy dress ball, and Nora was to go as a Neapolitan fisher girl and dance the tarantella. To divert her husband's attention from the mailbox outside, Nora practiced her dance before Torvald and Dr. Rank, an old friend. Nora was desperate, not knowing quite which way to turn. She had thought of Mrs. Linde, with whom Krogstad had at one time been in love. Mrs. Linde promised to do what she could to turn Krogstad from his avowed purpose. Nora thought also of Dr. Rank, but when she began to confide in him he made it so obvious that he was in love with her that she could not tell her secret. However, Torvald had promised her not to go near the mailbox until after the ball.

What bothered Nora was not her own fate, but Torvald's. She pictured herself as already dead, drowned in icy black water. She pictured the grief-stricken Torvald taking upon himself all the blame for what she had done and being disgraced for her sake. But the reality did not quite correspond with Nora's picture. Mrs. Linde, by promising to marry Krogstad and look after his children, succeeded in persuading him to withdraw all accusations against the Helmers, but she realized that Nora's affairs had come to a crisis and that sooner or later Nora and Torvald would have to come to an understanding.

This crisis came when Torvald read Krogstad's letter after their return from the ball. He accused Nora of being a hypocrite, a liar, and a criminal, of having no religion, no morality, no sense of duty. He declared that she was unfit to bring up her children. He informed her that she might remain in his household but she would no longer be a part of it.

Then another letter arrived from Krogstad, declaring that he intended to take no action against the Helmers. Torvald's whole attitude changed, and with a sigh of relief he boasted that he was saved. For the first time Nora saw her husband for what he was—a selfish, pretentious hypocrite was no regard for her position in the matter. She reminded him that no marriage could be built on inequality, and announced her intention of leaving his house forever. Torvald could not believe his ears and pleaded with her to remain. But she declared she was going to try to become a reasonable human being, to understand the world—in short, to become a woman, not a doll to flatter Torvald's selfish vanity. She went out with irrevocable finality, slammed the door of her doll house behind her.

Critical Evaluation

Although Henrik Ibsen was already a respected playwright in Scandinavia, it was *A Doll's House* (*Et Dukkehjem*) that catapulted him to international fame. This drama, the earliest of Ibsen's social-problem plays, must be read in its historical context in order to understand its impact not only on modern dramaturgy but also on society at large.

Most contemporary theater up to the time, including Ibsen's earlier work, fell into two general categories. One was the historical romance; the other was the so-called well-made (or "thesis") play, a contrived comedy of manners revolving around an intricate plot and subplots but ultimately suffocated by the trivia of its theme and dialogue as well as by its shallow characterization. An occasional poetic drama—such as Ibsen's own *Brand* and *Peer Gynt*—would also appear, but poetic form was often the only distinction between these plays and historical romances, since the content tended to be similar.

Into this dramaturgical milieu, *A Doll's House* injected natural dialogue and situations, abstinence from such artificial conventions as the soliloquy, the "aside," or observance of the "unities" of time and place, and insistence upon the strict logical necessity of the outcome without wrenching events into a happy ending. These theatrical innovations—now so familiar that twentieth century audiences hardly notice them—constitute Ibsen's fundamental contribution to the form of realistic drama.

Realism in the theater emphasizes believability; the guiding question is, "Could this event actually have happened in the lives of real people?" There is no attempt to achieve the comprehensiveness of, say, photographic reality; rather, realism is selective, striving for representative examples in recognizable human experience. And through selectivity, realism implicitly assumes a critical stance. Thus, the Helmers' domestic crisis had, and still has, a there-but-for-the-grace-of-God-go-I impact on theater audiences. Since *A Doll's House* was first produced, drama has not been the same. And it is for that reason that Ibsen is called the father of modern drama.

Ibsen's influence on modern drama was twofold, for he combined both technique and content in the realism of his *A Doll's House*. Specifically, Ibsen elevated playmaking to a level above mere entertainment by validating the respectability of plays about serious social issues. And one of the most volatile issues of his day was the position of women, for at that time women throughout virtually all of Western civilization were considered by law and by custom chattel of fathers and husbands. Women were denied participation in public life; their access to education was limited; their social lives were narrowly circumscribed; they could not legally transact business, own property, or inherit. In the mid-nineteenth century, chafing under such restrictions, women began to demand autonomy. They pushed for the right to vote and the opportunity for higher education and entry into the professions. By the last two decades of the nineteenth century, open defiance developed as women began engaging in such traditionally men's sports as bicycling, hunting, and golf. Their demands and their behavior predictably evoked cries of outrage from men.

Against this turbulent background, Ibsen presented *A Doll's House*. The response was electric. On the strength of the play, suffragists construed Ibsen as a partisan supporter, while their opposition accused the playwright of propagandizing and being an *agent provocateur*. Yet Ibsen was neither a feminist nor a social reformer in the more general sense. (Indeed, Ibsen personally deplored the kind of emancipation and self-development which brought women out of the domestic sphere into the larger world; he saw women's proper role as motherhood, and motherhood only.) His apparent feminist sympathies were but a facet of his realism. His own responsibility extended no further than describing the problems as he saw them; he did not attempt to solve them. Nevertheless, he had a sharp eye and many sharp words for injustice, and it was the injustice of Torvald's demeaning treatment of Nora—a deplorably common occurrence in real life, Ibsen conceded—that provided the impetus for the play.

In the raging debate over the morality of Nora's behavior, however, it is altogether too easy to neglect Torvald and his dramatic function in the play. For this smug lawyer-bank manager is meant to represent the social structure at large, the same social structure that decreed an inferior position for women. Torvald is, in effect, a symbol for society: male-dominated and authoritarian. Thus, he establishes "rules" for Nora—the petty prohibition against macaroons, for one; he also requires her to act like an imbecile and insists upon the rightness, empirical as well as ethical, of his view in all matters. (In fact, Ibsen remarks in his "Notes" for the play that men make the laws and judge a woman's conduct from a man's point of view, "as though she were not a woman but a man.") His righteous refusal to borrow money is a particularly ironic example, and his contemptuous attitude toward Nora's intelligence and sense of responsibility—he calls her *his* "little lark," *his* "little squirrel," *his* "little featherbrain," *his* "little spendthrift," and so on—actually reflects men's prevailing view toward women: that they are owned property, playthings, dolls to be housed in toy mansions and be indulged, but only sparingly.

In this Neanderthal context, it is difficult not to view Torvald as a thorough-going villain. But like society, Torvald is not completely devoid of redeeming grace—else why would Nora have married him to begin with; why would she commit forgery at great personal risk and use her utmost ingenuity to save his life and to protect him from shame; why would she continue to sacrifice for him, if he possessed not a shred of virtue to elicit from her a feeling of genuine love? For Nora is both sensible and sensitive, despite Torvald's disparaging insinuations, and her awareness of her own worth is gradually awakened as the play unfolds—and with it her sense of individual responsibility. When at last she insists on her right to individual self-development, the spoiled girl-doll becomes a full-fledged woman. She slams the door of the doll house in a gesture symbolic of a biblical putting away of childish things and takes her rightful place in the adult world. Needless to say, that slam shook the very rafters of the social-domestic establishment, and the reverberations continue to the present time. So powerful an echo makes a powerful drama.

DON JUAN

Type of work: Epic poem
Author: George Gordon, Lord Byron (1788–1824)
Type of plot: Social satire
Time of plot: Late eighteenth century
Locale: Spain, Turkey, Russia, England
First published: By cantos, 1819–1824

This unfinished epic satire is written in ottava rima *and contains 16,000 lines in its sixteen cantos. Rather than following the epic tradition, the poem becomes a vehicle for digression on any subject; Byron, through his hero, gives his views on wealth, power, society, chastity, poets, diplomats, and England. For this reason the poem holds a high place among literary satires.*

Principal Characters

Don Juan (jũ′an), the young son of Donna Inez and Don José, a hidalgo of Seville. He is a handsome, mischief-making boy whose education, after his father's death, is carefully supervised by his mother, who insists that he read only classics expurgated in the text but with all the obscenities collected in an appendix. He is allowed to associate only with old or ugly women. At the age of sixteen he learns the art of love from Donna Julia, a young matron. The ensuing scandal causes Donna Inez to send her son to Cadiz, there to take ship for a trip abroad. The vessel on which he is a passenger sinks after a storm; he experiences a romantic interlude with the daughter of a Greek pirate and slave trader; he is sold to the Turks; he takes part in the siege of Ismail, a Turkish fort on the Danube River; he becomes the favorite of the Empress Catherine of Russia; and he is sent on a diplomatic mission to England, where he becomes a critical observer of English society.

Donna Inez, Don Juan's mother, a domineering and short-sighted woman who first tries to protect her son from the facts of life but later rejoices in his good fortune and advancement when he becomes the favorite of Empress Catherine of Russia.

Don José, Don Juan's father, a gallant man often unfaithful to his wife, with whom he quarrels constantly. He dies while his son is still a small boy.

Donna Julia, Don Juan's first love, a woman of twenty-three married to a fifty-year-old husband, Don Alfonso. She is forced to enter a convent after her irate husband discovers his wife and her young lover in her bedchamber. In a long letter, written on the eve of Don Juan's departure from Spain, she professes her undying love for him.

Don Alfonso, the cuckold husband who discovers Don Juan hiding in a closet in his wife's bedroom.

Haidée, the second love of Don Juan. A tall, lovely child of nature and passion, she finds him unconscious on the seashore following the sinking of the ship on which he had sailed from Spain. Filled with love and sympathy, she hides and protects him. This idyllic island romance ends when Lambro, her pirate father, returns from one of his expeditions and finds the two sleeping together after a great feast which Lambro has watched from a distance. Don Juan, wounded in a scuffle with Lambro's men, is bound and put aboard one of the pirate's ships. Shortly afterward Haidée dies lamenting her vanished lover, and his child dies with her.

Lambro, Haidée's father, "the mildest-manner'd man that ever scuttled ship or cut a throat." Returning from one of his piratical expeditions, he surprises the young lovers and sends Don Juan, wounded in a fight with Lambro's men, away on a slave ship. Later he regrets his hasty action when he watches his only child die of illness and grief.

Gulbeyaz, the sultana of Turkey. Having seen Don Juan in the slave market where he is offered for sale, along with an Italian opera troupe sold into captivity by their disgusted impresario, she orders one of the palace eunuchs to buy the young man. She has him taken to the palace and dressed in women's clothes. Even though she brings her strongest weapon, her tears, to bear, she is unable to make Don Juan her lover.

The Sultan of Turkey, the father of fifty daughters and four dozen sons. Seeing the disguised Don Juan in his wife's apartments, he orders the supposed female slave to be taken to the palace harem.

Baba, the African eunuch who buys Don Juan at the sultana's command. He later flees with Don Juan and John Johnson from Constantinople.

Lolah, Katinka, and **Dudú,** three girls in the sultan's harem. Dudú, lovely and languishing, has the disguised Don Juan for her bedfellow. Late in the night she awakes screaming after a dream in which she reached for a golden apple and was stung by a bee. The next morning jealous Gulbeyaz orders Dudú and Don Juan executed, but they escape in the company of Johnson and Baba.

John Johnson, a worldly Englishman fighting with the Russians in the war against the Turks. Captured, he is bought in the slave market along with Don Juan. The two escape and make their way to the Turkish lines before Ismail. Johnson is recognized by General Suwarrow, who welcomes him and Don Juan as allies in the attack on Ismail.

Leila, a ten-year-old Moslem girl whose life Don Juan saves during the capture of Ismail. He becomes her protector.

General Suwarrow (Souvaroff), the leader of the Russian forces at the siege and taking of Ismail.

Catherine, empress of Russia, to whose court Don Juan is sent with news of the Turkish victory at Ismail. Voluptuous and rapacious in love, she receives the young man with great favor and he becomes her favorite. After he becomes ill she reluctantly decides to send him on a diplomatic mission to England.

Lord Henry Amundeville, an English politician and the owner of Norman Abbey. Don Juan meets the nobleman in London and the two become friends.

Lady Adeline Amundeville, his wife, who also becomes Don Juan's friend and mentor. She advises him to marry because she is afraid that he will become seriously involved with the notorious Duchess of Fitz-Fulke. During a house party at Norman Abbey she sings a song telling of the Black Friar, a ghost often seen wandering the halls of the Abbey.

The Duchess of Fitz-Fulke, a woman of fashion notorious for her amorous intrigues. She pursues Don Juan after his arrival in England and finally, disguised as the ghostly Black Friar of Norman Abbey, succeeds in making him her lover.

Miss Aurora Raby, a young Englishwoman with whom Don Juan contemplates matrimony. Although she seems completely unimpressed by his attentions, he is piqued by her lack of interest.

Pedrillo, Don Juan's tutor. When the ship on which he and his master sail from Cadiz sinks after a storm, they are among those set adrift in a longboat. When the food runs out, the unlucky pedagogue is eaten by his famished companions. Although Don Juan considers the man an ass, he is unable to help eat the hapless fellow.

Zoe, Haidée's maid.

Lady Pinchbeck, a woman of fashion who, after Don Juan's arrival in London, takes Leila under her protection.

The Story

When Don Juan was a small boy, his father died, leaving the boy in the care of his mother, Donna Inez. Donna Inez was a righteous woman who had made her husband's life miserable. She had her son tutored in the arts of fencing, riding, and shooting, and she herself attempted to rear him in a moral manner. But even though young Don Juan read widely in the sermons and lives of the saints, he did not seem to absorb from his studies the qualities his mother thought essential.

At sixteen, he was a handsome lad much admired by his mother's friends. Donna Julia, in particular, often looked pensively at the youth. Donna Julia was just twenty-three and married to a man of fifty. Although she loved her husband, or so she told herself, she thought often of young Don Juan. One day, finding herself alone with him, she gave herself to the young man.

The young lovers spent long hours together during the summer, and it was not until November that Don Alfonso, her husband, discovered their intrigue. When Don Alfonso found Don Juan in his wife's bedroom, he tried to throttle him. But Don Juan overcame Don Alfonso and fled, first to his mother's home for clothes and money. Then Donna Inez sent him to Cadiz to begin a tour of Europe. The good lady prayed that the trip would mend his ways.

Before his ship reached Leghorn a storm broke it apart. Don Juan spent many days in a lifeboat without food or water. At last the boat was washed ashore, and Don Juan fell exhausted on the beach and slept. When he awoke, he saw bending over him a beautiful girl who told him that she was called Haidée and that she was the daughter of the ruler of the island, one of the Cyclades. Her father, Lambro, was a pirate, dealing in jewels and slaves. Because she knew her father would sell Don Juan to the first trader who came by, Haidée hid Don Juan in a cave and sent her maids to wait on him.

When Lambro left on another expedition, Haidée took Don Juan from the cave and they roamed together over the island. Haidée heaped jewels and fine foods and wines on Don Juan, for he was the first man she had ever known except her father and her servants. Although Don Juan still tried to think of Donna Julia, he could not resist Haidée. A child of nature and passion, she gave herself to him with complete freedom. Again Don Juan lived an idyllic existence, until Haidée's father returned unexpectedly. Don Juan again fought gallantly, but at last he was overcome by the old man's servants and put aboard a slave ship bound for a distant market. He never saw Haidée again, and he never knew that she died giving birth to his child.

The slave ship took Don Juan to a Turkish market, where he and another prisoner were purchased by a black eunuch and taken to the palace of a sultan. There Don Juan was made to dress as a dancing maiden and present himself to the sultana, the fourth and favorite wife of the sultan. She had passed by the slave market and had seen Don Juan and wanted him for a lover. In order to conceal his sex from the sultan, she forced the disguise on Don Juan. But even at the threat of death, Don Juan would not become her lover, for he still yearned for Haidée. Perhaps his constancy might have wavered, if the sultana had not been an infidel, for she was young and beautiful.

Eventually Don Juan escaped from the palace and joined the army of Catherine of Russia. The Russians were at war with the sultan from whose palace Don Juan had fled. Don Juan was such a valiant soldier that he was sent to St. Petersburg, to carry the news of a Russian victory to Empress Catherine. Catherine also cast longing eyes on the handsome stranger, and her approval soon made Don Juan the toast of her capital.

In the midst of his luxury and good fortune, Don Juan grew ill. Hoping that a change of climate would help her favorite, Catherine resolved to send him on a mission to England. When he reached London he was well received, for he was a polished young man, well versed in fashionable etiquette. His mornings were spent in business, but his afternoons and evenings were devoted to lavish entertainment. He conducted himself with such decorum, however, that he was much sought after by proper young ladies and much advised by older ones. Lady Adeline Amundeville, made him her protégé, and advised him freely on affairs of the heart. Another, the Duchess of Fitz-Fulke, advised him too, but her suggestions were of a more personal nature and seemed to demand a secluded spot where there was no danger from intruders. Because of the Duchess Fitz-Fulke's attentions to Don Juan, Lady Adeline began to talk to him about selecting a bride from the chaste and suitable young ladies attentive to him.

Don Juan thought of marriage, but his interest was stirred by a girl not on Lady Adeline's list. Aurora Raby was a plain young lady, prim, dull, and seemingly unaware of Don Juan's presence. Her lack of interest served to spur him on to greater efforts, but a smile was his only reward from the cold maiden.

His attention was diverted from Aurora Raby by the appearance of the ghost of the Black Friar, who had once lived in the house of Lady Adeline, where Don Juan was a guest. The ghost was a legendary figure reported to appear before births, deaths, or marriages. To Don Juan, the ghost was an evil omen, and he could not laugh off the tightness about his heart. Lady Adeline and her husband seemed to consider the ghost a great joke. Aurora Raby appeared to be a little sympathetic with Don Juan, but the Duchess of Fitz-Fulke merely laughed at his discomfiture.

The second time the ghost appeared, Don Juan followed it out of the house and into the garden. It seemed to float before him, always just out of his reach. Once he thought he had grasped it, but his fingers touched only a cold wall. Then he seized it firmly and found that the ghost had a sweet breath and full, red lips. When the monk's cowl fell back, the Duchess of Fitz-Fulke was revealed.

On the morning after, Don Juan appeared at breakfast, wan and tired. Whether he had overcome more than the ghost, no one will ever know. The duchess, too, came down, seeming to have the air of one who had been rebuked.

Critical Evaluation

George Gordon Byron, who became the sixth Lord Byron by inheriting the title from his uncle, William, was born on January 22, 1788. Because his father, the notorious "Mad Jack" Byron, deserted the family, young Byron was brought up in his mother's native Scotland, where he was exposed to Presbyterian concepts of predestination which distorted his religious views throughout his life. In 1801 he entered Harrow, a public school near London; in 1808 he received the Master of Arts degree from Cambridge; in 1809 he took his seat in the House of Lords. From June 1809 to July 1811, Byron traveled in Europe in the company of his friend Hobhouse. In 1812 he met Lady Caroline Lamb, who later became his mistress; in 1813 he spent several months with his half sister, Augusta Leigh, who later bore a daughter who may have been Byron's. Byron married Annabella Milbanke in 1815; she bore him a daughter, Ada, a year later and left him shortly thereafter. In 1816 Byron left England, never to return. That year found him in Switzerland with the Shelleys, where in 1817 Clare Clairmont bore his illegitimate daughter Allegra. After 1819 Countess Teresa Guicciola, who sacrificed her marriage and social position for Byron, became his lover and comforter. Byron died on April 19, 1824, in Missolonghi, where he had hoped to help Greece gain independence from Turkey.

Don Juan, an "epic" poem written in *ottava rima*, is permeated throughout with Byronic philosophy. Its episodic plot, narrated in first person by its author, tells the story of young Juan, who, victimized by a narrow-minded and hypocritical mother, an illogical educational system, and his own fallible humanity, loses his innocence and faith and becomes disillusioned with man and his institutions. The poem's rambling style allows for Byron's numerous digressions, in which he satirizes many aspects of English life: English government and its officials, religion and its confusions and hypocrisies, society and its foibles, war and its irrationality, woman and her treachery, man and his inhumanity to his fellows. Even English poets feel the fire of Byron's wrath. Thus Byron has been accused of a completely negative view in *Don Juan*— anti-everything and pro-nothing. Though it is true that to Byron all is relative, because there can be no absolutes in a world without reason, sanity, or justice, the philosophy of *Don Juan* is not wholly pessimistic. Admittedly, the undertone, especially in the digressions, is often sardonic; yet the overtone, created by a flippant refusal to take Juan's story (or life) too seriously and by extensive use of exaggerated feminine rhyme, such as "intellectual" and "hen-peck'd you all," is essentially comic. Thus the zest and the laughter in *Don Juan* belie the idea of total despair and lend an affirmation of life despite its ironies; the lapses into lyricism reveal a heart that sings despite the poet's attempt to stifle emotion with sophistication.

In *Don Juan*, Byron's philosophical confusion seems to be caused by his natural affinity for a Platonic, idealistic view, which has been crushed under the weight of a realism he is too honest and too perceptive to ignore. Though he denies that he discusses metaphysics, he comments that nothing is stable or permanent; all is mutable and subject to violent destruction. Yet Byron, in calling the world a "glorious blunder," is not totally blind to its temporary beauties. During the Juan-Haidée romance, the lovers live in an Edenic world of beautiful sunsets and warm, protective caves. Still, Juan's foreboding and Haidée's dream are reminders that nature's dangers always lurk behind its façade of beauty. And even Haidée, "Nature's bride," pursued pleasure and passion only to be reminded that "the wages of sin is death."

Byron's view of the nature of man is closely akin to his complex view of natural objects. Man has his moments of glory, integrity, and unselfishness. For example, Juan, the novice, does not flee from the horror of battle; he shuns cannibalism even though he is starving; he refuses to be forced to love the sultana; he risks his life to save young Leila. Often Byron emphasizes man's freedom of mind and spirit. Yet he believes that man's self-deceit is the chief factor in his decadence; his false ideas of glory lead to bloodshed. Ironically, Suwarrow lectures his soldiers on "the noble art of killing"; man kills because "it brings self-approbation." In fact, Byron suggests that man is more destructive than nature or God. Still, he does not condemn man; some taint at the heart of nature and of man turns "simple instinct and passion" to guilt; besides,

society's corruption in turn corrupts man. Lord Henry as the elder sophisticate is perhaps the best example of man's inability to retain his innocence; caught in the trap of his own greed and hypocrisy and of society's political game, Lord Henry finds that he cannot turn back, even though "the fatigue was greater than the profit." Byron also strikes out against political corruption. He had strong hopes for England's budding liberalism: a "king in constitutional procession" had offered great promise in leading the world to political freedom and morality. Yet Byron boldly declares England's failure to fulfill this promise.

Byron does, however, offer positive values in *Don Juan*. He believes that momentary happiness and glory and love *are* worth living for. Although "A day of gold from out an age of iron/ Is all that life allows the luckiest sinner," it is better than nothing. Man must fight, though he knows that he can never redeem the world and that defeat and death are certain. Since hypocrisy is one of the worst sins, man should be sincere. To Byron, the creative act is especially important, for it is man's only chance to transcend his mortality.

Throughout *Don Juan*, then, one follows man through his hapless struggle with life. Born in a fallen state, educated to hypocrisy and impracticality, cast out into a world of false values and boredom, man follows the downward path to total disillusionment. He learns, however, to protect himself from pain by insulating himself with the charred shell of burned-out passion and crushed ideals. Blindly, he stumbles toward that unknown and unknowable end—death. Yet he goes not humbly but defiantly, not grimly but with gusto.

Therefore, Byron's philosophy, despite its harshness, is one which embraces life, seeking to intensify and electrify each fleeting, irrevocable moment. It is a philosophy of tangibles, though they are inadequate; of action, though it will not cure man's ills; of honesty, though it must recognize man in his fallen state. And, though death is inevitable and no afterlife is promised, Byron maintains his comic perspective: "Carpe diem, Juan, . . . play out the play."

DON QUIXOTE DE LA MANCHA

Type of work: Novel
Author: Miguel de Cervantes Saavedra (1547–1616)
Type of plot: Picaresque romance
Time of plot: Late sixteenth century
Locale: Spain
First published: *El ingenioso hidalgo don Quixote de la Mancha*, Part 1, 1605; part 2, 1615 (English translation, 1612–1620)

One of the best-loved novels of all time, Don Quixote *was intended to be a satire on the exaggerated chivalric romances of Cervantes' time. However, the author soars above this purpose in his wealth of fancy and in his irrepressible high spirit as he pokes fun at social and literary conventions of his day. The novel offers a good cross-section of Spanish life, thought, and feeling at the end of the chivalric age as it parades a variegated assortment of minor characters— shepherds, innkeepers, students, priests, and nobles—through its pages. Contrasting characterizations of Don Quixote, the visionary idealist, and Sancho Panza, the practical realist, symbolize the duality of the Spanish character in this essentially humane novel.*

Principal Characters

Don Quixote (dōn kĭ·hō'tā), possibly a gentle but impoverished man named Alonso Quixano (or perhaps Quixana) of Argamasilla, in the Spanish province of La Mancha. Driven mad by reading many romances of chivalry, he determines to deck himself out in rusty armor and a cardboard helmet and to become a knight-errant. Under the name of "Don Quixote" he will roam the world, righting wrongs. His squire calls him "The Knight of the Sorrowful Countenance." He has moments of lucidity, especially at the end of the novel when a victorious enemy forces him to give up his questing. He returns home, repents of his folly, and dies.

Sancho Panza (sän'chō pän'thä), a paunchy rustic at first described as "long-legged." He is persuaded by promises of governorship of an island to become squire and attendant of the knight. He is the best drawn of the 669 characters in this 461,000 word novel. He does get his island, but he abdicates upon news of the approach of a hostile army.

Rocinante (rrō·thē·nän'tā), the nag that carries Don Quixote on his journeying. His companion is Dapple, the donkey of Sancho Panza.

Aldonza Lorenzo (äl·dōn'thä lō·rän'thō), a sweaty peasant girl of Toboso, whom Don Quixote idealizes under the name of **Dulcinea del Toboso;** he chooses her to be his Queen of Love and Beauty, the inspiration of his knightly questing.

Antonia Quixana (än·tō'nyä kē·hä'nä), Don Quixote's niece, who by the terms of his dying will can marry only a man who is not given to reading books of chivalry.

Teresa Cascajo (tā·rä'sä käs·kä'hō), also called **Juana Gutiérrez** (hwä'nä gōōtyä'rräth), the wife of Sancho Panza.

An Innkeeper, the fat master of a roadside inn which Don Quixote mistakes for a fortress. He dubs Don Quixote a knight.

Andrés (än·dräs'), an unpaid servant, temporarily saved form a beating in Don Quixote's first attempt at righting wrongs.

Pedro Pérez (pā'drō pā'rāth), the curate who burns the knight's library of chivalric romances in an attempt to cure him of his madness.

Master Nicolás (nē·kō·läs'), the village barber, who assists in burning the books. Dressed in woman's clothes, he impersonates Dulcinea in an effort to persuade Don Quixote to leave the Sierra Morena.

Cardenio (kär·dā'nyō), who meets Don Quixote in the Sierra Morena and tells his sad story.

Dorotea (dō·rō·tä'ä), another ill-starred wanderer with a melancholic tale. She pretends to be a damsel in distress in order to persuade the knight to go home.

Ginés de Pasamonte (hē·nās' dā pä·sämōn'tā), a criminal condemned to the galleys. Don Quixote rescues him and a dozen more from the chain gang, only to be stoned by them.

Two Friars, acting as escort for a noble lady in a coach. The knight believes they are abducting her and attacks the Biscayan squire and the retinue. They beat up Sancho Panza.

Roque Guinart (rō'kä gē·närt'), a man driven to banditry by bad luck. He captures Don Quixote and Sancho. Refusing to be persuaded by them to turn knight-errant, he sends his prisoners to a neighboring bandit and recommends them as entertaining persons.

Master Pedro (pä'drō), the owner of a divining ape and a puppet show whose characters the knight mistakes for real people. He tries to rescue the leading lady.

A Barber, whose shaving basin Don Quixote mistakes for Mambrino's golden helmet.

A Carter, taking caged lions from the Governor of Oran to King Philip. In outfacing one of them, Don Quixote achieves his only successful adventure in the novel.

A Duke and his Duchess, who invite Don Quixote and Sancho Panza to their palace and play jokes on them, such as a supposed ride through space on a magic wooden horse, Clavijero. They make Sancho governor of an island, a village owned by the Duke.

Samson Carrasco (säm′sōn kä·rräs′kō), a neighbor who disguises himself as the Knight of the Mirrors and the Knight of the White Moon. He eventually overcomes Don Quixote and sentences him to abandon knight-errantry and return home. There Don Quixote dies after denouncing knight-errantry as nonsense, never realizing that he himself has been a true knight and a gallant gentleman.

The Story

A retired and impoverished gentleman named Alonzo Quixano lived in the Spanish province of La Mancha. He had read so many romances of chivalry that his mind became stuffed with fantastic accounts of tournaments, knightly quests, damsels in distress, and strange enchantments, and he decided one day to imitate the heroes of the books he read and to revive the ancient custom of knight-errantry. Changing his name to Don Quixote de la Mancha, he had himself dubbed a knight by a rascally publican whose miserable inn he mistook for a turreted castle.

For armor he donned an old suit of mail which had belonged to his great-grandfather. Then upon a bony old nag he called Rosinante, he set out upon his first adventure. Not far from his village he fell into the company of some traveling merchants who thought the old man mad and beat him severely when he challenged them to a passage at arms.

Back home recovering from his cuts and bruises, he was closely watched by his good neighbor, Pedro Perez, the village priest, and Master Nicholas, the barber. Hoping to cure him of his fancies, the curate and the barber burned his library of chivalric romances. Don Quixote, however, believed that his books had been carried off by a wizard. Undaunted by his misfortunes, he determined to set out on the road again with an uncouth rustic named Sancho Panza as his squire. As the mistress to whom he would dedicate his deeds of valor, he chose a buxom peasant wench famous for her skill in salting pork. He called her Dulcinea del Toboso.

The knight and his squire had to sneak out of the village under cover of darkness, but in their own minds they presented a brave appearance: the lean old man on his bony horse and his squat, black-browed servant on a small ass, Dapple. The don carried his sword and lance, Sancho Panza a canvas wallet and a leather bottle. Sancho went with the don because in his shallow-brained way he hoped to become governor of an isle.

The don's first encounter was with a score of windmills on the plains of Montiel. Mistaking them for monstrous giants, he couched his lance, set spurs to Rosinante's thin flanks, and charged full tilt against them. One of the whirling vanes lifted him from his saddle and threw him into the air. When Sancho Panza ran to pick him up, he explained that sorcerers had changed the giants into windmills.

Shortly afterward he encountered two monks riding in company with a lady in a coach escorted by men on horseback. Don Quixote imagined that the lady was a captive princess. Haughtily demanding her release, he unhorsed one of the friars in an attempted rescue. Sancho was beaten by the lady's lackeys. Don Quixote bested her Biscayan squire in a sword fight, sparing the man's life on the condition that he go to Toboso and yield himself to the peerless Dulcinea. Sancho, having little taste for violence, wanted to get on to his isle as quickly as possible.

At an inn, Quixote became involved in an assignation between a carrier and a servant girl. He was trounced by the carrier. The don, insulted by the innkeeper's demand for payment, rode away without paying. To his terror, Sancho was tossed in a blanket as payment for his master's debt.

The pair came upon dust clouds stirred up by two large flocks of sheep. Don Quixote, sure that they were two medieval armies closing in combat, intervened, only to be pummeled with rocks by the indignant shepherds, whose sheep he had scattered.

At night the don thought a funeral procession was a parade of monsters. He attacked and routed the mourners and was called the Knight of the Sorry Aspect by Sancho. The two came upon a roaring noise in the night. Quixote, believing it to be made by giants, wanted to attack immediately, but Sancho judiciously hobbled Rosinante so he could not move. The next day, they discovered that the noise came from the pounding of a mill.

Quixote attacked an itinerant barber and seized the poor barber's bowl, which he declared to be the famous golden helmet of Mambrino, and his packsaddle, which he believed to be a richly jeweled caparison.

Next, the pair came upon a chain gang being taken to the galleys. The don interviewed various prisoners and decided to succor the afflicted. He freed them, only to be insulted by their remarks concerning his lady, the fair Dulcinea. Sancho, afraid of what would ensue from their releasing of the galley slaves, led Quixote into the mountains for safety. There they came upon a hermit, a nobleman, who told them a long story of unrequited love. Quixote and the hermit fought over the virtues of their inamoratas. Deciding to do penance and to fast for the love of Dulcinea, Quixote gave a letter to Sancho to deliver to the maiden. When Sancho returned to the village, Don Quixote's friends learned from Sancho the old man's whereabouts. They returned with Sancho to the mountains, hoping they could trick Don Quixote into returning with them. The priest devised a scheme whereby a young peasant woman would pose as a distressed princess. Don Quixote, all but dead from hunger and exposure, was easily deceived, and the party started homeward.

They came to the inn where Sancho had been tossed in the blanket. The priest explained the don's vagaries to the alarmed innkeeper, who admitted that he, too, was addicted to the reading of romances of chivalry. At the inn, Don Quixote fought in his sleep with ogres and ran his sword through two of the innkeeper's precious wineskins. The itinerant barber stopped by and demanded the return of his basin and packsaddle. After the party had sport at the expense of the befuddled barber, restitution was made. An officer appeared with a warrant for the arrest of the don and Sancho for releasing the galley slaves. The priest explained his friend's mental condition, and the officer departed.

Seeing no other means of getting Don Quixote quietly home, his friends disguised themselves and placed the don in a cage mounted on an oxcart. He was later released under oath not to attempt to escape. A canon joined the party and sought to bring Quixote to his senses by logical argument against books of knight-errantry. The don refuted the canon with a charming and brilliant argument and went on to narrate a typical romance of derring-do. Before the group reached home, they came upon a goatherd who told them a story, but because of a misunderstanding the goatherd beat Quixote.

Sometime later the priest and the barber visited the convalescing Don Quixote to give him news of Spain and of the world. When they told him there was danger of an attack on Spain by the Turks, the don suggested that the king assemble all of Spain's knights-errant to repulse the enemy. At this time, Sancho entered despite efforts to bar him. He brought word that a book telling of their adventures had appeared. The sight of Sancho inspired the don to sally forth again. His excuse was a great tournament to be held at Saragossa.

Failing to dissuade Don Quixote from going forth again, his friends were reassured when a village student promised he would waylay the flighty old gentleman.

Don Quixote's first destination was the home of Dulcinea in nearby El Toboso. While the don waited in a forest, Sancho saw three peasant girls riding out of the village. He rode to his master and told him that Dulcinea with two handmaidens approached. Frightened by the don's fantastic speech, the girls fled. Don Quixote swore

that Dulcinea had been enchanted.

Benighted in a forest, the knight and his squire were awakened by the arrival of another knight and squire. The other knight boasted that he had defeated in combat all Spanish knights. The don, believed the knight to be mistaken, challenged him. They fought by daylight and, miraculously, Don Quixote unhorsed the Knight of the Wood, who was Samson Carrasco, the village student, in disguise. His squire was an old acquaintance of Sancho. The don declared the resemblances were the work of magicians and continued on his way. Upset by his failure, Carrasco swore vengeance on Don Quixote.

Sancho filled Quixote's helmet with curds which he procured from shepherds. When the don suddenly clapped on his helmet at the approach of another adventure, he thought his brains were melting. This new adventure took the form of a wagon bearing two caged lions. Quixote, ever intrepid, commanded the keeper to open one cage—he would engage a lion in combat. Unhappily, the keeper obeyed. Quixote stood ready, but the lion yawned and refused to come out.

The don and Sancho joined a wedding party and subsequently attended a wedding festival at which the rejected lover tricked the bride into marrying him instead of the rich man she had chosen.

Next, the pair were taken to the Caves of Montesinos, where Quixote was lowered underground. He was brought up an hour later asleep, and, upon awakening, he told a story of having spent three days in a land of palaces and magic forests where he had seen his enchanted Dulcinea.

At an inn, Quixote met a puppeteer who had a divining ape. By trickery, the rascal identified the don and Sancho with the help of the ape. He presented a melodramatic puppet show which Don Quixote, carried away by the make-believe story, demolished with his sword. The don paid for the damage done and struck out for the nearby River Ebro. He and Sancho took a boat and were carried by the current toward some churning mill wheels, which the don thought were a beleaguered city awaiting deliverance. They were rescued by millers after the boat had been wrecked and the pair thoroughly soaked.

Later, in a forest, the pair met a huntress who claimed knowledge of the famous knight and his squire. They went with the lady to her castle and were welcomed by a duke and his duchess who had read of their previous adventures and who were ready to have great fun at the pair's expense. The hosts arranged an elaborate night ceremony to disenchant Dulcinea, who was represented by a disguised page. To his great discomfort, Sancho was told that he would receive five hundred lashes as his part of the disenchantment. Part of the jest was a ride through space on a magic wooden horse. Blindfolded, the pair mounted their steed, and servants blew air in their faces from bellows and thrust torches near their faces.

Sancho departed to govern his isle, a village in the domains of the duke and duchess, while the female part of the household turned to the project of compromising Quixote in his worship of Dulcinea. Sancho governed for a week. He made good laws and delivered wise judgments, but at the end of a week, he yearned for the freedom of the road. Together he and his master proceeded toward Saragossa. Don Quixote changed their destination to Barcelona, however, when he heard that a citizen of that city had written a spurious account of his adventures.

In Barcelona, they marveled at the city, the ships, and the sea. Don Quixote and Sancho were the guests of Moreno, who took them to inspect the royal galleys. The galley which they visited suddenly put out to sea in pursuit of pirates, and a fight followed. Sancho was terrified.

There came to Barcelona a Knight of the White Moon, who challenged Don Quixote to combat. After the old man had been overcome, the strange knight, in reality the student Carrasco, sentenced him to return home. Don Quixote went back, determined next to follow a pastoral shepherd life. At home, the tired old man quickly declined. Before he died, he renounced as nonsense all to do with knight-errantry, not realizing that in his high-minded, noble-hearted nature he himself had been a great chivalrous gentleman.

Critical Evaluation

It has been said that *Don Quixote de la Mancha* is "the best novel in the world, beyond comparison." This belief was, is, and certainly will be shared by lovers of literary excellence everywhere. Miguel de Cerantes' avowed purpose was to ridicule the books of chivalry which enjoyed popularity even in his day, but he soared beyond this satirical purpose in his wealth of fancy and in his irrepressible high spirits as he pokes fun at social and literary conventions of his day. The novel provides a cross-section of Spanish life, thought, and feeling at the end of the chivalric age.

"For my absolute faith in the details of their histories and my knowledge of their features, their complexions and their deeds and their characters enable me by sound philosophy to deduce their features, their complexions, and their statures," says Don Quixote, declaring his expertise in knight-errantry. This declaration affords a key to understanding Cervantes' *Don Quixote de la Mancha*, for it demonstrates both the literal and the symbolic levels of the novel—and the distinction between those levels is crucial to grasping the full import of the story. The literal level is superficial; it reveals the obvious. The symbolic level, however, probes much deeper; it reveals the significance. In fact, the symbolic level deals, as all good literature must, with values. Thus, Don Quixote's declaration must be considered on both levels, and when set in context, it will lend insight into the novel as a whole.

On the literal level, Don Quixote is eminently qualified by his extensive reading to assert familiarity with the history, the deeds, and the character of virtually every knight whose existence was recorded. Indeed, his penchant for reading books of chivalry is established on the first page of the first chapter of the book. Even his niece and his housekeeper refer frequently to his reading habits. Moreover, the inventory of the don's library, made just before the books were burned, reveals the extent of his collection, and earlier mention of his omnivorous reading leads to the assumption that he had read all of them. Further evidence of Don Quixote's erudition is his ready knowledge of the rules of knight-errantry and his recalling the legend of Mambrino's helmet in connection with his oath of knighthood as well as elsewhere in the novel. Later, after an encounter with Yanguesan herdsmen, there is evidence, in a very lucid and pragmatic statement for a presumably insane old man, of Don Quixote's having read Machiavelli, followed by the don's citation of the misfortunes which befell his hero, Amadis of Gaul.

Other adventures provide internal evidence of Quixote's knowledge about the history of chivalry. A thrashing by muleteers jogs the don's memory to analogies between his plight and similar outrages visited upon the Marquis of Mantua, Baldwin, Abindarraez, and Don Roderigo de Narvaez. After his lance is broken by a windmill, Don Quixote remembers the makeshift tree-limb weapon used by Diego Perez de Vargas when the latter's weapon was broken in battle. At another time, he explains and defends the code of knight-errantry to fellow travelers, citing Arthurian legend, the ever-present Amadis of Gaul, the stricter-than-monastic rules of knight-errantry, and the noble families of Italy and Spain who contributed to the tradition. In fact, incredible as it may seem, just before the don attacks the herd of sheep, he attributes to each sheep a title and an estate culled from his reservoir of reading—or from his overactive imagination. In addition, to rationalize his own designation as the Knight of the Sorry Aspect, he recalls the sobriquets of other knights-errant. In an attempt to inculcate Sancho Panza with the proper respect for his master, Don Quixote even relates biographical incidents from the lives of the squires of Amadis of Gaul and Sir Galaor. Significantly, almost craftily, he mentions that Gandalin, Amadis' squire, was also Count of the Firm Isle—a blatant inducement for Sancho to remain in the don's service. Yet, all in all, on the literal level, Don Quixote's mastery of chivalric lore seems to serve only as a rationalization for his ill luck.

On the symbolic level, more questions are raised than are answered. Quixote claims to have reached a "sound philosophy." But, is reliance on reading alone—as he has done—a valid basis for "sound philosophy," or has the don become so absorbed in his books that he is unable to formulate or express the applicability of his reading? Can literature serve as a basis for understanding reality, as Don Quixote avers? In lieu of a clear-cut answer, Cervantes offers a paradox. Early in the text, Don Quixote learns from Sancho that the Squire has never read any histories because he is illiterate; but later, trying to divert the don's attention with a story, Sancho under questioning, admits that although he had not seen the person in question, "the man who told me this story said it was so true and authentic . . . I could swear on my oath that I had seen it all." The issues of verisimilitude and credibility are not really resolved in this novel. Consequently, these issues generate further questions about distinctions between reality and fantasy. Sancho represents empirical, commonsensical reality; the don stands for whimsy and unfettered imagination. Whose view of the world is more accurate? Cervantes is ambiguous, at best, about the answer. The question persists, however, as Luigi Pirandello's *Henry IV* (1922) vividly testifies. Readers are left to ponder this paradox which Emily Dickinson has so succinctly described: "Much madness is divinest sense."

Another issue raised on the symbolic level involves the possible immorality of reading "too many" books. Books, in this sense, are a symbol of education, and this facet of *Don Quixote de la Mancha* may be a veiled protest against the *Index Librorum Prohibitorum*. The literal lesson emphasizes the corruptive power of books (and, therefore, education); however, the symbolic implication—given Cervantes' sympathetic treatment of Don Quixote—is that books and education are liberating influences on the human psyche. Thus, the symbolic purport of *Don Quixote de la Mancha* may be a parody of the Church's monopoly of literacy in the Middle Ages, with the uninhibited don a reproach to the insensitive, book-burning priest.

To be sure, Don Quixote becomes a tragic figure toward the end of the novel, but not for the failure of his philosophy; rather, it is society's failure to accommodate a deviation from the norm. Herein lies another symbolic level of the novel: society's intolerance of deviance. For Cervantes certainly did not make the don contemptible nor did he treat him with contempt. Such treatment would have been repellent after the tender tolerance of the first part of the story. Despite the satirical thrust of the novel on the symbolic level, the don himself is a sympathetic character throughout the story. Although he strives to push time back, his efforts are depicted as noble. The sympathy he evokes is that popular sympathy for the underdog who defies all odds and is broken in the attempt in contrast to the protagonist who has everything in his favor and succumbs to a surfeit of success.

Cervantes' novel is a complex web of tangled skeins, subject to many more interpretations than those suggested here. Suffice it to say that *Don Quixote de la Mancha* is unequivocally judged the finest Spanish novel ever written and one of the greatest works in world literature.

DRACULA

Type of work: Novel
Author: Bram Stoker (1847–1912)
Type of plot: Horror romance
Time of plot: Nineteenth century
Locale: Transylvania and England
First published: 1897

This work is a classic of the gothic novel genre, and its principal character, Count Dracula, the vampire, continues to live on in contemporary entertainment media. Using the rhetorical device of letters and diaries and staging scenes full of Gothic horror, such as mysterious gloomy castles and open graves at midnight, the overall effect of the novel is one of excitement, realism, and horror.

Principal Characters

Count Dracula, a vampire. A corpse during the day, he comes to life at night. He has lived for centuries by sucking blood from living people. He pursues his victims in many harrowing episodes, and is pursued in turn from England to Rumania. There his body, in transport home to his castle, is overtaken and a stake driven through the heart, making it permanently dead.

Jonathan Harker, an English solicitor. He goes to Castle Dracula to transact business with the Count, whose nocturnal habits and total absence of servants puzzle Harker. Harker finds himself a prisoner in the castle, comes one day upon Dracula's corpse, and is occasionally victimized by the vampire. Then the coffinlike boxes are carried away and Harker finds himself left alone, still a prisoner. Later, after he has escaped, he is able to throw light on certain strange happenings in England.

Mina Murray, Harker's fiancée. She joins in the pursuit of Dracula; in a trance, she is able to tell the others that Dracula is at sea, on his return voyage.

Lucy Westenra, a lovely friend whom Mina visits at the time of Harker's trip to Rumania. She is the repeated victim of Dracula, now in England, who appears sometimes in werewolf guise. Finally she dies and becomes a vampire also.

Dr. Van Helsing, a specialist from Amsterdam called to aid the failing Lucy. His remedies are effective, but a fatal attack comes after he leaves; he then returns to England to still her corpse as well as to hunt Dracula.

Dr. Seward, Lucy's former suitor, who attends her during her illness. Until he makes a midnight visit to her empty tomb, he does not believe Van Helsing's advice that the dead girl's soul can be saved only if a stake is driven through her heart.

Arthur Holmwood, a young nobleman and Lucy's fiancée. As he kisses the dying Lucy, her teeth seem about to fasten on his throat. He goes with Seward and Van Helsing to the empty tomb and joins them in tracking down Dracula.

The Story

On his way to Castle Dracula in the province of Transylvania in Rumania, Jonathan Harker, an English solicitor, was apprehensive. His nervousness grew when he observed the curious, fearful attitude of the peasants and the coachman after they learned of his destination. He was on his way to transact business with Count Dracula, and his mission would necessitate remaining at the castle for several days.

Upon his arrival at the castle, Harker found comfortable accommodations awaiting him. Count Dracula was a charming host, although his peculiarly bloodless physical appearance was somewhat disagreeable to Harker's English eyes. Almost immediately, Harker was impressed with the strange life of the castle. He and the Count discussed their business at night, as the Count was never

available during the daytime. Although the food was excellent, Harker never saw a servant about the place. While exploring the castle, he found that it was situated high at the top of a mountain with no accessible exit other than the main doorway, which was kept locked. He realized with a shock that he was a prisoner of Count Dracula.

Various harrowing experiences ensued. While Harker half dozed in the early morning hours, three phantom women materialized and attacked him, attempting to bite his throat. Then the Count appeared and drove them off, whispering fiercely that Harker belonged to him. Later, Harker thought he saw a huge bat descending the castle walls, but the creature turned out to be Count Dracula. In the morning Harker, trying frantically to escape, stumbled into an old chapel where a number of coffinlike boxes of earth were stored. Harker opened one, and beneath the cover lay the Count, apparently dead. In the evening, however, the Count appeared as usual, and Harker demanded that he be released. The Count obligingly opened the castle door. A pack of wolves surrounded the entrance. The Count, laughing hysterically, left poor Harker a prisoner in his room.

The next day Harker, weak and sick from a strange wound in his throat, saw a pack cart, loaded with the mysterious boxes, drive from the castle. Dracula was gone and Harker was alone, a prisoner with no visible means of escape.

Meanwhile, Harker's fiancée, Mina Murray, had gone to visit her beautiful and charming friend Lucy Westenra in England. Lucy was planning to marry Arthur Holmwood, a young nobleman. One evening, early in Mina's visit, a storm blew up and a strange ship was driven aground. The only living creature aboard was a gray wolflike dog. The animal escaped into the countryside.

Soon afterward, Lucy's happiness began to fade because of a growing tendency to sleepwalk. One night, Mina followed her friend during one of her spells and discovered Lucy in a churchyard. A tall, thin man who was bending over Lucy disappeared at Mina's approach. Lucy could remember nothing of the experience when she awoke, but her physical condition seemed much weakened. Finally, she grew so ill that Mina was forced to call upon Dr. Seward, Lucy's former suitor. Lucy began to improve under his care, and when Mina received a report from Budapest that her missing fiancé had been found and needed care, she felt free to end her visit.

When Lucy's condition suddenly grew worse, Dr. Seward asked his old friend, Dr. Van Helsing, a specialist from Amsterdam, for his professional opinion. Examining Lucy thoroughly, Van Helsing paused over two tiny throat wounds that she was unable to explain. Van Helsing was concerned about Lucy's condition, which pointed to unusual loss of blood without signs of anemia or hemorrhage. She was given blood transfusions at intervals, and someone sat up with her at night. She improved but expressed fear of going to sleep at night because her dreams had grown so horrible.

One morning, Dr. Seward fell asleep outside her door. When he and Van Helsing entered her room, they found Lucy ashen white and in a worse condition than ever. Van Helsing quickly performed another transfusion; she rallied, but not as satisfactorily as before. Van Helsing then secured some garlic flowers and told Lucy to keep them around her neck at night. When the two doctors called the next morning, Lucy's mother had removed the flowers because she feared their odor might bother her daughter. Frantically, Van Helsing rushed to Lucy's room and found her in a coma. Again, he administered a trans-

fusion, and her condition improved. She said that with the garlic flowers close by she was not afraid of nightly flapping noises at her window. Van Helsing sat with her every night until he felt her well enough to leave. After cautioning her to sleep with the garlic flowers about her neck at all times, he returned to Amsterdam.

Lucy's mother continued to sleep with her daughter. One night, the two ladies were awakened by a huge wolf that crashed through the window. Mrs. Westenra fell dead of a heart attack, and Lucy fainted, the wreath of garlic flowers slipping from her neck. Seward and Van Helsing, who had returned to England, discovered her half dead in the morning. They knew she was dying and called Arthur. As Arthur attempted to kiss her, Lucy's teeth seemed about to pierce his throat. Van Helsing drew him away. When Lucy died, Van Helsing put a tiny gold crucifix over her mouth, but an attendant stole it from her body.

Soon after Lucy's death, several children of the neighborhood were discovered far from their homes, their throats marked by small wounds. Their only explanation was that they had followed a pretty lady. When Jonathan Harker returned to England, Van Helsing went to see him and Mina. After talking with Harker, Van Helsing revealed to Dr. Seward his belief that Lucy had fallen victim to a vampire, one of those strange creatures who can live for centuries on the blood of their victims and breed their kind by attacking the innocent and making them vampires in turn. According to Van Helsing, the only way to save Lucy's soul was to drive a stake through the heart of her corpse, cut off her head, and stuff her mouth with garlic flowers. Dr. Seward protested violently. The next midnight Arthur, Dr. Seward, and Van Helsing visited Lucy's tomb and found it empty. When daylight came, they did as Van Helsing had suggested with Lucy's corpse, which had returned to its tomb.

The men, with Mina, tried to track down Dracula in London in order to find him before he victimized anyone else. Their object was to remove the boxes of sterilized earth he had brought with him from Transylvania so that he would have no place to hide in the daytime. At last, the hunters trapped Dracula, but he escaped them. By putting Mina into a trance, Van Helsing was able to learn that Dracula was at sea, and it was necessary to follow him to his castle. Wolves gathered about them in that desolate country. Van Helsing drew a circle in the snow with a crucifix, and the travelers rested safely within the magic enclosure. The next morning, they overtook a cart carrying a black box. Van Helsing and the others overcame the drivers of the cart and pried open the lid of Dracula's coffin. As the sun began to set, they drove a stake through the heart of the corpse. The vampire was no more.

Critical Evaluation

Legend is inextricably twined with Bram Stoker's novel *Dracula*, for the novel is based on the legend. It is impossible to separate the two: The reader will inevitably supply legendary associations between the lines of the novel; but more often than not, readers tend to forget that both legend and novel were based on reality. This is not to say that vampires do or did roam Transylvania or elsewhere. However, the prototype for the Dracula legend was a verifiable historical figure, Prince Vlad Tepes, ruler of Transylvania and Walachia (now Rumania) in the mid-fifteenth century. Tepes, nicknamed "The Impaler," earned a bloody reputation by spearing his victims (some 100,000 of them in a six- to ten-year reign, so it is reported) on wooden sticks, a tactic that served to deter domestic criminals and potential outside invaders alike. He assumed the name Dracula, the meaning of which has been variously interpreted. The subjects of his small kingdom were convinced that such blood lust as he exhibited could be found only in a human vampire; hence Vlad Tepes, self-proclaimed Dracula, was the basis for the legend that Stoker captured so well.

Vampirism has been traced by historians, studied by scholars, embellished by artists and writers, and feared by the superstitious. In Western culture, vampirism has been associated mainly with the Transylvania region of Eastern Europe; however, the vampire phenomenon in one form or another is attested in all parts of the world from ancient times onward. Outside Europe, the vampire has appeared in the ancient cultures of the Middle East and the Mediterranean, in China as well as throughout Asia, in several African cultures, and in Aztec civilization and later in Mexico. Some references are in allegedly official reports and in religious works on demonology; others occur in folklore and in literature, drama, painting, and sculpture. Clearly, the vampire was no nineteenth century European invention, but the Romantic obsession with Gothic horror certainly stimulated a spate of vampiric literature among its other supernatural preoccupations. A short story, "The Vampyre," by John Polidori, was published in 1819. The melodrama *Les Vampires*, by Charles Nodier and Carmouche, was first produced in Paris in 1820. *Varney the Vampire*, or *The Feast of Blood* (authorship is disputed; either John Malcolm Rymer or Thomas Peckett Prest), a long novel, appeared in 1847 Joseph Sheridan Le Fanu's redoubtable "Carmilla" first saw print in 1871; but it was Stoker's *Dracula*, published in 1897, that surpassed them all and remains the paragon of vampire stories even today.

Drawing primarily upon European sources, Stoker produced a terrifying and credible tale by eliminating the inconsistencies and the contradictions common to legendary matter. Wisely avoiding some of the more outlandish explanations of vampirism, for example, Stoker portrayed the trait as transmitted from vampire to victim, who in turn became a vampire, and so on. To evade straining credulity, Stoker required prolonged contact between vampire and victim before the victim was irrevocably enlisted in the ranks. Thus, Jonathan Harker, whose sustenance of Count Dracula is brief, recovers with no lasting ill effects; but Lucy Westenra is literally drained and consequently becomes a vampire herself. As a result—and given the perilous circumstances—Van Helsing is compelled to restrain forcibly Lucy's ertswhile fiancé Arthur from giving her a deathbed kiss on her frothing, fanged mouth. Stoker also conceded the vampire's power to exercise a species of demonic possession, without physical contact, as the affliction of Mina Murray Harker illustrates.

In like manner, Stoker employed only the most conventional techniques for repelling vampires: garlic and the crucifix. The requirements for vampire survival were equally simplified from the vast complexity of alternatives that accumulated in the legend. Stoker limited his vampires to nocturnal activity; mandated, of course, the periodic sucking of blood (allowing for moderate stretches of hibernation or abstinence); insisted upon daylight repose in a coffin filled with Transylvania soil; and claimed vampiric invulnerability to ordinary human weapons.

Finally, Stoker's methods for the total annihilation of vampires were similarly conventional without resort to esoteric impedimenta. He stipulated that a wooden stake be driven through the vampire's heart (although Dracula was dispatched with a bowie knife); that the vampire's head be cut off; and that the vampire's mouth be stuffed with garlic flowers.

Stoker's recounting of the vampire legend has become the "standard version" in Western culture. Countless short stories and novels have spun off from the Stoker novel—the enormous success of Ann Rice's *Interview with the Vampire* (1976) and its sequels attests the continuing appeal of the vampire theme. Similarly, a number of theatrical and film adaptations have been mounted, but the classic stage and screen performances of Bela Lugosi, based upon Stoker's *Dracula*, have never been equaled. Lugosi's 1932 portrayal of Dracula still spellbinds motion-picture audiences as no other production has been able to do; and in this atmosphere of at least semicredulity, reported sightings of vampiric activity—much like reported sightings of flying saucers or unidentified flying objects—continue to the present.

In the meanwhile, Vlad Tepes's castles in Walachia and the Carpathians have been refurbished by the Rumanian government as tourist attractions, and the historical Dracula is being hailed as a national hero who strove to upgrade the moral fiber of his subjects. In many ways, therefore, Stoker's Dracula lives on to influence the present as powerfully—albeit in a different manner—as he influenced the past.

DRAMATIC MONOLOGUES AND LYRICS OF BROWNING

Author: Robert Browning (1812–1889)
First published: *Dramatic Lyrics*, 1842; *Dramatic Romances and Lyrics*, 1845; *Men and Women*, 1855

Much of Browning's finest writing was done during his thirties, years which comprise most of the poems in the volumes *Dramatic Lyrics*, *Dramatic Romances and Lyrics*, and *Men and Women*. The intentions and procedures of these three volumes are similar, so that most often one's comments on the first two hold good for the third as well. In fact, Browning himself in a later collected edition reshuffled many of these poems, breaking down the divisions between individual books but preserving always the dominating premise that the poems should be, as he said, "though often Lyric in expression, always Dramatic in principle, and so many utterances of so many imaginary persons, not mine." During his middle years, we see Browning striving to write poems at once less sentimental and more objective than those of his early hero Shelley. He developed his own form of the dramatic monologue in the attempt to overcome subjectivity and vagueness, and his success here is in the nature of an overcompensation. The poems in these volumes, "always Dramatic in principle," are brilliant but somehow chilly.

Browning's verse-play, *Pippa Passes*, published in 1841, immediately precedes *Dramatic Lyrics* and by its superb rendering of the spirit of Italy—a country which is for Browning always the dialectical counterpart of England, a kind of anti-England—the play foreshadows the skeptical attitude conveyed by the poems. In "The Bishop Orders His Tomb at Saint Praxed's Church," in "My Last Duchess," and in the immense narrative poem *The Ring and the Book* the poet was later to draw implicit and explicit contrasts between contemporary England and Renaissance Italy. His habitual approach is in this way argumentative and skeptical, the counterbalancing of opposing countries, times, sexes, and beliefs—as is suggested even by many of the titles in these volumes: "Meeting at Night" against "Parting at Morning," "Love in a Life" against "Life in a Love," "The Italian in England" against "The Englishman in Italy." The method permits Browning to end an elegant dialogue between two Venetian lovers, "In a Gondola," with a vicious stabbing. Alternately, he can present the interior monologue of a warped person, allowing the character to condemn himself by his (or her) words: as is the case of the female poisoner, crossed in love, in "The Laboratory," or the deranged murderer who speaks in "Porphyria's Lover." Perhaps the best of these interior monologues is the "Soliloquy of the Spanish Cloister," in which a splenetic monk grumbles against his abbot:

> GR-R-R—there go, my heart's abhorrence!
> Water your damn flower-pots, do!
> If hate killed men, Brother Lawrence,
> God's blood, would not mine kill you!
> What? your myrtle-bush wants trimming?
> Oh, that rose has prior claims—
> Needs its leaden vase filled brimming?
> Hell dry you up with its flames!

The lines are characteristic: Not only does the voice contradict the speaker's appearance and vocation, but the very exclamations and dashes render the punctuation histrionic and serve to define a particular habit of mind.

The monologues which imply a listener are psychologically more complex. "My Last Duchess" and "The Bishop Orders His Tomb at Saint Praxed's Church" appeared in 1842 and 1845, respectively, and are models, in these earlier volumes, of the kind of irony and immediacy which the dramatic method at its best is capable of generating:

> That's my last Duchess painted on the wall,
> Looking as if she were alive, I call
> That piece a wonder, now: Fra Pandolf's hands
> Worked busily a day, and there she stands.

Browning consciously follows Donne in beginning poems with arresting first lines. Here, much of the Duke's ruthlessness is conveyed at the very outset by his exquisitely casual reference, with the possessive "my," to his dead wife, by his evident pleasure at being able now to consider her as an art object, not as an intractable life-study:

> She had
> A heart—how shall I say?—too soon made glad,
> Too easily impressed; she liked what-e'er
> She looked on, and her looks went everywhere.

Subtly, Browning manages to turn the Duke's criticism of his former wife, his specious yet elegantly phrased "how shall I say?" claim that she was too much alive, too indiscriminately joyous, into an exposure of his own monstrous pride in "a nine-hundred-years-old name." Flexible couplets with unobtrusive rhymes are the fit medium for his self-justifying logic and for the vicious sweetness which informs even his dealings with his present auditor, the envoy of the woman who will probably be Ferrara's next Duchess ("Will't please you rise?"

addressed to the envoy is a command in the guise of a question). By tracing a logic of association in the blank verse of "The Bishop Orders His Tomb at Saint Praxed's Church," Browning focuses in a similar way on an incident of crucial importance for the self-revelation of his title character, the delirious churchman whose dying words concern pagan luxury and worldly pomp rather than Christian salvation.

Two dramatic monologues from the *Men and Women* volume, "Fra Lippo Lippi" and "How it Strikes a Contemporary," are explicitly concerned with aesthetics and the process of composition in poetry and painting. If we read between the lines of these poems, looking for the passages which most accord with Browning's actual practice, it is clear that he believes the best art is a universalizing of individual experience; and that to this end the poet or painter must be first of all curious, preeminently a noticer. Indeed, the verbs "notice," "mark," "see" are common in Browning's dramatic lyrics, where to notice a unique scene or situation is to exert an individual consciousness, and where to notice intensely is the first step in separating the apparent from the real and in beginning to write a book that in words from *The Ring and the Book* "shall mean beyond the facts." Accordingly, a collection of "so many utterances of so many imaginary persons" would escape the charge of subjectivity, yet taken as a whole it would convey a meaning beyond the mathematical sum of the dramatic lyric voices involved. These speakers reveal themselves far beyond what the occasion warrants, and the poems are essentially more dramatic and romantic than lyric. Browning takes definite pleasure in the vivid selfhood of his speakers, and pleasure as well in the multiple vision of the artist who can create and embody conflicting viewpoints while remaining himself uncommitted.

Browning's interest in conflict, incongruity, even in the grotesque, has its natural complement in his dramatic technique. The range of styles and effects is as various as the range of complexity among his characters. "An Englishman in Italy" exhibits a cataloguing, descriptive style, for instance in the request that one observe a fishing skiff from Amalfi, with alien English eyes watching

> . . . Our fisher arrive,
> And pitch down his basket before us,
>   All trembling alive
> With pink and gray jellies, your seafruit;
>   You touch the strange lumps,
> And mouths gape there, eyes open, all manner
>   Of horns and lumps. . . .

In "The Pied Piper of Hamelin," and in "Incident of the French Camp," Browning manages well two very different kinds of narrative. The mode of "Pictor Ignotus," an early monologue which looks ahead to "Andrea Del Sarto"

and "Fra Lippo Lippi," is one of ratiocination, following a proud artist's ebb and flux of thought:

> O human faces, hath it spilt, my cup?
>   What did ye give me that I have not saved?
> Nor will I say I have not dreamed (how well!)
>   Of going—I, in each new picture,—forth,
> As, making new hearts beat and bosoms swell,
>   To Pope or Kaiser, East, West, South, or
>   North. . . .

There is also the lyric outcry of "Home-Thoughts, From Abroad," with its famous lines, "Oh, to be in England/ Now that April's there." Browning's metrical range is diverse and experimental as well; in "Boot and Saddle" and "How They Brought the Good News From Ghent to Aix" he brilliantly turns the difficult anapestic meter to his own purposes, for both poems succeed in conveying by a kind of metrical imitation the excitement of a fast ride on a horse ("I galloped, Dirck galloped, we galloped all three"). Finally, it accords well with Browning's perspective, his prizing of unique objects and irreducible selfhood, that he should have created a new metrical or stanzaic form for almost every separate poem.

These earlier poems are a true representation of Browning in that they show him to be intellectually ingenious but no philosopher; an experimenter with both social and literary norms but by no standard a Victorian radical; a writer aware of evil and violence, but for the most part a cautious optimist. The later poems and *The Ring and the Book* bear out one's sense that his major achievement is in fact in these dramatic poems of his middle years, where the view of truth as relative is first impressively demonstrated in dramatic monologues. There is, of course, something deeply subversive in the notion that different points of view are equally valid, in the oblique yet damaging criticisms of Victorian sexual and religious conventions conveyed in some of these poems, in the attacks on bureaucracy such as the telling poem written against the "official" Wordsworth, "The Lost Leader." The dramatic monologue, at once objective and subjective, public and private in its methods, was the main vehicle used by Browning for criticism of Victorian society and manners; the monologue permitted ethical pronouncements to be made through someone else's voice, as it were, ventriloquially.

Thus in "My Last Duchess," in "Bishop Blougram's Apology," in many of his best poems, Browning is a public writer with disturbing private tendencies: He never pushes exposure or criticism past the point of pleasure, and his work as a whole gives an effect of hard impersonal brilliance. Browning was typically a man of his age in believing that the poet was a moral agent in his society, a "Maker-see" whose concerns were norms and value, the discovery and presentation of a heightened reality. Yet in wishing to write poems which would mean "beyond the facts" he settled on a method which from the start excluded personal directness. Because all his sincerities and critiques had to be conveyed indirectly, these poems for all their peculiar triumphs will be found to lack the keynote of passionate personal despair which is the most profound theme in the finest Victorian poetry.

DREAM OF THE RED CHAMBER

Type of work: Novel
Author: Ts'ao Hsüeh-ch'in (c. 1715–1763), with a continuation by Kao Ou
Type of plot: Domestic chronicle
Time of plot: c. 1729–1737
Locale: Peking
First published: *Hung-lou meng*, 1792 (English translation, 1929)

First published anonymously, this greatest of Chinese novels is now ascribed to Ts'ao Hsüeh-ch'in, who wrote the first eighty chapters, and Kao Ou, who expanded the work with forty additional chapters based on notes left by Ts'ao Hsüeh-ch'in at his death in 1763. The portrait of Pao-yu, the petted, spoiled younger son of a powerful aristocratic family already in financial decline at the time of his birth, is probably largely autobiographical. The long and complicated plot, containing over four hundred characters, is at once a family history, a lively comedy of manners, and a moral fable.

Principal Characters

Madame Shih, called **called the Matriarch,** the widow of Chia Tai-shan and the oldest living ancestress of the family Chia. In her eighties, she rules with authority and grace her large families in two palace compounds. Although she shows favoritism to her favorite grandson, she is fair in her judgments and unselfish in her actions. She sacrifices her personal wealth to aid her decadent descendants, but she herself never compromises her integrity.

Chia Cheng, her younger son. A man of strict Confucian principles, he manages to keep his integrity in spite of calumnious actions against him. Extremely autocratic and strong-willed, he is puritanical as well. Although he loves his talented son, Chia Cheng cannot condone his frivolous ways or his lack of purpose; hence he disciplines the delicate boy too severely.

Madame Wang, Chia Cheng's wife.

Pao-yu, Chia Cheng's son by Madame Wang and the favorite of the Matriarch. Born with a jade tablet of immortality in his mouth, the boy is thought by all to be favored by the gods and distinguished among mortals. He is extremely handsome, sensitive, and perceptive, through delicate in health. He is also lazy, self-indulgent, effeminate—in short all the things his father does not want him to be—and he lives surrounded by faithful maidservants whose loving care is most touching. His character develops as he associates with his beloved cousin, Black Jade, and her cousin, Precious Virtue. His loss of the jade amulet causes him great pain and trouble, especially when his parents and grandmother decide on the wrong wife for him. When Black Jade dies of a broken heart, he turns to scholarship and distinguishes himself and his family, renewing their fortune before he disappears in the company of a Buddhist monk and a lame Taoist priest. His filial piety in redeeming the reputation

and fortune of the Chias atones for all the trouble he caused his family. Precious Virtue, his wife, bears him a son to carry on the family line.

Tai-yu, called **Black Jade,** another of the Matriarch's grandchildren, a girl born into mortality from the form of a beautiful flower. Delicate in health and gravely sensitive, the beautiful and brilliant child comes to live in the Matriarch's home after her mother dies. Immediately she and Pao-yu sense their intertwined destinies, and their mutual love and respect develop to uncanny depths, to the point that manifestation of her dream appears as stigmata on Pao-yu's body. Given to jealousy and melancholy, she finally wastes away to the point that the Matriarch will not allow Pao-yu to have her in marriage. Black Jade dies in consequence, at the time when Pao-yu marries Precious Virtue, disguised as Black Jade.

Pao-chai, called **Precious Virtue,** the demure and reserved niece of Black Jade's mother, brought into the Matriarch's pavilion as a companion to her favored grandchildren. Obedient to her benefactress' wishes, devoted to the handsome Pao-yu, loyal to Black Jade, and generous to all the many Chia relatives, Pao-chai well fits her name. Her virtues are the more remarkable in the face of the many trials placed before her, especially in giving herself in marriage to one who loves another. She is the model Chinese wife and companion, a great contrast to her brother Hsueh Pan, a reckless libertine.

Hsi-feng, called **Phoenix,** the efficient but treacherous wife of Chia Lien. At first a careful manager of the estate, she eventually indulges her greedy nature, lends money at high interest, and finally brings disgrace upon the Chia family. Her jealous nature causes tragedy and unhappiness among the loving members of the households, but she dies repentant.

Chia Lien, the husband of Phoenix and the son of

Chia Sheh by an unnamed concubine, an idle, lecherous man unfaithful to his wife. After the death of Phoenix he marries Ping-er, called Patience, a devoted maid of the household.

Chia-chieh, the young daughter of Phoenix and Chia Lien.

Chia Sheh, the Matriarch's older son and master of the Yungkuofu, one of the two great palace compounds of the Chia family. He is a man of very ordinary talents, holds no important official post, and takes little part in the affair of his household.

Madame Hsing, the wife of Chia Sheh.

Ying-chun, called **Welcome Spring,** the daughter of Chia Sheh by an unnamed concubine. Although the Matriarch and Chia Cheng oppose the match, Chia Sheh marries her to Sun Shao-tsu. Her husband beats her and she is miserable in her marriage.

Chia Gen, master of the Ningkuofu. A man of no moral scruples, he carries on an intrigue with his daughter-in-law, Chin-shih. He helps to bring disgrace on the Chia family when he is accused of corrupting the sons of noble families and of turning the Ningkuofu into a gambling resort.

Chia Ging, Chia Gen's aged father. He has renounced the world and retired to a Taoist temple.

Yu-shih, the wife of Chia Gen.

Chia Jung, Chia Gen's son. He involves himself in several family intrigues.

Chin-shih, the wife of Chia Jung. She dies after a long illness, possibly a suicide. Before her death she carries on an affair with her father-in-law.

Hsi-chun, called **Compassion Spring,** the daughter of Chia Ging.

Chia Chiang, the Matriarch's great-grandson. An orphan, he grows up in the household of Chia Gen and is a close friend of Chia Jung.

Chin Chung, the brother of Chin-shih. He and Pao-yu become good friends. He dies while still a schoolboy.

Chih-neng, a young nun at Iron Sill Temple, in love with Chin Chung.

Cardinal Spring, the daughter of Chia Cheng and Madame Wang. She brings great honor to the Chia family when she becomes an Imperial Concubine.

Chao Yi-niang, Chia Cheng's concubine. Jealous of Pao-yu and hating Phoenix, she secretly pays to have a spell put on them. Both become desperately ill and their coffins are prepared. Then a Buddhist monk and a lame Taoist priest miraculously appear and restore the power of Pao-yu's jade tablet. Pao-yu and Phoenix recover.

Chia Huan, Chia Cheng's son by Chao Yi-niang. Like his mother, he resents the favoritism shown to Pao-yu.

Tan-chun, called **Quest Spring,** Chia Cheng's daughter by Chao Yi-niang. She marries the son of an important frontier official.

Hsueh Yi-ma, a widow, the sister of Madame Wang. After her husband's death she goes with her son and daughter to live with the Chia family in the Yungkuofu. Precious Virtue, her daughter, becomes the bride of Pao-yu.

Hsueh Pan, a drunkard and libertine always in pursuit of girls and young men. His purchase of a maid, Lotus, involves him in controversy and a lawsuit. Eventually he marries Cassia, a shrew, and is unfaithful to her. Cassia dies, accidentally poisoned, while he is living in exile on the frontier. After his return he makes Lotus his chief wife.

Cassia, Hsueh Pan's selfish, quarrelsome, disobedient wife. While her husband is exiled she tries to seduce his cousin, Hsueh Kuo, but he repulses her. She then tries to poison Lotus, her husband's maid, but drinks the poison by mistake and dies.

Hsueh Kuo, Hsueh Pan's cousin. Incapable of disloyalty, he spurns Cassia's attempts to make her his lover.

Lotus, Hsueh Pan's maid. Stolen from her family while a child, she later attracts the attention of Hsueh Pan, who buys her but soon becomes indifferent to her beauty and grace. Married to her master after his wife's death and his return from exile, Lotus dies in childbirth.

Chen Shih-yin, the father of Lotus. After his daughter has been stolen and he has lost all his possessions in a fire, he and his wife go to live with her family. One day he disappears in the company of a lame Taoist priest and is never seen again.

Feng-shih, Cheng Shih-yin's wife and the mother of Lotus. After her husband's disappearance she supports herself as a seamstress.

Lin Ju-hai, the well-born descendant of an ancient family of Soochow, the Matriarch's son-in-law and the father of Black Jade. A widower without a male heir, he decides to give his daughter the education that in those times only sons of noble families received.

Chia Yu-tsun, a scholar befriended by Chen Shih-yin. He becomes Black Jade's tutor in the household of Lin Ju-hai. Later he is appointed to the post of provincial prefect.

Hsiang-yun, called **River Mist,** a grandniece of the Matriarch. She lives with her Chia relatives for a time, but after Black Jade dies and Pao-yu and Precious Virtue are married she returns to her own family.

Yu Lao-niang, the stepmother of Yu-shih.

Er-chieh, the daughter of Yu Lao-niang by a previous marriage. Chia Lien, enamored of the girl, makes her his secret concubine and installs her with her sister, San-chieh, in a separate house. Phoenix, learning of her husband's second establishment, pretends to be reasonable and without jealousy. Secretly hating her rival, she finds an accomplice in a maid from the other household. The maid insults her mistress and treats her with such abuse that Er-chieh commits suicide by swallowing gold.

San-chieh, the sister of Er-chieh. When Chia Gen and Chia Lien decide to find a husband for her, she announces that the only man she will marry is Liu Hsiang-lien, a handsome young actor. He changes his mind, however, after a formal engagement has been arranged. San-chieh, grief-stricken, kills herself with his sword.

Liu Hsiang-lien, a handsome young actor. Although a female impersonator, he is not effeminate in mind or habits, and he rejects Hsueh Pan's suit when that licentious young nobleman pursues him. He breaks his betrothal to San-chieh after hearing gossip about her, and the girl commits suicide. Conscience-stricken, he cuts off his hair and goes away with a lame Taoist priest.

Hsi-jen, called **Pervading Fragrance,** Pao-yu's devoted maid and concubine. After the disappearance of her master she wishes only to remain faithful to his memory, but her brother arranges her marriage to a son of the Chiang family. To her surprise, her bridegroom is Chiang Yu-han, once called Chi-kuan, an actor who had been Pao-yu's close friend.

Chiang Yu-han, a young actor whose professional name is Chi-kuan, a friend of Pao-yu. Accused of seducing the handsome player, Pao-yu is beaten severely by his stern father. Chiang Yu-han later marries Pervading Fragrance, his friend's loyal maid.

Golden Bracelet, a maid accused of attempting to seduce Pao-yu. Sent back to her family, she drowns herself.

Liu Lao-lao, a poor relation of Madame Wang. Visiting the Yungkuofu from time to time, she grows prosperous from gifts that the Chias give her.

Pan-er, her grandson, a shy boy.

Exquisite Jade, a pious, fastidious nun living in the Yungkuofu. Bandits who break into the compound seize her and take her away beyond the frontier.

Chia Lan, Pao-yu's young kinsman who also distinguishes himself in the Imperial Examinations.

Chia Jui, an oaf who tries to force his attentions on Phoenix.

A Buddhist Monk and **A Taoist Priest,** lame in one leg, mysterious figures, possibly messengers of the Immortals, who appear suddenly and mysteriously in times of revelation or crisis.

Faith, Ching-wen, called **Bright Design, Sheh-yueh,** called **Musk Moon, Oriole, Tzu-chuan,** called **Purple Cuckoo, Autumn Sky,** and **Snow Duck,** maids in the Yungkuofu.

Chiao Ta, a privileged old family servant.

The Story

Ages ago, in the realm of the Great Void, the Goddess Nügua, whose task it was to repair the Dome of Heaven, rejected a stone which she found unsuited to her purpose. Because she had touched it, however, the stone became endowed with life, so that thereafter it could move as it pleased. In time, it chanced on a crimson flower in the region of the Ethereal, where each day it watered the tender blossoms with drops of dew. At last the plant was incarnated as a beautiful young girl. Remembering the stone that had showered the frail plant with refreshing dew, she prayed that in her human form she might repay it with the gift of her tears. Her prayers were to be granted, for the stone, too, had been given life in the Red Dust of earthly existence. At his birth, the piece of jade was miraculously found in the mouth of Pao-yu, a younger son of the rich and powerful house of Chia, which by imperial favor had been raised to princely eminence several generations before.

At the time of Pao-yu's birth, the two branches of the Chia family lived in great adjoining compounds of palaces, pavilions, and parks on the outskirts of Peking. The Matriarch, an old woman of great honor and virtue, ruled as the living ancestress over both establishments. Chia Ging, the prince of the Ningkuofu, had retired to a Taoist temple some time before, and his son Chia Gen was master in his place. The master of the Yungkuofu was Chia Sheh, the older son of the Matriarch. Chia Cheng, her younger son and Pao-yu's father, also lived with his family and attendants in the Yungkuofu. A man of upright conduct and strict Confucian morals, he was a contrast to the other members of his family, who had grown lax and corrupt through enervating luxury and the abuse of power.

Pao-yu, the possessor of the miraculous jade stone and a boy of great beauty and quick wit, was his grandmother's favorite. Following her example, the other women of the family—his mother, aunts, sisters, cousins, and waiting maids—doted on the boy and pampered him at every opportunity, with the result that he grew up girlish and weak, a lover of rouge pots and feminine society. His traits of effeminacy infuriated and disgusted his austere father, who treated the boy with undue severity. As a result, Pao-yu kept as much as possible to the women's quarters.

His favorite playmates were his two cousins, Black Jade and Precious Virtue. Black Jade, a granddaughter of the Matriarch, had come to live in the Yungkuofu after her mother's death. She was a lovely, delicate girl of great poetic sensitivity, and she and Pao-yu were drawn to each other by bonds of sympathy and understanding that seemed to stretch back into some unremembered past. Precious Virtue, warmhearted and practical, was the niece of Pao-yu's mother. She was a girl as good as her brother Hsueh Pan was vicious, for he was always involving the family in scandal because of his pursuit of maidens and young boys. Pao-yu's favorite waiting maid was Pervading Fragrance. She slept in his chamber at night, and it was with her that he followed a dream vision and practiced the play of cloud and rain.

When word came that Black Jade's father was ill and

wished to see her before his death, the Matriarch sent the girl home under the escort of her cousin Chia Lien. During their absence, Chin-shih, the daughter-in-law of Chia Gen, died after a long illness. By judicious bribery, the dead woman's husband, Chia Jung, was made a chevalier of the Imperial Dragon Guards in order that she might be given a more elaborate funeral. During the period of mourning, Chia Gen asked Phoenix, Chia Lien's wife, to take charge of the Ningkuofu household. This honor gave Phoenix a position of responsibility and power in both palaces. From that time on, although she continued to appear kind and generous, she secretly became greedy for money and power. She began to accept bribes, tamper with the household accounts, and lend money at exorbitant rates of interest.

One day a great honor was conferred on the Chias. Cardinal Spring, Pao-yu's sister and one of the emperor's concubines, was advanced to the rank of an Imperial consort of the second degree. Later, when it was announced that she would pay a visit of filial respect to her parents, the parks of the two compounds were transformed at great expense into magnificent pleasure grounds, called the Takuanyuan, in honor of the consort's visit. Later, at Cardinal Spring's request, the pavilions in the Takuanyuan were converted into living quarters for the young women of the family. Pao-yu also went there to live, passing his days in idle occupations and writing verses. His pavilion was close to that of Black Jade, who had returned to the Yungkuofu after her father's death.

Pao-yu had a half brother, Chia Huan. His mother, jealous of the true-born son, paid a sorceress to bewitch the boy and Phoenix, whom she also hated. Both were seized with fits of violence and wild delirium. Pao-yu's coffin had already been made when a Buddhist monk and a lame Taoist priest suddenly appeared and restored the power of the spirit stone. Pao-yu and Phoenix recovered.

A short time later a maid was accused of trying to seduce Pao-yu. When she was dismissed, she drowned herself. About the same time, Chia Cheng was informed that his son had turned the love of a young actor away from a powerful patron. Calling his son a degenerate, Chia Cheng almost caused Pao-yu's death by the severity of the beating which the angry father administered.

As Phoenix became more shrewish at home, Chia Lien dreamed of taking another wife. Having been almost caught in one infidelity, he was compelled to exercise great caution in taking a concubine. Phoenix learned about the secret marriage, however, and by instigating claims advanced by the girl's former suitor she drove the wretched concubine to suicide.

Black Jade, always delicate, became more sickly.

Sometimes she and Pao-yu quarreled, only to be brought together again by old ties of affection and understanding. The gossip of the servants was that the Matriarch would marry Pao-yu to either Black Jade or Precious Virtue. While possible marriage plans were being discussed, a maid found in the Takuanyuan a purse embroidered with an indecent picture. This discovery led to a search of all the pavilions, and it was revealed that one of the maids was involved in a secret love affair. Suspicion also fell on Bright Design, one of Pao-yu's maids, and she was dismissed. Proud and easily hurt, she died not long afterward. Pao-yu became even moodier and more depressed after Bright Design's death. Outraged by the search, Precious Virtue left the park and went to live with her mother.

A begonia tree near Pao-yu's pavilion bloomed out of season. This event was interpreted as a bad omen, for Pao-yu lost his spirit stone and sank into a state of complete lethargy. In an effort to revive his spirits, the Matriarch and his parents decided to marry him at once to Precious Virtue rather than to Black Jade, who continued to grow frailer each day. Pao-yu was allowed to believe, however, that Black Jade was to be his wife. Black Jade, deeply grieved, died shortly after the ceremony. Knowing nothing of the deception that had been practiced, she felt that she had failed Pao-yu and that he had been unfaithful to her, so the flower returned to the Great Void.

Suddenly a series of misfortunes overwhelmed the Chias as their deeds of graft and corruption came to light. When bailiffs took possession of the two compounds, the usury Phoenix had practiced was disclosed. Chia Gen and Chia Sheh were arrested and sentenced to banishment. The Matriarch, who took upon herself the burden of her family's guilt and surrendered her personal treasures for expenses and fines, became ill and died. During her funeral services, robbers looted the compound and later returned to carry off Exquisite Jade, a pious nun. Phoenix also died, neglected by those she had dominated in her days of power. Through the efforts of powerful friends, however, the complete ruin of the family was averted, and Chia Cheng was restored to his official post.

In the end, however, the despised son became the true redeemer of his family's honor and fortunes. After a Buddhist monk had returned his lost stone, Pao-yu devoted himself earnestly to his studies and passed the Imperial Examinations with such brilliance that he stood in seventh place on the list of successful candidates. The emperor was so impressed that he wished to have the young scholar serve at court; but Pao-yu was nowhere to be found. The tale was that he became a bodhisattva and disappeared in the company of a Buddhist monk and a Taoist priest.

Critical Evaluation

Chinese readers consider the *Dream of the Red Chamber* (also available in English translation as *The Story of the Stone*) the greatest of their novels. Published anonymously in 1792 and for a long time a matter of scholarly dispute, the book is now ascribed to Ts'ao Hsüeh-ch'in (or Cao Xueqin, as his name is sometimes transliterated), who completed the first eighty chapters before his death in 1763, and Kao Ou, who added forty more as an expansion of Ts'ao Hsüeh-ch'in's original notes. (Manuscript copies of the first eighty chapters of the novel were apparently circulated before the publication of the complete 120-chapter version in 1792.) There is internal evidence to show that Ts'ao Hsüeh-ch'in may have drawn on his own experience and family background in creating the character of Pao-yu, the pampered younger son of an aristocratic and powerful family, which was in gradual financial decline at the time of his birth. Like Pao-yu, Ts'ao Hsüeh-ch'in was petted by his family and spoiled by luxury; unlike Pao-yu, he failed to pass the Imperial Examinations which would have raised him to some official position.

Dream of the Red Chamber is within a single framework a long and extremely complicated domestic chronicle—the novel contains more than four hundred characters—that is a lively comedy of manners, a realistic fable of moral seriousness, and a metaphysical allegory. The title is capable of expressing several meanings. In the view of Professor Chi-Chen Wang, it may be translated as "Dreams of Young Maidens," since the younger women of the Chia clan lived in the traditional "red chamber" of a palace compound. The term may also be interpreted as a reference to the metaphor "Red Dust," which in Buddhist usage is a designation for the material world with all of its pleasures, follies, and vices.

On the metaphysical level of the novel, the stone and the flower, originally located in the Ethereal, suffer a fall when they enter earthly reality in the Red Dust. Here the novel may be read as an allegory endorsing a Taoist-Buddhist system of otherworldly values (represented by the mysteriously recurring priest and monk) and rejecting the this-worldly view of Confucianism (represented by Chia Cheng). Interestingly enough, this novel's critique of feudalist and Confucian China has won praise from Marxist readers.

The Ethereal stone's fortunes translate into a novel of manners when the stone falls into earthly existence as the protagonist, Chia Pao-yu. In this mode, the novel becomes, through its portrayal of the Chia family, a brilliantly realistic document of upper-class life during the Ching Dynasty. It encompasses financial affairs and sexual aberrations, fraternal jealousies, and tragic suicides. The Chia fortunes reach their apogee when Cardinal Spring becomes the emperor's concubine. The Takuanyuan Garden, built to honor Cardinal Spring, symbolizes the halcyon days; it becomes the domain of the younger Chia generation led by Pao-yu. Here their way of life is carefree, innocent, almost Edenic; but, just as Pao-yu must grow into adulthood, so evil invades this Eden. The fall begins when an indecent purse is found. A general search ensues, scandals surface, a tragic death results. Analogous disasters overtake the family. Their financial dealings incur the emperor's displeasure; Imperial Guards ransack the Chia compound. Then bandits raid the garden itself. Finally, Pao-yu chooses to deny the folly of this world and join the Buddhist priest and the Taoist monk journeying presumably to the Ethereal.

To Western readers, this novel will seem episodic; Chinese novels, however, did not aim to tell a particular story but to weave a rich tapestry of life. This latter purpose Ts'ao Hsüeh-ch'in achieves brilliantly, and his novel remains widely appreciated for its skillful interweaving of philosophical allegory with unblinking realism.

DUINO ELEGIES

Type of work: Poetry
Author: Rainer Maria Rilke (1875–1926)
First published: 1923

For the reader who must rely on a prose translation of Rainer Maria Rilke's culminating work, the story and the man behind its appearance may overshadow the poem itself. Nothing of the elegiac quality of the original German can be translated which is as deeply affecting as the inspiration which produced the work, or the philosophy of the man who wrote it—a craftsman, a visionary, and one of the greatest poets of the twentieth century.

In October, 1911, Rilke visited his friend, Princess Marie von Thurn und Taxis-Hohenlohe, at Schloss Duino, near Trieste. He remained at the castle, alone throughout the winter, until April, and there he composed the first, the second, and parts of several other elegies. The opening stanza, "Who, if I cried, would hear me among the angelic orders?" came to him while walking in a storm along a cliff two hundred feet above the raging sea, a romantic interlude worthy of an atmospheric passage in a Gothic novel. Rilke conceived the plan of all ten elegies as a whole, though ten years elapsed before the poem found its final form.

The First Elegy, like the first movement of a musical work, presents the central theme and suggests the variations that follow. From the opening line to the last, Rilke invokes the Angels, not those of Christianity but of a special order immersed in time and space, a concept of being of perfect consciousness, of transcendent reality. As a symbol appearing earlier in Rilke's poetry, the Angel represents to him the perfection of life in all the forms to which he aspired, as high above man as God is above this transcending one. Nearest to this angelic order are the Heroes—later he praises Samson—and a woman in love, especially one who dies young, as did Gaspara Stampa (1523–1554), whom Rilke celebrates as a near-perfect example. Like the lover, man must realize each moment to the fullest rather than be distracted by things and longings. With this contrast of Man and Angels, of Lovers and Heroes, and with the admission of life's transcience, the poet suggests the meaning of life and death as well as words can identify such profound things.

If the introduction or invocation is a praise of life, the Second Elegy is a lament for life's limitations. We moderns must, at best, content ourselves with an occasional moment of self-awareness, of a glimpse at eternity. Unlike the Greeks, we have no external symbols for the life within. In love, were we not finally satiated, we might establish communication with the Angels; but finally our intuitions vanish and we have only a fleeting glance at reality.

Rilke began the Third Elegy at Duino and completed it in Paris the following year; during an intervening visit to Spain he composed parts of the Sixth, Ninth, and Tenth Elegies. In the third section he confronts the physical bases of life, especially love. He suggests that woman is always superior in the love act, man a mere beginner led by blind animal passion, the libido a vicious drive. Sublime love is an end in itself, but often human love is a means to escape life. Even children have a sort of terror infused into their blood from this heritage of doubt and fear. From this view of mortality Rilke would lead the child away, as he says in powerful though enigmatic conclusion,

> . . . Oh gently, gently
> show him daily a loving, confident task done,—
> guide him
> close to the garden, give him those counter-
> balancing nights. . . .
> Withhold him. . . .

Perhaps the advent of war made the Fourth Elegy the most bitter of all, written as it was from Rilke's retreat in Munich in 1915. The theme of distraction, our preoccupation with fleeting time and time serving, makes this part a deep lament over the human condition. We are worse than puppets who might be manipulated by unseen forces, Angels. Our attempts to force destiny, to toy with fate, cause us to break from heaven's firm hold. We must be as little children, delighted within ourselves by the world without, and with our attention and energies undivided, alone. Here, we will find our answer to death as the other side of life, a part of life and not the negation or end of it.

The Fifth Elegy, the last to be composed, was written at the Château de Muzot in 1922. Rilke was inspired by Picasso's famous picture of the acrobats, *Les Saltim banques*. Its owner, Frau Hertha Koenig, had allowed Rilke the privilege of living in her home in 1915 in order to be near his favorite painting. Either the poet imperfectly remembered the details of the painting when the poem was finally written or else he included recollections of acrobats who had so delighted him during his Paris years. Regardless of influences, however, this poem is remarkable in its merging of theme and movement with a painting, emphasizing Rilke's conviction that a poem must celebrate all the senses rather than appeal to eye or ear alone.

The acrobats, symbolizing the human condition, travel about, rootless and transitory, giving pleasure neither to themselves nor the spectators. Reality to the acrobat, as to man, is best discovered in the arduousness of the task; but routine often makes the task a mockery, especially if death is the end. If death, however, is the other side of life and makes up the whole, then life forces are real and skillfully performed to the inner delight of performers and spectators, living and dead alike.

The Hero, Rilke asserts in the Sixth Elegy, is that fortunate being whose memory, unlike that of long-forgotten lovers, is firmly established by his deeds. He, being single-minded and single-hearted, has the same destiny as the early departed, those who die young without losing their view of eternity. The great thing, then, is to live in the flower of life, with the calm awareness that the fruit, death, is the unilluminated side of life. For the Hero, life is always beginning.

In the Seventh Elegy, the poet sings the unpremeditated song of existence:

> Don't think that I'm wooing!
> Angel, even if I were, you'd never come.
>   For my call
> is always full of 'Away!' Against such a powerful
> current you cannot advance. Like an outstretched
> arm is my call. And its clutching, upwardly
> open hand is always before you
> as open for warding and warning,
> aloft there, Inapprehensible.

From this viewpoint, Rilke attempts in the Eighth Elegy, dedicated to his friend Rudolph Kassner, to support his belief in the "nowhere without no," the "open" world, timeless, limitless, inseparable "whole." "We," con-trasted to animals, are always looking away rather than toward this openness.

The theme of creative existence Rilke continues in the Ninth Elegy, possibly begun at Duino but certainly finished at Muzot. Here he suggests that the life of the tree is superior in felicity to the destiny of man. We should, perhaps, rejoice in spite of the limiting conditions of man by overcoming this negation of the flesh with a reaffirmation of the spirit. Then death holds no fears since it is not opposite to life, not an enemy but a friend. This work may represent the author's own transformation from the negating, inhibiting conditions of the Great War to a renewed faith in life.

The Tenth Elegy, the first ten lines of which came to Rilke in that burst of creativity at Duino, contains a satiric portrait of the City of Pain where man simply excludes suffering, pain, death, from his thoughts; where distractions, especially the pursuit of money, are the principal activities. This semi-existence the poet contrasts with that in the Land of Pain, Life-Death, where there is continuous progress through glimpses of a deeper reality to the primal source of joy.

> And we, who have always thought
> of happiness climbing, would feel
> the emotion that almost startles
> when happiness falls.

Perhaps Rilke means that by complete submission or attunement to universal forces one is suspended or even falls into the "open." This deeply realized philosophy he developed in the *Sonnets to Orpheus* (1923), a work which complements the *Duino Elegies*, though it does not surpass them in deep emotional undertones and sheer power of expression.

EAST OF EDEN

Type of work: Novel
Author: John Steinbeck (1902–1968)
Type of plot: Regional chronicle
Time of plot: 1865–1918
Locale: California
First published: 1952

East of Eden *is an ambitious but not altogether successful attempt to present three stories simultaneously: a panoramic history of the Salinas Valley (symbolic of America as a whole); a melodramatic chronicle of two families in the valley; and a symbolic re-creation of the Cain and Abel story. In each story the theme is the same: good and evil are always in conflict, but man's freedom and glory lie in his ability to choose the good to direct his own life.*

Principal Characters

Adam Trask, a settler in the Salinas Valley. He marries Cathy Ames in Connecticut and moves west where he and their twin sons, Caleb and Aron, are deserted by her.

Cathy Ames, Adam Trask's innocent appearing but evil wife. Deserting Adam and their twin sons, Caleb and Aron, she becomes the proprietress of a notorious brothel.

Aron Trask, smugly religious, idealistic twin son of Adam Trask and Cathy Ames. Unable to face the knowledge of his parents' past, he joins the army and is killed in France.

Caleb Trask, impulsive twin son of Adam Trask and Cathy. Rejected in an effort to help his father, he takes revenge by revealing to his brother Aron the secret of their mother's identity. He later accepts responsibility for the disillusioned Aron's death.

Abra Bacon, Aron Trask's fiancée. Disturbed because she feels unable to live up to Aron's idealistic image of her, she finally turns to the more realistic Caleb Trask.

Charles Trask, Adam Trask's half brother.

Samuel Hamilton, an early settler in the Salinas Valley.

Liza Hamilton, Samuel Hamilton's wife.

Lee, Adam Trask's wise and good Chinese servant.

Faye, proprietress of a Salinas brothel. Her death is engineered by Cathy Ames as she seeks to gain full control of Faye's establishment.

Will Hamilton, business partner of Caleb Trask.

The Story

The soil of the Salinas Valley in California is rich, although the foothills around it are poor, and life in the valley is barren during the long dry spells. The Irish-born Hamiltons, arriving after American settlers had displaced the Mexicans, settled on the barren hillside. There Sam Hamilton, full of talk, glory, and improvident inventions, and Liza, his dourly religious wife, brought up their nine children.

In Connecticut, Adam Trask and his half brother Charles grew up, mutually affectionate in spite of the differences in their natures. Adam was gentle and good; Charles, roughly handsome with a streak of wild violence. After Adam's mother had committed suicide, his father had married a docile woman who gave birth to Charles. Adam loved his stepmother but hated his father, a rigid disciplinarian whose fanatic militarism had begun with a fictitious account of his own war career and whose dream was to have a son in the army. To fulfill his dream, he chose Adam, who could gain the greater strength that comes from the conquest of weakness as Charles could not. Charles, however, whose passionate love for his father went continually unnoticed, could not understand this final rejection of himself. In violent despair, he beat Adam almost to death.

Adam served in the cavalry for five years. Then, although he hated regimentation and violence, he reenlisted, for he could neither accept help from his father, who had become an important figure in Washington, nor return to the farm Charles now ran alone. Afterward, he wandered through the West and the South, served time for vagrancy, and finally came home to find his father dead and himself and Charles rich. In the years that followed, he and Charles lived together, although their bickering and inbred solitude drove Adam to periodic wanderings. Feeling that their life was one of pointless industry, he talked of moving west but did not.

Meanwhile, Cathy Ames was growing up in Massachusetts. She was a monster, born unable to comprehend goodness but with a sublimely innocent face and a consummate knowledge of how to manipulate or deceive people to serve her own ends. After a thwarted attempt to leave home, she burned her house, killing her parents and leaving evidence to indicate that she had been murdered. She then became the mistress of a man who ran a string of brothels and used his insatiable love for her to torment him. When he realized her true nature, he took her to a deserted spot and beat her savagely. Near death, she crawled to the nearest house—the Trasks'—where Adam and Charles cared for her. Adam found her innocent and beautiful; Charles, who had a knowledge of the evil in himself, recognized the evil in her and wanted her to leave. Cathy, needing temporary protection, enticed Adam into marrying her, but on their wedding night, she gave him a sleeping draught and went to Charles.

Feeling that Charles disapproved of Cathy, Adam decided to carry out his dream of going west. He was so transfigured by his happiness that he did not take Cathy's protests seriously; as his ideal of love and purity, she could not disagree. Adam bought a ranch in the richest part of the Salinas Valley and worked hard to ready it for his wife and the child she expected. Cathy hated her pregnancy, but she knew that she had to wait calmly to get back to the life she wanted. After giving birth to twin boys, she waited a week; she then shot Adam, wounding him, and walked out.

Changing her name to Kate, Cathy went to work in a Salinas brothel. Her beauty and seeming goodness endeared her to the proprietress, Faye, and Kate gradually assumed control of the establishment. After Faye made a will leaving Kate her money and property, Kate slyly engineered Faye's death. Making her establishment one which aroused and purveyed to sadistic tastes, she became legendary and rich.

Adam was like a dead man for a year after his wife left him, unable to work his land or even to name his sons. Finally, Sam Hamilton woke him by deliberately angering him, and Sam, Adam, and Lee, the Chinese servant and a wise and good man, named the boys Caleb and Aron. As the men talked of the story of Cain and Abel, Lee concluded that rejection terrifies a child most and leads to guilt and revenge. Later, after much study, Lee discovered the true meaning of the Hebrew word *timshel* (thou mayest) and understood that the story meant in part that man can always choose to conquer evil.

Sam, grown old, knew that he would soon die. Before he left his ranch, he told Adam of Kate and her cruel, destructive business. Adam, disbelieving in her very existence, visited her and suddenly knew her as she really was. Though she tried to taunt him, telling him that Charles was the true father of his sons, and to seduce him, he left her a free and curiously exultant man. Yet he could not tell his sons that their mother was not dead.

Caleb and Aron were growing up very differently. Aron was golden haired and automatically inspired love, yet he remained single-minded and unyielding; Caleb was dark and clever, a feared and respected leader left much alone. When Adam moved to town, where the schools were better, Aron fell in love with Abra Bacon. Abra told Aron that his mother was still alive, but he could not believe her because to do so would have destroyed his faith in his father and thus in everything.

About this time, Adam had the idea of shipping lettuce packed in ice to New York, but the venture failed. Aron was ashamed of his father for failing publicly. Caleb vowed to return the lost money to his father.

As they faced the problems of growing into men, Aron became smugly religious, which was disturbing to Abra because she felt unable to live up to his idealistic image of her. Caleb alternated between wild impulses and guilt. Learning that Kate was his mother, he began following her until she, noticing him, invited him to her house. As he talked to her, he knew with relief that he was not like her; she felt his knowledge and hated him. Kate herself, obsessed by the fear that one of the old girls had discovered Faye's murder, plotted ways to destroy this menace. Although Caleb would accept Kate's existence, he knew that Aron could not. To get the boy away from Salinas, Caleb talked him into finishing high school in three years and beginning college. Adam, knowing nothing of Caleb's true feelings, was extravagantly proud of Aron.

World War I began. Caleb went into the bean business with Will Hamilton and made a fortune because of food shortages. With growing excitement, he planned an elaborate presentation to his father of the money once lost in the lettuce enterprise. First he tried to persuade Aron, who seemed indifferent to his father's love, not to leave college. Caleb offered money to Adam, but Adam rejected it in anger because his idealistic nature would not allow him to accept money made as profit from the war. He wanted Caleb's achievements to be like his brother's. In a black mood of revenge, Caleb took Aron to meet his mother. After her sons' visit, Kate, who was not as disturbed by those she could hurt as she was by someone like Caleb, made a will leaving everything to Aron. Then, overburdened by age, illness, and suspicion, she committed suicide.

Unable to face his new knowledge of his parents' past, Aron joined the army and went to France. Adam did not recover from the shock of his leaving. Abra turned to Caleb, admitting that she loved him rather than Aron, whose romantic stubbornness kept him from facing reality. When the news of Aron's death arrived, Adam had another stroke. As he lay dying, Caleb, unable to bear his guilt any longer, told his father of his responsibility for Aron's enlisting and thus his death. Lee begged Adam to forgive his son. Adam weakly raised his hand in benediction and, whispering the Hebrew word *timshel*, died.

Critical Evaluation

The expressed concern of *East of Eden* is philosophical—the nature of the conflict between good and evil. In this conflict, love and the acceptance or rejection it brings to the individual play an important role, yet one has always the opportunity to choose the good. In this freedom lies man's glory. The book's defects stem from the author's somewhat foggy and sentimental presentation of its philosophy and his tendency to manipulate or oversimplify characters and events for symbolic purposes.

In most of his other works, John Steinbeck was concerned with social issues from a realistic or a naturalistic point of view, portraying human travail with relentless accuracy through an intensive examination of a short time span. In *East of Eden*, however, Steinbeck departs from his customary literary style to write an epic portrait which ranges less intensively over a much broader time span of about seventy years. Although depictions of characters and events are really no less vivid than in his other novels, Steinbeck's *East of Eden* is certainly less structured, a looser novel than his dedicated readers had come to expect. Thus, despite some quite explicit sex scenes, disappointed reader expectation accounts in large measure for the failure of *East of Eden* to win immediate popular or critical acclaim. It simply was not what people had come to expect of Steinbeck.

The novel is, however, respectable if not brilliant. In fact, it is, in many ways, a historical romance in its panoramic sweep of significant history overlaid with specific human problems. The story ranges from the Civil War to World War I, from the East Coast to the West Coast, over several generations of two families. It displays all of the conventional elements of historical romance. Genuinely historical events and people provide the backdrop, even the shaping forces that mold the fictional characters' lives and determine their destiny. These characters thus appear to have only partial control over their lives, at best, and external factors consequently determine, to a large extent, what they must cope with in order to survive. They appear to be buffeted mercilessly by fate.

However, Steinbeck's philosophical commitment to free will aborts the naturalistically logical conclusion. As a result, both Charles and Adam Trask appear to select freely their own paths in life, the former indulging fantasies of evil and the latter choosing to disregard everyone's evil inclinations, including his own. So, too, is Cathy made to seem capable of choice and responsible for it. Likewise, the other major characters are depicted as having the capacity for moral choice and for living with the consequences. Yet it is just this aspect of *East of Eden* that flies in the face of the reader's expectations of "typical" Steinbeck and flies in the face of both logic and reality. Finally, it is Steinbeck's own ambivalence about free will and determinism that constitutes the major weakness in *East of Eden*.

THE EDUCATION OF HENRY ADAMS

Type of work: Novelized autobiography
Author: Henry Adams (1838–1918)
Type of plot: Intellectual and social history
Time of plot: 1838–1905
Locale: America, England, France
First published: 1907

The theme of this autobiography is the process of technological growth and the multiplication of mechanical forces which led, during the author's own lifetime, to a degeneration of moral relationships between men and to the lapsing of their pursuits into money seeking or complete lassitude. The book is a masterpiece of intellectual writing, tracing intimately the author's thought processes and his moral and emotional maturation.

The Story

Henry Brooks Adams was born of the union of two illustrious Massachusetts families, the Brookses and the Adamses, and he was, in addition, the grandson and the great-grandson of presidents. His wealth and social position should have put him among the leaders of his generation.

Although the period of mechanical invention had begun by 1838, Henry Adams was raised in a colonial atmosphere. He remembered that his first serious encounter with his grandfather, John Quincy Adams, occurred when he refused to go to school, and that gentleman led him there by the hand. For Henry Adams, the death of the former president marked the end of his eighteenth century environment.

Charles Francis Adams, Henry's father, was instrumental in forming the Free-Soil party in 1848, and he ran on its ticket with Martin Van Buren. Henry considered that his own education was chiefly a heritage from his father, an inheritance of Puritan morality and interest in politics and literary matters. In later life, looking back on his formal education, he concluded that it had been a failure. Mathematics, French, German, and Spanish were needed in the world in which he found himself an adult, not Latin and Greek.

He had opportunity to observe the use of force in the violence with which the people of Boston treated the antislavery Wendell Phillips, and he had seen black slaves restored to the South.

Prompted by his teacher, James Russell Lowell, he spent nearly two years abroad after his graduation from college. He enrolled to study civil law in Germany, but finding the lecture system atrocious, he devoted most of his stay to enjoying the paintings, the opera, the theater in Dresden.

When he returned to Boston in 1860, Henry Adams settled down briefly to read Blackstone. In the elections that year, however, his father became a Congressman, and Henry accompanied him to the capital as his secre-

tary. There he met John Hay, who was to become his best friend.

In 1861 President Lincoln named Charles Francis Adams minister to England. Henry went with his father to Europe. The Adams party had barely disembarked when they were met by bad news. England had recognized the belligerency of the Confederacy. The North was her undeclared enemy. The battle of Bull Run proved so crushing a blow to American prestige that Charles Francis Adams felt he was in England on a day-to-day sufferance. The Trent Affair and the second battle of Bull Run were equally disastrous abroad. Finally, in 1863, the tide began to turn. Secretary Seward sent Thurlow Weed and William Evarts to woo the English, and they were followed by announcements of victories at Vicksburg and Gettysburg. Charles Francis Adams remained in England until 1868, for Andrew Johnson had too many troubles at home to make many diplomatic changes abroad.

At the end of the war Henry Adams had no means of earning a livelihood. He had, however, developed some taste as a dilettante in art, and several of his articles had been published in the *North American Review*. On his return to America, Henry Adams was impressed by the fact that his fellow-countrymen, because of the mechanical energy they had harnessed, were all traveling in the same direction. Europeans, he had felt, were trying to go in several directions at one time. Handicapped by his education and by his long absence from home, he had difficulty in adapting himself to the new industrial America. He achieved some recognition with his articles on legal tender and his essays in the *Edinburgh Review*, and he hoped that he might be offered a government position if Ulysses S. Grant were elected president. But Grant, a man of action, was not interested in reformers or intellectuals like Henry Adams.

In 1869 Adams went back to Quincy to begin his investigation of the scandals of the Grant administration, among them Jay Gould's attempts to obtain a corner on gold,

Senator Charles Sumner's efforts to provoke war with England by compelling her cession of Canada to the United States, and the rivalries of Congressmen and Cabinet members.

He decided it would be best to have his article on Gould published in England, to avoid censorship by the powerful financier. Gould's influence was not confined to the United States, however, and Adams was refused by two publications. His essay on Gould was finally published by the *Westminster Review*.

Adams became assistant professor of medieval history at Harvard and taught in Cambridge for seven years. During that time he tried to abandon the lecture system by replacing it with individual research. He found his students apt and quick to respond, but he felt that he needed a stone against which to sharpen his wits. He gave up his position in 1871 and went west to Estes Park with a Government Geological Survey. There he met Clarence King, a member of the party with whom he could not help contrasting himself. King had a systematic, scientific education and could have his choice of scientific, political, or literary prizes. Adams felt his own limitations.

After his flight from Harvard, he made his permanent home in Washington, where he wrote a series of books on American history. In 1893 he visited the Chicago Exhibition. From his observations of the steamship, the locomotive, and the newly invented dynamo, he concluded that force was the one unifying factor in American thought. Back in Washington, he saw the gold standard adopted, and concluded that the capitalistic system and American intervention in Cuba offered some signs of the direction in which the country was heading. During another visit to the Exhibition in 1900 Adams formulated an important theory. In observing the dynamo, he decided that history is not merely a series of causes and effects, of men acting upon men, but the record of forces acting upon men. For him, the dynamo became the symbol of force acting upon his own time, as the Virgin had been the symbol of force in the twelfth century.

During the next five years Henry Adams saw his friends drop away. Clarence King was the first to go. He lost his fortune in the panic of 1893 and died of tuberculosis in 1901. John Hay, under William McKinley, became American minister to England, and then Secretary of State. He was not well when he accepted the President's appointments, and the enormous task of bringing England, France, and Germany into accord with the United States and of attempting to keep peace, unsuccessfully, between Russia and Japan caused his death in 1905.

Adams considered that his education was continuous during his lifetime. He had found the tools which he had been given as a youth utterly useless, and he had to spend all of his days forging new ones. As he grew older, he found the moral standards of his father's and grandfather's times disintegrating, so that corruption and greed existed on the highest political levels. According to his calculations, the rate of change, due to mechanical force, was accelerating, and the generation of 1900 could rely only on impersonal forces to teach the generation of 2000. He himself could see no end to the multiplicity of forces which were so rapidly dwarfing mankind into insignificance.

Critical Evaluation

"Education" is both the theme and the metaphor of *The Education of Henry Adams*. In the preface, Adams notes that the object of his "study is the garment, not the figure," and he goes on to say that his specific object "is to fit young men, in universities or elsewhere, to be men of the world, equipped for any emergency; and the garment offered to them is meant to show the faults of the patchwork fitted on their fathers." Thus, by recounting the way in which he educated himself, he intends to educate others—a typical goal of autobiographers such as Benjamin Franklin, St. Augustine, and Jean Jacques Rousseau, all of whom are cited by Adams in his book.

Adopting the voice of a third-person narrator and following a strict chronological order in telling the story, including using parenthetical dates for each chapter title, suggests that the educated man is indeed sharing his knowledge with the uneducated and is doing this with complete objectivity. This apparent objectivity is misleading, however. Not only is the book more theory than it is narrative; it also does not recount Adams' life with the objectivity one might expect from the tone and chronological approach. For example, complete silence surrounds all that happened to Adams from 1872 to 1891. He concludes one chapter, titled "Failure (1871)," and begins the next chapter, titled "Twenty Years After (1892)," with no explanation of what occurred during that hiatus. Critics have speculated about this silence, suggesting that perhaps Adams simply did not want to write about his marriage and his wife Marian's suicide, or perhaps Adams wanted to emphasize the contrast between what he had been at the age of thirty-three and what he had become by the age of fifty-three. Whatever the reason for the gap, Adams apparently felt that his readers did not need the details to complete their education.

What Adams did give his audience was an autobiography that moves from the self into abstraction, that theorizes about four areas that were critical to his becoming educated: politics, science, nature, and psychology. Each influence helped Adams become a skeptical, observing individual who attempted to educate others.

In addition to showing his family's role in helping him see the role of politics in his life, Adams devotes an important section of his autobiography to examining President Ulysses S. Grant and the lessons Adams learned from that politician. Adams had hoped for some kind of political office from Grant, but not realizing that goal, he speculates on why that loss was probably his gain and a step toward his being educated. Adams explains how he came to see Grant as a "pre-intellectual, archaic" type, who "would have seemed so even to the cave-dwellers." Though Adams felt that he himself did not suit the twentieth century, he came to understand that he possessed what Grant lacked—namely, the ability to think. That quality was one aspect of the educated man.

Another quality was the ability to live without absolute certainty, the ability to use the scientific method to understand the incompleteness of truth. Describing himself as a Darwinian, he explains that he "was the first in an infinite series to discover and admit to himself that he really did not care whether truth was, or was not, true." In other words, in his educational process, he learned that the process of examination, the inclination to be skeptical about absolutes, was essential.

Equally critical, and related to his understanding of science, was Adams' recognition of what governed nature: chaos. Whereas order was the dream of man, chaos, according to Adams, was the order of nature. Thus Adams came to learn that his simplistic notion of an orderly nature needed to be replaced with a more sophisticated sense of the lack of unity and uniformity in nature.

The final influence upon Adams was what he called "the new psychology," which, like Adams' understanding of science and nature, pointed to complexity and a lack of unity. Thus, he pointed to the new psychology as being "convinced that it had actually split personality not only into dualism, but also into complex groups, like telephonic centres and systems, that might be isolated and called up at will." Added to the three other influences, this new way of viewing psychological realities shaped Adams' education, so that he came to realize that his earlier beliefs in unity were being replaced by an awareness of multiplicity.

In coming to this understanding, Adams makes dramatic use of dialectic, emphasizing the tension between opposites. His chapter titles demonstrate this when, for example, he juxtaposes "Quincy" to "Boston," "Political Mortality" to "The Battle of the Rams," and "The Height of Knowledge" to "The Abyss of Ignorance." The most famous of his oppositions occurs in one chapter, "The Dynamo and the Virgin," in which Adams explores the dynamo as the symbol of the twentieth century, contrasted with the Virgin, the symbol of force acting upon medieval times. The chapter in which he explores this particular opposition is actually a condensed version of two books written by Adams in which he carefully explores first unity and then multiplicity. The first book, *Mont-Saint-Michel and Chartres*, is also one of the finest introductions to the Middle Ages, and the second, *The Education of Henry Adams*, continues to be one of the best analyses of twentieth century intellectual history.

In his autobiographical study of opposites and the way in which they contribute to a person's education, Adams determined that the aim of education was the ability to cope, and the aim of education in the twentieth century was the ability to cope with a particularly important phenomenon: multiplicity. As he put it, "The child born in 1900 would, then, be born into a new world which would not be a unity but a multiple." *The Education of Henry Adams* chronicles one man's coming to this realization and his effort to help others become educated as well.

ELECTRA

Type of work: Drama
Author: Euripides (480–406 B.C.)
Type of plot: Classical tragedy
Time of plot: After the fall of Troy
Locale: Argos
First presented: c. 413 B.C.

Euripides' Electra is a psychological study of a woman's all-consuming hatred for her mother and stepfather on the one hand, and her love for her murdered father and exiled brother on the other. The plot revolves around the attempts of Electra—who has been forced to marry a farmer so that she will have no power—to spur her brother Orestes on to murder her enemies.

Principal Characters

Electra (ē·lek′trə), the daughter of Agamemnon and Clytemnestra. On his return from the Trojan War, Agamemnon was slain by Clytemnestra and Aegisthus, her lover, who now rules in Argos. For his own safety Orestes, Electra's brother, was smuggled out of the kingdom; Electra remained, was saved from death at the hands of Aegisthus by Clytemnestra, and was married to a poor farmer by Aegisthus. The farmer, out of respect for the house of Agamemnon, has never asserted his marital rights. In her first appearance Electra is thus the slave princess, unwashed and in rags, longing for attention and some emotional outlet, morbidly attached to her dead father and powerfully jealous of Clytemnestra. Orestes appears and, posing as a friend of the exiled brother, discusses with Electra the conduct of their mother and Aegisthus. In her speech to him she betrays herself as a woman whose desire for revenge has through continuous brooding become a self-centered obsession; her motive for the murder of Clytemnestra has now become hatred for her mother rather than love for her father, and she is an ugly and perverted being. Her expression of joy in the thought of murdering her mother causes Orestes not to reveal his identity until an old servant recognizes him. Electra takes no part in plotting vengeance on Aegisthus but arranges the murder of her mother. She sends a message that she has been delivered of a son and needs Clytemnestra to aid in the sacrifices attending the birth. When the body of Aegisthus is brought in, Electra condemns him. The language in her speech is artificial and stilted; it contrasts sharply with her passionate condemnation of Clytemnestra shortly after. Electra never realizes that she is committing exactly the same atrocity for which she wishes to punish her mother. She leads her mother into the house and guides Orestes' sword when he hesitates. It is only after the deed is committed that she feels the burden of what she has done. At the end of the play she is given by the gods in marriage to Pylades.

Orestes (ō·rĕs′tēz), Electra's brother. He returns secretly from exile under compulsion from Apollo to kill Aegisthus and his mother. Guided by the oracle, he does not share Electra's extreme lust for revenge. He kills Aegisthus by striking him in the back as he is preparing a sacrifice to the Nymphs and then, driven on by Electra, stabs his mother when she enters the house of Electra. The gods reveal that he will be pursued by the Furies of blood-guilt for his actions, but that he will find release at Athens before the tribunal of the Areopagus, where Apollo will accept responsibility for the matricide.

Clytemnestra (klī′təm·nĕs′trə), the regal mother of Electra, who took Aegisthus as her lover before Agamemnon returned from Troy. Together the pair plotted the murder of the husband. Her attempt to justify the murder on the grounds that Agamemnon had sacrificed her daughter Iphigenia is unsuccessful. Her cruelty, vanity, and sordid private affairs alienate her from any great sympathy, but she has saved the life of Electra and has enough affection to answer Electra's request that she help in the sacrifice to celebrate the birth of her daughter's son. She is murdered by Orestes, at his sister's urging.

A Farmer, a Mycenaean to whom Aegisthus has given Electra in marriage. He understands and accepts his station in life with nobility. Electra acknowledges her gratitude for his understanding behavior.

Pylades (pĭl′ə·dēz), a mute character. He is the faithful friend who accompanies Orestes during his exile and is given Electra as a wife by the gods.

An Old Man, a former servant in the house of Agamemnon who is still faithful to Electra. Summoned by her, he recognizes Orestes and helps to devise a plan for the murder of Aegisthus.

Castor (kăs′tər) and **Polydeuces** (pŏl′ĭ·dū′sēz), the Dioscuri, brothers of Clytemnestra. They appear at the end of the play to give Electra in marriage and to foretell the future of Orestes.

The Story

After Agamemnon, king of Argos, had returned home from the Trojan War, his wife, Clytemnestra, and her lover, Aegisthus, murdered him in cold blood during the homecoming banquet. Afterward Aegisthus and Clytemnestra were married, and Aegisthus became king. Orestes, young son of Agamemnon, was sent by a relative to Phocis before Aegisthus could destroy him. Electra, the daughter, remained, but was given in marriage to an old peasant, lest she marry a warrior powerful enough to avenge her father's death.

One day, after Electra and the peasant had gone out to do the day's work, Orestes came in disguise with his best friend, Pylades, to the farm to seek Electra. They heard her singing a lament for her lot and for the death of her father. A messenger interrupted her lament with word that a festival would be held in honor of the Goddess Hera and that all Argive maidens were to attend. Electra said she preferred to remain on the farm away from the pitying eyes of the people of Argos. The messenger advised her to pay honor to the gods and to ask their help.

Electra mistook Orestes and Pylades for friends of her brother and told them the story of her grief. She urged that Orestes avenge the death of Agamemnon and the ill treatment of himself and Electra. Aegisthus, meanwhile, had offered a reward for the death of Orestes.

The peasant returned from his work and asked Orestes and Pylades to remain as his guests. Electra sent her husband to bring the relative who had taken Orestes away from Argos. On his way to the peasant's cottage, the old foster father noticed that a sacrifice had been made at the tomb of Agamemnon and that there were some red hairs on the grave. He suggested to Electra that Orestes might be in the vicinity, but Electra answered that there was no chance of his being in Argos. When Orestes came out of the cottage, the old man recognized a scar on his forehead; thus brother and sister were made known to each other.

At the advice of the old peasant, Orestes planned to attend a sacrificial feast over which Aegisthus would preside. Electra sent her husband to tell Clytemnestra that she had given birth to a baby. Electra and Orestes invoked the aid of the gods in their venture to avenge the death of their father.

Orestes and Pylades were hailed by Aegisthus as they passed him in his garden. The pair told Aegisthus that they were from Thessaly and were on their way to sacrifice to Zeus. Aegisthus informed them that he was preparing to sacrifice to the nymphs and invited them to tarry. At the sacrifice of a calf, Orestes plunged a cleaver into Aegisthus' back while Aegisthus was examining the entrails of the beast. Orestes then revealed his identity to the servants, who cheered the son of their former master. Orestes carried the corpse of Aegisthus back to the cottage where it was hidden after Electra had reviled it.

At the sight of Clytemnestra approaching the peasant's hut, Orestes had misgivings about the plan to murder her. He felt that matricide would bring the wrath of the gods upon his head. But Electra, determined to complete the revenge, reminded Orestes that an oracle had told him to destroy Aegisthus and Clytemnestra.

Clytemnestra defended herself before Electra with the argument that Agamemnon had sacrificed Iphegenia, their child, as an offering before the Trojan venture and that he had returned to Argos with Cassandra, princess of Troy, as his concubine. Electra indicted her mother on several counts and said that it was only just that she and Orestes murder Clytemnestra. The queen entered the hut to prepare a sacrifice for Electra's supposed firstborn; within, she was killed by Orestes, who moaned in distress at the violence and bloodshed and matricide in which the gods had involved him.

The Dioscuri, twin sons of Zeus and brothers of the half-divine Clytemnestra, appeared to the brother and sister, who were overcome with mixed feelings of hate and love and pride and shame at what they had done. The twin gods questioned the wisdom of Apollo, whose oracle had advised this violent action; they decreed that Orestes should give Electra to Pylades in marriage and that Orestes himself should be pursued by the Furies until he could face a trial in Athens, from which trial he would emerge a free man.

Critical Evaluation

Electra is a compelling example of Euripides' dramaturgy, but it also affords us a means of comparing his purpose and techniques with those of Aeschylus and Sophocles, for each of them used the same legend and presented roughly the same action. Aeschylus in *The Libation-Bearers* (part of his trilogy, the *Oresteia*), Sophocles in *Electra*, and Euripides in his *Electra* all treat Orestes' return to Argos, his presentation of himself to his sister Electra, their planning of the revenge against Aegisthus and Clytemnestra, and the execution of that revenge. Each treatment is unique, showing the distinct temper of mind of these three tragedians.

With Aeschylus the twin murders of Aegisthus and Clytemnestra are the culminating crimes in a family polluted by generations of kin slayings. Regicide and matricide are evils instigated by Apollo to punish and purge the earlier murder of Agamemnon. Orestes alone takes on the burden of these crimes. A minor character, Electra offers him encouragement to the deed, but her gentle nature prevents her from being an actual accomplice. Aeschylus shows us Orestes' revenge as an act of divine justice, a crime that will in time earn an acquittal.

Sophocles takes a different view of the matter. The regicide and matricide are justifiable for him in human terms mainly, as the proper retribution for Agamemnon's killing. Electra is portrayed as a hard, bitter, determined young woman who aids her brother as a rightful duty. This perspective is similar to that in Homer's *Odyssey*.

Euripides, however, calls both points of view into question. He sees the murders of Aegisthus and Clytemnestra as wholly unmitigated evils that are neither humanly nor divinely justifiable. Euripides says in effect that no killing is permissible for any reason. And he carries this logic to its ultimate conclusion—that killers have as much right to live as anyone else no matter how twisted their psyche or how questionable their motives. This is a radical stand, but it is based on Euripides' firm belief in the value of every human life. This conviction shines through the whole of *Electra* and makes the idea of just retribution a mockery. One has the impression that Euripides would have liked to abolish all courts and prisons, turning justice into a matter of individual conscience. What is interesting is the way he works out these ideas dramatically.

Whereas Aeschylus and Sophocles concentrate on royalty and heroes, Euripides does not hesitate to depict an honorable peasant or to show ignoble blue bloods. In fact, the entire action of *Electra* takes place in front of a peasant's hut. To Euripides each life had worth, but the index to that worth was strength of character. Position, wealth, power, beauty, and physique were nothing to him. He was chiefly interested in an accurate, realistic psychology—a direct consequence of his beliefs.

Each of the main characters is shown as a clearly defined personality in relation to a specific environment. Euripides tends to concentrate on the sordid aspects in *Electra* as the legend would seem to demand, yet it is here that his faith in human dignity reveals its power. We find it easy to love good people, but to love people as warped by circumstances as Electra, Orestes, or Clytemnestra requires moral courage. Euripides had it, and he portrayed their pain as though it were his own.

Electra has fallen from lavish prosperity to squalor in a forced, loveless marriage to a peasant. She is slovenly and full of self-pity and spite. Further, she envies her mother, Clytemnestra, who lives in luxury and power, and she hates Aegisthus. Her single passion is to kill them both, and when she discovers Orestes, she uses him to obtain revenge. Orestes himself is a neurotic vagabond of no status, with authorization from Apollo to kill his mother and her lover, yet he declaims pompously about nobility of character.

Clytemnestra seems like a housewife in queen's clothing, operating by a retaliatory logic. She takes a lover because her husband had a mistress, and she kills Agamemnon because he killed their daughter Iphigenia. But none of this has made her happy. And when she visits Electra out of motherly concern, she is hacked to death by her two children. Even Aegisthus appears to be decent. It is precisely their ordinariness that makes the realistic descriptions of their murders so hideously sickening. We feel with Euripides that they deserve to live.

Once their passion for revenge is spent, Orestes and Electra are filled with self-revulsion, having arrived at the depths of a nightmarish degradation. Then Euripides brings two gods on stage, Castor and Polydeuces, to settle the matter. This *deus ex machina* ending puts the action in a new light. Apollo is directly responsible for the murders, just as Zeus is responsible for the Trojan War. These are not wise or just gods by human standards, and an individual person has infinitely more worth than their abominable edicts. Euripides is supremely confident in his position, and he does not shrink from judging gods by it.

Consistent with his faith in man's value, he allows Orestes and Electra a good measure of compassion in the end. These two share in the blood-guilt and will be exiled. Orestes will be driven mad by the Furies, but even they deserve to live, Euripides says in essence, and in time they will win forgiveness. The belief in human dignity has rarely had such a steadfast champion as Euripides.

EMMA

Type of work: Novel
Author: Jane Austen (1775–1817)
Type of plot: Social comedy
Time of plot: Early nineteenth century
Locale: Surrey, England
First published: 1816

In this novel about a headstrong, snobbish, intellectually proud young woman, Austen's genius for ironic comedy is displayed at its peak. The plot involves finding the proper husband for the heroine, but behind the deceptively simple and everyday events lies the author's moral vision of a world in which social responsibility and familial obligation are key virtues, and compromise a necessary response to the irreconcilable opposites encountered in life.

Principal Characters

Emma Woodhouse, the younger daughter of the wealthy owner of Hartfield and the most important young woman in the village of Highbury. Good-hearted, intelligent, but spoiled, she takes under her protection Harriet Smith, a seventeen-year-old girl of unknown parentage, who is at school in the village. Given to matchmaking, Emma breaks up the love affair between Harriet and Robert Martin, a worthy farmer, because she thinks Harriet deserves better, and persuades her to fall in love with the vicar, Mr. Elton. To her dismay, Elton proposes to her rather than to Harriet and is indignant when she refuses him. Next, Emma becomes interested in Frank Churchill, an attractive young man who visits his father in Highbury, and thinks him in love with her; but it develops that he is secretly engaged to Jane Fairfax. Emma had never really cared for Churchill, but she thinks him a possible match for Harriet. She becomes really concerned when she discovers that Harriet's new interest is in Mr. Knightley, an old friend of the Woodhouse family. She now realizes that Knightley is the man she has always loved and happily accepts his proposal. Harriet marries her old lover, Martin, and the matrimonial problems are solved.

George Knightley, a landowner of the neighborhood, sixteen years Emma's senior, and an old family friend. Honorable, intelligent, and frank, he has always told Emma the truth about herself. When she thinks that he may marry someone else, she realizes that she has always loved him and accepts his proposal.

John Knightley, George's brother, married to Emma's older sister.

Isabella Knightley, née **Woodhouse,** John Knightley's wife and Emma's sister, a gentle creature absorbed in her children.

Henry Woodhouse, father of Emma and Isabella, kindly and hospitable but an incurable hypochondriac.

Mr. Weston, a citizen of Highbury who has married Anne Taylor, Emma's former governess.

Anne Weston, née **Taylor,** Emma's former governess, a sensible woman whom Emma regards highly.

Frank Churchill, Mr. Weston's son by a former marriage. He has been adopted by and taken the name of his mother's family. His charm attracts Emma briefly, but she is not seriously interested. He is secretly engaged to Jane Fairfax.

Jane Fairfax, a beautiful and accomplished orphan, who visits her family in Highbury. Emma admires but cannot like her, finding her too reserved. The mystery of her personality is solved when it is learned that she is engaged to Churchill.

Mrs. Bates and **Miss Bates,** grandmother and aunt of Jane Fairfax. Poor but worthy women, they are intolerably loquacious and boring.

Harriet Smith, the illegitimate daughter of a tradesman. Young, pretty, and impressionable, she is taken up by Emma Woodhouse, rather to her disadvantage, for Emma gives her ideas above her station. She is persuaded to refuse the proposal of Robert Martin and to believe that Mr. Elton, the vicar, is in love with her. When Elton proves to be interested in Emma, Harriet is deeply chagrined. After considering the possibility of Harriet as a match for Churchill, Emma finds to her dismay that Harriet is thinking of Knightley. This discovery makes Emma realize how much she has always loved him. After Emma and Knightley are engaged, Harriet is again proposed to by Robert Martin; she happily marries him.

Robert Martin, the honest young farmer who marries Harriet Smith.

The Rev. Philip Elton, vicar of the parish. A conceited, silly man, he proposes to Emma Woodhouse, who has thought him in love with Harriet Smith. Emma's refusal makes him her enemy.

Augusta Elton, née **Hawkins,** the woman Elton marries after being refused by Emma. She is vulgar, pretentious, and officious.

The Story

A rich, clever, and beautiful young woman, Emma Woodhouse was no more spoiled and self-satisfied than one would expect under such circumstances. She had just seen her friend, companion, and former governess, Miss Taylor, married to a neighboring widower, Mr. Weston. While the match was suitable in every way, Emma could not help sighing over her loss, for now only she and her father were left at Hartfield, and Mr. Woodhouse was too old and too fond of worrying about trivialities to be a companion for his daughter.

The Woodhouses were the great family in the village of Highbury. In their small circle of friends, there were enough middle-aged ladies to make up card tables for Mr. Woodhouse, but there was no young lady to be a friend and confidante to Emma. Lonely for her beloved Miss Taylor, now Mrs. Weston, Emma took under her wing Harriet Smith, the parlor boarder at a nearby boarding school. Although not in the least brilliant, Harriet was a pretty seventeen-year-old girl with pleasing, unassuming manners and a gratifying habit of looking up to Emma as a paragon.

Harriet was the natural daughter of some mysterious person; Emma, believing that the girl might be of noble family, persuaded her that the society in which she had moved was not good enough for her. She encouraged her to give up her acquaintance with the Martin family, respectable farmers of some substance though of no fashion. Instead of thinking of Robert Martin as a husband for Harriet, Emma influenced the girl to aspire to Mr. Elton, the young rector.

Emma believed from Mr. Elton's manner that he was beginning to fall in love with Harriet, and she flattered herself upon her matchmaking schemes. The brother of a London lawyer married to Emma's older sister and one of the few people who could see Emma's faults, Mr. Knightley was concerned about her intimacy with Harriet. He warned her that no good could come of it for either Harriet or herself, and he was particularly upset when he learned that Emma had influenced Harriet to turn down Robert Martin's proposal of marriage. Emma herself suffered from no such qualms, for she was certain that Mr. Elton was as much in love with Harriet as Harriet—through Emma's instigation—was with him.

Emma suffered a rude awakening when Mr. Elton, finding her alone, asked her to marry him. She suddenly realized that what she had taken for gallantries to Harriet had been meant for herself; he had taken what Emma had intended as encouragement to his suit of her friend as encouragement to aspire for her hand. His presumption was bad enough, but the task of breaking the news to Harriet was much worse.

Another disappointment now occurred in Emma's circle. Frank Churchill, who had promised for months to come to see his father and new stepmother, again put off his visit. Churchill, Mr. Weston's son by a first marriage, had taken the name of his mother's family. Mr. Knightley believed that the young man now felt superior to his father. Emma argued with Mr. Knightley, but found herself secretly agreeing with him.

Although the Hartfield circle was denied Churchill's company, it did acquire an addition in the person of Jane Fairfax, niece of the garrulous Miss Bates. Jane rivaled Emma in beauty and accomplishment; this was one reason why, as Mr. Knightley hinted, Emma had never been friendly with Jane. Emma blamed Jane's reserve for their somewhat cool relationship.

Soon after Jane's arrival, the Westons received a letter from Churchill setting another date for his visit. This time he actually appeared, and Emma found him a handsome, well-bred young man. He frequently called upon the Woodhouses and also upon the Bates family, because of prior acquaintance with Jane Fairfax. Emma rather than Jane was the recipient of his gallantries, however, and Emma could see that Mr. and Mrs. Weston were hoping that the romance would prosper.

About this time, Jane Fairfax received the handsome gift of a pianoforte, anonymously given. It was presumed to have come from some rich friends with whom Jane, an orphan, had lived, but Jane seemed embarrassed with the present and refused to discuss it. Emma wondered if it had come from Mr. Knightley, after Mrs. Weston pointed out to her his seeming preference and concern for Jane. Emma could not bear to think of Mr. Knightley's marrying Jane Fairfax; after observing them together, she concluded to her own satisfaction that he was motivated by friendship, not love.

It was now time for Frank Churchill to end his visit, and he departed with seeming reluctance. During his last call at Hartfield, he appeared desirous of telling Emma something of a serious nature; but she, believing him to be on the verge of a declaration of love, did not encourage him because in her daydreams she always saw herself refusing him and their love ending in quiet friendship.

Mr. Elton returned to the village with a hastily wooed and wedded bride, a lady of small fortune, extremely bad manners, and great pretensions to elegance. Harriet, who had been talked into love by Emma, could not be so easily talked out of it; but what Emma had failed to accomplish, Mr. Elton's marriage had, and Harriet at last began to recover. Her recovery was aided by Mr. Elton's rudeness to her at a ball. When he refused to dance with her, Mr. Knightley, who rarely danced, offered himself as a partner, and Harriet, without Emma's knowledge, began to think of him instead of Mr. Elton.

Emma began to think of Churchill as a husband for Harriet, but she resolved to do nothing to promote the match. Through a series of misinterpretations, Emma thought Harriet was praising Churchill when she was really referring to Mr. Knightley.

The matrimonial entanglement was further complicated because Mrs. Weston continued to believe that Mr. Knightley was becoming attached to Jane Fairfax. In his turn, Mr. Knightley saw signs of some secret agreement between Jane Fairfax and Frank Churchill. His suspicions were finally justified when Churchill confessed to Mr. and Mrs. Weston that he and Jane had been secretly engaged since October. The Westons' first thought was for Emma, for they feared that Churchill's attentions to her might have had their effect. Emma assured Mrs. Weston that she had at one time felt some slight attachment to Churchill, but that time was now safely past. Her chief concerns now were that she had said things about Jane to Churchill which she would not have said had she known of their engagement, and also that she had, as she believed, encouraged Harriet in another fruitless attachment.

When she went to break the news gently to Harriet, however, Emma found her quite unperturbed by it; after a few minutes of talking at cross-purposes, Emma learned that it was not Churchill but Mr. Knightley upon whom Harriet had now bestowed her affections. When she told Emma that she had reasons to believe that Mr. Knightley returned her sentiments, Emma suddenly realized the state of her own heart; she herself loved Mr. Knightley. She now wished she had never seen Harriet Smith. Aside from the fact that she wanted to marry Mr. Knightley herself, she knew a match between him and Harriet would be an unequal one, hardly likely to bring happiness.

Emma's worry over this state of affairs was soon ended when Mr. Knightley asked her to marry him. Her complete happiness was marred only by the fact that she knew her marriage would upset her father, who disliked change of any kind; she was also aware that she had unknowingly prepared Harriet for another disappointment. The first problem was solved when Emma and Mr. Knightley decided to reside at Hartfield with Mr. Woodhouse as long as he lived. Harriet's problem, however, still remained; but when Mr. Knightley was paying attention to her, he was really trying to determine the real state of her affections for his young farm tenant. Consequently, Mr. Knightley was able to announce one morning that Robert Martin had again offered himself to Harriet and had been accepted. Emma was overjoyed that Harriet's future was now assured. She could always reflect that all parties concerned had married according to their stations, a prerequisite for their true happiness.

Critical Evaluation

Jane Austen had passed her fortieth year when her fourth published novel, *Emma*, appeared in 1816, the year before her death. Although *Pride and Prejudice* has always been her most popular novel, *Emma* is generally regarded as her greatest. In this work of her maturity, she deals once more with the milieu she preferred: "3 or 4 Families in a Country Village is the very thing to work on." The seventh of eight children of a learned clergyman, she had grown to womanhood in her native Hampshire village of Steventon. She spent the remainder of her life, except for brief intervals in Bath and Southampton, in another Hampshire village, Chawton, and was thoroughly familiar with the world she depicted.

The action of *Emma* cannot be properly considered apart from the setting of Highbury, a populous village only sixteen miles from London. Its physical attributes are presented in such circumstantial detail that it becomes a real entity. London seems far away, not because of the difficulty of travel but because of the community's limited views. It is a village where a light drizzle keeps its citizens at home, where Frank Churchill's trip to London for the alleged purpose of getting a haircut is foppery and foolishness, where the "inconsiderable Crown Inn" and Ford's "woollen-draper, linen-draper, and haberdasher's shop united" dominate the main street. Emma's view of the busiest part of town, surveyed from the doorway of Ford's, sums up the life of the village:

Mr. Perry walking hastily by, Mr. William Cox letting himself in at the office door, Mr. Cole's carriage horses returning from exercise . . . a stray letter boy on an obstinate mule . . . the butcher with his tray, a tidy old woman . . . two curs quarreling over a dirty bone, and a string of dawdling children round the baker's little bow-window.

The novel concerns the interrelationship between such an inconsequential place and Emma Woodhouse, a pretty and clever young lady almost twenty-one years old, who is rich and has few problems to vex her. Ironically, her world is no bigger than the village of Highbury and a few surrounding estates, including her father's Hartfield; nevertheless, in that small world, the Woodhouse family is the most important one. As the author states, the real dangers for Emma are "the power of having rather too much her own way, and a disposition to think a little too well of herself."

Moreover, these dangers are unperceived by Emma. Thus, in the blind exercise of her power over Highbury, she involves herself in a series of ridiculous errors, mistakenly judging that Mr. Elton cares for Harriet rather than for herself; Frank Churchill for herself rather than for Jane Fairfax; Harriet for Frank rather than for Mr. Knightley; and Mr. Knightley for Harriet rather than for herself. It is the triumph of Austen's art that however absurd or obvious Emma's miscalculations, they are convincingly a part of Emma's charming egotism. The reader finally agrees with Mr. Knightley that there is always "an anxiety, a curiosity in what one feels for Emma."

Emma's vulnerability to error can in part be attributed to inexperience, her life circumscribed by the boundaries of Highbury and its environs. Although Emma's only sister lives in London, no mention is made of visits there. She has never been to the seacoast, nor even to Box Hill, a famous scenic attraction nearby. She is further restricted by her valetudinarian father's gentle selfishness, which resists any kind of change and permits a social life limited to his own small circle, exclusive to the degree of admitting only four people as his closest acquaintances and only three to the second group.

Nevertheless, Emma's own snobbery binds her to the conclusion that she has no equals in Highbury. Mr. Knightley well understands the underlying assumption of superiority in Emma's friendship for Harriet Smith: "How can Emma imagine she has anything to learn herself, while Harriet is presenting such a delightful inferiority?" Emma fears superiority in others as a threat. Of the capable farmer Robert Martin, Harriet's wooer, she observes: "But a farmer can need none of my help, and is therefore in one sense as much above my notice as in every other way he is below it." Her resolution to like Jane Fairfax is repeatedly shattered by the praise everybody else gives Jane's superior attractions.

While Emma behaves in accordance with her theory that social rank is too important to be ignored, she fails to perceive that she is nearly alone in her exclusiveness. Indeed, the Eltons openly assume airs of superiority, and Jane Fairfax snubs Emma. Emma's increasing isolation from Highbury is epitomized in her resistance to the Cole family, good people of low rank who have nevertheless come to be regarded socially as second only to the Woodhouse family. Snobbishly sure that the Coles will not dare to invite the best families to an affair, she finds only herself uninvited. Therefore, ironically, she images her power in Highbury to be flourishing even as it is already severely diminished.

Emma's task is to become undeceived and to break free of the limitations imposed by her pride, by her father's flattering tyranny, and by the limited views of Highbury. She must accomplish all this without abandoning her self-esteem and intelligence, her father, or society. The author prepares for the possibility of a resolution from the beginning, especially by establishing Mr. Knightley as the person who represents the standard of maturity that Emma must assume. Emma is always half aware of his significance, often putting her folly to the test of his judgment.

There are brief, important occasions when the two, united by instinctive understanding, work together to create or restore social harmony; however, it is not until Harriet presumes to think of herself as worthy of his love that Emma is shocked into recognition that Mr. Knightley is superior to herself as well as to Harriet.

Highbury itself, which seems so confined, also serves to enlarge Emma's views simply by proving to be less fixed than it appears. As John Knightley observes: "Your neighbourhood is increasing, and you mix more with it." Without losing her desire for social success, Emma increasingly suffers from it. She is basically deficient in human sympathy, categorizing people as second or third rank in Highbury or analyzing them to display her own wit. She begins to develop in sensitivity, however, as she experiences her own humiliations. While still disliking Jane, she is capable of "entering into her feelings" and granting a moment of privacy. Her rudeness to Miss Bates is regretted, not only because Mr. Knightley is displeased but also because she perceives that she has been brutal, even cruel to Miss Bates.

Despite her love of small schemes, Emma shares an important trait with Mr. Knightley, one which he considers requisite for a prospective wife—an "open temper," the one quality lacking in the admirable Jane. Emma's disposition is open, her responsiveness to life counteracting the conditions in herself and her circumstances, which tend to be constricting. Her reaction to news of Harriet's engagement to Robert Martin is characteristic: she is "in dancing, singing, exclaiming spirits; and till she had moved about, and talked to herself, and laughed and reflected, she could be fit for nothing rational." Too ready to laugh at others, she can as readily laugh at herself. Impulsive in her follies, she is quick to make amends. She represents herself truthfully as she says, in farewell to Jane, "Oh! if you knew how much I love everything that is decided and open!"

A fully realized character who develops during the course of the action, Emma is never forced by the author to be other than herself, despite her new awareness. Once Harriet is safely bestowed upon Robert Martin, she complacently allows their friendship to diminish. The conniving to keep her father reasonably contented is a way of life. If he wishes to marry her, Mr. Knightley is required to move into Hartfield. Serious reflection upon her past follies is inevitably lightened by her ability to laugh at them—and herself. The novel is complete in every sense, yet Emma is so dynamic a characterization that one shares Mr. Knightley's pleasure in speculation: "I wonder what will become of her!"

AN ENEMY OF THE PEOPLE

Type of work: Drama
Author: Henrik Ibsen (1828–1906)
Type of plot: Social criticism
Time of plot: Late nineteenth century
Locale: Southern Norway
First presented: 1883

In An Enemy of the People *Ibsen relates the story of a doctor who is rejected by society for upsetting the status quo and the financial security of a Norwegian coastal town when he exposes the health hazards of the local Baths, a lucrative tourist attraction. Ibsen uses Dr. Stockmann to dramatize the problem of an individual faced with personal disaster if he speaks out against majority opinion.*

Principal Characters

Dr. Thomas Stockmann, the medical officer of the Municipal Baths, a conscientious man of science and the enemy of illness and deceit. Because Stockmann discovers that the healing waters, the principal source of income for the town, are polluted, causing the users to contract typhoid fever and gastric illnesses, he incurs the censure of the town and is proclaimed an "enemy of the people." Stockmann is the one honest man in public life in the town. When he realizes that all his associates would prefer concealing the fact that the Baths are polluted, he is at first amazed and then infuriated. Denied all means of spreading his information through the press or in public meeting, he at last calls a meeting in the home of a ship's captain, Captain Horster. Before Stockmann can speak, however, the group elects a chairman, Aslaksen, who permits Stockmann's brother, Peter, mayor of the town, to make a motion forbidding the doctor to speak on the matter of the Baths because unreliable and exaggerated reports might go abroad. Aslaksen seconds the motion. Stockmann then speaks on the moral corruption of the town and manages to offend everyone, including his wife's adoptive father, Morten Kiil, a tanner whose works are one of the worst sources of water pollution. Morten Kiil buys up the bath stock the next day and proposes that the doctor call off the drive because he has bought it with money which Kiil had planned to leave Mrs. Stockmann and the children. Stockmann rejects the suggestion. He thinks of leaving the town and going to America, but when Captain Horster is discharged for permitting Stockmann to speak in his house, he cannot sail on Horster's ship and decides to remain in the town, educate the street urchins, and rear his own sons to be honest men. He says that only the middle class opposes him and that the poor people will continue to call on him. In his decision, he is cheered by his young schoolteacher daughter, Petra, and by Mrs. Stockmann and one of the boys. Although Petra, and by Mrs. Stockmann and one of the boys. Although Stockmann is not an especially personable character, he is an excellent representation of the frustrations which confront the reformer.

Peter Stockmann, the mayor of the town and brother of Dr. Stockmann. Peter Stockmann is a typical willfully blind public official who would rather poison the visitors of his town than cut its income. Under the pretense of concern for the town he is able to win others to his side. He ruins his brother but suggests that he will reinstate him if he recants.

Hovstad, the editor of the *People's Messenger*. At first, Hovstad supports Dr. Stockmann and plans to print his article about the Baths. However, when he learns that public opinion is against Stockmann, he deserts him until he hears that Morten Kiil has bought up the bath stock. Then he offers to support Stockmann again, because he thinks that Stockmann will cash in on the Baths and he wants to be in on the deal. Because Hovstad starts off as a forthright newspaper man, he is a disappointment when he abruptly changes character and sides.

Aslaksen, a printer. Aslaksen begins as a volunteer supporter of Stockmann's proposal to clean up the Baths. As chairman of the Householders' Association, he promises the support of the majority in the town, but as soon as matters become difficult, and when Dr. Stockmann grows more emotional than Aslaksen thinks is in keeping with his idea of moderation, he turns against the doctor. He comes with Hovstad to try to cash in on the profits which they think Stockmann expects to make with Morten Kiil.

Petra, the daughter of Dr. and Mrs. Stockmann. An earnest young woman, a teacher, Petra is the first to discover Hovstad's insincerity. Petra refused to translate an English story for Hovstad to print because its theme is that a supernatural power looks after the so-called good people in the world and that everything happens for the best, while all the evil are punished; she has no such belief. When Hovstad tells her that he is giving his readers exactly the kind of story they want, Petra is distressed.

When he blurts out a few minutes later that the reason he is supporting Dr. Stockmann is that he is Petra's father, Petra tells him that he has betrayed himself, that she will never trust him again. Because she supports her father, she loses her job. Her employer tells her that a former guest in the Stockmann home has revealed Petra's emancipated views. Petra is her father's true child.

Mrs. Stockmann, the doctor's wife and his loyal supporter. At first she does not want her husband to go against the wishes of his brother, but she soon gives her full approval. She is not presented as a woman of strong personality.

Morten Kiil, a tanner, Mrs. Stockmann's adoptive father. Although described by other characters as an "old badger," a man of wealth whose influence and money Dr.

Stockmann hates to lose because of his wife and children, Morten Kiil seems to live more by reputation than by representation in the play. He goes against Dr. Stockmann and buys up all the bath stock with money he had intended leaving to Mrs. Stockmann.

Captain Horster, a ship's captain who befriends Dr. Stockmann, the only person outside the Stockmann family who remains loyal to the doctor. He allows Stockmann to attempt his public speech about the Baths to an audience assembled in his house.

Ejlif and

Morten, the two young sons of the Stockmanns.

Billing, a sub-editor. He agrees with Aslaksen and Hovstad.

The Story

All the citizens of the small Norwegian coastal town Christiania were very proud of the Baths, for the healing waters were making the town famous and prosperous. Dr. Thomas Stockmann, the medical officer of the Baths, and his brother Peter, the mayor and chairman of the Baths committee, did not agree on many things, but they did agree that the Baths were the source of the town's good fortune. Hovstad, the editor of the *People's Messenger*, and Billing, his sub-editor, were also loud in praise of the Baths. Business was good and the people were beginning to enjoy prosperity.

Then Dr. Stockmann received from the university a report stating that the waters of the Baths were contaminated. Becoming suspicious when several visitors became ill after taking the Baths, he had felt it his duty to investigate. Refuse from tanneries above the town was oozing into the pipes leading to the reservoir and infecting the waters. This meant that the big pipes would have to be relaid, at a tremendous cost to the owners or to the town. When Hovstad and Billing heard this news, they asked the doctor to write an article for their paper about the terrible conditions. They even spoke of having the town give Dr. Stockmann some kind of testimonial in honor of his great discovery.

Dr. Stockmann wrote up his findings and sent the manuscript to his brother so that his report could be acted upon officially. Hovstad called on the doctor again, urging him to write some articles for the *People's Messenger*. It was Hovstad's opinion that the town had fallen into the hands of a few officials who did not care for the people's rights, and it was his intention to attack these men in his paper and urge the citizens to get rid of them in the next election.

Aslaksen, a printer who claimed to have the compact majority under his control, also wanted to join in the fight to get the Baths purified and the corrupt officials defeated. Dr. Stockmann could not believe that his brother would

refuse to accept the report, but he soon learned that he was wrong. Peter went to the doctor and insisted that he keep his knowledge to himself because the income of the town would be lost if the report were made public. He said that the repairs would be too costly, that the owners of the Baths could not stand the cost, and that the townspeople would never allow an increase in taxes to clean up the waters. He even insisted that Dr. Stockmann write another report, stating that he had been mistaken in his earlier judgment. He felt this action necessary when he learned that Hovstad and Billing knew of the first report. When the doctor refused either to change his report or withhold it, Peter threatened him with the loss of his position. Even his wife pleaded with him not to cross his powerful brother; he was sustained in his determination to do right only by his daughter Petra.

Hovstad, Billing, and Aslaksen were anxious to print the doctor's article so that the town could know of the falseness of the mayor and his officials. They thought his words so clear and intelligible that all responsible citizens would revolt against the corrupt regime. Aslaksen did plead for moderation, but he promised to fight for what was right.

Peter Stockmann appeared at the office of the *People's Messenger* and cleverly told Aslaksen, Hovstad, and Billing that the tradespeople of the town would suffer if the doctor's report were made public. He said that they would have to stand the expense and that the Baths would be closed for two years while repairs were being made. The two editors and the printer then turned against Dr. Stockmann and supported Peter, since they felt that the majority would act in this way.

The doctor pleaded with them to stand by the promises they had given him, but they were the slaves of the majority opinion which they claimed to mold. When they refused to print his article, the doctor called a public meeting in the home of his friend, Captain Horster. Most of the citizens who attended were already unfriendly to him because the mayor and the newspaper editors had spread the news that he wanted to close the Baths and ruin the town. Aslaksen, nominated as chairman by the mayor, so controlled the meeting that a discussion of the Baths was ruled out of order.

Dr. Stockmann took the floor, however, and in ringing tones told the citizens that it was the unbelievable stupidity of the authorities and the great multitude of the compact majority that caused all the evil and corruption in the world. He said that the majority destroyed the freedom and truth everywhere because the majority was ignorant and stupid. The majority was really in slavery to ideas which had long outlived their truth and usefulness. He contended that ideas become outdated in eighteen or twenty years at the most, but the foolish majority continued to cling to them and deny new truths brought to them by the intelligent minority. He challenged the citizens to deny that all great ideas and truths were first raised by the persecuted minority, those few men who dared to stand out against the prevailing opinions of the many. He said that the real intellectuals could be distinguished as easily as could a thoroughbred animal from a crossbreed. Economic and social position had no bearing on the distinction. It was a man's soul and mind that separated him from the ignorant masses.

His challenge fell on deaf ears. As he knew from the beginning, the majority could not understand the meaning of his words. By vote they named him an enemy of the people. The next day they stoned his house and sent him threatening letters. His landlord ordered him to move. He lost his position as medical director of the Baths, and his daughter Petra was dismissed from her teaching position. In each case the person responsible for the move against him stated that it was only public opinion that forced the move. No one had anything against him or his family, but no one would fight the opinion of the majority. Even Captain Horster, a friend who had promised to take the Stockmanns to America on his next voyage, lost his ship because the owner was afraid to give a ship to the man, the only man, who had stood by the radical Dr. Stockmann.

Then the doctor learned that his father-in-law had bought up most of the now undesirable Bath stock with the money which would have gone to Mrs. Stockmann and the children. The townspeople accused the doctor of attacking the Baths so that his family could buy the stock and make a profit, and his father-in-law accused him of ruining his wife's inheritance if he persisted in his stories about the uncleanliness of the Baths. Reviled and ridiculed on all sides, Dr. Stockmann determined to fight back. He could open a school. Starting only with any urchins he could find on the streets, he would teach the town and the world that he was stronger than the majority, that he was strong because he had the courage to stand alone.

Critical Evaluation

Sometimes called "the father of realism" in modern drama, Norwegian playwright Henrik Ibsen unleashes in *An Enemy of the People* a savage attack on majoritarian democracy and its tendency to sacrifice truth on the altar of financial success or power. Widely praised—and at times disparaged—as a "provincial dramatist," Ibsen was frequently led by his social conscience into open controversy in his homeland, and often engendered undisguised public outrage toward the themes and the moral conflicts with which he imbued his plays. His reputation as a social dramatist is in some ways overshadowed by his equally electrifying stage technique, a technique born of his iconoclastic view of the theater and his rejection of the classical model of dramaturgy. Because Ibsen's innovative staging techniques became so conventional in the twentieth century, it is difficult to realize just how revolutionary they were in turn-of-the-century stage direction. His strong realism—exemplified in *An Enemy of the People* in the minutiae of everyday detail, the precision of dialogue, the painfully honest portrayal of the psychological makeup of his characters—requires of his actors and his readers their utmost energy and resilience.

It appears that Ibsen completed *An Enemy of the People* as a response to the savagely negative critical response to his earlier play, *Ghosts* (1881), though both plays were begun at roughly the same time. Hearing a news item regarding a Hungarian scientist who had discovered and exposed the poisoned water in the town's water supply and was then unceremoniously pilloried for his discovery, Ibsen adapted its essential core for his drama. In *An Enemy of the People*, Ibsen probes the tensions between the individual and society, specifically between majority rule and minority dissent, and the stage becomes a window through which the audience may witness a living dialectic. Artfully using G. W. F. Hegel's thesis-antithesis-synthesis formula, Ibsen posits the individual-as-thesis in conflict with society's antithetical opposition, the clash eventually yielding a synthesis that in some sense resolves the dramatic plot conflicts without relieving the tension or friction between the dissenter and his social context.

Ibsen's keen sense of everydayness, the vivid capturing of the details of the then-emergent "modern age," gives *An Enemy of the People* its stability and moral force. Christiania, ostensibly the town in which the story takes place, is on the verge of renown and legendary status as a healing oasis whose soothing waters symbolize the humanitarianism of its people. On the surface, Dr. Stockmann, a rather self-effacing personality, is an ebullient, community-minded scientist. He lives in the best of all worlds—a town whose income is built almost entirely on the Baths, which supply life-giving nurture to tourists who travel there for health reasons–enjoying a quality of life he himself has had a part in discovering and now oversees. He basks in the success of his township's "natural" benevolence. Yet, the same scientific rigor that certifies Dr. Stockmann's judgment and accredits him as an authority also brings him grief when the contamination of the same Baths is revealed to him. When Dr. Stockmann blithely reports the findings to his brother Peter and to fellow citizens, always assuming their equal concern for the "health" of the tourist trade, he discovers a different kind of concern, and the play's fundamental theme emerges: his animated opposition to his brother Peter's credo, "The individual must subordinate himself to Society as a whole or more precisely to those authorities responsible for the well-being of that society."

An Enemy of the People is thus Ibsen's cynical answer to the question, "What happens when the truth conflicts with the will of the majority?" In his response, Dr. Stockmann is at once both an aristocrat and an anarchist; when the majority is right, to be one of the establishment has honor and dignity—he may protect, within certain boundaries, the welfare of his people and his clients. When he becomes an outsider, however, he is quick to become uncooperative and obstinate in his stand for the truth. His willingness to start over after his defeat—to begin a school that will reeducate the young in ethical behavior—marks him as one willing to subvert the social order at any cost, even if it means isolation and alienation from the public at large. His family, initially and understandably cautious, takes up his cause with fervor. Yet, he is not completely admirable; Ibsen himself referred to Stockmann as a muddlehead, an innocent, absent-minded professor type, uncomfortable and shy in public yet lavishly hospitable and extravagant with his own resources. Consequently, while Stockmann appears to be a classical hero who invites the spectator's identification at the play's start, later he reveals that he is not. He is, in fact, impetuous and uninhibited. Stockmann is not a savvy and brooding clinical observer of human life and its folly but a common, compassionate man genuinely shocked by what has transpired among people he thought he knew well. Thus he remains a prototypical nineteenth century hero: His defiant confidence at the end of the play, while in some ways not foreshadowed, marks him essentially as a gullible optimist who is incredulous (as a truly good man would be) at the turn of events which displaces his sudden heroism with equally sudden villainy in the public eye. This newfound boldness and stubborn insistence on standing alone may be seen simply as the other side of the charm and naïveté he displays at the beginning of the play.

Another key theme is the failure of each of the town's major institutions—the press, the Householders' Association, and the town council itself—to stand with integrity on the side of honor. Each betrays its selfishness when the town's livelihood is threatened. Petra, Dr. Stockmann's daughter, uncovers the jadedness of the newspaper she works for early in the play, when she refuses to translate a short story whose message she finds patronizing: "It's all about a supernatural power that's supposed to watch over all the so-called good people, and how everything is for the best and how the wicked people get punished in the end." Her editor Hovstad's reply, "You're absolutely right, of course. But an editor cannot always do what he wants. After all, politics is the most important thing in life—at least, for a newspaper it is," manifests his shallow concern for veracity. With one eye on the truth and the other on subscriptions, Hovstad's priorities are clear, and it is no surprise that he later must fire Petra for her insubordination. Despite his tabloid-like response to Dr. Stockmann's alarming report and his initial desire to expose to the populace its unscrupulous politicians, Hovstad's reluctance to buck the tide and thus print all the news fit to print demonstrates that even in a democracy the media can be coopted. When the mayor, Dr. Stockmann's own brother, and businessman extraordinaire Aslaksen conspire against them, the family's illusions of the goodness and mercy they thought to be characteristic of their friends and colleagues is shattered beyond repair. Built into their culture's hitherto disguised authoritarian community is an ethical malaise wherein outworn conventions strangle the life of the individual—compelling choices without a moral basis, thereby corrupting and stultifying the society in which they live.

While *An Enemy of the People* is rightly considered Ibsen's most militant play, it is technically, in an odd way, also a species of comedy: a play designed to bring, with humor as well as pathos, a stumbling protagonist to a fitting end. There are no tragic deaths in the play, save that of the principle of minority rights and altruistic concern for the welfare of all in a democracy. Yet it is just this juxtaposition of dramatic form with dramatic irony that gives the play its ideological impact. Declaring that to be a poet is most of all to "see," and thus deliberately conflating the role of the *poet* ("to make") with that of the biblical *prophet* ("to see") into one office, Ibsen peered into the fading Lutheran culture of *fin de siècle* Norway and, gazing bleakly heavenward, discovered only an empty sky bereft of divine comfort or direction. Fast closing industrialization had brought to his country a more ruthless sense of profit and production, a fact mirrored in the malice and errant democracy depicted in the town of Christiania in *An Enemy of the People*. As American playwright Arthur Miller, who adapted his work for the American stage, has suggested, every Ibsen play in effect begins with the words, "Now listen here." This preaching, even pontificating posture would seem to border on propaganda, and would do so in the hands of a less skillful dramatist. The quality that prevents *An Enemy of the*

People from devolving into a political tract is Ibsen's dialectical narrative, a strategy that forces his characters to discover the truth about themselves and others onstage in the course of the action, and not in exposition or soliloquy. The audience learns of Dr. Stockmann's stalwart character, and the weaknesses of his brother's, through a temporal confrontation that unfolds before the audience's (and the characters') eyes as it happens. As neither brother is a classical hero or villain—one whose fate is fixed by the gods or by fatal flaws neither can transcend—their destinies rest, rather, in the moral choices they make when they are confronted with life's challenges and then called to stand alone for the truth against the majority. This single dramatized fact is perhaps Ibsen's main legacy both to the theater and to twentieth century democracy.

AN ENQUIRY CONCERNING HUMAN UNDERSTANDING

Type of work: Philosophical treatise
Author: David Hume (1711–1776)
First published: 1748

"Philosophical decisions," says Hume toward the end of his *Enquiry*, "are nothing but the reflections of common life, methodised and corrected." This simple, homely epigram conceals a great deal. For one thing, the *Enquiry* is actually a sort of popularized revision of ideas that were systematically developed in Book I of his precocious *Treatise of Human Nature* (1739–1740), which, although it was completed before the author was twenty-five, has been characterized as one of the most profound, thoroughly reasoned, and purely scientific works in the history of philosophy. Secondly, Hume's method for correcting the reflections of common life actually involves a thorough attack on the obscurities of metaphysical idealists.

Born in an age of reason, Hume at first shared the optimism of those who were certain that pure reason could unlock the secrets of nature, and as he read Bacon, Newton, Hobbes, and Locke, he longed for fame equal to theirs. But, as he reported in a letter to Sir Gilbert Elliot, though he "began with an anxious search after arguments, to confirm the common opinion; doubts stole in, dissipated, returned; were again dissipated, returned again; and it was a perpetual struggle of restless imagination against inclination, perhaps against reason." That last, "perhaps against reason," is the crucial phrase, for no philosopher before Hume used reason so brilliantly in an attack against the certainties of reason. The twelve essays of the *Enquiry* reflect his three principal attacks: (1) against rationalism, the doctrine of innate ideas, faith in ontological reasoning and an ordered universe; (2) against empiricism, both the kind that led to Lockean dualism and Berkeleyan idealism, on the ground that neither the physical nor the spiritual can be proved; and (3) against deism, based on universal axioms and the law of causality. It is not surprising that since Hume religions have largely made their appeals to faith rather than to reason.

Considering what remains when such thoroughgoing skepticism rejects so much of the beliefs of rational men, Hume himself readily admitted (in the fourth essay, "Sceptical Doubts Concerning the Operations of the Understanding") that as a man he was quite satisfied with ordinary reasoning processes, but that as a philosopher he had to be skeptical. For reasoning was not based on immediate sense experience. "The most lively thought is still inferior to the dullest sensation," he asserted in his second essay, "The Origin of Ideas." Unless the mind is "disordered by disease or madness," actual perceptions have the greatest "force and vivacity," and it is only on such matters of basic mental fact rather than on the abstract relations of ideas, as in mathematics, that we must depend for certainties about life. For example, no amount of reasoning could have led Adam in the Garden of Eden to believe that fluid, transparent water would drown him or that bright, warm fire would burn him to ashes. "No object ever discovers [reveals], by the qualities which appear to the senses, either the causes which produced it, or the effects which arise from it." In dealing with this idea, Hume is quite dogged and persistent; he backs every argument into a corner, into some "dangerous dilemma." What is more he enjoys himself immensely while doing it—"philosophers that give themselves airs of superior wisdom and sufficiency, have a hard task when they encounter persons of inquisitive dispositions," he says. Concerning cause and effect, he argues that we expect similar effects from causes that appear similar; yet this relationship does not always exist and, though it is observed, it is not reasoned. Furthermore, it is merely an arbitrary assumption, an act of faith, that events which we remember as having occurred sequentially in the past will continue to do so in the future. Causation thus was merely a belief, and belief he had defined as a "lively idea related to or associated with a present impression."

This seemed to Hume not an impractical philosophical idea, but a momentous discovery of great consequence. Since causation was an *a priori* principle of both natural and moral philosophy, and since causation could not be reasonably demonstrated to be true, a tremendous revolution in human thought was in preparation. Only in the pure realm of ideas, logic, and mathematics, not contingent upon the direct sense awareness of reality, could causation safely (because arbitrarily) be applied—all other sciences are reduced to probability. The concluding essay, "Of the Academical or Sceptical Philosophy," reaches grand heights of eloquence, when Hume argues that *a priori* reasoning can make anything appear to produce anything: "The falling of a pebble may, for aught we know, extinguish the sun; or the wish of a man control the planets in their orbits. . . ." Hume further claims that

when we run over libraries, persuaded of these principles, what havoc must we make? If we take in hand any volume; of divinity or school metaphysics, for instance; let us ask, *Does it contain any abstract reasoning concerning quantity or number?* No. *Does it contain any experimental reasoning concerning matter of fact and existence?* No. Commit it then to the flames: for it can contain nothing but sophistry and illusion.

The polemic vigor of the essays stems in large part from the bitter experiences Hume had in the years immediately preceding the publication of the *Enquiry*. In 1744 he had sought to fill a vacancy in the chair of Ethics and Pneumatical Philosophy at Edinburgh University, but to his astonishment his *Treatise* was invoked to prevent the appointment: "Such a popular clamor has been raised against me in Edinburgh, on account of Scepticism, Heterodoxy, and other hard names . . . that my Friends find some Difficulty in working out the Point of my Professorship." Then he was dismissed without full salary as tutor to the mad son of the Marquis of Annandale. These experiences helped sharpen the hard cutting edge of his thought and prose style.

After refining his conception of reason and its modes of function, Hume applies it to four crucial problems: "Liberty and Necessity," "Reason of Animals," "Miracles," and "Particular Providence and a Future State."

Concerning liberty and necessity, Hume argues that since the subject relates to common life and experience (unlike topics such as the origin of worlds or the region of spirits), only ambiguity of language keeps the dispute alive. For a clear definition, he suggests that it be consistent with plain matters of fact and with itself. Difficulty arises when philosophers approach the problem by examining the faculties of the soul rather than the operations of body and brute matter. In the latter, men assume that they perceive cause and effect, but in the functioning of their minds they feel no connection between motive and action. However, we cannot invoke the doctrine of cause and effect without, ultimately, tracing all actions—including evil ones—to the Deity whom men refuse to accept as the author of guilt and moral turpitude in all his creatures. As a matter of fact, freedom and necessity are matters of momentary emotional feeling "not to be controuled or altered by any philosophical theory or speculation whatsoever."

The "Reason of Animals" consists—as it does in children, philosophers, and mankind in general—not so much in logical inferences as in experience of analogies and sequential actions. Observation and experience alone teach a horse the proper height which he can leap or a greyhound how to meet the hare in her tracks and the least expenditure of energy. Hume's learning theory here seems to be based on the pleasure-pain principle and forms the background for some theories of twentieth century psychology. However, Hume ends this essay with a long qualification in which he cites the instincts, unlearned knowledge derived from the original hand of nature, and then adds this curious final comment: "The experimental reasoning itself, which we possess in common with beasts, and on which the whole conduct of life depends, is nothing but a species of instinct or mechanical power, that acts in us unknown as ourselves."

The essay on miracles is perhaps the most spirited of the entire collection and it is the one which Hume expected, correctly, would stir the greatest opposition. Nevertheless, he was certain that his argument would be, for the wise and the learned, "an everlasting check to all kinds of superstitious delusion, and consequently . . . useful as long as the world endures." Events can be believed to happen only when they are observed, and all reports of events not directly observed must be believed only to the degree that they conform with probability, experimentally or experientially derived. A miracle is a violation of the laws of nature; therefore it violates all probability; therefore it is impossible. History gives no instance of any miracle personally attended to by a sufficient number of unquestionably honest, educated, intelligent men. Despite the surprise, wonder, and other pleasant sensations attendant upon reports of novel experiences, all new discoveries that achieve credibility among men have always resembled in fundamentals those objects and events of which we already have experience. The most widespread belief in miracles exists among primitive people. Finally, since there is no objective way of confirming miracles, believers have no just basis for rejecting those claimed by all religions. "So that, on the whole, we may conclude, that the *Christian Religion* not only was at first attended with miracles, but even at this day cannot be believed by any reasonable person without one. Mere reason is insufficient to convince us . . . to believe what is most contrary to custom and experience."

In the 1777 posthumous edition of the *Enquiry* appeared the announcement that these unsystematic essays be *alone* regarded as containing Hume's philosophical sentiments and principles. Despite the fact that professional philosophers, especially the logical positivists, still prefer the earlier *Treatise of Human Nature*, it is well that the *Enquiry* with its livelier style and popular appeal stands as his personal testament. In it he said that he would be "happy if . . . we can undermine the foundations of an abstruse philosophy, which seems to have hitherto served only as a shelter to superstition, and a cover to absurdity and error." The irony is that he succeeded so well in undermining reason that he opened the door to the Romanticism of the late eighteenth and early nineteenth centuries. But his voice has outlasted that babel and his humanistic skepticism survives. "Be a philosopher," he cautioned himself, "but amidst all your philosophy, be still a man."

THE EPIC OF GILGAMESH

Type of work: Poem
Author: Unknown
Type of plot: Heroic adventure
Time of plot: Remote antiquity
Locale: The ancient world
First transcribed: c. 2,000 B.C.

Written almost four thousand years ago, this epic contains many of the themes found in the later epic literary tradition of Achilles, Odysseus, Samson, Beowulf, Roland, and King Arthur. Although two-thirds god, Gilgamesh experiences from his human nature love and conflict, joy and sorrow, courage and fear, and ultimately the horror and mystery of death. Although of heroic stature, he is also a sympathetic human figure who must learn through his suffering and errors.

Principal Characters

Gilgamesh, king of Uruk, a demigod. He is the wisest, strongest, and handsomest of mortals. In earth-shaking combat he overcomes Engidu, who has been fashioned by Aruru to be his rival. After the battle the heroes become inseparable friends and companions through a series of heroic exploits. When Engidu dies, the grieving Gilgamesh seeks for and finds his friend in the land of the dead.

Engidu, a demigod formed by Aruru to be a rival to Gilgamesh. Vanquished by Gilgamesh, he becomes the hero's inseparable companion and goes with him to conquer Khumbaba. Accidentally touching the portal of the gate to Khumbaba's lair, he receives a curse from which he eventually dies. Allowed to meet the grief-stricken Gilgamesh in the underworld, he reveals to his friend the terrors of death.

Utnapishtim, a mortal possessing the secret of life. After Engidu's death Gilgamesh receives from Utnapishtim the secret—a magic plant—only to lose it on his homeward journey.

Aruru, a goddess who fashions Engidu from clay.

Anu, chief of the gods.

Ninsun, a goddess and adviser to Gilgamesh.

Ishtar, a fertility goddess in love with Gilgamesh.

Siduri, the divine cupbearer.

Ur-Shanabi, the boatman on the waters of death.

Ea, lord of the depths of the waters.

Khumbaba, a fearful monster.

The Story

Gilgamesh was the wisest, strongest and most handsome of mortals, for he was two-thirds god and one-third man. As king of the city-state of Uruk he built a monumental wall around the city, but in doing so he overworked the city's inhabitants unmercifully, to the point where they prayed to the gods for relief.

The god Anu listened to their plea and called the goddess Aruru to fashion another demigod like Gilgamesh in order that the two heroes might fight, and thus give Uruk peace. Aruru created the warrior Engidu out of clay and sent him to live among the animals of the hills.

A hunter of Uruk found Engidu and in terror reported his existence to Gilgamesh. Gilgamesh advised the hunter to take a priestess to Engidu's watering place to lure Engidu to the joys of civilization and away from his animal life. The priestess initiated Engidu into civilization with her body, her bread, and her wine. Having forsaken his animal existence, Engidu and the priestess started for Uruk. On their arrival she told him of the strength and wisdom of Gilgamesh and of how Gilgamesh had told the goddess Ninsun about his dreams of meeting Engidu, his equal, in combat.

Engidu challenged Gilgamesh by barring his way to the temple. An earth-shaking fight ensued in which Gilgamesh stopped Engidu's onslaught. Engidu praised Gilgamesh's strength and the two enemies became inseparable friends.

Gilgamesh informed Engidu of his wish to conquer the terrible monster, Khumbaba, and challenged him to go along. Engidu replied that the undertaking was full of peril for both. Gilgamesh answered that Engidu's fear of death deprived him of his might. At last Engidu agreed to go with his friend. Gilgamesh then went to the elders and they, like Engidu, warned him of the perils he would encounter. Seeing his determination, the elders gave him their blessing. Gilgamesh then went to Ninsun and she also warned him of the great dangers, but to no avail. Then she took Engidu aside and told him to give Gilgamesh special protection.

Upon climbing the cedar mountain to reach Khumbaba, Gilgamesh related three terrible dreams to Engidu, who shored up Gilgamesh's spirit by placing a favorable interpretation on them. On reaching the gate to the cedar wood where Khumbaba resided, the pair were stopped by the watchman, who possessed seven magic mantles. The two heroes succeeded in overcoming him. Accidentally, Engidu touched the magic portal of the gate; immediately he felt faint and weak, as if afraid of death. The champions entered the cedar wood and with the aid of the sun god slew Khumbaba.

Upon their return to Uruk after their victory, the goddess Ishtar fell in love with Gilgamesh and asked him to be her consort. But Gilgamesh, being wiser than her previous consorts, recalled all of the evil things she had done to her earlier lovers. Ishtar then angrily ascended to heaven and reported his scornful refusal to Anu. Threatening to destroy mankind, she forced Anu to create a monster bull that would kill Gilgamesh.

Anu formed the bull and sent it to Uruk. After it had slain five hundred warriors in two snorts, Engidu jumped on its back while Gilgamesh drove his sword into its neck. Engidu then threw the bull's thighbone in Ishtar's face, and Gilgamesh held a feast of victory in his palace.

Engidu, still ailing from touching the portal to the cedar wood, cursed those who had shown him civilization. He related his nightmares to Gilgamesh, grew faint-hearted, and feared death. Since he had been cursed by touching the gate, he died. Gilgamesh mourned his friend six days and nights; on the seventh he left Uruk to cross the steppes in search of Utnapishtim, the mortal who had discovered the secret of life.

Upon reaching the mountain named Mashu, he found scorpion men guarding the entrance to the underground passage. They received him cordially when they learned he was seeking Utnapishtim, but they warned him that no one had ever found a way through the mountain.

Gilgamesh traveled the twelve miles through the mountain in pitch darkness, and at last he entered a garden. There he found Siduri, the cup-bearing goddess, who remarked on his haggard condition. Gilgamesh explained that his woeful appearance had been caused by the loss of Engidu, and that he sought Utnapishtim. The goddess advised him to live in pleasure at home and warned him of the dangers ahead.

Gilgamesh went on his way, seeking the boatman Ur-Shanabi, who might possibly take him across the waters of death. On finding Ur-Shanabi's stone coffers, Gilgamesh broke them in anger, but he made up for them by presenting the boatman with huge poles. Ur-Shanabi then ferried Gilgamesh across the waters of death.

Utnapishtim, meeting Gilgamesh on the shore, also spoke of his haggard condition. Gilgamesh told him about the loss of Engidu and his own search for the secret of life. Utnapishtim replied that nothing was made to last forever, that life was transient, and that death was part of the inevitable process.

Gilgamesh then asked how Utnapishtim had found the secret of eternal life, and Utnapishtim told him the story of the Great Flood.

Utnapishtim had been told in a dream of the gods' plans to flood the land. So he built an ark and put his family and all kinds of animals on it. When the flood came, he and those on the ark survived, and when the flood subsided he found himself on Mount Nisser. After the waters had returned to their normal level, he gave thanks to the gods, and in return the god Ea blessed him and his wife with the secret of life everlasting.

After finishing his story Utnapishtim advised Gilgamesh to return home, but before going he had Ur-Shanabi bathe and clothe Gilgamesh in a robe that remained clean as long as he lived. As Gilgamesh was leaving Utnapishtim gave him the secret of life, a magic plant which grew at the bottom of the waters of death. However, as Gilgamesh bathed in a pool on his way home, an evil serpent ate the plant.

On arriving home Gilgamesh went to Ninsun to inquire how he could reach Engidu in the land of the dead. Although Ninsun directed him, he failed in his attempt because he broke some of the taboos that she had laid out for him. Deeply disappointed, he made one final appeal to the god Ea, the lord of the depths of the waters, and Engidu was brought forth. Gilgamesh asked Engidu what happened to one after death, and Engidu laid bare the full terrors of the afterworld. Worms, neglect, and disrespect were the lot of the dead.

Critical Evaluation

The Epic of Gilgamesh belongs to that group of Ancient Near Eastern myths which may be termed "societal." Each nation had its societal myth to justify and sustain its particular social system and to fulfill several crucial functions: to validate prevailing social patterns, to provide rules and acceptable models for living, to supply divine sanction for the existing power structure, and to prove to the individual that the laws and customs of his country were superior of those of other countries. Thus the myth served the purpose of preserving the *status quo*. Particularly in the case of hero tales like the Gilgamesh epic, the heroes were models of proper and improper behavior whose feats dramatized just what should or should not be attempted. Through the events narrated in this chronicle of the life of King Gilgamesh, therefore, one may make several assumptions concerning the Babylonian social system which the tale was intended to substantiate.

The action in *The Epic of Gilgamesh* falls into three major phases of the hero's development. In the first phase, King Gilgamesh is a proud tyrant who rejects the concept of the king as a loving and concerned shepherd of his people; instead, he drives his subjects so cruelly that they petition the god Anu for relief. Since Gilgamesh is two-thirds god himself, a powerful chastisement is necessary, and Anu commissions the king's mother, the goddess Aruru, to create a foe powerful enough to fight with Gilgamesh and thus redirect his energies and interests. This creation—in many ways the sophisticated king's uncivilized alter ego—is named Engidu. After Engidu and Gilgamesh engage in a colossal battle of strength and endurance, they become inseparable friends, and the hero embarks on the second phase of his career. In this phase Gilgamesh rises above the level of pure selfishness and brute force and goes in search of romantic adventures which will bring meaning to his life and lasting fame to himself and his accepted brother. During the course of his adventures, Gilgamesh mocks and insults and goddess of love, Ishtar, and scornfully rejects her offer to become his lover, but escapes death at her hands because of his own divinity and great strength. Soon after, however, Engidu dies a slow and painful death, prompting Gilgamesh to undertake the final stage of his travels. In this stage, the hero, horrified at the terrible death of his friend and fearing a similar end for himself, departs on a journey to find immortality. This search ultimately terminates in failure when a serpent eats the plant of everlasting life which the hero has located on the bottom of the sea. After an interview with the spirit of Engidu in which his friend reveals to him that nothing awaits man after death but worms and mud, Gilgamesh reaches the conclusion that the only course left open for him is to return to his city of Uruk and fulfill his role of king and shepherd to his people.

The message conveyed through this societal myth is clear: if a heroic demigod cannot acquire immortality and is led to accept his ordained role, there is nothing for the humble Babylonian citizen to do but acknowledge the inevitability of death and likewise embrace the role assigned to him by the social system, no matter how lowly. And while the myth reinforces the Near Eastern belief that there is no life after death, it also offers some practical advice, through the words of a barmaid whom Gilgamesh meets on his travels, on how to make the most of this life:

> Make every day a day of joy.
> Dance, play, day and night . . .
> Cherish the child who grasps your hand.
> Let your wife rejoice in your bosom
> For this is the fate of man.

ESSAIS

Type of work: Essays
Author: Michel Eyquem de Montaigne (1533–1592)
First published: Books 1–II, 1580; I–II, revised, 1582; I–III, 1588; I–III, revised, 1595

Montaigne began his essays as a stoical humanist, continued them as a skeptic, and concluded them as a human being concerned with man. Substantially, this evolution is the one upon which Montaigne scholars are agreed. Surely these three phases of his thought are apparent in his *Essais*, for one may find, in these volumes, essays in which Montaigne considers how a man should face pain and die, such as "To Philosophize Is to Learn to Die"; essays in which the skeptical attack on dogmatism in philosophy and religion is most evident, such as the famous "Apology for Raimond Sebond"; and essays in which the writer makes a constructive effort to encourage men to know themselves and to act naturally for the good of all men, as in "The Education of Children."

Montaigne retired to his manor when he was thirty-eight. Public life had not satisfied him, and he was wealthy enough to live apart from the active life of his times and to give himself to contemplation and the writing of essays. He did spend some time in travel a few years later, and he was made mayor of Bordeaux, but most of his effort went into the writing and revision of his *Essais*, the attempt to essai, or test, the ideas which came to him.

An important essay in the first volume is "That the Taste for Good and Evil Depends in Good Part upon the Opinion We Have of Them." The essay begins with a paraphrase of a quotation from Epictetus to the effect that men are bothered more by opinions than by things. The belief that all human judgment is, after all, more a function of the human being than of the things judged suggested to Montaigne that by a change of attitude human beings could alter the values of things. Even death can be valued, provided the man who is about to die is of the proper disposition. Poverty and pain can also be good provided a person of courageous temperament develops a taste for them. Montaigne concludes that "things are not so painful and difficult of themselves, but our weakness or cowardice makes them so. To judge of great and high matters requires a suitable soul. . . ."

This stoical relativity is further endorsed in the essay "To Study Philosophy Is to Learn to Die." Montaigne's preoccupation with the problem of facing pain and death was caused by the death of his best friend, Etienne de la Boétie, who died in 1563 at the age of thirty-three, and then the deaths of his father, his brother, and several of his children. In addition, Montaigne was deeply disturbed by the Saint Bartholomew Day massacres. As a humanist, he was well educated in the literature and philosophy of the ancients, and from them he drew support

of the stoical philosophy suggested to him by the courageous death of his friend La Boétie.

The title of the essay is a paraphrase of Cicero's remark "that to study philosophy is nothing but to prepare one's self to die." For some reason, perhaps because it did not suit his philosophic temperament at the time, perhaps because he had forgotten it, Montaigne did not allude to a similar expression attributed by Plato to Socrates, the point then being that the philosopher is interested in the eternal, the unchanging, and that life is a preoccupation with the temporal and the variable. For Montaigne, however, the remark means either that the soul in contemplation removes itself from the body, so to speak, or that philosophy teaches us how to face death. It is the latter interpretation that interested him.

Asserting that we all aim at pleasure, even in virtue, Montaigne argued that the thought of death is naturally disturbing. He refers to the death of his brother, Captain St. Martin, who was killed at the age of twenty-three when he was struck behind the ear by a tennis ball. Other instances enforce his claim that death often comes unexpectedly to the young; for this reason the problem is urgent. With these examples before us, he writes, how can we "avoid fancying that death has us, every moment, by the throat?" The solution is to face death and fight it by becoming so familiar with the idea of death that we are no longer fearful. "The utility of living," he writes, "consists not in the length of days, but in the use of time. . . ." Death is natural, and what is important is not to waste life with the apprehension of death.

In the essay "Of Judging the Death of Another," Montaigne argues that a man reveals his true character when he shows how he faces a death which he knows is coming. A "studied and digested" death may bring a kind of delight to a man of the proper spirit. Montaigne cites Socrates and Cato as examples of men who knew how to die.

Montaigne's most famous essay is his "Apology for Raimond Sebond," generally considered to be the most complete and effective of his skeptical essays. Yet what Montaigne is skeptical of is not religion, as many critics have asserted, but of the pretensions of reason and of dogmatic philosophers and theologians. When Montaigne asks "Que sais-je?" the expression becomes the motto of his skepticism, "What do I know?"—not because he thinks that man should give up the use of the intellect and imagination, but because he thinks it wise to recognize the limits of these powers.

The essay is obstensibly in defense of the book entitled *Theologia naturalis: sive Liber creaturarum magistri Raimondi de Sebonde*, the work of a philosopher and theologian of Toulouse, who wrote the book about 1430.

Montaigne considers two principal objections to the book: the first, that Sebond is mistaken in the effort to support Christian belief upon human reasons; the second, that Sebond's arguments in support of Christian belief are so weak that they may easily be confuted. In commenting upon the first objection, Montaigne agrees that the truth of God can be known only through faith and God's assistance, yet Montaigne argues that Sebond is to be commended for his noble effort to use reason in the service of God. If one considers Sebond's arguments as an aid to faith, they may be viewed as useful guides.

Montaigne's response to the second objection takes up most of the essay, and since the work is, in some editions, over two hundred pages long, we may feel justified in concluding from length alone the intensity of Montaigne's conviction. Montaigne uses the bulk of his essay to argue against those philosophers who suppose that by reason alone man can find truth and happiness. The rationalists who attack Sebond do not so much damage the theologian as show their own false faith in the value of reason. Montaigne considers "a man alone, without foreign assistance, armed only with his own proper arms, and unfurnished of the divine grace and wisdom . . ." and he sets forth to show that such a man is not only miserable and ridiculous but grievously mistaken in his presumption. Philosophers who attempt to reason without divine assistance gain nothing from their efforts except knowledge of their own weakness. Yet that knowledge has some value; ignorance is then not absolute ignorance. Nor is it any solution for the philosopher to adopt the stoical attitude and try to rise above humanity, as Seneca suggests; paradoxically, the only way to rise is by accepting suffering and the common lot of humankind with a spirit of Christian faith.

In the essay "Of the Education of Children," Montaigne writes that the only objective he had in writing the essays was to discover himself. In giving his opinions concerning the education of children Montaigne shows how the study of himself took him from the idea of philosophy as a study of what is "grim and formidable" to the idea of philosophy as a way to the health and cheerfulness of mind and body. He claims that "The most manifest sign of wisdom is a continual cheerfulness," and that "the height and value of true virtue consists in the facility, utility, and pleasure of its exercise. . . ." Philosophy is "that which instructs us to live." The aim of education is to lead the child so that he will come to love nothing but the good, and the way to this objective is an education that takes advantage of the youth's appetites and affections. Though his love of books led Montaigne to live in such a manner that he was accused of slothfulness and "want of mettle," he justifies his education by pointing out that this is the worst men can say of him.

Not all of Montaigne's essays reflect the major stages of his transformation from stoic and skeptic to a man of good will. Like Bacon, he found satisfaction in working out his ideas concerning the basic experiences of life. Thus he wrote of sadness, of constancy, of fear, of friendship (with particular reference to La Boétie), of moderation, of solitude, of sleep, of names, of books. These essays are lively, imaginative, and informed with the knowledge of a gentleman well trained in the classics. Yet it is when he writes of pain and death, referring to his own long struggle with kidney stones and to the deaths of those he loved, and when he writes of his need for faith and of man's need for self-knowledge, that we are most moved. In such essays the great stylist, the educated thinker, and the struggling human being are one. It was in the essaying of himself that Montaigne became a great essayist.

AN ESSAY CONCERNING HUMAN UNDERSTANDING

Type of work: Philosophical treatise
Author: John Locke (1632–1704)
First published: 1690

Locke's purpose in *An Essay Concerning Human Understanding* was to inquire into the origin and extent of human knowledge, and his answer—that all knowledge is derived from sense experience—became the principal tenet of the new empiricism which has dominated Western philosophy ever since. Even George Berkeley (1685–1753), who rejected Locke's distinction between sense qualities independent of the mind and sense qualities dependent on the mind, proposed an idealistic philosophy in response to Locke's provocative philosophy and gave it an empirical cast which reflected Western man's rejection of innate or transcendental knowledge.

An Essay Concerning Human Understanding is divided into four books: Book I, "Of Innate Notions"; Book II, "Of Ideas"; Book III, "Of Words"; and Book IV, "Of Knowledge, Certain and Probable."

In preparation for his radical claim that all ideas are derived from experience, Locke began his *Essay* with a careful consideration of the thesis that there are innate ideas, that is, ideas which are a necessary part of man's convictions and are, therefore, common to all men. Locke's attack on this claim is from two directions. He argues that many of the ideas which are supposed to be innate can be and have been derived naturally from sense experience, that not all men assent to those ideas which are supposed to be innate. He maintained that even if reason enables men to discover the truth of certain ideas, those ideas cannot be said to be innate; for reason is needed to discover their truth.

In Book II, "Of Ideas," Locke considers the origin of such ideas as those expressed by the words "whiteness," "hardness," "sweetness," "thinking," "motion," "man," and the like. The second section states his answer.

Let us then suppose the mind to be, as we say, white paper void of all characters, without any ideas. How comes it to be furnished? . . . Whence has it all the *materials* of reason and knowledge? To this I answer, in one word, from *experience*. . . . Our observation, employed either about *external sensible objects, or about the internal operations of our minds perceived and reflected on by ourselves, is that which supplies our understandings with all the materials of knowledge.*

The two sources of our ideas, according to Locke, are *sensation* and *reflection*. By the senses we come to have perceptions of things, thereby acquiring the ideas of yellow, white, cold, for example. Then, by reflection, by consideration of the mind in operation, we acquire the ideas of thinking, doubting, believing, knowing, willing, and so on. By sensation we acquire knowledge of external objects; by reflection we acquire knowledge of our own minds.

Ideas that are derived from sensation are simple; that is, they present "one uniform appearance," even though a number of simple ideas may come together in the perception of an external object. The mind dwells on the simple ideas, comparing them to each other, combining them, but never inventing them. By a "simple idea" Locke meant what some modern and contemporary philosophers have called a "sense-datum," a distinctive, entirely differentiated item of sense experience, such as the odor of some particular glue, or the taste of coffee in a cup. He called attention to the fact that we use our sense experience to imagine what we have never perceived, but no operation of the mind can yield novel simple ideas.

By the "quality" of something Locke meant its power to produce an idea in someone sensing the thing. The word "quality" is used in the *Essay* in much the same way the word "characteristic" or "property" has been used by other, more recent, writers, for Locke distinguished between primary and secondary qualities. Primary qualities are those which matter has constantly, whatever its state. As primary qualities Locke names solidity, extension, figure, motion or rest, and number. By secondary qualities Locke meant the power to produce various sensations which have nothing in common with the primary qualities of the external objects. Thus, the power to produce the taste experience of sweetness is a secondary quality of sugar, but there is no reason to suppose that the sugar itself possesses the distinctive quality of the sensation. Colors, tastes, sounds, and odors are secondary qualities of objects.

Locke also referred to a third kind of quality or power, called simply "power," by which he meant the capacity to affect or to be affected by other objects. Thus, fire can melt clay; the capacity to melt clay is one of fire's powers, and such a power is neither a primary nor a secondary quality.

Locke concluded that primary ideas resemble external objects, but secondary ideas do not. It is this particular claim which has excited other professional philosophers, with Berkeley arguing that primary qualities can be understood only in terms of our own sensations, so that whatever generalization can be made about secondary qualities would have to cover primary qualities as well, and other philosophers arguing that Locke had no ground for maintaining that primary ideas "resemble" primary qualities, even if the distinction between primary and secondary qualities is allowed.

Complex ideas result from acts of the mind, and they fall into three classes: ideas of modes, of substances, and of relations. *Modes* are ideas that are considered to be incapable of independent existence since they are affections of substance, such as the ideas of triangle, gratitude, and murder. To think of *substances* is to think of "particular things subsisting by themselves," and to think in that manner involves supposing that there is a support, which cannot be understood, and that there are various qualities in combination which give various substances their distinguishing traits. Ideas of *relations* are the result of comparing ideas with each other.

After a consideration of the complex ideas of space, duration, number, the infinite, pleasure and pain, substance, relation, cause and effect, and of the distinctions between clear and obscure ideas and between true and false ideas, Locke proceeded to a discussion, in Book III, of words and essences. Words are signs of ideas by "arbitrary imposition," depending upon observed similarities which are taken as the basis for considering things in classes. Words are related to "nominal essences," that is, to obvious similarities found through observation, and not to "real essences," the actual qualities of things. Locke then discussed the imperfections and abuses of words.

In Book IV Locke defined knowledge as "the perception of the connection of and agreement, or disagreement and repugnancy, of any of our ideas." An example cited is our knowledge that white is not black, Locke arguing that to know that white is not black is simply to perceive that the idea of white is not the idea of black.

Locke insisted that knowledge cannot extend beyond the ideas we have, and that we determine whether ideas agree or disagree with each other either directly, by intuition, or indirectly, by reason or sensation. Truth is defined as "the joining or separating of signs, as the things signified by them do agree or disagree one with another." For example, the proposition "White is not black" involves the separation by "is not" of the signs "white" and "black," signifying the disagreement between the ideas of white and black. Since the ideas are different, the proposition is true. Actually to have compared the ideas and to have noted their disagreement is to know the fact which the true proposition signifies.

Locke devoted the remaining chapters of Book IV to arguing that we have knowledge of our existence by intuition, of the existence of God by demonstration, and of other things by sensation. Here the influence of Descartes is clearly evident. But it is the empiricism of the earlier parts of the book which won for Locke the admiration of philosophers.

ESSAY ON MAN

Type of work: Philosophical verse essay
Author: Alexander Pope (1688–1744)
First published: 1733–1734

Pope's *Essay on Man* stands as the intellectual landmark of the eighteenth century because it embodies the cosmological, theological, and ethical thought of its age. Heavily influenced by Pope's friend Lord Bolingbroke, whose philosophy was congenial to Pope, the *Essay on Man* actually sums up the leading principles of the time, principles whose origins may be traced to Plato, Aristotle, Leibnitz, and others, but which were commonplace ideas by Pope's day. Arthur Lovejoy's *The Great Chain of Being* provides the essential background for a thorough understanding of the traditions upon which Pope drew.

The central conception of this poem rests, however, upon the ideas of plenitude, gradation, and continuity. Plenitude, for Pope, meant the overwhelming fullness of creation, of a universe inhabited by all possible essences created by God out of His own goodness. The abundance and variety of creation is also marked by gradation, the notion that there exists a graduated chain or rank among creation, moving from the lowest created thing up to God. This chain implies, of course, subordination of lower creatures to higher because each step up the ladder marks a slight variation upon the preceding step. Thus man is superior by virtue of his reason to lower beings. The ordered harmony of the entire creation depends upon the proper ordering of parts. Continuity, this ordered continuum of creation, is for Pope the principle of social and divine love which ties together all forms of creation in measured rule.

Epistle I explains the relationship of man to the universe. Man's knowledge of the universe must be limited to this world only; however, because evil exists on earth, we should not question God's ways or His justice. It is enough to know that God, because of His infinite goodness, created a perfect system and that man is merely a small part of the gigantic whole. God created the universe in one vast chain; somewhere along this chain man's place may be found. The imperfections in his nature man pretends to find are not really imperfections, for God created man suited to his place and rank in creation. Our happiness here consists in two things: our ignorance of the future and our hope for better things in the future. "Hope springs eternal in the human breast:/ Man never Is, but always to be blest."

Man's chief error is his pride which causes him to aspire to be better than he is, to question Providence about the fitness of things. Such pride inverts the real order since we are the judged, not the judges. We must not presume to doubt the justice of God's dispensations.

Another error is that man sees himself wrongly as the final cause of all creation, as though all nature exists to serve him alone.

Equally unjust is our wish for the strength of wild beasts or the power of angels, because God made the earth and all its inhabitants in a graduated scale; at the bottom are the lowest of creatures, man stands in the middle, and above men are multitudes of angels and, finally, God.

> Vast chain of Being! which from God began,
> Natures ethereal, human, angel, man,
> Beast, bird, fish, insect, what no eye can see,
> No glass can reach; from Infinite to thee,
> From thee to Nothing.

Each animal is subordinated to the ranks above and superior to those below. Man, by virtue of his reason, rules all creation below, but he is not of ethereal substance, as an angel is, and does not possess angelic power. Therefore it is absurd to claim another's place since each is a part of the whole ordained by God. To break this vast chain at any point would destroy the whole and violate God's plan. Man should not view creation as imperfect because he can envision only a part of it. His middle place on the scale implies a limited perception of the complete plan, and what he sees as evil is actually from God's larger vision, partial evil contributing ultimately to His universal good.

> All partial Evil, universal Good:
> And, spite of Pride, in erring Reason's spite,
> One truth is clear, WHATEVER IS, IS RIGHT.

Epistle II discusses the nature and state of man as an individual whose tragic situation is that he is in this middle state, both god and beast, both spirit and body. In human nature two principles, self-love and reason, operate often at odds with one another. Neither is entirely good or bad; when each does its function properly and works in conjunction with the other, good results occur. Pope compares these two principles to the mechanism of a watch; within men self-love is the spring, reason the balance wheel. Without one man could not act; without the other action would be aimless. Without self-love men would vegetate; without reason men would consume themselves in lawless passion. Self-love motives, inspires, while reason checks, advises. Self-love judges by present good and reason by future consequences. Reason through time acquires power to control impulsive self-love.

The passions are modes of self-love and are good as long as they conform to reason's dictates. The Ruling Passion, often dominates all others and determines the character of a man. No virtue arising from any passion can be wholly without value if subdued, as lust may be turned to gentle love, anger to zeal.

Although man possesses both vice and virtue, Heaven compensates by converting individual defects into the strength of all. Our weaknesses motivate mutual reliance. And since each man is given his due portion of happiness and misery no one should wish to exchange his state for another's. Each should rest content with his own lot.

Epistle III discusses the role of man in society. Pope sees the whole universe as one comprehensive society, a complex system of interrelations cementing all creation. Each part relates to others but rank in the chain of being confers power and control over inferior ranks. But with rule comes responsibility, and man, the imperial race, must care for his underlings as God cares for him.

Whether ruled by animal instinct or human reason, each enjoys that power best suited to his place. Although God set the necessary bounds for each species, alloting to each its particular share of happiness, his design ensures the happiness of the whole rather than of the part. The happiness of all depends upon maintaining the proper relations among the individuals; each should love itself and others.

In the primitive state of society, self-love and social love existed. Man's reason then learned useful rules from instinct. Reason observed principles of government from monarchical bees and republican ants. Man constructed his own cities and societies and soon common interest suggested the need for a ruler, who was chosen for his virtues in learning and arms. True religion and government were united in love. Superstition and tyranny arose to invert nature's order, but man's self-love taught him to protect his interests by erecting governments and laws, finding private good in public. Self-love directed to social love returned general social harmony. It is this charity that renders particular forms of government and religion unessential, for charity always seeks the happiness of all, linking self-love with social love, enlisting all ranks of

creation into a harmonious order.

Epistle IV views man in relation to happiness. Since God works by general laws, he intends all to be happy, not merely a few. Because order is Heaven's first law, there can be only one result: that some beings will be greater than others. Yet, if Heaven intended all to be equally happy, to be greater is not to be happier. True happiness is not located in external condition or possessions. God compensates those who lack them with hope for the future; those who have them fear the future.

Individual bliss on earth rests on three possessions: health, peace, and competence. To good or bad men fortune may bestow its blessings, but gifts of fortune dispose the individual as he obtains them to enjoy them less. In achieving bliss the virtuous man has most advantages. We must not impute injustice to God because the virtuous man often finds calamities his reward for virtue. Calamity occurs through fortune or natural law; God does not dispense with his laws merely to favor a special person. Virtue, moreover, is not rewarded with material gifts.

Virtue's reward is not earthly and external. Its reward resides in the peace and joy of the heart. Earthly recompense would either be disdained as unworthy or would destroy the very virtue that prompted it. No shame or honor arises from one's station in life. True honor comes from faithful employment of one's responsibility. It is character that distinguishes a man, not his worldly fortune or fame. History teaches that those who attained worldly prizes frequently paid dearly for them. What deeds made the hero often corrupted the man.

Only true virtue is happiness. It is the sole thing a man may possess without loss to himself. Heaven's bliss is bestowed on him who avoids the extremism of sect and who observes in the creation the presence of God and the divine chain that links all to God. Such a man knows that true happiness belongs not to the individual but to the whole creation, that the source of all faith, law, morality, and happiness is love of God and of man. Self-love, transcending self in pursuing social love and divine, showers blessings upon all things. Self-love awakens the virtuous mind, and like a pebble dropped into water, stirring ripples on the surface, ever embraces wider and wider spheres, from friend, to parent, to neighbor, until it encompasses all living creation.

THE ESSAYS OF EMERSON

Type of work: Philosophical essays
Author: Ralph Waldo Emerson (1803–1882)
First published: First Series, 1841; Second Series, 1844

Emerson's *Essays* proclaim the self-reliance of a man who believed himself representative of all men since he felt himself intuitively aware of God's universal truths. He spoke to a nineteenth century that was ready for an emphasis on individualism and responsive to a new optimism that linked God, nature, and man into a magnificent cosmos.

Emerson himself spoke as one who had found in Transcendentalism a positive answer to the static Unitarianism of his day. He had been a Unitarian minister for three years at the Old North Church in Boston (1829-1832), but he had resigned because in his view the observance of the Lord's Supper could not be justified in the Unitarian Church.

Transcendentalism combined Neoplatonism, a mystical faith in the universality and permanence of value in the universe, with a pervasive moral seriousness akin to the Calvinist conviction and with a Romantic optimism that found evidence of God's love throughout all nature. Derivative from these influences was the faith in man's creative power, the belief that the individual, by utilizing God's influence, could continue to improve his understanding and his moral nature. Knowledge could come to man directly, without the need of argument, if only he had the courage to make himself receptive to God's truth, manifest everywhere.

Through his essays and addresses, Emerson became not only the leading Transcendentalist in America but also one of the greatest of American philosophers. The latter accomplishment may be attributed more to the spirit of his philosophy than to its technical excellence, for Emerson had little respect for logic, empiricism, and linguistic analysis—features common to the work of other great American philosophers such as Charles Sanders Peirce, William James, and John Dewey. Nor can Emerson be compared in his method to such a philosopher as Alfred North Whitehead, for Emerson disdained speculative adventures: he believed himself to be affirming what nature told him, and nature spoke directly of God and of God's laws.

Emerson's *Nature* (1836) was the first definitive statement of his philosophical perspective, and within this work may be found most of the characteristic elements of Emerson's thought. The basic idea is that nature is God's idea made apparent to men. Thus, "the whole of nature is a metaphor of the human mind." Moreover, "the axioms of physics translate the laws of ethics," and "This relation between the mind and matter is not fancied by some poet, but stands in the will of God, and so is free to be known by all men." Emerson asserted emphatically that "day and night, river and storm, beast and bird, acid and alkali, preexist in necessary Ideas in the mind of God"; hence he agreed with those who supposed that nature reveals spiritual and moral truths. Not only does nature reveal truths; it also disciplines men, rewarding them when nature is used properly, punishing them when it is abused.

One secret of Emerson's charm was his ability to translate metaphysical convictions into vivid images. Having argued that nature is the expression of God's idea, and having concluded that "The moral law lies at the center of nature and radiates to the circumference," he illustrated the moral influence of nature by asking, "Who can guess how much firmness the sea-beaten rock has taught the fishermen?" The danger in Emerson's method, however, was that readers tended to forget that his idealism was philosophically, not merely poetically, intended; he believed literally that only spirit and its ideas are real. He admitted the possibility that nature "outwardly exists," that is, that physical objects corresponding to his sensations exist, but he pointed out that since he was not able to test the authenticity of his senses, it made no difference whether such outlying objects existed. All that he could be sure of was his ideas, and these ideas, whether directly or indirectly, came from God. For Emerson, then, idealism was not only a credible philosophy, but also the only morally significant one.

If nature is God's idea made apparent to men, it follows that the way to God's truth is not by reason or argument but by simple and reverent attention to the facts of nature, to what man perceives when his eye is innocent. Emerson criticized science not because it was useless but because more important matters, those having a moral bearing, confronted man at every moment in the world of nature; the individual needed only to intuit nature, to see it as it was without twisting it to fit his philosophy or his science, in order to know God's thoughts. Thus, in the essay "Nature" Emerson wrote that "Nature is the incarnation of a thought, and turns to a thought again. . . . The world is mind precipitated. . . ." He added, with assurance, "Every moment instructs, and every object; for wisdom is infused into every form."

The ideas which Emerson had endorsed in *Nature* found explicit moral application in the address titled "The American Scholar," delivered before the Phi Beta Kappa Society at Cambridge in 1837. Emerson defined the scholar as "Man Thinking," and he declared that the main influences of the scholar's education are nature, books, and action. The duties of a scholar all involve self-trust; he must be both free and brave. The rewards of such freedom and bravery are inspiring: the mind is altered by the truths uncovered, and the whole world will come to honor the independent scholar. It was in this address that Emerson said that "the ancient precept, 'Know thyself,' and the modern precept, 'Study nature,' become at last one maxim."

The essay "Self-Reliance," included in the First Series, emphasizes the importance of that self-trust to which Emerson referred in his Phi Beta Kappa address. It is understandable that this emphasis seemed necessary to Emerson. If nature reveals the moral truths which God intends for man's use, then three elements are involved in the critical human situation: nature, man, and man's attitude toward nature. It is possible to be blind to the truths about us; only the man who is courageous enough to be willing to be different in his search and convictions is likely to discover what is before every man's eyes. Emerson emphasized self-reliance not because he regarded the self, considered as a separate entity, important, but because he believed that the self is part of the reality of God's being and that in finding truth for oneself, provided one faces nature intuitively, one finds what is true for all men. "To believe your own thought, to believe that what is true for you in your private heart is true for all men—that is genius," Emerson wrote in "Self-Reliance"; he added that it is a kind of genius that is possible for anyone who is willing to acquire it.

Believing that each man's mind is capable of yielding important truth, Emerson distinguished between goodness and the name of goodness. He urged each man to work and act without being concerned about the mere opinions of others. "Whoso would be a man, must be a nonconformist," and whoever would advance in the truth should be willing to contradict himself, to be inconsistent: "A foolish consistency is the hobgoblin of little minds, adored by little statesmen and philosophers and divines."

That Emerson's philosophy was not an endorsement of selfish behavior is clear from his emphasis upon the use of the mind as an instrument for the intuitive understanding of universal truths and laws, but it is possible to misinterpret "Self-Reliance" as a joyous celebration of individuality. A sobering balance is achieved by the essay "The Over-Soul," in which Emerson subordinates the individual to the whole: "Meantime within man is the soul of the whole . . . the eternal One." Using language reminiscent of Platonism, Emerson wrote that the soul "gives itself, alone, original and pure, to the Lonely, Original and Pure, who, on that condition, gladly inhabits, leads and speaks through it."

Emerson valued the poet because the poet uses his imagination to discern the meanings of sensuous facts. The poet sees and expresses the beauty in nature because he recognizes the spiritual meaning of events; he takes old symbols and gives them new uses, thereby making nature the sign of God. In the essay "The Poet," Emerson wrote that the poet's insight is "a very high sort of seeing," a way of transcending conventional modes of thought in order to attend directly to the forms of things.

It is a misunderstanding of Emerson to regard him as a sentimental mystic, as one who lay on his back and saw divinity in every cloud. Emerson's transcendental insight is more akin to the intelligence of the Platonic philosopher who, having recognized his own ignorance, suddenly finds himself able to see the universal in the jumble of particular facts. Emerson may be criticized for never satisfactorily relating the life of contemplation to the life of practical affairs, but he cannot be dismissed as an iconoclastic mystic. For him the inquiring soul and the heroic soul were one, and the justification of self-reliance and meditation was in terms of the result, in the individual soul, of the effort to recognize the unity of all men. In "Experience," Emerson chooses knowing in preference to doing, but it is clear that he was rejecting a thoughtless interest in action and results. In "Character" and again in "Politics," he emphasized the importance of coming to have the character of transcending genius, of spirit which has found moral law in nature and has adapted it for use in the world of men. The transforming power of spirit properly educated and employed was something Emerson counted on, and he was concerned to argue that such power is not easily achieved.

Emerson defended democracy as the form of government best fitted for Americans, whose religion and tradition reflect a desire to allow the judgments of citizens to be expressed in the laws of the state. But he cautioned that "Every actual State is corrupt," and added, "Good men must not obey the laws too well." Here the independent spirit, concerned with the laws of God, demands heroism and possibly, like Thoreau, civil disobedience.

Scholars have written innumerable articles and books attempting to account for Emerson's influence—which continues to be profound—on American thought. If agreement is ever reached, it seems likely that it will involve acceptance of the claim that Emerson, whatever his value as a philosopher, gave stirring expression to the American faith in the creative capacity of the individual soul.

THE ESSAYS OF THOREAU

Author: Henry David Thoreau (1817–1862)
First published: From 1842 to after Thoreau's death

To the nonspecialist, Thoreau's significant works could be numbered on the fingers of both hands. Of these undoubtedly the first to come to mind would be *Walden*, his most famous book, and perhaps *A Week on the Concord and Merimack Rivers*. But almost as famous and perhaps even more influential have been several of his essays, which were written on various occasions for different purposes, and generally on rather widely ranging subjects. More than his two famous books, his essays vary in quality from the nearly banal to the profound, from the useless to the useful. To the reader genuinely interested in the life and writings of one of America's greatest and most influential writers—as well as perhaps our most outstanding true Transcendentalist—all his works are fascinating. But since many do concern closely related subjects and treat these topics in a similar manner, a selection of the works can give the heart of the essays.

Thoreau's earliest essay, possibly, is one named "The Seasons," written when he was only eleven or twelve years old. As would be expected, it is of importance only to the close specialist. There are also in existence at least twenty-eight essays and four book reviews that Thoreau wrote while a student at Harvard. These, too, are of greater interest to the student interested in the young Harvardian than to the readers looking for the Thoreau of mature ideas and style.

His first published essay was "Natural History of Massachusetts," printed in 1842. This work does more than promise the later man. It is, in fact, the mature thinker and observer already arrived. Drawn chiefly from entries in his journals, which he had begun to keep after graduation from Harvard in 1837, it reveals his characteristics of Transcendentalism and his keen eye for observation, an eye that was to make him acclaimed by many people as one of America's best early scientists. It reveals Thoreau's pleasure in viewing the world around him and his detachment from the world of men. He believes, for example, that one does not find health in society but in the world of nature. To live and prosper, a person must stand with feet firmly planted in nature. He believes, also, that society is corrupting, is inadequate for man's spiritual needs; when considered as members of a society, especially a political organization, men are "degraded." As a scientist, Thoreau catalogues many aspects of natural phenomena in Massachusetts; he notes, for example, that 280 birds live permanently in that state or summer there or visit it passingly.

Among Thoreau's best essays is another early one, "A Winter Walk," published in 1843, the material of which was taken mainly from his journal for 1841. As was generally the case with Thoreau, this essay is lyrical and ecstatic, the lyricism being augmented by the inclusion of various bits of Thoreau's own poetry. Thematically the essay is strung on a long walk on a winter's day and the observations and meditations of the author as he progresses. Both his observations and meditations are mature, virtually as vivid and sound as those given in the later *Walden*. His reactions to the physical walk are immediate and sharply detailed. He likes to walk through the "powdery snow," and he feels that man should live closer to nature in order to appreciate life fully. In a Wordsworthian-pantheistic point of view, he feels that plants and animals and men, if they would conform, find in nature only a "constant nurse and friend."

Thoreau's most famous essay is "Resistance to Civil Government," published in 1849 and renamed, after Thoreau's death, "Civil Disobedience," the title by which it is known today. As is often the case, this essay grew directly from an experience by the author, this time Thoreau's one-night imprisonment for nonpayment of his taxes, taxes which he claimed would go to finance the Mexican War and were therefore, in his mind, immoral. The influence of this essay has been profound, far-reaching, and long-lasting. It served Gandhi as a guidebook in his campaign to free India from British rule; it also served the British Labour party in England during its early days; it offered model and hope for the European resistance against Nazi Germany, and it has aided, more recently, the struggle for civil rights in the South.

The essay is a bristling and defiant reaffirmation of the individualism of man, of his moral obligation to restate his individualism and to act on it. Government, any government, is at best an expediency. Thoreau heartily accepts the precept "That government is best which governs least," a thesis which logically leads to the conclusion "That government is best which governs not at all." Government, however, still exists, but it is not unchangeable: "A single man can bend it to his will." Government, in Thoreau's eyes, was far from pure and beneficent. He felt that he could not have as his government those institutions which enslaved certain races and colors. Therefore he felt compelled to resist his government. He felt that ten men—even one—could abolish slavery in America if they would allow themselves to go to prison for their belief and practice. Men of goodwill must unite. Every good man must constitute a majority of one to resist tyranny and evil. Democracy may not be the ultimate in systems of government, he concludes, in a ringing statement of man's political position: "There will never be a really free and enlightened State, until the State comes to recognize the individual as a higher and independent power, from which all its own power and authority are derived, and treats him accordingly."

One of Thoreau's notable essays is "A Plea for Captain John Brown," published in 1860, one of three on the same person, the other two being "After the Death of John Brown," delivered at the Concord memorial services for Brown, held the day the raider of Harper's Ferry was hanged, and "The Last Days of John Brown," written for a memorial service on July 4, 1860. The earliest essay of the three justifies the actions of Brown because generally he tried to put Thoreau's convictions into action.

"Walking," published in 1862, was taken from his journal written some ten years earlier and used as material for lectures in the early 1850s. It is an enthusiastic reaction to the joys of walking, "for absolute freedom and wildness," in which Thoreau in effect boasts that the course of progress is always westward, drawn probably from the mere fact, as has been pointed out, that around Concord the best walking country was to the southwest. Extremely lyrical, the essay sometimes surfaces into sheer nonsense, as in the statement that "Above all, we cannot afford not to live in the present. He is blessed over all other mortals who loses no moment of the passing life in remembering the past." Such comments caused a more deeply dedicated thinker, Herman Melville, to react with great scorn and frequently to satirize Thoreau's easy optimism.

"Life Without Principle," published more than a year after Thoreau's death in 1863, was likewise drawn from the journals during the author's most powerful decade, in the early 1850s. Delivered in 1854 as "Getting a Living," it is a ringing statement on the dignity and real worth of the individual, of the man. It is the voice of the self-reliant man calling all individuals to the assertion of their self-reliance so that they can live like men and live

fully. Thoreau feels that most men misspend their lives, especially those who are concerned merely with getting money: "The ways by which you may get money almost without exception lead downward. To have done anything by which you earned money *merely* is to have been truly idle or worse." To be born wealthy is disastrous—as he says in one of his pithy statements—it is rather "to be stillborn." The wise man cannot be tempted by money. He must be free, as Thoreau was convinced, feeling that his "connection with and obligation to society are still very slight and transient."

The world must be composed of individuals and must live not for the moment but for eternity. "Read not the Times. Read the Eternities." America must reform. "Even if we grant that the American has freed himself from a political tyrant, he is still the slave of an economical and moral tyrant." In other ways America has not lived up to her potential. She is not the land of the free. "What is it to be free from King George and continue to be the slaves of King Prejudice? What is it to be born free and not to live free?"

The everyday routines of life are necessary, to be sure, but they should be "unconsciously performed, like the corresponding functions of the physical body" so that the mind—the better parts of men—can rise to the greater and noble aspects of living so that they will not discover at death that life has been wasted.

This essay is Thoreau at his best. He is characteristically the Transcendentalist, the individualist, voicing his opinion without reserve, pithily and most tellingly. Thoreau was perhaps more than other nineteenth century American writer circumscribed in his subjects for writing. Therefore his essays are repetitious. He liked to brag that he was widely traveled in Concord. But, though perhaps narrow in breadth, Thoreau's writings are shafts reaching to the essence of man's being. And a half dozen essays represent him truthfully and succinctly.

ETHAN FROME

Type of work: Novel
Author: Edith Wharton (1862–1937)
Type of plot: Domestic tragedy
Locale: Late nineteenth century
First published: 1911

Unrepresentative though it is of Wharton's works, Ethan Frome *is the most critically acclaimed and most popular. Wharton's terse depiction of Ethan's wasted talents and passions becomes a cynical fable describing the triumph of a trivial, conventional society over the ambitious, creative individual.*

Principal Characters

Ethan Frome, a farmer frustrated in his ambition to become an engineer or a chemist and in his marriage to a nagging, sour, sickly wife. He falls in love with his wife's good and lovely cousin, Mattie Silver, who comes to live with them. When his wife finally drives the girl away, Ethan insists on taking her to the station. Ethan and Mattie decide to take a sleigh ride they have promised themselves, and, in mutual despair over the impending separation, they resolve to kill themselves by running the sled against a tree. Yet they are not killed, only permanently injured, and Ethan's wife is to look after them for the rest of their lives.

Zenobia Pierce Frome (Zeena), Ethan's wife, a distant cousin who nursed his mother during a long illness. The marriage is loveless, and Zeena is sickly and nagging.

Mattie Silver, Zeena's cousin, who comes to live with the Fromes. She returns Ethan's love. Once when Zeena spends a night away from home, she and Ethan spend a happy evening together, not making love but sitting quietly before the fire, as Ethan imagines happily married couples do. Mattie feels that she would rather die than leave Ethan, but in the crash she suffers not death but a permanent spinal injury. She must submit thereafter to being nursed by Zeena.

Ruth Varnum and **Ned Hale,** a young engaged couple whom Ethan observes stealing a kiss. On his night alone with Mattie he tells her wistfully about it; it is as close as he comes to making advances.

The Story

Ethan Frome was twenty-one years old when he married Zenobia Pierce, a distant cousin who nursed his sick mother during her last illness. It was a wedding without love. Zenobia, called Zeena, had no home of her own, and Ethan was lonely, so they were married. Zeena's talkativeness, which had been pleasing to Ethan during his mother's illness, quickly subsided, however, and within a year of their marriage Zeena developed the sickliness that was to plague her husband all her life. Ethan became increasingly dissatisfied with his life. He was an intelligent and ambitious young man who had hoped to become an engineer or a chemist, yet he found himself chained to a wife he detested and a farm he could not sell.

The arrival of Mattie Silver brightened the gloomy house considerably. Mattie, Zeena's cousin, had come to Starkfield partly because she had no other place to go and partly because Zeena felt in need of a companion around the house. Ethan saw in Mattie's goodness and beauty every fine quality that Zeena lacked.

When Zeena suggested that Ethan help Mattie find a husband, he began to realize how much he was attracted to the girl. When he went to a church social to bring Mattie home and saw her dancing with the son of a rich Irish grocer, he realized that he was jealous. On his way home with her, Ethan felt his love for Mattie more than ever, for on that occasion as on others, she flattered him by asking him questions about astronomy. His dreams of happiness were short-lived, however, for when he reached home, Zeena was her nagging, sour self. The contrast between Zeena and Mattie impressed him more and more.

One day, Ethan returned from his morning's work to find Zeena dressed in her traveling clothes. She was going to visit a new doctor in nearby Bettsbridge. Ordinarily, Ethan would have objected to the journey because of the expensive remedies that Zeena was in the habit of buying on such trips. On this occasion, however, he was overjoyed at the news of Zeena's proposed departure, for he realized that he and Mattie would have the house to themselves overnight.

With Zeena out of the way, Ethan became a changed man. Later in the evening, before supper, Ethan and Mattie sat quietly before the fire, just as Ethan imagined happily married couples would do. During supper, the cat broke Zeena's favorite pickle dish, which Mattie had used to brighten the table. In spite of the accident, they spent the rest of the evening happily. They talked about going sledding together, and Ethan told shyly—and perhaps wistfully—how he had seen Ruth Varnum and Ned Hale, a young engaged couple, stealing a kiss earlier in the evening.

In the morning Ethan was happy, but not because of anything out of the ordinary the night before. In fact, when he went to bed, he remembered sadly that he had not so much as touched Mattie's fingertips or looked into her eyes. He was happy because he could imagine what a wonderful life he would have if he were married to Mattie. He got glue to mend the pickle dish, but Zeena's unexpected return prevented him from repairing it. His spirits were further dampened when Zeena told him that the Bettsbridge doctor considered her quite sick. He had advised her to hire someone to relieve her of all household duties, someone stronger than Mattie. She had already engaged the new girl. Ethan was dumbfounded by this development. In her insistence that Mattie be sent away, Zeena gave the first real hint that she might have been aware of gossip about her husband and Mattie.

When Ethan told Mattie of Zeena's decision, the girl was as crestfallen as Ethan. Zeena interrupted their lamentations, however, by coming downstairs for something to eat. After supper, she required stomach powders to relieve a case of heartburn. In getting the powders, which she had hidden in a spot supposedly unknown to Mattie, Zeena discovered the broken pickle dish, which had been carefully reassembled in order to give the appearance of being unbroken. Having detected the deception and learned that Mattie was responsible for the broken dish, Zeena called Mattie insulting names and showed plainly that the girl would be sent away at the earliest possible moment.

Faced with the certainty of Mattie's departure, Ethan thought of running away with her. Yet his poverty, as well as his sense of responsibility to Zeena, offered no solution to his problem, only greater despair. On the morning Mattie was to leave Starkfield, Ethan, against the wishes of his wife, insisted on driving Mattie to the station. The thought of parting was unbearable to both. They decided to take the sleigh ride that Ethan had promised Mattie the night before. Down the hill they went, narrowly missing a large elm tree at the bottom. Mattie, who had told Ethan that she would rather die than leave him, begged until Ethan agreed to take her down the hill a second time and run the sled into the elm. They failed, however, to hit the tree with force sufficient to kill them. The death they sought became a living death, for in the accident Mattie suffered a permanent spinal injury and Ethan an incurable lameness. The person who then received Mattie into her home, who waited on her, and who cooked for Ethan was—Zeena.

Critical Evaluation

When Edith Wharton wrote the introduction to an edition of *Ethan Frome* published in the 1920's, she pointed out that the picture of New England presented in the regional fiction popular a decade earlier "bore little . . . resemblance to the harsh and beautiful land" that she had known from her life in Massachusetts; the "granite" of the landscape had been left out. The attempt to remedy this omission, she goes on to suggest, accounts for the grimness of *Ethan Frome*, a tragic story of thwarted passion, in which the starkness of the natural world and the limited lives of the people who inhibit it are inextricably intertwined.

Certainly, the New England landscape is the most striking feature of Wharton's novella. The "outcroppings of slate that nuzzled up through the snow like animals pushing out their noses to breathe," the majestic, mute hills that separate small communities from one another, the poor, farmed-over fields where *Ethan Frome* can barely scratch out a living—all of these suggest a physical and mental terrain that holds little promise for those doomed to spend "too many winters" within its bounds. The blazing blue skies of deep winter and the hard glitter of the snowy hills are beautiful, but they are invariably followed by sunless cold and pitiless storms, which serve to isolate still more the already remote villages and farms. The faint curls of smoke that rise from the chimneys of the scattered frame structures, the only signs of life in winter, suggest that human beings and their affairs are feeble and powerless in the face of nature's indifference and force.

Like Hawthorne and Melville, Wharton depicts a natural world that is profoundly ambiguous. Beautiful as it may seem to the outsider who narrates the story, or to Mattie and Ethan themselves when they wander in the woods together or picnic on a summer day, nature is as treacherous as the elm tree that fails to provide the oblivion the lovers have chosen. Ethan, trapped in his desolate farmhouse, at first by his mother, then by Zeena, and finally by the momentary impulse which causes him to turn the sled away from the tree at the crucial instant, was doomed from the start by the climate and the land. The contrast the narrator describes between the farmer's noble, striking head and his twisted body embodies the tragic relationship in this harsh world between human aspirations and the forces that make a mockery of them.

Warmth, color, and passion are equally doomed in this northern place. In Ethan, whose stiff, heroic mien represents an incarnation of the "frozen woe" of the landscape, all sentient response has been buried. He seeks Mattie as a plant seeks sunlight, instinctively. Yet from the beginning, when he stands beside the church, within which the iron flanks of the stove "looked as though they were heaving with volcanic fires," he is an outsider who can only look through barred windows at the source of heat and light. The little study where he spends the last night before Mattie leaves is unheated, and the chill that creeps into him as he contemplates his doomed future is a foretaste of that future.

In a life devoid of sensual resources, individual objects take on symbolic importance. The breaking of Zeena's pickle dish, a pivotal event in the plot, marks a critical step toward the ironic consummation of the lovers' passion. Zeena's anger is clearly a reaction to her accurate perception of the situation between the lovers, yet the event is effective also because of the abject poverty of the senses it reveals. Zeena is cruel, but she as much as Ethan is a victim of environment; by breaking the garish bit of glass, Mattie has destroyed—and, through her relationship with Ethan, is still destroying—what little Zeena has.

Ethan Frome was written when Wharton's powers as a writer were at their height. Like *The Custom of the Country* (1913) and *The Age of Innocence* (1920), novels that were to follow shortly, *Ethan Frome* displays the author's confident control of her materials and style. The structure of the story, in particular, shows how successfully Wharton had learned the lesson taught by her friend Henry James that the way in which a story is told is at least as important as the story itself. The relatively straightforward tale of the doomed love of Ethan and Mattie is presented to the reader by a narrator who is, we are told, basing his story on a superficial observation of town life and a few incomplete conversations with townspeople, who have described to him events of thirty years before. This complex narrative structure enables the writer to present convincingly a story of the interior life of people who would be unlikely to speak of it themselves and who are in fact characterized by their isolation from the outside world. The timeless, legendary quality

of the affair is enhanced by Wharton's decision to set it in the past, and the townsfolk, Harmon Gow and Mrs. Hale, not only act as a kind of Greek chorus, interpreting the action to the narrator, but also serve as a bridge to a present time in which power stations and the modern technology they represent will make the kind of isolation that destroyed Ethan and his companions unlikely.

It was when the narrator looked through the doorway into the farmhouse kitchen, he tells us, that he first "began to put together" his vision of Ethan Frome's story. He withholds from the reader the knowledge of what he saw within the dingy kitchen, thereby whetting curiosity. His imaginative reconstruction of the love affair and the accident that led to the scene he has just witnessed may in fact tell us more about him, the narrator, than about the unsympathetic group he is contemplating. He projects his own fantasies and fears onto the dark silences of the community that has remained essentially impenetrable to him as an outsider. What he sees are the twisted remnants of a thwarted passion, enfeebled by poverty and buried beneath the icy reserves of the archetypal New England character. The heat of Ethan and Mattie's brief kisses and the breathless, rushed descent of the sled on the Corbury road are emblematic of the deep eroticism that, denied its natural outlets, twists and destroys its possessors.

Other Wharton novels present their readers with similar visions of denied emotion and unfulfilled passions. Biographers suggest that these had their source in the deep frustrations and isolation of the author's early years, and in the failure of a love affair which had awakened her to the possibilities of the sensual life. Whatever the source, the bleakness and pessimism of Wharton's vision is realized with great power in this New England tale. Although begun in France and finished well after Wharton had become a member of a cosmopolitan and largely expatriate set, *Ethan Frome* is a very American novel. It remains, in the judgment of many readers, one of her simplest and most striking works.

ETHICS

Type of work: Philosophy
Author: Benedictus de Spinoza (1632–1677)
First published: 1677

The complete Latin title of Spinoza's masterpiece is *Ethica ordine geometrico demonstrata*. A geometric demonstration of ethics is a novelty in the history of thought, but this work is famous not because of, but in spite of, its novelty of method. The principal advantage of the method is that it reveals Spinoza's thought as clearly as possible, and although the demonstrations may not satisfy critics who concern themselves only with definitions and logical form, they have a strong persuasive force upon those who, already committed to the love of the good and of God, need clarity and structure in their thoughts.

Spinoza begins with definitions, proceeds to axioms (unproved but obviously acceptable), and then to propositions and demonstrations. Obviously, if one must find fault with Spinoza's argument, any place is vulnerable, for one can quarrel about the definitions, doubt the truth of the axioms, or question the validity of the demonstrations. But in order to reject the book it would be necessary to question the integrity and wisdom of Spinoza's spirit, and that would be not only difficult but impertinent to do.

It has long been regarded an error in philosophy to attempt to deduce what men ought to do from a study of what men do. What Spinoza attempts is a deduction of what men ought to do from a study of what must be, according to his definitions and axioms. The primary criticism of his method, then, is not that he errs—although most critics find errors in Spinoza—but that he tries to use logical means to derive ethical truths. The criticism depends on the assumption that ethical truths are either matters of fact, not of logic, or else that they are not truths at all but, for example, emotive expressions.

Spinoza begins the *Ethics* with definitions of "cause," "finite," "substance," "attribute," "mode," "free," "eternity," and "God," the latter term being defined to mean "Being absolutely infinite, that is to say, substance consisting of infinite attributes, each one of which expresses eternal and infinite essence." To understand this definition one must relate it to the definitions of the terms within it—such as "substance," "finite," and "attribute"—but one must also resist the temptation to identify the term, so defined, with any conventionally used term. Spinoza's God is quite different from anyone else's God, at least in conception. The point of the definition is that what Spinoza means by "God" is whatever is "conceived through itself" (is substance), has no limit to its essential characteristics (has infinite attributes), and maintains its character eternally. As one might suspect, the definition of "God" is crucial.

The axioms contain such logical and semantical truths as "I. Everything which is, is either in itself or in another"; "II. That which cannot be conceived through another must be conceived through itself"; "VI. A true idea must agree with that of which it is the idea," and "VII. The essence of that thing which can be conceived as not existing does not involve existence." At first the axioms may be puzzling, but they are not as extraordinary as they seem. The last axiom, for example, number VII, means only that anything which can be thought of as not existing does not by its nature *have* to exist.

The propositions begin as directly implied by the definitions: "I. Substance is by its nature prior to its modifications" follows from the definitions of "substance" and "mode," and "II. Two substances having different attributes have nothing in common with one another" is another consequence of the definition of "substance." As the propositions increase, the proofs become longer, making reference not only to definitions but also to previous propositions and their corollaries. For those interested in technical philosophy the proofs are intriguing even when they are unconvincing, but for others they are unnecessary; the important thing is to get at Spinoza's central idea.

Proposition XI is important in preparing the way for Spinoza's main contention: "XI. God or substance consisting of infinite attributes, each one of which expresses eternal and infinite essence, necessarily exists." Although one may be tempted to seize upon this proposition as an instrument to use against atheists, it is necessary to remember that the term "God" is a technical term for Spinoza and has little, if anything, to do with the object of religious worship.

Proposition XIV soon follows with the startling claim that "Besides God no substance can be nor can be conceived." A corollary of this proposition is the idea that God is one; that is, everything that exists, all of nature, is God. Individual things do not by their natures exist, but only through God's action; and God is not only the cause of their existence but also of their natures. (XXIV, XXV.) We might expect, consequently, that a great deal of the universe is contingent; that is, it depends upon something other than itself and need not be as it is. But Spinoza argues in Proposition XXIX that "In Nature, there is nothing contingent, but all things are determined from the necessity of the divine nature to exist and act in a certain manner." Consequently, man's will is not free but necessary. (XXXII.) This was one of the ideas that made Spinoza unpopular with both Jews and Christians.

Having used Part One of the *Ethics* to develop the conception of God, Spinoza goes on in Part Two, after presenting further definitions and axioms, to explain the nature and origin of mind. Here again Spinoza concludes that "In the mind there is no absolute or free will . . ." (XLVIII.) In this section he also develops the idea that God is a thinking and extended being.

In Part Three, "On the Origin and Nature of the Emotions," Spinoza argues that emotions are confused ideas. "Our mind acts at times and at times suffers," he contends in Proposition I of Part Three; "insofar as it has adequate ideas, it necessarily acts; and insofar as it has inadequate ideas, it necessarily suffers." Perhaps it is well to note that Spinoza defines "emotion" as any modification of the body "by which the power of acting of the body itself is increased, diminished, helped, or hindered, together with the ideas of these modifications."

By this time in his book Spinoza has created the idea that God, as both thinking and extended substance, is such that all nature is both thinking and extended (since everything that is must be part of God). Another way of putting it is that everything that exists does so both as body and as idea. Thus, the human being exists as both body and idea. If, then, the human being, as idea, does not adequately comprehend the modifications of the human body, the mind suffers.

In Part Four, "Of Human Bondage; or of the Strength of the Emotions," Spinoza defines the good as "that which we certainly know is useful to us," and in a series of propositions he develops the idea that each person necessarily desires what he considers to be good, that in striving to preserve his being a man acquires virtue, and that the desire to be happy and to live well involves desiring to act, to live, "that is to say, actually to exist." In this attempt to relate man's freedom to his will to act and in the identification of the good with the striving toward existence, Spinoza anticipated much of the more significant work of the twentieth century Existentialists.

In Proposition XXVIII of Part IV, Spinoza writes that "The highest good of the mind is the knowledge of God, and the highest virtue of the mind is to know God." This claim has been prepared for by previous propositions relating the good to what is desired, the desire to action, action to being, and being to God. Because of the intri-

cacy of Spinoza's argument it becomes possible for him to argue that to seek being, to seek the good, to use reason, and to seek God are one and the same. To use reason involves coming to have adequate ideas, having adequate ideas involves knowing the nature of things, knowing the nature of things involves knowing God.

Although it might seem that Spinoza's philosophy, for all its references to God, is egoistic in that this crucial phase of his argument depends upon the claim that each man seeks to preserve his own being, a full examination of Part IV will show that Spinoza manages to transcend the egoistic base of action by arguing that to serve the self best one uses reason; but to use reason is to seek an adequate idea of God and, consequently, to seek what is good for all men. In fact, Spinoza specifically states that whatever causes men to live in harmony with one another is profitable and good, and that whatever brings discord is evil.

The highest happiness or blessedness of man, according to Spinoza, is "the peace of mind which springs from the intuitive knowledge of God." This conclusion is certainly consistent with Spinoza's ideas that man's good consists in escaping from the human bondage of the passions, that to escape from the passions is to understand the causes that affect the self, that to understand the causes involves action, and that action leads to God.

When man through rational action comes to determine himself, he participates in the essence of all being; he becomes so at one with God that he possesses an intellectual love of God, which is man's blessedness and virtue. The eternal is known only by the eternal; hence, in knowing God, man makes himself eternal—not in any finite or individual way, but as part of God's being.

Divested of its formal trappings and of those respects in which philosophic imagination outruns credibility—for example, the claim that everything is both thought and extension—Spinoza's philosophy of ethics tells the reader that happiness consists in understanding the causes of things. It might be argued that this idea, so familiar in philosophy, puts more simply than any other concept the kind of faith that makes a man a philosopher. But to understand the causes of things is, as Spinoza concludes, "as difficult as it is rare."

EUGENE ONEGIN

Type of work: Poem
Author: Alexander Pushkin (1799–1837)
Type of plot: Impressionistic romance
Time of plot: Nineteenth century
Locale: Russia
First published: 1833

Pushkin's lyric poem describing the eccentric life of Eugene Onegin reworks the Don Juan legend familiar to readers of Byron. Regarded as the inspiration for the great Russian novels of the nineteenth century, Pushkin's romantic lyric has the world-weary Onegin duel with and kill his only friend and spurn the love of a worthy woman, only to fall in love with her after she has despaired and married another.

Principal Characters

Tatyana Larin (tä·tyä′nə lä′rĭn), also called **Tanya Larina** (tän′yä lä′rĭn·ə), the reserved, withdrawn older daughter of the well-to-do Larin family. Her parents despair of her marriage prospects, but she falls in love at first sight with Eugene Onegin and, unable to write grammatical Russian, sends him a passionate letter written in French. Although he fails to encourage her, she turns down several other proposals of marriage. When her family takes her to Moscow, she picks up beauty hints at a ball and attracts the attentions of a retired general, who persuades her to marry him. Years later she again sees Eugene, who falls in love with her and writes her pleading letters. She reads them and preserves them to read again, but she gives him no encouragement and remains faithful to her general to the end of her life.

Eugene Onegin (ĕu·gĕ′nĭy ô·nĕ′gĭn), the hero of this narrative poem, with many resemblances to its author. Brought up in the aristocratic tradition, he is a brilliant, witty man of the world. Successful in many light love affairs, he is bored with living. City life, with its opera and ballet, has lost its appeal. A stay on the country estate willed to him by his uncle wearies him after several days. He is finally persuaded by his friend, Vladimir Lensky, to accompany him on a visit to the Larin family. There he finds the conversation dull, the refreshment too simple and too abundant, and Tatyana unattractive. Visiting her later, after receiving her love letter, he tells her frankly that he would make her a very poor husband because he has had too many disillusioning experiences with women. He returns to the lonely estate and the life of an anchorite.

When Vladimir takes him under false pretenses to Tatyana's birthday party, he gets revenge by flirting with her sister Olga, engaged to Vladimir. His jealous friend challenges him to a duel. Eugene shoots Vladimir through the heart.

Olga Larin (ōly′gə lä′rĭn), also called **Olenka** (ô·lĕn′kə), the pretty and popular younger daughter of the Larin family, betrothed to Vladimir Lensky. At a ball she dances so often with Onegin that her fiancé gets angry. Though she assures him that she means nothing by her flirtation, he challenges Onegin to a duel and is killed. Later she marries an army officer.

Vladimir Lensky (vlä·dĭ′mĭr lĕn′skĭy), a German-Russian friend of Eugene, brought up in Germany and influenced by romantic illusions of life and love. Although his reading of Schiller and Kant sets him apart from most other young Russians, he and Eugene have much in common. He tries to get his friend interested in Tatyana Larin, even to inviting him to her big birthday party, which he describes as an intimate family affair. In resentment Eugene avoids Tatyana and devotes himself to Olga. After the challenge is given, Vladimir is too proud to acknowledge his misjudgment and is killed.

M. Guillot (gĭl·yō′), Eugene's second in the duel.

Zaretsky (zä·rĕt′skĭy), Vladimir's second.

The Prince (called **Gremin** in the operatic version), a fat, retired general and Eugene's friend. Seeing Tatyana at a ball in Moscow, he falls in love with her and proposes. She accepts. Later he invites Eugene to his house, where the latter meets Tatyana again.

The Story

Eugene Onegin was brought up in the aristocratic tradition. Although he had little classical background, he had a flashing wit and he was well-read in economics. He had become an accomplished man of the world by the time he reached young manhood. In fact, he had been so successful in love and so accustomed to the social life of Moscow that he habitually felt a supreme boredom with life. Even the ballet had lately failed to hold his attention.

Eugene's father had led the usual life. He gave balls

regularly and tried his best to keep up his social position by borrowing recklessly. Just as he was declared a bankrupt, Eugene received word that his uncle was dying. Since he was the heir, he left in haste to attend the dying man. Grumbling at the call of duty, he was nevertheless thankful to be coming into an inheritance.

His uncle died, however, before he arrived. After the relatives had departed, Eugene settled down to enjoy his uncle's handsome country estate. The cool woods and the fertile fields charmed him at first, but after two days of country life his old boredom returned. He soon acquired a reputation as an eccentric. If neighbors called, Eugene found himself obliged to leave on an urgent errand. After a while the neighbors left him to himself.

Vladimir Lensky, however, remained his friend. At eighteen, Vladimir was still romantic and filled with illusions of life and love. He had been in Germany, where he was much influenced by Kant and Schiller. In Russia his German temperament set him apart. He and Eugene became more and more intimate.

The Larins had two daughters, Olga and Tatyana. Olga was pretty and popular, and although she was the younger, she was the leader in their group. Tatyana was reserved and withdrawn, but a discerning observer would have seen her real beauty. She made no effort to join in the social life. Olga had been long betrothed to Vladimir; the family despaired of a marriage for Tatyana.

On Vladimir's invitation, Eugene reluctantly agreed to pay a visit to the Larins. When the family heard that the two men were coming, they immediately thought of Eugene as a suitor for Tatyana. He, however, was greatly bored with his visit. The refreshments were too ample and too rustic, and the talk was heavy and dull. He paid little attention to Tatyana.

After he left, Tatyana was much disturbed. Having fallen deeply in love, she had no arts with which to attract Eugene. After confiding in her dull-witted nurse, she wrote Eugene a passionate, revealing love letter. She wrote in French, for she could not write Russian grammatically.

Eugene, stirred by her letter, paid another visit to the Larins and found Tatyana in a secluded garden. He told her the brutal truth: He was not a good man for a husband, for he had too much experience with women and too many disillusionments. Life with him would not be at all worthy of Tatyana. The girl, making no protest, suffered in silence.

On his lonely estate Eugene lived the life of an anchorite. He bathed every morning in a stream, read, walked and rode in the countryside, and slept soundly at night. Only Vladimir called occasionally.

That winter the Larins celebrated Tatyana's name-day. When Vladimir represented the gathering as only a small family affair, Eugene consented to go. He felt betrayed when he found the guests numerous, the food heavy, and the ball obligatory. For revenge, he danced too much with

Olga, preventing Vladimir from enjoying his fiancée's company. Vladimir became jealously angry and challenged Eugene to a duel. Through stubbornness Eugene accepted the challenge.

Before the duel, Vladimir went to see Olga. His purpose was to reproach her for her behavior, but Olga, as cheerful and affectionate as ever, acted as if nothing had happened. More lighthearted but somewhat puzzled, Vladimir prepared to meet Eugene on the dueling ground.

When the two friends met, Eugene shot Vladimir through the heart. Remorseful at last, Eugene left his estate to wander by himself. Olga soon afterward married an army man and left home.

In spite of the scandal, Tatyana still loved Eugene. She visited his house and made friends with his old housekeeper. She sat in his study reading his books and pondering his marginal notes. Eugene had been especially fond of *Don Juan* and other cynical works, and his notes revealed much about his selfishness and disillusionment. Tatyana, who had hitherto read very little, learned much bitterness from his books and came to know more of Eugene.

At home, Tatyana's mother did not know what to do. The girl seemed to have no interest in suitors and had refused several proposals. On the advice of relatives, the mother decided to take Tatyana to Moscow, where there were more eligible men. They were to visit a cousin for a season in hopes that Tatyana would become betrothed.

From her younger cousins Tatyana learned to do her hair stylishly and to act more urbanely in society. At a ball a famous general, a prince, was attracted to Tatyana. In spite of the fact that he was obese, she accepted his proposal.

After more than two years of wandering, Eugene returned to Moscow. Still indifferent to life, he decided to attend a fashionable ball, simply to escape from boredom for a few hours. He was warmly greeted by his host, whom he had known well in former times. While the prince was reproaching him for his long absence, Eugene could not keep from staring at a queenly woman who dominated the gathering. She looked familiar. When he asked the prince about her, he was astounded to learn that she was Tatyana, his host's wife.

The changed Tatyana showed no traces of the shy rustic girl who had written so revealingly of her love. Eugene, much attracted to her, frequently went to her house, but he never received more than a cool reception and a distant hand to kiss.

Finally Eugene began to write her letters in which he expressed his hopeless longing. Still Tatyana gave no sign. All that winter Eugene kept to his gloomy room, reading and musing. At last, in desperation, he called on Tatyana unannounced and surprised her rereading his letters.

Tatyana refused to give in to his importunate declarations. Why had he scorned the country girl, and why did he now pursue the married woman? She would rather listen to his brutal rejection than to new pleadings. She had once been in love with Eugene and would gladly have been his wife; perhaps she was still in love with him. Perhaps she had been wrong in listening to her mother, who had been insistent that she marry the prince. But now she was married, and she would remain faithful to her husband until she died.

Critical Evaluation

Pushkin called *Eugene Onegin* a "novel in verse." Well aware of European literary models, and especially attracted to Lord Byron's long narrative poems *Childe Harold's Pilgrimage* and *Don Juan*, Pushkin mixed the distinct qualities of prose and verse into a landmark work of Romantic literature.

Pushkin follows the novel-of-manners tradition in several respects. In *Eugene Onegin* he offers a picture of Russian society as well as a tale of individuals. The story moves from the Europeanized salons of St. Petersburg to the gentry's country estates to the aristocratic circles of Moscow. It alternates scenes of social occasions and private interviews. Like a novel of manners, *Eugene Onegin* concerns characters that the reader is meant to care about. Penetrating the recesses of Tatyana's and Eugene's hearts, and presenting their love letters for inspection, Pushkin allows the reader to see events, themselves, and others through their eyes as well as the narrator's. Finally, like a novelist, Pushkin arranges his characters as paired reflections (Vladimir is a younger Eugene, Tatyana a deeper Olga) who switch positions like dancers in a minuet (for example, in the city Eugene loves Tatyana as vainly as she loves him in the country).

Pushkin is a novelist, then, but he is also a poet. He has a poet's care for the exact arrangement of words. He tells the story in eight books composed of 399 stanzas; each stanza has fourteen lines (three quatrains and a couplet) of iambic tetrameter with a complicated pattern of varying rhymes. Like a sonneteer arranging a sequence, Pushkin the poet carefully crafts each stanza internally even as he fits it into the unfolding narrative.

Eugene Onegin brims with lyrical passages about the beauty of the countryside as the seasons change, the glorious ideals of youth, and the power of romantic passion. Though these lyrical sections digress from the narrative development, they add texture and atmosphere to preceding and following scenes. Like all great poets, Pushkin has an eye for symbol and metaphor. All the characters reveal themselves by the books they read: Eugene remains, like the cynical hero in Byron's works, aloof from life; Tatyana expects love to be the permanent exchange of noble souls described by epistolary novelists; Lensky explores the heights and depths of emotion glorified by romantic and sentimental poems. The seasons likewise mirror the state of the characters' hearts. It is in the spring that Eugene first arrives in the country to start a new life; the fateful name-day party and duel occur in winter; in the spring come Olga's wedding and Tatyana's visits to Eugene's estate; Tatyana's marriage and Eugene's hopeless proposition are winter events.

At times the poet-narrator intrudes upon the world of the characters, reminding readers of the literary conventions that dictate how a novel in verse develops. He shares with them the agonies and ecstasies of writing this story. He juxtaposes the characters' individual emotional reactions to events with a transcendent objectivity hard won by his own experience. The narrator's intrusion is another of the complexities that enrich *Eugene Onegin* and reward repeated readings.

The presence of an intrusive narrator suggests that *Eugene Onegin* contains strong autobiographical elements. Pushkin wrote the work over a period of eight years (1832–1831). He began the work while in virtual exile on the family estate after a youth of living rakishly and writing passionate poetry, a life-style that had cost him a government commission. Vladimir and Eugene are versions of him: Lensky his youthful dedication to poetry, Onegin his weariness with society. Not until 1826 did Pushkin live and work again in St. Petersburg; in 1830 he reluctantly reentered government service after marrying a beautiful, ambitious younger woman. During these years he wrote the middle parts of *Eugene Onegin* in fitful bursts, completing it only in 1830 during three intensely creative months of isolation at a country estate. The poem's movement from city to country mirrors Pushkin's own journey. His caricatures of country bumpkins and city pseudosophisticates mirror his own hesitant participation in Russian society. The poem's attention to the varieties of love—its innocence, intensity, and mercurial nature—mirrors his own experience of requited and unrequited affection.

Eugene Onegin concerns as much the state of Russia's soul, however, as it does the state of Pushkin's own soul. In Tatyana and Onegin Pushkin created characters who had a deep influence on other Russian writers of the nineteenth century. Tatyana is the prototype of the spiritual, melancholy woman who needs a love more profound than any man can give her. She anticipates heroines like Ivan Turgenev's Anna Odintzov (*Fathers and Sons*) and Leo Tolstoy's Anna Karenina. Eugene is the first of the superfluous men, like Ivan Goncharov's Oblomov and Tolstoy's Ivan Ilyich, who despairingly realize that their lives have no meaning outside the social role they play. Though attracted passionately to each other, these melancholy women and superfluous men cannot save themselves or their lovers. Their efforts to connect fail by chance, by choice, or by circumstance. The world about them is no help. Country society is dull, cliquish, and petty; city society cares only for status, reputation, and show. The community offers the individual no pattern for spiritual health or emotional communion. Indeed, it isolates individuals and insulates them from true feeling by providing conventional expectations and roles.

Technically, Pushkin's novel in verse highlights the literary conventions that manipulate readers; thematically, the work depicts the social conventions that manipulate women and men. Though rooted in the experience of a writer now dead and mirroring a society now equally dead, *Eugene Onegin* remains a powerful work for modern readers. It takes up universal themes and eternal hopes and fears. Tatyana embodies the unflinching hope that demands that life and love measure up to expectations while Eugene embodies the constant fear that life and love can never meet those expectations. The poet-narrator embodies the continuing desire to control this chaos of hopes and fears with the inexhaustible resources of art.

EUGÉNIE GRANDET

Type of work: Novel
Author: Honoré de Balzac (1799–1850)
Type of plot: Naturalism
Time of plot: Early nineteenth century
Locale: Saumur, France
First published: 1833 (English translation, 1859)

Considered one of Balzac's most powerful works, Eugénie Grandet *delineates the character of a miser whose calculating and inhumane parsimoniousness cripples the lives of his wife and his only child, Eugénie. The tale is told simply with an abundance of realistic detail characteristic of French naturalists such as Zola.*

Principal Characters

Eugénie Grandet (oe·zhä·nē′ grän·dä′), the young heiress to a fortune, who lives in the world but is not of it. Reared without a childhood in the penurious surroundings of Saumur, a provincial French town, Eugénie, for a brief period, lives for the love of her cousin, newly orphaned and a guest in the Grandet home. Strong of character and handsome in appearance, she pledges herself to young Charles Grandet and remains true to him throughout her life. As an obedient daughter of parents and church, she tries to live righteously but defies her father in the matter of love. Her kind ministrations to both her dying parents, her lifelong devotion to her one loyal friend, and her constancy of memory make her one of the most steadfast and pitiable of heroines. Her good deeds and her loving devotion to the poor whom she serves give her life tragic beauty.

Monsieur Grandet (mə·syoe′ grän·dä′), her father, one of the most miserly figures in all literature. The author of the family tragedy, Goodman Grandet, as Balzac satirically calls him, is unyielding in his niggardliness without seeming to realize his great fault. He appears to be trying to clear his brother's good name by not allowing him to fall into bankruptcy, but in reality he profits from the delaying action. His towering anger at the least "extravagance" finally puts his devoted wife on her deathbed, and his unrelenting love of gold destroys the loving confidence of his daughter. Shrewd and grasping in his business deals, he has no redeeming features. Ironically enough, his fortune is finally put to good purposes through his daughter, who makes restitution for his wrongs.

Madame Grandet, his long-suffering wife, whose piety is taxed by the burden of her husband's stinginess. Accustomed to her hard lot and strengthened by her religion, Madame Grandet bows under her heavy yoke of work and harsh treatment until she takes up the cause of her daughter's right to love and devotes herself to the memory of that love. Still she prays for reconciliation, and when it comes she dies happy, without knowing her dowry is the reason for the deathbed forgiveness.

Charles Grandet (shärl), the dandified cousin of the heroine, who loses his fortune through his father's suicide but who regains a fortune through unscrupulous dealings financed, ironically, by Eugénie's gift of money to him. Heroic only in his unselfish grief for his father and generous only once in bestowing his love, Charles reveals a twisted mind tutored by a corrupt society. Outwardly prepossessing, inwardly vacillating, he chooses to disregard the one fine thing that was given him, a dowry of unselfish love, and bases his life on treachery, lechery, and adultery.

Nanon (nà·nōṅ′), the faithful servant who loyally defends the indefensible in her master because it was he who raised her a full step in the social order. Large and mannish, Nanon manages the entire Grandet household with such efficiency as to cause admiration from the master, himself efficient and desperately saving. Her devotion to him, however, does not preclude rushing to the defense of his wife and daughter, the victims of his spite. Finally she marries the gamekeeper and together they rule the Grandet holdings for their mistress Eugénie.

Monsieur Cruchot (mə·syoe′ krü·shō′), a notary and petty government official who becomes husband in name only to Eugénie. He feels that by marrying the name and inheriting the fortune his own name will become illustrious. His untimely death ends the reign of self-seeking misers.

Monsieur de Grassins (mə·syoe′ də gràsäṅ′), the provincial banker sent to Paris to act for M. Grandet at the time of his brother's bankruptcy. Attracted to the exciting life in the capital, he fails to return to Saumur.

The Story

In the French town of Saumur, old Grandet was a prominent personality, and the story of his rise to fortune was known throughout the district. He was a master cooper who had married the daughter of a prosperous wood merchant. When the new French Republic offered for sale the church property in Saumur, Grandet used his savings and his wife's dowry to buy an old abbey, a fine vineyard, and several farms. Under the Consulate he became mayor and grew still more wealthy. In 1806, he inherited three fortunes from his wife's mother, her grandfather, and her grandmother. By this time he owned the abbey, a hundred acres of vineyard, thirteen farms, and the house in which he lived. In 1811, he bought the nearby estate of an impoverished nobleman.

He was known for his miserliness, but he was respected for the same reason. His manners were simple, his table was meager, but his speech and gestures were the law of the countryside. His household consisted of his wife, his daughter, Eugénie, and a servant, Nanon. Old Grandet had reduced his wife almost to slavery, using her as a screen for his devious financial dealings. Nanon, who did all the housework, was gaunt and ugly but of great strength. She was devoted to her master because he had taken her in after everyone else had refused to hire her because of her appearance. On each birthday, Eugénie received a gold piece from her father and a winter and a summer dress from her mother. Each New Year's Day, Grandet would ask to see the coins and would gloat over their yellow brightness.

He begrudged his family everything except the bare necessities of life. Every day he would carefully measure and dole out the food for the household—a few lumps of sugar, several pieces of butter, and a loaf of bread. He forbade the lighting of fires in the rooms before the middle of November. His family, like his tenants, lived under the austere circumstances he imposed upon them.

The townspeople wondered whom Eugénie would marry. There were two rivals for her hand. One of them, M. Cruchot, was the son of the local notary. The other, M. de Grassins, was the son of the local banker. On Eugénie's birthday, in the year 1819, both called at the Grandet home. During the evening, there was an unexpected knock at the door, and in came Charles Grandet, the miser's nephew. Charles's father had amassed a fortune in Paris, and Charles himself, dressed in the most fashionable Parisian manner, was an example of Parisian customs and habits for these awkward, gawking provincials whom he tried to impress with his superior airs.

Eugénie outdid herself in an effort to make the visitor welcome, even defying her father in the matter of heat, candlelight, and other luxuries for Charles. Grandet was polite enough to his nephew that evening, as he read a letter Charles had brought from his father. Grandet's brother announced in a letter that he had lost his fortune, and he was about to commit suicide, and that he entrusted Charles to his brother's care. The young man was quite unaware of what his father had written, and when informed next day of his father's failure and suicide, he burst into tears and remained in his room for several days. Finally he wrote to a friend in Paris and asked him to dispose of his property and pay his debts. He gave little trinkets to Eugénie, her mother, and Nanon. Grandet looked at them greedily and said he would have them appraised. He informed his wife and daughter that he intended to turn the young man out as soon as his father's affairs were settled.

Charles felt there was a stain on his honor. Grandet felt so too, especially since he and his late brother had the same family name. In consultation with the local banker, M. de Grassins, he arranged a plan whereby he could save the family reputation without, at the same time, spending a penny. M. de Grassins went to Paris to act for Grandet. He did not return but lived a life of pleasure in the capital.

Meanwhile, Eugénie fell in love with Charles. Sympathizing with his penniless state, she decided to give him her hoard of coins so that he could go to the Indies and make his fortune. The two young people pledged everlasting love to each other, and Charles left Saumur.

On the following New Year's Day, Grandet asked to see Eugénie's money. Her mother, who knew her daughter's secret, kept silent. In spite of Eugénie's denials, Grandet guessed what she had done with the gold. He ordered her to stay in her room, and he would have nothing to do with either her or her mother. Rumors began to arise in the town. The notary, M. Cruchot, told Grandet that if his wife died, there would have to be a division of property—if Eugénie insisted on it. The village whispered that Mme. Grandet was dying of a broken heart and the maltreatment of her husband. Realizing that he might lose a part of his fortune, Grandet relented and forgave them both. When his wife died, he tricked Eugénie into signing over her share of the property to him.

Five years passed with no word from Charles to brighten Eugénie's drab existence. In 1827, when Grandet was eighty-two years old, he was stricken with paralysis. He died urging Eugénie to take care of his money.

Eugénie lived with old Nanon, still waiting for Charles to return. One day a letter came. Charles no longer wished to marry her. Instead, he hoped to marry the daughter of a titled nobleman and secure by royal ordinance his father-in-law's title and coat of arms. Eugénie released Charles, but M. de Grassins hurried to Charles and told him that his father's creditors had not been satisfied. Until they were, his fiancée's family would not allow a marriage. Learning of his predicament, Eugénie herself paid the debt, and Charles was married.

Eugénie continued to live alone. The routine of the house was exactly what it had been while Grandet lived. Suitors came again. Young de Grassins was now in disgrace because of the loose life his father was living in Paris, but M. Cruchot, who had risen to a high post in the provincial government, continued to press his suit. At last Eugénie agreed to marry him, providing he did not demand the prerogatives of marriage, for she would be his wife in name only. They were married only a short time before M. Cruchot died. To her own property Eugénie added his. Nanon herself had married, and she and her husband stayed with Eugénie. Convinced that Nanon was her only friend, the young widow resigned herself to a lonely life. She lived as she had always lived in the bare old house. She had great wealth, but, lacking everything else in life, she was indifferent to it.

Critical Evaluation

Eugénie Grandet is part of Honoré de Balzac's grand design, *La Comédie Humaine*. Some say it is one of the best parts. Rather late in his prolific writing career, Balzac conceived the idea of arranging his novels, stories, and studies in a certain order. He described his plan in *Avant-Propos* (1842, although he claimed the idea originated in 1833), where he named the project *La Comédie Humaine* (*The Human Comedy*). Influenced by Georges Louis Leclerc de Buffon, Étienne Geoffroy Saint-Hilaire, and Jean Lamarck, all naturalists, Balzac sought to apply their scientific principles—especially the taxonomic system—to literature, particularly for the purpose of organizing information. Balzac firmly believed that "social species" could be classified just as "zoological species" were, and he attempted to classify his fifty-odd previously written works as well as his future writings to fit such a scheme. To accommodate his plan, he adopted eight major topic headings: Scenes from Private Life, Scenes from Provincial Life, Scenes from Parisian Life, Scenes from Political Life, Scenes from Military Life, Scenes from Rural Life, Philosophical Studies, and Analytical Studies. The works were arranged, rearranged, and arranged again, ad infinitum. *Eugénie Grandet* was finally a Scene of Provincial Life. As a consequence of this ambitious organizational plan, Balzac exercised Procrustean prerogatives, tailoring his earlier output to his new standards. The results were predictably disastrous, but the literary qualities of the novels themselves—notably *Eugénie Grandet*—are irrefutable testimony to the triumph of art over science.

Balzac realized his goal of presenting typical human species in spite of, not because of, his "scientific" system of taxonomy. As the unsurpassed historian of the French middle class during the first half of the nineteenth century, he incarnated the stereotypes which were novel then but are well known today: the snob, the provincial, the prude, the miser, the lecher, and a great many others. He did so on the strength of his artistic skill and not by virtue of scientific analysis, for Balzac was not a systematic philosopher or a scientist but an artist. He wrote fine novels—even though they are often marred by his insensitivity to language and his proclivity for excessive details—which outlined the essential characteristics of the nineteenth century French middle class more clearly than anyone else has ever done. Matching Juvenal and Martial, Balzac satirized avarice, ambition, lust, vanity, and hypocrisy. Greed, however, was his *bête noire* and Monsieur Grandet his archetype. The author himself was something of a prototype.

Money is a pervasive theme in Balzac's novels, where its evil effects are resoundingly deplored. The figure of the greedy miser furnishes Balzac with one of his best characters, Grandet. Ironically, the novel reflects Balzac's own preoccupation with money and his desire to earn vast sums of it. Like many of his characters, he wanted wealth and social position. Early in his career, he was poor and constantly in debt; but even after his novels began earning him sizable sums, he was still constantly in debt because he lived an extravagant life-style well beyond his means. He never did learn how to manage money. When he was writing, he lived like a monk, working furiously for long hours with virtually no time out even for eating. When the novel was completed, however, Balzac devoted that same energy to nonstop revelry. His feasts were legendary, his capacity for fine foods gargantuan—one hundred oysters as an hors d'oeuvre, for example. His drinking and other debauches were no less excessive. He would agree with Monsieur Grandet that money is power and power is all that matters; therefore, money is the only important factor in life.

Balzac, however, wanted money for what it would buy, and Grandet wanted money for its own sake. Balzac cultivated the Dionysian life-style with the same single-minded dedication with which Grandet cultivated abstemiousness. Therein lies the difference between author and character. The former enjoyed a grand style; the latter took pleasure from self-denial. Yet Grandet dominates the novel just as he dominates his family. To be sure, the novel is entitled *Eugénie Grandet*, and it depicts the sterility of provincial life. Balzac's neat categories notwithstanding, Grandet dominates the story. He is the overwhelming force that determines the destiny of his wife—who is ultimately killed by his penny-pinching vindictiveness—and his daughter—who is emotionally warped by his miserly indoctrination. The novel is thus as much about Grandet as it is about Eugénie.

Monsieur Grandet is what literary critics call an undeveloped or a "flat" character. He undergoes no change in the course of the novel. From start to finish, he is venal and miserly. He experiences no enlightenment. In fact, Eugénie is the only character who undergoes change as she moves from innocence to experience. The others remain as they were at the beginning. More important, the emotional power which Grandet exercises as his prerogative kills his wife and permanently damages Eugénie. Although Eugénie knows nothing of Grandet's machinations in accumulating his fortune, she is nevertheless shaped by her father's influence. Grandet thus exerts his wishes even beyond the grave, since his training of Eugénie—implicit or explicit—is reflected in her behavior long after he is dead. She adopts his parsimonious living habits, although she is publicly charitable. Seemingly without effort, she increases her fortune rather than depletes it. Her father taught her well. In this way, Grandet rivals Eugénie as the novel's protagonist.

Eugénie would not be what she is without having grown up with such a father. The cause-effect matrix of this interpersonal relationship illustrates one of Balzac's major premises (which was to become a tenet of late nineteenth century literary naturalism): that the combined effects of genetics and environment cannot be surmounted. This phenomenon is labeled "determinism"—more precisely, "mechanistic determinism," to distinguish it from its religious counterpart of predestination. Eugénie is born into a given social environment with a given genetic makeup. She is unable to change those factors, yet they are the twin determinants of her fate. The novel traces her development up to the time when she accepts that fate which was foreordained at the outset: She is very, very rich and very, very unhappy. The inescapable forces of determinism thus work through to their inevitable conclusion.

Eugénie Grandet is an unusually moving novel, for the reader can hardly fail to sympathize with Eugénie while despising her father. It comes as something as a shock, then, to realize that Eugénie bore her father no malice. Even her vengeance of Charles's betrayal is so subtle that it is untainted; Charles is oblivious to subtlety, and the reader does not begrudge Eugénie her one, lone exercise of financial power. Balzac's incredible prestidigitation is at work here, manipulating the readers so that they accept the novel's point of view without imposing extraneous judgments. Truly, *Eugénie Grandet* is a tribute to the novelist's craft and art.

"THE EVE OF ST. AGNES"

Type of work: Poem
Author: John Keats (1795–1821)
Type of plot: Chivalric romance
Time of plot: Middle Ages
Locale: A castle
First published: 1820

The plot of Keats's poem is built around an ancient superstition that a maiden who retires to her bed on St. Agnes Eve after practicing a particular ritual will be awakened in her dreams by her lover. An example of English Romanticism at its best, the poem is matchless in its musical verse and vivid in its descriptions of color, sight, and sound.

Principal Characters

Madeline, a young virgin, first shown preoccupied at a ball given in the castle of her noble father. Eager to carry out the ritual of St. Agnes' Eve and thereby see her future husband in a dream, she leaves the revelry and retires to her room where, falling asleep, she dreams of Porphyro, the son of an enemy house. Awakening to find him beside her bed, she is at first frightened; but after he tells her "This is no dream, my bride," she steals with him out of the castle, past the sleeping, drunken wassailers, and away into the stormy night.

Porphyro (pôr′fĭ·rō), her gallant young knight, who comes from his home across the moors, slips into the castle full of his enemies, and with the aid of Angela, an understanding old nurse, goes to Madeline's chamber before she prepares for bed. After she is asleep, he emerges from the closet where he has hidden himself, sets a table loaded with exotic foods, and wakes his beloved with a song, "La belle dame sans merci," to the accompaniment of Madeline's lute. He persuades his beloved to leave her home of hate and flee with him.

Angela, an old beldame, Madeline's nurse and Porphyro's friend. Convinced, after Porphyro has revealed his plan, that the young lover's intentions are honorable, she hides him in Madeline's bedchamber and provides the dainties for a feast. She dies "palsy-twitched."

The Beadsman, an aged supplicant who at the beginning of the poem is telling his rosary with cold-numbed fingers in the castle chapel. He closes the story by sleeping forever unsought for "among his ashes cold."

The Story

A cold St. Agnes' Eve it was—so cold that the owl with all its feathers shivered, so cold that the old Beadsman's fingers were numb as he told his rosary and said his prayers. Passing by the sculptured figures of the dead, he felt sorry for them in their icy graves. As he walked through the chapel door, he could hear the sound of music coming from the castle hall. He sadly turned again to his prayers.

The great hall of the castle was a scene of feasting and revelry, but one among the merry throng was scarcely aware of her surroundings. The lovely Madeline's thoughts were on the legend of St. Agnes' Eve, which told that a maiden, if she followed the ceremonies carefully and went supperless to bed, might there meet her lover in a dream.

Meanwhile, across the moonlit moors came Porphyro. He entered the castle and hid behind a pillar, aware that his presence meant danger, because his family was an enemy of Madeline's house. Soon the aged crone, Angela, came by and offered to hide him, lest his enemies find him there and kill him.

He followed her along dark arched passageways, out of sight of the revelers. When they stopped, Porphyro begged Angela to let him have one glimpse of Madeline. He promised on oath that if he so much as disturbed a lock of her hair, he would give himself up to the foes who waited below. He seemed in such sorrow that the poor woman gave in to him. She took Porphyro to the maiden's chamber and there hid him in a closet where was stored a variety of sweetmeats and confections brought from the feast downstairs. Angela then hobbled away, and soon the breathless Madeline appeared.

She came in with her candle, which blew out, and kneeling before her high arched casement window, she began to pray. Watching her kneel there, her head a halo of moonlight, Porphyro grew faint at the sight of her beauty. Soon she disrobed and crept into bed, where she lay entranced until sleep came over her.

Porphyro stole from the closet and gazed at her in awe as she slept. For an instant a door opened far away, and the noises of another world, boisterous and festive, broke in; but soon the sounds faded away again. In the silence he brought dainty foods from the closet—quinces, plums, jellies, candies, syrups and spices that perfumed the chilly room. Madeline slept on, and Porphyro began to play a soft melody on a lute. Madeline opened her eyes and thought her lover a vision of St. Agnes' Eve. Porphyro, not daring to speak, sank upon his knees until she spoke, begging him never to leave her or she would die.

St. Agnes' moon went down. Outside the casements, sleet and ice began to dash against the windowpanes. Porphyro told her that they must flee before the house awakened. Madeline, afraid and trembling, followed her lover down the cold, gloomy corridors, through the wide deserted hall, and past the porter, asleep on his watch. So they fled—into the wintry dawn.

Critical Evaluation

Keats wrote "The Eve of St. Agnes" in January and February of 1819, the first of an astonishing spate of masterpieces that belied his failing health and emotional turmoil, and which ended abruptly one year later when it became apparent that his illness was fatal. "La Belle Dame Sans Merci," "Lamia," and six great odes were all written before October of that year. The near circumstance of his death seems to throw into a kind of relief the luscious descriptions of physical reality in this and other poems. More striking still is the poet's refusal to take comfort in the simplistic assurances of any religious or philosophical system that denied either the complexity of mind or the reality and importance of the senses. "The Eve of St. Agnes" manifests Keats's characteristic concern with the opposition and subtle connection of the sensual world to the interior life. He shared this preoccupation with other Romantic poets, notably Coleridge and Wordsworth, taking as his subject the web of an antithesis at the heart of human experience; like them, he cloaked his meditations in sensuous imagery.

In this and other ways, Keats and all the Romantics abandoned the poetic theory of the century before. Eighteenth century poetry was formal, didactic, and objective in stance. Its chief aim was to show to the world (that is, to mankind) a picture of itself for its own improvement and edification. Its chief ornament was art: puns, wordplay, satiric description, and so forth. In short, what eighteenth century poets saw as virtue in poetry was logic and rigid metrics. Nineteenth century poets wrote from a radically different philosophical base, due in part to the cataclysmic political changes surrounding the American and French revolutions. Before these upheavals occurred, a belief in order and measure extended into all facets of life, from social relations to literature; extremes were shunned in all things as unnatural, dangerous, and perhaps blasphemous.

After 1789, when the social order in France turned upside down, an expectation of the millennium arose in England, especially in liberal intellectual circles; the old rules of poetry were thrown off with the outworn social strictures, and a new aesthetic bloomed in their place. Its ruling faculty was imagination: Romantic poets frequently stated that poems ought to be composed on the inspiration of the moment, thereby faithfully recording the purity of the emotion. In fact, Keats and his contemporaries labored hard over their creations; they exerted themselves not to smoothness of meter but to preserving the grace of spontaneity while achieving precision in observation of natural and psychological phenomena. Poets saw themselves as charting hitherto unexplored reaches of human experience, extremes of joy and dejection, guilt and redemption, pride and degradation. They wrote meditations, confessions, and conversations, in which natural things were seen to abet internal states. And they wrote ballads and narratives, such as "The Eve of St. Agnes," set in the past or in distant parts of the world and using archaic language and rhythms to make the related events seem even more strange and wonderful. Over and over they described epiphanous moments when the human consciousness becomes one with nature, when all is made new, when divinity animates the inanimate, and the lowest creature seems wondrous. This way of seeing was thought to be a return to an earlier consciousness lost in early childhood—the theme of Wordsworth's seminal "Ode: Intimations of Immortality."

In "The Eve of St. Agnes," Keats attempts, among other things, to maintain this elevated state of mind throughout the narrative. He sets the story in medieval times, so that the familiar Romeo-and-Juliet characters take on charm from their quaint surroundings, and from the archaic language in which they speak and are described. Its verse form is the Spenserian stanza, smooth yet free, with its slightly asymmetric rhyme scheme that avoids the monotony of couplet or quatrain, and the piquant extension of the ninth line which gives to the whole an irregularity echoing ordinary speech. The first five stanzas contrast the Beadsman, coldly at his prayers, with the "argent revelry" making gaudy the great hall. This imagery of cold and warmth, silver and scarlet, chastity and sensuality continues throughout the poem, a comment on the plot.

That the poem is named for a virgin martyr yet tells the story of an elopement is likewise significant; for the point of the poem, on the one hand, is that piety and passion are opposing but inseparable drives. Each without the other has no point of reference. Porphyro without Madeline becomes the gross Lord Maurice, the savage Hildebrand; Madeline without Porphyro becomes the Beadsman with his deathlike abrogation of sensuality. Instead, Porphyro is made to faint at the celestial beauty of Madeline at her prayers, Madeline to be wooed by songs and colors and things to eat. But what fruits! Not mere groceries, but the glowing essence of fruitfulness, tribute to a love match of the meditative and emotional faculties that, when accomplished in one individual, fulfills the whole human potential.

The other theme, or perhaps the other face of the same theme, is the relentless press of quotidian misery on the poetic personality, another favorite arena of reflection among the Romantics, and one that was poignantly near Keats's heart, menaced by tuberculosis as he was, and his younger brother having died of the disease the previous winter. The lovers are shown, unearthly fair, escaping from a house where wrath and drunkenness hold sway, bound for a dream-vision of happiness. Significantly, the poet does not follow them to their southern sanctuary. Instead he relates the wretched end of Angela, who dies "palsy-twitched" in her sleep; the cold sleep of the Beadsman among the ashes; the drunken nightmares of the Baron and his guests. The ending, in short, is not unreservedly happy, but partakes of that bittersweet emotion which in the midst of joy acknowledges wretchedness, the mark of a mind that strives for aesthetic detachment while believing in its duty to the rest of humankind.

EVERYMAN

Type of work: Drama
Author: Unknown
Type of plot: Moral allegory
Time of plot: Any time
Locale: Any place
Earliest extant version: 1508

Thanks to the preservation of four printed versions from the sixteenth century, this is one of the few morality plays to survive into the present. In addition, it has contemporary appeal, having been produced several times within the twentieth century. Written to teach moral lessons to the illiterate masses, the characters of the play are personifications of virtue and vice.

Principal Characters

God, who has decided to have a reckoning of all men.

Death, summoned to receive God's instructions to search out Everyman. Death agrees to give Everyman some time to gather together companions to make the journey with him.

Everyman, whom Death approaches and orders to make the long journey to Paradise in order to give an accounting for his life.

Good-Deeds, the one companion who can and will make the entire journey with Everyman. Everyman finds Good-Deeds too weak to stir, but after Everyman accepts penance, Good-Deeds is fit for the journey.

Knowledge, the sister of Good-Deeds. Knowledge offers to guide Everyman, but cannot go with him into the presence of his Maker.

Confession, who lives in the house of salvation. Confession gives penance to Everyman.

Discretion, Strength, Beauty, and **The Five Wits,** companions who go part of the way with Everyman.

Fellowship, Kindred, and **Goods,** to whom Everyman turns for companions. All offer to help, but refuse when they learn the nature of the journey.

A Messenger, who appears in prologue to announce a moral play to the audience. He warns that man should look to the end of his life.

A Doctor, who appears at the end to remind the audience that only Good-Deeds will avail at the final judgment.

The Story

One day a Messenger appeared to announce a moral play on the summoning of Everyman. In the beginning of his life, he declared, man should look to the ending, for we shall see how all earthly possessions avail little in the final reckoning. At first sin looks sweet, but in the end it causes the soul to weep in pain.

Then God spoke. All living creatures were unkind to Him. They lived with no spiritual thought in their worldly possessions. The Crucifixion was a lesson they had forgotten. Man had turned to the Seven Deadly Sins, and every year his state grew worse. Therefore, God had decided to have a reckoning of all men, lest mankind should become more brutish than the beasts.

At an imperative summons Death came to receive his instructions. He was ordered to search out every man and tell him that he had to make a pilgrimage to his final reckoning. Death promised to be cruel in his search for each man who lived outside God's law.

Spying Everyman walking unconcernedly about his business, his mind on fleshly lust and treasure, Death bade him stand still and asked him if he had forgotten his Maker. Then Death announced that God had dispatched him in all haste to warn Everyman. Everyman was to make a long journey, and he was to take with him his full book of accounts. He was to be very careful, for he had done many bad deeds and only a few good ones. In Paradise he would soon be forced to account for his life.

Everyman protested that death was farthest from his thoughts at the time. Death was adamant, setting no store by worldly goods or rank, for when he summoned all men must obey. Everyman cried in vain for respite. Then he asked if he must go on the long journey alone. Death assured him that he could take any companions who would make the journey with him. Reminding him that his life was only his on loan, Death said he would return very shortly; in the meantime Everyman would have an opportunity to find possible companions for his journey.

Weeping for his plight and wishing he had never been born, Everyman thought of Fellowship, with whom he had spent so many agreeable days in sport and play. Fortunately he saw Fellowship close by and spoke to him. Seeing Everyman's sad countenance, Fellowship asked his trouble. Everyman told him he was in deep sorrow because he had to make a journey. Fellowship reminded him of their past friendship and vowed that he would go anywhere with him, even to Hell. Greatly heartened, Everyman told him of Death's appearance and his urgent summons. Fellowship thought of the long trip from which there would be no return and decided against accompanying Everyman. He would go with him in sport and play, he declared, or to seek lusty women, but he definitely refused to go on that pilgrimage.

Cast down by this setback, Everyman thought of Kindred. Surely the ties of blood were strong. His Kindred swore that they would help him in any way they could, but when they heard that Everyman had to account for his every deed, good or bad, they knew at once the last journey he had in mind. They refused in one voice to go with him. Everyman appealed directly to his favorite cousin, who said he would have gone willingly if it had not been for a cramp in his toe.

Still reflecting on his woes, Everyman thought of turning to Goods. All his life he had loved Goods. Goods heard his plea and offered to help him, but when asked to go on that journey to the highest judge of all, Goods promptly refused. Everyman reminded him that money is supposed to right all wrongs. Goods disagreed with him. Anyway, if Everyman took Goods with him he would be the worse off, for worldly goods were not given, only lent.

Everyman became ashamed of having sought unworthy companions. Calling aloud to Good-Deeds, he asked again for help. Good-Deeds answered feebly, for he was lying on the cold ground, bound by sins. Good-Deeds already knew of the projected journey and wanted to go along, but he was too weak to stir. It was revealed that Good-Deeds had a sister, Knowledge, who would stay with Everyman until Good-Deeds could regain strength.

Promptly Knowledge offered to go with him and guide him in his great need. Knowledge led him to Confession, who lived in the house of salvation, to ask for strength for Good-Deeds. Confession in pity gave penance to Everyman to shrive his soul. Accepting penance joyfully, Everyman scourged his flesh and afterward Knowledge bequeathed him to his Savior. Thankfully Good-Deeds rose from the ground, delivered from sickness and woe. Declaring himself fit for the journey, Good-Deeds promised to help Everyman count his good works before the judgment throne. With a smile of sympathy Knowledge told Everyman to be glad and merry, for Good-Deeds would be his true companion. Knowledge gave a garment to Everyman to wear, a garment of sorrow which would deliver him from pain.

Asking Good-Deeds if his account were ready, Everyman prepared to start his pilgrimage. Good-Deeds reminded him that three other companions would go part of the way: Discretion, Strength, and Beauty. Knowledge proposed also the Five Wits, who would be his counselors. After Kindred had called the new companions together, Everyman, now well fortified, set out on his last journey.

Knowledge said that their first stop must be to see the priest, who would give Everyman unction and ointment, for priests perform the seven unctions as intermediaries of God. Surely priests were man's best hope on earth, in spite of the many weak and venal people who somehow were invested with holy orders.

After receiving the last rites from the priest, Everyman prepared to meet Death. Again he was troubled, however, for one by one his companions left him. Even Knowledge refused to go with him into the presence of his Maker. Only Good-Deeds stayed with Everyman until the end. So it is with every man who must die. Knowledge, Strength, Beauty—all the other companions are a help in the journey, but only Good-Deeds can face death.

The Angel greeted Everyman as an elected spouse of Jesus. Taking him on high, he announced that Everyman was thus exalted by reason of his singular virtue. When Everyman's soul was taken from his body, his reckoning was crystal clear. So shall it be with every man, if he will only live well before his doom.

Finally a Doctor appeared to remind all men that on the last journey, Beauty, Strength, Discretion, and the Five Wits forsake every man at the end; only Good-Deeds avail at the final judgment.

Critical Evaluation

The morality play, of which *Everyman* is the best extant example, and the mystery play are the two principal kinds of medieval drama. The mystery play is a dramatic recreation of a story from Scripture, and its aim is the elucidation of the revelation contained in the Bible. The morality play is an allegorical form, peopled by personified abstractions, such as Beauty, Justice, and Fortitude, and types such as Everyman, Priest, and King. In addition, the subject matter is admonitory, particularly concerning man's last end. As Albert Baugh has pointed out, it is difficult to discover precise sources for the subject matter or the dramatic method. There are, however, certain parallels in medieval sermons, which often bolstered moral exhortations with allegorical examples. Indeed, allegory is pervasive in medieval literature as is, for that matter, concern about a happy death, but how these evolved into the particular form of the morality play is hard to tell.

Few morality plays have survived, and only *Everyman* is well enough thought of to be dignified with modern performance. One reason for the unpopularity of the genre is the limitation placed on dramatic complication by the static nature of the personifications. The characters are of necessity simple and there is no possibility of change except perhaps in a central type like Everyman. All characters are partially—and most characters are completely—frozen as what they are. As a result, there can be little psychological insight and little of the diverse movement that invigorates earlier and later drama.

Like all forms of allegory, the method is essentially intellectual. The active involvement of the spectator is not through emotion so much as it is in the discovery of the meanings of characters and the significance of the configurations in which they are arranged. Allegory engages the mind and *Everyman* succeeds well in representing a complex, highly specific, theological system, while generating, by juxtaposition and order, sufficient immediacy to give force to the moral exhortation. The structure is elegant and compact; there is no attempt to catalog the deficiencies of Everyman's past life. Rather the play focuses on the poignant hour of death and implies what Everyman is and what he ought to be at that critical moment.

Because of the allegorical method, it is easy to trivialize the significance of the play by reducing it to the identification of the personifications. But one thereby misses the awesome power of its abstractions and the complex view of life that is represented. A play about the reaction to imminent death, *Everyman*, in its configurations of characters, implies much about how life should be lived. When God initiates the action, we begin with the premise that all men are to be called to give an account of their actions. As the plot develops, it would perhaps be more accurate to refer to the central character as Anyman, but the use of the name Everyman implies that the experience is not random, not what might happen, but is paradigmatic of what will happen and how we ought to respond.

As Everyman turns to his valued, habitual companions for comfort on his difficult and dangerous journey, it is important that the playwright does not present a pageant of specific sins. Instead, in Fellowship, Kindred, and Goods, we have summary abstractions, which are not particular sins in themselves, but rather examples of the distractions which divert man away from positive direction toward God and salvation. Thus, Everyman's fail-ures are represented not by a static series of vices, but by the vital enticements which have taken too much of his attention. The conception is a Dantean analysis of sin as a turning away from God, the end toward Whom we ought to tend, in favor of the preoccupations of this world.

In the theology of the play, salvation obviously cannot come by faith alone, since it is imperative that Everyman be accompanied to judgment by Good Deeds. However, Good Deeds is so infirm, because of Everyman's prior misdirection, that a prior step is necessary: Everyman is entrusted to Knowledge for guidance. The implication is that knowledge of the institutional Church and its remedies is necessary for the successful living of the good life. Knowledge first directs Everyman to Confession, one of the tangible means of repentance and regeneration. When Confession has been completed, Good Deeds begins to revive since contrition and amendment free the accumulated merits of past virtuous actions.

Knowledge also summons other attainments which can travel at least part way with Everyman. Beauty, Strength, Discretion, and Five Wits are all auxiliary human accomplishments which can help and comfort men along their way, though none can persevere to the final moment of judgment. As they fall away, one by one, we are watching the process of death. Of course Beauty is the first to depart in this telescoped version of man's death. Of course Strength follows as life ebbs. The last of the attainments to leave is Five Wits, the sensual means through which man acquires whatever understanding he gains in life.

In the end, even Knowledge, the representative of the human intellect, which builds on sense and is a higher power than sense, cannot go the whole distance with Everyman. The respect for Knowledge in the play's implied theological system is enormous: Knowledge plays the pivotal role in informing Everyman of the way to salvation. Yet, in the final analysis, only Good Deeds can descend into the grave with Everyman because it is only the efficacious result of knowledge in right living that merits eternal reward.

An examination of the abstractions and of the arrangement of them reveals in *Everyman* the complex shape of medieval Christianity. The play suggests a means to salvation everywhere consistent with the prescriptions of the medieval church; there is an ultimate accountability, but man has the capacity, through faith and reason, to direct himself toward God by using the institution of the Church to enable him to do the good which is required of all men.

A FABLE

Type of work: Novel
Author: William Faulkner (1897–1962)
Type of plot: Religious allegory
Time of plot: 1918
Locale: Western Front in France
First published: 1954

Like many of Faulkner's other novels, A Fable *is steeped in mythic allusions, both biblical and pagan. Yet, the work still has a life of its own, a statement equally true for Faulkner's other works. Nine years in the writing, the novel obviously alludes to the events of Christ's Passion and Crucifixion; these elements are interwoven into a narrative set during World War I. The work departs, as does* The Wild Palms, *from Faulkner's ambitious and spectacularly successful development of his own mythic creation, Yoknapatawpha County.*

Principal Characters

The Corporal, a Christlike soldier. Accompanied by his twelve squad members, the Corporal brings about a cease-fire along the entire Western front by preaching peace on earth. His story bears a strong, yet often subtle resemblance to the life of Christ, the Passion, and the Crucifixion as events unfold which correspond in some degree to the birth, the betrayal, the denial, the Last Supper, and the death of Christ. Refusing an offer of freedom, the Corporal is executed between two murderers and buried at his sister's farm. Shellfire destroys the grave, but ironically his body is recovered and placed in the Unknown Soldier's tomb. These events suggest resurrection and immortality of a sort.

The Marshal, commander in chief of the Allied Armies in France. As a young man stationed in the Middle East he had seduced a woman and fathered a son who turns out to be the Corporal who instigated the mutiny. The old man never seems surprised by the turn of events and apparently is omniscient. He offers the Corporal an opportunity to escape, but must order his execution when he refuses.

General Gragnon, the French division commander. When his regiment refuses to attack the German line, he arrests the entire three thousand and insists upon his own arrest. While in prison he is executed by a brutal American soldier named Buchwald.

The Quartermaster General, the Marshal's former fellow student. After the Corporal's execution, he loses faith in the cause for which the Marshal stands.

The Runner, a former officer. Sympathizing with the Corporal's aims, he is crippled in a surprise barrage while fraternizing with the Germans. At the Marshal's funeral he throws a medal obtained at the Corporal's grave at the caisson and shouts his derision and defiance.

Marthe, the Corporal's half sister.

Marya, the Corporal's feeble-minded half sister.

Polchek, the soldier in the Corporal's squad who betrays him.

Pierre Bouc, the soldier in the Corporal's squad who denies him.

The Corporal's Wife, a former prostitute.

Buchwald, the American soldier who executes General Gragnon.

The Reverend Tobe Sutterfield, an American black preacher.

David Levine, a British flight officer who commits suicide.

The Story

On a Monday in May, 1918, a most unusual event took place on a battlefield in France where French and German troops faced one another after four years of trench warfare. At dawn, the regiment under the command of General Gragnon refused to attack. Another unbelievable event occurred when the Germans, who were expected to take advantage of the mutiny, did not move either. At noon, the whole sector of the front stopped firing, and soon the rest of the front came to a standstill. Division Commander Gragnon requested execution of all three thousand mutineers; he also demanded his own arrest.

On Wednesday, the lorries carrying the mutinous regiment arrived at headquarters in Chaulnesmont, where the dishonor brought on the town aroused the people to noisy demonstration. Relatives and friends of the mutineers knew that a corporal and his squad of twelve, moving in a mysterious way behind the lines, had succeeded in spreading their ideas about peace on earth and good will toward men among the troops. Four of the thirteen men were not Frenchmen by birth; among those only the Corporal spoke French, and he was the object of the crowd's fury.

This situation created uncertainty among the Allied generals because a war ended by mutiny was not reconcilable with military principles. To clarify the confusion, a conference to which a German general was invited took place, and an agreement was reached for continuation of the war.

To young Flight Officer David Levine, the unsuspected pause in war meant tragedy. Determined to find glory in battle but realizing that he might miss his opportunity, he committed suicide. To another soldier, the Runner, the truce at the front was a welcome sign. A former officer, he had rejected submissive principles and abuse of authority by superiors, and he had been returned to the ranks. Having heard about the Corporal from the Reverend Tobe Sutterfield, an American black preacher who had arrived under unexplainable circumstances in France, the Runner tried to show once again the power of the Corporal's ideas. He forced a sentry, who profiteered by collecting fees for life insurance among the soldiers, to leave the trenches and join a British battalion in a peaceful walk toward the German line. When they showed their empty hands, the Germans also came unarmed to meet the French. A sudden artillery barrage by French and German guns, however, killed the sentry and crippled the Runner.

The man to decide the fate of the mutineers was the commander in chief of the Allied Armies, an aged French marshal. The orphaned son of a prominent family, he had attended France's St. Cyr. There his unselfish attitude combined with his devotion to studies had made him an outstanding and beloved student. Especially attracted to him was the man who was now his quartermaster general. After leaving school, the Marshal had been stationed in the Sahara, where he incurred blood-guilt by sacrificing a brutal legionnaire to tribal justice. Later, he spent several years in a Tibetan monastery. In the Middle East, he had met a married woman with two daughters. His affair with her resulted in the birth of a son in a stable at Christmas. The mother died in childbirth, and Marthe, one of the daughters, cared for the boy. When World War I broke out, the Marshal became the Allied commander and the hope of France.

The mutinous troops were kept in a former factory building while awaiting trial. The Marshal, not surprised by the court proceedings, seemed to anticipate all answers. Marthe and Marya, the Corporal's half sisters, and his wife arrived in Chaulnesmont and, in an interview with the Marshal, revealed that the Corporal was the Marshal's son. Marthe had married a French farmer, Dumont, and

her half brother had grown up on her farm. Soon after the outbreak of war, he had enlisted in the army and received a medal for bravery in action. He had married a former prostitute from Marseilles. Again, the old Marshal was not surprised and seemed to know every detail.

On Thursday, a meal was served to the squad during which it became known that soldier Polchek had betrayed the Corporal. Another soldier, Pierre Bouc, denied his leader thrice. After the meal, the Corporal was called away to meet the Marshal. On a hill overlooking the town, the Marshal tried to explain the futility of his son's martyrdom. When he promised a secret ocean passage to allow him to escape the death penalty, the Corporal refused the offer. Later the Marshal made a last attempt to influence his son with the help of an army priest. Recognizing his own unworthiness before the humble Corporal, the priest committed suicide. On the same evening, General Gragnon was executed by an American soldier named Buchwald.

On Friday, the Corporal was tied to a post between two criminals. Shot, he fell into a coil of barbed wire that lacerated his head. The Corporal's body and his medal were buried on the Dumont farm near St. Mihiel. After the burial, a sudden artillery barrage plowed the earth, leaving no trace of the Corporal's grave.

After the war, a unit was sent to reclaim a body to be placed in the Unknown Soldier's tomb under the Arc de Triomphe in Paris. As a reward, the soldiers were promised brandy. Near Verdun, they obtained a body and drank the brandy. While they were guarding the coffin, an old woman approached. Having lost her mind because her son had not returned from the war, she had sold her farm in order to search for him. Knowing about the mission of the soldiers, she wanted to look at the body. Convinced that the dead soldier was her son, she offered all her money for the corpse; the soldiers accepted and bought more brandy with the money. They secured another body from a field adjoining the Dumont farm. Thus, the body of the Corporal reached Paris. Four years later, the Runner visited the Dumont farm and picked up the medal.

Six years later, the Marshal's body was carried to the Arc de Triomphe, with dignitaries of the Western world following the coffin on foot to pay their respects to the dead leader. As soon as the eulogy started, a cripple made his way through the crowd. It was the Runner, who threw the Corporal's medal at the caisson before an angry mob closed in and attacked him. Rescued by the police, he was dragged into a side street, where a few curious onlookers gathered around the injured cripple. While he lay in the gutter, a man resembling the old Quartermaster General stepped forward to comfort the Runner, who declared that he would never die.

Critical Evaluation

A Fable is probably the most ambitious, though not the most successful, work of one of the twentieth century's most ambitious novelists. By juxtaposing elements of the Passion of Christ to a story of trench mutiny in World War I, William Faulkner attempts to combine two very different types of narrative: an allegorical "fable" based upon parallels between the events of his story and those of the original "myth" as well as a realistic narrative of war, politics, and personal relationships.

Most of the similarities to Christ's life and death are obvious. The Corporal, who was born in a stable and is thirty-three years old, leads a mutinous group of twelve followers, and the events surrounding his capture and execution suggest the Passion: one disciple betrays him for money, another denies him three times; the followers have a "Last Supper"; the Corporal is executed between two thieves in a manner that suggests Christ's Crucifixion; he acquires a crown of thorns; he is mourned by women who resemble Mary Magdalene and Mary; and his body vanishes three days after burial. It is necessary, however, to remember that *A Fable* is *not* the Passion retold in modern dress. Faulkner does not simply update or interpret Christian myth: he *uses* it. Therefore, any attempt to come to terms with *A Fable* must consider the unique, personal vision that Faulkner presents in his book.

Some critics have faulted the novel on the grounds that the Corporal's personality is insufficiently developed. It is true that he is not strongly individualized, but to present the character in greater detail would risk either the creation of a purely symbolic figure or one too humanized to maintain the Christ parallel. Instead, the Corporal remains a silent, mysterious embodiment of man's spiritual side; the concrete presentation of his "meaning" is entrusted to other characters. The most important thing is that, for all the biblical allusions, the Corporal is not the chosen Son of God, but is definitely a son of man—specifically of the Marshal—and the thematic center of the novel is dramatized in the conflict between the Corporal and his father-Marshal antagonist.

In the novel's most powerful and important scene, the final confrontation between the two men, the Marshal defines their basic natures as

> two articulations . . . not so much to defend as to test two inimical conditions which . . . must contend and one of them—perish: I champion of the mundane earth . . . while you champion of an esoteric realm of man's baseless and his infinite capacity—no passion—for unfact.

Thus, *A Fable* is not really about man's relationship to God, or even to society, but to himself. Each of these men stands for one aspect of the human personality, and the conflict between them can be seen in several ways: son versus father, youth versus age, idealist versus realist, common man versus authority, heart versus mind. In short, the major conflict of the book is, in the words of Faulkner's Nobel Prize speech, "the human heart in conflict with itself"—man's basic dualism: the major theme of Faulkner's late fiction.

If the Corporal remains the shadowy incarnation of man's spiritual side, the Marshal, both in his symbolic and his realistic functions, is a much more vivid and complicated character. On the literal level, it is he, as the supreme commander of the Allied Armies in France, who masterminds the successful military counterstrategy; symbolically, as the primary representative of secular power, the Marshal represents everything in human society that denies personal autonomy and spiritual freedom to man.

Any attempt to pin down the Marshal's symbolic antecedents more precisely is very difficult. At times he suggests Satan, at times Pilate or Caesar, or simply military authority, but in the central confrontation scene, his role seems to most closely resemble that of the "Grand Inquisitor," who appears in the greatest of earlier "Second Coming" fictions, Ivan Karamazov's parable in Fyodor Dostoevski's *The Brothers Karamazov.*

Like the Grand Inquisitor, the Marshal faces a Christ surrogate who poses a threat to the established order. Likewise, the Marshal makes an offer to his antagonist of life and freedom in return for betrayal, which he knows in advance will be refused. The Marshal's background also resembles the Inquisitor's in that he, too, began life with a spiritual quest by renouncing the world in favor of the desert and the mountains. Like the Inquisitor—and Christ—the Marshal was tempted and, like the Inquisitor—*but unlike Christ*—he accepted the temptations and the view of life they represented in return for temporal power.

Thus, although he knows and understands man's duality, the Marshal rejects the spiritual and creative side of man and accepts him only as a mundane, earthbound creature who needs security and control rather than individual freedom and spiritual fulfillment. Further, on the practical level, he commits himself to the human institution that fixes and formalizes this view of man. Like the Inquisitor, the Marshal justifies his actions on the grounds that they are what man needs and wants. He taunts his opponent with the notion that he, not the Corporal, is the true believer in man: "after the last ding dong of doom has rung and died there will still be one sound more; his voice, planning still to build something higher and faster and louder. . . . I don't fear man, I do better: I respect and admire him. . . . Because man and his folly—they will prevail."

These words echo the Nobel Prize speech but differ in one important respect from the novelist's own; in the address, Faulkner went on to add: "He is immortal, not because he alone among creatures has an inexhaustible voice, but because he has a soul, a spirit capable of compassion and sacrifice and endurance." This statement defines the essence of the conflict between the Marshal and the Corporal and their visions.

If the Marshal's view of mankind is correct, then the military hierarchy, the rituals and institutions it supports, and the war itself are things man creates for himself and needs for survival. The Corporal's mutiny is, therefore, not only foolish, but even destructive to man's well-being. On the other hand, if the Corporal's vision is true, such things are artificial, malevolent restraints on man's potential. The mutiny in this context becomes a necessary act in the struggle to cast off the life-denying lies and organizations imposed on him and to fulfill his own human and spiritual capacities by taking control of his own destiny. Because the immediate secular power belongs to the Marshal, the earthbound view seems to win, but the question Faulkner raises is whether the impact of the Corporal's actions and martyrdom does not postulate the ultimate triumph of the spiritual vision.

To answer that question, Faulkner attempts to work out the implications of the Corporal's ethic in the actions of several other characters and especially in the attempt of the English Runner to foment a second and wider mutiny. Here lies the primary critical problem of the book: Do these secondary actions establish and elaborate the novel's main thrust, or do they obscure and finally bury it?

Although he borrows Christian symbolism, Faulkner is clearly not presenting a conventionally religious message. He affirms the human spirit, but his attitude toward its ultimate fate is ambiguous. If the Corporal dies a heroic martyr, the other witnesses to the human spirit—the English Runner, the Sentry, the Reverend Sutterfield, the Quartermaster General—suffer dubious or ignominious fates, and even the Corporal's death has no clear effect beyond stimulating the Runner's quixotic gestures. Faulkner postulates *hope* and *faith* as vital elements in man's fulfillment, but they are presented as ends in themselves; it is unclear what man should hope *for* or have faith *in*.

It seems likely that Faulkner began to write *A Fable* with a number of abstract concepts in mind rather than a special set of human experiences. (In his best works, in contrast, the meanings grow out of concrete situations.) Consequently, the novel is not completely satisfying on either the realistic or the symbolic level. Yet, even with these problems, *A Fable* is a powerful novel. If it fails to fulfill completely Faulkner's most ambitious intentions, it does present separate characters and scenes that are powerful and memorable, and if all of Faulkner's concepts are not completely clear, his dramatization of man's basic duality is stimulating and provocative.

THE FAERIE QUEENE

Type of work: Poem
Author: Edmund Spenser (1552?–1599)
Type of plot: Allegorical epic
Time of plot: The Arthurian Age
Locale: England
First published: Books 1–3, 1590; books 4–6, 1596

The Faerie Queene *is the first sustained poetic creation in English after Chaucer. For this lengthy epic, Spenser created his own form, known as the Spenserian stanza: nine lines, eight of five feet, and one of six, rhyming ababbcbcc. The characters and plot are completely allegorical, representing such concepts as chastity and its trials, and lust and its conquests. Most importantly, however, the richness of characterization and detail of plot, as well as the beauty of its language, give* The Faerie Queene *much more than historical significance.*

Principal Characters

Gloriana, the Faerie Queene, an idealized portrait of Queen Elizabeth. Although she does not appear in the extant portion of the poem, many of the knights set out upon their quests from her court, and they often praise her virtue and splendor.

Prince Arthur, the legendary British hero, who represents Magnificence, the perfection of all virtues. He rides in search of Gloriana, who had appeared to him in a vision, and, on his way, aids knights in distress.

The Red Cross Knight, the hero of book 1, where he represents both England's patron, Saint George, and Christian man in search of Holiness. He sets out confidently to rescue Una's parents from the dragon of evil, but he is attacked by forces of sin and error which drive him to the point of suicide. He is restored in the House of Holiness by the teachings and offices of the Church and, refreshed by a fountain and a tree, symbolizing the sacraments of baptism and communion, he triumphs in his three-day combat with the dragon.

Una, the daughter of the King and Queen of the West, Adam and Eve; she personifies Truth and the Church. She advises her knight wisely, but she cannot protect him from himself. Deserted, she is aided by a lion and a troop of satyrs, and is finally restored to the Red Cross Knight, who is betrothed to her after his victory over the dragon.

The Dwarf, her companion, Common Sense.

Error, the Red Cross Knight's first adversary, a monster who lives in the wandering wood.

Archimago, a satanic figure who uses many disguises in his attempts to lure the knights and ladies of the poem into sin and disaster.

Duessa, his accomplice, whose attractive appearance hides her real hideousness. She represents variously Falsehood, the Roman Catholic church, and Mary, Queen of Scots.

Sans Foy, Sans Loy, and **Sans Joy,** Saracen knights, who attack Una and her knight.

Fradubio, a knight betrayed by Duessa and transformed into a tree.

Kirkrapine, a church robber, slain by Una's lion when he tries to enter the cottage where she has taken refuge.

Abessa, his mistress.

Corceca, her blind mother.

Lucifera, mistress of the House of Pride.

Malvenu, her porter.

Vanity, her usher.

Night, the mother of falsehood, to whom Duessa appeals for help.

Aesculapius, the physician of the gods.

Sylvanus, the leader of the satyrs, who rescues Una from Sans Loy.

Satyrane, a valiant, gentle knight who is half nobleman, half satyr.

Despair, an emaciated creature who drives warriors to suicide with his sophistic recitals of their sins.

Trevisan, one of his intended victims.

Dame Coelia, a virtuous matron who lives in the House of Holiness.

Fidelia, Speranza, and **Charissa,** her daughters, Faith, Hope, and Charity.

Contemplation, a holy hermit who gives the Red Cross Knight a vision of the City of God, then sends him back into the world to complete his quest.

Guyon, the Knight of Temperance, the sternest of the Spenserian heroes, who must violently destroy Acrasia's power and all its temptations that lead men to intemperance.

Palmer, his faithful companion, who stands for Reason or Prudence.

Acrasia, the Circelike mistress of the Bower of Bliss. She lures men to their ruin in her world of debilitating luxuriance and turns them into animals.

Amavia, the desolate widow of one of her victims.

Ruddymane, her baby, whose hands cannot be cleansed of his dying mother's blood.

Medina, Perissa, and **Elissa,** sisters who personify the mean, the deficiency, and the excess of temperance.

Sir Huddibras, a malcontent, Elissa's lover.

Braggadocio, a vain-glorious braggart who masquerades as a knight on Guyon's stolen horse.

Trompart, his miserly companion.

Belphoebe, a virgin huntress, reared by the goddess Diana, who cannot respond to the devotion offered by Prince Arthur's squire, Timias. She is another of the figures conceived as a compliment to Elizabeth.

Furor, a churlish fellow whom Guyon finds furiously beating a helpless squire.

Occasion, his mother, a hag.

Phedon, the maltreated squire, who falls into Furor's hands through his jealousy of his lady, Pryene, and his friend Philemon.

Pyrochles and **Cymochles,** intemperate knights defeated by Guyon.

Atin, Pyrochles' servant.

Phaedria, a coquette who lures knights to her island, where she lulls them into forgetfulness of their quests.

Mammon, the god of riches, who sits in rusty armor surveying his hoard of gold.

Philotime, his daughter, who holds the golden chain of ambition.

Alma, the soul, mistress of the castle of the body where Guyon and Prince Arthur take refuge.

Phantastes and **Eumnestes,** guardians, respectively, of fantasy and of memory.

Maleger, the captain of the shadowy forces who attacked the bulwarks of the House of Alma.

Verdant, a knight released by Guyon from Acrasia's clutches.

Grille, one of Acrasia's victims. He reviles Guyon and the Palmer for restoring his human form.

Britomart, the maiden knight, heroine of the book of Chastity. She subdues the forces of lust as she travels in search of Artegall, with whom she fell in love when she saw him in a magic mirror. Her union with him represents the alliance of justice and mercy as well as Spenser's ideal of married chastity, which surpasses the austere virginity of Belphoebe.

Malecasta, the lady of delight, beautiful and wanton, who entertains Britomart in Castle Joyous.

Glauce, Britomart's nurse, who accompanies her as her squire.

Merlin, the famous magician, whom Glauce and Britomart consult to learn the identity of the knight in the mirror.

Marinell, the timid son of a sea nymph and Florimell's lover.

Cymoent, his mother.

Florimell, the loveliest and gentlest of the ladies in Faerie Land. She is pursued by many evil beings, men and gods, before she is wed to Marinell.

Timias, Prince Arthur's squire, who is healed of severe wounds by Belphoebe. Although he falls in love with her, he can never win more than kindness as a response.

Crysogene, the mother of Belphoebe and Amoret, who were conceived by the sun.

Argante, a giantess, one of the figures of lust.

Ollyphant, her brother and lover.

A Squire of Dames, Argante's prisoner.

Snowy Florimell, Braggadocio's lady, a creature made by a witch with whom Florimell had stayed.

Proteus, the shepherd of the sea, who rescues Florimell from a lecherous fisherman.

Panope, an old nymph, his housekeeper.

Paridell, a vain, lascivious knight.

Malbecco, a miserly, jealous old man.

Hellenore, his young wife, who runs away with Paridell.

Scudamour, the knight most skilled in the art of courtly love. He wins Amoret at the court of Venus, but she is taken from him almost immediately.

Amoret, his beautiful bride, who is taken prisoner at her own wedding by Busirane, who represents her own passions and the confining forces of the rigid code of love in which she has grown up.

Busirane, her captor.

Venus, the goddess of love and a personification of the creative force in nature, Amoret's foster mother.

Adonis, her lover.

Diana, the divine huntress, the virgin goddess who raises Belphoebe.

Ate, Discord, a malicious old woman.

Blandamour, a fickle knight.

Sir Ferraugh, one of the suitors of Snowy Florimell.

Cambello, one of the knights of friendship.

Canacee, his sister, a wise and beautiful lady who is won by Triamond.

Cambina, Cambello's wife.

Priamond, Diamond, and **Triamond,** brothers who fight for the hand of Canacee. The first two are killed, but their strength passes into their victorious surviving brother.

Artegall, the knight of Justice, Britomart's beloved.

Talus, the iron man, The Red Cross Knight's implacable attendant, who upholds justice untempered by mercy.

Aemylia, a lady imprisoned with Amoret by a villainous churl and rescued by Belphoebe.

Corflambo, a mighty pagan who corrupts his enemies by filling them with lust.

Poeana, his rude, tyrannical daughter.

Amyas, the Squire of Low Degree, Aemylia's suitor.

Placidas, another squire loved by Poeana. Encouraged by Prince Arthur, Placidas marries Poeana and reforms her.

Druon and **Claribell,** pugnacious companions of Blandamour and Paridell.

Thames and **Medway,** the river-god and goddess whose marriage is attended by the famous waterways of the world.

Neptune, the sea god to whom Marinell's mother pleads for Florimell's release from Proteus.

Grantorto, a tyrant who holds Irena's country in his power. He is the emblem of the political strength of the Roman Catholic church.

Irena, his victim, who appeals to the Faerie Queene for help.

Sir Sanglier, a cruel lord, chastened by Talus.

Pollente, a Saracen warrior who extorts money from travelers.

Munera, his daughter, the keeper of his treasury.

Giant Communism, Artegall's foe. He tries to weigh everything in his scales, but he learns, before Talus hurls him into the sea, that truth and falsehood, right and wrong, cannot be balanced.

Amidas and **Bracidas,** brothers whose dispute over a treasure chest is settled by Artegall.

Philtera, Bracidas' betrothed, who weds his wealthy brother.

Lucy, Amidas' deserted sweetheart and Bracidas' wife.

Sir Turpine, a knight whom Artegall discovers bound and tormented by Amazon warriors.

Radigund, Queen of the Amazons. She captures Artegall and dresses him in woman's clothes to humiliate him, then falls in love with him and tries unsuccessfully to win him.

Clarinda, her attendant, who comes to love Artegall as she woos him for her mistress.

Dolon, Deceit, a knight who tries to entrap Britomart.

Mercilla, a just and merciful maiden queen whose realm is threatened by a mighty warrior.

The Souldan, her enemy, thought to represent Philip of Spain. He is destroyed by the brilliant light of Prince Arthur's diamond shield.

Malengin, an ingenious villain who transforms himself into different shapes at will. Talus crushes him with his iron flail.

Belgae, a mother who loses twelve of her seventeen children to the tyrant Geryoneo and appeals to Mercilla for help.

Geryoneo, her enemy, the power of Spain, who is slain by Artegall.

Burbon, a knight rescued by Artegall as he fights Grantorto's men to rescue his lady, Flourdelis, France.

Sir Sergis, Irena's faithful adviser.

Calidore, the knight of Courtesy, sent to destroy the Blatant Beast, malicious gossip.

Briana, a proud lady who abuses the laws of hospitality by demanding the hair and beards of ladies and gentlemen who pass her castle.

Crudor, the disdainful knight for whom she weaves a mantle of hair.

Tristram, a young prince reared in the forest, who impresses Prince Arthur by his instinctive courtesy.

Aldus, a worthy old knight.

Aladine, his son.

Priscilla, Aladine's lady.

Serena, a noble lady, severely wounded by the Blatant Beast.

Calepine, her knight.

Sir Turpine, a discourteous gentleman who refuses aid to Calepine and Serena.

Blandina, his wife, who tries to assuage his cruelty.

The Salvage Man, a "noble savage," another untaught practitioner of courtesy.

Matilde, a childless noblewoman who adopts a baby rescued by Calidore from a bear.

Mirabella, a proud, insolent lady.

Disdaine and **Scorne,** her tormentors.

Pastorella, a nobleman's daughter who grows up with shepherds. Calidore falls in love with her and with her rustic life.

Meliboee, her wise foster father, who warns Calidore that happiness is not to be found in one place or another but in oneself.

Coridon, Pastorella's shepherd admirer.

Colin Clout, a shepherd poet who pipes to the graces on Mount Acidale.

Sir Bellamour, Calidore's friend, Pastorella's father.

Claribell, his wife.

Melissa, her maid, who discovers Pastorella's true identity.

Mutability, a proud Titaness who challenges the power of Cynthia, the moon-goddess.

Cynthia, her rival.

Mercury, the messenger of the gods.

Jove, the king of the gods.

Mollana, a nymph and an Irish river.

Faunus, a satyr who pursues her.

Dame Nature, a great veiled figure who hears Mutability's arguments and judges, finally, that order reigns in all change.

The Story

Gloriana, the Fairy Queen, was holding her annual twelve-day feast. As was the custom, anyone in trouble could appear before the court and ask for a champion. The fair lady Una came riding on a white ass, accompanied by a dwarf. She complained that her father and mother had been shut up in a castle by a dragon. The Red Cross Knight offered to help her, and the party set out to rescue Una's parents.

In a cave the Red Cross Knight encountered a horrible creature, half serpent, half woman. Although the foul stench nearly overpowered him, the knight slew the monster. After the battle, the Red Cross Knight and Una lost their way. A friendly stranger who offered them shelter was really Archimago, the wicked magician. By making the Red Cross Knight dream that Una was a harlot, Archimago separated Una from her champion.

Una went on her way alone. Archimago quickly assumed the form of the Red Cross Knight and followed her to do her harm. Meanwhile the Red Cross Knight fell into the company of Duessa, an evil enchantress. They met the great giant Orgoglio, who overcame the Red Cross Knight and made Duessa his mistress. Prince Arthur, touched by Una's misfortunes, rescued the Red Cross Knight from Orgoglio and led him to Una. Once again Una and her champion rode on their mission.

At last they came to Una's kingdom, and the dragon who had imprisoned her parents came out to do battle. After two days of fighting, the Red Cross Knight overthrew the dragon. After the parents had been freed, the Red Cross Knight and Una were betrothed.

Still hoping to harm the Red Cross Knight, Archimago told Sir Guyon that the Red Cross Knight had despoiled a virgin of her honor. Shocked, Guyon set out to right the wrong. The cunning Archimago disguised Duessa as a young girl and placed her on the road, where she told a piteous tale of wrong done by the Red Cross Knight and urged Guyon to avenge her. When Guyon and the Red Cross Knight met, they lowered their lances and began to fight. Fortunately the signs of the Virgin Mary on the armor of each recalled them to their senses, and Guyon was ashamed that he had been tricked by the magician.

In his travels Guyon fell in with Prince Arthur, and the two visited the Castle of Alma, the stronghold of Temperance. The most powerful enemy of Temperance was the demon Maleger. In a savage battle Prince Arthur vanquished Maleger. Guyon went on to the Bower of Bliss, where his arch enemy Acrasy was living. With stout heart Guyon overthrew Acrasy and destroyed the last enemy of Temperance.

After sending Acrasy back to the fairy court under guard, Guyon and Prince Arthur went on their way until on an open plain they saw a knight arming for battle. With Prince Arthur's permission, Guyon rode against the strange knight, and in the meeting Guyon was unhorsed by the strong lance of his opponent. Ashamed of his fall, Guyon snatched his sword and would have continued the fight on foot.

The palmer, attending Guyon, saw that the champion could not prevail against the stranger, for the strange knight was enchanted. When he stopped the fight, the truth was revealed; the strange knight was really the lovely Britomart, a chaste and pure damsel, who had seen the image of her lover, Artegall, in Venus' looking glass and had set out in search of him. With the situation explained, Britomart joined Guyon, Prince Arthur, and Arthur's

squire, Timias, and the four continued their quest.

In a strange wood they traveled for days, seeing no one, but everywhere they met bears, lions, and bulls. Suddenly a beautiful lady on a white palfrey galloped out of the brush. She was Florimell, pursued by a lustful forester who spurred his steed cruelly in an attempt to catch her. The three men joined the chase, but out of modesty Britomart stayed behind. She waited a long time; then, despairing of ever finding her companions again, she went on alone.

As she approached Castle Joyous she saw six knights attacking one. She rode into the fight and demanded to know why they were fighting in such cowardly fashion. She learned that any knight passing had to love the lady of Castle Joyous or fight six knights. Britomart denounced the rule and with her magic lance unhorsed four of the knights. She entered Castle Joyous as a conqueror.

After meeting the Red Cross Knight in the castle, Britomart resolved to go on as a knight-errant. She heard from Merlin, whom she visited, that she and Artegall were destined to have illustrious descendants.

Meanwhile Timias had been wounded while pursuing the lustful forester. Belphoebe, the wondrous beauty of the Garden of Adonis, rescued him and healed his wounds. Timias fell in love with Belphoebe.

Amoret, the fair one, was held prisoner by a young knight who attempted to defile her. For months she resisted his advances. Then Britomart, hearing of her sad plight, overcame the two knights who guarded Amoret's prison and freed her. Greatly attracted to her brave rescuer, Amoret set out with Britomart.

At a strange castle a knight claimed Amoret as his love. Britomart jousted with him to save Amoret, and after winning the tourney Britomart was forced to take off her helmet. With her identity revealed, Britomart and Amoret set off together in search of their true loves.

Artegall, in search of adventure, joined Scudamour, a knight-errant. They met Amoret and Britomart, who was still disguised as a knight. Britomart and Artegall fought an indecisive battle during which Artegall was surprised to discover that his opponent was his lost love, Britomart. The two lovers were reunited at last, but in the confusion Amoret was abducted by Lust. With the help of Prince Arthur, Scudamour rescued Amoret from her loathsome captor. He wooed Amoret in the Temple of Love, where they found shelter.

Artegall, champion of true justice, was brought up and well trained by Astraea. When Artegall was of age, Astraea gave him a trusty groom, and the new knight set out on his adventures. Talus, the groom, was an iron man who carried an iron flail to thresh out falsehood. Irena, who asked at the fairy court for a champion against the wicked Grantorto, set out with Artegall and Talus to regain her heritage. With dispatch Artegall and Talus overcame Grantorto and restored Irene to her throne.

Later Artegall entered the lists against a strange knight

who was really the disguised Amazon, Radigund. Artegall wounded Radigund, but when he saw that his prostrate foe was a comely woman, he threw away his weapons. The wounded Amazon then rushed on the defenseless Artegall and took him prisoner. Artegall was kept in shameful confinement until at last Talus informed Britomart of his fate. Britomart went to her lover's rescue and slew Radigund.

Continuing his quest, Artegall met two hags, Envy and Detraction, who defamed his character and set the Blatant Beast barking at his heels. But Artegall forbade Talus to beat the hags and returned to the fairy court.

The Blatant Beast, defamer of knightly character and the last remaining enemy of the fairy court, finally met his match. The courteous Calidore, the gentlest of all the knights, conquered the beast and led him, tamed, back to the court of the Fairy Queen.

Critical Evaluation

Although Spenser completed only six books, and part of a seventh, of the twelve projected books of *The Faerie Queene*, the bulk of what he did finish is so great that this epic is universally regarded as one of the masterpieces of English literature. The grand conception and execution of the poem reflect both the life of the poet and his participation in the life and ideals of his age. Spenser was committed to public service in the expansive period of Elizabethan efflorescence. A gentleman poet and friend of the great, Spenser never received the preferment he hoped for, but he remained devoted to Elizabeth, to England, and to late sixteenth century optimism. Even during his lifetime, Spenser was honored as a poet by the court and by other men of letters. To the present, Spenser's allegorical imagination and his control of language have earned him a reputation as "the poet's poet."

Like other Elizabethan poets, Spenser produced ecologues and a sonnet sequence, but *The Faerie Queene* is his great accomplishment. In a famous letter to Sir Walter Raleigh, Spenser explained the ambitious structure and purpose of his poem. It was to be composed of twelve books, each treating one of Aristotle's moral virtues as represented in the figure of a knight. The whole was to be a consistent moral allegory and the twelve books taken together would describe the circumscribing Aristotelian virtue of magnanimity, which Spenser called Magnificence.

At some point Spenser apparently decided to modify this plan. By the fourth book the simple representation of one virtue in one hero has broken down, though each book still does define a dominant virtue. More significantly, virtues are included which are not in Aristotle. Spenser is true to Aristotle, however, in consistently viewing virtue as a mean between extremes, as a moderate path between many aberrations of excess and defect.

The poem owes many debts to other antecedents. It is filled with references to and echoes of the Bible and the Greek and Latin classics. It is suffused with the spirit and much of the idealized landscape and atmosphere of medieval romance. However, its greatest debts are to the writers of the Continental Renaissance, particularly Ariosto. Ariosto's loosely plotted *Orlando Furioso* was the most influential single model and Spenser borrows freely, but where Ariosto was ironic or skeptical, Spenser transforms the same material into a serious medium for his high ethical purposes. Moreover, while allegory is a dimension added to Ariosto by his critics, Spenser is motivated throughout by his allegorical purpose: "To fashion a gentleman or noble person in vertuous and gentle discipline." In this aim, he is within the Renaissance tradition of writing courtesy books, such as Castiglione's *The Courtier*, which were guides to conduct for the gentleman who would seek excellence in behavior and demeanor. *The Faerie Queene* is a courtesy book turned to the highest of purposes—the moral formation of the ideal Christian gentleman.

Book 1, the story of Red Cross Knight, the Knight of Holiness, is the truest to the original structural intention. Red Cross is assigned to Una to relieve her kingdom of a menacing dragon. Through the book Red Cross's chivalric exploits gradually develop in him the virtue he represents, so that he can ultimately kill the dragon. Book 2 also makes its demonstration in a relatively straightforward way. Sir Guyon, the Knight of Temperance, despite temporary setbacks and failures, eventually gains the knowledge of what true temperance is by seeing how it is violated both by excess and defect, by self-indulgence and by inhuman austerity. Ultimately Guyon can reject the opulent pleasures of the sensuous Bower of Bliss.

In book 3 the allegorical method begins to change, probably because the virtues represented are more sophisticated in concept and more difficult to define. This complexity is mirrored in plot as earlier characters reappear and subsequent characters make brief entries. The result is an elaborate suspense and an intricate definition of virtues by means of examples, comparisons, and contrasts.

Book 3 deals with Chastity, book 4 with Friendship; both incorporate Renaissance platonic notions of love. Chastity is infinitely more than sexual abstinence, because by the perception of beauty and experience of love man moves closer to divine perfection. The concept of mutuality is emphasized in book 3 by the fact that Scudamour cannot accomplish his quest without Britomart's contribution to his development. Book 4 further explores platonic love by defining true friendship through a series of examples and counterexamples which culminate in the noblest kind of friendship, that between a man and a woman.

In book 5, the adventures of Artegall, Spenser develops a summary statement of his political philosophy. Justice is relentless and inexorable; it is not only a matter of abstract principle but also of wise governing. After the stringency of the Book of Justice, book 6 is a softer, more pastoral treatment of the chivalric ideal of Courtesy in the person of Sir Calidore.

Spenser's allegory is enlivened by the meanderings of plot as well as by the fullness and appeal of his personifications. In addition to the well-wrought moral allegory, there is sporadic political allegory, as Elizabeth occasionally becomes visible in Una or Britomart or Belphoebe, or as contemporary events are evoked by the plot. At every point Spenser's style is equal to his noble intentions. The verse form, the Spenserian stanza, is an ingenious modification of the rhyme royal stanza, in which the last line breaks the decasyllabic monotony with a rhythmically flexible Alexandrine. The diction has often been called archaic but is perhaps more a capitalizing on all the sources of Elizabethan English, even the obsolescent, in the service of the beauty of sound. Alliteration and assonance further contribute to a consummate aural beauty which not only reinforces sense but also provides a pervasive and distinctly Spenserian harmony.

"THE FALL OF THE HOUSE OF USHER"

Type of work: Short story
Author: Edgar Allan Poe (1809–1849)
Type of plot: Gothic romance
Time of plot: Nineteenth century
Locale: The House of Usher
First published: 1839

The twins Madeline and Roderick are the last of the Ushers and symbolic of two warring facets of the human character: sensuality and intellect. The story follows Roderick's descent into madness and culminates in his entombment of his still-living sister. As she fights her way from the premature grave, a final apocalypse occurs. Battered by an almost supernatural storm, the Usher Castle and its occupants literally crumble and sink into a miasmic swamp. Truly one of Poe's finest short stories, The Fall of the House of Usher *ranks with the best in the genre.*

Principal Characters

Roderick Usher, a madman. Excessively reserved in childhood and thereafter, Usher is the victim not only of his own introversion but also of the dry rot in his family, which because of inbreeding has long lacked the healthy infusion of vigorous blood from other families. His complexion is cadaverous, his eyes are lustrous, his nose is "of a delicate Hebrew model," his chin is small and weak though finely molded, his forehead broad, and his hair soft and weblike. (The detailed description of Usher's face and head in the story should be compared with the well-known portraits of Poe himself.) In manner Usher is inconsistent, shifting from excited or frantic vivacity to sullenness marked by dull, guttural talk like that of a drunkard or opium addict. It is evident to his visitor, both through his own observation and through what Usher tells him, that the wretched man is struggling desperately but vainly to conquer his fear of fear itself. His wide reading in his extensive library, his interest in many art objects, his playing the guitar and singing to its accompaniment, his attempts at conversation and friendly communication with his guest—all seem piteous efforts to hold on to his sanity. The battle is finally lost when Madeline, risen from her grave and entering through the doors of the guest's apartment, falls upon Usher and bears him to the floor "a corpse, and a victim to the terrors he has anticipated."

Madeline, his twin sister, a tall, white-robed, wraith-like woman who succumbs to catalepsy, is buried alive, escapes from her tomb, confronts her brother in her bloodstained cerements, and joins him in death.

The Narrator, Usher's visitor and only personal friend, who has been summoned to try to cheer up Usher but who himself is made fearful and nervously excited by the gloomy, portentous atmosphere of the Usher home. Having witnessed the double deaths of Usher and Madeline, the narrator flees in terror and, looking back, sees the broken mansion fall into the tarn below.

The Story

As the visitor approached the House of Usher, he was forewarned by the appearance of the old mansion. The fall weather was dull and dreary, the countryside shady and gloomy, and the old house seemed to fit perfectly into the desolate surroundings. The windows looked like vacant eyes staring out over the bleak landscape.

The visitor had come to the House of Usher in response to a written plea from his boyhood friend, Roderick Usher. The letter had told of an illness of body and mind suffered by the last heir in the ancient line of Usher, and although the letter had strangely filled him with dread, the visitor had felt that he must go to his former friend. The Usher family, unlike most, had left only a direct line of descent, and perhaps it was for this reason that the family itself and the house had become one—the House of Usher.

As he approached closer, the house appeared even more formidable to the visitor. The stone was discolored and covered with fungi. The building gave the impression of decay, yet the masonry had not fallen. A barely discernible crack extended in a zigzag line from the roof to the foundation, but otherwise there were no visible breaks in the structure.

The visitor entered the house, gave his things to a servant, and proceeded through several dark passages to the study of the master. There he was stunned at the appearance of his old friend. Usher's face looked cadaverous, his eyes were liquid and lips pallid. His weblike hair was untrimmed and floated over his brow. All in all, he was a depressing figure. In manner, he was even more morbid. He was afflicted with great sensitivity and strange fear. There were only a few sounds, a few odors, a few foods, and a few textures in clothing that did not fill him with terror. In fact, he was haunted incessantly by unnamed fears.

Even more strangely, he was imbued with the thought that the house itself exerted great influence over his morale and that it had obtained influence over his spirit. Usher's moodiness was heightened by the approaching death of his sister, Lady Madeline. His only living relative, she was wasting away from a strange malady that baffled the doctors. Often the disease revealed its cataleptic nature. The visitor saw her only once, on the night of his arrival. Then she passed through the room without speaking, and her appearance filled him with awe and foreboding.

For several days, the visitor attempted to cheer the sick master of Usher and restore him to health, but it seemed, rather, that the hypochrondria suffered by Usher affected his friend. More and more, the morbid surroundings and the ramblings of Usher's sick mind preyed upon his visitor. More and more, Usher held that the house itself had molded his spirit and that of his ancestors. The visitor was helpless to dispel this morbid fear and was in danger of subscribing to it himself, so powerful was the influence of the gloomy old mansion.

One day, Usher informed his friend that Madeline was dead. It was his intention to bury her in one of the vaults under the house for a period of two weeks. The strangeness of her malady, he said, demanded the precaution of not placing her immediately in the exposed family burial plot. The two men took the encoffined body into the burial vault beneath the house and deposited it upon a trestle. Turning back the lid of the coffin, they took one last look at the lady, and the visitor remarked on the similarity of appearance between her and her brother. Then Usher told him that they were twins and that their natures had been singularly alike. The man then closed the lid, screwed it down securely, and ascended to the upper room.

A noticeable change now took possession of Usher. He paced the floors with unusual vigor. He became more pallid, while his eyes glowed with even greater wildness.

His voice was little more than a quaver, and his words were utterances of extreme fear. He seemed to have a ghastly secret that he could not share. More and more, the visitor felt that Usher's superstitious beliefs about the malignant influence of the house were true. He could not sleep, and his body began to tremble almost as unreasonably as Usher's.

One night, during a severe storm, the visitor heard low and unrecognizable sounds that filled him with terror. Dressing, he had begun to pace the floor of his apartment when he heard a soft knock at his door. Usher entered, carrying a lamp. His manner was hysterical and his eyes those of a madman. When he threw the window open to the storm, they were lifted almost off their feet by the intensity of the wind. Usher seemed to see something horrible in the night, and the visitor picked up the first book that came to hand and tried to calm his friend by reading. The story was that of Ethelred and Sir Launcelot, and as he read, the visitor seemed to hear the echo of a cracking and ripping sound described in the story. Later, he heard a rasping and grating, of what he knew not. Usher sat facing the door, as if in a trance. His head and his body rocked from side to side in a gentle motion. He murmured some sort of gibberish, as if he were not aware of his friend's presence.

At last, his ravings became intelligible. He muttered at first but spoke louder and louder until he reached a scream. Madeline was alive. He had buried Madeline alive. For days, he had heard her feebly trying to lift the coffin lid. Now she had escaped her tomb and was coming in search of him. At that pronouncement, the door of the room swung back and on the threshold stood the shrouded Lady Madeline of Usher. There was blood on her clothing and evidence of superhuman struggle. She ran to her terrified brother, and the two fell to the floor in death.

The visitor fled from the house in terror. He gazed back as he ran and saw the house of horror split asunder in a zigzag manner, down the line of the crack he had seen as he first looked upon the old mansion. There was a loud noise, like the sound of many waters, and the pond at its base received all that was left of the ruined House of Usher.

Critical Evaluation

More than a century after his death, Edgar Allan Poe probably remains—both in his life and his work—America's most controversial writer. Numerous biographical and critical studies have not succeeded in dispelling the myth of Poe promulgated by his hostile first biographer, who portrayed him as a self-destructive, alcoholic, almost demonic creature. Even today, after much serious research and analysis, the "true" Poe remains enigmatic and elusive—the same can be said of his works. Fellow writers

such as D. H. Lawrence, Henry James, T. S. Eliot, Charles Baudelaire, and Aldous Huxley have differed greatly in assessing the merits of Poe's works, with opinions ranging from extravagant eulogy to total dismissal. And no work of his has excited more diverse opinion or been given more conflicting analyses than his short story "The Fall of the House of Usher."

The problem is that there are many completely different, yet seemingly valid, interpretations of the tale; contradictory readings that can "explain" all of the story's numerous ambiguities. And yet, obviously, as one prominent Poe critic has lamented, "they cannot all be right." Is there any way of choosing between these views or of synthesizing the best of them into a single one? Perhaps the task is not impossible if two important facts about the author are remembered: He was an adroit, conscious craftsman and critic who worked out his ideas with mathematical precision, and yet he was essentially a lyric poet.

These diverse readings can be divided roughly into three primary types: natural or psychological, supernatural, and symbolic. In the first approach, the analysis has usually focused on the unreliable narrator as he chronicles Roderick Usher's descent into madness. As an artist, intellectual, and introvert, Usher has become so reclusive that his prolonged isolation, coupled with the sickness of his sister, has driven him to the edge of madness; along with the narrator, the reader sees him go over the edge. Or perhaps the tale is simply a detective story minus a detective; Usher manipulates the narrator into helping him murder Madeline and then goes insane from the emotional strain. The crucial fantastic elements in the story—Madeline's return from the tomb and the collapse of the house into the tarn—are logically explained in terms of the narrator's mounting hysteria, the resulting hallucination, and the natural destructiveness of the storm.

According to the second general view, the actions of the characters can be explained only by postulating a supernatural agency: The Usher curse is working itself out; the house is possessed and is destroying the occupants; Roderick is a demon drawing vitality from his sister until, as a Nemesis figure, she returns to punish him; Madeline is a vampire claiming her victim.

In the third view, the story is seen as an allegory: Roderick as intellect is suppressing sensuality (Madeline) until it revolts; Madeline is a Mother figure who returns from the grave to punish Usher-Poe for deserting her and for having incest desires; Roderick is the artist who must destroy himself in order to create; the entire story is a symbolic enactment of the Apocalypse according to Poe.

As a critic and a writer, Poe was thoroughly aware of the machinery of the Gothic romance, and "The Fall of the House of Usher" is a veritable catalog of devices from the genre—the haunted mansion, the artistic hero-villain, the twins motif, suggestions of vampirism—and all of the physical paraphernalia—dank crypts, violent electrical storms. It does not follow, however, that because Poe utilizes the conventions of the form, he is also holding himself to the substance of them. It is precisely because he does not commit himself exclusively to either a rational, supernatural, or symbolic reading of the tale that he is able to provoke emotional reactions by indirection and implication that would be impossible if he fixed his meaning more precisely. The technique is essentially that of the lyric poet who uses the power of image, atmosphere, and suggestion to evoke emotions and to produce the desired single effect on the reader—which was Poe's stated aim as a short-story writer.

"I feel that the period will sooner or later arrive," says Roderick Usher, "when I must abandon life and reason together, in some struggle with the grim phantasm, FEAR." Thus, Poe underscores "fear" as the central emotion he wishes to provoke, and the story can best be discussed in terms of how he develops this response.

The tale divides into five distinct parts: first, the description of the house and the background of the narrator's relationship to Usher; second, his meeting with Roderick Usher that ends with his glimpse of Lady Madeline; third, the survey of Usher's art, that is, music, painting, the recitation of the poem "The Haunted Palace," Roderick's theory of "sentience," and the description of the library; fourth, Madeline's "death" and entombment; and fifth, her return from the crypt counterpointed against the narrator's reading of "The Mad Trist" story which culminates in the death of the twins, the narrator's flight, and the collapse of the house into the tarn. Each of these phases not only furthers the plot line but also intensifies the emotions provoked in the reader by means of the narrator's progressive hysteria and the growing distortion of the atmosphere.

The narrator is quickly characterized as a skeptic, who attempts to explain everything rationally, but who is, at the same time, quite susceptible to unexplained anxieties and undefined premonitions. His first glimpse of the Usher mansion provokes "a sense of unsufferable gloom." As he describes it, the house resembles a giant face or skull with "eye-like windows" and hairlike "minute fungi" that almost seem to hold the decayed building together, as well as a "barely perceptible fissure" that threatens to rip it apart. He is even more horrified when he looks into the tarn (a small, stagnant lake in front of the house) and sees the house's inverted reflection in the black water. Thus, in the first paragraph of the tale, readers are introduced to three crucial elements: the subjective reactions of the narrator, which begin with this furtive, general uneasiness and will end in complete hysteria; the central image of a huge, dead, decaying object that is, paradoxically, very alive; and the first of many reflections or doubles that reinforce and intensify the atmosphere and implications of the story.

When the narrator meets his old friend Roderick Usher, the other side of the death-life paradox is suggested. Whereas the dead objects seem "alive," the "live" things seem dead. All the peripheral characters—the two servants, the doctor, the "living" Madeline—are shadows. Roderick, with his "cadaverous" complexion, "large, liquid and luminous eyes," "thin and very pallid" lips, and "hair of more than web-like softness," seems more zombie than human. Moreover, his description mirrors that of the house's exterior: his eyes are like the windows; his hair resembles the fungi.

Roderick does, however, have a definable personality. For all of the spectral hints, Poe never abandons the possibility that Roderick's character and fate can be explained naturally. Although Usher's behavior is violent and erratic, perhaps manic-depressive by modern clinical standards, tenuous rationalizations are provided for everything he does.

Nor does Roderick's role as an artist resolve the questions about his character. The extended catalogue of his artistic activities may seem digressive in terms of Poe's strict single-effect theory, but it is, in fact, the necessary preparation for the story's harrowing finale. Each of Roderick's artistic ventures conforms to both his realistic personality and the otherworldliness of the situation; they can either signal his descent into psychosis or his ineffectual attempts to understand and withstand the incursion of supernatural forces. His dirges suggest death; his abstract painting of a vaultlike structure previews Madeline's interment. When he recites "The Haunted Palace" poem, he is either metaphorically recounting his own fall into madness, or he is, literally, talking about "haunting." Roderick's statements about the sentience of all vegetable things—that is, the conscious life in all inanimate matter—brings a notion that has previously been latent in the reader's mind to the surface. Finally, Roderick's exotic library, made up almost entirely of books about supernatural journeys, suggests either a perversely narrow and bizarre taste or an attempt to acquire the knowledge needed to defend against demonic intruders.

Nevertheless, for all of the mounting intensity of suggestion and atmosphere, the actual story does not begin until almost two-thirds of the narrative has been completed. When Roderick announces that Lady Madeline "is no more," the pace quickens. It is at this point that the narrator notices the "striking similitude between the brother and sister" and so emphasizes the "twin theme," the most important reflection or double in the tale. As they entomb her, the narrator takes note of the "mockery of a faint blush upon the bosom and the face." Does this suggest a trace of life and implicate Roderick, consciously or unconsciously, in her murder? Or, does it hint at an "undead" specter who, knowing that she will return from the grave, mocks the attempt to inter her?

Nowhere is the value of indirection in the maximizing of suspense more evident than in the last sequence of the story. Having established the literary context of the narrative, Poe then counterpoints the reading of a rather trite medieval romance against Madeline's actual return from the crypt. At the simplest level, "The Mad Trist" tale is a suspense-building device that magnifies the reader's excitement as he awaits Madeline's certain reappearance. Thematically, it suggests a parallel—either straight or ironic, depending on the reader's interpretation—between the knight Ethelred's quest and Madeline's return from the tomb. Reinforced by the violent storm, the narrator's frenzy, and Usher's violence, Madeline's return, her mutually fatal embrace of her brother, the narrator's flight, and the disintegration of the house itself, all fuse into a shattering final effect, which is all that Poe claimed he wanted, and a provocative insight into—what? The collapse of a sick mind? The inevitable self-destruction of the hyperintroverted artistic temperament? The final end of aristocratic inbreeding? Or incest? Or vampirism? Or the end of the world?

Although the meaning of "The Fall of the House of Usher" remains elusive, the experience of the story is powerful, disturbing, and lasting. And that, in the final analysis, is where its greatness lies and why it must be considered one of the finest short stories of its kind ever written.

A FAREWELL TO ARMS

Type of work: Novel
Author: Ernest Hemingway (1899–1961)
Type of plot: Impressionistic realism
Time of plot: World War I
Locale: Northern Italy and Switzerland
First published: 1929

This story of a tragic love affair is set on the Italian front during World War I. Hemingway tells his tale with an abundance of realistic detail. Rather than a celebration of the "Triumph of victory and the agony of defeat," the author's vision is uncompromisingly disillusioned. Not only is war useless, but efforts to maintain any meaningful relationship with individuals in the modern world are equally doomed.

Principal Characters

Lieutenant Frederic Henry, an American who has volunteered to serve with an Italian ambulance unit during World War I. Like his Italian companions, he enjoys drinking, trying to treat the war as a joke, and (it is implied) visiting brothels. Before the beginning of a big offensive he meets Catherine Barkley, one of a group of British nurses assigned to staff a hospital unit. Henry begins the prelude to an affair with her but is interrupted by having to go to the front during the offensive; he is wounded, has an operation on his knee, and is sent to recuperate in Milan, where he again meets Miss Barkley, falls in love with her, and sleeps with her in his hospital room. When Henry returns to the front, he knows Catherine is pregnant. In the retreat from Caporetto, Henry is seized at a bridge across the Tagliamento River and realizes he is about to be executed for deserting his troops. He escapes by swimming the river. At Stresa he rejoins Catherine and, before he can be arrested for desertion, the two lovers row across Lake Como to Switzerland. For a few months they live happily at an inn near Montreux—hiking, reading, and discussing American sights (such as Niagara Falls, the stockyards, and the Golden Gate) that Catherine must see after the war. Catherine is to have her baby in a hospital. Her stillborn son is delivered by Caesarian section and that same night Catherine dies. Lieutenant Henry walks back to his hotel through darkness and rain. As developed by Hemingway, Henry is a protagonist who is sensitive to the horrors and beauties of life and war. Many of his reactions are subtly left for the reader to supply. At the end of the novel, for instance, Henry feels sorrow and pity for the dead baby strangled by the umbilical cord, but the full, unbearable weight of Catherine's death falls upon the reader.

Catherine Barkley, the nurse whom Frederic Henry nicknames "Cat." She had been engaged to a childhood sweetheart killed at the Somme. When she falls in love with Henry she gives herself freely to him. Although they both want to be married, she decides the ceremony would not be a proper one while she is pregnant; she feels they are already married. Catherine seems neither a deep thinker nor a very complex person; but she enjoys life, especially good food, drink, and love. She has a premonition that she will die in the rain; the premonition is tragically fulfilled at the hospital in Lausanne.

Lieutenant Rinaldi, Frederick Henry's jokingly cynical friend. Over many bottles they share their experiences and feelings. Although he denies it, Rinaldi is a master of the art of priest-baiting. He is very fond of girls, but he teases Henry about Catherine, calling her a "cool goddess."

The Priest, a young man who blushes easily but manages to survive the oaths and obscenities of the soldiers. He hates the war and its horrors.

Piani, a big Italian soldier who sticks by Henry in the retreat from Caporetto after the others in the unit have been killed or have deserted. With other Italian soldiers he can be tough but with Henry he is gentle and tolerant of what men suffer in wartime.

Helen Ferguson, a Scottish nurse who is Catherine Barkley's companion when Frederic Henry arrives in Stresa. She is harsh with him because of his affair with Catherine.

Count Greffi, ninety-four years old, a contemporary of Metternich and a former diplomat with whom Frederic Henry plays billiards at Stresa. A gentle cynic, he says that men do not become wise as they grow old; they merely become more careful.

Ettore Moretti, an Italian from San Francisco serving in the Italian army. Much decorated, he is a professional hero whom Frederic Henry dislikes and finds boring.

The Story

Lieutenant Frederic Henry was a young American attached to an Italian ambulance unit on the Italian Front. An offense was soon to begin, and when Henry returned to the Front from leave, he learned from his friend, Lieutenant Rinaldi, that a group of British nurses had arrived in his absence to set up a British hospital unit. Rinaldi introduced him to Nurse Catherine Barkley.

Between ambulance trips to evacuation posts at the Front, Henry called on Miss Barkley. He liked the frank young English girl in a casual sort of way, but he was not in love with her. Before he left for the Front to stand by for an attack, she gave him a St. Anthony medal.

At the Front, as Henry and some Italian ambulance drivers were eating in a dugout, an Austrian projectile exploded over them. Henry, badly wounded in the legs, was taken to a field hospital. Later, he was moved to a hospital in Milan.

Before the doctor was able to see Henry in Milan, the nurse prohibited his drinking wine, but he bribed a porter to bring him a supply which he kept hidden behind his bed. Catherine Barkley came to the hospital, and Henry knew that he was in love with her. The doctors told Henry that he would have to lie in bed six months before they could operate on his knee. Henry insisted on seeing another doctor, who said that the operation could be performed the next day. Meanwhile, Catherine managed to be with Henry constantly.

After his operation, Henry convalesced in Milan with Catherine Barkley as his attendant. Together they dined in out-of-the-way restaurants, and together they rode about the countryside in a carriage. Henry was restless and lonely at nights and Catherine often came to his hospital room.

Summer passed into autumn. Henry's wound had healed, and he was due to take convalescent leave in October. He and Catherine planned to spend the leave together, but he came down with jaundice before he could leave the hospital. The head nurse accused him of bringing on the jaundice by drink, in order to avoid being sent back to the Front. Before he left for the Front, Henry and Catherine stayed together in a hotel room; already she had disclosed to him that she was pregnant.

Henry returned to the Front with orders to load his three ambulances with hospital equipment and go south into the Po valley. Morale was at a low ebb. Rinaldi admired the job that had been done on the knee and observed that Henry acted like a married man. War weariness was all-pervasive. At the Front, the Italians, having learned that German divisions had reinforced the Austrians, began their terrible retreat from Caporetto. Henry drove one of the ambulances loaded with hospital supplies. During the retreat south, the ambulance was held up several times by wagons, guns, and trucks which extended in stalled lines for miles. Henry picked up two straggling Italian sergeants. During the night, the retreat was halted in the rain for hours.

At daybreak, Henry cut out of the long line and drove across country in an attempt to reach Udine by side roads. The ambulance got stuck in a muddy side road. The sergeants decided to leave, but Henry asked them to help dislodge the car from the mud. They refused and ran. Henry shot and wounded one; the other escaped across the fields. An Italian ambulance corpsman with Henry shot the wounded sergeant through the back of the head. Henry and his three comrades struck out on foot for Udine. On a bridge, Henry saw a German staff car with German bicycle troops crossing another bridge over the same stream. Within sight of Udine, one of Henry's group was killed by an Italian sniper. The others hid in a barn until it seemed safe to circle around Udine and join the mainstream of the retreat toward the Tagliamento River.

By that time, the Italian army was nothing but a frantic mob. Soldiers were throwing down their arms and officers were cutting insignia of rank from their sleeves. At the end of a long wooden bridge across the Tagliamento, military carabinieri were seizing all officers, giving them drumhead trials, and executing them by the riverbank. Henry was detained, but in the dark of night he broke free, plunged into the river, and escaped on a log. He crossed the Venetian plain on foot, then jumped aboard a freight train and rode to Milan, where he went to the hospital in which he had been a patient. There he learned that the English nurses had gone to Stresa.

During the retreat from Caporetto, Henry had made his farewell to arms. He borrowed civilian clothes from an American friend in Milan and went by train to Stresa, where he met Catherine, who was on leave. The bartender of the hotel in which Henry was staying warned Henry that authorities were planning to arrest him for desertion the next morning; he offered his boat by means of which Henry and Catherine could escape to Switzerland. Henry rowed all night. By morning, his hands were so raw that he could barely stand to touch the oars. Over his protests, Catherine took a turn at the rowing. They reached Switzerland safely and were arrested. Henry told the police that he was a sportsman who enjoyed rowing and that he had come to Switzerland for the winter sports. The valid passports and the ample funds that Henry and Catherine possessed saved them from serious trouble with the authorities.

During the rest of the fall and winter, the couple stayed at an inn outside Montreux. They discussed marriage, but Catherine would not be married while she was pregnant. They hiked, read, and talked about what they would do together after the war.

When the time for Catherine's confinement approached, she and Henry went to Lausanne to be near a hospital. They planned to return to Montreux in the spring. At the hospital, Catherine's pains caused the doctor to use an anaesthetic on her. After hours of suffering she delivered a dead baby. The nurse sent Henry out to get something to eat. When he went back to the hospital, he learned that Catherine had had a hemorrhage. He went into the room and stayed with her until she died. There was nothing he could do, no one he could talk to, no place he could go. Catherine was dead. He left the hospital and walked back to his hotel in the dark. It was raining.

Critical Evaluation

Ernest Hemingway once referred to *A Farewell to Arms* as his *Romeo and Juliet*. Without insisting on a qualitative comparison, several parallels are obvious. Both works are about "star-crossed" lovers, both show erotic flirtations that rapidly develop into serious, intense, mature love affairs, and both describe the romances against a backdrop of social and political turmoil. Whether *A Farewell to Arms* finally qualifies as tragic is a matter of personal opinion, but it certainly represents, for Hemingway, an attempt to broaden his concerns from the aimless tragicomic problems of the expatriates in *The Sun Also Rises* (1926) to the fundamental question of life's meaning in the face of human mortality.

Frederic Henry begins the affair as a routine wartime seduction, "a game, like bridge, in which you said things instead of playing cards." He feels mildly guilty, especially after learning about Catherine's vulnerability because of the loss of her lover in combat, but he still foresees no complications from the temporary arrangement. It is not until he is wounded and sent to her hospital in Milan that their affair deepens into love—and from that point on, they struggle to free themselves in order to realize it. Yet they are constantly thwarted, first by the impersonal bureaucracy of the military effort, then by the physical separation imposed by the war itself, and, finally, by the biological "accident" that kills Catherine at the point where their "separate peace" at last seems possible.

As Henry's love for Catherine grows, his disillusionment with the war also increases. From the beginning of the book, Henry views the military efforts with ironic detachment, but there is no suggestion that, prior to his meeting with her, he has had any deep reservations about his involvement. Hemingway's attitude toward war was always an ambiguous one. Like Henry, he felt that "abstract words such as glory, honor, courage, or hallow were obscene." For the individual, however, war could be the necessary test. Facing imminent death in combat, one either demonstrated "grace under pressure" and did the "one right thing" or one did not; one either emerged from the experience as a whole person with self-knowledge and control, or one came out of it lost and broken.

There is little heroism in this war as Henry describes it. The hero's disengagement from the fighting is made most vivid in the extended "retreat from Caporetto," generally considered one of the great sequences in modern fiction. The retreat begins in an orderly, disciplined, military manner. Yet as it progresses, authority breaks down, emotions of self-preservation supersede loyalties, and the neat military procession gradually turns into a panicking mob. Henry is caught up in the momentum and carried along with the group in spite of his attempts to keep personal control and fidelity to the small band of survivors he travels with. Upon reaching the Tagliamento River, Henry is seized, along with all other identifiable officers, and held for execution. After he escapes by leaping into the river—an act of ritual purification as well as physical survival—he feels that his trial has freed him from any and all further loyalty to the Allied cause.

Henry then rejoins Catherine, and they complete the escape together. In Switzerland, they seem lucky and free at last. Up in the mountains, they hike, ski, make love, prepare for the baby, and plan for their postwar life together. Yet even in their most idyllic times, there are ominous hints; they worry about the baby; Catherine jokes about her narrow hips; she becomes frightened by a dream of herself "dead in the rain."

Throughout the novel, Hemingway associates the plains and rain with death, disease, and sorrow; the mountains and the snow with life, health, and happiness. Catherine and Frederic are safe and happy in the mountains, but it is impossible to remain there indefinitely. Eventually everyone must return to the plains. When Catherine and Henry descend to the city, it is, in fact, raining, and she does, in fact, die.

Like that of Romeo and Juliet, the love between Catherine and Henry is not destroyed by any moral defect in their own characters. Henry muses that Catherine's fate is the price paid for the good nights in Milan, but such a price is absurdly excessive. Nor, strictly speaking, is the war responsible for their fate, any more than the Montague-Capulet feud directly provokes the deaths of Shakespeare's lovers. Yet the war and the feud provide the backdrop of violence and the accumulation of pressures that coerce the lovers into actions which contribute to their doom. In the final analysis, both couples are defeated by bad luck—the illness that prevents the friar from delivering Juliet's note to Romeo, the accident of Catherine's anatomy that prevents normal childbearing. Thus, both couples are "star-crossed." But if a "purpose" can be vaguely ascertained in Shakespeare's version—the feud is ended by the tragedy—there is no metaphysical justification for Catherine's death; it is, in her own words, "a dirty trick"—and nothing more.

Hemingway does not insist that the old religious meanings are completely invalid but only that they do not work for his people. Henry would like to visit with the priest in his mountain village, but he cannot bring himself to do it. His friend Rinaldi, a combat surgeon, proclaims atheism, hedonism, and work as the only available meanings. Count Greffi, an old billiard player Henry meets in Switzerland, offers good taste, cynicism, and the fact of a long, pleasant life. Catherine and Henry have each other: "You are my religion," she tells him.

All of these things fail in the end. Religion is only for others, patriotism is a sham, hedonism becomes boring, culture is a temporary distraction, work finally fails (the operation on Catherine was "successful"), even love cannot last (Catherine dies; they both know, although they will not admit it, that the memory of it will fade).

All that remains is a stoic acceptance of the above facts with dignity and without bitterness. Life, like war, is absurd. Henry survives because he is lucky; Catherine dies because she is unlucky. There is no guarantee that the luck ever balances out and, since everyone ultimately dies, it probably does not matter. What does matter is the courage, dignity, and style with which one accepts these facts as a basis for life, and, more important, in the face of death.

THE FATHER

Type of work: Drama
Author: August Strindberg (1849–1912)
Type of plot: Psychological realism
Time of plot: Mid-nineteenth century
Locale: Sweden
First presented: 1887

The antagonism between the sexes concerned Strindberg in all of his works. In The Father, *the captain is driven to insanity by his wife and rejected by his own daughter. In the beginning of their relationship, his love for his wife was as a son for his mother. When he became her lover, she rebelled and planted in his mind the fear that he was not the father of their daughter, Bertha. Falling into insanity and finally suffering a stroke, the Captain is rejected by wife, daughter, and mother.*

Principal Characters

The Captain, a captain of cavalry who is the chief sufferer in this domestic tragedy. He was rejected by his mother and consequently sought a mother-figure in marriage. Driven to raving madness by his wife, he is straitjacketed and suffers a stroke.

Laura, his wife. Accepting the maternal side of her relationship with her husband, she loathes her role as wife and takes vengeance on her husband by destroying him. In her efforts to prove him mad, she resorts to forgery and to misrepresentation of his scientific interests, which in fact she does not understand. She also exploits a suspicion she has planted in his mind that their daughter is not his.

Bertha, their daughter and a chief object of conflict.

Margaret, the Captain's old nurse. She tries to reassure him periodically; it is she who at last calms him enough to slip a straitjacket on him.

Dr. Östermark, the new village doctor, to whom Laura goes with her "evidence" of her husband's insanity.

Auditor Safberg, a freethinker with whom the Captain intends to board Bertha so that she will be educated away from the influence of her mother and of her grandmother, who is bent on teaching her spiritualism.

Nöjd, a trooper in difficulties because he got a servant girl in trouble. His relatively trivial problem suggests to Laura the weapon she successfully uses against her husband.

Emma, the servant girl in trouble.

Ludwig, who Nöjd claims may well be the father of Emma's child.

The Pastor, Laura's brother, before whom Nöjd is called. His sympathy for Nöjd is greater than the Captain's. Later, when the Pastor sees through Laura's scheme, she dares him to accuse her.

The Story

When a trooper named Nöjd got a servant girl in trouble, the Captain sent an orderly to bring Nöjd to face the Pastor. The culprit, vague about his affair with Emma, hinted that the paternity of her child was uncertain. The Pastor told Nöjd that he would have to support the child, but the soldier claimed that Ludwig should contribute also, since it was possible that Ludwig was the real father. The Captain declared angrily that the case would go to court. After Nöjd had gone, the Captain berated the Pastor for his gentle treatment of the soldier. The Pastor said he thought it a pity to saddle Nöjd with the support of a child if he were not the real father.

The Captain was married to the Pastor's sister Laura. In his house, complained the Captain, there were too many women: his mother-in-law, a governess, his old nurse Margaret, his daughter Bertha. The Captain, worried about his daughter's education, which was being influenced in all directions by the people around her, deplored the incessant struggle between men and women.

After the Pastor had gone, Laura entered to collect her household money. His affairs near bankruptcy, the Captain reminded her that a father had the sole control of his children. When Laura brought up the subject of Nöjd's affair, the Captain admitted that the paternity would be difficult to determine. Laura scoffingly claimed that if such were the case even the child of a married woman could be any other man's offspring.

Laura confided to Dr. Östermark, the new village doctor, her suspicion that her husband was mentally ill. He bought books he never read, and he tried to fathom events on other planets by peering through a microscope. He had become a man who could not stand by his decisions, although he was most vehement when he first uttered one.

Speaking privately with his old nurse, the Captain expressed his fear that his family was plotting against him and that something evil was about to happen. The family quarrel was clearly outlined when Bertha complained to her father that her grandmother was trying to teach her spiritualism and had even told the girl that the Captain, who was a meteorologist by profession, was a charlatan. Bertha agreed with her father that she ought to go away to study, but Laura boasted that she could persuade Bertha to stay home. She hinted again that she could prove the Captain was not Bertha's father.

Dr. Östermark explained to Laura that she had been mistaken about her husband; he had used a spectroscope, not a microscope, to examine the elements on other planets. Still, the doctor said, he would watch the Captain for further signs of insanity. Laura also told the doctor that the Captain feared he was not Bertha's father; quite obviously Laura had planted this idea in the Captain's mind. When he began to worry over his daughter's paternity, old Margaret tried to reassure him.

It became impossible for the Captain to allow his wife to continue her persecution of him. She had intercepted some of his mail, thereby thwarting him in the progress of his scientific ventures. He further accused her of spreading among his friends the idea that he was insane. Afraid that under such provocation he might lose his reason, he appealed to his wife's selfishness. It would be in her best interest for him to remain sane, he said, since insanity might lead to his suicide, which would invalidate her right to collect his life insurance. She could assure his sanity by confessing that Bertha was not his child, a suspicion which was undermining his sanity.

When she refused to admit a sin of which she was not guilty, he reminded her that in doing so she would gain sole control of Bertha's future. The tables were turned. Now the Captain began to believe that Bertha was not his child and Laura began to insist that she was. The Captain, recalling the circumstances of Bertha's birth, recollected how a solicitor had told Laura that she had

no right of inheritance without a child. At that time the Captain had been ill. When he recovered, Bertha had been born.

The Captain understood the power his wife held over him. At first he had loved her as he would love a mother, but she had loathed him after he became her lover. Laura showed him a letter she had forged in which he confessed his insanity and said that she had sent the letter to court. Boasting that she had employed him only as a breadwinner, she declared that she would use his pension for Bertha's education. In anger, the Captain hurled a lamp at her.

Laura succeeded in locking her husband in another room while she examined his private papers. Although the Pastor saw through her scheme, she dared him to accuse her. The doctor arrived with a straitjacket shortly before the Captain, armed with literary evidence of cases in which a child's paternity had been questioned, burst into the room. His talk was so erratic and his raving about conjugal fidelity so wild that when the doctor told him he was insane, the Captain acknowledged his own madness.

Bertha, accusing him of a deliberate attempt to injure her mother, announced that he was not her father if he behaved so badly. The Captain, in reply, told her that her soul was in two parts; one was a reflection of his own, and to preserve it he intended to destroy the part which was not his. He seized a revolver but found it empty. Bertha ran out screaming.

Old Margaret soothed the raving man by talking softly to him of his childhood, and when he was off guard she slipped the straitjacket on him. Seeing him seated, helpless and dejected, on the sofa, Laura nearly repented the course she had taken, as the Captain piteously described his life of torment with mother, wife, and child, all of whom had rejected him. After she had assured him that Bertha was his own child, the Captain, calling to old Margaret for comfort, suffered a stroke. As he lay unconscious, Bertha ran to her mother, who caressed her and called the girl her own daughter.

Critical Evaluation

The plays of August Strindberg have exerted a powerful and pervasive influence on modern drama. His insights into naturalism, in such early plays as *The Father* and *Miss Julie* (1888) were central in the shaping of that dramatic movement, while his later experiments with expressionism, in works such as the *To Damascus* trilogy (1898–1904), *A Dream Play* (1902), and *The Ghost Sonata* (1907), have profoundly affected nonrealistic approaches to the modern stage.

The relationship between Strindberg's own life and his writing becomes apparent in an examination of *A Mad-*

man's Defense (1893), an autobiographical novel. Written between 1887 and 1888, it chronicles fourteen years of Strindberg's life, including his fateful meeting with and marriage to Siri Von Essen. Strindberg intended the work as an exposé of Siri's attempts to confine him for mental treatment, but, in reality, it presents a clear picture of enveloping paranoia and acute mental instability.

Strindberg's first-person narrator portrays his wife as doubtful of his sanity. (Indeed, in 1886 Siri consulted a Swiss doctor about Strindberg's instability.) Based on her conviction, Maria attempts to provoke behavior that can be used as evidence to justify confinement. When she sides with critics of her husband's book, he calls her a traitor. He escapes to Paris, but she follows him and insists on a retreat in Switzerland. Once there, she convinces the doctor, guests, proprietor, and servants that their new guest is, indeed, insane.

Beginning to doubt his sanity, the narrator turns his suspicions on his wife. He studies her behavior and comes to believe that she is an adulteress trying to cover her wrongdoings and gain his insurance money. He then rifles through her letters seeking evidence and makes her face his strenuous cross-examinations. Her denials simply intensify his agitation and instability. The parallels to *The Father* are clear.

Moreover, Strindberg's account closely parallels the events that surrounded the publication of the first volume of *Married* (1884). In this collection of short stories dealing with the husband-wife relationship, Strindberg is scornful of the "emancipated" woman, believing that such a woman wants not equality with her mate but domination over him. The ideal role for the woman, Strindberg believes, is that of wife and mother—anything else can only be destructive.

This view of woman clearly had its origins in Strindberg's personal experience. Having been unwanted at birth and rejected as a child, Strindberg grew up as a stranger in his own home. Thus, what Strindberg sought in a mate (he went though three stormy marriages) was not only a wife but also a substitute mother. Naturally, his ideal of the wife-mother was shattered over and over again, leading to an absolute confusion of roles. When Strindberg first met Siri, he described her as "a deliciously girlish mother." During their trial separation, Strindberg stated that he felt "like an embryo prematurely detached from the umbilical cord." This attitude is echoed in *The Father*, when Laura tells the Captain (II, v): "I loved you as if you were my child. But you know, you must have felt it, when your sexual desires were aroused, and you came forward as my lover, I was reluctant, and the joy I felt in your embrace was followed by such revulsion that my very blood knew shame. The son became the lover— oh!"

Strindberg's disillusion led him naturally into bitter antifeminism. Actually, his philosophy paralleled that of many contemporaries, particularly those in France—a country he frequented during "exile" periods. The literary atmosphere there in the 1870s was extremely misogynistic. In the theater, the character of the femme fatale, as popularized by such actresses as Sarah Bernhardt, was popular. The female was seen as a parasitic being who lived off of the productivity of the more talented and imaginative male.

The source for the question of paternity that is central to *The Father* is provided by Strindberg's personal correspondence. When Strindberg married Siri, she was pregnant and had not long before their marriage shared the company of her first husband, Baron Wrangel. After Strindberg became actively paranoid, his remembrance of that situation provoked him to harbor doubts about the paternity of his children. That the suspicion was in his mind was confirmed by his reaction to Henrik Ibsen's play *The Wild Duck* (1891): He considered suing Ibsen for slander on the grounds that Ibsen had used him as a model for the protagonist, Hjalmar Ekdal, who doubts the paternity of his child. Strindberg and Siri were also at odds about the future occupations of their two daughters. Siri wished them to become actresses, while Strindberg wanted them to be trained as midwives. Both of these two personal conflicts became central issues in *The Father*.

Although Strindberg's own experiences provided the major inspiration for *The Father*, he was also deeply influenced by the literary and cultural milieu of his time. The novels of the Goncourt brothers, particularly Edmond's *Chérie* (1884), may have directly affected the play. A naturalistic play with the same analytical emphasis, *Thérèse Raquin* (1867), by Émile Zola, may also have provided Strindberg with some insight. Furthermore, before he began writing *The Father*, he studied contemporary theories of psychiatry and hypnotism. After finishing *The Father*, he articulated the results of these researches in an essay series titled *Vivisektioner* (1887). The titles of two of the essays reveal the influence of these studies on *The Father*: "The Battle of the Brains" and "Psychic Murder."

The battle between Laura and the Captain is actually a Darwinian struggle for power, with survival going to the "fittest"—a central concept in the naturalistic school. The Captain states that the battle with his wife is "to eat or to be eaten." At one point, the discussion becomes overtly Darwinistic:

Captain: I feel in this battle one of us must succumb.
Laura: Who?
Captain: The weaker, of course.
Laura: And the stronger is right?
Captain: He is always right because he has the power.
Laura: Then I am right.

The amorality of action—with the end justifying the means—the detached scientific tone, the emphasis on the psychological, and the objectivity of the playwright are among the play's naturalistic tendencies.

Zola, however, pointed out that despite his psychological emphasis and scientific attitude, Strindberg had failed to give the play a social setting—that is, he had failed to emphasize the importance of heredity and environment in his characterizations. Although he had attributed the Captain's initial weakness to his early rejection, Strindberg had gone no further in demonstrating the power of environmental influences. In spite of this weakness, Zola encouraged Strindberg in his pursuits. Strindberg presented perhaps the first important naturalistic drama with his next play, *Miss Julie*, in which the power of heredity and milieu are dramatized in the destruction of a willful aristocratic female by her father's brazen valet.

Thus, at the time he wrote *The Father*, Strindberg was a man of mental and emotional complexity who stood on the brink of developing one of the most important movements in modern dramatic literature: naturalism. In the third section of his autobiography, Strindberg expresses an awareness of his position in the development of the modern drama. He saw himself as spanning the gap between Romanticism and naturalism and being "like the blindworm, which retains rudimentary lizard feet inside its skin." But this dependence on his background was no detriment to his dramatic career. Rather than holding him back, his reliance on autobiography, controlled and polished, became the driving force in his naturalistic writings and, in a different way, was to become the substance of his later experiments with expressionism.

His influence was felt not only on the Continent but also in the United States, for though never awarded the coveted Nobel Prize, he was noted by Eugene O'Neill in his acceptance speech for the Nobel Prize as one of O'Neill's foremost literary inspirations. Since that time, Strindberg's reputation has grown until he is generally regarded today to be, along with Henrik Ibsen and Anton Chekhov, one of the three giants most responsible for the shape, direction, and power of the modern theater.

FATHERS AND SONS

Type of work: Novel
Author: Ivan Turgenev (1818–1883)
Type of plot: Social criticism
Time of plot: 1859
Locale: Russia
First published: *Ottsy i deti*, 1862 (English translation, 1867)

Fathers and Sons *differs from most nineteenth century Russian novels in that the characters are simply drawn and the plot is straightforward. Still, the work operates on two levels. On the one hand, Turgenev dramatizes the universal conflicts which arise between any two generations. On the other, he vividly portrays the unsettled state of Russian peasantry before the Revolution. His discussions of political anarchy make the work an important document in Russian political history.*

Principal Characters

Yevgeny Vassilyitch Bazarov (ĕv·gĕ′ nĭy vä·sĭ′lĭch bä·zä′rəf), a nihilistic young medical school graduate and Arkady's closest friend. Arrogant and ruthless, Bazarov believes only in the power of the intellect and science. As a revolutionary, he feels himself far superior to Nikolai Kirsanov and his brother. To him, they are hopelessly antiquated humanitarians. He tells them: "You won't fight—and yet you fancy yourselves gallant chaps—but we mean to fight. . . . We want to smash other people."

Arkady Kirsanov (är·kä′dĭy kĭr·sä′nəf), Nikolai's son and Bazarov's naïve young disciple. For a time he worships his leader and echoes everything that Bazarov says; however, Arkady lacks the necessary ruthlessness required for a revolutionary spirit. He is unable to believe, as Bazarov does, that a good chemist "is twenty times as useful as any poet." After Bazarov's death he marries Katya and settles down to a prosaic life on the family estate.

Nikolai Petrovitch Kirsanov (nĭ′kô·lī pĕt·rō′vĭch kĭr·sä′nəf), Arkady's gentle music-loving father. Possessing a liberal, well-meaning spirit, he is happy to free his serfs and to rent them farm land. In his ineffectual way he attempts to run the estate profitably. Unfortunately, the newly freed serfs take every opportunity to cheat him out of his rent.

Pavel Kirsanov (pä′vĕl kĭr·sä′nəf), Nikolai's brother. A dandified patrician, he has little liking for Bazarov or his revolutionary ideals. Believing strongly in the aristocratic way of life, he considers Bazarov a charlatan and a boor. In his own heart, however, Pavel knows that the new must supplant the old. Finally, dissatisfied with pro-

vincial life, he moves to Dresden, where he is much sought after by the aristocrats.

Katya Loktiv (kä′tyä lôk·tĭf′), Anna Odintsov's attractive young sister. Although she is shy and somewhat afraid of her sister, Katya becomes interested in Arkady. When he asks her to marry him, she readily accepts his proposal and shortly afterward becomes his wife.

Anna Odintsov (än′nä ·dĭn′tsəf), a haughty young aristocrat, a widow. Because of her beauty even the unsentimental Bazarov falls in love with her. At first he interests her, but he is never able to pierce her cold exterior for long. She does show some feeling for him as he is dying and even brings a doctor to his deathbed. Unable to help him, she yields enough to kiss his forehead before he dies.

Vasily Bazarov (vä·sĭ′lĭy bä·zä′rəf), a village doctor, the father of young Bazarov. Like the other fathers, he is unable to bridge the gulf between his generation and his son's; in fact, he has no desire to do so. Doting on his son, the old man thinks Yevgeny to be beyond reproach.

Arina Bazarov (ä·rĭ′nə bä·zä′rəf), Yevgeny Bazarov's aging mother. In her way the old woman, although quite superstitious, is clever and interesting. She also loves her son deeply. When he dies, she becomes, like her husband, a pathetic, broken figure.

Fenitchka Savishna (fĕ·nĭ·ch′kə sä·vĭsh′nə), Nikolai's young mistress. At Pavel's urging, Nikolai finally marries her and thereafter lives a happy life with the gentle, quiet girl.

The Story

At a provincial posting station, Kirsanov waited impatiently for his son, Arkady, who had completed his education at the university in St. Petersburg. Kirsanov reflected that Arkady had probably changed, but he hoped his son had not grown away from him entirely. Arkady's mother was dead, and the widower was strongly attached to his son.

At last the coach appeared, rolling along the dusty road. Arkady jumped out, but he was not alone. Lounging superciliously behind was a stranger whom Arkady introduced as Bazarov, a fellow student. Something in Arkady's manner told Kirsanov that here was a special attachment. In a low aside, Arkady begged his father to be gracious to his guest.

Feeling some qualms about his unexpected guest, Kirsanov was troubled during the trip home. He was hesitant about his own news but finally told Arkady that he had taken a mistress, Fenichka, and installed her in his house. To his great relief, Arkady took the news calmly and even congratulated his father on the step. Later, Arkady was pleased to learn that he even had a little half brother.

Kirsanov soon found he had good reason to distrust Bazarov, who was a doctor and a clever biologist. Arkady seemed too much under his influence. Worse, Bazarov was a nihilist. At the university the liberal thinkers had consciously decided to defy or ignore all authority—state, church, home, pan-Russianism. Bazarov was irritating to talk to, Kirsanov decided, because he knew so much and had such a sarcastic tongue.

Pavel, Kirsanov's older brother, was especially irritated by Bazarov. Pavel was a real aristocrat, bound by tradition, who had come to live in retirement with his younger brother after a disappointing career as an army officer and the lover of a famous beauty, Princess R_____. With his background and stiff notions of propriety, Pavel often disagreed with Bazarov.

Luckily, Bazarov kept busy most of the time. He collected frogs and infusoria and was always dissecting and peering into a microscope. He would have been an ideal guest, except for his calmly superior air of belonging to a generation far surpassing Pavel's. Kirsanov, loving his son so much, did his best to keep peace, but all the while he regretted the nihilism which had so greatly affected Arkady.

Kirsanov was harassed by other troubles. Soon, by law, the serfs would be freed. Kirsanov strongly approved of this change and had anticipated the new order by dividing his farm into smaller plots which the peasants rented on a sharecropping basis. With their new independence, however, the peasants cheated him more than ever and were slow in paying their rent.

Arkady and Bazarov, growing bored with quiet farm life, went to visit in the provincial capital, where they had introductions to the governor. In town, they ran into Sitnikoff, a kind of polished jackal who felt important because he was one of the nihilist circle. Sitnikoff introduced them into provincial society.

At a ball, the two friends met and were greatly taken by a young widow, Madame Odintzov. Arkady did not dance, but he sat out a mazurka with her. They became friends at once, especially when she found that Arkady's mother had been an intimate friend of her own mother. After the ball, Madame Odintzov invited the two men to visit her estate.

Arkady and Bazarov accepted the invitation promptly. In a few days, they settled down to the easy routine of favored guests in a wealthy household. Katya, Madame Odintzov's young sister, was especially attracted to Arkady. Bazarov, older and more worldly, became the good friend of the widow.

Although Bazarov, as a good nihilist, despised home and family life, he made a real effort to overcome his scruples; but when he finally began to talk of love and marriage to Madame Odintzov, he was politely refused. Chagrined at his rejection, he induced Arkady to leave with him at once. The two friends then went on to Bazarov's home.

Vasily, Bazarov's father, was glad to see his son, whom he both feared and admired. He and his wife did all they could to make the young men comfortable. At length Arkady and Bazarov quarreled, chiefly because they were so bored. Abruptly they left and impulsively called again on Madame Odintzov. She received them coolly. Feeling that they were unwelcome, they went back to the Kirsanov estate.

Because Bazarov was convinced that Arkady was also in love with Madame Odintzov, his friendship with Arkady became greatly strained. Arkady, thinking constantly of Katya, returned by himself to the Odintzov estate to press his suit of the younger sister.

At the Kirsanov home, Bazarov became friendly with Fenichka. He prescribed for her sick baby and even for her. Out of friendship, Fenichka spent much of her time with Bazarov. One morning, as they sat in a garden, Bazarov kissed her unexpectedly, to her distress and confusion. Pavel witnessed the scene by accident and became increasingly incensed at the strange nihilist.

Although Pavel did not consider Bazarov a gentleman, he challenged him to a duel with pistols. In the encounter, Pavel was wounded in the leg, and Bazarov left the house in haste, never to return. Pavel recovered from his wound, but he felt a never-ending shame at being wounded by a low nihilist. He urged Kirsanov to marry Fenichka, and he returned to his old life. He spent the rest of his days as an aging dandy in Dresden.

Bazarov stopped briefly at the Odintzov home. Still convinced that Arkady was in love with Madame Odintzov, he attempted to help his friend in his suit. Madame Odintzov ridiculed him, however, when Arkady made his request for the hand of Katya. With a sense of futility, Bazarov took his leave and rejoined his own family.

Vasily was the local doctor, and he eagerly welcomed his son as a colleague. For a time, Bazarov led a successful life, helping to cure the ailments of the peasants and pursuing his research at the same time. When one of his patients contracted typhus, he accidentally scratched himself with a scalpel he had used. Although Vasily cauterized the wound as well as he could, Bazarov became ill with a fever. Sure that he would die, he summoned Madame Odintzov to his side. She came gladly and helped to ease him before his death.

Madame Odintzov eventually made a good marriage with a lawyer. Arkady was happy managing his father's farm and playing with the son born to him and Katya. Kirsanov became a magistrate and spent most of his life settling disputes brought about by the liberation of the serfs. Fenichka, at last a respected wife and mother, found great happiness in her daughter-in-law, Katya.

Critical Evaluation

In *Fathers and Sons*, Ivan Turgenev attempted to examine the forces of change operating, for the most part in isolation and frustration, in mid-nineteenth century Russia. The storm of protest and outrage produced from the moment the novel appeared indicates that he had indeed touched a sensitive nerve in Russian society. In fact, Turgenev never really got over the abuse upon him; his periods of exile in Germany, France, and Italy were all the more frequent and of longer duration after the publication of the novel. One wonders at the excitement occasioned by *Fathers and Sons*, for a cooler reading undertaken more than a hundred years later indicates that Turgenev clearly attempted and achieved a balanced portrait of conservative and revolutionary Russia—a triumphant achievement in political fiction, where the passions of the moment so often damage the artistic effort.

The subtlety and rightness of Turgenev's technique is most clearly seen in the central character Bazarov. A pragmatist, scientist, and revolutionary ideologue, Bazarov is a prefiguration of twentieth century man. Bazarov is put into relationship with every important character, and it is from these relationships that the reader gets to know him and to understand more about him than he understands. A master of literary impressionism, Turgenev liked to do an "atmospheric" treatment of his characters, vividly rendering visual, auditory, and other sense impressions in a nicely selected setting. This technique admits all sorts of lively and contradictory details and prevents the novel—and Bazarov—from flattening out into mere ideology and political polemic. Most of all, for all of his roughness and bearishness, Turgenev really liked Bazarov and sympathized with him ("with the exception of [his] views on art, I share almost all his convictions," he wrote).

Bazarov's chief conflict is with Pavel Kirsanov, a middle-aged bachelor with refined Continental tastes and a highly developed sense of honor. Pavel stands for everything Bazarov despises: an old-world emphasis upon culture, manners, and refinement, and an aristocratic and elitist view of life. He represents the traditions which Bazarov vainly struggles to destroy in his efforts to bring a democratic, scientific, and utilitarian plan of action into widespread use. For Bazarov, "a good chemist is more useful than a score of poets," because the chemist attacks the central problem of poverty, disease, and ignorance. The old humanism represented by Pavel is, for him, a manifestation of ignorance which perpetrates and countenances needless suffering, particularly for the lower classes. His rude and sneering treatment of Pavel is undercut by his participation in the duel, which is an absurd custom of the upper classes he despises. Bazarov is the loser in the duel and he knows it. His passion, which he tries to cover up with a cold, clinical attitude, leads him into it.

His relationship with Madame Odintzov shows that Bazarov is at heart a romantic, though he would hardly admit it. This cool and cultured widow provokes the most ardent response from him—despite his contention that women are mere instruments of amusement and pleasure. With Madame Odintzov, however, Bazarov has unfortunately chosen an inadequate object for his passion. She is lovely but cold and detached and is unable to respond to him.

Bazarov's romanticism, however, is chiefly frustrated in social and political matters. He deeply believes that conditions can be changed and that he and others can work together to that end. When readers look at these "others," they see how painful and tragic his situation is. Arkady, his schoolmate and friend, is a kindly fellow who imitates Bazarov's revolutionary attitudes. He is in awe of his friend's rough manner, but he does not understand that Bazarov really intends to follow his ideas to the end. Rather, Arkady is not even dimly aware at first that he is incapable of supporting Bazarov all the way. Like most men, Arkady is conventional and conforming out of natural adaptability. His marriage to Katya is a model of bourgeois comfort and serves to underline Bazarov's loneliness and ineffectuality. Like his father before him, Arkady chooses domestic satisfactions and a life of small compromises over the absurd "heroism" of his schoolfellow. The Kirsanov homestead remains, on the whole, ill-managed and unimproved. No revolution in land management has occurred even though the peasants are about to be freed. Life goes on in a muddle despite the passionate efforts of one or two enlightened persons to reform it.

Bazarov's curious and potentially violent behavior to Arkady when they are lying in a haystack suggests that he knows that Arkady cannot follow him. Furthermore, this scene reveals that Bazarov is full of violent distaste for those who pretend to be reformers. He cannot spare them ridicule, and his frustrated energies burst forth in threatening gestures. He is a leader without followers, a general without an army. Nevertheless, he loves his parents, two kindly old representatives of the traditional way of life, for they do not pretend to be anything they are not.

Bazarov's death is a form of suicide. His willingness to take no immediate steps to prevent the spread of infection after he has carelessly cut himself suggests that he has seen the absurdity of his position and, to some extent at least, given in to it. In his delirium, he states that Russia needs a cobbler, a tailor, a butcher more than she needs him. Nevertheless, for Turgenev, Bazarov was "the real hero of our time."

FAUST

Type of work: Dramatic poem
Author: Johann Wolfgang von Goethe (1749–1832)
Type of plot: Philosophical allegory
Time of plot: Timeless
Locale: The world
First published: 1790–1831

A seminal work in the Romantic Movement, Faust *dissects the philosophical problem of human damnation brought about by the desire for knowledge and personal happiness. A basically good man and a man of genius, Faust sells his soul to the Devil in a contract stipulating that only when he finds an experience so great that he wishes it to endure forever can the Devil take his soul. He finally reaches his goal, but the experience is one in which he helps his fellow man. Thus Mephistopheles loses despite his efforts.*

Principal Characters

Faust (foust), a perpetual scholar with an insatiable mind and a questing spirit. The middle-aged Faust, in spite of his enthusiasm for a newly discovered source of power in the sign of the macrocosm, finds his intellectual searches unsatisfactory and longs for a life of experiences in the world of man. On the brink of despair and a projected suicide, he makes a wager with the Devil that if he ever lies on his bed of slothfulness or says of any moment in life, "Stay thou art so fair," at that moment will he cease to be. He cannot be lured by the supernatural, the sensual, the disembodied spiritual, but he does weaken in the presence of pure beauty and capitulates to humanitarian action. He displays himself as a sensual man in his deep love for Gretchen (Margarete), only to be goaded to murder by her brother, who sees not selfless love in their actions, but only sin. Faust aspires to the love of Helen of Troy, but he is finally disconsolate when she appears. As an old man he returns to his early vision of being a man among men, working and preparing for a better world to be lived here on earth. His death is not capitulation, though he thinks at this point man can cry "stay," and he has never taken his ease or been tempted by a life of sloth. His death is his victory and his everlasting life is to be lived resourcefully among the creators.

Mephistopheles (mĕf·ĭ·stŏf′ə·lēz), the Devil incarnate and Lucifer in disguise of dog and man. Portrayed here as a sophisticate, cynic, and wit, he is most persuasive and resourceful. He works magic, manages miracles, creates spirits and situations for Faust's perusal and delectation. His persistence is the more remarkable for the ability of Faust to withstand and refute, though Mephistopheles often expresses resentment. Somehow more attractive than God and the archangels, he powerfully represents the positive force of evil in its many and attractive guises.

Gretchen, sometimes called **Margarete,** an innocent, beautiful young maiden. A foil for the Devil, Gretchen remarkably personifies womanly love without blemish or fear. She gives herself to Faust, who swears he cannot molest her, with an earthy abandon and remains for a time unearthly innocent in her raptures, until the forces for morality convince her she has sinned deeply and that she must pay first by destroying her child and then by being sacrificed to the state, suffering death for her transgressions. Brooding over her brother's death, she refuses solace from her lover.

Valentin, a soldier and Gretchen's brother, killed by Faust with the aid of Mephistopheles.

Wagner (väg′nər), Faust's attendant, an unimaginative pedant. Serving as a foil for Faust, Wagner expresses himself in scholarly platitudes and learns only surface things. He aspires not to know all things but to know a few things well, or at least understandably; the unobtainable he leaves to Faust. He serves as the Devil's advocate, however, in the temptation of Faust by helping Mephistopheles create Homunculus.

Homunculus (hō·mŭng′kyōō·ləs), a disembodied spirit of learning. This symbol of man's learning, mind separated from reality, interprets for Mephistopheles, and accurately, what Faust is thinking. The spirit discloses Faust's near obsession with ideal beauty, and thus Faust was given the temptress, Helen of Troy.

Helen of Troy, who appears as a wraith at first and then with form. Representing the classical concept of eternal or ideal beauty, aesthetic, complete, Helen very nearly succeeds where Gretchen failed. She finally seems to Faust only transitory beauty, no matter how mythological and idealized. After this final experience Faust denounces such hypothetical pursuits and returns to deeds.

Dame Marthe Schwerdtlein, Gretchen's neighbor and friend, an unwitting tool in the girl's seduction.

The Story

While three archangels were singing the praise of God's lofty works, Mephistopheles, the Devil, appeared and said that he found conditions on earth to be bad. The Lord tacitly agreed that man had his weaknesses, but He slyly pointed out that His servant Faust could not be swayed from the path of righteousness. Mephistopheles made a wager with the Lord that Faust could be tempted from his faithful service. The Lord knew that He could rely on the righteous integrity of Faust, but that Mephistopheles could lead Faust downward if he were able to lay hold of Faust's soul. Mephistopheles considered Faust a likely victim, for Faust was trying to obtain the unobtainable.

Faust was not satisfied with all the knowledge he had acquired. He realized man's limits, and he saw his own insignificance in the great macrocosm. In this mood, he went for a walk with his servant, Wagner, among people who were not troubled by thoughts of a philosophical nature. In such a refreshing atmosphere, Faust was able to feel free and to think clearly. Faust told Wagner of his two souls, one which clung to earthly things and another which strove toward supersensual things that could never be attained as long as his soul resided within his fleshly body. Feeling so limited in his daily life and desiring to learn the meaning of existence, Faust was ready to accept anything which would take him to a new kind of life.

Mephistopheles recognized that Faust was ready for his attack. In the form of a dog, Mephistopheles followed Faust to his home when the scholar returned to his contemplation of the meaning of life. After studying the Bible, he concluded that man's power should be used to produce something useful. Witnessing Faust's struggle with his ideas, the dog stepped forth in his true identity. But Faust remained unmoved by the arguments of Mephistopheles.

The next time Mephistopheles came, he found Faust much more receptive to his plot. Faust had decided that, although his struggles were divine, he had produced nothing to show for them. Faust was interested in life on this earth. At Mephistopheles' suggestion that he could peacefully enjoy a sensual existence, Faust declared that if ever he could lay himself in sloth and be at peace with himself, or if ever Mephistopheles could so rule him with flattery that he became self-satisfied, then let that be the end of Faust. But Faust had also renounced all things that made life worthwhile to most men. So he further contracted with Mephistopheles that if ever he found experience so profound that he would wish it to endure, then Faust would cease to be. This would be a wager, not the selling of a soul.

After two trials Mephistopheles had failed to tempt Faust with cheap debauchery. The next offering he presented was love for a woman. First Faust was brought to the Witch's Kitchen, where his youth was restored. Then a pure maiden, Gretchen, was presented to Faust, but when he saw her in her own innocent home, he vowed he could not harm her. Mephistopheles wooed the girl with caskets of jewels which she thought came from Faust, and Faust was so tempted that he returned to Gretchen. She surrendered herself to him as a fulfillment of her pure love.

Gretchen's brother convinced her that her act was a shameful one in the eyes of society. Troubled by Gretchen's grief, Faust finally killed her brother. Gretchen at last felt the full burden of her sin. Mephistopheles showed Faust more scenes of debauchery, but Faust's spirit was elevated by the thought of Gretchen and he was able to overcome the evil influence of the devil. Mephistopheles had hoped that Faust would desire the moment of his fulfillment of love to endure. However, Faust knew that enduring human love could not satisfy his craving. He regretted Gretchen's state of misery, and he returned to her; but she had killed her child and would not let her lover save her from the death to which she had been condemned.

Mephistopheles brought Faust to the emperor, who asked Faust to show him the most beautiful male and female who had ever existed—Paris, and Helen of Troy. Faust produced the images of these mythological characters, and at the sight of Helen, his desire to possess her was so strong that he fainted, and Mephistopheles brought him back in a swoon to his own laboratory. Mephistopheles was unable to comprehend Faust's desire for the ideal beauty that Helen represented.

With the help of Wagner, Mephistopheles created a formless spirit of learning, Homunculus, who could see what was going on in Faust's mind. Homunculus, Mephistopheles, and Faust went to Greece, where Mephistopheles borrowed from the fantastic images of classical mythology one of their grotesque forms. With Mephistopheles' intervention, a living Helen was brought to Faust. It seemed now, with the attainment of this supreme joy of beauty in Helen, that Faust would cry for such a moment to linger forever, but he soon realized that the enjoyment of transitory beauty was no more enduring than his other experiences.

With a new knowledge of himself, Faust returned to his native land. Achievement was now his goal, as he reaffirmed his earlier pledge that his power should be used to produce something useful to man. The mystical and magical powers which Faust had once held were banished so that he could stand before nature alone. He obtained a large strip of swamp land and restored it to productivity.

Many years passed. Now old and blind, Faust realized he had created a vast territory of land occupied by people who would always be active in making something useful for themselves. Having participated in this achievement,

Faust beheld himself as a man standing among free and active people as one of them. At the moment when he realized what he had created, he cried out for this moment, so fair to him, to linger on. Faust had emerged from a self-centered egoist into a man who saw his actions as a part of a creative society.

He realized that life could be worth living, but in that moment of perception he lost his wager to Mephistopheles. The devil now claimed Faust's soul, but in reality

he too had lost the wager. The Almighty was right. Although Faust had made mistakes in his life, he had always remained aware of goodness and truth.

Seeing his own defeat, Mephistopheles attempted to prevent the ascension of Faust's soul to God. Angels appeared to help Faust, however, and he was carried to a place in Heaven where all was active creation—exactly the kind of afterlife that Faust would have chosen.

Critical Evaluation

Faust, Goethe's masterwork, virtually summarizes his entire career, stretching from the passionate storm and stress of his youth through his classical phase in his middle years and ending with his mature philosophical style. Its composition occupied him from the time of his first works in the 1770s until his death in 1832, and each of its various sections reveals new interests and preoccupations, as well as different stylistic approaches. Yet the work as a whole possesses a unity that testifies to the continuing centrality of the Faust subject in Goethe's mind.

The first scenes composed, those of Faust in his study and the Gretchen scenes, embody the spirit of the twenty-three-year-old Goethe, full of university parodies on the one hand and titanic projects on the other, a desire to fathom the depths of knowledge, to pass beyond all limitations, typical of the brilliant young writers of this period. In fact, *Faust* was originally one of a planned series of dramas about heroic figures who transgress society's rules—Julius Caesar, Prometheus, and Götz von Berlichingen among them.

Goethe stresses the tragedy of the scholar whose emotional life is not fulfilled and who quests after limitless knowledge, only to find himself frustrated by mortal limitations. The scenes with Gretchen provide for an emotional release, but leave Faust with a sense of guilt for the destruction of purity. The theme of the unwed mother was a popular one among young poets of this period, and represented a revolt against traditional bourgeois values, giving occasion for much social criticism. In the Gretchen scenes, Goethe, who as a student himself had romances with simple small-town girls, evokes great sympathy for Gretchen, who acts always out of sincere emotion and desires only the good. His theme of the corruption of all human questing because of the inherent imperfections of man's knowledge and will receives here its first expression, though with no philosophical elaboration. Neither Faust nor Gretchen wills evil, yet evil comes through Mephistopheles, who in his every utterance is the cynic, opposed to Faust's idealist hopes and exposing the coarse reality that in his view is the sole aspect of man's life on earth. When *Faust* was first published as a fragment in 1790, these elements, dating back to the 1770s, constituted the work.

Between 1797 and 1806, under Schiller's encouragement, Goethe returned to *Faust* and created the Prologue in Heaven and the pact with Mephistopheles, both of which are crucial to the philosophical aspect of the work. Mephistopheles is no longer the absolute opponent of God, but is included in the divine framework; he is a necessary force in creation, a gadfly. The *Faust* action now becomes a wager between God and Mephistopheles, which God necessarily must win. Thus the old blood contract between Faust and Mephistopheles must make Faust deny his very nature by giving up his quest for ever higher satisfactions, by giving him a moment of absolute fulfillment. Damnation, for Goethe, is the cessation of man's striving toward the absolute, and this striving is good, no matter what mistakes man makes in his limited understanding. This is made clear in the Prologue: God recognizes that man will err as long as he strives, but He states that only by seeking after the absolute, however confusedly, can man fulfill his nature. Mephistopheles sees only the confusion, the futility of the results, and the coarseness of man's life. He is blind to the visionary, poetic quality of Faust, the quality which animates his quest. This relationship established in part 1 will continue until the end of the play. In each episode, Faust begins with an idealistic vision of what he seeks, but he never attains it. Seen externally, Mephistopheles is always right—it is only internally that Faust's quest has meaning.

In the original Faust story, Faust meets Helen of Troy, and this episode occupied Goethe in the period of his fascination with the classical world. The third act of part 2 is the union of Faust, the northern, modern, Romantic quester, with Helen, representative of classical harmony and ideal beauty. In this act, Goethe imitates first the style of Greek tragedy, then brings Faust and Helen together in an idyllic realm of fantasy filled with music. This music—Goethe actually wanted an operatic interlude—underlines the purely aesthetic nature of this experience. Helen cannot be the end of Faust's seeking; their relationship can exist only in the mythical Arcadia, where reality, symbolized perhaps by Helen's husband, Menelaus, cannot intrude. The act was subtitled "Classic-Romantic Phantasmagoria," and Goethe followed it immediately with a scene in which Faust sees visions of

Helen and Gretchen and is drawn toward the latter in spite of Helen's ideal perfection. Gretchen, however tragic, is real.

The final sections of *Faust* were composed between 1825 and 1831. In them, Faust's appearances at court are developed and the final scenes of Faust's redemption return to the framework established in the Prologue. Faust's last days are still unsatisfied and his quest is as violent as ever—his merchant ships turn to piracy and a gentle old couple are killed to make room for his palace. But his final vision is that of all humanity, striving onward to turn chaos to order, seeking a dimly imagined goal which is represented in the final scene by an endless stairway. Here, on the path toward the Divine, Faust is to continue to strive, and his life is redeemed by divine love, represented by Gretchen, who in spite of her crimes is also here, a penitent, praying for Faust. On earth all is transitory and insufficient. Only from the point of view of the Divine does all the confused striving attain meaning—meaning which was, in fact, implicit in the stanzas of the three archangels sung at the opening of the work, 12,000 lines earlier.

FLOWERS OF EVIL

Type of work: Poetry
Author: Charles Baudelaire (1821–1867)
First published: 1857

"Small hands washed, scoured, cared for like the hands of a woman—and with that, the head of a maniac, a voice cutting like a voice of steel"—thus did the observant but uncharitable Goncourt brothers describe Charles Baudelaire, who had already become the subject of innumerable legends in the Paris of the Second Empire. It was said that he had dyed his hair green; that he had been heard to remark in a café: "Have you ever eaten a baby? I find it pleasing to the palate!" But unfortunately for seekers after the sensational, most of the Baudelaire legends have been disproved by later research. Like Poe, he enjoyed creating mystifications about himself.

Flowers of Evil, the volume on which Baudelaire's fame rests, was published in 1857, although some of the poems had appeared in magazines as much as fifteen years earlier, when the author was ruining himself financially by attempting to be a dandy of the boulevards. The book immediately become famous—or notorious—because of a prosecution brought against author and publisher on the grounds of offense against public morals. In the same year a similar charge had been brought against Flaubert for his *Madame Bovary*. Possibly because of the ridiculous position in which the government had found itself in the earlier case, the prosecution of Baudelaire was halfhearted, and the fine of three hundred francs was never paid. Actually, there were only six poems found to be objectionable (the subject of two of them being lesbianism); they were reprinted in a new edition published in Belgium, and are now included in all the standard texts and in some of the English translations.

When Barbey d'Aurevilly wrote of Baudelaire: "His present book is an anonymous drama in which he takes all the parts," he was saying no more than that the poet was a Romantic. No young man of his generation could escape the "Byronic attitude" that had been the Englishman's legacy to Europe—to be grand, gloomy, and peculiar was expected. In addition to international Byronism, however, Baudelaire had been exposed to other influences at that time unusual in France. As a boy, he had learned English; hence, he came to know authors such as De Quincey and the Gothic novelists. Most important, he encountered the works of Poe about 1846 and translated much of that work between 1856 and 1865. It was through this translation that Poe began to have an influence upon French literature far greater than any he has ever exerted in America. Baudelaire's admiration of Poe was immense: He called him "the incomparable Poet, the irrefutable philosopher—who must always be quoted in regard to the mysterious maladies of the mind. . . . The Master of the Horrible, the Prince of Mystery." And yet a reading of Baudelaire's poetry does not greatly remind us of that of Poe; the American was not so preoccupied with sex nor do his ethereal, idealized females suggest the tigerish women with smoldering eyes whose nude charms—"ingenuousness united to lubricity"—Baudelaire loved to describe. What Poe gave him was a general interest in the macabre and a feeling for compression, the latter a welcome reaction against the overwhelming verbosity of much Romantic poetry.

Baudelaire's style, at least as it appeared to a contemporary, was described by Gautier as "ingenious, complicated, learned, full of shades and of investigations, always pushing back the limits of language, borrowing all technical vocabularies, taking its colors from all palettes. . . . This decadent style is the last word of language called upon to express everything and pushed to the utmost." It is a "gamy" style like that of late Latin, suitable for the "haggard phantoms of insomnia." This, it must be confessed, rather melodramatic description well indicates the peculiar appeal that Baudelaire held for his contemporaries, who felt that "since Louis XIV French poetry has been dying of correctness."

As for his subject matter, the word "morbid" has been applied to it with unfailing regularity. D'Aurevilly called Baudelaire an "atheistic and modern Dante" whose Muse descended into Hell as surely as Dante's had ascended therefrom. The Romantic indulgence in sensation for its own sake he carried to the point at which pleasure becomes revulsion. In what is perhaps his most famous poem, "A Voyage to Cytherea," after the gay opening of the ship setting sail for the island of Venus, we are brought up sharply by

Look at it; after all, it's a poor land,

and are carried remorselessly through the description of the gibbet from which dangles a "ridiculous hanged man" torn by birds, to the final stanza:

In thine isle, O Venus, I found only upthrust
A Calvary symbol whereon mine image hung,
—Give me, Lord God, to look upon that dung,
My body and my heart, without disgust!

Added to all of this was the attitude of world-weariness inherited from Byron. Baudelaire compares himself to a king in whose veins "the green waters of Lethe flow"; to someone who, in a former life, lived among "vast porticoes," tended by slaves whose only task was to discover their master's secret grief. There were also the blasphemies ("Les Litanies de Satan") and the meticulous descriptions of the revolting ("Une Charogne").

Much of Baudelaire's pyrotechnics—even that part which was sincere and not merely intended to shock the bourgeoisie—has lost its effect. A modern reader, accustomed to clinically precise analyses of sex, is not particularly shocked by his lubricities; his blasphemies seem rather juvenile. One wonders what all the fuss was about.

But to contemporary poets, English as well as French, he is important as a counter-Romantic in a Romantic age; As the first modern, to quote Peter Quennell, "He had enjoyed a sense of his own age, had recognized its pattern while the pattern was yet incomplete." He enormously extended the frontiers of poetry by showing that it need not be limited to the conventionally "poetic." And there are few readers who will not be forced to admit the truth of the last line of his "Preface":

Hypocrite reader—my likeness—my brother!

FOR WHOM THE BELL TOLLS

Type of work: Novel
Author: Ernest Hemingway (1899–1961)
Type of plot: Impressionistic realism
Time of plot: 1937
Locale: Spain
First published: 1940

The novel's title, an allusion to lines from John Donne's poem, "No Man Is An Island," tells the story of a young American, fighting voluntarily against Franco's Fascist forces in Spain, who leads a band of guerrillas in what turns out to be a totally useless military exploit. The entire novel encompasses only a seventy-two-hour time period during which Robert Jordan loses his comrades in battle, falls in love, is wounded too badly to continue, and finally prepares to make a suicidal stand for his cause.

Principal Characters

Robert Jordan, an American expatriate school teacher who has joined the Loyalist forces in Spain. Disillusioned with the world and dissatisfied with his own country, Jordan has come to Spain to fight and die, if necessary, for a cause he knows is vital and worthwhile, that of the native, peasant, free soul against the totalitarian cruelty of Franco and his Fascists. He is, however, aware of the contrast between his ideals and the realities he has found among narrow, self-important, selfish, bloodthirsty men capable of betrayal and cruelty as well as courage. He also finds love, devotion, generosity, selflessness in the persons of Anselmo, Pilar, and especially Maria. The latter he loves with the first true selflessness of his life, and he wishes to avenge her cruel suffering and someday make her his wife in a land free of oppression and cruelty. With bravery, almost bravado, he carries out his mission of blowing up a bridge and remains behind to die with the sure knowledge that in Maria and Pilar his person and ideals will survive. Successful for the first time in his life, in love and war, he awaits death as an old friend.

Maria, a young and innocent Spanish girl cruelly ravaged by war and men's brutality. Befriended by Pilar, a revolutionary, Maria finds a kind of security in the guerrilla band and love in her brief affair with Robert Jordan. As his common-law wife almost all memory of her rape and indignities disappear, and at a moment of triumph for their forces it looks as if they will live to see their dreams of the future fulfilled. Elemental in her passions and completely devoted to her lover, she refuses to leave him and must be forced to go on living. The embodiment of Jordan's ideals, she must live.

Pilar, the strong, almost masculine leader of the guerrilla group with whom Jordan plans to blow up the bridge. Although a peasant and uneducated, Pilar has not only deep feeling but also a brilliant military mind; she is somewhat a Madame Defarge of the Spanish Civil War. Her great trial is her murderous, traitorous husband whom she loves but could kill. Without fear for herself, she has sensitive feelings for Maria, who is suffering from her traumatic experiences as the victim of Fascist lust and cruelty behind the lines. Greatly incensed by inhumanities, Pilar valorously carries out her mission in destroying the bridge, the symbol of her vindictiveness.

Pablo, Pilar's dissolute, drunken, treacherous husband, a type of murderous peasant for whom nothing can be done but without whom the mission cannot be successfully carried out. A hill bandit, Pablo feels loyalty only to himself, kills and despoils at random, is given to drinking and whoring at will. Nevertheless he displays a kind of generosity, even after he has stolen the detonators and peddled them to the enemy, when he comes back to face almost certain death and to go on living with the wife whom he loves and fears. This admixture of cunning, cruelty, and bravado finally leads the band to safety. Pablo represents that irony of ways and means which war constantly confuses.

Anselmo, the representative of peasant wisdom, devotion to duty, high-minded, selfless love for humanity, and compassion for the human condition. Hating to kill but not fearing to die, Anselmo performs his duty by killing when necessary, but without rancor and with a kind of benediction; He dies as he lived, generously and pityingly. While the others of the guerrilla band are more of Pablo's persuasion, brutally shrewd and vindictive in loyalty, Anselmo tempers his devotion to a cause with a larger view. Aligned with Pilar and Jordan in this larger vision, he displays disinterested but kind loyalty that is almost pure idealism, all the more remarkable for his age, background, and experience. The benign, almost Christlike Anselmo dies that others may live and that Robert Jordan may know how to die.

El Sordo, a Loyalist guerrilla leader killed in a Fascist assault on his mountain hideout.

General Golz, the Russian officer commanding the

Thirty-fifth Division of the Loyalist forces.

Karkov, a Russian journalist.

Andrés, a guerrilla sent by Robert Jordan with a dispatch for General Golz.

André Marty, the commissar who prevents prompt

delivery of the dispatch intended for General Golz.

Rafael, a gypsy.

Agustín, Fernando, Primitivo, and **Eladio,** other members of the guerrilla band led by Pablo and Pilar.

The Story

At first, nothing was important but the bridge, neither his life nor the imminent danger of his death—just the bridge. Robert Jordan was a young American teacher who was in Spain fighting with the Loyalist guerrillas. His present and most important mission was to blow up a bridge that would be of great strategic importance during a Loyalist offensive three days hence. Jordan was behind the Fascist lines, with orders to make contact with Pablo, the leader of the guerrilla band, and with his wife Pilar, who was the strongest figure among the partisans. While Pablo was a weak and drunken braggart, Pilar was strong and trustworthy. She was a swarthy, raw-boned woman, vulgar and outspoken, but she was so fiercely devoted to the Loyalist cause that Jordan knew she would carry out her part of the mission regardless of her personal danger.

The plan was for Jordan to study the bridge from all angles and then to make final plans for its destruction at the proper moment. Jordan had blown up many bridges and three trains, but this was the first time that everything must be done on a split-second schedule. Pablo and Pilar were to assist Jordan in any way they could, even in rounding up other bands of guerrillas if Jordan needed them to accomplish his mission.

At the cave hideout of Pablo and Pilar, Jordan met a beautiful young girl named Maria, who had escaped from the Fascists. Maria had been subjected to every possible indignity that a woman could suffer. She had been starved, tortured, and raped, and she felt unclean. At the camp, Jordan also met Anselmo, a loyal old man who would follow orders regardless of his personal safety. Anselmo hated having to kill but, if he were so ordered, faithful Anselmo would do so.

Jordan loved the brutally shrewd, desperate, loyal guerrillas, for he knew that their cruelties against the Fascists stemmed from poverty and ignorance. But he abhorred the Fascists' cruelty, for the Fascists came largely from the wealthy, ambitious people of Spain. Maria's story of her suffering at their hands filled him with such hatred that he could have killed a thousand of them, even though he, like Anselmo, hated to kill.

The first night he spent at the guerrilla camp destroyed his cold approach to the mission before him, for he fell deeply in love with Maria. She came to his sleeping bag that night, and although they talked little, he knew after she left that he was no longer ready to die. He told Maria that one day they would be married, but he was afraid of

the future—and fear was dangerous for a man on an important mission.

Jordan made many sketches of the bridge and laid his plans carefully. There his work was almost ruined by Pablo's treachery. On the night before the blowing up of the bridge, Pablo deserted after stealing and destroying the explosives and the detonators hidden in Jordan's pack. Pablo returned, repentant, on the morning of the mission, but the damage had been done. The loss of the detonators and the explosives meant that Jordan and his helper would have to blow the bridge with hand grenades, a much more dangerous method. Pablo had tried to redeem himself by bringing another small guerrilla band and their horses with him. Although Jordan despised Pablo by that time, he forgave him, as did Pilar.

At the bridge, Jordan worked quickly and carefully. Each person had a specific job to do, and each did his work well. First Jordan and Anselmo had to kill the sentries, a job Anselmo hated. Pablo and his guerrillas attacked the Fascist lines approaching the bridge, to prevent their crossing before the bridge was demolished. Jordan had been ordered to blow up the bridge at the beginning of a Loyalist bombing attack over the Fascist lines. When he heard the thudding explosions of the bombs, he pulled the pins and the bridge shot high into the air. Jordan got to cover safely, but Anselmo was killed by a steel fragment from the bridge. As Jordan looked at the old man and realized that he might be alive if Pablo had not stolen the detonators, he wanted to kill Pablo. Yet he knew that his duty was otherwise, and he ran to the designated meeting place of the fugitive guerrillas.

There he found Pablo, Pilar, Maria, and the two remaining gypsy partisans. Pablo, herding the extra horses, said that all the other guerrillas had been killed. Jordan knew that Pablo had ruthlessly killed the other men so that he could get their horses. When he confronted Pablo with his knowledge, Pablo admitted the slaughter, but shrugged his great shoulders and said that the men had not been of his band.

The problem now was to cross a road that could be swept by Fascist gunfire, the road that led to safety. Jordan knew that the first two people would have the best chance, since probably they could cross before the Fascists were alerted. Because Pablo knew the road to safety, Jordan put him on the first horse. Maria was second, for Jordan was determined that she should be saved before the others. Pilar was to go next, then the two remaining guerrillas, and last of all Jordan. The first four crossed safely, but Jordan's horse, wounded by Fascist bullets, fell on Jordan's leg. The others dragged him across the road and out of the line of fire, but he knew that he could not go on; he was too badly injured to ride a horse. Pablo and Pilar understood, but Maria begged to stay with him. Jordan told Pilar to take Maria away when he gave the signal, and then he talked to the girl he loved so much. He told her that she must go on, that as long as she lived, he lived also. But when the time came, she had to be put on her horse and led away.

Jordan, settling down to wait for the approaching Fascist troops, propped himself against a tree, with his sub-machine gun across his knees. As he waited, he thought over the events that had brought him to that place. He knew that what he had done was right, but that his side might not win for many years. He knew, too, that if the common people kept trying, kept dying, someday they would win. He hoped they would be prepared when that day came, that they would no longer want to kill and torture, but would struggle for peace and for good as they were now struggling for freedom. He felt at the end that his own part in the struggle had not been in vain. As he saw the first Fascist officer approaching, Robert Jordan smiled. He was ready.

Critical Evaluation

In 1940 Ernest Hemingway published *For Whom the Bell Tolls* to wide critical and public acclaim. The novel became an immediate best-seller, erasing his somewhat flawed performance in *To Have and Have Not* (1937). During the 1930s, Hemingway enjoyed a decade of personal publicity that put most American authors in his shade. These were the years of his African safari which produced *Green Hills of Africa* (1935) and his *Esquire* column (1933–1936). Wherever he went, he was news. In 1940, he was divorced by his second wife, Pauline Pfeiffer, and then married Martha Gellhorn. He set fishing records at Bimini in marlin tournaments. He hunted in Wyoming and fished at Key West, where he bought a home. In 1937, when the Spanish Civil War broke out, Hemingway went to Spain as a correspondent with a passionate devotion to the Spain of his early years. Not content merely to report the war, he became actively involved with the Loyalist Army in its fight against Franco and the generals. He wrote the script for the propaganda film *The Spanish Earth* (1937), which was shown at the White House at a presidential dinner. The proceeds of the film were used to buy ambulances for the Loyalists. In 1939, with the war a lost cause, Hemingway wrote *For Whom the Bell Tolls* just as World War II was beginning to destroy Europe.

In order to understand Hemingway's motive in writing *For Whom the Bell Tolls*, it is necessary to know the essence of the quotation from John Donne, from which Hemingway took his theme: "Any man's death diminishes me, because I am involved in Mankinde; And therefore never send to know for whom the bell tolls; It tolls for thee." Hemingway wanted his readers to feel that what happened to the Loyalists in Spain in 1937 was a part of that crisis of the modern world in which everyone shares.

Even more than *A Farewell to Arms*, Hemingway here has focused the conflict of war on a single man. Like Frederic Henry, Robert Jordan is an American in a European country fighting for a cause that is not his by birth. Henry, however, just happened to be in Italy when World War I broke out; he had no ideological commitment to the war. Robert Jordan has come to Spain because he believes in the Loyalist cause. Although the Loyalists have Communist backing, Jordan is not a Communist. He believes in the land and the people, and ultimately this belief costs him his life. Jordan's death is an affirmation. One need only compare it with the earlier novels to see this novel as a clear political statement of what a man must do under pressure.

For Whom the Bell Tolls is a circular novel. It begins with Robert Jordan belly-down on a pine forest in Spain observing a bridge he has been assigned to destroy. At the conclusion, Jordan is once again belly-down against the Spanish earth; this time snow covers the pine needles, and he has a broken leg. He is carefully sighting on an enemy officer approaching on horseback, and "he could feel his heart beating against the pine needle floor of the forest." Between the opening and closing paragraphs, two hundred thousand words have passed covering a time period of only seventy hours. At the center of all the action and meditation is the bridge. It is the focal point of the conflict to which the reader and the characters are drawn back again and again.

In what was his longest novel to that point, Hemingway forged a tightly unified plot: a single place, a single action, and a brief time—the classical unities. Jordan's military action takes on other epic qualities associated with the Greeks. His sacrifice is not unlike that of Leonidas at the crucial pass or Thermopylae, during the Persian Wars. There, too, heroic action was required to defend an entry point, and there, too, the leader died in an action that proved futile in military terms but became a standard measure of courage and commitment.

Abandoning somewhat the terse, clipped style of his earlier novels, Hemingway makes effective use of flashbacks to delineate the major characters. Earlier central characters seemed to exist without a past. Yet if Robert Jordan's death was to "diminish mankind," then the reader had to know more about him. This character development takes place almost within suspended time. Jordan and Maria try to condense an entire life into those seventy hours. The reader is never allowed to forget time altogether, for the days move, light changes, meals are eaten, and snow falls. Everything moves toward the time when the bridge must be blown, but this time frame is significant only to Jordan and the gypsy group. It has little reference to the rest of the world. Life, love, and death are compressed into those seventy hours, and the novel becomes a compact cycle suspended in time.

The novel has more fully developed characters than the earlier Hemingway novels. In the gypsy camp, each person becomes important. Pilar is often cited as one of Hemingway's better female characters, just as Maria is often criticized as being unbelievable. However, Maria's psychological scars are carefully developed. She has been raped by the Fascists and has seen her parents and village butchered. She is just as mentally unstable as were Brett Ashley and Catherine Barkley. Jordan, too, is a wounded man. He lives with the suicide of his father and the killing of his fellow dynamiter. The love of Jordan and Maria makes each of them whole again.

The bridge is destroyed on schedule, but, through no fault of Jordan's, its destruction is meaningless in military terms. Seen in the context of the military and political absurdities, Jordan's courage and death were wasted. However, the bridge was more important for its effect upon the group. It gave them a purpose and a focal point; it forged them into a unity, a whole. They can take pride in their accomplishment in spite of its cost. Life is ultimately a defeat no matter how it is lived; what gives defeat meaning is the courage that a man is capable of forging in the face of death's certainty. One man's death does diminish the group, for they are involved together. Jordan's loss is balanced by the purpose he has given to the group.

Just as the mountains are no longer a safe place from the Fascists with their airplanes, Hemingway seems to be saying that no man and no place are any longer safe. It is no longer possible to make a separate peace as Frederic Henry did with his war. When Fascist violence is loose in the world, a man must take a stand. Jordan does not believe in the Communist ideology that supports the Loyalists, but he does believe in the earth and its people. He is essentially the nonpolitical man caught in a political conflict that he cannot avoid. He does the best he can with the weapons available to him.

FOUR QUARTETS

Type of work: Poetry
Author: T. S. Eliot (1888–1965)
First published: *Four Quartets*, 1943

At age sixty and already an elder statesman of letters, T. S. Eliot was awarded the British Order of Merit and the Nobel Prize in Literature in 1948, five years after publishing what would be his last masterpiece, *Four Quartets*. Musing on the Nobel committee's choice, he surmised that they made their selection having considered "the entire corpus" of his work. Although he would go on to write three more plays, several volumes of essays, and some more poetry, *Four Quartets* was to remain the capstone of his career as a poet, the masterpiece of his maturity, very different in style from the masterpiece of his poetic apprenticeship, "The Love Song of J. Alfred Prufrock" (1917) and from his renowned and no longer disputed chef d'oeuvre, *The Waste Land* (1922). Quite simply, some of his poetic concerns had changed, as had his mode of expression.

More seemingly direct and more apparently accessible than Eliot's early work, *Four Quartets* exhibits a certain simplicity of statement that leads into the depth of his thought. The sequence, like some of his earlier poetry, grew incrementally over an eight-year period. "Burnt Norton" (1935), the first of the quartets, was formed from lines originally intended for the verse drama *Murder in the Cathedral* (1935) and contains themes common to the play. Its title refers to a specific country house with a rose garden in the Cotswolds. "East Coker" (1940) invokes the place from which Eliot's forebears emigrated in the seventeenth century; Eliot would be buried in East Coker, Somerset, in 1965. "The Dry Salvages" is also linked to Eliot's own geography: In his youth his family spent summers in New England, principally in Rockport and Gloucester, Massachusetts, on Cape Ann, near the rocks known as the Dry Salvages (a corruption, Eliot speculates, of *les trois sauvages*). Finally, "Little Gidding" (1942), which some have called Eliot's *Paradiso*, recalls the seventeenth century High Church religious community founded near Huntingdon by Nicholas Ferrar. Each of the poems is a meditation about place or inspired by place; together they form a devotional sequence linked by considerations of time, place, memory, consciousness of the self and of others, transcendence, and the act of writing.

Eliot has endowed the poems, each a quartet, with musical qualities and repetitive motifs. All of Eliot's poetry should be read aloud, and *Four Quartets* in particular should be heard. Walter Pater, to whom Eliot owed many debts he was eager to conceal, once wrote that "all art continually aspires to the condition of music." In these poems, Eliot's verbal art seems to aspire to that condition, so that in every phrase and sentence that is right, one finds "the complete consort dancing together."

Structurally, the poems follow the five-part plan Eliot had used in a more startling way in *The Waste Land*. These five movements, patterned on the form of a musical quartet or sonata, concern the varied relationships between time and eternity, the meaning of history, and the experience of Joycean epiphanies. C. K. Stead has provided lengthy and useful analyses of each of the poems by probing each according to a naming of the parts. The first part of each poem is concerned with the movement of time in which fleeting moments of eternity are caught. The second part examines worldly experience, which leads to an inevitable dissatisfaction. In the third part, the speaker seeks purgation in the world and seeks to divest the soul of love for created things. Part 4, the briefest, is a lyric prayer for or affirmation of the need for spiritual intercession. The final part deals with the problems of attaining artistic wholeness, which become analogs for, and blend into, the problems of achieving spiritual health.

"Burnt Norton" begins with two epigraphs from the fragments of the great philosopher of flux, Heraclitus. These are central to the concerns of Eliot as a modern-day poet-philosopher of the Word. Heraclitus' fragments mark him as a profound thinker who assigned the divine attribute of eternity to the universal Logos (word). This Logos Eliot would also find resonating in the later Logos of St. John's Gospel. Heraclitus did not believe that the universe began in time but that there exists a perpetual stream of creation in which "all things are an exchange for fire and fire for all things" in a world order that "was, is, and will be everliving fire being kindled in measures and quenched in measures." That for which Heraclitus is generally renowned becomes the more important for Eliot as he reflects, desiderative and expectant, upon his own craft in these poems: Heraclitus was the first Greek writer to explore the nature of discourse and to find an intelligible principle of the universe not only in the Logos but also in the depths of the philosophic soul, depths which deepen even as the soul attempts to fathom them. In particular, Eliot cites two sentences from H. Diels's *Die Fragmente der Vorsokratiker*, likely from the fifth edition of 1934. The first may be loosely translated, "While the Law of Reason (Logos) is common, the majority of people live as though they had an understanding (wisdom) of their own." The second is a paradox fundamental to Eliot's poem: "The way upward and downward are one and the same."

The poem opens with a reflection on the nature of time and leads to the proposition "If all time is eternally present/ All time is unredeemable," a notion that puts in question the need for a redemption and possibly the lack of such a need in a cosmos ruled by the redemptive Logos. The mix of memory and desire leads to the rose garden: Directed by the bird "into our first world," one finds that "the leaves are full of children,/ Hidden excitedly, containing laughter." This, possibly one of those brief encounters with eternity, is ended by the bird: "Go, go, go, said the bird: human kind/ Cannot bear very much reality."

Part 2 focuses upon individual humanity and the tension between an ascending spirit and a descending body. Eliot continues to pit Heraclitean opposites against each other "at the still point of the turning world. . . . Where past and future are gathered." Here is "inner freedom from the practical desire," "release from action and suffering, release from the inner/ And the outer compulsion." The human condition of incompleteness and temporality is an unsatisfactory one. What redeems the time and releases one from it is consciousness, but only in time can memory function. Paradoxically, he concludes, "Only through time time is conquered." Here, as in Heraclitus, the philosophic soul adds to its depths as it seeks to plumb them.

The poem's third part reveals "a place of disaffection," a twilight that has neither the light that turns shadow into transient beauty nor the darkness that purifies the soul. Indeed, spiritual purification is the speaker's goal with his command to "descend lower . . ./ Into the world of perpetual solitude" and his enumeration of necessary negations in abstention to achieve a present "while the world moves/ In appetency, on its metalled ways/ Of time past and time future." The search for purgation reiterates the Heraclitean virtue of desiccation, the "dry soul" approaching the condition of fire.

The short lyric that is part 4 celebrates the darkness in which the soul may be purified and places the speaker in the lower depths, below the sunflower's tendrils and the yew's fingers. Here, in the darkness "the light is still/ At the still point of the turning world." The questions in this section of the poem may hint at the need for intercession, but the mention of the "kingfisher's wing" is a more obvious allusion to the celebrated image Gerard Manley Hopkins had used for Christ.

In part 5 the speaker muses that "words move, music moves/ Only in time" and continues to meditate on the temporal nature of music, words, silence, ends and beginnings. Here Eliot examines the adequacy and inadequacy of words and moves to consider the Johanine Logos as he reflects that "the word in the desert/ Is most attacked by voices of temptation." In a further contrast

between desire (movement) and love (a stillness that impels motion), he finds the latter timeless except for the temporality that is necessary to the difference between unbeing and being. Finally, to draw the sequence full circle to part 1, there is the "hidden laughter/ Of children in the foliage" and a repetition, without attribution, of the bird's directives, and the closing statement "Ridiculous the waste sad time/ Stretching before and after." The questions of artistic wholeness and spiritual health involve a consideration of words as part of the Word and of love as a timeless present. By association, love participates in Logos; also by association, the laughter of children in the past in the rose garden becomes present and eternal in the remembered words "Quick now, here, now, always—" and has a connection, however tenuous, with love and Logos.

This type of analysis is only one among many possible approaches to the poem in itself and as part of a sequence. Some have read "Burnt Norton" as the first of a series which features God the Father and concerns the element of air, with "East Coker" focusing on God the Son (earth), "The Dry Salvages" dealing with Mary the Mother of God (water), and "Little Gidding" devoted to God the Spirit (fire). While this scheme offers suggestive possibilities, it presents a somewhat limited view of the poem and the sequence as a whole. What it does suggest is a range of possible interpretations suggested by the text.

To use Stead's fivefold analyses as applied to "Burnt Norton" in considering its three companion pieces is to develop a deep and rich appreciation of the poet at work in exploring his own consciousness. "East Coker" pursues the poet's beginning in his end (part 1), especially in light of family history, and is a much more explicit meditation on the role of the poet as craftsman of words (part 5). Like the speaker of Dante's *The Divine Comedy*, he is in the middle way; in his case he has spent twenty years—"years largely wasted, the years of *l'entre deux guerres*"—trying to learn to use words. "The Dry Salvages" recalls Eliot's youthful life in America not only in Massachusetts but also in St. Louis, Missouri, alongside the "strong brown god," the river. This poem, more than the first two, is explicitly concerned with religious thought, with direct references to God and the Annunciation (part 2), Krishna (part 3), and a prayer to the Queen of Heaven, "Figlia del tuo figlio" (daughter of your son). Again, the work of the poet in search of artistic wholeness and spiritual health becomes the clear focus of part 5, as the speaker considers varied attempts to communicate, spiritually and at times fantastically. He does offer a clue to his sense of his own purpose in probing language and time and eternity: "The point of intersection of the timeless/ With time, is an occupation for the saint." It is also an occupation for the poet and for his readers.

The most anthologized poem of the *Four Quartets*, "Little Gidding," contains Eliot's most mature and virtually final poetic statement. Musing on the place Little Gidding and its significance—historically, as a seat of spiritual life in the seventeenth century, and currently, as a source of spiritual strength—he finds "the intersection of the timeless moment/ Is England and nowhere. Never and always." Part 2 describes another sort of spiritual encounter reminiscent of Eliot's earlier dramatic poetry. Here, in Dantean fashion, he encounters the shade "of some dead master" whose burden is a total disillusion expressed in a disclosure of "the gifts reserved for age." He offers these observations as one poet to another, "since our concern was speech, and speech impelled us/ To purify the dialect of the tribe."

Part 3 contains echoes of Dame Julian of Norwich, a fourteenth century mystic, as the speaker reflects upon the inevitability of sin and the mystic knowledge of forgiveness based upon beseeching. The lyrical part 4 combines the "dove" of part 2, which had been a bomber, with the descent of the Spirit at Pentecost and the Her-aclitean fire foreshadowed in the epigraph to "Burnt Norton," as the speaker reflects upon love and fire. Finally, in some of his most memorable lines, a paean on poetic practice as a unifying, health-giving activity, Eliot achieves a synthetic vision, summarizes the varied strands of the poem, and ends at an unqualified affirmation. He unifies the sequence in the poem's closing lines by echoing the moments of insight he had revealed in the earlier poems and earlier in this one.

Eliot once wrote that his favorite author, Dante, is "a poet to whom one grows up over a lifetime." Eliot himself has achieved something of that stature: He is a poet to whom one returns without exhausting meaning or the possibility of meaning, especially when one reads his later poetry in light of the earlier work. In particular, *Four Quartets* is a sequence to which a reader may return after few or many years, exploring it anew and coming away with fresh insight.

FRANKENSTEIN: Or, The Modern Prometheus

Type of work: Novel
Author: Mary Wollstonecraft Shelley (1797–1851)
Type of plot: Gothic romance
Time of plot: Eighteenth century
Locale: Europe
First published: 1818

Victor Frankenstein, a brilliant inventor, actually succeeds in creating life. His creature, animate but lacking all human graces, is alone and scorned by mankind. Bitterly he accuses his creator and threatens to murder at will unless Victor creates a mate for him. Victor does, but in a moment of conscience, he destroys her. The monster avenges himself by strangling Victor's bride. Following the creature in an attempt to destroy him, Victor dies of exposure at the North Pole. The story hints in part at the possible dangers inherent in the pursuit of pure science; it also portrays the injustice of a society which persecutes such outcasts as Victor's creature.

Principal Characters

Victor Frankenstein, a native of Geneva who early evinces a talent in natural science. Having concluded his training at the university at Ingolstadt, he works until he discovers the secret of creating life. He makes a monster from human and animal organs found in dissecting rooms and butcher shops. The monster brings only anguish and death to Victor and his friends and relatives. Having told his story, he dies before his search for the monster is complete.

The Monster, an eight-foot-tall synthetic man endowed by its creator with human sensibilities. Rebuffed by man, it turns its hate against him. Its program of revenge accounts for the lives of Frankenstein's bride, his brother, his good friend, and a family servant. Just after Victor dies, the monster appears and tells the explorer that Frankenstein's was the great crime, for he had created a man devoid of friend, love, or soul.

Robert Walton, an English explorer who, on his ship frozen in a northland sea of ice, hears the dying Frankenstein's story and also listens to the monster's account of, and reason for, its actions.

Elizabeth Lavenza, Victor's foster sister and later his bride, who is strangled by the monster on her wedding night.

William, Victor's brother, who is killed by the monster while seeking revenge on its creator.

Henry Clerval, Victor's friend and a man of science who is killed by the monster to torment Frankenstein.

Justine Moritz, a family servant tried and condemned for William's murder.

The Story

Walton was an English explorer whose ship was held fast in polar ice. As the company looked out over the empty ice field, they were astonished to see a sledge drawn by dogs speeding northward. The sledge driver looked huge and misshapen. That night, an ice floe carried to the ship another sledge, one dog, and a man in weakened condition. When the newcomer learned that his was the second sledge sighted from the ship, he became agitated.

Walton was greatly attracted to the man during his convalescence, and as they continued fast in the ice, the men had leisure time to get acquainted. At last, after he had recovered somewhat from exposure and hunger, the man told Walton his story.

Victor Frankenstein was born of good family in Geneva. As a playmate for their son, the parents had adopted a lovely little girl of the same age. Victor and Elizabeth grew up as brother and sister. Much later another son, William, was born to the Frankensteins.

At an early age, Victor showed promise in the natural sciences. He devoured the works of Paracelsus and Albertus Magnus and thought in his ignorance that they were the real masters. When he grew older, his father decided to send Victor to the university at Ingolstadt. There he soon learned all that his masters could teach him in the field of natural science. Engaged in brilliant and terrible research, he stumbled by chance on the secret of creating life. Once he had gained this knowledge, he could not rest until he had employed it to create a living being. By haunting the butcher shops and dissecting rooms, he soon had the necessary raw materials. With great cunning, he fashioned an eight-foot monster and endowed him with life.

As soon as he had created his monster, however, he

was subject to strange misgivings. During the night, the monster came to his bed. At the sight of the horrible face, he shrieked and frightened the monster away. The horror of his act prostrated him with a brain fever. His best friend, Henry Clerval, arrived from Geneva and helped to nurse him through his illness. He was unable to tell Clerval what he had done.

Terrible news came from Geneva. William, Victor's young brother, was dead by the hand of a murderer. He had been found strangled in a park, and a faithful family servant, Justine, had been charged with the crime. Victor hurried to Geneva.

At the trial, Justine told a convincing story. She had been looking for William in the countryside and, returning after the city gates had been closed, had spent the night in a deserted hut; but she could not explain how a miniature from William's neck came to be in her pocket. Victor and Elizabeth believed the girl's story, but despite all of their efforts, Justine was convicted and condemned.

Depressed by these tragic events, Victor went hiking over the mountainous countryside. Far ahead on the glacier, he saw a strange, agile figure that filled him with horrible suspicions. Unable to overtake the figure, he sat down to rest. Suddenly, the monster appeared before him. The creature demanded that Victor listen to his story.

When he left Victor's chambers in Ingolstadt, everyone he met screamed and ran away. Wandering confusedly, the monster finally found shelter in an abandoned hovel adjoining a cottage. By great stealth, he remained there during daylight and at night sought berries for food. Through observation, he began to learn the ways of man. Feeling an urge to friendship, he brought wood to the cottage every day; but when he attempted to make friends with the cottagers, he was repulsed with such fear and fury that his heart became bitter toward all men. When he saw William playing in the park, he strangled the boy and took the miniature from his neck. Then

during the night, he came upon Justine in the hut and put the picture in her pocket.

Presently, the monster made a horrible demand. He insisted that Victor fashion a mate for him who would give him love and companionship. The monster threatened to ravage and kill at random if Victor refused the request; but if Victor agreed, the monster promised to take his mate to the wilds of South America where they would never again be seen by man. It was a hard choice, but Victor felt that he must accept.

Victor left for England with his friend Clerval. After parting from his friend, he went to the distant Orkneys and began his task. He was almost ready to animate the gross mass of flesh when his conscience stopped him. He could not let the two monsters mate and spawn a race of monsters. He destroyed his work.

The monster was watching at a window. Angered to see his mate destroyed, he forced his way into the house and warned Victor that a terrible punishment would fall upon the young man on his wedding night. Then the monster escaped by sea. Later, to torment his maker, he fiendishly killed Clerval.

Victor was suspected of the crime. Released for lack of evidence, he went back to Geneva. He and Elizabeth were married there. Although Victor was armed and alert, the monster got into the nuptial chamber and strangled the bride. Victor shot at him, but he escaped again. Victor vowed eternal chase until the monster could be killed.

That was Victor's story. Weakened by exposure, he died there in the frozen North with Elizabeth, William, Justine, and Clerval unavenged. Then the monster came to the dead man's cabin, and Walton, stifling his fear, addressed the gigantic, hideous creature. Victor's was the greater crime, the monster said. He had created a man, a man without love or friend or soul. He deserved his punishment. After his speech, the monster vanished over the ice field.

Critical Evaluation

Although Mary Wollstonecraft Shelley wrote other novels, such as *The Last Man* (1824) and *Lodore* (1835), she is remembered in literary history as the author of *Frankenstein*. The subject for her book arose in a discussion between her husband, the poet Percy Bysshe Shelley, and Lord Byron. Shelley, like Victor Frankenstein, fancied himself an amateur scientist as well as a professional humanitarian; and both Shelleys suffered from the hatred of conventional people when they outraged the public sense of decency. One theme of the novel, accordingly, is the unjust persecution of an outcast from society. The revenge of that outcast, the creature of Frankenstein, has become part of the popular imagination.

Frankenstein superficially resembles Ann Radcliffe's *The Mysteries of Udolpho* (1794), Matthew Gregory Lewis'

The Monk (1796), and Charles Robert Maturin's *Melmoth the Wanderer* (1820). Like these romances of suggested or actual physical horror, Shelley's novel is steeped in sentimental melancholy. Unlike most Gothic novels, however, *Frankenstein: Or, The Modern Prometheus* is at least partially philosophical and offers a scientific rather than supernatural explanation for the horror.

Indeed, for its serious ideas the novel more closely resembles *St. Leon* (1799) by Mary Shelley's father, William Godwin. As an illustration of the humanitarian philosophy of Jean Jacques Rousseau, *Frankenstein* shows the destructive results of undeveloped affection. The creature (who is at the time of his composition a "monster" only to the fearful and ignorant) craves but is denied ordinary human tenderness. Rejected as a man, he becomes a vengeful monster. Although he is given vital existence by science, he is never fully alive. Victor Frankenstein's science (or rather pseudoscience of vitalism, a belief in the "vital spark") is unable to produce a creature capable of attracting love. Instead, his scientific genius creates death—a theme that appears rarely in nineteenth century literature but is a major one in the twentieth century.

Readers familiar with the popular motion picture adaptations of *Frankenstein* are likely to be surprised when they come upon Mary Shelley's novel. The book is considerably richer in details, fuller in its development of minor characters, and more complicated in plot structure than later adaptations and parodies; it also treats the crea-ture from a significantly different point of view. Contrary to the popular stereotypes of the Frankenstein monster, he is articulate and, at least in the beginning, quite sympathetic. His revenge, although excessive, is motivated. From a modern reader's assessment, he is a monster too sentimental to be wholly frightening. *Frankenstein*, for all of its appeal to modern readers, represents the culmination of a tradition of Gothic horror on the one hand and sentimentalism on the other. Given a different philosophical orientation, much of that horror is bound to be misunderstood. What is remarkable, to be sure, is that so much survives.

GARGANTUA AND PANTAGRUEL

Type of work: Mock-heroic chronicle
Author: François Rabelais (c. 1494–1553)
Type of plot: Burlesque romance
Time of plot: Renaissance
Locale: France
First published: *Gargantua et Pantagruel*, 1567 (first complete edition): *Gargantua*, 1534 (English translation, 1653); *Pantagruel*, 1532 (English translation, 1653); *Tiers Livre*, 1546 (*Third Book*, 1693); *Le Quart Livre*, 1552 (*Fourth Book*, 1694); *Le Cinquiesme Livre*, 1564 (*Fifth Book*, 1694)

Gargantua and Pantagruel is a vast mock-heroic panorama about an amiable dynasty of giants who are prodigious eaters and drinkers, gay and earthy. Discursive and monumental, the work demonstrates the theme that the real purpose of life is to expand the soul by exploring the sources of varied experience.

Principal Characters

Gargantua, an affable prince, a giant—as an infant over 2,000 ells of cloth are required to clothe him—who has many adventures. He travels over Europe and other parts of the world fighting wars from which all prisoners are set free, straightening out disputes in other kingdoms, and helping his friends achieve their goals.

Pantagruel, Gargantua's giant son, who once got an arm out of his swaddling clothes and ate the cow that was nursing him. Pantagruel was born when his father was 400 years old. Accepting with good nature the responsibility of aiding the oppressed, he spends a good deal of his time traveling the earth with his companion Panurge. In their travels they visit a land where all citizens have noses shaped like the ace of clubs and a country in which the people eat and drink nothing but air.

Panurge, a beggar and Pantagruel's companion, who knows sixty-three ways to make money and two hundred fourteen ways to spend it. He speaks twelve known and unknown languages, but he does not know whether he should marry. Finally, he decides to consult the Oracle of the Holy Bottle to find the answer to his question. The trip to the island of the Holy Bottle is filled with adventures for Panurge and Pantagruel. The Oracle, when finally consulted, utters one word, "trinc." Panurge takes this pronouncement, translated as "drink," to mean that he should marry.

Friar John of the Funnels, a lecherous, lusty monk who fights well for Gargantua when the latter finds himself at war with King Picrochole of Lerné. To reward the friar for his gallantry, Gargantua orders workers to build the Abbey of Thélème, which has been Friar John's dream. Here men and women live together and work to accumulate wealth.

Grandgousier, the giant king who is Gargantua's father.

Gargamelle, Gargantua's mother who, taken suddenly in labor, bears Gargantua from her left ear.

Picrochole, King of Lerné, who invades Grandgousier's country. His army is repulsed by Gargantua, with the aid of Friar John and other loyal helpers. The prisoners captured are all allowed to go free.

Anarchus, King of Dipsody, who invades the land of the Amaurots. His army is overcome by Pantagruel, who makes the King a crier of green sauce.

Bacbuc, the priestess who conducts Panurge to the Oracle of the Holy Bottle and translates the Oracle's message for him.

Holofernes and **Joberlin Bridé,** Gargantua's first teachers.

The Story

Grandgousier and Gargamelle were expecting a child. During the eleventh month of her pregnancy, Gargamelle ate too many tripes and then played tag on the green. That afternoon in a green meadow, Gargantua was born from his mother's left ear.

Gargantua was a prodigy, and with his first breath, he began to clamor for drink. Seventeen thousand nine hundred and thirteen cows were needed to supply him with milk. For his clothing, the tailors used nine hundred ells of linen to make his shirt and eleven hundred and five ells of white broadcloth to make his breeches. Eleven hundred cowhides were used for the soles of his shoes.

At first Gargantua's education was in the hands of two masters of the old school, Holofernes and Joberlin Bridé. When Grandgousier observed that his son was making no progress, however, he sent him to Paris to study with Ponocrates. Aside from some mishaps, as when he took the bells from the tower of Notre Dame to tie around his horse's neck, Gargantua did much better with his studies in Paris.

Back home a dispute arose. The bakers of Lerné refused to sell cakes to the shepherds of Grandgousier. In the quarrel, a shepherd felled a baker, and King Picrochole of Lerné invaded the country. Grandgousier baked cartloads of cakes to appease Picrochole but to no avail, for no one dared oppose Picrochole except doughty Friar John of the Funnels. Finally, Grandgousier asked Gargantua to come to his aid.

Gargantua fought valiantly. Cannonballs seemed to him as grape seeds, and when he combed his hair, cannonballs dropped out. After he had conquered the army of Lerné, he generously set all the prisoners free.

All of his helpers were rewarded well, but for Friar John. Gargantua built the famous Abbey of Thélème, where men and women could be together, could leave when they wished, and where marriage and the accumulation of wealth were encouraged.

When he was more than four hundred years old, Gargantua had a son, Pantagruel. A remarkable baby, Pantagruel was hairy as a bear at birth and of such great size that he cost the life of his mother. Gargantua was sorely vexed between weeping for his wife and rejoicing for his son.

Pantagruel required the services of four thousand six hundred cows to nurse him. Once he got an arm out of his swaddling clothes and, grasping the cow nursing him, he ate the cow. Afterward, Pantagruel's arms were bound with anchor ropes. One day, the women forgot to clean his face after nursing, and a bear came and licked the drops of milk from the baby's face. By a great effort, Pantagruel broke the ropes and ate the bear. In despair, Gargantua bound his son with four great chains, one of which was later used to bind Lucifer when he had the colic. Pantagruel, however, broke the five-foot beam that constituted the footboard of his cradle and ran around with the cradle on his back.

Pantagruel showed great promise as a scholar. After a period of wandering, he settled down in Paris. There he was frequently called on to settle disputes between learned lawyers. One day he met a ragged young beggar. On speaking to him, Pantagruel received answers in twelve known and unknown tongues. Greatly taken by this fluent beggar, Pantagruel and Panurge became great friends. Panurge was a merry fellow who knew sixty-three ways to make money and two hundred fourteen ways to spend it.

Pantagruel learned that the Dipsodes had invaded the land of the Amaurots. Stirred by this danger to Utopia, he set out by ship to do battle. By trickery and courage, Pantagruel overcame the wicked giants. He married their king, Anarchus, to an old lantern-carrying hag and made the king a crier of green sauce. Now that the land of Dipsody had been conquered, Pantagruel transported a colony of Utopians there numbering 9,876,543,210 men, besides many women and children. All of these people were very fertile. Every nine months, each married woman bore seven children. In a short time, Dipsody was populated by virtuous Utopians.

For his services and friendship, Panurge was made Laird of Salmigondin. The revenue from this lairdship amounted to 6,789,106,789 gold royals a year, but Panurge managed to spend his income well in advance. Then, intending to settle down, Panurge began to reflect seriously on marriage, and he consulted his lord Pantagruel. They came to no conclusion in the matter because they got into an argument about the virtues of borrowing and lending money. Nevertheless, the flea in his ear kept reminding Panurge of his contemplated marriage, and he set off to seek other counsel.

Panurge consulted the Sibyl of Panzoult, the poet Raminagrobis, Herr Tripa, and Friar John. When all the advice he received proved contradictory, Panurge prevailed on Pantagruel and Friar John to set out with him to consult the Oracle of the Holy Bottle. From Saint Malo, the party sailed in twelve ships for the Holy Bottle, located in Upper India. The Portuguese sometimes took three years for that voyage, but Pantagruel and Panurge cut that time to one month by sailing across the Frozen Sea north of Canada.

The valiant company had many adventures on the way. On the Island of the Ennasins, they found a race of people with noses shaped like the ace of clubs. The people who lived on the Island of Ruach ate and drank nothing but wind. At the Ringing Islands, they found a strange race of Siticines who had long ago turned into birds. On Condemnation Island, they fell into the power of Gripe-men-all, Archduke of the Furred Law-cats, and Panurge was forced to solve a riddle before the travelers were given their freedom.

At last they came to the island of the Holy Bottle. Guided by a Lantern from Lanternland, they came to a large vineyard planted by Bacchus himself. Then they went underground through a plastered vault and came to marble steps. Down they went, a hundred steps or more. Panurge was greatly afraid, but Friar John took him by the collar and heartened him. At the bottom they came to a great mosaic floor on which was shown the history of Bacchus. Finally they were met by the priestess Bacbuc, who was to conduct them to the Bottle. Panurge knelt to kiss the rim of the fountain. Bacbuc threw something into the well, and the water began to boil. When Panurge sang the prescribed ritual, the Oracle of the Holy Bottle pronounced the word "trinc." Bacbuc looked up the word in a huge silver book. It meant drink, a word declared to be the most gracious and intelligible she had ever heard from the Holy Bottle. Panurge took the word as a sanction for his marriage.

Critical Evaluation

Partly because France's greatest comic prose writer was a legend even in his own lifetime, most of the facts of François Rabelais' life remains hazy. A monk, doctor of medicine, and writer, Rabelais transferred from the Franciscan to the Benedictine order with the Pope's express permission, because the latter order was both more tolerant and more scholarly. The year 1532 found him in Lyons, at that time the intellectual center of France, where he published his first creative work, book 2 (*Pantagruel*). As a satirist and humanist, Rabelais labored between the two religious extremes of Roman Catholicism and Genevan Protestantism; he had the mixed blessings of being attacked, alike, by Scaliger, St. Francis de Sales, and Calvin. All of them warned against his heretical impiety; he was, first and last, an iconoclast. Yet, like Erasmus, he attempted to steer a middle course—the attitude that led Thomas More to his death in the same period. This may have made Rabelais unpopular with his more radical contemporaries, such as Martin Luther and Ignatius Loyola; but it also made him one one of the most durable and most human comic writers of this century—and of all time.

In Rabelais, the spirit of comedy blends with the spirit of epic to produce a novel work without parallel or close precedent. The chronicles are universally inclusive, expressing the Renaissance ambition to explore and chart all realms of human experience and thought; and the mood of the narrator matches the scope of the narration. Rabelais, as Alcofibras, attributes his infinite exuberance to his literal and symbolic inebriation, which he invites his readers to share. His curiosity, realism, joy, and unpredictability are all things to all men—as long as the reader, whoever he may be, is willing to be intoxicated by a distillation of strong wit and language. As a genre, the chronicles may be compared to the "institute" so popular during the Renaissance (such as Niccolò Machiavelli's *The Prince*, 1532, Baldassare Castiglione's *The Courtier*, 1528, Roger Ascham's *The Schoolmaster*, 1570); they have also been considered a parody of medieval adventure romances. In the end, however, Rabelais' work beggars generic typology. Its narrative includes history, fable, myth, drama, lyric, comedy, burlesque, novel, and epic; just as its sources include sculpture, jurisprudence, pedagogy, architecture, painting, medicine, physics, mathematics, astronomy, chemistry, theology, religion, music, aeronautics, agriculture, botany, athletics, and psychological counseling. All of these elements are thrown together, with characteristic flair and mad abandon, into a savory stew.

It is a consistency of flavor, of authorial mood, that holds together this diverse and variegated work. That flavor is not one of thought, for Rabelais is no great thinker. As his translator Jacques LeClerq says, "his ideas are primitive, fundamental and eternal in their simplic-

ity." The unifying idea is the philosophy of Pantagruelism: "Do As Thou Wilt." The world of Pantagruel is a world in which no restrictions on sensual or intellectual exploration can be tolerated; excessive discipline is regarded as evil and inhuman. In true epicurean fashion, Rabelais has no patience for inhibitions; man lives for too brief a time to allow himself the luxury of denial. The Abbey of Thélème is the thematic center of the work, with its credo that instinct forms the only valid basis for morality and social structure. Rabelais ignores the dangers of the anarchy this credo implies; he is talking about the mind, not the body politic. The dullest thing imaginable is the unimaginative, conforming mind. His satirical pen is lifted against all who affect *freedom* of any kind in any fashion: against the hypocrites, militarists, abusers of justice, pedants, and medieval scholastics.

The reader of these gigantic chronicles, then, must not expect a plot. Anything so regular is anathema to Pantagruelism. Readers should also realize that the characters themselves are not the focus of the author's art but are, in fact, largely indistinguishable from one another. One of the most amusing elements of the book is that they are also indistinguishably large; Pantagruel's mouth, described in book 2, chapter 32, one of the finest chapters in European literature, is, at times, large enough to contain kingdoms and mountain ranges, at other times, no larger than a dovecote. The exception is Panurge, the normal-size man. He is an unforgettable character who makes so strong an impression, even on the author, that he cannot be forgotten. The third, fourth, and fifth books, in fact, are based on his adventures—just as Shakespeare wrote *The Merry Wives of Windsor* to exploit the beloved character of Falstaff. Panurge is the heroic companion of Pantagruel, in the best epic tradition; he also has the cunning of Ulysses, the drunken mirth of Falstaff, the roguishness of Jack Wilton and Tyl Ulenspiegel (his numerous pockets filled with innumerable tricks), the cynical but lighthearted opportunism of Chaucer's Pardoner, the magic powers of Shakespeare's Puck or Ariel. He is the wise fool of Erasmus and King Lear, and a Socratic gadfly who bursts the pretensions and illusions of all he encounters. The chapter entitled "How Panurge Non-plussed the Englishman Who Argued by Signs" is a literary tour de force, concentrating into one vivid, raucous chapter the comic spirit forever to be known as Rabelaisian. Important in other ways are "How Pantagruel Met a Limousin Who Spoke Spurious French," for its attack on unfounded affectation; and Gargantua's letter to Pantagruel, expressing the entire range of Renaissance learning, juxtaposed with the chapter introducing Panurge, who personifies Renaissance wit.

Rabelais' chaotically inventive style, filled with puns, wordplays, and synonyms, as well as with neologisms of his own creation, makes him one of the most difficult of all writers to translate accurately. His language reflects the rich variety of sixteenth century France, and he was to first to observe invariable rules in the writing of French prose—called, by Pasquier, "the father of our idiom." His syntax is flexible, supple, expansive, sparkling with vitality and the harmony of an ebullient character, complex and original. Rabelais did for French vocabulary what Chaucer did for English, fortifying it with eclecti-

cally selected terms of the soil, mill, tavern, and market, as well as scholarly terms and phrases gleaned from nearly all languages. As his comic theme reflects the universal as well as the particular, Rabelais' language combines the provincial with the popular—in a stew fit for the mouths of giants. A gargantuan appetite has nothing to do with gluttony..

GERMINAL

Type of work: Novel
Author: Émile Zola (1840–1902)
Type of plot: Naturalism
Time of plot: Nineteenth century
Locale: France
First published: 1885 (English translation, 1885)

One of the first novels dealing with the conflict between capital and labor, the book is still a work of fiction and not a manifesto. The events of the novel are based on an actual strike which occurred in France in 1884. Most notable about the work is Zola's ability to portray mob scenes; the emotions and movements of masses of people are so successfully rendered that the characters become believable results of the events which mold them.

Principal Characters

Étienne Lantier, a trained mechanic from Paris who becomes a miner and falls under the influence of socialism, which he believes is the workers' only hope. He organizes the miners, only to lose his popularity when a strike is settled and the people go back to work. His suffering, even the loss of his lover in a mine accident, only persuades him that he must continue his revolutionary work. He is the illegitimate son of Gervaise Macquart.

Catherine Maheu, a girl who works as a miner. She is loved by Lantier, even though she is forced to take another man as her lover. She eventually becomes Lantier's mistress, sharing his miserable, lonely life until she dies of suffocation after an accident in the mine where she and Lantier work.

Vincent Maheu, an elderly miner nicknamed Bonnemort because of his many escapes from accidental death in the mines.

Toussaint Maheu (known simply as Maheu), Vincent's son, the father of seven children. He becomes Lantier's friend and works with him in the mine. He is killed by soldiers during a strike at the mine.

La Maheude, Maheu's wife.

Zacharie Maheu, son of Maheu. He is a young miner who marries his mistress after she presents him with two children.

Philomène Levaque, Zacharie's mistress and, later, his wife.

Souvarine, a Russian anarchist who becomes Lantier's friend.

M. Hennebeau, director of the Montsou mines. He refuses to make any concessions to the miners and imports strikebreakers to operate the closed mines.

Paul Négrel, an engineer, nephew of M. Hennebeau. He feels compassion for the miners and leads a rescue party to save them after an accident traps Lantier and others below the surface of the ground.

Chaval, a miner who seduces Catherine Maheu. He is jealous of his rival, Lantier, and their mutual animosity ends in a fight below the surface of the ground in which Chaval is killed.

Dansaert, head captain of the mine in which Lantier works.

Cécile Grégoire, daughter of a mine stockholder, fiancée of Négrel. She is strangled to death by old Vincent Maheu (Bonnemort), who has become senile.

Maigrat, a rapacious storekeeper who extends credit to the women who grant him amorous favors.

M. Grégoire, a mine stockholder who justifies low pay for the workers by asserting that they spend their money only for drink and vice.

Jeanlin Maheu, an eleven-year-old who works in a mine until he is crippled in an accident. He murders a mine guard, but his crime is hidden by Lantier.

Alzire Maheu, a deformed sister of Catherine. The little girl dies of starvation during the strike.

Pluchart, a mechanic who persuades Lantier to join the workers' international movement.

The Story

Étienne Lantier set out to walk from Marchiennes to Montsou looking for work. On the way, he met Vincent Maheu, another workman, called Bonnemort because of successive escapes from death in the mines. Nearing sixty years old, Bonnemort suffered from a bad cough because of particles of dust from the mine pits.

Bonnemort had a son, Maheu, whose family consisted of seven children. Zacharie, Maheu's eldest son, twenty-one years old, Catherine, sixteen years old, and Jeanlin, eleven years old, worked in the mines. Étienne, too, was given a job in the mine. He descended the mine shaft along with Maheu, Zacharie, Chaval, Levaque, and Catherine. At first he mistook the latter for a boy. During lunchtime, Chaval roughly forced the girl to kiss him. This act angered Étienne, although the girl insisted that the brute was not her lover.

The head captain, Dansaert, came with M. Négrel, M. Hennebeau's nephew, to inspect Étienne, the new worker. Although there was bitterness among the workers, danger lurking in the shafts, and so little· pay that it was hardly worth working, Étienne decided to stay in the mine.

M. Grégoire had inherited from his grandfather a share in the Montsou mines. He lived in peace and luxury with his wife and only daughter, Cécile. A marriage had been arranged between Cécile and Négrel.

One morning, La Maheude (Maheu's wife) and her younger children went to the Grégoires to seek help. They were given warm clothing but no money, since the Grégoires believed working people would only spend money in drinking and nonsense. La Maheude had to beg for some groceries and money from Maigrat, who ran the company shop and who would extend credit only if he received a woman's caresses in return. He had Catherine in mind. Catherine, however, escaped him, met Chaval that night, and allowed him to seduce her. Étienne witnessed the seduction and was disillusioned by the young girl.

Étienne so quickly and expertly adapted himself to the mine that he earned the profound respect of Maheu. He made friends with the other workers. Only toward Chaval was he hostile, for Catherine now openly behaved as the man's mistress. At the place where Étienne lived, he would chat with Souvarine, a quiet Russian who espoused Nihilism, the abolition of all forms of government. Étienne discussed a new movement he had heard about from his friend Pluchart, a Lille mechanic. It was an international trade-union movement to strengthen the workers. Étienne had come to loathe the working and living conditions of the miners and their families, and he hoped to collect a fund to sustain the forthcoming strike. He discussed his plan with Rasseneur, with whom he boarded.

After Zacharie married his mistress Philomène Levaque, the mother of his two children, Étienne came to the Maheu household as a boarder. Night after night he urged the family to accept his socialistic point of view. As the summer wore on, he gained prestige among the neighbors, and his fund grew. As the secretary, he drew a small fee and was able to put aside money for himself. He began to take on airs.

The threat of strike was provoked when the company lowered the wages of the workers. As a final blow to the Maheus, a cave-in struck Jeanlin, leaving him a cripple. Catherine went to live with Chaval, who had been accusing her of sleeping with Étienne. In December, the miners struck.

While the Grégoires and the Hennebeaus were at dinner arranging the plans for the marriage between Cécile and Négrel, the miners' delegation came to see M. Hennebeau, but he refused to give any concessions. The strike wore on through the weeks while the workers slowly starved. Étienne preached socialism, and the strikers listened; as their misery increased, they became more adamant in their resistance to M. Hennebeau. The long weeks of strike at the Montsou mines ended in a riot when the people advanced to other pits to force the workers to quit their labors and join the strike. The mob destroyed property throughout the day and raged against their starvation.

Catherine had remained faithful to Chaval, but when, during the riot, he turned renegade and ran to get the gendarmes, she deserted him to warn her comrades, especially Étienne.

Étienne went into hiding, assisted by Jeanlin, who had become a street urchin and a thief. The Maheu family fared poorly. Crippled Alzire, one of the younger children, was dying of starvation. Everywhere neighbors quarreled fretfully over trifles. Étienne frequently slipped into Maheu's house for a visit; for the most part, however, he wandered alone at night. After the strike had been in force for two months, there was a rumor that the company was bringing strikebreakers, Borain workers, to the pits. Étienne began to despair. He suggested to the Maheus that the strikers bargain with M. Hennebeau, but La Maheude, who once had been so sensible and had resisted violence, shouted that they should not give in to the pressure of the mine director's demands.

One night at Rasseneur's, while Étienne was discussing matters with Souvarine, Chaval and Catherine entered. The animosity between Étienne and Chaval flared up, and they fought. Chaval was overpowered and ordered Catherine not to follow him but to stay with Étienne. Left alone, Catherine and Étienne were embarrassed and confused. Étienne had no place to take the girl. It was not possible for her to go home, since La Maheude could not forgive her for having deserted the family and for working during the strike. Resignedly, Catherine went back to her lover.

After Catherine had gone, Étienne walked by the pits, where he was a witness to the murder of a guard by little Jeanlin. Étienne dragged the body away and hid it.

When the strikebreakers began to work, the strikers stormed the entrance to the pit and threatened the soldiers on guard. After a while, the soldiers fired into the mob. Twenty-five workers were wounded, and fourteen were killed. Maheu was among those killed.

Company officials came to Montsou to settle the strike. The Borain workers were sent away. Étienne's popularity ended. He brought Catherine home and began to stay at Maheu's house again. The bleak house of mourning filled Étienne with remorse.

Souvarine resolved to leave Montsou. Before he went, he sneaked into the pit and committed enough damage to cause a breakdown in the shafts. That same morning,

Étienne and Catherine decided that they must go back to work. Chaval managed to be placed on the same work crew with Étienne and Catherine. Repeatedly the two men clashed; Chaval still wanted Catherine.

Water began rushing into the shaft. Chaval, Étienne, and the rest were trapped below when the cage made its last trip up and did not come down again. The people above waited and watched the mine slowly become flooded by subterranean torrents of water.

Négrel set about to rescue the entombed workers; as long as they were below, they must be assumed to be still alive. At last, he and a rescue party heard faint thumpings from the trapped workers. The men began to dig. An explosion injured several of them and killed Zacharie.

Meanwhile, the trapped workers had scattered, trying to find a place of safety. Étienne and Catherine came upon Chaval in the gallery to which he had climbed. There the animosity between the two men led to a fight, which ended when Étienne killed Chaval. Alone, the two lovers heard the rescuers' tapping. For days they continued to answer the tapping. Catherine died before the men outside reached them, but Étienne was still alive when help came.

After six weeks in a hospital, Étienne prepared to go to Paris, where more revolutionary work awaited him.

Critical Evaluation

When Émile Zola's novel *Germinal* appeared in 1885, as the thirteenth of a projected series of twenty interrelated novels designed to give "the natural and social history of a family under the Second Empire," it was acclaimed by some as the most impressive and powerful of the series that far, and dismissed by others as a deliberately sensational catalogue of the horrors of sex and violence prevalent in French coal-mining communities. A century later, the initial ambivalence about *Germinal*'s reputation has largely dissipated, and most critics willingly grant it a place among the greatest novels of the nineteenth century, in any language.

To know that *Germinal* gives a painstakingly detailed account of daily life in a coal-mining community of northern France, in accordance with Zola's well-known literary theory of naturalism, and that the novel's central action, the account of a strike among the miners of Montsou, was given extraordinary authenticity because Zola paid a personal visit to a mine under strike conditions and took careful notes for his novel, is to deepen one's appreciation for the value of the novel as a social and historical document. None of that kind of information, however, can explain why *Germinal* stands out as a major work of literary art. To evaluate *Germinal* fairly as literature, one must go beyond its acknowledged realism and consider the range and believability of its characters, the ingenuity and force of its structure, and the scope and significance of its themes.

The cast of characters in this monumental novel is unusually large, for Zola wished to represent as many facets as possible of social and economic life in the northern region of France, near the Belgian border, where the novel's action takes place. The central figure of the novel is actually an outsider to the mining country, a Parisian mechanic named Étienne Lantier, who comes to the region in March of 1866 looking for work of any nature, because times are bad. Lantier is also the sole link in the novel to the other novels of Zola's vast series, since he is a member of the Rougon-Macquart family that Zola invented as a focus for his series. Lantier accepts menial work in the Montsou mine, but with his education and native intelligence he quickly becomes a skilled and respected miner and emerges within months as a leader who helps organize a union among the miners.

The miners, who live in small company-built houses, are chiefly represented by one family, named Maheu, consisting of Toussaint Maheu and his wife (called La Maheude); Maheu's father, Vincent Maheu (called Bonnemort); and Maheu and La Maheude's seven children, ranging in age from an infant daughter to an adult son named Zacharie who is a full-time miner like his father and grandfather before him. The reader is given some knowledge of several other families, neighbors of the Maheus in the mining village, who add to the variety of types and ways of living found among the miners, though life is generally hard and impoverished for all. A different social level is represented by a character named Rasseneur, a former miner, now the proprietor of a tavern, and ambitious to be a leader of the miners; a strange foreigner, Souvarine, who works as an engineer in the mines, keeps largely to himself, and harbors anarchist principles brought from his Russian homeland; and a sinister figure named Maigrat, who runs the company store in the village and abuses his power by demanding sexual favors of the miners' wives and daughters in exchange for credit.

Ownership and management of the mines is represented by four individuals: the director of Montsou, Hennebeau, who is tormented by an adulterous wife; Hennebeau's nephew, Paul Négrel, employed as chief engineer in the mines; Deneulin, an independent owner of a small mine in the area; and Grégoire, a stockholder in the Montsou mine, who lives a very comfortable bourgeois life solely on the income he derives from his inherited mining stock. An array of marginal figures, involved in one way or another in the life of the mining community, also people the novel's pages, and there is frequent mention of the Montsou mine's board of directors, remote and mysterious in its Paris headquarters, yet the source of all the decisions that most directly affect life in Montsou.

Zola places this carefully balanced cast of characters in a series of actions, arising out of tensions between labor and management, which escalate relentlessly in hostility and violence. The protests begin as a dispute about working conditions and develop into a full-scale strike, followed by the use of troops to break the strike; the crisis culminates in Souvarine's attempt, based on anarchist principles, to destroy the mine by sabotage. The most notable feature of the novel's action is that most of the events are sprawling crowd scenes of increasing complexity as the novel progresses, which allowed Zola to demonstrate impressive mastery of that special kind of writing. This series of major actions, forming a crescendo of emotional intensity, allows all levels of the small community to come into cooperation or confrontation with one another and to display all that is good, and all that is bad, in their natures as well as in their respective situations.

Zola is at great pains to preserve some kind of balance in the distribution of good and evil traits, so as not to oversimplify the moral and political issues the novel raises. Those on the side of labor are neither always virtuous nor always ignorant; those on the side of capital are neither always inhuman nor always rational. There is blame and praise enough to assign to all levels of the community. The result is that, as the action builds to an ever higher emotional pitch from section to section of the novel, the reader, having no clear villain and no clear hero on whom to focus, is overwhelmed by a sense of helplessly witnessing an inevitable tragedy for which no individual or group bears the ultimate responsibility. Zola certainly tried to depict in *Germinal* the central crisis of industrialized society in that era: the clash between capital and labor. Constrained, however, by the principle of objectivity inherent in his quasi-scientific literary theory, which he called naturalism, Zola was careful to show the crisis as complex, multifarious, unpredictable, and hence hardly reducible to any black-and-white formula ranging all virtue on one side and all villainy on the other.

The attempt at a semblance of objectivity in *Germinal* was for Zola an artistic imperative, but it did not imply neutrality or indifference on his part with respect to the social and economic struggle of his time. The socialist tendencies Zola had developed by 1885 were publicly known and are perhaps expressed in the vaguely ambiguous closing scene of the novel, in which Lantier, resorted to health after the mine cave-in and flood that nearly killed him, leaves Montsou for Paris to continue the struggle as a union organizer, full of hope that he and his mining comrades will eventually triumph in the name of social justice. What makes the hope seem just a bit ambiguous is that Lantier thinks of himself and his comrades in violent terms, as a "black avenging army," forecasting more death and destruction before a better world can be attained.

Zola's last-minute choice of the title *Germinal* is one possible clue to the significance of the ambiguity in the ending. As a title, *Germinal* evokes the French Revolution, since it is the name of a month in the revolutionary calendar that was invented after 1789. Zola's thought was perhaps that the industrial crisis of his time, depicted in his novel, had brought France once again to the same political and social situation that had existed in 1789. His novel was therefore intended as a warning, perhaps, of a new revolution about to burst forth, with social justice as its admirable goal but with the attendant threat of volatile and unpredictable violence as well, as in the well-remembered aftermath of 1789.

THE GOLDEN BOWL

Type of work: Novel
Author: Henry James (1843–1916)
Type of plot: Psychological realism
TIme of plot: c. 1900
Locale: England and the Continent
First publIshed: 1904

The Golden Bowl is a meticulous, involved, and incredibly detailed exploration of the subtleties of thought and nuances of emotion of a small circle of wealthy, cultured Americans living in Europe. James's collection of psychological shades and discriminations are at times almost overwhelming to the reader. A forerunner of psychological expressionism, the novel describes characters who live in a world shut off from homely realities, a world that will not tolerate crudities.

Principal Characters

Maggie Verver, the motherless daughter of an American millionaire. For a number of years the Ververs have spent much of their time abroad, where Mr. Verver has devoted himself to acquiring a magnificent art collection for the museum he plans to build in American City. Sharing her father's quiet tastes and aesthetic interests, Maggie has become his faithful companion, and they have created for themselves a separate, enclosed world of ease, grace, and discriminating appreciation, a connoisseurship of life as well as of art. Even Maggie's marriage to Prince Amerigo, an Italian of ancient family, does not change greatly the pattern of their lives, a pattern that she believes complete when Mr. Verver marries her best friend, Charlotte Stant. What Maggie does not know is the fact that before her marriage the Prince and Charlotte, both moneyless and therefore unable to marry, had been lovers. Several years later the Prince, bored by his position as another item in the Verver collection, and Charlotte, restless because she takes second place beside her elderly husband's interest in art, resume their former intimacy. Maggie finds her happiness threatened when her purchase of a flawed gold-and-crystal bowl leads indirectly to her discovery of the true situation. Her problem is whether to disclose or conceal her knowledge. Deeply in love with her husband and devoted to her father, she decides to remain silent. Her passivity becomes an act of drama because it involves a sense of ethical responsibility and a moral decision; her predicament is the familiar Jamesian spectacle of the innocent American confronting the evil of European morality, in this case complicated by Maggie's realization that she and her father are not without guilt, that they have lived too much for themselves. In the end her generosity, tact, and love resolve all difficulties. Mr. Verver and his wife leave for America and Maggie regains her husband's love, now unselfishlessly offered.

Prince Amerigo, a young Italian nobleman, handsome, gallant, sensual, living in England with his American wife. A man of politely easy manners, he is able to mask his real feelings under an appearance of courteous reserve. Though he has loved many women, he has little capacity for lies or deception in his dealings with them; he objects when Charlotte Stant, his former mistress, wishes to purchase a flawed golden bowl as a wedding gift to his wife, for he wants nothing but perfection in his marriage. He and Charlotte are often thrown together after she marries his father-in-law, and they become lovers once more. When his wife learns, through purchase of the same flawed bowl, the secret of his infidelity, he tries to be loyal to all parties concerned, and he so beautifully preserves the delicate harmony of family relationships that no outsiders except their mutual friends, the Assinghams, know of the situation. Maggie, his wife, is able to save her marriage because his delicacy in the matter of purchased and purchasable partners makes tense situations easier. After Mr. Verver and his wife return to America, the Prince shows relief as unselfish as it is sincere; their departure allows him to be a husband and a father in his own right.

Charlotte Stant, the beautiful but impecunious American girl who needs a wealthy husband to provide the fine clothes and beautiful things she believes necessary for her happiness. Because Prince Amerigo is poor, she becomes his mistress but never considers marrying him. After his marriage to Maggie Verver, her best friend, Mr. Verver proposes to Charlotte. She accepts him and, though Mr. Verver cannot understand her claim of unworthiness, but she declares herself prepared to be as devoted as possible, as a wife and as a stepmother to her good friend. Often left in the Prince's company while Maggie and her father pursue their interest in art, she resumes her affair with her former lover. When the truth is finally revealed, Charlotte, determined to prove her loyalties to all concerned, persuades Mr. Verver to return with her to America. Her poised and gracious farewell to Maggie and the Prince is more than a demonstration of her ability to keep up appearances; it shows the code of responsibility she has assumed toward her lover, her friend, and her husband.

Adam Verver, a rich American who has given over the pursuit of money in order to achieve the good life for himself and his daughter Maggie. In his innocence he believes that this end may be attained by seeing and collecting the beautiful art objects of Europe. A perfect father, he cannot realize that there is anything selfish in the close tie that exists between himself and his daughter, and he tries to stand in the same relationship with his son-in-law, Prince Amerigo, and Charlotte Stant, his daughter's friend, whom he marries. All he really lives for is to provide for Maggie and his grandson the life of happiness and plenty he envisions for them. When he finally realizes that the pattern of his life has been a form of make-believe, he sacrifices his own peace of mind and agrees to return with his wife to make the United States his permanent home.

Fanny Assingham, the friend of Maggie and Adam Verver, Prince Amerigo, and Charlotte Stant, and the guardian angel of their secret lives. As one who senses the rightness of things, she helps to bring about both marriages with a sensitive understanding of the needs of all, a delicacy she will not allow to be disrupted by Maggie's discovery of her husband's infidelity. Her belief is that even wickedness is more to be condoned than wrongness of heart. She helps to resolve the situation between Maggie and Prince Amerigo when she hurls the golden bowl, symbol of Maggie's flawed marriage and the Prince's guilt, to the floor and smashes it.

Colonel Robert Assingham, called **Bob,** a retired army officer who understands his wife's motives and the interest she takes in the Verver family but who manages to keep himself detached from her complicated dealings with the lives of others.

The Principinio, the small son of Prince Amerigo and his wife Maggie.

The Story

Maggie Verver was the daughter of a wealthy American widower who had devoted all his life to his daughter. The Ververs lived a lazy life. Their time was spent in collecting items to decorate their own existence and to fill a museum that Mr. Verver was giving to his native city back in the United States. They had few friends, Maggie's only confidante was Mrs. Assingham, the American-born wife of a retired British Army officer.

It was Mrs. Assingham who introduced the Ververs to Prince Amerigo, a handsome, quiet young Italian nobleman who struck Maggie's fancy. When she informed her father that she would like to marry the Prince, Mr. Verver provided a handsome dowry so that the wedding might take place.

A few days before the wedding, a painful scene occurred in Mrs. Assingham's home, where the Prince and Charlotte Stant, deeply in love with each other, met to say good-bye. Each was penniless, and a marriage had been out of the question. Since both were friends of Maggie, the present situation was painful for them. As a farewell lark, they spent the last afternoon in searching for a wedding present for Charlotte to present to Maggie. In a tiny shop, they discovered a golden bowl which Charlotte wished to purchase as a remembrance for the Prince from her. He refused it because of superstitious fears that a crack in the golden bowl might bring bad luck.

After the wedding of the Prince and Maggie, the lives of the pair coincided with the life that the Ververs had been living for years. Maggie and her father spent much of their time together. The Prince, although he did not complain, was really only a convenience that they had purchased because Maggie had reached the age when she needed to have a husband.

After a year and a half, a baby was born to the Prince and Maggie, but the child made no apparent difference in the relationships between the woman and her father or the woman and her husband. Maggie decided that her father also needed a wife. She went to Mrs. Assingham and told her friend that she planned to have Charlotte Stant marry her father. Charlotte was a quiet person aware of the love between Maggie and her father, and she was the sort of person who would be thankful to marry a wealthy man. Neither Maggie nor Mrs. Assingham puts this into words, but it was tacitly understood.

Mr. Verver, anxious to please his daughter in this as in everything else, married Charlotte a short time later. This second marriage created a strange situation. Maggie and her father both took houses in London where they could be together a great deal of the time. The association of father and daughter left the Prince and Charlotte together much of the time. Maggie encouraged them to go out, to represent her and her father at balls and dinners. Maggie, however, did not know that her husband and her stepmother had been intimate before her own marriage to the Prince.

Several years went by in this manner, but slowly the fact that there was something strange in the relationships dawned upon Maggie's sensitive feelings. She eventually went to Mrs. Assingham and poured out her suspicions. Mrs. Assingham, in full knowledge of the circumstances, decided to keep silent.

Maggie resolved to say nothing of her suspicions to anyone else. Yet her attitude of indifference and her insistence in throwing the Prince and Charlotte together, aroused their suspicions that she knew they had been sweethearts and that she suspected them of being lovers after marriage.

Each one of the four speculated at length as to what

the other three knew or suspected. Yet their mutual confidence and love prevented each one of them from ever asking anything of the others.

One day, Maggie went shopping for some unusual art object to present to her father on his birthday. She accidentally happened into the same shop where the Prince and Charlotte had gone several years before, and she purchased the golden bowl that they had passed over because of its flaw. The following day, the shopkeeper visited her. The name and address had told him that she was the wife of the Prince who had passed up the bowl years before. He knew that the existence of the crack would quickly come to the attention of the Prince, and so he had hastened to inform Maggie of the flaw and to return part of the purchase price. He also told her of the Prince's first visit to the shop and of the young woman who had been with him. Maggie then knew that the Prince and Charlotte had known each other before her marriage and that they had spent an afternoon together the day before she was married. She was upset. Again, she confided in Mrs. Assingham.

Having learned that there was no serious relationship between the Prince and Charlotte, Mrs. Assingham informed Maggie that she was making a great ado over nothing at all. To back up her remark, she raised the bowl above her head and smashed it to the floor, where it broke into several pieces. As she did so, the Prince entered the room and saw the fragments of the bowl. After Mrs. Assingham's departure, he tried to learn how much Maggie knew. Maggie and her husband agreed to say nothing to either Maggie's father or to Charlotte.

Charlotte, too, began to sense that something had disturbed Maggie, and she shrewdly guessed what it was. Then Maggie tried to realign the relationships of the four by proposing that she and Charlotte stay together for a while and that the Prince and her father go to the Continent to buy art objects. This proposal was gently put forward and as gently rebuffed by the other three.

Maggie and her father began to realize that their selfishness in continuing the father-daughter relationship that they had had before her marriage was wrong. Shortly after that selfishness had been brought into the open and discussed by Maggie and Mr. Verver, Charlotte told Maggie that she wished to return to America and to take her husband with her. She bluntly informed Maggie that she was afraid that if Mr. Verver continued to live so close to his daughter, he would lose interest in his wife. Mr. Verver agreed to accompany Charlotte back to the United States. It was a difficult decision for him to make. He realized that once he was away, Charlotte would never agree to his coming back to Europe to live.

On an autumn afternoon, Mr. Verver and Charlotte went to have tea with Maggie and the Prince before leaving England. It was almost heartbreaking to Maggie to see her father's carriage take him out of sight and to know that her old way of life had really ended. The only thing that kept her from breaking down completely was the look on the Prince's face as he turned her face away from the direction her father's carriage had taken. At that moment, seeing his eyes, Maggie knew she had won her husband for herself and not for her money.

Critical Evaluation

The Golden Bowl, along with *The Ambassadors* and *The Wings of the Dove*, is one of the novels of the triad of works upon which the high reputation of Henry James's "major phase" rests. In these novels, James's already complex style reaches new levels of sophistication as the writing becomes more and more intricate and convoluted, accommodating ever more subtle levels of analysis of character and event. Gradually the "center of consciousness" in the mind of a character, which had been essential to James's earlier works, gives way to an omniscient point of view, and a narrative voice that is James's own. Though it hardly appears so to the eye, James's style of this period is essentially oral—he had developed the habit of dictating his material to a secretary—and reflects his characteristically ponderous manner of speech. Seeming to move endlessly to circle or enfold a subject or an idea without ever touching it directly, James's technique in these late novels has been admired highly by critics who place a premium on style, while frequently being disparaged by those who stress content and clarity of thought. For James himself, the art of the novel was

everything in writing, and there is little doubt that in *The Golden Bowl*, his artistry reached a peak.

With this novel, James continues the subject matter of the "international theme," which had characterized his work from its beginning, by dealing with a group of Americans in Europe. Adam Verver, in particular, can be seen as an avatar of the American Adam who recurs in James's fiction, often, as here, in search of European culture, which he will take back to his culturally barren homeland. Prince Amerigo is linked by his name to the historic connection between America and Europe and, by his marriage to Maggie, might be seen as dramatizing a new dependence of the Old World upon the New. Yet, *The Golden Bowl* ultimately is less an international novel than such works as *The American*, *Daisy Miller*, or *The Ambassadors* because its concerns are finally more with individuals than with cultures. Though the Ververs begin in America and Adam returns there at the novel's end, neither his experience nor that of Maggie or Charlotte is essentially contingent upon the sort of conflict of cultural values that is at the heart of James's international novels and stories. Rather, the problems of love and marriage at the heart of *The Golden Bowl* are truly universal; neither their nature nor their solution depends upon an American perspective.

Like many of James's works, *The Golden Bowl* began in his notebooks with the recording of an anecdote he had heard concerning a young woman and her widower father, each of whom had taken spouses, who learned their partners were engaged in an affair. From this scant beginning, James crafted his longest and most elaborate novel, not by greatly complicating the essential material of this simple plot but by scrupulous elaboration of the conflicts and resolutions resulting from the complex relations among his four central characters. By making his characters members of the wealthy leisure class, James frees them from the mundane worries of the world so he can focus his, and their, entire attention on the one particular problem without regard to external complications. Ultimately, the novel seeks to pose moral and philosophical questions that transcend either the psychological or social levels of the work to confront the basic question of Maggie's adjustment to a less-than-perfect world.

The golden bowl is James's metaphor for the marriage between Amerigo and Maggie, and perhaps, in its larger implications, for life itself. The bowl, not really "golden" at all, but crystal gilded with gold leaf, has the superficial appearance of perfection, but is, in fact, cracked. As a symbol of Maggie's "perfect" marriage, the bowl very clearly illustrates the flaw at the heart of the relationship—a flaw that no doubt existed even before the Prince and Charlotte resume their old love affair and that represents a potential threat to the marriage. Both Maggie

and her father are guilty of treating the Prince as nothing more than one of the valuable objects they have come to Europe to purchase—they have bought the perfect marriage for Maggie. Unlike art, however, human relationships are not subject to purchase, nor can they, as in the case of Adam's marriage to Charlotte, be arranged for convenience without regard to the human factors concerned. In fact, both Maggie and her father tend to live in a small, supremely selfish world. Insulated by their money from the actuality of life, they isolate themselves from the real complexities of daily existence. Their world is, in effect, itself more "art" than "life."

The resolution of the novel results from Maggie's positive act, although in the earlier parts of the novel, she is more passive than active. The marriage itself, for example, seems more of an arrangement between the Prince and Adam Verver than a particular choice of Maggie's—Adam wants the perfect marriage for his daughter, and Prince Amerigo wants access to the Verver millions, so they come to an agreement between themselves. Maggie apparently has little to say about it, and even, judging from her relationship to the Prince throughout most of the novel, no very great interest in the marriage. Her real desire seems to be to continue life with her father, rather than to begin an independent life with her husband. Only when confronted with the Prince's infidelity does Maggie recognize that she must confront this reality for all their sakes. In choosing to separate from her father in order to begin making the best of her imperfect marriage, Maggie discovers a latent ability to confront the world as it really is and to rise above the romantic idealism that had characterized her life with her father.

THE GOOD EARTH

Type of novel: Novel
Author: Pearl S. Buck (1892–1973)
Type of plot: Social chronicle
Time of plot: Early twentieth century
Locale: Northern China
First published: 1931

With a detached, pastoral style, this novel follows the cycles of birth, marriage, and death in the Chinese peasant family of Wang Lung. The good years of plentiful harvest, marriage, and healthy children are balanced by the times of near starvation and stillborn progeny. Wang Lung finally finds himself a wealthy man, but his grown sons for whom he has worked so hard have no respect for their father's love of the good earth; they plan to sell his hard-earned property as soon as he dies.

Principal Characters

Wang Lung, an ambitious farmer who sees in the land the only sure source of livelihood. But at the end of his life his third son has left the land to be a soldier and his first and second sons callously plan to sell the land and go to the city as soon as Wang dies.

O-lan, a slave bought by Wang's father to marry Wang. She works hard in their small field with Wang, and during the civil war violence she loots in order to get money to buy more land. She dies in middle age of a stomach illness.

Nung En, their oldest son, who, when he covets his father's concubine, Lotus Blossom, is married to the grain merchant Liu's daughter.

Nung Wen, their second son, apprenticed to Liu.

The Fool, their feebleminded daughter.

Liu, a grain merchant in the town.

The Uncle, who brings his wife and shiftless son to live on Wang's farm. Secretly a lieutenant of a robber band, he also brings protection.

Lotus Blossom, Wang Lung's concubine, who is refused entrance into the house by O-Lan.

Ching, a neighbor hired by Wang Lung as overseer, as the farm is extended.

Pear Blossom, a pretty slave taken by Wang after the death of his wife.

The Story

His father had chosen a slave girl to be the bride of Wang Lung, a slave from the house of Hwang, a girl who would keep the house clean, prepare the food, and not waste her time thinking about clothes. On the morning he led her out through the gate of the big house, they stopped at a temple and burned incense. That was their marriage.

O-lan was a good wife. She thriftily gathered twigs and wood, so that they would not have to buy fuel. She mended Wang Lung's and his father's winter clothes and scoured the house. She worked in the fields beside her husband, even on the day she bore their first son.

The harvest was a good one that year. Wang Lung had a handful of silver dollars from the sale of his wheat and rice. He and O-lan bought new coats for themselves and new clothes for the baby. Together they went to pay their respects, with their child, at the home in which O-lan had once been a slave. With some of the silver dollars Wang Lung bought a small field of rich land from the Hwangs.

The second child was born a year later. It was again a year of good harvest.

Wang Lung's third baby was a girl. On the day of her birth crows flew about the house, mocking Wang Lung with their cries. The farmer did not rejoice when his little daughter was born, for poor farmers raised their daughters only to serve the rich. The crows had been an evil omen. The child was born feebleminded.

That summer was dry, and for months no rain fell. The harvest was poor. After the little rice and wheat had been eaten and the ox killed for food, there was nothing for the poor peasants to do but die or go south to find work and food in a province of plenty. Wang Lung sold their furniture for a few pieces of silver. After O-lan had borne their fourth child, found dead with bruises on its neck, the family began their journey. Falling in with a crowd of refugees, they were lucky. The refugees led them to a railroad, and with the money Wang Lung had received for his furniture they traveled on a train to their new home.

In the city they constructed a hut of mats against a wall, and while O-lan and the two older children begged, Wang Lung pulled a ricksha. In that way they spent the winter, each day earning enough to buy rice for the next.

One day an exciting thing happened. There was to be a battle between soldiers in the town and an approaching enemy. When the wealthy people in the town fled, the poor who lived so miserably broke in the houses of the rich. By threatening one fat fellow who had been left behind, Wang Lung obtained enough money to take his family home.

O-lan soon repaired the damage which the weather had done to their house during their absence; then, with jewels which his wife had managed to plunder during the looting of the city, Wang Lung bought more land from the house of Hwang. He allowed O-lan to keep two small pearls which she fancied. Now Wang Lung had more land than one man could handle, and he hired one of his neighbors, Ching, as overseer. Several years later he had six men working for him. O-lan, who after their return from the south, had borne him twins, a boy and a girl, no longer went out into the fields to work but kept the new house he had built. Wang Lung's two oldest sons were sent to school in the town.

When his land was flooded and work impossible until the water receded, Wang Lung began to go regularly to a tea shop in the town. There he fell in love with Lotus and brought her home to his farm to be his concubine. O-lan would have nothing to do with the girl, and Wang Lung was forced to set up a separate establishment for Lotus in order to keep the peace.

When he found that his oldest son visited Lotus often while he was away, Wang Lung arranged to have the boy marry the daughter of a grain merchant in the town. The wedding took place shortly before O-lan, still in the prime of life, died of a chronic stomach illness. To cement the bond between the farmer and the grain merchant, Wang Lung's second son was apprenticed to Liu, the merchant, and his youngest daughter was betrothed to Liu's young

son. Soon after O-lan's death Wang Lung's father followed her. They were buried near one another on a hill on his land.

When he grew wealthy, an uncle, his wife, and his shiftless son came to live with Wang Lung. One year there was a great flood, and although his neighbors' houses were pillaged by robbers during the confusion, Wang Lung was not bothered. Then he learned that his uncle was second to the chief of the robbers. From that time on, he had to give way to his uncle's family, for they were his insurance against robbery and perhaps murder.

At last Wang Lung coaxed his uncle and aunt to smoke opium, and so they became too involved in their dreams to bother him. But there was no way he could curb their son. When the boy began to annoy the wife of Wang Lung's oldest son, the farmer rented the deserted house of Hwang, and he, with his own family, moved into town. The cousin left to join the soldiers. The uncle and aunt were left in the country with their pipes to console them.

After Wang Lung's overseer died, he did no more farming himself. From that time on he rented his land, hoping that his youngest son would work it after his death. But he was disappointed. When Wang Lung took a slave young enough to be his granddaughter, the boy, who was in love with her, ran away from home and became a soldier.

When he felt that his death was near, Wang Lung went back to live on his land, taking with him only his slave, young Pear Blossom, his feebleminded first daughter, and some servants. One day as he accompanied his sons across the fields, he overhead them planning what they would do with their inheritance, with the money they would get from selling their father's property. Wang Lung cried out, protesting that they must never sell the land because only from it could they be sure of earning a living. He did not know that they looked at each other over his head and smiled.

Critical Evaluation

Pearl Buck referred to herself as "mentally bifocal" with respect to her American and Chinese ways of looking at things. The daughter of American missionaries in China, Buck came to know that land better than any other. She spent her formative years in China, and that time was extremely significant in developing her ideas, viewpoints, and philosophy. She attended schools both in China and the United States and made several trips back and forth, some unwillingly as when she and her parents were expelled from China during the Boxer Rebellion of 1900.

Buck began her writing as a girl in China with articles and short stories. There is no doubt that she had a gift

for making the strange, unknown, and distant appear familiar. Until the time of her first published success, *East Wind, West Wind,* very little had been written about simple Chinese life although China was becoming of increasing interest to businessmen, diplomats, and missionaries. Nevertheless, the general public thought of the Chinese in rather strange terms, not as people with whom they could easily identify. Buck's feeling for the fundamental truths of life transcended any preconceived notions that the reading public may have had about China, and portrayed her people as understandable human beings who struggled for happiness and success like anyone else.

The Good Earth was published in 1931 and is probably

Buck's most popular and widely read novel. It depicts a simple picture, the cycle of life from early years until death. Some Americans who first read the book thought the simple detailed descriptions of everyday Chinese life were "too Chinese" and, therefore, unappealing. Then, too, some Chinese felt that the author's portrayal of their people was inaccurate and incomplete. Most Chinese intellectuals objected to her choice of the peasant farmer as a worthy subject of a novel. They preferred to have the Western world see the intellectual and philosophical Chinese, even though that group was (and is) in the minority. Buck's only answer to such criticism was that she wrote about what she knew best; these were the people whom she came to love during her years in the interior of China.

The theme of *The Good Earth* is an uncomplicated one with universal appeal. The author tries to show how man can rise from poverty and relative insignificance to a position of importance and wealth. In some ways, the story is the proverbial Horatio Alger tale that so many Americans know and admire. The distinctive feature of this novel is its setting. Wang Lung, the main character around whom the action in the novel resolves, is a poor man who knows very little apart from the fact that land is valuable and solid and worth owning. Therefore, he spends his entire life trying to acquire as much land as he can in order to ensure his own security as well as that of his family and descendants for generations to come. Ironically, he becomes like the rich he at first holds in awe. He has allowed himself to follow in their path, separating himself from the land. The earth theme appears repeatedly throughout the book. Wang Lung's greatest joy is to look out over his land, to hold it in his fingers, and to work it for his survival. Even at the end of the novel he returns to the old quarters he occupied on his first plot of land so that he can find the peace he knows his kinship with the land can bring him.

Buck's style is that of a simple direct narrative. There are no complicated literary techniques such as foreshadowing, flashbacks, or stream of consciousness. Neither are there any involved subplots to detract from the main story line. Wang Lung is, as has been noted, the central character, and all the other characters and their actions relate in one way or another to him. *The Good Earth* is structured upon characterization; it is a book of dramatic

episodes which are projected through the sensitivities and experiences of those characters. It may be said that a strength of the author's characterization is her consistency, that is to say, all of her characters act and react in keeping with their personalities. None is a mere stereotype, as their motives are too complex. O-lan is typically good, but there are aspects of her personality which give her depth, dimension, and originality. When she does some seemingly dishonest thing such as steal the jewels she found at the home of the plundered rich, or kill the small baby girl born to her in ill health, she is consistent with her character in the context of these situations. She is realistic, and she sees both acts as producing more good than evil.

One of the most obvious and significant Chinese customs which appears repeatedly in the novel is the submission of the wife in all things to the will of the man. Girls were born only to be reared for someone else's house as slaves, while boys were born to carry on family names, traditions, and property. Such were the conditions in China when Buck wrote *The Good Earth*. Since that time, along with many other changes, the status of women in China has improved, although the old ways die hard.

The novel may be criticized as having no climax. True enough, there is no single momentous decision. Instead, dramatic interest is sustained by well-placed turning points which give the story new direction. One such point is Wang Lung's marriage to O-lan, which is followed by their first satisfying years together. Later, in the face of poverty, destitution, and little hope of recovery, Wang Lung demands and receives the handful of gold from the rich man and is thus able to get back to his land. At this point we see how very much Wang Lung's land means to him and what he is willing to do to have it back. In the closing pages of the novel, the quiet servitude and devotion of Pear Blossom, his slave, brings him the only peace and contentment he is to know in his last years.

The success of *The Good Earth* is apparent. Pearl Buck won the Pulitzer Prize for it and it has been dramatized as well as made into a motion picture. It is widely read in many languages, undoubtedly because of its universal appeal as a clear portrayal of one man's struggle for survival, success, and ultimate happiness.

THE GRAPES OF WRATH

Type of work: Novel
Author: John Steinbeck (1902–1968)
Type of plot: Social criticism
Time of plot: 1930s
Locale: Southwest United States and California
First published: 1939

A bitter chronicle of the exodus of farm families from the Dust Bowl during the 1930s, this work is a harsh indictment of our capitalistic economy. Searching for work in California, the Joads begin their long journey. Treated like enemies by the businessmen along their path, the older members of the family die, and those remaining are herded into migrant camps where the poor help one another to survive.

Principal Characters

Tom Joad, Jr., an ex-convict. Returning to his home in Oklahoma after serving time in the penitentiary for killing a man in self-defense, he finds the house deserted, the family having been pushed off the land because of dust bowl conditions and in order to make way for more mechanized farming. With Casy, the preacher, he finds his family and makes the trek to California in search of work. During labor difficulties Tom kills another man when his friend Casy, who is trying to help the migrant workers in their labor problems, is brutally killed by deputies representing the law and the owners. He leaves his family because, as a "wanted" man, he is a danger to them, but he leaves with a new understanding which he has learned from Casy; it is no longer the individual that counts but the group. Tom promises to carry on Casy's work of helping the downtrodden.

Tom Joad, Sr., called **Pa,** an Oklahoma farmer who finds it difficult to adjust to new conditions while moving his family to California.

Ma Joad, a large, heavy woman, full of determination and hope, who fights to hold her family together. On the journey to California she gradually becomes the staying power of the family.

Rose of Sharon Rivers, called **Rosasharn,** the married, teenage daughter of the Joads. Her husband leaves her, and she bears a stillborn baby because of the hardships she endures. As the story ends she gives her own milk to save the life of a starving man.

Noah, the slow-witted second son of the Joads. He finally wanders off down a river when the pressures of the journey and his hunger become too much.

Al, the third son of the Joads. In his teens, he is interested in girls and automobiles. He idolizes his brother Tom.

Ruthie, the pre-teenage daughter of the Joads.

Winfield, the youngest of the Joads.

Uncle John, the brother of Tom Joad, Sr. He is a lost soul who periodically is flooded with guilt because he let his young wife die by ignoring her illness.

Grampa Joad, who does not want to leave Oklahoma and dies on the way to California. He is buried with little ceremony by the roadside.

Granma Joad, also old and childish. She dies while crossing the desert and receives a pauper burial.

Jim Casy, the country preacher who has given up the ministry because he no longer believes. He makes the trek to California with the Joads. He assumes the blame and goes to jail for the "crime" of a migrant worker who has a family to support. He is killed as a "red" while trying to help the migrant workers organize and strike for a living wage.

Connie Rivers, Rosasharn's young husband, who deserts her after arriving in California.

Floyd Knowles, a young migrant worker with a family, called a "red" because he asks a contractor to guarantee a job and the wages to be paid. He escapes from a deputy sheriff who is attempting to intimidate the workers. Tom Joad trips the deputy and Jim Casy kicks him in the back of the head.

Muley Graves, a farmer who refuses to leave the land, although his family has gone. He remains, abstracted and lonely, forced to hide, and is hunted and haunted.

Jim Rawley, the kind, patient manager of a government camp for the migrant worker.

Willy Feeley, a former small farmer like the Joads; he takes a job driving a tractor over the land the Joads farmed.

Ivy Wilson, a migrant who has car trouble on the way to California with his sick wife Sairy. The Joads help them and the two families stay together until Sairy becomes too ill to travel.

Sairy Wilson, Ivy's wife. When the Wilsons are forced to stay behind because of her illness, she asks Casy to pray for her.

Timothy Wallace, a migrant who helps Tom Joad find work in California.

Wilkie Wallace, his son.

Aggie Wainwright, the daughter of a family living in a boxcar with the Joads while they work in a cotton field. Al Joad plans to marry her.

Jessie Bullitt, Ella Summers, and **Annie Littlefield,** the ladies' committee for Sanitary Unit Number Four of the government camp for migrant workers.

The Story

Tom Joad was released from the Oklahoma state penitentiary where he had served a sentence for killing a man in self-defense. He traveled homeward through a region made barren by drought and dust storms. On the way, he met Jim Casy, a former preacher; the pair went together to the home of Tom's family. They found the Joad place deserted. While Tom and Casy were wondering what had happened, Muley Graves, a die-hard tenant farmer, came by and disclosed that all the families in the neighborhood had gone to California or were going. Tom's folks, Muley said, had gone to a relative's place to prepare for going west. Muley was the only sharecropper to stay behind.

All over the southern Midwest states, farmers, no longer able to make a living because of land banks, weather, and machine farming, had sold or were forced out of the farms they had tenanted. Junk dealers and used-car salesmen profiteered on them. Thousands of families took to the roads leading to the promised land, California.

Tom and Casy found the Joads at Uncle John's place, all busy with preparations for their trip to California. Assembled for the trip were Pa and Ma Joad; Noah, their mentally backward son; Al, the adolescent younger brother of Tom and Noah; Rose of Sharon, Tom's sister, and her husband, Connie; the Joad children, Ruthie and Winfield; and Granma and Grampa Joad. Al had bought an ancient truck to take them west. The family asked Jim Casy to go with them. The night before they started, they killed the pigs they had left and salted down the meat so that they would have food on the way.

Spurred by handbills which stated that agricultural workers were badly needed in California, the Joads, along with thousands of others, made their tortuous way, in a worn-out vehicle, across the plains toward the mountains. Grampa died of a stroke during their first overnight stop. Later, there was a long delay when the truck broke down. Small business people along the way treated the migrants as enemies; and, to add to their misery, returning migrants told the Joads that there was no work to be had in California, that conditions were even worse than they were in Oklahoma. But the dream of a bountiful West Coast urged the Joads onward.

Close to the California line, where the group stopped to bathe in a river, Noah, feeling he was a hindrance to the others, wandered away. It was there that the Joads first heard themselves addressed as *Okies*, another word for tramps.

Granma died during the night trip across the desert. After burying her, the group went into a Hooverville, as the migrants' camps were called. There they learned that work was all but impossible to find. A contractor came to the camp to sign up men to pick fruit in another county. When the Okies asked to see his license, the contractor turned the leaders over to a police deputy who had accompanied him to camp. Tom was involved in the fight that followed. He escaped, and Casy gave himself up in Tom's place. Connie, husband of the pregnant Rose of Sharon, suddenly disappeared from the group. The family was breaking up in the face of its hardships. Ma Joad did everything in her power to keep the group together.

Fearing recrimination after the fight, the Joads left Hooverville and went to a government camp maintained for transient agricultural workers. The camp had sanitary facilities, a local government made up of the transients themselves, and simple organized entertainment. During the Joads' stay at the camp, the Okies successfully defeated an attempt of the local citizens to give the camp a bad name and thus to have it closed to the migrants. For the first time since they had arrived in California, the Joads found themselves treated as human beings.

Circumstances eventually forced them to leave the camp, however, for there was no work in the district. They drove to a large farm where work was being offered. There they found agitators attempting to keep the migrants from taking the work because of unfair wages offered. The Joads, however, thinking only of food, were escorted by motorcycle police into the farm. The entire family picked peaches for five cents a box and earned in a day just enough money to buy food for one meal. Tom, remembering the pickets outside the camp, went out at night to investigate. He found Casy, who was the leader of the agitators. While Tom and Casy were talking, deputies, who had been searching for Casy, closed in on them. The pair fled but were caught. Casy was killed. Tom received a cut on his head, but not before he had felled a deputy with an ax handle. The family concealed Tom in their shack. The rate for a box of peaches dropped, meanwhile, to two-and-a-half cents. Tom's danger and the futility of picking peaches drove the Joads on their way. They hid the injured Tom under the mattresses in the back of the truck, and then they told the suspicious guard at the entrance to the farm that the extra man they had had with them when they came was a hitchhiker who had stayed behind to pick.

The family found at last a migrant crowd encamped in abandoned boxcars along a stream. They joined the camp and soon found temporary jobs picking cotton. Tom, meanwhile, hid in a culvert near the camp. Ruthie innocently disclosed Tom's presence to another little girl. Ma, realizing that Tom was no longer safe, sent him away. Tom promised to carry on Casy's work in trying to improve the lot of the downtrodden everywhere.

The autumn rains began. Soon the stream that ran beside the camp overflowed and water entered the boxcars. Under these all but impossible conditions, Rose of Sharon gave birth to a dead baby. When the rising water made their position no longer bearable, the family moved from the camp on foot. The rains had made their old car useless. They came to a barn, which they shared with a boy and his starving father. Rose of Sharon, bereft of her baby, nourished the famished man with the milk from her breasts. So the poor kept each other alive in the Depression years.

Critical Evaluation

The publication of John Steinbeck's *The Grapes of Wrath* caused a nationwide stir in 1939. This account of the predicament of migrant workers was taken more as social document than as fiction. Some saw it as an exposé of capitalist excesses; others, as a distorted call to revolution. Frequently compared to *Uncle Tom's Cabin*, it was awarded the Pulitzer Prize for Literature in 1940.

Recent literary critics, taking a second look at the novel, have often lumped it with a number of other dated books of the 1930s as "proletarian fiction." A careful reader, however, recognizes that beneath this outraged account of an outrageous social situation lies a dynamic, carefully structured story that applies not only to one era or society but also to the universal human predicament.

As a social document, the novel presents such a vivid picture of oppression and misery that one tends to doubt its authenticity. Steinbeck, however, had done more than academic research. He had journeyed from Oklahoma to California, lived in a migrant camp, and worked alongside the migrants. (Peter Lisca reports that after the novel appeared, the workers sent Steinbeck a patchwork dog sewn from scraps of their clothing and wearing a tag labeled "Migrant John.") Before making the motion picture, which still stands as one of the great films of the era, Darryl F. Zanuck hired private detectives to verify Steinbeck's story; they reported that conditions were even worse than those depicted in the book. The political situation was a powder keg; Freeman Champney has remarked that "it looked as if nothing could avert an all-out battle between revolution and fascism in California's great valleys."

Social injustice was depicted so sharply that Steinbeck himself was accused of being a revolutionary. Certainly, he painted the oppressive economic system in bleak colors. Warren French argues convincingly, however, that Steinbeck was basically a reformer, not a revolutionary; that he wanted to change the attitudes and behavior of people—both migrants and economic barons—not overturn the private enterprise system. Indeed, Steinbeck observes that ownership of land is morally edifying to a man.

Steinbeck once declared that the writer must "set down his time as nearly as he can understand it" and that he should "serve as the watchdog of society . . . to satirize its silliness, to attack its injustices, to stigmatize its faults." In *The Grapes of Wrath*, he does all these things, then goes further to interpret events from a distinctly American point of view. Like Whitman, he expresses love for all men and respect for manual labor. Like Jefferson, he asserts a preference for agrarian society in which men retain a close, nourishing tie to the soil: his farmers dwindle psychologically as they are separated from their land, and the California owners become oppressors as they substitute ledgers for direct contact with the soil. Like Emerson, Steinbeck demonstrates faith in the common man and in the ideal of self-reliance. He also develops the Emersonian religious concept of an oversoul. The preacher Jim Casy muses ". . . maybe that's the Holy Sperit—the human sperit—the whole shebang. Maybe all men got one big soul ever'body's a part of it." Later, Tom Joad reassures Ma that even if he isn't physically with her, "Wherever they's a fight so hungry people can eat, I'll be there. Wherever they's a cop beatin' up a guy, I'll be there. . . . I'll be in the way kids laugh when they're hungry an' they know supper's ready. . . ."

This theme, that all men essentially belong together and are a part of one another and of a greater whole that transcends momentary reality, is what removes *The Grapes of Wrath* from the genre of timely proletarian fiction and makes it an allegory for all men in all circumstances. Warren French notes that the real story of this novel is not the Joads' search for economic security but their education, which transforms them from self-concern to a recognition of their bond with the whole human race. At first, Tom Joad is intensely individualistic, interested mainly in making his own way; Pa's primary concern is keeping bread on his table; Rose of Sharon dreams only of traditional middle-class success; and Ma, an Earth-Mother with a spine of steel, concentrates fiercely upon keeping the "fambly" together. At the end, Tom follows Casy's example in fighting for human rights; Pa, in building the dike, sees the necessity for all men to work together; Rose of Sharon forgets her grief over her stillborn child and unhesitatingly lifts a starving man to her milk-filled breast; and Ma can say "Use' ta be the fambly was fust. It ain't so now. It's anybody. Worse off we get, the more we got to do." Thus the Joads have overcome that separation which Paul Tillich equates with sin, that alienation from others which existentialists are so fond of describing as the inescapable human condition.

It is interesting to note how much *The Grapes of Wrath*,

which sometimes satirizes, sometimes attacks organized Christian religion, reflects the Bible. In structure, as critics have been quick to notice, it parallels the story of the Exodus to a "promised land." Symbolically, as Peter Lisca observes, the initials of Jim Casy are those of Jesus Christ, another itinerant preacher who rebelled against traditional religion, went into the wilderness, discovered his own gospel, and eventually gave his life in service to others.

The novel's language, too, is frequently biblical, especially in the interchapters, which, like a Greek chorus, restate, reinforce, and generalize from the specific happenings of the narrative. The cadences, repetitions, and parallel lines all echo the patterns of the Psalms—Ma Joad's favorite book.

Even the title of the novel is biblical; the exact phrase is Julia Ward Howe's, but the reference is to Jeremiah and Revelation. The grapes have been a central symbol throughout the book: first of promise, representing the fertile California valleys, but finally of bitter rage as the midwesterners realize that they have been lured west with false bait and that they will not partake of this fertility. The wrath grows, a fearsome, terrible wrath; but, as several interchapters make clear, better wrath than despair, because wrath moves to action. Steinbeck would have his people act, in concert and in concern for one another—and finally prevail over all forms of injustice.

GREAT EXPECTATIONS

Type of work: Novel
Author: Charles Dickens (1812–1870)
Type of plot: Mystery romance
Time of plot: Nineteenth century
Locale: England
First published: 1860–1861

From two events, Miss Havisham's desertion by her fiancé on her wedding day, and the youngster Pip's aid to an escaped prisoner, Dickens weaves a story of vindictiveness on the one hand and gratitude on the other. The motives combine to affect the life of young Pip, for Miss Havisham has marked him as an object of her vindictiveness, while a prisoner has sworn to reward the boy. The novel, though resolved on a hopeful note, is primarily gloomy in tone, focusing on the constant pressures placed on the orphan boy, Pip.

Principal Characters

Philip Pirrip, called **Pip,** an orphan and the unwanted ward of his harsh sister, Mrs. Joe. Although seemingly destined for the blacksmith shop, he sees his fortunes improve after he meets a convict hiding in a graveyard. Afterward, through Miss Havisham, he meets Estella, the eccentric old woman's lovely young ward. Thinking Miss Havisham is his benefactor, he goes to London to become a gentleman. Unfortunately for his peace of mind, he forgets who his true friends are. Finally, after Magwitch dies and the Crown confiscates his fortune, Pip understands that good clothes, well-spoken English, and a generous allowance do not make one a gentleman.

Miss Havisham, a lonely, embittered old spinster. When her lover jilted her at the altar, she refused ever to leave her gloomy chambers. Instead, she has devoted her life to vengeance. With careful indoctrination she teaches Estella how to break men's hearts. Just before her death she begs Pip to forgive her cruelty.

Estella, Miss Havisham's ward. Cold, aloof, unfeeling, she tries to warn Pip not to love her, for she is incapable of loving anyone; Miss Havisham has taught her too well. But years later Pip meets her in the garden near the ruins of Satis House, Miss Havisham's former home. She has lost her cool aloofness and found maturity. Pip realizes that they will never part again.

Joe Gargery, Pip's brother-in-law. Even though he is married to the worst of shrews, Mrs. Joe, he manages to retain his gentle simplicity and his selfless love for Pip. After he marries Biddy, he finds the domestic bliss which he so richly deserves.

Mrs. Georgiana Maria Gargery, commonly called **Mrs. Joe,** Pip's vituperative sister, who berates and misuses him and Joe with impunity. When she verbally assails Joe's helper, Orlick, she makes a mortal enemy who causes her death with the blow of a hammer. Later he tries to do the same for Pip.

Abel Magwitch, alias **Mrs. Provis,** Pip's benefactor.

When Pip helps him, an escaped convict, Magwitch promises to repay the debt. Transported to New South Wales, he eventually makes a large fortune as a sheep farmer. When he returns illegally to England years later, the escaped felon reveals himself as Pip's real patron. Casting off his distaste, Pip finds a real affection for the rough old man and attempts to get him safely out of England before the law apprehends him once more. Recaptured, Magwitch dies in prison.

Mr. Jaggers, a criminal lawyer employed by Magwitch to provide for Pip's future. He is a shrewd man with the ability to size up a person at a glance. To him, personal feelings are unimportant; facts are the only trustworthy things. Although completely unemotional, he deals with Pip and Magwitch honestly throughout their long association.

Herbert Pocket, Miss Havisham's young relative and Pip's roommate in London. Almost always cheerful and uncomplaining, he is constantly looking for ways to improve his prospects. With Pip's aid he is able to establish himself in a profitable business.

John Wemmick, Mr. Jaggers' efficient law clerk. Dry and businesslike in the office, he keeps his social and business life completely separate. As a friend, he proves himself completely loyal to Pip.

Biddy, Joe Gargery's wife after the death of Mrs. Joe. A gentle, loving girl, she is a good wife to him.

Compeyson, a complete villain, the man who jilted Miss Havisham and betrayed Magwitch. He is killed by Magwitch as the two struggle desperately just before the ex-convict is recaptured.

The Aged, John Wemmick's deaf old father. In their neat little home, his chief pleasures are reading the newspaper aloud and listening to his son's nightly firing of a small cannon.

Dolge Orlick, Joe Gargery's surly helper in the blacksmith shop. After an altercation with Mrs. Joe, he attacks her with a hammer. Later he plots to kill Pip, his hated enemy. Only the timely arrival of Herbert Pocket and Startop prevents the crime.

Molly, Mr. Jaggers' housekeeper, a woman of strange, silent habits, with extraordinarily strong hands. A murderess, she is also revealed as Magwitch's former mistress and Estella's mother.

Matthew Pocket, Miss Havisham's distant relative and Pip's tutor during his early years in London. He is also Herbert Pocket's father.

Mrs. Belinda Pocket, a fluttery, helpless woman, the daughter of a knight who had expected his daughter to marry a title.

Alick, Joe, Fanny, and **Jane,** other children of the Pockets.

Sarah Pocket, another relative of Miss Havisham, a withered-appearing, sharp-tongued woman.

Uncle Pumblechook, a prosperous corn chandler and Joe Gargery's relative. During Pip's childhood he constantly discusses the boy's conduct and offers much platitudinous advice.

Clara Barley, a pretty, winning girl engaged to Herbert Pocket. Magwitch is hidden in the Barley house while Pip is trying to smuggle the former convict out of England.

Old Bill Barley, Clara's father. A former purser, he is afflicted by gout and bedridden.

Mr. Wopsle, a parish clerk who later becomes an actor under the name of Mr. Waldengarver. Pip and Herbert Pocket go to see his performance as Hamlet.

Bentley Drummle, called **The Spider,** a sulky, rich boy notable for his bad manners. He is Pip's rival for Estella's love. After marrying her, he treats her cruelly. Pip meets him while Drummle is being tutored by Mr. Pocket.

Startop, a lively young man tutored by Mr. Pocket.

Mr. Trabb, a village tailor and undertaker.

Trabb's Boy, a young apprentice whose independence is a source of irritation to Pip.

Mr. John (Raymond) Camilla, a toady.

Mrs. Camilla, his wife, Mr. Pocket's sister. She and her husband hope to inherit a share of Miss Havisham's fortune.

Miss Skiffins, a woman of no certain age but the owner of "portable property," who marries John Wemmick.

Clarriker, a young shipping broker in whose firm, Clarriker & Company, Pip secretly buys Herbert Pocket a partnership.

Pepper, also called **The Avenger,** Pip's servant in the days of his great expectations.

The Story

Little Pip had been left an orphan when he was a small boy, and his sister, much older than he, had grudgingly reared him in her cottage. Pip's brother-in-law, Joe Gargery, on the other hand, was kind and loving to the boy. In the marsh country where he lived with his sister and Joe, Pip wandered alone. One day, he was accosted by a wild-looking stranger who demanded that Pip secretly bring him some food, a request which Pip feared to deny. The stranger, an escaped prisoner, asked Pip to bring him a file to cut the iron chain that bound his leg. When Pip returned to the man with a pork pie and file, he saw another mysterious figure in the marsh. After a desperate struggle with the escaped prisoner, the stranger escaped into the fog. The man Pip had aided was later apprehended. He promised Pip that he would somehow repay the boy for helping him.

Mrs. Joe sent Pip to the large mansion of strange Miss Havisham upon that lady's request. Miss Havisham lived in a gloomy, locked house where all the clocks had been stopped on the day her bridegroom failed to appear for the wedding ceremony. She often dressed in her bridal robes; a wedding breakfast molded on the table in an unused room. Pip went there every day to visit the old lady and a beautiful young girl, named Estella, who delighted in tormenting the shy boy. Miss Havisham enjoyed watching the two children together, and she encouraged Estella in her haughty teasing of Pip.

Living in the grim atmosphere of Joe's blacksmith shop and the uneducated poverty of his sister's home, Pip was eager to learn. One day, a London solicitor named Jaggers presented him with the opportunity to go to London and become a gentleman. Both Pip and Joe accepted the proposal. Pip imagined that his kind backer was Miss Havisham herself. Perhaps she wanted to make a gentleman out of him so that he would be fit someday to marry Estella.

In London Pip found a small apartment set up for him. Herbert Pocket, a young relative of Miss Havisham, was his living companion. When Pip needed money, he was instructed to go to Mr. Jaggers. Although Pip pleaded with the lawyer to disclose the name of his benefactor, Jaggers advised the eager young man not to make inquiries; when the proper time arrived, Pip's benefactor would make himself known.

Soon Pip became one of a small group of London dandies, among them a disagreeable chap named Bentley Drummle. Joe Gargery came to visit Pip, much to Pip's disturbance; by now, he had outgrown his rural background, and he was ashamed of Joe's manners. Herbert Pocket, however, cheerfully helped Pip to entertain the uncomfortable Joe in their apartment. Simple Joe loved Pip very much, and after he had gone, Pip felt ashamed of himself. Joe had brought word that Miss Havisham wanted to see the young man, and Pip returned with his brother-in-law. Miss Havisham and Estella noted the changes in Pip, and when Estella had left Pip alone with the old lady, she told him he must fall in love with the beautiful girl. She also said it was time for Estella to come to London, and she wished Pip to meet her adopted daughter when she arrived. This request made Pip feel more certain he had been sent to London by Miss Havisham to be groomed to marry Estella.

Estella had not been in London long before she had many suitors. Of all the men who courted her, she seemed to favor Bentley Drummle. Pip saw Estella frequently. Although she treated him kindly and with friendship, he knew she did not return his love.

On his twenty-first birthday, Pip received a caller, the man whom Pip had helped in the marsh many years before. Ugly and coarse, he told Pip it was he who had been financing Pip ever since he had come to London. At first, the boy was horrified to discover he owed so much to this crude former criminal, Abel Magwitch. He told Pip that he had been sent to the Colonies where he had grown rich. Now he had wanted Pip to enjoy all the privileges he had been denied in life, and he had returned to England to see the boy to whom he had tried to be a second father. He warned Pip that he was in danger should his presence be discovered, for it was death for a prisoner to return to England once he had been sent to a convict colony. Pip detested his plight. Now he realized Miss Havisham had had nothing to do with his great expectations in life, but he was too conscious of his debt to consider abandoning the man whose person he disliked. He determined to do all in his power to please his benefactor. Magwitch was using the name Provis to hide his identity. Furthermore, Provis told Pip that the man with whom Pip had seen him struggling long ago in the marsh was his enemy, Compeyson, who had vowed to destroy him. Herbert Pocket, a distant cousin of Miss Havisham, told Pip that the lover who had betrayed her on her wedding day was named Arthur Compeyson.

Pip went to see Miss Havisham to denounce her for having allowed him to believe she was helping him. On his arrival, he was informed that Estella was to marry Bentley Drummle. Since Miss Havisham had suffered at the hands of one faithless man, she had reared Estella to inflict as much hurt as possible upon the many men who loved her. Estella reminded Pip that she had warned him not to fall in love with her, since she had no compassion for any human being. Pip returned once more to visit Miss Havisham after Estella had married. An accident started a fire in the old, dust-filled mansion; although Pip tried to save the old woman, she died in the blaze that also badly damaged her gloomy house.

From Provis' story of his association with Compeyson and from other evidence, Pip had learned that Provis was Estella's father; but he did not reveal his discovery to anyone but Jaggers, whose housekeeper, evidently, was Estella's mother. Pip had also learned that Compeyson was in London and plotting to kill Provis. In order to protect the man who had become a foster father to him, Pip arranged to smuggle Provis across the channel to France with the help of Herbert Pocket. Pip intended to join the old man there. Elaborate and secretive as their plans were, Compeyson managed to overtake them as they were putting Provis on the boat. The two enemies fought one last battle in the water, and Provis killed his enemy. He was then taken to jail, where he died before he could be brought to trial.

When Pip fell ill shortly afterward, it was Joe Gargery who came to nurse him. Older and wiser from his many experiences, Pip realized that he no longer needed to be ashamed of the kind man who had given so much love to him when he was a boy. His sister, Mrs. Joe, had died and Joe had married again, this time very happily. Pip returned to the blacksmith's home to stay awhile, still desolate and unhappy because of his lost Estella. Later, Herbert Pocket and Pip set up business together in London.

Eleven years passed before Pip went to see Joe Gargery again. Curiosity led Pip to the site of Miss Havisham's former mansion. There he found Estella, now a widow, wandering over the grounds. During the years, she had lost her cool aloofness and had softened a great deal. She told Pip she had thought of him often. Pip was able to foresee that perhaps he and Estella would never have to part again. The childhood friends walked hand in hand from the place that had once played such an enormous part in both of their lives.

Critical Evaluation

G. K. Chesterton once observed that all Charles Dickens' novels could be titled "Great Expectations," for they are full of an unsubstantial yet ardent expectation of everything. Nevertheless, as Chesterton pointed out with irony, the only book to which Dickens gave the actual title was one in which most of the expectations were never realized. To the Victorians, the word *expectations* had the specific meaning of a potential legacy as well as the more general meaning still attached to it today. In that closed society, one of the few means by which a person born of the lower or lower-middle class could rise dramatically to wealth and high status was through the inheritance of valuables. A major theme of the Victorian social novel involved the hero's movement through the class structure, and often the vehicle for that movement was money, either bestowed before death or inherited. Unlike many nineteenth century novels that rely upon the stale plot device of a surprise legacy to enrich the fortunate protagonists, *Great Expectations* probes deeply into the ethical and psychological dangers of advancing through the class system by means of wealth acquired from the toil of others.

Although the story of Pip's expectations dominates the bulk of the novel, he is not the only person who waits to benefit from another's money. His beloved Estella, the ward of Miss Havisham, is wholly dependent upon the caprices of the unstable old woman. Moreover, other characters are the mysterious instrumentalities of legacies. The solicitor Jaggers, who acts as the legal agent for both Miss Havisham and Abel Magwitch, richly benefits from his services. Even his lackey Mr. Wemmick, a mild soul who changes his personality from lamb to wolf to please his employer, earns his living from the legal machinery of the courts. Just as the source of Pip's money is revealed at last to be socially corrupted, so the uses of tainted wealth inevitably bring about corruption.

In *Bleak House* (1852–1853), Dickens had already explored with great skill the ruthless precincts of the law courts. His next three novels—*Hard Times* (1854), *Little Dorrit* (1855–1857), and *A Tale of Two Cities* (1859)— were not so well sustained and, despite memorable scenes, were less popular with the critics and the public alike. *Great Expectations* (1860–1861, first published serially in *All the Year Round*) recovered Dickens' supremacy with his vast reading audience. Serious, controlled, and nearly as complex structurally as *Bleak House*, the novel also reminded Victorian readers of *David Copperfield* (1849–1850). Both are apprenticeship novels that treat the life-education of a hero. *Great Expectations* is somewhat less autobiographical than *David Copperfield*, but it repeats the basic formula of the genre: the story of an honest, rather ingenuous but surely likable young man who, through a series of often painful experiences, learns important lessons about life and himself. These lessons are always designed to reveal the hero's limitations. As he casts off his weaknesses and better understands the dangers of the world, he succeeds by advancing through the class system and ends up less brash, a chastened but wiser man.

Great Expectations differs from *David Copperfield* in the ways that the hero matures to self-knowledge. In the beginning, both David and Pip are young snobs (Pip more than David). Both suffer the traumas of a shattered childhood and troubled adolescence; but David's childhood suffering is fully motivated on the basis of his separation from loved ones. An innocent, he is the victim of evil that he does not cause. Pip, on the other hand, suffers from a childhood nightmare that forms a pattern of his later experience. An orphan like David, he lives with his brutal sister and her husband, the gentle blacksmith Joe Gargery. For whatever abuse Pip endures from Mrs. Joe, he is more than compensated by the brotherly affection of this simple, generous man. He also wins the loving sympathy of Biddy, another loyal friend. Nevertheless,

he is not satisfied, and when he comes upon the convicts in the fog and is terrified, he feels a sense of guilt— misplaced but psychologically necessary—as much for his crimes against his protectors as for the theft of a pork pie. Thereafter, his motives, cloudy as the scene of his childhood terror, are weighted with secret apprehension and guilt. To regain his lost innocence, he must purge himself of the causes of this guilt.

Pip's life apprenticeship, therefore, involves his fullest understanding of "crimes" against his loved ones and the ways to redeem himself. The causes of his guilt are— from lesser to greater—his snobbish pride, his betrayal of friends and protectors, and finally his participation in the machinery of corruption.

As a snob, he not only breaks the social mold into which he has been cast but lords it over the underlings and unfortunates of the class system. Because of his presumed great expectations, he believes himself to be superior to the humbler Joe and Biddy. He makes such a pompous fool of himself that Trabb's boy—that brilliant comic invention, at once naughty boy and honest philosopher—parodies his absurd airs and pretensions. His snobbery, however, costs him a dearer price than humiliation by an urchin. He falls in love with Estella, like himself a pretender to high social class, only to be rejected in place of a worthless cad, Bentley Drummle. Finally, his fanciful dreams of social distinction are shattered forever when he learns the bitter truth about his benefactor, who is not the highborn Miss Havisham but the escaped convict Magwitch, the wretched stranger of his terror in the fog.

As Pip comes to understand the rotten foundations for his social position, he also learns terrible truths about his own weaknesses. Out of foolish pride, he has betrayed his most loyal friends, Joe and Biddy. In a sense, he has even betrayed Miss Havisham. He has mistaken her insanity for mere eccentricity and allowed her to act out her fantasies of romantic revenge. When he tries to confront her with the reality of her life, he is too late. She dies in flames. He is almost too late, in fact, to come to the service of his real benefactor, Magwitch. He is so disturbed with the realization of the convict's sacrifice that he nearly flees from the old man, now disguised as "Provis," when he is in danger. At best, he can return to Magwitch gratitude, not love, and his sense of guilt grows from his understanding that he cannot ever repay his debt to a man he secretly loathes.

Pip's final lesson is that, no matter how pure might be his motives, he has been one of the instruments of social corruption. In a sense, he is the counterpart to the malcontent Dolge Orlick. Like Orlick, as a youth he had been an apprentice at the forge; but whereas he was fortunate to move upward into society, Orlick, consumed by hatred, failed in every enterprise. In chapter 53, a climactic scene of the novel, Orlick confronts his enemy and blames Pip for all of his failures. He even accuses

Pip of responsibility for the death of Mrs. Joe. The charge is paranoiac and false: Orlick is the murderer. In his almost hallucinatory terror, however, Pip can psychologically accept Orlick's reasoning. As a child, Pip had hated his sister. If he had not been the active instrument of her death, he nevertheless profited from it. Similarly, Pip profited from the hard-earned toil of Magwitch. Indeed, most of the success he had enjoyed, thanks to the astute protection of Mr. Jaggers, had come not as his due but for a price, the payment of corrupted money. Since he had been the ignorant recipient of the fruits of corruption, his psychological guilt is all the greater.

Nevertheless, Pip, though chastened, is not over-whelmed by guilt. During the course of his apprenticeship to life, he has learned something about himself, some valuable truths about his limitations. By the end of the novel, when his apprenticeship is over and he is a responsible, mature being, he has cast off petty pride, snobbery, and the vexations of corrupted wealth. Although he has lost his innocence forever, he can truly appreciate Herbert Pocket, Joe, and Biddy, who have retained their integrity. When he turns to Estella, also chastened by her wretched marriage to the sadistic Drummle, he has at least the hope of beginning a new life with her, one founded upon an accurate understanding of himself and the dangers of the world.

THE GREAT GATSBY

Type of work: Novel
Author: F. Scott Fitzgerald (1896–1940)
Type of plot: Social criticism
Time of plot: 1922
Locale: New York City and Long Island
First published: 1925

Jay Gatz changes his name to Gatsby and amasses great wealth by dubious means solely to please Daisy, a socialite. Wooed earlier by the penniless Gatsby, Daisy had rejected him for her social equal, Tom Buchanan. Yet no matter how high Gatsby rises, he is doomed, for the wealthy Buchanans are not worthy of Gatsby's sincerity and innocence. Though Gatsby plans to take the blame for a hit-and-run murder committed by Daisy, Tom Buchanan tells the victim's husband that Gatsby was driving, and the husband murders Gatsby. The Buchanans retreat into the irresponsibility their wealth allows them.

Principal Characters

Nick Carraway, the narrator. A young midwesterner who was dissatisfied with his life at home, he was attracted to New York and now sells bonds there. He is the most honest character of the novel and because of this trait fails to become deeply fascinated by his rich friends on Long Island. He helps Daisy and Jay Gatsby to renew a love they had known before Daisy's marriage, and he is probably the only person in the novel to have any genuine affection for Gatsby.

Jay Gatsby, a fabulously rich racketeer whose connections outside of the law are only guessed at. He is the son of poor parents from the Middle West. He has changed his name from James Gatz and becomes obsessed with a need for making more and more money. Much of his time is spent in trying to impress and become accepted by other rich people. He gives lavish parties for people he knows nothing about and most of whom he never meets. He is genuinely in love with Daisy Buchanan and becomes a sympathetic character when he assumes the blame for her hit-and-run accident. At his death he has been deserted by everyone except his father and Nick.

Daisy Buchanan, Nick's second cousin. Unhappy in her marriage because of Tom Buchanan's deliberate unfaithfulness, she has the character of a "poor little rich girl." She renews an old love for Jay Gatsby and considers leaving her husband, but she is finally reconciled to him. She kills Tom's mistress in a hit-and-run accident after a quarrel in which she defends both men as Tom accuses Gatsby of trying to steal her from him; but she allows Gatsby to take the blame for the accident and suffers no remorse when he is murdered by the woman's husband.

Tom Buchanan, Daisy's husband. The son of rich midwestern parents, he reached the heights of his career as a college football player. Completely without taste, culture, or sensitivity, he carries on a rather sordid affair with Myrtle Wilson. He pretends to help George Wilson, her husband, but allows him to think that Gatsby was not only her murderer but also her lover.

Myrtle Wilson, Tom Buchanan's mistress. She is a fat, unpleasant woman who is to highly appreciative of the fact that her lover is a rich man that she will suffer almost any degradation for him. While she is with Rom, her pretense that she is rich and highly sophisticated becomes ludicrous.

George Wilson, Myrtle's husband, and a rather pathetic figure. He runs an auto repair shop and believes Tom Buchanan is really interested in helping him. Aware that his wife has a lover, he never suspects who he really is. His faith in Tom makes him believe what Buchanan says, which, in turns, causes him to murder Gatsby and then commit suicide.

Jordan Baker, a friend of the Buchanans, a golfer. Daisy introduces Jordan to Nick and tries to throw them together, but when Nick realizes that she is a cheat who refuses to assume the elementary responsibility of the individual, he loses all interest in her.

Meyer Wolfshiem, a gambler and underworld associate of Gatsby.

Catherine, Myrtle Wilson's sister, who is obviously proud of Myrtle's rich connection and unconcerned with the immorality involved.

Mr. and Mrs. McKee, a photographer and his wife who try to use Nick and Tom to get a start among the rich people of Long Island.

Mr. Gatz, Jay Gatsby's father who, being unaware of the facts of Jay's life, thought his son had been a great man.

The Story

Young Nick Carraway decided to forsake the hardware business of his family in the Middle West in order to sell bonds in New York City. He took a small house in West Egg on Long Island and there became involved in the lives of his neighbors. At a dinner party at the home of Tom Buchanan, he renewed his acquaintance with Tom and Tom's wife, Daisy, a distant cousin, and he met an attractive young woman, Jordan Baker. Almost at once he learned that Tom and Daisy were not happily married. It appeared that Daisy knew her husband was unfaithful.

Nick soon learned to despise the drive to the city through unkempt slums; particularly, he hated the ash heaps and the huge commercial signs. He was far more interested in the activities of his wealthy neighbors. Near his house lived Jay Gatsby, a mysterious man of great wealth. Gatsby entertained lavishly, but his past was unknown to his neighbors.

One day, Tom Buchanan took Nick to call on his mistress, a dowdy, plump, married woman named Myrtle Wilson, whose husband, George Wilson, operated a second-rate automobile repair shop. Myrtle, Tom, and Nick went to the apartment that Tom kept, and there the three were joined by Myrtle's sister Catherine and Mr. and Mrs. McKee. The party settled down to an afternoon of drinking, Nick unsuccessfully doing his best to get away.

A few days later, Nick attended another party, one given by Gatsby for a large number of people famous in speakeasy society. Food and liquor were dispensed lavishly. Most of the guests had never seen their host before.

At the party, Nick met Gatsby for the first time. Gatsby, in his early thirties, looked like a healthy young roughneck. He was offhand, casual, and eager to entertain his guests as extravagantly as possible. Frequently he was called away by long-distance telephone calls. Some of the guests laughed and said that he was trying to impress them with his importance.

That summer, Gatsby gave many parties. Nick went to all of them, enjoying each time the society of people from all walks of life who appeared to take advantage of Gatsby's bounty. From time to time, Nick met Jordan Baker there, and when he heard that she had cheated in an amateur golf match, his interest in her grew.

Gatsby took Nick to lunch one day and introduced him to a man named Wolfshiem, who seemed to be Gatsby's business partner. Wolfshiem hinted at some dubious business deals that betrayed Gatsby's racketeering activities, and Nick began to identify the sources of some of Gatsby's wealth.

Jordan Baker told Nick the strange story of Daisy's wedding. Before the bridal dinner, Daisy, who seldom drank, became wildly intoxicated and kept reading a letter that she had just received and crying that she had changed her mind. After she had become sober, however, she went through with her wedding to Tom without a murmur. Obviously, the letter was from Jay Gatsby. At the time, Gatsby was poor and unknown; Tom was rich and influential.

Gatsby was still in love with Daisy, however, and he wanted Jordan and Nick to bring Daisy and him together again. It was arranged that Nick should invite Daisy to tea the same day he invited Gatsby. Gatsby awaited the invitation nervously.

On the eventful day, it rained. Determined that Nick's house should be presentable, Gatsby sent a man to mow the wet grass; he also sent over flowers for decoration. The tea was a strained affair at first, and Gatsby and Daisy were shy and awkward in their reunion. Afterward, they went over to Gatsby's mansion, where he showed them his furniture, clothes, swimming pool, and gardens. Daisy promised to attend his next party.

When Daisy disapproved of his guests, Gatsby stopped entertaining. The house was shut up and the bar crowd turned away.

Gatsby informed Nick of his origin. His true name was Gatz, and he had been born in the Middle West. His parents were poor. When he was a boy, he had become the protégé of a wealthy old gold miner and had accompanied him on his travels until the old man died. He had changed his name to Gatsby and was daydreaming of acquiring wealth and position. In the war, he had distinguished himself. After the war, he had returned penniless to the States, too poor to marry Daisy, whom he had met during the war. Later, he became a partner in a drug business. He had been lucky and had accumulated money rapidly. He told Nick that he had acquired the money for his Long Island residence after three years of hard work.

The Buchanans gave a quiet party for Jordan, Gatsby, and Nick. The group drove into the city and took a room in a hotel. The day was hot and the guests uncomfortable. On the way, Tom, driving Gatsby's new yellow car, stopped at Wilson's garage. Wilson complained because Tom had not helped him in a projected car deal. He said he needed money because he was selling out and taking his wife, whom he knew to be unfaithful, away from the city.

At the hotel, Tom accused Gatsby of trying to steal his wife and also of being dishonest. He seemed to regard Gatsby's low origin with more disfavor than his interest in Daisy. During the argument, Daisy, sided with both men. On the ride back to the suburbs, Gatsby drove his own car, accompanied by Daisy, who temporarily would not speak to her husband.

Following them, Nick, Jordan, and Tom stopped to investigate an accident in front of Wilson's garage. They discovered an ambulance picking up the dead body of Myrtle Wilson, struck by a hit-and-run driver in a yellow car. They tried in vain to help Wilson and then went on to Tom's house, convinced that Gatsby had struck Myrtle Wilson.

Nick learned that night from Gatsby that Daisy had been driving when the woman was hit. Gatsby, however, was willing to take the blame if the death should be traced to his car. He explained that a woman had rushed out as though she wanted to speak to someone in the yellow car and Daisy, an inexpert driver, had run her down and then collapsed. Gatsby had driven on.

In the meantime, George Wilson, having traced the yellow car to Gatsby, appeared on the Gatsby estate. A few hours later, both he and Gatsby were discovered dead. He had shot Gatsby and then killed himself.

Nick tried to make Gatsby's funeral respectable, but only one among all of Gatsby's former guests attended along with Gatsby's father, who thought his son had been a great man. None of Gatsby's racketeering associates appeared.

Shortly afterward, Nick learned of Tom's part in Gatsby's death. Wilson had visited Tom and had threatened Tom with a revolver, forcing him to reveal the name of the owner of the hit-and-run car. Nick vowed that his friendship with Tom and Daisy was ended. He decided to return his people in the Middle West.

Critical Evaluation

F. Scott Fitzgerald, the prophet of the Jazz Age, was born in St. Paul, Minnesota, to the daughter of a self-made Irish immigrant millionaire. His father was a ne'er-do-well salesman who had married above his social position. From his mother, Fitzgerald inherited the dream that was America—the promise that any young man could become anything he chose through hard work. From his father, he inherited a propensity for failure. This antithesis pervaded his own life and most of his fiction. Educated in the East, Fitzgerald was overcome with the glamour of New York and Long Island. To him, it was the "stuff of old romance," "the source of infinite possibilities." His fiction focused primarily on the lives of the rich. With the family fortune depleted by his father, Fitzgerald found himself in his early twenties an army officer in love with a Southern belle, Zelda Sayre, who was socially above him. She refused his first proposal of marriage because he was too poor. Fitzgerald was determined to have her. He wrote and published *This Side of Paradise* (1920), on the basis of which Zelda married him.

Their public life for the next ten years epitomized the dizzy spiral of the 1920s—wild parties, wild spending—and, following the national pattern, they crashed spectacularly in the 1930s. Zelda went mad and was committed finally to a sanitarium. Fitzgerald became a functional alcoholic. From his pinnacle in the publishing field during the 1920s, when his short stories commanded as much as fifteen hundred dollars, he fell in the 1930s to writing lukewarm Hollywood scripts. He died in Hollywood in 1940, almost forgotten and with most of his work out of print. Later revived in academic circles, Fitzgerald's reputation in American letters rests primarily on a single novel—*The Great Gatsby*.

Fitzgerald once said, "America's great promise is that something's going to happen, but it never does. America is the moon that never rose." This indictment of the America Dream could well serve as an epigraph for *The Great Gatsby*. Jay Gatsby pursues his dream of romantic success without ever understanding that it has escaped him. He fails to understand that he cannot recapture the past (his fresh, new love for Daisy Buchanan) no matter how much money he makes, no matter how much wealth he displays.

The character of Gatsby was never intended by Fitzgerald to be a realistic portrayal; he is a romantic hero, always somewhat unreal, bogus, and absurd. No matter the corrupt sources of his wealth such as bootlegging and gambling (and these are only hinted at), he stands for hope, for romantic belief—for innocence. He expects more from life than the other characters who are all more or less cynical. He is an eternal juvenile in a brutal and corrupt world.

To underscore the corruption of the American Dream, Fitzgerald's characters all are finally seen as liars. Buchanan's mistress lies to her husband. Jordan Baker is a pathological liar who cheats in golf tournaments. Tom Buchanan's lie to his mistress Myrtle's husband results in the murder of Gatsby. Daisy, herself, is basically insincere; she lets Gatsby take the blame for her hit-and-run accident. Gatsby's whole life is a lie: he lies about his past and his present. He lies to himself. Nick Carraway, the midwestern narrator, tells readers that he is the only completely honest person he knows. He panders for Gatsby, however, and in the end, he turns away from Tom Buchanan, unable to force the truth into the open. He knows the truth about Gatsby but is unable to tell the police. His affirmation of Gatsby at the end is complex; he envies Gatsby's romantic selflessness and innocence at the same time that he abhors his lack of self-knowledge.

The Great Gatsby incorporates a number of themes and motifs that unify the novel and contribute to its impact. The initiation theme governs the narrator Nick Carraway, who is a young man come East to make his fortune in stocks and bonds and who returns to the Midwest sadly disillusioned. The frontier theme is also present. Gatsby believes in the "green light," the ever-accessible future in which one can achieve what one has missed in the past. The final paragraphs of the novel state this important theme as well as it has ever been stated. Class issues are very well presented. Tom and Daisy seem accessible, but when their position is threatened, they close the doors, retreating into their wealth and carelessness, letting others like Gatsby pay the price in hurt and suffering. The carelessness of the rich and their followers is seen in the recurring motif of the bad driver.

Automobile accidents are ubiquitous. At Gatsby's first party, there is a smashup with drunk drivers. Jordan Baker has a near accident after which Nick calls her "a rotten driver." Gatsby is stopped for speeding but is able to fix the ticket by showing the cop a card from the mayor of New York. Finally, Myrtle Wilson is killed by Daisy, driving Gatsby's car. Bad driving becomes symbolic of pervasive irresponsibility and self-indulgence.

Settings in the novel are used very well by Fitzgerald, from the splendid mansions of Long Island through the wasteland of the valley of ashes presided over by the eyes of Dr. T. J. Eckleburg (where the Wilsons live) to the New York of the Plaza Hotel or Tom and Myrtle Wilson's apartment. Most important, however, is Fitzgerald's use of Nick as a narrator. Like Conrad before him—and from whom he learned his craft—Fitzgerald had a romantic sensibility that controlled fictional material best through the lens of a narrator. Like Marlow in Conrad's *Heart of Darkness*, Nick relates the story of an exceptional man who fails in his dream. He is both attracted and repelled by a forceful man who dares to lead a life he could not sustain. Like Marlow, he pays tribute to his hero, who is also his alter ego. Gatsby's tragedy is Nick's education. His return to the Midwest is a moral return to the safer, more solid values of the heartland. Fitzgerald himself was unable to follow such a path, but he clearly felt that the American Dream should be pursued with less frantic, orgiastic, prideful convulsions of energy and spirit.

GULLIVER'S TRAVELS

Type of work: Simulated record of travel
Author: Jonathan Swift (1667–1745)
Type of plot: Social satire
Time of plot: 1699–1713
Locale: England and various fictional lands
First published: 1726

One of the masterpieces of satire among the world's literature, Gulliver's Travels *is written in the form of a travel journal divided into four sections, each of which describes a different voyage of ship's physician Lemuel Gulliver. In each section he visits a different fantastical society—Lilliput, Brobdingnag, Laputa, and Houyhnhnmland—and records the facts and customs of the country. Through Gulliver's adventures and observations, Swift aims his at times savage satire against the English people generally and the Whigs particularly, against various political, academic, and social institutions, and against man's constant abuse of his greatest gift, reason.*

Principal Character

Lemuel Gulliver, a surgeon, sea captain, traveler and the narrator of these travel accounts, the purpose of which is to satirize the pretensions and follies of man. Gulliver is an ordinary man, capable of close observation; his deceptively matter-of-fact reportage and his great accumulation of detail make believable and readable a scathing political and social satire. On his first voyage he is shipwrecked at Lilliput, a country inhabited by people no more than six inches tall, where pretentiousness, individual as well as political, is ridiculed. The second voyage ends in Brobdingnag, a land of giants. Human grossness is a target here. Moreover, Gulliver does not find it easy to make sense of English customs and politics in explaining them to a king sixty feet high. On Gulliver's third voyage pirates attack the ship and set him adrift in a small boat. One day he sees and goes aboard Laputa, a flying island inhabited by incredibly abstract and absent-minded people. From Laputa he visits Balnibari, where wildly impractical experiments in construction and agriculture are in progress. Then he goes to Glubbdubdrib, the island of sorcerers, where he is shown apparitions of such historical figures as Alexander and Caesar, who decry the inaccuracies of history books. Visiting Luggnagg, Gulliver, after describing an imaginary immortality of constant learning and growing wisdom, is shown a group of immortals called Struldbrugs, who are grotesque, pitiable creatures, senile for centuries, but destined never to die. Gulliver's last journey is to the land of the Houyhnhnms, horselike creatures in appearance, possessed of great intelligence, rationality, restraint, and courtesy. Dreadful humanlike creatures, called Yahoos, impart to Gulliver such a loathing of the human form that, forced to return at last to England, he cannot bear the sight of even his own family and feels at home only in the stables.

The Story

Lemuel Gulliver, a physician, took the post of ship's doctor on the *Antelope*, which set sail from Bristol for the South Seas in May, 1699. When the ship was wrecked in a storm somewhere near Tasmania, Gulliver had to swim for his life. Wind and tide helped to carry him close to a low-lying shore where he fell, exhausted, into a deep sleep. Upon awakening, he found himself held to the ground by hundreds of small ropes. He soon discovered that he was the prisoner of humans six inches tall. Still tied, Gulliver was fed by his captors; then he was placed on a special wagon built to his size and drawn by fifteen hundred small horses. Carried in this manner to the capital city of the small humans, he was exhibited as a great curiosity to the people of Lilliput, as the land of the diminutive people was called. He was kept chained to a huge Lilliputian building into which he crawled at night to sleep.

Gulliver soon learned the Lilliputian language, and through his personal charm and natural curiosity, he came into good graces at the royal court. At length, he was given his freedom, contingent upon his obeying many rules devised by the emperor prescribing his deportment in Lilliput. Now free, Gulliver toured Mildendo, the capital city, and found it to be similar to European cities of the time.

Learning that Lilliput was in danger of an invasion by the forces of the neighboring empire, Blefuscu, he offered his services to the emperor of Lilliput. While the enemy fleet awaited favorable winds to carry their ships the eight hundred yards between Blefuscu and Lilliput, Gulliver took some Lilliputian cable, waded to Blefuscu, and brought back the entire fleet by means of hooks attached to the cables. He was greeted with great acclaim, and the emperor made him a nobleman. Soon, however, the emperor and Gulliver quarreled over differences concerning the fate of the now helpless Blefuscu. The emperor wanted to reduce the enemy to the status of slaves; Gulliver championed their liberty. The pro-Gulliver forces prevailed in the Lilliputian parliament; the peace settlement was favorable to Blefuscu. Gulliver, however, was now in disfavor at court.

He visited Blefuscu, where he was received graciously by the emperor and the people. One day, while exploring the empire, he found a ship's boat washed ashore from a wreck. With the help of thousands of Blefuscu artisans, he repaired the boat for his projected voyage back to his own civilization. Taking some cattle and sheep with him, he sailed away and was eventually picked up by an English vessel.

Back in England, Gulliver spent a short time with his family before he shipped aboard the *Adventure*, bound for India. The ship was blown off course by fierce winds. Somewhere on the coast of Great Tartary a landing party went ashore to forage for supplies. Gulliver, who had wandered away from the party, was left behind when a gigantic human figure pursued the sailors back to the ship. Gulliver was caught in a field by giants threshing grain that grew forty feet high. Becoming the pet of a farmer and his family, he amused them with his human-like behavior. The farmer's nine-year-old daughter, who was not yet over forty feet high, took special charge of Gulliver.

The farmer displayed Gulliver first at a local market town. Then he took his little pet to the metropolis, where Gulliver was put on show to the great detriment of his health. The farmer, seeing that Gulliver was near death, sold him to the queen, who took a great fancy to the little curiosity. The court doctors and philosophers studied Gulliver as a quaint trick of nature. He subsequently had adventures with giant rats the size of lions, with a dwarf thirty feet high, with wasps as large as partridges, with apples the size of Bristol barrels, and with hailstones the size of tennis balls.

He and the king discussed the institutions of their respective countries, the king asking Gulliver many questions about Great Britain that Gulliver found impossible to answer truthfully without embarrassment.

After two years in Brobdingnag, the land of the giants, Gulliver miraculously escaped when a large bird carried his portable quarters out over the sea. The bird dropped the box containing Gulliver, and he was rescued by a ship that was on its way to England. Back home, it took Gulliver some time to accustom himself once more to a world of normal size.

Soon afterward, Gulliver went to sea again. Pirates from a Chinese port attacked the ship. Set adrift in a small sailboat, Gulliver was cast away upon a rocky island. One day, he saw a large floating mass descending from the sky. Taken aboard the flying island of Laputa, he soon found it to be inhabited by intellectuals who thought only in the realm of the abstract and the exceedingly impractical. The people of the island, including the king, were so absentminded that they had to have servants following them to remind them even of their trends of conversation. When the floating island arrived above the continent of Balnibari, Gulliver received permission to visit that realm. There he inspected the Grand Academy, where hundreds of highly impractical projects for the improvement of agriculture and building were under way.

Next, Gulliver journeyed by boat to Glubbdubdrib, the island of sorcerers. By means of magic, the governor of the island showed Gulliver such great historical figures as Alexander, Hannibal, Caesar, Pompey, and Sir Thomas More. Gulliver talked to the apparitions and learned from them that history books were inaccurate.

From Glubbdubdrib, Gulliver ventured to Luggnagg. There he was welcomed by the king, who showed him the Luggnaggian immortals, or Struldbrugs—beings who would never die.

Gulliver traveled on to Japan, where he took a ship back to England. He has been away for more than three years.

Gulliver became restless after a brief stay at his home, and he signed as captain of a ship that sailed from Portsmouth in August, 1710, destined for the South Seas. The crew mutinied, keeping Captain Gulliver prisoner in his cabin for months. At length, he was cast adrift in a long-boat off a strange coast. Ashore, he came upon and was nearly overwhelmed by disgusting half-human, half-ape creatures who fled in terror at the approach of a horse. Gulliver soon discovered, to his amazement, that he was in a land where rational horses, the Houyhnhnms, were masters of irrational human creatures, the Yahoos. He stayed in the stable house of a Houyhnhnm family and learned to subsist on oaten cake and milk. The Houyhnhnms were horrified to learn from Gulliver that horses in England were used by Yahoolike creatures as beasts of burden. Gulliver described England to his host, much to the candid and straightforward Houyhnhnm's mystification. Such things as wars and courts of law were unknown to this race of intelligent horses. As he did in the other lands he visited, Gulliver attempted to explain the institutions of his native land, but the friendly and benevolent Houyhnhnms were appalled by many of the things Gulliver told them.

Gulliver lived in almost perfect contentment among the horses, until one day his host told him that the Houyhnhnm Grand Assembly had decreed Gulliver either be treated as an ordinary Yahoo or be released to swim back to the land from which he had come. Gulliver built a canoe and sailed away. At length, he was picked up by a Portuguese vessel. Remembering the Yahoos, he became a recluse on the ship and began to hate all mankind. Landing at Lisbon, he sailed from there to England; but

on his arrival, the sight of his own family repulsed him. He fainted when his wife kissed him. His horses became his only friends on earth.

Critical Evaluation

It has been said that Dean Jonathan Swift hated humanity but loved individual men. His hatred is brought out in this caustic political and social satire aimed at the English people, representing mankind in general, and at the Whigs in particular. By means of a disarming simplicity of style and of careful attention to detail in order to heighten the effect of the narrative, Swift produced one of the outstanding pieces of satire in world literature. Swift himself attempted to conceal his authorship of the book under its original title: *Travels into Several Remote Nations of the World, in Four Parts, by Lemuel Gulliver, First a Surgeon, and then a Captain of Several Ships*.

When Swift created the character of Lemuel Gulliver as his narrator for *Gulliver's Travels*, he developed a personality with many qualities admired by an eighteenth century audience and still admired by many readers. Gulliver is a decent sort of person: hopeful, simple, fairly direct, and full of good will. He is a scientist, a trained doctor; and, as any good scientist should, he loves detail. His literal-minded attitude makes him a keen observer of the world around him. Furthermore, he is, like another famous novel character of the eighteenth century— Robinson Crusoe—encouragingly resourceful in emergencies. Why is it, then, that such a seemingly admirable, even heroic character, should become, in the end, an embittered misanthrope, hating the world and turning against everyone, including people who show him kindness?

The answer lies in what Swift meant for his character to be, and Gulliver was certainly not intended to be heroic. Readers often confuse Gulliver the character with Swift the author, but to do so is to miss the point of *Gulliver's Travels*. The novel is a satire, and Gulliver is a mask for Swift the satirist. In fact, Swift does not share Gulliver's values especially his rationalistic, scientific responses to the world and his belief in progress and the perfectibility of man. Swift, on the contrary, believed that such values were dangerous to mankind and that to put such complete faith in the material world, as scientific Gulliver did, was folly. As Swift's creation, Gulliver is a product of his age, and he is designed as a character to demonstrate the great weakness underlying the values of the "Age of Enlightenment," the failure to recognize the power of that which is irrational in man.

Despite Gulliver's apparent congeniality in the opening chapters of the novel, Swift makes it clear that his character has serious shortcomings, including blind spots about human nature and his own nature. Book 3, the least readable section of *Gulliver's Travels*, is in some ways the most revealing part of the book. In it Gulliver complains, for example, that the wives of the scientists he is observing run away with the servants. The fact is that Gulliver—himself a scientist—gives little thought to the well-being of his own wife. In the eleven years covered in Gulliver's "travel book," Swift's narrator spends a total of seven months and ten days with his wife.

Therefore, Gulliver, too, is caught up in Swift's web of satire in *Gulliver's Travels*. Satire as a literary form tends to be ironic; the author says the opposite of what he means. Consequently, readers can assume that much of what Gulliver observes as good and much of what he thinks and does are the opposite of what Swift thinks.

As a type of the eighteenth century, Gulliver exhibits its major values: belief in rationality, in the perfectibility of man, in the idea of progress, and in the Lockean philosophy of the human mind as a *tabula rasa*—or blank slate, at the time of birth—controlled and developed entirely by the differing strokes and impressions made on it by the environment. Swift, in contrast to Gulliver, hated the abstraction that accompanied rational thinking; he abhorred the rejection of the past that resulted from a rationalist faith in the new and improved; and he cast strong doubts on man's ability to gain knowledge through reason and logic.

The world Gulliver discovers during his travels is significant in Swift's satire. The Lilliputians, averaging not quite six inches in height, display the pettiness and the smallness Swift detects in much that motivates human institutions, such as church and state. It is petty religious problems that lead to continual war in Lilliput. The Brobdingnagians continue the satire in part 2 by exaggerating man's grossness through their enlarged size. (Swift divided human measurements by a twelfth for the Lilliputians and multiplied the same for the Brobdingnagians.)

The tiny people of part 1 and the giants of part 2 establish a pattern of contrasts that Swift follows in part 4 with the Houyhnhnms and the Yahoos. The Yahoos, "their heads and breasts covered with a thick hair, some frizzled and others lank," naked otherwise and scampering up trees like nimble squirrels, represent the animal aspect of man when it is viewed as separate from the rational. The Houyhnhnms, completing the other half of the split, know no lust, pain, or pleasure. Their rational temperaments totally rule their passions, if they have any at all. The land of the Houyhnhnms is a Utopia to Gulliver, and he tells the horse-people that his homeland is unfortunately governed by Yahoos.

But what is the land of the Houyhnhnms really like, how much a Utopia? Friendship, benevolence, and equality are the principal virtues there. Decency and civility guide every action. As a result, each pair of horses mates to have one colt of each sex; after that, they no longer stay together. The marriages are arranged to ensure pleasing color combinations in the offspring. To the young, marriage is "one of the necessary actions of a reasonable being." After the function of the marriage has been fulfilled—after the race has been propagated—the two members of the couple are no closer to each other than to anybody else in the whole country. It is this kind of "equality" that Swift satirizes. As a product of the rational attitude, such a value strips life of its fullness, denies the power of emotion and instinct, subjugates all to logic, reason, the intellect, and makes all dull and uninteresting—as predictable as a scientific experiment.

By looking upon the Houyhnhnms as the perfect creatures, Gulliver makes his own life back in England intolerable:

> I . . . return to enjoy my own speculations in my little garden at Redriff; to apply those excellent lessons of virtue which I learned among the Houyhnhnms; to instruct the Yahoos of my own family as far as I shall find them docible

animals; to behold my figure often in a glass, and thus if possible habituate myself by time to tolerate the sight of a human creature.

When Gulliver holds up rational men as perfect man and when he cannot find a rational man to meet his ideal, he concludes in disillusionment that mankind is totally animalistic, like the ugly Yahoos. In addition to being a satire and a parody of travel books, *Gulliver's Travels* is an initiation novel. As Gulliver develops, he changes; but he fails to learn an important lesson of life, or he learns it wrong. His naïve optimism about progress and rational man leads him to bitter disillusionment.

It is tragically ironic that Swift died at the age of seventy-eight after three years of living without his reason; a victim of Ménière's disease, he died "like a rat in a hole." For many years, he had struggled against fits of deafness and giddiness, symptoms of the disease. As a master of the language of satire, Swift remains unequaled. He gathered in *Gulliver's Travels*, written late in his life, all the experience he had culled from both courts and streets. For Swift knew people, and, as individuals, he loved them; but when they changed into groups, he hated them, satirized them, and stung them into realizing the dangers of the herd. Gulliver never understood this.

HAMLET, PRINCE OF DENMARK

Type of work: Drama
Author: William Shakespeare (1564–1616)
Type of plot: Romantic tragedy
Time of plot: c. 1200
Locale: Elsinore, Denmark
First presented: 1602

One of the most popular and highly respected plays ever written, Hamlet *owes its greatness to the character of the Prince, a man of thought rather than action, a philosophical, introspective hero who is swept along by events rather than exercising control of them. Through the medium of some of the most profound and superb poetry ever composed, Shakespeare transforms a conventional revenge tragedy into a gripping exploration of the universal problems of mankind. In Hamlet's struggle with duty, morality, and ethics are mirrored the hopes, fears, and despair of all mankind.*

Principal Characters

Hamlet (hăm′lət), prince of Denmark. Generally agreed to be Shakespeare's most fascinating hero, Hamlet has been buried under volumes of interpretation, much of it conflicting. No brief sketch can satisfy his host of admirers nor take into account more than a minute fraction of the commentary now in print. The character is a mysterious combination of a series of literary sources and the phenomenal genius of Shakespeare. Orestes in Greek tragedy is probably his ultimate progenitor, not Oedipus, as some critics have suggested. The Greek original has been altered and augmented by medieval saga and Renaissance romance; perhaps an earlier "Hamlet," written by Thomas Kyd, furnished important material; however, the existence of such a play has been disputed. A mixture of tenderness and violence, a scholar, lover, friend, athlete, philosopher, satirist, and deadly enemy, Hamlet is larger than life itself. Torn by grief for his dead father and disappointment in the conduct of his beloved mother, Hamlet desires a revenge so complete that it will reach the soul as well as the body of his villainous uncle. His attempt to usurp God's prerogative of judgment leads to all the deaths in the play. Before his death he reaches a state of resignation and acceptance of God's will. He gains his revenge but loses his life.

Claudius (klô′dĭ·ŭs), king of Denmark, husband of his brother's widow, Hamlet's uncle. A shrewd and capable politician and administrator, he is courageous and self-confident; but he is tainted by mortal sin. He has murdered his brother and married his queen very soon thereafter. Although his conscience torments him with remorse, he is unable to repent or to give up the throne or the woman that his murderous act brought him. He has unusual self-knowledge and recognizes his unrepentant state. He is a worthy and mighty antagonist for Hamlet, and they destroy each other.

Gertrude, queen of Denmark, Hamlet's mother. Warmhearted but weak, she shows deep affection for Hamlet and tenderness for Ophelia. There are strong indications that she and Claudius have been engaged in an adulterous affair before the death of the older Hamlet. She loves Claudius, but she respects Hamlet's confidence and does not betray him to his uncle when he tells her of the murder, of which she has been obviously innocent and ignorant. Her death occurs after she drinks the poison prepared by Claudius for Hamlet.

Polonius (pə·lō′nĭ·ŭs), Lord Chamberlain under Claudius, whom he has apparently helped to the throne. An affectionate but meddlesome father to Laertes and Ophelia, he tries to control their lives, He is garrulous and self-important, always seeking the devious rather than the direct method in politics or family relationships. Hamlet jestingly baits him but he apparently has some affection for the officious old man and shows real regret at killing him. Polonius' deviousness and eavesdropping bring on his death; Hamlet stabs him through the tapestry in the mistaken belief that Claudius is concealed there.

Ophelia, Polonius' daughter and Hamlet's love. A sweet, docile girl, she is easily dominated by her father. She loves Hamlet but never seems to realize that she is imperiling his life by helping her father spy on him. Her gentle nature being unable to stand the shock of her father's death at her lover's hands, she loses her mind and is drowned.

Laertes (lā·ûr′tēz), Polonius' son. He is in many ways a foil to Hamlet. He also hungers for revenge for a slain father. Loving his dead father and sister, he succumbs to Claudius' temptation to use fraud in gaining his revenge. This plotting brings about his own death but also destroys Hamlet.

Horatio (hō·rā′·shĭ·ō), Hamlet's former schoolmate and loyal friend. Well balanced, having a quiet sense of humor, he is thoroughly reliable. Hamlet trusts him implicitly and confides in him freely. At Hamlet's death, he wishes to play the antique Roman and die by his own hand; but he yields to Hamlet's entreaty and consents to remain alive to tell Hamlet's story and to clear his name.

Ghost of King Hamlet. Appearing first to the watch, he later appears to Horatio and to Hamlet. He leads Hamlet away from the others and tells him of Claudius' foul crime. His second appearance to Hamlet occurs during the interview with the queen, to whom he remains invisible, causing her to think that Hamlet is having hallucinations. In spite of Gertrude's betrayal of him, the ghost of murdered Hamlet shows great tenderness for her in both of his appearances.

Fortinbras (fôr′tĭn·bräs), prince of Norway, son of old Fortinbras, the former king of Norway, nephew of the present regent. Another foil to Hamlet, he is resentful of his father's death at old Hamlet's hands and the consequent loss of territory. He plans an attack on Denmark, which is averted by his uncle after diplomatic negotiations between him and Claudius. He is much more the man of action than the man of thought. Hamlet chooses him as the next king of Denmark and expresses the hope and belief that he will be chosen. Fortinbras delivers a brief but emphatic eulogy over Hamlet's body.

Rosencrantz (rō·zĕn′krănz) and **Guildenstern** (gĭl′dən·stèrn), the schoolmates of Hamlet summoned to Denmark by Claudius to act as spies on Hamlet. Though hypocritical and treacherous, they are no match for him, and in trying to betray him they go to their own deaths.

Old Norway, uncle of Fortinbras. Although he never appears on the stage, he is important in that he diverts young Fortinbras from his planned attack on Denmark.

Yorick (yŏr′ĭk), King Hamlet's jester. Dead some years before the action of the play begins, he makes his brief appearance in the final act when his skull is thrown up by a sexton digging Ophelia's grave. Prince Hamlet reminisces and moralizes while holding the skull in his hands. At the time he is ignorant of whose grave the sexton is digging.

Reynaldo (rā·nôl′dō), Polonius' servant. Polonius sends him to Paris on business, incidentally to spy on Laertes. He illustrates Polonius' deviousness and unwillingness to make a direct approach to anything.

First Clown, a gravedigger. Having been sexton for many years, he knows personally the skulls of those he has buried. He greets with particular affection the skull of Yorick, which he identifies for Hamlet. He is an earthy humorist, quick with a witty reply.

Second Clown, a stupid straight man for the wit of the First Clown.

Osric (ŏz′rĭk), a mincing courtier. Hamlet baits him in much the same manner as he does Polonius, but without the concealed affection he has for the old man. He brings Hamlet word of the fencing match arranged between him and Laertes and serves as a referee of the match.

Marcellus (mär·sĕl′ŭs) and **Bernardo** (bər·när′dō), officers of the watch who first see the Ghost of King Hamlet and report it to Horatio, who shares a watch with them. After the appearance of the Ghost to them and Horatio, they all agree to report the matter to Prince Hamlet, who then shares a watch with the three.

Francisco (frăn·sĭs′kō), a soldier on watch at the play's opening. He sets the tone of the play by imparting a feeling of suspense and heartsickness.

First Player, the leader of a troop of actors. He produces "The Murder of Gonzago" with certain alterations furnished by Hamlet to trap King Claudius into displaying his guilty conscience.

A Priest, who officiates at Ophelia's abbreviated funeral. He refuses Laertes' request for more ceremony, since he believes Ophelia has committed suicide.

Voltimand (vŏl′tĭ·mänd) and **Cornelius** (kôr·nēl′yŭs), ambassadors sent to Norway by Claudius.

The Story

Three times the ghost of Denmark's dead king had stalked the battlements of Elsinore Castle. On the fourth night Horatio, Hamlet's friend, brought the young prince to see the specter of his father, two months dead. Since his father's untimely death, Hamlet had been grief-stricken and in an exceedingly melancholy frame of mind. The mysterious circumstances surrounding the death of his father had perplexed him; then too, his mother had married Claudius, the dead king's brother, much too hurriedly to suit Hamlet's sense of decency.

That night Hamlet saw his father's ghost and listened in horror to what it had to say. He learned that his father had not died from the sting of a serpent, as had been supposed, but that he had been murdered by his own brother, Claudius, the present king. The ghost added that Claudius was guilty not only of murder but also of incest and adultery. But the spirit cautioned Hamlet to spare Queen Gertrude, his mother, so that heaven could punish her.

The ghost's disclosures should have left no doubt in Hamlet's mind that Claudius must be killed. But the introspective prince was not quite sure that the ghost was his father's spirit, for he feared it might have been a devil sent to torment him. Debating with himself the problem of whether or not to carry out the spirit's commands, Hamlet swore his friends, including Horatio, to secrecy concerning the appearance of the ghost, and he told them not to consider him mad if his behavior seemed strange to them.

Meanwhile Claudius was facing not only the possibility of war with Norway, but also, and much worse, his own conscience, which had been much troubled since his hasty marriage to Gertrude. In addition, he did not like the melancholia of the prince, who, he knew, resented the king's hasty marriage. Claudius feared that Hamlet would take his throne away from him. The prince's strange behavior and wild talk made the king think that perhaps Hamlet was mad, but he was not sure. To learn the cause of Hamlet's actions—madness or ambition—Claudius commissioned two of Hamlet's friends, Rosencrantz and Guildenstern, to spy on the prince. But Hamlet saw through their clumsy efforts and confused them with his answers to their questions.

Polonius, the garrulous old chamberlain, believed that Hamlet's behavior resulted from lovesickness for his daughter, Ophelia. Hamlet, meanwhile, had become increasingly melancholy. Rosencrantz and Guildenstern, as well as Polonius, were constantly spying on him. Even Ophelia, he thought, had turned against him. The thought of deliberate murder was revolting to him, and he was constantly plagued by uncertainty as to whether the ghost were good or bad. When a troupe of actors visited Elsinore, Hamlet saw in them a chance to discover whether Claudius were guilty. He planned to have the players enact before the king and the court a scene like that which, according to the ghost, took place the day the old king died. By watching Claudius during the performance, Hamlet hoped to discover for himself signs of Claudius' guilt.

His plan worked. Claudius became so unnerved during the performance that he walked out before the end of the scene. Convinced by the king's actions that the ghost was right, Hamlet had no reason to delay in carrying out the wishes of his dead father. Even so, Hamlet failed to take advantage of his first real chance after the play to kill Claudius. He came upon the king in an attitude of prayer and could have stabbed him in the back. Hamlet did not strike because he believed that the king would die in grace at his devotions.

The queen summoned Hamlet to her chamber to reprimand him for his insolence to Claudius. Hamlet, remembering what the ghost had told him, spoke to her so violently that she screamed for help. A noise behind a curtain followed her cries, and Hamlet, suspecting that Claudius was eavesdropping, plunged his sword through the curtain, killing old Polonius. Fearing an attack on his own life, the king hastily ordered Hamlet to England in company with Rosencrantz and Guildenstern, who carried a warrant for Hamlet's death. But the prince discovered the orders and altered them so that the bearers should be killed on their arrival in England. Hamlet then returned to Denmark.

Much had happened in that unhappy land during Hamlet's absence. Because Ophelia had been rejected by her former lover, she went mad and later drowned. Laertes, Polonius' hot-tempered son, returned from France and collected a band of malcontents to avenge the death of his father. He thought that Claudius had killed Polonius, but the king told him that Hamlet was the murderer and even persuaded Laertes to take part in a plot to murder the prince.

Claudius arranged for a duel between Hamlet and Laertes. To allay suspicion of foul play, the king placed bets on Hamlet, who was an expert swordsman. At the same time, he had poison placed on the tip of Laertes' weapon and put a cup of poison within Hamlet's reach in the event that the prince became thirsty during the duel. Unfortunately, Gertrude, who knew nothing of the king's treachery, drank from the poisoned cup and died. During the contest, Hamlet was mortally wounded with the poisoned rapier, but the two contestants exchanged foils in a scuffle, and Laertes himself received a fatal wound. Before he died, Laertes was filled with remorse and told Hamlet that Claudius was responsible for the poisoned sword. Hesitating no longer, Hamlet seized his opportunity to act, and fatally stabbed the king. Then the prince himself died. But the ghost was avenged.

Critical Evaluation

Hamlet has remained the most perplexing, as well as the most popular, of Shakespeare's major tragedies. Performed frequently, the play has tantalized critics with what has become known as the Hamlet mystery. The mystery resides in Hamlet's complex behavior, most notably his indecision and his reluctance to act.

Freudian critics have located his motivation in the psychodynamic triad of the father-mother-son relationship. According to this view, Hamlet is disturbed and eventually deranged by his Oedipal jealousy of the uncle who has done what, we are to believe, all sons long to do themselves. Other critics have taken the more conventional tack of identifying Hamlet's tragic flaw as a lack of courage or moral resolution. In this view, Hamlet's indecision is a sign of moral ambivalence which he overcomes too late.

The trouble with both of these views is that they presuppose a precise discovery of Hamlet's motivation. However, Renaissance drama is not generally a drama of motivation either by psychological set or moral predetermination. Rather, the tendency is to present characters, with well delineated moral and ethical dispositions, who are faced with dilemmas. It is the outcome of these conflicts, the consequences, which normally hold center stage. What we watch in *Hamlet* is an agonizing confrontation between the will of a good and intelligent man and the uncongenial role which circumstance calls upon him to play.

The disagreeable role is a familiar one in Renaissance drama—the revenger. The early description of Hamlet, bereft by the death of his father and the hasty marriage of his mother, makes him a prime candidate to assume such a role. One need not conclude that his despondency is Oedipal in order to sympathize with the extremity of his grief. His father, whom he deeply loved and admired, is recently deceased and he himself seems to have been finessed out of his birthright. Shakespeare, in his unfortunate ignorance of Freud, emphasized Hamlet's shock at Gertrude's disrespect to the memory of his father rather than love of mother as the prime source of his distress. The very situation breeds suspicion, which is reinforced by the ghastly visitation by the elder Hamlet's ghost and the ghost's disquieting revelation. The ingredients are all there for bloody revenge.

However, if Hamlet were simply to act out the role that has been thrust upon him, the play would be just another sanguinary potboiler without the moral and theological complexity which provides its special fascination. Hamlet has, after all, been a student of theology at Wittenberg. Hamlet's knowledge complicates the situation. First of all, he is aware of the fundamental immorality of the liaison between Gertrude and Claudius. Hamlet's accusation of incest is not an adolescent excess but an accurate theological description of a marriage between a widow and her dead husband's brother.

Hamlet's theological accomplishments do more than exacerbate his feelings. For the ordinary revenger, the commission from the ghost of the murdered father would be more than enough to start the bloodletting. But Hamlet is aware of the unreliability of otherworldly apparitions, and consequently he is reluctant to heed the ghost's injunction to perform an action which is objectively evil. In addition, the fear that his father was murdered in a state of sin and is condemned to hell not only increases Hamlet's sense of injustice but also, paradoxically, casts further doubt on the reliability of the ghost's exhortation. Is the ghost, Hamlet wonders, merely an infernal spirit goading him to sin?

Thus, Hamlet's indecision is not an indication of weakness, but the result of his complex understanding of the moral dilemma with which he is faced. He is unwilling to act unjustly, yet he is afraid that he is failing to exact a deserved retribution. He debates the murky issue and becomes unsure himself whether his behavior is caused by moral scruple or cowardice. He is in sharp contrast with the cynicism of Claudius and the verbose moral platitudes of Polonius. The play is in sharp contrast with the moral simplicity of the ordinary revenge tragedy. Hamlet's intelligence has transformed a stock situation into a unique internal conflict.

He believes that he must have greater certitude of Claudius' guilt if he is to take action. The device of the play within a play provides greater assurance that Claudius is suffering from a guilty conscience, but it simultaneously sharpens Hamlet's anguish. Having seen a re-creation of his father's death and Claudius' response, Hamlet is able to summon the determination to act. However, he once again hesitates when he sees Claudius in prayer because he believes that the king is repenting and, if murdered at that moment, will go directly to heaven. Here Hamlet's inaction is not the result of cowardice nor even of a perception of moral ambiguity. Rather, after all of his agonizing, Hamlet once decided on revenge is so thoroughly committed that his passion cannot be satiated except by destroying his uncle body and soul. It is ironic that Claudius has been unable to repent and that Hamlet is thwarted this time by the combination of his theological insight with the extreme ferocity of his vengeful intention.

That Hamlet loses his mental stability is clear in his behavior toward Ophelia and in his subsequent meanderings. Circumstance had enforced a role whose enormity has overwhelmed the fine emotional and intellectual balance of a sensitive, well-educated young man. Gradually he regains control of himself and is armed with a cold determination to do what he decides is the just thing. Yet, even then, it is only in the carnage of the concluding scenes that Hamlet finally carries out his intention. Having concluded that "the readiness is all," he strikes his uncle only after he has discovered Claudius' final scheme to kill him and Laertes, but by then he is mortally wounded.

The arrival of Fortinbras, who has been lurking in the background throughout the play, superficially seems to indicate that a new, more direct and courageous order will prevail in the place of the evil of Claudius and the weakness of Hamlet. But Fortinbras' superiority is only apparent. He brings stasis and stability back to a disordered kingdom, but he does not have the self-consciousness and moral sensitivity which destroy and redeem Hamlet.

Gerald Else has interpreted Aristotle's notion of *katharsis* to be not a purging of the emotions but a purging of a role of the moral horror, the pity and fear, ordinarily associated with it. If that is so, then Hamlet, by the conflict of his ethical will with his role, has purged the revenger of his horrific bloodthirstiness and turned the stock figure into a self-conscious hero in moral conflict.

HEART OF DARKNESS

Type of work: Novella
Author: Joseph Conrad (Józef Teodor Konrad Korzeniowski, 1857–1924)
Type of plot: Symbolic romance
Time of plot: Late nineteenth century
Locale: The Belgian Congo
First published: 1902

Both an adventure story and the account of a philosophical and moral quest, this tale takes the reader on a symbolic journey into the blackness central to the heart and soul of man. A vagueness at its core has detracted little from the story's power and continued popularity.

Principal Characters

Marlow, the narrator and impartial observer of the action, who becomes the central figure when the story is interpreted psychologically. He makes a trip into the center of Africa which becomes, symbolically, a journey toward the essential meaning of life. After talking with Kurtz, with whom he identifies himself, he is able to see deeply into his own being.

Mr. Kurtz, manager of an inland trading station in the Belgian Congo. After having arrived in the Congo with high ideals and a self-imposed mission to civilize the natives, he is instead converted by them to savagery.

His awareness of his downfall and his conviction that evil is at the heart of everything is revealed in a long talk which he has with Marlow.

The District Manager, an avowed enemy of Mr. Kurtz. His only interest is in collecting as much ivory as possible, and he is totally unaware of the central darkness.

A Russian Traveler, an admirer and disciple of Mr. Kurtz, but one who thought Kurtz lived before his time.

Kurtz's Fiancée, whom Marlow allows to retain her belief in Kurtz's goodness and power.

The Story

A group of men were sitting on the deck of the cruising yawl, *The Nellie*, anchored one calm evening in the Thames estuary. One of the seamen, Marlow, began reflecting that the Thames area had been, at the time of the invading Romans, one of the dark and barbarous areas of the earth. Dwelling on this theme, he then began to tell a story of the blackest, most barbarous area of the earth that he had experienced.

Through his aunt's connections, Marlow had once secured a billet as commander of a river steamer for one of the trading companies with interests in the Belgian Congo. When he went to Belgium to learn more about the job, he found that few of the officials of the company expected him to return alive. In Brussels, he also heard of the distinguished Mr. Kurtz, the powerful and intelligent man who was educating the natives and at the same time sending back record shipments of ivory.

The mysterious figure of Mr. Kurtz fascinated Marlow. In spite of the ominous hints that he gathered from various company officials, he became more and more curious about what awaited him in the Congo. During his journey, as he passed along the African coast, he reflected that the wilderness and the unknown seemed to seep right out to the sea. Many of the trading posts and

stations the ship passed were dilapidated and looked barbaric. Finally, Marlow arrived at the seat of the government at the mouth of the river. Again, he heard of the great distinction and power of Mr. Kurtz who had an enormous reputation because of his plans to enlighten the natives and his success in gaining their confidence. Marlow also saw natives working in the hot sun until they collapsed and died. Marlow had to wait impatiently for ten days at the government site because his work would not begin until he reached the district manager's station, two hundred miles up the river. At last, the expedition left for the district station.

Marlow arrived at the district station to find that the river steamer had sunk a few days earlier. He met the district manager, a man whose only ability seemed to be the ability to survive. The district manager, unconcerned with the fate of the natives, was interested only in getting out of the country; he felt that Mr. Kurtz's new methods were ruining the whole district. The district manager also reported that he had not heard from Kurtz for quite some time but had received disquieting rumors about his failing health.

Although he was handicapped by a lack of rivets, Marlow spent months supervising repairs to the antiquated river steamer. He also overheard a conversation which revealed that the district manager was Kurtz's implacable enemy, who hoped that the climate would do away with his rival.

The steamer was finally ready for use, and Marlow, along with the district manager, sailed to visit Kurtz at the inner station far up the river. The journey was difficult and perilous; the water was shallow; there were frequent fogs. Just as they arrived within a few miles of Kurtz's station, natives attacked the vessel with spears and arrows. Marlow's helmsman, a faithful native, was killed by a long spear when he learned from his window to fire at the savages. Marlow finally blew the steamboat whistle, and the sound frightened the natives away. The district manager was sure that Kurtz had lost control over the blacks. When they docked, they met an enthusiastic Russian traveler who told them that Kurtz was gravely ill.

While the district manager visited Kurtz, the Russian told Marlow that the sick man had become corrupted by the very natives he had hoped to enlighten. He still had power over the natives, but instead of his changing them, they had debased him into an atavistic savage. Kurtz attended native rituals, had killed frequently in order to get ivory, and had hung heads as decorations outside his hut. Later Marlow met Kurtz and found that the man had, indeed, been corrupted by the evil at the center of experience. Marlow learned from the Russian that Kurtz

had ordered the natives to attack the steamer, thinking that, if they did so, the white men would run away and leave Kurtz to die among his fellow savages in the wilderness. Talking to Marlow, Kurtz showed his awareness of how uncivilized he had become and how his plans to educate the natives had been reversed. He gave Marlow a packet of letters for his fiancée in Belgium and the manuscript of an article, written sometime earlier, in which he urged efforts to educate the natives.

The district manager and Marlow took Kurtz, now on a stretcher, to the river steamer to take him back home. The district manager contended that the area was now ruined for collecting ivory. Full of despair and the realization that devouring evil was at the heart of everything, Kurtz died while the steamer was temporarily stopped for repairs.

Marlow returned to civilization. About a year later, he went to Belgium to see Kurtz's fiancée. She still thought of Kurtz as the splendid and powerful man who had gone to Africa with a mission, and she still believed in his goodness and power. When she asked Marlow what Kurtz's last words had been, Marlow lied and told her that Kurtz had asked for her at the end. In reality, Kurtz, who had seen all experience, had in his final words testified to the horror of it all. This horror was not something, Marlow felt, that civilized ladies could, or should, understand.

Critical Evaluation

In one sense, *Heart of Darkness* is a compelling adventure tale of a journey into the blackest heart of the Belgian Congo. The story presents attacks by the natives, descriptions of the jungle and the river, and characterizations of white men who, sometimes with ideals and sometimes simply for profit, invade the jungles to bring out ivory. The journey into the heart of the Congo, however, is also a symbolic journey into the blackness central to the heart and soul of man, a journey deep into primeval passion, superstition, and lust. Those who, like the district manager, undertake this journey simply to rob the natives of ivory, without any awareness of the importance of the central darkness, can survive. Similarly, Marlow, who is only an observer, never centrally involved, can survive to tell the tale; but those who, like Kurtz, are aware of the darkness, who hope with conscious intelligence and a humane concern for all mankind to bring light into the darkness, are doomed, are themselves swallowed up by the darkness and evil they had hoped to penetrate. Conrad manages to make his point, a realization of the evil at the center of human experience, without ever breaking the closely knit pattern of his narrative or losing the compelling atmospheric and psychological force of the tale. The wealth of natural symbols, the clear development of character, and the sheer fascination of

the story make this a novella that has been frequently praised and frequently read ever since its publication in 1902. *Heart of Darkness* is, in both style and insight, a masterful work.

Christened Jósef Teodor Konrad Nalecz Korzeniowski by his Polish parents, Joseph Conrad was able to write of the sea and sailing from firsthand knowledge. He left the cold climate of Poland early in his life to travel to the warmer regions of the Mediterranean, where he became a sailor. He traveled a great deal: to the West Indies, Latin America, Africa. Eventually, he settled in England and perfected a remarkably subtle yet powerful literary style in his adopted language.

Criticism of Conrad's work in general and *Heart of Darkness* in particular has been both extensive and varied. Many critics concern themselves with Conrad's style; others focus on the biographical aspects of his fiction; some see the works as social commentaries; some are students of Conrad's explorations into human psychology; many are interested in the brooding, shadowy symbolism that hovers over all the works. E. M. Forster censured him as a vague and elusive writer who never quite clearly discloses the philosophy that lies behind his tales. Such a judgment, however, ignores Conrad's intentions as a writer of fiction. Partly as Conrad's mouthpiece, the narrator of *Heart of Darkness* states in the first few pages of the novel:

> The yarns of seamen have a direct simplicity, the whole meaning of which lies within the shell of the cracked nut. But Marlow was not typical (if his propensity to spin yarns be excepted), and to him the meaning of an episode was not inside like a kernel but outside, enveloping the tale which brought It out only as a glow brings out a haze, in the likeness of one of those misty halos that sometimes are made visible by the spectral illumination of moonshine.

The mention of the narrator brings up one of the most complex and intriguing features of *Heart of Darkness*: its carefully executed and elaborately conceived handling of point of view. Readers can detect that the novella is in truth two narratives, inexorably woven together by Conrad's masterful craftsmanship. The outer frame of the story—the immediate setting—involves the unnamed narrator, who is apparently the only one on the *Nellie* profoundly affected by Marlow's tale, but it is the inner story that constitutes the bulk of the novella. Marlow narrates, and the others listen passively. The narrator's closing words show his feeling at the conclusion of Marlow's recounting of the events in the Congo:

> Marlow ceased, and sat apart, indistinct and silent, in the pose of a meditating Buddha. Nobody moved for a time. "We have lost the first of the ebb," said the Director suddenly. I raised my head. The offing was barred by a black bank of clouds, and the tranquil waterway leading to the uttermost ends of the earth flowed sombre under an overcast sky—seemed to lead into the heart of an immense darkness.

Since Marlow's narrative is a tale devoted primarily to a journey to the mysterious dark continent (the literal heart of darkness, Africa), a superficial view of the tale is simply that it is essentially an elaborate story involving confrontation with exotic natives, treacherous dangers of the jungle, brutal savagery, and even cannibalism. Such a view, however, ignores larger meanings with which the work is implicitly concerned: namely, social and cultural implications; psychological workings of the cultivated European left to the uncivilized wilderness; and the richly colored fabric of symbolism that emerges slowly but inevitably from beneath the surface.

Heart of Darkness can also be examined for its social and cultural implications. It is fairly obvious that a perverted version of the "White Man's Burden" was the philosophy adopted by the ivory hunters at the Inner Station. Kurtz's "Exterminate the brutes!" shows the way a white man can exploit the helpless savage. The futile shelling from the gunboat into the jungle is also vividly portrayed as a useless, brutal, and absurd act perpetrated against a weaker, more uncivilized culture than the one that nurtured Kurtz.

Here the psychological phenomena of Marlow's tale emerge. Kurtz, a man relieved of all social and civilized restraints, goes mad after committing himself to the total pursuit of evil and depravity. His observation "The horror! the horror!" suggests her final realization of the consequences of his life. Marlow also realizes this and is allowed (because he forces restraint upon himself) to draw back his foot from the precipice of madness. The experience leaves Marlow sober, disturbed, meditative, and obsessed with relating his story in much the same way Coleridge's Ancient Mariner must also relate his story.

On a symbolic level, the story is rich; a book could easily be written on this facet of the novel. A mention of some of the major symbols must suffice here: the Congo River that reminded Marlow early in his youth of a snake as it uncoiled its length into the darkness of Africa and furnished him with an uncontrollable "fascination of the abomination"; the symbolic journey into man's own heart of darkness reveals the blind evil of man's own nature, the irony of the quest when the truth is revealed not in terms of light but in terms of darkness (the truth brings not light but rather total darkness). The entire symbolic character of the work is capsuled at the end of Marlow's tale when he is forced to lie to Kurtz's intended spouse in order to preserve her illusion; the truth appears to Marlow as an inescapable darkness, and the novel ends with the narrator's own observation of darkness.

Heart of Darkness is one of literature's most somber fictions. It explores fundamental questions about man's nature: his capacity for evil; the necessity for restraint; the effect of physical darkness and isolation on a civilized soul; and the necessity of relinquishing pride for one's own spiritual salvation. Forster's censure of Conrad may be correct in many ways, but it refuses to admit that through such philosophical ruminations Conrad has allowed generations of readers to ponder humanity's own heart of darkness.

HEDDA GABLER

Type of work: Drama
Author: Henrik Ibsen (1828–1906)
Type of plot: Social criticism
Time of plot: Late nineteenth century
Locale: Norway
First presented: 1890

Perhaps the most perfectly structured play of the modern theater, Hedda Gabler *was the summing up of Ibsen's dramatic theories and skills. Within this flawless structure he created an unforgettable character, a woman filled with contradictions; she is both ruthless and afraid, desperate and tormented. The economy of writing and the compression of style in the play contribute greatly to its emotional impact.*

Principal Characters

Hedda Gabler Tessman, the exciting but unenthusiastic bride of George Tessman, who holds a scholarship for research into the history of civilization. Back from a six-month wedding trip during which George studied civilization, Hedda is dangerously bored. The daughter of General Gabler, she keeps as her prize possession her father's pistols, with which she plays on occasion. She also plays with people: with George's Aunt Julia, whose new bonnet Hedda pretends to think belongs to the servant; with George, who has bought her a villa which she pretended to want and who now must buy her a piano because her old one does not suit her new home; with an old school acquaintance, Mrs. Elvsted, who has rescued Hedda's talented former lover, Eilert Lovberg, from drink; with Eilert Lovberg, whom she cannot bear to see rescued by Mrs. Elvsted; with Judge Brack, who outmaneuvers her and pushes her over the brink of endurance to her death. Hedda is a complete egocentric, caring for no one, careless of life for herself and for others. Badly spoiled, she seems to gain her only pleasure from making everyone miserable. Eilert Lovberg she finds more amusing than anyone else, even though she had dismissed him when she was free. When she realizes that he has destroyed his career, she gives him a pistol and tells him to use it—beautifully. When the pistol discharges accidentally and injures him fatally in the boudoir of Mademoiselle Diana, and when Judge Brack convinces her that he knows where Eilert got the pistol, Hedda takes its mate, goes to her room, and shoots herself in the temple, but not before she has seen Mrs. Elvsted quietly gain a hold on George Tessman.

George Tessman, Hedda's husband, a sincere, plodding young man dazzled by his bride but devoted to his work. When Hedda burns Eilert's manuscript, which George has found, she tells George that she did so to keep Eilert from surpassing him; but in reality she burned it because Eilert wrote it with Mrs. Elvsted and they call it their "child." George's surprised horror at her deed turns to warm delight when he thinks that Hedda loves him enough to destroy the manuscript for his sake. When Mrs. Elvsted says that she has notes for the manuscript, George says that he is just the man to work on someone else's manuscript and that they can put the book together again. Sincerely delighted that he can help restore the lost valuable book, he plans to work evenings with Mrs. Elvsted, to the disgust of Hedda, who in cold, calm rage and despair shoots herself.

Eilert Lovberg, a former suitor of Hedda who has written a book in the same field as Tessman's. He could easily win the appointment which Tessman expects, but he decides not to compete with him. Since Hedda broke up their association after it threatened to become serious, he has been living with the family of Sheriff Elvsted, teaching the Elvsted children and writing another book. His manuscript completed, he comes to town. In his writing and in his reform from his old wild ways, he has been inspired by Mrs. Elvsted. Eilert shows the effects of hard living. As soon as Hedda has an opportunity, she reasserts her control over him, destroying his confidence in Mrs. Elvsted and persuading him to resume his drinking. Hedda says that he will return "with vine leaves in his hair—flushed and fearless." Instead, he returns defeated, having lost his manuscript. He tells Thea Elvsted that all is over between them, because he has destroyed the manuscript, but he has merely lost it and is ashamed to tell her so. After leaving Judge Brack's party he had gone to the rooms of Mademoiselle Diana, a red-haired entertainer whom he had known in his riotous days. There, missing his manuscript, he had accused Diana and her friends of robbing him. When the police appeared, he struck a constable and was carried off to the police station. Released the next day, he goes in despair to Mademoiselle Diana's rooms to look for his lost manuscript. Here the gun discharges, killing him. Wanting the manuscript desperately because he claimed it contained his "true self" and dealt with the future, he had planned to deliver lectures on it after Tessman's appointment had gone through.

Judge Brack, a friend of the family, a sly man whom Tessman trusts. Hedda agrees to the apparently harmless arrangement to keep her entertained. After Eilert Lovberg's death, Judge Brack tells Hedda that he knows the true story, but there is no danger if he says nothing. When Hedda protests that she will now be his slave, a thought which she cannot bear, he replies that he will not abuse the advantage he now holds. He is incredulous when he hears that Hedda has killed herself.

Thea Elvsted, the wife of Sheriff Elvsted, a sweet-faced woman with blonde hair, born to inspire men, although, unfortunately, not her husband. She rescues Eilert, works with him, preserves his notes, seeks to preserve him, and after his death and Hedda's will no doubt inspire Tessman. When Eilert comes to town, Mrs. Elvsted, who is in love with him, follows him because she is afraid that he will relapse into his old ways. Because she and Hedda had known each other in school, she comes to see Hedda. Mrs. Elvsted had been afraid of her when they were girls because Hedda sometimes pulled her hair and threatened to burn it off. However, she confides to Hedda the story of her love for Eilert and thus helps to bring about his death and Hedda's.

Miss Juliana Tessman (Aunt Julia), Tessman's aunt, who is eternally hoping for an offspring for Hedda and George. Her constant, veiled remarks about sewing and the use for the two empty rooms are lost on George and ignored by Hedda. With her sister, Rina, now dying, Aunt Julia had reared George. She serves in the play to remind George of his past and to irritate Hedda. She is a sweet, good woman who loves her nephew and wants to help the helpless.

The Story

When aristocratic Hedda Gabler, daughter of the late General Gabler, consented to marry Doctor George Tessman everyone in Hedda's set was surprised and a little shocked. Although George was a rising young scholar soon to be made a professor in the university, he was hardly considered the type of person Hedda would marry. He was dull and prosaic, absorbed almost exclusively in his dusty tomes and manuscripts, while Hedda was the beautiful, spoiled darling of her father and of all the other men who had flocked around her. But Hedda was now twenty-nine, and George was the only one of her admirers who was willing to offer her marriage and a villa which had belonged to the widow of a cabinet minister.

The villa was somewhat beyond George's means, but with the prospect of a professorship and with his Aunt Juliana's help, he managed to secure it because it was what Hedda wanted. He arranged a long wedding tour lasting nearly six months because Hedda wished that also. On their honeymoon George spent most of his time delving into libraries for material on his special field, the history of civilization. Hedda was bored. She returned to the villa hating George. Then it began to look as if George might not get the professorship, in which case Hedda would have to forego her footman and saddlehorse and some of the other luxuries she craved. George's rival for the post was Eilert Lovberg, a brilliant but erratic genius who had written a book, acclaimed a masterpiece, in George's own field. Hedda's boredom and disgust with her situation was complete. She found her only excitement in practicing with the brace of pistols which had belonged to General Gabler, the only legacy her father had left her.

George discovered that Eilert had written another book, more brilliant and important than the last, a book written with the help and inspiration of a Mrs. Elvsted, whose devotion to the erratic genius had reformed him. The manuscript of this book Lovberg brought with him one evening to the Tessman villa. Hedda proceeded to make the most of this situation. In the first place, Thea Elvsted was Hedda's despised schoolmate, and her husband's former sweetheart. The fact that this mouselike creature had been the inspiration for the success and rehabilitation of Eilert Lovberg was more than Hedda could bear. For Eilert Lovberg had always been in love with Hedda, and she knew it. In the distant past, he had urged her to throw in her lot with him and she had been tempted to do so but had refused because his future had been uncertain. Now Hedda felt a pang of regret mingled with anger that another woman possessed what she had lacked the courage to hold for herself.

Her only impulse was to destroy, and circumstances played into her hands. When Lovberg called at the Tessman Villa with his manuscript, George was on the point of leaving with his friend, Judge Brack, for a bachelor party. They invited Lovberg to accompany them, but he refused, preferring to remain at the villa with Mrs. Elvsted and Hedda. But Hedda, determined to destroy the handiwork of her rival, deliberately sent Lovberg off to the party. All night, Hedda and Mrs. Elvsted awaited the revelers' return. George was the first to appear with the story of the happenings of the night before.

The party had ended in an orgy, and on the way home Lovberg had lost his manuscript, which George recovered and brought home. In despair over the supposed loss of his manuscript, Lovberg had spent the remainder of the evening at Mademoiselle Diana's establishment. When he finally made his appearance at the villa, George had gone. Lovberg told Mrs. Elvsted he had destroyed his manuscript, but later he confessed to Hedda that it was lost and that, as a consequence, he intended to take his own life. Without revealing that the manuscript was at that moment in her possession, Hedda urged him to do the deed beautifully, and she pressed into his hand a memento of their relationship, one of General Gabler's pistols—the very one with which she had once threatened Lovberg.

After his departure, Hedda coldly and deliberately threw the manuscript into the fire. When George returned and heard from Hedda's own lips the fate of Lovberg's manuscript, he was unspeakably shocked; but half believing that she burned it for his sake, he was also flattered. He resolved to keep silent and devote his life to reconstructing the book from the notes kept by Mrs. Elvsted.

Except for two circumstances, Hedda would have been safe. The first was the manner in which Lovberg met his death. Leaving Hedda, he had returned to Mademoiselle Diana's, where instead of dying beautifully, as Hedda had planned, he became embroiled in a brawl in which he was accidentally killed. The second was the character of Judge Brack, a sophisticated man of the world, as ruthless in his way as Hedda was in hers. He had long admired Hedda's cold, dispassionate beauty, and had wanted to make her his mistress. The peculiar circumstances of Eilert Lovberg's death gave him his opportunity. He had learned that the pistol with which Lovberg met his death was one of a pair belonging to Hedda. If the truth came out, there would be an investigation followed by scandal in which Hedda would be involved. She could not face either a public scandal or the private ignominy of the judge's proposal. So while her husband and Mrs. Elvsted were beginning the long task of reconstructing the dead Lovberg's manuscript, Hedda calmly went to her boudoir and with the remaining pistol she died beautifully—as she had urged Lovberg to do—by putting a bullet through her head.

Critical Evaluation

In *Hedda Gabler*, Henrik Ibsen constructed a complex play which caused considerable bewilderment among contemporary critics. Some found fault; some simply confessed puzzlement. *Hedda Gabler*, as one of Ibsen's later plays, was, for example, often judged in the context of his earlier work instead of evaluated on its own merits. Hence, when the broad social issues treated in earlier plays were found lacking or deficient in *Hedda Gabler*, the latter play was pronounced inferior. The most common misperception of *Hedda Gabler*, however, stemmed from a tendency to see the play through its title and hence its protagonist. "How," it was asked, "could Ibsen present a 'heroine' so totally devoid of any redeeming virtues?" Again, critics who raised the question misconstrued the play—and drama criticism, as well—for a protagonist need not be a heroine or a hero.

Modern critical opinion has focused more carefully on the structure of the play. Hence, one critic has called attention to a typical Ibsen device which the critic characterizes as "retrospective action"—a theatrical method noted by many other critics but without the apt label. As a theatrical device, Ibsen's dramatic innovation operates thus: the problem of exposition—revealing the crucial events which preceded the present action in the play (motion pictures solve the problem through flashbacks)—is handled in the first few scenes by having the major characters, reunited with other characters after a long absence, recapitulate past activities to bring the other characters up to date. Hence, the Tessmans, returning from their extended honeymoon, reveal much of themselves in conversation with Juliana and others. Yet, despite this sophisticated surmounting of theatrical obstacles, the play is not without structural weaknesses. Lovberg's apocalyptic attitude is unconvincing; Ibsen's view of scholarly enterprise as a batch of notes in someone's briefcase is ludicrous; and Hedda's potential disaffiliation with the play poses a threat to dramatic unity. These disabilities notwithstanding, the play holds up under critical review because dialogue, characterization, and theme carry it through.

For the verbal polish and linguistic sensitivity of the dialogue, Ibsen's method of playwriting is largely responsible. After completing a play, Ibsen would rest, letting his mind lie fallow. Then he would begin incubating ideas for his next play. When he was ready to write, he wrote quickly, completing his first draft in about two months. Next, the draft was set aside for another two months or so to "age" properly, whereupon Ibsen would then attack the final job of refining each nuance to perfection, completing the job in two to three weeks and having the copy ready for the printer within a month's time; the following month, the play was off the press and ready for distribution. It was in the refining process that Ibsen sharpened his dialogue to crystal-clear perfection. He added to the play George Tessman's fussy expostulations—the characteristic, questioning "Hmm's?" and "Eh's"—Brack's inquisitorial manner, and striking imagery such as "vine leaves in his hair." Out of such stuff truly poetic dialogue is made, and Ibsen certainly made it. Few playwrights can match the exquisitely fine-tuned dialogue of *Hedda Gabler*.

As for characterization, one is hard put to resist the temptation to concentrate exclusively on Hedda without touching upon at least George, Lovberg, and Judge Brack. Yet the character of Hedda stands out in bold relief only by contrast with these other characters in the play. Thus the others must be given serious consideration at least as the medium for Hedda's development. Hedda's three major counterfoils are George Tessman, Eilert Lovberg, and Brack, but all of the men are rather static characters in the play. Although their personalities are revealed to us gradually as the play progresses, none of them undergoes any fundamental change. Thus, George Tessman begins and ends as a somewhat distracted "Mr. Chips" personality; Lovberg is revealed as an incurable incompetent; and Brack is exposed for the coldly calculating, manipulative Svengali he wants to be, on the face of it a perfect match for Hedda's own apparently predatory instincts. But against this background, Hedda dominates the scene: a creature of impulse and indulgence, her father's spoiled darling. Let us remember that the play is titled *Hedda Gabler*, not Hedda Tessman! Let us also remember Hedda's growing contempt for Tessman and her opportunism as it grows in inverse ratio to his declining prospects. And let us not forget that in the matrix of Lovberg's inelegant death, Tessman's ineffectuality, Brack's obscene proposition, and Hedda's unwanted pregnancy with Tessman's child, Hedda prefers an efficient suicide to a messy life. Hedda's life does not meet her exacting standards, but her suicide fulfills her sense of style in a way that living cannot. Ibsen's vivid insight into Hedda's personality thus constitutes the real meat of the play, for it is Hedda as an individual—not Hedda as a "case study" or Hedda as a "social issue" or Hedda as anything else— that constitutes the play *Hedda Gabler*.

How can we understand Hedda? Certainly she is more substantial than a mad housewife or an ex-prom queen. Inchoately, she desires, but she has not the sophistication to focus her desires. She is thus directionless. Her *angst* is as much an identity crisis as a lack of goals. She does not know what she wants, much less how to get it. Her apparent hardheadedness, which so attracts Brack, is no more than a mask for insecurity. Hers is not a problem of social justice but of private insight. She knows nothing of personal or political power; hence, she appears to use people, to exploit them—but, in reality, more out of naïveté than cold calculation, for she does not recognize or appreciate her influence. The metaphorical evolution of Hedda's personality—from self-indulgent child, to falsely confident adolescent, to desperate and despairing (and pregnant) woman who puts a bullet through her head—starkly depicts the life of an individual, not a symbol of a social issue. As such, *Hedda Gabler* is a problem play, not a social-problem play.

HENRY THE FOURTH, PART ONE

Type of work: Drama
Author: William Shakespeare (1564–1616)
Type of plot: Historical chronicle
Time of plot: 1400–1405
Locale: England
First presented: 1596

Through the antics of Falstaff and his mates, comedy and history join in this play. Woven into scenes of court and military matters, the humorous sequences are used to reveal Prince Hal's character and to bring into sharp relief the serious affairs of honor and history.

Principal Characters

King Henry the Fourth, England's troubled ruler. Haunted by his action in the deposition and indirectly in the death of his predecessor and kinsman, Richard II, and deeply disturbed by the apparent unworthiness of his irresponsible eldest son, he also faces the external problem of rebellion. He wishes to join a crusade to clear his conscience and to carry out a prophecy that he is to die in Jerusalem; it turns out that he dies in the Jerusalem chamber in Westminster.

Henry, Prince of Wales (Prince Hal, Harry Monmouth), later King Henry V. A boisterous youth surrounded by bad companions, he matures rapidly with responsibility, saves his father's life in battle, and kills the dangerous rebel, Hotspur. When he comes to the throne, he repudiates his wild companions.

Sir John Falstaff, a comical, down-at-the-heels follower of Prince Hal. Considered by many to be one of Shakespeare's finest creations, by some to be his greatest, Falstaff is a plump fruit from the stem of the "Miles Gloriosus" of Plautus. He is the typical braggart soldier with many individualizing traits. As he says, he is not only witty himself, but the cause of wit in other men. Innumerable pages have been written on whether or not he is a coward. He is a cynical realist, a fantastic liar, a persuasive rascal. Also, he is apparently a successful combat soldier. His colossal body, which "lards the lean earth as he walks along," appropriately houses his colossal personality. In the second part of the play, there is some decline of his character, perhaps to prepare the way for Prince Hal, as King Henry V, to cast him off.

Prince John of Lancaster, another of King Henry's sons, who also bears himself well in battle at Shrewsbury. He commands part of his father's forces in Yorkshire and arranges a false peace with the Archbishop of York and other rebels. When their troops are dismissed, he has them arrested and executed.

Thomas Percy, Earl of Worcester, a leading rebel against King Henry IV. He conceals the king's offer of generous terms from his nephew Hotspur, thereby causing the young

warrior's death. He is executed for treason.

Henry Percy, Earl of Northumberland, Worcester's brother. Having had an important share in the deposition of Richard II and the enthronement of Henry IV, he feels that he and his family are entitled to more power and wealth than they receive. He is also influenced to rebellion by his crafty brother and his fiery son. He fails his cause by falling ill or feigning illness before the Battle of Shrewsbury, and he does not appear there. Later he disconcerts Mowbray by withdrawing to Scotland, where he is defeated.

Hotspur (Henry Percy), son of Northumberland. A courageous, hot-tempered youth, he seeks to pluck glory from the moon. He is a loving, teasing husband, but his heart is more on the battlefield than in the boudoir. He rages helplessly at the absence of his father and Glendower from the Battle of Shrewsbury. In the battle he falls by Prince Henry's hand.

Edmund Mortimer, Earl of March, Hotspur's brother-in-law, designated heir to the English throne by Richard II. Captured while fighting against Glendower, he marries his captor's daughter. King Henry's refusal to ransom him leads to the rebellion of the Percys. He too fails to join Hotspur at Shrewsbury.

Owen Glendower, the Welsh leader. Hotspur finds his mystical self-importance irritating and almost precipitates internal strife among King Henry's opponents. Glendower also fails Hotspur at Shrewsbury. Some time later, Warwick reports Glendower's death to the ailing king.

Sir Richard Vernon, another rebel. He is with the Earl of Worcester when King Henry offers his terms for peace, and with great reluctance he agrees to conceal the terms from Hotspur.

Archibald, Earl of Douglas, a noble Scottish rebel. After killing Sir Walter Blunt and two others whom he mistakes for King Henry at Shrewsbury, he is prevented from killing the king by Prince Hal. After the battle, Prince Hal generously releases him without ransom.

Richard Scroop, Archbishop of York, a principal rebel. He thinks to make peace with King Henry and take later advantage of his weakness, but is tricked by Prince John and executed.

Sir Walter Blunt, a heroic follower of the king. At the Battle of Shrewsbury, he pretends to Douglas that he is the King, thus bringing death on himself.

Mistress Quickly, hostess of the Boar's Head Tavern in Eastcheap. She is a silly, voluble woman with a stupendous fund of malapropisms. Easily angered, but gullible, she is a frequent victim of Falstaff's chicanery.

Bardolph, the red-nosed right-hand man of Falstaff. His fiery nose makes him the butt of many witticisms. Like Falstaff, he is capable of sudden and violent action.

Poins, Prince Hal's confidant. Masked, he and the Prince rob Falstaff and the other robbers at Gadshill and endeavor to discountenance Falstaff at the Boar's Head Tavern afterward.

Gadshill and **Peto,** other members of the Prince's scapegrace following.

The Sheriff, who seeks Falstaff after the robbery. Prince Hal sends him away with the promise that Sir John will answer for his behavior.

Lady Percy, Hotspur's wife, Mortimer's sister. A charming and playful girl, she is deeply in love with her fiery husband and tragically moved by his death.

Lady Mortimer, daughter of Glendower. Speaking only Welsh, she is unable to understand her husband, to whom she is married as a political pawn.

Sir Michael, a follower of the Archbishop of York, for whom he delivers secret messages to important rebels.

The Story

King Henry, conscience-stricken because of his part in the murder of King Richard II, his predecessor, planned a pilgrimage to the Holy Land. He declared to his lords that war had been banished from England and that peace would reign throughout the kingdom.

But there were those of differing opinions. Powerful barons in the North remained disaffected after the accession of the new king. Antagonized by his failure to keep promises made when he claimed the throne, they recruited forces to maintain their feudal rights. In fact, as Henry announced plans for his expedition to the Holy Land, he was informed of the brutal murder of a thousand persons in a fray between Edmund Mortimer, proclaimed by Richard as heir to the crown, and Glendower, a Welsh rebel. Mortimer was taken prisoner. A messenger also brought word of Hotspur's success against the Scots at Holmedon Hill. The king expressed his commendation of the young knight and his regrets that his own son, Prince Henry, was so irresponsible and carefree.

But King Henry, piqued by Hotspur's refusal to release to him more than one prisoner, ordered a council meeting to bring the overzealous Hotspur to terms. At the meeting Henry refused to ransom Mortimer, the pretender to the throne, held by Glendower. In turn, Hotspur refused to release the prisoners taken at Holmedon Hill, and Henry threatened more strenuous action against Hotspur and his kinsmen.

In a rousing speech Hotspur appealed to the power and nobility of Northumberland and Worcester and urged that they undo the wrongs of which they were guilty in the dethronement and murder of Richard and in aiding Henry instead of Mortimer to the crown. Worcester promised to help Hotspur in his cause against Henry. Worcester's plan would involve the aid of Douglas of Scotland, to be sought after by Hotspur, of Glendower and Mortimer, to be won over through Worcester's efforts, and of the Archbishop of York, to be approached by Northumberland.

Hotspur's boldness and impatience were shown in his dealing with Glendower as they, Mortimer, and Worcester discussed the future division of the kingdom. Hotspur, annoyed by the tedium of Glendower's personal account of his own ill-fated birth and by the uneven distribution of land, was impudent and rude. Hotspur was first a soldier, then a gentleman.

In the king's opinion, Prince Henry was quite lacking in either of these attributes. In one of their foolish pranks Sir John Falstaff and his riotous band had robbed some travelers at Gadshill, only to be set upon and put to flight by the prince and one companion. Summoning the prince from the Boar's Head Tavern, the king urged his son to break with the undesirable company he kept, chiefly the ne'er-do-well Falstaff. Contrasting young Henry with Hotspur, the king pointed out the military achievements of Northumberland's heir. Congenial, high-spirited Prince Henry, remorseful because of his father's lack of confidence in him, swore his allegiance to his father and declared he would show the king that in time of crisis Hotspur's glorious deeds would prove Hotspur no better soldier than Prince Henry. To substantiate his pledge, the prince took command of a detachment that would join ranks with other units of the royal army—Blunt's, Prince John's, Westmoreland's, and the king's—in twelve days.

Prince Henry's conduct seemed to change very little. He continued his buffoonery with Falstaff, who had recruited a handful of bedraggled, nondescript foot soldiers. Falstaff's contention was that, despite their physical condition, they were food for powder and that little more could be said for any soldier.

Hotspur's forces suffered gross reverses through Northumberland's failure, because of illness, to organize an army. Also, Hotspur's ranks were reduced because Glendower believed the stars not propitious for him to march at that time. Undaunted by the news of his reduced forces, Hotspur pressed on to meet Henry's army of thirty thousand.

At Shrewsbury, the scene of the battle, Sir Walter Blunt carried to Hotspur the king's offer that the rebels' grievances would be righted and that anyone involved in the revolt would be pardoned if he chose a peaceful settlement. In answer to the king's message Hotspur reviewed the history of Henry's double-dealing and scheming in the past. Declaring that Henry's lineage should not continue on the throne, Hotspur finally promised Blunt that Worcester would wait upon the king to give him an answer to his offer.

Henry repeated his offer of amnesty to Worcester and Vernon, Hotspur's ambassadors. Because Worcester doubted the king's sincerity, because of previous betrayals, he lied to Hotspur on his return to the rebel camp and reported that the king in abusive terms had announced his determination to march at once against Hotspur. Worcester also reported Prince Henry's invitation to Hotspur that they fight a duel. Hotspur gladly accepted the challenge.

As the two armies moved into battle, Blunt, mistaken for the king, was slain by Douglas, who, learning his error, was sorely grieved that he had not killed Henry. Douglas, declaring that he would yet murder the king, accosted him after a long search over the field. He would

have been successful in his threat had it not been for the intervention of Prince Henry, who engaged Douglas and allowed the king to withdraw from the fray.

In the fighting Hotspur descended upon Prince Henry, exhausted from an earlier wound and his recent skirmish with Douglas. When the two young knights fought, Hotspur was wounded. Douglas again appeared, fighting with Falstaff, and departed after Falstaff had fallen to the ground as if he were dead. Hotspur died of his wounds and Prince Henry, before going off to join Prince John, his brother, eulogized Hotspur and Falstaff. The two benedictions were quite different. But Falstaff had only pretended lifelessness to save his life. After the prince's departure, he stabbed Hotspur. He declared that he would swear before any council that he had killed the young rebel.

Worcester and Vernon were taken prisoners. Because they had not relayed to Hotspur the peace terms offered by the king, they were sentenced to death. Douglas, in flight after Hotspur's death, was taken prisoner. Given the king's permission to dispose of Douglas, Prince Henry ordered that the valiant Scottish knight be freed.

The king sent Prince John to march against the forces of Northumberland and the Archbishop of York. He and Prince Henry took the field against Glendower and Mortimer, in Wales. Falstaff had the honor of carrying off the slain Hotspur.

Critical Evaluation

Although there is no evidence that the cycle of plays including *Richard the Second*, *Henry the Fourth, Part One* and *Part Two*, and *Henry the Fifth* were intended by Shakespeare to form a unit, there is much continuity, of theme as well as of personages. There is a movement from one grand epoch to another, from the Middle Ages to the Renaissance. The main aspects of his transition implied at the end of each play are projected into the next, where they are developed and explored.

The reader of *Henry the Fourth, Part One*, should be familiar with some aspects of *Richard the Second*, for in that play the broad lines of the entire cycle are drawn and the immediate base of *Henry the Fourth, Part One*, is formed. In *Richard the Second*, the legitimate king, Richard II, is deposed by Bolingbroke, who becomes Henry IV. This event, to include both historical perspectives, must be viewed as at once a usurpation and a necessary political expediency. It is a usurpation because unjustifiable, indeed unthinkable, from the strictly medieval view of what has been called "the great chain of being." This notion postulates that the universe is ordered, hierarchical, that everything is given a place by God, from angels to ants, and that station is immutable. In this world, formed by ritual, an anointed king is representative of God's Order. To depose him is to call in question

all order in the world. Tradition, especially ritual, presupposed and supported fixed order. Ritual in this larger sense is broken in *Richard the Second* first by the excesses of Richard himself and then, in a more definitive sense, by the usurping Bolingbroke. The irony of Bolingbroke's act, and the subject of *Henry the Fourth, Part One*, is the consequences of what was to have been a momentary departure from ordained ritual. As with Eve, the gesture of self-initiative was irrevocable, the knowledge and correlative responsibility gained at that moment inescapable.

At the opening of *Henry the Fourth, Part One*, then, we see the results of rebellion already installed; the security of the old system of feudal trust is forever lost. Those who helped the king to power are men instead of God, the guarantors of the "sacredness" (the term already anachronistic) of the crown. This means political indebtedness and, at this point in history, with the anxiety of lost certainty still sharp, terrible doubt as to whence truth, power, and justice rightfully emanate. The king is no longer sovereign as he must negotiate, in the payment of his political debts, the very essence of his station. At the historical moment of the play, distrust predictably triumphs. Men are guided by the most available counsel, a *personal* sense of justice, or merely, perhaps, their own interests and passions.

In the void left by the fallen hierarchical order Shakespeare dramatizes the birth of modern individualism and, as a model for this, the formation of a Renaissance king (Prince Hal), an entity now of uncertain, largely self-created identity.

Prince Hal's position in the play is central. He represents a future unstigmatized by the actual usurpation. However, he inherits, to be sure, the new political and moral climate created by it. Yet while Henry's planned crusade to the Holy Land will be forever postponed in order to defend his rule from his former collaborators, Hal looks to the future.

It is characteristic of Henry's uncertain world that he knows his son only through hearsay, rumor, and slander. Even the Prince of Wales is suspect. He is widely thought a wastrel, and the king even suspects his son would like him dead. But where is the pattern of virtue for Hal? The king, the usurper, is tainted, of ambiguous virtue at best. He has betrayed, perhaps out of political necessity, even those who helped him to the throne.

In this play Hal is clearly attracted to two figures, Hotspur and Falstaff. Both of these are removed from the medieval ritualistic structures that had once tended to integrate disparate aspects of life: courtesy, valor, honest exchange, loyalty, and the like. A new synthesis of this sort is symbolically enacted in Hal's procession through the experience of, and choices between, the worlds of Hotspur and Falstaff.

For Hotspur life is a constant striving for glory in battle. As has been remarked, time for him presses implacably, considered wasted if not intensely devoted to the achievement of fame. But his is an assertion of the individual enacted outside a traditional frame such as the medieval "quest." Hotspur's character is seen to be extremely limited, however breathtaking his élan may be. For it is finally morbid, loveless, incourteous, and even sexually impotent. He has not the patience to humor the tediousness of Glendower (which costs him, perhaps, his support); his speech is full of death and death's images; he mocks the love of Mortimer and has banished his wife from his bed, too absorbed by his planned rebellion.

Falstaff, on the other hand, is as quick to lie, to steal, to waste time with a whore or drinking wine, as Hotspur is to risk his life for a point of honor. Hal spends most of his time with him, and he seems at times a sort of apprentice to the older man in the "art" of tavern living. This means, for Hal, living intimately with common people, who naïvely call him "boy," and whose unpretentiousness strips him of the artificial defenses he would have among people who understand protocol.

The adventure with the robbery is the image of cowardice as the reputation of Hotspur is the image of valor. Yet both stories are in their ways celebrative. Falstaff's flexible ways are more human, certainly kinder than Hotspur's, kinder even than Hal's. Hal is awkward at joking sometimes, not being sensitive enough to know what is serious, what light. Hotspur has renounced sensitivity to human love; Falstaff has abandoned honor. In schematic terms, it is a synthesis of these two perspectives that Hal must, and in a way does, achieve.

HENRY THE FOURTH, PART TWO

Type of work: Drama
Author: William Shakespeare (1564–1616)
Type of plot: Historical chronicle
Time of plot: 1405–1413
Locale: England
First presented: 1597

As in Henry the Fourth, Part One, *comedy is an outstanding feature of this play, with Falstaff continuing to promise great things for his friends until the touching moment of his death. The pomp and drama common to Shakespeare's historical chronicles permeate the serious parts of the play, and the deathbed scene between Henry IV and Prince Henry is considered among the best in dramatic literature.*

Principal Characters

King Henry IV, England's troubled ruler. Haunted by his action in the deposition and indirectly in the death of his predecessor and kinsman, Richard II, and deeply disturbed by the apparent unworthiness of his irresponsible eldest son, he also faces the external problem of rebellion. He wishes to join a crusade to clear his conscience and to carry out a prophecy that he is to die in Jerusalem; it turns out that he dies in the Jerusalem chamber in Westminster.

Henry, Prince of Wales (Prince Hal, Harry Monmouth), later King Henry V. A boisterous youth surrounded by bad companions, he matures rapidly with responsibility, saves his father's life in battle, and kills the dangerous rebel Hotspur. When he comes to the throne, he repudiates his wild companions.

Sir John Falstaff, a comical, down-at-the-heels follower of Prince Hal. Considered by many to be one of Shakespeare's finest creations, by some to be his greatest, Falstaff is a plump fruit from the stem of the "Miles Gloriosus" of Plautus. He is the typical braggart soldier with many individualizing traits. As he says, he is not only witty himself but the cause of wit in other men. Innumerable pages have been written on whether or not he is a coward. He is a cynical realist, a fantastic liar, a persuasive rascal. Also, he apparently a successful combat soldier. His colossal body, which "lards the lean earth as he walks along," appropriately houses his colossal personality. In the second part of the play, there is some decline of his character, perhaps to prepare the way for Prince Hal, as King Henry V, to cast him off.

Prince John of Lancaster, another of King Henry's sons, who also bears himself well in battle at Shrewsbury. He commands part of his father's forces in Yorkshire and arranges a false peace with the Archbishop of York and other rebels. When their troops are dismissed, he has them arrested and executed.

Humphrey of Gloucester and **Thomas of Clarence,** other sons of Henry IV, brothers of Henry V.

Henry Percy, earl of Northumberland, Worcester's brother. Having had an important share in the deposition of Richard II and the enthronement of Henry IV, he feels that he and his family are entitled to more power and wealth than they receive. He is also influenced to rebellion by his crafty brother and his fiery son. He fails his cause by falling ill or feigning illness before the Battle of Shrewsbury, and he does not appear there. Later he disconcerts Mowbray by withdrawing to Scotland, where he is defeated.

Richard Scroop, Archbishop of York, a principal rebel. He thinks to make peace with King Henry and take later advantage of his weakness, but is tricked by Prince John and executed.

Sir Walter Blunt, a heroic follower of the king. At the Battle of Shrewsbury he pretends to Douglas that he is the king, thus bringing death on himself.

Mistress Quickly, hostess of the Boar's Head Tavern in Eastcheap. She is a silly, voluble woman with a stupendous fund of malapropisms. Easily angered, but gullible, she is a frequent victim of Falstaff's chicanery.

Bardolph, the right-hand man of Falstaff. His fiery nose makes him the butt of many witticisms. Like Falstaff, he is capable of sudden and violent action.

Poins, Prince Hal's confidant. Masked, he and the Prince rob Falstaff and the other robbers at Gadshill and endeavor to discountenance Falstaff at the Boar's Head Tavern afterward.

Peto, another member of the Prince's scapegrace following.

Pistol, a cowardly, loud-mouthed soldier who has a habit of quoting or misquoting snatches of drama. He swaggers and roars until Falstaff is forced to pink him in the shoulder, and Bardolph ejects him from the inn.

Page, a tiny and witty boy given to Falstaff, apparently to make a ridiculous contrast. He makes impudent and spicy remarks on several of the characters.

Doll Tearsheet, a frowzy companion of Sir John Falstaff. She flatters and caresses the old knight, but cannot abide Pistol.

The Lord Chief Justice, a stern man who has dared even to commit the Prince. After Mistress Quickly's complaints, he rebukes Falstaff and demands that he make restitution. Because Falstaff's reputation has increased since the Battle of Shrewsbury, the justice is more lenient than expected.

Justice Shallow, a garrulous old man. Before furnishing Falstaff with a roll of soldiers from his district, he pours out a flood of reminiscences about their wild youth.

Justice Silence, Shallow's cousin.

Davy, Shallow's servant.

Fang and **Snare,** two sergeants called in by the hostess to arrest Falstaff.

Ralph Mouldy, Simon Shadow, Thomas Wart, Francis Feeble, and **Peter Bullcalf,** country soldiers furnished to Falstaff's company.

Rumour, an abstraction who presents exposition at the beginning of the Second Part of "King Henry the Fourth."

Lady Northumberland, Hotspur's mother, Northumberland's troubled wife.

Lady Percy, Hotspur's wife and Mortimer's sister. A charming and playful girl, she is deeply in love with her fiery husband and tragically moved by his death.

Sir John Colville (Colville of the Dale), Lord Mowbray, Lord Hastings, Lord Bardolph, Travers, and **Morton,** rebels against King Henry IV.

The Earl of Westmoreland, The Earl of Warwick, The Earl of Surrey, Gower, and **Harcourt,** followers of King Henry IV.

The Story

After the battle of Shrewsbury many false reports were circulated among the peasants. At last they reached Northumberland, who believed for a time that the rebel forces had been victorious. But his retainers, fleeing from that stricken field, brought a true account of the death of Hotspur, Northumberland's valiant son, at the hands of Prince Henry, and of King Henry's avowal to put down rebellion by crushing those forces still opposing him. Northumberland, sorely grieved by news of his son's death, prepared to avenge that loss. Hope lay in the fact that the Archbishop of York had mustered an army, because soldiers so organized, being responsible to the church rather than to a military leader, would prove better fighters than those who had fled from Shrewsbury field. News that the king's forces of twenty-five thousand men had been divided into three units was encouraging to his enemies.

In spite of Northumberland's grief for his slain son and his impassioned threat against the king and Prince Henry, he was easily persuaded by his wife and Hotspur's widow to flee to Scotland, there to await the success of his confederates before he would consent to join them with his army.

Meanwhile, Falstaff delayed in carrying out his orders to proceed north and recruit troops for the king. Deeply involved with Mistress Quickly, he used his royal commission to avoid being imprisoned for debt. With Prince Henry, who had paid little heed to the conduct of the war, he continued his riotous feasting and jesting until both were summoned to join the army marching against the rebels.

King Henry, aging and weary, had been ill for two weeks. Sleepless nights had taken their toll on him, and in his restlessness he reviewed his ascent to the throne and denied, to his lords, the accusation of unscrupulousness brought against him by the rebels. He was somewhat heartened by the news of Glendower's death.

In Gloucestershire, recruiting troops at the house of Justice Shallow, Falstaff grossly accepted bribes and let able-bodied men buy themselves out of service. The soldiers he took to the war were a raggle-taggle lot.

Prince John of Lancaster, taking the field against the rebels, sent word by Westmoreland to the archbishop that the king's forces were willing to make peace, and he asked that the rebel leaders make known their grievances so that they might be corrected.

When John and the archbishop met for a conference, John questioned and criticized the archbishop's dual role as churchman and warrior. Because the rebels announced their intention to fight until their wrongs were righted, John promised redress for all. Then he suggested that the archbishop's troops be disbanded after a formal review; he wished to see the stalwart soldiers that his army would have fought if a truce had not been declared.

His request was granted, but the men, excited by the prospect of their release, scattered so rapidly that inspection was impossible. Westmoreland, sent to disband John's army, returned to report that the soldiers would take orders only from the prince. With his troops assembled and the enemy's disbanded, John ordered some of the opposing leaders arrested for high treason and others, including the archbishop, for capital treason. John explained that his action was in keeping with his promise to improve conditions and that to remove rebellious factions was the first step in his campaign. The enemy leaders were sentenced to death. Falstaff took Coleville, the fourth of the rebel leaders, who was sentenced to execution with the others.

News of John's success was brought to King Henry as he lay dying, but the victory could not gladden the sad, old king. His chief concern lay in advice and admonition to his younger sons, Gloucester and Clarence, regarding their future conduct, and he asked for unity among his sons. Spent by his long discourse, the king lapsed into unconsciousness.

Prince Henry, summoned to his dying father's bedside, found the king in a stupor, with the crown beside him. The prince, remorseful and compassionate, expressed regret that the king had lived such a tempestuous existence because of the crown and promised, in his turn, to wear the crown graciously. As he spoke, he placed the crown on his head and left the room. Awaking and learning that the prince had donned the crown, King Henry immediately assumed that his son wished him dead in order to inherit the kingdom. Consoled by the prince's strong denial of such wishful thinking, the king confessed his own unprincipled behavior in gaining the crown. Asking God's forgiveness, he repeated his plan to journey to the Holy Land to divert his subjects from revolt, and he advised the prince, when he should become king, to involve his powerful lords in wars with foreign powers, thereby relieving the country of internal strife.

The king's death caused great sorrow among those who loved him and to those who feared the prince, now Henry V. A short time before, the Lord Chief Justice, acting on the command of Henry IV, had alienated the prince by banishing Falstaff and his band, but the newly crowned king accepted the Chief Justice's explanation for his treatment of Falstaff and restored his judicial powers.

Falstaff was rebuked for his conduct by Henry, who stated that he was no longer the person Falstaff had known him to be. Until the old knight learned to correct his ways, the king banished him, on pain of death, to a distance ten miles away from Henry's person. He promised, however, that if amends were made Falstaff would return by degrees to the king's good graces. Undaunted by that reproof, Falstaff explained to his cronies that he yet would make them great, that the king's reprimand was only a front, and that the king would send for him and in the secrecy of the court chambers they would indulge in their old foolishness and plan the advancement of Falstaff's followers.

Prince John, expressing his admiration for Henry's public display of his changed attitude, prophesied that England would be at war with France before a year had passed.

Critical Evaluation

The third play in Shakespeare's second tetralogy, *Henry the Fourth, Part Two*, is based primarily upon Raphael Holinshed's *Chronicles* and an anonymous play, *The Famous Victories of Henry V.* Yet it offers a galaxy of well-rounded characters for whom Shakespeare makes slender use of sources. Clearly a sequel to *Part One*, the play resolves the conflict between the king and the rebellious nobles, a struggle between local and national rule, and continues the development of Prince Hal as an ideal future king. The denial of characters' expectations and assumptions, often marked by dramatic reversals, represents a unifying motif of the play.

Retaining the main plot of the rebellion and the subplot involving Falstaff and his companions found in *Part One*, the drama limits action in favor of rhetoric. As the rebels, under the able leadership of the Archbishop of York, regroup following Shrewsbury, the king's divided army prepares to move against two centers of rebel strength, York and Wales, arousing expectations of decisive battles. Instead, the king returns to London, grievously ill, and later learns that his Welsh enemy Glendower has died, ending the threat in the west. In York, Prince John, a capable but ruthless general, forces the rebels into a deceptive truce and sends their leaders, including the archbishop, to immediate execution. The expected military actions having been averted, the king consolidates his rule, only to discover that he is too ill to continue.

An important theme of the play concerns orderly succession, and while the major characters are troubled by the prospect of Hal as king, their pessimistic expectations prove groundless. Except for Warwick, the king's counselors fear disorder and chaos when Hal succeeds his father.

In an early scene (act 1, scene 2), Falstaff, who has escaped punishment for theft only through holding a military commission, attempts to intimidate the Chief Justice, who has sought to admonish Falstaff about his behavior. The Chief Justice, who sent Hal to prison and thus expects least from his reign, represents a father figure in the drama. Courageous, loyal, and devoid of self-interest, he is the antithesis of Falstaff, a pseudo-father figure. Falstaff, as witty, fertile, and energetic as ever, continues to intimidate and outwit those of his own class, the frequenters of the Boar's Head Tavern and the country bumpkins led by Justice Shallow, yet when he attempts to hold his own with those connected with the court, he is clearly beyond his depth. Falstaff intimates that the king is dying, that Hal will be the next king, and that Hal as Falstaff's friend will act against the Chief Justice. Unmoved by any personal threat, the Chief Justice demonstrates his commitment to law as an ideal. This scene enables the reader to assess the mettle of the Chief Justice and anticipates Prince Hal's three important rhetorical confrontations: with the king, his real father; with the Chief Justice, a just and wise father figure; and with Falstaff, a pseudo-father figure who must be rejected.

In the climactic (act 4, scene 4), Hal is summoned to the dying king's bedside. The king's doubts about him are reinforced when Hal, thinking his father dead, takes the crown from the pillow to meditate on the pain and grief it has brought. Regaining consciousness, the king notices that the crown is missing and concludes that Hal has seized it prematurely. When he returns, the king denounces him for ingratitude, citing numerous instances from the past. But his sense of personal injury gives way to a more important concern—the future of the nation under Hal's rule. He has long considered Hal as foolish and indiscreet as the deposed Richard, and he fears that Hal will recklessly give power and office to Falstaff and friends like him. As a consequence, the unity that the king has achieved will degenerate into riot and anarchy. In an eloquent response, Hal convinces the dying king that he is mistaken about the crown and about Hal's intentions, assuring the king that he intends to follow his example. Following the speech, the king gives Hal advice about governance, urging him to retain trusted counselors like Warwick and the Chief Justice and to involve the nation in a foreign war in order to unify it.

As if to demonstrate how mistaken the king has been in his expectations, Shakespeare introduces an old prophecy. The king has always believed that he would die in Jerusalem. He casually inquires the name of the chamber where he first collapsed and learns that it is called Jerusalem. Recognizing that the prophecy meant something other than he thought, he orders that he be returned there to die.

Following the king's death, all those around Hal, especially the princes, express fear of the future. To reassure them, he deliberately singles out the Chief Justice, who is convinced that he has the most to lose. Formally, he greets the new king. Now assuming the role of the injured party, that of his father in the earlier confrontation, Hal asks whether he can be expected to forget the indignity suffered at the hands of the Chief Justice. The Chief Justice recounts the episode in detail and argues that authority and justice demanded Hal's commitment to prison. Pointedly, he asks Hal to explain how his sentence was unjust. The king's response, moving in its dignity, reassures the Chief Justice that he was correct, confirms him in his office, retains him as counselor, and assures those present that Hal will follow the example of his father.

In remote Gloucestershire, visiting Justice Shallow to extort money from him, Falstaff learns of Hal's succession and immediately sets out with his companions to see the king, assuming that the king longs for him and confidently offering Justice Shallow his choice of offices. Arriving in time for the coronation procession, Falstaff thrusts himself forward and addresses the king with impudent familiarity: "God save thee, my sweet boy!" Hal coldly turns aside and asks the Chief Justice to speak to him. This move astonishes Falstaff, who is confident that the Chief Justice will be punished for his transgressions, and he again directs his speech to Hal. Speaking in his royal person, the king denounces Falstaff as a misleader of youth with too many appetites and banishes him from his company. Incredulous at this reversal and denial of his expectations, Falstaff thinks that the king will send for him in private, but even Justice Shallow discerns the finality of the king's tone.

At the drama's end, the Chief Justice and Prince John approve the handling of Falstaff and suggest that Hal will lead the nation to war with France in order to unify it, as the former king had advised. Hal faces an aristocracy united in support of the monarch, now that the rebel threat has been eliminated. He has separated himself from those who would weaken his authority internally and has gained the loyalty of the king's counselors. It remains for him to unite the commoners through a foreign war, as his father had recommended and as he will do in *Henry the Fifth*.

HENRY THE FIFTH

Type of work: Drama
Author: William Shakespeare (1564–1616)
Type of plot: Historical romance
Time of plot: Early part of the fifteenth century
Locale: England and France
First presented: 1600

In The Life of Henry the Fifth, *Shakespeare skillfully combined poetry, pageantry, and history in his effort to glorify England and Englishmen. Although the characters are larger than life, they also are shown to be flawed like other men; even Henry at last achieves a necessary element of humility.*

Principal Characters

Henry the Fifth, king of England from 1413 to 1422, the wild "Prince Hal" of the "Henry IV" plays. Since his accession to the throne, he has grown into a capable monarch whose sagacity astonishes his advisers. The question of state that most concerns him is that of his right, through his grandfather, Edward III, to certain French duchies and ultimately to the French crown. His claim to the duchies is haughtily answered by the Dauphin of France, who sends Henry a barrel of tennis balls, a jibe at the English king's misspent youth. Having crushed at home a plot against his life fomented by his cousin, the Earl of Cambridge, abetted by Lord Scroop and Sir Thomas Gray, and having been assured by the Archbishop of Canterbury that his claim to the French crown is valid, Henry invades France. After the capture of Harfleur, at which victory he shows mercy to the inhabitants of the town, the king meets the French at Agincourt in Picardy. The French take the impending battle very lightly, since they outnumber the English. Henry spends the night wandering in disguise around his camp, talking to the soldiers to test their feelings and to muse on the responsibilities of kingship. In the battle on the following day, the English win a great victory. The peace is concluded by the betrothal of Henry to the Princess Katharine, daughter of the French king, and the recognition of his claim to the French throne. To Shakespeare, as to most of his contemporaries, Henry was a great national hero, whose exploits of two centuries earlier fitted in well with the patriotic fervor of a generation that had seen the defeat of the Spanish Armada.

Charles the Sixth, the weak-minded king of France.

Queen Isabel, his wife.

Lewis, the dauphin of France, whose pride is humbled at Agincourt.

Katharine of France, daughter of Charles VI. As part of the treaty of peace, she is betrothed to Henry V, who woos her in a mixture of blunt English and mangled French.

Edward, duke of York, the cousin of the king, though called "uncle" in the play. He dies a hero's death at Agincourt.

Richard, Earl of Cambridge, the younger brother of York. Corrupted by French gold, he plots against the life of Henry and is executed for treason.

Lord Scroop and **Sir Thomas Gray,** fellow conspirators of Cambridge.

Philip, duke of Burgundy, the intermediary between Charles VI and Henry V. He draws up the treaty of peace and forces it on Charles.

Montjoy, the French herald who carries the haughty messages from the French to Henry.

Pistol, a soldier, addicted to high-flown language and married to Mistress Quickly, once hostess of a tavern in Eastcheap. Later, Fluellen proves him a coward. When he learns of his wife's death, he resolves to return to England to become a cutpurse.

Nell Quickly, once hostess of the Boar's Head Tavern in Eastcheap and now married to Pistol. It is she who gives the famous account of the death of Falstaff. She dies while Pistol is in France.

Bardolph, now a soldier, formerly one of Henry's companions in his wild youth. In France, his is sentenced to be hanged for stealing a pax.

Fluellen, a Welsh soldier, tedious and long-winded. By a trick, the king forces him into a fight with Williams.

Michael Williams, a soldier who quarrels with Henry while the king is wandering incognito through the camp. They exchange gages to guarantee a duel when they next meet. When the meeting occurs, the king forgives Williams for the quarrel.

John, duke of Bedford, the "John of Lancaster" of the "Henry IV" plays and the younger brother of Henry V.

Humphrey, Duke of Gloucester, youngest brother of Henry V.

The Story

Once the toss-pot prince of Falstaff's tavern brawls, Henry V was now king at Westminster, a stern but just monarch concerned with his hereditary claim to the crown of France. Before the arrival of the French ambassadors, the young king asked for legal advice from the Archbishop of Canterbury. The king thought that he was the legal heir to the throne of France through Edward III, whose claim to the French throne was, at best, questionable. The Archbishop assured Henry that he had as much right to the French throne as did the French king; consequently, both the Archbishop and the Bishop of Ely urged Henry to press his demands against the French.

When the ambassadors from France arrived, they came, not from Charles, the king, but from his arrogant eldest son, the Dauphin. According to the ambassadors, the Dauphin considered the English monarch the same hotheaded, irresponsible youth he had been before he ascended the throne. To show that he considered Henry an unfit ruler whose demands were ridiculous, the Dauphin presented Henry with some tennis balls. Enraged by the insult, Henry told the French messengers to warn their master that the tennis balls would be turned into gunstones for use against the French.

The English prepared for war. The Dauphin remained contemptuous of Henry, but others, including the French Constable and the ambassadors who had seen Henry in his wrath, were not so confident. Henry's army landed to lay siege to Harfleur, and the king threatened to destroy the city, together with its inhabitants, unless it surrendered. The French governor had to capitulate because help promised by the Dauphin never arrived. The French, meanwhile, were—with the exception of King Charles—alarmed by the rapid progress of the English through France. That ruler, however, was so sure of victory that he sent his herald, Montjoy, to Henry to demand that the English king pay a ransom to the French, give himself up, and have his soldiers withdraw from France. Henry was not impressed by this bold gesture, and retorted that if King Charles wanted him, the Frenchman should come to get him.

On the eve of the decisive battle of Agincourt, the English were outnumbered five to one. Henry's troops were on foreign soil and ridden with disease. To encourage them, and also to sound out their morale, the king borrowed a cloak and in this disguise walked out among his troops, from watch to watch and from tent to tent. As he talked with his men, he told them that a king is but a man like other men, and that if he were a king he would not want to be anywhere except where he was, in battle with his soldiers. To himself, Henry mused over the cares and responsibilities of kingship. Again he thought of himself simply as a man who differed from other men only in ceremony, itself an empty thing.

Henry's sober reflections on the eve of a great battle, in which he thought much English blood would be shed, were quite different from those of the French, who were exceedingly confident of their ability to defeat their enemy. Shortly before the conflict began, Montjoy again appeared before Henry to give the English one last chance to surrender. Henry again refused to be intimidated. He was not discouraged by the numerical inferiority of his troops, for, as he reasoned in speaking with one of his officers, the fewer troops the English had, the greater would be the honor to them when they won.

The following day the battle began. Because of Henry's leadership, the English held their own. When French reinforcements arrived at a crucial point in the battle, Henry ordered his men to kill all their prisoners so that the energies of the English might be directed entirely against the enemy in front of them, not behind. Soon the tide turned. A much humbler Montjoy approached Henry to request a truce for burying the French dead. Henry granted the herald's request, and at the same time learned from him that the French had conceded defeat. Ten thousand French had been killed, and only twenty-nine English.

The battle over, nothing remained for Henry to do but to discuss with the French king terms of peace. Katharine, Charles's beautiful daughter, was Henry's chief demand, and while his lieutenants settled the details of surrender with the French, Henry made love to the princess and asked her to marry him. Though Katharine's knowledge of English was slight and Henry's knowledge of French little better, they were both acquainted with the universal language of love. French Katharine consented to become English Kate and Henry's bride.

Critical Evaluation

Henry the Fifth is the last play in the cycle including *Richard the Second*, *Henry the Fourth, Part One* and *Part Two*, and *Henry the Fifth*. The three plays dealing with the reign of King Henry VI, mentioned in the epilogue of *Henry the Fifth*, were written much earlier and are not ordinarily grouped with this cycle. *Henry the Fifth* is itself almost a break with this cycle. However, there are important, if in some ways superficial, elements of continuity.

These elements of continuity are the great historical transition represented by the movement from the reign of Richard II to that of Henry V. Richard and, progressively, the two Henrys, are associated by Shakespeare with the medieval, then the Renaissance, even modern, worldviews. The second dominant element is the formation of Prince Hal, who becomes Henry V, as a Renaissance king.

In *Richard the Second*, the king, Richard, is deposed by Bolingbroke, who becomes Henry IV. What is important is the act of rupturing, symbolized by this usurpation, of an entire conception of humanity governed by ritual and tradition. This conception is sometimes referred to as "the great chain of being." It asserts an utterly planned cosmos which is considered the manifestation of God. To challenge and finally replace this world is a force not clearly understood by its protagonists, but nevertheless defines their own practical and political ambitions as individuals.

The two *Henry the Fourth* plays are continuations of Shakespeare's exploration of the shift in political perspective. The rebellions which follow Henry IV's usurpation had been predicted by Richard II, and seem, indeed, a kind of natural consequence to the break in the structure of authority.

But while his father is engaged morally by that break even to a death troubled by remorse for his "crime," the education of Prince Hal is pursued in a subplot mainly situated in taverns and places of public amusement. Hal's progress, in a few words, is between two extremes of individualism (characteristic of the Renaissance): the obsessive and bloody quest for glory in the person of Hotspur, and the pleasure-seeking, nearly total, incontinence of Falstaff. What he learns from each of them could be said to be the sense of valor and honor of the one, and the wittiness and humanity of the other. But this is so, in a way, only "theoretically," for the nature of the prince in *Henry the Fifth*, as king, is quite removed from either the thesis or the antithesis which precedes him.

An explanation for this can be found symbolically in the two scenes at the end of *Henry the Fourth, Part Two*, where Hal, after his father's death but before his own coronation, takes as his own his father's Lord High Justice, and banishes Falstaff. The Chief Justice had expected—among all who feared Hal would become an irresponsible king—the worst personal damage, as he had punished Hal's rebels in the name of Henry IV. Shakespeare seems to imply, in a very modern sense, that Hal was assuming fully his father's Law. In the historical perspective it is secular law, in contrast to the divine mandate of Richard II.

The opening scenes of *Henry the Fifth* show how secular, indeed, how free and easy, the new law has become. Individualism, in the form of self-interest, rules, but in an orderly, legalistic way. The bishops made the ancient laws fit the needs of their own financial interests and the ambition (concerning the French throne) of King Henry V.

These scenes already suggest a sense of *fait accompli* to the broad transitional process which is, at base, the rise of the bourgeoisie. Thus the play is a kind of break with the others. As a whole it is a kind of apotheosis of the powerful though incipient undercurrent of the times, the collective mentality we have come to ascribe to the bourgeoisie. This play has a lack of moral depth, which derives, perhaps, from a contradiction in bourgeois society. There is the economic base of cutthroat competition and an ideological superstructure of supposedly harmonious relations between men and nations. The loss of the sacred system of exploitation made the contradiction more apparent. The dynamic individualism of the new culture takes on the authority of the old order but sublimates the sense of responsibility into platitudes of doubtful logic.

The bishop is one example of this. The ease with which Henry allows his conscience to be soothed in those scenes is another. Later, he rather cavalierly blames the citizens of Harfleur for the impending destruction of their city, with all the barbaric effects he will not even try to control, by his invading army. Likewise, he shuns, by pure sophistry, any responsibility for the deaths, or souls, of his soldiers. He skirts the question of the justice of the king's cause with the assertion that, in any case, each man's soul is his own worry before God.

Shakespeare presents, then, a society in triumph, but one of atrophied moral sensitivity, escaping always in bad faith. The need to compensate for inner insecurity is shown in the aggressive, even hostile and puerile, clumsiness of Henry's wooing of Katharine. He tells her, on the one hand, that he will not be very hurt if she rejects him, and on the other hand, that she and her father are, in effect, his conquered subjects and have no real choice in the matter. This does not constitute a definite condemnation by Shakespeare of this society, but he does not wholly praise it either. In *Henry the Fifth*, more than in the other plays of the cycle, the moral opacity of the action leaves judgment to the reader's, or spectator's, understanding of history.

HERCULES AND HIS TWELVE LABORS

Type of work: Classical myth
Source: Folk tradition
Type of plot: Heroic adventure
Time of plot: Remote antiquity
Locale: Mediterranean region
First transcribed: Unknown

Not born a god, Hercules achieved godhood at the time of his death because he devoted his life to the service of his fellowmen. Some authorities link Hercules with the sun, as each labor took him farther from his home and one of his tasks carried him around the world and back. Whatever their origin, the adventures remain fascinating stories which can support varied interpretations.

Principal Characters

Hercules (hûr′kyə·lēz), the son of Jupiter and Alcmena. He is a mortal. As a child, he is the object of Juno's jealousy. Through her influence he is commanded to carry out twelve labors, in hopes that he will be killed in accomplishing one of them: (1) he must strangle the Nemean lion; (2) he must kill the nine-headed hydra; (3) he must capture the dread Erymanthian boar; (4) he must capture a stag with golden antlers and brazen feet; (5) he must get rid of the carnivorous Stymphalian birds; (6) he must cleanse the stables of Augeas; (7) he must capture the sacred bull of Minos; (8) he must drive away the carnivorous mares of Diomedes; (9) he must secure the girdle of Hippolyta, queen of the Amazons; (10) he must bring back the oxen belonging to the monster Geryoneus; (11) he must bring back the golden apples of the Hes-perides; and (12) he must bring back Cerberus, the three-headed dog of the Underworld.

Jupiter, (jōō′pə·tər), king of the gods, Hercules' father.

Alcmena (ălk·mē′nē), a mortal woman, Hercules' mother.

Juno (jōō′nō), Jupiter's wife. Jealous of mortal Alcmena, she hopes to cause Hercules' death and thus be avenged.

Eurystheus (yōō·rĭs′thōōs), Hercules' cousin. Acting for Juno, he assigns the twelve labors.

Rhadamanthus (răd′ə·măn′thəs), Hercules' tutor, killed by Hercules when he punishes the boy.

Amphitryon (ăm·fĭt′rĭ·ən), Hercules' foster father. He rears the boy as a shepherd, high in the mountains.

The Story

Hercules was the son of a mortal, Alcmena, and the god Jupiter. Because Juno was hostile to all children of her husband by mortal mothers, she decided to take revenge upon the child. She sent two snakes to kill Hercules in his crib, but the infant strangled the serpents with ease. Then Juno caused Hercules to be subject to the will of his cousin, Eurystheus.

As a child, Hercules was taught by Rhadamanthus, who one day punished the child for misdeeds. Hercules immediately killed his teacher. For this act, his foster father, Amphitryon, took Hercules away to the mountains to be reared by rude shepherds. Early in youth, Hercules began to attract attention for his great strength and courage. He killed a lion single-handedly and took heroic part in a war. Juno, jealous of his growing success, called on Eurystheus to use his power over Hercules. Eurystheus then demanded that Hercules carry out twelve labors. The plan was that Hercules would perish in one of them.

In the first labor Juno had sent a lion to eat the people of Nemea. The lion's hide was so protected that no arrow could pierce it. Knowing that he could not kill the animal with his bow, Hercules met the lion and strangled it with his bare hands. Thereafter he wore the lion's skin as a protection when he was fighting, for nothing could penetrate that magic covering.

In the second labor, Hercules had to meet the Lernaean hydra. This creature lived in a swamp, and the odor of its body killed all who breathed its fetid fumes. Hercules began the battle but discovered that for every head he severed from the monster two more appeared. Finally he obtained a flaming brand from a friend and burned each head as he severed it. When he came to the ninth and invulnerable head, he cut it off and buried it under a rock. Then he dipped his arrows into the body of the hydra so that he would possess more deadly weapons for use in future conflicts.

Hercules captured the Erymanthian boar in his third labor and brought it back on his shoulders. The sight of the wild beast frightened Eurystheus so much that he hid in a large jar. With a fine sense of humor, the hero deposited the captured boar in the same jar. While on this trip, Hercules incurred the wrath of the centaurs by drinking wine which they had claimed for their own. In order to escape from them, he had to kill most of the half-horse men.

In the fourth labor, Hercules had to capture a stag with antlers of gold and hooves of brass. In order to capture this creature, Hercules pursued it for a whole year.

In the fifth labor, Hercules faced the carnivorous Stymphalian birds. Hercules alarmed them with a bell, shot many of them with his arrows, and caused the rest to fly away.

In the sixth labor, Augeas, king of Elis, had a herd of three thousand oxen whose stables had not been cleaned for thirty years. Commanded to clean the stables, Hercules diverted the rivers Alpheus and Peneus through them and washed them clean in one day. Augeas refused the agreed payment and as a result, Hercules later declared war on him.

In the seventh labor, Neptune had given a sacred bull to Minos, king of Crete. Minos' wife, Pasiphaë, fell in love with the animal and pursued it around the island. Hercules overcame the bull and took it back to Eurystheus by making it swim the sea while he rode upon its back.

Hercules' eighth labor was to drive away the mares of Diomedes fed on human flesh. Usually Diomedes found food for them by feeding to them all travelers who landed on his shores. Diomedes tried to prevent Hercules from driving away his herd. He was killed, and his body was fed to his own beasts.

In his ninth labor, Admeta, daughter of Eurystheus, persuaded her father to send Hercules for the girdle of Hippolyta, queen of the Amazons. The Amazon queen was willing to give up her girdle, but Juno interfered by telling the other Amazons that Hercules planned to kidnap their queen. In the battle that followed, Hercules killed Hippolyta and took the girdle from her dead body.

In the tenth labor, Geryoneus, a three-bodied, three-headed, six-legged, winged monster possessed a herd of oxen. Ordered to bring the animals to Eurystheus, Hercules traveled beyond the pillars of Hercules, now Gibraltar. He killed a two-headed shepherd dog and a giant herdsman, and finally slew Geryoneus. He loaded the cattle on a boat and sent them to Eurystheus. He returned afoot across the Alps. He had many adventures on the way, including a fight with giants in the Phlegraean fields, near the present site of Naples.

His eleventh labor was more difficult, for his task was to obtain the golden apples in the garden of the Hesperides. No one knew where the garden was, and Hercules set out to roam until he found it. In his travels, he killed a giant, a host of pygmies, and burned alive some of his captors in Egypt. In India he set Prometheus free. At last, he discovered Atlas holding up the sky. Hercules assumed this task, releasing Atlas to go after the apples. Atlas returned with the apples and reluctantly took up his burden. Hercules brought the apples safely to Eurystheus.

His twelfth, however, was his most difficult labor. After many adventures, he brought the three-headed dog Cerberus from the underworld. He was forced to carry the struggling animal in his arms because he had been forbidden to use weapons of any kind. Afterward, he took Cerberus back to the king of the underworld. So ended the labors of this mighty ancient hero.

Critical Evaluation

Hercules (Latin form of Greek "Herakles," meaning "Hera's, or Juno's, fame") rightfully deserved to rule Mycenae and Tiryns, but because of the machinations of Juno, his cousin Eurystheus had become his lord. Driven mad by Juno, Hercules killed his own wife and children and was required by the Delphic oracle to atone for his crime by becoming King Eurystheus' vassal. Eurystheus originally assigned ten *athloi* (ordeals for a prize), but he refused to count both the killing of the hydra, since Hercules had been assisted by his nephew Iolaus, and the cleansing of the Augean stables, since Hercules had demanded payment. These *athloi* required twelve years and are described above essentially according to Apollodorus, the first or second century mythographer (the third and fourth labors are reversed as are the fifth and sixth). Sometimes the last two labors are reversed, which subtracts from the supreme accomplishment of conquering death, as it were, by returning from Hades. The same twelve exploits were sculpted nearly life-size on the metopes of the Temple of Zeus at Olympia in the mid-fifth century B.C.; four scenes have been reconstructed from the fragments. Euripides perhaps reflects an earlier tradition, which begins with Homer, when he lists encounters with the Centaurs, with Cycnus the robber, and with pirates in place of the boar, the stables, and the bull (*Herakles Mad*).

Nevertheless, the twelve labors are not the extent of Hercules' fame. Apollodorus, Pausanias, and Diodorus Siculus detail the "life" of this folk hero; Ovid briefly recounts the labors and death of the hero in book 9 of the *Metamorphoses* (c. A.D. 8). From their accounts, and from numerous other sources, readers have a wealth of exploits accomplished before, during, and after the labors. Among those before is Hercules' fathering a child by each of the fifty daughters of King Thespius. During the labors, Hercules performed a number of well-known *parerga*, or "side deeds," such as joining Jason's Argonauts in quest of the Golden Fleece. He never completed the journey, however, since he was left at Mysia looking for his lost squire and boy-love Hylas. Among other *parerga* are his rescue of Alcestis from Death after she had volunteered to die in place of her husband, King Admetus of Pherae (see Euripides' *Alcestis*). He also rescued Hesione, daughter of King Laomedon of Troy, who was to have been sacrificed to Poseidon's sea-monster. In Italy he killed the fire-breathing Cacus who had stolen the cattle of Geryon(es) which Hercules was driving back to Eurystheus (see Vergil's *Aeneid*). In Libya, he lifted the giant Antaeus from his mother Earth, from whom he derived his strength, and crushed him. He rescued Prometheus from the rock in the Caucasus and Theseus from the Underworld.

After the labors, Hercules sought to marry Iole, daughter of Eurytus, king of Oechalia, and the man who had taught him archery. Eurytus refused, and Hercules killed the king's son, for which he was sold into slavery to Omphale, queen of Lydia. There he performed numerous feats, including killing a great snake, fathering a child on Omphale, and burying the body of the fallen Icarus, who had flown too near the sun. Freed, Hercules went on to seek revenge on Laomedon and Augeas for their refusal to honor their debts for services rendered. He later married Deianira, whom he soon had to rescue from the lustful Nessus, who instructed Deianira to dip Hercules' tunic into the dying centaur's blood. The wearing of the tunic, she was told, would prevent Hercules (notorious for his *amours*) from loving another. Soon Hercules returned to Oechalia, where he murdered Eurytus and abducted Iole. In desperation and ignorance, Deianira sent the tunic, and as soon as Hercules put it on it began to sear his flesh (since Nessus' blood had been poisoned by an arrow which long ago had been dipped in the Hydra's blood). Hercules' horrible death is vividly described in Euripides' *Trachiniae*.

By the twelve labors, Hercules earned the immortality promised by the Delphic oracle, and so when Hercules died (having mounted his own funeral pyre), Jupiter persuaded all the gods, including Juno, to accept him into the pantheon. He took Hebe ("Youth") to wife and was thereafter universally honored. If Hercules' mythic origins are indeed solar, it is appropriate that he enjoyed apotheosis, or deification, and allegorical union with Youth, since the sun, having passed through the twelve zodiacal constellations, returns each year, renewed in strength. On the other hand, Hercules may well have been the original male consort to a pre-Greek mother goddess (Hera), as his name would imply. Whatever his origins, throughout the ancient world in religion and literature, he was welcomed as the ultimate folk hero, simple but not obtuse, powerful but humane, whose myths symbolized the pains and indignities that even great men, beloved of Jupiter, must undergo to attain undying glory. On him, the Athenians modeled their local hero, Theseus. Numerous other localities variously worshipped Hercules as a hero, if not a god. The Cynics and Stoics admired his attention to duty and hardy self-reliance.

In art, Hercules is a favorite subject—his broad, muscled shoulders draped with the skin of a Nemean lion. Although he gained fame for his archery and physical strength, he is usually represented wielding a knotted club. In Roman art representations of his strength tend toward brutishness, so that he becomes more the gladiator than the noble demigod who courageously submitted to the will and whims of the lesser. More than any other figure, Hercules drew together the mythic experiences of Olympians and Titans, monsters and men, death and immortality.

THE HISTORY

Type of work: History
Author: Herodotus (484–c. 425 B.C.)
Time: 500-479 B.C.
Locale: Greece, Egypt, Asia Minor
First transcribed: c. 430 B.C.

Principal Personages

Croesus, king of Lydia
Solon, an Athenian statesman
Cyrus the Great, king of Persia
Darius, Cyrus' cousin
Xerxes, Darius' son and successor
Leonidas, king of Sparta

"Heredotus, beyng of the citye of Halicarnassus in Greece, wrote and compiled an History to the end that nether tract of time might overwhelme and bury in silence the actes of humayne kind; nor the worthye and renowed adventures of the Grecians and Barbarians (as well others as chiefly those that were done in warre) might want the due reward of immortale fame." So did the unknown "B.R." begin his translation of two of the nine books of Herodotus, "entitled with the names of the nine Muses."

As the first to use the word "history," Herodotus deserves Cicero's title, "Father of History." To be sure, this son of wealthy upper-class parents did not have the historian's critical attitude toward his sources. Interesting anecdotes of the wars between the Greeks and the Persians of the fifth century B.C. found their way into his pages whether he could verify them or not, but he does sometimes hedge and tag certain items as hearsay. From his quotations, he must have read widely. From the details in his descriptions and the comments like "this I saw," he must have visited most of the places he mentions. The true greatness of Herodotus lies in the fact that he was the first important writer to depart from the verse of Homer and others, to produce Europe's first prose literature. Some predecessors had chronicled the beginnings of their small communities or states, but the writings of Herodotus embrace a vaster panorama, not only Greece, but Egypt, Sardis, and Babylon as well. And he looked for the reasons back of the events. His aim was to trace the early rivalries between Greek and barbarian; in the process he recounted the story of many tribes, described the lands they inhabited, and reported many of their interesting customs. Those who want greater accuracy can consult Thucydides (c. 455–400 B.C.), who wrote a half-century later. His work is more objective, but it lacks the color of Herodotus' account.

The Persians maintained that the Phoenicians origi-

nally started the quarrel by kidnapping women from Argos. Later the Hellenes raided the port of Tyre and abducted Europa, the king's daughter. The wars actually started, however, when Croesus, whose magnificent court was visited by Solon, desired to enlarge his empire by conquering some of the Ionian cities of Asia Minor. When he consulted the oracles, he was persuaded at Delphi to gather his allies for an attack on the mainland. The invasion resulted in a stalemate, however, and Croesus returned to Lydia, where his capital, Sardis, was surprised and captured by the Persians. Only a rainstorm, sent by the gods, saved him as he was being burned to death. The same miracle persuaded Cyrus to free his captive after taking possession of some of his vassal states. With them, Cyrus went on to capture Babylon. However, the Massagetae, under Queen Tomyris, were too strong in their resistance and strategy. Book 1, titled Clio, ends with the death of Cyrus.

Book 2, called Euterpe, tells how Cambyses, the son of Cyrus, became king and planned to march against Egypt. The rest of the book is a tourist's guide and history of Egypt from its beginnings to the coronation of Amasis.

Book 3, called Thalia, tells how Cambyses marched against Amasis. The Egyptian king having died in the meantime, the mercenary army of his son was no match for the Persian, who then betrayed his incipient insanity by dishonoring his slain enemies.

Book 4, called Melpomene, introduces Darius, cousin of and successor to Cambyses, who let the barbarous Scythians outwit him into making peace with them.

The next volume, whose Muse is Terpsichore, begins with a plan that failed. Two Paeonian nobles, wishing to be named rulers over their people, brought their beautiful sister to Sardis, where Darius saw her, carrying water on her head, leading a horse, and spinning. Anxious to spread such industry throughout his empire, he had the Paeonians sent throughout Asia Minor. But the book deals largely with the revolt in Ionia, the growth of Athens, and its expedition, encouraged by Aristagoras, against Sardis. Although the capital was captured and burned, Darius rallied and defeated the invaders at Salamis, in Cyprus.

Erato is the Muse of book 6, which tells of a battle fought between 353 Ionian triremes and six hundred Babylonian ships. By dissension among the enemy rather than by his strength Darius defeated them and went on to besiege and conquer Miletus. Again Greek bickering helped him during his march to Athens, but the Athenians, rallying and with a few Plataeans, successfully engaged the forces of Darius at Marathon, on September 14, 450 B.C. The Persians were driven back with a loss of 6,400 dead. The Athenians lost only 192 in the battle.

Book 7, named after Polymnia, Muse of the Sublime Hymn, tells in considerable detail how Darius prepared to revenge his defeat. Fate delayed him; rebellious Egypt sidetracked him, and death ended all his plans. The uncertain Xerxes, succeeding his father to the throne, undertook the Egyptian campaign. After a quick victory, at the head of twenty thousand soldiers he marched on Athens. It took seven days for Xerxes' army to cross the Hellespont bridge, erected by his engineers, and Xerxes, reviewing them, lamented that none would be alive a hundred years hence.

Many Greek cities were quick to surrender. Only Athens, as Herodotus boasts, dared confront the host of Xerxes. Themistocles interpreted the oracle's counsel to defend the city with "wooden walls" as advice to use the two hundred warships originally built for an attack on Egypt. Nature, however, provided a better defense in an east wind that wrecked four hundred Persian galleys along with uncounted transports and provision carriers. However, neither armed forces nor natural obstacles halted Xerxes' army until it reached the Pass of Thermopylae. There, for a day, the Athenians and Spartans checked the Persian host until a traitor revealed another path to the invader. The next day the Persians were again on the march, leaving all the defenders and twenty thousand of their own troops dead behind them.

In book 8, titled Urania, there is an account of Xerxes' march into Athens and the firing of the Acropolis. But the "wooden walls" of the Athenian fleet were victorious at Salamis on September 20, 480 B.C. Winner of the greatest glory was the Persian queen Artemis, who used the confusion of battle to get revenge on another Persian by ramming and sinking his ship. Because Xerxes thought she was attacking an enemy and the Athenians believed she had changed loyalties, everybody lauded her.

Fearing that the Greeks might sail on to destroy his bridge, Xerxes ordered a retreat. From the Asian mainland he sent demands for a peace treaty, promptly refused by both Athens and Sparta.

Calliope is the Muse presiding over book 9. Here the account tells how Mardonios renewed the attack against the Greeks in the hope of sending word of victory back to Xerxes in Sardis. Though temporarily checked by the Thebans, he again entered Athens, whose citizens had fled to Salamis to assemble their allies. When they marched back, Mardonios burned what was left of Athens and retreated.

Except for cavalry skirmishes, neither side wanted to engage in battle until the sacrifices were propitious, but Mardonios' patience broke first, and he fell into a trap at Plataea, where he was killed and his army routed; there were twenty thousand Persian and Boeotian casualties against ninety-one Spartans and fifty-two Athenians killed.

At Thermopylae, Leonidas, the Spartan king, had been crucified and beheaded by the Persians. Certain Greeks wanted to dishonor Mardonios in the same way, but they were told that dishonoring a dead enemy was worthy only of barbarians. Some of the fleeing Persians were pursued and killed at Mycale. Their defeat ended Xerxes' ambitious plan to crush the Hellenes.

THE HISTORY OF THE DECLINE AND FALL OF THE ROMAN EMPIRE

Type of work: History
Author: Edward Gibbon (1737–1794)
Time: 180–1461
Locale: Italy, Persia, Germany, Constantinople, Greece, Africa, Arabia, Turkey
First published: 1776–1788

Gibbon's *The History of the Decline and Fall of the Roman Empire* is the definitive history of the Roman empire from the end of its golden age to its final political and physical disintegration. The massive character of the work, testifying to the years devoted to its composition by its scholar-author, is the first, but most superficial sign, of its greatness. The style—urbane, dramatic, polished—assures its eminent place in literature. Finally, as history, the work stands or falls on the accuracy and depth of its report of events covering more than twelve centuries; and in this respect *The Decline and Fall of the Roman Empire* continues to prevail as the most authoritative study on this theme ever written. Later scholars have challenged minor points or added to the material of the history, but Gibbon's work stands as the source of all that is most relevant in the story of Rome's declining years.

The account begins with a critical description of the age of the Antonines. Gibbon concentrates on the period from 96 to 180, a time which he describes as "a happy period," during the reigns of Nerva, Trajan, Hadrian, and the two Antonines. The first three chapters are prefatory to the body of the work; they establish the claim that Rome was then at the height of its glory as an Empire—it was strong, prosperous, active, with worldwide influence. After the death of Marcus Aurelius, and with the ascent of Commodus (180–192), the Empire began its long and gradual decline. The body of Gibbon's work is devoted to a careful recital of the events that followed.

Gibbon was more interested in recounting the principal events of the Empire's history than he was in analyzing events in an effort to account for the downfall of Rome. But he did not entirely ignore the question of causes. At the close of his monumental history he reports four principal causes of Rome's decline and fall: "I. The injuries of time and nature. II. The hostile attacks of the barbarians and Christians. III. The use and abuse of the materials. And, IV. The domestic quarrels of the Romans."

It is customary for commentators on Gibbon to emphasize the reference to the opposing influences of Christianity and barbarism; and, in particular, some critics have been inclined to charge Gibbon with a lack of sympathetic understanding of the early Christian church. It is clear from Gibbon's narrative and summary statement, however, that the Christian contribution to the eventual downfall of Rome was only part of a complex of causes, and it seems unlikely that the Christian effort would have succeeded if the Roman Empire had not already been in decline.

In any case, it is not so much what Gibbon says as his way of saying it that has proved irritating. In the first place, Gibbon writes as if he were located in Rome; his view of events is from the Roman perspective, although it does not always exhibit a Roman bias. Secondly, his objectivity, when it is achieved, has been offensive to some who so cherish the Christian church that they cannot tolerate any discussion of its faults; it is as if such critics were demanding that Gibbon maintain historical impartiality about the Romans but not about the Christians.

When the *Decline and Fall* first appeared, the chapters on Christianity—chapters 15 and 16—immediately became the objects of critical attack. Gibbon seems to have anticipated this response, for he wrote, "The great law of impartiality too often obliges us to reveal the imperfections of the uninspired teachers and believers of the Gospel; and, to a careless observer, *their* faults may seem to cast a shade on the faith which they professed." Perhaps this word of caution would have pacified the critics had not Gibbon immediately brought into play his urbane sarcasm, so distasteful to the insistently pious: "The theologian may indulge the pleasing task of describing Religion as she descended from Heaven, arrayed in her native purity. A more melancholy duty is imposed on the historian. He must discover the inevitable mixture of error and corruption which she contracted in a long residence upon earth, among a weak and degenerate race of beings."

Obviously, there is no truly impartial judge. Gibbon's tone is acceptable, even proper, to those who share his skepticism; but to others more emotionally involved in the Christian faith Gibbon seems cynical to the point of gross distortion.

Gibbon asks how the Christian faith came to achieve its victory over Rome and the other religions of the world. He rejects as unsatisfactory an answer which attributes Christianity's force to the truth of its doctrine and the providence of God. Five causes of the rapid growth of the Christian church are then advanced: "I. The inflexible, and, if we may use the expression, the intolerant zeal of the Christians. . . . II. The doctrine of a future life. . . . III. The miraculous powers ascribed to the primitive church. IV. The pure and austere morals of the Christians. V. The union and discipline of the Christian republic, which gradually formed an independent and increasing state in the heart of the Roman empire."

In his comments on these five causes Gibbon discusses Jewish influences on the Christian faith and explains how the Roman religion had failed to be convincing in its mythology and doctrine of a future life; but although he admits the persuasive power of the Christian use of the claim of immortality, he speaks with skeptical condescension of the efforts of philosophers to support the doctrine of a future life, and he is sarcastic when he mentions "the mysterious dispensations of Providence" which withheld the doctrine from the Jews only to give it to the Christians. When he speaks of the miracles, Gibbon leaves the impression that the pagans failed to be convinced because no such events actually took place. "The lame walked, the blind saw, the sick were healed, the dead were raised," he writes; but he adds that "the laws of Nature were frequently suspended for the benefit of the church."

Gibbon argues that the emperors were not as criminal in their treatments of the Christians as some Christian apologists have argued. He maintains that the Romans acted only with caution and reluctance after a considerable amount of time and provocation, and that they were moderate in their use of punishments. He offers evidence in support of his claim that the stories of martyrdom were often exaggerated or wholly false, and that in many cases the Christians sought martyrdom by provoking the Romans to violence. Gibbon concludes by casting doubt on the numbers of those punished by death, and he insists that the Christians have inflicted more punishments on one another than they received from the Romans.

Discussion of Gibbon's chapters on Christianity sometimes tends to turn attention away from the historian's virtues: the inclusiveness of his survey, the liveliness of his account, and his careful documentation of historical claims. Gibbon did not pretend that he was without moral bias, but his judgments of the tyrannical emperors are defended by references to their acts. It was not enough for Gibbon to discover, for example, that Septimus Severus was false and insincere, particularly in the making of treaties; the question was whether Severus was forced, by the imperious demands of politics, to be deceitful. Gibbon's conclusion was that there was no need for Severus to be as false in his promises as he was; consequently, he condemns him for his acts. In similar fashion he reviews the tyrannical behavior of Caracalla, Maximin, and other emperors before the barbarian invasion of the Germans.

Gibbon names the Franks, the Alemanni, the Goths, and the Persians as the enemies of the Romans during the reigns of Valerian and Gallienus, when a weakened Empire was vulnerable to attack both from within and without. Perhaps the Empire would have wholly disintegrated at that time had not Valerian and Gallienus been succeeded by Claudius, Aurelian, Probus, and Diocletian, described as "great princes" by Gibbon and as "Restorers of the Roman world."

Several chapters of this massive work are devoted to a recital and discussion of the acts and influence of Constantine I, who reunited the Empire which had been divided under Diocletian and, as a consequence of his conversion to the Christian faith, granted tolerance to the Christians by the Edict of Milan. As a result, the bishops of the church came to have more and more influence on matters of state.

The date 476 is significant as marking the end of the West Roman Empire with the ascent to power of Odoacer, the barbarian chieftain. The remainder of Gibbon's classic story of Rome's decline is the story of the increase of papal influence, the commencement of Byzantine rule, the reign of Charlemagne as emperor of the West, the sacking of Rome by the Arabs, the retirement of the popes to Avignon, the abortive efforts of Rienzi to restore the government of Rome, the return of the popes and the Great Schism, and the final settlement of the ecclesiastical state.

HISTORY OF THE PELOPONNESIAN WAR

Type of work: History
Author: Thucydides (455?–c. 400 B.C.)
Time: 431–411 B.C.
Locale: Greece and the Mediterranean
First transcribed: c. 431–400 B.C.

Principal Personages

Pericles, founder of Athenian democracy
Thucydides, an Athenian general and historian
Demosthenes, the famous orator
Alcibiades, an Athenian general and turncoat
Nicias, an Athenian general
Archidamus, king of Sparta
Brasidas, a Spartan general

In writing his *History of the Peloponnesian War*, Thucydides, content to look for human causes behind results, refused to credit the gods with responsibility for the acts of man. Impartially he chronicled the clash of a military and a commercial imperialism: the land empire of the Spartans confronting the Athenian maritime league. Some have attributed to him an attitude of moral indifference, such as is revealed in his report of the debate between Athenian and Melian ambassadors, but he wrote with no intention of either moralizing or producing a cultural history. He was a military man interested in the vastly different political and economic patterns of Athens and Sparta. Seeing in the modes and ideals of their cultures an explanation of their ways of warfare, he wrote for intelligent readers rather than the ignorant masses.

The eight books of Thucydides' history, divided into short paragraph-chapters, provide a few facts about their author. For instance, in book 4, he refers to himself as "Thucydides, son of Olorus, who wrote this history." He must have been wealthy, for, discussing Brasidas' attack on Amphipolis, he states that the Spartan "heard that Thucydides had the right of working goldmines in the neighboring district of Thrace and was consequently one of the leading men of the city." He also tells frankly of his failure as the commander of a relief expedition to that city and of his twenty years' exile from Athens as punishment. Apparently he spent the years of his exile in travel among the sites of the battles he describes, thereby increasing the accuracy of his details. Students of warfare find that he gives descriptions of the tricks and stratagems of both siege and defense. Not until 404, after the war had ended, did he return to Athens. By tradition he was killed about 400 B.C., either in Thrace for the gold he carried, or in Athens for publicly writing his opinions.

"Thucydides the Athenian wrote the history of the war in which the Peloponnesians and the Athenians fought against one another" are the opening words of this masterpiece of Greek history. "He began to write when they first took up arms, believing it would be great and memorable above all previous wars." After this beginning Thucydides drops into the first person to explain the rivalry of Athens and Sparta, the two great states of Hellas then at the height of their power. He was proud of the advances made by his native Athens over the ways of the barbarians. "In ancient times the Hellenes carried weapons because their homes were undefended and intercourse unsafe." But swords, like the old-fashioned linen undergarments and the custom of binding the hair in knots, had gone out of style by his time.

Rivalry between the two cities was an old story; it had kept Spartans from fighting beside Athenians at Marathon. It took a commercial form, however, when the Lacedaemonians demanded that their allies, the Megarians, be allowed to market their products in Athens. Pericles, orator, statesman, and patron of the arts, took the first step toward breaking his own Thirty Years' Truce, agreed upon in 445 B.C. In a fiery oration he declared that to yield to the Spartans would reduce the Athenians to vassals.

The final break, according to Thucydides, came later. He dates the year (431) according to the calendars of the three leading states: Chrysis had been high priestess of Argos for forty-eight years; Aenesias was ephor of Sparta; and Pythodorus was concluding his archonship in Athens. In that year Thebes, at the invitation of disgruntled Plataean citizens, made a surprise attack on Plataea, a Boeotian ally of Athens.

To understand the situation fully, it is necessary to keep in mind a clash of political concepts that the historian does not mention. In 445 B.C., under Pericles, Athens had become a radical democracy whose policy was to send help to any democratically inclined community. Sparta and its allies were just as eager to promote their conservative oligarchy. To both, self-interest was paramount.

Violation of the truce by Thebes, says Thucydides, gave Athens an excuse to prepare for war. Its walled city could be defeated only by a fleet and Sparta had no fleet. On the other hand, landlocked Sparta could withstand anything except a full-scale land invasion, and Athens had no army. The Lacedaemonians begged their friends in Italy and Sicily to collect and build ships, and Athens sent ambassadors to raise armies and completely surround Sparta. Thucydides was honest enough to admit that public opinion largely favored the Spartans, who posed as the liberators of Hellas.

Sparta moved first by invading the Isthmus of Corinth in 431 B.C. Strife during the winter and summer of the first year (as the historian divided his time) consisted largely of laying waste the fields around the fortified cities. Like many primitive peoples, the Greeks stopped fighting during planting and harvesting. (The entries frequently begin with: "The following summer, when the corn was coming into ear.") The war was also halted for their games, not only the Olympic games of 428 but the Delian, Pythian, and Isthmian games as well.

In the summer of the next year a plague broke out in Athens and raged intermittently for three years. Seven chapters of Book II provide a vivid description, "for I myself was attacked and witnessed the suffering of others." The seriousness of the plague protected Athens because enemy troops were afraid to approach its walls.

The most vivid part of Thucydides' history deals with the Syracuse campaign of 416. An embassy from Egesta, Sicily, sought Athenian help against its rival city of Selinus. The ambitious Alcibiades thought this would be a good excuse for Athens to annex Syracuse. With Alcibiades, Nicias, and Lamachus sharing the command, the best-equipped expeditionary force ever sent from a Greek city sailed for Sicily with 134 triremes, 5,100 hoplites or heavy-armed infantry, 480 archers, and 820 slingers.

Alcibiades had left behind bitter enemies who accused him of defacing sacred statues on the day the fleet sailed.

Though there was no evidence against him, he was ordered home to defend himself. Fearing treachery, he fled to Sparta, where he was warmly welcomed. Informed of the Athenian expedition, the Lacedaemonians sent a military adviser to Syracuse. The Persians offered to outfit a fleet for Alcibiades to lead against Athens. His patriotism outweighed his injured pride, however, and eventually he returned to Athens and won several victories for the city before another defeat sent him again into exile. This occurred, however, after the period covered by Thucydides' history.

Meanwhile, in the campaign before Syracuse, Nicias disregarded the advice of Demosthenes and was defeated on both land and sea. "Of all the Hellenic actions on record," writes Thucydides, "this was the greatest, the most glorious to the victor, and the most ruinous to the vanquished. Fleet and army vanished from the face of the earth; nothing was saved, and out of the many who went forth, few returned home. This ended the Sicilian expedition."

The account of the expedition practically ends Thucydides' history. There is another book, but it does not rise to the dramatic pitch of book 7. Though he lived eleven years after these events and four years after the end of the war, Thucydides did not chronicle its last stages, perhaps because they were too painful. After Alcibiades had been exiled a second time, Sparta starved the Athenians into surrender, and with this defeat their glory faded. For the next thirty years Sparta was the supreme power in Hellas.

As Macaulay wrote, Thucydides surpassed all his rivals as the historian of the ancient world. Perhaps not as colorful as Herodotus, "the Father of History," he was certainly more accurate; and while the annals of Tacitus contain excellent character delineation, the Roman's pages are "cold and poor." Thucydides may be superficial in his observations and shallow in his interpretation of events, but he did accumulate facts and dates and he presented them in a three-dimensional picture of people and places. For this reason his work has survived for more than two thousand years.

THE HOUSE OF THE SEVEN GABLES: A Romance

Type of work: Novel
Author: Nathaniel Hawthorne (1804–1864)
Type of lot: Psychological romance
Time of plot: 1850
Locale: Salem, Massachusetts
First published: 1851

Woven into the ingenious plot of this novel is the theme that the sins of the fathers are passed on to the children in succeeding generations. The book reflects the author's interest in New England history and his doubts about a moribund New England that looked backward to past times.

Principal Characters

Colonel Pyncheon, a stern Massachusetts magistrate who, during the famous witchcraft trials of the seventeenth century, sent to his death a man whose property he coveted for himself. Cursed by his innocent victim, the Colonel died on the day his big new house, the House of the Seven Gables, built on his victim's land, was officially opened to guests.

Matthew Maule, Colonel Pyncheon's victim, who swore that his unjust accuser should drink blood, as Colonel Pyncheon did when he died.

Thomas Maule, the son of Matthew Maule. As the head carpenter building the House of the Seven Gables, young Maule took an opportunity to build a secret recess in which was hidden the deed by which the Pyncheons hoped to claim a vast domain in Maine.

Jaffrey Pyncheon, one of Colonel Pyncheon's nineteenth century descendants and a man like his ancestor in many ways. A judge, a member of Congress at one time, a member of many boards of directors, and an aspirant to the governorship of his state, he is a rich man who through his own efforts has multiplied the fortune he inherited from his uncle. Although he tries to present himself in a good light, Jaffrey Pyncheon is a hard man and not entirely honest. He destroys one of his uncle's wills, which names his cousin Clifford as heir, and he stands by while his cousin is wrongly sent to prison for a murder he did not commit. Convinced that his wronged cousin knows of additional family wealth hidden by their uncle, Jaffrey threatens the broken man with confinement in an insane asylum if the hiding place of the remaining wealth is not revealed. Fortunately for his cousin, Jaffrey dies of natural causes induced by emotion while making his threats.

Clifford Pyncheon, Jaffrey's unfortunate cousin, who serves a thirty-year prison term for allegedly murdering his uncle, who really died of natural causes. A handsome, carefree, beauty-loving man at one time, he emerges from prison three decades later a broken, pale, and emaciated wreck of a human being, content to hide away in the House of the Seven Gables, where he is looked after by his sister Hepzibah and their young cousin Phoebe. Clifford's mind is weakened and his spirit so broken by misfortune that he actually does strange, if harmless, acts, so that Jaffrey's threat to force Clifford into an asylum could be made good. At Jaffrey's unexpected death Clifford feels a great release after having been oppressed by his cousin for so long. Clifford, his sister, and Phoebe Pyncheon inherit Jaffrey's fortune and have the promise of a comfortable life in the future.

Hepzibah Pyncheon, Clifford's spinster sister, who lived alone for many years in shabby gentility in the House of the Seven Gables while her brother was in prison. She has few friends, for she seldom leaves the house, and she is so nearsighted that she always wears a frown, making people think she is a cross and angry woman. After the return of her brother from prison, she sets up a little shop in her house to try to provide for herself and Clifford, to whom she is devoted. Opening the shop is very difficult for her, as she dislikes meeting people and believes that entering trade is unladylike for a member of the Pyncheon family.

Phoebe Pyncheon, a young, pretty, and lively girl from the country. She comes to live with Hepzibah when her mother, a widow, remarries. Phoebe takes over the little cent-shop and makes it a profitable venture for Hepzibah. Phoebe also brings new life to the House of the Seven Gables by cheering it with her beauty and song, as well as by tending the neglected flowers and doing other homely tasks. She is highly considerate of her elderly cousins and spends much of her time entertaining Clifford.

Mr. Holgrave, a liberal-minded young daguerreotypist who rents a portion of the House of the Seven Gables from Hepzibah. An eager, energetic young man of twenty-two, he falls in love with Phoebe Pyncheon, and they are engaged to be married. When Phoebe inherits a third of Jaffrey's large fortune, Holgrave decides to become more conservative in his thinking. It is he who reveals the secret recess hiding the now-useless deed to the vast tract of land in Maine. He knows the secret because he is a descendant of Thomas Maule. In fact, his name is Maule, but he hides his true identity by assuming for a time the name of Holgrave.

Uncle Venner, an old handyman befriended by the Pyncheons. He is one of the few persons of the town to accept Hepzibah and Clifford as friends when they are in unfortunate circumstances.

The Story

The House of the Seven Gables was a colonial house built in the English style of half-timber and half-plaster. It stood on Pyncheon Street in quiet Salem. The house had been built by Colonel Pyncheon, who had wrested the desirable site from Matthew Maule, a poor man executed as a wizard. Because Colonel Pyncheon was responsible and because he was taking the doomed man's land, Maule, at the moment of his execution, declared that God would give the Pyncheons blood to drink. Despite this grim prophecy, the Colonel had his house, and its builder was Thomas Maule, son of the old wizard.

Colonel Pyncheon, dying in his great oak chair just after the house had been completed, choked with blood so that his shirtfront was stained scarlet. Although doctors explained the cause of his death as apoplexy, the townsfolk had not forgotten old Maule's prophecy. The time of the Colonel's death was inauspicious. It was said that he had just completed a treaty by which he had bought huge tracts of land from the Indians, but this deed had not been confirmed by the general court and was never discovered by any of his heirs. Rumor also had it that a man was seen leaving the house about the time Colonel Pyncheon died.

More recently, another startling event had occurred at the House of the Seven Gables. Jaffrey Pyncheon, a bachelor, had been found dead in the Colonel's great oak armchair, and his nephew, Clifford Pyncheon, had been sentenced to imprisonment after being found guilty of the murder of his uncle.

These events were in the unhappy past, however, and in 1850, the House of the Seven Gables was the home of Miss Hepzibah Pyncheon, an elderly, single woman, who let one wing of the old house to a young man of radical tendencies, a maker of daguerreotypes, whose name was Mr. Holgrave.

Miss Hepzibah was about to open a shop in one of the rooms of her house. Her brother Clifford was coming home from the state prison after thirty years, and she had to earn money in some way to support him. On the first day of her venture as a storekeeper, Miss Hepzibah proved to be a failure. The situation was saved, however, by the arrival of young Phoebe Pyncheon from the country. Soon she was operating the shop at a profit.

Clifford arrived from the prison a broken man of childish, querulous ways. Once he tried to throw himself from a big arched window which afforded him almost his only contact with the outside world. He was fond of Phoebe, but Miss Hepzibah irritated him with her sullen scowling. For acquaintances, Clifford had Uncle Venner, a handyman who did odd jobs for the neighborhood, and the tenant of the house, Mr. Holgrave, the daguerreotypist.

The only other relative living in town was the highly respected Judge Pyncheon, another nephew of old Jaffrey Pyncheon, for whose murder Clifford had spent thirty years in prison. He was, in fact, the heir of the murdered man, and he had been somehow involved with Clifford's arrest and imprisonment. For these reasons, Clifford refused to see him when the Judge offered to give Clifford and Hepzibah a home at his countryseat.

Meanwhile, Phoebe had become friendly with Mr. Holgrave. In turn, he thought that she brought light and hope into the gloomy old house, and he missed her greatly when she returned to her home in the country. Her visit was to be a brief one, however, for she had gone only to make some preparations before coming to live permanently with Miss Hepzibah and Clifford.

Before Phoebe returned from the country, Judge Pyncheon visited the House of the Seven Gables and, over Miss Hepzibah's protest, insisted on seeing Clifford, who, he said, knew a family secret which meant great wealth for the Judge. When at last she went out of the room to summon her brother, Judge Pyncheon sat down in the old chair by the fireplace, over which hung the portrait of the Colonel Pyncheon who had built the house. As the Judge sat in the old chair, his ticking watch in his hand, an unusually strong family likeness could be noted between the stern Judge and his Puritan ancestor in the portrait. Unable to find Clifford to deliver the Judge's message, Miss Hepzibah returned. As she approached the door, Clifford appeared from within, laughing and pointing to the chair where the Judge sat dead of apoplexy under the portrait of the old Colonel. His shirt front was stained with blood. The wizard's curse had been fulfilled once more; God had given him blood to drink.

The two helpless old people were so distressed by the sight of the dead man that they crept away from the house without notifying anyone and departed on the train. The dead body of the Judge remained seated in the chair.

It was some time before the body was discovered by Holgrave. When Phoebe returned to the house, he admitted her. He had not yet summoned the police because he wished to protect the old couple as long as possible. While he and Phoebe were alone in the house, Holgrave declared his love for her. They were interrupted by the return of Miss Hepzibah and the now calm Clifford. They had decided that to run away would not solve their problem.

The police attributed the Judge's death to natural causes, and Clifford, Miss Hepzibah, and Phoebe became the heirs to his great fortune. It now seemed certain that Jaffrey Pyncheon had also died of natural causes, not by Clifford's hand, and that the Judge had so arranged the evidence to make Clifford appear a murderer.

In a short time, all the occupants of the House of the Seven Gables were ready to move to the Judge's country estate which they had inherited. They gathered for the last time in the old room under the dingy portrait of Colonel Pyncheon. Clifford said he had a vague memory of something mysterious connected with the picture. Holgrave offered to explain the mystery and pressed a secret spring near the picture. When he did so, the portrait fell to the floor, disclosing a recess in the wall. From this niche, Holgrave drew out the ancient Indian deed to the lands which the Pyncheons had claimed. Clifford then remembered he had once found the secret spring. It was this secret that Judge Pyncheon had hoped to learn from Clifford.

Phoebe asked how Holgrave happened to know these facts. The young man explained his name was not Holgrave, but Maule. He was, he said, a descendant of the wizard, Matthew Maule, and of Thomas Maule, who built the House of the Seven Gables. The knowledge of the hidden Indian deed had been handed down to the descendants of Thomas Maule, who built the compartment behind the portrait and secreted the deed there after the Colonel's death. Holgrave was the last of the Maules, and Phoebe the last of the Pyncheons. Matthew Maule's curse had been expiated.

Critical Evaluation

In reputation, *The House of the Seven Gables* usually stands in the shadow of its predecessor, *The Scarlet Letter*. It is, however, a rich and solid achievement, a Gothic romance whose characters are among Nathaniel Hawthorne's most complex. The author himself thought it, in comparison with the earlier work, "more characteristic of my mind, and more proper and natural for me to write."

In his preface, Hawthorne explicitly states his moral: "The truth, namely that the wrong-doing of one generation lives into the successive ones, and, divesting itself of every temporary advantage, becomes a pure and uncontrollable mischief." This sentiment echoes the biblical adage that "The fathers have eaten sour grapes, and the children's teeth are set on edge." Hawthorne's interest in the heritage of sin was probably whetted by the history of his own family. His first American ancestor, William Hathorne (Nathaniel himself added the *w* to the family name), was a soldier and magistrate who once had a Quaker woman publicly whipped through the streets. William's son John, having, as Nathaniel said, "inherited the persecuting spirit," was a judge at the infamous Salem witch trials, during which a defendant cursed another of the three judges with the cry, "God will give you blood to drink!" Thenceforth, as Hawthorne noted, although the family remained decent, respectable folk, their fortunes began to decline.

The fate of the Pyncheon family of the novel is considerably more dramatic. Matthew Maule's curse on Colonel Pyncheon, who has persecuted him for witchcraft and wrested from him the land on which the seven-gabled house is to be built, is precisely that which Judge John Hathorne had heard in a similar trial. It is apparently fulfilled on the day of the housewarming when Colonel Pyncheon dies of apoplexy, the hemorrhage rising through his throat to stain his white shirt. Hawthorne would have readers believe, however, that such sins as Pyncheon's are not so easily paid for. The family occupies the mansion, but misfortune is their constant lot. There are repeated apoplectic deaths, sometimes heralded by an ominous gurgling in the throat; greed leads Judge Jaffrey Pyncheon, like his ancestor, to participate in a trumped-up trial, this time against his own cousin; and years of pride and isolation have thinned the family blood so that, like the scrawny chickens that peck in the Pyncheon garden, they are an unattractive, ineffectual lot. Judge Pyncheon is a monster who hides his avarice and callousness behind a façade of philanthropy and civic service. Clifford, like Hawthorne's Young Goodman Brown, is a sensitive soul who is unmanned by his confrontation with evil; after years of imprisonment, he is poised on the brink of madness. Hepzibah, a spinster who has spent most of her life waiting for her brother's release, is virtually helpless either to resolve her precarious financial situation or to deal with her malevolent cousin.

Only young Phoebe possesses both goodness and energy. It is significant that she is the "country cousin" whose father married beneath his rank; Hepzibah observes that the girl's self-reliance must have come from her mother's blood. Thus Hawthorne casts his vote for the energizing effects of a democratic, as opposed to an aristocratic, social system; he has Holgrave, the daguerreotypist, support this view with the comment that families should continually merge into the great mass of humanity, without regard to ancestry.

Holgrave is the other fully vital character in the novel. He is one of Hawthorne's most charming creations: a perceptive, adventurous man who has been, it seems, almost everywhere and done almost everything. His conversations with Phoebe reveal him as a radical who believes that the past "lies upon the Present like a giant's dead body," preventing any generation's true fulfillment—a thesis frequently expressed by Hawthorne's contemporary, Ralph Waldo Emerson. Holgrave goes so far as to suggest that institutional buildings should "crumble to ruin once in twenty years, or thereabouts, as a hint to the people to examine into and reform the institutions which they symbolize." He is also a psychologist; his daguerreotypes, which go beyond mere pictorial likeness to expose personality, symbolize his insight into human nature.

At the end of the novel, readers are led to believe that the curse is broken as Phoebe, the last the Pyncheons, plans to marry Holgrave, who turns out to be a descendant of old Matthew Maule. The curse's effects can all be explained naturally: Holgrave observes that perhaps old Maule's prophecy was founded on knowledge that apoplectic death had been a Pyncheon trait for generations. Avarice and cruelty can certainly be passed on by example; and pride, isolation, and inbreeding can account for the "thin-bloodedness" of the once-aristocratic family. Now, as Phoebe, whose blood has already been enriched by plebeian stock, and Holgrave, who has escaped the stifling influence of his own declining family by traveling widely, replace a tradition of hatred with that of love, it seems plausible that the curse may indeed have run its course. Perhaps the chain of ugly events—what Chillingworth of *The Scarlet Letter* termed "dark necessity"—can be terminated by positive acts of good will.

The novel is replete with Gothic characteristics: mystery, violence, a curse, gloomy atmosphere, archaic diction, and visits from the spirit world. Yet, though it is not realistic, it demonstrates what Henry James called Hawthorne's "high sense of reality," in that it reveals profound truths about how the effects of the sins of the fathers are felt by children for generations to come. The ending discloses that, although he recognized the deterministic effects of heredity, environment, and man's predisposition to evil, Hawthorne was essentially a hopeful man who believed that the individual possesses a residuum of will that can cope with and perhaps change "dark necessity."

THE HUNCHBACK OF NOTRE DAME

Type of work: Novel
Author: Victor Hugo (1802–1885)
Type of plot: Historical romance
Time of plot: Fifteenth century
Locale: France
First published: *Notre-Dame de Paris*, 1831 (English translation, 1833)

In this masterpiece of romantic writing, Hugo tells of the love of a grotesquely ugly, hunchbacked deaf-mute for a mysteriously beautiful gypsy dancer. The compelling theme of the novel is that God has created in man an imperfect image of Himself, an image fettered with numerous handicaps, but one which has the potential to transcend its limitations and achieve spiritual greatness.

Principal Characters

Quasimodo (kä·zē·mô′do), a bellringer abandoned in infancy at Notre Dame Cathedral on Quasimodo Sunday, and now deaf from the din of the bells he rings. He is also unspeakably ugly, with tusk-like teeth and a wen over one eye, bristling red hair and eyebrows, and a snoutlike nose. Because of his horrible appearance, the Paris crowd selects him King of Fools for the Epiphany celebrations of 1482. During the carnival he sees Esmeralda, the gypsy who dances before him. When he is later pilloried and beaten, she brings him a drink. From then on he is her devoted slave and on several occasions saves her from Archdeacon Frollo, his benefactor. When she is hanged, through Frollo's scheming, he hurls the priest from the bell tower, then weeps at the death of the only two people he has ever loved. Years later, when the vault of Montfaucon, burial place of criminals, is opened, a skeleton of a woman in white is found in the arms of a misshapen man with a crooked spine. The bones disintegrate into dust when touched.

Esmeralda (ĕz·mä·räl′dä), a lovely and kindhearted gypsy who possesses an amulet by which she hopes to find her family. She and her goat Djali dance to earn their living. Attracted to Captain Phoebus after he saves her from kidnapping, she agrees to a rendezvous in a house on the Pont St. Michel. There the officer is stabbed by Frollo, but Esmeralda is accused of the crime. Under torture, she confesses to everything and is sentenced to be hanged. With Quasimodo's help, however, she escapes while confessing to Frollo and takes sanctuary in the church. Gringoire deceives her into leaving when the mob attacks Notre Dame. For a time she hides in the cell of a madwoman, in reality her mother from whom the gypsies had stolen her. Soldiers of Captain Phoebus' company find her there. Clothed in white, she is hanged at dawn.

Pierre Gringoire (pyâr′ grăn·gwär′), a penniless and stupid Parisian poet who falls in love with Esmeralda.

He writes a play to entertain the Flemish ambassadors at the Palace of Justice. Captured later by thugs and threatened with hanging, he is freed when Esmeralda promises to marry him, but the marriage is never consummated. At Frollo's bidding, Gringoire tempts the girl from her sanctuary and she is captured.

Captain Phoebus de Châteaupers (fā·büs′ də shà·tō·pĕrs′), loved by Esmeralda. He reveals to Frollo his rendezvous with her and is stabbed by the jealous priest. When Esmeralda is accused of the crime, Phoebus allows her be tried for his attempted murder because he is fearful for his reputation if he appears. Soon he forgets the gypsy and marries his cousin, Fleur-de-Lys.

Claude Frollo (klōd frô·yō′), the archdeacon of Notre Dame, once an upright priest but now a student of alchemy and necromancy as well as a pursuer of women. Determined to possess Esmeralda, he sends Quasimodo in disguise to seize her. Her rescue by Captain Phoebus makes him try to kill the officer. When Esmeralda is accused of the crime, he offers to save her if she will give herself to him. Failing to possess her, he shakes with evil laughter as he looks down from Notre Dame at her hanging in the Place de Grève. Here he is found by Quasimodo and hurled to his death on the pavement below.

The Dauphin Charles (dō·fằn′ shärl), of France, whose marriage to Margaret of Flanders occasions the celebration at the beginning of the novel.

Charles, Cardinal de Bourbon (shärl′, kàr·dē·nàl′ də bōōr·bôň′), who provides the dramatic entertainment for the visiting Flemish guests.

Tristan (trĕs·tằn′), who directs Captain Phoebus' soldiers in search of Esmeralda.

Jacques Charmolue (zhäk shär·mô·lü′), the king's attorney in the Ecclesiastical Court that tries Esmeralda for witchcraft.

Philippe Lheulier (fē·lēp′ lû·lyā′), the king's Advocate Extraordinary, who accuses her.

Gudule (gü·dül'), an ex-prostitute whose daughter Agnes had been stolen by gypsies. She has gone mad and for fifteen years has lived in a cell. She fondles constantly a shoe that her baby had worn. When Esmeralda takes refuge there, she produces its companion, and mother and daughter are briefly reunited.

The Story

Louis XI, king of France, was to marry his oldest son to Margaret of Flanders, and in early January, 1482, the king was expecting Flemish ambassadors to his court. The great day arrived, coinciding both with Epiphany and the secular celebration of the Festival of Fools. All day long, raucous Parisians had assembled at the great Palace of Justice to see a morality play and to choose a Prince of Fools. The throng was supposed to await the arrival of the Flemish guests, but when the emissaries were late Gringoire, a penniless and oafish poet, ordered the play to begin. In the middle of the prologue, however, the play came to a standstill as the royal procession passed into the huge palace. After the procession passed, the play was forgotten, and the crowd shouted for the Prince of Fools to be chosen.

The Prince of Fools had to be a man of remarkable physical ugliness. One by one the candidates, eager for this one glory of their disreputable lives, showed their faces in front of a glass window, but the crowd shouted and jeered until a face of such extraordinary hideousness appeared that the people acclaimed this candidate at once as the Prince of Fools. It was Quasimodo, the hunchback bellringer of Notre Dame. Nowhere on earth was there a more grotesque creature. One of his eyes was buried under an enormous wen. His teeth hung over his protruding lower lip like tusks. His eyebrows were red bristles, and his gigantic nose curved over his upper lip like a snout. His long arms protruded from his shoulders, dangling like an ape's. Though he was deaf from long years of ringing Notre Dame's thunderous bells, his eyesight was acute.

Quasimodo sensed that he had been chosen by popular acclaim, and he was at once proud and suspicious of his honor as he allowed the crowd to dress him in ridiculous robes and hoist him above their heads. From this vantage point, he maintained a dignified silence while the parade went through the streets of Paris, stopping only to watch the enchanting dance of a gypsy girl, La Esmeralda, whose grace and charm held her audience spellbound. She had a little trained goat with her that danced to her tambourine. The pair were celebrated throughout Paris, though there were some who thought the girl a witch, so great was her power in captivating her audience.

Late that night the poet Gringoire walked the streets of Paris. He had no shelter, owed money, and was in desperate straits. As the cold night came on, he saw Esmeralda hurrying ahead of him. Then a black-hooded man came out of the shadows and seized the gypsy. At the same time, Gringoire caught sight of the hooded man's partner, Quasimodo, who struck Gringoire a terrible blow. The following moment a horseman came riding from the next street. Catching sight of Esmeralda in the arms of the black-hooded man, the rider demanded that he free the girl or pay with his life. The attackers fled. Esmeralda asked the name of her rescuer. It was Captain Phoebus de Chateaupers. From that moment Esmeralda was hopelessly in love with Phoebus.

Gringoire did not bother to discover the plot behind the frustrated kidnapping, but had he known the truth he might have been more frightened than he was. Quasimodo's hooded companion had been Claude Frollo, archdeacon of Notre Dame, a man who had once been a pillar of righteousness, but who now, because of loneliness and an insatiable thirst for knowledge and experience, had succumbed to the temptations of necromancy and alchemy.

Frollo had befriended Quasimodo when the hunchback had been left at the gates of Notre Dame as an unwanted baby; Quasimodo was slavishly loyal to him. He acted without question when Frollo asked his aid in kidnapping the beautiful gypsy. Frollo, having admired Esmeralda from a distance, planned to carry her off to his small cell in the cathedral, where he could enjoy her charms at his leisure.

As Quasimodo and Frollo hurried back to the cathedral, Gringoire continued on his way and found himself in a disreputable quarter of Paris. Captured by thugs, he was threatened with death if none of the women in the thieves' den would marry him. When no one wanted the pale, thin poet, a noose was lowered about his neck. Suddenly Esmeralda appeared and volunteered to take him, but Gringoire enjoyed no wedding night. Esmeralda's heart belonged to Phoebus; she had rescued the poet only out of pity.

In those days the courts of Paris often picked innocent people from the streets, tried them, and convicted them with little regard for justice. Quasimodo had been seen in his role as the Prince of Fools and had been watched as he stood before the gypsy girl while she danced. There was a rumor that Esmeralda was a witch, and most of Paris suspected that Frollo, Quasimodo's only associate, was a sorcerer. Consequently, Quasimodo was brought into a court, accused of keeping questionable company, and sentenced to a severe flogging and exposure on the pillory. Quasimodo endured his disgrace stoically, but after his misshapen back had been torn by the lash, he was overcome with a terrible thirst. The crowd jeered and threw stones. They hated and feared Quasimodo because of his ugliness.

Presently Esmeralda mounted the scaffold and put her flask to Quasimodo's blackened lips. This act of kindness moved him deeply and he wept. At that same time Frollo had happened upon the scene, caught sight of Quasimodo, and departed quickly. Later Quasimodo was to remember this betrayal.

One day Phoebus was entertaining a lady in a building overlooking the square where Esmeralda was dancing. The gypsy was so smitten with Phoebus that she had taught her goat to spell out his name with alphabet blocks. When she had the animal perform this trick, the lady called her a witch and a sorceress. Phoebus, however, followed the gypsy and arranged for a rendezvous with her for the following night.

Meanwhile, Gringoire happened to meet Frollo, who was jealous of the poet because he was rumored to be Esmeralda's husband. Gringoire, however, explained that Esmeralda did not love him; she had eyes and heart only for Phoebus.

Desperate to preserve Esmeralda for himself, Frollo trailed the young gallant and asked him where he was going. Phoebus said that he had a rendezvous with Esmeralda. The priest offered him money in exchange for an opportunity to conceal himself in the room where this rendezvous was to take place, ostensibly to discover whether Esmeralda was really the girl whose name Phoebus had mentioned. It was a poor ruse at best, but Phoebus was not shy at lovemaking and agreed to the bargain. When he learned that the girl was really Esmeralda, Frollo leaped from concealment and wounded Phoebus with a dagger. Esmeralda could not see her lover's assailant in the darkness, and when she fainted, Frollo escaped. A crowd gathered, murmuring that the sorceress had slain Phoebus. They took the gypsy off to prison.

Now tales of Esmeralda's sorcery began to circulate. At her trial, she was convicted of witchcraft, sentenced to do penance on the great porch of Notre Dame and from there to be taken to a scaffold in the Place de la Grève and publicly hanged.

Captain Phoebus was not dead, but he had kept silent rather than implicate himself in a case of witchcraft. When Esmeralda was on her way to Notre Dame, she caught sight of him riding on his beautiful horse and called out to him, but he ignored her completely. She then felt that she was doomed.

When she came before Frollo to do penance, he offered to save her if she would be his; but she refused. Quasimodo suddenly appeared on the porch, took the girl in his arms, and carried her to sanctuary within the church. Esmeralda was now safe as long as she remained within the cathedral walls.

Quasimodo hid her in his own cell, where there was a mattress and water, and brought her food. He kept the cell door locked so that if her pursuers did break into the sanctuary, they could not reach her. Aware that she would be terrified of him if he stayed with her, he entered her cell only to bring her his own dinner.

Frollo, knowing that the gypsy was near him in the cathedral, secured a key to the chamber and stole in to see Esmeralda one night. She struggled hopelessly, until suddenly Quasimodo entered and dragged the priest from the cell. With smothered rage, he freed the trembling archdeacon and allowed him to run away.

One day a mob gathered and demanded that the sorceress be turned from the cathedral. Frollo was jubilant. Quasimodo, however, barred and bolted the great doors. When the crowd charged the cathedral with a battering ram, Quasimodo threw stones from a tower where builders had been working. When the mob persisted, he poured melted lead upon the crowd below. Then the mob secured ladders and began to mount the façade, but Quasimodo seized the ladders and pushed them from the wall. Hundreds of dead and wounded lay below him.

The king's guards joined the fray. Looking down, Quasimodo thought that the soldiers had arrived to protect Esmeralda. He went to her cell, but to his amazement, he found the door open and Esmeralda gone.

Frollo had given Gringoire the key to her chamber and had led the poet through the cathedral to her cell. Gringoire convinced her that she must fly, since the church was under siege. She followed him trustingly, and he led her to a boat where Frollo was already waiting. Frightened by the violence of the priest, Gringoire fled. Once more, Frollo offered to save Esmeralda if she would be his, but she refused him. Fleeing, she sought refuge in a cell belonging to a madwoman. There the soldiers found her and dragged her away for her execution the next morning at dawn.

Meanwhile, Quasimodo roamed the cathedral searching for Esmeralda. Making his way to the tower which looked down upon the bridge of Notre Dame, Quasimodo came upon Frollo, who stood shaking with laughter as he watched a scene far below. Following the direction of the priest's gaze, Quasimodo saw a gibbet erected in the Place de la Grève and on the platform a woman in white. It was Esmeralda. Quasimodo saw the noose lowered over the girl's head and the platform released. The body swayed in the morning breeze. Then Quasimodo picked up Frollo and thrust him over the wall on which he had been leaning. At that moment, Quasimodo understood everything that the priest had done to ensure the death of Esmeralda. He looked at the crushed body at the foot of the tower and then at the figure in white upon the gallows. He wept.

After the deaths of Esmeralda and Claude Frollo, Quasimodo was not to be found. Then in the reign of Charles VIII, the vault of Montfaucon, in which the bodies of criminals were interred, was opened to locate the remains of a famous prisoner who had been buried there. Among the skeletons were those of a woman who had been clad in white and of a man whose bony arms were wrapped tightly around the woman's body. His spine was crooked, one leg was shorter than the other, and it was evident that he had not been hanged, for his neck was unbroken. When those who discovered these singular remains tried to separate the two bodies, they crumbled into dust.

Critical Evaluation

Victor Hugo, leader of the French Romantic movement, not only could tell a gripping story but also could endow his essentially Romantic characters with a realism so powerful that they have become monumental literary figures. *The Hunchback of Notre Dame* has every quality of a good novel: an exciting story, a magnificent setting, and deep, lasting characterizations. Perhaps the compelling truth of this novel lies in the idea that God has created in man an imperfect image of Himself, an image fettered by society and by man's own body and soul, but one which, in the last analysis, has the freedom to transcend these limitations and achieve spiritual greatness.

Hugo was inspired to write *The Hunchback of Notre Dame* when he accidentally discovered the Greek word for "fate" carved into an obscure wall of one of the Notre Dame cathedral's towers. Each personality in the novel is built around a "fixed idea": Claude Frollo embodies the consuming, destructive passion of lust; Esmeralda, virgin beauty and purity; Quasimodo, unshakable devotion and loyalty. Hugo's characters do not develop but simply play out their given natures to their inevitable conclusions.

In analyzing the character of archdeacon Claude Frollo, it is helpful to understand Hugo's theory that the advent of Christianity in Western Europe marked a new era in literature and art. Because Christianity viewed man as a creature half animal and half spirit—the link between beast and angel—writers could present the ugly and lowly as well as the beautiful and sublime. They could attain a new synthesis —more meaningful because realistic—not achieved by writers of antiquity, who only depicted idealized, larger-than-life subjects on the grounds that "art should *correct* nature." Claude Frollo excludes all human contact from his life and locks himself up with his books; when he has mastered all the legitimate branches of knowledge, he has nowhere to turn in his obsession but to the realm of alchemy and the occult. He is ultimately destroyed, along with those around him, because in denying his animal nature and shutting off all avenues for the release of his natural drives and affections, he falls into the depths of a lustful passion that amounts to madness.

As the novel develops, Quasimodo, the hunchback of the novel's title, is increasingly trapped between his love for the gypsy girl Esmeralda and his love for the archdeacon, his master and protector. These two loyalties finally create an irreconcilable conflict; a choice must be made. When the priest destroys the gypsy, the bell ringer hurls his master from the heights of Notre Dame: a fitting death for Frollo, symbolic of his descent in life from the sublime to the bestial. In Quasimodo, Hugo dramatized his belief that the grotesque and the sublime must coexist in art and literature, as they do in life; the modern writer, he says, "will realize that everything in creation is not humanly beautiful, that the ugly exists beside the beautiful, the unshapely beside the graceful . . . and [he] will ask . . . if a mutilated nature will be the more beautiful for the mutilation." Esmeralda is the embodiment of innocence and beauty. She is held in reverence even by the criminal population of Paris, who vaguely equate her in their minds with the Virgin Mary. Her beauty, however, is too innocent and pure to exist amid the brutality and sinfulness of her world. Of all the men in the book, only one is worthy of Esmeralda: the hunchbacked Quasimodo, who loves her so totally and unselfishly that he would rather die than go on living after she is executed. Appropriately, it is Esmeralda and Quasimodo who are finally "married" in the charnel-house at Montfaucon; theirs is the perfect union of physical and spiritual beauty.

Almost more than by any of the human characters, the novel is dominated by the presence of the cathedral itself. The hero, Quasimodo, understands Notre Dame: He is in tune with her "life." Like her deformed bell ringer, Notre Dame is both ugly and beautiful, both strong and vulnerable, both destructive and life-giving. Quasimodo's monstrous face hides a loving, faithful spirit, while his twisted body conceals a superhuman strength; Notre Dame's beautiful sanctuary is enclosed by a rough exterior encrusted with gargoyles, while her vulnerable treasures are guarded by doors that six thousand maddened vagrants cannot batter down. The cathedral and the ringer work together, almost as one entity, to protect Esmeralda in her room hundreds of feet above the city; to repulse invaders with hurled stones and molten lead; to dash the blasphemous student Jehan to death against the massive walls; and to cast off the priest whose lustfulness defiles the purity of the place.

Setting was all-important to Hugo. As the foremost French Romanticist of the nineteenth century, he was fascinated by the medieval period and strove to reconstruct it in such a way that it would live again in his novel. Hugo believed that a description built on exact, localized details would recapture the mood of a historical period; he also believed that setting was as crucial as characterization in engraving a "faithful representation of the facts" on the minds of his readers. Early in the novel, therefore, Hugo devotes an entire section to a description of the cathedral and the city of Paris; and throughout the book, he offers brief passages of historical background which add verisimilitude to his narrative.

In the preface to his play *Cromwell* (1827), Hugo wrote, "The place where this or that catastrophe took place becomes a terrible and inseparable witness thereof; and the absence of silent characters of this sort would make the greatest scenes in history incomplete in the drama." Thus, in *The Hunchback of Notre Dame*, not only does the cathedral live almost as a personality but so also does the Place de la Grève spread its influence over the lives of all the characters. The cathedral and the square are the two focal points not only of the setting but also of the plot and the theme of the novel; the former embodies the spiritual and beautiful, the latter the lowly and cruel. It is the cathedral that enfolds the humble and loyal Quasimodo and the compassionate Esmeralda, while the square, the scene of poverty, suffering, and grisly death, with its Rat-Hole and its gibbet, claims Esmeralda's lunatic mother and Claude Frollo as its victims.

HUNGER

Type of work: Novel
Author: Knut Hamsun (Knut Pedersen, 1859–1952)
Type of plot: Impressionistic realism
Time of plot: Late nineteenth century
Locale: Norway
First published: *Sult*, 1890 (English translation, 1899)

In Hunger *we find a striking study of a man's mind under stress; realistic in subject, the novel's form and treatment are highly impressionistic. This is the novel that established Hamsun's reputation.*

Principal Characters

The Narrator, a young man down on his luck who writes articles and plays. He is paid so little for his work, however, that he is desperately hungry most of the time. He tells his story in the feverish state of mind that hunger produces. It is a story of his encounters in the town with girls, beggars, pawnbrokers, old friends, policemen, editors, potential employers. Sick with hunger, he is eventually turned out of his room and, finally and violently, out of the house itself. His story ends when he throws into his landlady's face a crumpled envelope containing a half sovereign and a letter from a woman.

An Old Cripple, a penniless beggar to whom the narrator gives a halfpenny after he has pawned his waistcoat to get the money.

Two Women, who are strolling about the town. They take the narrator for a madman because he tells the younger one that she is losing her book, when the fact of the matter is that she carries no book with her. Later, the younger woman—now **The Lady in Black**—befriends the narrator because she is an adventuresome girl who is intrigued with the idea of odd experiences, including those madmen might provide for her.

A Company Manager, an employer who refuses to give the narrator a job as a bookkeeper because he made a careless mistake on his application.

A Policeman, an officer who sends the narrator to the police barracks as a homeless man.

A Pawnbroker, a merchant who laughs at the narrator when he appears at the pawnshop to sell the buttons from his coat.

An Editor, a kindly gentleman who likes the narrator's work but cannot accept his sketch on Correggio. He offers the narrator money, certain that the narrator can repay the obligation with his writing, but the narrator refuses the advance.

A Young Clerk, a boy who gives the narrator change for a crown when he has given the boy only a florin with which to buy a candle. The narrator profits by the clerk's mistake by renting a room in a hotel and buying two full meals.

A Landlady, a woman with a family who patiently waits for the narrator to pay his rent. She finally rents his room to a sailor but allows the narrator to sleep in the house. She throws him out of the house, however, when he protests the children's cruel game of sticking straws into the nose of the paralyzed grandfather who lies in a bed before the fire.

A Beautiful Girl, dressed in silk, who appears to the narrator in a dream. She offers him erotic pleasure.

The Story

I awoke at six o'clock and lay awake in my bed until eight. Hungry, I searched in my packet of odds and ends, but there was not even a crumb of bread. I knew that I should have gone out early to look for work, but I had been refused so often I was almost afraid to venture out again.

At last I took some paper and went out, for if the weather permitted I could write in the park. There were several good ideas in my head for newspaper articles. In the street an old cripple with a big bundle was using all of his strength to keep ahead of me.

When I caught up with him, he turned around and whined for a halfpenny to buy milk. Not having a cent on me, I hurried back to the pawnbroker's dark shop. In the hall I took off my waistcoat and rolled it in a ball. The pawnbroker gave me one and six for it. I found the old cripple again and gave him his halfpenny. He stared at me with his mouth open as I hurried away.

Two women, one of them young, were idly strolling about. When I told the young woman that she would lose her book, she looked frightened and they hurried on. Seeing them standing before a shop window, I went up to them again and told the younger woman that she was losing her book. She looked herself over in a bewildered way; she had no book. I kept following them, but they put me down as a harmless madman.

In the park I could not write a thing. Little flies stuck to my paper. All afternoon I tried to brush them off. Then I wrote an application for a job as bookkeeper. After a day or two, I went to see the man in person. He laughed at my desire to become a bookkeeper because I had dated my letter 1848, years before I was born. I went home discouraged.

On my table was a letter. I thought it a notice from my landlady, for I was behind in my rent. But no, my story had been accepted. The editor said it would be printed right away. He had included half a sovereign in payment. I had written a masterpiece, and I had a half sovereign.

A few weeks later I went out for an evening walk and sat in a churchyard with a new manuscript. At eight o'clock, when the gates were closed, I meant to go straight home to the vacant tinker's workshop which I had permission to occupy, but I stumbled around hardly knowing where I was. I felt feverish because I had not eaten for several days. At last I sat down and dozed off. I dreamed that a beautiful girl dressed in silk waited for me in a doorway and led me down a hall, she holding my hand. We went into a crimson room where she clasped me tightly and begged me to kiss her.

A policeman woke me up and advised me to go to the police barracks as a homeless man. When I got there, I lied about my name and said that it was too late for me to get back to my lodgings. The officer believed me and gave me a private room. In the morning, thinking I was only a young rake instead of a destitute, the police gave me no breakfast ticket. I drank a lot of water, but I could scarcely keep it down.

Faint with hunger, I cut the buttons from my coat and tried to pawn them, but the pawnbroker laughed at me. On the way out, I met a friend bringing his watch to pawn. He fed me and gave me five shillings.

I went to see an editor who critically read my sketch on Correggio. He was kind, saying that he would like to publish my work but that he had to keep his subscribers in mind. He asked if I could write something more to the common taste. When I prepared to leave, he also asked me if I needed money. He was sure I could write it out. Although I had not eaten a real meal for some time, I thanked him and left without an advance payment.

A lady in black stood every night on the corner by my tinker's garret. She would look intently at my lodging for a while and then pass on. After several days, I spoke to her and accompanied her on her walk. She said she had no special interest in my poor garret or in me. When she lifted her veil, I saw that she was the woman I had followed and spoken to about the book. She was merry with me and seemed to enjoy my company.

One night she took me to her home. Once inside, we embraced; then we sat down and began to talk. She confessed that she was attracted to me because she thought I was a madman. She was an adventurous girl, on the lookout for odd experiences. I told her the truth about myself, that I acted oddly because I was so poor. Much of the time I was so hungry that I had a fever. She found my story hard to believe, but I convinced her. She was sympathetic for a moment. I had to leave, for her mother was returning, and I never saw her again.

I awoke sick one morning. All day I shivered in bed. Toward night I went down to the little shop below to buy a candle, for I felt I had to write something. A boy was alone in the store. I gave him a florin for my candle, but he gave me change for a crown. I stared stupidly at the money in my hand for a long time, but I got out without betraying myself.

I took a room in a real hotel and had a chamber to myself and breakfast and supper. About the time my money was gone, I started on a medieval play. The landlady trusted me for quite a while, for I explained that I would pay her as soon as my play was finished. One night she brought a sailor up to my room and turned me out, but she let me go down and sleep with the family.

For some time I slept on a sofa in the entryway; once in a while a servant gave me bread and cheese. In my nervous condition it was hard to be meek and grateful. The break came one evening when the children were amusing themselves by sticking straws into the nose and ears of the paralyzed grandfather who lay on a bed before the fire. I protested against their cruel sport. The landlady flew at me in a rage and ordered me out.

I wandered down to the docks and got a berth on a Russian freighter going to England. I came back to the hotel for my possessions and on the step met the postman. He handed me a letter addressed in a feminine hand. Inside was a half sovereign. I crumpled the envelope and coin together and threw them in the landlady's face.

Critical Evaluation

Knut Hamsun's *Hunger* is part of the literary tradition of impressionistic realism. This so-called "modernistic" school deals in part with subjective reality, and it is particularly in this regard that Hamsun's position in the movement is most secure.

Hunger grew out of the same general environment that produced at the end of the nineteenth century Sigmund Freud and his works. Hamsun delves into the subconscious of his protagonist and comes up with an excellent depiction of madness as seen from inside the mind of the madman. The fact that this madness derives from hunger is significant, because this story of a young journalist literally starving to death is autobiographical to some extent. When Hamsun first presented the manuscript of his work for publication, the editor was so struck by his emaciation that he paid Hamsun an advance on the work, without even bothering to read the title. The story told by the editor is closely paralleled in the novel.

On one level, this is a madman's story of a madman, but on another, it is an account of life in a large city of the industrial age. The city where the action takes place, Christiania, is like any city where people try to sell their art, their literature, or their journalism and discover that there is no market for the best they have to offer. Like modern-day Los Angeles and New York, Christiania is presented as a city full of people who seek fame and fortune but who find instead that they are not capable of reaching their goals. Characteristically, this sort of person often becomes discouraged and is obliged to seek employment in a field far removed from his original ambition. The protagonist of *Hunger* finds himself in just this situation. He is unable to make a career for himself in the environment of a large city of the industrial age.

What lifts this novel from a mere story about a poor boy doing poorly in the big city is Hamsun's description of the internal workings of the human mind. He demonstrates the foolish pride and motiveless behavior that come from a tenuous existence such as the protagonist of the novel leads. The starving man in this novel is one who lies, as the saying goes, even when it is not necessary. He has no regular habits and is at the mercy of his own strange whims. The incident of his persistence in telling a strange woman on the street that she has lost her nonexistent book is a case in point. He lies to save his pride time and again, even in the face of starvation.

Hamsun explains that at the stage when the body is starving, the mind falters and mistakes the inconsequentials of life for life's necessities and cannot distinguish between the two. Hamsun terrifyingly depicts in this book the odd sort of seemingly lucid logic that is to an impartial observer nothing but the worst sort of nonsense.

While Hamsun is able to depict the workings of such a mind broken by the stress of hunger, he does not present a full picture of the book's protagonist. Yet, because of this omission, his study of psychological pressure is all the more vivid and effective. The reader does not know much about the young man in the novel, only that he is starving and periodically reduced to chewing on wood shavings or bits of cloth. Hamsun focuses the reader's full attention upon the issue of the mind, and he does so in a masterful fashion.

On yet a third level, this book is also a portrait of a failure. Indeed, the book is a collection of episodes that are united only by the underlying themes. The book is divided into four sections, each one describing the thoughts and actions of the protagonist as he suffers the effects of starvation at different times. There is, strictly speaking, no beginning or end to the novel. At the end of each section there is a stroke of good luck. The protagonist sells a story or gets a loan. Then the novel immediately jumps to the next episode in his life when he is starving, and the cycle begins again.

At the end of the book the young writer joins the crew of a steamship bound for England. The effect of this ending, however, is one not of escape but of pessimism. There is a flaw in this man's character, one that Hamsun only hints at, that damns him to a continuing cycle of luck and hunger. It is a cycle that the reader at the end of the novel feels can lead eventually only to death.

ILIAD

Type of work: Poem
Author: Homer (c. ninth century B.C.)
Type of plot: Heroic epic
Time of plot: Trojan War
Locale: Troy
First transcribed: Sixth century B.C.

Set during a three-day period in the Trojan War, the Iliad *tells the story of the wrath of Achilles against King Agamemnon. The battle episodes reveal the true characters of the warriors, their strengths and their weaknesses. These figures emerge as human beings not of one era, but of all eras and for all time.*

Principal Characters

Achilles (ə·kǐ′lēz), the son of Peleus and the Nereid Thetis, prince of the Myrmidons, and mightiest of the Achaian warriors at the siege of Troy. At his birth his mother had dipped him in the Styx so that all parts of his body are invulnerable to hurt except the heel by which she held him. A young man of great beauty, strength, courage, and skill in battle, he nevertheless possesses two tragic flaws, an imperious will and a strong sense of vanity. Enraged because King Agamemnon orders him to surrender the maid Briseis, whom Achilles had taken as his own prize of war, he quarrels bitterly with the commander of the Greek forces and withdraws from the battlefield. When the Trojan host attacks, driving the Greeks back toward their ships, Achilles remains sulking in his tent. So great is his wrath that he refuses to heed all entreaties that he come to the aid of the hard-pressed Greeks. When the Trojans begin to burn the Greek ships he allows his friend Patroclus, dressed in the armor of Achilles, to lead the warlike Myrmidons against the attackers. Patroclus is killed by Hector, the Trojan leader, under the walls of the city. Seeing in the death of his friend the enormity of his own inaction, Achilles puts on a new suit of armor made for him by Hephaestus and engages the Trojans in fierce combat. Merciless in his anger and grief, he kills Hector and on successive days drags the body of the vanquished hero behind his chariot, while King Priam, Hector's father, looks on from the walls of the city. When the sorrowing king visits the tent of Achilles at night and begs for the body of his son, Achilles relents and permits Priam to conduct funeral rites for Hector for a period of twelve days. In a later battle before the walls of Troy an arrow shot by Paris, King Priam's son, strikes Achilles in the heel and causes his death.

Hector (hek′tėr), the son of King Priam and Queen Hecuba. As the commander of the Trojan forces he is the greatest and most human of the heroes, an ideal figure in every respect: a skilled horseman, a brave soldier, an able leader, a man devoted to his family and his city, and the master of his emotions under every circumstance. His courage in battle, his courtesy in conference, his submission to the gods, and his sad fate at the hands of revengeful Achilles provide an admirable contrast to the actions of the blustering, cunning, cruel, rapacious Greeks.

Andromache (ăn·drŏm′ə·kē), the devoted wife of Hector and the mother of Astyanax. After the fall of Troy, she was taken into captivity by Neoptolemus, the son of Achilles. Still later, according to the *Aeneid*, she married Helenus, the brother of Hector, and ruled with him in Pyrrhus.

Astyanax (ăs·tī′ə·năks), the young son of Hector and Andromache. During the sack of Troy Neoptolemus killed the child by hurling him over the city wall.

Agamemnon (ăg′ə·mĕm′nŏn), king of Mycenae and the older brother of King Menelaus, husband of the lovely Helen whose infidelity brought about the Trojan War. Courageous and cunning, but often rash and arrogant, as in his treatment of Achilles, he is the commander of the Greeks in the war. He stands as a symbol of the capable leader, without the heroic qualities of the more dramatic warriors who fight under his command. He is killed by his wife Clytemnestra after his return from Troy.

Menelaus (mĕ′nə·lā′əs), king of Sparta and husband of beautiful but faithless Helen, seduced and abducted by Paris, prince of Troy, in fulfillment of a promise made by Aphrodite. He stands more as a symbol than as a man, a victim of the gods and an outraged husband who avenges with brave deeds the wrong done to his honor. At the end of the war he takes Helen back to Sparta with him, and in the *Odyssey* she is shown presiding over his royal palace.

Helen (hĕ′lən), the wife of King Menelaus of Sparta and for nineteen years after her abduction the consort of Paris. Being confined within the walls of Troy, in the company of doting elders, she plays a minor part in the story; and because she is the victim of Aphrodite's promise to Paris, she does not suffer greatly for her actions. Her attempts at reconciliation unwittingly aid the Greek cause in the capture of Troy.

Paris (pâ′rĭs), the son of King Priam and Queen Hecuba. Called to judge a dispute between Aphrodite, Hera, and Athena, he awarded the prize, the golden apple of discord, to Aphrodite, who in turn promised him the most beautiful woman in the world as his wife. Although his love for Helen, the bride he stole from her husband, has become proud devotion to a principle, Paris nevertheless places himself in jeopardy as a champion of the Trojan cause and offers to meet King Menelaus, the injured husband, in single combat. Aphrodite, fearful for the safety of her favorite, watches over him and saves him from harm. An arrow from his bow strikes Achilles in the heel and kills the Achaian warrior. One story says that Paris was slain by a poisoned arrow from the bow of Philoctetes.

Priam (prī′ăm), king of Troy and the beneficent father of a large family. While not a ruler of Agamemnon's stature, he is a man of shrewdness and quiet strength who suffers much at the hands of fate and the rivalry of the gods. Although he does not condone the abduction of Helen by Paris, he is fair in his judgment of both because he knows that they are victims of Aphrodite's whims. His devotion to his son Hector and his pity for all who suffer in the war elevate him to noble stature.

Hecuba (hĕ′kŭ·bə), the wife of King Priam. Her fate is tragic. She witnesses the death of her sons, the enslavement of her daughter Cassandra, who is carried into captivity by Agamemnon, and the sacrifice of her daughter Polyxena to appease the shade of Achilles.

Calchas (kăl′kəs), the seer and prophet of the Greeks. After many animals and men have been slain by the arrows of Apollo, Calchas declares that the destruction is a divine visitation because of Agamemnon's rape of Chryseis, the daughter of Chryses, a priest of Apollo. He counsels that the maid be returned to her father without ransom.

Chryseis (krī′sĭ·əs), a maiden seized by the Greeks during the plundering of Chrysa and given to Agamemnon as a prize of war. Forced by the intervention of Apollo to send the girl back to Chryses, her father, Agamemnon announces that he will in turn take any other maid he desires. His choice is Briseis, the slave of Achilles. Agamemnon's demand leads to a quarrel between the two Greeks.

Briseis (brī′sĭ·əs), a captive slave taken by Achilles as a prize of war. Agamemnon's announcement that he intends to take the girl into his own tent leads to a quarrel between the two men. Forced to surrender Briseis, Achilles and his followers retire from the battlefield and refuse to engage in the fierce fighting that follows. Agamemnon returns the girl to Achilles shortly before the sulking warrior undergoes a change of mood and returns to the fighting in order to avenge the death of his friend Patroclus.

Patroclus (pă·trō′kləs), the noble squire and loyal friend of Achilles. His death at the hands of Hector is merci-lessly and horribly revenged when Achilles and Hector meet in hand-to-hand combat and the Greek warrior kills his Trojan rival. Reasonable in argument and courageous in the face of great odds, Patroclus distinguishes himself in battle and is sublime in his willingness to die for a cause and a friend.

Odysseus (ō·dĭs′ūs), the crafty, middle-aged warrior who with Diomedes scouts the Trojan camp, captures a Trojan spy, Dolon, and kills Rhesus, a Thracian ally of the Trojans. Although a minor figure in the story, he serves as a foil to haughty Agamemnon and sulking Achilles. He and Nestor are the counselors who interpret rightly the will of the gods.

Diomedes (dī′ō·mē′dēz), a valiant Argive warrior who dashes so often and fearlessly between the Greek and Trojan lines that it is difficult to tell on which side he is fighting. He is the companion of Odysseus on a night-scouting expedition in the Trojan camp, and he is the slayer of Pandarus. In hand-to-hand fighting he attacks Aeneas so fiercely that the gods wrap the Trojan in a veil of mist to protect him from Diomedes' onslaught.

Dolon (dō′lən), a Trojan spy captured and put to death by Odysseus and Diomedes.

Nestor (nĕs′tėr), the hoary-headed king of Pylos and a wise counselor of the Greeks. Though the oldest of the Greek leaders, he survives the ten years of war and returns to his own land, where Telemachus, the son of Odysseus, visits him.

Machaon (mə·kā′ən), the son of Asclepius, the famous physician of the ancient world. He is the chief surgeon in the Greek forces. He heals Menelaus after the king of Sparta has been wounded by an arrow from the bow of Pandarus.

Ajax (ā′jăks), the son of Telamon of Salamis and half brother of Teucer. A warrior of great physical size and strength, he uses his mighty spear to hold off the Trojans attempting to burn the Greek ships after breaching the rampart around the vessels. According to a later story he goes mad when Agamemnon, acting on the advice of Athena, awards the armor of dead Achilles to Odysseus.

Teucer (tōō′sĕr), the half brother of Ajax and a mighty bowman. He helps Ajax defend the Greek ships from the attacking Greeks. During one of the Trojan onslaughts he kills the charioteer of Hector.

Glaucus (glô′kəs), a Lycian ally of the Trojans. Meeting him in battle, Diomedes recognizes the Lycian as a guest-friend by inheritance. To seal a covenant between them, they exchange armor, Glaucus giving up his gold armor, worth a hundred oxen, for the brass armor of Diomedes, worth only nine oxen.

Sarpedon (sär·pē′dən), leader of the Lycian allies fighting with the Trojans. He is killed by Patroclus.

Aeneas (ē·nē′əs), the son of Anchises and Aphrodite. A warrior descended from a younger branch of the royal house of Troy, he commands the Trojan forces after the death of Hector. Earlier, while trying to protect the fallen body of his friend Pandarus, Aeneas is struck down by Diomedes, who would have slain him if the gods had not hidden the Trojan in a misty cloud. The wounds of Aeneas are miraculously healed in the temple of Apollo and he returns to the battle.

Pandarus (păn′də·rəs), a Lycian ally of the Trojans and a skilled archer. After Paris has been spirited away from his contest with Menelaus, Pandarus aims at the king of Sparta and would have pierced him with an arrow if Athena had not turned the shaft aside. Diomedes kills Pandarus.

Cassandra (kă·săn′drə), the daughter of King Priam and Queen Hecuba. Gifted with second sight, she is never to have her prophecies believed because she has rejected the advances of Apollo. She becomes Agamemnon's captive after the fall of Troy.

Helenus (hĕ′lə·nəs), the son of King Priam and Queen Hecuba. Like his sister Cassandra, he possesses the gift of second sight. He eventually marries Andromache, the wife of his brother Hector.

Deïphobus (dē·ī′fə·bəs), the son of King Priam and Queen Hecuba. He becomes the husband of Helen after the death of Paris and is killed during the sack of Troy.

Antenor (ăn·tē′nər), the Trojan elder who advises that Helen be returned to the Greeks in order to avoid bloodshed.

Polydamus (pŏ·lĭ·dă′məs), a shrewd, clear-headed leader of the Trojans.

Aphrodite (ă·frō·dī′tē), the goddess of Love. Because Paris had awarded her the fated golden apple and Aeneas is her son, she aids the Trojans during the war.

Apollo (ə·pŏ′lō), the god of Poetry, Music, and Prophecy, as well as the protector of flocks and the patron of bowmen. He fights on the side of the Trojans.

Athena (ə·thē·nə), also called **Pallas Athena,** the goddess of Wisdom. She aids the Achaians.

Poseidon (pŏ·sī′dən), the god of the Sea and Earthquakes. The enemy of the Trojans, he aids the Achaians.

Ares (ā′rēz), the god of War. Because of Aphrodite, he fights on the side of the Trojans.

Hera (hîr′ə), the consort of Zeus and the enemy of the Trojans.

Zeus (zōōs), the supreme deity. He remains for the most part neutral during the war.

Thetis (thē′tĭs), a Nereid, the mother of Achilles, whom she aids in his quarrel with Agamemnon.

Hephaestus (hē·fĕs′təs), the artificer of the gods. At the request of Thetis he makes the suit of armor which Achilles is wearing when he slays Hector.

The Story

The Greeks were camped outside the walls of Troy, in the tenth year of their siege on that city. Agamemnon, king of the Achaians, wanted the maid, Briseis, for his own, but she was possessed by Achilles, the son of Zeus. When Achilles was forced to give up the maid, he withdrew angrily from the battle and returned to his ship. But he won from Zeus the promise that the wrong which he was enduring would be revenged on Agamemnon.

That evening Zeus sent a messenger to the Greek king to convey to him in a dream an order to rise and marshal his Achaian forces against the walls of Troy. When the king awoke, he called all his warriors to him and ordered them to prepare for battle. All night long the men armed themselves in battle array, making ready their horses and their ships. The gods appeared on earth in the disguise of warriors, some siding with the Greeks, some hastening to warn the Trojans. With the army mustered, Agamemnon began the march from the camp to the walls of the city, while all the country around was set on fire. Only Achilles and his men remained behind, determined not to fight on the side of Agamemnon.

The Trojan army came from the gates of the city ready to combat the Greeks. Then Paris, son of King Priam and Helen's lover, stood out from the ranks and suggested that he and Menelaus settle the battle in a fight between them, the winner to take Helen and all her possessions, and friendship to be declared between the warring nations. Menelaus agreed to these words of his rival, and before the warriors of both sides, and under the eyes of Helen, who had been summoned to witness the scene from the walls of Troy, he and Paris began to battle. Menelaus was the mightier warrior. As he was about to pierce his enemy, the goddess Aphrodite, who loved Paris, swooped down from the air and carried him off to his chamber. She summoned Helen there to minister to her wounded lord. Then the victory was declared for Menelaus.

In the heavens the gods who favored the Trojans were much disturbed by this decision. Athena appeared on earth to Trojan Pandarus and told him to seek out Menelaus and kill him. He shot an arrow at the unsuspecting king, but the goddess watching over Menelaus deflected the arrow so that it only wounded him. When Agamemnon saw that treacherous deed, he revoked his vows of peace and exhorted the Greeks once more to battle. Many Trojans and many Greeks lost their lives that day, because of the foolhardiness of Pandarus.

Meanwhile Hector, son of King Priam, had returned to the city to bid farewell to Andromache, his wife, and to his child, for he feared he might not return from that day's battle. He rebuked Paris for remaining in his chambers with Helen when his countrymen were dying because of his misdeeds. While Paris made ready for battle, Hector said good-bye to Andromache, prophesying that Troy would be defeated, himself killed, and Andromache taken captive. Then Paris joined him and they went together into the battle.

When evening came, the Greeks and the Trojans retired to their camps. Agamemnon instructed his men to build a huge bulwark around the camp and in front of the ships, for fear the enemy would press their attack too close. Zeus then remembered his promise to Achilles to avenge the wrong done to him by Agamemnon. He summoned all the gods and forbade them to take part in the war. The victory was to go to the Trojans.

The next day Hector and the Trojans swept through the fields slaughtering the Greeks. Hera, the wife of Zeus, and many of the other goddesses were not content to watch the defeat of their mortal friends. But when they attempted to intervene, Zeus sent down his messengers to warn them to desist.

Fearing his armies would be destroyed before Achilles would relent, Agamemnon sent Odysseus to Achilles and begged the hero to accept gifts and be pacified. But Achilles, still wrathful, threatened to sail for home at the break of day. Agamemnon was troubled by the proud refusal of Achilles. That night he stole to the camp of the wise man, Nestor, to ask his help in a plan to defeat the Trojans. Nestor told him to awaken all the great warriors and summon them to a council. It was decided that two warriors should steal into the Trojan camp to determine its strength and numbers. Diomedes and Odysseus volunteered. As they crept toward the camp, they captured and killed a Trojan spy; then they stole into the camp of the enemy, spied upon it, and as they left, took with them one of the king's horses.

The next day the Trojans pressed hard upon the Greeks and slaughtered many. Both Diomedes and Odysseus were wounded and many warriors killed. Achilles watched the battle from his ship but made no move to take part in it. He sent his friend Patroclus to Nestor to learn how many had been wounded. The old man sent back a despairing answer, pleading that Achilles give up his anger and help his fellow Greeks. At last the Trojans broke through the walls of the enemy, and Hector was foremost in an attack upon the ships.

Meanwhile many of the gods plotted to aid the Greeks. Hera lulled Zeus to sleep, and Poseidon urged Agamemnon to resist the onrush of the Trojans. In the battle that day Hector was wounded by Aias, but as the Greeks were about to seize him and bear his body away the bravest of the Trojans surrounded their hero and covered him with their shields until he could be carried to safety.

When Zeus awakened and saw what had happened, his wrath was terrible, and he ordered Apollo to restore Hector to health. Once again the walls were breached and the Trojans stormed toward the ships, eager to fire them. Zeus inspired the Trojans with courage and weakened the Greeks with fear. But he determined that after the ships were set afire he would no longer aid the Trojans but would allow the Greeks to have the final victory.

Patroclus went to his friend Achilles and again pleaded with him to return to the fight. Achilles, still angry, refused. Then Patroclus begged that he be allowed to wear the armor of Achilles so that the Greeks would believe their hero fought with them, and Achilles consented. Patroclus charged into the fight and fought bravely at the gates of the city. But there Hector mortally wounded Patroclus and stripped from his body the armor of Achilles.

All that day the battle raged over the body of Patroclus. Then a messenger carried to Achilles word of his friend's death. His sorrow was terrible, but he could not go unarmed into the fray to rescue the body of Patroclus.

The next morning his goddess mother, Thetis, brought him a new suit of armor from the forge of Hepaestus. Then Achilles decked himself in the glittering armor which the lame god of fire had prepared for him and strode forth to the beach. There he and Agamemnon were reconciled before the assembly of the Greeks, and he went out to battle with them. The whole plain was filled with men and horses in fierce battle. Achilles in his vengeance pushed back the enemy to the banks of the River Xanthus, and there were so many Trojan bodies choking the river that at length the god of the river spoke to Achilles, ordering him to cease throwing their bodies into his waters. Proud Achilles mocked him and sprang into the river to fight with the god. Feeling himself overpowered, he struggled out upon the banks, but still the wrathful god pursued him. Achilles then called on his mother to help him, and Thetis, with the aid of Hepaestus, quickly subdued the angry river-god.

As Achilles drew near the walls of Troy, Hector girded on his armor. Amid the wailing of all the Trojan women, he came from the gates to meet the Greek warrior. He fled three times around the city walls before he turned to face Achilles' fatal spear. Then Achilles bound Hector's body to his chariot and dragged it to the ships, a prey for dogs and vultures.

In the Trojan city there was great grief for the dead hero. The aged King Priam resolved to drive a chariot into the camp of Achilles and beg that the body of his son Hector be returned to him. The gods, too, asked Achilles to curb his wrath and restore the Trojan warrior to his own people, and so Achilles received King Priam with respect, granted his request, and agreed to a twelve-day truce that both sides might properly bury and mourn their dead. Achilles mourned for Patroclus as the body of his friend was laid upon the blazing funeral pyre. The body of mighty Hector was also burned and his bones were buried beneath a great mound in the stricken city.

Critical Evaluation

The earliest extant work of European literature, Homer's epic poem, the *Iliad*, is also one of the most enduring creations of Western culture. Of the author, or possibly authors, we know nothing for certain. Tradition says that Homer was a Greek of Asia Minor. Herodotus surmised that Homer lived in the ninth century B.C., which seems reasonable in the light of modern scholarship and archaeology. The poet drew on a large body of legend about the siege of Troy, material with which his audience was familiar, and which had been part of a bardic tradition. Homer himself may not have transcribed the two epics attributed to him, but it is probable that he gave the poems their present shape.

The *Iliad* was originally intended to be recited or chanted, rather than read. Its poetic style is vivid, taut, simple, direct, full of repeated epithets and elaborate visual similes. The treatment is serious and dignified throughout, and the total effect is one of grandeur. With Homer we are clearly in the presence of a great poet.

His greatness also reveals itself in the action of the *Iliad*, where, within the scope of a few weeks in the tenth year of the siege of Troy, Homer gives the impression of covering the whole scope of the war by a few deft incidents. The appearance of Helen on the walls of Troy forcibly reminds the reader that she was the cause of the war. The catalogue of ships and warriors calls to mind the first arrival of the Greek army at Troy. The duel between Paris and Menelaus would properly have come in the first years of the war, but its placement in the poem suggests the breakdown of diplomacy which leads to the bloodbath of fighting. And Hector's forebodings of his own death and of the fall of Troy as he talks to his wife, not to mention his dying forecast of Achilles' death, all point to the future of the war and its conclusion. Homer thus gives the rather narrow scope of the poem's immediate action much greater breadth.

However, the *Iliad* is not a mere chronicle of events in the Trojan War. It deals with one specific, and crucial, set of sequences of the war: the quarrel of Achilles with his commander, Agamemnon; Achilles' withdrawal from the war; the fighting in his absence; Agamemnon's futile attempt to conciliate Achilles; the Trojan victories; Patroclus' intervention and death at Hector's hands; Achilles' re-entry to the war to avenge his friend's murder; the death of Hector; and Priam's ransom of Hector's body from Achilles.

This sequence is important in its effect on the war as a whole for two reasons. Without Achilles, their ablest fighter, the Greeks are demoralized even though they have many other powerful warriors. It is plain that Achilles will die before Troy is taken, so the Greeks will have to capture Troy by other means than force in his absence. The second reason is that the climax of the poem, the killing of Hector, prefigures the fall of Troy, for as long as Hector remained alive the Greeks were unable to make much headway against the Trojans.

Achilles is the precursor of the tragic hero according to Aristotle's definition. Young, handsome, noble, courageous, eloquent, generous, and of unsurpassed prowess, his tragic flaw lies in the savage intensity of his emotions. He knows he will die young. In fact, he has chosen to die at Troy, and thereby win a lasting reputation, rather than grow old peacefully. It is precisely his pride, his supreme skill in warfare, and his lust for future glory that make him so ferocious when he is crossed. He has a hard time restraining himself from killing Agamemnon, and a harder time bearing Agamemnon's insult. He puts pride before loyalty when his Greek comrades are being overrun. And only when the war touches him personally, after he has allowed his friend Patroclus to enter the combat and be slain, does he come to terms with Agamemnon. Then his rage against the Trojans and Hector consumes him, and he is merciless in his vengeance, slaughtering Trojans by scores, gloating over Hector's corpse and abusing it, and sacrificing twelve Trojan nobles on Patroclus' funeral pyre. His humanity is restored in the end when, at Zeus's command, he allows old King Priam to ransom Hector's body. Trembling with emotion, he feels pity for the old man and reaches out his hand to him. It is the most moving moment in the epic.

If Achilles lives by a rigid code of personal honor and fights to win a lasting reputation, he has nothing to lose by dying. Life is worthless to him except insofar as it allows him to prove his own value. Yet, paradoxically, this very ethic makes his life more intense and tragic than it might have been. Hector, by contrast, is fighting on the defensive for a city he knows is doomed, and his responsibilities as a leader tend to burden him. He has others to think about, even though he foresees their fate, and all of this hinders his becoming a truly effective warrior like Achilles. Whereas Achilles' life seems tragic, Hector's life is one of pathos of a man fighting heroically against overwhelming odds.

The gods play a prominent part in the *Iliad*, and they are thoroughly humanized, having human shapes, sexes, and passions. Although they have superhuman powers, they behave in an all-too-human fashion—feasting, battling, fornicating, cheating, protecting their favorites from harm. Just as the Greek army is a loose confederation under Agamemnon, so the gods are subject to Zeus. What is interesting is the way superhuman and human forces interact. Divinity penetrates human action through oracles, dreams, visions, inspiration; it shows itself in inspired warfare where a hero seems invincible, and in miraculous interventions where a wounded hero is spirited away and healed. However, the gods are not omnipotent. Zeus can merely delay the death of a man, but in the end must bow to Fate. Further, men have free will; they are not mere puppets. Achilles has deliberately chosen his destiny. Men, finally, have more dignity than the gods because they choose their actions in the face of death, while the gods have no such necessity, being immortal. It is death that gives human decisions their meaning, for death is final and irrevocable. The *Iliad* is a powerful statement of what it means to be human in the middle of vast and senseless bloodshed.

THE IMPORTANCE OF BEING EARNEST

Type of work: Drama
Author: Oscar Wilde (1856–1900)
Type of plot: Comedy of manners
Time of plot: Late nineteenth century
Locale: London and Hertfordshire
First published: 1895

A play built on a pun and plotted around a misunderstanding over the name Ernest, this comic masterpiece is an attack on "earnestness": the Victorian false seriousness which results in priggishness, hypocrisy, and so-called piety.

Principal Characters

Algernon Moncrieff, called **Algy,** a young man of fashion, considerable worldly charm, and a confirmed Bunburyist; that is, he uses an imaginary sick friend's name and condition as an excuse to leave London when he finds his aristocratic aunt, Lady Bracknell, too domineering or her dinner parties too dull. He delights in the artificial, the trivial, the faddish, and he employs them for his own amusement, the only thing about which, as he insists, he is ever serious. Out for a jape, he poses as John Worthing's fictitious brother Ernest in order to court his friend's ward, Cecily Cardew. Though genuinely in love, he never abandons his pose of reckless pretense or his cynically amusing observations on country and city life, manners, fashions, and relatives.

John Worthing, J.P., called **Jack,** Algernon Moncrieff's friend, who poses as Ernest in order to win the hand of Algy's cousin, the Honorable Gwendolen Fairfax, Lady Bracknell's daughter. Also a Bunburyist, he has invented a fictitious brother Ernest, a reprobate who is always getting into scrapes, as an excuse for his frequent visits to London. Jack is serious about most things, especially love. He was a foundling, brought up by a wealthy man who made Jack the guardian of his benefactor's granddaughter, Cecily Cardew. When Jack proposes to Gwendolen he arouses Lady Bracknell's displeasure because he cannot trace his family tree. All he knows is that he had been found abandoned in a leather bag left at Victoria Station. Finally his parentage is traced, and he learns that he is the long-lost son of Lady Bracknell's sister, that Algy is his younger brother, and that his Christian name really is Ernest. This last fact is the most pleasing, for Gwendolen could not possibly love him under any other name.

Lady Augusta Bracknell, Algernon Moncrieff's aunt, a strong-willed woman of fashion who lives only by society's dictates. The hostess at numerous dinner parties to which her nephew is always invited but which he seldom attends, she dominates the lives of all about her in the same compulsive fashion that makes her move only in the best circles. Although Jack Worthing is an eligible young bachelor of means, she rejects his suit of Gwendolen and advises him to find some acceptable relatives as quickly as possible. Although witty in her pronouncements, she never deviates into good sense about the artificial world she inhabits with other snobs and pretenders, but her sense of social superiority is punctured when she learns that her daughter's rejected suitor is her own nephew.

The Honorable Gwendolen Fairfax, Lady Bracknell's daughter, in love with Jack Worthing, whose name she believes to be Ernest. Although she moves in the same conventional snobbish social world with her mother, her outlook is whimsical and rebellious. Determined to marry the man of her choice, she is pleased to discover that Worthing, his parentage revealed, can offer her not only the right name and devotion but also family connections and wealth. She accommodates herself to her good fortune.

Cecily Cardew, an eighteen-year-old girl given to romantic dreams and a diary of fictitious events. She is the ward of Jack Worthing, who had been adopted by her eccentric grandfather. Lovely, determined, rusticated, she is seemingly without guile, but she is in reality as poised as her newly discovered friend, Gwendolen Fairfax. The dupe of her guardian's story that he has a wicked brother named Ernest in the city, she is charmed and won when that supposed roué, as impersonated by Algy Moncrieff, appears in the country. She is also pleased that the man she intends to marry is named Ernest. After learning the truth, she decides that she still loves him, in spite of his having such a name as Algernon.

Miss Letitia Prism, the forgetful authoress of a sentimental three-volume romance, the governess of Cecily Cardew and, earlier, of Jack Worthing. Bent on marriage herself, she contrives to keep her charge's mind on the serious business of learning inconsequentials. In the end she is revealed as the absentminded nurse who twenty-eight years before had placed the infant Ernest Moncrieff in a leather handbag deposited in the cloakroom at Victoria station and the manuscript of her novel in a perambulator.

The Reverend Frederick Chasuble, D.D., an Anglican clergyman who is amenable to performing any rite for anyone at any time, in much the same way that he fits one sermon into many contexts. Delightful in his metaphorical allusions, he meets his match in Miss Prism, whose allusions contain direct revelation of matrimonial intent.

The Story

Algernon Moncrieff, nephew of the aristocratic Lady Bracknell, was compelled by necessity to live a more or less double life, or he would have been completely at the mercy of his Aunt Augusta. To escape from her incredibly dull dinner parties, he had emulated that lady's husband by inventing a wholly fictitious friend named Bunbury, whose precarious state of health required Algy's absence from London whenever his aunt summoned him to attendance.

Algy's friend Jack Worthing was also forced by circumstances into a similar subterfuge for quite a different reason. He had under his care a young ward named Cecily Cardew, who lived at Jack's country place in Hertfordshire under the admirable tutelage of a stern governess, Miss Prism. Jack thought it necessary to preserve a high moral tone in the presence of Cecily and her governess. To escape from this atmosphere of restraint, he invented an imaginary brother named Ernest, who was supposed to be quite a reprobate and whose name and general mode of behavior Jack took over during his frequent trips to London.

To complicate matters, Jack had fallen in love with Gwendolen Fairfax, the daughter of Algy's aunt, Lady Bracknell. Moreover, Gwendolen had fallen in love with him, particularly with his name, Ernest, of which she was very fond. When Lady Bracknell learned "Ernest's" intentions toward Gwendolen, she naturally wanted to know something about his family history. Since Ernest, however, could supply nothing more definite than the fact that he had been found in a leather bag at the Victoria Railway Station, and that his true parentage was quite unknown, Lady Bracknell refused to consider his marriage to her daughter.

Jack realized that the time had come to put an end to Ernest. He even went so far as to appear at the manor house in Hertfordshire in deep mourning for his brother Ernest. His friend Algy, however, "Bunburying" as usual, had preceded him, posing as Earnest. Cecily took an immediate interest in Algy, the supposed brother of her guardian. When Jack and Algy came face to face, Jack promptly announced that his brother Ernest had been unexpectedly called back to London and was leaving at once. Algy, having meanwhile fallen in love with Cecily, refused to leave. Cecily, in turn, confessed that it had always been her dream to love someone whose name was Ernest.

Algy, realizing that his hopes of marrying Cecily depended on his name, decided to have himself rechristened Ernest, and to that effect he called upon the local clergyman, the Reverend Frederic Chasuble, D.D. Jack, however, had preceded him with a like request. Dr. Chasuble had an engagement for two christenings at five-thirty that afternoon.

In the meantime, Gwendolen arrived at the manor house. Because of the mix-up in names, both Gwendolen and Cecily believed that they were in love with the same man, the nonexistent Ernest.

When Jack and Algy appeared together, the real identities of the two pretenders were established. Both girls became furious. At first Jack and Algy upbraided each other for their mutual duplicity, but they finally settled down to tea and consoled themselves by vying with one another to see who could eat the last muffin on the plate. Cecily and Gwendolen at last decided to forgive their suitors, after Algy had admitted that the purpose of his deception was to meet Cecily, and Jack maintained that his imaginary brother was an excuse to go to London to see Gwendolen. Both girls agreed that in matters of grave importance—such as marriage—style and not sincerity was the vital thing.

Lady Bracknell, arriving in search of her daughter, discovered her nephew engaged to Cecily. Afraid that the girl, like her guardian, might possibly have only railway station antecedents, Lady Bracknell demanded to know Cecily's origin. She was informed that Cecily was the granddaughter of a very wealthy man and the heiress to one hundred and thirty thousand pounds. When she willingly gave her consent to the marriage, Jack refused to allow the match, pointing out that Cecily could not marry without his consent until she came of age, and that according to her grandfather's will she would not come of age until she was thirty-five. However, he said he would give his consent the moment Lady Bracknell approved of his marriage to Gwendolen.

There were, however, some objections to Jack as a suitable husband for Gwendolen, the main one being the question of his parentage. The mystery was cleared up to Lady Bracknell's satisfaction by the revelation that Miss Letitia Prism, Cecily's governess, was the nurse who had left Lord Bracknell's house with a perambulator containing a male infant which she had placed in a leather handbag and left in the cloakroom of the Victoria Station. The infant was the son of Lady Bracknell's sister, a circumstance which made Jack Algy's older brother. Jack's

Christian name still had to be determined. It turned out to be—Ernest. The Reverend Chasuble was relieved of his two christenings that afternoon, and Gwendolen was happy that she was actually going to marry a man named Ernest.

Critical Evaluation

The object of unreserved praise since its opening in 1895, Oscar Wilde's last play stands as the triumphant culmination of his career as a playwright. *Lady Windermere's Fan* (1892), *A Woman of No Importance* (1893), and *An Ideal Husband* (1895) had brought Wilde repeated success on the London stage, exposing with epigrammatic wit the shallow and often evil social façades of the time. Then, with the highly desirable Ernest and the incomparable Bunbury, Wilde thrust evil off the stage entirely in favor of fantasy.

Some have claimed that *The Importance of Being Earnest* had no peer since Richard Sheridan's plays (an Irish link); others choose Alexander Pope's *The Rape of the Lock* (1712) as the work nearest in time worthy of comparison. Still others go so far as to deny any genuine comparison possible, finding the play utterly unique, one of a kind, and perfect in itself. Nevertheless, it is worth knowing what Victorian stage conventions are parodied and burlesqued in *The Importance of Being Earnest*, particularly the long-popular melodrama, as well as Gilbert and Sullivan musicals. There has been considerable critical effort expended in sorting out the play's position in the comic genre, whether high or low, farce, parody, or satire, but there has been wholehearted agreement that Wilde achieved his aim of writing brilliant language. Wilde's range allowed him to maneuver language from aphorism to pun and back again, always carrying forward the plot and developing the theme: No life can be lived in earnest without due regard for nonsense.

Wilde was intent, as his biographer Richard Ellmann documents, upon working a renaissance in cultural values in the English-speaking world. His speaking tour of America had had that purpose, and his theatrical ventures were likewise meant to challenge the mindless and complacent Victorian social assumptions. Undoubtedly, Lady Bracknell's thoughts on education were intended to be representative, in their inane way, of prevailing attitudes: "Ignorance is like a delicate exotic fruit; touch it and the bloom is gone. The whole theory of modern education is radically unsound. Fortunately, in England, at any rate, education produces no effect whatsoever." The plays that had been holding the stage since the Theater Act of 1843 were of two sorts, each for a separate audience: the suspense-packed, sentimental, morally simplistic melodramas, which incorporated the formulas of the romance, were the popular fare for the lower middle class; the spectacular Shakespearean stagings were for the fashionable upper middle class.

Wilde felt confident of his ability to challenge the likes of Arthur Pinero and Henry Arthur Jones, and his assurance was borne out in a succession of well-attended and acclaimed plays, the last of which he drafted in three weeks. George Bernard Shaw, the only newspaper critic who disliked *The Importance of Being Earnest*, was also intent on something new for the London stage, which he found in the plays of Henrik Ibsen. Wilde identified his chief difference from Shaw and Ibsen as one of purpose, his being a "verbal ricochet" expressing "a conflict between our artistic sympathies and our moral judgment." For Wilde, brilliant dialogue was essential to the examination of cultural values he had in mind.

Thematically, the play explicitly confronts the hypocrisy and sentimentality at the heart of Victorian values. The play's subtitle reveals Wilde's intention: *A Trivial Play for Serious People*. the trivial pursuit of both Jack and Algy is a game called Bunburying. When Jack vows that he will get rid of his invented brother Ernest once he has married Gwendolen, Algy sagely warns that a married couple need a Bunbury more than ever. The women in the play indulge in their own particular trivialities, one of which is keeping fictionalized diaries, and another (a coincidence necessary to both theme and plot), an irrational attachment to the name Ernest. "We live in an age of ideals," Gwendolen explains to her Ernest (actually Jack) in act 1; and though she may have confused ideals with romantic nonsense, she is unshakably determined to marry someone of that name because it "inspires absolute confidence." It is not simply that the serious contends with the frivolous in the play, but that the serious becomes the frivolous, and vice versa. As act 1 comes to a close, Jack is warning Algy that his friend Bunbury will get him into "a serious scrape one day." To which Algernon replies, "I love scrapes. They are the only things that are never serious." When Jack protests, "You never talk anything but nonsense," Algy insists, "Nobody ever does."

What is abundantly clear as the play proceeds is that everyone is laboring, some more or less consciously, under a pretense of earnestness, motivated by the need for social acceptance, a universal need. Furthermore, no one is really fooling anybody else. Algy sees through Jack's story about an aunt named Cecily who gave him his cigarette case, Lady Bracknell sees through her nephew Algy's story about the ailing Bunbury, and Gwendolen sees through Ernest/Jack's comments on the weather. If these individuals are living by fictions, they are shared fictions; everyone accepts Lane's explanation that there were no cucumbers in the market, "not even for ready money"—even though the audience watched as Algy and Jack devoured a plateful of cucumber sandwiches not five minutes earlier.

In act 2, the two men are still competing, this time for the title of greatest pretender, as Jack appears in darkest mourning for his recently departed brother Ernest, and then Algy, dressed in one of his Bunburying suits as the younger brother himself, the prodigal home for forgiveness. The women, surviving their initial shock at hearing their fiancés' actual Christian names, decide to crush firmly any doubts they feel about the men's integrity. Gwendolen sums the matter up neatly: "In matters of grave importance, style, not sincerity is the vital thing." Finally, the play that begins by throwing a satirical light on social fabrications of all kinds ends with the protagonist apologizing for unknowingly, all his life, telling the truth. Paradoxically, hypocrisy and misrepresentation, however ridiculous, are central to social well-being.

The Importance of Being Earnest is a play that needs to be listened to, either on recording or in live performance, for the considerable impact of its language. Wilde had been practicing his epigrammatic talents since his Oxford days, and he began playing aphorisms off of platitudes as early as *Lady Windermere's Fan*. A Wilde trademark is the unexpected reversal of a well-worn phrase, as in this plea from Algy that Jack account for the inscription, "From little Cecily," in his cigarette case: "Now produce your explanation, and pray make it improbable." When Jack promises a perfectly simple explanation, Algy pompously intones, "The truth is rarely pure and never simple." With something as seemingly simple as a shift in emphasis, a play on words, or a shifting tone of voice, Wilde keeps the laughter coming, as when Lady Bracknell, upon hearing that Jack has lost his parents, comments suspiciously, "To lose one parent, Mr. Worthing, may be regarded a misfortune. To lose both looks like carelessness." Ingeniously clever plotting is matched by scintillating dialogue—sparkling repartee, devilish maxims, delightful non sequiturs—and over all looms the gigantic pun of earnest/Ernest.

It is dangerous to attempt the classification of Wilde's masterpiece beyond the level of comedy, but it is important to make the attempt. Can it really be a farce with such a prominent plot, an upper-class social scheme, and such intellectual amusement? On the other hand, how can the burlesque be ignored? The question becomes a test of taste and intelligence when the distinction between trivializing the serious and satirizing the sentimental and meretricious emerges. When Lady Bracknell learns that Cecily Cardew is to inherit one hundred thirty thousand pounds, she want a closer look at the young woman: "There are distinct social possibilities in your profile," the indomitable matron says to Mr. Worthing's ward, "The two weak points in our age are its want of principle and its want of profile." The scope of the satire here is broader than social hypocrisy; in Lady Bracknell's relentless matchmaking, civilization itself is the target. The answer could be that Wilde was drawing on his considerable resources within the broadest reaches of comedy to express what he had come to believe at Oxford, that truth implied its opposite, that for a thing to be true in art, its opposite had also to be true.

One solution to the question of genre, and a valid one, is the comedy of manners, a category that accommodates the highly sophisticated society, the satire, and the wit, and can even be adapted to self-parody. As H. G. Wells perceptively noted in his review of the play, so much of what is funny about *The Importance of Being Earnest* is its theatrical satire. The romance formula reaches preposterous dimensions when Jack and Algy, instead of a duel, engage in a muffin-eating contest, the befuddled attempts at being rechristened parody the stock regeneration theme, and the wicked brother is merely Algy. It was the mediocrity of late Victorian fantasies, of their theater, that Wilde was scoring, while presenting them with the real thing.

IN MEMORIAM

Type of work: Elegy
Author: Alfred, Lord Tennyson (1809–1892)
First published: 1850

In Memoriam A.H.H., Obiit MDCCC-XXXIII, unquestionably one of the greatest elegies of English literature, records the intellectual, emotional, religious, and aesthetic changes Tennyson underwent in a sixteen-year period following the early and tragic death of his closest friend, Arthur Henry Hallam, in Vienna, on September 15, 1833. The year *In Memoriam* was first published, 1850, was also the year Tennyson married Emily Sellwood and succeeded Wordsworth as Poet Laureate.

In Memoriam represents the chief Victorian conflict between science and faith more than any work of its era; and Tennyson's attempt to reconcile the religious doubts arising from his personal sorrow and the effects of pre-Darwinian theories of evolution was hailed by thinkers of his time as an intellectual landmark. The cyclic change, the turn from private grief and despair to the larger public vision and concern for wider, social issues, that can be found in this poem reflects Tennyson's growing acceptance and reconciliation with the problems of his age.

It appears that Tennyson did not conceive publishing the one-hundred-thirty-one lyrics of *In Memoriam* until late in the 1840s, when he brought them together as one poem, arranging them so as to reflect in the three-year time scheme of the poem the sixteen-year period of his life which they actually represent. Since these lyrics were written over a long time span, they vary considerably in tone and mood, thus dramatizing lyrically Tennyson's psychological condition. Though many organizational schemes have been offered, the most generally accepted scheme views the poem as illustrating a movement from initial grief (I-XXVII); to philosophic doubt and despair (XXVIII-LXXVII); to rising hope (LXXVIII-CIII); to affirmation of faith (CIV-CXXXI). But the actual growth is more subtle than this and requires close attention to repeated images, such as the two yew tree poems or the two visits to Hallam's house.

The "Prologue," dated 1849, and addressed to "Strong Son of God, immortal Love," expresses the poet's conviction that faith, not knowledge, leads to a harmonious union of the intellectual and the spiritual. The first section then relates the poet's nearly complete self-absorption in grief, but even here we notice a change, evident for example in the difference between "I held it truth" (I) to "I hold it true" (XXVII). Though Love provides a "higher life" for man hereafter, few can find immediate comfort for present loss in this promise of future tranquility. Nevertheless, the poet affirms his belief that "T'is better to have loved and lost/ Than never to have loved at all." This acceptance of his experience despite its accompanying sorrow comes only after intervening poems reveal the true depth of his despair; his identification, for instance, with the yew tree, a symbol of death, shows the poet's marked conviction that he, like the yew tree which is not subject to seasonal changes, is imprisoned in grief and can merely endure in "stubborn hardihood."

This fellowship with "Sorrow" (III) induces an intellectual despair and alienates him from comforting Love.

> "The stars," she whispers, "blindly run;
> A web is woven across the sky;
> From out waste places comes a cry,
> And murmurs from the dying sun. . . ."

In one sense this conception of the universe as a blindly run mechanism is the central intellectual conflict of the poem. In his deep melancholy, Tennyson questions not only the justice of Hallam's tragic death but also the justice of the entire creation.

Like a passenger of a "helmless bark" Tennyson moves alternately from numbed despair to self-awareness (IV), and finds composing poetry an anodyne for pain (V). Poems IX-XVII constitute a group unified by the poet's meditation upon the return from Italy by ship of Hallam's body. A "calmer grief" now pervades his heart (XI).

The pain of grief "slowly forms the firmer mind" (XVIII), but locked in his heart remain the deeper sorrows that words cannot relieve (XX). He writes not to parade his emotions publicly, but because he must (XXI).

The second section commences with the first Christmas celebration some three months after Hallam's death. The poet hears the bells' message of "peace and goodwill" but almost wishes never to hear them again. Yet even in his despondency, the bells recall his happy youth, and, touching pain with joy, ease his misery. In the renewal of "old pastimes in the hall" they make a "vain pretense" (XXX), but find consolation in the thought of an afterlife for the dead, though what that afterlife may be "remaineth unrevealed" (XXXI).

The second yew tree poem illustrates a lightening of his burden, for he now sees the tree with "fruitful cloud," subject to change like his grief. The group of poems from XXXI to XLVIII shows Tennyson wrestling with questions about the afterlife and the possibility of a reunion with Hallam. These speculations are not meant to solve the problems, he tells us (XLVIII), but were "Short swallow-flights of song" which soothed his mind.

In LIV Tennyson expresses the vague "trust that somehow good/ Will be the final goal of ill." But the two following poems call in doubt this qualified optimism, so that all he can permit himself is to "faintly trust the larger hope" (LV). In his agitated state of mind the poet views Nature "red in tooth and claw" (LVI). The remaining portion of this section deals with the former relationship of the poet with Hallam.

The third section opens with the second Christmas and finds the poet with the sense of the abiding presence of his friend. His subdued grief allows him to treasure their friendship.

> Which masters Time indeed, and is
> Eternal, separate from fears.

Tennyson contemplates the possibility of a visitation by Hallam and experiences a "mystic trance" in XCV, when "The dead man touch'd" him "from the past." The third section concludes with a four-poem series relating to the Tennyson family's removal from Somersby, with its pleasant and sorrowful associations.

With the fourth and final section the poet turns from the past and his personal grief to the future of mankind; this change is signaled by the famous lyric "Ring out, wild bells" (CVI). Tennyson resolves not to allow sorrow to alienate him from society (CVIII). Hallam's qualities emerge clearly for the first time; in a series of poems Tennyson praises his friend, particularly for his attributes of leadership and dedication to social good.

Tennyson draws an important distinciton in CXIV of the difference between knowledge and wisdom; with wisdom man does not fear death since wisdom is "of the soul," while knowledge must learn to submit to wisdom and "know her place." Acknowledging "Love" as his "lord and king." Tennyson proclaims that "all is well" (CXXVII). His optimism is buttressed by his knowledge that Hallam

> O'erlook'st the tumult from afar,
> And smilest, knowing all is well.

As the elegy draws to a close the poet more strongly feels the certainty of cosmic design: "That all, as in some piece of art,/ Is toil coöperant to an end" (CXXVIII). He feels more confident of Hallam's omnipresence: "Thy voice is on the rolling air;/ I hear thee where the waters run" (CXXX). His love, though founded on their previous earthly relationship, is "vaster passion" now that Hallam's presence is spiritual and diffused through "God and Nature." The elegy concludes with the poet's self-confident assertion of the permanence of the "living will" which purifies our "deeds" and of the "faith" in truths not to be "proved" until our deaths.

In the "Epilogue" Tennyson celebrates the marriage of his friend, Edward Lushington, to the poet's sister.

THE INTERPRETATION OF DREAMS

Type of work: Psychological study
Author: Sigmund Freud (1856–1939)
First published: 1900

In March, 1931, in a foreword to the third English edition of *The Interpretation of Dreams*, Freud expressed the opinion that the volume contained the most valuable of all the discoveries he had been fortunate enough to make.

The author's estimation of his work concurs with that of most students and critics. The ideas that dreams are wish-fulfillments, that the dream disguises the wishes of the unconscious, that dreams are always important, always significant, and that they express infantile wishes—particularly for the death of the parent of the same sex as that of the dreamer—all appear in this masterpiece of psychological interpretation. Here the Oedipus complex is first named and explained, and the method of psychoanalysis is given impetus and credibility by its application to the analysis of dreams.

It is a common criticism of Freud to say that the father of psychoanalysis, although inspired in this and other works, went too far in his generalizations concerning the basic drives of the unconscious. Freud is charged with regarding every latent wish as having a sexual object, and he is criticized for supposing that dreams can be understood as complexes of such universally significant symbols as umbrellas and boxes.

Although Freud argues that repressed wishes that show themselves in disguised form in dreams generally have something to do with the unsatisfied sexual cravings of childhood—for dreams are important and concern themselves only with matters we cannot resolve by conscious deliberation and action—he allows for the dream satisfaction of other wishes that reality has frustrated: the desire for the continued existence of a loved one already dead, the desire for sleep as a continuation of the escape from reality, the desire for a return to childhood, the desire for revenge when revenge is impossible.

As for the charge that Freud regarded dreams as complexes of symbols having the same significance for all dreamers, this is clearly unwarranted. Freud explicitly states that "only the context can furnish the correct meaning" of a dream symbol. He rejects as wholly inadequate the use of any such simple key as a dream book of symbols. Each dreamer utilizes the material of his own experience in his own way, and only by a careful analytical study of associations—obscured by the manifest content of the dream—is it possible to get at the particular use of symbols in an individual's dream. It is worth noting, Freud admits, that many symbols recur with much the same intent in many dreams of different persons, but this knowledge must be used judiciously. The agreement in the use of symbols is only partly a matter of cultural tendencies; it is largely attributable to limitations of the imagination imposed by the material itself: "To use long, stiff objects and weapons as symbols of the male genitals, or hollow objects (chests, boxes, etc.) as symbols of the female genitals, is certainly not permitted by the imagination."

It is not surprising that most of the symbols discussed by Freud, either as typical symbols or as symbols in individual cases, are sexually significant. Although Freud did not regard all dreams as the wish-fulfillments of repressed sexual desires, he did suppose that a greater number of dreams have a sexual connotation: "The more one is occupied with the solution of dreams, the readier one becomes to acknowledge that the majority of the dreams of adults deal with sexual material and give expression to erotic wishes." Freud adds, "In dream-interpretation this importance of the sexual complexes must never be forgotten, though one must not, of course, exaggerate it to the exclusion of all other factors."

The technique of dream interpretation is certainly not exhausted, according to Freud, by the technique of symbol interpretation. Dreams involve the use of the images dreamed, the *manifest* dream-content, as a way of disguising the unconscious "dream-thoughts," or *latent* dream-content. The significance of a dream may be revealed only after one has understood the dramatic use of the symbolism of the dream, the condensation of the material, the displacement of the conventional meaning of a symbol or utterance, or even a displacement of the "center" of the dream-thoughts; that is, the manifest dream may center on a matter removed from the central concern of the latent dream. As Freud explains the problems of dream interpretation, making numerous references to dream examples, it becomes clear that dream interpretation must be at least as ingenious as dream-work—and there is nothing more ingenious.

Freud begins *The Interpretation of Dreams* with a history of the scientific literature of dream problems from ancient times to 1900. He then proceeds to make his basic claim: that dreams are interpretable as wish-fulfillments. To illustrate this point, he begins with an involved dream of his own, justifying his procedure by arguing that self-analysis is possible and, even when faulty, illustrative.

A problem arises with the consideration of painful dreams. If dreams are wish-fulfillments, why are some dreams nightmares? Who wishes to be terrified? Freud's answer is that the problem arises from a confusion between the manifest and the latent dream. What is painful, considered as manifest, may, because of its disguised significance, be regarded as satisfactory to the unconscious. When one realizes, in addition, that many suppressed wished are desires for punishment, the painful dream presents itself as a fulfillment of such wishes. To understand the possibility of painful dreams, it is necessary to consider Freud's amended formula: "The dream is the (disguised) fulfillment of a (suppressed or repressed) wish."

In describing the method most useful in enabling a person to recall his dream by facilitating memory and by inhabiting the censorship tendency of the person recounting the dream, Freud presents what has become known as the psychoanalytic method of free association. He suggests that the patient be put into a restful position with his eyes closed, that the patient be told not to criticize his thoughts or to withhold the expression of them, and that the patient continue to be impartial about his ideas. This problem of eliminating censorship while recounting the dream is merely an extension of the problem of dealing with the censorship imposed by the dreamer while dreaming. The dreamer does not want to acknowledge his desires; for one reason or another he has repressed them. The fulfillment of the suppressed desire can be tolerated by the dreamer only if he leaves out anything which would be understandable to the waking mind. Consequently, only a laborious process of undoing the dream-work can result in some understanding of the meaning the censor tries to hide.

Among the interesting subsidiary ideas of Freud's theory is the idea that the dream-stimulus is always to be found among the experiences of the hours prior to sleeping. Some incident from the day becomes the material of the dream, its provocative image. Yet although the dream-stimulus is from the day preceding sleep, the repressed wish which the dream expresses and fulfills is from childhood, at least in the majority of cases: "The deeper we go into the analysis of dreams, the more often are we put on to the track of childish experiences which play the part of dream-sources in the latent dream-content." To explain the difficulty of getting at the experiences in childhood which provide the latent dream-content, Freud argues for a conception of dreams as stratified: In the dream layers of meaning are involved, and it is only at the lowest stratum that the source in some experience of childhood may be discovered.

Among the typical dreams mentioned by Freud are the embarrassment dream of nakedness, interpreted as an exhibition dream, fulfilling a wish to return to childhood (the time when one ran about naked without upsetting anyone); the death-wish dream in which one dreams of the death of a beloved person, interpreted as a dream showing repressed hostility toward brother or sister, father or mother; and the examination dream in which one dreams of the disgrace of flunking an examination, interpreted

as reflecting the ineradicable memories of punishments in childhood.

Of these typical dreams, the death-wish dream directed to the father (by the son) or to the mother (by the daughter) is explained in terms of the drama of *Oedipus* by Sophocles. In the old Greek play, Oedipus unwittingly murders his own father and marries his mother. When he discovers his deeds, he blinds himself and exiles himself from Thebes. The appeal of the drama is explained by Freud as resulting from its role as a wish-fulfillment. The play reveals the inner self, the self which directed its first sexual impulses toward the mother and its first jealous hatred toward the father. These feelings have been repressed during the course of our developing maturity, but they remain latent, ready to manifest themselves only in dreams somewhat more obscure than the Oedipus drama itself. Freud mentions *Hamlet* as another play in which the same wish is shown, although in *Hamlet* the fulfillment is repressed. Freud accounts for Hamlet's reluctance to complete the task of revenge by pointing out that Hamlet cannot bring himself to kill a man who accomplished what he himself wishes he had accomplished: the murder of his father and marriage to his mother.

In his discussion of the psychology of the dream process, Freud calls attention to the fact that dreams are quickly forgotten—a natural consequence, if his theory is correct. This fact creates problems for the analyst who wishes to interpret dreams in order to discover the root of neurotic disturbances. Yet, the self that forgets is the same self that dreamed, and it is possible by following the implications of even superficial associations to get back to the substance of the dream.

Realizing that many people would be offended by his ideas, Freud attempted to forestall criticism by insisting on the universal application of his theory and by claiming that dreams themselves—since they are not acts—are morally innocent, whatever their content. To a degree, intellectual historians and scholars accept the universal application of his theory, but they criticize his attempt to link his method of dream interpretation to his theory of neurosis. His most vociferous critics complain that once he fastened on a particular theory about the meaning of a patient's dream, he demanded very little to substantiate that theory and, in fact, discounted evidence that might contradict it. They point to the famous case of Dora to illustrate Freud's stubborn adherence to his theory.

Dora came to Freud suffering from convulsions and fainting fits, catarrh, shortness of breath, and a dragging leg. Freud analyzed her dreams and concluded that all of her symptoms were the result of hysterical thinking on her part. His critics charge that his failure to put Dora through a physical examination or to investigate parallel symptoms in her tubercular and syphilitic father demonstrate the weakness of Freud's theory and his blind spot with respect to its application.

There is still little question but that Freud's contribution to psychology will remain one of the great discoveries of the human mind. It is more commonly accepted a century later, however, that Freud's contribution is more to the realm of the philosophic than to the scientific. It is no longer accepted with certainty that Freud discovered a cure for neurosis or that he was able to translate the language of the unconscious. Through his own self analysis, however, he revealed to the world a mind so brilliant and complex that legions of analysts follow respectfully, if not blindly, in his footsteps.

IVANHOE: A Romance

Type of work: Novel
Author: Sir Walter Scott (1771–1832)
Type of plot: Historical romance
Time of plot: 1194
Locale: England
First published: 1819

For a hundred and fifty years, Ivanhoe has held its charm in the popular mind as the epitome of chivalric novels. Among its characters are two of the most popular of English heroes, Richard the Lion-Hearted and Robin Hood. It may not be Scott's greatest novel, but it is without doubt his most popular.

Principal Characters

Cedric the Saxon, the rude, warlike master of Rotherwood, a small landholder during the reign of Richard I. Obstinately hoping for Saxon independence, he wishes his ward, Lady Rowena, to marry Athelstane of Coningsburgh, a descendant of the ancient Saxon kings, and he disinherits his son, Wilfred of Ivanhoe, for learning Norman customs. When Ivanhoe returns from the Crusades and falls wounded after winning the tournament at Ashby-de-la-Zouche, Cedric allows him to be cared for by strangers. Captured by Normans, Cedric is taken to Torquilstone Castle, but he escapes and helps the besiegers take the castle. In the end he becomes somewhat reconciled to the marriage of Ivanhoe and Rowena and with Norman rule under King Richard I.

Wilfred of Ivanhoe, the chivalrous, disowned hero, a Crusader. Returning home disguised as a pilgrim, he befriends a Jew, Isaac of York, and his daughter Rebecca on the way to the tournament at Ashby. After defeating his opponents in the tourney he reveals his true identity and faints from loss of blood while accepting the prize from Rowena. Captured with the Jew, along with Cedric and his party, he is cared for by Rebecca at Torquilstone and is rescued by the disguised King Richard. He repays Rebecca's kindness by defending her when she is accused of witchcraft. After Athelstane relinquishes his claim to Rowena, Ivanhoe marries her and enjoys prosperity under Richard's rule.

Lady Rowena, Cedric's beautiful ward. At Rotherwood she inquires of Ivanhoe's exploits from the disguised knight himself, becomes the tournament queen at his request, and learns his identity after he is declared victor. Seized by Norman knights, she is saved from the advances of a captor and the Torquilstone fire by the timely intervention of Richard, Cedric, and Robin Hood. Happy when Athelstane disclaims her, she weds Ivanhoe.

Isaac of York, an avaricious but kindly Jew. He supplies Ivanhoe with a horse and armor for the tournament and takes him off to be cared for after the knight has been wounded. Isaac is taken prisoner and about to be tortured for his gold when rescuers lay siege to the castle. He is set free but forced to pay a ransom. Learning of his daughter's abduction at the hands of haughty Sir Brian de Bois-Guilbert, he sends for Ivanhoe to rescue her. Sick of England, he and his daughter move to Spain.

Rebecca, the generous, lovely Jewess who returns Ivanhoe's payment for the horse and armor and nurses his wound. She is carried off by an enamored Templar during the siege. Accused of witchcraft at Templar headquarters, she is rescued from burning by the exhausted Ivanhoe's defense.

Sir Brian de Bois-Guilbert (brē·äṅ də bwä'-gēl·bĕr'), the fierce and passionate Templar who kidnaps Rebecca, deserts her because of Templar politics, and fights a fatal battle against her defender, Ivanhoe.

Richard the Lion-Hearted, an audacious, hardy king. Secretly returning to England, he saves Ivanhoe's life at the tournament and leads the siege of Torquilstone. After thwarting an ambush, he throws off his disguise of the "Black Sluggard" and claims his rightful throne.

Robin Hood (Locksley), the famed outlaw. He wins an archery contest, supports Richard during the siege of Torquilstone, and becomes a loyal subject of the restored King.

Athelstane of Coningsburgh (ath'əl·stān), the sluggish Saxon knight who half-heartedly woos Rowena and loses fights with Richard and Bois-Guilbert.

Maurice de Bracy, an ambitious Norman who captures Rowena; however, he possesses too much honor to pursue his designs on her.

Reginald Front de Boeuf (rĕ·zhē·nàl' frôn' də bėf'), the savage Norman who seizes Isaac for his gold. He dies of a wound inflicted by Richard amid the flames of Torquilstone.

Prince John, Richard's haughty, unscrupulous brother, who has tried to usurp the throne with the aid of the Norman nobles.

Lucas de Beaumanoir (lü·kä′ də bō·må·nwår′), the bigoted, ascetic head of the Templars who presides over Rebecca's trial on a charge of witchcraft. His Order is disbanded by Richard because of treasonous activities and plotting against the king and the realm.

Philip and **Albert Malvoisin** (ål·běr′ mål·vwå·zăn′), Templars executed by King Richard for treason.

Waldemar Fitzurse (vål·dəmår′ fïts·ėrs′), Prince John's wily, aspiring follower, who is banished by Richard.

Aymer (ā′mėr), the comfort-loving Prior of Jorvaulx,

who is captured by Robin Hood and forced to pay a ransom.

Ulrica (ōōl·rē′kə), the Saxon hag who burns Torquilstone in order to be revenged on the Normans.

Gurth, Cedric's swineherd and Ivanhoe's loyal servant, who is given his freedom.

Wamba, Cedric's quick-witted jester; he helps Cedric escape Torquilstone by dressing him in a priest's robe.

Friar Tuck, Robin Hood's hefty, hearty follower, a hedge priest who treats Richard to a meal.

The Story

Night was drawing near when Prior Aymer of Jorvaux and the haughty Templar, Brian de Bois-Guilbert, overtook a swineherd and a fool by the roadside and asked directions to Rotherwood, the dwelling of Cedric the Saxon. The answers of these serfs so confused the Templar and the Prior that they would have gone far afield had it not been for a pilgrim from the Holy Land whom they encountered shortly afterward. The pilgrim was also traveling to Rotherwood, and he brought them safely to Cedric's hall, where they claimed lodging for the night. The custom of the rude days afforded hospitality to all benighted travelers, and so Cedric gave a grudging welcome to the Norman lords.

There was a feast at Rotherwood that night. On the dais beside Cedric the Saxon sat his ward, the lovely Lady Rowena, descendant of the ancient Saxon princes. It was the old man's ambition to wed her to Athelstane of Coningsburgh of the line of King Alfred. Because his son, Wilfred of Ivanhoe, had fallen in love with Rowena, Cedric had banished him, and the young knight had gone with King Richard to Palestine. None in the banquet hall that night suspected that the pilgrim was Ivanhoe himself.

Another traveler who had claimed shelter at Rotherwood that night was an aged Jew, Isaac of York. Hearing some orders the Templar muttered to his servants at the feast's end, Ivanhoe warned the Jew that Bois-Guilbert had designs on his moneybag or his person. Without taking leave of their host the next morning, the disguised pilgrim and Isaac of York left Rotherwood and continued on to the nearby town of Ashby de la Zouche.

Many other travelers were also on their way to the town, for a great tournament was to be held there. Prince John, regent of England in King Richard's absence, would preside. The winner of the tournament would be allowed to name the Queen of Love and Beauty and receive the prize of the passage of arms from her hands.

Ivanhoe attended the tournament with the word *Disinherited* written upon his shield. Entering the lists, he struck the shield of Bois-Guilbert with the point of his lance and challenged the knight to mortal combat. In the first passage, both knights splintered their lances, but neither was unhorsed. At the second passage, Ivanhoe's

lance struck Bois-Guilbert's helmet and upset him. Then one by one, Ivanhoe vanquished five knights who had agreed to take on all comers. When the heralds declared the Disinherited Knight victor of the tourney, Ivanhoe named Rowena the Queen of Love and Beauty.

In the tournament on the following day, Ivanhoe was pressed hard by three antagonists, but he received unexpected help from a knight in black, whom the spectators had called the Black Sluggard because of his previous inactivity. Ivanhoe, because of his earlier triumphs during the day, was named champion of the tournament once more. In order to receive the gift from Lady Rowena, Ivanhoe had to remove his helmet. When he did so, he was recognized. He received the chaplet, his prize, kissed the hand of Lady Rowena, and then fainted from loss of blood. Isaac of York and his daughter, Rebecca, were sitting nearby, and Rebecca suggested to her father that they nurse Ivanhoe until he was well. Isaac and his daughter started for their home with the wounded knight carried in a horse litter. On the way, they joined the train of Cedric the Saxon, who was still ignorant of the Disinherited Knight's identity.

Before the travelers had gone far, however, they were set upon and captured by a party led by three Norman knights, Bois-Guilbert, Maurice de Bracy, and Reginald Front de Boeuf. They were imprisoned in Front de Boeuf's castle of Torquilstone. De Bracy had designs upon Lady Rowena because she was an heiress of royal lineage. The Templar desired to possess Rebecca. Front de Boeuf hoped to extort a large sum of money from the aged Jew. Cedric was held for ransom. The wounded knight was put into the charge of an ancient hag named Ulrica.

Isaac and his daughter were placed in separate rooms. Bois-Guilbert went to Rebecca in her tower prison and asked her to adopt Christianity so that they might be married; but the plot of the Norman nobles with regard to their prisoners was thwarted by an assault on the castle by Richard the Lion-Hearted, The Black Sluggard of the tournament at Ashby, in company with Robin Hood and his outlaws. Ulrica aided the besiegers by starting a fire within the castle walls. Robin Hood and his men took the prisoners to the forest along with the Norman nobles.

In the confusion, however, Bois-Guilbert escaped with Rebecca, and Isaac made preparation to ransom her from the Templar. De Bracy was set free, and he hurried to inform Prince John that he had seen and talked with Richard. John plotted to make Richard his prisoner.

Isaac went to the establishment of the Knights Templar and begged to see Bois-Guilbert. Lucas de Beaumanoir, the grand master of the Templars, ordered Isaac admitted to his presence. Isaac was frightened when the grand master asked him his business with the Templar. When he told his story, the grand master learned of Bois-Guilbert's seizure of Rebecca. It was suggested that Bois-Guilbert was under a spell cast by Rebecca. Condemned as a witch, she was sentenced to be burned at the stake. In desperation she demanded, as was her right, a champion to defend her against the charge. Lucas de Beaumanoir agreed and named Bois-Guilbert champion of the Temple.

The day arrived for Rebecca's execution. A pile of wood had been laid around the stake. Seated in a black chair, Rebecca awaited the arrival of her defender. Three times the heralds called upon her champion to appear. At the third call, a strange knight rode into the lists and announced himself as Rebecca's champion. When Bois-Guilbert realized that the stranger was Ivanhoe, he at first refused combat because Ivanhoe's wounds were not completely healed. Nevertheless, the grand master gave orders for the contest to begin. As everyone expected, the tired horse of Ivanhoe and its exhausted rider went down at the first blow, so that Ivanhoe's lance merely touched the shield of the Templar. Then to the astonishment of all, Bois-Guilbert reeled in his saddle and fell to the ground. Ivanhoe arose from where he had fallen and drew his sword. Placing his foot on the breast of the fallen knight, he called upon Bois-Guilbert to yield himself or die on the spot. There was no answer from Bois-Guilbert; he was dead, a victim of the violence of his own passions. The grand master declared that Rebecca was acquitted of the charge against her.

At that moment, the Black Knight appeared, followed by a band of knights and men-at-arms. It was King Richard, who had come to arrest Rebecca's accusers on a charge of treason. The grand master saw the flag of the Temple hauled down and the royal standard raised in its place.

King Richard had returned in secret to reclaim his throne. Robin Hood became his true follower. Athelstane let go his claims to Lady Rowena's hand so that she and Ivanhoe could be married. Reconciled at last with his son, Cedric the Saxon gave his consent, and Richard himself graced their wedding. Isaac and Rebecca left England for Granada, hoping to find in that foreign land greater happiness than could ever be theirs in England.

Critical Evaluation

For more than a hundred and fifty years, *Ivanhoe* has held its charm in the popular mind as the epitome of chivalric novels. It has among its characters two of the most popular of English heroes, Richard the Lion-Hearted and Robin Hood, and tells a story of chivalric romance. It has sufficient action and color to appeal to a great number of people. Although *Ivanhoe* may not be Sir Walter Scott's greatest novel, it is without doubt his most popular.

Scott himself wrote that he left the Scottish scenes of his previous novels and turned to the Middle Ages in *Ivanhoe* because he feared the reading public was growing weary of the repetition of Scottish themes in his books. Since he was fascinated with history all of his life, it was logical that Scott should turn to the past for subject matter. Many faults have been found with the historical facts of the book; Robin Hood, if he lived at all, belonged to a later century than that represented in the novel, and by the time of Richard I, the distinction between Saxons and Normans had faded. Nevertheless, the thrilling story, the drama and action, still grip the reader, whatever liberties Scott took with history.

Scott's four great chivalric novels all possess similar structures in that they all focus on a moment of crisis between two great individuals, a moment that determines the survival of one of the opposed pair. In *Ivanhoe*, the symbolic contrast is between Richard the Lion-Hearted and his brother John. The struggle between these two helps to raise one of the principal questions of the novel: the decadence of chivalry. For generations of juvenile readers, *Ivanhoe* represented the glory of chivalric adventure, but Scott actually entertained serious doubts about the chivalric tradition. At several strategic points in *Ivanhoe*, passages occur that unequivocally damn the reckless inhumanity of romantic chivalry.

The novel is divided into three parts, each reaching its climax in a great military spectacle. The first part ends with the Ashby tournament, the second with the liberation from the castle of Front de Boeuf, and the third with the trial by combat to acquit Rebecca. The beginning chapters draw together all of the character groups for the tournament, Ivanhoe being present only as the mysterious palmer. The problem of seating at the tournament provides a sketch of the cultural animosities that divided the world of the novel.

Richard is the moral and political center of the book, and, therefore, the proper object of Ivanhoe's fidelity. The captive king does not appear until he fights the mysterious Black Knight during the second day of the tournament. He saves Ivanhoe and then disappears until the scene of his midnight feast with Friar Tuck. The reader's impression of him is of a fun-loving, heroic fighter. The Friar thinks of him as a man of "prudence and of counsel." Richard possesses a native humanity and a love of life, as well as the heroic chivalric qualities. He is always ready to act as a protector of others.

John, by contrast, is an ineffectual ruler whose own followers despise him. His forces quickly disintegrate, and his followers abandon him for their own selfish ends. He is a petulant, stupid man, incapable of inspiring loyalty. It is inevitable that the historical climax of the novel should be the confrontation between Richard and John. The chivalric code has become completely corrupt in the England left to John's care. Both the narrator and the characters make clear that chivalry is no more than a mixture of "heroic folly and dangerous imprudence."

Rebecca speaks against chivalry, asking during the bloody siege of the castle if possession by a "demon of vainglory" brings "sufficient rewards for the sacrifice of every kindly affection, for a life spent miserably that yet may make others miserable?" (Rebecca is antichivalric, yet she is the most romantic character in the book, suggesting the traditional chivalric attitudes toward women.) The narrator speaks most sharply of the chivalric code at the end of the tournament:

> This ended the memorable field of Ashby-de-la-Zouche, one of the most gallantly contested tournaments of that age; for although only four knights, including one who was smothered by the heat of his armor, had died upon the field, yet upwards of thirty were desperately wounded, four or five of whom never recovered. Several more were disabled for life; and those who escaped best carried the marks of the conflict to the grave with them. Hence it is always mentioned in the old records as the 'gentle and joyous passage of arms at Ashby.'

An argument has been made that Scott's historical novels, such as *Ivanhoe*, are inferior to his earlier novels based on his direct, personal knowledge of the Scottish customs, characters, and land. Even in the historical novels, however, Scott's characters are colorful, full of vitality, and realized with amazing verisimilitude. Scott's knowledge of the past about which he was writing was so deep that he could draw upon it at will to clothe out his fictions. He did not find it necessary to research a novel such as *Ivanhoe* in order to write it; the historical lore was already part of him. Years before, at the time when he was beginning the Waverley series, he had written a study about chivalry. His prolific writing did not seem to exhaust his resources.

Scott was one of the most prolific writers in the history of British fiction; only Trollope could stand up against his record. Scott's novels were published anonymously, although their authorship came to be an open secret. Scott's friends found it difficult to believe that he was the author of the novels, for he lived the life of a county magistrate and landowner, spending hours daily on these occupations as well as entertaining lavishly and writing poetry and nonfiction works. His secret was that he would rise early and finish novel-writing before breakfast. In time, his compulsive working injured his health, and while he was writing *Ivanhoe*, he was tortured by a cramp of the stomach and suffered such pain that he could not physically hold the pen but was forced to dictate much of the story.

Like many great novels, *Ivanhoe* betrays a complexity of attitude on the part of the author. Although much of the book makes clear Scott's severe view of the code of chivalry, it also reveals Scott's attraction to the Romantic traditions of the period. Through the characters of Rebecca and Rowena, Ivanhoe and Richard, Scott dramatized his ambivalent feelings about the chivalric period. The tension created through these mixed feelings, coupled with the dramatic (if historically inaccurate) story and the vast accumulation of detail as to costume and social customs and historical anecdotes, produced a work of enduring value.

JANE EYRE: An Autobiography

Type of work: Novel
Author: Charlotte Brontë (1816–1855)
Type of plot: Psychological romance
Time of plot: 1800
Locale: Northern England
First published: 1847

The poetry and tension of Jane Eyre *marked a new development in adult romanticism in fiction, just as Jane herself was a new kind of heroine, a woman of intelligence and passion, but one lacking in the charm, beauty, and grace usually associated with romantic heroines. Likewise, the strange and unconventional hero, Rochester, is a new type, who sets the often eerie, moody, or even violently passionate atmosphere of the novel.*

Principal Characters

Jane Eyre, a plain child with a vivid imagination, intelligence, and great talent in art and music. Left an orphan in childhood, she is forced to live with her aunt Reed, who was the sister-in-law of her father. At the Reed home she is mistreated and spurned, and is finally sent to a charity home for girls. Her education completed, she teaches at the school for several years and then takes a position as a private governess to the ward of Mr. Rochester. After a strange, tempestuous courtship she and Mr. Rochester are to be married, but the revelation that his insane first wife still lives prevents the wedding. After each has suffered many hardships, Jane and Mr. Rochester are eventually married.

Edward Fairfax Rochester, a gentleman of thirty-five, the proud, sardonic, moody master of Thornfield. Before Jane Eyre's arrival to become a governess in his household he visits Thornfield only occasionally. After he falls in love with Jane, much of his moroseness disappears. When they are separated because the presence of his insane wife becomes known, Mr. Rochester remains at Thornfield. His wife sets fire to the house and Mr. Rochester loses his eyesight and the use of an arm during the conflagration, in which his wife dies. Summoned, she believes, by his call, Jane Eyre returns a short time later and the two are married.

Adele Varens, the illegitimate daughter of Mr. Rochester and a French opera singer, his ward upon her mother's death. She is pale, small-featured, extremely feminine, and not especially talented.

Mrs. Fairfax, the elderly housekeeper at Thornfield. She has been extremely kind to Jane and is delighted that she and Mr. Rochester are to be married.

Grace Poole, a stern woman with a hard, plain face, supposedly a seamstress at Thornfield but actually the keeper of mad Mrs. Rochester. Occasionally she tipples too much and neglects her post.

Bertha Mason Rochester, Mr. Rochester's insane wife, kept in secret on an upper floor at Thornfield. She had lied and her family had lied when Mr. Rochester met her in Jamaica while traveling, for she was even then demented. During Jane's stay at Thornfield Mrs. Rochester tries to burn her husband in bed. Finally she burns the whole house and herself, and seriously injures her husband.

Mrs. Reed, an exacting, clever, managing woman, the guardian of Jane Eyre. She hates her charge, however, misuses her, and locks her in dark rooms for punishment. At her death she repents of her actions. Her children turn out badly.

Eliza Reed, her older daughter, a penurious, serious girl who eventually becomes a nun.

John Reed, the son, a wicked child who torments Jane Eyre and then blames her for his own bad deeds. He ends up as a drunk in London and dies in disgrace.

Georgiana Reed, the younger daughter, a pretty, spoiled child who later becomes very fat. She makes a poor marriage.

Bessie Leaven, Mrs. Reed's governess, pretty, capricious, hasty-tempered. Before Jane Eyre leaves the Reed house, Bessie has become fond of her.

Robert Leaven, Bessie's husband and Mrs. Reed's coachman.

Abbot, the Reed's bad-tempered maid.

Mr. Lloyd, an apothecary called in when Jane Eyre becomes sick and feverish after having been locked in a dark room. He suggests that she be sent off to school.

Mr. Brocklehurst, a strict clergyman and the master of Lowood School. He forces the girls to wear short, uncurled hair and plain wrappers, and he feeds them on a starvation diet.

Maria Temple, the supervisor of Lowood School, a pretty, kind woman who tries against tremendous odds to make her pupils' lot as easy and pleasant as possible. She is interested in Jane Eyre's talents and is responsible for her getting a teaching position later at Lowood.

Miss Smith, Miss Scratcherd, and **Miss Miller,** teachers at Lowood School.

Helen Burns, a clever thirteen-year-old pupil at Lowood School, constantly ridiculed and punished by her teachers because she is not neat and prompt. She dies during a fever epidemic.

Miss Gryce, a fat teacher at Lowood School and Jane Eyre's roommate when they both teach there.

Mary Ann Wilson, one of Jane Eyre's fellow students, a witty and original girl.

John and **Leah,** the house servants at Thornfield Hall.

Sophie, the French maid.

Mrs. Eshton, a guest at a house party given by Mr. Rochester. Once a handsome woman, she still has a well-preserved style.

Mr. Eshton, her husband, a magistrate of the district.

Amy Eshton, their older daughter, rather small, naïve, and childlike in manner.

Louisa Eshton, the younger daughter, a taller and more elegant young woman.

Lady Lynn, another woman whose family is invited to the Thornfield house party; she is large, stout, haughty-looking, and richly dressed.

Mrs. Dent, another guest, less showy than the others, with a slight figure and a pale, gentle face.

Colonel Dent, her husband, a soldierly gentleman.

The Dowager Lady Ingram, another guest, a proud, handsome woman with hard, fierce eyes.

Blanche Ingram, her daughter, a young woman with an elegant manner and a loud, satirical laugh, to whom Mr. Rochester is reported engaged.

Mary Ingram, her sister.

Henry Lynn and **Frederick Lynn,** gentlemen at the party, two dashing sparks.

Lord Ingram, Blanche's brother, a tall, handsome young man of listless appearance and manner.

Mr. Mason, Mr. Rochester's brother-in-law. During a visit to see his sister, she wounds him severely. He halts the marriage of Jane Eyre and Mr. Rochester.

Diana Rivers and **Mary Rivers,** daughters of the family with which Jane Eyre takes refuge after running away from Thornfield. They turn out to be her cousins, their mother having been Jane's aunt. At first they do not know that Jane is a relative because she calls herself Eliot.

St. John Rivers, their brother, a complex religious-minded man who wishes to marry Jane but plans to live with her in platonic fashion while they devote their lives to missionary work in India.

Hannah, the Rivers' housekeeper, a suspicious but kind woman.

Rosamund Oliver, a beautiful, kind heiress, the sponsor of the school in which St. John Rivers find Jane a post. Miss Oliver is coquettish and vain, but she holds real affection for Rivers.

Mr. Oliver, her father, a tall, massive-featured man.

Alice Wood, an orphan, one of Jane's pupils in the school where she teaches after leaving Thornfield.

The Story

Jane Eyre was an orphan. Both her father and mother had died when Jane was a baby, and the little girl passed into the care of Mrs. Reed of Gateshead Hall. Mrs. Reed's husband, now dead, had been the brother of Jane Eyre's mother; on his deathbed, he had directed Mrs. Reed to look after the orphan as she would her own three children. At Gateshead Hall, Jane knew ten years of neglect and abuse. One day, a cousin knocked her to the floor. When she fought back, Mrs. Reed punished her by sending her to the gloomy room where Mr. Reed had died. There Jane lost consciousness. Furthermore, the experience caused a dangerous illness from which she was nursed slowly back to health by sympathetic Bessie Leaven, the Gateshead Hall nurse.

Feeling that she could no longer keep her unwanted charge in the house, Mrs. Reed made arrangements for Jane's admission to Lowood School. Early one morning without farewells, Jane left Gateshead Hall and rode fifty miles by stage to Lowood, her humble possessions in a trunk beside her.

At Lowood, Jane was a diligent student, well liked by her superiors, especially by Miss Temple, the mistress, who refused to accept without proof Mrs. Reed's low estimate of Jane's character. During the period of Jane's schooldays at Lowood, an epidemic of fever caused many deaths among the girls. It also resulted in an investigation that caused improvements at the institution. At the end of her studies, Jane was retained as a teacher. When Jane grew weary of her life at Lowood, she advertised for a position as a governess. She was engaged by Mrs. Fairfax, housekeeper at Thornfield, near Millcote.

At Thornfield, the new governess had only one pupil, Adele Varens, a ward of Jane's employer, Mr. Edward Rochester. From Mrs. Fairfax, Jane learned that Mr. Rochester traveled much and seldom came to Thornfield. Jane was pleased with the quiet country life, with the beautiful old house and gardens, the well-stocked library, and her own comfortable room.

While she was out walking, Jane met Mr. Rochester for the first time, going to his aid after his horse had thrown him. She found her employer a somber, moody man, quick to change in his manner toward her, brusque in his speech. He commended her work with Adele, however, and confided that the girl was the daughter of a French dancer who had deceived him and deserted her daughter. Jane felt that this experience alone could not account for Mr. Rochester's moody nature.

Mysterious happenings occurred at Thornfield. Alarmed by a strange noise one night, Jane found Mr. Rochester's door open and his bed on fire. When she attempted to arouse the household, he commanded her to keep quiet about the whole affair. She also learned that Thornfield had a strange tenant, a woman who laughed like a maniac and who stayed in rooms on the third floor of the house. Jane believed that this woman was Grace Poole, a seamstress employed by Mr. Rochester.

Mr. Rochester attended numerous parties at which he was obviously paying court to Blanche Ingram, daughter of Lady Ingram. One day, the inhabitants of Thornfield were informed that Mr. Rochester was bringing a party of houseguests home with him. The fashionable Miss Ingram was among the party guests. During the house party, Mr. Rochester called Jane to the drawing room, where the guests treated her with the disdain that they thought her humble position deserved. To herself, Jane had already confessed her interest in her employer, but it seemed to her that he was interested only in Blanche Ingram. One evening while Mr. Rochester was away from home, the guests played charades. At the conclusion of the game, a gypsy fortuneteller appeared to read the palms of the lady guests. During her interview with the gypsy, Jane discovered that the so-called fortuneteller was Mr. Rochester in disguise.

While the guests were still at Thornfield, a stranger named Mason arrived to see Mr. Rochester on business. That night, Mason was mysteriously wounded by the strange inhabitant of the third floor. The injured man was taken away secretly before daylight.

One day, Robert Leaven came from Gateshead to tell Jane that Mrs. Reed, now on her deathbed, had asked to see her former ward. Jane returned to her aunt's home. The dying woman gave Jane a letter, dated three years before, from John Eyre in Madeira, who asked that his niece be sent to him for adoption. Mrs. Reed confessed that she had told him that there had been an epidemic at Lowood. The sin of keeping the news from Jane—news that would have meant relatives, adoption, and an inheritance—had become a heavy burden on the conscience of the dying woman.

Jane went back to Thornfield, which she now looked upon as her home. One night in the garden, Edward Rochester embraced her and proposed marriage. Jane accepted and made plans for a quiet ceremony in the village church. She also wrote to her uncle in Madeira, explaining Mrs. Reed's deception and telling him she was to marry Mr. Rochester.

Shortly before the date set for the wedding, Jane had a harrowing experience. She awakened to find a strange, repulsive-looking woman in her room. The intruder tried on Jane's wedding veil and then ripped it to shreds. Mr. Rochester tried to persuade Jane that the whole incident was only her imagination, but in the morning she found the torn veil in her room. As the vows were being said at the church, a stranger spoke up declaring the existence of an impediment to the marriage. He presented an affirmation, signed by the Mr. Mason who had been wounded during this visit to Thornfield. The document stated that Edward Fairfax Rochester had married Bertha Mason, Mr. Mason's sister, in Spanish Town, Jamaica, fifteen years before. Mr. Rochester admitted this fact; then he conducted the party to the third-story chamber at Thornfield. There they found the attendant Grace Poole and her charge, Bertha Rochester, a raving maniac. Mrs. Rochester was the woman Jane had seen in her room.

Jane felt that she must leave Thornfield at once. She notified Mr. Rochester and left quietly early the next morning, using all of her small store of money for the coach fare. Two days later, she was set down on the moors of a north midland shire. Starving, she actually begged for food. Finally, she was befriended by the Reverend St. John Rivers and his sisters, Mary and Diana, who took Jane in and nursed her back to health. Assuming the name of Jane Elliot, she refused to divulge any of her history except her connection with the Lowood institution. Reverend Rivers eventually found a place for her as mistress in a girls' school.

Shortly afterward, St. John Rivers received word from his family solicitor that John Eyre had died in Madeira, leaving Jane Eyre a fortune of twenty thousand pounds. Because Jane had disappeared under mysterious circumstances, the lawyer was trying to locate her through the next of kin, St. John Rivers. Jane's identity was now revealed through her connection with Lowood School, and she learned, to her surprise, that St. John and his sisters were really her own cousins. She then insisted on sharing her inheritance with them.

When St. John decided to go to India as a missionary, he asked Jane to go with him as his wife—not because he loved her, as he frankly admitted, but because he admired her and wanted her services as his assistant. Jane felt indebted to him for his kindness and aid, but she hesitated to accept his proposal.

One night, while St. John was awaiting her decision, she dreamed that Mr. Rochester was calling her name. The next day, she returned to Thornfield by coach. Arriving there, she found the mansion gutted—a burned and blackened ruin. Neighbors told her that the fire had broken out one stormy night, set by the madwoman, who died while Mr. Rochester was trying to rescue her from the roof of the blazing house.

Mr. Rochester was blinded during the fire and now lived at Ferndean, a lonely farm some miles away. Jane Eyre went to him at once, and there they were married. For both, their story had an even happier ending. After two years, Mr. Rochester regained the sight of one eye, so that he was able to see his first child when it was put in his arms.

Critical Evaluation

Charlotte Brontë was always concerned that her work be judged on the basis of its art and not because of her sex. This fact explains the choice of the pseudonym that she continued to use even after her authorship was revealed, often referring in her letters to Currer Bell when speaking of herself as writer. *Jane Eyre*, her first published novel, has been called "feminine" because of the Romanticism and deeply felt emotions of the heroine-narrator. It would be more correct, however, to point to the feminist qualities of the novel: a heroine who refuses to be placed in the traditional female position of subservience, who disagrees with her superiors, who stands up for her rights, who ventures creative thoughts; more important, a narrator who comments on the role of women in the society and the greater constraint experienced by them. Those feminine emotions often pointed to in Jane Eyre herself are surely found as well in Rochester, and the continued popularity of this work must suggest the enduring human quality of these emotions.

Brontë often discussed the lack of passion in her contemporaries' work and especially in that of Jane Austen, about whom she said, "Her business is not half so much with the human heart as with the human eyes, mouth, hands and feet." Coldness, detachment, excessive analysis, and critical distance were not valued by Brontë. The artist must be involved in her subject, she believed, and must have a degree of inspiration not to be rationally explained. Such a theory of art is similar to that of the Romantic poets, an attitude not altogether popular in the mid-nineteenth century.

In *Jane Eyre*, therefore, Brontë chose the exact point of view to suit both her subject matter and her artistic theory, the first-person narrator. The story is told entirely through the eyes of the heroine Jane Eyre. This technique enables Brontë to deliver the events with an intensity that involved the reader in the passions, feelings, and thoughts of the heroine. A passionate directness characterizes Jane's narration: conversations are rendered in direct, not indirect, dialogue; actions are given just as they occurred with little analysis of either event or character. In a half-dozen key scenes, Brontë shifts to present tense instead of the immediate past, so that Jane Eyre narrates the event as if it were happening just at the present moment. After Jane flees Thornfield and Rochester, when the coachman puts her out at Whitcross having used up her fare, she narrates to the moment: "I am alone. . . . I am absolutely destitute." After a long description of the scene around her and her analysis of her situation, also narrated in the present tense, she reverts to the more usual past tense in the next paragraph: "I struck straight into the heath." Such a technique adds greatly to the immediacy of the novel's action and further draws the reader into the situation.

Like all Brontë's heroines, Jane Eyre has no parents and no family that accepts or is aware of her. She, like Lucy Snowe (*Villette*) and Caroline Helstone (*Shirley*), leads her life cut off from society, since family was the means for a woman to participate in society and community. Lacking such support, Jane must face her problems alone. Whenever she forms a close friendship (Bessie at Gateshead, Helen Burns and Miss Temple at Lowood, Mrs. Fairfax at Thornfield), she discovers that these ties can be broken easily—by higher authority, by death, by marriage—since she is not "kin." Cutting her heroines off so radically from family and community gave Brontë the opportunity to make her women independent and to explore the Romantic ideal of individualism.

Jane Eyre is a moral tale, akin to a folk or fairy tale, with nearly all ambiguities—in society, character, and situation—omitted. Almost all choices that Jane must make are easy ones, and although she grows and matures her character does not change significantly. Her one difficult choice is refusing to become Rochester's mistress and deciding to leave Thornfield alone and penniless instead. That choice was difficult precisely because she had no family or friends to influence her with their disapproval. No one would be hurt if she consented; that is, no one but Jane herself, and it is her own self-love that helps her to refuse.

Again like a fairy tale, *Jane Eyre* is full of myth and superstition. Rochester often calls Jane his "elf," "changeling," or "witch"; there are mysterious happenings at Thornfield; Jane is inclined to believe the gypsy fortuneteller (until Rochester reveals himself) and often thinks of the superstitions she has heard; the weather often presages mysterious or disastrous events. Most important, at the climax of the story when Jane is about to consent to be the unloved wife of St. John Rivers, she hears Rochester calling her—at precisely the time, readers learn later, that he had in fact called to her. This event is never rationally explained, and readers must accept Jane's judgment that it was a supernatural intervention.

Numerous symbolic elements pervade the novel; most often something in nature symbolizes an event or person in Jane's life. The most obvious example is the chestnut tree, which is split in two by lightning on the night that Jane accepts Rochester's marriage proposal, signifying the rupture of their relationship. The two parts of the tree, however, remain bound, as do Jane and Rochester despite their physical separation.

Likewise, the novel is full of character foils and parallel situations. Aunt Reed at Gateshead is contrasted with Miss Temple at Lowood; the Reed sisters at the beginning are contrasted with the Rivers sisters—cousins all—at the end; Rochester's impassioned proposal and love is followed by St. John's pragmatic proposition. Foreshadowing is everywhere in the book, so that seemingly chance happenings gain added significance as the novel unfolds, and each previous event is echoed in the next.

Therefore, the novel's well-crafted structure and carefully chosen point of view add to the strong and fascinating character of Jane herself, making *Jane Eyre* not a typical Victorian novel but a classic among English novels.

JASON AND THE GOLDEN FLEECE

Type of work: Classical legend
Source: Folk tradition
Type of plot: Heroic adventure
Time of plot: Remote antiquity
Locale: Ancient Greece
First transcribed: Unknown

The story of Jason and the pursuit of the Golden Fleece has been repeated in story and song for more than thirty centuries; its form has often changed, but its substance remains unchanged. The peculiar poignancy of the myth lies in the contrast between the image of the youthful Jason, strong and arrogant, and the aged Jason, a homeless outcast who wanders until he is killed by the falling prow of his old ship, the Argo.

Principal Characters

Jason (jā′sən), a Greek prince whose father has been driven from his throne. Jason is commanded to regain the throne, but to do so he must bring back the Golden Fleece for the usurper, his uncle Pelias. Jason bravely sets out and brings back the Golden Fleece. Although Pelias refuses to keep his promise, he dies that same night, leaving the throne to Jason.

Pelias (pē′lĭ·əs), Jason's cruel uncle, who usurps his brother's throne and plots to kill Jason. When Jason brings back the Golden Fleece to Iolcus, Pelias does not want to fulfill his bargain and give up the throne, but death takes him the same night.

Chiron (kī′rŏn), a centaur. He is Jason's foster father and tutor.

Herakles (hěr′ə·klēz) and **Orpheus** (ôr′fĭ·əs), Jason's companions on the quest for the Golden Fleece.

Argus (är′gəs), another of Jason's companions on the quest for the Golden Fleece. He builds the ship "Argo" for Jason.

Zetes (zē′tēz) and **Calais** (kă′lā·əs), sons of the North Wind, companions of Jason.

Phineus (fĭ′nĕ·əs), the blind king of Salmydessa, saved from the Harpies by Jason.

Aeetes (ē·ē′tēz), king of Colchis, who agrees to give up the Golden Fleece if Jason can accomplish deeds beyond mortal skill and strength.

Medea (mĭ·dē·ə), a princess of Colchis. She falls in love with Jason, aids him in gaining the Golden Fleece, and returns with him to become his queen in Iolcus.

The Story

In ancient Greece there lived a prince named Jason, son of a king who had been driven from his throne by a wicked brother named Pelias. To protect the boy from his cruel uncle, Jason's father took him to a remote mountaintop where he was raised by Chiron the Centaur, whom many say was half man and half horse. When Jason had grown to young manhood, Chiron the Centaur told him Pelias had seized his brother's crown. Jason was instructed to go and win back his father's kingdom.

Pelias had been warned to beware of a stranger who came with one foot sandaled and the other bare. It happened that Jason had lost one sandal in a river he crossed as he came to Iolcus, where Pelias ruled. When Pelias saw the lad, he was afraid and plotted to kill him; but he pretended to welcome Jason. At a great feast he told Jason the story of the golden fleece.

In days past a Greek king called Athamas banished his wife and took another, a beautiful but wicked woman who persuaded Athamus to kill his own children; but a golden ram swooped down from the skies and carried the children away. The girl slipped from his back and fell into the sea, but the boy came safely to the country of Colchis. There the boy let the king of Colchis slaughter the ram for its golden fleece. The gods were angered by these happenings and placed a curse on Athamus and all of his family until the golden fleece should be returned to Colchis.

As Pelias told Jason the story, he could see that the young prince was stirred, and he was not surprised when Jason vowed that he would bring back the golden fleece. Pelias promised to give Jason his rightful throne when he returned from his quest, and Jason trusted Pelias and agreed to the terms. He gathered about him many great heroes of Greece—Hercules, the strongest and bravest of all heroes; Orpheus, whose music soothed savaged beasts; Argus, who with the help of Juno built the beautiful ship *Argo*; Zetes and Calais, sons of the North Wind, and many other brave men.

They encountered great dangers on their journey. One of the heroes was drawn under the sea by a nymph and was never seen again by his comrades. They visited Salmydessa where the blind King Phineus was surrounded by Harpies, loathsome creatures, with the faces of women and the bodies of vultures. Zetes and Calais chased the creatures across the skies, and the heroes left the old king in peace.

Phineus had warned the heroes about the clashing rocks through which they must pass. As they approached the rocks, they were filled with fear, but Juno held the rocks back and they sailed past the peril. They rowed along the shore until they came to the land of Colchis.

Aeetes, king of Colchis, swore never to give up the treasure, but Jason vowed that he and his comrades would do battle with Aeetes. Then Aeetes consented to yield the treasure if Jason would yoke to the plow two wild, fire-breathing bulls and sow a field with dragon's teeth. When a giant warrior sprang from each tooth, Jason must slay each one. Jason agreed to the trial.

Aeetes had a beautiful daughter Medea, who had fallen in love with the handsome Jason, and she brewed a magic potion which gave Jason godlike strength; thus it was that he was able to tame the wild bulls and slay the warriors. Aeetes promised to bring forth the fleece the next day, but Jason saw the wickedness in the king's heart and warned his comrades to have the *Argo* ready to sail.

In the night Medea secured the seven golden keys that unlocked the seven doors to the cave where the golden fleece hung, and she led Jason to the place. Behind the seven doors, he found a hideous dragon guarding the treasure. Medea's magic caused the dragon to fall asleep, and Jason seized the fleece. It was so bright that night seemed like day.

Fearing for her life, Medea sailed away from her father's house with Jason and the other heroes. After many months, they reached their homeland, where Jason placed the treasure at the feet of Pelias. The fleece, however, was no longer golden. Pelias was wrathful and swore not to give up his kingdom, but in the night the false king died. Afterward, Jason wore the crown, and the enchantress Medea reigned by his side.

Critical Evaluation

The journey of the Argonauts ("Sailors of the *Argo*"), or Minyae, may well be one of the oldest Greek adventure myths. Homer alludes to it, and it is placed in the generation preceding the Trojan War. (The roster of heroes includes Telamon, the father of Ajax, and Peleus, the father of Achilles.) No doubt its folktale theme of a sea journey to inhospitable lands in quest of a valuable prize was the model for the adventures of Odysseus, Hercules, Theseus, and others. Compare, for example, the dragon-guarded golden fleece with the dragon-guarded golden apples of the Hesperides (the eleventh labor of Hercules); the beautiful young princess who aids her father's enemy and is eventually cast aside (as was Ariadne by Theseus); the journey to Aeaea, the island of Circe (Odysseus); a kingdom usurped (Hercules) and regained with a vengeance (Odysseus). Typical of such tales is the accomplishment of an impossible task, a confrontation with death and the fantastically inhuman, all to prove one's nobility of birth and right to reign. The retrieval of the fleece, then, is not the subject of this myth but the occasion; it is a device by which the hero becomes involved with the heroic. Furthermore, the entire expedition would not have come about were it not for Hera, whom Pelias had refused to honor. Her tortuous plan was to have Jason sent off to Colchis so that he would bring back with him the sorceress Medea who would kill Pelias (which she did, by convincing the old king's daughters to kill him so that she might rejuvenate him).

Despite the age of this myth, the earliest extensive literary account is found in Pindar's *Pythian Ode 4* (462 B.C.), and it was not until the third century B.C.

that the myth received formal expanded treatment by Apollonius Rhodius, who revived the epic genre. His romantic effort, the *Argonautica* not only would be the model for other versions of the quest but also would greatly influence Roman epic poets, notably Vergil.

Apollonius' work, despite its obvious stylistic and structural inferiority to Homer's poems, nevertheless contains some very charming, if not masterful, descriptions and characterizations. The first two books are devoted to the voyage from Thessaly to Colchis. Among the more prominent episodes are the Argonauts' landfall at Lemnos, where they are entertained for a year by the women who, having once been plagued with a malodor, killed their men because they had taken Tracian brides. Reaching the Asian mainland, they soon were forced to fight six-armed giants and were involved in two other battles before rescuing the prophet-king Phineus. Book 3 contains the arrival at Colchis and Medea's falling in love with Jason. Unlike the *Iliad*, in which Hera and Athena are at odds with Aphrodite, the *Argonautica* portrays them as allies who instigate the mischievous Eros (Cupid) to fire a shaft into the Princess Medea. Torn between filial loyalty and her uncontrollable passion, she soon yields to love. Her escape with Jason and their eventual arrival at Iolchus (book 4) include the murder of Medea's brother Absyrtus and the necessary expiation on Circe's island, Aeaea. Apollonius had Jason kill Absyrtus through Medea's treachery; in the earlier version, Medea herself murders her brother and scatters the butchered remains over the sea in order to delay the pursuing Colchians, who have to gather the pieces for burial.

The exact return route supposedly taken by the Argonauts was disputed in ancient times. Doubtless the various versions were based on the trade routes begun in the Mycenaean age. Apollonius takes the Argonauts from the mouth of the river Phasis on the Black Sea to the Ister (Danube), overland to the Adriatic, where they are confronted by Absyrtus; then to the Eridanus (Po?) overland to the Rhone to the Tyrrhenian Sea and Circe's island. Other accounts include a return by the same route as they came, sailing east up the Phasis to the world-encircling river Ocean, then southwest to Africa and overland to the Mediterranean (Pindar's version) and sailing up the Phasis, through Russia, and over northern sea routes past Britain and through the Pillars of Hercules. Apollonius includes in the journey the perils of the Sirens, Scylla and Charybdis, and the Wandering Rocks; Medea and Jason, like Odysseus, are given refuge in hospitable Phaeacia on the west coast of Greece, but only after the young lovers marry to void Aeetes' claim to his daughter.

The myth receives brief attention in Ovid's *Metamorphoses* (c. A.D. 8) and would have been retold at length in the Latin hexameters of Valerius Flaccus (first century A.D.), but his *Argonautica* is incomplete. Jason's adventure, nevertheless, is included in Apollodorus' *The Library*, the invaluable (Greek) collection of myths (second century A.D.). Like most myths, the search for the fleece was subject to the rationalizing minds of classical writers: Strabo the geographer theorized that the Argonauts were an expedition in search of alluvial gold; but whatever the origins of the myth, it stands out as a magnificent prototype of the perilous search for the marvelous prize. In a sense, this search is also the theme of the Trojan cycle, in which the greatest figures of a distant glorious age attempt to retrieve the most beautiful mortal woman. The voyage of the *Argo*, however, like the wanderings of Odysseus, belongs to that entertaining genre, *Märchen*, which attends to the unnatural, the exotic, the romantic. Jasonlike heroes are not only seen in the many local legends of ancient Greece but also in history (Alexander's oriental conquests were romanticized). Comparisons may be drawn between Jason and Celtic heroes, and between the Fleece and the Grail.

Classical authors seemed to be more concerned with Medea than with Jason. Euripides' masterpiece *Medea* (431 B.C.) deals with Jason's cruel rejection of the woman who sacrificed all—even murdered—for him. Her vengeance, to deprive Jason of the things he loves most, requires that she kill not only the girl he intends to marry but also Jason's (and Medea's) sons as well. Her refuge in Athens as wife of aging King Aegeus is brief; she escapes to Colchis after an unsuccessful attempt to poison Theseus. Nothing is known of her death—if she died at all. Jason, however, overcome with grief, loneliness, and shame returned to the rotting hulk of the *Argo* which he had beached at Corinth. There he was struck by a falling beam and died.

JUDE THE OBSCURE

Type of work: Novel
Author: Thomas Hardy (1840–1928)
Type of plot: Philosophical realism
Time of plot: Nineteenth century
Locale: Wessex
First published: 1895

Hardy's sexual frankness and unconventional treatment of the theme of marriage in this novel outraged readers when the book was first published; now Jude the Obscure *is seen as one of the author's most powerful achievements. A somber, at times grim novel, it is rich in its portrayal of suffering, powerful in its evocation of nature, and tragic in its vision of a universe where men are powerless to avert the fates inflicted by impersonal external forces.*

Principal Characters

Jude Fawley, a village stonemason who is thwarted in every attempt to find success and happiness. His chief desire from the time of his youth is to become a religious scholar, but because of his sensuous temperament he is forced into an early marriage. After his first wife leaves him he falls in love with his cousin and lives with her illegally for several years. The weight of social disapproval dooms their life together. After the tragic death of their children his cousin leaves him also, and Jude, having turned to drink, dies a miserable death.

Arabella Donn, a country girl who tricks Jude into his first marriage. She has nothing in common with Jude and soon leaves him to go to Australia. She later returns but makes no immediate demands on him, preferring to marry another and advance her station in life. After the death of her second husband and the separation of Jude and his cousin, she tricks him into marrying her a second time. But instead of helping to brighten the last of his life she increases his misery and is planning her next marriage even before his death.

Sue Bridehead, Jude's cousin. Although priding herself on being a free-thinker, she marries a much older man out of a sense of obligation and leaves him shortly afterward because of her revulsion toward him. She lives with Jude for several years and bears him three children. She is a strong influence on him and through her unorthodox thought becomes the primary reason for his giving up his attempts to enter the ministry. After the tragic death of her children, she undergoes a complete change in personality; now wanting to conform, she returns to her first husband.

Richard Phillotson, a village schoolmaster who instills in Jude his first desires to learn. He falls in love with Sue after she becomes his assistant and marries her in spite of obvious differences in age, thought, and belief. When she expresses her desire to live with Jude, he allows her a divorce, although it causes his own downfall. He gladly remarries her when she wants to come back to him, even though he is fully aware that she does not love him.

Little Father Time, the son of Jude and Arabella. He is a precocious child who seems to feel the weight of the world on his shoulders. Having been sent to Jude by Arabella when she married the second time, he is bothered by a sense of being unwanted and feels that he is a source of anxiety for his elders. This feeling becomes so intensified that he hangs himself and the two younger children.

Drusilla Fawley, Jude's great-grandaunt, who raises him after the death of his parents. During his youth she constantly warns him against ever marrying because the Fawleys have never had successful marriages.

Anny and **Sarah,** friends of Arabella. They give her the idea of tricking Jude into marriage.

Mr. Donn, Arabella's father. Although he has nothing to do with the first trick on Jude, he helps Arabella carry out the second one.

Gillingham, a friend and confidant of Phillotson, whose advice Phillotson never takes.

Mrs. Edlin, a neighbor of Drusilla Fawley; she is always ready to help Jude and Sue when they need her.

Vilbert, a quack doctor. He serves as Jude's first source of disillusionment about life.

Cartlett, Arabella's second husband.

The Story

In the nineteenth century, eleven-year-old Jude Fawley said good-bye to his schoolmaster, Richard Phillotson, who was leaving the small English village of Marygreen for Christminster to study for a degree. Young Jude was hungry for learning and yearned to go to Christminster too, but he had to help his great-grandaunt, Drusilla Fawley, in her bakery. At Christminster, Phillotson did not forget his former pupil. He sent Jude some classical grammars, which the boy studied eagerly.

Anticipating a career as a religious scholar, Jude apprenticed himself, at age nineteen, to a stonemason engaged in the restoration of medieval churches in a nearby town. Returning to Marygreen one evening, he met three young girls who were washing pigs' chitterlings by a stream bank. One of the girls, Arabella Donn, caught Jude's fancy, and he arranged to meet her later. The young man was swept off his feet and tricked into marriage, but he soon realized that he had married a vulgar country girl with whom he had nothing in common. Embittered, he tried unsuccessfully to commit suicide; when he began to drink, Arabella left him.

Now free, Jude decided to carry out his original purpose. With this idea in mind, he went to Christminster, where he took work as a stonemason. He had heard that his cousin, Sue Bridehead, lived in Christminster, but he did not seek her out because his aunt had warned him against her and because he was a married man. Eventually, he met her and was charmed. She was an artist employed in an ecclesiastical warehouse. Jude also met Phillotson, again working as a simple schoolteacher. At Jude's suggestion, Sue became Phillotson's assistant. The teacher soon lost his heart to his bright and intellectually independent young helper. Jude was hurt by evidence of intimacy between the two. Disappointed in love and ambition, he turned to drink and was dismissed by his employer. He went back to Marygreen.

At Marygreen, Jude was persuaded by a minister to enter the church as a licentiate. Sue, meanwhile, had won a scholarship to a teacher's college at Melchester; she wrote Jude and asked him to come to see her. Jude worked at stonemasonry in Melchester in order to be near Sue, even though she told him she had promised to marry Phillotson after her schooling. Dismissed from college after an innocent escapade with Jude, Sue influenced him away from the church with her unorthodox beliefs. Shortly afterward, she married Phillotson. Jude was despondent and returned to Christminster, where he came upon Arabella working in a bar. Jude heard that Sue's married life was unbearable. He continued his studies for the ministry and thought a great deal about Sue.

Succumbing completely to his passion for Sue, Jude at last forsook the ministry. His Aunt Drusilla died, and at the funeral, Jude and Sue realized that they could not remain separated. Sympathizing with the lovers, Phillotson released Sue, who now lived apart from her husband. The lovers went to Aldbrickham, a large city where they would not be recognized. Phillotson gave Sue a divorce and subsequently lost his teaching position. Jude gave Arabella a divorce so that she might marry again.

Sue and Jude now contemplated marriage, but they were unwilling to be joined by a church ceremony because of Sue's dislike for any binding contract. The pair lived together happily, and Jude continued his simple stonework. One day, Arabella appeared and told Jude that her marriage had not materialized. Sue was jealous and promised Jude that she would marry him. Arabella's problem was solved by eventual marriage, but out of fear of her husband, she sent her young child by Jude to live with him and Sue. The pathetic boy, nicknamed Little Father Time, joined the unconventional Fawley household.

Jude's business began to decline, and he lost a contract to restore a rural church when the vestry discovered that he and Sue were unmarried. Forced to move on, they traveled from place to place and from job to job. At the end of two and a half years of this itinerant life, the pair had two children of their own and a third on the way. They were a family of five, including Little Father Time. Jude was in failing health, and became a baker; Sue sold cakes in the shape of Gothic ornaments at a fair in a village near Christminster. At the fair, Sue met Arabella, who was now a widow. Arabella reported Sue's poverty to Phillotson, who was once more the village teacher in Marygreen.

Jude took his family to Christminster, where the celebration of Remembrance Week was under way. Utterly defeated by failure, Jude still had a love for the atmosphere of learning that pervaded the city.

The family had difficulty finding lodgings and were forced to separate. Sue's landlady, learning that Sue was an unmarried mother and fearful that she might have the trouble of childbirth in her rooming house, told Sue to find other lodgings. Sue's attitude turned bitter, and she told Little Father Time that children should not be brought into the world. When she returned from a meal with Jude, she found that the boy had hanged the two babies and himself. She collapsed and gave premature birth to a dead baby.

Her experience brought about a change in Sue's point of view. Believing she had sinned and wishing now to conform, she asked Jude to live apart from her. She also expressed the desire to return to Phillotson, whom she believed, in her misery, to be still her husband. She returned to Phillotson, and the two remarried. Jude was utterly lost and began drinking heavily. In a drunken stupor, he was again tricked by Arabella into marriage. His lungs failed; it was evident that he would die soon. Arabella would not communicate with Sue, whom Jude desired to see once more, and so Jude traveled in the rain to see her. The lovers had a last meeting. She then made complete atonement for her past mistakes by becoming Phillotson's wife completely. This development was reported to Jude, who died in desperate misery of mind and body. Fate had grown tired of its sport with a luckless man.

Critical Evaluation

A unique transitional figure between the literary worlds of the Victorian and the modern, Thomas Hardy was an undistinguished architect whose novels and poems were to become his chief profession. Although his rustic characters and some of his poems exhibit a humorous hand at work, invading most of his creations are a brooding irony reflecting life's disappointments and a pessimistic belief that man is a victim of a neutral force that darkly rules the universe. Hardy divided his novels into three groups: Novels of Ingenuity (such as *Desperate Remedies*); Romances and Fantasies (for example, *A Pair of Blue Eyes*); and Novels of Character and Environment. This last class includes his best and most famous works, *Tess of the D'Urbervilles*, *The Return of the Native*, *Far from the Madding Crowd*, *The Mayor of Casterbridge*, and *Jude the Obscure*.

First published in a modified form as an 1894 serial in *Harper's*, *Jude the Obscure* is considered by many critics to be Hardy's top-ranking novel. Today, however, it is read less often than many of his works, and it was the outraged reception of *Jude the Obscure* that turned Hardy from the novel to a concentration on poetry. His disgust at the critical reaction was bitter and enduring.

The best explanation of the book's basic framework was stated by Hardy himself in his preface: the novel, meant for adults, was intended "to tell, without a mincing of words, of a deadly war waged between flesh and spirit; and to point to the tragedy of unfulfilled aims." To these, readers may add two other important themes: an attack on convention and society and an examination of man's essential loneliness.

The flesh-spirit division bedevils Jude throughout the novel. His relationship with Arabella represents his strong sexual propensities, while his attraction to intellectual pursuits and his high principles reveal his spiritual side. His obsession with Sue is a reflection of both sides of his personality, for while he is attracted by her mind and emotion, he is also drawn to her physically. At the crucial moments of his life, Jude's fleshly desires are strong enough to supersede his greatest ambitions. His initial attempt at a university career is halted when he succumbs to Arabella, and his plans for the ministry end when he kisses Sue and decides that as long as he loves another man's wife he cannot be a soldier and servant of a religion that is so suspicious of sexual love.

"The tragedy of unfulfilled aims" is forcefully present in both Jude and Sue. For years Jude, in a truly dedicated and scholarly fashion, devotes himself to preparing to enter Christminster (Hardy's name for Oxford). Even when he frees himself from the sexual entanglement with Arabella, his hopes for an education are dashed, for the master of the college advises him to "remain in your own sphere." Through no fault of his own and despite his seeming ability, he is again denied what he so desperately

seeks. The fact of his birth as a poor person is unchangeable, and Jude must accept its results. His second great desire, a spiritual (as well as sexual) union with Sue, is also doomed. When Jude first sees Sue's picture, he thinks of her as a saint, and he eventually derives many of his maturing intellectual concepts from her. His passion for Sue is true and full; yet Sue's deeply flawed character necessitates her self-destruction as well as the destruction of Jude. She drains Jude while simultaneously serving as a source of his growth, for she is irresponsible, cold, and cruel. She is an imperfect being, afraid not only of her physical side but of her very ideas. She tells Jude that she does not have the courage of her convictions, and when he adopts her iconoclastic stance, she abandons it and demonstrates how conventional she really is. Her pagan shouts, her free thought, her brave spirit prove as much a sham as Christminster's promises. Her tragedy, the gap between what she is and what she might have been, is not hers alone but is shared by Jude and becomes his.

As an attack on convention and society, *Jude the Obscure* focuses on three major areas: the British university system, marriage, and religion. Jude's exclusion from Christminster is an indictment of the structure of an institution that allegedly symbolizes the noble part of man's mind yet actually stands only for a closed, tightly knit social club. In its criticism of marriage, a union that Hardy said should be dissolved by either side if it became a burden, the novel reveals how false is the view of marriage as a sacred contract. Marriage, as in Jude's merger with Arabella, is often the fruit of a temporary urge, but its harvest can be lifelong and ruinous. Sue's fear of marriage also suggests that the bond can be one of suffocation. Perhaps most important are the novel's charges against Christianity. The fundamental hollowness and hypocrisy of Christianity, Hardy asserts, damn it dreadfully. A farmer thrashes Jude for lovingly letting the birds feed, and the sounds of the beating echo from the church tower that the same farmer had helped finance. Hardy's scorn for such inconsistencies is evident throughout the book, and he proposes that the only valuable part of Christianity is its idea that love makes life more bearable.

Mirroring the development of these themes is the final impression that the book is also a cry of loneliness. Jude's hopelessness is in the final analysis a result of his alienation not only from Arabella and Sue but from his environment. Used in connection with Jude, the word "obscure," in addition to conveying his association with darkness, his lack of distinction in the eyes of the world, and his humble station, suggests that he is not understood, that he is hidden from others and is only faintly perceptible. In Hardy's world, the happiest people are those who are most in touch with their environment, a condition that usually occurs in the least reflective characters. Jude, however, is always grasping for the ideal and ignores the unpleasantness about him as much as he possibly can; this inevitably places him on the path to isolation. Hardy hints that such is the price man must pay for the refusal to accept his status without questioning.

All the ills that Hardy ascribes to this world are, he feels, merely a reflection of the ills of the universe. Man ruins society because he is imperfect and caught in the grip of a fatal and deterministic movement of the stars. Defending his dark outlook, Hardy tells us: "If a way to the better there be, it demands a full look at the worst." In a philosophy which he terms evolutionary meliorism, Hardy further amplifies this concept in both a brighter and a more pessimistic vein. That philosophy proposes not only that man may improve, but that he *must* find the way to that better condition if he is to survive.

JULIUS CAESAR

Type of work: Drama
Author: William Shakespeare (1564–1616)
Type of plot: Romantic tragedy
Time of plot: 44 B.C.
Locale: Rome
First presented: 1601

The story of Brutus rather than of Caesar, this drama transforms history into a tragedy of character. Brutus emerges as a forerunner of Hamlet, while Caesar appears as a rather shallow individual and the so-called villain Cassius develops into a sympathetic figure.

Principal Characters

Marcus Brutus (mär′kŭs brōō′tŭs), one of the leading conspirators who intend to kill Julius Caesar. Although defeated in the end, Brutus is idealistic and honorable, for he hopes to do what is best for Rome. Under Caesar, he fears, the Empire will have merely a tyrant. Something of a dreamer, he, unlike the more practical Cassius, makes a number of tactical errors, such as allowing Marcus Antonius to speak to the citizens of Rome. Finally, defeated by the forces under young Octavius and Antonius, Brutus commits suicide. He would rather accept death than be driven, caged, through the streets of Rome.

Caius Cassius (kā′yŭs kăs′ĭ·ŭs), another leading conspirator, one of the prime movers in the scheme. A practical man, and a jealous one, he is a lean and ambitious person. Some of his advice to Brutus is good. He tells Brutus to have Antonius killed. When this is not done, the conspirators are doomed to defeat. Like Brutus, Cassius commits suicide when his forces are routed at Philippi. To the last a brave man, he has fought well and courageously.

Julius Caesar (jōōl′yŭs sē′zər), the mighty ruler of Rome, who hopes to gain even more power. As portrayed in the play, he is a somewhat bombastic and arrogant man, possibly even a cowardly one. From the first he mistrusts men who, like Cassius, have "a lean and hungry look." Finally reaching for too much power, he is stabbed by a large number of conspirators led by Brutus and Cassius.

Marcus Antonius (mär′kŭs ăn·tō′nĭ·ŭs), also **Mark Antony,** the close friend of Caesar. Although he denies it, he has a great ability to sway a mob and rouse them to a feverish pitch. As a result of his oratorical abilities, he, with the help of a mob, forces the conspirators to ride for their lives to escape the maddened crowd. Later, along with Octavius and Lepidus, he is to rule Rome.

Calpurnia (kăl·pėr′nĭ·ə), the wife of Caesar. Afraid because she has had frightful dreams about yawning graveyards and lions whelping in the streets, she begs her arrogant husband not to go to the Capitol on the day of the assassination.

Portia (pôr′shə), wife of Brutus. When she learns that her husband has been forced to flee for his life, she becomes frightened for his safety. As matters worsen, she swallows hot coals and dies.

Decius Brutus (dē′shŭs brōō′tŭs), one of the conspirators against Julius Caesar. When the others are doubtful that the superstitious Caesar will not come to the Capitol, Decius volunteers to bring him to the slaughter; for he knows Caesar's vanities and will play upon them until he leaves the security of his house.

Publius (pŭb′lĭ·ŭs), **Cicero** (sĭs′ə·rō), and **Popilius Lena** (pō·pĭl′ĭ·ŭs lē′nə), Senators.

A Soothsayer. At the beginning of the play, he warns Caesar to beware the Ides of March. For his trouble he is called a dreamer.

Artemidorus of Cnidos (är′tə·mĭ·dō′rus of nī′dŏs), a teacher of rhetoric who tries to warn Caesar to beware of the conspirators led by Brutus and Cassius. Like the soothsayer, he is ignored.

Casca (kăs′kə), **Caius Ligarius** (kā′yŭs lĭ·gā′rĭ·ŭs), **Cinna** (sĭn′ə), and **Metellus Cimber** (mĕ·tĕl′ŭs sĭm′bər), the other conspirators.

Flavius (flā′vĭ·ŭs) and **Marullus** (mă·rŭl′ŭs), tribunes who speak to the crowd at the beginning of the play.

Pindarus (pĭn′dȧa·rŭs), Cassius' servant. At his master's orders he runs Cassius through with a sword.

Strato (strā′tō), servant and friend to Brutus. He holds Brutus' sword so that the latter could run upon it and commit suicide.

Marcus Aemilius Lepidus (mär′kŭs ē·mĭl′ĭ·ŭs lĕp′ĭ·dŭs), the weakest member of the triumvirate after the deaths of Brutus and Cassius.

Lucius (lōō′shĭ·ŭs), Brutus' servant.

Young Cato, Messala (mĕ·sā′lə), and **Titinius** (tĭ·tĭn′ĭ·ŭs), friends of Brutus and Cassius.

The Story

At the feast of Lupercalia all Rome rejoiced, for the latest military triumphs of Julius Caesar were being celebrated during that holiday. Yet tempers flared and jealousies seethed beneath this public gaiety. Flavius and Marallus, two tribunes, coming upon a group of citizens gathered to praise Caesar, tore down their trophies and ordered the people to go home and remember Pompey's fate at the hands of Caesar.

Other dissatisfied noblemen discussed with concern Caesar's growing power and his incurable ambition. A soothsayer, following Caesar in his triumphal procession, warned him to beware the Ides of March. Cassius, one of the most violent of Caesar's critics, spoke at length to Brutus of the dictator's unworthiness to rule the state. Why, he demanded, should the name of Caesar have become synonymous with that of Rome when there were so many other worthy men in the city?

While Cassius and Brutus were speaking, they heard a tremendous shouting from the crowd. From aristocratic Casca they learned that before the mob Marcus Antonius had three times offered a crown to Caesar and three times the dictator had refused it. Thus did the wily Antonius and Caesar catch and hold the devotion of the multitude. Fully aware of Caesar's methods and the potential danger that he embodied, Cassius and Brutus, disturbed by this new turn of events, agreed to meet again to discuss the affairs of Rome. As they parted, Caesar arrived in time to see them, and he became suspicious of Cassius. Cassius did not look content; he was too lean and nervous to be satisfied with life. Caesar much preferred to have fat, jolly men about him.

Cassius' plan was to enlist Brutus in a plot to overthrow Caesar. Brutus himself was one of the most respected and beloved citizens of Rome; if he were in league against Caesar, the dictator's power could by curbed easily. But it would be difficult to turn Brutus completely against Caesar, for Brutus was an honorable man and not given to treason, so that only the most drastic circumstances would make him forego his loyalty. Cassius plotted to have certain false papers denoting widespread public alarm over Caesar's rapidly growing power put into Brutus' hands. Then Brutus might put Rome's interests above his own personal feelings.

Secretly, at night, Cassius had the papers laid at Brutus' door. Their purport was that Brutus must strike at once against Caesar to save Rome. The conflict within Brutus was great. His wife Portia complained that he had not slept at all during the night and that she had found him wandering, restless and unhappy, about the house. At last he reached a decision. Remembering Tarquin, the tyrant whom his ancestors had banished from Rome, Brutus agreed to join Cassius and his conspirators in their attempt to save Rome from Caesar. He refused, however, to sanction the murder of Antonius, planned at the same

time as the assassination of Caesar. The plan was to kill Caesar on the following morning, March fifteenth.

On the night of March fourteenth, all nature seemed to misbehave. Strange lights appeared in the sky, graves yawned, ghosts walked, and an atmosphere of terror pervaded the city. Caesar's wife Calpurnia dreamed she saw her husband's statue with a hundred wounds spouting blood. In the morning she told him of the dream and pleaded that he not go to the Senate that morning. When she had almost convinced him to remain at home, one of the conspirators arrived and persuaded the dictator that Calpurnia was unduly nervous, that the dream was actually an omen of Caesar's tremendous popularity in Rome, the bleeding wounds a symbol of Caesar's power going out to all Romans. The other conspirators then arrived to allay any suspicion that Caesar might have of them and to make sure that he attended the Senate that day.

As Caesar made his way through the city, more omens of evil appeared to him. A paper detailing the plot against him was thrust into his hands, but he neglected to read it. When the soothsayer again cried out against the Ides of March, Caesar paid no attention to the warning.

At the Senate chamber Antonius was drawn to one side. Then the conspirators crowded about Caesar as if to second a petition for the repealing of an order banishing Publius Cimber. When he refused the petition, the conspirators attacked him, and he fell dead of twenty-three knife wounds.

Craftily pretending to side with the conspirators, Antonius was able to reinstate himself in their good graces, and in spite of Cassius' warning he was granted permission to speak at Caesar's funeral after Brutus had delivered his oration. Before the populace Brutus, frankly and honestly explaining his part in Caesar's murder, declared that his love for Rome had prompted him to turn against his friend. Cheering him, the mob agreed that Caesar was a tyrant who deserved death. Then Antonius rose to speak. Cleverly and forcefully he turned the temper of the crowd against the conspirators by explaining that even when Caesar was most tyrannical, everything he did was for the people's welfare. Soon the mob became so enraged over the assassination that the conspirators were forced to flee from Rome.

Gradually the temper of the people changed, and they became aligned in two camps. One group supported the new triumvirate of Marcus Antonius, Octavius Caesar, and Aemilius Lepidus. The other group followed Brutus and Cassius to their military camp at Sardis.

At Sardis, Brutus and Cassius quarreled constantly over various small matters. In the course of one violent disagreement Brutus told Cassius that Portia, despondent over the outcome of the civil war, had killed herself. Cassius, shocked by this news of his sister's death, allowed himself to be persuaded to leave the safety of the camp at Sardis and meet the enemy on the plains of Philippi. The night before the battle Caesar's ghost appeared to Brutus in his tent and announced that they would meet at Philippi.

At the beginning of the battle the forces of Brutus were at first successful against those of Octavius. Cassius, however, was driven back by Antonius. One morning Cassius sent one of his followers, Titinius, to learn if approaching troops were the enemy or the soldiers of Brutus. When Cassius saw Titinius unseated from his horse by the strangers, he assumed that everything was lost and ordered his servant Pindarus to kill him. Actually, the troops had been sent by Brutus. Rejoicing over the defeat of Octavius, they were having rude sport with Titinius. When they returned to Cassius and found him dead, Titinius also killed himself. In the last charge against Antonius, the soldiers of Brutus, tired and discouraged by these new events, were defeated. Brutus, heartbroken, asked his friends to kill him. When they refused, he commanded his servant to hold his sword and turn his face away. Then Brutus fell upon his sword and died.

Critical Evaluation

The first of Shakespeare's so-called "Roman plays"—which include *Coriolanus* and *Antony and Cleopatra*—*Julius Caesar* also heralds the great period of his tragedies. The sharply dramatic and delicately portrayed character of Brutus is a clear predecessor of Hamlet and Othello. With *Titus Andronicus* and *Romeo and Juliet*, *Julius Caesar* is one of the three tragedies written before the beginning of the sixteenth century. It is, however, more historical than the four great tragedies—*Hamlet*, *Othello*, *Macbeth*, and *King Lear*—being drawn in large part from Sir Thomas North's wonderfully idiomatic translation of Plutarch's *Lives of the Noble Grecians and Romans* (1579). A comparison of the Shakespearean text with the passages from North's chapters on Caesar, Brutus, and Antony reveals the remarkable truth of T. S. Eliot's statement: "Immature poets borrow; mature poets steal." For in example after example, Shakespeare has done little more than rephrase the words of North's exuberant prose to fit the rhythm of his own blank verse. The thievery is nonetheless a brilliant one, and not without originality on Shakespeare's part.

Shakespeare's originality, found in all his "historical" plays, is analogous to that of the great classical Greek playwrights. Aeschylus, Sophocles, and Euripides faced a dramatic challenge very unlike that offered to modern writers, who are judged by their capacity for sheer invention. Just as the Greek audience came to the play with full knowledge of the particular myth involved in the tragedy to be presented, so the Elizabethan audience knew the story of the assassination of Julius Caesar. Shakespeare, like his classical predecessors, had to work his dramatic art within the restrictions of known history. He accomplished this by writing "between the lines" of Plutarch, offering insights into the mind of the characters that Plutarch does not mention—insights which become, on the stage, dramatic motivations. An example is Caesar's revealing hesitation about going to the Senate because of Calpurnia's dream, and the way he is swayed by Decius into going after all. This scene shows the weakness of Caesar's character in a way not found in a literal reading of Plutarch. A second major "adaptation" by Shakespeare is a daring, dramatically effective telescoping of historical time. The historical events associated with the death of Caesar and the defeat of the conspirators actually took three years; Shakespeare condenses them into three tense days, following the Castolvetrian unity of time (though not of place).

Although prose is used in the play by comic and less important characters or in purely informative speeches or documents, the general mode of expression is Shakespeare's characteristic blank verse, with five stressed syllables per line and generally unrhymed. The iambic pentameter, a rhythm natural to English speech, has the effect of making more memorable lines such as Flavius' comment about the commoners ("They vanish tongue-tied in their guiltiness") or Brutus' observation, "Men at some time are masters of their fates." As in most of the tragedies, Shakespeare here follows a five-part dramatic structure, consisting of the exposition (to act 1, scene 2), complication (1.2 to 2.4), climax (3.1), consequence (3.1–5.2), and denouement (5.3–5.5).

The primary theme of *Julius Caesar* is a combination of political and personal concerns, the first dealing with the question of justifiable revolutions—revealing with the effectiveness of concentrated action the transition from a republic of equals to an empire dominated by great individuals (like Antony, influenced by the example of Caesar himself, and Octavius, who comes to his own at the end of the play). The personal complication is the tragedy of a noble spirit involved in matters it does not comprehend; that is, the tragedy of Brutus. For, despite the title, Brutus, not Caesar, is the hero of this play. It is true that Caesar's influence motivates the straightforward and ultimately victorious actions of Antony throughout the play, accounting for Antony's transformation from an apparently secondary figure into one of solid stature. But it is the presence of Brutus before the eyes of the audience as he gradually learns to distinguish ideals from reality that dominates the sympathy of the audience. Around his gentle character, praised at last even by Antony, Shakespeare weaves the recurrent motifs of honor and honesty, freedom and fortune, ambition and pride. Honor is the theme of Brutus' speech to the crowd in the Forum, honor as it interacts with ambition: "As Caesar loved me, I weep for him; as he was fortunate, I rejoice at it; as he was valiant, I honour him, but, as he was ambitious, I slew him." After the deed Brutus comments, "Ambition's debt is paid." One of the great, dramatically successful ironies of the play is that Antony's Forum speech juxtaposes the same two themes: "Yet Brutus says he was ambitious/ And Brutus is an honourable man." By the time Antony is finished, the term "honour" has been twisted by his accelerating sarcasm until it becomes a curse, moving the fickle crowd to change their opinion entirely and call for death to the conspirators.

The conjunction of Brutus and Antony in this particular scene (act 3, scene 2) reveals the telling difference between their dramatic characterizations. Though Caesar may have had too much ambition, Brutus' problem is that he has too little; Brutus is a man of ideals and words, and therefore cannot succeed in the corridors of power. Cassius and Antony, in contrast, have no such concern with idealistic concepts or words like honor and ambition; yet there is a distinction even between them. Cassius is a pure *doer*, a man of action, almost entirely devoid of sentiment or principle; Antony, however, is both a doer of deeds and a speaker of words—and therefore prevails over all in the end, following in the footsteps of his model, Caesar. To underline the relationships among these similar yet different characters and the themes that dominate their actions Shakespeare weaves a complicated net of striking images: monetary (creating a tension between Brutus and Cassius); the tide image ("Thou are the ruins of the noblest man/ That ever lived in the tide of times")

connected with the theme of fortune; the stars (Caesar compares himself, like Marlowe's Tamburlaine, to a fixed star while Cassius says, "The fault, dear Brutus, is not in our stars,/ But in ourselves, that we are underlings"); and the wood and stones used to describe the common people by those who would move them to their own will.

Julius Caesar, in yet another way, marks the advance of Shakespeare's artistry in its use of dramatic irony. In this play the Shakespearean audience becomes almost a character in the drama, as it is made privy to knowledge and sympathies not yet shared by all the characters on the stage. This pattern occurs most notably in Decius' speech interpreting Calpurnia's dream, showing the ability of an actor to move men to action by duplicity that is well managed. The pattern is also evident when Cinna mistakes Cassius for Metellus Cimber, foreshadowing the mistaken identity scene that ends in his own death; when Cassius, on two occasions, gives in to Brutus' refusal to do away with Mark Antony; and, most effectively of all, in the two Forum speeches when Antony addresses two audiences, the one in the theater (that knows his true intentions), and the other the Roman crowd whose ironic whimsicality is marked by the startling shift of sentiment, from admiration following Brutus' speech ("Let him be Caesar!") to the immediate and very opposite feeling after Antony's ("Die, honourable men!"). The effect of the irony is to suggest the close connection between functional politics and the art of acting. Antony, in the end, wins out over Brutus—as Bolingbroke does over Richard II—because he can put on a more compelling act.

DAS KAPITAL

Type of work: Political economy
Author: Karl Marx (1818–1883)
First published: Vol. I, 1867; Vols. II and III, edited by Friedrich Engels, 1885–1894

If Marx was right, the Russian Revolution was inevitable and the worldwide growth of communism is also inevitable; therefore, even if *Das Kapital* had never been written, the world would have been split by revolution and by the emergence of communism as a dynamic political force. But it may be that Marx was mistaken, and that the emergence of communism would not have been possible had it not been for the labors of Marx in the British Museum which resulted in the writing and publication of *Das Kapital*. Even if economic injustice had resulted in a revolutionary uprising of the proletariat in Russia or elsewhere, it probably would not have taken the form it did, or occurred when it did, or had the subsequent worldwide effect that it has had, had Marx not written *Das Kapital*. To write that this book has been world-shaking, then, is but to speak the truth.

Many of Marx's revolutionary ideas had already been expressed in the *Communist Manifesto* (1848) which he wrote with Friedrich Engels, but *Das Kapital* was more than another call to arms; it was an attempt to base communism on a theory of political economy which could be scientifically and dialectically defended. The *Manifesto* is a passionate document, an outline of a political philosophy, and something of a prophecy; but *Das Kapital* is a scholar's treatise, the product of years of research and reflection, a work of economic theory that continues to challenge professional economists. This contrast is illuminating, for the Communist movement has always been characterized by contrast: the intellectual leads the laborers; the reasoned defense is supplemented by violence and murder, and the scholar's program comes alive in revolution and the threat of war.

In the *Manifesto*, Marx and Engels argued that the history of all societies has been a history of class struggles, that the struggle had become one between the bourgeois class and the proletariat, that all the injustices of society result from the economic advantage the bourgeoisie have over the proletariat, that the proletariat would finally rebel and take over the means of production, forming a classless society, a dictatorship of the proletariat.

In *Das Kapital*, Marx uses a dialectic method which was inspired by Hegel, even though it is put to a different use. Marx claimed that his dialectic method was the "direct opposite" of Hegel's, that with Hegel the dialectic "is standing on its head" and "must be turned right side up again, if you would discover the rational kernel within the mystical shell." The method is not mysterious; it involves attending to the conflicting aspects of matters under consideration in order to be able to attain a better idea of the whole. Thus, Marx describes his "rational" dialectic as including "in its comprehension and affirmative recognition of the existing state of things, at the same time, also, the recognition of the negation of that state, of its inevitable breaking up. . . ." He went on to maintain that his account regarded "every historically developed social form as in fluid movement, and therefore takes into account its transient nature not less than its momentary existence. . . ."

In Marx the dialectic method led to "dialectical materialism," the theory that history is the record of class struggles, the conflict of economic opposites.

Das Kapital begins with a study of commodities and money. Marx distinguishes between *use* value and value, the latter being understood in terms of exchange value but involving essentially the amount of labor that went into the production of the commodity; thus, "that which determines the magnitude of the value of any article is the amount of labour socially necessary, or the labour time socially necessary for its production."

Money results from the use of some special commodity as a means of exchange in order to equate different products of labor. Money serves as "a universal measure of value." According to Marx, it is not money that makes commodities commensurable, but the fact of their being commensurable in terms of human labor that makes money possible as a measure of value.

Money begets money through the circulation of commodities: this is Marx's general formula for capital. Money is the first form in which capital appears precisely because it is the end product of a circulatory process which begins with the use of money to purchase commodities for sale at higher than the purchase price.

Capital would not be possible without a change of value. If money were used to purchase a commodity sold at the initial price, no profit would be made, no capital made possible. To explain the surplus value that emerges in the process, Marx reminds the reader that the capitalist buys labor power and uses it. The material of production belongs to the capitalist; therefore the product of the productive process also belongs to him. The product has a use-value, but the capitalist does not intend to use the product; his interest is in selling it for a price greater than the sum of the costs of its production, including the cost of labor. The realization of surplus value is possible, finally, only by some sort of exploitation of the laborer; somehow or other the capitalist must manage to make the cost of labor less than the value of labor.

One way of increasing surplus value is by increasing the productiveness of labor without decreasing the work day, but the problem which then arises is the problem of keeping the price of commodities up. One solution takes the form of using large numbers of laborers and dividing them for special tasks. The capitalist takes advantage of lower prices of commodities by paying labor less and purchasing materials more cheaply. At the same time, through a division of labor, he achieves greater productiveness without a corresponding rise in labor cost. In other words, the capitalist hires an individual and puts him to work in cooperation with others; he pays for the labor power of that individual, but he gains the value that comes from using that power cooperatively.

Marx rejects the idea that machinery is introduced in order to make work easier. He argues that "Like every other increase in the productiveness of labour, machinery is intended to cheapen commodities, and, by shortening that portion of the working day, in which the labourer works for himself, to lengthen the other portion that he gives, without an equivalent, to the capitalist. In short, it is a means for producing surplus value."

Marx concluded that the possibility of the growth of capital depended upon using labor in some way that would free the capitalist from the need to pay for the use of labor power. He decided that capital is "the command over unpaid labour. All surplus value . . . is in substance the materialisation of unpaid labour."

Capitalist production, according to Marx, "reproduces and perpetuates the condition for exploiting the labourer. It incessantly forces him to sell his labour-power in order to live, and enables the capitalist to purchase labour-power in order that he may enrich himself." Accordingly, the division between men which is described in terms of classes is inevitable in a capitalistic society.

Marx explains the self-destruction of the capitalistic society by arguing that from the exploitation of laborers the capitalist, if he has the economic power, passes to the exploitation of other capitalists and, finally, to their expropriation: "One capitalist always kills many." The monopolistic tendencies of capitalists finally hinder the modes of production, and the mass exploitation of workers reaches such a peak of misery and oppression that an uprising of the proletariat destroys the capitalist state. Thus, "capitalist production begets, with the inexorability of a law of Nature, its own negation." The transformation into the socialized state is much quicker and easier than the transformation of the private property of the workers into capitalist private property, for it is easier for the mass of workers to expropriate the property of a few capitalists than for the capitalists to expropriate the property of the laborers.

Das Kapital has often been criticized as an economic study written in the style of German metaphysics. It is generally regarded, particularly by those who have never read it, as an extremely difficult book, both in content and style. By its nature it is a complex, scholarly work, but it is also clear and direct in the exposition of Marx's ideas; and it is lightened by numerous hypothetical cases which illustrate in a vivid manner the various points which Marx makes. In its consideration of the work of other scholars it is respectful if not acquiescent. Perhaps the primary fault of this momentous work is not that it is too difficult, but that it is too simple: to argue that capital is made possible by exploitation of labor may be to ignore the ways in which profit can be realized and labor paid to the satisfaction of both the capitalist and the laborer.

KIDNAPPED: Being Memoirs of the Adventures of David Balfour in the Year 1751

Type of work: Novel
Author: Robert Louis Stevenson (1850–1894)
Type of plot: Adventure romance
Time of plot: 1751
Locale: Scotland
First published: 1886

This tale of high adventure, told simply but colorfully, is woven around a true incident; Stevenson's characters, from all classes, noble and ignoble, are skillfully drawn, and develop convincingly as they pass through kidnappings, battles at sea, murders, and other adventures.

Principal Characters

David Balfour, who tries to claim the inheritance of his dead father. He partially succeeds after many adventures, beginning with his kidnapping aboard the *Covenant* at the behest of his wicked uncle.

Ebenezer Balfour of Shaws, David's uncle, an unscrupulous man hated by his neighbors. He holds the Balfour possessions.

Captain Hoseason, master of the *Covenant,* who shanghais David to prevent his claiming his inheritance.

Alan Breck Stewart, a Jacobite rescued when the *Covenant* sinks his small ship. He becomes friendly with David.

Mr. Riach, the second mate of the *Covenant,* David's only friend aboard.

Mr. Shuan, the first mate of the *Covenant,* who while drunk beats to death the cabin boy, Ransome. David inherits Ransome's job aboard ship.

Mr. Rankeillor, the family lawyer, who reveals Ebenezer's treachery to David.

Mr. Campbell, the minister of Essendean, who carries a letter to David from his dead father.

Colin of Glenure, called **The Red Fox,** who hunts Alan for conspiracy against King George. His death is blamed on Alan.

The Story

When David Balfour's father died, the only inheritance he left his son was a letter to Ebenezer Balfour of Shaws, who was his brother and David's uncle. Mr. Campbell, the minister of Essendean, delivered the letter to David and told him that if things did not go well between David and his uncle he was to return to Essendean, where his friends would help him. David set off in high spirits. The house of Shaw was a great one in the Lowlands of Scotland, and David was eager to take his rightful place among the gentry. He did not know why his father had been separated from his people.

As he approached the great house, he began to grow apprehensive. Everyone of whom he asked the way had a curse for the name Shaws and warned him against his uncle; but he had gone too far and was too curious to turn back before he reached the mansion. What he found was not a great house. One wing was unfinished, and many windows were without glass. No friendly smoke came from the chimneys, and the closed door was studded with heavy nails.

David found his Uncle Ebenezer even more forbidding than the house, and he began to suspect that his uncle had cheated his father out of his rightful inheritance.

When his uncle tried to kill him, he was sure of Ebenezer's villainy. His uncle promised to take David to Mr. Rankeillor, the family lawyer, to get the true story of David's inheritance, and they set out for Queen's Ferry. Before they reached the lawyer's office, David was tricked by Ebenezer and Captain Hoseason into boarding the *Covenant*, and the ship sailed away with David a prisoner, bound for slavery in the American Colonies.

At first, he lived in filth and starvation in the bottom of the ship. The only person who befriended him was Mr. Riach, the second officer. Later, however, he found many of the roughest seamen to be kind at times. Although kind when he was drunk, Mr. Riach was mean when he was sober, while Mr. Shuan, the first officer, was gentle except when he was drinking. It was while he was drunk that Mr. Shuan beat to death Ransome the cabin boy, because the boy had displeased him. After Ransome's murder, David became the cabin boy, and for a time life on the *Covenant* was a little better.

One night, the *Covenant* ran down a small boat and cut her in two. Only one man was saved, Alan Breck Stewart, a Scottish Highlander and Jacobite with a price on his head. Alan demanded that Captain Hoseason set him ashore among his own people, and the captain agreed. When David overheard the captain and Mr. Riach planning to seize Alan, he warned Alan of the plot. Together, the two of them held the ship's crew at bay, killing Mr. Shuan and three others and wounding many more, including Captain Hoseason. Afterward, Alan and David were fast friends and remained so during the rest of their adventures. Alan told David of his part in the rebellion against King George and of the way he was hunted by the king's men, particularly by Colin of Glenure, known as the Red Fox. Alan was the king's enemy while David was loyal to the monarch, yet out of mutual respect, they swore to help each other in time of trouble.

It was not long before they had to prove their loyalty. The ship broke apart on a reef. David and Alan, separated at first, soon found themselves together again, deep in the part of the Highlands controlled by Alan's enemies. When Colin of Glenure was murdered, the blame fell on Alan. To be caught meant they would both hang. Therefore, they began an attempt to escape to the Lowlands and to find Mr. Rankeillor, their only chance for help. They hid by day and traveled by night. Often they went for several days without food and with only a flask of rum for drink. They were in danger not only from the king's soldiers, but also from Alan's own people. There was always the danger that a trusted friend would betray them for the reward offered. David, however, was to learn the meaning of loyalty. Many of Alan's clan endangered themselves to help the hunted pair.

When David was too weak to go on and wanted to give up, Alan offered to carry him. They finally reached Queen's Ferry and Mr. Rankeillor. At first, Mr. Rankeillor was skeptical when he heard David's story, but it began to accord so well with what he had heard from others that he was convinced of the boy's honesty; and he told David the whole story of his father and his Uncle Ebenezer. They had both loved the same woman, and David's father had won her. Because he was a kind man and because Ebenezer had taken to his bed over the loss of the woman, David's father had given up his inheritance as the oldest son in favor of Ebenezer. The story helped David realize why his uncle had tried to get rid of him. Ebenezer knew that his dealings with David's father would not stand up in the courts, and he was afraid that David had come for his inheritance.

With the help of Alan and Mr. Rankeillor, David was able to frighten his uncle so much that Ebenezer offered him two-thirds of the yearly income from the land. Because David did not want to submit his family to public scandal in the courts and because he could better help Alan if the story of their escape were kept quiet, he agreed to the settlement. In this way, he was able to help Alan reach safety and pay his debt to his friend.

So ended the adventures of David Balfour of Shaws. He had been kidnapped and sent to sea; he had known danger and untold hardships; he had traveled the length of his native island; but now he had come to take his rightful place among his people.

Critical Evaluation

Robert Louis Stevenson directed many of his works to young readers in deference to nineteenth century Romanticism's idealization of the presumed innocence of childhood and the fecundity of children's imaginations. It was his strong personal conviction that youngsters were an important segment of the reading public. *Kidnapped* was originally published as a serial in a boys' magazine, and Stevenson first won fame as a novelist with a children's adventure story, *Treasure Island* (1883).

A large part of the popular appeal of *Kidnapped* lies with the historical-romantic nature of the plot. Typical of such plots, the novel revolves around a genuine historical incident, the murder of Colin Campbell, the Red Fox of Glenure; and other historical figures appear— King George among them. Nevertheless, nonhistorical incidents and characters—David Balfour's trials and Alan Stewart's escapades, for example—constitute the largest part of the novel, although the pivotal action in the plot is tied to actual history. This intertwining of history and fantasy has the effect of both personalizing history and making fantasy credible to the reader.

An additional factor that enhances the verisimilitude of *Kidnapped* is the narrative technique. David Balfour

tells his own story in the first person. As a consequence, the reader develops a close rapport with the narrator and sympathizes with his plight. Most important, the first-person narration makes the story highly plausible.

Stevenson emphasized plot over characterization; his goal was to entertain—to transport the reader from mundane, daily existence to a believable world of excitement and adventure that the reader might otherwise never experience. To create this effect in *Kidnapped*, Stevenson combined the extraordinary with the commonplace. On the one hand, such extraordinary events as David's kidnapping, Alan's rescue, and the shipwreck take place. On the other hand, such commonplaces as family hostilities (David versus Ebenezer), drunken sailors and sober sailors, and Scottish feuds (Alan versus the monarchist Colin) lend a measure of realism to the unusual or extraordinary. This combination produces an exceptionally convincing tale.

Stevenson, however, does not ignore the impact of character development. His juxtaposition of David, the canny Lowlander, and Alan, the proud Highlander, brings the story to its highest pitch of excitement by synthesizing two opposing value systems into a compatible working unit. David and Alan have contradictory points of view and antithetical sociopolitical commitments; yet they work together and form a lasting bond on the basis of friendship and loyalty that transcend their differences. Here is Stevenson the novelist at his best—forsaking dogma and eschewing ideology in favor of humanistic values. Stevenson was a master storyteller. He wove this tale around the great and the small, the rich and the poor, men of virtue and scoundrels, and each character was truly drawn. A stolen inheritance, a kidnapping, a battle at sea, several murders—these are only a few of the adventures that befell the hero. It is easily understood why *Kidnapped* is a favorite with all who read it.

KIM

Type of work: Novel
Author: Rudyard Kipling (1865–1936)
Type of plot: Adventure romance
Time of plot: Late nineteenth century
Locale: British India
First published: 1901

Kim gives a vivid picture of the complexities of India under British rule. Kipling's vast canvas, crowded with action and movement, is painted in full detail, showing the life of the bazaar mystics, of the natives, and of the British military.

Principal Characters

Kimball O'Hara (Kim), the son of an Irish mother, who died in India when he was born, and an Irish father, who was color sergeant of the regiment called the Mavericks and who died and left Kim in the care of a half-caste woman. Kim grows up on the streets of Lahore and his skin becomes so dark that no one can tell he is white. He attaches himself to a Tibetan lama as a chela. Kim is caught by the chaplain of the Maverick regiment, who discovers his real identity. The lama pays for Kim's education, and Kim finally distinguishes himself as a member of the British Secret Service.

A Tibetan Lama, who becomes Kim's instructor and whose ambition it is to find the holy River of the Arrow that would wash away all sin. The lama pays for Kim's schooling. After Kim's education is complete, he accompanies the lama in his wanderings, though he is really a member of the secret service. In the end, the lama finds his holy river, a brook on the estate of an old woman who befriends him and Kim.

Mahbub Ali, a horse trader who is really a member of the British secret service. Mahbub Ali is largely responsible for Kim's becoming a member of the Secret Service.

Colonel Creighton, the director of the British Secret Service, who permits Kim to resume the dress of a street boy and do secret service work.

Hurree Chunder Mookerjee, a babu, and also a member of the secret service. He is Kim's confederate in securing some valuable documents brought into India by spies for the Russians.

The Story

Kim grew up on the streets of Lahore. His Irish mother had died when he was born. His father, a former color-sergeant of an Irish regiment called the Mavericks, died eventually of drugs and drink and left his son in the care of a half-caste woman. Young Kimball O'Hara then became Kim, and under the hot Indian sun, his skin grew so dark that one could not tell he was a white boy.

One day a Tibetan lama, in search of the holy River of the Arrow that would wash away all sin, came to Lahore. Struck by the possibility of exciting adventure, Kim attached himself to the lama as his chela. His adventures began almost at once. That night at the edge of Lahore, Mahbub Ali, a horse trader, gave Kim a cryptic message to deliver to a British officer in Umballa. Kim did not know that Mahbub was a member of the British Secret Service. He delivered the message as directed and then lay in the grass and watched and listened until he learned that his message meant that eight thousand men would go to war.

Out on the big road, the lama and Kim encountered many people of all sorts. Conversation was easy. One group in particular interested Kim, an old lady traveling in a family bullock cart attended by a retinue of eight men. Kim and the lama attached themselves to her party. Toward evening, they saw a group of soldiers making camp. It was the Maverick regiment. Kim, whose horoscope said that his life would be changed at the sign of a red bull in a field of green, was fascinated by the regimental flag, which was just that, a red bull against a background of bright green.

Caught by a chaplain, the Reverend Arthur Bennett, Kim accidentally jerked loose the amulet that he carried around his neck. Mr. Bennett opened the amulet and discovered three papers folded inside, including Kim's baptismal certificate and a note from his father asking that the boy be taken care of. Father Victor arrived in time to see the papers. When Kim had told his story, he was informed that he would be sent away to school. Kim parted sadly from the lama; he was sure, however, that he would soon escape. The lama asked that Father Victor's name and address and the costs of Kim's schooling be written down and given to him. Then he disappeared.

Kim, pretending to prophesy, told the priests what he had heard at Umballa. They and the soldiers laughed at him; but the next day his prophecy came true, and eight thousand soldiers were sent to put down an uprising in the north. Kim remained in camp.

One day, a letter arrived from the lama. He enclosed enough money for Kim's first year at school and promised to provide the same amount yearly. He requested that the boy be sent to St. Xavier's for his education. Meanwhile, the drummer who was keeping an eye on Kim had been cruel to his charge. When Mahbub Ali came upon the two boys, he gave the drummer a beating and began talking to Kim. While they were thus engaged, Colonel Creighton came up and learned from Mahbub Ali, in an indirect way, that Kim would be, when educated, a valuable member of the secret service.

At last, Kim was on his way to St. Xavier's. Near the school he spied the lama, who had been waiting a day and a half to see him. They agreed to see each other often. Kim was an apt pupil, but he disliked being shut up in classrooms and dormitories. When vacation time came, he went to Umballa and persuaded Mahbub Ali to let him return to the road until school reopened.

Traveling with Mahbub Ali, he played the part of a horse boy and saved the trader's life when he overheard two men plotting to kill the horse dealer. At Simla, Kim stayed with Mr. Lurgan, who taught him a great many subtle tricks and games and the art of makeup and disguise. Just as Mahbub Ali had said, he was now learning the great game, as the work of the secret service was called. At the end of the summer, Kim returned to St. Xavier's and studied there for a total of three years.

In conference with Mr. Lurgan and Colonel Creighton, Mahbub Ali advised that Kim be permitted once more to go out on the road with his lama. Kim's skin was stained dark, and again he resumed the dress of a street boy. Given the password by Hurree Chunder Mookerjee, a babu who was another member of the secret service, Kim set out with his lama after begging a train ticket to Delhi.

Still seeking his river, the lama moved up and down India with Kim as his disciple. The two of them once more encountered the old woman they had met on the road three years before. A little later, Kim was surprised to see the babu, who told him that two of the five kings of the north had been bribed and that the Russians had sent spies down into India through the passes that the kings had agreed to guard. Two men, a Russian and a Frenchman, were to be apprehended, and the babu asked Kim's aid. Kim suggested to the lama a journey into the foothills of the Himalayas, and so he was able to follow the babu on his mission.

During a storm, the babu came upon the two foreigners. Discovering that one of their baskets contained valuable letters including a message from one of the traitorous kings, he offered to be their guide; in two days, he had led them to the spot where Kim and the lama were camped. When the foreigners tore almost in two a holy drawing made by the lama, the babu created a disturbance in which the coolies, according to plan, carried off the men's luggage. The lama conducted Kim to the village of Shamlegh. There Kim examined all the baggage that the coolies had carried off. He threw everything except letters and notebooks over an unscalable cliff, then he hid the documents on him.

In a few days, Kim and the lama set out again. At last, they came to the house of the old woman who had befriended them twice before. When she saw Kim's emaciated condition, she put him to bed, where he slept many days. Before he went to sleep, he asked that a strongbox be brought to him. He deposited his papers in it, locked the box, and hid it under his bed. When he woke up, he heard that the babu had arrived, and Kim delivered the papers to him. The babu told him that Mahbub Ali was also in the vicinity. They assured Kim that he had played his part well in the great game. The old lama knew nothing of these matters. He was happy because Kim had brought him to his river at last, a brook on the old lady's estate.

Critical Evaluation

Rudyard Kipling wrote many poems, short stories, and novels about India. Whether by design or accident, most of these works assumed a tone that implied acceptance of the caste system and a class-conscious society. This position is diametrically opposed to that of E. M. Forster, who in his classic novel, *A Passage to India*, castigated British colonial depredations. *Kim* is a remarkable exception to Kipling's Tory allegiance, for his novel paints an almost affectionate—not condescending—portrait of the Indian masses. It affords sympathetic insight into some of the most important aspects of Indian life, including among them popular beliefs, life in the streets, bazaars, and life on the road.

Popular beliefs are often labeled superstitions when such beliefs are strange or foreign to the one who applies the label, as though the labeler were hardly aware of the pejorative connotations of "superstition." The Tibetan lama thus believes that his search will ultimately lead him to the holy River of Arrow, which will wash away all sin. An Anglo-American reader might scoff a such naïveté, whether it is called popular belief or superstition, but Kipling lends both credibility and dignity to the lama's faith by allowing him to find the river at the end of the novel. In this way, as in others dealing with uniquely Indian beliefs, Kipling pays respect to a culture other than his own.

The teeming life on India's streets and in its bazaars is relatively common knowledge today. At the turn of the century, however, it was unfamiliar territory and therefore quite exotic. Although Kipling did nothing to diminish the exotic ambience of street life, neither did he gloss over its harsh realities. Particularly vivid is the depiction of Kim's early experiences in the streets of Lahore— opium, extortion, fighting, and the like.

With equal verisimilitude, Kipling described the rigors of travel and life on the road. There were dangers, such as the two men who plotted to kill Mahbub Ali; there were discomforts and inconveniences, such as having occasionally to sleep in the open. Nevertheless, a spirit of friendship and hospitality could also be found, as, for example, when the old woman gives the exhausted and emaciated Kim a resting place. All in all, the nostalgic tale captured a flavor of tolerance and humane feeling for the most part lacking in Kipling's other Indian literature.

KING LEAR

Type of work: Drama
Author: William Shakespeare (1564–1616)
Type of plot: Romantic tragedy
Time of plot: First century B.C.
Locale: Britain
First presented: c. 1605

The theme of filial ingratitude is portrayed in two parallel stories with overwhelming pathos in this majestic achievement, considered by many the greatest of Shakespeare's tragedies. The heights of terror and pity achieved through the poet's treatment of his story equal those of the great tragedies of antiquity. Although generally considered one of the noblest utterances of the human spirit, the play often proves to be difficult to stage. Its world is more legendary than concrete and its figures larger than life, although they are vehicles for universal feelings.

Principal Characters

Lear (lēr), king of Britain. Obstinate, arrogant, and hot-tempered, he indiscreetly plans to divide his kingdom among his daughters, giving the best and largest portion to Cordelia, his youngest and best-loved. When she refuses to flatter him with lavish and public protestations of love, he casts her off with unreasoning fury. Disillusioned and abandoned by his older daughters, his age and exposure to internal and external tempests drive him to madness. During his suffering, signs of unselfishness appear, and his character changes from arrogance and bitterness to love and tenderness. He is reunited with his true and loving daughter until her untimely murder parts them again.

Goneril (gŏn′ə·rĭl), Lear's eldest daughter. Savage and blunt as a wild boar, she wears the mask of hypocritical affection to gain a kingdom. She has contempt for her aged father, her honest sister, and her kindhearted husband. Her illicit passion for Edmund, handsome bastard son of the Earl of Gloucester, leads to Edmund's, Regan's, and her own death.

Regan (rē′gən), Lear's second daughter. Treacherous in a catlike manner, she seldom initiates the action of the evil sisters, but often goes a step further in cruelty. She gloats over Gloucester when his eyes are torn out and unintentionally helps him to see the light of truth. Her early widowhood gives her some advantage over Goneril in their rivalry for the person of Edmund, but she is poisoned by Goneril, who then commits suicide.

Cordelia (kôr·dēl′yə), Lear's youngest daughter. Endowed with her father's stubbornness, she refuses to flatter him as her sisters have done. In his adversity she returns to him with love and forgiveness, restoring his sanity and redeeming him from bitterness. Her untimely death brings about Lear's death.

The Earl of Kent, Lear's frank and loyal follower. Risking Lear's anger to avert his impetuous unreason, he accepts banishment as payment for truth. Like Cordelia, but even before her, he returns to aid Lear—necessarily in disguise—as the servant Caius. The impudence of Oswald arouses violent anger in him. For his master no service is too menial or too perilous.

The Earl of Gloucester, another father with good and evil children, a parallel to Lear and his daughters. Having had a gay past, about which he speaks frankly and with some pride, he believes himself a man of the world and a practical politician. He is gullible and superstitious and, deceived by Edmund, he casts off his loyal, legitimate son Edgar. His loyalty to the persecuted king leads to the loss of his eyes; but his inner sight is made whole by his blinding. He dies happily reconciled to Edgar.

Edgar (in disguise **Tom o' Bedlam**), Gloucester's legitimate son. He is forced into hiding by his credulous father and the machinations of his evil half brother. As Tom o' Bedlam he is with the king during the tempest, and later he cares for his eyeless father both physically and spiritually. Finally he reveals himself to Gloucester just before engaging in mortal combat with Edmund, who dies as a result of Edgar's wounding him.

Edmund, Gloucester's illegitimate younger son. A Machiavellian villain governed by insatiable ambition, he attempts to destroy his half brother and his father for his own advancement. Without passion himself, he rejoices in his ability to arouse it in others, particularly Lear's two evil daughters. He has a grim and cynical sense of humor. His heartlessness is demonstrated by his plotting the murders of Lear and Cordelia, in which he is only half successful. He shows signs of repentance at the time of his death, but hardly enough to color his villainy.

The Duke of Cornwall, Regan's husband. An inhuman monster, he aids in heaping hardships on the aged king and tears out Gloucester's eyes when the Earl is discovered aiding the distressed monarch. His death, brought on by his cruelty, leaves Regan free to pursue Edmund as a potential husband.

The Duke of Albany, Goneril's husband. Noble and kind, he is revolted by Goneril's behavior toward her father, by Gloucester's blinding, and by the murder of Cordelia. He repudiates Goneril and Regan and restores order to the kingdom.

The Fool, Lear's jester but "not altogether a fool." A mixture of cleverness, bitterness, and touching loyalty, he remains with the old king in his terrible adversity. His suffering rouses Lear's pity and leads to the major change from selfish arrogance to unselfish love in the old king. The fool's end is obscure; he simply vanishes from the play. The line which says "My poor fool is hanged" may refer to Cordelia.

Oswald, Goneril's doglike servant. Insolent, cowardly, and evil, he is still devoted to his mistress, whom ironically he destroys. His last act of devotion to her is to urge his slayer to deliver a letter from her to Edmund. Since the slayer is Edgar, the letter goes to the Duke of Albany as evidence of Goneril's and Edmund's falsehood.

The King of France, a suitor of Cordelia. Captivated by her character and loveliness, he marries her with only her father's curse for dowry. He sets up an invasion of England to restore the old king but is called back to France before the decisive battle, leaving the responsibility on his young queen.

The Duke of Burgundy, a suitor of Cordelia. Cautious and selfish, he rejects Cordelia when he finds out that she has been cast off by her father.

First Servant of Cornwall. Moved by Cornwall's inhuman cruelty, he endeavors to save Gloucester from being blinded. Although his appearance is brief, he makes a profound impression as a character, and his action in mortally wounding Cornwall alters the course of events and leads to the overthrow of the evil forces.

An Old Man, Gloucester's tenant. Helping the blinded man, he delivers him to the care of the supposed mad beggar, actually Edgar.

A Captain, employed by Edmund to murder Lear and Cordelia in prison. He hangs Cordelia but later is killed by the aged king, who is too late to save his beloved daughter.

A Doctor, employed by Cordelia to treat her father in his illness and madness. He aids in restoring Lear to partial health.

Curan, a courtier.

The Story

King Lear, in foolish fondness for his children, decided to divide his kingdom among his three daughters. Grown senile, he scoffed at the foresight of his advisers and declared that each girl's statement of her love for him would determine the portion of the kingdom she would receive as her dowry.

Goneril, the oldest and the duchess of Albany, spoke first. She said that she loved her father more than eyesight, space, liberty, or life itself. Regan, Duchess of Cornwall, announced that the sentiment of her love had been expressed by Goneril, but that Goneril had stopped short of the statement of Regan's real love. Cordelia, who had secretly confided that her love was more ponderous than her tongue, told her father that because her love was in her heart, not in her mouth, she was willing to sacrifice eloquence for truth. Lear angrily told her that truth alone could be her dowry and ordered that her part of the kingdom be divided between Goneril and Regan. Lear's disappointment in Cordelia's statement grew into a rage against Kent, who tried to reason Cordelia's case with his foolish king. Because of Kent's blunt speech he was given ten days to leave the country. Loving his sovereign, he risked death by disguising himself and remaining in Britain to care for Lear in his infirmity.

When Burgundy and France came as suitors to ask Cordelia's hand in marriage, Burgundy, learning of her dowerless fate, rejected her. France, honoring Cordelia for her virtues, took her as his wife, but Lear dismissed Cordelia and France without his benediction. Goneril and Regan, wary of their father's vacillation in his weakened mental state, set about to establish their kingdoms against change.

Lear was not long in learning what Goneril's and Regan's statements of their love for him had really meant. Their caustic comments about the old man's feebleness, both mental and physical, furnished Lear's Fool with many points for his philosophical recriminations against the king. Realizing that his charity to his daughters had made him homeless, Lear cried in anguish against his fate. His prayers went unanswered, and the abuse he received from his daughters hastened his derangement.

The Earl of Gloucester, like Lear, was fond of his two sons. Edmund, a bastard, afraid that his illegitimacy would deprive him of his share of Gloucester's estate, forged a letter over Edgar's signature, stating that the sons should not have to wait for their fortunes until they were too old to enjoy them. Gloucester, refusing to believe that Edgar desired his father's death, was told by Edmund to wait in hiding and hear Edgar make assertions which could easily be misinterpreted against him. Edmund, furthering his scheme, told Edgar that villainy was afoot and that Edgar should not go unarmed at any time.

To complete his evil design, he later advised Edgar to flee for his own safety. After cutting his arm, he then told his father that he had been wounded while he and Edgar fought over Gloucester's honor. Gloucester, swearing that Edgar would not escape justice, had his son's description circulated so that he might be apprehended.

Edmund, meanwhile, allied himself with Cornwall and Albany to defend Britain against the French army mobilized by Cordelia and her husband to avenge Lear's cruel treatment. He won Regan and Goneril completely by his personal attentions to them and set the sisters against each other by arousing their jealousy.

Lear, wandering as an outcast on the stormy heath, was aided by Kent, disguised as a peasant. Seeking protection from the storm, they found a hut where Edgar, pretending to be a madman, had already taken refuge. Gloucester, searching for the king, found them there and urged them to hurry to Dover, where Cordelia and her husband would protect Lear from the wrath of his unnatural daughters.

For attempting to give succor and condolence to the outcast Lear, Gloucester was blinded when Cornwall, acting on information furnished by Edmund, gouged out his eyes. While he was at his grisly work, a servant, rebelling against the cruel deed, wounded Cornwall. Regan killed the servant. Cornwall died later as the result of his wound. Edgar, still playing the part of a madman, found his father wandering the fields with an old retainer. Without revealing his identity, Edgar promised to guide his father to Dover, where Gloucester planned to die by throwing himself from the high cliffs.

Goneril was bitterly jealous because widowed Regan could receive the full attention of Edmund, who had been made Earl of Gloucester. She declared that she would rather lose the battle to France than to lose Edmund to Regan. Goneril's hatred became more venomous when Albany, whom she detested because of his kindliness toward Lear and his pity for Gloucester, announced that he would try to right the wrongs done by Goneril, Regan, and Edmund.

Cordelia, informed by messenger of her father's fate, was in the French camp near Dover. When the mad old king was brought to her by faithful Kent, she cared for her father tenderly and put him in the care of a doctor skilled in curing many kinds of ills. Regaining his reason, Lear recognized Cordelia, but the joy of their reunion was clouded by his repentance for his misunderstanding and mistreatment of his only loyal daughter.

Edgar, protecting Gloucester, was accosted by Oswald, Goneril's steward, on his way to deliver a note to Edmund. After Edgar had killed Oswald in the fight which followed, Edgar delivered the letter to Albany. In it Goneril declared her love for Edmund and asked that he kill her husband. Gloucester died, feeble and brokenhearted after Edgar had revealed himself to his father.

Edmund, commanding the British forces, took Lear and Cordelia prisoners. As they were taken off to prison, he sent written instructions for their treatment.

Albany was aware of Edmund's ambition for personal glory and arrested him on a charge of high treason. Regan, interceding for her lover, was rebuffed by Goneril. Regan, suddenly taken ill, was carried to Albany's tent. When Edmund, as was his right, demanded a trial by combat, Albany agreed. Edgar, still in disguise, appeared and in the fight mortally wounded his false brother. Learning from Albany that he knew of her plot against his life, Goneril was desperate. She went to their tent, poisoned Regan, and killed herself.

Edmund, dying, revealed that he and Goneril had ordered Cordelia to be hanged and her death to be announced as suicide because of her despondency over her father's plight. Edmund, fiendish and diabolical always, was also vain. While he lay dying he looked upon the bodies of Goneril and Regan and expressed pleasure that two women were dead because of their jealous love for him.

Albany dispatched Edgar to prevent Cordelia's death, but he arrived too late. Lear refused all assistance when he appeared carrying her dead body in his arms. After asking forgiveness of heartbroken Kent, whom he recognized at last, Lear, a broken, confused old man, died in anguish. Edgar and Albany alone were left to rebuild a country ravaged by bloodshed and war.

Critical Evaluation

King Lear's first entrance in act 1 is replete with ritual and ceremony. He is full of antiquity, authority, and assurance as he makes his regal way through the ordered court. When he reveals his intention to divide his kingdom into three parts for his daughters, he exudes the confidence generated by his long reign. The crispness and directness of his language suggest a power, if not imperiousness, which, far from senility, demonstrate the stability and certainty of long, unchallenged sway. The rest of the play acts out the destruction of that fixed order and the emergence of a new, tentative balance.

In the opening scene Lear speaks as king and father. The absolute ruler has decided to apportion his kingdom as a gift rather than as a bequest to his three heirs. In performing this act, which superficially seems both reasonable and generous, Lear sets in motion a chain of events which lay bare his primary vulnerabilities not only as a king and a father but also as a man. In retrospect it is foolish to expect to divest oneself of power and responsibility and yet retain the trappings of authority. However, this is exactly what Lear anticipates because of his excessive confidence in the love of his daughters. He asks too much, he acts too precipitately, but he is punished, by an inexorable universe, out of all proportion to his errors in judgment.

When he asks his daughters for a declaration of love,

as a prerequisite for a share of the kingdom, he is as self-assured and overbearing a parent as he is a monarch. It is thus partly his own fault that the facile protestations of love by Goneril and Regan are credited; they are what he wants to hear because they conform to the ceremonial necessities of the occasion. Cordelia's honest response, born of a genuine love, are out of keeping with the formalities. Lear has not looked beneath the surface. He has let the ritual appearances replace the internal reality or he has at least refused to distinguish between the two.

The asseverations of Goneril and Regan soon emerge as the cynical conceits that they are, but by then Lear has banished Cordelia and the loyal Kent, who saw through the sham. Lear is successively and ruthlessly divested of all the accoutrements of kingship by the villainous daughters, who finally reduce him to the condition of a ragged, homeless madman. Paradoxically, it is in this extremity, on the heath with Edgar and the Fool, that Lear comes to a knowledge of himself and of his community with all humanity that he had never achieved amid the glories of power. Buffeted by the natural fury of the storm, which is symbolic of the chaos and danger that come with the passing of the old order, Lear sees through his madness the common bond of humanity.

The experience of Lear is mirrored in the Gloucester subplot on a more manageable, human level. Gloucester too suffers filial ingratitude but it is not raised to a cosmic level. He too mistakes appearance for reality in trusting the duplicitous Edmund and disinheriting the honest Edgar, but his behavior is more clearly the outgrowth of an existing moral confusion reflected in his ambivalent and unrepentant affection for his bastard. His moral blindness leads to physical blindness when his faulty judgment makes him vulnerable to the villains. In his blindness he finally sees the truth of his situation, but his experience is merely as a father and a man.

Lear's experience parallels Gloucester's in that his figurative madness leads to a real madness in which he finally recognizes what he has lacked. He sees in Edgar, himself a victim of Gloucester's moral blindness, the natural state of man, stripped of all external decoration, and he realizes that he has ignored the basic realities of the human condition. His experience finally transcends Gloucester's because he is a king, preeminent among men. He not only represents the occupational hazards of kingship but also the broadly human disposition to prefer pleasant appearances to troubling realities. However, because of his position, Lear's failure brings down the whole political and social order with him.

Lear has violated nature by a culpable ignorance of it. The result is familial discord, physical suffering, and existential confusion. Brought low, Lear begins to fashion a new view of himself, of human love, and of human nature. In his insanity, Lear assembles the bizarre court of mad king, beggar, and fool which reasserts the common bonds of all men. Once these realizations have come, the evil characters, so carefully balanced against the good in this precarious world, begin to kill each other off and succumb to the vengeance of regenerated justice.

However, it is a mark of Shakespeare's uncompromising view of reality that there is no simple application of poetic justice to reward the good and punish the wicked, for the good die too. It is true that Edgar finishes off his brother in trial by combat and that the machinations of Goneril and Regan result in the destruction of both, but the redeemed Lear and Cordelia, the perfection of selfless love, also die. That Lear should die is perhaps no surprise. The suffering that he has endured in his confrontation with the primal elements does not allow an optimistic return to normal life and prosperity. He has, on our behalf, looked into the eye of nature and there is nothing left but to die.

The death of Cordelia is more troublesome, at least tonally, because she is a perfectly innocent victim of the evil and madness that surround her. But Shakespeare refuses to save her. She dies gratuitously, not because of any internal necessity of the plot, but because the message to save her is too late. The dramatist has created his own inevitability in order to represent the ruthless consequences of the evil and chaos that have been loosed. When Lear enters with the dead Cordelia, he accomplishes the final expiation of his unknowing.

Out of these sufferings and recognitions comes a new moral stasis. Yet the purged world does not leave us with great confidence in future stability. Kent is old and refuses kingship. Edgar assumes authority but, despite his rectitude, there is an unsettling doubt that he has the force or stature to maintain the new order in a volatile world where evil and chaos are always rumbling beneath the surface.

THE LAST OF THE MOHICANS: A Narrative of 1757

Type of work: Novel
Author: James Fenimore Cooper (1789–1851)
Type of plot: Historical romance
Time of plot: 1757
Locale: Northern New York State
First published: 1826

This novel remains the most popular of Cooper's Leatherstocking Tales, a classic story of the French and Indian War. The battles and exciting pursuits which constitute the book's plot are rounded out by interesting Indian lore and descriptions of the wilderness.

Principal Characters

Natty Bumppo, called **Hawkeye,** the hardy, noble frontier scout in his prime during the French and Indian Wars. Traveling with his Indian companions, Chingachgook and his son Uncas, in Upper New York, he befriends an English soldier, a Connecticut singing master, and their two female charges. When the travelers are ambushed by hostile Huron warriors, he leaves the party to get help, in turn ambushes their captors with the aid of Chingachgook and Uncas, and leads the group to Fort William Henry, besieged by the French. In the massacre of English that takes place after the garrison is forced to surrender, the girls are captured again by Indians. Hawkeye assists once more in the escape of one of the girls; however, a renegade Huron chief, Magua, claims the other as his reluctant wife. In the ensuing fighting the girl and Hawkeye's friend, the noble young Uncas, are killed. Hawkeye shoots Magua in return. In the end he and Chingachgook return sorrowfully to the wilderness.

Chingachgook (chĭn·găch'gōōk), a courageous, loyal Mohican Chief, Hawkeye's inseparable friend. An implacable enemy of the Hurons, he is decorated as Death. Left to protect the English Colonel after the massacre, he joins the final battle with intense ferocity, only to see his son die. His grief is relieved somewhat by Hawkeye's companionship.

Uncas (ŭn'kəs), Chingachgook's stalwart son, the last of the Mohicans. A young and handsome chieftain, he falls in love with Cora Munro while protecting her and proves invaluable in tracking her after she has been captured. When a Delaware chief awards her to Uncas' rival, Magua, he follows them and is killed avenging her murder.

Major Duncan Heyward, the young English officer in charge of escorting the Munro girls from Fort Edward to Fort William Henry. Brave, good-looking and clever, he falls in love with Alice Munro and eventually succeeds in rescuing her from the Hurons. He finally marries her with Colonel Munro's blessing.

Magua (mä'gū·ə), "Le Renard Subtil," the handsome, renegade Huron chief. Both cunning and malicious, he seeks to avenge himself on Colonel Munro by turning his spirited daughter Cora into a servile squaw. Twice thwarted by Hawkeye and his companions, he wins Cora by putting his case before Tamenund, a Delaware chieftain. This victory, however, is short lived. Cora is killed by another Huron and Magua, after killing Uncas, is shot by Hawkeye.

Cora Munro, the Colonel's beautiful older daughter. She is independent, equal to every situation, and bears up well under the strain of a capture, a massacre, and the threat of marrying Magua. Her love for Uncas, however, remains unrequited when she is carried off by Magua and then stabbed.

Alice Munro, the Colonel's younger daughter, a pale, immature, but lovely half sister of Cora. Frail and clinging, she excites Heyward's protective feelings during their adventures, and he marries her.

Colonel Munro, the able but unsuccessful defender of Fort William Henry and the affectionate father of Cora and Alice. After surrendering to the French he is forced to watch helplessly the slaughter of the men, women, and children from the fort. His sorrow is doubled when Cora is killed.

David Gamut, a mild, ungainly singing master who accompanies Heyward and the Munro girls. His schoolbook piety contrasts with Hawkeye's natural pantheism. A rather ineffective person, he is nevertheless useful to Hawkeye, for the Hurons believe him insane and let him pass without trouble.

The Marquis de Montcalm, the skilled, enterprising general who captures Fort William Henry and then allows the defeated English to be massacred by savage Hurons.

Tamenund (tä·mə·nŭnd'), the old Delaware chief who foolishly decides to give Cora to Magua.

Hard Heart, the Delaware chief whom Magua flatters to gain Cora.

General Webb, the incompetent commander of Fort Edward. He refused to aid Colonel Munro.

A Huron Chief. He calls on Heyward, who is impersonating a witch doctor, to cure a relative, and he is duped when his captives are released.

The Story

Major Duncan Heyward had been ordered to escort Cora and Alice Munro from Fort Edward to Fort William Henry, where Colonel Munro, father of the girls, was commandant. In the party was also David Gamut, a Connecticut singing master. On their way to Fort William Henry they did not follow the military road through the wilderness. Instead, they placed themselves in the hands of a renegade Huron known as Magua, who claimed that he could lead them to their destination by a shorter trail.

It was afternoon when the little party met the woodsman, Hawkeye, and his Delaware Mohican friends, Chingachgook and his son Uncas. To their dismay, they learned they were but an hour's distance from their starting point. Hawkeye quickly decided Magua had been planning to lead the party into a trap. His Mohican comrades tried to capture the renegade, but Magua took alarm and fled into the woods.

At Heyward's urging the hunter agreed to guide the travelers to their destination. The horses were tied and hidden among some rocks along a river. Hawkeye produced a hidden canoe from among some bushes and paddled the party to a rock at the foot of Glenn's Falls. There they prepared to spend the night in a cave.

That night a band of Iroquois led by Magua surprised the party. The fight might have been a victory for Hawkeye if their supply of powder and ball had held out. Unfortunately, their ammunition had been left in the canoe which, unnoticed until it was too late, was stolen by one of the enemy who had ventured to swim the swirling river. The only hope then lay in the possibility of future rescue, for the capture of the rock and the little group was a certainty. Hawkeye, Chingachgook, and Uncas escaped by floating downstream, leaving the girls and Major Heyward to meet the savages.

Captured, Cora and Alice were allowed to ride their horses, but Heyward and David were forced by their captors to walk. Although they took a road paralleling that to Fort William Henry, Heyward could not determine the destination the Indians had in mind. Drawing close to Magua, he tried to persuade him to betray his companions and deliver the party safely to Colonel Munro. The Huron agreed, if Cora would come to live with him among his tribe as his wife. When she refused, the enraged Magua had everyone bound. He was threatening Alice with his tomahawk when Hawkeye and his friends crept silently upon the band and attacked them. The Iroquois fled, leaving several of their dead behind them. The party, under David's guidance, sang a hymn of thanksgiving and then pushed onward.

Toward evening they stopped at a deserted blockhouse to rest. Many years before, it had been the scene of a fight between the Mohicans and the Mohawks, and a mound still showed where bodies lay buried. While Chingachgook watched, the others slept.

At moonrise they continued on their way. It was dawn when Hawkeye and his charges drew near Fort William Henry. They were intercepted and challenged by a sentinel of the French under Montcalm, who was about to lay siege to the fort. Heyward was able to answer him in French and they were allowed to proceed. Chingachgook killed and scalped the French sentinel. Through the fog which had risen from Lake George and through the enemy forces which thronged the plain before the fort, Hawkeye led the way to the gates of the fort.

On the fifth day of the siege, Hawkeye who had been sent to Fort Edward to seek help was intercepted on his way back and a letter he carried was captured. Webb, the commander of Fort Edward, refused to come to the aid of Munro.

Under a flag of truce, Montcalm and Munro held a parley. Montcalm showed Webb's letter to Munro and offered honorable terms of surrender. Colonel Munro and his men would be allowed to keep their colors, their arms, and their baggage, if they would vacate the fort the next morning. Helpless to do otherwise, Munro accepted these terms. During one of the parleys Heyward was surprised to see Magua in the camp of the French. He had not been killed during the earlier skirmish.

The following day the vanquished English started their trip back to Fort Edward. Under the eyes of the French and their Indian allies, they passed across the plain and entered the forest. Suddenly an Indian grabbed at a brightly colored shawl worn by one of the women. Terrified, she wrapped her child in it. The Indian darted toward her, grabbed the child from her arms, and dashed out its brains on the ground. Then under the eyes of Montcalm, who did nothing to discourage or hold back his savage allies, a monstrous slaughter began.

Cora and Alice, entrusted to David Gamut's protection, were in the midst of the killing when Magua swooped down upon them and carried Alice away in his arms. Cora ran after her sister, and faithful David dogged her footsteps. They were soon atop a hill, from which they watched the slaughter of the garrison.

Three days later, Hawkeye, leading Heyward, Munro, and his Indian comrades, tracked the girls and David, following a path where they had found Cora's veil caught on a tree. Heyward was particularly concerned for the safety of Alice. The day before the massacre he had been given her father's permission to court her.

Hawkeye, knowing that hostile Indians were on their trail, decided to save time by traveling across the lake in a canoe which he discovered in its hiding place nearby. He was certain Magua had taken the girls north, where he planned to rejoin his own people. Heading their canoe in that direction, the five men paddled all day, at one point having a close escape from some of their intercepting enemies. They spent that night in the woods and the next day turned west in an effort to find Magua's trail.

After much searching Uncas found the trail of the captives. That evening, as the party drew near the Huron camp, they met David Gamut wandering about. He told his friends that the Indians thought him crazy because of his habit of breaking into song, and they allowed him to roam the woods unguarded. Alice, he said, was being held at the Huron camp. Cora had been entrusted to the care of a tribe of peaceful Delawares a short distance away.

Heyward, disguising his face with paint, went to the Huron camp in an attempt to rescue Alice, while the others set about helping Cora. Heyward was in the camp but a short time, posing as a French doctor, when Uncas was brought in as a captive. Called to treat an ill Indian woman, Heyward found Alice in the cave with his patient. He was able to rescue the girl by wrapping her in a blanket and declaring to the Hurons that she was his patient, whom he was carrying off to the woods for treatment. Hawkeye, attempting to rescue Uncas, entered the camp disguised in a medicine man's bearskin he had stolen. Uncas was cut loose and given the disguise, while the woodsman borrowed David Gamut's clothes. The singer was left to take Uncas' place while the others escaped, for Hawkeye was certain the Indians would not harm David because of his supposed mental condition. Uncas and Hawkeye fled to the Delaware camp.

The following day Magua and a group of his warriors visited the Delawares in search of their prisoners. The chief of that tribe decided the Hurons had a just claim to Cora because Magua wished to make her his wife.

Under inviolable Indian custom, the Huron was permitted to leave the camp unmolested, but Uncas warned him that in a few hours he and the Delawares would follow his trail.

During a bloody battle Magua fled with Cora to the top of a cliff. There, pursued by Uncas, he stabbed and killed the young Mohican and was in his turn sent to his death by a bullet from Hawkeye's long rifle. Cora too was killed by a Huron. Amid deep mourning by the Delawares, she and Uncas were laid in their graves in the forest. Colonel Munro and Heyward conducted Alice to English territory and safety. Hawkeye returned to the forest. He had promised to remain with his sorrowing friend Chingachgook forever.

Critical Evaluation

The Last of the Mohicans is the second title published in what was to become a series of five entitled collectively the Leatherstocking Tales. When Cooper published the first of these "romances," as he called them to distinguish them from the somewhat more realistic contemporary novels, he had no plan for a series with a hero whose life would be shown from youth to old age and death. In *The Pioneers* (1823) Natty Bumppo or Leatherstocking is in his early seventies. Responding to a suggestion from his wife, Cooper went back in *The Last of the Mohicans* to Natty's early thirties when he was called Hawkeye. The great popularity of *The Last of the Mohicans* led Cooper then to move chronologically beyond *The Pioneers* and to picture in *The Prairie* (1827) the last of Natty's life when he was in his eighties, living as a trapper and finally dying on the Great Plains far from his early home. At the time, Cooper did not intend to revive Natty in further romances. One minor romance of the forest, *The Wept of Wish-ton-Wish* (1829), was followed by a stream of nautical novels, socio-political novels, and nonfictional works of social and political criticism extending until 1840, when Cooper finally answered the pleas of many literary critics and readers and revived the hero whose death he had so touchingly portrayed at the end of *The Prairie*. In *The Pathfinder* (1840), Natty is called Pathfinder and the action shifts from land to the waters of Lake Ontario and back again. Pleased by the resounding praise he gained for having brought back his famed hero, Cooper decided to write one final romance about him in which Natty would be younger than in any of the earlier books. In *The Deerslayer* (1841), Natty is in his early twenties and goes by the nickname Deerslayer. In 1850, Cooper brought out a new edition of all five Leatherstocking Tales arranged according to the order of events in Natty Bumppo's life: *The Deerslayer*, *The Last of the Mohicans*, *The Pathfinder*, *The Pioneers*, *The Prairie*. For this edition he wrote a preface in which he remarked (prophetically, as it turned out): "If anything from the pen of the writer of these romances is at all to outlive himself, it is, unquestionably, the series of *The Leather-Stocking Tales*." Despite many complaints from Mark Twain and later critics about Cooper's style, plots, structure, characterization, and dialogue, the Leatherstocking Tales continue to be read, both in the United States and in many foreign countries, and they seem assured of a long life to come.

In Cooper's day, *The Last of the Mohicans* was the most popular of the five tales, and it has continued to be so. It has been filmed by American and British companies, and the British version was serialized on American television. Structurally, the novel is superior to the other tales, with three major plot actions and a transitional though bloody interlude (the massacre after the surrender of Fort William Henry). Cooper's action-filled plot, with bad characters chasing good ones or good characters chasing bad ones, has since become standard in many action novels as well as motion pictures and television dramas.

Romantic love was conventional in the plots of novels in Cooper's day. His portrayal of Duncan Heyward and the Munro sisters, Cora and Alice—who carry most of the love interest in *The Last of the Mohicans*—shows no originality. They are all genteel characters and they speak in a stiff, formalized manner that seems unreal to present-day readers. Duncan is gentlemanly and the two "females" (as Cooper repeatedly calls them) are ladylike. Cooper contrasts Cora and Alice as he does the pairs of women who keep turning up in his books. Cora, the dark one, is passionate, independent, and unafraid, even defiant; blonde Alice is timid and easily frightened into faints— she resembles the sentimentalized helpless girls of popular early nineteenth century fiction.

Cooper does much better with his forest characters. Hawkeye is talkative, boastful, superstitious, scornful of the book learning he does not possess, and inclined to be sententious at times. Yet he is brave, resourceful, and loyal to his two Indian friends. His French nickname, La Longue Carabine, attests to his shooting skill. He is religious but sometimes seems more pantheistic than Christian in any formal sense. Hawkeye's arguments with David Gamut oppose his generalized beliefs and Gamut's narrow Calvinism. With his dual background of white birth and early education by Moravian missionaries on the one side and his long experience of living with the Indians on the other, he is, as Balzac called him, "a moral hermaphrodite, a child of savagery and civilization."

Chingachgook and Uncas are idealized representatives of their race. As "good" Indians, they are dignified, taciturn, even noble despite their savage ways. Uncas is lithe, strong, and handsome; he reminds the Munro sisters of a Greek statue. Magua is the "bad" Indian, sullen, fierce, cunning, and treacherous. His desire for Cora as his squaw is motivated by his wish to avenge a whipping ordered by Colonel Munro.

In addition to the love theme, which provides for the marriage of Heyward and Alice, Cooper includes others. Related to the love theme is miscegenation, which Cooper has been accused of evading by killing off both Cora, who is part black, and Uncas, who had wanted to marry her. Another theme is suggested by the title of the romance. Chingachgook is left mourning for his son, the last of the Mohican sagamores. He grieves also because he foresees the eventual vanishing of his race. Both he and Hawkeye despair as they envision the end of their way of life in the great American wilderness, which will gradually disappear.

It is easy to complain of Cooper's faulty style, his verbosity, his heavy-handed humor (with David Gamut), his improbable actions, the insufficient motivation of his characters, the inconsistency and inaccuracy of his dialogue, yet many readers willingly suspend their disbelief or modify their critical objections in order to enjoy the rush of action which makes up so much of *The Last of the Mohicans*. They sorrow over the deaths of Cora and Uncas, and their sympathies go out to Chingachgook and Hawkeye in the loss of what had meant so much in their lives. Also, especially in a time when ecologists are fighting to preserve some of the natural beauty of our country, they enjoy Cooper's respect for nature found in his descriptions of the northeastern wilderness as it was in the eighteenth century.

LAZARILLO DE TORMES

Type of work: Novel
Author: Unknown
Type of plot: Picaresque romance
Time of plot: Sixteenth century
Locale: Spain
First published: 1553 (English translation, 1576)

This early picaresque novel is actually a series of brief sketches which gave a vivid picture of the stratagems used by the poor to stay alive. Without a trace of self-pity, the author shows the humorous side of continual penury and want. The book greatly influenced later picaresque tales such as Gil Blas.

Principal Characters

Lazarillo de Tormes (lä·thä·rē′lyō thä tôr′mäs), so named because he was born in a mill over the River Tormes. Bereaved at an early age by the death of his father, Lazarillo is given by his impoverished mother to his first master, a blind beggar whose cruelty is precisely the kind of education the unfortunate lad needs to strip away his naïveté and prepare him for a cruel world which promises only hardships for him. Treated cruelly, Lazarillo learns all the tricks of providing himself with food and drink. Becoming sharp and witty, although keeping his good nature, he develops the ability to please people and impress them. He is a kindhearted, generous lad, though his environment might well train him in the opposite direction. He is what may be best described as one of nature's gentlemen. Given an opportunity by a kindly chaplain, Lazarillo settles down to a respectable career as a town crier. A diligent worker, he saves enough money to become respectable. Another friend, the archpriest of St. Savior's Church, in Toledo, provides Lazarillo with an opportunity to marry an honest and hardworking woman who gives her husband no trouble, though gossip, until silenced by Lazarillo, tries to make out that the young woman is the Archpriest's mistress. By his wit, competence, and industry Lazarillo thrives and becomes a government inspector of wines at Toledo, a post which provides him with comfort and self-respect, if not affluence or great honor.

Antonia Pérez Goncales (än·tō′nyä pā′räth gōn·thä′läs), Lazarillo's mother. A good but poor woman, she faces adversity following the death of her husband. To help her keep alive and provide for her small son, she takes a Moorish lover, by whom she has a dark-skinned child. After her lover's conviction of theft she is thrown upon her own meager resources, at which time she tries to provide for Lazarillo by putting him in the service of a blind beggar.

Thome Goncales (tō′mä gōn·thä′läs), Lazarillo's father, a miller. Convicted of fraud and theft, he enters military

service and is killed shortly thereafter, in a battle with the Moors, while Lazarillo is a small child.

The Zayde (thä′ē·thä), a stable master for the Comendador de la Magdalena. He is a Moor who becomes the lover the Lazarillo's mother. Being a poor man, the Zayde steals to provide for his mistress and the two children, Lazarillo and his half brother. His thievery discovered, the unhappy man is punished brutally and forbidden to see his adopted family.

The Blind Beggar, Lazarillo's first master. He treats Lazarillo cruelly from the first, beating the boy and starving him. He is a clever man who imparts his knowledge of human nature to the boy. No better master could have been found to acquaint Lazarillo with the rigors of life for a poor boy in sixteenth century Spain, though Lazarillo realizes this fact only later in life. As a boy he becomes bitter toward the man because of brutality and starvation.

The Penurious Priest, Lazarillo's second master, who also starves the lad and keeps up a battle for months to prevent his acolyte from stealing either food or money; he has little success against the ingenious Lazarillo.

The Proud Squire, Lazarillo's third master. A man of honor, he starves himself rather than admit he is without money. Lazarillo joins him in the expectation of finding a rich master, only to learn he must beg on behalf of his master as well as for himself. Eventually the squire, besieged by creditors, disappears.

The Friar, Lazarillo's fourth master, who is so busy and walks so far each day that Lazarillo leaves him after a few days.

The Seller of Papal Indulgences, a hypocritical pardoner who knows, like Chaucer's famous Pardoner, all the tricks to part poor Christians from their money. He is a fraud in every way, but he has little effect on the quite honest Lazarillo.

The Chaplain, Lazarillo's sixth master and first real benefactor. He gives Lazarillo work as his water carrier, enters into a partnership with the lad, and provides Lazarillo with a mule and the other necessities of his work.

The Archpriest of St. Savior's Church, a good and benevolent clergyman who helps Lazarillo to preferment

and becomes his friend. He introduces Lazarillo to his future wife.

Lazarillo's Wife, a former servant of the archpriest. She gives birth to Lazarillo's child, a daughter.

The Story

Lazarillo's surname came from the peculiar circumstance of his birth. His mother happened to stay the night at the mill where his father was employed. Lazarillo was born on the mill floor just over the river Tormes, after which he was named.

He had reached his ninth year when his father was caught taking flour from customers' sacks. After being soundly punished, the father joined an army that was preparing to move against the Moors. He became a mule driver for a gentleman soldier and was killed in action.

Lazarillo's mother opened an eating house near a nobleman's estate. The widow soon made the acquaintance of Zayde, a black groom who frequently visited them. At first Lazarillo was afraid of the black man, but he quickly learned that Zayde's visits meant food and firewood. One consequence was a bit displeasing: Lazarillo acquired a small, dark brother to look after.

The nobleman's steward began to miss horseshoes and brushes as well as other supplies. When he was asked directly about the thefts, Lazarillo told all that he knew of Zayde's peccadillos. Zayde was soundly flogged, and boiling fat was poured on his ribs. To avoid further scandal, Lazarillo's mother set up a new eating house in a different neighborhood.

When Lazarillo was fairly well grown, his mother apprenticed him to a blind man who wanted a boy to lead him about. Though old, the blind man was shrewd and tough. As they were leaving the city, they passed by a stone bull. When the blind man told the boy to put his ear to the statue and listen for a peculiar noise, Lazarillo obeyed. Then the old man knocked the boy's head sharply against the stone, hard enough so his ears rang for three days. Lazarillo was forced to learn a few tricks for himself in order to survive.

The blind man, when they squatted over a fire to cook a meal, kept his hand over the mouth of his wine jug. Lazarillo bored a tiny hole in the jug, and, lying down, let the liquid trickle into his mouth. Then he stopped up the hole with beeswax. When the suspicious old man felt the jug, the wax melted and he found the hole. Giving no sign, the next night he again put the jug in front of him and Lazarillo again lay down expecting to guzzle wine once more. Suddenly the blind man raised the jug and brought it down with great force in Lazarillo's face. All the boy's teeth were loosened.

On another occasion, Lazarillo seized a roasting sausage from the spit and substituted a rotten turnip. When the blind man bit into his supposed sausage, he roared with rage and scratched the boy severely with his long nails. Resolved to leave his master, Lazarillo guided him to the shores of a brook. Telling the blind man he must run and leap, he placed his master behind a stone pillar. The old man gave a mighty jump, cracked his head on the stone, and fell down senseless. Lazarillo left town quickly.

His next master was a penurious priest who engaged him to assist at mass. Unfortunately, the priest watched the collection box like a hawk, and Lazarillo had no chance to filch a single coin. For food, the priest allowed him an onion every fourth day. If it had not been for an occasional funeral feast, the boy would have starved to death.

The priest kept his fine bread securely locked in a chest. Luckily, Lazarillo met a strolling tinker who made him a key. Then to avoid suspicion, he gnawed each loaf to make it look as if rats had got into the chest. The alarmed priest nailed up the holes securely, but Lazarillo made new holes. Then the priest set numerous traps from which Lazarillo ate the cheese. The puzzled priest was forced to conclude that a snake was stealing his bread.

Fearing a search while he was asleep, Lazarillo kept his key in his mouth while he was in bed. One night the key shifted so that he was blowing through the keyhole. The resulting whistle awoke the priest. Seizing a club, he broke it over Lazarillo's head. After his head had been bandaged by a kind neighbor, Lazarillo was dismissed. Hoping to find employment in a larger city, he sought further fortune in Toledo.

One night while his pockets were full of crusts he had begged on the city streets, a careless young dandy, a real esquire, engaged Lazarillo as a servant. Thinking himself lucky to have a wealthy master, Lazarillo followed him to a bare, mean house with scarcely a stick of furniture. After waiting a long time for a meal, the boy began to eat his crusts. To his surprise, his master joined him. The days went by, both of them living on what Lazarillo could beg.

At last the esquire procured a little money and sent Lazarillo out for bread and wine. On the way he met a funeral procession. The weeping widow loudly lamented her husband and cried out that the dead man was going to an inhospitable house where there was no food or furniture. Thinking they were going to bring the corpse to his esquire's house, Lazarillo ran home in fear. His master disabused him of his fear and sent him back on his errand.

At last the master left town. Lazarillo was forced to meet the bailiffs and the wrathful landlord. After some difficulty, he persuaded the bailiffs of his innocence and was allowed to go free.

His next master was a bulero, a dealer in papal indulgences, who was an accomplished rogue. Rumors began to spread that his indulgences were forged, and even the alguazil accused him publicly of fraud. The wily bulero prayed openly for his accuser to be confounded, and forthwith the alguazil, falling down in a fit, foamed at the mouth and grew rigid. The prayers and forgiveness of the bulero were effective, however, and little by little the alguazil recovered. From that time on the bulero earned a rich harvest selling his papal indulgences. Lazarillo, now wise in roguery, wondered how the bulero worked the trick; but he never found out.

Four years of service with a chaplain who sold water enabled Lazarillo to save a little money and buy respectable clothes. At last he was on his way to some standing in the community. On the strength of his new clothes, he was appointed to a government post which would furnish him an income for life. All business matters of the town passed through his hands.

The archpriest of Salvador, seeing how affluent Lazarillo had become, gave him a wife from his own household. The woman made a useful wife, for the archpriest frequently gave them substantial presents. Lazarillo's wife repaid the holy man by taking care of his wardrobe; but evil tongues wagged, and the archpriest asked Lazarillo if he had heard stories about his wife. Lazarillo disclosed that he had been told that his wife had borne three of the archpriests' children. The archpriest advised him sagely to think of his profit more and his honor less. Lazarillo was content, for surely the archpriest was an honorable man.

Lazarillo was now so influential that it was said that he could commit any crime with impunity. His happiness increased when his wife presented him with a baby daughter. The good lady swore that it was truly Lazarillo's child.

Critical Evaluation

In the fifteenth and sixteenth centuries, the Spanish novel began to develop into a modern form. This early novel form—particularly during the sixteenth century, the Spanish Golden Age of literature—evolved into four types. The earliest was the novel of chivalry. *Amadís de Gaul*, written in about the mid-fourteenth century but not published until 1508, is one of the best known of this type. Next in chronological order was the dramatic novel—a novel in dialogue—of which *La Celestina* (1499) is the prime exemplar. The other two types appeared at approximately the same time, mid-sixteenth century. One was the pastoral novel, the first and greatest being Jorge de Montemayor's *La Diana* (1559; *Diana*, 1596). The other was the picaresque novel, exemplified by *Lazarillo de Tormes (La vida de Lazarillo de Tormes y de sus fortunas y adversidades)*.

Lazarillo de Tormes is generally conceded to be the earliest and the best of the picaresque novels. Episodic in form, the picaresque novel is usually told in the first person, the story dealing with the life of a *pícaro* or rogue, who is both narrator and protagonist. In spite of much scholarly investigation, the origin of the terms *picaresque* and *pícaro* is still doubtful, and etymological research has so far proved fruitless. *Pícaro*, however, is understood to designate a wandering knave, a poor adventurer, who lives by his wits on the fringes of a class-conscious society and who must subordinate the luxury of ethics to the necessities of survival—in other words, the very essence of Lazarillo. Since the *pícaro* typically serves several masters sequentially and in the course of his service observes their weaknesses and those of others, the picaresque novel becomes an ideal vehicle for depicting a wide cross-section of society and, with its satirical tone, manages to attack broad segments of that society in the process. Yet these picaresque elements of satire, parody, caricature, and the like were not unique to picaresque novels; they also existed in earlier literature—such as Juan Ruiz, the Archpriest of Hita's *El libro de buen amor* and Fernando de Rojas' *La Celestina*—which influenced the development of the picaresque novel. Still, it was in the picaresque novel that society was held up to most careful scrutiny and given the most scathing denunciation.

In addition, *Lazarillo de Tormes* is often thought, by virtue of its form, to be autobiographical. The likelihood of such an eventuality, however, is slim. The anonymous author refers to Latin authors—improbable for a real-life Lazarillo—and reveals a distinct influence of the philosopher Erasmus—equally improbable for Lazarillo, whose formal education might charitably be described as lacking; but the intrinsically fascinating adventures of Lazarillo need no autobiographical buttress. The instant and enduring popularity of the novel—three editions from 1554 alone are extant—is testimony to its compelling qualities as literature. So, too, is the number of translations: French, English, Dutch, German, and Italian versions appeared within less than seventy years of *Lazarillo de Tormes'* first publication; others followed. Imitation is another gauge of the novel's popularity and influence: in addition to Lesage's *Gil Blas* (1715–1735), among many others, there were even two sequels to *Lazarillo de Tormes*. Perhaps the ultimate accolade, however, was that the novel was placed on the *Index librorum prohibitorum* for its anticlericalism. (This anticlericalism is routinely attributed to the influence of Erasmus.) The work's popularity and influence evidently posed a threat to the Roman Catholic church.

As a character, Lazarillo is not original, cut from the whole cloth of the author's imagination. Before becoming the novel's protagonist, he was a character in folklore, with his name appearing in early proverbs and anecdotes. In fact, a quarter century before *Lazarillo de Tormes* was published, Lazarillo had a cameo role in Francisco Delicado's novel *La lozana andaluza* (1528), which features a *pícara*, a female rogue after the *La Celestina* model. Following *Lazarillo de Tormes*, however, Lazarillo himself became such a staple that the very name itself became a generic term. Most particularly, the name was associated with the first episode in the novel: Lazarillo's service to the blind man. Hence, *un lazarillo* is, even now, a term used to designate a guide for blind persons.

The most important aspect of *Lazarillo de Tormes*, however, is satiric, and this satire is precisely targeted. All in all, Lazarillo serves seven masters before becoming his own master, so to speak. The story is thus divided into seven *tratados* (treatises or chapters), each dealing with a particular employer. The first is the blind beggar; the next, a priest; the third, a nobleman; the fourth, a friar; the fifth, a seller of indulgences; the sixth, a chaplain; the last, a constable. After narrating his unconventional background, Lazarillo launches his attack on social stratification, beginning with the blind man and continuing through the penniless nobleman and the constable; but his harshest commentary is reserved for the clergy—priest, friar, seller of indulgences, and chaplain—whose duplicity and venality are a constant source of amazement and embarrassment to him. Lazarillo's implicit and explicit criticism of the clergy constitutes the preponderant thrust of the novel. Yet Lazarillo's observations are astute, and the account accurately reflects contemporary conditions. Nevertheless, in such perceptivity lies a challenge to the status quo, a challenge which those in power must suppress, as they did by banning the novel.

Above all, *Lazarillo de Tormes* conveys a mood, a temper, a tenor: a cynical antidote to idealistic worldviews, secular or religious, which characterized the medieval age of faith. In this sense, the novel is refreshingly Renaissance, breathing clear air into a musty, closed era and musty, closed minds. It wafts a clarity which should, but does not, make the blind man see, the exploiter turn philanthropist, the self-seeking cleric become true shepherd, and so on. The unalloyed power of this novel in fact stems from its lack of malice: It deplores corruption, but it does not hate. Although it focuses on the lower levels of society, it is not Balzacian social criticism designed to reform. Although it attacks clerical depredations, it is not sacrilegious. Still, *Lazarillo de Tormes* is, in the last analysis, more than a bitter tale of personal privation. It is a realistic commentary—counterfoil to the competing idealism of somewhat earlier chivalric romances—on life as it is actually lived by common people who have neither privilege nor power but try to exercise those prerogatives in order to maintain or improve their positions in a hostile environment. Beyond cynicism and despair, it offers hope for better things to come, for Lazarillo ultimately gets his foot on the bottom rung of the ladder to respectable success. As town crier, he has a steady, assured income, even if his wife is a hand-me-down mistress of the archpriest of Salvador. Lazarillo is willing thus to compromise. The reader must finally respect Lazarillo's judgment.

LEAVES OF GRASS

Type of work: Poetry
Author: Walt Whitman (1819–1892)
First published: *Leaves of Grass*, 1855

Having been at one time or another an office boy, printer, teacher, newspaper editor and reporter, manager of a printing office and stationery store, and builder of houses, Walt Whitman was thirty-six when his first book of poems, *Leaves of Grass*, was published, in July, 1855, a publication for which he himself paid. That same month he sent a copy of the book of twelve poems to Ralph Waldo Emerson, famous essayist, poet, and spokesman for Transcendentalism, whom the younger poet had never met but by whose essays he had been greatly influenced. While certainly the gesture of a writer looking for approval from his mentor, Whitman's act also represented his salute to Emerson, and Transcendentalism, as well as his gratitude to the great man for showing him the way to his own unprecedented, authentically American kind of poetry.

Whitman's "leaves" would multiply. By the time of his death in 1892, *Leaves of Grass* contained 383 poems, including the magnificent threnody to Abraham Lincoln titled "When Lilacs Last in the Dooryard Bloomed," in addition to the great "Out of the Cradle Endlessly Rocking," "Calamus," and "Passage to India." Space limitations preclude discussion of the final 1888 edition of *Leaves of Grass*, but the essence of Whitman's poetic achievement, as well as his historical place and importance in American literature, can be gleaned from the first edition. In fact, even if Whitman had never published any poetry after 1855, his influence would remain apparent in the work of such twentieth century poets as Hart Crane, Robinson Jeffers, Carl Sandburg, Charles Olson, and Allen Ginsberg. And well it should, for his first book of untitled free-verse poems would prove to be not only the single greatest poetic triumph to emerge from Transcendentalism but also the first collection of poetry uniquely American in vision, voice, form, and substance—the kind of poetry Emerson had envisioned but failed to write.

Emerson was not the first nineteenth century American to note that, after two centuries, America still had not produced poetry uniquely its own. There was Orestes Brownson who, in 1838, wrote of American writers, "We are now the literary vassals of England, and continue to do homage to the mother country. Our literature is tame and servile, wanting in freshness, freedom, and originality. We write as Englishmen, not as Americans." Even earlier, in 1826, complaining that "rhymes add nothing to poetry, but rather detract from its beauty," Sampson Reed had asserted that "the poet should be free and unshackled as the eagle whose wings, as he soars in

the air, seem merely to serve the office of a helm, while he moves on simply by the agency of the will." Whitman would prove himself to be such a "free and unshackled" poet, in the first poem (later titled "Song of Myself") of the 1855 edition of *Leaves of Grass*:

I fly the flight of the fluid and swallowing soul,
My course runs below the soundings of plummets.

I help myself to material and immaterial,
No guard can shut me off, no law can prevent me.

I anchor my ship for a little while only,
My messengers continually cruise away or bring
    their returns to me.

For those "returns," both "material and immaterial," Whitman's persona in the poems—like the poems themselves—became a crucible for apotheosis, wherein any division between subject and object would be resolved, all categories fused into one; that oneness was to be voiced by the transcendent persona's self. Like Emerson's concept of the human-deifying "transparent eyeball," the self in Whitman's poetry is essentially a transpersonal soul or universal spirit. From childhood to adulthood, the "Walt Whitman" in *Leaves of Grass* has developed his identity through a metaphysical merging with everything around him, as the poet makes clear in the tenth poem (to be titled "There Was a Child Went Forth") of the 1855 edition:

There was a child went forth every day,
And the first object he looked upon and received
    with wonder or pity or love or dread, that
    object he became,
And that object became part of him for the day or
    a certain part of the day. . . . or for many years
    or stretching cycles of years.

Such a "child," whether eight or eighty, "who went forth every day, and who now goes and will always go forth every day," realizes immortality insofar as he slips free of the shackles of personality, of what Emerson calls "mean egotism," enters into a timeless union with all around him and becomes—again Emerson's words—"part or parcel of God."

Besides a healthy irreverence for secondhand customs and beliefs, especially those transplanted to America from England, essential to Transcendentalism was a denunciation by its adherents of institutionalized, traditional religion. Transcendentalists expressed a desire to mend the supposed split between God and man in order to glorify God-Man, and they insisted that Christ be seen as a historical personage, a man, and—though wiser—no more or less godlike than other humans. Poetry Emerson believed to be the best vehicle for expressing human awareness of the Universal Being, for "poetry was all written before time was, and whenever we are so finely organized that we can penetrate into that region where the air is music, we hear those primal warblings and attempt to write them down." Emerson's attempts at such poetry, however, remained cramped within the traditional prosody adopted from English poets; in 1835 he admitted that though he was "born a poet," his talent was "of a low class without doubt." Whitman, however, was determined to capture in his poetry "those primal warblings," as he indicates in "Song of Myself": "To me the converging objects of the universe perpetually flow,/ All are written to me, and I must get what the writing means." Later in the poem, he says, "Through me the afflatus surging and surging . . . through me the current and index./ I speak the password primeval." To his readers Whitman makes an implicit promise: "Stop this day and night with me and you shall possess the origin of all poems./ You shall possess the good of the earth and sun," of the terrestrial and celestial.

"My singing," said Emerson, "is for the most part in prose. Still am I a poet in the sense of a perceiver and dear lover of the harmonies that are in the soul and in matter." Emerson's singing in prose and his remarkable ability as an essayist to articulate what he perceived and conceived inspired Whitman to a feverishly intense responsiveness. In "The American Scholar" (1841), Emerson had asserted that the ideal American scholar-poet, "Man Thinking," should be "the world's eye" and "the world's heart." In "Song of Myself," Whitman is the ideal become real: "With the twirl of my tongue I encompass worlds and volumes of worlds./ Speech is the twin of my vision." Elsewhere (in the fourth poem, later titled "The Sleepers") he asserts, "I dream in my dream all the dreams of other dreamers,/ And I become the other dreamers." Emerson claimed that the "one thing in the world, of value, is the active soul," and that "the soul active sees absolute truth and utters truth, or creates. In this action it is genius. . . . In its essence it is progressive." Whitman responds (in the twelfth poem of the 1855 edition, later titled "Great Are the Myths"): "O truth of the earth! O truth of things! I am determined to press the whole way toward you,/ Sound your voice! I scale mountains or dive in the sea after you." Believing that the world is the "shadow of the soul, or *other* me," as Man Thinking, scholar-poet Emerson claimed to "embrace the common," to "explore and sit at the feet of the familiar, the low." Whitman was equal to such an embrace, exploration, and reverential humility—was in fact the personification of such in his poems, especially in "The Sleepers" and "Song of Myself": "What is commonest and cheapest and nearest and easiest is Me," and in "all people I see myself, none more and not one a barleycorn less."

"We have listened too long to the courtly muses of Europe. The spirit of the American freeman is already suspected to be timid, imitative, tame," Emerson had said in "The American Scholar." Three years later, in "The Poet," he asserted that the ideal American poet would be "representative," that "He stands among partial men for the complete man, and apprises us not of his wealth, but of the common wealth." Eleven years later, he would open *Leaves of Grass* and witness in the first poem the "barbaric yawp" of the actualized ideal: "I am the poet of the woman the same as the man,/ And I say it is as great to be a woman as to be a man." Furthermore, "I am large . . . I contain multitudes," the representative and democratic I of Whitman's poems announces. "Neither a servant nor a master am I," he sings in the second poem (to be titled "A Song for Occupations"); "I will be even with you, and you shall be even with me."

Emerson had said in "The American Scholar" that the world is the soul's shadow, and in "The Poet" he claimed that "the Universe is the externization of the soul." Undoubtedly this would be one of the most salient and liberating Emersonian premises for the younger poet, for it is endlessly all-encompassing, the truths one might discover through it countless and its realm incomprehensibly expansive. In fact, in the 1850s America itself seemed expansive enough to be viewed as "the externization of the soul," and this is how Whitman portrayed it, his persona the embodiment of a harmonious microcosmic and macrocosmic union. He is introduced in "Song of Myself" as "Walt Whitman, an American, one of the roughs, a kosmos,/ Disorderly fleshy and sensual . . . eating drinking and breeding,/ No sentimentalist . . . no stander above men and women or apart from them."

The American poetry Emerson had envisioned in 1844 would not depend upon meters, he said; rather its form would derive organically from its content, for "a meter-making argument . . . makes a poem,—a thought so passionate and alive that like the spirit of a plant or an animal it has an architecture of its own." He also maintained that in American poetry thought should make "everything fit for use. The vocabulary of an omniscient man would embrace words and images excluded from polite conversation." Although Emerson would be incapable of embracing or employing such "words and images" in his poetry, one of the hallmarks of Whitman's is that he did employ them:

> I keep as delicate around the bowels as around the
>   head and heart,
> Copulation is no more rank to me than death is.
>
> I believe in the flesh and the appetites,
> Seeing hearing and feeling are miracles, and each
>   part and tag of me is a miracle.

> Divine am I inside and out, and I make holy
> whatever I touch or am touched from;
> The scent of these arm-pits is aroma finer than
> prayer. . . .

Most modern readers would consider the above passage from "Song of Myself" tame in its celebration of the flesh, but in 1855 it was audacious and bold. Nevertheless, Whitman set out to celebrate in poetry what he called, in a letter to Emerson (1856), "the divinity of sex . . . I say that the body of a man or woman, the main matter, is so far quite unexpressed in poems; but that body is to be expressed, and sex is."

As a poet Whitman proved himself to be the kind of superior student Emerson had called for in his essays—one who surpasses his teacher. The creator of a revolutionary form of poetry and the uniquely representative American persona of the "barbaric yawp," Whitman was justified in singing, in "Song of Myself," "I am an acme of things accomplished, and I an encloser of things to be."

"THE LEGEND OF SLEEPY HOLLOW"

Type of work: Tale
Author: Washington Irving (1783–1859)
Type of plot: Regional romance
Time of plot: Eighteenth century
Locale: New York State
First published: 1819–1820

American literature's first great writer, Irving was responsible for two trends in American letters: one toward local color and the legendary tale, the other toward the historical novel. This tale belongs to the first trend and has fascinated and delighted readers for almost two hundred years.

Principal Characters

Ichabod Crane, a schoolmaster of Sleepy Hollow, near Tarry Town on the Hudson. He dreams of a comfortable marriage to Katrina. Because of his belief in ghosts, he is frightened from the area by a ghostly rider.

Gunpowder, Ichabod's gaunt horse.

Katrina Van Tassel, a rosy-cheeked student in Ichabod's singing classes.

Mynheer Van Tassel, her wealthy farmer father.

The Headless Horseman, a legendary apparition, supposedly a Hessian cavalryman whose head was shot off by a cannonball.

Abraham Van Brunt, called **Brom Bones,** who is in love with Katrina. Disguised as the Headless Horseman, he pursues Ichabod and throws a pumpkin at him. Ichabod leaves Sleepy Hollow permanently.

The Story

Near Tarry Town on the Hudson is a little valley which, years ago, was the quietest place in the world. A drowsy influence hung over the place and people so that the region was known as Sleepy Hollow, and the lads were called Sleepy Hollow boys. Some said that the valley was bewitched. It was true that marvelous stories were told there.

The main figure to haunt the valley was a headless horseman. Some said the specter was the apparition of a Hessian horseman who had lost his head from a cannonball, but, whatever it was, it was often seen in the valley and adjacent countryside in the gloom of winter nights. The specter was known to all as the Headless Horseman of Sleepy Hollow.

In the valley, years ago, there lived a schoolteacher called Ichabod Crane. He looked like a scarecrow because of his long, skinny frame and his snipelike nose. As was the custom in that fertile Dutch countryside, he boarded with the parents of his pupils a week at a time. Fortunately for him, the Dutch larders were full and the tables groaning with food, for the schoolmaster had a wonderful appetite. He was always welcome in the country homes because in small ways he made himself useful to the farmers. He was patient with the children, and he loved to spend the long winter nights with the families of his pupils, exchanging tales of ghosts and haunted places while ruddy apples roasted on the hearths.

Ichabod believed heartily in ghosts, and his walks home after an evening of tale-telling were often filled with fear. His only source of courage at those times was his voice, loud and nasal as it made the night resound with many a psalm tune.

The schoolteacher picked up a little odd change by holding singing classes. In one of his classes, he first became aware of a plump and rosy-cheeked girl named Katrina Van Tassel. She was the only child of a very substantial farmer, and that fact added to her charms for the ever-hungry Ichabod. Since she was not only beautiful but also lively, she was a great favorite among the lads in the neighborhood.

Abraham Van Brunt was Katrina's favorite squire. The Dutch first shortened his name to Brom and then called him Brom Bones when he became known for the tall and powerful frame of his body. He was a lively lad with a fine sense of humor and a tremendous amount of energy. When other suitors saw his horse hitched outside Katrina's house on a Sunday night, they went on their way. Brom Bones was a formidable rival for the gaunt and shaggy Ichabod. Brom would have liked to carry the battle into the open, but the schoolteacher knew better than to tangle with him physically. Brom Bones could do little but play practical jokes on lanky Ichabod.

The whole countryside was invited one fall evening to a quilting frolic at Mynheer Van Tassel's. For the occasion, Ichabod borrowed a horse from the farmer with whom he was then living. The horse, called Gunpowder, was as gaunt as Ichabod himself, but the steed still had a fair amount of spirit. The two of them were a sight as they jogged happily along to the party.

Ichabod was well pleased by every prospect he saw on the Van Tassel farm, the most prosperous holding for miles around. Perhaps Ichabod might be able to sell it and, with the proceeds, go farther west. It was a pretty picture he saw as he passed fields full of shocks of corn and pumpkins, granaries stuffed with grain, and meadows and barnlots filled with sleek cattle and plump fowl.

The party was a merry one with many lively dances. Ichabod was at his best when he danced with Katrina. After a time, he went out on the dark porch with the men and exchanged more Sleepy Hollow ghost stories—but the food was best of all. Ichabod did credit to all the cakes and pies, meats and tea.

After the others left, he tarried to pay court to Katrina, but it was not long before he started home crestfallen on the gaunt Gunpowder. All the stories he had heard came back to him, and as he rode along in the darkness, he became more dismal. He heard groans as the branches of the famed Major André tree rubbed against one another. He even thought he saw something moving beneath it.

When he came to the bridge over Wiley's Swamp,

Gunpowder balked. The harder Ichabod urged him on, the more the horse bucked. Then, on the other side of the marsh, Ichabod saw something huge and misshapen.

The figure refused to answer him when he called. Ichabod's hair stood straight on end. Because it was too late to turn back, however, the schoolmaster kept to the road. The stranger—it looked like a headless horseman, but it seemed to hold its head on the pommel—kept pace with him, fast or slow. Ichabod could not stand going slowly, and he whipped Gunpowder to a gallop. As his saddle loosened, he nearly lost his grip, but he hugged the horse around the neck. He could not even sing a psalm tune.

When he reached the church bridge, where by tradition the headless specter would disappear in a flash of fire and brimstone, Ichabod heard the horseman close in on him. As he turned to look, the spirit threw his head at him. Ichabod tried to dodge, but the head tumbled him into the dust.

In the morning, a shattered pumpkin was found near the bridge. Gunpowder was grazing at the farmer's gate nearby. Ichabod, however, was never seen in Sleepy Hollow again. In the valley, they say that Brom Bones, long after he had married the buxom Katrina, laughed heartily whenever the story was told of the horseman who had thrown his head at the schoolteacher during that ghostly midnight pursuit.

Critical Evaluation

Washington Irving was by inclination an amused observer of people and customs. By birth, he was in a position to pursue that inclination. Son of a New York merchant in good financial standing, he was the youngest of eleven children, several of whom helped him to take prolonged trips to Europe for his health and fancy. He was responsible for two trends in American literature: one, toward the legendary tale, steeped in local color; the other, toward the historical novel. "The Legend of Sleepy Hollow" belongs to the first trend.

The two best-known of Irving's stories are "Rip Van Winkle" and "The Legend of Sleepy Hollow," both of which appeared originally in *The Sketch Book of Geoffrey Crayon, Gent.*, a collection of tales and familiar essays. Both stories are based on German folklore, which Irving adapted to a lower New York State setting peopled with Dutch farmers.

In "The Legend of Sleepy Hollow," the Dutch farmers make up most of the folkloric elements, for Ichabod Crane is an outsider, a Yankee schoolmaster among the canny Dutch settlers. As an outsider, and a peculiar-looking one at that, Ichabod Crane becomes the butt of local humor and the natural victim for Brom Bones's practical jokes. Most of the humorous sallies of the Sleepy Hollow boys are in the vein of good-natured ribbing. Yet Brom

Bones's practical jokes are somewhat more serious because of the rather unequal rivalry between Brom and Ichabod for the hand of Katrina Van Tassel. It is in the relationship between Brom and Ichabod that the common folk theme of the scapegoat is most clearly seen.

Other folk themes appear in the story as well. Among them is the belief that one can ward off evil spirits with religious symbols; thus, Ichabod sings psalms on his fear-filled homeward treks after evenings of storytelling. The distinction of having a special ghost—one with a definite identity—to haunt a specific locality is a matter of honor and prestige, highly respected as a folkloric theme. Here, the putative Hessian, the Headless Horseman of Sleepy Hollow, fills the role with grace, wit, and style. The character of the comely wench, over whose favors men wrangle, dispute, and plot, is as common a catalyst in folklore as in life; hence, Katrina Van Tassel functions as fulcrum and folk theme in "The Legend of Sleepy Hollow."

These and other themes from folklore and legend appear in "The Legend of Sleepy Hollow" as well as other tales by Washington Irving, for legendary material was one of Irving's two major interests, the other being history, a closely related field. As far as Irving's work is concerned, the two interests seem to feed upon each other to the mutual benefit of both: his historical writings are enlivened by his cultural perceptions, and his stories are made more vivid by his knowledge of history. One of the first professional writers in America, and among the first to exercise a significant influence in Great Britain and the Continent, Irving has been called the father of American literature.

LEVIATHAN: Or, The Matter, Form, and Power of a Commonwealth, Ecclesiastical and Civil

Type of work: Philosophy of politics
Author: Thomas Hobbes (1588–1679)
First published: 1651

To appreciate the range of Hobbes's subject matter in the Leviathan one may first consider the entire title: *Leviathan: Or, The Matter, Form, and Power of a Commonwealth, Ecclesiastical and Civil*. In considering the "matter, form, and power" of the commonwealth, or state, Hobbes was doing far more than describing governments as he found them. His goal was to explain the origin of political institutions and to define their powers and proper limits. To this end he drew an analogy between man and the commonwealth. In drawing the analogy he first described man, giving to the description a thoroughly mechanistic bias. He then proceeded to explain the state as man's artful creation, designed to put an end to the continual state of war that is man's lot in his natural state.

The state, "that great Leviathan," is but an "Artificial Man," writes Hobbes. The sovereign is an artificial soul, the officers of the state are artificial joints, reward and punishment are nerves, wealth and riches are strength; the people's safety is the business of artificial man; the laws are its reason and will; concord, its health; sedition, its sickness; and civil war, its death.

According to Hobbes men's ideas originate in sense, that is, they are derived from sense impressions. All sensation is a result of external bodies pressing upon the sense organs. Imagination is "nothing but decaying sense," the effect of sense impressions after the external body has ceased to press upon the organs. If one wants to emphasize the past cause of the impression, one calls the fading image a "memory" image; if one wishes to emphasize the image as one not now related to any present cause, one calls it "fancy" or "imagination."

The passions are the "interior beginnings of voluntary motions," according to Hobbes. Since for Hobbes everything can be understood in terms of bodies in motion, it is not surprising that even the emotions are simply motions inside the body. Motion toward something is desire; motion away, aversion. In terms of these two basic motions, Hobbes defined the other passions.

While for Hobbes all knowledge stems from sense experience, true wisdom is the product of reason, from which one obtains such immutable truths as found in geometry. Hobbes believed that the way to true knowledge is through definition. From these ideas, Hobbes developed a complex theory of language and naming. Names serve as signs of man's thinking processes. Some names refer to objects, others refer to more abstract entities. For Hobbes, to say that something is "infinite" is simply to mean that one cannot conceive of its boundaries. Names such as "man" or "tree" refer to objects and indicate something more definite than words such as "infinite." This, however, is not to say that objects which can be called "tree" or "man" partake of some universal form of "treeness" or "manness." Thus, Hobbes denied the Platonic doctrine of forms.

After considering the intellectual virtues and defects, the two kinds of knowledge (knowledge of observed fact, and the conditional knowledge of science), and the powers and manners of men, Hobbes considered the question of religion. Hobbes was careful to delineate in his philosophy the proper domains of faith and of knowledge. He outlined a theory to explain the roots of religion and of superstition and spent much time interpreting the Scriptures. His primary aim in this area was to analyze religion to understand how it served as a source of civil discord. Thus, Hobbes was interested in religion primarily as it affected the state.

Hobbes's notion of God is complex. God's nature is incomprehensible to man. He must exist, since existence must be an attribute of God, that is, a part of God's definition. Through reason one can know what God is not, that is, finite, figured, having parts, and so on. Words such as "infinite" or "incomprehensible" are really no more than expressions of an inability to grasp the essence of God. Words such as "holy" or "most high," on the other hand, are simply expressions of man's admiration or reverence for God. Thus, rational arguments about God are pointless and a dishonor to Him.

For Hobbes, the differences between men are not so marked as the similarities, and there is no natural sanction for one man's assuming authority over another. Because men are similar, they sometimes come to desire the same thing; if they cannot both enjoy the object of their desire, they become enemies and war over the object. There are three principal causes of conflict between men: competition, diffidence, and glory. While men have no common power over them to keep them all in check, they are in "that condition which is called Warre; and such a warre, as is of every man, against every man." There are many inconveniences to war, and the fact that in a state of war there is no injustice (since there is no natural law governing action) in no way makes that state of affairs satisfactory. In order to secure peace, men enter upon certain agreements by which they bring about a transferring of rights. It is possible for men to make such agreements, or contracts, because they have certain natural rights to use their power however they choose in order to preserve themselves.

Hobbes argues, in the second part of *Leviathan*, that the commonwealth is brought into being in order to enable men to escape from the state of war. Loving liberty and dominion over others, men agree to make some person sovereign over them all to work for their peace and benefit. The sovereign is not bound by the contract or covenant; the contract is among those who are to be ruled. If the ruler turns out to be a despot, it must be remembered that it is better to be ruled in a commonwealth than to be in a state of nature and, consequently, a continual state of war.

Hobbes considers three kinds of commonwealth: monarchy, democracy, and aristocracy—the latter being ruled by an assembly of part of the commonwealth. There are certain advantages to the monarchial form of government, according to Hobbes: A monarch combines the private and public interest; he is better able to consult with men who have knowledge he needs; the only inconstancy the monarch has to put up with is his own; he cannot disagree with himself; and although it is sometimes inconvenient to have power vested in one man, particularly when the monarch may be an infant because of succession, the disadvantages are no greater than they are in other forms of government.

The subjects in a commonwealth are not entirely subject to the sovereign. The basic principle is that they cannot be compelled to act against that natural inclination toward self-preservation which the commonwealth is supposed to serve. They cannot be bound to injure themselves or to wage war—although this is a dubious right since the sovereign is free to imprison or execute them for disobedience. If the sovereign is not able to protect his subjects, the subjects are absolved of obedience to him.

The civil law of a commonwealth is made up of those rules that prescribe what is right and wrong for the subjects; and since the commonwealth itself is no lawmaker, the sovereign must be the legislator. He is not subject to civil law, and only he can abrogate the law. Since an undeclared law is no law at all, and since law is not binding unless it is clearly commanded by the sovereign, the sovereign must make the law known and understood, and he must see to it that it be known as his law. The only laws that need not be published are laws of nature, and they can be contained in one sentence: "Do not that to another, which thou thinkest unreasonable to be done by another to thy selfe."

Hobbes regarded crime as resulting from some defect of the understanding, or from some error of reasoning, or from some force of the passions. He declares that "No law, made after a Fact done, can make it a Crime," and that although ignorance of natural law is no excuse, ignorance of civil law may excuse a man provided he had not

the opportunity to hear the law declared. Punishment is not fundamentally retributive in Hobbes' scheme: "A Punishment, is an Evil inflicted by the publique Authority, on him that hath done, or omitted that which is Judged by the same Authority, to be a Transgression of the Law; to the end that the will of men may thereby the better be disposed to obedience."

Like anything made by men, a commonwealth can perish. Its infirmities result from what Hobbes calls an "Imperfect Institution"—errors in the creation of the commonwealth. Perhaps the sovereign is not given enough power, or every man is allowed to be a judge, or conscience is authoritative in moral judgment, or supernatural inspiration is given precedence over reason, or the sovereign is held to be subject to civil law, or it is supposed that every man has some absolute property which the sovereign cannot touch, or it is supposed that sovereign power can be divided. Other difficulties, such as the lack of money, the presence of monopolies and corrupt politicians, the popularity of certain subjects, the greatness of a town, or the invasion by a foreign power can lead to the dissolution of the commonwealth.

Part 3 of *Leviathan* is concerned with showing the relations between a Christian commonwealth and commonwealths in general. Hobbes uses hundreds of biblical references, as interpreted by him, to support his conclusion that it is possible to reconcile our obedience to God with our obedience to a civil sovereign, for either the sovereign is a Christian or he is not a Christian. If he is a Christian, then, even if he may sometimes err in supposing that some act is God's will, the proper thing for the subject, who has no right to judge, is to obey. If the sovereign is an infidel, then the subject must obey because the law of nature justifies the sovereign's power in a commonwealth, and to disobey would be to disobey the laws of nature which are the laws of God. No church leader, even a pope, can rule the sovereign; and this situation is not contrary to God's law, for the Church works through civil government.

The concluding section, "Of the Kingdome of Darknesse," argues that spiritual darkness has not been completely eliminated from the Church—by which Hobbes means the Church of Rome. His principal attack on the Church of Rome is based on his claim that the Scripture is misinterpreted in order to justify the assumption of temporal power by the popes.

Although Hobbes maintains that his entire argument is based upon a study of nature and of man's natural inclinations, it is clear that a large part of his discourse is an expression of his own preference for absolute monarchy. On this account he tends to overlook the possibility of restraining the power of a sovereign by democratic procedures. Nevertheless, *Leviathan* is a remarkable attempt to explain and justify the institution of government, and it remains one of the masterpieces of political thought.

LIFE IS A DREAM

Type of work: Drama
Author: Pedro Calderón de la Barca (1600–1681)
Type of plot: Romantic melodrama
Time of plot: Sixteenth century
Locale: Poland
First presented: 1635

A play filled with vigor and brilliance, Life Is a Dream *uses its Polish setting as freely as Shakespeare used the seacoast of Bohemia or the forest of Arden. A gothic quality in the mountain scenes suggests the popular atmosphere of eighteenth century fiction. There is considerable psychological insight in this metaphysical melodrama.*

Principal Characters

Segismundo (sā·hēs·mōōn′dō), heir to the throne of Poland, who has been imprisoned in a tower on the Russian frontier because horrible portents at his birth and later predictions by astrologers have convinced his father, King Basilio, that the boy will grow up into a monster who will destroy the land. Finally because the king sees his land split over the matter of succession, Segismundo is drugged and transported from his prison to the Court of Warsaw. There, uncouth and inexperienced, he behaves boorishly. He accuses the court of wronging him and scorns his father's explanations thus: "What man is so foolish as to lay on the disinterested stars the responsibility for his own actions?" Impossible as a king, he is again drugged and returned to his tower, where he is told it was all a dream. Later liberated by an army recruited by Rosaura, in revenge on the ambitious Astolfo, he thinks he is still dreaming. So why should he strive in a dream for something that disappears upon awakening? On that account he will not accept the throne when his followers overthrow King Basilio. He treats everybody kindly and generously, marries Estrella, and forces Astolfo to keep his promise and marry Rosaura.

Rosaura (rro·sä′ōō·rä), a Russian woman traveling with her servant Fife to the Court of Warsaw to seek the Pole who had promised to marry her. Crossing the Russian-Polish boundary, disguised as a man for protection against bandits, she loses her horse and her way. She finds and sympathizes with a young man, chained to the doorway of a tower and bemoaning his fate. He warns her to flee, which she does, after giving him the sword she has been carrying.

Clotaldo (klō·täl′dō), a Polish general and guardian of the imprisoned Segismundo. He captures Rosaura and

Fife but sends them on their way. He recognizes the sword as one he had left in Russia with a noblewoman with whom he had been in love, and he supposes the disguised Rosaura is his own son. However, duty to his king seals his lips. When Segismundo returns to his tower prison from his unfortunate experiences in Warsaw, Clotaldo assures the Prince that life is a dream and that in dreams men's evil thoughts and ambitions are unchecked. Awake, one can control his passions and behave like a sane individual. Later, when Segismundo gets a second chance, Clotaldo is unharmed because of his earlier advice.

King Basilio (bä·sē·lyō), the father of Segismundo, faced by the problem of succession to the Polish throne. Claimants are Astolfo, his nephew, and Estrella, his niece; their rival supporters form political factions that will disrupt the country in civil war. Calling an assembly, King Basilio announces that his son, who supposedly died with his mother, is really alive. With the consent of the claimants, he will send for the prince and see what sort of king he might make.

Astolfo (äs·tōl′fō), one claimant for the Polish throne. While in Russia, he had contracted matrimony with Rosaura, but now he wants to marry Estrella so that he can be sure of becoming king of Poland. When Segismundo awakes from his drugged sleep, he manhandles Astolfo for daring to touch the attractive Estrella.

Estrella (ĕs·trä′lyä), a princess whom Segismundo embraces, to the consternation of the courtiers. Eventually, after his second visit to the court, where he acts with proper dignity because of his conviction that life is a dream, Estrella becomes his queen.

Fife (fē′fä), the "gracioso," or comic servant of Rosaura, who adds humor and philosophy to the comedy.

The Story

One night, in the wild, mountainous country between Poland and Russia, a Russian noblewoman, Rosaura, and her servant, Fife, found themselves in distress. Their horses had bolted, and they feared that they would have

to make on foot the remainder of their journey to the royal court of Poland. Rosaura, for protection through that barbarous frontier country, was disguised as a man.

Their weary way brought them at last to a forbidding

fortress. There they overheard a young man, chained to the doorway of the castle, deliver a heart-rending soliloquy in which he lamented the harshness of his life. Rosaura approached the youth, who greeted her eagerly, with the excitement of one who had known little of sympathy or kindness during his brief span of years. At the same time he warned her to beware of violence. No sooner had he spoken these words than a shrill trumpet blast filled the night. Rosaura tossed her sword to the captive before she and Fife hid themselves among the rocks.

Clotaldo, a Polish general and the keeper of the youth, galloped up to the young man. Seeing the sword in his prisoner's hand, he ordered his men to seek the stranger who must be lurking nearby. Apprehended, Rosaura explained that she and Fife were Russian travelers on their way to the Polish court and that they were in distress because of the loss of their horses. Fife inadvertently hinted that Rosaura was really a woman. But the sword interested Clotaldo most of all, for he recognized the weapon as one which he had owned years before and which he had left in the keeping of a young noblewoman with whom he had been deeply in love. He decided that Rosaura must be his own son, but torn between his sworn duty to his king and his paternal obligation toward his supposed son, he decided at last to say nothing for the time being. The fact that Rosaura possessed the sword obligated him to protect the travelers and to escort them safely through the mountains.

Meanwhile, in King Basilio's royal castle, the problem of succession to the Polish throne was to be decided. To this purpose, the king welcomed his nephew Astolfo and his niece Estrella, cousins. The problem of the succession existed because it was generally believed that the true heir, King Basilio's son, had died with his mother in childbirth many years before. The need for a decision was pressing; both Astolfo and Estrella were supported by strong rival factions which in their impatience were threatening the peace of the realm.

King Basilio greeted his niece and nephew with regal ceremony and then startled them with the news that his son Segismundo was not really dead. The readings of learned astrologers and horrible portents which had accompanied Segismundo's birth had led the superstitious king to imprison the child in a mountain fortress for fear that otherwise the boy might grow up to be a monster who would destroy Poland. Now, years later, King Basilio was not sure that he had done right. He proposed that Segismundo be brought to the court in a drug-induced sleep, awakened after being dressed in attire befitting a prince, and observed carefully for evidence of his worthiness to wear his father's crown. Astolfo and Estrella agreed to that proposal.

In accordance with the plan, Segismundo, who dressed in rough wolfskins in his captivity, was drugged, taken to the royal castle, and dressed in rich attire. Awaking, he was disturbed to find himself suddenly the center of attention among obsequious strangers. Force of habit caused him to recall sentimentally his chains, the wild mountains, and his former isolation. Convinced that he was dreaming, he sat on the throne while his father's officers and the noble courtiers treated him with the respect due his rank. When they told him that he was the heir to the throne, he was mystified and somewhat apprehensive, but before long he began to enjoy his new feeling of power.

Clotaldo, his former guard and tutor, appeared to confirm the fact that Segismundo was really the prince. The young man then demanded an explanation of his lifelong imprisonment. Clotaldo patiently explained King Basilio's actions in terms that Segismundo might understand, but the youth, blinded by the sudden change in his fortunes, could see only that he had been grievously mistreated by his father. Declaring that he would have revenge for his unwarranted imprisonment, he seized Clotaldo's sword, but before he could strike the old general, Rosaura appeared out of the crowd, took the weapon from him, and reproved him for his rashness.

Segismundo, in a calmer mood, was introduced to Astolfo, whose courtly bearing and formal speech the prince could not bear. Sick of the whole aspect of the court, he ordered the guards to clear the audience hall. But again he was mollified, this time by the appearance of Estrella and her ladies in waiting. Unaccustomed to feminine society, he behaved in a boorish manner, even attempting to embrace Estrella. The courtiers advised him to behave in a manner befitting a prince, and Astolfo, who hoped to marry his beautiful cousin, cautioned Segismundo about his behavior toward the princess. Unfamiliar with the formalities of court life, Segismundo lost all patience. Holding all present responsible for his long exile, he reminded them of his exalted position and defied anyone to touch Estrella. When Astolfo did not hesitate to take her by the hand, Segismundo seized Astolfo by the throat.

At this crucial moment in Segismundo's test, King Basilio entered the throne room and saw his son behaving like a wild beast. Crushed, he feared that the forecast had been true after all. Segismundo faced his father with shocking disrespect. Pressed for an explanation of his son's imprisonment, the king tried to prove that it had been written in the stars. Segismundo scoffed at the folly of man in putting responsibility for his actions on the disinterested heavens. Then he cursed his father and called the guards to seize the king and Clotaldo. But at a trumpet blast the soldiers quickly surrounded Segismundo himself and took him prisoner.

Having failed the test of princehood, Segismundo was drugged and returned in chains to the mountain fortress. In his familiar surroundings once more, he had full opportunity to reflect on his late experiences. When he spoke to Clotaldo about them, the old general assured him that all had been a dream. Since the prince had been drugged before he left the fortress and before he returned, he was quite convinced that he had suffered an unpleasant dream. Clotaldo assured him that dreams reveal the true character of the dreamer. Because Segismundo had conducted himself with violence in his dream, there was great need for the young man to bridle his fierce passions.

Meanwhile Rosaura, aware of Segismundo's plight and anxious to thwart the ambitions of Astolfo, who had once promised to marry her, stirred up a faction to demand the prince's release. The rebels invaded the mountains and seized the fortress they failed, however, to seize Clotaldo, who had already returned to the royal castle to report to King Basilio. When the rebel army carried the sleeping Segismundo out of the fortress and awakened him with trumpet blasts, the unhappy prince would not be persuaded that his new experience was real, and he doubted the assurance that he had been rescued from his imprisonment. The rebel leader finally convinced him that it would be well for him to join the dream soldiers and fight with them against King Basilio's very real army, which was approaching.

Clotaldo was taken prisoner by Segismundo's forces, but the young prince, remembering the advice to curb his passions, ordered the old general's release. A great battle then took place, in which Segismundo proved his princely valor and chivalric bearing. King Basilio, defeated but refusing Clotaldo's and Astolfo's pleas to flee to safety, in admiration surrendered his crown to his son.

King of Poland in his own right, Segismundo ordered the marriage of Astolfo to Rosaura, who had, in the meantime, been revealed as Clotaldo's daughter. Estrella became Segismundo's queen. The young king made Clotaldo his trusted adviser.

Critical Evaluation

A dramatic genius and eminent mind of Spain's "Golden Century," Calderón resembled the gaunt, ascetic figures of El Greco's canvases. He was calm, withdrawn, reserved and courtly, and, as time went on, ever more religious and theological. Calderonian theater mirrored Christian principles but was best known for its "Cape and Sword" dramas featuring the delicate Spanish "point of honor." At one time, Calderón rivaled Shakespeare in European esteem.

Orphaned as an adolescent, Calderón wrote his first book while still a lad. He was sixteen years old when Cervantes and Shakespeare died. Between 1615 and 1619 he attended the famous Golden Century universities of Alcalá de Henares and Salamanca "the Golden." Even though declining at this time, Spain was still great, its red and gold flag floating over an immense world empire and its citizens excelling in many aspects of human activity. During his first literary phase following graduation, Calderón wrote poetry and one-act, sacred allegorical plays called *autos sacramentales*. He wrote his first major play in 1623, entitling it *Love, Honor, and Power*. As Calderón's star truly began to rise in drama—at which Spaniards were then considered Europe's masters—the "giants" of the Spanish Golden Age drama, such as Lope de Vega, Tirso de Molina, and Alarcón were closing their careers. El Greco had died in 1614, but Spain's most famous painting masters, including Ribera, Zurbarán, and Velásquez, produced some of their richest canvases during Calderón's ascendancy.

Calderón became a skilled swordsman, soldier, playwright, courtier, and eventually priest and theologian. He produced his masterpiece, *Life Is a Dream*, when he was thirty-five years old, whereas Shakespeare's *Hamlet* and Goethe's *Faust* were products of their respective author's ripest maturity. *Life Is a Dream* premiered at the Royal Court of Spain, and in the same year of 1635 Calderón was appointed Court dramatist upon the death of Lope de Vega. He was made a Knight of Santiago in 1637 (Spain had three great exclusive military-monastic orders dating from its earliest, medieval crusades against the Moors: Santiago, Calatrava, and Alcántara) and spent much of his life at the Royal Court, where intrigues and points of honor were rife. He eventually became the last giant literary figure of the vanishing Golden Age, far outliving all other greats. Information on the last three decades of his life is scant, but he is known to have lived calmly and in almost mystic seclusion.

Life Is a Dream has mysterious appeal, a will-o'-the-wisp lure. It is a metaphysical drama difficult to interpret, but moves its audiences deeply. It merits its fame as one of Spain's greatest plays, but puzzles commentators who strain to summarize it or probe its mysteries. Its verses are lyrical and beautiful, and it is prismatic, since new meanings can be derived from each rereading. Its basic theme is that life is a dream, filled with chaos, beauty, and torment. Thus it is partially based on the awakened sleeper theme (which Calderón did not originate; it dates from antiquity). Segismundo, Prince of Poland, represents man, but the play also stresses the evanescent nature of human life and the vanity of human affairs. It also emphasizes that salvation can be gained through good works and that, despite a strain of divine predestination, free will defeats astrological fatalism. Human bestiality is conquered by reason, while threads of freedom, grace, sin, and unreality are also a part of the play. The dramatic scenes in the tower and palace have often been praised. *Life Is a Dream* has basked in international fame for more than three centuries and still rates as one of Spain's most representative plays.

Oddly, few critics have detected that Calderón seems

to have set his masterpiece in Poland because the latter nation was akin to Spain in its devout Catholicism, rich seventeenth century culture, and, above all, its heroic historic role as a defender of Christendom's "marches" against nonbelievers (in Poland's case against pagan invaders from the endless East; in Spain's against Moors, Turks, and all anti-Catholics). George Tyler Northrup was evidently the first scholar to notice that Calderón borrowed much for *Life Is a Dream* from *Yerros de la Naturaleza y Acierto de la Fortuna*, a work that he and Antonio Coello wrote in 1634, also set in Poland. Most of the characters in *Life Is a Dream*, excepting Astolfo and Estrella, had their prototypes in *Yerros de la Naturaleza y Aciertos de la Fortuna*.

Calderón was Spain's most poetic dramatist. He was thus influenced by the stylistic obscurities of the Cordoban bard, Góngora, "the Prince of Darkness." "Gongorism" was richly obscure and featured classical-mythological references, metaphors, contrived words, strained comparisons, and the flaunting of erudition. Other features of the Spanish Golden Century have to be studied to understand Calderón. To appreciate his "Cape and Sword" theater, for example, the modern reader must comprehend the "point of honor" with which Spain was obsessed. A Spaniard's honor was a cherished possession while personal dignity and family honor were also sacred. Men were expected to be vehement defenders of their families, and Spanish husbands were obsessed with wifely fidelity; indeed, they were prone to avenge even supposed breaches of it by dispatching their spouses.

The erudite Menéndez y Pelayo labeled Calderón a less spontaneous dramatist than Lope de Vega. He also felt that Calderón was Tirso de Molina's inferior in characterization, but Menéndez y Pelayo also rated Calderón above everyone in conceptual grandeur, poetry, symbolism, and Christian depth. In short, alleged Menéndez, Calderón was history's greatest playwright after Sophocles and Shakespeare.

Calderón died on Pentecost Sunday in 1681, while writing an *auto*. He had ordered that his coffin be left ajar so as to stress the corruptible nature of the human body. His death left a void in Spanish literature, which declined into a long sterility; Calderón's theater, however, especially *Life Is a Dream*, has remained popular with Spanish and foreign audiences.

THE LIFE OF SAMUEL JOHNSON, LL.D.

Type of work: Biography
Author: James Boswell (1740–1795)
Time of plot: Eighteenth century
Locale: England
First published: 1791

To lovers of English literature, May 16 is a red-letter day second only to April 23, the birth and death date of William Shakespeare, for this is the anniversary of the momentous meeting of James Boswell and Samuel Johnson in the back room of Tom Davies' bookshop in 1763, and the appearance, twenty-eight years later, of the consequence of that encounter, Boswell's immortal *Life of Samuel Johnson, LL.D.*, perhaps the greatest biography in the English language.

Boswell had a great subject, but others shared this advantage without being able to utilize it as well. Barely a day after Johnson's death on December 13, 1784, the *St. James Chronicle* for December 14–16 reported,

Biographers are very busy in preparing Materials for the Life of Dr. Samuel Johnson. Many, we are told, are the Candidates, but the principal which are mentioned are Sir John Hawkins, and James Boswell, Esq. his itinerant Companion through the Highlands of Scotland.

Biographers were busy indeed. Less than two weeks later, William Cooke brought out his *Life of Samuel Johnson, LL.D.* (December 27, 1784), and the next month saw the publication of Thomas Tyers' "Biographical Sketch of Dr. Johnson" in the *Gentleman's Magazine* for January, 1785. Boswell's two chief rivals for the role of principal biographer were Hester Lynch Thrale Piozzi, who brought out her *Anecdotes of the Late Samuel Johnson LL.D.* in 1786, and Sir John Hawkins, whose *Life of Dr. Samuel Johnson* appeared the following year.

Hester Thrale Piozzi had known Johnson nearly as long as Boswell had; after their first meeting in January, 1765, Johnson had spent as much time at the Thrale homes in Streatham and Southwark as he did in the various residences he occupied in the last two decades of his life. Piozzi therefore knew him intimately; in fact, after the death of her first husband, Johnson hoped to become her second. Her marriage to an Italian music master instead effectively ended her friendship with Johnson, and while her book contains valuable information, it is colored by that final rift. Moreover, Johnson could be a difficult houseguest, a fact that affected her portrait.

Hawkins, too, could be less than charitable. Like Piozzi, he had spent considerable time with Johnson: The two had met in the 1740s, and in December, 1784, a group of London booksellers turned to him to edit Johnson's works and to write what they assumed would be the official life. This choice was logical, since Johnson had named Hawkins his literary executor; hence, he would have access to unpublished materials not available to anyone else. Hawkins is the source for the story of Johnson's celebration of Charlotte Lennox's first novel, *The Life of Harriet Stuart* (1750), and for the account of his stabbing his dropsical legs to remove fluid, but Hawkins also revealed— or invented—many faults. Hawkins maintained that he was writing a biography, not a panegyric, but George Colman the Elder expressed the general sentiment toward the work when he wrote in the *St. James Chronicle* for June 12–14, 1787,

Thee, Johnson, both dead and alive we may note
  In the fam'd Biographical Line,
When living the Life of a SAVAGE [Richard Savage]
  you wrote,
  Now many a Savage writes thine.

Within a year Hawkins' book was largely forgotten, not to be reprinted in its entirety until the twentieth century.

Boswell, too, refused to ignore Johnson's flaws. When Hannah More asked him in 1785 to play down Johnson's "asperities," Boswell replied that "he would not cut off his claws, nor make a tiger a cat, to please anybody." Yet is is clear that Boswell's work is written "with admiration and reverence," the last four words of the *Life*. Such an attitude could occasionally distort the record as much as Piozzi's lack of charity. Thus, Boswell, who did not meet Johnson until after the death of Tetty, Johnson's wife, refused to include any material suggesting marital difficulties. Hawkins, who knew the couple, paints a darker but probably truer picture of the marriage.

In general, though, Boswell's account is accurate. As early as 1764, within a year of meeting Johnson, he wrote to him, "It shall be my study to do what I can to render your life happy; and if you die before me, I shall endeavor to do honor to your memory." For almost as long as the two knew each other, then, Boswell was thinking of writing the *Life*, and by 1773 Johnson had accepted Boswell's role as his biographer. A copious diarist who was also blessed with an excellent memory—even Piozzi, who cared little for Boswell, granted him that—he was indefatigable in tracking down information about his subject.

As he truly said, "I have spared no pains in obtaining materials concerning him, from every quarter where I could discover that they were to be found"; he offered as an example "that I have sometimes been obliged to run half over London, in order to fix a date correctly."

Boswell has been accused of occupying too prominent a place in the *Life*, a charge to which he himself was sensitive. In 1785 he had produced a kind of trial run of the biography with his *Journal of a Tour to the Hebrides*, the account of his trip with Johnson to the Scottish Highlands in 1773. In response to criticism of that work, Boswell promised to place himself more in the background in the longer work, which nonetheless remains a dual biography. Although Boswell spent fewer than five hundred days with Johnson over the course of their twenty-year friendship, the *Life* suggests that they were inseparable. Boswell creates this effect by focusing on those times when they were together: Less than a fifth of the book deals with the fifty-four years of Johnson's life before their meeting, and, conversely, more than a hundred pages are devoted to the last year of his life.

Yet he never allows himself to eclipse his subject. Boswell's wife, who found Johnson coarse, once remarked of her husband's relationship with the older man that she had often seen a man leading a bear, but never before had she observed a bear leading a man. In the *Life* Boswell always lets the bear lead, or at least appear to lead. Recognizing Johnson's genius, he drew on and expanded the technique pioneered by William Mason in his *Memoirs of the Life and Writings of Mr. Thomas Gray* (1775), which incorporates the poet's letters and observations. Some 30 percent of Boswell's *Life* consists of Johnson's letters—334 of them, sometimes edited—publications, manuscripts ranging from legal briefs to prayers and meditations that first reached the public in the biography and famous conversations. When Sir Arthur Conan Doyle created his detective pair, he modeled them on Boswell and Johnson, giving Watson Boswell's role of recording companion.

Boswell not only enriched his book with Johnson's comments but also provided an immeasurable gift to posterity. As great as Johnson is as a writer, he was equally gifted as a speaker, and most people who quote Johnson—he is among the most quoted of Englishmen—are actually quoting from the *Life*:

Sir, a woman preaching is like a dog's walking on his hind legs. It is not done well; but you are surprised to find it done at all.

I look upon it, that he who does not mind his belly will hardly mind anything else.

A decent provision for the poor is the true test of civilization.

Patriotism is the last refuge of a scoundrel.

In lapidary inscriptions a man is not upon oath.

No man but a blockhead ever wrote except for money.

When a man is tired of London, he is tired of life; for there is in London all that life can afford.

It is better to live rich, than to die rich.

Clear your mind of cant.

The list could go on, and in the fifteenth edition of *Bartlett's Familiar Quotations* (1980) it does, with some hundred entries drawn from Boswell's work. "I am absolutely certain," Boswell wrote to William Temple in February, 1788,

that my mode of biography, which gives not only a *History* of Johnson's *visible* progress through the world, and of his publications, but a *view* of his mind in his letters and conversations, is the most perfect that can be conceived, and will be more of a Life than any work that has ever yet appeared.

Readers who have called for more than two hundred editions of the work since it first appeared have vindicated the method.

To elicit comments, Boswell was willing to risk angering his great friend. Johnson was terrified of death; once, when Boswell pursued the topic too diligently, Johnson replied, "Give us no more of this," and added "sternly, 'Don't let us meet to-morrow.' " On another occasion Boswell's probing brought forth the rebuke, "Sir, you have but two topics, yourself and me. I am sick of both." Boswell's recording of such reactions prompted nineteenth century critics such as Thomas Babington Macaulay to call him a great fool, but Boswell's genius lies in part in his readiness to play the fool to reveal his subject.

More characteristic of Boswell is his role as stage manager, introducing Johnson into various situations to see how he would react and so reveal his nature. The trip to the Scottish Highlands is a classic example of Boswell's ability to maneuver Johnson into new conditions and then observe (and record) what happens. Another instance is his arranging Johnson's meeting with the rakish, Whiggish John Wilkes, whose principles and life Johnson detested. Boswell notes that "they had even attacked one another with some asperity in their writings." Boswell knew that if he asked Johnson to dine with Wilkes, he would meet with an absolute refusal, so instead he told Johnson that Edward Dilly would love to have him to dinner but feared he might object to Wilkes's presence. Johnson responded as Boswell hoped, saying that he could dine with anyone on occasion.

Boswell knew how to describe scenes as well as create them, often incorporating what are essentially stage directions. Of a visit to Dr. William Adams, Master of Pembroke College, Oxford, which Johnson had attended for a little more than a year, Boswell wrote, "We walked with Dr. Adams into the master's garden, and into the common room. JOHNSON. (after a reverie of meditation), "Ay! Here I used to play at draughts with Phil. Jones and Fludyer." When Boswell mentioned that their friend Thomas Percy was writing an account of the wolf, Johnson replied, " 'I should like to see *The History of the Grey Rat, by Thomas Percy, D.D. . . . .'* (laughing immoderately)." On another occasion, Johnson responds to Boswell "in an animated tone." These comments let the reader see and hear Johnson; they animate the words on the page.

Boswell's dramatic sense informs even the structure of the biography, which is loosely assembled around a variety of scenes like the visit to Dr. Adams or the dinner with Wilkes. Chronology is merely a convenient thread on which to string these various gems. As the life unfolds, Johnson, though unchanging, emerges as a three-dimensional figure, for Boswell not only offers his own observations and allows Johnson to display himself but also presents others' perceptions, recording the views of Oliver Goldsmith, Edmund Burke, and many others. The cast of Boswell's *Life* is almost as great as that of a nineteenth century Russian novel.

The effect of the biography is also similar to that of *War and Peace* (1865–1869) or *Anna Karenina* (1875–1877). Just as those novels provide a social history of Russia, so the *Life* serves as a portrait of late eighteenth century England. On the title page Boswell claimed that his book exhibits "*a View of Literature and Literary Men in Great-Britain, for Near Half a Century,*" and the book has shaped posterity's view of Johnson's literary world quite as much as it has created an image of Johnson himself.

That the *Life* did establish a picture of Johnson is undeniable; when one speaks of Boswell's Johnson one is referring at once to the book and to its central figure. It is always "Dr." Johnson, though he did not receive an honorary LL.D. until 1765 and shied away from the title after he got it. Johnson is always in vigorous middle age, always at the pinnacle of the literary world rather than struggling up its slopes, in comfortable circumstances and hence slovenly by choice rather than by necessity. In dedicating the work to Sir Joshua Reynolds, Boswell was not merely directing the book to one of Johnson's closest friends; he was also choosing someone who shared his own view of portraiture. Reynolds maintained that the artist should present not the model itself but rather a mental image or impression of that model. Boswell's Johnson is heroic—in the "Advertisement to the Second Edition" Boswell compares him to Odysseus—at once larger than life and quintessentially human.

Asked whether he had assumed a task greater than he had anticipated in agreeing to compile his *Dictionary of the English Language* (1755), Johnson replied, "Sir, I knew very well what I was undertaking,—and very well how to do it,—and have done it very well." (One may note parenthetically that, again, posterity retains this observation only because of Boswell.) For seven years, in declining health and fortune, Boswell labored at a biography that must have seemed unending, but even if he did not realize at first what he was undertaking, in the end he too did it very well indeed. His work completed, in the "Advertisement to the Second Edition" he boasted, "I have Johnsonised the land," and so he had. Edmund Burke and Macaulay are but two of many who have noted that great as Johnson was, he appears still greater in Boswell's book, and many who have never knowingly read a page of Johnson have encountered his ideas and words because of the *Life*. Robert Anderson, himself a biographer of Johnson, summed up Boswell's achievement well when he wrote in the *Gentleman's Magazine* (1795),

With some venial exceptions on the score of egotism and indiscriminate admiration, his work exhibits the most copious, interesting, and finished picture of the life and opinions of an eminent man that was ever executed, and is justly esteemed one of the most instructive and entertaining books in the English language.

LIFE ON THE MISSISSIPPI

Type of work: Reminiscence
Author: Mark Twain (Samuel L. Clemens, 1835–1910)
Type of plot: Regional romance
Time of plot: Mid-nineteenth century
Locale: Mississippi River region
First published: 1883

Despite its loose and fragmented structure, Life on the Mississippi *is a vivid, dramatic, and extremely interesting collection of reminiscences. Like the mighty river with which it is concerned, the book has become part of the American tradition.*

The Story

When Mark Twain was a boy, he and his comrades in Hannibal, Missouri, had one great ambition; they hoped to become steamboatmen. They had other ambitions, too, such as joining the circus or becoming pirates, but these soon passed. Only the ambition to be a steamboatman remained, renewed twice each day when the upriver and the downriver boats put in at the rickety wharf and woke the sleepy village to bustling life. Through the years, boy after boy left the river communities, to return later, swaggering in his importance as a worker on a steamboat. Mark Twain saw these boys often, and the fact that some of them had been considered as undeniably damned in the eyes of the pious folk shook Twain's convictions profoundly. He wondered why these boys who flouted Sunday School maxims and ran away from home should win the rewards of adventure and romance that meeker town boys never knew.

Mark Twain, too, had this dream of adventure. His ambition was a lofty one. He determined to become a cub-pilot. While in Cincinnati, he heard that a government expedition was exploring the Amazon. With thirty dollars he had saved he took a boat bound for New Orleans. His intention was to travel on to the headwaters of the Amazon. But the ship was grounded at Louisville, and during the delay Mark came to the attention of Mr. Bixby, the most famous pilot on the Mississippi River. He prevailed upon Bixby to teach him how to navigate.

At first the adventure was a glorious one. But soon Mark found that the more he knew about the river, the less romantic it seemed. Though he was a dutiful student, he discovered that he could not remember everything Bixby told him, regardless of how important this information seemed to be. Furthermore, to his astonishment and despair, his instructor told him that the river was changing its course continually; that there were no such things as permanent landmarks; that the river channel was never the same, but always variable. There were times when the young cub-pilot was frightened, especially when he narrowly missed hitting another ship, or

trimmed the boat too close to shore. But worse was the experience of piloting in the dead of night, with no landmarks to observe and only deep blackness all around.

Bixby claimed the secret of navigation was not to remember landmarks, which changed, but to learn the shape of the river and then to steer by the shape in one's head.

It was undeniably an interesting life. The pilot had to be on the lookout for rafts sailing the river at night without lights. Often a whole family would be on a raft, and they would shout imprecations at the steamboat which had just barely missed dumping them all into the river. Then there was the fascinating behavior of the river itself. Prosperous towns would be isolated by a new cutoff and reduced to insignificance; towns and islands in one state would be moved up or down and into another state, or, as sometimes happened, into an area that belonged to no state at all!

The river pilot reigned supreme on his boat. The captain was theoretically the master; but as soon as the boat got under way, the pilot was in charge, and only a very foolhardy captain would have interfered. The importance of the pilot in river navigation eventually led to the formation of a pilots' association. At first the idea seemed ridiculous. But the union grew as, one by one, all the good pilots joined. As a result pilots could make their own terms with the owners. Not only were wages guaranteed but pilots secured better working conditions, pensions, and funds for their widows and orphans. Within a few years the association was the most indestructible monopoly in the country. But its days were numbered. First of all, the railroads came in and river transportation was gradually abandoned in favor of rail traffic. Then, too, the Civil War reduced navigation to a mere trickle and dealt a deathblow to river commerce. The steamboat was no longer an important means of transportation.

From then on the river was different. It seemed very different to Mark Twain when he returned after many years away from it, and saw the changes with nostalgic regret. He traveled once more on the Mississippi, but this time as a passenger and under an assumed name. He listened tolerantly to the man who told him wild and improbable stories about the river, and to a fellow traveler who explained, very explicitly, how everything worked.

Mark Twain decided to search for a large sum of money left by a murderer whom he had met in Germany. He and his companions made plans about the ten thousand dollars soon to be in their possession, and they asked to get off their boat at Napoleon to look for it. Unfortunately, the Arkansas River, years before, had swept the whole town into the Mississippi.

On his return to the river, Mark Twain learned many things he had not known. He witnessed the vast improvements in navigation and in the construction of the boats, improvements that made navigation easier and safer. He talked to the inhabitants of Vicksburg, who described their life during the bombardment of the town by Union forces. He visited Louisiana and expressed horror at the sham castles that passed for good architecture. He read Southern newspapers and saw in them, as in so many Southern traditions, the romantic sentimentality of Sir Walter Scott, an influence that he regretted, hated, and held responsible for the South's lack of progress. He came in contact with a cheerful and clever gambler; he heard about senseless feuds that wiped out entire families; he saw new and large cities that had grown up since he had left the river; he met such well-known writers as Joel Chandler Harris and George W. Cable; he had an experience with a spiritualist who grew rich on the credulous and the superstitious; he witnessed tragedy, and lost friends in steamboat explosions.

The river would never be the same again. The age of mechanization had arrived to stay. The days of the old river pilots, such as Mr. Bixby, were now a thing of the past. America was growing up, and with that growth the color and romance of the Mississippi had faded forever.

Critical Evaluation

Twain's book is not really a novel or regional romance. Generically, it is beyond classification—unless the reader is willing to be objective (and humorously enough inclined) to see it for what it is: an open-ended reminiscence, as rambling and broad as its subject, the Mississippi River. Readers of *The Adventures of Huckleberry Finn* (1884) will remember the dramatic role of the river in that work. Many critics feel the river is the structural foundation of *The Adventures of Huckleberry Finn*. T. S. Eliot and Lionel Trilling calling the river a "God." It watches over Huck and Jim but also demands wrecked houses and drowned bodies as propitiating sacrifices. In *Life on the Mississippi* the river is seen with the eyes of a comic reporter, not the creative vision of a dramatic and philosophical novelist posing as a juvenile romancer. Nevertheless, the same characteristics that determine the river's symbolic function in *The Adventures of Huckleberry Finn* are singled out and examined here: the dangerous and changing channels, the mud-infested villages, the floods. One way of reading *Life on the Mississippi* is to see it as the objective research from which Twain ultimately fashioned the art of his greatest story. Indeed, *Life on the Mississippi* and *The Adventures of Huckleberry Finn* stand in relation to each other much in the same way as the chapters describing whaling relate to the story of Ahab and his mad hunt in Melville's *Moby Dick* (1851).

The primary quality of the Mississippi River basin is its enormous size. How can such a geographic miracle be contained in a memoir? Twain begins by recalling his youth as an apprentice pilot. Even here the foreshadowing of Huckleberry Finn is astonishing: Twain learns to pilot down the same river on which Huck effortlessly floats his raft. Twain must master every curve, point, and bar. The feats of memory necessary to perform the skills of the river pilot are almost superhuman. "Nothing short of perfection will do." Just as Twain recalls first the map of the river as his mind mastered it, in *The Adventures of Huckleberry Finn* Twain had to strain his creative memory to bring back the Mississippi of his boyhood.

There is something humbling about the later chapters in *Life on the Mississippi*. True, they are fragmented and often look like padding. But there is an undeniable charm in their rambling quality: they seem to attest to Twain's continual deference to the giant and changing river. Although he learned its every curve as a youth, its natural evolution and the effect of social and technological "progress" astonishes him so much that he is reduced to gathering tall tales and newspaper clippings.

"LIGEIA"

Type of work: Short story
Author: Edgar Allan Poe (1809–1849)
Type of plot: Gothic romance
Time of plot: Early nineteenth century
Locale: Germany and England
First published: 1838

Poe considered this tale of terror combined with fantasy his best story. Ligeia *embodies perfectly the author's belief that in a perfect piece of writing, all elements—plot, setting, and characterization—must be fused and subordinated to a single effect.*

Principal Characters

The Narrator, a learned man enslaved by the memory of a woman whose powerful will once triumphed over death itself to return to him whom she so passionately loved. Half insane through grief after Ligeia's death and addicted to opium, he nevertheless remarries. Forgetful of Ligeia for a month, he abandons himself to Lady Rowena; but memory returns, and love turns to hatred and loathing. He witnesses (or so he believes) the dropping of poison into some wine he gives Rowena when she is ill. After Rowena's death he is awed by the rising of her corpse which he recognizes not as that of Rowena but of his lost Ligeia.

Ligeia, his first wife, a beautiful woman of rare learning and musically eloquent voice. Tall and slender, she is quietly majestic whether in repose or walking with "incomprehensible lightness and elasticity." Her features are "strange" rather than classically regular: the skin pale, forehead broad, luxuriously curly hair glossy and black. Her nose is slightly aquiline; and when her short upper lip and her voluptuous under one part in a radiant smile, her teeth gleam brilliantly. Her eyes are most notable: unusually large and luminously black, with long and jetty lashes and slightly irregular black brows. Though Ligeia

is outwardly calm and speaks in a low, distinct, and melodious voice, she has a passionately intense will which shows in the fierce energy of her wild words. Her knowledge of classical and modern European languages leads her (and her worshipping husband) into extensive metaphysical investigations. When Ligeia falls ill her wild eyes blaze, her skin turns waxen, and the veins in her forehead swell and sink. Though her voice drops lower, she struggles fiercely against the Shadow. Moments before her death, she shrieks and fiercely protests against the Conquering Worm in the poem which her husband has read to her. With her dying breath, she murmurs that man submits to death only through feebleness of will. When Lady Rowena later dies, Ligeia, through the power of her will, returns from death and enters the body of her successor.

Lady Rowena Trevanion, the second wife, fair-haired and blue-eyed. She falls ill and slowly dies, wasting away while she becomes increasingly irritable and fearful, her fear being increased by mysterious sounds and sights she is aware of. (Her illness may be compared to that which for five years tortured and finally killed Virginia Poe, the author's young wife.)

The Story

He could not remember when he had first met Ligeia, and he knew nothing of her family except that it was old. Ligeia herself, once his wife, he could remember in every detail. She was tall and slender. Ethereal as a shadow, her face was faultless in its beauty, her skin like ivory, her features classic. Crowning the perfect face and body was raven-black, luxuriant hair. Her eyes, above all else, held the key to Ligeia's mystery. Larger than ordinary, those black eyes held an expression unfathomable even to her husband. It became his all-consuming passion to unravel the secret of that expression.

In character, Ligeia possessed a stern will that never

failed to astound him. Outwardly she was placid and calm, but she habitually uttered words of such wildness that he was stunned by their intensity. Her learning was immense. She spoke many languages, and in metaphysical investigations, she was never wrong. Her husband was engrossed in a study of metaphysics, but it was she who guided him, she who unraveled the secrets of his research. With Ligeia, he knew that he would one day reach a goal of wisdom undreamed of by others.

Then Ligeia fell ill. Her skin became transparent and waxen, her eyes wild. Knowing that she must die, he watched her struggles against the grisly reaper, a conflict frightening in its passion. Words could not express the intense resistance with which she fought death. He had always known she loved him, but in those last days she abandoned herself completely to love. From her heart, she poured forth phrases of idolatry. And on the last day of her life, she bade him repeat to her a poem she had composed not long before. It was a morbid thing about death, about the conquering of Man by the Worm. As he finished repeating the melancholy lines, Ligeia leaped to her feet with a shriek, then sank onto her deathbed. In a scarcely audible whisper, she repeated a proverb that had haunted her before: that man did not yield to death save through the weakness of his own will. So Ligeia died.

Crushed with sorrow, her husband left his desolate home by the Rhine and retired to an old and decayed abbey in a deserted region in England. He left the exterior of the building in its sagging state, but inside he furnished the rooms lavishly and weirdly. He had become the slave of opium, and the furnishings took on the shapes and colors of his fantastic dreams. One bedchamber received the most bizarre treatment of all, and it was to this chamber that he led his new bride, the blue-eyed Lady Rowena Trevanion, of Tremaine.

The room was in a high turret of the abbey. It was of immense proportions, lighted by a single huge window. The pane had a leaden hue, giving a ghastly luster to all objects within the room. The walls, the floors, the furniture were all covered with a heavy, arabesque tapestry, black figures on pure gold. The figures changed as one looked at them from different angles, their appearance being changed by an artificial current of air that constantly stirred the draperies.

In rooms such as this, he spent a bridal month with Lady Rowena. It was easy to perceive that she loved him but little, and he hated her with a passion more demoniac than human. In his opium dreams, he called aloud for Ligeia, as if he could restore her to the earthly life she had abandoned. He reveled in memories of her purity and her love.

In the second month of her marriage, Rowena grew ill, and in her fever she spoke of sounds and movements in the chamber, fantasies unheard and unseen by her husband. Although she recovered, she had recurring attacks of the fever, and it became evident that she would soon succumb. Her imaginings became stronger, and she grew more insistent about the sounds and movements in the tapestries.

One night in September, she became visibly weaker and unusually agitated. Seeking to calm her, her husband stepped across the room to get some wine, but he was arrested midway by the sense of something passing lightly by him. Then he was startled to see on the gold carpet a shadow of angelic aspect. Saying nothing to Rowena, he poured the wine into a goblet. As she took the vessel, he distinctly heard a light footstep upon the carpet and saw, or thought he saw, three or four drops of a ruby-colored liquid fall into the goblet from an invisible source.

Immediately Rowena grew worse, and on the third night, she died. As he sat by her shrouded body in that bridal chamber, he thought of his lost Ligeia. Suddenly, he heard a sound from the bed upon which the corpse of his wife lay. Going closer, he perceived that Rowena had a faint color. It was unmistakable; Rowena lived. Unable to summon aid, he watched her with mounting terror. Then a relapse came, and she sank into a death pallor more rigid than before. All night this phenomenon recurred. Rowena returned briefly from the dead, only to sink once more into oblivion. Each time he saw again a vision of Ligeia.

Toward morning of that fearful night, the enshrouded figure rose from the bed and tottered to the center of the chamber. Terrified, he fell at her feet. She unwound the burial cerements from her head and there streamed down raven-black hair unknown to the living Rowena. Then the spectral figure slowly opened her eyes. He screamed in one last mad shout. He could not be mistaken. Staring at him were the full black eyes of his lost love, the Lady Ligeia.

Critical Evaluation

First published in the *Baltimore American Museum* in September, 1838, "Ligeia" was included in Edgar Allan Poe's *Tales of the Grotesque and Arabesque* (1839–1840). The final text appeared in the *Broadway Journal* in 1845. "Ligeia" is one of Poe's most famous tales, and it is also among his most brilliantly written—he himself once declared it his best. He apparently considered it an "arabesque," a term Poe seems to have used to refer to tales which, though incredible, or scarcely credible on the realistic level of meaning, are told "seriously" or without the tone of mockery or satire that Poe used in his "grotesques," such as "King Pest," with its fantastic group of characters, "every one of whom seemed to possess a

monopoly of some particular portion of physiognomy," or "A Predicament," in which a lady writer tells in shuddering detail how she felt when the minute hand of a giant clock cut off her head. Critics since Poe have called "Ligeia" a tale of terror, since the narrator is frightened and horrified by what he sees, or thinks he sees, at the story's end. Similar terror is experienced by Roderick Usher in "The Fall of the House of Usher." Readers see it also in a number of Poe's narrators during the harrowing experiences they undergo in other tales.

The narrator of "Ligeia" should not be directly identified in any way with Poe. He is simply the nameless husband of Ligeia (and later of Rowena). Poe often employs a first-person narrator whose name is not given to the reader; he uses such narrators in "The Pit and the Pendulum," "The Tell-Tale Heart," "The Black Cat," and many other tales. Telling the story from a first-person point of view increases the final dramatic "effect," a predetermined element which, Poe declared in his famous review of Hawthorne's *Twice-Told Tales*, should always be the aim of a serious artist in short fiction.

Two themes in "Ligeia" appear elsewhere in Poe's tales. Psychic survival through reincarnation is the theme in an early tale, "Morella," in which a bereaved husband learns that his dead wife has taken over the body and the character of the daughter who was born just before the mother died. In the climactic closing scene of "Ligeia," the supposedly dead first wife, Ligeia, has (or seems to have) appropriated the body of the second wife, Rowena. A second theme, that of premature burial, appears in the early tale, "Berenice," and in such later tales as "The Fall of the House of Usher" and "The Premature Burial."

In fictional technique, "Ligeia" well illustrates Poe's skill in achieving the unity of impression which, like his "predetermined effect," he regarded as of primary importance in telling a tale. Throughout, the tone of the narrator is intensely serious as he tells of his two marriages. He dwells on his love for and passionate adoration of the beautiful, mysterious, intellectual Ligeia. There is foreshadowing when he speaks of his suffering and of the loss "of her who is no more." The final scene is prepared for in several ways. The description of Ligeia at the beginning emphasizes "the raven-black, the glossy, the luxuriant, and naturally-curling tresses," and her eyes are repeatedly mentioned: "Those eyes! those large, those shining, those divine orbs!" The brief, hectic excitement of the second marriage, to the "fair-haired and blue-eyed Lady Rowena Trevanion, of Tremaine," is quickly followed by the husband's obsessed memories of "the beloved, the august, the beautiful, the entombed" Ligeia. In the second paragraph of the tale, Ligeia's beauty of face is described as "the radiance of an opium dream." This anticipates the actual opium dreams which result from the husband's addiction following his loss of Ligeia and which accompany his loathing and hatred of Rowena. These dreams are filled with Ligeia, and the intensity of the husband's longing for his lost love is climaxed by her return as the story ends. When she opens her eyes, he is sure of her identity, and he shrieks ". . . these are the full, and the black, and the wild eyes—of my lost love—. . . of the LADY LIGEIA."

The theme of psychic survival is suggested first in the epigraph from Joseph Glanvill, with its final sentence, "Man doth not yield himself to the angels, nor unto death utterly, save only through the weakness of his feeble will." This theme first appears in the story itself when the narrator recalls having read the passage from Glanvill, which he quotes. He connects Glanvill's words with Ligeia when he speaks of her "*intensity* in thought, action, or speech"

as "a result, or at least an index" of her "gigantic volition." After she fell ill, he was struck by "the fierceness of resistance with which she wrestled with the Shadow." He recalls that just before she died, she asked him to repeat a poem she had written some days before, a symbolic poem portraying life as a tragic drama with "its hero, the conqueror Worm," which finally devours each actor. As he concluded the poem, Ligeia shrieked and pleaded, "O God! O Divine Father! . . . shall this conqueror be not once conquered?" Her last murmured words were Glanvill's: "*Man doth not yield him to the angels, nor unto death utterly, save only through the weakness of his feeble will.*" Yet her own fierce will to live did not save her from death—or so her husband thought. He left Germany, moved to England, purchased a decaying abbey, extravagantly refurnished its interior, and led to its high turret bedroom his new bride, the fair-haired and blue-eyed Rowena. Though entombed, Ligeia continued to "wrestle with the Shadow." She filled her husband's memories and in final triumph replaced her blonde successor. Or did she?

"Ligeia" has achieved considerable twentieth century fame as the subject of many widely divergent interpretations. It has been argued that Ligeia is not a real woman but symbolically "the very incarnation of German idealism, German Transcendentalism provided with an allegorical form." One critic has suggested that Ligeia never existed at all but was merely imagined by a madman. Another has called her a witch and still another a "revenant—a spirit who has spent immemorial lifetimes on earth." As for the husband, he has been termed a liar and even a murderer, who killed Rowena, his second wife, by poisoning her with the "ruby drops" which fall into her wine glass.

Perhaps the most acceptable interpretation of the story is a literal one. The narrator marries the beautiful, brilliant Ligeia, and they live happily in Germany until she dies of a mysterious disease. He then marries Rowena in England but soon turns against her. Rowena suffers spells of illness, and her husband endlessly dreams of his lost Ligeia for whom he longs deeply. His increasing use of opium causes his dreams to become so confused with reality that in a final frightening hallucination, he believes he sees standing before him the beloved dark-haired and large-eyed Ligeia who has taken over the body of her fair-haired successor. By the strength of her intense will, Ligeia *has* defeated Death, the Conquering Worm.

Dramatically, the scene achieves the effect for which the Glanvill quotation prepared readers. That the return of Ligeia is only imagined is also prepared for by the narrator's repeated references to his drug addiction:

I had become a bounden slave in the trammels of opium. . . .
I was habitually fettered in the shackles of the drug. . . .
I was wild with the excitement of an immoderate dose of opium. . . . Wild visions, opium-engendered, flitted,

shadowlike, before me . . . passionate waking visions of Ligeia . . . a crowd of unutterable fancies . . . had chilled me into stone.

In his numbed state he has regained his intensely desired Ligeia, but surely it is a drug-induced "fancy" that shocks him into shrieking the words which end the story.

THE LYRIC POETRY OF LORD BYRON

Type of work: Poetry
Author: George Gordon, Lord Byron (1788–1824)
First published: *Fugitive Pieces*, 1806; *Poems on Various Occasions*, 1807; *Hours of Idleness*, 1807; *Poems Original and Translated*, 1808; *Childe Harold's Pilgrimage I-II*, 1812; *Hebrew Melodies*, 1815; *Poems*, 1816; *The Prisoner of Chillon and Other Poems*, 1816. Additional lyrics have gradually been gathered into the various collected editions, culminating in the seven-volume *The Complete Poetical Works*, edited by Jerome J. McGann, which began appearing in 1980.

Whatever other poetic forms Lord Byron eventually mastered, until the end of his career he continually returned to the short lyric, the mode with which he had begun. This most passionate of poets found the lyric capable of expressing passion, whether personal or, as in the case of *Hebrew Melodies*, dramatically distanced, with an unequaled clarity and intensity. In his lyrics, the sometimes unclassifiable Byron is at his most straightforwardly Romantic. His most characteristic lyric poetry is haunted by a melancholy knowledge of the fleeting nature of friendship and love and by a sensitivity to the evanescence of beauty, innocence, and joy. As many critics have pointed out, much of Byron's poetry displays a nostalgic longing for uncorrupted Paradise, and this is certainly true of the lyrics. The lyrics frequently manifest a sense of some perfection which has been lost or is about to be lost, and despite moments of exultation in things of undeniable worth which the world has not yet tarnished, the poet's common mood is weary disappointment with the fallenness of life.

Even in the poems written during Byron's teens and early twenties, not normally a period of world-weary sadness, a dominant theme is the melancholy nature of fallen mortal existence, with mortality itself the direct focus of several poems. In "On the Death of Young Lady," for example, the grieving poet returns to the tomb of a beloved cousin to "scatter flowers on the dust I love" and to lament that "not worth nor beauty have her life redeem'd" from the pitiless "King of Terrors." "Epitaph on a Friend" reiterates this conviction of the relentlessness of death and emphasizes its blindness both to the worth of its victim and to the grief of the devoted mourner:

> What fruitless tears have bathed thy honour'd bier!
> What sighs re-echo'd to thy parting breath,
> Whilst thou was struggling in the pangs of death!
> Could tears retard the tyrant in his course;
> Could sighs avert his dart's relentless force;
> Could youth and virtue claim a short delay,
> Or beauty charm the spectre from his prey;
> Thou still hadst lived to bless my aching sight,
> Thy comrade's honour and thy friend's delight.

An additional point to notice about both poems is that

the one significant remnant of the lost relationship is the poet's tormenting memory of the beloved dead and his sorrow over the fact of separation—a linking of memory with sorrow which occurs throughout Byron's earliest published lyrics and, with greater sophistication, throughout much of his later poetry as well.

In this fallen world, a sorrowful separation can occur through other means than death, of course, and the young Byron rings many variations on the theme of the temporary nature of earthly love and friendship. As the opening stanza of "To D——" implies, for instance, flawed human nature can destroy affection:

> In thee I fondly hoped to clasp
>   A friend whom death alone could sever;
> Till envy, with malignant grasp,
>   Detach'd thee from my breast forever.

In "To Emma," unavoidable circumstance is to blame. The loved one is leaving the hallowed place where she and the poet have known each other since childhood; as a result, their shared joys will end, and the very landscape will lose its power to please:

> These times are past—our joys are gone,
>   You leave me, leave this happy vale;
> These scenes I must retrace alone:
>   Without thee what will they avail?

Mutable human circumstance is also the culprit in "On a Distant View of the Village and School of Harrow on the Hill," and the sad realization of what has been lost is associated even more strongly with the landscape of the fondly remembered past. In this beloved place, Byron tells us, the "loved recollection" of "scenes of my childhood" "embitters the present, compared with the past."

In "To Caroline," mutability, this time in the form of the aging process, is once more the enemy. Here, even before time's ravages have begun, the poet bemoans their inevitable effect on love and beauty:

> Yet still this fond bosom regrets, while adoring,
>   That love, like the leaf, must fall into the sere;
> That age will come on, when remembrance, deploring,

Contemplates the scenes of her youth with a tear;

That the time must arrive, when, no longer retaining
  Their auburn, those locks must wave thin to the
    breeze,
When a few silver hairs of those tresses remaining,
  Prove nature a prey to decay and disease.

If remembrance were less persistent for the Byronic persona or less often tainted by a sense of disillusionment and decline, melancholy would not so frequently pervade Byron's lyric verse. The usual pattern is for early experience, enshrined forever in idyllic memory, to outshine later events and for initial hope to give way repeatedly to disappointment. This does not imply, however, that the feeling heart, having gained and then lost some Edenic ideal, ceases thereafter to seek beauty, joy, and fulfillment; it simply means that each attempt is likely to bring defeat, whatever the momentary impression of triumph. Indeed, a general assumption in Byron's poetry, both early and late, is that one taste of Paradise inspires the doomed longing for more.

The paradisiacal quality of innocent passion which makes it one of those human experiences most worthy of repetition is directly asserted in the following lines from "The First Kiss of Love," another of Byron's early lyrics: "Some portion of paradise still is on earth,/ And Eden revives in the first kiss of love."

Unfortunately, while much of the Byronic persona's energy is dedicated to reexperiencing the intensity of this first passionate moment with an unfallen Eve, even the very young Byron expresses the worldly man's distrust of the descendants of Eve the temptress—sometimes, in fact, at the very moment when he admits their irresistible allure. In "To Woman," he writes,

Woman! experience might have told me
That all must love thee who behold thee:
Surely experience might have taught
Thy firmest promises are nought;
But, placed in all thy charms before me,
All I forget, but to adore thee.

The lessons of the past are momentarily ignored when passion reasserts its sway, but passion inevitably fails, and memory gathers in still another justification for disillusionment:

Oh memory! thou choicest blessing
When join'd with hope, when still possessing;
But how much cursed by every lover
When hope is fled and passion's over.

Contained in a poem written in late 1805 or early 1806, when Byron was about eighteen years old, these lines express sentiments which remain prominent in much of his later verse.

The persistent, if sometimes conventionally phrased, sense of loss which pervades the various poems quoted above, all of them dating from before Byron's twenty-first birthday, is intensified to a moving elegiac grief in the two poems entitled "To Thyrza," probably composed in late 1811 after Byron had learned of the death of John Edleston, a Cambridge choirboy for whom he had felt a homosexual attraction. In Edleston's youth and in the angelic beauty of his singing voice, Byron found that combination of the innocent and beautiful which always appealed to his longings for Paradise, and in the Thyrza poems, he describes a love which is both intensely private and thoroughly free of appetitive selfishness:

Ours too the glance none saw beside;
  The smile none else might understand;
The whisper'd thought of hearts allied,
  The pressure of the thrilling hand;
The kiss so guiltless and refin'd
  That Love each warmer wish forbore;
Those eyes proclaim'd so pure a mind,
  Ev'n passion blush'd to plead for more.

In the proper elegiac manner, but with overtones of a distinctively Byronic melancholy, he also portrays the burden of misery that he alone must bear as bereft survivor:

Oft have I borne the weight of ill
  But never bent beneath till now!
Well hast thou left in life's best bloom
  The cup of woe for me to drain.

Manifesting the Byronic stamp, too, are the following lines from the second of the poems:

Then bring me wine, the banquet bring;
  Man was not form'd to live alone:
I'll be that light unmeaning thing
  That smiles with all, and weeps with none.
It was not thus in days more dear,
  It never would have been, but thou
Hast fled, and left me lonely here;
  Thou'rt nothing, all are nothing now.

With the death of innocent love, the celebration of life continues, but with honest joy replaced by insincerity and cynical abandon.

In the *Hebrew Melodies* of 1815, written largely but not wholly on Old Testament themes, a different aspect of Byron's lyric gift is prominent: his capacity, reminiscent of the similar power of his friend Thomas Moore, to produce a mellifluous verbal beauty through the subtle interaction of sound, rhythm, and imagery. The best example of this capacity is the opening stanza of "She Walks in Beauty," perhaps the most widely read of Byron's poems:

She walks in beauty, like the night
  Of cloudless climes and starry skies;
And all that's best of dark and bright
  Meet in her aspect and her eyes:
Thus mellow'd to that tender light
  Which heaven to gaudy day denies.

Despite the emphasis on an alluring verbal beauty in this
and the volume's other poems—intended, in the oldest
lyric tradition, for musical accompaniment—*Hebrew
Melodies* still manifests many of the thematic concerns
of the poems previously analyzed. The "cloudless climes
and starry skies" of the lines above, for example, suggest
that spiritual purity which Byron had long associated
with true beauty and love, and the poem's final stanza
makes the concern with untainted innocence explicit:

And on that cheek, and o'er that brow,
  So soft, so calm, yet eloquent,
The smiles that win, the tints that glow,
  But tell of days in goodness spent,
A mind at peace with all below,
  A heart whose love is innocent!

Furthermore, the subject matter of many of the book's
more scripturally oriented poems, the struggles and the
glorious memories of an exiled people, fits perfectly with
Byron's usual preoccupation with the fallen.

Although much of Byron's creative energy had been
shifting, and was to shift further, toward the production
of long poems and poetic dramas, the short lyric remained
an important mode of immediate self-expression for him
during the years following the publication of *Hebrew
Melodies*, particularly when his emotions were stirred by
some new avatar of innocent beauty and love and his
sense of troubled exile from Paradise at its strongest.

For a time, his half sister Augusta came to embody
such innocent perfection, and in several poems of 1816,
the year when he began his exile from the false paradise
of England, he addressed his passionate outpourings to
her. In the first of two poems titled "Stanzas to Augusta,"
his half sister's "unbroken light" is said to have "watch'd"
him in the troubled darkness of this world "as a seraph's
eye." Elsewhere in the same poem, she is likened to "a
lovely tree" remaining firmly protective in a world of
chaotic storms. In the second of the two poems, he writes
that "the love which my spirit hath painted/ It never hath
found but in *thee*." She is that most unlikely of creatures
in a fallen, mutable world, the loving human being who
will never betray:

Though human, thou didst not deceive me,
  Though woman, thou didst not forsake,
Though loved, thou forborest to grieve me,
  Though slander'd, thou never couldst shake;
Though trusted, thou didst not disclaim me,

Though parted, it was not to fly,
Though watchful, 't was not to defame me,
  Nor, mute, that the world might belie.

As he declares in the "Epistle to Augusta," although he
may be a wanderer with "a world to roam through," he
will always have "a home with thee."

From the beginning, Byron's lyrics are pervaded by
this sense of the passionate exile's desire for the sanctuary
of love and beauty, a sanctuary reminiscent of all that
the fallen world has lost. If any element in Byron's lyrical
amalgam becomes more prominent in the years of his
actual exile from his homeland, it is the weariness of the
passionate man's quest for an acceptable fulfillment.
Anticipations of this theme occur even in the adolescent
poems, but in the final decade, it receives more eloquent
and more convincing expression. In the well-known "So,
We'll Go No More A Roving" of 1817, for example, the
poet tells us that "though the heart be still as loving,/
And the moon be still as bright," he will suspend his
search for love,

For the sword outwears its sheath,
  And the soul wears out the breast,
And the heart must pause to breathe,
  And love itself have rest.

The weariness deepens as the years advance. In "To
the Countess of Blessington," written in 1823, only a few
months before his death at Missolonghi, he confesses to
spiritual exhaustion:

I am ashes where once I was fire,
  And the bard in my bosom is dead;
What I loved I now merely admire,
  And my heart is as grey as my head.

The same exhaustion is implied in "On This Day I Complete My Thirty-sixth Year," an even later poem:

My days are in the yellow leaf;
  The flowers and fruits of love are gone;
The worm, the canker, and the grief
    Are mine alone!

Nevertheless, exhaustion can still give way to energy if
that energy is properly redirected, if the private desires
of the lover give way to the public dedication of the
soldier:

Tread those reviving passions down,
  Unworthy manhood!—unto thee
Indifferent should the smile or frown
    Of beauty be.

Restoring the glory of Greece is an ambition superior to

seeking an elusive reunion with an undiscoverable Eve, even if the only result of such heroism is "a soldier's grave."

These two ambitions are not so different, however, and in Byron's end is his beginning. The wish for a return to Paradise and the wish for a return to the glory that was Greece are both expressions of Romantic dissatis-faction with the world as it now exists and of Romantic faith that the innocent past was more perfect than the fallen present. Whatever he may be in his nonlyric moments, in his longing for some lost perfection and in his willingness to consume himself in seeking what he knows to be beyond attainment, the lyric Byron is the quintessential Romantic.

THE LYRIC POETRY OF JOHN MILTON

Author: John Milton (1609–1674)
First published: "On the Morning of Christ's Nativity," 1629; "L'Allegro," 1631; "Il Penseroso," 1631; *Lycidas*, 1637; all published in *Poems*, 1645

While John Milton's reputation rests primarily upon his long works, *Paradise Lost, Paradise Regained*, and *Samson Agonistes*, his lyric poetry, written for the most part before he reached the age of forty, shows the same genius at work and reveals the wide range of his interests and abilities. He worked with many different verse forms and traditions adapted from his study of Latin, Greek, Hebrew, French, and Italian; many of his youthful lyrics are either translations from one of these languages or from original poems. He did a fine English version of the famous Horatian ode "To Pyrrha," translated many of the Psalms from Hebrew into English verse, and at seventeen composed an elegy for the vice-chancellor of Cambridge and a long poem commemorating the discovery of the Gunpowder Plot. He mastered the style and spirit of classical literature, as well as its verse forms and vocabulary. The influence of the Greeks and the Romans is pervasive in both his pastoral poem, *Lycidas* and his great epic.

Milton's twenty-one sonnets, composed at intervals over a thirty-year period, illustrate remarkably well the variety of tones at his command. Five of the first six were written in Italian, and all six show his temporary immersion in the Petrarchan tradition. He proclaims himself the servant of the Muse and Love and sings the praises of his anonymous lady in terms that belie the traditional concept of Milton as the stern Puritan moralist.

More characteristic of Milton's work is the better-known "How Soon Hath Time," a poem in which he muses on the fact that he has reached his twenty-third birthday and still has little notion of where life will take him. He is, however, prepared to follow the will of God:

> Yet be it less or more, or soon or slow,
>   It shall be still in strictest measure ev'n
> To that same lot, however mean or high,
> Toward which Time leads me, and the will of Heav'n;
> All is, if I have grace to use it so,
> As ever in my great task-Master's eye.

Some ten years after the composition of this poem, Milton returned to the sonnet form to write a witty piece addressed to whatever "Captain or Colonel or Knight in Arms" who might come to his house during the Civil War. He asks, tongue in cheek, that his home be spared, as that of the great poet Pindar was when Alexander the Great conquered his homeland. This poem is especially interesting as one of the very few pieces showing Milton in a mildly humorous frame of mind.

The same period saw Milton using the sonnet to pay graceful tribute to virtuous ladies and to a friend, the composer Henry Lawes, to praise leaders of the Parliamentary cause—Fairfax, Cromwell, and Vane—and to issue harsh-sounding tirades against critics of his treatises:

> I did but prompt the age to quit their clogs
> By the known rules of ancient liberty,
> When straight a barbarous noise environs me
> Of Owls and Cuckoos, Asses, Apes and Dogs.

The massacre of a group of Waldensians in the Piedmont occasioned one of his finest poems, which rises above his protest about a specific incident as a defense of all seekers after religious truth. Milton seldom surpassed the power of the opening lines: "Avenge, O Lord, thy slaughter'd Saints, whose bones lie scatter'd on the Alpine mountains cold."

Milton's mastery of the sonnet form is shown most clearly in "On His Blindness," where he grapples with the question of how, sightless, he can exercise his God-given poetic talents:

> When I consider how my light is spent,
> Ere half my days, in this dark world and wide,
> And to that one Talent which is death to hide,
> Lodg'd with me useless, though my Soul more bent
> To serve therewith my Maker, and present
> My true account, lest he returning chide;
> "Doth God exact day-labor, light denied,"
> I fondly ask; But patience to prevent
> That murmur, soon replies, "God doth not need
> Either man's work or his own gifts; who best
> Bear his mild yoke, they serve him best; his State
> Is Kingly. Thousands at his bidding speed
> And post o'er Land and Ocean without rest:
> They also serve who only stand and wait."

The sonnets formed only a small part of Milton's poetic achievement. His early works, in addition to translations and Latin verses, included speeches for allegorical pageants presented at Cambridge and portions of entertainments for noble families. *Arcades*, composed in 1632, when Milton was twenty-four, forshadows *Comus* in its pastoral, allegorical theme and in its mellifluous speeches and songs:

Nymphs and Shepherds dance no more
By sandy *Ladon's* Lillied banks.
On old *Lycaeus* or *Cyllene* hoar,
Trip no more in twilight ranks.
Though *Erymanth* your loss deplore,
A better soil shall give ye thanks.

Even at this stage in his poetic development, Milton knew the incantatory effect of resounding classical names, which were to be used often in *Paradise Lost*.

Before he was thirty, Milton wrote four poems that reveal fully that gift that was to make him one of England's two or three greatest poets. "On the Morning of Christ's Nativity" belongs to the Baroque tradition in its rich imagery, its religious intensity, and its musical quality. All Milton's learning comes into play as he portrays the exodus of the pagan deities at the birth of Christ:

Peor and *Baalim*
Forsake their Temples dim,
With that twice-batter'd god of *Palestine*,
and mooned *Ashtaroth*
Heav'n's Queen and Mother both,
Now sits not girt with Tapers' holy shine,
The Libyc *Hammon* shrinks his horn,
In vain the *Tyrian* Maids their wounded *Thammuz*
mourn.

The dynamic, turbulent quality of the portion of the poem from which this stanza is taken contrasts sharply with the serene, pastoral tone of the beginning and end of the hymn, where Milton is describing the birth of the Christ Child at Bethlehem:

But peaceful was the night
Wherein the Prince of light
His reign of peace upon the earth began:
The Winds, with wonder whist,
Smoothly the waters kiss't,
Whispering new joys to the mild Ocean,
Who now hath quite forgot to rave,
While Birds of Calm sit brooding on the charmed wave.

Milton has been criticized by some who believe that these contrasting tones destroy the unity of the poem, yet by emphasizing both the peaceful and the forceful aspects of the Incarnation, he has attempted to capture one of the central paradoxes of the Christian faith. He sets forth this paradox in more philosophical terms, reminiscent of Edmund Spenser's *Hymnes*, in the four introductory stanzas of the Nativity ode.

That glorious Form, that Light unsufferable,
And that far-beaming blaze of Majesty,
Wherewith he wont at Heav'n's high Council-Table,
To sit the midst of Trinal Unity,

He laid aside; and here with us to be, Forsook the
Courts of everlasting Day,
And chose with us a darksome House of mortal Clay.

The interests that were to culminate in *Paradise Lost* are already evident in this poem, composed nearly thirty-five years before the great epic.

"L'Allegro" and "Il Penseroso" are companion pieces setting forth the pleasures of the cheerful man and the pensive one. Writing in the same tetrameter line in both poems, Milton has carefully worked out parallel, but contrasting, sections. The man of mirth seeks the company of gay rural people in the daytime and frequents the city at night, attending the theater "if Jonson's learned Sock be on, or sweetest Shakespeare, fancy's child, warble his native Wood-notes wild." The melancholy man prefers solitude; his favorite time of day is evening, when he can wander alone in the woods, contemplating the stars. He spends his days in the cloister with his books and looks forward to ending his life in a hermitage. The mirthful man listens for the lark, the herald of morning; the pensive one awaits the song of the nightingale. Both men love music, but the latter is moved by the organ's peals and the anthems of a choir, while the former seeks a more romantic melody:

And ever against eating Cares,
Lap me in soft Lydian Airs,
Married to immortal verse,
Such as the meeting soul may pierce
In notes, with many a winding bout
Of linked sweetness long drawn out,
With wanton heed, and giddy cunning,
The melting voice through mazes running;
Untwisting all the chains that tie
The hidden soul of harmony.

Even the rhythms of the two poems echo the contrast the poet is making. The address to mirth that begins "L'Allegro" moves rapidly, joyfully:

Haste thee, Nymph, and bring with thee
Jest and youthful Jollity,
Quips and Cranks, and wanton Wiles,
Nods and Becks, and Wreathèd Smiles,
Such as hang on Hebe's cheek,
And love to live in dimple sleek.

Summoning melancholy, the poet shapes his words to a slower, statelier pace:

Come pensive Nun, devout and pure,
Sober, steadfast, and demure,
All in a robe of darkest grain,
Flowing with majestic train.

Seldom, if ever, has the essence of a mood been so clearly conveyed as it is in "L'Allegro" and "Il Penseroso," through an almost perfect fusion of idea, image, and sound. Milton understood the appeals of both the active and the contemplative life, and he makes both paths equally attractive to his reader.

It is in *Lycidas*, the pastoral elegy written on the death of a young Cambridge student, Edward King, who was a promising poet, that Milton's assimilation of the classical tradition is most evident. The detachment and the artificiality of the Greek and Latin pastoral made the form appropriate for lamenting an acquaintance; Milton did not know King well enough to feel deep personal grief. More important, the pastoral elegy as it was developed by Theocritus, Vergil, and their imitators traditionally encompassed discussions of literature and society. *Lycidas* has as much to say about Milton's poetic ambitions and his distress at the state of religion in his time as it does about the death of King.

The poem includes many conventions of the pastoral elegy: the lament of nature for the dead poet; the appeal to the sea nymphs who might have saved him; the reminiscences of his brother shepherd, who watched his flock and played his pipes with him; and the final turn from grief to joy with the realization that Lycidas lives again, immortal, as the genius, the guardian spirit, of the shore. The image of the poet as shepherd was so often used in Renaissance lyrics that it became a popular cliché; Milton adopts, too, the traditional Christian concept of Christ as the good shepherd to integrate his criticism of the clergy into the poem.

The lament for Lycidas is framed by two brief sections focusing attention on the narrator, the shepherd poet who is Milton himself. He first addresses the prematurely withered laurels and myrtles, plants associated with poetic fame, and declares his intention to sing of his dead friend. After the exalted conclusion of the lament, when Lycidas' immortality is proclaimed, a second voice enters to describe the departure of the shepherd-singer:

> At last he rose, and twitch't his Mantle blue:
> Tomorrow to fresh Woods, and Pastures new.

These lines suggest that perhaps even then Milton was contemplating greater things as a poet; the conventional classical pattern was to serve one's apprenticeship by writing pastoral poetry in preparation for the masterwork, the epic.

The main section of *Lycidas* falls into three parts. The first includes the mourning of the singer and his meditations on mortality. If Lycidas can die so young, why seek fame through writing? Apollo answers his question; it is not human, but divine, acclaim that is to be desired:

> "Fame is no plant that grows on mortal soil,
> Nor in the glistering foil
> Set off to th' world, nor in broad rumor lies,
> But lives and spreads aloft by those pure eyes
> And perfect witness of all-judging Jove;
> As he pronounces lastly on each deed,
> Of so much fame in Heav'n expect thy meed."

The second part introduces a procession of mourners: a herald of the sea who protests his innocence in the shepherd's drowning; Camus, the god of the river that runs through Cambridge, lamenting his loss; and finally St. Peter, who voices Milton's disgust with the priests of his time:

> He shook his Mitred locks, and stern bespake:
> "How well could I have spar'd for thee, young swain,
> Enough of such as for their bellies' sake,
> Creep and intrude and climb into the fold?
> Of other care they little reck'ning make,
> Than how to scramble at the shearers' feast,
> And shove away the worthy bidden guest.
> Blind mouths! that scarce themselves know how to hold
> A Sheep-hook, or have learn'd aught else the least
> That to the faithful Herdman's art belongs!"

A calmer tone prevails in the third part, in which Milton calls on the valleys round about to bloom with flowers for the shepherd's hearse. His quiet grief is expressed in the famous lines:

> Look homeward, Angel, now, and melt with ruth;
> And, O ye Dolphins, waft the hapless youth.

At this point there is an abrupt change as the poet proclaims Lycidas' immortality, and the elegy ends on a joyful note.

A study of Milton's shorter poems brings a new awareness of the poet's genius. He was the master of many voices—the lyric, the philosophic, and the satiric—even in his early works, which show little evidence of an inexperienced pen at work. Few writers have had so fine a mastery of the English language, and perhaps no other Englishman has surpassed him as a writer of Latin, Italian, and Greek verse. He would stand as one of his country's most remarkable literary men if his fame rested solely on the works discussed here.

LYSISTRATA

Type of work: Drama
Author: Aristophanes (c. 448–335 B.C.)
Type of plot: Utopian comedy
Time of plot: Fifth century B.C.
Locale: Athens
First presented: 411 B.C.

Lysistrata is based on a highly comic assumption—probably popular even in the time of Aristophanes—that is as impossible as it is comic: the idea that women might coerce their men into laying down their weapons produced a bawdy and delightful work of art.

Principal Characters

Lysistrata (lī·sĭs′trə·tə), an idealistic Athenian woman who is not content to stand submissively by and witness the obvious wastes war brings to the land. In her effort to bring a permanent peace to Greece, she demonstrates qualities that mark her as one of the archetypal revolutionaries because of her relentless fervor, cunning, and intractability. In addition to the traits of a revolutionary, Lysistrata possesses a healthy supply of Aristophanes' inimitable wit and humor, qualities lacking in the ordinary stage conception of a revolutionist. She reasons and persuades the women of Greece to cast their lots with her so that by simply refusing the men sexual satisfaction she can bring them to her terms: abolition of war and the relinquishment of the treasury to women. Amid the rollicking ribaldry of man laughing at his own precious taboo—sex—Lysistrata's plan to seize and occupy the Acropolis of Athens with her army of celibate women weathers a storm of protest, succeeds, and wrecks the framework of a society dominated by men.

Cleonice (klē·ō·nī′sē), a lusty Athenian friend of Lysistrata. At first reluctant to go along with so devastating and sacrificing a plan, she is eventually browbeaten by Lysistrata into accepting the challenge to save Greece from the total ruin of war, and she partakes of the solemn oath, binding herself to refrain from sharing the marriage bed with her husband. Constantly on hand, Cleonice adds much zest by ribald commentary and turns out to be one of Lysistrata's main supporters.

Myrrhiné (mĭ·rē′nē), one of Lysistrata's captains, representing Anagyra. Just as the idealism of Lysistrata is wearing thin and the torment of self-denial is weakening the ranks of the women, Myrrhiné's husband appears and, acting under orders from Lysistrata, she subjects him to unendurable, teasing torture. This episode is not only one of the play's funniest but also the point at which Lysistrata's strategy turns toward success.

Lampito (lăm′pĭ·tō), a woman of Sparta who agrees to Lysistrata's plan. Her loyalty and resourcefulness bring success in that land. Lampito, typical of the Athenian's concept of Spartan women, is athletic, bold, well proportioned. A key figure throughout the play, she steps forward at the very inception of Lysistrata's plan to be the major seconding voice. Her example assures the revolt of the women.

Cinesias (sĭ·nē′sĭ·əs), the husband of Myrrhiné. Exhibiting all symptoms of lust, he begs his wife to return to him.

A Child, the infant son of Myrrhiné and Cinesias, brought by his father in an attempt to bribe his mother into deserting the women's cause.

A Magistrate, a pompous representative of law and order who seeks to treat the revolutionaries as silly housewives to be spanked and sent to their kitchens. Much to his chagrin, he discovers them in no mood to be so treated. After seeing his force of Scythian policemen rebuffed, and completely defeated by Lysistrata's determined female logic, he becomes the echo and image of Aristophanes' laughter at the ineffectuality of the law when pitted against organized femininity.

A Chorus of Old Men who lead the first unsuccessful attempt to dislodge the women from the Acropolis. They toil uphill with smoke faggots and engage in much humorous comment upon the character of women in general; their efforts are confined mostly to threats and ineffectual maneuvering as the women prove too much for them.

A Chorus of Women, antagonists of the old men. The women establish a swift rapport with them, not only turning their smoke faggots into uselessness by soaking them but also besting them in a verbal exchange of ridicule and insult.

A Spartan Herald, also suffering the pangs of thwarted love.

Spartan Envoys, with whom the Athenian women conclude a treaty of peace.

The Story

The Second Peloponnesian War was in progress when Lysistrata, an Athenian woman, summoned women from Athens, Sparta, and all other Greek cities involved in the war. She wished to have them consider her carefully thought out plan for ending hostilities between Athens and Sparta. The women arrived one by one, curious about the purpose of the meeting. Since their husbands were all away at war, they looked with enthusiasm for any scheme which would bring their men back to them.

Lysistrata declared that the war would end immediately if all the Greek women refrained, from that time on, until the fighting stopped, from lying with their husbands. This suggestion took the women by complete surprise, and they objected strenuously. But Lampito, a Spartan woman, liked the idea. Although the others finally agreed to try the plan, they did so without enthusiasm.

Over a bowl of Thracian wine, Lysistrata led her companions in an oath binding them to charm their husbands and their lovers, but not to lie with them unless forced. Some of the women returned to their native lands to begin their continent lives. Lysistrata went to the Acropolis, citadel of Athens.

While the younger women had been meeting with Lysistrata, the older women had marched upon the Acropolis and seized it. The old men of the city laid wood around the base of the Acropolis and set fire to it with the intention of smoking out the women, who, in turn, threatened the old men with pots of water. During an exchange of scurrilous vituperation the women threw water on their opponents.

When a magistrate and his men attempted to break open a gate of the citadel, Lysistrata, now in command, emerged and suggested that the magistrate use common sense. When the indignant magistrate ordered his Scythians to seize Lysistrata and bind her hands, the Scythians advanced reluctantly and were soundly trounced by the fierce defenders.

Asked why they had seized the Acropolis, the women replied that they had done so in order to possess the treasury. Since they now controlled the money, and since it took money to wage war, they believed that the war must soon end.

The male pride of the old men was deeply wounded when Lysistrata declared that the women had assumed all civil authority and would henceforth provide for the safety and welfare of Athens. The magistrate could not believe his ears when he heard Lysistrata say that the women, tired of being homebodies, were impatient with the incompetence of their husbands in matters which concerned the commonweal. For rebuking the women, the magistrate received potfuls of water poured on his head. The ineffectual old men declared that they would never submit to the tyranny of women. The women answered that the old men were worthless, that all they could do was to legislate the city into trouble.

Despite their brave talk and their bold plan, however, the women proved to be weak in the flesh, and disaffection thinned their ranks. Some, caught as they deserted, offered various excuses in the hope of getting away from the strictures imposed by Lysistrata's oath. One woman simulated pregnancy by placing the sacred helmet of Athena under her robe. Some of the women claimed to be frightened by the holy snakes and by the owls of the Acropolis. As a last desperate measure, Lysistrata resorted to a prophecy, which was favorable to their project, and the women returned reluctantly to their posts.

When Cinesias, the husband of Myrrhiné, one of Lysistrata's companions, returned from the war and sought his wife, Lysistrata directed Myrrhiné to be true to her oath. Begging Myrrhiné to come home, Cinesias used various appeals, without success. Although Myrrhiné consented to his request for a moment of dalliance with her, she put him off with trifling excuses. At last, in spite of his pleas, she retired into the citadel.

A messenger arrived from Sparta, where Lampito and her cohorts had been successful, and declared that the men of Sparta were prepared to sue for peace. As the magistrate arranged for a peace conference, the women looked once more upon the old men of Athens with a kindness that cooled the ire of the indignant old fellows.

On their arrival in Athens, the Spartan envoys were obviously in need of the favors of their wives. Indeed, so desperate were they that they were ready to agree to any terms. Lysistrata rebuked the Spartans and the Athenians for warring upon each other; they had, she declared, a common enemy in the barbarians, and they shared many traditions. While she spoke, a nude maiden, representing the goddess of peace, was brought before the frustrated men. Lysistrata reminded the men of the two countries that they had previously been friends and allies and again insisted that war between the two was illogical. The men, their eyes devouring the nude maiden, agreed absently with everything Lysistrata said, but when she asked for an agreement, contention immediately arose because one side asked for conditions unsatisfactory to the other.

The women, seeing that any appeal to reason was futile, feasted the envoys and filled them with intoxicating liquors. Sated and eager for further physical satisfaction, the men signed a peace agreement and dispersed hastily, with their wives, to their homes.

Critical Evaluation

Lysistrata is the most frequently produced Greek drama in the modern theater. Reasons for its current vogue are not hard to find, for the play deals openly with sex, feminism, and pacifism—all major preoccupations of the late twentieth century. A popular slogan of our time, Make Love, Not War, sums up perfectly Aristophanes' attitude in this comedy. Our era has largely taken up *Lysistrata* for its ideology, rather than for its intrinsic value as a play. Yet it does provide some amusing, bawdy, and skeptical entertainment.

In structure the drama is smooth and straightforward. First the problem is presented: the women are sick of having their husbands absent because of the Peloponnesian War. The solution is that they avoid sex with their husbands, but at the same time tease them, until the men decide to settle the war from sheer frustration. Out of that solution everything else follows—the women capture the treasury; the old men try to force the women into submission; when force fails the two sides hold an inconclusive debate in which the magistrate, a chief warmonger, is dressed like a woman and then as a corpse by hostile females; then the women begin to defect from their oath of chastity; after a desperate effort Lysistrata regains her influence over the women; and the men agree to seek peace. When negotiation fails between the Athenians and the Spartans, the diplomats are tricked into a peace settlement through feasting and drinking. Given the basic idea, almost all of this action is predictable. If it amuses, it is never surprising enough to produce laughter. Perhaps the best and most comic idea in the play is that diplomats should never negotiate when they are sober. Cleverness and greed are inimical to peace, while drink and festivity promote good will.

Sex is a traditional subject for comedy and particularly the battle of the sexes. In fact, Greek comedy evolved in part from phallic farce, and there are phallic jokes in *Lysistrata*, although this element is not prominent. The implicit humor of the play's central idea rests in the belief of Aristophanes and his audience that the Athenian women were inveterate tipplers and lechers. Of course, the audience consisted largely of men, to whom the idea of women taking over the affairs of state would have seemed irresistibly comic. The slapstick and banter between the chorus of old men and the chorus of women simply restate the age-old contest between male and female. The male chorus puts the matter succinctly when it says, in effect, "We can't live with 'em, and we can't live without 'em."

Yet *Lysistrata* carries a more important theme than sexuality, which is merely shown as a weapon to bring about peace. At the time this play was first produced in 411 B.C., Athens had been through twenty hard years of war with Sparta, and the end of this conflict was still seven years in the future. The seriousness of the war is brought out very forcefully when Lysistrata tells the magistrate that sons have perished in battle, and that many young women will never find mates because of this. The fact that the chorus consists of old men underscores the point that many Athenian youths had died in the Peloponnesian War. Here the drama becomes absolutely serious and reveals Aristophanes' true feelings about the war with no trace of buffoonery. The dramatist clearly regards Lysistrata as something of a heroine and not a butt for humor. When men have failed so badly to govern the affairs of the city, he says it's time for the women to take over. But all the while Aristophanes and his audience are fully aware of the weaknesses of women. So in essence, the playwright is scolding the Athenian men by telling them that if they cannot put an end to the war in twenty years, they might as well give up.

Today the play is presented on stage or in print as straight drama, entirely spoken. Yet *Lysistrata* was originally presented as a musical comedy with choreography, colorful costumes, and masks. The actors were all male, as in the theater of Shakespeare's time. This type of presentation tended to soften the strength of Aristophanes' biting wit, and it gave the play an air of spectacle and of festivity.

MACBETH

Type of Work: Drama
Author: William Shakespeare (1564–1616)
Type of plot Romantic tragedy
Time of plot: Eleventh century
Locale: Scotland
First presented: 1606

This shortest of Shakespeare's four major tragedies was written to be performed for King James I and was designed to appeal to the monarch's fascination with witchcraft and supernatural phenomena. The play explores the nature of ambition and the complexities of moral responsibility through the story of a nobleman driven to murder at the instigation of his power-hungry wife. Macbeth's doom is fixed at this first evil act, after which he descends deeper and deeper into degradation in an attempt to conceal the crime and guarantee the invulnerability of his new position of power.

Principal Characters

Macbeth (măk·bĕth′), thane of Glamis, later thane of Cawdor and king of Scotland. A brave and successful military leader, potentially a good and great man, he wins general admiration as well as the particular gratitude of King Duncan, whose kinsman he is. Meeting the three weird sisters, he succumbs to their tempting prophecies; but he also needs the urging of his wife to become a traitor, a murderer, and a usurper. He is gifted, or cursed, with a powerful and vivid imagination and with fiery, poetic language. Gaining power, he grows more and more ruthless, until finally he loses even the vestiges of humanity. He dies desperately, cheated by the ambiguous prophecies, in full realization of the worthlessness of the fruits of his ambition.

Lady Macbeth, the strong-willed, persuasive, and charming wife of Macbeth. Ambitious for her husband's glory, she finds herself unable to kill King Duncan in his sleep, because he resembles her father. As Macbeth becomes more inhuman, she becomes remorseful and breaks under the strain. In her sleepwalking, she relives the events of the night of the king's murder and tries to wash her hands clean of imaginary bloodstains.

Banquo (băn′kwō, băng′kō), Macbeth's fellow commander. A man of noble character, seemingly unmoved by the prophecy of the three weird sisters that he will beget kings, he is not completely innocent; he does not disclose his suspicions of Macbeth, and he accepts a place in Macbeth's court. After being murdered by Macbeth's assassins, Banquo appears at a ceremonial banquet. His blood-spattered ghost, visible only to Macbeth, unnerves the king completely. In the final vision shown Macbeth by the three weird sisters, Banquo and his line of kings appear.

The Three Weird Sisters, the three witches, sinister hags who seem more closely allied to the Norns or Fates than to conventional witches. To Macbeth they make prophetic statements which are true but deceptive. Their

prophecy of his becoming thane of Cawdor is immediately fulfilled, tempting him to take direct action to carry out the second prophecy, that he shall be king. They lull him into false security by telling him that he has nothing to fear until Birnam Wood comes to Dunsinane, and that he cannot be killed by any man born of woman.

Macduff (mk·dŭf′), thane of Fife. He and Lennox arrive at Macbeth's castle just after the murder of King Duncan, and Macduff discovers the body. A brave but prudent man, he flees Scotland and offers his help to Malcolm. Underestimating the villainy of Macbeth's character, he is thunderstruck at hearing of the atrocious murder of his wife and children. He becomes a steel-hearted avenger. Before killing Macbeth, he deprives him of his last symbol of security, for as a Cesarean child he was not actually born of woman. He presents Macbeth's head to Malcolm and proclaims the young prince king of Scotland.

Duncan (dŭng′kən), king of Scotland. Gentle and trusting, he shows great kindness to Macbeth. His murder by Macbeth is therefore almost incredibly fiendish.

Malcolm (mĬ′kəm), King Duncan's eldest son. Far more cautious and shrewd than his father, he leaves for England to escape possible assassination. He is reluctant to give his trust to Macduff but finally, realizing his loyalty, accepts his aid in taking the throne of Scotland.

Donalbain (dŏn′əl·bān), King Duncan's younger son. After consulting with Malcolm, he agrees to take a separate path, going to Ireland so that the potential heirs to the throne would not be accessible to a common assassination.

Fleance (flē′əns), the son of Banquo. He escapes the murderers who kill his father and lives to haunt Macbeth with the three weird sisters' prophecy that kings will spring from Banquo's line.

Ross, a nobleman of Scotland. He is Duncan's messenger to Macbeth, bringing him word of his new title,

Thane of Cawdor. He also bears news to his kinswoman, Lady Macduff, of her husband's departure from Scotland. His third and most terrible office as messenger is to carry word to Macduff of the destruction of his entire family. He fights in Malcolm's army against Macbeth.

Lennox, a nobleman of Scotland. He is Macduff's companion when the latter brings the message to King Duncan at Macbeth's castle. He also deserts Macbeth and joins forces with Malcolm.

Lady Macduff, a victim of Macbeth's most horrible atrocity. She is human and pathetic.

A Boy, the son of Macduff, a brave and precocious child. He faces Macbeth's hired murderers without flinching and dies calling to his mother to save herself.

Siward (sē′wərd, sē′ərd), earl of Northumberland, the general of the English forces supporting Malcolm. He is the type of the noble father accepting stoically the death of a heroic son.

Young Siward, the general's courageous son. He dies fighting Macbeth hand to hand.

A Scottish Doctor. Called in to minister to Lady Macbeth, he is witness of her sleepwalking in which she relives the night of the murder.

A Gentlewoman, an attendant to Lady Macbeth. She is with the Doctor and observes Lady Macbeth during the sleepwalking scene.

A Sergeant (also called **Captain** in the Folio text), a wounded survivor of the battle at the beginning of the play. He reports to King Duncan the heroism of Macbeth and Banquo.

A Porter, a comical drunkard. Roused by the knocking on the castle door, he pretends to be the gatekeeper of Hell and imagines various candidates clamoring for admission. The audience, knowing of Duncan's murder, can realize how ironically near the truth is the idea of the castle as Hell.

Hecate (hĕk′ə·tē, hĕk′ət), patroness of the Witches. It is generally accepted among Shakespearean scholars that Hecate is an addition to the play by another author, perhaps Thomas Middleton, author of "The Witch."

A Messenger. He brings word that Birnam Wood is apparently moving. His message destroys one of Macbeth's illusions of safety.

Seyton, an officer attending Macbeth. He brings word of Lady Macbeth's death.

Menteith, Angus, and **Caithness,** Scottish noblemen who join Malcolm against Macbeth.

The Story

On a lonely heath in Scotland, three witches sang their riddling runes and said that soon they would meet Macbeth.

Macbeth was the noble thane of Glamis, recently victorious in a great battle against Vikings and Scottish rebels. For his brave deeds, King Duncan intended to confer upon him the lands of the rebellious thane of Cawdor. But before Macbeth saw the king, he and his friend Banquo met the three weird witches upon the dark moor. The wild and frightful women greeted Macbeth by first calling him thane of Glamis, then thane of Cawdor, and finally, King of Scotland. Too, they prophesied that Banquo's heirs would reign in Scotland in years to come.

When Macbeth tried to question the three hags, they vanished. Macbeth thought very little about the strange prophecy until he met one of Duncan's messengers, who told him that he was now thane of Cawdor. This piece of news stunned Macbeth, and he turned to Banquo to confirm the witches' prophecy. But Banquo, unduped by the witches, thought them evil enough to betray Macbeth by whetting his ambition and tricking him into fulfilling the prophecy. Macbeth did not heed Banquo's warning; the words of the witches as they called him king had gone deep into his soul. He pondered over the possibility of becoming a monarch and set his whole heart on the attainment of this goal. If he could be thane of Cawdor, perhaps he could rule all of Scotland as well. But as it was now, Duncan was king, with two sons to rule after him. The problem was great. Macbeth shook off his ambitious dreams to go with Banquo to greet Duncan.

A perfect ruler, Duncan was kind, majestic, gentle, strong; Macbeth was fond of him. But when Duncan mentioned that his son Malcolm would succeed him on the throne, Macbeth saw the boy as an obstacle in his own path, and he hardly dared admit to himself how this impediment disturbed him.

On a royal procession, Duncan announced that he would spend one night at Macbeth's castle. Lady Macbeth, who knew of the witches' prophecy, was even more ambitious than her husband, and she saw Duncan's visit as a perfect opportunity for Macbeth to become king. She determined that he should murder Duncan and usurp the throne.

That night there was much feasting in the castle. After everyone was asleep, Lady Macbeth told her husband of her plan for the king's murder. Horrified at first, Macbeth refused to do the deed. But on being accused of cowardice by his wife, and having bright prospects of his future dangled before his eyes, Macbeth finally succumbed to her demands. He stole into the sleeping king's chamber and plunged a knife into his heart.

The murder was blamed on two grooms whom Lady Macbeth had smeared with Duncan's blood while they were asleep. But the deed was hardly without suspicion in the castle, and when the murder was revealed, the dead king's sons fled, Malcolm to England, Donalbain to Ireland. Macbeth was proclaimed king. But Macduff, a nobleman who had been Duncan's close friend, also carefully noted the murder, and when Macbeth was crowned king, Macduff suspected him of the bloody killing.

Macbeth began to have horrible dreams; his mind was never free from fear. Often he thought of the witches' second prophecy, that Banquo's heirs would hold the throne, and the prediction tormented him. Macbeth was so determined that Banquo would never share in his own hard-earned glory that he resolved to murder Banquo and his son, Fleance.

Lady Macbeth and her husband gave a great banquet for the noble thanes of Scotland. At the same time, Macbeth sent murderers to waylay Banquo and his son before they could reach the palace. Banquo was slain in the scuffle, but Fleance escaped. Meanwhile in the large banquet hall Macbeth pretended great sorrow that Banquo was not present. But Banquo was present in spirit, and his ghost majestically appeared in Macbeth's own seat. The startled king was so frightened that he almost betrayed his guilt when he alone saw the apparition. Lady Macbeth quickly led him away and dismissed the guests.

More frightened than ever, thinking of Banquo's ghost which had returned to haunt him, and of Fleance who had escaped but might one day claim the throne, Macbeth was so troubled that he determined to seek solace from the witches on the dismal heath. They assured Macbeth that he would not be overcome by man born of woman, nor until the forest of Birnam came to Dunsinane Hill. They warned him to beware of Macduff. When Macbeth asked if Banquo's children would reign over the kingdom, the witches disappeared. The news they gave him brought him cheer. Macbeth felt he need fear no man, since all were born of women, and certainly the great Birnam forest could not be moved by human power.

Then Macbeth heard that Macduff was gathering a hostile army in England, an army to be led by Malcolm, Duncan's son, who was determined to avenge his father's murder. So terrified was Macbeth that he resolved to murder Macduff's wife and children in order to bring the rebel to submission. After this slaughter, however, Macbeth was more than ever tormented by fear; his twisted mind had almost reached the breaking point, and he longed for death to release him from his nightmarish existence.

Before long Lady Macbeth's strong will broke. Dark dreams of murder and violence drove her to madness. The horror of her crimes and the agony of being hated and feared by all of Macbeth's subjects made her so ill that her death seemed imminent.

On the eve of Macduff's attack on Macbeth's castle, Lady Macbeth died, depriving her husband of all courage she had given him in the past. Rallying, Macbeth summoned strength to meet his enemy. Meanwhile, Birnam Wood had moved, for Malcolm's soldiers were hidden behind cut green boughs, which from a distance appeared to be a moving forest. Macduff, enraged by the slaughter of his innocent family, was determined to meet Macbeth in hand-to-hand conflict.

Macbeth went to battle filled with the false courage given him by the witches' prophecy that no man born of woman would overthrow him. Meeting Macduff, Macbeth began to fight him, taunting him at the same time about his having been born of woman. But Macduff had been ripped alive from his mother's womb. The prophecy was fulfilled. Macbeth fought with waning strength, all hope of victory gone, and Macduff, with a flourish, severed the head of the bloody King of Scotland.

Critical Evaluation

Not only is *Macbeth* by far the shortest of William Shakespeare's great tragedies but also it is anomalous in several structural respects. Like *Othello*, and very few other Shakespearean plays, *Macbeth* is without the complications of a subplot. Consequently, the action moves forward in a swift and inexorable rush. More significantly, the climax, the murder of Duncan, takes place very early in the play. The result is that attention is focused on the manifold consequences of the crime rather than on the ambiguities or moral dilemmas which precede or occasion it.

Thus, the play is not like *Othello*, where the hero commits murder only after long plotting by the villain, nor is it like *Hamlet*, where the hero spends most of the play in moral indecision. It is more like *King Lear*, where destructive action flows from the central premise of the division of the kingdom. But *Macbeth* is much different from *King Lear* in that it does not raise monumental, cosmic questions of good and evil in nature; instead it

explores the moral and psychological effects of evil in the life of one man. For all the power and prominence of Lady Macbeth, the drama remains essentially the story of the lord, who commits regicide and thereby enmeshes himself in a complex web of consequences.

When Macbeth first enters, he is far from the villain whose experiences the play subsequently describes. He has just returned from a military success that has covered him with glory in defense of the crown. He is rewarded by the grateful Duncan, with preferment as thane of Cawdor. This excellence and honor, which initially qualify him for the role of hero, ironically intensify the horror of the murder Macbeth soon commits.

His fall is rapid, and his crime is more clearly a sin than is usually the case in tragedy. It is not mitigated by mixed motives or insufficient knowledge. Moreover, the sin is regicide, an action viewed by the Renaissance audience as exceptionally foul since it struck at God's representative on earth. The sin is so boldly offensive that many have tried to find extenuation in the impetus given Macbeth by the witches. However, the witches do not control behavior in the play. They are symbolic of evil and prescient of crimes which are to come, but they neither encourage nor facilitate Macbeth's actions. They are merely a reminder of the ambition which is already within Macbeth. Indeed, when he discusses the witches' prophecy with Lady Macbeth, it is clear that the possibility has been discussed before.

Nor can we shift responsibility to Lady Macbeth, despite her goading of her husband. In one, perhaps amoral, way, she is merely acting out the role of the good wife, encouraging her husband to do what she believes is in his best interests. In any case, she is rather a catalyst and supporter; she does not make the grim decision for Macbeth, and he never tries to lay the blame on her.

When Macbeth proceeds on his bloody course, there is little extenuation in his brief failure of nerve. He is an ambitious man, overpowered by his high aspirations. Nevertheless, we view Macbeth with much sympathy. Despite the clearcut evil of his actions, we never feel the distaste we deserve for villains such as Iago or Cornwall, perhaps because Macbeth is not evil incarnate, but a human being who has sinned, no matter how serious the transgression. In addition, we are as much affected by what Macbeth says about his actions as by the deeds themselves. Both substance and setting emphasize the great evil, but Macbeth does not go about his foul business easily. He knows what he is doing, but his agonizing reflections show a man increasingly out of control of his own moral destiny.

Although Lady Macbeth demonstrated greater courage and resolution at the time of the murder of Duncan, it is she who falls victim to the physical manifestations of remorse and literally dies of guilt. Macbeth, who starts more tentatively, becomes stronger, or perhaps more inured, as he faces the consequences of his initial crime. The play examines the effects of evil on Macbeth's character and on his subsequent moral behaviour. The later murders flow naturally out of the first. Evil breeds evil in that, to protect himself and consolidate his position, Macbeth is almost forced to murder again. Successively, he kills Banquo, attempts to murder Fleance, and brutally exterminates Macduff's family. As his crimes increase, Macbeth's freedom seems to decrease, but his moral responsibility does not. His actions become more cold-blooded as his options disappear. His growing resolution and steadfastness in a precarious predicament are admirable, but his specific actions are repugnant.

Shakespeare does not allow Macbeth any convenient moral excuses. The dramatist is aware of the notion, from contemporary faculty psychology, of the dominant inclination. The idea is that any action performed makes it more likely that the person will perform other such actions. The operation of this phenomenon is apparent as, in the face of complications, Macbeth finds it increasingly easier to rise to the gruesome occasion. However, the dominant inclination never becomes a total determinant of behavior, so Macbeth is left without the excuse of loss of free will. But it does become ever more difficult to break the chain of events which are rushing him toward moral and physical destruction.

As he degenerates, he becomes more deluded about his invulnerability and more emboldened. What he gains in will and confidence is counterbalanced and eventually toppled by the iniquitous weight of the events he set in motion and felt he had to perpetuate. When he dies, he seems almost to be released from the imprisonment of his own evil.

MADAME BOVARY

Type of Work: Novel
Author: Gustave Flaubert (1821–1880)
Type of plot: Psychological realism
Time of plot: Mid-nineteenth century
Locale: France
First published: 1857 (English translation, 1886)

This masterpiece of realism is an in-depth psychological study of a beautiful but bored and restless woman whose romantic fantasies and yearnings lead her to seek diversion from the monotony of her married life. Madame Bovary was one of the first novels of its kind to come out of France and caused a great deal of controversy among contemporary readers and critics; some were shocked at the presentation of the spoiled, romantic adulteress, while others saw the novel as moral and applauded Flaubert's skill and honesty of treatment.

Principal Characters

Emma Bovary (ĕ′mȧ bô·vȧ·rē′), a sentimental young woman whose foolishly romantic ideas on life and love cause her to become dissatisfied with her humdrum husband and the circumstances of her married life. Her feeling of disillusionment leads her first into two desperate, hopeless love affairs and then to an agonizing and ugly death from arsenic. Filled with fiery, indefinite conceptions of love which she is capable of translating only into gaudy bourgeois displays of materialism, she is unable to reconcile herself to a life of tedium as the wife of a country doctor. In her attempt to escape into a more exciting world of passion and dreams, she drifts into shabby, sordid affairs with Rodolphe Boulanger and Léon Dupuis. The first of these lovers, an older man, dominates the affair; the second, inexperienced and young, is dominated. Because Emma brings to both of these affairs little more than an unsubstantial and frantic desire to escape from her dull husband and the monotony of her life, the eventual collapse of her romantic dreams, the folly of her passionate surrender to passion and intrigue, and her death, brought on by false, empty pride, are inevitable.

Charles Bovary (shärl bô·vȧ·rē′), Emma's well-meaning but docile and mediocre medical husband. An unimaginative clod without intelligence or insight, he is unable to understand, console, or satisfy the terrible needs of his wife. Every move he makes to become a more important figure in her eyes is frustrated by his inadequacy as a lover and a doctor, for he is as much a failure in his practice as he is in his relations with Emma. Her suicide leaves him grief-stricken and financially ruined as a result of her extravagance. Soon after her death, he discovers in the secret drawer of her desk the love letters sent her by Rodolphe and Léon, and he learns of her infidelity for the first time. When he dies, the sum of twelve francs and seventy-five centimes is his only legacy to his small daughter.

Rodolphe Boulanger (rô·dôlf′ bōō·län-zhā′), Emma Bovary's first lover. A well-to-do bachelor and the owner of the Château La Huchette, he is a shrewd, suave, and brittle man with considerable knowledge of women and a taste for intrigue. Sensing the relationship between Emma and her husband, he makes friends with the Bovarys, sends them gifts of venison and fowl, and invites them to the chateau. On the pretext of concern for Emma's health, he suggests that they go riding together. He finds Emma so easy a conquest that after a short time he begins to neglect her, partly out of boredom, partly because he cannot see in himself the Byronic image Emma has created in her imagination; she never sees Rodolphe as the loutish, vulgar man he is. After he writes her a letter of farewell, on the pretext that he is going on a long journey, Emma suffers a serious attack of brain fever.

Léon Dupuis (lā·ōȧn′ dü·püe′), a young law clerk infatuated with Emma Bovary but without the courage to declare himself or to possess her. With him she indulges in progressively lascivious behavior in her attempt to capture the excitement and passion of the romantic love she desires. Léon, because he lacks depth and maturity, merely intensifies Emma's growing estrangement from her everyday world. When Léon, who never realizes the encouragement Emma offers him, goes off to continue his studies in Paris, she is filled with rage, hate, and unfulfilled desire, and a short time later she turns to Rodolphe Boulanger. After that affair she meets Léon once more in Rouen, and they become lovers. Oppressed by debts, living only for sensation, and realizing that she is pulling Léon down to her own degraded level, Emma ends the affair by committing suicide.

Monsieur Lheureux (lœ·rœ′), an unscrupulous, corrupt draper and moneylender who makes Emma the victim of his unsavory business deals by driving her deeper and deeper into debt. Her inability to repay the exorbitant loans he has made her in secret forces the issue of suicide on her as her only escape from her baseless world.

Monsieur Homais (ə·mĕ′), a chemist, presented in a masterpiece of ironic characterization. A speaker in clichés, the possessor of a wholly trite "Scientific Outlook" on society, he regards himself as a Modern Man and a Thinker. His pomposity and superficial ideals become one of the remarkable facets of the novel, as Flaubert sketches the hypocrisy and mediocrity of Charles Bovary's friend. Homais epitomizes the small-town promoter, raconteur, and self-styled liberal.

Hippolyte Tautain (ê·pô·lēt′ tō·tăn′), a witless, club-footed boy operated on by Charles Bovary at the insistence of M. Homais, who wishes to bring greater glory to the region by proving the merits of a new surgical device. Bovary's crude handling of the operation and the malpractice involved in the use of the device cause the boy to lose his leg. The episode provides Flaubert with an excellent commentary on both Homais and Bovary.

Théodore Rouault (tā·ô·dôr′ rōō·ȧl′), Emma Bovary's father, a farmer. Charles Bovary first meets Emma when he is summoned to set Rouault's broken leg.

Berthe Bovary (bĕrt bô·vȧ·rē′), the neglected young daughter of Emma and Charles Bovary. Orphaned and left without an inheritance, she is sent to live with her father's mother. When that woman dies, the child is turned over to the care of an aunt, who puts her to work in a cotton-spinning factory.

Captain Binet (bē·nā′), the tax collector in the town of Yonville-l'Abbaye.

Justin (zhüs·tăn′), the assistant in the shop of Mr. Homais. Emma persuades her young admirer to admit her to the room where poisons are kept. There, before horrified Justin can stop her, she secures a quantity of arsenic and eats it.

Madame Veuve Lefrançois (vœv′ lə·frään-swȧ′), the proprietress of the inn in Yonville-l'Abbaye. Hippolyte Tautain is the hostler at her establishment.

Heloise Bovary (ĕ·lō·ēz′ bô·vȧ·rē′), Charles Bovary's first wife, a woman much older than he, who had deceived the Bovarys as to the amount of property she owned. Her death following a severe hemorrhage frees Charles from his nagging, domineering wife, and soon afterward he marries young Emma Rouault.

The Story

Charles Bovary was a student of medicine who married for his own advancement a woman much older than he. She made his life miserable with her nagging and groundless suspicions. One day Charles was called to the bedside of Monsieur Rouault, who had a broken leg, and there he met the farmer's daughter, Emma, a beautiful but restless girl whose early education in a French convent had given her an overwhelming desire for broader experience. Charles found his patient an excellent excuse to see Emma, whose charm and grace had captivated the young doctor. His whining wife, Héloise, however, soon began to suspect the true reason for his visits to the Rouault farm. She heard rumors that in spite of Emma's peasant background, the girl conducted herself like a gentle-woman. Angry and tearful, Héloise made Charles swear that he would not visit the Rouault home again. Then Héloise's fortune was found to be nonexistent. A violent quarrel over her deception and a stormy scene between Héloise and Charles's parents brought on an attack of an old illness. Héloise died quickly and quietly.

Charles felt guilty because he had so few regrets at his wife's death. At old Rouault's invitation, he went once more to the farm and again fell under the influence of Emma's charms. As old Rouault watched Charles fall more deeply in love with his daughter, he decided that the young doctor was dependable and perfectly respectable, and so he forced the young man's hand, telling Charles he could have Emma in marriage and giving the couple his blessing.

During the first weeks of marriage Emma occupied herself with changing their new home and busied herself with every household task she could think of to keep herself from being utterly disillusioned. Emma realized that even though she thought she was in love with Charles, the rapture which should have come with marriage had not arrived. All the romantic books she had read during her early years had led her to expect more from marriage than she received, and the dead calm of her feelings was a bitter disappointment. The intimacy of marriage disgusted her. Instead of a perfumed, handsome lover in velvet and lace, she found herself tied to a dull-witted husband who reeked of medicines and drugs.

As she was about to give up all hope of finding any joy in her new life, a noble patient whom Charles had treated invited them to a ball at his château. At the ball Emma danced with a dozen partners, tasted champagne, and received compliments on her beauty. The contrast between the life of the Bovarys and that of the nobleman was painfully evident. Emma became more and more discontented with Charles. His futile and clumsy efforts to please her only made her despair at his lack of understanding. She sat by her window, dreamed of Paris, moped, and became ill.

Hoping a change would improve her condition, Charles took Emma to Yonville, where he set up a new practice and Emma prepared for the birth of a child.

When her daughter was born, Emma's chief interest in the child was confined to laces and ribbons for its dresses. The child was sent to a wet nurse, where Emma visited her, and where, accidentally, she met Léon Dupuis, a law clerk bored with the town and seeking diversion. Charmed with the youthful mother, he walked home with her in the twilight, and Emma found him sympathetic to her romantic ideas about life. Later Léon visited the Bovarys in company with Homais, the town chemist. Homais held little soirees at the local inn, to which he invited the townsfolk. There Emma's acquaintance with Léon ripened. The townspeople gossiped about the couple, but Charles Bovary was not astute enough to sense the interest Emma took in Léon.

Bored with Yonville and tired of loving in vain, Léon went to Paris in order to complete his studies. Brokenhearted, Emma deplored her weakness in not giving herself to Léon, fretted in her boredom, and once more made herself ill.

She had not time to become as melancholy as she was before, however, for a stranger, Rodolphe Boulanger, came to town. One day he brought his farm tenant to Charles for bloodletting. Rodolphe, an accomplished lover, saw in Emma a promise of future pleasure. Emma realized when Rodolphe began courting her that if she gave herself to him her surrender would be immoral. Nevertheless, she rationalized her doubts by convincing herself that nothing as romantic and beautiful as love could be sinful.

Deceiving Charles, Emma met Rodolphe, rode over the countryside with him, listened to his urgent avowals of love, and finally succumbed to his persuasive appeals. She felt guilty at first, but later she identified herself with adulterous heroines of fiction and believed that, like them, she had known true romance. Sure of Emma's love, Rodolphe no longer found it necessary to continue his gentle lover's tricks. He no longer bothered to maintain punctuality in his meetings with Emma; and though he continued to see her, she began to suspect that his passion was fading.

Meanwhile Charles became involved in Homais' attempt to cure a boy of a clubfoot with a machine Charles had designed. Both Homais and Charles were convinced that the success of their operation would raise their future standing in the community. After weeks of torment, however, the boy contracted gangrene, and his leg had to be amputated. Homais' reputation was undamaged, for he was by profession a chemist, but Bovary, a doctor, was looked upon with suspicion. His practice began to fall away.

Disgusted with Charles's failure, Emma, in an attempt to hold Rodolphe, scorned her past virtue, spent money recklessly on jewelry and clothes, and plunged her husband deeply in debt. She finally secured Rodolphe's word that he would take her away, but on the very eve of what was to be her escape, she received from him a letter so hypocritically repentant of their sin that she read it with sneers. Then, in horror over the realization that she had lost him, she almost threw herself from the window. She

was saved when Charles called to her. She became gravely ill with brain fever and lay near death for several months.

Her convalescence was slow, but she was finally well enough to go to Rouen to the theater. The tender love scenes behind the footlights made Emma breathless with envy. Once more, she dreamed of romance. In Rouen she met Léon Dupuis again.

This time Léon was determined to possess Emma. He listened to her complaints with sympathy, soothed her, and took her driving. Emma, whose desire for romance still consumed her, yielded herself to Léon with regret that she had not done so before.

Charles Bovary grew concerned over his increasing debts. In addition to his own financial worries, his father died, leaving his mother in ignorance about the family estate. Emma used the excuse of procuring a lawyer for her mother-in-law to visit Léon in Rouen, where he had set up a practice. At his suggestion she secured a power of attorney from Charles, a document which left her free to spend his money without his knowledge of her purchases.

Finally, in despair over his debts, the extent of which Emma only partly revealed, Charles took his mother into his confidence and promised to destroy Emma's power of attorney. Deprived of her hold over Charles's finances and unable to repay her debts, Emma threw herself upon Léon's mercy with all disregard for caution. Her corruption was so complete that she had to seek release in pleasure or go out of her mind.

In her growing degradation, Emma began to realize that she had brought her lover down with her. She no longer respected him, and she scorned him when he was unable to give her the money she needed to pay her bills. When her name was posted publicly for a debt of several thousand francs, the bailiff prepared to sell Charles's property to settle her creditors' claims. Charles was out of town when the debt was posted, and Emma, in one final act of self-abasement, appealed to Rodolphe for help. He, too, refused to lend her money.

Knowing that the framework of lies with which she had deceived Charles was about to collapse, Emma Bovary resolved to die a heroine's death and swallowed arsenic bought at Homais' shop. Charles, returning from his trip, arrived too late to save her from a slow, painful death.

Pitiful in his grief, Charles could barely endure the sounds of the hammer as her coffin was nailed shut. Later, feeling that his pain over Emma's death had grown less, he opened her desk, to find there the carefully collected love letters of Léon and Rodolphe. Broken with the knowledge of his wife's infidelity, scourged with debt, and helpless in his disillusionment, Charles died soon after his wife, leaving a legacy of only twelve francs for the support of his orphaned daughter. The Bovary tragedy was complete.

Critical Evaluation

Gustave Flaubert's genius lay in his detailed descriptions. *Madame Bovary*, so true in its characterizations, so vivid in its setting, so convincing in its plot, is ample testimony to the realism of his work. This novel was one of the first of its type to come out of France, and its truth shocked contemporary readers. Condemned on the one hand for picturing the life of a romantic adulteress, Flaubert was acclaimed on the other for the honesty and skill with which he handled his subject. Flaubert does not permit Emma Bovary to escape the tragedy which she brings upon herself. Emma finds diversion from the monotony of her life, but she finds it at the loss of her own self-respect. The truth of Emma's struggle is universal and challenging.

From the time of Charles Baudelaire to the present, many critics have noted, either approvingly or disapprovingly, Flaubert's application of an accomplished and beautifully sustained style to a banal subject matter in *Madame Bovary*. In Flaubert's own time, many readers objected to vulgarity as well as banality in the use of an adulteress as heroine. Baudelaire, however, offered a telling defense against this criticism in his acknowledgment that the logic of the work as a whole provides an indictment of the protagonist's immoral behavior.

Flaubert himself viewed his book as "all cunning and stylistic ruse." His intention was to write "a book about nothing, a book with no exterior attachment . . . a book which would have almost no subject." Flaubert's goals, however, were not as purely aesthetic as they might initially seem in that he did not mean to eschew significance entirely. Rather, he meant that any subject matter, no matter how trivial, could be raised to art by language and pattern. Like Stendhal and Honoré de Balzac, he believed that quotidian matters could be treated seriously, but Flaubert goes further than his predecessors in refusing to provide narrative guidance and interpretation.

Erich Auerbach has observed that Flaubert seems simply to pick scenes which are significant and to endow them with a language that allows them to be interpreted. As a result, many commentators have seen Flaubert as the first modern novelist, even a precursor of the anti-novelist, because of his unwillingness to deal with subject matter in the traditional manner. Certainly, he represents a break with the past to the extent that the novel had been essentially narration. Although he does retain the story, he makes the novel over, in his own words, into "a coloration, a nuance."

At the heart of the novel is a provincial dreamer, a romantic who distorts her environment and ultimately destroys herself with wish fulfillments born of the desperate boredom of her circumscribed situation. Her romantic illusions, however, are not the theme of the novel so much as they are the prime example of the human stupidity which dominates all the characters. Charles is trapped by his subhuman complacency as much as Emma is by her vain imaginings. The surrounding figures, more types than fully developed characters, represent contemporary failures—the irresponsible seducer, the usurer, the inadequate priest, the town rationalist. Each is isolated from the others by his own obsession or deficiency, and all contribute to the overwhelming stagnation which smothers Emma.

Martin Furnell has divided the novel into three parts, each of which is controlled by an action and a dominant image. In the first part, Emma marries Charles, and the dominant image is in her visit to Le Vaubyessard. The marriage is the central fact of her discontent, while the visit ostensibly provides her with a view of the opulent life she so desperately and nonspecifically craves. In the second part of the novel, she is seduced by the conscienceless landowner Rodolphe, and the dominant image is the Comices Agricoles, the elaborate fair with its rustic and vulgar trappings. To Emma, as she is succumbing to Rodolphe, the Comices Agricoles is the very symbol of the limitations of her life. Naturally, she is not capable of consciously making such an interpretation. If she were, her perception might save her. Moreover, what she does not realize is that her affair is as banal as the fair. The third part of the novel describes her seduction by Léon, and the dominant image is the meeting in Rouen Cathedral. The cathedral becomes both church and boudoir, populated not only by images of saints but also by a statue of Diane de Poitiers, a notable adulteress. Once again, Emma reaches out to the grand but is compromised by her own limitations and those of her situation.

The dominant images, which reveal the ambiguity as well as the frustration of her predicament, are reinforced and refined by a series of recurrent minor images. A striking example is the plaster statue of a curé which deteriorates as Emma is progressively debased. The image is extended by a contract of the curé's statue with a statue of Cupid: love and sexuality rise as the holy man disintegrates. Later, the damage to the curé's foot reminds the reader of Charles's peasant boots, which resemble a clubfoot, and of the amputation of Hippolyte's leg as a result of Charles's desperate desire to please Emma. As these complex images recur, they bind together the varieties of stupidity and vanity.

Even more revolutionary than the use of imagery is the point of view, the series of perspectives from which Flaubert narrates the story. He does not assume the stance of the distanced observer but repeatedly shifts the point of view to avail himself of multiple angles of vision. The narrative begins and ends with scenes focused on Charles. Although Flaubert never allows Charles a first-person presentation, the reader sees the beginning of the novel—and, indeed, is introduced to Emma—from Charles's perspective. The reader finally returns to view the debris of the conclusion from the vantage point of this uncomprehending victim.

Most of the novel is seen from Emma's perspective, but there is such a deft playing off of Emma's perceptions against the narrator's control that the reader is able to analyze her perceptions in a broader context rather than simply accept them as fact. The details of Charles's eating habits, for example, become both a sign of his bovinity, to Emma and the reader, and a sign of Emma's discontent, to the reader. Looking out from Emma's or Charles's eyes, the reader is granted insights that are beyond the mental capacity of either character: Flaubert presents what they perceive as a means of representing what they fail to perceive. An advantage of this method is that, while the reader becomes aware of Emma's shortcomings, a sympathy develops: The reader recognizes the oppressiveness of Emma's circumstances, the triviality of her evil, and the relative sensitivity of her kind of stupidity.

Thus, apparently subjective presentations, controlled and ordered by Flaubert's selection of image and detail, reveal what the characters themselves do not understand. Emma's romantic idealism is the prime example. If Flaubert cannot make tragedy out of these ingredients, he can quite powerfully describe, in his miniscule characters, personal and social frustration on a grand scale.

THE MAGIC MOUNTAIN

Type of work: Novel
Author: Thomas Mann (1875–1955)
Type of Plot: Philosophical chronicle
Time of plot: 1907–1914
Locale: Davos, Switzerland
First published: *Der Zauberberg*, 1924 (English translation, 1927)

This novel, concerned with perspectives of history and philosophy in our time, is considered one of the great intellectual achievements of the twentieth century. Modern ideologies and beliefs are represented by characters such as the Italian humanist, the absolutist Jewish Jesuit, a German doctor, a Polish scientist, and the hedonistic Mynheer Peeperkorn.

Principal Characters

Hans Castorp (häns cäs′tōrp), a young German of middle-class and commercial background. He is a sedate, sensible, correct young man, appreciative of good living, but without particular ambition or aspiration. This spiritual lack, Mann suggests, is allied to physical illness. About to enter a shipbuilding firm, Hans goes to make a three-week visit to the International Sanatorium Berghof, where his cousin is a patient. There he learns that he himself has contracted tuberculosis, and he spends seven years at the sanatorium. Spiritually unattached to his own time and place, he resigns himself rather easily to his new role as an inmate of the "magic mountain," where the spiritual conflicts and defects of modern Europe are polarized and where time and place are allied to eternity and infinity. His experience takes on the significance of a spiritual journey. He is exposed to a threadbare version of Western liberalism and rationalism (in the person of Settembrini); to the lure of irrational desire (in the person of Madame Cauchat); to Catholic absolutism and mysticism (in the person of Naphta, whose arguments with Settembrini make up a large part of the second portion of the novel). Finally (in the person of Mynheer Peeperkorn) he feels the attraction of a strong, vital personality that makes the intellectual strife of Settembrini and Naphta sound quite hollow. Lost in a snowstorm that quickly becomes a symbol of his passage through uncharted spiritual regions, Hans attains a vision of an earthly paradise and of blood sacrifice—the two opposed forces life has revealed to him—and he achieves a further revelation of the importance of goodness and love. Ironically, after he returns to the sanatorium, he forgets; the vision has literally led him beyond himself and his capacity. He now dabbles in spiritualism and, in a famous passage, also soothes himself with romantic music that, he feels, contains at its heart the death wish. It is a snatch of this music that Hans has on his lips when, at the conclusion of the novel, he is glimpsed on a battlefield of World War I.

Ludovico Settembrini (lōō′dō·fē′kō sĕ′tĕm·brē′nē), an Italian humanist, man of letters, apostle of reason, progress, equality, and the brotherhood of man, as well as a fiery Italian nationalist. His case is incurable; no longer able to return to the land of action (a fact that has obvious symbolic connotations), he spends his energy in hollow eloquence and in ineffectual writing for the International League for the Organization of Progress.

Leo Naphta (lā′ō näf′tä), an apostate Jew converted to Catholicism, educated by the Jesuits, brilliant in his defense of the immaterial, the spiritual, the authoritarian, the medieval. He gets the better of Settembrini in his many arguments with the Italian, but it becomes clear that Naphta's rigidity is essentially a form of death. Toward the end of the novel, having goaded Settembrini into a duel, Naphta turns his gun on himself.

Clavdia Chauchat (kläf′dē·ä kō·shä′), a Russian, married but refusing to carry a ring on her finger, wandering about Europe from sanatorium to sanatorium. Her manners are in many ways the antithesis of what Hans has learned to accept as ladylike; but that very difference seems to attract him once he has begun to lose his ties with Hamburg, and on a carnival night they consummate the passion she has aroused in him. She leaves the sanatorium for a time but returns in the company of Mynheer Peeperkorn.

Mynheer Peeperkorn (mēn′hâr pā′pėr-kōrn), an enormously wealthy, burly ex-planter. He is inarticulate (thus enforcing the difference between him, on the one hand, and Settembrini and Naphta, on the other), but exudes a strength of personality that engages the respect of Hans, who allies himself with the Dutchman. But Peeperkorn, feeling the approach of impotence, kills himself (another facet of nineteenth century individualism gone).

Joachim Ziemssen (yō′äkh·ĭm zēm′sĕn), Hans's cousin, soldierly, courteous, brave. A foil to Hans, he refuses to yield to the magic of the mountain, keeps track of time, anxious to return to the flatland so that he can pursue his career as a soldier. Though in love with an inmate, Marusja, he, unlike Castorp, refuses to yield to his passion. Finally he insists on leaving, though not fully cured, is gloriously happy for a while, but returns to the sanatorium to die.

Marusja (mä·roos′yä), a pretty young Russian girl, silently adored by Joachim Ziemssen.

Hofrat Behrens (hōk′rät bâ′rĕns), the chief medical officer at the sanatorium. His wife had died there some years before, and he stayed on when he found himself tainted with the disease. He is a mixture of melancholy and forced jocularity.

Dr. Krokowski (krō·kŏf′skē), a foil to Behrens. If Behrens represents the medical point of view, Krokowski represents the psychoanalytical.

Frau Stöhr (frou stœr), a middle-aged woman who irks Castorp at the dinner table by her boring conversation, yet he welcomes her gossip about Clavdia Chauchat.

Miss Robinson, an elderly English spinster and table companion of Castorp.

Fräulein Engelhart (froi′līn ăng′ĕl·härt), a school mistress from Königsberg, another table companion of Castorp.

Dr. Leo Blumenkohl (lā′ō blōō′mĕn-kōl′), a physician from Odessa. The advanced stage of his illness causes him to be the quietest person at Castorp's table.

Herr Albin (hâr äl′bēn), a patient who, unable to take his illness philosophically, creates excitement by demonstrating suicidal intentions.

Tous Les Deux (tōō lä dœ), an old Mexican woman known by this name because her conversation consists of only a few French phrases which always contain the words "tous les deux."

Sister Bertha (bâr′tä), formerly **Alfreda Schildknecht** (äl·frä′dä shĭld′knäsht), a talkative nurse who tries to explain her frustrations to reluctant Hans Castorp and Joachim Ziemssen.

Adriatica von Mylendonk (ä·drē·ä′tĭ·cä fŏn mē′lĕn·dŏnk), the directress of the sanatorium, who surprises Castorp by her businesslike manner.

The Story

Hans Castorp had been advised by his doctor to go to the mountains for a rest. Accordingly, he decided to visit his cousin, Joachim Ziemssen, who was a patient in the International Sanatorium Berghof at Davos-Platz in the mountains of Switzerland. He planned to stay there for three weeks and then return to his home in Hamburg. Hans had just passed his examinations and was now a qualified engineer; he was eager to get started in his career. His cousin was a soldier by profession. His cure at the sanatorium was almost complete. Hans thought Joachim looked robust and well.

At the sanatorium, Hans soon discovered that the ordinary notions of time did not exist. Day followed day almost unchangingly. He met the head of the institution, Dr. Behrens, as well as the other patients, who sat in groups at dinner. There were, for example, two Russian tables, one of which was known as the bad Russian table. A couple who sat at the latter table had the room next to Hans. Through the thin partitions, he could hear them— even in the daytime—chase each other around the room. Hans was rather revolted, because he could hear every detail of their lovemaking.

There was another patient who interested him greatly, a merry Russian woman, supposedly married, named Clavdia Cauchat. Every time she came into the dining room, she would bang the door, an act which annoyed Hans a great deal. Hans also met Settembrini, an Italian, a humanist writer and philosopher. Settembrini introduced him to a Jew, Naphta, who turned out to be a converted Jesuit and a cynical absolutist. Because the two men spent their time in endless discussions, Settem-

brini finally left the sanatorium to take rooms in the village, in the house where Naphta lodged.

From the very first day of his arrival, Hans felt feverish and a bit weak. When his three weeks were almost up, he decided to take a physical examination. The examination proved that he had tuberculosis and so he stayed on as a patient. One day, defying orders, he went out skiing and was caught in a snowstorm. The exposure aggravated his condition.

His interest in Clavdia was heightened when he learned that Dr. Behrens, who liked to dabble in art, had painted her picture. Furthermore, the doctor gave Hans an X-ray plate of Clavdia's skeletal structure. Hans kept the plate on the bureau in his room.

He spent most of his free time with Joachim or with Settembrini and Naphta. The Italian and the Jesuit were given to all sorts of ideas, and Hans became involved in a multitude of philosophical discussions on the duration of time, God, politics, astronomy, and the nature of reality. Joachim, who was rather humorless and unimaginative, did not enjoy those talks; but Hans, since he himself had become a patient at the sanatorium, felt more at home and was not quite so attached to Joachim. Besides, it was Clavdia who interested him.

On the occasion of a carnival, when some of the restrictions of the sanatorium had been lifted, Hans declared his love for Clavdia. She thought him foolish and refused his proposal. The next day she left for Russia. Hans was in despair and became listless. Joachim grew even more impatient with the progress of his cure when the doctor told him that he was not yet well and would have to remain on the mountain for six more months. Wanting to rejoin his regiment, Joachim, in defiance of the doctor's injunctions, left the sanatorium. The doctor told Hans that he could leave too; but Hans knew that the doctor was angry when he said it, and he remained.

Before long Joachim returned, his condition now so serious that his mother was summoned to the sanatorium. He died shortly afterward. Clavdia Cauchat also returned. She had been writing to the doctor, and Hans had heard of her from time to time, but she did not return alone. As a protector, she had found an old Dutchman named Mynheer Peeperkorn, an earthy, hedonistic planter from Java. Hans became very friendly with Peeperkorn, who soon learned that the young engineer was in love with Clavdia. The discovery did not affect their friendship at all, a friendship that lasted until the Dutchman died.

For a time the guests amused themselves with spiritualist seances. A young girl, a new arrival at the sanatorium, claimed that she was able to summon anyone from the dead. Hans took part in one meeting and asked that Joachim be called back from the dead. Dr. Krokowski, the psychologist at the sanatorium, however, was opposed to the seances and broke up the sessions. Then Naphta and Settembrini got into an argument. A duel was arranged between the two dialecticians. When the time came, the Italian said he would fire into the air.

When he did so, Naphta became more furious than ever. Realizing that Settembrini would not shoot at him, Naphta turned the pistol on himself and pulled the trigger. Dying, he fell face downward in the snow.

Hans Castorp had come to the sanatorium for a visit of three weeks. That stay turned out to be more than seven years. During that time he saw many deaths, many changes in the institution. He became an old patient, not just a visitor. The sanatorium became another home in the high, thin air of the mountaintop. For him time, as measured by minutes, or even years, no longer existed. Time belonged to the flat, busy world below.

Then an Austrian archduke was assassinated. Newspapers brought the world suddenly to the International Sanatorium Berghof, with news of war declared and troop movements. Some of the patients remained in neutral Switzerland. Others packed to return home. Hans Castorp said good-bye to Settembrini, who was his best friend among the old patients, and the disillusioned humanist wept at their parting. Hans was going back to Germany to fight. Time, the tragic hour of his generation, had overtaken him at last, and the sanatorium was no longer his refuge. Dodging bullets and bombs in a frontline trench, he disappeared into the smoky mists that hid the future of Europe.

Critical Evaluation

The Magic Mountain, begun in 1912 but written largely after World War I, was actually planned as a novella, inspired by Thomas Mann's own brief stay at the sanatorium at Davos, Switzerland. In fact, his early novella "Tristan" lays much of the groundwork for the later novel. *The Magic Mountain*, however, grew in bulk and complexity to become a veritable mirror of European society in the period leading up to World War I. It lies directly in the tradition of the German *Bildüngsroman*, or novel of development, which goes back to Goethe's Wilhelm Meister novels. In this genre, a relatively unformed character is exposed to manifold aspects of life and various influences, often quite conscious attempts to educate or mold his attitude. In a gradual process, his character achieves form, erroneous goals are cast aside, and the true calling and, more important, the right relationship to life are found. Hans Castorp is just such a character when he arrives from the flatlands for a brief visit at Berghof. Mann emphasizes his bourgeois background and the lack of firm convictions and direction in his life. For Mann, the North German type—Hans is from Hamburg—had always represented the solid, respectable middle-class life. Yet Hans is also something of a quester, curious and adventuresome in the spiritual and intellectual realm. He observes the new world of the sanatorium avidly and becomes involved with the personalities there,

inquiring and holding long conversations. The narrative voice of the novel, as in most of Mann's works, has a certain degree of ironic distance, but the pace of the work is very much tied to Hans's own experience of events and temporal rhythms. The three weeks of his planned visit stretch out to seven years, and the work becomes the record of the growth of his character in a microcosm of European society.

Mann's style had developed out of nineteenth century realism, and he observes and describes reality lovingly and with minute care. Yet his work becomes increasingly symbolic in his major novels, and the structure of these novels becomes increasingly expressive of symbolic values. Thus, the character development of Hans reflects the problems of European thought as a whole, and the various ideas to which he is exposed represent various intellectual and spiritual currents of the epoch. Hans initially falls prey to a fascination with death, a dangerous attraction to the irresponsible freedom of the mountain world, the temptation to turn inward and to fall in love with sickness. He studies the illness whose symptoms he himself soon exhibits. He visits the "moribundi" and has long talks with Behrens and Krokowski, two of the doctors. Here life is seen as a process of decay, and even the intellect and the emotions are reduced to unconscious urges in the new psychology of Freud. Hans crystallizes these ideas in his feverish love for Clavdia Cauchat, who represents the Russian temperament—the urge to lose oneself, to give in to the emotions, to live life for the sake of life. She is contrasted to Settembrini, the Italian intellectual, educator, and humanist. He is an optimist, believing in the perfectability of man by reason, and he opposes the fascination with death that Hans manifests. Settembrini is again contrasted to Naphta, his intellectual opponent, an irrationalist, a Jew turned Jesuit, with a highly Nietzschean viewpoint. He is a pessimist, deriding Settembrini's optimism and ridiculing his arguments as inconsistent. Neither figure is meant to convert Hans; their arguments cancel each other, as does so much else in the novel. Hans finds his own position midway between the various opposing forces. This occurs primarily in the chapter "Snow." If the magic mountain is a timeless realm above the immediate concerns of the world, "Snow" is a hermetic world within that realm. Hans loses his way in a snowstorm, and exhausted, and in danger of death, he has a dream, a vision in which he sees juxtaposed an idyllic world of tropical paradise, peopled by gentle and happy folk, while in a temple there is performed a terrible ritual of human sacrifice. Here the two poles of human life are symbolized, and Hans's response is clear and decisive: Life is inseparably bound up with death, the horrible is real and cannot be denied; but for the sake of goodness and love, man must not grant death dominion over his thoughts.

It is following this chapter that the figure of Mynheer Peeperkorn dominates the novel for a time, a figure of great vitality, simple in his thoughts but of powerful personality, in love with his life force, yet terrified of losing it, who commits suicide finally rather than face decay. He, like the other figures, represents an aspect of contemporary European thought and attitudes. Indeed, his traits, like those of Settembrini and Naphta, were drawn from life, from figures known to Mann. Thus, the novel has something of the autobiographical and represents a stage in Mann's own thought. In the realm he has constructed, all these aspects—*Bildüngsroman*, intellectual autobiography, and symbolic portrait of the prewar era—merge. This is made possible in part by the very foundation of the novel, the mountain. The small community is elevated above the flatlands, in the rarefied Alpine air, remote from the problems of the world and the demands of everyday life. Time is dissolved, the rhythm of the novel moves from sequences of hours to days, weeks, months, and finally years, all rendered indistinguishable by the precise daily routine. In this world outside of time, Hans can grow, can hover between conflicting opinions. Here he has freedom, most essentially in the "Snow" chapter, where even space is obliterated. Yet in contrast to the earlier romantic outlook, this elevated position of freedom in isolation is not seen as a good thing, for though it provides an aesthetic space in which ideal development can occur, it is divorced from life, and life is the value which Hans's development leads him to affirm—life, with all of its horror as well as its beauty. The European world saw itself plunged into World War I, Thomas Mann saw himself jolted out of his apolitical aesthetic stance, and thus it is only fitting that Hans Castorp, too, must come down from the mountain to the world of time and action, even if only to be lost among the havoc of a world at war.

MAHABHARATA

Type of work: Poem
Author: Unknown
Type of plot: Heroic epic
Time of plot: Remote antiquity
Locale: Ancient India
First transcribed: Fifth century B.C.(?)

This tremendous poetic effort is one of two national epics of the Hindu people, the second being the Ramayana. *It is both a history of prehistoric times and a compendium of materials that throws light on the religious, social, political, ethical, and moral ideals and practices of an old and memorable people.*

Principal Characters

Yudhishthira, Bhima, Arjuna, Nakula, and **Sahadeva,** King Pandu's five sons, known as the Pandavas. When Yudhishthira, the most capable of the brothers, is named heir apparent, their cousins, the Kauravas, take exception, and the Pandavas are forced into exile. In disguise, Arjuna wins the hand of Princess Draupadi, who becomes the wife of all five. Finally, after many heroic and romantic adventures, the Pandavas and the Kauravas engage in a mighty war of heroes, and Yudhishthira becomes king. Later, weary of earthly pomp, the Pandavas, with Draupadi, renounce the world and set out for the dwelling place of the gods on high.

King Pandu, father of the Pandavas.

Kind Dhritarashtra, the brother of King Pandu and father of the Kauravas.

Draupadi, a princess whose hand is won by Arjuna in a trial of strength. In a mysterious fashion, she becomes the wife of all the Pandavas.

King Drupada, Draupadi's father.

Duryodhana, the unscrupulous leader of the Kauravas and enemy of the Pandavas.

Bhishma, Dhritarashtra's wise uncle and adviser.

Krishna of Dvaraka, the Pandavas' cousin, counselor, and friend.

The Story

Among the descendants of King Bharata (after whose name India was called Bharata-varsha, land of the Bharatas) there were two successors to the throne of Hastinapura. Of these, the elder, Dhritarashtra, was blind and gave over the reins of government to his younger brother Pandu. But Pandu grew weary of his duties and retired to hunt and enjoy himself. Again Dhritarashtra took control, aided by the advice and example of his wise old uncle, Bhishma. Upon Pandu's death, his five sons were put under the care of his younger brother, who had one hundred sons of his own.

At first the king's household was peaceful and free from strife, but gradually it became apparent that Pandu's sons were far more capable of ruling than any of Dhritarashtra's heirs. Of the Pandavas, the name given to the five descendants of Pandu, all were remarkably able, but the oldest, Yudhishthira, was judged most promising and therefore was chosen heir apparent to the throne of the old blind king. To this selection of their cousin as the future king, the king's own sons took violent exception. Accordingly, they persuaded their father to allow the Pandavas to leave the court and live by themselves. As a result of a trap set by the unscrupulous Duryodhana,

leader of the king's sons, the five brothers escaped to the forest with their mother. There they spent some time in rustic exile.

In the meantime King Drupada had announced that the hand of his daughter, Princess Draupadi, would be given to the hero surpassing all others in a feat of strength and skill, and he had invited throngs of noblemen to compete for his daughter's hand. In disguise, the Pandavas set out for King Drupada's court.

More than two weeks were spent in celebrating the approaching nuptials of the princess before the trial of strength which would reveal the man worthy of taking the lovely princess as his wife. The test was to grasp a mighty bow, fit an arrow, bend the bow, and hit a metal target with the arrow. Contestant after contestant failed in the effort to bend the huge bow. Finally Arjuna, third of the sons of Pandu, came forward and performed the feat with little effort to win the hand of the princess. But in curious fashion Princess Draupadi became the wife of all five of the brothers. At this time, also, the Pandavas met their cousin on their mother's side, Krishna of Dvaraka. This renowned Yadava nobleman they accepted as their special counselor and friend, and to him they owed much of their future success and power.

Hoping to avert dissension after his death, King Dhritarashtra decided to divide his kingdom into two parts, giving his hundred sons, the Kauravas, one portion and the Pandavas the other. Thus it came about that Dhritarashtra's sons ruled in Hastinapur and the five sons of Pandu in Indraprastha.

The dying king's attempt to settle affairs of government amicably resulted in peace and prosperity for a brief period. Then the wily Duryodhana, leader of the Kauravas, set another trap for the Pandavas. On this occasion he enticed Yudhishthira, the oldest of the brothers, into a game of skill at dice. When the latter lost, the penalty was that the five brothers were to leave the court and spend the next twelve years in the forest. At the end of that time they were to have their kingdom and holdings once again if they could pass another year in disguise, without having anyone recognize them.

The twelve-year exile was one of many romantic and heroic adventures. All five brothers were active in stirring events; Arjuna, in particular, traveled far and long, visited the sacred stream of the Ganges, was courted by several noble ladies, and finally married Subhadra, sister of Krishna.

When the long time of exile was over, the Pandavas and Kauravas engaged in a war of heroes. Great armies were assembled; mountains of supplies were brought together. Just before the fighting began, Krishna stepped forth and sang the divine song, the *Bhagavad-Gita*, in which he set forth such theological truths as the indestructibility of the soul, the necessity to defend the faith, and other fundamental precepts of the theology of Brahma. By means of this song Arjuna was relieved of his doubts concerning the need to make his trial by battle.

The war lasted for some eighteen consecutive days, each day marked by fierce battles, single combats, and bloody attacks. Death and destruction were everywhere—the battlefields were strewn with broken bodies and ruined weapons and chariots. The outcome was the annihilation of all the pretensions of the Kauravas and their allies to rule over the kingdom. Finally Yudhishthira came to the throne amid great celebrations, the payment of rich tribute, and the ceremonial horse sacrifice.

Later the death of their spiritual and military counselor, Krishna, led the five brothers to realize their weariness with earthly pomp and striving. Accordingly, Yudhishthira gave up his duties as ruler. The five brothers then banded together, clothed themselves as hermits, and set out for Mount Meru, the dwelling place of the gods on high. They were accompanied by their wife Draupadi and a dog that joined them on their journey. As they proceeded, one after the other dropped by the way and perished. At last only Yudhishthira and the faithful dog remained to reach the portals of heaven. But when the dog was refused admission to that holy place, Yudhishthira declined to enter without his canine companion. Then the truth was revealed—the dog was in reality the god of justice himself, sent to test Yudhishthira's constancy.

But Yudhishthira was not content in heaven, for he soon realized that his brothers and Draupadi had been required to descend to the lower regions and there expiate their mortal sins. Lonely and disconsolate, he decided to join them until all could be united in heaven. After he had spent some time in that realm of suffering and torture, the gods took pity on him. Along with his brothers and Draupadi, he was transported back to heaven, where all dwelt in perpetual happiness.

Critical Evaluation

There are six facets of the *Mahabharata* which require closer examination. First is the problem of language. Second is the question of literary form. Third is the matter of structure. Fourth is the debate about interpretation. Fifth is the analysis of the contents. And last is a partial list of analogs.

In regard to the language problem, modern readers usually rely on translations and should know about variations between one English translation and another. These variations are not inaccuracies; rather, they are the result of translators' differing points of view, all of which may lend insight into the work. The serious student may thus consult more than one translation before evaluating the poem.

Second is the question of literary form. The *Mahabharata* is classified as a heroic (or "folk") epic to distinguish it from the literary epic and the mock epic. But in some formal respects, it does not follow the pattern of the Western epic. Whereas the Greek heroic epic contains twenty-four books and the English literary epic has twelve, the *Mahabharata* consists of eighteen books. The number eighteen does not appear to be arbitrary. The Bhagavad-Gita (book 6, chapters 25–42) is a microcosm, divided into eighteen chapters; and the war in which Duryodhana and his forces were defeated lasted eighteen days. Also while most Western heroic epics are nationalistic in tone, the *Mahabharata* is concerned with a story of conflict primarily for high moral purpose, a struggle between Good and Evil. In most other formal respects, it follows traditional epic formulas.

Third is the matter of structure. The *Mahabharata* is not a unified epic poem but a collection of poetry which includes myths, legends, secular as well as religious tales and advice, folk wisdom, and religious poetry, among other things. And there is an appendix, the *Harivamsa*, a genealogy of the god Hari (Vishnu), of whom Krishna was the eighth avatar. As an anthology, this Hindu poem is structurally similar to the Judeo-Christian Bible. Although there is no bible, as such, in Hinduism, there is still a great quantity of sacred literature, including the *Mahabharata* as well as the Vedas, the *Brahmanas*, the Upanishads, the *Puranas*, and the *Ramayana*. To the pious Hindu, the most familiar is the Gita.

Fourth, as regards interpretation, a distinction must be made between literal and figurative readings of the text. The main story is very likely based upon a historical event: a war between two neighboring peoples, the Kurus and the Panchalas, who inhabited the west and east point of the Madhyadesa (the "middle land" between the Ganges and the Jumna) respectively, with the war ending in the overthrow of the Kuru dynasty. But later recensions transformed history into legend and theology. Hence, the *Mahabharata* may be construed both literally and figuratively. For instance, the Gita is literally a dialogue between Arjuna and Krishna. Yet the circumstances and setting— the impending battle, Arjuna's ethical reservations, and the question-answer format—are merely devices to dramatize Krishna's ethical and metaphysical sermon (compare The Sermon on the Mount). So the figurative or allegorical interpretation, which develops the idea of Good striving for supremacy over Evil, sees Arjuna as the individual soul and Krishna as the external Supreme Spirit which resides in each heart. Arjuna's chariot stands for the mortal Body. King Dhritarashtra's blindness represents ignorance, and his hundred sons are the evil tendencies of mankind. The battle, then, becomes a perennial one between the power of Good and the power of Evil. And the warrior who heeds the advice of the Supreme Spirit speaking from within will succeed physically in battle and spiritually in attaining the Highest Good.

Fifth is the analysis of the contents. While the *Mahabharata* is cast in the framework of an epic feud between the Kauravas (Evil) and the Pandavas (Good), this feud occupies only twenty to twenty-five percent of the work. Also included are the theosophic Gita and the Harivamsa. Consequently, approximately seventy percent of the poem is composed of philosophy, poems, and stories, primarily of a legendary or mythological nature. Among the best-known of the legends is the tale of Sakuntala (book 1), whose son Bharata founded the Great Bharata dynasty of Indian kings. Sakuntala's story also appears in a separate poetic drama, *Sakuntala*, by Kalidasa (c. fifth century A.D.). Another popular tale is that of Savitri, whose love for her husband and devotion to her father-in-law triumphed over Yama, the god of death. In both of these legends, women have prominent roles, they are evidence of the high place women held in ancient Indian culture. The *Mahabharata* also provided ethical guidance and in time became an authoritative treatise on dharma (truth, duty, righteousness), inculcating the divine origin of Brahman institutions, the caste system, and the superiority of the priestly caste.

Finally, the Western reader may find it helpful to note analogs between the *Mahabharata* and Western literature in order to compare cultural concepts and assumptions. As noted above, the *Mahabharata* and the Bible share a similar format. The story of Savitri and the story of Ruth have much in common. The polyandry of Princess Draupadi with the Pandavas is reflected in the levirate marriages of the Old Testament. Likewise, the game of dice between Duryodhana and Yudhishthira also occurs in both the Bible (compare the "casting of lots") and Western folklore and literature. Equally common is the identity change or the disguise as manifested in, among other incidents, the discovery that Yudhishthira's faithful dog was in reality the god of justice. Such changes are also seen in Ovid's *Metamorphoses*, in *The Second Shepherd's Play*, in Shakespeare's *As You Like It* and *Twelfth Night*, and in many folktales. And the parallel between King Dhritarashtra and King Lear is quite clear. The richest source of analogs to the *Mahabharata* is found in Greek mythology. The bow-and-arrow feat of strength for the hand of Princess Draupadi is mirrored in the test of Penelope's suitors. The twelve-year exile and wandering of the Pandavas has its parallel in the *Odyssey*, just as the battle between the Pandavas and the Kauravas is echoed in the *Iliad*. And where Mount Meru was the dwelling place of the Hindu gods, Mount Olympus was the Greek counterpart; as Yudhishthira descended into the lower regions, so the Greek Orpheus descended into the underworld. These and other analogs suggest that the Hindu epic and its Western counterparts alike are rooted in archetypes of the collective unconscious.

MAIN STREET

Type of work: Novel
Author: Sinclair Lewis
Type of plot: Social satire
Time of plot: c. 1910–1920
Locale: Small midwestern town
First published: 1920

In this portrait of a typical small midwestern town called Gopher Prairie, Lewis satirizes the smug complacency, narrow-mindedness, hypocrisy, and resistance to change of the small-town mentality. Despite its social criticism, however, Main Street *reflects Lewis' affection for his home town of Sauk Center, Minnesota, upon which Gopher Prairie was based.*

Principal Characters

Carol Kennicott, an idealistic girl eager to reform the world. Interested in sociology and civic improvement, she longs to transform the ugliness of midwestern America into something more beautiful. Having married Dr. Will Kennicott, she moves to his home in Gopher Prairie, Minnesota, a hideous small town indistinguishable from hundreds of similar communities. There she shocks and angers the townspeople by her criticisms and by her attempts to combat the local smugness. To its citizens Gopher Prairie is perfection; they can see no need for change. To her, it is an ugly, gossipy, narrow-minded village, sunk in dullness and self-satisfaction. Her efforts to change the town fail, and she drifts into a mild flirtation with Erik Valborg, a Swedish tailor with artistic yearnings. Frightened by the village gossip, she and Kennicott take a trip to California; but on her return she realizes that she must get away from both her husband and Gopher Prairie. After some argument, she and her small son leave for Washington, where she stays for more than a year. The flight is a failure, for she finds Washington only an agglomeration of the small towns of America. She returns to Gopher Prairie, realizing that it is her home. Her crusade has failed; she can only hope that her children will accomplish what she has been unable to do.

Dr. Will Kennicott, Carol's husband, a successful physician in Gopher Prairie. Though he loves Carol, he is dull and unimaginative, unable to enter her world or to understand her longings. He is the typical self-satisfied citizen of a small town.

Guy Pollock, a lawyer. Though sensitive and intellectual, he is the victim of the "village virus" that has deprived him of all initiative. At first he appears to Carol as the most hopeful person in town, but he disappoints her with his timidity and conventionalism.

Vida Sherwin, a teacher in the high school. Though better educated, she is as satisfied with the Gopher Prairie standards as are the other citizens. She marries Raymond Wutherspoon.

Raymond Wutherspoon, a sales clerk in the Bon Ton Store. A pallid, silly man, he marries Vida Sherwin. He goes to France during World War I and returns as a major.

Erik Valborg, a tailor in Gopher Prairie, the son of a Swedish farmer. Handsome and esthetically inclined, he attracts Carol, and they have a mild flirtation. But gossip drives him from the town; he goes to Minneapolis and is last seen playing small parts in the movies.

Bea Sorenson, a farm girl who comes to Gopher Prairie to find work. She is as much fascinated by the town as Carol is repelled. She becomes the Kennicotts' hired girl and Carol's only real friend. She marries Miles Bjornstam and has a son. She and the little boy both die of typhoid fever.

Miles Bjornstam, the village handy man and radical, one of the few genuine people in Gopher Prairie and one of the few who understand Carol. He marries Bea Sorenson; when she and their child die, he leaves the town.

Mrs. Bogart, the Kennicotts' neighbor. She is the epitome of village narrow-mindedness.

Sam Clark, a hardware dealer and solid citizen.

Percy Bresnahan, born in Gopher Prairie but now a successful automobile manufacturer in Boston. He visits his home for occasional fishing trips and stoutly maintains that it is God's country. Heavy-handed, jocular, and thoroughly standardized, he is the forerunner of George F. Babbitt.

James Blauser, known as "Honest Jim." A professional hustler and a promoter, he is hired to start a campaign for a Greater Gopher Prairie. Not much is accomplished.

Hugh, Will and Carol's first child, on whom she lavishes her attention.

The Story

When Carol Milford was graduated from Blodgett College in Minnesota, she determined to conquer the world. Interested in sociology, and village improvement in particular, she often longed to set out on a crusade of her own to transform dingy prairie towns to thriving, beautiful communities. When she met Will Kennicott, a doctor from Gopher Prairie, and listened to his praise of his hometown, she agreed to marry him. He had convinced her that Gopher Prairie needed her.

Carol was essentially an idealist. On the train, going to her new home, she deplored the rundown condition of the countryside and wondered about the future of the northern Middle West. Will did not listen to her ideas sympathetically. The people were happy, he said. Through town after town they traveled, Carol noting with sinking heart the shapeless mass of hideous buildings, the dirty depots, the flat wastes of prairie surrounding everything, and she knew that Gopher Prairie would be no different from the rest.

Gopher Prairie was exactly like the other towns Carol had seen, except that it was a little larger. The people were as drab as their houses and as flat as their fields. A welcoming committee met the newlyweds at the train. To Carol, all the men were alike in their colorless clothes; overfriendly, overenthusiastic. The Kennicott house was a Victorian horror, but Will said he liked it.

Introduced to the townsfolk at a party held in her honor, Carol heard the men talk of motorcars, train schedules, "furriners," and praise Gopher Prairie as God's own country. The women were interested in gossip, sewing, and cooking, and most of them belonged to the two women's clubs, the Jolly Seventeen and the Thanatopsis Club. At the first meeting of the Jolly Seventeen, Carol incurred the member's resentment when she stated that the duty of a librarian was to get people to read. The town librarian staunchly asserted that her primary trust was to preserve the books.

Carol did many things which were to cause her great unhappiness. She hired a maid and paid her the overgenerous sum of six dollars a week. She gave a party with an Oriental motif. Sometimes she even kicked off a slipper under the table and revealed her arches. The women frowned on her unconventional behavior. Worse, she redecorated the old Kennicott house and got rid of the mildew, the ancient bric-a-brac, and the dark wallpaper. Will protested against her desire to change things.

Carol also joined the Thanatopsis Club, for she hoped to use the club as a means of awakening interest in social reform. The women of Gopher Prairie, however, while professing charitable intentions, had no idea of improving social conditions. When Carol mentioned that something should be done about the poor people of the town, everyone firmly stated that there was no real poverty in Gopher Prairie. Carol also attempted to raise funds for a new city hall, but no one could see that the ugly old building needed to be replaced. The town voted against appropriating the necessary funds.

Will Kennicott bought a summer cottage on Lake Minniemashie. There Carol enjoyed outdoor life and during the summer months almost lost her desire for reform. When September came, however, she hated the thought of returning to Gopher Prairie.

Carol resolved to study her husband. He was well thought of in the town, and she romanticized herself as the wife of a hardworking, courageous country doctor. She fell in love with Will again on the night she watched him perform a bloody but successful operation upon a poor farmer. Carol's praise of her husband, however, had little effect. Will was not the romantic figure she had pictured. He accepted his duties as a necessary chore, and the thought that he had saved the life of a human being did not occur to him. His interest in medicine was identical with his interest in motorcars. Once more, Carol turned her attention to Gopher Prairie.

Carol, trying to interest the Thanatopsis Club in literature and art, finally persuaded the members to put on an amateur theatrical, but enthusiasm soon waned. Carol's choice of a play, Shaw's *Androcles*, was vetoed, and *The Girl from Kankakee* put in its place. Carol considered even that choice too subtle for Gopher Prairie, but at least the town's interest in the theater had been revived.

After three years of marriage, Carol discovered that she was pregnant. Almost immediately, the neighborhood became interested in her condition. When her son was born, she resolved that some day she would send little Hugh away from Gopher Prairie, to Harvard, Yale, or Oxford.

With a new son and the new status of motherhood, Carol found herself more a part of the town, but she devoted nine-tenths of her attention to Hugh and had little time to criticize the town. She wanted a new house, but she and Will could not agree on the type of building. He was satisfied with a square frame house. Carol had visions of a Georgian mansion, with stately columns and wide lawns, or a white cottage like those at Cape Cod.

Then Carol met a tailor in town, an artistic, twenty-five-year-old aesthete with whom she imagined herself in love. She often dropped by his shop to see him, and one day Will warned her that the gossip in town was growing. Ashamed, Carol promised she would not see him again. The tailor left for Minneapolis.

Carol and Will decided to take a trip to California. When they returned three months later, Carol realized that her attempt to escape Gopher Prairie had been unsuccessful. For one thing, Will had gone with her. What she needed now was to get away from her husband. After a long argument with Will, Carol took little Hugh and went off to Washington, where she planned to do war work.

Yet hers was an empty kind of freedom. She found the people in Washington an accumulation of the population of thousands of Gopher Prairies all over the nation. Main Street had merely been transplanted to the larger city. Disheartened by her discovery, Carol had too much pride to return home.

After thirteen months, Will went to get her. He missed her terribly, he said, and begged her to come back. Hugh was overjoyed to see his father, and Carol realized that inevitably she would have to return to Gopher Prairie.

Home once more, Carol found that her furious hatred for Gopher Prairie had burned itself out. She made friends with the clubwomen and promised herself not to be snobbish in the future. She would go on asking questions—she could never stop herself from doing that—but her questions now would be asked with sympathy rather than with sarcasm. For the first time, she felt serene. In Gopher Prairie, she felt at last that she was wanted. Her neighbors had missed her. For the first time, Carol felt that Gopher Prairie was her home.

Critical Evaluation

Sinclair Lewis frequently had difficulty in determining in his own mind whether his works were meant as bitterly comic satires of American life and values or whether they were planned as complex novels centering around the lives of the series of characters he made famous. One of the difficulties of reading Lewis is that these two conflicting sorts of writing are both present in many of his works, and frequently at odds with each other. This is demonstrably true of *Main Street*, which cannot simply be called a satire of life in small-town America. For all the satire of small-town attitudes and values, Lewis is not unequivocal in his attack as a satirist might be expected to be. Actually, he finds quite a lot of value in the best Main Street has to offer, and he seems to see Carol Kennicott's reconciliation with Gopher Prairie at the end of the novel as a triumph more than a failure on her part. Thus, though *Main Street* is, as it has been frequently called, a revolt against the village, it is a revolt marked by the complexity of Lewis' attitude toward Gopher Prairie and toward its real-life counterpart, Sauk Center, Minnesota, where Lewis spent his early years.

Lewis' characters, particularly Will and Carol Kennicott, are another complication in this novel which prevents it from being simply a satire. Unlike the one-dimensional characters typical of satire, the Kennicotts develop into somewhat rounded characters who demand attention and sympathy in their own rights. Carol in particular, as the central figure of the novel, is developed more novelistically than satirically as Lewis traces her development from a very naïve and foolishly idealistic young woman into a more tolerant and understanding human being. Ironically, for the reader to adopt only the critical and satiric portrait of the small town that lies at the surface of *Main Street* would be for him to embrace the same overly simplistic attitudes that characterized Carol at the beginning of the novel, and which she must escape as evidence of her maturity.

During the early part of the century, Americans tended to accept on faith the premise that all that was best in life was epitomized by the small-town environment. Though by no means the first author to attack this premise, Lewis with *Main Street* achieved the widespread popularity which

gave new prominence to this revolt against the small town. Lewis, himself a small-town boy, knew at first hand the discrepancy between the vision of the village as a Utopia and the actuality of its bleak cultural and moral atmosphere. As Lewis makes clear in his prologue, *Main Street* is an analogue for all such towns, and by his treatment of Gopher Prairie, Lewis sought to strike a satiric blow at the very heartland of America. Rather than a Utopia, Lewis discovers in the provincial mentality of the small town a surfeit of hypocrisy, bigotry, ignorance, cruelty, and, perhaps most damning of all, a crippling dullness and conformity which is essentially hostile to any possibility of intellectual or emotional life. Ironically, though, even while ruthlessly exposing these negative qualities of the small town, Lewis finds, particularly in the matter-of-fact courage and determination of Will Kennicott, some of the very qualities which have given the small town its reputation as the strength of America. The fact is, Lewis was himself ambivalent in his attitude toward the village, and this indecisiveness creeps into the novel to mitigate his castigation of middle America.

The action of the novel centers around Carol Kennicott's discovery of the nature of life and society in Gopher Prairie and culminates with her eventual compromise with the town. For Lewis' purposes, Carol is an excellent device that enables him to expose the bleak heart of the midwestern town by contrasting its qualities and values with her own. Young, educated, intelligent, and idealistic, Carol can bring vision to Gopher Prairie. In that role she performs well. It is when she performs as a character in her own right that readers begin to see that Lewis' attitude is more complicated than simply approving Carol's values against those of the town. Carol's idealism is accompanied by a naïveté and intolerance which prevents her from accomplishing the reforms she advocates because she can only hope to change Gopher Prairie by becoming part of it. The polarization she brings about by trying too much too soon makes it improbable that she should ever be able to realize her ambitions for the town unless she learns to accommodate to—though not necessarily to approve of—its values. After running away to Washington only to discover that the values of the city are not too different from those of the village, Carol is in a better position to adopt a more tolerant attitude toward the villagers. As readers see her at the end of the novel, she has made an effort to come to terms with her environment by working to evolve realistic reforms rather than seeking a radical overthrow of entrenched values and institutions. In losing her naïveté, Carol gains in terms of her ability to confront reality and even to change it over a period of time.

Actually, most of Carol's reforms are too superficial to cure what Lewis called the village virus. Her concern is more with manners than values, and she would only substitute the slick sophistication of the city for the provincial dullness she finds so intolerable. The perfect foil to her is Will Kennicott, who, while epitomizing all the worst of the town's boorishness, goes about his daily medical practice with a quiet efficiency, determination, and even courage that Lewis clearly admires. Will's presence makes it impossible simply to accept Carol's assessment of the vulgarity of the town as Lewis' final word. It is Gopher Prairie that finally triumphs as Carol reconciles herself to its full reality.

MEASURE FOR MEASURE

Type of work: Drama
Author: William Shakespeare (1564–1616)
Type of plot: Tragicomedy
Time of plot: Sixteenth century
Locale: Vienna
First presented: c. 1603

Written when Shakespeare was also creating his major tragedies, Measure for Measure *has been called the darkest of his dark comedies. The shape of the play is comic, but its substance veers very close to tragedy. Before they are allowed a happy ending, the characters must all face the truth of their own morality and the fact of their personal mortality.*

Principal Characters

Angelo (ăn′jĕ·lō), a Viennese nobleman, the duke's deputy, a man who is cold, arrogant, and unbending in the certainty of his own virtuous life. He refuses to look with sympathy upon the offense of Claudio and stands firm, like Shylock, for justice untempered with mercy. He is shocked to find himself tempted by Isabella, but he dismisses all moral scruples and attempts to seduce her, promising to free her brother if she will yield to him. Once he thinks he has had his will he orders Claudio's execution to take place. Faced with the duke's knowledge of his behavior, he, still in character, asks death as the fitting recompense for his sins; mercy is still no part of his character, although it is that quality, meted out by the duke in accord with the pleas of Isabella and Mariana, which ultimately saves him.

Vincentio (vēn·chĕn′sē·ō), Duke of Vienna, a rather ambiguous figure who acts at times as a force of divine destiny in the lives of his subjects. He has wavered in the enforcement of his state's unjust laws, and, pretending to go on a trip to Poland, he leaves the government in Angelo's hands to try to remedy this laxity as well as to test Angelo's "pale and cloistered virtue." He himself moves quietly to counteract the effects of Angelo's strict law enforcement on Isabella, Claudio, and Mariana.

Isabella (ēz·ə·bĕl′ə), a young noblewoman who emerges from the nunnery where she is a postulant to try to save the life of her condemned brother. Her moral standards, like Angelo's, are absolute; she is appalled to find herself faced with two equally dreadful alternatives: to watch her brother die, knowing that it is in her power to save him, or to surrender herself to Angelo. She cannot entirely comprehend Claudio's passionate desire to live, no matter what the cost. Virtue is, for her, more alive than life itself, and she cannot help feeling a certain sense of justice in his condemnation, although she would save him if she could do so without causing her own damnation. She learns, as Angelo does not, to value mercy, and she is able at the end of the play to join Mariana on her knees to plead for the deputy's life.

Claudio (klô′dĭ·ō), Isabella's brother, condemned to death for getting his fiancée with child. He finds small consolation in the duke's description of death, and he makes a passionate defense of life, describing the horrors of the unknown.

Escalus (ĕs′kə·lŭs), a wise old Viennese counselor, left by the duke as Angelo's adviser. He deals humorously and sympathetically with the rather incoherent testimony of Elbow, the volunteer constable.

Mariana (mä·rē·ä′nȧ), a young woman betrothed to Angelo and legally his wife when he rejected her because of difficulties over her dowry. She agrees, at the duke's request, to take Isabella's place in the garden house where Angelo had arranged to meet her. Claiming him as her husband at the duke's reentry into the city, she asks mercy for his betrayal of Claudio and Isabella.

Lucio (lū′shĭ·o), a dissolute young man who brags of his desertion of his mistress and gives the disguised duke bits of malicious gossip about himself. He is condemned for his boasting and his slander to marry the prostitute he has abandoned.

Mrs. Overdone, a bawd.

Pompey, her servant.

Juliet, Claudio's fiancée.

Elbow, a clownish volunteer constable whose malapropisms make enforcement of the law more than difficult.

Francisca (frăn·sĭsf′kə), a nun of the order Isabella is entering.

Froth, a laconic patron of Mrs. Overdone's establishment.

Provost (prŏv′əst), an officer of the state who pities Claudio and helps the duke save him, thus disobeying Angelo's orders.

Abhorson, the hangman, a man of rather macabre humor.

Barnardine, a long-term prisoner freed by the merciful duke.

Friar Thomas and **Friar Peter,** religious men who aid the duke.

The Story

The growing political and moral corruption of Vienna were a great worry to its kindly, temperate ruler, Duke Vincentio. Knowing that he himself was as much to blame for the troubles as anyone because he had been lax in the enforcement of existing laws, the duke tried to devise a scheme whereby the old discipline of civic authority could be successfully revived.

Fearing that reforms instituted by himself might seem too harsh for his people to accept without protest, he decided to appoint a deputy governor and to leave the country for a while. Angelo, a respected and intelligent city official, seemed just the man for the job. The duke turned over the affairs of Vienna to Angelo for a time and appointed Escalus, a trustworthy old official, second in command. The duke than pretended to leave for Poland, but actually he disguised himself in the habit of a friar and returned to the city to watch the outcome of Angelo's reforms.

Angelo's first act was to imprison Claudio, a young nobleman who had gotten his betrothed, Juliet, with child. Under an old statute, now revived, Claudio's offense was punishable by death. The young man was paraded through the streets in disgrace and finally sent to prison. At his request, Lucio, a rakish friend, went to the nunnery where Isabella, Claudio's sister, was a young novice about to take her vows. Through his messenger, Claudio asked Isabella to plead with the new governor for his release. At the same time Escalus, who had known Claudio's father well, begged Angelo not to execute the young man. But the new deputy remained firm in carrying out the duties of his office, and Claudio's well-wishers held little hope for their friend's release.

The duke, disguised as a friar, visited Juliet and learned that the punishment of her lover was extremely unfair, even under the ancient statutes. The young couple had been very much in love, had been formally engaged, and would have been married, except for the fact that Juliet's dowry had become a matter of legal dispute. There was no question of seduction in the case at all.

Isabella, going before Angelo to plead her brother's cause, met with little success at first, even though she had been thoroughly coached by the wily Lucio. Nevertheless, the cold heart of Angelo was somewhat touched by Isabella's beauty, and by the time of the second interview he had become so passionately aroused as to forget his reputation for saintly behavior. After telling Isabella frankly that she could obtain her brother's release only by yielding herself to his lustful desires, Angelo threatened Claudio's death otherwise.

Shocked at these words from the deputy, Isabella asserted that she would expose him in public. Angelo, amused, asked who would believe her story. At her wit's end, Isabella rushed to the prison, where she told Claudio of Angelo's disgraceful proposition. When he first heard the deputy's proposal, Claudio was also revolted by the idea, but as images of death continued to terrify him he finally begged Isabella to placate Angelo and give herself to him. Isabella, horrified by her brother's cowardly attitude, lashed out at him with a scornful speech, but was interrupted by the duke in his disguise as a friar. Having overheard much of the conversation, he drew Isabella aside from her brother and confided that it would still be possible for her to save Claudio without shaming herself.

The friar told Isabella that, five years before, Angelo had been betrothed to Mariana, a high-born lady. The marriage had not taken place, however, because Mariana's brother, with her dowry, had been lost at sea. Angelo had consequently broken off his vows and hinted at supposed dishonor in the poor young woman. The friar suggested to Isabella that she plan the requested rendezvous with Angelo in a dark and quiet place and then let Mariana act as her substitute. Angelo would be satisfied, Claudio released, Isabella still chaste, and Mariana provided with the means to force Angelo into marriage.

Everything went as arranged, with Mariana taking Isabella's place at the assignation, but cowardly Angelo, fearing public exposure, broke his promise to release Claudio and ordered the young man's execution. Once again the good friar intervened. He persuaded the provost to hide Claudio and then to announce his death by sending Angelo the head of another prisoner who had died of natural causes.

On the day before the execution a crowd gathered outside the prison and discussed the coming events. One of the group was Lucio, who accosted the disguised duke as he wandered down the street. Very furtively Lucio told the friar that nothing like Claudio's execution would have taken place if the duke had been ruler. Lucio went on confidentially to say that the duke cared as much for the ladies as any other man and also drank in private. In fact, said Lucio, the duke bedded about as much as any man in Vienna. Amused, the friar protested against this gossip, but Lucio angrily asserted that every word was true.

To arouse Isabella so that she would publicly accuse Angelo of wrongdoing, the duke allowed her to believe that Claudio was dead. Then the duke sent letters to the deputy informing him that the royal party would arrive on the following day at the gates of Vienna and would expect a welcoming party there. Also, the command ordered that anyone who had had grievances against the government while the duke was absent should be allowed to make public pronouncement of them at that time and place.

Angelo grew nervous upon receipt of these papers from the duke. The next day, however, he organized a great crowd and a celebration of welcome at the gates of the city. In the middle of the crowd were Isabella and Mariana, heavily veiled. At the proper time the two women stepped forward to denounce Angelo. Isabella called him a traitor and virgin-violator; Mariana claimed that he would not admit her as his wife. The duke, pretending to be angry at these tirades against his deputy, ordered the women to prison and asked that someone apprehend the rascally friar who had often been seen in their company.

Then the duke went to his palace and quickly changed to his disguise as a friar. Appearing before the crowd at the gates, he criticized the government of Vienna severely. Escalus, horrified at the fanatical comments of the friar, ordered his arrest and was seconded by Lucio, who maintained that the friar had told him only the day before that the duke was a drunkard and a frequenter of bawdy houses.

At last, to display his own bravado, Lucio tore away the friar's hood. When the friar stood revealed as Duke Vincentio, the crowd fell back in amazement.

Angelo, realizing that his crimes would now be exposed, asked simply to be put to death without trial. The duke ordered him first to marry Mariana. After telling Mariana that Angelo's goods, legally hers, would secure her a better husband, the duke was surprised when she entreated for Angelo's pardon. Finally, because Isabella also pleaded for Angelo's freedom, the duke relented. He did, however, send Lucio to prison. Claudio was released and married to Juliet. The duke himself asked Isabella for her hand.

Critical Evaluation

Measure for Measure is one of those troubled plays, like *All's Well That Ends Well* and *Troilus and Cressida*, composed during the same years that Shakespeare was writing his greatest tragedies. Not tragedies, or comedies, or histories, these dark and often bitter dramas have frequently been described as problem plays. Not the least of the problems is that of literary classification, but the term generally refers to plays which examine a thesis. The main concern in this play is a rather grim consideration of the nature of justice and morality in both civic and psychological contexts.

The tone of this and the other problem plays is so gloomy and pessimistic that critics have tended to try to find biographical or historical causes for their bleakness. Some have argued that they reflect a period of personal disillusionment for the playwright, but there is no external evidence to corroborate this supposition. Others have laid the blame on the ghastly decadence of the Jacobean period. However, although other dramatists, such as Marston and Dekker, did write comparable plays around the same time, the historical evidence suggests that the period was, on the contrary, rather optimistic. What is clear is that Shakespeare has created a world as rotten as Denmark but without a tragic figure sufficient to purge and redeem it. The result is a threatened world, supported by comic remedies rather than purified by tragic suffering. Consequently, *Measure for Measure* remains a shadowy, ambiguous, and disquieting world even though it ends with political and personal resolutions.

The immediate source of the play seems to be George Whetstone's *History of Promos and Cassandra* or Whetstone's narrative version of the same story in his *Heptameron of Civil Discourses*. Behind Whetstone are narrative and dramatic versions by Cinthio, from whom Shakespeare derived the plot of *Othello*. However, *Measure for Measure* is such an eclectic amalgamation of items from a wide variety of literary and historical loci that a precise identification of sources is impossible. Indeed, the plot is essentially a conflation of three ancient folk tales, which J. W. Lever calls the Corrupt Magistrate, the Disguised Ruler, and the Substituted Bedmate. Shakespeare integrates these with disparate other materials into a disturbing, indeterminate analysis of justice, morality, and integrity.

The title of the play comes from the biblical text: "With what measure ye mete, it shall be measured to you again." As the play develops and expands on this quotation, we find that we cannot be satisfied with a simple but generous resolution "to do unto others what you would have them do unto you," because the play pursues its text so relentlessly that any easy confidence in poetic justice is undermined. We cannot be sure that good intentions and a clean heart will preserve us. In the final analysis, the action tends to support the admonition to "judge not that ye be not judged," a sentiment which can express either Christian charity or cynical irresponsibility.

Yet, we are in a world in which the civil authorities must judge others. Indeed, that is where the play begins. Vienna, as the duke himself realizes, is in a moral shambles. Bawdry and licentiousness of all sorts are rampant in the city, and the duke accepts responsibility for laxity in enforcing the law. Corruption seethes through the whole society down to the base characters, who are engaged less in a comic subplot than in a series of vulgar exemplifications of a pervasive moral decay. The duke intends to let Angelo, renowned for probity and puritanical stringency, act as vice-regent and, through stern measures, set the state right.

The chilling irony is that Angelo almost immediately falls victim to the sexual license he is supposed to eliminate. To compound the irony, Claudio, whom Angelo condemns for impregnating Juliet, had at least acted out of love with a full intention to marry. Things do not turn out to be as they seemed. Not only is justice not done, it is itself threatened and mocked. Perfect justice yields to temptation while apparent vice is extenuated by circumstances.

Isabella also does not behave as we would expect.

Called upon to intercede for her brother, she is faced with Angelo's harsh proposition. The dilemma is especially nasty since the choice is between *her* honor and *Claudio's* life. For her, neither is a noble alternative and, of course, Claudio is not strong enough to offer himself up for her and turn the play into a tragedy. Unfortunately, when Claudio is reluctant, she behaves petulantly rather than graciously. True, her position is intolerable, but she does spend more time speaking in defense of her virtue than acting virtuously. For all her religious aspirations, which are eventually abandoned, she is not large enough to ennoble her moral context.

The duke is always lurking in the background, watching developments, capable of intervening so as to avoid disaster. Indeed, we are tempted to blame him for being so slow to step in. Of course, if the duke had intervened earlier, or had never withdrawn, we would have had "business as usual" rather than a play which examines the ambiguities of guilt and extenuation, justice and mercy. He allows the characters to act out the complex patterns of moral responsibility which are the heart of the play.

For example, when Angelo, thinking that he is with Isabella, is in fact with Mariana, his act is objectively less evil than he thinks because he is really with the woman to whom he had earlier plighted troth. Yet, in intention, he is more culpable than Claudio, whom he had imprisoned. Such are the intricate complications of behavior in the flawed world of *Measure for Measure*.

The justice that the duke finally administers brings about a comic resolution. Pardons and marriages unravel the complications which varying degrees of evil have occasioned, but no one in the play escapes untainted. The duke, after a period of moral spectatorship which borders on irresponsibility, restores order. Angelo loses his virtue and reputation but gains a wife. Isabella abandons her extreme religious commitment but finds herself more human, and is rewarded with a marriage proposal. Everything works out—justice prevails, tempered with mercy—but we are left with the unsettling suggestion that tendencies toward corruption and excess may be inextricably blended with what is best and most noble in humankind.

MEDEA

Type of work: Drama
Author: Euripides (480–406 B.C.)
Type of plot: Classical tragedy
Time of plot: Remote antiquity
Locale: Corinth
First presented: 431 B.C.

Medea is one of the most fascinating, complex, and dynamic heroine-villainesses in dramatic literature. Few characters have been able to provoke such a range of emotional reactions: sympathy for her pain; wonder at the intensity of her emotions; admiration for her purpose, intellect, and style as a manipulator; fear, when her plan is understood; and horror as it is mercilessly carried out.

Principal Characters

Medea (mĭ·dē′ə), a princess of Colchis and the wife of Jason. Medea had aided Jason in avoiding the traps laid for him by her father, King Aeetes of Colchis, while regaining the Golden Fleece. Fleeing with Jason, she had murdered her own brother to aid in the escape. In Jason's hereditary kingdom of Iolcus, where they first settled but where Pelias, Jason's uncle, had cheated him of his rights, Medea tricked the daughters of Pelias into murdering their father. For this deed Medea, Jason, and their two children were exiled. The play is set in Corinth, where they came after leaving Iolcus and where Jason has put Medea aside in order to marry Glauce, the daughter of Creon, king of Corinth. It is at this point that the action of the play begins. The dramatic development, centering around Medea, is perhaps the finest example in Greek drama of character development. Medea changes from a woman overwhelmed with sorrow at her husband's desertion to a woman dominated by a fury of revenge in which every other feeling, even love for her children, is sacrificed to a desire to hurt Jason. The opening situation of the play is concerned with a sympathetic presentation of the sorrowful plight of Medea. She has given up home and position for Jason and can belong to no other except through him; these facts are conveyed by the nurse before Medea appears. Medea cries out violently against Jason before she appears and foreshadows the destruction of the children. Yet when she appears she is proud but courteous and self-possessed. She expresses her ills as those of all women, but greater, and she asks the Chorus not to betray her if she finds the means of vengeance. They promise secrecy. Creon appears to pronounce a sentence of exile on Medea and the children because he is afraid of her power as a sorceress. She is able only to convince him to grant her a one-day respite. When Creon leaves, Medea reveals her more barbaric and violent side in a terrible speech in which she decides to poison Creon and his daughter. At the appearance of Jason, Medea reveals her full fury as a betrayed mistress and becomes less sympathetic. Blinded by jealousy, she exhibits passion unchecked and untamed. Aegeus, king of Athens, suddenly appears and promises refuge to Medea if she can make her way to his city alone. Assured of a place of refuge, she calls Jason to her and, feigning sweetness and repentance, forgives him, asking only that he obtain a pardon for the children through the princess, his wife. She then gives them a poisoned robe and a golden crown to present to the princess and they leave. When the children return, the struggle between Medea's love for them and her passion for revenge reaches a height in a speech in which the latter triumphs. A messenger enters with news of the death of the princess and Creon, and Medea enters the house. Immediately the screams of the children are heard. Jason enters and Medea appears above the house, in a chariot supplied by her grandfather Helios, god of the sun, with the bodies of her children. She has destroyed the house of Jason and her revenge is complete.

Jason (jā′sən), king of Iolcus, the incarnation of a moderation and wisdom that is negative, not rooted in emotion. He is presented first as the faithless husband and is unreservedly condemned by the Chorus and servants. He loves neither Medea nor Creon's daughter. His only passion is his love for his children, which arouses some sympathy for him.

The Two Children of Medea and Jason. Silent except for the offstage screams as they are murdered, they are central to the plot as Medea's only successful means of revenge against Jason.

Creon (krē′ŏn), king of Corinth. His sentence of exile expresses the fear of Medea's power as a sorceress.

Aegeus (ē′jōōs, ē′jĭ·əs), king of Athens, who offers Medea a place of refuge. His appearance is a coincidence, but it provides a glimpse of Medea as she was before the disaster, a princess renowned for wisdom. The scene also emphasizes the child-motive: Aegeus had gone to Delphi because he is childless and thus he is already in the position in which Jason is left at the end of the play.

A Nurse, Medea's devoted servant. Desperately anxious, she identifies herself completely with the cause of her mistress. She speaks the prologue.

A Chorus of Corinthian Women. Sympathetic to the suffering of Medea, they swear secrecy to her revenge, though realizing the horror of the means.

The Tutor to Medea's Children. He is a good and faithful slave. He clearly condemns Jason's conduct.

A Messenger, who brings the news of the death of Creon and his daughter.

The Story

When Medea discovered that Jason had deserted her and married Glauce, the daughter of Creon, she vowed a terrible vengeance. Her nurse, although she loved Medea, recognized that a frightful threat now hung over Corinth, for she knew that Medea would not let the insult pass without some dreadful revenge. She feared especially for Medea's two sons, since the sorceress included her children in the hatred which she now felt for their father.

Her resentment increased still further when Creon, hearing of her vow, ordered her and her children to be banished from Corinth. Slyly, with a plan already in mind, Medea persuaded him to allow her just one day longer to prepare herself and her children for the journey. She had already decided the nature of her revenge; the one problem that remained was a place of refuge afterward. Then Aegeus, King of Athens and a long-time friend of Medea, appeared in Corinth on his way home from a journey. Sympathetic with her because of Jason's brutal desertion, he offered her a place of refuge from her enemies in his own kingdom. In this manner Medea assured herself of a refuge, even after Aegeus should learn of the deeds she intended to commit in Corinth.

When the Corinthian women came to visit her, Medea told them of her plan, but only after swearing them to absolute secrecy. At first she had considered killing Jason, his princess, and Creon, and then fleeing with her children. But after she had considered, she felt that revenge would be sweeter should Jason live to suffer long afterward. Nothing could be more painful than to grow old without a lover, without children, and without friends, and so Medea planned to kill the king, his daughter, and her own children.

She called Jason to her and pretended that she forgave him for what he had done, recognizing at last the justice and foresight he had shown in marrying Glauce. She begged his forgiveness for her earlier rage and asked that she be allowed to send her children with gifts for the new bride, as a sign of her repentance. Jason was completely deceived by her supposed change of heart and expressed his pleasure at the belated wisdom she was showing.

Medea drew out a magnificent robe and a fillet of gold, presents of her grandfather, Helios, the sun god, but before she entrusted them to her children she smeared them with a deadly drug. Shortly afterward, a messenger came to Medea and told her to flee. One part of her plan had succeeded. After Jason and the children had left, Glauce had dressed herself in her wonderful robe and walked through the palace. But as the warmth and moisture of her body came in contact with the drug, the fillet and gown clung to her body and seared her flesh. She tried frantically to tear them from her, but the garments only wrapped more tightly around her, and she died in a screaming agony of flames. When Creon rushed in and saw his daughter writhing on the floor, he attempted to lift her, but was himself contaminated by the poison. His death was as agonized as hers had been.

Meanwhile the children had returned to Medea. As she looked at them and felt their arms around her, she was torn between her love for them and her hatred of Jason; between her desire for revenge and the commands of her mother-instinct. But the barbarian part of her nature—Medea being not a Greek, but a barbarian from Colchis—triumphed. After reveling in the messenger's account of the deaths of Creon and his daughter, she entered her house with the children and barred the door. While the Corinthian women stood helplessly outside, they listened to the shrieks of the children as Medea killed them with a sword. Jason appeared, frantically eager to take his children away lest they be killed by Creon's followers for having brought the dreadful gifts. When he learned Medea had killed his children, he was almost insane with grief. As he hammered furiously on the barred doors of the house, Medea suddenly appeared above, holding the bodies of her dead children in a chariot which Helios, the sun god, had sent her. Jason alternately cursed her and pleaded with her for one last sight of his children as Medea taunted him with the loneliness and grief to which he was doomed. She told him that her own sorrow would be great, but it was compensated for by the sweetness of her revenge.

The chariot, drawn by winged dragons, carried her first to the mountain of the goddess Hera. There she buried her children. Then she journeyed to Athens, where she would spend the remainder of her days feeding on the gall and wormwood of her terrible grief and revenge.

Critical Evaluation

Commonly regarded as Euripides' greatest work, *Medea* is a powerful study of an impassioned love turned into furious hatred. As a tragedy this play is completely un-Aristotelian in concept and technique, but it has a nerve-jarring impact. It also reveals the extent to which Euripides diverges from his fellow tragedians, Aeschylus and Sophocles, in his depiction of human pain. With *Medea* there is no comforting philosophy to put the tragic agony at a safe psychological distance. Instead, Euripides tries to make Medea as realistic as possible and shows her fiery lust for vengeance in naked action with nothing to mitigate its effect. We are witnesses to a hideous passion, and we cannot be certain whether Euripides approves of it or condemns it. He simply presents it objectively so that we understand Medea, but he leaves it to us to determine his meaning.

Euripides was probably in his fifties when this play was first produced in 431 B.C., an age when a sensitive man is fully aware of the agony that life can inflict on a person. What struck him most was the universality of suffering. Confronted with pain, every other human reality seemed to dissolve. Medea's consuming hatred, kingship, laws, culture, self-esteem, and even motherly love have become meaningless. In *Medea* Euripides portrays a very important aspect of terrible suffering; namely, the desire of the sufferer to create the identical agony in the person who caused it. The dramatist recognized the crucial link between anguish and hate. Reports of Euripides say that he was a bookish recluse, but it is understandable that a man as vulnerable to human misery as he was should shut himself off from people.

He turned to the old legend of Jason and the Golden Fleece to illustrate his preoccupation. Euripides takes up the story after all Jason's successes have been accomplished with Medea's help. Jason has deserted Medea to marry the Greek princess, Glauce, leaving Medea with two small sons. As the nurse remarks in her opening monologue, Medea is not one to take such a betrayal lightly. Although Medea is prostrate with bitter grief and hoping to die as the play begins, the nurse knows how murderous her mistress really is, and she fears for the safety of Medea's sons. A common technique of Euripides is to use the opening speech or section to explain the background of the action and to suggest the climactic development.

Medea is a barbarian princess and sorceress who is accustomed to having her own way in everything. Furthermore, as a barbarian she is free of the restraints that civilization imposes. Jason is a Greek, subject to law, rationality, and practical calculation. As a result, he seems cold and indifferent, set beside Medea, who is a creature of passion. But this is merely a surface appearance. Eu-ripides exposes the inner layers of their psyches with unflinching honesty in the course of the play.

As a woman of passion, Medea is wholly committed to Jason as the object of her emotional life, whether in love or hate. When she loved Jason she did not hesitate to kill her brother, betray her father and country, or instigate Pelias' murder for Jason's sake. And she is equally amoral in her hatred. The drama consists of the unfolding of her plans for revenge and their ultimate execution. When Medea first appears on stage before a chorus of sympathetic women, she is the image of the wronged woman, and we feel pity for her. At the end of the play, after a bloodbath that takes four lives and leaves Jason in total desolation, we feel only horror.

These murders are as coldly calculated as any in *Macbeth*, and Medea feels no penitence whatever. It is precisely the icy manner in which she goes about the killings that inspires dread. She caters to Creon in order to gain time to kill him and his daughter, Glauce. Medea plans to kill Jason too, but when she sees Aegeus heartsick at being childless, she determines to render Jason childless, wifeless, and friendless. Medea pretends a reconciliation with Jason to slay Creon and Glauce in a loathsome fashion. And then, after hesitating to kill her sons because of temporary softness, she butchers them without mercy. Medea is a practitioner of black magic, a cold-blooded murderess, and a total monster; but under Euripides' spell we understand her.

The passion by which she lives makes her both sub-human and superhuman. When Euripides finally has her escape in a dragon-drawn chariot through the air, we come to realize that Medea is a piece of raw nature—female, barbaric, violent, destructive, inhumanly powerful, and beyond all moral standards. Jason becomes entangled with a force that crushes his dignity and detachment, that tears his successes to tatters. At the end he is in exactly the same position as Medea. Both are bereaved of mate, children, and friends. Both are free to grow old without comfort. And both are utterly empty inside, except that Jason is now filled with the same burning hatred that possessed Medea.

This play operates on several levels. The antagonism between Jason and Medea can be read as the enmity between man and woman, between intelligence and passion, between civilization and barbarism, or between man and nature. In each instance the woman, the passions, the barbarian, the forces of nature—all embodied in Medea—have the power to turn and reduce the masculine elements to nothing. *Medea* is a strong, depressing, fearsome drama in which Euripides presents his vision of life as starkly as possible.

MEDITATIONS

Type of work: Philosophical discourse
Author: Marcus Aurelius Antoninus (121–180)
First published: 1558, composed c. 171–180

The book of Marcus Aurelius Antoninus, emperor of Rome from 161 to 180, has been called *The Thoughts* and *The Reflections*, but most commonly *Meditations*. The true title of the work is unknown. Its history is mysterious, but scholars have never doubted its authenticity. When Marcus Aurelius was fifty years of age, perhaps older, he adopted the habit of composing notes, or memoranda, for his own benefit. From his boyhood, the emperor had been of a philosophic turn of mind, and he chose to write in Greek, the language of the philosophers. Although his reflections have inspired and comforted many thousands of readers, they are clearly intended for self-improvement only. The emperor's behavior, well documented by historians, indicates that he lived by those precepts he recorded.

For more than a thousand years, *Meditations* remained an obscure work, going unmentioned by other writers for centuries at a time. Suidas, the ancient lexicographer, cites the book under several words in his dictionary. He names Marcus Aurelius Antoninus as the author, indicating that it deals with the conduct of the emperor's own life, but he gives no title. Other writers of late antiquity mention a work by Marcus Aurelius as well. It was not until the fifteenth century that the work came to be valued as a treasure, and not until 1558 that it was published in Zurich by Xylander, in a Latin version. Before the end of the sixteenth century, Antonio de Guevara, a Spanish bishop, had based a sort of romance on the life and character of Marcus Aurelius, *Archontorologion: Or, The Diall of Princes, Containing the Golden and Famovs Booke of Marcvs Avrelivs, Sometime Emperovr of Rome*. Its purpose was to put before Emperor Charles V the model of antiquity's wisest and most virtuous prince.

Though nothing of the manuscript's early history is known for certain, reasonable inferences can be drawn. The emperor's notes were not abstract speculation. They were his philosophical response to the burdens he bore as ruler of a great state, and especially as commander in chief of armies fighting constant, protracted, and inconclusive wars on several frontiers. Since he was recording his most personal views in the form of self-admonition, it is improbable that he dictated to an amanuensis. Therefore, when the emperor died of the plague or some other contagious malady while campaigning along the upper Danube, it is likely that he left behind a manuscript in his own hand. The same would be true even if, as some scholars have suggested, the emperor was writing for his

unworthy son and successor, Commodus, rather than for himself. Some unknown person preserved, and probably copied, the manuscript.

The *Meditations* of Marcus Aurelius comprises twelve books. Whether this division was made by the emperor or by some later editor is not known. The contents are random, except that the writer devotes book 1 to an acknowledgment of the good qualities transmitted to him by grandparents, parents, sister, kinsmen, teachers, friends, and the gods. An inscription at the end of book 1 indicates that it was written among the Quadi at the Granua. An inscription at the end of book 2 indicates that it was written in Carnuntum. If these notes are genuine, the emperor may well have been the one who divided the work into books.

The *Meditations* represents the last great statement of the Stoic philosophy. The thoughts expressed are reminiscent of the *Discourses* and the *Enchiridion* of the first century Stoic philosopher Epictetus. They are practical statements of ethical behavior, undergirded by a deep religious faith. The central premise is that man's fate is chosen by the gods, for the gods can naturally choose better than man. Man's obligation is to respond to what the gods send him in those ways which are closest to nature. That which follows nature is good, that which departs from nature is evil, and the gods have given man the ability to distinguish between the two. Those vicissitudes to which man can find no natural response he must simply bear with dignity. A recurrent theme throughout the *Meditations* is that contentment never comes from the circumstances of man's life; it can come only from within. The Stoicism of Marcus Aurelius is modified somewhat by the philosophies of Plato and Aristotle, with which the emperor was clearly familiar.

When considered on its literary merits alone, the *Meditations* suffers by comparison to the greatest works of antiquity. The text is repetitious, and the writing style is undistinguished. Likewise, when judged purely as a writer, Aristotle suffers by comparison to Plato, since the former's work survived largely through lecture notes while the latter's dialogues were presumably finished, polished creations. Marcus Aurelius was not writing for posterity. He was writing for himself, or perhaps for his son who would be the next emperor. The power of the book lies in the character of its author and the clarity with which it expresses that character. Like all rulers in all times, Marcus Aurelius was surrounded by schemers, backbiters, flatterers, and gossips. The biographer Capitolinus and the historian Dion Cassius recount stories of the infidelities and lewdness of Faustina, the empress. Marcus Aurelius speaks only of his wife's virtue and gentle spirit, and of his deep love for her. In his attitude toward his son, the emperor could perhaps be faulted for an excess of high-mindedness, since Commodus proved himself lacking in his father's virtue and capacity.

Of the seduction of fame and the blandishments of flatterers, the emperor writes:

> But perhaps the desire of the thing called fame will torment thee.—See how soon everything is forgotten, and look at the chaos of infinite time on each side of [the present], and the emptiness of applause, and the changeableness and want of judgment in those who pretend to give praise, and the narrowness of the space within which it is circumscribed [and be quiet at last]. For the whole earth is a point, and how small a nook in it is this thy dwelling, and how few are there in it, and what kind of people are they who will praise thee.

A few lines further, he returns to his oft-repeated assertion that all life is change, and the particular circumstances of one's life are important only in regard to one's inner response to them. "Things do not touch the soul, for they are external and remain immovable; but our perturbations come only from the opinion which is within. . . . The universe is transformation: life is opinion."

The Stoicism of Marcus Aurelius posits no afterlife, nor does it suggest that there are any likely rewards on earth for virtuous behavior. Death—obliteration—is repeatedly cited as the fact which gives the lie to every human vanity. "This is the chief thing: Be not perturbed, for all things are according to the nature of the universal; and in a little time thou wilt be nobody and nowhere, like Hadrianus and Augustus." Along with the troubles the gods send to man, for whatever good reasons of their own, they send him the capacity to bear them:

> Do not disturb thyself by thinking of the whole of thy life. Let not thy thoughts at once embrace all the various troubles which thou mayest expect to befall thee: but on every occasion ask thyself, What is there in this which is intolerable and past bearing? for thou wilt be ashamed to confess.

Marcus Aurelius states that one should not hate one's enemies but, rather, should attempt to win them over to reason and the right. Nor should one blame another whose behavior has been base:

> But most of all when thou blamest a man as faithless or ungrateful, turn to thyself. For the fault is manifestly thy own, whether thou didst trust that a man who had such a disposition would keep his promise, or when conferring

thy kindness thou didst not confer it absolutely, nor yet in such a way as to have received from thy very act all the profit.

For Marcus Aurelius, there is a oneness to all things—physical, spiritual, and ethical: "There is one universe made up of all things, and one god who pervades all things." This belief informs life with an ultimate simplicity beneath all of its complexities. The author reduces the multifarious questions of honor, duty, and ethical behavior to this admonition: "Thou wilt give thyself relief, if thou doest every act of thy life as if it were the last." Men seek retreats from the affairs of the world—country houses, seashores, mountains—when they should retire into themselves. "Let thy principles be [such that they] will be sufficient to cleanse the soul completely, and to send thee back free from all discontent with the things to which thou returnest." All things are as they should be, if man can accept them as such. "Everything harmonizes with me which is harmonious to thee, O Universe." This harmony is not difficult to achieve if man will only follow the way of life which is natural and obvious: "Go straight on, following thy own nature and the common nature; and the way of both is one."

The Stoics, a sect founded by the Greek philosopher Zeno of Citium in the fourth century B.C., were waning in influence by the emperor's day. Their philosophy must have seemed especially austere when contrasted with the eternal life promised by the Christian sect, which was, at least in retrospect, clearly in the ascendancy. For example, here is Marcus Aurelius on happiness: "If thou holdest to this, expecting nothing, fearing nothing, but satisfied with thy present activity according to nature . . . thou wilt live happy."

Marcus Aurelius was the last of Rome's "good emperors." He was the embodiment of Plato's philosopher-king. Throughout the Christian era, attempts have been made to associate the *Meditations* with Christian thought. Such efforts are understandable, for the emperor's self-admonitions to virtuous conduct for its own sake, steadfastness, magnanimity, and forbearance are congenital to the mind of the Christian apologist. The weight of evidence, however, indicates otherwise. Marcus Aurelius seems to have known little about the Christians, and what he knew he did not like. At times during his reign, Christians were persecuted, especially by provincial governors. The state of constant warfare, aggravated by widespread pestilence, caused the populace to demand a scapegoat, and the Christians had renounced the ancient gods of Rome. The historical record is unclear, but it seems likely that the emperor—as tolerant as the ruler of a besieged empire could afford to be—acquiesced in these persecutions rather than instigating them. Still, he clearly regarded the Christians as fanatical troublemakers. He should be viewed, then, not as an incipient Christian but as the voice of paganism's last great moral pronouncements.

Marcus Aurelius was an able general, but he was not a military figure of the stature of Julius Caesar. He was a clear and disciplined thinker but not a brilliant one, like Plato or Aristotle. He was a competent writer of prose but not a master stylist, like Cicero. In the final analysis, the author of the *Meditations* was great because he was good.

THE MERCHANT OF VENICE

Type of work: Drama
Author: William Shakespeare (1564–1616)
Type of plot: Tragicomedy
Time of plot: Sixteenth century
Locale: Venice
First presented: c. 1596

In The Merchant of Venice *Shakespeare fuses a number of diverse, even contradictory, dramatic styles, ranging from folktale to romantic comedy to borderline tragedy, to create one of his most popular and moving plays. The encounter between the greedy Jew Shylock and the wise, fine Portia gives the play a grave beauty.*

Principal Characters

Shylock (shī′lŏk), a rich Jewish moneylender. He hates Antonio for often lending money at lower interest than the usurer demands; hence, when Antonio wishes to borrow three thousand ducats to help Bassanio, Shylock prepares a trap. Seemingly in jest, he persuades Antonio to sign a bond stating that, should the loan not be repaid within three months, a pound of flesh from any part of his body will be forfeited to Shylock. Next, Shylock has bad news when he learns that his daughter, Jessica, has eloped with Lorenzo, taking with her much of his money; good news when he learns that Antonio's ships have been lost at sea. Antonio being ruined and the loan due, Shylock brings the case before the duke. He refuses Bassanio's offer of six thousand ducats and demands his pound of flesh. But Portia, Bassanio's wife, disguised as a lawyer, claims that Shylock must have the flesh but can take not a single drop of blood with it. Further, she maintains that Shylock, an alien, has threatened the life of a Venetian; therefore, half of his fortune goes to Antonio, the other half to the state. However, Shylock is allowed to keep half for Jessica and Lorenzo if he will become a Christian. The character of Shylock has become one of the most controversial in Shakespearian drama. Is he a villain or a tragic figure? Does the author intend the audience to regard him as an example of Jewish malevolence or to sympathize with him as a persecuted man?

Portia (pōr′shə), an heiress whose father had stipulated in his will that any suitor must win her by choosing from among three caskets of gold, silver, and lead the one containing her portrait. The Prince of Morocco and the Prince of Aragon choose respectively the gold and the silver casket and find only mocking messages; Bassanio, whom she loves, selects the lead casket and wins her. Learning of Antonio's misfortune, she offers her dowry to buy off Shylock and goes to Venice disguised as a lawyer. When Shylock refuses the money and rejects her plea for mercy, she outwits him by showing that he is entitled to a pound of Antonio's flesh but cannot shed any blood in obtaining it, thus saving Antonio and ruining Shylock.

Antonio (ăn·tō′nĭ·ō), the merchant of Venice. Rich and generous, he wishes to aid his impecunious friend Bassanio to woo Portia. Having no ready money, he borrows three thousand ducats from Shylock with the proviso that if the debt cannot be repaid within three months, Shylock can have a pound of his flesh. His ships are apparently lost at sea, and he is saved from death only by Portia's cleverness. At the end of the play, he learns that some of his ships have returned and that he is not ruined.

Bassanio (bă·sä′nĭ·ō), the friend of Antonio, in need of money in order to woo Portia. To help him, Antonio concludes his almost fatal bargain with Shylock. Bassanio chooses the right casket at Portia's home and thus is able to marry her.

Gratiano (grä·shĭ·ä′nō, grä·tyä′nō), a friend of Bassanio. He marries Nerissa, Portia's waiting woman.

Nerissa (nĕ·rĭs′ə), Portia's clever waiting woman. She marries Gratiano.

Jessica (jĕs·ĭ′kə), the daughter of Shylock. She elopes with Lorenzo, taking with her much of Shylock's money and jewels. Her marriage is a heavy blow to her father.

Lorenzo (lô·rĕn′zō), a Venetian who marries Jessica.

The Prince of Morocco, a tawny Moor, one of Portia's suitors. He chooses the gold casket, in which he finds a skull and some mocking verses.

The Prince of Aragon, another of Portia's wooers. He chooses the silver casket, in which he finds the portrait of a blinking idiot.

Tubal (tū′bəl), a Jew and friend of Shylock.

Launcelot Gobbo (lôn′sə·lŏt gŏb′bō), a clown, Shylock's comic servant. Hating his master, he changes to the service of Bassanio. He acts as a messenger between Jessica and Lorenzo.

Old Gobbo, Launcelot's father, "sand-blind."

The Story

Bassanio, meeting his wealthy friend Antonio, revealed that he had a plan for restoring his fortune, carelessly spent, and for paying the debts he had incurred. In the town of Belmont, not far from Venice, there lived a wealthy young woman named Portia, who was famous for her beauty. If he could secure some money, Bassanio declared, he was sure he could win her as his wife.

Antonio replied that he had no funds at hand with which to supply his friend, as they were all invested in the ships which he had at sea, but he would attempt to borrow some money in Venice.

Portia had many suitors for her hand. According to the strange conditions of her father's will, however, anyone who wished her for his wife had to choose among three caskets of silver, gold, and lead the one which contained a message that she was his. Four of her suitors, seeing that they could not win her except under the conditions of the will, departed. A fifth, a Moor, decided to take his chances. The unfortunate man chose the golden casket, which contained only a skull and a mocking message. For his failure he was compelled to swear never to reveal the casket he had chosen and never to woo another woman.

The Prince of Aragon was the next suitor to try his luck. In his turn he chose the silver casket, only to learn from the note it bore that he was a fool.

True to his promise to Bassanio, Antonio arranged to borrow three thousand ducats from Shylock, a wealthy Jew. Antonio was to have the use of the money for three months. If he should be unable to return the loan at the end of that time, Shylock was to have the right to cut a pound of flesh from any part of Antonio's body. In spite of Bassanio's objections, Antonio insisted on accepting the terms, for he was sure his ships would return a month before the payment would be due. He was confident that he would never fall into the power of the Jew, who hated Antonio because he often lent money to others without charging the interest Shylock demanded.

That night Bassanio planned a feast and a masque. In conspiracy with his friend Lorenzo, he invited Shylock to be his guest. Lorenzo, taking advantage of her father's absence, ran off with the Jew's daughter, Jessica, who did not hesitate to take part of Shylock's fortune with her.

Shylock was cheated not only of his daughter and his ducats but also of his entertainment, for the wind suddenly changed and Bassanio set sail for Belmont.

As the days passed, the Jew began to hear news of mingled good and bad fortune. In Genoa, Jessica and Lorenzo were making lavish use of the money she had taken with her. The miser flinched at the reports of his daughter's extravagance, but for compensation he had the news that Antonio's ships, on which the latter's fortune depended, had been wrecked at sea.

Portia, much taken with Bassanio when he came to woo her, would have had him wait before he tried to pick the right casket. Sure that he would fail as the others had, she hoped to have his company a little while longer. Bassanio, however, was impatient to try his luck. Not deceived by the ornateness of the gold and silver caskets, but philosophizing that true virtue is inward virtue, he chose the lead box. In it was a portrait of Portia. He had chosen correctly.

To seal their engagement, Portia gave Bassanio a ring. She declared he must never part with it, for if he did it would signify the end of their love.

Gratiano, a friend who had accompanied Bassanio to Belmont, spoke up. He was in love with Portia's waiting woman, Nerissa. With Portia's delighted approval, Gratiano planned that both couples should be married at the same time.

Bassanio's joy at his good fortune was soon blighted. Antonio wrote that he was ruined, all his ships having failed to return. The time for payment of the loan being past due, Shylock was demanding his pound of flesh. In closing, Antonio declared that he cleared Bassanio of his debt to him. He wished only to see his friend once more before his death.

Portia declared that the double wedding should take place at once. Then her husband, with her dowry of six thousand ducats, should set out for Venice in an attempt to buy off the Jew.

After Bassanio and Gratiano had gone, Portia declared to Lorenzo and Jessica, who had come to Belmont, that she and Nerissa were going to a nunnery, where they would live in seclusion until their husbands returned. She committed the charge of her house and servants to Jessica and Lorenzo.

Instead of taking the course she had described, however, Portia set about executing other plans. She gave her servant, Balthasar, orders to take a note to her cousin, Doctor Bellario, a famous lawyer of Padue, in order to secure a message and some clothes from him. She explained to Nerissa that they would go to Venice disguised as men.

The Duke of Venice, before whom Antonio's case was tried, was reluctant to exact the penalty which was in Shylock's terms. When his appeals to the Jew's better feelings went unheeded, he could see no course before him except to give the money-lender his due. Bassanio also tried to make Shylock relent by offering him the six thousand ducats, but, like the duke, he met with only a firm refusal.

Portia, dressed as a lawyer, and Nerissa, disguised as her clerk, appeared in the court. Nerissa offered the duke a letter from Doctor Bellario. The doctor explained that he was very ill, but that Balthasar, his young representative, would present his opinion in the dispute.

When Portia appealed to the Jew's mercy, Shylock answered with a demand for the penalty. Portia then declared that the Jew, under the letter of the contract, could not be offered money in exchange for Antonio's release. The only alternative was for the merchant to forfeit his flesh.

Antonio prepared his bosom for the knife, for Shylock was determined to take his portion as close to his enemy's heart as he could cut. Before the operation could begin, however, Portia, examining the contract, declared that it contained no clause stating that Shylock could have any blood with the flesh.

The Jew, realizing that he was defeated, offered at once to accept the six thousand ducats, but Portia declared that he was not entitled to the money he had already refused. She stated also that Shylock, an alien, had threatened the life of a Venetian citizen. For that crime Antonio had the right to seize half of his property and the state the remainder.

Antonio refused that penalty, but it was agreed that one half of Shylock's fortune should go at once to Jessica and Lorenzo. Shylock was to keep the remainder, but it too was to be willed the couple. In addition, Shylock was to undergo conversion. The defeated man agreed to those terms.

Pressed to accept a reward, Portia took only a pair of Antonio's gloves and the ring which she herself had given Bassanio. Nerissa, likewise, managed to secure Gratiano's ring. Then the pair started back for Belmont, to be there when their husbands returned.

Portia and Nerissa arrived home shortly before Bassanio and Gratiano appeared in company with Antonio. Pretending to discover that their husbands' rings were missing, Portia and Nerissa at first accused Bassanio and Gratiano of unfaithfulness. At last, to the surprise of all, they revealed their secret, which was vouched for by a letter from Doctor Bellario. For Jessica and Lorenzo they had the good news of their future inheritance, and for Antonio a letter, secured by chance, announcing that some of his ships had arrived safely in port.

Critical Evaluation

Through the years *The Merchant of Venice* has been one of Shakespeare's most popular and most frequently acted plays. Not only has it an interesting and fast-moving plot, but also it evokes an idyllic, uncorrupted world reminiscent of folktale and romance. From the beginning, the play is bathed in light and music. The insistently improbable plot is complicated only by the evil influence of Shylock, and he is disposed of by the end of act 4. Yet Shakespeare uses this fragile vehicle to make some significant points about justice, mercy, and friendship, three typical topics of conversation during the Renaissance. Although some critics have suggested that the play contains all of the elements of tragedy only to be rescued by a comic resolution, the tone of the whole play creates a benevolent world in which, despite some opposition, we are always sure that things will work out for the best.

The story is based on ancient tales, which could have been drawn from many sources. It is actually two stories—the casket-plot, involving the choice by the suitor and his reward with Portia, and the bond-plot, involving the loan and the attempt to exact a pound of flesh. Shakespeare's genius here lies in the combination of the two. Although they intersect from the start in the character of Bassanio, who occasions Antonio's debt and is a suitor, they fully coalesce when Portia comes to Venice in disguise to make her plea and judgment for Antonio. At that point the bond-plot is unraveled by the casket-heroine and we have only the celebratory conclusion of the fifth act still to enjoy.

The most fascinating character to both audiences and critics has always been Shylock, the outsider, the anomaly in this felicitous world. Controversy rages over just what kind of villain Shylock is and just how villainous Shakespeare intended him to be. The matter has been complicated by a contemporary desire to try to absolve Shakespeare of the common medieval and Renaissance malady of anti-Semitism. Consequently, some commentators on the play have argued that in Shylock Shakespeare takes the stock character of the Jew, like Marlowe's Barabas in *The Jew of Malta*, and fleshes him out with complicating human characteristics. Some have gone so far as to argue that even in villainy he is represented as a victim of the Christian society, the grotesque product of hatred and ostracism. Regardless of Shakespeare's personal views, the fact remains that in his hands Shylock becomes much more than a stock character.

The more significant dramatic question is: just what sort of character is Shylock and what sort of role is he called upon to play? Certainly he is an outsider both in appearance and action, a stranger to the light and gracious world of Venice and Belmont. His language has a stridency and an unabashed materialism which isolate him from the other characters. He has no part in the network of beautiful friendships which unite the rest of the characters in the play. He is not wholly a comic character; despite his often appearing ridiculous, he poses too serious a threat to be dismissed lightly. Nor is he a cold and terrifying villain like Iago or Edmund, or even an engaging villain like Richard III; he is too ineffectual and too grotesque. He is a malevolent force, but he is finally overcome by the more generous world in which he lives. That he is treated so badly by the Christians is the kind of irony that ultimately protects Shakespeare from charges of mindless anti-Semitism. Still, on the level of the romantic plot, he is also the serpent in the garden, deserving summary expulsion and the forced conversion which is, ironically, both a punishment and a charity.

The rest of the major characters have much more in common with each other as sharers in the common civilization of Venice. As they come into conflict with Shylock and form relationships with one another, they act out the ideals and commonplaces of high Renaissance culture. Antonio, in his small but pivotal role, is afflicted with a fashionable melancholy and a gift for friendship. It is a casually generous act of friendship which sets the bond-plot in motion. Bassanio frequently comments on friendship and knows how to accept generosity gracefully. But Bassanio is also a Renaissance lover as well as a model Renaissance friend. He is quite frankly as interested in Portia's money as in her wit and beauty; he unselfconsciously represents a cultural integration of love and gain quite different from Shylock's materialism. And when he chooses the leaden casket, he does so for precisely the right traditional reason—a distrust of appearances, a recognition that the reality does not always correspond. To be sure, his success as suitor is never really in doubt, but is rather danced out like a ballet. Everyone

knows, or ought to know, that lead should be preferred to gaudy gold and silver, and indeed the greatest treasure of all, a portrait of Portia, is inside. In addition, the third suitor is always the successful one in folktale. What the ballet provides is another opportunity for the expression of the culturally correct sentiments.

Portia too is a culture heroine. She is not merely an object of love, but a witty and intelligent woman whose ingenuity resolves the central dilemma. That she too is not what she seems to be in the trial scene is another reminder of the familiar appearance/reality theme. More important, she has the opportunity to discourse on the nature of mercy as opposed to strict justice and to give an object lesson that he who lives by the letter of the law will perish by it.

With Shylock safely, if a bit harshly, out of the way, the last act is an amusing festival of vindication of the cultural values. The characters have had their opportunity to comment on the proper issues—love, friendship, justice, and the disparity between appearance and reality. Now each receives his appropriate reward as the play concludes with marriages, reunions, and the pleasantly gratuitous recovery of Antonio's fortune. There is no more trouble in paradise among the people of grace.

METAMORPHOSES

Type of work: Poetry
Author: Ovid (Publius Ovidius Naso, 43 B.C.–A.D. 17)
First published: c. A.D. 8

Ovid had published two books, the *Ars amatoria* (c. 2 B.C.; *Art of Love*) and *Remedia amoris* (before A.D. 8; *Cure for Love*), which with their erotic content flouted the gravity of Emperor Augustus' moral reformation. The poet appears also to have been privy or accessory to some morally questionable activity on the part of Augustus' granddaughter Julia. It was possibly for either or both of these offenses, and certainly for still another which no historian has been able to identify, that Ovid was exiled in A.D. 8 to Tomis (modern Constanţa), a frontier town on the west coast of the Black Sea. At this time, whether in spiteful resentment over his expulsion or from dissatisfaction with the poem's compositional state, he commanded the destruction of his *Metamorphoses*. If the directive was carried out, at least a single available copy was preserved; thus one of the greatest literary achievements of Roman antiquity remained extant.

It is difficult to believe that Ovid wanted the work destroyed by reason of its imperfection. The faults that can be discerned in it are patently venial and do not impair the fluidity and profundity that perennially ingratiate it to readers. Questionable lines or troublesome cruces may have owed more to the errors of copyists than to Ovid's hand. Questions about contradictions—for example, the continuance of Lycaon's lineage after Lycaon and everyone else except Deucalion and Pyrrha were drowned in the Flood—are not material in the context of myth; and the context of the *Metamorphoses* is myth. It is the mythological history of the world from the Creation to the time of Augustus. It is written in fifteen books, comprising 11,992 lines of dactylic hexameter, the meter of classical epic. Each segment of each book includes an episode of myth, and each mythic episode includes at least one metamorphosis. The music of the metric, the unobtrusive transition from story to story, the ingenious use of rhetorical and syntactical figures, and the resultant compendium of Greek and Roman myth, interlaced with natural and human history, all attest a literary masterwork that a proven poet would be unlikely to choose to destroy as a failure in artistry.

Its uniqueness among epics is variously evident. While it begins with the epic conventions of statement and invocation of divine muse, it does not leap *in medias res*, as epics by standard definition do. Moreover, it does not center its narrative upon a contest of antagonists (like Achilles and Hector in the *Iliad*), a hero (like Odysseus in the *Odyssey*), or a bonded pair in mission (like Aeneas and Achates in Vergil's *Aeneid*). It is closer in texture to the *Aeneid* than to the Greek epics, not only because Vergil and Ovid wrote in Latin but also because the two Roman poets both moved their episodic narratives toward a grand terminus that was the city of Rome itself, a city that was for both poets also an empire and a conceptual efflorescence of human destiny. Where Vergil sees Rome as the culmination of human history, however, Ovid views Rome as the manifestation of ameliorative change.

Ovid is true to his theme of change; and it is with this theme that he differs from all ancient writers of epic except possibly Lucretius (c. 98–55 B.C.), if one accepts as an epic his poeticized scientific treatise *De rerum natura* (c. 60 B.C.; *On the Nature of Things*), Lucretius elucidates change, among other facts of physicality, in his epitome of Epicurus' materialistic theory of atomism. Ovid illustrates Pythagoras' theory of constant change: He assigns to Pythagoras the words *omnia mutantur nihil interit* (everything changes, nothing dies) and adopts the Pythagorean theory of number, by which the earth was proved to be a sphere.

The theme of change is expressed and rhetorically exemplified in the first four lines of the poem. Here Ovid speaks of forms materializing as various bodies, not of bodies changing physical form, because his abstract constant, like Plato's forms, is taken as the insubstantial reality of all concretions. He uses the rhetorical device of chiasmus (symmetrically balanced word order, such as *abba*), to intimate the cyclic nature of change and that of anaphora (repetitively balanced word order, such as *abab*) to intimate the linear continuity of change.

The episodes of the fifteen books are similarly balanced in both symmetrical and repetitive sequences. In the first book, physical chaos becomes order, God creates humankind, and humankind is destroyed and restored; the symmetrical reverse appears in the last book, as Pythagoras teaches that life is destroyed and restored, as a created human (Julius Caesar) becomes a god, and as political disorder becomes order. The first two books contain a notable repetitive sequence in describing the destruction of the earth by the Flood, followed by its restoration, and then the destruction of the earth by the descent of the sun, again followed by the earth's restoration. Ovid incorporates the excesses of change in this sequence, showing an earth that fails from too much water and the same earth failing from not enough water. His echo of the Greek concept of the golden mean reverberates in books 5 and 6, where humans hubristically challenge gods: In their excessive pride the Pierides (challenging the Muses in song), Arachne (challenging Minerva in weaving), and Niobe (challenging Latona in maternity) are all appropriately transformed, the Pierides into magpies, Arachne into a spider, and Niobe into a mountain whose melting snows constitute tears shed for her slain children. The golden mean reverberates as well in book 8, in the figure of Icarus, who is cautioned by his father, Daedalus, not to fly too high or too low on the wings that Daedalus has fashioned of feathers and wax. "Proceed in the middle path" is the father's warning, but Icarus flies too high and is destroyed. The story of Icarus is in thematic balance with the story of Phaëton in book 2: Phaëton, assuming in his pride that he can do what in fact he has not the skill to do, drives the chariot of the sun too low and brings about the above-mentioned dehydration of the earth.

The moral content of the *Metamorphoses*, along with its currents of history and science (or philosophy—the two were not differentiated in classical antiquity) is overshadowed by the sensual character, a carryover from his amatory works, of Ovid's mythography. Indeed, during the Middle Ages dependence upon the text for mythological information had to be justified by a specially contrived moralistic reading: Compilations of *Ovide moralisé* (moralized Ovid) were produced in poetry and prose in the fourteenth and fifteenth centuries in France.

Actually, the moral fabric of Ovid's epic is more integumentary than interstitial. Apart from the kind of allegorical inference that justifies the inclusion of the Song of Songs in the Bible, Ovid's moral underpinnings can be seen in his story of the Four Ages—Golden, Silver, Bronze, and Iron—during which human life moved from golden bliss to iron-hard travail, suffering duress in proportion to human moral failings. Ovid adapted the story of the Five Ages, and indeed much else, from the Greek didactic poet Hesiod (late eighth century B.C.), eliminating the post-Bronze pre-Iron Heroic Age as well as Hesiod's alternative account of the deterioration of human morals, the story of Pandora's box. The story of the Flood is moralistic; likewise, there are many stories of transformation in the context of morality, particularly the series of episodes in books 9 through 11, in which models of righteousness alternate with examples of immorality. The righteous include Iolaus, Iphis, Ganymede, Hyacinthus, Pygmalion, and Atalanta. Immorality is exemplified by Byblis, seeker of incestuous relations with her brother the murderous Cerastae; horned women, transformed into bulls; the profane Propoetides, who became the first prostitutes and were changed into stone; Myrrha, who seduced her father; Orpheus, who loses his wife, Eurydice, through his possessiveness and is slain by Bacchantes in punishment for his subsequent misogyny; and Midas, the prototype of material greed.

The morally oriented metamorphoses are not consistently matters of reward and punishment. Some are retributive, particularly those by which the wrongdoer is translated into her or his excess: Lycaon becomes his rapacity in the body of a wolf; Ascalaphus becomes a screech owl, the embodiment of his inability to maintain discreet silence; the Sibyl, avid for long years of life, becomes those years as her body and all but her voice disintegrate in time. Some are remunerative: Hercules, Aeneas, Romulus, Hersilia, and Julius Caesar are all deified for their achievements. Virtue is not, however, regularly rewarded, nor vice regularly punished: Echo, who helps Jupiter to conceal his amours and whose love is not requited by the insufferably vain Narcissus, becomes, like the sibyl, a disembodied voice; Semele, beloved by Jupiter, is, like the great Achilles, reduced to ashes. In the *Metamorphoses*, morality, like time and physicality, is a symptom of change, not a determinant of evaluative quality.

The moral current of Ovid's epic moves generally from an unregenerate humankind punished by the Flood toward a gradually improving humankind whose greatest representatives merit apotheosis. This current is inseparable from the flow of the narrative. Books 1 and 2 move from the Creation and the modes of control exercised by Jupiter and Apollo to the Theban-centered myths of Greece in books 3 and 4 and the exploits of Perseus in books 4 and 5; books 5 and 6 offer their studies in hubris; books 7 through 9 focus on the figures of Jason, Theseus, and Hercules, the last more exemplary than the second, the second more than the first. After the specific examples of moral goodness and badness in books 10 and 11, the epic glides into the Trojan War (book 12) and the exploits of Ulysses (book 13) and Aeneas (book 14) in the Ovidian rehearsal of the *Iliad*, *Odyssey*, and *Aeneid*. Book 15 resolves the direction of the work with its highly moralistic Pythagorean peroration and its conclusion in Roman history from Romulus to Augustus. The accolade to Augustus at the end of the poem clearly had no effect upon the emperor's decision to exile the poet, and this may account in part for Ovid's order to destroy the manuscript.

The Pythagorean essay calls for vegetarianism and a respect for nature in its cycles of change. The invocation of the epic, directed to *di* (gods) as both inclusive of the Muses and productive of changes, is iterated in Pythagoras' intimations that change is divinely ordained; it is a universal force, the foremost representatives of which, throughout the epic, are Jupiter and Apollo.

The temple to Jupiter on Rome's Capitoline Hill was balanced by the temple to Apollo, constructed on the adjacent Palatine Hill by order of Augustus, ostensibly in gratitude for the emperor's naval victory at Actium in 30 B.C. Ovid maintains an effective Jupiter-Apollo equipollence in the *Metamorphoses*. In book 1 the series of episodes from the Creation to the Flood center on Jupiter; the series is followed by the stories of the postdiluvian Python, slain by Apollo, and Daphne, pursued by Apollo; and book 1 concludes with a framing story of Jupiter and

Io. In book 2 the framing story of Apollo's impetuous son Phaëton is followed by the episode in which Jupiter pursues Callisto, which in turn is followed by Apollo's affair with Coronis and the birth of his son Aesculapius, who will reappear in book 15 as the healer of Rome. The Jupiter-Apollo-Jupiter and Apollo-Jupiter-Apollo sequences are the initial means of emphasizing Rome's culminate gods; the second means of emphasis is the constant reference to stones, symbolic of Jupiter, and serpents, symbolic of Apollo. Each of the fifteen books includes specific references to both stones and serpents; in book 15 Aesculapius, the son of Apollo, glides in the body of a serpent over the stone steps of his father's temple to travel to Rome and relieve the city of suffering wrought by plague.

Ovid's beneficent Aesculapius ends his journey to Rome by residing on Tiber Island, which in modern times became, suitably, the site of a hospital. Like Aesculapius' journey from Delphi over the Ionian and Mediterranean seas to the Tiber River and Rome, Ovid's *Metamorphoses*, in winding its way through the ages to modern times, lavished its own beneficence on literary traditions, from his contemporaries to the medieval moralizers to enlightened neo-Augustans such as Alexander Pope. T. S. Eliot's use of Ovid's Sophoclean Teresias theme for the focal configuration of *The Waste Land* (1922) substantiates the claim that, in its epical amalgamation of Greco-Roman lyric and didactic mythography, the *Metamorphoses* required no moralizing apologists any more than it ever needed critical apologists for its artistry.

MIDDLEMARCH: A Study of Provincial Life

Type of Work: Novel
Author: George Eliot (Mary Ann Evans, 1819–1880)
Type of plot: Psychological realism
Time of plot: Nineteenth century
Locale: England
First published: 1871–1872

Middlemarch is the most comprehensive and sweeping of George Eliot's novels and is usually considered her masterpiece. Structuring the book around four major plotlines—the story of Dorothea Brooke, the story of Lydgate's marriage, the history of Mary Garth, and the fall of banker Bulstrode—the author creates a dynamic pattern that encompasses an entire spectrum of life, attitudes, and events in early nineteenth century England.

Principal Characters

Dorothea Brooke (Dodo), the sensitive and well-bred heroine who, in her desire to devote herself to something meaningful, marries an arid clerical scholar, Edward Casaubon. After Casaubon's death Dorothea, against the advice of friends and family, marries Will Ladislaw, an impulsive artist and political thinker. Dorothea also befriends the progressive young doctor of Middlemarch, Tertius Lydgate.

The Rev. Edward Casaubon, the clergyman at Lowick, near Middlemarch. Casaubon is a gloomy, severe, unimaginative, and unsuccessful scholar who soon destroys Dorothea's enthusiasm. He is so jealous of Dorothea's friendship with his cousin, Will Ladislaw, that he adds a codicil to his will depriving Dorothea of his property should she marry his younger relative.

Will Ladislaw, Casaubon's young cousin, whose English heritage is mixed with alien Polish blood. Ladislaw is forceful, imaginative, energetic, and unconventional. An artist and a liberal, he represents an appropriate object of devotion for Dorothea, although many in Middlemarch are shocked by his views. After marrying Dorothea, he becomes a member of Parliament.

Celia Brooke, called **Kitty,** Dorothea's younger sister, a calm and placid young lady. She has none of Dorothea's aspirations, but a great deal of affection. She marries Sir James Chettam, a staid landowner.

Sir James Chettam, the owner of Freshitt Hall. A conservative gentleman, Sir James loves, first, Dorothea, then Celia, whom he happily weds.

Dr. Tertius Lydgate, a young doctor who comes to Middlemarch to establish a new hospital along progressive lines and to pursue scientific research. His noble career is destroyed by his improvident marriage and consequent debts.

Rosamond Vincy Lydgate, the beautiful, spoiled, and selfish daughter of the mayor of Middlemarch. Once married, she insists on living in a style that her husband, Dr. Lydgate, cannot afford.

Mr. Arthur Brooke, of Tipton Grange, the genial, rambling, and ineffectual uncle of Dorothea and Celia. His vague benevolence leads him to run for Parliament and he is soundly beaten.

Fred Vincy, Rosamond's brother, equally spoiled but less selfish. Although Fred gets into debt as a student and rebels against his family's plans to establish him as a respectable vicar, he later reforms, becomes an industrious farmer, and marries Mary Garth.

Mary Garth, the level-headed, competent daughter of a large, old-fashioned family securely tied to the land. She takes care of her aged, ailing relative, Peter Featherstone, before she marries Fred Vincy, her childhood sweetheart.

Mr. Walter Vincy, the mayor of Middlemarch and a prosperous manufacturer. Mr. Vincy, who loves comfort and genial company, is neither wise nor sympathetic in dealing with the problems his children face.

Mrs. Lucy Vincy, his wife, a warm, sentimental woman who spoils her children and has vast pretentions to social gentility. She objects to Fred's relationship with the simple, commonplace Garths.

Mr. Nicholas Bulstrode, the enormously pious, evangelical, wealthy banker of Middlemarch. Bulstrode uses his public morality and his money to control events in Middlemarch; however, the questionable connections and the shady early marriage that built up his fortune are eventually revealed.

Mrs. Harriet Vincy Bulstrode, his wife and the sister of Mayor Vincy. Although she seems to care only for social prestige, she loyally supports her husband after his disgrace.

Peter Featherstone, the wealthy aged owner of Stone Court. He tries to give his fortune to Mary Garth while she is nursing him during his final illness, but she refuses. His capricious will, cutting off all his grasping relatives, brings to Middlemarch strangers who precipitate Bulstrode's disgrace.

The Rev. Camden Farebrother, the vicar of St. Botolph's, a genial and casual clergyman. An expert whist-player and a friend of Lydgate, he is also, unsuccessfully, in love with Mary Garth.

The Rev. Humphrey Cadwallader, of Freshitt and Tipton, another genial clergyman who is particularly fond of fishing.

Mrs. Elinor Cadwallader, his wife, a talkative woman always acquainted with the latest scandal.

Caleb Garth, Mary's father, a stalwart and honest surveyor, land agent, and unsuccessful builder. He pays Fred Vincy's debts.

Susan Garth, his loyal, devoted wife, who educates her children with scholarly care and insight.

Mrs. Selina Plymdale, a Middlemarch gossip, friendly with the Vincys and the Bulstrodes.

Ned Plymdale, her son, a disappointed suitor of Rosamond Vincy.

Borthrop Trumbull, a florid auctioneer and cousin to old Featherstone.

John Raffles, an old reprobate and blackmailer who enters Middlemarch because he has married the mother of Featherstone's unexpected heir and periodically appears to get money. Just before he dies he reveals Bulstrode's sordid past.

Joshua Rigg, an enigmatic man who inherits Featherstone's house and money. He must adopt Featherstone's name as well.

Mr. Tyke, an evangelical clergyman, supported by Bulstrode and Lydgate for the post of chaplain at the new hospital.

Naumann, a German artist and a friend of Will Ladislaw.

Mrs. Jane Waule, the widowed, avaricious sister of Peter Featherstone.

Solomon Featherstone, her wealthy and equally avaricious brother.

Jonah Featherstone, another of Peter's disappointed brothers.

Mrs. Martha Cranch, a poor sister of Peter Featherstone, also neglected in his will.

Tom Cranch, her unintelligent and unenterprising son.

Ben Garth, the active, athletic son of the Garths.

Letty Garth, the Garths' very bright younger daughter.

Alfred Garth, the son for whose engineering career the Garths are saving the money they use to pay Fred Vincy's debts.

Christy Garth, the Garths' oldest son, who becomes a scholar and tutor.

Mrs. Farebrother, the mother of the Reverend Mr. Camden.

Miss Henrietta Noble, her pious, understanding sister.

Miss Winifred Farebrother, Camden's sister, who idolizes him.

The Dowager Lady Chettam, Sir James's stiff and formal mother.

Arthur Chettam, the child of Sir James and Celia.

Sir Godwin Lydgate, of Quallingham in the north of England, Lydgate's distant and distinguished cousin. Rosamond appeals to him for money, but is denied.

Tantripp, Dorothea's faithful and understanding maid.

Mme. Laure, a French actress whom Lydgate once loved.

Dr. Sprague and **Dr. Minchin,** conservative Middlemarch physicians.

Mr. Wrench, at first physician to the Vincys, replaced by the more competent and progressive Lydgate.

Mr. Standish, the local lawyer who represents Peter Featherstone.

Mr. Mawmsey, a Middlemarch grocer.

Mrs. Mawmsey, his wife, a Middlemarch gossip.

Harry Toller, a local brewer.

Miss Sophy Toller, his daughter, who finally marries Ned Plymdale.

Edwin Larcher, a local businessman.

Mrs. Larcher, his wife, a local gossip.

Mr. Bambridge, a horse dealer who swindles Fred Vincy.

Mr. Horrock, his friend.

Mr. Hawley, a local citizen who frequently comments on people and events.

Mr. Chichely, another local citizen.

Dagley, an insolent farmer on Arthur Brooke's land.

Pinkerton, Mr. Brooke's political opponent in the election for Parliament.

The Story

Dorothea Brooke and her younger sister, Celia, were young women of good birth, who lived with their bachelor uncle at Tipton Grange near the town of Middlemarch. So serious was Dorothea's cast of mind that she was reluctant to keep jewelry she had inherited from her dead mother, and she gave all of it to her sister. Upon reconsideration, however, she did keep a ring and bracelet.

At a dinner party where Edward Casaubon, a middle-aged scholar, and Sir James Chettam both vied for her attention, she was much more attracted to the serious-minded Casaubon. Casaubon must have had an inkling that his chances with Dorothea were good; for the next morning, he sought her out. Celia, who did not like his complexion or his moles, escaped to other interests.

That afternoon, Dorothea contemplated the wisdom of the scholar. As she was walking, she encountered Sir James by chance; he was in love with her and mistook her silence for agreement, supposing she might love him in return.

When Casaubon made his proposal of marriage by

letter, Dorothea accepted him at once. Mr. Brooke, her uncle, thought Sir James a much better match; Dorothea's acceptance of Casaubon's proposal merely confirmed his bachelor views that women were difficult to understand. He decided not to interfere in her plans, but Celia felt that the event would be more like a funeral than a marriage and frankly said so.

Casaubon took Dorothea, Celia, and Mr. Brooke to see his home so that Dorothea might order any necessary changes. Dorothea intended to defer to Casaubon's tastes in all things and said she would make no changes in the house. During the visit, Dorothea met Will Ladislaw, Casaubon's second cousin, who did not seem in sympathy with his elderly cousin's marriage plans.

While Dorothea and her new husband were traveling in Italy, Tertius Lydgate, an ambitious yet poor young doctor, was meeting pretty Rosamond Vincy, to whom he was much attracted. Fred Vincy, Rosamond's brother, had indicated that he expected to receive a fine inheritance when his uncle, Mr. Featherstone, died. Vincy, meanwhile, was pressed by a debt he was unable to pay.

Lydgate became involved in petty local politics. When the time came to choose a chaplain for the new hospital of which Lydgate was the head, the young doctor realized that it was to his best interest to vote in accordance with the wishes of Nicholas Bulstrode, an influential banker and founder of the hospital. A clergyman named Tyke received the office.

In Rome, Ladislaw encountered Dorothea and her middle-aged husband. Dorothea had begun to realize too late how pompous and incompatible she found Casaubon. Seeing her unhappiness, Ladislaw first pitied and then fell in love with his cousin's wife. Unwilling to live any longer on Casaubon's charity, Ladislaw announced his intention of returning to England and finding some kind of gainful occupation.

When Fred Vincy's note came due, he tried to sell a horse at a profit, but the animal turned out to be vicious. Caleb Garth, who had signed his note, now stood to lose a hundred and ten pounds because of Fred's inability to raise the money. Fred fell ill, and Lydgate was summoned to attend him. Lydgate used his professional calls to further his suit with Rosamond.

Dorothea and her husband returned from Rome in time to hear of Celia's engagement to Sir James Chettam. Will Ladislaw included a note to Dorothea in a letter he wrote to Casaubon. This attention precipitated a quarrel that was followed by Casaubon's serious illness. Lydgate, who attended him, urged him to give up his studies for the present time. Lydgate confided to Dorothea that Casaubon had a weak heart and must be guarded from all excitement.

Meanwhile, all the relatives of old Mr. Featherstone were waiting impatiently for his death, but he hoped to circumvent their desires by giving his fortune to Mary Garth, daughter of the man who had signed Fred Vincy's

note. When she refused it, he fell into a rage and died soon afterward. When his will was read, it was learned he had left nothing to his relatives; most of his money was to go to Joshua Riggs, who was to take the name of Featherstone, and a part of his fortune was to endow the Featherstone Almshouses for old men.

Plans were made for Rosamond's marriage with Lydgate. Fred Vincy was ordered to prepare himself finally for the ministry, since he was to have no inheritance from his uncle. Mr. Brooke had gone into politics; he now enlisted the help of Ladislaw in publishing a liberal paper. Mr. Casaubon had come to dislike Ladislaw intensely after his cousin had rejected further financial assistance, and he had forbidden Ladislaw to enter his house.

Casaubon died suddenly. A codicil to his will gave Dorothea all of his property as long as she did not marry Ladislaw. This strange provision caused Dorothea's friends and relatives some concern because, if publicly revealed, it would appear that Dorothea and Ladislaw had been indiscreet.

Upon the advice of his Tory friends, Mr. Brooke gave up his liberal newspaper and thus cut off his connection with Ladislaw. Ladislaw realized that Dorothea's family was in some way trying to separate him from Dorothea, but he refused to be disconcerted about the matter. He resolved to stay on in Middlemarch until he was ready to leave. When he heard of the codicil to Casaubon's will, he was more than ever determined to remain so that he could eventually disprove the suspicions of the village concerning him and Dorothea.

Meanwhile, Lydgate and Rosamond had married, and the doctor had gone deeply in debt to furnish his house. When he found that his income did not meet his wife's spendthrift habits, he asked her to help him economize. He and his wife began to quarrel. His practice and popularity decreased.

A disreputable man named Raffles appeared in Middlemarch. Raffles knew that Ladislaw's grandfather had amassed a fortune as a receiver of stolen goods and that Nicholas Bulstrode, the highly respected banker, had once been the confidential clerk of Ladislaw's ancestor. More than that, Bulstrode's first wife had been his employer's widow. Upon money inherited from her, money that should have gone to Ladislaw's mother, Bulstrode had built his own fortune.

Bulstrode already had been blackmailed by Raffles, and he reasoned that the scoundrel would tell Ladislaw the whole story. To forestall trouble, he sent for Ladislaw and offered him an annuity of five hundred pounds and liberal provision in his will. Ladislaw, feeling that his relatives had already tainted his honor, refused; he was unwilling to be associated in any way with the unsavory business. Ladislaw decided to leave Middlemarch and went to London without the assurance that Dorothea loved him.

Lydgate drifted deeper into debt. When he wished to

sell what he could and take cheaper lodgings, Rosamond managed to make him hold on, to keep up the pretense of prosperity a little longer. At the same time, Bulstrode gave up his interest in the new hospital and withdrew his financial support.

Faced at last with the seizure of his goods, Lydgate went to Bulstrode and asked for a loan. The banker advised him to seek aid from Dorothea and abruptly ended the conversation; but when Raffles, in the last stages of alcoholism, returned to Middlemarch and Lydgate was called in to attend him, Bulstrode, afraid the doctor would learn the banker's secret from Raffles' drunken ravings, changed his mind and gave Lydgate a check for a thousand pounds. The loan came in time to save Lydgate's goods and reputation. When Raffles died, Bulstrode felt at peace at last. Nevertheless, it soon became common gossip that Bulstrode had given money to Lydgate and that Lydgate had attended Raffles in his final illness. Bulstrode and Lydgate were publicly accused of malpractice in Raffles' death. Only Dorothea took up Lydgate's defense. The rest of the town was busy with gossip over the affair. Rosamond was anxious to leave Middlemarch to avoid public disgrace. Bulstrode also was anxious to leave town after his secret, which Raffles had told while drunk in a neighboring village, became known; but he became ill,

and his doctors would not permit him to leave his bed.

Sympathetic with Lydgate, Dorothea was determined to give her support to the hospital and to try to convince Rosamond that the only way Lydgate could recover his honor was by remaining in Middlemarch. Unfortunately, she came upon Will Ladislaw, to whom poor Rosamond was pouring out her grief. Dorothea was afraid that Rosamond was involved with Ladislaw, and she left abruptly. Angered at the false position Rosamond had put him in, Ladislaw explained that he had always loved Dorothea, but from a distance. When Dorothea forced herself to return to Lydgate's house on the following morning, Rosamond told her of Ladislaw's declaration. Dorothea realized she was willing to give up Casaubon's fortune for Ladislaw's affection.

Despite the protests of her family and friends, they were married several weeks later and went to London to live. Lydgate and Rosamond lived together with better understanding and prospects of a happier future. Fred Vincy became engaged to Mary Garth, with whom he had long been in love. For a time, Dorothea's family disregarded her, but they were finally reconciled after Dorothea's son was born and Ladislaw was elected to Parliament.

Critical Evaluation

Modestly subtitled "A Study of Provincial Life," George Eliot's *Middlemarch* has long been recognized as a work of great psychological and moral penetration. Indeed, the novel has been compared with Tolstoy's *War and Peace* and Thackeray's *Vanity Fair* for its nearly epic sweep and its perspective of early nineteenth century history. These comparisons, however, are partly faulty. Unlike *War and Peace, Middlemarch* lacks a philosophical bias, a grand *Weltanschauung* that oversees the destinies of nations and generations. Unlike *Vanity Fair*, Eliot's novel is not neatly moralistic. In fact, much of *Middlemarch* is morally ambiguous in the modern sense of the term. Eliot's concept of plot and character derives from psychological rather than philosophical or social necessity. This is another way of saying that *Middlemarch* despite its Victorian trappings of complicated plot and subplot, its slow development of character, its accumulated detail concerning time and place, its social density is—in many other respects—a "modern" novel that disturbs as well as comforts the reader.

At the height of her powers, Eliot published *Middlemarch* in eight books, from December 1871 to December 1872, eight years before her death. She had already achieved a major reputation with *Adam Bede* (1859), *The Mill on the Floss* (1860), and *Silas Marner* (1861). Nevertheless, her most recent fiction, *Felix Holt, Radical* (1866) and *The Spanish Gypsy* (1868), both inferior to

her best writing, had disappointed her public. *Middlemarch,* however, was received with considerable excitement and critical acclaim. Eliot's publisher, Blackwood, was so caught up with the action as he received chapters of her novel by mail that he wrote back to her asking questions about the fates of the characters as though they were real people with real histories. Eliot, in fact, researched the material for her novel scrupulously. Her discussion of the social climate in rural England directly before the passage of the Reform Bill of 1832 is convincingly detailed; she accurately describes the state of medical knowledge during Lydgate's time; and she treats the dress, habits, and speech of Middlemarch impeccably, creating the metaphor of a complete world, a piece of provincial England that is a microcosm of the greater world beyond.

The theme of the novel itself, however, revolves around the slenderest of threads: the mating of "unimportant" people. This theme, which engages the talents of other great writers as well—such as Jane Austen, Thomas Hardy, Henry James, D. H. Lawrence—allows Eliot the scope to examine the whole range of human nature. She is concerned with the mating of lovers, because they are most vulnerable in love, most nearly the victims of their romantic illusions. Each of the three sets of lovers in *Middlemarch*—Dorothea Brooke/Edward Casaubon/Will Ladislaw; Rosamond Vincy/Tertius Lydgate; and Mary

Garth/Fred Vincy—mistakes illusion for reality. Eventually, all come to understand themselves better, whether or not they are completely reconciled with their mates. Each undergoes a sentimental education, a discipline of the spirit that teaches the heart its limitations.

The greater capacity Eliot's characters have for romantic self-deception, the greater their suffering and subsequent tempering of spirit. Mary Garth—plain, witty, honest—is too sensible to arouse the reader's psychological curiosity to the same degree that one is interested in the proud Dorothea, rash Ladislaw, pathetic Casaubon, ambitious Lydgate, or pampered Rosamond. Mary loves simply, directly. Fred, her childhood sweetheart, is basically a good lad who must learn the lessons of thrift and perseverance from his own misfortunes. He "falls" in class, from the status of an idle landowner to that of a decent but socially inferior manager of property. In truth, what he seems to lose in social prominence he more than recovers in the development of his moral character. Moreover, he wins as a mate the industrious Mary, who will strengthen his resolve and make of him an admirable provider like her father Caleb.

Dorothea, on the other hand, more idealistic and noble-hearted than Mary, chooses the worst possible mate as her first husband. Edward Casaubon, thirty years her senior, is a dull pedant, cold, hopelessly ineffectual as a scholar, absurd as a lover. Despite his intellectual pretensions, he is too timid, fussy, and dispirited ever to complete his masterwork, "A Key to All Mythologies." Even the title of his project is an absurdity. He conceals as long as possible his "key" from Dorothea, fearing that she will expose him as a sham. Nevertheless, it is possible that she might have endured the disgrace of her misplaced affection were Casaubon only more tender, reciprocating her own tenderness and self-sacrifice; but Casaubon, despotic to the last, tries to blight her spirit when he is alive and, through his will, to restrict her freedom when he is dead.

Dorothea's second choice of a mate, Will Ladislaw, is very nearly the opposite of Casaubon. A rash, sometimes hypersensitive lover, he is capable of intense affection, above all of self-sacrifice. He is a worthy suitor for Dorothea, who finds greatness in his ardor if not his accomplishments; yet Will, allowing for his greater vitality, is after all a logical successor to Casaubon. Dorothea had favored the elderly scholar because he was unworldly, despised by the common herd. In her imagination, he seemed a saint of intellect. In time, she comes to favor Will because he is also despised by most of the petty-minded bigots of Middlemarch, because he has suffered from injustice, and because he seems to her a saint of integrity. A Victorian St. Theresa, Dorothea is passive, great in aspiration rather than deed. Psychologically, Dorothea requires a great object for her own self-sacrifice and therefore she chooses a destiny that will allow her the fullest measure of heroism.

Quite the opposite, Tertius Lydgate is a calculating, vigorous, and ambitious young physician who attempts to move others to his own iron will. His aggressive energy contrasts with Dorothea's passiveness. Like her, however, he is a victim of romantic illusion. He believes that he can master, through his intelligence and determination, those who possess power. Nevertheless, his choice of a mate, Rosamond Vincy, is a disastrous miscalculation. Rosamond's fragile beauty conceals a petulant, selfish will equal to his own. She dominates him through her own weakness rather than strength of character. Insensitive except to her own needs, she offers no scope for Lydgate's sensitive intelligence. In his frustration, he can only battle with himself. He comes to realize that he is defeated not only in his dreams of domestic happiness but also in his essential judgment of the uses of power.

For Eliot, moral choice does not exist in a vacuum; it requires an encounter with power. To even the least sophisticated dwellers in Middlemarch, power is represented by wealth and status. As the widow Mrs. Casaubon, Dorothea depends upon her personal and inherited fortune for social prestige. When she casts aside her estate under Casaubon's will to marry Ladislaw, she also loses a great measure of status. At the same time, she acquires moral integrity, a superior virtue for Eliot. Similarly, when Mary Garth rejects Mr. Featherstone's dying proposition to seize his wealth before his relatives make a shambles of his will, she chooses morally, justly, and comes to deserve the happiness that she eventually wins. Lydgate, whose moral choices are most nearly ambiguous, returns Bulstrode's bribe to save himself from a social embarrassment, but his guilt runs deeper than mere miscalculation. He has associated himself, first through his choice of Tyke instead of the worthier Farebrother as vicar, with Bulstrode's manipulation of power. Lydgate's moral defeat is partial, for at least he understands the extent of his compromise with integrity. Bulstrode's defeat is total, for he loses both wealth and social standing. As for Middlemarch, that community of souls is a small world, populated with people of good will and bad, mean spirits and fine, and is the collective agent of moral will. After all, it is the town that endures, the final arbiter of moral judgment in a less than perfect world.

A MIDSUMMER NIGHT'S DREAM

Type of work: Drama
Author: William Shakespeare (1564–1616)
Type of plot: Romantic comedy
Time of plot: Remote antiquity
Locale: Athens
First presented: 1595

A Midsummer Night's Dream is probably the most purely romantic of Shakespeare's comedies. Although the magic of Puck explains the lovers' erratic behavior, they are really responding to the essential capriciousness of young love in this pastoral romp that spoofs not only the vagaries of romance but the nature of reality itself.

Principal Characters

Theseus (thē′sē·ŭs), duke of Athens, a wise, temperate ruler, Although he mistrusts the fantasy and imagination of "lunatics, lovers and poets," he can perceive with good humor the love and duty inspiring the abortive dramatic efforts of his subjects, and he tries to teach his bride and queen, Hippolyta, the value of their good intentions.

Hippolyta (hĭ·pŏl′ĭ·tə), Theseus' bride, queen of the Amazons, the maiden warriors whom he has conquered. She is a woman of regal dignity, less willing than her lord to be tolerant of the faults of Peter Quince's play, although she is more ready than he to believe the lovers' description of their night in the forest.

Titania (tĭ·tā′nĭ·ə), the imperious queen of the fairies. She feuds with her husband Oberon over her "little changeling boy," whom the king wants as his page. Enchanted by Oberon's flower, "love in idleness," she becomes enamored of Bottom the Weaver in his ass's head and dotes on him until her husband takes pity on her and frees her from the spell. She is quickly reconciled with him and they join in blessing the marriage of Theseus and Hippolyta, their favorites among mortals.

Oberon (ō′bə·rŏn), king of the fairies, who gleefully plots with Puck to cast a spell on the fairy queen and take away her changeling. Once he has stolen the child, he repents his mischief and frees Titania from her ridiculous dotage. He teases her for her fondness for Theseus and is, in return, forced to confess his own affection for Hippolyta.

Puck (pŭk), the merry, mischievous elf, Robin Goodfellow, of English folk legend and Oberon's servant. He brings about the confusion of the young Athenians on Midsummer Eve as he tries to carry out Oberon's wishes; the king has taken pity on Helena and hopes to turn Demetrius' scorn for her into love. Puck simply enchants the first Athenian he sees, Lysander, and with great amusement watches the confusion which follows, commenting, "Lord, what fools these mortals be!"

Hermia (hĕr′mĭ·ə), a bright, bold young Athenian maiden. She defies her father and flees into the Athenian wood to elope with her beloved Lysander. She shows herself a small spitfire when she finds Demetrius and Lysander, through Puck's machinations, suddenly rivaling each other for Helena's affection rather than hers.

Helena (hĕl′ə·nə), a maiden who mournfully follows Demetrius, spaniel-like, in spite of the scorn with which he repulses her affection. When she suddenly finds both Demetrius and Lysander at her feet, she can only believe that they are teasing her.

Demetrius (də·mē′trĭ·ŭs), a rather fickle Athenian youth. He deserts his first love, Helena, to win the approval of Hermia's father for marriage with her, but he cannot win Hermia herself. His affections are returned, by Oberon's herb, to Helena, and he is wed to her on his duke's marriage day.

Lysander (lī·săn′dər), Hermia's sweetheart, who plans their elopement to escape Theseus' decree that the girl must follow her father's will or enter a nunnery. He brashly argues with Demetrius, first over Hermia, then over Helena, before he is happily wed to his first love.

Nick Bottom, a good-natured craftsman and weaver. He is so enthralled by the prospect of Quince's play, "Pyramus and Thisbe," that he longs to play all the other parts in addition to his assigned role of the hero. He is supremely complacent as Titania's paramour and takes for granted the services of the fairies, who scratch the ass's ears placed on his head by Puck. He marvels at his "most rare vision" after his release from the fairy spell.

Peter Quince, a carpenter, director of the infamous play of "tragical mirth" presented in honor of Theseus' wedding. Completely well-meaning, he illustrates, as he mangles his prologue, the "love and tongue-tied simplicity" of which Theseus speaks.

Snug, a joiner, **Snout,** a tinker, **Flute,** a bellows-maker, and **Starveling,** a tailor, the other craftsmen-actors who portray, respectively, **Lion, Wall, Thisbe,** and **Moonshine.**

Egeus (ē·jē′ŭs), Hermia's father. He is determined that his daughter shall marry Demetrius, not Lysander, whom she loves.

Philostrate (fĭ′lŏs·trāt), Theseus' master of the revels.
Peaseblossom, Cobweb, Moth, and **Mustardseed,** Titania's fairy attendants, who wait on Bottom.

The Story

Theseus, the Duke of Athens, was to be married in four days to Hippolyta, Queen of the Amazons, and he ordered his Master of the Revels to prepare suitable entertainment for the nuptials. But other lovers of ancient Athens were not so happy as their ruler. Hermia, in love with Lysander, was loved also by Demetrius, who had her father's permission to marry her. When she refused his suit, Demetrius took his case to Theseus and demanded that the law be invoked. Theseus upheld the father, which meant that Hermia must marry Demetrius, be placed in a nunnery, or be put to death. Hermia swore that she would enter a convent before she would consent to become Demetrius' bride.

Lysander plotted with Hermia to steal her away from Athens, take her to the home of his aunt, and there marry her. They were to meet the following night in a woods outside the city. Hermia confided the plan to her good friend Helena. Demetrius had formerly been betrothed to Helena, and although he had switched his love to Hermia he was still desperately loved by the scorned Helena. Helena, willing to do anything to gain even a smile from Demetrius, told him of his rival's plan to elope with Hermia.

Unknown to any of the four young people, there were to be others in that same woods on the appointed night, Midsummer Eve. A guild of Athenian laborers was to meet there to practice a play the members hoped to present in honor of Theseus and Hippolyta's wedding. The fairies also held their midnight revels in the woods. Oberon, king of the fairies, desired for his page a little Indian prince, but Oberon's queen, Titania, had the boy. Loving him like a son, she refused to give him up to her husband. In order to force Titania to do his bidding, Oberon ordered his mischievous page, called Puck or Robin Goodfellow, to secure the juice of "love in idleness," a purple flower once hit by Cupid's dart. This juice, when placed in the eyes of anyone sleeping, caused that person to fall in love with the first creature seen on awakening. Oberon planned to drop some of the juice in Titania's eyes and then refuse to lift the charm until she gave him the boy.

While Puck was on his errand, Demetrius and Helena entered the woods. Making himself invisible, Oberon heard Helena plead her love for Demetrius and heard the young man scorn and berate her. They had come to the woods to find the fleeing lovers, Lysander and Hermia. Oberon, pitying Helena, determined to aid her. When Puck returned with the juice, Oberon ordered him to find the Athenian and place some of the juice in his eyes so that he would love the girl who doted on him.

Puck went to do as he was ordered, while Oberon squeezed the juice of the flower into the eyes of Titania as she slept. But Puck, coming upon Lysander and Hermia as they slept in the woods, mistook Lysander's Athenian dress for that of Demetrius and poured the charmed juice into Lysander's eyes. Lysander was awakened by Helena, who had been abandoned deep in the woods by Demetrius. The charm worked perfectly; Lysander fell in love with Helena. That poor girl, thinking that he was mocking her with his ardent protestations of love, begged him to stop his teasing and return to the sleeping Hermia. But Lysander, pursuing Helena, left Hermia alone in the forest. When she awakened she feared that Lysander had been killed, for she believed that he would never have deserted her otherwise.

Titania, in the meantime, awakened to a strange sight. The laborers, practicing for their play, had paused not far from the sleeping fairy queen. Bottom, the comical but stupid weaver who was to play the leading role, became the butt of another of Puck's jokes. The prankster clapped an ass's head over Bottom's own foolish pate and led the poor fool a merry chase until the weaver was at the spot where Titania lay sleeping. Thus when she awakened she looked at Bottom, still wearing the head of an ass. She fell instantly in love with him and ordered the fairies to tend his every want. This turn pleased Oberon mightily. When he learned of the mistake Puck had made in placing the juice in Lysander's eyes, however, he tried to right the wrong by placing love juice also in Demetrius' eyes, and he ordered Puck to have Helena close by when Demetrius awakened. His act made both girls unhappy and forlorn. When Demetrius, who she knew hated her, also began to make love to her, Helena thought that both men were taunting and ridiculing her. And poor Hermia, encountering Lysander, could not understand why he tried to drive her away, all the time protesting that he loved only Helena.

Again Oberon tried to set matters straight. He ordered Puck to lead the two men in circles until weariness forced them to lie down and go to sleep. Then a potion to remove the charm and make the whole affair seem like a dream was to be placed in Lysander's eyes. Afterward he would again love Hermia, and all the young people would be united in proper pairs. Titania, too, was to have the charm removed, for Oberon had taunted her about loving an ass until she had given up the prince to him. Puck obeyed the orders and placed the potion in Lysander's eyes.

The four lovers were awakened by Theseus, Hippolyta, and Hermia's father, who had gone into the woods to watch Theseus' hounds perform. Lysander again loved Hermia and Demetrius still loved Helena, for the love juice remained in his eyes. Hermia's father persisted in his demand that his daughter marry Demetrius, but since that young man no longer wanted her and all four were happy with their partners, he ceased to oppose Lysander's suit. Theseus gave them permission to marry on the day set for his own wedding to Hippolyta.

Titania also awakened and, like the others, thought that she had been dreaming. Puck removed the ass's head from Bottom and that poor bewildered weaver made his way back to Athens, reaching there just in time to save the play from ruin, for he was to play Pyramus, the hero. The Master of the Revels tried to dissuade Theseus from choosing the laborer's play for the wedding night. Theseus, however, was intrigued by a play that was announced as both tedious and brief as well as merry and tragic. So Bottom and his troupe presented *Pyramus and Thisbe*, much to the merriment of all the guests.

After the play all the bridal couples retired to their suites, and Oberon and Titania sang a fairy song over them, promising that they and all their children would be blessed.

Critical Evaluation

Written at the same time as many of Shakespeare's sonnets (1594–1595), *A Midsummer Night's Dream* shares with them the dual concerns of love and poetry. Like the sonnets, too, the play examines these issues from a variety of perspectives, though always with a light touch, in keeping with the festive mood of Midsummer Night (June 23).

Shakespeare's genius delights in variety. *Romeo and Juliet* (1594–1595) treats the tragedy of a pair of star-crossed lovers; here Shakespeare explores the comic possibilities of a similar situation. *A Midsummer Night's Dream* offers not one but five sets of ill-sorted lovers, their very multiplicity a comic device. Theseus has won Hippolyta in battle, wooing her with his sword. For him the four days before their marriage seem endless, but she, less eager to wed, fears that the time will pass all too quickly. Demetrius and Lysander both love Hermia, while Helena, in love with Demetrius, lacks a suitor. The fairy king and queen, Oberon and Titania, have become estranged, and Pyramus and Thisbe of the play-within-the-play are divided by parental animosity. Before the true lovers can be united, Shakespeare will reveal the odd metamorphoses, aptly symbolized by the transformation of Bottom into an ass, that love can work.

For love can, as readily as Puck, set an ass's head on anyone, or like a false light in the darkness waylay the unwary. Before the play ends Demetrius will pursue Hermia while Lysander seeks Helena, both men will woo Helena and flee from Hermia, and Titania will fall in love with a very odd-looking mortal. There is no logic to these shifts of fancy, for, as Lysander points out in the case of human lovers, the men are equal in birth and fortune, while Hermia and Helena differ only in height. In the typical Greek New Comedy (and its Roman counterparts) from which this play derives, a father wants to marry his child to a rich old suitor, while the child loves a poor, good-looking, young one. In such cases one can understand the motivation of each party. The parent seeks money, the son or daughter love. Here, however, Egeus behaves as arbitrarily as Helena or Demetrius, whimsi-cally choosing one suitor over the other. Aptly, Theseus finally tells Egeus, "I will overbear your will," since it is mere willfulness that has prompted him to prefer Demetrius. As Titania's falling in love with the transmogrified Bottom reveals, under love's spell reason vanishes, and one behaves as if asleep.

Other images reinforce this message. Most of the action unfolds at night, when the rational world of daylight yields to dream. Just as Mercutio in *Romeo and Juliet* equates love with the enchantment of Queen Mab, so here the spells of Puck and Oberon, relying of drops squeezed into sleepers' eyes, highlight love's blindness. As Helena remarks on the traditional iconography of Cupid,

> Nor hath Love's mind of any judgement taste;
> Wings and no eyes figure unheedy haste:
> And therefore is Love said to be a child,
> Because in choice he is so oft beguil'd.

The thick fogs that Puck raises to mislead the quarreling lovers in act 3 provide yet another objective correlative to the lovers' muddled state of mind. Over all shines that symbol of fickleness, mutability, and lunacy, the moon, which in this play changes even more rapidly than usual—now full, now dark, now new.

Hearing the strange account of the night's adventures, Theseus rejects the story with the comment that "the lunatic, the lover and the poet/ Are of imagination all compact." Certainly that view has some merit, but so has Hippolyta's; she sees that from these strange fancies emerges "something of great constancy." In *Romeo and Juliet*, Mercutio puns on the fact "that dreamers often lie," to which Romeo replies, "In bed asleep, while they do dream things true." Though Helena is right when she says, "Love looks not with the eyes," from this confusion and seeming blindness the proper couples emerge united, and the fairy masque at the play's conclusion mirrors the dance of life that results. Even the dead lovers, Pyramus and Thisbe, revive, for in the comic world death holds no sway; the very "graves all gaping wide,/ Every one lets forth his sprite,/ In the church-way paths to glide."

As Theseus' comment about the lunacy of lovers is a valid but partial view, so, too, is his association of poets and madness. In literature as in love, he is a realist who regards even the finest theater as "but shadows." For the rude mechanicals, on the other hand, these shadows are reality. Bottom and Starveling worry that the staged death of Pyramus will be too gruesome for the spectators. Snout is concerned lest the lion frighten the ladies, and Peter Quince will not let Bottom have that part because he would roar so fiercely that he "would fight the duchess and the ladies, that they would shriek; and that were enough to hang us all." Since their play calls for moonlight, the would-be actors consult an almanac to be sure that the moon will shine on the night of the performance.

Such literal-mindedness seems as foolishly naïve as Theseus' utter rejection of illusion and imagination, but both attitudes confront the audience with the question of what is reality. Bottom wonders whether he was turned into an ass, whether he has been the lover of the fairy queen, or whether all that was a dream. The spectators feel more certain; after all, they have seen the action unfold. Or have they? In his last speech, Puck dismisses all that has happened as a sleeper's vision. The play's very title embodies this ambiguity. Is it a midsummer night's dream or *A Midsummer Night's Dream*, something that exists apart from the spectator's imagination or not? Theseus, that arch-rejecter of illusion, is himself the product of the poet's brain. And what of the spectators of the spectators of Peter Quince's play? Already in this early comedy Shakespeare suggests the view that Prospero will express in *The Tempest* (1611) when he rejects any distinction between fact and fancy: "We are such stuff/ As dreams are made on, and our little life/ Is rounded with a sleep."

In Shakespeare's capacious soul, and in the plays that emanate from it, contraries coexist. The title of the mechanicals' play, "The Most Lamentable Comedy, and Most Cruel Death of Pyramus and Thisbe," is but another indication of life's, and art's, motley web. Yet from such contradictions of comedy and tragedy, dream and reality, emerges something of great constancy, at once an entertainment and a view of life as a midsummer night's dream.

THE MISANTHROPE

Type of work: Drama
Author: Molière (Jean Baptiste Poquelin, 1622–1673)
Type of plot: Comedy of manners
Time of plot: Seventeenth century
Locale: Paris
First presented: 1666

The basic question in The Misanthrope—*whether Alceste is an honest man behaving decently in a corrupt society, or a self-righteous, egocentric prig refusing to abide by the elementary rules of social discourse—has stimulated a long and continuing debate, a debate that may reveal more about the social attitudes and mores of the critics than about the play itself.*

Principal Characters

Alceste (ȧl·sĕst'), an outspoken, rigidly honest young man disgusted with society. Protesting against injustice, self-interest, deceit, roguery, he wants honesty, truthfulness, and sincerity. He hates all men because they are wicked, mischievous, hypocritic, and generally so odious to him that he has no desire to appear rational in their eyes. He would cheerfully lose a law case for the fun of seeing what people are and to have the right to rail against the iniquity of human nature. In love with a young widow, Célimène, he is not blind to her faults but feels that his sincere love will purify her heart. He controls his temper with her, for he deems her beneath his anger. Despite her coquetry, he will excuse her if she joins him in renouncing society and retiring into solitude. Seeing himself deceived on all sides and overwhelmed by injustice, he plans to flee from vice and seek a nook—with or without Célimène—where he may enjoy the freedom of being an honest man.

Célimène (sā·lē·mĕn'), a young widow loved by Alceste, though she embodies all qualities he detests. She is a flirt, a gossip with a satirical wit demonstrated in caustic sketches of her friends, a woman anxious for flattery. Not certain that she truly loves Alceste, she feels that he may be too jealous to deserve her love. In the end she scornfully rejects his invitation to grow old and bury herself in the wilderness with him.

Philinte (fē·lȧṅt'), a friend of Alceste. Believing in civilization, tact, conformity, he is a man of good sense and sober rationality who takes men as they are. Where Alceste says that Oronte's sonnet is very badly written, Philinte flatters him for the sentiment of the poem. Though he admits that trickery usually wins the day, he sees in it no reason to withdraw from society.

Oronte (ô·rôṅt'), a young fop who claims that he stands well in the court and offers to use his influence there for Alceste. When his offer of friendship and influence is rejected and his sonnet ridiculed, he brings charges against Alceste. Though in love with Célimène, he rejects his love when he learns of her ridicule of him, and admits he has been duped.

Éliante (ā·lē·äṅt'), Célimène's cousin, a woman whose ideas are similar to Philinte's and who marries him at the end. Though she enjoys gossip, she is sincere, as even Alceste admits, and favors people who speak their minds.

Arsinoé (ȧr·sē·nô·ā'), a friend of Célimène, an envious prude who offers advice on honor and wisdom. Though a flatterer, she is also outspoken at times.

Acaste (ä·cȧst') and **Clitandre** (klē·tändr'), noblemen and fops. Both desire the love of Célimène, who ridicules them.

Basque (bȧsk), a servant to Célimène.

Dubois (dü·bwä'), Alceste's servant.

An Officer of the Maréchaussée (mȧ-rā·shō·sā'), who delivers a summons to Alceste.

The Story

Alceste had been called a misanthrope by many of his friends, and he took a rather obstinate delight in the name. this characteristic led him to quarrel heatedly with his good friend Philinte, who accepted uncritically the frivolous manners of the day. When Philinte warmly embraced a chance acquaintance, as was customary, Alceste maintained that such behavior was hypocritical, especially since Philinte hardly knew the man.

Philinte reminded Alceste that his lawsuit was nearly ready for trial, and that he would do well to moderate his attitude toward people in general. His opponents in the suit were doing everything possible to curry favor, but Alceste insulted everyone he met and made no effort to win over the judges.

Philinte also taunted Alceste on his love for Célimène, who, as a leader in society, was hypocritical most of the time. Alceste had to admit that his love could not be explained rationally.

Oronte interrupted the quarrel by coming to visit Alceste, who was puzzled by a visit from suave and elegant Oronte. Oronte asked permission to read a sonnet he had lately composed, as he was anxious to have Alceste's judgment of its literary merit.

After some affected hesitation, Oronte read his mediocre poem. Alceste, too honest to give false praise, condemned the verses and even satirized the poor quality of the writing. Oronte instantly took offense at this criticism, and a new quarrel broke out. Although the argument was indecisive, there were hints of a possible duel.

Alceste then went to call on Célimène. As soon as he saw her, he began perversely to upbraid her for her frivolous conduct and her hypocritical attitude toward other people. Although Célimène could slander and ridicule with a keen wit and a barbed tongue while a person was absent, she was all flattery and attention when talking with him. This attitude displeased Alceste.

The servant announced several callers, including Éliante. To Alceste's dismay, they all sat down for an interminable conversation. The men took great delight in naming over all their mutual acquaintances, and as each name was mentioned, Célimène made unkind remarks. The only gentle person in the room was Éliante, whose good sense and kind heart were in striking contrast with Célimène's caustic wit. Éliante was overshadowed, however, by the more brilliant Célimène. The men all declared they had nothing to do all day, and each swore to outstay the other, to remain longer with Célimène. Alceste determined to be the last to leave.

A guard appeared, however, to summon Alceste before the tribunal. Astonished, Alceste learned that his quarrel with Oronte had become public knowledge, and the authorities intended to prevent a possible duel. Loudly protesting that except for an order direct from the king nothing could make him praise the poetry of Oronte, Alceste was led away.

Arsinoé, an austere woman who made a pretense of great virtue, came to call on Célimène. She took the opportunity to warn Célimène that her conduct was creating a scandal, because her many suitors and her sharp tongue were hurting her reputation. Célimène spoke bitingly of Arsinoé's strait-laced character.

Arsinoé decided to talk privately with Alceste, with whom she was half in love. She comforted him as best she could for being so unfortunate as to love Célimène, and complimented him on his plain dealings and forthright character. Carried away by the intimacy of her talk, Arsinoé offered to do much for Alceste by speaking in his favor at court. But the two concluded that the love of Alceste for Célimène, though unsuitable from almost every point of view, was a fast tie.

Éliante and Philinte were in the meantime discussing Alceste and his habit of antagonizing his friends through his frankness. Philinte told her of Alceste's hearing before the tribunal. He had insisted that Oronte's verses were bad, but he had nothing more to say. Éliante and Philinte began to discover a mutual liking. If Éliante ever lost her fondness for Alceste, Philinte intended to offer himself as a lover.

Alceste received an unflattering letter, purporting to come from Célimène, which described him in malicious terms. After much coy hesitation, Célimène admitted that she had sent the letter and expressed surprise at Alceste's indignation. Other suitors appeared, each holding a letter and each much upset. On comparing notes, they found that they had all been ridiculed and insulted.

Meanwhile, Alceste had made up his mind to ask Éliante to marry him, but reconsidered when he realized that his proposal would seem to spring from a desire to avenge himself on Célimène. To the misanthrope there seemed to be no solution except to go into exile and live a hermit's life.

When Célimène's suitors clamored for an explanation, she told them that she had written the letters because she was tired of the niceties of polite conversation. For once she decided to say what she really thought. This confession was shocking to the suitors who thought frankness and rudeness were unpardonable crimes. Hypocrisy, flattery, cajolery, extravagances—these were the marks of a gentle lady. Protesting and disdainful, they left together, never to return.

Only Alceste remained. Even the coquettish and malicious heart of Célimène was touched. When Alceste repeated his vows of fidelity and asked her once more to marry him, she almost consented. But when Alceste revealed that he wanted them to go into exile and lead quiet, simple lives, she refused. Célimène could never leave the false, frivolous society she loved.

Now completely the misanthrope, Alceste stalked way with the firm resolve to quit society forever, to become a hermit, far removed from the artificial sham of preciosity. Philinte and Éliante, more moderate in their views, however, decided that they would marry.

Critical Evaluation

In a letter to a friend, Jean Jacques Rousseau, the eighteenth century writer and philosopher, stated that "the character of Alceste in [*The Misanthrope*] is that of a fair, open and . . . truly honest man [and] the poet makes him a subject of ridicule." To what extent are these statements true?

If one examines the play closely, one finds that although Alceste is subject to ridicule, so is the society he ridicules. In other words, Molière validates Alceste's criticism of the follies of the age: the hypocrisy of court life, the absurd manners required by all who attempt to appear at court, the dishonest practice of bribing judges in order to win a law suit, the ludicrous poetry written by those with no talent simply because writing poetry was one of the acts required of a gentleman of the time, the delight in gossiping even if the gossip were to destroy the good name of an individual. Molière attacks all of these practices through Alceste.

And all of these attacks are seen to be valid because these practices are not observed in the behavior of those who represent the golden mean: Philinte (Alceste's best friend) and Éliante (who loves Alceste and is, in turn, loved by Philinte). They leave the gossiping, the poetry writing, the absurd activities to others. However, there is an important distinction between their behavior and Alceste's. They are willing to acknowledge certain social customs as essential to maintaining a stable society and accept those who practice these customs. Alceste, on the contrary, not only refuses to conform but delights in condemning all those who do not conform.

Thus, although Molière would agree with Alceste's view of society (as shown by the assent of Philinte and Éliante), he would disagree with his excessive manner in attacking the social fabric. this leads to the first part of Rousseau's statement (that is, Alceste is "fair, open and truly honest"). For Molière takes great pains to show us that Alceste is none of these.

The opening scene of the play shows him condemning his friend Philinte for having shown civility to a man he hardly knows. Alceste calls Philinte's action a crime and declares he would rather die than commit such an indignity. Alceste insists that acts of friendship should be reserved for those who are one's true friends. He declares that friendship has no meaning if it must be shared. His extreme reaction to Philinte's harmless act would seem to indicate that what Alceste resents most about the actions is that it reduces his relationship with Philinte to the same level as all other relationships; he insists that he wants to be singled out, chosen for his virtues, valued for himself. His attitude is hardly fair to Philinte, who fails to view his action as a criminal offense and maintains that in order to survive in society, one must sometimes compromise.

Although Alceste appears to be "open and truly honest," we find that his actions belie Rousseau's statement. When asked by Oronte to comment on a sonnet he has written, Alceste attacks it mercilessly. The poem is, obviously, of little merit, but Alceste again overreacts. One cannot help but wonder if Alceste's reaction to the poem stems from his knowledge that it was written to Célimène, whom he loves, by a rival, whom he detests.

It is, above all, in his relationship with Célimène, that we must question Alceste's openness and honesty. If he truly despises the falseness of his society, how can one account for his love for Célimène, the epitome of the falseness of that society? It is Célimène who recites nasty gossip about people, behind their backs, in the famous medallion scene. It is Célimène who leads on a number of suitors by writing loving letters to all of them. It is Célimène who is the quintessence of the hypocrisy of the society Alceste condemns. Yet, he loves her with a passion that overcomes his reason—a situation that serves as a source for comedy as well as tragedy in seventeenth century French drama.

Alceste is aware of all of Célimène's faults yet can do nothing to control his passion. The modest, reasonable Éliante would seem to be a more likely choice for his affections, but Célimène is the recipient of all his love. And, as with his friend Philinte, he refuses to share her love with anyone else. When she acknowledges that she enjoys her way of life, he chastises her in the extreme manner he used to criticize Philinte in the opening scene of the play. And can one call a man "fair" who, when he believes he has found proof that Célimène is untrue to him, turns to Éliante asking her to help him revenge himself on Célimène by accepting his heart? Éliante, fortunately, is reasonable enough to realize that Alceste is speaking in a moment of unreasonable anger and suggests that he not use her to seek revenge on Célimène.

The supreme example of Alceste's succumbing to the hypocrisy he professes to detest is presented in act 4, scene 3. He confronts Célimène with what he believes to be her treachery. Rather than give him the answer he desires—that is, that she loves only him—she agrees with his charges. He is brought to a point of ultimate despair and begs her to *pretend* that she loves him, that such pretense will suffice. At this point, the comedy closely approaches tragedy, for we find Alceste, the upholder of truth and honesty, begging for deception.

The seventeenth century belief in the overwhelming power of uncontrollable passion can account, in part, for Alceste's behavior. However, one can find examples throughout the play clearly demonstrating that although Alceste is correct in upbraiding society for its hypocritical behavior, much of his criticism is directed at those whose esteem he desires. It would thus seem that part of his protest rests in his fear that if all are treated with the same courtesy, how can one "set the worthy man apart"? He wishes to be loved and honored for himself and not merely because society deems such behavior correct. He wants to be set apart: to be Philinte's *best* friend (and not share the social niceties that Philinte bestows on others), to be Célimène's only lover (and not share her company with that of other men).

It would thus appear that not only is the first part of Rousseau's statement incorrect, but Molière's title as well.

Alceste is no misanthrope (his fondness for Philinte and Éliante and his love for Célimène are obvious). He does, however, abhor the sham of society. But although Alceste's ridicule of society is shown to be valid, his behavior is shown to be ridiculous. Thus the second part of Rousseau's statement is correct.

LES MISÉRABLES

Type of work: Novel
Author: Victor Hugo (1802–1885)
Type of plot: Social chronicle
Time of plot: c. 1815–1835
Locale: France
First published: 1862 (English translation, 1862)

In this ultimate "pursuit" novel, Jean Valjean, an essentially innocent man, is tracked relentlessly for most of his lifetime by an implacable, abstract "justice" in the person of the fanatical Inspector Javert. With this action as the spine, Hugo then ranges widely to describe early nineteenth century France with a sweep, power, and concreteness that give the novel epic stature.

Principal Characters

Jean Valjean (zhäṅ′ väl·zhäṅ′), a convict of unusual strength, originally sentenced to five years in prison for stealing a loaf of bread for his sister's starving family. Attempts to escape have kept him in the galleys for nineteen years before he is released in 1815. Police Inspector Javert is sure he will be back for his passport, proclaiming him an ex-convict and preventing him from getting work. He stops at the home of the Bishop of Digne, who treats him well despite Jean's attempts to rob him of some silverware. Eventually, calling himself Father Madeleine, a man with no previous history, he appears in the town of M. sur M. His discovery of a method for making jet for jewelry brings prosperity to the whole village, and the people elect him mayor. Then his conscience forces him to confess his former identity to save a prisoner unjustly arrested. Again he escapes from the galleys and from Inspector Javert, until he is betrayed by a blackmailer. In the end he dies peacefully, surrounded by those he loves and with his entangled past revealed. His final act is to bequeath to Cosette the Bishop's silver candlesticks, which he had kept for years while trying to deserve the Bishop's confidence.

Fantine (fäṅ·tēn′), a beautiful girl of Paris whose attempts to find a home for her illegitimate daughter Cosette have put her into the power of money-mad M. Thénardier. Unable to meet his demands for more money after the foreman of Father Madeleine's factory fires her upon learning of her earlier history, she turns prostitute, only to have M. Javert arrest her. By this time she is dying of tuberculosis. Father Madeleine promises to look after eight-year-old Cosette.

Cosette (kō·zĕt′), Fantine's daughter, who grows up believing herself the daughter of Father Madeleine. She is seen and loved by a young lawyer, Marius Pontmercy; but Valjean, fearing he will be compelled to reveal her story and his own if she marries, plans to take her away. Cosette hears from Pontmercy again as she is about to leave for England with her supposed father. She sends him a note which brings his answer that he is going to seek death at the barricades.

Felix Tholomyès (fā·lēks′ tô·lô·myĕs′), a carefree, faithless student, Fantine's lover and Cosette's father.

M. Javert (zhä·vĕr′), a police inspector with a strong sense of duty that impels him to track down the man whom he considers a depraved criminal. Finally, after Valjean saves his life at the barricades, where the crowd wants to kill him as a police spy, he struggles between his sense of duty and his reluctance to take back to prison a man who could have saved himself by letting the policeman die. His solution is to drown himself in the Seine River.

Marius Pontmercy (mă·ryüs′ pōṅ′-mĕr·sē′), a young lawyer of good blood, estranged from his aristocratic family because of his liberal views. His father, an army officer under Napoleon, had expressed a deathbed wish that his son try to repay his debt to Sergeant Thénardier, who had saved his life at Waterloo. Marius' struggle between obligations to a rascal and his desire to protect the father of the girl he loves sets M. Javert on Jean Valjean's tracks. A farewell letter from Cosette sends him to die at the barricade during a street revolt. After he has been wounded, Valjean saves him by carrying him underground through the sewers of Paris. Eventually Marius marries Cosette and learns, when the old man is dying, the truth about Jean Valjean.

M. Thénardier (tā·när·dyā′), an unscrupulous, avaricious innkeeper, a veteran of Waterloo, who bleeds Fantine of money to pay for the care of Cosette. Later he changes his name to Jondrette and begins a career of begging and blackmail while living in the Gorbeau tenement in Paris. Jean Valjean becomes one of his victims. He even demands money to let Valjean out of the sewers beneath Paris while Valjean is carrying wounded Marius Pontmercy to a place of safety.

Mme. Thénardier, a virago as cruel and ruthless as her husband.

Eponine Thénardier (ā·pô·nēn′), their older daughter, a good-hearted but pathetic girl. Marius Pontmercy first meets her when she delivers one of her father's begging, whining letters. In love with Marius, she saves his life by interposing herself between him and an aimed musket during the fighting at the barricade. Before she dies she gives him a letter telling where Cosette can be found.

Azelma (ă·zĕl·mȧ′), their younger daughter.

Little Gavroche (gȧ·vrôsh′), the Thénardiers' son, a street gamin. He is killed while assisting the insurgents in the fighting at the barricade.

Charles François Bienvenu Myriel (shȧrl frän·swȧ′ byän·vənü′ mē·ryĕl′), Bishop of Digne, a good-hearted, devout churchman who gives hospitality to Jean Valjean after the ex-convict's release from the galleys. When Valjean repays him by stealing some of the Bishop's silverware, the old man tells the police that he had given the valuables to his guest and gives him in addition a pair of silver candlesticks. His saintliness turns Valjean to a life of honesty and sacrifice.

Father Fauchelevent (fōsh·lə·vän′), a bankrupt notary, turned carter, jealous of Father Madeleine's success in M. sur M. One day his horse falls and the old man is pinned beneath his cart. The accident might have proved fatal if Father Madeleine, a man of tremendous strength, had not lifted the vehicle to free the trapped carter. This feat of strength, witnessed by M. Javert, causes the policeman to comment significantly that he had known only one man, a galley slave, capable of doing such a deed. Father Madeleine's act changes Father Fauchelevent from an enemy to an admiring friend. After his accident the old man becomes a gardener at the convent of the Little Picpus in Paris. Jean Valjean and Cosette, fleeing from the police, take refuge in the convent garden. Old Fauchelevent gives them shelter and arranges to have Valjean smuggled out of the convent grounds in the coffin of a dead nun. Later he helps Valjean to get work as a workman at the convent.

Little Gervaise (zhĕr·vĕs′), a young Savoyard from whom Jean Valjean steals two francs. The deed arouses his conscience, and he weeps because he cannot find the boy to return his money. This is the crime of which Champmathieu is later accused.

Champmathieu (chän·mȧ·tyœ′), an old man arrested for stealing apples. When he is taken to the departmental prison at Arras a convict there identifies him as Jean Valjean, a former convict, and he is put on trial for the theft of two francs stolen from a Savoyard lad eight years before. After a struggle with his conscience, Jean Valjean appears at the trial and confesses his identity. Champmathieu, convinced that all the world is mad if Father Madeleine is Jean Valjean, is acquitted. Javert arrests Valjean as the real culprit, but his prisoner escapes a few hours later after pulling out a bar of his cell window.

M. Gillenormand (zhĕl·nôr·män′), the stern grandfather of Marius Pontmercy. A royalist, the old man never became reconciled with his Bonapartist son-in-law. He and his grandson quarrel because of the young man's political views and reverence for his dead father. Turned out of his grandfather's house, Marius goes to live in the Gorbeau tenement.

Théodule Gillenormand (tā·ô·dül′), M. Gillenormand's great-grandnephew, a lieutenant in the lancers. He spies on Marius Pontmercy and learns that his kinsman is a regular visitor at his father's tomb.

Courfeyrac (kōōr·fā·rȧk′) and **Enjolas** (än·zhô·lȧ′), friends of Marius Pontmercy and members of the friends of the A.B.C., a society supposed to be interested in the education of children but in reality a revolutionary group. Both are killed in the uprising of the citizens in June, 1832, Courfeyrac at the barricades; Enjolas is in the house where the insurgents make their last stand.

M. Maboef (mȧ·bœf′), an aged churchwarden who had known Marius Pontmercy's father. A lover of mankind and a hater of tyranny, he marches unarmed to the barricades with the young friends of the A.B.C. He is killed during the fighting.

The Story

In 1815, in France, a man named Jean Valjean was released after nineteen years in prison. He had been sentenced to a term of five years because he stole a loaf of bread to feed his starving sister and her family, but the sentence was later increased because of his attempts to escape. During his imprisonment he astonished others by his exhibitions of unusual physical strength.

Freed at last, he started out on foot for a distant part of the country. Innkeepers refused him food and lodging because his yellow passport revealed that he was a former convict. Finally he came to the house of the Bishop of Digne, a saintly man who treated him graciously, fed him, and gave him a bed. During the night Jean stole the bishop's silverware and fled. He was immediately captured by the police, who returned him and the stolen goods to the bishop. Without any censure, the priest not only gave him what he had stolen but also added his silver candlesticks to the gift. The astonished gendarmes released his silver candlesticks to the gift. The astonished gendarmes released the prisoner. Alone with the bishop, Jean was confounded by the churchman's attitude, for the bishop asked only that he use the silver as a means of living an honest life.

In 1817, a beautiful girl named Fantine lived in Paris. She gave birth to an illegitimate child, Cosette, whom she left with Monsieur and Madame Thénardier to rear with their own children. As time went on, the Thénardiers demanded more and more money for Cosette's support yet treated the child cruelly and deprived her even of necessities. Meanwhile, Fantine had gone to the town of M—— and obtained a job in a glass factory operated by Father Madeleine, a kind and generous man whose history was known to no one, but whose good deeds and generosity to the poor were public information. He had arrived in M—— a poor laborer, and by a lucky invention he was able to start a business of his own. Soon he built a factory and employed many workers. After five years in the city, he was named mayor and was beloved by all the citizens. He was reported to have prodigious strength. Only one man, Javert, a police inspector, seemed to watch him with an air of suspicion. Javert was born in prison. His whole life was influenced by that fact, and his fanatical attitude toward duty made him a man to be feared. He was determined to discover the facts of Father Madeleine's previous life. One day he found a clue while watching Father Madeleine lift a heavy cart to save an old man who had fallen under it. Javert realized that he had known only one man of such prodigious strength, a former convict named Valjean.

Fantine had told no one of Cosette, but knowledge of her illegitimate child spread and caused Fantine to be discharged from the factory without the knowledge of Father Madeleine. Finally Fantine became a prostitute in an effort to pay the increasing demands of the Thénardiers for Cosette's support. One night Javert arrested her while she was walking the streets. When Father Madeleine heard the details of her plight and learned that she had tuberculosis, he sent Fantine to a hospital and promised to bring Cosette to her. Just before the mayor left to get Cosette, Javert confessed that he had mistakenly reported to the Paris police that he suspected Father Madeleine of being the former convict, Jean Valjean. He said that the real Jean Valjean had been arrested at Arras under an assumed name. The arrested man was to be tried two days later.

That night Father Madeleine struggled with his own conscience, for he was the real Jean Valjean. Unwilling to let an innocent man suffer, he went to Arras for the trial and identified himself as Jean Valjean. After telling the authorities where he could be found, he went to Fantine. Javert came there to arrest him. Fantine was so terrified that she died. After a day in prison, Jean Valjean escaped.

Valjean, some time later, was again imprisoned by Javert. Once more he made his escape. Shortly afterward he was able to take Cosette, a girl of eight, away from the Thénardiers. He grew to love the child greatly, and they lived together happily in the Gorbeau tenement on the outskirts of Paris. When Javert once more tracked them down, Valjean escaped with the child into a convent garden, where they were rescued by Fauchelevant, whose life Valjean had saved when the old peasant fell beneath

the cart. Fauchelevant was now the convent gardener. Valjean became his helper, and Cosette was put into the convent school.

Years passed. Valjean left the convent and took Cosette, her schooling finished, to live in a modest house on a side street in Paris. The old man and the young girl were little noticed by their neighbors. Meanwhile the blackguard Thénardier had brought his family to live in the Gorbeau tenement. He now called himself Jondrette. In the next room lived Marius Pontmercy, a young lawyer estranged from his aristocratic grandfather because of his liberal views. Marius was the son of an officer whose life Thénardier had saved at the battle of Waterloo. The father, now dead, had asked his son to repay Thénardier for his deed. Marius never suspected that Jondrette was really his father's benefactor. When the Jondrettes were being evicted from their quarters, however, he paid their rent from his meager resources.

During one of his evening walks, Marius met Cosette and Valjean. He fell in love with the girl as he continued to see her in the company of her white-haired companion. At last he followed her to her home. Valjean, noticing Marius, took Cosette to live in another house.

One morning Marius received an urgent letter delivered by Eponine Jondrette. His neighbors were again asking for help, and he began to wonder about them. Peeping through a hole in the wall, he heard Jondrette speak of a benefactor who would soon arrive. When the man came, Marius recognized him as Cosette's companion. He later learned Cosette's address from Eponine, but before he saw Cosette again he overheard the Jondrettes plotting against the man whom he believed to be Cosette's father. Alarmed, he told the details of the plot to Inspector Javert.

Marius was at the wall watching when Valjean came to give Jondrette money. While they talked, numerous heavily armed men appeared in the room. Jondrette then revealed himself as Thénardier. Horrified, Marius did not know whom to protect, the man his father had requested him to befriend or the father of Cosette. Threatened by Thénardier, Valjean agreed to send to his daughter for more money, but he gave a false address. When this ruse was discovered, the robbers threatened to kill Valjean. Marius threw a note of warning through the hole in the wall as Javert appeared and arrested all but Valjean, who made his escape through a window.

Marius finally located Cosette. One night she told him that she and her father were leaving for England. He tried, unsuccessfully, to get his grandfather's permission to marry Cosette. In despair, he returned to Cosette and found the house where she had lived empty. Eponine met him there and told him that his revolutionary friends had begun a revolt and were waiting for him at the barricades. Because Cosette had disappeared, he gladly followed Eponine to the barricades, where Javert had been seized as a spy and bound. During the fighting Eponine gave her life to save Marius. As she died, she gave him a note which Cosette had given her to deliver. In the note, Cosette told him where she could be found.

In answer to her note, Marius wrote that his grandfather would not permit his marriage, that he had no money, and that he would be killed at the barricade. Valjean discovered the notes and set out for the barricades. Finding Javert tied up by the revolutionists, he freed the inspector. The barricades fell. In the confusion Valjean came upon the wounded Marius and carried him into the Paris sewers.

After hours of wandering, he reached a locked outlet. There Thénardier, unrecognized in the dark, met him and agreed to open the grating in exchange for money. Outside Valjean met Javert, who took him into custody. Valjean asked only that he be allowed to take Marius to his grandfather's house. Javert agreed to wait at the door, but suddenly he turned and ran toward the river. Tormented by his conscientious regard for duty and his reluctance to return to prison the man who had saved his life, he drowned himself in the Seine.

When Marius recovered, he and Cosette were married. Valjean gave Cosette a generous dowry; and for the first time Cosette learned that Valjean was not her real father. Valjean told Marius only that he was an escaped convict, believed dead, and he begged to be allowed to see Cosette occasionally. Gradually Marius banished him from the house. Then Marius learned from Thénardier that it was Valjean who had rescued Marius at the barricade. Marius and Cosette hurried to Valjean's lodgings, to find him on his deathbed. He died knowing that his children loved him and that all his entangling past was now clear. He bequeathed the bishop's silver candlesticks to Cosette, with his last breath saying that he had spent his life in trying to be worthy of the faith of the Bishop of Digne. He was buried in a grave with no name on the stone.

Critical Evaluation

Essentially a detective story in plot, *Les Misérables* is a unique combination of melodrama and morality. It is filled with unlikely coincidences, with larger-than-life emotions and giantlike human beings, yet it all manages to ring true and move the reader. An epic of the people of Paris, with a vital and fascinating re-creation of the swarming Parisian underground, the novel suggests the crowded, absorbing novels of Charles Dickens and Fyodor Dostoevski. The main theme of man's ceaseless combat with evil clearly emerges from the suspenseful plot, while the book as a whole gives a dramatic picture of the ebb and flow of life.

Victor Hugo claimed that the huge book was a "religious" work, and certainly religion does play an important part in the story. From the very beginning, the struggle between good and evil is foremost in the tale. Another theme which is of equal importance is that of fate or "destiny." However one attempts to chisel the "mysterious block" of which his life is made, Hugo writes, the "black vein of destiny" reappears continually. One can never be certain what fate has in store until the last breath of life disappears. Mortals never are safe from the tricks of destiny, from the seemingly endless struggle.

The breathless pace of the novel probably has accounted for his tremendous popularity. The story is filled with dramatic and surprising action, many of the scenes ending with suspenseful episodes in the tradition of the melodramatic nineteenth century stage for which Hugo also wrote. Despite its digressions, the story moves quickly and excitingly, as the characters race across the countryside and through the narrow streets and alleys of Paris.

The characterizations, while on a grand—even epic—scale, are lifelike and believable. Many of the novel's characters seem possessed by strange obsessions or hatreds, but Hugo makes it clear that they have been warped by society and their earlier lives. Although a Romantic novel, *Les Misérables* has much in common with the naturalistic school which was to come into being a few decades later.

Perhaps the most terrifying and fascinating of all the characters who flood through the book's pages is Inspector Javert. Javert is clever but not intelligent. He is consumed by the malice that often dwells within the narrow, ignorant individual. He can conceive of no point of view other than his own. Sympathy, mercy, and understanding require an insight that he does not possess. For him there is no such thing as an extenuating circumstance. He clings with mindless, insane tenacity to his belief in "duty." At his hands, justice is warped beyond recognition.

The casual reader can still be moved by the author's search for justice in *Les Misérables*, and the more sophisticated can admire the novel's complex structure. Like so many of the greatest literary works, *Les Misérables* can be enjoyed many times by different kinds of readers and on many different levels.

An important, if implied, theme of *Les Misérables* is the attainment of salvation through good works. Many of the characters of the novel give charity to those less fortunate. The dramatic opening scenes in which the convict Jean Valjean learns of goodness through the charity of the priest establish the importance of this theme. Later, Jean Valjean and Cosette give anonymous charity to others. Marius, in his goodness, gives charity to the disreputable Thénardier family.

Other biblical virtues are dramatized in the novel, but none so effectively as that of love. By love, Hugo means not only romantic love but also love of humanity, the love of a kindhearted human being for another human being, the love that must be connected with genuine charity. Jean Valjean learns what love is during the course of the novel. Hugo makes it clear that a man cannot exist without love, for if he tries, he becomes warped and less than a man. Jean Valjean grows as a person, becomes a good and honorable man after he has found the love of the helpless little girl. By devoting his life to her, he finds the necessity of a meaning outside of his own life. Jean Valjean comes to value his own existence more because the girl is dependent upon him and loves him.

Victor Hugo knew how to write effectively and with simplicity of the joys and sorrows of the average man and woman. His poetry and fiction have always been popular with the common people, although they have at times been out of critical favor. The public mind was much moved by the generosity of his ideas and the warmth of their expression; more than a century after its publication, *Les Misérables* is still a favorite book with many people around the world. Much of Hugo's poetry and drama is no longer read or produced, but *Les Misérables* and *The Hunchback of Notre Dame* (1831) will endure as long as people read.

The novel covers a time span of more than twenty years—from the fall of the first Napoleon to the revolts of a generation later. The most exciting scenes, described with breathless precision and dramatic flair, are those at the barricades. The characters are swept up in an action bigger than they are. Skillfully, Hugo weaves Marius and Javert, Eponine and the others, into the battles along the streets of Paris. Always Hugo's eye catches the details of the passing spectacle, from the old woman who props up a mattress in front of her window to stop the stray bullets to the dynamic flood of humanity coursing down the boulevards. It is here that Hugo's skill as a master of narrative is fully displayed. Never, however, does he lose sight of the pathos of the individuals' struggles; the reader never forgets the principal characters and their plight amid the chaotic scenes. Perfectly, Hugo balances between the two elements which compose his masterpiece. The final scenes of the novel move relentlessly and excitingly to their inevitable conclusion. Perhaps Dostoevski probed deeper or Dickens caught the humor of life more fully, but Hugo was their equal in his ability to portray the human struggle of those caught up in the forces of history.

MISS JULIE

Type of work: Drama
Author: August Strindberg (1849–1912)
Type of plot: Naturalism
Time of plot: Nineteenth century
Locale: A country estate in Sweden
First presented: 1888

No author has portrayed the "battle of the sexes" with more intensity than August Strindberg, and Miss Julie *is one of his most forceful examples. The play strips the action down to an elemental struggle between the aristocratic, romantic, haughty Julie and the poor, realistic, grasping Jean, with survival at stake. But, in the end, the irrational inner drives overwhelm and destroy* both *of them in what is surely one of the most brutal short plays in the literature.*

Principal Characters

Miss Julie, a headstrong young woman, the daughter of a count. She has derived from her mother a hatred of men and of woman's subservient role. As the drama begins, the household servants are scandalized over the circumstances of Miss Julie's broken engagement: she had made her fiancé jump over her horsewhip several times, giving him a cut with the whip each time, and he had left her. Subsequently, she takes advantage of her father's absence to join the holiday dancing of the servants. She makes love to her father's not unwilling valet, Jean, and then shifts helplessly and impractically from one plan of action to another: running off alone; running off with the valet; a suicide pact when they become tired of each other; taking his fiancée, who naturally objects to being deserted, with them. When Jean kills Miss Julie's pet finch, at her command, her love turns to hate. Then, ecstatic at the thought of freedom through suicide, she takes her lover's razor and leaves the room.

Jean, Miss Julie's lover and her father's valet. His first suggestion is that they go to Como, Italy, to open a hotel. Later he brings Miss Julie his razor and indicates it as one answer to her plea for advice. The return of his master, the count, reduces him again to the menial attitudes of a servant.

Christine, a cook and Jean's fiancée. She loves him and does not intend to lose him to Miss Julie. She refuses Miss Julie's offer to go along with them to Como and announces as she leaves for church that she has spoken to the stable men about not letting anyone have horses until after the count's return.

The Story

Miss Julie's broken engagement to the county attorney was quite a scandal to the servants in the house. Miss Julie, daughter of a count, had made the man actually jump over her horsewhip several times, giving him a cut with the whip each time. He had finally put an end to such conduct and the engagement by snatching the whip, breaking it, and striding away from the manor.

On Midsummer Eve, a great holiday held throughout the Swedish countryside a few weeks later, Miss Julie entered into the festivities and danced with the servants. She dared to do so because her father had gone to the city and was not expected to return. Although the servants disliked her entrance into their fun, they were powerless to make their dislike known; she was their mistress. Her father's valet, Jean, left the festivities after dancing once with Miss Julie. He retreated to the kitchen, where his fiancée, Christine the cook, gave him a little supper.

But Miss Julie gave Jean no peace. She came into the kitchen and dragged him out to dance with her again, even though she knew that he had promised to dance with Christine. After dancing another time with Miss Julie, Jean escaped once more to the kitchen. He was afraid that Christine was angry. She assured him, however, that she did not blame him for what had happened. Just then Miss Julie returned to the kitchen and demanded that Jean dance with her again after he had changed from his livery into a tailcoat. While he was changing, Christine fell asleep in a chair. When he returned, Miss Julie asked him to get her something to drink. Jean got a bottle of beer for her and another for himself.

After finishing the beer, Miss Julie teased Christine by trying to wake her up. Christine, moving as if asleep, went to her own room. After she had gone, Miss Julie began to ogle Jean, who warned his mistress that it was dangerous to flirt with a man as young as he. But Miss Julie paid no attention to him. Jean, falling in with her mood, told about his early life as a cotter's child and how, even as a small child, he had been in love with his young mistress. They talked so long that the other servants came to look for the valet. Rather than expose themselves to the comments and the scandal of having drunk together in the kitchen, Jean and Miss Julie went into Jean's room. They were there a long time, for the servants stayed in the kitchen and danced and sang. During that time Miss Julie gave herself to Jean.

After the servants had gone, neither Jean nor Miss Julie knew just what to do. They agreed only that it was best for them to leave the country. Jean suggested that they go to Como, Italy, to open a hotel. Miss Julie asked Jean to take her in his arms again. He refused, saying that he could not make love to her a second time in her father's house, where she was the mistress and he the servant. When she reminded him of the extravagant language he had used a little while before, he told her the time had come to be practical.

To cheer her, Jean offered Miss Julie a drink of wine from a bottle he had taken from the count's cellar. She saw whose it was and accused Jean of stealing. An argument followed, with bitter words on both sides. When they had both calmed a little, Miss Julie tried to tell Jean how she had come to be what she was. She said that she had been brought up to do a man's work by her mother, because her mother had hated to be a slave to men. She told also how her mother had revenged herself on Miss Julie's father by taking a brick manufacturer as her lover and how her mother's lover had stolen great sums of money from the count. From her mother, said Miss Julie, she had learned to hate men and to wish to make them her slaves. He understood then why she had treated her fiancé as she had with the whip. Miss Julie ended her recital with the recommendation that she and Jean go abroad at once. To her suggestion that when they ceased enjoying each other they should commit suicide, Jean, far more practical, advised her to go away by herself. Miss Julie, helpless in the urgency of the situation, did as Jean suggested and prepared to leave.

While Miss Julie was upstairs dressing, Christine came into the kitchen. It was morning. Seeing the glasses on the table, she knew that Miss Julie and Jean had been drinking together. She guessed the rest, and Jean admitted what had happened. Christine, angry at Miss Julie, told Jean that fine people did not behave so with the servants. Christine urged him to go away with her as soon as possible. Loving him, she did not intend to lose him to her mistress.

Christine persuaded Jean to get ready to go to church with her, since it was Sunday morning. When they were both dressed, Miss Julie and Jean met in the kitchen. The mistress carried a bird cage. When Jean said she could not take her pet finch with her, she ordered him to kill it. Seeing her bird die, Miss Julie's love turned to hate. Despising him for killing in cold blood the pet she had loved so much, she raged at Jean and told him that her father would soon return. Then he would learn what had happened. Miss Julie declared she would welcome her father's discovery; she wished now only to die.

When Christine appeared ready for church, she told Miss Julie bluntly that she would not allow her mistress to run off with the man who had promised to become her husband. Miss Julie then tried to persuade Christine to go with them to Como. While the two women talked, Jean left the room. He returned a few moments later with his razor. Christine, refusing to join in the flight, left for church after saying that she had spoken to the men at the stables about not letting anyone have horses until the count's return.

After Christine's departure, Miss Julie asked Jean what he would do if he were in her position. He indicated the razor in his hand. At that moment the valet's bell rang. The count had returned. Jean, answering the bell, received instructions to have boots and coffee ready in half an hour. His master's voice reduced Jean once again to the mental attitudes of a servant. Miss Julie, almost in a state of trance, was filled with ecstasy at the thought of freeing herself by committing suicide. She took the razor Jean gave her and left the kitchen with it in her hand.

Critical Evaluation

Miss Julie was written by August Strindberg to be produced in Paris by André Antoine's avant-garde Thèâtre Libre. This "naturalistic tragedy" is recognized as one of the greatest works of the Swedish playwright. Strindberg's power, complexity, and originality of technique and vision have led playwrights such as Eugene O'Neill to see him as the father of modern drama.

Strindberg's achievements are all the more remarkable in view of the squalor of his upbringing. Born in Stockholm into a bankrupt family, one of twelve children, Strindberg was neglected by even his own mother. After her death when he was thirteen, his stepmother added harshness to neglect. This early experience developed in

him a strong, life-long quarrel with any conventional authority figure, evidenced in his rejection of traditional stage techniques and the rejection of traditional beliefs and conventions of society in his plays. His private life was equally unconventional. His three marriages were each characterized by intense love-hate relationships. In addition to private tensions, Strindberg was prosecuted for blasphemy upon the publication of his short stories, *Married* (1886–1888). The combination of these tensions produced an unstable psychological state with spells of insanity and delusions of persecution. Between the years 1894–1896 the increasing violence of his hallucinations led to the crisis known as the "Inferno period."

The inner torment of this psychological crisis gave rise to a shift in technique from the psychological naturalism of *The Father* and *Miss Julie* to symbolistic and expressionistic departures from external reality in the imaginative brilliance of dramas such as *A Dream Play* and *Ghost Sonata*.

While in Paris in 1883, Strindberg became familiar with the doctrine of literary naturalism espoused by Émile Zola, and he successfully applied this approach to drama, even sending a copy of his first naturalistic play to Zola for comments. The long foreword Strindberg wrote for *Miss Julie* explains his use of naturalistic doctrine in the play, but Strindberg's final formulation of dramatic naturalism is found in his essay, "On Modern Drama and Modern Theater" (1889). There he suggests that the true essence of naturalism is a presentation of the polarization of the basic conflicts of life—love and hate, life and death—through the Darwinian principle of survival of the fittest found in both personal relationships and class conflicts. Strindberg's knowledge of psychology contributes in creating his powerful authentic dramas, which remain as moving in our time as when they were created.

Strindberg utilized numerous important innovations in both the writing and the production of his plays. His dialogue, like Chekhov's, is meant to reproduce the pauses, wanderings, and flatness of everyday speech. He wrote *Miss Julie* to be presented in only one act without intermission to capitalize on the emotional involvement of the audience. In addition, he calls for music, mime, ballet, and improvisation to utilize the full range of actors' talents. He calls for new lighting techniques to illuminate faces better, allowing them to use less makeup and to appear more natural. Finally, he asks for a return to a smaller, more intimate theater with closer audience relationship.

Julie's complex motivations are ample evidence of Strindberg's art. We see her as a product of heredity and environment. Her mother was a low-born woman, full of hatred for woman's conventional place in society. She brought Julie up as a boy, creating in her a fascination with animals and a loathing for the opposite sex which causes self-disgust when her natural instincts attract her sexually to men. In addition, her mother suffered from strange attacks of mental instability which seems to carry over into Julie. Added to these problems is the biological determinant of Julie's menstrual cycle, which makes her more emotionally unstable than usual. There is also the strong element of chance: her father's absence frees Julie and Jean from customary restraints, and it is chance that leads the couple into the locked room. The sensual excitement of the Midsummer Eve celebration contributes to the seduction and to Julie's final tragedy.

Jean's motivation, although less complex than Julie's, is also conditioned by his environment, his biological drives, his psychological desires, and his social aspirations. At the same time that he can despise the weaknesses of the old aristocrats, he finds himself unable to break his social conditioning. Only in the count's absence could Jean have brought himself to seduce Julie.

An added complication is the class conflict in which the decaying aristocracy, which Julie represents, must, by law of nature, be destroyed to make way for a stronger lower class that is more fit for survival in the modern world. Some things of value, such as sensitivity and honor, are lost; these are the qualities that break Julie and her father, while brutality and lack of scruples ensure Jean's final triumph. He survives because of his animal virility, his keen physical senses, and his strength of purpose. Religion has been discarded by the aristocracy as meaningless, and it is used by the working class to ensure their innocence. Love is seen as another romantic illusion created by the aristocracy to be used, as Julie uses it, to explain animal instincts in an acceptable manner. Jean, the pragmatic realist from the lower class, has no such need for excuses for sexual release.

To underline his themes and characterizations, Strindberg uses recurring animal imagery which links man with his animal nature, a technique which may be seen in the dreams of Julie and Jean, the foreshadowing effect of Julie's mother, Julie's attitude toward her dog, and the brutal death of Julie's beautiful, caged bird.

Miss Julie follows Aristotle's analysis of tragedy, moving audiences to pity, fear, and catharsis. Pity is aroused by the characters' inherent weaknesses and the social class structure they inhabit; fear is aroused when we realize that the same fate could overcome any of us; catharsis is produced when we realize that the old, decaying order must give way to the newer and stronger order for life to continue.

MRS. DALLOWAY

Type of work: Novel
Author: Virginia Woolf (1882–1941)
Type of plot: Psychological realism
Time of plot: 1920s
Locale: London
First published: 1925

Mrs. Dalloway traces a single day in the life of two characters, Clarissa Dalloway and Septimus Smith, largely through their impressions, thoughts, and feelings. For Clarissa the day culminates with a successful party; for Septimus it ends in suicide. In the complex psychological relationship between the two, Virginia Woolf suggests provocative ideas about the nature and meaning of life, love, time, and death.

Principal Characters

Clarissa Dalloway, a woman fifty-two years old and chic, but disconcerted over life and love. The June day in her late middle years is upsetting to Mrs. Dalloway, uncertain as she is about her daughter and her husband's love, her own feelings for them and her former fiancé, lately returned from India. Years before Peter Walsh had offered her agony and ecstasy, though not comfort or social standing, and so she had chosen Richard Dalloway. Now, seeing Peter for the first time in many years, her belief in her motives and her peace of mind are gone. Engaged in preparations for a party, she knows her life is frivolous, her need for excitement neurotic, and her love dead. Meeting her best friend, Sally Seton, also makes her realize that their love was abnormal as is her daughter's for an older woman. Although she knows that her husband's love for her is very real and solid, she feels that death is near, that growing old is cruel, that life can never be innocently good again.

Richard Dalloway, her politician husband, a Conservative Member of Parliament. Never to be a member of the Cabinet of a Prime Minister, Richard is a good man who has improved his character, his disposition, his life. Loving his wife deeply but silently, he is able only to give her a conventional bouquet of roses to show his feeling, a fortunate gift because roses are the one flower she can stand to see cut. Devoted to his daughter, he sees her infatuation as a passing thing, an adolescent emotional outlet. He is gently persuasive among his constituents and colleagues and in thought and deed a thoroughly good man.

Peter Walsh, a widower lately returned from India to make arrangements for the divorce of a major's wife, a woman half his age whom he plans to marry, again an action to fill the void left by Clarissa. Perceptive and quick to understand motives for unhappiness, Peter sees his return to England as another step in his failure to live without Clarissa. Unnerved by seeing her again, he blurts out his recent history, and he continues the cruel probe all day and that night at her party.

Septimus Warren Smith, a war casualty who commits suicide on the night of Mrs. Dalloway's party and delays the arrival of one of the guests, a doctor. A poet and a brave man, Septimus brings back to England an Italian war bride whom he cannot really love, all feeling having been drained from him by the trauma of war. Extremely sensitive to motives, Septimus sees his doctors as representing the world's attempt to crush him, to force him into conventionality. Feeling abandoned and unable to withstand even the devotion of his lovely wife, he jumps to his death, a martyr to the cause of individuality, of sensitivity to feelings and beauty.

Lucrezia Smith, called **Rezia,** the Italian wife whom Smith met in Milan and married after the war. Desperately in love with her husband, she tries to give him back his former confidence in human relations, takes him to doctors for consultation, and hopes to prevent his collapse and suicide.

Elizabeth Dalloway, the daughter who has none of her mother's charm or vivacity and all of her father's steady attributes. Judged to be handsome, the sensible seventeen-year-old appears mature beyond her years; her thoughtfulness directly contradicts her mother's frivolity. She is until this day enamored of Miss Kilman, a desperate and fanatical older woman who is in love with Elizabeth but conceals her feeling under the guise of religiosity and strident charity. On the day of the party Elizabeth sees Miss Kilman's desire for power and escapes from the woman's tyranny of power and need. That night Elizabeth blossoms forth in womanly radiance so apparent that her father fails to recognize her.

Doris Kilman, Elizabeth Dalloway's tutor and friend, an embittered, frustrated spinster whose religious fanaticism causes her to resent all the things she could not have or be. With a lucid mind and intense spirit, largely given to deep hatreds of English society, she represents a caricature of a perversion of womanly love and affection.

Lady Rosseter, née **Sally Seton,** the old friend with whom Mrs. Dalloway had believed herself in love when she was eighteen. Sally has always known that Clarissa made the wrong choice and has always been aware of the shallowness of her friend's existence. Mellowed now, Sally and Peter Walsh can see the pattern of life laid out before them at this gay party, and they console each other for loss of girlhood friend and beloved.

Dr. Holmes, Septimus Smith's physician. Brisk and insensitive, he fails to realize the seriousness of his patient's condition. Puzzled because Smith does not respond to prescriptions of walks in the park, music halls, and bromides at bedtime, he sends him to consult Sir William Bradshaw.

Sir William Bradshaw, a distinguished specialist who devotes three-quarters of an hour to each of his patients. Ambitious for worldly position but apathetic as a healer, he shuts away the mad, forbids childbirth, and advises an attitude of proportion in sickness and in health. Because of Septimus Smith's suicide he and his wife arrive late at Mrs. Dalloway's party.

Lady Millicent Bruton, a fashionable Mayfair hostess. A dabbler in charities and social reform, she is sponsoring a plan to have young men and women immigrate to Canada.

Hugh Whitbread, a friend of the Dalloways and a minor official at Court.

The Story

Mrs. Clarissa Dalloway went to make last-minute preparations for an evening party. During her day in the city, she enjoyed the summer air, the many sights and people, and the general bustle of London. She met Hugh Whitbread, now a court official and a handsome and sophisticated man. She had known Hugh since her youth, and she knew his wife, Evelyn, as well, but she did not particularly care for Evelyn. Other people came down to London to see paintings, to hear music, or to shop. The Whitbreads came down to consult doctors, for Evelyn was always ailing.

Mrs. Dalloway went about her shopping. While she was in a flower shop, a luxurious limousine pulled up outside. Everyone speculated on the occupant behind the drawn curtains of the car. Everywhere the limousine went, it was followed by curious eyes. Mrs. Dalloway, who had thought that the queen was inside, felt that she was right when the car drove into the Buckingham Palace grounds.

The sights and sounds of London reminded Mrs. Dalloway of many things. She thought back to her youth, to the days before her marriage, to her husband, and to her daughter Elizabeth. Her daughter was indeed a problem and all because of that horrid Miss Kilman who was her friend. Miss Kilman was a religious fanatic, who scoffed at the luxurious living of the Dalloways and felt sorry for Mrs. Dalloway. Mrs. Dalloway hated her. Miss Kilman was not at all like the friend of her own girlhood. Sally Seton had been different. Mrs. Dalloway had really loved Sally.

Mrs. Dalloway wondered what love really was. She had loved Sally, but she had loved Richard Dalloway and Peter Walsh, too. She had married Richard, and then Peter had left for India. Later, she learned that he had married someone he met on shipboard. She had heard little about his wife since his marriage. The day, however, was wonderful and life itself was wonderful. The war was over, and she was giving a party.

While Mrs. Dalloway was shopping, Septimus Smith and his wife were sitting in the park. Septimus had married Lucrezia while he was serving in Italy, and she had given up her family and her country for him. Now he frightened her because he acted so strangely and talked of committing suicide. The doctor said that there was nothing physically wrong with him. Septimus, one of the first to volunteer for war duty, had gone to war to save his country, the England of Shakespeare. When he got back, he was a war hero and was given a good job at the office. They had nice lodgings, and Lucrezia was happy. Septimus began reading Shakespeare again. He was unhappy; he brooded. He and Lucrezia had no children. To Septimus, the world was in such horrible condition that it was unjust to bring children into it.

When Septimus began to have visitations from Evans, a Comrade who had been killed in the war, Lucrezia became even more frightened and called in Dr. Holmes. Septimus felt almost completely abandoned by that time. Lucrezia could not understand why her husband did not like Dr. Holmes, for he was so kind and so interested in Septimus. Finally, she took her husband to Sir William Bradshaw, a wealthy and noted psychiatrist. Septimus had had a brilliant career ahead of him. His employer spoke highly of his work. No one knew why he wanted to kill himself. Septimus said that he had committed a crime, but his wife said that he was guilty of absolutely nothing. Sir William suggested a place in the country where Septimus would be by himself, without his wife. It was not, Sir William said, a question of preference. Since he had threatened suicide, it was a question of law.

In the meantime, Mrs. Dalloway returned home. Lady Bruton had invited Richard Dalloway to lunch. Mrs. Dalloway had never liked Millicent Bruton; she was far too clever. Then Peter Walsh came to call, and Mrs. Dalloway was surprised and happy to see him again. She introduced him to Elizabeth, her daughter. He asked Mrs. Dalloway if she were happy; she wondered why. When he left, she called out to him not to forget her party. Peter thought about Clarissa Dalloway and her parties; that was all life meant to her. He had been divorced from his wife and had come to England. Life was far more complicated for him. He had fallen in love with another woman, one who had two children, and he had come to London to arrange for her divorce and to get some sort of a job. He hoped Hugh Whitbread would find him one, something in the government.

That night, Clarissa Dalloway's party was a great success. At first, she was afraid that it would fail; but at last the prime minister arrived, and her evening was complete. Peter was there, and Peter met Lady Rossetter. Lady Rossetter turned out to be Sally Seton. She had not been invited but had just dropped in. She had five sons, she told Peter. They chatted. Then Elizabeth came in, and Peter noticed how beautiful she was.

Later, Sir William Bradshaw and his wife entered. They were late, they explained, because one of Sir William's patients had committed suicide. Feeling altogether abandoned, Septimus Smith had jumped out of a window before they could take him into the country. Clarissa was upset. Here was death, she thought. Although Smith was completely unknown to her, she somehow felt it was her own disaster, her own disgrace. The poor young man had thrown away his life when it became useless. Clarissa had never thrown away anything more valuable than a shilling into the Serpentine. Yes, once she had stood beside a fountain while Peter Walsh, angry and humiliated, had asked her whether she intended to marry Richard; and Richard had never been prime minister. Instead, the prime minister came to her parties. Now she was growing old. Clarissa Dalloway, knew herself at last for the beautiful, charming, inconsequential person she was.

Sally and Peter talked on. They thought idly of Clarissa and Richard and wondered whether they were happy together. Sally agreed that Richard had improved. She left Peter and went to talk with Richard. Peter was feeling strange. A sort of terror and ecstasy took hold of him, and he could not be certain what it was that excited him so suddenly. It was Clarissa, he thought. Even after all these years, it must be Clarissa.

Critical Evaluation

Mrs. Dalloway comes midway in Virginia Woolf's career and near the beginning of her experiments with form and technique (just after *Jacob's Room*, her first experimental novel). The book is really two stories—Clarissa Dalloway's and Septimus Smith's—and the techniques by which Woolf united these two narrative strands are unusual and skillful. While writing the novel, Woolf commented in her diary on her new method of delineating character. Instead of explaining the characters' pasts chronologically, she uses a "tunneling process": "I dig out beautiful caves behind my characters." The various characters appear in the present without explanation: various sense impressions—a squeaky hinge, a repeated phrase, a particular tree—call to their minds a memory, and past becomes present. Such an evocation of the past is reminiscent of Proust, but Woolf's method does not involve the ego of the narrator. Woolf's "caves" reveal the past and at the same time give characters' reactions to present events. Woolf is then able to connect the "caves" and also her themes by structural techniques, both spatial and temporal.

Unlike that of Joyce, Woolf's handling of the stream-of-consciousness method is always filtered and indirect; the narrator is in command, telling the reader, "Clarissa thought" or "For so it had always seemed to her." This ever-present narrative voice generally helps the reader by clarifying the characters' inner thoughts and mediating the commentary of the novel; at times, however, it blurs the identity of the speaker. Woolf's use of this narrative voice becomes more prominent in *To the Lighthouse* (1927) but disappears in *The Waves* (1931).

With its disparate characters and various scenes of street life, the structure of the book seems at first to lack unity. Woolf, however, uses many devices, both technical and thematic, to unite those elements. The day (in mid-June, 1923), moving uninterruptedly from the early morning to the late evening, is a single whole. Although the book is not divided into chapters or sections headed by titles or numbers, Woolf notes some of the shifts in time or scene by a short blank space in the manuscript. More often, however, the transition from one group of characters to another is accomplished by the remarking of something public, something common to the experience of both, something seen or heard. The world of Clarissa and her friends alternates with the world of Septimus Smith; and the sight of the motorcar, the sight and sound of the skywriting plane, the running child, the woman singing, the omnibus, the ambulance, and the clock striking are the transitions connecting those two worlds. Moreover, the striking of the clocks ("first a warning, musical; then the hour, irrevocable") is noted at various other times to mark a shift from one character's consciousness to another within Clarissa's group. The exact time is given periodically, signaling the day's progress (noon comes at almost the exact center of the book) and stressing the irrevocable movement toward death, one of the book's themes. Usually at least two clocks are described as striking—first Big Ben, a masculine symbol; then a few seconds later, St. Margaret's, a feminine symbol, suggesting again the two genders of all existence, united in the echoes of the bells, "the leaden circles."

The main thematic devices used to unify the book are the similarity between Clarissa and Septimus and the repetition of key words and phrases in the minds of various characters. The likeness between Clarissa and Septimus is most important, as each helps to explain the other, although they never meet. Both are lonely and contemplate suicide. Both feel guilty for their past lives, Septimus because he "cannot feel" the death of Evans, Clarissa because of her rejection of Peter and her tendency to dominate others. Both have homosexual feelings, Septimus for Evans, Clarissa for Sally Seton. More important, both want desperately to bring order out of life's chaos. Septimus achieves this momentarily with the making of Mrs. Peters' hat, and Clarissa creates a harmonious unity with her successful party. Septimus understands that the chaos will return and so takes his own life uniting himself with Death, the final order. Septimus' suicide forces Clarissa to see herself in a new and honest way, understanding for the first time her schemings for success. Clarissa "felt somehow very like him"; she does not pity him but identifies with his defiant "embracing" of death.

Certain phrases become thematic because they are so often repeated, gaining richer overtones of meaning at each use, as different characters interpret the phrases differently. "Fear no more," "if it were now to die," the sun, the waves—these are some of the phrases and images appearing over and over, especially in the thoughts of Septimus and Clarissa.

All the disparate strands of the story are joined at Clarissa's party, over which she presides like an artist over her creation. Not inferior to the painter Lily Briscoe— another observant character in *To the Lighthouse*—as a creator, Clarissa's great talent is "knowing people almost by instinct," and she is able triumphantly to combine the right group of people at her party. Not only Clarissa but Richard and Peter also come to a new realization about themselves at the party. Richard, who has been unable to verbalize his love for Clarissa, is finally able to tell his daughter Elizabeth that he is proud of her. At the end, Peter realizes that the terror and excitement he feels in Clarissa's presence indicate his true feeling for her.

The two figures who are given unfavorable treatment—Sir William, the psychiatrist, and Miss Kilman, the religious fanatic—insist on modes of existence inimical to the passionate desire of Clarissa and Septimus for wholeness. Claiming that Septimus "lacks proportion," Sir William nevertheless uses his profession to gain power over others and, as Clarissa understands, makes life "intolerable" for Septimus. Miss Kilman's life is built on evangelical religion; she considers herself superior to Clarissa, whom she wants to humiliate. She proudly asserts that she will have a "religious victory," which will be "God's will."

The real action of the story is all within the minds of the characters, but Woolf gives these inner lives a reality and harmony that reveals the excitement and oneness of human existence. Clarissa and Septimus are really two aspects of the same being—the feminine and the masculine—united in Clarissa's ultimate awareness. *Mrs. Dalloway* remains the best introduction to Woolf's characteristic style and themes.

MOBY DICK: Or, The Whale

Type of work: Novel
Author: Herman Melville (1819–1891)
Type of plot: Symbolic allegory
Time of plot: Early nineteenth century
Locale: High seas
First published: 1851

Herman Melville brought many disparate elements together in Moby Dick: Or, The Whale, *a realistic picture of the whaling industry, an adventure-romance of the sea, an epic quest, a Faustian bargain, and metaphysical speculation. Although it is unlikely that any one interpretation of Ahab's obsessive pursuit of the white whale will ever be generally accepted, the depth, sweep, and power of the author's vision guarantees the novel's stature as one of the world's proven masterpieces.*

Principal Characters

Ishmael, a philosophical young schoolmaster and sometime sailor who seeks the sea when he becomes restless, gloomy, and soured on the world. With a new-found friend Queequeg, a harpooner from the South Seas, he signs aboard the whaler *Pequod* as a seaman. Queequeg is the only person on the ship to whom he is emotionally and spiritually close, and this closeness is, after the initial establishment of their friendship, implied rather than described. Otherwise Ishmael does a seaman's work, observes and listens to his shipmates, and keeps his own counsel. Having been reared a Presbyterian (as was Melville), he reflects in much of his thinking the Calvinism out of which Presbyterianism grew; but his thought is also influenced by his knowledge of literature and philosophy. He is a student of cetology. Regarding Ahab's pursuit of Moby Dick, the legendary white whale, and the parts played by himself and others involved, Ishmael dwells on such subjects as free will, predestination, necessity, and damnation. After the destruction of the *Pequod* by Moby Dick, Ishmael, the lone survivor, clings to Queequeg's floating coffin for almost a day and a night before being rescued by the crew of another whaling vessel, the *Rachel*.

Queequeg, Starbuck's veteran harpooner, a tattooed cannibal from Kokovoko, an uncharted South Seas island. Formerly a zealous student of Christianity, he has become disillusioned after living among so-called Christians and, having reverted to paganism, he worships a little black idol, Yojo, that he keeps with him. Although he appears at ease among his Christian shipmates, he keeps himself at the same time apart from them, his only close friend being Ishmael. In pursuit of whales he is skilled and fearless. When he nearly dies of a fever he has the ship's carpenter build him a canoe-shaped coffin which he tries out for size and comfort; then, recovering, he saves it for future use. Ironically it is this coffin on which Ishmael floats after the sinking of the *Pequod* and the drowning of Queequeg.

Captain Ahab, the proud, defiant, megalomaniacal captain of the "Pequod." He is a grim, bitter, brooding, vengeful madman who has only one goal in life: the killing of the white whale that had deprived him of a leg in an earlier encounter. His most prominent physical peculiarity is a livid scar that begins under the hair of his head and, according to one crewman, extends the entire length of his body. The scar symbolizes the spiritual flaw in the man himself. His missing leg has been replaced by one of whalebone for which a small hole has been bored in the deck. When he stands erect looking out to sea, his face shows the indomitable willfulness of his spirit, and to Ishmael he seems a crucifixion of a "regal overbearing dignity of some mighty woe." Ahab is in complete, strict command of his ship, though he permits Starbuck occasionally to disagree with him. Ahab dies caught, like Fedallah the Parsee in a fouled harpoon line that loops about his neck and pulls him from a whaleboat.

Starbuck, the first mate, tall, thin, weathered, staid, steadfast, conscientious, and superstitious, a symbol of "mere unaided virtue or right-mindedness." He dares to criticize Ahab's desire for vengeance, but he is as ineffectual as a seaman trying to halt a storm. Ahab once takes his advice about repairing some leaking oil casks; but when Starbuck, during a typhoon off Japan, suggests turning home, Ahab scorns him. Starbuck even thinks of killing or imprisoning Ahab while the captain is asleep, but he cannot. Having failed to dissuade Ahab from the pursuing of Moby Dick, Starbuck submits on the third day to Ahab's will, though feeling that in obeying Ahab he is disobeying God. When he makes one final effort to stop the doomed Ahab, the captain shouts to his boatmen, "Lower away!"

Stubb, the second mate, happy-go-lucky, indifferent to danger, good-humored, easy; he is a constant pipe-smoker and a fatalist.

Flask (King-Post), the young third mate, short, stout, ruddy. He relishes whaling and kills the monsters for the fun of it or as one might get rid of giant rats. In his shipboard actions, Flask is sometimes playful out of Ahab's sight but always abjectly respectful in his presence.

Fedallah, Ahab's tall, diabolical, white-turbaned Parsee servant. He is like the shadow of Ahab or the two are like opposite sides of a single character and Ahab seems finally to become Fedallah, though retaining his own appearance. The Parsee prophesies that Ahab will have neither hearse nor coffin when he dies. Fedallah dies caught in a fouled harpoon line which is wrapped around Moby Dick.

Moby Dick, a giant albino sperm whale that has become a legend among whalers. He has often been attacked and he has crippled or destroyed many men and boats. He is both a real whale and a symbol with many possible meanings. He may represent the universal spirit of evil, God the indestructible, or indifferent Nature; or perhaps he may encompass an ambiguity of meaning adaptable to the individual reader. Whatever his meaning, he is one of the most memorable nonhuman characters in all fiction.

Pip, the bright, jolly, genial little Negro cabin boy who, after falling from a boat during a whale chase, is abandoned in midocean by Stubb, who supposes that a following boat will pick him up. When finally taken aboard the *Pequod,* he has become demented from fright.

Tashtego, an American Indian, Stubb's harpooner. As the *Pequod* sinks, he nails the flag still higher on the mast and drags a giant seabird, caught between the hammer and the mast, to a watery grave.

Daggoo, a giant African, Flask's harpooner.

Father Mapple, a former whaler, now the minister at the Whaleman's Chapel in New Bedford. He preaches a Calvinistic sermon on Job filled with seafaring terms.

Captain Peleg and **Captain Bildad,** fighting, materialistic Quakers, who are the principal owners of the *Pequod.*

Elijah, a madman who warns Ishmael and Queequeg against shipping with Captain Ahab.

Dough-Boy, the pale, bread-faced, dull-witted steward who deathly afraid of Queequeg, Tashtego, and Daggoo does his best to satisfy their enormous appetites.

Fleece, the ship's cook. At Stubb's request he preaches a sermon to the voracious sharks and ends with a hope that their greed will kill them. He is disgusted also by Stubb's craving for whale meat.

Bulkington, the powerfully built, deeply tanned, soberminded helmsman of the *Pequod.*

Perth, the ship's elderly blacksmith, who took up whaling after losing his home and family. He makes for Ahab the harpoon intended to be Moby Dick's death dart, which the captain baptizes in the devil's name.

Captain Gardiner, the skipper of *Rachel* for whose lost son Captain Ahab refuses to search.

The Story

Ishmael was a schoolmaster who often felt that he must leave his quiet existence and go to sea. Much of his life had been spent as a sailor, and his voyages were a means for ridding himself of the restlessness which frequently seized him. One day, he decided that he would sign on a whaling ship, and packing his carpetbag, he left Manhattan and set out, bound for Cape Horn and the Pacific.

On his arrival in New Bedford, he went to the Spouter Inn near the waterfront to spend the night. There he found he could have a bed only if he consented to share it with a harpooner. His strange bedfellow frightened him when he entered the room, for Ishmael was certain that the stranger was a savage cannibal. After a few moments, however, it became evident that the native, whose name was Queequeg, was a friendly person, for he presented Ishmael with an embalmed head and offered to share his fortune of thirty dollars. The two men quickly became friends and decided to sign on the same ship.

Eventually they signed on the *Pequod,* a whaler out of Nantucket, Ishmael as a seaman, Queequeg as a harpooner. Although several people seemed dubious about the success of a voyage on a vessel such as the *Pequod,* which was reported to be under so strange a man as Captain Ahab, neither Ishmael nor Queequeg had any intention of giving up their plans. They were, however, curious to see Captain Ahab.

For several days after the vessel had sailed, there was no sign of the captain, as he remained hidden in his cabin. The running of the ship was left to Starbuck and Stubb, two of the mates, and though Ishmael became friendly with them, he learned very little about Ahab. One day, as the ship was sailing southward, the captain strode out on deck. Ishmael was struck by his stern, relentless expression. In particular, he noticed that the captain had lost a leg and that instead of a wooden leg, he now wore one cut from the bone of the jaw of a whale. A livid white scar ran down one side of his face and was lost beneath his collar, so that it seemed as though he were scarred from head to foot.

For several days, the ship continued south looking for the whaling schools. The sailors began to take turns on masthead watches to give the sign when a whale was sighted. Ahab appeared on deck and summoned all his men around him. He pulled out an ounce gold piece, nailed it to the mast, and declared that the first man to sight the great white whale, known to the sailors as Moby Dick, would have the gold. Everyone expressed enthusiasm for the quest except Starbuck and Stubb, Starbuck especially deploring the madness with which Ahab had directed all his energies to this one end. He told the captain that he was like a man possessed, for the white whale was a menace to those who would attempt to kill him. Ahab had lost his leg in his last encounter with Moby Dick; he might lose his life in the next meeting; but the captain would not listen to the mate's warning. Liquor was brought out, and at the captain's orders, the crew drank to the destruction of Moby Dick.

Ahab, from what he knew of the last reported sighting of the whale, plotted a course for the ship that would bring it into the area where Moby Dick was most likely to be. Near the Cape of Good Hope, the ship came across a school of sperm whales, and the men busied themselves harpooning, stripping, melting, and storing as many as they were able to catch.

When they encountered another whaling vessel at sea, Captain Ahab asked for news about the white whale. The captain of the ship warned him not to attempt to chase Moby Dick, but it was clear by now that nothing could deflect Ahab from the course he had chosen.

Another vessel stopped them, and the captain of the ship boarded the *Pequod* to buy some oil for his vessel. Captain Ahab again demanded news of the whale, but the captain knew nothing of the monster. As the captain was returning to his ship, he and his men spotted a school of six whales and started after them in their rowboats. While Starbuck and Stubb rallied their men into the *Pequod*'s boats, their rivals were already far ahead of them. The two mates, however, urged their crew until they outstripped their rivals in the race, and Queequeg harpooned the largest whale.

Killing the whale was only the beginning of a long and arduous job. After the carcass was dragged to the side of the boat and lashed to it by ropes, the men descended the side and slashed off the blubber. Much of the body was usually eaten by sharks, who swarm around it snapping at the flesh of the whale and at each other. The head of the whale was removed and suspended several feet in the air, above the deck of the ship. After the blubber was cleaned, it was melted in tremendous try-pots and then stored in vats below deck.

The men were kept busy, but their excitement increased as their ship neared the Indian Ocean and the probable sporting grounds of the white whale. Before long, they crossed the path of an English whaling vessel, and Captain Ahab again demanded news of Moby Dick. In answer, the captain of the English ship held out his arm, which from the elbow down consisted of sperm whalebone. Ahab demanded that his boat be lowered at once, and he quickly boarded the deck of the other ship. The captain told him of his encounter and warned Captain Ahab that it was foolhardy to try to pursue Moby Dick. When he told Ahab where he had seen the white whale last, the captain of the *Pequod* waited for no civilities but returned to his own ship to order the course changed to carry him to Moby Dick's new feeding ground.

Starbuck tried to reason with the mad captain, to persuade him to give up this insane pursuit, but Ahab seized a rifle and in his fury ordered the mate out of his cabin.

Meanwhile, Queequeg had fallen ill with a fever. When it seemed almost certain he would die, he requested that the carpenter make him a coffin in the shape of a canoe, according to the custom of his tribe. The coffin was then placed in the cabin with the sick man, but as yet there was no real need for it. Not long afterward Queequeg recovered from his illness and rejoined his shipmates. He used his coffin as a sea chest and carved many strange designs upon it.

The sailors had been puzzled by the appearance early in the voyage of the Parsee, Fedallah. His relationship to the captain could not be determined, but that he was highly regarded was evident. Fedallah had prophesied that the captain would die only after he had seen two strange hearses for carrying the dead upon the sea, one not constructed by mortal hands and the other made of wood grown in America. He also said that the captain himself would have neither hearse nor coffin for his burial.

A terrible storm arose one night. Lightning struck the masts so that all three flamed against the blackness of the night, and the men were frightened by this omen. It seemed to them that the hand of God was motioning them to turn from the course to which they had set themselves and return to their homes. Only Captain Ahab was undaunted by the sight. He planted himself at the foot of the mast and challenged the god of evil which the fire symbolized for him. He vowed once again his determination to find and kill the white whale.

A few days later, a cry rang through the ship. Moby Dick had been spotted. The voice was Captain Ahab's, for none of the sailors, alert as they had been, had been able to sight him before their captain. Then boats were lowered and the chase began, with Captain Ahab's boat in the lead. As he was about to dash his harpoon into the mountain of white, the whale suddenly turned on the boat, dived under it, and split it into pieces. The men were thrown into the sea, and for some time the churning of the whale prevented rescue. At length, Ahab ordered the rescuers to ride into the whale and frighten him away, so he and his men might be picked up. The rest of that day was spent chasing the whale, but to no avail.

The second day, the men started out again. They caught up with the whale and buried three harpoons in his white flanks, but he so turned and churned that the lines became twisted, and the boats were pulled every which way, with no control over their direction. Two of them were splintered, and the men had to be hauled out of the sea, but Ahab's boat had not as yet been touched. Suddenly, Ahab's boat was lifted from the water and thrown high into the air. The captain and the men were quickly picked up, but Fedallah was nowhere to be found.

When the third day of the chase began, Moby Dick seemed tired, and the *Pequod*'s boats soon overtook him. bound to the whale's back by the coils of rope from the harpoon poles, they saw the body of Fedallah. The first part of his prophecy had been fulfilled. Moby Dick, enraged by his pain, turned on the boats and splintered them. On the *Pequod*, Starbuck watched and turned the ship toward the whale in the hope of saving the captain and some of the crew. The infuriated monster swam directly into the *Pequod*, shattering the ship's timbers. Ahab, seeing the ship founder, cried out that the *Pequod*—made of wood grown in America—was the second hearse of Fed-

allah's prophecy. The third prophecy, Ahab's death by hemp, was fulfilled when rope from Ahab's harpoon coiled around his neck and snatched him from his boat. All except Ishmael perished. He was rescued by a passing ship after clinging for hours to Queequeg's canoe coffin, which had bobbed to the surface as the *Pequod* sank.

Critical Evaluation

Although his early adventure novels—*Typee* (1846), *Omoo* (1847), *Redburn* (1849), and *White Jacket* (1850)—brought Herman Melville a notable amount of popularity and financial success during his lifetime, it was not until nearly fifty years after his death—in the 1920s and 1930s—that he received universal critical recognition as one of the greatest nineteenth century American authors. Melville took part in the first great period of American literature—the period that included Poe, Emerson, Hawthorne, Whitman, and Thoreau. For complexity, originality, psychological penetration, breadth, and symbolic richness, Melville achieved his greatest artistic expression with the book he wrote when he was thirty, *Moby Dick: Or, The Whale*. Between the time of his birth in New York City and his return there to research and write his masterpiece, Melville had circled the globe of experience—working as a bank messenger, salesman, farmhand, schoolteacher (like his narrator, Ishmael), engineer and surveyor, bowling alley attendant, cabin boy, and whaleman in the Pacific on the *Acushnet*. His involvement in a mutinous Pacific voyage, combined with J. N. Reynolds' accounts of a notorious whale called "Mocha Dick" (in the *Knickerbocker Magazine*, 1839), certainly influenced the creation of *Moby Dick*.

The intertangled themes of this mighty novel express the artistic genius of a mind that, according to Hawthorne, "could neither believe nor be comfortable in unbelief." Many of those themes are characteristic of American Romanticism: the "isolated self" and the pain of self-discovery, the insufficiency of conventional practical knowledge in the face of the "power of blackness," the demonic center of the world, the confrontation of evil and innocence, the fundamental imperfection of man coupled with his Faustian heroism, the search for the ultimate truth, and the inadequacy of human perception. The conflict between faith and doubt was one of the major issues of the century, and *Moby Dick*, as Eric Mottram points out, is part of "a huge exploration of the historical and psychological origins and development of self, society and the desire to create and destroy gods and heroes." *Moby Dick* is, moreover, a work that eludes classification, combining elements of the psychological and picaresque novel; sea story and allegory; the epic of "literal and metaphorical quest"; the satire of social and religious events; the emotional intensity of the lyric genre, both

in diction and metaphor; Cervantian romance; Dantesque mysticism; Rabelaisian humor; Shakespearean drama (both tragedy and comedy), complete with stage directions; journalistic travel book; and scientific treatise on cetology. Melville was inspired by Hawthorne's example to give his story the unifying quality of a moral parable, although his own particular genius refused to allow that parable an unequivocal, single rendering. Both in style and theme, Melville was also influenced by Spenser, Shakespeare, Dante, Cervantes, Robert Burton, Sir Thomas Browne, Thomas Carlyle, and vastly miscellaneous reading in the New York Public Library (as witnessed by the two "Etymologies" and the marvelous "Extracts" that precede the text itself, items from the writer's notes and files that he could not bear to discard). It was because they did not know how to respond to its complexities of form and style that the book was "broiled in hell fire" by contemporary readers and critics. Even today, the rich mixture of its verbal texture—an almost euphuistic flamboyance balanced by dry, analytical expository prose—requires a correspondingly receptive range on the part of the reader.

Perhaps the most remarkable thing about the plot of the novel is that Moby Dick does not appear physically until after five hundred pages and is not even mentioned by name until nearly two hundred pages into the novel. Yet whether it be the knowledge of reality, an embodiment of the primitive forces of nature, the deep subconscious energies of mankind, fate or destiny inevitably victorious over illusory free will, or simply the unknown in experience, it is the question of what Moby Dick stands for that tantalizes the reader through the greater part of the novel. In many ways, the great white whale may be compared to Spenser's "blatant beast" (who, in *The Faerie Queene*, also represents the indeterminable elusive quarry, and also escapes at the end to continue haunting the world).

It is not surprising that *Moby Dick* is often considered to be "the American epic." The novel is replete with the elements characteristic of that genre: the piling up of classical, biblical, historical allusions to provide innumerable parallels and tangents that have the effect of universalizing the scope of action; the narrator's strong sense of the fatefulness of the events he recounts, and his corresponding awareness of his own singular importance as the narrator of momentous, otherwise unrecorded, events; Queequeg as Ishmael's "heroic companion"; the "folk" flavor provided by countless proverbial statements; the leisurely pace of the narrative, with its frequent digressions and parentheses; the epic confrontation of life and death on a suitably grand stage (the sea), with its consequences for the human city (the *Pequod*); the employment of microcosms to explicate the whole (for example, the painting in the Spouter Inn, the Nantucket pulpit, the crow's nest); epithetical characterization; a cyclic notion of time and events; an epic race of heroes, the Nantucket whalers with their biblical and exotic names; the mystical power of objects like Ahab's chair, the doubloon, or the *Pequod* itself; the alienated, sulking hero (Ahab); the use of lists to enhance the impression of an all-inclusive compass. Finally, *Moby Dick* shares the usually didactic purpose of the epic; on one level, its

purpose is to teach the reader about whales; on another level, it is to inspire the reader to become, himself, a heroic whaleman.

All this richness of purpose and presentation is somehow made enticing by Melville's masterly invention of his narrator. Ishmael immediately establishes a comfortable rapport with the reader in the unforgettable opening lines of the novel. He is both an objective observer of and a participant in the events recounted, both spectator and narrator. Yet he is much more than the conventional wanderer/witness. As a schoolmaster and sometime voyager, he combines book learning with firsthand experience, making him an informed observer and a convincing, moving reporter. Simply by surviving, he transcends the Byronic heroism of Ahab, as the wholesome overcomes the sinister.

LE MORTE D'ARTHUR

Type of work: Chronicle
Author: Sir Thomas Malory (1400?–1471)
Type of plot: Chivalric romance
Time of plot: Golden Age of chivalry
Locale: Britain
First published: c. 1469; printed 1485

Le Morte d'Arthur *is a monumental work which made the Arthurian cycle available for the first time in English. Malory took a body of legends, which had gone from the folklore of Celtic Britain into French literature by way of Brittany, gave those tales a typically English point of view, and added, amended, and deleted for his own purposes, to produce a work which has had tremendous influence on literature ever since.*

Principal Characters

Arthur (är'thər), king of Britain and head of the Round Table, a brave, just, and temperate ruler. He values the fellowship of his men above revenge for his queen's infidelity, and he closes his eyes to her love for Launcelot until Mordred and Agravaine force him to act.

Queen Guenevere (gwĕn'ə·vĭr), a jealous, passionate woman whose fury drives her lover Launcelot mad. She repents after the king is betrayed by Mordred, and she dies in a convent.

Launcelot du Lake (lôn'sə·lŏt dü lāk), the greatest of all the knights except those who achieve the Grail quest. He is, himself, granted a vision of the Grail, but his love for the queen bars him from success in spite of his deep and sincere penitence.

Tristram (trĭs'trəm), the great Cornish knight who is the faithful and devoted lover of Isolde, the wife of his uncle, King Mark. Like Launcelot, he adheres firmly for the knightly code of honor and continues to fight for his country even after Mark has tried to have him murdered.

Isolde (ĭ·sōd'), an Irish princess, married to King Mark for political reasons although she has loved Tristram from the time she cured him of a wound incurred while he jousted with her brother.

Mark, the cowardly, jealous king of Cornwall, who becomes increasingly bitter and vengeful toward Tristram.

Isolde la Blanche Mains (ĭ·sōd' ləblänsh män), Tristram's wife, Princess of Brittany.

Gawain (gä'wĭn), Arthur's nephew. He stands for virtue and justice untempered by mercy in his uncle's final contest with Launcelot, but he dishonors his fellowship earlier by beheading a lady and killing Lamorak de Galis when that knight was unarmed.

Sir Kay, Arthur's sardonic, mocking foster brother and seneschal.

Galahad (găl'ə·hăd), Launcelot's son, the best of the knights, who sits in the Siege Perilous and draws Balin's sword from a great stone as a prelude to his successful Grail quest. He dies after a vision in which he receives

the sacrament from St. Joseph of Arimathaea.

Percival (pûr'sə·vəl) and **Bors de Ganis** (bôrs də gä'nĭs), virtuous knights who accompany Galahad on the quest of the Grail. Bors alone returns to Arthur's court to describe their visions.

Palamides (păl·ə·mē'dēz), a valiant pagan knight, for many years Tristram's deadly enemy and Isolde's secret admirer. He is finally won over by his rival's courage and honor and signifies his new friendship by being christened.

Lamorak de Galis (lăm'ə·răk də gä'lĭs), a knight famous for his strength and valor, who is surpassed only by Launcelot and Tristram. He is killed by Gawain and his brothers for his affair with their mother.

Mordred (môr'drĕd), Arthur's son by his sister, an ill-tempered, evil knight who eventually destroys the fellowship of the Round Table and his royal father.

Agravaine (ăg'rə·vān) and **Gaheris** (gä'hėr·ĭs), Gawain's brothers, participants in Mordred's plots and in the slaying of their mother and Lamorak.

Gareth (găr'ĭth), a tall, handsome young man who undertakes his first quest as "Beaumains," the kitchen boy, but later reveals himself as the brother of Gawain.

Linet (lĭ·nĕt'), the damsel whose quest Gareth fulfills. She mocks and criticizes the inexperienced young knight until after he has rescued her sister.

Liones (lī·ə·nĕs'), Linet's sister, later Gareth's bride.

Balin le Sauvage (bā'lĭn lə sō·văzh'), a Northumbrian knight, fated by the acquisition of a magic sword to kill his beloved brother, Balan.

Dinadan (dĭn'ə·dăn'), Tristram's commonsensical, witty companion, who scorns love.

King Pelles (pĕl'ēz), the Fisher King of the Grail legends at some points, although his identity is often unclear. He understands the mysteries of the Sangreal and arranges the conception of Galahad, the knight who is to achieve the quest and cure the wounded king.

Elaine (ĭ·lān'), Pelles' daughter and Galahad's mother,

who loves Launcelot in spite of his rejection of her.

Elaine le Blanc the fair maid of Astolat who perishes of love for Launcelot.

King Evelake (ĕv·ə·lāk'), an ancient ruler, converted by St. Joseph of Arimathaea. He lives generations beyond his time to have the promised sight of the knight who will complete the Grail quest.

Merlin (mûr'lĭn), the magician whose spell allows King Uther Pendragon to enter Tingtail Castle in the shape of the rightful Duke of Cornwall, husband of the lovely Igraine, Arthur's mother. In return, Uther promises that the child thus conceived will be turned over to Merlin, to be reared under his charge.

Nimue (nĭm·ōō·ē'), the Lady of the Lake, Merlin's mistress, who serves as a *deus ex machina* for several of the knights.

Morgan le Fay (môr'gən lə fā), Arthur's half sister, who continually devises evil for him and his knights.

Pellinore (pel'ĭ·nōr), a bold knight who single-mindedly pursues the Questing Beast.

Gouvernail (gŭv·ėr·nāl'), Tristram's tutor and constant companion.

Brangwaine (brăng'wān), Isolde's maid and confidante.

Ector de Maris (ĕk'tər də mař'ĭs), **Lionel** (lī'ən·ĕl), **Dodinas le Sauvage** (dō·dē'năs lə sō-vazh'), **Sagramore** (săg'rə·mōr), **Breunor le Noire** (brė'nōr lə nwär), and **Safere** (să·fĭr'), brave and honorable knights.

Meliogrance (mē'lyō·grăns'), a treacherous nobleman who kidnaps Guenevere, then accuses her of treason with Launcelot when she refuses to yield to him.

The Story

King Uther Pendragon saw and loved Igraine, the beautiful and chaste Duchess of Cornwall. His desires, however, were checked by Igraine's husband. King Uther made war on Cornwall, and in that war, the duke was killed. By means of magic, King Uther caused Igraine to become pregnant; the couple were subsequently married. The child, named Arthur, was raised by a noble knight, Sir Ector. After the death of King Uther, Arthur proved his right to the throne by removing a sword from an anvil that was imbedded in a rock. From the Lady of the Lake, he received his famous sword, Excalibur. When the independent kings of Britain rebelled and made war on the young king, they were defeated. Arthur ruled over all Britain.

King Arthur married Guinevere, the daughter of King Leodegrance, who presented the Round Table and a hundred knights to Arthur as a wedding gift. Merlin the magician was enticed by one of the Ladies of the Lake into eternal imprisonment under a rock.

Five foreign kings invaded Arthur's realm and were defeated after a long war. To show his gratitude to God for his victory, King Arthur founded the Abbey of the Beautiful Adventure at the scene of his victory.

Sir Accolon was the paramour of Morgan le Fay, enchantress sister of King Arthur. He fought Arthur with Excalibur, which Morgan le Fay had procured from Arthur by black magic. Arthur was nearly overcome; but in the fight, their swords were accidentally exchanged, and the King defeated Accolon.

King Lucius of Rome sent ambassadors to Britain to demand tribute of King Arthur. When Arthur refused to pay, he was promised aid in war by all the knights of his realm. In the war that followed, the British defeated Lucius and conquered Germany and Italy. Arthur was crowned Emperor of Rome.

Back in England, Sir Launcelot, a knight of the Round Table and Queen Guinevere's favorite, set out on adventures to further the honor and glory of himself and of his queen. After many long and arduous adventures, all of them triumphant, Sir Launcelot returned to Camelot, the seat of King Arthur, and was acclaimed the first knight of all Christendom.

Elizabeth, queen of King Meliodas of Liones, died in giving birth to a son, who was named Tristram because of the sad circumstances surrounding his birth. Young Tristram was sent to France with his preceptor, Gouvernail, where he was trained in all the accomplishments of knighthood. The King of Ireland demanded tribute from King Mark of Cornwall. Sir Tristram thus defended the sovereignty of King Mark, his uncle, by slaying the Irish champion, Sir Marhaus, but he was wounded in the contest. He was nursed by Isolde, princess of Ireland. Tristram and Isolde fell in love and promised to remain true to each other. Later, King Mark commissioned Sir Tristram to return to Ireland to bring back Isolde, whom the King had contracted to marry. During the return voyage from Ireland to Cornwall, Tristram and Isolde drank a love potion and swore undying love. Isolde married King Mark, and Sir Tristram later married Isolde la Blanche Mains, daughter of King Howels of Brittany. Unable to remain separated from Isolde of Ireland, Tristram joined her secretly. At last, fearing discovery and out of his mind for love of Isolde, Tristram fled into the forest. In a pitiful condition, he was carried back to the castle, where a faithful hound revealed his identity to King Mark. King Mark then banished Tristram from Cornwall for ten years. The knight went to Camelot, where he won great renown at tourneys and in knightly adventures. King Mark heard of Tristram's honors and went in disguise to Camelot to kill Tristram. Sir Launcelot recognized King Mark and took him to King Arthur, who ordered the Cornish sovereign to allow Sir Tristram to return to Cornwall. In

Cornwall, King Mark attempted unsuccessfully to get rid of Tristram. Tristram, however, managed to avoid all the traps set for him, and he and Isolde escaped to England and took up residence in Castle Joyous Guard.

An old hermit prophesied to King Arthur that a seat which was vacant at the Round Table would be occupied by a knight not yet born—one who would win the Holy Grail.

After Sir Launcelot was tricked into an affair with Elaine, the daughter of King Pelles, the maid gave birth to a boy named Galahad. Some years later, a stone with a sword imbedded in it appeared in a river. A message on the sword stated that the best knight in the world would remove it. All the knights of the Round Table attempted to withdraw the sword without success. Finally, an old man brought a young knight to the Round Table and seated him in the vacant place at which the young knight's name, Sir Galahad, appeared magically after he had been seated. Sir Galahad withdrew the magic sword from the stone and set out, with Arthur's other knights, in quest of the Holy Grail. During his quest, he was joined part of the time by his father, Sir Launcelot. Sir Launcelot tried to enter the Grail chamber and was stricken for twenty-four days as a penance for his years of sin. A vision of Christ came to Sir Galahad; he and his comrades received communion from the Grail. They came to a city in the near east where they healed a cripple. Because of this miracle, they were thrown into prison by the pagan king. When the king died, Sir Galahad was chosen king; he saw the miracles of the Grail and died in holiness.

There was great rejoicing in Camelot after the questing knights returned. Sir Launcelot forgot the promises he had made during the quest and began to consort again with Guinevere.

One spring while traveling with her attendants, Guinevere was captured by a traitorous knight, Sir Meliagr-

ance. Sir Launcelot rescued the queen and killed the evil knight. Enemies of Launcelot reported Launcelot's love for Guinevere to King Arthur. A party championing the king's cause engaged Launcelot in combat. All members of the party except Mordred, Arthur's natural son, were slain. Guinevere was sentenced to be burned, but Sir Launcelot and his party saved the queen from the stake and retired to Castle Joyous Guard. When King Arthur besieged the castle, the pope commanded a truce between Sir Launcelot and the king. Sir Launcelot and his followers went to France, where they became rulers of that realm. King Arthur invaded France with the intent of overthrowing Sir Launcelot; in Arthur's absence, Mordred seized the throne of Britain and tried to force Guinevere to become his queen. Guinevere escaped to London, where she took refuge in the Tower. Hearing of the disaffection of Sir Mordred, King Arthur returned to England and in a great battle drove the usurper and his false knights back to Canterbury.

At a parley between King Arthur and Sir Mordred, an adder caused a knight to draw his sword. This action brought on a pitched battle in which Mordred was killed and King Arthur was mortally wounded. On his deathbed, King Arthur asked Sir Bedivere to cast Excalibur back into the lake from which the sword had come. Sir Bedivere hid the sword twice but was reproached by the king each time. Finally, Sir Bedivere threw the sword into the lake, where it was caught by a hand and withdrawn under the water.

King Arthur died and was carried on a barge down the river to the Vale of Avalon. When Sir Launcelot returned from France to avenge his king and queen, he learned that Guinevere had become a nun. Sir Launcelot retired to a hermitage and took holy orders. Sir Constantine of Cornwall was chosen king to succeed King Arthur.

Critical Evaluation

The author of *Le Morte d'Arthur* was the unusual Sir Thomas Malory of Newbold Revel. The strange circumstances of his life contributed significantly to the shape and meaning of his masterwork. Born about 1400, he served with Richard Beauchamp, Earl of Warwick, was knighted in 1442, and was elected a Member of Parliament in 1445. For whatever reasons of military adventure, Malory turned to a life of irresponsible violence and spent most of his last twenty years in prison until his death in 1471. It was during his imprisonment that Malory composed, translated, and adapted his great rendering of the Arthurian material. His active, fifteenth century life accounts for many of the differences between his vigorous narrative and its contemplative, ruminative antecedents in chivalric literature. Malory lived just a little past the age of chivalry, at a time when its elegance and leisure had to be rationalized.

Malory is the most influential of all Arthurian writers. He was the source and delight of Spenser and the wellspring of Tennyson's *Idylls of the King*. First printed by Caxton in one volume in 1485, *Le Morte d'Arthur* has been consistently popular since, except during the Augustan period of the early eighteenth century. Caxton's printing is the source of all extant versions except a manuscript discovered in 1934 in the Fellows' Library of Winchester College. The Winchester manuscript, which seems generally more reliable than Caxton, not only made the identity of the author more certain but also showed that Caxton had condensed the original.

Malory's *Le Morte d'Arthur* is itself a condensation, adaptation, and rearrangement of earlier materials. It is based primarily on the French Arthurian Prose Cycle (1225–1230) known as the Vulgate, a conglomeration of courtly stories of Launcelot, ostensibly historical accounts of the court of Arthur and stories of the quest for the Holy Grail. Eugène Vinaver, the foremost editor and critic of Malory, has explained that the differences between the Vulgate and Malory's narrative are good indicators of the nature of Malory's achievement.

The primary structure of the Vulgate is episodic, and its narrative movement is largely flashbacks. Episodes prepare for and elucidate other episodes that may have occurred earlier. It did not grow by accretion; its shape is a reflection of an alternative aesthetic. The result is a web of themes in which forward movement of the narrative is subordinated to the demonstration and clarification of the dominant ideals of the work. Malory took this source, added material from the fourteenth century English *Alliterative Morte d'Arthur* and, to a lesser extent, from the *Stanzaic Morte*, and fashioned a new kind of fictional structure. The result is not simply condensation but a disentanglement of the elements of the narrative and a recombination of them into an order, an emphasis, and a significance entirely alien to the sources.

Vinaver has identified two primary ways in which Malory transformed the structure of the narrative. First, certain episodes are formed into self-contained units, almost short stories, by detachment from their context and the excision of extraneous detail. For example, in the Vulgate the incidents grouped together by Malory as the story of the Knight of the Cart appeared long before the Grail quest; Malory puts them long after and organizes them as an exemplum of Launcelot's noble ideals rather than as a prefiguration of his amatory commitment. Consequently, Malory gives the episode a different significance by omission and shortening. Malory's second mode of transformation is to fashion a coherent narrative from bits and pieces taken from his sources. In the story of the Fair Maid of Astolat, for example, he organizes details into a sequential form.

The most striking change in the sources is Malory's imposition of a consistently forward chronological movement. The courtly digressions and the significant configurations of explanatory episodes are gone. Instead, there is a straightforward narrative that alters both the tone and meaning of the original. Malory had no comprehension of or sympathy for the tradition of courtly love that permeated his sources. Where its vestiges cannot be omitted, Malory translates them into something more compatible with his genius. Therefore, Lancelot is no longer the "knight of the cart" because of courtly self-debasement for the beloved but because of a dedication to chivalric ideals. The elegance and controlled artificiality of his antecedents are changed by Malory into directness and moral earnestness. Launcelot becomes a christianized, somewhat sentimentalized, figure who is the model of the moderation that leads to supernatural rewards. Similarly, in the story of Pelles and Ettard, Malory makes Pelles' behavior more practical than courtly. After Ettard's infidelity, Malory substitutes the poetic justice of her death and Pelles' happiness for the courtly self-abnegation demonstrated by Pelles in the Vulgate.

Sometimes Malory's fiction suffers from the tension between his sources and his rendering of them. Not all the courtly and mysterious elements are completely rationalized into the new intention and some undecipherable oddities result. *Le Morte d'Arthur*, however, remains a vigorous and compelling narrative, full of the spirit of adventurous knighthood. As Vinaver has shown in detail, Malory has substituted outdoor images for courtly affectation, the real English countryside for the conventional French, vigorous speech for conventional dialogues, and direct human relationships for the elaborate rituals of courtly love. All of this is accomplished in a blunt and lively prose which is the antithesis of the intricacies of the French sources and is perfectly suited to Malory's more direct structure and more forthright moral attitude.

MOURNING BECOMES ELECTRA

Type of work: Drama
Author: Eugene O'Neill (1888–1953)
Type of plot: Romantic tragedy
Time of plot: Shortly after the Civil War
Locale: New England
First presented: 1931

In Mourning Becomes Electra, *a trilogy (*Homecoming, The Hunted, The Haunted*) loosely based on Aeschylus'* Oresteia, *O'Neill dramatizes his conviction that the Greek concept of fate could be replaced by the modern notion of psychological—especially Freudian—determination. The Mannons are driven to their self-destructive behavior by inner needs and compulsions they can neither understand nor control. Such, O'Neill believed, was the material of contemporary tragedy.*

Principal Characters

Lavinia Mannon, daughter of Christine and Ezra Mannon. Tall, flat-breasted, angular, and imperious in manner. Lavinia is fond of her father and fiercely jealous of her mother. While Ezra was fighting in the Civil War Christine had been having an affair with Captain Adam Brant. Unconscious desire to have Adam for herself leads Lavinia to demand that Christine give up Brant or face a scandal which would ruin the family name. Unable to go on living with a husband she despises, Christine plots with Adam to poison Ezra when he returns. Ezra is murdered and Lavinia discovers her mother's guilt. When her brother Orin returns, wounded and distraught, from the war, Lavinia tries to enlist his aid in avenging their father's death. Orin refuses until Lavinia proves Christine's guilt by a ruse. Blaming Adam for the murder, Orin goes to Adam's ship and shoots him. When Orin reveals to Christine what he has done, she kills herself. Orin and Lavinia then close the Mannon house and voyage to the South Seas. Symbolically liberated from the repressiveness of the New England Puritan tradition, Lavinia blossoms into a duplicate of her voluptuous mother. She plans to marry and start a new life. But Orin, hounded by his guilt and going mad, threatens to reveal the Mannons' misdeeds and tries to extort from Lavinia a lover's promise never to leave him. Lavinia agrees but ruthlessly drives Orin to suicide. Now convinced that the Mannon blood is tainted with evil, she resolves to punish herself for the Mannons' guilt. She orders the house shuttered and withdraws into it forever.

Christine Mannon, Lavinia's mother, tall, beautiful, and sensual. Fearing that she will be killed or arrested for her husband's murder, she makes plans with Adam Brant to flee the country and sail for a "happy island." Orin kills Brant. When Orin taunts her with his deed, Christine goes into the Mannon house and shoots herself.

Orin Mannon, Lavinia's brother, a young idealist who has been spiritually destroyed by the war. Progressively degenerating under the burden of his guilt, Orin conceives that Lavinia has taken the place of his beloved mother. Resolved that Lavinia shall never forget what they have done, Orin writes a history of the Mannon family and uses the manuscript to force Lavinia to promise never to leave him.

General Ezra Mannon, Christine's husband, a tall, big-boned, curt, and authoritative aristocrat. Cold, proud, and unconsciously cruel, Ezra always favored Lavinia over Christine and Orin. When he returns from the war, he tries desperately to make Christine love him, but too late. She reveals her infidelity, causing Ezra to have a heart attack. When he asks for medicine, she gives him poison.

Captain Adam Brant, Christine's lover, the captain of a clipper ship. The son of Ezra Mannon's uncle and a servant girl, Marie Brantôme, Adam has sworn to revenge himself on the Mannons, who had allowed his mother to die of poverty and neglect. His first approaches to the Mannon house were motivated by this desire for revenge, but he falls deeply in love with Christine.

Captain Peter Niles, of the U.S. Artillery, a neighbor, Lavinia's intended. Lavinia is forced by Orin to give up her plans to marry Peter and leave behind her the collective guilt of the Mannon family.

Hazel Niles, Peter's sister and Orin's fiancée. She persists in trying to help the erratic Orin lead a normal life. As she becomes aware that Lavinia and Orin share some deep secret, she fears Lavinia will ruin Peter's life and demands of Lavinia that she not marry him.

Seth Beckwith, the Mannon's gardener, a stooped but hearty old man of seventy-five. Seth serves as commentator and chorus throughout the play.

Amos Ames, Louisa, his wife, and **Minnie,** Louisa's cousin, townsfolk who act as the chorus in *Homecoming*.

Josiah Borden, manager of the shipping company, **Emma,** his wife, and **Everett Hills, D. D.,** Congregational minister, the chorus in *The Hunted*.

The Chantyman, a drunken sailor who carries on a suspense-building conversation with Adam Brant as Brant waits for Christine to join him on his ship.

Joe Silva, Ira Mackel, and **Abner Small,** the chorus in *The Haunted*.

Avahanni, a Polynesian native with whom Lavinia carried on a flirtation. Lavinia's falsely telling Orin that Avahanni had been her lover helps drive Orin to suicide.

The Story

The Civil War was over, and in their New England home Christine and Lavinia Mannon awaited the homecoming of old Ezra Mannon and his son Orin. Lavinia, who adored her father, detested Christine because of Ezra's love for his wife. Christine, on the other hand, jealously guarded Orin's love because she hated her husband and her daughter. In this house of hidden hatred, Seth, the gardener, watched the old mansion and saw that Lavinia also despised Captain Brant, who was a steady caller at the Mannon home.

The Mannons, descended from old New England stock, had their family skeleton. Dave Mannon, Ezra's brother, had run off with an Indian woman named Marie Brantôme. Seth, seeing the antagonism between Lavinia and her mother, disclosed to Lavinia that Captain Brant was the son of Marie and Dave Mannon.

Embittered by her mother's illicit romance with Brant and jealous of Christine's hold on Ezra, Lavinia forced Christine to send her lover away. But Christine was too powerful a woman to succumb to her daughter's dominance. She urged the grudge-bearing Brant to send her some poison. It was common knowledge that Ezra had heart trouble, and Christine was planning to rid herself of the husband whom she hated so that she would be free to marry Brant. Lavinia cruelly reminded her mother that her favorite offspring was Orin, who was born while Ezra had been away during the Mexican War.

The family jealousies were obvious by the time Ezra came home. Ezra, a kind, just man, realized that Christine shrank from him while she attempted to pretend concern for his health. That night in their bedroom Ezra and Christine quarreled over their failing marriage. Ezra had a heart attack, and when he gasped for his medicine Christine gave him the poison instead. As he lay dying in Lavinia's arms, the helpless man feebly but incoherently accused Christine of guilt in his murder. Lavinia had no proof, but she did suspect her mother's part in Ezra's death.

Peter and Hazel Niles, cousins of the Mannons, came to the mansion after Ezra's death. Peter was a rejected suitor of Lavinia, and Hazel was in love with Orin. Lavinia spied upon her mother constantly. When Orin came home, the two women vied for his trust, Lavinia trying to create suspicion against her mother and Christine attempting to regain her son's close affection. Uncomfortable under her daughter's look of silent, sneering accusation, Christine finally realized that Lavinia had found the box of poison. While Hazel, Peter, and Christine tried to make a warm welcome for Orin, Lavinia hovered over the group like a specter of gloom and fatality. Able to get Orin alone before Lavinia could speak to him, Christine told her son about Lavinia's suspicions concerning Captain Brant and Ezra's death, and she tried to convince Orin that Lavinia's distraction over Ezra's death had warped her mind.

Orin, whose affection for his mother had made him dislike Ezra, believed Christine, but the returned soldier swore that if he ever discovered that the story about Captain Brant were true, he would kill Brant. Desperately, Christine told Lavinia that Orin's trust had been won, that Lavinia need not try to take advantage of his credulity; but Lavinia stared at her mother in silent defiance. Under her daughter's cold stare Christine's triumphant manner collapsed into a pathetic plea that Lavinia should not endanger Brant's life, for Orin had threatened to kill him.

Lavinia slyly hinted the truth to Orin, and his old childhood trust in his sister led him to believe her story in part, unwillingly however, for he was still influenced by love for his mother. Lavinia hinted that Christine might run to Brant at the first opportunity. Orin agreed to wait for proof, and if sufficient proof were offered, then to kill Brant. Lavinia instructed Orin to maintain his pretense that he believed her to be mad.

Shortly after Ezra's funeral, Christine did go to Brant. Orin and Lavinia had pretended to be paying a call on a nearby estate, but they followed their mother to Brant's ship, where they overheard the lovers planning to run off together. Although Orin was consumed with jealous hatred of Brant, Lavinia restrained him from impulsive action. When Christine had gone, Orin went into the cabin and shot Brant. Then the brother and sister rifled the ship's cabin and Brant's pockets to make the death appear to have been a robbery and murder.

Orin and Lavinia returned to the Mannon mansion and told Christine what they had done. At the sight of his mother's grief Orin fell to his knees, pleading with her to forgive him and to give him her love. Fearing he had lost his mother's affection, the bewildered boy rushed from the room, but Lavinia faced her mother victoriously. Christine went into the house and shot herself. Orin, in a frenzy of grief, accused himself of his mother's murder.

Lavinia took her brother on a long sea trip to help him overcome his feeling of guilt. When they returned, Orin was completely under Lavinia's control, reciting in toneless speech the fact that Christine had been an adulteress and a murderess and that Orin had saved his mother from public hanging. He was changed in appearance and spirit; it was plain that strange thoughts of grief and guilt preyed on his mind. During the trip Lavinia had grown to look and behave like Christine.

Lavinia was now able to accept Peter's love, but when Orin saw his sister in Peter's embrace, he became angered for a brief moment before he congratulated Peter and Lavinia. When Orin became engaged to Hazel, Lavinia was afraid to leave Orin alone with the girl for fear he would say too much about the past.

Orin began to write a family history, urged by a remorseful desire to leave a record of the family crimes. Becoming jealous of Lavinia's engagement to Peter, he threatened to expose her if she married him. Orin kept hinting to Lavinia that, like Christine, she was planning to poison him as Christine had poisoned the man who held her in bondage. Finally, driven to distraction by Orin's morbid possessive attitude toward her and by his incessant reminding of their guilt, Lavinia suggested to the crazed mind that he kill himself. As Peter held Lavinia in his arms, Orin went to the library to clean his pistol. His death was assumed to have been an accident.

Hazel suspected some vile and sinister fact hidden in Orin's accidental death. She went to Lavinia and pleaded with her not to ruin Peter by marrying him, but Lavinia denied that there was any reason to put off the marriage. While she spoke, however, Lavinia realized that the dead Mannons would always rule her life. The others had been cowards, and had died. She would live. She sent Peter away. Then she ordered Seth the gardener to board up the windows of the mansion. Alone, the last surviving Mannon, Lavinia entered the old house to spend the rest of her life with the dead.

Critical Evaluation

Eugene O'Neill, America's first dramatist to win international recognition, was awarded the Nobel Prize in Literature in 1936. One of the most ambitious playwrights since Aeschylus and Shakespeare, he introduced the European movements of realism, naturalism, and expressionism to the American stage as devices to express his comprehensive interest in all of life. His plays often make stringent demands on the actors and audience: the long monologues of *The Iceman Cometh* and *Strange Interlude*, the unrelenting despair of *Long Day's Journey into Night*, and the five-hour production length of *Mourning Becomes Electra*.

O'Neill, of Irish Catholic stock, literally grew up in the theater. He was born in a New York hotel while his father, the famous actor, James O'Neill, was starring in *The Count of Monte Cristo*. His mother, suffering from the pains of Eugene's birth, began taking morphine and soon became an addict. Many of O'Neill's plays deal with the intense love-hate relationships and tensions of his mother, father, brother, and himself. The most intensive and explicit of these is the powerful *Long Day's Journey into Night*, published posthumously in 1956. Before becoming a playwright, he briefly attended Princeton, worked as a sailor, and had a bout with tuberculosis. While in the sanatorium, he decided to become a playwright.

O'Neill's plays are bound together by consistent concerns. Embedded in them the reader will find a rejection of Victorian gentility, of materialism and opportunism, and of Puritan beliefs. He shared the postwar disillusionment with others of his generation who discovered that the Great War to end all wars had been a death trap for young men. His plays exhibit a keen sense of loss of the individual's relationship with his family, his nation, his society's values, nature, and God. Science, materialism, religion all fail to give O'Neill's heroes a satisfying meaning for life, or comfort from the fear of death. Still, they engage in often heroic struggles against total alienation. Many of O'Neill's strongest plays center on the question of whether illusions are, after all, the only thing that make reality bearable. He also consistently incorporated popular Freudian psychology in an attempt to project the subconscious levels of his characters. *Mourning Becomes Electra*, a trilogy consisting of *Homecoming, The Hunted,* and *The Haunted*, although set at the end of the American Civil War, is an adaptation of the greatest of Aeschylus' trilogies, the *Oresteia*.

Mourning Becomes Electra illustrates the struggle between the life-force and death, in which attempts to express natural sensual desires and love of others or even of life itself are overcome by the many forms of death: repression derived from the Puritan religion, death-in-life engendered by society's values, isolation, war, and actual physical death. This struggle is present not only in the plot structure, where each play culminates in actual death, but also in the setting, the actors' faces, stances, and costumes, and repetitive refrains. Darkness, associated with death, pervades the plays: *Homecoming*, for instance, begins with the sunset, moves into twilight, and ends in the dark of night; *The Hunted* takes place during night; *The Haunted* spans two evenings and a late afternoon, indicating the inevitable coming of night, darkness, and death as Lavinia retreats to rejoin the host of dead Mannons.

The Mannon house itself, seen by the audience at the beginning of each play, stands amid the beauty and abundance of nature. It has a white Greek temple portico which, O'Neill directs, should resemble "an incongruous white mask fixed on the house to hide its somber grey ugliness." That the house is an ironic inversion of the affirmation and love of this life associated with the Greeks is soon obvious. Christine thinks of the house as a tomb of cold gray stone, and even Ezra compares it to a "white meeting house" of the Puritans, a temple dedicated to duty, denial of the beauty of life and love—to death. The house itself is not only alienated from nature but also isolated from the community, built on the foundations of pride and hatred and Puritan beliefs. Its cold façade and isolation symbolize the family which lives within it, whose name indicates their spiritual relationship to Satan's chief helper, Mammon. The "curse" of this house stems from the effects of materialism, Puritanism, alienation, and repression of all that is natural—a death-in-life.

The stiff, unnatural bearing of the Mannons and the look of their faces are further evidence that the family is dead in the midst of life. Even the townspeople comment on the Mannons' "secret look." Their dead, masklike faces—in portraits of Orin and Ezra, on Christine's face when she is about to commit suicide, on Lavinia's face after Orin's death—all indicate the Mannons' denial of life, their repression of their sensual natures, and their refusal or inability to communicate with others. The dark costumes of all the family also indicate the hold that death has on them and accentuates the green satin worn first by Christine and later by Lavinia as they struggle to break out of their tomb and reach life.

The instinct of love and life survives strongest in the women, but even they are defeated. The search for pure love through a mother-son relationship is futile, for the Oedipal complex leads beyond the bounds of a pure relationship, as Orin finally realizes. Family love, too, fails, as is evident in the relationships between Christine and Lavinia and Ezra and Orin. Even love between men and women fails—as in the cases of Christine and Ezra and Lavinia and Peter—to triumph over the alienation and loneliness of the Mannon world.

The leitmotif of the South Sea islands, symbols of escape from the death cycle of heredity and environment of New England society, is present throughout the three plays. The islands represent a return to mother earth, a hope of belonging in an environment far removed from Puritan guilt and materialism. Brant has been to these islands; Ezra wishes for one; Orin dreams of being on one with Christine; Christine wants to go to an island; Orin and Lavinia do finally travel to the islands. However, they come to realize that they cannot become a permanent part of the island culture, but must return to the society to which they belong by birth and upbringing. As symbols of escape, then, the islands, too, finally fail.

The Mannons try all avenues of escape from their deathly isolation. David Mannon attempted to escape with Marie Brantôme, but finally turned to drinking and suicide. Ezra "escaped" through concentrating on his business

and then on the business of death—war—before he realized the trap of death. Christine focuses her attempts to escape first on her son and then on Brant. Orin tries to escape through his mother's love, then through Hazel's, and finally, in desperation, suggests an incestuous relationship with Lavinia. Lavinia does not see the dimensions of the death trap and does not desire escape until her trip to the islands, where she experiences the abundance of guilt-free life. After her return, she is willing to let Orin die, just as Christine let Ezra die, in order to be free to love and live. But then, too late, she feels the curse of the guilt associated with the Puritan beliefs and realizes that she cannot escape. Lavinia learns that Orin was right: the killer kills part of himself each time he kills until finally nothing alive is left in him. She underscores this in her last conversation with Peter, remarking, "Always the dead between [us]. . . . The dead are too strong." Death itself is the only real escape for the alienated, guilt-ridden Mannons.

Compared to its source, Aeschylus' *Oresteia*, O'Neill's themes and characterization seem shallow. Christine, who goads Ezra into a heart attack because of her hatred of his attitude toward their sexual relationship and her love of Brant, is no match for Clytemnestra, who revenges the death of her daughter, her insulted pride, and hatred of Agamemnon with a bloody knife. The weak, neurotic Orin is likewise a lesser character than Orestes, whose strong speech of triumphant justice over his mother's slain body breaks only with his horrified vision of the Furies. Yet Ezra is more human than Agamemnon, and Lavinia's complexities far outstrip Electra's: her recognition and acceptance of her fate is in the noble tradition of the tragic hero.

The radical difference in the intentions of the two playwrights accounts for some of these disparities. Aeschylus, whose major themes are concerned with the victory of man's and the gods' laws, concludes his trilogy with the establishment of justice on earth and the reconciliation of Orestes with society and the gods, affirming that good has come out of evil, order from chaos, and wisdom from suffering. In *Mourning Becomes Electra*, however, the curse is not lifted, but confirmed at the end, as Lavinia gives up her futile struggle against the psychological effects of Puritanical guilt. O'Neill's major concerns are with the detrimental effects of the materialism; the alienation of man from meaningful relationships with others, nature, and God; the death heritage of Puritanical beliefs; and the psychological "furies" that drive us all. Although the psychological analysis of these representative members of American society may be oversimplified occasionally, in the hands of a good director and cast *Mourning Becomes Electra* is one of the few works by an American dramatist that can truly be said to evoke the tragic emotions of pity, fear, and perhaps even awe in a modern audience.

MUCH ADO ABOUT NOTHING

Type of work: Drama
Author: William Shakespeare (1564–1616)
Type of plot: Romantic comedy
Time of plot: Thirteenth century
Locale: Italy
First presented: 1598

Much Ado About Nothing *focuses on two love affairs, the rivalry between the reluctant Beatrice and the confirmed bachelor Benedick, and the more serious courtship between Hero and Claudio. The former is one of the wittiest romantic conflicts in dramatic literature; the latter narrowly avoids catastrophe by means of a necessary, if contrived, manipulation of the plot to achieve a happy ending.*

Principal Characters

Don Pedro (pä′drō, pē′drō), Prince of Aragon. A victorious leader, he has respect and affection for his follower Claudio, for whom he asks the hand of Hero. Deceived like Claudio into thinking Hero false, he angrily shares in the painful repudiation of her at the altar. On learning of her innocence, he is deeply penitent.

Don John, the bastard brother of Don Pedro. A malcontent and a defeated rebel, he broods on possible revenge and decides to strike Don Pedro through his favorite, Claudio. He arranges to have Don Pedro and Claudio witness what they think is a love scene between Hero and Borachio. When his evil plot is exposed, he shows his guilt by flight. All in all, he is a rather ineffectual villain, though his plot almost has tragic consequences.

Claudio (klô′dĭ·ō), a young lord of Florence. A conventional hero of the sort no longer appealing to theater audiences, he behaves in an unforgivable manner to Hero when he thinks she is faithless; however, she—and apparently the Elizabethan audience—forgives him. He is properly repentant when he learns of her innocence, and he is rewarded by being allowed to marry her.

Benedick (bĕn′ə·dĭk), a witty young woman-hater. A voluble and attractive young man, he steals the leading role from Claudio. He spends much of his time exchanging sharp remarks with Beatrice. After being tricked by the Prince and Claudio into believing that Beatrice is in love with him, he becomes devoted to her. After Claudio's rejection of Hero, Benedick challenges him; but the duel never takes place. His witty encounters with Beatrice end in marriage.

Hero (hē′rō), the daughter of Leonato. A pure and gentle girl, extremely sensitive, she is stunned by the false accusation delivered against her and by Claudio's harsh repudiation of her in the church. Her swooning is reported by Leonato as death. Her character contains humor and generosity. She forgives Claudio when he repents.

Beatrice (bē′ə·trĭs), Hero's cousin. Although sprightly and witty, she has a serious side. Her loyal devotion to Hero permits no doubt of her cousin to enter her mind; she turns to her former antagonist, Benedick, for help when Hero is slandered and insists that he kill his friend Claudio. When all is clear and forgiven, she agrees to marry Benedick, but with the face-saving declaration that she does so for pity only.

Leonato (lē·ō·nä′tō), Governor of Messina, father of Hero. A good old man, he welcomes Claudio as a prospective son-in-law. He is shocked by the devastating treatment of his daughter at her wedding. Deeply angry with the Prince and Claudio, he at first considers trying to kill them but later consents to Friar Francis' plan to humble them. When Hero is vindicated, he forgives them and allows the delayed marriage to take place.

Conrade (kŏn′răd), a tale-bearing, unpleasant follower of Don John.

Borachio (bō·rä′kē·ō), another of Don John's followers. He is responsible for the idea of rousing Claudio's jealousy by making him think Hero has received a lover at her bedroom window. He persuades Margaret to wear Hero's gown and pretend to be Hero. His telling Conrade of his exploit is overheard by the watch and leads to the vindication of Hero. Borachio is much disgruntled at being overreached by the stupid members of the watch; however, he confesses and clears Margaret of any willful complicity in his plot.

Friar Francis, a kindly, scheming cleric. He recommends that Hero pretend to be dead. His plan is successful in bringing about the repentance of Don Pedro and Claudio and in preparing the way for the happy ending.

Dogberry, a self-important constable. Pompous, verbose, and prone to solecisms, he fails to communicate properly with Leonato; hence he does not prevent Hero's humiliation, though his watchmen have already uncovered the villains.

Verges (vėr′jĕs), a headborough. An elderly, bumbling man and a great admirer of his superior, the constable, he seconds the latter in all matters.

Margaret, the innocent betrayer of her mistress, Hero. She does not understand Borachio's plot and therefore is exonerated, escaping punishment.

Ursula (ėr′sū·lə), a gentlewoman attending Hero. She is one of the plotters who trick the sharp-tongued Beatrice into falling in love with Benedick.

First Watchman and **Second Watchman,** plain, simple-minded men. Overhearing Borachio's boastful con-

fession to Conrade, they apprehend both and bring them before the constable, thereby overthrowing clever malice and radically changing the course of events.

Antonio (ăn·tō′nĭ·ō), Leonato's brother. He plays the role of father to Leonato's supposed niece (actually Hero), whom Claudio agrees to marry in place of his lost Hero.

Balthasar (băl′thə·zăr), an attendant to Don Pedro.

A Sexton, who serves as recorder for Dogberry and the watch during the examination of Conrade and Borachio.

The Story

Don Pedro, Prince of Arragon, arrived in Messina accompanied by his bastard brother, Don John, and his two friends, Claudio and Benedick, young Italian noblemen. Don Pedro had been successful over his brother in battle. Reconciled, the brothers planned to visit Leonato before returning to their homeland. On their arrival in Messina, young Claudio was immediately smitten by the lovely Hero, daughter of Leonato. In order to help his faithful young friend in his suit, Don Pedro assumed the guise of Claudio at a masked ball and wooed Hero in Claudio's name. Thus he gained Leonato's consent for Claudio and Hero to marry. The bastard Don John tried to cause trouble by persuading Claudio that Don Pedro meant to betray him and keep Hero for himself, but the villain was foiled in his plot and Claudio remained faithful to Don Pedro.

Benedick, the other young follower of Don Pedro, was a confirmed and bitter bachelor who scorned all men willing to enter the married state. No less opposed to men and matrimony was Leonato's niece, Beatrice. These two were at each other constantly, each one trying to gain supremacy by insulting the other. Don Pedro, with the help of Hero, Claudio, and Leonato, undertook the seemingly impossible task of bringing Benedick and Beatrice together in matrimony in the seven days remaining before the marriage of Hero and Claudio.

Don John, thwarted in his first attempt to cause disharmony, now formed another plot. With the help of a servingman, he arranged to make it appear that Hero was unfaithful to Claudio. The servingman was to gain entrance to Hero's chambers when she was away. In her place would be her attendant, assuming Hero's clothes. Don John, posing as Claudio's true friend, would inform him of her unfaithfulness and lead him to Hero's window to witness her wanton disloyalty.

In the meantime Don Pedro carried out his plan to get Benedick and Beatrice to stop quarreling and fall in love with each other. When Benedick was close by, thinking himself unseen, Don Pedro, Claudio, and Leonato would talk of their great sympathy for Beatrice, who loved Benedick but was unloved by him. To each other, the three told sorrowful tales of the love letters Beatrice wrote to Benedick and then tore up. Sadly they said that Bea-

trice beat her breast and sobbed over her unrequited love for Benedick. Meanwhile Hero and her servingwoman would, when Beatrice was nearby but thought herself unseen, tell tales of poor Benedick, who pined and sighed for the heartless Beatrice. Thus both the unsuspecting young people decided not to let the other suffer. Each would sacrifice principles and accept the other's love.

As Benedick and Beatrice were ready to admit their love for each other, Don John was successful in his base plot to ruin Hero. He told Claudio that he had learned of Hero's duplicity and he arranged to take him and Don Pedro to her window that very night, when they might witness her unfaithfulness. Dogberry, a constable, and the watch apprehended Don John's followers and overheard the truth of the plot, but in their stupidity the petty officials could not get their story told in time to prevent Hero's disgrace. Although Don Pedro and Claudio did indeed witness the feigned betrayal, Claudio determined to let her get to the church on the next day still thinking herself beloved. There, instead of marrying her, he would shame her before all the wedding guests.

All happened as Don John had hoped. Before the priest and all the guests Claudio called Hero a wanton and forswore her love for all time. The poor girl protested her innocence, but to no avail. Claudio said that he had seen with his own eyes her foul act. Then Hero swooned and lay as if dead. Claudio and Don Pedro left her thus with Leonato, who also believed the story and wished his daughter really dead in her shame. But the priest, believing the girl guiltless, persuaded Leonato to believe in her too. The priest told Leonato to let the world believe Hero dead while they worked to prove her innocent. Benedick, also believing in her innocence, promised to help unravel the mystery. Then Beatrice told Benedick of her love for him and asked him to kill Claudio and so prove his love for her. Benedick challenged Claudio to a duel. Don John fled the country after the successful outcome of his plot, but Benedick swore that he would find Don John and kill him as well as Claudio.

At last Dogberry and the watch got to Leonato and told their story. Claudio and Don Pedro heard it also, and Claudio wanted to die and to be with his wronged Hero. Leonato allowed the two sorrowful men to continue to think Hero dead. In fact, they all attended her funeral. Leonato said that he would be avenged if Claudio would marry his niece, a girl who much resembled Hero. Although Claudio still loved the dead Hero, he agreed to marry the other girl in order to let Leonato have the favor he had so much right to ask.

When Don Pedro and Claudio arrived at Leonato's house for the ceremony, Leonato had all the ladies masked. He brought forth one of them and told Claudio that she was to be his wife. After Claudio promised to be her husband, the girl unmasked. She was, of course, Hero. At first Claudio could not believe his senses, but after he was convinced of the truth he took her to the church immediately. Then Benedick and Beatrice finally declared their true love for each other. They too went to the church after a dance in celebration of the double nuptials to be performed. Best of all, word came that Don John had been captured and was being brought back to Messina to face his brother, Don Pedro. But his punishment must wait the morrow. Tonight all would be joy and happiness.

Critical Evaluation

Much Ado About Nothing has in fact very much to do with "noting" (an intended pun on "nothing") or with half seeing, with perceiving dimly or not at all. Out of all the misperceptions arises the comedy of Shakespeare's drama. Indeed if it can be said that one theme preoccupies Shakespeare more than any other it is that of perception. It informs not only his great histories and tragedies but his comedies as well. For example, an early history such as *Richard II*, which also involves tragic elements, proceeds not only from the title character's inability to function as a king but also from his failure to apprehend the nature of the new politics. Both Othello and King Lear are perfect representatives of the tragic consequences of the inability to see. Hindered by their egos they act in their own small worlds, oblivious to the reality that demands recognition. When they fail to take the real into account, whether it is the nature of evil or their own limitation, they must pay the full cost—their lives.

Although in *Much Ado About Nothing* the blindness of Leonato, Don Pedro, Claudio and Benedick very nearly results in tragedy, it is the comic implications that emerge from mere noting rather than clear seeing which Shakespeare is concerned with. Yet if his mode is comic, his intention is serious. Besides the characters' inability to perceive Don John's obvious villainy, their superficial grasp of love, their failure to understand the nature of courtship and marriage, reveal their moral stupidity. Going further we see that the whole society is filled with a kind of civilized shallowness. The play begins as an unspecified war ends, and immediately we are struck by Leonato's and the messenger's lack of response to the casualty report. To the governor of Messina's question "How many gentlemen have you lost in this action?" the messenger replies "But few of any sort, and none of name." Leonato comments that "A victory is twice itself, when the achiever brings home full numbers." The heroes of the war, Don Pedro, Claudio, and Benedick, return in high spirits and good humor, seemingly untouched by their experiences, seeking comfort, games, and diversion.

Only Beatrice is unimpressed by the soldiers' grand entrance, for she knows what they are. Between their "noble" actions, they, like Benedick, are no more than seducers, "valiant trencher" men, or gluttons and leeches. Or like Claudio they are vain young boys ready to fall in love on a whim. Even the stately Don Pedro is a fool who proposes to Beatrice on impulse after he has wooed the childish Hero for the inarticulate Claudio. After witnessing their behavior we look back to Beatrice's initial cynicism—"I had rather hear my dog bark at a crow, than a man swear he loves me"—and applaud it as wisdom.

Yet at last, Beatrice is as susceptible to flattery as Benedick. Like her eventual lover and husband, she is seduced by Don Pedro's deception, the masque he arranges to lead both Beatrice and Benedick to the altar. Both of them, after hearing that they are adored by the other, pledge their love and devotion. To be sure the scenes in which they are duped are full of innocent humor; but the comedy must not lead us astray of Shakespeare's rather bitter observations on the foppery of human love—or at least courtship as it is pursued in Messina.

Nor is their foppery and foolishness the end of the matter. Don John realizes that a vain lover betrayed is a cruel and indeed inhuman tyrant. With little effort he convinces Claudio and Don Pedro that the innocent Hero is no more than a common jade. Yet rather than break off the engagement in private, they wait until all meet at the altar to accuse the girl of "savage sensuality." Without compunction they leave her in a swoon believing her dead. Even the father, Leonato, would have her dead rather than shamed. It is at this moment that the witty and sophisticated aristocrats of Messina are revealed as grossly hypocritical, for beneath their glittering and refined manners lies a moronic and vicious ethic.

In vivid contrast to the decorous soldiers and politicians are Dogberry and his watchmen, who function— we are well reminded—as more than a slapstick diversion. Hilarious clowns as they attempt to ape their social betters in manner and speech, they are yet possessed by a common sense or—as one critic has observed—by an instinctual morality that enable them immediately to uncover the villainy of Don John's henchmen, Conrade and Borachio. As the latter says to the nobleman, Don Pedro, "I have deceived even your very eyes: what your wisdoms could not discover, these shallow fools have brought to light." Like the outspoken and bawdy Margaret, who knows that underlying the aristocrats' courtly manners in the game of love is an unacknowledged lust, Dogberry and his bumbling followers get immediately to the issue and recognize villainy—even if they use the wrong words to describe it.

Still, Shakespeare does not force the point to any great conclusion. After all, we are not dealing here with characters of monumental stature; certainly they cannot bear revelations of substantial moral consequence. If they show compunction for their errors, they exhibit no significant remorse and are quite ready to get on with the rituals of their class. It finally does not seem to matter to Claudio that he marries Hero or someone who looks very much like her. And even Beatrice has apparently, once and for all, lost her maverick edge and joins the strutting Benedick in the marriage dance. At least all ends well for those involved, if through no very great fault of their own—for everyone, that is, except Don John; and one suspects he should be concerned, for Benedick promises "brave punishments." If our illustrious heroes can be cruel to a young virgin, what can a real villain hope for?

MY ÁNTONIA

Type of work: Novel
Author: Willa Cather (1873–1947)
Type of plot: Regional chronicle
Time of plot: Late nineteenth and early twentieth centuries
Locale: Nebraska prairie
First Published: 1918

My Ántonia is the story of a Bohemian girl whose family came from the Old Country to settle on the open prairies of Nebraska. While she lives on her farm and tills the soil, she is a child of the prairie, but when Ántonia goes to the city, she faces heartbreak, disillusionment, and social ostracism. Only after her return to the land, which is her heritage, does she find peace and meaning in life.

Principal Characters

Ántonia Shimerda, a young immigrant girl of appealing innocence, simple passions, and moral integrity, the daughter of a Bohemian homesteading family in Nebraska. Even as a child she is the mainstay of her gentle, daydreaming father. She and Jim Burden, the grandson of a neighboring farmer, become friends, and he teaches her English. After her father's death her crass mother and sly, sullen older brother force her to do a man's work in the fields. Pitying the girl, Jim's grandmother finds work for her as a hired girl in the town of Black Hawk. There her quiet, deep zest for life and the Saturday night dances lead to her ruin. She falls in love with Larry Donovan, a dashing railroad conductor, and goes to Denver to marry him, but he soon deserts her and she comes back to Black Hawk, unwed, to have her child. Twenty years later Jim Burden, visiting in Nebraska, meets her again. She is now married to Cuzak, a dependable, hardworking farmer, and the mother of a large brood of children. Jim finds her untouched by farm drudgery or village spite. Because of her serenity, strength of spirit and passion for order and motherhood, she reminds him of stories told about the mothers of ancient races.

James Quayle Burden, called **Jim,** the narrator. Orphaned at the age of ten, he leaves his home in Virginia and goes to live with his grandparents in Nebraska. In that lonely prairie country his only playmates are the children of immigrant families living nearby, among them Ántonia Shimerda, with whom he shares his first meaningful experiences in his new home. When his grandparents move into Black Hawk he misses the freedom of life on the prairie. Hating the town, he leaves it to attend the University of Nebraska. There he meets Gaston Cleric, a teacher of Latin who introduces the boy to literature and the greater world of art and culture. From the university he goes on to study law at Harvard. Aided by a brilliant but incompatible marriage, he becomes the legal counsel for a Western railroad. Successful, rich, but unhappy in his middle years and in the failure of his marriage, he recalls his prairie boyhood and realizes that he and Ántonia Shimerda have in common a past that is all the more precious because it is lost and almost incommunicable, existing only in memories of the bright occasions of their youth.

Mr. Shimerda, a Bohemian farmer unsuited to pioneer life on the prairie. Homesick for the Old World and never happy in his Nebraska surroundings, he find his loneliness and misery unendurable, lives more and more in the past, and ends by blowing out his brains.

Mrs. Shimerda, a shrewd, grasping woman whose chief concern is to get ahead in the world. She bullies her family, accepts the assistance of her neighbors without grace, and eventually sees her dream of prosperity fulfilled.

Ambrož Shimerda, called **Ambrosch,** the Shimerdas' older son. Like his mother, he is insensitive and mean. Burdened by drought, poor crops, and debt, he clings to the land with peasant tenacity. Even though he repels his neighbors with his surly manner, sly trickery, and petty dishonesties, everyone admits that he is a hard worker and a good farmer.

Yulka Shimerda, Ántonia's younger sister, a mild, obedient girl.

Marek Shimerda, the Shimerdas' youngest child. Tongue-tied and feebleminded, he is eventually committed to an institution.

Mr. Burden, Jim Burden's grandfather, a Virginian who has bought a farm in Nebraska. Deliberate in speech and action, he is a just, generous man; bearded like an ancient prophet, he sometimes speaks like one.

Mrs. Burden, his wife, a brisk, practical woman who gives selfless love to her orphan grandson. Kindhearted, she gives assistance to the immigrant families of the region, and without her aid the needy Shimerdas would not have survived their first Nebraska winter.

Lena Lingard, the daughter of poor Norwegian parents, from childhood a girl attractive to men. Interested in clothes and possessing a sense of style, she is successful as a designer and later becomes the owner of a dress shop in San Francisco. She and Jim Burden become good friends while he is a student at the University of Nebraska. Her sensuous beauty appeals greatly to his youthful imagination, and he is partly in love with her before he goes to study at Harvard.

Tiny Soderball, a girl of all work at the hotel in Black Hawk. She moves to Seattle, runs a sailors' boarding house for a time, and then goes to Alaska to open a hotel for miners. After a dying Swede wills her his claim, she makes a fortune from mining. With a comfortable fortune put aside, she goes to live in San Francisco. When Jim Burden meets her there, she tells him the thing that interests her most is making money. Lena Lingard is her only friend.

Wycliffe Cutter, called **Wick,** a miserly moneylender who has grown rich by fleecing his foreign-born neighbors in the vicinity of Black Hawk. Ántonia Shimerda goes to work for him and his suspicious, vulgar wife. Making elaborate plans to seduce Ántonia, he puts some of his valuables in his bedroom and tells her that she is to sleep there, to guard them, while he and his wife are away on a trip. Mrs. Burden sends her grandson to sleep in the Cutter house, and Wick, returning ahead of his wife, is surprised and enraged to find Jim Burden in his bed. Years later, afraid that his wife's family will inherit his money if he should die first, he kills her and then himself.

Mrs. Cutter, a woman as mean and miserly as her husband, whom she nags constantly. He murders her before committing suicide.

Larry Donovan, a railroad conductor and gay ladies' man. He courts Ántonia Shimerda, promises to marry her if she will join him in Denver, seduces her, and then goes off to Mexico, leaving her pregnant.

Mrs. Steavens, a widow, the tenant on the Burden farm. She tells Jim Burden, home from Harvard, the story of Ántonia Shimerda's betrayal by Larry Donovan.

Otto Fuchs, the Burdens' hired man during their farming years. Born in Austria, he came to America when a boy and lived an adventurous life as a cowboy, a stage driver, a miner, and a bartender in the West. After the Burdens rent their farm and move into Black Hawk he resumes his drifting life.

Jake Marpole, the hired man who travels with young Jim Burden from Virginia to Nebraska. Though a kind-hearted man, he has a sharp temper and is violent when angry. He is always deeply ashamed if he swears in front of Mrs. Burden.

Christian Harling, a prosperous, straitlaced grain merchant and cattle buyer, a neighbor of the Burden family in Black Hawk.

Mrs. Harling, his wife, devoted to her family and to music. She takes a motherly interest in Ántonia Shimerda, who works for her as a hired girl for a time, but feels compelled to send her away when the girl begins to go to the Saturday night dances attended by drummers and town boys.

Peter and **Pavel,** Russian neighbors of the Burden family and Mr. Shimerda's friends. Just before he dies Pavel tells a terrible story of the time in Russia when, to save his own life, he threw a bride and groom from a sledge to a pack of wolves.

Anton Jelinek, the young Bohemian who makes the coffin for Mr. Shimerda's funeral. He becomes a friend of the Burdens and later a saloon proprietor.

Cuzak, Anton Jelinek's cousin, the sturdy farmer who marries Ántonia Shimerda. Though he has had many reverses in his life, he remains good-natured. Hardworking, dependable, considerate, he is a good husband to Ántonia.

Rudolph, Anton, Leo, Jan, Anna, Yulka, Nina, and **Lucie,** Ántonia's children by Cuzak.

Martha, Ántonia's daughter by Larry Donovan. She marries a prosperous young farmer.

Gaston Cleric, the young Latin teacher who introduces Jim Burden to the classics and the world of ideas. When he accepts an instructorship at Harvard, he persuades Jim to transfer to that university.

Genevieve Whitney Burden, Jim Burden's wife. Though she does not figure in the novel, her presence in the background helps to explain her husband's present mood and his nostalgia for his early years in Nebraska. Spoiled, restless, temperamental, independently wealthy, she leads her own life, interests herself in social causes, and plays patroness to young poets and artists.

The Story

Jim Burden's father and mother died when he was ten years old, and the boy made the long trip from Virginia to his grandparents' farm in Nebraska in the company of Jake Marpole, a hired hand who was to work for Jim's grandfather. Arriving by train late at night in the prairie town of Black Hawk, the boy noticed an immigrant family huddled on the station platform. He and Jake were met by a lanky, scar-faced cowboy named Otto Fuchs, who drove them in a jolting wagon across the empty prairie to the Burden farm.

Jim grew to love the vast expanse of land and sky. One day Jim's grandmother suggested that the family pay a visit to the Shimerdas, an immigrant family just arrived in the territory. At first the newcomers impressed Jim unfavorably. The Shimerdas were poor and lived in a dugout cut into the earth. The place was dirty. The children were ragged. Although he could not understand her speech, Jim made friends with the oldest girl, Ántonia.

Jim found himself often at the Shimerda home. He did not like Ántonia's surly brother, Ambrosch, or her grasping mother, but Ántonia, with her eager smile and great, warm eyes won an immediate place in Jim's heart. One day her father, his English dictionary tucked under his arm, cornered Jim and asked him to teach the girl English. She learned rapidly. Jim respected Ántonia's father. He was a tall, thin, sensitive man, a musician in the Old Country. Now he was saddened by poverty and burdened with overwork. He seldom laughed any more.

Jim and Ántonia passed many happy hours on the prairie. Then tragedy struck the Shimerdas. During a severe winter, Mr. Shimerda, broken and beaten by the prairie, shot himself. Ántonia had loved her father more than any other member of the family, and after his death she shouldered his share of the farm work. When spring came, she went with Ambrosch into the fields and plowed like a man. The harvest brought money. The Shimerdas soon had a house, and with the money left over they bought plowshares and cattle.

Because Jim's grandparents were growing too old to keep up their farm, they dismissed Jake and Otto and moved to the town of Black Hawk. There Jim longed for the open prairie land, the gruff, friendly companionship of Jake and Otto, and the warmth of Ántonia's friendship. He suffered at school and spent his idle hours roaming the barren gray streets of Black Hawk.

At Jim's suggestion, his grandmother arranged with a neighbor, Mrs. Harling, to bring Ántonia into town as her hired girl. Ántonia entered into her tasks with enthusiasm. Jim saw a change in her. She was more feminine; she laughed oftener; and though she never shirked her duties at the Harling house, she was eager for recreation and gaiety.

Almost every night she went to a dance pavilion with a group of hired girls. There in new, handmade dresses, the immigrant girls gathered to dance with the village boys. Jim Burden went, too, and the more he saw of the hired girls the better he liked them. Once or twice he worried about Ántonia, who was popular and trusting. When she earned a reputation for being a little too gay, she lost her position with the Harlings and went to work for a cruel moneylender, Wick Cutter, who had a licentious eye on her.

One night, Ántonia appeared at the Burdens and begged Jim to stay in her bed for the night and let her remain at the Burdens. Wick Cutter was supposed to be out of town, but Ántonia suspected that, with Mrs. Cutter also gone, he might return and harm her. Her fears proved correct, for as Jim lay awake in Ántonia's bed Wick returned and went to the bedroom where he thought Ántonia was sleeping.

Ántonia returned to work for the Harlings. Jim, eager to go off to college, studied hard during the summer and passed his entrance examinations. In the fall he left for the state university and although he found there a whole new world of literature and art, he could not forget his early years under the blazing prairie sun and his friendship with Ántonia. He heard little of Ántonia during those years. One of her friends, Lena Lingard, who had also worked as a hired girl in Black Hawk, visited him one day. He learned from her that Ántonia was engaged to be married to a man named Larry Donovan.

Jim went on to Harvard to study law, and for years heard nothing of his Nebraska friends. He assumed that Ántonia was married. When he made a trip back to Black Hawk to see his grandparents, he learned that Ántonia, deceived by Larry Donovan, had left Black Hawk in shame and returned to her family. There she worked again in the fields until her baby was born. When Jim went to see her, he found her still the same lovely girl, though her eyes were somber and she had lost her old gaiety. She welcomed him and proudly showed him her baby.

Jim thought that his visit was probably the last time he would see Ántonia. He told her how much a part of him she had become and how sorry he was to leave her again. Ántonia knew that Jim would always be with her, no matter where he went. He reminded her of her beloved father, who, though he had been dead many years, still lived nobly in her heart. She told Jim good-bye and watched him walk back toward town along the familiar road.

It was twenty years before Jim Burden saw Ántonia again. On a Western trip he found himself not far from Black Hawk, and on impulse he drove out in an open buggy to the farm where she lived. He found the place swarming with children of all ages. Small boys rushed forward to greet him, then fell back shyly. Ántonia had married well, at last. The grain was high, and the neat farmhouse seemed to be charged with an atmosphere of activity and happiness. Ántonia seemed as unchanged as she was when she and Jim used to whirl over the dance floor together in Black Hawk. Cuzak, her husband, seemed to know Jim before they were introduced, for Ántonia had told all her family about Jim Burden. After a long visit with the Cuzaks, Jim left, promising that he would return the next summer and take two of the Cuzak boys hunting with him.

Waiting in Black Hawk for the train that would take him East, Jim found it hard to realize the long time that had passed since the dark night, years before, when he had seen an immigrant family standing wrapped in their shawls on the same platform. All his memories of the prairie came back to him. Whatever happened now, whatever they had missed, he and Ántonia had shared precious years between them, years that would never be forgotten.

Critical Evaluation

The character of the pioneer woman Ántonia Shimerda represents a complexity of values, an axis about which *My Ántonia* revolves. The novel in turn illustrates two classical themes of American literature. Written in 1918, it reaches back into the nineteenth century and beyond for its artistic and moral direction.

Willa Cather, the product of a genteel Virginia upbringing, found herself early in life transplanted to the frontier and forced to confront those vast blank spaces over which men had not yet succeeded in establishing the domination of custom and convention. She saw a few brave settlers confronting the wilderness, meeting the physical challenge as well as the moral one of having to rely on their instincts without benefit of civilized constraints; for her these people, particularly the women, were a race apart. Ántonia, with her noble simplicity, is among other things a monument to that vigorous race.

She is also an embodiment of a long tradition of fictional heroes of British and American romance. At the time the novel was written, literature and criticism in America were undergoing a change of direction. The thrust of literature in the new century owed much to the developing sciences; Sinclair Lewis and Theodore Dreiser appeared on the scene with their sociological novels, signaling the rise of naturalism. Fictional characters would henceforth be viewed as interpreting in their acts the flaws and beauties of laws, institutions, and social structures. *My Ántonia* fits an older mold, a form in which the effects of colonial Puritanism can be detected. Specifically, the mode demands that the hero overcome or try to overcome the strictures and hazards of his situation by his own wit, strength, or courage. This convention draws from the very wellspring of American life, the democratic belief in the wholeness and self-sufficiency of the individual, that is, in personal culpability, and in the absolute value of the personal conscience. Cather makes no real indictment of the society that scorns and undervalues Ántonia and the other hired girls; the social conventions are, with the land, simply the medium through which she fulfills her destiny. It is the peculiarly American sense of starting out brand-new in a new land, that sense of moral isolation, that adds poignance to the struggles of the individual against the vagaries of fortune. This theme of American newness and innocence, which R.B.W. Lewis calls "the theme of the American Adam," has as a natural concomitant elements of temptation and fortunate fall. The serpent in Ántonia's story is the town of Black Hawk, where she quarrels with her benefactors and runs afoul of Larry Donovan. Seduced and abandoned, she returns to the land; but her experience has made her better able, as she tells Jim Burden, to prepare her children to face the world.

But if the town is Ántonia's downfall in terms of one theme, it is the gray backdrop against which she shines in terms of another; in the same way the prairie is her antagonist in one sense, and the natural force of which she is the flower in another. Jim Burden first finds her, significantly, actually living in the earth. Early on she begins to take on characteristics of the land: "Her neck came up strongly out of her shoulders, like the bole of a tree out of the turf. . . . But she has such splendid color in her cheeks—like those big dark red plums." She works the land; she makes gardens; she nourishes the Harling children with food and stories. Her connection with the fertile earth is insisted upon. And the earth, the virgin land, is in this novel the source of physical vigor and the best resource of the soul. Jim Burden describes his first experience of the land as a feeling of cosmic unity: "Perhaps we feel like that when we die and become part of something entire, whether it is sun and air, or goodness and knowledge. At any rate, that is happiness; to be dissolved into something complete and great." The people who live on the prairie seem to him open and giving like the land; for instance, he says of Ántonia that "everything she said seemed to come right out of her heart." By contrast, the life of the town is pinched and ungenerous: "People's speech, their voices, their very glances, became furtive and repressed. Every individual taste, every natural appetite, was bridled by caution."

Ántonia, in all her acts, shows the naturalness and boundless generosity of the plains; gives freely of her strength and loyalty to her surly brother, to Jim and the Harling children, to Larry Donovan, and to her husband Cuzak; and showers love and nurturance upon her children. She alludes several times to her dislike of towns and cities and to her feeling of familiar friendship with the country. Toward the end of the book the figure of Ántonia and the infinite fertility of the land come together symbolically in an extremely vivid and moving image. Ántonia and her children have been showing Jim Burden the contents of their fruit cellar, and as they step outside, "[the children] all came running up the steps together, big and little, tow heads and gold heads and brown, and flashing little naked legs; a veritable explosion of life out of the dark cave into the sunlight." The cave might be the apotheosis of Ántonia's first home on the prairie, the latter redeeming the former by its fruitfulness.

Above all, the novel celebrates the early life on the plains of which Jim Burden and Ántonia were a part. The long digressions about Peter and Pavel, Blind D'Arnault, the Cutters and others, the profoundly elegiac descriptions of Jake Marpole and Otto Fuchs, the sharply-caught details of farm life, town life, landscape—these things are bent to the re-creation of a simpler and better time, a hard life now gone beyond recall, but lovingly remembered.

NAUSEA

Type of work: Novel
Author: Jean-Paul Sartre (1905–1980)
Type of plot: Philosophical realism
Time of plot: The 1930s
Locale: France
First published: *La Nausée*, 1938 (English translation, 1949)

In Nausea, *Sartre's first novel, the philosopher-novelist-dramatist delineates his Existentialist philosophy through a minute analysis of the interior life of Antoine Roquentin, a mild-mannered French historian. Roquentin experiences nausea and feels existence to be oppressive when he learns that life has no intrinsic meaning. Finding or making meaning thus becomes the object of Roquentin's life.*

Principal Characters

Antoine Roquentin (än·twàn′ rô·kän-tän′), a philosophical man who has settled down in Bouville, a town by the sea, to write a biography of the Marquis de Rollebon, an eighteenth century European politician. During the third year of work on the book, Roquentin notices that he has become the victim of a strange affliction; what he calls "a sweetish sickness" settles over him from time to time. Repelled by the malady, he seeks to rid himself of it by spending time with the few people he knows and by stopping work on the Rollebon book. No one can help him. In despair, he goes to Paris, hoping to be able to write a novel, knowing that he is never to solve the problems of his life.

Ogier P. (ô·zhyä′ pā′), an acquaintance whom Roquentin calls "the Self-Taught Man." To rid himself of loneliness and despair, Roquentin unprofitably spends some time with Ogier P. Roquentin witnesses a scene in which Ogier P., discovered to be a homosexual, is ordered to leave a library.

Anny (à·nē′), an English girl whom Roquentin had known before he began work on the biography. They meet in Paris. She has aged, however, and she insults Roquentin and leaves Paris with the man who is keeping her.

Françoise (frän·swàz′), a woman who operates a café called the Rendez-vous des Cheminots. She and Roquentin were once lovers on a purely physical level. When Roquentin visits her to say good-bye before he moves to Paris, he finds that she has a new lover and has no time for him.

The Story

Antoine Roquentin, a thirty-year-old Frenchman, after traveling though Central Europe, North Africa, and the Orient, settled down in the seaport town of Bouville to finish his historical research on the Marquis de Rollebon, an eighteenth century figure in European politics whose home had been at Bouville. For three years Roquentin searched the archives of the Bouville library in order to reconstruct the nobleman's life. All Roquentin's energies were concentrated on his task; he knew few people in Bouville, except by sight, and he lived more in the imaginary world he had created for the Marquis de Rollebon than in the actual world.

In the third year of his residence in Bouville during the winter of 1932, Roquentin began to have a series of disturbing psychological experiences, which he termed the Nausea. He felt that there was something new about commonplace articles; even his hands seemed to take on new aspects, to have an existence all their own. It was then that Roquentin's loneliness seemed a terrible thing to him, for there was no one to whom he could speak of his experiences. His only acquaintances were Ogier P., nicknamed by Roquentin the Self-Taught Man because he was instructing himself by reading all the books in the library, and a woman named Françoise, who operated a café called the Rendez-vous de Cheminots. Françoise, who had become fond of Roquentin, was the outlet for his physical sexuality, beyond which their acquaintance had not gone. Roquentin, in his loneliness, began to think of Anny, an English girl who had traveled with him some years before and whom he had loved; but he had not heard from her in more than three years. Worst of all, the Nausea came more and more often to plague Roquentin; it passed from objects into his body through his hands, and the only way he could describe it was that it seemed like a sweetish sickness.

One evening, shortly after the Nausea had first appeared, Roquentin went to the café, only to find that Françoise was gone for a time. He watched four men playing cards and wanted to vomit; for the first time, the Nausea had crept upon him in a place where there were bright lights and many people. As he listened to the music playing on a battered old phonograph, however, the Nausea vanished. He felt as if he were inside the music.

Strangely enough, as the days passed, the Self-Taught Man made an effort be friendly with Roquentin. Learning that the latter had traveled a great deal, he asked to see some of the photographs Roquentin had collected and to hear some of Roquentin's adventures. He even went to Roquentin's room one evening for that specific purpose. These friendly overtures were not entirely welcomed by Roquentin, who was immersed in his psychological problems, but he acquiesced in setting a date to have dinner with the Self-Taught Man a few days later.

In the interval before the dinner engagement, the book about the Marquis de Rollebon came to a halt. One day, Roquentin suddenly stopped writing in the middle of a paragraph and knew that he would write no more, although he had spent more than three years' labor on the work. Roquentin suddenly felt cheated, as if his very existence had been stolen by the Marquis de Rollebon during those years, so that the marquis had been living in place of himself. The feeling was caused partially by the discovery on Roquentin's part that he could never know for certain the truth about the notorious marquis, who had used men for his own ends during his life.

With the discovery that he was going to write no more, Roquentin also found that there was little or no purpose in his life. Indeed, there seemed to be no reason for his existence at all. For three years Roquentin had not reacted to his own existence because he had been working; now it was thrust upon him with disquieting abruptness.

Soon Roquentin received an unexpected letter from Anny, which had been forwarded from his old address in Paris. She wrote that she was to be in Paris for a few days and wished to see him. Roquentin looked forward to seeing her and planned to leave Bouville for the first time in three years to visit with her in Paris.

The following Wednesday, Roquentin and the Self-Taught Man met for their dinner engagement. During the dinner, a rather stiff affair, the Self-Taught Man tried to convince Roquentin that he, like the Self-Taught Man, ought to be a socialist and a humanist, that in the humanity of the world was to be found the true reason for the universe. Roquentin became so disquieted that the Nausea came over him during the discussion, and he abruptly left the restaurant.

When he visited Anny, he found her changed; she had gained weight, but the changes that bothered him the most were those he felt rather than saw. The interview was a dismal failure; Anny accused him of being worthless to her and finally thrust him from the room. Later he saw Anny getting on a train with the man who kept her, and he went back to Bouville with a sense of numbness. He believed that both he and Anny had outlived themselves. All that was left, he felt, was eating and sleeping, an existence not unlike that of an inanimate object.

Roquentin remained in Bouville only a few days more. Unhappy and lonesome, he sought out the Self-Taught Man, finding him in the library reading to two young boys. Roquentin also sat down to read. He never did get to open the conversation, for in the ensuing minutes, the Self-Taught Man revealed himself as a homosexual and was brutally ordered out of the library by a librarian. The only other person to whom Roquentin wished to say goodbye was the congenial woman who owned the Rendezvous des Cheminots. When he went to see her, however, she could give him only a moment, for another man claimed her time.

Roquentin went to the railway station for the train that was to take him to Paris. His only hope was that he might write a novel that would make people think of his life as something precious and legendary, though he knew that the work on such a book, unlike his attempts at the history of the Marquis de Rollebon, could not keep from him the troublesome problems of existence.

Critical Evaluation

Jean-Paul Sartre published his first novel, *Nausea*, in 1938, just as his existential philosophical system was taking clear shape in his mind. This book, both a work of philosophy and a novel in the form of a diary, explores the relationship of Antoine Roquentin to his reality—his surroundings, his acquaintances, and his relationships. Bound to Bouville (literally, "Mudville") by his research, Roquentin comes to perceive his total alienation from the world of bourgeois falsehoods and self-deceptions, but he is unable to attain an affirmation of his own authenticity. Some readers find existential literature repellent because those who wrote it (such as Sartre himself, Simone de Beauvoir, Albert Camus) often deal with negative atti-

tudes and the failures of their characters to achieve satisfaction and the fulfillment of their beings. *Nausea* is no exception, for Roquentin thinks of himself as a thing reflected in the trap of a mirror. The Nausea which sometimes overcomes him when he confronts real objects (a stone, a piece of paper) helps to free him from this static conception of himself and sets him on the road to self-discovery.

Sartre's effort to blend philosophy with literature is regarded by most critics as successful: Abstract ideas are exemplified through specific incidents or circumstances, and psychological subtleties are illustrated by the use of precise dramatic details. Roquentin's first perception of his own absurdity, for instance, occurs when he studies the shape of a muddy stone he has picked up from the ground and is unable to throw. The pebble seems to possess more inherent "reality" than he himself does. The stone *is*, while Roquentin is *becoming*. Nausea seizes Roquentin as he recognizes his own shapelessness and understands that he must somehow find and establish his own identity and being. Men are not stones; they shape themselves as they wish to become and to appear to others, making philosophical progress as they face moral dilemmas.

Roquentin finds himself more than ill at ease among his fellowmen: He is an absolute outsider. His contempt for the middle class and its values is wittily expressed as he watches the regular Sunday morning parade of prosperous townsfolk on the Rue Tournebride; he laughs inwardly at their greetings and handshakes, their smiles and gestures of courtesy, their superficial self-satisfaction. The irony reaches brilliant heights when he later studies the portraits of the illustrious forebears of the townsfolk and overhears the naïve conversation of a couple who are expressing reverence for the dignity of these "great" men. In a long passage of harsh, cynical satire Roquentin mocks and reviles the complacency of those who have not known his Nausea. During his three years in Bouville, Roquentin has not established a significant friendship with anyone. He constantly watches people in public places, seeking in the faces and behavior of these strangers some sign of authenticity, but usually discovers only some form of falseness or self-deception. He endures his existence in a state of unbridgeable loneliness, finding consolation only in his work.

Roquentin's relationship with the Self-Taught Man he meets at the library is curiously indifferent. For a long time their contact is limited to conventional exchanges. Roquentin takes no pleasure in the other's visit to his room to look at photographs; he reluctantly accepts an invitation to dinner, but there, suffering from an illusion of order and meaning in the world, the Self-Taught Man annoys Roquentin with a long harangue extolling the glories of humanism and socialism. Roquentin leaves abruptly in disgust, no longer able to tolerate the mouthing of commonplace ideas. The Nausea comes again shortly thereafter, as loneliness overcomes him.

Pleased at receiving an unexpected letter from his former mistress Anny, Roquentin realizes that he may still love her and can perhaps resolve his spiritual dilemmas with her aid. When he visits her in Paris, however, it becomes obvious that no such thing can happen. He finds her aged, and she has grown weary with life; she no longer seeks to derive "perfect moments" from "privileged situations" (a striving that Roquentin had never understood), for she feels she has outlived herself. In spite of Roquentin's attempt to renew their affair, Anny rejects him, thus shattering his only hope for fulfillment through love. The split is final, and Roquentin, disillusioned, lonely, and alone, fears he too may have outlived himself, with only his work left to give meaning to his life.

His research project, however, has become ever more boring to him as he has sought to discover the "real" Marquis de Rollebon hidden behind the historical documents, the personality behind the facts. Roquentin is unable to discern any unity among the diverse and conflicting impressions furnished by contemporaries who knew the marquis. As Rollebon the man eludes him, Roquentin experiences first curiosity, then frustration, and finally ennui with the task he has set himself. Rollebon seems to be as shapeless as Roquentin himself, and his failure to discover the reality of the eighteenth century politician eventually drives the historian to abandon his project altogether. He comes finally to question the very existence of the past, since everything seems to be in doubt. His own definition of himself as a historian is shattered as he stares at his reflection in a mirror, seeing himself reduced to a mere image, lacking substance and essence.

The only pleasure and joy which Roquentin had ever experienced in Bouville came to him from listening to an old, worn record of an American popular song in one of his favorite cafés. The sound of the saxophone and the black woman's voice singing the banal lyrics had somehow transformed him and carried him into a superior realm, driving away the Nausea temporarily. Now he imagines a Jewish-American in a hot New York apartment creating the music and the black woman bringing it to life with her voice. Though unknown and perhaps ultimately insignificant, these two had saved themselves through artistic creation. He wonders if he might justify his own existence in a similar way, by writing a novel in which he would attempt to clarify his past and rid himself of its repugnance. He is uncertain of the outcome as he prepares to move to Paris, but not without hope: No longer a stone, he senses the possibility, through creative effort, of beginning to become.

NEW ATLANTIS

Type of work: Essay
Author: Sir Francis Bacon (1561–1626)
Type of plot: Utopian voyage
Time of plot: Sixteenth century
Locale: New Atlantis, an island in the Pacific Ocean
First published: 1627

The English Renaissance produced two classic treatments of the ideal state concept, Thomas More's Utopia *and Francis Bacon's* New Atlantis. *Since Bacon was both a devout believer and a great scientist, it is not surpisting that his perfect society is based on a harmonious collaboration between religion and science.*

The Story

Traveling from Peru to the Orient, the narrator and his companions seemed hopelessly lost in the South Sea when they came upon an island and sailed into the harbor of one of its large cities. Its inhabitants stood on the shores with clubs, as if warning them not to land. A small boat came toward them, carrying a governmental official, who presented them with a scroll inscribed in Hebrew, Latin, Greek, and Spanish, promising any assistance they might need but forbidding them to land. Noticing with amazement and joy that the document bore the sign of the cross, the travelers asked permission to bring their sick companions to land. The voyagers offered merchandise in return for aid.

A few hours later another citizen, evidently of high rank, invited the whole company to land, if they would swear as Christians that they were not pirates and had killed no one in the past three months. They were given rooms in the city at the House of Strangers, where special cells and medicines were provided for the sick crew members.

The Governor of the House of Strangers, impressed by their gentlemanly behavior, invited them to remain in the city for six weeks and offered to answer their questions about his country. He was delighted when they inquired about his homeland's conversion to Christianity. He told them that one night, about twenty years after Christ's ascension, a large cross on a pillar of light appeared on the sea. The people of the city of Renfusa rowed out toward it, only to find that they could not move closer than about sixty yards away. A wise man prayed for an explanation of the sign and was able to sail on. The cross disappeared, but he found a chest containing the Old and New Testaments, even the books not written at that time, and a letter from Saint Bartholomew explaining that he had been ordered in a vision to send the ark to sea. The Testaments were themselves miraculous; they could be understood by everyone, no matter what his language, and through them the kingdom was converted.

On succeeding days the governor told how his people

knew the languages and literature of Europe yet remained unknown to its inhabitants. About three thousand years before, he said, navigation was widespread, and his country traded with Phoenicia, China, and the mighty kingdom of Atlantis, later named America. Within one hundred years, however, Atlantis was destroyed by flood, and only a few mountain-dwelling savages survived. The bulk of New Atlantis' commerce ceased, and its wise king, Salomon, perceiving that his land was self-sufficient, forbade communication with foreigners. He set strict regulations on the entrance of strangers and allowed only a chosen few to visit other nations.

To improve the welfare of his country, he established Salomon's House, a society of scientists named for the Hebrew king, to study all "the works and creatures of God," and he ordered that every twelve years six fellows of the House should go to gather information from other countries and bring back "books, instruments, and patterns of every kind." The governor added that he was not permitted to tell how these men concealed their identity during their travels.

The narrator was invited to a great family feast, given in honor of every man who had thirty living descendants. The tersan, the father, sat in state under a canopy of ivy decorated with silver and silk. As his family stood around him, a herald presented a scroll announcing honors from the king and a cluster of green grapes, one for each descendant. The latter was given to the worthiest son, henceforth called the Son of the Vine.

A second outstanding occasion for the narrator was a visit from a father of Salomon's House, who described his society, founded for "the knowledge of causes and secret motions of things and the enlarging of the bounds of human empire to the effecting of all things possible."

Among the elaborate experiments the society used to extend knowledge were processes of refrigeration, the production of artificial metals, the study of soils, grafting, and crossbreeding of plants and animals.

The fathers of Salomon's House studied the weather

from tall observation towers; heat in a variety of furnaces; light and color in "perspective houses," in which they also developed powerful telescopes and fine microscopes. They conveyed sound in trunks and pipes over long distances, and they had "some degrees of flying in the air" as well as "boats for going under water." In Salomon's house each member was assigned a function:

traveling, collecting experiments from books, making them, compiling results, finding practical applications for results, or formulating laws and axioms from experimental data.

The father of Salomon's House completed his discourse, blessed the narrator, and gave him permission to write down these observations about his order.

Critical Evaluation

Published after his death, Francis Bacon's *New Atlantis* reflects his world and its concerns. Bacon, whose life spanned the reigns of Elizabeth I and James I, in many ways exemplified the ideal Renaissance man, for he was a lawyer, a statesman, and an author. Bacon became Lord Chancellor of England, the highest political office in the state, but he also pursued philosophical and educational interests. *New Atlantis* itself was a product of the post-Columbian discoveries and explorations. Bacon generally wrote in Latin, and his works were almost always nonfiction. *New Atlantis* is an exception to both, although it has been pointed out that it is a fictionalized version of *The First Book of the Advancement of Learning*, which argued that mankind's proper study was not theology but the natural world, which could be examined and understood through scientific investigation.

New Atlantis was only one of a number of utopian tales or fables written during the sixteenth and seventeenth centuries. In England, Bacon's work was preceded by Thomas More's *Utopia*. Also from that era was *The City of the Sun*, by Tommaso Campanella, and Johann Valentin Andreae's *Christianopolis*. One might even include *The Tempest*, by Bacon's contemporary William Shakespeare. All, to some degree, are concerned with the implications of the scientific study of nature in the creation of the ideal society. Unlike many other utopian tales, *New Atlantis* contains considerable fictional historical background in Bacon's description of Bensalem. Also, unlike most other contemporary writers of utopian tales, Bacon establishes in the island of Bensalem a definite place where science is studied and nature dissected. What is particularly distinctive in *New Atlantis* is the fact that the scientific institution, Salomon's House, although so important to Bensalem, is also isolated from the surrounding society. Bacon long advocated the establishment of a college or some other institution devoted to scientific inquiry, but James I was more interested in theology than science. Salomon's House, in its physical isolation, possibly reflects Bacon's belief that the most productive study of science is initially done by a community of investigators isolated from possible interference by those less knowledgeable and perhaps less responsible.

Another theme discussed by critics of *New Atlantis* is the essentially conservative nature of Bensalem society.

Although its founding long predated the Christian era, the people of the island were early converted to that religion; Bacon's utopia is a Christian land. Science prospers in that Christian world, not only abstractly but for the benefit of the entire society. Unlike some of his Renaissance peers, Bacon was not entirely enamored with the ancient Greeks and Romans. It is revealing that his fictional institution's names, Salomon's House and the College of the Six Days' Works, allude to the Jewish past, which is also part of the Christian inheritance, more than to the classical world. Bacon was no atheist nor agnostic, and like most intellectuals of his day he believed that his religious beliefs were perfectly reconcilable to the latest scientific findings. It was one of the wise men from Salomon's House who was first made aware of the true meaning of the miracle that brought Christianity to the island; later, one of the characters notes that the College of the Six Days' Works "is dedicated to the study of the works and creatures of God." It could be argued that *New Atlantis* does not merely reflect Bacon's own religious beliefs but also attempts to portray a world in which traditional religious and social beliefs and institutions are buttressed rather than threatened by science and its investigations.

It has often been claimed that *New Atlantis* was left incomplete by Bacon, particularly that he developed no elaborate political structure for his utopia. It is possible that Bacon simply did not live long enough to develop an ideal polity for his utopian world. Bacon's first editor claimed that Bacon envisioned completing *New Atlantis* by including a framework of laws and a discussion of the ideal commonwealth. The work alludes to some sort of king, distantly in the background; Bacon was always a strong defender of the powers of the English monarchy. Also left undeveloped is the relationship of Salomon's House to the rest of Bensalem. Undoubtedly its governors have great influence, but in *New Atlantis* Bacon leaves this power generalized and implicit. It has been argued that Bacon envisioned a character such as himself as the mediator between the college and the society. A statesman with a broad knowledge of the possible ramifications of science would be the most suitable person to guide the community in the scientific study of nature and to give practical application to the resulting discoveries.

Bacon was impatient with the scholars of the Middle

Ages. Argument for the sake of argument did not find favor with this philosopher-statesman of Renaissance England. In *New Atlantis*, the narrator is shown the various laboratories of Salomon's House, all of which are intended to provide important benefits to society; knowledge for the sake of knowledge is insufficient. Bacon has been often called a prophet of science rather than a scientist himself. The College of the Six Days' Work, as Bacon presents it, shows the reader not so much the process of scientific investigation as its implied practical outcome. The college, though isolated, functions only to improve the general state of humanity.

Finally, commentators on *New Atlantis* have questioned whether Bacon's utopian community would have ultimately been beneficial to the future of humanity. In the twentieth century the destructive possibilities of science have been perceived, and modern utopian tales often dwell more on the negative impact of science than on its positive contributions to human society. Some critics have argued that Bacon was aware of the double-edged nature of the investigation of nature and knew that there was an element of hubris in opening the Pandora's box of science, but that he considered enlightened leadership, as shown by the governors of Salomon's House, a possible solution. Others have claimed that *New Atlantis* is in reality a work of its own time, the early seventeenth century, which still stood, naïvely and optimisticallly, at the dawn of the scientific revolution.

THE NIBELUNGENLIED

Type of work: Saga
Author: Unknown
Type of plot: Heroic epic
Time of plot: The Germanic legend, with the Burgundian story added from historical events of about 437
Locale: North Central Europe
First transcribed: c. 1200

Chief among the battle sagas of Germanic peoples, The Nibelungenlied *has merged and remerged with countless other legends and myths. In it are echoes of the ancient worship of the pagan gods along with elements of Christian ritual, as well as tales, like the battle of Siegfried and the dragon, that go back to prehistoric myths. Even in the modern era, the saga persists in poetry, music, and fiction.*

Principal Characters

Siegfried (sēg′frēd), a prince of Niderland whose heroic achievements include the winning of the great treasure hoard of the Nibelung. Having bathed in the blood of a dragon he slew, Siegfried is invulnerable except for a spot between his shoulders where a linden leaf had fallen. He goes to Burgundy and there wins Kriemhild as his wife. Later he is treacherously killed by a Burgundian knight.

Kriemhild (krēm′hĭld), the beautiful sister of the king of Burgundy. She marries Siegfried, and is subsequently tricked into revealing the secret of his vulnerability. After a long period of widowhood and mourning, she becomes the wife of the king of the Huns. Still seeking vengeance for Siegfried's death, she invites the whole Burgundian court to Hunland. In the final bloody combat all the Burgundians are killed, and Kriemhild herself is slain by her husband's order.

Gunther (gŏŏn′tėr), king of Burgundy. He promises that Siegfried shall marry Kriemhild in return for aiding him in winning Brunhild. With Siegfried's aid, Gunther overcomes Brunhild in her required feats of skill and strength. After the double wedding, Siegfried is again needed to impersonate Gunther in subduing Brunhild, who has determined never to let Gunther share her bed. Gunther is killed in the final blood bath in Hunland.

Brunhild (brŏŏn′hĭld), the daughter of Wotan, won by Gunther with Siegfried's help. Wishing to see Siegfried again, she plans a hunting party to which he and Kriemhild are invited. A great rivalry develops between the women; Kriemhild takes revenge by telling Brunhild the true story of her wedding night. Though Gunther and Siegfried settle the quarrel to their own satisfaction, it becomes a source of trouble among Gunther's brothers.

Hagen (hä′gen), a retainer of the Burgundians and a crafty and troublemaking knight. It is he who slays Siegfried. Hoping to get the Nibelungen treasure, now Kriemhild's, for himself, he orders it dropped into the Rhine. He is slain by Kriemhild herself and with him dies the secret of the treasure's hiding place.

Gernot (gâr′nôt) and **Giselher** (gē′sĕ·lėr), brothers of Kriemhild and Gunther. Convinced by Hagen that Siegfried has stained the honor of their house, they plot with Hagen to kill him. Later they fall victim to Brunhild's revenge.

Etzel (ăt′săl), also known as **Attila,** king of the Huns and Kriemhild's second husband.

Ortlieb (ôrt′lēb), Kriemhild's small son. Etzel gives him to the Burgundians as a hostage, and he is killed by Hagen when the fighting begins.

Dankwart (dänk′värt), the brother of Hagen. He too is killed in Hunland.

Sir Dietrich (dēt′rish), a knight who warns the Burgundians that Kriemhild still plots vengeance. As a result, they refuse to give up their weapons.

Sir Bloedel (blō′dăl), a knight who comes to Dankwart's quarters demanding vengeance for Kriemhild. He is killed by Dankwart and thus the final bloody combat begins.

Iring (ĭ′rĭng), one of Kriemhild's heroes.

Hildebrand (hēl′dĕ·bränd), a retainer of Etzel. At a sign from Etzel, he ends Kriemhild's life.

Hunold (hōō′nōld), a Burgundian hero.

Queen Uta (ōō′tä), the mother of Kriemhild.

King Siegmund (sēg′mōōnd), the father of Siegfried.

Queen Sieglind (sēg′lĭnd), the mother of Siegfried.

Ludger lōōd′gėr), king of the Saxons. After spending a year in the Burgundian court, Siegfried aids Gunther in overcoming the Saxons. In the celebrations that follow, Ludger sees Kriemhild for the first time.

Gelfrat (gălf′rät), a Burgundian slain by Dankwart in a quarrel at the start of the journey to Hunland. This and other evil omens are ignored.

Albric (äl′brĭk), a dwarf from whom Siegfried won the cloak of invisibility.

The Story

In Burgundy there lived a noble family which numbered three brothers and a sister. The sons were Gunther, who wore the crown, Gernot, and Giselher; the daughter was Kriemhild. About them was a splendid court of powerful and righteous knights, including Hagen of Trony, his brother Dankwart, and mighty Hunold. Kriemhild dreamed one night that she reared a falcon which then was slain by two eagles. When she told her dream to Queen Uta, her mother's interpretation was that Kriemhild should have a noble husband but that unless God's protection followed him he might soon die.

Siegfried was born in Niderland, the son of King Siegmund and Queen Sieglind. In his young manhood he heard of the beautiful Kriemhild, and, although he had never seen her, he determined to have her for his wife. Undeterred by reports of her fierce and warlike kinsmen, he made his armor ready for his venture. Friends came from all parts of the country to bid him farewell, and many of them accompanied him as retainers into King Gunther's land. When he arrived at Gunther's court, Hagen, who knew his fame, told the brothers the story of Siegfried's first success, relating how Siegfried had killed great heroes and had won the hoard of the Nibelung, a treasure of so much gold and jewels that five score wagons could not carry all of it. He also told how Siegfried had won the cloak of invisibility from the dwarf Albric and how Siegfried had become invisible from having bathed in the blood of a dragon he had slain.

Gunther and his brothers admitted Siegfried to their hall after they had heard of his exploits, and the hero stayed with them a year. In all that time, however, he did not once see Kriemhild.

The Saxons led by King Ludger threatened to overcome the kingdom of the Burgundians. Siegfried pledged to use his forces in overcoming the Saxons, and in the battle he led his knights and Gunther's troops to a great victory. In the following days there were great celebrations at which Queen Uta and her daughter Kriemhild appeared in public. On one of these occasions Siegfried and Kriemhild met and became betrothed.

King Gunther, wanting to marry Brunhild, Wotan's daughter, told Siegfried that if he would help him win Brunhild then he might wed Kriemhild. Gunther set out at the head of a great expedition, all of his knights decked in costly garments in order to impress Brunhild. Her choice for a husband, however, was not for a well-dressed prince but for a hero. She declared that the man who would win her must surpass her in feats of skill and strength. With Siegfried's aid Gunther overcame Brunhild, and she agreed to go with Gunther as his wife.

Siegfried was sent on ahead to announce a great celebration in honor of the coming marriage of Gunther to Brunhild. A double ceremony took place, with Kriemhild becoming the bride of Siegfried at the same time.

At the wedding feast Brunhild burst into tears at the sight of Kriemhild and Siegfried together. Gunther tried to explain away her unhappiness, but once more, Gunther needed Siegfried's aid, for Brunhild had determined never to let Gunther share her bed. Siegfried went to her chamber and there overpowered her. Thinking she had been overcome by Gunther, she was thus subdued to Gunther's wit and will.

Brunhild bore a son, who was named for Siegfried. As time passed she wished once more to see Siegfried, who had returned with Kriemhild to his own country. Therefore, she instructed Gunther to plan a great hunting party to which Siegfried and Kriemhild should be invited.

At the meeting of the two royal families, there was great rivalry between Brunhild and Kriemhild. They vied with each other by overdressing their attendants and then argued as to the place each should have in the royal procession. Finally, Kriemhild took revenge when she told Brunhild the true story of her wedding night. Accusing Brunhild of acting the part of a harlot, she said that Brunhild had slept first with Siegfried, then with her husband, Gunther. For proof, she displayed Brunhild's ring and girdle, both of which Siegfried had won from Brunhild the night he had overcome her. Brunhild, furious and desirous of revenge, sought out her husband and confronted him with the story of her humiliation and betrayal.

Gunther and Siegfried soon settled to their own satisfaction the wanton quarrel between the two women, but Hagen, the crafty one, stirred up trouble among Gunther's brothers with his claim that Siegfried had stained the honor of their house, and then plotted to trap Siegfried and destroy him. When it was reported that the Saxons were to attack Gunther's knights, Kriemhild unwittingly revealed Siegfried's one vulnerable spot. While bathing in the dragon's blood, he had failed to protect a portion of his body the size of a linden leaf because a leaf had fallen down between his shoulders. The villainous Hagen asked her to sew a token on the spot so that he could protect Siegfried during the fighting.

Hagen sent men to say that the Saxons had given up the attack. Then, the fear of battle over, Gunther rode out to hunt with all of his knights. There, deep in the forest, as Siegfried was bending over a spring to drink, he was struck in the fatal spot by an arrow from Hagen's bow. Before he died Siegfried cursed the Burgundians and their tribe forever. Indifferent to the dying man's curse, Hagen carried home the body of the dead hero.

He placed Siegfried's body in the path where Kriemhild would see it on her way to church, but a chamberlain discovered the body before she passed. Kriemhild knew instinctively whose hand had done the deed. A thousand knights headed by Siegmund, his father, mourned the dead hero, and everyone claimed vengeance. The widow

gave vast sums of money to the poor in honor of Siegfried. When Siegmund prepared to leave for Niderland,
he asked Kriemhild to go with him. She refused but allowed
him to take Siegfried's son with him. She was determined
to stay with the Burgundians. Queen Brunhild, however,
offered no compassion. The Nibelungen hoard was given
to Kriemhild, for it was her wedding gift; however, by
order of Hagen, who planned to get possession of the
treasure, all of it was dropped to the bottom of the Rhine.
In the years that followed Kriemhild remained in mourning for Siegfried.

At last the mighty Etzel, king of the Huns, sought to
marry Kriemhild. After a long courtship he won Kriemhild and took her to his land to be his wife. Etzel was
rich and strong, and after her long years of mourning,
Kriemhild again occupied a position of power and honor.
Now she began to consider how she might avenge herself
for the death of Siegfried. Hoping to get Hagen in her
power, she sent a messenger to her brothers, saying that
she longed to see all of them again.

When they received her message, the brothers and Hagen
set out. Old Queen Uta told them that in a dream she had
seen a vision of dire foreboding, but the Burgundians
refused to heed her warning. Furthermore, Hagen received
a token from some mermaidens, who said none of the
knights would return from Hunland. He disregarded the
prediction. Then a quarrel broke out among the Burgundians, and Dankwart slew Gelfrat. Three evil omens now
attended the coming journey, but still the brothers refused
to turn back. At last the Burgundians came to Etzel's
castle.

Gunther and his brothers were put into separate apartments. Dankwart and Hagen were sent to other quarters.
Warned by Sir Dietrich that Kriemhild still plotted vengeance for Siegfried's death, Hagen urged them all to take
precautions. When Kriemhild asked them to give her

their weapons, Hagen replied that it could not be. The
Burgundians decided to post a guard to prevent a surprise
attack while they slept.

The court went to mass. At the services the Huns were
displeased to see that Gunther and his party jostled Queen
Kriemhild.

In honor of the Burgundians, a great tournament was
held for all the knights. So bad was the feeling between
the Burgundians and the Huns that King Etzel was forced
to intervene in order to keep the peace. To appease the
brothers, Etzel gave them Kriemhild's small son, Ortlieb,
as a hostage. Sir Bloedel, however, pressed into Dankwart's quarters demanding justice for Kriemhild.

In a few minutes he had aroused the anger of Dankwart, who rose from his table and killed Bloedel. For
this deed the angered Huns killed Dankwart's retainers.
Dankwart, at bay, ran to Hagen for help. Hagen, knowing
that he would not live to seek his vengeance on Kriemhild
later, slaughtered the little prince, Ortlieb. Then a mighty
battle followed in which Hagen and Gunther managed to
kill most of their adversaries.

Kriemhild now urged her heroes to kill Hagen. The
first to take up the challenge was Iring. After he had
wounded Hagen, he rushed back to Kriemhild for praise.
Hagen recovered quickly and sought Iring to kill him.

The battle continued, and many knights from both sides
fell in the bloody combat. Outnumbered, the Burgundians fell one by one. Kriemhild herself slew Hagen, the
last of the Burgundians to survive. He died without
revealing the location of the treasure.

King Etzel grieved to see so many brave knights killed.
At a sign from him, Hildebrand, one of his retainers,
lifted his sword and ended the life of Kriemhild as well.

So died the secret of the new hiding place of the Nibelungen treasure hoard.

Critical Evaluation

The material which forms the subject matter of the
Germanic heroic epics is derived from historical events
which became part of an oral tradition and were passed
down, sometimes for centuries, in the form of sagas,
before being established in written form. The historical
events which lie behind the Nibelung saga are to be found
in the fifth and sixth centuries, the period of the tribal
wanderings at the end of the Roman Empire. The Burgundians, under King Gundahari, whose capital was at
Worms, were in fact destroyed by the Huns in 437. The
Siegfried figure is probably of Merovingian origin and
may derive from an intermarriage between the Burgundian and Frankish royal houses. The record of these events,
mingled with purely legendary elements, is preserved in
a number of works: Besides *The Nibelungenlied*, the
Scandinavian *Poetic Edda* (ninth to twelfth centuries) is

the most important. It was upon this latter source rather
than the Germanic version that Richard Wagner based
his four-part music drama, *The Ring of the Nibelung*
(1876). There are four main themes in the saga tradition:
the adventures of the young Siegfried, Siegfried's death,
the destruction of the Burgundians, and the death of Attila.
These elements occurred as separate works in the early
stages of composition. In the present version of the saga
composed by an anonymous German author around the
year 1200, the various elements are woven together into
a unified plot, linking the death of Siegfried with the
destruction of the Burgundians through the motive of
revenge. Traces of the older separate versions are evident, however, in such inner inconsistencies as the transformation of the character of Kriemhild, who appears
initially as a model courtly figure but becomes the blood-

thirsty avenger of her husband's death in the second part. It is a mark of the artistic talent of the anonymous author that he fuses the core episodes with such care and achieves a plausible and aesthetically satisfying work.

The Nibelungenlied is the product of the brilliant period of the Hohenstaufen dynasty of the Holy Roman Empire, a time when the courtly culture of Germany was at its height. The poet was probably of Austrian origin: The importance of the splendid court at Vienna and the noble figure of Bishop Pilgrim of Passau indicate that the poet may have enjoyed the patronage of these courts. That the poet remains anonymous is a tradition of the heroic epic form, evolving from the anonymous court singer of the wandering Germanic tribes. Whereas the writers of Arthurian epics and religious epics name themselves and often discuss their work in a prologue, the composer of the heroic epic remains outside his work, presenting his material more as history and without the self-conscious comments and digressions found in works such as *Parzival* (c. 1200–1210) or *Tristan and Isolde* (c. 1210), both of whose poets name themselves and go into some detail regarding their intentions and artistic conceptions. The work, written in four-line stanzas, bears the signs of its history of oral presentation—frequent repetition of rhyme words, the use of formulaic descriptions and filler lines, and general looseness of composition. The poem was not conceived as a written work but represents a written record of an oral performance tradition. Even after assuming written form, the work would be read aloud to an audience, books being a scarce and expensive commodity in this period.

The purpose of the work, like that of courtly poetry in general, was to mirror courtly society in its splendor, color, and activity and to present within that framework images of an idealized world in which larger-than-life figures act out the social rituals of the time and provide for the audience models of courtly behavior, of honor, fortitude, and noble bearing under great stress. Repeatedly in the work one observes long passages devoted to description of the court festivities—banquets, tourna-

ments, processions—all filled with details of clothing and jewelry, splendid utensils, and weapons. Questions of etiquette and precedence provide some of the central conflicts of the work, while the lyrical episodes of the love between Siegfried and Kriemhild may be seen as an embodiment of the idealized conception of love celebrated by the Minnesänger. Although the grim events of the old dramatic saga material at times conflict with the more cultivated ideal of the thirteenth century, the poet succeeds even here in transforming the traditional material. Elements related to fairy-tale tradition—the stories of Siegfried's youth, the battle with the dragon, the magic aura surrounding Brunhild on her island—are largely suppressed.

The idealizing elements are developed, both in the first part, where Siegfried and Kriemhild stand out brightly against the menacing forces of the Burgundian court, especially Hagen, and in the second part, where, despite the atmosphere of betrayal and carnage, the high points are moments of fortitude and courage and the preservation of ethical integrity. Rüdiger, who finds himself torn between feudal loyalty to King Etzel and his loyalty to and friendship with the Burgundians, to one of whom his daughter is engaged, is one of the greatest of these figures. The episode in which he finds himself obliged to fight against the Burgundian Gernot, to whom he has given the sword which now will kill him, is one of the most poignant scenes in the work.

The chain of crime and revenge finds cessation and resolution only in the lament for the fallen warriors, and it is in this tragic sense of the inevitable suffering that follows joy that the work preserves its links to the ancient Germanic heroic outlook, establishing its individuality against the more generally optimistic outlook of the Arthurian sagas. Here the fatalistic confrontation with destructive forces is opposed to the affirmation of order and the delight of life typical of much literature of the Hohenstaufen period. It is the tension between these two attitudes that provides much of the power of the work and lifts it into the realm of universal validity.

NICHOLAS NICKLEBY

Type of work: Novel
Author: Charles Dickens (1812–1870)
Type of plot: Sentimental romance
Time of plot: Early nineteenth century
Locale: England
First published: 1838–1839

In spite of a general disorganization and confusion in the plotting and the relative simplicity of the characterizations, Nicholas Nickleby *remains one of Dickens' finest early triumphs by virtue of its energy, comedy, and social realism. His portrayal of Wackford Squeers's mismanaged private school, based upon firsthand research, stimulated much public discussion and indignation, and eventually led to important reforms.*

Principal Characters

Nicholas Nickleby, the handsome, warm-hearted, enterprising son of a widow whose husband's death left her and her two children impoverished as the result of unwise speculations. Through the grudging influence of his uncle, a shrewd, miserly London businessman, he secures a post as an assistant master at Dotheboys Hall, a wretched school for boys, at a salary of five pounds a year. Finding conditions at the school impossible to tolerate, he thrashes Wackford Squeers, his employer, quits the place in disgust, and returns to London in the company of Smike, a half-starved, broken-spirited drudge, and now his loyal friend, whom he saved from the schoolmaster's brutality. After being cleared of a false charge of thievery brought by his uncle and the vindictive Squeers, he sets out again in the hope of bettering his fortune. He becomes an actor in a traveling troupe but is called back to London on behalf of his sister Kate, who has become the victim of the unwelcome attentions of Sir Mulberry Hawk and Lord Frederick Verisopht, two notorious rakes. After disabling one of her pursuers he finds work with the generous Cheeryble brothers, and his fortunes improve, so that he is able to provide a home for his mother and sister. He falls in love with Madeline Bray and rescues her from marriage to an elderly miser. After the romantic and financial complications of this situation have been unraveled, Nicholas and Madeline are married.

Kate Nickleby, his refined, pretty sister. After her arrival in London she first finds work with a dressmaker and later becomes a companion to Mrs. Julia Witterly, a vulgar, silly middle-class woman; meanwhile her uncle uses her as a snare to entrap two lustful noblemen. After Nicholas goes to work for the Cheeryble brothers, her future becomes secure. In love with Frank Cheeryble, the nephew of her brother's benefactors, she marries him when she is convinced at last that the young man is truly in love with her.

Mrs. Nickleby, their mother, an ineffective but well-meaning woman who is constantly building castles in Spain for her son and daughter. Because of her poor judgment, she becomes the dupe of several coarse, mean people.

Ralph Nickleby, the miserly, treacherous uncle who finds ignominious work for both Nicholas and Kate and then attempts to use them to further his greed for wealth. After his schemes have been exposed and the unfortunate Smike has been revealed as the son whom he supposed dead, he hangs himself.

Smike, Ralph Nickleby's lost son, who had been abandoned by a former clerk to the harsh care of Wackford Squeers. Flogged and starved until he resembles a scarecrow, he turns away from Dotheboys Hall to share the fortunes of Nicholas Nickleby. When Nicholas joins a theatrical troupe, Smike plays the apothecary in *Romeo and Juliet.* Recaptured by Squeers, he escapes with the aid of John Browdie, a stout-hearted Yorkshireman, and finds sanctuary with Nicholas once more. He falls in love with Kate Nickleby, despairingly because he is dying of tuberculosis. After his death it is revealed that he was the son of Ralph Nickleby.

Madeline Bray, a beautiful girl whose devotion to her selfish, dissolute father leads her to accept the proposal of Arthur Gride. Her father dying suddenly, Nicholas and Kate save her from the clutches of Gride and his friend, Ralph Nickleby. Later a lost will, concealed by Gride, is recovered, and Madeline becomes an heiress. She and Nicholas Nickleby are married after both experience reversals of fortune.

Walter Bray, Madeline's father. For his own selfish purposes, he plans to marry his daughter to an unwelcome and much older suitor, Arthur Gride.

Edwin and **Charles Cheeryble,** two benevolent brothers who make Nicholas Nickleby a clerk in their countinghouse, establish his family in a comfortable cottage, help to thwart the schemes of Ralph Nickleby, and finally bring about the marriages of Nicholas to Madeline

Bray and Kate Nickleby to their nephew.

Frank Cheeryble, the gentlemanly nephew of the Cheeryble brothers. He marries Kate Nickleby after the uncles have set right her mistaken belief that Frank loves Madeline Bray.

Wackford Squeers, the brutal, predatory proprietor of Dotheboys Hall and an underling of Ralph Nickleby. Thrashed by Nicholas Nickleby for his treatment of Smike and his cruelty to the helpless boys entrusted to his care, he tries to get revenge with Ralph's help. Arrested for stealing the will which provides for Madeline Bray's inheritance, he is sentenced to transportation for seven years.

Mrs. Squeers, his wife, a worthy helpmeet for her cruel, rapacious husband.

Fanny Squeers, their daughter, a twenty-three-year-old shrew. She is at first attracted to Nicholas Nickleby, her father's underpaid assistant, but later turns against him when he rebuffs her advances and declares that his only desire is to get away from detested Dotheboys Hall.

Wackford Squeers (Junior), a nasty boy who combines the worst traits of his parents.

Newman Noggs, Ralph Nickleby's eccentric, kind-hearted clerk and drudge. Ruined by Ralph's knavery, he enters the miser's employ in order to unmask his villainies. He aids Nicholas Nickleby and Smike on several occasions and is instrumental in securing Madeline Bray's inheritance. After Ralph's death he is restored to respectability.

Brooker, a felon, at one time Ralph Nickleby's clerk, later his enemy. He makes Ralph believe that his son is dead as part of a scheme for extorting money from his former employer. He reveals Smike's true identity and thus causes Ralph's suicide.

Arthur Gride, Madeline Bray's miserly old suitor, who makes Ralph Nickleby his accomplice in keeping the girl's inheritance a secret. He is later killed by robbers.

Lord Frederick Verisopht, a gullible young rake, the ruined dupe of Sir Mulberry Hawk. Enamored of Kate Nickleby, he tries to seduce her. Later he quarrels with Sir Mulberry and is killed in a duel by his mentor in vice.

Sir Mulberry Hawk, a man of fashion, a gambler, and a knave, severely punished by Nicholas Nickleby for his attempt to ruin the young man's sister. Sir Mulberry quarrels with his foolish dupe, Lord Frederick Verisopht, and kills him in a duel.

Tom Linkinwater, the Cheerybles' chief clerk, a man as amiable and cheerful as his employers. He marries Miss La Creevy.

Miss Linkinwater, his sister.

Miss La Creevy, a spinster of fifty springs, a miniature painter, and the landlady of the Nicklebys when they first come to London. She marries Tom Linkinwater.

Peg Sliderskew, Arthur Gride's wizened, deaf, ugly old housekeeper. She steals her master's papers, including the will bequeathing money to Madeline Bray. Squeers,

hired by Ralph Nickleby to secure the document, is apprehended by Newman Noggs and Frank Cheeryble while in the act of pocketing it.

Mr. Snawley, a smooth-spoken hypocrite who sends his two stepsons to Dotheboys Hall. Ralph Nickleby's tool, he commits perjury by swearing that Smike is his son, abducted by Nicholas Nickleby. Later, when his guilt is revealed, he confesses, implicating Ralph and Squeers as his confederates.

Mrs. Snawley, his wife.

Madame Mantalini, the owner of a fashionable dressmaking establishment in which Kate Nickleby works for a time. She goes bankrupt because of her husband's extravagance.

Alfred Mantalini, born Muntle, a spendthrift. When cajolery and flattery fail to get him the money he wants, he resorts to threats of suicide in order to obtain funds from his wife. Eventually his wasteful, foppish habits bring her to bankruptcy, and she secures a separation. Imprisoned, he is befriended by a sympathetic washerwoman who secures his release. Before long she tires of his idleness and airy manners, and she puts him to work turning a mangle "like a demd old horse in a demnition mill."

Mr. Kenwigs, a turner in ivory who lives with his family in the same boarding house with Newman Noggs.

Mrs. Kenwigs, his wife, a woman genteelly born.

Morleena Kenwigs, their older daughter. Her attendance at a dancing school helps to establish her mother's pretensions to gentility.

Mr. Lillyvick, Mrs. Kenwigs' uncle and a collector of water rates. At a party he meets Henrietta Petowker, an actress from the Theatre Royal, follows her to Portsmouth, and marries her. His marriage brings dismay to his niece and her husband, who had regarded themselves as his heirs. After his fickle wife deserts him, he makes a will in favor of the Kenwigses' children.

Henrietta Petowker, an actress who marries Mr. Lillyvick and then elopes with a captain on half-pay.

Matilda Price, a Yorkshire lass and Fanny Squeers's friend, engaged to John Browdie. The two women quarrel when Matilda flirts with Nicholas Nickleby, whom Fanny has marked as her own.

John Browdie, a hearty, open-handed young Yorkshireman who becomes jealous of Nicholas Nickleby when Matilda Price, his betrothed, flirts with the young man. Later, realizing that Nicholas was completely innocent, John lends him money to return to London. He releases Smike from the custody of Wackford Squeers.

Miss Knag, the forewoman in Madame Mantalini's dressmaking establishment. She is kind to Kate Nickleby at first but later turns against her. She takes over the business when Madame Mantalini goes bankrupt.

Celia Bobster, the girl whom Newman Noggs mistakes for Madeline Bray and at whose house Nicholas Nickleby calls before the error is discovered.

Mr. Bobster, her hot-tempered father.

Mrs. Julia Witterly, a woman of middle-class background and aristocratic pretense, who hires Kate Nickleby as her companion.

Henry Witterly, her husband. He believes that his wife is "of a very excitable nature, very delicate, very fragile, a hot-house plant, an exotic."

Mr. Bonney, Ralph Nickleby's friend and a promoter of the United Improved Hot Muffin and Crumpet Baking and Punctual Delivery Company, of which Ralph is a director.

Mr. Gregsby, a member of Parliament, a pompous politician to whom Nicholas Nickleby applies for a position as a private secretary. Nicholas declines the situation after Mr. Gregsby explains fully the duties and responsibilities he expects a secretary to assume.

Vincent Crummles, the manager of a traveling theatrical company which Nicholas Nickleby and Smike join for a time; Nicholas adapts plays and acts in them, and Smike plays the part of the apothecary in *Romeo and Juliet*. Nicholas and his employer become close friends.

Mrs. Crummles, his wife.

Ninetta Crummles, their daughter, billed as the "Infant Phenomenon."

Miss Snevellicci, Mr. and Mrs. Snevellicci, her parents, **Miss Belvawney, Mrs. Grudden, Thomas Lenville, Miss Bravassa, Miss Ledbrook,** and **The African Knife Swallower,** members of the Crummles theatrical troupe.

Tomkins, Belling, Graymarsh, Cobbey, Bolder, Mobbs, Jennings, and **Brooks,** pupils at Dotheboys Hall.

Mr. Curdle, an amateur critic of the drama and the author of a sixty-four-page pamphlet on the deceased husband of the nurse in *Romeo and Juliet*.

Pyke, a servant of Sir Mulberry Hawk.

Captain Adams and **Mr. Westwood,** seconds in the duel between Sir Mulberry Hawk and Lord Frederick Verisopht.

The Story

When Nicholas Nickleby was nineteen years old, his father died a bankrupt. A short time after their bereavement, Nicholas, his sister Kate, and their mother went to London. There they hoped to get aid from the late Mr. Nickleby's brother Ralph; but Ralph Nickleby, a moneylender and miser, refused to help them except on his own terms. Ralph and his ways had to be accepted by the other Nicklebys, although they were not sure where life was taking them with Ralph as their protector.

Ralph Nickleby first secured a position for Nicholas as assistant to Wackford Squeers, who operated a boys' boarding school in Yorkshire. When Nicholas arrived at the school, he found it a terrible place where the boys were starved and mistreated almost beyond human imagination. Nicholas nevertheless had to put up with the situation, for his uncle had warned him that any help given to his sister and mother depended upon his remaining at the school where he had been placed. A crisis arose, however, when Wackford Squeers unmercifully beat an older boy named Smike, who was little better than an idiot. Nicholas interfered by taking the whip from Squeers and beating the schoolmaster in place of the boy. Immediately afterward, Smike and Nicholas left the school and headed toward London.

In London, meanwhile, Mrs. Nickleby and Kate had been lodged in an old weatherbeaten cottage belonging to Ralph Nickleby, who hoped to use Kate to attract young Lord Verisopht into borrowing money at high rates. He also found work for Kate in a dressmaking establishment, where there was a great deal of labor and almost no pay. Kate did not mind the work at the dressmaker's, but she bitterly resented the leers that she had to endure when invited to her uncle's home to dine with Lord Ver-

isopht and Sir Mulberry Hawk. Not long after she had taken the job, the dressmaker went bankrupt; Kate then found work for herself as companion to a rich but neurotic woman.

When Nicholas arrived in London, he sought out Newman Noggs, his uncle's clerk, who had promised aid if it became necessary. Newman Noggs helped Nicholas to clear himself of false charges brought by Wackford Squeers and Ralph Nickleby, for the latter had denounced Nicholas as a thief.

With some notion of becoming sailors, Nicholas and Smike decided to go to Bristol. On the way, they met Vincent Crummles, a theatrical producer, and they joined his troupe. Both Smike and Nicholas were successful as actors. In addition, Nicholas adapted plays for the company to produce. After some weeks, however, Nicholas received a letter from Newman Noggs warning him that his presence was required in London. Upon his arrival in London, Nicholas accidentally met Sir Mulberry Hawk and Lord Verisopht at a tavern, where they were speaking maliciously of Kate. Nicholas remonstrated with them and caused Sir Mulberry's horse to bolt. The baronet, thrown from his carriage and severely injured, vowed to take revenge.

Kate, meanwhile, had been exposed to the continued attentions of Sir Mulberry and Lord Verisopht, for Mrs. Nickleby, who failed to see them as villains, courted their favor and invited them into Kate's company. The future seemed very bleak indeed, until Nicholas, while looking for work at an employment agency, became acquainted with a kindly man who offered him a job. The man turned out to be one of the Cheeryble brothers, great workers of philanthropy. The Cheeryble brothers gave Nicholas a job in their countinghouse at a decent salary, rented him a cottage reasonably, and helped him to furnish it for himself, Kate, and their mother. Suddenly, the fortunes of the little family seemed much improved.

One day, a beautiful young woman came into the Cheeryble brothers' office, and Nicholas fell in love with her. Shortly afterward, Kate also fell in love with Frank Cheeryble, nephew of Nicholas' employers. Only Smike seemed unhappy; he, too, had fallen in love with Kate. Worse adventures were in store for him, however, for Wackford Squeers and Ralph Nickleby conspired to have Smike sent back to Squeers's school. Smike, recaptured after one escape, ran away a second time, and Nicholas managed to keep the lad from Squeers's clutches, much to the idiot's relief. But Smike's new happiness was short-lived. Sick with tuberculosis, he died a few months later.

By then, Nicholas had discovered that his beloved's name was Madeline Bray and that her father was a bankrupt ne'er-do-well who lived off the little income she made by sewing and painting. Unknown to Nicholas, Ralph Nickleby and a fellow miser, Arthur Gride, were planning to force Madeline into a marriage with Gride, who was seventy years old. Fortunately, Madeline's father died just an hour before he was to hand his daughter over to the old miser. Nicholas arrived on the scene and took the girl to his home, to be cared for by Kate and his mother.

Meanwhile, Gride's housekeeper, an old crone, left in a fit of jealousy and stole some of her employer's papers. One of the documents was a will which, if known, would have made Madeline Bray a rich woman. Ralph learned of the will and had Squeers steal it from her. When he did, however, Frank Cheeryble and Newman Noggs caught

him and turned him over to the police. The prisoner then confessed his part in the plot and also the conspiracy between Ralph and Gride to get Madeline's fortune.

As if Ralph Nickleby's fortunes were all against him, an old employee appeared and revealed to the Cheeryble brothers that Smike had been Ralph's son. Having always believed that the child had died in infancy, Ralph, when given the news, went home and hanged himself.

Nicholas thought that Frank Cheeryble was in love with Madeline; he asked the Cheeryble brothers to see that she was taken care of elsewhere. Kate, who also believed that Frank was in love with Madeline, gave up seeing him. The Cheeryble brothers, in their goodhearted way, took the situation under observation and soon learned the true state of affairs. They then proceeded to unravel the lovers' troubles. They revealed to Nicholas that Frank was in love with Kate, and Frank readily admitted his love. While one Cheeryble brother did that, the other told the girls how matters stood. All four were, of course, exceedingly glad to have their affairs in order, and they were married shortly thereafter.

Years passed, and both couples prospered. Nicholas had invested his wife's fortune in the Cheeryble brothers' firm, and he later became a partner in the house along with Frank Cheeryble. Newman Noggs, the Nickleby clerk who had helped Nicholas many times, was restored to respectability; he had been a wealthy gentleman before he had fallen into Ralph Nickleby's hands. Old Gride, who had tried to marry Madeline for her money, was murdered by robbers; Lord Verisopht was killed in a duel, and Sir Mulberry Hawk came to a violent end. Therefore, the righteous prospered, and the villains received their just desserts.

Critical Evaluation

During the 1830s, the English heard many rumors that certain private schools in the north of England were badly mismanaged. Charles Dickens made a trip to investigate the terrible conditions that were said to exist. The results of his findings appear in the academy run by Wackford Squeers in *Nicholas Nickleby*, a school where boys are not taught a thing but are simply whipped, starved, and cowed in order to keep their spirits and the proprietor's expenses down. It has been claimed that the credit can be given to Dickens alone for arousing the wave of indignation that forced many institutions to close or to change. This novel, which also contains the Cheeryble brothers, the first of a series of exceptionally virtuous characters, was the first of Dickens' novels to have a truly complex plot. As such, it was a fitting antecedent for such later novels as *A Tale of Two Cities* and *Great Expectations*.

Although Prime Minister Gladstone and Thomas Arnold, headmaster of Rugby, objected to *Nicholas*

Nickleby on the grounds that the novel was insufficiently edifying, more Victorian readers—including Dickens' rival, Thackeray—admired it; from its initial sale of fifty thousand copies, the book was one of Dickens' triumphs. The first of his novels in which the love story is the main subject, *Nicholas Nickleby* still retains many picaresque elements that appeared in *The Pickwick Papers* (1836–1837) and *Oliver Twist* (1837–1838). The characters still tend to be eccentrics dominated by a single passion (almost in the manner of Ben Jonson's "humours" characters, although lacking Jonson's theory of the psychology of humours); the minor characters in particular seem to be grotesques. Nevertheless, there is a vitality in the farcical elements of the novel that is delightful, despite the excesses. The influence of Smollett, in both the comedy and the tendency to realistic detail, is still strong in this early novel; Dickens' greatest strength in *Nicholas Nickleby* lies in the marvelous descriptions of people and places. Although the influence of the popular melodrama still colors the plot, Dickens breathes new life into old stock situations.

The reader feels the tremendous force of life, of the changing times, of youth and growth, on every page. Tales within tales seem to blossom; countless life stories crowd the chapters. It is a young man's creation, indignant, farcical, and romantic in turn; and it is filled with vivid scenes. At this stage of his career, Dickens was still attempting to provide something for everybody.

Dickens, however, was not wholly successful in working out the psychology of the novel because of his complicated, melodramatic plot. As critic Douglas Bush has observed, the characters of Dickens' early fiction are given over to self-dramatization. Mrs. Nickleby, in particular, evades the responsibilities of her troubled life by nearly withdrawing into a blissful vision of the past. As she sees herself, she is a romantic heroine, although her admirer is a lunatic neighbor who throws cucumbers over the wall. Like many other characters of the book—among them Vincent Crummles, Smike, and Nicholas himself—she is isolated in her own imagination and locked in an often inimical world. Her eccentricity, like that of most of the minor characters, is an outward symbol of estrangement from the hostile social mechanisms of convention, order, and mysterious power. Nicholas succeeds in love and fortune, not so much by his own resources but through chance—good luck with the Cheeryble brothers, for example—and through his own amiable disposition. At this point in his development as a novelist, Dickens was unable to create—as he eventually would in David Copperfield, Pip, and other protagonists—a hero who is fully aware of his isolation and confronts his sense of guilt. The reader must accept Nicholas on the level of the author's uncomplicated psychology: as a genial, deserving fellow whose good luck, good friends, and honest nature reward him with happiness, affection, and prosperity.

NINETEEN EIGHTY-FOUR

Type of work: Novel
Author: George Orwell (Eric Blair, 1903–1950)
Type of plot: Political satire
Time of plot: 1984
Locale: London
First published: 1949

Nineteen Eight-Four, along with Aldous Huxley's Brave New World *and Yevgeni Zamyatin's* We, *must be considered one of the three great early anti-utopian novels, a genre that has become disturbingly popular in contemporary literature. Orwell's vision is especially bleak because it is not simply a flight of fancy but is, rather, the logical projection of the social, cultural, and historical environment that Orwell observed when writing the book in 1948.*

Principal Characters

Winston Smith, a citizen of Oceania. He is an intelligent man of thirty-nine, a member of the Outer Ring of the Party who has a responsible job in the Ministry of Truth, where he changes the records to accord with the aims and wishes of the Party. He is not entirely loyal, however, for he keeps a secret journal, takes a mistress, and hates Big Brother. Caught in his infidelities to the Party, he is tortured until he is a broken man; he finally accepts his lot, eventually even loving Big Brother.

Mrs. Smith, Winston's wife, a devoted follower of the Party and active member of the Anti-Sex League. Because she believes procreation a party duty, she leaves her husband when the union proves childless.

Julia, a bold, good-looking young woman who, though she wears the Party's red chastity belt, falls in love with Winston and becomes his mistress. She, like her lover, rebels against Big Brother and the Party. Like Winston, too, she is tortured and brainwashed and led to repent her political sins.

O'Brien, a member of the Inner Party. He leads Winston and Julia to conspire against the Party and discovers all their rebellious acts and thoughts. He is Winston's personal torturer and educator, who explains to Winston why he must accept his lot in the world of Big Brother.

Mr. Charrington, a member of the thought police who disguises himself as an old man running an antique shop in order to catch such rebels as Winston and Julia. He is really a healthy man of thirty-five.

The Story

In externals, at least, Winston Smith was well adjusted to his world. He drank the bitter victory gin and smoked the vile victory cigarettes. In the morning, he did his exercises in front of the telescreen, and when the instructor spoke to him over the two-way television, he bent with renewed vigor to touch the floor. His flat was dingy and rickety, but at thirty-nine years old, he was scarcely old enough to remember a time when housing had been better. He had a fair job at the Ministry of Truth, since he had a good mind and the ability to write newspeak, the official language. He was a member of the outer ring of the Party.

One noon, by giving up his lunch at the ministry, he had a little free time to himself. He went to an alcove out of reach of the telescreen and furtively took out his journal. It was a noble book with paper of fine quality unobtainable at present. It was an antique, bought on an illicit trip to a secondhand store run by old Mr. Charrington. Although it was not illegal to keep a diary, for there were no laws in Oceania, it made him suspect. He wrote ploddingly about a picture he had seen of the valiant Oceania forces strafing shipwrecked refugees in the Mediterranean.

Musing over his writing, Winston found to his horror that he had written a slogan against Big Brother several times. He knew his act was a crime, even if the writing was due to gin; even to think such a slogan was a crime. Everywhere he looked, on stair landings and on storefronts, were posters showing Big Brother's all-seeing face, and citizens were reminded a hundred times a day that Big Brother was watching every move.

At the Ministry of Truth, Winston plunged into his routine. He had the job of rewriting records. If the Party made an inaccurate prediction on the progress of the war, if some aspect of production did not accord with the published goals of the ninth three-year plan, Winston corrected the record. All published material was constantly changed so that all history accorded with the wishes and aims of the Party.

There was a break in the day's routine for a two-minute

hate period. The face of Goldstein, the enemy of the Party, would appear on the big telescreen, and a government speaker would work up the feelings of the viewers. Goldstein supposedly headed a great conspiracy against Oceania, and Winston loudly and dutifully drummed his heels as he took part in the group orgasm of hate.

A bold, dark-haired girl, wearing the red chastity belt, seemed often to be near Winston in the workrooms and in the commissary. He was afraid that she might be a member of the thought police. Seeing her outside the ministry, he decided she was following him. For a time, he played with the idea of killing her. One day, she slipped a note to him at work; the little paper announced that she loved him.

Winston was troubled. He had been married, but his wife belonged to the Anti-Sex League. For her, procreation was a Party duty. When they produced no children, his wife left him. Now this girl, Julia, spoke of love. Carefully making their conversation look like chance, Winston had a few private words with her in the lunchroom. She quickly named a place in the country for a rendezvous. Winston met her in a woods, far from a telescreen, and she eagerly took him for a lover. Julia boasted that she had been the temporary mistress of several Party members and that she had no patience with the Anti-Sex League, although she worked diligently for it. She also bought sweets on the black market.

On another visit to Mr. Charrington's antique shop, the proprietor showed Winston an upstairs bedroom still preserved as it was before the Revolution. Although it was madness, Winston rented the room. Thereafter, he and Julia had a comfortable bed for their brief meetings. Winston felt happy in the old room; there was no telescreen to spy on them.

At work, Winston sometimes saw O'Brien, a kindly looking member of the Inner Party. Winston deduced from a chance remark that O'Brien was not in sympathy with all the aims of the Party. When they could, Winston and Julia went to O'Brien's apartment. He assured them that Goldstein was really the head of a conspiracy and that eventually the Party would be overthrown. Julia told him of her sins against Party discipline, and Winston recounted his evidence that the Party distorted facts in public trials and purges. O'Brien then enrolled them in the conspiracy and gave them Goldstein's book to read.

After an exhausting hate week directed against the current enemy, Eurasia, Winston read aloud to the dozing Julia, both comfortably lying in bed, from Goldstein's treatise. Suddenly, a voice rang out and ordered them to stand in the middle of the room. Winston grew sick when he realized that a hidden telescreen had spied on their actions. Soon the room was filled with truncheon-wielding policemen. Mr. Charrington came in, no longer a kindly member of the simple proletariat, but a keen, determined man of thirty-five years. Winston knew then that Mr. Charrington belonged to the thought police. One of the guards hit Julia in the stomach, and the others hurried Winston off to jail.

Winston was tortured for days—beaten, kicked, and clubbed until he confessed his crimes. He willingly admitted to years of conspiracy with the rulers of Eurasia and told everything he knew of Julia. In the later phases of his torture, O'Brien was at his side constantly. O'Brien kept him on a kind of rack with a doctor in attendance to keep him alive. He told Winston that Goldstein's book was a Party production, written in part by O'Brien himself.

Through it all, the tortured man had one small triumph; he still loved Julia. O'Brien knew Winston's fear of rats and brought in a large cage filled with rodents; he fastened it around Winston's head. In his unreasoning terror, Winston begged him to let the rats eat Julia instead.

Only one hurdle was left. Winston still hated Big Brother and said so. O'Brien patiently explained that the Party wanted no martyrs for the strengthened opposition; nor did the leaders want only groveling subjection. Winston must also think right. The proletariat, happy in their ignorance, must never have a leader to rouse them. All Party members must think and feel as Big Brother directed.

When Winston was finally released, he was bald and his teeth were gone. Because he had been purged and because his crime had not been serious, he was even given a small job on a subcommittee. Mostly he sat solitary in taverns and drank victory gin. He even saw Julia once. She had coarsened in figure, and her face was scarred. They had little to say to each other.

One day, a big celebration was going on in the tavern. Oceania had achieved an important victory in Africa. Suddenly, the doddering Winston felt himself purged. He believed. Now he could be shot with a pure soul, for at last he loved Big Brother.

Critical Evaluation

Nineteen Eight-Four was first published in England in June, 1949, seven months before the death of its author, George Orwell, of tuberculosis. While his personal suffering certainly enhanced his fears regarding the future of the West, the world situation of the era most assuredly affected him more deeply. It was a world wherein the West had experienced within a thirty-year period World War I, the Depression, World War II, and the beginnings of the Cold War. It was also a world wherein totalitarian dictatorships had destroyed and were destroying human freedoms and humankind. The excesses of Benito Mussolini's Fascism and Adolf Hitler's Germany were well known; the excesses of Joseph Stalin's Communist dictatorship in the Soviet Union were just being discovered.

Orwell had long had grave concerns for the future of this world, and he was not alone. Intellectuals had been predicting the imminent demise of Western civilization for over a generation, beginning with Oswald Spengler's *The Decline of the West* (1918-1922). The catastrophes of the succeeding years had done little to alter Spengler's predictions. By 1948, the West was even more severely weakened, and vast stretches of Europe lay in ruins. This, coupled with the agitation for freedom within the colonial holdings of the Western nations, created an angst-filled preoccupation not only with decline but also regarding the future.

In the 1930s, Orwell had been a social commentator of no small repute. *Down and Out in Paris and London* (1933) and *The Road to Wigan Pier* (1937) had demonstrated his enormous talent for portraying in prose the social problems of the age. While his own proposals for solutions to human misery were unimposing, he had astutely noted that leftist theories were just as tyrannical as fascist theories, a theme that preoccupied him for the rest of his life. *Homage to Catalonia* (1938), which recorded his observations on the Spanish Civil War, was his first indictment of totalitarianism. As a participant in the conflict, he had witnessed at first hand the ruthless extermination of individual liberties by the Fascists and the Communists alike. He also witnessed, upon his return to Great Britain, the lies being reported regarding events in Spain. From that point onward, Orwell dedicated himself to attacking lies and threats to human liberty.

It was the expedient lie which drew Orwell's greatest wrath. He knew that the manipulation of minds through the manipulation of words was just as dangerous as the threat of force. The propaganda ministry of Nazi Germany had molded the minds of a generation of Germans. The true state of Stalin's Soviet Union lay hidden behind the invective of the dictator. Control of the media resulted in the control of the mind, just as control of the secret police resulted in the control of the body. Orwell feared that the inevitable result of such controls would be absolute control by the state over the masses. He inveighed against this brainwashing and thought/body control in his short novel *Animal Farm* (1945). While Orwell contended that his work applied to totalitarianism of all types, it was no coincidence that Napoleon the Pig bore an uncanny resemblance to Joseph Stalin and that the lie "All animals are equal, but some animals are more equal than others" became the focal point of this biting social satire.

Over the next four years Orwell worked, despite his worsening illness, on what was to become his magnum opus. *Nineteen Eighty-Four* describes a world devastated by nuclear war; the three superpowers that survived maintained their power through thought control and secret police. Never-ending local wars were used to fan the nationalism of the population and to justify the dismal, regimented world that remained. Orwell was not claim-

ing that his "sour utopian" future would be; he was only detailing a future that could be, if trends manifest in the 1940s remained unchanged. *Nineteen Eighty-Four* detailed a world monitored and manipulated by Big Brother, Orwell's version of an immortal totalitarian leader. Within the state, all aspects of life were regimented and controlled by ubiquitous, two-way telescreens.

It was a world without hope. Even working for the Brotherhood, the nonexistent resistance organization, was described in hopeless terms: "You will work for a while, you will be caught, you will confess, and then you will die." When Winston Smith, Orwell's antihero, told his torturers that he represented the human spirit that would prevail, he was told to look in a mirror. The guardian of the human spirit had become, through the excesses of the police state, totally physically dominated. The final surrender which followed was absolute; when he betrayed Julia, his lover and confidante, he also betrayed his own human integrity. The state had won; Winston had accepted and had been accepted. The state had triumphed over individualism.

The monolithic state used thought control of every type to brainwash the inhabitants of Oceania. Smith worked in the Ministry of Truth, where he used Newspeak to simplify news for the masses. Truth was distorted as expediency dictated, and oxymorons such as "War is Peace" or "Freedom is Slavery" made nonsense of language. It was this characteristic of totalitarianism which most concerned Orwell. He believed that only human nature, with its innate love of liberty, had saved humankind from tyranny. Orwell feared that even human nature would wither from an onslaught of mass suggestion. His warning was that the word must not be perverted and subverted; truth and ideals must never be abandoned.

What of this novel of the future which has been translated into over sixty languages, with tens of millions of copies in print? Orwell's monolithic, totalitarian state has never come into existence. Too many variables have rendered his view of the future improbable for the West. The renaissance of Europe, the lack of a nuclear holocaust, and the growth of individual freedom have combined to block his dismal portrait of the future. Even in the dictatorships, there has not yet been the development of monolithic, totalitarian states. Fragmentation and competition have continued to exist in even the most dictatorial of states. The kind of absolute control envisioned by Orwell has never existed; this does not mean, however, that it will never exist. New inventions have made possible alternative methods of control: Computers, two-way television, and other technical intrusions could assist a Big Brother of the future.

Some literary critics have defined *Nineteen Eighty-Four* as a first-rate political document instead of as a novel. While it is true that the political theme predominates, *Nineteen Eighty-Four* is, from beginning to end, a remarkable novel. Moreover, the word "Orwellian" has been, although it should not be, construed as a synonym for "dictatorship." Rather, Orwell's story was about truth and decency. The reader is asked to beware the loss of human dignity and of communication, for if, as Orwell feared, newspeak becomes the norm, then tyranny cannot be far behind.

NOSTROMO: A Tale of the Seaboard

Type of work: Novel
Author: Joseph Conrad (Józef Teodor Konrad Korzeniowski, 1857–1924)
Type of plot: Psychological romance
Time of plot: Early twentieth century
Locale: Costaguana, on the north coast of South America
First published: 1904

Using the San Tomé mine as his focal point, Conrad presents a group of fascinating characters, representing a cross section of attitudes, character types, and economic levels, who contend with one another and with themselves for the silver and all it implies economically, politically, and morally. The result is a powerful, panoramic vision of man, both as a solitary individual and as a social animal, caught up in forces, both external and internal, that he can neither understand nor contain.

Principal Characters

Nostromo (nŏs·trō'mō), the nickname of **Gian' Battista,** the "incorruptible" hero of the people after saving a valuable cargo of silver from revolutionists by hiding it on a barren island at the harbor entrance. Later he realizes that it can be his because the lighter on which he transported the silver is reported sunk in a collision with a troopship at night. He grows rich slowly by returning to the island occasionally for some of the silver. When a lighthouse is established on the island, he is still able to visit his hoard of silver because his friends, the Violas, are made keepers of the light. He chooses to love Giselle, the younger Viola daughter, rather than the more stable and idealistic Linda. Mistaken for a despised suitor of Giselle, he is shot by old Viola while on a night visit to see Giselle. Nostromo dies feeling that he has been betrayed and wishing to confess to Mrs. Gould. Because she refuses to listen, his secret is kept and his famed uncorruptibility remains intact.

Charles Gould, The manager of the San Tomé silver mine, which he idealizes as a civilizing force that will bring progress to contented but backward Sulaco, a city in the Occidental Province of the Republic of Costaguana, as well as atonement for the death of his father. But silver, the incorruptible metal, is a corrupting influence politically and morally. It separates Gould from his wife Emilia, attracts politicians from the interior, and provokes a revolution.

Doña Emilia, Charles Gould's wife, supplanted in his affections by his "redemption idea" of the mine. Childless, she is a victim of a "subtle unfaithfulness" created by the mine. In turn, she is gracious, kind, unselfish, and lives for others.

Martin Decoud (màr·tăn' də·kö'), a young Creole intellectual, skeptic, and amateur journalist recently returned from Paris. He falls in love with patriotic Antonia Avellanos and fathers the idea of a separate Occidental Republic. He escapes from the revolutionists on the lighter bearing the silver but commits suicide when left alone on the island to face all the silence and indifference of nature.

Dr. Monygham, a doctor of introspective temperament. Under torture during the former dictatorship of Guzman Bento, he had betrayed friends, a deed that weighs on his conscience. He risks his life during this revolution for the safety of others in order to earn restoration to the human community.

Captain Mitchell, the superintendent of the Oceanic Steam Navigation Company, a "thick, elderly man, wearing high pointed collars and short sidewhiskers, partial to white waistcoats, and really very communicative under his air of pompous reserve." He narrates part of the story.

Giorgio Viola (jôr'jō vē·ō'lä), a veteran of Garibaldi's army and keeper of the Casa Viola, a restaurant and hotel in Sulaco. Believing wholeheartedly in the human bond of liberty, he had risked his life in Italy in the hope of bringing freedom to men. He wishes to make Nostromo his son.

Teresa, the portly, ill wife of Viola, anxious for the future of her husband and daughters.

Giselle, the sensuous, blonde younger daughter of Viola, in love with Nostromo.

Linda, the idealistic, dark older daughter of Viola, also in love with Nostromo.

President Ribiera (rē·bē·ā'rä), the beneficent dictator of Costaguana, defeated by revolutionary forces.

Don José Avellanos (dōn hō·sā' ä·vä·yä'-nōs), an idealistic, cultured, dignified, patriotic statesman who has survived many changes in his country and the author of "Fifty Years of Misrule," a history of the republic. He dies of disappointment.

Antonia Avellanos (ăn·tō'nyä), his beautiful, freeminded, patriotic daughter, in love with Decoud.

Father Corbelàn (kŏr·bä·län'), the fanatical uncle of

Antonia Avellanos. His appearance suggests something unlawful behind his priesthood, the idea of a chaplain of bandits. He is Costaguana's first Cardinal Archbishop.

General Montero (mōn·tā′rō), a rural hero and a former Minister of War, the leader of the revolution.

Pedro Montero (pā′drō), his brother, a savage with a genius for treachery. He is the leader of the rebel army from the interior.

Don Pépé (dōn pā′pā), the faithful overseer of the San Tomé mine, under orders to blow up the mine if the revolutionaries try to seize it.

Father Roman (rō·män′), the faithful padre of the workers of the mine.

Colonel Sotillo (sō·tē′yō), one of the leaders of the revolution. Cowardly and traitorous, he hurries his army into Sulaco in the hope of gaining personal advantage.

Señor Hirsch, a craven and fearful hide merchant who tries to escape from Sulaco by secreting himself on the lighter with Nostromo and Decoud while they are transporting the silver. When the lighter and Sotillo's ship collide in the darkness, he leaps aboard the rebels' vessel.

There he is tortured for confession and finally killed by Sotillo.

Hernández (ĕr·nän′dēs), a man mistreated in an earlier revolution and now the leader of a robber band. During the revolt he becomes a general, pledged to Father Corbelàn.

General Barrios (bär′ryōs), a brave, trustworthy, unpretentious soldier who has lived heroically and loves to talk of the adventurous life of his past. He is the commander of the Occidental military district.

Don Juste Lopez (dōn hūs′tā lō′pĕz), the president of the provincial assembly. He thinks that resistance to Pedro Montero will be useless but that formalities may still save the republic.

Fuentes (fwēn′tās), a nominee for the post of political chief of Sulaco. Eager to take office, he sides with Pedro Montero.

Gamacho (gä·mä′chō), the commander of the Sulaco national guard. He throws his lot with the revolutionists.

Basilio (bä·sē′lyō), Mrs. Gould's head servant.

Luis (lōō′ēs), a mulatto servant at the Casa Viola.

The Story

The Republic of Costaguana was in a state of revolt. Under the leadership of Pedrito Montero, rebel troops had taken control of the eastern part of the country. When news of the revolt reached Sulaco, the principal town of the western section that was separated from the rest of the country by a mountain range, the leaders began to lay defense plans.

The chief interest of the town was the San Tomé silver mine in the nearby mountains, a mine managed by Charles Gould, an Englishman who, although educated in England, had been born in Sulaco, his father having been manager before him. Gould had made a great success of the mine. The semiannual shipment of silver had just come down from the mine to the customhouse when the telegraph operator from Esmeralda, on the eastern side of the mountains, sent word that troops had embarked on a transport under command of General Sotillo and that the rebels planned to capture the silver ingots as well as Sulaco.

Gould decided to load the ingots on a lighter and set it afloat in the gulf pending the arrival of a ship that would take the cargo to the United States. The man to guide the boat would be Gian' Battista, known in Sulaco as Nostromo (our man) for he was considered incorruptible. His companion would be Martin Decoud, editor of the local newspaper, who had been drawn from Paris and kept in Sulaco by the European-educated Antonia Avellanos, to whom he had just become engaged. Decoud had incurred the anger of Montero by denouncing the revolutionists in his paper. Decoud also had conceived a plan for making the country around Sulaco an independent state, the Occidental Republic.

When Nostromo and Decoud set out in the black of the night, Sotillo's ship, approaching the port without lights, bumped into their lighter. Nostromo made for a nearby uninhabited island, the Great Isabel, where he cached the treasure. Then, he left Decoud behind and rowed the lighter to the middle of the harbor, pulled a plug, and sank her. He swam the remaining mile to the mainland.

Upon discovering that the silver had been spirited away, Sotillo took possession of the customhouse, where he conducted an inquisition. The next day, Sulaco was seized by Montero, who considered Sotillo of little worth.

When the Europeans and highborn natives who had not fled the town discovered that Nostromo was back, they took it for granted that the silver had been lost in the harbor. They asked Nostromo to take a message to Barrios, who commanded the Loyalist troops on the eastern side of the mountains. In a spectacular engine ride up the side of the mountain and a subsequent six-day horseback journey through the mountain passes, Nostromo succeeded in delivering his message, and Barrios set out with his troops by boat to relieve the town of Sulaco.

Coming into the harbor, Nostromo sighted a boat that he recognized as the small craft attached to the lighter that had carried him and Decoud to Great Isabel. He dived overboard and swam to the boat. Barrios went on to Sulaco and drove the traitors out. Meanwhile, Gould had planted dynamite around the silver mine to destroy it in case of defeat, for he was determined to keep the mine from the revolutionists at any cost.

Nostromo rowed the little boat over to Great Isabel,

where he discovered that Decoud was gone and that he had taken four of the ingots with him. He correctly guessed that Decoud had killed himself, for there was a bloodstain on the edge of the boat. Decoud had been left to himself when Nostromo returned to the mainland, and each day he had grown more and more lonely until finally he dug up four of the ingots, tied them to himself, went out into the boat, shot himself, and fell overboard, the weight of the ingots carrying him to the bottom of the harbor. Now Nostromo could not tell Gould where the silver was, for he would himself have been suspected of stealing the four missing ingots. Since everyone thought the treasure was in the bottom of the sea, he decided to let the rumor stand and sell the ingots one by one and so become rich slowly.

In gratitude for his many services to the country, the people provided Nostromo with a boat in which he hauled cargo as far north as California. Sometimes he would be gone for months while he carried out his schemes for disposing of the hidden silver. One day on his return, he saw that a lighthouse was being built on Great Isabel. He was panic stricken. Then he suggested that the keeper should be old Giorgio Viola, in whose daughter Linda he was interested. He thought that with the Violas on the island no one would suspect his frequent visits. Linda had a younger sister, Giselle, for whom the vagabond Ramirez was desperate. Viola would not allow her to receive his attentions and kept her under close guard. He would not permit Ramirez to come to the island.

To make his comings and goings more secure, one day Nostromo asked Linda to be his wife. Almost at once he realized that he was really in love with Giselle. In secret meetings, he and Giselle confessed their mutual passion.

Linda grew suspicious. Giselle begged Nostromo to carry her away, but he said he could not do so for a while. He finally told her about the silver and how he had to convert it into money before he could take her away.

Obsessed by hate of Ramirez, Viola began patrolling the island at night with his gun loaded. One night as Nostromo was approaching Giselle's window, old Viola saw him and shot him. Hearing her father say that he had shot Ramirez, Linda rushed out, but Giselle ran past her and reached Nostromo first. It was she who accompanied him to the mainland. In the hospital, Nostromo asked for the kind Mrs. Gould, to whom he protested that Giselle was innocent and that he alone knew about the hidden treasure. Mrs. Gould, however, would not let him tell her where he had hidden it. It had caused so much sorrow that she did not want it to be brought to light again. Nostromo refused any aid from Dr. Monygham and died without revealing the location of the ingots.

Dr. Monygham went in the police galley out to Great Isabel, where he informed Linda of Nostromo's death. She was thoroughly moved by the news and whispered that she—and she alone—had loved the man and that she would never forget Nostromo. Al Linda in despair cried out Nostromo's name, Dr. Monygham observed that as triumphant as Nostromo had been in life, this love of Linda's was the greatest victory of all.

The region about Sulaco finally did become the Occidental Republic. The San Tomé mine prospered under Gould's management, the population increased enormously, and the new country flourished with great vigor. Although Decoud, the country's first planner, and Nostromo, the hero of its inception, were dead, life in the new country went on richly and fully.

Critical Evaluation

Joseph Conrad has always been known among the mass of readers as a great teller of sea stories. He is also a pertinent, even prophetic, commentator on what he called "land entanglements"—particularly on the subject of political revolution. Conrad's father was an active revolutionary in the cause of Polish independence; he died as a result of prolonged imprisonment for revolutionary "crimes." Three of Conrad's best novels are studies in political behavior: *Nostromo, The Secret Agent*, and *Under Western Eyes. Nostromo* is by far the most ambitious and complex of these works. It has a very large international cast of characters of all shapes and sizes, and it employs the typical Conradian device of an intentionally jumbled (and sometimes confusing) chronology. As typical of Conrad, the physical setting is handled superbly; the reader is drawn into the book through the wonderfully tactile descriptions of the land and sea. The setting in South America is also particularly appropriate to Conrad's skeptical consideration of progress achieved either by Capitalism or revolution.

Nostromo is a study in the politics of wealth in an underdeveloped country. The central force in the novel is the silver of the San Tomé mine—a potential of wealth so immense that a humane and cultured civilization can be built upon it. At least this is the view of the idealistic Charles Gould, the owner and developer of the mine. There are other views. From the start, Gould is ready to maintain his power by force if necessary. He remembers how the mine destroyed his father. The mine attracts politicians and armed revolutionaries from the interior, but Gould is willing to blow up his treasure and half of Sulaco, the central city, in order to defeat the revolution. He succeeds, but Conrad intends for the reader to regard his success as partial at best. His obsession with the mine separates him from his wife. As with Conrad's other heroes, the demands of public action distort and cancel out his capacity for private affection.

One of the magnificences of the first half of *Nostromo* is that Gould and his silver are seen from so many angles. For old Giorgio Viola, who was once a member of Garibaldi's red shirts, Gould's idealization of material interests is wrong because it has the potential of violating a pure and disinterested love of liberty for all humanity. Viola, however, is as ineffectual as the austere and cultured leader of Sulaco's aristocracy, Don José Avellanos, whose unpublished manuscript "Thirty Years of Misrule" is used as gun wadding at the height of the revolution. Ranged against Avellanos and Viola, at the other end of the spectrum, are those sanguinary petty tyrants, Bento, Montero, and Sotillo, who want to run the country entirely for their own personal advantage. Sotillo represents their capacity and blind lust for Gould's treasure. The most interesting characters, however, are those who occupy the middle of the spectrum. Of these, two—Martin Decoud, the dilettante Parisian boulevardier, and Dr. Monygham—are central to any understanding of the novel. Between them they represent Conrad's own point of view most fully.

Decoud may be the object of some of Conrad's most scourging irony, but his skeptical pronouncements accord well with the facts of Sulaco's politics as Conrad presents them in the early stages of the novel. Decoud saves the mine by arranging for a new rifle to be used in defense of Gould's material interests, but he does not share Gould's enthusiasm that the mine can act as the chief force in the process of civilizing the new republic. He views the whole business of revolution and counterrevolution as an elaborate charade, a comic opera.

The most trenchant charge against Gould is made by the other deeply skeptical character, Dr. Monygham. His judgment upon material interests is one of the most famous passages in the book:

> There is no peace and rest in the development of material interests. They have their law and their justice. But it is founded on expediency, and is inhuman; it is without the continuity and the force that can be found only in a moral principle. . . . The time approaches when all that the Gould Concession stands for shall weigh as heavily upon the people as the barbarism, cruelty, and misrule of a few years back.

It is clear that Conrad intends for his readers to take Monygham's judgment at face value. The trouble is that the facts of Costaguana's post-revolutionary state do not agree with it. The land is temporarily at peace and is being developed in an orderly fashion by the mine as well as other material interests, and the workers seem better off as a result. Monygham is of course hinting at the workers' revolt against the suppression of material interests, but this revolt seems so far in the future that his judgment is robbed of much of its power. This surely accounts for part of the "hollowness" that some critics have found in the novel.

The last section of the novel is concerned with Gould's successful resistance to the attempts of both church and military to take over the mine and the moral degradation of the "incorruptible" man of the people, Nostromo. In this latter case, Conrad abandons the richness and density of his panoramic view of South American society and gives us a semiallegorical dramatization of the taint of the silver within the soul of a single character.

Nostromo's fate is clearly related to the legend of the two gringos which begins the book, for the silver that he has hidden has this same power to curse his soul as the "fatal spell" cast by the treasure on the gringos. ("Their souls cannot tear themselves away from their bodies mounting guard over the discovered treasure. They are now rich and hungry and thirsty. . . .") The result of Conrad's absorption with Nostromo at the end of the novel is twofold. First, readers are denied a dramatization of the changing social conditions that would support Monygham's judgment. Second, and more important, the novel loses its superb richness and variety and comes dangerously close to insisting on the thesis that wealth is a universal corruptor, even that "money is the root of all evil."

For roughly two-thirds of its length, *Nostromo* gives readers one of the finest social panoramas in all fiction. The ending, however, suggests that underneath the complex texture of the novel lies a rather simplistic idea: that both "material interests" and revolution are doomed to failure. Although set in South America, *Nostromo* suggests a world in which systems and conditions change very little because men do not.

"ODE TO APHRODITE"

Type of work: Poem
Author: Sappho (fl. c. 600 B.C.)
First published: Early sixth century B.C.

The "Ode" (or "Prayer") "to Aphrodite" is the first poem in the standard edition of Sappho's work by Edgar Lobel and Denys Page (1955, 1963) and in earlier editions by Theodor Bergk (1843), Ernest Diehl (1924–1925, 1935), and J. M. Edmonds (1928). Translators do not regularly give it this pride of place; Susy Q. Groden (1975) does, but Mary Barnard (1958) and Willis Barnstone (1962, 1965) do not. There is, indeed, nothing to warrant the kind of primacy that translators, following editors, always accord to Pindar's *Olympian I* and almost always to Catullus' dedicatory poem to Cornelius Nepos except the assumption, hardly to be questioned, that this is the only complete poem of Sappho's that has survived.

The canon of Sappho amounts to a collection, apart from this one complete ode, of more than two hundred fragments, some of them no more than a single word or a letter or two. Except for two fragments each in excess of thirty lines but discontinuous because of lengthy lacunae, the "Ode to Aphrodite" is Sappho's longest extant work. The poem comprises seven four-line stanzas composed in the meter invented by Sappho and named for her, the sapphic. About twenty percent of the fragments ascribed to Sappho are in this meter.

The Sapphic stanza consists of three lines in the following scheme: $-\breve{}-x-\breve{}\;\breve{}-\breve{}-$, followed by one line in the scheme called adonic ($-\breve{}\;\breve{}-x$). The macron (–) denotes a long syllable, the equivalent of a half-note in music; the micron ($\breve{}$) denotes a short syllable, the equivalent of a quarter-note in music; and x indicates that the syllable may be long or short. The adonic is so called because its model is Sappho's line *ō tŏn Ădōnĭn* (O, [poor] Adonis).

In the following translation of the "Ode to Aphrodite" no attempt is made to reproduce the metric of the first three lines of each stanza, but a pentasyllabic fourth line is used to suggest the adonic:

Colorfully throned immortal Aphrodite
daughter of Zeus, designer of deceptions,
please do not, great queen, make me
   heartsick with grief now;

but, hearing my words from afar and
heeding them, come as you did before,
driving your chariot from your father's
   palace all golden,

with birds of beauty and swiftness
speeding through heaven on racing wings

and bringing you through the space of the sky
   over the dark earth.

Their swiftness prevailed and, Lady of Rapture,
smiling with your immortal visage,
you asked what my trouble was and why I
   called for your help then:

"Whom exactly," you asked, "am I
to persuade to return to the sphere
of your affection? Who, dear Sappho, is
   treating you badly?

"If she runs from you now, she'll run after you
soon; if she now spurns your gifts, she'll be
giving you gifts; and, willing or not, she will
   presently love you."

Come to me now, Aphrodite; dispel
the worries that irritate and offend me;
fulfill the wishes of my heart; and
   fight here beside me.

The poem is a prayer for a renewal of confidence that the person whom Sappho loves will requite that love. Sappho identifies herself in this poem; the name Sappho (Psappho) appears in only three other fragments. A previous prayer seems to have been answered satisfactorily, but the current situation is clouded over with doubt and uneasiness; reassurance is needed. Presumably the current situation involves the same beloved, in which case Sappho's anxiety has been heightened by a rival. The subject of the earlier prayer was a woman, and the context of the poem is female homosexuality. This is not the context of all of Sappho's poetic constructions; one fragment reads, "Sweet mother, I cannot stay at the loom:/ svelte Aphrodite has melted my will away/ and filled me with longing for a boy," and another is a call to the speaker's lost virginity. The speaker may not be Sappho in either of these heterosexual contexts; but the likelihood is that in all of the first-person fragments Sappho is expressing herself and her own feelings. In her sensual and sexual pursuits Sappho could be, and perhaps should be, identified as a bisexual: She had a husband, Cercylas, and a daughter named Cleïs (after Sappho's mother), and she was rumored, whether accurately or not, to be romantically involved with the poet Alcaeus. Still, it is the preponderantly homosexual ambience of the fragments that has contributed to the English language the word "lesbian." Sappho was in habitat a Lesbian; her home was the city of Mytilene on the island of Lesbos.

The text of the poem is preserved partially on papyrus and partially in quotation by ancient writers and scholiasts. This is the case with all of the fragments; no unitary text of Sappho's collected or representative poems appears ever to have been published in antiquity. The "Ode to Aphrodite" was preserved by the critic Dionysius of Halicarnassus (late first century B.C.), who quoted it as an example of smoothly flowing verse composition with a sonantal euphony resulting from avoidance of excessive use of consonants. The consensus is that Dionysius quoted the poem in its entirety and thereby provided posterity with Sappho's only complete extant poem. The more famous poem that begins *Phainetai moi kēnos isos theoisin* (that man seems to me to be on a par with gods), preserved by "Longinus" (first century A.D.) and imitated by Catullus (c. 85-54 B.C.), is missing at lest one stanza. There is, moreover, only one crux in the "Ode to Aphrodite": The fifth stanza contains a lacuna of a letter, perhaps two, which appears to be resolved by a reading in a fragmentary papyrus copy of the poem. There is some variance in the handling of the passage by editors and translators, but the sense of the passage is not irremediably obscured: Sappho rehearses Aphrodite's response, in part, to the poet's earlier prayer; the goddess had asked whom she was to persuade, or whom Persuasion was to move, to return the affection of the suppliant.

The poem follows the ancient literary conventions of prayer. It opens with an invocation to the deity, who is complimented by epithets and recognition of attributes and is then reminded of having answered a previous call for help. Sappho varies the formula slightly, introducing a preludial plea between the invocation and the reminder. The reminder, or the sanction, is the major part of the poem, taking up five of the seven stanzas. It is itself in two parts: a lyrical description of the goddess' physical approach to the suppliant, followed by a citation of the goddess' verbal response. The prayer concludes peremptorily with Sappho's plea.

The symmetrical balance of immortal-daughter-designer of deceptions with queen-father-immortal establishes the focal apposition of *doloploke* (designer of deceptions) and *potnia* (queen). Aphrodite is invoked as the queen of deception-designing or wiles-weaving. The focal emphasis defines the substance of the prayer: Aphrodite, queen of deception, make my beloved blind to any attraction but me. Sappho realizes that her appeal to her beloved can be sustained only by the persuasiveness of Aphroditean cosmetic mystery. It is the plight of many an erotically or sensually inclined person whose desire exceeds her or his desirability and who cannot become resigned to the inequity of the amatory situation.

The fourteenth line, which is the midpoint and the focal line of the poem, reads literally, "smiling with [respect to your] immortal face." This is one of the early instances in literature of the eternal smile, which, turned inward, like that of the Buddha, radiates serenity, but turned outward toward humankind, like that of the Etruscan Apollo of Veii, signals cruelty or indifference. As suppliant, Sappho wants Aphrodite to be *symmachos* (a fighter at her side) so that the smile, directed inward when the goddess first appeared to Sappho, will now be directed outward toward her rival. Sappho understands that the goddess or, figuratively, the force of love and sensuality is regent and militant, like Ishtar, the Babylonian counterpart of Aphrodite, who is goddess of both love and war; Aphrodite's paramour, moreover, is Ares, the god of war.

The juxtaposition of "designer of deceptions" and "queen" at the focal hinge of a symmetrical sequence and the location of the eternal smile at the focus of this poem which culminates in a calling of Aphrodite to arms produce a powerful portrait of the force of love, to which the poet entrusts herself in an exquisitely worded suppliant address. In doing so, she experiences the substance of her hopes.

"Longinus" selected Sappho's *Phainetai moi* to illustrate the sublimity of pathos (emotion) presented in such a way as to include both the subjective experience of incipient jealousy and the objective comprehension of the experience. The poem exceeds the sum of its parts. Much the same thing could be said about the "Ode to Aphrodite." It has all the fluency of expression that Dionysius found in it, yet this is not the extent of its quality. It is a prayer that becomes, by means of its perfect utterance, its own answer; it is a wish expressed so well that its very expression constitutes its fulfillment. The flow of vocalic music expedites the ode's smooth progression from arrested grief and passivity to aggressively active participation in the immortal force of love. The ode may be viewed as complete because this progression is impeccably completed. Beyond that, however, each of the parts of the ode—the invocation, the reminder, the speech of Aphrodite, and the precise plea—is complete in itself. The ode is more than the sum of its parts, and each of the parts is more than its own aggregation. The fragments of Sappho's poetry retain a value analogous to that of the fragments of a gold bar. If only a fragment of the "Ode to Aphrodite" had been preserved, there would be less gold, but the quality of the remaining gold would not be changed.

Each stanza of the ode frames a dominant image—throne, chariot, birds, eternal smile, persuasion, gifts, battle—in the manner of a Japanese haiku. Each stanza is therein a veritable poem, just as each line is a passage of music. The image of battle in the final stanza is projected in regimented word order: The stanza begins and ends with an imperative—come, fight (literally, "a companion-fighter be")—and contains two interior imperatives (dispel, fulfill); it also contains two symmetrically balanced ranks of words. Ultimately it is the irrefragable unity of form and content that lends distinction to every part, every fragment of Sappho's poetry.

One of her fragments is the following invitation, which, with its soft music and exquisitely framed imagery, creates the erotically religious serenity to which the addressee is invited:

> Come to this holy temple, where
> there is a pretty apple orchard and
> altars which, among the apple trees, are
>   smoking with incense.

and through the branches of the trees there is
a rustling sound of cool water; roses lend
their shadows to the grove, and sleep flows down
   from
    whispering tree leaves;

the grazing-meadow here has blossomed
with lotus flowers; and sweetest odors
issue from the anises—

This fragment creates the sound, the scene, and the mood to which the "Ode to Aphrodite" expresses the militant desire to return.

ODYSSEY

Type of work: Poem
Author: Homer (c. Ninth century B. C.)
Type of plot: Heroic epic
Time of plot: Years immediately following Trojan War
Locale: Greece and Mediterranean lands
First transcribed: Sixth century B. C.

The Iliad, *an epic about an incident in the Trojan War, and the* Odyssey, *concerned with Odysseus' difficulties in getting home after the war had been won by the Greeks, are the great epic masterpieces of Western literature and a storehouse of Greek folklore and myth. The* Odyssey, *with its sagacious, magnificent hero, its romantic theme, and its frequent change of scene, has enjoyed greater popularity than the* Iliad.

Principal Characters

Odysseus (ō·dĭ′sĭ·əs, ō·dĭs′ūs), a roving veteran of the Trojan War who, having incurred the anger of Poseidon by blinding the sea-god's son Polyphemus, a gigantic Cyclops, is fated to roam for ten years before he can return to his homeland of Ithaca. Leaving Troy, he and his followers sail first to Ismarus. In the sack of the Ciconian city Odysseus spares the life of Maro, priest of Apollo, who in turn gives the conqueror some jars of potent wine. Gales then drive the Greeks to the country of the Lotus-eaters, from which they sail to the land of the fierce Cyclops. There Ulysses and twelve of his band are captured by Polyphemus. After Odysseus frees himself and his companions by a clever ruse, leaving the Cyclops maimed and blinded the band journeys to the Isle of Aeolus. In the land of the Laestrygones man-eating giants destroy all but one of his ships and devour their crews. At Aeaea, Odysseus outwits the enchantress Circe and frees his men after she has turned them into swine. In the dark region of the Cimmerians he consults the shade of Tiresias, the Theban prophet, to learn what awaits him in Ithaca. Following the advice of Circe, Odysseus escapes the spell of the Sirens, passes safely between Scylla and Charybdis, and arrives at Thrinacia. There his remaining comrades are drowned for their impiety in eating cattle sacred to Hyperion. Cast adrift, Odysseus floats to the island of Ogygia, where for seven years he lives with the lovely nymph Calypso. Finally the gods take pity on him and order Calypso to release him. On a makeshift raft he continues his voyage. After his raft has been wrecked by Poseidon, he battles the waves until he arrives, exhausted, on the island of Drepane. Here Nausicaä, daughter of the king of the Phaeacians, finds him and leads him to the royal palace. Warmly received by King Alcinoüs, Odysseus takes part in celebration games and tells the story of his adventures. Alcinous gives Odysseus rich gifts and returns the wanderer by ship to Ithaca. There, in disguise, he meets his son Telemachus, now grown to manhood, routs and kills the suitors who throng his palace, and is reunited with his loyal wife Penelope. Odysseus is the ideal Greek hero, eloquent at the council board, courageous in battle, resourceful in danger, crafty in wisdom. He is the darling of the goddess Athena, who aids him whenever it is in her power to do so.

Penelope (pě·ně′lō·pē), his devoted wife, a model of domestic fidelity, skilled in handicrafts. Still attractive in spite of twenty years of anxiety and grief during the absence of Odysseus, she is by custom forced to entertain importunate, insolent suitors whom she puts off from year to year by various stratagems. Until betrayed by her false servants, she would weave by day a burial robe for Laertes, her father-in-law, and at night she would unravel her work. The return of Odysseus is for her an occasion of great joy, but first she tests his knowledge of the construction of their wedding bed in order to avoid being duped by a plausible stranger. Although she is noteworthy for her forbearance and fidelity, there are occasions when she complains bitterly and laments her sad fate.

Telemachus (tə·lě′mə·kəs), the son of Odysseus and Penelope, grown to handsome young manhood during his father's absence. Also favored by Athena, he accuses the suitors of being parasites, journeys to other lands in search of news of his father, and returns to fight bravely by the side of Odysseus when the one hundred and twelve suitors of Penelope are routed and put to death. His comeliness, manly bearing, and good manners show him to be his father's son when he meets wise King Nestor and King Menelaus.

Athena (ə·thē′nə), also called **Pallas Athena,** the goddess of Wisdom and the patroness of arts and crafts. Moved by pity and admiration, she becomes the benefactress of Odysseus and pleads with Zeus, her father, to release the hero from the seven-year embrace of the nymph Calypso. Assuming various disguises and aiding him in many ways, she watches over the homeward journey and eventual triumph of Odysseus. Her divine intervention assures peace between him and the angry families of the slain suitors.

Poseidon (pō·sī′dən), the earth-shaking god of the sea. The blinding of his giant son, the Cyclops Polyphemus, arouses his anger against Odysseus, and he prevents as long as possible the return of the hero to Ithaca.

Laertes (lā·ûr′tēz), the aged father of Odysseus. Withdrawn from the royal palace, he tends his vineyards and herds during his son's absence. Still vigorous, he helps Odysseus and Telemachus repulse a band of angry citizens in their attempt to avenge the death of the suitors.

Eumaeus (ū·mē′əs), the devoted swineherd in whose hut disguised Odysseus takes refuge on his return to Ithaca. Despising the suitors, he fights bravely against them alongside Odysseus, Telemachus, and Philoetius, the neatherd. Though of lowly occupation, he is of noble birth, and he is both slave and devoted friend to Odysseus.

Philoetius (fĭ·lē′tĭ·əs), the neatherd and a trusted servant in the household of Odysseus. Forced to provide cattle for the feasts of the suitors, he resents their presence in his master's hall, and he yearns for the return of the absent hero. In the great battle in which the suitors are killed, he fights bravely by the side of Odysseus, Telemachus, and Eumaeus.

Eurycleia (ū·rĭ·klē′ə), the aged nurse of both Odysseus and Telemachus. She recognizes her master by a scar on his thigh and reveals to him his faithless servants who have consorted with the suitors during his absence. Taken as a bondservant by Odysseus' father, she is loyal to the royal household and most vindictive in her revenge.

Polyphemus (pŏ·lĭ·fē′məs), one of the Cyclops, giants with one eye in the center of the forehead, and the sons of Poseidon. When Odysseus and twelve of his companions seek hospitality in his cave, the monster makes prisoners of the band and eats six of them. Wily Odysseus saves himself and his remaining companions by giving Polyphemus some of Maro's strong wine to drink and then, while the Cyclops is asleep, putting out his eye with a heated, pointed shaft. The Greeks escape from the cave by hiding beneath the bodies of Polyphemus' sheep when the giant turns his flock out to pasture.

Circe (sêr′sē), an enchantress, the daughter of Helios and Perse. Arriving at Aeaea, Odysseus sends Eurylochus, his lieutenant, and twenty-two men ashore to explore the island. When they come to Circe's palace, she invites them to feast with her. But Eurylochus, almost as crafty as his master, remains outside, and through a window he sees the sorceress serve the men drugged food and then transform them into swine. Odysseus, on his way to rescue his companions, encounters the god Hermes, who gives him a flower named moly as a charm against the powers of the enchantress. Her power destroyed by the magic herb, Circe frees her captives from her magic spell and entertains Odysseus and his companions for a year. At the end of that time Odysseus wishes to leave Circe's bed and continue his journey. Though reluctant, she con-

sents to his going, but first she advises him to consult the shade of Tiresias in order to learn what the future holds for the wanderers.

Eurylochus (ū·rĭ′lə·kəs), the lieutenant of Odysseus. He reports to Odysseus that the enchantress Circe has turned half of his band into swine. It is at his suggestion that the Greeks kill some of Hyperion's sacred cattle and eat them while Odysseus is sleeping. To punish their act of impiety, Zeus causes the Greek ship to founder and all but Odysseus are drowned.

Tiresias (tə·rē′sĭ·əs), the prophet of Thebes. In the land of the Cimmerians, acting on the advice of Circe, Odysseus summons the aged seer's shade from the dead. Tiresias tells him not to harm the sacred cattle of Hyperion, otherwise Odysseus will encounter many difficulties and delays on his homeward journey: he will find trouble in the royal house when he arrives there, he will be forced to make a journey into a land so far from the sea that its people will mistake an oar for a winnowing fan, he will be forced to make a rich sacrifice to Poseidon in that distant land, and in his old age he will meet death coming to him out of the sea.

Calypso (kə·lĭp′sō), the divine nymph who lives on the island of Ogygia, where Odysseus is washed ashore after his ship has foundered and his companions have drowned. For seven years he lives as her bondsman and husband, until Zeus sends Hermes to her with the message that Odysseus is to be released to return to his own land. Although she wishes him to stay with her and offers him immortality and youth in return, she yields to Odysseus' own wishes and the divine command of Zeus. She teaches Odysseus how to build a raft and allows him to set sail before a favorable breeze.

Nausicaä (nô·sĭ′kĭ·ə), the maiden daughter of King Alcinoüs and Queen Arete. Finding Odysseus on the seashore, where he is sleeping exhausted by buffeting waves after Poseidon has destroyed his raft, she befriends the hero and conducts him to her father's palace. There Odysseus tells the story of his adventures and hardships to an admiring, pitying, audience. Moved by the wanderer's plight, King Alcinoüs gives him rich gifts and returns him to Ithaca in a Phaeacian ship.

Alcinoüs (ăl·sĭ′nō·əs), king of the Phaeacians. He entertains Odysseus after the hero has been washed ashore on the island of Drepane, and he returns his guest to Ithaca in one of the royal ships.

Arete (â·rē′tē), the wife of Alcinoüs. She is famous for her kindness, generosity, and wisdom.

Nestor (nĕs′tẽr), the wise king of Phylos. Telemachus, seeking to rid the royal palace of his mother's insolent suitors, journeys to Nestor's country in search of his father.

Peisistratus (pī·sĭs′trə·təs), the noble youngest son of King Nestor. A skilled charioteer, he accompanies Telemachus when the son of Odysseus travels to Sparta in an effort to get word of his father from King Menelaus and Helen, his queen.

Menelaus (mĕ·nə·lā′əs), king of Sparta. Menelaus receives Telemachus hospitably and entertains him lavishly, but he has no information that will help the young man in his search for his father.

Helen (hĕ′lən), the wife of Menelaus and the cause of the war with Troy. Older but still beautiful, she presides over her husband's palace with queenly dignity. When Telemachus takes leave of the royal pair, she gives him a rich robe for his bride to wear on his wedding day.

Antinoüs (ăn·tĭ′nō·əs), the leader of the suitors for the hand of Penelope. Insolent and obstreperous, he leads more gullible young men to their corruption and destruction. He mocks Telemachus, berates Penelope, and tauntingly insults Odysseus disguised as a beggar. Because of his arrogance, he is the first of the suitors to die.

Eurymachus (ū·rĭ′mə·kəs), the most treacherous of the suitors. Charming in speech but cunning in his design to destroy Telemachus and marry Penelope, he deserves his death at the hands of Odysseus.

Noëmon (nō·ē′mən), one of the most generous and least offensive of the suitors. He lends Telemachus his own ship in which to sail to Pylos.

Theoclymenus (thē·ə·klĭ′mə·nəs), a young warrior who has fled from Argos after killing a kinsman. As Telemachus is about to set sail from Pylos, the fugitive asks to be taken aboard the vessel in order to escape the wrath of the dead man's brothers. Telemachus takes the stranger back to Ithaca and gives him shelter. At a feast in the palace Theoclymenus foretells the destruction of the suitors.

Peiraeus (pī·rē′əs), the loyal and gallant friend of Telemachus. He goes with the son of Odysseus to Pylos.

Mentor (mĕn′tər), one of the elders of Ithaca, wise in counsel. Athena assumes his form on several occasions.

Melanthius (mĕ·lăn′thĭ·əs), the treacherous goatherd who taunts disguised Odysseus and later tries to aid the suitors. On orders from Odysseus, he is hanged by Eumaeus and Philoetius and later dismembered.

Melantho (mĕ·lăn′thō), Penelope's faithless maid, the mistress of Eurymachas.

Medon (mē′dən), the herald. Because of his kindness to young Telemachus, his life is spared when the other suitors are killed.

Phemius (fē′mĭ·əs), the unwilling bard of the suitors. Telemachus asks that his life be spared and Odysseus grants him mercy.

Eurynome (ū·rĭ′nō·mē), the housekeeper of the royal palace in Ithaca.

Maro (mă′rō), the priest of Apollo whose life is spared when the Greeks raid the Ciconian city of Ismarus. In gratitude he gives Odysseus the wine with which the hero makes the Cyclops drunk.

Elpenor (ĕl·pē′nôr), one of Odysseus' companions whom Circe transformed into swine and then restored to human form. He climbs upon the roof of her palace, and, dazed by wine, falls to his death. Appearing among the shades in the land of the Cimmerians, he begs Odysseus to give him proper burial.

Haliserthes (hăl·ĭ·sĕr′thēz), an elder of Ithaca able to interpret the flight of birds. Seeing two eagles fighting in midair, he predicts that Odysseus will return and rend the unruly suitors like a bird of prey.

Irus (ī′rŭs), the nickname of Arnaeus, a greedy vagabond whom disguised Odysseus strikes down with a single blow when the two men fight, urged on by the amused suitors, to decide who will be allowed to beg in the palace.

Hermes (hûr′mēz), the messenger of the gods. He gives Odysseus the herb moly to protect him against Circe's spell and brings to the nymph Calypso Zeus's command that the hero be allowed to return to his own country.

Zeus (zōōs), the ruler of the Olympian deities and the father of Athena.

The Story

Of the Greek heroes who survived the Trojan War only Odysseus had not returned home, for he had been detained by the god Poseidon because of an offense that he had committed against the god of the sea.

At a conclave of the gods on Olympus, Zeus decreed that Odysseus should be allowed at last to return to his home and family in Ithaca. The goddess Athena was sent to Ithaca where, in disguise, she told Telemachus, Odysseus' son, that his father was alive. She advised the youth to rid his home of the great number of suitors suing for the hand of his mother, Penelope, and to go in search of his father. The suitors refused to leave the house of Odysseus, but they gave ready approval to the suggestion that Telemachus begin a quest for his father, since the venture would take him far from the shores of Ithaca.

The youth and his crew sailed to Pylos, where the prince questioned King Nestor concerning the whereabouts of Odysseus. Nestor, a wartime comrade of Odysseus, advised Telemachus to go to Lacedaemon, where Menelaus, who reigned there as king, could possibly give him the information he sought. At the palace of Menelaus and Helen, for whom the Trojan War had been waged, Telemachus learned that Odysseus was a prisoner of the nymph Calypso on her island of Ogygia, in the Mediterranean Sea.

Meanwhile Zeus sent Hermes, the messenger of the gods, to Ogygia, with orders that Calypso was to release Odysseus. When the nymph reluctantly complied, the hero constructed a boat in four days and sailed away from his island prison. But Poseidon, ever the enemy of Odysseus, sent great winds to destroy his boat and wash him ashore on the coast of the Phaeacians. There he was found by Nausicaä, daughter of King Alcinoüs of the Phaeacians, when she went down to the river mouth with her handmaidens to wash linen. The naked Odysseus awoke, saw Nausicaä and her maidens, and asked them where he was. Frightened at first by this stranger hiding behind the shrubbery, Nausicaä soon perceived that he was no vulgar person. She told him where he was, supplied him with clothing, and gave him food and drink. Then she conducted him to the palace of King Alcinoüs and Queen Arete. The royal pair welcomed him and, at his asking, promised to provide him with passage to his native land. At a great feast the minstrel Demodocus sang of the Trojan War and of the hardships suffered by the returning Greeks, and Alcinoüs saw that the stranger wept during the singing. At the games which followed the banquet and songs, Odysseus was goaded by a young Phaeacian athlete into revealing his great strength. Later, at Alcinoüs' insistence, Odysseus told the following story of his wandering since the war's end.

When Odysseus left Ilium he was blown to Ismarus, the Cicones' city, which he and his men sacked. Then they were blown by an ill wind to the land of the Lotus-eaters, where Odysseus had difficulty in getting his men to leave a slothful life of ease. Arriving in the land of the Cyclops, the one-eyed monsters who herded giant sheep, Odysseus and twelve of his men were caught by a Cyclops, Polyphemus, who ate the men one by one, saving Odysseus until last. But the wily hero tricked the giant into a drunken stupor, blinded him with a sharpened pole, and fled back to his ship. On an impulse, Odysseus disclosed his name to the blinded Polyphemus as he sailed away. Polyphemus called upon his father, Poseidon, to avenge him by hindering the return of Odysseus to his homeland.

Odysseus' next landfall was Aeolia, where lived Aeolus, the god of the winds. Aeolus gave Odysseus a sealed bag containing all the contrary winds, so that they could not block his homeward voyage. But the crew, thinking that the bag contained treasure, opened it, releasing all the winds, and the ship was blown back to Aeolia. When he learned what had happened, Aeolus was very angry that Odysseus' men had defied the gods by opening the bag of winds. He ordered them to leave Aeolia at once and denied them winds for their homeward journey. They rowed for six days and then came to the land of the Laestrigonians, half men, half giants, who plucked members of the crew from the ship and devoured them. Most managed to escape, however, and came to Aeaea, the land of the enchantress Circe. Circe changed the crew members into swine, but with the aid of the herb moly, which Hermes gave him, Odysseus withstood Circe's magic and forced her to change his crew back into men. Reconciled to the great leader, Circe told the hero that he could not get home without first consulting the shade of Tiresias, the blind Theban prophet. In the dark region of the Cimmerians, Odysseus sacrificed sheep. There-

upon appeared spirits from Hades, among them the shade of Tiresias, who warned Odysseus to beware of danger in the land of the sun-god.

On his way home Odysseus was forced to sail past the isle of the Sirens, whose hypnotic voices drew men to their death on treacherous rocks. By sealing the sailors' ears with wax and by having himself tied to the ship's mast, Odysseus passed the Sirens safely. Next, he sailed into a narrow sea passage guarded by the monsters, Scylla and Charybdis. Scylla's six horrible heads seized six of the crew, but the ship passed safely through the narrow channel. On the island of the sun god, Hyperion, the starving crew slaughtered some of Hyperion's sacred cows, despite a warning from their leader. The sun-god caused the ship to be wrecked in a storm, all of the crew being lost but Odysseus, who was ultimately washed ashore on Ogygia, the island of Calypso.

His story finished, Odysseus received many gifts from Alcinoüs and Arete. They accompanied him to a ship they had provided for his voyage to Ithaca and bade him farewell, and the ship brought him at last to his own land.

Odysseus hid in a cave the vast treasure he had received from his Phaeacian hosts. The goddess Athena appeared to him and counseled him on a plan by which he could avenge himself on the rapacious suitors. The goddess, after changing Odysseus into an old beggar, went to Lacedaemon to arrange the return of Telemachus from the court of Menelaus and Helen.

Odysseus went to the rustic cottage of his old steward Eumaeus, who welcomed the apparent stranger and offered him hospitality. The faithful servant disclosed the unpardonable behavior of Penelope's suitors and told how Odysseus' estate had been greatly reduced by their greed and love of luxury.

Meanwhile, Athena advised Telemachus to leave the ease of the Lacedaemon court and return home. On his arrival he went first to the hut of Eumaeus in order to get information from the old steward. There, Athena having transformed Odysseus back to his heroic self, son and father were reunited.

After pledging his son to secrecy, Odysseus described his plan of attack. Eumaeus and Odysseus, again disguised as a beggar, went to Odysseus' house where a meal was in progress. Reviled by the suitors, who had forgotten that hospitality to a stranger was a practice demanded by Zeus himself, Odysseus bided his time, even when arrogant Antinoüs threw a stool which struck Odysseus on the shoulder.

Odysseus ordered Telemachus to lock up all weapons except a few which were to be used by his own party; the women servants were also to be locked in their quarters. Penelope questioned Odysseus concerning his identity but Odysseus deceived her with a fantastic tale. When Eurycleia, ancient servant of the king, washed the beggar's feet and legs, she recognized her master by a scar on his thigh, but she did not disclose her secret.

Penelope planned an impossible feat of strength to free herself of her suitors. One day, showing the famous bow of Eurytus, and twelve battle-axes, she said that she would give her hand to the suitor who could shoot an arrow through all twelve ax handles. Telemachus, to prove his worth, attempted but failed to string the bow. One after another the suitors failed even to string the bow. Finally Odysseus asked if an old beggar might attempt the feat. The suitors laughed scornfully at his presumption. Then Odysseus strung the bow with ease and shot an arrow through the twelve ax shafts. Throwing aside his disguise, he next shot Antinoüs in the throat. There ensued a furious battle, in which all the suitors were killed by Odysseus and his small party. Twelve women servants who had been sympathetic with the suitors were hanged in the courtyard.

Penelope, in her room, heard what Odysseus, the erstwhile beggar, had done, and husband and wife were happily reunited after years of separation.

Critical Evaluation

The *Odyssey* is undoubtedly the most popular epic of Western culture. Its chief character, Odysseus (Ulysses), has inspired more literary works than any other legendary hero. From Homer to Joyce, Kazantzakis, and after, Odysseus has been a central figure in European literature, and one who has undergone many sea changes. The *Odyssey* has the ingredients of a perennial best-seller: pathos, sexuality, violence; a strong, resourceful hero with a firm purpose braving many dangers and hardships to accomplish it; a romantic account of exploits in strange places; a more or less realistic approach to characterization; a soundly constructed plot; and an author with a beautiful gift for description. It is, in fact, one of the greatest adventure stories of all time.

Of the poet, or poets, who wrote the poem there is only conjecture. Tradition says that Homer lived in Chios or Smyrna in Ionia, a part of Asia Minor; and it is probable that he, or they, composed this epic late in the ninth century B.C. The *Odyssey* was originally sung or recited, as evidenced by its style and content, and it was based on legend, folktale, and free invention, forming part of a minstrel tradition similar to that of the Middle Ages.

The style of the poem is visual, explanatory, repetitive, and stately. Like the *Iliad*, it has extended similes and repeated epithets, phrases, and sentences. Homer, whoever he was, wanted his audience to visualize and understand everything that happened. He grasped the principles of rhetoric, and he composed in a plain, direct fashion that possesses great eloquence and dignity.

Homer also had mastered certain crucial problems of organization. When the audience knows the broad outlines of the story one is going to tell, as Homer's did, it becomes necessary to introduce diversions from the main action, to delay the climax as long as the audience can bear. In this manner the leisurely development of the plot stirs one's anticipation and gives the climactic scene redoubled force. But the intervening action must have interest on its own and must have a bearing on the main action. The *Odyssey* shows remarkable ability on all of these counts.

If the subject of the *Iliad* was the wrath of Achilles during the Trojan War, the subject of the *Odyssey* is the homecoming of Odysseus ten years after the Trojan War ended. The immediate action of the poem takes place in no more than a few weeks, dramatizing the very end of Odysseus' wanderings and his restoration of order at home. Yet Homer allows Odysseus to narrate his earlier adventures, from the sack of Troy to his confinement on Calypso's island, which extends the magnitude of the poem. Through Nestor and Menelaus, Homer places Odysseus' homecoming into the wider context of the returns of all the major heroes from Troy, most of which were disastrous. Thus, the epic has a sweeping scope condensed into a very brief span of time.

The Telemachy (those first four books dealing with the travels and education of Telemachus) sets the stage for Odysseus' return. The gods make the arrangements, and then we are shown the terrible situation in Odysseus' palace, where the suitors are devouring Odysseus' substance, bullying his sons, and growing very impatient with Penelope. They intend to kill Odysseus if he should ever return, and they arrange an ambush to kill Telemachus. Their radical abuse of hospitality is contrasted with the excellent relations between guest and host when Telemachus goes to visit Nestor and then Menelaus. In an epic whose theme is travel the auxiliary theme must be the nature of hospitality. In Odysseus' journeyings his best host is Alcinoüs and his worst is the savage Cyclops. Between these two extremes there are all sorts of gradations, which depend on whether the host helps or hinders Odysseus on his long way home.

At first Telemachus is a disheartened young man trying to be hospitable in a house where it is impossible. Then Athena, as Mentes, puts pluck into him with the idea that his long-lost father is alive and detained. Telemachus calls an assembly to state his grievances and then undertakes a hazardous trip to learn of his father. He plainly has the makings of a hero, and he proves himself his father's true son when he helps slay the rapacious suitors, after displaying some tact and cunning of his own.

Odysseus is the model of the worldly, well-traveled, persevering man who overcomes obstacles. He has courage, stamina, and power, but his real strength lies in his brain, which is shrewd, quick-witted, diplomatic, and resourceful. He is also very eloquent and persuasive. He needs all of these qualities to survive and make his way home. His mettle is tested at every turn, either by dangers or temptations to remain in a place. Calypso even offers him immortality, but he is steadfast in his desire to return home. Athena may intercede for him with Zeus and aid and advise him, yet the will to return and the valor in doing so are Odysseus' alone. The one thing Odysseus finds truly unbearable in his travels is stasis, being stranded for seven years, even though he has an amorous nymph for company.

A good deal of the book is taken up with Odysseus' preparations, having arrived at Ithaca, for killing the suit-ors. The point is that the suitors are the most formidable enemy Odysseus has encountered, since they number well over a hundred and there are only he and Telemachus to face them. It is here that his true strategic and tactical cunning comes in handy—the previous wanderings being a long prologue to this climactic exploit. After nine chapters in which nothing much happens, the killing of the suitors, their henchmen, and maids is stunning in its exalting, deliberate violence. The house of Odysseus is at last purged of its predators, and our emotions are restored to an equilibrium. One final, weak chapter is used to tidy up the plot. But we have already seen Odysseus in his full glory.

OEDIPUS AT COLONUS

Type of work: Drama
Author: Sophocles (495?–406 B.C.)
Type of plot: Classical tragedy
Time of plot: Remote antiquity
Locale: Colonus, near Athens
First presented: 401 B.C.

Although the second day of the Theban Plays chronologically, Oedipus at Colonus *was the last one written and may be taken as the thematic climax of the trilogy. In the end Oedipus accepts the fact of his guilt and its consequences, but he insists on his essential innocence with passion and conviction, making a powerful affirmation of human dignity in the face of an incomprehensible universe.*

Principal Characters

Oedipus (ĕd′ə·pəs, ē′də·pəs), the former king of Thebes, now a wanderer, blind and in rags because he had been fated unwittingly to murder his father and marry his mother. *Oedipus Tyrannus* is Sophocles' version of Oedipus' discovery of these horrible crimes. After the suicide of his wife and mother, Jocasta, Oedipus, who had blinded himself in the moment of anguish which came with his full realization of who he was and what he had done, had lived for a time quietly in Thebes until his banishment by the regent Creon, his brother-in-law, with the acquiescence of his sons, Polynices and Eteocles. During his years of wandering he has endured hardship and pain, but from them he has gained spiritual authority and strength; he is aware that his special suffering has conferred upon him a special grace and that, although he is an object of disdain while alive, his dead body will confer divine benefits on the land in which it lies. Although changes have occurred, his personality is the same as that portrayed in *Oedipus Tyrannus*; he is still intelligent, courageous, and irascible, but to these characteristics has been added a new dimension of strength and knowledge. Through the horrible afflictions that the gods have visited upon him, he has become as nearly godlike as a man can be.

Antigone (ăn·tĭg′ə·nē), Oedipus' elder daughter and her father's guide since childhood. Although passionately devoted to him, she also is capable of love for Polynices, her brother, who wronged both her father and her. After the death of Oedipus, she returns to Thebes to try to mend the breach between Polynices and Eteocles, her other brother.

Ismene (is·mē′nē), Oedipus' younger daughter. Searching for her father and sister, she overtakes them at Colonus. She brings Oedipus word that the Oracle of Delphi has predicted that in the struggle between his sons for the mastery of Thebes the victory will go to Eteocles if the body of Oedipus rests in Theban soil, to Polynices if the blind, aged exile is buried in Attica. More pious than Antigone, Ismene shares her sister's courage and devotion.

Creon (krē′ŏn), Oedipus' brother-in-law and regent of Thebes during the minority of the sons of Oedipus. Because the presence of Oedipus will ensure victory for the Theban forces over the army of Polynices, Creon attempts to persuade Oedipus to return to his native city. Failing, he tries to take Antigone and Ismene by force but is thwarted by Theseus. Creon is articulate and clever, but these virtues are subordinate to his own self-interest.

Theseus (thē′sōōs, thē′sĭ·əs), king of Athens and protector of Oedipus, for whom he feels a deep sympathy and by whom he is convinced that Athens will prosper in a future war against Thebes if Oedipus' body is buried in Athenian soil. He is a man of high integrity, religious yet practical, honorable yet outspoken.

Polynices (pŏl′ə·nē′sēz), the elder son of Oedipus (although Aeschylus and Euripides make him the younger). Exiled after conflict with Eteocles, his brother, he has raised an army in Argos to regain his former place in Thebes. Like Creon, he wants Oedipus for the divine sanction the deposed king will give to his cause. He recognizes and admits his guilt for the wrongs he has done his father; but his penitence comes too late; and Oedipus, in cursing him, predicts that he and Eteocles will fall by each other's hand. He is sympathetically presented, but it is clear that he is not acting out of a desire to be reconciled with Oedipus, but a desire to recapture the throne of Thebes.

A Chorus of Elders of Colonus. The songs of the chorus contain some of the best of Sophocles' poetry, including the famous ode in praise of Colonus and Attica.

The Story

Many years had passed since King Oedipus had discovered to his horror that he had murdered his father and had married his own mother, who had given birth to his children. Having blinded himself and given up his royal authority in Thebes, he had been cared for by his faithful daughters, Antigone and Ismene. When internal strife broke out in Thebes, Oedipus, believed to be the cause of the trouble because of the curse the gods had put upon his family, was banished from the city.

He and Antigone wandered far. At last they came to an olive grove at Colonus, a sacred place near Athens. A man of Colonus warned the strangers that the grove in which they had stopped was sacred to the Furies. Oedipus, having known supreme mortal suffering, replied that he knew the Furies well and that he would remain in the grove. Disturbed, the man of Colonus stated that he would have to report this irregularity to Theseus, king of Athens and overlord of Colonus. Oedipus replied that he would welcome the king, for he had important words to say to Theseus.

The old men of Colonus were upset at Oedipus' calm in the grove of the Furies, whom they feared. From a discreet distance, they inquired about the identity of the blind stranger, and they were horror-stricken to learn that he was the infamous king of Thebes, whose dreadful story the whole civilized world had heard. Fearing the terrible wrath of the gods, they ordered him to be off with his daughter. Oedipus was able to quiet them, however, by explaining that he had suffered greatly, even though he had never consciously sinned against the gods. Furthermore, to the mystification of the old men, he hinted that he had strange powers and that he would bring good fortune to the land that would provide for him a place of refuge.

Ismene, another daughter of Oedipus, arrived in the grove at Colonus after searching throughout all Greece for her father and sister. She brought to Oedipus the unhappy news that his two sons, Polynices and Eteocles had fought for supremacy in Thebes. Polynices, defeated, had been banished to Argos, where he was now gathering a host to return to Thebes to regain control. Ismene also informed her father that the Oracle of Delphi had prophesied that Thebes was doomed to terrible misfortune if Oedipus should be buried anywhere but in that city. With this prophecy in mind, the Thebans hoped that Oedipus would return from his exile. But Oedipus, mindful of his banishment and of the faithlessness of his sons, declared to Ismene that he would remain in Colonus and that the land of Attica would be his tomb.

Having been informed of the arrival of Oedipus, Theseus went to Colonus and welcomed the pitiful old man and his daughters. Oedipus, offering his body to Attica and Colonus, prophesied that Attica would have good fortune if he were buried in its soil. Theseus, who had also known exile, was sympathetic; he promised to care for Oedipus and to protect the fearful old man from seizure by any Theban interloper.

After Theseus had returned to Athens, Creon, the former regent of Thebes, came to the grove with his followers. Deceitfully he urged Oedipus to return with him to Thebes, but Oedipus, aware of Creon's motives, reviled him for his duplicity. Oedipus cursed Thebes for the way it had repudiated him in his great suffering. Creon's men, at the command of their leader, seized Antigone and Ismene and carried them away. Blind Oedipus and the aged men of Colonus were too old and feeble to prevent their capture. Then Creon attempted to seize Oedipus. But by that time the alarm had been sounded, and Theseus returned to confront Creon, Creon had to order the rescue of Antigone and Ismene. Asked to explain his actions, Creon weakly argued that he had come to rid Attica of the taint which Oedipus surely would place upon the kingdom if its citizens offered shelter to any of the cursed progeny of Cadmus. Having checked Creon, Theseus rescued the two daughters of Oedipus.

In the meantime Polynices, older son of Oedipus, had been searching for Oedipus. Hoping to see the prophecy of the Delphic Oracle fulfilled for his own selfish ends, the young man came to the olive grove and professed repentance and filial devotion, begging Oedipus to return with him to Argos. Oedipus, knowing that his son wished only to ensure the success of his expedition against his brother Eteocles, who was in authority at Thebes, heard Polynices out in silence; then he scathingly denounced both sons as traitors. Furthermore, with vehement intensity he prophesied that Polynices and Eteocles would die by violence. Polynices, impressed by his father's words but still ambitious and arrogant, ignored Antigone's pleas to spare their native city. He departed, convinced that he was going to certain death.

Three rolls of thunder presaged the impending death of old Oedipus. Impatiently, but at the same time with a certain air of resignation, Oedipus called for Theseus. Guiding the king and his two daughters to a nearby grotto, he predicted that as long as his burial place remained a secret known only to Theseus and his male descendants Attica would successfully resist all invasions. After he had urged Theseus to protect Antigone and Ismene, he dismissed his daughters. Only Theseus was with him when Oedipus suddenly disappeared. Antigone and Ismene tried to return to their father's tomb, but Theseus, true to his solemn promise, prevented them. He did, however, second them in their desire to return to Thebes, that they might prevent the dreadful bloodshed which threatened their native city because of Polynices and Eteocles.

Critical Evaluation

Written when Sophocles was about ninety and approaching death, *Oedipus at Colonus* is the dramatist's valedictory to the stage, to Athens, and to life. In its transcendent spiritual power it is reminiscent of Shakespeare's last great play, *The Tempest*. It was probably inevitable that Sophocles, a great Athenian patriot, should have written this play, a story dealing with the legendary past of his birthplace. Indeed, two of the high points of this drama are magnificent odes in praise of Colonus and Attica. *Oedipus at Colonus* represents the culmination of Sophocles' handling of the Cadmean legend, which he had treated earlier in *Antigone* and *Oedipus Tyrannus*. At the same time it is his last, luminous affirmation of human dignity in the face of an incomprehensible universe.

The theme of the suppliants, or refugees pleading for protection, was common in Greek tragedy. Both Aeschylus and Euripides had written patriotic dramas on this subject earlier. The pattern was simple. People threatened with capture sue a powerful but democratic king for aid and receive it. *Oedipus at Colonus* is remarkably similar in its patriotic content to Euripides' *The Suppliants*. Each play treats the Theban myth and features an aspect of the war of Seven Against Thebes; each conforms to the formula stated above; and each presents Theseus and Athens in a heroic light, as the defenders of the weak from tyrannical force. When Sophocles wrote his play, Athens was in the final throes of the disastrous Peloponnesian War, which would result in Athens' defeat at the hands of Sparta. In its arrogance of power, the city had become rapacious and had undergone moral degeneration. So Sophocles' purpose in writing this play, at least from a civic viewpoint, was to remind the Athenians of their legendary respect for the rights of the helpless, a respect that up to that point had kept them safe from invaders. With the Greek tragedians, civic welfare depended directly on moral rectitude. By defending Oedipus and his daughters, Theseus ensures the safety of Athens for generations. Sophocles shows Theseus acting disinterestedly, out of concern for these suppliants, as a model ruler. The playwright wished to inspire his fellow citizens with virtues they had cast aside: piety, courage in a good cause, manliness.

Yet Sophocles' patriotism went beyond state morality. In his two beautiful choral odes on Colonus and Attica, there is an intense, wistful passion for the land itself and for the life it supported and for man's activities on it. There was, for Sophocles, something holy about the entire place. It is not accidental that the entire action of this play takes place before a sacred grove. Sophocles wanted his audience to feel the presence of divinity. The specific goddesses were the hideous and awesome Furies who judged and punished evildoers. As agents of divine justice, they presided invisibly over all that occurs in *Oedipus at Colonus*.

The center of this play, however, is not Theseus or Athens but a frightful beggar who has suffered terribly in his long life—the blind Oedipus. Although Oedipus is reconciled to exile, beggary, and blindness, he is still proud and hot-tempered; and he cannot forgive the two men who inflicted exile and penury on him, Creon and Polynices. Oedipus has paid in full for the infamous deeds he committed in ignorance. He rightly insists upon his innocence, not of killing his father, marrying his mother, and having children by her, but of knowingly doing these things. Fate led him into that trap and the Furies punished him for it. His nobility consists in bearing his suffering with dignity. Even if he is the weakest and most pitiful of men in his blindness, and though he must be led around by a young teenage girl, there is true manliness in him.

By contrast Creon is a man who lives by expediency, using force when persuasion fails, and who tamely submits when Theseus gains the upper hand. In pursuing a reasonable goal, namely the defense of Thebes, he is willing to use any means, including kidnapping Oedipus' only supports, his two daughters. His ruthlessness is highly distasteful. But even more unpleasant is Polynices' whining plea for Oedipus' aid in attacking Thebes. It stems from selfish ambition rather than concern for his poor father. One feels that the curses Oedipus levels at Creon, Polynices, Eteocles, and Thebes are justified and apt. In dishonoring a helpless blind man they incur calamity.

In this play Oedipus is a man preparing for death, as Sophocles must have been as he wrote it. Despite his hard destiny, and despite his power to curse men who have shamed him, Oedipus carries in his breast a profound blessing. In the end the Furies who hounded him bestow upon him a tremendous potency in death, the power to protect Athens for a long time, just as Athens had protected him. We never learn the ultimate reason for his suffering, but the manhood with which he faced it was the sole blessing he himself received, and that was all he needed. His mysterious and fearsome apotheosis amid flashes of lightning and earth tremors is the tribute the gods pay to Oedipus' supreme courage. Sophocles here wrote his last and most sublime testament on man's ability to take unmerited pain and transform it into glory.

OEDIPUS TYRANNUS

Type of work: Drama
Author: Sophocles (495?–406 B.C.)
Type of plot: Classical tragedy
Time of plot: Remote antiquity
Locale: Thebes
First presented: c. 429 B. C.

Oedipus Tyrannus is the first (chronologically; the second in order of composition) of the Theban Plays, which dramatize the effects of Oedipus' crime upon himself and his house. In finally realizing his guilt, in assuming the personal responsibility for his acts of patricide and incest, and in accepting blindness and exile to expiate those acts, Oedipus achieves a tragic stature that is, perhaps, unequaled in dramatic literature.

Principal Characters

Oedipus (ĕd′ə·pəs, ē′də·pəs), King of Thebes. A foundling, he had been reared by Polybus and Merope, King and Queen of Corinth. In that city he had enjoyed a place of honor until a drunken Corinthian at a banquet accused him of being a bastard. To settle the matter, he went to the oracle at Pytho, who revealed that he was destined to lie with his mother and murder his father. To avoid this curse, he fled Corinth. During his travels he was thrust out of the road by an old man in a carriage. Angered, Oedipus returned the old man's blow and killed him. Later he overcame the Sphinx by answering a riddle which the monster put to all whom it encountered, killing those who could not solve it. As a reward Oedipus was made King of Thebes and was given the hand of Queen Jocasta, whose former husband, King Laius, was believed killed in an encounter with highway robbers. When the action of the play begins, Oedipus has ruled well for many years, but a plague of unknown origin has recently fallen upon the city. His subjects appeal to him as one especially favored by the gods to help them, but Oedipus is powerless to do so. He is essentially a good man, courageous, intelligent, and responsible, but he is also short tempered, tragically weak in judgment, and proud of his position and past achievements, for which he gives the gods little credit. As the action progresses and the question of his responsibility for the plague is raised, he becomes obsessed with finding out who he is, regardless of repeated warnings that knowledge of his identity will bring disaster on himself and on those whom he loves.

Jocasta (jō·kăs′tə), wife of Oedipus and mother of his sons, Eteocles and Polynices, and his daughters, Antigone and Ismene. She, too, has a sense of the responsibilities of her position and is deeply concerned with the welfare of her husband. As bits of information relating to his identity are revealed, her sense of foreboding grows; and when the truth finally becomes apparent to her, she hangs herself, overwhelmed by the enormities she has unwittingly committed.

Creon (krē′ŏn), Jocasta's brother and a powerful Theban noble. Sent by Oedipus to ask the Delphic Oracle what can be done to save the city from the plague, he returns with word that it will be raised when the city no longer harbors the murderer of king Laius, Jocasta's former husband. When it later appears that Oedipus may be the murderer, the king violently accuses his brother-in-law of treacherously seeking the throne; but Creon defends himself as reasonably as he can until Jocasta calms her husband. Creon is presented as a calm, pious man, with a less tyrannical view of kingship than that of Oedipus.

King Laius (Lāə′us) Jocasta's former husband, he is killed on the road by Oedipus, who does not know Laius' true identity. Later it is revealed that Laius is Oedipus' father.

Tiresias (tī·rē′sĭ·əs), a blind prophet who alone knows what Oedipus' fate has been and will be. Oedipus consults him in an effort to find the murderer of King Laius and loses his patience when the old man at first refuses to answer. Becoming angry in turn, Tiresias reveals that Oedipus' seeming good fortune in vanquishing the Sphinx has actually caused him unknowingly to commit incest with his mother and to bring pollution upon Thebes. Furious, Oedipus sends the blind seer away.

The First Messenger, an old man who comes from Corinth with word that Polybus and Merope are dead and that the people of that city want Oedipus to return as their king. This information, under the circumstances, is received joyfully by Oedipus, for if his parents have died naturally, the Oracle's prediction that he is doomed to murder his father has been proved false. But the messenger goes on to say that Polybus and Merope were in reality Oedipus' foster parents; he himself had received the infant Oedipus from a Theban shepherd and given him to them.

A Herdsman, an old Theban who has voluntarily exiled himself from his native city. He is forced by Oedipus to confess that years before he had been ordered to expose the infant son of King Laius and Jocasta, but, pitying the child, he had given him to a Corinthian. He also had been the one survivor when King Laius was killed by a young man after a quarrel on the road. His information thus makes the web of evidence complete; Oedipus now knows that the old man whom he killed was Laius, his father, and that his wife Jocasta is also his mother.

The Second Messenger, a Theban who reports the immediate results of the shepherd's revelation: Jocasta has hanged herself and Oedipus blinded himself with the brooches which fastened her robe.

The Story

Thebes having been stricken by a plague, the people asked King Oedipus to deliver them from its horrors. Creon, brother of Jocasta, Oedipus' queen, returned from the oracle of Apollo and disclosed that the plague was punishment for the murder of King Laius, Oedipus' immediate predecessor, to whom Jocasta had been his wife. Creon further disclosed that the citizens of Thebes would have to discover and punish the murderer before the plague would be lifted. The people, meanwhile, mourned their dead, and Oedipus advised them, in their own interest, to search out and apprehend the murderer.

Asked to help find the murderer, Tiresias, the ancient, blind seer of Thebes, told Oedipus that it would be better for all if he did not tell what he knew. He said that coming events would reveal themselves. Oedipus raged at the seer's reluctance to tell the secret until the old man, angered, said that Oedipus was the one responsible for the afflictions of Thebes, that Oedipus was the murderer, and that the king was living in intimacy with his nearest kin. Oedipus accused the old man of being in league with Creon, whom he suspected of plotting against his throne. Tiresias answered that Oedipus would be ashamed and horrified when he learned the truth about his true parentage, a fact Oedipus did not know. Oedipus defied the seer, saying that he would welcome the truth as long as it freed his kingdom from the plague. Suspicious, Oedipus threatened Creon with death, but Jocasta and the people advised him not to do violence on the strength of rumor or momentary passion. Oedipus yielded, and Creon was banished.

Jocasta, grieved by the enmity between her brother and Oedipus, told her husband that an oracle had informed King Laius that he would be killed by his own child, the offspring of Laius and Jocasta. Jocasta declared Laius could not have been killed by his own child because soon after the child was born it was abandoned on a deserted mountainside. When Oedipus heard from Jocasta that Laius had been killed by robbers at the meeting place of three roads, he was deeply disturbed. Learning that the three roads met in Phocis, he began to suspect that he was, after all, the murderer. Hesitating to reveal his crime, he became more and more convinced of his own guilt.

Oedipus told Jocasta he had believed himself the son of Polybus of Corinth and Merope, until at a feast a drunken man had announced that the young Oedipus was not really Polybus' son. Disturbed, he had gone to consult the oracle of Apollo, who had told him he would sire children by his own mother and he would kill his own father. Leaving Corinth, at a meeting place of three roads, Oedipus had been offended by a man in a chariot. He killed the man and all of his servants but one. Thereafter he had come to Thebes and had become the new king by answering the riddle of the Sphinx, a riddle which asked what went on all fours before noon, on two legs at noon, and on three legs after noon. Oedipus had answered, correctly, that Man walks on all fours as an infant, on two legs in his prime, and with the aid of a stick in his old age. With the kingship, he also won the hand of Jocasta, King Laius' queen.

The servant who had reported that King Laius had been killed by robbers was summoned. Oedipus awaited his arrival fearfully. Jocasta assured her husband that the entire matter was of no great consequence, that surely the prophecies of the oracles would not come true.

A messenger from Corinth announced that Polybus was dead and that Oedipus was now king. Because Polybus had died of sickness, not by the hand of his son, Oedipus and Jocasta were at ease for the time being. Oedipus told the messenger he would not go to Corinth for fear of siring children by his mother, Merope, thus fulfilling the prophecy of the oracle.

The messenger then revealed that Oedipus was not really the son of Polybus and Merope, but a foundling whom the messenger, at that time a shepherd, had taken to Polybus. The messenger related how he had received the baby from another shepherd, who was a servant of the house of King Laius. Jocasta, realizing the dreadful truth, did not wish any longer to see the old servant who had been summoned, but Oedipus, desiring to have the matter out regardless of the cost, called again for the servant. When the servant appeared, the messenger recognized him as the herdsman from whom he had received the child years before. The old servant then confessed he had been ordered by King Laius to destroy the boy, but out of pity he had given the infant to the Corinthian to rear as his foster son.

Oedipus, now all but mad from the realization of what he had done, entered the palace to discover that Jocasta had hanged herself by her hair. He removed her golden brooches and with them pierced his eyes. Blinded, he would not be able to see the results of the horrible prophecy. Then he displayed himself, blind and bloody and miserable, to the Thebans and announced himself as the murderer of their king and the defiler of his own mother's bed. He cursed the herdsman who had saved him from death years before.

Creon, having returned, ordered the attendants to lead Oedipus back into the palace. Oedipus asked Creon to have him conducted out of Thebes where no man would

ever see him again. Also, he asked Creon to give Jocasta a proper burial and to see that the sons and daughters of the unnatural marriage should be cared for and not be allowed to live poor and unmarried because of any shame attached to their parentage. Creon led the wretched Oedipus away to his exile of blindness and torment.

Critical Evaluation

Oedipus Tyrannus is the most famous of the ancient Greek tragedies. Aristotle considered it the supreme example of tragic drama and largely modeled his theory of tragedy on it. He mentions the play no less than eleven times in his *Poetics*. Freud in this century used the story to name the Oedipus complex, which denotes the rivalry of male children with their fathers for the affection of their mother, and Jean Cocteau adapted the tale to the modern stage in *The Infernal Machine*. Yet no matter what changes the Oedipus myth has undergone in two and a half millennia, the finest expression of it is still this tragedy by Sophocles.

Brilliantly conceived and written, *Oedipus Tyrannus* is a drama of self-discovery. Sophocles achieves an amazing compression and force by limiting the dramatic action to the day on which Oedipus learns the true nature of his birth and destiny. The fact that we already know these dark secrets, that Oedipus has unwittingly slain his true father and married his actual mother, begetting children with her, does nothing to destroy our suspense. We are drawn into Oedipus' search for the truth with all the tautness of a mystery story, and because we already know the truth we are aware of all the ironies in which Oedipus is enmeshed. Our knowledge enables us to fear the final revelation but also to pity this man as his past is gradually and relentlessly uncovered to him.

The excellence of the plot is thoroughly integrated with the characterization of Oedipus, for it is he who impels the action forward in his concern for Thebes. Through his rashness and ignorance everything is brought to light, and he must face the consequences of all that he has done. He is flawed by a hot temper and impulsiveness, but without those traits his heroic course of self-discovery would never have occurred.

Fate for Sophocles is not something essentially outside man but something inherent in his character and yet transcendant as well. Oracles and prophets in this play may show the will of the gods and indicate future events, but it is the individual character of a man that gives substance to them. Moreover, there is an element of freedom in man, an ability to choose, where the compulsions of character and the compulsions of the gods are powerless. It is in how a man meets the necessities of his destiny that freedom lies. He can succumb to fate's blows like a victim, plead extenuating circumstances, or he can shoul-

der the full responsibility for what he does. In the first case he is merely pitiful, while in the second he is tragic—possessed of a greatness of soul that nothing can conquer. We will see these issues as they appear in *Oedipus Tyrannus*.

A crucial point is that Oedipus is entirely unaware that he has killed his father and wedded his mother. He himself is the cause of the plague on Thebes, and in vowing to find the murderer of Laius and exile him he unconsciously pronounces judgment on himself. As king and as the hero who saved Thebes from the Sphinx, Oedipus is public spirited. Believing in his own innocence, he is angry and incredulous when the provoked Tiresias accuses him of the crime, so he naturally jumps to the conclusion that Tiresias and Creon are conspirators against him. As plausible as that explanation may be, Oedipus maintains it with irrational vehemence, not even bothering to investigate it before he decides to have Creon put to death. Every act of his is performed in rashness, from his hot-tempered killing of Laius, to his investigation of the murder, to his violent blinding of himself, to his insistence on being exiled. He is a man of great pride and passion intent on serving Thebes, but until the evidence of his guilt begins piling up, he does not have the least tragic stature. He is merely a blind man sitting on the powder-keg of his past.

Ironically, his past is revealed to him by people who wish him well and who want to reassure him. Each time a character tries to comfort him with information, the information serves to damn him more thoroughly. Jocasta, in proving how false oracles can be, suggests to Oedipus unknowingly that he really did kill Laius, thus corroborating the oracles. The messenger from Corinth in reassuring Oedipus about his parentage brings his true parentage into question, but he says enough to convince Jocasta that Oedipus is her son. It is at this point that Oedipus' true heroism starts to emerge, for he determines to complete the search for the truth, knowing that he killed Laius and knowing that the result of his investigation may be utterly damning. His rashness here is no longer a liability but part of his absolute integrity.

Having learned the full truth of his dark destiny, his last act as king is to blind himself over the dead body of Jocasta, his wife and mother. It is a terrible, agonizing moment, even in description, but in his depths of pain

Oedipus is magnificent. He does not submit passively to his woe or plead that he committed his foul acts in ignorance, although he could do so with justice. He blinds himself in a rage of penitence, accepting total responsibility for what he did and determined to take the punishment of exile as well. As piteous as he appears in the final scene with Creon, there is more public spirit and more manhood in his fierce grief and his resolution of exile than in any other tragic hero in the history of the theater. He has unraveled his life to its utmost limits of agony and found there an unsurpassed grandeur of soul.

THE OLD MAN AND THE SEA

Type of work: Novella
Author: Ernest Hemingway (1899–1961)
Type of plot: Symbolic romance
Time of plot: Mid-twentieth century
Locale: Cuba and the Gulf Stream
First published: 1952

On the surface an exciting but tragic adventure story, The Old Man and the Sea *enjoys near-perfection of structure, restraint of treatment, and evocative simplicity of style. On a deeper level, the book is a fable of the unconquerable spirit of man, a creature capable of snatching spiritual victory from circumstances of disaster and apparent defeat: On yet another level, it is a religious parable which unobtrusively utilizes Christian symbols and metaphors.*

Principal Characters

Santiago, an old Cuban fisherman. After more than eighty days of fishing without a catch, the old man's patient devotion to his calling is rewarded. He catches a marlin bigger than any ever brought into Havana harbor. But the struggle to keep the marauding sharks from the fish is hopeless, and he reaches shore again with only a skeleton, worthless except as a symbol of his victory.

Manolin, a young Cuban boy devoted to Santiago, with whom he fishes until forbidden by his father after Santiago's fortieth luckless day. He begs or steals to make sure that Santiago does not go hungry.

The Story

For eighty-four days, old Santiago had not caught a single fish. At first a young boy, Manolin, had shared his bad fortune, but after the fortieth luckless day, the boy's father told his son to go in another boat. From that time on, Santiago worked alone. Each morning he rowed his skiff out into the Gulf Stream, where the big fish were. Each evening he came in empty-handed.

The boy loved the old fisherman and pitied him. If Manolin had no money of his own, he begged or stole to make sure that Santiago had enough to eat and fresh bait for his lines. The old man accepted his kindness with humility that was like a quiet kind of pride. Over their evening meals of rice or black beans, they would talk about the fish they had taken in luckier times or about American baseball and the great DiMaggio. At night, alone in his shack, Santiago dreamed of lions on the beaches of Africa, where he had gone on a sailing ship years before. He no longer dreamed of his dead wife.

On the eighty-fifth day, Santiago rowed out of the harbor in the cool dark before dawn. After leaving the smell of land behind him, he set his lines. Two of his baits were fresh tunas the boy had given him, as well as sardines to cover his hooks. The lines went straight down into deep dark water.

As the sun rose, he saw other boats in toward shore, which was only a low green line on the sea. A hovering man-of-war bird showed him where dolphin were chasing some flying fish, but the school was moving too fast and too far away. The bird circled again. This time Santiago saw tuna leaping in the sunlight. A small one took the hook on his stern line. Hauling the quivering fish aboard, the old man thought it a good omen.

Toward noon, a marlin started nibbling at the bait, which was one hundred fathoms down. Gently the old man played the fish, a big one, as he knew from the weight on the line. At last, he struck to settle the hook. The fish did not surface. Instead, it began to tow the skiff to the northwest. The old man braced himself, the line taut across his shoulders. Although he had his skill and knew many tricks, he waited patiently for the fish to tire.

The old man shivered in the cold that came after sunset. When something took one of his remaining baits, he cut the line with his sheath knife. Once the fish lurched suddenly, pulling Santiago forward on his face and cutting his cheek. By dawn, his left hand was stiff and cramped. The fish had headed northward; there was no land in sight. Another strong tug on the line sliced Santiago's right hand. Hungry, he cut strips from the tuna and chewed them slowly while he waited for the sun to warm him and ease his cramped fingers.

That morning the fish jumped. Seeing it leap, Santiago knew he had hooked the biggest marlin he had ever seen. Then the fish went under and turned toward the east. Santiago drank sparingly from his water bottle during the hot afternoon. Trying to forget his cut hand and aching back, he remembered the days when men had called him

El Campéon, and he had wrestled with a giant black man in the tavern at Cienfuegos. Once an airplane droned overhead on its way to Miami.

Close to nightfall, a dolphin took the small hook he had rebaited. He lifted the fish aboard, careful not to jerk the line over his shoulder. After he had rested, he cut fillets from the dolphin and also kept the two flying fish he found in its maw. That night he slept. He awoke to feel the line running through his fingers as the fish jumped. Feeding line slowly, he tried to tire the marlin. After the fish slowed its run, he washed his cut hands in seawater and ate one of the flying fish. At sunrise, the marlin began to circle. Faint and dizzy, he worked to bring the big fish nearer with each turn. Almost exhausted, he finally drew his catch alongside and drove in the harpoon. He drank a little water before he lashed the marlin to the bow and stern of his skiff. The fish was two feet longer than the boat. No catch like it had ever been seen in Havana harbor. It would make his fortune, he thought, as he hoisted his patched sails and set his course toward the southwest.

An hour later, he sighted the first shark. It was a fierce Mako, and it came in fast to slash with raking teeth at the dead marlin. With failing might, the old man struck the shark with his harpoon. The Mako rolled and sank, carrying the harpoon with it and leaving the marlin mutilated and bloody. Santiago knew the scent would spread. Watching, he saw two shovel-nosed sharks closing in. He struck at one with his knife lashed to the end of an

oar and watched the scavenger sliding down into deep water. He killed the other while it tore at the flesh of the marlin. When the third appeared, he thrust at it with the knife, only to feel the blade snap as the fish rolled. The other sharks came at sunset. At first, he tried to club them with the tiller from the skiff, but his hands were raw and bleeding and there were too many in the pack. In the darkness, as he steered toward the faint glow of Havana against the sky, he heard them hitting the carcass again and again. Yet the old man thought only of his steering and his great tiredness. He had gone out too far and the sharks had beaten him. He knew they would leave him nothing but the stripped skeleton of his great catch.

All lights were out when he sailed into the little harbor and beached his skiff. In the gloom, he could just make out the white backbone and the upstanding tail of the fish. He started up the shore with the mast and furled sail of his boat. Once he fell under their weight and lay patiently until he could gather his strength. In the shack, he fell on his bed and went to sleep.

There the boy found him later in the morning. Meanwhile other fishermen, gathered about the skiff, marveled at the giant marlin, eighteen feet long from nose to tail. When Manolin returned to Santiago's shack with hot coffee, the old man awoke. The boy, he said, could have the spear of his fish. Manolin told him to rest, to make himself fit for the days of fishing they would have together. All that afternoon, the old man slept, the boy sitting by his bed. Santiago was dreaming of lions.

Critical Evaluation

The Old Man and the Sea is one of the true classics of its generation. The qualities of Ernest Hemingway's short novel are those that readers associate with many great stories of the past: near perfection of form within the limitations of its subject matter, restraint of treatment, regard for the unities of time and place, and evocative simplicity of style. Also, like most great stories, it can be read on more than one level of meaning. First, it is an exciting but tragic adventure story. On another level, the book is a fable of the unconquerable spirit of man, a creature capable of snatching spiritual victory from circumstances of disaster and material defeat. On still another, it is a parable of religious significance, its theme supported by the writer's unobtrusive handling of Christian symbols and metaphors. Like Coleridge's Ancient Mariner, Hemingway's Cuban fisherman allows the imagination of his creator to operate simultaneously in two different worlds of meaning and value, the one real and dramatic, the other moral and devotionally symbolic.

Hemingway began his career as a journalist with the *Kansas City Star* in 1917, and later he was a wartime foreign correspondent for the *Toronto Star*. His first important collection of short stories, *In Our Time*, appeared

in 1925, to be followed, in 1926, by what many consider to be his finest novel, *The Sun Also Rises*. During his long stay among other American expatriates in Paris, Hemingway was influenced by Gertrude Stein, Ezra Pound, and James Joyce. From their models, from his journalistic background, and from his admiration for Mark Twain, Hemingway developed his own characteristic style. The Hemingway style, further expressed in *A Farewell to Arms* (1929), then gradually sinking toward stereotypical stylization in *Death in the Afternoon* (1932), *The Green Hills of Africa* (1935), and *For Whom the Bell Tolls* (where it reaches its lowest point of self-caricature, undermining his most ambitious novel), is marked by consistent elements: understatement created by tersely realistic dialogue; use of everyday speech and simple vocabulary; avoidance of the abstract; straightforward sentence structure and paragraph development; spare and specific imagery; objective, reportorial viewpoint; and emphasis on "the real thing, the sequence of emotion and fact to make the emotion." This last, Wordsworthian, technique accounts for Hemingway's position as the most gifted of the Lost Generation writers.

Accompanying these stylistic traits is a set of consistent thematic concerns that have become known as the Hemingway "code"; obsession with all outdoor pursuits and sports; identification with the primitive; constant confrontation with death; fascination with violence, and with the skillful control of violence; what he calls "holding the purity of line through the maximum of exposure." The typical Hemingway hero, existential in a peculiarly American way, faces the sterility and failure and death of his contemporary world with steady-handed courage and a stoical resistance to pain that allows him a fleeting, but essentially human, nobility and grace.

After a decade of silence, while Hemingway was preoccupied with the turmoil of World War II, he published *Across the River and into the Trees* (1950)—an inferior book that led many to believe his genius had dried up. Two years later, however, drawing from his experiences in Cuba, *The Old Man and the Sea* appeared. It was awarded the Pulitzer Prize and led to a Nobel Prize for Literature (1954) for his "mastery of the art of modern narration." As a kind of ultimate condensation of the Hemingway code, this short novel attains an austere dignity. Its extreme simplicity of imagery, symbolism, setting, and character stands in stark contrast with the epic sprawl of Herman Melville's masterpiece *Moby Dick*— a work with which it nevertheless has much in common.

Hemingway displays his genius of perception by using, without apology, the most obvious symbolic imagery; in fact, he creates his desired impact by admitting the ordinary (in the way of Robert Frost, whose "An Old Man's Winter's Night" resembles this book). An example is the statement that the old man's furled sail each evening "looked like a flag of permanent defeat." Here the admission of the obvious becomes ironic, since the old man is not, as he himself declares, *defeated*—although he is "destroyed." Aside from the two overt image-symbols of the lions on the beach and of "the great DiMaggio" ("who does all things perfectly even with the pain of the bone spur in his heel"), the implicit image of Christ stalks through the work until the reader understands that it is not, after all, a religious symbol, but a secular one that affirms that each man has his own agonies and crucifixion. As for setting, three elements stand out: the sea itself, which the old man regards as feminine and not as an enemy but as the *locus* in which man plays his little part, with security and serenity derived from acceptance of her inevitable capriciousness; the intrusions of the outside world, with the jet plane high overhead and the tourist woman's ignorant comment at the end that shows total insensitivity to the common man's capacity for tragedy, and the sharks, which make "everything wrong"

and stand for the heroic absurdity of human endeavors.

The old man's character is revealed in two ways: by the observations of the narrator and by his own monologue. The latter device might seem theatrical and out of place if Hemingway had not taken pains to set up its employment openly: "He did not remember when he had first started to talk aloud when he was by himself." The words he says to no one but himself reveal the old man's mind as clearly as, and even more poignantly than, the narrator's knowledge of his thoughts. He is seen as the unvanquished (whose eyes are as young as the sea); with sufficient pride to allow humility; with unsuspected, though simple, introspection ("I am a strange old man"); with unquestioning trust in his own skills and in the folklore of his trade; with almost superhuman endurance; and with a noble acceptance of the limitations forced upon him by age. Before the drama is over, the old man projects his own qualities onto the fish—his strength, his wisdom—until his initial hunter's indifference turns to pity, and the fish becomes "friend" and "brother." "But I must kill him," the old man says; "I am glad we do not have to try to kill the stars. . . . It is enough to live on the sea and kill our true brothers." Killing with dignity, as it done also in the bullring, is an accepted part of the human condition. Only the graceless, undignified sharks (like the hyenas in "The Snows of Kilimanjaro") are abhorrent, diminishing the tragic grandeur of the human drama.

The Old Man and the Sea is a direct descendant of *Moby Dick*. The size, strength, and mystery of the great marlin recall the presence of the elusive white whale; similarly, the strength, determination (like Ahab, the old man does not bother with eating or sleeping), and strangeness of Hemingway's hero may be compared to the epic qualities of Melville's. Yet the differences are as important as the similarities. In Melville, both the whale and Ahab have sinister, allusive, and unknown connotations that they seem to share between them and that are not revealed clearly to the reader—in the fashion of Romanticism. In contrast, Hemingway's realism does not present the struggle as a pseudosacred cosmic one between forces of darkness but as an everyday confrontation between the strength of an ordinary man and the power of nature. Hemingway's fish is huge, but he is not solitary and unique; the old man is not the oldest or the greatest fisherman. Finally, neither the old man nor the fish is completely victorious. The fish does not kill the old man; neither does the old man become older or wiser; the fish only makes him very tired.

THE OLD WIVES' TALE

Type of work: Novel
Author: Arnold Bennett (1867–1931)
Type of plot: Naturalism
Time of plot: Nineteenth century
Locale: England and Paris
First published: 1908

In this novel about the effects of passing time on human lives, Bennett offers striking character portraits of two sisters whose lives and personalities are in sharp contrast to each other. Set in the transitional era of the Industrial Revolution, the author uses colorful detail and events such as the siege of Paris primarily as background for the development of character.

Principal Characters

Sophia Baines, a high-spirited girl, the one member of the family strong enough to stand up against her father. Because she detests keeping a shop and domestic obligations, her parents finally allow her to become a schoolteacher. After her father's death, brought on by her carelessness, Sophia voluntarily returns to the shop as a penance. A brief, disillusioning marriage to Gerald Scales is followed by a period in which Sophia has a long, successful business career in Paris. After a twenty-seven-year absence, she returns to Bursley (one of the "Five Towns" made famous by Arnold Bennett) and renews her dominance over her sister Constance. Sophia's death is, according to the sister, simply an expression of God's punishment for her willful ways.

Constance Baines, her older sister. A perfect foil for Sophia, Constance follows her sister in all things, short of violating her parents' iron rule. She angers her mother, however, when she marries Samuel Povey. She is extraordinarily capable, except in managing her son; this phase of her life is distinguished by failure. In later years, life becomes more than the obese Constance cares to cope with, and she submits, with martyrdom, to sciatica, rheumatism, and Sophia.

John Baines, their father, the bed-ridden but influential proprietor of a draper's shop. He dominates the entire family in matters both domestic and business. Whether from fear or respect, some member of his household has for many years constantly attended him. With his death, a new era begins for the family.

Mrs. Baines, his wife, who in actuality is the proprietor of the shop. Stern, authoritarian, and ever suspicious, she keeps the entire ménage in line, except Sophia. By the time of Mrs. Baines's death, Constance is ready to step into her place.

Samuel Povey, first an apprentice in the shop, later the proprietor, after his marriage to Constance. Under an appearance of quiet diffidence, he conceals an aggressive personality. Deeply involved in the tragic life of his brother,

he is respected and renowned throughout the community.

Charles Critchlow, the close friend and legal adviser to the Baines family. Indomitable and apparently indestructible, he is still on hand to deliver his acid estimate of Sophia when she returns to Bursley after her long absence.

Aunt Maria, a distant cousin of John Baines, who narrowly escapes being a nonentity by her availability to attend the invalid John. She is called "Aunt" as a convenience to the family.

Harriet Maddock, Mrs. Baines' sister, an overbearing, self-righteous widow assigned the care of Sophia, particularly to distract the young woman from marrying Gerald. That Sophia, even in successful maturity, is never able to face her aunt because of Sophia's childhood theft from her, speaks for the older woman's uncompromising will.

Gerald Scales, Sophia's husband, whom she met as a commercial traveler in the shop. Soon after their runaway marriage, Sophia sees him as unscrupulous and unstable. They part, in Paris, in less than a year, and Gerald is not seen again until he reappears to die, an "old" man of less than sixty and a dissolute failure.

Maggie, a long-time servant in the Baines' household. Engaged and then having her engagement broken eleven times, she finally marries a man of even lesser talents than hers.

Aline Chetwynd, the self-conscious, old-maid schoolteacher who is entrusted with Sophia's education. It is she who persuades Mrs. Baines that Sophia should not be wasted by a life in the shop.

Elizabeth Chetwynd, her older sister. Her marriage to the Rev. Archibald Jones lends prestige to Aline in her association with Mrs. Baines.

Lily Holl, Maggie's granddaughter, engaged to Dick Povey. Except for a fluke, Lily and Dick might have inherited a good share of Constance's wealth.

Dick Povey, Samuel Povey's crippled nephew, who

commands much sympathy and attention from his uncle. Dick's scheming attentions to Constance seem a poor reward for her husband's earlier care of the young man.

Cyril Povey, Constance and Samuel's son. Thoroughly spoiled as a child and thoughtless and inconsiderate as a man, he is wholly indifferent to his mother's need for his affection.

Maria Insull, the assistant in the shop after Sam Povey's death; she marries Charles Critchlow.

Matthew Peel-Swynnerton, an occupant of the Pension Frensham, Sophia's fashionable tourist hotel in Paris. He is instrumental in reuniting Constance and Sophia.

The Story

Sixteen-year-old Constance Baines was a plump, pleasant girl with a snub nose. Sophia, aged fifteen, was a handsome girl with imagination and daring. The first symptoms of her rebelliousness and strong individuality came when she announced her desire to be a teacher in 1864.

Mr. and Mrs. Baines owned a draper's shop, and their income was adequate. They were most respectable and were therefore horrified at their daughter's unconventional plan, for it had been taken for granted that she as well as Constance would assist in the shop. When Sophia was four years old, John Baines, the father, had suffered a stroke of paralysis that had left him an invalid whose faculties were greatly impaired. Prodded by his capable wife, he tried to dissuade Sophia from pursuing teaching, but his opposition only strengthened Sophia's purpose.

When Sophia had been left alone to care for her father one day, she saw a handsome young man, a representative of a wholesale firm, enter the store. She instantly invented an errand to take her into the shop. She learned that his name was Gerald Scales. When Sophia returned to her father's room, he had slipped off the bed, had been powerless to move himself, and had died of asphyxia. Mr. Baines's old friend, Mr. Critchlow, was called immediately; having seen Sophia in the shop with Gerald, he instantly accused her of killing her father. Presumably as a gesture of repentance but actually because she hoped for an opportunity to see Gerald again, Sophia offered to give up her plans to teach.

Sophia worked in millinery while Constance assisted Samuel Povey, the clerk, a small quiet man without dignity and without imagination. He and Constance gradually fell in love.

After two years, Gerald returned. By artful contriving, Sophia managed to meet him alone and to initiate a correspondence. Mrs. Baines recognized Sophia's infatuation and sent her off to visit her Aunt Harriet. Several weeks later, Sophia ran off with Gerald Scales. She wrote her mother that they were married and planning to live abroad. A short time later, Constance and Samuel Povey were married. Mrs. Baines turned over the house and shop to them and went to live with her sister.

The married life of Constance held few surprises, and the couple soon settled into a routine tradesman's existence. Nothing further was heard of Sophia except for an occasional Christmas card giving no address. After six years of marriage a son, Cyril, was born. Constance centered her life on the baby, more so since her mother died shortly after his birth. Povey also devoted much attention to the child, but he made his wife miserable by his insistence on discipline. When, after twenty years of marriage, Povey caught pneumonia and left Constance a widow, she devoted herself entirely to Cyril. He was a charming, intelligent boy, but he seemed indifferent to his mother's efforts to please him. When he was eighteen years old, he won a scholarship in art and was sent to London. His mother was left alone.

Life had not been so quiet for Sophia, however. In a London hotel room, after her elopement, she had suffered her first disillusionment when Gerald began to make excuses for delaying their marriage; but after Sophia refused to go to Paris with him except as his wife, he reluctantly agreed to the ceremony. Gerald had inherited twelve thousand pounds. He and Sophia lived lavishly in Paris. Gerald's weakness, his irresponsibility, and lack of any morals or common sense soon became apparent. Realizing that Gerald had little regard for her welfare, Sophia took two hundred pounds in bank notes from his pocket and hid them in case of an emergency. As Gerald lost more money at gambling, they lived in shabbier hotels, wore mended clothes, and ate sparingly. When their funds were nearly exhausted, Gerald suggested that Sophia should write to her family for help. When Sophia refused, Gerald abandoned her.

The next day, she awoke ill and was visited by Gerald's friend, Chirac, who had come to collect money Gerald had borrowed from him. Chirac had risked his own reputation by taking money from the cash box of the newspaper where he was employed. Sophia unhesitatingly used some of the notes she had taken from Gerald to repay Chirac. When she again became ill, Chirac left her in the care of a middle-aged courtesan, Madam Faucault, who treated Sophia kindly during her long illness.

Madame Faucault was deeply in debt. Sophia rented Madame Faucault's flat and took in roomers and boarders. At that time, France was at war with Germany, and the siege of Paris soon began. Food was scarce. Only by hard work and the most careful management was Sophia able to feed her boarders. She grew hard and business-like. When the siege was lifted and Paris returned to normal, Sophia bought the pension Frensham at her own price. This pension was well known for its excellence and respectability, and under Sophia's management, it prospered. She did not hear from her husband again. By the Exhibition year, she had built up a modest fortune from the two hundred pounds she had stolen from Gerald.

One day, Cyril Povey's young English friend came to stay at the pension Frensham. Sophia's beauty and dignity intrigued him, and he learned enough about her to recognize her as his friend's aunt. On his return to England, he hastily informed both Cyril and Constance of Sophia's situation.

Constance immediately wrote Sophia a warm, affectionate letter begging her to come to England for a visit. Meanwhile in Paris, Sophia had suffered a slight stroke; when she was offered a large sum for the pension Frensham, she reluctantly let it go. Soon afterward, she visited England.

Although Sophia had intended to make only a short visit, the sisters lived together for nine years. On the surface, they got along well together, but Sophia had never forgiven her sister for her refusal to move from the ugly, inconvenient old house. Constance, on her part, silently resented Sophia's domineering ways.

Their tranquil existence was interrupted by a telegram to Sophia, informing her that Gerald Scales was very ill in a neighboring town. She went to him at once, but on her arrival, she learned that he was already dead. He was shabby, thin, and old. Sophia was greatly shocked when she saw Gerald; part of her shock was the fact that she no longer had any feeling for the man who had both made and ruined her life. She suffered another stroke while driving home and lived only a few hours. Cyril was left all of Sophia's money. He had continued to live in London on an allowance, completely absorbed in his art, still secretive and indifferent in his attitude toward his mother. When Constance died several years later, he was abroad and did not return in time for the funeral. When the servants went off for Constance's burial, only Sophia's old poodle was left in the house. She waddled into the kitchen to see if any food had been left in her dish.

Critical Evaluation

Late nineteenth century literary naturalism insists on the determining forces of heredity and environment; realism also concentrates objectively on the social and historical conditions of experience, but it allows for a greater independence in the principal characters. Frank Norris' novel *McTeague* is a typical naturalist phenomenon: Everything he is, from gentle dentist to brutal drunk, is the result of his biological and social background. Flaubert is a realist. His Emma Bovary, although corrupted by sentimental fantasies and trapped by her provincial life, pits her misguided energy against her fate and achieves tragic significance. Arnold Bennett's fiction is marked by a blending of these two literary movements. He cultivated detachment and technique in his writing because he felt that the English novel had neglected what he called a "scientific" eye; satire and sentiment, from Fielding to Dickens, had colored the author's presentation of reality. Bennett turned to France for new models; by absorbing realism and naturalism, he became a master of the "impressions of the moment," but he retained an English sense for the uniqueness of character.

The Old Wives' Tale is his masterpiece. The title is revealing in that, instead of describing a superstitious tale, it dramatizes his objectivity by forcing readers to interpret the phrase literally. The novel is about two women who become old; their story, despite its inevitability, is far more wondrous in its simple reality than any fantastic or "superstitious" tale. What is remarkable about them is that despite their having lived entirely different lives, they emerge, at the end, remarkably similar. This is primarily because of the moral fiber woven into their characters from earliest childhood. Neither woman "has any imagination," but each has the stability of a rock. Constance leads a conventional life and never leaves St. Luke's square; Sophia runs off with an attractive salesman, is deserted in Paris, and runs a successful boardinghouse during the siege of Paris and the Commune. Despite the difference of circumstance in their lives, they remain the self-reliant, middle-class daughters of John Baines. Critic John Wain calls the result "the effect Bennett was aiming at: a parallelism amid contrast." This pattern is illustrative of what Bennett meant by technique and craftsmanship; it also reveals the interweaving of naturalist and realist values.

The "judicial murder" of Daniel Povey in the prison at Stafford parallels the public execution of the murderer Rivain, which Sophia and Gerald take in as an unusual "attraction." This and many other parallels in the plot—for example, young Cyril's theft from the till at the shop and Sophia's prudent appropriation of Gerald's two hundred pounds—are done so cleverly that they never seem forced or artificial. Life is simply like this, says Bennett, and the range and sureness of his story vindicate his method.

Bennett's respect for his ordinary characters is intense. He admires their capacity for survival and never underestimates their souls. In the midst of bourgeois contentment, Constance is never free from a strange sadness. She lacks the imaginative power of a Hamlet, but she feels a similar anguish: "The vast inherent melancholy of the universe did not exempt her." Her simple and undistinguished husband, Samuel Povey, dies of toxemia contracted from pneumonia. His death is oddly heroic, because the illness that kills him is a cruelly ironic reward for his selfless dedication to his poor cousin Daniel. Bennett is unequivocal in his praise. He concedes that he thought Povey a "little" man easy to ridicule but that his honesty finally earns a great deal of respect. The last of his life displays a touch of greatness that all souls, insist Bennett, have in common.

It is important that readers understand that Constance's melancholy, Samuel's humility, and Sophia's passionate nature are secondary to what Bennett felt was the mainstream running through all of their natures: the blind will to survive. Fossette, the aged poodle, is the emblem of that instinct at the close of the novel. The great enemy of man and beast is time, and it always wins in the end. Readers may object to assigning Bennett such a cold view of life. To end on a comparison between Fossette and Sophia seems out of keeping with Bennett's fondness and respect for his characters. Nevertheless, readers remember that what Bennett praises the most in Sophia is precisely her pluck, her ability to survive in a totally alien environment. Her emotional life is not a rich one, and the last glimpse of Gerald Scales as an old man does not rekindle her feelings. On the contrary, it paves the way for the stroke that kills her. Unlike Povey's death, which

was senseless but pathetic because of his selflessness, Sophia's death is the result of an unbearable knowledge; she confronts her own death in Gerald's death, which strikes her as overwhelming in its sheer physical meaning. Once a handsome and vital young man who had excited her passions and moved her to abandon respectability, he is now a withered and aged corpse. Sophia is not concerned with his moral weakness or the grief that he caused her. All she can think of is that a young man, once proud and bold, has been reduced to a horribly decimated version of his former self. The cruelty of time itself, which has made a mockery of all the feelings of love and hatred they shared, shatters her self-confidence. She can no longer separate herself from the mortality around her. When the inevitability of death becomes apparent, even to someone without imagination like Sophia, the will to survive is gone. Suddenly the full weight of her life, the great struggle for survival in Paris, descends with crushing force. It is more than she can stand. Although she fears death, she begs for its deliverance. She can take no more.

Despite all the pressures and forces that shape *The Old Wives' Tale*, it does not end until the hearts of its protagonists stop beating.

ON LIBERTY

Type of work: Philosophical essay
Author: John Stuart Mill (1806–1873)
First published: 1859

John Stuart Mill, the English Utilitarian, here concerns himself with the problem of defining the limits of the power of the state in interfering with the liberty of persons. The result is one of the most important statements in the history of Western democracy. The essay is distinguished by its clarity and the orderly arrangement of its persuasive argument. Throughout the book can be discerned Mill's interest in the happiness and rights of men everywhere and his serious concern lest that happiness be threatened by governmental power unwisely used.

Mill states his purpose concisely:

The object of this Essay is to assert one very simple principle, as entitled to govern absolutely the dealings of society with the individual in the way of compulsion and control, whether the means used be physical force in the form of legal penalties, or the moral coercion of public opinion. That principle is, that the sole end for which mankind are warranted, individually or collectively, in interfering with the liberty of action of any of their number, is self-protection. That the only purpose for which power can be rightfully exercised over any member of a civilized community, against his will, is to prevent harm to others.

Another statement of the author's intention is found in the last chapter, "Applications," in which Mill states that two maxims together form "the entire doctrine" of the essay. The first maxim is "that the individual is not accountable to society for his actions, in so far as these concern the interests of no person but himself," and the second is "that for such actions as are prejudicial to the interests of others, the individual is accountable, and may be subjected either to social or to legal punishment, if society is of the opinion that the one or the other is requisite for its protection."

It would be an error of interpretation of Mill's intention to suppose that he is explicitly objecting to all efforts of government to improve the condition of its citizens. What Mill objects to is the restriction of human liberty for the sake of human welfare; he has nothing against welfare itself. On the contrary, as a Utilitarian, he believes that a right act is one which aims at the greatest happiness of the greatest number of persons; and it is precisely because the restriction of human liberty is so destructive to human happiness that he makes a plea for a judicious use of restrictive power, justifying it only when it is used to prevent harm, or unhappiness of whatever sort, to others than the person being restricted.

Restricting a man's liberty for his own good, for his happiness, is not morally justifiable. Mill permits, even encourages, "remonstrating" and "reasoning" with a person who is determined to act against his own best interests, but he does not approve of using force to keep him from it.

After reviewing some of the acts which a person may rightfully be compelled to do—such as to give evidence in court, to bear a fair share of the common defense, and to defend the helpless—Mill asserts that society has no right to interfere when a man's acts concern, for the most part, only himself. This statement means that a man must be free in his conscience, thought, and feeling, and that he must have freedom of opinion and sentiment on all subjects. This latter freedom involves freedom of the press. In addition, each man should be free to do what he likes and to enjoy what he prefers—provided what he does is not harmful to others. Finally, each man should be free to unite with others for any purpose—again, provided no one is harmed by this action.

Certainly this theme is pertinent, for at any time there is either the present or the possible danger of government interference in human affairs. Mill admits that his principal thesis has the "air of a truism," but he goes on to remind the reader that states have often felt justified in using their power to limit the liberty of citizens in areas which Mill regards as sacrosanct. In the context of Mill's philosophic work, *On Liberty* remains one of his most important essays, sharing honors with his *Utilitarianism*.

In perhaps the most carefully articulated part of his argument, in chapter 2, "On the Liberty of Thought and Discussion," Mill considers what the consequences of suppressing the expression of opinion would be if the suppressed opinion were true; and then, having countered a series of objections to his arguments against suppression, he continues by considering what the consequences of suppressing opinion would be if the opinion were false.

Suppressing true opinion is clearly wrong, particularly if the opinion is suppressed on the grounds that it is false. Silencing the expression of opinion on the grounds that the opinion is false is a sign of an assumption of infallibility. A moment's thought shows that the assumption may be mistaken, and that suppressing opinion may very well make discovery of error impossible.

In response to the objection that it is permissible to suppress opinion, even true opinion, because the truth always triumphs, Mill answers that the idea that truth always wins out is a "pleasant falsehood" proved false by experience. To the objection that at least we no longer put men to death for expressing their opinions, Mill counters with the argument that other kinds of persecution continue to be practiced, destroying truth and moral courage.

If the opinion suppressed be false, Mill continues, the prevailing and true opinion, lacking opposition, becomes a dead dogma. When ideas are not continually met by opposing ideas they tend to become either meaningless or groundless, or both. Beliefs which at one time had force and reasons behind them may come to be nothing but empty words.

The argument in favor of freedom of opinion and the press closes with the claim that most opinions are neither wholly true nor wholly false, but mixtures of the two; and that only in free discussion can the difference be made out.

In order to reinforce his central contention—that it is always wrong to hinder the freedom of an individual when what he does is not harmful to others—Mill devotes a chapter to an argument designed to show that development of individuality is essential to man's happiness. Since there is nothing better than happiness, it follows that individuality should be fostered and guaranteed. Mill supports Baron Wilhelm von Humboldt's injunction that every human being aim at "individuality of power and development," for which there are two prerequisites: "freedom and the variety of situations."

There is a refreshing pertinence to Mill's discussion of the value of individuality. We are reminded of Emerson's defense of nonconformism when we read that "originality is the one thing which unoriginal minds cannot feel the use of," and "He who lets the world, or his own portion of it, choose his plan of life for him, has no need of any other faculty than the ape-like one of imitation." Mill argues that only if uncustomary acts are allowed to show their merits can anyone decide which mode of action should become customary; and, in any case, the differences among men demand that differences of conduct be allowed so that each man can become what is best for him.

In his discussion of the harm that results from a state's interference with the rights of an individual to act in ways that concern only himself, Mill reviews some of the consequences of religious intolerance, prohibition, and other attempts to restrict liberty for the common good. In each case, he argues, the result is not only failure to achieve the goal of the prohibitive act but some damage to the character of the state and its citizens.

As if he were writing for our times, Mill closes by saying that "a State which dwarfs its men, in order that they may be more docile instruments in its hands even for beneficial purposes—will find that with small men no great thing can be accomplished."

ON THE NATURE OF THINGS

Type of work: Didactic epic
Author: Lucretius (Titus Lucretius Carus, c. 98 B.C.–55 B.C.)
First transcribed: First century B.C.

On the Nature of Things (*De rerum natura*) is justly renowned as the greatest poetic monument of Epicurean philosophy. It is outstanding both as a scientific explanation of the poet's atomic theory and as a fine poem. Vergil himself was much influenced by Lucretius' dactylic hexameter verse, and echoes passages of *On the Nature of Things* in the *Georgics*, a didactic epic modeled on Lucretius' poem, and in the *Aeneid*.

Lucretius, following his master Epicurus' doctrine, believed that fear of the gods and fear of death were the greatest obstacles to peace of mind, the object of Epicurean philosophy. He felt that he could dispel these unfounded terrors by explaining the workings of the universe and showing that phenomena interpreted as signs from the deities were simply natural happenings. His scientific speculations were based on Democritus' atomic theory and Epicurus' interpretation of it. Lucretius outlined the fundamental laws of this system in the first book of his poem.

According to Lucretius, everything is composed of small "first bodies," tiny particles made up of a few "minima" or "least parts" which cannot be separated. These "first bodies," atoms, are solid, indestructible, and of infinite number. They are mixed with void to make objects of greater hardness or softness, strength or weakness.

Lucretius "proves" these assertions by calling upon the reader's reason and his observation of nature, pointing out absurdities that might come about if his point were not true. For example, he substantiates his statement that nothing can be created from nothing by saying, "For if things came to being from nothing, every kind might be born from all things, nought would need a seed. First men might arise from the sea, and from the land the race of scaly creatures, and birds burst forth from the sky." These proofs, which may fill fifty or one hundred lines of poetry, are often unconvincing, but they reveal the author's knowledge of nature and his imaginative gifts.

The universe is infinite in the Epicurean system. Lucretius would ask a man who believed it finite, "If one were to run on to the end . . . and throw a flying dart, would you have it that that dart . . . goes on whither it is sped and flies afar, or do you think that something can check and bar its way?" He ridicules the Stoic theory that all things press toward a center, for the universe, being infinite, can have no center. Lucretius is, of course, denying the law of gravity. He often contradicts what science has since proved true, but he is remarkably accurate for his time.

Book 2 opens with a poetic description of the pleasure of standing apart from the confusion and conflicts of life: "Nothing is more gladdening than to dwell in the calm high places, firmly embattled on the heights by the teaching of the wise, whence you can look down on others, and see them wandering hither and thither." Lucretius is providing this teaching by continuing his discussion of atoms, which he says move continuously downward like dusty particles in a sunbeam. They have a form of free will and can swerve to unite with each other to form objects. Lucretius adds that if the atoms could not will motion for themselves, there would be no explanation for the ability of animals to move voluntarily.

The poet outlines other properties of atoms in the latter part of the second book: they are colorless, insensible, and of a variety of shapes which determine properties of the objects the atoms compose. Sweet honey contains round, smooth particles; bitter wormwood, hooked atoms.

While Lucretius scorns superstitious fear of the gods, he worships the creative force of nature, personified as Venus in the invocation of book 1. Nature controls the unending cycle of creation and destruction. There are gods, but they dwell in their tranquil homes in space, unconcerned for the fate of men.

A passage in praise of Epicurus precedes book 3, the book of the soul. Lucretius says that fear of death arises from superstitions about the soul's afterlife in Hades. This fear is foolish, for the soul is, like the body, mortal. The poet describes the soul as the life force in the body, composed of very fine particles which disperse into the air when the body dies. Since man will neither know nor feel anything when his soul has dissolved, fear of death is unnecessary.

A man should not regret leaving life, even if it has been full and rich. He should die as "a guest sated with the banquet of life and with calm mind embrace . . . a rest that knows no care." If existence has been painful, then an end to it should be welcome.

The introductory lines of book 4 express Lucretius' desire to make philosophy more palatable to his readers by presenting it in poetry. His task is a new one: "I traverse the distant haunts of the Pierides (the Muses), never trodden before by the foot of man."

The poet begins this book on sensation with an explanation of idols, the films of atoms which float from the surfaces of objects and make sense perception possible. Men see because idols touch their eyes, taste the bitter salt air because idols of hooked atoms reach their tongues. Idols become blunted when they travel a long distance, causing men to see far-off square towers as round.

Lucretius blames the misconceptions arising from visual phenomena like refraction and perspective on men's reason, not their senses, for accuracy of sense perception is an important part of his theory: "Unless they [the reports of the senses] are true, all reason, too, becomes false."

A second eulogy of Epicurus introduces the fifth book, for some readers the most interesting of all. In it Lucretius discusses the creation of the world and the development of human civilization. Earth was created by a chance conjunction of atoms, which squeezed out sun, moon, and stars as they gathered together to form land. The world, which is constantly disintegrating and being rebuilt, is still young, for human history does not go back beyond the Theban and Trojan wars.

The poet gives several explanations for the motion of stars, the causes of night, and eclipses. Since proof can come only from the senses, any theory which does not contradict perception is possible.

Lucretius presents the curious idea that the first animals were born from wombs rooted in the earth. Monsters were created, but only strong animals and those useful to man could survive. A delightful picture of primitive man, a hardy creature living on nuts and berries and living in caves, follows. Lucretius describes the process of civilization as men united for protection, learned to talk, use metals, weave, and wage war. Problems arose for them with the discovery of wealth and property, breeding envy and discord. It was at this point that Epicurus taught men the highest good, to free them from their cares.

The sixth book continues the explanation of natural phenomena which inspired men to fear the gods: thunder, lightning, clouds, rain, earthquakes. Lucretius rambles over a great many subjects, giving several explanations for many of them. He concludes the poem with a vivid description of the plague of Athens, modeled on Thucydides' account.

ON THE ORIGIN OF SPECIES

Type of work: Science
Author: Charles Darwin (1809–1882)
First published: 1859

On the Origin of Species by Means of Natural Selection: Or, The Preservation of Favoured Races in the Struggle for Life was first published in London, England, in 1859. The work presented Charles Robert Darwin's theory regarding the evolution of species. According to Darwin, life was a "struggle for existence" in which only the fittest survived. Favorable variations within organisms resulted in some organisms having a competitive advantage over other organisms. Darwin believed that positive variations, when passed to succeeding generations, in turn resulted not only in the evolution of entirely new species but also in the extinction of other, less favored species.

The idea of evolution was not new, and its origins may be found in an earlier age. The scientific revolution which had begun in the seventeenth century had resulted from the quest for laws determining the functioning of the physical world. These efforts provided the foundations for the technological revolution that followed. Throughout the eighteenth century, scientists applied the new learning to practical needs, thereby making possible the Industrial Revolution. It was believed by many that through the application of science, progress toward a better world would occur. For some, science became the new religion.

While the technological revolution was occurring, other scientists were investigating other areas. Regarding evolution, most scientists agreed that, contrary to some interpretations of the biblical story of Creation, the earth and its creatures had evolved. Charles Lyell, for example, in *The Principles of Geology* (1830), noted that the earth's geological processes appeared to have been gradual and evolutionary rather than cataclysmic and revolutionary. Thomas Malthus, in *Essay on the Principle of Population* (1798), described the intense competition for subsistence, concluding that the competition for food had resulted in the survival of the strong. While these and other works strongly influenced Darwin's ideas, none provided substantive data that could prove or disprove the theory of evolution. Providing such data was to be Darwin's great contribution.

Between 1831 and 1837, Darwin served as a naturalist on the HMS *Beagle*, a British vessel which explored the South Pacific and the South American coast. Before his departure, he had been convinced that evolution had occurred, but he did not know how or why. As nothing was known of heredity during his time, he could base his observations only upon the vague idea that characteristics, either acquired or inherited, had something to do with the evolution of species. What he wished to accomplish on his journey was the development of a theory that would more accurately explain that process. Moreover, he intended to acquire raw data that would support his conclusions. This he did, recording in dozens of notebooks his extensive observations on the nature and character of fossils and on the comparisons between species separated by time or geography.

Upon his return to England, he continued acquiring data. First he studied the breeding and artificial selection of farm animals. Then in 1838, he read Malthus and received the inspiration for his belief in the "survival of the fittest." Malthus had proposed that overcrowding and struggle were caused by more offspring being produced than could survive. Natural selection meant that survivors would usually be more capable of surviving a particular condition. With this as his hypothesis, Darwin continued to accumulate data. He was determined not to publish anything until he had conclusive evidence one way or the other. Indeed, he researched and studied for twenty more years before finally publishing his findings. Even then, it was only when he learned that another biologist, Alfred Russel Wallace, was working on a similar theory, that he finally agreed to publish *On the Origin of Species*.

While Darwin did not propose anything startlingly new, he provided an immense amount of data to support his hypothesis regarding evolution. Moreover, his lucid writing style transmitted his ideas to scientists and laymen alike. The first four chapters of his work dealt with his perception of artificial and natural selection in the struggle for existence. The fifth chapter dealt with species variation and modification in ways other than natural selection. The next five chapters noted problems in believing in or comprehending the processes of evolution and natural selection. The remaining chapters provided his evidence for evolution and his conclusions. On the first day of issue, the entire edition of 1,250 copies was sold out.

While others debated the merits and demerits of his theory, Darwin himself continued to research his subject, publishing *The Descent of Man and Selection in Relation to Sex* in 1871. He had concluded that man was just as much a product of natural selection as any other animal. Yet Darwin's ignorance of heredity led him to continue explaining evolution in terms of acquired characteristic evolutionary changes. Only after the work of Gregor Johann Mendel on genes and their role was discovered and applied in the early twentieth century, and only after

Sir Ronald Fisher, in the 1930s, proved that variation in organisms occurs fortuitously did the modern understanding of evolution occur. Still, Darwin's pioneering work was a major contribution to the field of biology. Just as important was his ability to present his ideas cogently and coherently, so that his theory was widely disseminated. Thus, *On the Origin of Species* is one of the most significant works of the nineteenth century.

Almost immediately upon its publication, a storm of controversy arose. Darwinism, which was the application of Darwin's theories, had an impact upon science, upon religion, and upon studies of society. The shy and retiring Darwin was interested primarily in the biological implications of evolution, at a time when science was treated reverently by many, a work such as *On the Origin of Species* was assured of having ramifications other than biology. Disciples of Darwin's ideas zealously promoted evolution, using it to validate many of the ideas that had grown out of the Industrial Revolution. Yet the most immediate impact of Darwinism was felt by organized religion.

The nineteenth century was an age in which formal religion had played an important role. Darwinism posed two significant problems for faithful Christians. The first was the challenge to the story of Creation in Genesis. If Darwin was correct, the Creator could not have made the heavens and the earth, and all that was in them, within the span of a single week. Moreover, if the Genesis account could not be taken literally, other parts of the Bible might also be only symbolic or perhaps even false. A second problem posed was that of the nature of man's soul. As Benjamin Disraeli asked in 1864, "Is man an ape or an angel?" If man merely had evolved as other animals had, was there any special relationship between man and God? For many, Darwin's evolutionary theory was incompatible with Christian teaching.

The debate between evolutionists and creationists began almost as soon as *On the Origin of Species* was published. The Roman Catholic church, for example, condemned many of the scientific works of the period, including *On the Origin of Species*. After proclaiming the dogma of papal infallibility in 1870, the pope declared evolution to be untrue, calling any compromise between science and theology a heresy. Only after World War I did the Catholic church become more permissive with regard to evolution. Still, the debate continued. The 1925 Scopes "Monkey Trial" in Dayton, Tennessee, was ultimately resolved in favor of the teaching of evolution. Even in the late twentieth century, in certain Fundamentalist circles the evolution-creation issue remains very much alive.

The theory that organisms had evolved led many to believe and to attempt to prove that groups in society were also selected. Indeed, the subtitle of Darwin's work, *The Preservation of Favoured Races in the Struggle for Life*, led some to cite Darwinism as justification for

exploitation, imperialism, and racism. While Darwin himself did not accept such extrapolations, many of his followers and disciples did. Social Darwinists, as they were called, distorted Darwin's ideas and applied "scientific laws" to societies. Darwin did not believe in the ideas of the Social Darwinists, and it is incorrect to attribute to him these concepts.

Of all the applications of Darwinism, the field of Social Darwinism was to have the greatest impact. Herbert Spencer, for example, in his ten-volume *Synthetic Philosophy* (1860–1896), in which he coined the phrase Social Darwinism, applied Darwin's findings to virtually every aspect of human society. Spencer stated that within a society groups compete with each other and superior groups naturally dominate inferior groups. Thus, Social Darwinism maintained that exploitation, nationalism, bigotry, and racism had been validated by science.

Given the worship of science in the nineteenth century, it is not surprising that such distortions were as popular as they were. Social Darwinism gave scientific sanction to laissez-faire capitalism, with its upholding of competition. John D. Rockefeller, an American industrialist, wrote that big business was "merely a survival of the fittest . . . the working out of a law of nature and a law of God." While this statement on the surface appears to reflect simply a belief in the free enterprise system, it was used to justify greed, illegal business tactics, and exploitation. The struggle for survival in the economic jungle was one-sided and unfair, but, according to Social Darwinists, that was exactly the way it was supposed to be.

Nationalists who believed in the supremacy of the state used Social Darwinism to justify militarism and war. They reasoned that if species evolved, then nations too would evolve into superior and inferior groupings. As proof of superiority that could be demonstrated only on the battlefield, military preparedness was an absolute necessity. Success on the battlefield meant the dominance by one and the subservience by the other. War was construed to be a "biological necessity." Thus, in the late nineteenth century, European nations vied to see which could build the biggest and best army. This competition led ultimately to the total wars of the twentieth century.

Social Darwinism was also used to justify the neoimperialism of the late nineteenth century. Between 1870 and 1900, much of the nonwhite population of the world was colonized and exploited by Western European nations. Justification for such activities was usually stated to be the superiority of the white race over inferior races. Exploitation of "inferior" races was permissible, just as exploitation of workers was acceptable to capitalists. Another justification for imperialism has been called the "White Man's Burden": It was the responsibility of the white man to take care of those less fortunate races which had not evolved as rapidly as the white races.

Extreme forms of nationalism and imperialism were

embodied in the new religion of militant nationalism. Literature exemplifying this dogma was filled with descriptions of superior and inferior races. One of the earliest racist writers, Arthur de Gobineau, in his *Essay on the Inequality of the Human Races* (1853–1855), proclaimed the superiority of the white races. Furthermore, he declared that within the white races there were superior groups, such as Aryan Germanic groups, and inferior national groups, such as Slavs and Jews. This message, "proved" by Darwin's theory, became popular by the end of the nineteenth century. Its long-term impact can most clearly be seen in the actions of Adolf Hitler and the Nazis of the Third Reich. The final solution of "the Jewish question" was, to the Nazis, merely the "survival of the fittest." To the Jews, it became the Holocaust.

Nevertheless, Charles Darwin's *On the Origin of Species* was an important contribution to the advancement of biology. Yet the significance of his work also lies in the extrapolations from his work that others proposed. Some used Darwinism to attack organized religion; others used it to justify racism, imperialism, and militarism. While Darwin himself remained a virtual recluse and a nonparticipant in the various debates during his lifetime, his ideas were misunderstood and misapplied by others who sought to justify man's inhumanity to man.

ORATIONS

Type of work: Speeches
Author: Marcus Tullius Cicero (106–43 B.C.)
First transcribed: 80–43 B.C.

When one thinks of the greatness of Rome and especially of its government, the name of Cicero is likely to come to mind. While a figure like Julius Caesar may symbolize the military greatness of imperial Rome, Cicero is a symbol of Roman justice and law, of the Roman Senate and its traditions, and of Roman greatness in philosophy and literature. Cicero is important in literature primarily for his orations and his numerous writings about oratory and rhetoric. As the author of these writings Cicero set a pattern in public speaking that is still alive in European culture. More than that, because of what he wrote and said and because of the viewpoints he held and defended, even dying for them, Cicero became historically one of the great advocates of culture and conservatism.

Cicero took ten years to prepare himself as a lawyer before he appeared on behalf of a client in public. In those years of preparation he held, as he did all his life, that a thorough education is necessary for success in any activity. There have been exponents of oratory who claim that manner is everything; Cicero disagreed, believing that matter is as inescapably a factor in oratorical success as is manner. In the *Orator*, one of his most mature pieces of writing on the art of oratory, Cicero wrote that his own success, like that of any orator, was more to be credited to his study of the philosophers than to his study of earlier rhetoricians, and that no one can express wide views, or speak fluently on many and various subjects, without philosophy. Although Cicero tried to make a science of rhetoric and saw profit in his own attempts at its systemization, he also realized that no simple set of formulas could ever make a great orator. As he put it, an eloquent man should be able to speak "of small things in a lowly manner, of moderate things in a temperate manner, and of great things with dignity."

In Cicero's time there were two prevalent styles in oratory, the Attic and the Asian. In the latter type, Cicero himself discerned two varieties, the one epigrammatic and euphuistic, dependent upon artful structure rather than importance of content, and the other characterized by a swift and passionate flow of speech in which choice of words for precise and elegant effect was a dominant factor. Cicero found both styles wanting in some degree and built his own style upon an eclectic combination of the two.

Fifty-eight speeches by Cicero are still extant, although not all have complete texts. The number of his speeches is unknown, but more than forty are known to have been lost. Not all the speeches Cicero wrote were delivered; sometimes he wrote them for an occasion which did not occur. His second *Philippic* is an example of such a speech. Marcus Antonius was so enraged by Cicero's first speech against him after the death of Julius Caesar that Cicero's friends persuaded the orator to leave the city of Rome temporarily. While absent from Rome, living at a villa near Naples, Cicero wrote the second *Philippic*, which was not spoken in the Senate or even published immediately. A copy was sent, however, to Brutus and Cassius, who enjoyed its invective against their enemy.

Not all of Cicero's speeches are of equal interest to a modern reader. His earliest extant oration, containing relatively little of interest, was delivered in a law court on behalf of Publius Quinctius. Cicero appeared for the defense, as he usually did, and spoke against Quintus Hortensius, the greatest lawyer in Rome at the time. Although Cicero won his case, it is difficult for a modern reader to retain interest in a case decided two thousand years ago when the stuff of the argument is largely points of law. But this speech, along with other early efforts, provided the opportunity for Cicero to prove himself. He made such a reputation that he was chosen to prosecute Caius Verres, who was accused of tyranny and maladministration in Sicily. Once again the famous Hortensius was Cicero's legal opponent. In the second oration he made against Verres, Cicero managed to produce such overwhelming evidence against the defendant that he went voluntarily into banishment. The evidence included chicanery designed to prevent the case from coming to trial, and even Hortensius could find little to say for the defendant. Although Cicero had no occasion to deliver five additional speeches he had written for the trial, scholars have judged that they are among Cicero's best and have found them excellent sources for material about Sicilian government, history, and art. Another of Cicero's noteworthy speeches is the one given in defense of Aulus Cluentius, who was tried and acquitted on a charge of having poisoned his father-in-law, who had tried a few years before to poison Cluentius.

Cicero's intent was to move his hearers, and his devices to ensure victory in court were not always above reproach, as his speech in defense of Lucius Flaccus indicates. The defendant was accused of extortion while an administrator in Asia, and apparently Cicero could find little to say in his client's defense beyond impugning the Jews and Greeks who were witnesses against him, members of groups not much in favor in Rome. Of even greater interest is Cicero's defense of Aulus Licinius Archias, a poet of Greek descent whose status as a Roman citizen had been questioned. In this oration Cicero developed a long passage in praise of literature, saying that literature and its creators are of paramount interest to a nation because they afford excellent material for speeches, because they make great deeds immortal by preserving them in writing, and because they give readers a useful and refreshing pastime.

Not all of Cicero's speeches were intended for courtroom presentation. Some were written for delivery in the Senate and some with a view to Cicero's own benefit. In 58 B.C. Cicero was exiled temporarily as a result of his activities in crushing the conspiracy of Catiline. When Pompey recalled him to Rome a year later, he thanked the Roman Senate in one speech for his recall; in another he thanked the Roman people generally; and in a third he made a request to the Senate for the return of his home, which had been taken over by Clodius for the state.

The most famous of Cicero's speeches are those he wrote against Marcus Antonius after the death of Julius Caesar. Cicero, a conservative, had not been favorable to the autocracy of Caesar and rejoiced when Caesar was assassinated. During an eight-month period in 44–43 B.C., when Marcus Antonius presumed to try to succeed Caesar, Cicero directed fourteen orations against him. These orations, passionate and sincere, are called the *Philippics*, after the famous speeches of Demosthenes against Philip, the father of Alexander the Great. In his first speech, Cicero spoke with some moderation, speaking only of Antonius' public life and appealing to his sense of patriotism. In later speeches, especially the second *Philippic*, he made all sorts of attacks on Antonius' private life, accusing him of almost every conceivable type of immorality. Eventually Antonius had his revenge: when he, Lepidus, and Octavianus formed their triumvirate, Cicero was put to death.

Perhaps Cicero's most significant legacy was his formulation of the principles of rhetoric. In the Middle Ages and the Renaissance, rhetoric played a vital part in the curriculum, which remained strongly based in oratory, and Cicero's influence on this discipline was great.

ORESTEIA

Type of work: Drama
Author: Aeschylus (525–456 B.C.)
Type of plot: Classical tragedy
Time of plot: After the fall of Troy
Locale: Argos
First presented: 458 B.C.

Aeschylus won first prize with this trilogy about the doomed descendants of the cruel and bloody Atreus. The atmosphere of the play is one of doom and revenge, as the playwright delves into the philosophical issue of the problem of evil and human suffering.

Principal Characters

Agamemnon (ă′ge·mĕm′nŏn), of the doomed House of Atreus, King of Argos and leader of the Greek expedition against Troy. When the Greeks were detained at Aulis, he had been commanded by the gods to sacrifice his daughter Iphigenia, so that the fleet might sail. This deed brought him the hatred of his wife Clytemnestra, who plots his death. On his return to Argos after the fall of Troy, she persuades him to commit the sin of pride by walking on purple carpets to enter his palace. Once within the palace, he is murdered in his bath by Clytemnestra and her lover Aegisthus.

Clytemnestra (klī′təm·nĕs′trə), daughter of Leda and wife of Agamemnon. Infuriated by his sacrifice of their daughter Iphigenia, she murders him and rules Argos with her lover, Aegisthus, until she is killed by her son Orestes.

Cassandra (kă·săn′drə), the daughter of King Priam of Troy. She is fated always to prophesy truth but never to be believed. Captured by Agamemnon and brought to Argos, she foretells the king's death and is then killed by Clytemnestra.

Aegisthus (ē·jĭs′thəs), cousin of Agamemnon and the lover of Clytemnestra. After Agamemnon's death he rules Argos with her until he is slain by Orestes.

Orestes (ō·rĕsf′tez), the son of Agamemnon and Clytemnestra. After his father's murder, he is driven by his mother and her lover from his heritage of Argos. Returning from exile, he meets his sister Electra at their father's tomb and tells her that he has been commanded by the oracle of Apollo to avenge Agamemnon by killing his murderers. This revenge he carries out, but he is driven mad by the Furies, who pursue him to the Delphi, where he takes refuge in the temple of Apollo. Athena, the goddess of wisdom, appears. Unable to decide the case, she calls in twelve Athenian citizens to act as judges. It is argued against Orestes that Clytemnestra, in killing

Agamemnon, had not slain a blood relative of her family and thus did not deserve death. Apollo argues that Clytemnestra, having only nourished the father's seed in her womb, was no blood relation of Orestes, and therefore the latter was innocent. The judges vote six to six, and Orestes is declared free of blood-guilt.

Electra (ē·lĕk′trə), the daughter of Agamemnon and Clytemnestra and sister of Orestes. After the murder of her father and the exile of her brother, she is left alone to mourn Agamemnon's death and to perform the rites at his tomb. There she meets Orestes, who has returned to Argos, but at first does not recognize him. Convinced at last of his identity, she urges him to avenge their father by killing their mother and her lover.

The Furies or *Eumenides* (ū·men′ĭ·dēz), children of Night, whose duty it is to dog the footsteps of murderers and to drive them mad. They pursue Orestes but are balked by the judges' decision that he is innocent. They rail against the younger gods who have deprived them of their ancient power. They are pacified by Athena, who promises them great honor and reverence if they will remain at Athens as beneficent deities.

Athena (ə·thē′nə), the goddess of wisdom and patron of Athens, she is always on the side of mercy. She defends the new law against the old in the case of Orestes, pacifies the Furies, and changes them into the Eumenides or "gracious ones."

Apollo (ə·pŏl′ō), the god of poetry, music, oracles, and healing. It is he who commands Orestes to avenge his father's death by killing his guilty mother. He then appears at Orestes' trial and defends the accused with the argument that, by killing his mother, Orestes was not guilty of shedding family blood, for the mother, being only the nourisher of the seed, is no relation to her child. Family relationship comes only through the father.

The Story

The house of Atreus was accursed because in the great palace at Argos the tyrant, Atreus, had killed the children of Thyestes and served their flesh to their father at a royal banquet. Agamemnon and Menelaus were the sons of Atreus. When Helen, wife of Menelaus, was carried off by Paris, Agamemnon was among the Greek heroes who went with his brother to battle the Trojans for her return. But on the way to Troy, while the fleet lay idle at Aulis, Agamemnon was prevailed upon to sacrifice his daughter, Iphigenia, to the gods. Hearing of this deed, Clytemnestra, his wife, vowed revenge. She gave her son, Orestes, into the care of the King of Phocis, and in the darkened palace nursed her consuming hate.

In her desire for vengeance she was joined by Aegisthus, surviving son of Thyestes, who had returned from his long exile. Hate brought the queen and Aegisthus together in a common cause; they became lovers as well as plotters in crime.

The ship of Menelaus having been delayed by a storm, Agamemnon returned alone from the Trojan wars. A watchman first saw the lights of his ship upon the sea and brought to his queen the news of the king's return. Leaving his men quartered in the town, Agamemnon drove to the palace in his chariot, beside him Cassandra, captive daughter of the king of Troy and an augeress of all misfortunes to come, who had fallen to Agamemnon in the division of the spoils. She had already warned the king that some evil was to befall him.

Agamemnon, however, had no suspicions of his homecoming, as Clytemnestra came to greet him at the palace doorway, her armed retainers about her, magnificent carpets unrolled for the feet of the conqueror of Troy. Agamemnon chided his queen for the lavishness of her reception and entered the palace to refresh himself after his long journey. He asked Clytemnestra to receive Cassandra and to treat his captive kindly.

After Agamemnon had retired, Clytemnestra returned and ordered Cassandra, who had refused to leave the chariot, to enter the palace. When Cassandra persisted in remaining where she was, the queen declared she would not demean herself by bandying words with a common slave and a madwoman. She reentered the palace. Cassandra lifted her face toward the sky and called upon Apollo to tell her why she had been brought to this cursed house. She informed the spectators in front of the palace that Clytemnestra would murder Agamemnon. She lamented the fall of Troy, recalled the butchery of Thyestes' children, and the doom that hung over the sons of Atreus, and foretold again the murder of Agamemnon by his queen. As she entered the palace, those outside heard the death cry of Agamemnon within.

A moment later Clytemnestra appeared in the doorway, the bloody sword of Aegisthus in her hand. Behind her lay the body of the king, entangled in the rich carpets.

Clytemnesta defended herself before the citizens, saying she had killed the king for the murder of Iphigenia and had also killed Cassandra, with whom Agamemnon had shamed her honor. Her deed, she told the citizens defiantly, had ended the bloody lust of the house of Atreus.

Then she presented Aegisthus, son of Thyestes, who asserted that his vengeance was just and that he intended to rule in the palace of Agamemnon. Reproaches were hurled at the guilty pair. There were cries that Orestes would avenge his father's murder. Aegisthus and Clytemnestra, in a fury of guilty horror, roared out their self-justification for the crime and defied the gods themselves to end their seizure of power.

Orestes, grown to manhood, returned from the land of Phocis to discover that his mother and Aegisthus had murdered his father. He mourned his father's death and asked the king of the gods to give him ability to take vengeance upon the guilty pair. Electra, daughter of Agamemnon, also mourned and cursed the murderers. Encountering her brother, she did not at first recognize him, for he appeared in the disguise of a messenger who brought word of the death of Orestes. They met at their father's tomb, where he made himself known to his sister. There he begged his father's spirit to give him strength in his undertaking. Electra assured him nothing but evil could befall any of the descendants of Atreus and welcomed the quick fulfillment of approaching doom.

Learning that Clytemnestra had once dreamed of suckling a snake which drew blood from her breast, Orestes saw in this dream the image of himself and the deed he intended to commit. He went to the palace in disguise and killed Aegisthus. Then he confronted Clytemnestra, his sword dripping with the blood of his mother's lover, and struck her down.

Orestes displayed the two bodies to the people and announced to Apollo that he had done the deed required of him. But he realized that he must suffer for his terrible crime. He began to go mad as Furies, sent by his mother's dead spirit, pursued him.

The Furies drove Orestes from land to land. Finally he took refuge in a temple, but the Pythian priestess claimed the temple was profaned by the presence of the horrible Furies, who lay asleep near Orestes. Then Apollo appeared to tell Orestes that he had put the Furies to sleep so the haunted man could get some rest. He advised Orestes to visit the temple of Pallas Athena and there gain full absolution for his crime.

While Orestes listened, the ghost of Clytemnestra spitefully aroused the Furies and commanded them to torture Orestes again. When Apollo ordered the Furies to leave, the creatures accused him of the murder of Clytemnestra and Aegisthus and the punishment of Orestes. The god confessed he had demanded the death of Agamemnon's murderers. He was told that by his demands he had caused an even greater crime, matricide. Apollo said Athena should decide the justice of the case.

In Athens, in the temple of the goddess, Orestes begged Athena to help him. Replying the case was too grave for her to decide alone, she called upon the judges to help her reach a wise decision. There were some who believed the ancient laws would be weakened if evidence were presented, and they claimed Orestes deserved his terrible punishment.

When Orestes asked why Clytemnestra had not been persecuted for the murder of Agamemnon, he was told her crime had not been the murder of a blood relative, as his was. Apollo was another witness at the trial. He claimed the mother was not the true parent, that the father, who planted the seed in the mother's womb, was the real parent, as shown in the tracing of descent through the male line. Therefore, Orestes was not guilty of the murder of a true member of his blood family.

The judges decided in favor of Orestes. There were many, however, who in an angry rage cursed and condemned the land where such a judgment might prevail. They cried woe upon the younger gods and all those who tried to wrest ancient rights from the hands of established tradition. But Athena upheld the judgment of the court and Orestes was freed from the anger of the Furies.

Critical Evaluation

The *Oresteia* won first prize in the Athenian drama competition when it was initially presented in 458 B.C. This was the thirteenth time Aeschylus had been awarded the highest honors in a career of forty-one years as a tragedian. He was foremost in establishing the drama as an art form capable of exploring the most compelling problems of human existence. And this dramatic trilogy—the only one in Greek drama to survive intact—was a fitting climax to his life. The *Oresteia* is not merely a magnificent work, it is one of the supreme achievements of classical culture.

In it Aeschylus took up the theme of the ancestral curse, as he had done in *Seven Against Thebes*, but here he uses that theme to probe the metaphysical problem of evil. The question amounts to this: In a divinely ordered universe why are atrocities committed, and what is the reason for human suffering? Aeschylus brought all of his dramatic skill, all of his lofty genius for poetry, and all of his intelligence and feeling to bear on the issue. And he came as close as any writer ever has to expressing the profoundest truths of human life.

The legend of the dynasty of Atreus is a series of crimes, each committed in retaliation against a close relative. The murder of kin was the most hideous sin a person could perform, according to Greek morality. The blood curse was brought on the house of Atreus when Atreus murdered his nephews, and from there on the history of the family is one of slaughter. *Agamemnon*, the first play in the trilogy, reveals the homecoming and murder of Agamemnon by his wife Clytemnestra and his cousin Aegisthus, who is also her lover. The second play, *The Libation-Bearers*, shows Orestes' arrival in Argos and his revenge upon his mother and Aegisthus for killing Agamemnon. Then he is pursued by the Furies. And in the final play, *The Eumenides* (or "The Kindly Ones"), the curse is put to rest when Orestes is absolved in guilt in the Athenian law court of Athena.

The action of this trilogy is simple enough, but it is in the way Aeschylus develops the action, with layer upon layer of meaning, that these dramas engross us. The curse theme operates on several planes at once, and it is given concrete expression in the recurring images of the web, the net, the coiling snake full of venom.

On the simplest level the *Oresteia* is a revenge trilogy. Agamemnon kills his daughter Iphigenia, which enables him to make war on Troy. When he returns Clytemnestra kills him in retaliation, aided by Aegisthus, who wants to avenge his father, Thyestes. Then Orestes slays the two of them to avenge Agamemnon, for which the Furies persecute him. Conceivably this chain of butchery could continue forever, if it were not for the intervention of the gods.

Yet on the personal plane crime begets crime not because of any abstract law, but because human motives require it. Aeschylus' characters have freedom of choice and must take full responsibility for what they do. However, their personalities are such that their deeds seem inevitable. On this level character is fate and impels acts of violence. Agamemnon brings Troy to rubble because family honor and his own pride demand it, but in the process he kills his daughter and nearly wipes out the youth of Greece. The tragedy of the Trojan War is repeatedly emphasized, and Agamemnon is in large measure responsible for that waste of life. He is rather a monster, grown fat and arrogant in his power.

Clytemnestra is equally prideful. Her vanity is injured when Agamemnon brings his mistress, Cassandra, home, and out of personal honor she avenges Iphigenia. Also, she is tied by sex to Aegisthus, a demagogue who turns tyrant.

Here another level of meaning becomes visible—that of political intrigue and the lust for power. Agamemnon is king. With him out of the way Clytemnestra and Aegisthus become co-rulers of Argos. Agamemnon went to Troy fully aware of the wealth and fame in store for him, and Orestes knows, as well, that Argos will fall to him when he kills his mother and her lover. Every act of vengeance in these plays carries some motive of gain.

We see the inevitable sequence of events. Power or the drive for power breeds insolence and crime, which brings retribution. Orestes breaks this chain. Why? Because he was encouraged to the crime by Apollo; because he feels pain and remorse afterward; because he does not take over Argos once the crime is committed; and because the gods feel compassion for such a man, even if the Furies do not.

Now the final level of meaning emerges—the divine revelation. That this occurs in the Areopagus is Aeschylus' patriotic salute to the notion that Athenian law had supernatural sanction. God, or Fate, tempers retribution with mercy in the end, and the vengeful Furies are placated with an honorary position as tutelary goddesses. If Orestes is absolved by a sophism about paternal lineage, this merely underscores the fact that Athena and Apollo, as the agents of Zeus, have compassion for him and would use any legal pretext to get him off the hook. Man must learn by suffering, Aeschylus says, and Orestes has shown himself to be the only character in the trilogy who is able to learn by agony. Success makes men proud and amoral, but pain teaches men the true way to live. As a vindication of divine justice the *Oresteia* is splendid, and as a depiction of the cumulative power of evil it is unsurpassed.

ORLANDO FURIOSO

Type of work: Poem
Author: Ludovico Ariosto (1474–1533)
Type of plot: Chivalric romance
Time of plot: Eighth century
Locale: France, Spain, Africa
First published: 1516; enlarged edition, 1532

Consisting as it does of a great number of stories and episodes, this masterpiece of early Italian literature contains too many shifts of scene and incident to enjoy a controlling interior unity. The world of chivalry and the world of fantasy mingle in the poem's three main stories: the account of the wars of Charlemagne, the tale of Orlando's hopeless love for Angelica and his later madness, and the love story of Rogero and Bradamant, the supposed heirs of the great house of Este.

Principal Characters

Orlando, the renowned nephew of King Charlemagne and the mightiest paladin among his Twelve Peers. While Paris is under siege by the Saracens, he dreams an evil dream concerning his beloved Angelica, the beautiful princess of Cathay who has caused great dissension among Christian and pagan champions alike. Forsaking his knightly duties, he passes through the enemy lines and goes in search of the damsel. His quest takes him into many lands, and after many strange adventures he is driven mad by the distractions of love and jealousy. Throwing away his armor, he wanders naked and raving among savage beasts, so that all knights are filled with pity when they hear of his sad state. He recovers his sanity after Astolpho, an English knight, finds the wits of his deranged friend in a vial in the region of the moon. His mind restored, Orlando once more engages in valorous deeds and champions the Christian cause. One of his feats is the rescue of Rogero, a gallant Saracen knight now converted to Christianity, who has been cast away on a desert island.

Angelica, the princess of Cathay who by her great beauty bewitches Orlando, Rinaldo, Ferraù, and Rogero, but in the end marries none of these paladins; her true love is Medoro, a Saracen knight of lowly birth whom she nurses back to health after he has been wounded in battle. The cause of many misfortunes to others, she herself falls victim to an enchanter's magic and is carried to the island of Ebuda, where she is about to be offered as a sacrifice to a giant orc when she is saved by Rogero, the Saracen knight who forgets his own loved Bradamant and falls under the spell of Angelica's charms. To keep her from harm, Rogero gives her a magic ring, but faithless Angelica uses it to make herself invisible and flees from him. After she has saved the life of Medoro, she returns with him to Cathay.

Rinaldo, one of King Charlemagne's Twelve Peers, second only to Orlando in loyalty, bravery, and knightly honor. His chivalric adventures are wonderful and strange but not always related to his quest for Angelica, whom he finally disdains. On several occasions he is called upon to engage in single combat for the honor of the king. Rejoicing when he learns that Rogero has received Christian baptism, he promises the hand of his sister Bradamant to the Saracen hero. Later he withstands the wishes of his parents and champions the right of Bradamant to marry her beloved.

Rogero, a noble Saracen knight in love with Bradamant, the sister of Rinaldo. After many marvelous adventures, which include his rescue of Bradamant from the enchanted castle in which Atlantes, a magician, holds him prisoner, his ride on a flying hippogryph, his slaying of the giantess Eriphilia, his rescue of Angelica from the monstrous orc, his forgetting of Bradamant while he woos and loses Angelica, his victory over Mandricardo, his sojourn on a desert island, and his Christian baptism, he is finally restored to his beloved Bradamant. At the feast celebrating the wedding of the happy couple envoys appear to make Rogero king of Bulgaria. Rogero and Bradamant, according to Ariosto, were the ancestors of the noble d'Este family of Ferrara.

Bradamant, a maiden knight, the sister of Rinaldo and later the wife of Rogero. In Ariosto's version of this chivalric story, she is always the romantic heroine, fighting on the side of right, vanquishing evil knights, and rescuing the unfortunate. Her steadfastness in her love for Rogero, the Saracen champion, contrasts sharply with the fickleness of Angelica, while her prowess on the field of battle rivals that of the bravest knights, including her own Rogero, who wins her from his princely rival after defeating her in single combat. The story ends with an account of the happy wedding festivities of Bradamant and Rogero, now turned Christian.

Astolpho, the English knight who restores Orlando's wits. Also a rider on the flying hippogryph, he engages in marvelous adventures, among them a journey to the fabled land of Prester John and a trip to the region of the moon, where the senses of poets and others are stored. Astolpho finds there the vial containing Orlando's lost wits and returns them to the hero, who regains his sanity after inhaling the contents of the vial.

Ferraù, a brave Saracen knight. Also under Angelica's spell, he battles with Rinaldo, his rival. While the two men fight, Angelica runs away. Ferraù returns to Spain to aid his king repel an invasion.

Sacripant, the king of Circassia. When Angelica meets him in the forest, she begs him to protect a damsel in distress. They are overtaken by Rinaldo, who battles with Sacripant and splinters his shield. Angelica flees once more when she sees Sacripant overthrown.

Count Pinabel, a treacherous knight whom Bradamant encounters while she is searching for Rogero. Pinabel tells her that Rogero and other knights are the captives of Atlantes, a magician whose enchanted castle stands high in the Pyrenees. Later he tries to kill Bradamant by pushing her into a deep cave.

Melissa, a seeress whom Bradamant finds in Merlin's cave, into which Count Pinabel pushed her. Melissa foretells the noble house that will spring from the union of Bradamant and Rogero, and she tells the maiden knight that Rogero can be freed from the spell of the magician Atlantes only with the aid of a magic ring.

Brunello, a dwarf to whom Agramant, king of Africa, has entrusted the magic ring used by Bradamant to free Rogero and his fellow knights from the spell cast upon them by the magician Atlantes.

Atlantes, the aged magician who puts Rogero under the magic spell from which Bradamant frees her lover. He is the owner of the flying hippogryph on which Rogero, after his release, is carried to the land of Alcina, a wicked sorceress.

Alcina, the evil sorceress under whose spell Rogero falls. He is saved by Melissa, a seeress, who gives him a magic ring to protect him from Alcina's power. Alcina also cast a spell on Astolpho, a brave English knight.

Agramant, king of Africa and the enemy of King Charlemagne. When it is decided to end the siege of Paris by a battle of champions, Agramant chooses Rogero as the greatest of his knights. Rinaldo is the defender of the Christians. During the combat Agramant treacherously breaks his oath and attacks the French forces. When the Saracens are routed, Rogero, who has promised to accept Christian baptism after the battle, remains with his defeated king, much to the distress of Bradamant, his beloved.

Rodomont, a fierce and vengeful Saracen warrior, the enemy of all Christians and a cause of dissension among the Saracens. After a quarrel with Mandricardo, prince of Tartary, Rodomont leaves King Agramant's camp. He meets Isabella, princess of Galicia, who is grieving for the death of Zerbino, her beloved knight, whom Rodomont had slain. In a drunken frenzy, Rodomont kills Isabella. Overcome by remorse, he builds a bridge over the river near her tomb and there challenges all traveling knights to combat in honor of the dead Princess. He is overcome by mad Orlando and by Bradamant. At the wedding feast of Rogero and Bradamant, Rodomont brashly appears to accuse the Saracen knight of apostasy. Rogero kills him.

Dardinello, king of Zumara, a Saracen leader killed when the Saracen besiegers of Paris are routed.

Cloridan and **Medoro,** brothers, brave young Saracen knights who, grieving for the death of their overlord, King Dardinello, kill many Christian knights to avenge their leader's death. Cloridan is killed by a band of Scottish knights and Medoro is left for dead on the field where Angelica finds him. She nurses him back to health in the nearby hut of a friendly herdsman.

Zerbino, prince of Scotland, the leader of the knights who kill Cloridan. The lover of Isabella, princess of Galicia. Zerbino is killed by fierce Rodomont.

Mandricardo, Prince of Tartary, with whom Rodomont quarrels over Doralice, a Spanish prince. Mandricardo is killed by Rogero following an argument over the Tartar's right to wear the escutcheon of Hector, the Trojan hero.

Gradasso, a Saracen king killed in a battle between pagans and Christians.

Sobrino, a Saracen king who becomes a Christian after his defeat at Lipadusa.

Brandimart, a Christian knight held prisoner by Rodomont. Defeated by Bradamant, the maiden knight, Rodomont promises to release him along with other Christian captives. Brandimart fights with Orlando, Oliver, and Bradamant against the Saracen kings at Lipadusa and is killed in battle.

Flordelice, the faithful wife of Brandimart.

Doralice, the Spanish princess who causes a quarrel between Rodomont and Mandricardo.

Leo, the son of Constantine, the emperor of Greece. When the parents of Bradamant shut her away in a castle in an attempt to make her accept the noble young Greek as her husband, Rogero becomes jealous and decides to kill Leo. Captured while fighting with the Bulgarians against the Greeks, the young Saracen is imprisoned by Theodora, the emperor's sister, in revenge for the death of her son, slain by Rogero. Leo, learning of Rogero's plight, rescues him and hides him in his own house. Later, unaware of Rogero's identity, he asks him to act as his champion, after Bradamant has declared that she will marry only a knight who can withstand her in combat. Rogero and Bradamant meet and Rogero is the victor. Disconsolate because he has won the hand of his beloved for his benefactor, Rogero wanders off into the forest. There Leo, having renounced his claim to Bradamant after hearing the story of the lovers' trials, finds the young Saracen and returns him to his betrothed.

Theodora, the sister of Emperor Constantine of Greece. To avenge the death of her son, she imprisons the Saracen

knight Rogero, his slayer.

Eriphilia, a giantess slain by Rogero.

The Story

It happened that in the old days, as Charlemagne and his paladins battled against the Saracens, the great press of their enemies scattered the Christians and drove them back toward Paris. Then Angelica, the damsel whose beauty and deceit had caused so much dissension among her lovers, Christian and Saracen alike, escaped during the confusion and fled into a nearby wood.

As she rode deeper into the forest, her desire being to reach the nearest seaport from which she could take ship to return to her own land of Cathay, she saw walking toward her Rinaldo of France, the lover whom she hated. Immediately she fled from him as fast as she could ride and in her flight came upon Ferraù, a Saracen knight, weary after the battle. While Rinaldo and Ferraù fought for the maid, she rode away. They followed, both upon the Saracen's horse, until they came to a fork in the path, where they parted. A short time later Rinaldo saw his own lost horse, Bayardo, but the animal ran from him in the direction Angelica had taken, the knight in pursuit.

Angelica rode for a day and a night, until at last from weariness she lay down and slept. While she rested, Sacripant, Circassia's king, came riding through the forest. Awaking, Angelica pretended love for him and begged his aid. But before they had traveled far, Rinaldo overtook them. The two knights fought with fury until Sacripant's shield was splintered.

Seeing her champion overthrown, Angelica fled again until she met a white-bearded hermit, a magician, who put a spell upon her, so that she fell down in a deep sleep upon the seashore. There some travelers saw her and carried her by boat to the dread island of Ebuda, where each day a beautiful maiden was sacrificed to a monstrous orc sent by an angry sea god to harry the island. When the day came for Angelica to be the orc's victim, the islanders stripped her of all ornaments except one bracelet before they tied her to a rock on the sands.

The unhappy lovers who would have died for Angelica knew nothing of her plight. But Orlando, paladin of France, dreamed an evil dream as he lay behind the walls of Paris after that city had been besieged by the Saracens. Forgetful of his duties to King Charlemagne, he arose and passed at night through enemy lines to begin his search for Angelica, a quest which would take him into many lands and finally drive him mad.

Meanwhile Bradamant, the maiden knight, Rinaldo's sister, rode through the land in search of Rogero, the gallant Saracen whom she loved. During her travels she met Count Pinabel, who told her that Rogero had been imprisoned, along with many other brave knights, in the

enchanted castle of old Atlantes, high in the Pyrenees. But Pinabel proved a treacherous knight intent on killing Bradamant. Leading her to the entrance of a cave, he pushed her headlong into the deep cavern.

Luckily, a tree broke her fall. Regaining consciousness, she found herself in the wizard Merlin's cave. There Melissa, a seeress, foretold a happy life for Bradamant and Rogero and related the history of the noble house they would found. The next day Melissa led Bradamant from the cave after telling the maiden that she could free Rogero with the aid of a magic ring given by Agramant, king of Africa, to Brunello, his faithful dwarf.

Bradamant found Brunello, as Melissa had directed. Armed with the ring, she caused the disenchantment of Rogero and all the other knights whom Atlantes held in his power. Released, the knights tried to capture the flying hippogryph, the old magician's steed. Rogero was successful in the chase, but when he mounted upon its back the creature soared high into the air. Bradamant grieved to see her lover carried skyward from her sight.

The hippogryph flew with Rogero to the realm of Alcina, a sorceress. There he saw Astolpho, a daring English knight, whom Alcina had enchanted. Later he slew Eriophilia, a giantess. Bradamant encountered Melissa again and from her learned that Rogero had yielded to Alcina's evil beauty. Melissa had herself conveyed to that strange land. There she reproved Rogero and gave him a magic ring by which he was able to break Alcina's spell. Mounting the hippogryph, he passed over many lands and came at last to the island of Ebuda, where he saw a beautiful maiden chained to a rock beside the sea.

The damsel was Angelica. She saw him check his flying steed, watched him as he prepared to battle the dreadful orc rising from the waves. Rogero put upon her finger the magic ring to keep her from all harm. Then he blinded the monster with the dazzling brightness of his shield. Leaving Ebuda, they rode away on the flying steed until they came to lesser Britain. By that time Rogero had forgotten Bradamant; he swore he would be Angelica's true knight forever.

But faithless Angelica made herself invisible by means of the magic ring and fled from him. Disconsolate, Rogero prepared to mount the hippogryph but found that the beast had flown back to its master. While he was returning to his own land, he saw Bradamant in the power of a giant. Following that false vision, conjured up by old Atlantes, he was lured to another enchanted palace in which the magician held captive many noble knights and ladies. Atlantes had been Rogero's tutor; he wished to keep the young knight safe from hurt in battle.

At Paris, meanwhile, the Saracens under fierce Rodomont had been defeated by the Christian champions. Rinaldo himself had killed in hand-to-hand combat Dardinello, king of Zumara. While Charlemagne's knights celebrated their victory, two Saracen youths mourned beside the body of Dardinello, their dead lord. One was Cloridan, a brave hunter; the other was Medoro, his brother. That night, like silent angels of death, they killed many Christian warriors to avenge their king. At daybreak they met prince Zerbino of Scotland and his men. The Scottish knights killed Cloridan and left Medoro for dead upon the field.

There Angelica, journeying under the protection of the magic ring, found him. Taking him to a herdsman's hut nearby, she nursed him until his wounds had healed, for she who had been wooed by the most famous of knights had fallen in love with that young Saracen of humble birth. When they left the hut to continue their travels, Angelica had only the bracelet left from her perilous experience on Ebuda with which to reward the herdsman. She and Medoro finally reached Cathay, and Angelica made him a king in that far land.

In his search for Angelica, Orlando came one day to the herdsman's hut. When the peasant told him the story of Medoro and Angelica, and displayed the bracelet, Orlando, recognizing the jewel, thought this heart would break. That night, in sudden madness, he saddled his horse and rode away. At last he threw away his armor, tore his clothes, and raged naked through the forest. There was great grief when it was known that Orlando, greatest of knights, lived like the wild beasts he fought with his bare hands.

Once more the Saracens besieged Paris, but as good fortune would have it dissension broke out in the attackers' camp between Rodomont and Mandricardo, a prince of Tartary, over Doralice the Spanish princess. Because Doralice chose Mandricardo as her knight, Rodomont left King Agramant's camp and traveled until he met Isabella, a princess of Galicia, who was mourning her dead lover, Zerbino, whom Mandricardo had slain. While drunk, Rodomont killed Isabella. Grief-stricken, he built a bridge across a river near her tomb and there challenged all passing knights in honor of the dead woman. Twice, however, he was overthrown, once by a naked madman, Orlando, and again by Bradamant.

Bradamant fought with Rodomont on the plea of Flordelice, whose husband, Brandimart, had been imprisoned by the Saracen. Defeated, Rodomont promised to release all his Christian prisoners, including Brandimart. Bradamant took Rodomont's horse, Frontino, which had once been Rogero's property and asked Flordelice to deliver it to Rogero.

For, in the meantime, Rogero had been freed from the enchantment of Atlantes. His deliverer was Astolpho, whom Melissa had released from Alcina's power. By the blast of a magic horn, Astolpho put Atlantes to flight. Then, mounting the wizard's hippogryph, he flew to the land of Prester John. From there he journeyed to the regions of the moon, where St. John showed him many wonders, including some mysterious vials containing Orlando's lost wits. With that vial he flew down to Nubia, where, after proper ceremonies, he held the vial to Orlando's nose and the madman's senses returned to his head. Orlando and Astolpho led a Nubian army against Biserta and sacked that city.

Rogero, returning to the Saracen camp, quarreled with Mandricardo over the Tartar's right to wear the escutcheon of Trojan Hector, and Rogero killed Mandricardo in single combat. As dissension continued in the Saracen camp, Agramant withdrew his army from the walls of Paris. Then it was decided to settle the war by a battle between champions. Rinaldo was named defender of the Christians. Agramant chose Rogero as his bravest knight. But in the midst of the combat Agramant broke his oath and attacked Charlemagne's knights. Although he had promised Bradamant that he would accept Christianity after the combat, Rogero, seeing the rout of the Saracens, chose to follow his defeated king. After many adventures, separated from his comrades, he was cast away on a desert isle. There a holy man baptized him, and there he lived while Orlando, Oliver, and Brandimart fought with the Saracen kings—Agramant, Gradasso, Sobrino—and overcame them at Lipadusa. Agramant, Gradasso, and Brandimart were killed in the fight. Old Sobrino survived to turn Christian.

On his return voyage Orlando stopped at the desert isle and rescued Rogero. Great was the rejoicing when the knights learned that Rogero had been baptized. Rinaldo, who was among the paladins, gladly promised his sister to Rogero.

But Bradamant's parents wished her to marry Leo, son of the Emperor Constantine of Greece, and to force her to their will they shut her up in a strong castle. Separated from his love, Rogero decided that Leo should die. On his way to challenge his rival, he joined an army of Bulgarians and fought with them against Constantine's troops. When the Greeks fled, he pursued them until he found himself alone in enemy country. Captured, he was imprisoned by Theodora, the emperor's sister, whose son he had slain. When Leo, a courteous knight, heard what had happened, he rescued Rogero and hid him in his own house.

Word came that Bradamant had vowed to wed only a knight who could withstand her in combat. Leo, unaware of Rogero's true name but impressed by the Saracen's valor, asked him to be the prince's champion. Bradamant and Rogero fought, and Rogero was the victor. Then the sad knight went off into the forest alone. Leo found him there, almost dead from grief. When he learned who the strange knight really was, Leo gave up his own claim to Bradamant's hand and returned with Rogero to Charlemagne's court. There Bradamant and Rogero were reunited.

At a feast to celebrate their betrothal Rodomont appeared to accuse Rogero of apostasy, and Rogero slew the haughty Saracen in single combat. So the Christian knights cel-

ebrated the wedding of Rogero and Bradamant with all goodwill. There was even greater cause for rejoicing when ambassadors from Bulgaria appeared to announce that the grateful Bulgarians had named gallant Rogero as their king.

Critical Evaluation

Son of a minor Lombardian military official, Ludovico Ariosto was initially encouraged to study law but was finally allowed to pursue his preference for literature by studying the classics. However, as the eldest of ten children, he was obliged in his mid-twenties to undertake the management of family affairs upon the death of his father. Shortly thereafter, although it grated against his independent spirit, he accepted an appointment to serve Cardinal Ippolito d'Este, and some years later entered the service of the Cardinal's brother Alphonso, Duke of Ferrara, who assigned Ariosto, among other tasks, to a brief (1522–1525) governorship of a lawless mountain province in the central peninsula. These experiences, particularly the latter, did much to undermine Ariosto's health, yet he survived until his fifty-ninth year, when he succumbed to tuberculosis.

As for literary output, early translations of Plautus and Terence—from Latin to Italian—were followed by Ariosto's own Italian comedies, modeled after his classical mentors: *La Cassaria* (1508), *I Suppositi* (1509), *Il Negromante* (1520), *La Lena (1529),* and the unfinished *Gli Studenti*. In addition to his letters and some rather undistinguished Latin poems—posthumously edited for publication by his illegitimate son Virginio—Ariosto also wrote a number of pungent satires which rank not far behind his monumental *Orlando Furioso (Mad Orlando)* for literary merit.

Orlando Furiosos is Ariosto's complement to Boiardo's *Orlando Innamorato*, but Ariosto's version differs greatly from Boiardo's. In its first edition (1516), *Orlando Furioso* contained forty cantos; the final edition (1532) contained forty-six. In between those editions, much polishing, revising, and improving took place, for Ariosto's artistic instincts would not rest until he was satisfied with the nuance of each word, the sound of each rhyme, the beat of each metrical foot, and the synthesis of all into exactly the right action, character, or setting which he was striving to describe. Ariosto's dedication to artistic perfection was coupled with a certain independence of mind which enabled the poet to portray knightly adventures from a more realistic point of view than Boiardo's fabulary tale did. It is just these qualities which make *Orlando Furioso* superior to *Orlando Innamorato*.

One of Ariosto's motives in composing his epic was to glorify the noble house of Este, rulers of Ferrara and Modena, under whose patronage Ariosto served. Hence, the main plot line of *Orlando Furioso* deals with the

troubled romance between the pagan Saracen Rogero and the Christian French Bradamant. When at last they marry— having overcome many obstacles, not the least of which were Rogero's several infidelities—they found, so the story goes, the ancestral line of the Este family. One intriguing aspect of the Rogero-Bradamant union is its implication of marriage between pagan and Christian, despite the merely ceremonial ritual of Rogero's baptism and his killing of the Saracen Rodomont. But even more interesting is Bradamant's skill, resourcefulness, and courage as a warrior. Here is no clichéd helpless maiden in distress but a strong-minded and strong-armed knight who takes the initiative in finding her beloved Rogero, who takes part in wars, who defeats men in single combat, and who defiantly declares she will marry none but the man who can match her or best her in battle. Stereotypes crumble in the face of Rogero and Bradamant, singly or united. Stereotypes of epic behavior and stereotypes of real behavior alike cannot stand up under Ariosto's skillful characterization, for the poet—indeed, the artist—convinces us of the plausibility of Rogero's and Bradamant's actions. In doing so, Ariosto demonstrates his consummate facility for imaginatively transforming incredible magic into verisimilitude.

Orlando's story, although his name lends itself to the title of the poem, is secondary. To be sure, Orlando's quest for Angelica, launched by Boiardo, provides Ariosto's point of departure. But the thrust of Ariosto's title is that Orlando—under the dual stress of searching for Angelica and fulfilling his knightly obligations—has temporarily parted company with his rational faculties; Orlando is thus *Furioso*. In the pre-Freudian sixteenth century, Orlando's psychiatric problems are of far less import than the empirical and pragmatic problems of, say, Agramant and Charlemagne or Rogero and Bradamant. Thus, Orlando's anguish over Angelica's liaison with Medoro and his subsequent shedding of human appurtenances is merely a personal tragedy without cosmic or global significance. This epoch, the Renaissance, was a watershed in Western consciousness. For all of the emphasis that Renaissance thinkers placed on the individual, society was still paramount, as it was in the succeeding Age of Reason. Not until the Romantic Age did thoughtful people consider the plight of the individual seriously. Consequently, Orlando and his aberrations were simply not matters of overriding importance, and Ariosto quite properly played them down.

Moreover, since Ariosto was thoroughly a product of the Renaissance and reflected its values and priorities in his writings, this calculated demotion of Orlando's role in the epic signals another aspect of Renaissance attitudes. This aspect pertains to the Renaissance view of history, a view which differs considerably from the modern one. For Ariosto, like virtually all other Renaissance writers, felt no compelling obligation to strict historical accuracy as most modern readers understand that concept. Shakespeare thus wrote his Roman plays as Renaissance dramas, and Ariosto too signified his Renaissance bias in *Orlando Furioso*. Hence, Ariosto depicts the Saracen Rodomont as killing Isabella in a fit of drunkenness. But Saracens, as devout Moslems, were prohibited by the Koran from consuming any alcoholic

beverage. And certainly a Saracen Moslem—like Rodomont—battling Christian crusaders would honor the sumptuary proscriptions of the religion which he was defending. Ariosto also incorporates into his poem elements of his time, his place, and theology which have no precise precedents in eighth century Christianity or Islam. Thus Ariosto portrays, only half-skeptically, events influenced by Merlin, the seeress Melissa, a magic ring, a hippogryph, the giantess Eriphilia, the conjurer Atlantes, and various supernaturally endowed herdsmen and hermits, among others. This combination—a naïveté about historical factuality with an acceptance of the era's traditional credulity about magic—marks both Ariosto and *Orlando Furioso* as genuine products of the Renaissance.

ORPHEUS AND EURYDICE

Type of work: Classical myth
Source: Unknown
Type of plot: Allegory of grief
Time of plot: Remote antiquity
Locale: Thrace and the Underworld
First transcribed: Unknown

This story of immortal love and of the power and inexpressible beauty of music dates from antiquity and has continued to appear in literature and music throughout every age. Probably best known to modern readers are the famous operatic versions of the story, including those by Monteverdi, Haydn, and Gluck. As in many myths, scenes of lyrical beauty and spiritual insight are combined with scenes of savage cruelty in the story of Orpheus and Eurydice.

Principal Characters

Orpheus (ôr′fē·əs), the son of Apollo and the Muse Calliope. His father teaches him to play the lyre so that all nature stops to listen to his music. He goes to the Underworld to redeem the shade of his dead wife, Eurydice. His wish to have her returned to him is granted, providing he does not look back until he has left the Underworld. He does look back, however, and Eurydice disappears. Later Orpheus is killed by a group of Thracian maidens in a Bacchic frenzy. Upon his death he joins Eurydice in the Underworld.

Apollo (ə·pŏl′ō), a god and the father of Orpheus. He gives a lyre to his son and teaches him to play it beyond the power of any other mortal.

Eurydice (ū·rĭ′dĭ·sē), the mortal wife of Orpheus. Fleeing from a shepherd who desires her, she is bitten by a snake and dies. she is granted permission to return

to the world with Orpheus if he will not look back until they have left the Underworld. When he looks back, she disappears again.

Hades (hā′dēz) and **Proserpine** (Prō·sĕr′pə·nē), the King and Queen of the Underworld. Moved by Orpheus' music, they grant his request to take Eurydice back among the living, providing he does not look back at her while he is still in the Underworld.

Calliope (kə·līf′ə·pē), one of the Muses and Orpheus' mother.

Hymen (hī′mən), the god of marriage, who brings no happy omens to the wedding of Orpheus and Eurydice.

Tantalus (tăn′tə·ləs), **Ixion** (ĭk·sī′ən), **The Daughters of Danaus** (dăn′ĭ·əs), and **Sisyphus** (sĭs′ə·fəs), shades of the Underworld, who are spellbound by the beauty of Orpheus' music.

The Story

Orpheus, son of Apollo and the muse Calliope, grew up in Thrace, a land long noted for the purity and richness of its divine gift of song. His father presented him with a lyre and taught him to play it. So lovely were the songs of Orpheus that the wild beasts followed him when he played, and even the trees, the rocks, and the hills gathered near him. It was said that his music softened the composition of stones.

Orpheus charmed Eurydice with his music, but Hymen brought no happy omens to their wedding. His torch smoked so that tears came to their eyes. Passionately in love with his wife, Orpheus became mad with grief when Eurydice died. Fleeing from a shepherd who desired her, she had stepped upon a snake and died from its bite.

Heartbroken, Orpheus wandered over the hills composing and singing melancholy songs of memory for the lost Eurydice. Finally he descended into the Underworld and made his way past the sentries by means of his music. Approaching the throne of Proserpine and Hades, he sang

a lovely song in which he said love had brought him to the Underworld. He complained that Eurydice had been taken from him before her time and if they would not release her, he would not leave Hades. Proserpine and Hades could not resist his pleas. They agreed to set Eurydice free if Orpheus would promise not to look upon her until they should safely reach the Upperworld.

The music of Orpheus was so tender that even the ghosts shed tears. Tantalus forgot his search for water; Ixion's wheel stopped; the vulture stopped feeding on the giant's liver; the daughters of Danaus stopped drawing water; and Sisyphus himself stopped to listen. Tears streamed from the eyes of the Furies. Eurydice then appeared, limping. The two walked the long and dismal passageway to the Upperworld, and Orpheus did not look back toward Eurydice. At last, forgetting his vow, he turned, but as they reached out their arms to embrace Eurydice disappeared.

Orpheus tried to follow her, but the stern ferryman

refused him passage across the River Styx. Declining food and drink, he sat by the River Strymon and sang his twice-felt grief.

As he sang his melancholy songs, so sad that oaks moved and tigers grieved, a group of Thracian maidens attempted to console him, but he repulsed them. One day, while they were observing the sacred rites of Bacchus, they began to stone him. At first, the stones fell without harm when they came within the sound of the lyre. As the frenzy of the maidens increased, however, their shouting drowned out the notes of the lyre so that it no longer protected Orpheus. Soon he was covered with blood.

Then the savage women tore his limbs from his body and hurled his head and his lyre into the river. Both continued singing sad songs as they floated downstream. The fragments of Orpheus' body were buried at Libretha, and it is said that nightingales sang more sweetly over his grave than in any other part of Greece. Jupiter made his lyre a constellation of stars in the heavens. Orpheus joined Eurydice in the Underworld, and there, happy at last, they wandered through the fields together.

Critical Evaluation

The longest and most familiar version of this myth is found in Ovid's *Metamorphoses* (c. A.D. 8), and Ovid may well have been inspired by Vergil's less florid account, carefully placed at the dramatic end of his *Georgics* (c. 37–29 B.C.). In Vergil's work, Eurydice is bitten by a snake as she flees the lustful rustic deity, Aristaeus. There, the Orpheus-Eurydice theme was most appropriate to Vergil's subject of rebirth and fruitfulness through sacrifice and discipline; indeed, this myth, perhaps more than any other, illustrates that man can never achieve victory over death without divine aid and that human immortality can be gained only through art.

Through extraordinary powers of music, Orpheus was able to perform unnatural feats, such as moving beasts, trees, even rocks, and ultimately obtaining a rare favor from the rulers of the Dead; yet his lack of discipline, that is, his inability to obey the command of Proserpine and Hades to the letter, resulted in his failure to achieve victory over death for Eurydice. (Even if he had won, however, one must assume that death would have come again for them both.) Nevertheless, there is a hopeful side to the myth: Eventually the two lovers are permanently united in death. This may be satisfying romantically, but it is less important than Orpheus' literary legacy, symbolized by his severed head continuing to sing his beloved's name, harmoniously echoed by sympathetic nature. Orpheus, therefore, has achieved ultimate victory over death: His art has given him the life after death he sought for Eurydice. This is further symbolized in his burial by the Muses near Olympus, in Apollo's petrifying his head on Lesbos (an island renowned for its poets), and finally in the transformation of Orpheus' lyre into a constellation. Certainly Vergil, if not Ovid, had this victory in mind, since their versions broke with the tradition in which Orpheus succeeded in rescuing Eurydice from death.

Both parts of the original myth—the retrieval of Eurydice and the death of Orpheus—probably originated in preclassical poetry, perhaps in cultic Orphism. Orpheus himself was believed to be the earliest of poets, along with Musaeus (his son), Homer, and Hesiod. He is given a place among Jason's Argonauts. His remote Thracian origins lend mystery to his myth, and no doubt this had a bearing on the relatively restricted popularity of Orphism, which seems to have been more philosophy than religion. The aim of the Orphics was to lead a life of purity and purification, so that eventually the successively reincarnated soul, having purged itself of the Titanic (or earthly) element, would be pure spirit divinely born of Zeus through his son Dionysus and thus would be released from the cycle, eternally to wander the Elysian fields.

Exactly how Orpheus is connected with this cult is unclear and indeed confusing. In Ovid's version Orpheus refuses to love any other woman; furthermore, he turns his attention to boys, which is why the Thracian women murder him. Yet, these women were Bacchants, that is, Dionysian orgiasts, and in other versions Dionysus himself directs them to kill Orpheus because the bard, in his devotion to Apollo the sun-god, has prevented the wine-god's acceptance in Thrace. On the other hand, the oracle established in Lesbos in honor of Orpheus was suppressed by Apollo. If Orpheus was the poet-priest-prophet of Apollo who refused the frenzy of Dionysus, it may well be that he became the cultic model whose sacrifice ironically inspired others to accept Dionysus. Orphic mysteries seem to have resembled the orgies of Dionysus, but whereas the Dionysiac is striving for that momentary ecstatic union with the god, the Orphic is striving for eternal peace.

The descent of Orpheus into the Underworld obviously symbolizes an Orphic's death, which will be followed by a new life, repeated until the cycle is complete. Other symbolic interpretations aside, the descent and return would be frightening were they not so entertaining. Having conducted a whirlwind tour of the Underworld, including introductions to the king and queen, Ovid slowly leads readers back along the murky upward path until suddenly Orpheus' concern for Eurydice outstrips his easy promise. The pathos of this second separation is intensified by its swiftness and by Orpheus' inability even to regain passage across the Styx, much less to see or hear his love again.

Few love stories from classical antiquity have made such an impression on succeeding ages. This myth became the subject of the first secular drama in vernacular, *Orfeo* (1480; *Orpheus*), composed in the era of the Medicis by Angelo Poliziano (Politian). In 1600, the first Italian opera, *Euridice*, was composed. Christoph Gluck's *Orfeo ed Eurydice* (1762) is considered the first "modern" opera for its balance of music and tragic drama, although a happy ending was supplied: Amore (Love) brings Euridice back to prevent Orfeo's suicide. Twentieth century playwrights have adapted the story to their own settings and purposes, among them, Jean Anouilh and Tennessee Williams. Composers such as Jacques Offenbach, Darius Milhaud, and Igor Stravinsky have borrowed the theme. In film, Vinicius de Moraes' Brazilian masterpiece, *Black Orpheus* (1957), takes place in Rio de Janeiro during Carnival and deftly uses the primitive color of the celebration to heighten the frenzy of Orpheus' search for his love.

OTHELLO

Type of work: Drama
Author: William Shakespeare (1564–1616)
Type of plot: Romantic tragedy
Time of plot: Early sixteenth century
Locale: Venice and Cyprus
First presented: 1604

The Tragedy of Othello: The Moor of Venice is concerned with the nature of good and evil and the struggle between the two forces in the human soul. Alone of the four great tragedies, this play is weakly motivated in the sense that the obsessive hatred of the villain Iago, perhaps the most sadistic and consummately evil character in any literature, is not sufficiently explained by his having been passed over for a promotion in Othello's army. Despite its tragic ending, Othello displays some optimism in its depiction of the triumph of love over hate and of the love of one woman for another, which is instrumental in bringing the villain to poetic justice.

Principal Characters

Othello (ō·thĕl'ō), a Moorish general in the service of Venice. A romantic and heroic warrior with a frank and honest nature, he has a weakness which makes him vulnerable to Iago's diabolic temptation. He becomes furiously jealous of his innocent wife and his loyal lieutenant. His judgment decays, and he connives with Iago to have his lieutenant murdered. Finally he decides to execute his wife with his own hands. After killing her, he learns of her innocence, and he judges and executes himself.

Iago (ē·ä'gō), Othello's ancient (ensign). A satirical malcontent, he is envious of the appointment of Michael Cassio to the position of Othello's lieutenant. He at least pretends to suspect his wife Emilia of having an illicit affair with the Moor. A demi-devil, as Othello calls him, he destroys Othello, Desdemona, Roderigo, his own wife, and himself. He is Shakespeare's most consummate villain, perhaps sketched in Aaron the Moor in *Titus Andronicus,* Richard of Gloucester in *Henry VI* and *Richard III,* and Don John in *Much Ado about Nothing;* and he is echoed in Edmund in *King Lear* and Iachimo in *Cymbeline.* He contains strong elements of the Devil and the Vice in the medieval morality plays.

Desdemona (dĕz·dē·mō'nə), daughter of Brabantio and wife of Othello. An idealistic, romantic girl, she gives her love completely to her warrior husband. In her fear and shock at his violent behavior, she lies to him about her lost handkerchief, thus convincing him of her guilt. Even when she is dying, she tries to protect him from her kinsmen. One scholar has called her a touchstone in the play; each character can be judged by his attitude toward her.

Emilia (ē·mĭl'ĭ·ə), Iago's plainspoken wife. Intensely loyal to her mistress, Desdemona, she is certain that some malicious villain has belied her to the Moor. She does not suspect that her husband is that villain until too late

to save her mistress. She is unwittingly the cause of Desdemona's death; when she finds the lost handkerchief and gives it to Iago, he uses it to inflame the Moor's insane jealousy. Emilia grows in stature throughout the play and reaches tragic dignity when she refuses to remain silent about Iago's villainy, even though her speaking the truth costs her her life. Her dying words, clearing Desdemona of infidelity, drive Othello to his self-inflicted death.

Michael Cassio (kăs'ĭ·ō), Othello's lieutenant. Devoted to his commander and Desdemona, he is impervious to Iago's temptations where either is concerned. He is, however, given to loose living, and his behavior when discussing Bianca with Iago fires Othello's suspicions, after Iago has made Othello believe they are discussing Desdemona. Cassio's drinking on duty and becoming involved in a brawl lead to his replacement by Iago. He escapes the plot of Iago and Othello to murder him, and he succeeds Othello as Governor of Cyprus.

Brabantio (bra·băn'shĭ·ō), a Venetian senator. Infuriated by his daughter's elopement with the Moor, he appeals to the senate to recover her. Losing his appeal, he publicly casts her off and warns Othello that a daughter who deceives her father may well be a wife who deceives her husband. This warning plants a small seed of uncertainty in Othello's heart, which Iago waters diligently. Brabantio dies brokenhearted at losing Desdemona and does not learn of her horrible death.

Roderigo (rŏd·ə·rē'gō), a young Venetian suitor of Desdemona. The gullible victim of Iago, who promises him Desdemona's person, he aids in bringing about the catastrophe and earns a well-deserved violent death, ironically inflicted by Iago, whose cat's-paw he is. The degradation of Roderigo is in striking contrast to the growth of Cassio. Iago, who makes use of Roderigo, has profound contempt for him.

Bianca (be·ăn'kə), a courtesan in Cyprus. Cassio gives

her Desdemona's handkerchief, which Iago has planted in his chambers. She thus serves doubly in rousing Othello's fury.

Montano (mŏn·tä′nō), former Governor of Cyprus. He and Cassio quarrel in their cups (by Iago's machinations), and Montano is seriously wounded. This event causes Cassio's removal. Montano recovers and aids in apprehending Iago when his villainy is revealed.

Gratiano (grä·shĭ·ä′nō, grä·tyä′nō), the brother of

Brabantio. He and Lodovico come to Cyprus from Venice and aid in restoring order and destroying Iago.

Lodovico (lō·dō·vē′kō), a kinsman of Brabantio. As the man of most authority from Venice, he ends the play after appointing Cassio Governor of Cyprus to succeed the Othello.

The Clown, a servant of Othello. Among Shakespeare's clowns he has perhaps the weakest and briefest role.

The Story

Iago, an ensign serving under Othello, Moorish commander of the armed forces of Venice, was passed over in promotion, Othello having chosen Cassio to be his chief of staff. In revenge, Iago and his follower, Roderigo, aroused from his sleep Brabantio, senator of Venice, to tell him that his daughter Desdemona had stolen away and married Othello. Brabantio, incensed that his daughter would marry a Moor, led his serving-men to Othello's quarters.

Meanwhile, the Duke of Venice had learned that armed Turkish galleys were preparing to attack the island of Cyprus, and in this emergency he had summoned Othello to the senate chambers. Brabantio and Othello met in the streets, but postponed any violence in the national interest. Othello, upon arriving at the senate, was commanded by the duke to lead the Venetian forces to Cyprus. Then Brabantio told the duke that Othello had beguiled his daughter into marriage without her father's consent. When Brabantio asked the duke for redress, Othello vigorously defended his honor and reputation, and he was seconded by Desdemona, who appeared during the proceedings. Othello, cleared of all suspicion, prepared to sail for Cyprus immediately. For the moment, he placed Desdemona in the care of Iago, with Iago's wife, Emilia, to be attendant upon her during the voyage to Cyprus.

A great storm destroyed the Turkish fleet and scattered the Venetians. One by one the ships under Othello's command put in to Cyprus until all were safely ashore and Othello and Desdemona were once again united. Still vowing revenge, Iago told Roderigo that Desdemona was in love with Cassio. Roderigo, himself in love with Desdemona, was promised all of his desires by Iago if he would engage Cassio, who did not know him, in a personal brawl while Cassio was officer of the guard.

Othello declared the night dedicated to celebrating the destruction of the enemy, but he cautioned Cassio to keep a careful watch on Venetian troops in the city. Iago talked Cassio into drinking too much, so that when the lieutenant was provoked later by Roderigo, Cassio lost control of himself and engaged Roderigo. Cries of riot and mutiny spread through the streets. Othello, aroused by the commotion, demoted Cassio for permitting a fight to start. Cassio, his reputation all but ruined, welcomed Iago's

promise to secure Desdemona's goodwill and through her have Othello restore Cassio's rank.

Cassio impatiently importuned Iago to arrange a meeting between him and Desdemona. While Cassio and Desdemona were talking, Iago brought Othello into view of the pair and spoke vague innuendoes to his commander. Afterward Iago would, from time to time, ask questions of Othello in such manner that he led Othello to believe that there may have been some intimacy between Cassio and Desdemona before Desdemona had married him. These seeds of jealousy having been sown, Othello began to doubt the honesty of his wife.

When Othello complained to Desdemona of a headache, she offered to bind his head with the handkerchief which had been Othello's first gift to her. She dropped the handkerchief, inadvertently, and Emilia picked it up. Iago, seeing an opportunity to further his scheme, took the handkerchief from his wife and hid it later in Cassio's room. When Othello asked Iago for proof that Desdemona was untrue to him, threatening his life if he could not produce any evidence, Iago said that he had slept in Cassio's room and had heard Cassio speak sweet words in his sleep to Desdemona. He reminded Othello of the handkerchief and said that he had seen Cassio wipe his beard that day with the very handkerchief. Othello, completely overcome by passion, vowed revenge. He ordered Iago to kill Cassio, and he appointed the ensign his new lieutenant.

Othello asked Desdemona to account for the loss of the handkerchief, but she was unable to explain its disappearance. She was mystified by Othello's shortness of speech and his dark moods.

Iago continued to work his treachery on Othello to the extent that the Moor fell into fits resembling epilepsy. He goaded Othello by every possible means into mad rages of jealousy. In the presence of an envoy from Venice, Othello struck Desdemona, to the consternation of all except Iago. Emilia swore to the honesty of her mistress, but Othello, in his madness, could no longer believe anything good of Desdemona, and he reviled and insulted her with harsh words.

One night Othello ordered Desdemona to dismiss her attendant and to go to bed immediately. That same night

Iago persuaded Roderigo to waylay Cassio. When Roderigo was wounded by Cassio, Iago, who had been standing nearby, stabbed Cassio. In the scuffle Iago stabbed Roderigo to death as well, so as to be rid of his dupe. Then a strumpet friend of Cassio came upon the scene of the killing and revealed to the assembled crowd her relationship with Cassio. Although Cassio was not dead, Iago hoped to use this woman to defame Cassio beyond all hope of regaining his former reputation. Pretending friendship, he assisted the wounded Cassio to return to Othello's house. They were accompanied by Venetian noblemen who had gathered after the fight.

Othello, meanwhile, entered his wife's bedchamber and smothered her, after telling her, mistakenly, that Cassio had confessed his love for her and had been killed. Then Emilia entered the bedchamber and reported that Roderigo had been killed, but not Cassio. This infor-mation was made doubly bitter for Othello his murder of his wife. Othello told Emilia that he had learned of Desdemona's guilt from Iago. Emilia could not believe that Iago had made such charges.

When Iago and other Venetians arrived at Othello's house, Emilio asked Iago to refute Othello's statement. Then the great wickedness of Iago came to light and Othello learned how the handkerchief had come into Cassio's possession. When Emilia gave further proof of her husband's villainy, Iago stabbed her. Othello lunged at Iago and managed to wound him before the Venetian gentlemen could seize the Moor. Emilia died, still protesting the innocence of Desdemona. Mad with grief, Othello plunged a dagger into his own heart. The Venetian envoy promised that Iago would be tortured to death at the hand of the governor-general of Cyprus.

Critical Evaluation

Although *Othello* has frequently been praised as Shakespeare's most unified tragedy, uncluttered with subplots, many critics have found the central character to be the most unheroic of Shakespeare's heroes. Some have found him stupid beyond redemption; others have described him as a passionate being overwhelmed by powerful emotion; still others have found him self-pitying and insensitive to the enormity of his actions. But all of these denigrations pale before the excitement and sympathy generated in the action of the play for the noble Moor.

Othello is an exotic. It is unlikely that Shakespeare would have cared whether or not Othello was black. More to the point is the fact that he is a foreigner from a fascinating and mysterious land. Certainly he is a passionate man, but he is not devoid of sensitivity. Rather, his problem is that he is thrust into the sophisticated and highly cultivated context of Renaissance Italy, a land which had a reputation in Shakespeare's England for connivance and intrigue. If anything, Othello is natural man confronted with the machinations and contrivances of a super-civilized society. His instincts are to be loving and trusting, but he is cast into a society where these natural virtues make one extremely vulnerable

The prime source of that vulnerability is personified in the figure of Iago, perhaps Shakespeare's consummate villain. Iago is so evil, by nature, that he does not even need any motivation for his antagonism toward Othello. He has been passed over for promotion, but that is clearly a pretext for a malignant nature whose hatred for Othello needs no specific grounds. It is Othello, with his candor, his openness, his spontaneous and generous love, that Iago finds offensive. His suggestion that Othello has seduced his wife is an even flimsier fabrication to cover the essential corruption of his nature.

Iago sees other human beings only as victims or tools. He is the classic Renaissance atheist—an intelligent man, beyond moral scruple, who finds pleasure in the corruption of the virtuous and the abuse of the pliable. That he brings himself into danger is of no consequence, because, relying on wit, he believes that all can be duped and destroyed—and there is no further purpose to his life. For such a manipulator, Othello, a good man out of his cultural element, is the perfect target.

More so than in any other Shakespearean play, one character, Iago, is the stage manager of the whole action. Once he sets out to destroy Othello, he proceeds by plot and by innuendo to achieve his goal. He tells others just what he wishes them to know, sets one character against another, and develops an elaborate web of circumstantial evidence to dupe the vulnerable Moor. Edgar Stoll has argued that the extraordinary success of Iago in convincing other characters of his fabrications is simply a matter of the conventional ability of the Renaissance villain. Yet, there is more to the conflict than Iago's abilities, conventional or natural, for Othello is his perfect prey.

Othello bases his opinions and his human relationships on intuition rather than reason. His courtship with Desdemona is brief and his devotion absolute. His trust of his comrades, including Iago, is complete. It is not simply that Iago is universally believed. Ironically, he is able to fool everyone about everything except on the subject of Desdemona's chastity. On that subject it is only Othello that he is able to deceive. Roderigo, Cassio, and Emilia all reject Iago's allegations that Desdemona has been unfaithful. Only Othello is deceived, and he because Iago is able to make him play the game with unfamiliar rules.

Iago entices Othello to use Venetian criteria of truth rather than the intuition on which he should rely. Iago plants doubts in Othello's mind, but his decisive success comes when he gets Othello to demand "ocular proof." Although it seems that Othello is demanding conclusive evidence before jumping to the conclusion that his wife has been unfaithful, it is more important that he has accepted Iago's idea of concrete evidence. From that point on, it is easy for Iago to falsify evidence and create appearances that will lead to erroneous judgments. To be fair, Othello does not easily allow his jealousy to overpower his better judgment. Certainly, he gives vent to violent emotions in his rantings and his fits, but these are the result of his acceptance of what seems indisputable proof, documentary evidence. It takes a long time, and many falsifications, before Othello finally abandons his intuitive perception of the truth of his domestic situation. As Othello himself recognizes, he is not quick to anger, but, once angered, his natural passion takes over. Iago's contrivances eventually loose that force.

The crime that Othello commits is made to appear all the more heinous because of the extreme loyalty of his wife. It is not that she is an innocent. Her conversation reflects that she is a sophisticate, but there is no question of her total fidelity to her husband. The moral horror of the murder is intensified by the contrast between our perception of the extreme virtue of the victim with Othello's perception of himself as an instrument of justice. His chilling conviction reminds us of the essential probity of a man deranged by confrontation with an evil he cannot comprehend.

Some critics, such as T. S. Eliot, have argued that Othello never comes to an understanding of the gravity of his crime—that he realizes his error, but consoles himself in his final speech with cheering reminders of his own virtue. But that does not seem consistent with the valiant and honest military character who has thus far been depicted. Othello may have been grossly deceived, and he may be responsible for not clinging to the truth of his mutual love with Desemona, but, in his final speech, he does seem to face up to his error with the same passion that had followed his earlier misconception. As he had believed that his murder of Desdemona was divine retribution, he believes that his suicide is a just act. His passionate nature believes it is meting out justice for the earlier transgression. We are promised that Iago will be tortured unto death, but Shakespeare dismisses Iago's punishment in order to focus on Othello's final act of expiation.

"THE OVERCOAT"

Type of work: Story
Author: Nikolai Gogol (1809–1852)
Type of plot: Social criticism
Time of plot: Early nineteenth century
Locale: St. Petersburg, Russia
First published: "Shinel," 1842 (English translation, 1923)

Having worked briefly as a civil servant, Gogol had no fondness for bureaucratic officialdom, and in his long tale he uses the wretched, ill-paid government clerk, Akakii Akakiievich Bashmachkin, to dramatize his view of the system and its effects on people. Gogol, often considered the father of nineteenth century Russian realism, achieves realistic description that avoids both bitterness and pathos.

Principal Characters

Akakii Akakiievich Bashmachkin (ä·kä′kĭy ä·kä′kĭy·ĕ·vĭch bäsh·mä′hĭn), a humble, poorly paid, aging government clerk, short, pock-marked, with reddish, balding hair, dim and bleary eyes, and wrinkled cheeks. Possessing a high-sounding government grade of perpetual titular councilor, he is a mere copyist of documents. He loves his work, which he does with neat and painstaking thoroughness, and he even takes some of it home to do at night. Badly needing an overcoat to replace his old one, which the tailor refuses to repair, he plans to have a new one made, and for several months he lives in happy anticipation of getting it. When he wears it to the office he is pleased over the attention it gains him from his fellow clerks; but he is desolated when it is stolen after a party. Stammering and frightened by the domineering manner of a certain important personage to whom he applies for help in finding his coat, he goes home in a snowstorm, becomes ill, and dies in delirium. His ghost, after snatching overcoats from various people, finds the person of consequence wearing a fine overcoat and seizes it. Apparently the garment is a perfect fit, for Akakii never reappears to seize more coats.

Petrovich (pĕt·rō′vĭch), a one-eyed, pock-marked tailor given to heavy drinking, quoting high prices to his clients, and slyly watching to see what effects he has achieved.

A Certain Important Personage, a bureaucrat recently promoted to a position of consequence. With his equals he is pleasant, gentlemanly, and obliging, but with those below him he is reticent, rude, and very conscious of his superiority. Strict and a stickler for form, he tyrannizes his subordinates. The ghost of Akakii steals his overcoat.

The Story

In one of the bureaus of the government, there was a clerk named Akakii Akakiievich Bashmachkin. He was a short, pockmarked man with dim, watery eyes and reddish hair beginning to show spots of baldness. His grade in the service was that of perpetual titular councilor, a resounding title for his humble clerkship.

He had been in the bureau for so many years that no one remembered when he had entered it or who had appointed him to the post. Directors and other officials came and went, but Akakii Akakiievich was always to be seen in the same place, in the same position, doing the same work, which was the copying of documents. No one ever treated him with respect. His superiors regarded him with disdain; his fellow clerks made him the butt of their rude jokes and horseplay.

Akakii Akakiievich lived only for his work, without thought for pleasure or his dress. His frock coat was no longer the prescribed green but a faded rusty color. Usu-ally it had sticking to it wisps of hay or thread or bits of litter someone had thrown into the street as he was passing by, for he walked to and from work in complete oblivion of his surroundings. Reaching home, he would gulp his cabbage soup and perhaps a bit of beef, in a hurry to begin transcribing papers he had brought with him from the office. His labors finished, he would go to bed. Such was the life of Akakii Akakiievich, satisfied with his pittance of four hundred rubles a year.

Even clerks on four hundred a year, however, must protect themselves against the harsh cold of northern winters. Akakii Akakiievich owned an overcoat so old and threadbare that over the back and shoulders one could see through the material to the torn lining beneath. At last he decided to take it to Petrovich, a tailor who did a large business repairing the garments of petty bureaucrats. Petrovich shook his head over the worn overcoat and announced that it was beyond mending, fit only for footcloths. For one hundred and fifty rubles, he said, he would make Akakii Akakiievich a new overcoat, but he would not touch the old one.

When he left the tailor's shop, the clerk was in a sad predicament: He had no money for an overcoat and little prospect of raising so large a sum. Walking blindly down the street, he failed to notice the sooty chimney sweep who jostled him, blacking one shoulder, or the lime that fell on him from a building under construction. The next Sunday he went to see Petrovich again and begged the tailor to mend his old garment. The tailor surlily refused. Then Akakii Akakiievich realized that he must yield to the inevitable. He knew that Petrovich would do the work for eighty rubles. Half of that amount he could pay with money he had saved, one kopeck at a time, over a period of years. Perhaps in another year he could put aside a like amount by doing without tea and candles at night and by walking as carefully as possible to save his shoe leather. He began that very day to go without the small comforts he had previously allowed himself.

In the next year Akakii Akakiievich had some unexpected luck when he received a holiday bonus of sixty rubles instead of the expected forty which he had already budgeted for other necessities. With the extra twenty rubles and his meager savings, he and Petrovich bought the cloth for the new overcoat—good, durable stuff with calico for the lining and catskin for the collar. After some haggling it was decided that Petrovich was to get twelve rubles for his labor.

At last the overcoat was finished. Petrovich delivered it early one morning, and opportunely, for the season of hard frosts had already begun. Akakii Akakiievich wore the garment triumphantly to work. Hearing of his new finery, the other clerks ran into the vestibule to inspect it. Some suggested that the owner ought to give a party to celebrate the event. Akakii Akakiievich hesitated but was saved from embarrassment when a minor official invited the clerks, including Akakii, to drink tea with him that evening.

Wrapped in his warm coat, Akakii Akakiievich started off to the party. It had been years since he had walked out at night, and he enjoyed the novelty of seeing the strollers on the streets and looking into lighted shop windows.

The hour was past midnight when he left the party; the streets were deserted. His way took him into a des- olate square, with only the flickering light of a police sentry box visible in the distance. Suddenly two strangers confronted him and with threats of violence snatched off his overcoat. When he came to himself, in the snowbank where they had kicked him, the clerk ran to the policeman's box to denounce the thieves. The policeman merely told him to report the theft to the district inspector the next morning. Almost out of his mind with worry, Akakii Akakiievich ran all the way home.

His landlady advised him not to go to the police but to lay the matter before a commissioner whom she knew. That official gave him little satisfaction. The next day his fellow clerks took up a collection for him, but the amount was so small that they decided to give him advice instead. They told him to go to a certain important personage who would speed up the efforts of the police. Finally Akakii Akakiievich secured an interview, but the very important person was so outraged by the clerk's unimportance that he never gave the caller an opportunity to explain his errand. Akakii Akakiievich went home through a blizzard, which gave him a quinsy requiring bed rest. After several days of delirium, in which he babbled about his lost overcoat and a certain important person, he died. A few days later another clerk sat in his place and began doing the same work at the bureau.

Before long rumors began to spread through the city that the ghost of a government clerk seeking a stolen overcoat had been seen near Kalinkin Bridge. One night a clerk from the bureau saw him and almost died of fright. After Akakii Akakiievich began stripping overcoats from passersby, the police were ordered to capture the dead man. Once the police came near arresting him, but the ghost vanished so miraculously that thereafter the police were afraid to lay hands on any malefactors, living or dead.

One night, after a sociable evening, a certain important personage was on his way to visit a lady friend about whom his wife knew nothing. As he relaxed comfortably in his sleigh, he felt a firm grip on his collar. Turning, he found himself eye to eye with a wan Akakii Akakiievich. In his fright he threw off his overcoat and ordered his coachman to drive him home at once. The ghost of Akakii Akakiievich must have liked the important person's warm greatcoat: From that time on he never again molested passersby or snatched away their overcoats.

Critical Evaluation

With "The Diary of a Madman" (1835) and "The Nose" (1836), "The Overcoat" forms Gogol's St. Petersburg cycle of stories. They are united in four important ways. The setting is the depressing crowdedness of St. Petersburg; the protagonist of each tale is a petty bureaucrat in government service; the common theme is the importance of appearance in determining social status; and the distinguishing method is fantasy. All the stories reflect Gogol's perception that modern urban life is inhospitable to the individual. The city's size, complexity, and impersonality disorder the individual and destroy the sense of community. The St. Petersburg stories are the antithesis of Gogol's stories of Ukranian life, *Evenings on a Farm*, in which lords and serfs inhabit a stable, integrated environment.

Gogol's sources for "The Overcoat" indicate that he intended the tale as a parable of city life. He merged two stories of contemporary events in St. Petersburg with a sixteenth century hagiographical account. The idea of a clerk whose mental and physical health depends upon a valued possession came from an anecdote Gogol heard: A young clerk lost the shotgun he had scrimped to purchase and was roused from his grief only when friends purchased him another. The idea of a ghost stalking a certain important personage originated in newspaper accounts from the early 1830s of two nobles robbed on the street. The name for his protagonist Gogol apparently took from the legend of St. Akaky, who suffered humiliation, without protest, from his monastic superior till he died. His memory taught his haughty tormentor the virtue of humility.

Akakii Akakiievich experiences all the humiliation the complex, impersonal capital city can offer. He is a ninth-class clerk in a rigid bureaucracy, a pen-pusher doomed to run forever like one of Dante's sinners in the same circle of Hell. At the government office, even porters ignore him, and other copyists tease him. His pay is a pittance of four hundred rubles a month, insufficient to buy him—without sacrifice—a decent coat against the cold. Petrovich the tailor drives a hard bargain for a new overcoat with the poor clerk, reducing the price from exorbitant to merely inflated after Akakii beseeches him repeatedly. The new coat wins Akakii momentary respect from his fellow clerks and an invitation to a party, where the ninth-class clerk feels ill at ease amid the artificial camaraderie. The thieves who rob Akakii of his coat beat him painfully. A watchman who witnesses the mugging is no help: He pretends the hulking hoodlums are Akakii's playful friends. When Akakii reports the crime to the police commissioner, he is questioned about being out late rather than about the crime. Seeking the aid of a certain important personage, Akakii is kept waiting, though the personage actually has nothing to do, for decorum demands that clerks wait a sufficient time to see an important personage. During the interview the important personage shows no interest in the overcoat but does berate Akakii for violating proper bureaucratic channels. Frightened into a faint by the official's manner, the clerk is carried to his bed. In a few days, a fever brings death to Akakii, who murmurs "Your Excellency" at the last, as if he needed a superior's permission to die.

For exposing the callousness of czarist bureaucracy and exhibiting sympathy for an underdog, Gogol maintains a high reputation among modern Soviet critics. Yet many nineteenth century writers who exposed the poverty and oppression accompanying urbanization have slipped into obscurity, while Gogol remains actively read. What distinguishes Gogol is not so much his theme as his technique.

"The Overcoat" delights because of its narrative complexity. It is a tale of humiliation, but sympathy is not the only emotion the narrator conjures up. In fact, Gogol keeps the reader riveted by skillful changes of pace and perspective. Like a juggler who makes his repetitive feat more interesting by changing the objects he tosses, Gogol manipulates several perspectives in rapid succession.

The first juggling occurs after only four words. Using a standard opening, "Once in a department . . . ," the narrator immediately digresses into an argument with himself: Should he name the department? He can cite reasons to do so but also knows that bureaucracies are jealous of one another. Rather than cause trouble, the narrator decides not to mention the specific department.

As the narrator tells of Akakii's birth, he clearly has little sympathy for the protagonist, like the parents who name him after his father out of sheer boredom. The narrator does sympathize with Akakii because of the way his fellow clerks treat him, yet he confesses that Akakii deserves some of the blame. Though he copies documents well enough, he panics when asked to originate one. For relaxation he copies over that day's documents that he especially liked. Genetics and environment conspire to make Akakii the quintessential ninth-class clerk.

The narrator's introduction of the tailor Petrovich begins with a comic description, because this is the literary fashion of the day, The description is distinctive since it comes from Akakii's point of view. The copyist notices unusual things: the tailor's calloused big toe, his snuffbox on the table, his penchant for routinely insulting Germans. Through the description, the reader senses Akakii's anxiety that Petrovich controls his fate. Akakii faces a dilemma; he cannot go without a new overcoat, but he cannot afford one without sacrificing his few comforts. When the overcoat is finally finished, the narrative viewpoint switches to observers of the new garment: Petrovich and the other clerks. They admire the coat even more perhaps than Akakii does.

Once Akakii leaves the party, events are again recorded as his impressions. Tipsy with champagne, Akakii senses everything in a heightened fashion. A prostitute flashes past him like "a streak of lightning." A large open square possesses a "sinister emptiness." The hoodlum who robs him has a fist "as big as the clerk's head."

Akakii's visits to the commissioner and the certain important personage reflect their outlooks. The narrator records the pleasure they receive from making Akakii wait, putting him in his place, and observing his growing agitation. His despair is the measure of their importance: Even receptionists grow in stature when trembling ninth-class clerks approach obsequiously. Akakii is a completely insignificant person in this world. It is a reality of modern urban life, not a cause for lament. Yet the certain important personage later feels a twinge of regret that he dismissed the clerk so abruptly. That twinge grows into guilt that causes the certain important personage to believe that the man who steals his coat is Akakii's ghost. There is no ghost, of course, except in a moral sense.

By switching perspectives subtly and without formal transitions, Gogol enables the reader to perceive St. Petersburg as a cruel complex, but one constructed out of human hopes, fears, kindnesses, and humiliations. Akakii's story is pathetic, but it is also laughable. "The Overcoat" is not simply either sentimental or satirical; it hangs somewhere in between. The narrator controls the swing of the reader's reactions, never allowing them to stray too far to one side or to linger at one point. The constant motion creates a complex of reactions appropriate to the complex of the modern city.

Like other nineteenth century writers—for example, James Hogg and Edgar Allan Poe—Gogol explores how the psychological state of the perceiver influences the construct of reality. Gogol's genius is the ability to move from the storyteller's traditional "objective" perceptions to altered perceptions of characters without readers being conscious of the change until they are already entrapped.

PARADISE LOST

Type of work: Poem
Author: John Milton (1608–1674)
Type of plot: Epic
Time of plot: The Beginning
Locale: Heaven, Hell, and Earth
First published: 1667

Considered the greatest epic in modern literature, Milton's poem in twelve books tells of man's happiness in the Garden of Eden and of his first disobedience; within this story, the angel Raphael tells Adam the history of Satan and his band of rebellious angels. The poem ends with the expulsion from Paradise and a vision of mankind's coming misery, but Michael also offers the future hope of the Redeemer who will one day bring salvation to mankind.

Principal Characters

Adam, the first man and representative of mankind. Though gifted with reason and restraint, he allows an excessively passionate tenderness for Eve to blind him. Forewarned by the archangel Raphael of danger from Satan, he nevertheless yields to Eve's entreaty that she alone be trusted. When he learns that she has fallen, he chooses to join her rather than turn from her. His first reaction after his own fall is to rebuke and blame her for his own sin. After falling into almost suicidal despair, he repents, and when the archangel Michael foretells the future redemption of mankind by Christ, he accepts his fate with gratitude.

Eve, the first woman and representative of womanhood. Beautiful, gentle, and submissive, she holds Adam enthralled. She is horrified when Satan first approaches her in a dream, but piqued by what she considers Adam's lack of faith in her, she stubbornly insists on working alone, thereby leaving herself vulnerable to the serpent's temptation. Like Adam, after the Fall she is first lustful, then quarrelsome. Finally, she too accepts her fate with dignity and resignation.

Satan (Lucifer), chief of the fallen angels, adversary of God and man. A splendid conception, his heroism and grandeur are tainted by a perversion of will and accompanying perversion of intellect. Rebellious against God, he is incapable of understanding Him. A self-tormented spirit, conscious of his loss but unwilling to repent, he allows evil to eat away at him, tarnishing his splendor. His degradation is complete when he wills to enter the body of the serpent. His attempt to seduce man succeeds, but his triumph is temporary and hollow.

Beelzebub (bǐ·ĕl′zə·bŭb), Satan's chief lieutenant. Less confident and less splendid than his chief, he works his will and serves as his mouthpiece. In the council of the fallen angels in Pandemonium, he presents forcefully Satan's plan of indirect war on God through man. His proposal carries.

Moloch (mō′lŏk), fiercest of the fallen angels. Appro-priately worshipped in later years with human sacrifice, he is bloody-minded and desperate. If the fallen angels cannot win Heaven, he chooses either to make Heaven intolerable for the angels who did not fall or to anger God to the point that He will annihilate the fallen spirits.

Belial (bē′lǐ·əl), a fallen angel industrious only in vice. Smooth and oily, he favors peace at any price and expresses the hope that if the fallen angels do not call God's attention to themselves, He will forget them and allow their sufferings to decrease. He favors a proper course but for improper reasons, basing his surrender on sloth, not on acceptance of God's will.

Mammon (măm′ən), the materialistic fallen angel. Like Belial, he is opposed to a second war against Heaven, but he favors a plan of development of natural resources and exploitation of Hell to raise an empire that will rival Heaven.

Mulciber (Vulcan) (mŭl′sǐ·bər), Mammon's chief engineer and architect. Formerly the planner of many of Heaven's buildings, he is now architect of Pandemonium, Satan's palace in Hell.

Sin, Satan's daughter, born from his brain without a mother. She is the loathsome keeper of Hell's gates, through which she lets Satan pass to attack the world. She and her grisly son Death follow Satan to Earth to prey on mankind.

Death, son of Sin and Satan by their incestuous union. He ravishes Sin and begets a horde of hellhounds on her. His voraciousness is so great that he would devour his own mother, except for the fear that her death would involve his own destruction. His fierce reaction to Satan is mollified by the latter's offer of hosts of men and beasts for him to devour if Satan's assault on Earth succeeds.

God the Father, All-knowing and all-powerful, He foresees Satan's activities and man's fall, but extends to man His grace and brings forth good from evil.

Christ (Messiah), the only Son of God. He is first granted by His Father the overthrow of Satan and his legions in the War in Heaven, then granted His wish to sacrifice Himself to redeem man.

Michael (mī′kəl), the warrior angel. Chief of the angelic forces in the War in Heaven, he is a worthy opponent of Satan. He is God's messenger to Adam and Eve to tell them of their banishment from Paradise and their coming death; however, he is allowed by God's grace to foretell to Adam the future of the human race and the redemption to come.

Abdiel (ăb′dĭ·ĕl), angelic servant of God. Alone among Lucifer's angel hordes, he remains steadfast and is rewarded by God's own praise and the favor of striking the first blow against Satan in the war against the rebel angels. Clearly one of Milton's favorite creations in "Paradise Lost," he is perhaps an idealized version of the poet himself.

Raphael (răf′ĭəl, rā′fĭ·əl), God's messenger to Adam to warn him of Satan's presence in Paradise. Gracious and friendly, he still is capable of severe judgment and warns Adam particularly against unreasonable and passionate adoration of Eve.

Gabriel (gā′brĭ·əl), chief of the angelic guards in Paradise. He is a leader in the War in Heaven against the evil angels.

Uriel (yōōr′ĭ·əl), regent of the Sun. Even though an angel, he is incapable of seeing through the mask of a hypocrite and fails to recognize Satan in his disguise as a lesser angel. He directs the evil spirit to Paradise, but sees his actions in Paradise and hastily warns Gabriel that an evil spirit has gained entrance there.

Uzziel (ŭ·zĭ′ĕl, ŭz′ĭ·ĕl), **Ithuriel** (ĭ·thū′rĭ·əl), and **Zephon** (zē′fŏn), angel guards in Paradise.

The Story

In Heaven, Lucifer, unable to abide the supremacy of God, led a revolt against divine authority. Defeated, he and his followers were cast into Hell, where they lay nine days on a burning lake. Lucifer, now called Satan, arose from the flaming pitch and vowed that all was not lost, that he would have revenge for his downfall. Arousing his legions, he reviewed them under the canopy of Hell and decided his purposes could be achieved by guile rather than by force.

Under the direction of Mulciber, the forces of evil built an elaborate palace in which Satan convened a congress to decide on immediate action. At the meeting, Satan reasserted the unity of those fallen and opened the floor to a debate on what measures to take. Moloch advised war. Belial recommended a slothful existence in Hell. Mammon proposed peacefully improving Hell so that it might rival Heaven in splendor. His motion was received with great favor until Beelzebub, second in command, arose and informed the conclave that God had created Earth, which He had peopled with good creatures called humans. It was Beelzebub's proposal to investigate this new creation, seize it, and seduce its inhabitants to the cause of the fallen angels.

Announcing that he would journey to Earth to learn for himself how matters were there, Satan flew to the gate of Hell. There he encountered his daughter, Sin, and his son, Death. They opened the gate and Satan winged his way toward Earth.

God, in his omniscience, beheld the meeting in Hell, knew the intents of the evil angels, and saw Satan approaching the Earth. Disguised as various beasts, Satan acquainted himself with Adam and Eve and with the Tree of Knowledge, which God had forbidden to man.

Uriel, learning that an evil angel had broken through to Eden, warned Gabriel, who appointed two angels to hover about the bower of Adam and Eve. The guardian angels arrived too late to prevent Satan, in the form of a toad, from beginning his evil work. He had influenced Eve's dreams.

Upon awaking, Eve told Adam that in her strange dream she had been tempted to taste of the fruit of the Tree of Knowledge. God, seeing that danger to Adam and Eve was imminent, sent the angel Raphael to the garden to warn them. At Adam's insistence, Raphael related in detail the story of the great war between the good and the bad angels and of the fall of the bad angels to eternal misery in Hell. To Adam's further inquiries Raphael responded with an account of the creation of the world and of how Earth was created in six days, an angelic choir singing the praises of God on the seventh day. He cautioned Adam not to be too curious, that there were many things done by God which were not for man to understand or to attempt to understand. Adam then told how he had been warned against the Tree of Knowledge of Good and Evil, how he had asked God for fellowship in his loneliness, and how Eve was created from his rib.

After the departure of Raphael, Satan returned as a mist to the garden and entered the body of a sleeping serpent. In the morning, as Adam and Eve proceeded to their day's occupation, Eve proposed that they work apart. Adam, remembering the warning of Raphael, opposed her wishes, but Eve prevailed and the couple parted. Alone, Eve was accosted by the serpent, which flattered her into tasting the fruit of the Tree of Knowledge. Eve, liking what she tasted, took a fruit to Adam, who was horrified when he saw what Eve had done. Yet in his love for Eve, he also ate the fruit.

Having eaten, the couple knew lust for the first time, and after their dalliance they knew sickening shame. The guardian angels now deserted the transgressors and returned to God, who approved them, saying they could not have prevented Satan from succeeding in his mission.

Christ descended to Earth to pass judgment. Before Adam and Eve, who in their shame, had been reluctant to come out of their bower to face Him, Christ sentenced the serpent to be forever a hated enemy of humanity. He told Eve that her sorrow would be multiplied by the bearing of children and that she would be the servant of Adam to the end of time. Adam, said Christ, would eat in sorrow, his ground would be cursed, and he would eat bread only by toiling and sweating.

Meanwhile, Death and Sin, having divined Satan's success, left the gates of Hell to join their father on Earth. Within sight of Earth, they met Satan, who delegated Sin and Death as his ambassadors on Earth. Back in Hell, Satan proudly reported his accomplishments to his followers. He was acclaimed by hisses, however, as his cohorts became serpents, and Satan himself was transformed into a serpent before their reptilian eyes. Trees similar to the Tree of Knowledge appeared in Hell, but when the evil angels tasted the fruit, they found their mouths full of ashes.

God, angered at the disaffection of Adam and Eve, brought about great changes on Earth. He created the seasons to replace eternal spring, and the violence and misery of storms—winds, hail, ice, floods, and earthquakes. He caused all Earth's creatures to prey upon one another.

Adam and Eve argued bitterly until they realized that they must face their common plight together. Repenting their sins, they prayed to God for relief. Although Christ interceded for them, God sentenced them to expulsion from Eden and sent the angel Michael to Earth to carry out the sentence. Adam and Eve, lamenting their misfortune, contemplated suicide, but Michael gave them new hope when he brought to Adam a vision of life and death; of the rise and fall of kingdoms and empires; of the activities of Adam's and Eve's progeny through their evil days to the flood, when God would destroy all life except that preserved by Noah in the ark; and of the subsequent return to evil days and Christ's incarnation, death, resurrection, and ascension as mankind's redeemer.

Despite the violence, evil, and bloodshed in the vision, Adam and Eve were pacified when they saw that mankind would be saved. They walked hand in hand from the heights of Paradise to the barren plains below.

Critical Evaluation

With *Paradise Lost*, John Milton realized his longstanding ambition to write an epic poem based upon a classical model, following conventions established by Homer and Vergil. The task was formidable, for during the seventeenth century the epic was considered man's greatest creative achievement. For his theme, Milton chose a grand synthesis of the Christian religion based upon the Bible. Centering on the Fall of Adam and Eve and their restoration to God's favor, the epic ranges over time from the rebellion of Satan and his followers in Heaven until Judgment Day, offering a comprehensive account of Christian history, belief, and values. Primarily a Protestant epic, emphasizing moral choice and salvation through faith, it narrates the most significant biblical events and represents what the minor seventeenth century poet Samuel Barrow called "the story of all things."

Its characters range from the divine to the demonic, from God the Father and Christ to Satan and his followers. Yet the narrative focus centers upon Adam and Eve, initially flawless human beings who violate God's covenant, fall from grace, and are restored. Satan, the most thoroughly developed character, is created on a grand scale with a single-minded goal of revenge and most closely resembles the conventional epic hero. Yet the mythic hero is Christ, the character who performs the positive actions of the story—creation, judgment, and redemption. Adam, the human hero, undergoes a change of fortune through the Fall and is restored; he stands as Milton's long-suffering hero of faith and resignation, in the tradition of Prometheus and Job.

Structurally, the epic forms three major parts, each consisting of four books. In books 1 to 4, Milton introduces the characters, settings (Heaven, Hell, Chaos, and Earth), and major conflicts. Book 1 accounts for the fall of Satan and his millions of followers and its immediate aftermath; in book 2, a council in Hell determines the course of action for Satan: revenge through deception and seduction of mankind. In book 3, a contrasting council in Heaven establishes that man will fall and lays the groundwork for his redemption through the willing sacrifice of Christ. Book 4 introduces the human characters Adam and Eve, who lead an idyllic life in the Garden of Eden, their only restraint being God's prohibition against the fruit of the Tree of Knowledge. Satan briefly appears in the garden following his journey through Chaos but is driven away by angelic guards.

The middle books (5-8) concern the mission of the angel Raphael in the garden, sent by God to warn Adam about the danger posed by Satan. These books, sometimes referred to as "the education of Adam," prepare readers for the Fall of Man through a psychological treatment of character that makes it credible. Unfallen Adam learns of Satan's fall and punishment. In conversation with Raphael, Adam confesses his uxoriousness, and thus the reader is prepared for Adam to disobey God's commandment motivated by a desire to share Eve's fate. Through the use of exposition, the middle books introduce numerous epic conventions. Raphael's narrative of the War in Heaven, which includes events that took place before the beginning of book 1, is an extended account of warfare, a theme Milton associates with the demonic. In this section, Milton continues his strategy of balancing and contrasting books; Raphael's account of the destructive War is counterbalanced by the narrative of Creation in book 7.

The final section (9-12) narrates the Fall and restoration of Adam and Eve, following Satan's return to the garden and assumption of the form of the serpent. Satan cleverly deceives Eve, and Adam willingly disobeys God in order to share her fate. In the final two books, the archangel Michael illuminates for Adam human history from his own time until Judgment Day, allowing Adam to comprehend all the panorama of human suffering and unhappiness that results from the Fall and to recognize Christ as man's redeemer. At the end, both Adam and Eve are reconciled to the loss of Eden and depart as wayfaring, warfaring Christians.

Written in blank verse in which the verse paragraph, not the line, is the most significant unit, *Paradise Lost* achieves a dignified, sonorous tone while incorporating traditional epic conventions. Milton chose blank verse because he considered it the closest English equivalent to classical epic verse. Biblical, classical, and Renaissance allusions abound, particularly character and place names. Often the allusions have typological significance, for Milton follows the Christian tradition of viewing Old Testament figures as precursors to and types of Christ. He extends the device by citing classical myth for par-

allels to Christian events and beliefs. Among the striking stylistic elements, one finds heavy use of Latinate diction, epic similes, frequent inversions, and complex schemes of repetition. Classical allusions and imagery recur as significant motifs in the narrative.

Although he incorporates familiar epic conventions such as the invocation of the muse, the statement of theme, the roll call, the dream, settings on different levels, and different orders of being, Milton frequently associates these conventions with the demonic, in part because he rejects traditional heroism in warfare in favor of the hero who suffers and endures for the right. Like other epic poets, he speaks in the authorial persona or voice, not only in prologues but within the narrative, in order to guide the reader, to express approval or disapproval, or to admonish or caution.

Paradise Lost forms an encyclopedic and comprehensive mythology based upon the Bible. For more than two centuries, readers considered the poem a sound theological interpretation of history and, like Milton, believed that it chronicled actual events, except for those passages obviously intended as allegorical. Like other epics, it embodies a value system that advocates a code of living and answers the most profound questions that man can ask concerning values and beliefs. For modern readers, the epic stands as the greatest example of its genre in English literature and a synthesis of Christianity unsurpassed in poetry.

PARZIVAL

Type of work: Poem.
Author: Wolfram von Eschenbach (c. 1170–1220?)
Type of plot: Chivalric romance
Time of plot: The chivalric age
Locale: Western Europe
First published: Thirteenth century manuscript

Parzival, the masterpiece of Germany's greatest medieval poet, provided the basis of the great body of Wagner's operas written on knightly themes. Eschenbach was instrumental in raising the moral tone of the Arthurian legends by upholding in his poem such chivalric virtues as fidelity to the plighted word, charity to one's fellowman, and reverence for God. In terms of plot, it is interesting to note the poet's use of a precious stone of supernatural powers as the Grail, rather than the chalice used at the last supper.

Principal Characters

Gamuret (gä′mōō·rĕt), the younger son of King Gandein, who leaves Anjou to seek his fortune. He rescues Belakane and marries her.

Gandein (gän′dĕ·ēn′), king of Anjou.

Belakane (bĕ·lä·kä′nĕ), a Moorish queen who is falsely accused of killing Eisenhart, her lover.

Friedebrand (frē′dĕ·bränd), king of Scotland and uncle of Eisenhart. He besieges the castle of Belakane in an attempt to avenge his nephew.

Feirefis (fī′rä·fīs), the son of Gamuret and Belakane, who almost vanquishes Parzival. Together they fight in many tournaments.

Herzeleide (hĕr′tsĕ·lī·dĕ), **Queen of Waleis** (wä′līs), at whose tournament Gamuret is the victor. She marries him after the tourney.

Parzival (pär′zē·fäl), the son of Herzeleide and Gamuret.

Queen Kondwiramur (kön′dwē′rämōōr), whom Parzival marries and later deserts.

Lohengrin (lō′hĕn·grēn), the son of Kondwiramur and Parzival.

Jeschute (ya·shōō′tĕ), who gives Parzival a token.

Orilus (ō′rĭ·lōōs), the jealous husband of Jeschute. He fights Parzival but is pacified.

The Red Knight, who knights Parzival.

Gurnemanz (gōōr′nĕ·mänts), the prince of Graharz, who instructs Parzival in knightly precepts.

Baruch (bä′rōōkh), the ruler of Alexandria, for whom Gamuret fought and was finally slain.

King Kailet (kī′lăt), the companion of Gamuret in Spain.

Arthur, king of Britain.

Queen Guinevere, Arthur's wife.

Sir Kay (kā), the seneschal, defeated by Parzival.

Sir Gawain (gä′wīn), who introduces Parzival to Arthur's Round Table.

Orgeluse (ōr′gĕl·ōōsĕ), the wife of Gawain.

King Meljanz of Lys (mĕl′yänts), for whom Sir Gawain fights Duke Lippaut.

Antikonie (än·tī′kŏ·nē), the daughter of King Meljanz, who is courted by Gawain.

Gramoflanz (grä′mō·flänts), whom Parzival offers to fight because, unknowingly, he has wounded Sir Gawain while that knight was riding to do battle with Gramoflanz. The challenge is rejected because Gramoflanz refuses to meet any knight but Gawain.

Trevrezent (trāv′rĕ·zănt), a hermit who indicates that Parzival is the nephew of Amfortas, the Grail King, and himself.

Amfortas (äm·fōr′täs), the Fisher King who shows Parzival the mysteries of the Grail and is himself cured of his grievous wound miraculously.

Kondrie (kŏn′drē), Parzival's guide to the Grail Kingdom.

Repanse de Schoie (rĕ·pän′sĕ dĕ shoi′ĕ), the wife of Feirefis and mother of Prester John.

Sigune (sĭ·gō′nĕ), the woman who tells Parzival of his lineage.

The Story

Gamuret, younger son of King Gandein of Anjou, refused to live as a vassal in the kingdom of his older brother, notwithstanding the brother's love for Gamuret. The young man, given gifts of gold by his king-brother, as well as horses, equipment, and men-at-arms, left Anjou to seek his fortune across the world. Hoping to find for himself fame and love, Gamuret went first to battle for Baruch at Alexandria; from there he went to the aid of the Moorish Queen Belakane. Belakane had been falsely accused of causing the death of her lover, Eisenhart, and was besieged in her castle by two armies under the command of Friedebrand, king of Scotland and Eisenhart's uncle.

Gamuret, after raising the siege, became the husband of Belakane, who bore him a son named Feirefis. But Gamuret tired of being king of Assagog and Zassamank, and so he journeyed abroad again in search of fame. Passing into Spain, Gamuret sought King Kailet and found him near Kanvoleis. The two entered a tournament sponsored by Queen Herzeleide. Gamuret did valiant deeds and carried off all the honors of that tournament, thereby winning a great deal of fame as the victor.

Two queens who had watched the lists during the tournament fell in love with Gamuret, but Queen Herzeleide won his heart and married him. They loved each other greatly, but once again the call of honor was too great to let Gamuret remain a housed husband. Receiving a summons from Baruch, he went once more to Alexandria. In the fighting there he was treacherously killed and given a great tomb by Baruch. When news of his death reached the land of Waleis, Queen Herzeleide sorrowed greatly, but her sorrow was in part dissipated by the birth of a child by Gamuret. Queen Herzeleide named the boy Parzival.

Parzival was reared by his mother with all tenderness and love. As he grew older he met knights who journeyed through the world seeking honor. Parzival, stimulated by tales of their deeds, left his homeland in search of King Arthur of Britain. He hoped to become one of Arthur's knights and a member of the order of the Round Table. During his absence his smother, Queen Herzeleide, died. On his way to Arthur's court Parzival took a token from Jeschute and thus aroused the jealous anger of her husband, Orilus. Farther along on his journey, he met a woman named Sigune and from her learned of his lineage and his kinship with the house of Anjou. Still later Parzival met the Red Knight and carried that knight's challenge with him to King Arthur. Having been knighted by the king, Parzival set forth again in quest of knightly honor. Finding himself in the land of Graharz, he sought out Gurnemanz, prince of the land, who taught the young knight the courtesy and the ethics of knighthood.

From Graharz, Parzival journeyed to Pelrapar, which he found besieged by enemies. He raised the siege by overthrowing Kingron. After this adventure Parzival fell in love with Queen Kondwiramur, and the two were married. But Parzival, like his father before him, soon tired of the quiet life and parted from his home and queen to seek further adventures.

Parzival journeyed to the land of the Fisher King and became the king's guest. In that land he first beheld the fabulous bleeding spear and all the marvels of the Holy Grail. One morning he awoke to find the castle deserted. Parzival, mocked by a squire, rode away. Later he met

Orilus, who had vowed to battle the young knight for taking Jeschute's token. They fought and Parzival was the victor, but he was able to reconcile Orilus to Jeschute once again and sent the couple to find a welcome at the court of King Arthur.

Arthur, meanwhile, had gone in search of the Red Knight, whose challenge Parzival had carried. Journeying in search of King Arthur, Parzival had the misfortune to fall into a love-trance, during which he overthrew Gagramor and took vengeance on Sir Kay. He met Gawain, who took him back again to Arthur's court. There Parzival was inducted into the company of the Round Table.

At Arthur's court, both Gawain and Parzival were put to shame by two other knights. When in his anger and despair Parzival set out to seek the Holy Grail and Gawain rode off to Askalon, the whole company of the Round Table was dispersed.

While Parzival sought the Grail, Gawain had many adventures. He joined the knights of King Meljanz of Lys, who sought vengeance on Duke Lippaut. When the fighting was over, Gawain rode to Schamfanzon, where he was committed by the king to the care of his daughter Antikonie. Gawain wooed the maiden and thus aroused the wrath of the people of Schamfanzon. Gawain was aided, however, by the girl and Kingrimursel. After Gawain swore to the king that he would ask Scherules to send back some kinsmen to him, Gawain left, also to search for the Holy Grail.

Parzival, meanwhile, had traveled for many days in doubt and despair. In the forest of Monsalvasch he fought with a knight of the Holy Grail and passed on. Then, on Good Friday, he met a pilgrim knight who told him he should not bear arms during the holy season. The knight bade him seek out Trevrezent, a hermit, who showed Parzival how he had sinned in being wrathful with God and indicated to Parzival that he was a nephew to Amfortas, one of the Grail kings. The two parted in sorrow and Parzival resumed his search for the Grail.

Gawain, continuing his adventures, had married Orgeluse. When Gawain decided to battle Gramoflanz, King Arthur and Queen Guinevere agreed to ride to see that famous joust. Before the joust could take place Gawain and Parzival met and did battle, each unknown to his opponent. Gawain was defeated and severely injured by Parzival, who was filled with grief when he learned with whom he had fought. Parzival vowed to take Gawain's place in the combat with Gramoflanz, but the latter refused to do battle with anyone but Gawain himself.

Parzival, released from his vow, longed to return once again to his wife. One morning before dawn he secretly left the camp of King Arthur. On his way back to his wife Parzival met a great pagan warrior, who almost vanquished him. After the battle he learned the pagan knight was Feirefis, Parzival's half brother, the son of Gamuret and Belakane. The two rode back to King Arthur's court, where both were made welcome by the king. In company the half brothers went into the lists and won many honors together. At a feast of the Round Table Kondrie entered the great hall to announce Parzival's election to the Grail kingdom. Summoned to Monsalvasch, Parzival, his wife, and Lohengrin, Parzival's son,

were guided there by Kondrie. Feirefis, although he failed to see the Grail, was baptized and married to Repanse de Schoie. With her he returned to his kingdom, which was held later by his son, Prester John.

Critical Evaluation

The life of Wolfram von Eschenbach, author of *Parzival*, spanned the end of the twelfth and the beginning of the thirteenth centuries. It was a time of political and religious turbulence—the Crusades reached their height in the twelfth century—but it was also a time of a flowering of the arts in general, and literature in particular. At a time when Richard the Lion-Hearted and John ruled England, some of the greatest names in German literature were already writing. Among Wolfram's contemporaries were Hartmann von Aue, Gottfried von Strassburg, and the lyric poet Walter von der Vogelweide. The anonymous author of *The Song of the Nibelungs* also wrote at this time.

Wolfram was born about 1170, in Eschenbach, a small village on the border between Swabia and Bavaria. He was a knight, but of very limited means, and was therefore dependent on patronage for support during the composition of his works. He wrote *Parzival* somewhere between 1197 and 1215. His other works include a handful of lyrics, some fragments of a romance, and a poem, *Willehalm*, which was left unfinished. The date of Wolfram's death is not known, but it was probably before 1220.

The method of the composition of *Parzival* is in doubt, since Wolfram claimed not to be able to read or write. Since the poem comprises 24,810 lines, the oral composition of the work would have been a formidable task, but not one beyond possibility, or, for that matter, without precedent. In a time of near-universal illiteracy, what would today seem to be phenomenal feats of memory were taken for granted. The oldest works in many languages are poems of epic length composed orally and either learned by rote or re-created for recitation according to set formulas. It should be noted too that John Milton, prevented from writing by his blindness, composed *Paradise Lost* orally.

Wolfram's main source for his story was Chrétien de Troyes' *Li Contes del Gral*. This collection of Arthurian romances furnished Wolfram with the material for eleven of the sixteen books of his poem. The source of the initial two and final three books of *Parzival* remains a puzzle. Wolfram several times refers to a Provençal poet named Kyot, who supposedly gave him the correct version of the story. This Kyot is a mystery to scholars, though, for a variety of reasons. No Provençal poem on the Parzival theme has survived, if any ever existed. Kyot is a northern, not a southern, French name, and many critics believe

that Kyot is simply a joke of Wolfram's, as is, perhaps, his claim of illiteracy. Yet Wolfram's statements cannot be disposed of out of hand, since customarily medieval poets worked from sources rather than the product of their own imagination.

Despite their cloudiness, Wolfram's sources are clear in comparison with the origin of the subject matter of which his poem is only one part—the Arthurian romances. Myth and legend shaped the origin of these tales of King Arthur and his court, and their beginnings are buried in now-lost Welsh and Irish stories. During the twelfth century, corresponding to a great rise in interest, written versions of the Arthurian material began to appear. About 1135, Geoffrey of Monmouth, a Welshman, composed in Latin a long compilation of fancy called *The History of the King of Britain*, the last third of which is devoted to Arthur. In 1155, an Anglo-Norman named Wace used Geoffrey's book as the basis for his French poem, *Brut* (the poem's title refers to a mythical Brutus, great-grandson of Aeneas, to whom Geoffrey had attributed the founding of the line of British kings). But neither Geoffrey nor Wace are used by Chrétien de Troyes; the French poet may have had other materials, now lost, from which he worked.

One other bit of Arthurian material should be mentioned: the *Mabinogion*. The *Mabinogion* is a Welsh collection of stories; it was put in writing after 1300, but probably composed at least a century earlier. The *Mabinogion* includes a version of the story that interested Wolfram, but the hero is named Peredur. (Chrétien de Troyes, either following his sources or for reasons of his own, did not use the Welsh form of the name; Parzival is Wolfram's rendition of the form used by Chrétien, Perceval.) Critics believe that *Peredur* is the existing version closest to the oral Welsh stories from which all the written versions are ultimately derived.

The object of Parzival's quest is, of course, the Grail in Wolfram's poem, but what the Grail is forms a story in itself. In the Welsh folklore from which so many of the romances derive, we hear of two miraculous objects— a horn of plenty, and a dish which increases the food put in it. In Old French, the word for dish or platter was *graal*, and although Chrétien de Troyes used the word *graal*, the object of the quest, the Grail, is a jeweled relic. Nor is there a wonderful dish in *Parzival*. The grail in Wolfram's work is apparently a magical gem—but the motif of plenty does appear: whatever food one wishes for appears at once in front of the gem; whatever drink one desires appears in his cup. Wherever Wolfram got this detail of his story, the source is definitely not Chrétien de Troyes. The conception of the Grail as the cup used by Christ at the Last Supper comes from a different tradition.

The poem itself is divided into sixteen books of rhyming couplets, grouped into sections of thirty lines. The poem is difficult to read in the original, since an involved syntax is characteristic of Wolfram's style, and the dialect in which he wrote is not a direct ancestor of modern German. Even readers of modern German find it con-venient to use a translation.

When the Reformation came to Germany in the sixteenth century, Wolfram's poem was forgotten, and it did not again become popular until the nineteenth century. Wagner's opera *Parsifal* did much to recommend the poem to a wider audience. The careful structure of the poem, its wide-ranging action, its insightful handling of the growing character of Parzival himself, and its story—one that has fascinated readers of Western literature for almost a thousand years—place Wolfram's *Parzival* among the greatest works of our medieval heritage.

A PASSAGE TO INDIA

Type of work: Novel
Author: E. M. Forster (1879–1970)
Type of plot: Social criticism
Time of plot: About 1920
Locale: India
First published: 1924

A Passage to India can be read on two levels: political and mystic. Politically it deals with the tension between the British and the native Indians, as well as with the tension between Hindus and Muslims. Mystically it is concerned with the search for the infinite and eternal so characteristic of Oriental religion, and with the illogical and inexplicable in human life. The visit to the Marabar Caves illustrates the malignant side of mysticism, the Temple-Festival at the close, its benignity. Forster divides the novel into three sections which correspond to the three seasons of the Indian year: the Cold Weather, the Hot Weather, and the Rains.

Principal Characters

Dr. Aziz (ä·zēz′), an amiable, sensitive, and intelligent young Muslim doctor in Chandrapore, India. Ignored and snubbed by the English colony, he nevertheless becomes friendly with three English newcomers to India— Mr. Fielding, Mrs. Moore, and Miss Quested. When he takes them on a tour of the sinister Marabar Caves, Miss Quested becomes separated from the party and later she accuses him of attempted rape. Jailed and humiliated, he becomes markedly anti-British. After Miss Quested withdraws her charge at his trial, he wants to collect damages, but Fielding dissuades him. Suspicious of Fielding's motives, he breaks off the friendship. Two years later the two men meet again and each realizes that any true communion between them is impossible because of their racial differences.

Cecil Fielding, the principal of the government college, a middle-aged, maverick intellectual who resists the herd instinct of his fellow Englishmen. He has Indian friends; he defends Aziz against the English bigots, and when Miss Quested is ostracized after the trial he offers her the protection of his home. Tired of the whole situation, he takes a trip to England, marries, and then returns to India, where he finds Aziz less cordial than before.

Adela Quested, the priggish young woman who goes to India to marry Ronald Heaslop, the City Magistrate; she announces that she is eager to see the real India. Her trip to the Marabar Caves proves disastrous. Thinking that she has been the victim of an attempted attack, she accuses Aziz; however, she shows courage by retracting the charge at his trial. The scandal ruins her prospective marriage and causes her to be avoided by almost everyone. She returns to England alone.

Mrs. Moore, Ronald Heaslop's mother, a lovely, sensitive old woman who accompanies Miss Quested to India. She has great regard for Dr. Aziz, but at the Marabar Caves she has a strange psychic experience, an unhappy intuition that life is worthless. When she irritably defends Dr. Aziz to her son, he sends her home and she dies on the way.

Ronald Heaslop, the self-righteous city magistrate, a man coarsened by life in India. Wishing his mother and fiancée to have nothing to do with the natives, he finds himself in a position where he must reject both to preserve his own standards and vanity.

Professor Godbole, a gentle old teacher at the college, a friend of Dr. Aziz and Fielding. He represents the Hindu mystical aspects of India as opposed to the narrower nationalisms of the Muslims and British.

The Nawab Bahadur, a wealthy Muslim who, acting as an unofficial diplomat between the Muslims and English, does favors for the whites. When Dr. Aziz is tried, he rejects the British.

Hamidullah, Dr. Aziz' well-to-do, Anglophobic uncle, a Cambridge barrister who conducts his nephew's defense.

Mahmoud Ali, a family friend of Hamidullah and Dr. Aziz. Cynical and embittered toward the English, he makes an emotional, histronic defense of Dr. Aziz at the trial.

Mohammed Latif, a poor, sneaky relative of Hamidullah and Aziz.

Major Callendar, the civil surgeon, Dr. Aziz's brutal superior, who believes that "white is right."

Mr. Turton, a white official who is willing to extend courtesy to the native and nothing more; a man who has succumbed to power and race snobbery.

Mrs. Turton, his haughty wife, who comforts Adela Quested after the incident at the Marabar Caves.

Mr. McBryde, the chief of police, an intelligent man who treats Dr. Aziz decently but at the same time supervises the prosecution. He is provincial in his attitudes.

Miss Derek, a selfish young woman who takes advantage of her Indian employers.

Amritrao, Dr. Aziz' defense lawyer, imported from

Calcutta, who gets Miss Quested to withdraw her charges.

Mr. Das, Heaslop's subordinate, the judge at the trial, a Hindu who later becomes friendly with Dr. Aziz.

Ralph Moore, Mrs. Moore's odd son, a boy who finally gets Cecil Fielding and Dr. Aziz together again.

Stella Moore, Mrs. Moore's daughter, a sensitive girl who marries Cecil Fielding.

The Story

Dr. Aziz had been doubly snubbed that evening. He had been summoned to the civil surgeon's house while he was at supper, but when he arrived, he found that his superior had departed for his club without bothering to leave any message. In addition, two Englishwomen emerged from the house and took their departure in the hired tonga without even thanking him.

The doctor started back toward the city of Chandrapore afoot. Tired, he stopped at a mosque to rest and was furiously angry when he saw a third Englishwoman emerge from behind its pillars with, as he thought, her shoes on. Mrs. Moore, however, had gone barefoot to the mosque, and in a surge of friendly feelings, Dr. Aziz engaged her in conversation.

Mrs. Moore had newly arrived from England to visit her son, Ronald Heaslop, the City Magistrate. Dr. Aziz found they had common ground when he learned that she did not care for the civil surgeon's wife. Her disclosure prompted him to tell of the usurpation of his carriage. The doctor walked back to the club with her, although as an Indian, he himself could not be admitted.

At the club, Adela Quested, Heaslop's prospective fiancée, declared she wanted to see the real India, not the India which came to her through the rarified atmosphere of the British colony. To please the ladies, one of the members offered to hold what he whimsically termed a bridge party and to invite some native guests.

The bridge party was a miserable affair. The Indians retreated to one side of a lawn and although the conspicuously reluctant group of Anglo-Indian ladies went over to visit the natives, an awkward tension prevailed.

There was, however, one promising result of the party. The principal of the Government College, Mr. Fielding, a man who apparently felt neither rancor nor arrogance toward the Indians, invited Mrs. Moore and Adela to a tea at his house. Upon Adela's request, Mr. Fielding also invited Professor Godbole, a teacher at his school, and Dr. Aziz.

At the tea, Dr. Aziz charmed Fielding and the guests with the elegance and fine intensity of his manner. The gathering, however, broke up on a discordant note when the priggish and suspicious Heaslop arrived to claim the ladies. Fielding had taken Mrs. Moore on a tour of his school, and Heaslop was furious at him for having left Dr. Aziz alone with his prospective fiancée.

Adela was irritated by Heaslop's callous priggishness during her visit and informed him that she did not wish to become his wife; but before the evening was over, she changed her mind. In the course of a drive into the Indian countryside, a mysterious figure, perhaps an animal, loomed out of the darkness and nearly upset the car in which they were riding. Their mutual loneliness and a sense of the unknown drew them together, and Adela asked Heaslop to disregard her earlier rejection.

The one extraordinary aspect of the city of Chandrapore was a phenomenon of nature known as the Marabar Caves, located several miles outside the city. Mrs. Moore and Adela accepted the offer of Dr. Aziz to escort them to the caves; but the visit proved catastrophic for all. Entering one of the caves, Mrs. Moore realized that no matter what was said, the walls returned only a prolonged booming, hollow echo. Pondering that echo while she rested, and pondering the distance that separated her from Dr. Aziz, from Adela, and from her own children, Mrs. Moore saw that all her Christianity, all her ideas of moral good and bad, in short, all her ideas of life, amounted only to what was made of them by the hollow, booming echo of the Marabar Caves.

Adela entered one of the caves alone. A few minutes later she rushed out in a terrified state and claimed that she had been nearly attacked in the gloom. She also claimed that Dr. Aziz was the attacker, and the doctor was arrested.

There always had been a clear division between the natives and the Anglo-Indian community, but as the trial of Dr. Aziz drew nearer, the temper of each group demanded strict loyalty. When Mrs. Moore casually intimated to her son that she was perfectly certain Dr. Aziz was not capable of the alleged crime, he had her shipped off to a coastal port of embarkation at once, and when Fielding expressed an identical opinion at the club, he was promptly ostracized.

The tension that marked the opening of the trial had a strange resolution. The first sensational incident occurred when one of Dr. Aziz's friends pushed into the courtroom and shouted that Heaslop had smuggled his mother out of the country because she would have testified to the doctor's innocence. When the restless body of Indian spectators heard the name of Mrs. Moore, they worked it into a kind of chant, as though she had become a deity. The English colony was not to learn until later that Mrs. Moore had already died aboard ship.

The second incident concluded the trial. It was Adela's testimony. The effects of the tense atmosphere of the courtroom, the reiteration of Mrs. Moore's name, and the continued presence of a buzzing sound in her ears that had persisted since the time she left the caves, combined to produce a trancelike effect upon Adela. She virtually relived the whole of the crucial day as she recollected its events under the interrogation of the prosecuting attorney. When she reached the moment of her lingering in the cave, she faltered, dramatically changed her mind, and withdrew all charges.

Chandrapore was at once and for several hours thereafter a great bedlam. Anglo-India sulked while India exulted. So far as Anglo-India was concerned, Adela had crossed the line. Heaslop carefully explained that he could no longer be associated with her. After accepting Fielding's hospitality for a few weeks, she returned home. Despite Dr. Aziz's increased anglophobia, Fielding persuaded him not to press Adela for legal damages.

Two years later, the Muslim Dr. Aziz was court physician to an aged Hindu potentate who died on the night of the Krishna Festival. The feast was a frantic celebration, and the whole town was under its spell when Field-

ing arrived on an official visit. During the two years he had married again, and Dr. Aziz, assuming he had married Adela Quested, tried to avoid his old friend. When he ran into him accidentally, however, he found out it was Mrs. Moore's daughter, Stella, whom Fielding had married. The doctor's shame at his mistake only caused him to become more distant.

Before they parted for the last time, Dr. Aziz and Fielding went riding through the jungles. The misunderstanding between them had now been resolved, but they had no social ground on which to meet. Fielding had cast his lot with his countrymen by marrying an Englishwoman. The rocks that suddenly loomed before them, forcing their horses to pass in single file on either side, were symbolic of the different paths they would travel from that time on. The affection of two men, however sincere, was not sufficient to bridge the gap between their races.

Critical Evaluation

E. M. Forster was a member of the intellectually select Bloomsbury group, which flourished in London just before and after World War I. Educated at Cambridge, as were many of the group, Forster became one of England's leading novelists during the prewar Edwardian period. In the Bloomsbury group, his friends included Lytton Strachey, a biographer; Virginia Woolf, a novelist; Clive Bell, an art critic; Roger Fry, a painter; John Maynard Keynes, an economist; and G. E. Moore, the philosopher. The group rejected convention and authority, placing great faith in its own intellect and good taste. Forster wrote several good novels between 1905 and 1910: *Where Angels Fear to Tread*, *The Longest Journey*, *A Room with a View*, and *Howards End*. After a hiatus of fourteen years, he published *A Passage to India* in 1924. No other novels were published during his lifetime. A posthumous novel, *Maurice*, was published in 1970. Forster once confessed that he did not understand the post-World War I values and had nothing more to say. *A Passage to India*, however, belies this statement; it is a novel for all seasons, which is underlined by the fact that a major motion picture was made in 1984 based on the novel.

Forster's title comes from the Whitman poem by the same name. This choice is ultimately ironic, for Whitman's vision is of the total unity of all people. In the novel, the attempt to unite people fails at all levels.

The book is divided into three sections: Mosque, Cave, Temple. These divisions correspond to the three divisions of the Indian year: cool spring, hot summer, wet monsoon. Each section is dominated by its concomitant weather. Each section also focuses on one of the three ethnic groups involved: Muslim, Anglo-Indian, Hindu. The Cave could also be called "The Club." Just as the Mosque and the Temple are the Muslim and Hindu shrines,

so is the Club the true Anglo-Indian shrine. Forster, however, is not writing a religious novel. He realizes that religious-ethnic divisions control social modes of activity. The Muslims are emotional; the British rely on intellect. Only the Hindus, in the person of Godbole, have the capacity to love.

The novel is not merely a social or political commentary. Forster belittles social forms on all sides of the conflict. He favors neither Indians nor British. The bridge party, Fielding's tea party, and Aziz's cave party are all failures. More important than social forms are the relationships among individuals. The novel's theme is the search for love and friendship. It is primarily the male-male relationships that have the capacity for mutual understanding, and it is the male characters that are most clearly defined. The females, Mrs. Moore and Adela Quested, have no real possibility of finding friendship across ethnic lines. Mrs. Moore is too old; Adela is too British. Both women want to see the "real" India, but they are unprepared for it when the experience comes. Mrs. Moore, at the mosque and the first cave, Adela, at the cave and the courtroom, discover the real India, and both suffer an almost catatonic withdrawal.

The male characters are more complex. With his Muslim sensitivity, Aziz is determined to find humiliation no matter what the experience. He tries to be both physician and poet—healer of body and soul, but he is inept at both attempts. In the last section, readers see him abandoning both. More than a type, Aziz needs love and friendship. Ultimately he is incapable of establishing a satisfying relationship among his own people, with the Hindus, or, more important, with Cecil Fielding. Muslim sensitivity prevents him from accepting friendship when it is offered.

Out of the multiple failures of the first two sections of the novel there is only the relationship between Aziz and Fielding that holds any promise of reconciliation. Muslim and Anglo-Indian, they meet in the final section in the Hindu province. Both men desire friendship and understanding, but it is too late. In the final scene, the very land seems to separate them; they are not in tune with nature, which is renewing itself in the monsoon downpour. Neither man has come to accept the irrational. They are not ready, in the Hindu sense of love, to accept things as they are. Only Godbole, a Hindu, can accept India and her people for what they are. The nothingness of the caves and the apparent chaos of the people do not disturb the Hindu.

The most crucial scene in *A Passage to India* is the visit to the Marabar Caves. These caves puzzle and terrify both Muslims and Anglo-Indians and form the center of the novel. Only Godbole instinctively understands them. The Hindus possessed India before either Muslims or British. The caves are also elemental; they have been there from the beginnings of the earth. They are not Hindu holy places, but Godbole can respect them without fear. Cave worship is the cult of the female principle, the Sacred Womb, Mother Earth. The Marabar Caves, both womb and grave, demand total effacing of ego. The individual loses his identity; whatever is said returns to him as Ommm, the holy word.

The caves are terrifying and chaotic to those who rely on the intellect. The trip itself emphasizes the chaos that is India. Godbole can eat no meat; Aziz can eat no pork; the British must have their whiskey and port. The confusion of the departure epitomizes the confusion that pervades the novel. Significantly it is Godbole, the one man who might have helped, who is left out. Once in the caves, the party encounters the Nothingness that terrifies. Only Mrs. Moore seems to accept it on a limited scale, but the caves have reduced her will to live. She retreats from the world of experience; nothing matters anymore. She has come to India seeking peace; she finds it in death. Ironically, as her body is being lowered into the Indian Ocean, she is being mythified into the cult of Emiss Emoore.

The conclusion of the novel emphasizes the chaos of India, but it also hints at a pattern that the outsider, Muslims or British, cannot understand. The last chapters portray the rebirth of the God Shri Krishna. It is the recycling of the seasons, the rebirth and renewal of the earth which signals the renewal of the Hindu religious cycle. Godbole shows that man may choose to accept and participate in the seeming chaos, or he can fight against it. Man, however, must be in tune with the natural rhythms of the universe in order to receive true love and friendship. One must accept. Neither Fielding nor Aziz, products of Western civilization, can accept the confusion without attempting to impose order. They still rely on the rational. Although they have moved toward the irrational in the course of the novel, they have not moved far enough.

PENGUIN ISLAND

Type of work: Novel
Author: Anatole France (Jacques-Anatole-François Thibault, 1844–1924)
Type of plot: Fantasy
Time of plot: Ancient times to the present
Locale: Mythical Alca
First published: *L'Ile des pingouins*, 1908 (English translation, 1914)

Penguin Island, a satiric and ironic burlesque of history, is doubly amusing to those who are familiar with the history of France, although the universality of the themes presented makes the satire recognizable to any reader. Using as his starting point the story of a blinded monk who mistakenly baptizes a group of penguins, whom God then changes to men, France satirizes politics, sexual mores, the Church, and other social institutions.

Principal Characters

Maël (må·ĕl'), a Breton missionary monk who, in ancient times, preached to a group of penguins living on an island at the North Pole. The penguins were baptized and turned into men, and the island was towed to a point off the Breton coast. Thus began a society that is the author's satire of French history.

Kraken (krä·kän'), a clever penguin who lives by his wits and turns to his advantage the ignorance and superstitions of the peasant penguins. By constructing an imitation dragon and "Killing" it at an appropriate time, he wins the gratitude of the populace and thereafter accepts annual tribute from them.

Orberosia (ŏr·bā·rō·zyä'), Kraken's mistress and the most beautiful of the penguin women. She appears as a virgin who conquers a dragon in order that Maël's prophecy might be fulfilled. The "dragon" is one she and Kraken have fashioned. Orberosian is the island's first and most important saint.

Eveline Clarence (ã·və·lēn' klä'räns'), a beautiful, talented charmer who becomes a favorite at political social gatherings. She marries a rising politician and becomes the mistress of the prime minister. She lives a long, happy life and, when she dies, leaves her property to the Charity of St. Orberosia.

M. Hippolyte Cérès (mə;·syə;œ' ē·pô·lĭ' sā·rĕs'), Eveline's husband, who tires to ruin the prime minister's career when it becomes apparent that Eveline is his mistress. His action has some effect, for the prime minister is finally put out of office.

Father Agaric (à·gà·rēk') and **Prince des Boscénos** (dä bō·sā·nōs'), conspirators who attempt to destroy the republic and restore the monarchy. The revolution they

launch is short-lived, failing almost as soon as it begins.

Greatank (gr·à·tänk'), the most powerful of all the penguins, who establishes Penguinia's first government on the island of Alca, its system that of a clan or tribe ruled by a strong warrior.

Draco (drà·kō'), Kraken's son, who founds the first royal family of Penguinia.

Draco the Great a descendant of Draco who establishes a monastery in honor of Orberosia; thus the Middle Ages come to the island of Alca.

Trinco (trăn·ko'), the great soldier who takes command of the army of the republic after the monarchy has been abolished. He quickly conquers and loses most of the known world.

Johannes Talpa (zhō·än' tàl·pà'), a learned monk who chronicles the early history of the penguins.

Marbodius (màr·bō·dyüs'), a literary monk who leaves a record of his descent into Hell.

Viscountess Olive (ô·lēv'), a clever aristocrat who seduces Chatillon in order to gain his support for the royalists' cause. Viscount Cléna (klā·na'), a suitor whom Eveline rejects when she learns that he is of modest means.

God, a deity who finds it necessary to call the saints together in order to decide what to do about the penguins Maël has baptized.

Chatillon (shà·tē·yŏn'), an admiral used by Father Agaric and the prince to head the military forces in the unsuccessful revolution.

M. Paul Visire (mə;·syœ' pôl'vē·zēr'), Prime Minister of Penguinia and Eveline's lover.

Madame Clarence (klä·räns'), Eveline's mother.

Pyrot (pē·rō'), a scapegoat.

The Story

In ancient times, Maël, a Breton monk, was diligent in gathering converts to the Church. One day the Devil caused Maël to be transported in a boat to the North Pole, where the priest landed on an island inhabited by penguins. Being somewhat snow-blind, he mistook the birds for men, preached to them, and, taking their silence as a sign of willingness, baptized them into the Christian faith.

This error of the pious Maël caused great consternation in Paradise. God called all the saints together, and they argued whether the baptisms were valid. At last they decided that the only way out of the dilemma was to change the penguins into men. After this transformation had taken place, Maël towed the island back to the Breton coast so that he could keep an eye on his converts.

Thus began the history of Penguinia on the island of Alca. At first the penguins were without clothes, but before long the holy Maël put clothes on the females. Because this covering excited the males, sexual promiscuity was enormously increased. The penguins began to establish the rights of property by knocking one another over the head. Greatank, the largest and strongest penguin, became the founder of power and wealth. A taxation system was established by which all penguins were taxed equally. This system was favored by the rich, who kept their money to benefit the poor.

Kraken, a clever penguin, withdrew to a lonely part of the island and lived alone in a cave. Finally he took as his mistress Orberosia, the most beautiful of penguin women. Kraken gained great wealth by dressing up as a dragon and carrying off the wealth of the peaceful penguins. When the citizens banded together to protect their property, Kraken became frightened. It was predicted by Maël that a virgin would come to conquer the dragon. Kraken and Orberosia fashioned an imitation monster. Orberosia appeared to Maël and announced herself as the destined virgin. At an appointed time she revealed the imitation monster. Kraken sprang from a hiding place and pretended to kill it. The people rejoiced and thenceforth paid annual tribute to Kraken. His son, Draco, founded the first royal family of Penguinia.

Thus began the Middle Ages on the island of Alca. Draco the Great, a descendant of the original Draco, had a monastery established in the cave of Kraken in honor of Orberosia, who was now a saint. There were great wars between the penguins and the porpoises at that time, but the Christian faith was preserved by the simple expedient of burning all heretics at the stake.

The history of the penguins in that far time was chronicled by a learned monk named Johannes Talpa. Even though the battles raged about his very ears, he was able to continue writing in his dry and simple style. Little record was left of the primitive paintings on the isle of Alca, but later historians believed that the painters were careful to represent nature as unlike herself as possible. Marbodius, a literary monk, left a record of a descent into Hell similar to the experience of Dante. Marbodius interviewed Virgil and was told by the great poet that Dante had misrepresented him: Virgil was perfectly happy with his own mythology and wanted nothing to do with the God of the Christians.

The next recorded part of Penguinian history treated is of modern times, when rationalistic philosophers began to appear. In the succeeding generation their teachings took root; the king was put to death, nobility was abolished, and a republic was founded. The shrine of Saint Orberosia was destroyed. The republic, however, did not last long. Trinco, a great soldier, took command of the country; with his armies, he conquered and lost all the known world. The penguins were left at last with nothing but their glory.

Then a new republic was established. It pretended to be ruled by the people, but the real rulers were the wealthy financiers. Another republic of a similar nature, new Atlantis, had grown up across the sea at the same time. It was even more advanced in the worship of wealth.

Father Agaric and Prince des Boscénos, as members of the clergy and nobility, were interested in restoring the kings of Alca to the throne. They decided to destroy the republic by taking advantage of the weakness of Chatillon, the admiral of the navy. Chatillon was seduced by the charms of the clever Viscountess Olive, who was able to control his actions for the benefit of the royalists. An immense popular antirepublican movement was begun with Chatillon as its hero; the royalists hoped to reinstate the king in the midst of the uproar. The revolution, however, was stopped in its infancy, and Chatillon fled the country.

Eveline, the beautiful daughter of Madame Clarence, rejected the love of Viscount Cléna, after she had learned that he had no fortune. She then accepted the attentions of Monsieur Cérès, a rising politician. After a short time they were married. Monsieur Cérès received a portfolio in the cabinet of Monsieur Visire, and Eveline became a favorite in the social gatherings of the politicians. M. Visire was attracted by her, and she became his mistress. M. Cérès learned of the affair, but he was afraid to say anything to M. Visire, the prime minister. Instead, he did his best to ruin M. Visire politically, but with little success at first. Finally M. Visire was put out of office on the eve of a war with a neighboring empire. Eveline lived to a respectable old age and at her death left all of her property to the Charity of Saint Orberosia.

As Penguinia developed into an industrial civilization ruled by the wealthy class, the one purpose of life became the gathering of riches; art and all other nonprofit activities ceased to be. Finally, the downtrodden workmen revolted, and a wave of anarchy swept over the nation. All the great industries were demolished. Order was established at last, and the government reformed many of the social institutions, but the country continued to decline. Where before there had been great cities, wild animals now lived.

Then came hunters seeking wild animals. Later, shepherds appeared, and after a time farming became the chief occupation. Great lords built castles. The people made roads; villages appeared. The villages combined into large cities. The cities grew rich. An industrial civ-

ilization developed, ruled by the wealthy class. History was beginning to repeat itself.

Critical Evaluation

Penguin Island has been the most popular and most widely read of all Anatole France's books, though by no means the most admired by serious critics. The reason is not far to seek: *Penguin Island* is a clever satirical allegory which skims mockingly over the main landmark events of French history under the ironic guise of being a solemn historical narrative about an island civilization inhabited exclusively by penguins. This fantastic concept naturally gives rise to a lighthearted, comic approach which seems never to take itself seriously enough to probe deeply into the causes and meanings of history. Instead it is breezily anecdotal in method, sparing of detail and extremely sketchy in its narration, vague in its handling of historical time, and, above all, cast in a charmingly witty style by a narrator who appears to have his tongue in his cheek at all times. As a result, the book makes no obvious intellectual demands on the reader and is fun to read. At the same time, the book seems rather saucily cavalier, even trivializing, about French history, and as a novel it is disconcertingly negligent about such elements of craft as plot, characters, and structure. These weaknesses have been pointed out repeatedly by serious critics, who tend to be instinctively suspicious of any work that proves to be both popular and enjoyable. It can be argued, however, that *Penguin Island* earns its popularity honestly, by artfully concealing under an apparently frivolous surface an implied commentary on some of the most far-reaching issues in history and historiography. For the casual reader, *Penguin Island* can indeed be a merry romp, but for the more thoughtful reader it provides matter for much profound reflection.

It will be helpful, in assessing the enduring value of *Penguin Island*, to recall the circumstances of its composition. When it was published in 1908, France was a celebrated and practiced man of letters who, at the age of sixty-four, was at the peak of his late-blooming creative powers. That same year, he had at least completed and published, after a quarter century of intermittent effort, a life of Joan of Arc in two volumes, which was a seriously intended work of historiography. During the preceding decade, he had, for the only time in his career, become active in public life, intervening in the Dreyfus Affair and making political speeches in favor of the socialist point of view. During that same decade, his voluminous imaginative writing had also had an unwonted emphasis on history, politics, and current events. The evidence is that by 1908, France had become somewhat disenchanted with public life, and had perhaps exhausted himself physically and soured his interest in history by the long struggle to complete *The Life of Joan of Arc*. *Penguin Island*,

rapidly composed in a few months, was perhaps a means of relaxing for France, after so much earnest and carefully researched historical writing, and was perhaps also a means of exorcising his troubled disenchantment with public affairs. It was a work conceived in a light vein which, by treating history as comic fantasy, might restore a badly needed sense of proportion to his own outlook, grown too grimly serious because of the nature of the historical and current events with which he had been so deeply concerned for a full, turbulent decade. By mocking his own erudition and solemn preoccupation with politics and history—which is the underlying spirit of *Penguin Island*—France seems to have aimed to relieve himself of the burdens he had assumed for so long and to bid an ironic farewell to his own activism.

Perhaps the best evidence in *Penguin Island* that the author was trying to purge himself of his own high moral seriousness might be found in the way the Dreyfus Affair is represented in the book. Called "The Affair of the Eighty Thousand Trusses of Hay," and featuring "a middle-class Jew called Pyrot, desirous of associating with the aristocracy" who is accused of treason, the episode of modern Penguin history, which is a transparent parody of the Dreyfus Affair, is turned into pure farce. All sides in Penguinia's "Pyrot Affair" are roundly mocked, the Pyrotists as much as the anti-Pyrotists, the socialists as much as the capitalists, the heroes as much as the villains. Even the most disinterested defender of Pyrot's innocence, a man named Colomban (clearly a parodic equivalent of Émile Zola), is presented as a naïve simpleton. The net effect of this globally satirical representation is to put distance between the narrator (France) and the events being narrated. No longer the passionate moralist who had so eloquently defended Dreyfus and Zola during the actual affair, France wished, in writing *Penguin Island*, to see recent events from a safe distance and from a posture above the battle, perhaps to remind himself that, viewed under the aspect of eternity, the fierce passions aroused by the affair—in himself as well as in others—must appear ludicrously petty.

Indeed, the effect of the ironic narrative tone throughout *Penguin Island* is to place all human history and all the learned endeavors to recover that history in the same remote, slightly ludicrous perspective. By the inspired invention of a society of penguins baptized by a near-sighted priest and thus coopted into the human family, France contrived to make the very premise underlying his composition a parody of human history. Thus he plants in the minds of his more reflective readers, at least, grave doubts about the way historical events occur and even graver doubts about the way historians reconstruct and interpret those events. That the bantering tone conceals profound questions about the nature and meaning of history appears most clearly in the famous concluding chapter, "The Endless History," which predicts the future of Penguinia as a cyclical process of expansion, conflict, and devastation followed by a new expansion arising out of the ruins and launching the cycle again. The conception of history as an endlessly repeated cycle of greed and violence, from which nothing is ever learned, is symbolically expressed by the device of closing the chapter with exactly the same words as were used to begin it. Through the prism of hindsight, *Penguin Island* must be seen as an ingenious travesty of French history, entertaining as farce yet at the same time subtly disturbing as an implied meditation on the limits of historiography.

PENSÉES

Type of work: Philosophical reflections
Author: Blaise Pascal (1623–1662)
First published: 1670

Blaise Pascal, scientist and mathematician, became an active member of the society of Port Royal after his conversion as the result of a mystical experience in 1654. He was actively involved in the bitter debate between the Jansenists, with whom he allied himself, and the Jesuits, and the series of polemical letters titled *Provinciales* (1656–1657) is the result of that great quarrel. Wanting to write a defense of Catholic Christianity which would appeal to men of reason and sensibility, Pascal, about 1660, began to prepare his defense of the Catholic faith.

Like many other great thinkers whose concern was more with the subject of their compositions than with the external order and completeness of the presentation, he failed to complete a continuous and unified apology. When he died at thirty-nine he left little more than his notes for the projected work, a series of philosophical fragments reflecting his religious meditations. These form the *Pensées* as we know it. Despite its fragmentary character, the book is a classic of French literature, charming and effective in its style, powerful and sincere in its philosophic and religious protestations.

Philosophers distinguish themselves either by the insight of their claims or by the power of their justification. Paradoxically, Pascal distinguishes himself in his defense by the power of his claims. This quality is partly a matter of style and partly a matter of conviction. It was Pascal, in the *Pensées*, who wrote, "The heart has its reasons, which reason does not know," by which he meant not that emotion is superior to reason, but that in being compelled by a moving experience one submits to a superior kind of reasons. Pascal also wrote that "all our reasoning reduces itself to yielding to feeling," but he admitted that it is sometimes difficult to distinguish between feeling and fancy; nevertheless, he believed that the way to truth is by the heart, the feeling, and that the intuitive way of knowledge is the most important, not only because it is of the most important matters but also because it is essential to all reasoning, providing the first principles of thought. Much of the value of the *Pensées* results from the clarity with which Pascal presented his intuitive thoughts.

A considerable portion of the *Pensées* is taken up with a discussion of philosophical method, particularly in relation to religious reflection. The book begins with an analysis of the difference between mathematical and intuitive thinking and continues the discussion, in later sections, by considering the value of skepticism, of contradictions, of feeling, memory, and imagination. A number of passages remind the reader of the fact that a proposition which seems true from one perspective may seem false from another, but Pascal insists that "essential" truth is "altogether pure and altogether true." The power of skepticism and the use of contradictions in reasoning both depend upon a conception of human thinking which ignores the importance of perspective in determining a man's belief. Thus, from the skeptic's point of view nothing is known because we can be sure of nothing; but the skeptic forgets that "it is good to be tired and wearied by the vain search after the true good, that we may stretch out our arms to the Redeemer." Contradiction, according to Pascal, "is a bad sign of truth" since there are some things certain which have been contradicted and some false ideas which have not. Yet contradiction has its use: "All these contradictions, which seem most to keep me from the knowledge of religion, have led me most quickly to the true one."

Pascal had the gift of responding critically in a way that added value to both his own discourse and that of his opponent. Criticizing Montaigne's skepticism, he came to recognize the truth—a partial truth, to be sure—of much that Montaigne wrote. His acknowledgment of this is grudging; he writes that "it is not in Montaigne, but in myself, that I find all that I see in him," and also "What good there is in Montaigne can only have been acquired with difficulty." Yet, as T. S. Eliot has pointed out in an introduction to the *Pensées*, Pascal uses many of Montaigne's ideas, phrases, and terms, paralleling several parts of Montaigne's "Apology for Raimond Sebond."

Perhaps the most controversial part of the *Pensées* is Pascal's section on miracles. He quotes Saint Augustine as saying that he would not have been a Christian but for the miracles, and he argues that there are three marks of religion: perpetuity, a good life, and miracles. He writes, "If the cooling of love leaves the Church almost without believers, miracles will rouse them," and, "Miracles are more important than you think. They have served for the foundation, and will serve for the continuation of the Church till Antichrist, till the end." Although there are other passages which assert the importance of faith which is in no way dependent upon miracles, as, for example, "That we must love one God only is a thing so evident, that it does not require miracles to prove it," Pascal does seem unambiguously to assert that miracles are a way to faith. This idea is opposed by those who insist that belief in miracles presupposes a belief in God and the Gospels. Pascal had been profoundly affected by a miracle at Port

Royal, but his defense of the importance of miracles goes beyond that immediate reference with appeals to reason and authority as well as to feeling.

Pascal's "Proof of Jesus Christ" is interesting not because it pretends to offer demonstrations which would appeal to unbelievers, but because it uses persuasive references which throw a new light on the question of Jesus' status. He argues that because of unbelievers at the time of Christ we now have witnesses to Him. If Jesus had made His nature so evident that none could mistake it, the proof of His nature and existence would not have been as convincing as it is when reported by unbelievers. Pascal emphasizes the function of the Jews as unbelievers when he writes: "The Jews, in slaying Him in order not to receive Him as the Messiah, have given Him the final proof of being the Messiah. And in continuing not to recognize Him, they made themselves irreproachable witnesses."

Pascal's famous wager is presented in the *Pensées*. He makes an appeal to "natural lights"—ordinary human intelligence and good sense. God either exists or He does not. How shall you decide? This is a game with infinitely serious consequences. You must wager, but how shall you wager? Reason is of no use here. Suppose you decide to wager that God is. "If you gain, you gain all; if you lose, you lose nothing." Pascal concludes that there is everything to be said in favor of committing oneself to a belief in God and strong reasons against denying God. To the objection that a man cannot come to believe simply by recognizing that he will be extremely fortunate if he is right and no worse off if he is wrong, Pascal replies by saying that if an unbeliever will act as if he believes, and if he wants to believe, belief will come to him. This wager later inspired William James's *The Will to Believe*, in which the American pragmatist argued that Pascal's method is essentially pragmatic. James's objection to Pascal's wager is that the wager alone presents no momentous issue; unless one can relate the particular issue being considered to a man's concerns, the appeal of the wager is empty. If such proof would work for Pascal's God, it would work for any god whatsoever. However, James's use of the wager to justify passional decisions is much like Pascal's.

In a section titled "The Fundamentals of the Christian Religion," Pascal wrote that the Christian religion teaches two truths: that there is a God whom men can know and that by virtue of their corruption men are unworthy of Him. Pascal rejected cold conceptions of God which reduced Him to the author of mathematical truths or of the order of the elements. For Pascal the God of salvation had to be conceived as He is known through Jesus Christ. The Christian God can be known, according to Pascal, but since men are corrupt they do not always know God. Nature assists God to hide Himself from corrupt men, although it also contains perfections to show that Nature is the image of God.

In considering "The Philosophers," Pascal emphasizes thought as distinguishing men from brutes and making the greatness of man possible. "Man is neither angel nor brute," he writes, "and the unfortunate thing is that he who would act the angel acts the brute."

Thus in Pascal we find a man who is on the one hand eager to defend the Christian faith, on the other determined to indicate the shortcomings of men. He is remorselessly critical in his attacks on skeptics, atheists, and other critics of the Church, not simply because they err, but because they do so in disorder and without respect for the possibilities of man or the values of religion. In regard to skepticism he wrote that his thoughts were intentionally without order, because only thus could he be true to the disorderly character of his subject.

But it is not Pascal the bitter critic who prevails in the *Pensées*; it is, rather, the impassioned and inspired defender of the faith. Even those who do not share his convictions admire his style and the ingenuity of his thought, and much that is true of all mankind has never been better said than in the *Pensées*.

PÈRE GORIOT

Type of work: Novel
Author: Honoré de Balzac (1799–1850)
Type of work: Naturalism
Time of plot: c. 1819
Locale: Paris
First published: *Le Père Goriot*, 1835 (English translation, 1899)

A gallery of fascinating characters, each with his own intriguing history, is assembled in Mme. Vauquer's boarding-house. Among them is Father Goriot. Gradually, he squanders away his ample retirement funds to pay the bills of his two ungrateful and profligate daughters. Finally, he is buried in a pauper's grave, and his children do not even attend the funeral. Other stories and characters interweave within this larger frame. Most effective is the history of Eugène de Rastignac, a poor law student who is subtly transformed from a naïve provincial into a Parisian gentleman.

Principal Characters

Father Goriot (gô·ryō′), a lonely old lodger at the pension of Madame Vauquer in Paris. Known to the other boarders as Old Goriot, he is a retired manufacturer of vermicelli who sold his prosperous business in order to provide handsome dowries for his two daughters. During his first year at the Maison Vauquer, he occupied the best rooms in the house; in the second year he asked for less expensive quarters on the floor above, and at the end of the third year he moved into a cheap, dingy room on the third story. Because two fashionably dressed young women have visited him from time to time in the past, the old man has become an object of curiosity and suspicion; the belief is that he has ruined himself by keeping two mistresses. Actually Old Goriot is a man in whom parental love has become an obsession, a love unappreciated and misused by his two selfish, heartless daughters, who make constant demands on his meager resources. After a life of hard work, careful saving, and fond indulgence of his children, he has outlived his usefulness and is now in his dotage. Happy in the friendship of Eugène de Rastignac, the law student who becomes the lover of one of the daughters, he uses the last of his money to provide an apartment for the young man, a place where Old Goriot will also have his own room. But before the change can be made the daughters drive their father to desperation by fresh demands for money to pay their bills. He dies attended only by Eugène and Bianchon, a poor medical student, and in his last moments he speaks lovingly of the daughters who have ruined him and made him the victim of their ingratitude. The daughters send their empty carriages to follow his coffin to the grave.

Countess Anastasie de Restaud (à·nà·stà·zē′ də rĕs·tō′), the more fashionable of Old Goriot's daughters, constantly in need of money to indulge her extravagant tastes and to provide for her lover. Meeting her at a ball given by his distant relative, Madame de Beauséant, Eugène de Rastignac immediately falls in love with

Anastasie. When he calls on her he finds Old Goriot just leaving. His mention of his fellow lodger causes Anastasie and her husband to treat the young law student with great coldness, and he realizes that he is no longer welcome in their house. Later Madame de Beauséant explains the mystery, saying that Anastasie is ashamed of her humble origins and her tradesman father.

Baroness Delphine de Nucingen (dĕl·fēn′ də nü·săn·zhän′), Old Goriot's second daughter, the wife of a German banker. Like her sister Anastasie, she married for position and money, but her place in society is not as exalted as that of the Countess de Restaud, who has been received at court. As a result, the sisters are not on speaking terms. Madame de Beauséant, amused by Eugène de Rastignac's youthful ardor, suggests that he introduce her to the Baroness de Nucingen in order to win Delphine's gratitude and a place for himself in Parisian society. Delphine accepts the young man as her lover. Though self-centered and snobbish, she is less demanding than her sister; she has asked for less, given more of herself, and brought more happiness to her father. When Old Goriot is dying, she goes to the Maison Vauquer at Eugène's insistence, but she arrives too late to receive her father's blessing.

Eugène de Rastignac (oe·zhĕn′ də rås·tēnyàk′), an impoverished law student, the son of a landed provincial family. As ambitious as he is handsome, he is determined to conquer Paris. At first his lack of sophistication makes him almost irresistible to his relative, Madame de Beauséant, and Delphine de Nucingen, whose lover he becomes. He learns cynicism without losing his warm feelings; he never wavers in his regard for Old Goriot, and while he does not attend seriously to the law studies for which his family is making a great sacrifice, he manages to get on in fashionable society, where friendships and influence are important. The revelation of the ways of the world that he gains through the patronage of Madame de Beauséant, his love affair with Delphine, and his regard for Old Goriot, as well as the shabby activities in which he engages in order to maintain himself in the world of fashion, make him all the more ambitious and eager to succeed.

Madame Vauquer (vō·kā′), the sly, shabby, penurious owner of the Maison Vauquer, the perfect embodiment of the atmosphere that prevails in the pension. When Old Goriot first moves into her boardinghouse, she considers him as a possible suitor, but after he fails to respond to her coy attentions she makes him an object of gossip and ridicule.

Monsieur Vautrin (vō·trăń′), a man who claims to be a former tradesman living at the Maison Vauquer. Reserved, sharp-tongued, secretive, he observes everything that goes on about him and is aware of Old Goriot's efforts to provide money for his daughters. Knowing that Eugène de Rastignac desperately needs money in order to maintain himself in society, he suggests that the young man court Victorine Taillefer, another lodger, an appealing young girl whose father has disinherited her in favor of her brother. Vautrin says that he will arrange to have the brother killed in a duel, a death that will make Victorine an heiress. He gives Eugène two weeks to consider his proposition. Eugène considers Vautrin a devil, but in the end, driven to desperation by his mistress, he begins to court Victorine. True to Vautrin's word, Victorine's brother is fatally wounded in a duel. Vautrin's scheme fails when he is arrested and revealed as a notorious criminal, **Jacques Collin,** nicknamed **Trompe-la-Mort.** Though his identity has been betrayed within the pension, he swears that he will return and continue his climb to good fortune by the same unscrupulous means used by those who call themselves respectable.

Victorine Taillefer (vēk·tô·rēn′pr tà·yəfěr′), a young girl cast off by her harsh father, who has decided to make his son his only heir. She lives with Madame Couture at the Maison Vauquer.

Madame Couture (kōō·tür′), the widow of a public official and a lodger at the Maison Vauquer. A kind-hearted woman, she fills the place of a mother in the lonely life of Victorine Taillefer.

Monsieur Poiret (pwà·rā′), a lodger at the Maison Vauquer. Gondureau, a detective, confides in him that he suspects that Monsieur Vautrin is in reality the famous criminal, Trompe-la-Mort.

Mademoiselle Michonneau (mē·shô·nō′), an elderly spinster living at the Maison Vauquer. Disliking Monsieur Vautrin, her fellow boarder, she agrees to put a drug in his coffee. While Vautrin is asleep, she discovers the brand of a criminal on his shoulder. Acting on this information, the police appear and arrest Vautrin.

Gondureau (gōń·dü·rō′), the detective who is trying to track down **Jacques Collin,** called **Trompe-la-Mort,** a criminal who lives at the Maison Vauquer under the name of Vautrin. Gondureau arranges with Monsieur Poiret and Mademoiselle Michonneau to have Vautrin drugged in order to learn whether he bears a criminal brand on his shoulder.

Count Maxime de Trailles (màk·sēm′ də trà′yə), an arrogant but impecunious young nobleman, the lover of Anastasie de Restaud. For his sake she helps to impoverish her father.

Madame de Beauséant (də bō·sā·yän′), a relative of Eugène de Rastignac. Aristocratic and high-minded, she is the ideal of inherited culture and good manners—kind, reserved, warmhearted, beautiful. Though saddened by the loss of her lover, she treats Eugène with great kindness, receives Delphine de Nucingen for his sake, and introduces the young man into fashionable Parisian society.

Bianchon (byän·shōn′), a poor medical student living at the Maison Vauquer. Like Eugène de Rastignac, he befriends Old Goriot and attends him when the old man is dying. Bianchon extends friendship easily and allows warm human feelings to influence his relations with other people.

Sylvie (sēl·vē′), the plump cook at the Maison Vauquer.

Christophe (krēs·tôf′), Madame Vauquer's man of all work.

The Story

There were many conjectures at Madame Vauquer's boardinghouse about the mysterious Monsieur Goriot. He had taken the choice rooms on the first floor when he first retired from his vermicelli business, and for a time his landlady had eyed him as a prospective husband. When, at the end of his second year at the Maison Vauquer, he had asked to move to a cheap room on the second floor, he was credited with being an unsuccessful speculator, a miser, and a moneylender. The mysterious young women who flitted up to his rooms from time to time were said to be his mistresses, although he protested that they were only his two daughters. The other boarders called him Father Goriot.

At the end of the third year, Goriot moved to a still cheaper room on the third floor. By that time, he was often the butt of jokes at the boardinghouse table, and his daughters rarely visited him.

One evening the impoverished law student, Eugène de Rastignac, came home late from the ball his wealthy cousin, Madame de Beauséant, had given. Peeking through the mysterious Goriot's keyhole, he saw him molding some silver plate into ingots. The next day he heard his fellow boarder, Monsieur Vautrin, say that early in the morning he had seen Father Goriot selling a piece of silver to an old moneylender. What Vautrin did not know was that the money thus obtained was intended for Goriot's daughter, Countess Anastasie de Restaud, whom Eugène had met at the dance the night before.

That afternoon Eugène paid his respects to the countess. Father Goriot was leaving the drawing room when he arrived. The countess, her lover, and her husband received Eugène graciously because of his connections with Madame de Beauséant, but when he mentioned they had the acquaintance of Father Goriot in common, he was quickly shown to the door, the count leaving word with his servant that he was not to be at home if Monsieur de Rastignac called again.

After his rebuff, Eugène went to call on Madame de Beauséant, to ask her aid in unraveling the mystery. She quickly understood what had happened and explained that de Restaud's house would be barred to him because both of Goriot's daughters, having been given sizable dowries, were gradually severing all connection with their father and therefore would not tolerate anyone who had knowledge of Goriot's shabby circumstances. She suggested that Eugène send word through Goriot to his other daughter, Delphine de Nucingen, that Madame de Beauséant would receive her. She knew that Delphine would welcome the invitation and would be grateful to Eugène and become his sponsor.

Vautrin had another suggestion for the young man. Under Madame Vauquer's roof lived Victorine Taillefer, who had been disinherited by her wealthy father in favor of her brother. Eugène had already found favor in her eyes, and Vautrin suggested that for two hundred thousand francs he would have the brother murdered, so that Eugène might marry the heiress. He was to have two weeks in which to consider the offer.

Eugène escorted Madame de Beauséant to the theater next evening. There he was presented to Delphine de Nucingen, who received him graciously. The next day he received an invitation to dine with the de Nucingens and to go to the theater. Before dinner he and Delphine drove to a gambling house where, at her request, he gambled and won six thousand francs. She explained that her husband would give her no money, and she needed it to pay a debt she owed to an old lover.

Before long Eugène learned that it cost money to keep the company of his new friends. Unable to press his own family for funds, he would not stoop to impose on Delphine. Finally, as Vautrin had foreseen, he was forced to take his fellow boarder's offer. The tempter had just finished explaining the duel between Victorine's brother and his confederate which was to take place the following morning when Father Goriot came in with the news that he and Delphine had taken an apartment for Eugène.

Eugène wavered once more at the thought of the crime which was about to be committed in his name. He attempted to send a warning to the victim through Father Goriot, but Vautrin, suspicious of his accomplice, thwarted the plan. Vautrin managed to drug their wine at supper so that both slept soundly that night.

At breakfast, Eugène's fears were realized. A messenger burst in with the news that Victorine's brother had been fatally wounded in a duel. After the girl hurried off to see him, another singular event occurred. After drinking his coffee, Vautrin fell to the ground as if he had suffered a stroke. When he was carried to his room and undressed, it was ascertained by marks on his back that he was the famous criminal, Trompe-la-Mort. One of the boarders, an old maid, had been acting as an agent for the police; she had drugged Vautrin's coffee so that his criminal brand could be exposed. Shortly afterward the police appeared to claim their victim.

Eugène and Father Goriot were preparing to move to their new quarters, for Goriot was to have a room over the young man's apartment. Delphine arrived to interrupt Goriot's packing. She was in distress. Father Goriot had arranged with his lawyer to force de Nucingen to make a settlement so that Delphine would have an independent income on which to draw, and she brought the news that her money had been so tied up by investments it would be impossible for her husband to withdraw any of it without bringing about his own ruin.

Hardly had Delphine told her father of her predicament when Anastasie de Restaud drove up. She had sold the de Restaud diamonds to help her lover pay off his debts, and she had been discovered by her husband. De Restaud had bought them back, but as punishment he demanded control of her dowry.

Eugène could not help overhearing the conversation through the thin partition between the rooms; when Anastasie said that she still needed twelve thousand francs for her lover, he forged one of Vautrin's drafts for that amount and took it to Father Goriot's room. Anastasie's reaction was to berate him for eavesdropping.

The financial difficulties of his daughters and the hatred and jealousy they had shown proved too much for Father Goriot. At the dinner table, he looked as if he were about to have a stroke of apoplexy, and when Eugène returned from an afternoon spent with his mistress, Delphine, the old man was in bed, too ill to be moved to his new home. He had gone out that morning to sell his last few possessions, so that Anastasie might pay her dressmaker for an evening gown.

In spite of their father's serious condition, both daughters attended Madame de Beauséant's ball that evening, and Eugène was too much under his mistress' influence to refuse to accompany her. The next day, Goriot was worse. Eugène tried to summon his daughters. Delphine was still abed and refused to be hurried over her morning toilet. Anastasie arrived at his bedside only after Father Goriot had lapsed into a coma and no longer recognized her.

Father Goriot was buried in a pauper's grave the next day. Eugène tried to borrow burial money at each daughter's house, but each sent word that they were in deep grief over their loss and could not be seen. He and a poor medical student from the boardinghouse were the only mourners at the funeral. Anastasie and Delphine sent their empty carriages to follow the coffin. It was their final tribute to an indulgent father.

Critical Evaluation

Honoré de Balzac's writing career spanned thirty years, from the decisive point in 1819 when he elected to abandon the study of law until his untimely death in 1850. His work up until 1829 consisted of novels, stories, and sketches on a variety of philosophical and social themes. They are, on the whole, undistinguished; Balzac later averred that the decade from 1819 until he began work on *The Chouans* in 1829 constituted his apprenticeship in the art of fiction. Certainly, the works of the last twenty years of his life show the benefits of that long period of development, both in stylistic and tonal precision and in general weight and narrative direction.

Many critics contend that the generative idea for *The Human Comedy* came to Balzac as he was writing *Father Goriot*, because in the manuscript the name of the young student is Massiac until in the scene of the afternoon call at Madame de Beauséant's house "Massiac" is abruptly scratched out and "Rastignac" inserted. The character Eugène de Rastignac had appeared in a minor role in *The Wild Ass's Skin* (1831), and the assumption is that the decision to reintroduce him at an earlier stage of his life in *Father Goriot* betokens a flash of creative light that revealed to the author a cycle of interconnected novels depicting every aspect of society and having numerous characters in common—*The Human Comedy*. That the idea came to him quite so suddenly is doubtful, since, as Henry Reed has pointed out, he had already decided to ring in Madames de Langeais and de Beauséant and the moneylender Gobseck, all of whom appear in previous works. It is certain, however, that *Father Goriot* is the first work in which the device of repetition occurs and in which the uncertain fates of two main characters, Eugène and Vautrin, point so obviously to other stories.

The novel began as a short story about parental obsession and filial ingratitude. Its title is most often translated into English as *Father Goriot*, losing the significance of the definite article. Its inclusion is not grammatically necessary in French, but the sense is more truly rendered as *Goriot the Father*. The point is that the condition of fatherhood absorbs the whole life and personality of old Goriot. At one time both a husband and a businessman, he has lost or given up these roles; he lives only in the paternal relation, existing at other times, in the boarders' neat phrase, as "an anthropomorphous mollusc." He seems, at first, horribly victimized, so betrayed and ill-repaid by his harpy daughters that his situation excites the silent sympathy of even such hard gems of the *haute monde* as the Duchesse de Langeais and Madame de Beauséant. His gratitude to his offspring for their least notice, slightingly and ungraciously bestowed

as it may be, and his joyful self-sacrifice and boundless self-delusion fill the reader with pity. Was there ever, Balzac seems to ask, a parent so ill-used?

He is the author of his own distress. Balzac leaves no doubt that Goriot reared the two girls in such a way as to ensure that they would be stupid, vain, idle, and grasping women. "The upbringing he gave his daughters was of course preposterous." As he lies dying, his outburst of impotent rage reminds one of Lear; their situations are similar in that each in the folly of his heart wreaks his own ruin. Lear's abasement leads to self-recognition and moral rebirth, but Goriot clings to his delusion to the end, clings to it with a mad tenacity, demanding of unfeeling reality that it conform to his dream of the rewards due faithful parenthood. In fact, he is properly rewarded, for he has been a bad father, the worst of fathers. Parenthood being both privilege and trust, Goriot has enjoyed the first and betrayed the last, as he himself recognizes in a brief interval of lucidity: "The finest nature, the best soul on earth would have succumbed to the corruption of such weakness on a father's part." Indulging himself in the warmth of their goodwill, he has failed in his duty to their moral sense; they are, as adults, mirror images of his own monumental selfishness, made, as it were, of the very stuff of it: "It was I who made them, they belong to me."

To this "obscure but dreadful Parisian tragedy" is added the separate tales of Rastignac and Vautrin, each quite self-contained and yet bound to the other two by the most subtle bonds. One of these links is the recurrent reference to parenthood, good and bad. At every turn, some facet of the parent-child relation is held up for the reader's notice: the wretchedness of the cast-off child Victorine Taillefer, for example, so like Goriot's wretchedness; Madame de Langeais' disquisition on sons-in-law, later echoed by Goriot; the parental tone taken with Eugène both by Madame de Beauséant ("Why you poor simple child!" and in a different way by Vautrin ("You're a good little lad . . .") in giving him wicked worldly advice in contrast to the good but dull counsel of his own mother; the filial relationship that develops between Eugène and Goriot; even Vautrin's enormously ironic nicknames for his landlady ("Mamma Vauquer") and the police ("Father Cop").

Another element linking the *haute monde*, the Maison Vauquer, and the underworld is the fact that they are all partners in crime. Goriot, for example, made his original fortune in criminal collusion with members of the de Langeais family. Vautrin neatly arranges the death of Mademoiselle Taillefer's brother for the benefit of the half-willing Rastignac. The Baron de Nucingen invests Delphine's dowry in an illegal building scheme. Vautrin, Goriot, and Anastasie all resort to "Papa Gobseck" the moneylender. The reader hears a precept uttered by Madame de Beauséant ("in Paris, success is everything, it's the key to power") enunciated a few pages later by Vautrin ("Succeed! . . . succeed at all costs"). The reader is clearly meant to see that whatever differences exist among the various levels of society, they are differences not of kind but of degree. Corruption is universal.

PHAEDRA

Type of work: Drama
Author: Jean Racine (1639–1699)
Type of plot: Classical tragedy
Time of plot: Remote antiquity
Locale: Troezen, in ancient Greece
First presented: 1677

Racine based this tragedy on Euripides' Hippolytus but shifted his focus to the character of Phaedra, who appears only briefly in the Greek play. The playwright explores once again in Phaedra the problem of the extent to which human beings are capable of free will and therefore responsible for their actions.

Principal Characters

Phaedra, the second wife of Theseus and daughter of Minos and Pasiphae, the king and queen of Crete. Phaedra is descended from a line of women of unnatural passions. When she realizes that she has fallen in love with her stepson Hippolyte, she fights the double contagion of heredity and passion with courage and in silence until, unable to resist her love, she arranges to have Hippolyte banished from Athens. She bears Theseus's children, erects a temple to Venus, and makes sacrifices in order to appease the wrath of the goddess. When Theseus leaves her in Troezen with Hippolyte, Phaedra's passion feeds on her until, willing to die, she becomes exhausted and ill from her battle to suppress her illicit love. Word is brought of Theseus's death shortly after her nurse, Oenone, has forced Phaedra to confess her love aloud for the first time. In an unguarded moment, while asking Hippolyte to keep her own son safe now that Hippolyte may be heir to the Athenian throne, Phaedra rather hopefully reveals her passion to him and witnesses his contempt for her. Angry and ashamed, when Phaedra hears to her joy and to her dismay that Theseus has returned alive from his travels, she allows her nurse to accuse Hippolyte of attempted rape—mainly, Phaedra believes, to keep the stigma of her family history and its unnatural passions from falling even more heavily on her own children. Distraught by her guilt and her love, her fear and her fury, she confesses to Theseus that she has lied to him when it is too late to save Hippolyte, and after she herself has taken poison.

Theseus, the son of Aegeus, king of Athens, traditionally faithless to women but faithful to his wives. Theseus so loves his young wife and his own honor that he believes Phaedra's slender evidence instead of trusting what he knows to be the character of his son. Becoming one more figure in Racine's gallery of passion's fools, Theseus in a fury prays to Neptune to grant him the death of Hippolyte. Too autocratic to curb himself when rebuked for his cruel and misinformed curse on his son, he never-

theless begins to suspect that Hippolyte has not lied to him. As the evidence against Phaedra begins to accumulate—she is too distraught to prevent it from doing so—Theseus recovers from his jealous rage too late to save the life of his son.

Hippolyte, the son of Theseus and Antiope, queen of the Amazons. Like everyone about him, Hippolyte goes to extremes. Unpolished, chaste, pure, a hunter and a woodsman, he spurns women until he falls in love with Aricie, becoming willing to hand over Athens, which he is to inherit from his father, to Aricie, his father's enemy. Because Hippolyte is harsh in his judgment of Phaedra, she reacts violently against the proud boy. Theseus is also harsh in his judgment, no less an extremist than his son. Hippolyte's sense of honor prevents him from telling his father about Phaedra's indiscreet confession of her passion, and Theseus's own outraged sense of honor makes him violent in judging Hippolyte.

Aricie, a princess of an older royal dynasty of Athens, held captive by Theseus. Until Hippolyte confesses his love for her, Aricie is content with her lot. Theseus has forbidden her to marry for fear that she may give birth to sons able to contest Theseus's right to rule Athens. She graciously accepts sovereignty of Athens, if Hippolyte can obtain it for her, and his offer of marriage.

Oenone, Phaedra's nurse and friend since childhood. Loyal to her mistress and determined that Phaedra shall not die from stifled passion, she is even willing to further Phaedra's love for Hippolyte. Later, after Hippolyte has spurned Phaedra, Oenone becomes the agent of his destruction.

Theramene, the tutor of Hippolyte. Because of his somewhat lecherous approach to life and to history, Theramene highlights the purity and aloofness of Hippolyte's views. Hippolyte, who would like to strike the love element from historical narratives, is ironically unaware that love will be the chief element in his own history.

The Story

After the death of his Amazon queen, Theseus, slayer of the Minotaur, married Phaedra, the young daughter of the king of Crete. Phaedra, seeing in her stepson, Hippolyte, all the bravery and virtue of his heroic father, but in a more youthful guise, fell in love with him. In an attempt to conceal her passion for the son of Theseus, she treated him in an aloof and spiteful manner until at last Hippolyte decided to leave Troezen and go in search of his father, absent from the kingdom. To his tutor, Theramene, he confided his desire to avoid both his stepmother and Aricie, an Athenian princess who was the daughter of a family which had opposed Theseus. Phaedra confessed to Oenone, her nurse, her guilty passion for Hippolyte, saying that she had merely pretended unkindness to him in order to hide her real feelings.

Word came to Troezen that Theseus was dead. Oenone talked to Phaedra in an attempt to convince the queen that her own son, not Hippolyte, should be chosen as the new king of Athens. Aricie hoped that she would be chosen to rule. Hippolyte, a fair-minded young man, told Aricie that he would support her for the rule of Athens. He felt that Phaedra's son should inherit Crete and that he himself should remain master of Troezen. He also admitted his love for Aricie, but said that he feared the gods would never allow it to be brought to completion. When he tried to explain his intentions to his stepmother, she in turn dropped her pretense of hatred and distrust and ended by betraying her love for Hippolyte. Shocked, he repulsed her, and she threatened to take her own life. The people of Athens, however, chose Phaedra's son to rule over them, to the disappointment of Aricie. There were also rumors that Theseus still lived. Hippolyte gave orders that a search be made for his father.

Phaedra, embarrassed by all she had told Hippolyte, brooded over the injury she now felt and wished that she had never revealed her love. Phaedra was proud, and now her pride was hurt beyond recovery. Unable to over-come her passion, however, she decided to offer the kingdom to Hippolyte so that she might keep him near her. Then news came that Theseus was returning to his home. Oenone warned Phaedra that now she must hide her true feeling for Hippolyte. She even suggested to the queen that Theseus be made to believe that Hippolyte had tempted Phaedra to adultery. When Theseus returned, Phaedra greeted him with reluctance, saying that she was no longer fit to be his wife. Hippolyte made the situation no better by requesting permission to leave Troezen at once. Theseus was greatly chagrined at his homecoming.

When scheming Oenone told the king that Hippolyte had attempted to dishonor his stepmother, Theseus flew into a rage. Hippolyte, knowing nothing of the plot, was at first astonished by his father's anger and threats. When accused, he denied the charges, but Theseus refused to listen to him and banished his son from the kingdom forever. When Hippolyte claimed that he was really in love with Aricie, Theseus, more incensed than ever, invoked the vengeance of Neptune upon his son. Aricie tried to convince Hippolyte that he must prove his innocence, but Hippolyte refused because he knew that the revelation of Phaedra's passion would be too painful for his father to bear. The two agreed to escape together. Before Aricie could leave the palace, however, Theseus questioned her. Becoming suspicious, he sent for Oenone to demand the truth. Fearing that her plot had been uncovered, Oenone committed suicide.

Meanwhile, as Hippolyte drove his chariot near the seashore, Neptune sent a horrible monster, part bull and part dragon, which destroyed the prince. When news of his death reached the palace, Phaedra confessed her guilt and drank poison. Theseus, glad to see his guilty queen die, wished that memory of her life might perish with her. Sorrowfully, he sought the grief-stricken Aricie to comfort her.

Critical Evaluation

The issues of free will, predestination, and grace that interested Racine in the seventeenth century constituted a restatement, in theological terms, of a problem of universal concern. To what extent is man free to create his own existence and be responsible for his actions? Are the terms of human existence within the arena of human control, or are they preestablished by some external force? Can human suffering be justified as the result of one's actions, or is it the imposition of a capricious deity?

The specific manner in which these questions are answered depends upon one's view of human nature and human potential. When a person chooses between pre-destination and free will, he is either asserting or denying his belief in his ability to make wise and ethically sound decisions. Emphasis on the dignity of man and on his potential for choice often coincides with optimism regarding human behavior. Conversely, a belief in man as a depraved and irresponsible creature will be found in conjunction with a distrust of man's ability to act in a positive and meaningful way. This view of the human condition is presented by Racine in *Phaedra*, which shows man as predetermined or predestined.

Racine was reared by the Jansenists at Port-Royal, and he returned to Port-Royal after completing *Phaedra*. The Jansenists held ideas on the problem of free will and predestination in opposition to the dominant position of the Catholic church, a position that had been set forth by the Jesuits. The Jesuits attempted to bring salvation within the grasp of all men, whereas the Jansenists emphasized a rigid determinism. They rejected the Jesuit doctrine that man could attain his salvation through good works and insisted that man was predestined to salvation or damnation. This denial of free will was based on the conviction that after the Fall man was left completely corrupt and devoid of rational self-control. Man was incapable of participating in the process of regeneration because Original Sin had deprived him of his will. The passions had gained control of man, and they could only lead to evil. Human passion was seen as capable of leading to falsehood, crime, suicide, and general destruction. It was inevitable that the Jansenists would regard with alarm any doctrine that allowed for the activity of human free will. Only God's gift of mercy could save man, and that mercy was reserved for those who had been elected to salvation.

Phaedra manifests a similar distrust of the passions, a similar curtailment of free will, and a consequent emphasis upon man's lack of control. Human passion is depicted as controlling reason. The arena of human choice and responsibility is severely limited. Phaedra is pursued by an inexorable fate. In the preface to *Phaedra*, however, Racine suggests the possibility of free will. He states that Phaedra is "neither completely guilty nor completely innocent. She is involved, by her destiny and by the anger of the gods, in an illicit passion of which she is the first to be horrified. She makes every effort to overcome it." Does Phaedra actually make the effort Racine attributes to her? To what extent is she free to make a choice? To what extent is this merely the illusion of free will? In his preface, Racine insists that "her crime is more a punishment of the gods than an act of her will."

Phaedra's genealogy would seem to support the argument of fatalism. She is initially referred to, not by name, but as the daughter of Minos and Pasiphaë. Throughout the play, she gives the appearance of being overwhelmed by a cruel destiny that is linked to her past. She exhibits perfect lucidity regarding the full implications of her situation, yet she seems incapable of resolving her dilemma. She has made numerous but ineffective attempts to overcome her love for Hippolyte: She built a temple to Venus, sacrificed innumerable victims, and attempted to surmount her passion through prayer.

As the play opens, Phaedra resorts to her final effort—suicide. Ironically, her attempted suicide will serve only to add physical weakness to her already weakened emotional condition and prevent her from overcoming the temptations with which she will be confronted. The first temptation is offered by Oenone. By implying that her suicide would constitute betrayal of the gods, her husband, and her children, Oenone attempts to persuade Phaedra to reveal her love for Hippolyte. The news of Theseus's apparent death further tempts Phaedra by removing the crime of potential adultery. In addition, Phaedra is tempted to offer the crown to Hippolyte in order to protect her children and appeal to his political aspirations.

Her interview with Hippolyte, however, turns into a confession of love which unfolds without any semblance of rational control. Although she expresses shame at her declaration, her passion is presented as part of the destiny of her entire race. At the moment following the confession to Hippolyte, Phaedra prays to Venus, not as in the past to free her from passion, but to inflame Hippolyte with a comparable passion. Theseus's return presents Phaedra with a choice of either revealing or denying her love for Hippolyte. She allows Oenone to deceive Theseus. Yet is this actually a moment of choice, assuming that choice involves a rational action? On the contrary, Phaedra's statement to her nurse at the end of Act 3, scene 3, implies complete lack of control. Phaedra's final temptation is to refuse to confess her lies to Theseus. Once again, she is prevented from acting in a rational manner, for upon learning of Hippolyte's love for Aricie, she is overwhelmed by a blinding jealousy.

Despite Racine's enigmatic remarks in the preface, the pattern of temptation and defeat developed in the play eliminates entirely the possibility of free will. Although Phaedra wishes to overcome her passion, all of her efforts are in vain. The series of temptations in *Phaedra* serves to emphasize her lack of control and conspires to bring about her ruin. From the possibility of an early death with honor, Phaedra is led, through a series of defeats, to a guilty and dishonorable death.

Some have seen in the character of Phaedra, however, a striving to surpass limits and an awareness of her own condition that elevate her to tragic greatness. Despite her helplessness, she feels responsibility for her actions. Denied choice, she does not revel in her lostness but instead is engulfed in shame, as if moral decisions were really possible. Racine's Phaedra, then, is doomed not only to do wrong but also to take responsibility for that wrongdoing, vainly but heroically pursuing a mirage of freedom.

THE PICKWICK PAPERS

Type of work: Novel
Author: Charles Dickens (1812–1870)
Type of plot: Comic romance
Time of plot: 1827–1828
Locale: England
First published: 1836–1837 (serial), 1838 (book)

These sketches, originally published in serial form, were planned as prose accompaniments to caricatures by a popular artist. The title derives from the character of Mr. Pickwick, a naïve, generous, lovable old gentleman who reigns over the activities of the Pickwick Club. Many of the comic highlights in the work spring from the imperturbable presence of mind and ready wit of Sam Weller, whose cleverness and humor are indispensable to the Pickwickians.

Principal Characters

Mr. Samuel Pickwick, the stout, amiable founder and perpetual president of the Pickwick Club. An observer of human nature, a lover of good food and drink, and a boon companion, he spends his time traveling about the countryside with his friends, accepting invitations from local squires and dignitaries, pursuing Mr. Alfred Jingle in an effort to thwart that rascal's schemes, and promoting his friends' romances. The height of his development occurs at the Fleet Prison where, because of a breach of promise suit, he observes human suffering and learns to forgive his enemies. A rather pompously bustling and fatuous person at first, he grows in the course of events to be a truly monumental character.

Mr. Nathaniel Winkle, the sportsman of the group. Inept and humane, he finds himself involved in hunting misadventures, romances, and duels. In the end he wins Arabella Allen, his true love, over the objections of her brother, her suitor, and his own father.

Mr. Augustus Snodgrass, the poetic member of the Pickwick Club. Although he keeps extensive notes, he never writes verses. Eventually he gains his sweetheart, Emily Wardle, after several visits to Manor Farm.

Mr. Tracy Tupman, a rotund member of the Pickwick Club, so susceptible that he is constantly falling in and out of love. Longing for romance, he finds himself thwarted at every turn. His flirtation with Miss Rachel Wardle, ends dismally when she elopes with Mr. Alfred Jingle.

Mr. Wardle, the owner of Manor Farm, Dingley Dell, the robust, genial, but sometimes hot-tempered host of the four Pickwickians. A patriarch, he rescues his sister from Mr. Jingle at the cost of one hundred and twenty pounds, and he objects at first to his daughter's romance with Mr. Snodgrass. Finally he gives the young couple his blessing.

Miss Rachel Wardle, a spinster of uncertain age. She flirts coyly with the susceptible Mr. Tupman but abandons him for the blandishments of Mr. Jingle, who has designs on her supposed wealth. Mr. Pickwick and Mr. Wardle pursue the elopers, Mr. Wardle buys off the rascal, and Miss Wardle returns husbandless to Manor Farm.

Mrs. Wardle, the aged, deaf mother of Mr. Wardle and Miss Rachel.

Emily Wardle, Mr. Wardle's vivacious daughter, in love with Mr. Snodgrass, whom she eventually marries.

Isabella Wardle, another daughter. She marries Mr. Trundle.

Mr. Trundle, Isabella Wardle's suitor. Though frequently on the scene, he remains a minor figure in the novel.

Joe, Mr. Wardle's fat, sleepy young servant. He is characterized by his ability to go to sleep at any time and under almost any circumstances, a trait which both amuses and irritates his master.

Mrs. Martha Bardell, Mr. Pickwick's landlady. When he consults her as to the advisability of taking a servant, she mistakes his remarks for a proposal of marriage and accepts him, much to Mr. Pickwick's dismay. The misunderstanding leads to the famous breach of promise suit of Bardell vs. Pickwick. Mr. Pickwick, refusing to pay damages, is sent to the Fleet Prison. After his refusal to pay, Mrs. Bardell's attorneys, unable to collect their fee, have her arrested and also sent to the Fleet Prison. Her plight finally arouses Mr. Pickwick's pity, and he pays the damages in order to release her and to free himself to aid his friend Mr. Winkle, who has eloped with Arabella Allen.

Tommy Bardell, Mrs. Bardell's young son.

Serjeant Buzfuz, Mrs. Bardell's counsel at the trial, a bombastic man noted for his bullying tactics with witnesses.

Mr. Skimpin, the assistant counsel to Serjeant Buzfuz.

Mr. Dodson and **Mr. Fogg,** Mrs. Bardell's unscrupulous attorneys. Having taken the suit without fee, they have their client arrested and sent to prison when Mr. Pickwick refuses to pay damages after the suit has been decided against him.

Mr. Alfred Jingle, an amiable, impudent strolling player remarkable for his constant flow of disjointed sentences. He makes several attempts to marry women for their money, but Mr. Pickwick thwarts his plans in every case. He ends up in the Fleet Prison, from which he is rescued by Mr. Pickwick's generosity. He keeps his promise to reform.

Job Trotter, Mr. Jingle's cunning accomplice and servant. He is the only person whose wits prove sharper than those of Sam Weller.

Jem Huntley, a melancholy actor called **Dismal Jemmy,** Mr. Jingle's friend and Job Trotter's brother.

Sam Weller, Mr. Pickwick's jaunty, quick-witted, devoted Cockney servant. He and Mr. Pickwick meet at the inn to which Mr. Wardle has traced his sister and Mr. Jingle. Mr. Pickwick's decision to hire Sam as his valet leads to the famous breach of promise suit brought by Mrs. Bardell. Sam's aphorisms, anecdotes, and exploits make him one of Dickens' great comic creations, the embodiment of Cockney life and character.

Tony Weller, Sam Weller's hardy, affable father, a coachman who loves food, drink, and tobacco, and wants nothing from his shrewish wife except the opportunity to enjoy them.

Mrs. Susan Weller, formerly **Mrs. Clarke,** a shrew, a hypocrite, and a religious fanatic. At her death her husband inherits a small estate she has hoarded.

The Reverend Mr. Stiggins, called the **Shepherd,** a canting, hypocritical, alcoholic clergyman, greatly admired by Mrs. Weller, who gives him every opportunity to sponge off her husband.

Arabella Allen, a lovely girl whom Mr. Winkle first meets at Manor Farm. Her brother, Benjamin Allen, wants his sister to marry his friend Bob Sawyer, but Arabella rejects her brother's choice. After she marries Mr. Winkle in secret, Mr. Pickwick pays his friend's debts, effects a reconciliation between the young couple and Arabella's brother, and breaks the news of the marriage to Mr. Winkle's father.

Benjamin Allen, Arabella's coarse, roistering brother, a medical student. With no regard for his sister's feelings, he stubbornly insists upon her marriage to Bob Sawyer.

Mr. Winkle (Senior), a practical man of business, much opposed to his son's romance with Arabella Allen. He changes his mind when, through the services of Mr. Pickwick, he meets his daughter-in-law. He builds the couple a new house and makes his son an assistant in the family business.

Bob Sawyer, Benjamin Allen's friend and Arabella's unwelcome, oafish suitor. He hangs up his shingle in Bristol and practices medicine there. Eventually he and Benjamin Allen take service with the East India Company.

Bob Cripps, Bob Sawyer's servant.

Mrs. Mary Ann Raddle, Bob Sawyer's landlady, a shrew.

Mr. Raddle, her husband.

Mrs. Betsey Cluppins, Mrs. Raddle's sister and a friend of Mrs. Bardell.

Mr. Gunter, a friend of Bob Sawyer.

Jack Hopkins, a medical student, Bob Sawyer's friend. He tells Mr. Pickwick the story of a child who swallowed a necklace of large wooden beads that rattled and clacked whenever the child moved.

Peter Magnus, a traveler who journeys with Mr. Pickwick from London to Ipswich. He is on his way to make a proposal of marriage.

Miss Witherfield, his beloved, into whose room Mr. Pickwick, unable to find his own, accidentally blunders at the inn in Ipswich.

The Hon. Samuel Slumkey, a candidate for Parliament from the borough of Eatanswill. He is victorious over his opponent, Horatio Fizkin, Esq.

Mr. Slurk, the editor of "The Eatanswill Independent."

Mr. Pott, the editor of "The Eatanswill Gazette."

Mrs. Pott, his wife.

Mrs. Leo Hunter, a lady of literary pretensions, the author of "Ode to an Expiring Frog," whom Mr. Pickwick meets in Eatanswill.

Mr. Leo Hunter, who lives in his wife's reflected glory.

Count Smorltork, a traveling nobleman whom Mr. Pickwick meets at a breakfast given by Mrs. Leo Hunter.

Horatio Fizkin, Esq., defeated in the election at Eatanswill.

Mr. Perker, the agent for the Hon. Samuel Slumkey in the Eatanswill election, later Mr. Pickwick's attorney in the suit of Bardell vs. Pickwick. After his client has been sentenced to prison, Perker advises him to pay the damages in order to gain his freedom.

Serjeant Snubbin, Mr. Pickwick's lantern-faced, dull-eyed senior counsel in the breach of promise suit.

Mr. Justice Starleigh, the judge who presides at the trial of Bardell vs. Pickwick.

Mr. Phunky, the assistant counsel to Serjeant Snubbin; he is called an "infant barrister" because he has seen only eight years at the bar.

Thomas Groffin, a chemist, and **Richard Upwitch,** a grocer, jurors at the trial of Bardell vs. Pickwick.

Mr. Jackson and **Mr. Wicks,** clerks in the office of Dodson and Fogg.

Mr. Lowten, clerk to Mr. Perker.

Captain Boldwig, a peppery-tempered landowner on whose grounds the Pickwickians accidentally trespass while hunting.

Dr. Slammer, the surgeon of the 97th Regiment. At a charity ball in Rochester he challenges Mr. Jingle to a duel, but because the player is wearing a borrowed coat Mr. Winkle is the one actually called upon to meet the hot-tempered surgeon. Mr. Winkle, having been drunk, cannot remember what his conduct was or whom he might have insulted the night before. The situation is eventually resolved and Mr. Winkle and the doctor shake hands and part on friendly terms.

Lieutenant Tappleton, Dr. Slammer's second.

Colonel Bulder, the commanding officer of the military garrison at Rochester.

Mrs. Bulder, his wife.

Miss Bulder, his daughter.

Mrs. Budger, a widow, Mr. Tupman's partner at the charity ball in Rochester.

Mr. Dowler, a blustering, cowardly ex-army officer whom Mr. Pickwick meets at the White Horse Cellar. The Dowlers travel with Mr. Pickwick to Bath.

Mrs. Dowler, his wife.

Lord Mutanhed, a man of fashion and Mr. Dowling's friend, whom Mr. Pickwick meets in Bath.

The Hon. Mr. Crushton, another friend of Mr. Dowler.

Angelo Cyrus Bantam, Esq., a friend of Mr. and Mrs. Dowling and a master of ceremonies at Bath.

George Nupkins, Esq., the mayor of Ipswich, before whom Mr. Pickwick is brought on the charge, made by Miss Witherfield, that he is planning to fight a duel. The mayor has recently entertained Mr. Jingle who, calling himself Captain Fitz-Marshall, was courting Miss Henrietta Nupkins.

Mrs. Nupkins, the mayor's wife.

Henrietta Nupkins, their daughter, the object of one of Mr. Jingle's matrimonial designs.

Mary, Mrs. Nupkins' pretty young servant. She eventually marries Sam Weller and both make their home with Mr. Pickwick in his happy, unadventurous old age.

Mr. Jinks, the clerk of the mayor's court at Ipswich.

Daniel Grummer, the constable of the mayor's court at Ipswich.

Frank Simmery, Esq., a young stock broker.

Solomon Pell, an attorney who, to his profit, assists in settling the deceased Mrs. Weller's modest estate.

Miss Tomkins, mistress of Westgate House, a boarding school for young ladies, at Bury St. Edmunds. Mr. Pickwick, tricked into believing that Mr. Jingle is planning to elope with one of the pupils, ventures into the school premises at night and finds himself in an embarrassing situation.

Tom Roker, a turnkey at the Fleet Prison.

Smangle, Mivins, called **The Zephyr, Martin, Simpson,** and **The Chancery Prisoner,** inmates of the Fleet Prison during Mr. Pickwick's detention.

Mrs. Budkin, Susannah Sanders, Mrs. Mudberry, and **Mrs. Rogers,** Mrs. Bardell's friends and neighbors.

Anthony Humm, chairman of the Brick Lane Branch of the United Grand Junction Ebenezer Temperance Association. Mr. Weller takes his son Sam to a lively meeting of the association.

The Story

Samuel Pickwick, Esquire, was the founder and perpetual president of the justly famous Pickwick Club. To extend his own researches into the quaint and curious phenomena of life, he suggested that he and three other Pickwickians should make journeys to places remote from London and report on their findings to the stay-at-home members of the club. The first destination decided upon was Rochester. As Mr. Pickwick, Mr. Tracy Tupman, Mr. Nathaniel Winkle, and Mr. Augustus Snodgrass went to their coach, they were waylaid by a rough gang of cab drivers. Fortunately, the men were rescued by a stranger who was poorly dressed but of a magnificently friendly nature. The stranger, who introduced himself as Alfred Jingle, also appeared to be going to Rochester, and the party mounted the coach together.

After they had arrived at their destination, Mr. Tupman's curiosity was aroused when Mr. Jingle told him that there was to be a ball at the inn that evening and that many lovely young ladies would be present. Because his luggage had gone astray, said Mr. Jingle, he had no evening clothes and so it would be impossible for him to attend the affair. This was a regrettable circumstance because he had hoped to introduce Mr. Tupman to the many young ladies of wealth and fashion who would be present. Eager to meet these young ladies, Mr. Tupman

borrowed Mr. Winkle's suit for the stranger. At the ball, Mr. Jingle observed a doctor in faithful attendance upon a middle-aged lady. Attracting her attention, he danced with her, much to the anger of the doctor. Introducing himself as Dr. Slammer, the angry gentleman challenged Mr. Jingle to a duel.

The next morning, a servant identified Mr. Winkle from the description given of the suit the stranger had worn; he then told Mr. Winkle that an insolent drunken man had insulted Dr. Slammer the previous evening and that the doctor was awaiting his appearance to fight a duel. Mr. Winkle had been drunk the night before, and he decided he was being called out because he had conducted himself in an unseemly manner that he could no longer remember. With Mr. Snodgrass as his second, Mr. Winkle tremblingly approached the battlefield. Much to his relief, Dr. Slammer roared that he was the wrong man. After much misunderstanding, the situation was satisfactorily explained, and no blood was shed.

During the afternoon, the travelers attended a parade, where they met Mr. Wardle in a coach with his two daughters and his sister, Miss Rachel Wardle, a plump old maid. Mr. Tupman was impressed by the elder Miss Wardle and accepted for his friends Mr. Wardle's invitation to visit his estate, Manor Farm. The next day, the four Pickwickians departed for the farm, which was a distance of about ten miles from the inn where they were staying. They encountered difficulties with their horses and arrived at Manor Farm in a disheveled state, but they were soon washed and mended under the kind assistance of Mr. Wardle's daughters. In the evening, they played a hearty game of whist, and Mr. Tupman squeezed Miss Wardle's hand under the table.

The next day, Mr. Wardle took his guests rook hunting. Mr. Winkle, who would not admit he couldn't hunt, was given the gun to try his skill. He proved his inexperience, though, by accidentally shooting Mr. Tupman in the arm. Miss Wardle offered her aid to the stricken man. Observing that their friend was in good hands, the others went off to a neighboring town to watch the cricket matches. There Mr. Pickwick unexpectedly encountered Mr. Jingle, and Mr. Wardle invited the fellow to return to Manor Farm with his party.

Convinced that Miss Wardle had a great deal of money, Mr. Jingle misrepresented Mr. Tupman's intentions to Miss Wardle and persuaded the spinster to elope with him. Mr. Wardle and Mr. Pickwick pursued the couple to London. There, with the help of Mr. Wardle's lawyer, Mr. Perker, they went from one inn to another in an attempt to find the elopers. Finally, through a sharp-featured young man cleaning boots in the yard of the White Hart Inn, they were able to identify Mr. Jingle. They indignantly confronted him as he was displaying a marriage license. After a heated argument, Mr. Jingle resigned his matrimonial plans for the sum of one hundred and twenty pounds. Miss Wardle tearfully went back to Manor Farm. The Pickwickians returned to London, where Mr. Pickwick engaged as his servant Sam Weller, the sharp, shrewd young bootblack of the White Hart Inn.

Mr. Pickwick was destined to meet the villainous Mr. Jingle soon again. Mrs. Leo Hunter invited the learned man and his friends to a party. There Mr. Pickwick spied Mr. Jingle, who, upon seeing his former acquaintance, disappeared into the crowd. Mrs. Hunter told Mr. Pickwick that Mr. Jingle lived at Bury St. Edmonds. Mr. Pickwick set out in pursuit in company with his servant, Sam Weller, for the old gentleman was determined to deter the scoundrel from any fresh deceptions he might be planning. At the inn where Mr. Jingle was reported to be staying, Mr. Pickwick learned that the rascal was planning to elope with a rich young lady who stayed at a boarding school nearby. Mr. Pickwick agreed with the suggestion that in order to rescue the young lady he should hide in the garden from which Mr. Jingle was planning to steal her. When Mr. Pickwick sneaked into the garden, he found nothing of a suspicious nature; in short, he had been deceived, and the blackguard had escaped.

Mr. Pickwick's housekeeper was Mrs. Bardell, a widow. When he was about to hire Sam Weller, Mr. Pickwick had spoken to her in such a manner that she had mistaken his words for a proposal of marriage. One day, Mr. Pick-

wick was resting in his room when he received a notice from the legal firm of Dodgson and Fogg that Mrs. Bardell was suing him for breach of promise. The summons was distressing; but first, Mr. Pickwick had more important business to occupy his time. After securing the services of Mr. Perker to defend him, he went to Ipswich upon learning that Mr. Jingle had been seen in that vicinity. The trip to Ipswich was successful. The Pickwickians were able to catch Mr. Jingle in his latest scheme of deception and to expose him before he had carried out his plot.

At the trial for the breach of promise suit brought by Mrs. Bardell, lawyers Dodgson and Fogg argued so eloquently against Mr. Pickwick that the jury fined him seven hundred and fifty pounds. When the trial was over, Mr. Pickwick told Dodgson and Fogg that even if they put him in prison he would never pay one cent of the damages, since he knew as well as they that there had been no true grounds for suit.

Shortly afterward, the Pickwickians went to Bath, where fresh adventures awaited Mr. Pickwick and his friends. On that occasion, Mr. Winkle's weakness for the fair sex involved them in difficulties. In Bath, the Pickwickians met two young medical students, Mr. Allen and Mr. Bob Sawyer. Mr. Allen hoped to marry his sister Arabella to his friend Mr. Sawyer, but Miss Allen professed extreme dislike for her brother's choice. When Mr. Winkle learned that Arabella had refused Mr. Sawyer because another man had won her heart, he felt that he must be the fortunate man, because she had displayed an interest in him when they had met earlier at Manor Farm. Mr. Pickwick kindly arranged to have Mr. Winkle meet Arabella in a garden, where the distraught lover could plead his suit.

Mr. Pickwick's plans to further his friend's romance were interrupted, however, by a subpoena delivered because he had refused to pay money to Mrs. Bardell. Still stubbornly refusing to pay the damages, Mr. Pickwick found himself returned to London and lodged in Fleet Street prison. With the help of Sam Weller, Mr. Pickwick arranged his prison quarters as comfortably as possible and remained deaf to the entreaties of Sam Weller or Mr. Perker, who thought that he should pay his debt and regain his freedom. Dodgson and Fogg proved to be of lower caliber than even Mr. Pickwick had suspected. They had taken Mrs. Bardell's case without fee, gambling on Mr. Pickwick's payment to cover the costs of the case. When they saw no payment forthcoming, they had Mrs. Bardell also arrested and sent to the Fleet Street prison.

While Mr. Pickwick was trying to decide what to do, Mr. Winkle with his new wife, Arabella, came to the prison and asked Mr. Pickwick to pay his debts so that he could visit Mr. Allen with the news of Mr. Winkle's marriage to Arabella. Arabella felt that Mr. Pickwick was the only person who could arrange a proper reconciliation between her brother and her new husband. Kindness prevailed; Mr. Pickwick paid the damages to Mrs. Bardell so that he would be free to help his friends in distress.

Winning Mr. Allen's approval of the match was not difficult for Mr. Pickwick, but when he approached the elder Mr. Winkle, the bridegroom's father objected to the marriage and threatened to cut off his son without a cent. To add to Mr. Pickwick's problems, Mr. Wardle came to London to tell him that his daughter Emily was in love with Mr. Snodgrass and to ask Mr. Pickwick's advice. Mr. Wardle had brought Emily to London with him.

The entire party came together in Arabella's apartment. All misunderstandings happily ended for the two lovers, and a jolly party followed. The elder Mr. Winkle paid a call on his new daughter-in-law. Upon seeing what a charming and lovely girl she was, he relented his decision to disinherit his son, and the family was reconciled.

After Mr. Snodgrass had married Emily Wardle, Mr. Pickwick dissolved the Pickwick Club and retired to a home in the country with his faithful servant, Sam Weller. Several times, Mr. Pickwick was called upon to be a godfather to little Winkles and Snodgrasses; for the most part, however, he led a quiet life, respected by his neighbors and loved by all of his friends.

Critical Evaluation

Mr. Pickwick, the lovable, generous old gentleman of Charles Dickens' novel, is one of the best-known characters of fiction. Mr. Pickwick benignly reigns over all activities of the Pickwick Club; under every circumstance, he is satisfied that he has helped his fellow creatures by his well-meaning efforts. The height of this Dickensian comedy, however, lies in Sam Weller and his father. Sam's imperturbable presence of mind and his ready wit are indispensable to the Pickwickians. The novel has importance beyond humorous incidents and characterizations. It is the first novel of a literary movement to present the life and manners of lower and middle-class life.

When in 1836 a publisher proposed that Dickens write the text for a series of pictures by the sporting artist Robert Seymour, Dickens was experiencing the first thrill of fame as the author of *Sketches by Boz*. He was twenty-four years old and had been for some years a court reporter and free-lance journalist; *Sketches by Boz* was his first literary effort of any length. The work that the publisher proposed was of a similar kind: short, usually humorous descriptions of cosmopolitan life, sometimes illustrated, and published monthly. Although Dickens already had the plan of a novel in mind, he was in need of cash and accepted the offer as a stopgap. He made one stipulation: that he and not Seymour have the choice of scenes to be treated. He did this because he himself was no sportsman and as a cockney had little knowledge of the country beyond what his journalistic travels had shown him. It is evident that he viewed the enterprise as an expedient from the digressive character of the first few chapters.

Dickens was able to disguise his ignorance of country life by a canny selection of scenes and topics. Actual sporting scenes are kept to a minimum and treated with broad humor and slight detail. On the other hand, he knew country elections, magistrates, and newspapers well, and the chapters describing the Eatanswill election and dealing with Mr. Nupkins, the mayor of Ipswich, and Mr. Pott, the editor of the Eatanswill *Gazette*, abound in atmosphere and choice observation. Most useful of all was his intimate knowledge of stagecoach travel, of life upon the road, and of the inhabitants and manners of inns great and small. The device of a journey by coach unifies the first part of the novel, and a large portion of the action, including several key scenes, takes place in inns and public houses; for example, Mr. Pickwick meets Sam Weller at the White Hart Inn, Mrs. Bardell is apprehended at the Spaniards, Sam is reunited with his father at the Marquis of Granby, and the Wellers plot Stiggins' discomfiture at the Blue Boar.

A theme that Dickens developed in later works appears in embryo here: the quicksand quality of litigation. Readers note that every figure connected with the law is portrayed as venal if not downright criminal, except Mr. Perker, who is merely depicted as a remarkably cold fish. Another feature of later works anticipated here is the awkward treatment of women. The author's attitude toward women is extremely ambiguous. Two of the women in the novel are unqualifiedly good. Sam's Mary is described perennially as "the pretty housemaid," and the fact that Sam loves her appears to complete the list of her virtues in Dickens' view. As a character, she has neither depth nor ethical range; no more has Arabella Allen, the dark-eyed girl with the "very nice little pair of boots." She is distinguished at first by flirtatious archness and later by a rather servile docility. The daughters of old Wardle first come to the reader's attention in the act of spiting their spinster aunt and never redeem this impression. Other female characters are rather poorly developed. None has, as do some of the male figures such as Jingle and Trotter, a human dimension.

The author's sentiments about the institution of marriage are also curious. Mr. Winkle makes a runaway match, Mr. Snodgrass is only forestalled from doing so by a lack of parental opposition, and Mr. Tupman escapes after a ludicrously close call. Mr. Pickwick, the great advocate of heart over head, however, is not and never has been married, and in fact, he shows his greatest strength as a character in his struggle for justice in a breach-of-promise suit; while Mr. Weller, the other beneficent father-figure of the work, makes no bones about his aversion to the connubial state: " 'vether it's worth while goin' through so much, to learn so little. . . is a matter o' taste. *I* rayther think it isn't.' "

Angus Wilson, among others, contends that *Pickwick Papers*, like most first novels, is autobiographical, however well disguised. There is evidence for this position in the fact that Dickens' estimation of the women in his life also tended to extremes of adulation and contempt. More pertinent to the main thrust of the novel, which is the development of Pickwick from buffoon to "angel in tights," and the concurrent development of Sam, is the author's relationship to his father, whom he adored. The elder Dickens' imprisonment for debt in 1824 was the great trauma of the author's childhood; it was made the more galling by the fact that he, the eldest son, was put out to work at a blacking factory and was able to join the family circle in the prison only on Sundays. Scarcely more than a child, he felt unable either to aid or to comfort his father in his distress; at the same time, he felt that his father had abandoned him to an ungentle world.

As a young man, Dickens wrote into his first novel an account of those times as he would have wished them to be. Mr. Pickwick is the epitome of those qualities of Dickens senior that so endeared him to his son: unsinkable good spirits and kindness that does not count the cost. To these, Pickwick adds financial sense, ethical size, and most important, a sensitivity to the best feelings of his spiritual son, Sam Weller. Sam, in turn, bends all of his cockney keenness of eye and wit, all of his courage and steadfastness, to the service not only of this ideal father unjustly imprisoned but also of his immensely endearing shadow-father Tony Weller. Clearly, this material has its roots in Dickens' life; but it is just as clear that his genius tapped a universal longing of sons to see their fathers as heroes and themselves as heroic helpers.

THE PILGRIM'S PROGRESS

Type of work: Novel
Author: John Bunyan (1628–1688)
Type of plot: Religious allegory
Time of plot: Any time since Christ
Locale: Anywhere
First published: (Part I, 1678; Part II, 1684)

One of the most widely read books in English literature, The Pilgrim's Progress *is a prose allegory relating the journey and adventures of Christian, who flees the City of Destruction and sets out for the Celestial City. Since Bunyan, a devout Puritan, wished his book to be accessible to the common people, he wrote in a straightforward, unadorned prose that has simple grandeur and nobility appropriate to its subject matter. Much of the success of* The Pilgrim's Progress *is also the result of its vivid characterizations.*

Principal Characters

Christian, an example of all God-fearing Protestants, whose adventures are recounted as events in a dream experienced by the narrator. Originally called Graceless, of the race of Japhet, Christian becomes distressed with his life in the City of Destruction and insists that his wife and four children accompany him in search of salvation. When they refuse to leave, Christian determines to set out alone. His life thereafter consists of hardships, sufferings, and struggles to overcome obstacles—physical and emotional—which beset his path. At the outset, Christian's family and neighbors, Pliable and Obstinate, try to dissuade him from breaking away from his sins of the past. Then Evangelist appears with a parchment roll on which is inscribed, "Fly from the Wrath to Come." On his long journey, Christian finds that human beings he meets offer distractions and hindrance, even bodily harm and violence. Mr. Worldly Wiseman turns him aside from his set purpose until Evangelist intervenes. **Simple, Sloth, Presumption, Formalist, Hypocrisy, Timorous,** and **Mistrust** seek to dissuade or discourage Christian because of the rigors of the straight and narrow way. The Giant of the Doubting Castle and his wife beat and torture Christian and Hopeful. In the Valley of Humiliation Christian engages in mortal combat with a monstrous creature named Apollyon for more than half a day, but at last emerges triumphant. In many times of peril, Christian is fortunate in having companions who can assist him: Evangelist, who gets him out of difficulties or warns him of impending strife; **Help**, who comes to his aid when he falls into the Slough of Despond; Faithful, who is by his side at Vanity Fair; Hopeful, who comforts him at the Doubting Castle and encourages him to give up bravely at the River of Death. In this narrative of a pilgrim's adventures, Christian must constantly overcome temptations and dangers that would thwart his goal, impede his progress toward eternal life, or prevent him from reaching Heaven; but with the aid of his religious fervor and the advice and counsel of a few true friends, he achieves salvation.

Evangelist, Christian's adviser and guide, particularly in times of danger. Evangelist shows him the way to avoid destruction, directs him to the Wicket Gate, and warns him of people such as Mr. Worldly Wiseman and of the dangers at Vanity Fair.

Apollyon (à·pŏl′lyŏn), the fiend in the Valley of Humiliation. Apollyon has scales like a fish, feet like a bear, wings like a dragon, and a mouth like a lion; he spouts fire and smoke from his belly, and he discourses like a devil in his attempt to keep Christian from continuing his journey.

Giant Despair, the giant owner of Doubting Castle. He imprisons Christian and Faithful, beats them, and threatens death, until Christian uses a key of Promise to make their escape.

Faithful, Christian's traveling companion. Imprisoned, tortured, and put to death by the people of Vanity Fair, he is transported to the Celestial Gate in a chariot.

Hopeful, another wayfarer. He joins Christian at Vanity Fair and accompanies him through various adventures on the way to eternal salvation.

Good-Will, who tells Christian that if he knocks the gate that is blocking his way will be opened, so that he may see a vision of the Day of Judgment.

Ignorance, a native of the country of Conceit. Refusing to accept the beliefs of Christian and Hopeful, he continues on the journey until he is seized and thrust into Hell.

Mr. Worldly Wiseman, a dweller in the town of Carnal-Policy. He advises Christian to go to Legality and get relief from the burden of sins which Christian carries on his back.

Three Shining Ones, who clothe Christian with new raiment after his burdens fall off before the Cross.

Obstinate and **Pliable**, neighbors of Christian. Both

try to keep Christian from leaving the City of Destruction. Obstinate remains behind, but Pliable goes with Christian until he deserts him at the Slough of Despond.

Interpreter, who instructs Christian in the mysteries of faith.

Discretion, Prudence, Piety, and **Charity**, virgins who arm Christian with the sword and shield of faith.

Pope and **Pagan**, giants whose caves Christian must pass after reciting verses from the Psalms to protect himself from devils issuing from one of the gates of Hell.

Knowledge, Experience, Watchful, and **Sincere**, shepherds who point out the Celestial Gate to Christian and Hopeful.

The Story

One day, according to Bunyan, he lay down in a den to sleep; in his sleep, he dreamed that he saw a man standing in a field and crying out in pain and sorrow because he and his whole family as well as the town in which they lived were to be destroyed. Christian, for that was his name, knew of this catastrophe because he had read about it in the book he held in his hands, the Bible. Evangelist, the preacher of Christianity, soon came up to Christian and presented him with a roll of paper on which it was written that he should flee from the wrath of God and make his way from the City of Destruction to the City of Zion. Running home with this hope of salvation, Christian tried to get his neighbors and family to go away with him, but they would not listen and thought he was either sick or mad. Finally, he shut his ears to his family's entreaties to stay with them and ran off toward the light in the distance. Under the light, he knew he would find the wicket gate that opened into Heaven.

On his way, he met Pliant and Obstinate; Christian was so distracted by them that he fell in a bog called the Slough of Despond. He could not get out because of the bundle of sins on his back. Finally, Help came along and aided Christian out of the sticky mire. Going on his way, he soon fell in with Mr. Worldly Wiseman, who tried to convince Christian that he would lead a happier life if he gave up his trip toward the light and settled down to the comforts of a burdenless town life. Fearing that Christian was about to be led astray, Evangelist came up to the two men and quickly showed the errors in Mr. Worldly Wiseman's arguments.

Soon Christian arrived at a closed gate, where he met Good-Will, who told him that if he knocked the gate would be opened to him. Christian did so. He was invited into the gatekeeper's house by the Interpreter and learned from him the meaning of many of the Christian mysteries. He was shown pictures of Christ and Passion and Patience; Despair in a cage of iron bars; and finally, a vision of the Day of Judgment, when evil men will be sent to the bottomless pit and good men will be carried up to Heaven. Christian was filled with both hope and fear after having seen these things. Continuing on his journey, he came to the Holy Cross and the Sepulcher of Christ. There his burden of sins fell off, and he was able to take to the road with renewed vigor.

Soon he met Sloth, Simple, Presumption, Formalism,

and Hypocrisy, but he kept to his way and they kept to theirs. Later, Christian lay down to sleep for a while. When he went on again, he forgot to pick up the roll of paper Evangelist had given him. Remembering it later, he hurried back to find it. Running to make up the time lost, he suddenly found himself confronted by two lions. He was afraid to pass by them until the porter of the house by the side of the road told him that the lions were chained and that he had nothing to fear. The porter then asked Christian to come into the house. There he was well treated and shown some of the relics of biblical antiquity by four virgins, Discretion, Prudence, Piety, and Charity. They gave him good advice and sent him on his journey armed with the sword and shield of Christian faith.

In the Valley of Humiliation, Christian was forced to fight the giant devil Apollyon, whose body was covered with the shiny scales of pride. Christian was wounded in this battle, but after he had chased away the devil, he healed his wounds with leaves from the Tree of Life, which grew nearby. After the Valley of Humiliation came the Valley of the Shadow of Death, in which Christian had to pass one of the gates to Hell. In order to save himself from the devils who issued out of the terrible hole, he recited some of the verses from the Psalms.

After passing through this danger, he had to go by the caves of the old giants Pope and Pagan; when he had done so, he caught up with a fellow traveler, Faithful. As the two companions went along, they met Evangelist, who warned them of the dangers in the town of Vanity Fair.

Vanity Fair was a town of ancient foundation which since the beginning of time had tried to lure men away from the path to Heaven. Here all the vanities of the world were sold, and the people who dwelt there were cruel and stupid and had no love for travelers such as Christian and Faithful. After having learned these things, the two companions promised to be careful and went down into the town. There they were arrested and tried because they would buy none of the town's goods. Faithful was sentenced to be burned alive, and Christian was put in prison. When Faithful died in the fire, a chariot descended from Heaven and took him up to God. Christian escaped from the prison. Accompanied by a young man named Hopeful, who had been impressed by Faithful's reward, he set off once more.

They passed through the Valley of Ease, where they were tempted to dig in a mine whose silver was free to all. As they left the valley, they saw the pillar of salt that had once been Lot's wife. They became lost and were captured by a giant, Despair, who lived in Doubting Castle; there they were locked in vaults beneath the castle walls. Finally, Christian remembered he had a key called Promise in his pocket; with this they escaped from the prison.

They met four shepherds, Knowledge, Experience, Watchful, and Sincere, who showed them the Celestial Gate and warned them of the paths to Hell. Then the two pilgrims passed by the Valley of Conceit, where they were met by Ignorance and other men who had not kept to the straight and narrow path. They passed on to the country of Beulah. Far off they saw the gates of the city of Heaven, glistening with pearls and precious stones. Thinking that all their troubles were behind them, they lay down to rest.

When they went on toward the city, they came to the River of Death. They entered the river and began to wade through the water. Soon Christian became afraid; the more afraid he became, the deeper the waters rolled. Hopeful shouted to him to have hope and faith. Cheered by these words, Christian became less afraid, the water became less deep, and finally they both got across safely. They ran up the hill toward Heaven, and shining angels led them through the gates.

Critical Analysis

John Bunyan's *The Pilgrim's Progress* represents a work that is at once fascinating theology, political tract, and literary masterpiece. It is also a book that exemplifies the post-Gutenberg power of the press to elevate and make universal the experiences of one writer or thinker above centuries of tradition. As Bunyan's most famous work, it was a by-product of the Protestant Reformation, which—by making available to individuals copies of the Bible—inevitably multiplied interpretations of the Bible and, thereby, advanced the notion of Christian personal experience. When the King James Version of the Bible was published in 1611, English Christians were freed from the tyranny of monolithic biblical interpretation by autocratic churchmen. A Bible in the vernacular emancipated the spirit and the imagination of members of the Protestant churches, evoking new metaphors and symbols for the Christian's journey through the world. *The Pilgrim's Progress* undermines the notion of a normative brand of Christian discipleship or path to Heaven created by the institutional church. At the same time, *The Pilgrim's Progress* shares with the medieval tradition of mystery and morality plays the technique of allegory, wherein the author uses archetypal characters or situations to advance his narrative and confirm its meaning. This tradition is itself built upon the characteristic teaching of Christ, who used parables to teach his most poignant lessons to his first century audience. It should be noted, however, that the book was not written or published without risk to both Bunyan himself and the band of Christian Baptists to whom he ministered and for whom he wrote *The Pilgrim's Progress*. Writing the manuscript from jail (he was frequently incarcerated for preaching without a license), Bunyan discovered that even in Protestant England certain sects and denominations could be despised and regarded as heterodox. Bunyan's Puritanism—a call for the church to be separate from the world while at the same time claiming it for God, the only rightful king—continually brought him into conflict with his religious critics and rivals.

To call *The Pilgrim's Progress* a religious allegory is to draw attention to the fact that its characters and situations symbolize particular qualities and actions that should inform the Christian's life. Christian, the pilgrim of the story, is simultaneously Bunyan and any of his fellow Protestant believers as they face a world whose signposts and boundaries have been knocked down. What appears to be true may be misleading or, worse, a ruse of the Devil; the circumspect believer trusts not in his senses but in the revelation of God—namely, the Bible. In Christian, we find an undisguised proclamation of Bunyan's belief that salvation is a gift of God's mercy and not a laurel or achievement won by good works or adherence to either civil or Mosaic law. As a pilgrim, Christian is on a journey to the Celestial City, a journey that will comprise both his conversion and his eventual death. His progress toward that destination is measured by his triumphs over distractions, perilous spiritual battles, temptations to unbelief, and general weariness. His obstacles include not only himself but also erstwhile friends and associates such as Mr. Worldly Wiseman and demonic influences such as Apollyon, who appear to speak authoritatively about faith and discipleship but are deluded sirens attempting to waylay him in "the wilderness of the world." Bunyan makes it abundantly clear, however, that Christian's final success is conditional not on his own cleverness or artful dodging but on his enduring trust in the irresistible grace of God.

It is important, then, to see Bunyan's creation as a political defense of the Separatist church and a worthy attempt to work out its radical theology in allegory. Despite the attempts of critics in later ages to see in Christian an Everyman character, Bunyan is most likely writing about one of the elect—the man or woman whose life is touched by grace—and not the prototypical agnostic or uncommitted soul who searches for God out of his own curiosity. The Puritan believer that Bunyan depicts here defines his faith very particularly in terms of his relationship to four realms: selfhood, Scripture, church, and world. Regarding his own selfhood, the Puritan believer names himself as a sinful creature, called to abstain from all appearance of evil, casting a jaundiced eye toward anything that smacks of worldliness. As a reader of Scripture, he is, with few exceptions, a consistent literalist, conceiving of its mode of revelation in inerrant, monolithic, encyclopedically authoritative terms. As a member of the church, he embraces its separatism, its hardwon peculiarity and anachronistic nature in relation to the world; it is for him an outpost on the edge of chaos. As one in but not of the world, he views the cosmos as basically irredeemable without the intervention of God— occupied territory under the dominion of the Devil. He awaits rescue from another world.

As a representative Puritan writer, Bunyan is, one might say, much more interested in proclaiming the revelation of the Bible than in narrating events from imagined histories, as a William Shakespeare or Samuel Johnson might do. Consequently, for Bunyan, the range of characters and character traits, plot lines and resolutions, and options in form, diction, and tone are fixed in advance by the propriety of biblical modesty and decorum. The Puritan, in a word, mistrusts Western literacy, the great tradition of worldly inspired texts and endless textual analysis. A good, righteous text should speak for itself, univocally; as an author, Bunyan is undismayed by charges that his characters are stock or obvious. That is exactly his point of view. His confidence that Scripture has "thoroughly equipped him for every good work" encourages him to use its content as the sole source of his characterizations and plot. Thus, Bunyan projected the original readers of *The Pilgrim's Progress* as an interpretive community prepared to receive it as a work parallel in spirit and content to the Bible, a commentary or elaboration of sorts that sent them back to the real text, which could reveal the ultimate source of their faith and salvation.

Bunyan shares with Christians outside of his Puritanism an acceptance of the fact that all are exiles of Eden, but there is one difference: He does not want to return to the Garden. It is enough for him to know that Adam and Eve have eaten of the tree of knowledge of good and evil; he himself has no interest in digesting such fruit, rejecting the futile attempt to substitute other dramas, stories, and predicaments for the simple truth of the one true predicament: All are lost and without hope, save for

God's mercy. Other kinds of nondidactic narratives are read, or rather dismissed, as worldly competition for the allegiance and energy of the believer—secular attempts to undermine the authority of the Bible. The world is already full of texts to distract, annoy, and alienate mankind. What possible interest could the pilgrim take in stories that galvanize or privilege the polyphonic, problematic fiction of sinful post-Babel humanity? How could such cacophony yield anything salutary or illuminating?

Thus, Christian, Bunyan's stalwart protagonist, leaves the Garden behind; he does not seek a heaven on earth, which would be merely a Vanity Fair. While he and Faithful both understand that there is no way back to it, even for the born-again, and both are prepared for martyrdom, only Faithful is called to it. God has another destiny for Christian. Sacred history is a line leading to a final resolution, not a cycle and still less a random occurrence of unconnected events. Bunyan's agenda has nothing to do with broadening, pluralizing, or expanding. His focus is the Narrow Path, the Single Eye, the One Way. He is interested in winning souls, not granting them college degrees. Thus, in a sense, he creates in Christian a pilgrim who holds his faith unreflectively—not in the sense that it is unexamined but in the sense that he rejects attempts to validate it with secular wisdom. That is Christian's charm; trusting fully in what he believes, he is called to put his faith on the line and into play in dramatic confrontations with the voices of despair and unbelief. Bunyan demonstrates consistently that the pilgrim must resist attempts to objectify his faith and become self-conscious and prideful about it. If Christian's life is a significant story in any way, it is the same as anyone's might be: "Once I was lost, but now I'm found." His story—history—is God's story, not his. His heavenly commission is to announce the terms of the kingdom, not to debate its merits, as if it were somehow contingent. He and his brethren know that their true battle is against principalities and powers, not flesh and blood—and thus present themselves as perfect for development in an allegorical treatment.

Bunyan's narrative, like Bunyan himself, is unpretentious, earnest, and amazingly unsentimental. Defiant, insular, certain though the world says he has no right to certainty, he espouses a faith which cannot be artificially stimulated or enriched by civil religion or ritualistic piety. Christ and the Bible alone are the source of salvation and his guide through the perils of earthly life. Like his pilgrim, Bunyan is interested most of all not in the faith he holds but in the faith that holds him.

THE PIONEERS: Or, The Sources of the Susquehanna

Type of work: Novel
Author: James Fenimore Cooper (1789–1851)
Type of plot: Historical romance
Time of plot: 1793
Locale: New York State
First published: 1823

The Pioneers, the first of the Leatherstocking Tales, is a romantic story of life in Upstate New York ten years after the Revolutionary War. The novel is filled with scenes of hunting and trapping life, and the description of Templeton is based upon the author's memories of his boyhood home of Cooperstown. The portrayals of Natty Bumppo and Indian John point to the tragedy of frontiersmen and Indians in a rapidly disappearing West.

Principal Characters

Judge Marmaduke Temple, the principal citizen and landholder of Templeton, a settlement in upstate New York. He is at once shrewd and honorable, benevolent and just. While trying to kill a deer he shoots an unfamiliar, educated young hunter named Oliver Edwards, has his wound dressed, and offers him a position as a secretary. When the young man's friend, the old woodsman and hunter called Leatherstocking, is arrested for threatening to shoot an officer, the judge sentences and fines the old man but pays the fine himself. Later he learns that Edwards is in reality Edward Oliver Effingham, the son of an old friend who had entrusted him with personal effects and family funds years before. The judge restores the property and the money to Edwards. Meanwhile Edwards and Elizabeth Temple have fallen in love, and the judge gives the young couple his blessing.

Elizabeth Temple, the judge's spirited, pretty daughter. Although she respects Oliver Edwards' abilities, she maintains a feminine independence. Grateful to Leatherstocking for saving her life when a savage panther attacks her, she assists in his escape from jail after the old man has been arrested for resisting an officer. Her romance with her father's secretary develops after the young man and Leatherstocking save her from a forest fire. When Edwards' true identity is revealed and he declares his love, she readily marries him.

Natty Bumppo, called **Leatherstocking,** a hardy, simple, upright woodsman in his seventy-first year. Although disgusted by wanton killing of game, he defends his right to kill game for food. He shoots a deer out of season and is arrested for resisting the magistrate who tries to search his cabin. Sentenced to jail for a month, he escapes with the help of Oliver Edwards and Elizabeth Temple. Twice he rescues Elizabeth, once from a panther and again from fire. After he is pardoned by the governor, the lonely hunter, his last two old friends dead, moves west into unsettled territory.

Oliver Edwards, later revealed as **Edward Oliver Effingham,** the impoverished young hunter who lives with Leatherstocking in a cabin near Templeton. Believing that Judge Temple has appropriated his inheritance, he is planning to recover it when he accepts the position of secretary to the judge. In the meantime he falls in love with Elizabeth Temple. Having quit his post when Leatherstocking is arrested and jailed, he helps the old man to escape, aids Elizabeth during the fire, and finally reveals his true identity. Judge Temple immediately restores his inheritance and the young man and Elizabeth are married.

Indian John Mohegan, an old Mohican chief whose real name is Chingachgook. Lonely, aged, and grieving for the old life of the wilderness and his vanished people, he dies attended by Leatherstocking, his blood brother and loyal companion, and by Elizabeth Temple, Oliver Edwards, and Mr. Grant, in a cave where they have taken refuge from a forest fire.

Hiram Doolittle, the cowardly, trouble-making, greedy magistrate who informs on Leatherstocking for breaking the hunting law, gets a search warrant, and is roughly handled by the old hunter when he tries to force his way into Leatherstocking's cabin.

Richard Jones, the meddlesome, pompous sheriff, a frontier fop who indulges in the irresponsible killing of game, spreads rumors that Leatherstocking is working a secret mine, and leads a raggle-taggle posse to recapture the old woodsman after his escape from jail.

Major Edward Effingham, a hero of the French and Indian War (see *The Last of the Mohicans*), the aged and senile grandfather of the young man who calls himself Oliver Edwards. The major was Leatherstocking's commander in the war and became the owner of the land around Templeton before the American Revolution, thanks in part to a gift from the Delaware tribe. He gave all his property to his son, who, in turn, made his friend, Marmaduke Temple, into his partner and manager. Leatherstocking cares for him when communication between Temple and the Effinghams breaks down after the revolution. His identity revealed after the fire, the old man is taken to Judge Temple's home and nursed tenderly until his death.

Mr. Grant, a sincere, eclectic minister adept at appealing to the heterogeneous frontier faiths.

Louisa Grant, his timid daughter, Elizabeth's companion. She is inept when faced with danger.

Benjamin Penguillan, called **Ben Pump,** an ex-sailor and Judge Temple's salty majordomo. Out of sympathy he shares Leatherstocking's humiliation in the stocks and thrashes Magistrate Doolittle.

Elnathan Todd, the gigantic village doctor who dresses Oliver Edwards' wound; he is an awkward quack.

Monsieur le Quoi (mə·syœ′ lə kwà′), the village storekeeper, a friend of Judge Temple.

Major Hartmann, a German farmer, also a friend of Judge Temple.

Billy Kirby, a good-natured woodcutter and strong man who sympathizes with Leatherstocking but takes the side of the law.

Jotham Riddel, Magistrate Doolittle's good-for-nothing deputy.

Remarkable Pettibone, Judge Temple's housekeeper.

Squire Lippet, Leatherstocking's lawyer at the time of the old hunter's trial.

Mr. Van de School, the thick-witted prosecutor.

Agamemnon, Judge Temple's Negro servant.

The Story

On a cold December day in 1793, Judge Temple and his daughter Elizabeth were traveling by sleigh through a snow-covered tract of wilderness near the settlement of Templeton. Elizabeth, who had been away from her home attending a female seminary, was now returning to preside over her father's household in the community in which he had been a pioneer settler after the Revolutionary War. Hearing the baying of hounds, the judge decided that Leatherstocking, an old hunter, had started game in the hills, and he ordered his coachman to stop the sleigh so he could have a shot at the deer if it came in his direction. A few minutes later, as a great buck leaped into the road, the judge fired both barrels of his fowling piece at the animal, but apparently without effect. Then a third report and a fourth were heard, and the buck dropped dead in a snowbank.

At the same time Natty Bumppo, the old hunter, and a young companion appeared from the woodland. The judge insisted that he had shot the buck, but Leatherstocking, by accounting for all the shots fired, proved the judge could not have killed the animal. The argument ended when the young stranger revealed that he had been wounded by one of the shots fired by the judge. Elizabeth and her father then insisted that he accompany them into the village in their sleigh, so he could have his wound dressed as soon as possible.

The young man got into the sleigh with obvious reluctance and said little during the drive. In a short time the party arrived at the Temple mansion, where his wound was treated. In answer to the judge's questions, he gave his name as Oliver Edwards. His manner remained distant and reserved. After he had departed, a servant in the Temple home reported that Edwards had appeared three weeks before in the company of old Leatherstocking and that he lived in a nearby cabin with the hunter and an Indian known as Indian John.

Judge Temple, wishing to make amends for having accidentally wounded Edwards, offered him a position as his secretary. When Elizabeth added her own entreaties to those of her father, Edwards finally accepted the judge's offer, with the understanding that he would be free to terminate his employment at any time. For a while he attended faithfully and earnestly to his duties in Judge Temple's mansion during the day, but his nights he spent in Leatherstocking's cabin. So much secrecy surrounded his comings and goings, added to the reserve of Leatherstocking and his Indian friend, that Richard Jones, the sheriff and a kinsman of the judge, became suspicious. Among other things, he wondered why Natty always kept his cabin closed and never allowed anyone except the Indian and Edwards to enter it. Jones and some others decided that Natty had discovered a mine and was working it. Jones also suspected that Edwards was an Indian half-breed, his father a Delaware chief.

Hiram Doolittle, a meddlesome magistrate, believed Jones's tale of a secret silver mine somewhere on Temple's land. Hoping to provoke Leatherstocking into hunting out of season, Doolittle prowled around the cabin and set free the hunter's dogs. In the meantime Elizabeth and Louisa Grant, while walking in the woods, were attacked by a panther. Leatherstocking saved them by shooting the panther; however, he was unable to resist the temptation to shoot the deer his roving dogs had flushed out. Hoping to find evidence of silver, Doolittle charged Leatherstocking with breaking Judge Temple's newly instituted, strict game laws and persuaded the judge to sign a warrant to search the hunter's cabin.

But when Doolittle went to the cabin, Leatherstocking, rifle in hand, refused him entrance. Then the magistrate attempted to force his way over the threshold, but the old hunter seized him and threw him twenty feet down an embankment. As the result of his treatment of an officer, Leatherstocking was arrested. Found guilty, he was given a month's jail sentence, fined, and placed in the stocks for a few hours. When Elizabeth went to see what assistance she could give the humiliated old woodsman, she learned he was planning to escape. Edwards, who had given up his position with the judge, was planning to flee with his aged friend; he had provided a cart in which to carry the old hunter to safety. Elizabeth promised to meet Leatherstocking the following day on the top of a nearby mountain and to bring with her a can of gunpowder he needed.

The next day Elizabeth and her friend Louisa started out on their expedition to meet Leatherstocking. On the way Louisa changed her mind and turned back, declaring that she dared not walk unprotected through the woods where they had lately been menaced by a panther. Elizabeth went on alone until she came to a clearing in which she found old Indian John, now dressed in the war costume and feathers of a great Mohican chief. When she stopped to speak to the Indian, she suddenly became aware of dense clouds of smoke drifting across the clearing and discovered that the whole mountainside was ablaze. At that moment Edwards appeared, followed by Leatherstocking, who led them to a cave in the side of the mountain. There the old Indian died of exhaustion, and Elizabeth learned that he had been in earlier days Chingachgook, a great and noble warrior of the Mohican tribe.

When danger of the fire had passed, Edwards conducted Elizabeth down the mountainside until she was within hearing of a party of men who were looking for her. Before they parted, Edwards promised he would soon reveal his true identity.

The next day the sheriff led a posse up the mountain in search of Leatherstocking and those who had aided him in his escape from jail. Leatherstocking was again prepared to defend with his rifle the cave to which he had taken Elizabeth the day before, but Edwards declared that the time had now come to let the truth be known. He and Natty brought from the depths of the cave an old man seated in a chair. The stranger's face was grave and dignified, but his vacant eyes showed that his mind was gone. Edwards announced that the old man was really the owner of the property on which they stood. Judge Temple interrupted with a shout of surprise and greeted the old man as Major Effingham.

The young man told his story. His name, he said, was Edward Oliver Effingham, and he was the grandson of the old man who sat before them. His own father had been, before the Revolutionary War, a close friend of

Judge Temple. Temple had managed the aristocratic Effingham's property before the revolution. When they took opposite sides in the war, control of the property came to Temple, who held it in trust and developed it, always with the idea of returning their fair share to the Effinghams. Several years after the war, Temple lost contact with the Effingham family and came to believe they all had died in a shipwreck off Nova Scotia.

Because Temple had never met Edward Effingham's grandfather, he would not have recognized him, even had he seen the helpless old man who had been hidden in Leatherstocking's cabin on the outskirts of Templeton. During those years he was nursed faithfully by Leatherstocking and his Indian friend; by Leatherstocking because he had served with the major on the frontier years before, by Indian John because the major was an adopted member of the Mohican tribe.

Judge Temple ordered that the old man be carried to the Temple mansion at once, where he would receive the best of care. Old Major Effingham thought himself back home once more, and his eyes gleamed with joy. He died, happy and well cared for, soon afterward.

Edward Effingham also explained to the Judge that he believed Temple had stolen his father's property and the money left in trust years before. In his resentment he had come to Templeton to assist his grandfather and regain in some manner the property which he believed Judge Temple had unrightfully possessed.

Now the judge was glad to return to the heir of his friend the property he had developed for him. The reconciliation of the two men was followed in September by the marriage of Oliver and Elizabeth, which unified the two inheritances, and shortly thereafter by the death of the elder Effingham.

Elizabeth and Edward wanted to build a new cabin for Leatherstocking, to keep him near as a valued friend and teacher, but Leatherstocking was determined to move on westward into as yet unsettled wilderness where he would feel truly at home. He departed after a touching meeting at the monuments the Effinghams had erected to Major Effingham, the courageous old soldier, and Chingachgook, the last great Mohican chief and the major's adoptive father. All three wept as they parted, and Judge Temple's later efforts to find the old hunter and bring him back bore no fruit.

Critical Evaluation

The first of the Leatherstocking tales Cooper wrote, *The Pioneers* is the fourth, chronologically, in the life adventures of Cooper's most famous hero, Natty Bumppo, or Leatherstocking. *The Deerslayer* (1841) shows Bumppo's entry into manhood. *The Last of the Mohicans* (1826) and *The Pathfinder* (1840) recount two of his mature adventures. *The Pioneers* and *The Prairie* (1827) tell of

the frontiersman's old age and death. Though Cooper had begun writing novels in response to a challenge from his wife, his second effort, *The Spy*, became an international best-seller in 1821. Having proved he could write successfully and having discovered that he could supplement a diminished family income by writing novels, Cooper conceived and composed *The Pioneers* with self-confidence and a new vision of his artistic purposes. He said it was the first novel he wrote primarily to satisfy himself.

The Pioneers is a great novel on several levels, with memorable characters, absorbing and humorous adventures, rich portraits of pioneer life, and a unified vision of Cooper's hopes for a high American destiny. In a later novel, *Home As Found* (1838), Cooper outlined a three-phase process by which he saw America being transformed from wilderness into civilization. In a first, pastoral stage of natural democracy, settlers of all kinds and classes work together equally to establish a community. In a second, anarchic stage, the settlement overcomes the tyranny of subsistence, and in the freedom of this comparative wealth, people divide into groups with like interests. In this phase, there is contention among families and other groups for political and economic power. In the final phase, society establishes a new order, based on written law rather than necessity. Cooper believed that in America, this last phase would be uniquely republican, with a natural order of fluid class divisions based on talent and inclination, as opposed to the rigid hereditary class systems of Europe. *The Pioneers* details the transition from the end of the pastoral phase through the anarchic phase to the first blossoming of a mature American community. In *Home As Found*, Cooper envisioned this process taking one hundred years, but in *The Pioneers* the central transitions occur in a single year.

Before settlers can begin communities, frontiersmen must tame the wilderness. In 1793, Leatherstocking is obsolete in Templeton, for this wilderness is virtually tamed. However, he still has an important mission in the community: to help pass on a legacy to the settlers. He does this in part by teaching the heirs of the land, Oliver Effingham and Elizabeth Temple, obligations to the land and nature that are crucial to their future roles as natural aristocrats in a democratic republic.

This teaching takes place in the context of their becoming uniquely legitimate heirs of the land. Oliver's title derives from his grandfather, who received the land from a high council of the Delaware Indians, when he was made the adoptive son of Chingachgook (John Mohegan). In this way, Cooper transfers the land from the "best" of the local Indian tribes to a white frontier aristocrat, and Oliver stands in this hereditary line. Elizabeth is the heir of Marmaduke Temple, who took the land in trust when the Effinghams lost their title by being Tories in the American Revolution. Temple develops and enlarges this estate, holding it for the Effingham heirs out of friendship and loyalty. For Oliver to deserve his inheritance, he must be Americanized. For Elizabeth to deserve hers, she must fully understand the obligations of ownership. Leatherstocking's teaching effects both of these transformations.

With the help of Chingachgook, Leatherstocking teaches these young people the morality he has learned from the book of nature. This morality has its foundation in Christianity and "natural" democracy, values Leatherstocking learned in his brief childhood education and from his friendship with the Delaware Indians. In his life as a scout and hunter, Leatherstocking has learned to see how God's Providence operates in nature. He believes that written law inevitably corrupts the fundamental divine law as revealed in nature, so it is crucial that gentlefolk and future rulers learn to renew continually their understanding of law by worship in God's original temple.

One lesson nature has to teach the natural aristocracy is humility, a sense of human limitations and dependence on the will and mercy of God. Twice the citizens of Templeton commit ecological hubris, killing more passenger pigeons and more fish than they can reasonably consume. Both times, Leatherstocking rails against them like an Old Testament prophet, saying that though nature is made for people's use, it is not made to waste. He impresses upon Oliver and Elizabeth that people are stewards of God's gifts.

Another lesson nature teaches is that all God's creatures are blessed with different gifts. No person is complete in himself or herself. This places upon a community an obligation to protect the weak, to treasure the God-given gifts of those who are not economically and politically strong. Leatherstocking and Chingachgook demonstrate this faithfulness to community by protecting Oliver, his grandfather, and several other characters from natural dangers and the sins of the community in its anarchic phase. They teach a democratic *noblesse oblige* in which the powerful are directly responsible not merely for the economic support of the weak but also for enabling the weak to use their gifts and live valuable lives.

That all have different gifts and all are mutually dependent also implies the most important lesson for Oliver: that legally inheriting land does not fully legitimate ownership. His right to the land depends more upon his being worthy than upon his legal status. He learns from Leatherstocking that gentility is an achievement rather than an inheritance and, thereby, learns to recognize the true nobility of Judge Temple and his daughter, both of whom are "commoners" and American democrats.

The Pioneers is based on the experiences of Cooper's father, William, founder of Cooperstown, New York, and author of *A Guide in the Wilderness* (1810), a manual for frontier settlement. William was the model for Marmaduke Temple. Reflecting James and William Cooper's idealism, *The Pioneers* expresses one of the great traditions of the American dream, the ideal of America as a rational, Christian, agrarian utopia, ruled by statesmen chosen democratically from a natural aristocracy. This dream stands behind and informs a touching, amusing, exciting, and informative novel.

THE PLAGUE

Type of work: Novel
Author: Albert Camus (1913–1960)
Type of plot: Impressionistic realism
Time of plot: The 1940s
Locale: Oran, Algeria
First published: *La Peste,* 1947 (English translation, 1948)

In The Plague, *Camus places his characters in a scene of widespread death and horror in order to follow their responses and record their answers to the age-old question: "Why are we here?" As the bubonic plague sweeps through an Algerian port town, Camus focuses on the mind of a doctor, Bernard Rieux, whose decision in the face of hopeless calamity is to at least do what he can to alleviate human suffering for a few moments and to continue to hope for the possibility of future joy.*

Principal Characters

Bernard Rieux (bĕr·nȧr′ ryœ′), a physician and surgeon in Oran, where a plague is claiming as many as three hundred lives a day. Dr. Rieux, a thirty-five-year-old man of great patience, fortitude, and unselfishness, represents the medical profession during the long siege of disease and deaths which strike rich and poor alike and from which there is no reprieve. The plague means failure to Rieux because he can find no cure or relief for the sufferers. His attitude is characterized by his regard for his fellowmen and his inability to cope with injustice and compromise. Very much involved with mankind, he explains that he is able to continue working with the plague-stricken population only because he has found that abstraction is stronger than happiness. He is identified at the end of the book as the narrator of the story, and his account gives the pestilence the attributes of a character, the antagonist. Events of the plague are secondary to philosophies as he pictures the people's reactions, individually and collectively, to their plight. These run the range of emotions and rationality: escape, guilt, a spirit of lawlessness, pleasure, resistance. During the plague individual destinies become collective destinies because the plague and emotions are shared by all. Love and friendship fade because they ask something of the future, and the plague leaves only present moments. As the pestilence subsides, relieving the exile and deprivation, there is jubilation, followed by the stereotyped patterns of everyday living.

Madame Rieux (ryœ′), the doctor's wife. The victim of another ailment, Mme. Rieux is sent away to a sanitarium before the town is quarantined. Her absence from Rieux points up his unselfishness in staying on in Oran.

Raymond Rambert (rĕ·mōn′ rän·bĕr′), a journalist from Paris. Assigned to a routine story on Oran, he is caught in exile when the city is quarantined because of the plague. Rambert, wanting to return to his wife, resorts to various means in order to escape. A non-resident, alien to the plight of the people, he personifies those who feel no involvement with the problems of others. When escape from the city becomes a reality for him, Rambert declines his freedom and accepts Rieux's philosophy of common decency, which amounts merely to doing one's job. In this instance Rambert's job, according to Rieux, is to fight the plague. The journalist becomes a volunteer on the sanitation teams.

Father Paneloux (pȧ·n·lōo′), a Jesuit priest who represents the ecclesiastical thinking of people caught in the crisis represented by the plague. Preaching on the plague, he compares the present situation with the pestilences of the past and tells his parishioners that they have brought the plague upon themselves through their godlessness. Placing the scientific and the spiritual in balance, Paneloux and Rieux debate whether the man of God and the scientist can consort in contending with adversities. The two men are closer in their thinking than Rieux, a self-proclaimed atheist, and Paneloux, a heretic in some of his preaching, will concede. Paneloux is among those who succumb to the plague.

Jean Tarrou (zhän′ tȧ·rōo′), an enigma to his associate among the volunteers in fighting the plague. Addicted to simple pleasures but no slave to them, Tarrou has no apparent means of income. Little is known of his background until he tells Rieux of his beginnings. The son of a prosecutor, he had been horrified by the thought of the criminals condemned because of his father. He himself has been a political agitator. Tarrou becomes a faithful helper to Rieux, and as a volunteer he records the social aspects of the plague. In telling of the plague, Rieux borrows from these records. After the worst of the pestilence has passed, Tarrou dies from the plague.

Joseph Grand (zhō·zĕf′ grän′), a municipal clerk. Characterized by all the attributes of insignificance, Grand has spent twenty-two years in his job, to which he was temporarily appointed. He is unable to escape from his imprisonment because he cannot find the words with which to protest. He announces early in his acquaintance with Rieux that he has a second job, which he describes as a "growth of personality." The futility of this avocation, writing, is epitomized by Grand's continuing work on the first sentence of a novel which he anticipates will be the perfect expression of love. He dies after asking Rieux to burn his sheaf of papers, manuscripts with only an adjective or a verb changed from one writing to the next.

M. Cottard (Kô·tàr′), a dealer in wines and liquors, treated by Rieux after an attempt at suicide. His undercover deals and unsettled life are sublimated or furthered by his keen delight in gangster movies. He survives the plague, only to go berserk during a shooting affray with the police.

Dr. Richard (rē·shà′), chairman of the medical association in Oran. He is more interested in observing the code of the organization than in trying to reduce the number of deaths.

M. Othon (ō·tōń′), the police magistrate. His isola-tion after contracting the plague shows Rieux's impartiality in dealing with plague victims.

Jacques Othon (zhàk′ ō·tōń′), the magistrate's son, on whom the new serum is tried. The lengthy description of young Othon's illness illustrates the suffering of the thousands who die of the plague.

Madame Rieux (ryœ′), the doctor's mother, who comes to keep house for her son during his wife's absence. She is an understanding woman who reminds Tarrou of his own childhood and elicits his philosophical discussion of man's role in life.

García (gär·sē′ä), **Raoul** (rà·ōōl′), **Gonzales** (gōn·sä′lĕs), **Marcel** (màr·sĕl′), and **Louis** (lwē′), the men involved in Raymond Rambert's contemplated escape from Oran. The intricacies of illegality are shown as Rambert is referred from one of these men to another. From García, an accomplice of Cottard, to Marcel and Louis, guards at the city gate, each one must have his stipend, until finally the cost of escape becomes exorbitant.

The Story

For a few days Dr. Bernard Rieux gave little thought to the strange behavior of the rats in Oran. One morning he found three on his landing, each animal lying inert with a rosette of fresh blood spreading from the nostrils. The concierge grumbled about the strange happening, but Rieux was a busy doctor, and just then he had personal cares.

Madame Rieux was going away from Oran. She suffered from a lingering illness, and Rieux thought that a sanatorium in a different town might do her some good. His mother was to keep house for him while his wife was absent. Rambert, a persistent journalist, cut into his time. The newsman wanted to do a story for his metropolitan paper on living conditions among the workers in Oran. Rieux refused to help him, for he knew an honest report would be censored.

Day by day the number of dead rats increased in the city. After a time truckloads were carried away each morning. People stepped on the furry dead bodies whenever they walked in the dark. Rieux's first case of fever was the concierge who had grumbled about having to clean up the rats on the stair landing. He had a high temperature and painful swellings. Rieux was apprehensive. By telephone inquiries he learned that his colleagues had similar cases.

The prefect was averse to taking any drastic action because he did not want to alarm the population. Only one doctor was sure the sickness was bubonic plague; the others reserved judgment. When the deaths rose to thirty a day, however, even officialdom was worried. Soon a telegram came instructing the prefect to take drastic measures, and the news became widespread; Oran was in the grip of the plague.

Rieux had been called to Cottard's apartment by Grand, a clerk and former patient. Grand had cut down Cottard just in time to prevent his suicide by hanging. Cottard could give no satisfactory reason for his attempt to kill himself. Rieux was interested in him; he seemed rather an eccentric person.

Grand was another strange man. For many years, he had been a temporary clerk, overlooked in his minor post by succeeding bureaucrats who kept him on without investigating his status. Grand was too timid to call attention to the injustice of his position. Each evening he worked hard on his manuscript and seemed to derive much solace from it. Rieux was surprised when he saw the work. In all of those years, Grand had only the beginning sentence of his novel finished, and he was still revising it. He had once been married to Jeanne, but she had left him.

Tarrou was an engaging fellow, a political agitator who had been concerned with governmental upheavals over the whole continent. He kept a meticulous diary in which he told of the ravages and sorrows of the plague. One of his neighbors was an old man who each morning called the neighborhood cats to him and shredded paper for them to play with. Then, when all the cats were around him, he would spit on them with great accuracy. After the plague grew worse, the city authorities killed all cats and dogs to check possible agents of infection. The old man, deprived of his cats as targets, stayed indoors, disconsolate.

As the blazing summer sun dried the town, a film of dust rolled over everything. The papers were meticulous in reporting the weekly deaths. When the weekly total, however, passed the nine hundred mark, the press reported only daily tolls. Armed sentinels were posted to prohibit anyone from entering or leaving the town. Letters were forbidden. Since the telephone lines could not accommodate the increased traffic, the only communication with the outside was by telegraph. Occasionally Rieux had an unsatisfactory wire from his wife.

The disposal of the dead bodies presented a problem. The little cemetery was soon filled, but the authorities made more room by cremating the remains in the older graves. At last two pits were dug in an adjoining field, one for men and one for women. When those pits were filled, a greater pit was dug, and no further effort was made to separate the sexes. The corpses were simply dropped in and covered with quicklime and a thin layer of earth. Discarded streetcars were used to transport the dead to the cemetery.

Rieux was in charge of one of the new wards at the infirmary. There was little he could do, however, for the serum from Paris was not effective. He observed what precautions he could, and to ease pain he lanced the distended buboes. Most of the patients died. Castel, an older physician, was working on a new serum.

Father Paneloux preached a sermon on the plague in which he called Oran's pestilence a retribution. Monsieur Othon, the judge, had a son under Rieux's care by the time Castel's new serum was ready. The serum did the boy little good; although he did show unexpected resistance, he died a painful death. Father Paneloux, who had been watching as a lay helper, knew the boy was not evil; he could no longer think of the plague as a retribution. His next sermon was confused. He seemed to be saying that man must submit to God's will in all things. For the priest, this view meant rejection of medical aid. When he himself caught the fever, he submitted to Rieux's treatment, but only because he had to. Father Paneloux died a bewildered man.

Rambert, because he was not a citizen of Oran, tried his best to escape. Convinced that there was no legal means of leaving the city, he planned to leave with some illicit smugglers. Then the spirit of the plague affected him. He voluntarily stayed to help Rieux and the sanitation teams, for he realized that only in fighting a common evil could he find spiritual comfort.

Tarrou had left home early because his father was a prosecutor; the thought of the wretched criminals condemned to death because of his father's zeal horrified him. After he had been an agitator for years, he finally realized that the workings of politics often resulted in similar executions. He had fled to Oran just before the plague started. There he found an answer to his problem in organizing and directing sanitary workers.

Cottard seemed content with plague conditions. Wanted for an old crime, he felt safe from pursuit during the quarantine. When the plague eased a little, two officers came for him, but he escaped. He was recaptured in a street gunfight.

Grand caught the fever but miraculously recovered to work again on his manuscript. Tarrou, also infected, died in Rieux's house. As the colder weather of January came, the plague ended. Rieux heard by telegram that his wife had died.

The streets became crowded again as lovers, husbands, and wives were reunited. Rieux dispassionately observed the masses of humanity. He had learned that human contact is important for everyone. For himself, he was content to help man fight against disease and pain.

Critical Evaluation

In the decade and a half that followed the end of World War II, as the West strived to repair the physical, psychic, and spiritual damage wrought by that conflict, the voice of Albert Camus, with its reasoned yet passionate affirmation of human dignity in the face of an "absurd" universe—an absurdity made palpable by the Nazi horror—was one of the major artistic, philosophical, and moral sources of strength and direction.

The Plague is the most thorough fictional presentation of Camus' mature thinking. In earlier works—notably the play *Caligula* (1938), the novel *The Stranger* (1942), and the essay *The Myth of Sisyphus* (1942)—Camus articulated his concept of the "absurd." Man is absurd because he has neither metaphysical justification nor essential connection to the universe. He is part of no divine scheme and, since he is mortal, all of his actions, individual and collective, eventually come to nothing. The only question, then, is how can man deal with his absurdity?

Camus' answer lies in his concept of "revolt." Man revolts against his condition first by understanding it and then, in the face of his cosmic meaninglessness, creating his own human meanings. In the previously mentioned works, Camus explored the problem in terms of the individual; in *The Plague*, Camus extends his moral and philosophical analysis to the question of man as a social creature. What, Camus asks, in the face of an absurd universe, is man's relationship to, and responsibility for, his fellowman?

The paradox that lies at the center of Camus' revolt concept is that of heroic futility. One struggles in spite of—even because of—the fact that, ultimately, one must lose. If the idea of the absurd denies man's cosmic meaning, it affirms his common bond. Since all men must die, all men are brothers. Mutual cooperation, not self-indulgence, is the logical ethic that Camus derives from his absurd perspective. To give an artistic shape to these convictions, Camus chooses a "plague" as an appropriate metaphor for the human condition, since it intensifies this awareness of man's mortality and makes the common bond especially clear.

Camus carefully divides the novel into five parts which correspond to the progression of the pestilence. Parts 1 and 5 show life before the plague's onslaught and after its subsidence. Parts 2 and 4 concentrate on the details of communal and personal suffering and, in particular, on the activities and reactions of the main characters as they do battle with the disease. Part 3, the climax of the book, shows the epidemic at its height and the community reduced to a single collective entity, where time has stopped, personal distinctions are lost, and suffering and despair have become routine.

The story is narrated by Dr. Bernard Rieux, who waits until almost the end of the novel to identify himself, in a factual, impersonal, almost documentary style. His account is occasionally supplemented by extracts from the journal of Jean Tarrou, but these intrusions, while more subjective and colorful, are characterized by a running irony that also keeps the reader at a distance. Both narratives, however, are juxtaposed against vivid, emotionally charged scenes. This continual movement back and forth between narrative austerity and dramatic immediacy, and from lucid analysis to emotional conflict, gives *The Plague* much of its depth and impact.

Three of the principal characters—Rieux, Tarrou, and the clerk Joseph Grand—accept their obligation to battle the epidemic as soon as it is identified. Rieux is probably the character who comes the closest to speaking for Camus. As a medical doctor, he has devoted his life to the losing battle with disease and death, and so the plague is simply an intensification of his normal life. From the outset he accepts the plague as a fact and fights against it with all the skill, endurance, and energy he can muster. He finds his only "certitude" in his daily round. There is no heroism involved, only the logic of the situation; and even after the plague has retreated, Rieux has no conviction that his actions had anything to do with its defeat. Yet Rieux learns much from his experience and, as the narrator, his is Camus' final word on the meaning of the ordeal.

Unlike Rieux, whose ideas are the practical consequence of his professional experience, Jean Tarrou first had the philosophical revelation and then shaped his life to it. Seeing his father, a prosecuting attorney, condemn a man to death, Tarrou became enraged with the inhumanity of his society and turned to revolutionary politics. That too, he came to realize, inevitably involved him in condemning others to death. Thus he felt infected with the "plague"—defined as whatever destroys human life—long before coming to Oran, and it has reduced him to a purposeless existence colored only by the ironic observations he jots down in his journal. When the plague arrives, he quickly and eagerly organizes the sanitation squads; the crisis gives him the opportunity to side with

the victims of life's absurdity without fearing that his actions will inadvertently add to their misery. Such obvious, total commitments, however, are not available under normal conditions, and so Tarrou appropriately dies as one of the plague's last victims.

Both Rieux and Tarrou are too personally inhuman—Rieux with his abstract view of man, Tarrou with his desire for secular sainthood—to qualify as heroic. The most admirable person in the book is the clerk Joseph Grand, who accepts his role in the plague automatically, needing neither professional nor philosophical justifications, simply because "people must help each other." His greater humanity is further demonstrated by the fact that, while carrying out his commitment to the victims of the plague, he continues to show active grief over the loss of his wife and tenaciously revolts in his artistic attempt to write the perfect novel (even though he cannot manage the perfect first sentence).

Among the other principal characters, the journalist Raymond Rambert opts for "personal happiness"; Father Paneloux presents the Christian reaction to the pestilence; and Cottard acts out the role of the criminal.

Caught in Oran by accident when the plague breaks out, Rambert turns his energies to escape, exhausting every means, legal and otherwise, to rejoin his wife. It is in him that the issue of exile or separation from loved ones is most vividly presented. For most of the novel he rejects the view that the plague imposes a social obligation on all; he insists that individual survival and personal happiness are primary. Furthermore, although Rieux is the book's principal advocate of collective responsibility, the doctor admits to Rambert that happiness is as valid an option as service. Even when Rambert finally decides to remain voluntarily and continue the fight, the issue remains ambiguous. At the end, as Rambert embraces his wife, he still wonders if he made the right moral choice.

If Rieux accepts Rambert's happiness as a decent option, he does not extend that tolerance to Father Paneloux's Christian view of the epidemic. *The Plague* has been called the most anti-Christian of Camus' books, and that is probably correct, although it could be argued that the ethical values advocated are essentially Christian ones. As a system of beliefs, however, it is clear that Christianity—at least as understood by Paneloux—is tested by the pestilence and found wanting. If the priest's beliefs are inadequate, however, his actions are heroic, and it is this incongruity between his theological convictions and his existential behavior that gives his character and fate its special poignancy.

Near the beginning of the epidemic, he preaches a sermon in which he proclaims that it is a manifestation of divine justice. Later in the book, after he has become one of the most active fighters against the plague and a witness to the suffering and death of numerous innocents, Paneloux's simple vision of sin and punishment is shaken.

He preaches a second sermon in which he advocates a blind, total acceptance of a God who seems, from the human vantage point, to be indifferent, arbitrary, perhaps even evil. Thus driven to this extreme either/or position, Paneloux finally dies of the plague. Significantly, he is the only victim whose body is unmarked by the disease; he has been destroyed emotionally and spiritually because his religious vision was inadequate to the challenge, and he could not live without that theological justification.

The most ambiguous character of all is Cottard. As a criminal, he has lived in a constant state of fear and exile. Unable to endure such separation, he attempts to commit suicide near the beginning of the book. Once the plague sets in, and all are subjected to that same sense of fear and solitude, however, Cottard rejoins humanity and flourishes; the plague is his natural element. Once it dissipates and he is again faced with isolation, Cottard goes berserk.

Thus, Camus describes the various human reactions to the plague—acceptance, defiance, detachment, solitary rejection, social commitment, criminality. The only value of the epidemic, Rieux admits, is educational, but the price paid for the knowledge is much too high. Nevertheless, even in the midst of the ordeal, there are moments of supreme pleasure and meaningful human connection. Shortly before the plague's last onslaught that takes Tarrou's life, he and Rieux defy regulations and go for a short swim. For a few brief moments, they are at one with the elements and in natural instinctive harmony with each other. The interlude soon ends, however, and both men return to the struggle—Tarrou to die, Rieux to chronicle its passing. He finally concludes, therefore, that the only victory won from the plague amounts to "knowledge and memories" and the conviction that men are, on the whole, admirable.

POEM OF THE CID

Type of work: Poem
Author: Unknown
Type of plot: c. 1075
Locale: Fief of Bivar, to the north of Burgos, Spain
First transcribed: Twelfth century

This national epic of eleventh century Spain consists of 3,735 lines in three cantos which relate the major events of the life of Rodrigo Díaz de Vivar, known as the Cid. The Cid is drawn as a typical Spanish warrior: proud, ruthless, and calculating at the same time that he is kind to his vassals and generous to a fault. Of all the epics about this national hero, this poem is the masterpiece, unique in its qualities of realism and poetic excellence.

Principal Characters

The Cid (thēd), or **Ruy Díaz** (r̄wē dē′äth), lord of Bivar. Banished from Christian Spain by Alfonso VI of Castile, he enters, with a company of his vassals, on a series of heroic exploits designed to impress the king and cause him to revoke the edict of banishment. The royal favor is finally won but only after the Cid becomes powerful enough to be a threat to the throne. A period of happiness and peace lasts until the Cid is forced to subdue his treacherous sons-in-law, Diego and Fernando, princes of Carrión. When the princes are banished, the Cid is free to marry his daughters to the rulers of Aragón and Navarre. He rejoices to count among his family two kings of Spain, and he finally dies in peace as lord of Valencia.

Alfonso VI (äl·fōn′sō ses′tō), king of León. After banishing the Cid from Christian Spain, he reinstates the hero when his growing power becomes a threat to the throne.

Doña Elvira (dō′nyä ĕl·bē′rä) and

Doña Sol (dō′nyä sōl), the Cid's daughters, who are married to Diego and Fernando, princes of Carrión, by whom the noble ladies are robbed and beaten. They are finally married to the kings of Aragón and Navarre.

Diego (dyĕ′gō) and

Fernando González (fĕr·nän′dō gōn·thä′lĕth), princes of Carrión and the Cid's cowardly sons-in-law. Resentful of the scorn heaped on them by the Cid's vassals, they seek revenge on their lord by ostensibly taking his daughters on a triumphant tour to Carrión. On the way they beat and rob the ladies and leave them for dead. For this deed the princes are stripped of property and honor.

Doña Ximena (dō′nyä hē·mĕ′nä), the Cid's wife.

Martín Antolínez (mär·tēn′ än·tō·lē′nĕth), a lieutenant to the Cid.

Minaya Alvar Fáñez (mē·nä′yä äl·bär′ fä′nyĕth), the Cid's chief lieutenant and friend, who is the liaison between his banished lord and Alfonso VI.

Félix Muñoz (fĕ′lĕks mōō·nyōth′), the Cid's nephew, who rescues his uncle's daughters after they are robbed and beaten by their husbands.

Ramón (r̄ä·mōn′), count of Barcelona, who is subdued and taken prisoner by the Cid.

Bucar (bōō·kär′), king of Morocco.

Gonzalo Ansúrez (gōn·thä′lō än·sōō′rĕth), count of Carrión and the father of Diego and Fernando González.

García Ordóñez (gär·thē′ä ôr·dōnyĕth), lord of Grañón, who is the Cid's enemy.

Raquel (r̄ä·kĕl′) and

Vidas (bē′thäs), moneylenders who are swindled by the Cid, after his banishment, in an effort to finance his force of loyal vassals.

The Story

By royal edict, the Cid was banished from Christian Spain by King Alfonso VI of Castile. The royal edict allowed him nine days in which to leave the kingdom but forbade him from taking with him any of his wealth and goods. Anyone in the kingdom who would offer aid to the Cid would forfeit his estate.

Nevertheless, the Cid enlisted the aid of Martín Antolínez in swindling two moneylenders, Raquel and Vidas, in exchange for two large sealed coffers, supposedly loaded with the Cid's riches but containing only sand. The Cid

and a small force of vassals then rode away and made a secret camp. On the morning of his actual departure from the country, with a fair-sized group of loyal vassals, mass for all was said at the abbey where Doña Ximena, the Cid's wife, and his two infant daughters, Doña Elvira and Doña Sol, had been ordered to remain.

Becoming a soldier of fortune, the knight led his host in conquest of one Moorish territory after another, each time with a generous sharing of spoils and booty among his knights and vassals, even the lowliest. Thus he built up a larger and stronger force with every foray, and after each victory mass was said in thanksgiving.

The Cid fought his way to the eastern side of the peninsula, where he fought his most crucial battle and won his greatest victory when he took as his prisoner Count Ramón of Barcelona. After Count Ramón had been humbled and forced to give up all his property, he was granted his liberty.

Although Minaya Alvar Fáñez returned to King Alfonso with gifts and a glowing report of the Cid's successes, the king did not revoke his decree of banishment. Minaya's estates were restored, however, and he was granted freedom to come and go without fear of attack.

The Cid continued his campaigns against the Moorish territories in order to increase his favor with King Alfonso. After he had conquered the provinces of Valencia and Seville, his men grew tired of fighting, and many wished to return to Castile. The Cid, although still generous and understanding, proved himself master by threatening all deserters with death.

Again the Cid sent Minaya to King Alfonso with a gift of one hundred horses and a request that Doña Ximena and her daughters be permitted to join him in Valencia. Visibly softened by the Cid's obvious power, King Alfonso granted this request. In addition, he returned their former estates to the Cid's men.

Shortly after a triumphant reunion with his family in Valencia, the Cid overcame the king of Morocco. As a gesture of victory he sent the Moroccan's tent to King Alfonso. This dramatic gift earned the Cid's pardon and the request that he give his daughters in marriage to Diego and Fernando, the princes of Carrión.

At the victory feast, many marveled at the great length and abundance of the Cid's beard, for he had sworn at the time of his banishment that his beard would never again be cut. A mystical significance of power and success was now attached to the fullness of his beard.

The Cid had reservations about giving his daughters to the princes of Carrión. They were, he thought, too young for marriage. Also, he distrusted the two men. However, with a great show of humbleness and subservience, he returned Doña Elvira and Doña Sol to the king with word that Alfonso would honor the Cid by disposing of his daughters' future as the monarch saw fit.

After the weddings, the elaborate wedding feast, to which all the Cid's vassals as well as those of the territory of Carrión had been invited, lasted for more than two weeks. The Cid expressed some satisfaction in having his family united with noblemen as rich as Prince Diego and his brother Fernando. Two years of happiness followed.

One day one of hte Cid's pet lions escaped. Far from showing valor in the emergency, Diego hid from the lion under the bench on which the Cid was asleep, while Fernando fled into the garden and hid behind a wine press. After the Cid's vassals had easily subdued the lion, the favored princes became the butt of much crude humor

and scorn, but the Cid, choosing to ignore the evident cowardice of his daughters' husbands, made excuses for their pallor.

Once again the Cid was forced to war with the Moroccans, this time against mighty King Bucar. After a great battle, Bucar was killed and his vassals were subdued. The Cid was jubilant. As the spoils were divided, he rejoiced that at last his sons-in-law had become seasoned warriors. His vassals were half-amused, half-disgusted, because it was common knowledge among them that neither Diego nor Fernando had shown the slightest bravery in the conflict, and at one time the Cid's standard-bearer had been forced to risk his life in order to cover for Fernando's shocking cowardice.

Diego and Fernando were richly rewarded for their supposed valor, but their greed was not satisfied. Resentful and injured by the insults and scorn heaped on them by the Cid's vassals, they began a scheme for revenge by telling the Cid that, proud of their wives and their wealth, they would like to make a journey to Carrión in order to show off their wives and to sing the Cid's praises. In secret, they planned not to return. The noble and generous Cid, always ready to think the best of anyone, granted their request without question.

The Cid added further to the princes' treasure and sent them off with a suitable company of his own vassals as an escort of honor. Then, belatedly concerned for the safety of his daughters, he also sent with them his nephew, Félix Muñoz, after charging the young nobleman with the care of Doña Elvira and Doña Sol.

When they were safely away from Valencia, the princes sent the company on ahead and took their wives into the woods. There, with viciousness, they stripped the women of their rich garments and their jewels, whipped them, and left them, bleeding and wounded, to die. His suspicion aroused by the desire of the princes to separate their wives from the rest of the party, Félix Muñoz followed the princes' tracks and found the women. He nursed them back to consciousness and returned them to the Cid.

The princes' scheme of revenge rebounded to their further disgrace. Word of their wicked and dishonest acts spread quickly, and King Alfonso, in his great displeasure, swore to try them in Toledo. The Cid swore that to avenge the treatment his daughters had received, he would marry them to the richest in the land.

At the trial, the princes were first ordered to return the Cid's valued swords, which he had given them as tokens of his high regard. They they were ordered to return his gold. Having squandered it all, they were forced to give him equal value in horses and property.

In the meantime ambassadors from Aragón and Navarre had arrived to ask for the Cid's daughters as queens for their kings. The Cid was jubilant, but still he demanded that the princes of Carrión pay in full measure for their brutality: trial by combat with two of the Cid's chosen knights. King Alfonso warned the princes that if they injured their opponents in the least, they would forfeit their lives. Proved cravens in the fight, the princes were stripped of all honor and wealth.

Criticial Evaluation

The *Poem of the Cid* is an epic composed about 1140, some forty years after the death of Rodrigo (or Ruy) Díaz de Vivar, the hero whose exploits it narrates. It was created by a *juglar* (minstrel) from Medinaceli, the area where the Cid lived, and probably based on an earlier poem written by another *juglar* who was closer in time to the events of the narrative. The earliest extant text of the poem is a copy of earlier manuscripts, made in 1307 by the scribe Per Abbat and first published by Tomás Antonio Sánchez in 1779. The authoritative edition of the manuscript, which includes reconstructions of lost passages based on medieval chronicles that used the original poem as their source, was published in 1900 by Ramón Menéndez Pidal, the philogist and literary historian who has contributed most to an understanding of the development of the epic form in Spain. In the years 1897 to 1903, an annotated edition with an English translation was published by Archer M. Huntington, the founder of the Hispanic Society of America.

All specimens of the epic genre from Homer to the medieval European poems are related in their technique of expressing essential ideas by formulas that remain fairly consistent throughout the development of epic literature. While the *Poem of the Cid* is representative of the genre in its use of traditional themes, it is markedly different in its tone and the presentation of its subject matter. It is distinctive for its realistic portrayal of the historical material and for the absence of the exaggerations and fabulous elements that are common in other, contemporary epics.

This moderation of tone is evident in the development and resolution of the central conflict of the poem, the banishment of the Cid by the king of Aragón and Castile, Alfonso VI. The *Poem of the Cid* concentrates on the exemplary behavior of the hero rather than on the severe and unjust actions of the king. This unusual approach is evident in the fictitious episode of the king's decision to give the Cid's daughters in marriage to the treacherous princes of Carrión. Contrary to the usual development of epic narrative, the *Poem of the Cid* does not aggrandize the villains in order to make the hero's victory over them seem more significant. Rather, it portrays the princes as weak, envious cowards who eventually suffer as punishment a severe legal action rather than the bloody vengeance typical of the epic tradition. At every point, the poem concentrates on the loyalty and reasoned judgment of the Cid, limiting its condemnation of the Cid's enemies to a measured, ironic expression of contempt.

The *Poem of the Cid* is very thorough in its representation of the functioning of eleventh century society in

The Cid rejoinced that, once banished, he could now count two kings of Spain among his kinsmen. He died, Lord of Valencia, on the Day of Pentecost.

Christian Spain. There is a clear portrayal of the social classes, from the lowest, the *burgueses* (commoners) and the Jews engaged in monetary exchange, through the *escuderos* (squires), *caballeros* (those men who had received some kind of military honor), and *infanzones* (knights recognized for their accomplishments and financial holdings), to the *ricos hombres* (representatives of the most powerful families, from whom were chosen the counts who would govern the various regions of Spain). The importance of these social distinctions serves as a stimulus to the action of the poem, as the princes of Carrión, *ricos hombres*, agree to marry, beneath their station, the daughters of an *infanzón*—the Cid. They are portrayed as doing so only because they think that the daughters will bring a good dowry. The narrative of their subsequent dastardly behavior of beating and robbing their wives and the portrayal of their cowardice during the trial that follows, reflect the poem's hostility toward the higher nobility.

The flexibility of this apparently rigid social structure is evident in the fact that the Cid is allowed to arrange a second marriage for his daughters to the kings of Aragón and Navarre, after proving himself loyal in spite of Alfonso's arbitrary behavior. The resolution of the poem reaffirms the democratic ideal of this highly structured society, as King Alfonso responds to the Cid's devotion by showing greater respect for the loyal *infanzón* than for the more powerful nobility represented by the family of the princes.

The challenge to the established societal structure is a reflection of the popular origins of the *Poem of the Cid*. The Cid's stature as a national hero does not derive from the portrayal of his unwavering loyalty to the throne, but rather from the representation of the knight as the incarnation of a popular ideal, the possibility of achieving a position of honor through one's accomplishments in spite of the obstacles of a rigid class structure, treacherous enemies, and unjust superiors. The historical circumstances of the eleventh century, reflected so clearly in the *Poem of the Cid*, provided the material necessary to develop the narrative of a popular leader who is able to unify the people in a common cause, the reconquest of the Spanish lands from the Moorish invaders. Thus, the Cid's military exploits represent the process of solidifying the power of the king through the conquest of Moorish lands and the territories of Christian adversaries, and at the same time the process of restoring his favor with the king and resolving his own exile.

Most critics of the *Poem of the Cid* agree that the text

is lacking in the rich, brilliant descriptive passages that characterize other epic literature of the period but that it is superior in its use of irony and its perceptive psychological analysis. The versificaiton and assonant rhyme of the poem is often faulty, though scholars have determined that those faults are due to errors and alterations made by the various copyists that intervened between the original and the earliest extant manuscript.

POETICS

Type of work: Philosophical essay
Author: Aristotle (384–322 B.C.)
First transcribed: Fourth century B.C.

Although Aristotle's reputation as one of the greatest philosophers of all time rests principally on his work in metaphysics, he nowhere shows himself more the master of illuminating analysis and style than in *Poetics*. The conception of tragedy which Aristotle developed in this work has perpetuated the Greek ideal of drama through the ages.

Aristotle begins his essay with an exposition of the Greek idea that all poetry, or art, is representative of life. This conception—that art is imitative—is also to be found in Plato's *Republic*, a work in which Plato, who was Aristotle's teacher, portrays Socrates as urging that poets be banned from the ideal state, for, as imitators, they are too far removed from reality to be worthy of attention. For the Greeks the idea of poetry as imitative, or representational, was a natural one, since, as a matter of fact, much Grecian art was representational in content. Furthermore, "representation" meant not a literal copying of physical objects, although it was sometimes that, but a new use of the material presented by sense.

Aristotle's intention in *Poetics* is to analyze the essence of poetry and to distinguish its various species. The word "poetry" is used in translation as synonymous with "fine art." Among the arts mentioned by Aristotle are epic poetry, tragedy, comedy, dithyrambic poetry, flute playing, and lyre playing. These arts are all regarded as representative of life, but they are distinguished from one another by their means and their objects. The means include rhythm, language, and tune; but not all the arts involve all three, nor are these means used in the same way. For example, flute playing involves the use of rhythm and tune, but dancing involves rhythm alone.

When living persons are represented, Aristotle writes, they are represented as being better than, worse than, or the same as the average. Tragedy presents men somewhat better than average, while comedy presents men somewhat worse. This point alone offers strong evidence against a narrow interpretation of Aristotle's conception of art, for if men can be altered by the poet, made better or worse than in actual life, then poetry is not a mere uncreative copying of nature. Furthermore, a comment made later on in *Poetics* tells us that the poet in representing life represents things as they are, as they seem to be, or as they should be. This concept certainly allows the artist more freedom than the word "imitation" suggests.

The origin of poetry is explained by Aristotle as the natural consequence of man's love of imitation and of tune and rhythm. We enjoy looking at accurate copies of things, he says, even when the things are themselves repulsive, such as the lowest animals and corpses. The philosopher accounts for this enjoyment by claiming that it is the result of our love of learning; in seeing accurate copies, we learn better what things are. This view is in opposition to Plato's idea that art corrupts the mind since it presents copies of copies of reality (physical objects being considered as mere copies of the universal idea). Aristotle believed that universals, or characteristics, are to be found only in things, while Plato thought that the universals had some sort of separate existence.

Comedy represents inferior persons in that, laughable, they are a species of the ugly. The comic character makes mistakes or is in some way ugly, but not so seriously as to awaken pity or fear.

Epic poetry differs from tragedy in that it has a single meter and is narrative in form. A further difference resulted from the Greek convention that a tragedy encompass events taking place within a single day, while the epic poem was unlimited in that respect.

Tragedy is defined by Aristotle as a representation of a heroic action by means of language and spectacle so as to arouse pity and fear and thus bring about a catharsis of those emotions. The release, or catharsis, of the emotions of pity and fear is the most characteristic feature of the Aristotelian conception of tragedy. According to Aristotle, tragedy arouses the emotions by bringing a man somewhat better than average into a reversal of fortune for which he is responsible; then, through the downfall of the hero and the resolution of the conflicts resulting from the hero's tragic flaw, the tragedy achieves a purging of the emotions in the audience. The audience feels pity in observing the tragic hero's misadventures because he is a vulnerable human being suffering from unrecognized faults, and then fear results from the realization that the hero is much like ourselves: We, too, can err and suffer.

Aristotle defines "plot" as the arrangement of the events which make up the play, "character" as that which determines the nature of the agents, and "thought" as what is expressed in the speeches of the agents. "Diction" is the manner of that expression. Plot is the most important element in the tragedy, because a tragedy is a representation of action. The characters exist for the sake of the action; the action does not exist for the sake of the characters.

The two most important elements of the plot of a tragedy are "peripety," or reversal, and "discovery." By peripety, Aristotle meant a change of a situation into its opposite state of fortune—in tragedy, a change from a good state of affairs to a bad state of affairs. A discovery is a revelation of a matter previously unknown. The most effective tragedy, according to Aristotle, results from a plot which combines peripety and discovery in a single action, as in Sophocles' *Oedipus*.

To modern readers Aristotle's definitions of the beginning, middle, and end of a tragedy may seem either amusing or trivial, but they contain important dramatic truths. Aristotle defines the beginning as that which does not necessarily follow anything else but does necessarily give rise to further action. The end necessarily follows from what has gone before, but it does not necessarily lead to further events. The middle follows the beginning and gives rise to the end.

The sense of Aristotle's definitions is found once we realize that the important thing about the beginning of a play is not that it is the start but that, relative to the audience's interest and curiosity, no earlier event is needed and further events are demanded. Similarly, for the ending, the closing events of a play should not be merely the last events presented. They should appear necessary as a result of what has already happened, and, furthermore, they should not give rise to new problems which must be solved if the audience is to be satisfied.

Aristotle writes that anything that is beautiful not only must have parts orderly arranged but also must have parts of a large enough, but not too large, size. An animal a thousand miles long or something too small to be seen cannot be beautiful. A play should be as long as possible, allowing a change of fortune in a sequence of events ordered in some apparently inevitable way, provided the play can be understood as a whole.

In his conception of unity Aristotle emphasizes a point that continues to be useful to all who compose or criticize works of art: if the presence of a part makes no difference, it has no place in the work. This idea, known as the "unity of action," had an enormous influence on sixteenth and seventeenth century dramatists. Aristotle's emphasis on the logical connection between events in a dramatic plot was extended to a privileging of unities of time and place by Italian scholars. By the early seven-teenth century, dramatists in France had extrapolated Aristotle's unity into a theory of three unities: of time, place, and action. Playwrights such as Pierre Corneille and Jean Racine attempted to adhere to these principles, confining the action of their plays to a single day and setting while continuing to emphasize the logical connection of events. (In England, this neoclassical approach was less successful, despite the efforts of John Dryden and Ben Jonson.)

According to Aristotle, a good tragedy should not show worthy men passing from good fortune to bad, for that is neither fearful nor pitiful but shocking. But even worse is to show bad men experiencing good fortune, for such a situation irritates us without arousing pity and fear. The tragic hero, consequently, should be a man better than ourselves, but not perfect; and he should suffer from a flaw which shows itself in some mistaken judgment or act resulting in his downfall. There has been considerable discussion about the kind of flaw Aristotle meant, but it seems clear from the examples he gives that the flaw should be such that, given it, a man must inevitably defeat himself in action; nevertheless, it is not inevitable that man have that flaw. All men are vulnerable to the flaw, however; hence, the tragic hero arouses fear in all those who see the resemblance between the hero's situation and their own. The hero arouses pity because, as a human being, he cannot be perfect like the gods; his end is bound to be tragic.

Aristotle concludes his *Poetics* with a careful discussion of diction and thought, and of epic poetry. Among the sensible comments he makes is one to the effect that what is believable though not possible is better in a play than an event which is possible but not believable. Throughout the *Poetics*, Aristotle offers remarkably clear analyses of what Greek tragedy actually was and of what, according to Aristotle, it ought to be. He shows not only an adroit, analytical intellect but also an understanding of the practical problems of the art of poetry; and he is sophisticated enough to realize that most questions as to the value, length, beauty, and other features of a work of art are settled relative to the kind of audience the judge prefers.

THE POETRY OF BASHŌ

Type of work: Verse and poetic prose
Author: Matsuo Bashō (1644–1694)
First published: 1672–1748

No poet in Japan has had a greater effect upon his contemporaries or his posterity or has been accorded greater acclaim and honor than Matsuo Bashō. Throughout Japan, wherever his poetic wanderings took him there are stone memorials, more than three hundred altogether, inscribed with his compositions and many mounds believed to contain objects he owned. Although his remains were buried in a Buddhist temple, on his centennial and sesquicentennial anniversaries he was deified in at least three Shinto shrines, one of which was actually named after two of the words in his famous poem:

Furu-ike ya
  Kawazu tobi-komu
    Mizu no oto.

Many have tried, but no one has successfully translated this poem, which refers to the sound of the water when a frog jumps into a pond. Thus, the name of the shrine might be translated as "Shrine of the Jump-sound."

Born the third (some say the second) son of a warrior family, Bashō not only studied *haikai* poetry but also read widely in the Japanese and Chinese classics and poetry. He was a student of Zen Buddhism, calligraphy, and painting, and had at one time been a student of Taoism and of medicine. With this rich and varied background Bashō, after a few youthful indiscretions common to his age and society, developed into a man of high virtue, possibly because of the shock he experienced at the death of his feudal lord and fellow poet, the privations he met during his wanderings, and his serious studies in Zen Buddhism.

Haikai, the origins of which may be traced back to the very beginnings of Japanese poetry, developed from a form in which a series of seventeen-syllable poems or stanzas were linked together. During the middle of the sixteenth century, this form split into the seventeen-syllable *haiku* and linked verse (*renga*), the former a humorous, sometimes bawdy, type of epigram. By the middle of the seventeenth century, haiku had again split into two schools, one emphasizing the form itself, the other seeking greater freedom for the expression of wit and the unusual at the expense of form. Neither school, however, produced superior poetry.

Bashō lived in a peaceful period following a century of wars and internecine strife. More than half a century before, Ieyasu had unified Japan under the rule of his house. The warriors who had fought under him and their descendants now were busy with peaceful enterprises.

There was also a rising moneyed class made up of merchants in the urban trading centers of Osaka and Edo, now Tokyo. The concentration of power and resources in the shogunate, the concentration of cash money among the merchants, the philosophical clashes between the rigid codes of feudal loyalty on the one hand and the power of money on the other, and peaceful times produced three of the greatest literary figures in Japanese history almost at the same time. Bashō was the poet among them, and the only one who renounced material wealth for matters of the spirit.

In 1666, when Bashō was twenty-three, his feudal lord died. Bashō left feudal service in spite of the fact that such a step made him a semi-outcast from his society, and in 1672 he arrived in Edo already versed in the two schools of the haiku. For the rest of his life he devoted himself to bringing this form back to true poetry and, in the course of this effort, created a third school which is named after him. In the three centuries since, haiku poetry has had its vicissitudes, but each revival has been a movement back to Bashō. His influence is felt not only in his own school but also in the other two. His death anniversaries are still strictly observed by his followers, and admiration for him amounts to bare idolatry. The latest revival was begun by Masaoka Shiki (1867–1902), haiku poet and novelist, in the 1890's.

There is no single adequate word for the essence of Bashō's poetry, but it has been described as the illustration of an old man girding on his armor and fighting on the battlefield, or clothing himself in the richest brocades to attend a banquet. In either case he cannot hide the fact that he is beyond his physical prime. The liveliest of Bashō's haiku contain an element of lingering pathos, but such pathos is not to be gained by seeking it per se. It must be a development of one's nature as the result of the varied experiences of life.

The best of the poems by Bashō and his disciples are collected in the *Haikai Shichibu-shû* (*Seven Collected Works*) in twelve volumes. The seven collections contained are *Fuyu no Hi* (*Winter Days*); *Haru no Hi* (*Spring Days*); *Arano* (*Fields of Wilderness*); *Hisago* (*The Gourd*); *Saru Mino* (*Coats of Straw for Monkeys*); *Sumi-dawara* (*Bags of Charcoal*); and *Zoku Saru Mino* (*Saru Mino, Continued*).

Other well-known collections of his verse and prose writings include *Kai-oi*, a collection of sixty haiku in pairs, each like the two shells of a clam, which gives this collection its title. The verse of thirty-seven persons contains Bashō's comments as well. The preface is dated

1672, when Bashō was twenty-eight. The poems combine snatches of popular songs and expressions of the time, and Bashō's comments indicate that if he himself did not indulge in an unrestrained life in his youth, he was at least in sympathy with those who did. This work is representative of his earlier years.

The remaining books are accounts of his wanderings and journeys, each liberally sprinkled with poems. These include *Nozarashi Kikô* (*In the Face of Wind and Rain*), 1685, an account of a trip from Edo to the Kyoto-Nara-Ise area, particularly Nagoya in 1684–1685; *Kashima Kikô* (*Moon Viewing to Kashima*), 1687; *Oi no Obumi* (*Scraps from my Letterbox*), 1687, an account of a journey in the Yamato area, believed to show Bashō at his peak as a poet and philosopher; *Sarashina Kikô* (*Moon Viewing to Sarashina*), 1688, a brief work like the *Kashima Kikô* and similar in style; *Oku no Hoso-michi* (*The Narrow Road of Oku*), an account of a trip in 1689 from Edo to Sakata in northeastern Japan via Nikkô and Matsushima, and thence down toward the Japan Sea to Kanazawa, Tsuruga and then southward to Ise, covering about 1,467 miles in seven months. This work, the greatest of Bashō's travel accounts, inspired numerous followers, both of his own time and later (including at least one American), to make trips by the same route. The *Saga Nikki* (*Diary at Saga*), 1691, is Bashō's diary written during a month's stay in 1691 at the Rakushi-sha, a modest residence in Saga, near Kyoto. The style reveals Bashō at his best in describing his enjoyment of a simple, uncluttered life.

Selections from Bashō's poetry and prose are widely available in English translation. Indeed, much of his work is available in several different versions, so that the reader is not limited to the perspective of a single translator.

THE POETRY OF BLAKE

Type of work: Poetry
Author: William Blake (1757–1827)
First published: *Songs of Innocence*, 1789; *The Marriage of Heaven and Hell*, 1790; *Songs of Experience*, 1794; *The Book of Urizen*, 1794; *The Four Zoas*, 1797–1807; *Milton*, 1804–1808; *Jerusalem: The Emanation of the Giant Albion*, 1804–1820.

William Blake was one of the greatest of the English Romantic poets, although his reputation was not finally established until well over a century after his death in 1827. Dates for first publication of his works are problematic; he produced his own books and was not always systematic in dating them. It is known, however, that his first major poems were those of *Songs of Innocence*, which Blake published in the form of an illustrated book, using his original method of printing. *Songs of Innocence* drew on a well-established tradition of children's books, such as Isaac Watts's *Divine Songs for Children*, but Blake disliked the conventional religious and moral sentiments expressed in books such as these. He thought that their emphasis on discipline and hard work stifled the natural, joyful instincts of the child and perverted his or her growth into adulthood. *Songs of Innocence* was his affirmation of the integrity of the state of childhood, its innate value and goodness.

Although simple in form, many of the poems in *Songs of Innocence* have a more sophisticated content than might at first appear. At the time, Blake was immersed in the writings of the Swedish seer Emanuel Swedenborg, and many of these poems reveal a Swedenborgian sense of a spiritual reality underlying temporal phenomena. The world of childhood they depict is lit by what Blake later called the Divine Vision; the speakers in the poems possess a spontaneous sense of the presence of the divine, which guides and illumines particularly the weak and the insignificant. The first two stanzas of "Night" evoke the typical atmosphere of Innocence:

> The sun descending in the west,
> The evening star does shine;
> The birds are silent in their nest,
> And I must seek for mine.
> The moon like a flower
> In heaven's high bower,
> With silent delight,
> Sits and smiles on the night.
>
> Farewell, green fields and happy groves,
> Where flocks have took delight;
> Where lambs have nibbled, silent moves
> The feet of angels bright.
> Unseen they pour blessing,

> And joy without ceasing,
> On each bud and blossom,
> And each sleeping bosom.

The state of Innocence, although precious, is not a perfect state. The innocent lack self-knowledge and are open to exploitation. "Holy Thursday," for example, which describes thousands of poor children taking part in an annual service at St. Paul's Cathedral, is full of irony: The children walk to the service in regimented style, "two and two"; the "wands as white as snow" which the beadles carry can also be used to enforce discipline, and the "voice of song" which the children raise to heaven is at once a voice of protest and a plea for divine help. Read in this light, the moralistic tone of the speaker's final line, "Then cherish pity, lest you drive an angel from your door," becomes a disturbing realization of injustice. Similarly, the young, exploited chimney sweeper in the poem of that name finds comfort in the moral guidance he receives from an angel in a dream: "if he'd be a good boy,/ He'd have god for his father and never want joy." The promise is not fulfilled, however, and the angel's advice merges with that of the narrator in the final line: "So if all do their duty, they need not fear harm." The innocent are made to accept the specious arguments of the adult world.

In 1794, Blake published a companion collection, *Songs of Experience*, and issued it jointly with *Songs of Innocence*, with the subtitle *Showing the Two Contrary States of the Human Soul*. Many of the poems in *Songs of Experience* are direct counterparts to poems in *Songs of Innocence*. In the state of experience there is no sense of the divine comfort; the corruption and cruelty of human society, and the suffering they cause, are laid bare. In these poems Blake's voice often rings with the honest indignation of the prophet, and his targets are those which he fought against all his life: conventional education, morality, and religion, all of which he thought were based on a false and inadequate view of man. For Blake, man was not a miserable "worm of sixty withers" but the "eternal great Humanity Divine." In the state of Experience, however, the life-energy which flows with such freedom and joy in Innocence is stifled. "The Garden of Love" is an example:

> I went to the garden of love,
> And saw what I never had seen:

A chapel was built in the midst,
Where I used to play on the green.

And the gates of this chapel were shut,
And *Thou shalt not* writ over the door;
So I turned to the garden of love,
That so many sweet flowers bore,

And I saw it was filled with graves,
And tomb-stones where flowers should be—
And priests in black gowns were walking their rounds,
And binding with briars my joys and desires.

The "joys and desires" of the speaker include sexual desire, which Blake regarded as a pure and innocent expression of the life force. Many of the *Songs of Experience* poems are about sexual guilt, repression, and jealousy. Others, such as "A Poison Tree," portray the negative consequences that result when strong emotions are unexpressed and so allowed to fester.

The state of Experience encourages a self-centered, brooding approach to life. The contrast with Innocence can be clearly seen in the two poems titled "Nurse's Song." The nurse in the "innocent" poem is in touch with the children in her charge, and with her environment; she is ready to adapt to what the situation demands. The "experienced" nurse is dogmatic and inflexible in her views; she looks inward rather than outward, and the open dialogue of the first poem is replaced by the self-engrossed monologue of the second.

Blake's other achievements from this stage of his career include the delightful *The Book of Thel* and the impassioned *Visions of the Daughters of Albion*, both of which further probe the psychological states of Innocence and Experience. Most important, however, is *The Marriage of Heaven and Hell*, a wonderfully exuberant satire, full of daring thought and irrepressible vitality. Its key statement is "Without contraries is no progression"; it is an attempt to marry all the opposite values in life: reason and energy, body and soul, the spiritual and the material. Blake wanted to unify existence, which he believed had been falsely sundered by religious dualism, without destroying its essential polarity.

The Marriage of Heaven and Hell contains much of what is most striking in Blake's poetry, that sense of joy, delight, and bliss which challenges our limited perceptions of the world: "How do you know but every bird that cuts the airy way/ Is an immense world of delight, closed by your senses five?" Blake believed that this heightened perception was available to anyone who was prepared to exercise his imaginative faculties: "If the doors of perception were cleansed everything would appear to man as it is—infinite." The creative imagination had the power to channel infinity, to pour the energy of life itself into all its finite receptacles, because "Eternity is in love with the productions of Time."

It is important to understand that in *The Marriage of Heaven and Hell*, Blake reverses conventional religious categories. His Angels are the religiously orthodox, who condemn the physical energies as evil and think that a passive adherence to reason alone, which they identify with the soul, is good. To this view, Blake, in the form of the Devil, replies, "Man has no body distinct from his soul, for that called body is a portion of soul discerned by the five senses." All systems that teach otherwise only divide man against himself. In *The Marriage of Heaven and Hell*, the Devil embodies the creative imagination, the energy which is "eternal delight," and it is the Devil's "Proverbs of Hell" which supply much of the Blakean wisdom expressed in the book. (One of the best is "Prudence is a rich ugly old maid courted by incapacity.")

During the mid-1790's Blake wrote what have become known as the Lambeth prophecies, of which the most important is *The Book of Urizen*. Blake's first creation myth, it is a creative reworking of Milton's *Paradise Lost*, the Book of Genesis, and the *Mysterium Magnum* of Blake's mentor in esoteric matters, the seventeenth century German seer Jacob Boehme. Urizen, the personification of the faculty of reason, cuts himself off from the company of other Eternals and attempts to impose on them a uniform set of laws. They shun him, and in his isolation, cut off from the creative power of the imagination, he can create only a limited world in which the expansive, translucent joy of eternity has hardened into the opacity of material forms. Seen in this light, the act of creation is also a fall; this concept is tinged with Gnosticism and hard to reconcile with the exuberant celebration of physical life in *The Marriage of Heaven and Hell*, although the dislike of reason remains the same.

The fallen world occupied much of Blake's attention during the 1790's, as he developed an increasingly complex mythology in which the four basic elements (the Zoas) of man's constitution war among themselves, destroying the primal unity of the Eternal or Universal Man, who once embodied the entire universe within himself. The Zoas are Urizen (reason), Urthona (imagination, who becomes Los in the fallen world), Luvah (passion and desire), and Tharmas (a vague figure who is sometimes identified with instinct and sometimes with compassion). The Zoas in turn are divided from their female counterparts, Ahania, Enitharmon, Vala, and Enion, respectively. The conflict between the Zoas is the subject of the long, unfinished poem "Vala," which Blake revised and called *The Four Zoas* but still did not finish. The later version introduced a theme of redemption, in Blake's expression of his own idiosyncratic version of Christianity.

The Four Zoas is a confusing, even bewildering poem at times, and Blake never resolved the structural difficulties which his sprawling myth presented. Still, the poem has many magnificent passages, as in this evocation of the Eternal Man:

And in the cries of birth & in the groans of death his voice
Is heard throughout the universe: wherever a grass grows
Or a leaf buds, the Eternal Man is seen, is heard, is felt,
And all his sorrows, till he reassumes his ancient bliss.

In common with the other Romantic poets, Blake viewed the poet as a seer and prophet, and he believed that the arts were the chief means of communication with eternity. In his next major work, *Milton*, he explored the implications of these ideas and described how the spirit of poetry was handed down from one age to the next. He also took the opportunity to continue his argument with Milton. (Blake did not agree with Milton's conception of God or his explanation of the Fall in *Paradise Lost*.) In the poem, Milton is unhappy in heaven and decides to return to earth to correct his errors. His redeemed spirit enters Blake, who assumes Milton's prophetic mantle, and Blake realizes that he has also become one with Los, the Imagination. These two moments of visionary illumination transfigure all subsequent perception: The world of time and space reveals eternity. The poem thus becomes a record of one man's enlightenment. Although, like all Blake's long poems, *Milton* can be bewildering because of its proliferation of characters, the unfamiliar psychological states it describes, and its unusual narrative structure, it contains some of Blake's finest poetry, including the famous stanzas beginning "And did those feet in ancient

time," popularly known as "Jerusalem."

Blake's final long poem, *Jerusalem: The Emanation of the Giant Albion*, depicts the rising of all men to the experience of unity and enlightenment that Blake had described for one individual in *Milton*. The central figure is Albion, who represents England and who is also each individual man and the embodiment of all men. The poem therefore operates at a number of different levels: psychological, historical, and cosmological. Originally, Albion, like the Eternal Man in *The Four Zoas*, was a vast being who contained the universe within himself. He lived in a state of harmony and bliss. When *Jerusalem* begins, however, Albion has already fallen from this condition because he has rejected his feminine aspect, Jerusalem, who represents spiritual wholeness. Instead, he has embraced the female figure of Vala, who is nature experienced in isolation from eternity. As a result, Albion's universe becomes externalized; time and space take on an objective appearance, and Albion finds himself living in a world that is no longer his own and that is hostile to his desires. Helpless, he sinks into a sleep and must rely on the efforts of Los, who struggles, with divine aid, to re-create the structures of eternity in the fallen world. The poem ends with Albion rising from his sleep, becoming reunited with Jerusalem, and recovering his paradisiacal state of universal knowledge, power, and bliss.

THE POETRY OF DICKINSON

Type of work: Poetry
Author: Emily Dickinson (1830–1886)
First published: *Poems*, 1890; *Poems: Second Series*, 1891; *Poems: Third Series*, 1896; *The Single Hound*, 1914; *Further Poems*, 1929; *Unpublished Poems*, 1936; *Bolts of Melody: New Poems*, 1945; *The Poems of Emily Dickinson* (edited by Thomas H. Johnson), 1955; *The Complete Poems of Emily Dickinson* (edited by Thomas H. Johnson), 1960.

Few of America's great poets waited so long to achieve recognition as did Emily Dickinson. Though she wrote over 1,775 poems, during her lifetime only seven were published, and those anonymously. When she died, few beyond her circle of family and friends had heard of her, yet nearly seventy years after her death she was critically acclaimed as one of the leading poets of her time. Along with Walt Whitman, Dickinson is credited with bringing American poetry into the twentieth century, for her highly unusual style and her passion for expressing the truth helped to free nineteenth century verse from its limitations of image, meter, and rhyme.

To neighbors in her hometown of Amherst, Massachusetts, Dickinson was an eccentric figure, the spinster who always dressed in white and who, after her early thirties, never ventured beyond the family home or garden. She rarely received a visitor, and when she did, she would hide upstairs and sometimes send down a note or poem to her guest. Some biographers suggest that the reports of her reclusive life-style may be somewhat exaggerated, but it is nonetheless clear that Dickinson preferred to socialize through letters and to confide her deepest thoughts in her poems. One of Dickinson's long-time correspondents was Thomas Wentworth Higginson, poetry critic for *The Atlantic Monthly*, to whom she initially sent a few poems along with the earnest question whether he found the poems alive. His answer that there *was* life in the poetry she claimed had saved her life; yet Higginson, a conventional critic with traditional tastes, was generally lukewarm in his praise. He found her poems strange and unpolished, and his reservations may have contributed to her reluctance to have them published.

After Dickinson's death her sister discovered hundreds of poems in Emily's room, many hand-sewn into small booklike packets. Lavinia Dickinson persuaded Higginson and a family friend, Mabel Loomis Todd, to published the poems, which they did in 1890, 1891, and 1896. It is clear, however, that Dickinson's editors had no conception of the value of her work, for they freely made changes to it, smoothing out rhymes and meter, fixing punctuation, and revising diction—in short, making the poems more conventional. Her books sold widely but met with little critical success. Friends and relatives brought out more editions over the years, but each persisted in the practice of "correcting" her work. It was not until the 1950s, after her estate was given to Harvard University, that through the painstaking scholarship of Thomas H. Johnson, a more authentic version finally reached the public. Though some controversy still exists about the dates of composition and Dickinson's final editing choices on some poems, Johnson's edition *The Complete Poems of Emily Dickinson* (1960), along with its system for numbering the poems, is generally accepted as the standard.

Approaching Dickinson's work, what she called her "letter to the World," one should bear in mind the words of the critic Allen Tate: "All pity for Miss Dickinson's 'starved life' is misdirected. Her life was one of the richest and deepest ever lived on this continent." The evidence for this richness and depth, of course, is her poems. Though she often wrote about small and common things, her reach was always broad and high, always bringing her to confront, with searching honesty, the larger universal themes: nature, love, death and immortality, and God. What looked unpolished to her contemporaries—the sometimes awkward phrasing, the skewed rhymes, the short staccato bursts set off by dashes rather than the more grammatically polite comma—reveal a passionate thinker, a mind that would not rest, that was continually seeking answers, and for whom poems were not a polite parlor game but rather a lifeline. She searched for truth and knew that the nature of truth made it impossible to nail it down once and for all; one had to nail it down a hundred times. This is why it is difficult to summarize "Dickinson's themes," such as her view of death, because for Dickinson, trying to understand death, or love, or God, was a continuous quest. If something was understood, why would she need to write about it again and again?

This passion to understand accounts for the sheer volume of Dickinson's work, as well as its occasional unevenness. Generally it is some uncontrollable feeling, such as the pain of loss, or a mind-numbing despair, or even an ecstatic joy, that tornadolike sets Dickinson's poetic faculties into motion. Often her subject is so volatile that it cannot even be named, a fact reflected in her work by a frequent use of the pronoun "it." Within those poems attempting to define the "it," the argument often proceeds like a riddle, developed with a confusion of imagery. It is as though she gathers words like the flying debris at the outer edge of a storm—mixing her metaphors and throwing words together in unlikely pairs—to give her restless subject at least some shape; or, she mixes words just as various pigments are added to a base of paint, and shaken, to reach an appropriate, exact color. The evidence of Dickinson's various drafts and revisions confirms that word choices that seemed careless to her first critics were actually quite carefully made. The brevity of Dickinson's poems makes them appear simple, but reading them actually requires careful attention, often to what is *not* said. One of Dickinson's strategies is to make an unstated shift in perspective; she will frequently investigate her subject by turning all around it, considering it from differing attitudes and points of view. This approach is manifest in the poems as a sometimes unresolvable tension of opposites, an imbalance, a seeming resolution and then dissolution, a dance between what can and cannot be faced or named. The destination of this process, so turbulently awakened, is always to penetrate to the center of this storm, a place of mastery and calm, where meaning can be distilled. Her passion for meaning is what made this reclusive spinster such a literary revolutionary: Dickinson had to bend language and form in order to get at the truth. "Tell all the Truth," she admonished, "but tell it slant."

Dickinson's truth is primarily an inner one. She was one of the first American poets to carefully map the interior landscape of feeling, exploring the terrain of the subconscious before it was "discovered" decades later by Freud. Even in those poems that are descriptions of external reality, such as her nature poems, the inner life still carries the greater force. Her well-known "A narrow Fellow in the Grass" (#986) culminates most powerfully when it shifts its focus from the snake, the object observed, to the observer, who with "a tighter breathing" is feeling "Zero at the Bone." "There's a certain Slant of light" (#258), a description of a winter afternoon, projects the poet's despair onto the landscape; in this Dickinson is a forerunner of the twentieth century Imagists, creating imagery that is not ornamental but intrinsic. In poems like "I felt a Funeral, in my Brain" (#280) Dickinson openly explores the mind, detailing the disturbing loss of reason, when feeling has overtaken sense.

Dickinson's love poems reveal a passion that belies the quiet facts of her biography. They support the speculation that if Dickinson withdrew from society it was not because she was indifferent to it; rather, it was because she felt her attachments to friends and lovers so deeply. There has been much speculation about the identity of the man for whom Dickinson's unrequited love occasioned an outpouring of poems during her "flood years" of the early 1860's. Many believe it was Charles Wadsworth, a married preacher from Philadelphia who left for California in 1862. Of course knowing whom Dickinson wrote about is ultimately much less significant than the poetry he inspired, poems ranging from the exuberant "Wild Nights—Wild Nights!" (#249) to the despairing "I cannot live with you" (#640).

The subject which holds by far the greatest fascination for Dickinson is death, about which she wrote over five hundred poems. Sometimes she considers it from the point of view of the bereaved survivors, as in "The last Night that She lived" (#1100) and "There's been a Death, in the Opposite House" (#389). Other times she looks at it from the point of view of the person dying, as in "I heard a Fly buzz—when I died" (#465) and "Because I could not stop for Death" (#712). The latter poem's personification of Death as a gentleman caller demonstrates her typically atypical approach. Hers is not so much a morbid fascination as it is an intense and fearless curiosity. At times she sees death as a horrifying cessation, but at others it is a blissful release envied by the living. Death is for Dickinson the ultimate punctuation mark, which, appearing at the end of life's sentence, gives it all its meaning. It is a gateway through which one passes to a perhaps even greater type of existence. It is also a mystery about which one can never be completely convinced, which is perhaps why she keeps probing. This restless questioning also characterizes her religious poetry, which vacillates between faith in God and doubt, as when the initial conviction in "I know that He exists" (#338) unravels during the stanzas that follow.

Dickinson also wrote poems about her craft, among them #675, "Essential Oils":

> Essential Oils—are wrung—
> The Attar from the Rose
> Be not expressed by Suns—alone—
> It is the gift of Screws—
>
> The General Rose—decay
> But this—in Lady's Drawer
> Make Summer—When the Lady lie
> In Ceaseless Rosemary—

"Essential Oils" is about poetry, but more specifically, it represents the mastery of a particular question important not only to Dickinson but, in varying degrees, to all poets: the choice between the life of the common man, with its sphere of social relationships, and the life of the poet, with its demanding solitude. In "Essential Oils" the choice is distilled, and embodied, in the metaphor of the rose. There is the rose that blooms in a day, whose fragrance is drawn out of it by the attentions of the sun, and the rose that is taken from the garden, so that its essence may be concentrated into an enduring perfume. There is no doubt in the poem about which rose Dickinson prefers. She has passed that stage of the argument, has reached the still center of meaning, and so sustains throughout the conviction that begins the poem.

"Essential Oils," the volatile essence that imparts the characteristic odor of a plant, represents that very nature of a thing, which is incapable of removal without destroying the thing itself or its character. Poems, the volatile essence of the poet, become of life-and-death importance; without them the poet ceases to be herself. This necessity justifies the process by which they are gotten: They "are wrung," a verb that implies physical and emotional pressure, the process of suffering and pain. This is the poet's secret: Art "is the gift of Screws." As a metaphor for the poetic process, "screws" is an image of remarkable compression. It suggests not only the flower press but also the pain of the medieval torture device, and as a reference to the tools of the carpenter, it implies discipline and craftsmanship as well. The image also suggests, in its spiral shape narrowing to a point, an emblem for the poet's mind turning around a subject until it reaches its center, until meaning is screwed down. This process is compared to that other one which draws the odor from a bloom, the expressions of "Suns," which for Dickinson is a metaphor for the masculine principle, hence symbolizing the warm attentions of suitors; thus the essence of the rose becomes an image for a woman's sexual potential. A woman can express her being through a union with a man; but the poet—"alone"—realizes her identity through the creative process.

"The General Rose" is the common rose, different from the rose of the poet. "General" carries the connotation of military ranking, an ironic reference to the command a wife exerts over her household and the social superiority she may enjoy. In outward form, the first line of this stanza is very similar to the opening line of the first stanza: A modified noun is separated by a dash from its verb. Whereas "Essential" seems to justify and balance the pain in "wrung," however, in this line the emotional scales are tipped, and there is nothing in the "General Rose" to redeem it from "decay," the most negatively charged word in the poem. "But this" redirects the argument to the strength of the poet, her attar, the poems and fascicles she keeps in her bureau drawer. "Lady's drawer" as an image of limited space also suggests the artistic isolation and confinement that are necessary to preserving the poet's essence. The scents of poems "Make Summer"—summer for Dickinson being an emblem of fruition, when the potential of nature is realized. This fact masters death for the poet so that it can be described with a gentle euphemism, "When the Lady lie/ In Ceaseless Rosemary." Rosemary has long been associated with the power of memory and was often used to scent coffins. The poet lying in "Ceaseless Rosemary" will not be forgotten after her death; the line is a prophetic description of Dickinson's belated but nonetheless powerful impact on American letters.

THE POETRY OF DONNE

Type of work: Poetry
Author: John Donne (1572–1631)
Principal published works: *An Anatomy of the World: The First Anniversary,* 1611; *Of the Progress of the Soule: The Second Anniversary,* 1612; *Poems by J.D.,* 1633

In the early years of the twentieth century John Donne was first acknowledged to be a major English poet, and his achievement meaningfully evaluated. Pope "translated" Donne's *Satires* so thoroughly that they were unrecognizable, and Dryden misleadingly declared that Donne wrote "nice speculations of Philosophy" and not love poetry at all. Few poets of the nineteenth century—a notable exception is Gerard Manley Hopkins—show the influence of the metaphysical poets. Poets of the twentieth century, however, have learned much from Donne's poetic method, in which emotions are expressed through ideas defined in their emotional context. (T. S. Eliot's championing of Donne and the metaphysical poets was particularly influential.) Ironically, Donne and Dryden by writing in what are essentially speech rhythms and not in the current poetic mode revitalized the language of poetry in their generation.

Dryden was in error when he called Donne's poetry philosophical. Donne was not committed to a particular philosophic system, but he was interested in the fascinating, conflicting, and often disturbing philosophies of his period. The scholastic way of thought, in which systems tended toward synthesis and unity, was giving way to the European scientific renaissance, which was analytical. Ptolemaic astronomy was challenged by Copernicus; Aristotle was challenged by Galileo. What interested Donne, however, was not the ultimate truth of an idea but the fascination of ideas themselves. His images are drawn from whatever belief best expressed the emotion he had to communicate.

Donne was not the first man to write metaphysical poetry, and he was not the first poet to describe an emotional state by its intellectual equivalent. Prior to Donne such intellectualized poetry was confined, with the exception of some of Shakespeare's sonnets and Ben Johnson's poetry, to the drama and was most frequently found in the plays of Ford, Jonson, and Webster. Also the Elizabethan tradition of love poetry had already begun to be rivaled by witty and cynical courtly verse. Donne's own reaction against the Elizabethan tradition was as successful as it was complete.

In some poems, as in "The Indifferent," Donne celebrated variety in love, and in "Go and Catch a Falling Star" he insisted that no woman remained faithful. In addition to these poems of wit and fancy, in which Donne directly mocked literary convention, he also wrote serious love poems in which he surpasses in technique and effect his more fanciful verse. In "A Feaver" the world would not merely be a place of darkness after the lady's death; it would disintegrate:

> But yet thou canst not die, I know;
> To leave this world behinde, is death,
> But when thou from this world wilt
>   goe;
> The whole world vapours with thy
>   breath.

A further departure from the tradition in which the lady was invariably unattainable is the glory Donne finds in sexual as well as spiritual love. In only two or three poems does he praise platonic relationships, and the poems that describe a relationship in which the beloved woman is not the poet's mistress are extremely bitter and mocking, as, for example, in "The Apparition."

The element of hyperbole is central in the poems of consummated love and continued devotion, where it is one of the means by which the strength and sincerity of the poet's passion is conveyed. "The Good-Morrow" begins:

> I wonder, by my troth, what thou and I
> Did, till we lov'd? were we not wean'd
>   till then?

and continues:

> For love, all love of other sights con-
>   troules,
> And makes one little roome, an every
>   where.

At first Donne's images may amaze rather than delight; however, they communicate effectively the idea through which the emotion is conveyed.

The areas from which Donne's images were drawn—astronomy, geography, philosophy, and alchemy among others—were those of interest to educated readers of his time. Donne's images do not evoke general or remembered sensation but explain a particular sensation. In "A Valediction: Forbidding Mourning," the central idea is that love is not destroyed by death. Donne compares his love to "the trepidation of the spheres" which on earth is not destructive, although the lesser "moving of the earth brings harms and fears." Furthermore, his love is beyond the ordinary love and includes the soul (love to Donne always involved the entire being); thus separation by death is not a "breach" but an "expansion"—"Like gold to airy thinness beat." The most striking image in this poem is that of a pair of compasses: the mistress who stays alive is the "fixt foot" around which the dead soul revolves and which, invisibly, circles with it. The poem ends:

> Thy firmness drawes my circle just,
> And makes me end where I begunne.

The circle in Donne's poetry is always a symbol for infinity.

The rhythm of Donne's poetry is as varied and accurate in conveying the sense as the imagery he employs. Its texture is sinewy and often irregular. The speech cadences of the verse are heard in the mind and are essentially dramatic. It is not smooth verse, but it is exact and musical. The opening of "The Sunne Rising" is illustrative of his quick, tense quality:

> Busie old foole, unruly Sunne,
>   Why dost thou thus,
> Through windowes, and through cur-
>   taines call on us?
> Must to thy motions lovers seasons
>   run?

Compare these lines with the tranqulity and sensuousness of his close:

> Thine age askes ease, and since thy
>   duties bee
> To warme the world, that's done in
>   warming us.
> Shine here to us, and thou art every
>   where;
> This bed thy center is, these walls, thy
>   spheare.

"Aire and Angels" has lines in which the vowel sounds are long and the consonants soft, when love is contemplated, and short-voweled monosyllabic lines which express love's actuality. The sound in Donne's poetry not only echoes the sense but in part communicates the emotion.

The power and beauty of Donne's poetry is its synthesis of emotion, passion, and thought. "The Anniversarie," which was presumably written to his wife Ann More, is a triumphant expression of confidence in love. In the opening stanza of this poem Donne contrasts the mutability of kings, courts, and even the sun with their love:

> Only our love hath us decay;
> This, no to morrow hath, nor yesterday,

> Running it never runs from us away,
> But truly keeps his first, last, everlasting day.

The discussion of death in the second stanza of this poem is not, here or in other of his lyrics, a morbid preoccupation but, as is true of all Donne's poetry, an illustration of the all-embracing and inquiring quality of his mind. Death will not destroy love; love will increase in the souls released from the grave. In the third stanza the lovers themselves are kings and thus they will know physical change and decay; however, since the love in their souls after death is inviolate, so are they, while they live. The evolution of this paradoxical idea and the simplicity and directness of the language carry dramatic conviction. The poem ends:

> Let us love nobly, and live, and adde againe
> Yeares unto yeares, till we attaine
> To write threescore; this is the second of our raigne.

Probably the *Songs and Sonets* are the best known of Donne's poems, but some of the *Elegies* and religious verse are of the same quality. In 1615, Donne was ordained an Anglican priest and became Dean of St. Paul's Cathedral in London. The poetry that Donne wrote after his ordination was as passionate, as intellectually inquiring, and often as tormented as his love poetry. He spoke of God and the church in the same terms as he spoke of secular love. For many years before he became a priest he had studied theology and was converted to Protestantism, from the Catholic faith to which he had been born. He discussed the difficulty of finding true religion in his poetry and was apparently almost overwhelmed by the knowledge of his sinfulness.

The "Holy Sonnets" are vibrant and impassioned cries, infused with the knowledge of the need for grace. They, too, are highly personal and dramatic. Number XIV begins:

> Batter my heart, three person'd God; for, you
> As yet but knocke, breathe, shine, and seeke to mend;
> That I may rise, and stand, o'erthrow mee, and bend
> Your force, to breake, blowe, burn and make me new.

It ends:

> Take mee to you, imprison mee, for I
> Except you enthrall mee, never shall befree,
> Nor ever chast, except you ravish mee.

Sometimes the paradoxes in the religious poetry are superb and convincing, but occasionally the ideas are pursued to the point of tedium and a seeming detail is overelaborated. One of Donne's most successful devotional poems is "A Hymne to God the Father," on sin, fear, and forgiveness, which, with its repeated phrase "Wilt thou forgive," has a simplicity and humility which is equaled only by the poetry of George Herbert.

Donne was the greatest of the metaphysical poets. In some few of their poems he was equaled by Vaughan and Marvell and in religious poetry by Herbert. But the body of his work is poetry of a quality which, when compared with that of any other of these poets, is unsurpassed. When his images are understood in their function of communicating a state of mind, and his ideas in their power to give expression to emotions, Donne's poetry is appreciated for its wit, beauty, and perception.

THE POETRY OF FROST

Type of work: Poetry
Author: Robert Frost (1874–1963)
Principal published works: *A Boy's Will*, 1913; *North of Boston*, 1914; *Mountain Interval*, 1916; *New Hampshire: A Poem with Notes and Grace Notes*, 1923; *West-Running Brook*, 1928; *A Further Range*, 1936; *A Witness Tree*, 1942; *A Masque of Reason*, 1945; *Steeple Bush*, 1947; *A Masque of Mercy*, 1947; *How Not to be King*, 1951.

They would not find me changed from him they knew—
Only more sure of all I thought was true.

In a sense, this early prediction by Robert Frost is an accurate description of the course of his writing career: Frost's poetry did not change; it simply grew stronger. The dominant characteristics of his work—his impeccable ear for the rhythms of speech; his realistic handling of nature, transcending the ordinary love we ascribe to poets of the outdoors; his revelation of human character by means of dramatic events; his warm philosophy, which combines the viewpoint of a whimsical poet with that of a dirt farmer—all these qualities were apparent (at least to some readers) early in his career. And they were still there at the end, handled with greater precision, displaying more depth.

For an example of this strengthening process, this growth of sapling into tree, look first at the little poem "The Pasture," the last stanza of which invites the reader into Frost's *A Boy's Will*:

> I'm going out to fetch the little calf
> That's standing by the mother. It's so young,
> It totters when she licks it with her tongue.
> I sha'n't be gone long—You come too.

The Frost charm is evident in these lines, but there is also a somewhat juvenile, Rilevesque quality. When one compares "The Pasture" with "Come In," a much later and firmer treatment of the same general theme, the superior diction is immediately apparent in such magnificent lines as these:

> Far in the pillared dark
> Thrush music went—
> Almost like a call to come in
> To the dark and lament.

But equally apparent is a greater depth of psychological complexity, a stronger suggestion of the "death wish" that John Ciardi discusses in his controversial analysis of "Stopping by Woods on a Snowy Evening," the more famous lyric to which "Come In" is a superb companion piece.

Frost did not change, only grew surer; but there has been an amazing change, down through the years, in the attitude taken toward his poems. At first, his fellow Americans could not see this most American of writers as a poet at all; it was necessary for him to go to England to be hailed for his talent. Then, when the English had pointed him out to his compatriots, we cataloged him as another cold New England poet who saw everything in black and white. This astonishing judgment becomes especially egregious when we consider that *A Boy's Will* contains a poem of such warm understanding as "The Tuft of Flowers," and that *North of Boston*, his second volume, includes "The Death of the Hired Man," "Home Burial," and "The Fear," three dramatic poems that are intensely emotional. After Frost's reputation finally became established, the critics forced him into a third stage of his career: He was recognized as a major poet, but one not very interesting to talk or write about because his poetry was thought too simple and because he held aloof from the free-verse poets, whose efforts, he thought, lacked discipline. Near the end of his life, Frost entered a fourth period: His great talents were at last fully recognized, and he came to be regarded as a poet of far more depth and complexity than anyone had previously realized. Two of Frost's poems that are provocative enough to satisfy the most eager analyst are "Directive," with its Grail imagery, and "The Subverted Flower," with its tantalizing psychological horror.

But Frost will always be a poet more loved than analyzed. He expresses himself in such an attractive way that his readers identify themselves with the poet; they would like to be Frost. The descriptive lines one finds in "After Apple Picking," for example, have a perfection that seems the only, and inevitable, way of describing the dream that the poet feels coming on. Many other poems by Frost contain this same perfection of word choice. "Two Tramps in Mud Time" is so meticulously written (and yet so effortless, with its touches of the famous Frost wit) that the reader feels surrounded by April weather, and he clearly sees those two hulking tramps who stand around idly, waiting for the poet to hire them to chop his wood.

If Frost had limited his poetry to descriptive and philosophical lyrics, he would still rank as a major poet; fortunately, his poems are also full of people, characters who are understandable and vividly real. In "The Death of the Hired Man," four people come alive: Mary, the sympathetic wife; Warren, the practical, somewhat cynical husband; Harold Wilson, the boy "who studied Latin like the violin because he liked it"; and Silas, the hired man who has come "home" to die. Other people are scattered like old friends throughout the poems: Magoon, the timid professor, and Lafe, the burly bill collector, in "A Hundred Collars"; the casual witch in "The Witch of Coos"; the newlyweds who philosophize so well in "West-Running Brook"; the old farmer in "The Mountain," who lives at the foot of a mountain he refuses to climb simply because he sees no practical reason for doing so; and the dour farmer in "Brown's Descent," who takes a hilarious ride down a mountain on a slick crust of snow.

There are others equally memorable, but perhaps the outstanding character in all the poems is Frost himself. Everything he wrote is warmed by his own personality, and he emerges from his volumes as a great and charming man who felt deeply but who never broke the restraining tether of good taste. He is emotional but never overly sentimental, dramatic but never melodramatic, conservative but not reactionary, sometimes pessimistic but never defeated, humorous without being flippant.

Trying to summarize the beguiling effect of Frost's outlook on life is difficult, for his writing personality is many-sided. Certainly he strikes the reader as a man who looked at life in a way that was both poetic and practical. The concluding lines of "Birches" beautifully illustrate this remarkable blend. In the poem the speaker has expressed a desire "to get away from earth awhile" and then come back for a new start:

> I'd like to go by climbing a birch tree,
> And climb black branches up a snow-white trunk
> *Toward* heaven, till the tree could bear no more,
> But dipped its top and set me down again.
> That would be good both going and coming back.
> One could do worse than be a swinger of birches.

Frost's wise outlook is not always concerned with only the broad generalities of life; sometimes he becomes specific about the events of his time, as in "To a Thinker," which gives advice to a president, and in "U.S. 1946 King's X," which is a mordant piece of irony:

> Having invented a new Holocaust,
> And been the first with it to win a war,
> How they make haste to cry with fingers crossed,
> King's X—no fair to use it any more!

A poet must be more than a dramatist, an analyst of human emotion, a humorist, and a philosopher; he must above all be a poet. Frost meets this difficult test. He wrote in the rhythms of human speech; sounding as natural as a man talking to his neighbor, he composed great poetry. His approach seems casual and disarming, rather like that of a champion athlete who breaks records without straining, who never tries too hard.

Yet to claim perfection for anyone—athlete or poet—is absurd. Frost has his defects. At times he is like a kindly teacher whose whimsicality is so sly as to be irritating, whose wisdom sometimes descends to mere crankiness. But he has written magnificent poetry—simple, sure, strong. Evidence is this beautiful (but not often quoted) lyric called "Moon Compasses":

> I stole forth dimly in the dripping pause
> Between two downpours to see what there was.
> And a masked moon had spread down compass rays
> To a cone mountain in the midnight haze,
> As if the final estimate were hers,
> And as it measured in her calipers,
> The mountain stood exalted in its place.
> So love will take between the hands a face.

THE POETRY OF YEATS

Type of work: Poetry
Author: William Butler Yeats (1865–1939)
Principal published works: *Mosada: A Dramatic Poem*, 1886; *The Wanderings of Oisin*, 1889; *Poems*, 1895; *The Wind Among the Reeds*, 1899; *In the Seven Woods*, 1903; *The Green Helmet and Other Poems*, 1910; *Responsibilities*, 1914; *The Wild Swans at Coole*, 1917; *Michael Robartes and the Dancer*, 1920; *Later Poems*, 1922; *The Cat and the Moon and Certain Poems*, 1924; *The Tower*, 1928; *The Winding Stair*, 1933; *Collected Poems*, 1933; *The King of the Great Clock Tower*, 1934; *A Full Moon in March*, 1935; *New Poems*, 1938; *Last Poems and Plays*, 1940; *Collected Poems*, 1949

The conflict that the antimonies between dream and action caused in the mind of William Butler Yeats could not be resolved in the verse tradition of the Pre-Raphaelites. This was the poetry, together with that of Shelley and Keats and the plays of Shakespeare, with which he was most familiar. It was also the tradition to which he was closest in time. Because he did not have a background of a coherent culture on which to base his poetry—nor a personally satisfying faith at least—Yeats throughout his life had to create his own systems of thought and create, in fact, the convention in which he was to write.

In the introduction to *A Vision*, he said: "I wished for a system of thought that would leave my imagination free to create as it chose and yet make all it created, or could create, part of the one history, and that the soul's." His search for reality in belief and feeling was aided by his knowledge that the Romantic poets expressed faith in the power of the imagination. This knowledge also strengthened his conviction that the problems of human existence would never be solved by science and that answers would have to come from quite different disciplines. Therefore, both his philosophy and his actions were of paramount importance to him in the writing of poetry.

Yeats spent many years in the study of the occult: spiritualism, magic, mysticism, and theosophy. His feelings for Ireland and for the Pre-Raphaelites led him, early in his life, to the study and use of ancient Irish myths. His hopes of independence for Ireland and his periodic identification with Irish nationalism, also a part of the fabric of his verse, were influenced by his passion for Maud Gonne and his friendship with his patron, Lady Gregory. He believed the system expounded in *A Vision* was revealed to him by his wife's power as a medium. Thus for Yeats, as for all poets, the pattern of his relationships, interests, beliefs, and loyalties was the material of his poetry. However, great poetry is always the expression of one man's personality in such a way that it is generally or universally meaningful. Magic, nationalism, and myth partly formed Yeats's complex personality, and his prose writings in these areas are undoubtedly esoteric. Although it was through these studies that Yeats was able to write as he did, it is not through them that the reader appreciates his poetry. All Yeats's poetry can be enjoyed and understood when carefully read, without reference to any of his prose. Yeats, in fact, took care to make his work understandable, and one of the most interesting aspects in the study of his poetry is his lifelong preoccupation with clarity, simplicity, and exactness.

Clarity in particular was the goal toward which he worked throughout his career. For Yeats, symbol was the means by which the natural and the supernatural could be fused and the antimonies be resolved. Writing in many personae, or voices, he worked toward this unified expression of reality, with the result that the continuous development of his powers and his ultimate success are both rare and exciting achievements. Yeats's dedication to his art was such that to the end of his life his conscious goals were always in advance of the poems he had completed.

Yeats was a lyric poet, but his belief in and practice of "active virtue"—that is, following a discipline that one has forged oneself—makes his verse essentially dramatic. His first volumes of poetry express the sensibility of the Pre-Raphaelites; the lyrics are slight and the emotion, incompletely realized, often expresses his indecision between the life of dream and that of action. Twilight and longing predominate in these poems.

In his fourth volume, *In the Seven Woods*, published in 1903, Yeats began to find his true voice. Emotion is particularized, and he has started to speak with authority. His technique is more sure and his tone more varied. In "Adam's Curse," in which the poet discusses the labor of writing poetry with a women whom he loves, he uses common words and speech idioms which firmly link the poem to reality:

> Better go down upon your marrow-bones
> And scrub a kitchen pavement or break
> stones
> Like an old pauper, in all kinds of
> weather;
> For to articulate sweet sounds together
> Is to work harder than all these.

In his verse plays of this period Yeats was beginning

deliberately to eschew abstraction and to introduce more direct and bold speech into his work. His 1910 volume, *The Green Helmet and Other Poems*, shows this technique in his lyric verse, which is becoming more dramatic and assertive. In "No Second Troy" the use of Greek myth approximates a reconciliation between dream and reality.

The 1914 volume, *Responsibilities*, shows an increase in force. Here Yeats uses other voices, of beggars, fools, and hermits, to present his ideas. At that time he was encouraged further in his progress toward exactness of expression and the use of only the most meaningful images by his contact with Ezra Pound, who insisted that Yeats remove all abstractions from his verse. He appears to have learned quickly and well from the younger poet, and in subsequent poems he was able to integrate completely his theories of history and personality, and his feelings of despair for Ireland. He also learned to pare his images so that they are totally relevant to his emotion:

> Things fall apart, the centre cannot
>   hold;
> Mere anarchy is loosed upon the world,
> The blood-dimmed tide is loosed, and
>   everywhere
> The ceremony of innocence is drowned.

The Tower, published in 1928, contains several of Yeats's finest poems. The most brilliant and complex of these is "Sailing to Byzantium." The dazzling civilization of Byzantium, which had successfully withstood the power of Rome as Yeats would have liked Ireland to withstand that of England, became for him the symbol of eternal art and of the fusion of the creator with the work of art. The reconciliation of youth and age, passion and intellect, is effected by the symbolic representation of the wisdom of the inspired soul in a supernatural form. In this poem, natural birds sing of the cycle of human life and the created birds of Byzantium, of the cycle of history. The glory of the old and of the young is here presented with a single steady vision, and the conflict between them has been resolved:

> This is no country for old men. The young
> In one another's arms, birds in the trees
> —Those dying generations—at their
>   song,
> The salmon-falls, the mackerel-crowded
>   seas,
> Fish, flesh, or fowl, commend all sum-
>   mer long
> Whatever is begotten, born, and dies.

He continues:

> An aged man is but a paltry thing,
> A tattered coat upon a stick, unless

> Soul clap its hands and sing, and louder
>   sing. . . .

The poet has sailed to Byzantium that he may thus sing. His soul after death will not take "bodily form from any natural thing" but will be one of the singing birds of metal and enamel that the goldsmiths make to amuse the emperor,

> Or set upon a golden bough to sing
> To lords and ladies of Byzantium
> Of what is past, or passing, or to come.

Another unified vision of life which is not dependent upon the supernatural is communicated in the poem "Among School Children." The mastery of technique, which gives "Sailing to Byzantium" its tour de force brilliance, enables Yeats in this poem to communicate the feeling of the quiet after a storm. The poet visits a convent school where the children see him as an old man, and as the children stare in mild curiosity, he is reminded of the "Ledaean body" of a woman he had loved, and this vision causes him to feel so joined in sympathy with her that he can visualize her as she must have been as a child:

> For even daughters of the swan share
> Something of every paddler's heritage.

The vision of the childhood of the woman who caused him much pain leads him to the thought that women would not think motherhood worth while if they could see their progeny at sixty. His suggestion that mothers as well as nuns worship images returns the poem to the convent school setting. In the last stanza of the poem Yeats, by a unifying image of continuity and completeness, reconciles the opposing forces of age and youth at the level of reality.

The poems written in the three years before Yeats's death at seventy-four show no diminution of power. He was still intent on his search for unity and reality of expression. In "The Circus Animals' Desertion," he reviews his poetic output and says that until he was an old man the machinery of his poetry was still in evidence:

> My circus animals were still on show,
> Those stilted boys, that gilded chariot.

He lists his old themes: the Irish myths, his lost love, and his preoccupation with the theater, and he tells how he dramatized his love in his plays. He faces his own delight in dreams which he feared would inhibit him from reality: "This dream itself had all my thought and love." He speaks of the personae in which he wrote and of the characters of Irish history:

> Players and painted stage took all my
>   love
> And not those things they were the
>   emblems of.

The reversal and resolution of these ideas comes in the last verse where he evaluates the use of images in his poetry, by questioning their origin and finding that they indeed had their foundation in reality.

Thus his adolescent faith in the imagination had been justified and he could join the ranks of those whom he admired and who had fused the subjective and objective self into a meaningful whole: "The antithetical self comes to those who are no longer deceived, whose passion is reality."

The philosophy that Yeats so carefully constructed was the basis for a personal vision of life, which by unswerving dedication to craftsmanship and constantly renewed emotional and intellectual vitality he presented in his poetry in all its varied facets and with always increasing significance.

THE PORTRAIT OF A LADY

Type of work: Novel
Author: Henry James (1843–1916)
Type of plot: Psychological realism
Time of plot: About 1875
Locale: England, France, and Italy
First published: 1881

In this novel crowded with brilliantly subtle and penetrating character studies, James explores the ramifications of a naïve, young, high-minded American girl's first exposure and gradual acclimatization to the traditions and decadence of an older European culture. The reader follows step by step the mental process of Isabel Archer as she gravitates away from the staunch and stuffy American, Caspar Goodwood, and her frail, intelligent, and devoted cousin Ralph Touchett, into a marriage with Gilbert Osmond, a worthless, tyrannical dilettante. The Portrait of a Lady is an excellent example of the Jamesian technique of refracting life through the mind and temperament of an individual.

Principal Characters

Isabel Archer, the heroine of the novel. Orphaned at an early age and an heiress, she uses her freedom to go to Europe to be educated in the arts of life lacking in her own country. She draws the interest and adoration of many people, all of whom feel that they can make a contribution to her growth, or at least can use her. Isabel is somewhat unworldly at the time of her marriage to Gilbert Osmond. After three years of resisting the social mold imposed on her by Osmond and his Roman ménage, Isabel faces a dilemma in which her intelligence and honesty vie with her sense of obligation. Sensitive to her own needs as well as to those of others, she is aware of the complicated future she faces.

Gilbert Osmond, an American expatriate. He finds in Rome an environment suited to his artistic taste and devotes his time and tastes solely to pleasing himself.

Madame Merle, Isabel's friend. Madame Merle was formerly Osmond's mistress and is the mother of his daughter Pansy. A clever, vigorous woman of considerable perspicacity, she promotes Isabel's marriage to Osmond.

Ralph Touchett, Isabel's ailing cousin. He appreciates the fine qualities of Isabel's nature. Distressed by what he considers her disastrous marriage, he sees to it that his own and his father's estates come to Isabel.

Caspar Goodwood, Isabel's faithful American suitor. He has the simplicity and directness of American insight that Isabel is trying to supplement by her European "education." He does not understand why he fails with Isabel.

Lord Warburton, a friend of Ralph Touchett. Like all the other unsuccessful men in Isabel's life, he deeply admires the young American woman and is distressed by her marriage to Gilbert Osmond.

Henrietta Stackpole, an American journalist and a girlhood friend of Isabel. Henrietta is, in her own right, an amusing picture of the sensation-seeking uncritical American intelligence ranging over the length and breadth of Europe. She is eager to save Isabel.

Pansy Osmond, the illegitimate daughter of Osmond and Madame Merle. Pansy is unaware of her situation, and she welcomes Isabel as her stepmother; she feels that in Isabel she has an ally, as indeed she has. Determined to endure gracefully what she must, she feels increasingly the strictures of her father's dictates.

Edward Rosier, a suitor for Pansy's hand. This kind, pleasant man lacks means sufficient to meet Osmond's demands.

Countess Gemini, Osmond's sister. She is a woman who has been spoiled and corrupted by her European experience, and she finds Isabel's behavior almost boring in its simplicity. Several motives prompt her to tell Isabel about Osmond's first wife and his liaison with Madame Merle. She does not spare Isabel a clear picture of Osmond's lack of humanity.

Mrs. Touchett, Isabel's vigorous and sympathetic aunt. Mrs. Touchett is the one responsible for the invitation that brings Isabel to Europe and the world.

The Story

Isabel Archer, upon the death of her father, had been visited by her aunt, Mrs. Touchett. She proved so attractive to the older woman that Mrs. Touchett decided to give her the advantage of more cosmopolitan experience, and Isabel was quickly carried off to Europe so she might see something of the world of culture and fashion.

On the day the women arrived at the Touchett home in England, Isabel's sickly young cousin, Ralph Touchett, and his father were taking tea in the garden with their friend, Lord Warburton. When Isabel appeared, Warburton had been confessing to the two men his boredom and his distaste for his routine existence. The young nobleman was much taken with the American girl's grace and lively manner.

Isabel had barely settled at Gardencourt, her aunt's home, before she received a letter from an American friend, Henrietta Stackpole, a newspaperwoman who was writing a series of articles on the sights of Europe. At Ralph's invitation, Henrietta went to Gardencourt to spend some time with Isabel and to obtain material for her writing.

Soon after Henrietta's arrival, Isabel heard from another American friend. Caspar Goodwood, a would-be suitor, had followed her abroad. Learning her whereabouts from Henrietta, he wrote to ask if he might see her. Isabel was irked by his aggressiveness, and she decided not to answer his letter.

On the day she received the letter from Goodwood, Lord Warburton proposed to her. Not wishing to seem indifferent to the honor of his proposal, she asked for time to consider it. At last, she decided she could not marry the young Englishman, for she wished to see considerably more of the world before she married. She was afraid that marriage to Warburton, although he was a model of kindness and thoughtfulness, would prove stifling.

Because Isabel had not seen London on her journey with Mrs. Touchett and since it was on Henrietta Stackpole's itinerary, the two young women, accompanied by Ralph Touchett, went to the capital. Henrietta quickly made the acquaintance of a Mr. Bantling, who undertook to escort her around London. When Caspar Goodwood visited Isabel at her hotel, she again refused him, though his persistence made her agree that if he still wished to ask for her hand, he might visit her again after two years had passed.

While the party was in London, a telegram came from Gardencourt. Old Mr. Touchett was seriously ill with gout, and his wife was much alarmed. Isabel and Ralph left on the afternoon train. Henrietta remained with her new friend.

During the time Mr. Touchett lay dying and his family was preoccupied, Isabel was forced to amuse herself with a new companion. Madame Merle, an old friend of Mrs. Touchett, had come to Gardencourt to spend a few days. She and Isabel, thrown together a great deal, exchanged many confidences. Isabel admired the older woman for her ability to amuse herself, for her skill at needlework, at painting, at the piano, and for her ability to accommodate herself to any social situation. On the other hand, Madame Merle spoke enviously of Isabel's youth and intelligence, lamenting the life that had left her, at middle age, a widow with no children and no visible success in life.

When her uncle died, he left Isabel, at her cousin's instigation, half of his fortune. Ralph, greatly impressed with his young kinswoman's brilliance, had persuaded his father that she should be given the opportunity to fly as far and as high as she might. For himself, he knew he could not live long because of his pulmonary illness, and his legacy was enough to let him live in comfort.

As quickly as she could, Mrs. Touchett sold her London house and took Isabel to Paris with her. Ralph went south for the winter to preserve what was left of his health. In Paris, the new heiress was introduced to many of her aunt's friends among the American expatriates, but she was not impressed. She thought their indolent lives worthy only of contempt. Meanwhile, Henrietta and Mr. Bantling had arrived in Paris, and Isabel spent much time with them and Edward Rosier. She had known Rosier when they both were children and she was traveling abroad with her father. Rosier was another dilettante, living on the income from his inheritance. He explained to Isabel that he could not return to his own country because there was no occupation there worthy of a gentleman.

In February, Mrs. Touchett and her niece went to the Palazzo Crescentini, the Touchett house in Florence. They stopped on the way to see Ralph, who was staying in San Remo. In Florence they were joined once more by Madame Merle.

Unknown to Isabel or her aunt, Madame Merle also visited her friend, Gilbert Osmond, another American who lived in voluntary exile outside of Florence with his art collection and his young convent-bred daughter, Pansy. Madame Merle told Osmond of Isabel's arrival in Florence, saying that as the heir to a fortune, Isabel would be a valuable addition to Osmond's collection.

The heiress who had rejected two worthy suitors did not refuse the third. She was quickly captivated by the charm of the sheltered life Gilbert Osmond had created for himself. Her friends were against the match. Henrietta Stackpole, who was inclined to favor Caspar Goodwood, was convinced that Osmond was interested only in Isabel's money, as was Isabel's aunt. Mrs. Touchett had requested Madame Merle, the good friend of both parties, to discover the state of their affections; she was convinced that Madame Merle could have prevented the match. Ralph Touchett was disappointed that his cousin should have fallen in love so quickly. Caspar Goodwood, learning of Isabel's intended marriage when he revisited her two years later as agreed, could not persuade her to reconsider her step. Isabel was indignant when he commented on the fact that she did not even know her intended husband's antecedents.

After her marriage to Gilbert Osmond, Isabel and her husband established their home in Rome, in a setting completely expressive of Osmond's tastes. Before three years had passed, Isabel began to realize that her friends had not been completely wrong in their objections to her marriage. Osmond's exquisite taste had made their home one of the most popular in Rome, but his ceaseless effort to press his wife into a mold, to make her a reflection of his own ideas, had not made their marriage one of the happiest.

He had succeeded in destroying a romance between Pansy and Edward Rosier, who had visited the girl's stepmother and found the daughter attractive. He had not succeeded, however, in contracting the match he desired between Pansy and Lord Warburton. Warburton had found Pansy as pleasing as Isabel had once been, but he had dropped his suit when he saw that the girl's affections lay with Rosier.

Ralph Touchett, his health growing steadily worse, gave up his wanderings on the continent and returned to Gardencourt to die. When Isabel received a telegram from his mother telling her that Ralph would like to see her before his death, she felt it her duty to go to Gardencourt at once. Osmond reacted to her wish as if it were a personal insult. He expected that, as his wife, Isabel would want to remain at his side and that she would not disobey any wish of his. He also made it plain that he disliked Ralph.

In a state of turmoil after her conversation with her husband, Isabel met the Countess Gemini, Osmond's sister. The Countess, visiting the Osmonds, knew the situation between her brother and Isabel. An honest soul, she felt more sympathy for her sister-in-law than for her brother. To comfort Isabel, she told her the story of Gilbert's past. After his first wife had died, he and Madame Merle had an affair that lasted six or seven years. During that time, Madame Merle, a widow, had borne him a child, Pansy. Changing his residence, Osmond had been able to pretend to his new circle of friends that the original Mrs. Osmond had died in giving birth to the child.

With this news fresh in her mind and still determined to go to England, Isabel stopped to say good-bye to Pansy, who was staying in a convent where her father had sent her to recuperate from her affair with Rosier. There, too, she met Madame Merle. Madame Merle, with her keen perception, had no difficulty realizing that Isabel knew her secret. When she remarked that Isabel would never need to see her again, that she would go to America, Isabel was certain Madame Merle would also find in America much to her own advantage.

Isabel was in time to see her cousin before his death. She stayed on briefly at Gardencourt after the funeral, long enough to bid good-bye to Lord Warburton, who had come to offer condolences to her aunt and to reject a third offer from Caspar Goodwood, who knew of her husband's treatment. When she left to start her journey back to Italy, Isabel knew what she must do. Her first duty was not to herself, but to put her house in order.

Critical Evaluation

The Portrait of a Lady first appeared serially in England and America (*Macmillan's Magazine*, October, 1880–November, 1881; *Atlantic*, November, 1880–December, 1881); it was published as a book in 1881. Usually regarded as the major achievement of Henry James's early period of fiction writing, *The Portrait of a Lady* is one of the great novels of modern literature. In it, James demonstrates that he has learned well from two European masters of the novel. Turgenev had taught him how to use a single character who shapes the work and is seen throughout in relationship to various other characters. From George Eliot he had learned the importance of tightening the structure of the novel and giving the story an architectural or organic form that develops logically from the given materials. He advances in *The Portrait of a Lady* beyond Eliot in minimizing his own authorial comments and analysis and permitting his heroine to be seen through her own tardily awakening self-realization and also through the consciousness of the men and women who are closest to her. Thus his "portrait" of a lady is one which slowly grows stroke by stroke as touches are added that bring out both highlights and shadows, until Isabel Archer stands at the end of the novel as a woman whose experiences have brought her excitement, joy, pain,

and knowledge and have given her an enduring beauty and dignity.

Isabel is one of James's finest creations and one of the most memorable women in the history of the novel. A number of sources have been suggested for her. She may have been partly drawn from James's cousin Mary "Minny" Temple, whom he was later to immortalize as Milly Theale in *The Wings of the Dove*. She has been compared to two of Eliot's heroines, Dorothea Brooke in *Middlemarch* and Gwendolyn Harleth in *Daniel Deronda*; to Diana Belfield in an early romantic tale by James entitled "Longstaff's Marriage"; to Bathsheba Everdene in Thomas Hardy's *Far from the Madding Crowd*; and even to James himself, some of whose early experiences closely parallel those of Isabel. Yet, though James may have drawn from both real and fictional people in portraying Isabel Archer, she possesses her own identity; she grew from James's original "conception of a certain young woman affronting her destiny," as he later wrote in his preface to the novel. He visualized her as "an intelligent but presumptuous girl" who would yet be "complex" and who would be offered a series of opportunities for free choice in the affronting of that destiny. Because of her presumption that she knew more than she did about herself and the world, Isabel was to make mistakes, including the tragic error of misjudging the nature of Gilbert Osmond. But her intelligence, thought it was not sufficient to save her from suffering, would enable her to achieve a moral triumph in the end.

Of the four men in Isabel's life, three love her, and one uses her innocence to gain for himself what he would not otherwise have had. She refuses marriage to Lord Warburton because, though he offers her a great fortune, a title, an entry into English society, and an agreeable and entertaining personality, she believes she can do better. She turns down Caspar Goodwood, who also offers wealth, because she finds him stiff, and she is frightened by his aggressiveness. Her cousin, Ralph Touchett, does not propose because he does not wish her to be tied to a man who daily faces death. She does not even suspect the extent of his love and adoration until she is almost overwhelmed by learning it just as death takes him from her. She accepts Gilbert Osmond because she is deceived by his calculated charm and because she believes that he deserves what she can offer him: first, a fortune that will make it possible for him to live in idleness but surrounded by the objects of the culture she believes he represents; and second, a mother's love and care for his supposedly motherless daughter. Half of the novel is given over to Isabel's living with, adjusting to, and, finally, triumphing over the disastrous choice she has made.

In his preface, James uses an architectural figure to describe *The Portrait of a Lady*. He says the "large building" of the novel "came to be a square and spacious house." Much of what occurs in the novel does so in or near a series of houses, each of which relates significantly to Isabel or to other characters. The action begins at Gardencourt, the tudor English country house of Daniel Touchett which Isabel finds more beautiful than anything she has ever seen. The charm of the house is enhanced by its age and its natural setting beside the Thames above London. It contrasts greatly with the "old house at Albany, a large, square, double house" belonging to her grandmother which Isabel in her childhood had found romantic and in which she had indulged in dreams stimulated by her reading. Mrs. Touchett's taking Isabel from the Albany house to Gardencourt is a first step in her plan to "introduce her to the world." When Isabel visits Lockleigh, Lord Warburton's home, she sees it from the gardens as resembling "a castle in a legend," though inside it has been modernized. She does not view it as a home for herself, or its titled owner as her husband, despite the many advantages he offers. The front of Gilbert Osmond's house in Florence is "imposing" but of "a somewhat uncommunicative character," a "mask." It symbolizes

Osmond whose mask Isabel does not see through until she has married him. The last of the houses in *The Portrait of a Lady* is the Palazzo Roccanera, the Roman home of the Osmonds, which James first describes as "a kind of domestic fortress . . . which smelt of historic deeds, of crime and craft and violence." When Isabel later broods over it during her night-long meditation in chapter 42, it is "the house of darkness, the house of dumbness, the house of suffocation."

Isabel is first seen at Gardencourt on her visit with Mrs. Touchett, and it is here that she turns down the first of three proposals of marriage. It is fitting that she should be last seen here by turns with each of the three men who have loved her. Asserting the independence on which she has so long prided herself, she has defied her imperious husband by going to England to see the dying Ralph, whose last words tell her that if she has been hated by Osmond, she has been adored by her cousin. In a brief conversation with Lord Warburton after Ralph's death, Isabel turns down an invitation to visit him and his sisters at Lockleigh. Shortly afterward, a scene six years earlier is reversed. Then she had sat on a rustic bench at Gardencourt and looked up from reading Caspar Goodwood's letter implying that she would come to England and propose to her—only to see and hear Warburton preparing to offer his own proposal. Now Caspar surprises her by appearing just after she has dismissed Warburton. There follows the one sexually passionate scene in the novel. In it Isabel has "an immense desire to appear to resist" the force of Caspar's argument that she should leave Osmond and turn to him. She pleads with streaming tears, "As you love me, as you pity me, leave me alone!" Defying her plea, Caspar kisses her:

> His kiss was like white lightning, a flash that spread, and spread again, and stayed; and it was extraordinarily as if, while she took it, she felt each thing in his hard manhood that had least pleased her, each aggressive fact of his face, his figure, his presence, justified of its intense identity and made one with this act of possession.

Caspar had possessed her for a moment only. "But when darkness returned she was free" and she flees into the house—and thence to Rome, as Caspar learns in the brief scene in London with Henrietta Stackpole that closes the novel.

James leaves the reader to conclude that Isabel's love for Pansy Osmond has principally determined her decision to continue enduring a marriage that she had freely—though so ignorantly and foolishly—chosen.

A PORTRAIT OF THE ARTIST AS A YOUNG MAN

Type of work: Novel
Author: James Joyce (1882–1941)
Type of plot: Psychological realism
Time of plot: 1882–1903
Locale: Ireland
First published: 1916

This autobiographical novel follows the emotional and intellectual growth from childhood to young manhood of Stephen Dedalus, who is also the protagonist of the later, more complex Ulysses. *The development of artistic self-awareness necessitates young Stephen's rejection of the values of his upbringing, including blind patriotism and rigid Catholicism. The narration is in the stream-of-consciousness style which Joyce was instrumental in developing.*

Principal Characters

Stephen Dedalus (dě′a·ləs, dēdə·ləs), a young man who is, like his creator, sensitive, proud, and highly intelligent, but often confused in his attempts to understand the Irish national temperament. He is bewildered and buffeted about in a world of political unrest, theological discord, and economic decline. In this environment he attempts to resolve for himself the problems of faith, morality, and art. At the end, feeling himself cut off from nation, religion, and family, he decides to leave Ireland in order to seek his own fulfillment as an artist, the artificer that his name suggests.

Simon Dedalus, an easy-going, talkative, patriotic Irishman who reveres the memory of Parnell. During his lifetime he has engaged in many activities, as a medical student, an actor, an investor, and a tax collector, among others; but he has failed in everything he has tried. Stephen Dedalus' realization that his father is self-deluded and shiftless contributes greatly to the boy's growing disillusionment and unrest. Simon is almost the stereotyped, eloquent Irishman who drinks much more than is good for him.

Mrs. Dedalus, a worn, quiet woman who remains a shadowy background figure in the novel. A woman of deep faith, her son's repudiation of religious belief becomes a source of anxiety and grief adding to her other cares.

Mrs. Dante Riordan, Stephen Dedalus's aunt. An energetic defender of anything Catholic, she despises anyone whose views are opposed to her own. Her special targets are certain Irish patriots, particularly Parnell, and all enemies of priests. Her violent arguments with Simon Dedalus on politics and religion make a profound impression on young Stephen.

Eileen Vance, Stephen Dedalus' childhood love. He is not allowed to play with the little girl because she is a Protestant.

E— C—, called Emma Clery in the "Stephen Hero" manuscript but in this novel more the embodied image of Stephen Dedalus' romantic fancies and fantasies than a real person. She is the girl to whom he addresses his love poems.

Davin, a student at University College and the friend of Stephen Dedalus. He is athletic, emotionally moved by ancient Irish myth, and obedient to the church. To Stephen he personifies country, religion, and the dead romantic past, the forces in the national life that Stephen is trying to escape.

Lynch, an intelligent but irreverent student at University College. During a walk in the rain Stephen Dedalus tries to explain to Lynch his own views on art. Stephen's explanation of lyrical, epical, and dramatic literary forms helps to illuminate Joyce's own career as a writer.

Cranley, a student at University College. A casuist, he serves as an intellectual foil to Stephen Dedalus. To him Stephen confides his decision not to find his vocation in the church and the reasons for his inability to accept its rituals or even to believe its teachings.

Father Arnall, a Jesuit teacher at Clongowes Wood School. While Stephen Dedalus is attending Belvedere College, during a religious retreat, Father Arnall preaches an eloquent sermon on the sin of Lucifer and his fall. The sermon moves Stephen so deeply that he experiences a religious crisis, renounces all pleasures of the flesh, and for a time contemplates becoming a priest.

Father Dolan, the prefect of studies at Clongowes Wood School. A strict disciplinarian, he punishes Stephen Dedalus unjustly after the boy has broken his glasses and is unable to study. The beating he administers causes Stephen's first feeling of rebellion against priests.

Uncle Charles, Stephen Dedalus' great-uncle, a gentle, hearty old man employed to carry messages. When Stephen is a small boy, he accompanies Uncle Charles on his errands.

Nasty Roche, a student at Clongowes Wood School. His mocking reference to Stephen Dedalus' name gives Stephen his first impression of being different or alienated.

The Story

When Stephen Dedalus went to school for the first time, his last name soon got him into trouble. It sounded too Latin, and the boys teased him about it. The other boys saw that he was sensitive and shy, and they began to bully him. School was filled with unfortunate incidents for Stephen. He was happy when he became sick and was put in the infirmary away from the other boys. Once, when he was there just before the Christmas holidays, he worried about dying and death. As he lay on the bed thinking, he heard the news of Parnell's death. The death of the great Irish leader was the first date he remembered—October 6, 1891.

At home during the vacation, he learned more of Parnell. His father, Simon Dedalus, worshipped the dead man's memory and defended him on every count. Stephen's aunt, Dante Riordan, despised Parnell as a heretic and a rabble-rouser. The fierce arguments that they got into every day burned themselves into Stephen's memory. He worshipped his father, and his father said that Parnell had tried to free Ireland, to rid it of the priests who were ruining the country. Dante insisted that the opposite was true. A violent defender of the priests, she leveled every kind of abuse against Simon and his ideas. The disagreement between them became a problem which, in due time, Stephen would have to solve for himself.

Returning to school after the holidays, Stephen got in trouble with Father Dolan, one of the administrators of the church school he attended. Because he had broken his glasses, Stephen could not study until a new pair arrived. Father Dolan saw that Stephen was not working, and thinking that his excuse about the glasses was false, he gave the boy a beating. For once, the rest of the boys were on Stephen's side, and they urged him to complain to the head of the school. With fear and trembling, Stephen went to the head and presented his case. The head understood and promised to speak to Father Dolan about the matter. When Stephen told the boys about his conversation, they hoisted him in their arms like a victorious fighter and called him a hero.

Afterward, life was much easier for Stephen. Only one unfortunate incident marked the term. In the spirit of fun, one of his professors announced in class that Stephen had expressed heresy in one of his essays. Stephen quickly changed the offending phrase and hoped that the mistake would be forgotten. After class, however, several of the boys accused him not only of being a heretic but also of liking Byron, whom they considered an immoral man and therefore no good as a poet. In replying to their charges, Stephen had his first real encounter with the problems of art and morality. They were to follow him throughout his life.

On a trip to Cork with his father, Stephen was forced to listen to the often-told tales of his father's youth. They visited the places his father had loved as a boy. Each night, Stephen was forced to cover up his father's drunkenness and sentimental outbursts. The trip was an education in everything Stephen disliked.

At the end of the school year, Stephen won several prizes. He bought presents for everyone, started to redo his room, and began an ill-fated loan service. As long as the money lasted, life was wonderful. Then one night when his money was almost gone, he was enticed into a house by a woman wearing a long pink gown. He learned what love was at age sixteen.

Not until the school held a retreat in honor of Saint Francis Xavier did Stephen realize how deeply conscious he was of the sins he had committed with women. The sermons of the priests about heaven and hell, especially about hell, ate into his mind. At night, his dreams were of nothing but the eternal torture that he felt he must endure after death. He could not bear to make confession in school. At last, he went into the city to a church were he was unknown. There he opened his unhappy mind and heart to an understanding and wise old priest, who advised him and comforted his soul. After the confession, Stephen promised to sin no more, and he felt sure that he would keep his promise.

For a time, Stephen's life followed a model course. He studied Aquinas and Aristotle and won acclaim from his teachers. One day, the director of the school called Stephen into his office; after a long conversation, he asked him if he had ever thought of joining the order of the Jesuits. Stephen was deeply flattered. Priesthood became his life's goal.

When Stephen entered the university, however, a change came over his thinking. He began to doubt, and the longer he studied, the more confused and doubtful he became.

His problems drew him closer to two of his fellow students, Davin and Lynch, and farther away from Emma, a girl for whom he had felt affection since childhood. He discussed his idea about beauty and the working of the mind with Davin and Lynch. Because he would not sign a petition for world peace, Stephen won the enmity of many of the fellows. They called him antisocial and egotistic. Finally, not the peace movement, the Irish Revival, or the church itself could claim his support.

Davin was the first to question Stephen about his ideas. When he suggested to Stephen that Ireland should come first in everything, Stephen answered that to him Ireland was an old sow that ate her offspring.

One day, Stephen met Emma at a carnival, and she asked him why he had stopped coming to see her. He answered that he had been born to be a monk. When Emma said that she thought him a heretic instead of a monk, his last link with Ireland seemed to be broken. At least he was not afraid to be alone. If he wanted to find and to understand beauty, he had to leave Ireland, where there was nothing in which he believed. His friend's prayers, asking that he return to the faith, went unanswered. Stephen got together his belongings, packed, and left Ireland, intending never to return. He did intend to write a book someday that would make clear his views on Ireland and the Irish.

Critical Evaluation

A Portrait of the Artist as a Young Man by James Joyce is possibly the greatest example in the English language of the bildungsroman, a novel tracing the physical, mental, and spiritual growth and education of a young man. Other examples of this genre range from Goethe's *The Sorrows of Young Werther* and Flaubert's *A Sentimental Education* to D. H. Lawrence's *Sons and Lovers*. Published in 1916, the work stands stylistically between the fusion of highly condensed naturalism and symbolism found in *Dubliners* (1914) and the elaborate mythological structure, interior monologues, and stream of consciousness of *Ulysses* (1922). There is a consistent concern with entrapment, isolation, and rebellion against home, church, and nation in all three of these works.

The novel is basically autobiographical; but in the final analysis, the variants from, rather than the parallels with, Joyce's own life are of utmost artistic significance. The events of Stephen Dedalus' life are taken from the lives of Joyce, his brother Stanislaus, and his friend Byrne, covering the period between 1885 and 1902. The book begins with the earliest memories of his childhood, recounted in childlike language, and ends when Stephen is twenty-two years old with his decision to leave his native Dublin in search of artistic development to forge the conscience of his race. In the intervening years, like Joyce, Stephen attends the Jesuit Clongowes Wood School (which he must leave because of family financial difficulties), attends a day school in Dublin, has his first sexual experience, his first religious crisis, and finally attends University College, where he decides on his vocation as a writer. The dedication to pure art involves for Stephen, and Joyce, a rejection of the claims on him of duty to family, to the Catholic church, and to Irish nationalism, either of the political type or of the literary type espoused by the writers of the Irish Renaissance. In his characterization of Stephen, however, Joyce eliminates much of himself: his sense of humor; his graduation from the university before leaving Dublin; his desire to attend medical school in France; his deep concern for his mother's health; his affection for his father; and the lifelong liaison he established with Nora Barnacle, who left Ireland with Joyce in 1904. The effect of these omissions is to make a narrower, more isolated character of Stephen than Joyce himself.

On one level, *A Portrait of the Artist as a Young Man* is an initiation story in which an innocent, idealistic youth with a sense of trust in his elders slowly comes to realize that this is a flawed, imperfect world, characterized by injustice and disharmony. Stephen finds this fact at home, at school, at church, in relationships with women and friends, and in the past and present history of his nation. His pride, however, prevents him from seeing any shortcomings in himself. In the second portion of the novel, he becomes involved in the excesses of carnal lust; in the third portion, in the excesses of penitent piety, which also eventually disgust him. In the fourth section, in which he assumes the motto *Non serviam*, excessive intellectual pride. In the final portion of the novel, Stephen develops his aesthetic theory of the epiphany—a sudden revelation of truth and beauty—through the artistic goals of "wholeness, harmony, and radiance." His final flight from his actual home—family, church, nation— is still part of an almost adolescent rejection of the imperfections of this world and an attempt to replace it with the perfection of form, justice, and harmony of artistic creation.

Stephen Dedalus' very name is chosen to underline his character. His first name links him to Saint Stephen, the first martyr to Christianity; Stephen Dedalus sees himself as a martyr, willing to give up all to the services of art. His last name, Dedalus, is famous from classical antiquity. It was Daedalus, the Athenian exile, who designed the famous labyrinth in which the monstrous Minotaur was kept captive. Later, longing to return to his native land but imprisoned in his own labyrinth, Daedalus invented wings to enable himself and his son, Icarus, to escape. Stephen, the artist, sees Dublin as the labyrinth from which he must fly in order to become the great artificer Daedalus was. It is important to remember, however, that Daedalus' son, Icarus, ignored his father's instructions on how to use the wings; because of pride and the desire to exceed, he flew too close to the sun, and his wings melted. He plunged into the ocean and drowned. It is only later, in *Ulysses*, that Stephen recognizes himself as "lap-winged Icarus" rather than as Daedalus.

Joyce's technical skill is obvious in the series of interwoven recurrent symbols of the novel. The rose, for example, which is associated with women, chivalric love, and creativity, appears throughout the novel. In addition, water is found in almost every chapter of the novel: it can be the water that drowns and brings death; it can also be the water that gives life, symbolic of renewal as in baptism and the final choice of escape by sea.

The central themes of *A Portrait of the Artist as a Young Man*—alienation, isolation, rejection, betrayal, the Fall, the search for the father—are developed with amazing virtuosity. This development is the second, following

Dubliners, of the four major parts in Joyce's cyclical treatment of the life of man that moves, like the great medieval cyclical plays, from Fall to Redemption, from isolation and alienation to acceptance. Joyce's analysis of the human condition and of the relationship of art to life was further developed in *Ulysses* and *Finnegans Wake*. Joyce emphasized the importance of the word "young" in the title of this work, and his conclusion—in the form of Stephen's diary, which illustrates Stephen's own perceptions, words, and style—forces the reader to become more objective and detached in his judgment of Stephen. The reader recognizes in these final pages Stephen's triumph in escaping from the nets of Ireland; the reader also, however, realizes that Stephen's triumph is complicated by important losses and sacrifices.

THE POSSESSED

Type of work: Novel
Author: Fyodor Mikhailovich Dostoevski (1821–1881)
Type of plot: Psychological realism
Time of plot: Mid-nineteenth century
Locale: Russia
First published: Besy, 1871–1872 (English translation, 1913)

> The Possessed *is Dostoevski's answer to Turgenev's treatment of Russian nihilism in* Fathers and Sons. *Using a large number of characters representing all classes of Russian society, the author shows how an idle interest in nihilism brings on robbery, arson, and murder in a Russian community.*

Principal Characters

Stepan Trofimovich Verhovensky (stĕphān′ trô·fĭ·′mə·vĭch vĕr·hô·vĕn′skĭ), a former professor of history, a free thinker, a mild liberal, and an old-fashioned, dandified intellectual. The protégé of Varvara Petrovna Stavrogina, a wealthy provincial aristocrat, he has lived for years on her country estate, first as the tutor of her impressionable son, later as the companion and mentor of his temperamental, strong-willed friend. At times he and his patroness quarrel violently, but usually their relationship is one of mutual understanding and respect. One of the old man's claims to fame is the fact that a poem he had written in his student days was seized by the authorities in Moscow, and he still believes that he is politically suspect. Weak-willed, opinionated, hedonistic in a mild way, he has indulged his own tastes and personal comfort while allowing his only son to be reared by distant relatives. At the end, appalled by the revelation of his son's nihilistic and criminal activities, and seeing himself in the role of an intellectual buffoon in the service of Varvara Petrovna, he wanders off to search for the true Russia. Like Lear, he is ennobled by suffering, and he dies with a deeper knowledge of himself and his unhappy country, divided between the moribund tradition of the past and the revolutionary spirit of the younger generation. Dostoevsky seems to make Stepan Trofimovich an illustration of the way in which a generation of sentimental, theorizing, intellectual liberals bred a new generation of nihilists and terrorists who believed only in violence and destruction.

Pyotr Stepanovitch Verhovensky (pyō′tr stĕ·pän′ə·vĭch vĕr·hô·vĕn′skĭ), Stepan's nihilistic, revolutionary, despicable son, who has traveled widely and engaged in a number of political intrigues. Really an antihero, he is an early model of the modern, exacting, scientific, psychological fanatic and iconoclast. A monster in his capacity for irreligiosity, deception, and destruction, he undermines the moral integrity of his friend, Nikolay Vsyevoldovitch Stavrogin, creates discord between his father and Varvara Petrovna, conducts a campaign of terrorism

in the provincial town to which he returns after a number of years spent in study and travel, and foments criminal activities that include arson and murder. If his father's chief trait is self-delusion, Pyotr's is the ability to delude others and lead them to their ruin; and he is always sure of his mission, fanatical in his singleminded belief in dissent and destruction, and convinced that the end justifies any means. Filled with a sense of his own power, he is totally wicked and corrupt, although he is not without charm to those who do not know his real nature.

Varvara Petrovna Stavrogin (vär·vä′rə pet′rəv·nə stäv·rō′gən), a wealthy woman who indulges her son, befriends Stepan Trofimovitch, pays for the schooling of Pyotr Stepanovitch, and takes into her household as her companion the daughter of a former serf. Tall, bony, yellow-complexioned, she is impressive in her outspoken, autocratic behavior. Abrupt and unsentimental for the most part, she is also capable of deep feeling. Her strength of character is shown at the end of the novel when she begins to rebuild her life after revelations of Stepan Trofimovitch's dilettantish intellectualism, her son's weakness and waywardness, and the ruthless violence of the revolutionary group. Her final blow is her son's suicide.

Nikolay Vsyevolodovitch Stavrogin (nĭkô·lī′ vsyĕ·vô·lō′də·vĭch), the son of Varvara Petrovna. A mixture of the sensitive and the coarse, the sensual and the spiritual, he has lived abroad for a number of years. There he has engaged in revolutionary activities and debauchery with a number of women, including Marya Timofyevna Lebyadkin, the crippled, weakminded woman whom he married to show his mocking contempt for social conventions, and Marya Ignatyevna Shatov, who is carrying his child. His friendship with Pyotr Stepanovitch leads to the formation of a revolutionary group that he establishes in his native village. Though he is ostensibly the leader, his friend is the real power within the group, and Pyotr Stepanovitch's wild dream is to make Stavrogin a false pretender who will lead Russia back into barbarism. Handsome in appearance, Stavrogin makes his presence felt everywhere, and his reputation makes him feared. Loved by some, hated by others, he has lost all capacity for deep feeling; he tries only to experience violently contrasting sensations as a means of escaping boredom. The night Lizaveta Nikolaevna Tushin spends with him makes him see himself as a spiritually sterile and physically impotent man aged before his time. Hoping to escape from his condition of moral torpor, he asks Darya, the sister of Ivan Shatov, to start a new life with him. She agrees, but before they can leave the village he commits suicide.

Ivan Shatov (ē·vän' shä·tōf'), the liberated and liberal-minded son of a former serf on the Stavrogin estate. Tutored by Stepan Trofimovitch and sent away by Varvara Petrovna for further education, he has traveled and worked in America. Disillusioned by Pyotr Stepanovich and his revolutionary group, Shatov still worships Stavrogin for the image of idealism he evokes. He represents the emancipated, educated Russian who in spite of the disordered life about him clings to his elemental feelings for home, friends, the countryside, ideals of liberty, and passion for independence. Unable to accept the nihilism for which Pyotr Stepanovitch stands, he announces his intention to believe in a human Christ, a Christ of the people. When his wife, from whom he has been separated, returns to give birth to her child, Shatov welcomes her with joy and the child as a token of the future. Because of fears that Shatov will betray the activities of the revolutionary group, Pyotr Stepanovitch has him murdered. Dostoevski uses Shatov as a spokesman for some of his own views on politics and religion.

Marya Ignatyevna Shatov (mä'ryə ĭg·nä'tĕv·nə shä'tōf'), Ivan's wife, who returns to his home to bear her child, fathered, it is suggested, by Stavrogin.

Alexey Nilitch Kirillov (ä·lĕk·sā' nĭ'lĭch kĭ·rĭl'əf), a member of the revolutionary group. Existentialist in his beliefs, he is able neither to accept God nor to endure the human condition. He has reached a state of negation in which his only hope is to commit suicide and thus to become God by exercising his will over life and death. Before he shoots himself Pyotr Stepanovitch persuades him to sign a false confession to the murder of Shatov, killed by the revolutionaries because they are afraid he will betray them to the authorities after the murder of Ignat Lebyadkin and his sister.

Ignat Lebyadkin (ĭg·nät' lĕ·byät'kĭn), a retired army captain, pompous in manner, ridiculous in his pride, crafty in his schemes for extorting money from Stavrogin, his brother-in-law. A would-be gallant, he makes approaches to Lizaveta Nikolaevna Tushin. Pyotr Stepanovitch sees Lebyadkin and his sister as threats to his plans for Stavrogin, and he arranges to have them killed. Their bodies are found by horrified, indignant villagers in the smoldering embers of their house.

Marya Timofyevna Lebyadkin (mä'ryə tĭ·mō·fyĕv'nə), a girl of weak mind and a cripple, Captain Lebyad-

kin's sister, who Stavrogin has married in order to show his contempt for his position in society and to perpetrate a cruel joke on the girl and himself. He has kept the marriage secret, however, and the efforts to determine his relation with Marya agitate his family and friends after his return to the village. He treats her with a mixture of amused condescension and ironic gallantry.

Lizaveta Nikolaevna Tushin (lĭ·zä·vĕ'tə nĭ·kô·lä'ĕv·nə tū'shən), also called **Liza,** the daughter of Praskovya Ivanovna Drozdov, Varvara Petrovna's friend, by a previous marriage. High-spirited and unconventional, she is strongly attracted to Stavrogin and is for a time interested in the proposed publication of a magazine by the revolutionary band. On the night that Captain Lebyadkin and his sister are killed, she gives herself to Stavrogin, only to discover that he is no more than the empty shell of a man. Stopping by to view the smoking ruins of the Lebyadkin house, she is beaten to death by the angry villagers because of her association with Stavrogin.

Praskovya Ivanovna Drozdov (präskōv'yə ē·vän'ĕv·nə drōz'dəf), Lizaveta Nikolaevna's mother. She and Varvara Petrovna have reached an understanding for the marriage of Liza and Stavrogin, but the young people have quarreled, possibly over Darya Shatov, possibly because of Stavrogin's friendship with Pyotr Stepanovitch, while all were living in Switzerland. Not knowing the reason, Praskovya blames Stavrogin for the disagreement and is filled with resentment against him.

Darya Paulovna Shatov (dä'ryə päv'ləv·nə shä·tōf'), also called **Dasha** and **Dashenka,** Ivan Shatov's meek, pretty sister, who has grown up in the Stavrogin household, half companion, half servant to Varvara Petrovna. During a visit to Switzerland, her mistress leaves the girl behind as a companion to Liza. On her return Varvara Petrovna plans for a time to marry the girl to Stepan Trofimovitch, and Darya meekly consents. When Stavrogin, with whom she is secretly in love, asks her to go away with him, she readily agrees. He commits suicide before they can arrange for their departure.

Andrey Antonovitch von Lembke (ändrā' än·tô'nə·vĭch vən lĕm'kē), the new governor of the province.

Yulia Mikhailovna von Lembke (ū'lĭ·yə mē·hī'ləv·nə vən lĕm'kē), the governor's vulgar, ambitious wife.

Semyon Yakovelitch Karmazinov (sĕmyōn' yäkôv·lĕ·vĭch kär·mə·zī'nəf), a pompous, foolish, elderly writer who makes a ridiculous spectacle of himself at a literary fete. He is Dostoevski's satirical portrait of Turgenev.

Liputin (lĭ·pö'tyĭn), a slanderer and zealous reformer, **Erkel** (ĕr'kĕl), a youthful enthusiast, **Virginsky** (vĭr·jĭn'skē), a civil clerk, and **Shigalov** (shĭ'gə·lōf), his brother, members of the revolutionary group.

Lyamshin (lyäm'shən), the member of the group who confesses and reveals the activities of the band to the authorities.

Arina Prohorovna Virginsky (ä·rī'nə prô·hō'rəv·nə vĭr·jĭn'skē), a midwife.

Artemy Pavlovitch Gaganov (är·tyôm′ē päv·lə·vĭch gä·gä·nəf), the local aristocrat with whom Stavrogin fights a duel.

Andrey Antonovich Blum (än·drā′ äntô′nə·vĭch blöm), the assistant to Governor von Lembke.

Sofya Matveyevna Ulitin (sôf′yə mät·vēyĕf′nə ū′lĭ·tən), the young widow who aids Stepan Trofimovitch during his wanderings. She goes to live with Varvara Petrovna.

Anton Lavrentyevitch G————v (än·tōn′ läv·rĕn′tyē·vĭch), the friend of Stepan Trofimovitch and the narrator of this story of violence and passion.

The Story

Stepan Verhovensky, a self-styled progressive patriot and erstwhile university lecturer, was footloose in a provincial Russian town until Varvara Stavrogin hired him to tutor her only son, Nikolay. Although Stepan's radicalism, which was largely a pose, shocked Varvara, the two became friends. When Varvara's husband died, Stepan even looked forward to marrying the widow. They went together to St. Petersburg, where they moved daringly in radical circles. After attempting without success to start a literary journal, they left St. Petersburg, Varvara returning to the province and Stepan, in an attempt to assert his independence, going to Berlin. After four months in Germany, Stepan, realizing that he was in Varvara's thrall emotionally and financially, returned to the province in order to be near her.

Stepan became the leader of a small group that met to discuss progressive ideas. Among the group were Shatov, the independent son of one of Varvara's serfs, a liberal named Virginsky, and Liputin, a man who made everyone's business his business.

Nikolay Stavrogin, whom Stepan had introduced to progressivism, went on to school in St. Petersburg and from there into the army as an officer. He resigned his commission, however, returned to St. Petersburg, and went to live in the slums. When he returned home, at Varvara's request, he proceeded to insult the members of Stepan's group. He bit the ear of the provincial governor during an interview with that dignitary. Obviously mentally unbalanced, Nikolay was committed to bed. Three months later, apparently recovered, he apologized for his actions and again left the province.

Months later Varvara was invited to visit a childhood friend in Switzerland, where Nikolay was paying court to her friend's daughter, Lizaveta. Before the party returned to Russia, however, Lizaveta and Nikolay broke their engagement because of Nikolay's interest in Dasha, Varvara's servant woman. In Switzerland, Nikolay and Stepan's son, Pyotr, met and found themselves in sympathy on political matters.

Meanwhile, in the province there was a new governor, von Lembke. Stepan, lost without Varvara, visibly deteriorated during her absence. Varvara arranged with Dasha, who was twenty years old, to marry Stepan, who was age fifty-three. Dasha, who was the sister of Shatov, submitted passively to her mistress' wishes. Stepan reluctantly consented to the marriage, but he balked when he discovered from a member of his group that he was being used to cover up Nikolay's relations with the girl.

New arrivals in the province were Captain Lebyadkin and his idiot, crippled sister, Marya. One day Marya attracted the attention of Varvara in front of the cathedral, and Varvara took the cripple home with her. She learned that Nikolay had known the Lebyadkins in St. Petersburg. Pyotr assured Varvara, who was suspicious, that Nikolay and Marya Lebyadkin were not married.

By his personal charm and a representation of himself as a mysterious revolutionary agent returned from exile, Pyotr began to dominate Stepan's liberal friends and became, for his own scheming purposes, the protégé of Yulia, the governor's wife. Nikolay at first followed Pyotr in his political activities, but he turned against the revolutionary movement and warned Shatov that Pyotr's group was plotting to kill Shatov because of information he possessed. Nikolay confessed to Shatov that on a bet he had married Marya Lebyadkin in St. Petersburg.

As a result of a duel between Nikolay and a local aristocrat who hated him, a duel in which Nikolay emerged victorious without killing his opponent, Nikolay became a local hero. He continued to be intimate with Dasha, Lizaveta having announced her engagement to another man. Meanwhile, Pyotr sowed seeds of dissension among all classes in the town; he disclosed von Lembke's possession of a collection of radical manifestos; he caused a break between his father and Varvara; and he secretly incited the working people to rebel against their masters.

Yulia led the leaders of the town in preparations for a grand fête. Pyotr saw in the fête the opportunity to bring chaos into an otherwise orderly community. He brought about friction between von Lembke, who was an inept governor, and Yulia, who actually governed the province through her salon.

At a meeting of the revolutionary group, despair and confusion prevailed until Pyotr welded it together with mysterious talk of orders from higher revolutionary leaders. He talked of many other such groups engaged in like activities. Shatov, who attended the meeting, denounced Pyotr as a spy and a scoundrel and walked out. Pyotr disclosed to Nikolay his nihilistic beliefs and proposed that Nikolay be brought forward as the Pretender when the revolution had been accomplished.

Blum, von Lembke's secretary, raided Stepan's quarters and confiscated all of Stepan's private papers, among them some political manifestos. Stepan went to the governor to demand his rights under the law and witnessed in front of the governor's mansion the lashing of dissident workers who had been quietly demonstrating for redress of their grievances. Von Lembke appeased Stepan by saying that the raid on his room was a mistake.

The fête was doomed beforehand. Many agitators without tickets were admitted. Liputin read a comic and seditious poem. Karmazinov, a great novelist, made a fool of himself by recalling the follies of his youth. Stepan insulted the agitators by championing the higher culture. When an unidentified agitator arose to speak, the afternoon session of the fête became a bedlam, so that it was doubtful whether the ball would take place that night. Abetted by Pyotr, Nikolay and Lizaveta eloped in the afternoon to the country house of Varvara.

The ball was not canceled, but few of the landowners of the town or countryside appeared. Drunkenness and brawling soon reduced the ball to a rout which came to a sorry end when fire was discovered raging through some houses along the river. Captain Lebyadkin, Marya, and their servant were discovered murdered in their house, which remained unburned. When Pyotr informed Nikolay of the murders, Nikolay confessed that he had known of the possibility that violence would take place but that he had done nothing to prevent it. Horrified, Lizaveta went to see the murdered pair; she was beaten to death by the enraged townspeople because of her connections with Nikolay. Nikolay left town quickly and quietly.

When the revolutionary group met again, they all mistrusted one another. Pyotr explained to them that Fedka, a former convict, had murdered the Lebyadkins for robbery, but he failed to mention that Nikolay had all but paid Fedka to commit the crime. He warned the group against Shatov and said that a fanatic named Kirillov had agreed to cover up the proposed murder of Shatov. After

Fedka denounced Pyotr as an atheistic scoundrel, Fedka was found dead on a road outside the town.

At the same time, Marie, Shatov's wife, returned to the town. The couple had been separated for three years; Marie was ill and pregnant. When she began her labor, Shatov procured Virginsky's wife as midwife. The couple were reconciled after Marie gave birth to a baby boy, for the child served to regenerate Shatov and make him happy once more.

Shatov left his wife and baby alone in order to keep an appointment with the revolutionary group, an appointment made for the purpose of separating himself from the plotters. Attacked and shot by Pyotr, his body was weighted with stones and thrown into a pond. After the murder Pyotr went to Kirillov to get Kirillov's promised confession for the murder of Shatov. Kirillov, who was Shatov's neighbor and who had seen Shatov's happiness at the return of his wife, at first refused to sign, but Pyotr finally prevailed upon him to put his name to the false confession. Kirillov, morally bound to end his life, shot himself. Pyotr left the province.

Stepan, meanwhile, left the town to seek a new life. He wandered for a time among peasants and at last became dangerously ill. Varvara went to him, and the two friends were reconciled before the old scholar died. Varvara disowned her son. Marie and the baby died of exposure and neglect when Shatov failed to return home. One of the radical group broke down and confessed to the violence that had been committed in the town at the instigation of the completely immoral Pyotr. Liputin escaped to St. Petersburg, where he was apprehended in a drunken stupor in a brothel.

Nikolay wrote to Dasha, the servant, suggesting that the two of them go to Switzerland and begin a new life. Before Dasha could pack her things, however, Nikolay returned home secretly and hanged himself in his room.

Critical Evaluation

Fyodor Dostoevski was nearly fifty years old when the final version of *The Possessed* (also translated as *The Devils*) appeared. (His poverty had forced him to write the book first in serial form for a Moscow literary review.) Because the novel rages so wildly against liberalism and "atheistic" socialism, many readers decided that its once-progressive author had now become a confirmed reactionary. Dostoevski himself lent credibility to this notion by his public statements. In a famous letter to Alexander III, Dostoevski characterized *The Possessed* as a historical study of that perverse radicalism which results when the intelligentsia detaches itself from the Russian masses. In another letter he proclaimed that "He who loses his people and his nationality loses his faith in his country and in God. This is the theme of my novel."

Further, given the nature of Dostoevski's personal his-

tory, a movement toward thoroughgoing conservatism could seem almost predictable. An aristocrat by birth, Dostoevski involved himself deeply in the Petrashevski Circle, a St. Petersburg discussion group interested in utopian socialism. Part of this group formed a clandestine revolutionary cadre, and Dostoevski was arrested for his participation in the conspiracy. There followed a mock execution, four years of imprisonment, and another four years of enforced service as a private in the Siberian army. Although freed in 1858, Dostoevski remained under surveillance, and his right to publish was always in jeopardy. He thus had every inducement to prove to government censors his utter fidelity to the *ancien regime* and "safe" principles.

In fact, *The Possessed* is not a reactionary novel. Dostoevski does not defend the institutions of monarchy, aristocracy, or censorship. He upholds Russian orthodoxy in a way that suggests a theocratic challenge to the status quo. His exaltation of the peasantry affords no comfort for capitalism or imperialism. While appearing to embrace Russian nationalism, he presents an image of small-town culture which, to say the least, does not inspire Russophilia. His portrait of the ruling class is as devastating as any essay on the subject by Marx or Engels. Thus, Dostoevski's critique of radical political ideas proceeds from a basis other than that of extremist conservatism. But what is that basis?

The answer is partially revealed in Shatov's statement that half-truth is uniquely despotic. *The Possessed* is at once a criticism of a variety of political and philosophical half-truths and a searching toward a principle of Wholeness, a truth which will reunite and compose man's fragmented psyche, his divided social and political order, and his shattered relationship with God. Dostoevski does not describe that truth, partly because *the* truth is too mysterious and grand to be expressed in human language. Rather, he merely points to it by showing the defects and incompleteness in positions which pretend to be the truth.

It is through the enigmatic character of Stavrogin that Dostoevski most fully carries out his quest for Wholeness, for Stavrogin has embraced and discarded all the philosophies which Dostoevski deems inadequate. As a result, Stavrogin is the embodiment of pure negativity and pure emptiness. He is also pure evil, more evil still than Pyotr, who at least has his absolute devotion to Stavrogin as a ruling principle in his life. From Stepan Verhovensky, Stavrogin learned skepticism and the tolerant principles of "higher liberalism." In St. Petersburg, he advances to utopian socialism and a more passionate faith in salvation-through-science. The elitism and shallow rationalism of this faith, however, cause Stavrogin to take up messianic Russian populism. Yet he is led even beyond this stage to an investigation of orthodox theology. Unable to commit himself to the Christian faith, he perpetrates the hideous crime he later confesses to Father Tihon.

At each step in his development, Stavrogin trains disciples who both propagate his teachings and carry them out to their logical extremes. Pyotr belongs partly to Stavrogin's "Socialist period," while Shatov embraces the populist creed and Kirillov elaborates the themes of the theological phase. In Pyotr, Socialist criticism of traditional society has produced a monomaniacal fascination with the revolutionary destruction and violence by which the new order shall emerge. Modeling this character after the infamous Russian terrorist, Sergey Nechayev, Dostoevski suggests that Pyotr is the natural outcome of socialism's faith in the power of reason to establish absolute values. Shigolov's "rational" defense of a Socialist tyranny shows how thoroughly rational structures rely on nonrational premises. For Pyotr, then, the absence of rational certainties means that all behavior is permissible

and all social orders are equally valid. He thus chooses to fight for a society based on men's hunger for submission, their fear of death, their longing for a messiah. Like Machiavelli, he decides that only by founding society on the most wretched aspects of human nature can anything really lasting and dependable be built. As his messiah, Pyotr has chosen Stavrogin, whose awesome and arbitrary will could be the source of order in a new society.

Kirillov elevates Pyotr Verhovensky's fascination with strength of will into a theological principle. Kirillov is not content with man's limited transcendence of the determinisms of nature: He aspires to the total freedom of God. Paradoxically, this freedom can only be achieved through suicide, that act which overcomes the natural fear of death by which God holds man in thrall. Not until all men are prepared at every moment to commit suicide can humanity take full responsibility for its own destiny. The great drawback in Kirillov's view is that it causes him to suppress his feelings of love and relatedness to his fellowman. Shatov's nationalistic theology is an attempt to do justice to these feelings. Rebelling against Kirillov's isolated quest for godhood, Shatov wishes to achieve the same goal by submerging himself in the life of a "God-bearing people." Yet Shatov's creed remains abstract and sentimental until Marya returns, providing him with a real person to love.

The birth of Marya's child and Stepan Verhovensky's "discovery" of the Russian people—these are the symbols by which Dostoevski reveals his own answer to Nikolay Stavrogin. The child is for Shatov an unimaginable act of grace. Significantly, Kirillov experiences a sudden serenity and a confirmation of his mystical insight that "everything is good." For Dostoevski, the source of this grace is God, who brings exquisite order to the most corrupted human situations. Shatov's rapturous love stands in utter contradiction to Stavrogin's empty indifference. In that the child's real father is Stavrogin, Shatov's love is all the more wondrous. Stavrogin's final inability to respond to Liza's love is the logical result of his long struggle to free himself of dependency on his family, his people, his church. He boasts that he does not need anyone; from that claim comes spiritual and moral death. All that Stavrogin has touched is, in the end, dead—even Shatov.

The magnificence of Dostoevski's artistry is nowhere more apparent than in the conclusion to *The Possessed*. For he does not finally embody his great theme—human wholeness through human dependence—in a titanic character like Stavrogin or Kirillov, but in the all-too-human Stepan. This quixotic buffoon, who is both laughable and pitiable, ultimately attains the dignity he seeks. He himself, however, is surprised by it all, for it comes in a way he least expected it: through an encounter with his people, reunion with Varvara, and the administration of the sacrament.

PRAGMATISM: A New Name for Some Old Ways of Thinking

Type of work: Philosophical essays
Author: William James (1842–1910)
First published: 1907

No more illuminating or entertaining account of pragmatism has ever been written than William James's *Pragmatism: A New Name for Some Old Ways of Thinking*. But this is more than a popular exposition prepared for the academic audiences of Lowell Institute and Columbia University during the winter of 1906–1907, it is historic philosophy in the making. Although James was profoundly influenced by Charles Sanders Pierce, who invented the basic statement and name of pragmatism, he was in independent thinker with a distinctive creative direction of his own.

Pierce's essay, "How to Make Our Ideas Clear," introduced the pragmatic notion that ideas are clarified by considering what we would expect in the way of experience if we were to act in a certain manner. The whole of our conception of the "sensible effects" of an object is the whole of our conception of the objects, according to Peirce. This essay, clear, radical, entertaining, appeared in the *Popular Science Monthly* in January, 1878. But professional philosophers were not interested in theory advanced by a mathematician, particularly when the theory went against the prevailing idealism of American philosophers. It was not until James revived the idea in 1898 with a talk on "Philosophical Conceptions and Practical Results" that the pragmatic philosophy began to stir up controversy. With the lectures on meaning and truth which were published under the titles *Pragmatism* and *The Meaning of Truth,* the former in 1907 and the latter in 1909, James brought pragmatism into the forefront of American thought.

In his first lecture on "The Present Dilemma in Philosophy," James distinguished between the "tender-minded" and the "tough-minded" in temperament, the former inclining toward a philosophy that is rational, religious, dogmatic, idealistic, and optimistic, and the latter, the tough-minded, inclining toward a philosophy that is empirical, irreligious, skeptical, materialistic, and pessimistic. He then went on to state his conviction that philosophy can satisfy both temperaments by becoming pragmatic.

His lecture on the pragmatic method begins with one of the most entertaining anecdotes in philosophical discourse. James describes a discussion by a group of philosophers on this question: Does a man go around a squirrel that is on a tree trunk if the squirrel keeps moving on the tree so that the trunk is always between himself and the man? Some of the philosophers claimed that the man did not go around the squirrel, while others claimed that

he did. James settled the matter by saying "which party is right depends on what you *practically mean* by 'going round' the squirrel." It could be said that the man goes around the squirrel since he passes from the north of the squirrel to the east, south, and west of the squirrel. On the other hand, the man could be said not to go around the squirrel since he is never able to get on the various sides of the squirrel—on the right of him, then behind him, and so forth. "Make the distinction," James said, "and there is no occasion for any further dispute."

James then applied the method to a number of perennial philosophical problems, but only after a careful exposition of the meaning of pragmatism. He described the pragmatic method as a way of interpreting ideas by discovering their practical consequences—that is, the difference the idea's truth would make in our experience. He asks, "What difference would it practically make to anyone if this notion rather than that notion were true?" and he replies, "If no practical difference whatever can be traced, then the alternatives mean practically the same thing, and all dispute is idle."

In his lecture James argued that the pragmatic method was not new; Socrates, Aristotle, Locke, Berkeley, and Hume had used it. But what was new was the explicit formulation of the method and a new faith in its power. Pragmatism is to be understood, however, not as a set of grand theories but as a method which turns attention away from first principles and absolutes and directs it to facts, consequences, and results in our experience.

A bare declaration would hardly have been enough to make pragmatism famous. James devoted a considerable part of his lectures to brief examples of the application of the pragmatic method. He cited with approval Berkeley's analysis of matter as made up of sensations. Sensations, he said, "are the cash-value of the term. The difference matter makes to us by truly being is that we then get such sensations . . ." Similarly, Locke applied the pragmatic method, James claimed, when he discovered that unless by "spirit" we mean consciousness, we mean nothing by the term.

Is materialism or theism true? Is the universe simply matter acting and interacting, or is God involved? James considers this problem pragmatically and reaches a curious result. As far as the past is concerned, he says, it makes no difference. If rival theories are meant to explain what is the case and if it makes no difference in our experience which theory is true, then the theories do not differ in meaning. If one considers the difference now and in the future, however, the case is different: "Materialism means simply the denial that the moral order is eternal . . . spiritualism means the affirmation of an eternal moral order and the letting loose of hope."

To this kind of analysis some critics have answered with the charge that James is one of the "tender-minded" philosophers he spoke harshly of in his earlier lectures. But throughout the course of this series of lectures and in subsequent books James continued to use pragmatism as a way of combining the tough and tender temperaments. He extended the use of the term "difference" so that the meaning of an idea or term was no longer to be understood merely in terms of sense experiences, as Peirce had urged, but also in terms of passionate differences, of effects upon human hopes and fears. The essays in *Pragmatism* show this liberalizing tendency hard at work.

The temperate tone of James's suggestions concerning the religious hypothesis is clear in one of his later lectures in the book, "Pragmatism and Religion," in which he writes that "Pragmatism has to postpone dogmatic answer, for we do not yet know certainly which type of religion is going to work best in the long run." He states again that the tough-minded can be satisfied with "the hurlyburly of the sensible facts of nature." and that the tenderminded can take up a monistic form of religion; but for those who mix temperaments, as James does, a religious synthesis that is moralistic and pluralistic, allowing for human development and creativity in various directions, is to be preferred.

Pragmatism is important not only as a clear statement of the pragmatic method and as an illustration of its application to certain central problems but also as an exposition, although introductory, of James's pragmatic theory of truth. His ideas were developed more fully two years later in *The Meaning of Truth*.

Beginning with the common notion that truth is a property of ideas that agree with reality, James proceeded to ask what was meant by the term "agreement." He decided that the conception of truth as a static relation between an idea and reality was in error, that pragmatic analysis shows that true ideas are those which can eventually be verified, and that an idea is said to be verified when it leads us usefully to an anticipated conclusion. Since verification is a process, it becomes appropriate to say that truth "happens to" an idea, and that an idea "*becomes* true, is *made* true by events." A revealing summary statement is this: "'The true,' to put it very briefly, is only the expedient in the way of our thinking, just as 'the right' is only the expedient in the way of our behaving."

The ambiguity of James's account, an ambiguity which he did not succeed in removing, allows extremes of interpretation. On the one hand, a reader might take the tenderminded route, something in the manner of James himself, and argue that all kinds of beliefs about God, freedom, and immortality are true in so far as they lead a man usefully in the course of his life. On the other hand, a tough-minded reader might be inclined to agree with James that an idea is true if the expectations in terms of which the idea makes sense are expectations that would be met, if one acted—but he might reject James's suggestions that this means that a great many ideas which would ordinarily be regarded as doubtful "become true" when they satisfy the emotional needs of a believer.

One difficulty with which James was forced to deal because of his theory of truth resulted, it might be argued, not from his idea of truth as the "workableness" of an idea, but from his inadequate analyses of the meanings of certain terms such as "God," "freedom" and "design." James maintained that, pragmatically speaking, these terms all meant the same thing, namely, the presence of "promise" in the world. If this were so, then it would be plausible to suppose that if the idea that the world is promising works out, the idea is true. But if James's analysis is mistaken, if "God" means more than the possibility of things working out for the better, James's claim that beliefs about God are true if they work loses its plausibility.

Whatever its philosophic faults, *Pragmatism* is saved by its philosophic virtues. For the general reader it offers the rare experience of confronting first-rate ideas by way of a clear and entertaining, even informal, style.

THE PRELUDE: Or the Growth of a Poet's Mind

Type of work: Poem
Author: William Wordsworth (1770–1850)
First published: *The Prelude: Or, Growth of a Poet's Mind, An Autobiographical Poem*, 1850

The Prelude is William Wordsworth's most important work; many critics regard it as the central poem of the English Romantic age. In this sustained autobiographical meditation in blank verse, Wordsworth adapts—in fact, revolutionizes—the conventions of the epic tradition to explore and dramatize the growth of his mind as a poet. A poem about imagination, memory, and selfhood, *The Prelude* addresses at the same time the interactions between the self and the forces outside it—Nature, mankind, and God. It is the vivid self-portrait of a great poet who came of age during a time of political, social, and intellectual revolution, and it delineates the dilemmas faced by a mind seeking truth as traditional values and systems of belief were called into question.

The poem exists in several versions, none of which was called *The Prelude* by Wordsworth himself, who died leaving it untitled and unpublished. It was given its title by his widow, who published it in its final version in 1850, shortly after Wordsworth's death. Wordsworth viewed *The Prelude* as part of a projected philosophical poem, conceived as his magnum opus, called *The Recluse*. Wordsworth never completed *The Recluse*; feeling that it was "a thing unprecedented in Literary history that a man should talk so much about himself," he was also reluctant to publish *The Prelude* by itself.

While he did not publish it, he painstakingly polished it. The 1850 text of *The Prelude* is based on a manuscript finished in 1839, itself the final result of three complete reworkings and a great number of small revisions of a poem begun in 1798. Of most interest to modern readers are the 1805 *Prelude* (thirteen books)—a complete draft of the poem which includes, in the fictionalized episode of Vaudracour and Julia, an account of Wordsworth's love affair in France during the French Revolution—and the 1850 *Prelude* (fourteen books), the version most frequently published. The 1850 *Prelude* differs from the 1805 text in several ways. Most important are its suppression of the Vaudracour and Julia episode and its many stylistic and tonal alterations. Wordsworth changed individual passages of verse to make them, in turn, smoother or clearer or more elaborate or—what is most interesting—more in keeping with Christian orthodoxy and less boldly personal. Readers seeking to witness the "growth of a poet's mind" (Mary Wordsworth's subtitle for *The Prelude*) as fully as possible can best do so by studying the 1805 and 1850 versions comparatively. There are, in fact, a number of modern editions of *The Prelude* that print the texts of 1805 and 1850 on facing pages (references here will be to the 1850 version).

Wordsworth remarked in an 1805 letter that he began *The Prelude* "because I was unprepared to treat any more arduous subject, and diffident of my own powers." The first book of the poem dramatizes these feelings vividly. Although Wordsworth is self-consciously and preeminently a poet of memory, he departs from his usual practice at the opening to locate his concerns squarely in the present. Book 1 shows the poet in the process of discovering his own subject. It begins as Wordsworth, having escaped from the cares of the city, is contemplating his newfound freedom. "The earth is all before me," he exclaims, and goes on to celebrate the prospect of long months of leisure to enjoy himself and to write poetry. His celebration is short-lived, however, and he goes on to recount, in the past tense, how he soon felt thwarted, unable to compose a line. A time of self-examination ensued, during which Wordsworth found himself unable to choose a subject to write about, whether because of "some imperfection in the chosen theme" or because he felt inadequate to the task. His spirits droop; he feels "like a false steward who hath much received and renders nothing back."

At this point the poem takes a dramatic turn. Wordsworth reaches back to his early childhood, asking rhetorically whether Nature's fostering ministry to his growing soul was meant only to end in frustration. Clearly, it was not, for now his imagination becomes unblocked as he begins to muse upon childhood activities and to focus in detail upon a series of vivid memories—snaring woodcocks on a frosty night, plundering a raven's nest on a high, naked crag, stealing a boat in the moonlight and feeling admonished by the "unknown modes of being" that are a part of Nature. These and other recollections, fetching "invigorating thoughts from former years, "help to steady the poet in his present distress, to revive his mind, and to move him toward the subject of the rest of *The Prelude*. Whereas in the opening lines the earth was all before him, but he could not find a way to proceed, now at the closing of book 1, he knows where he is going—"The road lies plain before me"—and he is ready to address "a theme/ Single and of determined bounds: "the story of my life."

The process, dramatized in book 1, of turning to the past for aid in present difficulties is characteristically Wordsworthian, and later in the poem he will specifically articulate a theory of how "feeling comes in aid/ Of feeling, and diversity of strength/ Attends us, if but once we have been strong." This theory of the saving power of imaginative memory is one of Wordsworth's most famous ideas:

> There are in our existence spots of time,
> That with distinct pre-eminence retain
> A renovating virtue, whence, depressed
> By false opinion and contentious thought,
> Or aught of heavier or more deadly weight,
> In trivial occupations, and the round
> Of ordinary intercourse, our minds
> Are nourished and invisibly repaired.

Such moments take place "from our first childhood," and are chiefly to be found

> Among those passages of life that give
> Profoundest knowledge to what point, and how,
> The mind is lord and master—outward sense
> The obedient servant of her will.

These lines are quintessentially Romantic in their assertion of the primacy of the human imagination. Not all of *The Prelude* is equally assertive or thoroughly self-consistent, and much of its power and interest lie in Wordsworth's arguments with himself about the power of imagination as he formulates, discards, refines, and perfects hypotheses about it and about Nature. *The Prelude* is a poem of process and discovery, and of doubt as well as of assertion. Wordsworth's own life becomes a kind of test case on the subject of imagination, and many of *The Prelude*'s highest moments turn upon it.

From book 2 on, spurred by the turn his mind took toward early childhood in book 1, Wordsworth follows a roughly chronological narrative of his life, interrupted at significant moments by recurrence to relevant "spots of time." Up through book 6, Wordsworth addresses the birth and early growth of his imaginative powers. Books 7 through 11 treat their impairment, and books 12 through 14 detail their eventual restoration.

Describing his school days in book 2, Wordsworth recounts at the same time his developing relationship with Nature as he makes the effort to put himself in touch with the sources of his identity. The effort is not without difficulty; musing on his boyhood, he often seems to himself "two consciousnesses, conscious of myself/ And of some other Being." Like many other Romantic poems, *The Prelude* is deeply concerned with epistemology, with the investigation of the origin, nature, methods, and limits of human knowledge.

The third book of *The Prelude* takes Wordsworth into his university days at Cambridge. There, in the face of his dislike of the formal curriculum and methods of instruction, he learned more and more to depend upon his own inner resources, aided by the remembered examples of the poets Geoffrey Chaucer, Edmund Spenser,

and John Milton, and of great thinkers such as Sir Isaac Newton, "a mind for ever/ Voyaging through strange seas of Thought, alone."

Wordsworth's experiences at Cambridge point up one of his characteristic difficulties: He was uncomfortable in casual social situations and among large groups of people. Although a professed lover of mankind, he was essentially a solitary individual, and his most cherished human encounters were with other solitaries or with a few intimate friends and family members. In book 4, he celebrates his return home from Cambridge for summer vacation, reflecting that "when from our better selves we have too long/ Been parted by the hurrying world, . . ./ How gracious, how benign, is Solitude," especially when it has an "appropriate human centre." He illustrates this idea by describing a powerful encounter he had with a discharged soldier he met one evening on a road. Solitude also figures significantly in book 4, in Wordsworth's account of how one morning, witnessing a glorious sunrise, he experienced an epiphanic moment that left him with the conviction "that I should be, else sinning greatly,/ A dedicated Spirit." Most critics have viewed this episode as referring to Wordsworth's vocation as a poet.

Wordsworth moves even more deeply into his contemplation of the forces that shape human life and the desires that drive it in *The Prelude*'s fifth book. Subtitled "Books," it recognizes the human longing for emotional and spiritual growth and immortality beneath all imaginative endeavors, particularly literary creation, mathematical thought, and the education of children. Wordsworth contemplates these endeavors in the contexts of human frailty and error and of the frightening and inevitable reality of death. He ponders human life as a terrible struggle to survive in spite of threats both from within and from without—educational systems that maim the human spirit, untimely illnesses and accidents that kill, natural catastrophes that bring widescale destruction. Wordsworth delineates this struggle most suggestively in book 5, in his description of a dream about an impending deluge that threatens to drown the entire world.

Still, his faith in imagination holds steady. Indeed, Wordsworth's description in book 6 of a walking tour he took in the Alps shows how this faith was strengthened. Such tours were very popular in Wordsworth's day; in fact, they had become conventionalized. Tourists embarked in the anticipation of sublime emotional experiences at prescribed vistas and moments. Mont Blanc, for example, was not to be missed, and the very moment of crossing the Alps—of passing from an upward to a downward course—held the promise of great excitement. This very conventionalization of the sublime, however, depressed Wordsworth. He was "grieved" to find Mont Blanc "a soulless image on the eye." Climbing the road to the Simplon Pass, he and his companion lost their way, only to learn from a passerby native to the district that they had crossed the Alps unwittingly. At this point, Wordsworth breaks from his narrative of disappointment to an impassioned celebration of the creative power of the imagination. He recognizes that the human mind's power of expectation is infinitely greater than any earthly fulfillment could be, and that therefore the imagination is not tied to the earth:

> Our destiny, our being's heart and home,
> Is with infinitude, and only there;
> With hope it is, hope that can never die,
> Effort, and expectation, and desire,
> And something evermore about to be.

Wordsworth returns to his narrative to describe, in what has become one of the most celebrated passages of blank verse in the English language, how the landscape subsequently seemed transformed, in fact, apocalyptic in import:

> . . . The immeasurable height
> Of woods decaying, never to be decayed,
> The stationary blasts of waterfalls,
> And in the narrow rent at every turn
> Winds thwarting winds, bewildered and forlorn,
> The torrents shooting from the clear blue sky,
> The rocks that muttered close upon our ears,
> Black drizzling crags that spake by the way-side
> As if a voice were in them, the sick sight
> And giddy prospect of the raving stream,
> The unfettered clouds and region of the Heavens,
> Tumult and peace, the darkness and the light—
> Were all like workings of one mind, the features
> Of the same face, blossoms upon one tree;
> Characters of the great Apocalypse,
> The types and symbols of Eternity,
> Of first, and last, and midst, and without end.

The human mind and Nature, therefore, each in its own way, partake of and shadow forth the Divine and the eternal.

From the Alps in book 6, Wordsworth descends in the seventh book into London, a "monstrous ant-hill on the plain/ Of a too busy world." His spirits sink, pulled down by his remembered impressions of the dehumanization of city life and the victimization there of women and children. The hideous realities of London impinge upon and threaten the imagination, which seems there to have scant place in and little hope for changing human society. Wordsworth leaves this confused, alienated, and alien-

ating world of conflicting data, sense impressions, and moral problems to return in book 8 to the country, where the sources of his own identity lie. Book 8 provides a mental retrospect of the action of the whole poem thus far, and culminates in Wordsworth's assertion that his early love of Nature led him to the love of Man; its climactic image, appropriately, is one of man *in* Nature—a shepherd.

Wordsworth goes on in the next several books to recall his own hopes for humankind in general during the French Revolution. He shared these hopes with visionary thinkers like Jean Jacques Rousseau, who asserted the natural goodness of human nature. The initial events of the Revolution were heartening to Wordsworth and seemed to him to be in the natural course of things. When England went to war with France, however, and with the shock of the Reign of Terror and of France's new role as an aggressor against other nations, Wordsworth's expectations were shattered, his faith in humankind shaken. Having witnessed a split between the ideal and the real, between theory and fact, in the events in France, a comparable splitting occurred in his own soul. First his thoughts became divorced from his feelings, and, tyrannized by his abstract intellect's exhausting demand for formal proof of "all precepts, judgements, maxims, creeds," he "yielded up moral questions in despair." Next, he found himself out of touch with the physical world, as his "bodily eye" began to tyrannize over his imagination; he became overly concerned with the visual surfaces of the natural world and no longer experienced its moral, emotional, and spiritual power.

From book 12 on, Wordsworth narrates how his impaired imagination was restored, principally through the agency and examples of his beloved sister Dorothy and his wife Mary, and through his own remembrances of "spots of time" in his early life. His joyous account of this restoration leads him to conclude *The Prelude* triumphantly, with an apocalyptic vision he experienced ascending Mount Snowdon, a vision in which Nature became "the type/ Of a majestic intellect," the emblem of the human creative imagination, which is itself godlike. He assumes the role of prophetic poet, who will teach others of the beauty, power, and divine fabric of the mind of man.

The Prelude is epic in scope and victorious in outcome. Its battles, however, are not external but internal, as are its depths and heights. Its hero is not to be defined narrowly, as William Wordsworth, but broadly, as the human imagination.

PRIDE AND PREJUDICE

Type of work: Novel
Author: Jane Austen (1775–1817)
Type of plot: Comedy of manners
Time of plot: Early nineteenth century
Locale: Rural England
First Published: 1813

In this masterpiece, Austen follows an empty-headed mother's scheming to find suitable husbands for her five daughters. With gentle irony, the author re-creates in meticulous, artistic detail the manners and morals of the country gentry in a small English village, focusing on the intelligent, irrepressible heroine Elizabeth. Major and minor characters are superbly drawn, the plot is beautifully symmetrical, and the dazzling perfection of style shows Austen at her best.

Principal Characters

Elizabeth Bennet, a spirited and intelligent girl who represents "prejudice" in her attitude toward Fitzwilliam Darcy, whom she dislikes because of his pride. She is also prejudiced against him by Mr. Wickham, whose false reports of Darcy she believes, and hence rejects Darcy's haughty first proposal of marriage. But Wickham's elopement with her sister Lydia brings Elizabeth and Darcy together, for it is Darcy who facilitates the legal marriage of the runaways. Acknowledging her mistake in her estimation of Darcy, she gladly accepts his second proposal.

Fitzwilliam Darcy, the wealthy and aristocratic landowner who represents "pride" in the story. Attracted to Elizabeth Bennet in spite of her inferior social position, he proposes marriage but in so high-handed a manner that she instantly refuses. The two meet again while Elizabeth is viewing the grounds of his estate in Derbyshire; she finds him less haughty in his manner. When Lydia Bennet and Mr. Wickham elope, Darcy feels partly responsible and straightens out the unfortunate affair. Because Elizabeth now realizes his true character, he is accepted when he proposes again.

Jane Bennet, the oldest and most beautiful of the five Bennet sisters. She falls in love with Mr. Bingley, a wealthy bachelor. Their romance is frustrated, however, by his sisters with the help of Mr. Darcy, for the Bennets are considered socially undesirable. As a result of the change in the feelings of Darcy and Elizabeth Bennet toward each other, Jane and Bingley are finally married.

Mr. Bingley, a rich, good-natured bachelor from the north of England. He falls in love with Jane Bennet but is easily turned against her by his sisters and his friend, Mr. Darcy, who consider the Bennets vulgar and socially beneath them. When Darcy changes his attitude toward Elizabeth Bennet, Bingley follows suit and resumes his courtship of Jane. They are married at the end of the story.

Mr. Bennet, an eccentric and mildly sarcastic small landowner. Rather indifferent to the rest of his family, he loves and admires his daughter Elizabeth.

Mrs. Bennet, his wife, a silly, brainless woman interested only in getting her daughters married.

Lydia Bennet, the youngest daughter, a flighty and uncontrolled girl. At the age of fifteen she elopes with the worthless Mr. Wickham. Their marriage is finally made possible by Mr. Darcy, who pays Wickham's debts, but the two are never very happy.

Mary Bennet and **Catherine (Kitty) Bennet,** younger daughters of the family.

Mr. Wickham, the villain of the story, an officer in the militia. He has been brought up by the Darcy family and, having a certain charm, attracts Elizabeth Bennet, whom he prejudices against Mr. Darcy by misrepresenting the latter's treatment of him. Quite unexpectedly, he elopes with fifteen-year-old, flirtatious Lydia Bennet. Darcy, who has tried to expose Wickham to Elizabeth, feels responsible for the elopement and provides the money for the marriage by paying Wickham's debts. Wickham and Lydia soon tire of each other.

William Collins, a pompous, sycophantic clergyman, distantly related to Mr. Bennet and the heir to his estate, since the Bennets have no son. He proposed to Elizabeth. After her refusal he marries her friend, Charlotte Lucas.

Lady Catherine de Bourgh, Mr. Darcy's aunt and the patron of Mr. Collins. An insufferably haughty and domineering woman, she wants Darcy to marry her only daughter and bitterly resents his interest in Elizabeth Bennet. She tries to break up their love affair but fails.

Anne de Bourgh, Lady Catherine's spiritless daughter. Her mother has planned to marry her to Mr. Darcy in order to combine two great family fortunes.

Charlotte Lucas, Elizabeth Bennet's closest friend. Knowing that she will have few chances of marriage, she accepts the pompous and boring Mr. Collins shortly after

Elizabeth has refused him.

Caroline Bingley and **Mrs. Hurst,** Mr. Bingley's cold and worldly sisters. They succeed for a time in turning him against Jane Bennet.

Mr. Gardiner, Mrs. Bennet's brother, a London merchant.

Mrs. Gardiner, his sensible and kind wife.

The Story

The chief business of Mrs. Bennet's life was to find suitable husbands for her five daughters. Consequently, she was elated when she heard that Netherfield Park, one of the area's great houses, had been let to Mr. Bingley, a gentleman from the north of England. Gossip such as Mrs. Bennet loved reported him a rich and eligible young bachelor. Mr. Bennet heard the news with his usual dry calmness, suggesting in his mild way that perhaps Bingley was not moving into the country for the single purpose of marrying one of the Bennet daughters.

Mr. Bingley's first public appearance in the neighborhood was at a ball. With him were his two sisters, the husband of the older, and Mr. Darcy, Bingley's friend. Bingley was an immediate success in local society, and he and Jane, the oldest Bennet daughter—a pretty girl of sweet and gentle disposition—were attracted to each other at once. His friend, Darcy, however, seemed cold and extremely proud and created a bad impression. In particular, he insulted Elizabeth Bennet, a girl of spirit and intelligence and her father's favorite. He refused to dance with her when she was sitting down for lack of a partner; Elizabeth also overheard him say that he was in no mood to prefer young ladies slighted by other men. On future occasions, however, he began to admire Elizabeth in spite of himself. At a later ball, she had the satisfaction of refusing him a dance.

Jane's romance with Bingley flourished quietly, aided by family calls, dinners, and balls. His sisters pretended great fondness for Jane, who believed them completely sincere. Elizabeth was more critical and discerning; she suspected them of hypocrisy, and quite rightly, for they made great fun of Jane's relations, especially her vulgar, garrulous mother and her two illbred, officer-mad younger sisters. Miss Caroline Bingley, who was eager to marry Darcy and shrewdly aware of his growing admiration for Elizabeth, was especially loud in her ridicule of the Bennet family. Elizabeth herself became Caroline's particular target when she walked three muddy miles to visit Jane, who was sick with a cold at Netherfield Park after a ride through the rain to accept an invitation from the Bingley sisters. Until Jane was able to be moved home, Elizabeth stayed to nurse her. During her visit, Elizabeth received enough attention from Darcy to make Caroline Bingley long sincerely for Jane's recovery. Her fears were not ill-founded. Darcy admitted to himself that he would be in some danger from the charm of Elizabeth, if it were not for her inferior family connections.

Elizabeth now acquired a new admirer in Mr. Collins, a ridiculously pompous clergyman and a distant cousin of the Bennets, who would someday inherit Mr. Bennet's property because that gentleman had no male heir. Mr. Collins' patroness, Lady Catherine de Bourgh, had urged him to marry, and he, always obsequiously obedient to her wishes, hastened to comply. Thinking to alleviate the hardship caused the Bennet sisters by the entail which gave their father's property to him, Mr. Collins first proposed to Elizabeth. Much to her mother's displeasure and her father's joy, she firmly and promptly rejected him. He almost immediately transferred his affections to Elizabeth's best friend, Charlotte Lucas, who, twenty-seven years old and somewhat homely, accepted at once his offer of marriage.

During Mr. Collins' visit and on one of their many walks to Meryton, the younger Bennet sisters, Kitty and Lydia, met a fascinating new officer, Mr. Wickham, stationed with the regiment there. Outwardly charming, he became a favorite among the ladies, even with Elizabeth. She was willing to believe the story that he had been cheated out of an inheritance left to him by his godfather, Darcy's father. Her suspicions of Darcy's arrogant and grasping nature deepened when Wickham did not come to a ball given by the Bingleys, a dance at which Darcy was present.

Soon after the ball, the entire Bingley party suddenly left Netherfield Park. They departed with no intention of returning, as Caroline wrote Jane in a short farewell note which hinted that Bingley might soon become engaged to Darcy's sister. Jane accepted this news at face value and believed that her friend Caroline was telling her gently that her brother loved someone else and that she must cease to hope. Elizabeth, however, was sure of a plot by Darcy and Bingley's sisters to separate him and Jane. She persuaded Jane that Bingley did love her and that he would return to Hertfordshire before the winter was over. Jane almost believed her until she received a letter from Caroline assuring her that they were all settled in London for the winter. Even after Jane told her this news, Elizabeth remained convinced of Bingley's affection for her sister and deplored the lack of resolution that made him putty in the hands of his scheming friend.

About that time, Mrs. Bennet's sister, Mrs. Gardiner, an amiable and intelligent woman with a great deal of affection for her two oldest nieces, arrived for a Christmas visit. She suggested to the Bennets that Jane return to London with her for a rest and change of scene and—so it was understood between Mrs. Gardiner and Elizabeth—to renew her acquaintance with Bingley. Elizabeth was not hopeful for the success of the plan and pointed out that proud Darcy would never let his friend call on Jane in the unfashionable London street on which the Gardiners lived. Jane accepted the invitation, however, and she and Mrs. Gardiner set out for London.

The time drew near for the wedding of Elizabeth's friend, Charlotte Lucas, to the obnoxious Mr. Collins. Charlotte asked Elizabeth to visit her in Kent. In spite of her feeling that there could be little pleasure in such a visit, Elizabeth promised to do so. She felt that in taking such a husband Charlotte was marrying simply for the sake of an establishment, as was indeed the case. Since she herself could not sympathize with her friend's action, Elizabeth thought their days of real intimacy were over. As March approached, however, she found herself eager to see her friend, and she sent out with pleasure on the journey with Charlotte's father and sister. On their way, the party stopped in London to see the Gardiners and Jane. Elizabeth found her sister well and outwardly happy, although she had not seen Bingley and his sisters had paid only one call. Elizabeth was sure Bingley had not been told of Jane's presence in London and blamed Darcy for keeping it from him.

Soon after arriving at the Collins' home, the whole party was honored, as Mr. Collins repeatedly assured them, by a dinner invitation from Lady Catherine de Bourgh, Darcy's aunt and Mr. Collins' patroness. Elizabeth found Lady Catherine a haughty, ill-mannered woman and her daughter thin, sickly, and shy. Lady Catherine was extremely fond of inquiring into the affairs of others and giving them unasked advice. Elizabeth circumvented the meddling old woman's questions with cool indirectness and saw from the effect that she was probably the first who had dared to do so.

Soon after Elizabeth's arrival, Darcy came to visit his aunt and cousin. He called frequently at the parsonage, and he and Elizabeth resumed their conversational fencing matches. His rather stilted attentions were suddenly climaxed by a proposal of marriage; the proposal, however, was couched in such proud and condescending terms that Elizabeth indignantly refused him. When he requested her reason for such an emphatic rejection, she mentioned his part in separating Bingley and Jane and also his mistreatment of Wickham. He was angry and left abruptly; the next day, however, he brought a letter answering her charges. He did not deny his part in separating Jane and Bingley, but he gave as his reasons the improprieties of Mrs. Bennet and her younger daughters and also his sincere belief that Jane did not love Bingley. As for his alleged mistreatment of Wickham, he proved that he had in reality acted most generously toward the unprincipled Wickham, who had repaid his kindness by attempting to elope with Darcy's young sister. At first incensed at the proud tones in which he wrote, Elizabeth was at length forced to acknowledge the justice of all he said, and her prejudice against him began to weaken. Without seeing him again, she returned home.

She found her younger sisters clamoring to go to Brighton, where the regiment formerly stationed at Meryton had been ordered. When an invitation came to Lydia from a young officer's wife, Lydia was allowed to accept it over Elizabeth's protests. Elizabeth was asked by the Gardiners to go with them on a tour, which would take them into Derbyshire, Darcy's home county. She accepted, reasoning that she was not very likely to meet Darcy merely by going into the same county with him. While they were there, however, Mrs. Gardiner decided they should visit Pemberly, Darcy's home. Elizabeth made several excuses, but her aunt was insistent. Then, learning that the Darcy family was not at home, Elizabeth consented to go.

At Pemberly, an unexpected and embarrassing meeting took place between Elizabeth and Darcy. He was more polite than Elizabeth had ever known him to be, and he asked permission for his sister to call upon her. The call was duly paid and returned, but the pleasant intercourse between the Darcys and Elizabeth's party was suddenly cut short when a letter came from Jane telling Elizabeth that Lydia had run away with Wickham. Elizabeth told Darcy what had happened, and she and the Gardiners left for home at once. After several days, the runaway couple was located and a marriage arranged between them. When Lydia came home as heedless as ever, she told Elizabeth that Darcy had attended her wedding. Suspecting the truth, Elizabeth learned from Mrs. Gardiner that it was indeed Darcy who brought about the marriage by giving Wickham money.

Soon after Lydia and Wickham left, Bingley came back to Netherfield Park. Darcy came with him. Elizabeth, now more favorably inclined to him than ever before, hoped his coming meant that he still loved her, but he gave no sign. Bingley and Jane, on the other hand, were still obviously in love with each other, and they became engaged, to the great satisfaction of Mrs. Bennet. Soon afterward, Lady Catherine paid the Bennets an unexpected call. She had heard it rumored that Darcy was engaged to Elizabeth. Hoping to marry her own daughter to Darcy, she had charged down the stairs with characteristic bad manners to order Elizabeth not to accept his proposal. The spirited girl was not to be intimidated by the bullying Lady Catherine and coolly refused to promise not to marry Darcy. She was far from certain she would have another chance, but she had not long to wonder. Lady Catherine, unluckily for her own purpose, repeated to Darcy the substance of her conversation with Elizabeth, and he knew Elizabeth well enough to surmise that her feelings toward him had greatly changed. He returned to Netherfield Park, and he and Elizabeth became engaged. Pride had been humbled and prejudice dissolved.

Critical Evaluation

In 1813, her thirty-eighth year, Jane Austen became a published novelist for the second time with *Pride and Prejudice*. She had begun this work in 1796, her twenty-first year, calling it *First Impressions*. It had so delighted her family that her father had tried, without success, to have it published. Eventually putting it aside, she returned to it probably at about the time that her first published novel, *Sense and Sensibility,* appeared in 1811. No longer extant, *First Impressions* must have been radically altered; for *Pride and Prejudice* is not an apprenticeship novel, but a mature work, and it continues to be the author's most popular novel, perhaps because readers share Darcy's admiration for the "liveliness" of Elizabeth Bennet's mind.

The original title, *First Impressions,* focuses upon the initial errors of judgment from which the story develops, whereas the title *Pride and Prejudice,* besides suggesting the kind of antithetical topic that delighted rationalistic eighteenth century readers, indicates the central conflict involving the kinds of pride and prejudice that bar the marriages of Elizabeth Bennet and Darcy and Jane Bennet and Bingley but bring about the marriages of Charlotte Lucas and Collins and Lydia Bennet and Wickham.

As in all of Austen's novels, individual conflicts are defined and resolved within a rigidly delimiting social context, in which human relationships are determined by wealth and rank. Therefore, the much-admired opening sentence establishes the societal values that underlie the main conflict: "It is a truth universally acknowledged, that a single man in possession of a good fortune, must be in want of a wife." Mr. and Mrs. Bennet's opening dialogue concerning the eligible Bingley explores this truth. Devoid of individuality, Mrs. Bennet is nevertheless well attuned to society's edicts and therefore regards Bingley only in the light of society's "truth." Mr. Bennet, an individualist to the point of eccentricity, represents neither personal conviction nor social conviction. He views with equal indifference both Bingley's right to his own reason for settling there and society's right to see him primarily as a potential husband. Having repudiated society, Mr. Bennet cannot take seriously either the claims of the individual or the social order.

As the central character, Elizabeth, her father's favorite child and her mother's least favorite, must come to terms with the conflicting values implicit in her parents' antithetical characters. She is like her father in her scorn of society's conventional judgments, but she champions the concept of individual merit independent of money and rank. She is, indeed, prejudiced against the prejudices of society. From this premise, she attacks Darcy's pride, assuming that it derives from the causes that Charlotte Lucas identifies: "with family, fortune, every thing in his favour . . . he has a *right* to be proud."

Flaunting her contempt for money, Elizabeth indignantly spurns as mere strategy to get a rich husband or any husband Charlotte's advice that Jane ought to make a calculated play for Bingley's affections. She loftily argues, while under the spell of Wickham's charm, that young people who are truly in love are unconcerned about each other's financial standing.

As a champion of the individual, Elizabeth prides herself on her discriminating judgment, boasting that she is a student of character. Significantly, it is Darcy who warns her against prejudiced conclusions, reminding her that her experience is quite limited. Darcy is not simply the representative of a society that primarily values wealth and consequence—as Elizabeth initially views him—but he is also a citizen of a larger society than the village to which Elizabeth is confined by circumstance. Consequently, it is only when she begins to move into Darcy's world that she can judge with true discrimination both individual merit and the dictates of the society that she has rejected. Fundamentally honest, she revises her conclusions as new experiences warrant, in the case of Darcy and Wickham radically altering her opinion.

More significant than the obviously ironic reversals, however, is the growing revelation of Elizabeth's unconscious commitment to society. For example, her original condemnation of Darcy's pride coincides with the verdict of Meryton society. Moreover, she always shares society's regard for wealth. Even while denying the importance of Wickham's poverty, she countenances his pursuit of the ugly Miss King's fortune, discerning her own inconsistency only after she learns of his bad character. Most revealing, when Lydia Bennet runs off with Wickham, Elizabeth instinctively pronounces the judgment of society when she states that Wickham would never marry a woman without money.

Almost unconsciously, Elizabeth acknowledges a connection between wealth and human values at the crucial moment when she first looks upon Pemberley, the Darcy estate:

She had never seen a place for which nature had done more, or where natural beauty had been so little counteracted by an awkward taste. They were all of them warm in their admiration; and at that moment she felt that to be mistress of Pemberley might be something!

She is not entirely joking when she tells Jane that her love for Darcy began when she first saw his beautiful estate.

Elizabeth's experiences, especially her discoveries of the well-ordered Pemberley and Darcy's tactful generosity to Lydia and Wickham, lead her to differentiate between Charlotte's theory that family and fortune bestow a "*right* to be proud" and Darcy's position that the intelligent person does not indulge in false pride. Darcy's pride is real, but it is regulated by responsibility. Unlike his aunt, Lady Catherine de Bourgh, who relishes the distinction of rank, he disapproves less of the Bennets' undistinguished family and fortune than he does of the lack of propriety displayed by most of the family. Therefore, Elizabeth scarcely overstates her case when, at the end, she assures her father that Darcy has no improper pride.

Elizabeth begins by rejecting the values and restraints of society as represented by such people as her mother, the Lucases, Miss Bingley, and Lady Catherine, upholding instead the claims of the individual, represented only by her whimsical father. By the end of the novel, the heart of her conflict appears in the contrast between her father and Darcy. She loves her father and has tried to overlook his lack of decorum in conjugal matters, but she has been forced to see that his freedom is really irresponsibility, the essential cause of Jane's misery as well as Lydia's amorality. The implicit comparison between Mr. Bennet's and Darcy's approach to matrimony illustrates their different methods of dealing with society's restraints. Unrestrained by society, having been captivated by the inferior Mrs. Bennet's youth and beauty, Mr. Bennet consulted only his personal desires and made a disastrous marriage. Darcy, in contrast, defies society only when he has made certain that Elizabeth is a woman worthy of his love and lifetime devotion.

When Elizabeth confronts Lady Catherine, her words are declarative, not of absolute defiance of society but of the selective freedom which is her compromise, and very similar to Darcy's: "I am only resolved to act in that manner, which will, in my own opinion, constitute my happiness, without reverence to *you,* or to any person so wholly unconnected with me." Austen does not falsify the compromise. If Elizabeth dares with impunity to defy the society of Rosings, Longbourne, and Meryton, she does so only because Darcy is exactly the man for her and, further, because she can anticipate "with delight . . . the time when they should be removed from society so little pleasing to either, to all the comfort and elegance . . . at Pemberly." In a sense, her marriage to Darcy is a triumph of the individual over society; but, paradoxically, Elizabeth achieves her most genuine conquest of pride and prejudice only after she has accepted the full social value of her judgment that "to be mistress of Pemberley might be something!"

Granting the full force of the snobbery, the exploitation, the inhumanity of all the evils which diminish the human spirit and which are inherent in a materialistic society, the novel clearly confirms the cynical "truth" of the opening sentence. Nevertheless, at the same time, without evading the degree of Elizabeth's capitulation to society, it affirms the vitality, the independent life that is possible at least to an Elizabeth Bennet. *Pride and Prejudice,* like its title, offers deceptively simple antitheses that yield up the complexity of life itself.

THE PRINCE

Type of work: Philosophy of politics
Author: Niccolò Machiavelli (1469–1527)
Time: Fifteenth and sixteenth centuries
Locale: Principally Italy
First Published: 1532

Principal Personages

Cesare Borgia, Duke of Valentinois and Romagna
Francesco Sforza, Duke of Milan
Pope Alexander VI, Roderigo Borgia, father of Cesare and Lucrezia Borgia
Pope Julius II
Caterina Sforza, Countess of Forli
Louis XII, King of France

This is the book that gives meaning to the critical adjective "Machiavellian." It is an ingenious and fascinating study of the art of practical politics, composed by a man who never rose higher than the position of secretary to the Second Chancery in Florence. The success of his book is due partly to his wit and partly to his having known some of the most clever and powerful rogues of the Renaissance. His model for the "Prince" was Cesare Borgia, a man who used all means of conquest, including murder, to achieve and hold political position.

Machiavelli never pretended that his book was a guide to the virtuous. On the other hand, he did not set out to prescribe the way to wickedness. He meant his account to be a practical guide to political power, and through a combination of experience, logic, and imagination he constructed one of the most intriguing handbooks of Western civilization: a primer for princes.

In beginning a discussion concerned with the manners and attitudes of a prince—that is, a ruler of a state—Machiavelli writes:

Since . . . it has been my intention to write something which may be of use to the understanding reader, it has seemed wiser to me to follow the real truth of the matter rather than what we imagine it to be. For imagination has created many principalities and republics that have never been seen or known to have any real existence, for how we live is so different from how we ought to live that he who studies what ought to be done rather than what is done will learn the way to his downfall rather than to his preservation.

This passage makes it clear that Machiavelli intended to explain how successful politicians actually work rather than how they ought to work.

The Prince begins with a one-paragraph chapter that illustrates Machiavelli's logical approach to the problem of advising prospective princes. He claims that all states are either republics or monarchies. Monarchies are either hereditary or new. New monarchies are either entirely new or acquired. Acquired states have either been dominated by a prince or been free; and they are acquired either by a prince's own arms or by those of others; and they fall to him either by fortune or because of his own character and ability.

Having outlined the modes of the state, Machiavelli first discusses the problems connected with governing a hereditary monarchy, and then goes on to discuss mixed monarchies. In each case, as his argument develops, Machiavelli considers what the logical alternatives are, and what should be done in each case if the prince is to acquire and hold power. In writing of mixed monarchies, for example, having pointed out that acquired states are either culturally similar to the conquering state or not, he then considers each possibility. If the acquired state is culturally similar, it is no problem to keep it; but if the acquired state is different in its customs, laws, or language, then there is a problem to be solved. One solution might be to have the ruler go to the acquired territory and live there. As an example, Machiavelli refers to the presence of the Turkish ruler in Greece.

Another possibility for solving the problem that arises when an acquired territory differs culturally from the conquering state is the establishment of colonies. Colonies are inexpensive to acquire and maintain, he argues, because the land is acquired from a few landowners of the conquered territory and they are the only ones who complain. Such a plan is preferable to maintaining soldiers, for policing a new state is expensive and, in addition, offends the citizens being policed.

Thus, by the somewhat mechanical device of considering logical alternatives, Machiavelli uses his limited experience to build a guide to power. Not only did Machiavelli, through his diplomatic missions, come to know intimately such leaders as Louis XII, Julius II, the Emperor Maximilian, and Cesare Borgia but he also used his time to advantage, noting political tricks that actually worked and building up his store of psychological truths.

It is doubtful that any ruler or rebel ever succeeded simply because he followed Machiavelli to the letter, but many political leaders have found his treatise to be essential reading. (Indeed, shortly after Fidel Castro's overthrow of the Batista government in Cuba in 1959, a newspaper account reported that among the books on Castro's revolutionary reading list was *The Prince*.)

What is inspiring for the politically ambitious in *The Prince* is not the substance but the attitude, not the prescription but the unabashed, calculating, and aggressive air with which the author analyzes the means to power.

For the reader without political ambition *The Prince* is a sometimes amusing and sometimes frightening reminder of the realities of political fortune. For example, Machiavelli writes that anyone who helps another to power is bound to fall himself because he has contributed to the success either by his cleverness or his power, and no prince can tolerate the existence of either in another person close to him.

Machiavelli considers this question: Why did the kingdom of Darius, occupied by Alexander the Great, not rebel after Alexander's death? The answer is that monarchies are governed either by a prince and his staff or by a prince and a number of barons. A monarchy controlled by the prince through his representatives is very difficult to conquer, since the entire staff owes its existence to the prince and is, consequently, loyal. Once such a monarchy is captured, however, power is easily maintained. So it was in Alexander's case. A nation like the France of Machiavelli's day, in contrast, is ruled by a king and barons. The barons are princes of a sort over their portions of the state, and they maintain control over their subjects. It is easy to conquer such a state because there are always unhappy barons willing to join a movement to overthrow the king. Once conquered, however, such a state is difficult to hold because the barons may regroup and overthrow the new prince.

Sometimes power is acquired through crime, Machiavelli admits, and he cites a violent example: the murder of Giovanni Fogliani of Fermo by his nephew Oliverotto. Machiavelli advises that the cruelty necessary to attain power be kept to a minimum and not be continued, for the purely practical reason that the prince will lose power otherwise. The best thing to do, says the author, is to commit one's acts of cruelty all at once, not over an extended period.

This cold practicality is echoed in such injunctions as if one cannot afford to be generous, accept with indifference the name of miser; it is safer to be feared than to be loved, if one must choose; a prince need not have a morally praiseworthy character, but he must *appear* to have it; if a prince's military support is good, he will always have good friends; to keep power one must be careful not to be hated by the people; it is always wiser for a prince to be a true friend or a true enemy than to be neutral; a prince should never listen to advice unless he asks for it; and it is better to be bold than cautious.

Machiavelli's prime examples are Francesco Sforza and Cesare Borgia, particularly the latter. The author writes that he is always able to find examples for his points by referring to the deeds of Borgia. Considering the value of using auxiliary arms, the military force of another state, Machiavelli refers to Borgia's unfortunate experience with auxiliaries in the capture of Romagna. Finding the auxiliaries untrustworthy, Borgia turned to mercenaries, but they were no better, so he finally used only his own troops. Machiavelli's conclusion in regard to auxiliary troops is that "If any one . . wants to make sure of not winning he will avail himself of troops such as these."

After reviewing Cesare Borgia's rise to power (with the remark that "I could not suggest better precepts to a new prince than the examples of Cesare's actions"), Machiavelli concludes that "I can find nothing with which to reproach him, rather it seems that I ought to point him out as an example . . . to all those who have risen to power by fortune or by the arms of others." This praise follows a description of such acts as Borgia's killing of as many of the hapless lords he had despoiled "as he could lay hands on."

Machiavelli praises the actions of other leaders, such as Francesco Sforza and Popes Alexander VI and Julius II, but only Cesare Borgia wins unqualified praise. Sforza, for example, is recognized as having become Duke of Milan "by the proper means and through his own ability," but later on he is criticized because of a castle he built when he should have been trying to win the good will of the people.

The Prince concludes with a plea to the Medici family to free Italy from the "barbarians" who ruled the republic of Florence and kept Italy in bondage. Machiavelli makes a plea for liberation, expresses his disappointment that Borgia is not available because of a turn of fortune, and closes with the capitalized cry that "THIS BARBARIAN OCCUPATION STINKS IN THE NOSTRILS OF ALL OF US."

Unfortunately for the author, his plea to the Medici family did him no good, and he died with the Republic still in power. Perhaps he himself was not bold enough; perhaps he was not cruel enough. In any case, he left behind a work to be used by any leader willing to be both.

PROMETHEUS BOUND

Type of work: Drama
Author: Aeschylus (525–456 B.C.)
Type of plot: Classical tragedy
Time of plot: Remote antiquity
Locale: A barren cliff in Scythia
First presented: Date unknown

In this compelling drama, Aeschylus offers the spectacle of a demigod in conflict with his destiny and defiant in the face of severe punishment. The mood of the play is one of sharp irony and deep reflection, for the suffering of the legendary Fire-Bearer symbolizes man's inhumanity to man.

Principal Characters

Prometheus, (prə·mē′thē·ŭs, prə·mē′thōōs), a Titan, the son of Themis (Earth). In the revolt of Zeus against Kronos, he had sided with Zeus and had provided the counsel by which the older gods had been overthrown. Later he persuaded Zeus to spare mankind, whom Zeus had planned to destroy. But he has broken the command of the king of the gods by bringing to men the gift of fire and instructing them in all the arts and crafts. For this flouting of the will of Zeus he is carried, a prisoner, by Kratos (Might) and Bia (Force) to a rocky cliff in remote Scythia, there to be fastened by Hephaestus to the crag and to remain bound for eternity. His only comfort in his anguish is his secret foreknowledge of the eventual downfall of Zeus. His knowledge of the future remains to him; he prophesies to Io the torments that await her; tells her that her descendant, Herakles, will finally release him, and declares that Zeus himself will one day be deposed by his own son, whose future identity only he, Prometheus, knows. This secret he refuses to divulge to Hermes, who brings the command of Zeus that Prometheus must reveal this all-important name on pain of even worse torments. Defiant to the last, Prometheus is blasted by the thunderbolt of Zeus and sinks into the underworld as the play ends. Prometheus is depicted in this drama as the embodiment of stubborn resistance against the tyranny of Zeus, willing to bear any punishment rather than submit. To the modern mind, and especially to the writers of the Romantic period, he is the personification of the revolt against tyranny of any sort, the symbol of man's war against the forces of reaction and of his eternal quest for knowledge.

Io (ī′ō), the daughter of the river-god Inachus, She was beloved by Zeus, who changed her into a heifer to save her from the jealous wrath of Hera. But the latter, penetrating her rival's disguise, sent a gadfly to torment her throughout the world. Half-crazed with pain, she has wandered to Scythia, where she finds in Prometheus a fellow sufferer. He prophesies her future adventures and traces her descendants down to Herakles, who will deliver him from his chains.

Hermes (hûr′mēz), the messenger of Zeus, sent to wring from Prometheus the secret of the identity of that son of Zeus who will overthrow his father. In his attitude, Hermes has been called the personification of prudent self-interest. He fails in his errand, for the dauntless Prometheus reviles him as a mere lackey and refuses to divulge the secret.

Hephaestus (hē·fĕs′təs), god of fire and of metal-working. He has been ordered by Zeus to forge the chains that fasten Prometheus to the rock and to drive an adamantine wedge through his breast. This horrible task he performs reluctantly, bowing only to the superior power of Zeus.

Oceanus (ō·sē′ə·nəs), god of the sea. He comes to sympathize with Prometheus and to preach to him the virtue of humility. He even offers to intercede on his behalf with Zeus. But Prometheus warns him that, in comforting a rebel, he himself may be charged with rebellion and urges him to depart.

Kratos (Might) and **Bia (Force),** brute beings who symbolize the tyranny of Zeus, for they carry out his will. They drag the captive Prometheus to the cliff in Scythia and supervise Hephaestus as he chains the Titan to the rock. Kratos taunts the fallen Titan, reminding him that the name Prometheus—the Contriver—has a terrible irony, for no contrivance can release him.

The Story

Condemned by Zeus for giving fire to mere mortals, the Titan Prometheus was brought to a barren cliff in Scythia by Hephaestus, the god of fire, and two guards, Kratos and Bia. There he was to be bound to the jagged cliffs with bonds as strong as adamant. Kratos and Bia obeyed willingly the commands of Zeus, but Hephaestus experienced pangs of sorrow and was reluctant to bind his kinsman to the storm-beaten cliff in that waste region where no man came, where Prometheus would never hear the voice or see the form of a human being. He grieved that the Titan was doomed forever to be guardian of the desolate cliff. But he was powerless against the commands of Zeus, and so at last he chained Prometheus to the cliff by riveting his arms beyond release, thrusting a biting wedge of adamant straight through his heart, and putting iron girths on both his sides with shackles around his legs. After Hephaestus and Bia departed, Kratos remained to hurl one last taunt at Prometheus, asking him what possible aid mankind might now offer their benefactor. The gods who gave Prometheus his name, Forethinker, were foolish, Kratos pointed out, for Prometheus required a higher intelligence to do his thinking for him.

Alone and chained, Prometheus called upon the winds, the waters, mother earth, and the sun, to look on him and see how the gods tortured a god. Admitting that he must bear his lot as best he could because the power of fate was invincible, he was still defiant. He had committed no crime, he insisted; he had merely loved mankind. He remembered how the gods first conceived the plan to revolt against the rule of Kronos and seat Zeus on the throne. At first Prometheus did his best to bring about a reasonable peace between the ancient Titans and the gods. Failing to do so and to avoid further violence, he sided with Zeus, who through the counsel of Prometheus overthrew Kronos. Once on the throne, Zeus parceled out to the lesser gods their share of power, but ignored mortal man with the ultimate plan of destroying him completely and creating instead another race which would cringe and be servile to Zeus's every word. Among all the gods, only Prometheus objected to this heartless proposal, and it was Prometheus' courage, his act alone, which saved man from burial in the deepest black of Hades. It was he who taught blind hopes to spring within man's heart and who gave him the gift of fire. Understanding the significance of these deeds, he had sinned willingly.

Oceanus, brother of Prometheus, came to offer aid out of love and kinship, but he first offered Prometheus advice and preached humility in the face of Zeus's wrath. Prometheus remained proud, defiant, and refused his offer of help on the grounds that Oceanus himself would be punished were it discovered that he sympathized with a rebel. Convinced by Prometheus' argument, Oceanus took sorrowful leave of his brother.

Once more Prometheus recalled that man was a creature without language, ignorant of everything before Prometheus came and told him of the rising and setting of stars, of numbers, of letters, of the function of beasts of burden, of the utility of ships, of curing diseases, of happiness and lurking evil, of methods to bring wealth in iron, silver, copper, and gold out of the earth. In spite of his torment, he rejoiced that he had taught all arts to humankind.

Io, a young girl changed into a heifer and tormented by a stinging gadfly, came to the place where Prometheus was chained. Daughter of Inachus, a river-god, she was beloved by Zeus. His wife, Hera, out of jealousy, had turned Io into a cow and set Argus, the hundred-eyed monster, to watch her. When Zeus had Argus put to death, Hera set a gadfly to sting Io and drive her all over the earth. Prometheus prophesied her future wanderings to the end of the earth, predicting that the day would come when Zeus would restore her to human form and together they would conceive a son named Epaphus. Before Io left, Prometheus also named his own rescuer, Hercules, who with his bow and arrow would kill the eagle devouring his vital parts.

Hermes, messenger of Zeus, came to see Prometheus and threatened him with more awful terrors at the hands of angry Zeus. Prometheus, still defiant, belittled Hermes' position among the gods and called him a mere menial. Suddenly there was a turbulent rumbling of the earth, accompanied by lightning, thunder, and blasts of wind, as angry Zeus shattered the rock with a thunderbolt and hurled Prometheus into an abysmal dungeon within the earth. Such was the terrible fate of the Fire-Bearer who defied the gods.

Critical Evaluation

In several ways *Prometheus Bound* is something of a puzzle. We do not know the date of its production, although we can safely assume it came rather late in Aeschylus' career, possibly between 466 B.C. and 456 B.C., which was the year of his death. Nor do we know its exact place in the Aeschylean trilogy on Prometheus, because this is the only surviving play; we know only that it was followed by a last play entitled *Prometheus Unbound*. Further, it is the one extant play by Aeschylus to deal directly with a metaphysical problem by means of supernatural characters, but even the questions it raises are unresolved. This drama is a mystery centering on a mystery.

The situation of the play is static: Prometheus is fastened to a Scythian crag for enabling mankind to live when Zeus intended to destroy this ephemeral creature. Once Hephaestus wedges and binds him down, Prometheus is immobile. Thereafter the theatrical movement lies in his visitors—the chorus of nymphs, Oceanus, Io, and Hermes. Essentially this is a drama of ideas, and those ideas probe the nature of the cosmos. We may forget that the characters are mainly extinct Greek gods, but the issues that Aeschylus raises are still very much alive today.

The Greeks loved a contest, and *Prometheus Bound* is about a contest of wills. On the one side is Zeus, who is omnipotent in this world, while on the other is Prometheus, who has divine intelligence. Neither will give an inch, for each feels he is perfectly justified. Zeus rules by right of conquest, and Prometheus resists by right of moral superiority. On Zeus's side are might and force, the powers of compulsion and tyranny, but Prometheus has knowledge and prescience. The play consists of a strange debate between the two. Zeus in his inscrutability and majesty does not appear, but we see his agents enforcing his will.

The drama begins and ends with the exercise of Zeus's almighty power. That power is used simply to make Prometheus suffer. At first it binds him to a crag and finally it envelops him in a cataclysm. Zeus has a fearsome capacity to inflict pain, not merely on Prometheus but on Io as well. In both instances it seems due to disobedience. If Prometheus opposed Zeus by giving man the fire and skills he needed to survive, Io resisted Zeus's love. Because of this Zeus exiled her from her home and changed her into a cow, while jealous Hera forced her to flee from land to land, bitten by a gadfly. Thus Prometheus shows rebellion on the divine plane (he being a Titan), while Io rebels on the human level. The price of their rebellion is written in their flesh, and both regard Zeus as their persecutor. Aeschylus certainly disliked political tyranny, but it is a mistake to read this play merely as a parable of man's inhumanity to man. The issues go far deeper.

Prometheus knew what would come of his revolt. He made a great personal sacrifice when he supported mankind out of compassion. In a real sense he is a savior and a tremendous hero. His knowledge does not keep him from suffering like man, nor does it make him accept his pain calmly. He knows why he suffers but still defies his fate. He feels that his is right and Zeus is wrong. Moreover, he claims that Zeus is not the ultimate power, that Zeus is subservient to the Fates and the Furies.

Yet Prometheus holds the winning hand in this play and he knows it, for he possesses a secret that Zeus needs to retain his power. No matter how much suffering Zeus may have caused him, one day Zeus will have to come begging. That is Prometheus' only consolation in torment. Every counsel to moderation or humility is superficial and vain, for why should Prometheus give up the joy of seeing Zeus humbled just to alleviate his own agony? This motivation comes through clearly in the bitter dialogue with Hermes.

Thus Prometheus is not only self-rightous and vengeful, but he is full of arrogant pride. He chooses his pain; perhaps he even deserves it. No one justifies Zeus, for he is beyond any notion of justice, but Prometheus exults in justifying himself to any divinity who will listen. Yet we remember his services to man and feel compassion for him. He is an authentic tragic hero, arousing both pity and fear.

As a dramatic character Io represents the human condition. The daughter of a god, she is shut out of her home by Zeus's command, given an animal's body, and made to run over the face of the earth in pain, stung by the ghost of many-eyed Argus (conscience). In the distant future, however, she and Zeus will be reconciled.

We can only guess at the resolution of the Zeus-Prometheus conflict that Aeschylus unveiled in the lost *Prometheus Unbound*. Possibly Zeus gained in maturity after centuries of rule and decided to release the Titan freely, after which Prometheus gave him the secret. Just as man evolved through the gifts of Prometheus into a civilized creature, perhaps Zeus changed and made his reign one of wisdom and force. It is hard to believe that Prometheus would alter unless such a change had come about in Zeus. This, however, is only speculation. The debate between Prometheus and Zeus remains open. Is Prometheus a rebel because God is unjust? Or is it that he places himself above God, doing what pleases him in the knowledge that he must suffer for it. Aeschylus never solves this dilemma in the play—he merely shows it to us in the strongest dramatic terms. Tautly written, *Prometheus Bound* is profound precisely because it remains an enigma. In judging the debate we judge ourselves.

PROMETHEUS UNBOUND

Type of work: Poem
Author: Percy Bysshe Shelley (1792–1822)
Type of plot: Lyric drama
Time of plot: Remote antiquity
Locale: Mythical realm, Asia
First published: 1820

Valuable as a key to understanding Shelley's philosophy, Prometheus Unbound *uses the combined mediums of drama and poetry to expound the author's theory that universal love is the only solution to mankind's ills.*

Principal Characters

Prometheus, a Titan punished by Jupiter for having befriended mankind. He is chained to a rocky cliff for three thousand years while eagles tear at his heart, but he will not repudiate the curse he has pronounced on Jupiter. Aided by spirits and gods, Prometheus is finally unbound. His freedom heralds an age of sweetness and light for mankind.

Jupiter, chief of the gods, who has had Prometheus bound to the cliff. As Prometheus is released, Jupiter loses his power and falls, impotent, into darkness.

Demogorgon, the supreme god and ruler of all gods, who finally reverses prevailing circumstances, thus causing Jupiter's downfall and Prometheus' release from torment.

Panthea and **Ione,** two Oceanids. Panthea and Asia, Prometheus' wife, learn from Demogorgon that Prometheus will be set free. They are Demogorgon's interlocutors as he explains what will come to pass on earth.

Herakles, the hero famous for his strength. Herakles, before spirits friendly to Prometheus, releases the captive from his bonds and torment.

Mercury, the messenger of the gods, sent by Jupiter to Prometheus to learn from the captive how long Jupiter will reign.

Earth, Prometheus' mother.

Asia, Prometheus' wife.

Phantasma of Jupiter, a wraith who appears to Prometheus to repeat for him the forgotten curse he had put on Jupiter.

The Furies, agents of torment who come with Mercury to punish further the bound Titan.

The Spirit of the Hour, one of a group of Hours, figures who move in Demogorgon's realm to show the passing of time by Age, Manhood, Youth, Infancy, and Death. The Spirit of the Hour announces Prometheus' release to all mankind and describes the pleasant things that will occur on earth now that the Titan is free.

The Story

Prometheus, the benefactor of mankind, was bound to a rocky cliff by order of Jupiter, who was jealous of the Titan's power. Three thousand years of torture Prometheus suffered there, while heat and cold and many torments afflicted him. An eagle continually ate at his heart. But Prometheus still defied the power of Jupiter.

At last Prometheus asked Panthea and Ione, the two Oceanides, to repeat to him the curse he had pronounced upon Jupiter when Jupiter had first begun to torture him. Neither Earth, his mother, nor the Oceanides would answer him. At last the Phantasm of Jupiter appeared and repeated the curse. When Prometheus heard the words, he repudiated them. Now that he had suffered tortures and found that his spirit remained unconquered, he wished pain to no living thing. Earth and the Oceanides mourned that the curse had been withdrawn, for they thought Jupiter had at last conquered Prometheus' spirit.

Then Mercury approached with the Furies. Mercury told the captive that he would suffer even greater tortures if he did not reveal the secret which Prometheus alone knew—the future fate of Jupiter. Jupiter, afraid, wished to avert catastrophe by learning the secret, and Mercury promised that Prometheus would be released if he revealed it, but Prometheus refused. He admitted only that he knew Jupiter's reign would come to an end, that he would not be king of the gods for all eternity. Prometheus said that he was willing to suffer torture until Jupiter's reign ended. Although the Furies tried to frighten him by describing the pains they could inflict, they knew they had no power over his soul.

The Furies mocked Prometheus and mankind. They showed him visions of blood and despair on earth; they showed the Passion of Christ and men's disregard for His message of love. Fear and hypocrisy ruled; tyrants took the thrones of the world.

A group of spirits appeared and prophesied that Love would cure the ills of mankind. They prophesied also that Prometheus would be able to bring Love to earth and halt the reign of evil and grief.

When the spirits had gone, Prometheus acknowledged the power of Love, for his love for Asia, his wife, had enabled him to suffer pain without surrendering.

While Asia mourned alone in a lovely valley for her lost husband, Panthea appeared to tell of two dreams she had had. In one, she saw Prometheus released from bondage and all the world filled with sweetness. In the other dream she had received only a command to follow. Just then the echoes in the valley broke their silence. They called Asia and Panthea to follow them. The listeners obeyed.

Asia and Panthea followed the echoes to the realm of Demogorgon, the supreme power ruling the gods. They stopped on a pinnacle of rock, but spirits beckoned them down into Demogorgon's cave. There he told them that he would answer any question they put to him. When they asked who had made the living world, he replied that God had created it. Then they asked who had made pain and evil. Prometheus had given knowledge to mankind, but mankind had not eradicated evil with all the gifts of science. They asked whether Jupiter was the source of these ills, the evil master over man.

Demogorgon answered that nothing which served evil could be master, for only eternal Love ruled all. Asia asked when Prometheus would gain his freedom and bring Love into the world to conquer Jupiter. Demogorgon then showed his guests the passage of the Hours. A dreadful

Hour passed, marking Jupiter's fall; the next hour was beautiful, marking Prometheus' release. Asia and Panthea accompanied this spirit of the Hour in her chariot and passed by Age, Manhood, Youth, Infancy, and Death into a new paradise.

Meanwhile, Jupiter, who had just married Thetis, celebrated his omnipotence over all but the soul of man. Then Demogorgon appeared and pronounced judgment on Jupiter. Jupiter cried for mercy, but his power was gone. He sank downward through darkness and ruin.

At the same time Herakles approached Prometheus. In the presence of Asia, Panthea, the Spirit of the Hour, and Earth, the captive was set free. Joyfully, Prometheus told Asia how they would spend the rest of their days together with Love. Then he sent the Spirit of the Hour to announce his release to all mankind. He kissed Earth, and Love infused all of her animal, vegetable, and mineral parts.

The Spirit of Earth came to the cave where Asia and Prometheus lived and told them of the transformation that had come over mankind. Anger, pride, insincerity, and all the other ills of man had passed away. The Spirit of the Hour reported other wonders that had taken place. Thrones were empty, and each man was king over himself, free from guilt or pain. He was still, however, subject to chance, death, and mutability, without which he would oversoar his destined place in the world.

Later in a vision Panthea and Ione saw how all the evil things of the world lay dead and decayed. Earth's happiness was boundless, and even the moon felt the beams of Love from Earth as snow melted on its bleak lunar mountains. Earth rejoiced that hate, fear, and pain had left mankind forever. Man was now master of his fate and of all the secrets of Earth.

Critical Evaluation

"I have," Shelley conceded in the preface to *Prometheus Unbound*, "a passion for reforming the world." For *Queen Mab* (1813) he had chosen three epigraphs; the first of these, printed in capital letters, was Voltaire's battle cry, "Écrasez l'infame"—destroy the monster—and the poem envisions universal regeneration through revolution. By 1818, though he had lost none of his zeal for reformation, he no longer regarded social or political change as the means for inaugurating a new golden age. Both *The Revolt of Islam* (1818) and *Prometheus Unbound* present love as the agent of universal change; internal renewal leads to external betterment.

Shelley chose Aeschylus rather than Plato as his model because he wanted to do more than merely present his ideas. He observed that "didactic poetry is my abhorrence," and though *Prometheus Unbound* must strike readers as having a design upon them, it transcends political or moral propaganda. The work not only describes the

transformation of the world but also seeks to create the environment that will allow reform to occur. Since each person's heart and mind must change before the world can be regenerated, the poem attempts to move as well as educate, where prose could accomplish only the latter.

Any philosophical poem runs the risk of becoming inaccessibly abstract. Shelley recognized the danger: "The imagery which I have employed will be found in many instances to have been drawn from the operations of the human mind, or from those external actions by which they are expressed." William Blake, whose prophetic books convey a message similar to that of *Prometheus Unbound*, created a personal mythology to embody his ideas. Shelley's poem is no less mythopoeic. He rejected a mere imitation of Aeschylus or John Milton but relied on an already existing framework, much as the Hellenic dramatists drew from Homer but interpreted material in their own way. As Shelley remarked, "The Agamemnonian story was exhibited on the Athenian theatre with as many variations as dramas."

For Shelley as for William Blake, mankind suffers because it has fallen into division. In the Age of Saturn, Shelley's equivalent of Blake's Beulah Land (and the biblical Garden of Eden), life was calm and simple, but people lacked "wisdom, which is strength." Prometheus gave this gift to Jupiter and to mankind; Shelley here interprets Promethean fire as knowledge, and he claims, contrary to the conventional myth, that Jupiter did not succeed against Saturn because of his own might but through Prometheus' intelligence.

Both Jupiter and humanity failed to use this gift as they should. When Jupiter tortures Prometheus in the first act, hoping to win the Titan to his side, his greatest torment is the vision of Christ, because Christ, like Prometheus, wanted to help the world. Instead, his name has "become a curse"; in the name of the God of love people kill, torture, and oppress. Shaken, Prometheus nonetheless says that he pities man, and once he utters that word pity, the Fury vanishes. In *Jerusalem* (1804–1820), Blake wrote that humanity, divided by anger, "must be united by/ Pity." So in *Prometheus Unbound* hate prevents the regeneration of the world. Asia asks Demogorgon the question that theologians and philosophers have always attempted to answer: "But who rains down/ Evil, . . .?—/ not Jove." Like Milton, Shelley attributes evil to man himself, and he uses Prometheus as humanity's representative as well as its benefactor.

As long as Prometheus hated Jupiter, the god could torture him and man. Having learned through suffering, Prometheus declares, "I wish no living thing to suffer pain," and thereby sets in motion the inevitable revolution. Like his mentor and father-in-law, William Godwin, Shelley believed that history is an amoral force—here embodied by Demogorgon—that can benefit or harm the world depending on how it is directed. For millennia hate has ruled; now a new age begins through pity. As Prometheus represented man in his state of hatred and subjugation, so he now reflects a regenerate humanity. In his former condition he was divided from Asia, signifying a severing of love (Asia) from intellect (Prometheus) and, more generally, man's alienation from himself. Shelley, who knew Plato well, may have had in mind

the statement in the *Timaeus* that at first everyone was hermaphroditic, and in the union of man and woman each seeks to regain that perfect state. Prometheus' pity not only compels the fall of Jupiter but also brings back Asia, in a symbolic restoration of the ideal, unified universe.

Since the revocation of Prometheus' curse in the first act sets in motion all subsequent action, the work has little dramatic tension. It might therefore more accurately be styled an extended lyric than a lyrical drama, for the musicality and majesty of the lines are of the highest order, earning favorable comparisons with Dante and Milton. Asia's song in the fifth scene of the second act has been set to music at least five times, and the entire piece has been scored at least three. Shelley's vision of harmonious nature echoes throughout the poem, particularly in the fourth act, which portrays a cosmic union as Earth woos the moon and engenders life on that formerly barren realm, representing on a macrocosmic scale the same process that joins Prometheus and Asia and showing that love is so powerful that it can make the moon fruitful. In mythic terms, one sees Diana converting to Venus.

Though man can find grace within himself, grace sufficient to change the world—it is interesting that the atheist Shelley and the Puritan Milton parallel each other in so many ways—"chance and death and mutability" remain; only in death does one enter Plato's realm of pure forms. Hence, as the symbol of the "amphisbaenic snake" (a snake with a head at either end) indicates, this regenerative process is reversible. Retaining happiness requires "Gentleness, Virtue, Wisdom and Endurance." In the triumphant paean that concludes the work, Demogorgon urges mankind to adhere to these virtues and so "be/ Good, great and joyous, beautiful and free;/ This is alone Life, Joy, Empire and Victory."

Shelley called *Prometheus Unbound* "the most perfect of my productions," and to Edward John Trelawney he observed, "If that is not durable poetry, tried by the severest test, I do not know what is. It is a lofty subject, not inadequately treated, and should not perish with me." He was right. To paraphrase Samuel Johnson's rhetorical question about Alexander Pope, if *Prometheus Unbound* is not great poetry, where is great poetry to be found?

RAMAYANA

Type of work: Poem
Author: Valmiki (fl. fourth century B.C.)
Type of plot: Religious epic
Time of plot: Remote antiquity
Locale: India
First transcribed: c. 350 B.C.

Although relatively unknown to Western readers, the Ramayana *is extremely popular throughout India, where it holds great religious significance. To the Western reader the characters may appear to be human beings with supernatural powers, roughly equivalent to certain figures in Greek legend and myth, but to Hindus the characters of the* Ramayana *are gods. Rama is a reincarnation of the Hindu god Vishnu, and he and his wife Sita represent the ideal man and woman.*

Principal Characters

Rama, King Dasa-ratha's son, partly an incarnation of Vishnu. The handsomest and strongest of the king's four sons, he wins Sita for his bride by bending the mighty bow of King Janak. Though his aging father wishes him to become regent, he is forced by Queen Kaikeyi into a fourteen-year exile, from which he finally returns triumphant to his throne.

Sita, Rama's wife, daughter of King Janak and the Earth Mother. She accompanies her husband into exile and is abducted by Ravan. Although she manages to remain faithful to Rama during her captivity, rumors of unfaithfulness are spread abroad and believed by her husband and the people. Finally her virtue is proved, but the Earth Mother takes her away from those who have doubted her.

Dasa-ratha, Rama's father, king of the Kosalas, who wishes his son to be regent but must send him, instead, into exile because of an old promise made to Queen Kaikeyi.

Queen Kaikeyi, one of King Dasa-ratha's wives and the mother of Bharat. Promised two boons by her husband, she asks that Rama be sent into exile and that Bharat be made regent.

Bharat, Rama's half brother. Though forced into the regency by Queen Kaikeyi, he recognizes Rama's claim to the throne, which he holds for him.

Lakshman, Rama's loyal brother and companion during his exile.

Satrughna, another of Rama's half brothers.

Mandavi, Urmila, and **Srutka-kriti,** Rama's sisters-in-law.

King Janak, Sita's father, who offers her as a bride to the one who bends his mighty bow.

The Earth Mother, Sita's mother, who takes her daughter back among the gods when her virtue is questioned by Rama and his people.

Ravan, demon-king of Lanka. He abducts Sita but is finally overthrown by Rama.

Bharad-vaja, Valmiki, and **Agastya,** hermits and holy men.

Hanuman, a leader of the monkey people.

Manthara, Queen Kaikeyi's maid.

The Story

King Dasa-ratha of the Kosalas, who kept his court at Ayodhya, had four sons, though not all by the same mother. According to legend, the god Vishnu, in answer to King Dasa-ratha's supplications, had given a divine liquor to each of the king's wives, so that they might bring forth sons, each of whom was partly an incarnation of Vishnu. Of the sons born, Rama was the handsomest and strongest of all, his mother having drunk more of the magic beverage than Dasa-ratha's other wives.

When Rama grew to manhood he heard of Sita, beautiful, talented, and virtuous daughter of King Janak and the Earth Mother. King Janak was the possessor of a wondrous bow, a mighty weapon that had belonged to the gods, and King Janak resolved that whoever could bend the bow should have Sita for his wife. The king knew, of course, that no ordinary mortal could possibly accomplish the feat.

Rama and his brothers traveled to the court of King Janak and were granted permission to try drawing the mighty bow. With ease Rama bent the bow, with such strength that the weapon snapped in two. King Janak promised that Sita should be Rama's bride and that each of his half brothers, too, should have a noble bride from the people of Videha.

So Sita became the wife of Rama; her sister Urmila became the bride of Lakshman, Rama's favorite brother; Mandavi and Sruta-kriti, cousins of Sita, became the wives of Bharat and Satrughna, the other half brothers of Rama. When all returned to Ayodhya, Dasa-ratha, fearing the rivalry between his children might create unhappiness and tragedy in his house, sent Bharat and Satrughna to live with their mothers' people.

Years passed, and King Dasa-ratha grew old. Wishing to have the time and opportunity to prepare himself for the next life, he proposed that Rama, his favorite son, should become regent. The king's council and the populace rejoiced in the proposal, and plans were made to invest Rama with the regency and place him on the Kosala throne. Before the preparations had been completed, however, Manthara, a maid to Queen Kaikeyi, one of King Dasa-ratha's wives, advised the queen that Rama's succession to the throne should be prevented and that Bharat, Queen Kaikeyi's son, should become regent. The ill advice was heard, and Queen Kaikeyi remembered that she had been promised two boons by her husband. So when King Dasa-ratha came to her, she asked that Bharat should be made regent and that Rama should go into exile for fourteen years. King Dasa-ratha was sad, but he had given his word and he must fulfill his promises. Like a dutiful son, Rama heard his father's decision and prepared to go into exile. He expected to go alone, but his wife Sita and his brother Lakshman prepared to go with him to share his lonely and uncomfortable exile in the dismal Dandak forest. The Kosala people mourned his departure and accompanied him on the first day of his journey away from Ayodhya.

Leaving his native country, Rama journeyed south. He and his companions crossed the Ganges River and came to the hermitage of Bharad-vaja, a holy man. After visiting with him, they went on to the hill of Chitrakuta, where stood the hermitage of Valmiki, a learned and holy man. There they learned that King Dasa-ratha had died the day after Rama's departure from Ayodhya, remembering in his hour of death a curse laid on him by a hermit whose son he had accidentally killed. Rama stayed with Valmiki for a time. Bharat returned to Ayodhya to become regent, as his mother had planned. However, he recognized Rama's claim and set out on a journey to find Rama and to ask him to become King of the Kosalas. But Rama, having given his word, remained in exile as he had vowed to do. Bharat returned to Avodhya to place Rama's sandals on the throne as a symbol of Rama's right to the kingship.

In order that his kinsmen might not find him again, Rama left Valmiki's hermitage and after a long journey he established his own hermitage near the dwelling of Agastya, a holy and learned man. There Rama, Sita, and Lakshman lived in peace until they were disturbed by a demon-maiden, enamored of Rama, who had been repulsed in her addresses by both Rama and Lakshman. Spurned and seeking revenge, she went to her brother, Ravan, demon-king of Lanka (Ceylon) and asked his help. Ravan was a powerful being who through asceticism had achieved power even over the gods. His domination, according to legend, could be broken only by an alliance of men and the monkey people. Ravan sent a demon in the disguise of a deer to lead Rama astray while on the hunt. When Rama failed to return, Sita insisted that Lakshman go look for him. In the absence of the brothers, Ravan came and abducted Sita.

Rama, having learned what had happened, allied himself with the monkey people in order to make war upon the demons and win back his beloved wife. Hanuman, one of the monkey people's leaders, found Sita at Ravan's palace and led Rama and the forces of the monkey people to Ceylon. There Ravan's city was besieged and many battles were fought, with combat between the great leaders of both sides and pitched battles between the forces of good and evil. Finally Ravan and his demon forces were defeated, Ravan was killed, and Sita was rescued and restored to her husband. Sita, who had remained faithful to Rama throughout her captivity, proved in an ordeal by fire that she was still virtuous and worthy to be Rama's wife.

Rama, Sita, and Lakshman returned in triumph to Ayodhya, where Rama was welcomed and became king of the Kosala people. Rumors were spread, however, that Sita had not been faithful to her husband; at last Rama sent his wife away, and she went to live at the hermitage of Valmiki. Shortly after her arrival at the hermitage, she gave birth to Rama's sons.

More years passed and the two sons grew up, tutored in their youth by the wise Valmiki, who took his charges eventually to Ayodhya. There Rama, recognizing them as his sons, sent for Sita and had her conducted to his court. Since her virtue had been in doubt she was asked for a token that she had been true to her marriage vows. The earth opened to a great chasm, and the Earth Mother herself rose up on her throne to speak on behalf of Sita and to take her to the land of the gods. Thus Sita was taken away from the husband and the people who had doubted her.

Critical Evaluation

The *Ramayana* is one of two great Hindu epics; the other is the earlier *Mahabharata*. Whereas the *Mahabharata* is genuinely a heroic (or "folk") epic deriving from an oral tradition, the *Ramayana* is more nearly like a literary epic, written in conscious imitation of the heroic-folk tradition. But whatever the original may have been, the *Ramayana* has been altered many times by subsequent rewriting and recension. In its extant versions, the *Ramayana* contains about 24,000 couplets (less than one-fourth the length of the *Mahabharata*) and is divided into seven books, as compared with the eighteen books of *Mahabharata*. In terms of conventional Western epic form, the Greek heroic-folk epic contains twenty-four books; the English literary epic contains twelve. Of the seven books of the *Ramayana*, the central story is found in books two through six. Book 1 is introductory. Book 7 appears to be a species of an appendix called *Uttara*, or "Supplemental," and provides both epilogue to and critique of the foregoing six books. It also provides instruction for the recital of the *Ramayana* by minstrels in much the same way that medieval *enseignements* coached jongleurs in their repertoire and their performance. Finally, the *Ramayana*, like most Western epics and unlike the *Mahabharata*, has unity, which stems from concentration on one main story.

One of the major themes in the central narrative is the relationship between destiny and volition, with the consequent consideration of personal responsibility or the lack of it. The key questions ultimately revolve around the power of the gods, for the obligatory nature of human promises hinges upon belief in the divine prerogative of retribution. Hence, King Dasa-ratha rescinds his proposal that Rama should succeed him as regent in order to honor his prior promise of Queen Kaikeyi. So, too, Rama dutifully accepts Bharat as regent and goes into exile, in deference to the king's expressed wishes (really, the gods' demands). Just as Rama accepts his fate, so also his brother Lakshman and his wife Sita accept theirs. But while Lakshman simply does his duty and perseveres, Sita is subjected to the most stringent of tests. After being kidnaped by Ravan, she is called upon to prove her virtue. The trial being so debilitating, Sita is finally rescued by her Earth Mother. All of these claims upon human endurance require intervention by the gods. The message of the *Ramayana* thus seems to be that human volition is subservient to divine will. The corollary also appears to establish the social order as subject to the divine order.

Closely allied to the theme of free will versus fate is the theme of duty. One aspect of this theme of duty is Rama's behavior, often cited as a model for other men to emulate. Rama's submission to his father's decision, his acceptance of exile, and his fidelity to his promise to remain in exile all bespeak Rama's filial piety and deference to duty. This view of duty follows the pattern traditional for warriors, princes, and kings; as such, it is compatible with ideals presented in the *Mahabharata* as well as with Western ethical assumptions. The other, and more important, aspect of the theme of duty is less conventional as an issue proper to epic consideration, for it concerns not wars and the affairs of state, the usual epic

grist, but human love and domestic matters. This aspect of duty, then, deals with Sita's story, which, all things considered, constitutes the main plot line in the epic. Sita, like Rama, is held up as an exemplar of ideal behavior—for women. Her behavior is characterized by sweetness, tenderness, obedience, patient suffering, and, above all, faithfulness; her piety and self-sacrifice ultimately qualify her for relief from mortal travail by being reabsorbed into her Earth Mother. She endures all without complaint and thus becomes a model of the perfect woman, wife, and mother, her image of duty unalloyed.

The *Ramayana* also deals with typical Hindu motifs. There is, for example, the Brahman's curse which King Dasa-ratha remembered on his deathbed. Also, there is the asceticism, as exemplified in Valmiki's hermitage and in Rama's own abstemious life after leaving Valmiki's hermitage. In addition, this asceticism reflects another Hindu value; the emphasis on social order, which is manifested in the caste system. The orderly functioning of society, with all people acknowledging their proper places in it, is a high priority in the Hindu ethos. Furthermore, the concepts of truth and duty provide the definitive guidelines for action. Truth and duty go hand in hand to create twin obligations for Dasa-ratha and Bharat as well as Rama and Sita and every devout Hindu. And the didactic elements of the *Ramayana* reinforce these typical Hindu motifs; most explicitly, the teachings of Valmiki convey the precepts. But the implicit message of the plot and of the human interaction conveys the ethical and moral substance even more clearly. Thus the Hindu ideals of faith and conduct are both taught and demonstrated in the *Ramayana*.

In addition to the Hindu motifs as well as the themes of duty and free will versus fate, the *Ramayana* also presents an interesting juxtaposition of the natural and the supernatural. The central narrative begins with the natural or "real-world" events: the political machinations at the court of King Dasa-ratha; the banishment of Rama, Sita, and Lakshman; and the death of King Dasa-ratha and the subsequent dilemma of Bharat when Rama refuses the throne. But the next half of the narrative deals with the supernatural: the intrusion of the demon-maiden; the intervention of Ravan; the alliance with the monkey people; the real and allegorical battle between the forces of good and the forces of evil; and the Earth Mother's absorption of Sita. This combination of natural and supernatural worlds synthesizes the ethical and spiritual concerns of Hinduism, incorporating the concepts of fatalism and duty. Through this synthesis, the *Ramayana* goes beyond the confines of a national cultural epic to become part of the sacred literature of Hinduism. As such, it joins company with the *Mahabharata*, the Vedas, the *Brahmanas*, the Upanishads, and the *Puranas*. This religious perspective has made the *Ramayana* one of the best known and best loved works in India.

THE RAPE OF THE LOCK

Type of work: Poem
Author: Alexander Pope (1688–1744)
Type of plot: Mock-heroic epic
Time of plot: Early eighteenth century
Locale: London
First published: 1712

The Rape of the Lock, generally considered the most popular of Pope's writings as well as the finest satirical poem in the English language, was written at the suggestion of John Caryll, Pope's friend, ostensibly to heal a family row which resulted when an acquaintance of Pope, Lord Petre, playfully clipped a lock of hair from the head of Miss Arabella Fermor. Pope's larger purpose in writing the poem, however, was to ridicule the social vanity of his day and the importance that was attached to the affected manners.

Principal Characters

Belinda, the poetic name of Arabella Fermor, an upper-class English girl. She is a beautiful young woman, vain of her appearance, who loves her spaniel. Though she is normally quite agreeable, she flies into a horrid rage when Lord Petre snips off one of her treasured curls.

Lord Petre, a young nobleman, one of Belinda's suitors. He admires Belinda so much that he wants one of her curls as a keepsake and snips it off at a party when she bends her head over a cup. He refuses to return the curl, and it disappears to become a star.

Ariel, Belinda's guardian spirit. He tries to warn her that something dreadful may happen and sets a guard of sylphs to protect his charge, but he is unsuccessful in preventing the loss of the lock of hair.

Umbriel, a spirit who takes over when Ariel leaves Belinda. He is a melancholy gnome who receives horrible noises, tears, sorrows, and griefs from the queen of bad tempers. He pours his magic substances over Belinda, magnifying her rage and sorrow.

Thalestris, Belinda's friend, a militant girl. She fans Belinda's rage by saying that the girl's honor is at stake in the matter of the stolen curl. She demands that Belinda's brother force Lord Petre to give the lock.

Clarissa, one of Belinda's acquaintances, who wonders openly at the vanity of women and the foolishness of men.

Sir Plume, Belinda's brother, who considers the entire affair slightly ridiculous. Prodded by Thalestris, he demands that Lord Petre relinquish the lock, but Petre refuses.

Shock, Belinda's beloved spaniel.

Spleen, the queen of bad tempers and the source of detestable qualities in human beings. She supplies Umbriel with magical substances.

Betty, Belinda's maid.

The Story

At noon, when the sun was accustomed to awaken both lapdogs and lovers, Belinda was still asleep. She dreamed that Ariel appeared to whisper praises of beauty in her ear. He said that he had been sent to protect her because something dreadful—what, he did not know—was about to befall her. He also warned her to beware of jealousy, pride, and above all, men.

After Ariel had vanished, Shock, Belinda's lapdog, thought that his mistress had slept long enough, and he awakened her by the lappings of his tongue. Rousing herself, Belinda spied a letter on her bed. After she had read it, she promptly forgot everything that Ariel had told her, including the warning to beware of men. Aided by her maid, Betty, Belinda began to make her toilet. Preening before her mirror, she was guilty of the pride against which Ariel had cautioned her.

The sun, journeying across the sky, witnessed its brilliant rival, Belinda, boating on the Thames with her friends and suitors. All eyes were upon her; like the true coquette, she smiled at her swains but favored no one more than another. Lord Petre, one of Belinda's suitors, admired a lock of her hair and vowed that he would have it by fair means or foul. So set was he on getting the lock that before the sun rose that morning he had built an altar to Love and had thrown on it all the trophies received from former sweethearts, meanwhile asking Love to give him soon the prize he wanted and to let him keep it for a long time. Love, however, was to grant him only half his prayer.

Everyone except Ariel seemed happy during the cruise on the Thames. That sprite summoned his aides and reminded them that their duty was to watch over the fair

Belinda—one sylph to guard her fan, another her watch, a third her favorite lock. Ariel himself was to guard Belinda's lapdog, Shock. Fifty sylphs were dispatched to watch over the maiden's petticoat, in order to protect her chastity. Any negligent sylphs, warned Ariel, would be punished severely.

After her cruise on the Thames, Belinda, accompanied by Lord Petre and the rest of the party, visited one of the palaces near London. There Belinda decided to play ombre, a Spanish card game, with two of her suitors, including Lord Petre. As she played, invisible sylphs sat on her important cards to protect them. Coffee was served after the game. Sylphs guarded Belinda's dress to keep it from being spotted. The fumes from the coffee sharpened Lord Petre's wits, inspiring him to devise new stratagems for stealing Belinda's lock. One of his cronies handed him a pair of scissors. The sylphs, aware of Belinda's danger, attempted to warn her before Lord Petre could act, but as the maid bent her head over her coffee cup, he clipped the lock. Even Ariel was unable to warn Belinda in time. At the rape of her lock, Belinda shrieked in horror. Lord Petre cried out in triumph. He praised the steel used in the scissors, comparing it to the metal of the Greek swords that overcame the Trojans. Belinda's fury was boundless; Ariel wept bitterly and flew away.

Umbriel, a melancholy gnome, took advantage of the human confusion and despair to fly down to the center of the earth to find the gloomy cave of Spleen, the queen of bad tempers and the source of every detestable quality in human beings, including ill-nature and affectation. Umbriel asked the queen to touch Belinda with chagrin, for he knew that if she were gloomy and melancholy, bad temper would spread to half the world. Spleen granted Umbriel's request and collected in a bag horrible noises such as those uttered by female lungs and tongues. In a vial she put tears, sorrows, and griefs. She gave both containers to Umbriel.

When the gnome returned to Belinda's world, he found the girl disheveled and dejected. Pouring the contents of the magic bag over her, Umbriel caused Belinda's wrath to be magnified many times. One of her friends, Thalestris, fanned the flames of the maiden's anger by telling her that her honor was at stake and that behind her back her friends were talking about the rape of her lock. Thalestris then went to Belinda's brother, Sir Plume, and demanded that he confront Lord Petre and secure the return of the precious lock. Sir Plume considered the whole episode absurd, but he went to demand Belinda's lock. Lord Petre refused to give up his prize.

Next, Umbriel broke the vial containing human sorrows, and Belinda was almost drowned in tears. She regretted having entered society and having learned to play ombre, she longed for simple country life. Suddenly she remembered, too late, that Ariel had warned her of impending evil.

In spite of Thalestris' pleas, Lord Petre was adamant. Clarissa, another of Belinda's circle, wondered at the vanity of women and at the foolishness of men who fawn before them. Clarissa insisted that both men and women need good sense; in making her feelings known, however, she exposed the tricks and deceits of women and caused Belinda to frown. Calling Clarissa a prude, Thalestris gathered her forces to battle Belinda's enemies, including Clarissa and Lord Petre. Umbriel was delighted by this Homeric struggle. Belinda pounced upon Lord Petre, who was subdued when a pinch of snuff caused him to sneeze violently. She demanded the lock, but it could not be found. Some thought that it had gone to the moon, where love letters and other tokens of tender passions go, but the muse of poetry saw it ascend to heaven and become a star.

Critical Evaluation

When Robert Lord Petre cut off a lock of Arabella Fermor's hair one fateful day early in the eighteenth century, he did not know that the deed would gain worldwide fame, attracting attention over several centuries. Nor, perhaps, did he foresee the ill feeling his act would create between the Petre and Fermor families. The story would probably have been soon lost amid the trivia of family histories, had not John Caryll asked his good friend the poet Alexander Pope to write a little poem about the episode, one that would show the comic element of the family quarrel and thus help heal it.

What began as a trivial event became, under the masterly guidance of Pope's hand, one of the most famous poems in the English language, and perhaps the best example of burlesque we have. *The Rape of the Lock* was begun at Caryll's behest ("The verse, to Caryll, Muse! is due") in 1711; Pope spent about two weeks on it and produced a much shorter version than the one he wrote two years later; making more additions in 1717, he then developed the final draft of the poem as it now stands.

The poem as we have it uses the essentially trivial story of the stolen lock of hair as a vehicle for making some sophisticated comments on society and man. Pope draws on his own classical background—he had translated the *Iliad* and the *Odyssey*—to combine epic literary conventions with his own keen, ironic sense of the values and societal structures shaping his age. The entire poem, divided into five cantos, is written in heroic couplets. Pope makes the most of this popular eighteenth century verse form (rhymed iambic pentameter lines), using devices such as balance, antithesis, bathos, and puns.

The burlesque genre typically takes trivial subjects and elevates them to seemingly great importance; the effect is comic. Pope defines his tasks as showing "What dire offense from amorous causes spring,/ What mighty contests rise from trivial things." From the opening lines of the poem, suggestions of the epic tradition are clear. Pope knew well not only the *Iliad* and the *Odyssey* but also John Milton's *Paradise Lost*. The narrator of *The Rape of the Lock* harks back to Homer, raising the epic question early in the poem: "Say what strange motive, goddess! could compel/ A well-bred lord t'assault a gentle belle?" Pope's elaborate description of Belinda's toilet in canto 1 furthers comparison with the epic; it parodies the traditional epic passage describing warriors' shields. Belinda's makeup routine is compared to the putting on of armor: "From each she nicely culls with curious toil,/ And decks the goddess with the glittering spoil."

The effect of using epic conventions is humorous, but it also helps establish a double set of values in the poem, making the world of Belinda and Sir Plume at the same time trivial and significant. Epic conventions contribute to this double sense in each canto: Canto 1 features the epic dedication and invocation, canto 2 the conference of protective gods, canto 3 the games and the banquet, canto 4 the descent into the underworld, and canto 5 the heroic encounters and apotheosis. In the midst of a basically silly situation, there are characters such as Clarissa who utter the always sensible virtues of the eighteenth century:

> Oh! if to dance all night, and dress all day,
> Charmed the smallpox, or chased old age away,
> Who would not scorn what housewife's cares produce,
> Or who would learn one earthly thing of use?
> . . . .
> But since, alas! frail beauty must decay,
> . . . .
> And she who scorns a man must die a maid;
> What then remains but well our power to use,
> And keep good humor still what'er we lose?

In these lines from canto 5, Clarissa expresses the norm of Pope's satire: the intelligent use of reason to control one's temperamental passion.

The heroic couplet merges perfectly with the epic devices in the poem. As a verse form, the heroic couplet seems naturally to evoke larger-than-life situations; it is, therefore, profoundly to Pope's credit that he successfully applies such a stanzaic pattern to a trivial subject. The critic Maynard Mack has said that Pope "is a great poet because he has the gift of turning history into symbol, the miscellany of experience into meaning."

Pope, perhaps more than anyone else writing poetry in the eighteenth century, demonstrated the flexibility of the heroic couplet. Shaped by his pen, it contains pithy aphorisms, social commentary, challenging puns, and delightful bathos. (The last of these juxtaposes the serious with the trivial, as in the line "Wrapped in a gown for sickness and for show.") But the key, if there is a key, to the enduring popularity of *The Rape of the Lock* is the use of the heroic couplet to include—sometimes in great

cataloged lists—those minute, precise, and most revealing details about the age and the characters that peopled it. The opening lines of canto 3 illustrate Pope's expert use of detail. The passage describes court life at Hampton Court, outside London, and is a shrewd comment on the superficiality of the people there:

> Hither the heroes and the nymphs resort
> To taste awhile the pleasures of a court;
> In various talk the instructive hours they passed,
> Who gave the ball, or paid the visit last;
> One speaks the glory of the British Queen,
> And one describes a charming Indian screen;
> A third interprets motions, looks, and eyes;
> At every work a reputation dies.
> Snuff, or the fan, supply each pause of chat,
> With singing, laughing, ogling, and all that.

The poet's criticism of such life is clear by the swift juxtaposition of Hampton Court life to a less pretty reality in the following lines:

> Meanwhile, declining from the noon of day,
> The sun obliquely shoots his burning ray;
> The hungry judges soon the sentence sign,
> And wretches hang that jurymen may dine.

Though always its critic, Pope had a keen interest in the life of London's aristocracy. A Catholic by birth, he was not always in favor with the Crown, but before the queen's death in 1714 he enjoyed meeting with a group of Tories, including Jonathan Swift, John Arbuthnot, Francis Atterbury, and Thomas Parnell. Richard Steele and Joseph Addison, England's first newspaper editors, courted him on behalf of the Whig party, but he refused to become its advocate.

Forbidden by law from living within several miles of London, he lived much of his adult life at Twickenham, a village on the Thames. He transformed his dwelling there into an eighteenth century symbol, with gardening and landscaping; he included vineyards, and the house had a temple and an obelisk to his mother's memory. During the 1720s he built a grotto, an underpass connecting his property under a dividing road; it was a conversation piece, with, according to one contemporary, bits of mirror on the walls which reflected "all objects of the river, hills, woods, and boats, forming a moving picture in their visible radiations." For Pope, who suffered throughout his life from the effects of a disease contracted in childhood, one that permanently disfigured his spine, the grotto was a symbol of the philosophic life and mind. Pope enjoyed great literary fame even during his lifetime, and near the end of his life, when he entered a room whispers of "Mr. Pope, Mr. Pope" would buzz among the occupants.

THE RED AND THE BLACK

Type of work: Novel
Author: Stendhal (Marie-Henri Beyle, 1783–1842)
Type of plot: Psychological realism
Time of plot: Early nineteenth century
Locale: France
First published: *Le Rouge et le noir,* 1830 (English translation, 1898)

In this novel whose chief character is a villain, Stendhal analyzes the psychological undercurrents of Julien Sorel's personality, showing how struggle and temptation shaped his energetic but morbidly introspective nature. The novel is considered Stendhal's greatest work, equally for its portrait of Sorel and its satire of French society during the Bourbon restoration.

Principal Characters

Julien Sorel (zhü-lyăṅ' sô·rĕl'), a son of a lawyer but an opportunist whose brilliant intellect, great ambition, and self-pride elevate him for a time, only to defeat him in the end. The youthful protégé of a local priest in the French town of Verières, Julien becomes the beloved tutor of the mayor's children and the lover of that aristocratic official's wife. Brazen, hypocritical, but shrewd, this contradictory hero espouses Napoleonic sentiments yet believes that his own salvation is through the Church. Pushed by scandal into a seminary, he proudly stands aloof from its politics and manages to become a secretary to one of the first men in France. Though he is insensitive to all feelings, his intellect again raises him in esteem to the point where he seduces as well as is seduced by the nobleman's daughter, a lively, intellectual young woman. Playing both ends against the middle—the middle being a respected position and a respectable income—he brings about his own downfall through attempted murder of his first mistress after she has revealed his villainy to his noble benefactor.

Madame de Rênal (də rĕ·nàl'), Julien Sorel's first mistress and greatest love, a beautiful, compassionate, though bigoted woman. Although she vacillates always between religiosity and passion, she truly loves the ascetic-looking younger man and dies shortly after he has been executed for his attempt to kill her. Her allegiance to the tutor is the more remarkable because of her clever deceptions, necessary to prevent an immediate tragedy brought about by her husband's vindictiveness. In the end religiosity predominates; she is torn by anguish, remorse, and guilt and dies while embracing her children three days after the death of her lover.

Monsieur de Rênal (mə·syœ' də rĕ·nàl'), the miserly mayor and village aristocrat, who desperately seeks status by hiring a tutor for his children. Vulgar and greedy to an extreme, this boorish landowner is elevated by the Marquis de La Mole, who later became Julien's employer. He loses his wife to a commoner's love and his position to his republican enemy.

Mathilde de La Mole (mà·tēld' də là môl'), a proud, intelligent aristocrat destined to become a duchess but fated to love out of her class. Desirous of the unexpected and bored with the conventionality of her life, she at first seeks distraction in lovemaking with Julien Sorel. When he pretends boredom, she pursues him shamelessly. Her pregnancy sets off a chain of tragic events which will leave her unborn child without name or father. After Julien's execution her romantic nature causes her to initiate the deed of a famous ancestress; she buries her lover's head and decorates his cave tomb with marble so that it resembles a shrine.

The Marquis de La Mole (də là môl'), a peer of France and the wealthiest landowner in the province. He is a subtle, learned aristocrat who through caprice gambles on a young man's genius, through kindness makes a gentleman of him, and through pride in family negotiates his downfall. Although he admires his brilliant secretary, the marquis can never rid himself of his social ambitions for his beautiful and intelligent daughter, and to bring about Julien Sorel's downfall he conspires to gain incriminating evidence against the young man.

The Marquise de La Mole, an aristocrat proud of her noble ancestors.

The Comte de La Mole, their son, a pleasant young man conditioned to fashionable Parisian life, in which ideas are neither encouraged nor discussed.

Fouqué (foō·kā'), a bourgeois but devoted friend of Julien Sorel. Acting as ballast for his mercurial friend, he offers Julien a good position in his lumber business, financial support for his studies, and finally his whole fortune to free him after his arrest.

The Abbé Chélan (shā·läṅ'), the local parish priest, who teaches and advances the fortune of Julien Sorel. The first to discover the tragic duality of protégé's nature, he nevertheless supports him in his ambitions and grieves over his misadventures.

The Abbé Pirard (pē·ràr'), the director of the seminary at Besançon, where Julien Sorel studies. He obtains for his brilliant pupil the post of secretary to the Marquis de La Mole. An irascible Jansenist among Jesuits, this learned priest sees in Sorel genius and contradiction. In spite of these contradictions, Pirard helps to elevate the youth to the munificence of courtly Paris.

Monsieur Valenod (vȧ-lə·nō′), a provincial official

grown prosperous on graft. Jealous because Monsieur de Rênal has hired a tutor for his children and because his own advances to Madame de Rênal have been unsuccessful, he writes an anonymous letter that reveals the love affair between Julien Sorel and his employer's wife.

The Story

Julien Sorel was the son of a carpenter in the little town of Verrières, France. Napoleon had fallen, but he still had many admirers, and Julien was one of these. Julien pretended to be deeply religious. Now that Napoleon had been defeated, he believed that the church rather than the army was the way to power. Because of his assumed piety and his intelligence, Julien was appointed as tutor to the children of Monsieur de Rênal, the mayor of the village.

Madame de Rênal had done her duty all of her life. Although she was a good wife and a good mother, she had never been in love with her husband, a coarse man who would hardly inspire love in any woman. Madame de Rênal was attracted to the pale young tutor and fell completely in love with him. Julien, thinking it his duty to himself, made love to her in order to gain power over her. He discovered after a time that he had really fallen in love with Madame de Rênal.

When Julien went on a holiday to visit Fouqué, a poor friend, Fouqué tried to persuade Julien to go into the lumber business with him. Julien declined; he enjoyed too much the power he held over his mistress.

The love affair was revealed to Monsieur de Rênal by an anonymous letter written by Monsieur Valenod, the local official in charge of the poorhouse. He had become rich on graft, and he was jealous because Monsieur de Rênal had hired Julien as a tutor. He had also made unsuccessful advances to Madame de Rênal at one time.

The lovers were able to smooth over the situation to some extent. Monsieur de Rênal agreed to send Julien to the seminary at Besançon, principally to keep him from becoming tutor at Monsieur Valenod's house. After Julien had departed, Madame de Rênal was filled with remorse. Her conscience suffered because of her adultery, and she became extremely religious.

Julien did not get on well at the seminary, for he found it full of hypocrites. The students did not like him and feared his sharp intelligence. His only friend was the Abbé Pirard, a highly moral man.

One day Julien went to help decorate the cathedral and by chance found Madame de Rênal there. She fainted, but he could not help her because his duties called him elsewhere. The experience left him weak and shaken.

The Abbé Pirard lost his position at the seminary because he had supported the Marquis de La Mole, who was engaged in a lawsuit against Monsieur de Frilair, Vicar

General of Besançon. When the Abbé Pirard left the seminary, the marquis obtained a living for him in Paris. He also hired Julien as his secretary.

Julien was thankful for his chance to leave the seminary. On his way to Paris he called secretly upon Madame de Rênal. At first she repulsed his advances, conscious of her great sin. At last, however, she yielded once again to his pleadings. Monsieur de Rênal became suspicious and decided to search his wife's room. To escape discovery, Julien jumped out the window, barely escaping with his life.

Finding Julien a good worker, the marquis entrusted him with many of the details of his business. Julien was also allowed to dine with the family and to mingle with the guests afterward. He found the Marquise de La Mole to be extremely proud of her nobility. Her daughter, Mathilde, seemed to be of the same type, a reserved girl with beautiful eyes. Her son, the Comte de La Mole, was an extremely polite and pleasant young man. Julien, however, found Parisian high society boring. No one was allowed to discuss ideas.

Julien enjoyed stealing volumes of Voltaire from the marquis' library and reading them in his room. He was astonished when he discovered that Mathilde was doing the same thing. Before long, they began to spend much of their time together, although Julien was always conscious of his position as servant and was quick to be insulted by Mathilde's pride. The girl fell in love with him because he was so different from the dull young men of her own class.

After Julien had spent two nights with her, Mathilde decided that it was degrading to be in love with a secretary. Her pride was an insult to Julien. Smarting, he planned to gain power over her and, consequently, over the household.

Meanwhile the marquis had entrusted Julien with a diplomatic mission on behalf of the nobility and clergy who wanted the monarchy reestablished. On his mission Julien met an old friend who advised him how to win Mathilde again. Upon his return he put his friend's plan into effect.

He began to pay court to a virtuous lady who was often a visitor in the de La Mole home. He began a correspondence with her, at the same time neglecting Mathilde. Then Mathilde, thinking that Julien was lost to her, discovered how much she loved him. She threw herself at his feet. Julien had won; but this time he would not let her gain the upper hand. He continued to treat Mathilde coldly as her passion increased. In this way he maintained his power.

Mathilde became pregnant. She was joyful, for now, she thought, Julien would know how much she cared for him. She had made the supreme sacrifice; she would now have to marry Julien and give up her place in society. Julien, however, was not so happy as Mathilde over her condition, for he feared the results when Mathilde told her father.

At first the marquis was furious. Eventually, he saw only one way out of the difficulty; he would make Julien rich and respectable. He gave Julien a fortune, a title, and a commission in the army. Overwhelmed with his new wealth and power, Julien scarcely gave a thought to Mathilde.

Then the marquis received a letter from Madame de Rênal, whom Julien had suggested to the marquis for a character recommendation. Madame de Rênal was again filled with religious fervor; she revealed to the marquis the whole story of Julien's villainy. The marquis immediately refused to let Julien marry his daughter.

Julien's plans for glory and power were ruined. In a fit of rage he rode to Verrières, where he found Madame de Rênal at church. He fired two shots at her before he was arrested and taken off to prison. There he promptly admitted his guilt, for he was ready to die. He had his revenge.

Mathilde, still madly in love with Julien, arrived in Verrières and tried to bribe the jury. Fouqué arrived and begged Julien to try to escape, but Julien ignored the efforts of his friends to help.

He was tried, found guilty, and given the death sentence, even though his bullets had not killed Madame de Rênal. In fact, his action had only rekindled her passion for him. She visited him and begged him to appeal his sentence. The two were as much in love as they had been before. When Monsieur de Rênal ordered his wife to come home, Julien was left again to his dreams. He had lost his one great love—Madame de Rênal. The colorless Mathilde only bored and angered him by her continued solicitude.

Julien went calmly to his death on the appointed day. The faithful Fouqué obtained the body in order to bury it in a cave in the mountains, where Julien had once been fond of going to indulge in his daydreams of power.

According to a family legend a woman had once loved a famous ancestor of Mathilde's with an extreme passion. When the ancestor was executed, the woman had taken his severed head and buried it. Mathilde, who had always admired this family legend, did the same for Julien. After the funeral ceremony at the cave, she dug a grave with her own hands and buried Julien's head. Later, she had the cave decorated with Italian marble.

Madame de Rênal did not go to the funeral; but three days after Julien's death, she died while embracing her children.

Critical Evaluation

Stendhal's *The Red and the Black* is one of the most polished and refined stories in the literary crown of European literature. Stendhal took the French novel from the hands of Romantic writers such as Chateaubriand and honed it into a rapier of social criticism and philosophical exposition. It is the content of Stendhal's novels that marks him as a harbinger, one who influenced a century of Continental literary epigones. He was the first French writer to battle with the social and philosophical implications inherent in the modern creed known as liberalism. Because liberalism was the prevailing doctrine of the emergent French middle class, and because Stendhal sought to assess the social attitudes of that class, he must be considered as the first significant bourgeois novelist. *The Red and the Black* amalgamates the best of Stendhal's abilities as refiner and innovator.

Like each of Stendhal's novels *The Red and the Black* is autobiographical. Published in 1830, the work reflects the author's ideas rather than the outer events of his life. Thus to appreciate fully the novel, it is necessary to know the background of Stendhal's life and the broad social developments which determined the writer's complex and often contradictory *Weltanschauung*.

Stendhal was born into a provincial bourgeois family in Grenoble. His family background was a mixture of contradictions. The father was a businessman of the middle class whose aggressive, pragmatic, Philistine habits the son professed to loathe. His mother's aristocratic family, however, attracted him. To Stendhal, the family appeared to live a balanced, harmonious life with its social as well as cultural influences. It was a world of social hierarchy where all classes knew their place. Yet despite his preference for the world of the provincial aristocrat, Stendhal followed a life which was markedly bourgeois in orientation and philosophy. He implicitly accepted the liberal ideas articulated in the French Revolution and became an avid supporter of Napoleon, the personification of French liberalism. Napoleon championed the notion of a French civil service staffed by men of talent rather than of high birth as had been the case in the pre-Napoleonic world. The writer launched his career within Napoleon's regime. He marched through Europe within Napoleon's armies and was present in the retreat from Moscow. Following Napoleon's defeat, Stendhal exiled himself to Milan, Italy. He returned to Paris in 1821 and compromised his values to the ultraconservative political climate then existing in France. It was not a difficult compromise since the official values espoused in Paris were similar to those expressed by the maternal side of Stendhal's family. Stendhal's life in France between 1821 and 1830 was similar to that of the hero of *The Red and the Black*, Julien Sorel. He carried the social and intellectual baggage appropriate for survival in the intricate Parisian world.

Liberalism was the intellectual cloak of the French Revolution and Napoleon the child of the revolution. In Stendhal's France, the most important arrow in a liberal's quiver was his belief in self-determination. The liberal felt that man was basically reasonable and hence perfectible; he believed that man needed a society where talent could freely rise to its highest level of accomplishment and find expression in whatever political, economic, or intellectual manner deemed appropriate by the individual. This creed naturally appealed to those segments of French society which had been prevented by aristocratic privilege from assuming worthwhile positions in the French civil service. Stendhal aimed to make his mark in France by ascribing to this philosophy. Yet, however much Sten-

dhal might have believed in French liberalism, or thought he believed in it, he was still troubled—aristocrat that he partly was—by the lack of hierarchy in the liberal vision of society. Indeed, Julien's love affairs for Madame de Rênal, the wife of the provincial bourgeois mayor, and Mathilde de La Mole, the daughter of a French aristocrat, are symbolic of his own intellectual "affairs" with modern bourgeois liberalism and traditional aristocratic conservatism.

Was it possible to fuse such disparate social attitudes? Where were the limits on a person's right to individual self-determination? What were the social implications of such a philosophy? In an attempt to answer these questions, Stendhal wrote *The Red and the Black*. Stendhal's own confusion about his social values does not detract from the impact of his novel; in fact, it only enhances its historical value, for French society suffered from the same confusion. Thus, *The Red and the Black* is both a personal testament and a social document, a creative fusion of diverse and even contradictory elements into an artistic unity.

THE RED BADGE OF COURAGE

Type of work: Novel
Author: Stephen Crane (1871–1900)
Type of plot: Impressionistic realism
Time of plot: Civil War
Locale: A Civil War battlefield
First published: 1895

Marking a dramatic departure from the traditional treatment of war in fiction, this novel ignores powerful generals and historic victories and defeats in favor of probing the personal reactions of unknown foot soldiers fighting unknown enemies in skirmishes of indeterminate outcome. Henry Fleming is motivated not by courage or patriotism but by cowardice, fear, and finally egoism, and events in the novel are all filtered subjectively through his consciousness.

Principal Characters

Henry Fleming, a young recruit under fire for the first time in an unnamed battle of the Civil War, possibly Chancellorsville. A farm boy whose struggle with his emotions might be that of the eternal recruit in any battle of any war, Henry has dreamed of fighting heroically in "Greeklike" battles. Irritated and unnerved by his regiment's inactivity, he tortures himself with the fear that he may run away when the actual firing begins. He does so. Sheepishly rejoining his regiment, he learns that his cowardice is not known to his fellow soldiers. In the next attack he keeps firing after the others have stopped. When a color-bearer falls, he picks up the flag and carries it forward. Later he hears that the colonel has complimented his fierceness. Henry's psychological battle with himself is now ended; it has gone from fear to cowardice to bravery and, finally, to egotism.

Jim Conklin, "the tall soldier," a veteran who comforts Henry and squabbles with the braggart Wilson. He predicts that the regiment is about to move into battle. When it does so, he is mortally wounded. Henry and "the tattered man" find him stumbling to the rear, still on his feet, fearful of falling under the wheels of an artillery wagon. He wanders into a field, as if it were a place of rendezvous with death. Henry and the tattered man follow him, trying to bring him back. He brushes them off and, with a great convulsion, drops dead.

Wilson, "the loud one." At first he seems confident, absolutely sure of his courage. But as the battle begins he suddenly thinks he may be killed, and he turns a packet of letters over to Henry Fleming. After the first attack he asks for the return of the letters. Some of his loudness and swagger is now gone. He and Henry struggle to get the flag from the fallen color-bearer. Henry seizes it, but Wilson aids him in going forward and setting an example to the wavering troops.

"The Tattered Man," a soldier encountered by Henry Fleming just after he has run away. The man embarrasses the recruit by asking where he is wounded. Later he and Henry follow Jim Conklin into the field. The soldier is so impressed by the manner of Jim's death that he calls the dead man a "jim-dandy." Then he cautions Henry to "watch out fer ol' number one."

Lieutenant Hasbrouck, a young officer of Henry Fleming's company. He is shot in the hand in the early part of the battle but is able to drive a fleeing soldier back into the ranks and tries vainly to stop the disorganized retreat. He later compliments Henry and Wilson by calling them "wild cats."

Colonel MacChesnay, the officer who also compliments Henry Fleming and Wilson. He is berated by the general, shortly after Henry's advance with the flag, for not forcing the partial success of the charge to a complete one.

The Story

The tall soldier, Jim Conklin, and the loud soldier, Wilson, argued bitterly over the rumor that the troops were about to move. Henry Fleming was impatient to experience his first battle, and as he listened to the quarreling of the seasoned soldiers he wondered if he would become frightened and run away under gunfire. He questioned Wilson and Conklin, and each man stated that he would stand and fight no matter what happened.

Henry had come from a farm, where he had dreamed of battles and longed for army life. His mother had held him back at first. When she saw that her son was bored with the farm, she packed his woolen clothing and with a warning that he must not associate with the wicked kind of men who were in the military camps sent him off to join the Yankee troops.

One gray morning Henry awoke to find that the regiment was about to move. With a hazy feeling that death would be a relief from dull and meaningless marching, Henry was again disappointed. The troops made only another march. He began to suspect that the generals were stupid fools, but the other men in his raw regiment scoffed at his idea and told him to shut up.

When the fighting suddenly began, there was very little action in it for Henry. He lay on the ground with the other men and watched for signs of the enemy. Some of the men around him were wounded. He could not see what was going on or what the battle was about. Then an attack came. Immediately Henry forgot all his former confused thoughts, and he could only fire his rifle over and over; around him men behaved in their strange individual manner as they were wounded. Henry felt a close comradeship with the men at his side who were firing at the enemy with him.

Suddenly the attack ended. To Henry it seemed strange that the sky above should still be blue after the guns had stopped firing. While the men were recovering from the attack, binding wounds, and gathering equipment, another surprise attack was launched from the enemy line. Unprepared and tired from the first fighting, the men retreated in panic. Henry, sharing their sudden terror, ran too.

When the fearful retreat had ended, the fleeing men learned that the enemy had lost the battle. Now Henry felt a surge of guilt. Dreading to rejoin his companions, he fled into the forest. There he saw a squirrel run away from him in fright. The fleeing animal seemed to vindicate in Henry's mind his own cowardly flight; he had acted according to nature whose own creatures ran from danger. Then seeing a dead man lying in a clearing, Henry hurried back into the retreating column of wounded men. Most were staggering along in helpless bewilderment, and some were being carried on stretchers. Henry realized that he had no wound and that he did not belong in that group of staggering men. There was one pitiful-looking man, covered with dirt and blood, wandering about dazed and alone. Everyone was staring at him and avoiding him. When Henry approached him, the young boy saw that the soldier was Jim Conklin. He was horrified at the sight of the tall soldier. He tried to help Jim, but with a wild motion of despair Jim fell to the ground dead. Once more Henry fled.

His conscience was torturing him. He wanted to return to his regiment to finish the fight, but he thought that his fellow soldiers would point to him as a deserter. He envied the dead men who were lying all about him. They were already heroes; he was a coward. Ahead he could hear the rumbling of artillery. As he neared the lines of his regiment, a retreating line of men broke from the trees ahead of him. The men ran fiercely, ignoring him or waving frantically at him as they shouted something he

could not comprehend. He stood among the flying men, not knowing what to do. One man hit him on the head with the butt of a rifle.

Henry went on carefully, the wound in his head hurting him a great deal. He walked for a long while until he met another soldier, who led Henry back to his regiment. The first familiar man Henry met was Wilson. Wilson, who had been a terrible braggart before the first battle, had given Henry a packet of letters to keep for him in case he were killed. Now Henry felt superior to Wilson. If the man asked him where he had been, Henry would remind him of the letters. Lost was Henry's feeling of guilt; he felt superior now, his deeds of cowardice almost forgotten. No one knew that he had run off in terror. Wilson had changed. He no longer was the swaggering, boastful man who had annoyed Henry in the beginning. The men in the regiment washed Henry's head wound and told him to get some sleep.

The next morning Wilson casually asked Henry for the letters. Half sorry that he had to yield them with no taunting remark, Henry returned the letters to his comrade. He felt sorry for Wilson's embarrassment. He felt himself a virtuous and heroic man.

Another battle started. This time Henry held his position doggedly and kept firing his rifle without thinking. Once he fell down, and for a panicky moment he thought that he had been shot, but he continued to fire his rifle blindly, loading and firing without even seeing the enemy. Finally someone shouted to him that he must stop shooting, that the battle was over. Then Henry looked up for the first time and saw that there were no enemy troops before him. Now he was a hero. Everyone stared at him when the lieutenant of the regiment complimented his fierce fighting. Henry realized that he had behaved like a demon.

Wilson and Henry, off in the woods looking for water, overheard two officers discussing the coming battle. They said that Henry's regiment fought like mule drivers, but that they would have to be used anyway. Then one officer said that probably not many of the regiment would live through the day's fighting. Soon after the attack started, the color bearer was killed and Henry took up the flag, with Wilson at his side. Although the regiment fought bravely, one of the commanding officers of the army said that the men had not gained the ground that they were expected to take. The same officer had complimented Henry for his courageous fighting. He began to feel that he knew the measure of his own courage and endurance.

His outfit fought one more engagement with the enemy. Henry was by that time a veteran, and the fighting held less meaning for him than had the earlier battles. When it was over, he and Wilson marched away with their victorious regiment.

Critical Evaluation

The Red Badge of Courage, Stephen Crane's second novel (*Maggie: A Girl of the Streets* had appeared under a pseudonym in 1893) and his most famous work, has often been considered the first truly modern war novel. The war is the American Civil War, and the battle is presumed to be the one fought at Chancellorsville, though neither the war nor the battle is named in the novel. Nor is there mention of Abraham Lincoln or the principal battle generals, Joseph Hooker (Union) and Robert E. Lee and "Stonewall" Jackson (Confederate). This is by design, since Crane was writing a different kind of war novel. He was not concerned with the causes of the war, the political and social implications of the prolonged and bloody conflict, the strategy and tactics of the commanding officers, or even the real outcome of a battle in which the combined losses were nearly thirty thousand men (including "Stonewall" Jackson, mistakenly shot in darkness by one of his own men).

From beginning to end, the short novel focuses upon one Union Army volunteer. Though other characters enter the story and reappear intermittently, they are distinctly minor, and they are present primarily to show the relationship of Henry Fleming (usually called only "the youth") to one person, to a small group of soldiers, or to the complex war of which he is such an insignificant part.

Much of the story takes the reader into Henry's consciousness. We share his boyish dreams of glory, his excitement in anticipating battle action, his fear of showing fear, his cowardice and flight, his inner justification of what he has done, his wish for a wound to symbolize a courage he has not shown (the ironic gaining of his false "red badge"), his secret knowledge of the badge's origin, his "earning" the badge as he later fights fiercely and instinctively, his joy in musing on his own bravery and valiant actions, his anger at an officer who fails to appreciate his soldiery, and his final feeling that "the great death" is, after all, not a thing to be feared so much. Now, he tells himself, he is a man. In centering the story within the consciousness of an inexperienced youth caught in a war situation whose meaning and complexities he cannot understand, Crane anticipates Ford Madox Ford, Ernest Hemingway, and other later novelists.

Crane has been called a realist, a naturalist, an impressionist, and a symbolist. He is all of these in *The Red Badge of Courage*. Though young Stephen Crane had never seen a battle when he wrote the novel, he had read about the experience of war; he had talked with veterans and had studied history under a Civil War general; and he had imagined what it would be like to be a frightened young man facing violent death amid the confusion, noise, and turmoil of a conflict which had no clear meaning to him. Intuitively he wrote so realistically that several early reviewers concluded that only an experienced soldier could have written the book. After Crane had later seen the Greeks and Turks fighting in 1897 (he was a journalist reporting the war), he told Joseph Conrad, "My picture of war was all right! I have found it as I imagined it."

Although naturalistic passages appear in the novel, Crane portrays in Henry Fleming not a helpless chip floating on the indifferent ocean of life but a youth sometimes impelled into action by society or by instinct yet also capable of consciously willed acts. Before the first skirmish Henry wishes he could escape from his regiment and considers his plight:" . . . there were iron laws of tradition and law on four sides. He was in a moving box." In the second skirmish he runs "like a rabbit." When a squirrel in the forest flees after Henry throws a pine cone at him, Henry justifies his own flight: "There was the law, he said. Nature had given him a sign." But he is not content to look upon himself as on the squirrel's level. He feels guilt over his cowardice. When he carries the flag in the later skirmishes, he is not a terrified chicken or rabbit or squirrel but a young man motivated by pride, by a sense of belonging to a group, and by a determination to show his courage to an officer who had scornfully called the soldiers in his group a lot of "mule drivers."

From the beginning, critics have both admired and complained about Crane's impressionistic writing and his use of imagery and symbols in *The Red Badge of Courage*. Edward Garnett in 1898 called Crane "the chief impressionist of our day" and praised his "wonderful fervour and freshness of style." Joseph Conrad (himself an impressionist) was struck by Crane's "genuine verbal felicity, welding analysis and description in a continuous fascination of individual style," and Conrad saw Henry as "the symbol of all untried men." By contrast, one American critic in 1898 described the novel as "a mere riot of words" and condemned "the violent straining after effect" and the "absurd similes." Though H. G. Wells liked the book as a whole, he commented on "those chromatic splashes that at times deafen and confuse in the *Red Badge*, those images that astonish rather than enlighten."

Yet judging by the continuing popularity of *The Red Badge of Courage*, most readers are not repelled by Crane's repeated use of color—"blue demonstration," "red eyes," "red animal—war," "red sun"—or by his use of images— "dark shadows that moved like monsters," "The dragons were coming," guns that "belched and howled like brass devils guarding a gate." Only in a few passages does Crane indulge in "arty" writing—"The guns squatted in a row like savage chiefs. They argued with abrupt violence"—or drop into the pathetic fallacy—"The flag suddenly sank down as if dying. Its motion as it fell was a gesture of despair." Usually the impressionistic phrasing is appropriate to the scene or to the emotional state of Henry Fleming at a particular moment, as when, after he has fought, he believes, heroically, the sun shines "now bright and gay in the blue, enameled sky."

A brilliant work of the imagination, *The Red Badge* *of Courage* will endure as what Crane afterward wrote a friend he had intended it to be, "a psychological portrayal of fear."

REMEMBRANCE OF THINGS PAST

Type of work: Novel
Author: Marcel Proust (1871–1922)
Type of plot: Psychological realism
Time of plot: Late nineteenth and early twentieth centuries
Locale: France
First published: *Á la recherche du temps perdu*, 1913–1927 (English translation, 1922–1931, 1981): *Du côté de chez Swann*, 1913 (*Swann's Way*, 1922); *Á l'ombre des jeunes filles en fleurs*, 1919 (*Within a Budding Grove*, 1924); *Le Côté de Guermantes*, 1920–1921 (*The Guermantes Way*, 1925); *Sodome et Gomorrhe*, 1922 (*Cities of the Plain*, 1927); *La Prisonnière*, 1925 (*The Captive*, 1929); *Albertine disparue*, 1925 (*The Sweet Cheat Gone*, 1930); *Le Temps retrouvé*, 1927 (*Time Regained*, 1931).

The title of this seven-novel work reveals Proust's twofold concern of time lost and time recalled. The writing is distilled from memory, the structure determined entirely by moods and sensations evoked by time passing or seeming to pass, recurring or seeming to recur. For Proust the true realities of human experience are not contained in a reconstruction of remembered scenes and events, but in the capture of physical sensations and moods re-created in memory. Symphonic in design, the work unfolds without plot or crisis as the writer reveals the motifs of his experience from childhood to middle age, holds them for thematic effect, and drops them, only to return to them once more in the processes of recurrence and change.

Principal Characters

Marcel (màr·sĕl′), the narrator who tells the story of his life from unsettled childhood to disillusioned middle age. Dealing with time lost and time recalled, Marcel says, as he looks back to a crucial childhood experience when his mother spent the night in his room instead of scolding him for his insomnia, that memory eliminates precisely that great dimension of Time which governs the fullest realization of our lives. Through the years, from his memory of that childhood experience to his formulation of this concept of time, Marcel sees the principals of two social sets spurn each other, then intermingle with the change of fortunes. He experiences love in various forms: an innocent affair with a friend's daughter, an adolescent passion for the friend's coquettish wife, an intermittent love affair with a lesbian. He develops friendships and animosities among individuals in the different social levels on which he moves. Reminded, by seeing the daughter of his childhood sweetheart, that he is old, he realizes the futility of his life and senses the ravages of time on everyone he has known.

Monsieur Swann (swän′), a wealthy broker and aesthete, and a friend of Marcel's parents. Swann, having known the Comte de Paris and the Prince of Wales, moves from level to level in the social milieu. Having married beneath his station, he knows that wealth sustains his social position and keeps his fickle wife dependent on him. Jealous and unhappy in courtship and marriage, he manipulates social situations by cultivating officers and politicians who will receive his wife. He dies, his life having been an meaningless as Marcel sees his own to

be; in fact, Marcel sees in his own life a close parallel to that of his sensitive friend.

Madame Swann, formerly **Odette de Crécy,** a courtesan. A woman whose beauty is suggestive of Botticelli's paintings, she is attractive to both men and women. Stupid and uncomprehending, Odette continues affairs with other men after her comfortable marriage. She introduces Swann to the social set below his own. Despite her beginnings, she moves to higher levels and becomes a celebrated, fashionable hostess when she remarries after Swann's death.

Gilberte Swann (zhēl·bĕrt swän′), the Swann's daughter and Marcel's playmate in Paris. Their relationship develops into an innocent love affair, and they remain constant good friends after Gilberte's marriage to Marcel's close friend, Robert de Saint-Loup. The sight of Gilberte's daughter, grown up, reminds Marcel that he himself is aging.

Madame de Villeparisis (də vē·yə·pà·rē·zē′), a society matron and the friend of Marcel's grandmother. It is said that her father ruined himself for her, a renowned beauty when she was young. She has become a dreadful, blowsy, hunched-up old woman; her physical deterioration is comparable to the decline of her friends' spiritual selves.

Robert de Saint-Loup (rô·bĕr′ də săṅ′-lōō′), her nephew, whom she introduces to Marcel. Their meeting is the beginning of a friendship that lasts until Robert's death in World War I. In his courtship and marriage, Robert suffers from the same insecurity, resulting in jealousy, that plagues Swann and Marcel in their relations with women. He marries Gilberte Swann.

Monsieur de Charlus (mə·syœ′ də shår·lüs′), another of Mme. de Villeparisis' nephews, a baron. The baron, as he is usually referred to, is a sexual invert who has affairs with men of many different stations in life. In his aberration the baron is both fascinating and repulsive to Marcel, who makes homosexuality a chief discussion in the volume titled *Cities of the Plain*. The baron's depravity leads to senile old age.

Madame Verdurin (vĕr·dü·răṅ′), a vulgar person of the bourgeoisie who, with her husband, pretends to despise the society to which they have no entrée. Odette introduces Swann to the Verdurins. Mme. Verdurin crosses social lines as she comes into money and marries into the old aristocracy after her first husband dies. The middle-class Verdurins seem to surround themselves with talented individuals, and many of their guests become outstanding in their professions and arts.

The Prince and Princess de Guermantes (də gĕr·mäṅt′), members of the old aristocracy and the family used by Proust in the volume titled *The Guermantes Way*, to delineate the social classes, the Guermantes representing aristocratic group as opposed to the moneyed society described in *Swann's Way*. After the princess dies, the prince, ruined by the war, marries widowed Mme. Verdurin. Their union is further evidence of social mobility.

The Duke and Duchess de Guermantes, members of the same family. After Odette's rise on the social scale, the duchess is received in Odette's salon. In earlier years the duchess left parties to avoid meeting the vulgar social climber.

Albertine (ål·bĕr·tēn′), a lesbian attracted by and to Marcel. Over an extended period of time their affair takes many turns. Marcel seeks comfort from her when his grandmother dies; he is unhappy with her and wretched without her; his immaturity drives her from him and back to her home in Balbec. A posthumous letter to Marcel, after Albertine is killed in a fall from a horse, tells of her intention to return to him.

Marcel's Grandmother, a woman known and revered in both the aristocratic and the merely fashionable social sets. Marcel loves and respects her, and her death brings into focus for him the emptiness in the lives of his smart, wealthy friends.

Monsieur Vinteuil (väṅ·tē·yül′), an old composer in Combray. He dies in shame because of his daughter's association with a woman of questionable character. Unhappy in his own life, Vinteuil's music brings pleasure to many. Among those affected is Swann, moved to marry Odette, his mistress, because he associates the charm of Vinteuil's exquisite sonatas with the beauty of the cocotte. Marcel, also captured by the spirit of Vinteuil's music, senses its effect on various listeners.

Rachel (rå·shĕl′), a young Jewish actress who becomes famous. Although she is Robert de Saint-Loup's mistress, she despises him because of his simplicity, breeding, and good taste. Rachel likes the aesthetic charlatans she considers superior to her devoted lover.

Dr. Cottard (kôt·tår′), a social boor because of his tiresome punning and other ineptitudes, a guest at the Verdurins' parties. He becomes a noted surgeon, professionally admired.

Elstir (ĕl·stēr′), a young man Marcel meets at Verdurins'. He becomes a painter whose genius is admired.

Madame de Saint-Euverte (ə săṅ·tœ·vĕrt′), a hostess whose parties attract both the old and new friends of Swann, to his displeasure at times.

The Princess des Iaunes (dā lōn′), a long-time friend of Swann and guest in Mme. de Saint-Euverte's salon. She is distressed at her friend's unhappiness, caused by lowering himself to Odette's level.

Morel (mô·rĕl′), the musician who, at the Verdurins' party, plays Vinteuil's compositions. Morel is a protégé of the perverted Baron de Charlus.

Jupien (zhü·pyăṅ′), a tailor. After becoming the object of de Charlus' affection he establishes a house for affairs among men.

Monsieur de Norpoie (də nôr·pwå′), an ambassador who, as Marcel finally realizes, has been Mme. de Villeparisis' lover for many years.

Aunt Léonie (lā·ô·nē′), Marcel's aunt. At the end he likens himself to her as he recalls her from his childhood, when she had become an old hypochondriac.

The Story

All of his life Marcel found it difficult to go to sleep at night. After he had blown out the light, he would lie quietly in the darkness and think of the book he had been reading, of an event in history, of some memory from the past. Sometimes he would think of all the places in which he had slept—as a child in his great-aunt's house in the provincial town of Combray, in Balbec on a holiday with his grandmother, in the military town where his friend, Robert de Saint-Loup, had been stationed, in Paris, in Venice during a visit there with his mother.

He remembered always a night at Combray when he was a child. Monsieur Swann, a family friend, had come to dinner. Marcel had been sent to bed early, where he lay for hours nervous and unhappy until at last he heard Monsieur Swann leave. Then his mother had come upstairs to comfort him.

For a long time, the memory of that night was his chief recollection of Combray, where his family took him to spend a part of every summer with his grandparents and aunts. Years later, while drinking tea with his mother, the taste of a small sweet cake suddenly brought back all the impressions of his old days at Combray.

He remembered the two roads. One was Swann's way, a path that ran beside Monsieur Swann's park where the lilacs and hawthorns bloomed. The other was the Guermantes way, along the river and past the château of the Duke and Duchess de Guermantes, the great family of Combray. He remembered the people he saw on his walks. There were familiar figures like the doctor and the priest. There was Monsieur Vinteuil, an old composer who died brokenhearted and shamed because of his daughter's friendship with a woman of bad reputation. There were the neighbors and friends of his grandparents. Best of all, he remembered Monsieur Swann, whose story he pieced together slowly from family conversations and village gossip.

Monsieur Swann was a wealthy Jew accepted in rich and fashionable society. His wife, Odette de Crécy, was not received, however, for she was his former mistress and a prostitute with the fair, haunting beauty of a Botticelli painting. It was Odette who had first introduced Swann to the Verdurins, a vulgar family that pretended to despise the polite world of the Guermantes. At an evening party given by Madame Verdurin, Swann heard played a movement of Vinteuil's sonata and identified his hopeless passion for Odette with that lovely music. Swann's love was an unhappy affair. Tortured by jealousy, aware of the vulgarity and pettiness of the Verdurins, determined to forget his unfaithful mistress, he went to Madame de Saint-Euverte's reception. There he heard Vinteuil's music again. Under its influence he decided, at whatever price, to marry Odette.

After their marriage Swann drifted more and more into the bourgeois circle of the Verdurins. When he went to see his old friends in Combray and in the fashionable Faubourg Saint-Germain, he went alone. Many people thought him both ridiculous and tragic.

On his walks Marcel sometimes saw Madame Swann and her daughter, Gilberte, in the park at Combray. Later, in Paris, he met the little girl and became her playmate. That friendship, as they grew older, became an innocent love affair. Filled also with a schoolboyish passion for Madame Swann, Marcel went to Swann's house as much to be in her company as in Gilberte's, but after a time, his pampered habits and brooding, neurasthenic nature began to bore Gilberte. His pride hurt, he refused to see her for many years.

Marcel's family began to treat him as an invalid. With his grandmother, he went to Balbec, a seaside resort. There he met Albertine, a girl to whom he was immediately attracted. He also met Madame de Villeparisis, an old friend of his grandmother's and a connection of the Guermantes family. Madame de Villeparisis introduced him to her two nephews, Robert de Saint-Loup and Baron de Charlus. Saint-Loup and Marcel became close friends. While visiting Saint-Loup in a nearby garrison town, Marcel met his friend's mistress, a young Jewish actress named Rachel. Marcel was both fascinated and repelled by Baron de Charlus; he was not to understand until later the baron's corrupt and depraved nature.

Through his friendship with Madame de Villeparisis and Saint-Loup, Marcel was introduced into the smart world of the Guermantes when he returned to Paris.

One day, while he was walking with his grandmother, she suffered a stroke. The illness and death of that good and unselfish old woman made him realize for the first time the empty worldliness of his smart and wealthy friends. For comfort he turned to Albertine, who came to stay with him in Paris while his family was away. Nevertheless, his desire to be humored and indulged in all of his whims, his suspicions of Albertine, and his petty jealousy finally forced her to leave him and go back to Balbec. With her, he had been unhappy; without her, he was wretched. Then he learned that she had been accidentally killed in a fall from her horse. Later he received a letter, written before her death, in which she promised to return to him.

More miserable than ever, Marcel tried to find diversion among his old friends. They were changing with the times. Swann was ill and soon to die. Gilberte had married Robert de Saint-Loup. Madame Verdurin, who had inherited a fortune, now entertained the old nobility. At one of her parties Marcel heard a Vinteuil composition played by a musician named Morel, the nephew of a former servant and now a protégé of the notorious Baron de Charlus.

His health breaking down at last, Marcel spent the war years in a sanatorium. When he returned to Paris, he found still greater changes. Robert de Saint-Loup had been killed in the war. Rachel, Saint-Loup's mistress, had become a famous actress. Swann was also dead, and his widow had remarried and was now a fashionable hostess who received the Duchess de Guermantes. Prince de Guermantes, his fortune lost and his first wife dead, had married Madame Verdurin for her money. Baron de Charlus had grown senile.

Marcel went to one last reception at the Princess de Guermantes' lavish house. There he met the daughter of Gilberte de Saint-Loup; he realized how time had passed, how old he had grown. In the Guermantes' library, he happened to take down the novel by George Sand which his mother had read to him that remembered night in Combray, years before. Suddenly, in memory, he heard again the ringing of the bell that announced Monsieur Swann's departure and knew that it would echo in his mind forever. He saw then that everything in his own futile, wasted life dated from that far night in his childhood, and in that moment of self-revelation he saw also the ravages of time among all the people he had ever known.

Critical Evaluation

Remembrance of Things Past is not a novel of traditional form. Symphonic in design, it unfolds without plot or crisis as the writer reveals in retrospect the motifs of his experience, holds them for thematic effect, and drops them, only to return to them once more in the processes of recurrence and change. This varied pattern of experience brings together a series of involved relationships through the imagination and observation of a narrator engaged in tracing with painstaking detail his perceptions of people and places as he himself grows from childhood to disillusioned middle age. From the waking reverie in which he recalls the themes and characters of his novel to that closing paragraph with its slow, repeated echoes of the word *time*, Marcel Proust's novel is great art distilled from memory itself, the structure determined entirely by moods and sensations evoked by the illusion of time passing, or seeming to pass, recurring, or seeming to recur.

In *Remembrance of Things Past*, Proust, together with Leo Tolstoy (*War and Peace*, 1865–1869), Fyodor Dostoevski (*The Brothers Karamazov*, 1879–1880), Thomas Mann (*Joseph and His Brothers*, 1933–1943), and James Joyce (*Ulysses*, 1922), transformed the novel from a linear account of events into a multidimensional art. The breakthrough was not into Freudian psychology, or existentialism, or scientific determinism but into a realization that all things are, or may be, interwoven, bound by time, yet freed from time, open to every associational context.

What is reality? Certainly there is the reality of the sensory experience; yet any moment of sensory experience may have numerous successive or even simultaneous realities as it is relived in memory in different contexts, and perhaps the most significant reality—or realities—of a given act or moment may come long after the moment when the event first took place in time. Percy Shelley, in *A Defence of Poetry* (1840), said, "All things exist as they are perceived: at least in relation to the percipient." And things which may have seemed inconsequential at the moment of their occurrence may take on richly multifaceted meanings in relation to other events, other memories, other moments. The initial act is not as significant, not as real, as the perceptions of it which may come in new contexts. Reality *is* a context, made up of moods, of recollections joined by chance or design, sets of associations that have grown over the years. This concept of the notion of reality, one that had been taking shape with increased momentum since the Romantic movement, opened the way to "those mysteries . . . the presentiment of which is the quality in life and art which moves us most deeply."

The elusive yet pervasively important nature of reality applies not only to events, such as the taste of the madeleine (or small cake), but also to the absence of events, for the failure of Marcel's mother to give him his accustomed good-night kiss proved to be an occasion which memory would recall again and again in a variety of relationships. Thus reality can and inevitably for all people does sometimes include, if not indeed center on, the nonbeing of an event. That nonexistence can be placed in time and in successive times as surely as events that did happen; moreover "it"—that nothing where something might or should have been—may become a significant part of the contexts which, both in time and freed from time, constitute reality.

Such thematic variations and turns of thought have led some to identify Proust as a "dilettante." Perhaps, in its literal sense, the term is justified, for his mind might have delighted in what, to the reader, may be unexpected turns of thought. In this he is most closely to be associated with Thomas Mann, whose consideration of time in the first volume of *Joseph and His Brothers* leads the reader into labyrinthine but essential paths; or whose speculations about the God-man relationship in volume 2, in the section headed "Abraham Discovers God," lead the reader down a dizzying path of whimsical yet serious thought. The fact remains, however, that Mann and Proust have opened doors of contemplation that modern man cannot afford to ignore if he would increase his understanding of himself, the world in which he lives, and the tenuous nature of reality and of time.

What Proust does with time and reality he also does with character. Although he was a contemporary of Freud, and although Freudian interpretation could be applied to some of his characters in part, his concept of character is much too complex for reduction to ego, id, and the subconscious. Character, like reality, is a changing total context, not static and not a thing in itself to be held off and examined at arm's length. Baron de Charlus is at once a study of character in disintegration and a caricature, reduced in the end to a pitiable specimen, scarcely human. It is Marcel, however, who is seen most fully. His character is seen in direct statements, in his comments about others and about situations, in what others say to him or the way they say it, even in descriptive passages which would at first glance not seem to relate to character at all. "Only the exhaustive can be truly interesting," Mann said in the preface to *The Magic Mountain* (1924). Proust surely agreed. His detail is not of the catalogue variety, however; it works cumulatively, developmentally, with the thematic progression of symphonic music.

Finally the totality of the work is "the past recaptured." To understand this masterpiece in its full richness, one must become and remain conscious of the author, isolated in his study, drawing upon his recollections, associating and reassociating moments, events, personalities (his own always central), both to recapture the past as it happened and to discover in it the transcendent reality which supersedes the time-bound moment of the initial occurrence. The total work is a story, a succession of stories, and a study of the life process, which, as one comes to understand it, must greatly enrich one's own sense of self and of the life one lives.

REPUBLIC

Type of work: Philosophic dialogue
Author: Plato (427–347 B.C.)
Time: Fifth century B.C.
Locale: The Piraeus, Greece
First transcribed: Fourth century B.C.

The *Republic* is Plato's masterpiece, not only because it presents a fascinating defense of the author's conception of the ideal state but also because it gives us the most sustained and convincing portrait of Socrates as a critical and creative philosopher. Other dialogues, such as the *Phaedo* and the *Apology*, may be superior as studies of the personality and character of Socrates, but the *Republic* is unexcelled as an exhibition of the famed Socratic method being brought to bear on such questions as "What is justice?" and "What kind of state would be most just?"

Although the constructive arguments of this dialogue come from the mouth of Socrates, it is safe to assume that much of the philosophy is Platonic in origin. As a rough reading rule, we may say that the method is Socratic, but the content is provided by Plato himself. Among the ideas which are presented and defended in the *Republic* are the Platonic theory of Forms—the formal prototypes of all things, objective or intellectual—the Platonic conception of the nature and obligations of the philosopher, and the Platonic theory and criticism of poetry. But the central concern of the author is with the idea of justice in man and the state. The pursuit of this idea makes the *Republic* the longest of the dialogues with the exception of the *Laws*.

The dialogue is a discussion between Socrates and various friends while they are in the Piraeus for a festival. The discussion of justice is provoked by a remark made by an old man, Cephalus, to the effect that the principal advantage of being wealthy is that a man near death is able to repay what he owes to the gods and men, and is thereby able to be just in the hope of achieving a happy afterlife. Socrates objects to this conception of justice, maintaining that whether a person should return what he has received depends on the circumstances. For example, a man who has received dangerous weapons from his friends while sane should not, if he is just, return those weapons if his friend while mad demands them.

Polemarchus amends the idea and declares that it is just to help our friends and return to them what they are due, provided they are good and worthy of receiving the good. Enemies, on the other hand, should have harm done to them for, they are bad and unworthy and that is what they are due.

Socrates compels Polemarchus to admit that injuring anyone, even a wicked man, makes him worse; and since no just man would ever sanction making men worse, justice must be something other than giving good to the good and bad to the bad.

Thrasymachus then proposes the theory that justice is whatever is to the interest of the stronger party. His idea is that justice is relative to the law, and the law is made by the stronger party according to his interests. In rebuttal, Socrates maneuvers Thrasymachus into saying that sometimes rulers make mistakes. If this is so, then sometimes the law is against their interests; when the law is against the interests of the stronger party, it is right to do what is not to the interest of the stronger party.

The secret of the Socratic method is evident from analysis of this argument. The term "interest" or "to the interest of" is ambiguous, sometimes meaning what a man is interested in, what he wants, and at other times what he could want if he were not in error, as when we say, "But although you want it, it is not really to your interest to have it." Socrates adroitly shifts from one sense of the expression to the other so that Thrasymachus apparently contradicts himself. In this indirect way Socrates makes it clear both to the "victim" and to the onlookers that the proponent of the claim—in this case, Thrasymachus—has not cleared it of all possibility of misinterpretation.

Socrates then goes on to say that justice must be relative to the needs of those who are served, not to the desires of those who serve them. The physician, for example, as physician, must make the health of the patient his primary concern if he is to be just.

Socrates suggests that their understanding of justice would be clarified if they were to consider a concrete case, say the state: if by discussion they could come to understand what a state must be in order to be just, it might be possible to generalize and to arrive at an idea of justice itself.

Beginning with an account of what a state would have to be in order to fulfill its functions as a state, Socrates then proceeds to develop the notion of an ideal state by asking what the relations of the various groups of citizens to each other should be.

Every state needs three classes of citizens: the Guardians, who rule and advise the rest; the Auxiliaries, who provide military protection for the state; and the Workers, the husbandmen and other providers of food, clothing, and such useful materials.

In a just state these three classes of citizens function together, each doing its own proper business without interfering with the tasks of the other classes.

Applying this idea to the individual person, Socrates decides that a just man is one who gives to each of his functions its proper task, relating them to each other in a harmonious way. Just as the state has three distinct elements, the governing, the defending, and the producing bodies, so the individual person has three corresponding elements, the rational, the spirited, and the appetitive. By the spirited element Plato means the passionate aspect of man's nature, his propensity to anger or other irrational emotions. He so uses the term anger that he allows for what we call righteous indignation, the passionate defense of reason against desire. The rational element is the discerning and calculating side of man's nature, and it is what enables man to be wise and judicious. The appetitive side of man is his inclination to desire some things in preference to others.

A just man, then, is one who keeps each of the three elements of his nature doing its proper work with the rational element in command. A person is brave, says Socrates, if his spirited element remains always in the service of reason. He is wise if he is governed by reason, for reason takes into account the welfare of the entire person; and he is temperate if his spirit and appetive work harmoniously under the guidance of reason.

In order to discover those citizens best suited to be Guardians, Socrates proposed that the ideal state educate all its citizens in music and gymnastics, continually observing them to decide upon the sort of occupation for which they would best be fitted. He also argues that the Guardians and Auxiliaries should have no private property, and that they each should share a community of wives and children.

These obvious communal features of the ideal state have led many critics to dismiss Plato's conception as unacceptable. But it is well to remember that in the dialogue Socrates tells his listeners that he is not concerned about the practicality of his state; the conception of the state is constructed merely to bring out the nature of justice.

In considering the education of the Guardians, Socrates builds the conception of the philosopher as the true aristocrat or rational man, the ideal ruler for the ideal state. The philosopher is a lover of wisdom, and he alone manages to keep appetite and spirit in harmony with reason. Consequently, the Guardians of the state should be educated as philosophers, supplementing their training in arithmetic, geometry, astronomy, and music with training in the philosophic skills of dialectic. But the prospective Guardians should not be allowed to undertake philosophic education until they are old enough to take it seriously, not as mere amusement. After his philosophic training the prospective Guardian should take part in the active life of his times, so that at fifty he can assume political power with some knowledge of the actual matters with which he shall be concerned.

In connection with his discussion of the philosopher, Socrates introduced his famous myth of the cave. Men are like prisoners in a cave that faces away from the light. Unable to see themselves or anyone else because they are shackled, they observe only the shadows of things on the wall in front of them, not realizing that the reality is something quite different from the shadows. The philosopher is like a man who leaves the cave, comes to know things as they really are, and returns reluctantly to help the shackled men who think that shadows make up the true world.

The philosopher comes to know reality through a study of the Forms or Ideas of particular things. The world of our experience is like the world of shadows, but the world of Ideas is the true reality. For every class of objects, such as beds (Socrates' example), there is an Idea-bed, a form shared by all particular beds. The man who studies only the individual beds made by carpenters, or only the pictures of beds made by artists, knows only copies of reality (and, in the case of the imitative artist, only copies of copies); but the philosopher, making the effort to learn the Idea itself, comes closer to reality.

Socrates objects to poetry and to art whenever they are imitative, which they usually are. Although he admits that some poetry can be inspiring in the patriotic training of the Guardians, he stresses the point that imitative art is corrupting because it is misleading. Physical things, after all, are merely copies of the Forms, the Ideas; hence they are one step removed from reality. But works of art are copies of physical things; hence they are at least two steps removed from reality. Furthermore, the artist paints only a single aspect of a thing; hence strictly speaking, art is three steps removed from reality. It is on this account, as well as because of the immoral effect of the poetic style of all but the most noble poets, that Socrates recommends that imitative poets be banned from the state.

The *Republic* closes with Socrates' reaffirmation of his conviction that only the just man is truly happy, for only he harmonizes reason, appetite, and spirit by loving wisdom and the Form of the Good. The soul is immortal, he argues, because the soul's illness is injustice; yet injustice itself does not destroy a soul. Since the soul cannot be destroyed by any illness other than its own, it must be immortal. Socrates concludes by using a myth about life after death to show that the just and wise man will prosper both in this life and "during the journey of a thousand years."

THE RETURN OF THE NATIVE

Type of work: Novel
Author: Thomas Hardy (1840–1928)
Type of plot: Romantic tragedy
Time of plot: Mid-nineteenth century
Locale: Egdon Heath, in southern England
First published: 1878

In this novel Thomas Hardy creates two strong opposing forces: Egdon Heath, a somber tract of wasteland symbolic of an impersonal fate, and Eustacia Vye, a beautiful, romantic young woman representing the opposing human element. Her marriage to the idealistic Clym Yeobright is doomed both by the external forces of nature and the intense, differing needs of the two characters. Eustacia's death by drowning in the company of Wildeve, her lover, is the fitting symbolic end to her life.

Principal Characters

Clement Yeobright, called **Clym,** a native of Egdon Heath who returns to visit with his mother and cousin after having made a career for himself as a successful diamond merchant in Paris. His success and his education make him an outstanding figure among the humble people who live scattered about the wild heath, and his return for a visit is a great occasion for them. During his stay he decides to remain, finding that the heath and its people mean far more to him than worldly success in Paris; his intention is to become a teacher and open a school to educate the people among whom he grew up, a superstitious and ignorant, if lovable and kindly set. A sensitive and somewhat rash young man, he falls in love with Eustacia Vye, a beautiful and passionate woman. In her Clym sees a perfect helpmeet for a schoolmaster, but she sees in him only a chance to escape the heath and to live abroad. Clym and Eustacia Vye are married, over the protests of his mother. These protests arouse the anger of Clym, who after his marriage does not communicate with her. Disaster, in the form of partial blindness, strikes Clym, but he accepts his plight philosophically and turns to the homely task of furze cutting to earn a living. Unhappy in her lot, Eustacia turns against him. On one occasion she refuses to let his mother into the house, an inhospitable act that indirectly causes the death of the older woman. Stricken by his mother's death and, a short time later, by his wife's suicide, Clym becomes a lay preacher to the people of the heath.

Eustacia Vye, the self-seeking and sensuous young woman who marries Clym Yeobright. Unhappy on the heath, bored by life with her grandfather, she tries to escape. First she seeks an opportunity to do so by marrying Clym. When he cannot and will not leave the heath, she turns to a former fiancé, now a married man. At the last, however, she cannot demean herself by unfaithfulness to her husband; instead of running away with her lover she commits suicide by plunging into a millpond.

Damon Wildeve, a former engineer, still a young man, who settles unhappily upon the heath as keeper of the Quiet Woman Inn. Selfish and uninspired, when he loses Eustacia Vye to Clym Yeobright he marries Thomasin Yeobright, Clym's cousin, out of spite. The marriage is an unhappy one, for Wildeve still pursues Eustacia, also unhappy because her husband cannot give her the life she wishes. Wildeve's pursuit of illicit love ends in his own death, for he drowns while trying to save Eustacia's life after she throws herself into a pond rather than elope to Paris as his mistress.

Thomasin Yeobright, called **Tamsin,** Clym's cousin, reared with Clym by his mother. A simple and faithful girl who loves Damon Wildeve despite his treatment of her, she is also faithful to the conventions and clings to her marriage even after it turns out badly. At her husband's death she inherits a small fortune left by his uncle shortly before Wildeve's end. She finds happiness eventually in a second marriage and in her little daughter.

Diggory Venn, an itinerant young reddleman in love with Thomasin Yeobright. Once of good family and some little fortune, he has fallen upon evil days. His lonely existence gives him opportunity to act in his love's behalf, and he tries to circumvent Wildeve's pursuit of Eustacia Vye. Having saved up a little money, he becomes a dairyman and presents himself, after a decent time, as Thomasin's suitor, following her husband's death. His patience, love, and understanding are rewarded when she accepts him.

Mrs. Yeobright, Clym Yeobright's mother and Thomasin Yeobright's aunt. In her good sense she opposes both their marriages, although the young people misinterpret her motives as selfish. Being of a forgiving nature, she tries to be reconciled with her son and his wife, as she became with Thomasin and her husband. But Eustacia refuses her overtures and is indirectly the cause of the older woman's death; Mrs. Yeobright dies of exposure and snakebite after having been refused admittance to her son's home.

Captain Vye, Eustacia Vye's grandfather, a retired seaman who brings his granddaughter to live on the heath with no thought of how such a place will affect her. He is a self-contained old man with little knowledge of the intense personality of his charge; therefore he makes no effort to prevent her tragedy.

Johnny Nunsuch, a little boy who plays upon the heath and unwittingly becomes involved as a witness to the fate of the Yeobrights, Eustacia Vye, and Damon Wildeve. His testimony concerning Mrs. Yeobright's last words brings about the separation of Clym Yeobright and his wife.

Mrs. Nunsuch, Johnny's mother. Convinced that Eustacia Vye is a witch who has cast a spell upon the child, Mrs. Nunsuch, an uneducated, superstitious woman, resorts to black arts to exorcise the spell. On the night of Eustacia Vye's death she forms a doll in the girl's image and destroys it in a fire.

Granfer Cantle, an ancient, **Christian Cantle,** his elderly youngest son, **Olly Dowden, Sam,** a turf cutter, **Humphrey,** a furze cutter, and **Timothy Fairway,** residents of Egdon Heath. They voice much of the rural wisdom and observe the folk customs of the region.

The Story

Egdon Heath was a gloomy wasteland in southern England. Against this majestic but solemn, brooding background a small group of people were to work out their tragic drama in the impersonal presence of nature.

Fifth of November bonfires were glowing in the twilight as Diggory Venn, the reddleman, drove his van across the Heath. Tired and ill, Thomasin Yeobright lay in the rear of his van. She was a young girl whom Diggory loved, but she had rejected his proposal in order to marry Damon Wildeve, proprietor of the Quiet Woman Inn. Now Diggory was carrying the girl to her home at Blooms-End. The girl had gone to marry Wildeve in a nearby town, but the ceremony had not taken place because of an irregularity in the license. Shocked and shamed, Thomasin had asked her old sweetheart, Diggory, to take her home.

Mrs. Yeobright, Thomasin's aunt and guardian, heard the story from the reddleman. Concerned for the girl's welfare, she decided that the wedding should take place as soon as possible. Mrs. Yeobright had good cause to worry, for Wildeve's intentions were not wholly honorable. Later in the evening, after Wildeve had assured the Yeobrights, rather casually, that he intended to go through with his promise, his attention was turned to a bonfire blazing on Mistover Knap. There old Cap'n Vye lived with his beautiful granddaughter, Eustacia. At dusk, the girl had started a fire on the Heath as a signal to her lover, Wildeve, to come to her. Although he had intended to break with Eustacia, he decided to obey her summons.

Meanwhile, Eustacia was waiting for Wildeve in the company of young Johnny Nunsuch. When Wildeve threw a pebble in the pond to announce his arrival, Eustacia told Johnny to go home. The meeting between Wildeve and Eustacia was unsatisfactory for both. He complained that she gave him no peace. She, in turn, resented his desertion. Meanwhile, Johnny Nunsuch, frightened by strange lights he saw on the Heath, went back to Mistover Knap to ask Eustacia to let her servant accompany him home, but he kept silent when he came upon Eustacia and Wildeve. Retracing his steps, he stumbled into a sand pit where the reddleman's van stood. Diggory learned from the boy of the meeting between Eustacia and Wildeve. Later, he overheard Eustacia declare her hatred of the Heath to Wildeve, who asked her to run away with him to America. Her reply was vague, but the reddleman decided to see Eustacia without delay to beg her to let Thomasin have Wildeve.

Diggory's visit to Eustacia was fruitless. He then approached Mrs. Yeobright, declared again his love for her niece, and offered to marry Thomasin. Mrs. Yeobright refused the reddleman's offer because she felt that the girl should marry Wildeve. She confronted the innkeeper with vague references to another suitor, with the result that Wildeve's interest in Thomasin awakened once more.

Shortly afterward, Mrs. Yeobright's son, Clym, returned from Paris, and a welcome-home party gave Eustacia the chance to view this stranger about whom she had heard so much. Uninvited, she went to the party disguised as one of the mummers. Clym was fascinated by this interesting and mysterious young woman disguised as a man. Eustacia dreamed of marrying Clym and going with him to Paris. She even broke off with Wildeve, who, stung by her rejection, promptly married Thomasin to spite her.

Clym Yeobright decided not to go back to France. Instead, he planned to open a school. Mrs. Yeobright strongly opposed her son's decision. When Clym learned that Eustacia had been stabbed in church by a woman who thought that Eustacia was bewitching her children, his decision to educate these ignorant people was strengthened. Much against his mother's wishes, Clym visited Eustacia's home to ask her to teach in his school. Eustacia refused because she hated the Heath and the country peasants; as the result of his visit, however, Clym fell completely in love with the beautiful but heartless Eustacia.

Mrs. Yeobright blamed Eustacia for Clym's wish to stay on the Heath. When bitter feeling grew between mother and son, he decided to leave home. His marriage to Eustacia made the break complete. Later, Mrs. Yeobright relented somewhat and gave a neighbor, Christian Cantle, a sum of money to be delivered in equal portions to Clym and Thomasin. Christian foolishly lost the money to Wildeve in a game of dice. Fortunately, Diggory won the money from Wildeve, but, thinking that all of it belonged to Thomasin, he gave it to her. Mrs. Yeobright knew that Wildeve had duped Christian. She did not know that the reddleman had won the money away from the innkeeper, and she mistakenly supposed that Wildeve had given the money to Eustacia. She met Eustacia and asked the girl if she had received any money from Wildeve. Eustacia was enraged by the question; in the course of her reply to Mrs. Yeobright's charge, she said that she would never have condescended to marry Clym had she known that she would have to remain on the Heath. The two women parted angrily.

Eustacia's unhappiness was increased by Clym's near-blindness, a condition brought on by too much reading, for she feared that this meant she would never get to Paris. When Clym became a woodcutter, Eustacia's feeling of degradation was complete. Bored with her life, she went by herself one evening to a gypsying. There she accidentally met Wildeve and again felt an attraction to him. The reddleman saw Eustacia and Wildeve together, told Mrs. Yeobright of the meeting, and begged her to make peace with Eustacia for Clym's sake. She agreed to try.

Nevertheless, Mrs. Yeobright's walk at noon across the hot, dry Heath to see her son and daughter-in-law proved fatal. When she arrived in sight of Clym's house, she saw her son from a distance as he entered the front door. Then, while she rested on a knoll near the house, she saw another man entering, but she was too far away to recognize Wildeve. After resting for twenty minutes, Mrs. Yeobright went on to Clym's cottage and knocked. No one came to the door. Heartbroken by what she considered a rebuff by her own son, Mrs. Yeobright started

home across the Heath. Overcome by exhaustion and grief, she sat down to rest, and a poisonous adder bit her. She died without knowing that inside her son's house Clym had been asleep, worn out by his morning's work. Eustacia did not go to the door because, as she later explained to her husband, she had thought he would answer the knock. The real reason for Eustacia's failure to go to the door was fear of the consequences if Mrs. Yeobright found Eustacia and Wildeve together.

Clym awoke with the decision to visit his mother. Starting out across the Heath toward her house, he stumbled over her body. His grief was tempered by bewilderment over the reason for her being on the Heath at that time. When Clym discovered that Eustacia had failed to let his mother in and that Wildeve had been in the cottage, he ordered Eustacia out of his house. She went quietly because she felt in part responsible for Mrs. Yeobright's death.

Eustacia took refuge in her grandfather's house, where a faithful servant thwarted her in an attempt to commit suicide. In utter despair over her own wretched life and over the misery she had caused others, Eustacia turned to Wildeve, who had unexpectedly inherited eleven thousand pounds and who still wanted her to run away with him. One night, she left her grandfather's house in order to keep a prearranged meeting with the innkeeper; but in her departure, she failed to receive a letter of reconciliation which Thomasin had persuaded Clym to send to her. On her way to keep her rendezvous with Wildeve, she lost her way in the inky blackness of the Heath and either fell accidentally or jumped into a small lake and was drowned. Wildeve, who happened to be near the lake when she fell in, jumped in to save her and also was drowned.

(Originally, *The Return of the Native* ended with the death of Eustacia and of Wildeve; but in order to satisfy his romantic readers, Hardy made additions to the story in a later edition. The faithful Diggory married Thomasin. Clym, unable to abolish ignorance and superstition on the Heath by teaching, became in the end an itinerant preacher.)

Critical Evaluation

Thomas Hardy was born in Dorset, England, on June 2, 1840. Although he attended several grammar schools and studied French at King's College, Hardy had little formal education. Later, however, he read extensively in the Bible, the classics, and recent scientific publications. He was an architect's apprentice from 1856 to 1874 and later an ecclesiastical architect. During this time, he wrote poetry, which was not published until after he was a well-known novelist. His first novel, *Desperate Remedies*, was published in 1872. In 1872, he married Emma Gifford; after her death in 1912, he married Florence Dug-

dale. When storms of protest arose over the pessimism and the violation of strict Victorian sexual mores in *Tess of the D'Urbervilles* and *Jude the Obscure*, Hardy gave up the novel but continued to write poetry. He died on January 11, 1928, and his ashes were placed in the poets' corner at Westminster Abbey. Among his best works are *Far from the Madding Crowd* and *The Return of the Native*. In *The Return of the Native*, there is a strong conflict between nature or fate, represented by Egdon Heath, and human nature, represented by the characters in the novel, especially Eustacia. The title of the first chapter, "A Face on Which Time Makes But Little Impression," establishes the heath's role as much more significant than merely a setting for the action. The word "face" suggests that the heath assumes anthropomorphic proportions and becomes, in essence, a major character in the novel; somber and dark, "the storm was its lover, and the wind its friend." And, while the characters struggle and become tired and disillusioned—or die—the heath remains indifferent and unchanged.

The heath, then, is a symbol of permanence. Other aspects of the setting also become symbolic, and they intensify the somber tone of the novel. The dominance of dark imagery adds to the novel's pessimism: The bonfires on the heath provide small areas of light in the blackness of the night, yet the furze burns quickly and is soon extinguished, like the momentary happiness of Eustacia and Clym and the wild passion of Eustacia and Wildeve. The moon's eclipse on the night Clym proposes to Eustacia foreshadows the eclipse of their love. On the night of Eustacia's death, the violent storm echoes her violent emotions as she cries out against her fate.

Like his character Eustacia, Hardy often seems to blame fate for many of the catastrophes of life. Many critics believe that in this novel fate is completely dominant and that the characters are helpless victims of its malevolence. Such a view, however, seems inadequate. Admittedly, fate does play a significant role; for example, Eustacia accidentally meets Wildeve at the maypole dance. Mrs. Yeobright just happens to choose an extremely hot day to visit Clym, just happens to arrive when Wildeve is there, and just happens to be bitten by the adder when she collapses from fatigue. Eustacia does not receive Clym's letter because her grandfather believes she is asleep. Much of the novel's tragedy, however, can be traced to the characters' motivations, decisions, and actions.

Mrs. Yeobright may seem victimized by Eustacia's failure to open the door to her, but one must remember that Mrs. Yeobright never accepts Eustacia and attempts to turn Clym against her. She feels socially superior to Eustacia, distrusts her because she is a free spirit, calls her lazy and irresponsible, hints that she is behaving indiscreetly with Wildeve, and, in general, is jealous of her because she wants to keep Clym to herself. She refuses to attend Clym's wedding and treats Eustacia in a condescending manner as they speak together near the pool. She then harbors her grudge and keeps away from her son and his wife long enough for the gulf between them to widen greatly.

Clym, too, brings much of his trouble upon himself. He is flattered by Eustacia's attention and passion for him but never really sees her as an individual totally different from himself. Without regard for her hatred of the heath and her longing for the excitement of Paris, he assumes that she will be a vital part of his teaching mission. After their marriage, he ignores her and devotes his time to his studies, which, perhaps, helps to bring about the physical blindness that becomes symbolic of his blindness to reality. Martyring himself as a furze cutter, he intensifies Eustacia's hatred for the heath and fails to see that his physical fatigue and his degrading work deal a crushing blow to his marriage. Even his desire to teach is selfish and unrealistic; he tries to escape from life's conflicts into an abstraction of truth, and he desires to impose his views on others. The view of Clym at the end of the novel is ironic; as an itinerant preacher "less than thirty-three," he may suggest a Christ figure; yet in his self-righteousness, he fails to find the meaning of love.

Eustacia, who blames fate for her tragedy, is the novel's most ambiguous character; even the author seems to have ambivalent feelings toward her. She is an exciting, passionate "queen of the night" whose romanticism makes her long to "be loved to madness" by a man great enough to embody her dreams. Allowing her imagination to convince her that Clym can master this role, she marries him, hoping to manipulate him, as she had manipulated Wildeve, and thus get to Paris. After her marriage, however, her liaison with Wildeve is at first innocent; only after Clym banishes her from his house does she agree to accept Wildeve's offer to help her leave the heath. Despite her desperation, Eustacia refuses to be humbled. Realizing that a lack of money will cause her to lose her honor for a man who is "not great enough" to meet her desires, she drowns herself to avoid humiliation. It is more believable that she dies willingly than that her death is accidental because only in death does she seem to find peace.

Although Eustacia has lost in her battle with the heath, her struggle proves that she is a strong, defiant character who is defeated partly by forces beyond her control and partly by her own refusal to give up her dream. Despite her selfishness and hauteur, her lively spirit gives life to the novel and makes her, in the end, its tragic but unforgettable heroine.

REYNARD THE FOX

Type of work: Beast-epic
Author: Unknown
Type of plot: Satiric stories
Time of plot: Middle Ages
Locale: Europe
First transcribed: Eighth century (?)

Second in popularity only to the fables of Aesop is the old German tale Reynard the Fox. *In it we see that cunning always conquers force, that one who lives by his wits will never suffer. We grudgingly admire the villainous hero even while hoping he will get his just punishment. In some explications, Reynard represents the Church, Isengrim the baronial component, and Noble the monarchy.*

Principal Characters

Reynard, the fox. So crafty and persuasive a liar is he, that he is at last made high bailiff of the country, though he has flagrantly cheated and injured all of the animals, including the king. Thus is craftiness set above mere strength.

Noble, the lion, King of Beasts. He listens to the animals' grievances against Reynard, and even sentences the fox to death. But Reynard lies so cleverly about hidden treasure and treachery on the part of the others that the king frees him. Noble is similarly gulled a second time and on this occasion even makes Reynard high bailiff.

Isengrim, the wolf, whose children have been made blind by Reynard. Convinced of Isengrim's treason, the king gives the wolf's shoes to Reynard. After this, when the wolf and the fox are engaged in combat, Reynard persuades Isengrim to let him go with promises of rewards.

Tibert, the cat. He defends Reynard before the others until he has been tricked by the fox into jumping into a trap.

Bruin, the bear. Reynard's promises of honey lure him into a trap, and he is badly beaten before he escapes. Later Reynard convinces the king that Bruin is plotting to replace him as ruler. Noble gives Bruin's skin to Reynard.

Grimbard, the brock. He defends Reynard before the court, and even warns the fox of a plot against him.

Panther, who complains of Reynard to the king.

Chanticleer, the cock. His complaint is that Reynard deceived him into relaxing his vigilance by pretending to have given up eating flesh. Then Reynard eats Chanticleer's children.

Kyward, the hare. He accompanies Reynard on a "pilgrimage" and is eaten by him.

Bellin, the ram, who goes with Reynard and Kyward. Deceived into thinking he is carrying a letter, he brings Kyward's head to the king. The furious king then gives the stupid ram and all his lineage to the wolf and the bear, to atone for his misjudgment of them.

The Story

When Noble, the great Lion-king, held court during the Feast of the Pentecost, all the animals told the king of their grievances against Reynard the fox. The list of sins and crimes was almost as long as the list of animals present. First to complain was Isengrim the wolf, whose children had been made blind by the crafty fox. Panther told how Reynard had promised the hare that he would teach him his prayers, but when the hare had stood in front of Reynard as he was instructed, Reynard had grabbed him by the throat and tried to kill him. To Chanticleer the cock, Reynard had gone disguised as a monk, saying that he would never eat flesh again, but when Chanticleer relaxed his vigilance over his flock and believed the villain, Reynard had grabbed his children and eaten them.

So the complaints went on, with only Tibert the cat and Grimard the brock speaking in Reynard's defense. These two reminded the king of the crimes committed by the complainers, but the king was stern; Reynard must be brought to court to answer for his sins. Bruin the bear was sent to bring in the culprit. Bruin was strong and brave, and he promised the king that he would not be fooled by Reynard's knavery of flattering tongue.

When Bruin arrived at Reynard's castle and delivered the king's message, Reynard welcomed the bear and promised to accompany him back to court. In fact, Reynard said that he wished they were already at court, for he had abstained from meat and eaten so much of a new food, called honeycombs, that his stomach was swollen and uncomfortable. Bruin fell into the trap and begged to be taken to the store of honey. Reynard pretended to be reluctant to delay their trip to court, but at last he agreed to show Bruin the honey. The wily fox led Bruin into a trap in some tree trunks, where the poor bear was set upon by humans and beaten unmercifully. He escaped with his life and sadly made his way back to court, mocked by the taunts of his betrayer.

Enraged at the insult to his personal messenger, the king sent Tibert the cat to tell Reynard to surrender himself at once, under penalty of death. Tibert, however, fared no better. He was tricked into jumping into a net trap by the promise of a feast on mice and rats. He too escaped and returned to the court, no longer a defender of the traitorous Reynard. The next time the king sent Grimbard the brock to bring in the fox. He was also warmly received by Reynard's promise to accompany him to court. This time the evil fox actually kept his promise, confessing all of his sins to the brock as they journeyed.

At court, Reynard was confronted by all of his accusers. One by one they told of his horrible crimes against them. Reynard defended himself against them all, saying that he was a loyal and true subject of the king and the object of many lies and deceits. The king was unmoved and sentenced Reynard to death. On the gallows, the fox confessed his sins, saying that he was the more guilty because he did not steal from want, since money and jewels he had in great plenty. Hearing Reynard speak of his treasure, the greedy king wanted it for himself, and he asked Reynard where the jewels were hidden. The fox said that he would gladly tell him the hiding place, for the treasure had been stolen in order to save the king's life. Crafty Reynard told a slippery story about a treasure that the other animals were going to use to depose the king and make Bruin the ruler in his place. In order to save the life of his sovereign, Reynard had stolen the treasure from the traitors and now had it in his possession. The foolish king, believing the smooth liar, ordered Reynard released from the gallows and made a favorite at court. Bruin the bear and Isengrim the wolf were arrested for high treason.

Reynard said that he himself could not show the king the treasure because he had to make a pilgrimage to Rome to ask the pope to remove a curse from him. For his journey he was given the skin of the bear and the shoes of the wolf, leaving those two fellows in terrible pain. The king then put his mail around Reynard's neck and a staff in his hand and sent him on his way. Kyward the hare and Bellin the ram accompanied Reynard on the pilgrimage. They stopped at the fox's castle to bid his wife good-bye, and there Reynard tricked the hare, killed him, and ate all but the head. That he sent back to the king by the ram, that stupid animal thinking he was carrying a letter for the monarch. The king was so furious that he gave the ram and all of his lineage to the wolf and the bear to atone for the king's misjudgment of them.

Complaints against the fox again poured into the king's ear. At last he determined to lay siege to Reynard's castle until the culprit was captured. This time there would be no mercy. Grimbard the brock, however, hurried to the castle and warned Reynard of the plot. The crafty fellow went immediately to the court to plead his case before the king.

On the way he again confessed to the brock that he was guilty of many sins, but he made them seem mild in comparison with those of the animals now accusing him. To the king also he confessed that he had sinned, but he denied the worst of the crimes laid to his doing. His plea was that he would not have surrendered voluntarily had he been so guilty. His words were so moving that most of his accusers kept silent, fearing that the king would again believe Reynard and punish those who would condemn him. Only the wolf and the bear held fast to their accusations. With the help of his aunt, the ape, Reynard once more excused himself in the king's eyes and made the monarch believe that it was the injured who were the guilty. Again Reynard talked of lost jewels of great value, jewels which he would search for and present to the king.

Only Isengrim the wolf would not accept Reynard's lies. He challenged the fox to a fight. Reynard would have been hard put to fight with the wolf except that Isengrim's feet were still sore from Reynard's taking of his shoes sometime before. Furthermore, the ape shaved off Reynard's fur and covered him with oil so that the wolf could not get hold of him. Even so, Isengrim would have defeated him had he not listened to Reynard's oily promises of all the rewards Isengrim would receive were he to let Reynard go. At last the king stopped the fight and ordered all the animals to a great feast. There he forgave Reynard for all of his sins after taking the scamp's promise that he would commit no more crimes against his fellow animals. The king made Reynard high bailiff of the country, thus setting him above all the others. From that time on the mighty of the forest would bow to the cunning of the weak.

Critical Evaluation

Reynard the Fox is classified as a "beast epic." The underlying framework of this popular medieval literary form is a series of stories linked by the same characters— invariably, anthropomorphized animals (hence, "*beast epic*"). In *Reynard the Fox,* the character of Reynard provides the connective thread. The epic designation derives from the length of the series as well as from the use of typical epic devices such as the loose, rather episodic relationship among the stories. Accordingly, most versions of *Reynard the Fox* are lengthy, and the episodes are only vaguely related. In addition, the target of such beast epics is satire of the contemporary social and political scene. Indeed, *Reynard the Fox* satirizes human folly, the judicial system, and much else.

The origin of the form, however, is still subject to scholarly debate. Since *Reynard the Fox* is one of the most important examples of this genre, the debate, in this case, is quite significant. Some scholars maintain that the beast epic derived from the oral folk tradition of storytelling, later being formalized in writing by medieval scribes. Other scholars find precedents among classical Latin authors to explain the origin of the beast epic. Both schools of thought have defensible positions, and both take their stand on the same set of facts, since many versions of the *Reynard the Fox* stories are extant.

Some basic information emerges from the dispute. First, Ovid's *Metamorphoses* (c. A.D. 8) contains stories similar to those in the *Reynard the Fox* series. Second, *Aesop's Fables* includes specific Reynard episodes. Limited medieval access to such "classical" precedents, however, renders the influence of these models moot. The earliest manifestations of *Reynard the Fox* are stories about the animosity between Reynard and his enemy, Isengrim the wolf. These stories may be derived from popular French, English, Dutch, Low German, and Latin folktales. They seem to have initiated in the Low Countries, northern France, and northeastern Germany, although precedence cannot be definitely assigned. The earliest versions were predictably in verse, although the later redactions appeared in prose.

A rather short poetic rendering of *Reynard the Fox* stories was done in medieval Latin by an eighth century cleric, Paulus Diaconus (Paul the Deacon), from Charlemagne's court. Another medieval Latin version appeared about two hundred years later in *Ecbasis captivi*, attributed to a German monk in Toul. The basic "Isengrim" story—*Ysengrimus*—is attributed to Master Nivardus of Ghent, who wrote in Latin at about A.D. 1150, developing his stories from Aesopian fables.

The evolution of vernacular versions is still open to question; some scholars claim priority for France, and others insist upon Germanic primacy. The issue has not been resolved, but there is no question that twelfth and thirteenth century Flanders, West Germany, and northern France were fertile grounds for this literary form, especially for Reynard stories.

At approximately the same time that *Ysengrimus* was produced, there appeared in France a compilation called the *Roman de Renart*, from the hands of several authors (many, according to medieval custom, anonymous). This vernacular compilation dealt mostly but not exclusively with stories of the protagonist Reynard facing his antagonist Isengrim the wolf. The stories are usually arranged in chronological "branches" (to reflect the time when they were written), rather than in topical order; unfortunately, this arrangement tends to undermine the ideo-

logical impact of the stories. The didactic element was much stronger in the almost simultaneous (c. 1180) vernacular redaction of Heinrich der Glichesäre, surviving in an anonymous manuscript written c. 1240. Nevertheless, the most important Reynard series seems to be a Middle Dutch version (c. 1270) by Willem of Hulsterlo, minimizing Reynard's humanitarian acts (curing the sick lion and the like) while emphasizing his venality. Willem's version thus exposed Reynard rather than praised him, and it set the tone for many subsequent vernacular versions of the stories.

Reynard the Fox appeared in Latin, French, German, Flemish, Dutch and English versions—testimony to its popularity. It is evident, however, that questions about origins and the chronological order of various versions cannot be unequivocally answered with the information at hand. As is the case with much medieval history and literature, final answers must wait upon the discovery of further evidence, most likely from a presently unknown cache of medieval manuscripts—if such a cache exists.

In the meantime, it is still possible to evaluate the extant material on its own terms, because *Reynard the Fox* evolved as the archetype of the beast epic. The central focus of the series is a single significant episode—Reynard's healing of the sick lion, in most versions—and other stories are spin-offs from this episode, all involving moralistic messages. The cast of animals varies from story to story and from version to version: Fox, lion, and wolf are constants; badger, bear, stag, rooster, cat, hare, camel, bear, ant, and others appear occasionally. The didactic factor is another constant, and for the temper of the times, it is a remarkably pragmatic one.

Indeed, the Reynard series is a lesson in ethics and morality. None of the animals is a paragon of virtue. All are vulnerable or corruptible or both; not even King Lion is exempt. They live in a world which recognizes no moral codes and where survival depends upon wit and exploitation of others. Isengrim the wolf is doomed because he carries to extremes his penchant for besting everything and everybody. He is obsessed by the compulsion to surpass, a compulsion that blinds him to the necessary humanistic rituals required for survival. By contrast, Reynard is pliable, adaptable, and fundamentally amoral. He survives *because* he is flexible. Yet, in the process, he becomes venal, power-hungry, and oblivious to humanistic values. Significantly, Geoffrey Chaucer's "Nun's Priest's Tale" (in *The Canterbury Tales*, 1387–1400) relates a Reynard story—the fox's attempt and failure to abduct the rooster Chanticleer—to demonstrate the weakness and the power of flattery. Reynard's tactics thus become an object lesson in compromised integrity. Reynard is the ultimate opportunist, knowing no scruple but his own advancement at the expense of others. To be sure, Reynard is neither explicitly praised nor explicitly condemned in the context of medieval ethics or morality. Rather, he is held forth as an example—albeit, an implicit example of "what *not* to do." In this sense, the best didactic functions of the beast epic are upheld. For it is the didactic element in such works that constitutes their intended impact. Although scholarly disputes continue about the origins and the development of the beast epic, in the last analysis the more crucial point is the moral import of such stories. In this respect, *Reynard the Fox* succeeds extremely well.

RICHARD II

Type of work: Drama
Author: William Shakespeare (1564–1616)
Type of plot: Historical tragedy
Time of plot: Fourteenth century
Locale: England
First presented: c. 1595

Richard II *is profound both as a political vision and as a personal tragedy. Richard is an inept king—erratic, willful, arrogant, susceptible to flattery, blind to good advice—but a sensitive, deeply moving poet. The play demonstrates the inevitable result of his bad qualities (his dethroning by Bolingbroke), yet also reveals his growth as a human being.* Richard II *contains some of Shakespeare's most beautiful and moving verse.*

Principal Characters

King Richard II, a self-indulgent and irresponsible ruler. He neglects the welfare of his country and brings on his own downfall. He is insolent in his treatment of his dying uncle, John of Gaunt, and greedy in his seizure of the property of his banished cousin, Henry Boling-broke. To his lovely young queen he gives sentimental devotion. Being forced to give up the crown, he wallows in poetic self-pity, playing with his sorrow and theatrically portraying himself as a Christ-figure. But he dies well.

Henry Bolingbroke (bol'ĭn·brŏŏk), duke of Hereford (afterward **King Henry IV**), the son of John of Gaunt. Able and ambitious, roused to anger by Richard's injustice and ineptitude, he forces the latter to abdicate. Although as king he desires the death of his deposed and imprisoned cousin, he laments the death and banishes the murderer permanently from his presence.

John of Gaunt (gänt, gônt), duke of Lancaster, the uncle of King Richard. Grieved by the banishment of his son and his country's decline, he delivers a beautiful and impassioned praise of England and a lament for its degradation under Richard. Angered by Richard's insulting behavior, he dies delivering a curse on the young king which is later carried out.

Edmund of Langley, duke of York, uncle of the king. Eager to do right and imbued with patriotism and loyalty, he is torn and troubled by the behavior of Richard as king and Bolingbroke as rebel. As Protector of the Realm in Richard's absence, he is helpless before Bolingbroke's power and yields to him. He bestows his loyalty on Bolingbroke when he becomes King Henry IV.

Queen to King Richard, a gentle, loving wife. Grief-stricken, she angrily wishes that her gardener, from whom she hears the news of Richard's downfall, may henceforth labor in vain. She shares with the king a tender and sorrowful parting.

The Gardener, a truly Shakespearean creation, unlike any character in Marlowe's *Edward the Second*, source of much in Shakespeare's play. A homely philosopher, he comments on the king's faults and his downfall and is overheard by the queen. Tenderly sympathetic, he wishes the queen's curse on his green thumb might be carried out if it could give her any comfort; however, confident that it will not be, he memorializes her sorrow by planting flowers where her tears fell.

The Duke of Aumerle (ō·mērl'), son of the duke of York. One of Richard's favorites, scornful of Bolingbroke, he is accused of complicity in the murder of the Duke of Gloucester. His father discovers a document linking him to a plot to assassinate King Henry IV. Aumerle outrides his father to King Henry and gains promise of pardon, which is confirmed after the duchess pleads for her son.

The Duchess of York, the indulgent mother of Aumerle. She is frantic at her husband's determination to report their son's treason, and she pleads to King Henry on her knees.

Thomas Mowbray, duke of Norfolk, an enemy of Bolingbroke. Accused of plotting the Duke of Gloucester's death, he and Bolingbroke are prepared for combat in the lists when Richard breaks off the combat and banishes both. Mowbray dies in exile.

The Duchess of Gloucester, widow of the murdered duke. She pleads with John of Gaunt to avenge his dead brother and prays that Bolingbroke may destroy Mowbray as part of the revenge. York receives news of her death.

Bushy and **Green,** unpopular favorites of King Richard. They are captured and executed by Bolingbroke's followers.

Bagot (băg'ət), another of the king's unpopular favorites. At his trial before Bolingbroke, he declares Aumerle guilty of having Gloucester murdered.

The Earl of Northumberland, a strong supporter of Bolingbroke. He aids in the overthrow of Richard.

Henry Percy (Hotspur), the son of Northumberland.

At Bagot's trial he challenges Aumerle to combat, but nothing comes of it.

The Lord Marshall, who officiates at the abortive duel of Mowbray and Bolingbroke.

The Bishop of Carlisle, a supporter of King Richard. Objecting to Bolingbroke's seizure of the crown, he is accused of treason and banished.

The Abbot of Westminster, a conspirator against King Henry IV. He dies before he can be tried.

Sir Stephen Scroop, a loyal follower of King Richard. He brings unwelcome tidings of Bolingbroke's success to the king.

A Keeper, King Richard's jailer, who angers the king

and is beaten by him.

A Groom, a devoted servant of King Richard who visits the deposed monarch in prison.

The Earl of Salisbury, a follower of Richard executed by Northumberland.

The Duke of Surrey, a Yorkist and a friend of Aumerle.

Lord Berkeley, a follower of the Duke of York.

Lord Fitzwater, Lord Ross, and **Lord Willoughby,** supporters of Bolingbroke.

Sir Pierce of Exton, a savage and ambitious knight. He kills King Richard in hope of a splendid career under King Henry IV, but is disappointed, cast off, and banished by the king.

The Story

During the reign of Richard II, two young dukes, Henry Bolingbroke and Thomas Mowbray, quarreled bitterly; and in the end the king summoned them into his presence to settle their differences publicly. Although Bolingbroke was the oldest son of John of Gaunt, Duke of Lancaster, and therefore a cousin of the king, Richard was perfectly fair in his interview with the two men and showed neither any favoritism.

Bolingbroke accused Mowbray, Duke of Norfolk, of mismanaging military funds and of helping to plot the murder of the dead Duke of Gloucester, another of the king's uncles. All these charges Mowbray forcefully denied. At last Richard decided that to settle the dispute the men should have a trial by combat at Coventry, and the court adjourned there to witness the tournament.

Richard, ever nervous and suspicious, grew uneasy as the contest began. Suddenly, just after the beginning trumpet sounded, the king declared that the combat should not take place. Instead, calling the two men to him, he banished them from the country. Bolingbroke was to be exiled for six years and Mowbray for the rest of his life. At the same time Richard exacted promises from them that they would never plot against him. Still persistent in his accusations, Bolingbroke tried to persuade Mowbray to plead guilty, before he left England, to the charges against him. Mowbray, refusing to do so, warned Richard against the cleverness of Bolingbroke.

Not long after his son had been banished, John of Gaunt, Duke of Lancaster, became ill and sent for Richard to give him his dying advice. Although the Duke of York pointed out that giving advice to Richard was too often a waste of time, John of Gaunt felt that perhaps a dying man would be heeded while a living one would not. From his deathbed he criticized Richard's extravagance, for the mishandling of public funds had almost impoverished the nation. John of Gaunt warned Richard also that the kingdom would suffer for his selfishness.

Richard paid no attention to his uncle's advice. After the death of John of Gaunt, the king seized his lands and

wealth to use for capital in backing his Irish wars. His uncle, the aged Duke of York, attempted to dissuade the king from these moves because of Bolingbroke's anger and influence among the people. York's fears were soon confirmed. Bolingbroke, hearing that his father's lands had been seized by the king's officers, used the information as an excuse to terminate his period of banishment. Gathering about him troops and supplies, he landed in the north of England. There other unruly lords, the Earl of Northumberland and his son, Henry Percy (known as Hotspur) Lord Ross, and Lord Willoughby joined him.

Richard, heedless of all warnings, had set off for Ireland to pursue his foreign war. He left his tottering kingdom in the hands of the weak Duke of York, who was no match for the wily Bolingbroke. When the exiled traitor reached Gloucestershire, the Duke of York visited him at his camp. Caught between loyalty to Richard and his despair over the bankrupt state of the country, York finally yielded his troops to Bolingbroke. Richard, returning to England and expecting to find an army of Welshmen under his command, learned that they, after hearing false reports of his death, had gone over to Bolingbroke. Moreover, the strong men of his court, the Earl of Wiltshire, Bushy, and Green, had all been executed.

Destitute of friends and without an army, the sorrowing Richard took refuge in Flint Castle, where Bolingbroke went pretending to pay homage to the king. Making his usurped titles and estates his excuse, Bolingbroke took Richard prisoner and carried him to London. There Richard broke completely, showing little interest in anything, philosophizing constantly on his own downfall. Brought before Bolingbroke and the cruel and unfeeling Earl of Northumberland, Richard was forced to abdicate his throne and sign papers confessing his political crimes. Bolingbroke, assuming royal authority, ordered Richard imprisoned in the Tower of London.

During a quarrel among the young dukes of the court, the Bishop of Carlisle announced that Mowbray had made a name for himself while fighting in the Holy Land, had then retired to Venice, and had died there. When Bolingbroke affected great concern over that news, the Bishop of Carlisle turned on him and denounced him for his part in depriving Richard of the throne. Nevertheless, Bolingbroke, armed with numerous legal documents he had collected to prove his rights, ascended the throne. Richard predicted to the Earl of Northumberland that Bolingbroke would soon distrust his old aide because the nobleman had practice in unseating a king. Soon afterward Richard was sent to the dungeons at Pomfret Castle and his queen was banished to France.

At the Duke of York's palace the aging duke sorrowfully related to his duchess the details of the coronation procession of Henry IV. When the duke discovered, however, that his son Aumerle and other loyal followers of Richard were planning to assassinate Henry IV at Oxford, York immediately started for the palace to warn the new monarch. The duchess, frantic because of her son's danger, advised him to reach the palace ahead of his father, reveal his treachery to the king, and ask the royal pardon.

She herself finally pleaded for her son before the king and won Aumerle's release.

Having punished the conspirators, Henry IV grew uneasy at the prospect of other treasonable activities, for while Richard lived there was always danger that he might be restored to power. Henry IV, plotting the death of the deposed monarch, suggested casually to Sir Pierce Exton, a faithful servant and courtier, that he murder Richard at Pomfret.

There in his dungeon Richard quarreled with his keeper, according to Exton's plan, and in the struggle that ensued the knight drew his sword and struck down his unhappy prisoner. He then placed Richard's body in a coffin, carried it to Windsor Castle, and there presented it to Henry IV. Distressed over the news of mounting insurrection in the country, King Henry pretended innocence of the murder of Richard and vowed to make a pilgrimage to the Holy Land to atone for the death of his fallen cousin.

Critical Evaluation

Part of Shakespeare's second tetralogy of historical plays (with *1-2 Henry IV* and *Henry V*), *Richard II* is also his second experiment in the *de casibus* genre of tragedy—dealing with the fall of an incompetent but not unsympathetic king. It is also part of the "lyrical group" of plays written between 1593 and 1596, in which Shakespeare's gradual transformation from poet to playwright can be traced. The sources of the play include *The Chronicles of England, Scotland and Ireland* by Raphael Holinshed (second edition, 1587); the chronicles of Froissart, and Edward Hall; the *Mirror for Magistrates*; Samuel Daniels' poetic account, *The Civil Wars*; and an earlier play by an unknown author, *Thomas of Woodstock*. Nonetheless, *Richard II* demonstrates Shakespeare's own inventiveness, especially in the female roles.

Thematic interests in the play are associated, in one way or another, with the question of sovereignty. Bolingbroke's challenge to Richard brings into focus the divine right of kings, its historical basis, its social implications. Connected with this is the matter of a subject's duty of passive obedience, especially as seen in the character of Gaunt and of York. Richard's arbitrariness in the opening scenes suggests the dangers of irresponsible despotism; as we follow his thoughts and strange behavior through the play, contrasted with the caginess and certainty of Bolingbroke (whose thoughts are seen only as translated into effective action), he becomes a study of the complex qualities of the ideal ruler. In this last respect the play reflects the Renaissance fascination with defining optimum behavior in various social roles (for example, Machiavelli's *The Prince*, Ascham's *The Schoolmaster*, Elyot's *The Governor*). Yet Shakespeare's psychologi-

cal realism does not reach a falsely definitive conclusion. This uncertainty creates a tragic aura around Richard which makes him a most attractive character. In many ways, the play is not so much a contest for power as a struggle within Richard himself to adjust to his situation.

In this first play where Shakespeare makes his central figure an introspective, imaginative, and eloquent man, it is not surprising that some of his finest lyrical passages appear. *Richard II* is the only play Shakespeare wrote entirely in verse, supported by a regal formality of design and manner and a profuse and delicate metaphorical base. Intricately interwoven throughout the play are image-patterns centered on the eagle, the lion, the rose, the sun (which begins with Richard but moves to Bolingbroke), the state as theater, the earth as a neglected or well-tended garden, and the rise and fall of Fortune's buckets. The complicated imagery illustrates the subconscious workings of Shakespeare's imagination that will enrich the great tragedies to follow. As Henry Morley comments, the play is "full of passages that have floated out of their place in the drama to live in the minds of the people"— including Gaunt's great apostrophe to England (act 2, scene 1), York's description of "our two cousins coming into London," Richard's prison soliloquy (5,4), and his monologues on divine right (3,2) and on the irony of kingship (3,2).

So poetic is *Richard II* that critics speculate Shakespeare may have written the part for himself. As a lover of music, spectacle, domestic courtesy, and dignified luxury, Richard would be the ideal host to Castiglione's courtier. His whimsical personality is balanced, to great dramatic effect, by his self-awareness. Richard seems fascinated with the contradictory flow of his own emotions; and this very fascination is a large part of his tragic flaw. Similarly, Richard's sensitivity is combined with a flair for self-dramatization that reveals only too clearly his ineptitude as a strong ruler. He plays to the wrong audience, seeking the approval of his court rather than of the common people; he seems to shun the "vulgar crowd" in preference to the refined taste of a court that can appreciate his delicate character. The last three acts, emphasizing Richard's charm as a man, are obviously more central to the play's aesthetic than the first two, which reveal his weakness as a king. His sentimental vanity in the abdication scene is so effective that it was censored during Elizabeth's lifetime. The alternation of courage and despair in Richard's mind sets the rhythm of the play; Coleridge observes that "the play throughout is a history of the human mind." Richard's character is drawn with a skill equaled only by Shakespeare's depiction of King Lear.

When the king speaks of "the unstooping firmness of my upright soul" we understand that he is compensating verbally for his inability to act. Richard insists upon the sacramental nature of kingship, depending for his support on the formal, legal rituals associated with the throne; he is all ceremony and pathetically fatal pomp. Yet, from the outset, Richard contradicts even the logic of sovereign ceremony when he arbitrarily changes his decision and banishes the two opponents in the joust. Bolingbroke is quick to note the king's weakness, and steps into the power vacuum it creates. For Bolingbroke is the consummate actor who can be all things to all men by seeming so. He is impressed by the kingly power Richard wields: "Four lagging winters and four wanton springs/ End in

a word: such is the breath of kings." He likes what he sees and, in deciding to imitate it, surpasses Richard. Even when Bolingbroke is ceremonious, as he is when he bows his knee to Richard before the abdication, he is acting. And the difference is that he knows the most effective audience. Richard laments that he has seen Bolingbroke's courtship of the common people, "how he did seem to dive into their hearts." He recognizes the actor in Bolingbroke and fears its power. It is not coincidental that York compares the commoners to the fickle theater audience. As in so many plays of Shakespeare—*Hamlet*, *Richard III*, *King Lear*—the theater itself becomes a central image; Richard's monologues are a stark contrast to Bolingbroke's speeches not only because they reveal internal states but also because they are narcissistically oriented. They reach inward, toward secrecy and communicative impotency; Bolingbroke speaks actively, reaching outward toward the audience he wishes to influence. His role can be compared usefully to that of Antony in *Julius Caesar*, Richard's to that of Brutus. The tension between the two styles of speaking, moreover, no doubt reflects the transformation in Shakespeare himself that will make the plays to follow much more strikingly dramatic then they are sheerly poetic. The Bolingbroke of *Henry IV* is born in *Richard II*, his realistic, calculating, efficient, politically astute performance directly antithetical to Richard's impractical, mercurial, meditative, and inept behavior. Bolingbroke is an opportunist, favored by fortune. A man of action and of few words, Bolingbroke presents a clear alternative to Richard, when the two men appear together. If Richard is the actor as prima donna, Bolingbroke is the actor as director.

RICHARD III

Type of work: Drama
Author: William Shakespeare (1564–1616)
Type of plot: Historical chronicle
Time of plot: Fifteenth century
Locale: England
First presented: c. 1593

Richard III is one of the most fascinating villains in all literature. Despite his personal deformity, he exudes charm and wit, demonstrates a potent rhetorical power, and possesses a tactical ability that deceives and manipulates his adversaries with an ease that is as awesome as his ruthlessness is repugnant. In the end he is doomed by his own excessive ambition, but even in defeat his courage and style are impressive.

Principal Characters

Richard, Duke of Gloucester, afterward **King Richard III,** sinister and Machiavellian brother of King Edward IV. A fiendish and ambitious monster, he shows the grisly humor of the medieval Devil or the Vice of the morality plays. An effective hypocrite, he successfully dissembles his ambition and his ruthlessness until he has won his kingdom. His character in this play is consistent with that established in *King Henry VI*. The role furnishes great opportunities for an acting virtuoso and has long been a favorite with great actors.

King Edward IV, eldest son of the deceased Duke of York. An aging and ailing monarch with a sin-laden past and a remorseful present, he struggles futilely to bring about peace between the hostile factions of this court. Tricked by Richard into ordering the death of his brother Clarence, he tries too late to countermand the order. His grief over Clarence's death hastens his own.

George, Duke of Clarence, brother of King Edward and Richard. Guilty of treachery and perjury in placing his brother Edward on the throne, he is bewildered by his imprisonment and death. In prison he is troubled by terrible dreams, partly begotten by his guilty conscience, and he fears being alone. He has no idea that his fair-seeming brother Richard is responsible for his miseries until his murderers tell him so at the moment of his death.

Queen Margaret, the maleficent widow of the murdered King Henry VI. Her long curse delivered near the beginning of the play, in which she singles out her enemies, is almost a scenario of the play, which might well bear the subtitle of "The Widowed Queen's Curse."

The Duke of Buckingham, Richard's kinsman and powerful supporter. A cold and masterful politician, he is instrumental in placing Richard on the throne. Unwilling to consent to the murder of the helpless young princes, he loses favor, flees the court, rebels, and is captured and executed. As he goes to his death, he recalls the curses and prophecies of Queen Margaret, whose warning to him he has earlier ignored.

Edward, Prince of Wales, afterward **King Edward V,** older son of King Edward IV. A bright and brave boy, he furnishes pathos by his conduct and by his early violent death.

Richard, Duke of York, King Edward's second son. Impish and precocious, he bandies words even with his sinister uncle. He dies with his brother in the Tower of London.

Henry Tudor, Earl of Richmond, afterward **King Henry VII,** King Richard's major antagonist. A heroic figure, he leads a successful invasion against King Richard and kills him in hand-to-hand combat at the Battle of Bosworth Field. His concluding speech promises the healing of the wounds of civil war and the union of the houses of York and Lancaster by his forthcoming marriage with Elizabeth, daughter of King Edward IV.

Lord Thomas Stanley, Earl of Derby, stepfather of Richmond. Suspicious of Richard of Gloucester from the beginning, he remains a token supporter through fear. His heart is with Richmond; at the Battle of Bosworth Field he risks the life of his son George, a hostage to Richard, by failing to bring up his troops against Richmond. George Stanley's death is prevented by the killing of King Richard.

Lord Hastings, Lord Chamberlain under Edward IV. He is devoted to King Edward and his sons, though an enemy to Queen Elizabeth and her family. His loyalty prevents his becoming a tool of Richard in the campaign to set aside the claims of small Edward V. He trusts Richard to the point of gullibility and pays for his trust and his loyalty to Edward with his life.

Queen Elizabeth, wife of King Edward IV. A haughty and self-willed woman during her husband's reign, she has powerful enemies at court, including Hastings and Richard of Gloucester. After the murder of her small sons, she is a grieving, almost deranged mother. Her terror for her daughter's safety drives her to appear to consent to Richard's monstrous proposal for the hand of her daughter, his niece. The horrible match is prevented by Richard's death.

Elizabeth, daughter of Edward IV. Although she is not listed in the cast and has no lines, she is an important political pawn in the play. Richard seeks her hand to clinch his claim to the throne, and Richmond announces his forthcoming union with her.

Lady Anne, daughter-in-law of Henry VI. Although she hates Richard, murderer of her father-in-law and her husband, she succumbs to his wiles and marries him, becoming a pale, wretched victim. She shares sympathy with the Duchess of York and Queen Elizabeth. After Richard has had her murdered, her ghost appears to him and to Richmond, to daunt the one and encourage the other.

The Duchess of York, mother of Edward IV, Clarence, and Richard III. A loving grandmother to the children of Edward and Clarence, she hates and despises her son Richard, whom she sends to his last battle with a heavy curse, prophesying and wishing for him a shameful death.

Cardinal Bourchier (bou′chǝr, bōōr′-shǐ·ā), Archbishop of Canterbury. He enables Richard to gain possession of the little Duke of York in order to confine him in the Tower with his brother.

Thomas Rotherham (roth′ĕr′ǝm), Archbishop of York. He conducts Queen Elizabeth and the little Duke of York to sanctuary, but his kind action turns out to be in vain.

John Morton, Bishop of Ely. His gift to King Richard of strawberries from his garden is in grim contrast to the immediately following arrest and execution of Hastings.

The Duke of Norfolk (Jockey of Norfolk), a loyal follower of Richard III. In spite of a warning that Richard has been betrayed, Norfolk remains faithful and dies in battle.

Anthony Woodville (Earl Rivers), brother of Queen Elizabeth. An enemy of Hastings, he becomes reconciled with him at King Edward's entreaty. He is arrested and executed at Richard's commands.

The Marquess of Dorset and **Lord Grey,** Queen Elizabeth's sons by her first husband. Dorset escapes to join Richmond; Grey is executed by Richard's orders.

Sir Thomas Vaughan, one of Richard's victims. He is beheaded with Earl Rivers and Lord Grey.

Sir Thomas, Lord Lovel, Sir Richard Ratcliff, and **Sir William Catesby,** Richard's loyal henchmen. Catesby remains with the king almost to his death, leaving him only to try to find a horse for him.

Sir James Tyrrel, a malcontent. Ambitious and haughty, he engineers for Richard the murder of the little princes in the Tower. He is later remorseful for his crime.

Sir Robert Brackenbury, Lieutenant of the Tower. He resigns the keys to the murderers of Clarence when he sees their warrant. He is killed at Bosworth Field.

The Keeper in the Tower, a kind man. He does his best to ease Clarence's captivity.

Christopher Urswick, a priest. He acts as a messenger from Lord Derby to Richmond to inform him that young George Stanley is held as a hostage by the king.

The Lord Mayor of London. He allows himself to be used by Richard and his followers to help replace Edward V with Richard III.

Edward Plantagenet, Earl of Warwick, the young son of Clarence.

Margaret Plantagenet, the young daughter of Clarence.

The Earl of Surrey, the son of the Duke of Norfolk. He remains with King Richard's army.

The Earl of Oxford (John De Vere), one of the lords who join Richmond in his rebellion.

The Sheriff of Wiltshire. He conducts Buckingham to execution.

Tressel and **Berkeley,** gentlemen attending Lady Anne and the body of Henry VI.

Sir William Brandon, Sir James Blunt, and **Sir Walter Herbert,** supporters of Richmond.

Ghosts of Richard's Victims. These include, in addition to the characters killed in this play, King Henry VI and his son Edward, Prince of Wales. All appear to both Richard and Richmond. They rouse uncharacteristic terror in Richard and give refreshing encouragement to Richmond.

The Story

After the conclusion of the wars between the Houses of York and Lancaster, Edward IV was firmly established on the throne once again. Before long, however, his treacherous brother Richard, the hunchbacked Duke of Gloucester, resumed his own plans for gaining the throne. Craftily he removed one obstacle in his path when he turned the king's hatred against the third brother, the Duke of Clarence. Telling the king of an ancient prophecy that his issue would be disinherited by one of the royal line whose name began with the letter G, Richard directed suspicion against the Duke of Clarence, whose

name was George. Immediately Clarence was arrested and taken to the Tower. Richard, pretending sympathy, advised him that the jealousy and hatred of Queen Elizabeth were responsible for his imprisonment. After promising every aid in helping his brother to secure his freedom, Richard, as false in word as he was cruel in deed, gave orders that Clarence be stabbed in his cell and his body placed in a barrel of malmsey wine.

Hoping to insure his position more definitely, Richard then made plans to marry Lady Anne, widow of Prince Edward, son of the murdered Henry VI. The young Prince of Wales had also been slain by Richard and his brothers after the battles had ended; Lady Anne and Queen Margaret, Henry's widow, were the only remaining members of the once powerful House of Lancaster still living in England. Intercepting Lady Anne at the funeral procession of Henry VI, Richard attempted to woo her. In spite of her hatred and fear of her husband's murderer, she was finally persuaded to accept an engagement ring when Richard insisted that it was for love of her that he had murdered the Prince of Wales.

Richard went to the court, where Edward IV lay ill. There he affected great sorrow and indignation over the news of the death of Clarence, thus endearing himself to Lord Hastings and the Duke of Buckingham, who were friends of Clarence. Insinuating that Queen Elizabeth and her followers had turned the wrath of the king against Clarence and thus brought about his death, Richard managed to convince everyone except Queen Margaret, who knew well what had really happened. Openly accusing him, she attempted to warn Buckingham and the others against Richard, but they ignored her.

Edward IV, meanwhile, ailing and depressed, tried to make peace among the enemy factions in his realm, but before this end could be accomplished he died. His son, Prince Edward, was sent for from Ludlow to take his father's place. At the same time Richard imprisoned Lord Grey, Lord Rivers, and Lord Vaughan, followers and relatives of the queen, and subsequently had them executed.

Queen Elizabeth, frightened, sought refuge for herself and her second son, the young Duke of York, with the Archbishop of Canterbury. Richard, upon hearing of the queen's action, pretended much concern over the welfare of his brother's children and set himself up as their guardian. Managing to remove young York from the care of his mother, he had him placed in the Tower, along with Prince Edward. He announced that they were under his protection and that they would remain there only until Prince Edward had been crowned.

Learning from Sir William Catesby, a court toady, that Lord Hastings was a loyal adherent of the young prince, Richard contrived to remove the influential nobleman from the court. He summoned Hastings to a meeting called supposedly to discuss plans for the coronation of the new king. Although Lord Stanley warned Hastings that ill luck awaited him if he went to the meeting, the trusting nobleman paid no attention but kept his appointment with Richard in the Tower. There, in a trumped-up scene, Richard accused Hastings of treason and ordered his immediate execution. Then Richard and Buckingham dressed themselves in rusty old armor and pretended to the lord mayor that Hastings had been plotting against them; the lord mayor was convinced by their false protestations that the execution was justified.

Richard, with Buckingham, plotted to seize the throne for himself. Buckingham, speaking in the Guildhall of the great immorality of the late King Edward, hinted that both the king and his children were illegitimate. Shocked, a citizens' committee headed by the lord mayor approached Richard and begged him to accept the crown. They found him, well coached by Buckingham, in the company of two priests, with a prayer book in his hand. So impressed were they with his seeming piety that they repeated their offer after he had hypocritically refused it. Pretending great reluctance, Richard finally accepted, after being urged by Buckingham, the lord mayor, and Catesby. Immediate plans for the coronation were made.

Lady Anne, interrupted during a visit to the Tower with Queen Elizabeth and the old Duchess of York, was ordered to Westminster to be crowned Richard's queen. The three women heard with horror that Richard had ascended the throne, and they were all the more suspicious of him because they had been refused entrance to see the young princes. Fearing the worst, they sorrowed among themselves and saw only doom for the nation.

Soon after his coronation Richard suggested to Buckingham that the two princes must be killed. When Buckingham balked at the order, Richard refused to consider his request for elevation to the earldom of Hereford. Proceeding alone to secure the safety of his position, he hired Sir James Tyrrel, a discontented nobleman, to smother the children in their sleep. Then, to make his position still more secure, Richard planned to marry Elizabeth of York, his own niece and daughter of the deceased Edward IV. Spreading the news that Queen Anne was mortally ill, he had her secretly murdered. He then removed the threat from Clarence's heirs by imprisoning his son and by arranging a marriage for the daughter whereby her social position was considerably lowered.

But all these precautions could not stem the tide of threats that were beginning to endanger Richard. In Brittany, the Earl of Richmond, Henry Tudor, gathered an army and invaded the country. When news of Richmond's landing at Milford reached London, Buckingham fled from Richard, whose cruelty and guilt were finally becoming apparent to his closest friends and associates. Buckingham joined the forces of Richmond, but shortly afterward he was captured and executed by Richard.

In a tremendous final battle, the armies of Richmond and Richard met on Bosworth Field. There, on the night before the encounter, all the ghosts of Richard's victims appeared to him in his sleep and prophesied his defeat. At the same time they foretold the coming victory and success of the Earl of Richmond. These predictions held true, for the next day Richard, fighting desperately, was slain in battle by Richmond, after crying out the offer of his ill-gotten kingdom for a horse, his own having been killed under him. The earl mounted the throne and married Elizabeth of York, thus uniting the houses of York and Lancaster and ending the feud of those noble families forever.

Critical Evaluation

Richard III is the last of a series of four plays which began with the three parts of *Henry VI*. These plays, though not strictly speaking a tetralogy, trace the bloody conflicts between the Houses of Lancaster and York and interpret the events leading up to the establishment of the Tudor dynasty. Despite the painful experiences of Richard, the drama remains a history rather than a tragedy. Richard does not have the moral stature to be a tragic hero. A tragic hero may murder, but he does so in violation of his own nature; Richard, however, is quite at home when intriguing and slaughtering. Even as bloody a character as Macbeth implies an earlier Macbeth of nobler behavior. Richard is too intelligent and self-aware, too much in control of himself and those around him to raise any of the moral ambiguities or dilemmas which are necessary to tragedy. Nor does Richard come to any transcendent understanding of his actions.

Richard is, nevertheless, the dominating figure in the play and a fascinating character. All the other characters pale before him, and the play becomes primarily a series of encounters between Richard and the opponents who surround him. Physically, Richard is a small man with a humpback. Many commentators have suggested that his behavior is a compensation for his physical deformity. But Richard is not a paranoid; everyone really does hate him. The deformity, which is a gross exaggeration of the historical reality, is more likely a physical representation of the grotesque shape of Richard's soul in a Renaissance world which took seriously such correspondences. In any case, it makes for good theater by representing Richard and his plots as all the more grotesque.

Richard is also the master rhetorician in a play in which Shakespeare shows for the first time the full power of his language. In Richard's speeches and in the staccato exchanges among characters, there appears the nervous energy that informs the more ambitious later plays. From his opening soliloquy, Richard fascinates us not only with his language but also with his intelligence and candor. Up until the very end, he is the stage manager of all that occurs. As a villain, he is unique in his total control and in the virtuosity of his performance. Even Iago pales before him, for Richard, in soliloquies and asides, explains to the audience exactly what he is going to do and then carries it off expeditiously.

In his opening speech it is immediately clear that Richard will preside if not eventually prevail. He reveals not only his self-confident awareness of his own physical limitations and intellectual superiority, but also a disarming perception of his own evil and isolation. His honest villainy is more total than Iago's both in the way that he is able to convince every character that he is his only friend and in the full step-by-step disclosure of his intentions to the audience. Since everyone is against him, he almost generates our sympathy against our will. Anyway, there is no one else in the play to turn to.

The plot is the relentless working out of Richard's schemes to his final destruction. His first confrontation, with Anne, the widow of Henry VI's son, whom Richard had killed, is a model for Richard's abilities. The exchange begins with Anne heaping abuse on her husband's murderer and ends with Richard extracting from her a promise of marriage. Anne is overwhelmed more by the brilliance and audacity of Richard's rhetorical wit than by the logic of his arguments. Yet, the audience is left with the extreme improbability of the short time it takes Richard to be successful. The violation of probability, however, is as much a convention as Richard's speaking to the audience in soliloquy. It is one of the givens of the play. It is part of the definition of this villain that he could succeed in such a wildly improbable adventure. And repeatedly Richard is able to put those who hate him to his own uses in a perverse gratification of his ostensible desire for power and his submerged desire to be loved. Only his own mother is painfully able to see through to the total corruption of his heart.

For Richard, the path to kingship is clear: it is simply a matter of ingratiating himself to the right people and of murdering all of those who stand in his way. He contracts the murder of Clarence in the tower amid a good bit of gallows humor, which appropriately sets the grim tone. Like a good Machiavel, he both builds on past success and takes advantage of any fortuitous circumstances. Thus, he uses the death of Clarence to cast suspicion on Elizabeth and her party and to get the support of Buckingham, and he seizes on the death of Edward IV to have the influential nobles imprisoned and killed. Richard is clearing the political scene and the stage of obstacles. Nothing happens except at Richard's instigation, except for coincidences which he turns to his advantage. He eliminates Hastings and choreographs his own reluctant acceptance of the throne by implying that Edward's sons are bastards. Then he accomplishes the murder of the boys of his wife, Anne, the imprisonment of Clarence's son, and the discrediting of his daughter. He has efficiently removed all near claims to the throne by lies, innuendoes, and vigorous action.

So appealing is his virtuosity and so faithful is he in informing the audience of his plans that we share his apprehension as the tide of opposition swells under the leadership of Richmond. Shakespeare neatly figures the balance of power by setting up the opposing camps on opposite sides of the stage. The ominous appearances of the ghosts, to Richmond as well as Richard, portend that retribution is at hand. Although he is unnerved for the first time, Richard behaves with martial valor and struggles determinedly to the last. This show of courage, amid all of the recognitions of evil, is the final complication of our complex admiration for a consummate villain.

THE RIME OF THE ANCIENT MARINER

Type of work: Poem
Author: Samuel Taylor Coleridge (1772–1834)
Type of plot: Ballad fantasy
Time of plot: Late medieval period
Locale: A voyage around the Horn into the Pacific and then home to England
First published: 1798

Coleridge's intention in writing The Rime of the Ancient Mariner *was to make the supernatural seem real. To do so he carefully moves his reader from a realistic sea voyage, reinforced by concrete details from the everyday world, to a nighmarish otherworldly setting, where supernatural powers force the Ancient Mariner to undertake an allegorical quest for understanding and redemption.*

The Story

Three young gallants on their way to a wedding were stopped by an old gray-headed sailor who detained one of them. The Ancient Mariner held with his glittering eye a young man whose next of kin was being married in the church nearby and forced him to listen, against his will, to the old seaman's tale. The Ancient Mariner told how the ship left the home port and sailed southward to the equator. In a storm the vessel was blown to polar regions of snow and ice.

When an albatross flew out of the frozen silence, the crew hailed it as a good omen. The sailors made a pet of the albatross and regarded it as a fellow creature. One day the Ancient Mariner killed the bird with his crossbow. The superstitious sailors believed bad luck would follow.

Fair winds blew the ship northward until it reached the equator, where it was suddenly becalmed and lay for days without moving. The thirsty seamen blamed the Ancient Mariner and hung the dead albatross about his neck as a sign of his guilt.

In the distance a ship appeared, a skeleton ship which moved on the still sea where no wind blew. On its deck Death and Life-in-Death were casting dice for the crew and the Ancient Mariner. As a result of the cast, Death won the two hundred crew members, who dropped dead one by one. As the soul of each dead sailor rushed by, the Ancient Mariner was reminded of the whiz of his crossbow when he shot the albatross. Life-in-Death had

won the Ancient Mariner, who must now live on to expiate his sins. Furthermore, the curse lived on in the eyes of the men who died accusing him. One night the Ancient Mariner, observing the beauty of the water snakes around the ship, blessed these creatures in his heart. The spell was broken. The albatross fell from his neck into the sea.

At last the Ancient Mariner was able to sleep. Rain fell to quench his thirst. The warped vessel began to move, and the bodies of the dead crew rose to resume their regular duties as the ship sailed quietly on, moved by a spirit toward the South Pole.

The Ancient Mariner fell into a trance. He awoke to behold his own country, the very port from which he had set sail. Then the angelic spirits left the dead bodies of the crew and appeared in their own forms of light. Meanwhile, the pilot on the beach had seen the lights, and he rowed out with his son and a holy Hermit to bring the ship into harbor.

Suddenly the ship sank, but the pilot pulled the Ancient Mariner into his boat. Once ashore, the old man asked the Hermit to hear his confession and give him penance. The Ancient Mariner told the Wedding Guest that at uncertain times since that moment, the agony of his guilt returned, and he must tell the story of his voyage to one who must be taught love and reverence for all things God has made and loved.

The merry din of the wedding had ceased, and the Wedding Guest returned home a sadder and a wiser man.

Critical Evaluation

Critical opinion about *The Rime of the Ancient Mariner* runs the gamut from the sublime to the ridiculous; one commentator gives each line a gloss from the Bible, while another wonders why all the fuss is made about a bird. A modern critic (David Beres) finds in the poem a systematic description of an orally fixated, homosexual personality; another (Elder Olson) declares that the poem does not have to mean anything and that it stands simply as a beautiful object. A beautiful object it undeniably is, for read aloud its stanzas fall on the ear like music. But to view the poem simply as a travelogue is perverse. Samuel Taylor Coleridge's contemporaries, for all their bewilderment about it, never doubted its high import; Coleridge himself added the gloss to the fifth edition in order to make the allegory more accessible, so it seems reasonable to conclude that he did not intend it merely as a Gothic horror tale. But what did he intend?

Born the son of an Anglican minister, he turned to Unitarianism at Cambridge, but before writing *The Rime of the Ancient Mariner* he had returned to orthodox belief. Meanwhile he had absorbed certain tenets of Neoplatonism, which clearly helped to shape *The Rime of the Ancient Mariner*. For example, Coleridge and other Romantics believed that men were united with all living things in having been divinely created. They thought that palpable reality was but a screen beyond which a higher reality existed. In addition, the notion that places and elements were inhabited by tutelary spirits had acquired a vogue in literary circles at least at that time. Elements of Protestantism and Neoplatonism, then, formed the philosophical impulses of the poem.

The physical circumstance and details that are their vehicle are equally easy to trace. At the time of composition Coleridge had never been to sea, but it is known that some years previously—perhaps in preparation for a voyage to North America, where he and the poet Southey intended to set up a utopia—he had begun to read accounts of voyages around Cape Horn and to the hot climes of the Pacific. Navigational details of such voyages were familiar to everybody; the greater part of the descriptions of natural things, such as the green color of the polar ice and the sounds it makes, the phosphorescence clothing the "water-snakes," and the abrupt onset of night in the tropics, can be found almost verbatim in one or another chronicle or traveler's memoir of the time. The plot evolved strangely, from the smallest of seeds. A friend told the poet of a dream he had had of a skeleton craft worked by a ghostly crew. Coleridge decided to write a poem about this in collaboration with Wordsworth, in order to earn five pounds to pay for a walking tour. Wordsworth contributed a few lines and the suggestion that an albatross be the victim of the mariner's crime, before dropping out of the project, and Coleridge thereafter, in four months of sustained effort most uncharacteristic of him, completed the poem. It is the greatest of his poems—mysterious, ambiguous, and deliciously terrifying, defying pat interpretation.

Coleridge wanted to write a poem of which the virtue would "consist in the interesting of the affections by the dramatic truth of such emotions, as would naturally accompany [supernatural] situations, supposing them real." (Coleridge, quoted in *The Annotated Ancient Mariner* by Martin Gardner.) His first object, then, was to anchor the physical circumstances firmly in the known. To begin with, he employed the ballad form and strategic archaisms, as evocative and familiar as "Once upon a time." Then he set the tale upon the sea. No one in England can live farther from the sea than a hundred miles or so, and all Englishmen look on seafaring as their birthright. In addition, the navigational details in the poem are flawlessly correct: the sun overhead at noon when the ship is on the Equator, the frightful cold and emptiness of the polar passage, the sudden glare of the sun when the ice-fog is left behind, the trade winds blowing northeasterly that carried the ship north to the line again. Other details too—the warping of the deck in the calm, the thin rotting sails at the end of the voyage—all help to anchor the story in quotidian reality. At what point, then, does the ship pass into the spirit-haunted world of guilt, retribution, and rebirth? At the point farthest from home, the passage around Cape Horn. It is here that the Albatross appears, that Christlike creature that "loved the man/ who shot him with his bow." The act of shooting the albatross is so boldly stated, without any attempt at motivation or explanation, that it packs a tremendous emotional punch. Upon this act as on a pivot the entire plot turns; it is the reason for everything that follows. The reader is given notice that he is entering the realm of the supernatural. Yet it all happens so gradually that the sense of reality is preserved. The ship is becalmed in the tropics; what could be more ordinary?

The kind of suffering experienced by the mariner leaves no doubt about the Christian character of the allegory. The albatross is hung from his neck as a Christian wears a cross. He suffers the agonies of thirst, dryness being a universal symbol of spiritual drought, separation from the creative principle. He is brought by the grace of God to understand his kinship to the monsters of the calm, and so to all living things ("Sure my kind saint took pity on me,/ and I blessed them *unaware*). He is refreshed with rain, baptized anew when, by supernatural agency, the ship sinks in the home harbor. He is shriven of the guilt but not the memory of his crime, and like the Wandering Jew roams the world, telling his tale of death-in-life and rebirth in love.

"RIP VAN WINKLE"

Type of work: Tale
Author: Washington Irving (1783–1859)
Type of plot: Regional romance
Time of plot: Eighteenth century
Locale: New York State
First published: 1819–1820

Even though "Rip Van Winkle" was originally based on a Germanic folk tale, it has become, since its first appearance in Irving's Sketch Book, *a basic American myth. The story of Rip's escape from his shrewish wife and his domestic responsibilities into the mountains with his dog and gun, and his subsequent return has been a popular favorite since its publication.*

Principal Characters

Rip Van Winkle, who was born along the Hudson River, of an old Dutch family. To get away from his wife he goes into the Kaatskill mountains, where drink puts him to sleep for twenty years.

Dame Van Winkle, Rip's shrewish wife who is disgusted by Rip's lack of energy and thrift. She dies of a stroke in the midst of a fit of anger at a Yankee peddler.

Wolf, Rip's dog, chased with his master from the house by Dame Van Winkle.

Judith Van Winkle, Rip's daughter, who fails to recognize him after twenty years. Rip is relieved when she reports that Dame Van Winkle is dead.

Hendrick Hudson, the leader of the Little Men who return once every twenty years to bowl and drink. They provide Rip with liquor.

The Story

Along the reaches of the Hudson, not far from the Kaatskill mountains, there was a small, antique Dutch town. The mountains overshadowed the town, and there were times when the good Dutch burghers could see a hood of clouds hanging over the crests of the hills.

In that small town lived a man named Rip Van Winkle. He was beloved by all his neighbors, by the children and the dogs, but at home his life was made miserable by his shrewish wife. Though he was willing to help anyone else at any odd job that might be necessary, it was impossible for him to keep his own house or farm in repair. He was descended from a good old Dutch family, but he had none of the fine Dutch traits of thrift or energy.

He spent a great deal of his time at the village inn, under the sign of King George III, until his wife chased him from there. Then he took his gun and his dog Wolf and headed for the hills. Wolf was as happy as Rip to get away from home. When Dame Van Winkle berated the two of them, Rip raised his eyes silently to heaven, but Wolf tucked his tail between his legs and slunk out of the house.

One fine day in autumn, Rip and Wolf walked high into the Kaatskills after squirrels. As evening came on, he and his dog sat down to rest awhile before starting home. When Rip started down the mountainside, he heard his name called.

A short, square little man with a grizzled beard had called Rip to help carry a keg of liquor. The little man was dressed in antique Dutch clothes. Although he accepted Rip's help in carrying the keg, he carried on no conversation. As they ascended the mountain, Rip heard noises that sounded like claps of thunder. When they reached a sort of amphitheater near the top, Rip saw a band of little men, dressed and bearded like his companion, playing ninepins. One stout old gentleman, who seemed to be the leader, wore a laced doublet and a high-crowned hat with a feather.

The little men were no more companionable than the first one had been, and Rip felt somewhat depressed. Because they seemed to enjoy the liquor from the keg, Rip tasted it a few times while they were absorbed in their game. Then he fell into a deep sleep.

On waking, he looked in vain for the stout old gentleman and his companions. When he reached for his gun, he found only a rusty flintlock. His dog did not answer his call. He tried to find the amphitheater where the little men had played, but the way was blocked by a rushing stream.

The people he saw as he walked into town were all strangers to him. Since most of them, upon looking at him, stroked their chins, Rip unconsciously stroked his and found that his beard had grown a foot long.

The town itself looked different. At first, Rip thought the liquor from the keg had addled his head, for he had a hard time finding his own house. When he did locate it at last, he found it in a state of decay. Even the sign over the inn had been changed to one carrying the name of General Washington. The men gathered under the sign talked gibberish to him, and they accused him of trying to stir up trouble by coming armed to an election. When they let him ask for his old cronies, he named men who the loungers told him had moved away, or else they had been dead these twenty years.

Finally, an eager young woman pushed through the crowd to look at Rip. Her voice started a train of thought, and he asked who she was and who her father had been. When she claimed to be Rip Van Winkle's daughter Judith, he asked one more question about her mother. Judith told him that her mother had died after breaking a blood vessel in a fit of anger at a Yankee peddler. Rip breathed more freely.

Although another old woman claimed that she recognized him, the men at the inn only winked at his story until an old man, a descendant of the village historian, vouched for Rip's tale. He assured the men that he knew for a fact from his historian ancestor that Hendrick Hudson with his crew came to the mountains every twenty years to visit the scene of their exploits, and that the old historian had seen the crew in antique Dutch garb playing at ninepins just as Rip had related.

Rip spent the rest of his life happily telling his story at the inn until everyone knew it by heart. Even now when the inhabitants of the village hear thunder in the Kaatskills, they say the Hendrick Hudson and his crew are playing ninepins, and many a henpecked husband has wished in vain for a draught of Rip Van Winkle's quieting brew.

Critical Evaluation

The Sketch Book of Geoffrey Crayon, Gent. made Washington Irving the first American author to enjoy international fame. "Rip Van Winkle" is perhaps the best example in the collection of Irving's artistic movement away from the neoclassic cosmic interests of his earlier satirical writing toward a localized and sentimental Romanticism. In a sense, Irving's romanticism is more superficial than that of the great American Romantics such as Emerson and Poe. Irving is concerned more with capturing moods and emotions than with probing introspectively into metaphysical states. Even his later writing follows his early stylistic models, Addison and Goldsmith. Although he did not develop a style peculiarly his own, Irving nonetheless wrote with undeniable clarity, grace, and charm—making the "regional romance" a noteworthy and enjoyable American genre.

The author's introductory note calls Rip's adventure "A Posthumous Writing of Diedrich Knickerbocker," the imaginary historian Irving invented earlier for his *A History of New York by Diedrich Knickerbocker* (1809). The narrator's droll references to his own "scrupulous accuracy" and "precise truth," as well as the "confirmation" provided by Peter Vandervonk (a figure from the past parallel to the Dutchmen Rip meets in the mountains), add subtlety to the humorous claim of veracity. Never-

theless, the story clearly combines the literature of folk-fable with that of antifeminism. Rip is depicted, almost heroically, as a kind of Socrates: "a simple good-natured man," a great rationalizer, always willing to help others (consequently henpecked, because unwilling to do his own work), ever found at the inn—"a kind of perpetual club of the sages." From this ironic realism basis the story leaps into myth, with the appearance of the strange little man carrying the keg, whose sullenness somehow enhances his mysterious character and the story's naïve credibility. When Rip awakens to present reality, himself now a fabulous figure from the past, he finds things much the same as before. Irving's satirical point is that political and social revolutions are superficial. Change is a myth.

Like many of Irving's tales, "Rip Van Winkle" is said to be based on a common European legend. In adapting this source, however, Irving did not simply change the setting; he gave the story a distinctively American flavor. Americans are frequently characterized as optimistic, pragmatic, future-oriented; and yet as this story reveals, there is another strain in the national character. Here, even at the very beginning of American literature, there is a powerful undercurrent of nostalgia that plays against the story's ironic tone.

ROBIN HOOD'S ADVENTURES

Type of work: Folktales
Author: Unknown
Type of plot: Adventure romance
Time of plot: Thirteenth century
Locale: England
First published: c. 1490

Robin Hood, the legendary outlaw is a folk hero who has been celebrated in ballad and tale since the Middle Ages. The first collection of ballads dealing with his exploits, published about 1490, tells of Robin Hood's courage, skill at archery, and daring deeds in support of the poor. Although known chiefly as a children's hero today, Robin Hood has served as the prototype for a great many heroes of romantic fiction.

Principal Characters

Robin Hood, actually the young Earl of Huntingdon, whose father has been wrongly dispossessed of his estates. Robin Hood becomes an outlaw when he kills one of the king's stags after being taunted by foresters to show his skill with a longbow. Under sentence of death for killing the animal, the young nobleman flees to Sherwood Forest, where he gathers together a band of outlaws known as the Merry Men. Robin earns his place of leadership by outfighting and outshooting his comrades, all of whom become intensely loyal followers. Robin enjoys playing tricks on the authorities sent to capture him and gains support by helping the poor. Although eventually he is pardoned by Richard the Lion-Hearted and given back his title and estates, Robin becomes homesick for his old ways and returns to life in Sherwood Forest and outlawry. He is eventually killed by a cousin, the prioress at Kirkly Abbey, who bleeds him to death under the guise of giving him medical treatment.

Little John, a huge man who joins the Merry Men after being bested by Robin in a shooting match. As a lark, Little John spends six months in the service of the Sheriff of Nottingham, Robin Hood's enemy. Little John is with Robin at the time of the hero's death, though he arrives too late to save him. He buries Robin under the ancient oak where his last arrow fell.

Friar Tuck, a hedge priest who joins the Merry Men after a fight with Robin precipitated by the friar's ducking Robin in a stream.

Will Scarlet, one of the Merry Men. He participates with Robin and Little John in an archery match against the king's own men. In the match the outlaws appear as the queen's men and win for her.

Richard the Lion-Hearted, the king. He bests Robin in a fight and then pardons the outlaws, returning the rightful title and estates to their leader.

King John, who is infuriated when Robin Hood reverts to outlawry. He sends a force of men to capture Robin and his men.

The Sheriff of Nottingham, a crown officer who tries for years to capture Robin Hood. He is killed in a battle just before the death of Robin himself.

Sir Richard of the Lea, Robin Hood's friend, a knight once helped by Robin.

The Tinker, The Cook, Allan-a-Dale, and **George-a-Greene,** faithful followers of Robin Hood.

Maid Marian, a young girl vaguely associated with the Robin Hood cycle. Her importance in the story grew as the morris dance developed.

The Story

Before he became an outlaw, Robin Hood was the rightful Earl of Huntingdon. Because the times were so corrupt, his father had been dispossessed of his estates, and young Robin was driven into the forest. His method of protest was to organize a band of outlaws in Sherwood Forest and prey upon the rich to give to the poor.

The story about how he became an outlaw begins when he was on his way to a shooting match in Nottingham. Some of the king's foresters met him in Sherwood Forest and mocked his youth. Because one of the foresters wagered that he could not slay a deer, Robin Hood killed one of the king's stags. The penalty for his deed was death. When the foresters gave chase, Robin was forced to hide in the forest. There he found other landless, hunted men and became their leader.

While seeking adventure one day, Robin Hood encountered a tall stranger at a bridge. Calling his merry men after the stranger had tumbled him into the stream, Robin and his companions soon overcame the stranger. Then a shooting match took place between the two. Robin

Hood won the match, and the stranger good-naturedly acknowledged defeat and joined Robin's band. The outlaws called him Little John because he was so big.

The Sheriff of Nottingham was angered because Robin flouted his authority, and he issued a warrant for his arrest. This warrant was carried by a Tinker into the forest. When the Tinker met Robin Hood, however, he failed to recognize the fugitive because Robin was disguised. Robin took the Tinker to the Blue Board Inn, got him drunk, and stole the warrant. Later, the Tinker met Robin in the forest and fought with him. Robin Hood won the bout, and the Tinker happily joined the other merry men in Robin's band.

The Sheriff of Nottingham grew more and more enraged by Robin's boldness. When the king rebuked him for not capturing the outlaw, the sheriff devised another plan. Knowing that Robin Hood prided himself on his skill in archery, the sheriff proclaimed a shooting match in Nottingham Tower. There he hoped to catch Robin Hood and his men. They outwitted him, however, for they went to the match in disguise. As a tattered stranger, Robin won the golden arrow given as a prize. After he returned to Sherwood Forest, he sent the sheriff a note of thanks for the prize. This act infuriated the officer even more.

Now the band of outlaws lay low in the forest for a time. At last, Robin Hood sent one of his men to learn the sheriff's next plan. When he was captured, the band set out to rescue him. As he was being dragged forth to be hanged, Little John leaped into the cart and cut the prisoner's bonds. The other outlaws ran from their hiding places and overcame the sheriff's men.

Next Robin Hood bought some meat and took it to Nottingham to sell to the poor at half price. Disguised as a butcher, he was thought by most people to be either a foolish peasant or a wealthy nobleman in disguise. When Robin Hood offered to sell him a herd of cattle at a ridiculously low price, the sheriff gleefully accepted the offer. Then Robin took the sheriff to Sherwood Forest, took his money, showed him the king's deer, and told him that there stood his herd.

As a lark, Little John went to the Fair at Nottingham Tower, where he treated all the people to food and drink. He was asked to enter the sheriff's service because of his great size. Little John decided such employment might be fun. He found life in the sheriff's household so pleasant that he stayed six months, but he gradually grew bored and became arrogant toward the steward. The steward called the cook to fight Little John. Both men ate such a huge meal before fighting that neither could win. Finally, they decided to stop because they did not really dislike each other. Then Little John persuaded the cook to join the Band of Merry Men.

On another day, Robin Hood and his men went out to find Friar Tuck of Fountain Dale, supposedly a rich cur-

ate. Spying a strange monk singing and feasting beside a brook, Robin joined him. When Robin wished to go across the water, he persuaded the man to carry him on his back. On the return trip the monk, who was in reality Friar Tuck, dumped Robin into the water. After another great fight, with Robin the victor, the friar joyfully joined the outlaw band.

The queen had heard of Robin's prowess and was fascinated by stories told about him and his men; she invited him to come to London. In an attempt to outwit the king, she proposed an archery match at which she would put up three archers against his best three. If her team won, the king was to issue a pardon of forty days to certain prisoners. The king accepted the wager. The queen's archers were Robin Hood, Little John, and Will Scarlet, all in disguise. Naturally the outlaws won, although Will Scarlet was bested in his match. When the king learned that the queen's archers were Robin Hood and two of his men, he was angry, and they escaped capture only with the queen's help. The others returned safely to Sherwood Forest, but Robin Hood met with many dangerous adventures on the way. During his journey, he encountered Sir Richard of the Lea, a knight whom he had once aided, and Sir Richard advised him to return to London and throw himself on the queen's mercy. She persuaded the king to give Robin Hood safe escort back to Sherwood Forest and so pay the wager of the shooting match.

Returning from the Crusades, King Richard the Lion-Hearted decided to seek out Robin Hood and his outlaw band. With six others, all disguised as friars, Richard encountered Robin and his men and bested them. Richard then revealed himself and pardoned Robin and his men. Robin he restored to his rightful honors as the Earl of Huntingdon.

On a visit to Sherwood Forest several years later, Robin Hood became so homesick for his old life that he gave up his title and returned to live with the outlaws. His action infuriated John, the new king, and the Sheriff of Nottingham. They sent their men to capture the outlaws. During the fighting, the sheriff was killed. Robin Hood, ill and much depressed by this bloodshed, went to Kirkley Abbey, where his cousin was prioress, to be bled. She was a treacherous woman and had him bled too long, so that he lay dying. At last Little John, having pulled down bolts and bars to get to Robin, reached his leader's bedside. As Robin Hood lay dying in Little John's arms, he asked for his bow and arrows and said that he wished to be buried wherever his arrow fell. Then Robin shot an arrow through the window of the priory. Little John marked its flight, and Robin was buried beneath the ancient oak, which was his last target. His merry men disbanded after his death, but the stories of their brave deeds and the prowess of Robin Hood live on even to this day.

Critical Evaluation

Robin Hood's Adventures is one of the best-loved stories of all time. It has the elements that make for entertaining reading: romance, adventure, the stage of history, and lofty characters. As a work of prose fiction, however, it is quite unusual in one respect; comparatively few have actually read the book, whereas millions have heard about the story. Those who have not read the original have nevertheless come to know and love the characters of the Robin Hood legend through the countless other versions of the story in prose, fireside tales, motion pictures, and more recently television.

The Robin Hood story itself goes back well into the Middle Ages. Legends developed about a "good" outlaw who protected and supported the poor while he stole from the rich. Early legends, however, did not center on one bandit. There appear to have been several similar heroes of this type who eventually coalesced into the character of Robin Hood, Earl of Huntingdon, as he appears in this story. Whether the prototypes of Robin Hood were real, as some historians believe them to have been, is a moot point. It is the legend and not the reality of the story that has excited people for centuries.

Although the first recorded reference to Robin Hood occurred in the writings of the Scottish historian John of Fordun (died c. 1384), the first known compilation of prose and poetry of the Robin Hood legend came in 1490 with the publication of the *Lytel Geste of Robin Hood*, by Wynkyn de Worde, a noted British printer. If there were records for best-sellers in those days, certainly this tale would have been high on the list. It proved so popular that this version appeared again several decades later and has been reprinted and re-told for centuries. It was used as a basis for works of later novelists such as Sir Walter Scott in *Ivanhoe* and more recently on film in successful motion picture and television adaptations of the story. To the English especially, Robin Hood is a great hero. He and King Arthur are the most revered characters in British legends, and their popularity has spread and continues to thrive throughout the world.

Although *Robin Hood's Adventures* would hardly be classed as one of the great works of world literature, it is so entertaining that it may be read with delight over and over again. It is truly a case of the overall story being more important to its popularity than any of the individual elements of the work. The reader can forgive a lack of in-depth character analysis when he is made to feel as if he were riding through Sherwood Forest by Robin Hood's side.

The story line of the tale is quite simple: the underdog, Robin Hood, fights oppression and injustice in the form of the Sheriff of Nottingham and Prince John, to protect the poor and rally them around the good, but absent, King Richard I. Robin Hood represented an early attempt to personify *noblesse oblige*. He was a highborn man who helped the unfortunate. He did not condescend in his assistance, however, because he lived and worked among the poor in Sherwood Forest. By contrast, Prince John was a blatant representation of a powerful, oppressive leader. By persecuting Robin Hood, he inadvertently encouraged Robin's followers. King Richard, his brother, represents the colorful "good king" who was fighting in the Holy Land during the Third Crusade to overthrow the Muslims.

While this narrative makes for entertaining reading and is the basic plot outline for many works, it is quite far removed from historical fact. As the legends grew about Robin Hood, the actual historical events surrounding the reigns of Richard and John became blurred. In reality, Richard was rarely seen in England after he became king. He preferred traveling and fighting in other countries. John was not a particularly bad leader, merely unlucky. He was called John Lackland because he had the unfortunate habit of losing English territories to the French. For this reason, he became very unpopular and has had a bad reputation down through the centuries. Adding up the elements of John's unpopularity, Richard's swashbuckling image, and the possibility of real Robin Hood-type bandits existing in the period surrounding the signing of the *Magna Carta*, the legend has been expanded so that the historical truth has been buried in a good story. If one reads *Robin Hood's Adventures* as escapist literature, the facts may not matter, but one should bear in mind that the tale is not historically accurate.

ROBINSON CRUSOE

Type of work: Novel
Author: Daniel Defoe (1660–1731)
Type of plot: Adventure romance
Time of plot: 1660–1731
Locale: An island off the coast of South America and the Several Seas
First published: 1719

Like many famous stories, Robinson Crusoe is more known than read. The tale of the shipwrecked sailor who survives, rescues a servant (Friday), and eventually "civilizes" the island before being rescued, is universally familiar. Crusoe's adventures as a castaway actually occupy a modest portion of the book. The real story is that of a man who survives and prospers, whatever the environment, through hard work, intelligence, tenacity, and faith in his Protestant God.

Principal Characters

Robinson Crusoe, a self-sufficient Englishman who, after several adventures at sea and on land, is cast away on a small uninhabited island. A practical, far-sighted man of talents, he sets about to make his island home comfortable, utilizing all his knowledge. His prudence and industry, aided by an imaginative insight, enable him to pass twenty-four years alone, providing for himself in every way from the resources of the island itself and what he is able to salvage from the shipwreck that puts him in his predicament. A God-fearing man, he reads his Bible and gives thanks each day for his delivery from death.

Eventually he is rescued and returns to England after an absence of thirty-five years, only to go traveling again.

Mr. Crusoe, Robinson Crusoe's father, a middle-class Englishman. He wants his son to go into business and remain at home, rather than go to sea.

Friday, a savage rescued from cannibal captors by Robinson Crusoe. He proves an apt pupil and learns how to participate in his rescuer's life and labors. He learns to speak English and becomes a friend and companion, as well as a fellow laborer.

The Story

Robinson Crusoe was the son of a middle-class English family. Although his father desired that Robinson go into some business and live a quiet life, Robinson had such longing for the sea that he found it impossible to remain at home. Without his parents' knowledge, he took his first voyage. The ship was caught in a great storm, and Robinson was so violently ill and so greatly afraid that he vowed never to leave the land again should he be so fortunate as to escape death.

When he landed safely, however, he found his old longing still unsatisfied, and he engaged as a trader, shipping first for the coast of Africa. The ship on which he sailed was captured by a Turkish pirate vessel, and he was carried as a prisoner into Sallee, a Moorish port. There he became a slave, and his life was so unbearable that at the first opportunity he escaped in a small boat. He was rescued by a Portuguese freighter and carried safely to Brazil. There he bought a small plantation and began the life of a planter.

When another English planter suggested that they make a voyage to Africa for a cargo of slaves, Robinson once more gave way to his longing and sailed again. This voyage was destined to be the most fateful of all, for it

brought him his greatest adventure.

The ship broke apart on a reef near an island off the coast of South America; of the crew and passengers, only Robinson was saved. The waves washed him ashore, where he took stock of his unhappy plight. The island seemed to be completely uninhabited, and there was no sign of wild beasts. In an attempt to make his castaway life as comfortable as possible, he constructed a raft and brought away food, ammunition, water, wine, clothing, tools, sailcloth, and lumber from the broken ship.

He first set up a sailcloth tent on the side of a small hill. He encircled his refuge with tall, sharp stakes and entered his shelter by means of a ladder that he drew up after him. Into this area he carried all the goods he had salvaged, being particularly careful of the gunpowder. His next concern was his food supply. Finding that there was little that had not been ruined by rats or by water, he ate sparingly during his first days on the island.

Robinson found some ink and a quill among the things he had brought from the ship; before long, he began to keep a journal. He also added the good and evil of his situation and found that he had much for which to thank God. He began to make his shelter permanent. Behind his tent he found a small cave, which he enlarged and braced. With crude tools, he made a table and a chair, some shelves, and a rack for his guns. He spent many months on the work, all the time able to find wildfowl or other small game that kept him well supplied with food. He also found several springs that kept him supplied with water.

His life for the next twenty-four years was spent in much the same way as his first days on the island. He explored the island and built what he was pleased to call his summer home on the other side of it. He was able to grow corn, barley, and rice. He carefully saved the new kernels each year until he had enough to plant a small field. With these grains, he learned to grind meal and bake coarse bread. He caught and tamed wild goats to supply his larder and parrots for companionship. He made better furniture and improved his cave, making it even safer from intruders, whom he still feared, although he had seen no sign of any living thing except small game, fowl, and goats. He had also brought three Bibles from the ship, and he had time to read them carefully. At a devotional period each morning and night, he never failed to thank God for delivering him from the sea.

In the middle of Robinson's twenty-fourth year on the island, an incident occurred that altered his way of living. About a year and a half previously, he had observed some savages who had apparently paddled over from another island. They had come in the night and gorged themselves on some other savages, obviously prisoners. Robinson had found the bones and the torn flesh the next morning and had since been terrified that the cannibals might return and find him. Finally, a band of savages did return. While they prepared for their gruesome feast, Robinson shot some of them and frightened the others away. Able to rescue one of the prisoners, he at last had human companionship. He named the man Friday after the day of his rescue, and Friday became his faithful servant and friend.

After a time, Robinson was able to teach Friday some English. Friday told him that seventeen white men were prisoners on the island from which he came. Although Friday reported the men well treated, Robinson had a great desire to go to them, thinking that together they might find some way to return to the civilized world. He and Friday built a canoe and prepared to sail to the other island, but before they were ready for their trip, another group of savages came to their island with more prisoners. Robinson discovered that one of the prisoners was a white man and managed to save him and another savage, whom Friday found to be his own father. There was great joy at the reunion of father and son. Robinson cared for the old man and the white man, who was a Spaniard,

one of the seventeen of whom Friday had spoken. A hostile tribe had captured Friday's island, and now the white men were no longer safe.

Robinson dispatched the Spaniard and Friday's father to the neighboring island to try to rescue the white men. While waiting for their return, Robinson saw an English ship one day at anchor near shore. Soon he found the captain of the ship and two others, who had been set ashore by a mutinous crew. Robinson, Friday, and the three seamen were able to retake the ship, and Robinson was at last delivered from the island. He disliked leaving before the Spaniard and Friday's father returned, and he determined to go back to the island some day and see how they had fared. Five of the mutinous crew chose to remain rather than be returned to England to hang. Robinson and Friday went to England, Robinson returning to his homeland after an absence of thirty-five years. He arrived there, a stranger and unknown, in June of 1687.

Nevertheless, his adventures were not completed. When he visited his old home, he found that his parents had died, as had all of his family but two sisters and the two children of one of his brothers. Robinson now had no reason to remain in England. He went to Lisbon to inquire about his plantation. There he learned that friends had saved the income of his estate for him and that he was now worth about five thousand pounds sterling. Satisfied with the accounting, Robinson and Friday returned to England, where Robinson married and had three children.

After his wife died, Robinson sailed again in 1695 as a private trader on a ship captained by his nephew and bound for the East Indies and China. The ship put in at his castaway island, where he found that the Spaniards and the English mutineers had taken native wives from an adjoining island; consequently, the population was greatly increased. Robinson was pleased with his little group and gave a feast for them. He also presented them with gifts from the ship.

After he had satisfied himself that the colony was well cared for, Robinson and Friday sailed away. On their way to Brazil, some savages attacked the ship, and Friday was killed. From Brazil, Robinson went around the Cape of Good Hope and on to the coast of China. At one port, after the sailors had taken part in a massacre, Robinson lectured them so severely that the crew forced their captain, Robinson's nephew, to set him ashore in China, as they could no longer tolerate his preaching. There Robinson joined a caravan that took him into Siberia. At last, he reached England. Having spent the greater part of fifty-four years away from his homeland, he was glad to live out his life in peace and in preparation for that longer journey from which he would never return.

Critical Evaluation

The Life and Strange Surprising Adventures of Robinson Crusoe of York, Mariner as Daniel Defoe called his novel, is read as eagerly today as when it was first published. On the surface, an exotic novel of travel and adventure, *Robinson Crusoe* functions primarily as Defoe's defense of his bourgeois Protestantism. Crusoe's adventures—the shipwrecks, his life as a planter in South America, and his years of isolation on the island—provide an apt context for his polemic. A political dissenter and pamphleteer, Defoe saw his enemies as the Tory aristocrats whose royalism in government and religion blocked the rise of the middle class. Furthermore, like Jonathan Swift in *Gulliver's Travels,* Defoe presented England as religiously and politically corrupt in his novel. Each author was intent upon bringing about a moral revolution, using his hero as an exemplum. Gulliver, however, represents a moral failure, whereas Crusoe's adventures reveal his spiritual conversion, a return to the ethics and religion of his father. As one critic has said,

We read it [*Robinson Crusoe*] . . . in order to follow with meticulous interest and constant self-identification the hero's success in building up, step by step, out of whatever material came to hand, a physical and moral replica of the world he had left behind him. If *Robinson Crusoe* is an adventure story, it is also a moral tale, a commercial accounting and a puritan fable.

Significantly, Crusoe's origins are in northern England, in York, where he was born in the early part of the seventeenth century and where his father had made a fortune in trade. He is of the solid middle class, that class which was beginning to come to political power during the early eighteenth century, when Defoe published his book. Crusoe's father is an apologist for the mercantile, Puritan ethic, which he tries without success to instill in his son. As Crusoe says, "mine was the middle state," which his father

had found by long experience was the best state in the world, the most suited to human happiness, not exposed to the miseries and hardships, the labour and sufferings of the mechanick part of mankind, and not embarrased with the pride, luxury, ambition and envy of the upper part of mankind.

Its virtues and blessings were those of "temperance, moderation, quietness, health [and] society."

His father's philosophy, which is designed to buy man happiness and pleasure in both this life and the next, nevertheless fails to persuade the young Crusoe, who finds nothing but boredom amid the comforts of the middle class. He longs to go to sea, to follow a way of life that represents the antithesis of his father's. He seeks the

extremes of sensation and danger, preferring to live on the periphery rather than in the secure middle where all is mundane and sure. Crusoe's decision to become a sailor is an act of adolescent rebellion, yet it is also very much in the tradition of Puritan individualism. Not content with the wisdom of his class, the young man feels it is necessary to test himself, to discover himself and his own ethic.

Even after the first stage in his adventures, which culminates in Crusoe's amassing a modest fortune in South America, he refuses to follow his father's ethic and settle down. Intent on his own "inclination," as he says, he leaves his plantation and once again takes up the uncertain life of sea trade. It is at this point in the narrative that Crusoe is shipwrecked, abandoned alone on a tropical island without any hope of rescue.

Crusoe's first response to his isolation and the prospect of living the rest of his life alone is one of despair. His instinct to survive, however, remains dominant, and he sets to the task not only of staying alive but also of creating a humane, comfortable society. One of the first things he does is to mark time, to make a calendar. Despite all of his efforts to continue his own life and environment, he falls ill and it is at this point that he realizes his complete vulnerability, his absolute aloneness in the universe. Stripped of all his illusions, limited by necessity to one small place, Crusoe is thrown back upon himself, confronted by an immense emptiness. He asks desperately: "What is this earth and sea of which I have seen so much? Whence is it produced? And what am I and all the other creatures, wild and tame, human and brutal? Whence are we?"

All of these questions predate Crusoe's religious conversion, the central and most significant act of the novel. His answer to the questions is that all creation comes from God and that the state of all creation, including his own, is an expression of the will of God. Upon this act of faith, he rebuilds not only his own life but also his own miniature society that reflects in its simplicity, moderation, and comfort the philosophy his father had taught. Furthermore, his faith brings him to an acceptance of his own life and station, an acceptance that he was never able to enjoy before: "I acquiesced in the dispositions of Providence, which I began now to own and to believe ordered everything for the best." And later, after two years on the island, he says,

"It is now that I began sensibly to feel how much more happy this life I now led was, with all its miserable circumstances, than the wicked, cursed, abominable life I led all the past part of my days; and now I changed both my sorrows and my joys; my very desires altered, my affections changed their gusts, and my delights were perfectly new from what they were at my first coming."

Once the overwhelming question of the novel—"Whence are we?"—has been answered, the rest of the narrative and Crusoe's adventures justify to his religious faith and the middle-class Puritan ethic. In addition to this justification there remains the glorification of the self-reliant and self-directing man; he was a man unfamiliar to Defoe's readers, a new man who was beginning to appear on the fringes of the power structure and who was about to demand his place in a society that was evolving toward a new political structure that is now recognized as middle-class democracy.

ROMEO AND JULIET

Type of work: Drama
Author William Shakespeare (1564–1616)
Type of plot: Romantic tragedy
Time of plot: Fifteenth century
Locale: Verona, Italy
First presented: c. 1595

This famous story of star-crossed lovers, one of Shakespeare's most popular, is his great youthful tragedy. The play is passionate, witty, rapid, intensely lyrical, and romantically beautiful. Romeo and Juliet are personifications of young love; they are also the innocent victims of an angry, foolish society, embodied in the feuding families, and a malevolent providence that uses their deaths to force the feuding factions to reconciliation.

Principal Characters

Romeo (rō'mĭ·ō), the only son of old Montague, a nobleman of Verona. A romantic youth, inclined to be in love with love, he gives up his idealized passion for Rosaline when Juliet rouses in him a lasting devotion. His star-crossed young life ends in suicide.

Juliet (jōō'lĭ·ĕt), the only daughter of old Capulet. Little more than a child at the beginning of the play, she is quickly matured by love and grief into a young woman of profound grace and tragic dignity. Unable to find sympathy in her family and unable to trust her nurse, she risks death to avoid a forced marriage, which would be bigamous. Awakening in the tomb to find Romeo's body, she too commits suicide.

Montague (mŏn'tə·gū), Romeo's father, head of the house of Montague. An enemy of the Capulets, he is a good, reasonable man and father. In the family feud he seems more provoked than provoking. After the deaths of Romeo and Juliet he becomes reconciled with the Capulets.

Lady Montague, Romeo's gentle mother. Tender-hearted and peace-loving, she breaks down under the fury of the clashing houses and the banishment of her son and dies of grief.

Capulet (kăp'ū·lĕt), Juliet's fiery father. Essentially good-hearted but furiously unreasonable when thwarted in the slightest thing, he destroys the happiness and the life of his dearly loved daughter. He joins his former enemy in grief and friendship after her death.

Lady Capulet, Juliet's mother. Dominated by her husband, she fails to offer Juliet the understanding and affection the girl desperately needs.

The Nurse, Juliet's good-hearted, bawdy-tongued mentor. She aids the young lovers to consummate their marriage; but, lacking in moral principle, when Romeo is banished, she urges Juliet to marry Paris. Hence, Juliet has no one to turn to in her great distress and need.

Friar Laurence, a kindly, timorous priest. He marries the young lovers and tries to help them in their fearful adversity, but fails, thwarted by fate.

Benvolio (bĕn·vō'lĭ·ō), old Montague's nephew, the friend of Romeo and Mercutio. Less hot-headed than Mercutio, he tries to avoid quarrels even with the irreconcilable Tybalt. His account of the deaths of Mercutio and Tybalt saves Romeo from execution, but not from banishment.

Mercutio (mėr·kū'shĭ·ō), Romeo's volatile and witty friend. Poetically fanciful and teasing, he can be a savage foe. His angry challenge to Tybalt after Romeo has behaved with humility leads to various deaths and the final catastrophe. He has a superb death scene.

Paris (pă'rĭs), a young nobleman in love with Juliet. The hasty marriage planned by the Capulets between Paris and Juliet forces her to counterfeit death in order to avoid a bigamous union. The counterfeit becomes real for her—and for Paris and Romeo.

Escalus (ĕs'kə·lŭs), Duke of Verona, kinsman of Mercutio and Paris. A just, merciful ruler, he tries to arrange a peace between the feuding families. He joins them at the tomb which holds their dead children and presides over their reconciliation.

Peter, Capulet's stupid servant. Unable to read, he asks Romeo and Mercutio to help him with Capulet's invitation list, thus bringing about the meeting between Romeo and Juliet.

Friar John, a friend of Friar Laurence. Caught in a home visited by the plague, he is delayed too long to deliver Friar Laurence's letter to Romeo informing him about Juliet's counterfeit death. This is another of the fatal events that work constantly against the young lovers.

An Apothecary, a poverty-stricken old wretch. He illegally sells Romeo poison.

Balthasar (băl'thə·zär), Romeo's servant. He brings Romeo news of Juliet's supposed death and actual interment in the Capulet vault. He accompanies Romeo to the tomb and remains nearby, though ordered to leave the area by Romeo. His testimony added to that of Friar Laurence and Paris' page enables Duke Escalus and the others to reconstruct the events.

The Story

Long ago in Verona, Italy, there lived two famous families, the Montagues and the Capulets. These two houses were deadly enemies, and their enmity did not stop at harsh words, but extended to bloody duels and sometimes death.

Romeo, son of old Montague, thought himself in love with haughty Rosaline, a beautiful girl who did not return his affection. Hearing that Rosaline was to attend a great feast at the house of Capulet, Romeo and his trusted friend, Mercutio, donned masks and entered the great hall as invited guests. But Romeo was no sooner in the ballroom than he noticed the exquisite Juliet, Capulet's daughter, and instantly forgot his disdainful Rosaline. Romeo had never seen Juliet before, and in asking her name he aroused the suspicion of Tybalt, a fiery member of the Capulet clan. Tybalt drew his sword and faced Romeo. But old Capulet, coming upon the two men, parted them, and with the gentility that comes with age requested that they have no bloodshed at the feast. Tybalt, however, was angered that a Montaque should take part in Capulet festivities, and afterward nursed a grudge against Romeo.

Romeo spoke in urgent courtliness to Juliet and asked if he might kiss her hand. She gave her permission, much impressed by this unknown gentleman whose affection for her was so evident. Romeo then begged to kiss her lips and when she had no breath to object, he pressed her to him. They were interrupted by Juliet's nurse, who sent the young girl off to her mother. When she had gone, Romeo learned from the nurse that Juliet was a Capulet. He was stunned, for he was certain that this fact would mean his death. He could never give her up. Juliet, who had fallen instantly in love with Romeo, discovered that he was a Montague, the son of a hated house.

That night Romeo, too much in love to go home to sleep, stole to Juliet's house and stood in the orchard beneath a balcony that led to her room. To his surprise, he saw Juliet leaning over the railing above him. Thinking herself alone, she began to talk of Romeo and wished aloud that he were not a Montague. Hearing her words, Romeo could contain himself no longer but spoke to her. She was frightened at first, and when she saw who it was she was confused and ashamed that he had overheard her confession. But it was too late to pretend reluctance, as was the fashion for sweethearts in those days. Juliet freely admitted her passion, and the two exchanged vows of love. Juliet told Romeo that she would marry him and would send him word by nine o'clock the next morning to arrange for their wedding.

Romeo then went off to the monastery cell of Friar Laurence to enlist his help in the ceremony. The good friar was much impressed with Romeo's devotion. Thinking that the union of a Montague and a Capulet would dissolve the enmity between the two houses, he promised to marry Romeo and Juliet.

Early the next morning, while he was in company with his two friends, Benvolio and Mercutio, Romeo received Juliet's message, brought by her nurse. He told the old woman of his arrangement with Friar Laurence and bade her carry the word back to Juliet. The nurse kept the secret and gave his mistress the message. When Juliet appeared at the friar's cell at the appointed time, she and Romeo were married. But the time was short and Juliet had to hurry home. Before she left, Romeo promised that he would meet her in the orchard underneath the balcony after dark that night.

That same day, Romeo's friends Mercutio and Benvolio were loitering in the streets when Tybalt came by with some other members of the Capulet house. Tybalt, still holding his grudge against Romeo, accused Mercutio of keeping company with the hateful and villainous young Montague. Mercutio, proud of his friendship with Romeo, could not take insult lightly, for he was as hot-tempered when provoked as Tybalt himself. The two were beginning their heated quarrel when Romeo, who had just returned from his wedding, appeared. He was appalled at the situation because he knew that Juliet was fond of Tybalt, and he wished no injury to his wife's people. He tried in vain to settle the argument peaceably. Mercutio was infuriated by Romeo's soft words, and when Tybalt called Romeo a villain, Mercutio drew his sword and rushed to his friend's defense. But Tybalt, the better swordsman, gave Mercutio a mortal wound. Romeo could ignore the fight no longer. Enraged at the death of his friend, he rushed at Tybalt with drawn sword and killed him quickly. The fight soon brought crowds of people to the spot. For his part in the fray, Romeo was banished from Verona.

Hiding out from the police, he went, grief-stricken, to Friar Laurence's cell. The friar advised him to go to his wife that night, and then at dawn to flee to Mantua until the friar saw fit to publish the news of the wedding. Romeo consented to follow this good advice. As darkness fell, he went to meet Juliet. When dawn appeared, heartsick Romeo left for Mantua.

Meanwhile, Juliet's father decided that it was time for his daughter to marry. Having not the slightest idea of her love for Romeo, the old man demanded that she accept her handsome and wealthy suitor, Paris. Juliet was horrified at her father's proposal but dared not tell him of her marriage because of Romeo's part in Tybalt's death. She feared that her husband would be instantly sought out and killed if her family learned of the marriage.

At first she tried to put off her father with excuses. Failing to persuade him, she went in dread to Friar Laurence to ask the good monk what she could do. Telling her to be brave, the friar gave her a small flask of liquid which he told her to swallow the night before her wedding to Paris. This liquid would make her appear to be dead for a certain length of time; her seemingly lifeless body would then be placed in an open tomb for a day or two, and during that time the friar would send for Romeo, who should rescue his bride when she awoke from the powerful effects of the draught. Then, together, the two would be able to flee Verona. Juliet almost lost courage over this desperate venture, but she promised to obey the friar. On the way home she met Paris and modestly promised to be his bride.

The great house of the Capulets had no sooner prepared for a lavish wedding than it became the scene of a mournful funeral. For Juliet swallowed the strong liquid and seemed as lifeless as death itself. Her anguished family sadly placed her body in the tomb.

Meanwhile Friar Laurence wrote to Romeo in Mantua, telling him of the plan by which the lovers could make their escape together. But these letters failed to reach Romeo before word of Juliet's death arrived. He determined to go to Verona and take his last farewell of her as she lay in her tomb and there, with the help of poison procured from an apothecary, to die by her side.

Reaching the tomb at night, Romeo was surprised to find a young man there. It was Paris, who had come to weep over his lost bride. Thinking Romeo a grave robber, he drew his sword. Romeo, mistaking Paris for a hated Capulet, warned him that he was desperate and armed.

Paris, in loyalty to Juliet, fell upon Romeo, but Romeo with all the fury of his desperation killed him. By the light of a lantern, Romeo recognized Paris and, taking pity on one who had also loved Juliet, drew him into the tomb so that Paris too could be near her. Then Romeo went to the bier of his beautiful bride. Taking leave of her with a kiss, he drank the poison he had brought with him and soon died by her side.

It was near the time for Juliet to awaken from her deathlike sleep. The friar, hearing that Romeo had never received his letters, went himself to deliver Juliet from the tomb. When he arrived, he found Romeo dead. Juliet, waking, asked for her husband. Then, seeing him lying near her with an empty cup in his hands, she guessed what he had done. She tried to kiss some of the poison from his lips that she too might die, but failing in this, she unsheathed his dagger and without hesitation plunged it into her breast.

By this time a guard had come up. Seeing the dead lovers and the body of Paris, he rushed off in horror to spread the news. When the Capulets and Montagues arrived at the tomb, the friar told them of the unhappy fate which had befallen Romeo and Juliet, whose only sin had been to love. His account of their tender and beautiful romance shamed the two families, and over the bodies of their dead children they swore to end the feud of many years.

Critical Evaluation

One of the most popular plays of all time, *Romeo and Juliet* was Shakespeare's second tragedy (after *Titus Andronicus*, 1594, a failure), written during his first transitional period. Consequently, the play shows the sometimes artificial lyricism of early comedies such as *Love's Labour's Lost* (c. 1594) and *A Midsummer Night's Dream* (1595) while its character development predicts the direction of the playwright's artistic maturity. In his usual fashion, he bases his story on common sources: Masuccio Salernitano's *Novellino* (1476), William Painter's *The Palace of Pleasure* (1566–1567), and, especially, Arthur Brooke's poetic *The Tragical History of Romeus and Juliet* (1562). Shakespeare reduces the time of the action from the months it takes in Brooke to a few days.

In addition to following the conventional five-part structure of a tragedy, Shakespeare also employs his characteristic alternation, from scene to scene, between taking the action forward and retarding it, often with comic relief (as when the ribald musicians follow the "death" scene in act 4, scene 5), to heighten the dramatic impact. Although in many respects the structure recalls that of the *de casibus* genre (dealing with the fall of powerful men), its true prototype is Boethian tragedy as employed by Chaucer in *Troilus and Criseyde*—a fall into unhappiness, on the part of more or less ordinary people,

after a fleeting period of happiness. The fall is caused both traditionally and in the play by the workings of fortune. Insofar as *Romeo and Juliet* is a tragedy, it is a tragedy of fate rather than of tragic flaw. Although the two lovers have weaknesses, it is not their faults but their unlucky stars that destroy them. As the friar comments at the end, "A greater power than we can contradict/ Hath thwarted our intents."

Shakespeare succeeds in having the thematic structure closely parallel the dramatic form of the play. The principal theme is that of the tension between the two houses, and all the other oppositions of the play derive from that central one. Thus romance is set against revenge, love against hate, day against night, sex against war, youth against age, and "tears to fire." Juliet's soliloquy in act 3, scene 2 makes it clear that it is the strife between her family and Romeo's that has turned Romeo's love to death. If at times Shakespeare seems to forget the family theme in his lyrical fascination with the lovers, that fact only sets off their suffering all the more poignantly against the background of the senseless and arbitrary strife between the Capulets and Montagues. For the families, after all, the story has a classically comic ending; their feud is buried with the lovers—which seems to be the intention of the indefinite fate that compels the action.

The lovers, of course, never forget their families; their consciousness of the conflict leads to another central theme in the play, that of identity. Romeo questions his identity to Benvolio early in the play, and Juliet asks him, "Wherefore art thou Romeo?" At her request he offers to change his name and to be defined only as one star-crossed with her. Juliet, too, questions her identity, when she speaks to the slaying of Tybalt. Romeo later asks the friar to help him locate the lodging of his name so that he may cast it from his "hateful mansion," bringing a plague upon his own house in an ironic fulfillment of Mercutio's dying curse. Only when they are in their graves together, do the two lovers find peace from the persecution of being Capulet and Montague; they are remembered by their first names only, an ironic proof that their story had the beneficial political influence the prince wishes at the end.

Likewise, the style of the play alternates between poetic gymnastics and pure and simple lines of deep emotion. The unrhymed iambic pentameter is filled with conceits, puns, and wordplays, presenting both lovers as very literate youngsters. Their verbal wit, in fact, is not Shakespeare's rhetorical excess but part of their characters. It fortifies the impression we have of their spiritual natures, showing their love as an intellectual appreciation of beauty combined with a pure physical passion. Their first dialogue, for example, is a sonnet divided between them. In no other early play is the imagery as lush and complex, making unforgettable the balcony speech in which Romeo describes Juliet as the sun, Juliet's nightingale-lark speech, her comparison of Romeo to the "day in night," which Romeo then develops as he observes, at dawn, "more light and light, more dark and dark our woes."

At the beginning of the play Benvolio describes Romeo as a "love-struck swain" in the typical pastoral fashion. He is, as the cliché has it, in love with love (Rosaline's name is not even mentioned until much later). He is sheer energy seeking an outlet, sensitive appreciation seeking a beautiful object. Both Mercutio and the friar comment on his fickleness. But the sight of Juliet immediately transforms Romeo's immature and purely erotic infatuation to true and constant love. He matures more quickly than anyone around him realizes; only the audience understands the process, since Shakespeare makes Romeo as introspective and verbal as Hamlet in his monologues. Even in love, however, Romeo does not reject his former romantic ideals. When Juliet comments, "You kiss by th' book," she is being astutely perceptive; Romeo's death is the death of an idealist, though not of a foolhardy youth. He knows what he is doing, his awareness growing from his comment after slaying Tybalt, "O, I am Fortune's fool."

Juliet is equally quick-witted, and also has early premonitions of their sudden love's end. She is made uniquely charming by her combination of girlish innocence with a winsome foresight that is "wise" when compared to the superficial feelings expressed by her father, mother, and Count Paris. Juliet, moreover, is realistic as well as romantic. She knows how to exploit her womanly softness, making the audience feel both poignancy and irony when the friar remarks at her arrival in the wedding chapel "O, so light a foot/ Will ne'er wear out the everlasting flint!" It takes a strong person to carry out the friar's strategem after all; Juliet succeeds in the ruse partly because everyone else considers her weak both in body and will. She is a subtle actress, telling us after dismissing her mother and the nurse, "My dismal scene I needs must act alone." Her quiet intelligence makes our tragic pity all the stronger when her "scene" becomes reality.

Shakespeare provides his lovers with effective dramatic foils in the characters of Mercutio, the nurse, and the friar, but the play remains forever that of "Juliet and her Romeo."

THE SCARLET LETTER

Type of work: Novel
Author: Nathaniel Hawthorne (1804–1864)
Type of plot: Psychological romance
Time of plot: Early days of the Massachusetts Colony
Locale: Boston
First published: 1850

The Scarlet Letter is Hawthorne's masterpiece and his most profound exploration of sin, alienation, and spiritual regeneration. The novel traces the effects—social, moral, psychological, and spiritual—of Hester Prynne's adulterous relationship with the Reverend Arthur Dimmesdale on four people: the lovers themselves, their daughter Pearl, and Roger Chillingworth, Hester's husband.

Principal Characters

Hester Prynne, an attractive young woman living among the Puritans of Boston during the 1650s. She becomes a martyr because she, presumably a widow, bears a child out of wedlock; this sin results in her being jailed and then publicly exhibited on a pillory for three hours. When she is released from jail, she must wear for a lifetime a scarlet "A" upon her bosom. She becomes a seamstress, stitching and embroidering to earn a living for herself and for Pearl, her child. After her one act of sin, Hester behaves with such uncanny rectitude she seems an American Jeanne d'Arc, battling not against opposing armies and bigotry but against bigotry alone, the most formidable of antagonists. Hester refuses to name the child's father, who is the Reverend Arthur Dimmesdale, her minister; she does not quail when her supposedly dead husband, Roger Chillingworth, comes from out of the forest to witness her appearance on the pillory; and without complaint or self-pity she fights her way back to respectability and the rights of motherhood. Her situation is made more poignant (and heroic) by Dimmesdale's lack of sufficient moral courage to confess that he is Pearl's father. Hester seems to need no partner to share her guilt. Her life ends in tragedy (as it must) when Dimmesdale dies, but the reader feels that Hester—as strong as the oak in American clipper ships—will stoutly and resolutely make her way through life.

The Reverend Arthur Dimmesdale, a minister in Boston. Emotionally he is drawn and halved by the consequences of his sin with Hester, and he is pulled apart by responsibility. Should he confess and thus ruin his career or should he keep silent and continue the great good resulting from his sin-inspired sermons? Outwardly Dimmesdale is a living man, but inwardly he is the rubble and wreckage resulting from a Puritan conscience. One night he drags himself (along with Hester and Pearl) up to the pillory where he feels he should have stood long ago; but this confession is a sham, for only Roger Chil-

lingworth (hidden in the darkness) observes the trio. Finally, at the end of his Election Day sermon, he takes Hester and Pearl by the hand, ascends the pillory, confesses publicly, and sinks down dead. When his clothing is removed, Puritans see the stigma of an "A" on the skin of his chest. Hawthorne does not judge Dimmesdale's weakness or strength; he says simply, "This is Dimmesdale."

Roger Chillingworth, a "physician" who might better be called "Evil." Thought to have been killed by the Indians, he reenters Hester's life when she first stands on the pillory. Pretending to minister to the physically ailing Dimmesdale, he tries only to confirm his suspicion that the minister is Pearl's father. When Arthur and Hester, in a desperate act of hope, book passage on a ship to England, Chillingworth also signs up for the voyage, and Hester knows she can never escape him. Although motivated by his wife's bearing another man's child, Chillingworth nevertheless seems chillingly sinister in his revenge. Conniving, sly, monomaniacal, he is more a devilish force than a man.

Pearl, Hester's elfin, unpredictable daughter. She refuses to repeat the catechism for the governor and thus risks being taken from her mother. At a meeting of Hester and Arthur in the forest she treats the minister as a rival; when he kisses her on the brow, she rushes to a stream and washes away the unwelcome kiss.

Governor Bellingham, of the Massachusetts Colony. He thinks Hester is unfit to rear Pearl but is persuaded to allow them to remain together by the pleas of Dimmesdale.

The Reverend John Wilson, a stern divine. Early in the story he exhorts Dimmesdale to force Hester to reveal Pearl's father.

Mistress Higgins, the bitter-tempered sister of the governor; she is simply and literally a witch.

The Story

On a summer morning in Boston, in the early days of the Massachusetts Colony, a throng of curious people had gathered outside the jail in Prison Lane. They were there looking for Hester Prynne, who had been found guilty of adultery by a court of stern Puritan judges. Condemned to wear on the breast of her gown the scarlet letter, the "A" which stood for adulteress, she was to stand on the stocks before the meetinghouse, so that her shame might be a warning and a reproach to all who saw her. The crowd waited to see her ascend the scaffold with her child in her arms, and there for three hours bear her shame alone.

At last, escorted by the town beadle, the woman appeared. She moved serenely to the steps of the scaffold and stood quietly under the staring eyes that watched her public disgrace. It was whispered in the gathering that she had been spared the penalty of death or branding only through the intercession of the Reverend Arthur Dimmesdale, into whose church she had brought her scandalous sin.

While Hester stood on the scaffold, an elderly, almost deformed man appeared from the edge of the forest. When her agitation made it plain that she had recognized him, he put his finger to his lips as a sign of silence.

Hester's story was well known in the community. She was the daughter of an ancient house of decayed fortune, and when she was young, her family had married her to a husband who had great repute as a scholar. For some years, they had lived in Antwerp. Two years before, the husband had sent his wife alone across the ocean to the Massachusetts Colony, intending to follow her as soon as he could put his affairs in order. There had been news of his departure, but his ship had never been heard of again. Hester, a young, attractive widow, had lived quietly in Boston until the time of her disgrace.

The scaffold of the pillory on which Hester stood was situated next to the balcony of the church where all the dignitaries of the colony sat to watch her humiliation. The ministers of the town called on her to name the man who with herself was equally guilty, and the most eloquent of those who exhorted her was the Reverend Arthur Dimmesdale, her pastor. Still Hester refused to name the father of her child, and she was led back to the prison after her period of public shame had ended.

On her return to prison, Hester was found to be in a state of great nervous excitement. When at last medical aid was called, a man was found who professed knowledge of medicine. His name was Roger Chillingworth, he told the jailer, and he had recently arrived in town after a year of residence among the Indians. Chillingworth was the stranger who had appeared so suddenly from the forest while Hester stood on the scaffold that afternoon, and she knew him as her husband, the scholar Prynne. His ship had been wrecked on the coast, and he had been captive among the Indians for many months.

He also asked Hester to name the father of her child. When she refused, he stated that he would remain in Boston to practice medicine, swearing at the same time that he would devote the rest of his life to discovering the identity of the man who had dishonored him. He commanded Hester not to betray the relationship between them, and she swore she would keep his secret.

When Hester's term of imprisonment was over, she found a small house on the outskirts of town, far removed from other habitation. There with her child, who she had named Pearl, she settled down to earn a living from needlework, an outcast from society and still wearing the scarlet emblem on her breast.

Hester Prynne dressed her child in bright, highly ornamented costumes, in contrast to her own sober dress. As she grew up, Pearl proved to be a capricious, wayward child, hard to discipline. One day, Hester called on Governor Bellingham to deliver a pair of embroidered gloves. She also wanted to see him about the custody of Pearl, for there was a movement afoot among the strict church members to take the child away from her. In the garden of the governor's mansion, Hester found the governor, Dimmesdale, and old Roger Chillingworth. Because the perverse Pearl would not repeat the catechism, the governor was about to separate the child from her mother. Dimmesdale saved the situation, however, by a persuasive speech which resulted in the decision to let Hester keep Pearl, who seemed to be strangely attracted to the minister.

Roger Chillingworth had become intimately acquainted with Arthur Dimmesdale both as his parishioner and his doctor, for the minister had been in ill health ever since the physician had come to town. As the two men lodged in the same house, the physician came to know Dimmesdale's inmost thoughts and feelings. The minister was much perturbed by thoughts of conscience and guilt, but when he expressed these ideas in generalities to his congregation, the people thought him only the more righteous. Chillingworth, though, was now convinced that Dimmesdale was Pearl's father, and he conjured up for the sick man visions of agony, terror, and remorse.

One night, unable to sleep, Dimmesdale walked to the pillory where Hester Prynne had stood in ignominy. He went up the steps and stood for a long time in the same place. A little later Hester, who had been watching at a deathbed, came by with little Pearl. The minister called them to the scaffold, saying that they had been there before when he lacked courage to stand beside them. Thus the three stood together, Dimmesdale acknowledging himself as Pearl's father, and Hester's partner in sin. This striking tableau was not unobserved. Roger Chillingworth watched them from the shadows.

Hester Prynne was so shocked by Dimmesdale's feeble

and unhealthy condition that she was determined to see her former husband and plead with him to free the sick minister from his evil influence.

One day, she met the old physician gathering herbs in the forest and begged him to be merciful to his victim. Chillingworth, however, was inexorable; he would not forgo his revenge on the man who had wronged him. Hester then advised him that she would tell Arthur Dimmesdale their secret and warn him against his physician. A short time later, Hester and Pearl intercepted Dimmesdale in the forest as he was returning from a missionary journey to the Indians. Hester confessed her true relation with Chillingworth and warned the minister against the physician's evil influence. She and the clergyman decided to leave the colony together in secret, to take passage in a ship then in the harbor, and to return to the Old World. They were to leave four days later, after Dimmesdale had preached the Election Sermon.

Election Day, on which the new governor was to be installed, was a holiday in Boston, and the port was lively with the unaccustomed presence of sailors from the ship in the harbor. In the crowd was the captain of the vessel, with whom Hester had made arrangements for her own and Dimmesdale's passage. During the morning, the captain informed Hester that Roger Chillingworth had also arranged for passage on the ship. Filled with despair, Hester turned away and went with Pearl to listen to Dimmesdale's sermon.

Unable to find room within the church, she stood at the foot of the scaffold where at least she could hear the sound of his voice. As the procession left the church, everyone had only words of praise for the minister's inspired address. Dimmesdale walked like a man in a dream, and once he tottered and almost fell. When he saw Hester and Pearl at the foot of the scaffold, he stepped out of the procession and called them to him. Then, taking them by the hand, he climbed the steps of the pillory. Almost fainting, but with a voice terrible and majestic, the minister admitted his guilt to the watching people. With a sudden motion, he tore the ministerial band from across his breast and sank dying to the platform. When he thus exposed his breast, witnesses said that the stigma of the scarlet letter "A" was seen imprinted on the flesh above his heart.

Chillingworth, no longer able to wreak his vengeance on Dimmesdale, died within the year, bequeathing his considerable property to Pearl. For a time, Hester disappeared from the colony, but years later, she returned alone to live in her humble thatched cottage and to wear as before the scarlet emblem on her breast. The scarlet letter, which was once her badge of shame, however, became an emblem of her tender mercy and kindness— an object of veneration and reverence to those whose sorrows she alleviated by her deeds of kindness and mercy. At her death, she directed that the only inscription on her tombstone should be the letter "A."

Critical Evaluation

Since it was first published in 1850, *The Scarlet Letter* has never been out of print, nor indeed out of favor with literary critics. It is inevitably included in listings of the five or ten greatest American novels. Considered the best of Nathaniel Hawthorne's writings, it may also be the most typical—the strongest statement of his recurrent themes and an excellent example of his craftsmanship.

The main thematic emphasis in *The Scarlet Letter*, as in most of Hawthorne's work, is on sin and its effects upon both the individual and society. It is frequently noted that Hawthorne's preoccupation with sin springs from the Puritan-rooted culture in which he lived and from his awareness of two of his own ancestors who presided over bloody persecutions during the Salem witchcraft trials. It is difficult for readers from a more permissive era to conceive of the heavy import that seventeenth century New Englanders placed upon transgression of the moral code. As Yvor Winters had pointed out, the Puritans, believing in predestination, viewed the commission of any sin as evidence of the sinner's corruption and preordained damnation. The harsh determinism and moralism of those early years, however, had softened somewhat by Hawthorne's day; furthermore, he had worked out, perhaps during the twelve years he spent in contemplation

and semi-isolation, his own notions about man's will and his nature. Thus *The Scarlet Letter* proves him closer to Paul Tillich than to Cotton Mather or Jonathan Edwards. Like Tillich, Hawthorne saw sin not as an act but as a state—that which Existentialists refer to as alienation, and which Tillich describes as a threefold separation from God, other men, and self. This alienation needs no fire and brimstone as consequence; it is in itself a hell.

There is a certain irony in the way in which this concept is worked out in *The Scarlet Letter*. Hester Prynne's pregnancy forces her sin to public view, and she is compelled to wear the scarlet "A" as a symbol of her adultery. Yet, although she is apparently isolated from normal association with "decent" folk, Hester, having come to terms with her sin, is inwardly reconciled to God and self; and she ministers to the needy among her townspeople, reconciling herself with others until some observe that her "A" now stands for "Able." On the other hand, Arthur Dimmesdale, her secret lover, and Roger Chillingworth, her secret husband, move freely in society and even enjoy prestige: Dimmesdale as a beloved pastor, Chillingworth as a respected physician. But Dimmesdale's secret guilt gnaws so deeply inside him that he views himself with scorn as a hypocrite, and he is unable to make his peace with God or to feel at ease with his fellowman. For his part, Chillingworth has permitted revenge to permeate his spirit so much that his alienation is absolute; he refers to himself as a "fiend," unable to impart forgiveness or change his profoundly evil path. His is the unpardonable sin—unpardonable not because God will not pardon, but because his own nature has become so depraved that he cannot repent or accept forgiveness.

Hawthorne clearly distinguishes between sins of passion and those of principle. Finally, even Dimmesdale, traditional Puritan though he is, becomes aware of the difference:

> We are not, Hester, the worst sinners in the world. There is one worse than even the polluted priest! That old man's revenge has been blacker than my sin. He has violated, in cold blood, the sanctity of a human heart. Thou and I, Hester, never did so.

Always more concerned with the consequences than the cause of sin, Hawthorne anticipated Sigmund Freud's theories of the effects of guilt to a remarkable extent. Hester, whose guilt is openly known, grows through her suffering into an extraordinarily compassionate and understanding woman, a complete person who is able to come to terms with life—including sin. Dimmesdale, who yearns for the relief of confession, but hides his guilt to safeguard his role as pastor, is devoured internally. Again like Freud, Hawthorne recognized that spiritual turmoil may produce physical distress. Dimmesdale's well-being diminishes, and eventually he dies from no apparent cause other than continual emotional stress. *The Scarlet Letter* has links with a number of Hawthorne's shorter works. Dimmesdale reminds one of Young Goodman Brown, who, having once glimpsed the darker nature of mankind, must forevermore view humanity as corrupt and hypocritical; and of Parson Hooper in "The Minister's Black Veil," who continues to perform the duties of his calling with eloquence and compassion but is forever separated from the company of men by the veil which he wears as a symbol of secret sin. Chillingworth is essentially like Ethan Brand, the limeburner who found the unpardonable sin in his own heart: "The sin of an intellect that triumphed over the sense of brotherhood with man and reverence for God, and sacrificed everything to its mighty claims!"

Hawthorne's craftsmanship is splendidly demonstrated in *The Scarlet Letter*. The structure is carefully unified, with three crucial scenes at the beginning, middle, and end of the action taking place on the scaffold. The scarlet "A" itself is entwined into the narrative repeatedly, as a symbol of sin or of shame, as a reminder of Hester's ability with the needle and her ableness with people, and in Dimmesdale's case, as evidence of the searing effects of secret guilt. Several times there is forewarning or suggestion that is fulfilled later in the book: for example, notice is made that Pearl, the impish child of Hester and Dimmesdale, seems to lack complete humanity, perhaps because she has never known great sorrow; at the end of the story, when Dimmesdale dies, readers are told that "as [Pearl's] tears fell upon her father's cheek, they were the pledge that she would grow up amid human joy and sorrow, nor forever do battle with the world, but be a woman in it."

Hawthorne's skill as a symbolist is fully in evidence. As one critic has noted, there is hardly a concrete object in the book that does not do double duty as a symbol: the scarlet letter, the sunlight that eludes Hester, the scaffold of public notice, the armor in which Hester's shame and Pearl's elfishness are distorted and magnified—also serve as central symbols in this, the greatest allegory of a master allegorist.

SCEPTICISM AND ANIMAL FAITH

Type of work: Philosophy
Author: George Santayana (1863–1952)
First published: 1923

Scepticism and Animal Faith was written as an introduction to a system of philosophy, a system later made explicit in Santayana's four-volume *The Realms of Being: The Realm of Essence* (1927), *The Realm of Matter* (1930), *The Realm of Truth* (1938), *The Realm of Spirit* (1940). Despite the fact that the author believed that his ideas needed the extended treatment he gave them in these volumes, the introductory work remains the clearest, most concise, and most representative of Santayana's works. Almost every important contribution which the author made to philosophy can be found here; the advantage of this single work is that the reader can gain a synoptic vision of the relations of the ideas to one another, something he might fail to achieve if he centered his attention initially upon one of the volumes of *The Realms of Being* or *The Life of Reason* (1905–1906).

Santayana's principal thesis is that knowledge is faith "mediated by symbols." The symbols of human discourse, when man is talking to himself about the world of facts, are the elements in his experience: sensations, images, feelings, and the like. "The images in sense are parts of discourse, not parts of nature: they are the babble of our innocent organs under the stimulus of things," writes Santayana. Since we cannot be certain that the given elements, the essences, are signs of physical objects affecting us as physical organisms, there is a sense in which we cannot be said to be free of the possibility of error. Nevertheless, as animals, as active beings, we find ourselves compelled to take our experiences as the experiences of a living organism in the process of being shocked and stimulated by the world. Our belief in a nature of change is made possible by our interpretation of the given—the data, the essences—but it cannot be justified by the given: hence it is animal faith.

To prepare himself for the statement that all knowledge is the faith that certain given elements are signs of things and events, Santayana develops a thorough skepticism which ends with the cryptic statement that "Nothing given exists." To understand the meaning and ground of this claim it is necessary to understand Santayana's conception of the given—his theory of essences.

It is difficult to make all the proper qualifications in a brief description, but if one begins by supposing that essences are characteristics of actual and possible things, whether physical, psychical, mathematical, or whatever, a beginning has been made. If a person were to have two or three sense experiences of precisely the same sort—three sense images of a certain shade of yellow, for exam-

ple—that shade of yellow would be an essence that had been given to him in sense experience. Even if he had not had the experience, he could have had it; the essence is a character his experience might come to have. Essences, then, are universals, not particulars; they are characteristics which may or may not be the characteristics of existing things.

It makes sense to say of a particular thing that it is, or was, or shall be, but we cannot sensibly talk that way about the characteristics of things. Considered in themselves, as they must be, essences are immutable, eternal, never vague, and neither good nor bad. In Santayana's terms, the realm of essence "is simply the unwritten catalogue, prosaic and infinite, of all the characters possessed by such things as they happen to exist, together with the characters which all different things would possess if they existed."

If this definition of essence is kept clearly in mind, if an essence is simply a character but not necessarily the character of anything, then it becomes clear that if essences are given—and they are—then nothing given exists. If we are correct in our suppositions, then, whenever an essence is given, it is given to a self, that is, someone has an experience, and the experience has a certain character, and essence. The self that has experiences exists; the "intuition," that is, the apprehension of the character of the experience, exists; and, if the self is not mistaken in its interpretation of the given, of the "datum," a physical event or object exists as signified by the datum. In conventional language, there are persons, sense experiences, and the objects which give rise to the experiences. But it is improper now, and false, to say that the essence of the experience exists. To say this would violate Santayana's definition of essence and, accordingly, lead to a paradox. For example, if an essence is a character, and if on three occasions the same character were given, then the consequence of saying that on each occasion the essence existed is that the essence will have gone in and out of existence three times. If two persons have the same kind of experience—that is, intuit the same essence—then we would have to say that the essence is in two places at the same time. As long as one remembers that, by definition, an essence is a character considered as a character, it is clearly nonsense to think of essences as existing.

The discovery of essence is the reward of a relentless skepticism. In Santayana's view, we have no final justification for our claims about the existence of external objects, and all of our beliefs about selves and change and memory are open to critical challenge. "Scepticism may . . . be carried to the point of denying change and memory, and the reality of all facts," he writes.

But Santayana had no great affection for this ultimate skepticism. In his terms he was a "wayward sceptic," entertaining the notion of an ultimate skepticism only to show that critical challenge of our customary beliefs is possible. It is customary and unavoidable for a human being to suppose that he himself lives and thinks, and Santayana's rejoinder is "That he does so is true; but to establish that truth he must appeal to animal faith."

In order to discuss the human being in his response to the data of experience Santayana introduces his special senses of the terms "spirit," "psyche," and "intuition." Intuition is the apprehension of essence; the spirit is the cool contemplator, that which intuits; and psyche is the self that acts, has preferences, takes data as signs. Of course, when we begin to use these terms as descriptive of facts, we are expressing our own animal faith; when we say that the spirit confronts essences and that the psyche acts accordingly, taking the essences as signs of a physical world, we are saying what the ultimate skeptic cannot allow—but we are animals, and the psyche has other business than philosophy.

There is something appealing and liberating in Santayana's conception of animal faith. No one could be more careful than he in examining and challenging the pretensions of the pretenders to knowledge and wisdom: the paradox that knowledge is animal faith reveals that what we call "knowledge" is merely unwarranted, but stubborn, animal conviction. That same paradox brings out the positive side of Santayana's philosophy: as animals taking data as signs we make sense out of what would otherwise be a static complex of essences and give order both to our world and ourselves.

In the description of the consequences of animal faith in action, Santayana considered first the belief in discourse, which arises once one has given up "passive intuition." From the belief in discourse one passes to belief "in experience, in substance, in truth, and in spirit."

This progression of beliefs is a natural one, and the description of the life of reason in various areas was undertaken by Santayana in his earlier five-volume work *The Life of Reason*. *The Realms of Being* naturally followed *Scepticism and Animal Faith* as a careful elaboration of the terms "essence," "matter," "truth," and "spirit."

Unlike many philosophers, Santayana had self-confidence enough to know the limits of his inquiry. He did not pretend to be able to discover what the physicist, for example, can discover by acting on his scientific animal faith. Once we pass from the intuitive contemplation of essences to the recognition of the human use of data as signs, we soon come to the discovery of our assumptions of an experiencing self coming up against substance—the presumed cause of the data. The philosopher can clarify the idea of substance, explaining that it is extended, in space and time, with a structure, and so forth; and he can go on to identify substance with such homely examples as "the wood of this tree . . . the wind . . . the flesh and the bones of the man." But he need not, and Santayana does not, try to do what the physicist and the chemist do in their specialized ways.

By this practice, then, Santayana fulfilled the promise of his introduction to *Scepticism and Animal Faith*, in which he said: "Here is one more system of philosophy. If the reader is tempted to smile, I can assure him that I smile with him. . . . I am merely trying to express for the reader the principles to which he appeals when he smiles."

In this book, as in all his others, Santayana presents his ideas by means of a beautifully articulated, poetic style. Even if his vision of knowledge as animal faith had no value, this work would endure as the most fascinating portrayal of the realm of essence which has yet appeared in literature. That this moving survey of the timeless, changeless realm of essence should have come from a naturalistic philosopher is one of those pleasant paradoxes to which we turn with classic delight after coming from *Scepticism and Animal Faith*.

SHE STOOPS TO CONQUER

Type of work: Drama
Author: Oliver Goldsmith (1730–1774)
Type of plot: Comedy of situation
Time of plot: Eighteenth century
Locale: England
First presented: 1773

Oliver Goldsmith labeled She Stoops to Conquer *a "laughing comedy" to distinguish it from the "sentimental comedies" that dominated the theater in his day and which were, in his view, violations of the essential nature of the genre. In* She Stoops to Conquer, *he succeeded brilliantly, both artistically and commercially, in writing a comedy that is funny as well as insightful.*

Principal Characters

Mr. Hardcastle, a landed English gentleman. Sometimes grumpy, he is more often a hearty old squire with the habit of retelling the same jokes and stories to his guests. At first excited by the prospect of having Marlow as his son-in-law, he finds his patience severely strained by the apparent impudence of the young man, who is the son of Hardcastle's old friend, Sir Charles Marlow. When he receives incivilities in return for his hospitality, the old gentleman loses his self-control and orders Marlow and his party from the house. Finally, however, he realizes that he is the victim of a hoax and willingly accepts the young man as Kate's suitor.

Mrs. Hardcastle, his formidable wife. Her strongest desire, other than having her son Tony marry Constance Neville, is to have an annual social polishing in London. For a time she manages to thwart the romance of Hastings and Constance. Seeing that they are in love, she tries to circumvent their plans by taking Constance to Aunt Pedigree's. But this stratagem fails when her undutiful son Tony merely drives them around Mrs. Hardcastle's home for three hours, finally landing the unsuspecting old lady in a horse pond near her home. Finally, she is forced to acknowledge the fact that her beloved Tony has only one desire—to get his inheritance.

Tony Lumpkin, her son by her first marriage. He is a roistering young squire completely spoiled by his doting mother. In return for her parental laxness, the lazy, hard-drinking prankster, when he is not singing bawdy songs in low taverns, plagues the Hardcastle household with practical jokes. Although he is uncommonly healthy, his mother is certain that he is dying of some dread ailment. When he meets Hastings and Marlow, he gives them some wrong information, thus creating his masterpiece among tricks. By telling them that Mr. Hardcastle's home is an inn, he causes them to think Hardcastle is an

innkeeper and, what is worse, a windy, inquisitive old bore who takes unseemly social liberties with his guests. Hardcastle, on the other hand, is certain of their being impudent, cheeky young scamps.

Kate Hardcastle, Hardcastle's lovely young daughter. Like her stepmother, she also has social pretensions. Because of her stubbornness and desire to be a woman of fashion, her father makes her agree to wear fine clothes part of the day and ordinary clothes the rest of the time. Aware that Marlow is often improper with ordinary working girls, she disguises herself as a servant. Only then does she realize that he has qualities other than modesty and timidity. Liking this impetuous side of her suitor, Kate is now determined to have him as a husband.

Constance Neville, Kate's best friend. Early in the play, she learns of the joke which Tony has played on Marlow and Hastings, the man she loves. Entering into the spirit of the prank, she and Hastings plot their elopement. Unfortunately for their hopes, Mrs. Hardcastle is keeping a fortune in family jewels for Constance. In order to outwit the old lady, Constance acts out a part: she convinces Mrs. Hardcastle of her love for Tony, who actually dislikes Constance strongly. Finally, with the help of Kate's father, she is free to marry Hastings.

Young Marlow, Kate's reluctant suitor. Timid in the presence of ladies, Marlow is quite different with working girls. After mistaking Kate for a servant, he is mortified to learn her true identity. In his wounded pride, he plans to leave the house immediately; instead, she leads him away, still teasing him unmercifully.

Hastings, Marlow's best friend. With the help of Tony and Mr. Hardcastle, Hastings, a far more impetuous lover than Marlow, wins Constance as his bride.

Sir Charles Marlow, the father of young Marlow and Mr. Hardcastle's old friend.

The Story

Mrs. Hardcastle, the wife of Mr. Hardcastle by a second marriage, had by her first husband a son, Tony Lumpkin. Tony was a lazy, spoiled boy, but his mother excused his actions by imagining him to be sickly. Mr. Hardcastle vowed that his stepson looked the picture of good health.

Kate Hardcastle, Mr. Hardcastle's daughter, was headstrong. To overcome his daughter's wish to be a lady of importance, Mr. Hardcastle had struck a bargain with her whereby she wore ordinary clothes and played a country girl during part of the day; at other times she was allowed to appear in fine clothes. Knowing it was time for his daughter to marry, Mr. Hardcastle sent for Mr. Marlow, the son of his closest friend, to meet Kate. Kate was pleased by her father's description of the young man in all features except one. She did not like the fact that he was considered shy and retiring.

Mrs. Hardcastle hoped to arrange a match between Tony and Constance Neville, her ward and Kate's best friend. The two young people hated each other but pretended otherwise for Mrs. Hardcastle's sake. On the day of Mr. Marlow's expected arrival, Constance identified the prospective bridegroom as the friend of Hastings, the man whom Constance really loved. Constance described Marlow as being very shy with fashionable young ladies but quite a different character with girls of lower station.

En route to the Hardcastle home, Hastings and Marlow lost their way and arrived at an ale-house where Tony was carousing with friends. Recognizing the two men, Tony decided to play a trick on his stepfather. When Hastings and Marlow asked the way to the Hardcastle home, Tony told them that they were lost and would be wise to stop at an inn a short distance up the road. Marlow and Hastings arrived at their destination but thought it the inn Tony had described. Hardcastle, knowing nothing of their misconception, treated them as guests, while Hastings and Marlow treated him as an innkeeper, each party thinking the other extremely rude. Hardcastle decided that Marlow's apparent character was in contradiction to the modest personage who had been described to him.

When Hastings met Constance, she quickly recognized Tony's hand in the mischief, but Hastings and Constance kept the secret to themselves. Hastings explained to Marlow that the two young ladies had arrived at the inn after a long journey through the country. When Tony came home, Hastings took him aside and explained his desire to marry Constance, an arrangement quite satisfactory to the rascal. He promised to help the lovers and even to try to secure Constance's jewelry, which was in Mrs. Hardcastle's keeping. The bargain having been made, Tony went to his mother's room and stole the gems. He gave them to Hastings. When Constance asked for the jewels, Tony whispered to his mother that she should tell Constance they had been lost. Thinking it a capital plan,

Mrs. Hardcastle complied with Tony's suggestion, only to discover later that the gems actually were gone. Meanwhile, Kate, according to her agreement with her father, had put on a pleasant, simple dress.

Learning of Marlow's mistaken idea that he was at an inn, Kate decided to keep him in error. Marlow, seeing Kate in her simple dress, thought she was a serving-girl and revealed himself as a flirtatious dandy. As he was trying to kiss her, Mr. Hardcastle entered the room, and Marlow fled. Mr. Hardcastle remarked to Kate that obviously she now had proof that Marlow was no modest young man. Kate vowed she would convince her father Marlow had the kind of personality pleasing to them both. However, Marlow's continued impudence aroused Hardcastle to such an uncontrollable state that he ordered him to leave his house. Kate, thinking the time had come to enlighten her deceived suitor, told Marlow about the trick Tony had played. Marlow, still unaware of Kate's real identity, found himself more and more attracted to her, while Kate was discovering him to be a fine and honest person.

Hastings had given Marlow the jewels which Tony had stolen from Mrs. Hardcastle. To protect the valuables, Marlow had sent them to Mrs. Hardcastle, supposing her to be the innkeeper's wife. The servants, under Tony's instructions, then explained to the distraught lady that the jewels had been mislaid because of some confusion in the household.

Mrs. Hardcastle discovered that Hastings planned to elope with Constance. Enraged, she decided to punish Constance by sending her to visit her Aunt Pedigree. To add to the confusion, news came that Sir Charles, Marlow's father, was on his way to the Hardcastle home.

Tony offered to drive the coach for Mrs. Hardcastle, but instead of taking the ladies to the house of Aunt Pedigree, he drove them around in a circle for three hours until Mrs. Hardcastle believed they were lost. After hiding his terrified mother in the bushes, Tony took Constance back to Hastings. But Constance was determined not to leave without her jewels. When Mrs. Hardcastle at last discovered Tony's trick, she was furious.

Sir Charles, on his arrival, was greatly amused by Hardcastle's account of Marlow's mistake. Hardcastle assured Sir Charles that Marlow loved Kate, but Marlow insisted he was not interested in Miss Hardcastle. Kate promised the two fathers she would prove that Marlow loved her, and she told them to hide while she talked with Marlow. Still under the impression that Kate was a serving-girl, the wretched young man told her he loved her and wanted to marry her. Sir Charles and Hardcastle emerged from their hiding place satisfied that the marriage would be arranged. Marlow was upset to learn that the serving-girl with whom he had behaved was really Miss Hardcastle.

Mrs. Hardcastle reminded her husband that she had full control of Constance's fortune until Tony married her when he became of age. But if he should refuse her, Constance would be given control of her inheritance. It was then announced that Tony's real age had been hidden in the hope that the lad would improve his character.

Informed that he was already of age, Tony refused to marry Constance. Sir Charles assured Mrs. Hardcastle that Hastings was a fine young man, and Constance obtained her jewels from her guardian.

So Kate married Marlow, and Constance married Hastings. And Tony gained his freedom from his mother.

Critical Evaluation

Oliver Goldsmith was a poverty-haunted, irritable, and envious man with a great wit and generosity and an essentially lovable nature; all of these contradictory characteristics are reflected in his writings. Hopelessly impractical, especially in money matters, in talk often foolish, he wrote with genius and Irish liveliness in many different forms and left a legacy of at least four masterpieces that will last as long as the English language endures. Goldsmith was forced, like Dr. Johnson before him, to plod away as a literary hack, trying to survive in London's Grub Street literary world. He did editorial work for booksellers, wrote essays and criticism, and gradually gained a modest reputation. *The Citizen of the World* essays appeared in 1760 and 1761, bringing him more recognition; when they were republished, the charm and grace of the satire in these letters, and their humor and good sense, caused a sensation. Although this success eased somewhat the pinch of poverty, Goldsmith continued to find it necessary to write pamphlets and miscellaneous journalism. A philosophic poem, *The Traveler*, brought high praise from Johnson, and *The Deserted Village* was a wide success. In 1766 *The Vicar of Wakefield*, written to pay his rent, brought Goldsmith fame as a novelist. His collected essays was a further triumph, although his money troubles continued. *She Stoops to Conquer*, Goldsmith's second comedy, received a flattering public response, but the financial returns paid off no more than a fraction of the author's huge debts. The drudgery of his efforts to raise money with his pen caused his health to fail, and he finally died in 1774, only forty-four years old, a victim of his financial failure.

Goldsmith's writings reflected his whimsical, yet serious, nature. As he fluctuated from lighthearted foolishness to depths of depression, so his work demonstrates a somber, earthy thread running through the farce and sentiment. He belonged mainly to the neoclassical tradition, his style and vocabulary of the eighteenth century, but he avoided the ponderousness of his friend and mentor, Johnson. Even his sentimental streak was lightened with his Irish humor and wistfulness.

Of all of Goldsmith's varied writings, *She Stoops to Conquer* stands supreme, one of the most beloved comedies of all time. The humor and humanity of such characters as Kate Hardcastle and Tony Lumpkin had guaranteed the play's immortality. The sentimental drama, under the influence of such works as Steele's *The Conscious Lovers*, dominated the eighteenth century stage. The rising middle class craved this kind of drama, and it provided a conventional code of manners for these new prosperous theater-goers to emulate. In *She Stoops to Conquer*, Goldsmith tried to move toward real human motivation and escape the artificiality of the sentimental drama, which was in many respects a flight from reality. He satirized the posturings of the sentimental plays, but he did much more than that; his wit and style and shrewd eye for human foibles gave *She Stoops to Conquer* a vitality and sense of real life that has endured for more than two centuries.

With all of its polish, the eighteenth century was often crude and coarse and cruel; Goldsmith offered a more humane vision of human folly. At the conclusion of *She Stoops to Conquer*, the audience cannot help but be saner and more civilized, and to view its fellow mortals with a warmer sympathy. There is no viciousness in Goldsmith's comedy, as might be found in the plays of Sheridan, Congreve, or Molière. In *She Stoops to Conquer*, the emphasis is not on the outcome (which the audience never doubts) but on *how* the outcome will arrive. The basis of the plot is the sentimental conflict of the opposed love match and the subordinate trite plot complication (of the mistaken house as an inn, an incident which is said to have happened to Goldsmith in his youth). But Goldsmith takes these conventions and breathes new life into them, with a pace and humanity seldom approached in the drama. The characters are not cruel to one another; even Tony Lumpkin is essentially a goodhearted rogue. The conclusion is a happy one without anyone suffering or being left out in the cold. Unlike so many authors of comedies of manners, Goldsmith has no interest in punishing his characters.

Goldsmith was unlearned compared to his friends and compatriots Sheridan and Johnson, but he was a natural writer with a loathing for pretense and artificiality. If *She Stoops to Conquer* has any message, it is of the dangers of pretense and pretentiousness. Mr. Hardcastle's rule that Kate and her mother must dress plainly reflects this attitude of Goldsmith. The right of individuals to lead their own lives must be considered the second theme of the play, for both Kate and Marlow at last win their right to love and Tony wins his freedom from his mother.

Because of the failure of his previous play, *The Good Natur'd Man*, Goldsmith had difficulty getting *She Stoops to Conquer* produced. The great Garrick would have nothing to do with it, and general opinion was that it was too different from the prevailing mode to be a success. It was believed that only plays in the sentimental manner were wanted by audiences. After many difficulties, the comedy finally opened at Covent Garden, and Johnson himself led a party to see his friend's play through its hour of judgment. "I know of no comedy for many years," Johnson said, after, "that has answered so much the great end of comedy—making an audience merry." As usual, the Doctor was right, for, while one or two comedies of the time might be considered superior, none of them is merrier. There is, in *She Stoops to Conquer*, something of the quality of the great Elizabethan comedies, a humanity and humor that might have revolutionized the eighteenth century theater. But Goldsmith wrote no more plays, had no followers or imitators, and produced almost no effect on the drama of the day. Perhaps technically the play is not as perfect as those of Sheridan and lacks the sharp wit of the Restoration comedies, but it reflects the author's own rich and genial personality and will continue to be produced and read and loved as one of the kindliest and funniest of all comedies.

THE SICKNESS UNTO DEATH

Type of work: Philosophical treatise
Author: Søren Kierkegaard (1813–1855)
First published: 1849

Kierkegaard gave *The Sickness unto Death* a subtitle, "A Christian Psychological Exposition for Edification and Awakening," and he used the pseudonym "Anti-Climacus" when it appeared. Walter Lowrie, in an introduction to his translation of this work, calls *The Sickness unto Death* "one of the most important productions of that most productive period" of Kierkegaard's life. The subtitle and the pseudonym reflect not the wit and eccentricity of a pedant, but the conscience and intellect of a modest but nevertheless self-assured philosopher in the service of God. What is the "sickness unto death" which Kierkegaard reveals in his psychological exposition in so forceful a manner that the work has impressed the critics and affected the course of modern philosophic thought? It is the sickness of a self that wills to tear itself away from the Power which constituted it.

According to Kierkegaard, man is in despair, which he may not recognize, because he is always critically "sick unto death." For a spirit in such a condition, death is no escape; the sickness is "unto death" precisely because it is a despairful longing for death, not for extinction alone, but for the experience of not being the self that one is. It is as if man were longing for the experience of death—an impossible experience because death, considered as death, is the end of all experience. The self is not content to be itself; it is not content to relate itself to God; it cannot be satisfied with extinction—the result is, in Kierkegaard's view, "the sickness unto death."

Another way of understanding Kierkegaard's account of this dreadful malady of the spirit is through a consideration of what he means by health. Kierkegaard maintains that "to have a self, to be a self, is the greatest concession made to man, but at the same time it is eternity's demand upon him." Yet man's self is a relation between the infinite and the finite, the temporal and the eternal, freedom and necessity—and as a relation, a synthesis, the self cannot exist before the synthesis is achieved. For that reason, there is some sense in which, as Kierkegaard claims at the outset, "man is not yet a self": he has not achieved a synthesis with God, with the Power which constituted him. Sickness is this alienation; health is the elimination of despair, achieved when the self, recognizing its dependence on the Power which constituted it, wills to be itself.

To use language other than Kierkegaard's in the attempt to understand the central thesis upon which the value of the book depends, we can say that Kierkegaard is arguing that man, considered not as an animal but as a spirit, can realize himself only by being willing to admit that he becomes something worthy of the name "self" when he accepts the whole of his condition. This acceptance of limitations, of opposing powers, even of God's eminence, is not resignation; it is a willingness to live "no matter what," to be what one is in the world as it is.

It is tempting to make Kierkegaard's thesis broader than it is, to argue that the great Danish philosopher has more sense than to suppose that significant action is possible only by relating the self to God. But the term "God" is not a convenient symbol for power; for Kierkegaard, God is the Power which relates itself to every spirit and makes possible, through the self's acknowledgment of that relation, the existence of every self.

Atheistic Existentialists have found much that is helpful to them in Kierkegaard, but only by eliminating all references to God. Philosophers like Jean-Paul Sartre argue that in man "existence precedes essence," that only through action can man "make himself" into some particular self. "Authentic" existence is not given to a man, but he can create himself by the life he chooses and lives. For Kierkegaard also, health of the spirit is possible whenever man chooses to be himself—but only because to be himself man must relate himself to God, while for Sartre health of the spirit consists not in relating oneself to God, but in recognizing one's freedom from all such dependent relations. Sartre writes of the nausea and anguish which grip a man when he realizes his creative responsibility, but for Kierkegaard anguish is not the result of realizing one's own creative responsibility—it is the condition of a self which is not yet a self, of a man who tries to escape from God and, consequently, from himself.

The despair which is the sickness unto death may take any one of three forms: it may be the despair of not being conscious of having a self; it may be the despair of not willing to be oneself; or it may be the despair of willing to be oneself.

If a man is in despair, how can he fail to be conscious of it? Kierkegaard asserts that a man who is primarily sensuous can be in despair without being conscious of his condition. Such a man "lives in the sensuous categories agreeable/disagreeable, and says goodby to truth." A person who is sensuously happy will resent any attempt to take his happiness from him; he refuses to acknowledge the despair which is deep within him. This form of despair, unconscious despair, is the most common. Since the sickness of not being willing to be oneself before God is sinful, it is important that all who are in the anguish of dread come to be conscious of that dread as the first step toward creating a self which is a synthesis. Kierkegaard defines sin as follows: "Sin is this: *before God, or with the conception of God, to be in despair at not willing to be oneself, or in despair at willing to be oneself.*" Both kinds of despair are eliminated, of course, by being willing, before God, to be oneself.

The formula which enables a man to escape the sin, the offense, of dread is, at the same time, a definition of faith: "By relating itself to its own self and by willing to be itself, the self is grounded transparently in the Power which constituted it." The opposite of sin, according to Kierkegaard, is not virtue, but faith.

In order to emphasize his conviction that the opposition of faith to sin is a Christian concept which is fundamental to all ethical concepts, Kierkegaard stresses the importance of the qualifying phrase "before God." Man comes to have a reality, a self, "by existing directly in the sight of God," and because of this, man's sin—his not willing to be himself before God—concerns God. Kierkegaard admits that the notion of man's being invited to exist before God and of God's being concerned for man is unacceptable to many persons because it is both strange and demanding. Just as it would be puzzling and disturbing if an emperor were to invite a peasant to be his son-in-law, so it is puzzling and disturbing to suppose that God takes enough interest in each man to wish to have that man come to exist before him by willing to be himself before God. Yet this is the Christian idea, Kierkegaard insists, and it is an idea which illuminates the entire area of ethical being and action.

The despair at not willing to be oneself is called the despair of weakness, and the despair of willing to be oneself is called the despair of defiance. Such forms of despair result from a concern with self as if the self could exist by itself; this delusion is made possible by an absorption in matters that do not properly concern the spirit—matters of business or pleasure.

The sin of despair may give rise to new sins, to a continuation of sin. One may despair over one's sin, so concentrating attention upon it as to make impossible the emergence of faith, or one may despair of being forgiven. In the latter case, the sinner chooses, in weakness, to be a sinner, for he rejects the forgiveness which would enable him to be himself before God. Finally, one may commit the sin of abandoning Christianity, of declaring it to be false. This sin is "offensive warfare," according to Kierkegaard, and it is a sin against the Holy Ghost.

Kierkegaard's conception of God is often difficult to grasp, because he explains the relations between God and man in a dialectical way, claiming that one understands either only by appreciating the subtle effects that the actions and attitude of either have on the other and on the emergence of man's spiritual self. An interesting feature of his account is his conception of God as a being who "can do no other" than make the possibility of man's offense a part of man's condition. Dread must be possible for man because God is concerned to allow man the possibility of faith.

The influence of Kierkegaard in modern philosophy can be explained, paradoxically, by reference to modern man's loss of faith. A dissatisfaction with unexamined creeds quickly leads to the rejection of the creeds. Man is then in anguish over the void which he finds before him, and modern writers tell of "wastelands" and "lost generations." This metaphysical despair has been intensified in the twentieth century by the horrors of two world wars. Thus, it was during the period immediately following World War II that the Existentialists enjoyed their greatest influence, for they offered an alternative to suicidal despair, declaring that through action man creates his self. The Christian Existentialist turns his attention to God as the factor to which man must be related in order to be a self, while the atheistic Existentialist makes virtues out of lucidity, courage, and action. Of the Christian Existentialists, none has been more original and persuasive than Kierkegaard.

SILAS MARNER: The Weaver of Raveloe

Type of work: Novel
Author: George Eliot (Mary Ann Evans, 1819–1880)
Type of plot: Domestic realism
Time of plot: Early nineteenth century
Locale: England
First published: 1861

This charming tale of a poor dissenting weaver who, betrayed and unjustly accused, becomes bitter and miserly until redeemed and transformed by a foundling, is virtually perfect in structure, tone, and execution. As several critics have pointed out, the novel combines the emotional and moral satisfactions of the fairy tale with the solid intellectual appeal of the realistic narrative.

Principal Characters

Silas Marner, a weaver of Raveloe. As a resident of Lantern Yard, he had been simple, trusting, and religious until falsely accused of theft. He then loses his faith in religion and people. Turning away from humanity, he directs his stunted affections towards his steadily increasing pile of coins. However, when Eppie enters his life, he regains his belief in the fundamental goodness of man. In his bewildered fashion he accepts help from his Raveloe neighbors and decides to rear the motherless child who has captured his heart; under her influence he no longer despairs because of the stolen money.

Eppie (Hephzibah), Marner's adopted daughter. Fair-haired and blue-eyed, she captivates everyone who meets her, including young Aaron Winthrop, her future husband. After years of loneliness, Silas is sustained and his spirit nurtured by having her constantly near him. Even after she marries Aaron, she is determined to care for Marner, now frail and bent from years of unremitting toil at the loom.

Godfrey Cass, Eppie's real father and the weak son of Squire Cass, a prominent Raveloe landowner. Blackmailed by his brother Dunstan, he lacks the moral courage to acknowledge to the public that Eppie is his daughter. Instead, fearing disinheritance, he keeps silent for many years with his guilt gnawing at his soul. Later, however, when Dunstan's skeleton is found in the Stone Pits, he finally confesses to his wife Nancy his previous marriage to Molly, dead for sixteen years. Belatedly, he wants, with Nancy's consent, to accept Eppie as his daughter. Thinking Eppie will be overcome by his generosity, he is shocked by her determination to remain with Silas.

Dunstan Cass (Dunsey), Godfrey's dull-minded, spendthrift brother. Drunken and dissolute, he forces Godfrey to give him money by threatening to reveal the secret of Godfrey's marriage to Molly, a low-bred, common woman. After stealing Silas' gold, he falls into the Stone Pit. Years later his skeleton, the gold still beside it, is found wedged between two huge stones.

Nancy Lammeter, Godfrey's second wife, a lovely, decorous, and prim young woman. Although living by a narrow moral code, she surprises her husband, who has underestimated her, by courageously accepting the knowledge of his marriage to Molly.

Squire Cass, a prominent Raveloe landowner. Often lax in his discipline, he can be unyielding when aroused. At times this inflexibility of character makes both his sons and tenants fear his anger.

William Dane, Silas Marner's treacherous friend in Lantern Yard. While mouthing religious platitudes, he steals money from the church and implicates Marner, thus forcing the latter's exile from the village. By planting Silas' pocketknife at the scene of the crime, Dane can steal the money with impunity, knowing that his friend will receive the blame.

Aaron Winthrop, a sturdy young Raveloe citizen. For many years he has worshiped Eppie; when she promises to marry him, he is overjoyed. He promises Silas security and love in the old man's increasing feebleness.

Molly Cass, Godfrey's first wife. A drug addict who marries him when he is drunk, she later walks to Raveloe to expose him as her husband. Fortunately for Godfrey, she takes an overdose of laudanum and freezes to death in the snow, leaving her baby to toddle into the warmth and security of Silas' cottage.

Dolly Winthrop, Aaron's mother, the wife of Raveloe's wheelwright. She and her little son often visit Silas, and it is she who defends his right to keep Eppie when the villagers question Silas' suitability as a parent.

The Story

Silas Marner, the linen weaver, lived in the small community of Raveloe. Long years at his spinning wheel had left Silas extremely nearsighted so that his vision was limited to only those objects that were very bright or very close to him. Because of an unjust accusation of theft, Silas had left his former home at Lantern Yard and had become a recluse. For fifteen years, the lonely, shriveled man had lived for no purpose but to hoard the money he received in payment for his weaving. Night after night, he took his golden hoard from its hiding place in the floor of his cottage and let the shining pieces run through his fingers.

The leading man in Raveloe was Squire Cass, who had one fine son, Godfrey, and one wastrel son, Dunstan. It was said that Godfrey would marry Nancy Lammeter. Godfrey, however, had become involved in Dunstan's gambling debts. He had lent his spendthrift brother some of the squire's rent money, which Dunstan had lost in gambling. Since neither brother could raise the money, they decided that Dunstan must sell Godfrey's favorite horse, Wildfire, at a nearby fair. Godfrey's one fear was that this affair would harm his reputation in the neighborhood and his chance with Nancy. Another thing that weighed on Godfrey's conscience and prevented his declaration to Nancy was the fact that he was already married. Once he had been drunk in a tavern in a distant hamlet, and in that condition he had married a low-bred, common woman. Sober, he had fled back to Raveloe and kept his marriage a secret.

Dunstan rode Wildfire across the fog-dimmed fields and crippled the animal on a high jump. With no means of raising the money, half-drunk and fear-driven, Dunstan came to Silas Marner's cottage. He knew through the neighborhood gossip that the weaver had a hoard of gold hidden away. The cottage was empty, and instinct soon led the drunken boy to the hiding place of the gold. Stealing out of the cabin with his prize and stumbling through the night, Dunstan fell into an abandoned quarry pit and was killed.

The robbery of Silas' cottage furnished gossip for the entire community. Another mystery was the disappearance of Dunstan Cass. Godfrey was forced now to tell his father about the rent money he had given Dunstan and about the loss of the valuable horse, which had been found dead. Silas began to receive visitors from the neighborhood. One of his most frequent callers was Dolly Winthrop and her son Aaron, a charming little boy. Nevertheless, Silas could not be persuaded to come out of his hermitage; he secretly mourned the loss of his gold.

On New Year's Eve, a destitute woman died in the snow near Silas' cottage. She had with her a little yellow-haired girl who made her way toward the light shining through the cottage window and entered the house. Returning from an errand, Silas saw a golden gleam in front of his fireplace, a gleam that he mistook for his lost gold. On closer examination, he discovered a sleeping baby. He followed the child's tracks through the snow and discovered the body of the dead woman.

Godfrey was dancing happily with Nancy when Silas appeared to say that he had found a body. Godfrey went with the others to the scene and saw to his horror that the dead woman was his estranged wife. He told no one of her identity, and he did not have the courage to claim the baby for his own. Silas, with a confused association between the golden-haired child and his lost hoard, tenaciously clung to the child. After Dolly Winthrop spoke up in favor of his proper attitude toward children, the villagers decided to leave the baby with the old weaver.

Years passed. Under the spell of the child, who in her baby language called herself Eppie instead of the biblical Hephzibah that Silas had bestowed upon her, the cottage of the weaver of Raveloe took on a new appearance. Lacy curtains decorated the once drab windows, and Silas outgrew his shell of reticence. Dolly brought her son to play with Eppie. Silas was happy. After many years, he even returned to Lantern Yard, taking Eppie. He searched his old neighborhood hopefully but could find no one who could clear his blighted past.

Godfrey Cass married Nancy, but it was a childless union. For sixteen years, Godfrey secretly carried with him the thought of his child growing up under the care of Silas. At last, the old stone quarry was drained, and workmen found a skeleton identified by Dunstan's watch and seals. Beside the skeleton was Silas' lost bag of gold, stolen on the night of Dunstan's disappearance. With this discovery, Godfrey's past reopened its sealed doors. He felt that the time had come to tell Nancy the truth. When he confessed the story of Eppie's birth, Nancy agreed with him that they should go to Silas. When they revealed Eppie's parentage, the unselfish weaver opened the way for Eppie to take advantage of her wealthy heritage; but Eppie fled to the arms of the man who had been a father and a mother to her when no one else would claim her.

There was one thing remaining to complete the weaver's happiness. Eppie married Aaron Winthrop, her childhood playmate, while Silas beamed happily on the scene of her wedding.

Critical Evaluation

In four remarkable years, George Eliot published in succession *Scenes from Clerical Life* (1858), *Adam Bede* (1859), *The Mill on the Floss* (1860), and *Silas Marner* (1861). The last, a short novel or novella, is unlike the other works, for its narrative combines elements of myth—some critics have called it a fairy tale—with otherwise realistic details of English country life centering on the rustic village of Raveloe. Certainly the novel can be understood as a moral tale. Its message, however sentimental to a modern reader, is unambiguous: true wealth is love, not gold. As a myth of loss and redemption, the novel concerns the miser Silas Marner, who loses his material riches only to reclaim a greater treasure of contentment. Silas comes to learn that happiness is possible only for the pure and self-sacrificing. Because of his love for Eppie, he is transformed, as if by magic, from a narrow, selfish, bitter recluse into a truly human, spiritually fulfilled man.

The novel, however, has a dimension other than the moralistic. Eliot skillfully counterpoints the experiences of Silas with those of Godfrey Cass. Whereas Godfrey appears, when the reader first meets him, to be a fortunate man entirely the opposite of the sullen miser, his fortunes fail just as Silas' improve. The wealthy, genial Godfrey has a secret guilt—an unacknowledged marriage to a woman beneath him in social class and refinement. Silas, on the other hand, carries with him the smoldering resentment for a wrong that he had suffered (and suffered innocently) from his friend William Dane. Godfrey's sense of guilt festers, especially after he learns about the terrible circumstances of the woman's death.

Nevertheless, he remains silent, fearful of exposing his past. Eppie, the child of his brief union with the woman, becomes the miser's treasure and replaces the sterile gold stolen by Dunstan. Thereafter, the happiness of the old man is Godfrey's doom. His second wife, Nancy, is barren; and when he offers too late to adopt Eppie as his own child, she clings to her foster father. Silas' love has earned what Godfrey's power had failed to command.

By contrasting Silas' good fortune with Godfrey's disappointment, the author expands the mythic scope of her fiction. If some men—the pure and deserving—discover almost by accident the truths of happiness, others, maybe no less deserving, pass by their chances and endure misery. Silas is reformed not only spiritually but also psychologically. Once blasphemous, he returns to the Christian faith of his childhood, but his religious reaffirmation is not so important as the improvement of his psychological health. Freed of his neurotic resentment for past injustices, he becomes a friend to all, beloved of the village. The fate of Godfrey, whose history is realistic rather than marvelous, is quite the opposite. Without an heir, he shrinks within himself. He may endure his disgrace, even eventually make up to Eppie and her husband Aaron some of the material things he owes her; yet he cannot shake his sense of wrongdoing, appease his sorrow for betrayal, or make restitution for the evils of the past. Eliot, who once described her novel as "rather somber," balances her miraculous fable of rebirth for the favored Silas with another more common human story, that of the defeated Godfrey Cass.

SIR GAWAIN AND THE GREEN KNIGHT

Type of work: Poem
Author: Unknown
Type of plot: Chivalric romance
Time of plot: Sixth century
Locale: England
First transcribed: Fourteenth century manuscript

In this Arthurian romance the unknown poet combines two famous medieval motifs: the beheading story and the temptation story. In the climactic scene, Sir Gawain not only reveals his courage but also his human fallibility. The ideal of knightly conduct—of courtesy, courage, and loyalty—against which the poem's action must be measured, was a long-standing ideal, which was still taken seriously in theory, if frequently compromised in practice.

Principal Characters

Sir Gawain, the bravest, most virtuous of the Knights of the Round Table. He accepts the Green Knight's challenge to uphold the honor of Arthur's court and sets out in autumn on the quest which is essentially a test of his virtue. Temptation awaits him at the castle of Bercilak de Hautdesert, where he must resist the amorous attention of his hostess without violating the courtesy which he owes her as her guest and, at the same time, keep his bargain with his host to exchange whatever he receives at home for the game Bercilak kills while he hunts. Gawain is faithful for two days, but on the third he succumbs to his fear for his life and accepts from the lady a green girdle which protects its wearer from injury. This very human lapse brings him a mild wound from the Green Knight, and he returns to Arthur's court a chastened, shamefaced hero.

King Arthur, the merry young ruler of Britain who is prepared to fight for his own cause if none of his knights will challenge the Green Knight.

Guenivere, his beautiful young queen, the object of Morgan le Fay's hatred.

Sir Bercilak de Hautdesert, the good-humored knight who is Gawain's host. An avid sportsman and lover of good entertainment, he proposes to Gawain an exchange of the gains of each day as amusement for both of them; the bargain is in reality a part of his test of the knight's virtue, for it is he who is disguised as the Green Knight by the arts of Morgan le Fay.

The Lady, his charming wife and accomplice in the temptation of Gawain.

Morgan le Fay, Arthur's half sister, who had learned her skills in magic from Merlin. She is said to have plotted the appearance of the Green Knight at Arthur's court to frighten her enemy Guenivere.

The Story

On Christmas Eve many knights and fair ladies gathered in King Arthur's banquet hall, there to feast and enjoy the holiday festivities. Suddenly a stranger entered the room. He was a giant of a man, clad all in green armor, with a green face, hair, and beard. He advanced, gave his greetings, and then loudly issued his challenge. Was there a knight in the group who would dare to trade blows with the mighty Green Knight? He who accepted the challenge was to strike one blow with a battle-ax on this occasion. Then on New Year's morning, a year hence, the Green Knight would repay the blow, at his own castle in a distant land. Arrogantly, the Green Knight waited for an answer. From King Arthur's ranks answered the voice of Sir Gawain, the youngest and least battle-scarred of the knights. Sir Gawain accepted the challenge.

King Arthur and the other knights watched approvingly as Sir Gawain advanced, ax in hand, to confront the Green Knight. The stranger knelt down, bared his neck, and waited for the blow. Sir Gawain struck, sure and true, and the head of the Green Knight was severed from his body. While all gaped in amazement, he picked up his head in his hands, leaped upon his charger, and rode toward the gate. As he rode, the lips of the head shouted defiance at Sir Gawain, reminding him of their forthcoming tryst at the Green Chapel on the coming New Year.

The months passed quickly. Noble deeds were legion at the Round Table, and an atmosphere of gaiety pervaded King Arthur's castle. Then when autumn came, Sir Gawain departed on his promised quest, and with much concern the other knights saw him set forth. Sir Gawain, riding his horse Gringalet, went north and at last arrived in Wirral, a region wild and uncivilized. On his way he was often in danger of death, for he faced fire-puffing dragons, fierce animals, and savage wild men in his search for the Knight of the Green Chapel. At last, on Christmas Eve, Sir Gawain saw a great castle in the middle of the wilderness. He entered it and was made welcome.

His host offered Sir Gawain the entire facilities of the castle. In a beautifully furnished chamber which he occupied, Sir Gawain was served the finest dishes and the best wines. The lady of the castle, a lady more beautiful even than Queen Guenivere, sat with him as he ate. The next day was Christmas, and the lord of the castle led in the feasting. Expressing the wish that Sir Gawain would remain at the castle for a long time, the host assured the knight that the Green Chapel was only a short distance away, so that it would not be necessary for him to leave until New Year's Day. The lord of the castle also asked Sir Gawain to keep a covenant with him. During his stay Sir Gawain was to receive all the game that his host caught during the day's hunt. In return, Sir Gawain was to exchange any gifts he received at the castle while the host was away.

On the first morning that the host hunted, Sir Gawain was awakened by the lady of the castle. She entered his chamber, seated herself on his couch, and spoke words of love to him. But Sir Gawain resisted temptation and took nothing from the lady. That evening, when the host presented his bounty from the hunt, Sir Gawain answered truthfully that he had received nothing that day. The second morning the same thing happened. Sir Gawain remained chaste in spite of the lady's conduct. On the third morning, however, the day before Sir Gawain was to depart, she gave him an embroidered silk girdle which she said would keep him safe from any mortal blow. Then she kissed him three times and departed. That evening Sir Gawain kissed his host three times, but he did not mention the silken girdle he had received.

On New Year's morning Sir Gawain set forth from the castle and rode to the Green Chapel. He found it without difficulty; as he approached he heard the Green Knight sharpening his ax. When Sir Gawain announced that he was ready for the blow and bared his head, the Green Knight raised his ax high in the air in preparation for the stroke of death. But Sir Gawain jumped aside as the ax descended. The second time the Green Knight merely struck at Sir Gawain, not touching him at all. With the third blow he wounded Sir Gawain in the neck, drawing a great deal of blood. Then Sir Gawain shouted defiance and said that he had fulfilled the covenant. The Green Knight laughed loudly at that and began to praise Sir Gawain's courage.

To Sir Gawain's surprise, he revealed himself as the host of the castle and explained the blows. On the first two blows Sir Gawain escaped injury, because for two days he had faithfully kept the covenant. The third drew blood, however, because Sir Gawain had failed to reveal the gift of the girdle, the property of the host, Sir Bercilak de Hautdesert. Together with Morgan le Fay, King Arthur's half sister, the Green Knight had planned this whole affair to test the strength and valor of King Arthur's knights. They had devised the disguise of the Green Knight and persuaded Lady de Hautdesert to try tempting Sir Gawain. Sir Gawain had withstood the test of temptation well, his only fault the keeping of the girdle. The host forgave him for his act, however, because it was the love of life itself that had motivated Sir Gawain.

The two knights returned to the castle, and a few days later Sir Gawain journeyed back to King Arthur's court. As he rode, he gazed with shame at the girdle which he had procured from the host. It was to remain with Sir Gawain as a reminder of the moment when he yielded and succumbed to the weakness of the flesh.

At King Arthur's castle all the knights and ladies listened to the tale of Sir Gawain and the Green Knight, and then, to show their love for the young knight, they all donned silk girdles. This symbol became a traditional part of the costume of the Knights of the Round Table.

Critical Evaluation

Written in the dialect of the Northwest Midlands, *Sir Gawain and the Green Knight* uses the alliterative half lines of Old English poetry to weave its tale of Arthurian romance. The romance often tests codes of conduct, and the central concern of the work, fidelity, appears in the opening line's reference to Troy, which fell through deceit and betrayal. Troy serves as more than a classical allusion or even analogy, for supposedly the great-grandson of the Trojan Aeneas founded Britain; the fate that befell Troy awaits its new avatar of Arthur's court, if the English ruler and his followers are not careful. The role that a gift played in the destruction of the ancient city forms another link with this work.

Despite the lesson of history, Arthur's court is "reck-less" as it celebrates the Christmas season, and Morgan le Fay seizes the opportunity to test its merit by sending the Green Knight to Camelot. The giant courteously praises the king and knights:

> the praise of you, prince, is puffed up so high,
> And your court and your company are counted the best,
> Stoutest under steel-gear on steeds to ride,
> Worthiest of their works the wide world over,
> And peerless to prove in passages of arms,
> And courtesy here is carried to its height.

Every line contains a superlative, but is this reputation deserved or inflated?

Almost immediately one senses deficiencies in the supposed excellencies of Camelot. The Green Knight is carrying a holly bob, symbol of peace, but Arthur thinks that the intruder has come to fight. The Green Knight replies that he is not seeking combat, indicating that this adversary must be overcome by moral, not physical strength. Both seem absent from this supposedly ideal court, for no one takes up the challenge to trade blow for blow. Finally, Arthur himself must attempt to redeem the honor of his court. Yet even he seems incapable of acting. He swings the ax around but does not strike. At last his nephew Gawain, the greatest of the English knights, courteously and modestly asks to replace his king, thereby assuming the role of representative of the Arthurian world.

Physically strong, Gawain strikes off the giant's head at a blow. He has passed only the first and easiest test, however, because he has promised to seek out his opponent and submit to similar treatment, and he knows that his head, unlike the green giant's, is not replaceable. In setting out to fulfill his promise even though he faces almost certain death, he again upholds the honor of the knights. More challenges await him on his journey: Serpents, wolves, wild men and wild animals, cold, and nearly impassable woods provide numerous excuses for him to turn back. In addition, the Green Knight has not told Gawain where he can find the castle. Still, Gawain perseveres, until on Christmas Eve he finds a comfortable castle in which to pass the holidays.

Were he more perceptive, he might wonder at the flourishing state of the grounds, "fair and green" in the middle of winter. He does notice the hospitality. Even though he has come fully armed, he is greeted courteously; one recalls that Arthur's greeting of the Green Knight was less gracious. Gawain also observes that the lady of the castle is more beautiful than Guenivere. Compared to this world, Camelot again seems less worthy of the superlatives that have been lavished upon it.

Though Gawain has escaped the physical perils of nature, other dangers await him as the lord of the castle tests his human nature. Gawain seems imperceptive when his host proposes a game of exchanges; the reader or hearer will recall a similar entertainment almost a year earlier. Like the half lines of the poem that complement and modify each other, the structure of the poem relies on repetitions that are at once similar and different. The host's game reminds the audience that the earlier challenge also is largely moral, and Gawain has yet to fulfill the conditions of the first compact he made. The lord's hunting after Christmas parallels his lady's pursuit of Gawain, too, and raises the question whether he will fall prey to her. Gawain is beset by a dual threat. If he is true to the lord, how can he still chivalrously reject the lady? If he yields to the lady, he will betray his host. Furthermore, he has promised to reveal all that he receives in the castle; he is thus honor-bound to tell the lord of his adultery at the same time that he is honor-bound to protect his lover. Gawain escapes this dilemma in the only way possible, through passive obedience.

Gawain thus passes further tests, rejecting both lust and greed. He does not trust Providence sufficiently to resist the lady's last offer, a magic girdle that she claims will make him invincible. He might consider that this palladium is green and gold, the colors of the Green Knight, but he does not examine the gift closely. Urged by the lady—and his fears—to conceal the present, he does not exchange it that evening. Like his Trojan ancestors, he has accepted a gift that betrays him.

Believing himself protected by the magic girdle, Gawain goes to the ruined chapel to keep his appointment with the Green Knight. His guide, perhaps the shape-changing giant himself if not one of his servants, tempts Gawain again to break his pledge, speaking of the Green Knight's ferocity and promising to tell no one if Gawain flees. Gawain replies, "The Lord is strong to save:/ His servants trust in Him." So they do, and Gawain might recall that in his travels he passed Holy Head, where Saint Winifred had her head chopped off and then restored. He, however, actually has placed his trust in a talisman.

At last Gawain learns the biblical lesson that he who seeks to save his life shall lose it, that his faith was weak; the nick in the neck is an enduring physical sign of moral failing. Yet, as Bercilak recognizes, perfection is beyond human grasp. Gawain has sinned, but having undergone penance, he is redeemed. The girdle does in a sense save Gawain, though not in the way he had expected. He keeps it as a symbol not of immortality but of mortality, a reminder of his vulnerability and dependence on God.

Arthur had requested a story; *Sir Gawain and the Green Knight* is that tale. It is fitting for Christmas, for it tells of death and rebirth, physical in the case of Bercilak, spiritual for Gawain and, by implication, the court he represents. Like the Crucifixion, through penance the girdle is transformed from a sign of shame and defeat to one of victory. Worn openly—not concealed—by all the knights, it links them in a recognition of their common humanity. The poem fittingly ends, as it began, with references to the passing of time, reminding its audience that the only way to conquer death is to live uprightly and have faith in Him "that was crowned with thorn."

SONG OF ROLAND

Type of work: Tale
Author: Unknown
Type of plot: Chivalric romance
Time of plot: About A.D. 800
Locale: Western Europe
First published: *Chanson de Roland*, twelfth century

Loosely based upon an eighth century military incident involving a part of Charlemagne's army, The Song of Roland, one of the great medieval chansons de geste, *is a composite of several hero legends interlaced with Christian moral sentiments.*

Principal Characters

Emperor Charlemagne, also called **King Charles** and **Carlon,** represented as being two hundred years old, with a flowing white beard, regal bearing, and undiminished vigor. He presides democratically over his court in an orchard near Cordova and accepts the majority view in favor of what proves to be a false peace pact with the Saracens. His militant zeal for Christianizing pagans is offset by his humble submission to fate when his beloved nephew Roland and twenty thousand of his troops are killed by Moorish forces in the Pass of Roncevaux. He laments the deaths of his men before taking terrible vengeance on their conquerors, but he is completely unmoved by the pleas of Ganelon, the traitor knight.

Roland, Duke of the Marches of Brittany and nephew of Charlemagne. The favorite of his uncle, he glories in his post as leader of the emperor's rearguard, the exposed flank of the French army on its homeward march from Spain. Roland is the most outspoken of the Twelve Peers, a hater of all pagans, and the enemy of Ganelon, his stepfather; and his suggestion that Ganelon be sent to negotiate the truce proposed by the Saracens seems designed as a test of that knight's loyalty and honor. Brave in battle, Roland is also rash to the point of folly and lacking in foresight. He is the owner of the famous sword Durendal and the horn called Oliphant, both possessing supernatural powers. When Saracens attack the French force in the Pass of Roncevaux, he refuses to blow his horn and summon the main army until it is too late. Relying on his own Durendal and Christian supremacy over pagan knights, he dies by his simple chivalric code after facing the enemy and performing prodigious feats of valor.

Oliver, Roland's friend and fellow Peer. His prudence is balanced against Roland's impetuosity, but his warnings are unable to save the day when the Saracen army attacks the French forces at Roncevaux. After estimating the enemy's strength he urges Roland to blow his horn, Oliphant, in order to summon Charlemagne and the chivalry of France riding ahead. Dismounted, he dies with

honor, a ring of dead enemies piled about him.

Ganelon, also called **Guènes,** the traitor knight who nurses so deep a grudge against his stepson Roland that he conspires with Marsilion, the Saracen King of Saragossa, to betray the rearguard of the French army to the enemy. When Charlemagne hears the blast of Roland's horn, blown to summon aid of the emperor, Ganelon derides his ruler. Later he is arrested and charged with treason. After his champion has been defeated in an ordeal by combat, he is tied to four stallions that tear his body apart as they pursue a galloping mare.

Archbishop Turpin, the militant churchman of Rheims, killed at Roncevaux. He absolves Charlemagne's host of sin before the battle and urges all to die like Christian soldiers. It is he who finally persuades Roland to blow his horn, Oliphant (a blast that bursts Roland's temples and hurries his death), and it is he who survives long enough to arrange the bodies of the Twelve Peers so that Charlemagne will find them, avenge them, and give them Christian burial. Charlemagne orders his heart, like those of Roland and Oliver, preserved in urns.

Gerin, Gerier, Ives, Ivor, Othon, Berenger, Anseis, Samson, Gerard of Roussillon, and **Engelier of Bordeaux,** Charlemagne's Peers, also slain with Roland and Oliver.

Pinabel of Sorence, the knight who defends Ganelon, accused of treason, in an ordeal by battle.

Thierry, the younger brother of Duke Geoffrey of Anjou. He fights with and defeats Pinable of Sorence in the ordeal by battle that decides Ganelon's guilt.

Duke Naimon, Geoffrey, Duke of Anjou, Ogier the Dane, Count Jozeran of Provence, and **Antelme of Mayence,** Charlemagne's loyal vassels and trusted advisers.

Walter de Hum, a valorous French knight killed at Roncevaux.

Marsilion, also called **Marsile,** the Saracen King of Saragossa. Acting on the advice of one of his nobles, he sends envoys to Charlemagne with promises that he will sign a treaty of peace and receive Christian baptism if the emperor will withdraw his army from Spain. He leads the Saracen host against the French rearguard at Roncevaux. After Roland severs his sword hand as they struggle in hand-to-hand combat, Marsilion leaves the battle. Later he dies in his castle at Saragossa.

Blancandrin, the crafty Saracen knight who suggests the treacherous proposal that King Marsilion makes to Charlemagne. Ganelon plots with Blancandrin the destruction of the Twelve Peers and the French host at Roncevaux.

Adelroth, the nephew of King Marsilion, **Duke Falsaron, King Corsablis, Malprimis of Brigale, The Emir of Balaguet, The Lord of Moriana, Turgis of Tortelosa, Escremiz of Valterne, Estorgan, Estramarin, Margaris of Seville,** and **Chernubles of Munigre,** King

Marsilion's Twelve Champions killed by the Twelve Peers at Roncevaux.

Baligant, the Emir of Babylon and the ally of King Marsilion. He brings a mighty army to attack the French under Emperor Charlemagne. After a fierce battle that lasts from early morning until dusk the Emir and Charlemagne engage in single combat. Charlemagne, wounded, is heartened by Saint Gabriel. His strength renewed, he strikes with his sword the helmet of his enemy and cleaves him to his beard. The Saracens, seeing their leader dead, flee.

Aude, betrothed to Roland. Hearing that her lover is dead, she falls at Charlemagne's feet and dies.

Bramimond, the widow of King Marsilion. Charlemagne takes her with him when he returns to France, where she is baptized and given a Christian name, Juliana.

The Story

The boy Roland grew up far from his home country and lived with his penniless mother in a cave formerly occupied by a lonely monk. Nevertheless, his mother had taught him that some day he should be a brave hero like his father, Milon, and serve with the great army of Charlemagne. When he asked his mother to tell him the story of his birth, he learned that through his father he was descended from great heroes of old, Trojan Hector on one side and Wotan, king of the Norse gods, on the other. His father, Milon, having incurred the wrath of Charlemagne for taking the king's sister, the Princess Bertha, as his wife, had come to Italy and there had died fighting pagans in single-handed combat.

One summer, when he was still only a lad, his friend Oliver, the son of a local prince, met him, and the two watched the coming of the great Charlemagne into Italy, where the king was to receive the blessing of the pope at Rome.

Roland was impressed by the royal pageant but not overawed. That night, he walked into Charlemagne's banquet hall and demanded his rights for himself and his mother. Amused by the boy's daring, Charlemagne ordered that Bertha be brought to him. When the emperor recognized his long-lost sister, he rejoiced and gave her and her son a place of honor in his court.

Roland's boyhood years passed quickly and with increasing honors. At first he was merely a page in the court—attending the ladies, carrying messages, and learning court etiquette. He was permitted to accompany the king's knights during war with the Saxons, and he was present when the swan knight, of the race of Lohengrin, appeared at the court of Charlemagne.

When Roland was fourteen years old, he became a squire and made the acquaintance of Ogier the Dane, a hostage prince at Charlemagne's court. The two boys became great friends. Then, urged by a new queen, Ogier's

father, Duke Godfrey, planned a revolt against Charlemagne. In retaliation Charlemagne threatened to kill Ogier. Roland intervened and saved his friend's life.

In the meantime barbarians attacked Rome. In an effort to save the pope, Charlemagne ignored the rebellion of the Danes and set off to the south, taking Ogier with him as a prisoner. The great army was assisted on its passage across the Alps when a magnificent white stag appeared to lead the army through the mountain passes.

In the battles that followed, Charlemagne's army was divided. One force, led by the cowardly son of Charlemagne and the false knight Alory, attempted to retreat and placed the emperor's life in jeopardy. Roland and Ogier, aided by other squires, donned the garments of the cowards and saved the day. Charlemagne knighted them upon the battlefield.

One of the pagan knights proposed a personal combat. In this encounter Charlot, a son of Charlemagne, and Ogier met two barbarians, Prince Sadone and Karaheut. The pagans trapped Ogier and threatened to put him to death, but Charlot escaped. Karaheut, who was to have fought Ogier, rebelled against the unchivalrous action of his pagan prince and surrendered to Charlemagne, to be treated exactly as Ogier would be treated. Reinforcements came to the pagans, among them the giant king of Maiolgre. In a dispute over the marriage of Glorianda, a Danish prisoner, Ogier fought for Glorianda and put his enemy to rout. Charlemagne attacked at the same time. Ogier and Roland were reunited. The pope was restored to his throne.

Roland was invested with royal arms. His sword was the famous Durandal; his battle horn was the horn of his grandfather, Charles the Hammer. None but Roland could blow that horn. His armor was the best in the kingdom.

A new war began when Count Gerard refused homage to the emperor. Oliver, grandson of the count, was among the knights opposed to Charlemagne. After the French had besieged the fortress of Viana for seven months, it was decided to settle the war by encounter between a champion from each army. Roland was chosen to fight for Charlemagne. Unknown to him, his adversary was to be Oliver, his boyhood friend. When the two discovered each other's identity, they embraced.

A few weeks later on a boar hunt near Viana, Charlemagne was captured by Count Gerard. The two leaders declared a truce, and Count Gerard agreed to be a faithful liege man of the emperor thereafter. Roland met Oliver's sister, Alda, and became betrothed to her.

At Christmastime the Princess of Cathay arrived with her brothers at Charlemagne's court. She proposed a contest between a Christian knight and her brother Argalia. If one of Charlemagne's knights were the victor, he should have her hand in marriage. If the knight were defeated, he should become a hostage. Malagis, the wizard, discovered that the princess and her brothers really sought by sorcery to destroy Charlemagne. He visited the apartment of the foreigners but was discovered by them. They complained and Charlemagne, not understanding the wizard's desire to help him, sentenced Malagis to be imprisoned in a hollow rock beneath the sea forever.

The jousts began. After Argalia had defeated the first knight, Ferrau, the fierce Moor, began combat. Unhorsed, the Moor fought Argalia on foot and overpowered him. Then the princess became invisible, and Argalia rode away, the Moor in pursuit.

In the forest of Ardennes, the Moor discovered Argalia sleeping, killed him without honor, and seized his wonderful helmet. Roland, having followed them, discovered the murder of Argalia and sought the Moor to punish him for his unknightly deed.

Reinold of Montalban found the Princess of Cathay in the forest after he had drunk from the waters of the fountain of Merlin, and the effect of this water was to make him see the princess as an ugly crone. She thought him handsome, but he felt disgust and hurried away. Roland discovered the Moor and challenged him to combat, but the Moor suddenly remembered that his liege lord in Spain was in need of his help and did not remain to fight with Roland.

When the Princess of Cathay saw the Moor wearing her brother's helmet, she knew a tragedy had occurred, and she transported herself by magic to her father's kingdom.

Roland went on a quest to the Far East in search of the complete armor of Trojan Hector. Whether by chance or by evil design, he came to a fountain and there drank the water of forgetfulness. He was rescued by the Princess of Cathay and fought many battles for her sake, even though she was a pagan princess.

At last he came to the castle of the fairy queen, Morgan le Fay, where the armor of Trojan Hector was said to be hidden. Overcome for the first time, he failed to gain the armor and was ordered to return to the court of Charlemagne.

He arrived home in time to help the Danes resist an invasion of their country. When Ogier's father, Duke Godfrey, summoned help, Ogier and Roland set out for Denmark. The invaders fled. At the same time Ogier's father died, but Ogier, on the advice of Morgan le Fay, renounced his rights to his father's holdings in favor of his younger brother.

On his way back to France, Roland heard of a fierce orc said to be the property of Proteus. The orc devoured one beautiful maiden each day until Roland overcame it and was rewarded by Oberto, the king of Ireland, whose daughter he had saved.

In the meantime Charlemagne's forces were being attacked by the Saracens, and Roland set out to help Charlemagne's knights. On the way he was trapped in a wizard's castle. He was saved from this captivity by Bradamant, a warrior maiden. She, having won a magic ring from the Princess of Cathay, overcame the wizard and released all the knights and ladies held prisoner in the wizard's castle.

Ferrau, the Moorish knight, lost the helmet he had stolen from Argalia and vowed he would never again wear a helmet until he should wear that of Roland. By trickery he managed to get Roland's helmet.

Roland was set upon by Mandricardo, the fierce knight to whom fortune had awarded the arms of Trojan Hector. They fought for the possession of Durandal, Roland's sword, the only part of Trojan Hector's equipment which Mandricardo did not possess. At last Mandricardo was forced to flee for his life.

Roland visited the forest where the Princess of Cathay and Medoro, a Moorish prince, had fallen in love. Some declared it was jealousy for the princess, but others declared it was sheer exhaustion which caused Roland now to lose his mind. He cast his armor away from him and went wandering helplessly through the forest. Mandricardo seized Durandal and made Roland his prisoner.

Astolpho and Oliver set out from the court of Charlemagne to save Roland. Astolpho journeyed on the back of a flying horse to the fabulous land of Prester John. Having freed Prester John from a flock of harpies, Astolpho journeyed to the rim of the moon and there saw stored all the things lost on earth. There he found Roland's common sense, which he brought back with him and returned to Roland so that the knight became his former self.

In a battle against the Saracens, the wicked Ganelon betrayed the knights of Charlemagne. Greatly outnumbered, they fell one by one to their enemies.

Roland, unwilling to call for help, refused to use his famous horn to summon aid, and he died last of all. Charlemagne, discovering the dead hero, declared a great day of mourning. Alda, the betrothed of Roland, fell dead and was buried with many honors. Then Charlemagne died and was buried with great pomp. Only Ogier the Dane remained, and it is said that Morgan le Fay carried him to Avalon where he lives in company with Arthur of the Round Table.

Critical Evaluation

The *Song of Roland* is loosely associated with the romance literature—the adventure narratives—of medieval France. The romance is divided into three types on the basis of content. The first is the "Matter of Britain," dealing with Arthurian legend and Celtic lore. The second is the "Matter of Antiquity," taking its cue from the legends of Thebes, the legends of Troy (such as Geoffrey Chaucer's *Troilus and Criseyde*, 1382), and the legends about Alexander the Great. The third is the "Matter of France," focusing on stories of Charlemagne and his circle as well as stories of William of Orange, drawn from the *chansons de geste*, or songs of great deeds. It is here that the *Song of Roland* becomes important, for it is, properly speaking, one of the songs of great deeds.

The *chansons de geste* are epic in nature, although the precise origins of the form are unknown. A popular literary form between the eleventh and thirteenth centuries, they are written in French verse—as were early romances; late romances were written in prose—using first a ten-syllable than a twelve-syllable (Alexandrine) line and assonance. Rhyme was substituted for assonance in the late *chansons*. The lines are grouped in stanzas—called *laisses* or *tirades*—of varying lengths, and series of *chansons* developed into story cycles dealing with a particular person, such as Charlemagne, or a particular theme, such as the conflict between Christians and Saracens. Like the classical epics, the *chansons de geste* concentrate—as implied by the name—on battles, heroic feats, and knightly ideals. Scant notice is paid to women or the theme of love. These tales furnish the material for the medieval romance; however, in the romance, the emphasis shifts from the heroic to the chivalric, from war to love, and from tragic seriousness to lighthearted adventure. Thus the *Song of Roland*, a *chanson de geste*, is a narrative of knights in battle, but Lodovico Ariosto's sixteenth century *Orlando furioso* (1516, 1521, 1532) concerns itself with a smitten Roland (Orlando) gone mad over hopeless infatuation with the faithless Angelica, the Princess of Cathay.

Some verification for the events narrated in the *Song of Roland* is provided independently of the poem in the "Annales regni Francorum" of Einhard (or Eginhard), Charlemagne's biographer and chronicler. On this basis, it is possible to pinpoint the essential Roland story as a Basque ambush, in A.D. 778, of the rearguard of Charlemagne's army during a retreat through the Pyrenees. One unusual aspect of the story is that it tells of a defeat—not that defeat was a total stranger in the epic world of

It is also said that Charlemagne dwells inside a vast mountain cave with all of his heroes gathered around him. There they wait for the day when they shall march out to avenge the wrongs of the world.

chansons de geste, but rather the heroic ambience which pervaded the *chansons* precluded much talk of defeat. Several hypotheses have been offered to explain the apparent anomaly. One scholar traces the place-names mentioned in the poem to the pilgrimage route to the shrine of St. James of Compostella, theorizing that clerics on pilgrimage knitted the stories of Roland's defeat into an intrinsically Christian epic—in effect, an adaptation of history to a Christian poem. Another scholar construes the poem as a tribute to courage, loyalty, patriotism, and devotion in the face of overwhelming odds—in other words, a celebration of heroic ideals. A third scholar more plausibly approaches the problem by way of the poem's purpose. If, so the reasoning goes, the poem was written to glorify Charlemagne and Christianity, then Roland dies a martyr's death and Charlemagne's vengeance redounds to his credit as a Defender of the Faith. Whatever their other merits, these theories suggest two recurring themes in any reading of the *Song of Roland*: the religious and the heroic, both of them major preoccupations of the High Middle Ages.

The religious theme pits Christians against Saracens, imbuing the story with a strong crusading spirit. On the one hand, Charlemagne and his Peers display most, if not all, of the Seven Cardinal Virtues. Even the proud Roland dies humble and contrite, and Charlemagne's early indecision is resolved later in the poem when he becomes a courageous leader. The pagans, on the other hand, embody the Seven Deadly Sins. They are treacherous and greedy, fighting for personal glory or material gain rather than principle or faith. In this world of black-and-white morality, there are no good pagans, and the treasonous, deceitful Ganelon is severely punished for his perfidy. By contrast, the good Charlemagne is rewarded by the direct intervention of the Archangel Gabriel, who deals the pagan Saracens a final defeat by slaying their leader, Baligant, while God makes the sun stand still. Divine intervention even affects the trial of Ganelon. The Christian cause is never questioned, nor is there any doubt about its justice. The forced baptism of the Saracen captives is described without qualm, just as is the battlefield bloodshed. If contradictions appear to the modern reader, they certainly did not occur to the medieval mind, for religious faith—by no means the least of the Cardinal Virtues—obliterated any inconsistencies between, for example, the virtue of temperance and the slaughter of pagans.

The heroic theme in the *Song of Roland* is closely

linked to the religious, since most heroic deeds are performed in the name of religious principle. The hero's role, however, requires dedication to ideals that have only peripheral, if any, relationship to religious precepts. Loyalty and bravery, for example, are held in high esteem, but they are such basic heroic ideals that they are more implicit than explicit in the poem. Decision of major issues and even major battles by single combat is another heroic ideal which often manifests itself in the poem. In addition, the motifs of victory-defeat and treason-vengeance weigh heavily in the balance of heroic ideals. Still another factor, which the modern reader might call "team spirit," is the knightly obligation to subsume individual or personal honor and glory in furtherance of the cause. Thus Roland's early pride, especially his insistence upon the force to subdue the Saracens and his subsequent refusal to blow his horn to summon Charlemagne's aid until all were dead or dying, was later brought low. Finally Roland regretted his stubborn pride in a vivid demonstration of the need for that heroic ideal, teamwork. Not all is a self-evident exercise in primitive democracy. Charlemagne's word was still law, although the most powerful peers insisted upon a voice in decision making; nor is there

much attention paid to morality (as distinct from ethics) or to social courtesies. In fact, a pristine system of social and political justice characterized Charlemagne's court as an essential ingredient in the heroic ideal, quite apart from religious considerations altogether. Thus, the unique features of the heroic ideal are distinguishable from religious precepts.

All in all, the *Song of Roland* is a remarkable panorama of medieval life and thought, imaginatively perceived. To those who would say that it is false history, one can answer only with the cliché that fiction is often truer than history, for in the *Song of Roland* such is the case. The poem affords so vivid a picture of medieval reality that its historical accuracy is irrelevant; it presents psychological, emotional, and sociological realities that transcend factual data to reach a new plateau of reality, one reflecting the spirit of the times rather than the substance. In this sense the *Song of Roland* is, despite its ethical simplicities and its literary primitiveness, remarkably successful as a document of the medieval spirit, a characteristic that may explain its enduring popularity for nearly one thousand years.

SONNETS FROM THE PORTUGUESE

Type of work: Poetry
Author: Elizabeth Barrett Browning (1806–1861)
First published: 1850

When Elizabeth Barrett Browning finished *Sonnets from the Portuguese* in 1847, the book had no title and was intended as a private gift from wife to husband. At that time, the couple was living in Pisa, Italy. It was no easy thing to be married to the famous poet Robert Browning, and one of the many points of interest in this sequence of sonnets is the light they throw upon the uniquely productive marriage of Elizabeth and Robert Browning. It was Robert, after all, who suggested the title for the work, and it was he who prevailed upon Elizabeth to publish these famous love poems in 1850. A small edition had been printed in Reading, England, in 1847, but it was boldly marked "Not for Publication." The sequence as originally composed contained forty-three sonnets arranged in a carefully calculated order; for the 1856 edition of her *Poems*, however, Elizabeth Barrett Browning inserted a new sonnet after "Sonnet XLI," thus raising the total to forty-four and establishing the text as it has been subsequently reprinted in one edition after another.

This brief overview of the publication history of *Sonnets from the Portuguese* suggests that the work is the product of a highly systematic poet, one capable of working on a large scale, and one whose work was destined to become a classic of the English language. Elizabeth Browning's strategy and subsequent success depend upon highly successful psychological principles. The sonnets are arranged in a precise order that duplicates the emotional "graph" of her relationship with Robert. In general terms, the sonnets tell the story of her lonely withdrawal from society (the result of an overprotective father) prior to meeting Robert, her incredulity at his first professions of love, then her passionate and intimate involvement with him, and finally her triumphant celebration of their love.

More specifically, Sonnets I-X reveal her "melancholy years," which were characterized by her "heavy heart" and "frequent tears," while Sonnets XI-XIII represent her first, tentative steps toward full acceptance of Robert and his "vindicating grace," all of which she needs to "fashion into speech." Sonnets XIV-XL constitute the center of the book, where the lover-poet details the typical joys and frustrations of the lover. Sonnets XLI-XLIV represent the triumphant celebration and consummation of that love—and an appreciation of its value in the larger scheme of things.

The poet keeps this sequence under tight control by using a variety of rhetorical devices, chiefly transitional words like "yet" and "indeed" and transitional bridges created by repeating key words from the fourteenth line of one stanza in the first line of the succeeding sonnet. Even more interesting are the transitions effected by having one sonnet comment upon or answer its predecessor in some way (as occurs in the bridging word "love," which connects Sonnets I and II, or in the expanded meaning of "same heart" in the transition from Sonnet XXXIII to XXXIV).

Browning also employs a confessional tone that is revealed in diarylike private revelations, some of them suggesting a kind of dramatic honesty more typical of American poets like Emily Dickinson or Marianne Moore. For example, she likens Robert's love (in Sonnet I) to a force that physically pulls her "backward by the hair." Hers is a uniquely personal voice, original and unpredictable: she is unusually assertive, at least by nineteenth-century British standards, ordering her lover to "go" (in Sonnet V), to "love me for love's sake" (in Sonnet XIV), and to "choose" (in Sonnet XVII). She confesses many details of their relationship, telling the reader about exchanged locks of hair (in Sonnets XVIII and XIX), about her trembling hands in Robert's presence (in Sonnet XXIII), and about a secret letter (Sonnet XXVIII) and a pet name (Sonnet XXXIII). Finally, the poet maintains unity by self-consciously employing flower imagery (especially in the concluding Sonnet XLIV), a powerful stimulus for someone who lived the first twenty years of her life in Herefordshire in the beautiful environs of the Malvern Hills and who composed *Sonnets from the Portuguese* in Pisa, Italy.

A close reading of four of the more famous sonnets will serve to suggest the richness of the whole sequence. A sonnet sequence, after all, tells the story of an evolving relationship; it was a form well loved by Elizabeth Browning, who was quite familiar with the famous sequences of Dante, Petrarch, Sidney, and Shakespeare. No sequence can be stronger than its individual parts, however, and what distinguishes Browning's sequence is her remarkable psychological realism. In Sonnet XXI she documents the lover's need for constant reassurance and reinforcement. Like Juliet, she can never hear "I love you" too many times or grow tired of tender gestures motivated by love. Browning goes on to argue that good things are even better in abundance—never cloying or overpowering (as in the examples she adduces of stars and flowers):

> Say over again, and yet once over again,
> That thou dost love me. Though the word repeated

Should seem "a cuckoo-song," as thou dost treat it,
Remember, never to the hill or plain,
Valley and wood, without her cuckoo-strain
Comes the fresh Spring in all her green completed.
Belovèd, I, amid the darkness greeted
By a doubtful spirit-voice, in that doubt's pain
Cry, "Speak once more—thou lovest!" Who can fear
Too many stars, though each in heaven shall roll,
Too many flowers, though each shall crown the year?
Say thou dost love me, love me, love me—toll
The silver iterance!—only minding, Dear,
To love me also in silence with thy soul.

And ever since, it grew more clean and white,
Slow to world-greetings, quick with its "Oh, list,"
When the angels speak. A ring of amethyst
I could not wear here, plainer to my sight,
Than that first kiss. The second passed in height
The first, and sought the forehead, and half missed,
Half falling on the hair. O beyond meed!
That was the chrism of love, which love's own crown,
With sanctifying sweetness, did precede.
The third upon my lips was folded down
In perfect, purple state; since when, indeed,
I have been proud and said, "My love, my own."

The poem makes a daring reversal in its final two lines by undercutting the insistence on "the silver iterance" and reminding Robert that love truly thrives on the silence of the soul. Sonnet XXI is truly a remarkable document, a superb example of psychological fidelity coupled with spectacular poetic invention.

More of her powers of invention emerge in Sonnet XXXII, a poem which re-creates a moment in the early phases of the relationship when Elizabeth believed that Robert's love was simply too good to be true. At the same time she experienced a loss of self-esteem, feeling unworthy. Out of these rather shabby emotions and low self-image, the poet creates a startling image—that of the worn-out musical instrument which can be coaxed into beautiful utterances (here, by Robert) and thus transformed into a self-validated and lovely thing in the process (thereby saving face for Elizabeth):

And, looking on myself, I seemed not one
For such man's love!—more like an out-of tune
Worn viol, a good singer would be wroth
To spoil his song with, and which, snatched in haste,
Is laid down at the first ill-sounding note.
I did not wrong myself so, but I placed
A wrong on *thee*. For perfect strains may float
'Neath master-hands, from instruments defaced,—
And great souls, at one stroke, may do and [dote].

There is a noteworthy sensuousness in these lines as one considers the closeness between violin and the violinist, as well as the music (an ancient metaphor for love), the product of their mutual involvement.

This sensuousness is evident in many of the sonnets, especially Sonnet XXXVIII, which might easily by dubbed the Kissing Sonnet, since it offers a detailed account of Robert's first three efforts. Each kiss produces extraordinary results, especially the last one, which becomes the occasion for Elizabeth to claim Robert as passionately as he has already claimed her. The poem establishes an intense and believable mutuality:

First time he kissed me, he but only kissed
The fingers of this hand wherewith I write;

Especially clever are the poet's use of the word "folded" to describe the motion of kissing and of "purple state" to suggest the passionate intensity of Robert's lips. It is hard to find the equal of such descriptions in the poetry or the prose produced in Great Britain during the late 1840s.

Sonnet XLIII (the most famous and most frequently quoted and anthologized) is a rather specialized reworking of the Italian sonnet form, which Browning uses throughout the book. Whereas the typical Italian sonnet poses a question or states a problem in the octet (rhyming *abba abba*), then answers the question or solves the problem in the sextet (rhyming *cde cde*, and variants), Sonnet XLIII relies on a truncated octet, consisting of a single question, "How do I love thee?" followed by an inflated sextet in which the poet enumerates seven different answers to the question. All the answers serve to extend and amplify the emotion of love, linking it to religious feeling, to unconscious daily activities, to moral yearnings, to selflessness, to energy recaptured from lost ideals and embittered feelings, and—in her final stroke—to spiritual power available only in the afterlife. The poem exhausts all the glorious possibilities of temporal life (just as it exhausted the traditional sonnet form) because only eternity is capacious enough for her kind of love:

How do I love thee? Let me count the ways.
I love thee to the depth and breadth and height
My soul can reach, when feeling out of sight
For the ends of Being and ideal grace.
I love thee to the level of everyday's
Most quiet need, by sun and candle-light.
I love thee freely, as men strive for Right;
I love thee purely, as they turn from Praise.
I love thee with the passion put to use
In my old griefs, and with my childhood's faith.
I love thee with a love I seemed to lose
With my lost saints,—I love thee with the breath,
Smiles, tears, of all my life!—and, if God choose,
I shall but love thee better after death.

The sonnet has proved to be an extraordinarily resilient tool for the master poet, since it allows the artist to engage in an argument with himself or herself. The sonnet, like a concentrated diary entry, distills a moment of psychic and spiritual awareness and holds it up for inspection. A sequence of sonnets can replicate an entire emotional history. That is precisely what Elizabeth Barrett Browning achieved in *Sonnets from the Portuguese*. For those who have experienced love, *Sonnets from the Portuguese* will always be a reminder of this most poignant of all human emotions. More important, for those who have never loved—or never loved deeply enough—*Sonnets from the Portuguese* will do what literary art always does: beckon the reader to a life that is larger and deeper and more human than seemed possible beforehand. If the book accomplishes that task for successive generations of readers, then it becomes a classic, and *Sonnets from the Portuguese* eloquently meets that criterion. On its pages, an intensely private love affair is transformed into that rarest of phenomena—a truly universal work of art.

SONS AND LOVERS

Type of work: Novel
Author: D. H. Lawrence (1885–1930)
Type of plot: Psychological realism
Time of plot: Late nineteenth century
Locale: England
First published: 1913

Sons and Lovers is a partly autobiographical novel of education in which a young man's fixated Oedipal attachment to his mother destroys his chances for a successful romantic and sexual relationship with a girl of his own age.

Principal Characters

Walter Morel, an English collier in many ways typical of the literary image of the lower-class workingman. He is not interested in the arts, in matters of the intellect, or even greatly in his work, which for him is merely a source of income. He is a creature who lives for whatever pleasures he can find in eating, drinking and his bed. At first a warmly vital man, he later becomes rough and brutal to his family and fights with them verbally and physically. His wife, after the first glow of marriage fades, means little to him because of her puritanical attitudes and regard for culture, and he becomes alienated from his children. His one creative joy is mending odd bits of household equipment and his work clothing. A coal miner he has been since boyhood, and a coal miner he is content to be.

Gertrude Morel, Walter Morel's wife, a woman who has married beneath her class and who soon regrets her action. She is quickly disillusioned by her husband, and the glamour of their courtship soon fades. She discovers her husband has debts he tells her he has paid and that he constantly lies about the little money he brings home. He always saves out some money for his drinking, regardless of how little he earns at the mine. In her disillusionment Mrs. Morel turns to her children for understanding and affection, as well to protect them from their father's brutality when drunk. As the sons and daughter appear on the scene each becomes a focal point for the mother's love. She tries to help them escape the little mining community, and she succeeds. On her second son, Paul, she places a blight by centering her affections upon him and loving him too well, making him the recipient of love that should have been given to her husband. Her affection and attentions cause him to be stunted emotionally. She never realizes what she is doing to the talented young man but always believes that she is working in his best interest by keeping him at home and governing his affections. Her life, however, is cut short by cancer; Paul ends her terrible pain by giving her an overdose of opiates. Even after her death her influence lingers in his life, so that he shows little evidence of developing into an individual, fulfilled personality.

Paul Morel, the second child of Walter and Gertrude Morel. After his older brother goes off to London to take a job, Paul is the object of his mother's affection; she helps him find work as a clerk close to home so that he can continue to live with his family. He receives encouragement to study art and becomes a successful part-time painter and designer. But Paul's mother and her influence keep him from growing up. Though he fights against her ruling his life, he is trapped. He readily understands how she forces him to give up his love for Miriam Leivers, whom he courts for many years, but he fails to see that his ability to love any woman as an adult man has been crippled by his emotional attachment to his mother.

William Morel, Paul's older brother. When he leaves his family to go to London, his mother transfers her obsessive affections to Paul. William falls in love with a shallow, pseudo-sophisticated girl who takes his money readily, even for her personal clothing, and treats his family as her servants. Though he sees through the girl, William feels trapped into marrying her. A tragic marriage for him is averted only through his sudden and untimely death.

Miriam Leivers, a young farm girl with a highly spiritual yet possessive nature. She and Paul Morel are companions until their late teens, when Miriam falls in love with the young man. She spends a great deal of time with him, for he undertakes to educate her in French, algebra, and other subjects, but his mother objects strenuously to the girl, especially when Paul seems to return the girl's love. Of a highly romantic nature, Miriam is repelled by the physical aspects of love until she is slowly persuaded to give herself to her lover, who later breaks off his engagement to her, saying that in her need for a committed love she wants too much from him.

Clara Dawes, a handsome, married, but physically emancipated woman living apart from her husband. She becomes Paul Morel's mistress and comes as close as anyone can to helping him achieve the ability to love as an adult. At last even she despairs of him and, with his

help, is reconciled to her husband, from whom she has been separated many years.

Mrs. Radford, Clara Dawes' mother.

Baxter Dawes, Clara Dawes' husband. Though he and Paul Morel are bitter enemies for a time and have a fight in which Paul is badly beaten, Paul's mother's final illness drives the young man to feel sympathy for his rival, the wronged husband. Dawes, who is recuperating from typhoid fever, is helped financially and morally by Paul, who eventually brings the man and his wife together.

Anne Morel, Paul Morel's sister. She escapes her home by becoming a schoolteacher. She achieves a happy, successful marriage and goes to live in Sheffield.

Arthur Morel, the youngest of Mrs. Morel's children, much like his father. He enlists in the army but later Mrs. Morel buys him out of the service. He is trapped into marriage with a young woman he does not love.

Louisa Lily Denys Western (Gipsy), William Morel's shallow fiancée.

Mr. Leivers, a silent, withdrawn man, the owner of Willey Farm and Miriam's father.

Mrs. Leivers, his good, patient, meek wife. Her philosophy is that the smitten should always turn the other cheek.

Agatha, a schoolteacher, **Edgar, Geoffrey, Maurice,** and **Hubert Leivers,** Miriam's sister and brothers. Edgar is Paul Morel's good friend. The Leivers boys display a brooding, almost brutal nature in contrast to Miriam's romantic spirituality.

Thomas Jordan, a manufacturer of surgical appliances in Nottingham. Paul becomes a clerk in his factory.

Miss Jordan, Paul Morel's patroness. She encourages his interest in art.

Mr. Pappelworth, a senior clerk, in charge of the spiral department, in Mr. Jordan's factory. When he leaves to set up a business of his own, Paul Morel becomes the spiral overseer.

Fanny, a hunchback, a "finisher" in the spiral department at the Jordan factory. She sympathizes with Paul Morel in his adolescent moodiness and unhappiness.

The Story

Walter Morel, a collier, had been a handsome, dashing young man when Gertrude had married him. After a few years of marriage, however, he proved to be an irresponsible breadwinner and a drunkard, and his wife hated him for what he had once meant to her and for what he was now. Her only solace lay in her children—William, Annie, Paul, and Arthur—for she leaned heavily upon them for companionship and lived in their happiness. She was a good parent, and her children loved her. The oldest son, William, was successful in his work, but he longed to go to London, where he had promise of a better job. After he had gone, Mrs. Morel turned to Paul for the companionship and love she had found in William.

Paul liked to paint. More sensitive than his brothers and sister, he was closer to Mrs. Morel than any of the others. William brought a girl named Lily home to visit, but it was apparent that she was not the right kind of girl for him; she was too shallow and self-centered. Before long, William became aware of that fact, but he resigned himself to keeping the promise he had made to his fiancée.

When William became ill, Mrs. Morel went to London to nurse her son and was with him there when he died. Home once more after she had buried her first son, Mrs. Morel could not bring herself out of her sorrow. Not until Paul became sick did she realize that her duty lay with the living rather than with the dead. After this realization, she centered all of her attention upon Paul. The two other children were capable of carrying on their affairs without the constant attention that Paul demanded.

At age sixteen, Paul went to visit some friends of Mrs. Morel. The Leivers were a warmhearted family, and Paul easily gained the friendship of the Leivers children. Fifteen-year-old Miriam Leivers was a strange girl, but her inner charm attracted Paul. Mrs. Morel, like many others, did not care for Miriam. Paul went to work at a stocking mill, where he was successful in his social relationships and in his work. He continued to draw. Miriam watched over his work and with quiet understanding offered judgment concerning his success or failure. Mrs. Morel sensed that someday her son would become famous for his art.

By the time Miriam and Paul had grown into their twenties, Paul realized that Miriam loved him deeply and that he loved her; but for some reason, he could not bring himself to touch her. Then through Miriam he met Clara Dawes. For a long while, Mrs. Morel had been urging him to give up Miriam, and now Paul tried to tell Miriam that it was all over between them. He did not want to marry her, but he felt that he did belong to her. He could not make up his own mind.

Clara Dawes was separated from her husband, Baxter Dawes. Although she was five years Paul's senior, Clara was a beautiful woman whose loveliness charmed him. Although she became his mistress, she refused to divorce her husband and marry Paul. Sometimes Paul wondered whether he could bring himself to marry Clara if she were free. She was not what he wanted. His mother was the only woman to whom he could turn for complete understanding and love, for Miriam had tried to possess him and Clara maintained a barrier against him. Paul continued to devote much of his time and attention to making his mother happy. Annie had married and gone to live with her husband near the Morel home, and Arthur had married a childhood friend who bore him a son six months after the wedding.

Baxter Dawes resented Paul's relationship with his wife. Once he accosted Paul in a tavern and threatened him. Paul knew that he could not fight with Baxter, but he continued to see Clara.

Paul had entered pictures in local exhibits and had won four prizes. With encouragement from Mrs. Morel, he continued to paint. He wanted to go abroad, but he could not leave his mother. He began to see Miriam again. When she yielded herself to him, his passion was ruthless and savage. Their relationship, however, was still unsatisfactory, and he turned again to Clara.

Miriam knew about his love affair with Clara, but the girl felt that Paul would tire of his mistress and come back to her. Paul stayed with Clara, however, because he found in her an outlet for his unknown desires. His life was a great conflict. Meanwhile, Paul was earning enough money to give his mother the material possessions her husband had failed to provide. Mr. Morel stayed on with his wife and son, but he was no longer accepted as a father or a husband.

One day, it was revealed that Mrs. Morel had cancer and was beyond any help except that of morphine and then death. During the following months, Mrs. Morel declined rapidly. Paul was tortured by his mother's pain. Annie and Paul marveled at her resistance to death and wished that it would come to end her suffering. Paul dreaded such a catastrophe in his life, although he knew it must come eventually. He turned to Clara for comfort, but she failed to make him forget his misery. Then, visiting his mother at the hospital, Paul found Baxter Dawes recovering from an attack of typhoid fever. For a long time, Paul had sensed that Clara wanted to return to Dawes, and now, out of pity for Dawes, he brought about a reconciliation between the husband and wife.

When Mrs. Morel's suffering had mounted to a torturing degree, Annie and Paul decided that anything would be better than to let her live in agony. One night, Paul gave her an overdose of morphine, and Mrs. Morel died the next day.

Left alone, Paul was lost. He felt that his own life had ended with the death of his mother. Clara, to whom he had turned before, was now back with Dawes. Because they could not bear to stay in the house without Mrs. Morel, Paul and his father parted and each took different lodgings.

For a while, Paul wandered helplessly trying to find some purpose in his life. Then he thought of Miriam, to whom he had once belonged. He returned to her, but with the renewed association, he realized more than ever that she was not what he wanted. Once he had thought of going abroad. Now he wanted to join his mother in death. Leaving Miriam for the last time, he felt trapped and lost in his own indecision; but he also felt that he was free from Miriam after many years of passion and regret.

His mother's death was too great a sorrow for Paul to cast off immediately. Finally, after a lengthy inner struggle, he was able to see that she would always be with him and that he did not need to die to join her. With his newfound courage, he set out to make his own life anew.

Critical Evaluation

Although Freud was the first to provide a systematic analysis of the Oedipal relationship and its function in man's fate, this instinct has been a part of man's unconscious from his earliest beginnings as a social animal. The establishment of the taboo against a son's murdering his father and having a sexual relationship with his mother was man's initial step in the creation of civilization, because, according to Freud, this psychic drive lies deep in every man's subconscious or id as a reservoir of anarchistic energy. If man fails to acknowledge this biological compulsion and to incorporate its prohibition into his own ego, he invites annihilation, specifically in the form of castration by the father and generally in the loss of freedom and power.

One of the earliest and best-known dramatizations of this drive is Sophocles' play, *Oedipus Rex*. Without foreknowledge and culpable guilt, Oedipus murders his father and marries his mother. Since he has transgressed, however, he must be punished; he blinds himself, a form of castration. Shakespeare's *Hamlet* has also been explored and explicated, most notably by Ernest Jones, as a reenactment of the Oedipal myth. *Sons and Lovers*, based directly on D. H. Lawrence's own childhood experiences, is the most significant post-Freudian novel dealing with a young man's murderous feelings toward his father and his erotic attraction to his mother.

Although it would be overly simplistic to explain *Sons and Lovers* as a mere gloss on a psychological concept, Freud's "complex" does offer a convenient way to begin understanding the character and cultural situation of Lawrence's hero, Paul Morel. He is the youngest and adored son of a mother who has married beneath herself. Of the failed middle class, she is educated to a degree, refined with pretensions toward the higher matters of life. As a girl, she is attracted to Walter Morel, a miner who possesses a passionate exuberance she missed on the frayed edges of the middle class. Their marriage, however, soon disintegrates under the pressures of poverty and unfulfilled expectations. As the father and mother grow apart and the older children leave home, Mrs. Morel turns toward her youngest child, mapping out his life and intending to free him from the ignominy of the working class. Her ambitions for Paul are not untainted by her own frustrations, and it becomes clear that she wishes to live out her life through him.

Sensitive and frail, Paul finds his father's drunkenness and rough-edged masculinity repellent. Reared by his mother as if he were a fragile hot-house plant, he is further alienated by his father's vulgar habits and degrading job. Without any sympathy or understanding of his father's suffering or his hard and abrupt love for him, Paul withdraws and joins his mother in the domestic battle. Morel becomes enraged and disappointed by the loss of his son and wife and withdraws into self-pity and alcohol.

Bereft of his father's influence, Paul's life becomes dominated by his mother. Smothered by her warm maternity, cut off from the real world, he returns her ardent affection, and they form a relationship designed to hold off the horrors of reality. As he grows up, however, he discovers that he has traded his own "self" for security. His mother's protectiveness has cost him the power and freedom to relate to others. Every relationship he tries to create is inhibited by her jealousy and demands for his entire attention. Indeed, he comes to feel that every relationship he attempts to pursue is in some way a denial of her.

Paul's attraction to Miriam Leivers, which gradually develops into a love affair, is ironically both a rejection and a reaffirmation of his mother. Their immature love, which Mrs. Morel rightfully sees as a threat, is in some ways an acting out of the sexual implications of the mother-son relationship. In her passive dominance, Miriam unconsciously assumes for Paul the figure of his mother. Thus, if their love manages to remove him temporarily from his mother's sway, it also reinforces it. Both rela-

tionships are symbiotic; Paul draws sustenance from the women but loses the power of self-propulsion. It is evident that Paul does not completely acquiesce in the symbiosis in both his brutal sexual treatment of Miriam and his sexual ambivalence toward his mother.

Paul's connection with Clara and Baxter Dawes is much more interesting and complex. Clara provides him with an adult sexual experience unlike that which he had with Miriam. She is neither dominating nor submissive but demands that he meet her as an equal. He therefore must remain emotionally on his own; he is expected to give affection as well as receive it. Unfortunately, Paul cannot maintain such an independence, and this fact undermines their love. He cannot exist as a self-sufficient entity, and Clara will not tolerate an invasion of her self. Paul, however, does not understand this about their relationship until after Mrs. Morel's death. His subsequently successful attempt to reunite her with Baxter thus becomes his first sign of health; it is not only an admission that their romance is impossible but is also a reparation for having alienated her from Baxter.

Paul's act of reparation is also symbolic. Released from his mother's dominance by her death, a death that he hastened, he must continue his growth toward freedom and power by making peace with his father. Unable to confront him directly, Paul admits by bringing together Clara and Baxter the higher moral demands of marital love, a love he has helped to destroy—although innocently—between his father and mother. In this act, moreover, he negates the child in himself and salutes the reality of the father and husband.

THE SOUND AND THE FURY

Type of work: Novel
Author: William Faulkner (1897–1962)
Type of plot: Psychological realism
Time of plot: 1910–1928
Locale: Mississippi
First published: 1929

The Sound and the Fury, *an extremely complex yet rewarding novel, traces from 1910 to 1928 the decline of a once-aristocratic but now degenerated Southern family. Faulkner's method of narration, involving the consciousness of different members and servants of the Compson family, provides four distinct psychological points of view.*

Principal Characters

Jason Lycurgus Compson (III), grandson of a Mississippi governor, son of a Confederate general, and father to the last of the Compsons. Like his illustrious ancestors, his name suggested his passion, the classics. Unlike his forebears, he is unable to make a living or to fulfill his deepest ambition, the study of the Greek and Latin epigrammatists, but his stoic philosophy, culled from his reading, stands him in good stead. He speaks wisely, does little, drinks much, and is weary of his complaining wife, his wayward daughter, and his bickering sons.

Caroline Bascomb Compson, his wife, who resents the Compson lineage and feels that hers is more glorious. A neurotic woman with psychosomatic symptoms, she complains constantly of her grievances and ills. Reluctant to face reality and rejoicing that she was not born a Compson, she indulges her fancies and pretends to be an antebellum Southern gentlewoman. Her fortitude in tragedy is even more remarkable for all her complaining, but she victimizes her children and devoted servants to maintain her resentment and illnesses.

Candace Compson, their only daughter, affectionate, loyal, libido-driven. Called **Caddy,** a name which results in great confusion for her idiot brother whose playground is the pasture sold to a golf course where he hears her name, she herself is doomed, though devoted to her dead brother, her weak-minded brother, her own illegitimate daughter, her loving father. She is at odds with her mother, her vengeful brother Jason, and several husbands. So promiscuous is she, even urging her sensitive brother Quentin to abortive intercourse, that she does not really know the father of her child. As an adventuress she travels widely, and in the postlude to the novel appears as the consort of a Nazi officer in Paris.

Quentin Compson, her beloved brother for whom she names her child even before the baby's birth. Obsessed by a sense of guilt, doom, and death, he commits suicide by drowning in June, 1910, two months after his sister's marriage to a man he calls a blackguard. Because he is deeply disturbed by family affairs—the selling of a pas-

ture to pay for his year at Harvard, the loss of his sister's honor, the morbid despair he feels for his idiot brother, his hatred of the family vices of pride and snobbishness—his death is predictable, unalterable.

Jason Compson (IV), the only son to stay on in the old Compson place, loyal to his weak, querulous mother, determined to gain his full share of his patrimony, bitter over his deep failures. His tale is one of petty annoyances, nursed grievances, and egotistic aggressiveness in his ungenerous and self-assertive mastery of his niece and the black servants. This descendant of aristocrats is a small-town redneck, wily, canny, cunning, and deceitful. Not without reasons for his bitterness, he finally rids himself of his enervating responsibilities for a dying line by himself remaining a bachelor and having his idiot brother castrated.

Quentin, the daughter of Candace and her mother's own child. Reared by Dilsey, the black cook, Quentin is the last of anything resembling life in the old Compson house. As self-assertive as her uncle, she steals money he calls his (but which is rightfully hers) and elopes with a carnival pitchman. Beautiful in the wild way of her mother, she has never had affection from anyone except her morbid old grandmother and a brokenhearted servant. Her father may have been a young man named Dalton Ames.

Dilsey Gibson, the bullying but beloved black family retainer, cook, financier (in petty extravagances), and benefactress, who maintains family standards that no longer concern the Compsons. Deeply concerned for them, she babies the thirty-year-old Benjamin, the unfortunate Quentin, and the querulous old "Miss Cahline," though she resists the egocentric Jason. A woman whose wise, understanding nature is beyond limits of race or color, she endures for others and prolongs the lives of those dependent on her shrewdness and strength.

Benjamin Compson, called **Benjy,** at first named Maury after his mother's brother. He is an idiot who observes everything, smells tragedy, loves the old pasture, his sister Caddy, and firelight, but cannot compose his disordered thoughts into any coherent pattern of life or speech. Gelded by his brother Jason, he moans out his pitiful existence and is finally sent to the state asylum in Jackson.

Maury L. Bascomb, Mrs. Compson's brother. A bachelor, a drunkard, and a philanderer, he is supported by the Compsons. Benjy Compson was christened Maury, after his uncle.

Roskus, the Compsons' black coachman when the children were small.

T.P., a black servant who helps to look after Benjy

Compson. He later goes to Memphis to live.

Luster, a fourteen-year-old black boy who is thirty-three-year-old Benjy Compson's caretaker and playmate.

Frony, Dilsey's daughter.

Sydney Herbert Head, a young banker, Caddy Compson's first husband. He divorces her after he realizes that her daughter Quentin is not his child. The divorce ends young Jason Compson's hope of getting a position in Head's bank.

Shreve McCannon, Quentin Compson's Canadian roommate at Harvard.

The Story

The Compson family had once been a good one, but the present generation had done everything possible to ruin the name of Compson for all time. In the little Mississippi town in which they lived, everyone laughed and made slighting remarks when the name Compson was mentioned.

Mrs. Compson had come from what she considered good stock, but she thought she must have sinned terribly in marrying a Compson and now she was paying for her sins. For eighteen years she had been saying that she did not have long to live and would no longer be a burden to her family. Benjy was her greatest cross. He was an idiot who moaned, cried, and slobbered all day long. The only person who could quiet Benjy was Candace, his sister. When they were small, Candace loved Benjy very much and made herself his protector. She saw to it that the other children of the family and the black servants did not tease him. As Candace grew up, she continued to love Benjy, but she also loved every man she met, giving herself freely to any man who would have her. Mrs. Compson thought Candace was another cross she had to bear and did very little to force her daughter to have better morals.

Quentin, another son, was a moody, morose boy whose only passion was his sister Candace. He loved her not as a sister but as a woman, and she returned his love. Quentin was sent to school at Harvard. Although she loved Quentin in the spirit, Candace could not keep away from other men. Sydney Herbert Head was the one serious lover she had. He wanted to marry her. Head, a banker, promised to give her brother Jason a job in his bank after they were married. When Quentin learned that Candace was in a condition that made her marriage necessary, he was wild. He lied to his father and told him that he had had incestuous relations with Candace and that she must not be allowed to marry. His father did not believe him, and the family went along with their plans for the wedding. At last Quentin could stand no more. Two months after his sister's wedding, he drowned himself in the Charles River in Cambridge, Massachusetts. Mrs. Compson

resigned herself to one more cross.

When Candace had a baby too soon, Head threw her out of his house with her child. Her mother and father and her brother Jason would not let her come home, but they adopted the baby girl, Quentin. Jason believed that Quentin was the child of his brother Quentin and Candace, but the rest of the family refused to face such a possibility and accept it. They preferred to believe, and rightly, that Quentin was the child of some other lover who had deserted Candace. Candace stayed away from the little town for many years.

Quentin was as wild as her mother as she grew up. She, too, gave herself to any man in town and was talked about as her mother had been. Every month, Candace sent money to Mrs. Compson for Quentin's care. At first Mrs. Compson burned the checks, for she would have none of Candace's ill-gotten money. When Mr. Compson died, Jason became the head of the family. He blamed Quentin for his not getting the job in the bank, for if the child had not been born too soon, Head would not have left Candace and would have given Jason the job. Hating his sister, he wrote checks on another bank and gave those to his mother in place of the checks Candace had sent. The old lady was almost blind and could not see what she burned. Jason then forged her signature on the real checks and cashed them, using the money to gamble on the cotton market.

Quentin hated her Uncle Jason as much as he hated her, and the two were always quarreling. He tried to make her go to school and keep away from the men, but Mrs. Compson thought he was too cruel to Quentin and took the girl's side.

A show troupe came to town, and Quentin took up with one of the performers. Her grandmother locked her in her room each night, but she climbed out of the window to meet her lover. One morning, she did not answer when old Dilsey, the black woman who had cared for the family for years, called her to breakfast. Jason went to her room and found that all her clothes were gone. He also found that the three thousand dollars he had hidden in his room had been stolen. He tried to get the sheriff to follow the girl and the showman, but the sheriff wanted no part of the Compson family affairs. Jason set out to find the fugitives, but he had to give up his search when a severe headache forced him to return home for medicine.

Jason felt more than cheated. His money was gone, and he could not find Quentin so that he could punish her for stealing it. He forgot that the money really belonged to Quentin, for he had saved it from the money Candace had sent for the girl's care. There was nothing left for Jason but blind rage and hatred for everyone. He believed that everyone laughed at him because of his horrible family—because Benjy was an idiot, Candace a lost woman, Quentin a suicide, and the girl Quentin a village harlot and a thief. He forgot that he, too, was a thief and that

he had a mistress. He felt cursed by his family as his mother was cursed.

When he saw Benjy riding through town in a carriage driven by one of the black boys, he knocked the black boy down and struck Benjy with all his force, for there was no other way to show his rage. Benjy let out a loud moan and then settled back in the carriage. He very gently petted a wilted flower, and his face assumed a calm, quiet blankness, as if all the strife in the world were over and things were once more serene. It was as if he had understood what old Dilsey meant when she said she had seen the beginning and the end of life. Benjy had seen it all, too, in the pictures he could never understand but which flowed endlessly through his disordered mind.

Critical Evaluation

After early undistinguished efforts in verse (*The Marble Faun*, 1924) and fiction (*Soldier's Pay*, 1926; *Mosquitoes*, 1927), William Faulkner moved suddenly into the forefront of American literature in 1929 with the appearance of *Sartoris* and *The Sound and the Fury*, the first installments in the artistically complex and subtly satirical saga of Yoknapatawpha County that would be spun out further in *As I Lay Dying* (1930), *Light in August* (1932), *Absalom, Absalom!* (1936), *Go Down, Moses* (1942), *The Unvanquished* (1938), *Intruder in the Dust* (1948), the *Hamlet-Town-Mansion* trilogy (1940, 1957, 1959), and *Requiem for a Nun* (1951)—the last an extension of materials in *Sanctuary* (1931). Chiefly in recognition of the monumental literary importance of the Yoknapatawpha saga, Faulker was awarded the Nobel Prize in 1949.

The Sound and the Fury marked the beginning of the most fertile period of Faulkner's creativity, when he was in his early thirties. Both for its form and for its thematic significance this novel may well be considered Faulkner's masterpiece. Never again would his work demonstrate such tight, precise structure, combined with the complexities of syntax and punctuation that became his most characteristic stylistic trait. Furthermore, the themes recorded in his simple but not elegant Nobel Prize speech—"love and honor and pity and pride and compassion and sacrifice"—are already present in this novel with a forcefulness of characterization that could hardly be improved upon. It was in this novel that Faulkner found a way of embodying his peculiar view of time in an appropriate style, a style much influenced by Joycean stream of consciousness and by Faulkner's own stated desire ultimately to "put all of human experience between one Cap and one period." That concept of time, most emphatic in Quentin's section, can be summarized by Faulkner's statement that "there is no such thing as *was*; if *was* existed there would be no grief or sorrow." The contin-

uation of the past into the present, as a shaping influence that cannot be avoided, is the larger theme of Faulkner's life work.

In this novel, that theme is embodied specifically in the history of the decline of the aristocratic Compson family. Nearly twenty years after the original publication of the novel, at the instigation of his publisher Malcolm Cowley, Faulkner wrote the background history of the Compsons as an "appendix" that appears at the front of the book. The appendix records the noble origins of the Compson land, once the possession of a Chickasaw king named Ikkemotubbe, or "the man." After proceeding through the Compson succession—beginning with Quentin Maclachan Compson, who immigrated from Glasgow, and proceeding to Jason III, the "dipsomaniac" lawyer who could not tear himself away from the Roman classics long enough to preserve the vestiges of his family's good name, Faulkner presents terse but invaluable insights into the chief characters of *The Sound and the Fury*. Candace knew she was doomed and regarded her virginity as no more than a "hangnail," and her promiscuity represents the moral sterility of the family. Quentin III, who "identified family with his sister's membrane," convinced himself he had committed incest with her, but really loved only death—in his sublimation of emotions into a kind of latter-day courtly love mystique—and found his love in June, 1910, by committing the physical suicide that the destruction of his grandfather's watch symbolized. Benjy, the "idiot" whose "tale" forms the remarkable first section of the novel, "loved three things: the pasture . . . his sister Candace (who 'smelled like trees'), and firelight" and symbolizes both the mental deterioration of the family and, through his castration, its physical sterility. Jason IV, "the first sane Compson since before Culloden and (a childless bachelor) hence the last," commits Benjy to an asylum, sells the house, and displays the pathetically mediocre intelligence that alone is able to cope with the incursions of the modern world as symbolized by the Snopes family. Quentin IV, the child of Candace, "already doomed to be unwed from the instant the dividing egg determined its sex," is the last Compson and the final burden destined for Mrs. Compson, the personification, to Jason, of all the evil and insanity of his decaying, decadent family.

Benjy's section takes place on April 7, 1928, the day before Quentin IV steals her uncle's money. It is written with incredibly delicate perception, revealing the lucidity of a simpleminded innocence that can yet be accompanied by a terrible sharpness and consistency of memory. In its confusion of his father's funeral with Candace's wedding, in its constant painful reactivation—the sound of the golfers' cry of "caddie" causes him to bellow out his hollow sense of his sister's loss—Benjy's mind becomes the focus of more cruelty, compassion, and love than anyone but Dilsey imagines. Quentin III's section, taking place eighteen years earlier on the day of his suicide at Harvard, is one of the most sustained lyrical passages of twentieth century prose. The concentration of Quentin's stream of consciousness around the broken, handless watch is one of Faulkner's greatest achievements. Just as the leitmotif of Benjy's section was the smell of trees associated with Caddy's loss, the recurring refrain of Quentin's is the desperate rhetorical question, "Did you ever have a sister?" Jason's theme is hate, a hate as pitiful as is the diminution of Compson pride into pathetic vanity; and this third section of the novel may be the greatest for its evocation of deep, moving passions from even the most mediocre. The last section is focused on Dilsey, who "seed de first en de last" and who represents, to Faulkner, the only humanity that survives the fall of the house of Compson—the only humanity to endure.

SPOON RIVER ANTHOLOGY

Type of work: Poetry
Author: Edgar Lee Masters (1869–1950)
First published: 1915

Like Edward FitzGerald and a few other poets, Edgar Lee Masters established his reputation on the basis of one work, *Spoon River Anthology*. Masters was a prolific writer, producing many volumes of verse, several plays, an autobiography, several biographies, essays, novels, and an attempt to recapture his great success in a sequel, *The New Spoon River*; but except for a handful of individual poems from the other volumes, he will be remembered as the re-creator of a small Middle Western town which he calls Spoon River, but which was probably Lewiston, Illinois, where he studied law in his father's office and practiced for a year before moving on to Chicago.

In form and style *Spoon River Anthology* is not a work that sprang wholly out of Masters' imagination; it is modeled on *The Greek Anthology*, and the style of the character sketches owes a considerable debt to Browning. But Masters composed his book with such an effortless brilliance and freshness that decades after its first publication it still retains a kind of startling inevitability, as if this were the best and only way to present people in poetry. From their graveyard on the hill Masters lets more than two hundred of the dead citizens of Spoon River tell the truth about themselves, each person writing what might be his or her own epitaph. The secrets they reveal are shocking—stories of intrigue, corruption, frustration, adultery. Because of its frankness—mild by the standards of subsequent decades—*Spoon River Anthology* provoked howls of protest from disturbed readers who felt that it presented too sordid a picture of American small-town life. Distorted or not, Masters' approach to his subject undoubtedly helped open the way for dozens of novels whose authors seem to use grappling hooks to break that placid surface of life and dredge up secrets from the murk below.

Masters' book, however, is not a novel in verse, and while many of the poems are interrelated and a certain amount of suspense is created by having one character mention a person or incident to be further developed in a later epitaph, the anthology is not centered on a unifying theme. About the closest approach to such a theme is the tragic failure of the town's bank, chiefly attributed to Thomas Rhodes, its president, and his son Ralph, who confesses from the grave:

> All they said was true:
> I wrecked my father's bank with my loans
> To dabble in wheat; but this was true—

> I was buying wheat for him as well,
> Who couldn't margin the deal in his name
> Because of his church relationship.

Many people suffered from the bank's collapse, including the cashier, George Reece, who had the blame placed on him and served a term in prison; but a far more corroding effect was the cynicism generated in the citizens when they found that their leaders, the "stalwarts," were weak and culpable.

Masters has pictured many vivid characters in *Spoon River Anthology*. They range all the way from Daisy Fraser, the town harlot, who

> Never was taken before Justice Arnett
> Without contributing ten dollars and costs
> To the school fund of Spoon River!

to Lucinda Matlock, who

> Rambled over the fields where sang the larks,
> And by Spoon River gathering many a shell,
> And many a flower and medicinal weed—
> Shouting to the wooded hills, singing to the green
> valleys.
> At ninety-six I had lived enough, that is all,
> And passed to a sweet repose.

Others are the town physicians, Doc Hill and Doc Myers, both of whose lives are scarred; Petit, the poet whose "faint iambics" rattled on "while Homer and Whitman roared in the pines"; Ann Rutledge, from whose dead bosom the Republic blooms forever; Russian Sonia, a dancer who met old Patrick Hummer, of Spoon River, and went back with him to the town, where the couple lived twenty years in unmarried content; and Chase Henry, the town drunkard, a Catholic who was denied burial in consecrated ground but who won some measure of honor when the Protestants acquired the land where he was buried and interred banker Nicholas and wife beside the old reprobate.

Spoon River Anthology is weighted so heavily on the sordid side—abortions, suicides, adulteries—that the more cheerful and "normal" epitaphs come almost as a relief. Lucinda Matlock and Ann Rutledge fit this category; others are Hare Drummer, who delights in the memory of a happy childhood; Conrad Siever, content in his grave under an apple tree he planted, pruned, and tended; and

Fiddler Jones, who never could stick to farming and who ended up with "a broken laugh, and a thousand memories,/ And not a single regret."

One especially effective device that Masters makes use of in his collection is the pairing of poems so that the reader gets a startling jolt of irony. Thus when Elsa Wertman, a peasant girl from Germany, confesses that her employer, Thomas Greene, fathered her child and then reared it as his and Mrs. Greene's, we find in the next poem that Hamilton, the son, attributes his great success as a politician to the "honorable blood" he inherited from Mr. and Mrs. Greene. There is also Roscoe Purkapile, who ran away from his wife for a year, telling her when he came back that he had been captured by pirates while he was rowing a boat on Lake Michigan. After he told her the story,

> She cried and kissed me, and said it was cruel,
> Outrageous, inhuman!

However, when Mrs. Purkapile has her say in the next poem, she makes it known that she was not taken in by his cock-and-bull story, that she knew he was trysting in the city with Mrs. Williams, the milliner, and that she refused to be drawn into a divorce by a husband "who had merely grown tired of his marital vow and duty."

Masters displays an amazing variety of effects in these short poems. His use of free verse undoubtedly helps to achieve this variety, for a stricter form or forms might make the poems seem too pat, too artificial. Sometimes Masters lets his character's only remembrance of life be a simple, vivid description, as when Bert Kessler tells how he met his death. Out hunting one day, Bert killed a quail, and when he reached down by a stump to pick it up he felt something sting his hand, like the prick of a brier:

> And then, in a second, I spied the rattler—
> The shutters wide in his yellow eyes,
> The head of him arched, sunk back in the rings of him,
> A circle of filth, the color of ashes,
> Or oak leaves bleached under layers of leaves.
> I stood like a stone as he shrank and uncoiled
> And started to crawl beneath the stump,
> When I fell limp in the grass.

Bert tells of his death without comment, but when Harry Williams describes how he was deluded into joining the army to fight in the Spanish-American War, in which he was killed, the poem is full of bitterness, horror, and brutal irony.

To say that every poem in this volume is successful would be as foolish as to contend that each entry in Shakespeare's sonnet sequence is a masterpiece. Masters frequently strains for an effect; for instance, "Sexsmith the Dentist" seems to have been created so that Sexsmith may remark, at the end, that what we consider truth may be a hollow tooth "which must be propped with gold"; and Mrs. Kessler, a washerwoman, was probably included so that she might observe that the face of a dead person always looked to her "like something washed and ironed." And there are other poems in which the characters just do not come alive. One suspects that the poet wrote a number of philosophical lyrics, some of them marred by clichés and cloying rhetoric, and then titled them with names selected at random.

In the main, however, Masters has done a remarkable job in *Spoon River Anthology*. Anyone living in a small town will recognize in these poems the people he sees every day; and, though he may not like to admit it, when these people die they may carry to the grave secrets as startling and embarrassing as those revealed by the dead of Spoon River.

THE STRANGE CASE OF DR. JEKYLL AND MR. HYDE

Type of work: Novella
Author: Robert Louis Stevenson (1850–1894)
Type of plot: Fantasy
Time of plot: Nineteenth century
Locale: London
First published: 1886

This classic romantic adventure and fantasy has steadily maintained its popularity ever since it was first published in 1886. Based upon the dual personalities of a single man representing beauty and beast, the story reveals Stevenson's understanding of human nature and his mastery of English prose.

Principal Characters

Dr. Henry Jekyll, a London physician who leads a double life. He concocts a drug to change his personality at times to conform to his evil side. To protect himself, he then makes a will leaving his money to the incarnation of his other personality, Edward Hyde. Finally, after the medicine to restore his original personality has run out, he kills himself while in the person of Hyde.

Edward Hyde, the evil side of Dr. Jekyll, a trampler of children and the murderer of Sir Danvers Carew.

Dr. Hastie Lanyon, an intimate friend of Jekyll, who was once present at one of the transformations and who leaves a written description of it, to be opened after Jekyll's death.

Sir Danvers Carew, a kindly old man murdered by Hyde for the joy of doing evil.

Poole, Dr. Jekyll's servant, who vainly seeks the rare drug for the restorative needed by his master.

Mr. Utterson, Jekyll's lawyer, who holds, unopened, Lanyon's letter.

Richard Enfield, who has witnessed Hyde's cruelty and wants an investigation to learn why Hyde is Jekyll's heir.

The Story

Mr. Richard Enfield, and his cousin, Mr. Utterson, a lawyer, were strolling according to their usual Sunday custom when they came upon an empty building on a familiar street. Mr. Enfield stated that some time previously he had seen an ill-tempered man trample a small child at the doorway of the deserted building. He and other indignant bystanders had forced the stranger, who gave his name as Hyde, to pay over a sum of money for the child's welfare. Enfield remembered Hyde with deep loathing.

Utterson had reason to be interested in Hyde. When he returned to his apartment, he reread the strange will of Dr. Henry Jekyll. The will stipulated that in the event of Dr. Jekyll's death all of his wealth should go to a man named Edward Hyde.

Utterson sought out Hyde, the man whom Enfield had described, to discover if he were the same person who had been named heir to Dr. Jekyll's fortune. Suspicious of Utterson's interest, Hyde became enraged and ran into his house. Questioned, Dr. Jekyll refused to discuss the matter but insisted that in the event of his death the lawyer should see to it that Mr. Hyde was not cheated out of his fortune. The lawyer believed that Hyde was an extortioner who was getting possession of Dr. Jekyll's money

and who would eventually murder the doctor.

About a year later, Hyde was wanted for the wanton murder of a kindly old man, Sir Danvers Carew, but he escaped before he could be arrested. Dr. Jekyll presented the lawyer and the police with a letter signed by Hyde, in which the murderer declared his intention of making good his escape forever. He begged Dr. Jekyll's pardon for having ill-used his friendship.

About this time, Dr. Lanyon, who had been for years a great friend of Dr. Jekyll, became ill and died. A letter addressed to Utterson was found among his papers. Opening it, Utterson discovered an inner envelope also sealed and bearing the notice that it was not to be opened until after Dr. Jekyll's death. Utterson felt that it was somehow associated with the evil Hyde, but he could in no way fathom the mystery.

One Sunday, Enfield and Utterson were walking again in the street where Enfield had seen Hyde abusing the child. They now realized that the strange deserted building was a side entrance to the house of Dr. Jekyll, an additional wing used as a laboratory. Looking up at the window, they saw Dr. Jekyll sitting there. He looked disconsolate. Then his expression seemed to change, so that his face took on a grimace of horror or pain. Suddenly, he closed the window. Utterson and Enfield walked on, too overcome by what they had seen to talk further.

Not long afterward, Utterson was sitting by his fireside when Dr. Jekyll's manservant, Poole, sought entrance. He related that for a week something strange had been going on in Dr. Jekyll's laboratory. The doctor himself had not appeared. Instead, he had ordered his meals to be sent in and had written curious notes demanding that Poole go to all the chemical houses in London in search of a mysterious drug. Poole was convinced that his master had been slain and that the murderer, masquerading as Dr. Jekyll, was still hiding in the laboratory.

Utterson and Poole returned to Dr. Jekyll's house and broke into his laboratory with an ax. They entered and discovered that the man in the laboratory had killed himself by draining a vial of poison just as they broke the lock. The man was Edward Hyde.

They searched in vain for the doctor's body, certain it was somewhere about after they discovered a note of that date addressed to Utterson. In the note, Dr. Jekyll said he was planning to disappear, and he urged Utterson to read the note that Dr. Lanyon had left at the time of his death. An enclosure contained the confession of Henry Jekyll.

Utterson returned to his office to read the letters. The letter of Dr. Lanyon described how Dr. Jekyll had sent Poole to Dr. Lanyon with a request that Dr. Lanyon search for some drugs in Dr. Jekyll's laboratory. Hyde had appeared to claim the drugs. Then, in Dr. Lanyon's presence, Hyde had taken the drugs and had been transformed into Dr. Jekyll. The shock of this transformation had caused Dr. Lanyon's death.

Dr. Jekyll's own account of the horrible affair was more detailed. He had begun early in life to live a double life. Publicly, he had been genteel and circumspect; pri-

vately, however, he had practiced strange vices without restraint. Becoming obsessed with the idea that people had two personalities, he reasoned that men were capable of having two physical beings as well. Finally, he had compounded a mixture that transformed his body into the physical representation of his evil self. He became Hyde. In his disguise, he was free to haunt the lonely, narrow corners of London and to perform the darkest acts without fear of recognition.

He tried in every way to protect Hyde. He cautioned his servants to let him in at any hour; he took an apartment for him, and he made out his will in Hyde's favor. His life proceeded safely enough until he awoke one morning in the shape of Edward Hyde and realized that his evil nature had gained the upper hand. Frightened, he determined to cast off the nature of Hyde. He sought out better companions and tried to occupy his mind with other things. He was not strong enough, however, to change his true nature. He finally permitted himself to assume the shape of Hyde again, and on that occasion Hyde, full of an overpowering lust to do evil, murdered Sir Danvers Carew.

Dr. Jekyll renewed his effort to abandon the nature of Hyde. Walking in the park one day, he suddenly changed into Hyde. On that occasion, he had sought out his friend Dr. Lanyon to go to his laboratory to obtain the drugs that would change him back to the personality of the doctor. Dr. Lanyon had watched the transformation with horror. Thereafter the nature of Hyde seemed to assert itself constantly. When his supply of chemicals had been exhausted and could not be replenished, Dr. Jekyll, as Hyde, shut himself up in his laboratory while he experimented with one drug after another. Finally, in despair, as Utterson now realized, he killed himself.

Critical Evaluation

One of the great themes of British literature in the nineteenth century is that of the divided self. The theme is embodied in the works of such authors as Arthur Hugh Clough, Alfred, Lord Tennyson, Charles Dickens, Matthew Arnold, and Oscar Wilde. In the preface to his collected poems (1853) Arnold writes, "The calm, the cheerfulness, the disinterested objectivity have disappeared: the dialogue of the mind with itself has commenced; modern problems have presented themselves. . . ." The theme of human duality, however, is nowhere presented with more force and originality than in Robert Louis Stevenson's *Dr. Jekyll and Mr. Hyde*. The story has become part of Western folklore and has been popularized throughout the world through many motion picture and television adaptations. In its dramatization of the dark side of human nature, Stevenson's novel anticipates Sigmund Freud's study of the primitive

forces of the mind that dwell in what he termed the unconscious and the id.

The central fantasy of this novel lies in Dr. Jekyll's ability, through drinking a seemingly magical chemical potion, to separate the spontaneous, primitive, evil side of his character from that of his restrained, civilized, morally upright character. This fantasy resembles that of children's folklore, in which there coexists an evil witch and a fairy godmother. Unable to understand the ambiguity of a mother who both threatens and comforts, the child is better able to deal with two distinct mother figures.

Stevenson may well have been working out his own psychological problems in this book. As a youth he fought with his father and was torn between a family that insisted upon his adopting the life-style of the Edinburgh bourgeoisie and his own inclinations to seek the forbidden pleasure of a more bohemian existence. Henry Jekyll explains that his life has become unbearable because of the tension between the repressive nature of his middle-class character and his hidden desires for spontaneity and pleasure. He yearns to acquire a sense of peace by resolving this conflict through housing in separate identities these two forces struggling to dominate his soul.

After taking his chemical potion, he shrinks in size, and his actions resemble that of a rebellious son. He attacks Dr. Jekyll, his father figure, by destroying his portrait. Like a loving father, Dr. Jekyll does all that is in his power to protect Mr. Hyde from harm. Despite the ungratefulness and hatred exhibited toward him, Dr. Jekyll pities Mr. Hyde and suffers his outrageous behavior until their mutual deaths.

Viewed more broadly, however, the novel focuses upon the duality that exists within one person. Stevenson believed that there were two elements within the human soul and that all intelligent people experienced this duality at times. It would be a mistake to interpret the division of the soul simply into good and evil. Is not Dr. Jekyll, after all, responsible for Mr. Hyde, a creature that he conjures up at will? The interesting moral question arises— who is responsible for the murder of Sir Danvers Carew? Mr. Hyde is a depraved child of nature, an innocent, who, like an animal, seeks to fulfill himself without any of the restraints of social and moral codes. In a modern court of law he might be judged insane. Dr. Jekyll, on the other hand, is fully cognizant of his moral and social responsibilities and nevertheless continues with his dangerous experiments.

Dr. Jekyll's assertion that Mr. Hyde is "wholly evil," therefore, must be read in the light of Jekyll's own mis-understanding of himself. The novel makes clear that the separation of selves is finally impossible. Dr. Jekyll may carry on his customary respectable life and Mr. Hyde may continue to seek out new forbidden pleasures, but the fact remains that the two figures are inextricably bound together by love, pity, and hatred. It is, indeed, an appealing fantasy to believe that one can release his hidden desires for sensual pleasures and bear no responsibility for the outcome of that release. Stevenson's moral sense, however, makes clear that such a fantasy cannot be sustained, that moral and social judgment finally exacts a price for such a release, and the price that Dr. Jekyll pays is his own life.

The moral of the fable contained in *Dr. Jekyll and Mr. Hyde* is perhaps best summarized by Aldous Huxley, who recognized that both aspects of self, the rational and the spontaneous, must coexist if modern man and woman are to survive:

> The only satisfactory way of existing in the modern, highly specialized world is to live with two personalities. A Dr. Jekyll that does the metaphysical and scientific thinking, that transacts business in the city, adds up figures, designs machines . . . and a natural spontaneous Mr. Hyde to do the physical, instinctive living in the intervals of work. The two personalities should lead their unconnected lives apart, without poaching upon one another's preserves or inquiring too closely into one another's activities. Only by living discreetly and inconsistently can we preserve both the man and the citizen, both the intellectual and the spontaneous animal being, alive within us.

Dr. Jekyll and Mr. Hyde is one of popular classics of modern literature because it touches in readers a common nerve. Like Stevenson himself, the reader has experienced the powerful tensions between freedom and restraint, appetite and intellect, pleasure and moral propriety. The fantasy of dividing these opposing forces into separate personalities has an enormous appeal and, as Huxley has pointed out, the business of daily life requires that we coordinate the two selves within us in order to become productive members of society.

SUMMA THEOLOGICA

Type of work: Theological treatise
Author: Thomas Aquinas (c. 1225–1274)
First transcribed: c. 1265–1274

This towering edifice of thought, often called simply the *Summa*, stands as a bulwark against the forces of doubt and skepticism which invaded the Western world during the late Middle Ages, toward the close of which St. Thomas created this great summation of philosophical and theological knowledge. In it two of the mightiest forces in the realm of human thought met: Hellenism and Christianity. It was their first real encounter.

Simply stated, what St. Thomas did was to collect and synthesize the philosophical knowledge and thinking of previous eras and apply them to the Christian theology. This was, of course, an immensely ambitious task, and the wonder is that St. Thomas did so well with it. Though unfinished, because of the divine doctor's sudden death from illness, the *Summa* unites, or at least joins elements of thought from the Greek, Arabian, and Oriental traditions in a highly detailed fashion. St. Thomas thus became a historian of philosophy; but he was a critical historian, carefully weighing and evaluating each premise and conclusion.

The largest part of this previous thought is, as might be expected, that of the Greeks. St. Thomas is usually given credit for having reinterpreted the philosophy of Aristotle on a Christian basis. This statement is, however, something of an oversimplification, for St. Thomas' reading of Aristotle and other great Greek thinkers, including Plato, was a very special one. St. Thomas was himself a magnificent philosopher, and the *Summa* is unquestionably *his* book. What he did, in essence, was to organize the thought of Aristotle along Christian lines and to apply it to the problems and principles of religion. For example, some philosophers had interpreted Aristotle's *Physics* as a denial of Creation; St. Thomas saw it as merely falling short of this fundamental concept.

The *Summa* is an exceedingly long work, running into several volumes, a necessary length in order to approach the achievement of supplying Scholasticism, certainly the prevailing philosophical influence in the thirteenth century, to religion. In doing so, St. Thomas gave credit for ideas and lines of thought to many earlier thinkers, and he found the seeds of much thirteenth century belief in the works of previous philosophers. His work, then, is in the nature of a summary of past thinking on the highest subjects and a setting forth of the essential principles of Christian theology as he was able to formulate them from this past material and from his own conviction and thinking.

There are three main divisions of the *Summa*: the first dealing with God and the divine nature of the creation of man and the universe; the second, often called the *Moral Philosophy of St. Thomas*, treating man and the goal of his life and the ways of reaching that goal; the third devoted to Christ and His role as Saviour. Within this general framework virtually every possible subject pertaining to theology is discussed: good and evil, pleasure, knowledge, duty, property. The list is almost endless.

The method of attacking these questions is the Socratic one. A basic question is asked and the negative side of it is argued by a fictitious opponent; then St. Thomas undertakes to resolve the problem and explain the positive side of the contrived argument. This method, besides making for more interesting reading, tends to create an atmosphere giving fairer treatment to opposing beliefs.

The opening of the *Summa* presents a good example. Here St. Thomas poses the question of "Whether, Besides the Philosophical Sciences, Any Further Doctrine Is Required?" How fundamental is the divine doctor's approach can easily be seen; even before beginning his book, he wishes first to convince the reader of the necessity for any sacred doctrine at all. Following the question there are listed two chief objections to the writing of sacred doctrine; then St. Thomas explains the need for it and refutes each objection in turn. This tightly organized discussion is maintained throughout; in a book that is so closely reasoned it is essential.

Part of the reason for this clear organization was the fact that the *Summa* was not primarily intended for learned divines. Instead it was written for people whom St. Thomas called beginners, the common man in search of the truth. Also, such an intention probably had much to do with the style of the writing. Although the *Summa* is extremely long, it is praised for its economy of language, with no wasted words, no useless introduction of extraneous points of logic, and no pursuit of attenuated lines of reasoning past the point of common sense.

Although much of what St. Thomas has written in the *Summa* has long been accepted doctrine in the Roman Catholic church, there is for the average current reader considerable material that may strike him as remarkably up to date, for, theology aside, this book is pivotal in the history of Western philosophy.

Possibly the modern reader will not be as interested in the ethical elements—which are fairly familiar and do not seem to mark such a sharp break with earlier Greek views—as in the metaphysical and the epistemological aspects of the treatise. Two particularly important issues are raised by St. Thomas in these areas, and both are in opposition to Greek thought, especially that of Plato.

The first of these concerns the very nature of reality, which is the main point of inquiry in metaphysics. While Plato saw reality as made up of essences, largely perceived as abstractions in the mind (here the "way of knowing," the central question of epistemology, enters in), St. Thomas maintained that the basic statement was that something had *being*; that is, it had existence. This is, of course, the basis for an argument that has raged ever since among philosophers: Which is the supreme reality, essence or existence? Which is the more fundamental statement, *what* it is or *that* it is? Equally vital was St. Thomas' disagreement with the Platonic belief that man is really two separate things, a soul and a body. To St. Thomas man was a composite, a unity composed of soul and body, both essential to his nature as man.

This conflict connects with St. Thomas' convictions about the "way of knowing." Since reality is fundamentally existence rather than essence, in order to *know* this reality man must have a body—he must be able to perceive reality through the senses. Certainly St. Thomas' statements in this area would meet with much warmer approval by most readers today than would Platonic notions concerning reality as essences, known only by abstractions in the mind. The practicality of the Thomistic viewpoint makes it appeal to scientifically minded thinkers of today.

In building this great philosophical and theological structure, St. Thomas dealt with three of the most pressing problems in the thinking of the thirteenth century—the nature of being, of man, and of knowledge—and these three subjects parallel the divisions of philosophy as it is generally studied today: metaphysics, ethics, and epistemology. In approaching this skillful and subtle blending of theology and philosophy, the reader must be willing to do what nearly every philosophical writer demands: he must be agreeable to accepting certain general premises or principles. Without these, few philosophers can operate, and St. Thomas is no exception. He assumes certain beliefs in his reader (the prevailing beliefs toward the close of the Middle Ages) concerning theology and religion. Granting these convictions, the reader will find in the *Summa* well-documented (quotations are frequent) and carefully reasoned statements on both sides of every issue involved in Christian doctrine.

This work, which death ended as St. Thomas was working on the article about the Sacrament of Penance, has been widely translated into most modern languages and continues to be assiduously studied by all who wish to grasp the moment when, in the opinion of many, modern Christian theology began.

THE TALE OF GENJI

Type of work: Novel
Author: Lady Murasaki Shikibu (c. 978–c. 1030)
Type of plot: Court romance
Time of plot: Early medieval period
Locale: Japan
First transcribed: *Genji monogatari*, c. 1004 (English translation, 1925–1933)

Undoubtedly the finest example of medieval Japanese storytelling, The Tale of Genji *is the first and title volume of an extended court romance written by a cultured lady-in-waiting to the Empress Akiko.*

Principal Characters

Prince Genji, the handsome and popular son of the Emperor of Japan. This courtly romance of medieval Japan is primarily concerned with Genji's amours.

The Emperor of Japan, Genji's father.

Lady Kokiden, the Emperor's consort.

Kiritsubo, Genji's mother and the Emperor's concubine. Largely as a result of Lady Kokiden's antagonism to her, Kiritsubo dies during Genji's childhood.

Princess Aoi, who is married at the age of sixteen to twelve-year-old Genji. She is unhappy at first as a result of her husband's youth, and later because of his many amours. He does come to appreciate and love her, but her affliction results in her death in childbirth.

Fujitsubo, the Emperor's concubine and one of Genji's first paramours. She has a child by Genji, but fortunately for him the resemblance in looks is attributed to fraternity rather than to paternity. After Lady Kokiden's death, Fujitsubo is made official consort.

Utsusemi, a pretty young matron and another of Genji's paramours. Realizing that the affair cannot last, she ends it. While pursuing her again, Genji becomes distracted by another young woman.

Ki no Kami, a young courtier, at whose home Genji meets Utsusemi.

Yūgao, a young noblewoman in love with Genji. They live together in secret within the palace grounds for a time, until Yūgao dies tragically and strangely. Genji's friends act to avert a scandal.

Murasaki a young orphan girl of good family. Genji secretly rears her and, a year after Princess Aoi's death when Murasaki is of marriageable age, he makes her his wife.

The Story

When the Emperor of Japan took a beautiful gentlewoman of the bedchamber as his concubine, he greatly displeased his consort, the Lady Kokiden. The lot of the concubine, whose name was Kiritsubo, was not easy, despite the protection and love of the emperor, for the influence of Kokiden was very great. Consequently, Kiritsubo had little happiness in the birth of a son, although the child was beautiful and sturdy. Kiritsubo's son made Kokiden even more antagonistic toward the concubine, for Kokiden feared that her own son might lose favor in the emperor's eyes and not be elevated to the position of heir apparent. Because of her hard life among the women, Kiritsubo languished away until she died.

After his mother's death, the young child she had had by the emperor was put under the protection of the clan of Gen by the emperor, who gave the child the title of Prince Genji. The boy, spirited and handsome, was a popular figure at the court. Even Kokiden could not bear him a great deal of ill will, jealous as she was on behalf of her son. Genji won for himself a secure place in the emperor's eyes, and when twelve years old he was not only elevated to a man's estate but was also given in marriage to Princess Aoi, the daughter of the Minister of the Left, a powerful figure at court. Because of his age, Genji was not impressed with his bride nor was she entirely happy with her bridegroom, for she was four years older than he.

Genji was soon appointed a captain of the guard and in this capacity spent much of his time at the emperor's palace. Indeed, he really spent little time with his bride in their apartment in her father's home. He found that his good looks, his accomplishments, and his position made it very easy for him to have any woman he was disposed to love. His wife disliked this state of things and became very cool toward him. Genji, however, cared little what Princess Aoi said or did.

One of Genji's first amours was with a young gentlewoman named Fujitsubo, who, like his bride, was a few years older than he. His second adventure was at the home of a young courtier Ki no Kami. At the home of

Ki no Kami, who was honored to have the person of Prince Genji at his home, Genji went into the room of a pretty young matron, Utsusemi, and stole her away to his own quarters. The woman, because of Genji's rank and pleasing self, refused to be angered by his actions. In an effort to keep in touch with her, Genji asked that her brother be appointed a member of his train, a request that was readily granted. Utsusemi soon realized that such an affair could not long continue, and she broke it off; Genji named her his broom tree, after a Japanese shrub that at a distance promises shade but is really only a scrawny bush.

Once, a short time later, Genji made another attempt to renew the affair with Utsusemi, but she was not asleep when he entered her room and was able to run out ahead of him. With her was another very charming young woman who had failed to awaken when Utsusemi left and Genji came in. Genji, refusing to be irritated by Utsusemi, gently awakened the other girl and soon was on the most intimate of terms with her.

One day, while visiting his foster mother, Genji made the acquaintance of a young woman named Yūgao. She was living a rather poor existence, despite the fact that she came from a good family. After paying her several masked visits, Genji became tired of such clandestine meetings. He proceeded to make arrangements for them to stay for a time in a deserted palace within the imperial domains. The affair ended in tragedy, for during their stay Yūgao was strangely afflicted and died. Only through the good offices of his retainers and friends was Genji able to avoid a disastrous scandal.

Shortly after the tragic death of Yūgao, Genji fell ill of an ague. In order to be cured, he went to a hermit in the mountains. While staying with the hermit, he found a beautiful little girl, an orphan of a good family. Seeing something of himself in little Murasaki, who was pretty and talented, Genji resolved to take her into his care. At first Murasaki's guardians refused to listen to Genji's plans, until he was able to convince them that he had only the girl's best interests at heart and did not plan to make her a concubine at too early an age. Finally they agreed to let him shape the little girl's future, and he took her to his own palace to rear. Lest people misunderstand his motives, and for the sake of secrecy, Genji failed to disclose the identity of the girl and her age, even though his various paramours and his wife became exceedingly jealous of the mysterious stranger who was known to dwell with Genji.

Soon after his return to the emperor's court with Murasaki, Genji was requested to dance the "Waves of the Blue Sea" at the annual festival in the emperor's court. So well did he impress the emperor with his dancing and with his poetry that he was raised to higher rank. Had the emperor dared to do so, Genji would have been named as the heir apparent.

During this time, when Genji's star seemed to be in the ascendant, he was very worried, for he had made Fujitsubo, the emperor's concubine, pregnant. After the baby's birth, everyone noticed how like Genji the baby looked, but the likeness was, to Genji's relief, credited to the fact that they were both sons of the emperor himself. So pleased was the emperor that he made Fujitsubo his official consort after the unexpected death of Lady Kokiden.

Meanwhile Genji's marriage proceeded very badly, and he and his wife drifted farther and farther apart. Finally, however, she became pregnant, but her condition only seemed to make her sadder. During her pregnancy, Princess Aoi declined, filled with hallucinations that her rivals for Genji's affections were stealing her life from her by hatred and jealousy. So deep was her affliction that Princess Aoi died in childbirth, much mourned by Genji, who finally had come to appreciate and love her. A year after her death, however, when Murasaki, the girl he had reared, was of suitable age to marry, Genji took her for his wife and resolved to settle down.

Critical Evaluation

Lady Murasaki Shikibu was the daughter of a famous provincial governor and the widow of a lieutenant in the Imperial Guard. As a lady in waiting to the Empress Akiko, she was completely familiar with Nipponese court ritual and ceremony, and her knowledge of palace life is everywhere apparent in the adventures of her nobly born hero, Prince Genji. The novel is undoubtedly the finest example of medieval Japanese storytelling, and in it one can trace the very growth of Japanese literature about the year 1000. In the beginning, Lady Murasaki's romance is an adolescent affair, very much in the fairy-tale tradition of the old Japanese chronicles. As it progresses, it reaches the full-blown stage of the prose romance, and it can be compared satisfactorily with the medieval prose romances of western Europe. In both, the love affairs of the heroes are dominant. *The Tale of Genji*, however, imparts the qualities of Japanese culture—similar to and yet quite different from the medieval culture of Europe. Here are people whose main occupation, far from the arts of war and chivalry, was living well: enjoying nature and art in all its forms. Also, in place of idealized woman readers have the idealized man, with woman in a distinctly subordinate role.

The Tale of Genji (title for both the series and the first volume) comprises a long (more than eleven hundred pages), elegant, wittily ironical court romance that some critics have also described as a prototype of the novel. The whole book is in six parts, consisting of the title section, followed by "The Sacred Tree," "A Wreath of Cloud," "Blue Trousers," "The Lady of the Boat," and "The Bridge of Dreams." Murasaki's style, as noted above, improves as she continues her fiction (her first chapter crudely imitates the manner of old court romances); her characterizations become richer, more complex; and her full design—to fashion a moral picture of the emperor's court of her time—is made apparent. For some readers, *The Tale of Genji* is an incomparable re-creation of life in eleventh century Japan, with the smallest details of the customs, ceremonies, and manners of the aristocracy faithfully reproduced; for others, the book is an enchanting collection of interwoven stories, some slightly erotic, all vividly recounted; for still others, the book is a psychologically honest examination of passion and pretense, of the hearts of men and women.

The first section treats Genji, "The Shining One," as a child and as a young man, idealistic but often unwise, learning the arts of courtship and love. It also introduces Murasaki (who is certainly not the author, unless by ironic contrast), first as Genji's child-concubine then as his second wife. Her character, thus, is tentatively sketched. In the other parts of the book, she learns about the romantic and political intrigues of court life, becomes sophisticated in practicing her own wiles, and finally—in the section titled "Blue Trousers"—dies of a lingering, wasting disease. The early *Tale of Genji*, however, treats the hero and heroine as youthful, hopeful, and inexperienced, before they fully understand how to play the cynical games of love and dissembling.

In chapter 2 of *The Tale of Genji*, the author advances the main theme of her work, the romantic education of innocent lovers. The Equerry of the palace, To no Chujo, regales several noblemen, including Genji, with stories about the weakness of women. He has at last discovered that "there exists no woman of whom one can say: 'Here is perfection.' " Genji's youthful experiences tend to sup-

port this observation. Just twelve years old when he is married to the sixteen-year-old Princess Aoi, he is more amused by amorous adventures than by matrimonial responsibilities and comes to care for his wife only at the point of her untimely death. Nevertheless, with Fujitsubo (whom later he makes pregnant) he enjoys his first dalliance; thereafter he sports with the easily yielding but jealous Utsusemi; with a complaisant lady who happens, conveniently, to be sleeping in Utsusemi's bed; with the lower-class but refined Yūgao, who dies tragically; and finally, with the child Murasaki. Except for the last, each woman disappoints him. Murasaki, the most innocent and childlike of his lovers, is the only one spirited, imaginative, and beautiful enough to hold his affections.

Yet Murasaki also undergoes a romantic education. She must learn how to thrive in a world controlled by men, without becoming submissive to their power. When Genji brings her to the palace, he warns her: "Little girls ought to be very gentle and obedient in their ways." At this speech, the author wryly comments: "And thus her education was begun." Several years later, Genji takes sexual liberties with Murasaki, who is too innocent and confused either to oppose or enjoy his attentions. Indeed, her own innocence excites his desire. As the author explains, "It is in general the unexplored that attracts us, and Genji tended to fall most deeply in love with those who gave him least encouragement." When Genji decides to marry the girl, she has no choice in the matter; in fact, he criticizes her lack of enthusiasm for the arrangement, since she owes so much to his friendship. In the closed world of the emperor's palace, where court ladies at best play submissive parts, Lady Murasaki Shikibu shows how women must develop resources of their own—both of mind and heart—to live with dignity. By the end of *The Tale of Genji*, her heroine is already beginning to learn that lesson.

THE TAMING OF THE SHREW

Type of work: Drama
Author: William Shakespeare (1564–1616)
Type of plot: Comedy
Time of plot: Sixteenth century
Locale: Padua, Italy
First presented: c. 1593

A lusty, witty, well-crafted comedy, The Taming of the Shrew *abounds in vigorous, often ribald wordplay. Too farcical to be taken seriously as antifeminist, the work is a romp on the hoary subject of the battle of the sexes.*

Principal Characters

Katharina (kăt·ə·rē′nə), the shrew, the spirited elder daughter of Baptista, a well-to-do Paduan gentleman. She storms at her father, her mild young sister, and her tutors until she meets Petruchio, who ignores her protests of rage and marries her while she stands by in stunned amazement. She continues to assert her will, but she finds her husband's even stronger than her own and learns that submission is the surest means to a quiet life. Her transformation is a painful revelation to Lucentio and Hortensio, who must pay Petruchio their wagers and, in addition, live with wives who are less dutiful than they supposed.

Petruchio (pë·trōōch′ĭ·ō, pë·trōō′kē·ō), her masterful husband, who comes from Verona to Padua frankly in search of a wealthy wife. He is easily persuaded by his friend Hortensio to court Katharina and pave the way for her younger sister's marriage. Katharina's manners do not daunt him; in truth, his are little better than hers, as his long-suffering servants could testify. He meets insult with insult, storm with storm, humiliating his bride by appearing at the altar in his oldest garments and keeping her starving and sleepless, all the while pretending the greatest solicitude for her welfare. Using the methods of training hawks, he tames a wife and ensures a happy married life for himself.

Bianca (bē·än′kə, bē·än′kà), Katharina's pretty, gentle younger sister, for whose hand Lucentio, Hortensio, and Gremio are rivals. Although she is completely charming to her suitors, she is, in her own way, clever and strong-willed, and she chides her bridegroom for being so foolish as to lay wagers on her dutifulness.

Baptista (bàp·tēs′tà), her father, a wealthy Paduan. Determined to treat his shrewish daughter fairly, he refuses to let Bianca marry before her. Petruchio's courtship is welcome, even though its unorthodoxy disturbs him, and he offers a handsome dowry with Katharina, doubling it when he sees the results of his son-in-law's "taming," which gives him "another daughter." Bianca's marriage without his consent distresses and angers him, but his good nature wins out and he quickly forgives her, watch-

ing with delight as Petruchio demonstrates his success with Katharina.

Lucentio (lōō·chĕn′sē·ō), the son of a Pisan merchant, who comes to Padua to study. He falls in love with Bianca when he first hears her speak and disguises himself as Cambio, a schoolmaster, in order to gain access to her, while his servant masquerades as Lucentio. He reveals his identity to his lady and persuades her to wed him secretly, but he finds his happiness somewhat marred when she costs him one hundred crowns by refusing to come at his call.

Hortensio (hôr·tĕn′shĭ·ō), Petruchio's friend, who presents himself, disguised as a musician, as a teacher for Bianca. Convinced that Katharina is incorrigible, he watches Petruchio's taming of his wife with amusement and skepticism. He weds a rich widow after becoming disillusioned when he sees Bianca embracing the supposed Cambio. Thus he finds himself, like Lucentio, with a wife more willful than he has expected.

Gremio (grē′mĭ·ō, grē′mē·ō), an aging Paduan who hires the disguised Lucentio to forward his courtship of Bianca. His hopes are dashed when Tranio, as Lucentio, offers Baptista a large settlement for his daughter, and he is forced to become an observer of others' romances.

Vincentio (vĕn·chĕn′sē·ō), Lucentio's father. He is first bewildered, then angry, when he arrives in Padua to find an impostor claiming his name, his son missing, and his servant Tranio calling himself Lucentio. Overjoyed to find the real Lucentio alive, he quickly reassures Baptista that an appropriate settlement will be made for Bianca's marriage, saving his anger for the impostors who tried to have him imprisoned.

Tranio (trä′nē·ō), Lucentio's servant, who advises his master to follow his inclinations for pleasure, rather than study. He plays his master's part skillfully, courting Bianca to draw her father's attention away from her tutor and even providing himself with a father to approve his courtship. He recognizes trouble in the form of the real Vincentio and attempts to avert it by refusing to recognize his old master and ordering him off to jail. His ruse is unsuccessful, and only nuptial gaiety saves him from the force of Vincentio's wrath.

Grumio (grōō′mē·ō) and **Curtis** (kər′tĭs), Petruchio's long-suffering servants.

Biondello (bē·ŏn·dĕl′ō), Lucentio's servant, who aids in the conspiracy for Bianca's hand.

A Pedant, an unsuspecting traveler who is persuaded by Tranio to impersonate Vincentio.

Christopher Sly, a drunken countryman, found unconscious at a tavern by a lord and his huntsmen. They amuse themselves by dressing him in fine clothes and greeting him as a nobleman, newly recovered from insanity. Sly readily accepts their explanations, settles himself in his new luxury, and watches the play of Katharina and Petruchio with waning interest.

A Lord, the eloquent nobleman who arranges the jest.

Bartholomew, his page, who pretends to be Sly's noble wife.

The Story

As a joke, a beggar was carried, while asleep, to the house of a noble lord and there dressed in fine clothes and waited on by many servants. The beggar was told that he was a rich man who in a demented state had imagined himself to be a beggar, but who was now restored to his senses. The lord and his court had great sport with the poor fellow, to the extent of dressing a page as the beggar's rich and beautiful wife and presenting the supposed woman to him as his dutiful and obedient spouse. The beggar, in his stupidity, assumed his new role as though it were his own, and he and his lady settled down to watch a play prepared for their enjoyment.

Lucentio and Tranio, his serving man, had journeyed to Padua so that Lucentio could study in that ancient city. Tranio persuaded his master, however, that life was not all study and work and that he should find pleasures also in his new residence. On their arrival in the city, Lucentio and Tranio encountered Baptista and his daughters, Katharina and Bianca. These three were accompanied by Gremio and Hortensio, young gentlemen both in love with gentle Bianca. Baptista would not permit his younger daughter to marry, however, until someone should take Katharina off his hands. Although Katharina was wealthy and beautiful, she was such a shrew that no suitor would have her. Baptista, not knowing how to control his sharp-tongued daughter, announced that Gremio or Hortensio must find a husband for Katharina before either could woo Bianca. He charged them also to find tutors for the two girls, that they might be skilled in music and poetry.

Unobserved, Lucentio and Tranio witnessed this scene. At first sight Lucentio also fell in love with Bianca and determined to have her for himself. His first act was to change clothes with Tranio, so that the servant appeared to be the master. Lucentio then disguised himself as a tutor in order to woo Bianca without her father's knowledge.

About the same time, Petruchio came to Padua. He was a rich and noble man of Verona, come to Padua to visit his friend Hortensio and to find for himself a rich wife. Hortensio told Petruchio of his love for Bianca and of her father's decree that she could not marry until a husband had been found for Katharina. Petruchio declared that the stories told about spirited Katharina were to his liking, particularly the account of her great wealth, and he expressed a desire to meet her. Hortensio proposed that Petruchio seek Katharina's father and present his family's name and history. Hortensio, meanwhile, planned to disguise himself as a tutor and thus plead his own cause with Bianca.

The situation grew confused. Lucentio was disguised as a tutor and his servant Tranio was dressed as Lucentio. Hortensio was also disguised as a tutor. Petruchio was to ask for Katharina's hand. Also, unknown to anyone but Katharina, Bianca loved neither Gremio nor Hortensio and swore that she would never marry rather than accept one or the other as her husband.

Petruchio easily secured Baptista's permission to marry Katharina, for the poor man was only too glad to have his older daughter off his hands. Petruchio's courtship was a strange one indeed, a battle of wits, words, and wills. Petruchio was determined to bend Katharina to his will, but Katharina scorned and berated him with a vicious tongue. Nevertheless, she was obliged to obey her father's wish and marry him, and the nuptial day was set. Then Gremio and Tranio, the latter still believed to be Lucentio, vied with each other for Baptista's permission to marry Bianca. Tranio won because he claimed more gold and vaster lands than Gremio could declare. In the meantime, Hortensio and Lucentio, both disguised as tutors, wooed Bianca.

As part of the taming process, Petruchio arrived late for his wedding, and when he did appear he wore old and tattered clothes. Even during the wedding ceremony Petruchio acted like a madman, stamping, swearing, cuffing the priest. Immediately afterward, he dragged Katharina away from the wedding feast and took her to his country home, there to continue his scheme to break her to his will. He gave her no food and no time for sleep, while always pretending that nothing was good enough for her. In fact, he all but killed her with kindness. Before he was through, Katharina agreed that the moon was the sun, and that an old man was a woman.

Bianca fell in love with Lucentio, whom she thought to be her tutor. In chagrin, Hortensio threw off his disguise, and he and Gremio forswore their love for any woman so fickle. Tranio, still hoping to win her for himself, found an old pedant to act the part of Vincentio, Lucentio's father. The pretended father argued his son's cause with Baptista until that lover of gold promised his daughter's hand to Lucentio, as he thought, but in reality to Tranio. When Lucentio's true father appeared on the scene, he was considered an impostor and almost put in jail for his deceit. The real Lucentio and Bianca, meanwhile, had been secretly married. Returning from the church with his bride, he revealed the whole plot to Baptista and the others. At first Baptista was angry at the way in which he had been duped, but Vincentio spoke soothingly and soon cooled his rage.

Hortensio, in the meantime, had married a rich widow. To celebrate these weddings, Lucentio gave a feast for all the couples and the fathers. After the ladies had retired, the three newly married men wagered one hundred pounds each that his own wife would most quickly obey his commands. Lucentio sent first for Bianca, but she sent word that she would not come. Then Hortensio sent for his wife, but she too refused to obey his summons. Petruchio then ordered Katharina to appear, and she came instantly to do his bidding. At his request, she also forced Bianca and Hortensio's wife to go to their husbands. Baptista was so delighted with his daughter's meekness and willing submission that he added another twenty thousand crowns to her dowry. Katharina told them all that a wife should live only to serve her husband and that a woman's heart and tongue ought to be as soft as her body. Petruchio's work had been well done. He had tamed the shrew forever.

Critical Evaluation

The Taming of the Shrew is one of Shakespeare's most popular plays. The reasons for its enduring appeal are simple to determine: It has a well-crafted plot which moves briskly and engagingly through a variety of entertaining circumstances; its language is brilliant and witty, abounding with the wordplay and verbal virtuosity so characteristic of Shakespearean comedy; and its characters are appealing and believable, drawn from life and based on a keen understanding of human nature.

The plot of *The Taming of the Shrew* is more complex than many believe. The "taming" of Katharina (also called Kate) is not a simple matter of male dominance over the female through the institution of marriage but is rather related to the intricate Renaissance concern with degree, order, and the proper arrangement of the entire cosmos. E. M. W. Tillyard's classic study *Elizabethan World Picture* demonstrated that the Elizabethans were firmly committed to a belief in a hierarchy that ran through the entire course of nature. This hierarchy was mirrored in the larger world of politics and in the more intimate sphere of marriage: Just as the prince was ruler of the realm, so the husband was predestined to be lord of the family. In this sense, Petruchio's taming of Kate is actually her return into the proper order of things, and so, far from breaking her spirit, Petruchio actually frees her to achieve the utmost of her nature.

Petruchio's method was one that Shakespeare's audience would have found familiar; today we would call it "fighting fire with fire." Since Kate is willful, illtempered, and difficult, Petruchio pretends to be even more willful, more ill-tempered, and more difficult than she could ever conceive of being. At the same time, he counterpoises this approach by constant praise of those virtues which she conspicuously lacks during most of the play: patience, modesty, and gentleness. Once again, the title of the play can mislead, for Kate is not so much tamed as educated, and in the end she is a better and more fulfilled person for the lesson.

This development is paralleled in the plot of Lucentio and Bianca, Katharina's sister, as they struggle through difficulties to become and remain wed. The ironic counterpoint here is that while Kate is rather easily wed but slowly tamed, Bianca, who needs no taming, is a difficult marital prize for Lucentio to seize and hold. The expert fashion in which Shakespeare weaves these parallel plots closely together and has them comment upon one another is one of his finest dramatic achievements.

The plot of *The Taming of the Shrew* is not without its quirks, however, and the attentive reader will note numerous instances where the overt message of order and decorum is subverted. The questions must arise: Is Kate really "tamed?" Is Bianca actually the dutiful wife she appears to be? While subtle touches throughout the play cause doubts on these points, the most telling undercutting comes in the induction to the play, in which a beggar, Christopher Sly, is made to believe that he is a nobleman who has been out of his wits for fourteen years. This gulling, or fooling, of Christopher Sly frames the entire play and so casts doubts on the validity of the concepts of order and degree. If beggars can become lords, even in jest, then where is proper place, where is the great chain of being? Certainly it raises the possibility that Kate, while seeming to be tamed and submissive to Petruchio, might actually retain control of the situation.

The induction also includes two elements that will interest the careful reader of Shakespeare: It is a sequence of a play within (or actually before) a play, performed by a company of strolling actors, and thus looks forward to a similar but tragic performance in *Hamlet*; it contains numerous references to magic, dreams, and fairyland, themes which constitute the very atmosphere of Shakespearean comedy.

The language of *The Taming of the Shrew* is Shakespeare at his antic, comic acme. The words wing across the stage with a lively and darting air, as in act 2, scene 1, where Petruchio and Katharina exchange insults, or in the marvelous scene of act 4, scene 5, where the taming is complete and Katharina accepts her lord's assertion that the sun is the moon and a man is a woman. The verbal artistry alone rates *The Taming of the Shrew* as one of Shakespeare's prime accomplishments.

Highest accolades, however, must be awarded to Shakespeare's fashioning of the characters of this drama. Petruchio and Kate stamp themselves indelibly upon the reader or viewer, and even Christopher Sly, in his rela-

tively brief moment upon the stage, becomes a full-blooded and believable figure. With Kate, in particular, Shakespeare has achieved the most difficult task of a dramatist, that of altering a person's character during the course of a play. The transformation of Kate from a shrew to a loving wife can be explained in many ways, from the Elizabethan love of order to the necessities of a five-act drama, but in the end the change can only be regarded as the finest example of the perfect control Shakespeare exercised over his noisy, wonderful play.

TARTUFFE

Type of work: Drama
Author: Molière (Jean Baptiste Poquelin, 1622–1673)
Type of plot: Comedy
Locale: Paris
First presented: 1664

When Tartuffe: Or, the Hypocrite *was originally produced, Molière was attacked by critics for undermining the very basis of religion; instead, his comedy was meant to satirize false piety, not true devotion. The famous portrait of the hypocrite has been the ancestor of similar types, from Dickens' Mr. Pecksniff to Sinclair Lewis' Elmer Gantry.*

Principal Characters

Tartuffe (tär·tüf′), a religious hypocrite and impostor who uses religious cant and practices to play on the credulity of a wealthy man who befriends him. To gain money and cover deceit, he talks of his hair shirt and scourge, of prayers and distributing alms; and he disapproves of immodest dress. Before his first appearance, he is reported by some to be a good man of highest worth, by others to be a glutton, a drinker, and a hypocrite. Deciding that he wants his patron's daughter as his wife, he uses his seeming piety to convince his host to break his daughter's marriage plans. He then endeavors to seduce his host's wife by holding her hand, patting her knee, fingering her lace collar, and making declarations of love to her. When his conduct is reported to the husband by his wife and their son, the foolish man forgives Tartuffe and gives the hypocrite all his property. Another attempted seduction fails when the husband, hidden, overhears all that happens and orders Tartuffe out of the house. Tartuffe, boasting that the entire property is now his, has an eviction order served on his former patron. When a police officer arrives to carry out the eviction order, the tables are turned. Tartuffe is arrested at the order of the king, who declares him to be a notorious rogue.

Orgon (ôr·gōn′), a credulous, wealthy man taken in by Tartuffe, whom he befriends, invites into his home, and proposes as a husband for his daughter, already promised to another. Defending Tartuffe against the accusations of his family and servants, he refuses to believe charges that the scoundrel has attempted to seduce his wife. He then disowns his children and signs over all his property to Tartuffe. Only later, when he hides under the table, at the urging of his wife, and overhears Tartuffe's second attempt at seduction, is he convinced that he is harboring a hypocrite and scheming rascal. Orgon is saved from arrest and eviction when Tartuffe is taken away by police officers.

Elmire (ĕl·mēr′), Orgon's wife. Aware of the wickedness of Tartuffe, she is unable to reveal the hypocrite's true nature to her husband. When she finds herself the object of Tartuffe's wooing, she urges the son not to make the story public, for she believes a discreet and cold denial to be more effective than violent cries of deceit. Finally, by a planned deception of Tartuffe, she convinces her husband of that scoundrel's wickedness.

Dorine (dô·rēn′), a maid and a shrewd, outspoken, witty girl who takes an active part in exposing Tartuffe and assisting the lovers in their plot against him. Much of the humor of the play results from her impertinence. She objects straightforwardly to the forced marriage of Tartuffe to Mariane, and she prevents a misunderstanding between the true lovers.

Damis (dà·mē′), Orgon's son, regarded as a fool by his grandmother. His temper and indiscretion upset Tartuffe's carefully laid plans, as when, for example, he suddenly comes out of the closet in which he has listened to Tartuffe's wooing of Elmire and naïvely reports the story to his father. He is outwitted by Tartuffe's calm admission of the charge and his father's belief in Tartuffe's innocence, despite the confession.

Valère (và·lĕr′), Mariane's betrothed. He quarrels with her, after hearing that Orgon intends to marry the girl to Tartuffe, because she seems not to object to the proposal with sufficient force. In a comedy scene the maid, running alternately between the lovers, reconciles the pair, and Valère determines that they will be married. He loyally offers to help Orgon flee after the eviction order is served on him by the court.

Madame Pernelle (pĕr·nĕl′), Orgon's mother, an outspoken old woman. Like her son, she believes in the honesty and piety of Tartuffe, and she hopes that his attitude and teachings may reclaim her grandchildren and brother-in-law from their social frivolity. She defends Tartuffe even after Orgon turns against him. She admits her mistake only after the eviction order has been delivered.

Cléante (klā·änt′), Orgon's brother-in-law. He talks in pompous maxims and makes long tiresome speeches of advice to Orgon and Tartuffe. Both disregard him.

Monsieur Loyal (lwà·yàl′), a tipstaff of the court. He serves the eviction order on Orgon.

A Police Officer, brought in by Tartuffe to arrest Orgon. Instead, he arrests Tartuffe by order of the king.

Filipote (fē·lē·pôt′), Madame Pernelle's servant.

The Story

Orgon's home was a happy one. He himself was married to Elmire, a woman much younger than he, who adored him. His two children by a former marriage were fond of their stepmother, and she of them. Mariane, the daughter, was engaged to be married to Valère, a very eligible young man, and Damis, the son, was in love with Valère's sister.

Then Tartuffe came to live in the household. Tartuffe was a penniless scoundrel whom the trusting Orgon had found praying in church. Taken in by his cant and his pose of fervent religiousness, Orgon had invited the hypocrite into his home. As a consequence, the family was soon demoralized. Once established, Tartuffe proceeded to change their normal happy mode of life to a strictly moral one. He set up a rigid puritan regimen for the family, and persuaded Orgon to force his daughter to break her engagement to Valère in order to marry Tartuffe. He said she needed a pious man to lead her in a righteous life.

Valère was determined that Mariane would marry no one but himself, but unfortunately Mariane was too spineless to resist Tartuffe and her father. Confronted by her father's orders, she remained silent and remonstrated only weakly. As a result, Tartuffe was cordially hated by every member of the family, including Dorine, the saucy, outspoken servant, who did everything in her power to break the hold that the hypocrite had secured over her master. Dorine hated not only Tartuffe but also his valet, Laurent, for the servant imitated the master in everything. In fact, the only person besides Orgon who liked and approved of Tartuffe was Orgon's mother, Madame Pernelle, who was the type of puritan who wished to withhold from others pleasures she herself could not enjoy. Madame Pernelle highly disapproved of Elmire, maintaining that in her love for clothes and amusements she was setting her family a bad example which Tartuffe was trying to correct. Actually, Elmire was merely full of the joy of living, a fact that her mother-in-law was unable to perceive. Orgon himself was little better. When Elmire fell ill, and he was informed of this fact, his sole concern was for the health of Tartuffe. Tartuffe, however, was in fine fettle, stout and ruddy cheeked. For his evening meal, he consumed two partridges, half a leg of mutton and four flasks of wine. He then retired to his warm and comfortable bed and slept soundly until morning.

Tartuffe's designs were not really for the daughter, Mariane, but for Elmire herself. One day, after Orgon's wife had recovered from her illness, Tartuffe appeared before her. He complimented Elmire on her beauty, and even went so far as to lay his fat hand on her knee. Damis, Orgon's son, observed all that went on from the cabinet where he was hidden. Furious, he determined to reveal to his father all that he had seen. Orgon refused to believe him. Wily Tartuffe had so completely captivated Orgon that he ordered Damis to apologize to Tartuffe. When his son refused, Orgon, violently angry, drove him from the house and disowned him. Then to show his confidence in Tartuffe's honesty and piety, Orgon signed a deed of trust turning his estate over to Tartuffe's management, and announced his daughter's betrothal to Tartuffe.

Elmire, embittered by the behavior of this impostor in her house, resolved to unmask him. She persuaded Orgon to hide under a cloth-covered table and see and hear for himself the real Tartuffe. Then she enticed Tartuffe to make love to her, disarming him with the assurance that her foolish husband would suspect nothing. Emboldened, Tartuffe poured out his heart to her, leaving no doubt as to his intention of making her his mistress. Disillusioned and outraged when Tartuffe asserted that Orgon was a complete dupe, the husband emerged from his hiding place, denounced the hypocrite, and ordered him from the house. Tartuffe defied him, reminding him that the house was now his according to Orgon's deed of trust.

Another matter made Orgon even more uneasy than the possible loss of his property. This was a casket given him by a friend, Argas, a political criminal now in exile. It contained important state secrets, the revelation of which would mean a charge of treason against Orgon and certain death for his friend. Orgon had foolishly entrusted the casket to Tartuffe, and he feared the use that villain might make of it. He informed his brother-in-law Cléante that he would have nothing further to do with pious men; that in the future he would shun them like the plague. But Cléante pointed out that such rushing to extremes was the sign of an unbalanced mind. Because a treacherous vagabond was masquerading as a religious man was no good reason to suspect religion.

The next day Tartuffe made good this threat, using his legal right to force Orgon and his family from their house. Madame Pernelle could not believe Tartuffe guilty of such villainy, and she reminded her son that in this world virtue is often misjudged and persecuted. But when the sheriff's officer arrived with the notice for evacuation, even she believed that Tartuffe was a villain.

The crowning indignity came when Tartuffe took to the king the casket containing the state secrets. Orders were issued for Orgon's immediate arrest. But fortunately the king recognized Tartuffe as an impostor who had committed crimes in another city. Therefore, because of Orgon's loyal service in the army, the king annulled the deed Orgon had made covering his property and returned the casket unopened.

Critical Evaluation

Tartuffe was first produced in 1664 but was immediately censured by fanatical religious groups who viewed the play as an attack on religion. Despite three petitions to the king, Molière was unable to have the ban on the play lifted until 1669. Were the attacks on the play valid? According to Molière and to generations of readers and viewers since the seventeenth century, they were not.

In the preface to the 1669 edition of the play, Molière pointed out that he was not attacking religion, but took "every possible precaution to distinguish the hypocrite from the truly devout man." This is evident from Tartuffe's behavior throughout the play.

Tartuffe is not truly religious but an extreme example of false piety. His hypocrisy (or "imposture," as the subtitle to the 1669 version of the play depicts him) is evident from his first appearance on stage, when he asks his valet to hang up his hair shirt. His hypocrisy is further emphasized by his lusting after Elmire (act 3). Although Tartuffe's language is couched in religious terms, his earthly desires are plainly discernible. His hypocrisy is most clearly revealed at the end of the play when he betrays Orgon, exposing Orgon's political secrets, and utilizing Orgon's gifts to destroy the entire family.

Religious hypocrisy, however, is not the only source of comic criticism in the play. Lack of moderation in other areas of human behavior is also under attack. Both Orgon and his mother exhibit extreme behavior in their inability to see through Tartuffe's imposture. Their absurd devotion to Tartuffe is illustrated in two important scenes. The first (act 1) exposes Orgon's foolish devotion when he returns from a trip and is oblivious to Dorine's accounts of his wife's illness; his only concern is for the health and welfare of Tartuffe. When middle-aged Orgon, feeling jealous and resentful over the youth, passion, and high spirits of the other members of his family, establishes Tartuffe as the household's moral adviser, his admiration of that scoundrel reaches idolatrous proportions. Under Tartuffe's auspices, Orgon wildly distorts the spirit of Christianity to suit his own spiteful ends; as he so outrageously asserts to Cléante, "My mother, children, brother, and wife could die/ And I'd not feel a single moment's pain." A comic reversal of this situation is presented in act 5. After Orgon's eyes have seen Tartuffe's hypocrisy (in a scene in which Tartuffe attempts to seduce Elmire), he attempts to open his mother's eyes, only to be countered by her persistent devotion to Tartuffe.

Against the extreme comic figures of Tartuffe, Orgon, and Madame Pernelle, Molière opposes those who see through hypocrisy because they view the world through the eyes of reason. Dorine, Elmire, and, above all, Cléante represent Molière's examples of moderation triumphing over excess. It is Cléante who clearly points out in act 1 the distinction between false religious posturing and truly devout religious people. He cautions Orgon to distinguish between "artifice and sincerity . . . appearance and reality . . . false and true." He offers examples of "gentle and humane" religious people, particularly those who refrain from censuring others. When Orgon finally sees through Tartuffe's false appearance and is ready to condemn all "godly men," Cléante again warns him to learn to distinguish between "genuinely good men" and scoundrels like Tartuffe.

Cléante's advice indicates that the seventeenth century zealots who attacked the play were in error. Molière is not condemning true religion, only false piety.

THE TEMPEST

Type of work: Drama
Author: William Shakespeare
Type of plot: Romantic fantasy
Time of plot: Fifteenth century
Locale: An island in the sea
First presented: 1611

The Tempest, written toward the end of Shakespeare's career, is a work of fantasy and courtly romance. The story of a wise old magician, his beautiful, unworldly daughter, a gallant young prince, and a cruel, scheming brother, it contains all the elements of a fairy tale in which ancient wrongs are righted and true lovers live happily ever after. The play is also one of poetic atmosphere and allegory. Beginning with a storm and peril at sea, it ends on a note of serenity and joy. No other of Shakespeare's dramas holds so much of the author's mature reflection on life.

Principal Characters

Prospero, the former and rightful duke of Milan, now living on an island in the distant seas. Years before, he was deposed by his treacherous younger brother, Antonio, to whom he gave too much power, for Prospero was always more interested in his books of philosophy and magic than in affairs of state. Antonio had the aid of Alonso, the equally treacherous king of Naples, in his plot against his brother, and the conspirators set Prospero and his infant daughter, Miranda, adrift in a small boat. They were saved from certain death by the faithful Gonzalo, who provided the boat with food and Prospero's books. Eventually the craft drifted to an island which was formerly the domain of the witch Sycorax, whose son, the monster Caliban, still lived there. Through the power of his magic, Prospero subdued Caliban and freed certain good spirits, particularly Ariel, whom Sycorax had imprisoned. Now in a terrible storm the ship, carrying the treacherous king of Naples, his son Ferdinand, and Antonio, is wrecked; they with their companions are brought ashore by Ariel. Using Ariel as an instrument, Prospero frustrates the plots of Antonio and Sebastian against the king and of Caliban, Trinculo, and Stephano against himself. He also furthers the romance between Miranda and Ferdinand. Convinced at last that Antonio and Alonso have repented of the wrongs they have done him Prospero has them brought to his cell, where he reveals his identity and reclaims his dukedom. At the end of the story he has the satisfaction of releasing Ariel, abandoning his magic, and returning to Milan for the marriage of Miranda and Ferdinand. In the figure of Prospero, some readers have found Shakespeare's self-portrait; and in Prospero's burying of his books on magic, they have found a symbol of Shakespeare's renunciation of the stage.

Miranda, Prospero's daughter. Brought up on the island where her aged father is the only man she has ever seen, she falls instantly in love with Ferdinand. At the end of the play, they are to be married. The character of Miranda has often been taken as the depiction of complete innocence, untouched by the corruption of sophisticated life.

Ferdinand, prince of Naples, son of King Alonso. Separated from his father when they reach the island, he is capture by Prospero, who, to test him, puts him at menial tasks. He falls in love with Miranda and she with him. Prospero finally permits their marriage.

Alonso, king of Naples and father of Ferdinand. He aided the treacherous Antonio in deposing Prospero. When the castaways reach Prospero's island, Alonso is so grief-stricken by the supposed loss of his son that he repents of his wickedness and is forgiven by Prospero.

Antonio, Prospero's treacherous brother, who has usurped the dukedom of Milan. He is finally forgiven for his crime.

Sebastian, brother of Alonso. On the island he plots with Antonio to usurp the throne of Naples. Prospero discovers and frustrates the plot.

Gonzalo, a faithful courtier who saved the lives of Prospero and Miranda.

Ariel, a spirit imprisoned by Sycorax and released by Prospero, whom he serves faithfully. At the conclusion of the play, having carried out all Prospero's commands, he is given complete freedom.

Caliban, the monstrous son of Sycorax, now a servant of Prospero. He represents brute force without intelligence and can be held in check only by Prospero's magic. Some have seen in him Shakespeare's conception of the "natural man."

Stephano, a drunken butler who plots with Caliban and Trinculo against Prospero and is foiled by Ariel.

Trinculo, a clown, a companion of Stephano and later of Caliban.

The Story

When Alonso, king of Naples, was returning from the wedding of his daughter to a foreign prince, his ship was overtaken by a terrible storm. In his company were Duke Antonio of Milan and other gentlemen of the court. As the gale rose in fury, and it seemed certain the vessel would split and sink, the noble travelers were forced to abandon ship and trust to fortune in the open sea.

The tempest was no chance disturbance of wind and wave. It had been raised by a wise magician Prospero, as the ship sailed close to an enchanted island on which he and his lovely daughter Miranda were the only human inhabitants. Theirs had been a sad and curious history. Prospero was rightful duke of Milan. Being devoted more to the study of philosophy and magic than to affairs of state, he had given much power to ambitious Antonio, his brother, who twelve years before had seized the dukedom with the aid of the crafty Neapolitan king. The conspirators set Prospero and his small daughter adrift in a boat, and they would have perished miserably had not Gonzalo, an honest counselor, secretly stocked the frail craft with food, clothing, and the books Prospero valued most.

The helpless exiles drifted at last to an island which had been the refuge of Sycorax, an evil sorceress. There Prospero found Caliban, her son, a strange, misshapen creature of brute intelligence, able only to hew wood and draw water. Also obedient to Prospero's will were many good spirits of air and water, whom he had freed from torments to which the sorceress Sycorax had condemned them earlier. Ariel, a lively sprite, was chief of these.

Prospero, having used his magic arts to draw the ship bearing King Alonso and Duke Antonio close to his enchanted island, ordered Ariel to bring the whole party safely ashore, singly or in scattered groups. Ferdinand, King Alonso's son, was moved by Ariel's singing to follow the sprite to Prospero's rocky cell. Miranda, who remembered seeing no human face but her father's bearded one, at first sight fell deeply in love with the handsome young prince, and he with her. Prospero was pleased to see the young people so attracted to each other, but he concealed his pleasure, spoke harshly to them, and to test Ferdinand's mettle commanded him to perform menial tasks.

Meanwhile Alonso, Sebastian, Antonio, and Gonzalo wandered sadly along the beach, the king in despair because he believed his son drowned. Ariel, invisible in air, played solemn music, lulling to sleep all except Sebastian and Antonio. Drawing apart, they planned to kill the king and his counselor and make Sebastian tyrant of Naples. Watchful Ariel awakened the sleepers before the plotters could act. On another part of the island Caliban, carrying a load of wood, met Trinculo, the king's jester, and Stephano, the royal butler, both drunk. In rude sport they offered drink to Caliban. Tipsy, the loutish monster bewailed his thralldom to the "tyrant," Prospero. Caliban, Trinculo, and Stephano then schemed to kill Prospero and become rulers of the island—just as Sebastian and Antonio had plotted to murder Alonso. Stephano was to be king, Miranda his consort; Trinculo and Caliban would be viceroys. Unseen, Ariel listened to their evil designs and reported the plan to Prospero.

Meanwhile Miranda had disobeyed her father to interrupt Ferdinand's task of rolling logs and, the hidden magician's commands forgotten, the two exchanged lovers' vows. Satisfied by the prince's declarations of devotion and constancy, Prospero left them to their own happy company. He, with Ariel, went to mock Alonso and his followers by showing them a banquet which vanished before the hungry castaways could taste the rich dishes. Then Ariel, disguised as a harpy, reproached them for their conspiracy against Prospero. Convinced that Ferdinand's death was punishment for his own crime, Alonso was moved to repentance for his cruel deed.

Returning to his cave, Prospero released Ferdinand from his hard toil. While spirits dressed as Ceres, Iris, Juno, nymphs, and reapers entertained Miranda and the prince with a pastoral masque, Prospero suddenly remembered the schemes which had been devised by Caliban and the drunken servants. Told to punish the plotters, Ariel first tempted them with a display of kingly garments; then, urging on his fellow spirits in the shapes of fierce hunting dogs, he drove them howling with pain and rage through bogs and brier patches.

Convinced at last that the king of Naples and his false brother Antonio had repented their evil deed of years before, Prospero commanded Ariel to bring them into the enchanted circle before the magician's cell. Ariel soon returned, luring by strange, beautiful music the king, Antonio, Sebastian, and Gonzalo. At first they were astonished to see Prospero in the appearance and dress of the wronged duke of Milan. Prospero confirmed his identity, ordered Antonio to restore his dukedom, and severely warned Sebastian not to plot further against the king. Finally, he took the repentant Alonso into the cave, where Ferdinand and Miranda sat playing chess. There was a joyful reunion between father and son at this unexpected meeting, and the king was completely captivated by the beauty and grace of Miranda. During this scene of reconciliation and rejoicing, Ariel appeared with the master and boatswain of the wrecked ship; they reported the vessel safe and ready to continue the voyage. The three grotesque conspirators were driven in by Ariel, and Prospero released them from their spell. Caliban was ordered to prepare food and set it before the guests. Prospero invited his brother and the king of Naples and his train to spend the night in his cave.

Before he left the island, Prospero dismissed Ariel from his service, leaving that sprite free to wander as he wished. Ariel promised calm seas and auspicious winds for the voyage back to Naples and Milan, where Prospero would journey to take possession of his lost dukedom and to witness the marriage of his daughter and Prince Ferdinand.

Critical Evaluation

Earlier critics of *The Tempest* concerned themselves with meaning and attempted to establish symbolic representations for Prospero, Ariel, Caliban, and Miranda, suggesting such qualities as imagination, fancy, brute man, and innocence. Many considered the play in terms of its spectacle and music, comparing it to the masque or *commedia del l'arte*. A major group have read into Prospero's control and direction of all the characters, climaxed by the famous speech in which he gives up his magic wand, Shakespeare's own dramatic progress and final farewell to the stage.

Contemporary criticism seems to explore different levels of both action and meaning. Attention has been directed to various themes, such as illusion-reality, freedom-slavery, revenge-forgiveness, time and self-knowledge. Some Shakespearean scholars of the latter half of the twentieth century suggest that the enchanted isle upon which the shipwreck occurs is a symbol of life itself: an enclosed arena wherein are enacted the passions, dreams, conflicts, and self-discoveries of man. Such a wide-angled perspective satisfies both the casual reader who wishes to be entertained and the serious scholar who desires to examine different aspects of Shakespeare's art and philosophy.

This latter view is consonant with one of Shakespeare's major techniques in all his work: the microcosm-macrocosm analogy. The Elizabethans believed that the world of man (microcosm) mirrored the universe (macrocosm). In the major tragedies, this correspondence is shown in the pattern of order-disorder, usually with man's violent acts (such as Brutus' murder of Caesar, the usurpation of the throne by Richard III, Claudius' murder of Hamlet's father, Macbeth's killing of Duncan) being mirrored by a sympathetic disruption of order in the world of nature. Attendant upon such events are happenings such as unnatural earthquakes, appearance of strange beasts at midday, unaccountable storms, voices from the sky, witches, and other strange phenomena.

The idea that the world is but an extension of man's mind, and that the cosmic order in turn is reflected in man himself, gives validity to diverse interpretations of *The Tempest*. The initial storm, or "tempest," invoked by Prospero, which wrecks the ship, finds analogy in Antonio's long-past usurpation of Prospero's dukedom and his setting Prospero and his small daughter, Miranda, adrift at sea in a storm in the hope they would perish. Now, years later, the court party, including Alonso, Sebastian, Antonio, and Ferdinand, along with the drunken Stephano and Trinculo, are cast upon the island which will prove, with its "meanderings," pitfalls, and enchantments, a place where everyone will go through a learning process and most will come to greater self-knowledge.

Illusions upon this island, such as Ariel's disguises, the disappearing banquet, and the line of glittering costumes deluding Stephano, Trinculo, and Caliban, find counterparts in the characters' illusions about themselves. Antonio has come to believe he is the rightful duke; Sebastian and Antonio, deluded by ambition, plan to kill Alonso and Gonzalo and make Sebastian tyrant of Naples. The drunken trio of court jester, butler, and Caliban falsely see themselves as future conquerors and rulers of the island. Ferdinand is tricked into believing his father is drowned and that Miranda is a goddess. Miranda, in turn, nurtured upon illusions by her father, knows little of human beings and their evil. Even Prospero must come to see he is not master of the universe, and that revenge is no answer for injustice but that justice must be tempted by mercy.

It has been noted that the island is different things to different people. Here again is an illustration of the microcosm-macrocosm analogy. The characters of integrity see it as a beautiful place; for honest Gonzalo it is a possible Utopia. Sebastian and Antonio, whose outlook is soured by their villainy, characterize the island's air as perfumed by a rotten swamp. In like manner, the sense of freedom or slavery each character feels is again conditioned by his view of the island and his own makeup as well as by Prospero's magic. The most lovely expressions of the island's beauty and enchantment come from the half-human Caliban, who knew its offering far better than any before his enslavement by Prospero.

In few of his other plays has Shakespeare effected a closer relationship between the human and natural universe. Human beauty and ugliness, good and evil, gentleness and cruelty are matched with the external environment. Fortunately, in *The Tempest*, everything works toward a reconciliation of the best in both man and nature. This harmony is expressed, for example, by the delightful pastoral masque Prospero stages for the young lovers, Ferdinand and Miranda. In this entertainment, reapers and nymphs join in dancing, indicating the union of natural and supernatural. the coming marriage of Ferdinand and Miranda—the union of the children of two former enemies, signifying reunion, reconciliation, and a return to order after chaos—also foreshadows such harmony, as do the general repentance and forgiveness among the major characters. It may be true, as Prospero states in act 5, that upon the island "no man was his own," but he also confirms that understanding has come like a 'swelling tide'; and promises calm seas for the homeward journey, after which each man will take up the tasks and responsibilities of his station with improved perspective.

As Prospero renounces his magic, Ariel is free to return to the elements, and Caliban, true child of nature, is left to regain harmony with his unspoiled world. Perhaps the satisfaction Shakespeare's audience feels results from the harmony between man and nature that illumines the close of the play—a figurative return to innocence after the sins of the Fall. In this latter sense, *The Tempest* is Shakespeare's most idealistic play: a plea for the forgiveness, mercy, and love which are the only forces that can absolve man's sins and set the world right again.

TESS OF THE D'URBERVILLES: A Pure Woman Faithfully Presented

Type of work: Novel
Author: Thomas Hardy (1849–1928)
Type of plot: Philosophical realism
Time of plot: Late nineteenth century
Locale: England
First published: 1891

A powerful and tragic novel that shows how crass circumstances influence the destinies of people, Tess of the D'Urbervilles *is also a moral indictment of the smug Victorian attitude toward sexual purity.*

Principal Characters

Tess Durbeyfield, a naïve country girl. When her father learns that his family is descended from an ancient landed house, the mother, hoping to better her struggling family financially, sends Tess to work for the Stoke-d'Urbervilles, who have recently moved to the locality. In this household the innocent girl, attractive and mature beyond her years, meets Alec D'Urberville, a dissolute young man. From this time on she is the rather stoical victim of personal disasters. Seduced by Alec, she gives birth to his child. Later she works on a dairy farm, where she meets Angel Clare and reluctantly agrees to marry him, even though she is afraid of his reaction if he learns about her past. As she fears, he is disillusioned by learning of her lack of innocence and virtue. Although deserted by her husband, she never loses her unselfish love for him. Eventually, pursued by the relentless Alec, she capitulates to his blandishments and goes to live with him at a prosperous resort. When Angel Clare returns to her, she stabs Alec and spends a few happy days with Clare before she is captured and hanged for her crime.

Angel Clare, Tess's husband. Professing a dislike for effete, worn-out families and outdated traditions, he is determined not to follow family tradition and become a clergyman or a scholar. Instead, he wishes to learn what he can about farming, in hopes of having a farm of his own. When he meets Tess at a dairy farm, he teaches her various philosophical theories which he has gleaned from his reading. He learns that she is descended from the D'Urbervilles and is pleased by the information. After urging reluctant Tess to marry him, at the same time refusing to let her tell him about her past life, he persuades her to accept him; later he learns to his great mortification about her relations with Alec. Although he himself has confessed to an episode with a woman in London, he is not so forgiving as Tess. After several days he deserts her and goes to Brazil. Finally, no longer so provincial in his moral views, he remorsefully comes back to Tess, but he returns too late to make amends for his selfish actions toward her.

Alec D'Urberville, Tess's seducer. Lusting after the beautiful girl and making brazen propositions, he boldly pursues her. At first she resists his advancements, but she is unable to stop him from having his way in a lonely wood where he has taken her. For a time he reforms and assumes the unlikely role of an evangelist. Meeting Tess again, he lusts after her more than ever and hounds her at every turn until she accepts him as her protector. Desperate when Angel Clare returns, she kills her hated lover.

Jack Durbeyfield, a carter of Marlott, Tess's indolent father. After learning of his distinguished forebears, he gives up work almost entirely and spends much time drinking beer in the Rolliver Tavern. He thinks that a man who has grand and noble "skillentons" in a family vault at Kingsbere-sub-Greenhill should not have to work.

Joan Durbeyfield, Tess's mother. After her hard labor at her modest home, she likes to sit at Rolliver's Tavern while her husband drinks a few pints and brags about his ancestors. A practical woman in a harsh world, she is probably right when she tells Tess not to reveal her past to Angel Clare.

Sorrow, Tess's child by Alec D'Urberville. The infant lives only a few days. Tess herself performs the rite of baptism before the baby dies.

Eliza-Louisa, called **Liza-Lu,** Tess's younger sister. It is Tess's hope, before her death, that Angel Clare will marry her sister. Liza-Lu waits with Angel during the hour of Tess's execution for the murder of Alec D'Urberville.

Abraham, Hope, and **Modesty,** the son and young daughters of the Durbeyfields.

The Reverend James Clare, Angel Clare's father, a devout man of simple faith but limited vision.

Mrs. Clare, a woman of good works and restricted interests. She shows little understanding of her son Angel.

Felix and **Cuthbert Clare,** Angel Clare's conventional, rather snobbish brothers. They are patronizing in their attitude toward him and disapprove of his marriage to Tess Durbeyfield.

Mercy Chant, a young woman interested in church work and charity, whom Angel Clare's parents thought a proper wife for him. Later she marries his brother Cuthbert.

Mrs. Stoke-D'Urberville, the blind widow of a man who grew rich in trade and added the name of the extinct D'Urberville barony to his own. Her chief interests in life are her wayward son Alec and her poultry.

Car Darch, also called **Dark Car,** a vulgar village woman. Because of her previous relations with Alec D'Urberville she is jealous of Tess Durbeyfield. Her nickname is Queen of Spades.

Nancy, her sister, nicknamed Queen of Diamonds.

Mr. Tringham, the elderly parson and antiquarian who half-jokingly tells Jack Durbeyfield that he is descended from the noble D'Urberville family.

Richard Crick, the owner of Talbothays Farm, where Angel Clare is learning dairy farming. Farmer Crick also hires Tess Durbeyfield as a dairymaid after the death of her child. Tess and Angel are married at Talbothays.

Christiana Crick, Farmer Crick's kind, hearty wife.

Marian, a stout, red-faced dairymaid at Talbothays Farm. Later she takes to drink and becomes a field worker at Flintcomb-Ash Farm. She and Izz Huett write Angel Clare an anonymous letter in which they tell him that his wife is being pursued by Alec D'Urberville.

Izz Huett, a dairymaid at Talbothays Farm. In love with Angel Clare, she openly declares her feelings after he has deserted Tess. He is tempted to take Izz with him to Brazil, but he soon changes his mind. She and Marian write Angel a letter warning him to look after his wife.

Retty Priddle, the youngest of the dairymaids at Talbothays Farm. Also in love with Angel Clare, she tries to drown herself after his marriage.

Farmer Groby, the tight-fisted, harsh owner of Flintcomb-Ash Farm, where Tess works in the fields after Angel Clare has deserted her.

The Story

It was a proud day when Jack Durbeyfield learned that he was descended from the famous D'Urberville family. Durbeyfield had never done more work than was necessary to keep his family supplied with meager food and himself with beer, but from that day on, he ceased doing even that small amount of work. His wife joined him in thinking that such a high family should live better with less effort, and she persuaded their oldest daughter, Tess, to visit the Stoke-D'Urbervilles, a wealthy family that had assumed the D'Urberville name because no one else claimed it. It was her mother's hope that Tess would make a good impression on the rich D'Urbervilles and perhaps a good marriage with one of the sons.

When Tess met her supposed relatives, however, she found only a blind mother and a dapper son who made Tess uncomfortable by his improper remarks to her. The son, Alec, tricked the innocent young Tess into working as a poultry maid; he did not let her know that his mother was unaware of Tess's identity. After a short time, Tess decided to look for work elsewhere to support her parents and her brothers and sisters. She knew that Alec meant her no good. Alec, however, was more clever than she and managed at last to get her alone and then possessed her.

When Tess returned to her home and told her mother of her terrible experience, her mother's only worry was that Alec was not going to marry Tess. The poor girl worked in the fields, facing the slander of her associates bravely. Her trouble was made worse by the fact that Alec followed her from place to place, trying to possess her again. By traveling to different farms during the harvest season, Tess managed to elude Alec long enough to give birth to her baby without his knowledge. The baby did not live long, however, and a few months after its death, Tess went to a dairy farm far to the south to be a dairymaid.

At the dairy farm, Tess was liked and well treated. Angel Clare, a pastor's son who had rejected the ministry to study farming, was also at the farm. It was his wish to own a farm someday, and he was working on different kinds of farms so that he could learn something of the many kinds of work required of a general farmer. Although all the dairymaids were attracted to Angel, Tess interested him the most. He thought her a beautiful and innocent young maiden, as she was, for it was her innocence that had caused her trouble with Alec.

Tess felt that she was wicked, however, and rejected the attentions Angel paid to her. She urged him to turn to one of the other girls for companionship. It was unthinkable that the son of a minister would marry a dairymaid, but Angel did not care much about family tradition. Despite her pleas, he continued to pay court to Tess. At last, against the wishes of his parents, Angel asked Tess to be his wife. Not only did he love her, but he also realized that a farm girl would be a help to him on his own land. Although Tess was in love with Angel by this time, the memory of her night with Alec caused her to refuse Angel again and again. At last, his insistence, coupled with the written pleas of her parents to marry someone who could help the family financially, won her over, and she agreed to marry him.

On the night before the wedding, which Tess had postponed many times because she felt unworthy, she wrote Angel a letter, revealing everything about herself and Alec. She slipped the letter under his door; she was sure that when he read it, he would renounce her forever. In the morning, however, Angel acted as tenderly as before, and Tess loved him more than ever for his forgiving nature. When she realized that Angel had not found the letter, she attempted to tell him about her past. Angel only teased her about wanting to confess, thinking that such a pure girl could have no black sins in her history.

They were married without Angel's learning about Alec and her dead baby.

On their wedding night, Angel told Tess about an evening of debauchery in his own past. Tess forgave him and then told about her affair with Alec, thinking that he would forgive her as she had him; but such was not the case. Angel was at first stunned and then so hurt that he could not even speak to Tess. Finally, he told her that she was not the woman he loved, the one he had married, but a stranger with whom he could not live, at least for the present. He took her to her home and left her there. Then he went to his home and on to Brazil, where he planned to buy a farm. At first, Tess and Angel did not tell their parents the reason for their separation. When Tess finally told her mother, the ignorant woman blamed Tess for losing her husband by confessing something he need never have known.

Angel had left Tess some money and some jewels that had been given to him by his godmother. Tess put the jewels in the bank; she spent the money on her parents. When it was gone, her family went hungry once more, for her father still thought himself too highborn to work for a living. Again, Tess went from farm to farm, performing hard labor in the fields to get enough food to keep herself and her family alive.

While she was working in the fields, she met Alec again. He had met Angel's minister father and, repenting his evil ways, had become an itinerant preacher. The sight of Tess, for whom he had always lusted, caused a lapse in his new religious fervor, and he began to pursue her once again. Frightened, Tess wrote to Angel, sending the letter to his parents to forward to him. She told Angel that she loved him and needed him and that an enemy was pursuing her. She begged him to forgive her and to return to her.

The letter took several months to reach Angel. Meanwhile, Alec was so kind to Tess and so generous to her family that she began to relent in her feelings toward him. At last, when she did not receive an answer from Angel, she wrote him a note saying that he was cruel not to forgive her and that now she would not forgive his treatment of her. Then she went to Alec again and lived with him as his wife.

It was thus that Angel found her. He had come to tell her that he had forgiven her and that he still loved her. When he found her with Alec, however, he turned away, more hurt than before.

Tess, too, was bitterly unhappy. She now hated Alec because once again he had been the cause of her husband's repudiation of her. Feeling that she could find happiness only if Alec were dead, she stabbed him as he slept. Then she ran out of the house and followed Angel, who was aimlessly walking down a road leading out of the town. When they met and Tess told him what she had done, Angel forgave her everything, even the murder of Alec, and they went on together. They were happy with each other for a few days, although Angel knew that the authorities would soon find Tess.

When the officers finally found them, Tess was asleep. Angel asked the officers to wait until she awoke. As soon as she opened her eyes, Tess saw the strangers and knew that they had come for her and that she would be hanged, but she was not unhappy. She had had a few days with the husband she truly loved, and now she was ready for her punishment. She stood up bravely and faced her captors. She was not afraid.

Critical Evaluation

English fiction assumed a new dimension in the hands of Thomas Hardy. From its beginnings, it had been a middle-class genre; it was written for and about the bourgeois, with the working class and the aristocracy assuming only minor roles. The British novelist explored the workings of society in the space between the upper reaches of the gentry and the new urban shopkeepers. In the eighteenth century, Daniel Defoe treated the rogue on his or her way to wealth; Henry Fielding was concerned with the manners of the gentry; and Samuel Richardson dramatized romantic, middle-class sentimentality. In the nineteenth century, Jane Austen's subject matter was the comedy of manners among a very closely knit segment of the rural gentry; the farm laboring classes were conspicuous by their absence. After Walter Scott and his historical romances, the great Victorian novelists—the Brontës, Thackeray, Dickens, Trollope, and George Eliot—were all concerned with the nuances of middle-class feelings and morality, treating their themes either romantically or comically.

Although he certainly drew on the work and experience of his predecessors, Hardy opened and explored fresh areas: indeed, he was constantly hounded by critics and censors for his realistic treatment of sexuality and the problems of faith. After his last novel, *Jude the Obscure,* was attacked for its immorality, he was driven from the field. The final thirty years or so of his life were devoted entirely to poetry. Even more important than this new honesty and openness toward sex and religion, however, was Hardy's development of the tragic possibilities of the novel and his opening of it to the experience of the rural laborer and artisan. Moreover, his rendering of nature, influenced by Greek thought and Darwin's *On the Origin of the Species*, radically departed from the nineteenth century view of nature as benevolent and purposeful. Hardy's novels, written between 1868 and 1895, have a unity of thought and feeling challenging all the accepted truths of his time. He was part of and perhaps the most formidable spokesman for that group of artists—including the Rossettis, Swinburne, Wilde, Yeats, and Housman—which reacted against the materialism, pieties, and unexamined faith of the Victorian Age. As he said of the age in his poem "The Darkling Thrush": "The land's sharp features seemed to be/ The Century's corpse outleant. . . ." Finally, he can be viewed not only as the last Victorian but also as the first modern writer, defining the themes that were to occupy such great successors as Joseph Conrad and D. H. Lawrence.

Tess of the D'Urbervilles ranks as one of Hardy's finest achievements, along with *Far from the Madding Crowd, The Return of the Native, The Mayor of Casterbridge,* and *Jude the Obscure.* Together with the last novel mentioned, it forms his most powerful indictment of Victorian notions of virtue and social justice. Its subtitle, *A Pure Woman Faithfully Presented,* is itself a mockery of a moral sense that works in rigid categories. Mesmerized and seduced by Alec D'Urberville, the mother of a bastard child, the married mistress of Alec, and a murderess who is eventually hanged, Tess is yet revealed as an innocent victim of nature, chance, and a social and religious system that denies human feeling. Her purity is not only a matter of ethics—for Hardy finds her without sin—but also one of soul. Tess maintains a kind of gentle attitude toward everyone, and even when she is treated with the grossest injustice, she responds with forgiveness. It is not until the conclusion of the novel when she has been deprived once again of her beloved, Angel Clare (a love that the reader has great difficulty in accepting, since he lacks any recognizable human passion), that she

is ultimately overcome by forces beyond her control and murders Alec. Like her sister in tragedy, Sophocles' Antigone, she is driven by a higher justice to assert herself. That she must make reparation according to a law that she cannot accept does not disturb her, and like Antigone's, her death is a triumph rather than a defeat.

It is precisely at this point that Hardy most effectively challenges Victorian metaphysics. In Tess, readers witness a woman disposed of by irrational and accidental forces. The Victorians tried to deny such forces—not always easily, to be sure—through a devotion to reason in matters of law, science, and religion; these impulses were anomalies that could not be admitted if their worldview were to stand. To insist, moreover, as Tess does, that she is not to be judged by human law is a radical attack on a culture that rested uncertainly on a fragile social contract. To compound the enigma, Tess acquiesces in the judgment and gives her life—for society does not really take it—with a sense of peace and fulfillment.

Thus Hardy exposed the primitive passions and laws of nature to his readers. He called into question not only their idea of law but also their notion of human nature. Indeed, Hardy seems to suggest that no matter the success of politics in removing social abuses, there remains an element in man that cannot be legislated: his instinctual nature that drives him to demand justice for his being, despite the consequences. For Victorian civilization to accept Tess, therefore, would be to admit its own myopia—which it was not yet prepared to do.

THREE SISTERS

Type of work: Drama
Author: Anton Chekhov (1860–1904)
Type of plot: Impressionistic realism
Time of plot: Nineteenth century
Locale: Russia
First presented: 1901

Three Sisters, a poignant drama rich in perceptive character studies, treats the lassitude of the middle class with ironical scorn. Although Chekhov's male characters are weak-willed and incapable of action, his women, among them the three sisters, have hopes of achieving happiness, if only because they live on dreams.

Principal Characters

Andrey Prozorov (än·drä′ prô·zō′rəf), the son of a high-ranking Russian army officer. He studies to be a professor, but after his marriage he turns to gambling in order to forget his boorish wife, who takes a lover. He is an ineffective man who accomplishes nothing.

Natasha (nä·tä′shə), Andrey's ill-bred, selfish wife. She takes a local official, Protopopov, as her lover.

Masha (mä′shə), one of Andrey's sisters and the wife of Fyodor Kuligin. She once thought her husband clever, but she has been disillusioned. She falls in love with Vershinin, though he cannot leave his wife and children for her.

Fyodor Kuligin (fyō′dər kōō′lǐ·gǐn), Masha's husband, a rather ineffectual man who teaches in a high school.

Olga Prozorov (ōl′y·gə prô·zō′rəf), one of Andrey's sisters. She wants desperately to return to Moscow. She teaches languages in the town's high school and becomes headmistress, but she is unhappy with her lot.

Irina Prozorov (ĭr·ĭn′ə prô·zō′rəf), one of Andrey's sisters. Her hopes are dashed when Baron Tusenbach is killed by Captain Solyony in a duel, for she had thought she could escape the little garrison town by marrying Tusenbach.

Ivan Chebutykin (īv·än′ che·bōōt′ykǐn), an incompetent doctor and a friend of the Prozorovs.

Baron Tusenbach (tōō′sĕn·bäch), an army lieutenant in love with Irina Prozorov. He is killed in a duel by Captain Solyony, his rival for her affections.

Captain Vassily Solyony (vä·sǐ′lǐy sô·lyon′y), Baron Tusenbach's rival for Irina Prozorov's love. He kills Tusenbach in a duel over the young woman.

Alexandr Vershinin (al·eks′andr vershǐ′nǐn), an artillery commander. he believes that the world and people will get better and better. He falls in love with Masha but cannot leave his family for her.

Protopopov (prô·tô·pō′pəf), a local official who becomes Natasha Prozorov's lover.

The Story

On Irina's name day, her friends and family called to wish her happiness. It was exactly one year after the death of their father, who had been sent from Moscow eleven years before to this provincial town at the head of a brigade. Irina and Olga longed to go back to Moscow, and Masha would have liked to go too, except that she had been married to Kuligin, whom she once thought the cleverest of men. They all pinned their hopes on their brother Andrey, who was studying to become a professor.

An old army doctor, Chebutykin, brought Irina a samovar because he had loved her mother. Masha's husband gave Irina a copy of the history of the high school in which he taught; he said he wrote it because he had nothing better to do. When Irina told him that he had given her a copy for Easter, he merrily handed the new copy over to one of the army men who was calling.

Tusenbach and Solyony quarreled halfheartedly because Tusenbach and Irina had decided that what they needed for happienss was work. Tusenbach had never done anything but go to cadet school, and Irina's father had prepared her only in languages. Both had a desire to labor hard at something.

Vershinin, the new battery commander, came to call, reminding the girls that he had lived on the same street with them in Moscow. When he praised their town, they said they wanted to go to Moscow. They believed that they had been oppressed with an education which was useless in a dull provincial town. Vershinin thought that for every intelligent person then living, many more would appear later, and that the whole earth would be unimaginably beautiful two or three hundred years hence. He thought it might be interesting to relive one's life to see if one could improve on the first version.

Natasha came in while they were still sitting at the dinner table. Olga criticized her dress, and the men began to tease her about an engagement. Andrey, who could not stand having her teased, followed her out of the room and begged her to marry him. She accepted.

After their marriage, Andrey lost any ambition he ever had to become a professor and spent much of his time gambling in order to forget how ill-bred, rude, and self-ish Natasha really was. Irina, meanwhile, had taken a job in the telegraph office, and Olga was teaching in the high school. Tired when they came home at night, they let Natasha run the house as she pleased, even to moving Irina out of her own bedroom so that Natasha and Andrey's baby could have it.

Vershinin had fallen in love with Masha, though he felt bound to his neurotic wife because of his two daughters. Kuligin realized what was going on but cheerfully hoped Masha still loved him.

Tusenbach, afraid that life would always be difficult, decided to give up his commission and seek happiness in a workingman's life. Vershinin was convinced that by living, working, and struggling people create a better life all the time. Since his wife periodically tried to commit suicide, he did not look for happiness for himself but for his descendants.

Audrey asked Chebutykin to prescribe a cure for his shortness of breath, but the old doctor swore he had forgotten all the medical knowledge he had ever known.

Solyony fell in love with Irina, who would have nothing to do with him. He declared that he would have no happy rivals.

One night all gathered to have a party with some mummers who were to come in. Natasha, however, decided that the baby was not well and canceled the party at the last minute. Then Protopopov, the Chairman of the Rural Board, came by with his carriage to take Natasha riding while Audrey sat reading in his room.

A short time later, fire destroyed part of the town. Olga gave most of her clothes to those whose homes had been burned and, after the fire, invited the army people to sleep at the house. Natasha berated Olga for letting her old servant sit in her presence and finally suggested that Olga herself move out of the house. The old doctor became drunk because he had prescribed the wrong treatment for a woman who later had died. After the fire people wanted him to help them, but he could not. In disgust, he picked up a clock and smashed it.

Masha, more bored than before, gave up playing the piano. She was disgusted, too, because Andrey had mortgaged the house in order to give money to Natasha. Everyone but he knew that Natasha was having an affair with Protopopov, to whose Rural Board Andrey had recently been elected.

Irina, at twenty–four, could not find work to suit her, and she believed she was forgetting everything she had ever known. Olga persuaded her to consider marrying Tusenbach, even if he was ugly; with him, Irina might get to Moscow.

Masha confessed that she was in love with Vershinin and that he loved her, though he was unable to leave his children.

Andrey berated his sisters for treating his wife so badly and then confessed that he had mortgaged the house, which belonged to all four of them. He had so hoped they could all be happy together.

Irina heard a report that the brigade would move out of town. If that happened, they would have to go to Moscow because no one worth speaking to would be left.

On the day the first battery was to leave, the officers came to say their farewells to the sisters. Kuligin told Irina that Tusenbach and Solyony had had words because both of them were in love with her and she had promised to marry Tusenbach. Kuligin eagerly anticipated the departure of the brigade because he hoped that then Masha would again turn to him. Masha was bored and spiteful. She felt that she was losing, bit by bit, the small happiness she had.

Andrey wondered how he could love Natasha when he knew she was so vulgar. The old doctor claimed that he was tired of their troubles, and he advised Andrey to walk off and never look back. Yet the doctor, who was to be retired from the army in a year, planned to come back to live with them because he really loved them all.

Irina hoped to go off with Tusenbach. Olga intended to live at the school of which she was now headmistress. Natasha, expecting to be left in sole charge of the house, planned all sorts of changes to wipe away the memory of the sisters' having been there. Andrey wondered how his children could possibly overcome the deadening influence of their mother's vulgarity.

After Tusenbach had fought a duel with Solyony, Chebutykin returned to tell them that Tusenbach had been killed. So the sisters were left alone with their misery, each thinking that she must go on with her life, if only to find out why people suffer so much in a world that could be beautiful.

Critical Evaluation

In a seven-year span, Anton Chekhov wrote and saw produced four plays that established him as a brilliant and important playwright. The four are *The Sea Gull* (1896), *Uncle Vanya* (1897), *Three Sisters* (1901), and *The Cherry Orchard* (1904). Taken together, the plays present a portrait of provincial town life in late nineteenth century Russia; they are filled with varied, complex characters who express a broad range of attitudes about life, from world-weariness to foolish hopefulness. Dramatically, the plays are original and distinctive; Chekhov overthrows conventions about plot, stage action, and structure. The first productions by the Moscow Art Theater occasionally put the dramatist at odds with the director and performers who failed to grasp the play's subtle mood and innovative devices.

Of Chekhov's major plays, *Three Sisters* is perhaps the best. It is his most somber play, full of melancholy punctuated by moments of fragile beauty. Its titular heroines are attractive characters with whose struggles to improve their lives an audience easily sympathizes. Their fate, however, is not simply their own: It has ramifications for the nation during a time of historic change. *Three Sisters* is also Chekhov's most ingeniously crafted play, subtly interweaving the diverse actions and motivations of Masha, Olga, Irina, and Andrey into one account of the fall of the house of Prozorov.

Chekhov's theatrical premise is that real drama is found in the routine of everyday living rather than in contrived, complicated conflicts. Thus, the dramatist presents characters engaged in ordinary activities and conversing about normal interests. The playwright does not divide the cast into major and minor parts; all actors and actresses take approximately equal part in stage activity and in speaking. Many characters are on stage together, but they do not interact with every other character or defer their own stage business to so-called leading characters. Thus, in the opening scene three distinct activities occur simultaneously: Olga and Irina reminisce, Masha reads and whistles softly, Chebutykin and Tusenbach joke. The entrance of Solyony draws the characters together in a common conversation about work. When Vershinin enters, he engages each of the others in an extended but separate exchange, thus once more fragmenting stage activities. As the name-day party progresses, characters move about the rooms rearranging themselves in shifting groups of two or three. No one holds center stage; conversations develop stage right only to fade before conversation from stage left. The dialogues vary in mood: While one pair engages in serious discussion, another pair jokes, and a third makes each other's acquaintance. Chekhov's characters are choreographed like dancers.

No action emerges as the main plot with precedence over minor plot. Masha's growing affection for Vershinin is as important as the competition between Tusenbach and Solyony for Irina's hand in marriage; Olga's increasing commitment to her school teaching is as important as Andrey's marriage to Natasha. All four stories unfold together, their principals sometimes—but not always—interacting and influencing each other. Chekhov avoids the design of the well-made play, which puts plot within plot like Chinese boxes and resolves them all neatly at the denouement.

The unity of the four plots of *Three Sisters* derives from the common theme of dispossession. The prosperous house of Prozorov disintegrates and declines during the course of the play. Though in the end Irina, Masha, Olga, and Andrey are conscious that their expectations are frustrated, they are less conscious that they have lost control of their own property. The Prozorovs realize with sadness that their future is destroyed: Masha nobly gives up the love of Vershinin, Irina weeps for her slain fiancé, Olga accepts a permanent life at the school, and Andrey abandons plans to be a professor. They are less conscious that Natasha, by taking over the wealth and space of the household, has stolen from them both their past and their present. Natasha's theft is less noticeable because it seems natural that Andrey's marriage and fatherhood should bring gradual changes. The change is also less noticeable because the Prozorovs concentrate on impractical ideals. Natasha lacks the Prozorov sensibility about life's larger purposes, but she intently pursues life's immediate concerns: self, sexuality, and status.

The subtlety of Chekhov's dramatic art is evident in the way that Natasha's takeover of the Prozorov household is dramatized. In each act, there is a brief scene that emblemizes her growing ascendancy. At the end of act 1, Natasha joins the name-day party, but her garish dress and awkward manners are an embarrassment. Protectively, Andrey embraces her behind a screen: The future scholar finds Natasha sexually irresistible, whatever her social sophistication. At the opening of act 2, Natasha prowls the house possessively and interrupts Andrey's study with her worries. Why are Olga and Masha let out? Will the carnival carousers disturb them? Is the baby all right? Does little Bobik need his room now? Perhaps Irina could move in with Olga.

In act 3, Natasha openly asserts her authority. With a second child in the nursery and the house crowded, Natasha decides to dismiss Anfisa, Olga's elderly servant. When Olga protests, Natasha has a tantrum; Olga decides to live at the school with Anfisa. In act 4, Andrey pushes a child in a baby carriage; when he attempts to console Masha over Vershinin's departure, Natasha reprimands him noisily for disturbing the children. As Natasha surveys her realm from a window, a servant brings Andrey mortgage papers to sign: Without informing his sisters, he has plunged all of them into debt to support Natasha's expensive tastes. At the final curtain, the pathos is strong. The Prozorovs' plans for the future have collapsed, and their security in the present has evaporated.

The theme of dispossession—manifested in the characters' conversations about work, heritage, and family—reflects Chekhov's awareness of the changes occurring in Russia at the end of the nineteenth century. A century before, it had been a static society: A royal house ruled autocratically over a nation of serfs; an aristocracy knew the wealth, privilege, and leisure that flowed from loyal service to the royal house; the agricultural economy depended on the landowners and landworkers staying on their estates and villages. In Chekhov's time, change was under way. Serfdom had been abandoned, and some democratic political participation was being permitted. Aristocrats shared status with nouveau riche merchants, and industrialization drew workers from the land to the city. Chekhov's interest was not the cause or the value of these changes; he was not a sociologist or an economist.

His concern was one small consequence of these vast changes. A sense of beauty was dying: The leisure to cultivate aesthetic experience, to reflect upon serious questions, and to touch with another soul was being lost in the press of immediate needs. Those like the Prozorovs who require time to think, to feel, and to love are the first to be dispossessed in an era of change.

THROUGH THE LOOKING-GLASS, AND WHAT ALICE FOUND THERE

Type of work: Imaginative tale
Author: Lewis Carroll (Charles Lutwidge Dodgson, 1832–1898)
Type of plot: Fantasy
Time of plot: Nineteenth century
Locale: The dream world of an imaginative child
First published: 1871

Its plot structured around moves in a chess game, the story of this fantasy, which continues Alice's Adventures in Wonderland, *is set in a land peopled by live chessmen and talking insects, a land where everything happens backwards. Carroll's book may be read as a madcap children's fairy tale or interpreted as a complex, sophisticated adult fable laced with subtle ironies and inspired by inimitable humor.*

Principal Characters

Alice, an imaginative English child who has fantastic adventures in Looking-Glass House.

The White Kitten, a good kitten who is not responsible for Alice's adventures.

The Black Kitten, told by Alice to pretend that they can go through the mirror to Looking-Glass House.

Dinah, the kittens' mother.

The White Queen, a live chess piece. In Alice's adventures she becomes a sheep, gives Alice some needles, and tells the little girl to knit. She reappears throughout the story in various guises.

The White King, a live chess piece. He has Alice serve a cake which cuts itself.

Tiger Lily, Rose, and **Violet,** flowers Alice questions regarding which path to take.

Gnat, a pleasant insect as big as a chicken. He melts away.

The Red Queen, a live chess piece. She tells Alice

that one has to run to stay in the same place. Later she turns into the black kitten.

Tweedledum and **Tweedledee,** two odd, fat, little men. They speak in ambiguities and recite poems to Alice. They fight over a rattle until frightened away by a crow.

The Red King, a live chess piece. He dreams about Alice, says Tweedledee, and thus gives her reality.

Humpty Dumpty, who has a conversation in riddles with Alice. He explains to her the Jabberwocky poem.

The Lion and **the Unicorn,** who fight over the White King's crown.

The Red Knight, a live chess piece who claims Alice as his prisoner.

The White Knight, a live chess piece who also claims Alice as his prisoner. He leads Alice to a brook and tells her to jump into the next square in order to become a queen herself.

The Story

Alice was sure the whole thing was not the white kitten's fault. It must surely have been the fault of the black kitten. Dinah, the mother cat, had been washing the white kitten's face when it happened; she certainly had had nothing to do with it. The mischievous black kitten, however, had been unwinding Alice's yarn and in all ways acting naughty enough to cause the whole strange affair.

While the black kitten was curled up in Alice's lap playing with the yarn, Alice told it to pretend that the two of them could go right through the mirror and into Looking-Glass House. As she talked, the glass grew misty and soft; in a moment, Alice was through the mirror and in the Looking-Glass room. The place was very strange; although the room looked just the same as the real room she had seen in the mirror, the clock and the fire and the other things in the room seemed to be alive. Even the

chessmen, for Alice loved to play chess, were alive.

When Alice picked up the White Queen and set her on the table, the White Queen screamed in terror, thinking that a volcano had shaken her about. The White King had the same fear, but he was too astonished to cry out. They did not seem to see or hear Alice, and although she wanted to stay and watch them and read the king's rather funny poetry, she felt she must look at the garden before she had to go back through the Looking Glass. When she started down the stairs, she seemed to float, not even once touching the steps.

In the garden, every path Alice took led her straight back to the house. She asked Tiger Lily, Rose, and Violet whether there were any other people in the garden; she hoped they might help her find the right path. The flowers told her there was only one, and Alice found her to be the Red Queen—but a very strange chess figure, for the Red Queen was taller than Alice herself. As Alice walked toward the Red Queen, she once more found herself back at the door of the house. Then Alice figured out that in order to get to any place in this queer land, one must walk in the *opposite* direction. She did so and came face-to-face with the Red Queen.

The queen took Alice to the top of a hill. There, spread out below them, was a countryside that looked like a large chessboard. Alice was delighted and said that she would love to play on this board. Then the Red Queen told her that they would play and that Alice could be the White Queen's Pawn. They would start on the Second Square; but at that moment, the Red Queen grabbed Alice's hand and they started to run. Alice had never run so fast in her life, but although she was breathless from such fast running, the things around them never changed a tiny bit. When they finally stopped running, the queen told Alice that in this land one had to run as fast as she could to stay in the same place and twice as fast as she could to get somewhere else. Then the queen showed Alice the pegs in the Second Square and told her how to move. At the last peg, the Red Queen disappeared, leaving Alice alone to continue the game.

Alice started to run down the hill. The next thing she knew she was on a train filled with insects and having quite an unpleasant time because she did not have a ticket. All the insects talked unkindly to her, and to add to her discomfort, the train jumped over the brook and took them all straight up in the air. When she came down, she was sitting under a tree, talking to a Gnat. Gnat was as big as a chicken but very pleasant. He told her about the other insects that lived in the woods; then he too melted away, and Alice had to go on alone.

Turning a corner, she bumped into two fat little men, called Tweedledum and Tweedledee, the funniest little creatures she had ever seen. Everything they said seemed to have two meanings. It was fun to listen to the merry little men as they recited a long poem about a Walrus and a Carpenter and some Oysters. While they were explaining the poem to Alice, she heard a puffing noise, like the sound of a steam engine. Tweedledee told her it was the Red King snoring. Sure enough, they found him asleep. Tweedledee told Alice that the Red King was dreaming about her and that if he stopped dreaming Alice would be gone for good. Alice cried when they told her she was not real but only a part of the Red King's dream.

As she brushed her tears away, she saw Tweedledum staring in terror at something on the ground. It was an old broken rattle, over which the two foolish men got into a terrible fight—that is, they *talked* a terrible fight, but neither seemed very anxious to have a real battle. The Crow flew over and frightened them so that the funny men ran away into the wood. Alice ran too, and as she ran, she saw a shawl blowing about.

Looking for the owner of the shawl, Alice saw the White Queen running toward her. The White Queen was a very queer person; she lived backward and remembered things *before* they happened. For example, she hurt *before* she pricked her finger. While the queen was telling these strange things to Alice, the queen turned into a Sheep and was in a shop with Alice. It was a very curious shop; the shelves were full of things that disappeared when Alice looked at them. Sometimes the boxes went right through the ceiling. Then Sheep gave Alice some needles and told her to knit.

As she started to knit, the needles became oars, and she found herself and Sheep in a little boat rowing in a stream. The oars kept sticking in the water. Sheep explained that the crabs were catching them. Alice picked some beautiful, fragrant rushes that melted away as soon as she picked them. To her surprise, the river and boat soon vanished, and Alice and Sheep were back in the shop. She bought an egg, although in this shop two were cheaper than one, but when she started to get the egg, as Sheep would not reach it for her, the egg began to grow larger and larger and more and more real, with eyes, a nose, and a mouth. Then Alice could tell plain as day that the egg was Humpty Dumpty.

She had a queer conversation with Humpty Dumpty, a conversation filled with riddles. They took turns at choosing the topic to discuss, but most of the subjects turned into arguments, although Alice tried to be polite. Humpty Dumpty explained to Alice what the "Jabberwocky" poem meant, the one she had seen in the White King's book. Then while reciting another poem, Humpty Dumpty stopped right in the middle and said that was all. Alice thought it very queer but did not tell him so. She thought it time for her to leave, but as she walked away, there was a terrible crash that shook the whole forest.

Thousands of soldiers and horses came rushing toward her, and the riders constantly fell off their horses. Frightened, she escaped from the wood into the open. There she found the White King, who told her that he had sent the soldiers and horses and that the loud crash she had heard was the noise of the Lion and Unicorn fighting for the crown. She went with the king to watch the fight, which was indeed a terrible one. It was silly of them to fight for the crown, since it belonged to the White King and he had no notion of giving it away. After the fight, Alice met the Unicorn and the Lion. At the king's order, she served them cake, a very strange cake that cut itself when she carried the dish around.

A great noise interrupted the party. When it stopped, Alice thought she might have dreamed the whole thing until the Red Knight came along, followed soon by a White Knight. Each claimed her as a prisoner. Alice thought the whole business silly, since neither of them could do anything except fall off his horse and climb back on again, over and over and over. At last the Red Knight galloped off, and the White Knight told her that she would be a queen as soon as she crossed the next brook. He was supposed to lead her to the end of the wood, but she spent the whole journey helping him back on his horse each time he fell off. The trip was filled with more queer conversation. By that time, Alice was used to strange talk from her Looking-Glass friends. At last, they reached the brook. The knight rode away, and Alice jumped over the brook and into the last square of the chessboard. To her delight, when she reached that square she felt something tight on her head—a crown! She was a queen.

Soon she found the Red Queen and the White Queen confronting her; they were very cross because she also thought she was a queen. They gave her a test for queens which she must have passed, for before long they were calling her "Your Majesty" and inviting people to a party that she was to give. After a time, the Red Queen and the White Queen went to sleep. Alice watched them until they disappeared. Then she found herself before a doorway marked "Queen Alice." All of her new friends were there, including the queens who had just vanished. The party was the most amazing experience of all. Puddings talked, guests poured wine over their heads, and the White Queen turned into a leg of mutton. Alice was exasperated, so much so that she seized the tablecloth and jerked it and everything on it to the floor. Then she grabbed the Red Queen and shook her as she would a kitten. But what was this? It *was* a kitten she was shaking, the black kitten.

Alice talked to Dinah and both the kittens about the adventure they had all experienced, but the silly kittens did nothing but purr.

Critical Evaluation

It is rare for the sequel to a highly creative literary work to surpass the original. Nevertheless, such is the case with *Through the Looking-Glass, and What Alice Found There*, which in 1871 followed *Alice's Adventures in Wonderland*, published seven years earlier. For most readers, the two books are so closely entwined that they are considered a unit, and many of Lewis Carroll's most famous Looking-Glass creations (Tweedledee, Tweedledum, and Humpty Dumpty, for example) are often mistakenly placed in *Alice's Adventures in Wonderland*. Each book, however, is a distinct entity. *Through the Looking-Glass* is most attractive to adults, for in this second fantasy Lewis Carroll (the pen name for Oxford mathematics lecturer and tutor the Reverend Charles Lutwidge Dodgson) presented an even more sophisticated puzzle about reality and logic than he did in the earlier story. It is in *Through the Looking-Glass* that one finds conscious suggestion of the cruel questions rather delicately presented in *Alice's Adventures in Wonderland*.

The books share many characteristics: each has twelve chapters, and both merge the fairy tale with science. Alice is seven years old in the first book and is seven and one-half years old on her second venture. A slight shift in scene turns the pleasant outdoor summer setting of *Alice's Adventures in Wonderland* into the more somber indoor winter stage of *Through the Looking-Glass*. Corresponding to the card game of the first book is chess in *Through the Looking-Glass*, another game that involves kings and queens. Within the chess-and-mirror framework of the Looking-Glass world, Carroll has, however, constructed an intricate symbolic plan unlike the seemingly spontaneous movement of Wonderland.

Although medieval and Renaissance sportsmen sometimes enjoyed chess that used human players on a giant field, Carroll was apparently the first to use the idea in literature. Science fiction has since, of course, often employed the technique. In the game plan, Alice is a white pawn on a giant chessboard of life in which the rows of the board are separated by brooks and the columns by hedges. Alice never speaks to any piece who is not in a square beside her, as appropriate for the pawn that never knows what is happening except at its spot on the board. Alice remains in the queen's field except for her last move, by which time she has become a queen and captures the Red Queen (and shakes her into a kitten); as a result, she checkmates the Red King, who has slept throughout the game. Her behavior complements the personalities assigned to the other pieces, for each assumes the qualities of the figure it represents. As in chess, the queens are the most powerful and active beings, and the kings are impotent. Erratic and stumbling, the White Knight recalls the movement of the chess knight, which moves two squares in any direction, then again one square in a different direction.

Critics have noted inconsistencies in the chess game, charging that the White side makes nine consecutive moves; the White King is placed in an unnoticed check by the queen's castle; and the White Queen misses a chance to take the Red Knight. In a later explanatory note, however, Carroll said that the game is correct in relation to the moves, although the alternation of sides is not strictly consistent, and that the "castling" of the queens is merely his phrase to indicate that they have entered the palace. Not interested in the game as an example of chess strategy, Carroll conceived of it as a learning experience for a child who was to be a pawn warring against all the other pieces, controlled by an adult—an idea apparently stimulated by the chess tales Carroll had fashioned for Alice Liddell, a young friend who was learning the game. Alice, the daughter of the dean of Christ Church, Oxford, had also been, of course, the Alice whom he had placed in Wonderland.

Arising from Carroll's use of this structure has been the proposal that Alice is Everyman and that chess is Life. Like a human being who exists from birth to death only vaguely comprehending the forces directing his moves, Alice never understands her experience. Indeed, none of the pieces really assimilates the total concept of the game. Even the mobile queens do not really grasp the idea that beyond the board there is a room and people who are determining the game. Man's own reality thus becomes very unreal if he, like the chess pieces, has such a limited perception of the total environment.

Carroll pursues still another definition of reality when Alice confronts the Red King and is told that she exists merely as a part of his dreams, not as an objective being. Upsetting to Alice is the sage advice of Tweedledum and Tweedledee to the effect that if the king were to wake, Alice would vanish like the flame of a candle. The incident recalls Bishop Berkeley's empirical proposal that nothing exists except as it is perceived. Alice, like Samuel Johnson, who refuted Berkeley by painfully kicking a stone, insists that she is "real," for she cries "real" tears. When she leaves the world of the Looking-Glass and supposedly awakens, Carroll mischievously permits her to ask herself: Which dreamed it? His final poem apparently provides the answer, for the last words are: "Life, what is it but a dream?"

In examining the second structural device of the book, the mirror reversal theme, readers find that Carroll has achieved another *tour de force*. The reversals—including, for example, the Tweedle brothers, Alice's attempt to reach the Red Queen by walking backward, memory that occurs before the event, and running to stay in the same place—are not merely mind teasers. Scientists now seriously propose the existence of antimatter, which is, in effect, a mirror image of matter, just like Alice's Looking-Glass milk. And again readers wonder: Which is the real matter, the real milk?

Further developing this continuing paradox are Carroll's damaging attacks on our understanding of language. Humpty Dumpty (like the Tweedles, the Lion, the Unicorn, and Wonderland's Jack of Hearts, a nursery rhyme character) says a person's ideas are formulated in his mind; to express them, he may use any word he pleases. Alice and the White Knight debate the difference between the name of the song and the song, between what the name is and what the name is called. The fawn becomes frightened of Alice only when it realizes she is a "child." In these and many more incidents, Carroll explores how our language works, directly and indirectly making fun of our misconceptions: We see language as part of a totally objective system of reality, forgetting how language actually helps create that reality. His nonsense words and poems are his final jibe at our so-called logical language, for they are no more and no less disorderly than ordinary table talk.

THUS SPAKE ZARATHUSTRA

Type of work: Philosophical comments as parable and prophecy
Author: Friedrich Wilhelm Nietzsche (1844–1900)
First published: Parts I-III, 1883–1884; Part IV, 1891

Only a philosopher with a great ego (resulting from a fear of failure) and a great passion would have conceived the idea of putting his most radical thoughts into the mouth of a Persian mystic dead more than five centuries before the birth of Jesus. Zarathustra, or Zoroaster, was a Persian religious leader whose revolutionary religious activity stimulated the growth of the religion that bears his name: Zoroastrianism. Nietzsche fancied that he found similarities between his ideas and passions and those of Zarathustra, but whether he was justified in using the name of the Persian in order to give his paradoxical and poetic work a certain mystical quality is a problem that can be left to those who moralize about art. The important word to remember is "art"; *Thus Spake Zarathustra* is a work of art in which a radical inversion of traditional values is expressed in the guise of poetic prophetic writings.

Nietzsche's prologue, entitled "Zarathustra's Prologue," tells us that Zarathustra went up into the mountains when he was thirty and stayed there ten years. When he came down, he went to the market place of the nearest town and said, "*I teach you the Superman*. Man is something that is to be surpassed. What have you done to surpass man?"

The book is Nietzsche's attempt to help man surpass himself, to become Superman. Of course, Superman is the author's conception, and the qualities which make Superman distinctive can most readily be understood as the opposite to whatever is enervating and spiritless in traditional Christianity. It is easy to read Nietzsche as one who condemns whatever is generally regarded as worthwhile and virtuous; he condemns Christianity as fostering a "slave morality." But what he says makes some sense, whatever its excesses, if considered as having been stimulated by Christianity at its sentimental and dogmatic worst.

Nietzsche's basic idea is that the most important feature of all existence is will, an idea he received from Schopenhauer. But, unlike the pessimistic Schopenhauer, he did not believe that man's objective should be to abolish the will and, consequently, to be nothing; on the contrary, Nietzsche thought that man should seek to surpass himself, to strengthen his will, to rise above ordinary men, and to achieve greatness of will and being. For him pride is a great virtue and so is contempt of everything that ordinary men believe and worship.

Zarathustra speaks to the spectators of a rope-dancing performance and tells them to "remain true to the earth" and not to believe "those who speak unto you of super-earthly hopes!" He tells them that the greatest thing they can experience is "the hour of great contempt" in which they look with loathing upon their happiness, their reason, and their virtue. When the rope-dancer falls and is fatally injured, Zarathustra tells him not to worry about being dragged to hell; he assures the dying man that his soul will be dead before his body is. When the rope-dancer replies that if this is so, he is nothing more than an animal, Zarathustra objects by pointing out that the rope-dancer had made danger his calling, and he adds that "therein there is nothing contemptible."

Nietzsche's ideas have sometimes been compared to those of the Nazis, but it is probably more accurate to suppose that the virtues Nietzsche endorses are those which Hemingway extols in his novels. Both writers ask men to surpass themselves, to be courageous and proud, to face danger, to love action and to act, and to respect those who can kill and be killed; both writers regard love as important only when it is biologically compelling, and even then it is regarded as something of a nuisance.

Nietzsche is famous not only for his denunciation of Christianity but also for his attacks on women. In section 18 of the first part, Zarathustra gives his views on women:

> Everything in woman is a riddle, and everything in woman hath one solution—it is called pregnancy . . . . Two different things wanteth the true man: danger and diversion. Therefore wanteth he woman, as the most dangerous plaything. Man shall be trained for war, and woman for the recreation of the warrior: all else is folly.

Zarathustra concludes with a "little truth" which the old woman to whom he expressed his ideas gave him: "Thou goest to women? Do not forget thy whip!"

Although it is possible for the critic so to consider *Thus Spake Zarathustra* that it becomes sensible to speak of its philosophic content, it is more helpful to take the book as a prose poem, a passionate and sometimes incoherent injunction to men to become more than they have been and to go beyond the petty limits prescribed for them by conventional moralities.

Nevertheless, when the effort is made to extract from this curious book its philosophic claims, it soon becomes clear that for Nietzsche values make sense only if they are relative to the individual, not only in the respect that whatever is good or bad is so *to* a person, but also in the respect that whatever is good or bad (according to Nietzsche) is so *for* a person. There would be no point in telling the author that some men value the welfare of other persons; such sentimental attachment to others is what keeps a man from surpassing himself, Nietzsche believes. To be great, to surpass himself, a man must consider his own power and know how he can best use that power to extend himself and to satisfy himself. "One must learn to love oneself . . . with a wholesome and healthy love," he writes; moreover, he believes "that one may endure to be with oneself, and not go roving about." To be more than man, to discover oneself, involves giving up the moral habits and injunctions we learned "almost in the cradle." Nietzsche claims that with the words "brotherly love" there has been "the best lying and dissembling, and especially by those who have been burdensome to every one." And he argues that "He, however, hath discovered himself who saith: This is *my* good and evil: therewith hath he silenced the mole and dwarf who say: 'Good for all, evil for all.' " The conclusive statement of the relativity of values comes at the end of the section titled "The Spirit of Gravity," from which the quotations of this paragraph come: " 'This—is now *my* way,—where is yours?' Thus did I answer those who asked me 'the way.' For *the* way—it doth not exist!"

In "Old and New Tables" Nietzsche reaches the extreme point of demanding the destruction of old laws and commandments. Nietzsche venerates the creator of new values and, consequently, the destroyer of old ones. The creation of new values is important, not because it rights wrongs and liberates men, but because the creative process itself is an exercise of the will's power; it is the way to Superman. Nietzsche argues that the greatest danger to any man and to mankind comes from the good and the just; that is, from the defenders of the old morality. He writes that "The good *must* crucify him who deviseth his own virtue!"

Nietzsche argues that God is dead, the old God that preached brotherly love; man faces an abyss and before the response of petty men the higher man feels nothing but disgust. The proper response to the abyss is the creative act of a man who loves himself and takes pride in his power to create new values through his acts. "Doth not—man's *future* strive and struggle in you?" he asks.

These ideas are presented to the reader in the midst of strange accounts of Zarathustra's wanderings and encounters with the mass of the marketplace and with a few eccentric persons who in one way or another suggest the Superman ideal.

To suppose that Nietzsche created the ideal of the Superman as the destroyer of old values and the creator of the new, as the teacher of the virtue of pride, in order to justify a totalitarian state is to misread him. Because of the superficial resemblance of Nazi propaganda to Nietzschean utterances, it is easy to fall into the error of taking Nietzsche as an apologist for a state controlled by self-styled "supermen." Early in *Thus Spake Zarathustra*, Nietzsche condemns the state for its pretension to be identified with the people. Not only is it a lie to identify the state with the people but it is destructive of men to believe the lie. Only where the state falls does man rise and make Superman possible.

Many persons dismiss Nietzsche altogether, knowing only that he contemptuously dismissed Christianity. But throughout *Thus Spake Zarathustra* and *Beyond Good and Evil*, Nietzsche reveals a constant and impassioned concern for that part of each man that is lost because, in his opinion, of slavish obedience to a conventional, effeminate morality. His scorn of the "rabble"—"Life is a well of delight; but where the rabble also drink, there all fountains are poisoned"—is not so much a scorn of men and virtue as it is of those who pervert themselves and others in the name of virtue. He writes, "And many a one who cannot see man's loftiness, calleth it virtue to see their baseness far too well." Nietzsche creates Zarathustra as a liberator, as one who brings the new word that all men might be free—not to march onward in any regimented way, but to stream outward as individually creative beings. Much of what Emerson endorsed as "self-reliance" Nietzsche endorses as "the will to power."

If Nietzsche is to be criticized for his shortcomings, it would be better to call attention to the absence of development and order in his work. However one may sympathize with his love for the creative man, certain problems remain: How does one come to choose or to create the new law? Is it possible for a man desiring to be Superman—to surpass himself—to be free and creative in the wrong way, and thus to destroy himself?

Nietzsche's failure to clarify the procedure of value-creation is his greatest fault. His work remains a paean for an art he never elucidates.

THYESTES

Type of work: Drama
Author: Lucius Annaeus Seneca (c. 4 B.C.–A.D. 65)
Type of Plot: Tragedy of revenge
Time of plot: The Heroic Age
Locale: Greece
First presented: c. A.D. 60

Thyestes, wooden on the stage, is nevertheless a closet drama of horrific intensity. Remarkable for its scenes of terror, such as the banquet at which the father partakes of his own children, the Senecan tragedy was a landmark in dramatic history, influencing in particular many Elizabethan and Jacobean revenge plays.

Principal Characters

Atreus (ā′trĭ·əs), the oldest son of Pelops and the rightful ruler of Argos, who is the protagonist in the most fiendish revenge play in the history of the theater.

Thyestes (thĭ·ĕs′tēz), Atreus' brother, who seduces his wife and steals the golden ram, the symbol of power in the kingdom. Having been defeated and banished by Atreus, Thyestes accepts with forebodings his brother's invitation to return to Argos. There he is fed the bodies of his sons at a banquet. Learning the truth, his greatest regret is his inability to get similar vengeance on Atreus.

Tantalus (tăn′tə·ləs), a son of Thyestes.

Thyestes' Two Other Sons. They are murdered by their uncle, who roasts their bodies for their father's banquet.

Agamemnon (ă′gə·mĕm′nŏn) and **Menelaus** (mĕ′nə·lā′əs), sons of Atreus.

Megaera (mə·gā′rə), one of the Furies.

The Ghost of Tantalus, the former king of Argos, who is summoned back to witness the fury of his descendants.

Pelops (pē′lŏps), the father of Atreus and Thyestes and the son of Tantalus, who is sacrificed by his father to the gods.

The Story

Megaera, one of the Furies, summoned the ghost of Tantalus to return from Hades to Argos, where Tantalus in life had been king, to watch revenge, hate, and havoc spread across that kingdom. Tantalus was hesitant because of the part he had played in the story of his royal house, but Megaera forced him to witness the fate of his descendants.

The grandsons of Tantalus, the sons of Pelops, whom Tantalus had sacrificed to the gods, were at war with one another. The oldest of Pelops' sons, Atreus, was the rightful ruler of Argos, but his brother, Thyestes, had seduced Atreus' wife and carried her away. With them they took the golden ram, the symbol of power held by the ruler of the kingdom. Civil war broke out, and Thyestes was defeated. After his defeat he was exiled by Atreus.

But exile was not sufficient punishment for Thyestes. The fierce hatred of Atreus, burning over his brother's crimes and his own misfortune in the loss of his wife, demanded greater revenge. A tyrant who believed that death was a comfort to his subjects, Atreus brooded over fierce and final vengeance upon his younger brother. He felt that no act of revenge could be a crime when committed against a man who had worked against him as his brother had. Moreover, he felt that he, as a king, could do as he wished; private virtues were not for rulers.

When an attendant suggested that Atreus put Thyestes to the sword, Atreus said that death was only an end. He wanted Thyestes to suffer even greater torture. The punishment Atreus finally hit upon was a scheme to feed Thyestes' own children to him at a banquet.

Atreus took the first step toward accomplishing his revenge. He sent his own sons, Agamemnon and Menelaus, as emissaries of good will to Thyestes and asked the exile, through them, to return to a place of honor at his brother's side. Fearing that his sons, forewarned, might lack the discretion needed to act as friendly ambassadors, he did not tell them the part they were playing in his scheme of revenge.

Thyestes, trusting the king, returned to Argos with his three sons, including one named Tantalus, after his great-grandfather of famous memory. But when he looked again at familiar landscapes, Thyestes felt a sense of foreboding. His footsteps faltered, and his sons noted his apparent unwillingness to return. The offer of peace and half the kingdom seemed to Thyestes unlike his brother's earlier hatred and fury. He felt that there had been too much hate and bloodshed between them for real peace. But his sons, silencing his doubts, led him on to the court of Atreus.

Atreus, overjoyed to see his brother and nephews in

his power and apparently unmindful of the revenge plotted against them, concealed his hatred and welcomed them to the kingdom once again.

Atreus announced a great feast to celebrate his brother's homecoming. Then, taking the three sons of Thyestes aside, he led them to a grove behind the palace and there slew them with all the ceremony of a sacrifice to the gods. The first he stabbed in the neck, the second he decapitated, and the third he killed by a thrust through the body. The boys, knowing that appeals were useless, suffered death in silence. Atreus drew off their blood and prepared the carcasses like so much beef. The limbs he quartered and placed upon spits to roast; the bodies he hacked into small pieces and placed in pots to boil.

The fire seemed reluctant to burn as an accomplice to his deed, but Atreus stood by and acted as cook until the ghastly banquet was ready. As he cooked, the sky grew dark and an unnatural night settled across the face of the earth. The banquet prepared, Atreus felt that he was the equal of the gods themselves.

The feast began. After the banquet had progressed to the point that the guests were glutted by all they had eaten, Atreus prepared for Thyestes a drink of wine and blood drained from the bodies of Thyestes' sons.

All the while a premonition of evil hung like a cloud in the back of Thyestes' mind. Try as he would, he could not be gay and enjoy the feast, for vague terrors struck at his heart. When Atreus gave him the cup of blood and wine, he could not lift it to drink at first, and when he did try to drink the wine seemed to roll around the brim of the cup rather than pass through his lips. Filled with sudden fears, Thyestes demanded that Atreus produce his sons.

Atreus left and returned with the heads of the three sons on a platter. Thyestes, chilled with horror at the sight, asked where the bodies were. He feared that Atreus had refused them honorable burial and had left them for the dogs to eat. Atreus told Thyestes that he had eaten his own children. Then Thyestes realized why unnatural night had darkened the skies.

Still Atreus was not satisfied. He felt disappointed that he had not planned to force Thyestes to drink some of his children's blood while they were yet alive. The king bragged of what he had done and described how he himself had committed the murders and spitted the meat before the fires.

Atreus, enjoying his revenge, could never believe that the greatest weight upon Thyestes' mind was regret that he had not thought of such revenge and caused Atreus to eat of his own children

Critical Evaluation

Seneca's *Thyestes* is undoubtedly the most lurid, gruesome, and undramatic tragedy to survive from antiquity, and perhaps the most fiendish revenge play in the literature. It is spectacle rather than true drama. Whereas genuine tragedy arises from character conflicts or internal divisions within character, spectacle relies on sensational events carried out by characters who exist merely for the sake of the events and who have no actual existence of their own. This is certainly the case with every character in *Thyestes*. Each exists simply to emphasize the horror of Atreus' revenge on his brother Thyestes, where Thyestes is fed his own butchered sons at a hideous banquet.

Another important point of difference between true drama and spectacle is their use of language. The speech of authentic tragedy approximates, in a formal way, the devices of normal conversation to reveal passions. The language of spectacle, however, being florid and highly artificial, tends toward bombast. Spectacle operates by set pieces, rhetorical essays that develop simple ideas at great length, by tedious and lush descriptive passages, and by *sententiae*, or moralizing epigrams. Sencea used all three, and the result is that his characters speak in a highly unnatural way, instead of communicating they attitudinize.

This characteristic of Senecan drama had led many scholars to believe that Seneca wrote his plays for private recitation rather than public performance. In fact there is no reason for assuming that the plays were not produced. Spectacle, rhetorical overindulgence, and horrors were a part of public entertainment under the Roman Emperors Caligula, Claudius, and Nero, who ruled during Seneca's maturity. We know that Seneca's tragedies were staged in the Elizabethan period, and that they had immense influence on the dramas of Kyd, Marlowe, Shakespeare, Webster, and others.

The subject of *Thyestes* derives from Greek legend, and is based upon an incident that occurred in the tragic family descended from Tantalus. Although Sophocles, Euripides, Ennius, Accius, and Varius had dramatized the story of Thyestes earlier, none of their plays has survived to provide a basis of comparison. Seneca's treatment of the myth has some interest in its own right, but it also serves to illuminate his own biography.

He handles the figure of Thyestes rather sympathetically, making him the victim of Atreus' lunatic lust for revenge. Seneca plays down the fact that Thyestes seduced Atreus' wife, stole his symbol of power, and caused a civil war. When Thyestes appears on stage, he assumes the role of the Stoic hero, determined to bear whatever fate has in store for him, and he frankly prefers the hardships of exile to the pomp of power that Atreus has treacherously extended to him. Exile has tempered his character. And here we remember that Seneca himself underwent eight years of exile on Corsica, after being accused of an intrigue with Claudius' niece Julia. The parallel is striking, but it extends even further. Like Thyestes, Seneca was recalled from exile with the promise of power. He was to tutor and guide Nero in the art of statesmanship. When Nero became Emperor in A.D. 54, Seneca was able to exercise some control over him for the first five years of his reign; but then Nero began acting on his own, and Seneca retired from public life. *Thyestes* is Seneca's personal testament on the instability of power and the helplessness of those who incur the wrath of an absolute and maniacal ruler. The only solution Seneca finds in this play is the same one he found in life—to bear one's misfortune with Stoic dignity. Eventually Nero ordered Seneca to commit suicide for an alleged conspiracy. And Seneca met his death bravely.

Through the murky rhetoric of *Thyestes* three important themes emerge: cannibalism, the nature of kingship, and the necessity of maintaining a Stoic endurance in the face of a murderous disintegrating cosmos. The appearance of Tantalus and Megaera the Fury at the beginning is not accidental. Tantalus served his son, Pelops, as food for the gods, and as part of his eternal torment he must not only witness the kin murders of his descendants, he must abet them. Presumably he inspires the idea of the cannibalistic revenge in Atreus' mind, but Atreus carries it out with gloating satisfaction. Atreus is an unrelieved monster, raging with paranoid pride.

Against him Seneca sets the idea of kingship founded on morality and restraint. The aphoristic conversation between Atreus and the attendant in act 2, scene 1, is a debate on whether kings should serve the people or the people should be utterly subservient to the king. In the first case morality is the main law, and in the second the will of the the tyrant. The point is made that morality creates a stable kingdom, but tyranny is supremely unstable. Later, the chorus says that true kingship lies in self-control, not in wealth, power, or pomp.

Unfortunately these observations make no impression whatever on Atreus, who is intent on proving his godlike power over human life, much like the Roman Emperors Seneca knew. In striving to become like a god in his pride, Atreus becomes loathsomely bestial. Seneca constantly generalizes from the concrete situation of Atreus and Thyestes to the universe. When kings are corrupt, society is corrupted, and the rot extends throughout the cosmos. Nature mirrors human conditions in Seneca: the fire hesitates to boil the children; an unnatural night falls upon the banquet. The play is full of hyperbole about the disintegrating universe, rendered in very purple poetry. Against this profusion of rhetoric stand the pithy epigrams, like a Stoical element trying to bear up tightly against the frenetic declamations. The Stoic attitude can never prevail in a world full of crime, but it can enable a man to endure great stress with courage. Seneca, in *Thyestes*, embodied the shame of Rome and his own valor in a style eminently suited to his subject.

THE TIME MACHINE

Type of work: Novel
Author: H. G. Wells (1866–1946)
Type of plot: Fantasy
Time of plot: Late nineteenth century
Locale: England
First published: 1895

Wells's first novel, despite its exuberant style, is a delineation of unfulfilled hope in which the Time Traveler's dreams for a future founded upon scientific technology and social organization are dashed by a vision of humankind reduced to a level of brutality or effeteness, then finally extinguished.

Principal Characters

The Time Traveler, who exhibits his Time Machine one evening after dinner. The next week, his guests arrive for dinner but do not find him home. Informed that they are to proceed without him, they sit down to dinner. Later, dirty and limping, their host arrives. He has travelled to the year 802,701, the time of the sunset of humanity. He tells his guests what he found: The people, weak, rounded creatures about four feet high, are vegetarians called Eloi, living in enormous buildings. Underground live the predatory Morlocks, apelike creatures also descended from man. They were responsible for the disappearance of the Time Machine, but the Time Traveler says he managed to get it back and take off as the Morlocks sprang at him. Then, after quick and horrifying excursions ahead millions of years to that distant future time when the sun is dying and the earth is enveloped in bitter cold and deathly stillness, he hurried back to the present. Next day the Time Traveler silences his friends' doubts by departing again on his Time Machine; he does not return, and his friends can only wonder what mishap has made him a lost wanderer in time and space.

Weena, a girl of the Eloi. The Time Traveler saves her from drowning, and she becomes his friend and guide. After sightseeing, they find that they have walked too far to return that night. They build a fire on a hill to keep away the dark-loving Morlocks, but later the Time Traveler wakes to find the fire out and Weena missing.

The Story

After dinner, one evening, the Time Traveler led the discussion to the subject of the relationship of time and space. It was his theory that time was a fourth dimension, and that his concept could be proved. To the astonishment of his guests, he exhibited a model of his Time Machine, which, he declared, could travel backward or forward in time. One of the guests was invited to touch a lever. To the amazement of all, the machine disappeared. The Time Traveler explained that the instrument was no longer visible because it was traveling into the past at such great speed that it was below the threshold of visibility.

The following week the Time Traveler was not at home to greet his dinner guests when they arrived, but he had left word that they were to proceed without him. Everyone was at the table when their host came in, dirty from head to toe, limping, and with a cut on his chin. After he had changed his clothes and dined, he told his friends the story of the day's adventures.

That morning he had taken off on his Time Machine. As he reeled through space, the days shot past him like minutes, the rapid alternation of light and darkness hurting the Time Traveler's eyes. Landing and falling from his machine when he braked too suddenly, he found himself on the side of a hill. In the misty light he could see the figure of a winged sphinx on a bronze pedestal. As the sun came out, the Time Traveler saw enormous buildings on the slope. Some figures were coming toward him. One was a little man about four feet tall. Regaining his confidence, the Time Traveler waited to meet this citizen of the future.

Soon a group of these creatures gathered around the voyager. Without a common language, he and his new acquaintances had to communicate with signs. After they had examined the Time Machine, from which he had the presence of mind to remove the levers, one of them asked him if he had come from the sun.

The Time Traveler was led to one of the large buildings, where he was seated upon a cushion and given fruit to eat. Everyone was a vegetarian, animals having become extinct. When he had eaten, he tried to learn his new friends' language, but without much success. These people, who called themselves the Eloi, were not able to concentrate and tired quickly.

Free to wander about, the Time Traveler climbed a hill

and from the crest saw the ruins of an enormous granite structure. Looking at some of the creatures who were following him, he realized that all wore similar garb and had the same soft, rounded figures. Children could be distinguished only by their size.

The Time Traveler realized that he was seeing the sunset of humanity. In the society of the future there was no need for strength. The world was at peace and secure. The strong of body or mind would only have felt frustrated.

As he looked about to find a place to sleep, he saw that his Time Machine had disappeared. He tried to wake the people in the building in which he had dined, but he succeeded only in frightening them. At last he went back to the lawn and there, greatly worried over his plight, fell asleep.

The next morning he managed to trace the path the Time Machine made to the base of the sphinx, but the bronze doors in the pedestal were closed. The Time Traveler tried to intimate to some of the Eloi that he wished to open the doors, but they answered him with looks of insult and reproach. He attempted to hammer in the doors with a stone, but he soon stopped from weariness.

Weena, a young girl he rescued from drowning, became the Time Traveler's friend and guide. On the fourth morning, while he explored one of the ruins, he saw eyes staring at him from the dark. Curious, he followed a small, apelike figure to a well-like opening, down which it retreated. He was convinced that this creature was also a descendant of man, a subterranean species that worked below ground to support the dwellers in the upper world.

Convinced that the Morlocks, as the subterranean dwellers were called, were responsible for the disappearance of his Time Machine and hoping to learn more about them. he climbed down into one of the wells. At its bottom he discovered a tunnel which led into a cavern in which he saw a table set with a joint of meat. The Morlocks were carnivorous. He was able to distinguish, too, some enormous machinery.

The next day the Time Traveler and Weena visited a green porcelain museum containing animal skeletons, books, and machinery. Since they had walked a long distance, he planned to sleep in the woods that night with Weena and to build a fire to keep the dark-loving Morlocks away. When he saw three crouching figures in the brush, however, he changed his mind and decided he and Weena would be safer on a hill beyond the forest. He started a fire to keep their enemies at a distance.

When he awoke the fire had gone out, his matches were missing, and Weena had vanished. A fire he had started earlier was still burning, and while he slept it had set the forest on fire. Between thirty and forty Morlocks perished in the blaze while the Time Traveler watched.

When daylight returned, the Time Traveler retraced his steps to the sphinx. He slept all day and in the evening prepared to ram open the doors in the pedestal with the lever he had found in the porcelain palace. He found the doors open, his machine in plain view. As a group of Morlocks sprang at him, he took off through space.

The Time Traveler had his encounter with the Morlocks and the Eloi in the year 802,701. On his next journey he moved through millions of years, toward that time when the earth will cease rotating. He landed on a deserted beach, empty except for a flying animal, which looked like a huge white butterfly, and some crablike monsters. On he traveled, finally halting thirty million years after the time he had left his laboratory. In that distant age the sun was dying. It was bitter cold and it began to snow. All around was deathly stillness. Horrified, the Time Traveler started back toward his present.

That evening, as he told his story, his guests grew skeptical. In fact, the Time Traveler himself had to visit his laboratory to make sure his machine existed. The next day, however, all doubts ceased, for one of his friends watched him depart on his vehicle. It was this friend who wrote the story of the Time Traveler's experiences three years later. The Time Traveler had not reappeared during that time, and his friends speculated on the mishap which had made him a lost wanderer in space and time.

Critical Evaluation

With the publication of his first novel, *The Time Machine*, H. G. Wells made a name for himself as a writer of science fiction and a critic of his times, two characteristics he would continue to exhibit throughout his lengthy writing career. *The Time Machine* appeared in 1895, seven years after two other important utopian novels: William Morris' *News from Nowhere* and Edward Bellamy's *Looking Backward*. A number of late Victorian authors produced books of this type, largely in response to the events they witnessed in their own times. For some, a utopian fiction afforded the opportunity to describe what a culture could be if people would only become less selfish, less aggressive. Of more importance, however, are the utopian texts whose authors follow current trends to their logical conclusions in a not-too-distant or a far future. *The Time Machine* falls under this category and is an important novel, clearly demonstrating the effect of Charles Darwin and T. H. Huxley on Victorian England.

As a student of Huxley, the young Wells was exposed to the full impact of post-Darwinian thought. Victorian philosophers who applied Darwin's ideas concerning evolution to human culture perceived a struggle for survival that predicted the destruction of all that was good in human nature. This attitude clearly helped shape *The*

Time Machine, as did Wells's own experience of growing up in a lower-class family where the disparity between the haves and the have-nots was painfully obvious.

The Time Machine functions as both a warning of present dangers and a veiled prescription for halting the downward spiral toward the death of the human species. Wells accomplishes both these goals by taking his unnamed Time Traveler on a journey to the far reaches of time, well past what we must presume has been the height of human physical and cultural evolution. When this representative of late Victorian science, culture, and values comes to rest in the year 802,701 he thinks that he has landed in a new Eden. His surroundings are like a garden, but one going to ruin rather than one flourishing and productive. Like many people from his "home time," however, the Time Traveler only reads the surface of this future world, and for some time he incorrectly interprets what he sees as signs of the noble march of progress down through future eons. After he is jarred into examining his new surroundings more closely, however, he comes to see the frail Weena for what she really is: a member of the herd on which her keepers, the subterranean Morlocks, feed. What Wells shows us is a projection of Victorian laissez-faire values, a time when machines have destroyed human initiative—and, in being allowed to do so, have destroyed Homo sapiens as well.

In the year 802,701 things are obviously not perfect. Wells means for readers to understand that progress as defined in his own times by proponents of cultural evolution and the survival-of-the-fittest ethic will only produce negative results. At some point in the Eloi and Morlocks' past, a division of labor occurred with the capitalists (Eloi) coming to depend totally upon the laborers (Morlocks) to operate the machines that ran the world. Gradually, the Eloi grew weaker and more passive; the Morlocks, kept underground to tend the factories, grew more brutal. Both subspecies of Homo sapiens were caught in a destructive symbiotic relationship, destructive at least in terms of how "human" either group could be said to be. What the Time Traveler confronts in the year 802,701 is the result of human *de*volution, a degeneration brought about because people no longer needed to struggle to survive and thus lost initiative. The world of the frail Weena is not paradise regained but the very essence of a Darwinian hell. On the evidence of *The Time Machine* it is obvious that Wells had mastered his teacher Huxley's lesson: It is fallacious to assume that escape from pain and suffering is a desirable goal. In the year 802,701 it is clear that such an escape has been responsible for the destruction of the human will to survive. What remains is a pale, unquestioning lassitude.

This future garden world is only an overgrown ruin of former human greatness, for the Eloi and the Morlocks are certainly not human but something beyond, and something far less. The outward decay of the buildings mirrors the creatures' interior erosion. It is also no accident that language itself has declined to a very simple level, for language is what marks the human intellectual capacity to question, evaluate, and explore. Weena can do none of these things. Wells even confronts his Time Traveler with a sphinx, the enigmatic figure that Oedipus had met so many centuries in the past. And the beast's unstated riddle remains the same: What is man? *The Time Machine*, of course, is Wells's attempt to provide readers with an answer.

Although the Time Traveler's sojourn in the year 802,701 makes up the longest section of the book, it is not Wells's final statement. Having failed to protect Weena from the Morlocks, the Time Traveler again takes to his machine. His next stop is brief, but long enough for Wells to show us that the Darwinian struggle has not ended: Although no humans are in evidence, a gigantic crablike creature and a huge butterfly are at odds with each other. Again the Time Traveler escapes, this time to a point even further into the earth's future, the year 30,000,000. This time there can be no mistaking Wells's intention. The second law of thermodynamics is relentlessly at work: The earth is grinding to a halt, its face turned to a red, dying sun. In the eerie half light, the Time Traveler watches a huge, tentacled creature wait at the edge of a sluggish ocean. Life on land seems to have been reduced to lichens and simple plants; on earth, everything is floundering back toward the point of its origin: the slack-tided sea. The devolutionary, entropic metaphor extends to the rest of the universe as well, for the dying sun's increased gravitational pull is dragging the planets toward their destruction. At every stop in his journey, the Time Traveler has witnessed a world degenerating by degrees, and he has found nothing that offers any hope for reversing the process.

Yet he returns to his own present, to Victorian England, and makes a vain effort to convince his listeners that something must be done. His dinner guests scoff at his tales and refuse to heed his warnings. The only alternative remaining for the Time Traveler is to escape again into the future, with the hope that his individual efforts to produce a change will make the necessary difference. Wells leaves unanswered the question whether the Time Traveler succeeded, for the man never returns. Thus our future, insofar as the reader is concerned, remains in jeopardy, since we cannot know what effects the Time Traveler's warning might have had on future humans.

For this reason, *The Time Machine* must be read as a warning to his—and future—times: Those in power must work to change human destiny or face the doom awaiting the human race. The yearning for the status quo that seemed to be such a desirable result of industrial progress in Victorian England was the exact thing that would make the horrors of the Morlocks and the Eloi inevitable. To remain unthinking and unquestioning—as capitalist or as worker—would ensure the destruction of human vitality and the natural human impulse for good that Wells believed were the key ingredients of human progress. The technology-produced world of 802,701 is devoid of morality and empty of humans, a world in which the "highest" creatures, the Morlocks and the Eloi, seem able only to walk in place, do what they have been programmed to do, and wait for the end.

TO THE LIGHTHOUSE

Type of work: Novel
Author: Virginia Woolf (1882–1941)
Type of plot: Psychological realism
Time of plot: c. 1910–1920
Locale: The Isle of Skye in the Hebrides
First published: 1927

This major psychological novel, based in part on the author's own family background, is significant for its impressionistic evocation of setting and character; its effective use of stream-of-consciousness technique; its complex, unified structure; and its advancement of Woolf's theory of androgynous personality.

Principal Characters

Mr. Ramsay, a professor of philosophy, a metaphysician of high order, an author, and the father of eight. Not really first-rate, as he realized by the time he was sixty, he knew also that his mind was still agile, his ability to abstract strong. Loved by his wife, he is nonetheless offered sympathy and consolation for the things he is not. Lithe, trim, the very prototype of the philosopher, he attracts many people to him and uses their feelings to buoy him in his weaknesses. Not truly a father, his gift for the ironic and sardonic arouses fear and hatred rather than respect among his children. Broken by his wife's and oldest son's deaths, he continues to endure and sharpen his mind on the fine whetstone of wit.

Mrs. Ramsay, a beautiful woman even in her aging; she is warm, compassionate, and devoted to the old-fashioned virtues of hearth, husband, and children. With an aura of graciousness and goodness about her, ineffable but pervasive, Mrs. Ramsay gathers about her guests, students, friends, and family at their summer home on the Isle of Skye. Loving and tender to her children, polite and pleasant to her guests, she impresses upon them all the sanctity of life and marriage, the elemental virtues. Mrs. Ramsay's love and reverence of life have its effect on all her guests, even an atheistic student of her husband and an aloof poet, but especially on Lily Briscoe whose self-revelation at the end of the novel is due in part to Mrs. Ramsay's influence.

James, the Ramsays' youngest son and his mother's favorite, though the child most criticized by the professor because the boy robs him of sympathy that he desperately needs. Sensitive and austere, James at six and sixteen suffers most the loss of his mother, taken from him at first by a calculating father's demands and later by her death. He and his sister Camilla make a pact of war against their father's tyranny of demands and oversights. Finally, on a trip to the lighthouse, the symbol of what had been denied him by his father, Mr. Ramsay praises his son's seamanship.

Prue, who dies in childbirth, **Andrew,** killed in World War I, **Nancy, Roger, Rose, Jasper,** and **Camilla,** called **Cam,** the other children of Mr. and Mrs. Ramsay. All the children resent their father and his dominance. Mrs. Ramsay regrets that they must grow up and lose the sensitivity and imagination that will come with adulthood.

Lily Briscoe, an artist and friend of the family who more than any other loved and cared for the weeks spent with the Ramsays in the Hebrides. Desperately in need of assurance, Lily has withheld love and affection from others until the summer she spends at the Ramsay cottage where she observes life with its fixed center and raw edges. Completely won over by Mrs. Ramsay, Lily almost gets her chance at life, and had the war not interfered, she might have married. She is not really a great artist, but during a visit to the Ramsay home after the war she experiences a moment of fulfilled vision, a feeling of devotion to the oldest cause, of a sense of oneness with all time, of sympathy for the human condition, and she is able to express this fleeting moment in a painting she had begun before Mrs. Ramsay's death.

Augustus Carmichael, a minor poet with one major success, a hanger-on, the only one who does not at first love his hostess but who finally discovers her genius years after her death. Laughed at by all the Ramsay children because of his yellow-tinted beard, the result of taking opium, as they imagine, he soaks up love and life without himself giving anything. His late fame as a poet is a surprise to all who know him.

Minta Doyle and **Paul Rayley,** two handsome guests who become engaged through Mrs. Ramsay's quiet management. Minta is like the young Mrs. Ramsay and sends out an aura of love and passion, while Paul, with his good looks and careful dress, is a foil for all affections and strong feelings. But the marriage turns out badly; Minta leads her own life and Paul takes a mistress. No longer lovers, they can afford to be friends.

William Bankes, a botanist, the oldest friend of Professor Ramsay. An aging widower, he first comes to visit with the Ramsays out of a sense of duty, but he stays on enraptured with life. The object of Lily Briscoe's undisguised affections, he appears to Mrs. Ramsay almost willing to become domesticated in spite of his eccentricities and set ways. Nothing comes of this relationship except a broadening of Lily's views on life.

Charles Tansley, Mr. Ramsay's protégé, a boorish young man who eventually is won over to the warmth and love of Mrs. Ramsy. It is his opinionated conviction that women cannot paint or write. Interested in abstract thought, he makes his career in scholarship.

Mrs. McNab, the old charwoman who acts as caretaker of the Ramsay house in the Hebrides during the ten years it stands empty.

Mrs. Bast, the cottager who helps Mrs. McNab get the house ready for the return of the Ramsay family.

George Bast, her son, who catches the rats and cuts the grass surrounding the Ramsay house.

Macalister, the aged Scottish boatman who takes Mr. Ramsay, Cam, and James on an expedition to the lighthouse. He tells the voyagers tales of winter, storm, and death.

The Story

Mrs. Ramsay promised James, her six-year-old son, that if the next day were fair he would be taken on a visit to the lighthouse they could see from the window of their summer home on the Isle of Skye. James, the youngest of Mrs. Ramsay's eight children, was his mother's favorite. The father of the family was a professor of philosophy whose students often thought he was inspiring and one of the foremost metaphysicians of the early twentieth century; but his own children, particularly the youngest, did not like him because he made sarcastic remarks.

Several guests were visiting the Ramsays at the time. There was young Mr. Tansley, Ramsay's student, who was also unpopular with the children because he seemed to delight in their discomfiture. Tansley was mildly in love with his hostess, despite her fifty years and her eight children. There was Lily Bricoe, who was painting a picture of the cottage with Mrs. Ramsay and little James seated in front of it. There was old Mr. Carmichael, a ne'er-do-well who amused the Ramsay youngsters because he had a white beard and a mustache tinged with yellow. There was also William Bankes, an aging widower, and Prue, the prettiest of the Ramsay daughters.

The afternoon went by slowly. Mrs. Ramsay went to the village to call on a sick woman. She spent several hours knitting stockings for the lighthouse keeper's child, whom they were planning to visit. Many people wondered how the Ramsays, particularly the wife, managed to be as hospitable and charitable as they were, for they were not rich; Mr. Ramsay could not possibly make a fortune by expounding Locke, Berkeley, and Hume to students or by publishing books on metaphysics.

Mr. Carmichael, pretending to read, had actually fallen asleep early after lunch. The children, except for James, who was busy cutting pictures out of a catalogue, had busied themselves in a game of cricket. Mr. Ramsay and Mr. Tansley had passed the time in a pointless conversation. Miss Briscoe had only made a daub or two of paint on her canvas. For some reason, the lines of the scene refused to come clear in her painting. She then went for a walk with Mr. Bankes along the shore.

Even the dinner went by slowly. The only occasion of interest to the children, which was one of tension to their mother, came when Mr. Carmichael asked the maid for a second bowl of soup, thereby angering his host, who liked to have meals dispatched promptly. As soon as the children had finished, their mother sent the younger ones to bed. Mrs. Ramsay hoped that Mr. Bankes would marry Lily Briscoe. She also thought how Lily always became seasick, so it was questionable whether she would want to accompany them in the small sailboat if they should go to the lighthouse the following day. Then she thought about the fifty pounds needed to make some necessary repairs on the house.

After dinner, Mrs. Ramsay went upstairs to the nursery. James had a boar's skull that his sister detested. Whenever Camilla tried to remove it from the wall and her sight, he burst into a frenzy of screaming. Mrs. Ramsay wrapped the boar's skull in her shawl. Afterward, she went downstairs and joined her husband in the library, where they sat throughout the evening. Mrs. Ramsay knitted, while Mr. Ramsay read. Before they went to bed, it was agreed that the trip for the next day would have to be canceled. The night had turned stormy.

Night followed night. The trip to the lighthouse was never made that summer, and the Ramsays did not return to their summer home for some years. In the meantime, Mrs. Ramsay died quietly in her sleep. By now, her daughter Prue had been married and died in childbirth. World War I began, and Andrew Ramsay enlisted and was sent to France, where he was killed by an exploding shell.

Time passed. The wallpaper in the house came loose from the walls. Books mildewed. In the kitchen, a cup was occasionally knocked down and broken by old Mrs. McNab, who came to look after the house from time to time. In the garden, the roses and the annual flowers grew wild or died.

Mr. Carmichael published a volume of poems during the war. About the same time his book appeared, daffodils and violets bloomed on the Isle of Skye. Mrs. McNab looked longingly at a warm cloak left in a closet. She wished the cloak belonged to her.

At last the war ended. Mrs. McNab recieved a telegram requesting that the house be put in order. For several days, the housekeeper worked, aided by two cleaning women. When the Ramsays arrived, the cottage was in order once more. Several visitors came again to share a summer at the cottage. Lily Briscoe returned for a quiet vacation. Mr. Carmichael, the succesful poet, also arrived.

One morning, Lily Briscoe came down to breakfast and wondered at the quiet that greeted her. No one had been down ahead of her, although she had expected that Mr. Ramsay and the two youngest children, James and Camilla, would have eaten early and departed for the long-postponed sail to the lighthouse, to which the youngsters had not been looking forward with joyful anticipation. Very shortly, the three straggled down; all had slept past the time they had intended to arise. After a swift breakfast, they disappeared toward the shore. Lily Briscoe watched them go. She had set up her canvas with the intention of once again trying to paint her picture of the cottage.

The journey to the island where the lighthouse stood was not very pleasant, as the children had expected. They had never really liked their father; he had taken too little time to understand them. He was short and sharp when they did things that seemed foolish to him, although these actions were perfectly comprehensible to his son and daughter. James, especially, expected to be blamed caustically and pointlessly if the crossing were slow or not satisfactory in some other way, for he had been delegated to handle the sheets and the tiller of the boat.

Mr. Ramsay strode down to the beach with his off-spring, each carrying a paper parcel to take to the keepers of the lighthouse. They soon set sail and pointed the prow of the sailboat toward the black and white striped pillar of the lighthouse in the hazy distance. Mr. Ramsay sat in the middle of the boat, along with an old fisherman and his son. They were to take over the boat in case of an emergency, for Mr. Ramsay had little trust in James as a reliable seaman. James himself sat in the stern, nerves tingling lest his father look up from his book and indulge in unnecessary and hateful criticism. His nervous tension, however, was needless, for within a few hours the little party reached the lighthouse, and Mr. Ramsay sprang ashore like a youngster, smiled back at his children, and praised his son for his seamanship.

Critical Evaluation

Because of its unity of theme and technique, *To the Lighthouse* is probably Virginia Woolf's most satisfying novel. In theme, it is her most direct fictional statement about the importance of an androgynous artistic vision: that ideal which is neither masculine nor feminine but partakes of both. The book was almost contemporaneous with her important essay on women and fiction, *A Room of One's Own*, and *Orlando*, her androgynous fictitional biography. In *A Room of One's Own*, she appeals for androgynous creation, arguing that it is fatal for a writer to emphasize gender. For Woolf, the mind that blends female and male themes "is naturally creative, incandescent and undivided." Many of her protagonists and most of the artists in her novels have both traditional masculine and feminine characteristics: Bernard in *The Waves*, Eleanor in *The Years*, Miss La Trobe in *Between the Acts*, and Lily Briscoe in *To the Lighthouse*. Each of these characters has an androgynous *consciousness*, even as Orlando completes the *physical* change from male to female.

To the Lighthouse clearly shows the deficiencies of the purely masculine (Mr. Ramsay) and the purely feminine (Mrs. Ramsay) personalities, and, as well, holds up the androgynous vision as a way of unifying the two—in the person of Lily Briscoe, the artist. Mr. Ramsay, a philosopher, has those qualities associated with the empirical view, while Mrs. Ramsay employs a mythopoetic vision. Mr. Ramsay is concerned with the discovery of truth, and his mind functions in a logical, reasoned fashion, moving, as he says, from A to Z, step-by-step. He worries that he has only so far reached Q. Mrs. Ramsay cares about details, about people's feelings, about her relationship with her husband and children; and her mind jumps and skips with the association of ideas—she can move from A to Z in one leap.

Mr. Ramsay is deficient in the attention he gives to his children and his wife, in concern for financial details, in awareness of social and international situations. His character is satirized by Lily, who always pictures him as seeing the whole of reality in a phantom kitchen table (the table is a traditional object for philosophic speculation). Mrs. Ramsay is lacking as well: she attempts to direct and fashion people's lives (she engineers the engagement of Minta and Paul and tries to match Lily Briscoe and William Bankes); she does not want her children to grow up; she cannot understand mathematics or history; she too often relies on men and their "masculine intelligence." The dinner scene shows Mrs. Ramsay's main strengths and weaknesses. She orchestrates the whole, directs the conversation, worries about the *Boeuf en Daube*, thinks about the lateness of the hour, makes sure all the guests are involved. Nevertheless, she lets her mind wander, looking ahead to the next details. She is the unifier in the first part of the book, but she fails because her vision is too limited; the trip to the lighthouse is not made, and she dies before the Ramsays can return to the island.

Lily Briscoe and her art become the true unifier of the

story's disparate elements. During the dinner party, as she remembers Charles Tansley's dictum that "Women can't write, women can't paint," she suddenly envisions the way to give her picture coherence, and she moves the saltcellar to remind herself. Her painting, however, remains incomplete, and, like the trip to the lighthouse, is not accomplished until many years later. Lily, an unmarried professional, embodies both rational (masculine) and imaginative (feminine) characteristics. She analyzes art with William Bankes and still feels emotionally attuned with Mrs. Ramsay. Lily becomes the central figure in the final section; her visions of Mrs. Ramsay and of Mr. Ramsay and the children finally landing at the lighthouse enable her to complete her work, uniting the rational and the imaginative into the androgynous whole which the painting symbolizes.

The novel's structure is thematically as well as techincally brilliant. The work has three parts: the first, entitled "The Window" takes place about 1910, the last, entitled "The Lighthouse," about 1920. The middle section is entitled "Time Passes" and narrates the intervening time period. The window in the first section functions as a symbol of the female principle, as the narrator returns again and again to Mrs. Ramsay in her place near the open window. Mrs. Ramsay is the center and unifier of the family, and even as different characters participate in various activities, their thoughts and glances return to Mrs. Ramsay. The reddish-brown stocking she is knitting is another emblem of her unifying power; but, like the trip to the lighthouse and Lily's painting, it is not com-

pleted in the first section. The thoughts of different characters are narrated by means of interior monologue, and Woolf makes skillful use of the theory of association of ideas. Mrs. Ramsay's mind is most often viewed, however, and she is the most realistic of the characters.

Early in the novel, the lighthouse, in its faraway light-giving aspects, functions as a female symbol. Mrs. Ramsay identifies herself with that lighthouse: "she was stern, she was searching, she was beautiful like that light." In the last section, however, the lighthouse becomes a masculine principle; when seen from nearby it is a "tower, stark and straight . . . barred with black and white." Nevertheless, the male and female aspects become joined in that section as well; James thinks, "For nothing was simply one thing. The other Lighthouse was true too." James and Camilla, therefore, come to understand their father as well as their dead mother. The line that Lily Briscoe draws in the center of her picture—perhaps her image of the lighthouse—enables her to complete her painting, uniting the masculine and the feminine.

The center section, "Time Passes," is narrated from the viewpoint of the house itself, as the wind over the years peels wallpaper; rusts pots; brings mildew, dust, spider webs, and rats. Important events in the lives of the Ramsays are inserted prosaically into this poetic interlude by means of square brackets.

To the Lighthouse is a difficult work, but each successive reading brings new insights into Woolf's techiniques and themes.

TOM JONES

Type of work: Novel
Author: Henry Fielding (1707–1754)
Type of plot: Comic epic
Time of plot: Early eighteenth century
Locale: England
First published: 1749

Tom Jones, a major contribution to the history of the English novel, has been admired by many readers as the most meticulously crafted book of its type. With neoclassic objectivity, humor, and fine psychological delicacy, Fielding dissects the motives of his characters to reveal universal truths about human nature.

Principal Characters

Tom Jones, a foundling. Although befriended by his foster father, Squire Allworthy, Tom encounters many vicissitudes, some of them of his own making, for he is a somewhat wild and foolish, though good-hearted young man. His wild ways, exaggerated by enemies, including Master Blifil, cause Tom to be cast off by Squire Allworthy. After Tom's goodness and virtue eventually triumph over disastrous circumstances, the young man is reconciled with the squire and, even more important, with Sophia Western, the beautiful and virtuous woman he loves. He is acknowledged as the squire's nephew when the secret of his real parentage becomes known.

Squire Allworthy, an extremely just and virtuous country gentleman who becomes Tom's foster father after the infant is discovered in the squire's bed. Tom's enemies play upon the squire's gullibility, for Allworthy, like many another honest man, finds it difficult to believe that there is dishonesty in other people. Eventually he sees Tom's essential goodness, receives his as his nephew, and makes the young man his heir.

Sophia Western, the virtuous daughter of a domineering country squire. She loves Tom Jones, even to facing down her father and aunt when they try to marry her off to Master Blifil and Lord Fellamar. Though she loves Tom, she is disappointed by his escapades, particularly those of an amorous nature, and until she is convinced he can be a faithful husband she refuses to accept his suit.

Squire Western, Sophia's domineering, profane father, who loves his hounds, his horses, and his bottle almost as much as his only child. When he insists upon forcing her to marry Master Blifil, the husband of his choice, Sophia is forced into running away from home, placing herself and her virtue in the path of adventure and danger. The squire, though uncouth, is a good man at heart. Both he and Squire Allworthy are exceptionally well-drawn characters.

Master Blifil, the villainous son of the squire's sister Bridget. A great hypocrite, he hides his villainy under a cloak of seeming honesty and virtue. He plays false witness against Tom Jones many times. He becomes Sophia Western's suitor only because he wants her money and hates Tom, the man she loves. His villainy is done, too, in the face of his knowing that Tom is really an older half brother, not a foundling.

Bridget Blifil, Squire Allworthy's seemingly virtuous spinster sister. She bears Tom out of wedlock and lets his become a foundling. Later she marries and has another son, Master Blifil. On her deathbed she sends to her brother a letter telling the story of Tom's parentage. The letter is stolen and concealed by her legitimate son.

Captain Blifil, Bridget's husband, who marries her for her money. He dies of apoplexy, however, before he can enjoy any of his wife's money.

Mr. Partridge, a schoolteacher and barber-surgeon. Long Tom's loyal, if loquacious, companion, he is for many years suspected of being Tom's father.

Jenny Jones, later **Mrs. Waters,** a maid in Mr. Partridge's house, she is accused of being Tom's mother, and her surname is given to him. As Mrs. Waters she has a brief love affair with Tom, much to the horror of some of his acquaintances, who believed the supposed mother and son have committed incest. Through her testimony the identity of Tom's real mother becomes known.

Mr. Dowling, a not-so-honest lawyer. Through his testimony Tom's identity is proved, as he corroborates Jenny Jones's statements. He keeps the secret for years, thinking that he is following Mr. Allworthy's wishes.

Black George Seagrim, so-called because of his extremely black beard, a rustic and poacher. Though befriended by Tom, he steals from the young man and plays him ill turns.

Molly Seagrim, a young woman of easy virtue, Black George's daughter. Tom's escapades with her cause him grave trouble until her affairs with other men take some of the blame from him.

The Rev. Roger Thwackum, an Anglican clergyman retained by Mr. Allworthy to tutor Tom Jones and Master

Blifil during their boyhood. A self-righteous, bigoted man, he voices his prejudices at all times. He beats Tom often and severely, living up to his name.

Mr. Thomas Square, a deistically inclined philosopher who is a pensioner in Mr. Allworthy's household and Mr. Thwackum's opponent in endless debates over the efficacy of reason and religious insight. Though he dislikes Tom Jones, he makes a deathbed confession that clears Tom of some of his supposed misdeeds.

Lady Bellaston, a sensual noblewoman of loose morals who takes a fancy to Tom Jones and, when she is spurned, tries to do him a great deal of evil.

Mrs. Western, Lady Bellaston's cousin and Sophia's aunt. To satisfy her own social pretensions she tries to marry off Sophia to Lord Fellamar against the girl's will.

Mrs. Fitzpatrick, Sophia's cousin. They travel to London together.

Mr. Fitzpatrick, her jealous husband. Tom is jailed for wounding him in a duel.

Lord Fellamar, a licentious nobleman who makes love

to Sophia and, with Mrs. Western's approval, even attempts to ravish the girl in order to force her to marry him. Misled by Lady Bellaston's advice, he tries to have Tom Jones impressed into the naval service.

Mrs. Arabella Hunt, a pretty and wealthy widow who offers formally by letter to marry Tom Jones. His refusal of this handsome offer helps reestablish Tom with Sophia.

Honour Blackmore, Sophia's loyal, if somewhat selfish, maid, who shares in most of her mistress' adventures.

Mrs. Miller, Tom's landlady in London. Convinced of his virtue by his many good deeds she pleads on his behalf with Squire Allworthy and is instrumental in helping restore Tom to his foster father's good graces.

Nancy and **Betty Miller,** the landlady's daughters.

Mr. Nightingale, Tom's fellow lodger at the Miller house. Tom persuades the elder Nightingale to permit the son to marry Nancy.

Mr. Summer, a handsome young cleric befriended as a student by Mr. Allworthy. It was he who seduced Bridget Allworthy and fathered Tom Jones.

The Story

Squire Allworthy lived in retirement in the country with his sister Bridget. Returning from a visit to London, he was surprised upon entering his room to find an infant lying on his bed. His discovery caused astonishment and consternation in the household, for the squire himself was a childless widower. The next day, Miss Bridget and the squire inquired in the community to discover the baby's mother. Their suspicions were shortly fixed upon Jenny Jones, who had spent many hours in the squire's home while nursing Miss Bridget through a long illness. The worthy squire sent for the girl and in his gentle manner reprimanded her for her wicked behavior, assuring her, however, that the baby would remain in his home under the best of care. Fearing malicious gossip in the neighborhood, Squire Allworthy sent Jenny away.

Jenny Jones had been a servant in the house of a schoolmaster, Mr. Partridge, who had educated the young woman during her four years in his house. Because of Jenny's comely face, Mrs. Partridge was jealous of her. Neighborhood gossip soon convinced Mrs. Partridge that her husband was the father of Jenny's son, whereupon Squire Allworthy called the schoolmaster before him and talked to him at great length concerning morality. Mr. Partridge, deprived of his school, his income, and his wife, also left the country.

Shortly afterward, Captain Blifil won the heart of Bridget Allworthy. Eight months after their marriage, Bridget bore a son. The squire thought it would be advisable to rear the foundling and his sister's child together. The foundling had been named Jones, after his mother.

Squire Allworthy became exceedingly fond of the foundling. Captain Blifil died during his son's infancy,

and Master Blifil grew up as Squire Allworthy's acknowledged heir. Otherwise, he remained on even terms with the foundling so far as opportunities for advancement were concerned. Tom, however, was such a mischievous lad that he had only one friend among the servants, the gamekeeper, Black George, an indolent man with a large family. Mr. Thwackum and Mr. Square, who considered Tom a wicked soul, were hired to instruct the lads. Tom's many deceptions were always discovered through the combined efforts of Mr. Thwackum, Mr. Square, and Master Blifil, who disliked Tom more and more as he grew older. It had been assumed by all that Mrs. Blifil would dislike Tom, but at times she seemed to show greater affection for him than for her own son. In turn, the compassionate squire took Master Blifil to his heart and became censorious of Tom.

Mr. Western, who lived on a neighboring estate, had a daughter whom he loved more than anyone else in the world. Sophia had a special fondness for Tom because of a kind deed he had performed for her when they were still children. At the age of twenty, Master Blifil had become a favorite with the young ladies, while Tom was considered a ruffian by all but Mr. Western, who admired his ability to hunt. Tom spent many evenings at the Western home, with every opportunity to see Sophia, for whom his affections were increasing daily. One afternoon, Tom had the good fortune to be nearby when Sophia's horse ran away. When Tom attempted to rescue her, he broke his arm. He was removed to Mr. Western's house, where he received medical care and remained to recover from his hurt. One day, he and Sophia had occasion to be alone in the garden, where they exchanged confessions of love.

Squire Allworthy became mortally ill. The doctor assumed that he was dying and sent for the squire's relatives. With his servants and family gathered around him, the squire announced the disposal of his wealth, giving generously to Tom. Tom was the only one satisfied with his portion; his only concern was the impending death of his foster father and benefactor. On the way home from London to see the squire, Mrs. Blifil died suddenly. When the squire was pronounced out of danger, Tom's joy was so great that he became drunk through toasting the squire's health, and he quarreled with young Blifil.

Sophia's aunt, Mrs. Western, perceived her niece's interest in Blifil; wishing to conceal her affection for Tom, Sophia had given Blifil the greater part of her attention when she was with the two young men. Informed by his sister of Sophia's conduct, Mr. Western suggested to squire Allworthy that a match be arranged between Blifil and Sophia. When Mrs. Western told the young girl of the proposed match, Sophia thought that she meant Tom, and she immediately disclosed her passion for the foundling. Nevertheless, it was unthinkable that Mr. Western, much as he liked Tom, would ever allow his daughter to marry a man without a family and a fortune, and Mrs. Western forced Sophia to receive Blifil under the threat of exposing the girl's real affection for Tom. Sophia met Tom secretly in the garden, and the two lovers vowed constancy. Mr. Western discovered them and went immediately to Squire Allworthy with his knowledge.

Aware of his advantage, Blifil told the squire that on the day he lay near death, Tom was out drinking and singing. The squire felt that he had forgiven Tom's wrongs, but Tom's seeming unconcern for the squire's health infuriated the good man. He sent for Tom, reproached him, and banished him from his house.

With the help of Black George, the gamekeeper, and Mrs. Honour, Sophia's maid, Tom and Sophia were able to exchange love letters. When Sophia was confined to her room because she refused to marry Blifil, she bribed her maid to flee with her from her father's house. Tom, setting out to seek his fortune, went to an inn with a small company of soldiers. A fight followed in which he was severely injured, and a barber was summoned to treat his wound. When Tom had told the barber his story, the man surprisingly revealed himself to be Partridge, the schoolmaster, banished years before because he was suspected of being Tom's father. When Tom was well enough to travel, the two men set out together on foot.

Before they had gone far, they heard screams of a woman in distress and came upon a woman struggling with a soldier who had deceived her and led her to that lonely spot. Promising to take her to a place of safety, Tom accompanied the unfortunate woman to the nearby village of Upton, where the landlady of the inn refused to receive them because of the woman's torn and disheveled clothing. When she heard the true story of the woman's misfortune and had been assured that the woman

was the lady of Captain Waters, a well-known officer, she nevertheless relented. Mrs. Waters invited Tom to dine with her so that she could thank him properly for her rescue.

Meanwhile, a lady and her maid arrived at the inn and proceeded to their rooms. They were followed, several hours later, by an angry gentleman in pursuit of his wife. Learning from the chambermaid that there was a woman resembling his wife in the inn, he burst into Mrs. Waters' chambers, only to confront Tom Jones. At his intrusion, Mrs. Waters began to scream. Abashed, the gentleman identified himself as Mr. Fitzpatrick and retreated with apologies. Shortly after this disturbance had subsided, Sophia and Mrs. Honour arrived at the inn. When Partridge unknowingly revealed Tom's relationship with Mrs. Waters and the embarrassing situation that Mr. Fitzpatrick had disclosed, Sophia, grieved by Tom's fickleness, decided to continue on her way. Before leaving the inn, however, she had Mrs. Honour place on Tom's empty bed a muff that she knew he would recognize as hers.

Soon after setting out, Sophia overtook Mrs. Fitzpatrick, who had arrived at the inn early the previous evening and who had fled during the disturbance caused by her husband. Mrs. Fitzpatrick was Sophia's cousin, and they decided to go on to London together. In London, Sophia proceeded to the home of Lady Bellaston, who was known to her through Mrs. Western. Lady Bellaston sympathetized with Sophia.

Unable to overtake Sophia, Tom and Partridge followed her to London, where Tom took lodgings in the home of Mrs. Miller, a home Squire Allworthy patronized on his visits to the city. The landlady had two daughters, Nancy and Betty, and a lodger, Mr. Nightingale, who was obviously in love with Nancy. Tom found congenial residence with Mrs. Miller, and he became friends with Mr. Nightingale. Partridge, who still harbored a hope of future advancement, was still with Tom. Repeated visits to Lady Bellaston and Mrs. Fitzpatrick finally gave Tom the opportunity to meet Sophia during an intermission at a play. There Tom was able to allay Sophia's doubts as to his love for her. During his stay with the Millers, Tom learned that Mr. Nightingale's father objected to his marrying Nancy. Through the kindness of his heart, Tom persuaded the elder Nightingale to permit the marriage, to Mrs. Miller's great delight.

Mr. Western had learned of Sophia's whereabouts from Mrs. Fitzpatrick. He came to London and took Sophia from Lady Bellaston's house to his own lodgings. When Mrs. Honour brought the news to Tom, he was in despair. Penniless, he could not hope to marry Sophia, and now his beloved was in the hands of her father once more. Then Partridge brought news that Squire Allworthy was coming to London and was bringing with him Master Blifil to marry Sophia. In his distress, Tom went to see Mrs. Fitzpatrick but encountered her jealous husband on her doorstep. In the duel that followed, Tom wounded

Fitzpatrick and was carried off to jail.

There he was visited by Partridge, the friends he had made in London, and Mrs. Waters, who had been traveling with Mr. Fitzpatrick since their meeting in Upton. When Partride and Mrs. Waters met in Tom's cell, Partridge recognized her as Jenny Jones, Tom's reputed mother. Horrified, he revealed his knowledge to everyone, including Squire Allworthy, who by that time had arrived in London with Blifil.

At Mrs. Miller's lodgings, so many people had praised Tom's goodness and kindness that Squire Allworthy had almost made up his mind to forgive the foundling when news of Tom's conduct with Mrs. Waters reached his ears. Fortunately, however, the cloud was soon dispelled by Mrs. Waters herself, who assured the squire that Tom was no son of hers but the child of his sister Bridget and a student whom the squire had befriended. Tom's true father had died before his son's birth, and Bridget had concealed her shame by putting the baby on her brother's bed upon his return from a long visit to London. Later, she had paid Jenny liberally to let suspicion fall upon her former maid.

Squire Allworthy also learned that Bridget had claimed Tom as her son in a letter written before her death, a letter Blifil probably had destroyed. There was futher proof that Blifil had plotted to have Tom hanged for murder. Fitzpatrick, however, had not died, and he recovered sufficiently to acknowledge himself the aggressor in the duel; Tom was released from prison.

Upon these disclosures of Blifil's villainy, Squire Allworthy dismissed Blifil and made Tom his true heir. Once Tom's proper station had been revealed, Mr. Western withdrew all objections to his suit. Reunited, Tom and Sophia were married and retired to Mr. Western's estate in the country.

Critical Evaluation

Henry Fielding was a poet and a playwright, a journalist and a jurist, as well as a pioneer in the formal development of the modern novel. His early poetry may be disregarded, but his dramatic works gave Fielding the training that later enabled him to handle adeptly the complex plots of his novels. Although he wrote perhaps half a dozen novels (some attributions are disputed), Fielding is best remembered for *The History of Tom Jones, a Foundling*, as it was originally titled. This novel contains a strong infusion of autobiographical elements. The character Sophia, for example, was based on Fielding's wife Charlotte, who was his one great love. They eloped in 1734 and had ten years together before she died in 1744. Squire Allworthy combined traits of a former schoolmate from Eton named George Lyttleton (to whom the novel is dedicated), and a generous benefactor of the Fielding family named James Ralph. Moreover, Fielding's origins in a career army family and his rejection of that background shaped his portrayal of various incidental military personnel in this and his other novels; he had an anti-army bias. Fielding's own feelings of revulsion against urban living are reflected in the conclusion of *Tom Jones* (and in his other novels): the "happy ending" consists of a retreat to the country. Published a scant five years before Fielding's death, *Tom Jones* was a runaway best-seller, going through four editions within a twelve-month period.

The structure of the novel is carefully divided into eighteen books in a fashion similar to the epic form that Fielding explicitly praised. Of those eighteen books, the first six are set on the Somersetshire estate of Squire Allworthy. Books 7 through 12 deal with events on the road to London, and the culmination of the six books is laid in London. The very midpoint of the novel, books 9 and 10, covers the hilarious hiatus at the inn in Upton.

Apparent diversions and digressions are actually intentional exercises in character exposition, and all episodes are deliberately choreographed to advance the plot—sometimes in ways not evident until later. Everything contributes to the overall organic development of the novel.

This kind of coherence was intimately connected with Fielding's preoccupation with the craft of fiction. It is no accident that *Tom Jones* is one of the most carefully and meticulously written novels in the history of English literature. It is, in fact, remarkably free of inconsistencies and casual errors. Fielding saw his task as a novelist to be a "historian" of human nature and human events, and he felt obligated to emphasize the moral aspect of his work. More important, Fielding introduced each of his eighteen books with a chapter about the craft of prose fiction. Indeed, the entire novel is dotted with intercalary chapters on the craft of the novel and on literary criticism. The remainder of the novel applies the principles enunciated in the chapters on proper construction of prose fiction—an amazing tour de force. The detailed analyses in themselves constitute a substantial work of literary criticism; however, Fielding amplified these theories with his own demonstration of their application by writing a novel, *Tom Jones*, according to his own principles. So compelling a union of theory and practice rendered Fielding's hypotheses virtually unassailable.

As Fielding made practical application of his theories of craftsmanship, their validity became readily apparent in his handling of characterization. He viewed human nature ambivalently, as a combination of good and bad. Whereas the bad person had almost no hope of redemption, the fundamentally good person could be somewhat tinged with bad but nonetheless worthy for all that, according to Fielding. Therefore, the good person could occasionally be unwise (as Allworthy was) or indiscreet (as Jones often was) but still be an estimable human being, for such a person was more credible as a "good" person, Fielding thought, than the one who was without defect. Consequently, the villain Blifil is hopelessly wicked, but the hero Tom Jones is essentially good, although morally flawed. To succeed, Jones had to improve morally—to cultivate prudence and religion, as Squire Allworthy recommended. Some minor characters are not so fully psychologized—they are essentially allegorical, representing ideas (Thwackum and Square, for example)—yet overall, Fielding's command of characterization is impressive. At the same time, he does not allow character sketches to dominate the novel, for all of them are designed to contribute to the development of the story. Such a system of priorities provides insight into Fielding's aesthetic and epistemological predispositions.

Fielding subscribed to a fundamentally neoclassical set of values, ethically and aesthetically. He saw the novel as a mirror of life, not an illumination of life. He valued literary craftsmanship; he assumed a position of detached objectivity; he esteemed wit; and he followed the neoclassical unity of action: his plot brought Tom Jones full circle from a favored position to disgrace back to the good graces of Squire Allworthy and Sophia. In the course of the book, Fielding achieves aesthetic distance by commenting critically on the form of the novel. The easygoing development of the plot also reveals Fielding's detachment and objectivity, and the great variety in the types of characters which he presents is another indication of his neoclassical inclinations toward universality. Above all, however, it is Fielding's moral stance that unequivocally marks him as a neoclassicist.

TREASURE ISLAND

Type of work: Novel
Author: Robert Louis Stevenson (1850–1894)
Type of plot: Adventure romance
Time of plot: 1740s
Locale: England and the Spanish Main
First published: 1881–1882 (serial), 1883 (book)

A favorite boys' adventure story, Treasure Island *is also a kind of "education" novel concerning Jim Hawkins' rites of passage into the dangerous world of mature responsibilities. Stevenson's romance is noted for its swift, clearly depicted action; its memorable character types, especially Long John Silver; and its sustained atmosphere of menace.*

Principal Characters

Jim Hawkins, the principal narrator, a bright, courageous boy. His father owns the Admiral Benbow Inn, where Billy Bones hides. In Bones's sea chest, Jim finds a map of Captain Flint's buried treasure.

Dr. Livesey, who treats Jim's dying father and later the wounded mutineers on Treasure Island.

Squire Trelawney, who finances the treasure hunt and outsmarts the pirates.

Captain Smollett, captain of the expedition's ship, the *Hispaniola*.

Captain Bill Bones, who steals the map and sings, "Fifteen men on a dead man's chest." He dies of fright when the pirates bring him his death warning.

Black Dog, who discovers Bones's hiding place and is almost killed in their fight in the inn parlor.

Blind Pew, a deformed pirate who delivers the Black Spot death notice. He is trampled to death by the mounted revenue officers who attack the pirate gang searching for Bill Bones's sea chest.

Long John Silver, a one-legged ship's cook who owns a pet parrot called Captain Flint. He gathers a crew for the *Hispaniola*, from pirates whom he can control. Once he saves Jim from their fury. He manages to get back to the West Indies with a bag of coins.

Ben Gunn, a pirate marooned by Captain Flint on Treasure Island. He moves the treasure and thus can keep it from the pirates and turn it over to Squire Trelawney.

Israel Hands, a pirate shot by Jim after he tries to kill Jim with a knife.

The Story

Young Jim Hawkins always remembered the day the strange seaman, Bill Bones, came looking for lodgings at his father's inn, the Admiral Benbow. He came plodding up to the inn door, where he stood for a time and looked around Black Hill Cove. Jim heard him singing snatches of an old sea song: "Fifteen men on a dead man's chest, Yo-ho-ho, and a bottle of rum."

When he learned from Jim's father that the inn was a quiet one with little trade, he declared it was just the berth for an old seaman. From that time, the strange guest—a retired captain, he called himself—kept watch on the coast and the land road by day and made himself free in the taproom of the inn at night. There he drank and sang and swore great oaths while he told fearsome tales of the Spanish Main. Bones was wary of all visiting seamen, and he paid Jim Hawkins to be on the lookout for a one-legged sailor in particular. He was so terrible in his speech and manners that Jim's father, a sick man, never had the courage to ask for more than the one reckoning Bill Bones had paid the day he came to the

inn. He stayed on without ever clinking another coin into the inn till for his meals and lodging.

The one-legged sailor never came to the inn, but another seaman named Black Dog did. The two men fought in the inn parlor, to the terror of Jim and his mother, before Captain Bones chased his visitor up the road and out of sight. He fell down in a fit when he came back to the inn. Dr. Livesey came in to attend to Jim's father and cautioned Captain Bones to contain himself and drink less.

Jim's father died soon afterward. On the day of the funeral, a deformed blind man named Pew tapped his way up to the door of the Admiral Benbow. The man forced Jim to lead him to the captain. Bill Bones was so terrified when the blind man gave him the Black Spot, the pirates' death notice, that he had a stroke and died.

Jim and his mother took the keys to his sea chest from the dead man's pocket and opened it to find the money due them. As they were examining the contents, they heard the tapping of the blind man's stick on the road.

Jim pocketed an oilskin packet, and he and his mother left hurriedly by the back door of the inn as a gang of men broke in to search for Captain Bones's chest. Mounted revenue officers arrived and scattered the gang. Blind Pew was trampled to death by the charging horses.

Jim gave the packet to Dr. Livesey and Squire Trelawney. The three discovered that it contained a map locating the hidden treasure of the bloody buccaneer, Captain Flint. Squire Trelawney was intrigued and decided to outfit a ship in which to sail after the treasure. The doctor threw in his lot and invited Jim to come along as cabin boy.

In Bristol, Trelawney purchased a schooner, the *Hispaniola*, and hired Long John Silver as the ship's cook. Silver promised to supply a crew. Jim went to Bristol and met Silver, who had only one leg. He was alarmed when he saw Black Dog again in the inn operated by Silver, but Silver's smooth talk quieted Jim's suspicions.

After the *Hispaniola* had sailed, Captain Smollett, hired by Squire Trelawney to command the ship, expressed his dislike of the first mate and the crew and complained that Silver had more real authority with the crew than he did. One night Jim, in a barrel after an apple, overheard Silver discussing mutiny with members of the crew. Before Jim had a chance to reveal the plot to his friends, the island was sighted.

The prospects of treasure on the island caused the disloyal members of the crew to pay little attention to Captain Smollett's orders; even the loyal ones were hard to manage. Silver shrewdly kept his party under control. The captain wisely allowed part of the crew to go ashore; Jim smuggled himself along in order to spy on Silver and the men on the island. Ashore, Silver killed two of the crew who refused to join the mutineers. Jim, alone, met Ben Gunn, who was with captain Flint when the treasure was buried. Gunn told Jim that he had been marooned on the island three years before.

While Jim was ashore, Dr. Livesey went to the island and found Captain Flint's stockade. When he heard the scream of one of the men Silver murdered, he returned to the *Hispaniola*, where it was decided that the honest men would move to the fort within the stockade. Several dangerous trips in an overloaded boat completed the move. During the last trip, the mutineers aboard the ship unlimbered the ship's gun. Squire Trelawney shot one seaman from the boat.

In the meantime, the gang ashore saw what was afoot and made efforts to keep Jim's friends from occupying the stockade. Squire Trelawney and his party took their posts in the fort after the enemy had been repulsed. The mutineers on the *Hispaniola* fired round shot into the stockade but did little damage.

After leaving Ben Gunn, the marooned seaman, Jim made his way to the stockade. The *Hispaniola* now flew the Jolly Roger skull and crossbones. Carrying a flag of truce, Silver approached the stockade and offered to parley. He was admitted by the defenders and demanded the treasure chart in exchange for the safe return of Squire Trelawney's party to England. Captain Smollett would concede nothing, and Silver returned to his men in a rage. The stockade party prepared for the coming battle. A group of the pirates attacked from two sides, swarmed over the paling, and engaged the defenders in hand-to-hand combat. In the close fighting, the pirates were reduced to one man, who fled back to his gang in the jungle. The loyal party was reduced to Squire Trelawney, Dr. Livesey, Captain Smollett, and Jim.

During the lull after the battle, Jim sneaked off and borrowed Ben Gunn's homemade boat. He rowed out to the *Hispaniola* under cover of darkness and cut the schooner adrift. In trying to return to shore, he was caught offshore by coastal currents. Daylight had come, and Jim could see that the *Hispaniola* was also aimlessly adrift. When the ship bore down upon him, he jumped to the bowsprit. Ben Gunn's little boat was smashed. Jim found himself on board alone with pirate Israel Hands, who had been wounded in a fight with another pirate. Jim took command and proceeded to beach the ship. Pursued by Hands, he climbed quickly to a crosstree just before Hands threw his knife into the mast not more than a foot below Jim as he climbed. Jim had time to prime and reload his pistols, and he shot the pirate after he had pinned the boy to the mast with another knife throw.

Jim removed the knife from his shoulder, made the ship safe by removing the sails, and returned to the stockade at night, only to find it abandoned by his friends and now in the hands of the pirates. When Silver's parrot, Captain Flint, drew attention to the boy's presence, the pirates captured him. Dissatisfied with the buccaneer's methods of gaining the treasure, Silver's men grumbled. One attempted to kill Jim, who had bragged to them of his exploits on behalf of his friends. For reasons of his own, Silver, however, took the boy's side and swore he would also take the part of Squire Trelawney. Silver's disaffected mates met Silver, gave him the Black Spot, and deposed him as their chief. The pirate leader talked his way out of his difficulty by showing them, to Jim's amazement and to their delight, Captain Flint's chart of Treasure Island.

Dr. Livesey came under a flag of truce to the stockade to administer to the wounded pirates. He learned from Jim that Silver had saved the boy's life, and Jim heard, to his mystification, that the doctor had given Captain Flint's chart to Silver.

Following the directions of the chart, the pirates went to find the treasure. They approached the hiding place and heard a high voice singing the pirate chantey, "Yo-ho-ho, and a bottle of rum." The voice also spoke the last words of Captain Flint. The men were terrified until Silver recognized Ben Gunn's voice. Then the pirates found the treasure cache opened and the treasure gone. When they uncovered only a broken pick and some boards, they turned on Silver and Jim. At this moment, Jim's friends, with Ben Gunn, arrived to rescue the boy.

Early in his stay on the island Ben Gunn had discovered the treasure and carried it to his cave. After Dr. Livesey had learned all of this from Gunn, the stockade was abandoned and the useless chart given to Silver. Squire Trelawney's party moved to Gunn's safe and well-provisioned quarters.

The *Hispaniola* had been floated by a tide; conse-quently, the group left Treasure Island, leaving on it three escaped buccaneers. They sailed to a West Indies port where, with the connivance of Ben Gunn, John Silver escaped the ship with a bag of coins. A full crew was taken on, and the schooner voyaged back to Bristol. There the treasure was divided among the survivors of the adventure. "Drink and the devil had done for the rest."

Critical Evaluation

Although Robert Louis Stevenson produced a large variety of writings during his relatively short life, he is largely remembered now as the writer of one great horror story, *The Strange Case of Dr. Jekyll and Mr. Hyde* (1886), and two classics of juvenile fiction, *Treasure Island* and *Kidnapped* (1886). Such a view is undoubtedly unfair and slights many valuable literary accomplishments, but the fact that these three works have endured not only as citations in literary histories but as readable, exciting, essentially contemporary books is a tribute to their author's genius. *Treasure Island* remains Stevenson's supreme achievement. Although critics may debate its "seriousness," few question its status as the purest and most perfect of adventure stories. According to Stevenson, the book was born out of his fascination with a watercolor map he himself drew of an imagined treasure island.

When Jim Hawkins begins by stating that he is telling the story in retrospect, at the request of "Squire Trelawney, Dr. Livesey, and the rest of these gentlemen," readers are assured that all the principals survived the quest successfully. Although many exciting scenes will ensue and the heroes will face great danger on a number of occasions, readers know that they will overcome all such obstacles. Thus, the suspense centers on *how* they escape, not on their personal survival as such. At the same time, by denying details of either the precise time of the adventure (sometime prior to "17—") or the exact location, Stevenson sets readers imaginatively free to enjoy the story unencumbered by the specifics of when or where.

By introducing the mysterious, threatening Bill Bones into the serene atmosphere of the Admiral Benbow Inn, Stevenson immersed readers directly into the story. The strange secret of Bones's background and nature creates the novel's initial excitement, which is then intensified by his apparent fear and subsequent encounters with Black Dog and Blind Pew. In all, the sequence that begins with Bones's arrival and ends with Pew's death serves as an overture to the adventure and sets up most of the important elements in the story, especially Captain Flint's map, which directs the group to Treasure Island, and the warnings to beware of "the seafaring man with one leg," which prepares readers for the archvillain of the tale, Long John Silver.

In the classic adventure-story pattern, an ordinary individual, Jim Hawkins, living a normal, routine life, is suddenly thrust into an extraordinary and dangerous situation. Although the hero is involuntarily pressed into danger, he nevertheless can extricate himself and return the situation to normality only through his own efforts. The adventure story is, therefore, usually to some extent a "coming of age" novel, whether the hero be fourteen years old or sixty-four years old. Since *Treasure Island* is essentially a book for young readers, it is appropriate that it center on the transition of its hero from boyhood to manhood.

Near the beginning of the book, the death of Jim's father frees Jim to seek his fortune and places the responsiblity upon him to find it for the sake of his widowed mother. Without a father of his own, Jim can look to the other male father-figures as substitutes. He finds two: Dr. Livesey, who represents stability, maturity, and moral responsibility, and John Silver, who suggests imagination, daring, bravado, and energy. Between these two and, more important, through his own actions, Jim finds his own manhood along with the treasure.

Jim's education begins with the act of searching the belongings of the dead Bill Bones despite the proximity of Pew's pirate band. To accomplish this feat, however, he needs his mother's support. Once the *Hispaniola* sets sail, however, he is on his own. The next stage in his growth occurs when, crouching in the apple barrel, he overhears Silver reveal his plans to his coconspirators. Jim keeps calm, cooly informs his friends, and with them, devises survival tactics. His initial positive, independent action takes place when they first reach the island and he goes off on his own, without a specific plan; but he is sure that he can further the cause in some undetermined way. He wanders in the woods and meets Ben Gunn, rejoins his party at the stockade, and engages in his first combat.

Next, Jim makes a second solo trip, but this time he has a definite course of action in mind; he plans to board the *Hispaniola* and cut it loose to drift inland with the tide, thus depriving the pirates of a refuge and an escape route. His final test in action comes on board the boat, when he encounters the evil first mate, Israel Hands. When Hands tries to manipulate him, Jim sees through the deception and, acting with considerable courage and dexterity, manages to outmaneuver the experienced pirate. Finally, faced with an enraged adversary, Jim remains calm and, with a knife sticking in his own shoulder, still manages to shoot the villain.

His final test of manhood is not physical, however, but moral. Returning to the stockade, which he still believes to be occupied by his friends, Jim is captured by the pirates. Given the opportunity a short time later to talk privately with Dr. Livesey, Jim refuses to escape: "No . . . you know right well you wouldn't do the thing yourself, neither you, nor squire, nor captain, and no more will I. Silver trusted me, I passed my word, and back I go." Therefore, Jim puts his word above his life and consequently he signals the transition not just from boy to man but, more important to Stevenson, from boy to gentleman.

Although Jim's development is important to the novel, the most vivid and memorable element in the book remains the character of Long John Silver. All critics pointed out the obvious about him—he is both bad and good, cruel and generous, despicable and admirable. Some have tried to fuse these elements into a single character "type," a "hero-villain," in which the good and bad are traced back to a common source. Such an effort is probably wrong: Silver is both good and bad, and his role in the novel demands both kinds of actions. Rather than try to "explain" Silver psychologically, it is probably more profitable to analyze the ways in which Stevenson manipulates the readers' feelings toward the character.

In any pirate story aimed at youth, the author faces a moral and artistic dilemma. On the one hand, pirates can hardly be presented as moral exemplars or heroes; they must be criminals and cutthroats. On the other hand, they are the most romantically attractive and interesting characters to the young—or even adult—reader. Enhance their attractiveness and the book becomes morally distorted; mute it and the book becomes dull.

One solution for the dilemma is to mitigate their badness by introducing an element of moral ambiguity into the characterization and behavior of some of them without denying the evil effects of their actions and then to separate the "good-bad" villains from the "bad-bad" ones. Stevenson uses this technique in *Treasure Island*. Silver is separated from his purely villainous cronies and set against the truly evil figures, Israel Hands and George Merry, with the other faceless pirates remaining in the background.

Stevenson mitigates Silver's evil side with two simple strategies: he presents the ruthless, cruel aspects of Silver's character early in the novel and lets his better side reveal itself late in the book, and he keeps the "evil" Silver at a distance and gives readers an intimate view only of the relatively good Silver. Therefore, although readers never forget the viciousness of Silver's early words and deeds, they recede into the background more and more as the adventure goes on.

Readers are prepared for the bad Long John Silver by the many early warnings to beware of the one-legged man. Then readers see him manipulate Squire Trelawney and even Jim in their first encounters. Therefore, readers admire his role-playing but fear the conspiratorial evil that obviously lies behind it. Silver's treachery is evident in the apple barrel scene, especially in his callous "vote" to kill all the nonconspirators when given the chance. Silver reaches the peak of his villainy in the killing of a sailor who refuses to join the mutiny, first stunning the sailor with his crutch and then knifing him to death.

Even these two evidences of Silver's badness, however, are seen at a distance, from inside an apple barrel and from behind a clump of trees. When Silver moves to the center of the novel and assumes an intimate relationship with Jim, his character is softened, and by the time Silver and Jim become unwilling partners in survival, the pirate's image and status have considerably changed.

The early view of Silver suggests that he is not only evil but invincible. As he becomes less one-dimensionally evil, he also becomes increasingly vulnerable, and vulnerability always stimulates sympathy in a reader, regardless of the character's moral status. As the tide begins to turn against the pirates, Silver begins to lose control not only of the treasure-hunting expedition, but even of his own men. This erosion of power is signaled by an increasing emphasis on his own physical disability. The John Silver who must crawl on his hands and knees out of the stockade, after the failure of his "embassy," is a far cry from the Silver who can knock down an opponent with a flying crutch and then pounce on him like an animal.

Silver's glibness and adroitness in manipulating the good men of the *Hispaniola* were components of his villainy in the first parts of the book, but when Silver is threatened by a mutiny of his own men and must utilize those same talents to save himself and Jim, they become virtues. Although he is obviously motivated by an instinct for self-preservation, Silver does protect Jim from the others and conveys a feeling of honestly liking and wanting to help the lad.

Thus, the morally ambiguous ending of the novel is the only one artistically possible. John Silver has not been bad enough to hang, and it is hard to imagine his vitality stifled in prison; yet if he has edged away from the villains, he hardly qualifies as a hero. He is neither punished nor greatly rewarded for his machinations and heroics but left to seek another fortune elsewhere.

THE TRIAL

Type of work: Novel
Author: Franz Kafka (1883–1924)
Type of plot: Fantasy
Time of plot: Twentieth century
Locale: Germany
First published: *Der Prozess*, 1925 (English translation, 1937)

Left unfinished at the time of his death, Kafka's disturbing and vastly influential novel has been interpreted on many levels of structure and symbol; but most commentators agree that the book explores the themes of guilt, anxiety, and moral impotency in the face of some ambiguous external force.

Principal Characters

Joseph K., an employee in a bank. He is a man without particular qualitites or abilities, a fact which makes doubly strange his "arrest" by the officer of the court in the large city where K. lives. Joseph K.'s life is purely conventional and resembles the life of any other person of his class. Consequently, he tries in vain to discover how he has aroused the suspicion of the court. His honesty is conventional; his sins, with Elsa the waitress, are conventional; and he has no striking or dangerous ambitions. He is a man without a face; at the most, he can only ask questions, and he receives no answers that clarify the strange world of courts and court functionaries in which he is compelled to wander.

Frau Grubach, K.'s landlady. She has a high opinion of K. and is deeply shocked by his arrest. She can do nothing to help him.

Fraülein Bürstner, a respectable young woman who also lives in Frau Grubach's house. She avoids any close entanglement with K.

The Assistant Manager, K.'s superior at the bank. He invites K. to social occasions which K. cannot attend because of his troubles with the court. He is also eager to invade K.'s proper area of authority.

The Examining Magistrate, the official who opens the formal investigation of K.'s offense. He conducts an unruly, arbitrary, and unsympathetic hearing.

The Washerwoman, an amiable but loose woman who lives in the court building. She is at the disposal of all the functionaries.

The Usher, the subservient husband of the washerwoman. His submission to official authority is, like his wife's, a sign of the absorption of the individual into the system.

The Clerk of Inquiries, a minor official who reveals court procedures to newly arrested persons.

Franz and **Willem,** minor officers of the court, who must endure the attentions of The Whipper because K. has complained to the court about them.

Uncle Karl (Albert K.), K.'s uncle, who is determined that K. shall have good legal help in his difficulties.

Huld, the lawyer, an ailing and eccentric man, in league with the court. He keeps his great knowledge of the law half-hidden from K. K. finally dismisses the lawyer as a man whose efforts will be useless.

Leni, the notably promiscuous servant at the lawyer's house. Full of kind instructions to K., she tells him how to get along with the erratic Huld.

Block, a tradesman who has been waiting for five and a half years for Huld to do something for him. He lives at the lawyer's house in order to be ready for consultations at odd hours.

The Manufacturer, one of K.'s clients. He expresses sympathy for K.'s plight and sends K. to an artist acquaintance, Titorelli, as a means of influencing the court in K.'s favor.

Titorelli, an impoverished painter who lives in an attic just off the courts of justice. He paints many a magistrate in uneasy and yet traditional poses. He explains in great detail to K. the different kinds of sentences an accused person can receive. He also reveals the contrast between what the law is supposed to do and how it actually works.

The Prison Chaplain, whom K. encounters as the preacher at the Cathedral in the town. The Chaplain tells K. a long story about a door guarded by a Tartar; it is a door that somehow exists especially for K. Despite his sympathy, the Chaplain finally reveals himself as merely one more employee of the court.

The Story

Perhaps someone had been telling lies about Joseph K., for one morning he was arrested. The landlady's cook always brought him his breakfast at eight o'clock, but this morning she failed to appear. Joseph looked out of the window and noticed that the old lady across the way was peering into his room. Feeling uneasy, he rang the bell. At once a man entered dressed like a tourist. He advised Joseph to stay in his room, but Joseph failed to obey. In the next room he saw another strange man reading a book. The missing breakfast was explained by the empty dishes he saw. The two strangers had eaten it.

The two strangers had come to notify Joseph that he was under arrest. They were so sure of themselves and yet so considerate that Joseph was at a loss as to how to respond to them. They tried to take his underwear, saying it was of too good quality, but when he objected, they did not press him. They refused to tell him the reason for his arrest, saying only that he would be interrogated. Finally, after Joseph had dressed according to their directives, they led him to another room to be questioned by the Inspector.

To his dismay Joseph saw that the Inspector was occupying Fraülein Bürstner's room. The Inspector gave no further hint as to the reason for the arrest nor did he inquire into Joseph's defense. The latter at one point said that the whole matter was a mistake; but under pertinent if vague questioning, Joseph admitted that he knew little of the law. All he learned, really, was that someone in high authority had ordered his arrest.

Then Joseph was told that he could go to work as usual. His head fairly aching from bewilderment, Joseph went to the bank in a taxi. Arriving half an hour late, he worked all day long as diligently as he could. Frequently, however, he was interrupted by congratulatory callers, for this day was his thirtieth birthday.

He went straight home at nine-thirty to apologize for using Fraülein Bürstner's room. She was not in, however, and he settled down to anxious waiting. At eleven-thirty she arrived, tired from an evening at the theater. In spite of her uninterested attitude, he told her the whole story very dramatically. At last Fraülein Bürstner sank down exhausted on her bed. Joseph rushed to her, kissed her passionately many times, and returned to his room.

A few days later Joseph received a brief note ordering him to appear before the court for interrogation on the following Sunday. Oddly enough, although the address was given, no time was set for the hearing. By some chance Joseph decided to go at nine o'clock. The street was a rather mean one, and the address proved to be that of a large warehouse.

Joseph did not know where to report, but after trying many doors, he finally reached the fifth floor. There a bright-eyed washerwoman seemed to be expecting him and motioned him through her flat into a meeting hall. Joseph found the room filled with old men, most of them with long beards. They all wore badges.

When the judge asked Joseph if he were a house painter, he snappishly rejoined that he was the junior manager of a bank. Then the judge said he was an hour and ten minutes late. To this charge Joseph replied that he was present now, his appearance in court being the main thing. The crowd applauded. Encouraged, Joseph launched into a harangue damning the court, its methods, the warders who had arrested him, and the meeting time and place.

The judge seemed abashed. Then an interruption occurred. At the back of the room, a man clasped the washerwoman in his arms and screamed, all the while looking at the ceiling. Joseph dashed from the room, loudly refusing to have any more dealings with the court.

All that week Joseph awaited another summons. When none came, he decided to revisit the meeting hall. The washerwoman again met him kindly and expressed her disappointment that the court was not in session. She told him a little about the court and its methods. It seemed that the court was only a lower body which rarely interfered with the freedom of the accused people. If one were acquitted by the court, it meant little, because a higher court might rearrest the prisoner on the same charge. She seemed to know little of Joseph's particular case, although she said she knew as much as the judge. As she was speaking, a law student seized the washerwoman and carried her up the stairs.

The woman's husband kindly offered to lead Joseph up to the law offices, the inner sanctum of the court located in the attic. There Joseph found a number of people waiting for answers to petitions. Some of them had been waiting for years, and they were becoming a little anxious about their cases. The hot room under the roof made Joseph dizzy, and he had to sit down. The hostess tried to soothe him, and the director of public relations was very pleasant. Finally someone suggested that Joseph ought to leave and get some fresh air.

On his uncle's advice, Joseph hired an advocate, an old man who stayed in bed most of the time. His servant, Leni, took a liking to Joseph and would often kiss him while he was conferring with the advocate. Joseph liked best to dally with her in the kitchen. After some months, all the advocate had done was to think about writing a petition. In desperation Joseph discharged him from the case.

Leni was heartbroken. She was in her nightgown entertaining another client. This man, a businessman, Leni kept locked up in a small bedroom. The advocate warned Joseph of his high-handed behavior and pointed to the businessman as an ideal client. Disgusted, Joseph left the house.

Then Joseph went to see Titorelli, the court painter. Titorelli told him he could hope for little. He might get definitive acquittal, ostensible acquittal, or indefinite postponement. No one was ever really acquitted, but sometimes cases could be prolonged indefinitely. Joseph bought three identical paintings in return for the advice.

Even the priest at the cathedral, who said he was court chaplain, offered little encouragement when consulted. He was sure that Joseph would be convicted of the crime charged against him. Joseph still did not know what the crime was, nor did the priest.

At last two men in frock coats and top hats came for Joseph at nine o'clock on the evening before his thirty-first birthday. Somehow they twined their arms around his and held his hands tightly. They walked with him to a quarry. There one held his throat and the other stabbed him in the heart, turning the knife around twice.

Critical Evaluation

The Trial is one of the most effective and most widely discussed works to come out of central Europe between the world wars. Although the complex and ambiguous surface of the novel defies exact interpretation, the plight of Joseph K., consumed by guilt and condemned for a "crime" he does not understand by a "court" with which he cannot communicate, is a profound and disturbing image of man in the modern world. To some the court is a symbol of the Church as an imperfect bridge between the individual and God. To others, the symbolism represents rather the search of a sensitive Jew for a homeland that is always denied him. Although unfinished, *The Trial* is a powerful and provocative book.

As one of the pillars upon which Franz Kafka's reputation as a major twentieth century author rests, *The Trial* was among the works he ordered destroyed in his will. It survives only because his friend Max Brod, who possessed a manuscript of the unfinished novel, disobeyed Kafka and preserved it, along with *The Castle* (1926), *Amerika* (1913), and a host of fragments and shorter works. The salvaging of this novel from the manuscript was not an easy task, however, and controversy still exists as to the proper order of the chapters as well as over the placement and interpretation of a number of unfinished segments which are not included in the usual editions. Fortunately, both the beginning and the end of the novel are extant, and because of the peculiar structure of the work, minor changes in the order of the sections do not really alter one's understanding of it.

The novel is structured within an exact time frame: Exactly one year elapses between the arrest of Joseph K. (the K. clearly refers to Kafka himself, though the work is hardly autobiographical in the usual sense), which takes place on his thirtieth birthday, and his execution, which takes place on the night before his thirty-first birthday. Moreover, the novel tells almost nothing about Joseph K.'s past; there are no memories, no flashbacks, no expository passages explaining the background. As in so many of his works, Kafka begins *The Trial* with the incursion of a totally unexpected force into an otherwise uneventful life, and the situation never again returns to normal. Kafka felt that the moment of waking was the most dangerous moment of the day, a time when one was unprotected by the structures of one's life and open to such an incursion. Joseph K., in his vulnerable state, responds to the messengers of the court; from this point, there is no turning back. Yet the court is invisible—a hierarchy in which even the lowest members are somehow beyond his reach. There are no formal charges, no procedures, and little information to guide the defendant. Indeed, one of the most unsettling aspects of the novel is the constant uncertainty, the continual juxtaposition of alternative hypotheses, the multiple explanations for events, and the differing interpretations regarding cause and effect. The whole rational structure of the world is undermined, as perceived reality becomes the subject of detailed exegesis such as one might apply to sacred Scripture. Reality itself becomes a vague concept, since the reader is denied the guiding commentary of a narrator and sees everything from Joseph's point of view. The entire work is composed of Joseph's experiences; he is present in every scene. Secondary characters appear only as they relate to him, and the reader knows no more than he does. With Joseph, the reader receives information which may be misinformation, experiences bizarre, barely credible incidents, and moves from scene to scene as if in a trance. This narrowness of the point of view becomes oppressive, but it is highly effective as a technique; the reader, in effect, *becomes* Joseph K.

The body of the novel consists of Joseph's attempts to approach the court through a series of "helpers." These helpers, however, offer no encouragement to his possible defense or acquittal. Since there are no charges, a defense is virtually impossible. Their advice is simply to prolong the trial, to avoid a decision, to adjust to the idea of living on trial without seeking a judgment. It is for this reason that the order of the central chapters is not crucial: Aside from Joseph's increasing exhaustion, there is no real development, merely a series of false starts, leading him no closer to a solution. Whether or not there is any development in Joseph's position before his death is open to debate, and critics have disagreed strongly. In the next to last chapter, "In the Cathedral," Joseph is told the parable of the man who comes seeking entrance into the Law. His way is blocked by a doorkeeper, and the man's entire life is spent waiting. As he dies, he learns that this door, which he could never enter, was nevertheless meant for him alone. Typically, several possible interpretations are offered, but it is perhaps significant that the next chapter finds Joseph waiting for his executioners. Has he come to an acceptance? Does the paradox achieve meaning for him? However that may be, he does not have the strength to act, and he dies, as he thinks at the end, "like a dog."

One is left with the question of what it all means. This is perhaps the wrong question to ask, because it implies that there is a meaning which can be defined, or a key to understanding which generally involves assigning some allegorical value to the court, such as authoritarian society, man's alienation from a sense of wholeness and purpose in life, or the search for God's grace. Yet it is the genius of Kafka's works that their meanings are inexhaustible and veiled in an ultimately impenetrable mystery. His works admit of many interpretations, but the more specific the definition of the meaning of the work, the more inadequate it is to encompass the full amplitude of the novel. Kafka's works are less allegorical than symbolic; their symbolism lies in the construction of an image or an experience that is analogous to a human experience that lies far deeper than any of the specific problems offered as explanations for the work's meaning. In *The Trial*, Joseph K. is confronted with the need to justify his life and to justify it at a metaphysical level deeper than any *ex post facto* rationalization of his actions. It is a demand he cannot meet, and yet it is inescapable because it arises from within him. He is an Everyman, but he is stripped of his religion and on trial fro his life. For Kafka, the trial becomes a metaphor for life itself, and every sentence is a sentence of death.

TRISTAN AND ISOLDE

Type of work: Poem
Author: Gottfried von Strassburg (fl. late twelfth and early thirteenth centuries)
Type of plot: Romantic tragedy
Time of plot: The Arthurian period
Locale: Northern Europe, Ireland, England
First transcribed: c. 1210

Tristan and Isolde, the famous metrical romance attributed to the medieval German court poet Gottfried, belongs to the tradition of the Minnesang but differs from the line of chivalric tales in its emphasis upon ecstatic romantic love rather than knightly deeds of valor.

Principal Characters

Tristan (trĕs'tän), the courtly son of Rivalin and Blanchefleur. Orphaned at birth, he is reared by Rual the Faithful until he joins King Mark's court after his escape from Norwegian kidnappers. He serves his lord well by killing Duke Morolt and winning the hand of Isolde the Fair for Mark. However, Tristan and Isolde drink a love potion by accident and fall helplessly in love. The two lovers deceive Mark until Tristan is forced to flee. Later he marries Isolde of the White Hands, but it is a marriage in name only.

Isolde the Fair (ē·zōl'dĕ), the wife of King Mark and lover of Tristan.

Mark (märk), the vacillating King of Cornwall, uncle of Tristan, and cuckolded husband of Isolde the Fair.

Rivalin (rē·vä'lĭn, rĭ·vä'lēn), a lord of Parmenie. On his travels he marries Blanchefleur and fathers Tristan

before his death in battle against Duke Morgan.

Blanchefleur (bläṅsh·flœr'), the sister of King Mark, wife of Rivalin. Upon learning of Rivalin's death, she dies giving birth to Tristan.

Brangene (brän'gä·nĕ), the companion of Isolde and her substitute in Mark's wedding bed.

Rual the Faithful (rōō·äl'), the foster father of Tristan.

Duke Morolt (mŏ·rŏlt'), the brother of Queen Isolde. He is killed by Tristan when he demands tribute from Cornwall for Ireland.

Duke Morgan (mōr'găn), the enemy of Rivalin, later killed by Tristan.

Isolde of the White Hands (ē·zōl'dĕ), the wife of Tristan in name only.

Queen Isolde of Ireland, the mother of Isolde the Fair.

The Story

Rivalin, a lord of Parmenie, tired of baiting Duke Morgan, the wicked ruler, signed a year's truce and set off for Britain, where King Mark of Cornwall was establishing peace and order. Badly wounded while fighting in the defense of Cornwall, Rivalin was pitied and nursed back to health by Mark's sister Blanchefleur, whom he took back to Parmenie as his bride. Later, hearing of Rivalin's death at Duke Morgan's hand, Blanchefleur went into labor and died during the birth of her son. Rual, Rivalin's faithful steward, and his wife reared the boy out of loyalty to their dead lord and mistress and to thwart Duke Morgan's vindictiveness. The boy was named Tristan, in keeping with the sad events preceding his birth and a prophecy of grief to come.

Tristan's education was courtly, both at home and abroad; it included music, art, literature, languages, falconry, hunting, riding, knightly prowess with sword and spear, and jousting. These accomplishments he used to great advantage throughout his short life. He was loved deeply

by his foster parents, his stepbrothers, and the people of Parmenie as well.

Kidnapped by Norwegians, Tristan managed to make his way to Cornwall after an eight-day storm at sea. He immediately attached himself to King Mark's court as a hunter, later the master of the hunt. When his royal lineage was revealed, he became his uncle's knight and vassal.

Known far and wide as a doughty knight, Tristan returned to avenge his father's death by defeating and killing Duke Morgan; his lands he gave to Rual and his sons. Meanwhile, Duke Morolt of Ireland, who had exacted tribute from King Mark, demanded further payment or a fight to the death in single combat with the Cornish king. Tristan acted as King Mark's emissary to the Irish court, where his efforts to have Duke Morolt recall his demand for tribute were unsuccessful. Duke Morolt did agree, however, to let Tristan fight in King Mark's place. They met and fought in Cornwall. After wounding Tristan in the hip, Duke Morolt suggested that the young knight yield so that his sister Isolde, Queen of Ireland, could nurse him back to health. This offer was refused, and the fight waged fiercely again. Tristan finally sliced off Duke Morolt's head and hand.

Tristan, disguised as a beggar, went to Ireland to be cured. Calling himself Tantris, he ingratiated himself with Queen Isolde, who cured him of his hurt. Afterward he became the tutor in music and languages to her daughter, Isolde the Fair. When the young Isolde learned that he was the murderer of her uncle, the queen mother forgave him and allowed him to return to Cornwall.

In Cornwall, Tristan sang the praises of the Irish princess. Because King Mark had made the young knight his heir, some jealous noblemen, hoping to have Tristan slain, suggested that he return to Ireland and bring Isolde back as King Mark's bride. On his arrival in Ireland Tristan killed a dragon which had long ravished the kingdom. In gratitude, Queen Isolde entrusted her beautiful daughter to Tristan's care.

On the return voyage, Brangene, the faithful companion and cousin of Isolde the Fair, failed to guard carefully the love potion intended by the queen for Isolde and King Mark on their nuptial day. Tristan and the princess drank the potion and were thenceforth enslaved by love for each other. They both experienced conflicting duty and desire, turned red then white, became both depressed and exalted, and finally gave in to love. To deceive King Mark, Brangene stole into Isolde's bed so that Tristan and Isolde might meet in secret.

After some time had passed, Isolde grew apprehensive lest Brangene betray her, and she ordered her compan-

ion's death. Fortunately, the queen relented before Brangene could die, and all went on as before until the king was at last informed of Tristan's treachery. King Mark made many attempts to trap the lovers, meanwhile vacillating between trust and angry jealousy. Each time a trap was set, Tristan and Isolde proved their false innocence by some cunning ruse.

Finally the lovers were exiled. The king invited them to return, however, when he discovered them innocently asleep in a cave, a sword between them. Although King Mark urged propriety on their return to court, Tristan and Isolde almost immediately abandoned all caution, driven as they were by the caprices of love. Knowing that the king would have them killed if they were discovered, Tristan set out from Cornwall after accepting a ring from his beloved as a token of their fidelity to each other.

During his travels Tristan performed deeds of knightly valor in Germany, Champagne, and Normandy. In gratitude for his services in Normandy the duke gave him his daughter Isolde, called Isolde of the White Hands to distinguish her from Isolde the Fair, as his bride. Lovesick and dejected, Tristan accepted his bride in name only—the name Isolde.

(At this point Gottfried's narrative breaks off abruptly. From his source materials and from related versions, it is likely that Tristan was fatally wounded by a poison spear and that Isolde the Fair, summoned from Cornwall, arrived after her lover had died. Shock and grief caused her death also. King Mark, learning of the love potion, forgave them and ordered the lovers buried side by side in Cornwall.)

Critical Evaluation

Gottfried von Strassburg's *Tristan and Isolde* is unique in many ways. Though its material is courtly in nature, the poem ends tragically, rather than in the usual redemptive resolution, and the sphere of reference is not specifically courtly. In his prologue, Gottfried defines his audience as those "noble hearts" who share the sufferings and joys of love, and who are willing to accept the power of love as the central value in life. All other courtly values—honor, religious faith, feudal fidelity—are subordinated to the one overriding force of passion, conceived as an external objective force symbolized in the magic potion. Even Gottfried's conception of love departs from the courtly pattern, for rather than the usual unfulfilled longing and devoted service of the Minnesänger, love here is mutual and freely given, and cannot be contained within the conventions of courtly society. It is in fact a law unto itself and destructive of the social order.

The material of the legend, like that of the Arthurian sagas, may be traced back to Celtic origins, though no versions prior to the twelfth century are extant. In the late 1100's the story takes shape, and it is the French version by the Anglo-Norman poet Thomas of Britanny

(c.1160) that provided the direct source for Gottfried— and which enables us to guess as to the probable ending of Gottfried's unfinished work. In Thomas' version the approach is still distinctly courtly; Gottfried's departures from the norm may be attributed both to his own origin and to his time. Gottfried was most likely not a member of courtly society himself, but rather a member of the middle class of the important commercial city of Strassburg, wealthy and well-educated—as evidenced by his extensive knowledge of theology and law—and familiar with both French and German literature, as well as the Latin that was the universal language of higher education at the time. His work shows mastery of formal rhetorical devices and a knowledge of Latin literature remarkable for his time. His literary sophistication is evident in the extended discussion of German authors of his day that he inserts into the story at a point where Tristan's investiture would be discussed. It is in this literary excursus that he voices his praise of Hartmann von Aue and castigates Wolfram von Eschenbach for his excessively difficult and erratic style.

This critical attitude toward his courtly contemporaries

is reflected in his whole approach to the conventions of courtly romance and helps to explain the uniqueness of his work. He is not above mocking even the rituals of the Church, as when Isolde successfully passes a trial by fire through an elaborate ruse that enables her to avoid perjury on a technicality, but destroys the intent and integrity of the trial. "Christ," Gottfried says, "is as pliable as a windblown sleeve." One must in fairness point out that by 1210 such a mockery would not be terribly shocking to the educated classes, who would regard the whole idea of trial by fire as rather archaic and superstitious. What must have appeared virtually blasphemous to some, however, is the elevation of love to a quasi-religious significance. There is considerable borrowing from the language of mystical writers in Gottfried's discussion of love, both in the prologue, where the elevating and ennobling qualities generally ascribed to courtly love take on religious significance through the use of specifically religious metaphor, and in the body of the work, where both in his imagery and in his presentation of a scale of values, Gottfried stresses the sacred and transfiguring power of love. St. Bernard of Clairvaux in particular has been pointed out as a source of much of Gottfried's religious love imagery. Scholars are divided on the degree to which one should view this cult of love as an attempt to create a surrogate religion; there is no question, however, but that Gottfried viewed love's claims as exerting a powerful counter-force against the social and religions conventions of the time.

The turning away from the public, external values of the courtly epics toward the inner, personal, emotional values of *Tristan and Isolde* is consistent with the wider cultural trends of the time: the new grace and sensitivity evident in the sculptures of the North Portal at Chartres, and the break with the conventions of courtly love in the later songs of Walther von der Vogelweide, in whose poems we also find the development of an ideal of love in which physical consummation replaces the state of prolonged yearning which is the subject of the poetry of the earlier phase of courtly love. The mystical qualities of this love are portrayed in the scene in the Cave of Love, which is an elaborate allegory expressing the ideal state toward which love strives. But the sequence of trials and traps surrounding Tristan and Isolde depicts the reality experienced by the "noble hearts" whom Gottfried is addressing in his poem when they must live in a world which does not accord to the power of love its due respect.

In this world, the lovers are in fact far from ideal. Isolde uses her servant Brangene shamelessly and even considers murdering her to prevent possible exposure, while Tristan, banished from the court at last, falls in love with Isolde of the White Hands, lacking the sustaining power of fidelity that Isolde demonstrates. How Gottfried might have resolved this dichotomy can only be guessed, but viewing the work from the stance of the prologue, it is clear that Gottfried saw the company of "noble hearts" as forever torn between love's joy and sorrow, and accepting both as equally valid. It is precisely this quality of bitterness that separates love's votaries from the mundane world of pleasure seekers, and it is in relation to this ambivalent state that Gottfried explains the purpose of his work: sad stories of love do indeed increase the pain of a heart that already feels love's sadness, yet the noble heart cannot help but be drawn again and again to the contemplation of love. Like the sacraments of the Church, Gottfried's work offers mystical communion: "Their death is the bread of the living." In this insistence upon the centrality of love, Gottfried's romantic tragedy is both the culmination and turning point of the tradition of courtly love in Germany.

TRISTRAM SHANDY

Type of work: Humorous sensibility
Author: Lawrence Sterne (1713–1768)
Type of plot: Humorous sensibility
Time of plot: 1718–1766
Locale: Hall in England
First published: 1759–1767 (published in several books)

The Life and Opinions of Tristram Shandy, Gentleman *blends Rabelaisian prankishness, sound psychological insight, sensibility, neoclassic common sense, and much irreverent nonsense in a comic masterwork remarkable for its technical inventiveness.*

Principal Characters

Tristram Shandy, the narrator and ostensible hero of this literary farrago who details his early life, his father's opinions and eccentricities, his uncle's passion for the reenactment of Malborough's military campaigns and describes assorted oddities of mind and conduct. His mother having incurred some time before the expense of a needless trip to London for a lying-in, Tristram, according to the terms of his parents' marriage contract, is born at Shandy Hall on November 5, 1718. Various misfortunes befall him early in life: a broken nose, crushed by the doctor's forceps at birth; the wrong name, Tristram instead of Trismegistus, when he is christened by a stupid young curate; and the loss of his member, a heavy sash having fallen while he was relieving himself through an open window. Though crushed by these irreparable accidents, his father still insists that the boy shall have a proper education, and to this end Mr. Shandy writes a "Tristra-paedia" in imitation of the "Cyro-paedia" designed for the training of Cyrus the Great, as set forth in the stages Xenophon. Except for a few scattered hints, the reader learns almost nothing about Tristram's later life. Sterne devotes most of the novel to reporting humorous incidents and the sayings of the other characters.

Walter Shandy, Tristram's father, a crotchety retired turkey merchant who possesses an immense stock of obscure information gained by reading old books collected by his ancestors. As the result of his reading, he takes delight in lengthy discussions on unimportant topics. A man of acute sensibilities, alert to the minor pricks and vexations of life, he has developed a drollish but sharp manner of peevishness, but he is so open and generous in all other ways that his friends are seldom offended by his sharpness of tongue. He suffers from sciatica as well as loquacity.

Mrs. Shandy, a good-natured but rather stupid woman. Typical is her interruption of the moment of Tristram's conception on the first Sunday of March, 1718, by asking her husband if he has remembered to wind the clock. "I dare say" and "I suppose not" in agreement with Mr.

Shandy are her most brilliant remarks in conversation.

Toby Shandy, called **My Uncle Toby,** a retired army captain who had been wounded in the groin during the siege of Namur in 1698. Now retired to the country, he spends most of his time amid a large and complicated series of miniature fortifications and military emplacements on the bowling green behind Shandy Hall. There he follows with all the interest and enthusiasm of actual conflict the military campaigns of the Duke of Marlborough on the Continent. Occasionally forced into conversations with his brother, as on the night of Tristram's birth, he escapes the flood of Mr. Shandy's discourse by whistling "Lillibullero" to himself. Completely innocent on the subjects of women and sex, he is pursued by a neighbor, the Widow Wadman, whose intentions are matrimonial and whose campaign on the old soldier's heart is as strategically planned as his own miniature battles.

Widow Wadman, a buxom woman who lays siege to Uncle Toby's bachelor life and begs him to show her the exact spot where he was wounded. Eventually he indicates on a map the location of Namur. Her question kills her chance of a proposal when Corporal Trim tells his embarrassed master what the widow really wants to know.

Corporal Trim, the faithful and loquacious servant of Uncle Toby. He helps his master enact mimic battles on the bowling green.

Susannah, a vain and careless maid. Supposed to tell the curate to christen the sickly baby Trismegistus, after the minor philosopher admired by Mr. Shandy, she arrives on the scene so out of breath that she can say only the name is Tris-something, and the curate decides that the child is to be called Tristram. He is pleased because that is his own name.

Parson Yorick, a mercurial and eccentric clergyman completely innocent of the ways of the wicked world. He is in the habit of speaking his mind plainly, often to the discomfiture or resentment of the man toward whom his remarks are directed. Once a lover of fine horses, he rides about the countryside on a nag that would disgrace Don Quixote. His good horses were always spavined, or wind-broken, by anxious expectant fathers who would borrow the animals to fetch a midwife for their wives who were in labor. At the end of the novel he declares that the closing anecdote is a Cock and Bull story, "and one of the best of its kind, I ever heard." As Tristram relates, the epitaph on the clergyman's tombstone is a simple, brief inscription: Alas, poor YORICK!

Dr. Slop, a squat, bungling country doctor, the author of a book on midwifery. For a fee of five guineas, this "man-midwife" sits in the back parlor of Shandy Hall and listens to Mr. Shandy hold forth on various topics, including a treatise on oaths, while a midwife is attending Mrs. Shandy upstairs. When called in to assist at the birth, his forceps permanently flatten Tristram's nose.

Obadiah, the outdoors servant at Shandy Hall, an awkward, good-natured fellow.

Jonathan, Mr. Shandy's dull-witted coachman.

Le Fever, a poor lieutenant who falls sick while traveling to rejoin his regiment in Flanders. When Corporal Trim, who has visited the dying man at the village inn, reports to Uncle Toby that the poor fellow will never march again, the old soldier is so moved that he swears one of his rare oaths while declaring that Le Fever shall not die. The recording angel, making a note of the oath, drops a tear on the word and blots it out forever.

Tom, Corporal Trim's brother, who marries the widow of a Jew in Lisbon.

A Negress, a friend of Tom Trim, who motivates a discussion on slavery.

Mrs. Bridget, Widow Wadman's maid, ambitions to marry Corporal Trim.

Eugenius, the friend and adviser of Parson Yorick. He witnesses the clergyman's dying moments.

Master Bobby Shandy, Tristram's older brother, whose death at an early age is reported. His sudden death gives Corporal Trim a good opportunity to provide the servants of Shandy Hall with a dramatic illustration—he drops his hat—of man's mortality, the fact that he can be here one moment and gone the next. Trim's action causes Susannah, who has been thinking of the gown that may become hers when her mistress goes into mourning, to burst into tears.

The Story

Tristram Shandy, in telling the story of his earliest years, always believed that most of the problems of his life were brought about by the fact that the moment of his conception was interrupted when his mother asked his father if he had remembered to wind the clock. Tristram knew the exact date of his conception, the night between the first Sunday and the first Monday of March, 1718. He was certain of this date because, according to his father's notebook, Mr. Shandy set out immediately after this date to travel from Shandy Hall up to London. Before this date, Mr. Shandy had been seriously inconvenienced by an attack of sciatica.

Another complication of Tristram's birth was the marriage settlement of his parents. According to this settlement as quoted in full by Tristram, Mrs. Shandy had the privilege of going to London in preparation for childbirth. If Mrs. Shandy were to put Mr. Shandy to the expense of a trip to London on false pretenses, however, then the next child was to be born at Shandy Hall. The circumstance of a needless trip to London had occurred some time before, and Mr. Shandy stoutly insisted that Tristram should be born at Shandy Hall; the birth would be in the hands of a country midwife rather than in those of a London doctor.

On the night of Tristram's birth, his father and his Uncle Toby were sitting in the living room engaged in one of their interminable discussion and debates. Informed by Susannah, the maid, that Mrs. Shandy was about to deliver a child, they sent for the midwife. As an extra measure of safety, they also sent for Dr. Slop, a bungling country practitioner whom Mr. Shandy admired because he had written a five-shilling book on the history of midwifery. While the midwife attended Mrs. Shandy, the doctor, for a fee of five guineas, would drink a bottle of wine in the back parlor with Mr. Shandy and his brother, Toby.

Uncle Toby, who had been called the highest compliment ever paid human nature, had been a soldier until he was wounded during the siege of Namur in 1695. The wound, the exact position of which was to play such a large part in Tristram's story later on, forced him to retire to the country. There at the suggestion of his faithful servant Corporal Trim, he had built, on a bowling green behind Shandy Hall, a large and complicated series of model fortifications and military emplacements. Uncle Toby's entire time was spent playing soldier and thinking about this miniature battlefield. It was his hobbyhorse, and he rode it continually with great pleasure. Mr. Shandy was not impressed with his brother's hobby and kept him from discussing it by violent interruptions, so that he could continue, or start, one of his long a detailed digressions on obscure information.

As the two brothers awaited the arrival of the midwife and her rival Dr. Slop, Mr. Shandy asked Mrs. Shandy whether she preferred a midwife or a male doctor. Uncle Toby suggested naïvely that modesty might explain her choice. This innocent answer led Mr. Shandy into a long discussion of the nature of women and of the fact that everything has two handles. Because of his naïveté, it was impossible for Uncle Toby to understand such affairs.

Dr. Slop finally arrived with his bag of tools. The midwife was already in attendance when he went up to see about the birth of the child. Meanwhile, Corporal Trim read a sermon aloud to pass the time. In attending Mrs. Shandy, Dr. Slop unfortunately mistook Tristram's hip for his head. In probing with his large forceps, he flattened what Tristram always referred to as his nose. Tristram essentially blamed this mistake on the affair of the winding of the clock mentioned earlier. This, and a later incident concerning the falling of a window sash when Tristram, still a little boy, was relieving himself through a window, caused an anatomical peculiarity which he mentions often in his story of his life.

Between Tristram's birth and almost immediate baptism, Mr. Shandy entertained the company with a long story he had translated from the Latin of the old German writer, Slawkenbergius, a tale telling of the adventures of a man with an especially long nose. By the time Mr. Shandy had recovered from the bad news of the accident with the forceps and had asked about his child, he learned that it was very sickly and weak; consequently, he summoned Mr. Yorick, the curate, to baptize the child immediately. While rushing to get dressed to attend the ceremony, Mr. Shandy sent word to the parson by the maid, Susannah, to name the child Trismegistus, after an ancient philosopher who was a favorite of Mr. Shandy. Susannah forgot the name, however, and told Mr. Yorick to name the child Tristram. This name pleased the old man because it happened to be his own as well. When Mr. Shandy, still half unbuttoned, reached the scene, the evil had been done. Despite the fact that Mr. Shandy thought a proper name most important, his child was Tristram, a name Mr. Shandy believed the worst in the world. He lamented that he had lost three-fourths of his son in his unfortunate geniture, nose, and name. There remained only one-fourth—Tristram's education.

Tristram managed to give a partial account of his topsy-turvy boyhood between many sidelights on the characters of his family. Uncle Toby continued to answer most of his brother's arguments by softly whistling *Lillibullero*,

his favorite tune, and by going out to the little battlefield to wage small wars with his servant, Corporal Trim. The next important event in the family was the death of Master Bobby, Tristram's older brother, who had been away at Westminster school. Mr. Shandy reacted to this event in his usual way by calling up all the philosophic ideas of the past on death and discoursing on them until he had adjusted himself to the new situation. The tragic news was carried to the kitchen staff. Susannah, despite a desire to show grief, could think of nothing but the wonderful wardrobe of dresses she would inherit when her mistress went into mourning. The vision of all of Mrs. Shandy's dresses passed through her mind. Corporal Trim well demonstrated the transitory nature of life by dropping his hat, as if it had suddenly died; then he made an extemporaneous funeral oration.

After many more digressions on war, health, the fashions of ancient Roman dress, his father's doubts as to whether to get Tristram a tutor and whether to put him into long trousers, Tristram proceeded to tell the history of his Uncle Toby, both in war and in love. Near Shandy Hall lived the Widow Wadman, who, after laying siege to Uncle Toby's affections for a long period, almost got him to propose marriage to her. The gentle former soldier, who literally would not kill a fly, finally learned the widow's purpose when she began to pointedly inquire into the extent and position of his wound. First, he promised the widow that he would allow her to put her finger on the very spot where he was wounded, and then he brought her a map of Namur to touch. Uncle Toby's innocence balked her real question until Corporal Trim finally told his master that it was the spot on his body, not the spot on the surface of the world where the accident took place, that was the point of the Widow Wadman's interest. This realization so embarrassed the old man that the idea of marriage disappeared from his mind forever. Tristram concluded his story with Parson Yorick's statement that the book had been one of the cock and bull variety: the reader had been led on a mad but merry chase through the satirical and witty mind of the author.

Critical Evaluation

This masterpiece of eighteenth century narrative was written by a man who never reconciled his sentimental nature with his roguish tendencies and who never tried to reconcile them. Laurence Sterne was educated at Jesus College, Cambridge, where he met John Hall-Stevenson, a young aristocrat who shared and encouraged his taste for erotic subjects and exaggeration. After taking holy orders, Sterne received an ecclesiastical appointment in Sutton through family connections; but he was temperamentally completely unsuited for the clerical, pastoral life. In fact, the only part of religion he mastered was

sermon-writing, at that, he excelled. Eventually, he turned his pen to miscellaneous journalism in York periodicals. In 1759, *A Political Romance* appeared, including many elements that would characterize his Shandean masterpiece: allegory, levels of meaning, verbal fanfare, whimsical use of scholastic learning, profanity, and great stylistic versatility.

Nevertheless, it was the appearance of the first two volumes of *The Life and Opinions of Tristram Shandy, Gentleman* (commonly called *Tristram Shandy*) that made Sterne an instant celebrity, despite the immediate denunciation of Johnson, Richardson, Walpole, Goldsmith, and other literary establishment figures who condemned Sterne's iconoclastic style and frankly mercenary attitude for both ethical and artistic reasons. Sterne characterized the first part of his life's work as "taking on, not only the weak part of the sciences in which the true part of Ridicule lies, but everything else which I find laugh-at-able." The reader soon discovers that Sterne finds everything laughable, his comic vision as universal and as detailed as that of Rabelais and Cervantes, whose works strongly influenced Sterne. Like Rabelais' *Gargantua and Pantagruel*, moreover, Sterne's is a work held together only by the unswerving and exuberant force of the author's own personality. "'Tis a picture of myself," he admitted; indeed it is impossible to distinguish the profane minister from the "alleged" narrator, young Tristram—just as Rabelais makes his narrator Alcofibras tangible only when it suits his whim.

Tristram Shandy also has been called "a prolonged conversation" between Sterne and his reader, a conversation in which acquaintance becomes familiarity and, then, an enduring friendship. For this friendship to occur, however, the reader must accept certain ground rules and must be willing to adopt a rule he rarely embraces so willingly as he does here. In his endless comments to the reader (who is sometimes addressed in the plural, sometimes in the singular, sometimes as "your worship," sometimes as "Madam"), Sterne scolds readers for wanting to know everything at once (book 1, chapter 4), asks readers to help him sell his "dedication," assures readers that their company (of Sterne readers) will swell to include all the world and all time, and dismisses reader's objections with a mad swirl of his pen. He tells readers that he is quite aware that some will understand and others will not; indeed, the varying forms of address to the reader indicate his astute consciousness of the variety of his audience. He says the "cholerick" reader will toss the book away, the "mercurial will laugh most heartily at it," and the "saturnine" will condemn it as fanciful and extravagant. Like Cervantes, he is not interested (or so he claims) in apologizing for his work or for himself. Readers either take him or leave him. At the very beginning, as he begins one of his great digressions, he warns the strict reader that to continue may annoy him—only the curious need pass through the narrative line into this first of many excursions with him. "Shut the door," he directs the first kind of reader; if readers pass through it with him, they realize the door is never opened again. Only the reader who is willing to let "anything go" will remain on speaking terms with this most quixotic, irrepressible author.

The work itself, alternately characterized by Tristram as "vile" and as "rhapsodic," defies structural analysis. Sterne makes his formal principles clear from the beginning: "not to be in a hurry" but to follow every new thought in whatever direction it may beckon until he loses track of his starting point and has to flip back the pages to find his place; "to spend two years discussing one," just as Tristram's mental and emotional autobiography reflects his father's *Tristrapaedia* (the gargantuan work of pedagogy that takes so long in the writing that Tristram grows up before he can start following its directives); and "in writing what I have set about [to], shall confine myself neither to his [Horace's] rules, nor to any man's rules that ever lived." Sterne would have understood T. S. Eliot's dictum, "Immature poets borrow, mature poets steal." He not only steals—whether it is the actual music of Uncle Toby's "Lillibulero" or a medieval French theological tract on baptism—but also openly admits and boasts of his theft. The boast, however, is itself misleading since, as Shakespeare did with North's Plutarch, Sterne subtly but most effectively alters his thieveries to fit the chaotic image of his own work. At one point, in discussing the nature of digressions, Sterne characterizes that work as "digressive, and . . . progressive too—and at the same time." Digressions, he continues, are "the sunshine" of a writer's art, the very stuff of literary and fictional vitality. Life itself, in the ultimate reading, is nothing but a diverting digression for Sterne; the role of the author as he embraces it, is to make that essential human digression as diverting, as complicated, and as emotionally and intellectually rich as possible.

The greatness of his comic wit lies in its indefatigable mastery of making one detail relevant to another, a detail from Tristram's unfortunate life immediately provoking in "my father" a pointed consideration of Saxo Grammaticus' Danish history or causing Uncle Toby to expound its relationship to the siege of Navarre. Reading *Tristram Shandy* is an education in the esoteric and picayune minutiae of forgotten scholarship at the same time that it is a parody of the irrelevance of scholarship (also following closely in the spirit of Rabelais). By the time readers close even the first volume, they are convinced of the validity of Sterne's point of departure: Epictetus' statement that "not actions but opinions of actions are the concern of men." In other words, it is not what happens to the reader that matters but what the reader thinks of what happens to him. The relationship between the Shandean world and the real world is a very close, in fact a promiscuous, relationship; it is defined by Sterne's deliberate blurring of the line between fictional and real events and also by his thematic insistence on the interdependence of thought, feeling, and action. Thought without emotion, he would say, is futile; but feeling without reason is equally sterile. All the elements in human life, love, war, business, theology, religion, science, trade, and medicine are treated in an epic comprehensiveness, and everything is shown to be related absolutely to everything else. The texture of the style, however, is not the reassuring predictability of epic; instead, it is a collage of typographical caprice, gestures, dramatic devices, soliloquies, offhand obscenity, serious and mock-serious treatises. Sterne is like a magician juggling more balls than anyone can see, but he never loses control because his magic is as unflagging as it is electric. More than any other work of his century, Sterne's *Tristram Shandy* is a monument to the complexity, vitality, and *sprezzatura* of the mind.

THE TROJAN WOMEN

Type of work: Drama
Author: Euripides (c. 485–c. 406 B.C.)
Type of plot: Classical tragedy
Time of plot: Age of the Trojan War
Locale: Before the ruined walls of Troy
First presented: 415 B.C.

The Trojan Women (the Troades*) is not, strictly speaking, an Aristotelian tragedy, for it has no central tragic hero; neither is it simply a tragic pageant. The Greek warriors collectively constitute the tragic hero in that they commit hubris by defiling the Trojan temples and brutally murdering the innocent. In this powerful indictment of war, Euripides protests the Athenian massacres in Melos in 415 B.C.*

Principal Characters

Hecuba (hĕ′kū·bə), queen of Troy. Aged and broken by the fall of the city, she is the epitome of all the misfortune resulting from the defeat of the Trojans and the destruction of the city. She is first revealed prostrate before the tents of the captive Trojan women, with the city in the background. Her opening lyrics tell of the pathos of her situation and introduce the impression of hopelessness and the theme of the inevitable doom which war brings. The Greek herald enters with the news that each of the women has been assigned to a different master. Hecuba asks first about her children, Cassandra and Polyxena; then when she finds that she has been given to Odysseus, she rouses herself to an outburst of rebellious anger. Cassandra appears and recalls the prophecy that Hecuba would die in Troy. After Cassandra is led away, Andromache, who appears with news of the sacrifice of Polyxena, tries to console Hecuba with the idea that Polyxena is fortunate in death, but Hecuba in reproach and consolation points out to Andromache and the younger women of the chorus the hope of life. Her attempts to console the younger women, here and elsewhere, are her most endearing feature. The other important aspect of her character, the desire for vengeance against Helen, who has caused her sorrow, is shown in her reply to Helen's plea to Menelaus. Hecuba's reply is vigorous; she points to Helen's own responsibility for her actions and ends with a plea to Menelaus to kill Helen and vindicate Greek womanhood. Hecuba's last action is the preparation for burial of the body of Astyanax, the young son of Andromache and Hector killed by the Greeks out of fear. Her lament over the body is profoundly moving. At the end of the play, she is restrained from throwing herself into the ruins of the burning city.

Cassandra (kə·săn′drə), daughter of Hecuba, a prophetess chosen by Agamemnon as a concubine. When she first appears, wild-eyed and waving a torch above her head, she sings a parody of a marriage song in her own honor; but she soon calms down and prophesies the dreadful end of Agamemnon because of his choice and of the suffering of the Greeks. She views aggressive war as a source of unhappiness for the aggressor himself. As she leaves she hurls the sacred emblems of her divine office to the ground and looks forward to her triumph in revenge.

Andromache (ăn·drŏ′mə·kē), the wife of Hector. Allotted to Neoptolemus, the son of Achilles, she brings Hecuba news of the sacrifice of Polyxena and compares her fate in accepting a new lord to Polyxena's escape through death. When she learns of the Greeks' decision to kill Astyanax, her son by Hector, she gives expression to her tortured love as a mother. Unable to condemn the Greeks because they would refuse Astyanax burial, she curses Helen as the cause of misfortune.

Helen (hĭl′ən), the queen of Sparta abducted by Paris. Beautiful and insolent, her pleading before Menelaus is an attempt to place the blame for her actions on others: on Priam and Hecuba because they had refused to kill Paris at the oracle's command; on the goddess Aphrodite because she promised Helen to Paris at the time of the judgment; on the Trojan guards who had prevented her return to the Greeks. She departs, proud and confident.

Menelaus (mĕ·nə·lā′əs), king of Sparta and the husband of Helen, who has been returned to him, the man she wronged, to kill; but it is evident that he will not do so. His eagerness to assure others that Helen has no control over him and that he intends to kill her becomes almost comic.

Talthybius (tăl·thĭ′bĭ·əs), a herald of the Greeks. He appears three times: to fetch Cassandra, to execute Astyanax, and to bring back Astyanax's body for burial and set fire to the remains of Troy. A kindly man, he is unable to carry out the execution of Astyanax personally.

Astyanax (ăs·tī′ə·năks), the infant son of Andromache and Hector. He is flung from the highest battlement of Troy because the Greeks believe that a son of Hector is too dangerous to live.

A Chorus of Trojan Women. Their odes express a mood of pity and sorrow for the Trojans.

Poseidon (pō·sī′dən), the god of the sea and patron of Troy. He appears, at the beginning of the drama, to take official leave of the city; he had favored it, but the gods aiding the greeks had proved too strong, especially Pallas Athena. His monologue also gives the necessary background for the play.

Pallas Athena (păl′əs ə·thē′nə), the goddess of wisdom. She confronts Poseidon as he bids farewell to Troy and proposes a common vengeance against the Greeks, though she had favored them earlier. Because their impious behavior at the capture of Troy has alienated the gods, the Greeks are to be punished as they put to sea. This threat of retribution looms over the entire play.

The Story

On the second morning after the fall of Troy and the massacre of all its male inhabitants, Poseidon appeared to lament the ruins and vow vengeance against the Greeks. To his surprise, Pallas Athena, the goddess who had aided the Greeks, joined him in plotting a disastrous homeward voyage for the victors who had despoiled her temple in Troy. They withdrew as Hecuba rose from among the sleeping Trojan women to mourn the burning city and her dead sons and husband. The chorus joined her in chanting an anguished lament.

Talthybius, the herald of the Greeks, arrived to announce that Agamemnon had chosen Cassandra to be his concubine and that the other royal women of Troy had been assigned by lot—Polyxena to the tomb of Achilles, Andromache to Achilles' son Neoptolemus, and Hecuba herself to Odysseus, king of Ithaca and conceiver of the wooden horse that had led to the fall of the city. Amid the cries of the grieving women Cassandra appeared, bearing a flaming torch in each hand. The chorus was convinced that she had gone mad as she danced and prayed to Hymen, god of Marriage, that Agamemnon take her soon to Argos as his bride, for there she would cause his death and the ruin of his entire family. As for Odysseus, she foretold that he would suffer for ten more years on the seas before reaching his homeland. As Talthybius led her off, he observed that Agamemnon himself must have been mad to fall in love with the insane Cassandra.

Hecuba, broken with grief, collapsed to the ground. From the city came a Greek-drawn chariot loaded with the spoils of war and bearing Andromache and her infant son Astyanax. Cursing Helen, the cause of all their woe, Andromache called upon the dead Hector to come to her and announced enviously that Polyxena had just been killed upon the tomb of Achilles as a gift to the dead hero. Drawing upon her last remaining strength, Hecuba tried to comfort the distraught Andromache and urged that instead of mourning for Hector she win the love of Neoptolemus so that her son might grow to manhood and perhaps redeem Troy. At this point the reluctant herald Talthybius announced the Greeks' order that the son of so distinguished a warrior as Hector must not be permitted to reach manhood but must be killed at once by being hurled from the battlements of Troy. As Talthybius led away Andromache and her son, a fresh lament and cursing of Helen went up from the grieving women of Troy.

Suddenly King Menelaus came striding in the sunlight with his retinue to demand that his faithless wife Helen be dragged to him by her blood-reeking hair. Hecuba pleaded with him to slay Helen at once, lest her beauty and feminine wiles soften his will, but Menelaus remained determined to take her back to Greece, where the relatives of those who died for her sake might have the pleasure of stoning her to death. Helen approached, calm and dignified. Her plea for the right to speak being supported by Hecuba, she argued that she was not responsible for the fall of Troy. The first blame must be attributed to Priam and Hecuba, who refused to kill the infant Paris as the oracle commanded; the second to Aphrodite, who bewitched her into submitting to Paris; the third to Deiphobus and the Trojan guards who prevented her from escaping to the Greeks after she had come to her senses. Goaded on by the chorus of Trojan women, Hecuba jeered at these claims, insisting that the gods would not have been so foolish as Helen would have them believe, that her own lust drove her into Paris' arms, and that she could always have escaped Troy and her own shame by way of suicide. Helen, falling to her knees, pleaded with Menelaus not to kill her. Hecuba also knelt to beg Helen's immediate death and to warn Menelaus against taking her aboard his ship. Menelaus compromised: Helen would return to Greece on another ship and there pay for her shameful life. As Menelaus led her away, the chorus wailed that Zeus had forsaken them.

Talthybius then returned, bearing the crushed body of Astyanax on Hector's shield. He told Hecuba that Andromache, as she was being led aboard Neoptolemus' ship, had begged that the infant be given proper burial. The performance of that rite was more than Hecuba could bear, and she had to be restrained by force from throwing herself into the flames of the city. As the captive women were led off to the Greek ships, the great crash of Troy's collapsing walls was heard and the city was engulfed in smoke and darkness.

Critical Evaluation

The Trojan Women is a masterpiece of pathos, as well as a timeless and chilling indictment of the brutality of war. Yet to its original audience it was a highly topical play, one that clearly referred to an incident in the Peloponnesian War that occurred a few months before the tragedy was presented in 415 B.C. The people of Melos had tried to remain neutral in the Athenian conflict with Sparta, and Athens responded by massacring the grown males and enslaving the women and children. In *The Trojan Women,* Euripides shows Troy after the men have been slaughtered, with a handful of women waiting to be taken into bondage. The parallel is clear and painful, but Euripides does not stop with that. The women in their anguish have dignity, pride, and compassion, whereas their conquerors are vain, unscrupulous, empty. Further, the conquering Greeks are shown to be headed for disaster, since the gods have turned against them. When this play was produced, Athens was preparing a large fleet to take over Sicily, an expedition that ended in calamity. The prophecies of sea disasters in the play must have made the Athenian audience squirm. Indeed, the whole tragedy seems calculated to sting the consciences of the Athenians. That they allowed it to be produced is amazing. The fact that a nonentity named Xenocles won first prize that year, defeating Euripides, is scarcely surprising.

This play concluded a trilogy of tragedies on the legend of Troy. It was preceded by *Alexandros* (another name for Paris), which dealt with the refusal of Priam and Hecuba to murder their infant Paris, who would eventually bring about the destruction of Troy. This is important, because in *The Trojan Women* Hecuba sees the full consequences of her choice. *Alexandros* was followed by *Palamedes*, where Odysseus exacts a dire revenge on the clever Palamedes through treachery. *The Trojan Women* merges the Trojan and Greek lines of tragedy, showing them to be complementary aspects of a central agony. Since *Alexandros* and *Palamedes*, along with the satyr play *Sisyphus*, have not survived, we must rely on the *Troades* for Euripides' depiction of the Trojan War.

Euripides merely dramatizes a brief portion of the aftermath, about an hour or two the morning after Troy has been looted and burned and the Trojan men put to death, but in that time we see enough to realize that war is the most devastating, unheroic activity that man has ever devised. No one wins. The Greeks in their swollen vanity have committed atrocities against both the gods and human decency, and they are about to receive their just punishment, as Poseidon, Athena, and Cassandra point out. The action of the play consists of the revelation of those atrocities, one after the other, as they overwhelm the helpless old queen, Hecuba. It is primarily through Hecuba that we experience the enormity of Troy's fall. The chorus of captive women, Cassandra, Andromache, and Helen, serve to balance and counterpoint Hecuba's anguish, as well as contribute to it.

A brief time before, Hecuba was the proud queen of a great, wealthy city, and within the space of a night she has been reduced to a slave. Hecuba has witnessed her husband Priam's murder and knows that almost all of her children have been butchered. Longing for death, she experiences one dreadful thing after another. She learns that she is the prize of Odysseus, the vilest Greek of all, and that her daughters will be handed out as concubines. She sees her daughter Cassandra madly singing a marriage hymn, and she finally grasps that Cassandra, through prescience, is really singing a death song for herself and the commander of the Greeks, Agamemnon. Believing her daughter Polyxena to be alive, Hecuba learns from Andromache that the girl had her throat slit. Hecuba, trying to comfort Andromache with the prospect of Astyanax's growing to manhood, sees the little boy taken from Andromache to be smashed to death. Menelaus arrives to drag Helen off, and Helen, who caused the whole war, calmly faces him down, oblivious of Hecuba's accusations. Thus Hecuba loses the satisfaction of seeing her worst enemy killed. We know that shallow, worthless Helen will go unpunished. In her final anguish Hecuba must look upon her poor, mangled grandchild lying on the shield of her dead son Hector. The last ounce of torment is wrung from her, and she makes an abortive suicide attempt. Hecuba's stark pathos has been drawn out to an excruciating degree.

Yet the play is not a mere shapeless depiction of human pain. Hecuba's suffering is cumulative, and there is a pattern to the appearances of the chorus, Cassandra, Andromache, and Helen. The chorus of captive women serves to generalize Hecuba's grief. If Poseidon creates future misery for the Greeks, the chorus shows the past and present pain of the Trojans on a larger canvas. It places Hecuba's agony in perspective as one calamity among many. Moreover, Cassandra, Andromache, and Helen extend the portrayal of women as the spoils of war: Cassandra, the raped virgin and crazed bride of death; Andromache, the exemplary wife and mother turned into a childless widow and handed over to the son of the man who killed her husband; and brazen Helen, the faithless wife who has the knack of getting her own way in every circumstance. The contrast among these three could not be more striking.

Euripides takes pains in *The Trojan Women* to show that the only justice in war is punitive and nihilistic. War arises from numerous individual choices and leads to disaster for everyone, the conquered and the victors alike. With Thucydides the historian, Euripides shares the view that power corrupts, promoting arrogance and criminality. His vision of the suffering caused by the war is as valid today as it was when he wrote the play.

THE TURN OF THE SCREW

Type of work: Novella
Author: Henry James (1843–1916)
Type of plot: Moral allegory
Time of plot: Mid-nineteenth century
Locale: England
First published: 1898

More than a horrific ghost story, The Turn of the Screw *is an enigmatic and disturbing psychological novel that probes the sources of terror in neurosis and moral degradation.*

Principal Characters

The Governess, from whose point of view the story is told. Employed to look after his orphaned niece and nephew by a man who makes it clear that he does not wish to be bothered about them, she finds herself engaged in a struggle against evil apparitions for the souls of the children. There has been a good deal of the "Is-Hamlet-mad?" sort of inconclusive speculation as to whether *The Turn of the Screw* is a real ghost story or a study of a neurotic and frustrated woman. Probably both interpretations are true: the apparitions are real; the children are indeed possessed by evil; and the governess is probably neurotic.

Miles, a little boy, one of the governess' charges. At first he seems to be a remarkably good child, but gradually she learns that he has been mysteriously corrupted by his former governess and his uncle's former valet, whose ghosts now appear to maintain their evil control. Miles dies in the governess' arms during her final struggle to save him from some mysterious evil.

Flora, Miles's sister and feminine counterpart. The governess finally sends her away to her uncle.

Miss Jessel, the former governess, now dead. She appears frequently to the governess and to the children, who refuse to admit the appearances.

Peter Quint, the uncle's former valet, now dead. Drunken and vicious, he was also Miss Jessel's lover. The governess sees his apparition repeatedly.

Mrs. Grose, the housekeeper of the country estate where the story is set. Good-hearted and talkative, she is the source of what little concrete information the governess and the reader get as to the identities and past histories of the evil apparitions. Allied with the governess against the influence of Peter Quint and Miss Jessel, she takes charge of Flora when the child is sent to her uncle.

The Story

It was a pleasant afternoon in June when the governess first arrived at the country estate at Bly, where she was to take charge of Miles, age ten, and Flora, eight. She faced her new position with some trepidation because of the unusual circumstances of her situation. The two children were to be under her complete care, and the uncle who had engaged her had been explicit in the fact that he did not wish to be bothered with his orphaned niece and nephew. Her uneasiness disappeared, however, when she saw her charges, for Flora and Miles seemed incapable of giving the slightest trouble.

The weeks of June passed uneventfully. Then, one evening, while she was walking in the garden at twilight, the governess was startled to see a young man at a distance. The man looked at her challengingly and disappeared. The incident angered and distressed the young woman, but she decided the man was a trespasser.

On the following Sunday evening, the young woman was startled to see the same stranger looking in at her through a window. Once again he stared piercingly at her for a few seconds and then disappeared. This time the governess realized that the man was looking for someone in particular and that perhaps he boded evil for the children in her care. A few minutes later, the governess told the housekeeper, Mrs. Grose, of the incident and described the appearance. of the man. Mrs. Grose told her that it was a perfect description of Peter Quint, the valet to the governess' employer but that Mr. Quint was dead.

One afternoon shortly afterward, a second apparition appeared. This time the ghost of Miss Jessel, the former governess, appeared in the garden to both the governess and the little girl, Flora. The strange part of the situation was that the little girl refused to let the governess know that she had seen the figure and knew who it was, though it was obvious that she had understood the appearance fully.

The governess learned from the housekeeper that the two apparitions had been lovers while alive, though the girl had been of a very fine family and the man had been guilty of drunkenness and worse vices. For what evil purpose these two spirits wished to influence the seemingly innocent children, neither the housekeeper nor the governess could guess. The secrecy of the children about seeing the ghosts was maddening to the two women.

They both felt that the boy was continuing to see the two ghosts in private and concealed that fact, just as he had known of the illicit affair between the valet and the former governess in life and had helped them to conceal it. Yet, when in the presence of the children, the governess sometimes felt that it would be impossible for the two children to be influenced into evil.

The third time, the ghost of Quint appeared to the governess inside the house. Unable to sleep, she had sat reading late at night. Hearing someone on the stairs, she went to investigate and saw the ghost, which disappeared when faced by her unflinching gaze. Each night after that, she inspected the stairs, but she never again saw the ghost of the man. Once she glimpsed the apparition of Miss Jessel as it sat dejectedly on the lowest stair. Worse than the appearance of the ghosts was the discovery that the children had left their beds at night to wander on the lawn in communication with the spirits who were leading them to unknown evil. It became apparent to the governess that the children were not good within themselves. In their imaginations, they were living in a world populated by the evil dead restored.

In such an atmosphere, the summer wore away into autumn. In all that time, the children had given no sign of awareness of the apparitions. Knowing that her influence with the children was as tenuous as a thread which would break at the least provocation, the governess did not allude to the ghosts. She herself had seen no more manifestations, but she had often felt by the children's attitude that the apparitions were close at hand. What was worse for the distressed woman was the thought that what Miles and Flora saw were things still more terrible than she imagined, visions that sprang from their association with the evil figures in the past.

One day, Miles went to her and announced his desire to go away to school. The governess realized it was only proper that he be sent to school, but she feared the results of ghostly influences once he was beyond her care. Later,

opening the door of the schoolroom, she again saw the ghost of her predecessor, Miss Jessel. As the apparition faded, the governess realized that her duty was to stay with the children and combat the spirits and their deadly influence. She decided to write immediately to the children's uncle, contrary to his injunction against being bothered on their behalf. That night before she wrote, she went into Miles's room and asked the boy to let her help him in his secret troubles. Suddenly a rush of cold air filled the room, as if the window had been blown open. When the governess relighted the candle blown out by the draft, the window was still closed, and the drawn curtain had not been disturbed.

The following day, Flora disappeared. Mrs. Grose and the governess found her beside the garden pond. The governess, knowing she had gone there to see the ghost, asked her where Miss Jessel was. The child replied that she only wanted to be left alone. The governess could see the apparition of Miss Jessel standing on the opposite side of the pond.

The governess, afraid that the evil influence had already dominated the little girl, asked the housekeeper to take the child to London and to request the uncle's aid. In place of the lovable angelic Flora there had suddenly appeared a little child with a filthy mind and filthy speech, which she used in denouncing the governess to the housekeeper. The same afternoon, Mrs. Grose left with the child as the governess had requested.

That evening, immediately after dinner, the governess asked Miles to tell her what was on his mind before he left the dining room. When he refused, she asked him if he had stolen the letter she had written to his uncle. As she asked the question, she realized that standing outside the window, staring into the room, was the ghost of Peter Quint. She pulled the boy close to her, shielding him from any view of the ghost at the window, while he told her that he had taken the letter. He also informed her that he had already been expelled from one school because of his lewd speech and actions. Noting how close the governess was holding him, he suddenly asked if Miss Jessel were near. The governess, angry and distraught, shrieked at him that it was the ghost of Peter Quint, just outside the window. When Miles turned around, the apparition was gone. With a scream, he fell into the governess' arms. At first, she did not realize that she had lost him forever—that Miles was dead.

Critical Evaluation

One of the world's most famous ghost stories, *The Turn of the Screw* was first published serially in *Colliers' Weekly* from January 27, 1898, to April 16, 1898, and in book form, along with a second story, *Covering End*, late in 1898. In 1908, Henry James discussed at some length the origin and nature of the tale in the preface to volume

12 of *The Novels and Tales of Henry James*. Considerable critical discussion and controversy have been devoted to the story, especially since Edmund Wilson's 1934 essay on "The Ambiguity of Henry James," in which Wilson argues that "the governess who is made to tell the story is a neurotic case of sex repression, and that the ghosts

are not real ghosts but hallucinations of the governess." Since many critics have taken issue with Wilson and since Wilson later modified his interpretation, it is important to note briefly what James himself says about his story, his characters, and his theme in the preface. He calls *The Turn of the Screw* "a piece of ingenuity pure and simple, of cold artistic calculation, an *amusette* to catch those not easily caught . . . the jaded, the disillusioned, the fastidious." He terms the governess' account "her record of so many anomalies and obscurities." He comments that he purposely limited his revelation of the governess' character: "We have surely as much of her nature as we can swallow in watching it reflect her anxieties and inductions." He says he presented the ghosts as "real" ones, and he describes them as

> my hovering prowling blighting presences, my pair of abnormal agents . . . [who] would be agents in fact; there would be laid on them the dire duty of causing the situation to reek with the air of Evil. Their desire and their ability to do so, visibly measuring meanwhile their effect, together with their observed and described success—this was exactly my central idea.

Concluding his discussions of "my fable," James explains that he purposely did not specify the evils in which the ghosts either attempt to or actually involve Miles and Flora: "Only make the reader's general vision of evil intense enough, I said to myself . . . and his own experience, his own imagination, his own sympathy (with the children) and horror (of their false friends) will supply him quite sufficiently with all the particulars."

Thus, readers see that James conceived of the tale as one in which the governess, a young woman with limited experience and education but high moral principles, attempts to protect two seemingly innocent children from corruption by the malign ghosts of two former servants who in life were evil persons. His capitalizing of "Evil" and his use of the term "fable" to describe the story suggest a moral as well as an aesthetic intent in writing it. To interpret *The Turn of the Screw* in terms of Freudian psychology, as Wilson and some other critics have done, is to go beyond James and to find what he did not put there—consciously anyway. Admittedly, some of the "anomalies and obscurities" which puzzle and trouble the governess do lead the reader in the direction of a Freudian interpretation. The account is the governess' alone, and there is no proof that anyone else actually saw the ghosts though she believes that the children saw them and lied to her or tried otherwise to hide the truth from her. Before his reading of the governess' journal, Douglas admits that she was in love with her employer, the children's handsome uncle who showed no personal interest in her. Within the account itself, the reader who hunts may find apparent Freudian symbolism. For example, the

male ghost, Peter Quint, first appears standing on a tower when the governess has been deeply longing for her employer to appear and approve her care of the children. The female ghost, Miss Jessel, first appears by a lake and watches as little Flora, also watched absorbedly by the governess, plays a childish game:

> She had picked up a small flat piece of wood, Which happened to have in it a little hole that had evidently suggested to her the idea of sticking in another fragment that might figure as a mast and make the thing a boat. This second morsel . . . she was very markedly and intently attempting to tighten in its place.

Tenear-old Miles's repeated use of the word "dear" in speaking to the governess may suggest a precocious boy's sexual interest in his pretty governess.

One can go on, but it is important to remember that James's story was published in 1898 and that Freud's first significant work explaining psychoanalytic theory did not appe until 1905. Perhaps it is best to regard such details in the story as those cited as no more than coincidental, though they may seem suggestive to the post-Freudian reader of *The Turn of the Screw*.

Among the most difficult facts to explain away in developing the theory that the ghosts are mere hallucinations of a sexually frustrated young woman, is the governess' detailed description of a man she has never seen or heard of:

> He has no hat. . . . He has red hair, very red, close-curling, and a pale face, long in shape, with straight, good features and little, rather queer whiskers that are as red as his hair. His eyebrows are, somehow, darker; they look particularly arched. . . . His eyes are sharp—awfully. . . . His mouth's wide, and his lips are are thin, and except for his whiskers he's quite clean-shaven.

Mrs. Grose easily identifies him as the dead Peter Quint. She just as easily identifies Miss Jessel when the governess describes the person she later saw: "A figure of quite an unmistakable horror and evil: a woman in black, pale and dreadful—with such an air also, and such a face!—on the other side of the lake." It is difficult to argue convincingly that Peter Quint and Miss Jessel are not "real" ghosts.

The Turn of the Screw will continue to fascinate and to intrigue because James's "cold artistic calculation" has so filled it with suggestiveness and intentional ambiguity that it may be read at different levels and with new revelations at each successive reading. As Leon Edel has said, "The reader's mind is forced to hold to two levels of awareness: *the story as told*, and *the story to be deduced*."

TWELFTH NIGHT

Type of work: Drama
Author: William Shakespeare (1564–1616)
Type of plot: Romantic comedy
Time of plot: Sixteenth century
Locale: Ilyria
First presented: 1600

The principal charm of Twelfth Night, *one of Shakespeare's most delightful comedies, lies in its gallery of characters; the dour Puritan Malvolio; the clownish Sir Toby Belch and Sir Andrew Aguecheek; and the witty Maria. The original source of the plot was a novella by Bandello, based on an earlier work by Cinthio, but the story was translated into various secondary sources which Shakespeare probably used.*

Principal Characters

Viola (vē′ō·lə), who, with her twin brother Sebastian, is shipwrecked upon the coast of Ilyria. The twins are separated, and a friendly sea captain helps Viola to assume male clothes and to find service as the page **Cesario** (sĕ·zä′rĭ·ō), with Orsino, duke of Ilyria. Her new master is pleased with her and sends the disguised girl to press his suit for the hand of the Countess Olivia, with whom the duke is in love. Olivia, who has been in mourning for her brother, finally admits the page and instantly falls in love with the supposed young man. Cesario, meanwhile, has been falling in love with Orsino. So apparent is Olivia's feeling for Cesario that the countess' admirer, Sir Andrew Aguecheek, is persuaded that he must send a challenge to the page, which challenge Cesario reluctantly accepts. A sea captain, Antonio, a friend of Sebastian, chances upon the duel and rescues Viola, mistaking her for her brother whom he had found after the wreck and to whom he had entrusted his purse. In the ensuing confusion, Olivia marries the real Sebastian, thinking him to be Cesario. Viola and her brother are finally reunited. Viola marries Orsino, and all ends happily.

Sebastian (sĕ·băs′tyən), Viola's twin brother. Separated from her during the shipwreck, he makes his way to Duke Orsino's court, where he is befriended by Antonio. He is involved in a fight with Sir Andrew Aguecheek, who mistakes him for Cesario. When Olivia interferes and takes Sebastian to her home, she marries him, also thinking him to be Cesario. Thus he and Viola are reunited.

Orsino (ôr·sē′nō), duke of Ilyria (ĭ·lĭr′-ĭ·ə), in love with Olivia. He sends the disguised Viola to press his suit, not realizing that Viola is falling in love with him. But when Viola reveals herself as a girl, the duke returns her love and marries her.

Olivia (ō·lĭv′ĭ·ə), a rich countess, living in retirement because of the death of her brother. Orsino courts her through Cesario, but she rejects his suit and falls in love with the disguised Viola. When Sebastian, whom she

mistakes for Cesario, is brought to her after the fight with Sir Andrew, she marries him.

Malvolio (măl·vō′lĭ·ō), Olivia's pompous steward. Considering himself far above his station, he dreams of marrying the countess. He so angers the other members of her household by his arrogance that they play a trick on him. Maria, imitating Olivia's handwriting, plants a note telling him that to please the countess he must appear always smiling and wearing yellow stocking cross-gartered, affectations that Olivia hates. The countess considers him insane and has him locked in a dark room. He is finally released and leaves the stage vowing revenge. Some critics have seen Malvolio as Shakespeare's satiric portrait of the Puritan, but this interpretation is disputed by others.

Maria (mă·rē′ə), Olivia's lively waiting woman. It is she who, angered by the vanity of Malvolio, imitates Olivia's handwriting in the note that leads him to make a fool of himself. She marries Sir Toby Belch.

Sir Toby Belch (tō′bĭ bĕlsh), Olivia's uncle and a member of her household. His conviviality is constantly threatened by Malvolio so that he gladly joins in the plot against the steward. Sir Toby marries Maria.

Sir Andrew Aguecheek (ā·gū′chēk), a cowardly, foolish drinking companion of Sir Toby and suitor of Olivia. He is forced into a duel with Cesario but mistakenly becomes involved with Sebastian, who wounds him.

Antonio (ăn·tō′nĭ·ō), a sea captain who befriends Sebastian, though at great risk, for he has been forbidden to enter Ilyria. Having entrusted Sebastian with his purse, he is involved in the confusion of identities between Sebastian and Cesario. When he is confronted with the twins, Antonio helps to clear up the mystery of the mistaken identities.

Feste (fĕs′tə), a clown. He teases Malvolio during his confinement, but brings to Olivia the steward's letter explaining the trick that had been played on him.

The Story

Viola and Sebastian, identical twin brother and sister, were separated when the ship on which they were passengers was wrecked during a great storm at sea. Each, thinking the other dead, set out into the world alone, with no hope of being reunited.

The lovely and charming Viola was cast upon the shores of Ilyria, where she was befriended by a kind sea captain. Together they planned to dress Viola in men's clothing and have her take service as a page in the household of young Duke Orsino. This course was decided on because there was no chance of her entering the service of the Countess Olivia, a rich noblewoman of the duchy. Olivia, in deep mourning for the death of her young brother, would admit no one to her palace and would never think of interviewing a servant. So Viola, dressed in man's garb, called herself Cesario and became the duke's personal attendant. Orsino, impressed by the youth's good looks and pert but courtly speech, sent him as his envoy of love to woo the countess Olivia.

That wealthy noblewoman lived in a splendid palace with a servant, Maria, a drunken old uncle, Sir Toby Belch, and her steward, Malvolio. These three made a strange combination. Maria and Sir Toby were a happy-go-lucky pair who drank and caroused with Sir Andrew Aguecheek, an ancient nobleman who was much enamored of Olivia. In return for the grog supplied by Sir Andrew, Sir Toby was supposed to press Sir Andrew's suit of love with Olivia. Actually, however, Sir Toby never sobered up long enough to maintain his part of the bargain. All these affairs were observed with a great deal of disapproval by Malvolio, the ambitious, narrow-minded steward. This irritable, pompous individual could brook no jollity in those about him.

When Cesario arrived at the palace, Olivia finally decided to receive a messenger from Orsino. Instantly Olivia was attracted to Cesario and paid close attention to the page's addresses, but it was not love for Orsino that caused Olivia to listen so carefully. When Cesario left, the countess, feeling in a flirtatious mood, sent Malvolio after the page with a ring. With an abrupt shock, Viola, who enjoyed playing the part of Cesario, realized that Olivia had fallen in love with her disguise.

Meanwhile Maria with Sir Toby and Sir Andrew decided to stop Malvolio's constant prying into their affairs. Maria devised a scheme whereby Malvolio would find a note, supposedly written by Olivia, in which she confessed her secret love for the steward and asked him to wear yellow stockings tied with cross garters and to smile continually in her presence. Malvolio, discovering the note, was overjoyed. Soon he appeared in his strange dress, capering and bowing before the countess. Olivia, startled by the sight of her usually dignified steward behaving in such a peculiar fashion, decided he had lost his wits. Much to the amusement of the three conspirators, she

had him confined to a dark room.

As the days went by in the duke's service, Viola fell deeply in love with that sentimental nobleman, but he had eyes only for Olivia and pressed the page to renew his suit with the countess. When Cesario returned with another message from the duke, Olivia openly declared her love for the young page. Cesario insisted, however, that his heart could never be won by any woman. So obvious were Olivia's feelings for Cesario that Sir Andrew became jealous. Sir Toby and Maria insisted that Sir Andrew's only course was to fight a duel with the page. Sir Toby delivered Sir Andrew's blustering challenge, which Cesario reluctantly accepted.

While these events were taking place, Sebastian, Viola's twin brother, had been rescued by Antonio, a sea captain, and the two had become close friends. When Sebastian decided to visit the court of Duke Orsino at Ilyria, Antonio, although he feared that he might be arrested because he was the duke's enemy and had once fought a duel with Orsino, decided to accompany his young friend. Upon arrival in Ilyria, Antonio gave Sebastian his purse for safekeeping, and the two men separated for several hours.

During his wanderings about the city, Antonio happened upon the trumped-up duel between the unwilling Cesario and Sir Andrew. Mistaking the page for Sebastian, Antonio immediately went to the rescue of his supposed friend. When police officers arrived on the scene, one of them recognized Antonio and arrested him in the name of the duke.

Antonio, mistaking Viola in disguise for Sebastian, asked for the return of his purse, only to be surprised and hurt because the page disclaimed all knowledge of the captain's money. As Antonio was dragged protesting to jail, he shouted invectives at Sebastian for refusing him his purse. Thus Viola learned for the first time that her brother still lived.

The real Sebastian, meanwhile, had been followed by Sir Andrew, who never dreamed that the young man was not the same Cesario with whom he had just been fighting. Egged on by Sir Toby and Maria, Sir Andrew engaged Sebastian in a duel and was promptly wounded, along with Sir Toby. Olivia then interfered and had Sebastian taken to her home. There, having sent for a priest, she married the surprised but not unwilling Sebastian.

The officers were escorting Antonio past Olivia's house as Duke Orsino, accompanied by Cesario, appeared at the gates. Instantly Orsino recognized Antonio and demanded to know why the sailor had returned to Ilyria, a city filled with his enemies. Antonio explained that he had rescued and befriended the duke's present companion Sebastian, and because of his deep friendship for the lad had accompanied him to Ilyria despite the danger his visit involved. Then pointing to Cesario, he sorrowfully accused the supposed Sebastian of violating their friendship by not returning his purse.

The duke was protesting against this accusation when Olivia appeared and saluted Cesario as her husband. The duke also began to think his page ungrateful, especially since Cesario had been told to press Orsino's suit with Olivia. Just then Sir Andrew and Sir Toby came running looking for a doctor because Sebastian had wounded them. Seeing Cesario, Sir Andrew began to rail at him for his violence. Olivia dismissed the two old men quickly. As they left, the real Sebastian appeared and apologized for the wounds he had given the old men.

Spying Antonio, Sebastian joyfully greeted his friend. Antonio and the rest of the amazed group, unable to believe what they saw, stared from Cesario to Sebastian. Viola then revealed her true identity, explained her dis-

guise, and told how she and her brother had been separated. The mystery cleared up, Sebastian and Viola affectionately greeted each other. The duke, seeing the page whom he had grown so fond was in reality a woman, asked that Viola dress again in feminine attire. She was unable to do as he desired, she explained, because the kind sea captain to whom she had entrusted her clothes was held in prison through the orders of Malvolio. This difficulty was cleared up quickly, for Olivia's clown, Feste, pitying Malvolio, visited him in his confinement and secured a long letter in which the steward explained the reasons for his actions. The plot against him revealed, Malvolio was released. Then followed the freeing of the sea captain, the marriage of Viola and Orsino, and also that of Sir Toby and Maria. Only Malvolio, unhappy in the happiness of others remained peevish and disgruntled.

Critical Evaluation

Twelfth Night: Or, What You Will, was apparently written to be performed on that feast day, the joyous climax of the Renaissance Christmas season, although the feast has nothing intrinsic to do with the substance of the play. The subtitle perhaps suggests that it is a festive bagatelle to be lightly, but artfully, tossed off. Indeed, the play may have been written earlier and revised for the occasion; surely there are many signs of revision, as in the assignment of some songs to Feste which must originally have been intended for Viola. The tone of the play is consistently appropriate to the high merriment of the season. This is Shakespeare at the height of his comic powers, with nine comedies behind him, in an exalted mood to which he never returned, for this play immediately precedes the great tragedies and the problem plays. In *Twelfth Night*, he recombines many elements and devices from earlier plays, particularly *Two Gentlemen of Verona* and *The Comedy of Errors*, into a new triumph, unsurpassed in its deft execution.

It is a brilliant irony that this most joyous play should be compounded out of the sadnesses of the principal characters. Yet the sadnesses are, for the most part, the mannered sadnesses that the Elizabethans so much savored. Orsino particularly revels in a sweet melancholy which is reminiscent of that which afflicted Antonio at the beginning of *The Merchant of Venice*. His opening speech, which has often been taken too seriously, is not a grief-stricken condemnation of love. It owes much more to Petrarch. Orsino revels in love-longing and the bittersweet satiety of his romantic self-indulgence. He is in love with love, and he is loving every minute of it.

Set up at the other end of town, in balance with Orsino and his establishment, is the household of Olivia. Although her sadness for her brother's death initially seems more substantial than Orsino's airy fantasies, the fact is that she too is a Renaissance melancholic who is wringing

the last ounce of enjoyment out of her grief. Her plan to isolate herself for seven years of mourning is an excess, as is wittily pointed out by Feste among others. This plan, though, does provide an excellent counterbalance to Orsino's fancy and sets the plot in motion, since Orsino's love-longing is frustrated, or should we say gratified, by Olivia's being a recluse.

The point of contact, ferrying back and forth between the two, is Viola—as Cesario. She too is sad, but her sadness, like the rest of her behavior, is more direct and human. The sweet beauty which shines through her disguise is elevated beyond a vulgar joke by the immediate, though circumstantially ridiculous, response of Olivia to her human appeal. Viola's grief is not stylized and her love is for human beings rather than abstractions. She seems destined to unite the two melancholy dreamers, but what the play in fact accomplishes is the infusion of Viola, in her own person and in her alter ego, her brother, into both households. The outcome is a glorious resolution. It is, of course immaterial to the dreamy Orsino that he gets Viola instead of Olivia—the emotion is more important than the person. And Olivia, already drawn out of her study by the disguised Viola, gets the next best thing—Sebastian.

The glittering plot is reinforced by some of Shakespeare's best, most delicate dramatic poetry. Moreover, the drama is suffused with bittersweet music. The idyllic setting in Ilyria cooperates with language and imagery to create a most delightful atmosphere wholly appropriate to the celebration of love and the enjoyment of this world.

There is one notable briar in the rose garden, Malvolio, but he is perhaps the most interesting character in the play. Malvolio is called a puritan, and, though he is not a type, he does betray characteristics contemporarily associated with that sect. He is the sort of self-important, serious-minded person with high ideals who cannot bear the happiness of others. As Sir Toby puts it, "Dost thou think because thou art virtuous, there shall be no more cakes and ale?" Malvolio is in a tough spot in this joyous world and, against his will, he becomes part of the fun when he is duped and made to appear ridiculous. He is, however, the representative of a group, growing in power, whose earnestness threatened to take the joy out of life (and, incidentally, close the theaters). Yet, Shakespeare does not indulge in a satire on puritanism. As Dover Wilson has noted, he does not characteristically, avail himself of the critical powers of comedy except in a most indirect way.

Malvolio is ridiculous, but so are the cavaliers who surround him. The absurd Aguecheek and the usually drunken Sir Toby Belch are the representatives, on the political level, of the old order which Malvolio's confreres in the real world were soon to topple. Yet, if these characters are flawed, they are certainly more engaging than the inflated Malvolio. Shakespeare does not set up the contrast as a political allegory, with right on one side and wrong on the other. Nevertheless, Malvolio is an intrusion in the idyllic world of the play. He cannot love; his desire for the hand of Olivia is grounded in an earnest will to get ahead. He cannot celebrate; he is too pious and self-involved. What is left for him but to be the butt of the joke? That is his role in the celebration. Some critics have suggested that he has been treated too harshly. However, a Renaissance audience would have understood how ludicrous and indecorous it was for a man of his class to think for a moment of courting Olivia. His pompous and blustery language are the key to how alien he is to this festive context. When he has done his bit, Olivia casually mentions that perhaps he has been put upon, but this is the only gesture he deserves. He is the force that can ruin the celebration of all that is good and refined and joyful in Elizabethan society.

TWENTY THOUSAND LEAGUES UNDER THE SEA

Type of work: Novel
Author: Jules Verne (1828–1905)
Type of plot: Adventure romance
Time of plot: 1866–1867
Locale: The Seven Seas
First published: *Vingt Mille Lieues sous les mers*, 1870 (English translation 1874)

An imaginative romance prophetic of modern scientific inventions, most notably the submarine, Twenty Thousand Leagues Under the Sea *is an exciting adventure story that features the exploits of Captain Nemo of the* Nautilus.

Principal Characters

Captain Nemo, a mysterious man who designs and builds the submarine *Nautilus* on a desert island. It provides its own electricity and oxygen, and the sea supplies food for its crew. Nemo hates society but uses gold recovered from sunken ships to benefit the unfortunate.

Professor Pierre Aronnax (pyĕr' à·rônâx'), of the Paris Museum of Natural History, who heads an expedition aboard the American frigate *Abraham Lincoln* to track down a mysterious sea creature that has attacked and sunk ships all over the world.

Ned Land, a harpooner taken along on the theory that the killer is a gigantic newrhal. An explosion aboard the *Abraham Lincoln* tosses him, along with Aronnax and Conseil, aboard the *Nautilus,* where he and Nemo save each other's lives.

Conseil (kŏn·sĕy'), the servant of Aronnax, who shares their adventures aboard the *Nautilus* in the Atlantic, Pacific, and Polar Oceans. When a maelstrom overcomes the submarine in Norwegian waters, Aronnax, Land, and Conseil recover consciousness on an island, in ignorance of the fate of Captain Nemo or the *Nautilus*.

The Story

In different parts of the ocean, a number of ships had sighted a mysterious monster, gleaming with light, such as no man had ever seen before. After this monster had attacked and sunk several vessels, people all over the world were both amazed and alarmed. Finally an American frigate, the *Abraham Lincoln*, was fitted out to track down and destroy the mysterious sea creature. Among its passengers was Pierre Aronnax, Professor of Natural History in the Museum of Paris, who had published his opinion that the monster was a giant narwhal. One of the crew was Ned Land, an expert harpooner. For quite a while, the ship sailed without sighting anything even remotely resembling the reported terror of the seas.

The creature was sighted at last. When an opportunity presented itself, Ned Land threw his harpoon, but the monster was uninjured and Land realized that it was protected by a thick steel-like armor. During a pursuit in the darkness, a terrific explosion rocked the ship. Professor Aronnax, Ned Land, and Conseil found themselves floundering in the water. Aronnax fainted. Regaining consciousness, he discovered that they were aboard some sort of underwater craft. Later, two men came to greet them. The survivors from the ship spoke to them in various languages, but the men appeared not to understand. Then the captain of the vessel appeared and spoke to them in French. He revealed that his name was Nemo, that the vessel was a submarine, that they were, in effect, prisoners who would have every liberty aboard, except on occasions when they would receive orders to retire to their cabins.

Aronnax learned that the submarine *Nautilus* had been built in a complicated manner. Parts of it had been secured from various places and secretly assembled on a desert island. Then a fire had been set to destroy all traces of the work done there. The ship manufactured its own electricity, had provisions for quantities of oxygen which allowed it to remain submerged, and was as comfortable as any home. All food came from the ocean. There was fish, but fish such as Aronnax had never before tasted. There were cigars, not of tobacco but of a special seaweed. Captain Nemo showed them air guns, which allowed him and the crew to go hunting, as well as a device that permitted the crew to walk on the ocean floor.

In the Pacific, Captain Nemo invited the three survivors to a hunt in the marine forest of Crespo, where Ned Land saved Captain Nemo's life by killing a creature which was about to put an end to the captain. Later, the captain saved Land's life. In Ceylon they watched the pearl divers in the oyster beds. There Nemo saved an Indian from the jaws of a shark.

Off the coast of Borneo the three survivors decided to go ashore in the hope of bagging some land game. While they were hunting, they were attacked by natives. Although they managed to get back to the *Nautilus*, the savages remained clustered about the ship. Aronnax was alarmed, certain that the natives would board the submarine when the hatches were opened for oxygen the next morning. He took his problem to Captain Nemo, who was not at all worried. Instead he told the professor about an eighteenth century ship that had sunk with a full cargo of gold. The next morning, when the hatches were opened, the natives did try to come aboard, but the few who touched the rails let out a shriek and retreated in terror. Ned Land touched the rail and was paralyzed with shock; the rail was electrified.

The captain announced suddenly that he would enter the Mediterranean. Aronnax supposed that he would have to circle the Cape of Good Hope. To his astonishment, he learned that the captain had discovered a passage under the Isthmus of Suez. The submarine entered the Mediterranean through the underwater passage.

On one occasion, the three companions were ordered to go to their cabins. Some sort of encounter occurred, and later Aronnax was called upon to treat a crew member who had been injured. When the sailor died, he was buried in a coral forest on the ocean floor. By that time, the survivors had discovered that Captain Nemo had a tremendous fortune in gold salvaged from sunken vessels. Although the captain had some mysterious hatred against society, he nevertheless used the money to benefit his unfortunate fellowmen.

Ned Land grew to dislike the captain intensely. He told Aronnax that he would escape as soon as an opportunity presented itself. They thought such an opportunity had come when they rounded Spain, but their plan did not materialize. When they came close to Long Island, they thought the time for escape had come, but a sudden hurricane blew the ship off its course, toward Newfoundland.

On another occasion the captain astonished them by heading toward the South Pole. There the ship was endangered by an iceberg, and for several days, passengers and crew were in danger of their lives. Escaping, they headed northward. As the *Nautilus* approached the coast of Norway, it was suddenly drawn into the notorious maelstrom, the deathtrap for so many ships. Shortly before, the submarine had encountered a mysterious ship, which had attacked it. The submarine succeeded in sinking the unknown vessel. Aronnax believed that in this incident there was a clue to Captain Nemo's hatred of society.

The professor never knew what actually happened after the *Nautilus* was drawn into the maelstrom. When he awoke, he and his companions were safe and sound on a Norwegian island. They also had no idea how they had reached the island. They were the only men who now knew the secrets of the ocean—if Captain Nemo and his crew had perished.

Critical Evaluation

Jules Verne was a fascinating and gifted man about whom most readers of his works know relatively little. Americans usually base their opinions of Verne solely upon the inaccurate and shoddy translations of his works. Unfortunately, many of Verne's books were published and translated hurriedly in the last quarter of the nineteenth century, and they lost much of the detail and concern for accuracy which Verne had put into the French originals. Consequently, Jules Verne is regarded as a great storyteller, even the father of science fiction by many; but in no way do most people respect him as a writer who drew to the full extent on the science of his time. A study of Verne in his original French offers a much more impressive look at the author's expertise in his field. The plots of his books are structured around pages and pages of scientific notes, observations, and investigations made into his subject matter. *Twenty Thousand Leagues Under the Sea* is no exception. Before writing the book, Verne interviewed marine engineering specialists, scientists, fishermen, sailors—in short, everyone who could add new dimensions to the plans he had for a novel about the fascinating depths of the ocean floor and travel in that realm in an enclosed vessel. After much thought, Verne developed a plot around these many facts and used his fictional characters to bring it to life.

The basic outline of *Twenty Thousand Leagues Under the Sea* is a simple one. The greatest creation is Captain Nemo, whose name means "no one." He has rejected all that society represents and has taken refuge in his underwater realm. As captain of the *Nautilus*, he is the supreme commander who holds the fate of his three prisoners in his hands. He is, on the one hand, kind, patient, and cultured; on the other, he is vengeful and mysterious. His tragic flaw is the hatred he has for society, a hatred never fully explained. The senseless and unjust destruction of the warship in the last pages of the book makes Professor Aronnax all too eager to escape the *Nautilus* and the clutches of Captain Nemo.

Professor Aronnax is the most real character in the book. The professor narrates this story and answers the questions of his comrades while dispensing great amounts of information regarding things he has studied about marine life and the underwater world. The professor thus provided Verne with an outlet for some of the innumerable details which he collected for his story.

Conseil, the professor's servant whose devotion to his

master is unquestioned, is a simple character, pleasingly eccentric. Ned the harpooner represents the more physical, temperamental, and self-reliant personality. He is the common man whose makeup reflects extremes of good and bad. Ned's passions and his anger at being made a prisoner of Captain Nemo make him seem a little more normal than the rest.

Throughout the book, Verne combines science fiction with humor and fascinating characterization with vivid detail and description. Verne was not an especially great literary stylist, but he was, without doubt, a great researcher. In his enthusiasm for the discoveries of science and his communication of such findings through his writings, he foresaw the future's shape, and he built a valuable stepping-stone for writers of science fiction in the decades that followed.

TWO ESSAYS ON ANALYTICAL PSYCHOLOGY

Type of work: Psychological monographs
Author: Carl G. Jung (1875–1961)
First published: 1928

Two Essays on Analytical Psychology, now published in English as volume 1 of the *Collected Works*, has often been called the best introduction to Carl G. Jung's work that the beginning student can find. Both "On the Psychology of the Unconscious" and "Relations Between the Ego and the Unconscious" are 1928 revisions of essays that Jung wrote in 1912 and 1916. (Almost all of Jung's early work was revised extensively before its appearance in the collected edition to which he devoted his last years.)

"On the Psychology of the Unconscious" begins, as so many of Jung's monographs do, with a version of his famous criticism of Sigmund Freud and Alfred Adler. Jung, who was Freud's most famous disciple from 1909 to 1914, held differences in ideas that led to personal differences which have been continued with more than enough rancor by their followers even today. One crucial difference was Jung's belief that the Freudian libido was too narrowly concerned with sexual energy and that Adler's definition of libido as a will to power was also too simplistic. Jung called this basic reservoir of human drives "psychic energy." Jung, however, endorsed the cornerstone of Freud's theory, the dream analysis, calling this technique "the royal road to the unconscious." But Jung would have us rise above too exclusive a concern with sexuality or the will to power. These drives are more important to the young man than they are to the complete man over a long lifetime. Jung saw them as partial truths, and he proposed a theory of the psyche that would transcend both and contain other aspects.

Undoubtedly there is much to be said for Jung's criticism of Freud and Adler as being concerned too reductively with elective forces in the analysis of human motivation. But as time passed, Jung turned more to mythology and folklore for keys to understanding the unconscious of his patients. While Freud always stayed within the confines of the patient's personal experience from childhood on. More important, no matter how a person reacts to Jungian theory, he must acknowledge an unrelenting tendency in the Swiss psychologist to schematize. Again and again in Freud's productive career, his ideas about the unconscious and its significance changed because of the material presented him by his patients. In Jung's analysis, however, a few details from dreams led him to set up categories of psychological behavior and characterological type, drawn from his extensive research into primitive religions and the mysticism of Europe and the Near East. This tendency to formalize patterns of meaning from universal myths and legends has led many of Jung's critics to refuse him the name of scientist; they insist that he is another German philosopher, and a medieval one at that.

Like many makers of mystical systems, Jung insists that everything within the mind has a dual purpose. Conflict may be destructive to mental health, but it also is necessary to spiritual development. He believes that energy results from the tension of opposites. For the young, says Jung, the conflicts are outside—with parents, with society—and here, as noted, the analysis of Freud and Adler are most valuable. But the conflicts of mature man are within. Many are unable to form a significant self because they are unable or unwilling to come to satisfactory terms with the threatening or "shadow" aspects of the collective unconsciousness.

This last division of the mind is another great distinction between Jungian theory and Freudian. Jung postulates a racial or collective unconsciousness, containing what he (and Jacob Burkhardt) called "primordial images," figures containing those qualities dramatized in the great myths of past cultures. These images of daemonic power are not inherited in themselves but the thought patterns that produced them are. For Jung there is a personal unconsciousness such as Freud described, containing our repressed personal emotions. But the collective consciousness is, according to Jung, much more obscure and more powerful, charged with potential for good and evil. Jung also formulated a distinctive dream analysis. Every interpretation of a dream that equates a dream image with a real object he calls interpretation on the objective level. But he contrasted that view with his own subjective interpretation that brings the dreamer back to himself and is synthetic rather than analytic. This is the point at which the vast store of myth and legend material come in, as Jung examines dreams in terms of the struggle for mental health and significant life. The archetype of the hero is one of the most famous he describes, and he relates how both dreams and legends are parallel in their depiction of the lonely voyage of the hero, beneath or through the sea, to a cave or castle where he must battle a monster for the treasure. The hero image is the health-giving power of the unconscious, Jung says, and the monster is the shadow side—perhaps the dark mother, the feminine image in its nihilistic phase. The treasure or boon the hero can win is life itself, a process labeled by Jung as "individuation." For Jung, dreams are another form of the old legends; they are what they say and are not to be translated out of symbolism into psychological motivation, as they were by Freud. To analyze dreams we need to draw parallels from primitive material, because dreams come from the unconsciousness that contains remnants of man's experience in all preceding epochs of evolution. These images are the dominant powers of laws and principles. Prominent in this dark reservoir of the past, besides the hero, are figures Jung called the shadows—the wise old man, the mother, and child—and the anima and the animus, the images of the feminine and the masculine ideals respectively. Charged with power that is beyond good or evil, many of these images carry their own shadow or destructive charge. The wise old man in his malevolent role would appear as Satan or some other demon. The mother may be the generous, nurturing aspect of woman, or she may appear as dark chaos, the shape of devouring emotion into which the self can sink without a trace.

The all-important process of individuation is achieved, says Jung, by analyzing and compensating for these demonic powers that threaten psychic stability. The process, involving suffering and action, is often depicted in dreams by rectangles and circles—enclosures of perfection that Jung termed *mandalas*.

Much of this analysis is like philosophy, Jung admitted, but he added that it must be, for the psyche seeks expression that will involve its whole nature, not merely correct minor irritating obstacles that cause neurosis. One of the essential needs of man's irrational nature is the idea of God, Jung insisted. It is necessary for man's health that the image of the ideal be charged with power and projected outside himself into religious myth whose action he will imitate and whose standards he will uphold.

In "The Relation Between the Ego and the Unconscious," Jung sketches many of these concepts again. (Like the dreams of his patients, Jung's works seem endlessly moving back and forth over much the same ground.) Here, however, he also describes the function of the *persona*, the mask the psyche creates to mediate between the desire of the unconscious inner world and the conscious outer world. Individuation consists of the creation of an authentic self, living in dynamic but useful tension between those two forces. If the unconsciousness rides roughshod over the *persona*, psychosis results. If the unconsciousness is not expressed in some useful way, however, the power from the libido can never be harnessed and unending psychic paralysis, characterized by unceasing tension and anxiety, results. Man must use this dark power, which Jung calls *mana,* and not be used by it.

It is interesting to observe that although many literary people and humanists have become champions of Jung, few scientists have. Even though Jung seems so often in his analysis merely to substitute one system of metaphor for another, rather than bring us any basically new understanding of mental process, there can be no denying that, by joining comparative mythology to psychology, Jung has had extraordinary influence upon both the reading and the writing of literary works in this century.

THE TWO GENTLEMEN OF VERONA

Type of work: Drama
Author: William Shakespeare (1564–1616)
Type of plot: Romantic comedy
Time of plot: Sixteenth century
Locale: Italy
First presented: 1594

An early and comparatively immature romantic comedy, The Two Gentlemen of Verona *is charming and witty; but the characters seem superficial, and the hero's quick and sympathetic forgiveness of the friend who had betrayed him strikes a false note.*

Principal Characters

Valentine (văl′ən·tīn), a witty young gentleman of Verona. Scoffing at his lovesick friend Proteus, he goes with his father to Milan, where he enters the court of the duke and promptly falls in love with Silvia, the ruler's daughter. Planning to elope with her, he finds his plot betrayed to the duke, and he flees to a nearby forest to save his life. There he joins a band of outlaws and becomes their leader, a sort of Robin Hood. His concept of the superior claims of friendship over love is uncongenial to the modern reader, who finds it hard to forgive him when he calmly bestows Silvia upon Proteus, from whose clutches he has just rescued her, to testify to the depth of his renewed friendship for the young man.

Proteus (prō′tē·ŭs), his friend, a self-centered youth who fancies himself a lover in the best euphuistic tradition. He forgets his strong protestations of undying affection for Julia when he meets Valentine's Silvia in Milan. No loyalties deter him from betraying his friend's planned elopement to the duke, then deceiving the latter by trying to win the girl for himself while he pretends to be furthering the courtship of Sir Thurio. When Silvia resists his advances, he carries her off by force. Stricken with remorse when Valentine intervenes to protect her, he promises to reform. The constancy of his cast-off sweetheart, Julia, makes him recognize his faithlessness and her virtue, and they are happily reunited.

Julia (jōōl′yə), a young noblewoman of Verona. She criticizes her suitors with the humorous detachment of a Portia before she confesses to her maid her fondness for Proteus. She follows him to Milan in the disguise of the page Sebastian, and with dogged devotion she even carries Proteus' messages to her rival Silvia, in order to be near him. She reveals her identity almost unwittingly by fainting when Valentine relinquishes Silvia to Proteus as a token of his friendship. She regains the love of her fiancé by this demonstration of her love.

Silvia (sĭl′vĭ·ə), daughter of the Duke of Milan. She falls in love with Valentine and encourages his suit; she asks him to copy a love letter for her—directed to himself, although he does not realize this fact at first. Proteus' fickle admiration annoys rather than pleases her, and she stands so firm in her love for Valentine that his generous offer of her to Proteus seems almost intolerable.

Speed, Valentine's exuberant, loquacious servant, cleverer than his master at seeing through Silvia's device of the love letter. He is one of the earliest of Shakespeare's witty clowns, the predecessor of Touchstone, Feste, and the Fool in *King Lear.*

Launce (läns), Proteus' man, a simple soul, given to malapropisms and faux pas, in spite of his excellent intentions. His presentation to Silvia, in Proteus' name, of his treasured mongrel, Crab, a dog "as big as ten" of the creature sent by his master as a gift, does little to further Proteus' courtship. Inspired by his master's gallantry, he pays court to a milkmaid and gives great amusement to Speed by his enumeration of her virtues.

The Duke of Milan, Silvia's father, a strong-willed man who attempts to control his rash impulses. He welcomes and trusts Valentine, although he suspects his love for Silvia, until Proteus reveals the proposed elopement; then he cleverly forces Valentine into a position in which he must reveal his treachery. He finally consents to his daughter's marriage to Valentine as gracefully as possible, but one cannot forget that he is at this time the prisoner of the prospective bridegroom's men.

Sir Thurio (tōōrĭ·ō, thōō′rĭ·ō), a vain, unsuccessful suitor for the hand of Silvia, who despises him. Although he is willing to follow Proteus' expert instruction in the manners of courtship, he has no desire to risk his life for a woman who cares nothing for him, and he hastily departs when Valentine stands ready to defend his claim to Silvia's hand.

Lucetta (lōō·eĕt′ə), a clever, bright young woman who delights in teasing her mistress Julia, for whom she is friend and confidante as well as servant.

Sir Eglamour (ĕg′lə·mōōr), an elderly courtier. He serves as Silvia's protector when she prepares to flee from her father and marriage to Sir Thurio.

The Story

Valentine and Proteus, two longtime friends of great understanding, disagreed heartily on one point. Valentine thought the most important thing in life was to travel and learn the wonders of the world. Proteus, on the other hand, thought love the only thing worthwhile. The two friends parted for a time when Valentine traveled to Milan, to seek advancement and honor in the palace of the duke. He pleaded with Proteus to join him in the venture, but Proteus was too much in love with Julia to leave her side for even a short time. Julia was a noble and pure young girl, pursued by many, but Proteus at last won her heart, and the two were happy in their love.

Valentine journeyed to Milan, and there he learned his friend had been right in believing love to be all that is worthwhile. In Milan Valentine met the duke's daughter Silvia and fell instantly in love with her. Silvia returned his love, but her father wanted her to marry Thurio, a foolish man who had no charm but owned much land and gold. Valentine longed for Silvia, but he saw no chance of getting her father's consent to his suit. Then he learned that his friend Proteus was soon to arrive in Milan, sent there by his father, who, ignorant of Proteus' love affair, wished his son to educate himself by travel.

The two friends had a joyful reunion. Valentine proudly presented his friend to Silvia, and to Proteus he highly praised the virtue and beauty of his beloved. When they were alone, Valentine confided to Proteus that he planned to fashion a rope ladder and steal Silvia from her room and marry her, for her father would give her to no one but Thurio. Valentine, asking his friend to help him in his plan, was too absorbed to notice that Proteus remained strangely silent. The truth was that, at the first sight of Silvia, Proteus had forgotten his solemn vows to Julia, sealed before he left her with the double giving of rings, and he had forgotten too his oath of friendship with Valentine. He determined to have Silvia for his own. So, with protestations of self-hatred for the betrayal of his friend, Proteus told the duke of Valentine's plan to escape with Silvia from the palace and carry her away to be married in another land. The duke, forewarned, tricked Valentine into revealing the plot and banished him from Milan, on penalty of his life should he not leave at once.

While these events were taking place, Julia, thinking that Proteus still loved her and grieving over his absence, disguised herself as a page and traveled to Milan to see her love. She was on her way to Milan when Valentine was forced to leave that city and Silvia. Valentine, not knowing that his onetime friend had betrayed him, believed Proteus' promise that he would carry letters back and forth between the exile and Silvia.

With Valentine out of the way, Proteus next proceeded to get rid of Thurio as a rival. Thurio, foolish and gullible, was an easy man to trick. One night Proteus and Thurio went to Silvia's window to serenade her in Thu-

rio's name but Proteus sang to her and made love speeches also. Unknown to him, Julia, in the disguise of a page, stood in the shadows and heard him disown his love for her and proclaim his love for Silvia. Silvia scorned him, however, and swore that she would love no one but Valentine. She also accused him of playing false with Julia, for Valentine had told her the story of his friend's betrothal.

Calling herself Sebastian, Julia, still in the dress of a page, was employed by Proteus to carry messages to Silvia. One day he gave her the ring which Julia herself had given him and told her to deliver it to Silvia. When Silvia refused the ring and sent it back to Proteus, Julia loved her rival and blessed her.

Valentine, in the meantime, had been captured by outlaws, once-honorable men who had been banished for petty crimes and had taken refuge in the woods near Mantua. In order to save his own life, Valentine joined the band and soon became their leader. A short time later, Silvia, hoping to find Valentine, escaped from the palace and with the help of an agent arrived at an abbey near Milan. There she was captured by the outlaws. When her father heard of her flight, he took Thurio and Proteus, followed by Julia, to the abbey to look for her. Proteus, arriving first on the scene, rescued her from the outlaws before they were able to take her to their leader. Again Proteus proclaimed his love for her. When she scornfully berated him, he seized her and tried to force his attentions upon her. Unknown to Proteus, however, Valentine had overheard all that was said. He sprang upon Proteus and pulled him away from the frightened girl.

Valentine was more hurt and wounded by his friend's duplicity than by anything else that had happened. Yet such was Valentine's forgiving nature that when Proteus confessed his guilt and his shame over his betrayal, Valentine forgave him and received him again as his friend. In order to prove his friendship, he gave up his claim on Silvia. At that moment, Julia, still disguised, fainted away. When she was revived, she pretended to hand over to Silvia the ring Proteus had ordered her to deliver. Instead, however, she offered the ring Proteus had given her when they parted in Verona. Than Julia was recognized by all, and Proteus professed that he still loved her.

The outlaws appeared with the duke and Thurio, whom they had captured in the forest. Thurio gave up all claim to Silvia, for he thought a girl who would run off into the woods to pursue another man much too foolish for him to marry. Then her father, convinced at last of Valentine's worth, gave that young man permission to marry Silvia. During the general rejoicing Valentine begged one more boon. He asked the duke to pardon the outlaws, all brave men who would serve the duke faithfully if he would return them from exile. The duke granted the boon, and the whole party made its way back to Milan. There the two happy couples would share one wedding day.

Critical Evaluation

The Two Gentlemen of Verona is a play about love. The major source of conflict in the play is the dispute caused by the friction between two differing varieties of love: the attraction between man and woman (romantic love) and the bond between man and man (friendship). Even in modern times there is debate as to which of these types of love is the higher—the more refined, the more pure variety—and during the Renaissance this question was debated endlessly in a series of philosophical and artistic works which form the essential backdrop for Shakespeare's play. In a sense, *The Two Gentlemen of Verona* is Shakespeare's contribution to and comment upon an ongoing controversy over human affections and their proper place within a universal order.

Although *The Two Gentlemen of Verona* is one of Shakespeare's shorter plays, a glance at a Shakespearean concordance reveals that it uses this very word "love" more than does any other—even more than that supposedly most romantic of his works, *Romeo and Juliet*. Yet the love that runs through *The Two Gentlemen of Verona* is at first glance a puzzling one, for what sort of affection must Valentine have in order to offer Silvia to Proteus? In turn, what is Silvia's love that she seems silently to accept the barter? Moreover, if love is indeed the central theme of the play, why is Proteus so laggard in discovering not only Julia's devotion to him but his appreciation for her? On the one hand there is a simple enough answer: If these were not the complications involved, there would be no play. On the other hand, there is the matter of the contemporary worldview from which Shakespeare fashioned his comedy.

The series of changes in thought and attitudes so conveniently jumbled together and labeled as the Renaissance came to England at a relatively late date, and when it arrived it carried contradictory strains, two of the most prominent being courtly love and its counterpart, Neoplatonic love. Courtly love, as expressed most notably by Dante in his *Vita nuova,* emphasized the ennobling and uplifting effects of romantic love, the powerful and positive impact that a virtuous, usually virginal, woman could have on a lowly and often sinful male. Its underlying theme, explicit in Dante and always implicit in Shakespearean comedy, is that man is incomplete and imperfect without the love of a worthy woman. Critics have often speculated as to why Julia is so attracted to Proteus and why Silvia accepts the less-than-perfect and certainly less-than-appreciative Valentine. In the same vein, it could be asked of another of Shakespeare's plays, *All's Well That Ends Well,* why the clearly superior Helena so determinedly woos, outwits, and wins the undeserving Bertram. Such questions miss an essential point: According to the tenets of courtly love, it is precisely the fact that a virtuous woman chooses a man—however many or serious his faults—that ennobles him and raises him, despite those faults, to something approaching her level. This theme is clearly present in *The Two Gentlemen of Verona,* and Julia is the forerunner of her equally virtuous and even more accomplished sister Portia (*A Merchant of Venice*) and Viola (*As You Like It*). Indeed, like Viola, Julia disguises herself as a man in order to follow her lover on his adventures. So accomplished are Shakespeare's heroines in these comedies that they can embrace the social role of either sex and outshine men in their own sphere.

This view of relationships is one pole of the magnetic word "love" as it appears in *The Two Gentlemen of Verona*. The second pole concentrates on male friendship, a theme which was well known in Shakespeare's time because of the philosophy of Neoplatonism. Perhaps the most widely known exponent of this thought in Shakespeare's England was the Italian writer Marsilio Ficino (1433–1499), who developed and elaborated upon the concept of the ladder of love. According to Ficino, the truly noble mind progresses through a series of upward steps, beginning with earthly, physical love and leading ultimately to that final, transcendent love which can be equated with God. In such a system, the love between man and man, expressed as a friendship of souls, was higher than romantic love between man and woman, because it had no (or little) physical attraction and instead concentrated upon intellectual and spiritual affinities. This enabled the soul to mount the ladder toward contemplation of true, divine love. Within such a philosophy, it is allowable that Valentine could openly offer Silvia to his friend Proteus, without either shame or regret.

Yet this philosophy is not the one which guides *The Two Gentlemen of Verona*. It has enough potency to shape the play's plot, but it cannot determine its outcome or control its theme. A tough-minded sense of romantic, courtly love, embodied in Julia, is capable of outdueling the somewhat fragile male friendship of Valentine and Proteus. The triumph of Julia, however, is more than the victory of one philosophical system over another; instead, it is the triumph of common sense over all abstract forms of thought. In its ending, as in its characters and style, *The Two Gentlemen of Verona* looks forward to Shakespeare's later comedies, which are cast in the golden light of his deep understanding of human faults, needs, and values.

ULYSSES

Type of work: Novel
Author: James Joyce (1882–1941)
Type of plot: Psychological realism
Time of plot: June 16, 1904
Locale: Dublin
First published: 1922

A continuation of the story of Stephen Dedalus told in A Portrait of the Artist as a Young Man, *this major psychological novel is structured around Homeric parallels, so that the incidents, characters, and scenes of a single day in Dublin in 1904 correspond to those of the Odyssean myth.*

Principal Characters

Stephen Dedalus, a proud, sensitive young Irishman, a writer and teacher called **Kinch** (from "kinchin," child) by one of his friends. In his search for the nature and meaning of life, Stephen examines all phases of his existence. History, he says, is a nightmare from which he is trying to awake. As he looks back to his childhood, he can remember only his family's poverty and his father as a patron of taverns. His devotion to Ireland is not the answer to his search; she is an old sow, he believes, that eats her own young. His religion is not enough to make life purposeful. Stephen cannot dismiss his mother's deathbed prayer that he avow his belief, and his inability to comply frets him with remorse. Symbolically, Stephen is Telemachus, the son in search of a father. In effect, he finds a symbolic father in Leopold Bloom, an older man who takes care of Stephen after the young man has been in a street fight with British soldiers. Declining Bloom's invitation to live with him and his wife, Stephen goes out into the darkened street to return to the Tower where he is staying and to his dissolute life among the young men and students he knows.

Leopold Bloom, a Jewish advertising salesman who is, symbolically, Ulysses, the father of Telemachus. Bloom's yearning for a son stems from the long-past death of Rudy, his eleven-day-old son. A patient husband, he is cuckolded by his wife's business manager, but he is carrying on a furtive flirtation of his own. Bloom is Any Man, plodding through the daily routine of living—visiting bars, restaurants, newspaper offices, hospitals, and brothels of Dublin—because he hopes for something out of the ordinary but must be satisfied with the tawdry.

Malachi Mulligan, called **Buck,** a medical student and the friend of Stephen Dedalus. He points up Stephen's attitudes and philosophies, the two young men being opposites, the scientific and the philosophical. Buck, calloused to suffering and death by his medical training, says that death is a beastly thing and nothing else; it simply does not matter. According to Buck, Stephen's religious strain is all mockery; if it were not, Buck says,

Stephen could have prayed with his mother. Buck is doubtful that Stephen will ever produce any great writing. The model for Buck Mulligan was the Irish physician and poet, Oliver St. John Gogarty.

Marion Tweedy Bloom, called **Molly,** whose background differs greatly from her husband's. Brought up in the atmosphere of a military post in Gibraltar, Molly, a lush creature and second-rate concert singer, finds life with her husband and life in Dublin dull. Her escape from the reality of the humdrum comes through love affairs with other men. Her latest lover is Blazes Boylan, a virile younger man. Bloom's suggestion that Stephen Dedalus come to live with them gives Molly a momentary tingle as she contemplates the pleasure of having a still younger man in the house. Molly's thoughts and reverie make up the final section of the book, as she considers the present but finally lapses into reminiscences of a sexual experience of her girlhood. She is Penelope to Bloom's Ulysses.

Blazes Boylan, Molly's lover and the manager of a concert tour she is planning. The business aspect of their meetings does not delude Bloom.

Haines, a young Englishman who lives in the Tower with Stephen Dedalus, Buck Mulligan, and other students and artists. His indulgence in drinking orgies alienates more ascetic Stephen. Because Haines has considerably more money than the other young men, he is frequently the butt of their sarcasm. Haines is an anti-Semite who fears that England may be taken over by German Jews.

Paddy Dignam, Bloom's friend, who dies of a stroke.

Father Coffey, who performs the funeral rites over the body of Paddy Dignam.

Mrs. Breen, a neighbor, to whom Bloom gives the account of the funeral.

Mrs. Purefoy, another neighbor, who, Mrs. Breen reports, is in a maternity hospital. Bloom's visit to the hospital to inquire about her leads to his meeting with Stephen Dedalus, who is drinking with a group of medical students.

Davy Byrnes, a tavern owner whose establishment

attracts all types of people who discuss many subjects.

Barney Kiernan, the owner of a bar where Leopold Bloom gets into an argument with a patriotic Irishman and is ejected.

Mr. Deasy, the headmaster of the school where Stephen teaches. Deasy probably assesses Stephen's aptitudes rather exactly when he tells the younger man that he is more a learner than a teacher. In lamenting the influx of Jews in England, Deasy points out to Stephen that Ireland is the only country where Jews have not been persecuted—because she never let them in.

Talbot, Cochrane, Armstrong, Comyn, Edith, Ethel, and **Lily,** some of Stephen's pupils. Their indifference and ineptness are discouraging to their young teacher, giving rise to Deasy's prognosis of Stephen's career.

Milly, the Bloom's daughter. Her existence does not mitigate Bloom's longing for a son, nor does it lessen Molly's desire for romance and release from tedium.

Gertie MacDowell, a young girl who exhibits herself to Leopold Bloom on Sandymount shore.

Myles Crawford, a newspaper editor.

The Story

Buck Mulligan mounted the stairs of the old tower and prepared to shave on the morning of June 16, 1904. A moment later, Stephen Dedalus came to the stairhead and stood looking out over Dublin Bay. When Mulligan spoke of the sea glinting in the morning sunlight, Stephen had a sudden vision of his own mother; he had been called back from Paris to her deathbed a year before. He remembered how she had begged him to pray for her soul and how he, rebelling against the churchly discipline of his boyhood, had refused.

After breakfast, Stephen and Mulligan went off with Haines, a young Englishman who also lived in the old tower. Despite the Englishman's attempts to be friendly, Stephen disliked Haines, who was given to nightlong drunken sprees. Stephen felt that his own life was growing purposeless and dissolute through his association with Mulligan and other medical students.

Stephen was a teacher. Because it was a half-day holiday at school, the boys were restless. One of his pupils was unable to do his simple arithmetic problems, and in the boy Stephen saw for a moment an image of his own awkward youth. He was relieved when he could dismiss the class.

Later, he walked alone on the beach. He thought of literature and his student days, of his unhappiness in Dublin, his lack of money, his family sinking into poverty while his shabby genteel father made his daily round of the Dublin pubs. He saw the carcass of a dead dog rolling in the surf. Stephen remembered how a dog had frightened him in his childhood; he was, he thought wryly, not one of the Irish heroes.

Meanwhile, Leopold Bloom had crawled out to bed to prepare his wife's breakfast. He was a Jewish advertising salesman, and, for sixteen years, the patient, uncomplaining husband of Marion Tweedy Bloom, a professional singer of mediocre talent. He was vaguely unhappy to know that she was carrying on an affair with Blazes Boylan, a sporting Irishman who was managing the concert tour that she was planning.

Bloom munched his own breakfast and read a letter from his daughter Milly, who was working in a photographer's shop in Mullingar. Her letter reminded Bloom of his son Rudy, who had died when he was eleven days old. Bloom read Milly's letter again, wondering about a young student his daughter mentioned. For a moment, he was afraid that Milly might grow up like her mother.

Bloom set out on his morning walk. At the post office, he stopped to pick up a letter addressed to Henry Flower, Esq., a letter from a woman who signed herself Martha. Bloom was unhappy at home and was carrying on a flirtation by mail under another name. He idly wandered into a church and listened to part of the mass. Later he joined a party of mourners on their way to the funeral of an old friend, Paddy Dignam, who had died suddenly of a stroke. During the service, Bloom watched Father Coffey. He thought again of little Rudy and of his own father, a suicide victim.

The day's business for Bloom was a call at a newspaper office to arrange for the printing of an advertisement. While he was there, Stephen Dedalus also came to the office. The two men saw each other, but they did not speak.

Bloom left the newspaper building and walked across the O'Connell bridge. He met Mrs. Breen and gave her an account of Dignam's funeral. She told him that Mrs. Purefoy was in the maternity hospital in Holles Street. Bloom walked on, taking in the sights of Dublin on a summer day. At last he entered Davy Byrne's pub and ordered a cheese sandwich. Later he went to the National Library to look at some newspaper files. There Stephen, flushed with the drinks he had taken at lunch, was expounding to Buck Mulligan and some literary friends his own ingenious theory of Shakespeare's plays and the second-best bed of Shakespeare's will. Again, Bloom and Stephen saw each other but did not speak.

Bloom went to the Ormond Hotel for a late lunch. Blazes Boylan came into the bar before he left to keep an appointment with Molly.

Late that afternoon, Bloom got into a brawl in a pub where the talk was all about the money that Blazes Boylan had won in a boxing match. Bloom escaped from the jeering crowd and walked along the Sandymount shore.

In the dimming twilight, he watched young Gertie MacDowell. The moon rose. Bloom decided to stop by the hospital to ask about Mrs. Purefoy. As he walked slowly along the strand, a cuckoo clock struck nine in a priest's house that he was passing. Bloom suddenly realized that he had been cuckolded again, while he sat dreaming his amorous fantasies on the Dublin beach.

At the hospital, he learned that Mrs. Purefoy's baby had not yet been born. There he saw Stephen Dedalus again, drinking with Buck Mulligan and a group of medical students. Bloom was disturbed to find the son of his old friend, Simon Dedalus, in ribald, dissolute company.

Bloom went with the medical students to a nearby pub, where Stephen and Buck Mulligan began a drunken argument over the possession of the key to the old tower. When the group broke up, Stephen and one of the students went on to a brothel in the Dublin slums; Bloom followed them slowly. All were drunk by that time. Bloom had a distorted, lurid vision of his wife and Blazes Boylan together. Stephen was befuddled and thought that his dead mother suddenly appeared from the grave to ask him again to pray for her soul. Running headlong into the street, he was knocked down in a scuffle with two British soldiers. Bloom took Stephen home with him.

Exhausted by his wild night, Stephen remained silent and glum while Bloom talked about art and science. Bloom had begged him to spend the night, to leave Mulligan and his wild friends and come to live with the Blooms, but Stephen refused. The bells of St. George's Church were ringing as he walked off down the silent street.

Bloom went slowly to bed. As he drifted off to sleep, he told Molly firmly that she was to get up and prepare his breakfast in the morning.

Molly Bloom lay awake thinking of Blazes Boylan. She thought of the mysteries of the human body, of people she had known, of her girlhood at a military post on Gibraltar. She considered the possibility that Stephen Dedalus might come to live with her and her husband. Stephen was a writer—young, refined, not coarse like Boylan. She heard a far, shrill train whistle. She recalled all of her past lovers, Bloom's courtship, their years together, the rose she wore in her hair the day Bloom had asked her to marry him as they stood close under a Moorish arch. These wakeful, earthy Penelopean thoughts flowed on, while her tawdry Ulysses, Bloom, the far wanderer of a Dublin day, snored in the darkness by her side.

Critical Evaluation

Ulysses is an attempt at completely recapturing, so far as it is possible in fiction, the life of a particular time and place. The place is Dublin—its streets, homes, shops, newspaper offices, pubs, hospitals, brothels, and schools. The time is a single day in 1904. A continuation of the story of Stephen Dedalus as told in *A Portrait of the Artist as a Young Man*, the novel is also a series of remarkable Homeric parallels, with characters and scenes of a Dublin day corresponding to those of the Odyssean myth. Leopold Bloom is easily recognizable as Ulysses; Molly Bloom, his wife, as Penelope; and Dedalus himself as Telemachus, son of Ulysses—in James Joyce's novel, Bloom's spiritual son. The book is written in a variety of styles and techniques; the most important is the stream-of-consciousness method by which Joyce attempts to reproduce not only the sights, sounds, and smells of Dublin but also the memories, emotions, and desires of his people trapped in the drab modern world.

Approaching *Ulysses* for the first time, the reader should proceed aggressively. If comprehension lapses—even for pages at a time—it is better to push on. For one thing, it is a novel that must be reread. Many elements that appear early in the story make sense only after having read much further along. Bloom's potato talisman, for example, is mentioned in the fourth episode but remains unexplained until the fifteenth, often leaving readers feeling lost in a random flux. The persistent reader, however, will find that the novel is intricately structured.

Joyce himself provided the key to the structure of the novel in two very similar "schemas" which he provided to would-be expositors of *Ulysses*. These charts indicate for each of the eighteen episodes a title corresponding to an episode in the *Odyssey*; the time of day; a dominant color; a "technic" (the style of the episode: for example, "narrative, young," "catechism, personal," "monologue, male"); a dominant "art" (history, literature, philology); an organ of the body (adding up to a more or less complete person); a dominant symbol (in the first episode: "Hamlet, Ireland, Stephen"); and correspondences between Homeric and Joycean characters. These schemes can be found in their most complete form in Richard Ellmann's *Ulysses on the Liffey*.

The schemas have been a mixed blessing to Joycean criticism, for they are sometimes ambiguous or cryptic. Nevertheless, it is difficult to think of another major author whose critics have been so influenced, indeed dominated, by a single piece of external evidence. The schemas are at least suggestive with regard to three of the more salient (and problematic) aspects of the book. These three are the Homeric parallels, Stephen's theory about Shakespeare and art, and the episodic structure and use of style.

Shortly after the publication of *Ulysses*, the Homeric parallel was lauded by T. S. Eliot as having "the importance of a scientific discovery." The schemas and Joyce's notes make clear that he took the parallels very seriously, although the elaborate Homeric analogy is surely not, as Eliot thought, merely a backdrop to heighten "the immense panorama of futility that is the modern world."

Ulysses had been Joyce's favorite hero from his childhood. The quality he was to isolate as unique to the Greek hero was *completeness*. He observed that Ulysses had been a father, a son, a husband, a lover, a soldier who was at first a draft-dodger, and then a "hawk." Although this is a rather curious ideal, it suggests what may have been Joyce's purpose. The story of Ulysses constitutes such a full representation of a complexity of attitudes and values that Joyce was able to use it as a paradigm for the structure of a modern story. The *Odyssey* itself no doubt had been determined by the structure of Homer's intuitions about the nature of life. These intuitions correspond, in the abstract, to Joyce's own. Joyce's at times rather wide digressions from Homer's story suggest this kind of substratum "beneath" the Homeric substratum, which determines both in a manner similar to the combinatory processes of mathematical probability.

This ideal "complete" hero "beyond" even Ulysses would be the abstract person, possessor of the "organs of the body" of the schema. The schema supports this general contention in that the distribution of correspondences to Homer is not consistent. Bloom and Stephen are, in fact, only "in general" Ulysses and Telemachus. Correspondences listed on the schema indicate that in the first episode, for example, Stephen is Telemachus, but also Hamlet. In the ninth episode, Ulysses is "Jesus, Socrates, Shakespeare"; they are each important there. Furthermore, as has been remarked, Stephen is more like a youthful aspect of Ulysses than like Telemachus, who is almost a minor character in Homer. There is, then, no one-to-one impersonation of Homeric characters. Rather, there is a play of functions pointing to an essential human, the abstract "Ulysses" who belongs not exclusively to Homer but to the entire tradition of the Ulysses theme.

The ninth episode, "Scylla and Charybdis," contains Stephen's aesthetic theory. The action is presented as a parable of artistic creation based on Shakespeare's biography. The way the "Ulysses" of the schema functions is rather complex. The schema says that Scylla is "The Rock—Aristotle, Dogma" and Charybdis "The Whirlpool—Plato, Mysticism." "Ulysses," who must sail between these perils, is given as "Socrates, Jesus, Shakespeare." This aspect of "Ulysses" is manifested in Stephen's discourse; Bloom is not even immediately present. The course is the one the artist must take. It includes going between extremes of the inner and outer worlds of his personal experience. There is a struggle between the flux of everyday life and a permanent, repeated structure in the artist's self. This structure is compared to the mole that remains on Stephen's breast although all the molecules of his body have changed, and, in the parable, to a supposed psychological trauma in Shakespeare's youth that determined the structure of his plays and their themes of usurpation, humiliation, and, later, reconciliation. At the level of the individual artistic psyche, the theory recapitulates the determinism treated by the novel as historical and sociological.

As to the individual episodes, the schema names a variety of elements of style that make each unique. Joyce told friends that he intended each to be able to stand on its own. Various episodes are sometimes anthologized and read like short stories. "Circe," episode fifteen, has been produced as a play many times. There is narrational point of view in each episode, but it is clearly never the same. There is abundant exegetical literature for each episode, treating in detail the unity derived of its tone, style, and themes. For this overview, however, it is more important to note that the various episodic styles are part of a second structural principle in the novel.

Total autonomy *and* interdependence combine in the episodic structure; Stephen and Bloom, component elements of the "Ulysses" composite, partake of this combination and therefore avoid becoming mere allegorical types. They are, in fact, complete individuals. This pattern suggests the paradoxical doctrine of the Trinity, where three complete and equal Persons have one Essence. Of the Trinity, Joyce once said that when contemplating one Person, the others slip from view. So it is with Stephen and Bloom; for that matter, any individual episode in *Ulysses* seems capable of absorbing the reader's whole attention. It is, therefore, the overview that leads the reader best through the myriad captivations of Joyce's odyssey.

UTOPIA

Type of work: Humanistic treatise
Author: Sir Thomas More (1478–1535)
Time: Reign of Henry VII of England
Locale: Antwerp, England, Utopia
First published: 1516

Principal Characters

Thomas More, the narrator of "Utopia," who meets the fictional Raphael Hythloday while serving as Henry VII's ambassador in Flanders. More himself suggests in the first part of "Utopia" many reforms, including reform of the severe penal code of England at the time.

Peter Giles, a citizen of Antwerp, a learned and honest young man with whom Thomas More becomes acquainted. Peter Giles introduces Raphael Hythloday to the Englishman and listens with him to Hythloday's marvelous account of the island of Utopia.

Raphael Hythloday, a Portuguese mariner who is learned in the classical languages and in philosophy. He is a widely traveled man, having accompanied Amerigo Vespucci on some of the latter's voyages. He tells Thomas More that he is interested only in peaceful matters and so has attached himself to no monarch. He describes for Thomas More and Peter Giles the civilization on the island of Utopia and tells why he thinks it is the best state in the world.

How to make a better world for men to live in has fascinated the minds of thinkers in every age. From Plato to the present day, men have been thinking and writing about what the world would be like if men could create an earthly paradise. One of the most celebrated examples of such thought and writing is Sir Thomas More's *Utopia*, a work so famous in Western civilization that its title has come to stand for any idealized state. Originally written in Latin, the international language of medieval and Renaissance Europe, the book was widely read, and as early as 1551 a translation into English was made by Ralph Robinson, a London goldsmith.

The book is in two parts, with the second part, curiously enough, written first, in 1515, and the introductory half written in the following year. The book begins with a narrative framework in which More tells how he traveled to Antwerp on a royal mission and there met Peter Giles, a worthy citizen of Antwerp, who in turn introduced him to Raphael Hythloday, whose name in Greek means "a talker of nonsense." Hythloday proved to be more than a mere mariner, for in his conversation he appeared to More to be a man of ripe wisdom and rare experience. The fictional Hythloday was supposedly a companion of Amerigo Vespucci when that worthy was supposed to have made his voyages to America. It was on one of his voyages with Vespucci that Hythloday, according to his own account, discovered the fabled land of Utopia, somewhere in the oceans near the Western hemisphere.

Actually, the first part of *Utopia* does not deal with the legendary island; in it Hythloday tells how, during the reign of King Henry VII, he visited England, conversed with Cardinal Morton, and suggested to that churchman, who was Henry VII's chancellor, some reforms which might benefit England. Among the reforms the fictional Hythloday suggested were the abolishment of the death penalty for theft, the prevention of gambling, less dependence upon the raising of sheep for wool, the disuse of mercenary soldiers, cheaper prices for all commodities, and an end to the enclosure of the common lands for the benefit of great and wealthy landlords. Although Cardinal Morton is made to listen intently to Hythloday's suggestions, More introduces a lawyer who objects that Hythloday's reforms could not be undertaken and that they would not be deemed desirable by anyone who knew the history and customs of England.

In the first part of his *Utopia*, More is obviously pointing out some of the social and economic evils in sixteenth century European life. More than that, he is suggesting that only an outsider can see the faults with an objective eye. The introduction of the lawyer's objections, which are cut short by Cardinal Morton, suggest also that More discerned in sixteenth century society persons who opposed reform and who sought reasons for doing so. Part one of the *Utopia* is More's way of preparing the reader for the section in which his ideal realm is delineated.

In the second part, Hythloday expounds at length about the culture of the mythical land of Utopia, which he had visited during his travels. Hythloday describes Utopia as an island kingdom which is crescent shaped and about five hundred miles in perimeter, separated from other lands by an artificial channel constructed by its founder, the fabulous King Utopus, who saw that the Utopian experiment, if it were to succeed, must be isolated and protected from the encroachments of warlike and predatory neighbors. The island is divided into fifty-four shires, or counties, each with its own town, no town more than a day's walking journey from its neighbors. The central city, Amaurote, is the capital, the seat of the prince who is the island's nominal ruler.

The government of Utopia is relatively simple and largely vested in older men, in patriarchal fashion. Each unit of thirty families is ruled by one man chosen by election every year. Each ten groups of families elects a member of the island council. This council in turn elects the prince, who serves throughout his lifetime unless deposed because of tyranny. The council meets every three days to take up matters of consequence to the people, and no decision is made on the same day the problem is advanced, lest undue haste cause mistakes.

It is not in government alone that More introduces suggestions for reform in his *Utopia*. In this ideal state everyone works, each man having a trade or craft, except the unusually talented who are selected for training and service in the academy of learning. The workday is six hours long, with the time divided equally between the morning and the afternoon. Each person spends a two-year period working as a farmer in the shire outside the city in which he resides. Since everyone works, there is more than enough food and other commodities for the inhabitants. All goods are community-owned, with each person guarding what is given to him for the benefit of the commonwealth. The tastes of the people are simple; no one, having enough for himself, desires to have more than his fellows. Even the prince of Utopia is designated only by the symbol of a sheaf of grain, symbol of plenty. Each person is garbed in durable clothing of leather, linen, or wool. Jewelry is given to children to play with, so that everyone associates such baubles with childishness. Gold and silver are despised, being used for chamber pots, chains for slaves, and the marks of criminal conviction.

In the dialogue Sir Thomas More interjects some objections to the communal idea, but this is the only point on which he seems to have reservations. Yet even on this point, Hythloday's answers to his objections satisfy him.

Violence, bloodshed, and vice, says Hythloday, have been done away with in Utopia. Lest bloodshed of any kind corrupt the people, slaves are required to slaughter the cattle. Dicing and gambling are unknown. The people choose instead to labor for recreation in their gardens, improve their homes, attend humanistic lectures, enjoy music, and converse profitably with one another. The sick are provided for in spacious hospitals erected in each quarter of each city. In the event of a painful and incurable illness, the priests consult with the patient and encourage him to choose death administered painlessly by the authorities. Although no one is required to do so, everyone eats in mess halls where slaves prepare the meals under the supervision of the wives of the family group. At mealtime young and old eat together, except for children under five, and enlightening, pleasant conversation is encouraged.

The Utopian criminal is enslaved, rather than put to death, as he was in sixteenth century England. Adultery is regarded as a crime and punished by slavery. Marriage for love is encouraged but with prudence. Males must be twenty-two and women eighteen before marriage is permitted. The welfare of the family is a state matter, since the family is the basic unit of the Utopian state. The people are anxious for the commonwealth to be rich, for the Utopians buy off their enemies and use their wealth to hire foreign mercenary soldiers; they hope in this manner to encourage potential enemies to murder one another.

The Utopians are described as a religious people who practice toleration almost unknown in Catholic Tudor England. Some are Christians; others worship God in other ways. Atheism and militant sectarianism are alike forbidden.

Two points should be made in connection with Sir Thomas More's work. One is that his borrowings from Plato and other earlier authors did not prevent him from adding much that was his own in theory and practice. The second point is that in the centuries since the writing of *Utopia*, some of the author's ideas have been put into effect—unlikely as they may have appeared to his contemporaries. Society may never realize an Utopian ideal, but surely society today is closer to that ideal than in the sixteenth century. Perhaps some of the credit should go to Sir Thomas More.

VANITY FAIR: A Novel Without a Hero

Type of work: Novel
Author: William Makepeace Thackeray (1811–1863)
Type of plot: Social satire
Time of plot: Early nineteenth century
Locale: England and Europe
First published: 1847–1848 (serial), 1848 (book)

Thackeray's most famous novel, Vanity Fair: A Novel Without a Hero *is intended to expose social hypocrisy and sham. Moralistic and sentimental, the work also has redeeming strengths: its panoramic sweep—especially the scenes of the battle of Waterloo—and its creations of lifelike characters, chief among them Becky Sharp.*

Principal Characters

Rebecca Sharp, called **Becky,** an intelligent, beautiful, self-centered, grasping woman whose career begins as an orphaned charity pupil at Miss Pinkerton's School for Girls and continues through a series of attempted seductions, affairs, and marriages which form the background of the novel. Unscrupulous Becky is the chief exponent of the people who inhabit Vanity Fair—the world of pretense and show—but she is always apart from it because she sees the humor and ridiculousness of the men and women of this middle-class English world where pride, wealth, and ambition are the ruling virtues.

Amelia Sedley, Becky Sharp's sweet, good, gentle schoolmate at Miss Pinkerton's school. Although married to George Osborne, who subsequently dies in the Battle of Waterloo, Amelia is worshiped by William Dobbin. Amelia does not notice his love, however, so involved is she with the memory of her dashing dead husband. Eventually some of Amelia's goddesslike virtue is dimmed in Dobbin's eyes, but he marries her anyway and transfers his idealization of women to their little girl, Jane.

Captain William Dobbin, an officer in the British Army and a former schoolmate of George Osborne at Dr. Swishtail's school. He idolizes Amelia Sedley, George's wife, and while in the background provides financial and emotional support for her when she is widowed. After many years of worshiping Amelia from afar, he finally marries her.

George Osborne, the dashing young army officer who marries Amelia despite the fact that by so doing he incurs the wrath of his father and is cut off from his inheritance. George, much smitten with the charms of Becky Sharp, slips a love letter to Becky on the night before the army is called to the Battle of Waterloo. He is killed in the battle.

George Osborne, called **Georgy,** the small son of Amelia and George.

Captain Rawdon Crawley, an officer of the Guards, the younger son of Sir Pitt Crawley. He marries Becky Sharp in secret, and for this deception his aunt cuts him

out of her will. Charming but somewhat stupid, he is a great gambler and furnishes some of the money on which he and Becky live precariously. He lets Becky order their life, and even though she flirts outrageously after they are married, he does not abandon her until he discovers her in an intimate scene with the Marquis of Steyne. He dies many years later of yellow fever at Coventry Island.

Rawdon Crawley, the son of Rawdon and Becky. He refuses to see his mother in her later years, though he gives her a liberal allowance. From his uncle he inherits the Crawley baronetcy and estate.

Joseph Sedley, called **Jos,** Amelia's fat, dandified brother, whom Becky Sharp attempts unsuccessfully to attract into marrying her. A civil servant in India, the Collector of Boggley Wollah, Jos is rich but selfish and does nothing to rescue his father and mother from bankruptcy. Persuaded by Dobbin, finally, to take some family responsibility, he supports Amelia and her son Georgy for a few months before Dobbin marries her. For a time he and Becky travel on the Continent as husband and wife. He dies at Aix-la-Chapelle soon after Amelia and Dobbin's marriage. His fortune gone from unsuccessful speculations, he leaves only an insurance policy of two thousand pounds, to be divided between Becky and his sister.

Sir Pitt Crawley, a crusty, eccentric old baronet who lives at Queen's Crawley, his country seat, with his abused, apathetic second wife and two young daughters, Miss Rosalind and Miss Violet. Immediately after Lady Crawley's death Sir Pitt proposes marriage to Becky. His offer leads to the disclosure of her secret marriage to Rawdon Crawley, his younger son. Later, grown more senile than ever, Sir Pitt carries on an affair with his butler's daughter, Betsy Horrocks, much to the disgust of his relatives. He eventually dies, and his baronetcy and money go to Pitt, his eldest son.

Miss Crawley, Sir Pitt's eccentric sister, a lonely old maid. Imperious and rich, she is toadied to by everyone in the Crawley family and by Becky Sharp, for they see in her the chance for a rich living. She finally is won over by young Pitt Crawley's wife, Lady Jane, and her estate goes to Pitt.

Pitt Crawley, the older son of Sir Pitt Crawley. A most proper young man with political ambitions, he marries Lady Jane Sheepshanks, and after his brother's secret marriage so endears himself to Miss Crawley, his rich, domineering aunt, that he gains her money as well as his father's.

Lady Jane, Pitt Crawley's wife. Like Amelia Sedley, she is good, sweet, and kind, and is, above all else, interested in her husband's and their daughter's welfare.

The Reverend Bute Crawley, the rector of Crawley-cum-Snailby and Sir Pitt's brother. His household is run by his domineering wife.

Mrs. Bute Crawley, who dislikes Becky Sharp because she recognizes in her the same sort of ambition and craftiness that she herself possesses. She fails in her plans to gain Miss Crawley's fortune.

James Crawley, the son of the Bute Crawleys. For a time it looks as if this shy, good-looking young man will win favor with his aunt, but he ruins his prospects by getting very drunk on his aunt's wine and later smoking his pipe out the window of the guest room. Miss Crawley's maid also discovers that James has run up a tremendous bill for gin (to which he treated everyone in the local tavern in one of his expansive moods), and this fact combined with his smoking tobacco puts an end to the Bute Crawleys' prospects of inheriting Miss Crawley's money.

Horrocks, Sir Pitt Crawley's butler.

Betsy Horrocks, the butler's daughter and old Sir Pitt's mistress. She is done out of any inheritance by the interference of Mrs. Bute Crawley.

Mr. John Sedley, the father of Amelia and Joseph, a typical middle-class English merchant of grasping, selfish ways. After his failure in business his family is forced to move from Russell Square to a cottage kept by the Clapps, a former servant of the Sedleys. Never able to accept his poverty, Mr. Sedley spends his time thinking up new business schemes with which to regain his former wealth.

Mrs. John Sedley, the long-suffering wife of Mr. Sedley, and mother of Amelia and Joseph. She, like her daughter, is a sweet woman. Her only expression of wrath in the entire story comes when she turns upon Amelia after her daughter has criticized her for giving little Georgy medicine that has not been prescribed for him.

John Osborne, George Osborne's testy-tempered father, provincial, narrow, and mean. Never forgiving his son for marrying the penniless Amelia Sedley, Mr. Osborne finally succeeds in getting the widow to give up her adored Georgy to his care. Amelia regains her son, however, and when he dies Mr. Osborne leaves to his grandson a legacy of which Amelia is the trustee.

Jane, Maria, and **Frances Osborne,** George's sisters, who adore their young nephew. Maria finally marries Frederick Bullock, Esq., a London lawyer.

Mr. Smee, Jane Osborne's drawing teacher, who tries to marry her. Mr. Osborne, discovering them together, forbids him to enter the house.

Lord Steyne, Lord of the Powder Closet at Buckingham Palace. Haughty and well-born and considerably older than Becky, he succumbs to her charms. Her husband discovers them together and leaves her.

Wirt, the Osbornes' faithful maid.

Mrs. Tinker, the housekeeper at Queen's Crawley.

Lord Southdown, Lady Jane Crawley's brother, a dandified London friend of the Rawdon Crawleys.

Miss Briggs, Miss Crawley's companion and later Becky Sharp's. She fulfills Becky's need for a female companion so that the little adventuress will have some sort of respectability in the eyes of society.

Bowles, Miss Crawley's butler.

Mrs. Firkins, Miss Crawley's maid. Like the other servants, she is overwhelmed by the overbearing old lady.

Charles Raggles, a greengrocer, at one time an assistant gardener to the Crawley family. Having saved his money, he has bought a greengrocer's shop and a small house in Curzon Street. Becky and Rawdon live there for a time on his charity, for they are unable to pay their rent.

Lord Gaunt, son of Lord Steyne. He goes insane in his early twenties.

Major O'Dowd, an officer under whom George Osborne and William Dobbin serve. He is a relaxed individual, devoted to his witty and vivacious wife.

Mrs. O'Dowd, the Irish wife of Major O'Dowd. She is an unaffected, delightful female who tries to marry off her sister-in-law to William Dobbin.

Glorvina O'Dowd, the flirtatious sister of Major O'Dowd. She sets her cap for Dobbin, but because she is only and "frocks and shoulders," nothing comes of the match. She marries Major Posky.

General Tufto, the officer to whom Rawdon Crawley at one time serves as aide-de-camp. He is a typical army man with a mistress and a long-suffering wife.

Mrs. Tufto, his wife.

Mrs. Bent, his mistress.

Dolly, the housekeeper to the Rawdon Crawleys in London. She is the one who fends off tradesmen when they come to demand their money.

Mrs. Clapp, the landlady of the Sedleys after their move from Russell Square.

Polly Clapp, a young former servant of the Sedleys. She takes Dobbin to meet Amelia in the park after the former's ten-year absence in the Indian service.

Mary Clapp, another daughter of the Clapps and Amelia's friend.

Lady Bareacres, a snobby old aristocrat who cuts Becky socially in Brussels. Later Becky has her revenge when she refuses to sell her horses to the old woman so that she may flee from Napoleon's invading army.

Lady Blanche Thistlewood, Lady Bareacres' daughter and a dancing partner of George Osborne when they were very young.

Mr. Hammerdown, the auctioneer at the sale of the Sedley possessions.

Major Martindale, Lieutenant Spatterdash, and **Captain Cinqbars,** military friends of Rawdon Crawley who are captivated by his charming wife.

Tom Stubble, a wounded soldier who brings news of the Battle of Waterloo to Amelia Sedley and Mrs. O'Dowd. They care for him until he regains his health.

Mr. Creamer, Mrs. Crawley's physician.

Miss Pinkerton, the snobbish mistress of the academy for girls at which Amelia Sedley and Becky Sharp met. She dislikes Becky intensely.

Miss Jemima Pinkerton, the silly, sentimental sister of the elder Miss Pinkerton. She takes pity on Becky and tries to give her the graduation gift of the academy, a dictionary, but Becky flings it into the mud as her coach drives off.

Miss Swartz, the rich, woolly-haired mulatto student at Miss Pinkerton's School. Because of her immense wealth she pays double tuition. Later the Crawley family tries to marry off Rawdon to her, but he has already married Becky.

Mr. Sambo, the Sedley's black servant.

The Reverend Mr. Crisp, a young curate in Chiswick, enamored of Becky Sharp.

Miss Cutler, a young woman who unsuccessfully sets her cap for Joseph Sedley.

Mr. Fiche, Lord Steyne's confidential man. After Becky's fortunes have begun to decline, he tells her to leave Rome for her own good.

Major Loder, Becky's escort in the later phases of her career.

The Story

Becky Sharp and Amelia Sedley became good friends while they were students at Miss Pinkerton's School for Girls. It was proof of Amelia's good, gentle nature that she took as kindly as she did to her friend, who was generally disliked by all the other girls. Amelia overlooked the evidences of Becky's selfishness as much as she could.

After the two girls had finished their education at the school, Becky accompanied her friend to her home for a short visit. There she first met Joseph Sedley, Amelia's older brother Jos, who was home on leave from military service in India. Jos was a shy man, unused to women, and certainly to women as designing and flirtatious as Becky. His blundering and awkward manners did not appeal to many women, but Becky was happy to overlook these faults when she compared them with his wealth and social position. Amelia innocently believed that her friend had fallen in love with her brother, and she discreetly tried to further the romance.

To this end, she arranged a party at Vauxhall. Becky and Jos, along with Amelia and her admirer, George Osborne, were present. There was a fifth member of the group, Captain Dobbin, a tall, lumbering fellow, also in service in India. He had been in love with Amelia for a long time, but he recognized that dashing George Osborne was much more suitable for her. All the maneuvering of the flirtations Becky and the amiable Amelia, however, was not sufficient to corner Jos, who drank too much punch and believed that he had made a silly figure of himself at the party. A day or so later, a letter delivered to the Sedley household announced that Jos was ill and planned to return to India as soon as possible.

Since there was no longer any reason for Becky to remain with the Sedleys, she left Amelia, after many tears and kisses, to take a position as governess to two young girls at Queen's Crawley. The head of the household was Sir Pitt Crawley, a cantankerous old man renowned for his miserliness. Lady Crawley was an apathetic soul who lived in fear of her husband's unreasonable outbursts. Becky decided that she would have nothing to fear from her timid mistress and spent most of her time ingratiating herself with Sir Pitt and ignoring her pupils. Becky also showed great interest in Miss Crawley, a spinster aunt of the family, who was exceedingly wealthy. Miss Crawley paid little attention to Sir Pitt and his children, but she was fond of Rawdon Crawley, a captain in the army and a son of Sir Pitt by a previous marriage. She was so fond of her dashing young nephew that she supported him through school and paid all of his gambling debts with only a murmur.

During Becky's stay, Miss Crawley visited Sir Pitt only once, at a time when Rawdon was also present. The handsome young dragoon soon fell prey to Becky's wiles and followed her about devotedly. Becky also took care to ingratiate herself with the holder of the purse strings. Miss Crawley founded Becky witty and charming and did not attempt to disguise her opinion that the little governess was worth all the rest of the Crawley household put together. Becky, therefore, found herself in a very enviable position. Both Sir Pitt and his handsome son were obviously interested in her. Miss Crawley insisted that Becky accompany her back to London.

Becky had been expected to return to her pupils after only a short stay with Miss Crawley; but Miss Crawley was taken ill and refused to allow anyone but her dear Becky to nurse her. Afterward, there were numerous other excuses to prevent the governess from returning to her duties. Certainly, Becky was not unhappy. Rawdon

Crawley was a constant caller and a devoted suitor for Becky's hand. When the news arrived that Lady Crawley had died, no great concern was felt by anyone. A few days later, however, Sir Pitt himself appeared, asking to see Miss Sharp. Much to Becky's surprise, the baronet threw himself at her feet and asked her to marry him. Regretfully, she refused his offer. She was already secretly married to Rawdon Crawley.

Following this disclosure, Rawdon and his bride left for a honeymoon at Brighton. Chagrined and angry, old Miss Crawley took to her bed, changed her will, and cut off her nephew without a shilling. Sir Pitt raved with anger.

Amelia's marriage had also precipitated a family crisis. Her romance with George had proceeded with good wishes on both sides until Mr. Sedley lost most of his money through some unfortunate business deals. Then George's snobbish father ordered his son to break his engagement to a penniless woman. George, whose affection for Amelia was never stable, was inclined to accept this parental command; but Captain Dobbin, who saw with distress that Amelia was breaking her heart over George, finally prevailed upon the young man to go through with the marriage, regardless of his father's wishes. When the couple arrived in Brighton for their honeymoon, they found Rawdon and Becky living there happily in penniless extravagance.

Captain Dobbin also arrived in Brighton. He had agreed to act as intercessor with Mr. Osborne. Nevertheless, his hopes of reconciling father and son were shattered when Mr. Osborne furiously dismissed Captain Dobbin and took immediate steps to disown George. Captain Dobbin also brought the news that the army had been ordered to Belgium. Napoleon had landed from Elba. The Hundred Days had begun.

In Brussels, the two couples met again. George Osborne was infatuated with Becky. Jos Sedley, now returned from India, and Captain Dobbin were also stationed in that city; Captain Dobbin was in faithful attendance upon the neglected Amelia. Everyone was waiting for the next move that Napoleon would make; but in the meantime, the gaiety of the Duke of Wellington's forces was widespread. The Osbornes and Crawleys attended numerous balls. Becky, especially, made an impression upon military society, and her coquetry extended with equal effect from general to private. June, 1815, was a famous night in Brussels, for on that evening the Duchess of Richmond gave a tremendous ball. Amelia left the party early, brokenhearted at the attentions her husband was showing Becky. Shortly after she left, the men were given orders to march to meet the enemy. Napoleon had entered Belgium, and a great battle was impending.

As Napoleon's forces approached, fear and confusion spread throughout Brussels, and many of the civilians fled from the city, but Amelia and Becky did not. Becky was not alarmed, and Amelia refused to leave while George

was in danger. She remained in the city some days before she heard that her husband had been killed. Rawdon returned safely from the Battle of Waterloo. He and Becky spent a merry and triumphant season in Paris, where Becky's beauty and wit gained her a host of admirers. Rawdon was very proud of the son she bore him.

Amelia also had a child. She had returned to London almost out of her mind with grief, and only after her son was born did she show any signs of rallying.

When Becky grew bored with the pleasures of Paris, the Crawleys returned to London. There they rented a large home and proceeded to live well with little money. By this time, Becky was a master at this art, and so they lived on a grander scale than Rawdon's small winnings at cards would warrant. Becky had become acquainted with the nobility of England and had made a particular impression on rich old Lord Steyne. At last, all society began to talk about young Mrs. Crawley and her elderly admirer. Fortunately, Rawdon heard nothing of this ballroom and coffeehouse gossip.

Through the efforts of Lord Steyne, Becky eventually achieved her dearest wish, presentation at Court. Presented along with her was the wife of the new Sir Pitt Crawley. The old man had died, and young Sir Pitt, his oldest son and Rawdon's brother, had inherited the title. Since then, friendly relations had been established between the two brothers. If Rawdon realized that his brother had also fallen in love with Becky, he gave no sign, and he accepted the money his brother gave him with good grace; but more and more, he felt himself shut out from the happy life that Becky enjoyed. He spent much time with his son, for he realized that the child was neglected. Once or twice he saw young George Osborne, Amelia's son.

Amelia struggled to keep her son with her, but her pitiful financial status made it difficult to support him. Her parents had grown garrulous and morose with disappointment over their reduced circumstances. At length, Amelia sorrowfully agreed to let Mr. Osborne take the child and rear him as his own. Mr. Osborne still refused to recognize the woman his son had married against his wishes, however, and Amelia rarely saw the boy.

Rawdon was now deeply in debt. When he appealed to Becky for money, she told him that she had none to spare. She made no attempt to explain the jewelry and other trinkets she bought. When Rawdon was imprisoned for a debt, he wrote and asked Becky to take care of the matter. She answered that she could not get the money until the following day. An appeal to Sir Pitt, however, brought about Rawdon's release, and he returned to his home to find Becky entertaining Lord Steyne. Not long afterward, Rawdon accepted a post abroad, and he never returned to his unfaithful, scheming wife.

Amelia's fortunes had now improved. When Jos Sedley returned home, he established his sister and father in a more pleasant home. Mrs. Sedley had died, and Jos resolved to do as much as he could to make his father's last days happy. Captain Dobbin had returned from India and confessed his love for Amelia. Although she acknowledged him as a friend, she was not yet ready to accept his love. It was Captain Dobbin who went to Mr. Osborne and gradually succeeded in reconciling him to his son's wife. When Mr. Osborne died, he left a good part of his fortune to his grandson and appointed Amelia as the boy's guardian.

Amelia, her son, Captain Dobbin, and Jos Sedley took a short trip to the Continent. This visit was perhaps the happiest time in Amelia's life. Her son was with her constantly, and Captain Dobbin was a devoted attendant. Eventually, his devotion was to overcome her hesitation and they were to be married.

At a small German resort, they encountered Becky once more. After Rawdon left her, Becky had been unable to live down the scandal of their separation. Leaving her child with Sir Pitt and his wife, she crossed to the Continent. Since then, she had been living with first one considerate gentleman and then another. When she saw the prosperous Jos, she vowed not to let him escape as he had before. Amelia and Jos greeted her in a friendly manner, and only Captain Dobbin seemed to regard her with distrust. He tried to warn Jos about Becky, but Jos was a willing victim of her charms.

Becky traveled with Jos wherever he went. Although she could not get a divorce from Rawdon, Jos treated her as his wife, and despite Captain Dobbin's protests, he took out a large insurance policy in her name. A few months later, his family learned that he had died while staying with Becky at Aix-la-Chapelle. The full circumstances of his death were never established, but Becky came into a large sum of money from his insurance. She spend the rest of her life on the Continent, where she assumed the role of the virtuous widow and won a reputation for benevolence and generosity.

Critical Evaluation

When critics call William Makepeace Thackeray's characters in *Vanity Fair: A Novel Without a Hero* "life-like," they are milking that term for a subtler meaning than it usually conveys. His people are not true to life in the sense of being fully rounded or drawn with psychological depth. On the contrary, readers sometimes find their actions too farcical to be human (Jos Sedley's ignominious flight from Brussels after the Battle of Waterloo) or too sinister to be credible (the implication that Becky poisons Jos to collect his insurance is totally out of keeping with what readers learned about her in the previous sixty-six chapters; she may be a selfish opportunists, but she is not a murderer). Thackeray's characters *are* "lifelike" if "life" is defined as a typological phenomenon. When readers shrug their shoulders and say "that's life," they are indulging in a kind of judgment on the human race which is based on types, not individuals; on the common failings of all men and women, not on the unique goodness or evil of some. Insofar as all men share one another's weaknesses, every man is represented in *Vanity Fair*. Our banality levels us all. That is the satirical revelation that *Vanity Fair* provides. That is the way in which its characters are "lifelike."

Thackeray's general approach is comic satire; his method is that of the theatrical producer, specifically the puppeteer. In his prologue, he calls himself the "Manager of the Performance" and refers to Becky, Amelia, and Dobbin as puppets of varying "flexibility . . . and liveliness." Critics usually interpret this offhanded way of referring to his principal characters as a vindication of his own intrusions and asides, as a reminder to the reader that he, the author, is as much involved in the action as any of his characters. Nevertheless, readers should probably take a harder look at Thackeray's metaphor: he is a puppeteer because he must be one; *because* his people are puppets, someone must pull the strings. The dehumanized state of Regency and early Victorian society comes to accurate life through the cynical vehicle of Thackeray's puppeteering. Sentimentality and hypocrisy, closely related social vices, seem interchangeable at the end of the novel when Thackeray gathers all the remaining puppets: Amelia and Dobbin, a "tender little parasite" clinging to her "rugged old oak," and Becky, acting out her newfound saintliness by burying herself "in works of piety" and "having stalls at Fancy Fairs" for the benefit of the poor. "Let us shut up," concludes Thackeray, "the box and the puppets, for our play is played out."

Despite the predictability of all the characters' puppetlike behavior, they often exhibit just enough humanity to make their dehumanization painful. Thackeray wants readers to feel uncomfortable over the waste of human potential in the vulgar concerns of *Vanity Fair*. George Osborne lives like a cad, is arrogant about his spendthrift ways, unfaithful to his wife, and dies a hero, leading a charge against the retreating French at Waterloo. The reader is left with the impression that the heroism of his death is rendered irrelevant by the example of his life. Such satire is demanding in its moral vision precisely because it underscores the price of corruption: honor becomes absurd.

Rawdon Crawley's love for his little son slowly endows the father with a touch of decency, but he is exiled by the "Manager of the Performance" to Coventry Island, where he dies of yellow fever, "most deeply beloved and deplored." Presumably the wastrel, separated from his own, dies in a position of duty. Or are readers to pity him for having been forced, by his financial situation, to accept the position at Coventry as a bribe from Lord

Steyne? Thackeray is elusive; again, the suggestions of pathos are touched on so lightly that they hardly matter. The indifference itself is *Vanity Fair*'s reward. For all of his jocularity and beef-eating familiarity, the "Manager of the Performance" sets a dark stage. *Vanity Fair* is colorful enough: the excitement at Brussels over Waterloo, the gardens at Vauxhall, the Rhine journey; but it is a panoply of meretricious and wasteful human endeavor. Readers really do not need Thackeray's moralizing to convince them of the shabbiness of it all.

Astonishing is the fact that despite the novel's cynicism, it also has immense vitality. It is difficult to deny the attractiveness of the ephemeral—Bunyan made that perfectly clear in *Pilgrim's Progress*, and Thackeray simply updates the vision. What was allegory in Bunyan becomes realism in Thackeray; the modern writer's objectivity in no way detracts from the alluring effect achieved by Bunyan's imaginary Vanity Fair. Bunyan still operated in the Renaissance tradition of Spenserian façade; evil traps man through illusion, as exemplified in the trials of the Red Cross Knight. Thackeray drops the metaphor of illusion and shows corruption bared—and still it is attractive.

Becky Sharp is described as "worldliness incarnate" by Louis Kronenberger, but the reader cannot deny her charms. Thackeray calls his book "A Novel Without a Hero," but readers know better. Becky's pluck and ambition are extraordinary; her triumph is even more impressive because of the formidable barriers of class and poverty she has to scale. When she throws the Johnson's

dictionary out of the coach window as she leaves Miss Pinkerton's academy, readers are thrilled by her refusal to be patronized; her destructive and cruel manipulations of the Crawleys have all the implications of a revolutionary act. Thackeray actually emphasizes Becky's spirit and power by making virtuous Amelia so weak and sentimental. Although readers are tempted to see this as a contradiction of Thackeray's moral intention, they must remember that he understood very clearly that true goodness must be built on strength: "clumsy Dobbin" is Thackeray's somewhat sentimental example. The human tragedy is that most men and women cannot reconcile their energies with their ideals and that in a fallen world of social injustices, men must all sin in order to survive. It is ironic that precisely because Becky Sharp is such an energetic opportunist, readers almost believe her when she says, "I think I could have been a good woman if I had five thousand a year."

Vanity Fair, the best known of Thackeray's works, has joined the ranks of the classics, for in it Thackeray has created characters as great as any in English literature. Most of his people are not good people, but they were not intended to be. Thackeray shows that goodness often goes hand in hand with stupidity and folly and that cleverness is often knavery. A cynical story, this novel was intended to expose social hypocrisy and sham. Although Thackeray was frankly moralistic, his moral does not in any way overshadow a magnificent novel or the lifelike characters he created.

VOLPONE

Type of work: Drama
Author: Ben Jonson (1573?–1637)
Type of plot: Social satire
Time of plot: Sixteenth century
Locale: Venice
First presented: 1605

One of Ben Jonson's most effective "humours" comedies, Volpone *is intricately plotted and vigorous and savage in its satire of hypocrisy, mendacity, and greed. In this play the characters resemble predatory beasts.*

Principal Characters

Volpone (vŏl·pō′nä), the Fox, a Venetian magnifico. Delighting in foxlike trickery, Volpone scorns the easy gain of cheating widows and orphans and the hard gain of labor. He chooses for his victims Venice's leading crooked advocate, its most greedy and dishonest merchant, and its most hardened miser. The joy of the chase of gold and jewels belonging to other men is keener to him than the possession. He also delights in acting, both onstage and off. To fool others with disguises, makeup, and changes of voice is a passion with him. His three weaknesses are excessive trust of his unreliable parasite Mosca, his ungovernable desire for Corvino's virtuous wife Celia, and his overconfidence in his ability to deceive. When defeated, however, he shows a humorous and sporting self-knowledge and resignation to his punishment.

Mosca (mŏs′kä), the Gadfly, Volpone's malicious and witty parasite. Acting as the chief instrument of Volpone's trickery and the frequent instigator of additional pranks, he keeps the plot moving. Under cover of tormenting Volpone's victims, he often engages in annoying Volpone himself, almost always with impunity. His tantalizing of Volpone with sensuous descriptions of Celia sets in train the events that finally destroy both his master and himself. A master improviser of deceit and pranks, he becomes in love with his dear self, underestimates his master, and falls victim to his own overconfidence and greed. He whines and curses as he is dragged away to punishment.

Voltore (vŏl·tō′rä), the Vulture, an advocate. A ruthless and voracious scavenger seeking the spoils of the dead, he yearns for Volpone's wealth. He is willing to connive whenever gain is apparent. A dangerous man when thwarted, he helps Volpone gain acquittal in his first trail; then, tormented beyond endurance by Mosca, who pretends that Volpone is dead and has left Voltore nothing, the lawyer reverses himself and causes the collapse of Volpone's plans.

Corbaccio (kôr·bä′t·chō), the Raven, an aged miser. Feeble, stone-deaf, pathologically greedy, he is willing to risk his son's inheritance to have Volpone exchange wills with him; he is also willing to have Mosca administer poison in Volpone's sleeping draft to hasten the validation of the will.

Corvino (kôr·vē′nō), the Crow, the merchant husband of Celia. Mean-spirited, cowardly, and insanely jealous of his beautiful wife, he is the most repulsive of Volpone's victims. His greed is sufficient to counteract his jealousy, and he is willing to leave his wife in Volpone's hands in order to assure his future as Volpone's heir.

Celia (sēl′yä), Corvino's virtuous wife. Cursed with a repulsive and pathologically jealous husband, the heavenly Celia faces her slander and perils with noble fortitude.

Bonario (bō·nä′ryō), the good son of Corbaccio. He is the savior of Celia when she is helpless in Volpone's clutches.

Lady Politic Would-Be, a parrot-voiced, shallow-brained Englishwoman. She grates on Volpone's sensibilities so much that he is willing to lose the financial gain which she thrusts upon him. At any price he wishes to be rid of "my madam with the everlasting voice." Her unreasonable jealousy makes her a gullible tool when Mosca accuses her husband of having an affair with Celia; her resulting false testimony saves Volpone and convicts Celia and Bonario at the first trial.

Sir Politic Would-Be, a gullible, naïve traveler. Eager to be thought a member of the inner circle of state knowledge, Sir Pol has a sinister explanation for even the most commonplace actions. He furnishes the picture of the ridiculous English tourist on the Continent.

Peregrine (pĕr′ə·grĭn), a sophisticated traveler. He finds amusement, mixed with contempt, in the credulities and foibles of Sir Pol.

Androgyno (ăn·droj′ə·nō), the hermaphrodite.

Castrone (kä·strō′nē), the eunuch, and

Nano (nä′nō), the dwarf, household freaks kept by Volpone for amusement.

Avocatori (ä·vō′kä·tō′rē), the four judges. The ambition of the fourth, to marry his daughter to Mosca, stirs Volpone to make his confession, which saves Bonario and Celia and brings punishment on the evildoers.

The Story

Volpone and his servant, Mosca, were playing a cunning game with all who professed to be Volpone's friends, and the two conspirators boasted to themselves that Volpone acquired his riches not by the common means of trade but by a method which cheated no one in a commercial sense. Volpone had no heirs. Since it was believed he possessed a large fortune, many people were courting his favor in hopes of rich rewards after his death.

For three years, while the foxy Volpone feigned gout, catarrh, palsy, and consumption, valuable gifts had been given him. Mosca's role in the grand deception was to assure each hopeful donor that he was the one whom Volpone had honored in an alleged will.

To Voltore, one of the dupes, Mosca boasted that particular attention was being paid to Voltore's interests. When Voltore the vulture left, Corbaccio the crow followed. He brought a potion to help Volpone, or so he claimed. But Mosca knew better than to give his master medicine from those who were awaiting the fox's death. Mosca suggested that to influence Volpone, Corbaccio should go home, disinherit his own son, and leave his fortune to Volpone. In return for this generous deed, Volpone, soon to die, would leave his fortune to Corbaccio, whose son would benefit eventually.

Next came Corvino, who was assured by Mosca that Volpone, now near death, had named him in a will. After the merchant had gone, Mosca told Volpone that Corvino had a beautiful wife whom he guarded at all times. Volpone resolved to go in disguise to see this woman.

Sir Politic Would-Be and his wife were traveling in Venice. Peregrine, another English visitor, met Sir Politic on the street and gave him news from home. While the two Englishmen were trying to impress one another, Mosca and a servant came to the street and erected a stage for a medicine vendor to display his wares. Volpone, disguised as a mountebank, mounted the platform. While he haggled with Sir Politic and Peregrine over the price of his medicine, Celia appeared at her window and tossed down her handkerchief. Struck by Celia's beauty, Volpone resolved to possess her. Meanwhile Corvino brutally scolded Celia and told her that henceforth he would confine her to her room.

Mosca went to Corvino with news that physicians had recommended a healthy young girl sleep by Volpone's side and that other men were striving to be the first to win Volpone's gratitude in this manner. Not to be outdone, Corvino promised that Celia would be sent to Volpone.

Mosca also told Bonario, Corbaccio's son, that his father was about to disinherit him. He promised to lead Bonario to a place where he could witness his father's betrayal.

When Lady Politic Would-Be came to visit Volpone, she was so talkative Volpone feared she would make him actually sick. To relieve Volpone's distress, the servant told the lady that Sir Politic was in a gondola with a young girl. Lady Would-Be hurried off in pursuit of her husband. Volpone retired to a private closet while Mosca led Bonario behind a curtain so the young man could spy on Corbaccio. At that moment, eager to win favor with Volpone, Corvino arrived with Celia, and Mosca had to send Bonario off to another room so he would not know of her presence. Meanwhile Corvino had told Celia what she must do to prove her chastity. To quiet her fears and to guarantee the inheritance from Volpone, Corvino assured his distressed wife that Volpone was so decrepit he could not harm her.

When they were alone, Volpone leaped from his couch and displayed himself as an ardent lover. As he was about to force himself upon Celia, Bonario appeared from his hiding place and saved her. While Mosca and Volpone, in terror of exposure, bewailed their ruined plot, Corbaccio knocked. Volpone dashed back to his couch. As Mosca was assuring Corbaccio of Volpone's forthcoming death, Voltore entered the room and overheard the discussion. Mosca drew Voltore aside and assured the lawyer that he was attempting to get possession of Corbaccio's money so that Voltore would inherit more from Volpone. Mosca further explained that Bonario had mistaken Celia's visit and had burst in on Volpone and threatened to kill him. Taken in by Mosca's lies, Voltore promised to keep Bonario from accusing Volpone of rape and Corvino of villainy; he ordered the young man arrested.

Mosca proceeded with his case against Celia and Bonario. He had assured Corvino, Corbaccio, and Voltore, independently, that each would be the sole heir of Volpone. Now he added Lady Would-Be as a witness against Celia. In court Voltore presented Celia and Bonario as schemers against Corvino and he further showed that Bonario's father had disinherited his son and that Bonario had dragged Volpone out of bed and had attacked him. Both Corvino and Corbaccio testified against Celia and Bonario, while Mosca whispered to the avaricious old gentlemen that they were helping justice. To add to the testimony, Mosca presented Lady Would-Be, who told the court she had seen Celia beguiling Sir Politic in a gondola. Mosca promised Lady Would-Be that as a reward for her testimony her name would stand first on Volpone's list of heirs.

When the trial was over, Volpone sent his servants to announce that he was dead and that Mosca was his heir. While Volpone hid behind a curtain, Mosca sat at a desk taking an inventory of the inheritance as the hopefuls arrived. The next step in Volpone's plan was to escape from Venice with his loot. Mosca helped him disguise himself as a commodore. Mosca also put on a disguise.

Having lost his hopes for the inheritance, Voltore withdrew his false testimony at the trial, and Corbaccio and

Corvino trembled lest their cowardly acts be revealed. The court ordered Mosca to appear. Suspecting that Mosca planned to keep the fortune for himself, the disguised Volpone went to the court. When the dupes, learning that Volpone was still alive, began to bargain for the wealth Mosca held, Volpone threw off his disguise and exposed to the court the foolish behavior of Corbaccio, Corvino, and Voltore, and the innocence of Celia and Bonario.

The court then sentenced each conspirator according to the severity of his crime. Bonario was restored to his father's inheritance, and Celia was allowed to return to her father because Corvino had attempted to barter her honor for wealth.

The court announced that evil could go only so far and then it killed itself.

Critical Evaluation

Written during a period in which Ben Jonson had turned his hand largely to the making of entertaining masques and satirical anti-masques, *Volpone*'s success did something to make up for the failure of his tragedy, *Sejanus*. *Volpone* was performed by the King's Men in London and at the two universities, to which he later dedicated the play in his prologue. The play also led to Jonson's most fertile dramatic period, that of the five great comedies (including *Epicoene*, 1609; *The Alchemist*, 1610; *Bartholomew Fair*, 1614; and *The Devil Is an Ass*, 1616). Jonson was preeminent among the Elizabethans and Jacobeans as that rare combination of the academic and creative genius. He was a serious classicist who criticized Shakespeare's "little Latin and less Greek," modeling his own plays on those of the Romans. As a humanist he brought classical control and purity to English forms, further strengthening those forms with Italian imports (his comedies were influenced strongly by Machiavelli). More than anyone else at the time, Jonson followed the prescriptions of Sidney's *An Apologie for Poetrie* (1595). Like Sidney, he believed that the poet had a moral function in society; he viewed drama as a means of social education, paving the way for the great English satirists of the eighteenth century. His diverse artistic character makes Jonson both representative of his own age and a predecessor of the more rigorous classicism of the Augustans.

Jonson's style, as might be expected, is disciplined, formal, balanced, and classically simple and unembellished—a style that foreshadows the Cavalier school (who called themselves "the sons of Ben"). Though his dramatic verse is highly stylized, it is nevertheless vibrant and fast-moving; we hardly feel we are reading poetry. Rarely does Jonson allow himself the lyrical excursions of Shakespeare or the rhetorical complexity of Marlowe, though he was capable of both. There is a solidity, firmness, and straightforward clarity in his comedies equaled only by the classical French comic theater of Molière. In *Volpone* Jonson follows the Aristotelian unities, as proclaimed to the Renaissance by Castelvetro. The action of the play takes place in only one day (the unity of time); it occurs entirely in Venice (place); and with the exception of some of the exchanges between Peregrine and Sir Politic Would-Be, the action is unified structurally, all centered around the machinations of Volpone and his parasite, and their greedy suitors.

The satirical theme of the play is greed, the vice that dominates the actions of all the characters. Family bonds, marriage, and legal justice are not merely disregarded by Corbaccio, Corvino, and Voltore, they are made the means by which the characters' inhuman avarice destroys them. Actually, Jonson would insist that their greed is all too human, recalling what Spenser's Sir Calidore had exclaimed, "No greater crime to man/ Than inhumanitie." It is ironic that the Politic Would-Be's, though they too want Volpone's money, seem less offensive and morally corrupt simply because they do not sell their souls for hope of lucre. The passages in which they appear are a kind of relief. For though *Volpone* is a comedy it is so serious that it is almost equally tragic, foreshadowing Byron's Don Juan who said, "And if I laugh at any mortal thing, 'tis that I may not weep." *Volpone* may be a comedy insofar as it deals with particular figures in a particular situation; but its social application is in deadly earnest. Jonson has succeeded brilliantly in combining the stereotyped *dramatis personae* of Latin comedy, the Renaissance characters based on *humours* (which he himself used in his first comedy, *Every Man in His Humour*), the popular tradition of beast-fables (from which he derived the names of his characters), with astute psychological insight that makes them all come alive before our eyes. Although the plot of *Volpone* is original, it is based on the common Roman *captatores* theme dealt with by Horace, Juvenal, Pliny, Lucian, and Petronius. Jonson turns his fortune hunters loose in contemporary Venice—chosen, no doubt, because the English of the time regarded Italy as a country of crime and rampant passions (compare Nash's *The Unfortunate Traveller*)—and the audience understands that this kind of man is eternal. That is the point Jonson himself makes in defining the high moral purpose of comic satire in his preface to the two universities.

Another important theme is that of imitation, as a distortion of normal reality. Sir Politic Would-Be seeks to imitate Volpone, an imitation of an imitation in the sense that led Plato to expel the poets from his republic; the tragedy is that though Volpone can be imitated, he is not imitable. And no one in the play has a firm moral standard that prevents them all from degrading their humanity. Lady Would-Be attempts to cover her mental deformities with physical cosmetics, and the dressing scene remains one of the most familiar and most pathetic in the play. Carrying imitation even further, Volpone pretends to be a mountebank in a complicated and convincing scene that leads to the question of how can we distinguish between a real imitator and an imitation imitator? Indeed Volpone and Mosca are actors throughout. They are also directors, leading the fortune hunters, one by one, to give their best performances; in the process, they reveal how near beneath the surface lies the actor's instinct in all men. Any strong emotion can activate it: love of power in the case of Bolingbroke in *Richard the Second,* sheer ambition in *Macbeth*, jealousy in *Othello,* and greed in *Volpone*. *Volpone* creates chaos, associated with comedy from the time of Aristophanes, by confusing the identifying features of species, class, sex, and morals. Animals imitate men; men imitate animals.

Volpone is, of course, the guiding spirit who, like Marlowe's Jew of Malta, takes constant pleasure in his own mental agility and showmanship. Mosca is equally forceful; his only motive seems to be a delight in perpetrating perversities, and he accepts his inheritance only because it allows him to continue to be perverse. The three birds of prey, Corbaccio, Corvino, and Voltore, stumble over one another in their haste to devour the supposed carcass. If they are hideous caricatures, they are, in fact, caricatures of themselves—as the development of the play from the first scene demonstrates. Mosca and Volpone simply bring out the worst in them; they do not plant it—it is there. The sham trial in act 4 is the dramatic triumph of Jonson's career. When Corvino calls Voltore "mad" at the very point when the old man has become sane again, we see that we, too, have been beguiled by the terrible logic of greed.

WAITING FOR GODOT

Type of work: Drama
Author: Samuel Beckett (1906–   )
Type of plot: Tragicomedy
Time of plot: The present
Locale: A country road
First presented: 1952

In this comedy of the absurd, antic yet philosophically troubling, Beckett views the human condition through symbolism that has its roots in Freudian psychology, the Christian myth, and Existentialism. The two tramps vacillate between hope and despair; they are obsessed by uncertainty and dominated by the absurd.

Principal Characters

Vladimir (Didi) (vlȧ·dē·mēr′; dē·dē′) and **Estragon (Gogo)** (ĕs·trȧ·gōṅ′; gô·gō′), two tramps. In this play action is unimportant; the characters remain undeveloped as the tramps wait impatiently for Godot, who remains a mysterious entity, possibly a local land owner but also a symbol of man's spiritual seeking. They gnaw carrots, rest their tired feet, and engage in other simple activities while their conversations reveal the helplessness of their situation. Throughout the play there is every suggestion that the two live estranged from a state of grace which is hoped for but never realized. Often considering suicide, they are caught in a calm of inactivity between hope and despair in their longing for salvation, which is linked somehow with Godot. When the play ends, the two are still waiting for the promised appearance of Godot.

Pozzo (pō·zō′), a materialist. A rich, boisterous tyrant, he is obviously an expounder of Neitzschean doctrines and materialistic concepts. Pozzo admits that Lucky has taught him all the beautiful things he knows, but now his servant has become unbearable and is driving him mad. At first he drives his servant with a rope; however, when he reappears, blinded in symbolic fashion by his own worldly successes and romantic pessimism, he must be led by his mute servant.

Lucky (lü·kē′), Pozzo's servant. Born a peasant, he gives the impression of a new proletarian, the symbol of modern man's belief in the promises and miracles of science. Lucky first appears driven by Pozzo at the end of a rope. Ordered to think for the group, he delivers the wildest, most brilliantly sustained monologue of the play. When he next appears, he is leading the blind Pozzo, but he is mute.

A Boy, a messenger from Godot.

The Story

Estragon tried to take off his boot but failed. Vladimir agreed with him that it sometimes appeared that there was nothing one could do. They were glad to be reunited after a night apart. With Vladimir's help, Estragon succeeded in removing his painful boot. Vladimir, also in pain, could not laugh in comfort; he tried smiling instead but it was not satisfactory.

Vladimir mused on the one gospel account that said Christ saved one of the thieves. Estragon wanted to leave. They could not leave because they were waiting for Godot. They became confused about the arrangements and wondered if they were waiting at the right time, in the right place, and on the right day. They quarreled briefly but were, as always, reconciled.

They considered hanging themselves but decided that it would be safer to do nothing until they heard what Godot said. They did not know what they had asked Godot for. They concluded they had foregone their rights.

Vladimir gave Estragon a carrot, which he ate hungrily. They decided that although they were not bound to Godot, they were in fact unable to act.

Pozzo entered, driving Lucky, who was laden with luggage fastened by a rope around his neck. Estragon and Vladimir mistook him for Godot but accepted him as Pozzo. Although he attempted to intimidate them, he was glad of their company. After ordering Lucky to bring him his stool and his coat, he gave Lucky the whip. Lucky obeyed automatically. Vladimir and Estragon protested violently against Pozzo's treatment of Lucky. Pozzo deflected their outburst and the subject was dropped.

After smoking a pipe, Pozzo rose. He then decided he did not want to leave, but his pride almost prevented him from reseating himself. The tramps wanted to know why Lucky never put down the luggage. Pozzo said that Lucky was trying to make him keep the fellow. When Pozzo added that he would sell Lucky rather than throw him out, Lucky wept; but when Estragon tried to dry his tears, Lucky kicked him away. Then Estragon wept. Pozzo philosophized on this and said that Lucky had taught him all the beautiful things he knew, but that the fellow had now become unbearable and was driving Pozzo mad. Estragon and Vladimir then abused Lucky for mistreating his master.

Pozzo broke into a monologue on the twilight, alternating between the lyrical and the commonplace and ending with the bitter thought that everything happened in the world when one was least prepared. He decided to reward Estragon and Vladimir for praising him by making Lucky entertain them. Lucky executed a feeble dance which Estragon mocked but failed to imitate.

Estragon stated that there had been no arrivals, no departures, and no action, and that everything was terrible. Pozzo next decided that Lucky should think for them. For this Vladimir replaced Lucky's derby hat. Lucky's thought was an incoherent flood of words which resembled a dissertation on the possible goodness of God, the tortures of hell fire, the prevalence of sport, and the vacuity of suburbs. He desperately upset his listeners, who attacked him and silenced him by seizing his hat. Having restored Lucky to his position as carrier, Pozzo and the tramps said many farewells before he and Lucky finally left.

The Boy called to Vladimir and Estragon. He came with a message from Godot, who would come the next evening. The Boy, a goatherd, said that Godot was kind to him, but that he beat his brother, a shepherd. Vladimir asked the Boy to tell Godot only that he had seen them.

By the time the Boy left, night had fallen. Estragon decided to abandon his boots to someone else. Vladimir protested and Estragon said that Christ had gone barefoot. Once again they considered and rejected the idea of separating. They decided to leave for the night. They stayed where they were.

The following evening the boots were still there and the tree had grown some leaves. The tramps had spent the night separately. Vladimir returned first. When Estragon came back he said he had been beaten again, and Vladimir felt that he could have prevented such cruelty. Vladimir began to talk of the previous day, but Estragon could remember nothing but being kicked. Then they were overwhelmed by the thought of the whispering voices of the dead around them. They tried to break their silence but succeeded only in part. By a great effort Estragon recalled that the previous day had been spent chattering

inanities. He reflected that they had spent fifty years doing no more than that.

They discovered that the boots left behind by Estragon had been exchanged for another old pair. After finding Lucky's hat, which assured them that they had returned to the right place, they started a wild exchange of the three hats, shifting them from hand to hand. Finally Vladimir kept Lucky's hat and Estragon kept his own.

Once more Estragon decided to leave. To distract him, Vladimir suggested that they "play" Pozzo and Lucky. Puzzled, Estragon left, but he returned almost immediately because some people were coming. Vladimir was jubilant, convinced that Godot was arriving. They tried to hide, but there was nowhere for them to go. Finally Lucky entered with Pozzo, who was not blind. Lucky fell and dragged Pozzo with him. Pozzo cried for help. Vladimir passionately wished to act while there was the opportunity—to do one good thing as a member of the human race, a species that appalled him. Pozzo was terrified, and Vladimir also fell in his attempts to raise him. Estragon fell too while trying to lift Vladimir. As they fought and argued on the ground, they called Pozzo "Cain" and "Abel." When he responded to both names they concluded that he was all humanity. Suddenly they got up without difficulty.

Pozzo prepared to leave, but Vladimir wanted Lucky to sing first. Pozzo explained that Lucky was dumb. They wanted to know when he had been afflicted. Angry, Pozzo said that all their lives were merely momentary and time did not matter. He left with Lucky.

While Estragon slept, the Boy entered to say that Godot would come, not that night but the next. The message for Godot was that the Boy had seen Vladimir. The Boy left and Estragon awoke. He immediately wanted to leave. Vladimir insisted that they could not go far because they must return the next night in order to wait for Godot, who would punish them if they did not wait.

Estragon and Vladimir remarked that only the tree in the landscape was alive and considered hanging themselves again. Instead, they decided that if Godot did not come to save them the next night, they would hang themselves. At last the tramps decided to go. They remained immobile.

Critical Evaluation

Waiting for Godot (*En Attendant Godot*) is a landmark in modern drama. When it premiered in Paris, its originality stunned audiences; no one had seen or heard anything like it before. Initially, some were disgusted; some were puzzled; and some were wildly enthusiastic. Within a short time, audiences came to the theater prepared for a wholly new dramatic experience and went away with praises for the enigmatic Samuel Beckett. The play ran for more than three hundred performances in Paris, other

productions were mounted in London and major cities on the Continent, and it was widely translated and performed around the world. After a disastrous United States premiere in Miami, *Waiting for Godot* went on to a successful New York run, suggesting that the play was best received by an audience of sophisticated intellectuals.

Nevertheless, audience enthusiasm has not been matched by unalloyed critical acclaim. To be sure, many critics as well as eminent playwrights have paid high tribute to the play, but other critics, like some members of the first-night audience in Paris, have been repelled or baffled by *Waiting for Godot*, their reactions most often stemming from a misunderstanding of the play. In order to avert such misunderstanding, it is necessary to examine two crucial aspects of the play: its language and its philosophical orientation.

First, the language of the play is intimately connected to Beckett's own background in language studies and literary influences. Beckett was born in Dublin, Ireland, and took his A.B. degree in French and Italian at Trinity College. After teaching English in Paris for two years, he returned to Trinity to teach and complete his M.A. in French. Next, he traveled in England and on the Continent, and he wrote poems, short stories, and novels—in English. He at last settled permanently in Paris, except for a brief hiatus during World War II, and began writing in French in the late 1940s.

Of equal importance, during Beckett's first sojourn in Paris (1928–1930), was his meeting with James Joyce, a meeting which launched a long and mutually satisfying friendship between the two Irish expatriates and language experts. The influence of Joyce on Beckett's work is evident in the wordplay in *Waiting for Godot*, for puns, allusions, and linguistic "tricks" abound.

Great effort has been expended, for instance, in trying to decipher the word "Godot," as character and as concept. Beckett himself has declined to explain, but critics, undeterred, continue to speculate. The most common view sees Godot as God with the "-ot" as a diminutive suffix. The French title *En Attendant Godot* seems to lend support to this interpretation. Another suggestion is the analogy between Godot and Charlot (both utilizing the diminutive suffix), the latter an affectionate nickname for the Charlie Chaplin character in a derby hat, the kind of hat which plays a significant part in the stage business of *Waiting for Godot*. Some readings inevitably deteriorate into the preposterous—that Godot represents De Gaulle, for example. But the most likely explanation involves an allusion to a highly obscure source: Honoré de Balzac's comedy, *Le Faisseur* (also known as *Mercadet*). Balzac's play revolves around a character—named Godeau—who strongly influences the action of the play but who never appears on stage. The parallels between the Balzac work and *Waiting for Godot* are too close to attribute to mere coincidence, for Beckett, like Joyce, has a marked fondness for the esoteric literary allusion. It is possible, of course, to circumvent these literary contortions and simply view Godot as the objectification of a state of being: the *waiting*, bracketed by birth and death, which we call life.

In addition, Beckett plays other word games in *Waiting for Godot*. Estragon, for instance, begins a sentence which Vladimir then finishes. Yet the overwhelming monotony of the dialogue, reflecting the monotony in the characters' lives, is reminiscent of the exercise drills in old language texts of the "La plume de ma tante est sur la table" variety, further suggesting the debasement of language and the consequent breakdown of communication. (This point is a major preoccupation of another modern playwright, Eugene Ionesco.) And the non sequiturs which emerge from rapid-fire exchanges in the dialogue echo the music-hall comedians in the heyday of vaudeville. Thus Beckett's penchant for wordplay reveals the influence of his language training, of his friend James Joyce, and of his conviction that language in the modern world is both necessary and impotent.

The philosophical orientation of *Waiting for Godot* is another matter, however, for the years of Beckett's residence in France coincided with a period of great ferment in Existential philosophy, most of it centered in Paris. Beckett is not a formal or doctrinaire Existentialist, but he could hardly avoid being affected by Existentialism, for such ideas were part of his cultural milieu. There is no systematically Existential point of view in *Waiting for Godot*—as there is in, say, the plays of Jean-Paul Sartre and the novels of Albert Camus. Yet a generally Existential view of the human condition comes through very clearly in the play. Vladimir and Estragon, Lucky and Pozzo are psychically isolated from one another; despite physical proximity, they are alienated and lonely, as indicated by their failure to communicate meaningfully. And in that state of mind, each despairs, feeling helpless in the face of an immutable destiny. But, unlike the formal Existentialists, Estragon and Vladimir hope, and it is that hope which sustains them through their monotonous and immobile existence. Thus, they wait. They wait for Godot, who will surely bring them words of comfort and advice, and who will intervene to alter their destinies. By maintaining this hope, by waiting for Godot to come, Vladimir and Estragon elude the inevitable Existential logic which postulates hopelessness followed by a sense of futility, reducing humankind to absurdity. In this way, Vladimir and Estragon attain truly heroic proportions; they endure.

Beckett's play has been criticized, even by Estragon, because, as the tramp puts it, "Nothing happens." In fact, a great deal does happen—there is a lot of action, much coming and going. However, action in this sense is quite superficial, for all of it is meaningless. Yet that very action assumes a rhythm and a pattern which constitute the structure of the play. The repetitive movements and dialogue reinforce the quasi-Existential theme of the play: that life is a meaningless and monotonous performance of endlessly repeated routine. The pattern established in the first act is recapitulated in the second act, with only slight variation. Obviously the action in *Waiting for Godot* is not the action of conventional drama, but it is this unique fusion of theme and structure which accounts for the startling originality of the play and which rightly earns Beckett a place as one of the few genuine innovators in modern drama.

WALDEN

Type of work: Essays
Author: Henry David Thoreau (1817–1862)
Type of treatise: Autobiography and nature notes
Time of treatise: 1845–1847
Locale: Walden Pond, near Concord, Massachusetts
First published: 1854

More than a naturalist's record of finely observed phenomena, Walden *is a major philosophical statement on the American character, the uses of a life of simple toil, and the values of rugged independence.*

The Story

Early in the summer of 1845, Henry David Thoreau left his family home in the village of Concord, Massachusetts, to live for two years by himself in a rude house that he had constructed beside Walden Pond, in a far corner of Concord township. While there he wrote in his journal about many of the things he did and thought. He was not the owner of the land on which he settled, but he had received the owner's permission to build his house and to live there. His objective was really to live simply and think and write; in addition, he proved to himself that the necessities of food, clothing, shelter, and fuel could be rather simply obtained for a man who desired only what he needed.

As early as March, 1845, Thoreau went out to Walden Pond and cut the timber he needed for the framework of his house, doing all the labor himself. When that was done and the framing in place, Thoreau bought a shanty from an Irish railroad worker. He then tore down the shanty and used the boards for the sidings of the house, even making use of many of the nails already in the boards. By July, then, the house was ready for his occupancy. Before the advent of cold weather the following fall, Thoreau also built himself a fireplace and a chimney for cooking and heating purposes. He also lathed and plastered the interior of the one-room house, in order that it would be warm and comfortable during the cold New England winter.

Having done all the work himself, and having used native materials wherever possible, he had built the house for the absurdly low cost of twenty-eight dollars. In addition to providing himself with a place to live, Thoreau believed he had taught himself a great lesson in the art of living. He was also vastly pleased that he had provided himself with a place to live for less than a year's lodging had cost him as a student at Harvard College.

In order to get the money needed to build the house, Thoreau had planted about two and a half acres of beans, peas, potatoes, corn, and turnips, which he sold at harvest time. The land on which they were grown was lent by a neighbor who believed, along with everyone else,

that the land was good for nothing. In addition to selling enough produce to pay his building expenses, Thoreau had enough yield left from his gardening to provide himself with food. But he did not spend all his time working on the house or in the garden. One of his purposes in living at Walden Pond was to live so simply that he might have plenty of time to think, to write, and to observe nature; and so he spent only as much time in other labors as he had to. He had little respect for possessions and material things. He believed, for instance, that most men were really possessed by their belongings, and that such a literary work as the *Bhagavad-Gita* was worth more than all the towers and temples of the Orient.

Thoreau was quite proud of how little money he needed to live comfortably while at Walden Pond. The first eight months he was there he spent only slightly more than a dollar a month for food. In addition to some twenty-odd dollars he received for vegetables he raised, his income, within which he lived, was slightly more than thirteen dollars. His food consisted almost entirely of rye and Indian meal bread, potatoes, rice, a little salt pork, molasses, and salt. His drink was water. Seldom did he eat large portions of meat, and he never hunted. His interest in the animals that lived in the woods and fields near Walden Pond was the interest of a naturalist. Although he spent some time fishing, he felt that the time he had was too valuable to spend in catching fish to feed himself.

For the small amounts of cash he needed, Thoreau worked with his hands at many occupations, working only so long as was necessary to provide himself with the money his meager wants required. He kept as much time as possible free for thinking and studying. His study consisted more of man and nature than of books, although he kept a few well-selected volumes about him at all times.

While at Walden Pond, summer and winter, Thoreau lived independent of time: he refused to acknowledge days of the week or month. When he wished to spend some time observing certain birds or animals, or even the progress of the weather, he felt free to do so. About the only thing to remind him that men were rushing pell-mell to keep a schedule was the whistle of the Fitchburg Railway trains, which passed within a mile or so of his dwelling. Not that he disliked the railroad; he thought it, in fact, a marvel of man's ingenuity, and he was fascinated by the cargoes which the trains carried from place to place. But he was glad that he was not chained to the commerce those cargoes represented. As much as he sometimes enjoyed the sound of the train, he enjoyed far more the sounds of the birds and animals, most of which he knew, not only as a country dweller knows them, but as the naturalist knows them as well. The loons, the owls, the squirrels, the various kinds of fish in Walden Pond, the migratory birds, all of these were part of his conscious existence and environment.

People often dropped in to visit with Thoreau, who frankly confessed that he did not consider people very important. He failed, in fact, to tell who his most frequent visitors were. He preferred only one visitor at a time if he were an intelligent conversationalist. Whenever he had more visitors than could be accommodated

in his small house with its three chairs, he took them into his larger drawing room, the pine wood which surrounded his home. Few people, it seems, came to visit him, perhaps because he was a crusty kind of host, one who, if he had nothing better to do, was willing to talk, but who usually had more to occupy him than ordinary conversation.

During the winter months Thoreau continued to live comfortably at Walden Pond, though his activities changed. He spent more time at the pond itself, making a survey of its bottom, studying the ice conditions, and observing the animal life which centered about the pond, which had some open water throughout the year.

After two years of life at Walden, Thoreau left the pond. He felt no regret for having stayed there or for leaving; his attitude was that he had many lives to live and that he had finished with living at the pond. He had learned many lessons there, had had time to think and study, and had proved what he had set out to prove twenty-six months before, that living could be extremely simple and yet fulfill the individual.

Critical Evaluation

Few contemporaries of Henry David Thoreau would have predicted the enormous popularity his small volume, *Walden*, would win in our century. Author and work were virtually neglected during Thoreau's lifetime. Locally, he was considered the village eccentric; even his great friend and mentor Ralph Waldo Emerson was disappointed because his young disciple seemingly frittered away his talent instead of "engineering for all America." After Thoreau's death in 1862, his works attracted serious critical attention, but unfavorable reviews by James Russell Lowell and others severely damaged his reputation. Toward the turn of the century he began to win favorable attention again, mainly in Britain. During the Depression of the 1930s when most people were forced to cut the frills from their lives, *Walden*, whose author admonished readers voluntarily to "Simplify, simplify, simplify!" became something of a fad. In the 1960s, with new awareness of environment and emphasis on nonconformity, Thoreau was exalted as a prophet and *Walden* as the individualists' bible.

Walden can be approached in several different ways. Obviously it is an excellent nature book. During the Romantic era, many writers—Wordsworth, Byron, Shelley, Emerson, Whitman, to name a few—paid tribute to nature. But Thoreau went beyond simply rhapsodizing natural wonders. He was a serious student of the natural world, one who would spend hours observing a woodchuck or tribes of battling ants, who meticulously mapped Walden Pond, and who enjoyed a hilarious game of tag with a loon. Like Emerson, he saw nature as a master teacher. In his observations of nature, Thoreau was a

scientist; in his descriptions, a poet; in his interpretations, a philosopher and psychologist; and certainly he was an ecologist in his insistence on man's place *in* (not *over*) the natural universe, and on man's need for daily contact with the earth.

Walden may also be considered as a handbook for the simplification of life. As such, it becomes a commentary upon the sophistication or "refinement" of frequently distorted values and devotion to things of civilized society. Thoreau admits the necessities of food, shelter, clothing, and fuel, "for not till we have secured these are we prepared to entertain the true problems of life with freedom and a prospect of success." He then illustrates how we may strip these necessities to essentials for survival and health, ignoring the dictates of fashion or the yearning for luxury. "Most of the luxuries, and many of the so-called comforts of life," he asserts, "are not only not indispensable, but positive hindrances to the elevation of mankind." With relentless logic he points out how making a living has come to take precedence over living itself; how a man mortgages himself to pay for more land and fancier clothing and food than he really requires; how he refuses to walk to a neighboring city because it will take too long—but then must work longer than the walk would take in order to pay for a train ticket. He questions our dedication to "progress," noting that it is technological, not spiritual: "We are in great haste to construct a magnetic telegraph from Maine to Texas; but Maine and Texas, it may be, having nothing important to communicate."

Perhaps the most serious purpose of *Walden* and its

most powerful message is to call men to freedom as individuals. One looks at nature in order to learn about oneself; one simplifies one's life in order to have time to develop that self fully; and one must honor one's uniqueness if one is to know full self-realization. It is this emphasis on nonconformity that has so endeared Thoreau to the young, who have adopted as their call to life these words from the final chapter of *Walden*: "If a man does not keep pace with his companions, perhaps it is because he hears a different drummer. Let him step to the music which he hears, however measured or far away."

There is an ease, a clarity, a concreteness to Thoreau's prose that separates it from the more abstract, eloquent, and frequently involuted styles of his contemporaries. The ease and seeming spontaneity are deceptive. Thoreau revised the book meticulously during the five years it took to find a publisher; there are five complete drafts which demonstrate how consciously he organized not only the general outline, but every chapter and paragraph. For an overall pattern, he condensed the two years of his actual Walden experience into one fictional year, beginning and concluding with spring—the time of rebirth.

Pace and tone are also carefully controlled. Thoreau's sentences and paragraphs flow smoothly. The reader is frequently surprised to discover that sentences occasionally run to more than half a page, paragraphs to a page or more; syntax is so skillfully handled that one never feels tangled in verbiage. Tone varies from matter-of-fact to poetic to inspirational and is spiced with humor—usually some well-placed satire—at all levels. Even the most abstract topics are handled in concrete terms; Thoreau's ready use of images and figurative language prepares us for twentieth century Imagist poetry.

Taken as a whole, *Walden* is a first-rate example of organic writing, with organization, style, and content fused to form a work that today, over one hundred years after its publication, is as readable and perhaps even more timely than when it was written. In *Walden*, Thoreau reaches across the years to continue to "brag as lustily as Chanticleer . . . to wake my neighbors up."

WAR AND PEACE

Type of work: Novel
Author: Leo Tolstoy (1828–1910)
Type of plot: Historical romance
Time of plot: 1805–1813
Locale: Russia
First published: *Voyna i mir*, 1865–1869 (English translation, 1886)

This novel, often acclaimed as the greatest of its genre, is a panorama of Russian life in the Napoleonic era. War and Peace is a moving record of historical progress, and the dual themes of this vast work—Age and Youth, War and Peace—are shown as simultaneous developments of history.

Principal Characters

Pierre Bezuhov (pyěr′ bĕ·zōō′həf), the illegitimate son of wealthy Count Cyril Bezuhov. Clumsy, stout, and uncommonly tall, he is at first spurned by the social set but is much admired after his father leaves him a fortune. He is beguiled into a marriage with Hélène Kuragina, who in turn is unfaithful to him. For long years Pierre searches for peace of mind, a meaning in life. He seeks for it in philanthropy, in the dissipations of society, in wine, in heroic feats of self-sacrifice during the war with Napoleon. Finally he gains such a internal harmony through witnessing the horror of death on the battlefield and by learning to share the misery of the human race. At the conclusion of the novel he marries Natasha Rostova, whom he has long secretly loved.

Princess Natasha Rostova (nä·tä′shə rôs·tōv′ə), the beautiful daughter of Count Ilya Rostov. Regularly in attendance at all social functions, she is admired by a host of suitors. She becomes engaged to the wealthy and handsome Prince Andrey Bolkonsky; however, the marriage is postponed for a year at Andrey's father's request. During this engagement period, Natasha ruins the proposed marriage by attempting to elope with the rake Anatole Kuragin. When Andrey is mortally wounded, she faithfully cares for him and receives his forgiveness. Later she becomes the wife of Pierre Bezuhov.

Princess Hélène Kuragina (kōō·rä′gĭ·nə), "the most fascinating woman in Petersburg," who becomes Pierre Bezuhov's wife. Although she has no love for Pierre, she marries him for the advantage of wealth and social position. Marriage in no way hampers her amours, and she constantly entertains and encourages prosperous admirers. Essentially she is a superficial and shallow individual, seemingly unperturbed by the misery and suffering of the war around her. Her happiness is only a façade, however, for the tragedy of loneliness and isolation; unable to find the meaning of life in true love and affection, she takes her own life by an overdose of medicine.

Count Nikolay Rostov (nĭ·kô·läy′ rôs·tôf′), Natasha's handsome older brother, who distinguishes himself as a cavalry officer in the Russian army. It is long supposed that he will wed Sonya, his cousin, who lives with the Rostov family; however, the financial ruination of his family makes necessary a more profitable match with Princess Marya Bolkonskaya. When the Russian army is in retreat, he saves Marya from the rebellious peasants on her estate.

Princess Marya Bolkonskaya (mä′ryə vôl·kōn′skĭ·yə), Prince Andrey Bolkonsky's sister, who endures the eccentricities of a tyrannical father. The old prince, desirous of Marya as a nurse and companion, methodically destroys her chances of marriage by refusing to entertain would-be suitors. Resigned to her fate, she takes refuge in an intense religious conviction, entertaining and sponsoring "God's Folk," peasants who have had various mystical experiences. After the deaths of her father and brother, she desires the life of a recluse; but her admiration and love for Nikolay Rostov, whom she later marries, restores her to a normal life.

Sonya (sō′nyə), Nikolay Rostov's poor cousin, the affectionate companion of Natasha in the Rostov family. For the sake of allowing Nikolay to make a more advantageous marriage, she releases him from a childhood pledge.

Prince Andrey Bolkonsky (än·drä′ vôl·kōn′skĭy), a wealthy nobleman, the son of an eccentric father and the brother of Marya. At the battle of Austerlitz he fights valiantly, rallying the Russian troops by charging directly into the front line while waving the Russian flag. Missing in action, he is assumed dead, but he later returns after having been nursed to health by peasants of the countryside. He becomes engaged to Natasha Rostova, but the marriage is canceled as a result of Natasha's indiscretions. Although he swears never to fight again, his sense of duty compels him to enlist when France invades Russian soil. Again wounded, he dies in Natasha's arms, having been reconciled to her through her untiring devotion to him during his illness.

Princess Lise Bolkonskaya (lĭ′sə vôl·kōn′-skĭ·yə), the

beautiful and sensitive wife of Prince Andrey. She dies in childbirth.

Nikolushka Bolkonsky (nĭ·kō·lōō′shkə vôl·kōn′skĭy), the young son of Prince Andrey and his wife Lise. Count Nikolay Rostov and his wife Marya adopt the child after Prince Andrey's death.

Prince Nikolay Bolkonsky (nĭ·kô·läy′vôl·kōn′skĭy), the tyrannical and eccentric father of Andrey and Marya.

Prince Anatole Kuragin (ä·nä·tō′lĭy kōō′rə·gĭn), Hélène's brother, a profligate. Although previously forced into marriage, he woos Natasha Rostova and subjects her to scandal and ridicule.

Prince Vasily Kuragin (vä·sē′lĭy kōō′rə-gĭn), the head of the Kuragin family and the father of Anatole and Hélène.

Prince Hippolyte Kuragin (hĭ·pō′ly·tə kōō′rə·gĭn), his feeble-minded younger son.

Count Ilya Rostov (ēl·yə′ rôs·tôf′), a wealthy nobleman.

Countess Natalya Rostova (nä·täl′yə rôs-tōv′ə), his wife.

Countess Vera Rostova (vyĕ′rə rôs·tōv′ə), their older daughter.

Count Petya Rostov (pyē′tyə rôs·tōf′), their younger son.

Lieutenant Alphose Berg, an officer and intimate friend of the Rostov family. He marries the Countess Vera.

Prince Boris Drubetskoy (bô·rĭs′ drōō-bĕt′skōy), a fashionable and ambitious friend of the Rostovs, a successful staff officer.

Princess Anna Drubetskaya (än′nə drōō-bĕt′skī·yə), the mother of Prince Boris, an impoverished noblewoman.

Julie Karagina (zhōō′lī kä·rä′gĭ·nə), a wealthy young woman who marries Prince Boris Drubetskoy.

Anna Scherer (än′nə shä′rər), maid of honor to the Empress Marya Fedorovna. Her salon is a meeting place for the highest St. Petersburg society.

General Michael Kutuzov (mĭ·hä·ĭl′ kōō-tōō′zəf), appointed commander-in-chief of the Russian army in August, 1812. Obese and slovenly, he is disliked by his fellow officers, and his military tactics are considered obsolete. Yet it is to him that Czar Alexander I and all Russia turn when Napoleon boldly advances upon Russian soil. Even then, however, he is viciously criticized when, after a prolonged and costly battle at Smolensk, he chooses not to defend Moscow by what he considers a useless and hopeless encounter. His wily scheme of "time and patience" proves sound after Napoleon, his line overextended and the Russian winter fast approaching, is forced to withdraw his forces, which are virtually annihilated by hunger, cold, and guerrilla warfare.

Napoleon Bonaparte, the renowned commander of the French Grand Armée. Worshiped and admired by the French, feared by the Russians, he shatters the myth of his invincibility during his disastrous Russian campaign.

Mademoiselle Bourienne, a companion of Marya in the Bolkonsky family. In his senility, Count Bolkonsky finds her alluring and sympathetic.

The Story

In 1805, it was evident to most well-informed Russians that war with Napoleon was inevitable. Austria and Russia joined forces at the battle of Austerlitz, where they were soundly defeated by the French. In the highest Russian society, however, life went on quite as though nothing of tremendous import were impending. After all, it was really only by a political formality that Russia had joined with Austria. The fact that one day Napoleon might threaten the gates of Russia seemed ridiculous. Thus, soirees and balls were held, old women gossiped, and young women fell in love. War, though inevitable, was being waged on foreign soil and was, therefore, of little importance.

The attraction held by the army for the young noblemen of Russia was understandable enough, for the Russian army had always offered excellent opportunities for ambitious, politically inclined young men. It was a wholesome release for their energies. Young Nikolay Rostov, for example, joined the hussars simply because he felt drawn to that way of life. His family idolized him because of his loyalty to the czar, because of his courage, and because he was so handsome in his uniform. Natasha, his sister, wept over him, and Sonya, his cousin, promptly fell in love with him.

While young Nikolay was applauded in St. Petersburg society, Pierre Bezuhov, a friend of the Rostov family, was looked upon as something of a boor. He had just returned from Paris, where he had studied at the university, and he had not yet made up his mind what to do with his life. He would not join the army, for he saw no sense in a military career. His father gave him a liberal allowance, and he spent it frivolously at gambling. In truth, he seemed like a lost man. He would start long arguments, loudly shouting in the most conspicuous manner in the quiet drawing rooms, and then suddenly lapse into sullen silence. He was barely tolerated at soirees before his father died and left him millions. Then, suddenly, Pierre became popular, although he attributed his rise to some new personality development of his own. He was no longer sullen but loved everyone, and it was quite clear that everyone loved him. His most dogged follower was Prince Vassily Kuragin, the father of a beautiful, unmarried daughter, Hélène, who was recognized everywhere as a prospective leader of St. Petersburg society. Pierre was forced into marrying her by the crafty prince, who knew a good catch when he saw one. The marriage, however, was never a success.

Pierre Bezuhov's closest friend was Prince Andrey

Bolkonsky, an arrogant, somewhat cynical man who also despised his wife. Lise, the "Little Princess," as she was called, was pregnant, but Prince Andrey could endure the bondage of domesticity no longer. When he received a commission in the army, he left his wife at the family estate, Bleak Hills, in the care of his sister Marya and his tyrannical old father, and he went off to war. During his absence, Princess Lise bore him a son but died in childbirth. Prince Andrey returned after the battle of Austerlitz to find himself free once more, but he enjoyed no feeling of satisfaction in his freedom. Seeking Pierre, Prince Andrey turned to his friend for answers to some of the eternal questions of loneliness and despair that tortured him.

Meanwhile, Pierre had joined the brotherhood of Freemasons and through this contact had arrived at a philosophy of life which he sincerely believed to be the only true philosophy. Had Pierre realized that the order had initiated him solely because of his wealth, he would never have adopted their ideals. In true faith, however, Pierre restored some of Prince Andrey's lost courage by means of a wild if unreasoning enthusiasm. In the belief that he was now an unselfish, free individual, Pierre freed his peasants and set about improving his estate; but having absolutely no sense of business administration, he lost a great deal of money. Finally, with his affairs in almost hopeless disorder, he left an overseer in charge and retired to Bleak Hills and Prince Andrey's sane company.

Meanwhile, Nikolay Rostov was in the thick of the fighting. Napoleon had overcome the Prussian forces at Jena and had reached Berlin in October. The Russians once more had gone to the assistance of their neighbors, and the two opposing armies met in a terrible battle at Eylau in February, 1807. In June, Nikolay had entered the campaign at Friedland, where the Russians were beaten. In June of that year Nikolay naïvely thought the war was over, for Napoleon and Czar Alexander signed the Peace of Tilsit. What the young officer did not know was that Napoleon possessed a remarkable gift for flattery and had promised, with no intention of keeping his word, that Russia would be given a free hand with Turkey and Finland. For two years Nikolay enjoyed all the privileges of his post in the army, without having to endure any of the risks. Napoleon had gone to Spain.

After having served in minor skirmishes as an adjutant under General Kutuzov, leader of the Russian forces, Prince Andrey returned to the country. He had some business affairs to straighten out with Count Rostov, marshal of his district, and so he went to the Rostov estate at Otradnoe. There Andrey fell almost immediately under the spell of Count Rostov's lovely young daughter, Natasha. He fancied himself in love as he had never loved before. Once again he turned to Pierre for advice. Pierre, however, had experienced an unfortunate quarrel with his wife, Hélène. They were now separated, and Pierre had fought a senseless duel with an innocent man because he

had suspected his wife of being unfaithful; but at the sight of Prince Andrey, so hopelessly in love, Pierre's great heart was touched. He had always been fond of Natasha, whom he had known since childhood, and the match seemed to him ideal. With love once more flowing through his heart, he took his wife back, feeling very virtuous at his own generosity. Meanwhile he encouraged Prince Andrey in his suit.

Natasha had ignored previous offers of marriage. When dashing and wealthy Prince Andrey came upon the scene, however, she lost her heart to him instantly. He asked her parents for her hand, and they immediately consented to the match, an excellent one from their point of view. When Prince Andrey broke the news to his quarrelsome and dictatorial old father, however, the ancient prince said he would not give his blessing until a year had elapsed. He felt that Natasha had little money and was much too young to take charge of Prince Andrey's home and his son. Marya, Prince Andrey's sister, also disapproved of the match. She was jealous of her brother's fiancée.

Natasha was heartbroken but agreed to wait a year; Prince Andrey kept their betrothal a secret, in order, as he said, to let her have complete freedom. Natasha went to visit a family friend in Moscow. There her freedom was too complete. One night at the opera with Pierre's wife Hélène, who was now recognized as an important social leader, she met Hélène's disreputable brother, Anatole. Unknown to Natasha, Anatole had already been forced to marry a peasant girl, whom he had ruined. The young rake now determined to conquer Natasha. Aided by his unscrupulous sister, he forced his suit. Natasha became confused. She loved Prince Andrey, but he had joined the army again and she never saw him; and she loved Anatole, who was becoming more insistent every day. At last, she agreed to run away with Anatole and marry him. Anatole arranged with an unfrocked priest to have a mock ceremony performed.

On the night set for the elopement, Natasha's hostess discovered the plan. Natasha was confined to her room. Unfortunately, she had already written to Prince Andrey's sister asking to be relieved of her betrothal vows.

When Pierre heard the scandal, he forced Anatole to leave town. Then he went to see Natasha. Strangely, he was the only person whom she trusted and to whom she could speak freely. She looked upon him as if he were an older uncle, and she was charmed with his gruff, friendly disposition. Pierre realized that he felt an attraction toward Natasha he should not have had, since he was not free. Nevertheless, he managed to let her know his affection for her, and she was pleased over his attentions. She soon began to get well, although she was never again to be the frivolous girl whom Prince Andrey had loved.

Prince Andrey had suffered a terrible blow to his pride, but in the army there were many engrossing matters to take his attention away from himself. By 1810, the Franco-

Russian alliance had gradually dissolved. When France threatened to free Russia of responsibility for Poland, the czar finally understood that Napoleon's promises meant little. The dapper little French emperor had forsaken Russia in favor of Austria as the center of his European domination, had married Marie Louise, and in 1812, with his eyes unmistakably fixed on Moscow, had crossed the Nieman River. From June to August Napoleon enjoyed an almost uninterrupted march to Smolensk.

In Smolensk he found burned and wrecked houses. The city was deserted. By that time Napoleon began to run into fierce opposition. Old General Kutuzov, former leader of the army of the East and now in complete charge of the Russian forces, was determined to halt the French advance. Oddly enough, the tactics he had chosen actually kept the Russians from a decisive victory. If he had not attempted to halt the French but instead had drawn them deeper and deeper into Russia, lengthening their lines of communication and cutting them off in the rear, the Russians might have won their war earlier. It was odd, too, that Napoleon, in attempting to complete his march, also lessened his chances for victory. Both sides, it seemed, did the very things which would automatically ensure defeat.

Battle after battle was fought, with heavy losses on both sides before Napoleon finally led his forces to Borodino. There the most senseless battle in the whole campaign was fought. The Russians, determined to hold Moscow, which was only a short distance away, lost nearly their whole army. The French forces dwindled in proportion, but it was clear that the Russians got the worst of the battle. General Kutuzov, bitter and war-weary, decided, against his will, that the army could not hold Moscow. Triumphant Napoleon marched once more into a deserted city.

Prince Andrey was gravely wounded at Borodino. The Rostovs were already abandoning their estate to move into the interior, when many wagons loaded with wounded soldiers were brought to the house for shelter. Among these was Prince Andrey himself. Natasha nursed him and sent for Marya, his sister, and his son, Nikolushka. Old Prince Bolkonsky, suffering from the shock of having French soldiers almost upon his doorstep, had died of a stroke. Nikolay managed to move Marya and the boy to safer quarters. Although Prince Andrey welcomed his sister, it was evident that he no longer expected to recover. Natasha nursed him tenderly, and they once more declared their love for each other. When his wound festered, Prince Andrey knew at last that he was dying. He died one night in his sleep. United in tragedy, Marya and Natasha became close friends, and young Nikolay found Prince Andrey's sister attractive.

Meanwhile, Pierre Bezuhov had decided to remain in Moscow. Fired with thoughts of becoming a national hero, he hit upon the plan of assassinating Napoleon. Pierre, however, was captured as a prisoner of war when he attempted to rescue a Russian woman who was being molested by French soldiers.

Napoleon's army completely disintegrated in Moscow. After waiting in vain for peace terms from the czar, Napoleon decided to abandon Moscow and head for France. A ragged, irresponsible, pillaging group of men, who had once been the most powerful army in the world, gathered up their booty, threw away their supplies, and took the road back to Smolensk. Winter came on. Pierre Bezuhov, luckily, was robust and healthy. Traveling with the other prisoners, he learned from experience that happiness could consist of merely being warm and having enough to eat. His privations aged and matured him. He learned responsibility and gained courage. He developed a sense of humor at the irony of his plight. His simplicity and even temperament made him a favorite with French and Russians alike.

On the road to Smolensk, the French forces became completely demoralized. Cossacks charged out of the forests, cutting the lines, taking countless French prisoners, and rescuing the Russian captives. Many Frenchmen deserted. Others fell ill and died on the road. Pierre, free at last, returned to Orel, where he fell ill with fever. Later he learned of the deaths of Prince Andrey and his own wife. Hélène had died in St. Petersburg after a short illness. These shocks, coupled with the news of the defeat of the French, seemed to deprive him of all feeling. When he finally recovered, however, he was overwhelmed with a joyous sense of freedom of soul, a sense that he had at last found himself, that he knew himself for what he really was. He knew the sheer joy of being alive, and he was humble and grateful. He had discovered a faith in God that he had never known before.

Pierre returned to Moscow and renewed his friendships with Marya Bolkonskaya and the Rostovs. Once more Natasha charmed him, and Pierre suddenly realized that she was no longer a child. He loved her now, as always, and so when the opportunity presented itself, he dutifully asked her parents for Natasha's hand. At the same time, Nikolay Rostov entertained the thought of marrying Marya. Natasha and Pierre were married and were very happy. Natasha was an efficient wife who dominated her husband, much to the amusement of their friends, but Pierre loved her and respected her because she knew how to take charge of everything. She managed his estates as well as her household.

Nikolay, though not entirely sure that he loved Marya, knew that to marry her would be a wise thing. The Rostovs were now poor, since the old count had left his affairs in a deplorable state. At the insistence of his mother, Nikolay finally proposed to Marya, and the two families were joined. The union proved happier than Nikolay had expected. They adopted Prince Andrey's son, Nikolushka.

After eight years of marriage, Pierre and Natasha had four fine children, of whom they were very proud. Although society thought that Natasha carried her devotion to her husband and children to an extreme, Natasha and Pierre were happier than they had ever been before, and they found their lives together a fulfillment of all of their dreams.

Critical Evaluation

Leo Tolstoy's *War and Peace* is a panorama of Russian life in that active period of history known as the Napoleonic era. The whole structure of the novel indicates that Tolstoy was writing a new kind of book. He was not concerned with plot, setting, or even people, as such. His purpose was simply to show that the continuity of life in history is eternal. Each human life holds its influence on history, and the developments of youth and age, war and peace, are so interrelated that in the simplest patterns of social behavior vast implications are recognizable. Tolstoy seemed to feel a moral responsibility to present history as it was influenced by every conceivable human force. To do this, it was necessary for him to create not a series of simple, well-linked incidents but a whole evolution of events and personalities. Each character must change, must affect those around him; these people in turn must influence others, until imperceptibly, the whole historical framework of the nation changes. *War and Peace*, then, is a moving record of historical progress, and the dual themes of this vast novel—age and youth, war and peace—are shown as simultaneous developments of history.

War and Peace and *Anna Karenina* (1875–1877), two of the greatest works of fiction in Russian literature—or any literature—were both written when Tolstoy was at the height of his powers as a writer. He was busy managing his country estate as well as writing; his life had a healthy, even exuberant, balance between physical and intellectual activities. *War and Peace*, in particular, reflects the passionate and wide-ranging tastes and energies of this period of his life—before domestic strife and profound spiritual conversion brought about a turning away from the world as well as from art. The novel is huge in size and scope; it presents a long list of characters and covers a splendid variety of scenes and settings. It is, however, a carefully organized and controlled work—not at all the vast, shapeless "monster" many readers and some writers have supposed.

The basic controlling device involves movement between clusters of characters surrounding the major characters: Natasha, Kutuzov, Andrey, Pierre. The second ordering device is thematic and involves Tolstoy's lifelong investigation of the question: What is natural? This theme is offered in the first chapter at Anna Scherer's party, where readers encounter the artificiality of St. Petersburg society and meet the two chief seekers of the natural, Andrey and Pierre. Both Andrey and Pierre love Natasha, who is an instinctive embodiment of the natural in particularly Russian terms. Kutuzov is also an embodiment of Russian naturalness; only he can lead the Rus-

sian soldiers in a successful war against the French. The Russian character of Tolstoy's investigation of the natural or the essential is the main reason one speaks of *War and Peace* as a national epic. Yet, Tolstoy's characters also represent all men.

Natasha's group of characters centers in the Rostov family (the novel is, among many things, a searching study of family life). Count Ilya Rostov, a landowning nobleman, is a sympathetic portrait of a carefree, warmhearted rich man. His wife is somewhat anxious and less generous in spirit, but they are happily married and the family as a whole is harmonious. Natasha's brothers and sisters are rendered with great vividness: the passionate, energetic Nikolay; the cold, formal Vera; the youthful Petya; the sweet, compliant Sonya, cousin to Natasha and used by Tolstoy as a foil to her. Natasha herself is bursting with life. She is willful, passionate, proud, humorous, capable of great growth and change. Like all the major characters, she seeks the natural. She *is* the natural; her instincts are right and true. All of book 7, particularly chapter 7 when she sings and dances, dramatizes the essential Russianness of her nature. Her nearly consummated love affair with Anatole Kuragin, her loss of Andrey, and her final happy marriage to Pierre show how intensely life-giving she is. One of the great experiences of reading *War and Peace* is to witness her slow transition from slim, exuberant youth to thick-waisted motherhood. For Tolstoy, Natasha can do nothing which is not natural and right.

Kutuzov stands above the generals who cluster about him. Forgotten at the start of the war, he is called into action when all else seems to have failed. Unlike the other generals, many of them German, Kutuzov knows that battles are not won in the staff room by virtue of elaborate planning but by the spirit of the soldiers who actually do the fighting. Kutuzov alone knows that one must wait for that moment when the soldiers' spirit is totally committed to the battle. He knows that the forces of war are greater than any one man can control and that one must wait upon events and know when not to act as well as when to act. His naturalness is opposed to Napoleon's artificiality. A brilliant strategist and planner, Napoleon believes that he controls events. His pride and vanity are self-binding; he cannot see that if he invades Russia, he is doomed. Kutuzov's victory over Napoleon is a victory of the natural and the humble, for he is, after all, a man of the people. Furthermore, the figure of Kutuzov is very closely related to Tolstoy's philosophy of historical change and necessity.

The characters of Andrey and Pierre probably represent two sides of Tolstoy: the rational-spiritual versus the passionate-mystical, although these labels are far too simple. Andrey's group of characters centers in the Bolkonsky family; the merciless, autocratic, but brilliant General Bolkonsky, Andrey's father, and his sister Princess Marya, who is obedient, pious, and loving and who blossoms when she marries Nikolay Rostov. When readers first see Andrey, he is bored and even appears cynical; yet, like Pierre, he is searching for an answer to life, and he undergoes a series of awakenings which bring him closer to the natural. The first awakening occurs when he is wounded at Austerlitz and glimpses infinity beyond the blue sky; the second occurs at his wife's death; the third occurs when he falls in love with Natasha; and the last when he dies. In all of these instances, Andrey moves closer to what he conceives of as the essential. This state of mind involves a repudiation of the world and its petty concerns and passions. In all but one of these instances, death is involved. Indeed, Andrey's perception of the natural is closely related to his acceptance of death. He comes to see death as the doorway to infinity and glory and not as a fearful black hole. Death becomes part of the natural rhythm, a cycle which promises spiritual rebirth.

Pierre's group is composed of St. Petersburg socialites and decadents: the Kuragin family, composed of the smooth, devious Prince Vasily; his son, the rake Anatole, and daughter, the beautiful, corrupt Hélène, Pierre's first wife; the rake Dolokhov; and finally, in Pierre's third or fourth transformation, the peasant Platon Karataev. Unlike Andrey, Pierre's approach to life seems almost strategically disordered and open—he embraces all forms of life passionately and hungrily. Compared to Andrey's rigorous and discriminating mind, Pierre seems hopelessly naïve and chaotic.

Pierre, however, even more than Natasha, is capable of vital and creative change. As Andrey seems fitted to perceive intimations of essences beyond the world, Pierre seems fitted to find his essences in the world. He shucks off his mistaken connection with Hélène and her family and experiences the first of his own awakenings in the conversion to Freemasonry (one of several interesting "false" conversions in the novel, one other being Natasha's after she is rejected by Andrey). He, too, learns from death, both in his duel with Dolokhov and in his observations of the battle of Borodino. His two most important awakenings, however, occur in his love for Natasha and in his experience as a prisoner of the French. In the latter instance, he encounters the peasant Karataev, who teaches him to accept all things—even death—in good grace and composure of spirit. When Natasha encounters Pierre after this experience, she rightly recognizes that he has been transformed. All that is superficial and nonessential is gone from him. Their marriage is a union of two vital human beings tempered by suffering. At the end, there is more than a hint that Pierre is involved in efforts on the part of the aristocracy to modify the ossified system of government under the czars.

War and Peace, perhaps beyond any other work, shows the advantages of the long novel. After reading the book, the reader feels a sense of space and a sense of change through the passage of time which are impossible to transmit so vividly in shorter fiction. This great novel reveals the beauty and injustice, the size and complexity, of life itself.

THE WASTE LAND

Type of work: Poem
Author: T. S. Eliot (1888–1965)
First published: 1922

By the time T. S. Eliot startled the literary world with the publication of *The Waste Land* in *The Criterion* and *The Dial* (1922), he had already achieved considerable recognition as an innovative and prolific essayist and reviewer and a highly original poet of considerable depth and complexity. His earlier poems, particularly "The Love Song of J. Alfred Prufrock" (1917), "Portrait of a Lady" (1917), and "Gerontion" (1920), contain arresting images, dramatic situations and monologues, highly allusive language, and linguistic virtuosity reminiscent of the work of John Donne and Robert Browning. They also serve as preludes to the most famous poem of the twentieth century, one which has engendered more commentaries, exegeses, and speculations than any other, *The Waste Land*. Indeed, Eliot considered "Gerontion" to be a prologue to the longer work. It is useful, then, for readers coming to Eliot's work for the first time to read *The Waste Land* in the context of his earlier poetry, since those poems contain the seeds of the later work and, in many respects, introduce it. Thematically, they anticipate *The Waste Land*'s examination of aridity, the burden of history, the use of memory (personal history), a larger economy of spiritual dimensions, the problems raised by sexuality and love, and the quest to find meaning by ordering and reordering personal, historical, and mythic experience. Technically, they are of a piece with it in that they employ a stream of consciousness centered in various characters, an approach that owes much to Eliot's admiration for French Symbolist poetry, especially the poetry of Jules Laforgue and others he had found revealed to him in Arthur Symons' *The Symbolist Movement in Literature* (1899).

The Waste Land is a series of five poems that together form one poem. Each is separable, but all are joined together by the vision of the blind Tiresias, into whom Gerontion (the little old man) has been transformed. When he published the poem in book form, also in 1922, Eliot added some fifty notes to it, only some of which are helpful to reading the poem as a poem rather than as a compendium of literary and cultural allusions. One note (to line 218) helps readers to focus on the unified nature of the work by claiming that "what Tiresias *sees*, in fact, is the substance of the poem." Tiresias, he has noted, is the poem's "most important personage, uniting all the rest." The male characters, he suggests, melt into each other and are not wholly distinct from each other; likewise, " all the women are one woman, and the two sexes meet in Tiresias," the androgynous seer. Following Eliot's

clue, the reader may enter into the vision of the ancient Theban, his vision of the future which is the poet's present and, now, the reader's present and past. The vision is both temporal and timeless, linked to the post-World War I era of disillusion and transcending it in its universality and visionary quality.

This latter, dreamlike aspect is important to bear in mind when attempting to make sense of one's own experience of the poem. If one considers the work as a Symbolist poem, many of its historical and cultural elements diminish in importance. The archetypal elements of infertility, the barren land and the sterile sexuality, ritual death and rebirth are played out symbolically within the dreamscape in fragmented fashion. Indeed, a key to understanding the nature of the poem lies near its end (line 431): "These fragments I have shored against my ruins." The fragments of speech, action, thought, and emotion are the very words of the poem, shored up against the ruins of culture or of an individual sense of its dilapidation the reader is invited to share.

The poem's title, epigraph, and dedication merit attention. *The Waste Land* is a phrase common to the varied medieval tellings of the Grail Quest, a tale rooted in earlier myths of Indo-European culture. The land is a waste as a result of some grievous wrong that can be righted only by a naïve and sometimes reluctant adventurer (reader), who must ask the right question of its wounded ruler, the Fisher King, to free the land from its curse. Eliot refers to Jessie L. Weston's *From Ritual to Romance* (1920) as a clue to understanding the poem's title and to Sir James Frazer's *The Golden Bough* (1890–1915) for its detailed study of vegetation myths and rituals. The epigraph, in Latin and Greek, about the Cumean Sibyl, a seer who was granted immortality but not eternal youth, points to the necessity of inquiry (the boy asks what the Sibyl wants), the impossibility of her wish (to die), and the prophetic nature of the poem. The dedication, to Ezra Pound, "the better craftsman," directs the reader to Pound's poetry as a way of thanking the poet who "discovered" Eliot in 1914 and who had a principal hand in editing the poem. More important, the dedication points to Pound's innovative work as a context for reading and thinking about Eliot's poem. Thus, before reading the first line of the poem the reader is conditioned to think of ancient myths and modernist poetry.

Part 1, "The Burial of the Dead," presents the reader with a perplexing wealth of images, allusions in English, German, and French, the arcana of the Tarot, and varied voices mixing memory and desire in the paradoxical season of rebirth in which burial is remembered and reenacted. The speakers range from Marie to a biblical seer to Madame Sosostris, "famous clairvoyante," to Stetson and his acquaintance. The profusion of images, particularly those of water, vegetation, growth, aridity, decay, decomposition, and rebirth, imitates dream sequences and promotes a confusion of time and place, of incidents and meanings. Part 1 also foreshadows events of subsequent sections (such as the heap of broken images and death by water) and instills in the reader a disquietude. Familiar acts such as the rush-hour walk over London Bridge take on an aspect of Dantean menace, and the commonplace errand of delivering a horoscope becomes a dangerous business: "One must be so careful these days." Its concluding line, from Charles Baudelaire's *Flowers of Evil*, serves to startle the reader, now directly addressed as a reader who is both hypocrite and brother, into a sharp and eager observation and reflection on the lines preceding it. The keynotes of the section, as Bernard Bergonzi has observed, are movement in time across day, season, year, and centuries, and change from youth to age, from motion to stillness in death, and reluctant rebirth. These give the reader an emotional sense of the poem but not necessarily a rational sense of logical connections between the stanzas or verse paragraphs.

"A Game of Chess" (part 2) continues to meld the mythic with the banal, joining the story of Philomel and the tale of Lil, both of which involve unsatisfactory sexuality, while the entire sequence presents a disenchantment with worldly experience at both ends of the social spectrum. The sequence opens with evocations of royalty in the richly ornate, overwrought boudoir and proceeds to depict the emptiness of luxury and the means by which the speakers choose to while away their time. The scene shifts from mindless opulence to a gossipy late evening in a pub at closing time. Here one learns of Albert and Lil in a catty postwar monologue punctuated by the barman's call, which, for want of an apostrophe, becomes a plea for the advent of some long-awaited event: "HURRY UP PLEASE ITS TIME."

The title of the poem's third part, "The Fire Sermon," refers to a refining fire of purgation. This section introduces Tiresias as one among many voices, including those of the Fisher King, the three Thames-daughters, Saint Augustine, and the Buddha. The ordinary but sordid sexual encounters along the Thames, in a flat, in a canoe, in the heralded tryst of Sweeney and Mrs. Porter, and in Mr. Engenides' proposition conspire to equate sexuality with seaminess and to present it as a mindless and emotionless, automatic and animal impulse. Over against this view of the body is the exaltation of the soul, as Eastern and Western spirituality join at the end of the sequence in a burning away of the physical to free the spirit. As the omniscient narrator who foresees all, Tiresias subsumes the other voices; thus the unifying technique of the poem begins to work.

In the briefest, ten-line part of the poem, part 4, "Death by Water," the reader considers the drowned Phlebas the Phoenician and recalls the cards dealt by Madame Sosostris earlier with the warning to "fear death by water" (line 55). Phlebas serves as an appropriate memento mori and possibly as something of a model in the liberation of the soul: Two weeks dead, he "forgot" the usual concerns as he passed, in reverse, "the stages of his age and youth" and entered the whirlpool. In counterpoint to the burning of "The Fire Sermon," here "a current under sea/ Picked his bones in whispers" as water becomes a cleansing agent.

In part 5, "What the Thunder Said," the waste land, still parched, is haunted by a "dry sterile thunder without rain" until "a damp gust/ Bringing rain" arrives. The thunder speaks in the words of the Upanishads, "datta, dayadhvam, damyata" (give, sympathize, control). The thunder's words bring revitalizing rain and a wisdom that allows for the possibility of revivification. As Eliot had blended the journey of Jesus' disheartened disciples to Emmaus, the approach to the Chapel Perilous, and "the present decay of eastern Europe" in the beginning of this final part of the poem, so he introduces a more ancient spiritual element to begin to change the present state of spiritual decay and to retrieve the land from waste. How he does so is, characteristically, with words, words the thunder speaks, words presumably still reported by Tiresias, words the poet, after all, writes. The quest for spiritual health is, the poem suggests, achieved through the recovery of artistic wholeness.

Elsewhere, Eliot has written about seeing the end in the beginning and the beginning in the end. At the end of *The Waste Land*, one finds the possibility for beginning the poem anew, for reading it anew with the knowledge gleaned from Tiresias and with a sense of direction. In the last stanza, for example, the Fisher King, no longer fishing in the dull canal behind the gashouse as he did in part 3, has the arid plain behind him and is fishing on the shore. He poses himself a healing question that seems to precipitate a multivocal and multilingual chorus in the poem's concluding lines. If the Fisher King can contemplate "at least" setting his lands in order, this notion implies his ability to do so, and the words of the thunder seem to have had some effect. Immediately after the question is posed, as is so often the case in the Grail Quest narratives, the king and the land revive. The next line of the poem borrows from the children's nursery rhyme "London Bridge Is Falling Down" and heralds the destruction of the pathway to the burial of the dead (part 1). It is followed by a citation from Dante's *Purgatory* in which the lustful Arnaut Daniel leaps voluntarily into the refining fire (possibly glossing "The Fire Sermon"). Next, a phrase from the poem *Pervigilam Veneris* and the song of the nightingale (which in the Latin poem sadly silences the speaker) serve to recall Philomel (parts 1 and

2). An allusion to Gérard de Nerval's "El desdichado" suggests yet another approach to yet another tower, reinforcing the quest motif. The line that follows, as already noted, highlights the poet's act of shoring up verbal fragments against his ruins, just as the Fisher King shores up fragments to set his lands in order and Tiresias shores up fragmented visions into a continuous discourse. Eliot's citation from Thomas Kyd's *The Spanish Tragedy* may also be self-referential, since the mad Hieronymo proposes to "fit" together a play using poetic fragments in several languages. The penultimate line's repetition of what the thunder said reinforces the ostensibly salvific effect of these words, since the poem concludes with the repetition of "Shantih"—the formal ending, Eliot's note explains, to an Upanishad, equivalent to the phrase "the peace which passeth understanding." The journey from the cruelest month to this peace, while foreseen by Tiresias, is one which the reader may wish to undertake again with Tiresias as guide.

Eliot's mastery of the Symbolist poem and his virtuosity in the use of language mark *The Waste Land* as a singular achievement in English poetry of the twentieth century. His multiple allusions, suggesting a place in world literature and cultural traditions for his work, serve to make it, indeed, part of those traditions while adding to them. As is the case with the best poetry, *The Waste Land* is a poem to which readers return, to contemplate and to find a newly familiar voice of considerable relevance to succeeding generations.

THE WAVES

Type of work: Novel
Author: Virginia Woolf (1882–1941)
Type of plot: Psychological realism
Time of plot: The present
Locale: England
First published: 1931

A major psychological novel, The Waves *presents a series of interlocking dramatic monologues in which six characters, all of them more or less androgynous types, reveal the hidden essence of being at successive stages of their lives. The action is a record of time passing as the six characters trace the course of their memories and sensations from childhood to old age and death.*

Principal Characters

Percival, a childhood friend of the six central characters, who respect, admire, and love him; he is the symbol of the ordinary man, the conventional figure. Rather awkward, bumbling, but pleasant and accepted everywhere, Percival forms the light around whom the six-sided flower revolves, as Bernard put it. In love with the natural woman, Susan, he is beloved by Neville, the scholar, the lover of young men, the brilliant poet. A sportsman, a hale fellow, a poor scholar, and finally a soldier who dies in India, Percival represents a kind of norm in personality and conduct.

Bernard, the phrasemaker, the chronicler of the group of childhood friends as they grope toward death, the great adversary of all human life, he thinks. Through Bernard the rest of the characters see life, because in his attempt to grasp reality he is able to become whomever he meets or talks with. Though he sees himself as a failure, he does catch at essences and makes of these his unfinished stories, tales that Percival once saw through and would not let him finish. Deeply devoted to his best friend Neville, he nevertheless is all things to all the characters. A husband, father, provider, friend, he becomes, finally, a seer who tries to sum up the meaning of experiences all have shared.

Neville, the poet, the scrupulous artist, the lover of a single man, the sensitive genius who keeps his life carefully wrapped and labeled. Gaunt and handsome, gifted with the tongue of all great men and able to mimic them from Catulus to Shakespeare, he finds it difficult to survive the shock of Percival's death. He turns first to reproductions of the man and measures his time by the conversations with young, handsome men to whom he is a kind of Socrates. Lonely, introspective he finally finds diversion with frivolous Jinny. He has the ability to speak to them all, even Susan, who sees him as her antithesis.

Susan, the elemental woman, nature-loving and natural, a born mother and an implement of life. Disliking the pine and linoleum smells of school, civilization, she endures education, even travel, so that she may replace her dead mother, administer love to her earthy father, marry a farmer, and raise a family amid the natural, lovely, rural England where she can indulge in its sights, smells, sounds, and feelings. She has long loved Bernard and has been the object of Percival's love, but none know of these things until later. She resists social ways, dress, attitudes even to the point of boorishness, though she carries human feelings, love and jealousy, admiration and disgust, to their meetings.

Louis, the son of a Brisbane banker, a self-conscious outcast of the society of his friends but the most brilliant and egotistical one of the group. Endowed with self-knowledge, the result of fine breeding from the Hebrews in their Egyptian bondage through the present, Louis hides his endowments and very real gifts out of shame and fear of ridicule. In this way he finally becomes assertive and makes of business a romance, false but substantial. He fears all the others except Rhoda, whom he makes his mistress after these two outsiders are drawn together by their loneliness. All recognize his supremacy in subtle ways, and he is respected for this fierce inner being in spite of the discomfort it causes the group.

Rhoda, the plain, clumsy misfit who tries to imitate the world which despises her. Alone with her meager self, she longs for anonymity and retreats from reality early. Tolerated by Susan, avoided by Jinny, she has a kind of ease with Bernard and a negative attraction to Louis. Not gifted in any way, she denies the role life has created for her and commits suicide in middle life.

Jinny, the hedonist, the careful cultivator of externals, and the one who causes a rustle wherever she goes. Beautiful, she possesses physical vitality, which she burns out in a few brief years; Jinny has the superficial drive of appearances as opposed to the elemental in Susan. Assignations are her business; epicureanism is the method, and weariness is the result.

The Story

The waves rolled shoreward, and at daybreak, the children awoke. Watching the sunrise, Bernard, maker of phrases, seeker of causes, saw a loop of light—he would always think of it as a ring, the circle of experience giving life pattern and meaning. Neville, shy and passionate, imagined a globe dangling against the flank of day. Susan, lover of fields and seasons, saw a slab of yellow, the crusted loaf, the buttered slice, of tea time in the country. Rhoda, awkward, timid, heard wild cries of startled birds. Jinny, sensuous and pleasure loving, saw a tassel of gold and crimson. Louis, of a race that had seen women carry red pitchers to the Nile, heard a chained beast stamping on the sands.

While the others played, Louis hid among the currant bushes. Jinny, finding him there and pitying his loneliness, kissed him. Suddenly jealous, Susan ran away, and Bernard followed to comfort her. They walked across fields to Elvedon, where they saw a woman writing at a window. Later in the schoolroom, Louis refused to recite because he was ashamed of his Australian accent. Rhoda was unable to do her sums and had to stay in. Louis pitied her, for she was the one he did not fear.

The day brightened. Bernard, older now, yawned through the headmaster's speech in chapel. Neville leaned sideways to watch Percival, who sat flicking the back of his neck. A glance, a gesture, Neville realized, and one could fall in love forever. Louis, liking order, sat quietly. As long as the head talked, Louis forgot snickers at his accent, his memories of kisses underneath a hedge. Susan, Jinny, and Rhoda were in a school where they sat primly under a portrait of Queen Alexandra. Susan thought of hay waving in the meadows at home. Jinny pictured a gold and crimson party dress. Rhoda dreamed of picking flowers and offering them to someone whose face she never saw.

Time passed, and the last day of the term arrived. Louis went to work in London after his father, a Brisbane banker, failed. In his attic room, he sometimes heard the great beast stamping in the dark, but now the noise was that of city crowds and traffic. At Cambridge, Neville read Catullus and waited with uneasy eagerness for Percival's smile or nod. Bernard was Byron's young man one day, Shelley's or Dostoevski's the next. One day, Neville brought him a poem. Reading it, Bernard felt that Neville would succeed while he would fail. Neville was one person in love with one person, Percival. In this phrasemaking, Bernard became many people—a plumber, a horse breeder, an old woman in the street—as well as Byron's or Dostoevski's man. In Switzerland, Susan dreamed of newborn lambs in baskets, or marsh mists and autumn rains, of the lover who would walk with her beside dusty hollyhocks. At a ball in London, Jinny, dancing, felt as if her body glowed with inward fire. At the same ball, Rhoda sat and stared across the rooftops.

They all loved Percival; before he left for India, they met at a dinner party in London to bid him good-bye. Bernard, not knowing that Susan had loved him, was already engaged. Louis was learning to cover his shyness with brisk assurance; the poet had become a businessman. Rhoda was frightened by life. Waiters and diners looked up when Jinny entered—lovely and poised. Susan became dowdy, hated London. Neville, loving Percival in secret, dreaded the moment of parting that would carry him away. Here, thought Bernard, was the circle he had seen long ago. Youth was friendship and a stirring in the blood, like the notes of Percival's wild hunting song.

The sun passed the zenith, and shadows lengthened. When word came that Percival had been killed in India, Neville felt as if that doom had been his own. Nevertheless, he would go on, a famous poet and scholar after a time, but always as well a lonely man waiting in his rooms for the footstep on the stair of this young man or that whom he loved in place of Percival. Bernard was married then; his son had been born. He thought of Susan, whom Percival had loved. Rhoda also thought of Susan, engaged to her farmer in the country. She remembered the dream in which she had offered flowers to a man whose face had been hidden from her, and she knew at last that the man had been Percival.

Shadows grew longer over country and town. Louis, a wealthy, successful businessman, planned a place in Surrey with greenhouses and rare gardens, but he still kept his attic room where Rhoda often came; they had become lovers. Susan walked in the fields with her children or sat sewing by the firelight in a quiet room. Jinny groomed a body shaped for gaiety and pleasure. Neville measured time by the hours he spent waiting for the footstep on the stair, the young face at the door. Bernard tried to snare in phrases the old man on the train, the lovers in the park. The only realities, he thought, were in common things. He realized that he had lost friends by death—Percival was one—and others because he had not wished to cross the street. After Louis and Rhoda parted, his new mistress was a vulgar cockney actress. Rhoda, always in flight, went to Spain. Climbing a hill to look across the sea toward Africa, she thought of rest and longed for death.

Slowly, the sun sank. At Hampton Court, the six friends met again for dinner. They were old now, and each had gone a different way after Percival had died in India years before. Bernard felt that he had failed. He had wrapped himself in phrases; he had sons and daughters, but he had ventured no farther than Rome. He had not become rich, like Louis, or famous, like Neville. Jinny had lived only for pleasure, little enough, as she was learning. After dinner, Bernard and Susan walked by the lake. There was little of their true thoughts they could say to each other. Bernard, however, was still a maker of phrases.

Percival, he said, had become like the flower on the table where they ate—six-sided, made from their six lives.

So it seemed to him years later, after Rhoda had jumped to her death and the rest were old. He wondered what the real truth had been—the middle-class respectability of Louis, Rhoda's haunted imagination, Neville's passion for one love, Susan's primitivism, Jinny's sensuous plea-sures, his own attempt to catch reality in a phrase. He had been Byron's young man and Dostoevski's and also the hairy old savage in the blood. Once he had seen a loop of light, a ring; but he had found no pattern and no meaning, only the knowledge that death is the great adversary against whom man rides in the darkness where the waves break on the shore.

Critical Evaluation

The Waves owes nothing whatever to the traditional form of the novel. In this book, Virginia Woolf was attempting to give to fiction the subtle insights and revealing moments of perception that at one time were the sole domain of poetry. Her method is highly stylized. In a series of interlocking dramatic monologues, six characters reveal the hidden essence of being at successive stages of their lives. The action, if anything so fleeting and inward can be called action, is a record of time passing as the six characters trace the course of their memories and sensations from childhood to old age and death. There is nothing irrelevant here; everything is observation, sensation, and naked intuition.

Woolf looked at life with a poet's vision, and in this novel, she went even beyond Joyce in her use of symbols to make objects in the external world correspond to inner reality. Each section of her story is prefaced by a descriptive passage in which the movements of sun and waves through a single day stand for time and eternity. Uniting her people is the character of Percival, viewed only through their eyes, symbol of the natural man and also of the emotional certainty that all seek in life. At the end, Bernard summarizes the experiences of the group and sees in their lives man's challenge to death.

The six soliloquies, spoken by six different characters at different periods in their lives from childhood to old age, are not literally spoken aloud; in most cases, the characters are verbalizing their thoughts and inner feelings. Often the narration is in the present tense, as a character explains what he is doing at that moment. Characters do not usually speak to one another, although at times they almost seem to communicate telepathically; each person is set apart, alone, although each knows and thinks about the others. The soliloquies are too well ordered for random thought patterns and too sophisticated and artificial for actual speech; they evoke the atmosphere of a dreamworld. Each soliloquy is paralleled by the passing of a day from sunrise to sunset; descriptions of nature—of the sun, the sea, birds, and plants—precede each section and serve to make implicit comparisons with the characters' speeches. The most dominant of these images is that of the waves.

The characters have different qualities: Bernard is the leader and unifier; Jinny is an extrovert, Rhoda an introvert; Louis wanted desperately to succeed; Neville is a poet; Susan loves the country life. The quality of their speech, however, is not differentiated, and it is perhaps more correct to say that the six characters are all parts of one being; or the six may all be aspects of the personality of Woolf herself, or of the human personality. In addition to these main characters, there is Percival, a schoolfellow of the other six who dies in India in his midtwenties and who never speaks directly in the novel but appears as the others speak of him. He is a unifying element for the group, all of whom care deeply about him. He seems to have almost mythical powers over them as well, and his name is related to Parzival, the keeper of the Grail. They all look to him as their ideal and goal.

Woolf often uses Bernard to express ideas about the ambiguity of language, which is one of the book's major themes. A phrasemaker, Bernard comes to distrust words and believes in the experience that is inexpressible. Words have always enabled Bernard to create order from chaos, but he comes to understand that words may not capture the reality of the experience at all, but only an image of it; thus, he worries about the very process of telling the story. Actually, the "story" in *The Waves* is practically nonexistent. The crucial event is Bernard's renewal, as the wave of life's desires again rises in him; this reuniting with the cycle of life, death, and rebirth has been foreshadowed throughout the novel by the symbol of the waves. Thus, the shining ring that Bernard envisioned as a boy becomes an appropriate symbol for the oneness of art and life that Woolf has established by the end of the book.

THE WEALTH OF NATIONS

Type of work: Economic treatise
Author: Adam Smith (1723–1790)
First published: 1776

The classic statement of economic liberalism, the policy of laissez-faire, was written over a ten-year period by Adam Smith, a Scottish professor of moral philosophy, and published under the title *An Inquiry into the Nature and Causes of the Wealth of Nations*. Its power derived from its ideas which were useful in encouraging the rise of new business enterprise in Europe, but the ideas could not have taken hold so readily had it not been for the scope of Smith's work and the effectiveness of his style.

As a philosopher, Smith was interested in finding intellectual justification for certain economic principles which he came to believe, but as an economist and writer he was interested in making his ideas prevail in the world of business. He was reacting against oppressive systems of economic control that were restricting the growth of business; but although he concerned himself with general principles and their practical application, he was aware of the value of the individual, whether employer or laborer. There is no reason to believe Smith would have sanctioned monopolistic excesses of big business or any unprincipled use of the free-enterprise philosophy.

Smith began his work with the assumption that whatever a nation consumes is either the product of the annual labor of that nation or what is purchased with the products of labor. The wealth of the nations depends upon the proportion of the produce to the consumers, and that proportion depends partly upon the proportion of those who are employed to those who are not, and perhaps even more on the skill of the workers and the efficiency of the means of distribution.

Book 2 of *The Wealth of Nations* considers the question of how the skill of the laborers can best be increased; book 2 is a study of capital stock, since it is argued that the proportion of workers to non-laborers is a function of the amount of capital stock available; book 3 explains how Europe came to emphasize the industry of the towns at the expense of agriculture; book 4 presents various economic theories, some stressing the importance of industry in the towns, others, the importance of agriculture; and book 5 considers the revenue of the sovereign, or commonwealth, with particular attention paid to the sources of that revenue and the consequences of governmental debt.

In Smith's view, the productive power of labor is increased most readily by the division of labor, for by giving each worker a specific job to do he becomes more skillful, time is saved, and machinery is invented that further speeds the rate of production. Smith believed that as a result of the increase in production which followed the division of labor, a well-governed community was able to enjoy a "universal opulence which extends itself to the lowest ranks of people."

Smith regarded the division of labor as a necessary consequence of the human propensity to trade or exchange one thing for another. The propensity to trade is itself a consequence of a more fundamental human trait: self-love. Thus, for Smith, the basic motivating force of any economic system, including successful ones, is the self-interest of each person involved in the system.

Money originates as a means of facilitating exchange when the products of those who wish to barter are not desired by those with whom they choose to trade. To use Smith's example, if a butcher has all the bread and beer he needs, he will not accept more bread or beer in exchange for meat. But if the man with bread or beer can exchange it elsewhere for money—whether it be shells, tobacco, salt, or cattle, or the most favored medium of exchange, metal—he can then use the money to buy meat from the butcher.

Among the most important ideas in *The Wealth of Nations* is Smith's claim that labor is the real measure of the exchangeable value of commodities. Commodities have a value in use, but for the producer this value becomes unimportant, and he seeks to exchange what he has made for something that he needs. The amount of work he can purchase with his commodity is the real exchangeable value of that commodity. Thus Smith defines wealth as the power of purchasing labor. The nominal, as distinguished from the real, price of commodities is their money value.

Smith defined *natural* price as the average price of a commodity in a community, and *market* price as the actual selling price. He presents the familiar principle of supply and demand by stating that market price increases when the quantity of a commodity brought to market falls short of the demand.

Wherever there is perfect liberty the advantages and disadvantages of different uses of labor and stock must be either equal or tending to equality, according to Smith. However there are counterbalancing circumstances that affect equality: the agreeableness of the job, the cost of learning the business, the constancy of employment, the amount of trust that must be put in the employee, and the probability of success.

Smith makes a distinction between productive and

unproductive labor. Labor is productive when it adds to the value of something, unproductive when it does not. The labor of a manufacturer adds to the value of the material which is used, but the labor of a menial servant adds nothing to the value of the employer whom he serves. This distinction is important because it is by reference to the proportion of productive to unproductive labor that capital is explained.

There are four ways of using capital: for purchasing raw materials, for manufacturing, for transportation, and for distribution.

Adam Smith was confident that he could discover the natural order of economic matters, but to later critics it has appeared that he was mistaking his own preferred kind of economic situation for that which would prevail if economic relations among men were in no way affected by social habit. His inclination was to regard what would prevail in a civilized community free from governmental restraint as the natural state of affairs. This view is acceptable when he says, for example, "According to the natural course of things, therefore, the greater part of the capital of every growing society is, first, directed to agriculture, afterwards to manufactures, and last of all to foreign commerce;" but the following account of rent is more provocative: "Rent, considered as the price paid for the use of land, is naturally the highest which the tenant can afford to pay in the actual circumstances of the land." However, Smith wrote without any obvious interest in supporting one economic class against another, and his definitions of "natural" price, rent, and other economic factors are couched in neutral terms.

Smith's experiences as a teacher and philosopher are reflected most clearly in his account "Of the Expence of the Institutions for the Education of Youth." He is rather bitter about the quality of education when the teacher is not driven by economic necessity to do his best. In situations where the professor is responsible only to his colleagues, they are likely to allow one another to neglect their duties as teachers. The result is that "In the university of Oxford, the greater part of the public professors have, for these many years, given up altogether even the pretense of teaching." Smith favored giving the student a considerable part to play in the selection and retention of teachers, and he warned that if this were not done, the professors would devise ways of giving "sham-lectures" and would force their students to attend regularly and keep silent.

Smith thought that the wealthy and wellborn could see to the education of their young, but that the state should support education for those who could not otherwise afford it. He argued that it was important, particularly in free countries, that the public be educated in order to exercise the art of judgment.

In considering the revenue of the state, Smith proceeded on the principle that whatever expense was beneficial to the whole society could justly be defrayed by the general contribution of the whole society. Thus, defending the society, supporting the chief magistrate, administering justice, maintaining good roads and communications, supporting state institutions or public works, and, under certain circumstances, defraying the expenses of educational institutions and institutions for religious instruction are all properly supported by general contribution of the whole society.

Support of the institutions and activities of the state must come either from some fund belonging to the state or from the revenue of the people. Smith considers three sources of the revenue of individuals: rent, profit, and wages. His discussion of taxes is based upon four maxims: 1. The taxpayer ought to be taxed according to his ability to pay as determined by his revenue; 2. The tax should be certain in the sense that there should be no question as to the time, manner, or quantity of payment; 3. Taxes should be levied in a convenient manner, (for example, taxes on consumer goods are paid for when the goods are bought); 4. The tax should be economical in the sense that it should not be expensive to collect.

Adam Smith's *The Wealth of Nations* is a temperate, thorough, and even engrossing analysis of the economic facts of life in a free industrial society. Insofar as it is also a concrete proposal, it is not surprising that it has not won universal approval; but it is a masterpiece of its kind, and its influence on modern thought and practice has been historically significant.

THE WINTER'S TALE

Type of Work Drama
Author: William Shakespeare (1564–1616)
Type of plot: Tragicomedy
Time of plot: The legendary past
Locale: Sicilia and Bohemia
First presented: 1611

The motivating passion of this late Shakespearean play, a tragicomedy suffused by gentle melancholy, is unreasonable and cruel jealousy, the effects of which are moderated by the charming romance of the young lovers, Perdita and Florizel.

Principal Characters

Leontes (lē·ŏn′tēz), king of Sicilia. For many years a close friend of King Polixenes of Bohemia, Leontes, curiously, becomes insanely jealous of him. Afraid of becoming a cuckold, he imprisons Hermione, wrests her son away from her, and attempts to murder Polixenes. When he learns that Hermione is pregnant, he rails; he calls his daughter a bastard and forces Antigonus to leave the child alone in a deserted area. Finally, coming to his senses, he realizes the awful truth. Through his jealousy, he loses child, wife and friends.

Polixenes (pō·lĭks′ə·nēz), king of Bohemia. The innocent victim of Leontes' wrath, he flees to his kingdom, bewildered by his friend's outburst. Many years later he is to meet Leontes under much happier circumstances.

Hermione (hėr·mī′ə·nē), queen to Leontes and one of the noblest women in Shakespearean drama. Like Polixenes, she is baffled by Leontes' jealousy. Imprisoned, her children snatched away from her, she remains in hiding with Paulina, his devoted friend, until she is reunited with her family after sixteen years.

Perdita (pėr′dĭ·tə), daughter of Leontes and Hermione. Luckily for her, after she has been abandoned she is found by an old shepherd who protects her as his own child until she is of marriageable age. Meeting young Prince Florizel of Bohemia, she falls in love with him. Later she and her repentant father are reunited.

Paulina (pô·lē′nə), wife of Antigonus and lady in waiting to Hermione. Realizing the absurdity of Leontes' accusations, the courageous woman upbraids him

unmercifully for his blind cruelty to Hermione, whom she keeps hidden for sixteen years. Finally, through her efforts, husband and wife meet on a much happier note.

Camillo (kä·mĭl′ō), a lord of Sicilia and Leontes' trusted adviser, who realizes that Hermione is completely innocent of adultery. When ordered by Leontes to kill Polixenes, loyal, steadfast Camillo cannot murder a good king. Instead, he sails with Polixenes and serves him well for many years. Later, he returns to his beloved Sicilia.

Antigonus (ăn·tĭg′ə·nŭs), a lord of Sicilia and Paulina's husband. Much against his will, this unhappy man is forced to abandon Perdita in a deserted wasteland. Unfortunately for this good man, who is aware of the king's irrationality, he is killed and eaten by a bear; hence the fate and whereabouts of Perdita remain unknown for many years.

Autolycus (ô·tŏl′ĭ·kŭs), a rogue. A balladist, he is a delightful scoundrel. Quick with a song, he is equally adept at stealing purses and, in general, at living by his quick wit.

Florizel (flŏr′ĭ·zĕl), prince of Bohemia. In love with Perdita, he refuses to give her up, even though, in so doing, he angers his hot-tempered father who does not want to see his son marry a girl of apparent low birth.

An Old Shepherd, the reputed father of Perdita.

A Clown, his oafish son.

Dion (dīŏn) and **Cleomenes** (klē·ŏm′ə·nēz), lords of Sicilia.

Mamillius (mă·mĭl′ĭ·ŭs), the young prince of Sicilia, son of Leontes and Hermione.

The Story

Polixenes, king of Bohemia, was the guest of Leontes, king of Sicilia. The two men had been friends since boyhood, and there was much celebrating and joyousness during the visit. At last Polixenes decided that he must return to his home country. Although Leontes urged him

to extend his visit, Polixenes refused, saying that he had not seen his young son for a long time. Then Leontes asked Hermione, his wife, to do her part in persuading Polixenes to remain. Hermione did as her husband asked and finally Polixenes yielded to her pleas. The fact that

Polixenes had listened to Hermione's request after refusing his own urgings aroused Leontes' suspicion. Quickly he decided that Hermione and Polixenes were lovers and that he had been cuckolded.

Leontes was of a jealous disposition, even seeking constant reassurance that his son Mamillius was his own offspring. Jealously misjudging his wife and his old friend, Leontes was so angered by this latest turn of events that he ordered Camillo, his chief counselor, to poison Polixenes. All Camillo's attempts to dissuade Leontes from his scheme only strengthened the jealous man's feelings of hate. Nothing could persuade the king that Hermione was true to him. Eventually Camillo agreed to poison Polixenes, but only on condition that Leontes return to Hermione with no more distrust.

Polixenes himself had noticed a change in Leontes' attitude toward him. When he questioned Camillo, the sympathetic lord revealed the whole plot to poison him. Together they hastily embarked for Bohemia.

Upon learning that Polixenes and Camillo had fled, Leontes was more than ever convinced that his guest and his wife had been guilty of carrying on an affair. He conjectured that Polixenes and Camillo had been plotting together all the while and planning his murder. Moreover, he decided that Hermione, who was pregnant, was in all likelihood bearing Polixenes' child and not his. Publicly he accused Hermione of adultery and commanded that her son be taken from her. She herself was put into prison. Although his servants protested the order, Leontes' mind could not be changed.

In prison Hermione gave birth to a baby girl. Paulina, her attendant, thought that the sight of the baby girl might cause Leontes to relent in his harshness, and so she carried the child to the palace. Instead of forgiving his wife, Leontes became more incensed and demanded that the child be put to death. He instructed Antigonus, Paulina's husband, to take the baby to a far-off desert shore and there abandon it. Although the lord pleaded release from this cruel command, he was at length forced to put out to sea with the intention of leaving the child to perish on some lonely coast.

Leontes had sent two messengers to consult the Oracle of Delphi to determine Hermione's guilt. When the men returned, Leontes summoned his wife and the whole court to hear the verdict. The messengers read a scroll that stated that Hermione was innocent, as well as Polixenes and Camillo, that Leontes was a tyrant, and that he would live without an heir until that which was lost was found.

The king, refusing to believe the oracle, declared its findings false, and again accused Hermione of infidelity. In the midst of his tirade a servant rushed in to say that young Mamillius had died because of sorrow and anxiety over his mother's plight. On hearing this news Hermione fell into a swoon and was carried to her chambers. Soon afterward Paulina returned to say that her mistress was dead. At this news Leontes, who had already begun to believe the oracle after news of his son's death, beat his breast with self-rage. He reproached himself bitterly for his insane jealousy which had led to these unhappy events. In repentance the king swore that he would have the legend of the deaths of his son and wife engraved on their tombstones and that he himself would do penance thereafter.

Meanwhile Antigonus took the baby girl to a desert country near the sea. Heartsick at having to abandon her, the old courtier laid a bag of gold and jewels by her with instructions that she should be called Perdita, a name revealed to him in a dream. After Antigonus completed these tasks, he was attacked and killed by a bear. Later his ship was wrecked in a storm and all hands were lost. Thus no news of the expedition reached Sicilia. A kind shepherd who had found Perdita watched, however, the deaths of Antigonus and his men.

Sixteen years passed, bringing with them many changes. Leontes was a broken man, grieving alone in his palace. Little Perdita had grown into a beautiful and charming young woman under the care of the shepherd. So lovely was she that Prince Florizel, heir to the throne of Bohemia and the son of Polixenes, had fallen madly in love with her.

Unaware of the girl's background, and knowing only that his son was in love with a young shepherdess, Polixenes and Camillo, now his most trusted servant, disguised themselves and visited a sheep-shearing festival, where they saw Florizel, dressed as a shepherd, dancing with a lovely young woman. Although he realized that the shepherdess was of noble bearing, Polixenes revealed himself when Florizel was about to become engaged to Perdita, and in great rage he forbade the marriage and threatened to punish his son.

Florizel then made secret plans to elope with Perdita to a foreign country in order to escape his father's wrath. Camillo, pitying the young couple, advised Florizel to embark for Sicilia and to pretend that he was a messenger of goodwill from the king of Bohemia. Camillo supplied the young man with letters of introduction to Leontes. Camillo's plan was also to inform Polixenes of the lovers' escape, travel to Sicilia to find them, and thus enable himself to return home once more.

The poor shepherd, frightened by the king's wrath, decided to tell Polixenes how, years before, he had found the baby and a bag of gold and jewels by her side. Fate intervened, however, and the shepherd never reached the royal palace. Intercepted by the rogue Autolycus, he was put aboard the ship sailing to Sicilia.

Soon Florizel and Perdita arrived in Sicilia, followed by Polixenes and Camillo. When the old shepherd heard how Leontes had lost a daughter, he described the finding of Perdita. Leontes, convinced that Perdita and his own abandoned infant were the same, was joyfully reunited with his daughter. Polixenes immediately gave his consent to the marriage of Florizel and Perdita. The only sorrowful circumstance to mar the happiness of all concerned was the tragic death of Hermione.

One day Paulina asked Leontes to visit a newly erected statue of the dead woman in Hermione's chapel. Leontes, ever faithful to the memory of his dead wife—even to the point of promising Paulina never to marry again—gathered his guests and took them to view the statue. Standing in the chapel, amazed at the wonderful lifelike quality of the work, they heard strains of soft music. Suddenly the statue descended from its pedestal and was revealed as the living Hermione. She had spent sixteen years in seclusion while awaiting some word of her daughter. The happy family once more united, Hermione completely forgave her repentant husband. He and Polixenes were again the best of friends, rejoicing in the happiness of Perdita and Florizel.

Critical Evaluation

Written after *Cymbeline* and before *The Tempest, The Winter's Tale* is as hard to classify generically as is the fully mature dramatic genius of its author. Partaking of the elements of tragedy, the play yet ends in sheer comedy, just as it mingles elements of realism and romance. Shakespeare took his usual free hand with his source, Robert Greene's euphuistic romance *Pandosto: The Triumph of Time* (1588). Yet time remains the most crucial element in the play's structure, its clearest break with the pseudo-Aristotelian unities. The effect of time on Hermione, moreover, when the statue is revealed to be wrinkled and aged, heightens the pathos and credibility of the triumphant discovery and recognition scene. In order to allow that final scene full effect, Shakespeare wisely has Perdita's discovery and recognition reported to the audience secondhand in act 5, scene 2. In keeping with the maturity of Shakespeare's dramatic talent, the poetic style of this play is clear, rarely rhetorical, sparse in its imagery, but metaphorically sharp. Verse alternates with prose as court characters alternate with country personages.

Mamillius tells his mother, who asks him for a story, that "a sad tale's best for winter." Ironically the little boy's story is never told; the entrance of Leontes interrupts it, and Hermione's son, his role as storyteller once defined, strangely disappears. In his place the play itself takes over, invigorated by Mamillius' uncanny innocent wisdom that reflects a Platonic view of childhood. The story that unfolds winds within its skeins a multitude of themes, without losing sight of any of them. It presents two views of honor, a wholesome one represented by Hermione, and a demented view represented by Leontes. Like many of Shakespeare's plays, it treats of the unholy power of kings, kings who can be mistaken, but whose power, however mistaken, is final. Yet the finality here is spared, the tragic ending avoided. For the absolute goodness of Hermione, Paulina, Cammilo, the shepherd, and Florizel proves to be enough to overcome the evil of Leontes. Moving from the older generation's inability to love to the reflowering of love in the younger, the play spins out into a truly comic ending, with the reestablishment of community, royal authority, and general happiness in a triple *gamos*. The balance of tension between youth and age, guilt and innocence, death and rebirth, is decided in favor of life and the play escapes the clutches of remorseless tragedy in a kind of ultimate mystical vision of human life made ideal through suffering.

Leontes is a most puzzling character. His antifeminism, as expressed in his cynical speech on cuckoldry (act 1, scene 2), seems more fashionable than felt. He resembles, in his determined jealousy, Othello, and in his self-inflicted insanity, Lear. In fact, the words of Lear to Cordelia resound in Leontes' great speech, beginning, "Is whispering nothing?" and concluding, "My wife is nothing; nor nothing have these nothings,/ If this be nothing" (act 1, scene 2. It is almost impossible to sympathize with him further when he condemns even his helpless child in the face of Paulina's gentle pleas (act 2, scene 3); and we are not surprised that he at first denies the oracle itself (act 3, scene 2). Yet his sudden recognition of culpability is no more convincing than the unmotivated jealousy with which he begins the play. It is as if he changes too quickly for belief; and perhaps this is the reason for Hermione's decision to test his penitence with time, until it ripens into sincerity. Certainly his reaction to his wife's faint shows only a superficial emotion. Leontes is still self-centered, still regally assured that all can be put right with the proper words. Only after the years have passed in his loneliness does he realize it takes more than orderly words to undo the damage wrought by disorderly royal commands. His admission to Paulina that his words killed Hermione, in act 5, scene 1, paves the way for the happy ending.

Even the minor characters are drawn well and vividly. Camillo is the ideal courtier who chooses virtue in favor of favor. Paulina, like the nurse Anna in Euripides' *Hippolytus*, is the staunch helpmate of her mistress, especially in adversity, aided by magical powers that seem to spring from her own determined character. Her philosophy is also that of the classical Greeks: "What's gone and what's past help/ Should be past grief." But this play does not have the tragic Greek ending, because Paulina preserves her mistress rather than assisting her to destroy herself. Even the rogue Autolycus is beguiling, with his verbal witticisms, his frank pursuit of self-betterment, and his lusty and delightful songs. His sign is Mercury, the thief of the gods, and he follows his sign like the best rascals in Renaissance tradition, Boccaccio's Friar Onion,

Rabelais' Panurge, and Shakespeare's own Falstaff.

In Hermione and Perdita, Shakespeare achieves two of his greatest portraits of women. Hermione's speech reflects her personality, straightforward, without embroidery, as pure as virtue itself. Her reaction to Leontes' suspicion and condemnation is brief, but telling, "Adieu, my lord," she says, "I never wish'd to see you sorry; now/ I trust I shall." She combines the hardness of Portia with the gentleness of Desdemona—and Antigonus' oath in her defense recalls the character of Othello's wife. Like Chaucer's patient Griselda, Hermione loses all; but she strikes back with the most devastating weapon of all: time. Yet in the final scene of the play it is clear that her punishment of Leontes has made Hermione suffer no less than him. Perdita personifies, though never in a stereotypical way, gentle innocence: "Nothing she does or seems/ But smacks of something greater than herself/ Too noble for this place." Indeed, when Polixenes' wrath, paralleling Leontes' previous folly, threatens Perdita's life for a second time, the audience holds its breath because she is too good to be safe. When Shakespeare saves her, we rejoice, and the play abruptly ends on its highest note.

In its theme and structure, *The Winter's Tale* bears a striking resemblance to Euripides' *Alcestis*. In both plays, the "death" of the queen threatens the stability and happiness of society and, in both, her restoration, which is miraculous and ambiguous, restores order to the world of the court. Shakespeare, however, widens the comic theme by adding the love of the younger generation. So *The Winter's Tale* defies the forces of death and hatred both romantically and realistically. The sad tale becomes happy, as winter becomes spring.

WORKS AND DAYS

Type of work: Poetry
Author: Hesiod (fl. c. 735 B.C.)
First transcribed: Eighth century B.C.

Proof of the existence of a writer who flourished about 2,500 years ago is hard to find. Herodotus, who tended toward hyperbole, wrote that Hesiod lived "not more than 400 years before my time," putting him about 850 B.C. Most scholars, however, are inclined to place him a century later. Some scholars, believing that the author of *Theogony,* a genealogy of the gods (from which Aeschylus took his *Prometheus Bound*), could not have written *Works and Days* because the two works differ dramatically in concepts and styles, solve the problem by hypothesizing two writers with the same name.

At any rate, Homer and Hesiod have left the only Greek writing of the Epic age. Hesiod, in his *Theogony*, shows his indebtedness to the Homeric concept of Zeus, his power and his family life, as set forth in the *Iliad*. Working with some of Homer's earlier material, Hesiod the traditionalist tried also to combine the concepts of his own times. In *Works and Days*, he is no longer concerned with the past. To him the gods are contemporary, directly influencing life in Boeotia. He was talking about his own environment, and not writing a story of the past.

From internal evidence (lines 636-640), it is assumed that the author's father migrated across the Aegean from Cyme in Aeolia because of poverty. He settled at Ascra, a village of Boeotia, at the foot of Mt. Helicon. Ovid in referring to Hesiod used the adjective "ascraeus." The poet, himself heir to the traditions of minstrelsy in this colony of Hellas, says that he once sailed to Chalcis in Euboea where he competed in a poetry contest held by Amphidamas and won the prize, a tripod with handles, which he gave to the Muses of Helicon.

The poem also contains details of a lawsuit brought against Hesiod by his brother Perses. Apparently by bribery of the judges, Perses was awarded Hesiod's sheep, but the diligent Hesiod accumulated another fortune while Perses lost all he had and was forced to beg further help from the poet. Without hard feelings, Hesiod gave him assistance with the warning not to ask again and put his admonitions in a poem of 828 lines, of which the title well sums up its content: Rules for work and days on which luck is favorable.

Works and Days is neither a scientific treatise on farming nor a lesson on economic recovery through diligence, but rather a combination of moral precepts and an agricultural almanac. Under the symbols of Prometheus and Epimetheus (Forethought and Afterthought), Hesiod epitomized himself and his brother.

In epic style, Hesiod begins *Works and Days* with an appeal to the Muses of Pieria to sing of their father Zeus, who determines man's fame or dishonor, provides the good and the bad, destroys the mighty, and rewards the humble. The poet adds that there are two kinds of Strife on earth, one good and one bad. The good Strife, the elder daughter of Dark Night and of Zeus, the son of Chronos, makes men industrious so that they strive to imitate and surpass their neighbors.

Then addressing himself to his brother Perses, Hesiod begs him not to follow the other Strife, in marketplace or courthouse. First lay up food for a year, he advises, and then, if necessary, enter disputes of law. This section contains references to Perses' unbrotherly lawsuit to get more than his rightful share of their father's possessions.

Prometheus by craft recovered the fire that Zeus had taken from men, and in revenge Zeus created a woman of water and earth—Pandora. Pandora ("The All-Endowed") received all the lures provided by the gods to deceive men. She was eagerly accepted by Epimetheus, who had forgotten his brother's warning against gifts from the gods. Before her advent, men lived on earth free from wearying toil and deathly diseases. But Pandora removed the great lid from the jar and all the evils flew out and scattered over the earth.

Hesiod then tells another tale about the way gods and men came from the same seed. In the time of Chronos there existed a golden race of mortals, living like gods and ignorant of sorrow or old age. Everything good belonged to them; abundant flocks, fruits, the blessings of the gods. After the earth covered them, the gods created an inferior race of silver. After a hundred years of idiotic childhood, they came of age, only to kill one another off in warfare. A third race followed whose delight was war; they died and went to Hades. Then came the demi-gods, the heroes of Thebes and Troy, preceding the present race of iron, whose daily lot is weariness and woe. To them, might is right. They have no reverence for justice and oaths.

At this point in the poem, Hesiod tells the first animal fable in Greek literature, the tale of a hawk who flew high into the sky with a nightingale, lecturing her against the folly of trying to compete with stronger people. To Perses, he adds a warning that violence is a bad quality in a poor man. For him, justice is better.

A city that provides honest judgments, says Hesiod, is blessed by Zeus who protects it from war and famine. Its citizens never have to make sea voyages (which Hesiod hated); their earth provides their living. But an insolent city, even one with a single insolent citizen, is plagued by the gods because Justice, the daughter of Zeus, is quick with rewards or punishment.

Then follows a series of homilies as encouragement to the lazy and improvident Perses: "Work is no disgrace; it is idleness that is disgraceful," and "The idle envy the wealth of the hard worker and try to seize it violently. God-given wealth is better."

After these homilies the poet creates a sort of rhyming farmers' almanac: Plow when the Pleiades set (in November). After forty days they come back. Then sharpen your sickle. When the autumn rains come, cut your wood. Choose oak for ploughbeams, and bring home two, in case one breaks. Get two nine-year-old oxen to plow. A forty-year-old slave is most reliable in the fields. Have everything ready to start plowing when the cry of the crane is heard. If the cuckoo sings, plant quickly, for it will rain in three days. When winter comes, your slaves will need twice as much food, your oxen half their regular ration. Prune your grapes before the return of the swallow, sixty days after the sun turns. When Orion is overhead, it is time to harvest your grapes. Sun them for ten days, cover them for five, and then press out the wine.

His theories on husbandry extend into domestic life. The ideal time for a man to marry, he says, is at the age of thirty; for a woman, the fifth year after puberty. Marry a neighbor, but be sure the others will not laugh at your choice.

Finally, the poet records holy days and the lucky days for different tasks. He concludes that the wise man is the one who works blamelessly before the deathless gods, for he knows the propitious omens and avoids sin.

WUTHERING HEIGHTS

Type of work: Novel
Author: Emily Brontë (1818–1848)
Type of plot: Impressionistic romance
Time of plot: 1757–1803
Locale: The moors of northern England
First published: 1847

Published under the pseudonym Ellis Bell, this famous novel was once considered such a risk by its publishers that Emily Brontë had to defray the cost of publication until a sufficient number of copies had been sold. Despite some scenes of romantic exaggeration, Wuthering Heights *is an intriguing tale of revenge in which the main figures are controlled by their consuming passions.*

Principal Characters

Heathcliff, a dark-visaged, violently passionate, black-natured man. A foundling brought to the Earnshaw home at an early age, he is subjected to cruel emotional sufferings during his formative years. His chief tormentor is Hindley Earnshaw, who is jealous of his father's obvious partiality toward Heathcliff. These he endures with the sullen patience of a hardened, ill-treated animal, but just as the years add age his suffering adds hatred in Heathcliff's nature and he becomes filled with an inhuman, almost demonic, desire for vengeance against Hindley. This ambition coupled with his strange, transcendent relationship with Catherine, Hindley's sister, encompasses his life until he becomes a devastatingly wasted human, in fact, hardly human at all. He evaluates himself as a truly superior person who, possessing great emotional energies and capabilities, is a creature set apart from the human. Some regard him as a fiend, full of horrible passions and powers. In the end he dies empty, his will gone, his fervor exhausted, survived by Cathy and Hareton, the conventionalists, the moralists, the victims of his vengeful wraths.

Catherine Earnshaw, the sister of Hindley, later the wife of Edgar Linton and mother of young Cathy Linton. Catherine is spirited as a girl, selfish, wild, saucy, provoking and sometimes even wicked. But she can be sweet of eye and smile, and she is often contrite for causing pain with her insolence. In childhood she and Heathcliff form an unusually close relationship, but as her friendship with Edgar and Isabella Linton grows, she becomes haughty and arrogant. In spite of her devotion to Heathcliff she rejects him for fear marriage to him would degrade her. Instead, she accepts Edgar Linton's proposal. But her deep feeling for Heathcliff remains; he is her one unselfishness, and she insists that Edgar must at least tolerate him so that her marriage will not alter her friendship with Heathcliff. Her marriage is a tolerably happy one, possibly because Catherine becomes unspirited after Heathcliff's departure because of her rejection. Upon his return they become close friends again, despite his apparent vile character and foul treatment of her family. In their inhuman passion and fierce, tormented love they are lost to each other, each possessing the other's spirit as if it were his own. Her mind broken and anguished, Catherine finally dies in childbirth.

Hindley Earnshaw, the brother of Catherine Earnshaw, husband of Frances, and father of Hareton. As a child he is intensely jealous of Heathcliff and treats the boy cruelly. After the death of Frances, Hindley's character deteriorates rapidly; he drinks heavily and finally dies in disgrace, debt, and degradation as the result of Heathcliff's scheme of vengeance.

Edgar Linton, the husband of Catherine and father of Cathy. A polished, cultured man, he is truly in love with Catherine and makes her happy until Heathcliff returns to Wuthering Heights. He is a steady, unassuming person, patient and indulgent of both his wife and his daughter.

Cathy Linton, the daughter of Edgar and Catherine and wife of Linton Heathcliff. A bright, spirited affectionate girl, she pities Linton, becomes his friend, and through the trickery and bribery of Heathcliff is forced to marry the sickly young man. She becomes sullen and ill-tempered in Heathcliff's household, but she finds ultimate happiness with Hareton Earnshaw.

Hareton Earnshaw, the son of Hindley and Frances and the object of Heathcliff's revenge against Hindley. Under Heathcliff's instruction, or rather neglect, Hareton grows into a crude, gross, uneducated young man until Cathy, after Heathcliff's death, takes him under her charge and begins to improve his mind and manners. The two fall in love and marry.

Linton Heathcliff, the son of Heathcliff and Isabella and the husband of Cathy Linton. He is a selfish boy indulged and spoiled by his mother. After her death he returns to live with Heathcliff and at Wuthering Heights sinks into a weak-willed existence, a victim of his father's harsh treatment. Sickly since infancy, he dies at an early age, shortly after his marriage to Cathy Linton.

Isabella Linton, the sister of Edgar, Heathcliff's wife, and mother of Linton. A rather reserved, spoiled, often sulking girl, she becomes infatuated with Heathcliff, and in spite of her family's opposition and warnings she runs away with him. Later, regretting her foolish action, she leaves him and lives with her son Linton until her death.

Frances Earnshaw, the wife of Hindley; she dies of consumption.

Mr. Earnshaw, the father of Catherine and Hindley. He brings Heathcliff to Wuthering Heights after a business trip to Liverpool.

Mrs. Earnshaw, his wife.

Mrs. Ellen Dean, called **Nelly,** the housekeeper who relates Heathcliff's history to Mr. Lockwood and thereby serves as one of the books' narrators. A servant in the household at Wuthering Heights, she goes with Catherine to Thrushcross Grange when the latter marries Edgar Linton. Some years later she returns to live at Wuthering Heights as the housekeeper for Heathcliff. She is a humble, solid character, conventional, reserved, and patient. Although Hindley's disorderly home and Heathcliff's evil conduct distress her, often appall her, she does little to combat these unnatural personalities, perhaps through lack of imagination but certainly not from lack of will, for in the face of Heathcliff's merciless vengeance she is stanch and strong.

Mr. Lockwood, the first narrator, a foppish visitor from the city and Heathcliff's tenant. Interested in his landlord, he hears Mrs. Dean relate the story of the Earnshaw and Linton families.

Joseph, a servant at Wuthering Heights. He is forever making gloomy observations and predictions about other people and offering stern reprimands for their impious behavior.

Zillah, a servant at Wuthering Heights.

Mr. Green and **Mr. Kenneth,** lawyers in Gimmerton, a neighboring village.

The Story

In 1801, Mr. Lockwood became a tenant at Thrushcross Grange, an old farm owned by Mr. Heathcliff of Wuthering Heights. In the early days of his tenancy, he made two calls on his landlord. On his first visit, he met Heathcliff, an abrupt, unsocial man, surrounded by a pack of snarling, barking dogs. When he went to Wuthering Heights a second time, he met the other members of the strange household: a rude, unkempt but handsome young man named Hareton Earnshaw and a pretty young woman who was the widow of Heathcliff's son.

During his visit, snow began to fall; it covered the moor paths and made travel impossible for a stranger in that bleak countryside. Heathcliff refused to let one of the servants go with him as a guide but said that if he stayed the night he could share Hareton's bed or that of Joseph, a sour, canting old servant. When Mr. Lockwood tried to borrow Joseph's lantern for the homeward journey, the old fellow set the dogs on him, to the amusement of Hareton and Heathcliff. The visitor was finally rescued by Zillah, the cook, who hid him in an unused chamber of the house.

That night, Mr. Lockwood had a strange dream. Thinking that a branch was rattling against the window, he broke the glass in his attempt to unhook the casement. As he reached out to break off the fir branch outside, his fingers closed on a small ice-cold hand, and a weeping voice begged to be let in. The unseen presence said that her name was Catherine Linton, and she tried to force a way through the broken casement; Mr. Lockwood screamed.

Heathcliff appeared in a state of great excitement and savagely ordered Mr. Lockwood out of the room. Then he threw himself upon the bed by the shattered pane and begged the spirit to come in out of the dark and the storm. The voice, however, was heard no more—only the hiss of swirling snow and the wailing of a cold wind that blew out the smoking candle.

Ellen Dean satisfied part of Mr. Lockwood's curiosity about the happenings of that night and the strange household at Wuthering Heights. She was the housekeeper at Thrushcross Grange, but she had lived at Wuthering Heights during her childhood.

Her story of the Earnshaws, Lintons, and Heathcliffs began years before, when old Mr. Earnshaw was living at Wuthering Heights with his wife and two children. Hindley and Catherine. Once on a trip to Liverpool, Mr. Earnshaw had found a starving and homeless orphan, a ragged, dirty, urchin, dark as a gypsy, whom he brought back with him to Wuthering Heights and christened Heathcliff—a name that was to serve the fourteen-year-old boy as both a given and a surname. Gradually, the orphan began to usurp the affections of Mr. Earnshaw, whose health was failing. Wuthering Heights became a bedlam of petty jealousies; Hindley was jealous of both Heathcliff and Catherine; old Joseph, the servant, augmented the bickering; and Catherine was much too fond of Heathcliff. At last, Hindley was sent away to school. A short time later, Mr. Earnshaw died.

When Hindley Earnshaw returned home for his father's funeral, he brought a wife with him. As the new master of Wuthering Heights, he revenged himself on Heathcliff by treating him as a servant. Catherine became a wild and undisciplined hoyden who still continued her affection for Heathcliff.

One night, Catherine and Heathcliff tramped through the moors to Thrushcross Grange, where they spied on their neighbors, the Lintons. Attacked by a watchdog, Catherine was taken into the house and stayed there as a guest for five weeks until she was able to walk again. Thus she became intimate with the pleasant family of Thrushcross Grange—Mr. and Mrs. Linton and their two children, Edgar and Isabella. Afterward, the Lintons visited frequently at Wuthering Heights. The combination of ill-treatment on the part of Hindley and arrogance on the part of Edgar and Isabella made Heathcliff jealous and ill-tempered. He vowed revenge on Hindley, whom he hated with all the sullen fury of his savage nature.

The next summer, Hindley's tubercular wife, Frances, gave birth to a son, Hareton Earnshaw. A short time later, she died. In his grief, Hindley became desperate, ferocious, and degenerate. In the meantime, Catherine Earnshaw and Edgar Linton had become sweethearts. The girl confided to Ellen Dean that she really loved Heathcliff, but she felt it would be degrading for her to marry the penniless orphan. Heathcliff, who overheard this conversation, disappeared the same night and did not return for many years. Edgar and Catherine soon married and took up their abode at Thrushcross Grange with Ellen Dean as their housekeeper. There the pair lived happily until Heathcliff's return caused trouble between them. When he returned to the moors, Heathcliff was greatly improved in manners and appearance. He accepted Hindley's invitation to live at Wuthering Heights—an invitation offered by Hindley because he found in Heathcliff a companion at cards and drink, and he hoped to recoup his own dwindling fortune from Heathcliff's pockets.

Isabella Linton began to show a sudden, irresistible attraction to Heathcliff, much to the dismay of Edgar and Catherine. One night, Edgar and Heathcliff had a quarrel. Soon afterward, Heathcliff eloped with Isabella, obviously marrying her only to avenge himself and provoke Edgar. Catherine, an expectant mother, underwent a serious attack of fever. When Isabella and her husband returned to Wuthering Heights, Edgar refused to recognize his sister and forbade Heathcliff to enter his house. Despite this restriction, Heathcliff managed a final tender interview with Catherine. Partly as a result of this meeting, her child, named Catherine Linton, was born prematurely. The mother died a few hours later.

In the meantime, Isabella had found life with Heathcliff unbearable. She left him and went to London, where a few months later her child, Linton, was born. After Hindley's death, Heathcliff the guest became the master of Wuthering Heights, for Hindley had mortgaged everything to him. Hareton, the natural heir, was reduced to dependency on his father's enemy.

Twelve years after leaving Heathcliff, Isabella died, and her brother took the sickly child to live at Thrushcross Grange. Heathcliff soon heard of the child's arrival and demanded that Linton be sent to Wuthering Heights to live with his father. Young Catherine once visited Wuthering Heights and met her cousin Linton. Her father had tried to keep her in ignorance about the tenants of the place, for Heathcliff had been at pains to let it be known that he wished the two children, Cathy and Linton, to be married; and Heathcliff had his way. About the time that Edgar Linton became seriously ill, Heathcliff persuaded Cathy to visit her little cousin, who was also in extremely bad health. Upon her arrival, Cathy was imprisoned for five days at Wuthering Heights and forced to marry her sickly cousin Linton before she was allowed to go home to see her father. Although she was able to return to Thrushcross Grange before her father's death, there was not enough time for Edgar Linton to alter his will. Thus his land and fortune went indirectly to Heathcliff. Weak, sickly Linton Heathcliff died soon after, leaving Cathy a widow and dependent on Heathcliff.

Mr. Lockwood went back to London in the spring without seeing Wuthering Heights or its people again. Traveling in the region the next autumn, he had a fancy to revisit Wuthering Heights. He found Catherine and Hareton now in possession. He heard from Ellen Dean the story of Heathcliff's death three months before. He had died after four days of deliberate starvation, a broken man disturbed by memories of the beautiful young Catherine Earnshaw. His death freed Catherine Heathcliff and Hareton from his tyranny. Catherine was now teaching the ignorant boy to read and to improve his rude manners.

Mr. Lockwood went to see Heathcliff's grave. It was on the other side of Catherine Earnshaw's and her husband's. They lay under their three headstones: Catherine's in the middle, weather-discolored and half-buried, Edgar's partly moss-grown, Heathcliff's still bare. In the surrounding countryside, there was a legend that these people slept uneasily after their stormy, passionate lives. Shepherds and travelers at night claimed that they had seen Catherine and Heathcliff roaming the dark moors as they had done so many years before.

Critical Evaluation

Published under the pseudonym of Ellis Bell, *Wuthering Heights* was considered such a risk by its publishers that Emily Brontë had to defray the cost of publication until a sufficient number of copies had been sold. The combination of lurid and violent scenes in this novel must have been somewhat shocking to mid-nineteenth century taste. Despite its exaggerated touches, *Wuthering Heights* is an intriguing tale of revenge, and the main figures exist in a more than lifesize vitality of their own consuming passions. Brontë chose a suitable title for her novel: The word *wuthering* is a provincial adjective used to describe the atmospheric tumult of stormy weather.

In his influential critical study *The Great Tradition* (1948), F. R. Leavis calls *Wuthering Heights* a "sport." He cannot find a clear place for the book in his historical scheme of the English novel's development. The novel has eluded classification since its publication, and its characters and ideas continue to perplex and fascinate. The source of its energy lies in the powerful tension between its plot and its characters, between its organization and its themes. Dorothy Van Ghent (*The English Novel*, 1953) observes that in plot and design the book has rigorous "limitation," although its characters are passionately immoderate; as a result, the story is constantly explosive. Time and space force their restrictions on spirits straining to be free.

After an initial reading, the reader tends only to remember the most violent or emotional scenes and thinks back on the organization of the novel as merely a string of fiery events: Lockwood's dream, Cathy and Heathcliff fighting off the dogs of Thrushcross Grange, Heathcliff at Cathy's deathbed, or countless moments of cruelty and ecstasy involving all the characters. On closer analysis, the reader discovers the intricate interweaving of the novel's four parts into the core-story of Catherine and Heathcliff. The scheme can be summarized as follows: the establishment of the violently passionate relationship between Catherine and Heathcliff; Catherine's rejection of marriage with Heathcliff and her marriage to Edgar Linton and death in childbirth; Heathcliff's revenge; and Heathcliff's disintegration and death.

In addition to this four-part design, with its intricate changes in time and relationships among secondary characters, the novel is prescribed by the spatial and social polarity of Wuthering Heights and Thrushcross Grange. Without all of these defining and prescriptive forms, the metaphysical revolt that underlies the relationship between Catherine and Heathcliff would not have a sufficient antagonist; that is, the pressures designed to crush them help to make their haunting and demonic challenge to experience credible.

How do Catherine and Heathcliff do it? How does Brontë empower her protagonists to overcome time, space, and society? She makes their minds independent of empirical reality. Catherine confides to Ellen Dean that "dreams . . . have stayed with me . . . and changed my ideas; they've gone through and through me, like wine through water, and altered the colour of my mind." Unlike Lockwood, who is terribly frightened by his nightmare, Catherine associates her dreaming with self-definition. In Catherine's dream, the angels in Heaven are so offended by her "weeping to come back to earth . . . that they flung" her out "into the middle of the heath on the top of Wuthering Heights," where she wakes "sobbing for joy." Long before she dies physically, Catherine resurrects herself in her imagination; the irony of this religious vision is that it reverses traditional priorities: earth becomes a paradise to Heaven's misery. A "vision" of Nature replaces the phenomenal world of time and space.

Gods are realized in the minds of their worshipers. Catherine has only one worshiper, Heathcliff, but he is powerful enough to substitute for the multitudes. Heathcliff is Catherine's Faith because their souls are interchangeable ("Nelly, I am Heathcliff"); powerless to resist her intensity, Heathcliff is sanctified by her identification with him. The terms are diabolical: "you have treated me infernally," complains Heathcliff to Catherine after his return to Wuthering Heights. In response to Catherine's plea that he refrain from marrying Isabella Linton, Heathcliff lashes back: "The tyrant [and he means Catherine] grinds down his slaves and they don't turn against him, they crush those beneath them." The terms may be diabolical, but the actuality is seraphic. Brontë is similar to William Blake in the way she reverses the values of Heaven and Hell in order to dramatize and release a spiritually revolutionary moral energy.

When Heathcliff learns of Catherine's illness, he tells Ellen Dean that "existence after losing her would be hell." Indeed, the love Heathcliff and Catherine share is a new kind of emotional paradise, despite its pain and destiny of frustration; therefore, when Catherine lies ill on what will be her deathbed, Heathcliff is witness to a desacralized crucifixion. Afraid that Heathcliff will be harmed by Linton once he discovers them together, Catherine's words ring with beatific self-denial: "Kiss me again; and don't let me see your eyes. I forgive what you have done to me. I love my murderer—but *yours*! How can I?" When Ellen tells him shortly afterward of Catherine's death, Heathcliff demands that she haunt him to his dying day since life without her is inconceivable. Just as Catherine preferred Nature with Heathcliff to Heaven without him in her dreams, Heathcliff spends the rest of his life rejecting earthly possibilities and directs his spiritual and mental energies toward reunion with Catherine: "I cannot live without my soul!" When the time comes, he prepares for his death as if it were salvation: "Last night, I was on the threshold of hell. Today, I am within sight of my heaven."

These two lovers inhabit a psychic and emotional world entirely their own. Ellen Dean seems an honest observer, but her conventional imagination makes her finally a spiritual stranger to all the facts she so carefully relates. Lockwood is awed by the lovers' story, but he "sees" it at a great distance because of limitations of feeling and perception. Three generations of Lintons and Earnshaws together with the conflicts of class and religious differences embodied in the juxtaposition of "Heights" and "Grange" seem merely an insignificant background to the classless, timeless, and eerily universal passion of these two children of the moor.

Masterpieces of World Literature

TITLE INDEX

MASTERPIECES OF WORLD LITERATURE

AUTHOR INDEX

AUTHOR INDEX